The Bill James Handbook 2004

Baseball Info Solutions

Published by ACTA Publications

Cover by Tom A. Wright

Cover Photo by Scott Jordan Levy

Second Edition: December 2003

Published by: ACTA Publications, 4848 N. Clark Street, Chicago, IL 60640 (800-397-2282) www.actapublications.com

ISBN 0-87946-258-2

Printed in the United States of America

Acknowledgments

Bill James is always a busy man, but working for the Red Sox makes him busier than ever. Thanks, Bill, for finding time to use your sense of perfection to continue growing and improving your original Handbook design.

One of the visionaries for this project was John Dewan, who is dedicated to helping Baseball Info Solutions become an innovator in the collection, interpretation, commercialization, and dissemination of in-depth baseball statistics. He invests the breadth of his baseball expertise into generating original ideas and consulting on critical decisions. Thanks for taking the risk to back this start-from-scratch company.

Steve Moyer began this company with the idea of bringing fun back to statistics gathering. Thank you Steve! We needed that. And thanks for getting this baby from the crawling stage to walking on its feet, tall and proud.

Steve's brainchild wouldn't have left the crib without help form some very important staff members. Thanks to all for their dependable, extraordinary efforts!

We don't know where Damon Lichtenwalner gets all his expertise and energy. We are amazed by all you do and your database infrastructure genius. Ryan Galla, who joined the team full-time in the past year, has been a great addition with non-stop programming and guidance of the data collection. Andy Bausher's pitching knowledge is essential to having this book rise above all other publications. Pat Quinn has joined the team, and has provided valuable assistance during the final push to get the book out.

Mike Canter, though not officially on staff, we appreciate you for extending your "side project" for the second volume. You helped bring the book successfully through the prototype stage to an annual.

Greg Pierce, Andrew Yankech, and the rest of the ACTA staff never stop encouraging us and being there to help.

Our network of helpers throughout the country is essential. Thank you Bryce Babcock, Kevin Barge, Mike Brodhead, Darin Brown, Brad Burrow, Dennis Crowley, David Dick, Paul Galgon, Greg Gambler, Joe Glandon, Durward Hamil, Jared Haydt, David Houck, Darren James, Wes Koser, Vinay Kumar, Chippy Lichtenwalner, Randy Lillard, George Lindholm, Al Melchior, John Menna, Gus Papadopoulos, Scott Pianowski, Todd Radcliffe, Daryl Ravani, Gary Read, Tim Reyes, Joe Ritzo, Bob Routier, Kenn Ruby, G.C. Seibert, Wayne Sit, Karen Thomas, John Wagner, Trace Wood, and Todd Zola.

Last, but certainly not least, thanks to our friends in the baseball industry: Greg Ambrosius, Jim Callis, Chris Dahl, Jeff Erickson, Steve Goldstein, Steve Greenberg, John Hunt, Peter Kreutzer, Rob Neyer, Mat Olkin, Peter Schoenke, Ron Shandler, and Rick Wolf.

Dedication

For my three Baby Girls: my wife Michelle and my two daughters Harmony and Mary Lou (aka Shell, Wolf Girl and Monkey Lou). Thanks for your constant love and support. Here's to a great future.

Steve Moyer

Table of Contents

Introduction

Last year we created the first *The Bill James Handbook* and called it the "prototype for the future." This second book becomes the second annual. We met our commitment, stated in the first book, to begin making the book available November 1. That's within weeks of the end of the baseball season! We re-affirm our commitment to this same availability date for all the years to come.* We also commit to improving the book every year with thorough evaluation of reader input (info@baseballinfosolutions.com) and the insights of Bill James. This book is for the professional sports researcher, the fantasy league participant, and baseball fans who want to get baseball statistics accurately, easily, and now . . . *early*.

We continue to deliver on the high standard we set in our first volume. This year we added Bill James' Manager's Record and his Win Shares player evaluation statistic. Bill James' Manager's Record breaks new ground in understanding the tactical differences between managers during games. Bill's Win Shares already broke new ground by measuring the individual's contributions to his team. Now we bring it to this annual publication.

Just for fun, we offer our Alfred Hitchcockian riddle again: Where's Bill James? We hope you figured it out last year. Solve it this year and be the first one to email us at info@baseballinfosolutions.com with the correct answer and you will receive a free 2005 book next year.

---

* Major League Baseball releases the official statistics in December. That's too late for us. Even though our statistics are unofficial, they are no less accurate.

2003 Team Statistics

2003 American League Standings

Overall

EAST Team	W-L	Pct	GB	D1	LD1	LLd	CENTRAL Team	W-L	Pct	GB	D1	LD1	LLd	WEST Team	W-L	Pct	GB	D1	LD1	LLd
New York Yankees	101-61	.623	0.0	171	9/28	7.5	Minnesota Twins	90-72	.556	0.0	65	9/28	6.0	Oakland Athletics	96-66	.593	0.0	61	9/28	6.0
Boston Red Sox*	95-67	.586	6.0	13	6/11	2.5	Chicago White Sox	86-76	.531	4.0	24	9/14	2.0	Seattle Mariners	93-69	.574	3.0	135	8/26	8.0
Toronto Blue Jays	86-76	.531	15.0	0	-	0.0	Kansas City Royals	83-79	.512	7.0	106	8/29	7.5	Anaheim Angels	77-85	.475	19.0	4	4/16	0.0
Baltimore Orioles	71-91	.438	30.0	1	3/31	0.0	Cleveland Indians	68-94	.420	22.0	0	-	0.0	Texas Rangers	71-91	.438	25.0	2	3/31	1.0
Tampa Bay Devil Rays	63-99	.389	38.0	1	3/31	0.0	Detroit Tigers	43-119	.265	47.0	0	-	0.0							

* Clinched Wild Card Birth on 9/25. Division Clinch Dates: Oakland 9/23, Minnesota 9/23, New York 9/24.
D1 = Number of days a team had at least a share of first place of their division; LD1 = Last date the team had at least a share of first place; LLd = The largest number of games that a team led their division

East Division

Tm	AT Home	Road	VERSUS East	Cent	West	NL	LHS	RHS	CONDITIONS Day	Night	Grass	Turf	GAME 1-Rn	5+Rn	XInn	MONTHLY Apr	May	June	July	Aug	Sep	ALL-STAR Pre	Post
NYY	50-32	51-29	47-29	23-9	18-18	13-5	26-11	75-50	36-26	65-35	83-56	18-5	22-14	34-20	6-6	20-6	11-17	20-7	14-10	17-12	18-9	57-36	44-25
Bos	53-28	42-39	41-35	24-12	19-13	11-7	26-27	69-40	28-22	67-45	84-53	11-14	26-16	36-20	11-5	18-8	13-14	16-10	16-11	15-14	17-9	55-38	40-29
Tor	41-40	45-36	37-39	22-14	17-15	10-8	26-18	60-58	30-23	56-53	36-30	50-46	14-23	28-25	4-4	10-17	21-8	15-11	8-17	13-15	19-7	49-46	37-30
Bal	40-40	31-51	31-45	14-18	21-15	5-13	17-30	54-61	25-27	46-64	64-76	7-15	21-22	22-23	4-10	12-12	14-15	8-18	15-10	11-20	10-16	41-50	30-41
TB	36-45	27-54	34-42	12-20	14-22	3-15	17-29	46-70	14-34	49-65	21-47	42-52	23-28	11-27	7-7	9-17	11-16	5-21	14-12	13-16	10-17	32-60	31-39

Central Division

Tm	AT Home	Road	VERSUS East	Cent	West	NL	LHS	RHS	CONDITIONS Day	Night	Grass	Turf	GAME 1-Rn	5+Rn	XInn	MONTHLY Apr	May	June	July	Aug	Sep	ALL-STAR Pre	Post
Min	48-33	42-39	17-15	43-33	20-16	10-8	25-29	65-43	28-24	62-48	36-39	54-33	22-20	25-27	9-8	11-14	19-9	12-15	10-16	18-11	19-7	45-49	45-23
CWS	51-30	35-46	21-15	42-34	13-19	10-8	26-25	60-51	29-21	57-55	79-65	7-11	18-22	28-21	8-4	14-12	11-16	15-13	17-9	16-13	13-12	45-49	41-27
KC	40-40	43-39	12-20	46-30	16-20	9-9	24-24	59-55	27-29	56-50	75-70	8-9	18-22	25-28	5-4	16-7	10-19	15-12	15-11	13-15	13-15	51-41	32-38
Cle	38-43	30-51	14-18	35-41	13-23	6-12	19-31	49-63	22-31	46-63	58-88	10-6	15-25	17-20	7-11	7-19	14-12	13-15	11-16	16-13	7-18	41-53	27-41
Det	23-58	20-61	9-27	24-52	6-26	4-14	12-39	31-80	12-43	31-76	41-106	2-13	19-18	7-40	3-13	3-20	11-18	5-22	9-17	6-23	9-18	25-67	18-52

West Division

Tm	AT Home	Road	VERSUS East	Cent	West	NL	LHS	RHS	CONDITIONS Day	Night	Grass	Turf	GAME 1-Rn	5+Rn	XInn	MONTHLY Apr	May	June	July	Aug	Sep	ALL-STAR Pre	Post
Oak	57-24	39-42	28-13	25-20	34-24	9-9	26-19	70-47	39-24	57-42	91-55	5-11	25-20	26-19	10-4	17-10	14-13	15-12	16-11	20-9	14-11	54-39	42-27
Sea	50-31	43-38	18-23	32-13	33-25	10-8	33-16	60-53	29-16	64-53	83-64	10-5	16-15	36-17	6-6	17-10	19-8	17-10	13-14	14-15	13-12	58-35	35-34
Ana	45-37	32-48	15-30	26-15	25-33	11-7	28-26	49-59	22-24	55-61	70-77	7-8	16-20	28-22	2-4	13-13	13-13	14-13	12-15	14-15	11-15	49-43	28-42
Tex	43-38	28-53	22-23	21-20	24-34	4-14	21-35	50-56	17-22	54-69	64-80	7-11	17-20	18-36	5-7	12-14	12-15	7-20	13-14	17-12	9-16	38-55	33-36

Team vs. Team Breakdown

	EAST NYY	Bos	Tor	Bal	TB	CENTRAL Min	CWS	KC	Cle	Det	WEST Oak	Sea	Ana	Tex
New York Yankees	-	10	10	13	14	7	2	4	5	5	3	5	6	4
Boston Red Sox	9	-	10	10	12	2	5	5	4	8	3	5	6	5
Toronto Blue Jays	9	9	-	11	8	3	3	5	4	7	2	4	7	4
Baltimore Orioles	6	9	8	-	8	3	2	3	3	3	2	4	8	7
Tampa Bay Devil Rays	5	7	11	11	-	0	3	3	2	4	3	5	3	3
Minnesota Twins	0	4	3	4	6	-	10	8	10	15	8	3	4	5
Chicago White Sox	4	4	6	4	3	9	-	11	11	11	4	2	4	3
Kansas City Royals	2	1	1	4	4	11	8	-	13	14	2	4	3	7
Cleveland Indians	2	2	2	3	5	9	8	6	-	12	3	3	3	4
Detroit Tigers	1	1	2	3	2	4	8	5	7	-	3	1	1	1
Oakland Athletics	6	4	5	7	6	1	5	7	6	6	-	7	12	15
Seattle Mariners	4	2	3	5	4	6	7	5	6	8	12	-	11	10
Anaheim Angels	3	3	2	1	6	5	4	6	5	9	8	8	-	9
Texas Rangers	5	4	5	2	6	4	4	2	5	6	4	10	10	-

(read wins across and losses down)

2003 National League Standings

Overall

EAST

Team	W-L	Pct	GB	D1	LD1	LLd
Atlanta Braves	101-61	.623	0.0	156	9/28	15.0
Florida Marlins*	91-71	.562	10.0	0	-	0.0
Philadelphia Phillies	86-76	.531	15.0	14	4/28	1.0
Montreal Expos	83-79	.512	18.0	30	5/1	1.0
New York Mets	66-95	.410	34.5	2	4/8	0.0

CENTRAL

Team	W-L	Pct	GB	D1	LD1	LLd
Chicago Cubs	88-74	.543	0.0	78	9/28	3.0
Houston Astros	87-75	.537	1.0	92	9/25	4.0
St Louis Cardinals	85-77	.525	3.0	32	9/2	2.0
Pittsburgh Pirates	75-87	.463	13.0	10	4/14	1.0
Cincinnati Reds	69-93	.426	19.0	0	-	0.0
Milwaukee Brewers	68-94	.420	20.0	0	-	0.0

WEST

Team	W-L	Pct	GB	D1	LD1	LLd
San Francisco Giants	100-61	.621	0.0	182	9/28	15.5
Los Angeles Dodgers	85-77	.525	15.5	6	6/22	0.0
Arizona Diamondbacks	84-78	.519	16.5	0	-	0.0
Colorado Rockies	74-88	.457	26.5	0	-	0.0
San Diego Padres	64-98	.395	36.5	0	-	0.0

* Clinched Wild Card Birth on 9/26. Division Clinch Dates: San Francisco 9/17, Atlanta 9/18, Chicago 9/27.

D1 = Number of days a team had at least a share of first place of their division; LD1 = Last date the team had at least a share of first place; LLd = The largest number of games that a team led their division

East Division

Tm	Home	Road	East	Cent	West	AL	LHS	RHS	Day	Night	Grass	Turf	1-Rn	5+Rn	XInn	Apr	May	June	July	Aug	Sep	Pre	Post
Atl	55-26	46-35	41-35	27-12	23-9	10-5	24-13	77-48	36-13	65-48	88-52	13-9	17-25	37-19	7-10	17-9	20-8	14-11	20-8	16-12	14-12	61-32	40-29
Fla	53-28	38-43	48-28	19-20	15-17	9-6	27-11	64-60	19-23	72-48	85-67	6-4	30-23	25-22	6-4	14-14	12-16	16-11	11-7	14-14	18-8	49-46	42-25
Phi	49-32	37-44	39-37	21-18	18-14	8-7	14-17	72-59	27-23	59-53	34-37	52-39	20-18	30-17	10-3	15-12	13-13	16-9	15-13	13-16	13-13	52-40	34-36
Mon	52-29	31-50	35-41	20-16	19-13	9-9	21-20	62-59	29-27	54-52	28-41	55-38	22-24	15-18	9-8	16-10	16-12	12-15	10-17	16-13	12-12	49-45	34-34
NYM	34-46	32-49	27-49	17-22	17-14	5-10	18-25	48-70	21-31	45-64	61-82	5-13	15-28	18-25	1-6	11-15	14-14	10-16	9-18	15-12	7-19	40-53	26-42

Central Division

Tm	Home	Road	East	Cent	West	AL	LHS	RHS	Day	Night	Grass	Turf	1-Rn	5+Rn	XInn	Apr	May	June	July	Aug	Sep	Pre	Post
ChC	44-37	44-37	15-15	47-37	17-13	9-9	18-20	70-54	51-41	37-33	85-67	3-7	27-17	24-21	8-3	14-12	15-12	12-15	12-14	15-13	19-8	47-47	41-27
Hou	48-33	39-42	13-17	49-35	14-16	11-7	18-16	69-59	23-25	64-50	85-71	2-4	19-21	28-14	3-8	11-15	18-12	13-12	16-11	13-15	16-10	50-44	37-31
StL	48-33	37-44	17-13	46-38	12-19	10-8	19-17	66-60	37-24	48-53	83-73	2-4	14-25	24-20	7-6	12-12	14-15	16-11	13-14	16-12	13-13	49-45	36-32
Pit	39-42	36-45	15-18	39-45	16-17	5-7	20-25	55-62	24-35	51-52	70-80	5-7	24-27	17-23	5-5	11-14	12-16	10-14	15-13	13-15	13-15	41-50	34-37
Cin	35-46	34-47	14-19	34-50	14-19	7-5	16-29	53-64	22-33	47-60	63-90	6-3	30-21	9-29	15-5	11-15	15-13	12-13	11-17	10-18	10-16	43-50	26-43
Mil	31-50	37-44	14-22	37-47	12-18	5-7	16-22	52-72	23-34	45-60	66-87	2-7	25-21	15-35	6-10	9-17	12-16	12-13	11-17	16-12	8-18	37-56	31-38

West Division

Tm	Home	Road	East	Cent	West	AL	LHS	RHS	Day	Night	Grass	Turf	1-Rn	5+Rn	XInn	Apr	May	June	July	Aug	Sep	Pre	Post
SF	57-24	43-37	14-17	23-13	53-23	10-8	26-11	74-50	31-27	69-34	99-55	1-6	28-12	24-13	9-3	18-7	15-13	15-12	19-8	14-13	18-8	57-37	43-24
LA	46-35	39-42	16-16	23-13	35-41	11-7	24-16	61-61	26-14	59-63	83-73	2-4	26-23	17-17	6-10	13-14	17-10	14-11	9-18	17-11	14-13	49-44	36-33
Ari	45-36	39-42	16-16	23-16	34-42	11-4	27-21	57-57	29-25	55-53	79-74	5-4	30-25	26-16	8-8	12-15	13-14	20-6	11-16	14-14	14-12	52-42	32-36
Col	49-32	25-56	11-21	19-20	35-41	9-6	20-26	54-62	27-30	47-58	72-81	2-7	17-22	27-28	2-7	15-12	12-17	15-13	14-13	9-19	9-14	50-47	24-41
SD	35-46	29-52	10-22	13-23	33-43	8-10	17-30	47-68	19-31	45-67	62-93	2-5	21-20	16-31	8-8	10-16	6-23	12-15	14-12	13-15	9-16	35-61	29-37

Team vs. Team Breakdown

	Atl	Fla	Phi	Mon	NYM	ChC	Hou	StL	Pit	Cin	Mil	SF	LA	Ari	Col	SD
Atlanta Braves	-	9	9	12	11	4	5	4	7	3	4	2	4	5	6	6
Florida Marlins	10	-	13	13	12	2	1	3	2	4	7	1	2	5	2	5
Philadelphia Phillies	10	6	-	11	12	5	4	4	2	4	2	3	5	2	4	4
Montreal Expos	7	6	8	-	14	3	3	1	3	4	6	7	2	2	4	4
New York Mets	8	7	7	5	-	1	4	1	4	4	3	4	3	2	5	3
Chicago Cubs	2	4	1	3	5	-	9	8	10	10	10	4	2	4	3	4
Houston Astros	1	5	2	3	2	7	-	11	10	12	9	2	4	1	4	3
St Louis Cardinals	2	3	2	5	5	9	7	-	10	7	13	1	2	3	2	4
Pittsburgh Pirates	2	4	4	3	2	8	6	7	-	11	7	2	1	3	6	4
Cincinnati Reds	3	2	5	2	2	7	5	9	5	-	8	3	2	2	4	3
Milwaukee Brewers	2	2	4	0	6	6	8	3	10	10	-	1	2	3	1	5
San Francisco Giants	4	5	3	0	2	2	4	5	4	3	5	-	13	14	12	14
Los Angeles Dodgers	2	5	2	4	3	4	2	4	5	4	4	6	-	9	12	8
Arizona Diamondbacks	2	2	4	4	4	2	5	3	3	7	3	5	10	-	10	9
Colorado Rockies	0	4	2	3	2	3	2	4	3	2	5	7	7	9	-	12
San Diego Padres	1	1	3	2	3	2	3	2	2	3	1	5	11	10	7	-

(read wins across and losses down)

American League Batting

						BATTING													BASERUNNING					PERCENTAGES		
Tm	G	AB	H	2B	3B	HR	(Hm	Rd)	TB	R	RBI	TBB	IBB	SO	HBP	SH	SF	ShO	SB	CS	SB%	GDP	LOB	Avg	OBP	Slg
Bos	162	5769	1667	371	40	238	(111	127)	2832	961	932	620	61	943	53	24	64	5	88	35	.72	126	1224	.289	.360	.491
Tor	162	5661	1580	357	33	190	(94	96)	2573	894	853	546	40	1081	90	11	56	5	37	25	.60	146	1175	.279	.349	.455
NYY	163	5605	1518	304	14	230	(106	124)	2540	877	845	684	54	1042	81	25	35	7	98	33	.75	154	1239	.271	.356	.453
KC	162	5568	1526	288	39	162	(69	93)	2378	836	781	476	32	926	75	63	57	5	120	42	.74	128	1096	.274	.336	.427
Tex	162	5664	1506	274	36	239	(140	99)	2569	826	799	488	31	1052	75	24	42	11	65	25	.72	115	1141	.266	.330	.454
Min	162	5655	1567	318	45	155	(76	79)	2440	801	755	512	36	1027	63	42	52	5	94	44	.68	139	1166	.277	.341	.431
Sea	162	5561	1509	290	33	139	(69	70)	2282	795	759	586	34	989	53	35	46	10	108	37	.74	130	1202	.271	.344	.410
CWS	162	5487	1445	303	19	220	(130	90)	2446	791	766	519	27	916	58	43	41	8	77	29	.73	132	1074	.263	.331	.446
Oak	162	5497	1398	317	24	176	(88	88)	2291	768	742	556	52	898	59	22	53	6	48	14	.77	118	1130	.254	.327	.417
Bal	163	5665	1516	277	24	152	(79	73)	2297	743	695	431	32	902	54	51	40	12	89	36	.71	123	1121	.268	.323	.405
Ana	162	5487	1473	276	33	150	(68	82)	2265	736	687	476	42	838	56	50	50	12	129	61	.68	125	1086	.268	.330	.413
TB	162	5654	1501	298	38	137	(56	81)	2286	715	678	420	46	1030	56	32	50	10	142	42	.77	108	1129	.265	.320	.404
Cle	162	5572	1413	296	26	158	(69	89)	2235	699	660	466	25	1062	62	46	41	5	86	61	.59	128	1068	.254	.316	.401
Det	162	5466	1312	201	39	153	(67	86)	2050	591	553	443	24	1099	47	65	49	17	98	63	.61	114	1047	.240	.300	.375
AL	1135	78311	20931	4170	443	2499	(1222	1277)	33484	11033	10505	7223	536	13805	882	533	676	118	1279	547	.70	1786	15898	.267	.333	.428

American League Pitching

HOW MUCH THEY PITCHED						WHAT THEY GAVE UP												THE RESULTS									
Tm	G	CG	Rel	IP	BFP	H	R	ER	HR	SH	SF	HB	TBB	IBB	SO	WP	Bk	W	L	Pct.	ShO	Sv-Op	Hld	OAvg	OOBP	OSlg	ERA
Sea	162	8	366	1441.0	6025	1340	637	602	173	35	43	54	466	24	1001	35	4	93	69	.574	15	38-52	48	.247	.311	.388	3.76
Oak	162	16	364	1441.2	6078	1336	643	582	140	55	29	54	499	42	1018	41	10	96	66	.593	14	48-60	53	.246	.314	.376	3.63
CWS	162	12	361	1431.0	6067	1364	715	663	162	48	57	53	518	30	1056	39	4	86	76	.531	7	36-53	33	.253	.322	.404	4.17
NYY	163	8	367	1462.0	6209	1512	716	653	145	37	48	49	375	36	1119	33	0	101	61	.623	12	49-67	57	.265	.314	.407	4.02
Ana	162	5	375	1431.1	6161	1444	743	680	190	25	42	76	486	38	980	53	3	77	85	.475	9	39-52	56	.261	.327	.421	4.28
Min	162	7	399	1462.0	6246	1526	758	716	187	54	41	50	402	35	997	62	9	90	72	.556	8	45-64	65	.268	.319	.428	4.41
Cle	162	5	428	1459.1	6254	1477	778	682	179	52	46	64	501	37	943	48	7	68	94	.420	7	34-59	52	.264	.329	.426	4.21
Bos	162	5	437	1464.2	6355	1503	809	729	153	28	52	76	488	41	1141	44	0	95	67	.586	6	36-57	46	.263	.327	.415	4.48
Bal	163	9	425	1449.2	6366	1579	820	767	198	42	35	80	526	43	981	42	4	71	91	.438	3	41-62	66	.278	.346	.446	4.76
Tor	162	14	443	1435.0	6270	1560	826	748	184	29	38	57	485	46	984	56	2	86	76	.531	6	36-53	64	.276	.337	.441	4.69
TB	162	7	372	1436.2	6340	1454	852	787	196	39	65	95	639	37	877	64	9	63	99	.389	7	30-55	56	.264	.347	.440	4.93
KC	162	7	407	1438.2	6366	1569	867	808	190	36	65	66	566	33	865	61	9	83	79	.512	10	36-64	62	.279	.348	.450	5.05
Det	162	3	451	1438.2	6376	1616	928	847	195	48	60	56	557	35	764	52	5	43	119	.265	5	27-46	44	.286	.352	.461	5.30
Tex	162	4	494	1433.1	6413	1625	969	903	208	41	56	63	603	45	1009	52	8	71	91	.438	3	43-63	74	.288	.360	.473	5.67
AL	1135	110	5689	20225.0	87526	20905	11061	10168	2500	569	677	893	7111	522	13735	682	74	1123	1145	.495	109	538-807	776	.267	.332	.427	4.52

American League Fielding

							Fielding													
Team	G	Inn	PO	Ast	OFAst	E	(Throw	Field)	TC	DP	GDP	SB	CS	SB%	CPkof	PPkof	PB	UER	UERA	FPct
Seattle	162	1441.0	4323	1450	20	65	27	38	5838	159	131	62	32	.66	2	6	12	35	0.22	.989
Minnesota	162	1462.0	4386	1481	19	87	38	46	5954	114	93	70	27	.72	1	8	10	42	0.26	.985
Texas	162	1433.1	4300	1703	33	94	45	48	6097	168	139	96	45	.68	1	3	11	66	0.41	.985
Chicago	162	1431.0	4293	1588	29	93	44	47	5974	154	135	58	29	.67	3	8	13	52	0.33	.984
Baltimore	163	1449.2	4349	1683	31	105	43	61	6137	164	139	121	37	.77	3	5	12	53	0.33	.983
Tampa Bay	162	1436.2	4310	1580	32	103	39	63	5993	158	124	65	41	.61	0	5	9	66	0.41	.983
Oakland	162	1441.2	4325	1779	12	107	54	47	6211	145	128	91	43	.68	0	4	9	61	0.38	.983
Kansas City	162	1438.2	4316	1705	41	108	48	59	6129	143	118	95	42	.69	0	3	8	58	0.36	.982
Anaheim	162	1431.1	4294	1517	26	105	49	55	5916	138	113	80	48	.63	3	4	11	63	0.40	.982
Boston	162	1464.2	4394	1679	34	113	49	62	6186	130	109	101	35	.74	1	0	20	66	0.49	.982
New York	163	1462.0	4386	1578	31	114	48	65	6078	126	104	92	37	.71	4	2	13	63	0.39	.981
Toronto	162	1435.0	4305	1742	18	117	55	62	6164	161	141	126	32	.80	0	2	10	78	0.49	.981
Cleveland	162	1459.1	4378	1780	33	126	56	70	6284	178	149	84	43	.66	0	7	11	96	0.59	.980
Detroit	162	1438.2	4316	1813	25	138	55	82	6267	194	163	128	54	.70	1	7	11	81	0.51	.978
American League	1135	20225.0	60675	23078	384	1475	650	805	85228	2132	1786	1269	545	.70	19	64	160	893	0.40	.983

National League Batting

Tm	G	AB	H	2B	3B	HR	(Hm	Rd)	TB	R	RBI	TBB	IBB	SO	HBP	SH	SF	ShO	SB	CS	SB%	GDP	LOB	Avg	OBP	Slg
																			BASERUNNING					**PERCENTAGES**		
Atl	162	5670	1608	321	31	235	(111	124)	2696	907	872	545	46	933	49	65	49	4	68	22	.76	124	1170	.284	.349	.475
StL	162	5672	1580	342	32	196	(85	111)	2574	876	827	580	68	952	73	87	54	7	82	32	.72	136	1217	.279	.350	.454
Col	162	5518	1472	330	31	198	(113	85)	2458	853	814	619	46	1134	52	55	38	12	63	37	.63	140	1156	.267	.344	.445
Hou	162	5583	1466	308	30	191	(97	94)	2407	805	763	557	44	1021	81	61	38	5	66	30	.69	125	1185	.263	.336	.431
Phi	162	5543	1448	325	27	166	(83	83)	2325	791	757	651	56	1155	55	46	38	10	72	29	.71	120	1220	.261	.343	.419
SF	161	5456	1440	281	29	180	(82	98)	2319	755	713	593	79	980	40	76	39	6	53	37	.59	130	1188	.264	.338	.425
Pit	162	5581	1492	275	45	163	(81	82)	2346	753	711	529	42	1049	87	79	38	9	86	37	.70	112	1214	.267	.338	.420
Fla	162	5490	1459	292	44	157	(72	85)	2310	751	709	515	44	978	57	82	41	9	150	74	.67	114	1114	.266	.333	.421
ChC	162	5519	1431	302	24	172	(86	86)	2297	724	691	492	40	1158	50	40	46	10	73	31	.70	135	1114	.259	.323	.416
Ari	162	5570	1467	303	47	152	(79	73)	2320	717	696	531	63	1006	45	63	52	12	76	38	.67	126	1185	.263	.330	.417
Mil	162	5548	1423	266	24	196	(108	88)	2325	714	685	547	41	1221	71	62	40	7	99	39	.72	158	1155	.256	.329	.419
Mon	162	5437	1404	294	25	144	(81	63)	2180	711	682	522	57	990	45	72	40	8	100	39	.72	143	1102	.258	.326	.401
Cin	162	5509	1349	239	21	182	(97	85)	2176	694	669	524	34	1049	79	66	32	10	80	34	.70	102	1134	.245	.318	.395
SD	162	5531	1442	257	32	128	(55	73)	2147	678	641	565	34	1073	57	50	42	9	76	39	.66	142	1219	.261	.333	.388
NYM	161	5341	1317	262	24	124	(54	70)	1999	642	607	489	42	1035	54	78	45	10	70	31	.69	136	1086	.247	.314	.374
LA	162	5458	1328	260	25	124	(68	56)	2010	574	544	407	43	985	72	71	28	13	80	36	.69	121	1108	.243	.303	.368
NL	1295	88426	23126	4657	491	2708	(1352	1356)	36889	11945	11381	8666	779	16996	967	1093	660	141	1294	585	.69	2064	18567	.262	.332	.417

National League Pitching

Tm	G	CG	Rel	IP	BFP	H	R	ER	HR	SH	SF	HB	TBB	IBB	SO	WP	Bk	W	L	Pct.	ShO	Sv-Op	Hld	OAvg	OOBP	OSlg	ERA
	HOW MUCH THEY PITCHED					**WHAT THEY GAVE UP**												**THE RESULTS**									
LA	162	3	438	1457.2	6001	1254	556	511	127	62	19	40	526	35	1289	50	5	85	77	.525	17	58-66	81	.234	.306	.354	3.16
SF	161	7	461	1437.1	6090	1349	638	595	136	61	53	43	546	34	1006	68	8	100	61	.621	10	43-60	77	.250	.321	.386	3.73
Hou	162	1	502	1450.0	6176	1350	677	622	161	66	36	74	565	53	1139	40	4	87	75	.537	5	50-64	91	.248	.326	.397	3.86
ChC	162	13	420	1456.1	6227	1304	683	619	143	82	36	71	617	36	1404	63	3	88	74	.543	14	36-51	62	.241	.324	.372	3.83
Ari	162	7	452	1455.0	6230	1379	685	621	150	81	31	72	526	52	1291	51	9	84	78	.519	11	42-55	47	.250	.322	.388	3.84
Fla	162	7	395	1445.1	6165	1415	692	648	128	60	53	40	530	40	1132	50	11	91	71	.562	11	36-50	48	.258	.325	.396	4.04
Phi	162	9	437	1443.2	6195	1386	697	648	142	79	29	77	536	51	1060	53	4	86	76	.531	13	33-51	56	.253	.327	.401	4.04
Mon	162	15	437	1437.2	6171	1467	716	640	181	47	35	71	540	61	1028	71	4	83	79	.512	10	42-60	67	.264	.327	.423	4.01
Atl	162	4	489	1456.1	6247	1425	740	663	147	63	39	42	555	69	992	53	4	101	61	.623	7	51-71	75	.257	.327	.401	4.10
NYM	161	3	412	1413.1	6204	1497	754	704	168	63	43	45	576	71	907	45	7	66	95	.410	10	38-53	59	.273	.345	.438	4.48
StL	162	9	460	1463.2	6375	1544	796	748	210	68	45	65	508	36	969	53	1	85	77	.525	10	41-71	72	.271	.336	.452	4.60
Pit	162	7	457	1444.1	6293	1527	801	744	178	81	44	61	502	58	926	49	2	75	87	.463	10	44-68	77	.272	.336	.431	4.64
SD	162	2	473	1431.1	6303	1458	831	774	208	54	53	62	611	52	1091	64	3	64	98	.395	10	31-49	60	.264	.341	.437	4.87
Mil	162	5	460	1452.0	6459	1590	873	810	219	69	47	61	575	43	1034	57	8	68	94	.420	3	44-71	59	.279	.348	.462	5.02
Cin	162	4	475	1446.1	6423	1578	886	818	190	70	43	48	590	61	932	45	3	69	93	.426	5	38-64	60	.278	.349	.463	5.09
Col	162	3	500	1420.0	6364	1629	892	821	200	54	53	84	552	51	866	48	8	74	88	.457	4	34-54	76	.290	.359	.470	5.20
NL	1295	99	7268	23110.1	99923	23152	11917	10986	2707	1060	659	956	8778	793	17066	860	84	1306	1284	.504	150	661-958	1067	.262	.333	.418	4.28

National League Fielding

Team	G	Inn	PO	Ast	OFAst	E	(Throw	Field)	TC	DP	GDP	SB	CS	SB%	CPkof	PPkof	PB	UER	UERA	FPct
St Louis	162	1463.2	4391	1644	37	77	26	50	6112	138	114	55	24	.70	1	1	7	48	0.30	.987
Florida	162	1445.1	4336	1590	29	78	41	37	6004	162	139	70	25	.74	3	5	11	44	0.27	.987
San Francisco	161	1437.1	4312	1675	29	80	34	45	6067	163	137	67	29	.70	1	6	8	43	0.27	.987
Houston	162	1450.0	4350	1710	47	95	37	56	6155	149	126	86	48	.64	1	4	5	55	0.34	.985
Philadelphia	162	1443.2	4331	1694	25	97	44	50	6122	146	138	112	24	.82	0	0	16	49	0.31	.984
Montreal	162	1437.2	4313	1732	38	102	42	60	6147	152	140	40	38	.51	1	2	11	76	0.48	.983
San Diego	162	1431.1	4294	1633	40	102	50	50	6029	141	112	95	25	.79	1	1	15	57	0.36	.983
Chicago	162	1456.1	4369	1681	16	106	44	60	6156	157	136	70	42	.63	2	5	12	64	0.40	.983
Arizona	162	1455.0	4365	1884	22	107	40	66	6165	132	106	84	38	.69	1	3	15	64	0.40	.983
Milwaukee	162	1452.0	4356	1617	29	114	47	66	6087	142	121	100	37	.73	1	3	14	63	0.39	.981
Colorado	162	1420.0	4260	1784	30	116	48	67	6160	165	140	73	42	.63	1	1	11	71	0.45	.981
Los Angeles	162	1457.2	4373	1810	23	119	62	56	6302	164	139	117	75	.61	2	3	8	45	0.28	.981
Atlanta	162	1456.1	4369	1844	25	121	41	78	6374	166	145	91	34	.73	2	3	7	77	0.48	.981
Pittsburgh	162	1444.1	4333	1844	27	123	50	72	6300	159	141	69	26	.73	1	4	10	57	0.36	.980
New York	161	1413.1	4240	1655	30	118	41	77	6013	158	128	98	52	.65	0	7	5	50	0.32	.980
Cincinnati	162	1446.1	4339	1700	33	141	69	72	6180	152	126	77	28	.73	2	1	9	68	0.42	.977
National League	1295	23110.1	69331	27346	480	1696	716	962	98373	2446	2067	1304	587	.69	20	49	163	931	0.36	.983

Career Register

Beyond the obvious:

Age is seasonal age as of June 30, 2004.

For pitchers BFP is batters facing pitcher; TBB is total walks (both intentional and unintentional); Op is save opportunities; Hld is holds.

The Career Register includes Runs Created (RC) for batters and Component ERA (ERC) for pitchers. RC is a method of measuring every facet of a hitter's strengths and weaknesses, and combining those factors into one production number. It was invented by Bill James many years ago and he has revised the formula several times. ERC estimates what a pitcher's ERA should have been based upon his raw pitching statistics, such as Hits, Home Runs, and Walks Allowed, etc. It gives a good indication of whether or not a pitcher "deserved" his ERA, whether he was saved or deserted by pitchers that followed him, etc. ERC was also invented by Bill James. You can find complete definitions and formulas for each in the Baseball Glossary.

Players who have appeared in fewer than three major league seasons have full minor league statistics included. Other 2003 major leaguers who spent time in the minors last year have just their 2003 minor league totals included (indicated by an asterisk).

When a player led the league in a particular category, his register total will be in boldface.

Andy Abad

Bats: L **Throws:** L **Pos:** 1B-7; RF-1; PH-1; PR-1   **Ht:** 5'11" **Wt:** 196 **Born:** 8/25/72 **Age:** 31

Year Team	Lg	G	AB	H	2B	3B	HR	(Hm	Rd)	TB	R	RBI	RC	TBB	IBB	SO	HBP	SH	SF	SB	CS	SB%	GDP	Avg	OBP	Slg
1993 Red Sox	R	59	230	57	9	2	1	(-	-)	73	24	28	25	25	0	27	2	2	4	2	2	.50	2	.248	.322	.317
1994 Sarasota	A+	111	354	102	20	0	2	(-	-)	128	39	35	45	42	4	58	5	5	5	2	12	.14	9	.288	.367	.362
1995 Trenton	AA	89	287	69	14	3	4	(-	-)	101	29	32	33	36	2	58	3	6	3	5	7	.42	6	.240	.328	.352
1995 Sarasota	A+	18	59	17	3	0	0	(-	-)	20	5	10	7	6	0	13	0	0	0	4	3	.57	0	.288	.354	.339
1996 Sarasota	A+	58	202	58	15	1	2	(-	-)	81	28	41	35	37	1	28	3	2	2	10	3	.77	6	.287	.402	.401
1996 Trenton	AA	65	213	59	22	1	4	(-	-)	95	33	39	36	33	2	41	0	0	3	5	3	.63	4	.277	.369	.446
1997 Trenton	AA	45	165	50	13	0	8	(-	-)	87	37	24	36	33	3	27	2	0	1	2	4	.33	2	.303	.423	.527
1997 Pawtucket	AAA	68	227	62	7	0	9	(-	-)	96	28	32	37	36	1	47	2	1	1	3	2	.60	4	.273	.376	.423
1998 Pawtucket	AAA	111	365	112	18	1	16	(-	-)	180	71	66	76	68	2	70	3	4	5	10	6	.63	7	.307	.415	.493
1999 Pawtucket	AAA	102	377	112	21	4	15	(-	-)	186	61	65	70	51	5	50	2	2	3	7	2	.78	9	.297	.381	.493
2000 Sacramento	AAA	124	462	139	19	2	19	(-	-)	219	72	82	81	58	1	67	1	3	2	4	2	.67	12	.301	.379	.474
2001 Sacramento	AAA	124	462	139	19	2	19	(-	-)	219	72	82	81	58	1	67	1	3	2	4	2	.67	12	.301	.379	.474
2002 Calgary	AAA	111	352	106	28	2	11	(-	-)	171	50	70	68	57	1	44	4	0	2	0	3	.00	7	.301	.402	.486
2003 Pawtucket	AAA	134	504	153	35	3	13	(-	-)	233	78	93	83	55	8	67	4	3	7	0	3	.00	15	.304	.372	.462
2001 Oakland	AL	1	1	0	0	0	0	(0	0)	0	0	0	0	0	0	0	0	0	0	0	0	-	0	.000	.000	.000
2003 Boston	AL	9	17	2	0	0	0	(0	0)	2	1	0	0	2	0	5	0	0	0	0	1	.00	1	.118	.211	.118
2 ML YEARS		10	18	2	0	0	0	(0	0)	2	1	0	0	2	0	5	0	0	0	0	1	.00	1	.111	.200	.111

Paul Abbott

Pitches: R **Bats:** R **Pos:** SP-8; RP-2   **Ht:** 6'3" **Wt:** 204 **Born:** 9/15/67 **Age:** 36

Year Team	Lg	G	GS	CG	GF	IP	BFP	H	R	ER	HR	SH	SF	HB	TBB	IBB	SO	WP	Bk	W	L	Pct	ShO	Sv-Op	Hld	ERC	ERA
2003 Tucson*	AAA	11	8	1	1	54.2	242	63	29	24	3	1	3	4	12	0	50	3	0	3	4	.429	1	0- -	1	4.10	3.95
1990 Minnesota	AL	7	7	0	0	34.2	162	37	24	23	0	1	1	1	28	0	25	1	0	0	5	.000	0	0-0	0	5.53	5.97
1991 Minnesota	AL	15	3	0	1	47.1	210	38	27	25	5	7	3	0	36	1	43	5	0	3	1	.750	0	0-0	0	4.42	4.75
1992 Minnesota	AL	6	0	0	5	11.0	50	12	4	4	1	0	1	1	5	0	13	1	0	0	0	-	0	0-0	0	5.10	3.27
1993 Cleveland	AL	5	5	0	0	18.1	84	19	15	13	5	0	0	1	11	1	7	1	0	0	1	.000	0	0-0	0	6.28	6.38
1998 Seattle	AL	4	4	0	0	24.2	105	24	11	11	2	0	1	0	10	0	22	3	0	3	1	.750	0	0-0	0	3.85	4.01
1999 Seattle	AL	25	7	0	8	72.2	298	50	31	25	9	3	4	0	32	3	68	2	0	6	2	.750	0	0-2	3	2.65	3.10
2000 Seattle	AL	35	27	0	2	179.0	766	164	89	84	23	1	4	5	80	4	100	3	0	9	7	.563	0	0-0	4	4.09	4.22
2001 Seattle	AL	28	27	1	0	163.0	710	145	79	77	21	3	5	7	87	5	118	11	0	17	4	.810	0	0-0	0	4.33	4.25
2002 Seattle	AL	7	5	0	1	26.1	137	40	36	35	5	1	1	1	20	0	22	2	0	1	3	.250	0	0-0	0	9.89	11.96
2003 Kansas City	AL	10	8	0	0	47.2	214	47	29	28	8	2	1	2	26	2	32	2	1	1	2	.333	0	0-0	0	5.17	5.29
10 ML YEARS		142	93	1	17	624.2	2736	576	345	325	79	18	21	17	335	16	450	31	1	40	26	.606	0	0-2	7	4.45	4.68

Brent Abernathy

Bats: R **Throws:** R **Pos:** 2B-11; PH-2; PR-1   **Ht:** 6'1" **Wt:** 191 **Born:** 9/23/77 **Age:** 26

Year Team	Lg	G	AB	H	2B	3B	HR	(Hm	Rd)	TB	R	RBI	RC	TBB	IBB	SO	HBP	SH	SF	SB	CS	SB%	GDP	Avg	OBP	Slg
2003 Omaha*	AAA	92	368	107	22	0	7	(-	-)	150	60	40	53	34	3	38	4	6	4	13	7	.65	9	.291	.354	.408
2003 Durham*	AAA	1	5	3	0	0	0	(-	-)	3	0	1	2	0	0	0	0	0	0	0	0	-	0	.600	.600	.600
2001 Tampa Bay	AL	79	304	82	17	1	5	(3	2)	116	43	33	39	27	1	35	0	3	1	8	3	.73	3	.270	.328	.382
2002 Tampa Bay	AL	117	463	112	18	4	2	(2	0)	144	46	40	47	25	0	46	6	8	2	10	4	.71	8	.242	.288	.311
2003 TB-KC	AL	12	34	2	0	0	0	(0	0)	2	3	0	0	1	0	3	0	2	0	1	0	1.00	0	.059	.086	.059
2003 Tampa Bay	AL	2	7	0	0	0	0	(0	0)	0	1	0	0	0	0	0	0	0	0	1	0	1.00	0	.000	.000	.000
2003 Kansas City	AL	10	27	2	0	0	0	(0	0)	2	2	0	0	1	0	3	0	2	0	0	0	-	2	.074	.107	.074
3 ML YEARS		208	801	196	35	5	7	(5	2)	262	92	73	86	53	1	84	6	13	3	19	7	.73	13	.245	.295	.327

Bobby Abreu

Bats: L **Throws:** R **Pos:** RF-158   **Ht:** 6'0" **Wt:** 195 **Born:** 3/11/74 **Age:** 30

Year Team	Lg	G	AB	H	2B	3B	HR	(Hm	Rd)	TB	R	RBI	RC	TBB	IBB	SO	HBP	SH	SF	SB	CS	SB%	GDP	Avg	OBP	Slg
1996 Houston	NL	15	22	5	1	0	0	(0	0)	6	1	1	1	2	0	3	0	0	0	0	0	-	1	.227	.292	.273
1997 Houston	NL	59	188	47	10	2	3	(3	0)	70	22	26	25	21	0	48	1	0	0	7	2	.78	0	.250	.329	.372
1998 Philadelphia	NL	151	497	155	29	6	17	(10	7)	247	68	74	101	84	14	133	0	4	4	19	10	.66	6	.312	.409	.497
1999 Philadelphia	NL	152	546	183	35	11	20	(13	7)	300	118	93	131	109	8	113	3	0	4	27	9	.75	13	.335	.446	.549
2000 Philadelphia	NL	154	576	182	42	10	25	(14	11)	319	103	79	130	100	9	116	1	0	3	28	8	.78	12	.316	.416	.554
2001 Philadelphia	NL	162	588	170	48	4	31	(18	13)	319	118	110	125	106	11	137	1	0	4	36	14	.72	13	.289	.393	.543
2002 Philadelphia	NL	157	572	176	50	6	20	(8	12)	298	102	85	115	104	9	117	3	0	6	31	12	.72	11	.308	.413	.521
2003 Philadelphia	NL	158	577	173	35	1	20	(11	9)	270	99	101	119	109	13	126	2	0	7	22	9	.71	13	.300	.409	.468
8 ML YEARS		1008	3566	1091	250	40	136	(72	64)	1829	631	569	747	635	64	793	11	4	33	170	64	.73	69	.306	.409	.513

Jose Acevedo

Pitches: R **Bats:** R **Pos:** SP-4; RP-1   **Ht:** 6'0" **Wt:** 185 **Born:** 12/18/77 **Age:** 26

Year Team	Lg	G	GS	CG	GF	IP	BFP	H	R	ER	HR	SH	SF	HB	TBB	IBB	SO	WP	Bk	W	L	Pct	ShO	Sv-Op	Hld	ERC	ERA
2003 Louisville*	AAA	29	3	0	9	60.1	253	56	26	23	5	1	2	1	20	1	57	2	0	6	2	.750	0	0- -	1	3.34	3.43
2001 Cincinnati	NL	18	18	0	0	96.0	417	101	61	58	17	6	3	3	34	2	68	4	0	5	7	.417	0	0-0	0	4.84	5.44
2002 Cincinnati	NL	6	5	0	0	23.2	112	28	21	19	8	2	0	2	12	0	14	1	0	4	2	.667	0	0-0	0	7.81	7.23
2003 Cincinnati	NL	5	4	1	1	27.0	103	17	8	8	3	1	2	1	6	1	23	1	0	2	0	1.000	0	0-0	0	1.75	2.67
3 ML YEARS		29	27	1	1	146.2	632	146	90	85	28	9	5	6	52	3	105	6	0	11	9	.550	0	0-0	0	4.64	5.22

Juan Acevedo

Pitches: R **Bats:** R **Pos:** RP-39   **Ht:** 6'2" **Wt:** 228 **Born:** 5/5/70 **Age:** 34

Year Team	Lg	G	GS	CG	GF	IP	BFP	H	R	ER	HR	SH	SF	HB	TBB	IBB	SO	WP	Bk	W	L	Pct	ShO	Sv-Op	Hld	ERC	ERA
1995 Colorado	NL	17	11	0	0	65.2	291	82	53	47	15	4	2	6	20	2	40	2	1	4	6	.400	0	0-0	1	6.65	6.44
1997 New York	NL	25	2	0	4	47.2	215	52	24	19	6	2	5	4	22	2	33	0	1	3	1	.750	0	0-4	3	5.34	3.59
1998 St Louis	NL	50	9	0	29	98.1	394	83	30	28	7	8	1	4	29	2	56	3	0	8	3	.727	0	15-16	3	2.87	2.56
1999 St Louis	NL	50	12	0	21	102.1	457	115	71	67	17	4	6	4	48	3	52	5	0	6	8	.429	0	4-6	4	5.78	5.89
2000 Milwaukee	NL	62	0	0	18	82.2	347	77	38	35	11	1	1	1	31	9	51	3	2	3	7	.300	0	0-2	7	3.74	3.81
2001 Col-Fla	NL	58	0	0	20	60.1	282	68	35	28	6	3	3	2	35	9	47	1	0	2	5	.286	0	0-5	4	5.34	4.18
2002 Detroit	AL	65	0	0	48	74.2	314	68	33	22	4	5	5	5	23	3	43	2	0	1	5	.167	0	28-35	1	3.12	2.65
2003 NYY-Tor	AL	39	0	0	25	38.1	188	52	32	28	6	2	3	2	18	4	28	4	0	1	5	.167	0	6-8	4	6.79	6.57
2001 Colorado	NL	38	0	0	14	32.0	153	37	24	20	4	2	1	1	19	6	26	0	0	0	2	.000	0	0-5	3	5.62	5.63
2001 Florida	NL	20	0	0	6	28.1	129	31	11	8	2	1	2	1	16	3	21	1	0	2	3	.400	0	0-0	1	5.04	2.54
2003 New York	AL	25	0	0	19	25.2	125	34	24	22	5	2	3	2	10	3	19	2	0	0	3	.000	0	6-7	3	6.57	7.71
2003 Toronto	AL	14	0	0	6	12.2	63	18	8	6	1	0	0	0	8	1	9	2	0	1	2	.333	0	0-1	1	7.20	4.26
8 ML YEARS		366	34	0	165	570.0	2488	597	316	274	72	29	26	28	226	34	350	20	4	28	40	.412	0	53-76	27	4.66	4.33

Terry Adams

Pitches: R **Bats:** R **Pos:** RP-66   **Ht:** 6'3" **Wt:** 215 **Born:** 3/6/73 **Age:** 31

Year Team	Lg	G	GS	CG	GF	IP	BFP	H	R	ER	HR	SH	SF	HB	TBB	IBB	SO	WP	Bk	W	L	Pct	ShO	Sv-Op	Hld	ERC	ERA
1995 Chicago	NL	18	0	0	7	18.0	86	22	15	13	0	0	0	0	10	1	15	1	0	1	1	.500	0	1-1	0	4.95	6.50
1996 Chicago	NL	69	0	0	22	101.0	423	84	36	33	6	7	3	1	49	6	78	5	1	3	6	.333	0	4-8	11	3.20	2.94
1997 Chicago	NL	74	0	0	39	74.0	341	91	43	38	3	1	2	1	40	6	64	6	0	2	9	.182	0	18-22	11	5.49	4.62
1998 Chicago	NL	63	0	0	15	72.2	330	72	39	35	7	3	3	1	41	3	73	4	3	7	7	.500	0	1-7	13	4.55	4.33
1999 Chicago	NL	52	0	0	38	65.0	277	60	33	29	9	1	3	0	28	2	57	6	0	6	3	.667	0	13-18	3	4.00	4.02
2000 Los Angeles	NL	66	0	0	18	84.1	369	80	42	33	6	3	0	0	39	0	56	5	0	6	9	.400	0	2-7	15	3.77	3.52
2001 Los Angeles	NL	43	22	0	10	166.1	708	172	84	80	9	6	0	3	54	1	141	7	2	12	8	.600	0	0-1	4	3.74	4.33
2002 Philadelphia	NL	46	19	0	10	136.2	590	132	76	66	9	10	2	3	58	5	96	8	0	7	9	.438	0	0-1	12	3.71	4.35
2003 Philadelphia	NL	66	0	0	16	68.0	284	68	22	20	1	3	2	2	23	4	51	4	0	1	4	.200	0	0-0	16	3.35	2.65
9 ML YEARS		497	41	0	175	786.0	3408	781	390	347	50	34	15	11	342	28	631	46	6	45	56	.446	0	39-65	85	3.92	3.97

Jon Adkins

Pitches: R **Bats:** L **Pos:** RP-4   **Ht:** 6'0" **Wt:** 200 **Born:** 8/30/77 **Age:** 26

Year Team	Lg	G	GS	CG	GF	IP	BFP	H	R	ER	HR	SH	SF	HB	TBB	IBB	SO	WP	Bk	W	L	Pct	ShO	Sv-Op	Hld	ERC	ERA
1999 Modesto	A+	26	15	0	2	102.0	460	113	65	54	6	4	6	9	30	1	93	8	0	9	5	.643	0	1--	-	4.17	4.76
2000 Sacramento	AAA	1	1	0	0	4.0	19	6	4	4	2	0	0	0	1	0	2	0	0	0	1	.000	0	0--	-	9.51	9.00
2000 Modesto	A+	9	7	1	0	49.2	203	41	17	10	1	1	2	1	17	0	38	2	0	5	2	.714	0	0--	-	2.51	1.81
2001 Midland	AA	24	24	1	0	137.1	590	147	71	68	9	5	2	9	36	1	74	0	0	8	8	.500	1	0--	-	3.94	4.46
2001 Sacramento	AAA	3	2	0	0	12.2	60	17	9	6	1	1	0	0	8	0	7	0	0	1	0	1.000	0	0--	-	7.11	4.26
2002 Sacramento	AAA	20	20	0	0	97.0	457	139	74	65	9	3	4	6	33	0	76	2	0	7	6	.538	0	0--	-	6.63	6.03
2002 Modesto	A+	1	1	0	0	6.2	32	11	7	6	0	1	0	1	1	0	4	1	0	0	1	.000	0	0--	-	6.79	8.10
2002 Charlotte	AAA	8	7	1	1	46.1	196	47	20	19	4	0	1	2	12	0	31	1	0	4	2	.667	0	0--	-	3.68	3.69
2003 Charlotte	AAA	26	19	1	2	122.2	518	119	65	54	11	2	7	7	34	1	59	2	1	7	8	.467	1	1--	-	3.57	3.96
2003 Chicago	AL	4	0	0	2	9.1	42	8	5	5	1	1	1	1	7	0	3	0	0	0	0	-	0	0-0	0	5.27	4.82

Jeremy Affeldt

Pitches: L **Bats:** L **Pos:** SP-18; RP-18   **Ht:** 6'4" **Wt:** 215 **Born:** 6/6/79 **Age:** 25

Year Team	Lg	G	GS	CG	GF	IP	BFP	H	R	ER	HR	SH	SF	HB	TBB	IBB	SO	WP	Bk	W	L	Pct	ShO	Sv-Op	Hld	ERC	ERA
1997 Royals	R	10	9	0	0	40.0	171	34	24	20	3	2	3	5	21	0	36	4	2	2	0	1.000	0	0--	-	4.17	4.50
1998 Lansing	A	6	3	0	0	17.0	90	27	21	18	1	0	1	0	12	0	8	2	0	0	3	.000	0	0--	-	8.46	9.53
1998 Royals	R	12	9	0	0	56.0	241	50	24	18	1	3	0	8	24	0	67	7	0	4	3	.571	0	0--	-	3.61	2.89
1999 Chrlstn - WV	A	27	24	2	1	143.1	637	140	78	61	4	9	4	8	60	0	111	14	4	7	7	.500	1	0--	-	4.28	3.83
2000 Wilmington	A+	27	26	0	0	147.1	656	158	87	67	7	8	5	10	59	0	92	17	1	5	15	.250	0	0--	-	4.35	4.09
2001 Wichita	AA	25	25	0	0	145.1	621	153	74	63	9	6	5	10	46	0	128	3	1	10	6	.625	0	0--	-	4.11	3.90
2002 Wichita	AA	3	3	0	0	6.0	21	1	1	1	0	0	0	1	3	0	3	2	0	0	0	-	0	0--	-	0.90	1.50
2002 Kansas City	AL	34	7	0	4	77.2	353	85	41	40	8	2	1	3	37	4	67	5	2	3	4	.429	0	0-1	1	4.97	4.64
2003 Kansas City	AL	36	18	0	5	126.0	533	126	58	55	12	2	5	5	38	1	98	2	1	7	6	.538	0	4-4	3	3.82	3.93
2 ML YEARS		70	25	0	9	203.2	886	211	99	95	20	4	6	8	75	5	165	7	3	10	10	.500	0	4-5	4	4.25	4.20

Kurt Ainsworth

Pitches: R **Bats:** R **Pos:** SP-11; RP-3   **Ht:** 6'3" **Wt:** 192 **Born:** 9/9/78 **Age:** 25

Year Team	Lg	G	GS	CG	GF	IP	BFP	H	R	ER	HR	SH	SF	HB	TBB	IBB	SO	WP	Bk	W	L	Pct	ShO	Sv-Op	Hld	ERC	ERA
2003 Fresno*	AAA	1	1	0	0	2.0	10	2	1	1	0	0	0	0	2	0	1	0	0	0	0	-	0	0--	-	5.48	4.50
2001 San Francisco	NL	2	0	0	2	2.0	12	3	3	3	1	0	0	1	2	0	3	0	0	0	0	-	0	0-0	0	16.26	13.50
2002 San Francisco	NL	6	4	0	0	25.2	108	22	7	6	1	2	0	1	12	0	15	1	0	1	2	.333	0	0-0	0	3.34	2.10
2003 SF-Bal		14	11	0	0	68.1	298	72	34	31	8	2	2	1	27	0	52	2	0	5	5	.500	0	0-0	0	4.55	4.08
2003 San Francisco	NL	11	11	0	0	66.0	283	66	31	28	7	2	2	1	26	0	48	2	0	5	4	.556	0	0-0	0	4.19	3.82
2003 Baltimore	AL	3	0	0	2	2.1	15	6	3	3	1	0	0	0	1	0	4	0	0	0	1	.000	0	0-0	0	16.91	11.57
3 ML YEARS		22	15	0	4	96.0	418	97	44	40	10	4	2	3	41	0	70	3	0	6	7	.462	0	0-0	0	4.42	3.75

Antonio Alfonseca

Pitches: R **Bats:** R **Pos:** RP-60   **Ht:** 6'5" **Wt:** 250 **Born:** 4/16/72 **Age:** 32

Year Team	Lg	HOW MUCH HE PITCHED						WHAT HE GAVE UP												THE RESULTS							
		G	GS	CG	GF	IP	BFP	H	R	ER	HR	SH	SF	HB	TBB	IBB	SO	WP	Bk	W	L	Pct	ShO	Sv-Op	Hld	ERC	ERA
2003 Iowa*	AAA	3	0	0	2	3.2	19	6	2	2	0	1	0	1	0	5	0	0	0	0	1	.000	0	0- -	-	6.01	4.91
1997 Florida	NL	17	0	0	2	25.2	123	36	16	14	3	1	0	1	10	3	19	1	0	1	3	.250	0	0-2	6	6.41	4.91
1998 Florida	NL	58	0	0	27	70.2	316	75	32	32	10	7	6	3	33	9	46	1	0	4	6	.400	0	8-14	9	4.96	4.08
1999 Florida	NL	73	0	0	49	77.2	325	79	28	28	4	3	1	4	29	6	46	1	0	4	5	.444	0	21-25	5	3.96	3.24
2000 Florida	NL	68	0	0	62	70.0	311	82	35	33	7	3	1	1	24	3	47	0	2	5	6	.455	0	**45**-49	0	4.79	4.24
2001 Florida	NL	58	0	0	52	61.2	268	68	24	21	6	5	1	5	15	3	40	2	0	4	4	.500	0	28-34	0	4.24	3.06
2002 Chicago	NL	66	0	0	55	74.1	330	73	34	33	5	4	3	3	36	3	61	1	0	2	5	.286	0	19-28	6	4.12	4.00
2003 Chicago	NL	60	0	0	17	66.1	296	76	43	43	7	4	1	2	27	3	51	0	0	3	1	.750	0	0-4	9	5.05	5.83
7 ML YEARS		400	0	0	264	446.1	1969	489	212	204	42	27	13	19	174	30	310	6	2	23	30	.434	0	121-156	23	4.61	4.11

Edgardo Alfonzo

Bats: R **Throws:** R **Pos:** 3B-133; 2B-6; PH-3   **Ht:** 5'11" **Wt:** 187 **Born:** 11/8/73 **Age:** 30

Year Team	Lg	BATTING																			BASERUNNING				AVERAGES		
		G	AB	H	2B	3B	HR	(Hm	Rd)	TB	R	RBI	RC	TBB	IBB	SO	HBP	SH	SF	SB	CS	SB%	GDP	Avg	OBP	Slg
1995 New York	NL	101	335	93	13	5	4	(0	4)	128	26	41	37	12	1	37	1	4	4	1	1	.50	7	.278	.301	.382
1996 New York	NL	123	368	96	15	2	4	(2	2)	127	36	40	38	25	2	56	0	9	5	2	0	1.00	8	.261	.304	.345
1997 New York	NL	151	518	163	27	2	10	(4	6)	224	84	72	91	63	0	56	5	8	5	11	6	.65	4	.315	.391	.432
1998 New York	NL	144	557	155	28	2	17	(8	9)	238	94	78	85	65	1	77	3	2	3	8	3	.73	11	.278	.355	.427
1999 New York	NL	158	628	191	41	1	27	(11	16)	315	123	108	121	85	2	85	3	1	9	9	2	.82	14	.304	.385	.502
2000 New York	NL	150	544	176	40	2	25	(13	12)	295	109	94	122	95	1	70	5	0	6	3	2	.60	12	.324	.425	.542
2001 New York	NL	124	457	111	22	0	17	(6	11)	184	64	49	62	51	0	62	5	1	5	5	0	1.00	8	.243	.322	.403
2002 New York	NL	135	490	151	26	0	16	(8	8)	225	78	56	89	62	8	55	7	0	3	6	0	1.00	5	.308	.391	.459
2003 San Francisco	NL	142	514	133	25	2	13	(6	7)	201	56	81	75	58	4	41	4	3	7	5	2	.71	14	.259	.334	.391
9 ML YEARS		1228	4411	1269	237	16	133	(58	75)	1937	670	619	720	516	19	539	33	28	47	50	16	.76	82	.288	.363	.439

Chad Allen

Bats: R **Throws:** R **Pos:** LF-6; PH-4; RF-2; CF-1; DH-1; PR-1   **Ht:** 6'1" **Wt:** 195 **Born:** 2/6/75 **Age:** 29

Year Team	Lg	BATTING																			BASERUNNING				AVERAGES		
		G	AB	H	2B	3B	HR	(Hm	Rd)	TB	R	RBI	RC	TBB	IBB	SO	HBP	SH	SF	SB	CS	SB%	GDP	Avg	OBP	Slg
2003 Albuquerque*	AAA	91	337	109	30	2	8	(-	-)	167	45	53	56	18	0	48	6	5	4	11	10	.52	10	.323	.364	.496
1999 Minnesota	AL	137	481	133	21	3	10	(4	6)	190	69	46	61	37	1	89	2	1	2	14	7	.67	10	.277	.330	.395
2000 Minnesota	AL	15	50	15	3	0	0	(0	0)	18	2	7	6	3	0	14	1	0	1	0	2	.00	1	.300	.345	.360
2001 Minnesota	AL	57	175	46	13	2	4	(1	3)	75	20	20	23	19	1	37	0	0	1	1	2	.33	7	.263	.333	.429
2002 Cleveland	AL	5	10	1	1	0	0	(0	0)	2	0	0	0	0	0	2	0	1	0	0	0	-	1	.100	.100	.200
2003 Florida	NL	12	24	5	1	1	0	(0	0)	8	2	0	0	0	0	5	1	0	0	0	0	-	1	.208	.240	.333
5 ML YEARS		226	740	200	39	6	14	(5	9)	293	93	73	90	59	2	147	4	2	4	15	11	.58	20	.270	.326	.396

Luke Allen

Bats: L **Throws:** R **Pos:** PH-2   **Ht:** 6'2" **Wt:** 208 **Born:** 8/4/78 **Age:** 25

Year Team	Lg	BATTING																			BASERUNNING				AVERAGES		
		G	AB	H	2B	3B	HR	(Hm	Rd)	TB	R	RBI	RC	TBB	IBB	SO	HBP	SH	SF	SB	CS	SB%	GDP	Avg	OBP	Slg
1997 Great Falls	R+	67	258	89	12	6	7	(-	-)	134	50	40	48	19	1	53	0	1	0	12	11	.52	3	.345	.390	.519
1998 Sn Brnardino	A+	105	399	119	25	6	4	(-	-)	168	51	46	58	30	0	93	3	7	4	18	11	.62	4	.298	.349	.421
1998 San Antonio	AA	23	78	26	3	1	3	(-	-)	40	9	10	14	6	1	16	0	1	0	1	2	.33	0	.333	.381	.513
1999 San Antonio	AA	137	533	150	16	12	14	(-	-)	232	90	82	77	44	0	102	1	2	2	14	8	.64	8	.281	.336	.435
2000 San Antonio	AA	90	339	90	15	5	7	(-	-)	136	55	60	46	40	3	71	1	0	5	14	5	.74	10	.265	.340	.401
2001 Jacksonville	AA	125	486	141	32	6	16	(-	-)	233	74	73	80	42	3	111	1	1	5	13	3	.81	7	.290	.345	.479
2001 Las Vegas	AAA	2	9	2	1	0	0	(-	-)	3	1	0	0	0	0	0	0	0	0	0	0	-	1	.222	.222	.333
2002 Las Vegas	AAA	137	501	165	28	3	12	(-	-)	235	85	78	89	56	3	77	2	0	5	4	6	.40	12	.329	.395	.469
2003 Co Springs	AAA	127	438	120	21	3	6	(-	-)	165	65	45	55	51	4	78	0	0	5	9	12	.43	11	.274	.346	.377
2002 Los Angeles	NL	6	7	1	1	0	0	(0	0)	2	2	0	1	2	0	3	0	0	0	0	0	-	0	.143	.333	.286
2003 Colorado	NL	2	2	0	0	0	0	(0	0)	0	0	0	0	0	0	0	0	0	0	0	0	-	1	.000	.000	.000
2 ML YEARS		8	9	1	1	0	0	(0	0)	2	2	0	1	2	0	3	0	0	0	0	0	-	1	.111	.273	.222

Armando Almanza

Pitches: L **Bats:** L **Pos:** RP-51   **Ht:** 6'3" **Wt:** 240 **Born:** 10/26/72 **Age:** 31

Year Team	Lg	HOW MUCH HE PITCHED						WHAT HE GAVE UP													THE RESULTS							
		G	GS	CG	GF	IP	BFP	H	R	ER	HR	SH	SF	HB	TBB	IBB	SO	WP	Bk	W	L	Pct	ShO	Sv-Op	Hld	ERC	ERA
1999 Florida	NL	14	0	0	2	15.2	64	8	4	3	1	1	1	1	9	1	20	0	1	0	1	.000	0	0-0	3	2.09	1.72
2000 Florida	NL	67	0	0	8	46.1	216	38	27	25	3	2	2	2	43	6	46	1	0	4	2	.667	0	0-4	13	4.79	4.86
2001 Florida	NL	52	0	0	8	41.0	178	34	24	22	8	1	3	0	26	1	45	2	0	2	2	.500	0	0-2	12	4.73	4.83
2002 Florida	NL	51	0	0	10	45.2	191	36	22	22	8	3	3	0	23	1	57	2	1	3	2	.600	0	2-4	12	3.83	4.34
2003 Florida	NL	51	0	0	15	50.1	230	59	37	34	10	1	3	2	25	2	49	2	1	4	5	.444	0	0-2	6	6.42	6.08
5 ML YEARS		235	0	0	43	199.0	879	175	114	106	30	8	12	5	126	11	217	7	3	13	12	.520	0	2-12	46	4.73	4.79

Edwin Almonte

Pitches: R **Bats:** R **Pos:** RP-12   **Ht:** 6'3" **Wt:** 220 **Born:** 12/17/76 **Age:** 27

Year Team	Lg	HOW MUCH HE PITCHED						WHAT HE GAVE UP													THE RESULTS							
		G	GS	CG	GF	IP	BFP	H	R	ER	HR	SH	SF	HB	TBB	IBB	SO	WP	Bk	W	L	Pct	ShO	Sv-Op	Hld	ERC	ERA
1998 White Sox	R	5	0	0	2	9.2	37	6	5	1	0	0	0	1	1	0	8	0	0	0	0		0	0- -	-	1.18	0.93
1998 Bristol	R+	8	3	0	0	26.2	113	29	14	10	3	0	1	1	4	0	26	2	0	3	0	1.000	0	0- -	-	3.76	3.38
1999 Burlington	A	37	5	2	16	115.2	480	107	48	39	5	2	1	2	28	4	85	6	1	9	12	.429	0	5- -	-	2.69	3.03
2000 Winstn-Salm	A+	33	7	0	10	77.0	320	66	32	27	2	3	1	5	20	0	73	4	1	3	1	.750	0	2- -	-	2.52	3.16
2000 Birmingham	AA	7	6	0	0	39.2	159	45	22	20	5	0	1	1	9	0	21	2	0	1	3	.250	0	0- -	-	4.78	4.54
2001 Birmingham	AA	54	0	0	46	66.1	272	58	16	11	4	4	0	0	16	4	62	2	0	1	4	.200	0	36- -	-	2.44	1.49

12

Year Team	Lg	G	GS	CG	GF	IP	BFP	H	R	ER	HR	SH	SF	HB	TBB	IBB	SO	WP	Bk	W	L	Pct	ShO	Sv-Op	Hld	ERC	ERA
2002 Charlotte	AAA	50	0	0	44	60.1	238	52	16	15	6	3	1	2	12	2	56	0	0	2	3	.400	0	26--		2.73	2.24
2003 Charlotte	AAA	30	0	0	22	34.0	159	45	27	26	6	5	3	1	14	4	24	1	0	2	6	.250	0	14--		6.54	6.88
2003 Norfolk	AAA	16	0	0	14	17.2	77	16	5	5	0	1	1	1	6	0	14	0	0	1	1	.500	0	6--		2.76	2.55
2003 New York	NL	12	0	0	3	11.1	57	21	15	14	3	1	0	0	5	1	7	1	0	0	0	-	0	0-0	2	11.40	11.12

Erick Almonte

Bats: R **Throws:** R **Pos:** SS-31

Ht: 6'2" **Wt:** 180 **Born:** 2/1/78 **Age:** 26

Year Team	Lg	G	AB	H	2B	3B	HR	(Hm	Rd)	TB	R	RBI	RC	TBB	IBB	SO	HBP	SH	SF	SB	CS	SB%	GDP	Avg	OBP	Slg
1997 Yankees	R	52	180	51	4	4	3	(-	-)	72	32	31	26	21	1	27	0	1	2	8	2	.80	5	.283	.355	.400
1998 Greensboro	A	120	450	94	13	0	6	(-	-)	125	53	33	26	29	0	121	3	7	2	6	2	.75	17	.209	.260	.278
1999 Tampa	A+	61	230	59	8	2	5	(-	-)	86	36	25	26	18	0	49	2	5	2	3	1	.75	6	.257	.313	.374
1999 Yankees	R	9	30	9	2	0	2	(-	-)	17	5	9	6	3	0	10	0	0	2	1	0	1.00	1	.300	.343	.567
2000 Norwich	AA	131	454	123	18	4	15	(-	-)	194	56	77	66	35	0	129	3	12	3	12	2	.86	3	.271	.326	.427
2001 Columbus	AAA	97	345	99	19	3	12	(-	-)	160	55	55	57	44	1	90	2	7	2	4	5	.44	7	.287	.369	.464
2001 Norwich	AA	3	12	3	0	0	0	(-	-)	3	2	0	1	1	0	6	0	0	0	1	0	1.00	0	.250	.308	.250
2002 Columbus	AAA	66	221	52	10	1	9	(-	-)	91	25	28	26	15	0	60	0	0	2	2	1	.67	2	.235	.282	.412
2002 Norwich	AA	53	187	45	7	0	8	(-	-)	76	28	33	27	30	2	59	0	3	2	10	2	.83	6	.241	.342	.406
2003 Yankees	R	6	21	6	0	0	0	(-	-)	6	4	0	3	5	1	9	0	0	0	0	0	-	0	.286	.423	.286
2003 Columbus	AAA	48	179	43	11	1	4	(-	-)	68	26	26	20	17	2	46	1	2	0	4	3	.57	5	.240	.310	.380
2001 New York	AL	8	4	2	1	0	0	(0	0)	3	0	0	2	0	0	1	0	0	0	2	0	1.00	0	.500	.500	.750
2003 New York	AL	31	100	26	6	0	1	(0	1)	35	17	11	10	8	0	24	1	2	0	1	0	1.00	3	.260	.321	.350
2 ML YEARS		39	104	28	7	0	1	(0	1)	38	17	11	12	8	0	25	1	2	0	3	0	1.00	3	.269	.327	.365

Hector Almonte

Pitches: R **Bats:** R **Pos:** RP-35

Ht: 6'2" **Wt:** 190 **Born:** 10/17/75 **Age:** 28

Year Team	Lg	G	GS	CG	GF	IP	BFP	H	R	ER	HR	SH	SF	HB	TBB	IBB	SO	WP	Bk	W	L	Pct	ShO	Sv-Op	Hld	ERC	ERA
1997 Marlins	R	8	0	0	7	23.2	89	12	3	2	0	0	1	2	6	0	25	1	0	2	0	1.000	0	5--		1.15	0.76
1997 Kane County	A	8	1	0	3	14.0	59	11	6	6	1	1	2	1	6	0	10	2	0	1	1	1.000	0	1--		3.10	3.86
1998 Kane County	A	43	0	0	41	43.1	200	51	22	19	5	1	1	1	19	0	51	3	2	1	5	.167	0	21--		5.37	3.95
1999 Portland	AA	47	0	0	41	44.1	202	42	14	14	1	8	1	2	26	3	42	4	0	1	4	.200	0	23--		3.90	2.84
2000 Calgary	AAA	18	0	0	13	19.1	98	36	24	24	7	1	0	0	9	0	16	2	1	0	4	.000	0	0--		12.77	11.17
2000 Marlins	R	1	1	0	0	2.0	8	3	1	1	0	0	0	0	1	0	2	0	0	0	0	-	0	3--		8.24	4.50
2000 Brevard Cnty	A+	8	2	0	3	15.1	61	11	6	4	2	1	0	2	5	0	16	1	0	1	1	.500	0	0--		3.09	2.35
2000 Portland	AA	4	0	0	4	5.0	25	5	2	2	1	0	0	0	4	0	6	0	0	1	0	1.000	0	3--		6.09	3.60
2001 Calgary	AAA	18	0	0	11	24.2	123	36	29	23	6	0	2	0	15	0	21	2	0	0	0	-	0	0--		9.01	8.39
2003 Pawtucket	AAA	21	0	0	17	26.0	97	16	5	5	2	0	0	0	6	0	28	0	0	3	0	1.000	0	9--		1.54	1.73
1999 Florida	NL	15	0	0	0	15.0	67	20	0	7	1	0	0	0	6	0	8	0	0	0	2	.000	0	0-0	0	5.99	4.20
2003 Bos-Mon		35	0	0	9	36.2	175	43	29	29	5	2	2	2	24	3	32	6	0	1	2	.333	0	0-1	3	6.52	7.12
2003 Boston	AL	7	0	0	4	7.2	38	9	7	7	1	1	2	0	7	1	6	1	0	1	0	1.000	0	0-0	0	7.28	8.22
2003 Montreal	NL	28	0	0	5	29.0	137	34	22	22	4	1	0	2	17	2	26	5	0	1	1	.500	0	0-1	3	6.32	6.83
2 ML YEARS		50	0	0	9	51.2	242	63	29	36	6	2	2	2	30	3	40	6	0	1	4	.200	0	0-1	3	6.36	6.27

Roberto Alomar

Bats: B **Throws:** R **Pos:** 2B-139; PH-6

Ht: 6'0" **Wt:** 185 **Born:** 2/5/68 **Age:** 36

Year Team	Lg	G	AB	H	2B	3B	HR	(Hm	Rd)	TB	R	RBI	RC	TBB	IBB	SO	HBP	SH	SF	SB	CS	SB%	GDP	Avg	OBP	Slg
1988 San Diego	NL	143	545	145	24	6	9	(5	4)	208	84	41	68	47	5	83	3	16	0	24	6	.80	15	.266	.328	.382
1989 San Diego	NL	158	623	184	27	1	7	(3	4)	234	82	56	85	53	4	76	1	17	8	42	17	.71	10	.295	.347	.376
1990 San Diego	NL	147	586	168	27	5	6	(4	2)	223	80	60	76	48	1	72	2	5	5	24	7	.77	16	.287	.340	.381
1991 Toronto	AL	161	637	188	41	11	9	(6	3)	278	88	69	106	57	3	86	4	16	5	53	11	.83	5	.295	.354	.436
1992 Toronto	AL	152	571	177	27	8	8	(5	3)	244	105	76	109	87	5	52	5	6	2	49	9	.84	5	.310	.405	.427
1993 Toronto	AL	153	589	192	35	6	17	(8	9)	290	109	93	121	80	5	67	5	4	5	55	15	.79	13	.326	.408	.492
1994 Toronto	AL	107	392	120	25	4	8	(4	4)	177	78	38	67	51	2	41	2	7	3	19	8	.70	14	.306	.386	.452
1995 Toronto	AL	130	517	155	24	7	13	(7	6)	232	71	66	84	47	3	45	0	6	7	30	3	.91	16	.300	.354	.449
1996 Baltimore	AL	153	588	193	43	4	22	(14	8)	310	132	94	126	90	10	65	1	8	12	17	6	.74	14	.328	.411	.527
1997 Baltimore	AL	112	412	137	23	2	14	(10	4)	206	64	60	78	40	2	43	3	7	7	9	3	.75	10	.333	.390	.500
1998 Baltimore	AL	147	588	166	36	1	14	(7	7)	246	86	56	87	59	3	70	2	3	5	18	5	.78	11	.282	.347	.418
1999 Cleveland	AL	159	563	182	40	3	24	(12	12)	300	138	120	131	99	3	96	7	12	13	37	6	.86	13	.323	.422	.533
2000 Cleveland	AL	155	610	189	40	2	19	(8	11)	290	111	89	111	64	4	82	6	11	6	39	4	.91	19	.310	.378	.475
2001 Cleveland	AL	157	575	193	34	12	20	(7	13)	311	113	100	130	80	5	71	4	9	9	30	6	.83	9	.336	.415	.541
2002 New York	NL	149	590	157	24	4	11	(4	7)	222	73	53	74	57	4	83	1	6	1	16	4	.80	12	.266	.331	.376
2003 NYM-CWS		140	516	133	28	2	5	(3	2)	180	76	39	64	59	3	77	3	12	8	12	2	.86	17	.258	.333	.349
2003 New York	NL	73	263	69	17	1	2	(1	1)	94	34	22	36	29	2	40	2	4	4	6	0	1.00	8	.262	.336	.357
2003 Chicago	AL	67	253	64	11	1	3	(2	1)	86	42	17	28	30	1	37	1	8	4	6	2	.75	9	.253	.330	.340
16 ML YEARS		2323	8902	2679	498	78	206	(107	99)	3951	1490	1110	1517	1018	62	1109	49	145	96	474	112	.81	202	.301	.372	.444

Sandy Alomar Jr.

Bats: R **Throws:** R **Pos:** C-75; PH-3

Ht: 6'5" **Wt:** 235 **Born:** 6/18/66 **Age:** 38

Year Team	Lg	G	AB	H	2B	3B	HR	(Hm	Rd)	TB	R	RBI	RC	TBB	IBB	SO	HBP	SH	SF	SB	CS	SB%	GDP	Avg	OBP	Slg
1988 San Diego	NL	1	1	0	0	0	0	(0	0)	0	0	0	0	0	0	1	0	0	0	0	0	-	0	.000	.000	.000
1989 San Diego	NL	7	19	4	1	0	1	(1	0)	8	1	6	2	3	1	3	0	0	0	0	0	-	1	.211	.318	.421
1990 Cleveland	AL	132	445	129	26	2	9	(5	4)	186	60	66	60	25	2	46	2	5	6	4	1	.80	10	.290	.326	.418
1991 Cleveland	AL	51	184	40	9	0	0	(0	0)	49	10	7	10	8	1	24	4	2	1	0	4	.00	4	.217	.264	.266
1992 Cleveland	AL	89	299	75	16	0	2	(1	1)	97	22	26	26	13	3	32	5	3	0	3	3	.50	7	.251	.293	.324
1993 Cleveland	AL	64	215	58	7	1	6	(3	3)	85	24	32	28	11	0	28	6	1	4	3	1	.75	3	.270	.318	.395
1994 Cleveland	AL	80	292	84	15	1	14	(4	10)	143	44	43	48	25	2	31	2	0	1	8	4	.67	7	.288	.347	.490
1995 Cleveland	AL	66	203	61	6	0	10	(4	6)	97	32	35	30	7	0	26	3	1	1	3	1	.75	8	.300	.332	.478

Year Team	Lg	G	AB	H	2B	3B	HR	(Hm Rd)	TB	R	RBI	RC	TBB	IBB	SO	HBP	SH	SF	SB	CS	SB%	GDP	Avg	OBP	Slg
1996 Cleveland	AL	127	418	110	23	0	11	(3 8)	166	53	50	44	19	0	42	3	2	2	1	0	1.00	20	.263	.299	.397
1997 Cleveland	AL	125	451	146	37	0	21	(9 12)	246	63	83	78	19	2	48	3	6	1	0	2	.00	16	.324	.354	.545
1998 Cleveland	AL	117	409	96	26	2	6	(3 3)	144	45	44	33	18	0	45	3	5	3	0	3	.00	15	.235	.270	.352
1999 Cleveland	AL	37	137	42	13	0	6	(4 2)	73	19	25	23	4	0	23	0	1	2	0	1	.00	1	.307	.322	.533
2000 Cleveland	AL	97	356	103	16	2	7	(5 2)	144	44	42	45	16	1	41	4	4	4	2	2	.50	9	.289	.324	.404
2001 Chicago	AL	70	220	54	8	1	4	(1 3)	76	17	21	20	12	1	17	2	3	2	1	2	.33	6	.245	.288	.345
2002 CWS-Col		89	283	79	14	1	7	(5 2)	116	29	37	29	9	0	33	1	1	2	0	0	-	11	.279	.302	.410
2003 Chicago	AL	55	194	52	12	0	5	(3 2)	79	22	26	21	4	0	17	0	5	1	0	0	-	4	.268	.281	.407
2002 Chicago	AL	51	167	48	10	1	7	(5 2)	81	21	25	22	5	0	14	1	1	2	0	0	-	5	.287	.309	.485
2002 Colorado	NL	38	116	31	4	0	0	(0 0)	35	8	12	7	4	0	19	0	0	0	0	0	-	6	.267	.292	.302
16 ML YEARS		1227	4126	1133	229	10	109	(51 58)	1709	485	543	497	193	13	457	38	42	30	25	24	.51	122	.275	.311	.414

Moises Alou

Bats: R Throws: R Pos: LF-142; DH-9; PH-1   Ht: 6'3" Wt: 220 Born: 7/3/66 Age: 37

Year Team	Lg	G	AB	H	2B	3B	HR	(Hm Rd)	TB	R	RBI	RC	TBB	IBB	SO	HBP	SH	SF	SB	CS	SB%	GDP	Avg	OBP	Slg
1990 Pit-Mon	NL	16	20	4	0	1	0	(0 0)	6	4	0	1	0	0	3	0	1	0	0	0	-	1	.200	.200	.300
1992 Montreal	NL	115	341	96	28	2	9	(6 3)	155	53	56	53	25	0	46	1	5	5	16	2	.89	5	.282	.328	.455
1993 Montreal	NL	136	482	138	29	6	18	(10 8)	233	70	85	79	38	9	53	5	3	7	17	6	.74	9	.286	.340	.483
1994 Montreal	NL	107	422	143	31	5	22	(9 13)	250	81	78	92	42	10	63	2	0	5	7	6	.54	7	.339	.397	.592
1995 Montreal	NL	93	344	94	22	0	14	(4 10)	158	48	58	52	29	6	56	9	0	4	4	3	.57	9	.273	.342	.459
1996 Montreal	NL	143	540	152	28	2	21	(14 7)	247	87	96	81	49	7	83	2	0	7	9	4	.69	15	.281	.339	.457
1997 Florida	NL	150	538	157	29	5	23	(12 11)	265	88	115	97	70	9	85	4	0	7	9	5	.64	13	.292	.373	.493
1998 Houston	NL	159	584	182	34	5	38	(19 19)	340	104	124	130	84	11	87	5	0	6	11	3	.79	14	.312	.399	.582
2000 Houston	NL	126	454	161	28	2	30	(17 13)	283	82	114	104	52	4	45	2	0	9	3	3	.50	21	.355	.416	.623
2001 Houston	NL	136	513	170	31	1	27	(15 12)	284	79	108	104	57	14	57	3	0	8	5	1	.83	18	.331	.396	.554
2002 Chicago	NL	132	484	133	23	1	15	(7 8)	203	50	61	58	47	4	61	0	0	3	8	0	1.00	15	.275	.337	.419
2003 Chicago	NL	151	565	158	35	1	22	(14 8)	261	83	91	94	63	7	67	7	0	3	3	1	.75	16	.280	.357	.462
1990 Pittsburgh	NL	2	5	1	0	0	0	(0 0)	1	0	0	0	0	0	0	0	0	0	0	0	-	1	.200	.200	.200
1990 Montreal	NL	14	15	3	0	1	0	(0 0)	5	4	0	1	0	0	3	0	1	0	0	0	-	0	.200	.200	.333
12 ML YEARS		1464	5287	1588	318	31	239	(127 112)	2685	829	986	945	556	81	706	40	9	64	92	34	.73	143	.300	.367	.508

Juan Alvarez

Pitches: L Bats: L Pos: RP-9   Ht: 6'0" Wt: 175 Born: 8/9/73 Age: 30

Year Team	Lg	G	GS	CG	GF	IP	BFP	H	R	ER	HR	SH	SF	HB	TBB	IBB	SO	WP	Bk	W	L	Pct	ShO	Sv-Op	Hld	ERC	ERA
2003 Albuquerque*	AAA	51	0	0	15	52.0	245	69	38	34	9	4	4	3	24	1	43	2	2	3	2	.600	0	0- -	1	7.15	5.88
1999 Anaheim	AL	8	0	0	1	3.0	14	1	1	1	0	1	0	0	4	0	1	1	0	0	0	-	.000	0-0	1	3.04	3.00
2000 Anaheim	AL	11	0	0	3	6.0	38	14	9	9	3	0	1	0	7	1	2	1	0	0	0	-	-	0-0	0	21.26	13.50
2002 Texas	AL	52	0	0	12	39.2	173	35	22	21	7	2	2	3	21	0	30	0	1	0	4	.000	0	0-3	10	4.83	4.76
2003 Florida	NL	9	0	0	3	11.2	46	8	4	4	2	0	0	1	8	1	6	0	0	0	0	-	-	0-0	0	4.66	3.09
4 ML YEARS		80	0	0	19	60.1	271	58	36	35	12	3	3	4	40	2	42	2	1	0	5	.000	0	0-3	11	6.04	5.22

Victor Alvarez

Pitches: L Bats: L Pos: RP-5   Ht: 5'10" Wt: 150 Born: 11/8/76 Age: 27

Year Team	Lg	G	GS	CG	GF	IP	BFP	H	R	ER	HR	SH	SF	HB	TBB	IBB	SO	WP	Bk	W	L	Pct	ShO	Sv-Op	Hld	ERC	ERA
1997 Great Falls	R+	12	8	0	3	48.1	212	49	30	18	0	0	4	3	17	0	50	2	3	4	1	.800	0	0- -		3.44	3.35
1999 Vero Beach	A+	12	12	1	0	73.0	280	56	21	16	4	1	2	2	16	0	57	1	1	4	4	.500	0	0- -		2.12	1.97
1999 San Antonio	AA	9	9	0	0	56.1	234	58	27	23	5	3	1	2	10	0	43	1	0	4	3	.571	0	0- -		3.44	3.67
2000 Vero Beach	A+	4	4	0	0	22.2	94	17	14	13	6	0	0	0	11	0	20	1	0	1	1	.500	0	3-00	0	4.15	5.16
2000 San Antonio	AA	11	8	0	0	48.1	218	44	27	21	3	5	3	7	30	1	43	0	0	0	3	.000	0	0- -		4.74	3.91
2001 Jacksonville	AA	8	8	0	0	45.0	163	27	6	6	1	1	0	1	7	0	40	2	0	2	0	1.000	0	0- -		1.19	1.20
2001 Las Vegas	AAA	20	20	0	0	118.0	502	115	63	56	12	4	2	6	41	0	94	4	5	7	4	.636	0	0- -		3.97	4.27
2002 Las Vegas	AAA	34	15	0	8	122.2	526	132	69	64	11	5	4	3	39	1	106	4	1	10	7	.588	0	3- -		4.23	4.70
2003 Las Vegas	AAA	22	7	0	4	63.1	256	53	25	19	2	2	1	1	15	0	47	1	0	4	4	.500	0	1- -		2.24	2.70
2002 Los Angeles	NL	4	1	0	1	10.1	40	9	5	5	1	0	0	0	2	0	7	0	0	0	1	.000	0	0-0	0	2.70	4.35
2003 Los Angeles	NL	5	0	0	3	5.2	31	9	8	8	1	1	0	1	6	0	3	0	0	0	0	-	0	0-0	0	12.90	12.71
2 ML YEARS		9	1	0	4	16.0	71	18	13	13	2	1	0	1	8	0	10	0	0	0	2	.000	0	0-0	0	5.86	7.31

Wilson Alvarez

Pitches: L Bats: L Pos: SP-12; RP-9   Ht: 6'1" Wt: 245 Born: 3/24/70 Age: 34

Year Team	Lg	G	GS	CG	GF	IP	BFP	H	R	ER	HR	SH	SF	HB	TBB	IBB	SO	WP	Bk	W	L	Pct	ShO	Sv-Op	Hld	ERC	ERA
2003 Las Vegas*	AAA	8	8	0	0	47.0	181	36	9	7	1	2	2	4	6	0	33	0	0	5	1	.833	0	0- -		1.79	1.34
1989 Texas	AL	1	1	0	0	0.0	3	3	3	3	2	0	0	0	2	0	0	0	0	0	1	.000	0	0-0	0		
1991 Chicago	AL	10	9	2	0	56.1	237	47	26	22	9	3	1	0	29	0	32	2	0	3	2	.600	1	0-0	0	4.09	3.51
1992 Chicago	AL	34	9	0	4	100.1	455	103	64	58	12	3	4	4	65	2	66	2	0	5	3	.625	0	1-1	3	5.61	5.20
1993 Chicago	AL	31	31	1	0	207.2	877	168	78	68	14	**13**	6	7	**122**	8	155	2	1	15	8	.652	1	0-0	0	3.69	2.95
1994 Chicago	AL	24	24	2	0	161.2	682	147	72	62	16	4	3	0	62	1	108	3	0	12	8	.600	1	0-0	0	3.49	3.45
1995 Chicago	AL	29	29	3	0	175.0	769	171	96	84	21	6	5	2	93	4	118	1	2	8	11	.421	0	0-0	0	4.66	4.32
1996 Chicago	AL	35	35	0	0	217.1	946	216	106	102	18	5	4	9	97	3	181	2	0	15	10	.600	0	0-0	0	4.26	4.22
1997 CWS-SF		33	33	2	0	212.0	896	180	97	82	18	10	6	4	91	4	179	5	1	13	11	.542	1	0-0	0	3.30	3.48
1998 Tampa Bay	AL	35	25	0	0	142.2	624	150	78	75	18	1	2	9	68	0	107	4	0	6	14	.300	0	0-0	0	4.30	4.73
1999 Tampa Bay	AL	28	28	1	0	160.0	703	159	92	75	23	3	6	3	79	1	128	3	0	9	9	.500	0	0-0	0	4.87	4.22
2002 Tampa Bay	AL	23	10	0	3	75.0	338	80	47	44	13	2	4	3	36	3	56	2	0	2	3	.400	0	1-1	0	5.48	5.28
2003 Los Angeles	NL	23	12	1	2	95.0	377	80	27	25	5	2	1	5	23	1	82	1	0	6	2	.750	1	1-1	1	2.61	2.37
1997 Chicago	AL	22	22	2	0	145.2	613	126	61	49	9	6	5	3	55	1	110	4	0	9	8	.529	1	0-0	0	3.05	3.03
1997 San Francisco	NL	11	11	0	0	66.1	283	54	36	33	9	4	1	1	36	3	69	1	1	4	3	.571	0	0-0	0	3.86	4.48
12 ML YEARS		294	246	12	9	1603.0	6909	1484	786	700	171	54	36	45	767	27	1212	27	4	94	82	.534	5	3-3	6	4.13	3.93

Alfredo Amezaga

Bats: B **Throws:** R **Pos:** SS-24; 3B-13; PR-4; DH-1   **Ht:** 5'10" **Wt:** 165 **Born:** 1/16/78 **Age:** 26

Year Team	Lg	G	AB	H	2B	3B	HR	(Hm	Rd)	TB	R	RBI	RC	TBB	IBB	SO	HBP	SH	SF	SB	CS	SB%	GDP	Avg	OBP	Slg
1999 Butte	R+	8	34	10	2	0	0	(-	-)	12	11	5	6	5	0	5	1	0	0	6	2	.75	0	.294	.400	.353
1999 Boise	A-	48	205	66	6	4	2	(-	-)	86	52	29	36	23	2	29	5	3	1	14	3	.82	7	.322	.402	.420
2000 Lk Elsinore	A+	108	420	117	13	4	4	(-	-)	150	90	44	68	63	0	70	4	5	5	73	21	.78	4	.279	.374	.357
2001 Arkansas	AA	70	285	89	10	5	4	(-	-)	121	50	21	45	22	1	55	4	3	0	24	15	.62	0	.312	.370	.425
2001 Salt Lake	AAA	49	200	50	5	4	1	(-	-)	66	28	16	20	14	1	45	3	2	1	9	6	.60	2	.250	.307	.330
2002 Salt Lake	AAA	128	518	130	25	7	6	(-	-)	187	77	51	57	45	0	100	8	6	6	23	14	.62	15	.251	.317	.361
2003 Salt Lake	AAA	75	317	110	20	5	3	(-	-)	149	55	45	57	20	2	39	4	1	2	14	8	.64	3	.347	.391	.470
2002 Anaheim	AL	12	13	7	2	0	0	(0	0)	9	3	2	6	0	0	5	1	0	0	1	0	1.00	1	.538	.538	.692
2003 Anaheim	AL	37	105	22	3	2	2	(0	2)	35	15	7	7	9	0	23	1	5	0	2	2	.50	2	.210	.278	.333
2 ML YEARS		49	118	29	5	2	2	(0	2)	44	18	9	13	9	0	24	1	5	0	3	2	.60	3	.246	.305	.373

Brian Anderson

Pitches: L **Bats:** R **Pos:** SP-31; RP-1   **Ht:** 6'1" **Wt:** 183 **Born:** 4/26/72 **Age:** 32

Year Team	Lg	G	GS	CG	GF	IP	BFP	H	R	ER	HR	SH	SF	HB	TBB	IBB	SO	WP	Bk	W	L	Pct	ShO	Sv-Op	Hld	ERC	ERA
1993 Anaheim	AL	4	1	0	3	11.1	45	11	5	5	1	0	0	0	2	0	4	0	0	0	0	-	0	0-0	0	3.08	3.97
1994 Anaheim	AL	18	18	0	0	101.2	441	120	63	59	13	3	6	5	27	0	47	5	5	7	5	.583	0	0-0	0	5.05	5.22
1995 Anaheim	AL	18	17	1	0	99.2	433	110	66	65	24	5	5	3	30	2	45	1	3	6	8	.429	0	0-0	0	5.37	5.87
1996 Cleveland	AL	10	9	0	0	51.1	215	58	29	28	9	2	3	0	14	1	21	2	0	3	1	.750	0	0-0	1	4.96	4.91
1997 Cleveland	AL	8	8	0	0	48.0	199	55	28	25	7	0	5	0	11	0	22	1	0	4	2	.667	0	0-0	1	4.71	4.69
1998 Arizona	NL	32	32	2	0	208.0	845	221	100	100	39	8	3	4	24	2	95	3	6	12	13	.480	1	0-0	0	3.99	4.33
1999 Arizona	NL	31	19	2	4	130.0	549	144	69	66	18	4	0	1	28	3	75	0	2	8	2	.800	1	1-2	1	4.23	4.57
2000 Arizona	NL	33	32	2	0	213.1	876	226	101	96	38	6	6	3	39	7	104	1	4	11	7	.611	0	0-0	0	4.15	4.05
2001 Arizona	NL	29	22	1	1	133.1	571	156	93	77	25	7	4	1	30	2	55	2	1	4	9	.308	0	0-1	0	5.00	5.20
2002 Arizona	NL	35	24	0	1	156.0	659	174	86	83	23	6	8	1	32	3	81	2	5	6	11	.353	0	0-0	0	4.28	4.79
2003 Cle-KC	AL	32	31	2	0	197.2	821	212	110	83	27	4	12	4	43	3	87	3	1	14	11	.560	1	0-0	0	4.14	3.78
2003 Cleveland	AL	25	24	0	0	148.0	623	162	88	61	21	3	10	4	32	3	72	2	1	9	10	.474	0	0-0	0	4.29	3.71
2003 Kansas City	AL	7	7	2	0	49.2	198	50	22	22	6	1	2	0	11	0	15	1	0	5	1	.833	1	0-0	0	3.72	3.99
11 ML YEARS		250	213	10	9	1350.1	5654	1487	750	687	224	45	52	22	280	23	636	20	27	75	69	.521	3	1-3	3	4.43	4.58

Garret Anderson

Bats: L **Throws:** L **Pos:** LF-144; DH-15   **Ht:** 6'3" **Wt:** 228 **Born:** 6/30/72 **Age:** 32

Year Team	Lg	G	AB	H	2B	3B	HR	(Hm	Rd)	TB	R	RBI	RC	TBB	IBB	SO	HBP	SH	SF	SB	CS	SB%	GDP	Avg	OBP	Slg
1994 Anaheim	AL	5	13	5	0	0	0	(0	0)	5	0	1	2	0	0	2	0	0	0	0	0	-	0	.385	.385	.385
1995 Anaheim	AL	106	374	120	19	1	16	(7	9)	189	50	69	63	19	4	65	1	2	4	6	2	.75	8	.321	.352	.505
1996 Anaheim	AL	150	607	173	33	2	12	(7	5)	246	79	72	68	27	5	84	0	5	3	7	9	.44	22	.285	.314	.405
1997 Anaheim	AL	154	624	189	36	3	8	(5	3)	255	76	92	80	30	6	70	2	1	5	10	4	.71	20	.303	.334	.409
1998 Anaheim	AL	156	622	183	41	7	15	(4	11)	283	62	79	88	29	8	80	1	3	3	8	3	.73	13	.294	.325	.455
1999 Anaheim	AL	157	620	188	36	2	21	(10	11)	291	88	80	92	34	8	81	0	0	6	3	4	.43	15	.303	.336	.469
2000 Anaheim	AL	159	647	185	40	3	35	(20	15)	336	92	117	95	24	5	87	0	1	9	7	6	.54	21	.286	.307	.519
2001 Anaheim	AL	161	672	194	39	2	28	(13	15)	321	83	123	97	27	4	100	0	0	5	13	6	.68	12	.289	.314	.478
2002 Anaheim	AL	158	638	195	56	3	29	(13	16)	344	93	123	111	30	11	80	0	0	10	6	4	.60	11	.306	.332	.539
2003 Anaheim	AL	159	638	201	49	4	29	(12	17)	345	80	116	117	31	10	83	0	0	4	6	3	.67	15	.315	.345	.541
10 ML YEARS		1365	5455	1633	349	27	193	(91	102)	2615	703	872	813	251	61	732	4	12	49	66	41	.62	137	.299	.328	.479

Jason Anderson

Pitches: R **Bats:** L **Pos:** RP-28   **Ht:** 6'0" **Wt:** 170 **Born:** 6/9/79 **Age:** 25

Year Team	Lg	G	GS	CG	GF	IP	BFP	H	R	ER	HR	SH	SF	HB	TBB	IBB	SO	WP	Bk	W	L	Pct	ShO	Sv-Op	Hld	ERC	ERA
2000 Staten Island	A-	15	15	0	0	80.0	342	84	41	36	1	2	2	5	25	0	73	5	4	6	5	.545	0	0--	-	3.68	4.05
2001 Greensboro	A	23	19	1	3	124.0	530	127	68	52	9	3	8	3	40	1	101	8	0	7	9	.438	0	1--	-	3.80	3.77
2001 Staten Island	A-	7	7	0	0	48.0	184	32	9	9	2	0	0	4	12	0	56	1	1	5	1	.833	0	0--	-	1.87	1.69
2002 Tampa	A+	12	3	0	3	24.1	102	27	13	11	2	1	2	0	3	0	22	2	1	4	2	.667	0	1--	-	3.43	4.07
2002 Norwich	AA	16	0	0	10	19.1	72	14	2	2	1	1	0	0	5	1	21	3	0	1	1	.500	0	2--	-	1.94	0.93
2002 Columbus	AAA	26	0	0	25	34.1	138	26	13	12	3	2	1	1	11	0	28	0	1	5	1	.833	0	7--	-	2.55	3.15
2003 Columbus	AAA	6	0	0	6	7.2	29	3	0	0	0	1	0	0	2	0	13	0	0	0	0	-	0	3--	-	0.68	0.00
2003 Norfolk	AAA	10	5	0	4	23.1	91	18	8	7	3	0	0	0	7	0	9	1	1	1	3	.250	0	4--	-	2.76	2.70
2003 NYY-NYM		28	0	0	14	31.1	147	33	19	17	5	0	4	3	19	5	16	3	0	1	0	1.000	0	0-0	0	5.74	4.88
2003 New York	AL	22	0	0	12	20.2	100	23	13	11	3	0	2	2	14	4	9	3	0	1	0	1.000	0	0-0	0	6.19	4.79
2003 New York	NL	6	0	0	2	10.2	47	10	6	6	2	0	2	1	5	1	7	0	0	0	0	-	0	0-0	0	4.86	5.06

Jimmy Anderson

Pitches: L **Bats:** L **Pos:** SP-7; RP-1   **Ht:** 6'1" **Wt:** 218 **Born:** 1/22/76 **Age:** 28

Year Team	Lg	G	GS	CG	GF	IP	BFP	H	R	ER	HR	SH	SF	HB	TBB	IBB	SO	WP	Bk	W	L	Pct	ShO	Sv-Op	Hld	ERC	ERA
2003 Fresno*	AAA	8	8	0	0	43.1	209	65	36	31	3	4	2	3	15	0	17	2	1	1	4	.200	0	0--	-	6.86	6.44
2003 Louisville*	AAA	9	9	0	0	60.2	248	61	26	21	2	3	1	0	14	0	30	4	0	6	1	.857	0	0--	-	3.07	3.12
1999 Pittsburgh	NL	13	4	0	2	29.1	127	25	15	13	2	2	1	1	16	2	13	4	0	2	1	.667	0	0-0	0	3.62	3.99
2000 Pittsburgh	NL	27	26	1	0	144.0	648	169	94	84	13	5	3	7	58	2	73	6	0	5	11	.313	0	0-0	0	5.21	5.25
2001 Pittsburgh	NL	34	34	1	0	206.1	922	232	123	117	15	11	9	11	83	14	89	6	1	9	17	.346	0	0-0	0	4.69	5.10
2002 Pittsburgh	NL	28	25	1	1	140.2	636	167	91	85	20	5	4	5	63	5	47	4	0	8	13	.381	0	0-0	0	5.84	5.44
2003 Cincinnati	NL	8	7	0	1	38.2	184	60	39	38	8	0	3	0	14	1	13	0	0	1	5	.167	0	0-0	0	8.22	8.44
5 ML YEARS		110	96	3	4	559.0	2517	653	362	337	58	23	20	24	234	24	235	20	1	25	47	.347	0	0-0	0	5.28	5.43

Marlon Anderson

Bats: L **Throws:** R **Pos:** 2B-134; PH-18; DH-4; LF-3; PR-1   **Ht:** 5'11" **Wt:** 200 **Born:** 1/6/74 **Age:** 30

								BATTING												BASERUNNING				AVERAGES		
Year Team	Lg	G	AB	H	2B	3B	HR	(Hm	Rd)	TB	R	RBI	RC	TBB	IBB	SO	HBP	SH	SF	SB	CS	SB%	GDP	Avg	OBP	Slg
1998 Philadelphia	NL	17	43	14	3	0	1	(1	0)	20	4	4	7	1	0	6	0	0	1	2	0	1.00	0	.326	.333	.465
1999 Philadelphia	NL	129	452	114	26	4	5	(4	1)	163	48	54	49	24	1	61	0	2	4	13	2	.87	6	.252	.292	.361
2000 Philadelphia	NL	41	162	37	8	1	1	(1	0)	50	10	15	12	12	0	22	0	0	0	2	2	.50	5	.228	.282	.309
2001 Philadelphia	NL	147	522	153	30	2	11	(7	4)	220	69	61	72	35	5	74	2	10	5	8	5	.62	12	.293	.337	.421
2002 Philadelphia	NL	145	539	139	30	6	8	(4	4)	205	64	48	52	42	14	71	5	2	4	5	1	.83	16	.258	.315	.380
2003 Tampa Bay	AL	145	482	130	27	3	6	(2	4)	181	59	67	70	41	5	60	3	4	5	19	3	.86	6	.270	.328	.376
6 ML YEARS		624	2200	587	124	16	32	(19	13)	839	254	249	262	155	25	294	12	20	17	49	13	.79	45	.267	.316	.381

Matt Anderson

Pitches: R **Bats:** R **Pos:** RP-23   **Ht:** 6'4" **Wt:** 190 **Born:** 8/17/76 **Age:** 27

		HOW MUCH HE PITCHED						WHAT HE GAVE UP										THE RESULTS						
Year Team	Lg	G	GS	CG	GF	IP	BFP	H	R	ER	HR	SH	SF	HB	TBB	IBB	SO	WP	Bk	W	L	Pct	ShO	Sv-Op	Hld	ERC	ERA
2003 Toledo*	AAA	23	5	0	9	38.0	170	50	23	16	4	2	0	1	8	1	31	0	0	1	3	.250	0	3- -		5.20	3.79
1998 Detroit	AL	42	0	0	10	44.0	194	38	16	16	3	6	3	2	31	4	44	2	0	5	1	.833	0	0-4	6	4.38	3.27
1999 Detroit	AL	37	0	0	9	38.0	180	33	27	24	8	0	2	1	35	1	32	3	0	2	1	.667	0	0-2	3	6.34	5.68
2000 Detroit	AL	69	0	0	27	64.1	324	61	44	39	8	2	6	3	45	4	71	4	0	3	2	.600	0	1-1	9	4.02	4.72
2001 Detroit	AL	62	0	0	41	56.0	239	56	33	30	2	1	2	0	18	4	52	9	1	3	1	.750	0	22-24	9	3.19	4.82
2002 Detroit	AL	12	0	0	8	11.0	58	17	13	11	1	1	2	2	8	1	8	1	0	2	1	.667	0	0-2	0	9.52	9.00
2003 Detroit	AL	23	0	0	10	23.1	108	25	17	14	5	2	1	1	9	1	13	1	0	0	1	.000	0	3-4	4	5.09	5.40
6 ML YEARS		245	0	0	105	246.2	1103	230	150	134	27	12	16	9	146	15	220	20	1	15	7	.682	0	26-37	31	4.55	4.89

Kevin Appier

Pitches: R **Bats:** R **Pos:** SP-23   **Ht:** 6'2" **Wt:** 200 **Born:** 12/6/67 **Age:** 36

		HOW MUCH HE PITCHED						WHAT HE GAVE UP										THE RESULTS						
Year Team	Lg	G	GS	CG	GF	IP	BFP	H	R	ER	HR	SH	SF	HB	TBB	IBB	SO	WP	Bk	W	L	Pct	ShO	Sv-Op	Hld	ERC	ERA
1989 Kansas City	AL	6	5	0	0	21.2	106	34	22	22	3	0	3	0	12	1	10	0	0	1	4	.200	0	0-0	0	8.72	9.14
1990 Kansas City	AL	32	24	3	1	185.2	784	179	67	57	13	5	9	6	54	2	127	6	1	12	8	.600	3	0-0	0	3.34	2.76
1991 Kansas City	AL	34	31	6	1	207.2	881	205	97	79	13	8	6	2	61	3	158	7	1	13	10	.565	3	0-0	0	3.32	3.42
1992 Kansas City	AL	30	30	3	0	208.1	852	167	59	57	10	8	3	2	68	5	150	4	0	15	8	.652	3	0-0	0	2.41	2.46
1993 Kansas City	AL	34	34	5	0	238.2	953	183	74	68	8	3	5	1	81	3	186	5	0	18	8	.692	1	0-0	0	2.25	2.56
1994 Kansas City	AL	23	23	1	0	155.0	653	137	68	66	11	9	7	4	63	7	145	11	1	7	6	.538	0	0-0	0	3.31	3.83
1995 Kansas City	AL	31	31	4	0	201.1	832	163	90	87	14	3	4	8	80	1	185	5	0	15	10	.600	1	0-0	0	3.01	3.89
1996 Kansas City	AL	32	32	5	0	211.1	874	192	87	85	17	7	4	5	75	2	207	10	1	14	11	.560	1	0-0	0	3.41	3.62
1997 Kansas City	AL	34	34	4	0	235.2	972	215	96	89	24	4	4	4	74	2	196	14	1	9	13	.409	1	0-0	0	3.37	3.40
1998 Kansas City	AL	3	3	0	0	15.0	69	21	13	13	3	0	1	1	5	1	9	1	0	1	2	.333	0	0-0	0	7.33	7.80
1999 KC-Oak	AL	34	34	1	0	209.0	926	230	131	120	27	7	5	7	84	4	131	10	1	16	14	.533	0	0-0	0	4.99	5.17
2000 Oakland	AL	31	31	1	0	195.1	884	200	109	98	23	5	6	9	102	10	129	6	0	15	11	.577	1	0-0	0	4.89	4.52
2001 New York	NL	33	33	1	0	206.2	856	181	89	82	22	6	7	15	64	4	172	12	0	11	10	.524	1	0-0	0	3.38	3.57
2002 Anaheim	AL	32	32	0	0	188.1	795	191	89	82	23	1	8	7	64	2	132	7	0	14	12	.538	0	0-0	0	4.29	3.92
2003 Ana-KC	AL	23	23	0	0	111.2	499	120	69	67	21	1	1	8	43	4	55	6	1	8	9	.471	0	0-0	0	5.29	5.40
1999 Kansas City	AL	22	22	1	0	140.1	613	153	81	76	18	5	3	6	51	3	78	5	0	9	9	.500	0	0-0	0	4.83	4.87
1999 Oakland	AL	12	12	0	0	68.2	313	77	50	44	9	2	2	1	33	1	53	5	1	7	5	.583	0	0-0	0	5.32	5.77
2003 Anaheim	AL	19	19	0	0	92.2	422	105	60	58	17	0	1	8	36	4	50	4	1	7	7	.500	0	0-0	0	5.65	5.63
2003 Kansas City	AL	4	4	0	0	19.0	77	15	9	9	4	1	0	0	7	0	5	2	0	1	2	.333	0	0-0	0	3.56	4.26
15 ML YEARS		412	400	34	2	2591.1	10936	2418	1160	1072	232	67	72	79	930	51	1992	104	7	169	136	.554	12	0-0	1	3.58	3.72

Tony Armas Jr.

Pitches: R **Bats:** R **Pos:** SP-5   **Ht:** 6'4" **Wt:** 215 **Born:** 4/29/78 **Age:** 26

		HOW MUCH HE PITCHED						WHAT HE GAVE UP										THE RESULTS						
Year Team	Lg	G	GS	CG	GF	IP	BFP	H	R	ER	HR	SH	SF	HB	TBB	IBB	SO	WP	Bk	W	L	Pct	ShO	Sv-Op	Hld	ERC	ERA
1999 Montreal	NL	1	1	0	0	6.0	28	8	4	1	0	0	1	0	2	1	2	2	0	0	1	.000	0	0-0	0	4.53	1.50
2000 Montreal	NL	17	17	0	0	95.0	403	74	49	46	10	7	3	3	50	2	59	3	0	7	9	.438	0	0-0	0	3.49	4.36
2001 Montreal	NL	34	34	0	0	196.2	851	180	101	88	18	15	6	10	84	6	176	9	1	9	14	.391	0	0-0	0	3.95	4.03
2002 Montreal	NL	29	29	0	0	164.1	705	149	87	81	22	6	2	7	78	12	131	14	2	12	12	.500	0	0-0	0	4.19	4.44
2003 Montreal	NL	5	5	0	0	31.0	124	25	9	9	4	2	2	1	8	0	23	0	0	2	1	.667	0	0-0	0	2.84	2.61
5 ML YEARS		86	86	0	0	493.0	2111	436	250	225	54	30	14	21	229	21	391	28	3	30	37	.448	0	0-0	0	3.87	4.11

Bronson Arroyo

Pitches: R **Bats:** R **Pos:** RP-6   **Ht:** 6'5" **Wt:** 194 **Born:** 2/24/77 **Age:** 27

		HOW MUCH HE PITCHED						WHAT HE GAVE UP										THE RESULTS						
Year Team	Lg	G	GS	CG	GF	IP	BFP	H	R	ER	HR	SH	SF	HB	TBB	IBB	SO	WP	Bk	W	L	Pct	ShO	Sv-Op	Hld	ERC	ERA
2003 Pawtucket*	AAA	24	24	1	0	149.2	627	148	66	57	9	5	1	10	23	0	155	8	0	12	6	.667	1	0- -		3.01	3.43
2000 Pittsburgh	NL	20	12	0	1	71.2	338	88	61	51	10	5	2	4	36	6	50	3	1	2	6	.250	0	0-0	0	6.18	6.40
2001 Pittsburgh	NL	24	13	1	1	88.1	390	99	54	50	12	4	6	4	34	6	39	4	1	5	7	.417	0	0-0	2	5.09	5.09
2002 Pittsburgh	NL	9	4	0	1	27.0	123	30	14	12	1	1	1	0	15	3	22	0	0	2	1	.667	0	0-0	0	4.64	4.00
2003 Boston	AL	6	0	0	2	17.1	66	10	5	4	0	0	0	1	4	2	14	0	0	0	0	-	0	1-1	1	1.14	2.08
4 ML YEARS		59	29	1	5	204.1	917	227	134	117	23	10	9	9	89	17	125	7	2	9	14	.391	0	1-1	3	4.98	5.15

Miguel Asencio

Pitches: R **Bats:** R **Pos:** SP-8   **Ht:** 6'2" **Wt:** 160 **Born:** 9/29/80 **Age:** 23

		HOW MUCH HE PITCHED						WHAT HE GAVE UP										THE RESULTS						
Year Team	Lg	G	GS	CG	GF	IP	BFP	H	R	ER	HR	SH	SF	HB	TBB	IBB	SO	WP	Bk	W	L	Pct	ShO	Sv-Op	Hld	ERC	ERA
1999 Phillies	R	9	5	0	3	28.2	137	35	24	19	1	0	4	2	16	0	14	1	0	1	4	.200	0	0- -		5.71	5.97
2000 Clearwater	A+	5	5	0	0	33.0	132	22	10	10	2	0	0	0	17	0	24	1	1	2	1	.667	0	0-0	0	2.58	2.73
2000 Batavia	A-	7	7	1	0	39.2	165	32	23	22	3	1	1	3	17	0	28	2	0	2	2	.500	0	0- -		3.32	4.99

16

Year Team	Lg	G	GS	CG	GF	IP	BFP	H	R	ER	HR	SH	SF	HB	TBB	IBB	SO	WP	Bk	W	L	Pct	ShO	Sv-Op	Hld	ERC	ERA
2001 Clearwater	A+	28	21	2	1	155.1	649	124	62	49	7	3	6	2	70	1	123	9	2	12	5	.706	1	0--	-	2.86	2.84
2003 Wichita	AA	1	1	0	0	4.0	14	1	0	0	0	0	0	0	1	0	3	0	0	0	0	-	0	0--	-	0.40	0.00
2002 Kansas City	AL	31	21	0	7	123.1	557	136	73	70	17	2	6	3	64	2	58	7	0	4	7	.364	0	0-0	0	5.55	5.11
2003 Kansas City	AL	8	8	1	0	48.1	215	54	29	28	4	3	5	3	21	0	27	1	0	2	1	.667	0	0-0	0	5.08	5.21
2 ML YEARS		39	29	1	7	171.2	772	190	102	98	21	5	11	6	85	2	85	8	0	6	8	.429	0	0-0	0	5.42	5.14

Andy Ashby

Pitches: R Bats: R Pos: SP-12; RP-9   Ht: 6'1" Wt: 202 Born: 7/11/67 Age: 36

Year Team	Lg	G	GS	CG	GF	IP	BFP	H	R	ER	HR	SH	SF	HB	TBB	IBB	SO	WP	Bk	W	L	Pct	ShO	Sv-Op	Hld	ERC	ERA
1991 Philadelphia	NL	8	8	0	0	42.0	186	41	28	28	5	1	3	3	19	0	26	6	0	1	5	.167	0	0-0	0	4.54	6.00
1992 Philadelphia	NL	10	8	0	0	37.0	171	42	31	31	6	2	2	1	21	0	24	2	0	1	3	.250	0	0-0	0	6.17	7.54
1993 Col-SD	NL	32	21	0	3	123.0	577	168	100	93	19	6	7	4	56	5	77	6	3	3	10	.231	0	1-1	0	7.10	6.80
1994 San Diego	NL	24	24	4	0	164.1	682	145	75	62	16	11	3	3	43	12	121	5	0	6	11	.353	0	0-0	0	2.82	3.40
1995 San Diego	NL	31	31	2	0	192.2	800	180	79	63	17	10	4	11	62	3	150	7	0	12	10	.545	2	0-0	0	3.60	2.94
1996 San Diego	NL	24	24	1	0	150.2	612	147	60	54	17	6	2	3	34	1	85	3	0	9	5	.643	0	0-0	0	3.50	3.23
1997 San Diego	NL	30	30	2	0	200.2	851	207	108	92	17	13	6	5	49	2	144	3	0	9	11	.450	0	0-0	0	3.59	4.13
1998 San Diego	NL	33	33	5	0	226.2	939	223	90	84	23	8	5	7	58	8	151	7	0	17	9	.654	1	0-0	0	3.55	3.34
1999 San Diego	NL	31	31	4	0	206.0	862	204	95	87	26	10	1	7	54	4	132	6	0	14	10	.583	3	0-0	0	3.78	3.80
2000 Phi-Atl	NL	31	31	3	0	199.1	867	216	124	109	29	18	10	6	61	9	106	6	1	12	13	.480	1	0-0	0	4.52	4.92
2001 Los Angeles	NL	2	2	0	0	11.2	49	14	5	5	2	0	0	0	1	0	7	0	0	2	0	1.000	0	0-0	0	4.42	3.86
2002 Los Angeles	NL	30	30	0	0	181.2	771	179	85	79	20	7	6	8	65	3	107	2	0	9	13	.409	0	0-0	0	4.10	3.91
2003 Los Angeles	NL	21	12	0	5	73.0	318	90	42	42	8	7	2	3	17	2	41	5	0	3	10	.231	0	0-0	0	4.99	5.18
1993 Colorado	NL	20	9	0	3	54.0	277	89	54	51	5	3	3	3	32	4	33	2	3	0	4	.000	0	1-1	0	9.06	8.50
1993 San Diego	NL	12	12	0	0	69.0	300	79	46	42	14	3	4	1	24	1	44	4	0	3	6	.333	0	0-0	0	5.58	5.48
2000 Philadelphia	NL	16	16	1	0	101.1	455	113	75	64	17	11	9	5	38	5	51	4	0	4	7	.364	0	0-0	0	5.20	5.68
2000 Atlanta	NL	15	15	2	0	98.0	412	103	49	45	12	7	1	1	23	4	55	2	1	8	6	.571	1	0-0	0	3.84	4.13
13 ML YEARS		307	285	21	8	1808.2	7685	1856	922	829	205	99	51	61	540	49	1171	58	4	98	110	.471	7	1-1	0	4.03	4.13

Pedro Astacio

Pitches: R Bats: R Pos: SP-7   Ht: 6'2" Wt: 210 Born: 11/28/69 Age: 34

Year Team	Lg	G	GS	CG	GF	IP	BFP	H	R	ER	HR	SH	SF	HB	TBB	IBB	SO	WP	Bk	W	L	Pct	ShO	Sv-Op	Hld	ERC	ERA
2003 St.Lucie*	A+	4	4	0	0	17.1	70	15	6	4	0	1	0	1	3	0	15	0	0	0	2	.000	0	0--	-	2.12	2.08
1992 Los Angeles	NL	11	11	4	0	82.0	341	80	23	18	1	3	2	2	20	4	43	1	0	5	5	.500	4	0-0	0	2.78	1.98
1993 Los Angeles	NL	31	31	3	0	186.1	777	165	80	74	14	7	8	5	68	5	122	8	9	14	9	.609	2	0-0	0	3.24	3.57
1994 Los Angeles	NL	23	23	3	0	149.0	625	142	77	71	18	6	5	4	47	4	108	4	0	6	8	.429	1	0-0	0	3.71	4.29
1995 Los Angeles	NL	48	11	0	7	104.0	436	103	53	49	12	5	3	4	29	5	80	5	0	7	8	.467	1	0-1	2	3.76	4.24
1996 Los Angeles	NL	35	32	0	0	211.2	885	207	86	81	18	11	5	9	67	9	130	6	2	9	8	.529	0	0-0	0	3.69	3.44
1997 LA-Col	NL	33	31	2	2	202.1	862	200	98	93	24	9	7	9	61	0	166	6	3	12	10	.545	1	0-0	0	3.92	4.14
1998 Colorado	NL	35	34	0	0	209.1	938	245	160	145	39	12	3	17	74	0	170	2	0	13	14	.481	0	0-0	0	5.91	6.23
1999 Colorado	NL	34	34	7	0	232.0	1008	258	140	130	38	6	10	11	75	6	210	5	0	17	11	.607	0	0-0	0	5.08	5.04
2000 Colorado	NL	32	32	3	0	196.0	875	217	119	115	32	7	4	15	77	5	193	8	0	12	9	.571	0	0-0	0	5.42	5.27
2001 Col-Hou	NL	26	26	4	0	169.2	733	181	101	96	22	6	5	13	54	3	144	2	0	8	14	.364	1	0-0	0	4.68	5.09
2002 New York	NL	31	31	3	0	191.2	828	192	106	102	32	8	7	16	63	5	152	1	2	12	11	.522	1	0-0	0	4.57	4.79
2003 New York	NL	7	7	0	0	36.2	174	47	30	30	8	1	1	3	18	1	20	4	0	3	2	.600	0	0-0	0	7.42	7.36
1997 Los Angeles	NL	26	24	2	2	153.2	654	151	75	70	15	9	5	4	47	0	115	4	3	7	9	.438	1	0-0	0	3.67	4.10
1997 Colorado	NL	7	7	0	0	48.2	208	49	23	23	9	0	2	5	14	0	51	2	0	5	1	.833	0	0-0	0	4.72	4.25
2001 Colorado	NL	22	22	4	0	141.0	617	151	91	86	21	5	4	10	50	3	125	2	0	6	13	.316	1	0-0	0	4.94	5.49
2001 Houston	NL	4	4	0	0	28.2	116	30	10	10	1	1	1	3	4	0	19	0	0	2	1	.667	0	0-0	0	3.43	3.14
12 ML YEARS		346	303	30	9	1971.0	8482	2037	1073	1004	258	81	60	108	653	47	1538	52	16	118	109	.520	11	0-1	2	4.42	4.58

Garrett Atkins

Bats: R Throws: R Pos: 3B-19; PH-8   Ht: 6'3" Wt: 210 Born: 12/12/79 Age: 24

Year Team	Lg	G	AB	H	2B	3B	HR	(Hm	Rd)	TB	R	RBI	RC	TBB	IBB	SO	HBP	SH	SF	SB	CS	SB%	GDP	Avg	OBP	Slg
2000 Portland	AA	69	251	76	12	0	7	(-	-)	109	34	47	48	45	1	48	2	0	1	2	0	1.00	3	.303	.411	.434
2001 Salem	A+	135	465	151	43	5	5	(-	-)	219	70	67	93	74	10	98	8	2	6	6	4	.60	8	.325	.421	.471
2002 Carolina	AA	128	510	138	27	3	12	(-	-)	207	71	61	71	59	2	77	2	0	6	6	6	.50	12	.271	.345	.406
2003 Co Springs	AAA	118	439	140	30	1	13	(-	-)	211	80	67	78	45	2	52	3	0	5	2	4	.33	9	.319	.382	.481
2003 Colorado	NL	25	69	11	2	0	0	(0	0)	13	6	4	2	3	0	14	1	0	0	0	0	-	1	.159	.205	.188

Rich Aurilia

Bats: R Throws: R Pos: SS-123; PH-5; DH-1   Ht: 6'1" Wt: 185 Born: 9/2/71 Age: 32

Year Team	Lg	G	AB	H	2B	3B	HR	(Hm	Rd)	TB	R	RBI	RC	TBB	IBB	SO	HBP	SH	SF	SB	CS	SB%	GDP	Avg	OBP	Slg
1995 San Francisco	NL	9	19	9	3	0	2	(0	2)	18	4	4	7	1	0	2	0	1	0	1	0	1.00	1	.474	.476	.947
1996 San Francisco	NL	105	318	76	7	1	3	(1	2)	94	27	26	29	25	2	52	1	6	2	4	1	.80	1	.239	.295	.296
1997 San Francisco	NL	46	102	28	8	0	5	(1	4)	51	16	19	16	8	0	15	0	1	2	1	1	.50	3	.275	.321	.500
1998 San Francisco	NL	122	413	110	27	4	9	(5	4)	168	54	49	54	31	3	62	2	5	2	3	3	.50	3	.266	.319	.407
1999 San Francisco	NL	152	558	157	23	1	22	(9	13)	248	68	80	79	43	3	71	5	3	5	2	3	.40	16	.281	.336	.444
2000 San Francisco	NL	141	509	138	24	2	20	(12	8)	226	67	79	74	54	2	90	0	4	4	1	2	.33	15	.271	.339	.444
2001 San Francisco	NL	156	636	206	37	5	37	(15	22)	364	114	97	124	47	2	83	0	3	3	1	3	.25	14	.324	.369	.572
2002 San Francisco	NL	133	538	138	35	2	15	(4	11)	222	76	61	61	37	0	90	4	3	7	1	2	.33	15	.257	.305	.413
2003 San Francisco	NL	129	505	140	26	1	13	(6	7)	207	65	58	55	36	0	82	1	0	3	2	2	.50	18	.277	.325	.410
9 ML YEARS		993	3598	1002	190	14	126	(53	73)	1598	491	473	499	282	12	547	13	26	29	16	17	.48	86	.278	.331	.444

Brad Ausmus

Bats: R Throws: R Pos: C-143; PR-1   Ht: 5'11" Wt: 200 Born: 4/14/69 Age: 35

Year Team	Lg	G	AB	H	2B	3B	HR	(Hm	Rd)	TB	R	RBI	RC	TBB	IBB	SO	HBP	SH	SF	SB	CS	SB%	GDP	Avg	OBP	Slg
1993 San Diego	NL	49	160	41	8	1	5	(4	1)	66	18	12	19	6	0	28	0	0	0	2	0	1.00	2	.256	.283	.413
1994 San Diego	NL	101	327	82	12	1	7	(6	1)	117	45	24	36	30	12	63	1	6	2	5	1	.83	8	.251	.314	.358
1995 San Diego	NL	103	328	96	16	4	5	(2	3)	135	44	34	49	31	3	56	2	4	4	16	5	.76	6	.293	.353	.412
1996 SD-Det		125	375	83	16	0	5	(2	3)	114	46	35	32	39	1	72	5	6	2	4	8	.33	8	.221	.302	.304
1997 Houston	NL	130	425	113	25	1	4	(1	3)	152	45	44	51	38	4	78	3	6	6	14	6	.70	8	.266	.326	.358
1998 Houston	NL	128	412	111	10	4	6	(2	4)	147	62	45	51	53	11	60	3	3	1	10	3	.77	18	.269	.356	.357
1999 Detroit	AL	127	458	126	25	6	9	(5	4)	190	62	54	69	51	0	71	14	3	1	12	9	.57	11	.275	.365	.415
2000 Detroit	AL	150	523	139	25	3	7	(3	4)	191	75	51	68	69	0	79	6	4	2	11	5	.69	19	.266	.357	.365
2001 Houston	NL	128	422	98	23	4	5	(1	4)	144	45	34	38	30	6	64	1	6	2	4	1	.80	13	.232	.284	.341
2002 Houston	NL	130	447	115	19	3	6	(4	2)	158	57	50	43	38	3	71	6	2	3	2	3	.40	30	.257	.322	.353
2003 Houston	NL	143	450	103	12	2	4	(1	3)	131	43	47	42	46	1	66	4	4	5	5	3	.63	8	.229	.303	.291
1996 San Diego	NL	50	149	27	4	0	1	(0	1)	34	16	13	6	13	0	27	3	1	0	1	4	.20	4	.181	.261	.228
1996 Detroit	AL	75	226	56	12	0	4	(2	2)	80	30	22	26	26	1	45	2	5	2	3	4	.43	4	.248	.328	.354
11 ML YEARS		1314	4327	1107	191	29	63	(34	29)	1545	542	430	498	431	41	708	45	44	28	85	44	.66	131	.256	.328	.357

Jeff Austin

Pitches: R Bats: R Pos: SP-7   Ht: 6'0" Wt: 185 Born: 10/19/76 Age: 27

Year Team	Lg	G	GS	CG	GF	IP	BFP	H	R	ER	HR	SH	SF	HB	TBB	IBB	SO	WP	Bk	W	L	Pct	ShO	Sv-Op	Hld	ERC	ERA
2003 Louisville*	AAA	9	9	0	0	45.2	196	46	24	22	5	1	2	1	19	0	37	4	1	4	2	.667	0	0- -	-	4.40	4.34
2001 Kansas City	AL	21	0	0	9	26.0	117	27	17	16	4	1	2	1	14	2	27	3	0	0	0	-	0	0-0	1	5.31	5.54
2002 Kansas City	AL	10	0	0	6	11.0	52	14	6	6	0	0	2	0	6	1	6	1	0	0	0	-	0	0-0	0	5.24	4.91
2003 Cincinnati	NL	7	7	0	0	28.1	132	28	27	27	9	1	0	0	21	0	22	1	0	2	3	.400	0	0-0	0	7.11	8.58
3 ML YEARS		38	7	0	15	65.1	301	69	50	49	13	2	4	1	41	3	55	5	0	2	3	.400	0	0-0	0	6.08	6.75

Steve Avery

Pitches: L Bats: L Pos: RP-19   Ht: 6'4" Wt: 205 Born: 5/11/70 Age: 34

Year Team	Lg	G	GS	CG	GF	IP	BFP	H	R	ER	HR	SH	SF	HB	TBB	IBB	SO	WP	Bk	W	L	Pct	ShO	Sv-Op	Hld	ERC	ERA
2003 Toledo*	AAA	22	2	0	4	34.1	146	37	16	12	6	2	4	0	10	3	14	1	0	1	4	.200	0	0- -	-	4.50	3.15
1990 Atlanta	NL	21	20	1	1	99.0	466	121	79	62	7	14	4	2	45	2	75	5	1	3	11	.214	1	0-0	0	5.26	5.64
1991 Atlanta	NL	35	35	3	0	210.1	868	189	89	79	21	8	4	3	65	0	137	4	1	18	8	.692	1	0-0	0	3.25	3.38
1992 Atlanta	NL	35	35	2	0	233.2	969	216	95	83	14	12	8	0	71	3	129	7	3	11	11	.500	2	0-0	0	3.02	3.20
1993 Atlanta	NL	35	35	3	0	223.1	891	216	81	73	14	12	8	0	43	5	125	3	1	18	6	.750	1	0-0	0	2.92	2.94
1994 Atlanta	NL	24	24	1	0	151.2	628	127	71	68	15	4	6	4	55	4	122	5	2	8	3	.727	0	0-0	0	3.12	4.04
1995 Atlanta	NL	29	29	3	0	173.1	724	165	92	90	22	6	4	6	52	4	141	3	0	7	13	.350	1	0-0	0	3.73	4.67
1996 Atlanta	NL	24	23	1	0	131.0	567	146	70	65	10	7	3	4	40	8	86	5	0	7	10	.412	0	0-0	0	4.22	4.47
1997 Boston	AL	22	18	0	1	96.2	453	127	76	69	15	1	4	2	49	0	51	4	0	6	7	.462	0	0-0	1	7.01	6.42
1998 Boston	AL	34	23	0	4	123.2	546	128	74	69	14	3	0	4	64	0	57	7	0	10	7	.588	0	0-1	5	5.06	5.02
1999 Cincinnati	NL	19	19	0	0	96.0	426	75	62	55	11	3	6	1	78	0	51	4	1	6	7	.462	0	0-0	0	4.69	5.16
2003 Detroit	AL	19	0	0	5	16.0	71	19	11	10	5	1	0	0	7	1	6	0	0	2	0	1.000	0	0-1	1	7.02	5.63
11 ML YEARS		297	261	14	11	1554.2	6609	1529	800	723	148	71	47	26	569	27	980	47	9	96	83	.536	6	0-2	3	3.88	4.19

Luis Ayala

Pitches: R Bats: R Pos: RP-65   Ht: 6'2" Wt: 170 Born: 1/2/78 Age: 26

Year Team	Lg	G	GS	CG	GF	IP	BFP	H	R	ER	HR	SH	SF	HB	TBB	IBB	SO	WP	Bk	W	L	Pct	ShO	Sv-Op	Hld	ERC	ERA
1997 Saltillo	AAA	37	2	0	0	62.1	269	76	37	32	3	1	7	3	21	4	30	2	1	7	5	.583	0	0- -	-	4.99	4.62
1998 Saltillo	AAA	47	4	0	0	83.1	381	105	52	52	2	10	1	4	45	13	29	3	0	7	8	.467	0	7- -	-	5.65	5.62
1999 Saltillo	AAA	61	0	0	0	79.0	287	54	17	15	1	3	0	3	22	5	28	3	0	7	3	.700	0	41- -	-	1.76	1.71
2000 Saltillo	AAA	55	0	0	52	65.1	269	69	22	20	4	4	0	3	13	1	38	1	0	5	3	.625	0	25- -	-	3.59	2.76
2001 Salem	A+	33	0	0	33	40.0	164	34	11	9	2	3	2	0	11	0	34	0	0	1	2	.333	0	21- -	-	2.47	2.03
2001 Saltillo	AAA	13	0	0	12	13.1	61	19	14	6	0	1	0	2	5	0	10	2	1	0	1	.000	0	7- -	-	6.67	4.05
2002 Saltillo	AAA	49	0	0	43	53.2	225	43	16	10	2	2	0	7	15	0	43	0	0	3	5	.375	0	23- -	-	2.60	1.68
2002 Ottawa	AAA	6	0	0	3	7.2	32	7	3	3	1	0	0	0	4	0	6	0	0	0	0	-	0	0- -	-	4.48	3.52
2003 Expos	R	2	2	0	0	3.2	15	2	0	0	0	0	0	0	2	0	2	0	0	0	0	-	0	0- -	-	1.65	0.00
2003 Montreal	NL	65	0	0	24	71.0	288	65	27	23	8	3	1	5	13	3	46	1	0	10	3	.769	0	5-8	19	3.11	2.92

Manny Aybar

Pitches: R Bats: R Pos: RP-3   Ht: 6'1" Wt: 177 Born: 5/4/72 Age: 32

Year Team	Lg	G	GS	CG	GF	IP	BFP	H	R	ER	HR	SH	SF	HB	TBB	IBB	SO	WP	Bk	W	L	Pct	ShO	Sv-Op	Hld	ERC	ERA
2003 Fresno*	AAA	52	0	0	41	57.1	247	55	27	26	7	4	2	1	23	0	45	4	1	2	4	.333	0	17- -	-	4.06	4.08
1997 St Louis	NL	12	12	0	0	68.0	295	66	33	32	8	7	4	4	29	0	41	1	1	2	4	.333	0	0-0	0	4.40	4.24
1998 St Louis	NL	20	14	0	1	81.1	369	90	58	54	6	4	1	2	42	1	57	2	0	6	6	.500	0	0-0	0	5.04	5.98
1999 St Louis	NL	65	1	0	22	97.0	430	104	67	59	13	4	3	4	36	3	74	1	2	4	5	.444	0	3-5	12	4.68	5.47
2000 Col-Cin-Fla	NL	54	0	0	20	79.1	349	74	42	38	11	5	4	2	35	3	45	7	1	2	2	.500	0	0-1	1	4.08	4.31
2001 Chicago	NL	17	1	0	1	22.2	113	28	19	16	5	1	1	2	17	0	16	2	0	2	1	.667	0	0-0	2	8.38	6.35
2002 San Francisco	NL	15	0	0	4	14.1	63	16	6	4	1	0	0	1	3	2	11	0	1	1	0	1.000	0	0-0	1	3.71	2.51
2003 San Francisco	NL	3	0	0	1	3.0	16	4	2	2	1	0	1	0	3	0	2	0	0	0	0	-	0	0-0	0	10.72	6.00
2000 Colorado	NL	1	0	0	0	1.2	10	5	3	3	1	0	0	0	0	0	0	0	0	0	1	.000	0	0-0	0	21.12	16.20
2000 Cincinnati	NL	32	0	0	10	50.1	226	51	31	27	7	4	3	2	22	2	31	7	1	1	1	.500	0	0-0	1	4.57	4.83
2000 Florida	NL	21	0	0	10	27.1	113	18	8	8	3	1	1	0	13	1	14	0	0	1	0	1.000	0	0-1	0	2.53	2.63
7 ML YEARS		186	28	0	49	365.2	1635	382	227	205	45	21	14	15	165	9	246	13	5	17	18	.486	0	3-6	16	4.79	5.05

Brandon Backe

Pitches: R Bats: R Pos: RP-28

Ht: 6'0" Wt: 190 Born: 4/5/78 Age: 26

Year Team	Lg	G	GS	CG	GF	IP	BFP	H	R	ER	HR	SH	SF	HB	TBB	IBB	SO	WP	Bk	W	L	Pct	ShO	Sv-Op	Hld	ERC	ERA
1998 Princeton	R+	1	0	0	1	2.0	9	0	0	0	0	0	0	0	2	0	3	0	0	0	0	-	0	0--	-	0.84	0.00
1998 Princeton	R+	1	0	0	0	2.0	9	0	0	0	0	0	0	0	2	0	3	0	0	0	0	-	0	0--	-	0.84	0.00
2001 Chrlstn - SC	A	16	0	0	15	24.2	98	17	8	8	2	2	0	4	7	1	20	2	0	2	1	.667	0	7--	-	2.51	2.92
2001 Bakersfield	A+	17	0	0	12	24.2	97	13	7	3	1	0	2	0	8	0	33	2	0	1	0	1.000	0	3--	-	1.27	1.09
2001 Orlando	AA	14	0	0	1	22.0	94	20	14	14	1	0	0	4	11	0	20	2	0	1	0	1.000	0	0--	-	4.49	5.73
2002 Orlando	AA	20	14	3	4	92.1	400	91	58	48	9	2	1	5	37	1	45	9	0	4	6	.400	1	2--	-	4.19	4.68
2003 Durham	AAA	16	2	0	4	33.0	147	33	21	17	1	0	2	0	13	0	27	1	1	2	1	.667	0	0--	-	3.42	4.64
2002 Tampa Bay	AL	9	0	0	4	13.0	61	15	10	10	3	0	0	2	7	0	6	0	0	0	0	-	0	0-0	0	7.37	6.92
2003 Tampa Bay	AL	28	0	0	8	44.2	192	40	28	27	6	2	1	2	25	1	36	3	0	1	1	.500	0	0-0	5	4.64	5.44
2 ML YEARS		37	0	0	12	57.2	253	55	38	37	9	2	1	4	32	1	42	3	0	1	1	.500	0	0-0	5	5.22	5.77

Mike Bacsik

Pitches: L Bats: L Pos: SP-3; RP-2

Ht: 6'3" Wt: 190 Born: 11/11/77 Age: 26

Year Team	Lg	G	GS	CG	GF	IP	BFP	H	R	ER	HR	SH	SF	HB	TBB	IBB	SO	WP	Bk	W	L	Pct	ShO	Sv-Op	Hld	ERC	ERA
2003 Norfolk*	AAA	22	21	0	0	117.2	507	129	70	65	13	6	9	9	34	1	62	2	1	2	9	.182	0	0--	-	4.61	4.97
2001 Cleveland	AL	3	0	0	0	9.0	45	13	10	9	0	0	1	1	3	1	4	0	0	0	0	-	0	0-0	0	5.56	9.00
2002 New York	NL	11	9	1	1	55.2	247	63	29	27	8	5	1	4	19	3	30	0	0	3	2	.600	0	0-0	0	5.13	4.37
2003 New York	NL	5	3	0	1	17.2	85	28	21	20	5	0	1	0	8	0	12	0	0	1	2	.333	0	0-0	0	9.79	10.19
3 ML YEARS		19	12	1	2	82.1	377	104	60	56	13	5	3	5	30	4	46	0	0	4	4	.500	0	0-0	0	6.10	6.12

Carlos Baerga

Bats: B Throws: R Pos: PH-63; 1B-19; 2B-15; DH-6; 3B-5

Ht: 5'11" Wt: 215 Born: 11/4/68 Age: 35

Year Team	Lg	G	AB	H	2B	3B	HR	(Hm	Rd)	TB	R	RBI	RC	TBB	IBB	SO	HBP	SH	SF	SB	CS	SB%	GDP	Avg	OBP	Slg
1990 Cleveland	AL	108	312	81	17	2	7	(3	4)	123	46	47	36	16	2	57	4	1	5	0	2	.00	4	.260	.300	.394
1991 Cleveland	AL	158	593	171	28	2	11	(2	9)	236	80	69	81	48	5	74	6	4	3	3	2	.60	12	.288	.346	.398
1992 Cleveland	AL	161	657	205	32	1	20	(9	11)	299	92	105	103	35	10	76	13	2	9	10	2	.83	15	.312	.354	.455
1993 Cleveland	AL	154	624	200	28	6	21	(8	13)	303	105	114	104	34	7	68	6	3	13	15	4	.79	17	.321	.355	.486
1994 Cleveland	AL	103	442	139	32	2	19	(8	11)	232	81	80	74	10	1	45	6	3	8	8	2	.80	10	.314	.333	.525
1995 Cleveland	AL	135	557	175	28	2	15	(7	8)	252	87	90	87	35	6	31	3	0	5	11	2	.85	15	.314	.355	.452
1996 Cle-NYM		126	507	129	28	0	12	(5	7)	193	59	66	51	21	0	27	9	2	5	1	1	.50	23	.254	.293	.381
1997 New York	NL	133	467	131	25	1	9	(4	5)	185	53	52	53	20	1	54	3	3	5	2	6	.25	13	.281	.311	.396
1998 New York	NL	147	511	136	27	1	7	(3	4)	186	46	53	51	24	6	55	6	3	7	0	1	.00	21	.266	.303	.364
1999 SD-Cle		55	137	33	1	0	3	(2	1)	43	10	10	12	10	1	24	2	2	1	2	1	.67	5	.241	.300	.314
2002 Boston	AL	73	182	52	11	0	2	(1	1)	69	17	19	17	7	1	20	2	1	2	6	0	1.00	6	.286	.316	.379
2003 Arizona	NL	105	207	71	13	0	4	(4	0)	96	31	39	37	18	1	20	2	1	3	1	1	.50	6	.343	.396	.464
1996 Cleveland	AL	100	424	113	25	0	10	(5	5)	168	54	55	47	16	0	25	7	2	4	1	1	.50	15	.267	.302	.396
1996 New York	NL	26	83	16	3	0	2	(0	2)	25	5	11	4	5	0	2	2	0	1	0	0	-	8	.193	.253	.301
1999 San Diego	NL	33	80	20	1	0	2	(1	1)	27	6	5	9	6	0	14	2	1	0	1	0	1.00	2	.250	.318	.338
1999 Cleveland	AL	22	57	13	0	0	1	(1	0)	16	4	5	3	4	1	10	0	1	1	1	1	.50	3	.228	.274	.281
12 ML YEARS		1458	5196	1523	270	17	130	(56	74)	2217	707	744	706	278	41	551	62	25	66	59	24	.71	147	.293	.333	.427

Danys Baez

Pitches: R Bats: R Pos: RP-73

Ht: 6'3" Wt: 225 Born: 9/10/77 Age: 26

Year Team	Lg	G	GS	CG	GF	IP	BFP	H	R	ER	HR	SH	SF	HB	TBB	IBB	SO	WP	Bk	W	L	Pct	ShO	Sv-Op	Hld	ERC	ERA
2001 Cleveland	AL	43	0	0	8	50.1	202	34	22	14	5	0	1	3	20	4	52	3	0	5	3	.625	0	0-1	14	2.51	2.50
2002 Cleveland	AL	39	26	1	9	165.1	726	160	84	81	14	2	8	9	82	5	130	6	1	10	11	.476	0	6-8	0	4.35	4.41
2003 Cleveland	AL	73	0	0	46	75.2	318	65	36	32	9	6	1	4	23	0	66	5	0	2	9	.182	0	25-35	5	3.22	3.81
3 ML YEARS		155	26	1	63	291.1	1246	259	142	127	28	8	10	16	125	9	248	14	1	17	23	.425	0	31-44	19	3.72	3.92

Jeff Bagwell

Bats: R Throws: R Pos: 1B-158; PH-2

Ht: 6'0" Wt: 215 Born: 5/27/68 Age: 36

Year Team	Lg	G	AB	H	2B	3B	HR	(Hm	Rd)	TB	R	RBI	RC	TBB	IBB	SO	HBP	SH	SF	SB	CS	SB%	GDP	Avg	OBP	Slg
1991 Houston	NL	156	554	163	26	4	15	(6	9)	242	79	82	95	75	5	116	13	1	7	7	4	.64	12	.294	.387	.437
1992 Houston	NL	162	586	160	34	6	18	(8	10)	260	87	96	96	84	13	97	12	2	13	10	6	.63	17	.273	.368	.444
1993 Houston	NL	142	535	171	37	4	20	(9	11)	276	76	88	102	62	6	73	3	0	9	13	4	.76	20	.320	.388	.516
1994 Houston	NL	110	400	147	32	2	39	(23	16)	300	104	116	121	65	14	65	4	0	10	15	4	.79	12	.368	.451	.750
1995 Houston	NL	114	448	130	29	0	21	(10	11)	222	88	87	89	79	12	102	6	0	6	12	5	.71	9	.290	.399	.496
1996 Houston	NL	162	568	179	48	2	31	(16	15)	324	111	120	144	135	20	114	10	0	6	21	7	.75	15	.315	.451	.570
1997 Houston	NL	162	566	162	40	2	43	(22	21)	335	109	135	142	127	27	122	16	0	8	31	10	.76	10	.286	.425	.592
1998 Houston	NL	147	540	164	33	1	34	(20	14)	301	124	111	125	109	8	90	7	0	5	19	7	.73	14	.304	.424	.557
1999 Houston	NL	162	562	171	35	0	42	(12	30)	332	143	126	148	149	16	127	11	0	7	30	11	.73	18	.304	.454	.591
2000 Houston	NL	159	590	183	37	1	47	(28	19)	363	152	132	144	107	11	116	15	0	7	9	6	.60	14	.310	.424	.615
2001 Houston	NL	161	600	173	43	4	39	(21	18)	341	126	130	130	106	5	135	6	0	5	11	3	.79	20	.288	.397	.568
2002 Houston	NL	158	571	166	33	2	31	(16	15)	296	94	98	109	101	8	130	10	0	9	7	3	.70	16	.291	.401	.518
2003 Houston	NL	160	605	168	28	2	39	(22	17)	317	109	100	117	88	3	119	6	0	3	11	4	.73	25	.278	.373	.524
13 ML YEARS		1955	7125	2137	455	30	419	(213	206)	3909	1402	1421	1562	1287	148	1406	119	3	95	196	74	.73	207	.300	.411	.549

Paul Bako

Bats: L **Throws:** R **Pos:** C-69; PH-2   **Ht:** 6'2" **Wt:** 205 **Born:** 6/20/72 **Age:** 32

								BATTING												BASERUNNING				AVERAGES		
Year Team	Lg	G	AB	H	2B	3B	HR	(Hm Rd)	TB	R	RBI	RC	TBB	IBB	SO	HBP	SH	SF	SB	CS	SB%	GDP	Avg	OBP	Slg
1998 Detroit	AL	96	305	83	12	1	3	(2 1)	106	23	30	34	23	4	82	0	1	4	1	1	.50	3	.272	.319	.348
1999 Houston	NL	73	215	55	14	1	2	(2 0)	77	16	17	26	26	3	57	0	3	3	1	1	.50	4	.256	.332	.358
2000 Hou-Fla-Atl	NL	81	221	50	10	1	2	(2 0)	68	18	20	20	27	10	64	1	1	1	0	0	-	6	.226	.312	.308
2001 Atlanta	NL	61	137	29	10	1	2	(0 2)	47	19	15	15	20	2	34	0	0	0	1	0	1.00	3	.212	.312	.343
2002 Milwaukee	NL	87	234	55	8	1	4	(2 2)	77	24	20	19	20	3	46	0	3	0	0	2	.00	4	.235	.295	.329
2003 Chicago	NL	70	188	43	13	3	0	(0 0)	62	19	17	20	22	3	47	1	1	1	0	1	.00	2	.229	.311	.330
2000 Houston	NL	1	2	0	0	0	0	(0 0)	0	0	0	0	0	0	1	0	0	0	0	0	-	0	.000	.000	.000
2000 Florida	NL	56	161	39	6	1	0	(0 0)	47	10	14	16	22	7	48	1	1	1	0	0	-	4	.242	.335	.292
2000 Atlanta	NL	24	58	11	4	0	2	(2 0)	21	8	6	4	5	3	15	0	0	0	0	0	-	0	.190	.254	.362
6 ML YEARS		468	1300	315	67	8	13	(8 5)	437	119	119	134	138	25	330	2	9	9	3	5	.38	22	.242	.314	.336

Rocco Baldelli

Bats: R **Throws:** R **Pos:** CF-154; DH-2; PH-2; PR-2   **Ht:** 6'4" **Wt:** 187 **Born:** 9/25/81 **Age:** 22

								BATTING												BASERUNNING				AVERAGES		
Year Team	Lg	G	AB	H	2B	3B	HR	(Hm Rd)	TB	R	RBI	RC	TBB	IBB	SO	HBP	SH	SF	SB	CS	SB%	GDP	Avg	OBP	Slg
2000 Princeton	R+	60	232	50	9	2	3	(- -)	72	33	25	19	12	0	56	5	2	0	11	3	.79	3	.216	.269	.310
2001 Chrlstn - SC	A	113	406	101	23	6	8	(- -)	160	58	55	50	23	0	89	11	5	6	25	9	.74	7	.249	.303	.394
2002 Bakersfield	A+	77	312	104	19	1	14	(- -)	167	63	51	63	18	2	63	7	4	1	21	6	.78	2	.333	.382	.535
2002 Orlando	AA	17	70	26	3	1	2	(- -)	37	10	13	15	5	0	11	2	0	3	3	2	.60	1	.371	.413	.529
2002 Durham	AAA	23	96	28	6	1	3	(- -)	45	13	7	11	0	0	23	0	2	0	2	5	.29	1	.292	.292	.469
2003 Tampa Bay	AL	156	637	184	32	8	11	(2 9)	265	89	78	76	30	4	128	8	3	6	27	10	.73	10	.289	.326	.416

James Baldwin

Pitches: R **Bats:** R **Pos:** RP-10   **Ht:** 6'3" **Wt:** 235 **Born:** 7/15/71 **Age:** 32

		HOW MUCH HE PITCHED						WHAT HE GAVE UP												THE RESULTS						
Year Team	Lg	G	GS	CG	GF	IP	BFP	H	R	ER	HR	SH	SF	HB	TBB	IBB	SO	WP	Bk	W	L	Pct	ShO	Sv-Op	Hld	ERC	ERA
2003 Rochester*	AAA	5	5	0	0	29.2	114	25	11	8	2	0	0	0	3	0	18	0	0	0	2	.000	0	0--	-	2.01	2.43
2003 Omaha*	AAA	8	8	0	0	46.1	200	48	25	21	3	0	3	3	13	0	24	3	1	3	2	.600	0	0--	-	3.79	4.08
1995 Chicago	AL	6	4	0	0	14.2	81	32	22	21	6	0	0	0	9	1	10	1	0	0	1	.000	0	0-0	0	16.49	12.89
1996 Chicago	AL	28	28	0	0	169.0	719	168	88	83	24	2	2	4	57	3	127	12	1	11	6	.647	0	0-0	0	4.17	4.42
1997 Chicago	AL	32	32	1	0	200.0	879	205	128	117	19	3	6	5	83	3	140	14	3	12	15	.444	0	0-0	0	4.28	5.27
1998 Chicago	AL	37	24	1	3	159.0	712	176	103	94	18	3	5	10	60	2	108	5	1	13	6	.684	0	0-1	0	4.89	5.32
1999 Chicago	AL	35	33	1	1	199.1	886	219	119	113	34	4	7	7	81	1	123	11	1	12	13	.480	0	0-0	0	5.33	5.10
2000 Chicago	AL	29	28	2	0	178.0	758	185	96	92	34	6	5	8	59	3	116	4	1	14	7	.667	1	0-0	0	4.91	4.65
2001 CWS-LA		29	28	2	0	175.0	764	191	95	86	25	7	7	7	63	1	95	7	0	11	11	.476	1	0-0	0	4.94	4.42
2002 Seattle	AL	30	23	0	4	150.0	662	179	95	88	26	4	2	7	49	2	88	1	0	7	10	.412	0	0-0	0	5.70	5.28
2003 Minnesota	AL	10	0	0	3	15.0	69	21	10	9	6	0	2	0	4	1	7	0	0	1	0	1.000	0	1-2	1	8.09	5.40
2001 Chicago	AL	17	16	2	0	95.2	431	109	56	49	15	3	5	4	38	0	42	4	0	7	5	.583	1	0-0	0	5.44	4.61
2001 Los Angeles	NL	12	12	0	0	79.1	333	82	39	37	10	4	2	3	25	1	53	3	0	3	6	.333	0	0-0	0	4.35	4.20
9 ML YEARS		236	200	7	11	1260.0	5530	1376	756	703	192	29	36	48	465	17	814	55	7	79	70	.530	2	1-3	1	5.01	5.02

John Bale

Pitches: L **Bats:** L **Pos:** SP-9; RP-1   **Ht:** 6'4" **Wt:** 205 **Born:** 5/22/74 **Age:** 30

		HOW MUCH HE PITCHED						WHAT HE GAVE UP												THE RESULTS						
Year Team	Lg	G	GS	CG	GF	IP	BFP	H	R	ER	HR	SH	SF	HB	TBB	IBB	SO	WP	Bk	W	L	Pct	ShO	Sv-Op	Hld	ERC	ERA
2003 Norfolk*	AAA	8	0	0	1	13.2	55	11	5	5	0	1	1	0	3	0	15	0	0	0	1	.000	0	0--	-	1.78	3.29
2003 Louisville*	AAA	26	2	0	14	43.2	181	36	17	16	1	1	2	2	13	0	43	1	0	4	1	.800	0	4--	-	2.40	3.30
1999 Toronto	AL	1	0	0	0	2.0	10	2	0	3	1	0	0	0	2	0	4	0	0	0	0	-	0	0-0	0	9.87	13.50
2000 Toronto	AL	2	0	0	0	3.2	22	5	0	6	1	0	0	0	3	0	6	0	0	0	0	-	0	0-0	0	8.10	14.73
2001 Baltimore	AL	14	0	0	0	26.2	113	18	0	9	2	0	0	0	17	0	21	0	0	1	0	1.000	0	0-0	0	3.05	3.04
2003 Cincinnati	NL	10	9	0	0	46.1	195	50	24	23	7	1	2	2	12	2	37	1	0	1	2	.333	0	0-0	0	4.52	4.47
4 ML YEARS		27	9	0	0	78.2	340	75	24	41	11	1	2	2	34	2	68	1	0	2	2	.500	0	0-0	0	4.28	4.69

Grant Balfour

Pitches: R **Bats:** R **Pos:** RP-16; SP-1   **Ht:** 6'2" **Wt:** 185 **Born:** 12/30/77 **Age:** 26

		HOW MUCH HE PITCHED						WHAT HE GAVE UP												THE RESULTS						
Year Team	Lg	G	GS	CG	GF	IP	BFP	H	R	ER	HR	SH	SF	HB	TBB	IBB	SO	WP	Bk	W	L	Pct	ShO	Sv-Op	Hld	ERC	ERA
1997 Twins	R	13	12	0	0	67.0	275	73	31	28	1	0	1	4	20	0	43	3	2	2	4	.333	0	0--	-	4.06	3.76
1998 Elizabethton	R+	13	13	0	0	77.2	327	70	36	29	7	0	2	5	27	0	75	6	0	7	2	.778	0	0--	-	3.53	3.36
1999 Quad City	A	19	14	0	2	91.2	368	66	39	36	7	1	1	6	37	0	95	1	0	8	5	.615	0	1--	-	2.78	3.53
2000 Fort Myers	A+	35	10	0	13	89.0	392	91	46	42	8	3	1	8	34	2	90	10	1	8	5	.615	0	6--	-	4.37	4.25
2001 New Britain	AA	35	0	0	24	50.0	197	26	6	6	1	1	0	0	22	2	72	1	0	2	1	.667	0	13--	-	1.40	1.08
2001 Edmonton	AAA	11	0	0	2	16.1	73	18	11	10	2	3	1	0	10	1	17	2	0	2	2	.500	0	0--	-	5.79	5.51
2002 Edmonton	AAA	58	0	0	25	71.1	296	60	34	33	3	3	3	0	30	1	88	2	1	2	4	.333	0	8--	-	2.92	4.16
2003 Rochester	AAA	21	11	0	10	71.0	276	48	21	19	6	1	0	3	16	0	87	0	1	5	2	.714	0	5--	-	1.87	2.41
2001 Minnesota	AL	2	0	0	0	2.2	14	3	0	4	2	0	0	0	3	0	2	0	0	0	0	-	0	0-0	0	13.78	13.50
2003 Minnesota	AL	17	1	0	6	26.0	115	23	12	12	4	2	1	0	14	2	30	0	0	1	0	1.000	0	0-1	1	4.14	4.15
2 ML YEARS		19	1	0	6	28.2	129	26	12	16	6	2	1	0	17	2	32	0	0	1	0	1.000	0	0-1	1	4.89	5.02

Brian Banks

Bats: B **Throws:** R **Pos:** PH-53; LF-23; 1B-12; RF-10; DH-1; PR-1   **Ht:** 6'3" **Wt:** 210 **Born:** 9/28/70 **Age:** 33

								BATTING													BASERUNNING				AVERAGES		
Year Team	Lg	G	AB	H	2B	3B	HR	(Hm	Rd)	TB	R	RBI	RC	TBB	IBB	SO	HBP	SH	SF	SB	CS	SB%	GDP	Avg	OBP	Slg
1996 Milwaukee	NL	4	7	4	2	0	1	(0	1)	9	2	2	4	1	0	2	0	0	0	0	0	-	0	.571	.625	1.286
1997 Milwaukee	NL	28	68	14	1	0	1	(0	1)	18	9	8	8	6	0	17	0	0	1	0	1	.00	1	.206	.267	.265
1998 Milwaukee	NL	24	24	7	2	0	1	(0	1)	12	3	5	5	4	0	7	0	0	0	0	0	-	0	.292	.393	.500
1999 Milwaukee	NL	105	219	53	7	1	5	(4	1)	77	34	22	26	25	5	59	0	3	2	6	1	.86	2	.242	.317	.352
2002 Florida	NL	20	28	9	1	0	1	(1	0)	13	3	4	4	1	0	6	0	0	0	0	0	-	0	.321	.345	.464
2003 Florida	NL	92	149	35	6	2	4	(1	3)	57	14	23	19	25	1	38	2	2	2	2	1	.67	4	.235	.348	.383
6 ML YEARS		273	495	122	19	3	13	(6	7)	186	65	64	62	62	6	129	2	5	5	8	3	.73	7	.246	.330	.376

Rod Barajas

Bats: R **Throws:** R **Pos:** C-79; PH-1   **Ht:** 6'2" **Wt:** 229 **Born:** 9/5/75 **Age:** 28

								BATTING													BASERUNNING				AVERAGES		
Year Team	Lg	G	AB	H	2B	3B	HR	(Hm	Rd)	TB	R	RBI	RC	TBB	IBB	SO	HBP	SH	SF	SB	CS	SB%	GDP	Avg	OBP	Slg
2003 Tucson*	AAA	4	16	7	1	0	1	(-	-)	11	3	4	5	1	0	1	0	0	0	0	0	-	0	.438	.471	.688
2003 Lancaster*	A+	3	12	5	0	0	0	(-	-)	5	2	3	2	1	0	2	0	0	0	0	0	-	0	.417	.462	.417
1999 Arizona	NL	5	16	4	1	0	1	(1	0)	8	3	3	2	1	0	1	0	1	0	0	0	-	0	.250	.294	.500
2000 Arizona	NL	5	13	3	0	0	1	(1	0)	6	1	3	1	0	0	4	0	0	0	0	0	-	0	.231	.231	.462
2001 Arizona	NL	51	106	17	3	0	3	(2	1)	29	9	9	4	4	0	26	0	0	0	0	0	-	0	.160	.191	.274
2002 Arizona	NL	70	154	36	10	0	3	(1	2)	55	12	23	16	10	4	25	3	2	3	1	0	1.00	4	.234	.288	.357
2003 Arizona	NL	80	220	48	15	0	3	(3	0)	72	19	28	20	14	7	43	1	1	3	0	0	-	6	.218	.265	.327
5 ML YEARS		211	509	108	29	0	11	(8	3)	170	44	66	43	29	11	99	4	4	6	1	0	1.00	10	.212	.257	.334

Josh Bard

Bats: B **Throws:** R **Pos:** C-87; PH-8   **Ht:** 6'3" **Wt:** 215 **Born:** 3/20/78 **Age:** 26

								BATTING													BASERUNNING				AVERAGES		
Year Team	Lg	G	AB	H	2B	3B	HR	(Hm	Rd)	TB	R	RBI	RC	TBB	IBB	SO	HBP	SH	SF	SB	CS	SB%	GDP	Avg	OBP	Slg
2000 Salem	A+	93	309	88	17	0	2	(-	-)	111	40	25	40	32	1	33	1	1	2	3	1	.75	6	.285	.352	.359
2000 Co Springs	AAA	4	17	4	0	0	0	(-	-)	4	0	1	1	0	0	2	0	0	0	0	0	-	0	.235	.235	.235
2001 Carolina	AA	35	124	32	13	0	1	(-	-)	48	14	24	18	19	1	23	1	1	1	0	1	.00	1	.258	.359	.387
2001 Mahning VI	A-	13	44	12	4	0	2	(-	-)	22	7	8	8	6	0	2	1	0	0	0	1	.00	1	.273	.373	.500
2001 Akron	AA	51	194	54	11	0	4	(-	-)	77	26	25	26	16	1	27	2	1	1	0	0	-	4	.278	.338	.397
2001 Buffalo	AAA	1	4	0	0	0	0	(-	-)	0	0	0	0	0	0	1	0	0	0	0	0	-	0	.000	.000	.000
2002 Buffalo	AAA	94	344	102	26	2	6	(-	-)	150	36	53	46	20	0	45	0	3	3	0	0	-	13	.297	.332	.436
2003 Buffalo	AAA	35	115	38	7	0	5	(-	-)	60	14	21	22	14	1	17	1	0	0	1	2	.33	1	.330	.408	.522
2002 Cleveland	AL	24	90	20	5	0	3	(2	1)	34	9	12	7	4	0	13	0	1	0	0	0	-	6	.222	.255	.378
2003 Cleveland	AL	91	303	74	13	1	8	(5	3)	113	25	36	33	22	1	53	0	1	3	0	2	.00	9	.244	.293	.373
2 ML YEARS		115	393	94	18	1	11	(7	4)	147	34	48	40	26	1	66	0	2	3	0	2	.00	15	.239	.284	.374

Clint Barmes

Bats: R **Throws:** R **Pos:** SS-12; PR-1   **Ht:** 6'0" **Wt:** 175 **Born:** 3/6/79 **Age:** 25

								BATTING													BASERUNNING				AVERAGES		
Year Team	Lg	G	AB	H	2B	3B	HR	(Hm	Rd)	TB	R	RBI	RC	TBB	IBB	SO	HBP	SH	SF	SB	CS	SB%	GDP	Avg	OBP	Slg
2000 Asheville	A	19	81	14	4	0	0	(-	-)	18	11	4	5	10	0	13	1	2	1	4	1	.80	3	.173	.269	.222
2000 Portland	AA	45	181	51	6	4	2	(-	-)	71	37	16	26	18	0	28	5	0	1	12	9	.57	1	.282	.361	.392
2001 Asheville	A	74	285	74	14	1	5	(-	-)	105	40	24	34	17	0	37	7	3	3	21	7	.75	6	.260	.314	.368
2001 Salem	A+	38	121	30	3	3	0	(-	-)	39	17	9	14	15	0	20	4	2	0	4	1	.80	5	.248	.350	.322
2002 Carolina	AA	103	438	119	23	2	15	(-	-)	191	62	60	63	31	3	72	9	2	5	15	11	.58	3	.272	.329	.436
2003 Co Springs	AAA	136	493	136	35	1	7	(-	-)	194	63	54	60	22	2	63	9	4	5	12	7	.63	9	.276	.316	.394
2003 Colorado	NL	12	25	8	2	0	0	(0	0)	10	2	2	3	0	0	10	2	0	1	0	0	-	0	.320	.357	.400

Larry Barnes

Bats: L **Throws:** L **Pos:** PH-19; 1B-8; LF-2; PR-2   **Ht:** 6'1" **Wt:** 195 **Born:** 7/23/74 **Age:** 29

								BATTING													BASERUNNING				AVERAGES		
Year Team	Lg	G	AB	H	2B	3B	HR	(Hm	Rd)	TB	R	RBI	RC	TBB	IBB	SO	HBP	SH	SF	SB	CS	SB%	GDP	Avg	OBP	Slg
1995 Angels	R	56	197	51	8	3	3	(-	-)	74	42	37	30	27	0	40	5	1	2	12	5	.71	1	.259	.359	.376
1996 Cedar Rpds	A	131	489	155	36	5	27	(-	-)	282	84	112	105	58	5	101	6	1	6	9	6	.60	8	.317	.392	.577
1997 Lk Elsinore	A+	115	446	128	32	2	13	(-	-)	203	68	71	71	43	4	84	5	1	5	3	4	.43	6	.287	.353	.455
1998 Lk Elsinore	A+	51	183	45	11	2	7	(-	-)	81	32	33	27	22	2	49	1	0	0	2	0	1.00	3	.246	.330	.443
1998 Midland	AA	69	245	67	16	4	6	(-	-)	109	29	35	38	28	3	54	1	2	2	4	2	.67	5	.273	.348	.445
1999 Erie	AA	130	497	142	25	9	20	(-	-)	245	73	100	87	49	7	99	5	0	16	14	3	.82	7	.286	.346	.493
2000 Edmonton	AAA	103	397	102	22	11	7	(-	-)	167	56	54	56	48	5	81	0	0	3	3	6	.33	4	.257	.335	.421
2001 Salt Lake	AAA	100	404	117	21	8	18	(-	-)	208	78	73	69	29	1	90	1	0	2	6	1	.86	6	.290	.337	.515
2002 Salt Lake	AAA	114	452	142	29	11	20	(-	-)	253	71	95	85	28	5	90	4	0	8	8	1	.89	11	.314	.354	.560
2003 Salt Lake	AAA	82	302	83	20	3	15	(-	-)	154	43	57	50	23	3	61	2	0	4	4	1	.80	3	.275	.326	.510
2001 Anaheim	AL	16	40	4	0	0	1	(1	0)	7	2	2	1	1	0	9	0	0	0	0	0	-	1	.100	.122	.175
2003 Los Angeles	NL	30	38	8	2	0	0	(0	0)	10	2	2	4	1	0	9	0	0	0	0	0	-	0	.211	.231	.263
2 ML YEARS		46	78	12	2	0	1	(1	0)	17	4	4	5	2	0	18	0	0	0	0	0	-	1	.154	.175	.218

Michael Barrett

Bats: R **Throws:** R **Pos:** C-68; PH-5; PR-1   **Ht:** 6'2" **Wt:** 200 **Born:** 10/22/76 **Age:** 27

								BATTING													BASERUNNING				AVERAGES		
Year Team	Lg	G	AB	H	2B	3B	HR	(Hm	Rd)	TB	R	RBI	RC	TBB	IBB	SO	HBP	SH	SF	SB	CS	SB%	GDP	Avg	OBP	Slg
2003 Edmonton*	AAA	2	6	2	1	0	0	(-	-)	3	2	0	1	0	0	2	0	0	0	1	0	1.00	0	.333	.333	.500
1998 Montreal	NL	8	23	7	2	0	1	(0	1)	12	3	2	5	3	0	6	1	0	0	0	0	-	0	.304	.407	.522
1999 Montreal	NL	126	433	127	32	3	8	(5	3)	189	53	52	59	32	4	39	3	0	1	0	2	.00	18	.293	.345	.436
2000 Montreal	NL	89	271	58	15	1	1	(0	1)	78	28	22	19	23	5	35	1	1	0	0	1	.00	7	.214	.277	.288

Year Team		Lg	G	AB	H	2B	3B	HR	(Hm	Rd)	TB	R	RBI	RC	TBB	IBB	SO	HBP	SH	SF	SB	CS	SB%	GDP	Avg	OBP	Slg
													BATTING										BASERUNNING			AVERAGES		
2001 Montreal		NL	132	472	118	33	2	6	(3	3)	173	42	38	46	25	2	54	2	4	3	2	1	.67	14	.250	.289	.367
2002 Montreal		NL	117	376	99	20	1	12	(4	8)	157	41	49	49	40	7	65	1	6	5	6	3	.67	14	.263	.332	.418
2003 Montreal		NL	70	226	47	9	2	10	(5	5)	90	33	30	25	21	7	37	2	2	1	0	0	-	6	.208	.280	.398
6 ML YEARS			542	1801	456	111	9	38	(17	21)	699	200	193	203	144	25	236	10	13	11	8	7	.53	59	.253	.310	.388

Miguel Batista

Pitches: R **Bats:** R **Pos:** SP-29; RP-7   **Ht:** 6'2" **Wt:** 195 **Born:** 2/19/71 **Age:** 33

Year Team		Lg	G	GS	CG	GF	IP	BFP	H	R	ER	HR	SH	SF	HB	TBB	IBB	SO	WP	Bk	W	L	Pct	ShO	Sv-Op	Hld	ERC	ERA
					HOW MUCH HE PITCHED					WHAT HE GAVE UP												THE RESULTS					
1992 Pittsburgh		NL	1	0	0	1	2.0	13	4	2	2	1	0	0	0	3	0	1	0	0	0	0	-	0	0-0	0	20.26	9.00
1996 Florida		NL	9	0	0	4	11.1	49	9	8	7	0	3	0	0	7	2	6	1	0	0	0	-	0	0-0	0	2.77	5.56
1997 Chicago		NL	11	6	0	2	36.1	168	36	24	23	4	4	4	1	24	2	27	2	0	0	5	.000	0	0-0	0	5.09	5.70
1998 Montreal		NL	56	13	0	12	135.0	598	141	66	57	12	7	5	6	65	7	92	6	1	3	5	.375	0	0-0	3	4.70	3.80
1999 Montreal		NL	39	17	2	3	134.2	606	146	88	73	10	8	11	7	58	2	95	6	0	8	7	.533	1	1-1	0	4.62	4.88
2000 Mon-KC			18	9	0	2	65.1	310	85	68	62	19	1	2	2	37	2	37	4	0	2	7	.222	0	0-2	0	8.37	8.54
2001 Arizona		NL	48	18	0	6	139.1	581	113	57	52	13	9	3	10	60	2	90	6	0	11	8	.579	0	0-0	4	3.43	3.36
2002 Arizona		NL	36	29	1	2	184.2	790	172	99	88	12	5	8	6	70	3	114	9	2	8	9	.471	0	0-0	2	3.45	4.29
2003 Arizona		NL	36	29	2	5	193.1	822	197	85	76	13	10	6	8	60	3	142	7	0	10	9	.526	1	0-0	0	3.77	3.54
2000 Montreal		NL	4	0	0	0	8.1	49	19	14	13	2	1	1	2	3	0	7	0	0	0	1	.000	0	0-2	0	14.73	14.04
2000 Kansas City		AL	14	9	0	2	57.0	261	66	54	49	17	0	1	0	34	2	30	4	0	2	6	.250	0	0-0	0	7.50	7.74
9 ML YEARS			254	121	5	37	902.0	3937	903	497	440	84	47	39	40	384	23	602	41	3	42	50	.457	2	1-3	9	4.28	4.39

Tony Batista

Bats: R **Throws:** R **Pos:** 3B-154; DH-7; PH-1   **Ht:** 6'0" **Wt:** 205 **Born:** 12/9/73 **Age:** 30

Year Team		Lg	G	AB	H	2B	3B	HR	(Hm	Rd)	TB	R	RBI	RC	TBB	IBB	SO	HBP	SH	SF	SB	CS	SB%	GDP	Avg	OBP	Slg
													BATTING										BASERUNNING			AVERAGES		
1996 Oakland		AL	74	238	71	10	2	6	(1	5)	103	38	25	37	19	0	49	1	0	2	7	3	.70	2	.298	.350	.433
1997 Oakland		AL	68	188	38	10	1	4	(0	4)	62	22	18	14	14	0	31	2	3	0	2	2	.50	8	.202	.265	.330
1998 Arizona		NL	106	293	80	16	1	18	(9	9)	152	46	41	46	18	0	52	3	0	4	1	1	.50	7	.273	.318	.519
1999 Ari-Tor			142	519	144	30	1	31	(10	21)	269	77	100	87	38	4	96	6	3	7	4	0	1.00	12	.277	.330	.518
2000 Toronto		AL	154	620	163	32	2	41	(25	16)	322	96	114	94	35	1	121	6	0	3	5	4	.56	15	.263	.307	.519
2001 Tor-Bal			156	579	138	27	6	25	(14	11)	252	70	87	70	32	1	113	4	0	7	5	2	.71	9	.238	.280	.435
2002 Baltimore		AL	161	615	150	36	1	31	(14	17)	281	90	87	80	50	9	107	11	0	6	5	4	.56	13	.244	.309	.457
2003 Baltimore		AL	161	631	148	20	1	26	(10	16)	248	76	99	66	28	4	102	5	0	6	4	3	.57	20	.235	.270	.393
1999 Arizona		NL	44	144	37	5	0	5	(1	4)	57	16	21	21	16	3	17	2	0	2	2	0	1.00	1	.257	.335	.396
1999 Toronto			98	375	107	25	1	26	(9	17)	212	61	79	66	22	1	79	4	3	5	2	0	1.00	11	.285	.328	.565
2001 Toronto		AL	72	271	56	11	1	13	(9	4)	108	29	45	27	13	1	66	4	0	3	0	1	.00	2	.207	.251	.399
2001 Baltimore		AL	84	308	82	16	5	12	(5	7)	144	41	42	43	19	0	47	0	0	4	5	1	.83	7	.266	.305	.468
8 ML YEARS			1022	3683	932	181	15	182	(83	99)	1689	515	571	494	234	19	671	38	6	35	33	19	.63	86	.253	.302	.459

Rick Bauer

Pitches: R **Bats:** R **Pos:** RP-35   **Ht:** 6'6" **Wt:** 212 **Born:** 1/10/77 **Age:** 27

Year Team		Lg	G	GS	CG	GF	IP	BFP	H	R	ER	HR	SH	SF	HB	TBB	IBB	SO	WP	Bk	W	L	Pct	ShO	Sv-Op	Hld	ERC	ERA
					HOW MUCH HE PITCHED					WHAT HE GAVE UP												THE RESULTS					
2003 Ottawa*		AAA	7	7	0	0	36.2	150	31	10	10	1	1	1	3	13	0	21	0	0	3	1	.750	0	0- -	-	2.98	2.45
2001 Baltimore		AL	6	6	0	0	33.0	143	35	22	17	7	0	1	1	9	0	16	0	0	0	5	.000	0	0-0	0	4.74	4.64
2002 Baltimore		AL	56	1	0	15	83.2	358	84	41	37	12	2	2	4	36	4	45	4	0	6	7	.462	0	1-5	12	4.78	3.98
2003 Baltimore		AL	35	0	0	10	61.1	259	58	36	31	5	1	3	4	24	3	43	6	0	0	0	-	0	0-1	3	3.87	4.55
3 ML YEARS			97	7	0	25	178.0	760	177	99	85	24	3	6	9	69	7	104	10	0	6	12	.333	0	1-6	15	4.46	4.30

Danny Bautista

Bats: R **Throws:** R **Pos:** RF-59; CF-18; PH-11; LF-3; PR-1   **Ht:** 5'11" **Wt:** 204 **Born:** 5/24/72 **Age:** 32

Year Team		Lg	G	AB	H	2B	3B	HR	(Hm	Rd)	TB	R	RBI	RC	TBB	IBB	SO	HBP	SH	SF	SB	CS	SB%	GDP	Avg	OBP	Slg
													BATTING										BASERUNNING			AVERAGES		
2003 Tucson*		AAA	8	24	9	1	1	1	(-	-)	15	4	4	5	2	0	2	0	0	0	1	1	.50	2	.375	.423	.625
2003 El Paso*		AA	2	7	1	0	0	0	(-	-)	1	1	1	0	1	0	2	0	0	0	0	0	-	0	.143	.250	.143
1993 Detroit		AL	17	61	19	3	0	1	(0	1)	25	6	9	8	1	0	10	0	0	1	3	1	.75	1	.311	.317	.410
1994 Detroit		AL	31	99	23	4	1	4	(3	1)	41	12	15	9	3	0	18	0	0	0	1	2	.33	3	.232	.255	.414
1995 Detroit		AL	89	271	55	9	0	7	(3	4)	85	28	27	18	12	0	68	0	6	0	4	1	.80	6	.203	.237	.314
1996 Det-Atl			42	84	19	2	0	2	(1	1)	27	13	9	8	11	0	20	1	0	0	1	2	.33	4	.226	.323	.321
1997 Atlanta		NL	64	103	25	3	2	3	(1	2)	41	14	9	11	5	1	24	1	2	1	2	0	1.00	4	.243	.282	.398
1998 Atlanta		NL	82	144	36	11	0	3	(2	1)	56	17	17	15	7	0	21	0	3	2	1	0	1.00	4	.250	.281	.389
1999 Florida		NL	70	205	59	10	1	5	(3	2)	86	32	24	25	4	0	30	1	0	1	3	0	1.00	5	.288	.303	.420
2000 Fla-Ari			131	351	100	20	7	11	(5	6)	167	54	59	54	25	4	50	3	4	5	6	2	.75	11	.285	.333	.476
2001 Arizona		NL	100	222	67	11	2	5	(0	5)	97	26	26	31	14	1	31	1	2	0	3	2	.60	7	.302	.346	.437
2002 Arizona		NL	40	154	50	5	2	6	(4	2)	77	22	23	26	11	2	21	0	0	1	4	2	.67	4	.325	.367	.500
2003 Arizona		NL	88	284	78	16	3	4	(2	2)	112	29	36	33	21	2	50	4	2	3	3	2	.60	7	.275	.330	.394
1996 Detroit		AL	25	64	16	2	0	2	(1	1)	24	12	8	8	9	0	15	0	0	0	1	2	.33	1	.250	.342	.375
1996 Atlanta		NL	17	20	3	0	0	0	(0	0)	3	1	1	0	2	0	5	1	0	0	0	0	-	3	.150	.261	.150
2000 Florida		NL	44	89	17	4	0	4	(1	3)	33	9	12	8	5	0	20	0	0	0	1	0	1.00	1	.191	.234	.371
2000 Arizona		NL	87	262	83	16	7	7	(4	3)	134	45	47	46	20	4	30	3	4	5	5	2	.71	10	.317	.366	.511
11 ML YEARS			754	1978	531	94	18	51	(21	30)	814	253	254	238	114	10	343	11	19	14	31	14	.69	55	.268	.310	.412

Jay Bay

Bats: R **Throws:** R **Pos:** LF-24; CF-5; PH-2; RF-1   **Ht:** 6'2" **Wt:** 200 **Born:** 9/20/78 **Age:** 25

						BATTING													BASERUNNING				AVERAGES		
Year Team	Lg	G	AB	H	2B	3B	HR	(Hm | Rd)	TB	R	RBI	RC	TBB	IBB	SO	HBP	SH	SF	SB	CS	SB%	GDP	Avg	OBP	Slg
2000 Vermont	A-	35	135	41	5	0	2	(- | -)	52	17	12	21	11	0	25	1	0	1	17	4	.81	2	.304	.358	.385
2001 Jupiter	A+	38	123	24	4	1	1	(- | -)	33	12	10	11	18	1	26	2	1	1	10	3	.77	4	.195	.306	.268
2001 Clinton	A	87	318	115	20	4	13	(- | -)	182	67	61	80	48	0	62	4	1	2	15	2	.88	4	.362	.449	.572
2002 St.Lucie	A+	69	261	71	12	2	9	(- | -)	114	48	54	46	34	3	54	5	2	3	22	2	.92	4	.272	.363	.437
2002 Binghamton	AA	34	107	31	4	2	4	(- | -)	51	17	19	21	15	0	23	3	0	3	13	3	.81	2	.290	.383	.477
2002 Mobile	AA	23	81	25	5	2	4	(- | -)	46	16	12	19	13	1	22	1	0	0	4	2	.67	0	.309	.411	.568
2003 Portland	AAA	91	307	93	11	1	20	(- | -)	166	64	59	72	55	1	71	5	0	6	23	4	.85	3	.303	.410	.541
2003 SD-Pit	NL	30	87	25	7	1	4	(2 | 2)	46	15	14	19	19	0	29	1	0	0	3	1	.75	0	.287	.421	.529
2003 San Diego	NL	3	8	2	1	0	0	(0 | 1)	6	2	2	2	1	0	1	1	0	0	0	0	-	0	.250	.400	.750
2003 Pittsburgh	NL	27	79	23	6	1	3	(2 | 1)	40	13	12	17	18	0	28	0	0	0	3	1	.75	0	.291	.423	.506

Rod Beck

Pitches: R **Bats:** R **Pos:** RP-36   **Ht:** 6'1" **Wt:** 235 **Born:** 8/3/68 **Age:** 35

		HOW MUCH HE PITCHED						WHAT HE GAVE UP										THE RESULTS						
Year Team	Lg	G	GS	CG	GF	IP	BFP	H	R	ER	HR	SH	SF	HB	TBB	IBB	SO	WP	Bk	W	L	Pct	ShO	Sv-Op Hld	ERC	ERA
2003 Iowa*	AAA	21	0	0	9	30.2	122	25	3	2	2	4	1	0	7	0	26	1	0	1	1	.500	0	4-- -	2.27	0.59
1991 San Francisco	NL	31	0	0	10	52.1	214	53	22	22	4	4	2	1	13	2	38	0	0	1	1	.500	0	1-1 1	3.52	3.78
1992 San Francisco	NL	65	0	0	42	92.0	352	62	20	18	4	6	2	2	15	2	87	5	2	3	3	.500	0	17-23 4	1.44	1.76
1993 San Francisco	NL	76	0	0	71	79.1	309	57	20	19	11	6	3	3	13	4	86	4	0	3	1	.750	0	48-52 0	2.05	2.16
1994 San Francisco	NL	48	0	0	47	48.2	207	49	17	15	10	3	3	0	13	2	39	0	0	2	4	.333	0	28-28 0	4.17	2.77
1995 San Francisco	NL	60	0	0	52	58.2	255	60	31	29	7	4	3	2	21	3	42	2	0	5	6	.455	0	33-43 0	4.20	4.45
1996 San Francisco	NL	63	0	0	58	62.0	248	56	23	23	9	0	2	1	10	2	48	1	0	0	9	.000	0	35-42 0	2.95	3.34
1997 San Francisco	NL	73	0	0	66	70.0	281	67	31	27	7	1	0	2	8	2	53	1	0	7	4	.636	0	37-45 1	2.84	3.47
1998 Chicago	NL	81	0	0	70	80.1	349	86	33	27	11	2	5	2	20	4	81	2	0	3	4	.429	0	51-58 1	4.05	3.02
1999 ChC-Bos		43	0	0	27	44.0	196	50	29	29	5	2	2	1	18	3	25	1	0	2	5	.286	0	10-15 3	4.99	5.93
2000 Boston	AL	34	0	0	8	40.2	169	34	15	14	2	2	0	2	12	1	35	1	0	3	0	1.000	0	0-3 7	2.59	3.10
2001 Boston	AL	68	0	0	28	80.2	342	77	42	35	15	3	2	3	28	6	63	5	1	6	4	.600	0	6-11 15	4.25	3.90
2003 San Diego	NL	36	0	0	30	35.1	140	25	7	7	4	1	0	1	11	2	32	0	0	3	2	.600	0	20-20 1	2.35	1.78
1999 Chicago	NL	31	0	0	19	30.0	141	41	26	26	5	2	2	0	13	3	13	1	0	2	4	.333	0	7-11 1	6.75	7.80
1999 Boston	AL	12	0	0	8	14.0	55	9	3	3	0	0	0	1	5	0	12	0	0	0	1	.000	0	3-4 2	1.79	1.93
12 ML YEARS		678	0	0	509	744.0	3062	676	290	265	89	34	24	20	182	33	629	22	3	38	43	.469	0	286-341 33	3.14	3.21

Josh Beckett

Pitches: R **Bats:** R **Pos:** SP-23; RP-1   **Ht:** 6'5" **Wt:** 216 **Born:** 5/15/80 **Age:** 24

		HOW MUCH HE PITCHED						WHAT HE GAVE UP										THE RESULTS						
Year Team	Lg	G	GS	CG	GF	IP	BFP	H	R	ER	HR	SH	SF	HB	TBB	IBB	SO	WP	Bk	W	L	Pct	ShO	Sv-Op	ERC	ERA
2003 Carolina*	AA	1	1	0	0	4.0	15	4	2	2	1	0	0	0	0	0	7	0	0	0	0	-	0	0-- -	3.59	4.50
2003 Jupiter	A+	1	1	0	0	3.0	11	2	0	0	0	0	0	0	0	0	5	0	0	0	0	-	0	0-- -	0.91	0.00
2001 Florida	NL	4	4	0	0	24.0	99	14	9	4	3	0	0	1	11	0	24	1	0	2	2	.500	0	0-0 0	2.36	1.50
2002 Florida	NL	23	21	0	0	107.2	454	93	56	49	13	5	3	1	44	2	113	5	0	6	7	.462	0	0-0 0	3.50	4.10
2003 Florida	NL	24	23	0	1	142.0	601	132	54	48	9	5	1	2	56	4	152	6	1	9	8	.529	0	0-0 0	3.44	3.04
3 ML YEARS		51	48	0	1	273.2	1154	239	119	101	25	10	4	4	111	6	289	12	1	17	17	.500	0	0-0 0	3.37	3.32

Joe Beimel

Pitches: L **Bats:** L **Pos:** RP-69   **Ht:** 6'3" **Wt:** 215 **Born:** 4/19/77 **Age:** 27

		HOW MUCH HE PITCHED						WHAT HE GAVE UP										THE RESULTS						
Year Team	Lg	G	GS	CG	GF	IP	BFP	H	R	ER	HR	SH	SF	HB	TBB	IBB	SO	WP	Bk	W	L	Pct	ShO	Sv-Op Hld	ERC	ERA
2001 Pittsburgh	NL	42	15	0	9	115.1	511	131	72	67	12	3	1	6	49	4	58	3	0	7	11	.389	0	0-0 0	5.24	5.23
2002 Pittsburgh	NL	53	8	0	8	85.1	391	88	49	44	9	7	3	4	45	12	53	2	0	2	5	.286	0	0-1 5	4.65	4.64
2003 Pittsburgh	NL	69	0	0	11	62.1	275	69	35	35	7	3	5	4	33	6	42	0	1	1	3	.250	0	0-5 12	5.65	5.05
3 ML YEARS		164	23	0	28	263.0	1177	288	156	146	28	13	9	14	127	22	153	5	1	10	19	.345	0	0-6 17	5.14	5.00

Matt Belisle

Pitches: R **Bats:** B **Pos:** RP-6   **Ht:** 6'3" **Wt:** 195 **Born:** 6/6/80 **Age:** 24

		HOW MUCH HE PITCHED						WHAT HE GAVE UP										THE RESULTS						
Year Team	Lg	G	GS	CG	GF	IP	BFP	H	R	ER	HR	SH	SF	HB	TBB	IBB	SO	WP	Bk	W	L	Pct	ShO	Sv-Op	ERC	ERA
1999 Danville	R+	14	14	0	0	71.1	329	86	50	37	3	0	2	8	23	0	60	6	2	2	5	.286	0	0-- -	4.86	4.67
2000 Macon	A	15	15	1	0	102.1	392	79	37	27	7	2	3	4	18	0	97	7	0	9	5	.643	0	0-- -	2.11	2.37
2002 Greenville	AA	26	26	1	0	159.1	682	162	91	77	18	3	9	10	39	1	123	6	2	5	9	.357	0	0-- -	3.84	4.35
2003 Greenville	AA	21	21	1	0	125.1	532	128	59	49	5	8	5	6	42	2	94	3	2	6	8	.429	0	0-- -	3.74	3.52
2003 Richmond	AAA	3	3	0	0	20.0	77	17	6	5	1	0	1	2	0	0	10	0	0	1	1	.500	0	0-- -	1.94	2.25
2003 Louisville	AAA	4	4	0	0	26.0	108	31	15	11	2	0	1	5	0	0	15	0	0	1	3	.250	0	0-- -	4.52	3.81
2003 Cincinnati	NL	6	0	0	2	8.2	39	10	5	5	1	2	1	1	2	0	6	0	0	1	1	.500	0	0-1 0	4.73	5.19

David Bell

Bats: R **Throws:** R **Pos:** 3B-85; 2B-3   **Ht:** 5'10" **Wt:** 195 **Born:** 9/14/72 **Age:** 31

						BATTING													BASERUNNING				AVERAGES		
Year Team	Lg	G	AB	H	2B	3B	HR	(Hm	Rd)	TB	R	RBI	RC	TBB	IBB	SO	HBP	SH	SF	SB	CS	SB%	GDP	Avg	OBP	Slg
1995 Cle-StL		41	146	36	7	2	2	(1	1)	53	13	19	14	4	0	25	2	0	1	1	2	.33	0	.247	.275	.363
1996 St Louis	NL	62	145	31	6	0	1	(1	0)	40	12	9	9	10	2	22	1	0	1	1	1	.50	3	.214	.268	.276
1997 St Louis	NL	66	142	30	7	2	1	(1	0)	44	9	12	11	10	2	28	0	2	1	1	0	1.00	1	.211	.261	.310
1998 StL-Cle-Sea		132	429	117	30	2	10	(2	8)	181	48	49	53	27	4	65	2	1	5	0	4	.00	11	.273	.315	.422
1999 Seattle	AL	157	597	160	31	2	21	(11	10)	258	92	78	87	58	0	90	2	3	7	4	7	.64	7	.268	.331	.432
2000 Seattle	AL	133	454	112	24	2	11	(4	7)	173	57	47	54	42	0	66	6	6	4	2	3	.40	11	.247	.316	.381
2001 Seattle	AL	135	470	122	28	0	15	(7	8)	195	62	64	58	28	1	59	3	5	4	2	1	.67	8	.260	.303	.415

Year Team	Lg	G	AB	H	2B	3B	HR	(Hm	Rd)	TB	R	RBI	RC	TBB	IBB	SO	HBP	SH	SF	SB	CS	SB%	GDP	Avg	OBP	Slg
2002 San Francisco	NL	154	552	144	29	2	20	(7	13)	237	82	73	79	54	2	80	9	6	7	1	2	.33	18	.261	.333	.429
2003 Philadelphia	NL	85	297	58	14	0	4	(1	3)	84	32	37	26	41	1	40	4	0	6	0	0	-	7	.195	.296	.283
1995 Cleveland	AL	2	2	0	0	0	0	(0	0)	0	0	0	0	0	0	0	0	0	0	0	0	-	0	.000	.000	.000
1995 St Louis	NL	39	144	36	7	2	2	(1	1)	53	13	19	14	4	0	25	2	0	1	1	2	.33	0	.250	.278	.368
1998 St Louis	NL	4	9	2	1	0	0	(0	0)	3	0	0	1	0	0	3	0	0	0	0	0	-	0	.222	.222	.333
1998 Cleveland	AL	107	340	89	21	2	10	(2	8)	144	37	41	41	22	4	54	2	1	5	0	4	.00	8	.262	.306	.424
1998 Seattle	AL	21	80	26	8	0	0	(0	0)	34	11	8	11	5	0	8	0	0	3	0	0	-	3	.325	.365	.425
9 ML YEARS		965	3232	810	176	12	85	(35	50)	1265	407	388	391	274	12	475	29	23	36	15	17	.47	67	.251	.312	.391

Jay Bell

Bats: R **Throws:** R **Pos:** PH-27; 1B-14; 2B-14; 3B-14; SS-12; DH-1   **Ht:** 6'0" **Wt:** 184 **Born:** 12/11/65 **Age:** 38

Year Team	Lg	G	AB	H	2B	3B	HR	(Hm	Rd)	TB	R	RBI	RC	TBB	IBB	SO	HBP	SH	SF	SB	CS	SB%	GDP	Avg	OBP	Slg
1986 Cleveland	AL	5	14	5	2	0	1	(0	1)	10	3	4	4	2	0	3	0	0	0	0	0	-	0	.357	.438	.714
1987 Cleveland	AL	38	125	27	9	1	2	(1	1)	44	14	13	12	8	0	31	1	3	0	2	0	1.00	0	.216	.269	.352
1988 Cleveland	AL	73	211	46	5	1	2	(2	0)	59	23	21	17	21	0	53	1	1	2	4	2	.67	3	.218	.289	.280
1989 Pittsburgh	NL	78	271	70	13	3	2	(1	1)	95	33	27	27	19	0	47	1	10	2	5	3	.63	9	.258	.307	.351
1990 Pittsburgh	NL	159	583	148	28	7	7	(1	6)	211	93	52	71	65	0	109	3	39	6	10	6	.63	14	.254	.329	.362
1991 Pittsburgh	NL	157	608	164	32	8	16	(7	9)	260	96	67	84	52	1	99	4	30	3	10	6	.63	15	.270	.330	.428
1992 Pittsburgh	NL	159	632	167	36	6	9	(5	4)	242	87	55	79	55	0	103	4	19	2	7	5	.58	12	.264	.326	.383
1993 Pittsburgh	NL	154	604	187	32	9	9	(3	6)	264	102	51	102	77	6	122	6	13	1	16	10	.62	16	.310	.392	.437
1994 Pittsburgh	NL	110	424	117	35	4	9	(3	6)	187	68	45	64	49	1	82	3	8	3	2	0	1.00	15	.276	.353	.441
1995 Pittsburgh	NL	138	530	139	28	4	13	(8	5)	214	79	55	69	55	1	110	4	3	1	2	5	.29	13	.262	.336	.404
1996 Pittsburgh	NL	151	527	132	29	3	13	(7	6)	206	65	71	67	54	5	108	5	6	6	6	4	.60	10	.250	.323	.391
1997 Kansas City	AL	153	573	167	28	3	21	(10	11)	264	89	92	97	71	2	101	4	3	9	10	6	.63	13	.291	.368	.461
1998 Arizona	NL	155	549	138	29	5	20	(11	9)	237	79	67	83	81	3	129	7	5	3	3	5	.38	14	.251	.353	.432
1999 Arizona	NL	151	589	170	32	6	38	(21	17)	328	132	112	121	82	2	132	4	4	9	7	4	.64	9	.289	.374	.557
2000 Arizona	NL	149	565	151	30	6	18	(9	9)	247	87	68	89	70	0	88	3	6	5	7	3	.70	7	.267	.348	.437
2001 Arizona	NL	129	428	106	24	1	13	(6	7)	171	59	46	62	65	3	79	4	8	4	0	1	.00	9	.248	.349	.400
2002 Arizona	NL	32	49	8	1	0	2	(0	2)	15	3	11	6	5	0	9	1	0	1	0	0	-	2	.163	.250	.306
2003 New York	NL	72	116	21	1	0	0	(0	0)	22	11	3	7	22	1	38	2	1	1	0	0	-	4	.181	.319	.190
18 ML YEARS		2063	7398	1963	394	67	195	(95	100)	3076	1123	860	1061	853	25	1443	57	159	58	91	60	.60	165	.265	.343	.416

Rob Bell

Pitches: R **Bats:** R **Pos:** SP-18; RP-1   **Ht:** 6'5" **Wt:** 225 **Born:** 1/17/77 **Age:** 27

Year Team	Lg	G	GS	CG	GF	IP	BFP	H	R	ER	HR	SH	SF	HB	TBB	IBB	SO	WP	Bk	W	L	Pct	ShO	Sv-Op	Hld	ERC	ERA
2003 Durham*	AAA	12	12	0	0	71.2	297	72	33	32	10	4	1	0	15	1	48	5	0	6	4	.600	0	0- -		3.59	4.02
2000 Cincinnati	NL	26	26	1	0	140.1	618	130	84	78	32	8	2	1	73	6	112	11	0	7	8	.467	0	0-0	0	4.98	5.00
2001 Cin-Tex		27	27	0	0	149.2	670	176	115	111	32	3	9	7	64	1	97	9	0	5	10	.333	0	0-0	0	6.40	6.67
2002 Texas	AL	17	15	0	0	94.0	425	113	69	65	16	1	6	1	35	0	70	7	0	4	3	.571	0	0-0	0	5.67	6.22
2003 Tampa Bay	AL	19	18	0	0	101.0	441	103	64	62	15	2	2	5	39	1	44	0	0	5	4	.556	0	0-0	0	4.66	5.52
2001 Cincinnati	NL	9	9	0	0	44.1	188	46	28	27	9	0	1	3	17	1	33	1	0	0	5	.000	0	0-0	0	5.43	5.48
2001 Texas	AL	18	18	0	0	105.1	482	130	87	84	23	3	8	4	47	0	64	8	0	5	5	.500	0	0-0	0	6.82	7.18
4 ML YEARS		89	86	1	0	485.0	2154	522	332	316	95	14	19	14	211	8	323	27	0	21	25	.457	0	0-0	0	5.47	5.86

Mark Bellhorn

Bats: B **Throws:** R **Pos:** 3B-57; PH-28; 2B-20; SS-6; CF-3; RF-2; 1B-1   **Ht:** 6'1" **Wt:** 205 **Born:** 8/23/74 **Age:** 29

Year Team	Lg	G	AB	H	2B	3B	HR	(Hm	Rd)	TB	R	RBI	RC	TBB	IBB	SO	HBP	SH	SF	SB	CS	SB%	GDP	Avg	OBP	Slg
2003 Co Springs*	AAA	16	54	21	5	1	4	(-	-)	40	11	16	18	11	0	10	0	0	1	2	0	1.00	0	.389	.485	.741
1997 Oakland	AL	68	224	51	9	1	6	(3	3)	80	33	19	29	32	0	70	0	5	0	7	1	.88	1	.228	.324	.357
1998 Oakland	AL	11	12	1	1	0	0	(0	0)	2	1	1	1	3	0	4	1	0	0	2	0	1.00	0	.083	.313	.167
2000 Oakland	AL	9	13	2	0	0	0	(0	0)	2	2	0	1	2	0	6	0	0	0	0	0	-	0	.154	.267	.154
2001 Oakland	AL	38	74	10	1	2	1	(1	0)	18	11	4	3	7	0	37	0	1	0	0	0	-	1	.135	.210	.243
2002 Chicago	NL	146	445	115	24	4	27	(15	12)	228	86	56	80	76	3	144	6	2	0	7	5	.58	6	.258	.374	.512
2003 ChC-Col	NL	99	249	55	10	1	2	(1	1)	73	27	26	25	50	1	78	3	1	4	5	6	.45	3	.221	.353	.293
2003 Chicago	NL	51	139	29	7	1	2	(1	1)	44	15	22	17	29	1	46	1	0	4	3	3	.50	2	.209	.341	.317
2003 Colorado	NL	48	110	26	3	0	0	(0	0)	29	12	4	8	21	0	32	2	1	0	2	3	.40	1	.236	.368	.264
6 ML YEARS		371	1017	234	45	8	36	(20	16)	403	160	106	139	170	4	339	10	9	4	21	12	.64	11	.230	.345	.396

Ronnie Belliard

Bats: R **Throws:** R **Pos:** 2B-113; PH-7   **Ht:** 5'8" **Wt:** 197 **Born:** 4/7/75 **Age:** 29

Year Team	Lg	G	AB	H	2B	3B	HR	(Hm	Rd)	TB	R	RBI	RC	TBB	IBB	SO	HBP	SH	SF	SB	CS	SB%	GDP	Avg	OBP	Slg
2003 Co Springs*	AAA	6	19	5	1	0	0	(-	-)	6	2	0	2	0	0	1	0	0	0	0	0	-	0	.263	.263	.316
1998 Milwaukee	NL	8	5	1	0	0	0	(0	0)	1	1	0	0	0	0	0	0	0	0	0	0	-	0	.200	.200	.200
1999 Milwaukee	NL	124	457	135	29	4	8	(5	3)	196	60	58	72	64	0	59	0	6	4	4	5	.44	16	.295	.379	.429
2000 Milwaukee	NL	152	571	150	30	9	8	(4	4)	222	83	54	81	82	4	84	3	4	7	7	5	.58	12	.263	.354	.389
2001 Milwaukee	NL	101	364	96	30	3	11	(7	4)	165	69	36	56	35	2	65	5	4	2	5	2	.71	5	.264	.335	.453
2002 Milwaukee	NL	104	289	61	13	0	3	(0	3)	83	30	26	14	18	0	46	1	6	3	2	3	.40	8	.211	.257	.287
2003 Colorado	NL	116	447	124	31	2	8	(6	2)	183	73	50	70	49	0	71	2	6	1	7	2	.78	7	.277	.351	.409
6 ML YEARS		605	2133	567	133	18	38	(22	16)	850	316	224	293	248	6	325	11	26	17	25	17	.60	48	.266	.343	.398

Carlos Beltran

Bats: B **Throws:** R **Pos:** CF-130; DH-8; PH-4   **Ht:** 6'1" **Wt:** 190 **Born:** 4/24/77 **Age:** 27

				BATTING																BASERUNNING				AVERAGES		
Year Team	Lg	G	AB	H	2B	3B	HR	(Hm	Rd)	TB	R	RBI	RC	TBB	IBB	SO	HBP	SH	SF	SB	CS	SB%	GDP	Avg	OBP	Slg
2003 Wichita*	AA	3	9	3	2	0	0	(-	-)	5	3	1	2	2	0	3	0	0	0	1	0	1.00	0	.333	.455	.556
1998 Kansas City	AL	14	58	16	5	3	0	(0	0)	27	12	7	9	3	0	12	1	0	1	3	0	1.00	2	.276	.317	.466
1999 Kansas City	AL	156	663	194	27	7	22	(12	10)	301	112	108	100	46	2	123	4	0	10	27	8	.77	17	.293	.337	.454
2000 Kansas City	AL	98	372	92	15	4	7	(4	3)	136	49	44	43	35	2	69	0	2	4	13	0	1.00	12	.247	.309	.366
2001 Kansas City	AL	155	617	189	32	12	24	(7	17)	317	106	101	118	52	2	120	5	1	5	31	1	.97	7	.306	.362	.514
2002 Kansas City	AL	162	637	174	44	7	29	(19	10)	319	114	105	120	71	1	135	4	3	7	35	7	.83	12	.273	.346	.501
2003 Kansas City	AL	141	521	160	14	10	26	(10	16)	272	102	100	117	72	4	81	2	0	7	41	4	.91	8	.307	.389	.522
6 ML YEARS		726	2868	825	137	43	108	(52	56)	1372	495	465	507	279	11	540	16	6	34	150	20	.88	58	.288	.350	.478

Adrian Beltre

Bats: R **Throws:** R **Pos:** 3B-157; SS-1; PH-1   **Ht:** 5'11" **Wt:** 170 **Born:** 4/7/79 **Age:** 25

				BATTING																BASERUNNING				AVERAGES		
Year Team	Lg	G	AB	H	2B	3B	HR	(Hm	Rd)	TB	R	RBI	RC	TBB	IBB	SO	HBP	SH	SF	SB	CS	SB%	GDP	Avg	OBP	Slg
1998 Los Angeles	NL	77	195	42	9	0	7	(5	2)	72	18	22	20	14	0	37	3	2	0	3	1	.75	4	.215	.278	.369
1999 Los Angeles	NL	152	538	148	27	5	15	(6	9)	230	84	67	84	61	12	105	6	4	5	18	7	.72	4	.275	.352	.428
2000 Los Angeles	NL	138	510	148	30	2	20	(7	13)	242	71	85	85	56	2	80	2	3	4	12	5	.71	13	.290	.360	.475
2001 Los Angeles	NL	126	475	126	22	4	13	(4	9)	195	59	60	60	28	1	82	5	2	5	13	4	.76	9	.265	.310	.411
2002 Los Angeles	NL	159	587	151	26	5	21	(7	14)	250	70	75	74	37	4	96	4	1	6	7	5	.58	17	.257	.303	.426
2003 Los Angeles	NL	158	559	134	30	2	23	(13	10)	237	50	80	68	37	4	103	5	1	6	2	2	.50	13	.240	.290	.424
6 ML YEARS		810	2864	749	144	18	99	(42	57)	1226	352	389	391	233	23	503	25	13	26	55	24	.70	60	.262	.320	.428

Marvin Benard

Bats: L **Throws:** L **Pos:** PH-26; LF-17; RF-4; PR-1   **Ht:** 5'9" **Wt:** 191 **Born:** 1/20/71 **Age:** 33

				BATTING																BASERUNNING				AVERAGES		
Year Team	Lg	G	AB	H	2B	3B	HR	(Hm	Rd)	TB	R	RBI	RC	TBB	IBB	SO	HBP	SH	SF	SB	CS	SB%	GDP	Avg	OBP	Slg
2003 San Jose*	A+	3	9	2	0	0	0	(-	-)	2	2	0	1	0	0	2	1	0	0	0	0	-	0	.222	.300	.222
2003 Fresno*	AAA	14	50	11	3	0	1	(-	-)	17	8	8	4	1	0	4	1	0	0	2	0	1.00	2	.220	.250	.340
1995 San Francisco	NL	13	34	13	2	0	1	(0	1)	18	5	4	7	1	0	7	0	0	0	1	0	1.00	1	.382	.400	.529
1996 San Francisco	NL	135	488	121	17	4	5	(2	3)	161	89	27	57	59	2	84	4	6	1	25	11	.69	8	.248	.333	.330
1997 San Francisco	NL	84	114	26	4	0	1	(0	1)	33	13	13	11	13	0	29	2	0	1	3	1	.75	2	.228	.315	.289
1998 San Francisco	NL	121	286	92	21	1	3	(2	1)	124	41	36	51	34	1	39	2	4	1	11	4	.73	3	.322	.396	.434
1999 San Francisco	NL	149	562	163	36	5	16	(9	7)	257	100	64	93	55	2	97	6	1	1	27	14	.66	5	.290	.359	.457
2000 San Francisco	NL	149	560	147	27	6	12	(6	6)	222	102	55	81	63	0	97	6	2	2	22	7	.76	4	.263	.342	.396
2001 San Francisco	NL	129	392	104	19	2	15	(3	12)	172	70	44	56	29	2	66	4	1	3	10	5	.67	3	.265	.320	.439
2002 San Francisco	NL	65	123	34	9	2	1	(0	1)	50	16	13	14	7	0	26	1	0	0	5	1	.83	3	.276	.321	.407
2003 San Francisco	NL	46	71	14	3	1	0	(0	0)	19	5	4	3	4	0	9	0	1	1	1	0	1.00	3	.197	.237	.268
9 ML YEARS		891	2630	714	138	21	54	(22	32)	1056	441	260	373	265	7	454	25	15	10	105	43	.71	32	.271	.343	.402

Alan Benes

Pitches: R **Bats:** R **Pos:** SP-4; RP-3   **Ht:** 6'5" **Wt:** 235 **Born:** 1/21/72 **Age:** 32

		HOW MUCH HE PITCHED						WHAT HE GAVE UP											THE RESULTS						
Year Team	Lg	G	GS	CG	GF	IP	BFP	H	R	ER	HR	SH	SF	HB	TBB	IBB	SO	WP	Bk	W	L	Pct	ShO	Sv-Op	Hld	ERC	ERA
2003 Iowa*	AAA	19	17	2	0	114.0	498	129	74	68	13	9	5	1	44	1	81	5	0	7	7	.500	0	0- -		4.97	5.37
1995 St Louis	NL	3	3	0	0	16.0	76	24	15	15	2	1	0	1	4	0	20	3	0	1	2	.333	0	0-0	0	6.84	8.44
1996 St Louis	NL	34	32	3	1	191.0	840	192	120	104	27	15	9	7	87	3	131	5	1	13	10	.565	1	0-0	0	4.76	4.90
1997 St Louis	NL	23	23	2	0	161.2	666	128	60	52	13	5	4	4	68	3	160	9	2	9	9	.500	0	0-0	0	3.01	2.89
1999 St Louis	NL	2	0	0	2	2.0	7	2	0	0	0	0	0	0	0	0	2	0	0	0	0	-	0	0-0	0	2.31	0.00
2000 St Louis	NL	30	0	0	16	46.0	214	54	33	29	7	2	1	2	23	2	26	5	0	2	2	.500	0	0-1	2	5.96	5.67
2001 St Louis	NL	9	1	0	4	14.2	75	18	12	12	5	0	0	0	12	0	10	0	0	2	0	1.000	0	0-0	0	7.55	7.36
2002 Chicago	NL	7	7	0	0	39.1	167	42	22	19	3	1	2	0	12	1	32	2	0	2	2	.500	0	0-0	0	3.91	4.35
2003 ChC-Tex		7	4	0	1	23.1	115	37	22	21	2	0	1	0	14	0	20	0	2	0	3	.000	0	1-1	0	8.69	8.10
2003 Chicago	NL	3	0	0	1	8.1	36	8	2	2	0	0	0	0	6	0	9	0	1	0	0	-	0	1-1	0	4.60	2.16
2003 Texas	AL	4	4	0	0	15.0	79	29	20	19	2	0	1	0	8	0	11	0	1	0	3	.000	0	0-0	0	11.17	11.40
8 ML YEARS		115	70	5	24	494.0	2153	493	284	252	59	24	17	14	220	9	401	24	5	29	28	.509	1	1-2	2	4.49	4.59

Armando Benitez

Pitches: R **Bats:** R **Pos:** RP-69   **Ht:** 6'4" **Wt:** 229 **Born:** 11/3/72 **Age:** 31

		HOW MUCH HE PITCHED						WHAT HE GAVE UP											THE RESULTS						
Year Team	Lg	G	GS	CG	GF	IP	BFP	H	R	ER	HR	SH	SF	HB	TBB	IBB	SO	WP	Bk	W	L	Pct	ShO	Sv-Op	Hld	ERC	ERA
1994 Baltimore	AL	3	0	0	1	10.0	42	8	1	1	0	0	1	0	4	0	14	0	0	0	0	-	0	0-0	0	2.71	0.90
1995 Baltimore	AL	44	0	0	18	47.2	221	37	33	30	8	2	3	5	37	2	56	3	1	1	5	.167	0	2-5	6	5.06	5.66
1996 Baltimore	AL	18	0	0	8	14.1	56	7	6	6	2	0	1	0	6	0	20	1	0	1	0	1.000	0	4-5	1	1.78	3.77
1997 Baltimore	AL	71	0	0	26	73.1	307	49	22	20	7	2	4	1	43	5	106	1	0	4	5	.444	0	9-10	20	2.92	2.45
1998 Baltimore	AL	71	0	0	54	68.1	289	48	29	29	10	3	2	4	39	2	87	0	0	5	6	.455	0	22-26	3	3.63	3.82
1999 New York	NL	77	0	0	42	78.0	312	40	17	16	4	0	0	0	41	4	128	2	0	4	3	.571	0	22-28	17	1.69	1.85
2000 New York	NL	76	0	0	68	76.0	304	39	24	22	10	2	1	0	38	2	106	0	0	4	4	.500	0	41-46	0	2.08	2.61
2001 New York	NL	73	0	0	64	76.1	320	59	32	32	12	2	1	1	40	6	93	5	0	6	4	.600	0	43-46	0	3.67	3.77
2002 New York	NL	62	0	0	52	67.1	275	46	20	17	8	3	2	3	25	0	79	1	0	1	0	1.000	0	33-37	0	2.55	2.27
2003 NYM-NYY-Sea		69	0	0	49	73.0	312	59	27	24	6	0	1	0	41	3	75	3	1	4	4	.500	0	21-29	5	3.46	2.96
2003 New York	NL	45	0	0	40	49.1	209	41	18	17	5	0	1	0	24	1	50	3	1	3	3	.500	0	21-28	5	3.46	3.10
2003 New York	AL	9	0	0	2	9.1	39	8	4	2	0	0	0	0	6	1	10	0	0	1	1	.500	0	0-0	4	3.50	1.93
2003 Seattle	AL	15	0	0	7	14.1	64	10	5	5	1	0	0	0	11	1	15	0	0	0	0	-	0	0-1	0	3.40	3.14
10 ML YEARS		564	0	0	382	584.1	2438	392	211	197	67	14	15	15	314	24	764	16	2	30	31	.492	0	197-232	52	2.96	3.03

Gary Bennett

Bats: R **Throws:** R **Pos:** C-91; PH-7   **Ht:** 6'0" **Wt:** 208 **Born:** 4/17/72 **Age:** 32

					BATTING														BASERUNNING				AVERAGES		
Year Team	Lg	G	AB	H	2B	3B	HR	(Hm	Rd)	TB	R	RBI	RC	TBB	IBB	SO	HBP	SH	SF	SB	CS	SB%	GDP	Avg	OBP	Slg
1995 Philadelphia	NL	1	1	0	0	0	0	(0	0)	0	0	0	0	0	0	1	0	0	0	0	0	-	0	.000	.000	.000
1996 Philadelphia	NL	6	16	4	0	0	0	(0	0)	4	0	1	1	2	1	6	0	0	0	0	0	-	0	.250	.333	.250
1998 Philadelphia	NL	9	31	9	0	0	0	(0	0)	9	4	3	4	5	0	5	0	0	1	0	0	-	1	.290	.378	.290
1999 Philadelphia	NL	36	88	24	4	0	1	(0	1)	31	7	21	7	4	0	11	0	0	2	0	0	-	7	.273	.298	.352
2000 Philadelphia	NL	31	74	18	5	0	2	(0	2)	29	8	5	12	13	0	15	2	0	0	0	0	-	0	.243	.371	.392
2001 Phi-NYM-Col	NL	46	131	32	6	1	2	(2	0)	46	15	10	15	12	4	24	1	2	2	0	0	-	4	.244	.308	.351
2002 Colorado	NL	90	291	77	10	2	4	(2	2)	103	26	26	28	15	2	45	6	2	0	1	3	.25	10	.265	.314	.354
2003 San Diego	NL	96	307	73	15	0	2	(1	1)	94	26	42	32	24	3	48	2	3	2	3	0	1.00	8	.238	.296	.306
2001 Philadelphia	NL	26	75	16	3	1	1	(1	0)	24	8	6	7	9	1	19	0	1	1	0	0	-	1	.213	.294	.320
2001 New York	NL	1	1	1	0	0	0	(0	0)	1	0	0	1	0	0	0	0	0	0	0	0	-	0	1.000	1.000	1.000
2001 Colorado	NL	19	55	15	3	0	1	(1	0)	21	7	4	7	3	3	5	1	1	1	0	0	-	3	.273	.317	.382
8 ML YEARS		315	939	237	40	3	11	(5	6)	316	86	108	99	75	10	155	11	7	7	4	3	.57	27	.252	.313	.337

Joaquin Benoit

Pitches: R **Bats:** R **Pos:** SP-17; RP-8   **Ht:** 6'3" **Wt:** 205 **Born:** 7/26/77 **Age:** 26

		HOW MUCH HE PITCHED						WHAT HE GAVE UP										THE RESULTS							
Year Team	Lg	G	GS	CG	GF	IP	BFP	H	R	ER	HR	SH	SF	HB	TBB	IBB	SO	WP	Bk	W	L	Pct	ShO	Sv-Op	Hld	ERC	ERA
2003 Oklahoma*	AAA	6	6	0	0	33.0	134	28	17	14	3	0	0	2	11	0	31	1	0	2	1	.667	0	0--	-	3.27	3.82
2001 Texas	AL	1	1	0	0	5.0	26	8	6	6	3	0	1	0	3	0	4	0	0	0	0	-	0	0-0	0	13.11	10.80
2002 Texas	AL	17	13	0	2	84.2	405	91	51	50	6	4	3	5	58	2	59	7	0	4	5	.444	0	1-1	0	5.52	5.31
2003 Texas	AL	25	17	0	1	105.0	462	99	67	64	23	1	4	3	51	0	87	3	1	8	5	.615	0	0-0	0	5.03	5.49
3 ML YEARS		43	31	0	3	194.2	893	198	124	120	32	5	8	8	112	2	150	10	1	12	10	.545	0	1-1	0	5.46	5.55

Kris Benson

Pitches: R **Bats:** R **Pos:** SP-18   **Ht:** 6'4" **Wt:** 200 **Born:** 11/7/74 **Age:** 29

		HOW MUCH HE PITCHED						WHAT HE GAVE UP										THE RESULTS							
Year Team	Lg	G	GS	CG	GF	IP	BFP	H	R	ER	HR	SH	SF	HB	TBB	IBB	SO	WP	Bk	W	L	Pct	ShO	Sv-Op	Hld	ERC	ERA
1999 Pittsburgh	NL	31	31	2	0	196.2	840	184	105	89	16	6	7	6	83	5	139	2	1	11	14	.440	0	0-0	0	3.78	4.07
2000 Pittsburgh	NL	32	32	2	0	217.2	936	206	104	93	24	7	6	10	86	5	184	5	0	10	12	.455	1	0-0	0	3.97	3.85
2002 Pittsburgh	NL	25	25	0	0	130.1	575	152	76	68	18	5	3	3	50	8	79	3	1	9	6	.600	0	0-0	0	5.32	4.70
2003 Pittsburgh	NL	18	18	0	0	105.0	475	127	67	58	14	3	4	1	36	4	68	7	0	5	9	.357	0	0-0	0	5.20	4.97
4 ML YEARS		106	106	4	0	649.2	2826	669	352	308	72	21	20	20	255	22	470	17	2	35	41	.461	1	0-0	0	4.37	4.27

Jason Bere

Pitches: R **Bats:** R **Pos:** SP-2   **Ht:** 6'3" **Wt:** 225 **Born:** 5/26/71 **Age:** 33

		HOW MUCH HE PITCHED						WHAT HE GAVE UP										THE RESULTS							
Year Team	Lg	G	GS	CG	GF	IP	BFP	H	R	ER	HR	SH	SF	HB	TBB	IBB	SO	WP	Bk	W	L	Pct	ShO	Sv-Op	Hld	ERC	ERA
2003 Lake County*	A-	1	1	0	0	4.0	18	7	3	3	1	0	0	0	0	0	1	0	0	0	0	-	0	0--	-	8.42	6.75
2003 Buffalo*	AAA	3	3	0	0	14.2	53	9	1	1	0	0	0	0	3	1	17	0	0	1	0	1.000	0	0--	-	1.16	0.61
1993 Chicago	AL	24	24	1	0	142.2	610	109	60	55	12	4	2	5	81	0	129	8	0	12	5	.706	0	0-0	0	3.46	3.47
1994 Chicago	AL	24	24	0	0	141.2	608	119	65	60	17	4	4	1	80	0	127	2	0	12	2	.857	0	0-0	0	4.03	3.81
1995 Chicago	AL	27	27	1	0	137.2	668	151	120	110	21	4	7	6	106	6	110	8	0	8	15	.348	0	0-0	0	6.63	7.19
1996 Chicago	AL	5	5	0	0	16.2	93	26	19	19	3	1	1	0	18	1	19	2	0	0	1	.000	0	0-0	0	11.16	10.26
1997 Chicago	AL	6	6	0	0	28.2	123	20	15	15	4	1	1	3	17	0	21	1	0	4	2	.667	0	0-0	0	3.86	4.71
1998 CWS-Cin		27	22	0	2	127.1	588	137	91	80	17	4	7	3	78	0	84	8	0	6	9	.400	0	0-0	0	5.73	5.65
1999 Cin-Mil	NL	17	14	0	0	66.2	322	79	52	45	9	6	2	2	50	3	47	6	0	5	0	1.000	0	0-0	0	7.00	6.08
2000 Mil-Cle		31	31	0	0	169.1	767	180	107	103	25	12	6	5	89	7	142	5	1	12	10	.545	0	0-0	0	5.34	5.47
2001 Chicago	NL	32	32	2	0	188.0	801	171	99	90	24	7	6	1	77	7	175	6	0	11	11	.500	0	0-0	0	3.75	4.31
2002 Chicago	NL	16	16	0	0	85.2	379	98	63	54	13	3	7	3	28	1	65	5	0	1	10	.091	0	0-0	0	5.09	5.67
2003 Cleveland		2	2	0	0	6.2	28	5	3	3	0	1	1	0	2	0	1	0	0	0	0	-	0	0-0	0	1.70	4.05
1998 Chicago	AL	18	15	0	0	83.2	404	98	71	60	14	4	5	2	58	0	53	7	0	3	7	.300	0	0-0	0	6.90	6.45
1998 Cincinnati	NL	9	7	0	2	43.2	184	39	20	20	3	0	2	1	20	0	31	1	0	3	2	.600	0	0-0	0	3.65	4.12
1999 Cincinnati	NL	12	10	0	0	43.1	220	56	37	33	6	5	1	2	40	3	28	2	0	3	0	1.000	0	0-0	0	8.60	6.85
1999 Milwaukee	NL	5	4	0	0	23.1	102	23	15	12	3	1	1	0	10	0	19	4	0	2	0	1.000	0	0-0	0	4.26	4.63
2000 Milwaukee	NL	20	20	0	0	115.0	515	115	66	63	19	12	3	1	63	7	98	3	1	6	7	.462	0	0-0	0	5.06	4.93
2000 Cleveland	AL	11	11	0	0	54.1	252	65	41	40	6	0	3	4	26	0	44	2	0	6	3	.667	0	0-0	0	5.94	6.63
11 ML YEARS		211	203	4	2	1111.0	4987	1095	694	634	145	47	44	29	626	25	920	51	1	71	65	.522	0	0-0	0	4.93	5.14

Dave Berg

Bats: R **Throws:** R **Pos:** 2B-24; 3B-17; PH-11; PR-7; RF-5; DH-5; 1B-2; SS-1; LF-1   **Ht:** 5'11" **Wt:** 196 **Born:** 9/3/70 **Age:** 33

					BATTING														BASERUNNING				AVERAGES		
Year Team	Lg	G	AB	H	2B	3B	HR	(Hm	Rd)	TB	R	RBI	RC	TBB	IBB	SO	HBP	SH	SF	SB	CS	SB%	GDP	Avg	OBP	Slg
2003 Syracuse*	AAA	6	20	5	1	0	0	(-	-)	6	3	0	2	1	0	2	1	0	0	0	0	-	0	.250	.318	.300
1998 Florida	NL	81	182	57	11	0	2	(1	1)	74	18	21	32	26	1	46	0	4	3	3	0	1.00	1	.313	.393	.407
1999 Florida	NL	109	304	87	18	1	3	(1	2)	116	42	25	39	27	0	59	2	3	0	2	2	.50	7	.286	.348	.382
2000 Florida	NL	82	210	53	14	1	1	(1	0)	72	23	21	26	25	0	46	5	1	4	3	0	1.00	5	.252	.340	.343
2001 Florida	NL	82	215	52	12	1	4	(2	2)	78	26	16	22	14	0	39	2	2	2	0	1	.00	3	.242	.292	.363
2002 Toronto	AL	109	374	101	26	2	4	(3	1)	143	42	39	47	26	1	57	5	4	5	0	1	.00	6	.270	.322	.382
2003 Toronto	AL	61	161	41	6	1	2	(2	0)	61	26	18	13	11	0	34	0	1	1	0	1	.00	7	.255	.301	.379
6 ML YEARS		524	1446	391	87	6	18	(10	8)	544	177	140	179	129	2	281	14	15	15	8	6	.57	29	.270	.333	.376

Brandon Berger

Bats: R **Throws:** R **Pos:** RF-11; PH-2; DH-1; PR-1   **Ht:** 5'11" **Wt:** 205 **Born:** 2/21/75 **Age:** 29

Year Team	Lg	BATTING																	BASERUNNING				AVERAGES		
		G	AB	H	2B	3B	HR	(Hm | Rd)	TB	R	RBI	RC	TBB	IBB	SO	HBP	SH	SF	SB	CS	SB%	GDP	Avg	OBP	Slg
2003 Omaha*	AAA	62	226	61	16	3	12	(- | -)	119	43	53	44	31	1	58	6	0	4	6	1	.86	5	.270	.367	.527
2001 Kansas City	AL	6	16	5	1	1	2	(1 | 1)	14	4	2	5	2	0	2	0	0	0	0	0	-	0	.313	.389	.875
2002 Kansas City	AL	51	134	27	5	1	6	(5 | 1)	52	16	17	16	8	2	32	2	0	1	1	0	1.00	2	.201	.255	.388
2003 Kansas City	AL	13	32	7	0	0	0	(0 | 0)	7	3	3	4	5	0	4	0	1	0	0	0	-	0	.219	.324	.219
3 ML YEARS		70	182	39	6	2	8	(6 | 2)	73	23	22	25	15	2	38	2	1	1	1	0	1.00	2	.214	.280	.401

Lance Berkman

Bats: B **Throws:** L **Pos:** LF-153; CF-1   **Ht:** 6'1" **Wt:** 220 **Born:** 2/10/76 **Age:** 28

Year Team	Lg	BATTING																	BASERUNNING				AVERAGES		
		G	AB	H	2B	3B	HR	(Hm	Rd)	TB	R	RBI	RC	TBB	IBB	SO	HBP	SH	SF	SB	CS	SB%	GDP	Avg	OBP	Slg
1999 Houston	NL	34	93	22	2	0	4	(2	2)	36	10	15	12	12	0	21	0	0	1	5	1	.83	2	.237	.321	.387
2000 Houston	NL	114	353	105	28	1	21	(10	11)	198	76	67	76	56	1	73	1	0	7	6	2	.75	6	.297	.388	.561
2001 Houston	NL	156	577	191	55	5	34	(13	21)	358	110	126	144	92	5	121	13	0	6	7	9	.44	8	.331	.430	.620
2002 Houston	NL	158	578	169	35	2	42	(20	22)	334	106	128	132	107	20	118	4	0	3	8	4	.67	10	.292	.405	.578
2003 Houston	NL	153	538	155	35	6	25	(11	14)	277	110	93	115	107	13	108	9	1	3	5	3	.63	10	.288	.412	.515
5 ML YEARS		615	2139	642	155	14	126	(56	70)	1203	412	429	479	374	39	441	27	1	20	31	19	.62	36	.300	.407	.562

Adam Bernero

Pitches: R **Bats:** R **Pos:** RP-32; SP-17   **Ht:** 6'4" **Wt:** 205 **Born:** 11/28/76 **Age:** 27

Year Team	Lg	HOW MUCH HE PITCHED						WHAT HE GAVE UP											THE RESULTS						
		G	GS	CG	GF	IP	BFP	H	R	ER	HR	SH	SF	HB	TBB	IBB	SO	WP	Bk	W	L	Pct	ShO	Sv-Op	Hld	ERC	ERA
2000 Detroit	AL	12	4	0	4	34.1	141	33	18	16	3	2	1	1	13	1	20	1	0	0	1	.000	0	0-0	1	3.94	4.19
2001 Detroit	AL	5	0	0	4	12.1	56	13	13	10	4	0	1	1	4	0	8	1	0	0	0	-	0	0-0	0	5.79	7.30
2002 Detroit	AL	28	11	0	5	101.2	459	128	74	70	17	3	5	6	31	1	69	5	1	4	7	.364	0	0-0	0	5.95	6.20
2003 Det-Col		49	17	0	5	133.1	589	137	90	87	19	5	8	8	54	1	80	3	0	1	14	.067	0	0-2	5	4.77	5.87
2003 Detroit	AL	18	17	0	0	100.2	447	104	68	68	14	3	6	7	41	0	54	1	0	1	12	.077	0	0-0	0	4.83	6.08
2003 Colorado	NL	31	0	0	5	32.2	142	33	22	19	5	2	2	1	13	1	26	2	0	0	2	.000	0	0-2	5	4.58	5.23
4 ML YEARS		94	32	0	18	281.2	1245	311	195	183	43	10	17	16	102	3	177	10	1	5	22	.185	0	0-2	6	5.13	5.85

Angel Berroa

Bats: R **Throws:** R **Pos:** SS-158   **Ht:** 6'0" **Wt:** 175 **Born:** 1/27/78 **Age:** 26

Year Team	Lg	BATTING																	BASERUNNING				AVERAGES		
		G	AB	H	2B	3B	HR	(Hm	Rd)	TB	R	RBI	RC	TBB	IBB	SO	HBP	SH	SF	SB	CS	SB%	GDP	Avg	OBP	Slg
2001 Kansas City	AL	15	53	16	2	0	0	(0	0)	18	8	4	6	3	0	10	0	0	0	2	0	1.00	2	.302	.339	.340
2002 Kansas City	AL	20	75	17	7	1	0	(0	0)	26	8	5	8	7	1	10	1	0	0	3	0	1.00	1	.227	.301	.347
2003 Kansas City	AL	158	567	163	28	7	17	(6	11)	256	92	73	82	29	3	100	18	13	8	21	5	.81	13	.287	.338	.451
3 ML YEARS		193	695	196	37	8	17	(6	11)	300	108	82	96	39	4	120	19	13	8	26	5	.84	16	.282	.334	.432

Rafael Betancourt

Pitches: R **Bats:** R **Pos:** RP-33   **Ht:** 6'2" **Wt:** 176 **Born:** 4/29/75 **Age:** 29

Year Team	Lg	HOW MUCH HE PITCHED						WHAT HE GAVE UP											THE RESULTS						
		G	GS	CG	GF	IP	BFP	H	R	ER	HR	SH	SF	HB	TBB	IBB	SO	WP	Bk	W	L	Pct	ShO	Sv-Op	Hld	ERC	ERA
1997 Michigan	A	27	0	0	0	32.1	125	26	9	7	2	1	0	0	2	0	52	3	1	0	3	.000	0	11--	-	1.64	1.95
1998 Red Sox	R	4	3	0	0	5.0	22	6	5	4	1	0	1	0	1	0	4	1	1	0	2	.000	0	0--	-	5.00	7.20
1998 Sarasota	A+	20	0	0	4	28.0	111	22	12	11	2	1	0	0	6	0	33	0	0	3	1	.750	0	2--	-	2.10	3.54
1998 Trenton	AA	7	0	0	3	9.1	42	9	7	7	0	1	0	0	3	0	9	0	0	0	0	-	0	0--	-	2.67	6.75
1999 Sarasota	A+	6	0	0	5	7.0	25	5	0	0	0	0	0	0	1	0	6	0	0	0	0	-	0	4--	-	1.42	0.00
1999 Trenton	AA	39	0	0	30	54.2	218	50	24	22	7	4	2	0	10	0	57	0	1	6	2	.750	0	13--	-	3.00	3.62
2001 Trenton	AA	16	0	0	10	24.0	100	28	16	15	0	0	0	2	3	0	27	1	0	0	1	.000	0	4--	-	3.66	5.63
2003 Akron	AA	31	0	0	20	45.1	183	33	10	7	0	1	0	0	13	2	75	1	0	0	0	-	0	16--	-	1.61	1.39
2003 Buffalo	AAA	4	0	0	2	6.2	27	6	3	3	1	0	0	0	2	0	6	1	0	0	0	-	0	1--	-	3.55	4.05
2003 Cleveland	AL	33	0	0	13	38.0	154	27	11	9	5	1	1	1	13	2	36	1	0	2	2	.500	0	1-3	4	2.54	2.13

Rocky Biddle

Pitches: R **Bats:** R **Pos:** RP-73   **Ht:** 6'3" **Wt:** 230 **Born:** 5/21/76 **Age:** 28

Year Team	Lg	HOW MUCH HE PITCHED						WHAT HE GAVE UP											THE RESULTS						
		G	GS	CG	GF	IP	BFP	H	R	ER	HR	SH	SF	HB	TBB	IBB	SO	WP	Bk	W	L	Pct	ShO	Sv-Op	Hld	ERC	ERA
2000 Chicago	AL	4	4	0	0	22.2	105	31	25	21	5	0	2	0	8	0	7	2	0	1	2	.333	0	0-0	0	7.01	8.34
2001 Chicago	AL	30	21	0	1	128.2	571	137	87	77	16	4	3	8	52	3	85	6	0	7	8	.467	0	0-3	1	4.85	5.39
2002 Chicago	AL	44	7	0	9	77.2	339	72	42	35	13	0	1	5	39	4	64	5	0	3	4	.429	0	1-3	4	4.78	4.06
2003 Montreal	NL	73	0	0	58	71.2	327	71	43	37	10	4	1	6	40	5	54	8	0	5	8	.385	0	34-41	0	5.13	4.65
4 ML YEARS		151	32	0	68	300.2	1342	311	197	170	44	8	7	19	139	12	210	21	0	16	22	.421	0	35-47	9	5.05	5.09

Nick Bierbrodt

Pitches: L **Bats:** L **Pos:** RP-13; SP-5   **Ht:** 6'5" **Wt:** 214 **Born:** 5/16/78 **Age:** 26

Year Team	Lg	HOW MUCH HE PITCHED						WHAT HE GAVE UP											THE RESULTS						
		G	GS	CG	GF	IP	BFP	H	R	ER	HR	SH	SF	HB	TBB	IBB	SO	WP	Bk	W	L	Pct	ShO	Sv-Op	Hld	ERC	ERA
1996 Diamndbcks	R	8	8	0	0	38.0	175	25	9	7	1	0	0	0	13	0	46	2	0	1	1	.500	0	0--	-	1.74	1.66
1996 Lethbridge	R+	3	3	0	0	18.0	72	12	4	1	0	0	1	1	5	0	23	1	0	2	0	1.000	0	0--	-	1.57	0.50
1997 South Bend	A	15	15	0	0	75.2	340	77	43	34	4	3	1	9	37	0	64	6	1	2	4	.333	0	0--	-	4.67	4.04
1998 High Desert	A+	24	23	1	0	129.2	560	122	66	49	7	3	6	7	64	0	88	9	0	8	7	.533	0	0--	-	4.06	3.40
1999 El Paso	AA	14	14	2	0	76.0	341	78	45	39	3	2	1	8	37	0	55	5	0	5	6	.455	0	0--	-	4.55	4.62

Year Team	Lg	G	GS	CG	GF	IP	BFP	H	R	ER	HR	SH	SF	HB	TBB	IBB	SO	WP	Bk	W	L	Pct	ShO	Sv-Op	Hld	ERC	ERA
					HOW MUCH HE PITCHED						WHAT HE GAVE UP											THE RESULTS					
1999 Tucson	AAA	11	11	0	0	43.1	213	57	42	35	9	4	0	3	30	0	43	3	0	1	4	.200	0	0--	-	8.58	7.27
2000 Tucson	AAA	4	3	0	0	18.2	77	13	10	10	3	0	0	2	14	0	11	0	0	2	1	.667	0	0--	-	5.03	4.82
2000 Diamndbcks	R	4	3	0	0	8.0	34	4	4	4	0	0	0	1	5	0	10	1	0	0	0	-	0	0--	-	2.03	4.50
2000 El Paso	AA	7	7	0	0	35.1	166	37	30	28	1	2	1	3	24	0	36	5	0	1	3	.250	0	0--	-	5.22	7.13
2001 El Paso	AA	4	4	0	0	19.2	76	13	3	3	1	0	0	0	6	0	18	0	0	2	1	.667	0	0--	-	1.77	1.37
2001 Tucson	AAA	7	6	0	0	45.1	185	48	15	11	0	3	1	1	9	1	56	1	0	4	1	.800	0	0--	-	3.09	2.18
2002 Chrlstn - SC	A	1	1	0	0	5.0	23	5	4	2	0	0	0	0	2	0	2	1	0	0	0	-	0	0--	-	3.11	3.60
2003 Buffalo	AAA	16	1	0	5	27.0	121	22	10	9	1	2	0	2	18	2	31	1	0	2	2	.500	0	0--	-	3.73	3.00
2001 Ari-TB		16	16	0	0	84.1	389	100	59	52	17	0	2	4	39	1	73	3	0	5	6	.455	0	0-0	0	6.37	5.55
2003 TB-Cle	AL	18	5	0	4	43.1	222	64	47	44	9	2	5	5	27	3	29	4	1	0	2	.000	0	0-0	0	9.29	9.14
2001 Arizona	NL	5	5	0	0	23.0	108	29	21	21	6	0	1	0	12	0	17	0	0	2	2	.500	0	0-0	0	7.43	8.22
2001 Tampa Bay	AL	11	11	0	0	61.1	281	71	38	31	11	0	1	4	27	1	56	3	0	3	4	.429	0	0-0	0	5.99	4.55
2003 Tampa Bay	AL	13	5	0	1	35.1	189	59	41	38	9	2	3	5	23	3	20	4	1	0	2	.000	0	0-0	0	11.39	9.68
2003 Cleveland	AL	5	0	0	3	8.0	33	5	6	6	0	0	2	0	4	0	9	0	0	0	0	-	0	0-0	0	1.84	6.75
2 ML YEARS		34	21	0	4	127.2	611	164	106	96	26	2	7	9	66	4	102	7	1	5	8	.385	0	0-0	0	7.34	6.77

Larry Bigbie

Bats: L **Throws:** R **Pos:** LF-76; RF-5; PH-4; CF-2; PR-1   **Ht:** 6'4" **Wt:** 190 **Born:** 11/4/77 **Age:** 26

Year Team	Lg	G	AB	H	2B	3B	HR	(Hm	Rd)	TB	R	RBI	RC	TBB	IBB	SO	HBP	SH	SF	SB	CS	SB%	GDP	Avg	OBP	Slg
						BATTING															BASERUNNING				AVERAGES	
2003 Ottawa*	AAA	30	117	41	14	4	3	(-	-)	72	23	21	29	14	0	31	1	0	1	0	0	-	1	.350	.421	.615
2003 Orioles*	R	2	6	2	1	0	0	(-	-)	3	1	0	1	0	0	1	0	0	0	0	0	-	0	.333	.333	.500
2001 Baltimore	AL	47	131	30	6	0	2	(0	2)	42	15	11	14	17	1	42	0	1	0	4	1	.80	2	.229	.318	.321
2002 Baltimore	AL	16	34	6	1	0	0	(0	0)	7	1	3	1	1	0	11	0	0	1	1	0	1.00	1	.176	.194	.206
2003 Baltimore	AL	83	287	87	15	1	9	(4	5)	131	43	31	47	29	3	60	0	1	2	7	1	.88	2	.303	.365	.456
3 ML YEARS		146	452	123	22	1	11	(4	7)	180	59	45	62	47	4	113	0	2	3	12	2	.86	5	.272	.339	.398

Craig Biggio

Bats: R **Throws:** R **Pos:** CF-150; PH-3   **Ht:** 5'11" **Wt:** 185 **Born:** 12/14/65 **Age:** 38

Year Team	Lg	G	AB	H	2B	3B	HR	(Hm	Rd)	TB	R	RBI	RC	TBB	IBB	SO	HBP	SH	SF	SB	CS	SB%	GDP	Avg	OBP	Slg
						BATTING															BASERUNNING				AVERAGES	
1988 Houston	NL	50	123	26	6	1	3	(1	2)	43	14	5	11	7	2	29	0	1	0	6	1	.86	1	.211	.254	.350
1989 Houston	NL	134	443	114	21	2	13	(6	7)	178	64	60	64	49	8	64	6	6	5	21	3	.88	7	.257	.336	.402
1990 Houston	NL	150	555	153	24	2	4	(2	2)	193	53	42	68	53	1	79	3	9	1	25	11	.69	11	.276	.342	.348
1991 Houston	NL	149	546	161	23	4	4	(0	4)	204	79	46	79	53	3	71	2	5	3	19	6	.76	2	.295	.358	.374
1992 Houston	NL	162	613	170	32	3	6	(3	3)	226	96	39	95	94	9	95	7	5	2	38	15	.72	5	.277	.378	.369
1993 Houston	NL	155	610	175	41	5	21	(8	13)	289	98	64	105	77	7	93	10	4	5	15	17	.47	10	.287	.373	.474
1994 Houston	NL	114	437	139	44	5	6	(4	2)	211	88	56	94	62	1	58	8	2	2	39	4	.91	5	.318	.411	.483
1995 Houston	NL	141	553	167	30	2	22	(6	16)	267	123	77	116	80	1	85	22	11	7	33	8	.80	6	.302	.406	.483
1996 Houston	NL	162	605	174	24	4	15	(7	8)	251	113	75	105	75	0	72	27	8	8	25	7	.78	10	.288	.386	.415
1997 Houston	NL	162	619	191	37	8	22	(7	15)	310	146	81	139	84	6	107	34	0	7	47	10	.82	0	.309	.415	.501
1998 Houston	NL	160	646	210	51	2	20	(10	10)	325	123	88	135	64	6	113	23	1	4	50	8	.86	10	.325	.403	.503
1999 Houston	NL	160	639	188	56	0	16	(10	6)	292	123	73	117	88	9	107	11	5	6	28	14	.67	5	.294	.386	.457
2000 Houston	NL	101	377	101	13	5	8	(2	6)	148	67	35	63	61	3	73	16	7	5	12	2	.86	10	.268	.388	.393
2001 Houston	NL	155	617	180	35	3	20	(10	10)	281	118	70	109	66	4	100	28	0	6	7	4	.64	11	.292	.382	.455
2002 Houston	NL	145	577	146	36	3	15	(7	8)	233	96	58	73	50	2	111	17	9	2	16	2	.89	15	.253	.330	.404
2003 Houston	NL	153	628	166	44	2	15	(6	9)	259	102	62	97	57	3	116	27	3	2	8	4	.67	4	.264	.350	.412
16 ML YEARS		2253	8588	2461	517	51	210	(89	121)	3710	1503	931	1470	1020	65	1373	241	76	65	389	116	.77	112	.287	.375	.432

Casey Blake

Bats: R **Throws:** R **Pos:** 3B-140; 1B-31; PH-1; PR-1   **Ht:** 6'2" **Wt:** 205 **Born:** 8/23/73 **Age:** 30

Year Team	Lg	G	AB	H	2B	3B	HR	(Hm	Rd)	TB	R	RBI	RC	TBB	IBB	SO	HBP	SH	SF	SB	CS	SB%	GDP	Avg	OBP	Slg
						BATTING															BASERUNNING				AVERAGES	
1999 Toronto	AL	14	39	10	2	0	1	(0	1)	15	6	1	4	2	0	7	0	0	0	0	0	-	1	.256	.293	.385
2000 Minnesota	AL	7	16	3	2	0	0	(0	0)	5	1	1	2	3	0	7	1	0	0	0	0	-	0	.188	.333	.313
2001 Min-Bal	AL	19	37	9	1	0	1	(0	1)	13	3	4	5	4	1	12	0	0	0	3	0	1.00	0	.243	.317	.351
2002 Minnesota	AL	9	20	4	1	0	0	(0	0)	5	2	1	1	2	0	7	0	0	0	0	0	-	0	.200	.273	.250
2003 Cleveland	AL	152	557	143	35	0	17	(2	15)	229	80	67	68	38	1	109	10	8	8	7	9	.44	11	.257	.312	.411
2001 Minnesota	AL	13	22	7	1	0	0	(0	0)	8	1	2	4	3	1	8	0	0	0	1	0	1.00	0	.318	.400	.364
2001 Baltimore	AL	6	15	2	0	0	1	(0	1)	5	2	2	1	1	0	4	0	0	0	2	0	1.00	0	.133	.188	.333
5 ML YEARS		201	669	169	41	0	19	(2	17)	267	92	74	80	49	2	142	11	8	9	10	9	.53	13	.253	.310	.399

Hank Blalock

Bats: L **Throws:** R **Pos:** 3B-141; PH-7; 2B-4; PR-1   **Ht:** 6'1" **Wt:** 195 **Born:** 11/28/80 **Age:** 23

Year Team	Lg	G	AB	H	2B	3B	HR	(Hm	Rd)	TB	R	RBI	RC	TBB	IBB	SO	HBP	SH	SF	SB	CS	SB%	GDP	Avg	OBP	Slg
						BATTING															BASERUNNING				AVERAGES	
1999 Rangers	R	51	191	69	17	6	3	(-	-)	107	34	38	42	25	4	23	1	0	5	3	2	.60	7	.361	.428	.560
1999 Savannah	A	7	25	6	1	0	1	(-	-)	10	3	2	3	1	0	3	1	0	1	0	0	-	0	.240	.286	.400
2000 Savannah	A	139	512	153	32	2	10	(-	-)	219	66	77	85	62	3	53	5	0	11	31	8	.79	14	.299	.373	.428
2001 Charlotte	A+	63	237	90	19	1	7	(-	-)	132	46	47	53	26	7	31	1	0	4	7	4	.64	6	.380	.437	.557
2001 Tulsa	AA	68	272	89	18	4	11	(-	-)	148	50	61	59	39	1	38	2	0	2	3	3	.50	5	.327	.413	.544
2002 Oklahoma	AAA	95	387	119	32	1	8	(-	-)	177	63	62	62	34	1	61	1	1	2	2	1	.67	9	.307	.363	.457
2002 Texas	AL	49	147	31	8	0	3	(2	1)	48	16	17	14	20	1	43	1	2	2	0	0	-	2	.211	.306	.327
2003 Texas	AL	143	567	170	33	3	29	(18	11)	296	89	90	90	44	1	97	1	0	3	2	3	.40	17	.300	.350	.522
2 ML YEARS		192	714	201	41	3	32	(20	12)	344	105	107	104	64	2	140	2	2	5	2	3	.40	19	.282	.340	.482

Henry Blanco

Bats: R **Throws:** R **Pos:** C-52; PH-4; PR-1   **Ht:** 5'11" **Wt:** 220 **Born:** 8/29/71 **Age:** 32

Year Team	Lg	G	AB	H	2B	3B	HR	(Hm	Rd)	TB	R	RBI	RC	TBB	IBB	SO	HBP	SH	SF	SB	CS	SB%	GDP	Avg	OBP	Slg
1997 Los Angeles	NL	3	5	2	0	0	1	(0	1)	5	1	1	2	0	0	1	0	0	0	0	0	-	0	.400	.400	1.000
1999 Colorado	NL	88	263	61	12	3	6	(3	3)	97	30	28	32	34	1	38	1	3	2	1	1	.50	4	.232	.320	.369
2000 Milwaukee	NL	93	284	67	24	0	7	(3	4)	112	29	31	33	36	6	60	0	0	4	0	3	.00	9	.236	.318	.394
2001 Milwaukee	NL	104	314	66	18	3	6	(4	2)	108	33	31	30	34	6	72	2	5	2	3	1	.75	10	.210	.290	.344
2002 Atlanta	NL	81	221	45	9	1	6	(4	2)	74	17	22	16	20	5	51	1	2	5	0	2	.00	5	.204	.267	.335
2003 Atlanta	NL	55	151	30	8	0	1	(0	1)	41	11	13	13	10	2	21	1	3	1	0	0	-	3	.199	.252	.272
6 ML YEARS		424	1238	271	71	7	27	(14	13)	437	121	126	126	134	20	243	5	13	14	4	7	.36	31	.219	.295	.353

Nate Bland

Pitches: L **Bats:** L **Pos:** RP-22   **Ht:** 6'5" **Wt:** 190 **Born:** 12/27/74 **Age:** 29

Year Team	Lg	G	GS	CG	GF	IP	BFP	H	R	ER	HR	SH	SF	HB	TBB	IBB	SO	WP	Bk	W	L	Pct	ShO	Sv-Op	Hld	ERC	ERA
1993 Yakima	A-	16	13	0	1	63.1	272	54	34	20	2	0	1	0	29	1	43	3	1	4	6	.400	0	0--	-	2.95	2.84
1994 Great Falls	R+	2	1	0	1	9.1	37	6	2	1	0	1	0	1	3	0	12	1	0	0	0	-	0	0--	-	8.14	0.96
1994 Bakersfield	A+	12	9	0	0	50.1	228	58	31	30	0	3	0	1	27	0	19	2	1	2	6	.250	0	0--	-	4.87	5.36
1995 Bakersfield	A+	27	23	0	1	122.1	562	155	89	71	13	5	3	1	55	0	46	12	2	4	9	.308	0	0--	-	5.97	5.22
1996 Savannah	A	5	5	0	0	27.2	115	24	8	5	0	0	1	1	10	0	24	2	0	1	0	1.000	0	0--	-	2.70	1.63
1996 Vero Beach	A+	17	17	0	0	96.0	414	99	42	33	3	4	2	1	35	0	69	5	0	10	4	.714	0	0--	-	3.66	3.09
1997 San Antonio	AA	10	8	0	1	41.0	190	47	34	32	5	3	1	3	24	0	30	3	1	3	2	.600	0	0--	-	6.27	7.02
1997 Vero Beach	A+	17	14	0	0	82.2	356	85	35	35	7	4	3	4	38	0	67	5	0	7	7	.500	0	0--	-	4.71	3.81
1998 San Antonio	AA	26	0	0	5	45.1	203	56	21	14	0	0	2	2	14	0	34	3	0	4	2	.667	0	0--	-	4.48	2.78
2000 Sioux City	IND	27	0	0	0	42.0	180	35	18	17	0	0	0	0	19	0	45	0	0	1	0	1.000	0	6--	-	2.64	3.64
2002 Chico	IND	8	0	0	0	15.2	62	10	6	4	0	0	0	0	5	0	17	0	0	1	0	1.000	0	2--	-	1.46	2.30
2002 Binghamton	AA	15	0	0	8	24.2	98	16	9	7	0	1	0	1	8	3	19	0	0	2	1	.667	0	0--	-	1.48	2.55
2003 New Orleans	AAA	17	0	0	5	19.0	81	15	6	6	1	1	1	1	9	1	23	0	0	0	1	.000	0	1--	-	2.98	2.84
2003 Houston	NL	22	0	0	2	20.1	96	22	13	13	3	4	1	2	12	2	18	3	0	1	2	.333	0	0-1	3	5.85	5.75

Willie Bloomquist

Bats: R **Throws:** R **Pos:** 3B-37; SS-18; PR-16; LF-10; PH-9; 2B-7; 1B-3; DH-3; RF-1   **Ht:** 5'11" **Wt:** 180 **Born:** 11/27/77 **Age:** 26

Year Team	Lg	G	AB	H	2B	3B	HR	(Hm	Rd)	TB	R	RBI	RC	TBB	IBB	SO	HBP	SH	SF	SB	CS	SB%	GDP	Avg	OBP	Slg
1999 Everett	A-	42	178	51	10	3	2	(-	-)	73	35	27	29	22	0	25	1	0	1	17	5	.77	1	.287	.366	.410
2000 Lancaster	A+	64	256	97	19	6	2	(-	-)	134	63	51	59	37	2	27	0	1	1	22	12	.65	3	.379	.456	.523
2000 Tacoma	AAA	51	191	43	5	1	1	(-	-)	53	17	23	13	7	0	28	0	4	3	5	0	1.00	3	.225	.249	.277
2001 San Antonio	AA	123	491	125	23	2	0	(-	-)	152	59	28	46	28	0	55	1	7	4	34	9	.79	11	.255	.294	.310
2002 Tacoma	AAA	104	337	91	14	3	6	(-	-)	129	47	47	44	29	1	44	3	9	3	20	10	.67	5	.270	.331	.383
2002 Seattle	AL	12	33	15	4	0	0	(0	0)	19	11	7	10	5	0	2	0	0	0	3	1	.75	0	.455	.526	.576
2003 Seattle	AL	89	196	49	7	2	1	(1	0)	63	30	14	17	19	1	39	1	2	2	4	1	.80	6	.250	.317	.321
2 ML YEARS		101	229	64	11	2	1	(1	0)	82	41	21	27	24	1	41	1	2	2	7	2	.78	6	.279	.348	.358

Geoff Blum

Bats: B **Throws:** R **Pos:** 3B-83; 2B-25; PH-19; SS-11; 1B-6; LF-1; RF-1   **Ht:** 6'3" **Wt:** 200 **Born:** 4/26/73 **Age:** 31

Year Team	Lg	G	AB	H	2B	3B	HR	(Hm	Rd)	TB	R	RBI	RC	TBB	IBB	SO	HBP	SH	SF	SB	CS	SB%	GDP	Avg	OBP	Slg
1999 Montreal	NL	45	133	32	7	2	8	(0	8)	67	21	18	22	17	3	25	0	3	0	1	0	1.00	3	.241	.327	.504
2000 Montreal	NL	124	343	97	20	2	11	(5	6)	154	40	45	50	26	2	60	3	3	4	1	4	.20	4	.283	.335	.449
2001 Montreal	NL	148	453	107	25	0	9	(6	3)	159	57	50	49	43	8	94	10	3	5	9	5	.64	12	.236	.313	.351
2002 Houston	NL	130	368	104	20	4	10	(6	4)	162	45	52	61	49	5	70	1	1	2	5	0	1.00	15	.283	.367	.440
2003 Houston	NL	123	420	110	19	0	10	(6	4)	159	51	52	39	20	1	50	2	2	5	0	0	-	15	.262	.295	.379
5 ML YEARS		570	1717	450	91	8	48	(23	25)	701	214	217	221	155	19	299	16	12	16	13	9	.59	42	.262	.326	.408

Hiram Bocachica

Bats: R **Throws:** R **Pos:** CF-5; LF-1   **Ht:** 5'11" **Wt:** 165 **Born:** 3/4/76 **Age:** 28

Year Team	Lg	G	AB	H	2B	3B	HR	(Hm	Rd)	TB	R	RBI	RC	TBB	IBB	SO	HBP	SH	SF	SB	CS	SB%	GDP	Avg	OBP	Slg
2003 Toledo*	AAA	95	322	78	19	3	12	(-	-)	139	48	37	44	24	0	57	10	8	2	11	6	.65	5	.242	.313	.432
2000 Los Angeles	NL	8	10	3	0	0	0	(0	0)	3	2	0	1	0	0	2	0	0	0	0	0	-	0	.300	.300	.300
2001 Los Angeles	NL	75	133	31	11	1	2	(2	0)	50	15	9	15	9	0	33	1	0	0	4	1	.80	1	.233	.287	.376
2002 LA-Det		83	168	37	7	0	8	(2	6)	68	26	17	14	10	0	41	0	1	0	3	3	.50	3	.220	.264	.405
2003 Detroit	AL	6	22	1	1	0	0	(0	0)	2	1	0	0	0	0	7	0	0	0	0	0	-	0	.045	.045	.091
2002 Los Angeles	NL	49	65	14	3	0	4	(1	3)	29	12	9	7	5	0	19	0	0	0	1	1	.50	1	.215	.271	.446
2002 Detroit	AL	34	103	23	4	0	4	(1	3)	39	14	8	7	5	0	22	0	1	0	2	2	.50	2	.223	.259	.379
4 ML YEARS		172	333	72	19	1	10	(4	6)	123	44	26	30	19	0	83	1	1	0	7	4	.64	4	.216	.261	.369

Brian Boehringer

Pitches: R **Bats:** B **Pos:** RP-62   **Ht:** 6'2" **Wt:** 190 **Born:** 1/8/70 **Age:** 34

Year Team	Lg	G	GS	CG	GF	IP	BFP	H	R	ER	HR	SH	SF	HB	TBB	IBB	SO	WP	Bk	W	L	Pct	ShO	Sv-Op	Hld	ERC	ERA
1995 New York	AL	7	3	0	0	17.2	99	24	27	27	5	0	1	1	22	1	10	3	0	0	3	.000	0	0-1	0	11.86	13.75
1996 New York	AL	15	3	0	1	46.1	205	46	28	28	6	3	3	1	21	2	37	1	0	2	4	.333	0	0-1	4	4.42	5.44
1997 New York	AL	34	0	0	11	48.0	210	39	16	14	4	3	2	0	32	6	53	2	0	3	2	.600	0	0-3	5	3.74	2.63
1998 San Diego	NL	56	1	0	18	76.1	347	75	38	37	10	4	4	4	45	6	67	1	0	5	2	.714	0	0-1	5	5.06	4.36
1999 San Diego	NL	33	11	0	8	94.1	409	97	38	34	10	6	4	1	35	4	64	2	0	6	5	.545	0	0-2	3	4.12	3.24
2000 San Diego	NL	7	3	0	1	15.2	74	18	15	10	4	0	1	0	10	0	9	0	0	0	3	.000	0	0-1	0	7.15	5.74
2001 NYY-SF		51	0	0	17	69.0	311	67	35	28	7	2	4	5	29	5	60	0	0	0	4	.000	0	2-2	3	4.02	3.65

			HOW MUCH HE PITCHED						WHAT HE GAVE UP											THE RESULTS						
Year Team	Lg	G	GS	CG	GF	IP	BFP	H	R	ER	HR	SH	SF	HB	TBB	IBB	SO	WP	Bk	W	L	Pct	ShO	Sv-Op	Hld	ERC	ERA
2002 Pittsburgh	NL	70	0	0	20	79.2	328	65	30	30	5	6	3	2	33	6	65	1	0	4	4	.500	0	1-6	28	2.92	3.39
2003 Pittsburgh	NL	62	0	0	18	62.1	277	64	39	38	11	3	2	3	30	3	47	0	1	5	4	.556	0	0-3	15	5.26	5.49
2001 New York	AL	22	0	0	8	34.2	155	35	15	12	3	1	2	3	12	0	33	0	0	0	1	.000	0	1-1	1	4.03	3.12
2001 San Francisco	NL	29	0	0	9	34.1	156	32	20	16	4	1	2	2	17	5	27	0	0	0	3	.000	0	1-1	2	4.01	4.19
9 ML YEARS		335	21	0	94	509.1	2260	495	266	246	62	28	21	17	257	31	412	10	1	25	31	.446	0	3-20	65	4.49	4.35

Jeremy Bonderman

Pitches: R **Bats:** R **Pos:** SP-28; RP-5   **Ht:** 6'2" **Wt:** 210 **Born:** 10/28/82 **Age:** 21

			HOW MUCH HE PITCHED						WHAT HE GAVE UP											THE RESULTS						
Year Team	Lg	G	GS	CG	GF	IP	BFP	H	R	ER	HR	SH	SF	HB	TBB	IBB	SO	WP	Bk	W	L	Pct	ShO	Sv-Op	Hld	ERC	ERA
2002 Modesto	A+	25	25	1	0	144.2	627	129	77	58	15	6	7	5	55	1	160	9	3	9	8	.529	0	0- -	-	3.45	3.61
2002 Lakeland	A+	2	2	1	0	12.0	49	11	8	8	1	0	2	4	4	0	10	1	0	0	1	.000	0	0- -	-	5.42	6.00
2003 Detroit	AL	33	28	0	0	162.0	727	193	118	100	23	3	6	4	58	2	108	12	2	6	19	.240	0	0-0	0	5.39	5.56

Barry Bonds

Bats: L **Throws:** L **Pos:** LF-123; DH-6; PH-2   **Ht:** 6'2" **Wt:** 228 **Born:** 7/24/64 **Age:** 39

							BATTING											BASERUNNING				AVERAGES		
Year Team	Lg	G	AB	H	2B	3B	HR	(Hm | Rd)	TB	R	RBI	RC	TBB	IBB	SO	HBP	SH	SF	SB	CS	SB%	GDP	Avg	OBP	Slg
1986 Pittsburgh	NL	113	413	92	26	3	16	(9 | 7)	172	72	48	64	65	2	102	2	2	2	36	7	.84	4	.223	.330	.416
1987 Pittsburgh	NL	150	551	144	34	9	25	(12 | 13)	271	99	59	92	54	3	88	3	0	3	32	10	.76	4	.261	.329	.492
1988 Pittsburgh	NL	144	538	152	30	5	24	(14 | 10)	264	97	58	97	72	14	82	2	0	2	17	11	.61	3	.283	.368	.491
1989 Pittsburgh	NL	159	580	144	34	6	19	(7 | 12)	247	96	58	91	93	22	93	1	1	4	32	10	.76	9	.248	.351	.426
1990 Pittsburgh	NL	151	519	156	32	3	33	(14 | 19)	293	104	114	121	93	15	83	3	0	6	52	13	.80	8	.301	.406	.565
1991 Pittsburgh	NL	153	510	149	28	5	25	(12 | 13)	262	95	116	113	107	25	73	4	0	13	43	13	.77	8	.292	.410	.514
1992 Pittsburgh	NL	140	473	147	36	5	34	(15 | 19)	295	109	103	134	127	32	69	5	0	7	39	8	.83	9	.311	.456	.624
1993 San Francisco	NL	159	539	181	38	4	46	(21 | 25)	365	129	123	155	126	43	79	2	0	7	29	12	.71	11	.336	.458	.677
1994 San Francisco	NL	112	391	122	18	1	37	(15 | 22)	253	89	81	105	74	18	43	6	0	3	29	9	.76	3	.312	.426	.647
1995 San Francisco	NL	144	506	149	30	7	33	(16 | 17)	292	109	104	125	120	22	83	5	0	4	31	10	.76	12	.294	.431	.577
1996 San Francisco	NL	158	517	159	27	3	42	(23 | 19)	318	122	129	148	151	30	76	1	0	4	40	7	.85	11	.308	.461	.615
1997 San Francisco	NL	159	532	155	26	5	40	(24 | 16)	311	123	101	140	145	34	87	8	0	5	37	8	.82	13	.291	.446	.585
1998 San Francisco	NL	156	552	167	44	7	37	(21 | 16)	336	120	122	141	130	29	92	8	1	6	28	12	.70	15	.303	.438	.609
1999 San Francisco	NL	102	355	93	20	2	34	(16 | 18)	219	91	83	85	73	9	62	3	0	3	15	2	.88	6	.262	.389	.617
2000 San Francisco	NL	143	480	147	28	4	49	(25 | 24)	330	129	106	139	117	22	77	3	0	7	11	3	.79	6	.306	.440	.688
2001 San Francisco	NL	153	476	156	32	2	73	(37 | 36)	411	129	137	191	177	35	93	9	0	2	13	3	.81	5	.328	.515	.863
2002 San Francisco	NL	143	403	149	31	2	46	(19 | 27)	322	117	110	161	198	68	47	9	0	2	9	2	.82	4	.370	.582	.799
2003 San Francisco	NL	130	390	133	22	1	45	(23 | 22)	292	111	90	131	148	61	58	10	0	2	7	0	1.00	7	.341	.529	.749
18 ML YEARS		2569	8725	2595	536	74	658	(323 | 335)	5253	1941	1742	2233	2070	484	1387	84	4	84	500	140	.78	138	.297	.433	.602

Jung Bong

Pitches: L **Bats:** L **Pos:** RP-44   **Ht:** 6'3" **Wt:** 175 **Born:** 7/15/80 **Age:** 23

			HOW MUCH HE PITCHED						WHAT HE GAVE UP											THE RESULTS						
Year Team	Lg	G	GS	CG	GF	IP	BFP	H	R	ER	HR	SH	SF	HB	TBB	IBB	SO	WP	Bk	W	L	Pct	ShO	Sv-Op	Hld	ERC	ERA
1998 Braves	R	11	10	0	0	48.1	181	31	9	8	2	1	4	6	14	0	56	7	3	1	1	.500	0	0- -	-	2.10	1.49
1999 Macon	A	26	20	0	2	108.2	484	111	61	48	8	5	1	11	50	0	100	9	4	6	5	.545	0	1- -	-	4.67	3.98
2000 Macon	A	20	19	0	0	112.2	500	119	65	53	4	5	3	14	45	0	90	10	2	7	7	.500	0	0- -	-	4.44	4.23
2000 Myrtle Beach	A+	7	6	0	0	41.1	163	33	14	10	1	1	0	5	7	0	37	4	0	3	1	.750	0	0- -	-	2.21	2.18
2001 Myrtle Beach	A+	28	28	0	0	168.0	677	151	67	56	7	6	3	4	47	0	145	7	1	13	9	.591	0	0- -	-	2.87	3.00
2002 Greenville	AA	27	17	0	4	122.0	533	136	59	44	6	5	5	3	45	1	107	8	1	7	8	.467	0	2- -	-	4.35	3.25
2003 Richmond	AAA	3	3	0	0	11.1	49	11	7	7	1	0	0	0	3	0	15	0	0	1	2	.333	0	0- -	-	3.16	5.56
2002 Atlanta	NL	1	1	0	0	6.0	27	8	5	5	0	0	0	0	2	0	4	0	0	0	1	.000	0	0-0	0	5.03	7.50
2003 Atlanta	NL	44	0	0	14	57.0	247	56	32	32	8	3	1	2	31	6	47	6	1	6	2	.750	0	1-3	2	4.97	5.05
2 ML YEARS		45	1	0	14	63.0	274	64	37	37	8	3	1	2	33	6	51	6	1	6	3	.667	0	1-3	2	4.98	5.29

Aaron Boone

Bats: R **Throws:** R **Pos:** 3B-137; 2B-19; SS-5; PH-2   **Ht:** 6'2" **Wt:** 200 **Born:** 3/9/73 **Age:** 31

							BATTING											BASERUNNING				AVERAGES		
Year Team	Lg	G	AB	H	2B	3B	HR	(Hm | Rd)	TB	R	RBI	RC	TBB	IBB	SO	HBP	SH	SF	SB	CS	SB%	GDP	Avg	OBP	Slg
1997 Cincinnati	NL	16	49	12	1	0	0	(0 | 0)	13	5	5	3	2	0	5	0	1	0	1	0	1.00	1	.245	.275	.265
1998 Cincinnati	NL	58	181	51	13	2	2	(2 | 0)	74	24	28	27	15	1	36	5	3	2	6	1	.86	3	.282	.350	.409
1999 Cincinnati	NL	139	472	132	26	5	14	(7 | 7)	210	56	72	70	30	2	79	8	5	5	17	6	.74	6	.280	.330	.445
2000 Cincinnati	NL	84	291	83	18	0	12	(5 | 7)	137	44	43	50	24	1	52	10	2	4	6	1	.86	5	.285	.356	.471
2001 Cincinnati	NL	103	381	112	26	2	14	(10 | 4)	184	54	62	63	29	1	71	8	3	6	6	3	.67	9	.294	.351	.483
2002 Cincinnati	NL	162	606	146	38	2	26	(14 | 12)	266	83	87	86	56	4	111	10	9	4	32	8	.80	9	.241	.314	.439
2003 Cin-NYY		160	592	158	32	3	24	(13 | 11)	268	92	96	90	46	2	104	8	6	2	23	3	.88	13	.267	.327	.453
2003 Cincinnati	NL	106	403	110	19	3	18	(10 | 8)	189	61	65	66	35	2	74	5	3	0	15	3	.83	6	.273	.339	.469
2003 New York	AL	54	189	48	13	0	6	(3 | 3)	79	31	31	24	11	0	30	3	3	2	8	0	1.00	7	.254	.302	.418
7 ML YEARS		722	2572	694	154	14	92	(51 | 41)	1152	358	393	389	202	11	458	49	29	23	91	22	.81	46	.270	.332	.448

Bret Boone

Bats: R **Throws:** R **Pos:** 2B-159   **Ht:** 5'10" **Wt:** 190 **Born:** 4/6/69 **Age:** 35

							BATTING											BASERUNNING				AVERAGES		
Year Team	Lg	G	AB	H	2B	3B	HR	(Hm | Rd)	TB	R	RBI	RC	TBB	IBB	SO	HBP	SH	SF	SB	CS	SB%	GDP	Avg	OBP	Slg
1992 Seattle	AL	33	129	25	4	0	4	(2 | 2)	41	15	15	7	4	0	34	1	1	0	1	1	.50	4	.194	.224	.318
1993 Seattle	AL	76	271	68	12	2	12	(7 | 5)	120	31	38	35	17	1	52	4	6	4	2	3	.40	6	.251	.301	.443
1994 Cincinnati	NL	108	381	122	25	2	12	(5 | 7)	187	59	68	65	24	1	74	8	5	6	3	4	.43	10	.320	.368	.491
1995 Cincinnati	NL	138	513	137	34	2	15	(6 | 9)	220	63	68	70	41	0	84	6	5	5	5	1	.83	14	.267	.326	.429
1996 Cincinnati	NL	142	520	121	21	3	12	(7 | 5)	184	56	69	50	31	0	100	3	2	6	3	2	.60	9	.233	.275	.354
1997 Cincinnati	NL	139	443	99	25	1	7	(4 | 3)	147	40	46	42	45	4	101	4	4	5	5	5	.50	11	.223	.298	.332

Year Team	Lg	G	AB	H	2B	3B	HR	(Hm	Rd)	TB	R	RBI	RC	TBB	IBB	SO	HBP	SH	SF	SB	CS	SB%	GDP	Avg	OBP	Slg
1998 Cincinnati	NL	157	583	155	38	1	24	(13	11)	267	76	95	80	48	3	104	4	9	4	6	4	.60	23	.266	.324	.458
1999 Atlanta	NL	152	608	153	38	1	20	(9	11)	253	102	63	77	47	0	112	5	9	2	14	9	.61	11	.252	.310	.416
2000 San Diego	NL	127	463	116	18	2	19	(8	11)	195	61	74	63	50	7	97	5	0	7	8	4	.67	11	.251	.326	.421
2001 Seattle	AL	158	623	206	37	3	37	(19	18)	360	118	141	126	40	5	110	9	5	13	5	5	.50	11	.331	.372	.578
2002 Seattle	AL	155	608	169	34	3	24	(13	11)	281	88	107	96	53	4	102	6	2	6	12	5	.71	11	.278	.339	.462
2003 Seattle	AL	159	622	183	35	5	35	(16	19)	333	111	117	114	68	3	125	7	1	7	16	3	.84	17	.294	.366	.535
12 ML YEARS		1544	5764	1554	321	25	221	(109	112)	2588	820	901	825	468	28	1095	62	52	68	80	46	.63	138	.270	.328	.449

Chris Bootcheck

Pitches: R **Bats:** R **Pos:** RP-3; SP-1 **Ht:** 6'5" **Wt:** 200 **Born:** 10/24/78 **Age:** 25

		HOW MUCH HE PITCHED						WHAT HE GAVE UP										THE RESULTS						
Year Team	Lg	G	GS	CG	GF	IP	BFP	H	R	ER	HR	SH	SF	HB	TBB	IBB	SO	WP	Bk	W	L	Pct	ShO	Sv-Op	Hld	ERC	ERA
2001 R Cucamnga	A+	15	14	1	0	87.0	359	84	45	38	11	0	1	0	23	0	86	4	0	8	4	.667	0	0- -		3.56	3.93
2001 Arkansas	AA	6	6	1	0	36.1	161	39	25	22	3	0	0	3	11	0	22	1	1	3	3	.500	0	0- -		4.23	5.45
2002 Arkansas	AA	19	19	3	0	116.0	517	130	68	62	11	4	2	6	35	0	90	4	0	8	7	.533	0	0- -		4.45	4.81
2002 Salt Lake	AAA	9	9	1	0	58.0	247	64	29	25	5	1	2	2	16	0	38	1	0	4	3	.571	1	0- -		4.27	3.88
2003 Salt Lake	AAA	28	26	3	0	171.1	737	194	103	81	19	6	12	7	43	1	82	1	0	8	9	.471	0	0- -		4.49	4.25
2003 Anaheim	AL	4	1	0	2	10.1	53	16	13	11	5	0	0	0	6	0	7	0	0	0	1	.000	0	0-0	0	11.53	9.58

Pedro Borbon

Pitches: L **Bats:** L **Pos:** RP-7 **Ht:** 6'1" **Wt:** 230 **Born:** 11/15/67 **Age:** 36

		HOW MUCH HE PITCHED						WHAT HE GAVE UP										THE RESULTS						
Year Team	Lg	G	GS	CG	GF	IP	BFP	H	R	ER	HR	SH	SF	HB	TBB	IBB	SO	WP	Bk	W	L	Pct	ShO	Sv-Op	Hld	ERC	ERA
2003 Memphis*	AAA	7	0	0	4	8.2	32	6	3	3	1	1	0	1	0	0	6	1	0	0	1	.000	0	1- -		1.65	3.12
1992 Atlanta	NL	2	0	0	2	1.1	7	2	1	1	0	0	0	0	1	1	1	0	0	0	1	.000	0	0-0	0	5.90	6.75
1993 Atlanta	NL	3	0	0	0	1.2	11	3	4	4	0	1	0	0	3	0	2	0	0	0	-		0	0-0	0	14.26	21.60
1995 Atlanta	NL	41	0	0	19	32.0	143	29	12	11	2	3	1	1	17	4	33	0	1	2	2	.500	0	2-4	6	3.61	3.09
1996 Atlanta	NL	43	0	0	19	36.0	140	26	12	11	1	4	0	1	7	0	31	0	0	3	0	1.000	0	1-1	4	1.64	2.75
1999 Los Angeles	NL	70	0	0	11	50.2	220	39	23	23	5	0	3	1	29	1	33	1	0	4	3	.571	0	1-2	15	3.45	4.09
2000 Toronto	AL	59	0	0	6	41.2	213	45	37	30	5	2	7	5	38	5	29	0	0	1	1	.500	0	1-1	12	6.91	6.48
2001 Toronto	AL	71	0	0	14	53.1	217	48	24	22	8	2	2	4	12	3	45	0	0	2	4	.333	0	0-5	13	3.44	3.71
2002 Tor-Hou		72	0	0	9	50.1	232	53	32	30	10	3	6	3	25	8	50	1	0	4	4	.500	0	1-5	17	5.36	5.36
2003 St Louis	NL	7	0	0	3	4.0	28	14	9	9	2	0	0	1	2	2	0	0	0	0	1	.000	0	0-1		28.24	20.25
2002 Toronto	AL	16	0	0	6	12.2	60	12	8	7	3	0	1	1	6	3	11	1	0	1	2	.333	0	0-2	1	4.61	4.97
2002 Houston	NL	56	0	0	3	37.2	172	41	24	23	7	3	5	2	19	5	39	0	0	3	2	.600	0	1-3	16	5.63	5.50
9 ML YEARS		368	0	0	83	271.0	1211	259	154	141	33	15	19	16	134	24	224	1	0	16	16	.500	0	6-18	68	4.38	4.68

Joe Borchard

Bats: B **Throws:** R **Pos:** CF-16 **Ht:** 6'5" **Wt:** 220 **Born:** 11/25/78 **Age:** 25

		BATTING																	BASERUNNING				AVERAGES		
Year Team	Lg	G	AB	H	2B	3B	HR	(Hm | Rd)	TB	R	RBI	RC	TBB	IBB	SO	HBP	SH	SF	SB	CS	SB%	GDP	Avg	OBP	Slg
2000 White Sox	R	7	29	12	4	0	0	(- | -)	16	3	8	7	4	0	4	0	0	0	0	0	-	0	.414	.485	.552
2000 Winstn-Salm	A+	14	52	15	3	0	2	(- | -)	24	7	7	10	6	0	9	2	0	1	0	0	-	0	.288	.377	.462
2000 Birmingham	AA	6	22	5	0	1	0	(- | -)	7	3	3	2	3	0	8	0	0	1	0	0	-	1	.227	.308	.318
2001 Birmingham	AA	133	515	152	27	1	27	(- | -)	262	95	98	97	67	1	158	10	0	5	5	4	.56	13	.295	.384	.509
2002 Charlotte	AAA	117	438	119	35	2	20	(- | -)	218	62	59	72	49	2	139	4	0	2	2	4	.33	11	.272	.349	.498
2003 Charlotte	AAA	114	435	110	20	2	13	(- | -)	173	62	53	49	27	1	103	8	0	2	2	4	.33	14	.253	.307	.398
2002 Chicago	AL	16	36	8	0	0	2	(0 | 2)	14	5	5	5	1	0	14	0	0	0	0	0	-	0	.222	.243	.389
2003 Chicago	AL	16	49	9	1	0	1	(0 | 1)	13	5	5	2	5	0	18	0	0	3	0	1	.00	0	.184	.246	.265
2 ML YEARS		32	85	17	1	0	3	(0 | 3)	27	10	10	7	6	0	32	0	0	3	0	1	.00	0	.200	.245	.318

Pat Borders

Bats: R **Throws:** R **Pos:** C-7; 3B-2; PH-2; PR-2 **Ht:** 6'2" **Wt:** 200 **Born:** 5/14/63 **Age:** 41

		BATTING																	BASERUNNING				AVERAGES		
Year Team	Lg	G	AB	H	2B	3B	HR	(Hm	Rd)	TB	R	RBI	RC	TBB	IBB	SO	HBP	SH	SF	SB	CS	SB%	GDP	Avg	OBP	Slg
2003 Tacoma*	AAA	79	293	92	27	1	12	(-	-)	157	36	51	57	20	3	54	4	0	3	1	2	.33	12	.314	.363	.536
1988 Toronto	AL	56	154	42	6	3	5	(2	3)	69	15	21	18	3	0	24	0	2	1	0	0	-	5	.273	.285	.448
1989 Toronto	AL	94	241	62	11	1	3	(1	2)	84	22	29	22	11	2	45	1	1	2	2	1	.67	7	.257	.290	.349
1990 Toronto	AL	125	346	99	24	2	15	(10	5)	172	36	49	48	18	2	57	0	1	3	0	1	.00	17	.286	.319	.497
1991 Toronto	AL	105	291	71	17	0	5	(3	2)	103	22	36	26	11	1	45	1	6	3	0	0	-	8	.244	.271	.354
1992 Toronto	AL	138	480	116	26	2	13	(7	6)	185	47	53	52	33	3	75	2	1	5	1	1	.50	11	.242	.290	.385
1993 Toronto	AL	138	488	124	30	0	9	(6	3)	181	38	55	46	20	2	66	2	7	3	2	2	.50	18	.254	.285	.371
1994 Toronto	AL	85	295	73	13	1	3	(3	0)	97	24	26	25	15	0	50	0	1	0	1	1	.50	7	.247	.284	.329
1995 KC-Hou		63	178	37	8	1	4	(1	3)	59	15	13	14	9	2	29	0	0	0	0	0	-	4	.208	.246	.331
1996 StL-Ana-CWS		76	220	61	7	0	5	(3	2)	83	15	18	23	9	0	43	0	5	0	0	2	.00	4	.277	.306	.377
1997 Cleveland	AL	55	159	47	7	1	4	(0	4)	68	17	15	21	9	0	27	2	0	0	0	2	.00	5	.296	.341	.428
1998 Cleveland	AL	54	160	38	6	0	0	(0	0)	44	12	6	11	10	0	40	2	2	1	0	2	.00	3	.238	.289	.275
1999 Cle-Tor	AL	12	34	9	0	1	1	(1	0)	14	3	6	4	1	0	5	0	0	1	0	1	.00	0	.265	.286	.412
2001 Seattle	AL	5	6	3	0	0	0	(0	0)	3	1	0	1	0	0	1	0	1	0	0	0	-	0	.500	.500	.500
2002 Seattle	AL	4	4	2	1	0	0	(0	0)	3	0	1	1	0	0	1	0	0	0	0	0	-	0	.500	.500	.750
2003 Seattle	AL	12	14	2	1	0	0	(0	0)	3	1	1	1	0	0	5	0	0	0	0	0	-	0	.143	.200	.214
1995 Kansas City	AL	52	143	33	8	1	4	(1	3)	55	14	13	14	7	1	22	0	0	0	0	0	-	3	.231	.267	.385
1995 Houston	NL	11	35	4	0	0	0	(0	0)	4	1	0	0	2	1	7	0	0	0	0	0	-	1	.114	.162	.114
1996 St Louis	NL	26	69	22	3	0	0	(0	0)	25	3	4	7	1	0	14	0	1	0	0	1	.00	1	.319	.324	.362
1996 Anaheim	AL	19	57	13	3	0	2	(2	0)	22	6	5	8	5	0	11	0	1	0	0	0	-	0	.228	.267	.386
1996 Chicago	AL	31	94	26	1	0	3	(1	2)	36	6	6	11	5	0	18	0	3	0	0	0	-	2	.277	.313	.383
1999 Cleveland	AL	6	20	6	0	1	0	(0	0)	8	2	3	2	0	0	4	0	0	1	0	1	.00	0	.300	.300	.400
1999 Toronto	AL	6	14	3	0	0	1	(1	0)	6	1	3	2	1	0	1	0	0	0	0	0	-	0	.214	.267	.429
15 ML YEARS		1022	3070	786	157	12	67	(36	31)	1168	268	329	313	150	12	513	10	27	18	6	13	.32	88	.256	.291	.380

Mike Bordick

Bats: R **Throws:** R **Pos:** SS-69; 3B-22; 2B-13; PH-3; PR-1   **Ht:** 5'11" **Wt:** 175 **Born:** 7/21/65 **Age:** 38

Year Team	Lg	G	AB	H	2B	3B	HR	(Hm	Rd)	TB	R	RBI	RC	TBB	IBB	SO	HBP	SH	SF	SB	CS	SB%	GDP	Avg	OBP	Slg
1990 Oakland	AL	25	14	1	0	0	0	(0	0)	1	0	0	0	1	0	4	0	0	0	0	0	-	0	.071	.133	.071
1991 Oakland	AL	90	235	56	5	1	0	(0	0)	63	21	21	17	14	0	37	3	12	1	3	4	.43	3	.238	.289	.268
1992 Oakland	AL	154	504	151	19	4	3	(3	0)	187	62	48	69	40	2	59	9	14	5	12	6	.67	10	.300	.358	.371
1993 Oakland	AL	159	546	136	21	2	3	(2	1)	170	60	48	59	60	2	58	11	10	6	10	10	.50	9	.249	.332	.311
1994 Oakland	AL	114	391	99	18	4	2	(1	1)	131	38	37	43	38	1	44	3	3	5	7	2	.78	9	.253	.320	.335
1995 Oakland	AL	126	428	113	13	0	8	(2	6)	150	46	44	50	35	2	48	5	7	3	11	3	.79	8	.264	.325	.350
1996 Oakland	AL	155	525	126	18	4	5	(2	3)	167	46	54	52	52	0	59	1	4	5	5	6	.45	8	.240	.307	.318
1997 Baltimore	AL	153	509	120	19	1	7	(5	2)	162	55	46	39	33	1	66	2	12	4	0	2	.00	23	.236	.283	.318
1998 Baltimore	AL	151	465	121	29	1	13	(10	3)	191	59	51	60	39	0	65	10	15	4	6	7	.46	13	.260	.328	.411
1999 Baltimore	AL	160	631	175	35	7	10	(3	7)	254	93	77	82	54	1	102	5	8	10	14	4	.78	25	.277	.334	.403
2000 Bal-NYM	AL	156	583	166	30	1	20	(9	11)	258	88	80	84	49	0	99	3	4	5	9	6	.60	16	.285	.341	.443
2001 Baltimore	AL	58	229	57	13	0	7	(2	5)	91	32	30	29	17	1	36	6	2	3	9	3	.75	4	.249	.314	.397
2002 Baltimore	AL	117	367	85	19	3	8	(6	2)	134	37	36	40	35	0	63	3	6	2	7	4	.64	9	.232	.302	.365
2003 Toronto	AL	102	343	94	18	2	5	(2	3)	131	39	54	46	33	0	60	2	0	1	3	1	.75	8	.274	.340	.382
2000 Baltimore	AL	100	391	116	22	1	16	(6	10)	188	70	59	62	34	0	71	1	2	5	6	5	.55	12	.297	.350	.481
2000 New York	NL	56	192	50	8	0	4	(3	1)	70	18	21	22	15	0	28	2	2	0	3	1	.75	4	.260	.321	.365
14 ML YEARS		1720	5770	1500	257	30	91	(47	44)	2090	676	626	670	500	10	800	63	97	54	96	58	.62	145	.260	.323	.362

Toby Borland

Pitches: R **Bats:** R **Pos:** RP-7   **Ht:** 6'6" **Wt:** 210 **Born:** 5/29/69 **Age:** 35

		HOW MUCH HE PITCHED						WHAT HE GAVE UP											THE RESULTS							
Year Team	Lg	G	GS	CG	GF	IP	BFP	H	R	ER	HR	SH	SF	HB	TBB	IBB	SO	WP	Bk	W	L	Pct	ShO	Sv-Op	Hld	ERC	ERA
2003 Albuquerque*	AAA	9	0	0	9	9.2	44	6	5	4	1	1	0	3	6	0	12	4	0	1	1	.500	0	3- -	-	3.94	3.72
1994 Philadelphia	NL	24	0	0	7	34.1	144	31	10	9	1	1	0	4	14	3	26	4	0	1	0	1.000	0	1-1	0	3.50	2.36
1995 Philadelphia	NL	50	0	0	18	74.0	339	81	37	31	3	3	2	5	37	7	59	12	0	1	3	.250	0	6-9	11	4.62	3.77
1996 Philadelphia	NL	69	0	0	11	90.2	399	83	51	41	9	4	1	3	43	3	76	10	0	7	3	.700	0	0-2	10	3.89	4.07
1997 NYM-Bos		16	0	0	5	16.2	89	17	14	14	2	0	0	3	21	0	8	3	0	0	1	.000	0	1-2	1	8.72	7.56
1998 Philadelphia	NL	6	0	0	3	9.0	39	8	5	5	1	1	0	0	5	0	9	2	0	0	0	-	0	0-0	0	4.17	5.00
2001 Anaheim	AL	2	0	0	1	3.1	19	8	5	4	1	1	0	0	1	0	0	0	0	0	1	.000	0	0-1	0	14.71	10.80
2002 Florida	NL	15	0	0	3	13.2	62	14	8	8	3	0	2	3	5	0	11	2	0	1	0	1.000	0	0-0	1	5.85	5.27
2003 Florida	NL	7	0	0	1	9.2	40	3	3	2	0	0	1	0	8	1	4	0	0	0	0	-	0	0-0	0	1.40	1.86
1997 New York	NL	13	0	0	5	13.1	65	11	9	9	1	0	0	1	14	0	7	3	0	0	1	.000	0	1-2	1	5.68	6.08
1997 Boston	AL	3	0	0	0	3.1	24	6	5	5	1	0	0	2	7	0	1	0	0	0	0	-	0	0-0	0	23.38	13.50
8 ML YEARS		189	0	0	49	251.1	1131	245	133	114	20	10	6	18	134	14	193	33	0	10	8	.556	0	8-15	23	4.47	4.08

Joe Borowski

Pitches: R **Bats:** R **Pos:** RP-68   **Ht:** 6'2" **Wt:** 240 **Born:** 5/4/71 **Age:** 33

		HOW MUCH HE PITCHED						WHAT HE GAVE UP											THE RESULTS							
Year Team	Lg	G	GS	CG	GF	IP	BFP	H	R	ER	HR	SH	SF	HB	TBB	IBB	SO	WP	Bk	W	L	Pct	ShO	Sv-Op	Hld	ERC	ERA
1995 Baltimore	AL	6	0	0	3	7.1	30	5	1	1	0	0	0	0	4	0	3	0	0	0	0	-	0	0-0	0	2.32	1.23
1996 Atlanta	NL	22	0	0	8	26.0	121	33	15	14	4	5	0	1	13	4	15	1	0	2	4	.333	0	0-0	1	6.46	4.85
1997 Atl-NYY		21	0	0	9	26.0	123	29	13	12	2	1	0	0	20	5	8	0	0	2	3	.400	0	0-0	2	5.74	4.15
1998 New York	AL	8	0	0	6	9.2	42	11	7	7	0	0	0	0	4	0	7	0	0	1	0	1.000	0	0-0	0	5.74	6.52
2001 Chicago	NL	1	1	0	0	1.2	13	6	6	6	1	1	0	0	3	0	1	0	0	1	0	.000	0	0-0	0	39.91	32.40
2002 Chicago	NL	73	0	0	25	95.2	391	84	31	29	10	5	3	1	29	6	97	1	0	4	4	.500	0	2-6	12	3.05	2.73
2003 Chicago	NL	68	0	0	59	68.1	280	53	23	20	5	4	0	1	19	1	66	0	0	2	2	.500	0	33-37	1	2.26	2.63
1997 Atlanta	NL	20	0	0	8	24.0	111	27	11	10	2	1	0	0	16	4	6	0	0	2	2	.500	0	0-0	1	5.51	3.75
1997 New York	AL	1	0	0	1	2.0	12	2	2	2	0	0	0	0	4	1	2	0	0	0	1	.000	0	0-0	0	8.25	9.00
7 ML YEARS		199	1	0	110	234.2	1000	221	96	89	22	16	3	3	92	16	197	2	0	11	14	.440	0	35-43	16	3.62	3.41

Ricky Bottalico

Pitches: R **Bats:** L **Pos:** RP-2   **Ht:** 6'1" **Wt:** 215 **Born:** 8/26/69 **Age:** 34

		HOW MUCH HE PITCHED						WHAT HE GAVE UP											THE RESULTS							
Year Team	Lg	G	GS	CG	GF	IP	BFP	H	R	ER	HR	SH	SF	HB	TBB	IBB	SO	WP	Bk	W	L	Pct	ShO	Sv-Op	Hld	ERC	ERA
2003 Tucson*	AAA	31	0	0	6	39.1	170	39	24	16	4	0	2	1	16	1	28	2	0	2	2	.500	0	0- -	-	4.14	3.66
1994 Philadelphia	NL	3	0	0	3	3.0	13	3	0	0	0	0	0	0	1	0	3	0	0	0	0	-	0	0-0	0	3.05	0.00
1995 Philadelphia	NL	62	0	0	20	87.2	350	50	25	24	7	3	1	4	42	3	87	1	0	5	3	.625	0	1-5	20	2.17	2.46
1996 Philadelphia	NL	61	0	0	56	67.2	269	47	24	24	6	4	2	2	23	2	74	3	0	4	5	.444	0	34-38	0	2.29	3.19
1997 Philadelphia	NL	69	0	0	61	74.0	324	68	31	30	7	1	2	2	42	4	89	3	0	2	5	.286	0	34-41	0	4.29	3.65
1998 Philadelphia	NL	39	0	0	28	43.1	206	54	31	31	7	1	2	1	25	5	27	2	0	1	5	.167	0	6-7	3	6.63	6.44
1999 St Louis	NL	68	0	0	40	73.1	347	83	45	40	8	3	0	3	49	1	66	6	0	3	7	.300	0	20-28	8	6.16	4.91
2000 Kansas City	AL	62	0	0	50	72.2	319	65	40	39	12	3	1	2	41	3	56	5	1	9	6	.600	0	16-23	1	4.65	4.83
2001 Philadelphia	NL	66	0	0	18	67.0	281	58	31	29	11	7	4	4	25	2	57	5	0	3	4	.429	0	3-7	22	3.88	3.90
2002 Philadelphia	NL	30	0	0	6	27.1	128	33	16	14	3	2	1	2	13	2	24	2	0	0	3	.000	0	0-1	15	5.80	4.61
2003 Arizona	NL	2	0	0	0	1.2	10	3	1	1	0	0	0	0	2	1	2	0	0	1	0	1.000	0	0-0	1	10.00	5.40
10 ML YEARS		462	0	0	282	517.2	2247	464	244	232	61	24	13	20	263	23	485	27	1	28	38	.424	0	114-150	70	4.14	4.03

Rob Bowen

Bats: B **Throws:** R **Pos:** C-7; PH-1   **Ht:** 6'3" **Wt:** 225 **Born:** 2/24/81 **Age:** 23

		BATTING																		BASERUNNING				AVERAGES		
Year Team	Lg	G	AB	H	2B	3B	HR	(Hm	Rd)	TB	R	RBI	RC	TBB	IBB	SO	HBP	SH	SF	SB	CS	SB%	GDP	Avg	OBP	Slg
1999 Twins	R	29	77	20	4	0	0	(-	-)	24	10	11	12	20	0	15	0	1	3	2	2	.50	0	.260	.400	.312
2000 Elizabethton	R+	21	73	21	3	0	4	(-	-)	36	17	19	14	11	0	18	0	0	0	0	0	-	0	.288	.381	.493
2001 Quad City	A	106	385	98	18	2	16	(-	-)	168	47	70	53	37	2	112	2	2	3	4	0	1.00	11	.255	.321	.436
2002 Fort Myers	A+	100	342	63	12	1	10	(-	-)	107	52	49	27	38	0	69	5	2	5	1	0	1.00	12	.184	.272	.313
2002 Quad City	A	5	21	4	1	0	0	(-	-)	5	1	0	1	2	0	4	0	0	0	0	0	-	0	.190	.261	.238

Year Team	Lg	G	AB	H	2B	3B	HR	(Hm	Rd)	TB	R	RBI	RC	TBB	IBB	SO	HBP	SH	SF	SB	CS	SB%	GDP	Avg	OBP	Slg
2003 Rochester	AAA	30	105	27	7	0	6	(-	-)	52	14	17	17	11	1	25	1	0	0	0	0	-	3	.257	.333	.495
2003 New Britain	AA	42	134	41	13	0	1	(-	-)	57	17	16	22	13	0	24	2	1	0	0	0	-	0	.306	.376	.425
2003 Minnesota	AL	7	10	1	0	0	0	(0	0)	1	0	1	0	0	0	4	0	0	0	0	0	-	1	.100	.091	.100

Micah Bowie

Pitches: L Bats: L Pos: RP-6　　　　　　　　　　　　**Ht: 6'4" Wt: 210 Born: 11/10/74 Age: 29**

		HOW MUCH HE PITCHED						WHAT HE GAVE UP										THE RESULTS							
Year Team	Lg	G	GS	CG	GF	IP	BFP	H	R	ER	HR	SH	SF	HB	TBB	IBB	SO	WP	Bk	W	L	Pct	ShO	Sv-Op	Hld	ERC	ERA
2003 Modesto*	A+	2	2	0	0	2.0	6	0	0	0	0	0	0	0	0	0	3	0	0	0	0	-	0	0--	-	0.00	0.00
2003 Sacramento*	AAA	5	0	0	4	4.0	16	2	1	0	0	0	0	0	1	0	3	0	0	0	0	-	0	2--	-	0.88	0.00
1999 Atl-ChC	NL	14	11	0	2	51.0	265	81	60	58	9	3	3	2	34	2	41	4	2	2	7	.222	0	0-0	0	9.69	10.24
2002 Oakland	AL	13	0	0	4	12.0	55	12	2	2	1	0	0	1	8	1	8	0	0	2	0	1.000	0	0-0	3	5.26	1.50
2003 Oakland	AL	6	0	0	3	8.1	38	13	7	7	1	0	0	0	2	0	4	0	0	0	1	.000	0	0-0	0	7.15	7.56
1999 Atlanta	NL	3	0	0	2	4.0	23	8	6	6	1	0	0	0	4	0	2	0	0	0	1	.000	0	0-0	0	15.43	13.50
1999 Chicago	NL	11	11	0	0	47.0	242	73	54	52	8	3	3	2	30	2	39	4	2	2	6	.250	0	0-0	0	9.23	9.96
3 ML YEARS		33	11	0	9	71.1	358	106	69	67	11	3	3	3	44	3	53	4	2	4	8	.333	0	0-0	3	8.60	8.45

Brian Bowles

Pitches: R Bats: R Pos: RP-5　　　　　　　　　　　　**Ht: 6'5" Wt: 220 Born: 8/18/76 Age: 27**

		HOW MUCH HE PITCHED						WHAT HE GAVE UP										THE RESULTS							
Year Team	Lg	G	GS	CG	GF	IP	BFP	H	R	ER	HR	SH	SF	HB	TBB	IBB	SO	WP	Bk	W	L	Pct	ShO	Sv-Op	Hld	ERC	ERA
2003 Syracuse*	AAA	41	0	0	34	47.1	210	47	23	14	1	4	0	2	21	3	32	2	0	2	3	.400	0	14--	-	3.63	2.66
2001 Toronto	AL	2	0	0	0	3.2	15	4	0	0	0	0	0	0	1	0	4	1	0	0	0	-	0	0-0	0	3.55	0.00
2002 Toronto	AL	17	0	0	7	20.0	89	13	11	9	0	0	1	3	14	1	19	5	1	2	1	.667	0	0-1	1	3.00	4.05
2003 Toronto	AL	5	0	0	2	7.0	34	8	4	2	1	0	0	2	2	0	2	0	0	0	0	-	0	0-0	0	5.62	2.57
3 ML YEARS		24	0	0	9	30.2	138	25	15	11	1	0	1	5	17	1	25	6	1	2	1	.667	0	0-1	1	3.65	3.23

Jason Boyd

Pitches: R Bats: R Pos: RP-44　　　　　　　　　　　　**Ht: 6'3" Wt: 173 Born: 2/23/73 Age: 31**

		HOW MUCH HE PITCHED						WHAT HE GAVE UP										THE RESULTS							
Year Team	Lg	G	GS	CG	GF	IP	BFP	H	R	ER	HR	SH	SF	HB	TBB	IBB	SO	WP	Bk	W	L	Pct	ShO	Sv-Op	Hld	ERC	ERA
2003 Buffalo*	AAA	9	0	0	5	14.2	56	12	3	2	0	2	0	0	2	0	14	1	0	1	0	1.000	0	3--	-	1.67	1.23
1999 Pittsburgh	NL	4	0	0	0	5.1	24	5	2	2	0	0	1	1	2	0	4	1	0	0	0	-	0	0-0	0	3.53	3.38
2000 Philadelphia	NL	30	0	0	11	34.1	161	39	25	25	2	3	0	1	24	4	32	1	0	0	1	.000	0	0-1	2	5.71	6.55
2002 San Diego	NL	23	0	0	6	28.1	131	33	29	25	6	3	3	0	15	1	18	3	0	1	0	1.000	0	0-3	4	6.35	7.94
2003 Cleveland	AL	44	0	0	13	52.1	221	38	25	25	4	0	2	3	26	1	31	2	0	3	1	.750	0	0-1	8	2.98	4.30
4 ML YEARS		101	0	0	30	120.1	537	115	84	77	12	6	6	5	67	6	85	7	0	4	2	.667	0	0-5	14	4.51	5.76

Chad Bradford

Pitches: R Bats: R Pos: RP-72　　　　　　　　　　　　**Ht: 6'5" Wt: 203 Born: 9/14/74 Age: 29**

		HOW MUCH HE PITCHED						WHAT HE GAVE UP										THE RESULTS							
Year Team	Lg	G	GS	CG	GF	IP	BFP	H	R	ER	HR	SH	SF	HB	TBB	IBB	SO	WP	Bk	W	L	Pct	ShO	Sv-Op	Hld	ERC	ERA
1998 Chicago	AL	29	0	0	8	30.2	125	27	16	11	0	0	0	0	7	0	11	1	1	2	1	.667	0	1-3	9	2.16	3.23
1999 Chicago	AL	3	0	0	3	3.2	24	9	8	8	1	0	0	0	5	0	1	0	0	0	0	-	0	0-0	0	21.34	19.64
2000 Chicago	AL	12	0	0	5	13.2	52	13	4	3	0	0	0	0	1	1	9	0	0	1	0	1.000	0	0-0	2	2.01	1.98
2001 Oakland	AL	35	0	0	19	36.2	154	41	12	11	6	1	0	1	6	0	34	0	0	2	1	.667	0	1-4	4	4.36	2.70
2002 Oakland	AL	75	0	0	14	75.1	311	73	29	26	2	2	2	5	14	5	56	0	1	4	2	.667	0	2-5	24	2.77	3.11
2003 Oakland	AL	72	0	0	12	77.0	322	67	28	26	7	1	0	7	30	9	62	0	1	7	4	.636	0	2-5	23	3.50	3.04
6 ML YEARS		226	0	0	58	237.0	988	230	97	85	16	4	2	13	63	15	172	2	3	16	8	.667	0	6-17	62	3.32	3.23

Milton Bradley

Bats: B Throws: R Pos: CF-93; DH-8　　　　　　　　　　　　**Ht: 6'0" Wt: 190 Born: 4/15/78 Age: 26**

								BATTING												BASERUNNING				AVERAGES		
Year Team	Lg	G	AB	H	2B	3B	HR	(Hm	Rd)	TB	R	RBI	RC	TBB	IBB	SO	HBP	SH	SF	SB	CS	SB%	GDP	Avg	OBP	Slg
2000 Montreal	NL	42	154	34	8	1	2	(1	1)	50	20	15	14	14	0	32	1	1	1	2	1	.67	3	.221	.288	.325
2001 Mon-Cle		77	238	53	17	3	1	(0	1)	79	22	19	21	21	0	65	1	2	0	8	5	.62	7	.223	.288	.332
2002 Cleveland	AL	98	325	81	18	3	9	(4	5)	132	48	38	40	32	2	58	0	1	0	6	3	.67	12	.249	.317	.406
2003 Cleveland	AL	101	377	121	34	2	10	(4	6)	189	61	56	78	64	8	73	5	0	5	17	7	.71	10	.321	.421	.501
2001 Montreal	NL	67	220	49	16	3	1	(0	1)	74	19	19	20	19	0	62	1	2	0	7	4	.64	6	.223	.288	.336
2001 Cleveland	AL	10	18	4	1	0	0	(0	0)	5	3	0	1	2	0	3	0	0	0	1	1	.50	1	.222	.300	.278
4 ML YEARS		318	1094	289	77	9	22	(9	13)	450	151	128	153	131	10	228	7	4	6	33	16	.67	32	.264	.345	.411

Darren Bragg

Bats: L Throws: R Pos: RF-35; LF-29; PH-22; CF-21; PR-18　　　　　　　**Ht: 5'9" Wt: 180 Born: 9/7/69 Age: 34**

								BATTING												BASERUNNING				AVERAGES		
Year Team	Lg	G	AB	H	2B	3B	HR	(Hm	Rd)	TB	R	RBI	RC	TBB	IBB	SO	HBP	SH	SF	SB	CS	SB%	GDP	Avg	OBP	Slg
1994 Seattle	AL	8	19	3	1	0	0	(0	0)	4	4	2	1	2	1	5	0	0	0	0	0	-	0	.158	.238	.211
1995 Seattle	AL	52	145	34	5	1	3	(1	2)	50	20	12	19	18	1	37	4	1	2	9	0	1.00	4	.234	.331	.345
1996 Sea-Bos	AL	127	417	109	26	2	10	(7	3)	169	74	47	66	69	6	74	4	2	7	14	9	.61	5	.261	.366	.405
1997 Boston	AL	153	513	132	35	2	9	(3	6)	198	65	57	65	61	5	102	3	5	4	10	6	.63	16	.257	.337	.386
1998 Boston	AL	129	409	114	29	3	8	(3	5)	173	51	57	58	42	0	99	6	4	4	5	3	.63	16	.279	.351	.423
1999 St Louis	NL	93	273	71	12	1	6	(4	2)	103	38	26	41	44	1	67	3	5	0	3	0	1.00	6	.260	.369	.377
2000 Colorado	NL	71	149	33	7	1	3	(3	0)	51	16	21	16	17	1	41	0	0	3	4	1	.80	3	.221	.296	.342
2001 NYM-NYY		23	61	16	7	0	0	(0	0)	23	5	5	8	4	0	24	1	1	0	3	2	.60	0	.262	.318	.377
2002 Atlanta	NL	109	212	57	15	2	3	(2	1)	85	34	15	27	24	0	52	2	1	1	5	2	.71	4	.269	.347	.401

33

Year Team	Lg	G	AB	H	2B	3B	HR	(Hm	Rd)	TB	R	RBI	RC	TBB	IBB	SO	HBP	SH	SF	SB	CS	SB%	GDP	Avg	OBP	Slg
2003 Atlanta	NL	104	162	39	5	1	0	(0	0)	46	21	9	13	13	1	38	2	4	0	3	1	.67	1	.241	.305	.284
1996 Seattle	AL	69	195	53	12	1	7	(4	3)	88	36	25	35	33	4	35	2	1	4	8	5	.62	2	.272	.376	.451
1996 Boston	AL	58	222	56	14	1	3	(3	0)	81	38	22	31	36	2	39	2	1	3	6	4	.60	3	.252	.357	.365
2001 New York	NL	18	57	15	6	0	0	(0	0)	21	4	5	7	4	0	23	1	1	0	3	2	.60	0	.263	.323	.368
2001 New York	AL	5	4	1	1	0	0	(0	0)	2	1	0	1	0	0	1	0	0	0	0	0	-	0	.250	.250	.500
10 ML YEARS		869	2360	608	142	13	42	(23	19)	902	328	251	314	294	16	539	25	23	21	55	24	.70	52	.258	.343	.382

Russell Branyan

Bats: L **Throws:** R **Pos:** PH-27; 3B-20; LF-17; 1B-14; DH-1 **Ht:** 6'3" **Wt:** 195 **Born:** 12/19/75 **Age:** 28

Year Team	Lg	G	AB	H	2B	3B	HR	(Hm	Rd)	TB	R	RBI	RC	TBB	IBB	SO	HBP	SH	SF	SB	CS	SB%	GDP	Avg	OBP	Slg
2003 Louisville*	AAA	14	49	16	5	0	1	(-	-)	24	5	3	11	9	0	15	1	0	0	0	0	-	0	.327	.441	.490
1998 Cleveland	AL	1	4	0	0	0	0	(0	0)	0	0	0	0	0	0	2	0	0	0	0	0	-	0	.000	.000	.000
1999 Cleveland	AL	11	38	8	2	0	1	(0	1)	13	4	6	4	3	0	19	1	0	0	0	0	-	0	.211	.286	.342
2000 Cleveland	AL	67	193	46	7	2	16	(13	3)	105	32	38	34	22	1	76	4	0	1	0	0	-	2	.238	.327	.544
2001 Cleveland	AL	113	315	73	16	2	20	(11	9)	153	48	54	50	38	1	132	3	0	5	1	1	.50	2	.232	.316	.486
2002 Cle-Cin		134	378	86	13	1	24	(5	19)	173	50	56	49	51	3	151	2	0	4	4	3	.57	5	.228	.320	.458
2003 Cincinnati	NL	74	176	38	12	0	9	(7	2)	77	22	26	24	27	0	69	1	0	1	0	0	-	0	.216	.322	.438
2002 Cleveland	AL	50	161	33	4	0	8	(1	7)	61	16	17	14	17	0	65	0	0	2	1	2	.33	1	.205	.278	.379
2002 Cincinnati	NL	84	217	53	9	1	16	(4	12)	112	34	39	35	34	3	86	2	0	2	3	1	.75	2	.244	.349	.516
6 ML YEARS		400	1104	251	50	5	70	(36	34)	521	156	180	161	141	5	449	11	0	11	5	4	.56	10	.227	.318	.472

Dewon Brazelton

Pitches: R **Bats:** R **Pos:** SP-10 **Ht:** 6'4" **Wt:** 205 **Born:** 6/16/80 **Age:** 24

| | | HOW MUCH HE PITCHED | | | | | | WHAT HE GAVE UP | | | | | | | | | | THE RESULTS | | | | | | |
Year Team	Lg	G	GS	CG	GF	IP	BFP	H	R	ER	HR	SH	SF	HB	TBB	IBB	SO	WP	Bk	W	L	Pct	ShO	Sv-Op	Hld	ERC	ERA
2002 Orlando	AA	26	26	1	0	146.0	620	129	69	54	7	5	3	10	67	1	109	10	2	5	9	.357	0	0--	-	3.61	3.33
2002 Durham	AAA	1	1	0	0	5.0	20	5	0	0	0	0	0	0	1	0	6	0	0	1	0	1.000	0	0--	-	2.76	0.00
2003 Bakersfield	A+	9	9	0	0	49.2	230	62	33	29	4	0	0	3	19	0	42	4	1	1	5	.167	0	0--	-	5.49	5.26
2003 Orlando	AA	2	2	0	0	10.2	50	8	6	3	0	0	0	2	8	0	5	0	0	2	0	1.000	0	0--	-	3.86	2.53
2003 Durham	AAA	5	5	0	0	25.2	110	23	14	12	1	0	1	0	11	0	18	0	0	2	2	.500	0	0--	-	3.16	4.21
2002 Tampa Bay	AL	2	2	0	0	13.0	51	12	7	7	3	0	0	2	6	0	5	0	0	0	1	.000	0	0-0	0	6.29	4.85
2003 Tampa Bay	AL	10	10	0	0	48.1	225	57	49	37	9	2	2	3	23	1	24	1	0	1	6	.143	0	0-0	0	6.29	6.89
2 ML YEARS		12	12	0	0	61.1	276	69	56	44	12	2	2	5	29	1	29	1	0	1	7	.125	0	0-0	0	6.28	6.46

Troy Brohawn

Pitches: L **Bats:** L **Pos:** RP-12 **Ht:** 6'1" **Wt:** 190 **Born:** 1/14/73 **Age:** 31

| | | HOW MUCH HE PITCHED | | | | | | WHAT HE GAVE UP | | | | | | | | | | THE RESULTS | | | | | | |
Year Team	Lg	G	GS	CG	GF	IP	BFP	H	R	ER	HR	SH	SF	HB	TBB	IBB	SO	WP	Bk	W	L	Pct	ShO	Sv-Op	Hld	ERC	ERA
2003 Las Vegas*	AAA	1	0	0	0	4.0	16	3	2	2	1	0	1	0	1	0	1	0	0	1	0	1.000	0	0--	-	1.88	4.50
2001 Arizona	NL	59	0	0	10	49.1	220	55	27	27	5	2	4	1	23	2	30	2	0	2	3	.400	0	1-3	10	5.07	4.93
2002 San Francisco	NL	11	0	0	2	5.2	25	5	4	4	1	0	0	2	1	0	3	0	0	0	1	.000	0	0-0	3	4.37	6.35
2003 Los Angeles	NL	12	0	0	5	11.2	48	10	6	5	2	0	0	0	4	0	13	0	0	2	0	1.000	0	0-0	1	3.56	3.86
3 ML YEARS		82	0	0	17	66.2	293	70	37	36	8	2	4	3	28	2	46	2	0	4	4	.500	0	1-3	14	4.74	4.86

Ben Broussard

Bats: L **Throws:** L **Pos:** 1B-114; PH-4 **Ht:** 6'2" **Wt:** 220 **Born:** 9/24/76 **Age:** 27

Year Team	Lg	G	AB	H	2B	3B	HR	(Hm	Rd)	TB	R	RBI	RC	TBB	IBB	SO	HBP	SH	SF	SB	CS	SB%	GDP	Avg	OBP	Slg
1999 Billings	R+	38	145	59	11	2	14	(-	-)	116	39	48	55	34	2	30	4	0	1	1	0	1.00	0	.407	.527	.800
1999 Clinton	A	5	20	11	4	1	2	(-	-)	23	8	6	10	3	0	4	0	0	0	0	0	-	1	.550	.609	1.150
1999 Chattanooga	AA	35	127	27	5	0	8	(-	-)	56	26	21	17	11	1	41	3	0	1	1	0	1.00	0	.213	.291	.441
2000 Chattanooga	AA	87	286	73	8	4	14	(-	-)	131	64	51	60	72	3	78	6	0	2	15	2	.88	6	.255	.413	.458
2001 Mudville	A+	30	102	25	5	0	5	(-	-)	45	14	21	17	16	0	31	4	0	3	0	0	-	2	.245	.360	.441
2001 Chattanooga	AA	100	353	113	27	0	23	(-	-)	209	81	69	87	61	5	69	8	0	3	10	3	.77	5	.320	.428	.592
2002 Louisville	AAA	57	187	51	14	1	11	(-	-)	100	31	30	40	31	2	50	9	0	3	4	1	.80	4	.273	.396	.535
2002 Buffalo	AAA	42	153	37	8	0	5	(-	-)	60	30	21	23	24	2	30	3	1	1	0	0	-	4	.242	.354	.392
2003 Buffalo	AAA	32	120	30	2	1	3	(-	-)	43	17	15	14	9	0	29	1	0	2	3	0	1.00	1	.250	.303	.358
2002 Cleveland	AL	39	112	27	4	0	4	(2	2)	43	10	9	9	7	1	25	1	0	0	0	0	-	3	.241	.292	.384
2003 Cleveland	AL	116	386	96	21	3	16	(7	9)	171	53	55	53	32	2	75	5	3	3	5	2	.71	6	.249	.312	.443
2 ML YEARS		155	498	123	25	3	20	(9	11)	214	63	64	62	39	3	100	6	3	3	5	2	.71	9	.247	.308	.430

Jim Brower

Pitches: R **Bats:** R **Pos:** RP-46; SP-5 **Ht:** 6'3" **Wt:** 215 **Born:** 12/29/72 **Age:** 31

| | | HOW MUCH HE PITCHED | | | | | | WHAT HE GAVE UP | | | | | | | | | | THE RESULTS | | | | | | |
Year Team	Lg	G	GS	CG	GF	IP	BFP	H	R	ER	HR	SH	SF	HB	TBB	IBB	SO	WP	Bk	W	L	Pct	ShO	Sv-Op	Hld	ERC	ERA
1999 Cleveland	AL	9	2	0	1	25.2	113	27	13	13	8	1	1	1	10	1	18	0	0	3	1	.750	0	0-0	0	5.96	4.56
2000 Cleveland	AL	17	11	0	1	62.0	293	80	45	43	11	0	1	4	31	1	32	3	0	2	3	.400	0	0-0	0	6.95	6.24
2001 Cincinnati	NL	46	10	0	13	129.1	559	119	65	57	17	9	3	5	60	5	94	5	1	7	10	.412	0	1-2	2	4.21	3.97
2002 Cin-Mon	NL	52	0	0	23	80.1	344	77	40	39	7	2	1	4	32	2	57	1	0	3	2	.600	0	0-1	6	3.94	4.37
2003 San Francisco	NL	51	5	0	13	100.0	412	90	48	44	8	5	4	1	39	2	65	4	0	8	5	.615	0	2-3	2	3.45	3.96
2002 Cincinnati	NL	22	0	0	11	39.1	158	38	18	17	2	1	1	0	10	1	24	0	0	2	0	1.000	0	0-0	0	3.08	3.89
2002 Montreal	NL	30	0	0	12	41.0	186	39	22	22	5	1	0	4	22	1	33	1	0	1	2	.333	0	0-1	6	4.79	4.83
5 ML YEARS		175	28	0	51	397.1	1721	393	211	196	51	18	9	13	172	11	266	13	1	23	21	.523	0	3-6	10	4.47	4.44

Adrian Brown

Bats: B **Throws:** R **Pos:** CF-6; LF-3; PR-2   **Ht:** 6'0" **Wt:** 200 **Born:** 2/7/74 **Age:** 30

Year Team	Lg	G	AB	H	2B	3B	HR	(Hm	Rd)	TB	R	RBI	RC	TBB	IBB	SO	HBP	SH	SF	SB	CS	SB%	GDP	Avg	OBP	Slg
2003 Pawtucket*	AAA	122	482	136	16	3	5	(-	-)	173	81	32	62	48	1	81	0	3	0	34	11	.76	10	.282	.347	.359
1997 Pittsburgh	NL	48	147	28	6	0	1	(0	1)	37	17	10	10	13	0	18	4	2	1	8	4	.67	3	.190	.273	.252
1998 Pittsburgh	NL	41	152	43	4	1	0	(0	0)	49	20	5	16	9	0	18	0	4	0	4	0	1.00	3	.283	.323	.322
1999 Pittsburgh	NL	116	226	61	5	2	4	(2	2)	82	34	17	31	33	2	39	1	6	1	5	3	.63	5	.270	.364	.363
2000 Pittsburgh	NL	104	308	97	18	3	4	(2	2)	133	64	28	53	29	1	34	0	2	1	13	1	.93	1	.315	.373	.432
2001 Pittsburgh	NL	8	31	6	0	0	1	(0	1)	9	3	2	2	3	0	3	0	0	0	2	1	.67	1	.194	.265	.290
2002 Pittsburgh	NL	91	208	45	10	2	1	(0	1)	62	20	21	16	19	0	34	1	3	1	10	6	.63	5	.216	.284	.298
2003 Boston	AL	9	15	3	0	0	0	(0	0)	3	2	1	1	1	0	4	0	0	0	2	0	1.00	0	.200	.250	.200
7 ML YEARS		417	1087	283	43	8	11	(4	7)	375	160	84	129	107	3	150	6	17	4	44	15	.75	18	.260	.329	.345

Dee Brown

Bats: L **Throws:** R **Pos:** LF-17; RF-17; DH-10; PH-9   **Ht:** 6'0" **Wt:** 225 **Born:** 3/27/78 **Age:** 26

Year Team	Lg	G	AB	H	2B	3B	HR	(Hm	Rd)	TB	R	RBI	RC	TBB	IBB	SO	HBP	SH	SF	SB	CS	SB%	GDP	Avg	OBP	Slg
2003 Royals*	R	2	7	5	2	0	0	(-	-)	7	4	3	4	0	0	2	1	0	0	0	0	-	0	.714	.750	1.000
2003 Omaha*	AAA	12	47	13	2	0	2	(-	-)	21	6	9	7	4	0	9	1	0	1	1	0	1.00	1	.277	.340	.447
1998 Kansas City	AL	5	3	0	0	0	0	(0	0)	0	2	0	0	0	0	1	0	0	0	0	0	-	0	.000	.000	.000
1999 Kansas City	AL	12	25	2	0	0	0	(0	0)	2	1	0	0	2	0	7	0	0	0	0	0	-	0	.080	.148	.080
2000 Kansas City	AL	15	25	4	1	0	0	(0	0)	5	4	4	1	3	0	9	0	0	0	0	0	-	0	.160	.250	.200
2001 Kansas City	AL	106	380	93	19	0	7	(4	3)	133	39	40	34	22	4	81	1	1	2	5	3	.63	12	.245	.286	.350
2002 Kansas City	AL	16	51	12	3	1	1	(0	1)	20	5	7	4	4	0	20	0	0	0	0	0	-	0	.235	.291	.392
2003 Kansas City	AL	50	132	30	7	0	2	(1	1)	43	16	14	15	8	1	37	2	0	1	1	1	.50	0	.227	.280	.326
6 ML YEARS		204	616	141	30	1	10	(5	5)	203	67	65	54	39	5	155	3	1	3	6	4	.60	12	.229	.277	.330

Kevin Brown

Pitches: R **Bats:** R **Pos:** SP-32   **Ht:** 6'4" **Wt:** 200 **Born:** 3/14/65 **Age:** 39

Year Team	Lg	G	GS	CG	GF	IP	BFP	H	R	ER	HR	SH	SF	HB	TBB	IBB	SO	WP	Bk	W	L	Pct	ShO	Sv-Op	Hld	ERC	ERA
1986 Texas	AL	1	1	0	0	5.0	19	6	2	2	0	0	0	0	0	0	4	0	0	1	0	1.000	0	0-0	0	3.25	3.60
1988 Texas	AL	4	4	1	0	23.1	110	33	15	11	2	1	0	1	8	0	12	1	0	1	1	.500	0	0-0	0	6.33	4.24
1989 Texas	AL	28	28	7	0	191.0	798	167	81	71	10	3	6	4	70	2	104	7	2	12	9	.571	0	0-0	0	3.02	3.35
1990 Texas	AL	26	26	6	0	180.0	757	175	84	72	13	2	7	3	60	3	88	9	2	12	10	.545	2	0-0	0	3.54	3.60
1991 Texas	AL	33	33	0	0	210.2	934	233	116	103	17	6	4	13	90	5	96	12	3	9	12	.429	0	0-0	0	4.92	4.40
1992 Texas	AL	35	35	11	0	265.2	1108	262	117	98	11	7	8	10	76	2	173	8	2	21	11	.656	1	0-0	0	3.34	3.32
1993 Texas	AL	34	34	12	0	233.0	1001	228	105	93	14	5	3	15	74	5	142	8	1	15	12	.556	3	0-0	0	3.55	3.59
1994 Texas	AL	26	25	3	1	170.0	760	218	109	91	18	2	7	6	50	3	123	7	0	7	9	.438	0	0-0	0	5.49	4.82
1995 Baltimore	AL	26	26	3	0	172.1	706	155	73	69	10	5	2	9	48	1	117	3	0	10	9	.526	1	0-0	0	3.03	3.60
1996 Florida	NL	32	32	5	0	233.0	906	187	60	49	8	4	4	16	33	2	159	6	1	17	11	.607	3	0-0	0	2.00	1.89
1997 Florida	NL	33	33	6	0	237.1	976	214	77	71	10	5	1	14	66	7	205	7	1	16	8	.667	2	0-0	0	2.92	2.69
1998 San Diego	NL	36	35	7	0	257.0	1032	225	77	68	8	13	3	10	49	4	257	10	0	18	7	.720	3	0-0	1	2.35	2.38
1999 Los Angeles	NL	35	35	5	0	252.1	1018	210	99	84	19	7	1	7	59	1	221	4	1	18	9	.667	1	0-0	0	2.51	3.00
2000 Los Angeles	NL	33	33	5	0	230.0	921	181	76	66	21	13	4	9	47	1	216	4	0	13	6	.684	1	0-0	0	2.30	2.58
2001 Los Angeles	NL	20	19	1	0	115.2	465	94	41	34	8	5	0	2	38	2	104	3	1	10	4	.714	0	0-0	0	2.71	2.65
2002 Los Angeles	NL	17	10	0	0	63.2	277	68	36	34	9	2	0	5	23	1	58	2	0	3	4	.429	0	0-0	1	4.98	4.81
2003 Los Angeles	NL	32	32	0	0	211.0	856	184	67	56	11	12	2	5	56	2	185	5	1	14	9	.609	0	0-0	2	2.68	2.39
17 ML YEARS		451	441	72	1	3051.0	12644	2840	1235	1072	189	92	52	129	847	41	2264	96	15	197	131	.601	17	0-0	2	3.14	3.16

Eric Bruntlett

Bats: R **Throws:** R **Pos:** PH-12; SS-10; 2B-9; PR-2; 3B-1; LF-1; CF-1   **Ht:** 6'0" **Wt:** 200 **Born:** 3/29/78 **Age:** 26

Year Team	Lg	G	AB	H	2B	3B	HR	(Hm	Rd)	TB	R	RBI	RC	TBB	IBB	SO	HBP	SH	SF	SB	CS	SB%	GDP	Avg	OBP	Slg
2000 Martinsville	R+	50	172	47	11	4	1	(-	-)	69	40	21	34	30	0	22	11	1	0	14	1	.93	2	.273	.413	.401
2001 Round Rock	AA	123	503	134	23	3	3	(-	-)	172	84	40	63	50	1	76	8	5	3	23	7	.77	7	.266	.340	.342
2001 New Orleans	AAA	5	16	2	0	0	0	(-	-)	2	3	1	0	2	0	1	0	1	0	0	0	-	1	.125	.222	.125
2002 Round Rock	AA	116	464	123	21	2	2	(-	-)	154	81	48	58	56	0	61	10	4	8	35	12	.74	17	.265	.351	.332
2002 New Orleans	AAA	18	68	14	3	0	0	(-	-)	17	9	1	5	10	0	10	0	1	0	1	1	.50	3	.206	.308	.250
2003 New Orleans	AAA	84	324	84	10	0	2	(-	-)	100	48	27	37	35	0	51	3	3	5	9	4	.69	3	.259	.332	.309
2003 Houston	NL	31	54	14	3	0	1	(1	0)	20	3	4	5	0	0	10	0	1	1	0	0	-	1	.259	.255	.370

Brian Buchanan

Bats: R **Throws:** R **Pos:** PH-54; RF-29; 1B-24; LF-15; DH-4; PR-2   **Ht:** 6'4" **Wt:** 230 **Born:** 7/21/73 **Age:** 30

Year Team	Lg	G	AB	H	2B	3B	HR	(Hm	Rd)	TB	R	RBI	RC	TBB	IBB	SO	HBP	SH	SF	SB	CS	SB%	GDP	Avg	OBP	Slg
2000 Minnesota	AL	30	82	19	3	0	1	(1	0)	25	10	8	6	8	0	22	1	0	2	0	2	.00	3	.232	.301	.305
2001 Minnesota	AL	69	197	54	12	0	10	(7	3)	96	28	32	33	19	0	58	2	0	1	1	1	.50	2	.274	.342	.487
2002 Min-SD	AL	92	227	61	10	1	11	(7	4)	106	31	28	28	15	0	59	3	0	0	2	2	.50	6	.269	.322	.467
2003 San Diego	NL	115	198	52	10	2	8	(3	5)	90	29	29	27	24	1	51	3	0	3	6	2	.75	8	.263	.346	.455
2002 Minnesota	AL	44	135	34	5	1	5	(3	2)	56	19	15	11	6	0	33	2	0	0	2	1	.67	4	.252	.294	.415
2002 San Diego	NL	48	92	27	5	0	6	(4	2)	50	12	13	17	9	0	26	1	0	0	0	1	.00	2	.293	.363	.543
4 ML YEARS		306	704	186	35	3	30	(18	12)	317	98	97	94	66	1	190	9	0	6	9	7	.56	19	.264	.332	.450

Mark Budzinski

Bats: L Throws: L Pos: PH-3; CF-1   Ht: 6'2" Wt: 180 Born: 8/26/73 Age: 30

						BATTING																BASERUNNING				AVERAGES		
Year Team	Lg	G	AB	H	2B	3B	HR	(Hm	Rd)	TB	R	RBI	RC	TBB	IBB	SO	HBP	SH	SF	SB	CS	SB%	GDP	Avg	OBP	Slg
1995 Watertown	A-	70	253	64	12	8	3	(-	-)	101	50	25	45	52	1	49	8	3	2	15	5	.75	3	.253	.394	.399
1996 Columbus	A	74	260	68	12	4	3	(-	-)	97	42	38	45	59	4	68	4	2	1	12	3	.80	5	.262	.404	.373
1997 Kinston	A+	68	241	69	13	3	7	(-	-)	109	43	39	46	48	1	61	1	2	0	6	4	.60	3	.286	.407	.452
1998 Akron	AA	127	478	125	21	5	10	(-	-)	186	68	62	61	50	2	125	1	4	2	12	8	.60	9	.262	.331	.389
1999 Akron	AA	86	297	84	17	6	6	(-	-)	131	58	46	54	48	0	63	5	2	0	9	4	.69	3	.283	.391	.441
1999 Buffalo	AAA	47	133	38	7	3	2	(-	-)	57	24	17	22	22	2	36	0	2	0	4	2	.67	3	.286	.387	.429
2000 Akron	AA	18	71	17	2	0	1	(-	-)	22	7	5	7	6	1	20	1	1	0	3	2	.60	0	.239	.308	.310
2000 Buffalo	AAA	118	427	124	21	7	6	(-	-)	177	68	37	68	49	3	81	1	5	0	12	4	.75	2	.290	.365	.415
2001 Buffalo	AAA	122	438	112	26	4	2	(-	-)	152	69	39	49	28	2	125	7	9	4	13	4	.76	4	.256	.308	.347
2002 Iowa	AAA	12	32	9	2	1	0	(-	-)	13	6	4	5	3	1	5	0	0	0	1	0	1.00	0	.281	.343	.406
2002 W Tennessee	AA	114	427	127	19	6	4	(-	-)	170	68	36	68	51	3	85	5	1	2	21	7	.75	4	.297	.377	.398
2003 Indianapolis	AAA	46	159	43	7	1	1	(-	-)	55	27	12	21	16	0	39	1	4	1	7	2	.78	0	.270	.339	.346
2003 Louisville	AAA	74	259	71	15	3	1	(-	-)	95	53	15	39	37	0	56	3	2	1	10	4	.71	1	.274	.370	.367
2003 Cincinnati	NL	4	7	0	0	0	0	(0	0)	0	0	0	0	0	0	4	0	0	0	0	0	-	0	.000	.000	.000

Mark Buehrle

Pitches: L Bats: L Pos: SP-35   Ht: 6'2" Wt: 200 Born: 3/23/79 Age: 25

		HOW MUCH HE PITCHED						WHAT HE GAVE UP										THE RESULTS						
Year Team	Lg	G	GS	CG	GF	IP	BFP	H	R	ER	HR	SH	SF	HB	TBB	IBB	SO	WP	Bk	W	L	Pct	ShO	Sv-Op	Hld	ERC	ERA
2000 Chicago	AL	28	3	0	6	51.1	225	55	27	24	5	1	0	3	19	1	37	0	0	4	1	.800	0	0-2	3	4.56	4.21
2001 Chicago	AL	32	32	4	0	221.1	885	188	89	81	24	9	4	8	48	2	126	1	5	16	8	.667	2	0-0	0	2.79	3.29
2002 Chicago	AL	34	34	5	0	239.0	984	236	102	95	25	9	3	3	61	7	134	6	1	19	12	.613	2	0-0	0	3.53	3.58
2003 Chicago	AL	35	35	2	0	230.1	978	250	124	106	22	7	7	5	61	2	119	1	0	14	14	.500	0	0-0	0	4.10	4.14
4 ML YEARS		129	104	11	6	742.0	3072	729	342	306	76	26	14	19	189	12	416	8	6	53	35	.602	4	0-2	3	3.55	3.71

Ryan Bukvich

Pitches: R Bats: R Pos: RP-9   Ht: 6'3" Wt: 237 Born: 5/13/78 Age: 26

		HOW MUCH HE PITCHED						WHAT HE GAVE UP										THE RESULTS						
Year Team	Lg	G	GS	CG	GF	IP	BFP	H	R	ER	HR	SH	SF	HB	TBB	IBB	SO	WP	Bk	W	L	Pct	ShO	Sv-Op	Hld	ERC	ERA
2000 Spokane	A-	10	0	0	8	14.0	56	5	1	1	0	1	0	1	9	0	15	1	0	2	0	1.000	0	2--	-	1.44	0.64
2000 Chrlstn - WV	A	11	0	0	9	14.1	57	6	3	3	0	2	0	1	7	0	17	1	0	0	0	-	0	4--	-	1.29	1.88
2000 Wilmington	A+	2	0	0	0	2.0	15	3	4	4	0	1	0	1	5	2	3	1	0	0	1	.000	0	0--	-	14.54	18.00
2001 Wilmington	A+	37	0	0	29	57.2	248	41	16	11	1	0	2	4	31	0	80	5	1	0	1	.000	0	13--	-	2.68	1.72
2001 Wichita	AA	7	0	0	3	12.0	47	9	6	5	2	0	0	0	2	0	14	2	0	0	0	-	0	0--	-	2.26	3.75
2002 Wichita	AA	23	0	0	18	34.1	134	17	8	5	0	2	0	0	15	1	47	0	0	1	1	.500	0	8--	-	1.26	1.31
2002 Omaha	AAA	12	0	0	11	13.2	50	4	0	0	0	0	0	0	7	0	17	0	0	1	0	1.000	0	8--	-	0.91	0.00
2003 Omaha	AAA	34	0	0	21	36.2	171	39	21	20	2	1	2	0	25	0	44	6	0	1	2	.333	0	5--	-	5.18	4.91
2002 Kansas City	AL	26	0	0	2	25.0	121	26	19	17	2	4	3	1	19	3	20	1	0	1	0	1.000	0	0-1	5	5.39	6.12
2003 Kansas City	AL	9	0	0	6	10.1	52	12	11	11	2	1	1	0	9	0	8	1	0	1	0	1.000	0	0-0	0	7.65	9.58
2 ML YEARS		35	0	0	8	35.1	173	38	30	28	4	5	4	1	28	3	28	2	0	2	0	1.000	0	0-1	5	6.03	7.13

Kirk Bullinger

Pitches: R Bats: R Pos: RP-7   Ht: 6'2" Wt: 170 Born: 10/28/69 Age: 34

		HOW MUCH HE PITCHED						WHAT HE GAVE UP										THE RESULTS						
Year Team	Lg	G	GS	CG	GF	IP	BFP	H	R	ER	HR	SH	SF	HB	TBB	IBB	SO	WP	Bk	W	L	Pct	ShO	Sv-Op	Hld	ERC	ERA
2003 New Orleans*	AAA	55	0	0	45	65.0	263	56	18	14	3	1	2	3	14	4	46	0	0	3	3	.500	0	20--	-	2.41	1.94
1998 Montreal	NL	8	0	0	0	7.0	35	14	0	7	1	0	0	0	0	0	2	0	0	1	0	1.000	0	0-0	0	8.74	9.00
1999 Boston	AL	4	0	0	0	9	2	2	0	1	0	0	0	0	2	0	0	0	0	0	0	-	0	0-0	0	6.15	4.50
2000 Philadelphia	NL	3	0	0	0	3.1	14	4	0	2	0	0	0	0	0	0	4	0	0	0	0	-	0	0-0	0	2.89	5.40
2003 Houston	NL	7	0	0	3	8.0	33	7	6	6	2	0	0	0	1	0	5	0	0	0	0	-	0	0-0	1	3.06	6.75
4 ML YEARS		22	0	0	3	20.1	91	27	6	16	3	0	0	0	3	0	11	0	0	1	0	1.000	0	0-0	1	5.16	7.08

Nate Bump

Pitches: R Bats: R Pos: RP-32   Ht: 6'2" Wt: 185 Born: 7/24/76 Age: 27

		HOW MUCH HE PITCHED						WHAT HE GAVE UP										THE RESULTS						
Year Team	Lg	G	GS	CG	GF	IP	BFP	H	R	ER	HR	SH	SF	HB	TBB	IBB	SO	WP	Bk	W	L	Pct	ShO	Sv-Op	Hld	ERC	ERA
1998 Salem-Keizer	A-	2	2	0	0	8.0	31	5	0	0	0	0	0	2	3	0	8	1	0	0	0	-	0	0--	-	2.48	0.00
1998 San Jose	A+	11	11	0	0	61.2	240	37	13	12	2	1	1	2	24	0	61	2	0	6	1	.857	0	0--	-	1.77	1.75
1999 Shreveport	AA	17	17	1	0	92.1	394	85	40	34	9	6	0	5	32	0	59	2	0	4	10	.286	1	0--	-	3.59	3.31
1999 Portland	AA	8	8	0	0	43.0	203	57	38	29	3	1	2	5	12	0	33	1	0	6	2	.250	0	0--	-	5.58	6.07
2000 Portland	AA	26	26	3	0	149.2	663	169	85	76	16	5	4	15	49	1	98	5	0	8	9	.471	1	0--	-	5.00	4.57
2001 Portland	AA	11	8	0	2	54.2	228	55	41	32	10	2	1	3	10	0	41	0	0	4	5	.444	0	0--	-	4.01	5.27
2002 Portland	AA	20	20	3	0	127.2	525	110	56	48	5	3	1	8	29	0	81	2	1	7	6	.538	0	0--	-	2.52	3.38
2003 Albuquerque	AAA	15	15	0	0	85.1	368	89	48	42	4	3	1	7	24	1	52	1	0	6	5	.545	0	0--	-	3.77	4.43
2003 Florida	NL	32	0	0	8	36.1	166	34	21	19	3	1	1	7	20	0	17	0	0	4	0	1.000	0	0-0	6	4.94	4.71

Dave Burba

Pitches: R Bats: R Pos: RP-15; SP-2   Ht: 6'4" Wt: 240 Born: 7/7/66 Age: 37

		HOW MUCH HE PITCHED						WHAT HE GAVE UP										THE RESULTS						
Year Team	Lg	G	GS	CG	GF	IP	BFP	H	R	ER	HR	SH	SF	HB	TBB	IBB	SO	WP	Bk	W	L	Pct	ShO	Sv-Op	Hld	ERC	ERA
2003 Buffalo*	AAA	4	4	0	0	22.0	86	18	6	5	2	0	1	1	5	0	10	0	0	1	3	.250	0	0--	-	2.68	2.05
2003 Indianapolis*	AAA	10	9	0	0	50.2	225	65	37	30	4	1	1	1	16	0	34	4	0	5	4	.556	0	0--	-	5.39	5.33
1990 Seattle	AL	6	0	0	2	8.0	35	8	6	4	0	2	0	1	2	0	4	0	0	0	0	-	0	0-0	0	3.19	4.50
1991 Seattle	AL	22	2	0	11	36.2	153	34	16	15	6	0	0	0	14	3	16	1	0	2	2	.500	0	1-1	0	3.97	3.68
1992 San Francisco	NL	23	11	0	4	70.2	318	80	43	39	4	2	4	2	31	2	47	1	1	2	7	.222	0	0-0	0	4.71	4.97

Year Team	Lg	G	GS	CG	GF	IP	BFP	H	R	ER	HR	SH	SF	HB	TBB	IBB	SO	WP	Bk	W	L	Pct	ShO	Sv-Op	Hld	ERC	ERA
1993 San Francisco	NL	54	5	0	9	95.1	408	95	49	45	14	6	3	3	37	5	88	4	0	10	3	.769	0	0-0	10	4.44	4.25
1994 San Francisco	NL	57	0	0	13	74.0	322	59	39	36	5	3	1	6	45	3	84	3	0	3	6	.333	0	0-3	11	3.80	4.38
1995 SF-Cin	NL	52	9	1	7	106.2	451	90	50	47	9	4	1	0	51	3	96	5	0	10	4	.714	1	0-1	5	3.38	3.97
1996 Cincinnati	NL	34	33	0	0	195.0	849	179	96	83	18	5	12	2	97	9	148	9	1	11	13	.458	0	0-0	0	3.89	3.83
1997 Cincinnati	NL	30	27	2	1	160.0	706	157	88	84	22	6	3	9	73	10	131	6	0	11	10	.524	0	0-0	0	4.57	4.73
1998 Cleveland	AL	32	31	0	0	203.2	870	210	100	93	30	3	10	7	69	4	132	6	0	15	10	.600	0	0-0	0	4.50	4.11
1999 Cleveland	AL	34	34	1	0	220.0	940	211	113	104	30	2	3	8	96	3	174	13	0	15	9	.625	0	0-0	0	4.45	4.25
2000 Cleveland	AL	32	32	0	0	191.1	848	199	99	95	19	5	5	2	91	2	180	7	0	16	6	.727	0	0-0	0	4.62	4.47
2001 Cleveland	AL	32	27	1	4	150.2	684	188	112	104	16	5	7	3	54	2	118	6	0	10	10	.500	0	0-0	0	5.43	6.21
2002 Tex-Cle	AL	35	21	1	2	145.1	645	155	91	84	16	2	3	9	57	3	95	9	1	5	5	.500	0	0-2	1	4.69	5.20
2003 Milwaukee	NL	17	2	0	2	43.1	193	42	19	17	5	2	0	4	19	2	35	2	0	1	1	.500	0	0-0	0	4.40	3.53
1995 San Francisco	NL	37	0	0	7	43.1	191	38	26	24	5	3	1	0	25	2	46	2	0	4	2	.667	0	0-1	5	4.07	4.98
1995 Cincinnati	NL	15	9	1	0	63.1	260	52	24	23	4	1	0	0	26	1	50	3	0	6	2	.750	1	0-0	0	2.93	3.27
2002 Texas	AL	23	18	1	2	111.1	499	125	71	67	13	2	2	7	40	3	70	9	1	4	5	.444	0	0-1	0	4.90	5.42
2002 Cleveland	AL	12	3	0	0	34.0	146	30	20	17	3	0	1	2	17	0	25	0	0	1	0	1.000	0	0-1	1	4.01	4.50
14 ML YEARS		460	234	6	55	1700.2	7422	1707	921	850	194	47	52	56	736	51	1348	72	3	111	86	.563	1	1-7	27	4.42	4.50

Jamie Burke

Bats: R **Throws:** R **Pos:** C-4; 1B-1; DH-1; PH-1   **Ht:** 6'0" **Wt:** 195 **Born:** 9/24/71 **Age:** 32

								BATTING										BASERUNNING				AVERAGES		
Year Team	Lg	G	AB	H	2B	3B	HR	(Hm | Rd)	TB	R	RBI	RC	TBB	IBB	SO	HBP	SH	SF	SB	CS	SB%	GDP	Avg	OBP	Slg
2001 Salt Lake	AAA	100	404	117	21	8	18	(- | -)	208	78	73	69	29	1	90	1	0	2	6	1	.86	6	.290	.337	.515
2002 Salt Lake	AAA	88	316	96	12	4	8	(- | -)	140	47	44	46	20	1	37	4	0	3	1	3	.25	9	.304	.350	.443
2003 Charlotte	AAA	94	323	104	13	0	6	(- | -)	135	47	50	48	20	0	39	4	3	6	1	1	.50	9	.322	.363	.418
2001 Anaheim	AL	9	5	1	0	0	0	(0 | 0)	1	1	0	0	0	0	2	0	0	0	0	0	-	0	.200	.200	.200
2003 Chicago	AL	6	8	3	0	0	0	(0 | 0)	3	0	2	2	0	0	0	0	0	0	0	0	-	0	.375	.375	.375
2 ML YEARS		15	13	4	0	0	0	(0 | 0)	4	1	2	2	0	0	2	0	0	0	0	0	-	0	.308	.308	.308

John Burkett

Pitches: R **Bats:** R **Pos:** SP-30; RP-2   **Ht:** 6'3" **Wt:** 215 **Born:** 11/28/64 **Age:** 39

		HOW MUCH HE PITCHED						WHAT HE GAVE UP												THE RESULTS							
Year Team	Lg	G	GS	CG	GF	IP	BFP	H	R	ER	HR	SH	SF	HB	TBB	IBB	SO	WP	Bk	W	L	Pct	ShO	Sv-Op	Hld	ERC	ERA
1987 San Francisco	NL	3	0	0	1	6.0	28	7	4	3	2	1	0	1	3	0	5	0	0	0	0	-	0	0-0	0	8.25	4.50
1990 San Francisco	NL	33	32	2	1	204.0	857	201	92	86	18	6	5	4	61	7	118	3	3	14	7	.667	0	1-1	0	3.56	3.79
1991 San Francisco	NL	36	34	3	0	206.2	890	223	103	96	19	8	8	10	60	2	131	5	0	12	11	.522	1	0-0	1	4.22	4.18
1992 San Francisco	NL	32	32	3	0	189.2	799	194	96	81	13	11	4	4	45	6	107	0	0	13	9	.591	1	0-0	0	3.37	3.84
1993 San Francisco	NL	34	34	2	0	231.2	942	224	100	94	18	8	4	11	40	4	145	1	2	22	7	.759	1	0-0	0	3.07	3.65
1994 San Francisco	NL	25	25	0	0	159.1	676	176	72	64	14	12	5	7	36	7	85	2	0	6	8	.429	0	0-0	0	4.03	3.62
1995 Florida	NL	30	30	4	0	188.1	810	208	95	90	22	10	0	6	57	5	126	2	1	14	14	.500	0	0-0	0	4.53	4.30
1996 Fla-Tex		34	34	2	0	222.2	934	229	117	105	19	12	6	5	58	4	155	0	0	11	12	.478	1	0-0	0	3.68	4.24
1997 Texas	AL	30	30	2	0	189.1	828	240	106	96	20	4	7	4	30	1	139	1	0	9	12	.429	0	0-0	0	4.72	4.56
1998 Texas	AL	32	32	0	0	195.0	854	230	131	123	19	7	5	8	46	1	131	3	0	9	13	.409	0	0-0	0	4.55	5.68
1999 Texas	AL	30	25	0	1	147.1	656	184	95	92	18	5	3	3	46	1	96	4	0	9	8	.529	0	0-0	0	5.44	5.62
2000 Atlanta	NL	31	22	0	4	134.1	603	162	79	73	13	8	5	4	51	2	110	2	0	10	6	.625	0	0-1	0	5.28	4.89
2001 Atlanta	NL	34	34	1	0	219.1	902	187	83	74	17	6	7	6	70	13	187	5	1	12	12	.500	1	0-0	0	2.86	3.04
2002 Boston	AL	29	29	1	0	173.0	760	199	93	87	25	5	4	8	50	5	124	2	1	13	8	.619	1	0-0	0	4.95	4.53
2003 Boston	AL	32	30	1	1	181.2	785	202	108	104	20	4	6	9	47	1	107	3	0	12	9	.571	0	0-0	0	4.41	5.15
1996 Florida	NL	24	24	1	0	154.0	645	154	84	74	15	11	4	3	42	2	108	0	0	6	10	.375	0	0-0	0	3.64	4.32
1996 Texas	AL	10	10	1	0	68.2	289	75	33	31	4	1	2	2	16	2	47	0	0	5	2	.714	1	0-0	0	3.76	4.06
15 ML YEARS		445	423	21	8	2648.1	11324	2866	1374	1268	257	107	69	90	700	59	1766	33	8	166	136	.550	6	1-2	1	4.09	4.31

Morgan Burkhart

Bats: B **Throws:** L **Pos:** 1B-2; DH-2; PH-2   **Ht:** 5'11" **Wt:** 225 **Born:** 1/29/72 **Age:** 32

								BATTING										BASERUNNING				AVERAGES		
Year Team	Lg	G	AB	H	2B	3B	HR	(Hm	Rd)	TB	R	RBI	RC	TBB	IBB	SO	HBP	SH	SF	SB	CS	SB%	GDP	Avg	OBP	Slg
2003 Omaha*	AAA	104	382	96	18	0	17	(-	-)	165	54	57	63	50	5	67	17	0	2	2	0	1.00	5	.251	.361	.432
2000 Boston	AL	25	73	21	3	0	4	(1	3)	36	16	18	18	17	1	25	4	0	1	0	0	-	1	.288	.442	.493
2001 Boston	AL	11	33	6	1	0	1	(0	1)	10	3	4	2	1	0	11	0	0	0	0	0	-	0	.182	.206	.303
2003 Kansas City	AL	6	15	3	0	0	0	(0	0)	3	1	1	1	1	0	2	0	0	0	0	0	-	1	.200	.250	.200
3 ML YEARS		42	121	30	4	0	5	(1	4)	49	20	23	21	19	1	38	4	0	1	0	0	-	2	.248	.366	.405

Ellis Burks

Bats: R **Throws:** R **Pos:** DH-51; LF-2; PH-2   **Ht:** 6'2" **Wt:** 205 **Born:** 9/11/64 **Age:** 39

								BATTING										BASERUNNING				AVERAGES		
Year Team	Lg	G	AB	H	2B	3B	HR	(Hm	Rd)	TB	R	RBI	RC	TBB	IBB	SO	HBP	SH	SF	SB	CS	SB%	GDP	Avg	OBP	Slg
1987 Boston	AL	133	558	152	30	2	20	(11	9)	246	94	59	84	41	0	98	2	4	1	27	6	.82	1	.272	.324	.441
1988 Boston	AL	144	540	159	37	5	18	(8	10)	260	93	92	97	62	1	89	3	4	6	25	9	.74	8	.294	.367	.481
1989 Boston	AL	97	399	121	19	6	12	(6	6)	188	73	61	69	36	2	52	5	2	4	21	5	.81	8	.303	.365	.471
1990 Boston	AL	152	588	174	33	8	21	(10	11)	286	89	89	91	48	4	82	1	2	2	9	11	.45	18	.296	.349	.486
1991 Boston	AL	130	474	119	33	3	14	(8	6)	200	56	56	60	39	2	81	6	2	3	6	11	.35	7	.251	.314	.422
1992 Boston	AL	66	235	60	8	3	8	(4	4)	98	35	30	32	25	2	48	1	0	2	5	2	.71	5	.255	.327	.417
1993 Chicago	AL	146	499	137	24	4	17	(7	10)	220	75	74	76	60	2	97	4	3	8	6	9	.40	11	.275	.352	.441
1994 Colorado	NL	42	149	48	8	3	13	(7	6)	101	33	24	36	16	3	39	0	0	0	3	1	.75	3	.322	.388	.678
1995 Colorado	NL	103	278	74	10	6	14	(8	6)	138	41	49	49	39	0	72	2	1	1	7	3	.70	7	.266	.359	.496
1996 Colorado	NL	156	613	211	45	8	40	(23	17)	392	142	128	147	61	0	114	6	3	2	32	6	.84	19	.344	.408	**.639**
1997 Colorado	NL	119	424	123	19	2	32	(17	15)	242	91	82	82	47	0	75	3	1	2	7	2	.78	17	.290	.363	.571
1998 Col-SF	NL	142	504	147	28	6	21	(10	11)	250	76	76	89	58	1	111	5	6	9	11	8	.58	12	.292	.365	.496
1999 San Francisco	NL	120	390	110	19	0	31	(16	15)	222	73	96	84	69	2	86	6	0	4	7	5	.58	11	.282	.394	.569
2000 San Francisco	NL	122	393	135	21	5	24	(15	9)	238	74	96	94	56	5	49	1	0	8	5	1	.83	10	.344	.419	.606
2001 Cleveland	AL	124	439	123	29	1	28	(15	13)	238	83	74	85	62	2	85	5	0	9	5	1	.83	16	.280	.369	.542

(continued)

Year Team	Lg	G	AB	H	2B	3B	HR	(Hm	Rd)	TB	R	RBI	RC	TBB	IBB	SO	HBP	SH	SF	SB	CS	SB%	GDP	Avg	OBP	Slg
2002 Cleveland	AL	138	518	156	28	0	32	(16	11)	280	92	91	105	44	3	108	6	1	1	2	3	.40	13	.301	.362	.541
2003 Cleveland	AL	55	198	52	11	1	6	(2	4)	83	27	28	32	27	2	46	3	0	0	1	1	.50	4	.263	.360	.419
1998 Colorado	NL	100	357	102	22	5	16	(8	8)	182	54	54	60	39	0	80	2	2	5	3	7	.30	10	.286	.355	.510
1998 San Francisco	NL	42	147	45	6	1	5	(2	3)	68	22	22	29	19	1	31	3	4	4	8	1	.89	2	.306	.387	.463
17 ML YEARS		1989	7199	2101	402	63	351	(183	168)	3682	1247	1205	1312	790	33	1332	59	29	62	179	84	.68	170	.292	.364	.511

A.J. Burnett

Pitches: R Bats: R Pos: SP-4   **Ht: 6'4" Wt: 229 Born: 1/3/77 Age: 27**

| | | HOW MUCH HE PITCHED | | | | | | WHAT HE GAVE UP | | | | | | | | | | | | THE RESULTS | | | | | | |
Year Team	Lg	G	GS	CG	GF	IP	BFP	H	R	ER	HR	SH	SF	HB	TBB	IBB	SO	WP	Bk	W	L	Pct	ShO	Sv-Op	Hld	ERC	ERA
1999 Florida	NL	7	7	0	0	41.1	182	37	23	16	3	1	3	0	25	2	33	0	0	4	2	.667	0	0-0	0	4.00	3.48
2000 Florida	NL	13	13	0	0	82.2	364	80	46	44	8	6	3	2	44	3	57	2	0	3	7	.300	0	0-0	0	4.45	4.79
2001 Florida	NL	27	27	2	0	173.1	733	145	82	78	20	6	8	7	83	3	128	7	1	11	12	.478	1	0-0	0	3.76	4.05
2002 Florida	NL	31	29	7	0	204.1	844	153	84	75	12	9	4	9	90	5	203	14	0	12	9	.571	5	0-1	0	2.77	3.30
2003 Florida	NL	4	4	0	0	23.0	106	18	13	12	2	2	1	2	18	2	21	2	0	0	2	.000	0	0-0	0	4.36	4.70
5 ML YEARS		82	80	9	0	524.2	2229	433	248	225	45	24	19	20	260	15	442	25	1	30	32	.484	6	0-1	0	3.51	3.86

Jeromy Burnitz

Bats: L Throws: R Pos: LF-64; RF-50; CF-33; PH-1   **Ht: 6'0" Wt: 213 Born: 4/15/69 Age: 35**

Year Team	Lg	G	AB	H	2B	3B	HR	(Hm	Rd)	TB	R	RBI	RC	TBB	IBB	SO	HBP	SH	SF	SB	CS	SB%	GDP	Avg	OBP	Slg
2003 Binghamton*	AA	3	13	3	0	0	1	(-	-)	6	1	3	2	0	0	4	0	0	0	0	1	1.00	0	.231	.231	.462
1993 New York	NL	86	263	64	10	6	13	(6	7)	125	49	38	42	38	4	66	1	2	2	3	6	.33	2	.243	.339	.475
1994 New York	NL	45	143	34	4	0	3	(2	1)	47	26	15	17	23	0	45	1	1	0	1	1	.50	2	.238	.347	.329
1995 Cleveland	AL	9	7	4	1	0	0	(0	0)	5	4	0	2	0	0	0	0	0	0	0	0	-	0	.571	.571	.714
1996 Cle-Mil		94	200	53	14	0	9	(5	4)	94	38	40	37	33	2	47	4	0	2	4	1	.80	4	.265	.377	.470
1997 Milwaukee	NL	153	494	139	37	8	27	(18	9)	273	85	85	100	75	8	111	5	3	0	20	13	.61	8	.281	.382	.553
1998 Milwaukee	NL	161	609	160	28	1	38	(17	21)	304	92	125	102	70	7	158	4	1	7	7	4	.64	9	.263	.339	.499
1999 Milwaukee	NL	130	467	126	33	2	33	(12	21)	262	87	103	104	91	7	124	16	0	6	7	3	.70	11	.270	.402	.561
2000 Milwaukee	NL	161	564	131	29	2	31	(12	19)	257	91	98	94	99	10	121	14	0	9	6	4	.60	12	.232	.356	.456
2001 Milwaukee	NL	154	562	141	32	4	34	(16	18)	283	104	100	97	80	9	150	5	0	4	0	4	.00	8	.251	.347	.504
2002 New York	NL	154	479	103	15	0	19	(12	7)	175	65	54	48	58	5	135	10	1	2	10	7	.59	11	.215	.311	.365
2003 NYM-LA	NL	126	464	111	22	0	31	(10	21)	226	63	77	64	35	9	112	5	0	1	5	4	.56	5	.239	.299	.487
1996 Cleveland	AL	71	128	36	10	0	7	(4	3)	67	30	26	27	25	1	31	2	0	0	2	1	.67	3	.281	.406	.523
1996 Milwaukee	NL	23	72	17	4	0	2	(1	1)	27	8	14	10	8	1	16	2	0	2	2	0	1.00	1	.236	.321	.375
2003 New York	NL	65	234	64	18	0	18	(4	14)	136	38	45	44	21	6	55	4	0	0	1	4	.20	4	.274	.344	.581
2003 Los Angeles	NL	61	230	47	4	0	13	(6	7)	90	25	32	20	14	3	57	1	0	1	4	0	1.00	1	.204	.252	.391
11 ML YEARS		1273	4252	1066	225	23	238	(110	128)	2051	704	735	707	602	61	1069	65	6	33	63	47	.57	72	.251	.350	.482

Pat Burrell

Bats: R Throws: R Pos: LF-140; PH-6; DH-2   **Ht: 6'4" Wt: 222 Born: 10/10/76 Age: 27**

Year Team	Lg	G	AB	H	2B	3B	HR	(Hm	Rd)	TB	R	RBI	RC	TBB	IBB	SO	HBP	SH	SF	SB	CS	SB%	GDP	Avg	OBP	Slg
2000 Philadelphia	NL	111	408	106	27	1	18	(7	11)	189	57	79	69	63	2	139	1	0	2	0	0	-	5	.260	.359	.463
2001 Philadelphia	NL	155	539	139	29	2	27	(10	17)	253	70	89	86	70	7	162	5	0	4	2	1	.67	12	.258	.346	.469
2002 Philadelphia	NL	157	586	165	39	2	37	(18	19)	319	96	116	105	89	9	153	3	0	6	1	0	1.00	16	.282	.376	.544
2003 Philadelphia	NL	146	522	109	31	4	21	(9	12)	211	57	64	59	72	2	142	4	0	1	0	0	-	18	.209	.309	.404
4 ML YEARS		569	2055	519	126	9	103	(44	59)	972	280	348	319	294	20	596	13	0	13	3	1	.75	51	.253	.348	.473

Sean Burroughs

Bats: L Throws: R Pos: 3B-137; PH-10   **Ht: 6'2" Wt: 200 Born: 9/12/80 Age: 23**

Year Team	Lg	G	AB	H	2B	3B	HR	(Hm	Rd)	TB	R	RBI	RC	TBB	IBB	SO	HBP	SH	SF	SB	CS	SB%	GDP	Avg	OBP	Slg
1999 Fort Wayne	A	122	426	153	30	3	5	(-	-)	204	65	80	94	74	7	59	14	2	5	17	15	.53	10	.359	.464	.479
1999 R Cucamnga	A+	6	23	10	3	0	1	(-	-)	16	3	5	7	3	0	3	1	0	0	0	1	.00	1	.435	.519	.696
2000 Mobile	AA	108	392	154	29	4	2	(-	-)	157	46	42	60	58	6	45	3	4	4	6	8	.43	10	.393	.383	.401
2001 Portland	AAA	104	394	127	28	1	9	(-	-)	184	60	55	68	37	2	54	4	4	0	9	2	.82	13	.322	.386	.467
2002 Portland	AAA	50	179	54	16	2	2	(-	-)	80	29	23	30	21	0	16	3	0	2	1	0	1.00	5	.302	.380	.447
2002 San Diego	NL	63	192	52	5	1	1	(0	1)	62	18	11	14	12	1	30	1	1	0	2	0	1.00	6	.271	.317	.323
2003 San Diego	NL	146	517	148	27	6	7	(2	5)	208	62	58	67	44	4	75	11	2	4	7	2	.78	13	.286	.352	.402
2 ML YEARS		209	709	200	32	7	8	(2	6)	270	80	69	81	56	5	105	12	3	4	9	2	.82	19	.282	.343	.381

Brent Butler

Bats: R Throws: R Pos: 2B-20; PH-9; 3B-8; SS-4   **Ht: 6'0" Wt: 180 Born: 2/11/78 Age: 26**

Year Team	Lg	G	AB	H	2B	3B	HR	(Hm	Rd)	TB	R	RBI	RC	TBB	IBB	SO	HBP	SH	SF	SB	CS	SB%	GDP	Avg	OBP	Slg
2003 Co Springs*	AAA	54	205	68	19	1	6	(-	-)	107	37	27	39	19	1	20	4	0	0	0	1	.00	7	.332	.399	.522
2001 Colorado	NL	53	119	29	7	1	1	(0	1)	41	17	14	11	7	0	7	1	2	2	1	1	.50	4	.244	.287	.345
2002 Colorado	NL	113	344	89	18	4	9	(7	2)	142	55	42	42	10	3	40	5	4	4	2	6	.25	6	.259	.287	.413
2003 Colorado	NL	37	90	19	3	1	1	(1	0)	27	13	4	5	7	2	13	1	1	0	1	0	1.00	2	.211	.276	.300
3 ML YEARS		203	553	137	28	6	11	(8	3)	210	85	60	58	24	5	60	7	7	6	4	7	.36	12	.248	.285	.380

Mike Bynum

Pitches: L **Bats:** L **Pos:** RP-8; SP-5   **Ht:** 6'4" **Wt:** 200 **Born:** 3/20/78 **Age:** 26

Year Team	Lg	G	GS	CG	GF	IP	BFP	H	R	ER	HR	SH	SF	HB	TBB	IBB	SO	WP	Bk	W	L	Pct	ShO	Sv-Op	Hld	ERC	ERA
1999 Idaho Falls	R+	5	3	0	0	17.0	60	7	0	0	1	0	0	0	4	0	21	0	0	1	0	1.000	0	0- -	-	0.73	0.00
1999 R Cucamnga	A+	7	7	0	0	38.1	159	35	17	14	1	1	1	2	8	0	44	2	2	3	1	.750	0	0- -	-	2.57	3.29
2000 R Cucamnga	A+	21	21	0	0	126.0	517	101	55	42	4	3	5	8	51	0	129	7	1	9	6	.600	0	0- -	-	2.88	3.00
2000 Mobile	AA	6	6	0	0	34.0	144	31	12	11	2	1	2	2	16	0	27	1	1	3	1	.750	0	0- -	-	3.91	2.91
2001 Mobile	AA	16	15	0	0	84.1	368	90	53	47	14	4	3	3	35	0	69	0	0	2	7	.222	0	0- -	-	5.23	5.02
2002 Mobile	AA	6	5	0	0	33.0	123	17	5	3	0	0	0	3	7	0	29	2	0	4	0	1.000	0	0- -	-	1.10	0.82
2002 Portland	AAA	7	7	0	0	41.0	167	36	19	16	6	3	1	3	7	0	35	0	0	3	2	.600	0	0- -	-	3.10	3.51
2003 Portland	AAA	24	23	0	0	125.1	554	130	76	67	11	2	2	10	60	2	106	6	1	7	12	.368	0	0- -	-	4.89	4.81
2002 San Diego	NL	14	3	0	3	27.1	130	33	16	16	3	3	2	3	15	2	17	2	0	1	0	1.000	0	0-0	0	6.31	5.27
2003 San Diego	NL	13	5	0	3	36.0	165	44	35	35	14	1	0	1	15	0	35	0	0	1	4	.200	0	0-0	0	7.83	8.75
2 ML YEARS		27	8	0	6	63.1	295	77	51	51	17	4	2	4	30	2	52	2	0	2	4	.333	0	0-0	0	7.22	7.25

Marlon Byrd

Bats: R **Throws:** R **Pos:** CF-131; PH-7; PR-1   **Ht:** 6'0" **Wt:** 225 **Born:** 8/30/77 **Age:** 26

Year Team	Lg	G	AB	H	2B	3B	HR	(Hm	Rd)	TB	R	RBI	RC	TBB	IBB	SO	HBP	SH	SF	SB	CS	SB%	GDP	Avg	OBP	Slg
1999 Batavia	A-	65	243	72	7	6	13	(-	-)	130	40	50	49	28	1	70	5	0	3	8	2	.80	3	.296	.376	.535
2000 Piedmont	A	133	515	159	29	13	17	(-	-)	265	104	93	105	51	0	110	10	1	5	41	5	.89	7	.309	.379	.515
2001 Reading	AA	137	510	161	22	8	28	(-	-)	283	108	89	110	52	3	93	11	2	7	32	5	.86	7	.316	.386	.555
2002 Scrtn/WlksBr	AAA	136	538	160	37	7	15	(-	-)	256	103	63	95	46	2	98	11	2	5	15	1	.94	5	.297	.362	.476
2003 Scrtn/WlksBr	AAA	1	4	3	1	0	0	(-	-)	4	1	0	2	0	0	1	0	0	0	0	0	-	0	.750	.750	1.000
2003 Reading	AA	3	16	5	0	0	1	(-	-)	8	3	3	2	0	0	3	0	0	0	0	0	-	1	.313	.313	.500
2002 Philadelphia	NL	10	35	8	2	0	1	(-	-)	13	2	1	0	1	0	8	0	0	0	2	0	.00	0	.229	.250	.371
2003 Philadelphia	NL	135	495	150	28	4	7	(3	4)	207	86	45	71	44	3	94	7	4	3	11	1	.92	8	.303	.366	.418
2 ML YEARS		145	530	158	30	4	8	(4	4)	220	88	46	71	45	3	102	7	4	3	11	3	.79	8	.298	.359	.415

Paul Byrd

Pitches: R **Bats:** R **Pos:** SP   **Ht:** 6'1" **Wt:** 185 **Born:** 12/3/70 **Age:** 33

Year Team	Lg	G	GS	CG	GF	IP	BFP	H	R	ER	HR	SH	SF	HB	TBB	IBB	SO	WP	Bk	W	L	Pct	ShO	Sv-Op	Hld	ERC	ERA
1995 New York	NL	17	0	0	6	22.0	91	18	6	5	1	0	2	1	7	1	26	1	2	2	0	1.000	0	0-0	3	2.53	2.05
1996 New York	NL	38	0	0	14	46.2	204	48	22	22	7	1	1	0	21	4	31	3	0	1	2	.333	0	0-2	3	4.67	4.24
1997 Atlanta	NL	31	4	0	9	53.0	236	47	34	31	6	2	4	4	28	4	37	3	1	4	4	.500	0	0-0	1	4.15	5.26
1998 Atl-Phi	NL	9	8	2	0	57.0	233	45	19	17	6	2	1	0	18	1	39	2	0	5	2	.714	1	0-0	0	2.62	2.68
1999 Philadelphia	NL	32	32	1	0	199.2	872	205	119	102	34	5	6	17	70	2	106	11	3	15	11	.577	0	0-0	0	4.87	4.60
2000 Philadelphia	NL	17	15	0	0	83.0	371	89	67	60	17	3	1	3	35	2	53	1	0	2	9	.182	0	0-0	0	5.42	6.51
2001 Phi-KC		19	16	1	1	103.1	444	120	54	51	12	4	6	2	26	1	52	2	0	6	7	.462	0	0-0	0	4.62	4.44
2002 Kansas City	AL	33	33	7	0	228.1	935	224	111	99	36	2	13	7	38	1	129	3	1	17	11	.607	2	0-0	0	3.55	3.90
1998 Atlanta	NL	1	0	0	0	2.0	11	4	3	3	0	0	0	0	1	0	1	0	0	0	0	-	0	0-0	0	9.72	13.50
1998 Philadelphia	NL	8	8	2	0	55.0	222	41	16	14	6	2	1	0	17	1	38	2	0	5	2	.714	1	0-0	0	2.41	2.29
2001 Philadelphia	NL	3	1	0	1	10.0	45	10	9	9	1	2	2	1	4	0	3	1	0	1	0	1.000	0	0-0	0	4.36	8.10
2001 Kansas City	AL	16	15	1	0	93.1	399	110	45	42	11	2	4	1	22	1	49	1	0	6	6	.500	0	0-0	0	4.65	4.05
8 ML YEARS		196	108	11	30	793.0	3386	796	432	387	119	19	32	34	243	16	473	26	7	52	46	.531	3	0-2	7	4.21	4.39

Eric Byrnes

Bats: R **Throws:** R **Pos:** CF-82; LF-44; PH-5; PR-3; RF-2   **Ht:** 6'2" **Wt:** 210 **Born:** 2/16/76 **Age:** 28

Year Team	Lg	G	AB	H	2B	3B	HR	(Hm	Rd)	TB	R	RBI	RC	TBB	IBB	SO	HBP	SH	SF	SB	CS	SB%	GDP	Avg	OBP	Slg
2000 Oakland	AL	10	10	3	0	0	0	(0	0)	3	5	0	1	0	0	1	1	0	0	2	1	.67	0	.300	.364	.300
2001 Oakland	AL	19	38	9	1	0	3	(2	1)	19	9	5	7	4	0	6	1	0	0	1	0	1.00	0	.237	.326	.500
2002 Oakland	AL	90	94	23	4	2	3	(2	1)	40	24	11	10	4	0	17	3	1	2	3	0	1.00	3	.245	.291	.426
2003 Oakland	AL	121	414	109	27	9	12	(7	5)	190	64	51	68	42	4	71	2	0	2	10	2	.83	3	.263	.333	.459
4 ML YEARS		240	556	144	32	11	18	(11	7)	252	102	67	86	50	4	95	7	1	4	16	3	.84	6	.259	.326	.453

Jolbert Cabrera

Bats: R **Throws:** R **Pos:** 2B-59; CF-38; LF-31; PH-23; SS-9; 1B-8; 3B-5; RF-4; PR-2   **Ht:** 6'1" **Wt:** 190 **Born:** 12/8/72 **Age:** 31

Year Team	Lg	G	AB	H	2B	3B	HR	(Hm	Rd)	TB	R	RBI	RC	TBB	IBB	SO	HBP	SH	SF	SB	CS	SB%	GDP	Avg	OBP	Slg
1998 Cleveland	AL	1	2	0	0	0	0	(0	0)	0	0	0	0	0	0	1	0	0	0	0	0	-	0	.000	.000	.000
1999 Cleveland	AL	30	37	7	1	0	0	(0	0)	8	6	0	2	1	0	8	1	0	0	3	0	1.00	0	.189	.231	.216
2000 Cleveland	AL	100	175	44	3	1	2	(2	0)	55	27	15	16	8	0	15	2	1	1	6	4	.60	1	.251	.290	.314
2001 Cleveland	AL	141	287	75	16	3	1	(1	0)	100	50	38	32	16	0	41	6	1	2	10	4	.71	4	.261	.312	.348
2002 Cle-LA		48	84	12	2	0	0	(0	0)	14	8	8	3	7	0	15	1	1	1	1	1	.50	3	.143	.215	.167
2003 Los Angeles	NL	128	347	98	32	2	6	(4	2)	152	43	37	42	17	3	62	10	3	3	6	4	.60	10	.282	.332	.438
2002 Cleveland	AL	38	72	8	1	0	0	(0	0)	9	5	7	1	5	0	13	1	0	1	1	1	.50	3	.111	.177	.125
2002 Los Angeles	NL	10	12	4	1	0	0	(0	0)	5	3	1	2	2	0	2	0	1	0	0	0	-	0	.333	.429	.417
6 ML YEARS		448	932	236	54	6	9	(7	2)	329	134	98	95	49	3	142	20	6	7	26	13	.67	19	.253	.303	.353

Miguel Cabrera

Bats: R **Throws:** R **Pos:** LF-55; 3B-34; PH-1; PR-1   **Ht:** 6'2" **Wt:** 185 **Born:** 4/18/83 **Age:** 21

Year Team	Lg	G	AB	H	2B	3B	HR	(Hm	Rd)	TB	R	RBI	RC	TBB	IBB	SO	HBP	SH	SF	SB	CS	SB%	GDP	Avg	OBP	Slg
2000 Marlins	R	57	219	57	10	2	2	(-	-)	77	38	22	27	23	0	46	6	0	2	1	0	1.00	7	.260	.344	.352
2000 Utica	A-	8	32	8	2	0	0	(-	-)	10	3	6	3	2	0	6	0	0	0	0	0	-	0	.250	.294	.313
2001 Kane County	A	110	422	134	19	4	7	(-	-)	182	61	66	67	37	2	76	2	1	3	3	0	1.00	10	.318	.373	.431

Year Team	Lg	G	AB	H	2B	3B	HR	(Hm Rd)	TB	R	RBI	RC	TBB	IBB	SO	HBP	SH	SF	SB	CS	SB%	GDP	Avg	OBP	Slg
2002 Jupiter	A+	124	489	134	43	1	9	(- -)	206	77	75	67	38	2	85	9	1	8	10	1	.91	19	.274	.333	.421
2003 Carolina	AA	69	266	97	29	3	10	(- -)	162	46	59	63	31	7	49	2	0	4	9	4	.69	8	.365	.429	.609
2003 Florida	NL	87	314	84	21	3	12	(7 5)	147	39	62	52	25	3	84	2	4	1	0	2	.00	12	.268	.325	.468

Orlando Cabrera

Bats: R **Throws:** R **Pos:** SS-162   **Ht:** 5'10" **Wt:** 185 **Born:** 11/2/74 **Age:** 29

Year Team	Lg	G	AB	H	2B	3B	HR	(Hm Rd)	TB	R	RBI	RC	TBB	IBB	SO	HBP	SH	SF	SB	CS	SB%	GDP	Avg	OBP	Slg
1997 Montreal	NL	16	18	4	0	0	0	(0 0)	4	4	2	0	1	0	3	0	1	0	1	2	.33	1	.222	.263	.222
1998 Montreal	NL	79	261	73	16	5	3	(2 1)	108	44	22	34	18	1	27	0	5	1	6	2	.75	6	.280	.325	.414
1999 Montreal	NL	104	382	97	23	5	8	(6 2)	154	48	39	42	18	4	38	3	4	0	2	2	.50	9	.254	.293	.403
2000 Montreal	NL	125	422	100	25	1	13	(7 6)	166	47	55	43	25	3	28	1	3	3	4	4	.50	12	.237	.279	.393
2001 Montreal	NL	162	626	173	41	6	14	(7 7)	268	64	96	85	43	5	54	4	4	7	19	7	.73	15	.276	.324	.428
2002 Montreal	NL	153	563	148	43	1	7	(3 4)	214	64	56	62	48	4	53	2	9	4	25	7	.78	16	.263	.321	.380
2003 Montreal	NL	162	626	186	47	2	17	(8 9)	288	95	80	94	52	3	64	1	3	9	24	2	.92	18	.297	.347	.460
7 ML YEARS		801	2898	781	195	20	62	(33 29)	1202	366	350	360	205	20	267	11	29	24	81	26	.76	77	.269	.318	.415

Miguel Cairo

Bats: R **Throws:** R **Pos:** 2B-40; LF-22; PH-22; 3B-12; SS-7; RF-6; 1B-3; PR-1   **Ht:** 6'1" **Wt:** 200 **Born:** 5/4/74 **Age:** 30

Year Team	Lg	G	AB	H	2B	3B	HR	(Hm Rd)	TB	R	RBI	RC	TBB	IBB	SO	HBP	SH	SF	SB	CS	SB%	GDP	Avg	OBP	Slg
2003 Memphis*	AAA	3	13	3	1	0	0	(- -)	4	2	0	1	0	0	3	0	0	0	0	0	-	0	.231	.231	.308
1996 Toronto	AL	9	27	6	2	0	0	(0 0)	8	5	1	2	2	0	9	1	0	0	0	0	-	1	.222	.300	.296
1997 Chicago	NL	16	29	7	1	0	0	(0 0)	8	7	1	3	2	0	3	1	0	0	0	0	-	0	.241	.313	.276
1998 Tampa Bay	AL	150	515	138	26	5	5	(3 2)	189	49	46	58	24	0	44	6	11	2	19	8	.70	9	.268	.307	.367
1999 Tampa Bay	AL	120	465	137	15	5	3	(1 2)	171	61	36	57	24	0	46	7	7	5	22	7	.76	13	.295	.335	.368
2000 Tampa Bay	AL	119	375	98	18	2	1	(0 1)	123	49	34	42	29	0	34	2	6	5	28	7	.80	7	.261	.314	.328
2001 ChC-StL	NL	93	156	46	8	1	3	(2 1)	65	25	16	23	18	1	23	0	7	1	2	1	.67	4	.295	.366	.417
2002 St Louis	NL	108	184	46	9	2	2	(1 1)	65	28	23	18	13	2	36	3	6	2	1	1	.50	5	.250	.307	.353
2003 St Louis	NL	92	261	64	15	2	5	(2 3)	98	41	32	25	13	1	30	6	3	7	4	1	.80	6	.245	.289	.375
2001 Chicago	NL	66	123	35	3	1	2	(1 1)	46	20	9	17	16	1	21	0	7	1	2	1	.67	3	.285	.364	.374
2001 St Louis	NL	27	33	11	5	0	1	(1 0)	19	5	7	6	2	0	2	0	0	0	0	0	-	1	.333	.371	.576
8 ML YEARS		707	2012	542	94	17	19	(9 10)	727	265	189	228	125	4	225	26	40	22	76	25	.75	45	.269	.317	.361

Kiko Calero

Pitches: R **Bats:** R **Pos:** RP-25; SP-1   **Ht:** 6'1" **Wt:** 185 **Born:** 1/9/75 **Age:** 29

Year Team	Lg	G	GS	CG	GF	IP	BFP	H	R	ER	HR	SH	SF	HB	TBB	IBB	SO	WP	Bk	W	L	Pct	ShO	Sv-Op	Hld	ERC	ERA
1996 Spokane	A-	17	11	0	3	75.0	318	77	34	21	5	0	6	3	18	0	61	2	2	4	2	.667	0	1- -	-	3.51	2.52
1997 Wichita	AA	23	22	2	0	127.2	541	120	78	63	15	4	6	4	44	0	100	2	2	11	9	.550	0	0- -	-	3.76	4.44
1998 Lansing	A	4	4	0	0	16.2	76	19	7	7	1	0	0	2	7	0	10	1	1	1	0	1.000	0	0- -	-	5.15	3.78
1998 Wilmington	A+	17	17	0	0	97.2	409	74	33	31	7	1	3	7	51	1	90	6	0	7	3	.700	0	0- -	-	3.36	2.86
1998 Wichita	AA	3	3	0	0	14.0	72	23	16	15	2	1	0	1	6	0	5	0	0	1	0	1.000	0	0- -	-	8.68	9.64
1999 Wichita	AA	26	23	1	1	129.1	579	143	67	59	14	2	2	6	57	3	92	7	2	9	3	.750	1	1- -	-	5.07	4.11
2000 Wichita	AA	28	25	0	0	153.2	648	141	74	62	16	7	3	10	66	2	130	7	1	10	7	.588	0	0- -	-	4.11	3.63
2001 Wichita	AA	27	19	0	1	124.1	531	110	57	46	10	3	6	7	51	1	94	7	1	14	5	.737	0	0- -	-	3.54	3.33
2002 Wichita	AA	5	2	0	0	16.0	64	10	5	4	2	0	1	0	5	0	15	1	0	1	0	1.000	0	0- -	-	1.93	2.25
2002 Omaha	AAA	20	18	0	0	125.2	510	112	52	48	11	5	7	4	35	1	109	6	1	7	7	.500	0	0- -	-	3.11	3.44
2003 St Louis	NL	26	1	0	7	38.1	162	29	12	12	5	1	3	1	20	2	51	3	1	1	1	.500	0	1-4	1	3.44	2.82

Mickey Callaway

Pitches: R **Bats:** R **Pos:** RP-16; SP-7   **Ht:** 6'2" **Wt:** 200 **Born:** 5/13/75 **Age:** 29

Year Team	Lg	G	GS	CG	GF	IP	BFP	H	R	ER	HR	SH	SF	HB	TBB	IBB	SO	WP	Bk	W	L	Pct	ShO	Sv-Op	Hld	ERC	ERA
2003 Salt Lake*	AAA	7	4	0	0	21.1	85	22	8	7	1	1	1	0	6	0	10	1	0	1	0	1.000	0	0- -	-	3.66	2.95
2003 Oklahoma*	AAA	4	4	0	0	17.0	69	16	6	3	0	0	1	0	5	0	9	2	0	2	0	1.000	0	0- -	-	2.77	1.59
1999 Tampa Bay	AL	5	4	0	0	19.1	99	30	20	16	2	0	1	0	14	1	11	1	0	1	2	.333	0	0-0	0	8.89	7.45
2001 Tampa Bay	AL	2	0	0	2	5.0	20	3	4	4	2	0	0	0	2	0	2	0	0	0	0	-	0	0-0	0	3.65	7.20
2002 Anaheim	AL	6	6	0	0	34.1	147	31	20	16	4	1	0	3	11	0	23	2	0	2	1	.667	0	0-0	0	3.63	4.19
2003 Ana-Tex	AL	23	7	0	8	60.2	284	84	50	45	7	2	5	2	24	1	41	2	0	1	7	.125	0	0-0	0	6.62	6.68
2003 Anaheim	AL	17	4	0	8	38.1	184	57	32	29	7	0	2	1	16	1	22	0	0	1	4	.200	0	0-0	0	7.91	6.81
2003 Texas	AL	6	3	0	0	22.1	100	27	18	16	0	2	3	1	8	0	19	2	0	0	3	.000	0	0-0	0	4.55	6.45
4 ML YEARS		36	17	0	10	119.1	550	148	94	81	15	3	6	5	51	2	77	5	0	4	10	.286	0	0-0	0	5.94	6.11

Ron Calloway

Bats: L **Throws:** L **Pos:** LF-50; RF-47; PH-34; CF-2; PR-2   **Ht:** 6'1" **Wt:** 210 **Born:** 9/4/76 **Age:** 27

Year Team	Lg	G	AB	H	2B	3B	HR	(Hm Rd)	TB	R	RBI	RC	TBB	IBB	SO	HBP	SH	SF	SB	CS	SB%	GDP	Avg	OBP	Slg
1997 Lethbridge	R+	43	148	37	5	0	0	(- -)	42	23	9	12	14	0	29	3	0	2	5	8	.38	4	.250	.323	.284
1997 South Bend	A	9	25	7	1	0	0	(- -)	8	3	1	3	2	0	8	0	0	0	1	0	1.00	1	.280	.333	.320
1998 High Desert	A+	44	156	44	8	2	3	(- -)	65	30	27	21	12	0	38	2	2	2	4	.33	2		.282	.337	.417
1998 South Bend	A	69	251	66	12	2	3	(- -)	91	29	33	31	25	1	50	2	1	3	7	5	.58	3	.263	.331	.363
1999 High Desert	A+	60	196	62	14	1	3	(- -)	87	41	23	38	30	0	34	2	2	0	22	7	.76	3	.316	.412	.444
1999 El Paso	AA	11	32	7	0	0	0	(- -)	7	4	1	3	7	0	7	0	0	0	1	2	.33	0	.219	.359	.219
1999 Jupiter	A+	54	211	57	8	4	3	(- -)	82	30	25	23	15	0	45	2	4	0	5	6	.45	9	.270	.325	.389
2000 Jupiter	A+	135	530	147	24	6	6	(- -)	201	78	65	71	55	3	89	4	1	6	34	14	.71	13	.277	.346	.379
2001 Harrisburg	AA	74	279	92	22	4	9	(- -)	149	48	47	58	24	2	46	3	5	3	25	7	.78	2	.330	.385	.534

Year Team	Lg	BATTING																			BASERUNNING				AVERAGES		
		G	AB	H	2B	3B	HR	(Hm	Rd)	TB	R	RBI	RC	TBB	IBB	SO	HBP	SH	SF		SB	CS	SB%	GDP	Avg	OBP	Slg
2001 Ottawa	AAA	61	239	63	12	0	10	(-	-)	105	27	35	34	16	2	64	6	2	2		11	1	.92	6	.264	.323	.439
2002 Ottawa	AAA	128	447	118	21	5	14	(-	-)	191	72	60	59	44	3	89	6	4	5		16	12	.57	18	.264	.335	.427
2003 Montreal	NL	126	340	81	17	1	9	(5	4)	127	36	52	39	20	1	80	2	4	3		9	2	.82	13	.238	.282	.374

Mike Cameron

Bats: R **Throws:** R **Pos:** CF-147; PH-1   **Ht:** 6'2" **Wt:** 195 **Born:** 1/8/73 **Age:** 31

Year Team	Lg	BATTING																			BASERUNNING				AVERAGES		
		G	AB	H	2B	3B	HR	(Hm	Rd)	TB	R	RBI	RC	TBB	IBB	SO	HBP	SH	SF		SB	CS	SB%	GDP	Avg	OBP	Slg
1995 Chicago	AL	28	38	7	2	0	1	(0	1)	12	4	2	3	3	0	15	0	3	0		0	0	-	0	.184	.244	.316
1996 Chicago	AL	11	11	1	0	0	0	(0	0)	1	1	0	0	1	0	3	0	0	0		0	1	.00	0	.091	.167	.091
1997 Chicago	AL	116	379	98	18	3	14	(10	4)	164	63	55	63	55	1	105	5	2	5		23	2	.92	8	.259	.356	.433
1998 Chicago	AL	141	396	83	16	5	8	(5	3)	133	53	43	39	37	0	101	6	1	3		27	11	.71	6	.210	.285	.336
1999 Cincinnati	NL	146	542	139	34	9	21	(12	9)	254	93	66	96	80	2	145	6	5	3		38	12	.76	4	.256	.357	.469
2000 Seattle	AL	155	543	145	28	4	19	(5	14)	238	96	78	91	78	0	133	9	7	6		24	7	.77	10	.267	.365	.438
2001 Seattle	AL	150	540	144	30	5	25	(7	18)	259	99	110	96	69	3	155	10	1	13		34	5	.87	13	.267	.353	.480
2002 Seattle	AL	158	545	130	26	5	25	(7	18)	241	84	80	81	79	3	176	7	4	5		31	8	.79	8	.239	.340	.442
2003 Seattle	AL	147	534	135	31	5	18	(11	7)	230	74	76	81	70	1	137	5	1	2		17	7	.71	13	.253	.344	.431
9 ML YEARS		1052	3528	882	185	36	131	(57	74)	1532	567	510	550	472	10	970	48	24	37		194	53	.79	62	.250	.343	.434

Chris Capuano

Pitches: L **Bats:** L **Pos:** SP-5; RP-4   **Ht:** 6'2" **Wt:** 219 **Born:** 8/19/78 **Age:** 25

Year Team	Lg	HOW MUCH HE PITCHED						WHAT HE GAVE UP											THE RESULTS							
		G	GS	CG	GF	IP	BFP	H	R	ER	HR	SH	SF	HB	TBB	IBB	SO	WP	Bk	W	L	Pct	ShO	Sv-Op	Hld	ERC	ERA
2000 South Bend	A	18	18	0	0	101.2	408	68	35	25	2	4	1	5	45	0	105	2	2	10	4	.714	0	0--	-	2.23	2.21
2001 El Paso	AA	28	28	2	0	159.1	733	184	109	94	13	4	8	11	75	0	167	9	2	10	11	.476	2	0--	-	5.38	5.31
2002 Tucson	AAA	6	6	0	0	36.1	146	30	12	11	1	1	2	0	11	0	29	1	0	4	1	.800	0	0--	-	2.37	2.72
2003 Tucson	AAA	23	23	0	0	142.2	602	133	66	53	9	11	4	11	43	2	108	6	1	9	5	.643	0	0--	-	3.35	3.34
2003 Arizona	NL	9	5	0	2	33.0	139	27	19	17	3	4	1	6	11	1	23	3	0	2	4	.333	0	0-0	1	3.45	4.64

Chris Carpenter

Pitches: R **Bats:** R **Pos:** SP   **Ht:** 6'6" **Wt:** 215 **Born:** 4/27/75 **Age:** 29

Year Team	Lg	HOW MUCH HE PITCHED						WHAT HE GAVE UP											THE RESULTS							
		G	GS	CG	GF	IP	BFP	H	R	ER	HR	SH	SF	HB	TBB	IBB	SO	WP	Bk	W	L	Pct	ShO	Sv-Op	Hld	ERC	ERA
1997 Toronto	AL	14	13	1	1	81.1	374	108	55	46	7	1	2	2	37	0	55	7	1	3	7	.300	1	0-0	0	6.38	5.09
1998 Toronto	AL	33	24	1	4	175.0	742	177	97	85	18	4	5	5	61	1	136	5	0	12	7	.632	1	0-0	0	4.12	4.37
1999 Toronto	AL	24	24	4	0	150.0	663	177	81	73	16	4	6	3	48	1	106	9	1	9	8	.529	1	0-0	0	4.90	4.38
2000 Toronto	AL	34	27	2	1	175.1	795	204	130	122	30	3	1	5	83	1	113	3	0	10	12	.455	0	0-0	0	6.04	6.26
2001 Toronto	AL	34	34	3	0	215.2	930	229	112	98	29	3	1	16	75	5	157	5	0	11	11	.500	2	0-0	0	4.82	4.09
2002 Toronto	AL	13	13	1	0	73.1	327	89	45	43	11	1	4	4	27	0	45	3	0	4	5	.444	0	0-0	0	5.91	5.28
6 ML YEARS		152	135	12	6	870.2	3831	984	520	467	111	16	19	35	331	8	612	32	2	49	50	.495	5	0-0	0	5.16	4.83

Giovanni Carrara

Pitches: R **Bats:** R **Pos:** RP-23   **Ht:** 6'2" **Wt:** 235 **Born:** 3/4/68 **Age:** 36

Year Team	Lg	HOW MUCH HE PITCHED						WHAT HE GAVE UP											THE RESULTS							
		G	GS	CG	GF	IP	BFP	H	R	ER	HR	SH	SF	HB	TBB	IBB	SO	WP	Bk	W	L	Pct	ShO	Sv-Op	Hld	ERC	ERA
2003 Tacoma*	AAA	18	0	0	13	27.2	117	28	14	13	2	1	1	0	9	0	27	3	0	1	1	.500	0	5--	-	3.68	4.23
1995 Toronto	AL	12	7	1	2	48.2	229	64	46	39	10	1	2	1	25	1	27	1	0	2	4	.333	0	0-0	0	7.43	7.21
1996 Tor-Cin		19	5	0	4	38.0	188	54	36	34	11	1	0	2	25	3	23	1	0	1	1	.500	0	0-1	0	9.71	8.05
1997 Cincinnati	NL	2	2	0	0	10.1	49	14	9	9	4	1	0	0	6	1	5	0	0	0	1	.000	0	0-0	0	9.47	7.84
2000 Colorado	NL	8	0	0	2	13.1	72	21	19	19	5	0	1	1	11	2	15	0	0	0	1	.000	0	0-1	0	12.21	12.83
2001 Los Angeles	NL	47	3	0	2	85.1	348	73	30	30	12	6	1	1	24	3	70	0	0	6	1	.857	0	0-3	9	3.10	3.16
2002 Los Angeles	NL	63	1	0	13	90.2	387	83	34	33	14	6	2	6	32	4	56	1	0	6	3	.667	0	1-6	14	3.97	3.28
2003 Seattle	AL	23	0	0	7	29.0	137	40	22	22	6	1	0	2	14	0	13	0	0	2	0	1.000	0	0-0	4	8.10	6.83
1996 Toronto	AL	11	0	0	3	15.0	76	23	19	19	5	0	0	0	12	2	10	1	0	1	0	1.000	0	0-1	0	11.46	11.40
1996 Cincinnati	NL	8	5	0	1	23.0	112	31	17	15	6	1	0	2	13	1	13	0	0	0	0	1.000	0	0-0	0	8.62	5.87
7 ML YEARS		174	18	1	30	315.1	1410	349	196	186	62	16	6	13	137	14	209	3	0	17	11	.607	0	1-11	27	5.68	5.31

D.J. Carrasco

Pitches: R **Bats:** R **Pos:** RP-48; SP-2   **Ht:** 6'2" **Wt:** 190 **Born:** 4/12/77 **Age:** 27

Year Team	Lg	HOW MUCH HE PITCHED						WHAT HE GAVE UP											THE RESULTS							
		G	GS	CG	GF	IP	BFP	H	R	ER	HR	SH	SF	HB	TBB	IBB	SO	WP	Bk	W	L	Pct	ShO	Sv-Op	Hld	ERC	ERA
1998 Watertown	A-	13	1	0	6	31.2	145	36	23	19	3	1	0	2	14	0	38	1	0	1	1	.500	0	2--	-	5.20	5.40
1999 Williamsport	A-	18	4	0	6	51.2	212	43	20	17	2	1	3	3	23	0	49	7	4	4	2	.667	0	0--	-	3.27	2.96
1999 Lynchburg	A+	2	0	0	0	5.2	29	9	8	4	0	1	0	0	3	0	4	0	0	0	1	.000	0	0--	-	7.15	6.35
2000 Hickory	A	27	0	0	25	40.1	176	35	10	6	0	1	0	7	20	1	40	2	0	5	4	.556	0	6--	-	3.66	1.34
2000 Lynchburg	A+	8	0	0	6	10.1	45	16	5	4	1	1	0	0	8	0	10	1	0	1	0	1.000	0	0--	-	10.96	3.48
2000 Altoona	AA	9	0	0	3	14.0	68	16	14	13	0	0	0	1	13	0	10	1	0	1	1	.500	0	0--	-	6.73	8.36
2001 Lynchburg	A+	22	0	0	11	36.0	141	18	7	6	0	1	0	2	14	1	40	1	2	4	0	1.000	0	7--	-	1.29	1.50
2001 Altoona	AA	27	1	0	11	37.0	169	34	22	17	2	2	0	0	25	2	35	2	0	2	2	.500	0	1--	-	4.17	4.14
2002 Lynchburg	A+	55	0	0	44	72.2	286	52	18	13	1	4	4	6	18	1	83	2	0	4	4	.500	0	29--	-	1.86	1.61
2003 Kansas City	AL	50	2	0	21	80.1	355	82	44	43	8	1	4	4	40	4	57	6	0	6	5	.545	0	2-5	6	4.94	4.82

Hector Carrasco

Pitches: R **Bats:** R **Pos:** RP-40 · **Ht:** 6'2" **Wt:** 220 **Born:** 10/22/69 **Age:** 34

Year Team	Lg	G	GS	CG	GF	IP	BFP	H	R	ER	HR	SH	SF	HB	TBB	IBB	SO	WP	Bk	W	L	Pct	ShO	Sv-Op	Hld	ERC	ERA
2003 Ottawa*	AAA	33	0	0	16	44.2	181	32	11	11	2	4	3	0	20	2	47	7	1	4	2	.667	0	4- -		2.38	2.22
1994 Cincinnati	NL	45	0	0	0	56.1	237	42	0	14	3	0	0	0	30	0	41	0	0	5	6	.455	0	6-0	0	2.89	2.24
1995 Cincinnati	NL	64	0	0	0	87.1	391	86	0	40	1	0	0	0	46	0	64	0	0	2	7	.222	0	5-0	0	3.76	4.12
1996 Cincinnati	NL	56	0	0	0	74.1	325	58	0	31	6	0	0	0	45	0	59	0	0	4	3	.571	0	0-0	0	3.46	3.75
1997 Cin-KC		66	0	0	0	86.0	388	80	0	42	7	0	0	0	41	0	76	0	0	2	8	.200	0	0-0	0	3.66	4.40
1998 Minnesota	AL	63	0	0	0	61.2	287	75	0	30	4	0	0	0	31	0	46	0	0	4	2	.667	0	1-0	0	5.42	4.38
1999 Minnesota	AL	39	0	0	0	49.0	204	48	0	26	3	0	0	0	18	0	35	0	0	2	3	.400	0	1-0	0	3.66	4.78
2000 Min-Bos	AL	69	1	0	0	78.2	364	90	0	41	8	0	0	0	38	0	64	0	0	5	4	.556	0	1-0	0	5.13	4.69
2001 Minnesota	AL	56	0	0	0	73.2	317	77	0	38	8	0	0	0	30	0	70	0	0	4	3	.571	0	1-0	0	4.49	4.64
2003 Baltimore	AL	40	0	0	10	38.1	174	40	22	21	5	4	0	2	20	3	27	0	0	2	6	.250	0	1-3	8	5.09	4.93
1997 Cincinnati	NL	38	0	0	0	51.1	237	51	0	21	3	0	0	0	25	0	46	0	0	1	2	.333	0	0-0	0	3.84	3.68
1997 Kansas City	AL	28	0	0	0	34.2	151	29	0	21	4	0	0	0	16	0	30	0	0	1	6	.143	0	0-0	0	3.40	5.45
2000 Minnesota	AL	61	0	0	0	72.0	324	75	0	34	6	0	0	0	33	0	57	0	0	4	3	.571	0	1-0	0	4.31	4.25
2000 Boston	AL	8	1	0	0	6.2	40	15	0	7	2	0	0	0	5	0	7	0	0	1	1	.500	0	0-0	0	15.94	9.45
9 ML YEARS		**498**	**1**	**0**	**10**	**605.1**	**2687**	**596**	**22**	**283**	**45**	**4**	**0**	**2**	**299**	**3**	**482**	**0**	**0**	**30**	**42**	**.417**	**0**	**16-3**	**8**	**4.12**	**4.21**

Jamey Carroll

Bats: R **Throws:** R **Pos:** 3B-67; PH-19; PR-15; SS-14; 2B-11 · **Ht:** 5'10" **Wt:** 175 **Born:** 2/18/75 **Age:** 29

Year Team	Lg	G	AB	H	2B	3B	HR	(Hm	Rd)	TB	R	RBI	RC	TBB	IBB	SO	HBP	SH	SF	SB	CS	SB%	GDP	Avg	OBP	Slg
1996 Vermont	A-	54	203	56	6	1	0	(-	-)	64	40	17	25	29	0	25	0	3	2	16	11	.59	1	.276	.363	.315
1997 W Palm Bch	A+	121	407	99	19	1	0	(-	-)	120	56	38	41	43	0	48	4	8	4	17	11	.61	4	.243	.319	.295
1998 Jupiter	A+	55	222	58	5	0	0	(-	-)	63	40	14	25	24	1	26	5	2	1	11	4	.73	2	.261	.345	.284
1998 Harrisburg	AA	75	261	66	11	3	0	(-	-)	83	43	20	34	41	0	29	5	5	0	11	5	.69	4	.253	.365	.318
1999 Harrisburg	AA	141	561	164	34	5	5	(-	-)	223	78	63	78	48	2	58	5	5	4	21	10	.68	13	.292	.351	.398
2000 Ottawa	AAA	91	349	97	17	2	2	(-	-)	124	53	23	43	33	1	32	2	6	2	6	3	.67	9	.278	.342	.355
2000 Harrisburg	AA	45	169	49	5	3	0	(-	-)	60	23	18	20	12	0	13	0	1	1	8	2	.80	5	.290	.335	.355
2001 Ottawa	AAA	83	267	64	8	2	0	(-	-)	76	26	16	19	18	1	41	2	2	1	5	5	.50	8	.240	.292	.285
2002 Harrisburg	AA	3	9	4	0	0	0	(-	-)	4	1	1	3	3	0	0	0	0	0	0	0	-	0	.444	.583	.444
2002 Ottawa	AAA	117	421	118	19	2	8	(-	-)	165	57	49	54	37	1	39	3	7	1	6	10	.38	8	.280	.342	.392
2002 Montreal	NL	16	71	22	5	3	1	(1	0)	36	16	6	12	4	0	12	0	4	0	1	0	1.00	1	.310	.347	.507
2003 Montreal	NL	105	227	59	10	1	1	(1	0)	74	31	10	17	19	0	39	3	9	2	5	2	.71	10	.260	.323	.326
2 ML YEARS		**121**	**298**	**81**	**15**	**4**	**2**	**(2**	**0)**	**110**	**47**	**16**	**29**	**23**	**0**	**51**	**3**	**13**	**2**	**6**	**2**	**.75**	**11**	**.272**	**.328**	**.369**

Lance Carter

Pitches: R **Bats:** R **Pos:** RP-62 · **Ht:** 6'1" **Wt:** 190 **Born:** 12/18/74 **Age:** 29

Year Team	Lg	G	GS	CG	GF	IP	BFP	H	R	ER	HR	SH	SF	HB	TBB	IBB	SO	WP	Bk	W	L	Pct	ShO	Sv-Op	Hld	ERC	ERA
1999 Kansas City	AL	6	0	0	3	5.1	21	3	3	3	2	0	0	0	3	0	3	0	0	0	1	.000	0	0-0	0	4.22	5.06
2002 Tampa Bay	AL	8	0	0	7	20.1	79	15	3	3	2	0	0	0	5	1	14	0	0	2	0	1.000	0	2-2	0	2.12	1.33
2003 Tampa Bay	AL	62	0	0	55	79.0	328	72	39	38	12	1	6	4	19	6	47	0	0	7	5	.583	0	26-33	2	3.38	4.33
3 ML YEARS		**76**	**0**	**0**	**65**	**104.2**	**428**	**90**	**45**	**44**	**16**	**1**	**6**	**4**	**27**	**7**	**64**	**0**	**0**	**9**	**6**	**.600**	**0**	**28-35**	**2**	**3.16**	**3.78**

Sean Casey

Bats: L **Throws:** R **Pos:** 1B-144; PH-3 · **Ht:** 6'4" **Wt:** 225 **Born:** 7/2/74 **Age:** 29

Year Team	Lg	G	AB	H	2B	3B	HR	(Hm	Rd)	TB	R	RBI	RC	TBB	IBB	SO	HBP	SH	SF	SB	CS	SB%	GDP	Avg	OBP	Slg
1997 Cleveland	AL	6	10	2	0	0	0	(0	0)	2	1	1	1	1	0	2	1	0	0	0	0	-	0	.200	.333	.200
1998 Cincinnati	NL	96	302	82	21	1	7	(3	4)	126	44	52	45	43	3	45	3	0	3	1	1	.50	1	.272	.365	.417
1999 Cincinnati	NL	151	594	197	42	3	25	(11	14)	320	103	99	119	61	13	88	9	0	5	0	2	.00	15	.332	.399	.539
2000 Cincinnati	NL	133	480	151	33	2	20	(9	11)	248	69	85	91	52	4	80	7	0	6	1	0	1.00	16	.315	.385	.517
2001 Cincinnati	NL	145	533	165	40	0	13	(5	8)	244	69	89	86	43	8	63	9	0	3	3	1	.75	16	.310	.369	.458
2002 Cincinnati	NL	120	425	111	25	0	6	(3	3)	154	56	42	44	43	6	47	5	0	3	2	1	.67	11	.261	.334	.362
2003 Cincinnati	NL	147	573	167	19	3	14	(8	6)	234	71	80	82	51	4	58	2	0	3	4	0	1.00	19	.291	.350	.408
7 ML YEARS		**798**	**2917**	**875**	**180**	**9**	**85**	**(39**	**46)**	**1328**	**413**	**448**	**468**	**294**	**38**	**383**	**36**	**0**	**23**	**11**	**5**	**.69**	**88**	**.300**	**.369**	**.455**

Kevin Cash

Bats: R **Throws:** R **Pos:** C-34 · **Ht:** 6'0" **Wt:** 185 **Born:** 12/6/77 **Age:** 26

Year Team	Lg	G	AB	H	2B	3B	HR	(Hm	Rd)	TB	R	RBI	RC	TBB	IBB	SO	HBP	SH	SF	SB	CS	SB%	GDP	Avg	OBP	Slg
2000 Hagerstown	A	59	196	48	10	1	10	(-	-)	90	28	27	27	22	1	54	1	1	1	5	3	.63	7	.245	.323	.459
2001 Dunedin	A+	105	371	105	27	0	12	(-	-)	168	55	66	60	43	2	80	8	4	1	4	3	.57	11	.283	.369	.453
2002 Tennessee	AA	55	213	59	15	1	8	(-	-)	100	38	44	39	36	2	44	1	0	2	5	2	.71	4	.277	.381	.469
2002 Syracuse	AAA	67	236	52	18	0	10	(-	-)	100	27	26	30	25	0	72	2	2	1	0	1	.00	3	.220	.299	.424
2003 Syracuse	AAA	93	326	88	28	2	8	(-	-)	144	37	37	44	29	1	81	2	0	3	1	0	1.00	14	.270	.331	.442
2002 Toronto	AL	7	14	2	0	0	0	(0	0)	2	1	0	0	1	0	4	0	0	0	0	0	-	0	.143	.200	.143
2003 Toronto	AL	34	106	15	3	0	1	(1	0)	21	10	8	0	4	0	22	1	5	1	0	0	-	6	.142	.179	.198
2 ML YEARS		**41**	**120**	**17**	**3**	**0**	**1**	**(1**	**0)**	**23**	**11**	**8**	**0**	**5**	**0**	**26**	**1**	**5**	**1**	**0**	**0**	**-**	**7**	**.142**	**.181**	**.192**

Vinny Castilla

Bats: R **Throws:** R **Pos:** 3B-147; PH-1   **Ht:** 6'1" **Wt:** 205 **Born:** 7/4/67 **Age:** 36

Year Team	Lg	G	AB	H	2B	3B	HR	(Hm Rd)	TB	R	RBI	RC	TBB	IBB	SO	HBP	SH	SF	SB	CS	SB%	GDP	Avg	OBP	Slg
1991 Atlanta	NL	12	5	1	0	0	0	(0 0)	1	1	0	0	0	0	2	0	1	0	0	0	-	0	.200	.200	.200
1992 Atlanta	NL	9	16	4	1	0	0	(0 0)	5	1	1	2	1	1	4	1	0	0	0	0	-	0	.250	.333	.313
1993 Colorado	NL	105	337	86	9	7	9	(5 4)	136	36	30	34	13	4	45	2	0	5	2	5	.29	10	.255	.283	.404
1994 Colorado	NL	52	130	43	11	1	3	(1 2)	65	16	18	22	7	1	23	0	1	3	2	1	.67	3	.331	.357	.500
1995 Colorado	NL	139	527	163	34	2	32	(23 9)	297	82	90	94	30	2	87	4	4	6	2	8	.20	15	.309	.347	.564
1996 Colorado	NL	160	629	191	34	0	40	(27 13)	345	97	113	110	35	7	88	5	0	4	7	2	.78	20	.304	.343	.548
1997 Colorado	NL	159	612	186	25	2	40	(21 19)	335	94	113	110	44	9	108	8	0	4	2	4	.33	17	.304	.356	.547
1998 Colorado	NL	162	645	206	28	4	46	(26 20)	380	108	144	122	40	7	89	6	0	6	5	9	.36	24	.319	.362	.589
1999 Colorado	NL	158	615	169	24	1	33	(20 13)	294	83	102	93	53	7	75	1	0	5	2	3	.40	15	.275	.331	.478
2000 Tampa Bay	AL	85	331	73	9	1	6	(2 4)	102	22	42	22	14	3	41	3	0	6	1	2	.33	9	.221	.254	.308
2001 TB-Hou		146	538	140	34	1	25	(12 13)	251	69	91	70	35	3	108	4	0	4	1	4	.20	22	.260	.308	.467
2002 Atlanta	NL	143	543	126	23	2	12	(5 7)	189	56	61	36	22	4	69	7	0	6	4	1	.80	22	.232	.268	.348
2003 Atlanta	NL	147	542	150	28	3	22	(6 16)	250	65	76	70	26	3	86	3	1	6	1	2	.33	22	.277	.310	.461
2001 Tampa Bay	AL	24	93	20	6	0	2	(2 0)	32	7	9	7	3	0	22	1	0	0	0	0	-	3	.215	.247	.344
2001 Houston	NL	122	445	120	28	1	23	(10 13)	219	62	82	63	32	3	86	3	0	4	1	4	.20	19	.270	.320	.492
13 ML YEARS		1477	5470	1538	260	24	268	(148 120)	2650	730	881	785	320	51	825	44	7	55	29	41	.41	179	.281	.323	.484

Alberto Castillo

Bats: R **Throws:** R **Pos:** C-10; PH-2   **Ht:** 6'0" **Wt:** 200 **Born:** 2/10/70 **Age:** 34

Year Team	Lg	G	AB	H	2B	3B	HR	(Hm Rd)	TB	R	RBI	RC	TBB	IBB	SO	HBP	SH	SF	SB	CS	SB%	GDP	Avg	OBP	Slg
2003 Fresno*	AAA	12	34	8	1	0	0	(- -)	9	2	7	4	8	0	8	0	0	0	0	0	-	1	.235	.381	.265
1995 New York	NL	13	29	3	0	0	0	(0 0)	3	2	0	0	3	0	9	1	0	0	1	0	1.00	0	.103	.212	.103
1996 New York	NL	6	11	4	0	0	0	(0 0)	4	1	0	1	0	0	4	0	0	0	0	0	-	0	.364	.364	.364
1997 New York	NL	35	59	12	1	0	0	(0 0)	13	3	7	3	9	0	16	0	2	1	0	1	.00	3	.203	.304	.220
1998 New York	NL	38	83	17	4	0	2	(0 2)	27	13	7	7	9	0	17	1	6	0	0	2	.00	1	.205	.290	.325
1999 St Louis	NL	93	255	67	8	0	4	(2 2)	87	21	31	29	24	1	48	2	5	4	0	0	-	6	.263	.326	.341
2000 Toronto	AL	66	185	39	7	0	1	(1 0)	49	14	16	14	21	0	36	0	2	3	0	0	-	3	.211	.287	.265
2001 Toronto	AL	66	131	26	4	0	1	(0 1)	33	9	4	7	7	0	30	3	5	0	1	1	.50	2	.198	.255	.252
2002 New York	AL	15	37	5	1	1	0	(0 0)	8	3	4	1	1	0	12	0	3	0	0	0	-	2	.135	.158	.216
2003 San Francisco	NL	11	15	3	1	0	1	(1 0)	7	2	4	2	0	0	5	0	0	0	0	0	-	0	.200	.200	.467
9 ML YEARS		343	805	176	26	1	9	(4 5)	231	68	73	64	74	1	177	7	23	8	2	4	.33	17	.219	.287	.287

Luis Castillo

Bats: B **Throws:** R **Pos:** 2B-152; PH-1   **Ht:** 5'11" **Wt:** 190 **Born:** 9/12/75 **Age:** 28

Year Team	Lg	G	AB	H	2B	3B	HR	(Hm Rd)	TB	R	RBI	RC	TBB	IBB	SO	HBP	SH	SF	SB	CS	SB%	GDP	Avg	OBP	Slg
1996 Florida	NL	41	164	43	2	1	1	(0 1)	50	26	8	19	14	0	46	0	2	0	17	4	.81	0	.262	.320	.305
1997 Florida	NL	75	263	63	8	0	0	(0 0)	71	27	8	21	27	0	53	0	1	0	16	10	.62	6	.240	.310	.270
1998 Florida	NL	44	153	31	3	2	1	(0 1)	41	21	10	14	22	0	33	1	1	0	3	0	1.00	1	.203	.307	.268
1999 Florida	NL	128	487	147	23	4	0	(0 0)	178	76	28	78	67	0	85	0	6	3	50	17	.75	3	.302	.384	.366
2000 Florida	NL	136	539	180	17	3	2	(1 1)	209	101	17	95	78	0	86	0	9	4	62	22	.74	11	.334	.418	.388
2001 Florida	NL	134	537	141	16	10	2	(1 1)	183	76	45	67	67	0	90	1	4	3	33	16	.67	6	.263	.344	.341
2002 Florida	NL	146	606	185	18	5	2	(0 2)	219	86	39	80	55	4	76	2	4	1	48	15	.76	7	.305	.364	.361
2003 Florida	NL	152	595	187	19	6	6	(2 4)	236	99	39	83	63	0	60	2	15	1	21	19	.53	7	.314	.381	.397
8 ML YEARS		856	3344	977	106	31	14	(4 10)	1187	512	194	457	393	4	529	6	42	8	250	103	.71	41	.292	.367	.355

Juan Castro

Bats: R **Throws:** R **Pos:** 2B-56; 3B-30; SS-24; PH-10; 1B-1   **Ht:** 5'11" **Wt:** 195 **Born:** 6/20/72 **Age:** 32

Year Team	Lg	G	AB	H	2B	3B	HR	(Hm Rd)	TB	R	RBI	RC	TBB	IBB	SO	HBP	SH	SF	SB	CS	SB%	GDP	Avg	OBP	Slg
2003 Louisville*	AAA	9	32	7	0	0	1	(- -)	10	3	5	2	2	0	3	0	0	1	0	1	.00	2	.219	.257	.313
1995 Los Angeles	NL	11	4	1	0	0	0	(0 0)	1	0	0	1	1	0	1	0	0	0	0	0	-	0	.250	.400	.250
1996 Los Angeles	NL	70	132	26	5	3	0	(0 0)	37	16	5	8	10	0	27	0	4	0	1	0	1.00	3	.197	.254	.280
1997 Los Angeles	NL	40	75	11	3	1	0	(0 0)	16	3	4	2	7	1	20	0	2	0	0	0	-	2	.147	.220	.213
1998 Los Angeles	NL	89	220	43	7	0	2	(0 2)	56	25	14	12	15	0	37	0	9	2	0	0	-	5	.195	.245	.255
1999 Los Angeles	NL	2	1	0	0	0	0	(0 0)	0	0	0	0	0	0	1	0	0	0	0	0	-	0	.000	.000	.000
2000 Cincinnati	NL	82	224	54	12	2	4	(1 3)	82	20	23	20	14	1	33	0	4	2	0	2	.00	9	.241	.283	.366
2001 Cincinnati	NL	96	242	54	10	0	3	(0 3)	73	27	13	16	13	2	50	0	4	2	0	0	-	9	.223	.261	.302
2002 Cincinnati	NL	54	82	18	3	0	2	(0 2)	27	5	11	11	7	0	18	0	1	1	0	0	-	0	.220	.278	.329
2003 Cincinnati	NL	113	320	81	14	1	9	(4 5)	124	28	33	36	18	1	58	0	7	3	2	3	.40	7	.253	.290	.388
9 ML YEARS		557	1300	288	54	7	20	(5 15)	416	124	103	106	85	5	245	0	31	10	3	5	.38	35	.222	.267	.320

Ramon Castro

Bats: R **Throws:** R **Pos:** PH-27; C-18; DH-1   **Ht:** 6'3" **Wt:** 235 **Born:** 3/1/76 **Age:** 28

Year Team	Lg	G	AB	H	2B	3B	HR	(Hm Rd)	TB	R	RBI	RC	TBB	IBB	SO	HBP	SH	SF	SB	CS	SB%	GDP	Avg	OBP	Slg
1999 Florida	NL	24	67	12	4	0	2	(0 2)	22	4	4	6	10	3	14	0	0	1	0	0	-	1	.179	.282	.328
2000 Florida	NL	50	138	33	4	0	2	(0 2)	43	10	14	14	16	7	36	1	0	2	0	0	-	4	.239	.318	.312
2001 Florida	NL	7	11	2	0	0	0	(0 0)	2	0	1	0	1	0	1	0	0	0	0	0	-	0	.182	.250	.182
2002 Florida	NL	54	101	24	4	0	6	(4 2)	46	11	18	14	14	3	24	0	1	3	0	0	-	4	.238	.322	.455
2003 Florida	NL	40	53	15	2	0	5	(4 1)	32	6	8	8	4	0	11	0	0	0	0	0	-	0	.283	.333	.604
5 ML YEARS		175	370	86	14	0	15	(8 7)	145	31	45	42	45	13	86	1	1	6	0	0	-	6	.232	.313	.392

Frank Catalanotto

Bats: L Throws: R Pos: LF-60; RF-43; DH-19; PH-16; 1B-5; PR-1   Ht: 5'11" Wt: 195 Born: 4/27/74 Age: 30

						BATTING													BASERUNNING				AVERAGES		
Year	Team	Lg	G	AB	H	2B	3B	HR	(Hm | Rd)	TB	R	RBI	RC	TBB	IBB	SO	HBP	SH	SF	SB	CS	SB%	GDP	Avg	OBP	Slg
1997	Detroit	AL	13	26	8	2	0	0	(0 | 0)	10	2	3	4	3	0	7	0	0	0	0	0	-	0	.308	.379	.385
1998	Detroit	AL	89	213	60	13	2	6	(3 | 3)	95	23	25	30	12	1	39	4	0	5	3	2	.60	4	.282	.325	.446
1999	Detroit	AL	100	286	79	19	0	11	(6 | 5)	131	41	35	42	15	1	49	9	0	5	4	4	.43	5	.276	.327	.458
2000	Texas	AL	103	282	82	13	2	10	(6 | 4)	129	55	42	49	33	0	36	6	3	2	6	2	.75	5	.291	.375	.457
2001	Texas	AL	133	463	153	34	4	7	(4 | 7)	227	77	54	88	39	3	55	8	1	1	15	5	.75	5	.330	.384	.490
2002	Texas	AL	68	212	57	16	6	3	(2 | 1)	94	42	23	39	25	0	27	8	3	2	9	5	.64	3	.269	.364	.443
2003	Toronto	AL	133	489	146	34	6	13	(7 | 6)	231	83	59	84	35	1	62	6	2	3	2	2	.50	9	.299	.351	.472
	7 ML YEARS		639	1971	585	128	21	54	(28 | 26)	917	323	241	336	162	6	275	41	9	18	38	20	.66	31	.297	.359	.465

Roger Cedeno

Bats: B Throws: R Pos: RF-111; PH-26; CF-17; PR-4   Ht: 6'1" Wt: 205 Born: 8/16/74 Age: 29

						BATTING													BASERUNNING				AVERAGES		
Year	Team	Lg	G	AB	H	2B	3B	HR	(Hm | Rd)	TB	R	RBI	RC	TBB	IBB	SO	HBP	SH	SF	SB	CS	SB%	GDP	Avg	OBP	Slg
1995	Los Angeles	NL	40	42	10	2	0	0	(0 | 0)	12	4	3	3	3	0	10	0	0	1	1	0	1.00	1	.238	.283	.286
1996	Los Angeles	NL	86	211	52	11	1	2	(0 | 2)	71	26	18	26	24	0	47	1	2	0	5	1	.83	0	.246	.326	.336
1997	Los Angeles	NL	80	194	53	10	2	3	(3 | 0)	76	31	17	31	25	2	44	3	3	2	9	1	.90	1	.273	.362	.392
1998	Los Angeles	NL	105	240	58	11	1	2	(2 | 0)	77	33	17	27	27	2	57	0	3	1	8	2	.80	1	.242	.317	.321
1999	New York	NL	155	453	142	23	4	4	(4 | 0)	185	90	36	82	60	3	100	3	7	2	66	17	.80	5	.313	.396	.408
2000	Houston	NL	74	259	73	2	5	6	(3 | 3)	103	54	26	42	43	0	47	0	2	1	25	11	.69	6	.282	.383	.398
2001	Detroit	AL	131	523	153	14	11	6	(3 | 3)	207	79	48	76	36	1	83	2	6	5	55	15	.79	5	.293	.337	.396
2002	New York	NL	149	511	133	19	2	7	(2 | 5)	177	65	41	59	42	1	92	2	5	2	25	4	.86	10	.260	.318	.346
2003	New York	NL	148	484	129	25	4	7	(5 | 2)	183	70	37	51	38	3	86	1	2	2	14	9	.61	8	.267	.320	.378
	9 ML YEARS		968	2917	803	117	30	37	(22 | 15)	1091	452	243	397	298	12	566	12	30	16	208	60	.78	37	.275	.343	.374

Matt Cepicky

Bats: L Throws: R Pos: LF-3; PH-3; RF-1   Ht: 6'2" Wt: 215 Born: 11/10/77 Age: 26

						BATTING													BASERUNNING				AVERAGES		
Year	Team	Lg	G	AB	H	2B	3B	HR	(Hm | Rd)	TB	R	RBI	RC	TBB	IBB	SO	HBP	SH	SF	SB	CS	SB%	GDP	Avg	OBP	Slg
1999	Vermont	A-	74	323	99	15	5	12	(- | -)	160	50	53	52	20	1	49	1	0	0	10	9	.53	6	.307	.349	.495
2000	Jupiter	A+	131	536	160	32	7	5	(- | -)	221	61	88	72	24	4	64	2	1	5	32	13	.71	9	.299	.328	.412
2001	Harrisburg	AA	122	459	121	23	8	19	(- | -)	217	59	77	60	21	2	97	2	2	4	5	12	.29	6	.264	.296	.473
2002	Harrisburg	AA	109	419	116	25	2	16	(- | -)	193	54	76	61	33	4	94	2	1	8	7	1	.88	14	.277	.327	.461
2003	Edmonton	AAA	122	442	133	23	4	7	(- | -)	185	61	64	63	31	0	82	4	2	5	7	2	.78	12	.301	.349	.419
2002	Montreal	NL	32	74	16	3	0	3	(2 | 1)	28	7	15	8	4	1	21	0	0	0	0	0	-	6	.216	.256	.378
2003	Montreal	NL	5	8	2	1	0	0	(0 | 0)	3	0	0	0	0	0	2	0	0	0	0	0	-	0	.250	.250	.375
	2 ML YEARS		37	82	18	4	0	3	(2 | 1)	31	7	15	8	4	1	23	0	0	0	0	0	-	0	.220	.256	.378

Jaime Cerda

Pitches: L Bats: L Pos: RP-27   Ht: 6'0" Wt: 175 Born: 10/26/78 Age: 25

			HOW MUCH HE PITCHED						WHAT HE GAVE UP											THE RESULTS					
Year	Team	Lg	G	GS	CG	GF	IP	BFP	H	R	ER	HR	SH	SF	HB	TBB	IBB	SO	WP	Bk	W	L	Pct	ShO	Sv-Op	Hld	ERC	ERA
2000	Pittsfield	A-	20	1	0	8	47.0	176	33	6	3	0	2	0	0	6	0	51	2	0	4	1	.800	0	5--	-	1.28	0.57
2001	St.Lucie	A+	28	0	0	15	55.2	213	40	8	6	3	3	1	1	12	0	56	0	0	2	1	.667	0	6--	-	1.83	0.97
2001	Binghamton	AA	12	0	0	9	20.1	82	17	7	7	1	1	1	1	6	0	22	2	0	1	0	1.000	0	3--	-	2.72	3.10
2001	Norfolk	AAA	3	0	0	1	4.2	18	2	2	2	0	0	0	0	2	0	4	1	0	0	0	-	0	0--	-	1.08	3.86
2002	Binghamton	AA	14	0	0	5	31.2	121	21	8	8	0	1	1	0	10	0	33	2	0	5	1	.833	0	0--	-	1.59	2.27
2002	Norfolk	AAA	12	0	0	4	21.0	77	10	2	1	0	0	0	0	7	1	17	0	0	0	0	-	0	1--	-	1.03	0.43
2003	Norfolk	AAA	22	0	0	4	32.1	131	29	7	6	3	1	1	1	10	1	35	0	0	3	0	1.000	0	0--	-	3.29	1.67
2002	New York	NL	32	0	0	9	25.2	114	22	7	7	0	0	3	1	14	0	21	0	1	0	0	-	0	0-0	4	3.19	2.45
2003	New York	NL	27	0	0	9	32.1	144	32	21	21	4	2	2	0	20	1	19	3	1	1	1	.500	0	0-1	2	5.08	5.85
	2 ML YEARS		59	0	0	16	58.0	258	54	28	28	4	2	5	1	34	1	40	3	2	1	1	.500	0	0-1	6	4.21	4.34

Juan Cerros

Pitches: R Bats: R Pos: RP-11   Ht: 6'1" Wt: 200 Born: 9/25/76 Age: 27

			HOW MUCH HE PITCHED						WHAT HE GAVE UP											THE RESULTS					
Year	Team	Lg	G	GS	CG	GF	IP	BFP	H	R	ER	HR	SH	SF	HB	TBB	IBB	SO	WP	Bk	W	L	Pct	ShO	Sv-Op	Hld	ERC	ERA
1999	St.Lucie	A+	5	0	0	2	7.2	32	5	1	0	0	0	0	1	4	0	6	0	1	2	0	1.000	0	0--	-	2.52	0.00
2000	Binghamton	AA	50	2	0	23	74.2	327	71	33	29	8	0	3	4	30	1	52	6	0	10	4	.714	0	3--	-	3.98	3.50
2001	Binghamton	AA	13	0	0	7	18.1	86	24	10	10	2	0	0	0	7	0	14	3	0	1	2	.333	0	0--	-	5.74	4.91
2001	Norfolk	AAA	38	1	0	8	57.0	257	65	33	25	5	1	6	4	22	3	32	5	0	1	3	.250	0	1--	-	4.90	3.95
2002	Binghamton	AA	3	0	0	1	3.0	9	0	0	0	0	0	0	0	3	0	3	0	0	0	0	-	0	0--	-	0.00	0.00
2002	Norfolk	AAA	25	3	0	6	37.2	167	40	21	14	2	1	2	0	11	0	23	1	1	1	3	.250	0	2--	-	3.51	3.35
2003	Louisville	AAA	4	0	0	1	4.0	17	6	2	2	0	0	0	0	1	0	1	0	0	0	0	-	0	0--	-	4.76	4.50
2003	Cincinnati	NL	11	0	0	2	13.0	57	11	7	7	1	0	1	2	5	2	9	0	0	0	0	-	0	0-0	0	3.27	4.85

Shawn Chacon

Pitches: R Bats: R Pos: SP-23   Ht: 6'3" Wt: 212 Born: 12/23/77 Age: 26

			HOW MUCH HE PITCHED						WHAT HE GAVE UP											THE RESULTS					
Year	Team	Lg	G	GS	CG	GF	IP	BFP	H	R	ER	HR	SH	SF	HB	TBB	IBB	SO	WP	Bk	W	L	Pct	ShO	Sv-Op	Hld	ERC	ERA
2003	Co Springs*	AAA	1	1	0	0	3.0	13	5	2	2	1	0	0	0	2	0	2	1	0	0	0	-	0	0--	-	8.70	6.00
2001	Colorado	NL	27	27	0	0	160.0	711	157	96	90	26	6	3	10	87	10	134	6	0	6	10	.375	0	0-0	0	5.22	5.06
2002	Colorado	NL	21	21	0	0	119.1	537	122	84	76	25	5	2	7	60	3	67	0	1	5	11	.313	0	0-0	0	5.63	5.73
2003	Colorado	NL	23	23	0	0	137.0	596	124	73	70	12	10	5	12	58	4	93	8	0	11	8	.579	0	0-0	0	3.82	4.60
	3 ML YEARS		71	71	0	0	416.1	1844	403	253	236	63	21	10	29	205	17	294	14	1	22	29	.431	0	0-0	0	4.86	5.10

Jim Chamblee

Bats: R Throws: R Pos: 3B-1; PH-1   Ht: 6'4" Wt: 176 Born: 5/6/75 Age: 29

										BATTING											BASERUNNING				AVERAGES		
Year Team	Lg	G	AB	H	2B	3B	HR	(Hm	Rd)	TB	R	RBI	RC	TBB	IBB	SO	HBP	SH	SF	SB	CS	SB%	GDP	Avg	OBP	Slg
1995 Utica	A-	62	200	51	9	1	2	(-	-)	68	36	16	24	23	0	45	6	1	1	9	7	.56	5	.255	.348	.340
1996 Michigan	A	100	303	66	15	2	1	(-	-)	88	31	39	24	16	0	75	7	4	4	2	2	.50	1	.218	.270	.290
1997 Michigan	A	133	487	146	29	5	22	(-	-)	251	112	73	97	53	3	107	17	0	5	18	4	.82	8	.300	.384	.515
1998 Trenton	AA	136	489	118	33	3	17	(-	-)	208	71	65	76	62	1	144	16	6	4	9	5	.64	2	.241	.343	.425
1999 Pawtucket	AAA	127	464	127	21	3	24	(-	-)	226	84	88	79	43	2	126	13	4	3	5	3	.63	4	.274	.350	.487
2000 Pawtucket	AAA	127	407	105	26	4	17	(-	-)	190	72	56	68	50	1	129	7	2	2	8	3	.73	4	.258	.348	.467
2001 Pawtucket	AAA	103	378	91	22	0	10	(-	-)	143	40	32	44	31	4	104	6	5	1	8	5	.62	4	.241	.308	.378
2001 New Orleans	AAA	11	35	9	2	0	1	(-	-)	14	3	4	5	4	0	13	1	1	0	0	0	-	1	.257	.350	.400
2002 New Haven	AA	122	434	119	32	3	17	(-	-)	208	77	72	75	48	1	92	8	1	3	8	2	.80	5	.274	.355	.479
2002 Memphis	AAA	5	10	1	0	0	0	(-	-)	1	1	1	0	1	0	4	0	0	0	0	0	-	0	.100	.182	.100
2003 Louisville	AAA	85	263	75	13	4	5	(-	-)	111	31	35	41	29	0	59	5	4	1	2	0	1.00	6	.285	.366	.422
2003 Chattanooga	AA	28	102	34	7	0	4	(-	-)	53	16	16	22	9	0	27	5	0	0	3	1	.75	1	.333	.414	.520
2003 Cincinnati	NL	2	2	0	0	0	0	(0	0)	0	0	0	0	0	0	2	0	0	0	0	0	-	0	.000	.000	.000

Travis Chapman

Bats: R Throws: R Pos: 3B-1; PH-1   Ht: 6'2" Wt: 185 Born: 6/5/78 Age: 26

										BATTING											BASERUNNING				AVERAGES		
Year Team	Lg	G	AB	H	2B	3B	HR	(Hm	Rd)	TB	R	RBI	RC	TBB	IBB	SO	HBP	SH	SF	SB	CS	SB%	GDP	Avg	OBP	Slg
2000 Phillies	R	9	32	6	3	1	0	(-	-)	11	3	5	4	4	0	4	2	0	1	0	1	.00	0	.188	.308	.344
2000 Batavia	A-	49	174	55	10	2	1	(-	-)	72	23	28	28	12	0	24	7	2	2	0	1	.00	1	.316	.379	.414
2001 Clearwater	A+	96	329	101	22	0	4	(-	-)	135	39	50	55	44	3	39	11	2	6	3	1	.75	12	.307	.400	.410
2001 Reading	AA	7	22	4	0	0	1	(-	-)	7	3	3	2	0	0	5	2	0	0	0	0	-	0	.182	.250	.318
2002 Reading	AA	136	478	144	35	1	15	(-	-)	226	64	76	88	54	9	77	19	2	8	3	1	.75	11	.301	.388	.473
2003 Scrtn/WlksBr	AAA	134	478	130	36	0	12	(-	-)	202	62	82	70	44	1	97	15	0	6	2	2	.50	12	.272	.348	.423
2003 Philadelphia	NL	1	1	0	0	0	0	(0	0)	0	0	0	0	0	0	0	0	0	0	0	0	-	0	.000	.000	.000

Endy Chavez

Bats: L Throws: L Pos: CF-135; PH-10; PR-5   Ht: 6'0" Wt: 165 Born: 2/7/78 Age: 26

										BATTING											BASERUNNING				AVERAGES		
Year Team	Lg	G	AB	H	2B	3B	HR	(Hm	Rd)	TB	R	RBI	RC	TBB	IBB	SO	HBP	SH	SF	SB	CS	SB%	GDP	Avg	OBP	Slg
2001 Kansas City	AL	29	77	16	2	0	0	(0	0)	18	4	5	2	3	0	8	0	0	0	0	2	.00	3	.208	.238	.234
2002 Montreal	NL	36	125	37	8	5	1	(0	1)	58	20	9	14	5	0	16	0	7	1	3	5	.38	0	.296	.321	.464
2003 Montreal	NL	141	483	121	25	5	5	(4	1)	171	66	47	56	31	3	59	0	9	3	18	7	.72	7	.251	.294	.354
3 ML YEARS		206	685	174	35	10	6	(4	2)	247	90	61	72	39	3	83	0	16	4	21	14	.60	10	.254	.293	.361

Eric Chavez

Bats: L Throws: R Pos: 3B-154; PH-2   Ht: 6'1" Wt: 206 Born: 12/7/77 Age: 26

										BATTING											BASERUNNING				AVERAGES		
Year Team	Lg	G	AB	H	2B	3B	HR	(Hm	Rd)	TB	R	RBI	RC	TBB	IBB	SO	HBP	SH	SF	SB	CS	SB%	GDP	Avg	OBP	Slg
1998 Oakland	AL	16	45	14	4	1	0	(0	0)	20	6	6	7	3	1	5	0	0	0	1	1	.50	1	.311	.354	.444
1999 Oakland	AL	115	356	88	21	2	13	(8	5)	152	47	50	50	46	4	56	0	0	5	1	1	.50	7	.247	.333	.427
2000 Oakland	AL	153	501	139	23	4	26	(15	11)	248	89	86	86	62	8	94	1	0	5	2	2	.50	9	.277	.355	.495
2001 Oakland	AL	151	552	159	43	0	32	(14	18)	298	91	114	99	41	9	99	4	0	7	8	2	.80	7	.288	.338	.540
2002 Oakland	AL	153	585	161	31	3	34	(17	17)	300	87	109	105	65	13	119	1	0	2	8	3	.73	8	.275	.348	.513
2003 Oakland	AL	156	588	166	39	5	29	(12	17)	302	94	101	99	62	10	89	1	0	3	8	3	.73	14	.282	.350	.514
6 ML YEARS		744	2627	727	161	15	134	(66	68)	1320	414	466	446	279	45	462	7	0	17	28	12	.70	46	.277	.346	.502

Raul Chavez

Bats: R Throws: R Pos: C-16; PH-3   Ht: 5'11" Wt: 210 Born: 3/18/73 Age: 31

										BATTING											BASERUNNING				AVERAGES		
Year Team	Lg	G	AB	H	2B	3B	HR	(Hm	Rd)	TB	R	RBI	RC	TBB	IBB	SO	HBP	SH	SF	SB	CS	SB%	GDP	Avg	OBP	Slg
2003 New Orleans*	AAA	101	355	97	28	1	6	(-	-)	145	47	47	43	13	1	43	11	6	5	0	2	.00	11	.273	.315	.408
1996 Montreal	NL	4	5	1	0	0	0	(0	0)	1	1	0	0	1	0	1	0	0	0	1	0	1.00	1	.200	.333	.200
1997 Montreal	NL	13	26	7	0	0	0	(0	0)	7	0	2	2	0	0	5	0	0	1	1	0	1.00	0	.269	.259	.269
1998 Seattle	AL	1	1	0	0	0	0	(0	0)	0	0	0	0	0	0	0	0	0	0	0	0	-	0	.000	.000	.000
2000 Houston	NL	14	43	11	2	0	1	(0	1)	16	3	5	3	3	2	6	0	0	0	0	0	-	5	.256	.298	.372
2002 Houston	NL	2	4	1	1	0	0	(0	0)	2	1	0	1	1	0	0	0	0	0	0	0	-	0	.250	.500	.500
2003 Houston	NL	19	37	10	1	1	1	(0	1)	16	5	4	3	1	0	6	0	0	0	0	0	-	3	.270	.289	.432
6 ML YEARS		53	116	30	4	1	2	(0	2)	42	10	11	9	6	2	18	0	0	2	2	0	1.00	9	.259	.296	.362

Bruce Chen

Pitches: L Bats: L Pos: RP-14; SP-2   Ht: 6'2" Wt: 210 Born: 6/19/77 Age: 27

		HOW MUCH HE PITCHED							WHAT HE GAVE UP											THE RESULTS						
Year Team	Lg	G	GS	CG	GF	IP	BFP	H	R	ER	HR	SH	SF	HB	TBB	IBB	SO	WP	Bk	W	L	Pct	ShO	Sv-Op	Hld	ERC	ERA
2003 Pawtucket*	AAA	16	15	1	1	85.0	347	80	44	40	12	1	1	2	15	1	73	2	0	5	5	.500	1	1- -	-	3.22	4.24
1998 Atlanta	NL	4	4	0	0	20.1	91	23	9	9	3	1	0	1	9	1	17	0	0	2	0	1.000	0	0-0	0	5.55	3.98
1999 Atlanta	NL	16	7	0	3	51.0	214	38	32	31	11	1	1	2	27	3	45	0	0	2	2	.500	0	0-0	0	4.07	5.47
2000 Atl-Phi	NL	37	15	0	4	134.0	559	116	54	49	18	8	3	2	46	4	112	4	1	7	4	.636	0	0-0	0	3.35	3.29
2001 Phi-NYM	NL	27	27	0	0	146.0	634	146	90	79	29	4	7	1	59	4	126	5	0	7	7	.500	0	0-0	0	4.75	4.87
2002 NYM-Mon-Cin	NL	55	6	0	9	77.2	360	85	53	48	16	2	3	2	43	5	80	4	0	2	5	.286	0	0-0	1	5.99	5.56
2003 Hou-Bos	NL	16	2	0	4	24.1	110	26	16	15	6	3	3	2	10	1	20	0	0	0	1	.000	0	0-0	0	5.81	5.55
2000 Atlanta	NL	22	0	0	4	39.2	176	35	15	11	4	3	2	1	19	2	32	0	1	4	0	1.000	0	0-0	0	3.62	2.50
2000 Philadelphia	NL	15	15	0	0	94.1	383	81	39	38	14	5	1	1	27	2	80	4	0	3	4	.429	0	0-0	0	3.22	3.63
2001 Philadelphia	NL	16	16	0	0	86.1	381	90	53	48	19	2	4	1	31	4	79	2	0	4	5	.444	0	0-0	0	4.87	5.00
2001 New York	NL	11	11	0	0	59.2	253	56	37	31	10	2	3	0	28	0	47	3	0	3	2	.600	0	0-0	0	4.58	4.68

Year Team	Lg	G	GS	CG	GF	IP	BFP	H	R	ER	HR	SH	SF	HB	TBB	IBB	SO	WP	Bk	W	L	Pct	ShO	Sv-Op	Hld	ERC	ERA
2002 New York	NL	1	0	0	0	0.2	3	1	0	0	0	0	0	0	0	0	0	0	0	0	0	-	0	0-0	0	4.47	0.00
2002 Montreal	NL	15	5	0	4	37.1	179	47	29	29	9	0	0	1	23	3	43	3	0	2	3	.400	0	0-0	0	7.69	6.99
2002 Cincinnati	NL	39	1	0	5	39.2	178	37	24	19	7	2	3	1	20	2	37	1	0	0	2	.000	0	0-0	4	4.55	4.31
2003 Houston	NL	11	0	0	2	12.0	60	14	8	8	2	3	2	2	8	1	8	0	0	0	0	-	0	0-0	1	7.11	6.00
2003 Boston	AL	5	2	0	2	12.1	50	12	8	7	4	0	1	0	2	0	12	0	0	0	1	.000	0	0-0	0	4.40	5.11
6 ML YEARS		155	61	0	20	453.1	1968	434	254	231	83	19	17	10	194	18	400	13	1	20	19	.513	0	0-0	5	4.54	4.59

Chin-Feng Chen

Bats: R **Throws:** R **Pos:** PH-1   **Ht:** 6'1" **Wt:** 189 **Born:** 10/28/77 **Age:** 26

Year Team	Lg	G	AB	H	2B	3B	HR	(Hm	Rd)	TB	R	RBI	RC	TBB	IBB	SO	HBP	SH	SF	SB	CS	SB%	GDP	Avg	OBP	Slg
1999 Sn Brnardino	A+	131	510	161	22	10	31	(-	-)	296	98	123	119	75	6	129	5	0	7	31	7	.82	7	.316	.404	.580
2000 San Antonio	AA	133	516	143	27	3	6	(-	-)	194	66	67	70	61	3	131	1	3	1	23	15	.61	7	.277	.355	.376
2001 Vero Beach	A+	62	235	63	15	3	5	(-	-)	99	38	41	37	28	2	56	6	0	1	2	0	1.00	3	.268	.359	.421
2001 Jacksonville	AA	66	224	70	16	2	17	(-	-)	141	47	50	54	41	4	65	2	1	1	5	4	.56	7	.313	.422	.629
2002 Las Vegas	AAA	137	511	145	26	4	26	(-	-)	257	90	84	85	58	1	160	0	0	7	1	0	1.00	19	.284	.352	.503
2003 Las Vegas	AAA	133	474	133	30	5	26	(-	-)	251	84	86	86	59	1	106	2	0	4	6	4	.60	15	.281	.360	.530
2002 Los Angeles	NL	3	5	0	0	0	0	(0	0)	0	1	0	0	1	0	3	0	0	0	0	0	-	0	.000	.167	.000
2003 Los Angeles	NL	1	1	0	0	0	0	(0	0)	0	0	0	0	0	0	0	0	0	0	0	0	-	0	.000	.000	.000
2 ML YEARS		4	6	0	0	0	0	(0	0)	0	1	0	0	1	0	3	0	0	0	0	0	-	0	.000	.143	.000

Randy Choate

Pitches: L **Bats:** L **Pos:** RP-5   **Ht:** 6'1" **Wt:** 180 **Born:** 9/5/75 **Age:** 28

Year Team	Lg	G	GS	CG	GF	IP	BFP	H	R	ER	HR	SH	SF	HB	TBB	IBB	SO	WP	Bk	W	L	Pct	ShO	Sv-Op	Hld	ERC	ERA
2003 Columbus*	AAA	54	3	0	15	71.1	312	75	35	31	4	7	1	3	24	3	56	0	0	3	5	.375	0	1--	-	3.85	3.91
2000 New York	AL	22	0	0	6	12.0	75	14	10	9	3	0	1	1	8	0	12	1	0	0	1	.000	0	0-0	2	3.99	4.76
2001 New York	AL	37	0	0	13	48.1	207	34	21	18	0	2	1	9	27	2	35	3	0	3	1	.750	0	0-0	3	3.03	3.35
2002 New York	AL	18	0	0	11	22.1	101	18	18	15	1	0	0	3	15	0	17	4	0	0	0	-	0	0-0	4	4.13	6.04
2003 New York	AL	5	0	0	2	3.2	16	7	3	3	0	0	0	0	1	0	0	0	0	0	0	-	0	0-0	5	9.72	7.36
4 ML YEARS		82	0	0	32	91.1	399	73	52	45	4	2	2	13	51	2	64	8	0	3	2	.600	0	0-0	5	3.70	4.43

Hee Seop Choi

Bats: L **Throws:** L **Pos:** 1B-69; PH-13; PR-3   **Ht:** 6'5" **Wt:** 235 **Born:** 3/16/79 **Age:** 25

Year Team	Lg	G	AB	H	2B	3B	HR	(Hm	Rd)	TB	R	RBI	RC	TBB	IBB	SO	HBP	SH	SF	SB	CS	SB%	GDP	Avg	OBP	Slg
1999 Lansing	A	79	290	93	18	6	18	(-	-)	177	71	70	70	50	0	68	2	0	2	2	1	.67	8	.321	.422	.610
2000 Daytona	A+	96	345	102	25	6	15	(-	-)	184	60	70	66	37	5	78	6	0	5	4	1	.80	7	.296	.369	.533
2000 W Tennese	AA	36	122	37	9	0	10	(-	-)	76	25	25	30	25	0	38	0	0	1	3	1	.75	5	.303	.419	.623
2001 Iowa	AAA	77	266	61	11	0	13	(-	-)	111	38	45	36	34	1	67	0	0	4	5	1	.83	5	.229	.313	.417
2002 Iowa	AAA	135	478	137	24	3	26	(-	-)	245	94	97	102	95	4	119	6	0	7	3	2	.60	6	.287	.406	.513
2003 Iowa	AAA	18	66	17	4	1	6	(-	-)	41	12	16	13	9	0	19	1	0	1	0	1	.00	2	.258	.351	.621
2002 Chicago	NL	24	50	9	1	0	2	(1	1)	16	6	4	2	7	0	15	0	0	0	0	0	-	2	.180	.281	.320
2003 Chicago	NL	80	202	44	17	0	8	(5	3)	85	31	28	29	37	1	71	4	2	0	1	1	.50	2	.218	.350	.421
2 ML YEARS		104	252	53	18	0	10	(6	4)	101	37	32	31	44	1	86	4	2	0	1	1	.50	2	.210	.337	.401

Ryan Christenson

Bats: R **Throws:** R **Pos:** CF-59; PR-5   **Ht:** 6'0" **Wt:** 191 **Born:** 3/28/74 **Age:** 30

Year Team	Lg	G	AB	H	2B	3B	HR	(Hm	Rd)	TB	R	RBI	RC	TBB	IBB	SO	HBP	SH	SF	SB	CS	SB%	GDP	Avg	OBP	Slg
2003 Oklahoma*	AAA	52	195	61	15	1	5	(-	-)	93	30	24	38	28	0	45	1	2	1	11	1	.92	6	.313	.400	.477
1998 Oakland	AL	117	370	95	22	2	5	(2	3)	136	56	40	45	36	0	106	1	10	4	5	6	.45	1	.257	.321	.368
1999 Oakland	AL	106	268	56	12	1	4	(2	2)	82	41	24	26	38	0	58	1	8	4	7	5	.58	6	.209	.305	.306
2000 Oakland	AL	121	129	32	2	2	4	(3	1)	50	31	18	18	19	0	33	1	4	0	1	2	.33	1	.248	.349	.388
2001 Oak-Ari		26	8	1	1	0	0	(0	0)	2	4	1	1	1	0	2	0	0	0	1	0	1.00	0	.125	.222	.250
2002 Milwaukee	NL	22	58	9	4	0	1	(0	1)	16	5	3	1	5	0	13	0	3	0	0	0	-	1	.155	.222	.276
2003 Texas	AL	60	165	29	7	0	2	(2	0)	42	22	16	11	15	0	44	3	2	1	2	2	.50	3	.176	.255	.255
2001 Oakland	AL	7	4	0	0	0	0	(0	0)	0	1	0	0	0	0	1	0	0	0	0	0	-	0	.000	.000	.000
2001 Arizona	NL	19	4	1	1	0	0	(0	0)	2	3	1	1	1	0	1	0	0	0	1	0	1.00	0	.250	.400	.500
6 ML YEARS		452	998	222	48	5	16	(9	7)	328	159	102	102	114	0	256	6	27	9	16	15	.52	12	.222	.303	.329

Jason Christiansen

Pitches: L **Bats:** R **Pos:** RP-40   **Ht:** 6'5" **Wt:** 241 **Born:** 9/21/69 **Age:** 34

Year Team	Lg	G	GS	CG	GF	IP	BFP	H	R	ER	HR	SH	SF	HB	TBB	IBB	SO	WP	Bk	W	L	Pct	ShO	Sv-Op	Hld	ERC	ERA
2003 Fresno*	AAA	4	1	0	0	5.0	22	5	3	3	0	0	1	1	1	0	2	0	0	0	0	-	0	0--	-	3.28	5.40
2003 San Jose*	A+	5	1	0	0	4.2	20	5	1	1	0	0	1	0	3	0	2	0	0	0	0	-	0	0--	-	5.04	1.93
1995 Pittsburgh	NL	63	0	0	13	56.1	255	49	28	26	5	6	3	3	34	9	53	4	1	1	3	.250	0	0-4	12	3.89	4.15
1996 Pittsburgh	NL	33	0	0	9	44.1	205	56	34	33	7	2	3	1	19	2	38	4	1	3	3	.500	0	0-2	6	6.19	6.70
1997 Pittsburgh	NL	39	0	0	9	33.2	154	37	11	11	2	0	0	2	17	3	37	4	0	3	0	1.000	0	0-2	8	2.94	2.94
1998 Pittsburgh	NL	60	0	0	19	64.2	269	51	22	18	2	5	1	0	27	7	71	3	0	3	3	.500	0	6-10	15	2.39	2.51
1999 Pittsburgh	NL	39	0	0	17	37.2	158	26	17	17	2	2	1	2	22	4	35	0	0	2	3	.400	0	3-5	7	2.85	4.06
2000 Pit-StL	NL	65	0	0	19	48.0	210	41	29	27	3	4	1	2	27	5	53	3	0	3	8	.273	0	1-4	22	3.60	5.06
2001 StL-SF	NL	55	0	0	11	36.1	149	29	13	13	5	1	3	1	15	1	31	4	0	2	1	.667	0	3-4	11	3.41	3.22
2002 San Francisco	NL	6	0	0	2	5.0	21	8	3	3	1	1	0	0	2	0	1	0	0	1	0	1.000	0	0-0	6	6.48	5.40
2003 San Francisco	NL	40	0	0	7	26.0	115	25	15	15	3	0	0	1	11	0	22	2	0	0	1	.000	0	0-1	7	4.11	5.19
2000 Pittsburgh	NL	44	0	0	17	38.0	164	28	22	21	2	3	1	0	25	4	41	3	0	2	8	.200	0	1-3	13	3.11	4.97
2000 St Louis	NL	21	0	0	2	10.0	46	13	7	6	1	1	0	2	2	1	12	0	0	1	0	1.000	0	0-1	9	5.64	5.40

Year Team	Lg	HOW MUCH HE PITCHED						WHAT HE GAVE UP												THE RESULTS							
		G	GS	CG	GF	IP	BFP	H	R	ER	HR	SH	SF	HB	TBB	IBB	SO	WP	Bk	W	L	Pct	ShO	Sv-Op	Hld	ERC	ERA
2001 St Louis	NL	30	0	0	8	19.1	83	15	10	10	4	0	1	0	10	1	19	0	0	1	1	.500	0	3-3	4	4.12	4.66
2001 San Francisco	NL	25	0	0	3	17.0	66	14	3	3	1	1	2	0	5	0	12	4	0	1	0	1.000	0	0-1	7	2.62	1.59
9 ML YEARS		400	0	0	106	352.0	1536	320	172	163	30	20	12	12	174	31	341	24	2	17	22	.436	0	13-32	84	3.80	4.17

Vinnie Chulk

Pitches: R **Bats:** R **Pos:** RP-3   **Ht:** 6'2" **Wt:** 185 **Born:** 12/19/78 **Age:** 25

Year Team	Lg	HOW MUCH HE PITCHED						WHAT HE GAVE UP												THE RESULTS							
		G	GS	CG	GF	IP	BFP	H	R	ER	HR	SH	SF	HB	TBB	IBB	SO	WP	Bk	W	L	Pct	ShO	Sv-Op	Hld	ERC	ERA
2000 Medicine Hat	R+	14	13	0	0	68.2	295	75	36	29	5	0	2	2	20	0	51	3	0	2	4	.333	0	0--	-	4.11	3.80
2001 Dunedin	A+	16	1	0	4	34.2	157	38	16	12	2	2	2	0	13	1	50	4	0	1	2	.333	0	1--	-	4.00	3.12
2001 Tennessee	AA	24	1	0	7	43.0	169	34	15	15	5	5	4	2	8	1	43	1	0	2	5	.286	0	2--	-	2.45	3.14
2001 Syracuse	AAA	5	0	0	2	6.0	25	5	1	0	1	0	0	0	4	0	3	3	0	1	0	1.000	0	0--	-	4.98	0.00
2002 Tennessee	AA	25	24	0	1	152.0	626	133	55	50	12	3	2	5	53	0	108	6	0	13	5	.722	0	1--	-	3.24	2.96
2002 Syracuse	AAA	2	1	0	1	4.2	27	6	6	3	0	0	2	0	6	0	2	2	0	0	1	.000	0	0--	-	8.06	5.79
2003 Syracuse	AAA	23	21	1	1	119.1	524	118	70	56	14	6	6	5	46	0	90	5	0	8	10	.444	0	0--	-	4.17	4.22
2003 Toronto	AL	3	0	0	2	5.1	25	6	3	3	0	0	0	0	3	0	2	0	0	0	0	-	0	0-1	0	4.53	5.06

Alex Cintron

Bats: B **Throws:** R **Pos:** SS-93; 3B-16; 2B-9; PH-8   **Ht:** 6'2" **Wt:** 185 **Born:** 12/17/78 **Age:** 25

Year Team	Lg	BATTING																	BASERUNNING				AVERAGES		
		G	AB	H	2B	3B	HR	(Hm	Rd)	TB	R	RBI	RC	TBB	IBB	SO	HBP	SH	SF	SB	CS	SB%	GDP	Avg	OBP	Slg
2003 Tucson*	AAA	26	107	42	11	2	2	(-	-)	63	21	21	26	8	0	6	0	0	0	1	0	1.00	0	.393	.435	.589
2001 Arizona	NL	8	7	2	0	1	0	(0	0)	4	0	0	1	0	0	0	0	0	0	0	0	-	0	.286	.286	.571
2002 Arizona	NL	38	75	16	6	0	0	(0	0)	22	11	4	5	12	2	13	0	3	0	0	0	-	2	.213	.322	.293
2003 Arizona	NL	117	448	142	26	6	13	(6	7)	219	70	51	69	29	0	33	2	5	3	2	3	.40	7	.317	.359	.489
3 ML YEARS		163	530	160	32	7	13	(6	7)	245	81	55	75	41	2	46	2	8	3	2	3	.40	9	.302	.352	.462

Jeff Cirillo

Bats: R **Throws:** R **Pos:** 3B-85; PR-2; 1B-1   **Ht:** 6'1" **Wt:** 190 **Born:** 9/23/69 **Age:** 34

Year Team	Lg	BATTING																	BASERUNNING				AVERAGES		
		G	AB	H	2B	3B	HR	(Hm	Rd)	TB	R	RBI	RC	TBB	IBB	SO	HBP	SH	SF	SB	CS	SB%	GDP	Avg	OBP	Slg
2003 InlandEmpire*	A+	5	15	3	1	0	0	(-	-)	4	1	1	1	3	0	1	0	0	0	0	0	-	1	.200	.333	.267
2003 Tacoma*	AAA	5	17	6	3	0	2	(-	-)	15	7	6	6	3	0	3	1	0	0	0	0	-	0	.353	.476	.882
2003 Mariners*	R	6	24	7	0	0	0	(-	-)	7	2	0	3	4	0	2	1	0	0	0	1	.00	1	.292	.414	.292
1994 Milwaukee	NL	39	126	30	9	0	3	(1	2)	48	17	12	14	11	0	16	2	0	0	1	0	.00	4	.238	.309	.381
1995 Milwaukee	NL	125	328	91	19	4	9	(6	3)	145	57	39	55	47	0	42	4	1	4	7	2	.78	8	.277	.371	.442
1996 Milwaukee	NL	158	566	184	46	5	15	(6	9)	285	101	83	105	58	0	69	7	6	6	4	9	.31	14	.325	.391	.504
1997 Milwaukee	NL	154	580	167	46	2	10	(6	4)	247	74	82	91	60	0	74	14	4	3	4	3	.57	13	.288	.367	.426
1998 Milwaukee	NL	156	604	194	31	4	14	(6	8)	269	97	68	103	79	3	88	4	5	2	10	4	.71	26	.321	.402	.445
1999 Milwaukee	NL	157	607	198	35	1	15	(6	9)	280	98	88	111	75	4	83	5	3	7	7	4	.64	15	.326	.401	.461
2000 Colorado	NL	157	598	195	53	2	11	(9	2)	285	111	115	108	67	4	72	6	1	12	3	4	.43	19	.326	.392	.477
2001 Colorado	NL	138	528	165	26	4	17	(9	8)	250	72	83	89	43	6	63	5	1	9	12	2	.86	15	.313	.364	.473
2002 Seattle	AL	146	485	121	20	0	6	(2	4)	159	51	54	50	31	0	67	9	13	9	8	4	.67	12	.249	.301	.328
2003 Seattle	AL	87	258	53	11	0	2	(1	1)	70	24	23	22	24	1	32	5	4	2	1	1	.50	6	.205	.284	.271
10 ML YEARS		1317	4680	1398	296	19	102	(52	50)	2038	702	647	748	495	18	606	61	38	54	56	34	.62	132	.299	.369	.435

Brady Clark

Bats: R **Throws:** R **Pos:** RF-82; PH-40; LF-25; CF-6   **Ht:** 6'2" **Wt:** 195 **Born:** 4/18/73 **Age:** 31

Year Team	Lg	BATTING																	BASERUNNING				AVERAGES		
		G	AB	H	2B	3B	HR	(Hm	Rd)	TB	R	RBI	RC	TBB	IBB	SO	HBP	SH	SF	SB	CS	SB%	GDP	Avg	OBP	Slg
2003 Indianapolis*	AAA	9	34	9	3	0	0	(-	-)	12	4	3	3	2	0	6	0	0	0	1	0	1.00	3	.265	.306	.353
2000 Cincinnati	NL	11	11	3	1	0	0	(0	0)	4	1	2	1	0	0	2	0	0	0	0	0	-	0	.273	.273	.364
2001 Cincinnati	NL	89	129	34	3	0	6	(4	2)	55	22	18	21	22	1	16	1	4	1	4	1	.80	6	.264	.373	.426
2002 Cin-NYM	NL	61	78	15	4	0	0	(0	0)	19	9	10	6	7	2	11	1	1	0	1	2	.33	2	.192	.267	.244
2003 Milwaukee	NL	128	315	86	21	1	6	(5	1)	127	33	40	40	21	0	40	9	2	7	13	2	.87	12	.273	.330	.403
2002 Cincinnati	NL	51	66	10	3	0	0	(0	0)	13	6	9	4	6	2	9	1	1	0	1	2	.33	2	.152	.233	.197
2002 New York	NL	10	12	5	1	0	0	(0	0)	6	3	1	2	1	0	2	0	0	0	0	0	-	0	.417	.462	.500
4 ML YEARS		289	533	138	29	1	12	(9	3)	205	65	70	68	50	3	69	11	7	8	18	5	.78	20	.259	.331	.385

Howie Clark

Bats: L **Throws:** R **Pos:** 3B-13; PH-10; LF-4; DH-4; 2B-3; PR-3; 1B-2; SS-1; RF-1   **Ht:** 5'11" **Wt:** 180 **Born:** 2/13/74 **Age:** 30

Year Team	Lg	BATTING																	BASERUNNING				AVERAGES		
		G	AB	H	2B	3B	HR	(Hm	Rd)	TB	R	RBI	RC	TBB	IBB	SO	HBP	SH	SF	SB	CS	SB%	GDP	Avg	OBP	Slg
1992 Orioles	R	43	138	33	7	1	0	(-	-)	42	12	6	13	12	2	21	2	1	0	1	2	.33	2	.239	.309	.304
1993 Albany	A	7	17	4	0	0	0	(-	-)	4	2	1	1	0	0	3	0	0	0	1	0	1.00	1	.235	.235	.235
1993 Bluefield	R+	58	180	53	10	1	3	(-	-)	74	29	30	30	26	2	34	4	1	4	2	2	.50	4	.294	.388	.411
1994 Albany	A	108	353	95	22	7	2	(-	-)	137	56	47	53	51	3	58	7	4	1	5	4	.56	7	.269	.371	.388
1994 Frederick	A+	2	7	1	1	0	0	(-	-)	2	1	0	0	0	0	2	0	0	0	0	0	-	0	.143	.143	.286
1995 High Desert	A+	100	329	85	20	2	5	(-	-)	124	50	40	42	32	0	51	4	3	3	12	6	.67	4	.258	.329	.377
1996 Bowie	AA	127	449	122	29	3	4	(-	-)	169	55	52	61	59	1	54	2	10	7	2	8	.20	8	.272	.354	.376
1997 Bowie	AA	105	314	90	16	0	9	(-	-)	133	39	37	47	22	2	38	1	1	3	2	2	.50	7	.287	.351	.424
1998 Bowie	AA	88	276	79	16	0	9	(-	-)	122	37	45	43	29	2	42	3	0	1	1	1	.50	7	.286	.359	.442
1998 Rochester	AAA	30	95	22	4	1	3	(-	-)	37	13	8	10	9	0	11	0	0	0	1	2	.33	2	.232	.298	.389
1999 Rochester	AAA	79	279	82	19	4	6	(-	-)	127	33	28	45	34	2	24	1	1	2	1	2	.33	8	.294	.370	.455
1999 Bowie	AA	39	126	37	6	0	2	(-	-)	49	17	12	19	10	0	12	3	0	0	1	0	1.00	6	.294	.360	.389
2000 Bowie	AA	13	53	18	6	0	1	(-	-)	27	11	9	10	3	0	6	1	0	1	0	0	-	1	.340	.379	.509
2000 Rochester	AAA	54	189	54	10	0	3	(-	-)	73	25	21	29	26	0	14	1	1	1	3	1	.75	8	.286	.373	.386
2001 Yucatan	Mex	121	493	164	42	7	5	(-	-)	235	68	64	86	43	3	47	2	4	5	4	5	.56	12	.333	.385	.477

Year Team	Lg	G	AB	H	2B	3B	HR	(Hm	Rd)	TB	R	RBI	RC	TBB	IBB	SO	HBP	SH	SF	SB	CS	SB%	GDP	Avg	OBP	Slg
2001 Chico	IND	4	15	8	0	1	0	(-	-)	10	3	0	5	1	0	1	0	0	0	0	0	-	0	.533	.563	.667
2002 Rochester	AAA	108	418	129	21	4	7	(-	-)	179	57	43	64	41	2	28	2	2	5	3	4	.43	11	.309	.369	.428
2003 Syracuse	AAA	66	252	65	14	1	4	(-	-)	93	29	30	31	21	2	20	3	3	6	1	0	1.00	3	.258	.316	.369
2002 Baltimore	AL	14	53	16	5	0	0	(0	0)	21	3	4	3	3	0	6	2	0	0	0	0	-	5	.302	.362	.396
2003 Toronto	AL	38	70	25	3	1	0	(0	0)	30	9	7	12	3	0	6	2	2	0	0	1	.00	3	.357	.400	.429
2 ML YEARS		52	123	41	8	1	0	(0	0)	51	12	11	15	6	0	12	4	2	0	0	1	.00	8	.333	.383	.415

Jermaine Clark

Bats: L **Throws:** R **Pos:** LF-17; 2B-7; PH-2; PR-2; CF-1 **Ht:** 5'10" **Wt:** 175 **Born:** 9/29/76 **Age:** 27

Year Team	Lg	G	AB	H	2B	3B	HR	(Hm	Rd)	TB	R	RBI	RC	TBB	IBB	SO	HBP	SH	SF	SB	CS	SB%	GDP	Avg	OBP	Slg
1997 Everett	A-	59	199	67	13	2	3	(-	-)	93	42	29	46	34	1	31	3	3	2	22	3	.88	1	.337	.437	.467
1998 Wisconsin	A	123	448	145	24	13	6	(-	-)	213	81	55	88	57	4	64	2	4	1	40	14	.74	3	.324	.402	.475
1999 Lancaster	A+	126	502	158	27	8	6	(-	-)	219	112	61	85	58	2	80	2	8	3	33	15	.69	10	.315	.386	.436
2000 New Haven	AA	133	447	131	23	9	2	(-	-)	178	80	44	88	87	3	69	14	18	3	38	8	.83	7	.293	.421	.398
2001 Tacoma	AAA	74	216	54	7	3	1	(-	-)	70	36	26	26	27	0	39	3	3	1	13	2	.87	6	.250	.340	.324
2002 Tacoma	AAA	108	368	98	14	4	6	(-	-)	138	47	36	57	62	2	59	2	5	6	29	14	.67	3	.266	.370	.375
2002 Oklahoma	AAA	13	57	17	2	1	1	(-	-)	24	13	4	10	7	0	11	0	0	0	6	2	.75	0	.298	.375	.421
2003 Portland	AAA	50	160	40	2	2	4	(-	-)	58	27	10	23	22	1	24	1	2	1	14	3	.82	1	.250	.342	.363
2003 Oklahoma	AAA	49	171	38	6	4	6	(-	-)	70	24	24	22	16	0	26	1	4	1	11	1	.92	3	.222	.291	.409
2001 Detroit	AL	3	0	0	0	0	0	(0	0)	0	1	0	0	0	0	0	0	0	0	0	0	-	0	-	-	-
2003 Tex-SD		25	48	8	2	0	0	(0	0)	10	2	7	5	6	0	5	0	1	2	2	2	.50	1	.167	.250	.208
2003 Texas	AL	24	46	8	2	0	0	(0	0)	10	2	6	5	6	0	4	0	1	1	2	1	.67	1	.174	.264	.217
2003 San Diego	NL	1	2	0	0	0	0	(0	0)	0	0	1	0	0	0	1	0	0	1	0	1	.00	0	.000	.000	.000
2 ML YEARS		28	48	8	2	0	0	(0	0)	10	3	7	5	6	0	5	0	1	2	2	2	.50	1	.167	.250	.208

Tony Clark

Bats: B **Throws:** R **Pos:** 1B-80; PH-53; LF-1 **Ht:** 6'7" **Wt:** 245 **Born:** 6/15/72 **Age:** 32

Year Team	Lg	G	AB	H	2B	3B	HR	(Hm	Rd)	TB	R	RBI	RC	TBB	IBB	SO	HBP	SH	SF	SB	CS	SB%	GDP	Avg	OBP	Slg
2003 St.Lucie*	A+	1	4	1	0	0	0	(-	-)	1	0	0	0	0	0	1	0	0	0	0	0	-	0	.250	.250	.250
1995 Detroit	AL	27	101	24	5	1	3	(0	3)	40	10	11	11	8	0	30	0	0	0	0	-	-	2	.238	.294	.396
1996 Detroit	AL	100	376	94	14	0	27	(17	10)	189	56	72	55	29	1	127	0	0	6	0	1	.00	7	.250	.299	.503
1997 Detroit	AL	159	580	160	28	3	32	(18	14)	290	105	117	107	93	13	144	3	0	5	1	3	.25	11	.276	.376	.500
1998 Detroit	AL	157	602	175	37	0	34	(18	16)	314	84	103	107	63	5	128	3	0	5	3	3	.50	16	.291	.358	.522
1999 Detroit	AL	143	536	150	29	0	31	(12	19)	272	74	99	94	64	7	133	6	0	3	2	1	.67	14	.280	.361	.507
2000 Detroit	AL	60	208	57	14	0	13	(6	7)	110	32	37	35	24	2	51	0	0	0	0	0	-	10	.274	.349	.529
2001 Detroit	AL	126	428	123	29	3	16	(7	9)	206	67	75	74	62	10	108	1	0	6	0	1	.00	14	.287	.374	.481
2002 Boston	AL	90	275	57	12	1	3	(1	2)	80	25	29	18	21	0	57	1	0	1	0	0	-	11	.207	.265	.291
2003 New York	NL	125	254	59	13	0	16	(9	7)	120	29	43	30	24	2	73	1	0	1	0	0	-	8	.232	.300	.472
9 ML YEARS		987	3360	899	181	8	175	(88	87)	1621	482	586	531	388	40	851	15	0	27	6	9	.40	93	.268	.344	.482

Brandon Claussen

Pitches: L **Bats:** R **Pos:** SP-1 **Ht:** 6'2" **Wt:** 175 **Born:** 5/1/79 **Age:** 25

		HOW MUCH HE PITCHED						WHAT HE GAVE UP										THE RESULTS						
Year Team	Lg	G	GS	CG	GF	IP	BFP	H	R	ER	HR	SH	SF	HB	TBB	IBB	SO	WP	Bk	W	L	Pct	ShO	Sv-Op Hld	ERC	ERA
1999 Yankees	R	2	2	0	0	11.1	42	7	4	4	2	0	0	0	2	0	16	0	0	1	0	1.000	0	0--	1.79	3.18
1999 Staten Island	A-	12	12	1	0	72.0	295	70	30	27	4	3	0	3	12	2	89	4	4	6	4	.600	0	0--	2.87	3.38
1999 Greensboro	A	1	1	0	0	6.0	29	8	7	7	1	0	0	0	2	0	5	1	1	1	0	1.000	0	0--	5.90	10.50
2000 Greensboro	A	17	17	1	0	97.2	416	91	49	44	9	4	4	1	44	0	98	3	0	8	5	.615	0	0--	3.92	4.05
2000 Tampa	A+	9	9	1	0	52.1	220	49	24	18	1	1	0	2	17	0	44	2	1	2	5	.286	1	0--	3.04	3.10
2001 Tampa	A+	8	8	0	0	56.0	227	47	21	17	2	2	2	0	13	0	69	1	2	5	2	.714	0	0--	2.19	2.73
2001 Norwich	AA	21	21	1	0	131.0	554	101	42	31	6	7	6	5	55	0	151	5	3	9	2	.818	1	0--	2.66	2.13
2002 Columbus	AAA	15	15	0	0	93.1	408	85	47	34	4	7	3	1	46	3	73	2	0	2	8	.200	0	0--	3.48	3.28
2003 Tampa	A+	4	4	0	0	22.0	86	16	5	4	0	0	2	0	3	0	26	0	1	2	0	1.000	0	0--	1.33	1.64
2003 Columbus	AAA	11	11	1	0	68.2	275	53	28	21	4	1	6	1	18	0	39	0	2	2	1	.667	0	0--	2.17	2.75
2003 Louisville	AAA	3	3	0	0	15.2	65	17	13	13	3	1	0	0	6	0	16	0	0	1	0	1.000	0	0--	5.47	7.47
2003 New York	AL	1	1	0	0	6.1	28	8	2	1	1	0	0	0	1	0	5	0	0	1	0	1.000	0	0-0	4.89	1.42

Royce Clayton

Bats: R **Throws:** R **Pos:** SS-141; PH-5 **Ht:** 6'0" **Wt:** 185 **Born:** 1/2/70 **Age:** 34

Year Team	Lg	G	AB	H	2B	3B	HR	(Hm	Rd)	TB	R	RBI	RC	TBB	IBB	SO	HBP	SH	SF	SB	CS	SB%	GDP	Avg	OBP	Slg
1991 San Francisco	NL	9	26	3	1	0	0	(0	0)	4	0	2	0	1	0	6	0	0	0	0	0	-	1	.115	.148	.154
1992 San Francisco	NL	98	321	72	7	4	4	(3	1)	99	31	24	25	26	3	63	0	3	2	8	4	.67	11	.224	.281	.308
1993 San Francisco	NL	153	549	155	21	5	6	(5	1)	204	54	70	64	38	2	91	5	8	7	11	10	.52	16	.282	.331	.372
1994 San Francisco	NL	108	385	91	14	6	3	(1	2)	126	38	30	40	30	2	74	3	3	2	23	3	.88	7	.236	.295	.327
1995 San Francisco	NL	138	509	124	29	3	5	(2	3)	174	56	58	53	38	1	109	3	4	3	24	9	.73	7	.244	.298	.342
1996 St Louis	NL	129	491	136	20	4	6	(6	0)	182	64	35	56	33	4	91	1	2	4	33	15	.69	13	.277	.321	.371
1997 St Louis	NL	154	576	153	39	5	9	(5	4)	229	75	61	67	33	4	109	3	2	5	30	10	.75	19	.266	.306	.398
1998 StL-Tex		142	541	136	31	2	9	(2	7)	198	89	53	62	53	1	83	3	6	5	24	11	.69	16	.251	.319	.366
1999 Texas	AL	133	465	134	21	5	14	(6	8)	207	69	52	71	39	1	100	4	9	3	6	.57	6		.288	.346	.445
2000 Texas	AL	148	513	124	21	5	14	(9	5)	197	70	54	54	42	1	92	3	12	3	11	7	.61	21	.242	.301	.384
2001 Chicago	AL	135	433	114	21	4	9	(6	3)	170	62	60	50	33	2	72	3	9	7	10	7	.59	16	.263	.315	.393
2002 Chicago	AL	112	342	86	14	2	7	(4	3)	125	51	35	37	20	0	67	3	7	4	5	1	.83	7	.251	.295	.365
2003 Milwaukee	NL	146	483	110	16	1	11	(5	6)	161	49	39	36	49	10	92	3	4	4	5	2	.71	25	.228	.301	.333
1998 St Louis	NL	90	355	83	19	1	4	(1	3)	116	59	29	37	40	1	51	2	3	2	19	6	.76	10	.234	.313	.327
1998 Texas	AL	52	186	53	12	1	5	(1	4)	82	30	24	25	13	0	32	1	3	3	5	5	.50	6	.285	.330	.441
13 ML YEARS		1605	5634	1438	255	46	97	(54	43)	2076	708	573	615	435	31	1047	34	69	49	192	85	.69	165	.255	.310	.368

Roger Clemens

Pitches: R Bats: R Pos: SP-33   Ht: 6'4" Wt: 235 Born: 8/4/62 Age: 41

			HOW MUCH HE PITCHED						WHAT HE GAVE UP										THE RESULTS							
Year Team	Lg	G	GS	CG	GF	IP	BFP	H	R	ER	HR	SH	SF	HB	TBB	IBB	SO	WP	Bk	W	L	Pct	ShO	Sv-Op	Hld	ERC	ERA
1984 Boston	AL	21	20	5	0	133.1	575	146	67	64	13	2	3	2	29	3	126	4	0	9	4	.692	1	0-0	0	3.81	4.32
1985 Boston	AL	15	15	3	0	98.1	407	83	38	36	5	1	2	3	37	0	74	1	3	7	5	.583	1	0-0	0	2.96	3.29
1986 Boston	AL	33	33	10	0	254.0	997	179	77	70	21	4	6	4	67	0	238	11	3	24	4	.857	1	0-0	0	2.03	2.48
1987 Boston	AL	36	36	18	0	281.2	1157	248	100	93	19	6	4	9	83	4	256	4	3	20	9	.690	7	0-0	0	2.94	2.97
1988 Boston	AL	35	35	14	0	264.0	1063	217	93	86	17	6	3	6	62	4	291	4	7	18	12	.600	8	0-0	0	2.36	2.93
1989 Boston	AL	35	35	8	0	253.1	1044	215	101	88	20	9	5	8	93	5	230	7	0	17	11	.607	3	0-0	0	3.13	3.13
1990 Boston	AL	31	31	7	0	228.1	920	193	59	49	7	7	5	7	54	3	209	8	0	21	6	.778	4	0-0	0	2.33	1.93
1991 Boston	AL	35	35	13	0	271.1	1077	219	93	79	15	6	8	5	65	12	241	6	0	18	10	.643	4	0-0	0	2.23	2.62
1992 Boston	AL	32	32	11	0	246.2	989	203	80	66	11	5	5	9	62	5	208	3	0	18	11	.621	5	0-0	0	2.38	2.41
1993 Boston	AL	29	29	2	0	191.2	808	175	99	95	17	5	7	11	67	4	160	3	1	11	14	.440	1	0-0	0	3.53	4.46
1994 Boston	AL	24	24	3	0	170.2	692	124	62	54	15	2	5	4	71	1	168	4	0	9	7	.563	1	0-0	0	2.72	2.85
1995 Boston	AL	23	23	0	0	140.0	623	141	70	65	15	2	3	14	60	0	132	9	0	10	5	.667	0	0-0	0	4.67	4.18
1996 Boston	AL	34	34	6	0	242.2	1032	216	106	98	19	4	7	4	106	2	257	8	1	10	13	.435	2	0-0	0	3.52	3.63
1997 Toronto	AL	34	34	9	0	264.0	1044	204	65	60	9	5	2	12	68	1	292	4	0	21	7	.750	3	0-0	0	2.17	2.05
1998 Toronto	AL	33	33	5	0	234.2	961	169	78	69	11	8	2	7	88	0	271	6	0	20	6	.769	3	0-0	0	2.27	2.65
1999 New York	AL	30	30	1	0	187.2	822	185	101	96	20	10	5	9	90	0	163	8	0	14	10	.583	1	0-0	0	4.59	4.60
2000 New York	AL	32	32	1	0	204.1	878	184	96	84	26	1	2	10	84	0	188	2	1	13	8	.619	0	0-0	0	3.93	3.70
2001 New York	AL	33	33	0	0	220.1	918	205	94	86	19	4	4	5	72	1	213	14	0	20	3	.870	0	0-0	0	3.43	3.51
2002 New York	AL	29	29	0	0	180.0	768	172	94	87	18	5	5	7	63	6	192	14	0	13	6	.684	0	0-0	0	3.72	4.35
2003 New York	AL	33	33	1	0	211.2	878	199	99	92	24	3	6	5	58	1	190	5	0	17	9	.654	1	0-0	0	3.44	3.91
20 ML YEARS		607	606	117	0	4278.2	17653	3677	1672	1517	321	95	89	141	1379	52	4099	125	19	310	160	.660	46	0-0	0	2.98	3.19

Matt Clement

Pitches: R Bats: R Pos: SP-32   Ht: 6'3" Wt: 213 Born: 8/12/74 Age: 29

			HOW MUCH HE PITCHED						WHAT HE GAVE UP										THE RESULTS							
Year Team	Lg	G	GS	CG	GF	IP	BFP	H	R	ER	HR	SH	SF	HB	TBB	IBB	SO	WP	Bk	W	L	Pct	ShO	Sv-Op	Hld	ERC	ERA
1998 San Diego	NL	4	2	0	0	13.2	62	15	8	7	0	2	0	0	7	1	13	2	0	2	0	1.000	0	0-0	0	4.14	4.61
1999 San Diego	NL	31	31	0	0	180.2	803	190	106	90	18	7	6	9	86	2	135	11	0	10	12	.455	0	0-0	0	4.89	4.48
2000 San Diego	NL	34	34	0	0	205.0	940	194	131	117	22	12	5	16	125	4	170	23	0	13	17	.433	0	0-0	0	4.87	5.14
2001 Florida	NL	31	31	0	0	169.1	760	172	102	95	15	14	3	15	85	2	134	15	0	9	10	.474	0	0-0	0	4.84	5.05
2002 Chicago	NL	32	32	3	0	205.0	858	162	84	82	18	11	4	6	85	7	215	7	0	12	11	.522	2	0-0	0	2.96	3.60
2003 Chicago	NL	32	32	2	0	201.2	851	169	100	92	22	10	2	14	79	2	171	13	0	14	12	.538	1	0-0	0	3.47	4.11
6 ML YEARS		164	162	5	0	975.1	4274	902	531	483	95	56	20	60	467	18	838	71	0	60	62	.492	3	0-0	0	4.14	4.46

Greg Colbrunn

Bats: R Throws: R Pos: 1B-14; PH-5; DH-4   Ht: 6'0" Wt: 212 Born: 7/26/69 Age: 34

								BATTING												BASERUNNING				AVERAGES		
Year Team	Lg	G	AB	H	2B	3B	HR	(Hm	Rd)	TB	R	RBI	RC	TBB	IBB	SO	HBP	SH	SF	SB	CS	SB%	GDP	Avg	OBP	Slg
2003 Tacoma*	AAA	3	11	3	0	0	1	(-	-)	6	3	2	2	1	0	1	0	0	0	0	0	-	0	.273	.333	.545
2003 Everett*	A-	1	3	2	1	0	0	(-	-)	3	0	0	2	1	0	0	0	0	0	0	0	-	0	.667	.750	1.000
1992 Montreal	NL	52	168	45	8	0	2	(1	1)	59	12	18	18	6	1	34	2	0	4	3	2	.60	1	.268	.294	.351
1993 Montreal	NL	70	153	39	9	0	4	(2	2)	60	15	23	17	6	1	33	1	1	3	4	2	.67	1	.255	.282	.392
1994 Florida	NL	47	155	47	10	0	6	(3	3)	75	17	31	25	9	0	27	2	0	2	1	1	.50	3	.303	.345	.484
1995 Florida	NL	138	528	146	22	1	23	(12	11)	239	70	89	71	22	4	69	6	0	4	11	3	.79	15	.277	.311	.453
1996 Florida	NL	141	511	146	26	2	16	(7	9)	224	60	69	68	25	1	76	14	0	5	4	5	.44	22	.286	.333	.438
1997 Min-Atl		98	271	76	17	0	7	(3	4)	114	27	35	32	10	1	49	2	1	2	1	2	.33	8	.280	.309	.421
1998 Col-Atl	NL	90	166	51	11	2	3	(1	2)	75	18	23	26	10	0	34	4	0	0	4	3	.57	1	.307	.361	.452
1999 Arizona	NL	67	135	44	5	3	5	(2	3)	70	20	24	26	12	0	23	4	0	2	1	1	.50	3	.326	.392	.519
2000 Arizona	NL	116	329	103	22	1	15	(6	9)	172	48	57	66	43	2	45	10	0	3	0	1	.00	13	.313	.405	.523
2001 Arizona	NL	59	97	28	8	0	4	(4	0)	48	12	18	16	9	0	14	4	0	0	0	0	-	5	.289	.373	.495
2002 Arizona	NL	72	171	57	16	2	10	(3	7)	107	30	27	34	13	1	19	0	0	1	0	0	-	6	.333	.378	.626
2003 Seattle	AL	22	58	16	1	1	3	(1	2)	28	7	7	6	4	0	16	0	0	0	1	0	.00	3	.276	.323	.483
1997 Minnesota	AL	70	217	61	14	0	5	(2	3)	90	24	26	25	8	1	38	1	0	2	1	2	.33	7	.281	.307	.415
1997 Atlanta	NL	28	54	15	3	0	2	(1	1)	24	3	9	7	2	0	11	1	1	0	0	0	-	1	.278	.316	.444
1998 Colorado	NL	62	122	38	8	2	2	(1	1)	56	12	13	19	8	0	23	1	0	0	3	3	.50	1	.311	.359	.459
1998 Atlanta	NL	28	44	13	3	0	1	(0	1)	19	6	10	7	2	0	11	3	0	0	1	0	1.00	0	.295	.367	.432
12 ML YEARS		972	2742	798	155	12	98	(45	53)	1271	336	421	405	169	11	439	49	2	26	29	21	.58	80	.291	.340	.464

Lou Collier

Bats: R Throws: R Pos: 3B-2; LF-1; CF-1; PR-1   Ht: 5'10" Wt: 191 Born: 8/21/73 Age: 30

								BATTING												BASERUNNING				AVERAGES		
Year Team	Lg	G	AB	H	2B	3B	HR	(Hm	Rd)	TB	R	RBI	RC	TBB	IBB	SO	HBP	SH	SF	SB	CS	SB%	GDP	Avg	OBP	Slg
2003 Pawtucket*	AAA	103	392	115	19	4	14	(-	-)	184	58	69	61	32	4	94	8	0	6	8	7	.53	13	.293	.354	.469
1997 Pittsburgh	NL	18	37	5	0	0	0	(0	0)	5	3	3	0	1	0	11	0	0	0	1	0	1.00	1	.135	.158	.135
1998 Pittsburgh	NL	110	334	82	13	6	2	(1	1)	113	30	34	35	31	6	70	6	3	5	2	2	.50	8	.246	.316	.338
1999 Milwaukee	NL	74	135	35	9	0	2	(2	0)	50	18	21	17	14	0	32	1	1	2	3	2	.60	2	.259	.325	.370
2000 Milwaukee	NL	14	32	7	1	0	1	(0	1)	11	9	2	4	6	0	4	0	0	1	0	0	-	0	.219	.333	.344
2001 Milwaukee	NL	50	127	32	8	1	2	(1	1)	48	19	14	19	17	0	30	1	1	2	5	1	.83	0	.252	.340	.378
2002 Montreal	NL	13	11	1	1	0	0	(0	0)	2	3	0	0	1	1	3	1	1	0	0	0	-	0	.091	.231	.182
2003 Colorado	AL	4	1	0	0	0	0	(0	0)	0	0	0	0	0	0	0	0	0	0	0	1	.00	0	.000	.000	.000
7 ML YEARS		283	677	162	32	7	7	(4	3)	229	82	74	75	70	7	150	8	6	10	11	6	.65	12	.239	.314	.338

Jesus Colome

Pitches: R **Bats:** R **Pos:** RP-54 **Ht:** 6'4" **Wt:** 205 **Born:** 12/23/77 **Age:** 26

Year Team	Lg	G	GS	CG	GF	IP	BFP	H	R	ER	HR	SH	SF	HB	TBB	IBB	SO	WP	Bk	W	L	Pct	ShO	Sv-Op	Hld	ERC	ERA
2001 Tampa Bay	AL	30	0	0	9	48.2	209	37	22	18	8	2	2	2	25	4	31	2	0	2	3	.400	0	0-0	6	3.62	3.33
2002 Tampa Bay	AL	32	0	0	15	41.1	205	56	41	38	6	4	1	2	33	5	33	5	0	2	7	.222	0	0-5	3	8.53	8.27
2003 Tampa Bay	AL	54	0	0	24	74.0	334	69	37	37	9	2	4	3	46	5	69	7	0	3	7	.300	0	2-8	11	4.76	4.50
3 ML YEARS		116	0	0	48	164.0	748	162	100	93	23	8	7	7	104	14	133	14	0	7	17	.292	0	2-13	20	5.28	5.10

Bartolo Colon

Pitches: R **Bats:** R **Pos:** SP-34 **Ht:** 6'0" **Wt:** 235 **Born:** 5/24/73 **Age:** 31

Year Team	Lg	G	GS	CG	GF	IP	BFP	H	R	ER	HR	SH	SF	HB	TBB	IBB	SO	WP	Bk	W	L	Pct	ShO	Sv-Op	Hld	ERC	ERA
1997 Cleveland	AL	19	17	1	0	94.0	427	107	66	59	12	4	1	3	45	1	66	5	0	4	7	.364	0	0-0	0	5.53	5.65
1998 Cleveland	AL	31	31	6	0	204.0	883	205	91	84	15	10	2	3	79	5	158	4	0	14	9	.609	2	0-0	0	3.87	3.71
1999 Cleveland	AL	32	32	1	0	205.0	858	185	97	90	24	5	4	7	76	5	161	4	0	18	5	.783	1	0-0	0	3.68	3.95
2000 Cleveland	AL	30	30	2	0	188.0	807	163	86	81	21	2	3	4	98	4	212	4	0	15	8	.652	1	0-0	0	3.97	3.88
2001 Cleveland	AL	34	34	1	0	222.1	947	220	106	101	26	8	4	2	90	2	201	4	1	14	12	.538	0	0-0	0	4.24	4.09
2002 Cle-Mon	AL	33	33	8	0	233.1	966	219	85	76	20	19	6	2	70	5	149	4	0	20	8	.714	3	0-0	0	3.29	2.93
2003 Chicago	AL	34	34	9	0	242.0	984	223	107	104	30	5	8	5	67	3	173	8	3	15	13	.536	0	0-0	0	3.47	3.87
2002 Cleveland	AL	16	16	4	0	116.1	467	104	37	33	11	6	3	2	31	1	75	3	0	10	4	.714	2	0-0	0	3.09	2.55
2002 Montreal	NL	17	17	4	0	117.0	499	115	48	43	9	13	3	0	39	4	74	1	0	10	4	.714	1	0-0	0	3.48	3.31
7 ML YEARS		213	211	28	0	1388.2	5872	1322	638	595	148	53	28	26	525	25	1120	33	4	100	62	.617	7	0-0	0	3.85	3.86

Steve Colyer

Pitches: L **Bats:** L **Pos:** RP-13 **Ht:** 6'4" **Wt:** 205 **Born:** 2/22/79 **Age:** 25

Year Team	Lg	G	GS	CG	GF	IP	BFP	H	R	ER	HR	SH	SF	HB	TBB	IBB	SO	WP	Bk	W	L	Pct	ShO	Sv-Op	Hld	ERC	ERA
1998 Yakima	A-	15	12	0	2	65.1	302	72	46	36	2	1	1	4	36	0	75	5	0	2	2	.500	0	0- -	-	4.94	4.96
1999 Sn Brnardino	A+	27	25	1	0	145.2	644	145	82	76	12	3	7	8	86	0	131	8	3	7	9	.438	0	0- -	-	5.03	4.70
2000 Vero Beach	A+	26	18	1	2	95.1	442	97	74	61	9	2	7	7	68	0	80	6	0	5	7	.417	0	0- -	-	5.77	5.76
2001 Vero Beach	A+	24	24	0	0	120.1	524	101	62	53	16	4	4	7	77	0	118	3	1	4	8	.333	0	0- -	-	4.69	3.96
2002 Jacksonville	AA	59	0	0	46	62.2	284	50	29	24	6	4	3	2	40	3	68	4	0	5	4	.556	0	21- -	-	3.74	3.45
2003 Las Vegas	AAA	44	0	0	44	47.2	206	44	18	17	1	1	1	1	22	0	50	1	0	2	3	.400	0	23- -	-	3.40	3.21
2003 Los Angeles	NL	13	0	0	3	19.2	84	22	6	6	0	1	0	0	9	0	16	1	0	0	0	. -	0	0-0	0	4.44	2.75

Clay Condrey

Pitches: R **Bats:** R **Pos:** SP-6; RP-3 **Ht:** 6'3" **Wt:** 195 **Born:** 11/19/75 **Age:** 28

Year Team	Lg	G	GS	CG	GF	IP	BFP	H	R	ER	HR	SH	SF	HB	TBB	IBB	SO	WP	Bk	W	L	Pct	ShO	Sv-Op	Hld	ERC	ERA
1998 Padres	R	5	0	0	4	5.1	26	6	4	2	0	0	0	0	5	1	4	1	1	0	1	.000	0	0- -	-	5.82	3.38
1998 Idaho Falls	R+	18	0	0	17	24.2	111	31	12	7	2	1	1	1	4	0	19	3	0	2	1	.667	0	5- -	-	4.45	2.55
1999 Fort Wayne	A	42	0	0	39	47.2	202	40	24	20	5	0	2	0	19	4	47	4	1	2	3	.400	0	20- -	-	3.04	3.78
1999 R Cucamnga	A+	6	0	0	1	7.1	29	4	3	3	1	0	0	0	3	0	9	0	0	0	0	. -	0	0- -	-	1.98	3.68
2000 R Cucamnga	A+	18	0	0	9	20.2	85	18	9	8	1	1	0	2	7	0	21	2	1	1	1	.500	0	4- -	-	3.26	3.48
2000 Mobile	AA	35	0	0	19	43.2	195	41	27	26	4	3	2	5	20	0	25	1	0	2	2	.500	0	8- -	-	4.29	5.36
2001 Mobile	AA	27	0	0	23	33.2	144	33	23	17	1	4	2	0	15	4	21	0	0	2	2	.500	0	12- -	-	3.49	4.54
2001 Portland	AAA	39	0	0	13	53.0	231	63	37	28	7	4	3	4	13	1	45	2	0	1	3	.250	0	2- -	-	5.11	4.75
2002 Portland	AAA	25	23	0	0	133.2	552	128	55	52	12	6	3	5	40	1	73	2	3	10	4	.714	0	0- -	-	3.60	3.50
2003 Portland	AAA	11	11	0	0	63.0	261	64	34	29	7	1	4	0	12	0	46	4	0	3	3	.500	0	0- -	-	3.40	4.14
2002 San Diego	NL	9	0	0	2	26.2	106	20	7	5	1	2	2	2	8	1	16	1	1	1	2	.333	0	0-0	3	2.29	1.69
2003 San Diego	NL	9	6	0	0	34.0	167	43	32	32	7	3	0	3	21	4	25	0	0	1	2	.333	0	0-0	0	7.55	8.47
2 ML YEARS		18	9	0	2	60.2	273	63	39	37	8	5	2	5	29	5	41	1	1	2	4	.333	0	0-0	3	5.04	5.49

David Cone

Pitches: R **Bats:** L **Pos:** SP-4; RP-1 **Ht:** 6'1" **Wt:** 200 **Born:** 1/2/63 **Age:** 41

Year Team	Lg	G	GS	CG	GF	IP	BFP	H	R	ER	HR	SH	SF	HB	TBB	IBB	SO	WP	Bk	W	L	Pct	ShO	Sv-Op	Hld	ERC	ERA
2003 St.Lucie*	A+	3	3	0	0	12.2	51	10	4	4	1	0	1	0	3	0	6	3	0	0	1	.000	0	0- -	-	2.21	2.84
1986 Kansas City	AL	11	0	0	5	22.2	108	29	14	14	2	0	0	1	13	1	21	3	0	0	0	. -	0	0-0	0	6.48	5.56
1987 New York	NL	21	13	1	3	99.1	420	87	46	41	11	4	3	5	44	1	68	2	4	5	6	.455	0	1-1	2	3.87	3.71
1988 New York	NL	35	28	8	0	231.1	936	178	67	57	10	11	5	4	80	7	213	10	10	20	3	.870	4	0-0	1	2.34	2.22
1989 New York	NL	34	33	7	0	219.2	910	183	92	86	20	6	4	4	74	6	190	14	4	14	8	.636	2	0-0	0	2.89	3.52
1990 New York	NL	31	30	6	1	211.2	860	177	84	76	21	4	6	1	65	1	233	10	4	14	10	.583	2	0-0	0	2.87	3.23
1991 New York	NL	34	34	5	0	232.2	966	204	95	85	13	13	7	5	73	2	241	17	1	14	14	.500	2	0-0	0	2.85	3.29
1992 NYM-Tor		35	34	7	0	249.2	1055	201	91	78	15	6	9	12	111	7	261	12	1	17	10	.630	5	0-0	0	3.05	2.81
1993 Kansas City	AL	34	34	6	0	254.0	1060	205	102	94	20	7	9	10	114	2	191	14	2	11	14	.440	1	0-0	0	3.25	3.33
1994 Kansas City	AL	23	23	4	0	171.2	690	130	60	56	15	1	5	7	54	0	132	5	1	16	5	.762	3	0-0	0	2.57	2.94
1995 Tor-NYY	AL	30	30	6	0	229.1	954	195	95	91	24	2	3	6	88	2	191	11	1	18	8	.692	2	0-0	0	3.34	3.57
1996 New York	AL	11	11	1	0	72.0	295	50	25	23	4	1	3	2	34	0	71	4	1	7	2	.778	0	0-0	0	2.48	2.88
1997 New York	AL	29	29	1	0	195.0	805	155	67	61	17	3	2	4	86	2	222	14	2	12	6	.667	0	0-0	0	3.15	2.82
1998 New York	AL	31	31	3	0	207.2	866	186	89	82	20	4	4	15	59	1	209	6	0	20	7	.741	0	0-0	0	3.31	3.55
1999 New York	AL	31	31	1	0	193.1	827	164	84	74	21	5	6	11	90	2	177	7	1	12	9	.571	1	0-0	0	3.76	3.44
2000 New York	AL	30	29	0	0	155.0	733	192	124	119	25	6	8	9	82	3	120	11	0	4	14	.222	0	0-0	0	6.72	6.91
2001 Boston	AL	25	25	0	0	135.2	614	148	74	65	17	2	6	10	57	4	115	9	0	9	7	.563	0	0-0	0	4.06	4.31
2003 New York	NL	5	4	0	0	18.0	85	20	13	13	4	1	0	0	13	1	13	0	0	1	3	.250	0	0-0	0	6.98	6.50
1992 New York	NL	27	27	7	0	196.2	831	162	75	63	12	6	6	9	82	5	214	9	1	13	7	.650	5	0-0	0	3.04	2.88
1992 Toronto	AL	8	7	0	0	53.0	224	39	16	15	3	0	3	3	29	2	47	3	0	4	3	.571	0	0-0	0	3.08	2.55
1995 Toronto	AL	17	17	5	0	130.1	537	113	53	49	12	2	2	5	41	2	102	6	1	9	6	.600	2	0-0	0	3.12	3.38
1995 New York	AL	13	13	1	0	99.0	417	82	42	42	12	0	1	1	47	0	89	5	0	9	2	.818	0	0-0	0	3.63	3.82
17 ML YEARS		450	419	56	9	2898.2	12184	2504	1222	1115	258	76	82	106	1137	42	2668	149	32	194	126	.606	22	1-1	3	3.35	3.46

50

Jeff Conine

Bats: R **Throws:** R **Pos:** 1B-118; LF-31; RF-2; 3B-1   **Ht:** 6'1" **Wt:** 220 **Born:** 6/27/66 **Age:** 38

Year Team	Lg	G	AB	H	2B	3B	HR	(Hm	Rd)	TB	R	RBI	RC	TBB	IBB	SO	HBP	SH	SF	SB	CS	SB%	GDP	Avg	OBP	Slg
1990 Kansas City	AL	9	20	5	2	0	0	(0	0)	7	3	2	2	2	0	5	0	0	0	0	0	-	1	.250	.318	.350
1992 Kansas City	AL	28	91	23	5	2	0	(0	0)	32	10	9	10	8	1	23	0	0	0	0	0	-	1	.253	.313	.352
1993 Florida	NL	**162**	595	174	24	3	12	(5	7)	240	75	79	83	52	2	135	5	0	6	2	2	.50	14	.292	.351	.403
1994 Florida	NL	115	451	144	27	6	18	(8	10)	237	60	82	84	40	4	92	1	0	4	1	2	.33	8	.319	.373	.525
1995 Florida	NL	133	483	146	26	2	25	(13	12)	251	72	105	93	66	5	94	1	0	12	2	0	1.00	13	.302	.379	.520
1996 Florida	NL	157	597	175	32	2	26	(15	11)	289	84	95	99	62	1	121	4	0	7	1	4	.20	17	.293	.360	.484
1997 Florida	NL	151	405	98	13	1	17	(7	10)	164	46	61	55	57	3	89	2	0	2	2	0	1.00	11	.242	.337	.405
1998 Kansas City	AL	93	309	79	26	0	8	(4	4)	129	30	43	40	26	1	68	2	0	6	3	0	1.00	8	.256	.312	.417
1999 Baltimore	AL	139	444	129	31	1	13	(7	6)	201	54	75	64	30	0	40	3	1	7	0	3	.00	12	.291	.335	.453
2000 Baltimore	AL	119	409	116	20	2	13	(6	7)	179	53	46	58	36	1	53	2	0	4	4	3	.57	14	.284	.341	.438
2001 Baltimore	AL	139	524	163	23	2	14	(5	9)	232	75	97	89	64	6	75	5	0	8	12	8	.60	12	.311	.386	.443
2002 Baltimore	AL	116	451	123	26	4	15	(12	3)	202	44	63	61	25	6	66	2	0	10	8	0	1.00	16	.273	.307	.448
2003 Bal-Fla		149	577	163	36	3	20	(11	9)	265	88	95	85	50	5	70	5	1	13	5	0	1.00	16	.282	.338	.459
2003 Baltimore	AL	124	493	143	33	3	15	(8	7)	227	75	80	74	37	5	60	5	0	12	5	0	1.00	14	.290	.338	.460
2003 Florida	NL	25	84	20	3	0	5	(3	2)	38	13	15	11	13	0	10	0	1	1	0	0	-	2	.238	.337	.452
13 ML YEARS		1510	5356	1538	291	28	181	(93	88)	2428	694	852	823	518	35	931	32	2	79	40	22	.65	137	.287	.349	.453

Jason Conti

Bats: L **Throws:** R **Pos:** RF-19; PH-13; LF-1; CF-1   **Ht:** 5'11" **Wt:** 175 **Born:** 1/27/75 **Age:** 29

Year Team	Lg	G	AB	H	2B	3B	HR	(Hm	Rd)	TB	R	RBI	RC	TBB	IBB	SO	HBP	SH	SF	SB	CS	SB%	GDP	Avg	OBP	Slg
2003 Indianapolis*	AAA	121	456	113	17	3	10	(-	-)	166	57	40	48	24	1	120	8	6	4	13	8	.62	6	.248	.295	.364
2000 Arizona	NL	47	91	21	4	3	1	(1	0)	34	11	15	10	7	2	30	1	0	0	3	0	1.00	2	.231	.293	.374
2001 Arizona	NL	5	4	1	0	0	0	(0	0)	1	1	0	1	1	0	2	0	0	0	0	0	-	0	.250	.400	.250
2002 Tampa Bay	AL	78	222	57	15	2	3	(2	1)	85	26	21	25	18	1	55	1	4	0	4	2	.67	5	.257	.315	.383
2003 Milwaukee	NL	30	48	11	2	0	2	(1	1)	19	3	7	5	2	0	18	0	1	1	0	1	.00	1	.229	.255	.396
4 ML YEARS		160	365	90	21	5	6	(4	2)	139	41	43	41	28	3	105	2	5	1	7	3	.70	8	.247	.303	.381

Jose Contreras

Pitches: R **Bats:** R **Pos:** SP-9; RP-9   **Ht:** 6'4" **Wt:** 230 **Born:** 12/12/71 **Age:** 32

		HOW MUCH HE PITCHED						WHAT HE GAVE UP											THE RESULTS							
Year Team	Lg	G	GS	CG	GF	IP	BFP	H	R	ER	HR	SH	SF	HB	TBB	IBB	SO	WP	Bk	W	L	Pct	ShO	Sv-Op	Hld	ERC	ERA
2003 Columbus	AAA	3	3	0	0	15.0	56	10	2	2	1	0	0	1	2	0	18	0	0	2	0	1.000	0	0- -	-	1.60	1.20
2003 Staten Island	A-	1	1	0	0	7.0	23	2	0	0	0	0	0	0	0	0	15	0	0	0	0	-	0	0- -	-	0.19	0.00
2003 Tampa	A+	1	1	0	0	4.0	18	4	2	2	0	0	0	1	3	0	5	1	0	0	0	-	0	0- -	-	6.15	4.50
2003 Trenton	AA	1	1	0	0	1.2	8	1	0	0	0	0	0	0	2	0	3	0	0	0	0	-	0	0- -	-	3.97	0.00
2003 New York	AL	18	9	0	2	71.0	293	52	27	26	4	0	1	5	30	1	72	2	0	7	2	.778	0	0-1	1	2.71	3.30

Aaron Cook

Pitches: R **Bats:** R **Pos:** RP-27; SP-16   **Ht:** 6'3" **Wt:** 175 **Born:** 2/8/79 **Age:** 25

		HOW MUCH HE PITCHED						WHAT HE GAVE UP											THE RESULTS							
Year Team	Lg	G	GS	CG	GF	IP	BFP	H	R	ER	HR	SH	SF	HB	TBB	IBB	SO	WP	Bk	W	L	Pct	ShO	Sv-Op	Hld	ERC	ERA
1997 Rockies	R	9	8	0	0	46.0	208	48	27	16	1	2	0	5	17	0	35	3	3	1	3	.250	0	0- -	-	3.94	3.13
1998 Portland	A-	15	15	1	0	79.1	364	87	50	43	8	1	1	7	39	0	38	7	0	5	8	.385	0	0- -	-	5.35	4.88
1999 Asheville	A	25	25	2	0	121.2	561	157	99	87	17	2	1	9	42	0	73	15	0	4	12	.250	0	0- -	-	6.17	6.44
2000 Asheville	A	21	21	4	0	142.2	579	130	54	47	10	1	0	16	23	0	118	5	0	10	7	.588	2	0- -	-	2.97	2.96
2000 Salem	A+	7	7	1	0	43.0	196	52	33	26	4	1	1	7	12	0	37	3	0	1	6	.143	0	0- -	-	5.39	5.44
2001 Salem	A+	27	27	0	0	155.0	649	157	73	53	4	5	1	7	38	0	122	6	1	11	11	.500	0	0- -	-	3.24	3.08
2002 Carolina	AA	14	14	2	0	95.0	370	73	24	15	4	3	1	5	19	0	58	5	0	7	2	.778	2	0- -	-	2.04	1.42
2002 Co Springs	AAA	10	10	1	0	64.1	275	67	40	27	6	0	0	3	18	0	32	7	1	4	4	.500	0	0- -	-	3.97	3.78
2003 Co Springs	AAA	2	2	1	0	16.0	61	10	4	4	2	0	0	0	4	0	12	0	0	1	1	.500	0	0- -	-	1.80	2.25
2002 Colorado	NL	9	5	0	1	35.2	154	41	18	18	4	0	0	2	13	0	14	0	0	2	1	.667	0	0-0	1	5.31	4.54
2003 Colorado	NL	43	16	1	4	124.0	579	160	89	83	8	4	6	8	57	7	43	10	0	4	6	.400	0	0-0	1	5.95	6.02
2 ML YEARS		52	21	1	5	159.2	733	201	107	101	12	4	6	10	70	7	57	10	0	6	7	.462	0	0-0	2	5.81	5.69

Ron Coomer

Bats: R **Throws:** R **Pos:** PH-33; 1B-24; 3B-11; DH-4   **Ht:** 6'0" **Wt:** 215 **Born:** 11/18/66 **Age:** 37

Year Team	Lg	G	AB	H	2B	3B	HR	(Hm	Rd)	TB	R	RBI	RC	TBB	IBB	SO	HBP	SH	SF	SB	CS	SB%	GDP	Avg	OBP	Slg
2003 Vero Beach*	A+	3	10	5	1	0	0	(-	-)	6	1	2	3	0	0	1	0	0	1	0	0	-	0	.500	.455	.600
1995 Minnesota	AL	37	101	26	3	1	5	(2	3)	46	15	19	12	9	0	11	1	0	0	1	0	1.00	9	.257	.324	.455
1996 Minnesota	AL	95	233	69	12	1	12	(5	7)	119	34	41	38	17	1	24	0	0	3	3	0	1.00	10	.296	.340	.511
1997 Minnesota	AL	140	523	156	30	2	13	(4	9)	229	63	85	70	22	5	91	0	0	5	4	3	.57	11	.298	.324	.438
1998 Minnesota	AL	137	529	146	22	1	15	(6	9)	215	54	72	57	18	1	72	0	0	8	2	2	.50	**22**	.276	.295	.406
1999 Minnesota	AL	127	467	123	25	1	16	(6	10)	198	53	65	57	30	1	69	1	0	3	2	1	.67	16	.263	.307	.424
2000 Minnesota	AL	140	544	147	29	1	16	(3	13)	226	64	82	66	36	2	50	4	0	5	2	0	1.00	25	.270	.317	.415
2001 Chicago	NL	111	349	91	19	1	8	(3	5)	136	25	53	37	29	1	70	2	0	6	0	0	-	23	.261	.316	.390
2002 New York	AL	55	148	39	7	0	3	(2	1)	55	14	17	13	6	1	23	0	1	1	0	0	-	8	.264	.290	.372
2003 Los Angeles	NL	69	125	30	4	0	4	(2	2)	46	11	15	9	10	2	19	1	0	1	0	0	-	7	.240	.299	.368
9 ML YEARS		911	3019	827	151	8	92	(33	59)	1270	333	449	359	177	14	429	9	1	32	13	7	.65	131	.274	.313	.421

Alex Cora

Bats: L **Throws:** R **Pos:** 2B-141; SS-15; PH-6 **Ht:** 6'0" **Wt:** 180 **Born:** 10/18/75 **Age:** 28

Year Team	Lg	G	AB	H	2B	3B	HR	(Hm	Rd)	TB	R	RBI	RC	TBB	IBB	SO	HBP	SH	SF	SB	CS	SB%	GDP	Avg	OBP	Slg
1998 Los Angeles	NL	29	33	4	0	1	0	(0	0)	6	1	0	1	2	0	8	1	2	0	0	0	-	0	.121	.194	.182
1999 Los Angeles	NL	11	30	5	1	0	0	(0	0)	6	2	3	0	0	0	4	1	0	0	0	0	-	1	.167	.194	.200
2000 Los Angeles	NL	109	353	84	18	6	4	(2	2)	126	39	32	38	26	4	53	7	6	2	4	1	.80	6	.238	.302	.357
2001 Los Angeles	NL	134	405	88	18	3	4	(2	2)	124	38	29	30	31	6	58	8	3	2	0	2	.00	16	.217	.285	.306
2002 Los Angeles	NL	115	258	75	14	4	5	(4	1)	112	37	28	46	26	4	38	7	2	0	7	2	.78	3	.291	.371	.434
2003 Los Angeles	NL	148	477	119	24	3	4	(3	1)	161	39	34	46	16	3	59	10	9	2	4	2	.67	5	.249	.287	.338
6 ML YEARS		546	1556	375	75	17	17	(11	6)	535	156	126	161	101	17	220	34	22	6	15	7	.68	31	.241	.301	.344

Roy Corcoran

Pitches: R **Bats:** R **Pos:** RP-5 **Ht:** 5'10" **Wt:** 170 **Born:** 5/11/80 **Age:** 24

		HOW MUCH HE PITCHED						WHAT HE GAVE UP											THE RESULTS						
Year Team	Lg	G	GS	CG	GF	IP	BFP	H	R	ER	HR	SH	SF	HB	TBB	IBB	SO	WP	Bk	W	L	Pct	ShO	Sv-Op	Hld	ERC	ERA
2001 Expos	R	13	0	0	9	17.1	69	12	4	3	2	0	0	2	2	0	21	0	0	2	0	1.000	0	2--	-	1.91	1.56
2001 Jupiter	A+	1	0	0	0	2.0	8	0	0	0	0	0	0	0	2	0	0	0	0	0	0	-	0	0--	-	0.95	0.00
2002 Clinton	A	48	1	0	31	80.0	356	82	51	37	5	5	1	2	24	1	106	9	2	3	4	.429	0	11--	-	3.46	4.16
2003 Brevard Cnty	A+	28	0	0	25	33.0	131	19	8	7	1	6	1	2	11	1	35	0	0	5	3	.625	0	12--	-	1.52	1.91
2003 Harrisburg	AA	14	0	0	11	23.2	96	14	4	1	0	1	0	4	7	1	26	0	0	1	1	.500	0	3--	-	1.58	0.38
2003 Edmonton	AAA	2	0	0	1	2.0	6	0	0	0	0	0	0	0	0	0	1	0	0	0	0	-	0	0--	-	0.00	0.00
2003 Montreal	NL	5	0	0	2	7.1	31	7	2	1	0	0	0	0	3	0	2	1	0	0	0	-	0	0-0	1	3.20	1.23

Chad Cordero

Pitches: R **Bats:** R **Pos:** RP-12 **Ht:** 6'0" **Wt:** 195 **Born:** 5/18/82 **Age:** 22

		HOW MUCH HE PITCHED						WHAT HE GAVE UP											THE RESULTS						
Year Team	Lg	G	GS	CG	GF	IP	BFP	H	R	ER	HR	SH	SF	HB	TBB	IBB	SO	WP	Bk	W	L	Pct	ShO	Sv-Op	Hld	ERC	ERA
2003 Brevard Cnty	A+	19	0	0	13	26.1	103	17	8	6	1	4	2	1	10	0	17	0	0	1	1	.500	0	6--	-	2.00	2.05
2003 Montreal	NL	12	0	0	4	11.0	40	4	2	2	1	1	0	0	3	1	12	1	0	1	0	1.000	0	1-1	1	0.86	1.64

Francisco Cordero

Pitches: R **Bats:** R **Pos:** RP-73 **Ht:** 6'2" **Wt:** 200 **Born:** 5/11/75 **Age:** 29

		HOW MUCH HE PITCHED						WHAT HE GAVE UP											THE RESULTS						
Year Team	Lg	G	GS	CG	GF	IP	BFP	H	R	ER	HR	SH	SF	HB	TBB	IBB	SO	WP	Bk	W	L	Pct	ShO	Sv-Op	Hld	ERC	ERA
1999 Detroit	AL	20	0	0	4	19.0	91	19	7	7	2	2	4	0	18	2	19	1	0	2	2	.500	0	0-0	6	6.19	3.32
2000 Texas	AL	56	0	0	13	77.1	365	87	51	46	11	2	6	4	48	3	49	7	0	1	2	.333	0	0-3	4	6.15	5.35
2001 Texas	AL	3	0	0	2	2.1	12	3	1	1	0	0	0	0	2	1	1	1	0	0	0	-	0	0-0	1	5.73	3.86
2002 Texas	AL	39	0	0	25	45.1	177	33	12	9	2	0	0	2	13	1	41	1	0	2	0	1.000	0	10-12	1	2.11	1.79
2003 Texas	AL	73	0	0	36	82.2	352	70	33	27	4	3	4	2	38	6	90	0	0	5	8	.385	0	15-25	18	3.08	2.94
5 ML YEARS		191	0	0	80	226.2	997	212	104	90	19	7	14	8	119	13	200	10	0	10	13	.435	0	25-40	30	4.13	3.57

Wil Cordero

Bats: R **Throws:** R **Pos:** 1B-123; PH-10; DH-2; LF-1 **Ht:** 6'2" **Wt:** 200 **Born:** 10/3/71 **Age:** 32

Year Team	Lg	G	AB	H	2B	3B	HR	(Hm	Rd)	TB	R	RBI	RC	TBB	IBB	SO	HBP	SH	SF	SB	CS	SB%	GDP	Avg	OBP	Slg
1992 Montreal	NL	45	126	38	4	1	2	(1	1)	50	17	8	17	9	0	31	1	1	0	0	0	-	3	.302	.353	.397
1993 Montreal	NL	138	475	118	32	2	10	(8	2)	184	56	58	55	34	8	60	7	4	1	12	3	.80	12	.248	.308	.387
1994 Montreal	NL	110	415	122	30	3	15	(5	10)	203	65	63	74	41	3	62	6	2	3	16	3	.84	8	.294	.363	.489
1995 Montreal	NL	131	514	147	35	2	10	(2	8)	216	64	49	72	36	4	88	9	1	4	9	5	.64	11	.286	.341	.420
1996 Boston	AL	59	198	57	14	0	3	(2	1)	80	29	37	24	11	4	31	2	1	1	2	1	.67	8	.288	.330	.404
1997 Boston	AL	140	570	160	26	3	18	(11	7)	246	82	72	75	31	7	122	4	0	4	1	3	.25	11	.281	.320	.432
1998 Chicago	AL	96	341	91	18	2	13	(5	8)	152	58	49	47	22	0	66	3	1	4	2	1	.67	7	.267	.314	.446
1999 Cleveland	AL	54	194	58	15	0	8	(3	5)	97	35	32	34	15	0	37	6	0	2	2	0	1.00	7	.299	.364	.500
2000 Pit-Cle		127	496	137	35	5	16	(8	8)	230	64	68	70	32	1	76	7	0	1	1	2	.33	18	.276	.328	.464
2001 Cleveland	AL	89	268	67	11	1	4	(2	2)	92	30	21	22	22	2	50	4	2	3	0	0	-	8	.250	.313	.343
2002 Cle-Mon		72	161	43	9	0	6	(2	4)	70	22	30	27	17	0	29	2	0	4	2	0	1.00	4	.267	.337	.435
2003 Montreal	NL	130	436	121	27	0	16	(8	8)	196	57	71	68	49	5	90	4	0	3	1	1	.50	11	.278	.354	.450
2000 Pittsburgh	NL	89	348	98	24	3	16	(8	8)	176	46	51	55	25	1	58	4	0	1	1	2	.33	11	.282	.336	.506
2000 Cleveland	AL	38	148	39	11	2	0	(0	0)	54	18	17	15	7	0	18	3	0	0	0	0	-	7	.264	.310	.365
2002 Cleveland	AL	6	18	4	0	0	0	(0	0)	4	1	1	0	0	0	3	0	0	0	0	0	-	1	.222	.222	.222
2002 Montreal	NL	66	143	39	9	0	6	(2	4)	66	21	29	27	17	0	26	2	0	4	2	0	1.00	3	.273	.349	.462
12 ML YEARS		1191	4194	1159	256	19	121	(57	64)	1816	579	558	591	319	34	742	55	12	30	48	19	.72	108	.276	.333	.433

Marty Cordova

Bats: R **Throws:** R **Pos:** DH-5; LF-4 **Ht:** 6'0" **Wt:** 206 **Born:** 7/10/69 **Age:** 34

Year Team	Lg	G	AB	H	2B	3B	HR	(Hm	Rd)	TB	R	RBI	RC	TBB	IBB	SO	HBP	SH	SF	SB	CS	SB%	GDP	Avg	OBP	Slg
1995 Minnesota	AL	137	512	142	27	4	24	(16	8)	249	81	84	88	52	1	111	10	0	5	20	7	.74	10	.277	.352	.486
1996 Minnesota	AL	145	569	176	46	1	16	(10	6)	272	97	111	97	53	4	96	8	0	9	11	5	.69	18	.309	.371	.478
1997 Minnesota	AL	103	378	93	18	4	15	(4	11)	164	44	51	47	30	2	92	3	0	2	5	3	.63	13	.246	.305	.434
1998 Minnesota	AL	119	438	111	20	2	10	(6	4)	165	52	69	52	50	3	103	5	0	6	3	6	.33	14	.253	.333	.377
1999 Minnesota	AL	124	425	121	28	3	14	(9	5)	197	62	70	68	48	2	96	9	0	6	13	4	.76	22	.285	.365	.464
2000 Toronto	AL	62	200	49	7	0	4	(3	1)	68	23	18	21	18	0	35	3	0	0	3	2	.60	6	.245	.317	.340
2001 Cleveland	AL	122	409	123	20	2	20	(9	11)	207	61	69	69	23	0	81	8	0	2	0	3	.00	9	.301	.348	.506
2002 Baltimore	AL	131	458	116	25	2	18	(11	7)	199	55	64	62	47	3	111	3	2	3	1	6	.14	17	.253	.325	.434
2003 Baltimore	AL	9	30	7	1	0	1	(1	0)	11	5	4	7	8	1	5	1	0	0	1	0	1.00	1	.233	.410	.367
9 ML YEARS		952	3419	938	192	18	122	(69	53)	1532	480	540	510	329	16	730	50	2	33	57	36	.61	110	.274	.344	.448

Mark Corey

Pitches: R Bats: R Pos: RP-22   Ht: 6'3" Wt: 210 Born: 11/16/74 Age: 29

Year Team	Lg	HOW MUCH HE PITCHED						WHAT HE GAVE UP											THE RESULTS						
		G	GS	CG	GF	IP	BFP	H	R	ER	HR	SH	SF	HB	TBB	IBB	SO	WP	Bk	W	L	Pct	ShO	Sv-Op	Hld	ERC	ERA
2003 Nashville*	AAA	46	0	0	40	45.2	191	37	23	22	5	0	0	0	18	2	63	1	0	1	3	.250	0	30- -	-	2.99	4.34
2001 New York	NL	2	0	0	0	1.2	13	5	3	3	0	0	0	0	3	1	3	0	0	0	0	-	0	0-0	0	21.72	16.20
2002 NYM-Col	NL	26	0	0	8	22.0	114	32	23	21	9	1	0	3	16	2	21	1	0	0	3	.000	0	0-0	1	11.75	8.59
2003 Pittsburgh	NL	22	0	0	10	30.1	131	29	19	18	2	1	3	1	11	1	27	2	0	1	2	.333	0	0-0	4	3.47	5.34
2002 New York	NL	12	0	0	5	10.0	48	10	7	5	2	0	0	1	8	1	9	1	0	0	3	.000	0	0-0	0	4.56	4.50
2002 Colorado	NL	14	0	0	3	12.0	66	22	16	16	7	1	0	2	8	1	12	0	0	0	0	-	0	0-0	1	16.43	12.00
3 ML YEARS		50	0	0	18	54.0	258	66	45	42	11	2	3	4	30	4	51	3	0	1	5	.167	0	0-0	5	7.02	7.00

Rheal Cormier

Pitches: L Bats: L Pos: RP-65   Ht: 5'10" Wt: 187 Born: 4/23/67 Age: 37

Year Team	Lg	HOW MUCH HE PITCHED						WHAT HE GAVE UP											THE RESULTS						
		G	GS	CG	GF	IP	BFP	H	R	ER	HR	SH	SF	HB	TBB	IBB	SO	WP	Bk	W	L	Pct	ShO	Sv-Op	Hld	ERC	ERA
1991 St Louis	NL	11	10	2	1	67.2	281	74	35	31	5	1	3	2	8	1	38	2	1	4	5	.444	0	0-0	0	3.41	4.12
1992 St Louis	NL	31	30	3	1	186.0	772	194	83	76	15	11	3	5	33	2	117	4	2	10	10	.500	0	0-0	0	3.42	3.68
1993 St Louis	NL	38	21	1	4	145.1	619	163	80	70	18	10	4	4	27	3	75	6	0	7	6	.538	0	0-0	0	4.13	4.33
1994 St Louis	NL	7	7	0	0	39.2	169	40	24	24	6	1	2	3	7	0	26	2	0	3	2	.600	0	0-0	0	3.80	5.45
1995 Boston	AL	48	12	0	3	115.0	488	131	60	52	12	6	2	3	31	2	69	4	0	7	5	.583	0	0-2	9	4.56	4.07
1996 Montreal	NL	33	27	1	1	159.2	674	165	80	74	16	4	8	9	41	3	100	8	0	7	10	.412	1	0-0	0	3.93	4.17
1997 Montreal	NL	1	1	0	0	1.1	9	4	5	5	1	0	0	0	1	0	0	0	0	0	1	.000	0	0-0	0	27.46	33.75
1999 Boston	AL	60	0	0	7	63.1	275	61	34	26	4	1	3	5	18	2	39	1	0	2	0	1.000	0	0-3	15	3.33	3.69
2000 Boston	AL	64	0	0	12	68.1	293	74	40	35	7	5	2	0	17	2	43	1	0	3	3	.500	0	0-2	9	3.86	4.61
2001 Philadelphia	NL	60	0	0	16	51.1	222	49	26	24	5	3	0	4	17	4	37	1	0	5	6	.455	0	1-6	12	3.67	4.21
2002 Philadelphia	NL	54	0	0	7	60.0	268	61	38	35	6	0	2	4	32	6	49	4	0	5	6	.455	0	0-3	9	4.85	5.25
2003 Philadelphia	NL	65	0	0	21	84.2	327	54	18	16	4	4	0	1	25	2	67	0	1	8	0	1.000	0	1-4	14	1.63	1.70
12 ML YEARS		472	108	7	73	1042.1	4397	1070	523	468	99	46	29	40	257	27	660	33	4	61	54	.530	1	2-20	68	3.70	4.04

Nate Cornejo

Pitches: R Bats: R Pos: SP-32   Ht: 6'5" Wt: 240 Born: 9/24/79 Age: 24

Year Team	Lg	HOW MUCH HE PITCHED						WHAT HE GAVE UP											THE RESULTS						
		G	GS	CG	GF	IP	BFP	H	R	ER	HR	SH	SF	HB	TBB	IBB	SO	WP	Bk	W	L	Pct	ShO	Sv-Op	Hld	ERC	ERA
2001 Detroit	AL	10	10	0	0	42.2	217	63	38	35	10	2	0	3	28	4	22	1	0	4	4	.500	0	0-0	0	9.48	7.38
2002 Detroit	AL	9	9	1	0	50.0	230	63	33	28	6	1	1	2	18	0	23	2	0	1	5	.167	0	0-0	0	5.69	5.04
2003 Detroit	AL	32	32	2	0	194.2	842	236	111	101	18	7	6	3	58	8	46	1	0	6	17	.261	0	0-0	0	4.94	4.67
3 ML YEARS		51	51	3	0	287.1	1289	362	182	164	34	10	7	8	104	12	91	4	0	11	26	.297	0	0-0	0	5.70	5.14

Kevin Correia

Pitches: R Bats: R Pos: SP-7; RP-3   Ht: 6'3" Wt: 200 Born: 8/24/80 Age: 23

Year Team	Lg	HOW MUCH HE PITCHED						WHAT HE GAVE UP											THE RESULTS						
		G	GS	CG	GF	IP	BFP	H	R	ER	HR	SH	SF	HB	TBB	IBB	SO	WP	Bk	W	L	Pct	ShO	Sv-Op	Hld	ERC	ERA
2002 Salem-Keizer	A-	10	8	0	1	37.2	163	37	20	19	1	1	1	3	14	0	31	1	0	2	2	.500	0	0- -	-	3.66	4.54
2003 Norwich	AA	16	14	0	0	86.1	363	80	38	35	3	4	3	4	30	0	73	4	1	6	6	.500	0	0- -	-	3.23	3.65
2003 Fresno	AAA	3	3	0	0	19.0	74	16	8	6	3	0	0	0	2	0	23	2	0	1	0	1.000	0	0- -	-	2.47	2.84
2003 San Francisco	NL	10	7	0	1	39.1	173	41	16	16	6	1	1	4	18	1	28	2	0	3	1	.750	0	0-0	0	5.46	3.66

David Cortes

Pitches: R Bats: R Pos: RP-2   Ht: 5'11" Wt: 195 Born: 10/15/73 Age: 30

Year Team	Lg	HOW MUCH HE PITCHED						WHAT HE GAVE UP											THE RESULTS						
		G	GS	CG	GF	IP	BFP	H	R	ER	HR	SH	SF	HB	TBB	IBB	SO	WP	Bk	W	L	Pct	ShO	Sv-Op	Hld	ERC	ERA
1996 Eugene	A-	15	0	0	11	24.2	95	13	2	2	0	1	0	0	6	0	33	0	0	2	1	.667	0	4- -	-	0.98	0.73
1997 Macon	A	27	0	0	24	31.1	114	16	3	2	0	2	1	2	4	0	32	0	0	3	0	1.000	0	15- -	-	0.88	0.57
1997 Durham	A+	19	0	0	16	19.1	76	15	5	5	1	0	1	0	5	0	16	1	0	1	0	1.000	0	8- -	-	2.13	2.33
1997 Greenville	AA	3	0	0	1	5.0	20	4	1	1	1	0	0	0	1	0	7	0	0	1	0	1.000	0	0- -	-	2.80	1.80
1998 Richmond	AAA	29	0	0	17	44.2	181	37	15	14	2	3	1	0	14	3	46	1	0	3	3	.500	0	4- -	-	2.41	2.82
1998 Co Springs	AAA	6	0	0	0	7.0	37	14	6	6	0	0	0	0	2	0	5	0	0	1	0	1.000	0	0- -	-	8.76	7.71
1999 Richmond	AAA	47	0	0	42	45.2	198	50	19	17	2	2	1	0	14	5	42	2	0	2	3	.400	0	22- -	-	3.63	3.35
2001 Myrtle Beach	A+	9	0	0	8	10.2	49	11	7	7	2	1	0	0	5	0	9	2	0	0	2	.000	0	2- -	-	4.94	5.91
2001 Greenville	AA	14	0	0	6	17.2	85	19	18	16	2	1	0	1	11	2	10	3	1	0	3	.000	0	0- -	-	5.33	8.15
2001 Macon	A	10	0	0	4	12.2	61	14	11	10	1	0	1	1	5	0	8	2	0	1	0	1.000	0	0- -	-	4.43	7.11
2002 Tucson	AAA	3	0	0	0	4.0	16	3	0	0	0	0	0	0	0	0	1	0	0	0	0	-	0	0- -	-	1.06	0.00
2003 Buffalo	AAA	5	0	0	2	6.2	26	4	3	2	1	0	0	0	0	0	9	0	0	1	0	1.000	0	1- -	-	1.08	2.70
1999 Atlanta	NL	4	0	0	3	3.2	18	3	0	2	0	0	0	0	4	0	2	0	0	0	0	-	0	0-0	0	4.78	4.91
2003 Cleveland	AL	2	0	0	2	3.0	18	8	5	4	1	0	1	0	0	0	1	0	0	0	0	-	0	0-0	0	14.61	12.00
2 ML YEARS		6	0	0	2	6.2	36	11	5	6	1	0	1	0	4	0	3	0	0	0	0	-	0	0-0	0	8.99	8.10

Humberto Cota

Bats: R Throws: R Pos: PH-7; C-4   Ht: 6'0" Wt: 205 Born: 2/7/79 Age: 25

Year Team	Lg	BATTING																BASERUNNING				AVERAGES		
		G	AB	H	2B	3B	HR	(Hm | Rd)	TB	R	RBI	RC	TBB	IBB	SO	HBP	SH	SF	SB	CS	SB%	GDP	Avg	OBP	Slg
2003 Nashville*	AAA	62	200	41	9	0	8	(- | -)	74	23	27	21	20	1	59	2	0	0	2	0	1.00	4	.205	.284	.370
2001 Pittsburgh	NL	7	9	2	0	0	0	(0 | 0)	2	1	0	0	0	0	5	0	0	0	0	0	-	0	.222	.222	.222
2002 Pittsburgh	NL	7	17	5	1	0	0	(0 | 0)	6	2	0	1	1	1	4	0	0	0	0	0	-	0	.294	.333	.353
2003 Pittsburgh	NL	10	16	4	1	0	0	(0 | 0)	5	1	1	0	1	0	5	0	0	0	0	0	-	0	.250	.294	.313
3 ML YEARS		24	42	11	2	0	0	(0 | 0)	13	3	2	1	2	1	14	0	0	0	0	0	-	0	.262	.295	.310

53

Neal Cotts

Pitches: L Bats: L Pos: SP-4 Ht: 6'2" Wt: 200 Born: 3/25/80 Age: 24

Year Team	Lg	G	GS	CG	GF	IP	BFP	H	R	ER	HR	SH	SF	HB	TBB	IBB	SO	WP	Bk	W	L	Pct	ShO	Sv-Op	Hld	ERC	ERA
2001 Vancouver	A-	9	7	0	0	35.0	145	28	14	12	2	0	1	1	13	0	44	4	1	1	0	1.000	0	0- -	-	2.72	3.09
2001 Visalia	A+	7	7	0	0	31.0	139	27	14	8	0	0	1	3	15	0	34	0	0	3	2	.600	0	0- -	-	3.22	2.32
2002 Modesto	A+	28	28	0	0	137.2	611	123	72	63	5	1	3	5	87	0	178	7	2	12	6	.667	0	0- -	-	4.07	4.12
2003 Birmingham	AA	21	21	0	0	108.1	440	67	32	26	2	2	2	3	56	1	133	0	0	9	7	.563	0	0- -	-	2.11	2.16
2003 Chicago	AL	4	4	0	0	13.1	69	15	12	12	1	1	0	0	17	0	10	0	0	1	1	.500	0	0-0	0	8.43	8.10

Craig Counsell

Bats: L Throws: R Pos: 3B-57; SS-26; 2B-10; PH-8; PR-3; 1B-2 Ht: 6'0" Wt: 175 Born: 8/21/70 Age: 33

Year Team	Lg	G	AB	H	2B	3B	HR	Hm	Rd	TB	R	RBI	RC	TBB	IBB	SO	HBP	SH	SF	SB	CS	SB%	GDP	Avg	OBP	Slg
2003 Tucson*	AAA	5	23	10	2	0	0	(-	-)	12	8	2	5	1	0	3	0	0	0	0	0	-	0	.435	.458	.522
1995 Colorado	NL	3	1	0	0	0	0	(0	0)	0	0	0	0	1	0	0	0	0	0	0	0	-		.000	.500	.000
1997 Col-Fla	NL	52	164	49	9	2	1	(1	0)	65	20	16	24	18	2	17	3	3	1	1	1	.50	5	.299	.376	.396
1998 Florida	NL	107	335	84	19	5	4	(2	2)	125	43	40	48	51	7	47	4	8	1	3	0	1.00	5	.251	.355	.373
1999 Fla-LA	NL	87	174	38	7	0	0	(0	0)	45	24	11	12	14	0	24	0	5	2	1	0	1.00	2	.218	.274	.259
2000 Arizona	NL	67	152	48	8	1	2	(0	2)	64	23	11	25	20	0	18	2	1	1	3	3	.50	4	.316	.400	.421
2001 Arizona	NL	141	458	126	22	3	4	(4	0)	166	76	38	61	61	3	76	2	6	6	6	8	.43	9	.275	.359	.362
2002 Arizona	NL	112	436	123	22	1	2	(0	2)	153	63	51	63	45	3	52	1	4	3	7	5	.58	10	.282	.348	.351
2003 Arizona	NL	89	303	71	6	3	3	(3	0)	92	40	21	28	41	0	32	2	3	2	11	4	.73	4	.234	.328	.304
1997 Colorado	NL	1	0	0	0	0	0	(0	0)	0	0	0	0	0	0	0	0	0	0	0	0	-		-	-	-
1997 Florida	NL	51	164	49	9	2	1	(1	0)	65	20	16	24	18	2	17	3	3	1	1	1	.50	5	.299	.376	.396
1999 Florida	NL	37	66	10	1	0	0	(0	0)	11	4	2	1	5	0	10	0	2	0	0	0	-	1	.152	.211	.167
1999 Los Angeles	NL	50	108	28	6	0	0	(0	0)	34	20	9	11	9	0	14	0	3	2	1	0	1.00	1	.259	.311	.315
8 ML YEARS		658	2023	539	93	15	16	(10	6)	710	289	188	261	251	15	266	14	30	16	32	21	.60	39	.266	.349	.351

Carl Crawford

Bats: L Throws: L Pos: LF-137; CF-13; PH-5; DH-1; PR-1 Ht: 6'2" Wt: 219 Born: 8/5/81 Age: 22

Year Team	Lg	G	AB	H	2B	3B	HR	Hm	Rd	TB	R	RBI	RC	TBB	IBB	SO	HBP	SH	SF	SB	CS	SB%	GDP	Avg	OBP	Slg
1999 Princeton	R+	60	260	83	14	4	0	(-	-)	105	62	25	38	13	0	47	1	1	3	17	3	.85	5	.319	.350	.404
2000 Chrlstn - SC	A	135	564	170	21	11	6	(-	-)	231	99	57	87	32	1	102	3	9	1	55	9	.86	1	.301	.342	.410
2001 Orlando	AA	132	537	147	24	3	4	(-	-)	189	64	51	62	36	2	90	4	6	2	36	20	.64	3	.274	.323	.352
2002 Durham	AAA	85	353	105	17	9	7	(-	-)	161	59	52	55	20	5	69	2	4	4	26	8	.76	5	.297	.335	.456
2002 Tampa Bay	AL	63	259	67	11	6	2	(1	1)	96	23	30	34	9	0	41	3	6	1	9	5	.64	0	.259	.290	.371
2003 Tampa Bay	AL	151	630	177	18	9	5	(5	0)	228	80	54	78	26	4	102	1	1	3	55	10	.85	5	.281	.309	.362
2 ML YEARS		214	889	244	29	15	7	(6	1)	324	103	84	112	35	4	143	4	7	4	64	15	.81	5	.274	.304	.364

Joe Crede

Bats: R Throws: R Pos: 3B-151; PH-1 Ht: 6'2" Wt: 195 Born: 4/26/78 Age: 26

Year Team	Lg	G	AB	H	2B	3B	HR	Hm	Rd	TB	R	RBI	RC	TBB	IBB	SO	HBP	SH	SF	SB	CS	SB%	GDP	Avg	OBP	Slg
2000 Chicago	AL	7	14	5	1	0	0	(0	0)	6	2	3	2	0	0	3	0	0	1	0	0	-	0	.357	.333	.429
2001 Chicago	AL	17	50	11	1	1	0	(0	0)	14	1	7	4	3	0	11	1	0	1	1	0	1.00	1	.220	.273	.280
2002 Chicago	AL	53	200	57	10	0	12	(7	5)	103	28	35	31	8	0	40	0	0	1	0	2	.00	1	.285	.311	.515
2003 Chicago	AL	151	536	140	31	2	19	(11	8)	232	68	75	69	32	1	75	6	2	4	1	1	.50	10	.261	.308	.433
4 ML YEARS		228	800	213	43	3	31	(18	13)	355	99	120	106	43	1	129	7	2	7	2	3	.40	12	.266	.307	.444

Doug Creek

Pitches: L Bats: L Pos: RP-21 Ht: 6'0" Wt: 227 Born: 3/1/69 Age: 35

Year Team	Lg	G	GS	CG	GF	IP	BFP	H	R	ER	HR	SH	SF	HB	TBB	IBB	SO	WP	Bk	W	L	Pct	ShO	Sv-Op	Hld	ERC	ERA
1995 St Louis	NL	6	0	0	1	6.2	24	2	0	0	0	0	0	0	3	0	10	0	0	0	0	-	0	0-0	0	0.83	0.00
1996 San Francisco	NL	63	0	0	15	48.1	220	45	41	35	11	1	0	2	32	2	38	2	0	0	2	.000	0	0-1	7	5.80	6.52
1997 San Francisco	NL	3	3	0	0	13.1	64	12	12	10	1	0	0	0	14	0	14	0	0	1	2	.333	0	0-0	0	5.94	6.75
1999 Chicago	NL	3	0	0	2	6.0	32	6	7	7	1	0	1	0	8	1	6	1	0	0	0	-	0	0-0	0	8.01	10.50
2000 Tampa Bay	AL	45	0	0	8	60.2	265	49	33	31	10	2	3	2	39	2	73	3	0	1	3	.250	0	1-3	2	4.50	4.60
2001 Tampa Bay	AL	66	0	0	16	62.2	279	51	34	30	7	1	3	4	49	5	66	4	0	2	5	.286	0	0-3	15	4.84	4.31
2002 TB-Sea	AL	52	0	0	17	55.2	262	57	37	36	10	1	1	7	35	2	56	4	0	3	2	.600	0	0-2	5	6.19	5.82
2003 Toronto	AL	21	0	0	3	13.2	69	14	6	5	2	0	2	2	12	3	11	2	0	0	0	-	0	0-1	2	6.57	3.29
2002 Tampa Bay	AL	29	0	0	6	37.1	172	39	27	26	8	0	0	3	21	1	37	2	0	2	1	.667	0	0-2	4	6.15	6.27
2002 Seattle	AL	23	0	0	11	18.1	90	18	10	10	2	1	1	4	14	1	19	2	0	1	1	.500	0	0-0	1	6.22	4.91
8 ML YEARS		259	3	0	62	267.0	1215	236	170	154	42	5	10	17	192	16	274	16	0	7	14	.333	0	1-10	31	5.30	5.19

Jack Cressend

Pitches: R Bats: R Pos: RP-33 Ht: 6'1" Wt: 185 Born: 5/13/75 Age: 29

Year Team	Lg	G	GS	CG	GF	IP	BFP	H	R	ER	HR	SH	SF	HB	TBB	IBB	SO	WP	Bk	W	L	Pct	ShO	Sv-Op	Hld	ERC	ERA
2003 Akron*	AA	8	0	0	3	16.0	67	15	4	0	0	1	0	0	2	0	10	1	0	2	0	1.000	0	1- -	-	1.99	0.00
2003 Kinston*	A+	2	0	0	0	4.1	21	9	6	6	1	0	0	0	0	0	4	0	0	1	0	1.000	0	0- -	-	10.56	12.46
2003 Buffalo*	AAA	8	0	0	0	14.2	56	7	2	2	0	2	1	0	6	0	12	0	0	1	0	1.000	0	0- -	-	1.19	1.23
2000 Minnesota	AL	11	0	0	4	13.2	61	20	8	8	0	0	0	0	6	0	6	0	0	0	0	-	0	0-0	0	6.65	5.27
2001 Minnesota	AL	44	0	0	9	56.1	232	50	24	23	6	2	2	1	16	0	40	2	0	3	2	.600	0	0-2	5	3.13	3.67
2002 Minnesota	AL	23	0	0	0	32.0	154	40	25	21	6	1	2	1	19	4	22	1	0	0	1	.000	0	0-0	0	6.92	5.91
2003 Cleveland	AL	33	0	0	8	43.0	174	40	12	12	1	4	0	2	9	1	28	1	0	2	1	.667	0	0-1	5	2.67	2.51
4 ML YEARS		111	0	0	25	145.0	621	150	69	64	13	7	4	4	50	5	96	4	0	5	4	.556	0	0-3	10	4.06	3.97

Coco Crisp

Bats: B **Throws:** R **Pos:** CF-53; LF-39; DH-7; PH-3   **Ht:** 6'0" **Wt:** 185 **Born:** 11/1/79 **Age:** 24

Year Team	Lg	G	AB	H	2B	3B	HR	(Hm	Rd)	TB	R	RBI	RC	TBB	IBB	SO	HBP	SH	SF	SB	CS	SB%	GDP	Avg	OBP	Slg
1999 Johnson City	R+	65	229	59	5	4	3	(-	-)	81	55	22	39	44	0	41	2	8	2	27	6	.82	0	.258	.379	.354
2000 New Jersey	A-	36	134	32	5	0	0	(-	-)	37	18	14	15	11	0	22	1	5	0	25	3	.89	1	.239	.301	.276
2000 Peoria	A	27	98	27	9	0	0	(-	-)	36	14	7	15	16	0	15	0	4	0	7	3	.70	1	.276	.377	.367
2001 Potomac	A+	139	530	162	23	3	11	(-	-)	224	80	47	82	52	6	64	1	7	1	39	21	.65	8	.306	.368	.423
2002 Buffalo	AAA	4	21	5	1	0	0	(-	-)	6	3	2	1	0	0	2	0	0	0	1	0	1.00	2	.238	.238	.286
2002 New Haven	AA	89	355	107	16	1	9	(-	-)	152	61	47	56	36	1	56	0	5	1	26	10	.72	6	.301	.365	.428
2002 Akron	AA	7	32	13	1	0	1	(-	-)	17	9	4	8	3	1	3	0	1	0	4	0	1.00	0	.406	.457	.531
2003 Buffalo	AAA	56	225	81	19	6	1	(-	-)	115	42	24	49	26	0	24	5	9	2	20	8	.71	5	.360	.434	.511
2002 Cleveland	AL	32	127	33	9	2	1	(1	0)	49	16	9	19	11	0	19	0	3	2	4	1	.80	0	.260	.314	.386
2003 Cleveland	AL	99	414	110	15	6	3	(3	0)	146	55	27	46	23	1	51	0	7	3	15	9	.63	4	.266	.302	.353
2 ML YEARS		131	541	143	24	8	4	(4	0)	195	71	36	65	34	1	70	0	10	5	19	10	.66	4	.264	.305	.360

Tripp Cromer

Bats: R **Throws:** R **Pos:** PH-2; 2B-1   **Ht:** 6'2" **Wt:** 165 **Born:** 11/21/67 **Age:** 36

Year Team	Lg	G	AB	H	2B	3B	HR	(Hm	Rd)	TB	R	RBI	RC	TBB	IBB	SO	HBP	SH	SF	SB	CS	SB%	GDP	Avg	OBP	Slg
2003 New Orleans*	AAA	84	242	61	15	3	4	(Hm	Rd)	94	29	36	28	17	0	41	2	4	3	0	0	-	5	.252	.303	.388
1993 St Louis	NL	10	23	2	0	0	0	(0	0)	2	1	0	0	1	0	6	0	0	0	0	0	-	0	.087	.125	.087
1994 St Louis	NL	2	0	0	0	0	0	(0	0)	0	1	0	0	0	0	0	0	0	0	0	0	-	0	-	-	-
1995 St Louis	NL	105	345	78	19	0	5	(2	3)	112	36	18	26	14	2	66	4	1	5	0	0	-	14	.226	.261	.325
1997 Los Angeles	NL	28	86	25	3	0	4	(2	2)	40	8	20	12	6	3	16	0	2	1	0	1	.00	2	.291	.333	.465
1998 Los Angeles	NL	6	6	1	0	0	1	(0	1)	4	1	1	1	0	0	2	0	0	0	0	0	-	0	.167	.167	.667
1999 Los Angeles	NL	33	52	10	0	0	2	(1	1)	16	5	8	3	5	0	10	0	0	0	0	0	-	4	.192	.263	.308
2000 Houston	NL	9	8	1	0	0	0	(0	0)	1	2	0	1	1	0	1	0	1	0	0	0	-	0	.125	.222	.125
2003 Houston	NL	3	4	1	0	0	0	(0	0)	3	0	1	1	0	0	0	0	0	0	0	0	-	0	.250	.250	.750
8 ML YEARS		196	524	118	22	1	12	(5	7)	178	54	48	43	27	5	101	4	4	6	0	1	.00	20	.225	.266	.340

Bobby Crosby

Bats: R **Throws:** R **Pos:** SS-9; PH-3; PR-2; DH-1   **Ht:** 6'3" **Wt:** 195 **Born:** 1/12/80 **Age:** 24

Year Team	Lg	G	AB	H	2B	3B	HR	(Hm	Rd)	TB	R	RBI	RC	TBB	IBB	SO	HBP	SH	SF	SB	CS	SB%	GDP	Avg	OBP	Slg
2001 Modesto	A+	11	38	15	5	0	1	(-	-)	23	7	3	9	3	0	8	0	0	0	0	0	-	1	.395	.439	.605
2002 Modesto	A+	73	280	86	17	2	2	(-	-)	113	47	38	47	33	0	43	7	2	1	5	0	1.00	5	.307	.393	.404
2002 Midland	AA	59	228	64	16	0	7	(-	-)	101	31	31	32	19	1	41	0	3	1	9	2	.82	9	.281	.335	.443
2003 Sacramento	AAA	127	465	143	32	6	22	(-	-)	253	86	90	97	63	2	110	7	4	4	24	4	.86	16	.308	.395	.544
2003 Oakland	AL	11	12	0	0	0	0	(0	0)	0	1	0	0	1	0	5	1	0	0	0	0	-	0	.000	.143	.000

Bubba Crosby

Bats: L **Throws:** L **Pos:** PH-8; LF-1   **Ht:** 5'11" **Wt:** 185 **Born:** 8/11/76 **Age:** 27

Year Team	Lg	G	AB	H	2B	3B	HR	(Hm	Rd)	TB	R	RBI	RC	TBB	IBB	SO	HBP	SH	SF	SB	CS	SB%	GDP	Avg	OBP	Slg
1998 Sn Brnardino	A+	56	199	43	9	2	0	(-	-)	56	25	14	14	17	0	38	0	4	3	3	5	.38	3	.216	.274	.281
1999 Sn Brnardino	A+	96	371	110	21	3	1	(-	-)	140	53	37	55	42	3	71	6	4	1	19	8	.70	6	.296	.376	.377
2000 Vero Beach	A+	73	274	73	13	8	8	(-	-)	126	50	51	44	31	3	41	7	3	1	27	10	.73	9	.266	.355	.460
2000 Sn Brnardino	A+	3	12	3	0	0	0	(-	-)	3	2	2	0	0	0	4	0	0	0	1	0	1.00	1	.250	.250	.250
2001 Las Vegas	AAA	13	42	9	2	1	0	(-	-)	13	5	5	3	1	0	8	0	0	0	1	1	.50	0	.214	.233	.310
2001 Jacksonville	AA	107	384	116	22	5	6	(-	-)	166	68	47	64	37	2	60	8	7	7	22	6	.79	7	.302	.369	.432
2002 Las Vegas	AAA	73	279	73	12	1	9	(-	-)	114	26	36	36	19	1	47	2	3	1	3	1	.75	3	.262	.312	.409
2002 Jacksonville	AA	38	150	39	6	2	2	(-	-)	55	14	20	18	11	0	23	2	1	1	7	3	.70	2	.260	.317	.367
2003 Las Vegas	AAA	76	277	100	24	8	12	(-	-)	176	57	57	68	25	0	47	3	1	7	8	0	1.00	6	.361	.410	.635
2003 Columbus	AAA	16	63	19	2	1	2	(-	-)	29	9	8	12	6	0	12	1	0	1	3	0	1.00	1	.302	.366	.460
2003 Los Angeles	NL	9	12	1	0	0	0	(0	0)	1	0	1	0	0	0	3	0	0	0	0	0	-	0	.083	.083	.083

Mike Crudale

Pitches: R **Bats:** R **Pos:** RP-22   **Ht:** 6'0" **Wt:** 205 **Born:** 1/3/77 **Age:** 27

Year Team	Lg	G	GS	CG	GF	IP	BFP	H	R	ER	HR	SH	SF	HB	TBB	IBB	SO	WP	Bk	W	L	Pct	ShO	Sv-Op	Hld	ERC	ERA
1999 Johnson City	R+	24	0	0	8	33.0	142	29	15	12	1	1	0	1	14	0	36	5	0	1	1	.000	0	1- -	-	3.09	3.27
2000 Peoria	A	38	0	0	14	50.2	209	40	17	13	2	5	0	3	16	3	45	4	0	6	1	.857	0	5- -	-	2.37	2.31
2000 Potomac	A+	21	0	0	9	25.2	120	31	17	13	3	2	2	1	11	1	28	0	0	2	4	.333	0	2- -	-	5.49	4.56
2001 New Haven	AA	62	0	0	30	80.1	338	76	42	29	7	2	2	0	22	4	85	7	0	4	9	.308	0	9- -	-	3.08	3.25
2002 Memphis	AAA	13	0	0	13	14.2	57	10	3	3	1	0	0	0	5	1	16	2	0	1	0	1.000	0	7- -	-	2.00	1.84
2003 Memphis	AAA	32	0	0	29	29.1	131	34	19	18	7	0	0	0	11	1	23	2	0	5	5	.500	0	6- -	-	5.84	5.52
2003 Indianapolis	AAA	2	0	0	1	2.0	7	1	0	0	0	0	0	0	0	0	1	0	0	0	0	-	0	0- -	-	0.54	0.00
2002 St Louis	NL	49	1	0	14	52.2	213	43	11	11	3	3	6	1	14	2	47	3	0	3	0	1.000	0	0-1	6	2.35	1.88
2003 StL-Mil	NL	22	0	0	6	20.2	93	12	8	6	1	1	1	1	18	1	13	1	0	0	1	.000	0	0-1	4	3.20	2.61
2003 St Louis	NL	13	0	0	4	11.1	59	11	5	3	1	1	1	1	12	1	6	1	0	0	1	.000	0	0-1	1	6.37	2.38
2003 Milwaukee	NL	9	0	0	2	9.1	34	1	3	3	0	0	0	0	6	0	7	0	0	0	0	-	0	0-0	3	0.67	2.89
2 ML YEARS		71	1	0	20	73.1	306	55	19	17	4	4	7	2	32	3	60	4	0	3	1	.750	0	0-2	10	2.60	2.09

Deivi Cruz

Bats: R **Throws:** R **Pos:** SS-147; DH-4; PH-1   **Ht:** 6'0" **Wt:** 184 **Born:** 11/6/72 **Age:** 31

Year Team	Lg	G	AB	H	2B	3B	HR	(Hm	Rd)	TB	R	RBI	RC	TBB	IBB	SO	HBP	SH	SF	SB	CS	SB%	GDP	Avg	OBP	Slg
1997 Detroit	AL	147	436	105	26	0	2	(0	2)	137	35	40	31	14	0	55	0	14	3	3	6	.33	9	.241	.263	.314
1998 Detroit	AL	135	454	118	22	3	5	(5	0)	161	52	45	42	13	0	55	3	5	2	3	4	.43	11	.260	.284	.355
1999 Detroit	AL	155	518	147	35	0	13	(9	4)	221	64	58	64	12	0	57	4	14	5	1	4	.20	10	.284	.302	.427
2000 Detroit	AL	156	583	176	46	5	10	(1	9)	262	68	82	74	13	2	43	4	8	7	1	4	.20	25	.302	.318	.449
2001 Detroit	AL	110	414	106	28	1	7	(2	5)	157	39	52	42	17	0	46	4	1	2	4	1	.80	13	.256	.291	.379
2002 San Diego	NL	151	514	135	28	2	7	(3	4)	188	49	47	40	22	2	58	3	3	5	2	3	.40	20	.263	.294	.366
2003 Baltimore	AL	152	548	137	24	2	14	(7	7)	207	61	65	55	13	1	49	2	7	2	1	2	.33	13	.250	.269	.378
7 ML YEARS		1006	3467	924	209	13	58	(27	31)	1333	368	389	348	104	5	363	20	52	26	15	24	.38	101	.267	.290	.384

Enrique Cruz

Bats: R **Throws:** R **Pos:** PH-36; SS-13; PR-13; 2B-6; 3B-2   **Ht:** 6'1" **Wt:** 180 **Born:** 11/21/81 **Age:** 22

Year Team	Lg	G	AB	H	2B	3B	HR	(Hm	Rd)	TB	R	RBI	RC	TBB	IBB	SO	HBP	SH	SF	SB	CS	SB%	GDP	Avg	OBP	Slg
1999 Mets	R	54	183	56	14	2	4	(-	-)	86	34	24	35	28	0	41	1	0	1	0	0	-	3	.306	.399	.470
2000 Capital City	A	49	157	29	12	0	1	(-	-)	44	19	12	13	25	1	44	1	1	1	1	3	.25	1	.185	.299	.280
2000 Kingsport	R+	63	223	56	14	0	9	(-	-)	97	35	39	34	26	1	56	3	4	2	19	7	.73	3	.251	.335	.435
2001 Capital City	A	124	438	110	20	2	9	(-	-)	161	60	59	62	59	0	106	6	3	3	33	7	.83	7	.251	.346	.368
2002 St.Lucie	A+	124	467	136	21	2	6	(-	-)	179	69	45	57	32	2	76	2	3	5	33	16	.67	15	.291	.336	.383
2003 Milwaukee	NL	60	71	6	1	0	0	(0	0)	7	6	2	0	4	0	30	1	0	0	0	0	-	2	.085	.145	.099

Jacob Cruz

Bats: L **Throws:** L **Pos:** RF   **Ht:** 6'0" **Wt:** 210 **Born:** 1/28/73 **Age:** 31

Year Team	Lg	G	AB	H	2B	3B	HR	(Hm	Rd)	TB	R	RBI	RC	TBB	IBB	SO	HBP	SH	SF	SB	CS	SB%	GDP	Avg	OBP	Slg
1996 San Francisco	NL	33	77	18	3	0	3	(3	0)	30	10	10	10	12	0	24	2	1	0	0	1	.00	2	.234	.352	.390
1997 San Francisco	NL	16	25	4	1	0	0	(0	0)	5	3	3	0	3	0	4	0	0	1	0	0	-	3	.160	.241	.200
1998 SF-Cle		4	4	0	0	0	0	(0	0)	0	0	0	0	0	0	3	0	0	0	0	0	-	0	.000	.000	.000
1999 Cleveland	AL	32	88	29	5	1	3	(3	0)	45	14	17	14	5	0	13	1	1	1	0	2	.00	4	.330	.368	.511
2000 Cleveland	AL	11	29	7	3	0	0	(0	0)	10	3	5	5	5	0	4	1	0	1	1	0	1.00	4	.241	.361	.345
2001 Cle-Col		72	144	31	5	0	4	(2	2)	48	19	18	13	15	0	50	4	1	2	0	4	.00	4	.215	.303	.333
2002 Detroit	AL	35	88	24	3	1	2	(0	2)	35	12	6	11	13	0	20	3	1	2	3	1	.75	2	.273	.377	.398
1998 San Francisco	NL	3	3	0	0	0	0	(0	0)	0	0	0	0	0	0	2	0	0	0	0	0	-	0	.000	.000	.000
1998 Cleveland	AL	1	1	0	0	0	0	(0	0)	0	0	0	0	0	0	1	0	0	0	0	0	-	0	.000	.000	.000
2001 Cleveland	AL	28	68	15	4	0	3	(2	1)	28	12	11	7	5	0	23	3	0	0	0	2	.00	3	.221	.303	.412
2001 Colorado	NL	44	76	16	1	0	1	(0	1)	20	7	7	6	10	0	27	1	1	2	0	2	.00	1	.211	.303	.263
7 ML YEARS		203	455	113	20	2	12	(8	4)	173	61	59	53	53	0	118	11	4	7	4	8	.33	15	.248	.337	.380

Jose Cruz

Bats: B **Throws:** R **Pos:** RF-157; CF-3; PH-2   **Ht:** 6'0" **Wt:** 210 **Born:** 4/19/74 **Age:** 30

Year Team	Lg	G	AB	H	2B	3B	HR	(Hm	Rd)	TB	R	RBI	RC	TBB	IBB	SO	HBP	SH	SF	SB	CS	SB%	GDP	Avg	OBP	Slg
1997 Sea-Tor	AL	104	395	98	19	1	26	(11	15)	197	59	68	63	41	2	117	0	1	5	7	2	.78	5	.248	.315	.499
1998 Toronto	AL	105	352	89	14	3	11	(4	7)	142	55	42	55	57	3	99	0	0	4	11	4	.73	0	.253	.354	.403
1999 Toronto	AL	106	349	84	19	3	14	(8	6)	151	63	45	57	64	5	91	0	1	4	14	4	.78	6	.241	.358	.433
2000 Toronto	AL	162	603	146	32	5	31	(15	16)	281	91	76	91	71	3	129	2	2	3	15	5	.75	11	.242	.323	.466
2001 Toronto	AL	146	577	158	38	4	34	(15	19)	306	92	88	101	45	4	138	1	2	2	32	5	.86	8	.274	.326	.530
2002 Toronto	AL	124	466	114	26	5	18	(11	7)	204	64	70	72	51	1	106	0	1	4	7	1	.88	8	.245	.317	.438
2003 San Francisco	NL	158	539	135	26	1	20	(9	11)	223	90	68	71	102	6	121	0	2	7	5	8	.38	14	.250	.366	.414
1997 Seattle	AL	49	183	49	12	1	12	(7	5)	99	28	34	31	13	0	45	0	1	1	1	0	1.00	3	.268	.315	.541
1997 Toronto	AL	55	212	49	7	0	14	(4	10)	98	31	34	32	28	2	72	0	0	4	6	2	.75	2	.231	.316	.462
7 ML YEARS		905	3281	824	174	22	154	(73	81)	1504	514	457	510	431	24	801	3	9	25	91	29	.76	52	.251	.336	.458

Juan Cruz

Pitches: R **Bats:** R **Pos:** RP-19; SP-6   **Ht:** 6'2" **Wt:** 165 **Born:** 10/15/78 **Age:** 25

Year Team	Lg	G	GS	CG	GF	IP	BFP	H	R	ER	HR	SH	SF	HB	TBB	IBB	SO	WP	Bk	W	L	Pct	ShO	Sv-Op	Hld	ERC	ERA
2003 Iowa*	AAA	9	9	0	0	50.2	200	37	12	11	1	3	3	4	11	0	47	1	1	4	0	1.000	0	0- -	-	1.85	1.95
2001 Chicago	NL	8	8	0	0	44.2	185	40	16	16	4	2	0	2	17	1	39	0	0	3	1	.750	0	0-0	0	3.59	3.22
2002 Chicago	NL	45	9	0	14	97.1	431	84	56	43	11	7	8	7	59	4	81	1	0	3	11	.214	0	1-4	3	4.49	3.98
2003 Chicago	NL	25	6	0	3	61.0	284	66	44	41	7	7	2	7	28	0	65	4	0	2	7	.222	0	0-1	1	5.23	6.05
3 ML YEARS		78	23	0	17	203.0	900	190	116	100	22	16	10	17	104	5	185	5	0	8	19	.296	0	1-5	4	4.51	4.43

Nelson Cruz

Pitches: R **Bats:** R **Pos:** RP-13; SP-7   **Ht:** 6'1" **Wt:** 185 **Born:** 9/13/72 **Age:** 31

Year Team	Lg	G	GS	CG	GF	IP	BFP	H	R	ER	HR	SH	SF	HB	TBB	IBB	SO	WP	Bk	W	L	Pct	ShO	Sv-Op	Hld	ERC	ERA
2003 Co Springs*	AAA	4	4	0	0	15.0	72	24	18	12	3	2	1	3	0	0	10	0	0	1	2	.333	0	0- -	-	7.93	7.20
1997 Chicago	AL	19	0	0	11	26.1	116	29	19	19	6	1	0	0	9	1	23	3	0	0	2	.000	0	0-0	6	5.21	6.49
1999 Detroit	AL	29	6	0	10	66.2	295	74	44	42	11	2	4	3	23	1	46	2	0	2	5	.286	0	0-0	4	5.09	5.67
2000 Detroit	AL	27	0	0	12	41.0	172	39	14	14	4	0	2	3	13	3	34	2	0	5	2	.714	0	0-1	3	3.69	3.07
2001 Houston	NL	66	0	0	16	82.1	342	72	41	38	11	3	2	9	24	4	75	0	1	3	3	.500	0	2-4	10	3.59	4.15
2002 Houston	NL	43	5	0	11	78.1	360	90	44	39	12	5	3	6	29	4	61	4	0	2	6	.250	0	0-2	1	5.31	4.48
2003 Colorado	NL	20	7	0	1	53.2	235	65	43	43	15	1	2	3	11	2	38	3	0	3	5	.375	0	0-1	2	5.98	7.21
6 ML YEARS		204	18	0	55	348.1	1520	369	205	195	59	12	13	24	109	15	277	14	1	15	23	.395	0	2-8	25	4.75	5.04

Mike Cuddyer

Bats: R **Throws:** R **Pos:** RF-17; PH-8; 3B-7; 1B-5; 2B-1; LF-1; DH-1; PR-1   **Ht:** 6'2" **Wt:** 190 **Born:** 3/27/79 **Age:** 25

Year Team	Lg	G	AB	H	2B	3B	HR	(Hm	Rd)	TB	R	RBI	RC	TBB	IBB	SO	HBP	SH	SF	SB	CS	SB%	GDP	Avg	OBP	Slg
2003 Twins*	R	2	5	4	0	0	1	(-	-)	7	1	3	3	1	1	0	1	0	0	0	1	.00	0	.800	.857	1.400
2003 Rochester*	AAA	53	186	57	17	0	3	(-	-)	83	25	34	32	25	1	49	1	0	6	5	4	.56	4	.306	.381	.446
2001 Minnesota	AL	8	18	4	2	0	0	(0	0)	6	1	1	2	2	0	6	0	0	0	1	0	1.00	1	.222	.300	.333
2002 Minnesota	AL	41	112	29	7	0	4	(2	2)	48	12	13	14	8	0	30	1	1	1	2	0	1.00	3	.259	.311	.429
2003 Minnesota	AL	35	102	25	1	3	4	(1	3)	44	14	8	9	12	0	19	0	0	0	1	1	.50	6	.245	.325	.431
3 ML YEARS		84	232	58	10	3	8	(3	5)	98	27	22	25	22	0	55	1	1	1	4	1	.80	10	.250	.316	.422

Will Cunnane

Pitches: R **Bats:** R **Pos:** RP-20   **Ht:** 6'1" **Wt:** 205 **Born:** 4/24/74 **Age:** 30

Year Team	Lg	G	GS	CG	GF	IP	BFP	H	R	ER	HR	SH	SF	HB	TBB	IBB	SO	WP	Bk	W	L	Pct	ShO	Sv-Op	Hld	ERC	ERA
2003 Richmond*	AAA	15	0	0	7	21.0	74	11	2	0	0	0	3	0	2	0	19	1	0	1	0	1.000	0	2--	-	0.76	0.00
2003 Iowa*	AAA	12	0	0	3	16.1	73	17	5	4	0	2	1	0	8	3	16	3	0	1	0	.000	0	0--	-	3.55	2.20
1997 San Diego	NL	54	8	0	16	91.1	430	114	69	59	11	1	1	5	49	3	79	3	0	6	3	.667	0	0-2	4	6.48	5.81
1998 San Diego	NL	3	0	0	1	3.0	14	4	2	2	1	0	0	0	1	1	1	0	0	0	0	-	0	0-0	0	6.84	6.00
1999 San Diego	NL	24	0	0	2	31.0	130	34	19	18	8	2	0	0	12	3	22	3	0	2	1	.667	0	0-0	5	5.87	5.23
2000 San Diego	NL	27	3	0	4	38.1	169	35	21	18	2	1	1	1	21	0	34	1	0	1	1	.500	0	0-0	1	3.90	4.23
2001 Milwaukee	NL	31	1	0	6	51.2	238	66	34	31	6	7	1	2	22	6	37	0	0	3	0	.000	0	0-0	1	5.93	5.40
2002 Chicago	NL	16	0	0	2	26.1	115	27	16	16	5	1	0	1	13	1	30	1	0	1	1	.500	0	0-1	1	5.49	5.47
2003 Atlanta	NL	20	0	0	8	20.0	80	14	6	6	2	0	0	0	6	2	20	1	0	2	2	.500	0	3-3	5	2.00	2.70
7 ML YEARS		175	12	0	39	261.2	1176	294	167	150	35	12	3	9	124	16	223	9	0	12	11	.522	0	3-6	17	5.43	5.16

Jack Cust

Bats: L **Throws:** R **Pos:** DH-21; PH-6; LF-1   **Ht:** 6'1" **Wt:** 205 **Born:** 1/16/79 **Age:** 25

Year Team	Lg	G	AB	H	2B	3B	HR	(Hm	Rd)	TB	R	RBI	RC	TBB	IBB	SO	HBP	SH	SF	SB	CS	SB%	GDP	Avg	OBP	Slg
2003 Ottawa*	AAA	97	333	95	18	1	9	(-	-)	142	55	58	64	80	1	94	0	0	2	5	2	.71	9	.285	.422	.426
2001 Arizona	NL	3	2	1	0	0	0	(0	0)	1	0	0	1	1	0	0	0	0	0	0	0	-	0	.500	.667	.500
2002 Colorado	NL	35	65	11	2	0	1	(0	1)	16	8	8	6	12	0	32	0	0	1	0	1	.00	3	.169	.295	.246
2003 Baltimore	AL	27	73	19	7	0	4	(2	2)	38	7	11	18	10	0	25	1	0	0	0	0	-	0	.260	.357	.521
3 ML YEARS		65	140	31	9	0	5	(2	3)	55	15	19	25	23	0	57	1	0	1	0	1	.00	3	.221	.333	.393

Omar Daal

Pitches: L **Bats:** L **Pos:** SP-17; RP-2   **Ht:** 6'3" **Wt:** 204 **Born:** 3/1/72 **Age:** 32

Year Team	Lg	G	GS	CG	GF	IP	BFP	H	R	ER	HR	SH	SF	HB	TBB	IBB	SO	WP	Bk	W	L	Pct	ShO	Sv-Op	Hld	ERC	ERA
2003 Bowie*	AA	1	1	0	0	3.0	17	5	4	4	1	0	1	0	2	0	2	0	0	0	0	-	0	0--	-	13.15	12.00
1993 Los Angeles	NL	47	0	0	12	35.1	155	36	20	20	5	2	2	0	21	3	19	1	2	2	3	.400	0	0-1	7	5.29	5.09
1994 Los Angeles	NL	24	0	0	5	13.2	55	12	5	5	1	1	0	0	5	0	9	1	1	0	0	-	0	0-0	3	3.24	3.29
1995 Los Angeles	NL	28	0	0	8	20.0	100	29	16	16	1	1	1	1	15	4	11	0	1	4	0	1.000	0	0-1	4	7.85	7.20
1996 Montreal	NL	64	6	0	9	87.1	366	74	40	39	10	2	2	1	37	3	82	1	1	4	5	.444	0	0-4	9	3.44	4.02
1997 Mon-Tor	NL	42	3	0	6	57.1	270	82	48	45	7	7	1	2	21	3	44	2	0	2	3	.400	0	1-3	3	6.76	7.06
1998 Arizona	NL	33	23	3	4	162.2	664	146	60	52	12	9	6	3	51	3	132	0	1	8	12	.400	1	0-0	1	3.12	2.88
1999 Arizona	NL	32	32	2	0	214.2	895	188	92	87	21	4	7	7	79	3	148	3	2	16	9	.640	1	0-0	0	3.39	3.65
2000 Ari-Phi	NL	32	28	0	1	167.0	775	208	128	114	26	6	6	9	72	11	96	0	2	4	19	.174	0	0-0	0	6.17	6.14
2001 Philadelphia	NL	32	32	0	0	185.2	801	199	100	92	26	7	5	5	56	3	107	0	3	13	7	.650	0	0-0	0	4.45	4.46
2002 Los Angeles	NL	39	23	0	3	161.1	668	142	73	70	20	11	4	4	54	3	105	0	0	11	9	.550	0	0-0	1	3.42	3.90
2003 Baltimore	AL	19	17	0	1	93.2	434	134	69	66	11	8	3	2	30	1	53	2	0	4	11	.267	0	0-0	0	6.57	6.34
1997 Montreal	NL	33	0	0	6	30.1	150	48	35	33	4	5	1	2	15	3	16	1	0	1	2	.333	0	1-3	3	8.60	9.79
1997 Toronto	AL	9	3	0	0	27.0	120	34	13	12	3	2	0	0	6	0	28	1	0	1	1	.500	0	0-0	0	4.85	4.00
2000 Arizona	NL	20	16	0	1	96.0	460	127	88	77	17	3	5	7	42	11	45	0	1	2	10	.167	0	0-0	0	6.78	7.22
2000 Philadelphia	NL	12	12	0	0	71.0	315	81	40	37	9	3	1	2	30	0	51	0	1	2	9	.182	0	0-0	0	5.37	4.69
11 ML YEARS		392	164	5	41	1198.2	5183	1250	651	606	140	58	37	34	441	37	806	10	13	68	78	.466	2	1-9	29	4.40	4.55

Jeff D'Amico

Pitches: R **Bats:** R **Pos:** SP-29   **Ht:** 6'7" **Wt:** 250 **Born:** 12/27/75 **Age:** 28

Year Team	Lg	G	GS	CG	GF	IP	BFP	H	R	ER	HR	SH	SF	HB	TBB	IBB	SO	WP	Bk	W	L	Pct	ShO	Sv-Op	Hld	ERC	ERA
1996 Milwaukee	NL	17	17	0	0	86.0	367	88	53	52	21	3	6	0	31	0	53	1	1	6	6	.500	0	0-0	0	5.11	5.44
1997 Milwaukee	NL	23	23	1	0	135.2	585	139	81	71	25	4	4	8	43	2	94	3	1	9	7	.563	1	0-0	0	4.69	4.71
1999 Milwaukee	NL	1	0	0	1	1.0	4	0	0	0	0	0	0	0	0	0	1	0	0	0	0	-	0	0-0	0	1.95	0.00
2000 Milwaukee	NL	23	23	1	0	162.1	667	143	55	48	14	10	3	6	46	5	101	5	0	12	7	.632	1	0-0	0	3.01	2.66
2001 Milwaukee	NL	10	10	0	0	47.1	216	60	42	32	11	2	1	1	16	4	32	2	0	2	4	.333	0	0-0	0	6.30	6.08
2002 New York	NL	29	22	1	0	145.2	621	152	84	80	20	8	4	3	37	8	101	0	0	6	10	.375	1	0-0	0	3.96	4.94
2003 Pittsburgh	NL	29	29	2	0	175.1	765	204	104	93	23	11	6	7	42	6	100	6	0	9	16	.360	1	0-0	0	4.67	4.77
7 ML YEARS		132	124	5	2	753.1	3225	787	419	376	114	38	20	25	215	25	482	17	2	44	50	.468	4	0-0	0	4.30	4.49

Johnny Damon

Bats: L **Throws:** L **Pos:** CF-144; PH-4   **Ht:** 6'2" **Wt:** 190 **Born:** 11/5/73 **Age:** 30

Year Team	Lg	G	AB	H	2B	3B	HR	(Hm	Rd)	TB	R	RBI	RC	TBB	IBB	SO	HBP	SH	SF	SB	CS	SB%	GDP	Avg	OBP	Slg
1995 Kansas City	AL	47	188	53	11	5	3	(1	2)	83	32	23	29	12	0	22	1	2	3	7	0	1.00	2	.282	.324	.441
1996 Kansas City	AL	145	517	140	22	5	6	(3	3)	190	61	50	64	31	3	64	3	10	5	25	5	.83	4	.271	.313	.368
1997 Kansas City	AL	146	472	130	12	8	8	(3	5)	182	70	48	63	42	2	70	3	6	1	16	10	.62	5	.275	.338	.386
1998 Kansas City	AL	161	642	178	30	10	18	(11	7)	282	104	66	98	58	4	84	4	3	3	26	12	.68	4	.277	.339	.439

57

Year Team	Lg	G	AB	H	2B	3B	HR	(Hm	Rd)	TB	R	RBI	RC	TBB	IBB	SO	HBP	SH	SF	SB	CS	SB%	GDP	Avg	OBP	Slg
1999 Kansas City	AL	145	583	179	39	9	14	(5	9)	278	101	77	108	67	5	50	3	3	4	36	6	.86	13	.307	.379	.477
2000 Kansas City	AL	159	655	214	42	10	16	(10	6)	324	136	88	129	65	4	60	1	8	12	46	9	.84	7	.327	.382	.495
2001 Oakland	AL	155	644	165	34	4	9	(2	7)	234	108	49	79	61	1	70	5	5	4	27	12	.69	7	.256	.324	.363
2002 Boston	AL	154	623	178	34	11	14	(5	9)	276	118	63	100	65	5	70	6	3	5	31	6	.84	4	.286	.356	.443
2003 Boston	AL	145	608	166	32	6	12	(5	7)	246	103	67	90	68	4	74	2	6	6	30	6	.83	5	.273	.345	.405
9 ML YEARS		1257	4932	1403	256	68	100	(45	55)	2095	833	531	760	469	28	564	28	46	43	244	66	.79	49	.284	.347	.425

Vic Darensbourg

Pitches: L Bats: L Pos: RP-9   **Ht: 5'8" Wt: 170 Born: 11/13/70 Age: 33**

		HOW MUCH HE PITCHED						WHAT HE GAVE UP										THE RESULTS							
Year Team	Lg	G	GS	CG	GF	IP	BFP	H	R	ER	HR	SH	SF	HB	TBB	IBB	SO	WP	Bk	W	L	Pct	ShO	Sv-Op	Hld	ERC	ERA
2003 Co Springs*	AAA	20	0	0	10	22.2	96	24	13	9	1	3	0	0	5	1	15	1	0	2	2	.500	0	0--	-	3.22	3.57
2003 Edmonton*	AAA	11	0	0	0	13.2	60	12	3	3	0	0	0	2	7	0	11	1	0	1	1	.500	0	0--	-	3.69	1.98
1998 Florida	NL	59	0	0	10	71.0	287	52	5	29	5	3	3	0	30	6	74	4	0	0	7	.000	0	1-2	13	2.47	3.68
1999 Florida	NL	56	0	0	5	34.2	180	50	36	34	3	5	2	5	21	1	16	1	3	0	1	.000	0	0-1	10	7.90	8.83
2000 Florida	NL	56	0	0	17	62.0	274	61	32	28	7	3	6	2	28	1	59	1	0	5	3	.625	0	0-1	3	4.33	4.06
2001 Florida	NL	58	0	0	19	48.2	202	52	24	23	4	1	2	1	10	6	33	0	0	1	2	.333	0	1-3	11	3.52	4.25
2002 Florida	NL	42	0	0	13	48.1	233	61	34	33	10	2	3	2	26	4	33	0	0	1	2	.333	0	0-0	3	6.98	6.14
2003 Col-Mon	NL	9	0	0	3	9.0	46	17	9	8	2	1	0	0	1	0	4	0	0	0	0	-	0	0-0	1	9.00	8.00
2003 Colorado	NL	3	0	0	2	2.1	12	4	1	0	0	0	0	0	0	0	0	0	0	0	0	-	0	0-0	0	5.18	0.00
2003 Montreal	NL	6	0	0	1	6.2	34	13	8	8	2	1	0	0	1	0	4	0	0	0	0	-	0	0-0	1	10.54	10.80
6 ML YEARS		280	0	0	67	273.2	1222	293	140	155	31	15	16	10	116	18	219	6	3	7	15	.318	0	2-7	40	4.67	5.10

Brian Daubach

Bats: L Throws: R Pos: 1B-45; PH-33; DH-12; RF-9; LF-3   **Ht: 6'1" Wt: 233 Born: 2/11/72 Age: 32**

		BATTING																	BASERUNNING				AVERAGES		
Year Team	Lg	G	AB	H	2B	3B	HR	(Hm	Rd)	TB	R	RBI	RC	TBB	IBB	SO	HBP	SH	SF	SB	CS	SB%	GDP	Avg	OBP	Slg
1998 Florida	NL	10	15	3	1	0	0	(0	0)	4	0	3	1	1	0	5	1	0	0	0	0	-	0	.200	.294	.267
1999 Boston	AL	110	381	112	33	3	21	(11	10)	214	61	73	74	36	0	92	3	0	0	0	1	.00	5	.294	.360	.562
2000 Boston	AL	142	495	123	32	2	21	(10	11)	222	55	76	70	44	2	130	6	0	4	1	1	.50	6	.248	.315	.448
2001 Boston	AL	122	407	107	28	3	22	(11	11)	207	54	71	71	53	7	108	5	1	6	1	0	1.00	10	.263	.350	.509
2002 Boston	AL	137	444	118	24	2	20	(11	9)	206	62	78	76	51	4	126	7	0	4	2	1	.67	10	.266	.348	.464
2003 Chicago	AL	95	183	42	11	0	6	(4	2)	71	26	21	25	34	1	54	1	0	1	1	0	1.00	3	.230	.352	.388
6 ML YEARS		616	1925	505	129	10	90	(47	43)	924	258	322	317	219	14	515	23	1	15	5	3	.63	34	.262	.342	.480

Jeff DaVanon

Bats: B Throws: R Pos: RF-91; CF-31; PH-18; LF-8; PR-8   **Ht: 6'0" Wt: 185 Born: 12/8/73 Age: 30**

		BATTING																	BASERUNNING				AVERAGES		
Year Team	Lg	G	AB	H	2B	3B	HR	(Hm	Rd)	TB	R	RBI	RC	TBB	IBB	SO	HBP	SH	SF	SB	CS	SB%	GDP	Avg	OBP	Slg
2003 Salt Lake*	AAA	16	60	18	4	1	2	(-	-)	30	11	14	12	9	0	9	1	2	0	4	1	.80	1	.300	.400	.500
1999 Anaheim	AL	7	20	4	0	1	1	(1	0)	9	4	4	2	2	0	7	0	0	0	0	1	.00	0	.200	.273	.450
2001 Anaheim	AL	40	88	17	2	1	5	(3	2)	36	7	9	9	11	0	29	0	0	1	1	3	.25	1	.193	.280	.409
2002 Anaheim	AL	16	30	5	3	0	1	(0	1)	11	3	4	4	2	0	6	0	1	0	1	0	1.00	0	.167	.219	.367
2003 Anaheim	AL	123	330	93	16	1	12	(3	9)	147	56	43	56	42	0	59	1	4	5	17	5	.77	6	.282	.360	.445
4 ML YEARS		186	468	119	21	3	19	(7	12)	203	70	60	71	57	0	101	1	5	6	19	9	.68	7	.254	.333	.434

Ben Davis

Bats: B Throws: R Pos: C-73; PH-7; DH-1   **Ht: 6'4" Wt: 214 Born: 3/10/77 Age: 27**

		BATTING																	BASERUNNING				AVERAGES		
Year Team	Lg	G	AB	H	2B	3B	HR	(Hm	Rd)	TB	R	RBI	RC	TBB	IBB	SO	HBP	SH	SF	SB	CS	SB%	GDP	Avg	OBP	Slg
1998 San Diego	NL	1	1	0	0	0	0	(0	0)	0	0	0	0	0	0	0	0	0	0	0	0	-	0	.000	.000	.000
1999 San Diego	NL	76	266	65	14	1	5	(1	4)	96	29	30	27	25	3	70	0	0	2	2	1	.67	9	.244	.307	.361
2000 San Diego	NL	43	130	29	6	0	3	(1	2)	44	12	14	13	14	1	35	0	3	1	1	1	.50	2	.223	.297	.338
2001 San Diego	NL	138	448	107	20	0	11	(3	8)	160	56	57	54	66	5	112	4	1	7	4	4	.50	13	.239	.337	.357
2002 Seattle	AL	80	228	59	10	1	7	(1	6)	92	24	43	32	18	1	58	2	1	4	1	1	.50	6	.259	.313	.404
2003 Seattle	AL	80	246	58	18	0	6	(2	4)	94	25	42	29	18	2	61	0	1	4	0	0	-	5	.236	.284	.382
6 ML YEARS		418	1319	318	68	2	32	(8	24)	486	146	186	155	141	12	336	6	6	18	8	7	.53	35	.241	.313	.368

Doug Davis

Pitches: L Bats: R Pos: SP-20; RP-1   **Ht: 6'4" Wt: 190 Born: 9/21/75 Age: 28**

		HOW MUCH HE PITCHED						WHAT HE GAVE UP										THE RESULTS							
Year Team	Lg	G	GS	CG	GF	IP	BFP	H	R	ER	HR	SH	SF	HB	TBB	IBB	SO	WP	Bk	W	L	Pct	ShO	Sv-Op	Hld	ERC	ERA
2003 Oklahoma*	AAA	4	4	0	0	27.2	109	29	10	10	3	0	0	1	1	0	18	0	1	3	0	1.000	0	0--	-	3.22	3.25
2003 Indianapolis*	AAA	5	5	0	0	34.2	145	33	16	16	2	1	0	2	10	0	19	0	0	1	2	.333	0	0--	-	3.34	4.15
2003 Huntsville*	AA	1	1	0	0	6.0	26	5	2	2	0	0	0	1	3	0	6	2	0	1	0	1.000	0	0--	-	3.50	3.00
1999 Texas	AL	2	0	0	0	2.2	20	12	10	10	3	0	0	0	0	0	3	0	0	0	0	-	0	0-0	0	41.42	33.75
2000 Texas	AL	30	13	1	4	98.2	450	109	61	59	14	6	4	3	58	3	66	5	1	7	6	.538	0	0-3	2	5.93	5.38
2001 Texas	AL	30	30	1	0	186.0	828	220	103	92	14	4	6	3	69	1	115	7	2	11	10	.524	0	0-0	0	4.90	4.45
2002 Texas	AL	10	10	1	0	59.2	262	67	36	33	7	3	3	3	22	0	28	2	2	3	5	.375	1	0-0	0	5.05	4.98
2003 Tex-Tor-Mil	AL	21	20	1	0	109.1	491	123	55	49	16	6	2	1	51	1	62	7	0	7	8	.467	0	0-0	0	5.46	4.03
2003 Texas	AL	1	1	0	0	3.0	17	4	4	4	2	0	0	0	4	0	2	0	0	0	0	-	0	0-0	0	15.81	12.00
2003 Toronto	AL	12	11	0	0	54.0	250	70	33	30	6	3	0	1	26	1	25	6	0	4	6	.400	0	0-0	0	6.39	5.00
2003 Milwaukee	NL	8	8	1	0	52.1	224	49	18	15	8	3	2	0	21	0	35	1	0	3	2	.600	0	0-0	0	4.06	2.58
5 ML YEARS		93	73	4	4	456.1	2051	531	265	243	54	19	15	10	200	5	274	21	5	28	29	.491	1	0-3	2	5.42	4.79

J.J. Davis

Bats: R **Throws:** R **Pos:** RF-10; PH-9; PR-1 **Ht:** 6'5" **Wt:** 250 **Born:** 10/25/78 **Age:** 25

								BATTING												BASERUNNING				AVERAGES		
Year Team	Lg	G	AB	H	2B	3B	HR	(Hm Rd)	TB	R	RBI	RC	TBB	IBB	SO	HBP	SH	SF	SB	CS	SB%	GDP	Avg	OBP	Slg
1997 Pirates	R	45	165	42	10	2	1	(- -)	59	19	18	18	14	2	44	2	0	3	0	0	-	4	.255	.315	.358
1997 Erie	A-	4	13	1	0	0	0	(- -)	1	1	0	0	0	0	4	0	0	0	0	0	-	-	.077	.077	.077
1998 Augusta	A	30	106	21	6	0	4	(- -)	39	11	11	7	3	0	24	0	0	0	1	1	.50	4	.198	.220	.368
1998 Erie	A-	52	196	53	12	2	8	(- -)	93	25	39	32	20	1	54	2	0	2	4	1	.80	3	.270	.341	.474
1999 Hickory	A	86	317	84	26	1	19	(- -)	169	58	65	59	44	3	99	4	0	2	2	5	.29	3	.265	.360	.533
2000 Lynchburg	A+	130	485	118	36	1	20	(- -)	216	77	80	68	52	2	171	4	0	1	9	4	.69	11	.243	.319	.445
2001 Altoona	AA	67	228	57	13	3	4	(- -)	88	21	26	27	21	0	79	2	0	1	2	5	.29	1	.250	.317	.386
2001 Pirates	R	4	17	8	1	0	2	(- -)	15	3	6	6	1	0	2	0	0	0	0	0	-	1	.471	.500	.882
2002 Altoona	AA	101	348	100	17	3	20	(- -)	183	51	62	63	33	0	101	3	0	3	7	4	.64	3	.287	.351	.526
2003 Nashville	AAA	122	426	121	29	4	26	(- -)	236	68	67	78	35	4	85	4	0	3	23	6	.79	11	.284	.342	.554
2002 Pittsburgh	NL	9	10	1	0	0	0	(0 0)	1	1	0	0	0	0	4	1	0	0	0	0	-	1	.100	.182	.100
2003 Pittsburgh	NL	19	35	7	0	0	1	(1 0)	10	1	4	2	3	0	13	0	0	0	0	1	.00	0	.200	.263	.286
2 ML YEARS		28	45	8	0	0	1	(1 0)	11	2	4	2	3	0	17	1	0	0	1	1	.00	1	.178	.245	.244

Jason Davis

Pitches: R **Bats:** R **Pos:** SP-27 **Ht:** 6'6" **Wt:** 195 **Born:** 5/8/80 **Age:** 24

			HOW MUCH HE PITCHED					WHAT HE GAVE UP												THE RESULTS							
Year Team	Lg	G	GS	CG	GF	IP	BFP	H	R	ER	HR	SH	SF	HB	TBB	IBB	SO	WP	Bk	W	L	Pct	ShO	Sv-Op	Hld	ERC	ERA
2000 Burlington	R+	10	10	0	0	45.0	201	48	27	22	5	3	3	5	16	0	35	5	1	4	4	.500	0	0--	-	4.77	4.40
2001 Columbus	A	27	27	1	0	160.0	677	147	72	44	9	2	2	14	51	1	115	5	2	14	6	.700	0	0--	-	3.35	2.70
2002 Kinston	A+	17	17	1	0	99.2	442	107	64	46	7	7	3	8	31	2	68	6	0	3	6	.333	1	0--	-	4.13	4.15
2002 Akron	AA	10	10	0	0	59.0	250	63	26	23	2	1	1	5	16	0	45	3	2	6	2	.750	0	0--	-	3.90	3.51
2002 Cleveland	AL	3	3	0	0	14.2	60	12	3	3	1	1	0	0	4	0	11	0	1	1	0	1.000	0	0-0	0	2.40	1.84
2003 Cleveland	AL	27	27	1	0	165.1	696	172	101	86	25	7	3	8	47	4	85	9	2	8	11	.421	0	0-0	0	4.44	4.68
2 ML YEARS		30	29	1	0	180.0	756	184	104	89	26	8	3	8	51	4	96	9	3	9	11	.450	0	0-0	0	4.26	4.45

Gookie Dawkins

Bats: R **Throws:** R **Pos:** 2B-3; PR-1 **Ht:** 6'1" **Wt:** 180 **Born:** 5/12/79 **Age:** 25

								BATTING												BASERUNNING				AVERAGES		
Year Team	Lg	G	AB	H	2B	3B	HR	(Hm Rd)	TB	R	RBI	RC	TBB	IBB	SO	HBP	SH	SF	SB	CS	SB%	GDP	Avg	OBP	Slg
2003 Jacksonville*	AA	35	113	30	6	0	4	(- -)	48	12	20	16	10	0	12	2	7	1	3	2	.60	2	.265	.333	.425
2003 Las Vegas*	AAA	32	115	19	5	1	0	(- -)	26	5	12	5	9	1	26	0	2	1	3	1	.75	1	.165	.224	.226
2003 Omaha*	AAA	33	112	29	6	0	2	(- -)	41	18	18	11	7	0	24	1	2	2	2	3	.40	5	.259	.303	.366
1999 Cincinnati	NL	7	7	1	0	0	0	(0 0)	1	1	0	0	0	0	4	1	0	0	0	0	-	0	.143	.250	.143
2000 Cincinnati	NL	14	41	9	2	0	0	(0 0)	11	5	3	2	2	1	7	0	1	0	0	0	-	3	.220	.256	.268
2002 Cincinnati	NL	31	48	6	2	0	0	(0 0)	8	2	0	1	6	0	21	0	1	0	2	1	.67	1	.125	.222	.167
2003 Kansas City	AL	3	2	0	0	0	0	(0 0)	0	0	0	0	1	0	2	0	0	0	0	0	-	0	.000	.333	.000
4 ML YEARS		55	98	16	4	0	0	(0 0)	20	8	3	3	9	1	34	1	2	0	2	1	.67	4	.163	.241	.204

Joe Dawley

Pitches: R **Bats:** R **Pos:** RP-5 **Ht:** 6'4" **Wt:** 205 **Born:** 9/19/71 **Age:** 32

			HOW MUCH HE PITCHED					WHAT HE GAVE UP												THE RESULTS							
Year Team	Lg	G	GS	CG	GF	IP	BFP	H	R	ER	HR	SH	SF	HB	TBB	IBB	SO	WP	Bk	W	L	Pct	ShO	Sv-Op	Hld	ERC	ERA
1993 Bluefield	R+	20	0	0	15	30.2	143	34	20	12	1	2	1	1	14	3	30	3	1	3	1	.750	0	3--	-	4.18	3.52
1994 Bluefield	R+	11	2	0	5	23.2	110	20	18	15	2	0	1	1	18	0	18	4	0	1	2	.333	0	2--	-	4.55	5.70
1994 Albany	A	5	0	0	4	7.1	37	7	6	5	0	0	1	1	7	1	4	1	0	0	0	-	0	0--	-	5.28	6.14
1995 Frederick	A+	24	0	0	8	32.2	163	41	28	23	4	1	1	3	22	1	29	5	1	1	2	.333	0	1--	-	7.14	6.34
1995 Palm Spring	IND	15	0	0	1	28.0	128	28	14	12	2	0	1	2	9	0	20	1	1	1	0	1.000	0	0--	-	3.58	3.86
1996 Palm Spring	IND	27	0	0	18	33.2	146	26	14	6	3	0	0	1	18	1	29	2	1	2	1	.667	0	4--	-	3.27	1.60
1997 Chico	IND	41	0	0	35	41.1	196	42	24	20	2	0	2	2	18	2	51	2	1	1	4	.200	0	14--	-	3.70	4.35
1998 Chico	IND	45	0	0	41	43.0	196	43	22	16	2	2	2	0	27	2	36	5	0	2	4	.333	0	26--	-	4.44	3.35
1999 Greenville	AA	26	11	0	0	91.2	387	76	54	41	5	3	4	3	37	3	89	3	2	5	3	.625	0	0--	-	2.91	4.03
1999 Richmond	AAA	7	7	1	0	40.0	174	43	26	23	5	3	2	0	12	0	31	4	0	0	3	.000	0	0--	-	4.20	5.18
2001 Myrtle Beach	A+	5	0	0	2	10.0	34	4	2	2	0	0	0	0	0	0	16	0	0	1	0	1.000	0	0--	-	0.35	1.80
2001 Richmond	AAA	3	0	0	1	6.1	22	3	2	2	1	0	0	0	1	0	5	1	0	1	0	1.000	0	0--	-	1.23	2.84
2001 Greenville	AA	22	21	1	0	127.1	518	95	50	43	15	6	4	4	46	0	130	3	1	7	5	.583	0	0--	-	2.82	3.04
2002 Richmond	AAA	24	23	1	1	140.1	564	113	44	41	10	5	4	5	36	0	136	3	1	7	5	.563	1	0--	-	2.48	2.63
2003 Richmond	AAA	46	4	0	35	56.2	240	47	26	21	4	0	4	0	23	1	73	5	0	3	5	.375	0	23--	-	2.90	3.34
2002 Atlanta	NL	1	0	0	0	0.1	1	0	0	0	0	0	0	0	0	0	1	0	0	0	0	-	0	0-0	0	0.00	0.00
2003 Atlanta	NL	5	0	0	4	7.0	41	15	14	14	3	0	0	1	3	0	9	1	0	0	0	-	0	0-0	0	15.12	18.00
2 ML YEARS		6	0	0	5	7.1	42	15	14	14	3	0	0	1	3	0	9	1	0	0	0	-	0	0-0	0	14.05	17.18

Zach Day

Pitches: R **Bats:** R **Pos:** SP-23 **Ht:** 6'4" **Wt:** 185 **Born:** 6/15/78 **Age:** 26

			HOW MUCH HE PITCHED					WHAT HE GAVE UP												THE RESULTS							
Year Team	Lg	G	GS	CG	GF	IP	BFP	H	R	ER	HR	SH	SF	HB	TBB	IBB	SO	WP	Bk	W	L	Pct	ShO	Sv-Op	Hld	ERC	ERA
1996 Yankees	R	7	5	0	1	33.2	139	41	26	21	3	0	0	4	3	0	23	0	0	5	2	.714	0	0--	-	4.71	5.61
1997 Oneonta	A-	14	14	0	0	92.0	372	82	26	22	2	2	4	1	23	0	93	3	0	7	2	.778	0	0--	-	2.50	2.15
1998 Tampa	A+	18	17	0	0	100.0	479	142	89	61	5	3	2	6	32	4	69	5	0	5	8	.385	0	0--	-	5.86	5.49
1998 Greensboro	A	7	6	1	0	36.0	155	35	22	11	1	2	1	3	6	0	37	4	0	1	2	.333	0	0--	-	2.75	2.75
1999 Yankees	R	5	4	0	0	16.2	74	20	10	7	1	0	0	1	4	0	17	0	0	1	1	.500	0	0--	-	4.47	3.78
1999 Greensboro	A	2	2	0	0	8.0	42	14	11	2	0	1	0	0	1	0	4	0	0	0	1	.000	0	0--	-	6.62	2.25
2000 Greensboro	A	13	13	1	0	85.1	343	72	29	18	6	0	0	1	31	0	101	11	1	9	3	.750	1	0--	-	3.05	1.90
2000 Tampa	A+	7	7	0	0	34.1	150	33	22	16	2	0	0	1	15	1	36	1	0	4	3	.333	0	0--	-	3.73	4.19
2000 Akron	AA	8	8	0	0	46.0	192	38	20	18	1	4	0	3	21	0	43	4	0	4	2	.667	0	0--	-	3.13	3.52
2001 Akron	AA	22	22	2	0	136.2	572	123	57	47	8	3	1	4	45	1	94	7	0	9	10	.474	0	0--	-	3.08	3.10
2001 Buffalo	AAA	1	1	0	0	6.0	22	3	1	1	0	0	0	0	1	0	4	0	0	1	0	1.000	0	0--	-	0.80	1.50

Year Team	Lg	G	GS	CG	GF	IP	BFP	H	R	ER	HR	SH	SF	HB	TBB	IBB	SO	WP	Bk	W	L	Pct	ShO	Sv-Op	Hld	ERC	ERA
2001 Ottawa	AAA	6	5	0	0	26.2	120	38	23	22	2	0	1	2	8	0	15	3	0	2	2	.500	0	0--	-	6.59	7.43
2002 Ottawa	AAA	17	16	1	0	90.0	373	77	38	35	5	3	1	4	32	0	68	7	0	5	6	.455	0	0--	-	3.03	3.50
2003 Expos	R	1	1	0	0	2.1	12	3	3	1	0	0	1	0	1	0	3	1	0	0	0	-	0	0--	-	4.47	3.86
2003 Brevard Cnty	A+	1	1	0	0	5.1	19	3	1	1	0	0	0	0	1	0	3	0	0	0	0	-	0	0--	-	1.04	1.69
2002 Montreal	NL	19	2	0	5	37.1	153	28	18	15	3	1	1	1	15	2	25	1	0	4	1	.800	0	1-2	2	2.66	3.62
2003 Montreal	NL	23	23	1	0	131.1	580	132	64	61	8	2	5	10	59	3	61	13	0	9	8	.529	1	0-0	0	4.28	4.18
2 ML YEARS		42	25	1	5	168.2	733	160	82	76	11	3	6	11	74	5	86	14	0	13	9	.591	1	1-2	2	3.91	4.06

Valerio de los Santos

Pitches: L **Bats:** L **Pos:** RP-51 **Ht:** 6'2" **Wt:** 206 **Born:** 10/6/72 **Age:** 31

Year Team	Lg	G	GS	CG	GF	IP	BFP	H	R	ER	HR	SH	SF	HB	TBB	IBB	SO	WP	Bk	W	L	Pct	ShO	Sv-Op	Hld	ERC	ERA
1998 Milwaukee	NL	13	0	0	3	21.2	75	11	7	7	4	0	0	0	2	0	18	1	0	0	0	-	0	0-0	0	1.25	2.91
1999 Milwaukee	NL	7	0	0	3	8.1	43	12	6	6	1	0	0	1	7	0	5	1	0	0	1	.000	0	0-0	0	9.65	6.48
2000 Milwaukee	NL	66	2	0	15	73.2	320	72	43	42	15	2	1	1	33	7	70	3	1	2	3	.400	0	0-1	9	4.79	5.13
2001 Milwaukee	NL	1	0	0	0	1.0	5	1	1	1	0	0	0	0	1	0	1	0	0	0	0	-	0	0-0	0	5.48	9.00
2002 Milwaukee	NL	51	0	0	12	57.2	237	42	21	20	4	3	7	2	26	3	38	1	0	2	3	.400	0	0-0	7	2.70	3.12
2003 Mil-Phi	NL	51	0	0	6	52.0	228	45	31	26	8	7	4	5	25	0	39	2	0	4	3	.571	0	1-4	11	4.37	4.50
2003 Milwaukee	NL	45	0	0	5	48.0	205	38	24	22	8	6	4	4	22	0	35	1	0	3	3	.500	0	1-4	11	3.92	4.13
2003 Philadelphia	NL	6	0	0	1	4.0	23	7	7	4	0	1	0	1	3	0	4	1	0	1	0	1.000	0	0-0	0	10.26	9.00
6 ML YEARS		189	2	0	39	214.1	908	183	109	102	32	12	12	9	94	10	171	8	1	8	10	.444	0	1-5	27	3.87	4.28

Roger Deago

Pitches: L **Bats:** R **Pos:** SP-2 **Ht:** 5'10" **Wt:** 180 **Born:** 6/21/77 **Age:** 27

Year Team	Lg	G	GS	CG	GF	IP	BFP	H	R	ER	HR	SH	SF	HB	TBB	IBB	SO	WP	Bk	W	L	Pct	ShO	Sv-Op	Hld	ERC	ERA
2003 Mobile	AA	26	20	0	1	118.1	517	127	64	53	9	6	5	3	51	1	109	3	0	8	7	.533	0	0--	-	4.59	4.03
2003 San Diego	NL	2	2	0	0	10.1	49	11	9	9	0	1	1	0	8	0	10	3	0	0	1	.000	0	0-0	0	5.10	7.84

Rick DeHart

Pitches: L **Bats:** L **Pos:** RP-4 **Ht:** 6'1" **Wt:** 180 **Born:** 3/21/70 **Age:** 34

Year Team	Lg	G	GS	CG	GF	IP	BFP	H	R	ER	HR	SH	SF	HB	TBB	IBB	SO	WP	Bk	W	L	Pct	ShO	Sv-Op	Hld	ERC	ERA
2003 Omaha*	AAA	25	0	0	12	28.0	128	38	15	15	1	2	2	3	7	2	17	1	0	1	3	.250	0	1--	-	5.39	4.82
1997 Montreal	NL	23	0	0	0	29.1	130	33	0	18	7	0	0	0	14	0	29	0	0	2	1	.667	0	0-0	0	6.30	5.52
1998 Montreal	NL	26	0	0	0	28.0	134	34	0	15	3	0	0	0	13	0	14	0	0	0	0	-	0	1-0	0	5.37	4.82
1999 Montreal	NL	3	0	0	0	1.2	14	6	0	4	2	0	0	0	3	0	1	0	0	0	0	-	0	0-0	0	45.50	21.60
2003 Kansas City	AL	4	0	0	2	4.0	21	8	6	6	1	0	0	0	2	0	1	0	0	0	2	.000	0	0-0	0	12.83	13.50
4 ML YEARS		56	0	0	2	63.0	299	81	6	43	13	0	0	0	32	0	45	0	0	2	3	.400	0	1-0	0	7.01	6.14

Mike DeJean

Pitches: R **Bats:** R **Pos:** RP-76 **Ht:** 6'4" **Wt:** 219 **Born:** 9/28/70 **Age:** 33

Year Team	Lg	G	GS	CG	GF	IP	BFP	H	R	ER	HR	SH	SF	HB	TBB	IBB	SO	WP	Bk	W	L	Pct	ShO	Sv-Op	Hld	ERC	ERA
1997 Colorado	NL	55	0	0	15	67.2	295	74	34	30	4	3	1	3	24	2	38	2	0	5	0	1.000	0	2-4	13	4.29	3.99
1998 Colorado	NL	59	1	0	9	74.1	307	78	29	25	4	4	4	1	24	1	27	3	0	3	1	.750	0	2-3	11	3.92	3.03
1999 Colorado	NL	56	0	0	17	61.0	288	83	61	57	13	3	3	2	32	8	31	3	0	2	4	.333	0	0-4	9	7.77	8.41
2000 Colorado	NL	54	0	0	15	53.1	235	54	31	29	9	3	1	0	30	6	34	5	0	4	4	.500	0	0-4	7	5.22	4.89
2001 Milwaukee	NL	75	0	0	19	84.1	371	75	31	26	4	1	4	9	39	7	68	8	0	4	2	.667	0	2-4	8	3.56	2.77
2002 Milwaukee	NL	68	0	0	60	70.2	326	66	28	26	7	4	2	2	39	8	65	7	0	1	5	.167	0	27-30	0	3.74	3.12
2003 Mil-StL	NL	76	0	0	45	82.2	365	86	46	43	13	1	3	2	39	7	71	3	0	5	8	.385	0	19-27	10	5.00	4.68
2003 Milwaukee	NL	58	0	0	40	64.2	286	69	38	35	12	0	3	1	27	7	58	3	0	4	7	.364	0	18-26	5	5.02	4.87
2003 St Louis	NL	18	0	0	5	18.0	79	17	8	8	1	1	0	1	12	0	13	0	0	1	1	.500	0	1-1	5	4.89	4.00
7 ML YEARS		443	1	0	180	498.1	2187	516	260	236	54	19	18	19	227	39	334	31	0	24	24	.500	0	52-76	58	4.63	4.26

David DeJesus

Bats: L **Throws:** L **Pos:** CF-8; PH-2; RF-1; PR-1 **Ht:** 5'11" **Wt:** 170 **Born:** 12/20/79 **Age:** 24

Year Team	Lg	G	AB	H	2B	3B	HR	(Hm	Rd)	TB	R	RBI	RC	TBB	IBB	SO	HBP	SH	SF	SB	CS	SB%	GDP	Avg	OBP	Slg
2002 Wilmington	A+	87	334	99	22	6	4	(-	-)	145	69	41	61	48	2	42	13	10	5	15	6	.71	8	.296	.400	.434
2002 Wichita	AA	25	79	20	5	2	2	(-	-)	35	7	15	13	8	0	10	5	1	3	3	1	.75	3	.253	.347	.443
2003 Wichita	AA	17	71	24	4	0	2	(-	-)	34	14	10	13	9	0	8	2	0	1	1	3	.25	3	.338	.422	.479
2003 Omaha	AAA	59	215	64	16	3	5	(-	-)	101	49	23	41	34	2	30	9	5	2	8	4	.67	9	.298	.412	.470
2003 Kansas City	AL	12	7	2	0	1	0	(0	0)	4	0	0	2	1	0	2	1	1	0	0	0	-	0	.286	.444	.571

Carlos Delgado

Bats: L **Throws:** R **Pos:** 1B-147; DH-14 **Ht:** 6'3" **Wt:** 230 **Born:** 6/25/72 **Age:** 32

Year Team	Lg	G	AB	H	2B	3B	HR	(Hm	Rd)	TB	R	RBI	RC	TBB	IBB	SO	HBP	SH	SF	SB	CS	SB%	GDP	Avg	OBP	Slg
1993 Toronto	AL	2	1	0	0	0	0	(0	0)	0	0	0	0	1	0	0	0	0	0	0	0	-	0	.000	.500	.000
1994 Toronto	AL	43	130	28	2	0	9	(5	4)	57	17	24	20	25	4	46	3	0	1	1	1	.50	5	.215	.352	.438
1995 Toronto	AL	37	91	15	3	0	3	(2	1)	27	7	11	5	6	0	26	0	0	2	0	0	-	1	.165	.212	.297
1996 Toronto	AL	138	488	132	28	2	25	(12	13)	239	68	92	83	58	2	139	9	0	8	0	0	-	13	.270	.353	.490
1997 Toronto	AL	153	519	136	42	3	30	(17	13)	274	79	91	94	64	9	133	8	0	4	0	3	.00	8	.262	.350	.528
1998 Toronto	AL	142	530	155	43	1	38	(20	18)	314	94	115	117	73	13	139	11	0	6	3	0	1.00	8	.292	.385	.592

Year Team	Lg	G	AB	H	2B	3B	HR	(Hm	Rd)	TB	R	RBI	RC	TBB	IBB	SO	HBP	SH	SF	SB	CS	SB%	GDP	Avg	OBP	Slg
																								BATTING	BASERUNNING	AVERAGES
1999 Toronto	AL	152	573	156	39	0	44	(17	27)	327	113	134	121	86	7	141	15	0	7	1	1	.50	11	.272	.377	.571
2000 Toronto	AL	162	569	196	57	1	41	(30	11)	378	115	137	164	123	18	104	15	0	4	0	1	.00	12	.344	.470	.664
2001 Toronto	AL	162	574	160	31	1	39	(13	26)	310	102	102	126	111	22	136	16	0	3	3	0	1.00	9	.279	.408	.540
2002 Toronto	AL	143	505	140	34	2	33	(17	16)	277	103	108	118	102	18	126	13	0	8	1	0	1.00	8	.277	.406	.549
2003 Toronto	AL	161	570	172	38	1	42	(24	18)	338	117	145	147	109	23	137	19	0	7	0	0	-	9	.302	.426	.593
11 ML YEARS		1295	4550	1290	317	11	304	(157	147)	2541	815	959	995	758	116	1127	109	0	50	9	6	.60	82	.284	.395	.558

Wilson Delgado

Bats: B **Throws:** R **Pos:** PH-28; 3B-20; SS-20; 2B-13; PR-1   **Ht:** 5'11" **Wt:** 165 **Born:** 7/15/72 **Age:** 31

Year Team	Lg	G	AB	H	2B	3B	HR	(Hm	Rd)	TB	R	RBI	RC	TBB	IBB	SO	HBP	SH	SF	SB	CS	SB%	GDP	Avg	OBP	Slg
2003 Memphis*	AAA	26	86	20	2	0	2	(-	-)	28	11	12	9	10	1	15	0	0	0	2	1	.67	2	.233	.313	.326
1996 San Francisco	NL	6	22	8	0	0	0	(0	0)	8	3	2	4	1	0	5	2	0	0	1	0	1.00	0	.364	.440	.364
1997 San Francisco	NL	8	7	1	1	0	0	(0	0)	2	1	0	0	0	0	2	0	1	0	0	0	-	0	.143	.143	.286
1998 San Francisco	NL	10	12	2	1	0	0	(0	0)	3	1	1	1	1	0	3	0	0	0	0	0	-	0	.167	.231	.250
1999 San Francisco	NL	35	71	18	2	1	0	(0	0)	22	7	3	7	5	0	9	1	1	0	1	0	1.00	2	.254	.312	.310
2000 NYY-KC	AL	64	128	33	2	0	1	(0	1)	38	21	11	12	11	0	26	0	0	2	2	1	.67	2	.258	.312	.297
2001 Kansas City	AL	14	25	3	0	0	0	(0	0)	3	1	1	0	3	0	10	0	0	0	0	0	-	1	.120	.214	.120
2002 St Louis	NL	12	20	4	2	0	2	(2	0)	12	2	5	2	0	0	6	0	1	0	0	0	-	0	.200	.200	.600
2003 StL-Ana		62	127	29	3	0	0	(0	0)	32	12	7	6	11	0	18	1	0	1	0	0	-	5	.228	.293	.252
2000 New York	AL	31	45	11	1	0	1	(0	1)	15	6	4	5	5	0	9	0	0	1	1	0	1.00	1	.244	.314	.333
2000 Kansas City	AL	33	83	22	1	0	0	(0	0)	23	15	7	7	6	0	17	0	0	1	1	1	.50	1	.265	.311	.277
2003 St Louis	NL	43	77	13	3	0	0	(0	0)	16	8	3	3	0	0	10	1	0	1	0	0	-	4	.169	.207	.208
2003 Anaheim	AL	19	50	16	0	0	0	(0	0)	16	4	4	6	8	0	8	0	0	0	0	0	-	1	.320	.414	.320
8 ML YEARS		211	412	98	11	1	3	(2	1)	120	48	30	32	32	0	79	4	3	3	4	1	.80	10	.238	.297	.291

David Dellucci

Bats: L **Throws:** L **Pos:** RF-59; PH-21; CF-10; LF-6; PR-4   **Ht:** 5'11" **Wt:** 198 **Born:** 10/31/73 **Age:** 30

Year Team	Lg	G	AB	H	2B	3B	HR	(Hm	Rd)	TB	R	RBI	RC	TBB	IBB	SO	HBP	SH	SF	SB	CS	SB%	GDP	Avg	OBP	Slg
1997 Baltimore	AL	17	27	6	1	0	1	(0	1)	10	3	3	3	4	1	7	1	0	0	0	0	-	2	.222	.344	.370
1998 Arizona	NL	124	416	108	19	12	5	(1	4)	166	43	51	51	33	2	103	3	0	1	3	5	.38	6	.260	.318	.399
1999 Arizona	NL	63	109	43	7	1	1	(0	1)	55	27	15	24	11	0	24	3	0	0	2	0	1.00	3	.394	.463	.505
2000 Arizona	NL	34	50	15	3	0	0	(0	0)	18	2	2	6	4	0	9	0	0	0	2	0	.00	1	.300	.352	.360
2001 Arizona	NL	115	217	60	10	2	10	(5	5)	104	28	40	36	22	4	52	2	0	0	2	1	.67	2	.276	.349	.479
2002 Arizona	NL	97	229	56	11	2	7	(2	5)	92	34	29	26	28	5	55	1	0	3	2	4	.33	7	.245	.326	.402
2003 Ari-NYY		91	216	49	12	3	3	(3	0)	76	26	23	23	23	1	58	5	2	2	12	0	1.00	6	.227	.313	.352
2003 Arizona	NL	70	165	40	11	3	2	(2	0)	63	18	19	21	19	1	45	3	1	2	9	0	1.00	4	.242	.328	.382
2003 New York	AL	21	51	9	1	0	1	(1	0)	13	8	4	2	4	0	13	2	1	0	3	0	1.00	2	.176	.263	.255
7 ML YEARS		541	1264	337	63	20	27	(11	16)	521	163	163	169	125	13	308	15	2	6	21	12	.64	27	.267	.338	.412

Ryan Dempster

Pitches: R **Bats:** R **Pos:** SP-20; RP-2   **Ht:** 6'3" **Wt:** 215 **Born:** 5/3/77 **Age:** 27

		HOW MUCH HE PITCHED						WHAT HE GAVE UP										THE RESULTS							
Year Team	Lg	G	GS	CG	GF	IP	BFP	H	R	ER	HR	SH	SF	HB	TBB	IBB	SO	WP	Bk	W	L	Pct	ShO	Sv-Op	Hld	ERC	ERA
2003 Louisville*	AAA	2	2	1	0	13.2	55	13	5	5	1	0	1	0	3	0	9	1	1	1	1	.500	0	0- -	-	3.01	3.29
1998 Florida	NL	14	11	0	1	54.2	272	72	47	43	6	5	6	9	38	1	35	5	0	1	5	.167	0	0-1	0	8.14	7.08
1999 Florida	NL	25	25	0	0	147.0	666	146	77	77	21	3	6	6	93	2	126	8	0	7	8	.467	0	0-0	0	5.49	4.71
2000 Florida	NL	33	33	2	0	226.1	974	210	102	92	30	4	5	5	97	7	209	4	0	14	10	.583	1	0-0	0	4.04	3.66
2001 Florida	NL	34	34	2	0	211.1	954	218	123	116	21	15	7	10	112	5	171	5	0	15	12	.556	1	0-0	0	4.91	4.94
2002 Fla-Cin	NL	33	33	4	0	209.0	915	228	127	125	28	9	6	10	93	2	153	2	0	10	13	.435	0	0-0	0	5.35	5.38
2003 Cincinnati	NL	22	20	0	1	115.2	545	134	89	84	14	9	4	5	70	4	84	3	0	3	7	.300	0	0-0	0	6.11	6.54
2002 Florida	NL	18	18	3	0	120.1	521	126	66	64	12	7	3	7	55	1	87	0	0	5	8	.385	0	0-0	0	4.95	4.79
2002 Cincinnati	NL	15	15	1	0	88.2	394	102	61	61	16	2	3	3	38	1	66	2	0	5	5	.500	0	0-0	0	5.90	6.19
6 ML YEARS		161	156	8	2	964.0	4326	1008	565	537	120	45	34	45	503	21	778	27	0	50	55	.476	2	0-1	0	5.20	5.01

Joe DePastino

Bats: R **Throws:** R **Pos:** PH-2; C-1   **Ht:** 6'2" **Wt:** 210 **Born:** 9/4/73 **Age:** 30

Year Team	Lg	G	AB	H	2B	3B	HR	(Hm	Rd)	TB	R	RBI	RC	TBB	IBB	SO	HBP	SH	SF	SB	CS	SB%	GDP	Avg	OBP	Slg
1992 Red Sox	R	40	157	41	6	1	1	(-	-)	52	13	16	14	7	1	25	3	0	2	1	1	.50	7	.261	.302	.331
1993 Utica	A-	62	221	56	9	1	2	(-	-)	73	28	32	23	16	0	51	4	1	5	3	2	.60	4	.253	.309	.330
1994 Utica	A-	51	172	46	11	1	5	(-	-)	74	23	31	28	22	1	41	3	1	2	5	2	.71	1	.267	.347	.430
1995 Michigan	A	98	325	90	11	1	5	(-	-)	118	47	53	42	30	1	70	8	0	5	3	3	.50	5	.277	.348	.363
1996 Sarasota	A+	97	344	90	16	2	6	(-	-)	128	35	44	40	29	1	71	3	0	4	2	3	.40	7	.262	.321	.372
1997 Trenton	AA	79	276	70	14	1	17	(-	-)	137	51	55	45	32	0	63	7	0	1	1	2	.33	10	.254	.345	.496
1998 Trenton	AA	73	275	81	16	0	10	(-	-)	127	34	43	46	28	5	51	1	0	2	3	0	1.00	4	.295	.359	.462
1998 Pawtucket	AAA	9	33	8	1	0	0	(-	-)	9	1	4	2	0	0	8	1	0	0	1	1	.50	1	.242	.265	.273
1998 Red Sox	R	6	17	5	1	1	1	(-	-)	11	2	1	5	5	0	3	0	0	0	0	0	-	0	.294	.455	.647
1999 Pawtucket	AAA	77	257	65	13	0	13	(-	-)	117	35	52	38	27	0	40	1	0	1	1	1	.50	6	.253	.324	.455
1999 Trenton	AA	6	23	5	1	0	2	(-	-)	12	5	5	4	3	0	3	1	0	0	1	0	1.00	2	.217	.333	.522
2000 Rochester	AAA	20	71	18	3	0	0	(-	-)	21	7	5	7	8	0	16	1	0	0	1	1	.50	1	.254	.338	.296
2000 Bowie	AA	19	65	14	6	0	2	(-	-)	26	11	9	6	6	0	13	0	0	0	0	0	-	4	.215	.282	.400
2000 Round Rock	AA	5	18	8	0	1	2	(-	-)	16	3	4	5	0	0	2	0	0	0	0	0	-	0	.444	.444	.889
2002 Norfolk	AAA	70	248	74	15	3	5	(-	-)	110	24	27	34	12	1	47	3	1	1	4	0	1.00	6	.298	.338	.444
2003 Norfolk	AAA	84	277	74	16	0	2	(-	-)	96	26	22	29	20	2	51	2	1	1	2	1	.67	8	.267	.320	.347
2003 New York	NL	2	2	0	0	0	0	(0	0)	0	0	0	0	0	0	1	0	0	0	0	0	-	0	.000	.000	.000

Jorge DePaula

Pitches: R **Bats:** R **Pos:** RP-3; SP-1   **Ht:** 6'1" **Wt:** 160 **Born:** 11/10/78 **Age:** 25

		HOW MUCH HE PITCHED						WHAT HE GAVE UP												THE RESULTS							
Year Team	Lg	G	GS	CG	GF	IP	BFP	H	R	ER	HR	SH	SF	HB	TBB	IBB	SO	WP	Bk	W	L	Pct	ShO	Sv-Op	Hld	ERC	ERA
1999 Portland	AA	16	16	0	0	85.1	392	97	67	57	8	5	4	5	43	0	77	7	1	6	6	.500	0	0--	-	5.48	6.01
2000 Asheville	A	28	27	1	0	155.0	691	151	90	81	16	0	0	13	62	0	187	7	2	8	13	.381	1	0--	-	4.18	4.70
2001 Asheville	A	3	3	0	0	16.2	76	19	13	7	3	0	0	3	2	0	26	1	0	1	1	.500	0	0--	-	4.79	3.78
2001 Greensboro	A	8	8	0	0	55.2	221	35	19	17	2	1	0	4	21	0	67	2	3	6	1	.857	0	0--	-	1.98	2.75
2001 Tampa	A+	16	13	0	1	83.0	365	65	43	33	3	1	2	3	53	2	77	3	1	9	5	.643	0	0--	-	3.40	3.58
2002 Norwich	AA	27	26	6	0	175.0	710	141	74	67	11	7	6	5	52	0	152	6	3	14	6	.700	1	0--	-	2.54	3.45
2003 New York	AL	4	1	0	3	11.1	38	3	1	1	1	0	0	1	1	0	7	0	0	0	0	-	0	0-0	0	0.54	0.79

Mark DeRosa

Bats: R **Throws:** R **Pos:** PH-33; 2B-29; 3B-25; SS-20; PR-4; LF-2; DH-2; 1B-1   **Ht:** 6'1" **Wt:** 205 **Born:** 2/26/75 **Age:** 29

		BATTING																	BASERUNNING				AVERAGES		
Year Team	Lg	G	AB	H	2B	3B	HR	(Hm	Rd)	TB	R	RBI	RC	TBB	IBB	SO	HBP	SH	SF	SB	CS	SB%	GDP	Avg	OBP	Slg
1998 Atlanta	NL	5	3	1	0	0	0	(0	0)	1	2	0	0	0	0	1	0	0	0	0	0	-	0	.333	.333	.333
1999 Atlanta	NL	7	8	0	0	0	0	(0	0)	0	0	0	0	0	0	2	0	0	0	0	0	-	0	.000	.000	.000
2000 Atlanta	NL	22	13	4	1	0	0	(0	0)	5	9	3	2	2	0	1	0	0	0	0	0	-	0	.308	.400	.385
2001 Atlanta	NL	66	164	47	8	0	3	(3	0)	64	27	20	22	12	6	19	5	1	2	2	1	.67	3	.287	.350	.390
2002 Atlanta	NL	72	212	63	9	2	5	(3	2)	91	24	23	27	12	3	24	3	2	3	2	3	.40	5	.297	.339	.429
2003 Atlanta	NL	103	266	70	14	0	6	(3	3)	102	40	22	28	16	0	49	5	0	1	1	0	1.00	6	.263	.316	.383
6 ML YEARS		275	666	185	32	2	14	(9	5)	263	102	68	79	42	9	96	13	3	6	5	4	.56	14	.278	.330	.395

Elmer Dessens

Pitches: R **Bats:** R **Pos:** SP-30; RP-4   **Ht:** 6'0" **Wt:** 187 **Born:** 1/13/72 **Age:** 32

		HOW MUCH HE PITCHED						WHAT HE GAVE UP												THE RESULTS							
Year Team	Lg	G	GS	CG	GF	IP	BFP	H	R	ER	HR	SH	SF	HB	TBB	IBB	SO	WP	Bk	W	L	Pct	ShO	Sv-Op	Hld	ERC	ERA
1996 Pittsburgh	NL	15	3	0	1	25.0	112	40	23	23	2	3	1	0	4	0	13	0	0	0	2	.000	0	0-0	3	6.77	8.28
1997 Pittsburgh	NL	3	0	0	1	3.1	13	2	0	0	0	0	1	0	0	0	2	0	0	0	0	-	0	0-0	0	1.31	0.00
1998 Pittsburgh	NL	43	5	0	8	74.2	332	90	50	47	10	4	3	0	25	2	43	1	0	2	6	.250	0	0-1	6	5.19	5.67
2000 Cincinnati	NL	40	16	1	6	147.1	640	170	73	70	10	12	7	3	43	7	85	4	0	11	5	.688	0	1-1	1	4.31	4.28
2001 Cincinnati	NL	34	34	1	0	205.0	862	221	103	102	32	7	7	1	56	1	128	4	1	10	14	.417	1	0-0	0	4.49	4.48
2002 Cincinnati	NL	30	30	0	1	178.0	737	173	70	60	24	7	1	7	49	8	93	3	1	7	8	.467	0	0-0	0	3.82	3.03
2003 Arizona	NL	34	30	0	1	175.2	781	212	107	99	22	9	3	4	57	6	113	3	2	8	8	.500	0	0-0	0	5.19	5.07
7 ML YEARS		199	118	2	17	809.0	3477	908	426	401	100	42	22	16	234	24	477	15	4	38	43	.469	1	1-2	10	4.57	4.46

Einar Diaz

Bats: R **Throws:** R **Pos:** C-101; PR-2   **Ht:** 5'10" **Wt:** 190 **Born:** 12/28/72 **Age:** 31

		BATTING																	BASERUNNING				AVERAGES		
Year Team	Lg	G	AB	H	2B	3B	HR	(Hm	Rd)	TB	R	RBI	RC	TBB	IBB	SO	HBP	SH	SF	SB	CS	SB%	GDP	Avg	OBP	Slg
1996 Cleveland	AL	4	4	1	0	0	0	(0	0)	0	0	0	0	0	0	0	0	0	0	0	0	-	0	.000	.000	.000
1997 Cleveland	AL	5	7	1	1	0	0	(0	0)	2	1	1	0	0	0	2	0	0	0	0	0	-	0	.143	.143	.286
1998 Cleveland	AL	17	48	11	1	0	2	(1	1)	18	8	9	5	3	0	2	2	0	3	0	0	-	2	.229	.286	.375
1999 Cleveland	AL	119	392	110	21	1	3	(2	1)	142	43	32	46	23	0	41	5	6	1	11	4	.73	10	.281	.328	.362
2000 Cleveland	AL	75	250	68	14	2	4	(2	2)	98	29	25	30	11	0	29	8	6	0	4	2	.67	7	.272	.323	.392
2001 Cleveland	AL	134	437	121	34	1	4	(0	4)	169	54	56	53	17	0	44	16	8	0	1	2	.33	11	.277	.328	.387
2002 Cleveland	AL	102	320	66	19	0	2	(1	1)	91	34	16	14	17	1	27	6	6	2	0	1	.00	13	.206	.258	.284
2003 Texas	AL	101	334	86	14	1	4	(2	2)	114	30	35	30	9	0	32	10	4	4	3	1	.75	12	.257	.294	.341
8 ML YEARS		557	1789	463	104	5	19	(8	11)	634	199	174	178	80	1	177	47	30	10	19	10	.66	55	.259	.306	.354

Matt Diaz

Bats: R **Throws:** R **Pos:** PH-2; LF-1; DH-1   **Ht:** 6'1" **Wt:** 206 **Born:** 3/3/78 **Age:** 26

		BATTING																	BASERUNNING				AVERAGES		
Year Team	Lg	G	AB	H	2B	3B	HR	(Hm	Rd)	TB	R	RBI	RC	TBB	IBB	SO	HBP	SH	SF	SB	CS	SB%	GDP	Avg	OBP	Slg
1999 Hudson Val	A-	54	208	51	15	2	1	(-	-)	73	22	20	20	6	0	43	6	2	2	6	2	.75	5	.245	.284	.351
2000 St. Petersburg	A+	106	392	106	21	3	6	(-	-)	151	37	53	39	11	0	54	11	1	5	2	3	.40	21	.270	.305	.385
2001 Bakersfield	A+	131	524	172	40	2	17	(-	-)	267	79	81	94	24	3	73	14	4	5	11	5	.69	11	.328	.370	.510
2002 Orlando	AA	122	449	123	28	1	10	(-	-)	183	71	50	63	34	1	72	10	3	3	31	9	.78	11	.274	.337	.408
2003 Orlando	AA	60	227	87	21	0	5	(-	-)	123	32	41	50	19	6	24	8	1	3	9	5	.64	7	.383	.444	.542
2003 Durham	AAA	67	253	83	18	3	8	(-	-)	131	35	45	47	16	3	45	8	0	3	6	2	.75	8	.328	.382	.518
2003 Tampa Bay	AL	4	9	1	0	0	0	(0	0)	1	2	0	0	1	0	3	0	0	0	0	0	-	0	.111	.200	.111

R.A. Dickey

Pitches: R **Bats:** R **Pos:** RP-25; SP-13   **Ht:** 6'3" **Wt:** 205 **Born:** 10/29/74 **Age:** 29

		HOW MUCH HE PITCHED						WHAT HE GAVE UP												THE RESULTS							
Year Team	Lg	G	GS	CG	GF	IP	BFP	H	R	ER	HR	SH	SF	HB	TBB	IBB	SO	WP	Bk	W	L	Pct	ShO	Sv-Op	Hld	ERC	ERA
1997 Charlotte	A+	8	6	0	2	35.0	162	51	32	27	8	0	0	0	12	1	32	5	3	1	4	.200	0	0--	-	7.71	6.94
1998 Charlotte	A+	57	0	0	54	60.0	260	58	31	22	9	4	1	0	23	3	53	3	2	1	5	.167	0	38--	-	3.94	3.30
1999 Tulsa	AA	35	11	0	21	95.0	419	105	60	48	13	1	4	2	40	1	59	9	0	6	7	.462	0	10--	-	5.16	4.55
1999 Oklahoma	AAA	6	2	0	1	22.2	99	23	12	11	1	3	0	1	7	1	17	2	0	2	2	.500	0	0--	-	3.43	4.37
2000 Oklahoma	AAA	30	23	2	2	158.1	680	167	83	79	13	4	9	7	65	1	85	5	2	8	9	.471	0	1--	-	4.60	4.49
2001 Oklahoma	AAA	24	24	3	0	163.0	687	164	77	68	14	7	2	7	45	1	120	3	0	11	7	.611	0	0--	-	3.71	3.75
2002 Oklahoma	AAA	37	19	1	8	154.0	664	176	81	70	8	7	3	4	47	5	109	5	0	8	7	.533	0	0--	-	4.27	4.09
2003 Oklahoma	AAA	3	2	0	0	15.0	57	14	3	2	1	0	0	0	3	0	4	0	0	1	1	.500	0	0--	-	2.98	1.20
2001 Texas	AL	4	0	0	1	12.0	53	13	9	9	3	0	0	0	7	1	4	1	0	0	1	.000	0	0-0	0	6.57	6.75
2003 Texas	AL	38	13	1	6	116.2	513	135	68	66	16	4	3	5	38	5	94	5	2	9	8	.529	1	1-1	3	5.09	5.09
2 ML YEARS		42	13	1	7	128.2	566	148	77	75	19	4	3	5	45	6	98	6	2	9	9	.500	1	1-1	3	5.22	5.25

Mike DiFelice

Bats: R Throws: R Pos: C-58; PH-6

Ht: 6'2" Wt: 205 Born: 5/28/69 Age: 35

							BATTING													BASERUNNING				AVERAGES		
Year Team	Lg	G	AB	H	2B	3B	HR	(Hm	Rd)	TB	R	RBI	RC	TBB	IBB	SO	HBP	SH	SF	SB	CS	SB%	GDP	Avg	OBP	Slg
1996 St Louis	NL	4	7	2	1	0	0	(0	0)	3	0	2	1	0	0	1	0	0	0	0	0	-	0	.286	.286	.429
1997 St Louis	NL	93	260	62	10	1	4	(1	3)	86	16	30	23	19	0	61	3	6	1	1	1	.50	11	.238	.297	.331
1998 Tampa Bay	AL	84	248	57	12	3	3	(1	2)	84	17	23	19	15	0	56	1	3	2	0	0	-	12	.230	.274	.339
1999 Tampa Bay	AL	51	179	55	11	0	6	(5	1)	84	21	27	29	8	0	23	3	0	1	0	0	-	1	.307	.346	.469
2000 Tampa Bay	AL	60	204	49	13	1	6	(4	2)	82	23	19	21	12	0	40	0	5	2	0	0	-	8	.240	.280	.402
2001 TB-Ari		60	170	32	5	1	2	(0	2)	45	14	10	10	8	0	49	4	3	2	1	1	.50	3	.188	.239	.265
2002 St Louis	NL	70	174	40	11	0	4	(3	1)	63	17	19	17	17	3	42	1	2	3	0	0	-	4	.230	.297	.362
2003 Kansas City	AL	62	189	48	16	1	3	(1	2)	75	29	25	27	9	0	30	4	1	2	1	0	1.00	6	.254	.299	.397
2001 Tampa Bay	AL	48	149	31	5	1	2	(0	2)	44	13	9	10	8	0	39	3	2	2	1	1	.50	3	.208	.259	.295
2001 Arizona	NL	12	21	1	0	0	0	(0	0)	1	1	1	0	0	0	10	1	1	0	0	0	-	0	.048	.091	.048
8 ML YEARS		484	1431	345	79	7	28	(15	13)	522	137	155	147	88	3	302	16	20	13	3	2	.60	45	.241	.290	.365

Juan Dominguez

Pitches: R Bats: R Pos: SP-3; RP-3

Ht: 6'2" Wt: 180 Born: 5/18/80 Age: 24

		HOW MUCH HE PITCHED						WHAT HE GAVE UP										THE RESULTS							
Year Team	Lg	G	GS	CG	GF	IP	BFP	H	R	ER	HR	SH	SF	HB	TBB	IBB	SO	WP	Bk	W	L	Pct	ShO	Sv-Op	Hld	ERC	ERA
2003 Frisco	AA	9	9	0	0	55.1	220	35	17	16	2	0	1	1	21	0	54	1	0	5	0	1.000	0	0--	-	1.81	2.60
2003 Stockton	A+	16	9	0	0	63.1	266	55	27	20	3	0	1	6	16	0	72	3	1	4	0	1.000	0	1--	-	2.78	2.84
2003 Oklahoma	AAA	3	3	0	0	18.0	71	15	7	7	1	2	0	0	3	0	14	1	0	1	0	1.000	0	0--	-	2.09	3.50
2003 Texas	AL	6	3	0	1	16.1	73	16	14	13	5	1	1	0	12	0	13	1	0	0	2	.000	0	0-0	0	7.22	7.16

Brendan Donnelly

Pitches: R Bats: R Pos: RP-63

Ht: 6'3" Wt: 200 Born: 7/4/71 Age: 32

		HOW MUCH HE PITCHED						WHAT HE GAVE UP										THE RESULTS							
Year Team	Lg	G	GS	CG	GF	IP	BFP	H	R	ER	HR	SH	SF	HB	TBB	IBB	SO	WP	Bk	W	L	Pct	ShO	Sv-Op	Hld	ERC	ERA
1992 White Sox	R	9	7	0	1	41.2	191	41	25	17	0	0	2	8	21	0	31	6	0	0	3	.000	0	1--	-	4.35	3.67
1993 Geneva	A-	21	3	0	7	43.0	198	39	34	30	4	1	1	6	29	0	29	7	3	4	0	1.000	0	1--	-	5.15	6.28
1994 Ohio Valley	IND	10	0	0	1	13.2	59	13	5	4	1	0	0	3	4	0	20	1	0	1	1	.500	0	0--	-	4.10	2.63
1995 Chrlstn - WV	A	24	0	0	22	30.1	112	14	4	4	0	1	2	1	7	1	33	1	0	1	1	.500	0	12--	-	0.85	1.19
1995 Winstn-Salm	A+	23	0	0	14	35.1	138	20	6	4	1	2	0	2	14	2	32	0	1	1	2	.333	0	2--	-	1.63	1.02
1995 Indianapolis	AAA	3	0	0	0	2.2	18	7	8	7	2	0	1	0	2	0	1	2	0	1	1	.500	0	0--	-	26.41	23.63
1996 Chattanooga	AA	22	0	0	10	29.1	133	27	21	18	4	0	1	1	17	2	22	1	0	1	2	.333	0	0--	-	4.52	5.52
1997 Chattanooga	AA	62	0	0	21	82.2	359	71	43	30	6	4	3	1	37	4	64	9	0	6	4	.600	0	6--	-	3.34	3.27
1998 Chattanooga	AA	38	0	0	35	45.1	203	43	16	15	4	1	1	3	24	5	47	8	0	2	5	.286	0	13--	-	4.24	2.98
1998 Indianapolis	AAA	19	1	0	6	37.1	157	29	16	11	3	1	0	3	16	3	39	2	0	4	1	.800	0	0--	-	3.03	2.65
1999 Nashua	IND	3	0	0	3	3.0	11	1	1	1	1	0	0	0	3	0	4	0	0	0	0	-	0	0--	-	5.16	3.00
1999 Durham	AAA	37	1	0	10	62.0	247	53	23	21	5	0	4	4	18	61	5	0	0	5	5	.500	0	2--	-	1.64	3.05
1999 Altoona	AA	2	0	0	2	2.1	12	4	2	2	0	1	2	0	2	0	0	0	0	0	1	.000	0	1--	-	10.22	7.71
1999 Syracuse	AAA	5	0	0	2	9.1	39	8	4	3	1	2	0	1	4	1	9	1	0	0	1	.000	0	0--	-	3.31	2.89
2000 Syracuse	AAA	37	0	0	7	42.2	203	47	34	26	5	1	1	2	27	2	34	1	0	4	6	.400	0	0--	-	5.62	5.48
2000 Iowa	AAA	9	0	0	3	16.2	83	25	19	14	3	0	1	2	6	1	14	2	0	3	0	.000	0	1--	-	7.85	7.56
2001 Arkansas	AA	27	0	0	24	29.0	120	21	8	8	2	0	1	1	13	1	37	1	0	4	1	.800	0	12--	-	2.66	2.48
2001 Salt Lake	AAA	29	0	0	12	41.1	165	38	11	11	4	1	1	0	8	0	50	2	0	5	1	.833	0	1--	-	2.88	2.40
2002 Salt Lake	AAA	25	0	0	17	33.2	142	27	13	13	5	1	1	2	11	0	42	2	1	4	0	1.000	0	6--	-	3.18	3.48
2002 Anaheim	AL	46	0	0	11	49.2	199	32	13	12	2	3	1	2	19	3	54	1	0	1	1	.500	0	1-3	13	1.89	2.17
2003 Anaheim	AL	63	0	0	15	74.0	307	55	14	13	2	3	1	4	24	1	79	1	0	2	2	.500	0	3-5	29	2.12	1.58
2 ML YEARS		109	0	0	26	123.2	506	87	27	25	4	6	2	6	43	4	133	2	0	3	3	.500	0	4-8	42	2.02	1.82

Octavio Dotel

Pitches: R Bats: R Pos: RP-76

Ht: 6'0" Wt: 200 Born: 11/25/73 Age: 30

		HOW MUCH HE PITCHED						WHAT HE GAVE UP										THE RESULTS							
Year Team	Lg	G	GS	CG	GF	IP	BFP	H	R	ER	HR	SH	SF	HB	TBB	IBB	SO	WP	Bk	W	L	Pct	ShO	Sv-Op	Hld	ERC	ERA
1999 New York	NL	19	14	0	1	85.1	368	69	52	51	12	3	5	6	49	1	85	3	2	8	3	.727	0	0-0	0	4.30	5.38
2000 Houston	NL	50	16	0	25	125.0	563	127	80	75	26	7	8	7	61	3	142	6	0	3	7	.300	0	16-23	0	5.47	5.40
2001 Houston	NL	61	4	0	20	105.0	438	79	35	31	5	2	2	2	47	2	145	4	0	7	5	.583	0	2-4	14	2.62	2.66
2002 Houston	NL	83	0	0	22	97.1	376	58	21	20	7	3	7	4	27	2	118	2	0	6	4	.600	0	6-10	31	1.61	1.85
2003 Houston	NL	76	0	0	13	87.0	346	53	25	24	9	2	1	3	31	2	97	2	0	6	4	.600	0	4-6	33	2.02	2.48
5 ML YEARS		289	34	0	81	499.2	2091	386	213	201	59	17	23	22	215	10	587	17	2	30	23	.566	0	28-43	78	3.21	3.62

Sean Douglass

Pitches: R Bats: R Pos: RP-3

Ht: 6'6" Wt: 198 Born: 4/28/79 Age: 25

		HOW MUCH HE PITCHED						WHAT HE GAVE UP										THE RESULTS							
Year Team	Lg	G	GS	CG	GF	IP	BFP	H	R	ER	HR	SH	SF	HB	TBB	IBB	SO	WP	Bk	W	L	Pct	ShO	Sv-Op	Hld	ERC	ERA
2003 Ottawa*	AAA	27	27	0	0	143.0	624	142	67	54	6	2	5	6	58	4	118	10	0	10	8	.556	0	0--	-	3.71	3.40
2001 Baltimore	AL	4	4	0	0	20.1	94	21	12	12	3	0	1	1	11	0	17	1	1	2	1	.667	0	0-0	0	5.27	5.31
2002 Baltimore	AL	15	8	0	2	53.1	245	58	41	36	10	2	1	2	35	2	44	3	0	0	5	.000	0	0-0	0	6.56	6.08
2003 Baltimore	AL	3	0	0	0	8.0	44	14	12	12	2	0	0	1	6	0	3	0	0	0	0	-	0	0-0	0	12.56	13.50
3 ML YEARS		22	12	0	2	81.2	383	93	65	60	15	2	2	4	52	2	64	4	1	2	6	.250	0	0-0	0	6.76	6.61

Scott Downs

Pitches: L **Bats:** L **Pos:** SP-1   **Ht:** 6'2" **Wt:** 190 **Born:** 3/17/76 **Age:** 28

Year Team	Lg	G	GS	CG	GF	IP	BFP	H	R	ER	HR	SH	SF	HB	TBB	IBB	SO	WP	Bk	W	L	Pct	ShO	Sv-Op	Hld	ERC	ERA
1997 Williamsport	A-	5	5	0	0	23.0	93	15	11	7	0	1	1	0	7	0	28	0	2	0	2	.000	0	0--		1.44	2.74
1997 Rockford	A	5	5	0	0	36.0	128	17	5	5	1	1	0	1	8	0	43	2	2	3	0	1.000	0	0--		1.01	1.25
1998 Daytona	A+	27	27	2	0	161.2	713	179	81	70	12	7	7	4	55	0	117	12	4	8	9	.471	0	0--		4.31	3.90
1999 Fort Myers	A+	2	2	0	0	9.2	45	7	3	0	0	0	0	1	6	0	9	2	0	0	1	.000	0	0--		2.45	0.00
1999 Daytona	A+	7	7	1	0	48.0	185	41	12	10	2	0	0	1	11	0	41	3	1	5	0	1.000	1	0--		2.52	1.88
1999 W Tennesse	AA	13	12	1	0	80.0	319	56	13	12	2	1	0	1	28	0	101	1	0	8	1	.889	0	0--		1.95	1.35
2002 Brevard Cnty	A+	7	0	0	2	9.0	36	7	3	3	0	0	0	0	2	0	7	0	0	0	0	-	0	1--		1.68	3.00
2002 Ottawa	AAA	17	0	0	1	23.1	106	31	21	15	6	2	2	2	3	0	15	0	1	2	1	.667	0	0--		6.26	5.79
2003 Edmonton	AAA	21	21	3	0	121.2	502	119	67	58	13	2	7	1	39	0	54	1	0	8	9	.471	0	0--		3.82	4.29
2000 ChC-Mon	NL	19	19	0	0	97.0	442	122	0	57	13	0	0	0	40	0	63	0	0	4	3	.571	0	0-0		5.92	5.29
2003 Montreal	NL	1	1	0	0	3.0	17	5	5	5	2	0	0	0	3	2	4	0	1	0	1	1.000	0	0-0		15.01	15.00
2000 Chicago	NL	18	18	0	0	94.0	426	117	0	54	13	0	0	0	37	0	63	0	0	4	3	.571	0	0-0		5.78	5.17
2000 Montreal	NL	1	1	0	0	3.0	16	5	0	3	0	0	0	0	3	0	0	0	0	0	0	-	0	0-0		10.34	9.00
2 ML YEARS		20	20	0	0	100.0	459	127	5	62	15	0	0	0	43	2	67	0	1	4	4	.500	0	0-0		6.16	5.58

Darren Dreifort

Pitches: R **Bats:** R **Pos:** SP-10   **Ht:** 6'2" **Wt:** 211 **Born:** 5/3/72 **Age:** 32

Year Team	Lg	G	GS	CG	GF	IP	BFP	H	R	ER	HR	SH	SF	HB	TBB	IBB	SO	WP	Bk	W	L	Pct	ShO	Sv-Op	Hld	ERC	ERA
1994 Los Angeles	NL	27	0	0	15	29.0	148	45	21	20	0	3	0	4	15	3	22	1	0	0	5	.000	0	6-9	3	7.39	6.21
1996 Los Angeles	NL	19	0	0	5	23.2	106	23	13	13	2	3	1	0	12	4	24	2	1	1	4	.200	0	0-2	1	3.84	4.94
1997 Los Angeles	NL	48	0	0	15	63.0	265	45	21	20	3	5	2	1	34	2	63	3	1	5	2	.714	0	4-7	9	2.72	2.86
1998 Los Angeles	NL	32	26	1	0	180.0	752	171	84	80	12	11	6	10	57	2	168	9	0	8	12	.400	1	0-0		3.50	4.00
1999 Los Angeles	NL	30	29	1	0	178.2	773	177	105	95	20	8	2	7	76	2	140	9	4	13	13	.500	1	0-0		4.39	4.79
2000 Los Angeles	NL	32	32	1	0	192.2	842	175	105	89	31	9	0	12	87	1	164	17	3	12	9	.571	1	0-0		4.40	4.16
2001 Los Angeles	NL	16	16	0	0	94.2	416	89	62	54	11	7	1	6	47	0	91	10	0	4	7	.364	0	0-0		4.50	5.13
2003 Los Angeles	NL	10	10	0	0	60.1	261	58	29	27	6	3	1	0	25	0	67	3	1	4	4	.500	0	0-0		3.87	4.03
8 ML YEARS		214	113	3	35	822.0	3563	783	440	398	85	49	13	40	353	14	739	54	10	47	56	.456	3	10-18	13	4.12	4.36

Ryan Drese

Pitches: R **Bats:** R **Pos:** SP-8; RP-3   **Ht:** 6'3" **Wt:** 220 **Born:** 4/5/76 **Age:** 28

Year Team	Lg	G	GS	CG	GF	IP	BFP	H	R	ER	HR	SH	SF	HB	TBB	IBB	SO	WP	Bk	W	L	Pct	ShO	Sv-Op	Hld	ERC	ERA
2003 Frisco*	AA	2	2	0	0	9.0	38	10	4	4	1	0	0	2	0	0	8	0	0	1	1	.500	0	0--		4.09	4.00
2003 Oklahoma*	AAA	20	20	0	0	122.0	533	143	70	63	8	2	7	7	39	1	68	5	1	8	6	.571	0	0--		4.79	4.65
2001 Cleveland	AL	9	4	0	2	36.2	149	32	15	14	2	1	0	1	15	2	24	0	0	1	2	.333	0	0-0		3.27	3.44
2002 Cleveland	AL	26	26	1	0	137.1	635	176	104	100	15	3	9	6	62	1	102	11	0	10	9	.526	0	0-0		6.26	6.55
2003 Texas	AL	11	8	0	0	46.0	223	61	42	35	8	0	0	5	24	1	26	2	0	2	4	.333	0	0-0		7.60	6.85
3 ML YEARS		46	38	1	2	220.0	1007	269	161	149	25	4	9	12	101	4	152	13	0	13	15	.464	0	0-0	1	6.00	6.10

J.D. Drew

Bats: L **Throws:** R **Pos:** RF-53; PH-29; CF-26; LF-2   **Ht:** 6'1" **Wt:** 195 **Born:** 11/20/75 **Age:** 28

Year Team	Lg	G	AB	H	2B	3B	HR	(Hm Rd)	TB	R	RBI	RC	TBB	IBB	SO	HBP	SH	SF	SB	CS	SB%	GDP	Avg	OBP	Slg
2003 Palm Beach*	A+	8	19	7	0	0	1	(- -)	10	4	3	6	7	2	4	1	0	0	0	0	-	0	.368	.556	.526
1998 St Louis	NL	14	36	15	3	1	5	(4 1)	35	9	13	12	4	0	10	0	0	1	0	0	-	4	.417	.463	.972
1999 St Louis	NL	104	368	89	16	6	13	(5 8)	156	72	39	58	50	0	77	6	3	3	19	3	.86	4	.242	.340	.424
2000 St Louis	NL	135	407	120	17	2	18	(11 7)	195	73	57	80	67	4	99	6	5	1	17	9	.65	3	.295	.401	.479
2001 St Louis	NL	109	375	121	18	5	27	(15 12)	230	80	73	92	57	4	75	4	3	4	13	3	.81	6	.323	.414	.613
2002 St Louis	NL	135	424	107	19	1	18	(9 9)	182	61	56	65	57	4	104	8	3	4	8	2	.80	4	.252	.349	.429
2003 St Louis	NL	100	287	83	13	3	15	(7 8)	147	60	42	57	36	0	48	3	2	0	2	2	.50	6	.289	.374	.512
6 ML YEARS		597	1897	535	86	18	96	(51 45)	945	355	280	364	271	12	413	27	16	13	59	19	.76	27	.282	.377	.498

Tim Drew

Pitches: R **Bats:** R **Pos:** RP-5; SP-1   **Ht:** 6'1" **Wt:** 195 **Born:** 8/31/78 **Age:** 25

Year Team	Lg	G	GS	CG	GF	IP	BFP	H	R	ER	HR	SH	SF	HB	TBB	IBB	SO	WP	Bk	W	L	Pct	ShO	Sv-Op	Hld	ERC	ERA
2003 Edmonton*	AAA	27	15	0	6	93.1	429	128	80	75	10	4	4	3	35	2	54	5	1	5	9	.357	0	2--		6.44	7.23
2000 Cleveland	AL	3	3	0	0	9.0	51	17	12	10	1	0	2	1	8	0	5	0	0	1	0	1.000	0	0-0		12.94	10.00
2001 Cleveland	AL	8	6	0	0	35.0	173	51	39	31	9	1	2	4	16	0	15	5	0	0	2	.000	0	0-0		8.95	7.97
2002 Montreal	NL	7	1	0	3	16.0	64	12	8	5	1	1	1	0	2	0	10	0	0	1	0	1.000	0	2-3	1	1.57	2.81
2003 Montreal	NL	6	1	0	3	8.2	46	12	12	12	3	1	2	0	8	1	3	3	0	0	2	.000	0	0-0		10.57	12.46
4 ML YEARS		24	11	0	6	68.2	334	92	71	58	14	3	7	5	34	1	33	8	0	2	4	.333	0	2-3	1	7.57	7.60

Travis Driskill

Pitches: R **Bats:** R **Pos:** RP-20   **Ht:** 6'0" **Wt:** 225 **Born:** 8/1/71 **Age:** 32

Year Team	Lg	G	GS	CG	GF	IP	BFP	H	R	ER	HR	SH	SF	HB	TBB	IBB	SO	WP	Bk	W	L	Pct	ShO	Sv-Op	Hld	ERC	ERA
1993 Watertown	A-	21	8	0	7	63.0	276	62	38	29	4	3	6	5	21	0	53	6	0	5	4	.556	0	3--		3.70	4.14
1994 Columbus	A	62	0	0	59	64.1	267	51	25	18	2	5	1	1	30	4	88	6	0	5	5	.500	0	35--		2.75	2.52
1995 Kinston	A+	15	0	0	9	23.0	90	17	7	7	2	0	3	1	5	1	24	1	0	0	2	.000	0	0--		2.11	2.74
1995 Cantn-Akrn	AA	33	0	0	22	46.1	200	46	24	24	3	1	1	1	19	1	39	0	1	3	4	.429	0	4--		3.89	4.66
1996 Cantn-Akrn	AA	29	24	0	0	172.0	732	169	89	69	8	6	6	3	63	0	148	10	2	13	7	.650	2	0--		3.56	3.61
1997 Buffalo	AAA	29	24	1	1	147.0	645	159	86	76	22	6	6	3	60	0	102	15	1	8	7	.533	0	0--		5.06	4.65
1998 Akron	AA	5	4	0	1	26.1	109	27	12	10	4	0	1	0	7	0	16	0	0	3	0	1.000	0	0--		4.31	3.42

Year Team	Lg	G	GS	CG	GF	IP	BFP	H	R	ER	HR	SH	SF	HB	TBB	IBB	SO	WP	Bk	W	L	Pct	ShO	Sv-Op	Hld	ERC	ERA
				HOW MUCH HE PITCHED						**WHAT HE GAVE UP**												**THE RESULTS**					
1998 Buffalo	AAA	1	1	0	0	6.0	28	9	6	6	0	0	0	0	1	0	5	0	0	0	0	-	0	0- -	-	5.13	9.00
1999 Buffalo	AAA	31	18	0	3	132.1	561	146	78	71	21	5	5	6	32	2	90	4	1	9	8	.529	0	0- -	-	4.67	4.83
2000 New Orleans	AAA	28	28	2	0	179.1	774	201	101	80	15	5	3	7	45	0	113	6	0	12	11	.522	1	0- -	-	4.20	4.01
2001 New Orleans	AAA	28	28	1	0	178.2	735	175	83	75	21	6	5	6	33	2	145	5	1	11	5	.688	0	0- -	-	3.36	3.78
2002 Rochester	AAA	4	4	1	0	22.0	86	17	8	4	1	0	0	1	1	0	15	0	0	2	2	.500	1	0- -	-	1.53	1.64
2003 Ottawa	AAA	9	9	0	0	50.2	202	46	17	16	8	2	1	0	6	0	36	5	0	4	0	1.000	0	0- -	-	2.84	2.84
2002 Baltimore	AL	29	19	0	6	132.2	589	150	78	73	21	2	2	8	48	1	78	6	0	8	8	.500	0	0-0	0	5.36	4.95
2003 Baltimore	AL	20	0	0	6	48.0	215	62	35	32	8	3	2	1	9	2	33	3	0	3	5	.375	0	1-1	0	5.30	6.00
2 ML YEARS		49	19	0	12	180.2	804	212	113	105	29	5	4	9	57	3	111	9	0	11	13	.458	0	1-1	0	5.35	5.23

Eric DuBose

Pitches: L **Bats:** L **Pos:** SP-10; RP-7   **Ht:** 6'3" **Wt:** 231 **Born:** 5/15/76 **Age:** 28

Year Team	Lg	G	GS	CG	GF	IP	BFP	H	R	ER	HR	SH	SF	HB	TBB	IBB	SO	WP	Bk	W	L	Pct	ShO	Sv-Op	Hld	ERC	ERA
				HOW MUCH HE PITCHED						**WHAT HE GAVE UP**												**THE RESULTS**					
1997 Sth Oregon	A-	3	1	0	0	10.0	39	5	0	0	0	0	0	0	6	0	15	0	0	1	0	1.000	0	0- -	-	1.71	0.00
1997 Visalia	A+	10	9	0	0	38.1	194	43	37	30	4	2	0	5	28	0	39	6	3	1	3	.250	0	0- -	-	6.46	7.04
1998 Visalia	A+	17	10	0	4	72.0	307	56	34	27	5	1	2	5	35	0	85	8	2	6	1	.857	0	1- -	-	3.24	3.38
1998 Huntsville	AA	14	14	1	0	83.1	363	86	37	25	2	3	4	7	34	1	66	4	0	7	6	.538	1	0- -	-	4.10	2.70
1999 Midland	AA	21	14	0	3	77.0	361	89	57	47	10	2	4	7	44	1	68	8	0	4	2	.667	0	1- -	-	6.32	5.49
2000 Midland	AA	18	0	0	1	26.1	131	25	16	13	1	0	0	3	18	2	20	2	0	5	1	.833	0	1- -	-	4.36	4.44
2000 Visalia	A+	5	0	0	2	10.2	46	8	2	2	0	0	0	1	5	1	12	1	0	0	1	.000	0	1- -	-	2.45	1.69
2002 Rochester	AAA	1	0	0	0	0.1	5	1	2	1	0	0	0	0	2	0	0	0	0	0	0	-	0	0- -	-	35.68	27.00
2002 Bowie	AA	41	0	0	13	64.2	263	46	21	18	2	4	2	3	21	0	66	3	0	5	3	.625	0	3- -	-	2.02	2.51
2003 Ottawa	AAA	19	19	0	0	114.0	476	112	49	43	7	5	3	5	34	2	107	2	0	9	5	.643	0	0- -	-	3.52	3.39
2002 Baltimore	AL	4	0	0	2	6.0	25	7	2	2	1	0	0	1	1	0	4	0	0	0	0	-	0	0-0	0	5.59	3.00
2003 Baltimore	AL	17	10	1	3	73.2	305	60	33	31	6	2	3	5	25	2	44	0	1	3	6	.333	0	0-1	1	2.95	3.79
2 ML YEARS		21	10	1	5	79.2	330	67	35	33	7	2	3	6	26	2	48	0	1	3	6	.333	0	0-1	1	3.13	3.73

Justin Duchscherer

Pitches: R **Bats:** R **Pos:** SP-3; RP-1   **Ht:** 6'3" **Wt:** 190 **Born:** 11/19/77 **Age:** 26

Year Team	Lg	G	GS	CG	GF	IP	BFP	H	R	ER	HR	SH	SF	HB	TBB	IBB	SO	WP	Bk	W	L	Pct	ShO	Sv-Op	Hld	ERC	ERA
				HOW MUCH HE PITCHED						**WHAT HE GAVE UP**												**THE RESULTS**					
1996 Red Sox	R	13	8	0	2	54.2	232	52	26	19	0	3	3	3	14	0	45	4	6	0	2	.000	0	1- -	-	2.75	3.13
1997 Red Sox	R	10	8	0	0	44.2	190	34	18	9	0	2	1	3	17	0	59	5	4	2	3	.400	0	0- -	-	2.26	1.81
1997 Michigan	A	4	4	0	0	24.0	109	26	17	15	1	0	1	3	10	0	19	0	0	1	1	.500	0	0- -	-	4.64	5.63
1998 Michigan	A	30	26	0	2	142.2	627	166	87	76	9	7	3	13	47	3	106	7	1	7	12	.368	0	0- -	-	4.88	4.79
1999 Augusta	A	6	6	0	0	41.0	150	21	1	1	0	0	0	0	8	0	39	1	0	4	0	1.000	0	0- -	-	0.89	0.22
1999 Sarasota	A+	20	18	0	0	112.1	475	101	62	56	14	2	5	12	30	0	105	5	0	7	7	.500	0	0- -	-	3.55	4.49
2000 Trenton	AA	24	24	2	0	143.1	593	134	59	54	7	3	5	6	35	1	126	6	1	7	9	.438	2	0- -	-	2.95	3.39
2001 Trenton	AA	12	12	1	0	73.2	293	49	25	20	6	0	0	5	14	1	69	0	0	6	3	.667	1	0- -	-	1.69	2.44
2001 Tulsa	AA	6	6	1	0	43.1	176	39	14	10	3	1	2	2	10	0	55	0	0	4	0	1.000	1	0- -	-	2.91	2.08
2001 Oklahoma	AAA	7	7	1	0	50.2	205	48	20	16	6	2	1	4	10	0	52	0	0	3	3	.500	1	0- -	-	3.53	2.84
2002 Sacramento	AAA	14	11	0	0	63.0	279	73	45	39	7	0	2	2	17	0	52	1	0	2	4	.333	0	0- -	-	4.59	5.57
2003 Sacramento	AAA	24	23	0	0	155.0	623	151	59	56	12	1	8	2	18	0	117	2	0	14	2	.875	0	0- -	-	2.77	3.25
2001 Texas	AL	5	2	0	0	14.2	76	24	0	20	5	0	0	4	4	0	11	0	0	1	1	.500	0	0-0	0	8.77	12.27
2003 Oakland	AL	4	3	0	0	16.1	71	17	7	6	1	1	0	2	3	0	15	0	0	1	1	.500	0	0-0	0	3.58	3.31
2 ML YEARS		9	5	0	0	31.0	147	41	7	26	6	1	0	2	7	0	26	0	0	2	2	.500	0	0-0	0	5.91	7.55

Brandon Duckworth

Pitches: R **Bats:** R **Pos:** SP-18; RP-6   **Ht:** 6'2" **Wt:** 185 **Born:** 1/23/76 **Age:** 28

Year Team	Lg	G	GS	CG	GF	IP	BFP	H	R	ER	HR	SH	SF	HB	TBB	IBB	SO	WP	Bk	W	L	Pct	ShO	Sv-Op	Hld	ERC	ERA
				HOW MUCH HE PITCHED						**WHAT HE GAVE UP**												**THE RESULTS**					
2003 Reading*	AA	1	1	0	0	2.0	7	1	1	1	1	0	0	0	0	0	2	0	0	0	0	-	0	0- -	-	1.73	4.50
2003 Clearwater*	A+	2	2	0	0	9.0	32	3	1	1	1	0	0	0	2	0	11	0	0	0	0	-	0	0- -	-	0.81	1.00
2003 Scrtn/WlksBr*	AAA	3	3	0	0	18.2	82	21	11	7	3	1	0	2	4	0	14	0	0	2	1	.667	0	0- -	-	4.86	3.38
2001 Philadelphia	NL	11	11	0	0	69.0	289	57	29	27	2	7	3	6	29	5	40	2	0	3	2	.600	0	0-0	0	2.98	3.52
2002 Philadelphia	NL	30	29	0	0	163.0	725	167	103	98	26	7	3	7	69	5	167	10	0	8	9	.471	0	0-0	0	4.80	5.41
2003 Philadelphia	NL	24	18	0	2	93.0	424	98	58	51	12	9	1	10	44	3	68	5	0	4	7	.364	0	0-0	0	5.25	4.94
3 ML YEARS		65	58	0	2	325.0	1438	322	190	176	40	23	7	23	142	13	275	17	0	15	18	.455	0	0-0	0	4.53	4.87

Jeff Duncan

Bats: L **Throws:** L **Pos:** CF-52; PH-7; LF-1; PR-1   **Ht:** 6'2" **Wt:** 188 **Born:** 12/9/78 **Age:** 25

Year Team	Lg	G	AB	H	2B	3B	HR	(Hm	Rd)	TB	R	RBI	RC	TBB	IBB	SO	HBP	SH	SF	SB	CS	SB%	GDP	Avg	OBP	Slg
						BATTING															**BASERUNNING**			**AVERAGES**		
2000 Pittsfield	A-	53	186	45	3	5	2	(-	-)	64	39	13	30	34	0	46	4	4	0	20	3	.87	1	.242	.371	.344
2001 Capital City	A	88	318	69	16	8	3	(-	-)	110	49	23	45	46	0	97	3	4	2	41	3	.93	2	.217	.320	.346
2002 St.Lucie	A+	29	102	35	5	0	2	(-	-)	46	20	10	24	24	1	15	1	1	0	10	1	.91	4	.343	.472	.451
2002 Capital City	A	40	150	59	13	3	4	(-	-)	90	33	17	41	18	1	34	3	1	0	15	3	.83	1	.393	.468	.600
2003 Norfolk	AAA	4	15	4	1	0	2	(-	-)	11	2	4	4	1	0	7	0	1	0	1	0	1.00	0	.267	.313	.733
2003 Binghamton	AA	76	278	80	11	5	4	(-	-)	113	49	23	47	36	2	59	5	8	3	24	10	.71	0	.288	.376	.406
2003 New York	NL	56	139	27	0	2	1	(1	0)	34	13	10	13	17	3	41	2	8	0	4	2	.67	1	.194	.291	.245

Adam Dunn

Bats: L Throws: R Pos: LF-99; 1B-19; PH-6; RF-5; DH-2 **Ht:** 6'6" **Wt:** 240 **Born:** 11/9/79 **Age:** 24

								BATTING													BASERUNNING				AVERAGES		
Year Team		Lg	G	AB	H	2B	3B	HR	(Hm	Rd)	TB	R	RBI	RC	TBB	IBB	SO	HBP	SH	SF	SB	CS	SB%	GDP	Avg	OBP	Slg
2001 Cincinnati		NL	66	244	64	18	1	19	(8	11)	141	54	43	51	38	2	74	4	0	0	4	2	.67	4	.262	.371	.578
2002 Cincinnati		NL	158	535	133	28	2	26	(13	13)	243	84	71	97	128	13	170	9	1	3	19	9	.68	8	.249	.400	.454
2003 Cincinnati		NL	116	381	82	12	1	27	(16	11)	177	70	57	62	74	8	126	10	0	4	8	2	.80	4	.215	.354	.465
3 ML YEARS			340	1160	279	58	4	72	(37	35)	561	208	171	210	240	23	370	23	1	7	31	13	.70	16	.241	.379	.484

Erubiel Durazo

Bats: L Throws: L Pos: DH-121; 1B-33; PH-1 **Ht:** 6'3" **Wt:** 240 **Born:** 1/23/74 **Age:** 30

								BATTING													BASERUNNING				AVERAGES		
Year Team		Lg	G	AB	H	2B	3B	HR	(Hm	Rd)	TB	R	RBI	RC	TBB	IBB	SO	HBP	SH	SF	SB	CS	SB%	GDP	Avg	OBP	Slg
1999 Arizona		NL	52	155	51	4	2	11	(4	7)	92	31	30	38	26	1	43	1	0	3	1	1	.50	1	.329	.422	.594
2000 Arizona		NL	67	196	52	11	0	8	(3	5)	87	35	33	34	34	2	43	1	0	2	1	0	1.00	3	.265	.373	.444
2001 Arizona		NL	92	175	47	11	0	12	(4	8)	94	34	38	36	28	1	49	2	0	2	0	0	--	1	.269	.372	.537
2002 Arizona		NL	76	222	58	12	2	16	(11	5)	122	46	48	46	49	2	60	2	0	3	0	1	.00	1	.261	.395	.550
2003 Oakland		AL	154	537	139	29	0	21	(10	11)	231	92	77	91	100	12	105	2	0	6	1	1	.50	11	.259	.374	.430
5 ML YEARS			441	1285	347	67	4	68	(32	36)	626	238	226	245	237	18	300	8	0	16	3	3	.50	17	.270	.383	.487

Chad Durbin

Pitches: R Bats: R Pos: RP-2; SP-1 **Ht:** 6'2" **Wt:** 200 **Born:** 12/3/77 **Age:** 26

		HOW MUCH HE PITCHED						WHAT HE GAVE UP											THE RESULTS						
Year Team	Lg	G	GS	CG	GF	IP	BFP	H	R	ER	HR	SH	SF	HB	TBB	IBB	SO	WP	Bk	W	L	Pct	ShO	Sv-Op	Hld	ERC	ERA
2003 Akron*	AA	3	3	0	0	12.0	46	7	2	2	1	0	0	2	1	0	11	0	0	2	0	1.000	0	0--	-	1.46	1.50
2003 Buffalo*	AAA	10	10	1	0	58.2	241	51	30	30	9	1	0	5	16	0	64	2	0	3	6	.333	0	0--	-	3.60	4.60
2003 Mahning VI*	A-	2	2	0	0	12.0	46	9	4	3	1	0	0	2	3	0	8	0	0	1	1	.500	0	0--	-	2.93	2.25
1999 Kansas City	AL	1	0	0	0	2.1	9	1	0	0	0	0	0	0	1	0	3	1	0	0	0	-	0	0-0	0	0.00	0.00
2000 Kansas City	AL	16	16	0	0	72.1	349	91	71	66	14	1	3	0	43	1	37	7	0	2	5	.286	0	0-0	0	7.05	8.21
2001 Kansas City	AL	29	29	2	0	179.0	777	201	109	98	26	2	7	11	58	0	95	6	0	9	16	.360	0	0-0	0	5.15	4.93
2002 Kansas City	AL	2	2	0	0	8.1	43	13	11	11	3	0	0	1	4	0	5	0	0	1	0	1.000	0	0-0	0	10.58	11.88
2003 Cleveland	AL	3	1	0	0	8.2	45	18	12	7	2	0	0	0	3	0	8	2	0	0	1	.000	0	0-0	0	12.37	7.27
5 ML YEARS		51	48	2	0	270.2	1223	324	203	182	45	3	10	12	109	1	148	16	0	11	23	.324	0	0-0	0	5.96	6.05

Ray Durham

Bats: B Throws: R Pos: 2B-105; PH-7 **Ht:** 5'8" **Wt:** 180 **Born:** 11/30/71 **Age:** 32

								BATTING													BASERUNNING				AVERAGES		
Year Team		Lg	G	AB	H	2B	3B	HR	(Hm	Rd)	TB	R	RBI	RC	TBB	IBB	SO	HBP	SH	SF	SB	CS	SB%	GDP	Avg	OBP	Slg
1995 Chicago		AL	125	471	121	27	6	7	(1	6)	181	68	51	57	31	2	83	6	5	4	18	5	.78	8	.257	.309	.384
1996 Chicago		AL	156	557	153	33	5	10	(3	7)	226	79	65	87	58	4	95	10	7	7	30	4	.88	5	.275	.350	.406
1997 Chicago		AL	155	634	172	27	5	11	(3	8)	242	106	53	83	61	0	96	6	2	8	33	16	.67	14	.271	.337	.382
1998 Chicago		AL	158	635	181	35	8	19	(10	9)	289	126	67	110	73	3	105	6	6	3	36	9	.80	5	.285	.363	.455
1999 Chicago		AL	153	612	181	30	8	13	(7	6)	266	109	60	103	73	1	105	4	3	2	34	11	.76	9	.296	.373	.435
2000 Chicago		AL	151	614	172	35	9	17	(5	12)	276	121	75	100	75	0	105	7	5	8	25	13	.66	13	.280	.361	.450
2001 Chicago		AL	152	611	163	42	10	20	(9	11)	285	104	65	97	64	3	110	4	6	5	23	10	.70	10	.267	.337	.466
2003 San Francisco		NL	110	410	117	30	5	8	(5	3)	181	61	33	56	50	2	82	3	4	2	7	7	.50	4	.285	.366	.441
2002 CWS-Oak		AL	150	564	163	34	6	15	(11	4)	254	114	70	96	73	1	93	7	10	5	26	7	.79	15	.289	.374	.450
2002 Oakland		AL	54	219	60	14	4	6	(5	1)	100	43	22	35	24	1	34	2	2	1	6	2	.75	2	.274	.350	.457
2002 Chicago		AL	96	345	103	20	2	9	(6	3)	154	71	48	61	49	0	59	5	8	4	20	5	.80	13	.299	.390	.446
9 ML YEARS			1310	5108	1423	293	62	120	(52	68)	2200	888	539	789	558	16	874	53	48	45	232	82	.74	84	.279	.353	.431

Jayson Durocher

Pitches: R Bats: R Pos: RP-6 **Ht:** 6'3" **Wt:** 195 **Born:** 8/18/74 **Age:** 29

		HOW MUCH HE PITCHED						WHAT HE GAVE UP											THE RESULTS						
Year Team	Lg	G	GS	CG	GF	IP	BFP	H	R	ER	HR	SH	SF	HB	TBB	IBB	SO	WP	Bk	W	L	Pct	ShO	Sv-Op	Hld	ERC	ERA
1993 Expos	R	7	7	3	0	39.0	150	32	23	15	0	2	0	3	13	0	21	3	1	2	3	.400	2	0--	-	2.74	3.46
1994 Vermont	A-	15	15	3	0	99.0	422	92	40	34	0	0	3	2	44	1	74	11	1	9	2	.818	1	0--	-	3.24	3.09
1995 Albany	A	24	22	1	1	122.0	526	105	67	53	5	4	11	5	56	1	88	11	1	3	7	.300	1	0--	-	3.24	3.91
1996 W Palm Bch	A+	23	23	1	0	129.1	557	135	65	48	5	4	3	7	44	0	101	15	3	7	6	.538	1	0--	-	3.08	3.34
1997 W Palm Bch	A+	25	17	0	2	87.0	385	84	58	37	6	3	3	4	39	0	71	10	2	6	4	.600	0	0--	-	3.96	3.83
1998 Jupiter	A+	23	0	0	12	36.1	162	47	21	17	3	1	2	1	8	0	27	4	0	2	1	.667	0	5--	-	4.99	4.21
1998 Harrisburg	AA	10	0	0	4	11.1	48	10	8	5	0	1	1	0	6	0	12	1	0	0	1	.000	0	1--	-	3.29	3.97
1999 Harrisburg	AA	29	1	0	11	51.2	224	44	29	20	5	2	2	6	25	1	36	3	1	1	3	.250	0	4--	-	4.00	3.48
1999 Ottawa	AAA	17	0	0	6	35.2	146	17	12	6	2	3	1	1	20	2	22	3	0	1	3	.250	0	4--	-	1.71	1.51
2000 Las Vegas	AAA	31	0	0	18	40.0	187	44	25	22	2	2	3	3	25	3	38	6	0	3	5	.375	0	7--	-	5.33	4.95
2000 Mobile	AA	27	0	0	23	30.1	132	26	7	7	4	2	1	3	12	1	43	3	0	1	1	.500	0	14--	-	3.74	2.08
2001 Tulsa	AA	3	0	0	2	3.2	15	0	0	0	0	0	1	3	0	4	2	0	0	0	-	0	0--	-	1.10	0.00
2001 Oklahoma	AAA	31	0	0	20	39.2	176	34	25	22	5	3	0	3	23	1	52	1	0	4	1	.800	0	6--	-	4.41	4.99
2002 Indianapolis	AAA	20	0	0	9	26.1	115	19	9	8	3	0	0	2	15	0	39	2	0	1	0	1.000	0	0--	-	3.51	2.73
2003 Brewers	R	2	2	0	0	2.0	6	0	0	0	0	0	0	0	0	0	3	0	0	0	0	-	0	0--	-	0.00	0.00
2003 Indianapolis	AAA	7	3	0	2	7.0	30	7	2	2	0	0	0	0	1	0	9	1	0	0	0	-	0	0--	-	2.31	2.57
2002 Milwaukee	NL	39	0	0	10	48.0	189	27	13	10	3	0	1	2	21	2	44	1	0	1	1	.500	0	0-1	3	1.88	1.88
2003 Milwaukee	NL	6	0	0	0	7.1	33	9	9	9	4	0	0	1	2	0	7	2	0	2	0	1.000	0	0-0	0	9.04	11.05
2 ML YEARS		45	0	0	10	55.1	222	36	22	19	7	0	1	3	23	2	51	3	0	3	1	.750	0	0-1	3	2.65	3.09

Trent Durrington

Bats: R **Throws:** R **Pos:** 2B-5; 3B-4; PH-3; PR-3; DH-2; LF-1   **Ht:** 5'10" **Wt:** 188 **Born:** 8/27/75 **Age:** 28

				BATTING																BASERUNNING				AVERAGES		
Year Team	Lg	G	AB	H	2B	3B	HR	(Hm	Rd)	TB	R	RBI	RC	TBB	IBB	SO	HBP	SH	SF	SB	CS	SB%	GDP	Avg	OBP	Slg
2003 Salt Lake*	AAA	117	447	136	27	5	7	(-	-)	194	81	54	82	61	3	75	6	0	7	35	8	.81	6	.304	.390	.434
1999 Anaheim	AL	43	122	22	2	0	0	(0	0)	24	14	2	6	9	0	28	0	5	0	4	3	.57	1	.180	.237	.197
2000 Anaheim	AL	4	3	0	0	0	0	(0	0)	0	0	0	0	0	0	0	0	0	0	0	0	-	1	.000	.000	.000
2003 Anaheim	AL	12	14	2	0	0	0	(0	0)	2	5	1	0	3	0	0	0	0	0	1	1	.50	0	.143	.294	.143
3 ML YEARS		59	139	24	2	0	0	(0	0)	26	19	3	6	12	0	28	0	5	0	5	4	.56	2	.173	.238	.187

Jermaine Dye

Bats: R **Throws:** R **Pos:** RF-60; CF-3; DH-3; LF-1; PH-1   **Ht:** 6'5" **Wt:** 220 **Born:** 1/28/74 **Age:** 30

				BATTING																BASERUNNING				AVERAGES		
Year Team	Lg	G	AB	H	2B	3B	HR	(Hm	Rd)	TB	R	RBI	RC	TBB	IBB	SO	HBP	SH	SF	SB	CS	SB%	GDP	Avg	OBP	Slg
2003 Sacramento*	AAA	13	49	14	2	0	2	(-	-)	22	9	9	9	11	1	11	0	0	0	0	0	-	1	.286	.417	.449
1996 Atlanta	NL	98	292	82	16	0	12	(4	8)	134	32	37	36	8	0	67	3	0	3	1	4	.20	11	.281	.304	.459
1997 Kansas City	AL	75	263	62	14	0	7	(3	4)	97	26	24	26	17	0	51	1	1	1	2	1	.67	6	.236	.284	.369
1998 Kansas City	AL	60	214	50	5	1	5	(3	2)	72	24	23	17	11	2	46	1	0	4	2	2	.50	8	.234	.270	.336
1999 Kansas City	AL	158	608	179	44	8	27	(15	12)	320	96	119	106	58	4	119	1	0	6	2	3	.40	17	.294	.354	.526
2000 Kansas City	AL	157	601	193	41	2	33	(15	18)	337	107	118	125	69	6	99	3	0	6	1	0	.00	12	.321	.390	.561
2001 KC-Oak	AL	158	599	169	31	5	26	(16	10)	280	91	106	99	57	6	112	7	1	11	9	1	.90	8	.282	.346	.467
2002 Oakland	AL	131	488	123	27	1	24	(13	11)	224	74	86	71	52	2	108	10	0	5	2	0	1.00	15	.252	.333	.459
2003 Oakland	AL	65	221	38	6	0	4	(3	1)	56	28	20	10	25	2	42	3	0	4	1	0	1.00	11	.172	.261	.253
2001 Kansas City	AL	97	367	100	14	0	13	(8	5)	153	50	47	54	30	3	68	6	1	6	7	1	.88	2	.272	.333	.417
2001 Oakland	AL	61	232	69	17	1	13	(8	5)	127	41	59	45	27	3	44	1	0	5	2	0	1.00	6	.297	.366	.547
8 ML YEARS		902	3286	896	184	13	138	(72	66)	1520	478	531	490	297	22	644	29	2	40	19	12	.61	88	.273	.335	.463

Damion Easley

Bats: R **Throws:** R **Pos:** 3B-23; PH-8; 2B-4; DH-3   **Ht:** 5'11" **Wt:** 187 **Born:** 11/11/69 **Age:** 34

				BATTING																BASERUNNING				AVERAGES		
Year Team	Lg	G	AB	H	2B	3B	HR	(Hm	Rd)	TB	R	RBI	RC	TBB	IBB	SO	HBP	SH	SF	SB	CS	SB%	GDP	Avg	OBP	Slg
1992 Anaheim	AL	47	151	39	5	0	1	(1	0)	47	14	12	14	8	0	26	3	2	1	9	5	.64	2	.258	.307	.311
1993 Anaheim	AL	73	230	72	13	2	2	(0	2)	95	33	22	37	28	2	35	3	1	2	6	6	.50	5	.313	.392	.413
1994 Anaheim	AL	88	316	68	16	1	6	(4	2)	104	41	30	28	29	0	48	4	4	2	4	5	.44	8	.215	.288	.329
1995 Anaheim	AL	114	357	77	14	2	4	(1	3)	107	35	35	30	32	1	47	6	6	4	5	2	.71	11	.216	.288	.300
1996 Ana-Det	AL	49	112	30	2	0	4	(1	3)	44	14	17	16	10	0	25	1	5	1	3	1	.75	0	.268	.331	.393
1997 Detroit	AL	151	527	139	37	3	22	(12	10)	248	97	72	88	68	3	102	16	4	5	28	13	.68	18	.264	.362	.471
1998 Detroit	AL	153	594	161	38	2	27	(19	8)	284	84	100	94	39	2	112	16	0	2	15	5	.75	8	.271	.332	.478
1999 Detroit	AL	151	549	146	30	1	20	(12	8)	238	83	65	82	51	2	124	19	2	6	11	3	.79	15	.266	.346	.434
2000 Detroit	AL	126	464	120	27	2	14	(5	9)	193	76	58	69	55	1	79	11	4	1	13	4	.76	11	.259	.350	.416
2001 Detroit	AL	154	585	146	27	7	11	(4	7)	220	77	65	72	52	3	90	13	4	4	10	5	.67	10	.250	.323	.376
2002 Detroit	AL	85	304	68	14	1	8	(4	4)	108	29	30	29	27	3	43	11	1	3	1	3	.25	4	.224	.307	.355
2003 Tampa Bay	AL	36	107	20	3	1	1	(0	1)	28	8	7	3	2	0	18	0	1	0	0	0	-	3	.187	.202	.262
1996 Anaheim	AL	28	45	7	1	0	2	(1	1)	14	4	7	4	6	0	12	0	3	0	0	0	-	0	.156	.255	.311
1996 Detroit	AL	21	67	23	1	0	2	(0	2)	30	10	10	12	4	0	13	1	2	1	3	1	.75	0	.343	.384	.448
12 ML YEARS		1227	4296	1086	226	22	120	(63	57)	1716	591	513	562	401	17	749	103	34	31	105	52	.67	95	.253	.329	.399

Adam Eaton

Pitches: R **Bats:** R **Pos:** SP-31   **Ht:** 6'2" **Wt:** 190 **Born:** 11/23/77 **Age:** 26

		HOW MUCH HE PITCHED						WHAT HE GAVE UP										THE RESULTS					
Year Team	Lg	G	GS	CG	GF	IP	BFP	H	R	ER	HR	SH	SF	HB	TBB	IBB	SO	WP	Bk	W	L	Pct	ShO	Sv-Op	Hld	ERC	ERA
2000 San Diego	NL	22	22	0	0	135.0	583	134	63	62	14	1	3	2	61	3	90	3	0	7	4	.636	0	0-0	0	4.34	4.13
2001 San Diego	NL	17	17	2	0	116.2	499	108	61	56	20	3	2	5	40	3	109	3	0	8	5	.615	0	0-0	0	4.01	4.32
2002 San Diego	NL	6	6	0	0	33.1	142	28	20	20	5	2	2	2	17	0	25	2	0	1	1	.500	0	0-0	0	4.28	5.40
2003 San Diego	NL	31	31	1	0	183.0	789	173	91	83	20	5	5	7	68	6	146	7	1	9	12	.429	0	0-0	0	3.78	4.08
4 ML YEARS		76	76	3	0	468.0	2013	443	235	221	59	11	12	16	186	12	370	15	1	25	22	.532	0	0-0	0	4.03	4.25

Eric Eckenstahler

Pitches: L **Bats:** L **Pos:** RP-20   **Ht:** 6'7" **Wt:** 220 **Born:** 12/17/76 **Age:** 27

		HOW MUCH HE PITCHED						WHAT HE GAVE UP										THE RESULTS					
Year Team	Lg	G	GS	CG	GF	IP	BFP	H	R	ER	HR	SH	SF	HB	TBB	IBB	SO	WP	Bk	W	L	Pct	ShO	Sv-Op	Hld	ERC	ERA
2000 Oneonta	A-	8	0	0	4	11.0	46	7	3	2	0	0	1	1	2	0	13	1	0	0	0	-	0	0- -	1	1.71	1.64
2000 W Michigan	A	10	3	0	4	18.2	89	21	15	12	4	1	1	1	11	0	22	0	1	0	2	.000	0	1- -	1	6.58	5.79
2001 Lakeland	A+	4	0	0	2	6.0	22	3	1	1	0	0	0	1	2	0	7	2	0	1	0	1.000	0	1- -	1	1.54	1.50
2001 Erie	AA	46	0	0	18	64.2	289	65	32	28	7	1	1	3	31	4	73	3	1	4	2	.667	0	4- -	1	4.52	3.90
2002 Toledo	AAA	52	0	0	17	67.0	287	57	37	33	8	4	1	3	35	1	69	1	0	2	4	.333	0	0- -	3	4.06	4.43
2003 Toledo	AAA	39	0	0	9	42.2	186	32	21	15	2	4	0	7	25	3	40	4	0	3	6	.333	0	0- -	1	3.57	3.16
2002 Detroit	AL	7	0	0	2	8.0	39	14	5	5	1	0	0	0	2	0	13	0	0	1	0	1.000	0	0-0	0	8.30	5.63
2003 Detroit	AL	20	0	0	5	15.2	70	9	6	5	0	0	0	2	15	1	12	1	0	0	0	-	0	0-0	4	3.50	2.87
2 ML YEARS		27	0	0	7	23.2	109	23	11	10	1	0	0	2	17	1	25	1	0	1	0	1.000	0	0-0	4	5.04	3.80

David Eckstein

Bats: R **Throws:** R **Pos:** SS-116; DH-3; PH-1; PR-1   **Ht:** 5'8" **Wt:** 170 **Born:** 1/20/75 **Age:** 29

				BATTING																BASERUNNING				AVERAGES		
Year Team	Lg	G	AB	H	2B	3B	HR	(Hm	Rd)	TB	R	RBI	RC	TBB	IBB	SO	HBP	SH	SF	SB	CS	SB%	GDP	Avg	OBP	Slg
2001 Anaheim	AL	153	582	166	26	2	4	(3	1)	208	82	41	80	43	0	60	21	16	2	29	4	.88	11	.285	.355	.357
2002 Anaheim	AL	152	608	178	22	6	8	(3	5)	236	107	63	90	45	0	44	27	14	8	21	13	.62	7	.293	.363	.388
2003 Anaheim	AL	120	452	114	22	1	3	(1	2)	147	59	31	52	36	0	45	15	10	4	16	5	.76	9	.252	.325	.325
3 ML YEARS		425	1642	458	70	9	15	(7	8)	591	248	135	222	124	0	149	63	40	14	66	22	.75	27	.279	.350	.360

Jim Edmonds

Bats: L **Throws:** L **Pos:** CF-128; PH-9; DH-2; LF-1; PR-1   **Ht:** 6'1" **Wt:** 212 **Born:** 6/27/70 **Age:** 34

Year	Team	Lg	G	AB	H	2B	3B	HR	(Hm	Rd)	TB	R	RBI	RC	TBB	IBB	SO	HBP	SH	SF	SB	CS	SB%	GDP	Avg	OBP	Slg
1993	Anaheim	AL	18	61	15	4	1	0	(0	0)	21	5	4	4	2	1	16	0	0	0	0	2	.00	1	.246	.270	.344
1994	Anaheim	AL	94	289	79	13	1	5	(3	2)	109	35	37	38	30	3	72	1	1	1	4	2	.67	3	.273	.343	.377
1995	Anaheim	AL	141	558	162	30	4	33	(16	17)	299	120	107	100	51	4	130	5	1	5	1	4	.20	10	.290	.352	.536
1996	Anaheim	AL	114	431	131	28	3	27	(17	10)	246	73	66	88	46	2	101	4	0	2	4	0	1.00	8	.304	.375	.571
1997	Anaheim	AL	133	502	146	27	0	26	(14	12)	251	82	80	90	60	5	80	4	0	5	5	7	.42	8	.291	.368	.500
1998	Anaheim	AL	154	599	184	42	1	25	(9	16)	303	115	91	104	57	7	114	1	1	1	7	5	.58	16	.307	.368	.506
1999	Anaheim	AL	55	204	51	17	2	5	(3	2)	87	34	23	30	28	0	45	0	0	1	5	4	.56	3	.250	.339	.426
2000	St Louis	NL	152	525	155	25	0	42	(22	20)	306	129	108	126	103	6	167	6	1	8	10	3	.77	5	.295	.411	.583
2001	St Louis	NL	150	500	152	38	1	30	(16	14)	282	95	110	113	93	12	136	4	1	10	5	5	.50	8	.304	.410	.564
2002	St Louis	NL	144	476	148	31	2	28	(17	11)	267	96	83	102	86	14	134	8	0	6	4	3	.57	9	.311	.420	.561
2003	St Louis	NL	137	447	123	32	2	39	(17	22)	276	89	89	90	77	6	127	4	1	2	1	3	.25	11	.275	.385	.617
	11 ML YEARS		1292	4592	1346	287	17	260	(134	126)	2447	873	798	885	633	57	1122	37	6	41	46	38	.55	82	.293	.380	.533

Mike Edwards

Bats: R **Throws:** R **Pos:** PH-3; LF-2   **Ht:** 6'1" **Wt:** 185 **Born:** 11/24/76 **Age:** 27

Year	Team	Lg	G	AB	H	2B	3B	HR	(Hm	Rd)	TB	R	RBI	RC	TBB	IBB	SO	HBP	SH	SF	SB	CS	SB%	GDP	Avg	OBP	Slg
1995	Burlington	R+	43	130	22	2	0	0	(-	-)	24	20	5	6	17	0	35	2	0	0	5	2	.71	2	.169	.275	.185
1996	Burlington	R+	58	206	58	13	1	1	(-	-)	76	31	17	33	37	0	26	3	3	3	5	4	.56	4	.282	.394	.369
1997	Burlington	R+	60	236	68	16	2	4	(-	-)	100	50	41	41	38	1	53	1	0	2	10	5	.67	2	.288	.386	.424
1998	Columbus	A	124	497	146	34	4	8	(-	-)	212	82	81	77	55	2	95	3	3	2	16	6	.73	13	.294	.366	.427
1999	Kinston	A+	133	456	132	25	4	16	(-	-)	213	76	89	91	93	6	117	9	0	9	8	3	.73	12	.289	.413	.467
2000	Akron	AA	136	481	142	25	2	11	(-	-)	204	72	63	81	68	2	86	5	3	3	7	3	.70	9	.295	.386	.424
2001	Mahning VI	A-	20	71	26	5	0	6	(-	-)	49	19	24	21	12	0	7	1	0	0	0	1	.00	0	.366	.464	.690
2001	Akron	AA	29	111	37	7	3	6	(-	-)	68	21	24	25	13	1	28	0	0	0	0	0	-	3	.333	.403	.613
2001	Buffalo	AAA	3	9	2	0	0	0	(-	-)	2	1	1	0	1	0	3	0	0	0	0	0	-	1	.222	.300	.222
2002	Chattanooga	AA	119	424	130	19	2	11	(-	-)	186	57	60	64	41	1	57	10	6	5	9	11	.45	19	.307	.377	.439
2002	Louisville	AAA	15	57	23	5	1	2	(-	-)	36	7	8	15	6	0	9	0	0	0	0	1	-	1	.404	.460	.632
2003	Sacramento	AAA	125	436	130	23	4	14	(-	-)	203	78	95	76	60	0	78	6	1	4	5	2	.71	17	.298	.387	.466
2003	Oakland	AL	4	4	1	0	0	0	(0	0)	1	0	0	1	2	0	1	0	0	0	0	0	-	0	.250	.500	.250

Joey Eischen

Pitches: L **Bats:** L **Pos:** RP-70   **Ht:** 6'0" **Wt:** 210 **Born:** 5/25/70 **Age:** 34

			HOW MUCH HE PITCHED						WHAT HE GAVE UP										THE RESULTS							
Year	Team	Lg	G	GS	CG	GF	IP	BFP	H	R	ER	HR	SH	SF	HB	TBB	IBB	SO	WP	Bk	W	L	Pct	ShO	Sv-Op	Hld	ERC	ERA
1994	Montreal	NL	1	0	0	0	0.2	7	4	4	4	0	0	0	1	0	0	1	0	0	0	0	-	0	0-0	0	47.92	54.00
1995	Los Angeles	NL	17	0	0	8	20.1	95	19	9	7	1	0	0	2	11	1	15	1	0	0	0	-	0	0-0	1	3.97	3.10
1996	LA-Det		52	0	0	14	68.1	308	75	36	32	7	3	2	4	34	7	51	4	0	1	2	.333	0	0-2	2	5.15	4.21
1997	Cincinnati	NL	1	0	0	0	1.1	7	2	2	1	0	0	0	0	1	0	2	1	0	0	0	-	0	0-0	0	7.52	6.75
2001	Montreal	NL	24	0	0	7	29.2	131	29	17	16	4	1	0	1	16	1	19	1	0	0	1	.000	0	0-2	2	4.89	4.85
2002	Montreal	NL	59	0	0	18	53.2	217	43	11	8	1	3	2	2	18	5	51	6	1	6	1	.857	0	2-3	11	2.31	1.34
2003	Montreal	NL	70	0	0	18	53.0	221	57	27	18	7	3	0	3	13	1	40	3	0	2	2	.500	0	1-4	15	4.44	3.06
1996	Los Angeles	NL	28	0	0	11	43.1	198	48	25	23	4	3	1	4	20	4	36	1	0	1	1	.000	0	0-0	1	5.07	4.78
1996	Detroit	AL	24	0	0	3	25.0	110	27	11	9	3	0	1	0	14	3	15	3	0	1	1	.500	0	0-2	1	5.30	3.24
	7 ML YEARS		224	0	0	62	227.0	986	229	106	86	20	10	4	13	93	15	179	16	1	9	6	.600	0	3-11	31	4.23	3.41

Scott Elarton

Pitches: R **Bats:** R **Pos:** SP-10; RP-1   **Ht:** 6'8" **Wt:** 240 **Born:** 2/23/76 **Age:** 28

			HOW MUCH HE PITCHED						WHAT HE GAVE UP										THE RESULTS							
Year	Team	Lg	G	GS	CG	GF	IP	BFP	H	R	ER	HR	SH	SF	HB	TBB	IBB	SO	WP	Bk	W	L	Pct	ShO	Sv-Op	Hld	ERC	ERA
2003	Co Springs*	AAA	20	20	0	0	118.2	546	146	81	70	15	3	6	8	39	1	92	4	0	6	8	.429	0	0- -	-	5.48	5.31
1998	Houston	NL	28	2	0	7	57.0	227	40	21	21	5	1	1	1	20	0	56	1	0	2	1	.667	0	2-3	2	2.35	3.32
1999	Houston	NL	42	15	0	8	124.0	524	111	55	48	8	7	4	4	43	0	121	3	0	9	5	.643	0	1-4	5	3.16	3.48
2000	Houston	NL	30	30	2	0	192.2	855	198	117	103	29	5	7	6	84	1	131	8	0	17	7	.708	0	0-0	0	4.82	4.81
2001	Hou-Col	NL	24	24	0	0	132.2	595	146	105	104	34	7	2	6	59	2	87	5	0	4	10	.286	0	0-0	0	6.21	7.06
2003	Colorado	NL	11	10	0	0	51.2	253	73	46	36	13	3	4	4	20	3	20	3	0	4	4	.500	0	0-0	0	7.79	6.27
2001	Houston	NL	20	20	0	0	109.2	499	126	88	87	26	7	2	6	49	1	76	5	0	4	8	.333	0	0-0	0	6.42	7.14
2001	Colorado	NL	4	4	0	0	23.0	96	20	17	17	8	0	0	0	10	1	11	0	0	0	2	.000	0	0-0	0	5.18	6.65
	5 ML YEARS		135	81	2	15	558.0	2454	568	344	312	89	23	18	21	226	6	415	20	0	36	27	.571	0	3-7	7	4.73	5.03

Dave Elder

Pitches: R **Bats:** R **Pos:** RP-4   **Ht:** 6'0" **Wt:** 180 **Born:** 9/23/75 **Age:** 28

			HOW MUCH HE PITCHED						WHAT HE GAVE UP										THE RESULTS							
Year	Team	Lg	G	GS	CG	GF	IP	BFP	H	R	ER	HR	SH	SF	HB	TBB	IBB	SO	WP	Bk	W	L	Pct	ShO	Sv-Op	Hld	ERC	ERA
1997	Pulaski	R+	20	0	0	17	32.1	127	18	8	7	2	0	0	0	12	0	57	4	0	2	2	.500	0	6- -	-	1.56	1.95
1999	Charlotte	A+	24	1	0	16	44.1	186	33	15	14	2	4	0	2	25	0	42	4	0	4	2	.667	0	4- -	-	3.16	2.84
1999	Tulsa	AA	3	0	0	1	6.2	32	8	7	6	0	0	0	0	6	1	7	0	0	1	0	1.000	0	0- -	-	6.37	8.10
2000	Tulsa	AA	33	21	0	8	116.2	554	121	80	64	9	4	4	4	88	0	104	11	0	7	6	.538	0	3- -	-	5.63	4.94
2001	Tulsa	AA	13	13	0	0	72.0	308	64	28	24	1	0	3	6	43	0	78	3	0	4	6	.400	0	0- -	-	3.83	3.00
2001	Oklahoma	AAA	15	8	0	3	57.2	266	54	36	32	4	2	0	4	43	0	56	4	1	5	4	.556	0	1- -	-	5.15	4.99
2002	Akron	AA	23	1	0	18	36.0	142	19	8	8	1	1	1	0	18	2	42	1	0	2	1	.667	0	9- -	-	1.59	2.00
2002	Buffalo	AAA	22	1	0	15	34.0	145	32	11	10	1	1	1	0	14	0	42	2	0	3	1	.750	0	5- -	-	3.31	2.65
2003	Buffalo	AAA	8	0	0	6	12.2	47	5	6	6	0	1	0	0	6	0	17	0	0	0	0	-	0	6- -	-	1.12	0.00
2002	Cleveland	AL	15	0	0	4	23.0	100	18	10	8	1	1	2	1	14	3	23	0	0	0	2	.000	0	0-0	3	3.22	3.13
2003	Cleveland	AL	4	0	0	1	2.1	16	5	5	5	2	0	0	0	4	0	3	1	0	1	1	.500	0	0-1	0	27.02	19.29
	2 ML YEARS		19	0	0	4	25.1	116	23	15	13	3	1	2	1	18	3	26	1	0	1	3	.250	0	0-1	3	4.84	4.62

Cal Eldred

Pitches: R **Bats:** R **Pos:** RP-62   **Ht:** 6'4" **Wt:** 235 **Born:** 11/24/67 **Age:** 36

Year Team	Lg	G	GS	CG	GF	IP	BFP	H	R	ER	HR	SH	SF	HB	TBB	IBB	SO	WP	Bk	W	L	Pct	ShO	Sv-Op	Hld	ERC	ERA
1991 Milwaukee	NL	3	3	0	0	16.0	73	20	9	8	2	0	0	6	6	0	10	0	0	2	0	1.000	0	0-0	0	5.57	4.50
1992 Milwaukee	NL	14	14	2	0	100.1	394	76	21	20	4	1	0	2	23	0	62	3	0	11	2	.846	1	0-0	0	1.94	1.79
1993 Milwaukee	NL	36	36	8	0	258.0	1087	232	120	115	32	5	12	10	91	5	180	2	0	16	16	.500	1	0-0	0	3.62	4.01
1994 Milwaukee	NL	25	25	6	0	179.0	769	158	96	93	23	5	7	4	84	0	98	2	0	11	11	.500	0	0-0	0	3.97	4.68
1995 Milwaukee	NL	4	4	0	0	23.2	104	24	10	9	4	1	0	1	10	0	18	1	1	1	1	.500	0	0-0	0	4.91	3.42
1996 Milwaukee	NL	15	15	0	0	84.2	363	82	43	42	8	0	4	4	38	0	50	1	0	4	4	.500	0	0-0	0	4.33	4.46
1997 Milwaukee	NL	34	34	1	0	202.0	885	207	118	112	31	4	6	9	89	0	122	5	0	13	15	.464	1	0-0	0	5.00	4.99
1998 Milwaukee	NL	23	23	0	0	133.0	602	157	82	71	14	5	3	4	61	3	86	6	0	4	8	.333	0	0-0	0	5.54	4.80
1999 Milwaukee	NL	20	15	0	2	82.0	392	101	75	71	19	2	3	1	46	0	60	8	1	2	8	.200	0	0-0	0	7.13	7.79
2000 Chicago	AL	20	20	2	0	112.0	492	103	61	57	12	3	2	5	59	0	97	4	0	10	2	.833	1	0-0	0	4.36	4.58
2001 Chicago	AL	2	2	0	0	6.0	34	12	9	9	1	0	0	3	3	1	6	0	0	0	1	.000	0	0-0	0	14.25	13.50
2003 St Louis	NL	62	0	0	18	67.1	293	62	32	28	9	5	3	4	31	4	67	4	0	7	4	.636	0	8-14	11	4.25	3.74
12 ML YEARS		258	191	19	20	1264.0	5488	1234	676	635	159	31	40	47	541	13	856	36	2	81	72	.529	4	8-14	11	4.38	4.52

Mark Ellis

Bats: R **Throws:** R **Pos:** 2B-153; PH-2   **Ht:** 5'11" **Wt:** 180 **Born:** 6/6/77 **Age:** 27

Year Team	Lg	G	AB	H	2B	3B	HR	(Hm	Rd)	TB	R	RBI	RC	TBB	IBB	SO	HBP	SH	SF	SB	CS	SB%	GDP	Avg	OBP	Slg
1999 Spokane	A-	71	281	92	14	0	7	(--	--)	127	67	47	59	47	3	40	3	5	4	21	7	.75	1	.327	.424	.452
2000 Wilmington	A+	132	484	146	27	4	6	(--	--)	199	83	62	86	78	0	72	7	4	3	25	7	.78	11	.302	.404	.411
2000 Wichita	AA	7	22	7	1	0	0	(--	--)	8	4	4	4	5	0	5	0	0	0	1	0	1.00	0	.318	.444	.364
2001 Sacramento	AAA	132	472	129	38	0	10	(--	--)	197	71	53	70	54	4	78	5	5	5	21	7	.75	13	.273	.351	.417
2002 Sacramento	AAA	21	84	25	10	1	0	(--	--)	37	14	5	15	6	0	13	4	0	0	4	0	1.00	1	.298	.372	.440
2002 Oakland	AL	98	345	94	16	4	6	(6	0)	136	58	35	54	44	1	54	4	8	3	4	2	.67	3	.272	.359	.394
2003 Oakland	AL	154	553	137	31	5	9	(7	2)	205	78	52	69	48	4	94	7	9	5	6	2	.75	7	.248	.313	.371
2 ML YEARS		252	898	231	47	9	15	(13	2)	341	136	87	123	92	5	148	11	17	8	10	4	.71	10	.257	.331	.380

Robert Ellis

Pitches: R **Bats:** R **Pos:** SP-4   **Ht:** 6'5" **Wt:** 220 **Born:** 12/15/70 **Age:** 33

Year Team	Lg	G	GS	CG	GF	IP	BFP	H	R	ER	HR	SH	SF	HB	TBB	IBB	SO	WP	Bk	W	L	Pct	ShO	Sv-Op	Hld	ERC	ERA
2003 Oklahoma*	AAA	27	15	2	7	118.1	516	128	68	65	12	8	7	7	35	3	49	7	1	3	10	.231	0	3- --	-	4.30	4.94
1996 Anaheim	AL	3	0	0	3	5.0	19	0	0	0	0	0	0	0	4	0	5	1	0	0	0	-	0	0-0	0	0.64	0.00
2001 Arizona	NL	19	17	0	1	92.0	413	106	61	59	12	6	7	4	34	2	41	3	2	6	5	.545	0	0-0	0	5.17	5.77
2002 Los Angeles	NL	3	0	0	0	2.2	13	6	3	3	1	0	0	0	0	0	0	0	0	0	1	.000	0	0-0	0	13.68	10.13
2003 Texas	AL	4	4	0	0	18.1	89	26	17	17	7	0	2	1	10	0	8	0	0	1	1	.500	0	0-0	0	10.11	8.35
4 ML YEARS		29	21	0	4	118.0	534	138	81	79	20	6	9	5	48	2	54	4	2	7	7	.500	0	0-0	0	5.76	6.03

Jason Ellison

Bats: R **Throws:** R **Pos:** LF-3; PR-2; CF-1; PH-1   **Ht:** 5'10" **Wt:** 180 **Born:** 4/4/78 **Age:** 26

Year Team	Lg	G	AB	H	2B	3B	HR	(Hm	Rd)	TB	R	RBI	RC	TBB	IBB	SO	HBP	SH	SF	SB	CS	SB%	GDP	Avg	OBP	Slg
2000 Salem-Keizer	A-	74	300	90	15	2	0	(--	--)	109	67	28	44	29	0	45	7	4	1	13	7	.65	1	.300	.374	.363
2001 Hagerstown	A	130	494	144	38	3	8	(--	--)	212	95	55	85	71	3	68	10	13	5	19	15	.56	6	.291	.388	.429
2002 San Jose	A+	81	322	87	13	0	5	(--	--)	115	40	40	34	25	2	37	2	4	2	9	9	.50	10	.270	.325	.357
2002 Fresno	AAA	49	196	61	8	1	3	(--	--)	80	31	8	33	21	0	28	4	0	0	16	3	.84	4	.311	.389	.408
2003 Fresno	AAA	119	461	136	22	4	6	(--	--)	184	74	39	66	39	1	52	6	6	3	21	13	.62	7	.295	.356	.399
2003 San Francisco	NL	7	10	1	0	0	0	(0	0)	1	1	0	0	0	0	1	0	0	0	0	0	-	0	.100	.100	.100

Alan Embree

Pitches: L **Bats:** L **Pos:** RP-65   **Ht:** 6'2" **Wt:** 190 **Born:** 1/23/70 **Age:** 34

Year Team	Lg	G	GS	CG	GF	IP	BFP	H	R	ER	HR	SH	SF	HB	TBB	IBB	SO	WP	Bk	W	L	Pct	ShO	Sv-Op	Hld	ERC	ERA
2003 Sarasota*	A+	1	1	0	0	0.2	4	2	1	1	0	0	0	0	0	0	2	0	0	0	0	-	0	0- --	-	14.52	13.50
1992 Cleveland	AL	4	4	0	0	18.0	87	19	14	14	3	0	2	1	8	0	12	1	1	0	2	.000	0	0-0	0	5.25	7.00
1995 Cleveland	AL	23	0	0	8	24.2	111	23	16	14	2	2	2	0	16	0	23	1	0	3	2	.600	0	1-1	6	4.51	5.11
1996 Cleveland	AL	24	0	0	2	31.0	140	30	26	22	10	1	3	0	21	3	33	3	0	1	1	.500	0	0-0	1	6.58	6.39
1997 Atlanta	NL	66	0	0	15	46.0	190	36	13	13	1	4	1	2	20	2	45	3	1	3	1	.750	0	0-0	16	2.66	2.54
1998 Atl-Ari	NL	55	0	0	16	53.2	237	56	32	25	7	4	1	1	23	0	43	3	0	4	2	.667	0	1-3	12	4.71	4.19
1999 San Francisco	NL	68	0	0	13	58.2	244	42	22	22	6	3	2	3	26	2	53	3	0	3	2	.600	0	0-3	22	2.86	3.38
2000 San Francisco	NL	63	0	0	21	60.0	263	62	34	33	4	4	5	3	25	2	49	1	0	3	5	.375	0	2-5	9	4.24	4.95
2001 SF-CWS	AL	61	0	0	17	54.0	245	65	47	44	14	0	6	3	17	2	59	3	0	1	4	.200	0	0-3	9	6.20	7.33
2002 SD-Bos	AL	68	0	0	20	62.0	251	47	19	14	6	1	2	1	20	3	81	1	0	4	6	.400	0	2-7	18	2.48	2.03
2003 Boston	AL	65	0	0	15	55.0	221	49	26	26	5	0	2	0	16	3	45	0	0	4	1	.800	0	1-2	14	3.01	4.25
1998 Atlanta	NL	20	0	0	5	18.2	87	23	14	9	2	1	1	0	10	0	19	0	0	1	0	1.000	0	0-1	6	6.06	4.34
1998 Arizona	NL	35	0	0	11	35.0	150	33	18	16	5	3	0	1	13	0	24	3	0	3	2	.600	0	1-2	6	4.03	4.11
2001 San Francisco	NL	22	0	0	7	20.0	106	34	26	25	7	0	3	2	10	2	25	1	0	0	1	.000	0	0-1	0	11.29	11.25
2001 Chicago	AL	39	0	0	10	34.0	139	31	21	19	7	0	3	1	7	0	34	2	0	1	3	.333	0	0-2	9	3.61	5.03
2002 San Diego	NL	36	0	0	13	28.2	118	23	7	3	2	0	0	0	9	2	38	1	0	3	4	.429	0	0-2	10	2.38	0.94
2002 Boston	AL	32	0	0	7	33.1	133	24	12	11	4	1	2	1	11	1	43	0	0	1	2	.333	0	2-5	8	2.56	2.97
10 ML YEARS		497	4	0	127	463.0	1984	429	249	227	58	19	26	14	192	17	443	19	2	26	26	.500	0	7-24	107	3.96	4.41

Juan Encarnacion

Bats: R Throws: R Pos: RF-155; PH-1   Ht: 6'3" Wt: 215 Born: 3/8/76 Age: 28

Year Team	Lg	G	AB	H	2B	3B	HR	(Hm	Rd)	TB	R	RBI	RC	TBB	IBB	SO	HBP	SH	SF	SB	CS	SB%	GDP	Avg	OBP	Slg
1997 Detroit	AL	11	33	7	1	1	1	(1	0)	13	3	5	4	3	0	12	2	0	0	3	1	.75	1	.212	.316	.394
1998 Detroit	AL	40	164	54	9	4	7	(4	3)	92	30	21	31	7	0	31	1	0	3	7	4	.64	2	.329	.354	.561
1999 Detroit	AL	132	509	130	30	6	19	(6	13)	229	62	74	64	14	1	113	9	4	2	33	12	.73	12	.255	.287	.450
2000 Detroit	AL	141	547	158	25	6	14	(4	10)	237	75	72	76	29	1	90	7	3	4	16	4	.80	15	.289	.330	.433
2001 Detroit	AL	120	417	101	19	7	12	(4	8)	170	52	52	48	25	1	93	6	3	4	9	5	.64	9	.242	.292	.408
2002 Cin-Fla	NL	152	584	158	22	5	24	(8	16)	262	77	85	74	46	0	113	4	3	7	21	9	.70	18	.271	.324	.449
2003 Florida	NL	156	601	162	37	6	19	(6	10)	268	80	94	77	37	0	82	4	5	6	19	8	.70	17	.270	.313	.446
2002 Cincinnati	NL	83	321	89	11	2	16	(6	10)	152	43	51	42	26	0	63	1	3	3	9	4	.69	7	.277	.330	.474
2002 Florida	NL	69	263	69	11	3	8	(2	6)	110	34	34	32	20	0	50	3	0	4	12	5	.71	11	.262	.317	.418
7 ML YEARS		752	2855	770	143	35	96	(36	60)	1271	379	403	374	161	3	534	33	20	26	108	43	.72	74	.270	.313	.445

Morgan Ensberg

Bats: R Throws: R Pos: 3B-111; PH-23; DH-1   Ht: 6'2" Wt: 210 Born: 8/26/75 Age: 28

Year Team	Lg	G	AB	H	2B	3B	HR	(Hm	Rd)	TB	R	RBI	RC	TBB	IBB	SO	HBP	SH	SF	SB	CS	SB%	GDP	Avg	OBP	Slg
2000 Houston	NL	4	7	2	0	0	0	(-	-)	2	0	0	1	0	0	0	0	0	0	0	0	-	0	.286	.286	.286
2002 Houston	NL	49	132	32	7	2	3	(2	1)	52	14	19	13	18	0	25	3	0	0	2	0	1.00	8	.242	.346	.394
2003 Houston	NL	127	385	112	15	1	25	(16	9)	204	69	60	70	48	1	60	6	1	1	7	2	.78	10	.291	.377	.530
3 ML YEARS		180	524	146	22	3	28	(18	10)	258	83	79	84	66	1	86	9	1	1	9	2	.82	18	.279	.368	.492

Scott Erickson

Pitches: R Bats: R Pos: SP   Ht: 6'4" Wt: 230 Born: 2/2/68 Age: 36

Year Team	Lg	G	GS	CG	GF	IP	BFP	H	R	ER	HR	SH	SF	HB	TBB	IBB	SO	WP	Bk	W	L	Pct	ShO	Sv-Op	Hld	ERC	ERA
1990 Minnesota	AL	19	17	1	1	113.0	485	108	49	36	9	5	2	5	51	4	53	3	0	8	4	.667	0	0-0	0	4.07	2.87
1991 Minnesota	AL	32	32	5	0	204.0	851	189	80	72	13	5	7	6	71	3	108	4	0	20	8	.714	3	0-0	0	3.36	3.18
1992 Minnesota	AL	32	32	5	0	212.0	888	197	86	80	18	9	7	8	83	3	101	6	1	13	12	.520	3	0-0	0	3.75	3.40
1993 Minnesota	AL	34	34	1	0	218.2	976	266	138	126	17	10	13	10	71	1	116	5	0	8	19	.296	0	0-0	0	5.05	5.19
1994 Minnesota	AL	23	23	2	0	144.0	654	173	95	87	15	3	4	9	59	0	104	10	0	8	11	.421	1	0-0	0	5.61	5.44
1995 Min-Bal	AL	32	31	7	1	196.1	836	213	108	105	18	3	3	5	67	0	106	3	2	13	10	.565	2	0-0	0	4.48	4.81
1996 Baltimore	AL	34	34	6	0	222.1	968	262	137	124	21	5	5	11	66	4	100	1	0	13	12	.520	0	0-0	0	4.90	5.02
1997 Baltimore	AL	34	33	3	0	221.2	922	218	100	91	16	3	4	5	61	5	131	11	0	16	7	.696	2	0-0	0	3.40	3.69
1998 Baltimore	AL	36	36	11	0	251.1	1102	284	125	112	23	7	2	13	69	4	186	4	0	16	13	.552	2	0-0	0	4.40	4.01
1999 Baltimore	AL	34	34	6	0	230.1	995	244	127	123	27	7	6	11	99	4	106	10	0	15	12	.556	3	0-0	0	4.97	4.81
2000 Baltimore	AL	16	16	1	0	92.2	446	127	81	81	14	3	5	5	48	0	41	3	0	5	8	.385	0	0-0	0	7.50	7.87
2002 Baltimore	AL	29	28	3	0	160.2	719	192	109	99	20	3	7	8	68	2	74	5	0	5	12	.294	1	0-0	0	5.80	5.55
1995 Minnesota	AL	15	15	0	0	87.2	390	102	61	58	11	2	1	4	32	0	45	1	0	4	6	.400	0	0-0	0	5.29	5.95
1995 Baltimore	AL	17	16	7	1	108.2	446	111	47	47	7	1	2	1	35	0	61	2	2	9	4	.692	2	0-0	0	3.84	3.89
12 ML YEARS		355	350	51	2	2267.0	9842	2473	1235	1136	211	63	65	96	813	30	1226	65	3	140	128	.522	17	0-0	0	4.58	4.51

Darin Erstad

Bats: L Throws: L Pos: CF-66; PH-1   Ht: 6'2" Wt: 220 Born: 6/4/74 Age: 30

Year Team	Lg	G	AB	H	2B	3B	HR	(Hm	Rd)	TB	R	RBI	RC	TBB	IBB	SO	HBP	SH	SF	SB	CS	SB%	GDP	Avg	OBP	Slg
2003 Salt Lake*	AAA	7	27	11	0	0	0	(-	-)	11	6	4	5	2	0	1	0	0	0	1	0	1.00	0	.407	.448	.407
1996 Anaheim	AL	57	208	59	5	1	4	(1	3)	78	34	20	26	17	1	29	0	1	3	3	3	.50	3	.284	.333	.375
1997 Anaheim	AL	139	539	161	34	4	16	(8	8)	251	99	77	92	51	4	86	4	5	6	23	8	.74	5	.299	.360	.466
1998 Anaheim	AL	133	537	159	39	3	19	(9	10)	261	84	82	94	43	7	77	6	1	3	20	6	.77	2	.296	.353	.486
1999 Anaheim	AL	142	585	148	22	5	13	(7	6)	219	84	53	64	47	3	101	1	2	3	13	7	.65	16	.253	.308	.374
2000 Anaheim	AL	157	676	240	39	6	25	(11	14)	366	121	100	145	64	9	82	1	2	4	28	6	.78	8	.355	.409	.541
2001 Anaheim	AL	157	631	163	35	1	9	(3	6)	227	89	63	79	62	7	113	10	1	7	24	10	.71	8	.258	.331	.360
2002 Anaheim	AL	150	625	177	28	4	10	(2	8)	243	99	73	73	27	4	67	2	5	4	23	3	.88	9	.283	.313	.389
2003 Anaheim	AL	67	258	65	7	1	4	(1	3)	86	35	17	21	18	1	40	4	2	2	9	1	.90	8	.252	.309	.333
8 ML YEARS		1002	4059	1172	209	25	100	(42	58)	1731	645	485	594	329	36	595	28	19	32	143	46	.76	59	.289	.344	.426

Felix Escalona

Bats: R Throws: R Pos: SS-8; 2B-1; 3B-1   Ht: 6'0" Wt: 196 Born: 3/12/79 Age: 25

Year Team	Lg	G	AB	H	2B	3B	HR	(Hm	Rd)	TB	R	RBI	RC	TBB	IBB	SO	HBP	SH	SF	SB	CS	SB%	GDP	Avg	OBP	Slg
1996 Astros	R	28	75	11	2	0	1	(-	-)	16	8	9	4	8	0	31	4	1	1	1	2	.33	0	.147	.261	.213
1997 Astros	R	51	189	39	9	0	1	(-	-)	51	27	9	17	20	0	49	3	4	0	11	3	.79	1	.206	.292	.270
1997 Kissimmee	A+	3	9	2	0	0	0	(-	-)	2	6	0	2	1	0	2	3	0	0	0	0	-	0	.222	.462	.222
1998 Kissimmee	A+	3	4	0	0	0	0	(-	-)	0	0	0	0	1	0	1	0	0	0	0	0	-	0	.000	.000	.000
1998 Auburn	A-	51	149	31	5	0	1	(-	-)	39	22	17	11	11	0	33	6	1	4	4	2	.67	4	.208	.282	.262
1999 Michigan	A	116	396	114	29	4	6	(-	-)	169	78	47	61	29	0	60	17	7	3	7	7	.50	4	.288	.360	.427
2000 Michigan	A	64	251	65	14	1	6	(-	-)	99	42	35	34	22	1	49	4	3	2	7	0	1.00	3	.259	.326	.394
2000 Kissimmee	A+	42	143	36	5	1	0	(-	-)	43	19	8	14	9	0	21	6	3	1	5	3	.63	3	.252	.321	.301
2001 Lexington	A	130	536	155	42	2	16	(-	-)	249	92	64	88	30	2	85	16	5	5	46	12	.79	8	.289	.342	.465
2003 Ottawa	AAA	9	30	7	2	0	0	(-	-)	9	5	5	3	1	0	5	2	0	0	2	0	1.00	0	.233	.303	.300
2003 Orlando	AA	22	90	22	7	0	1	(-	-)	32	11	8	10	5	0	14	5	3	0	0	0	-	3	.244	.320	.356
2003 Bowie	AA	1	3	1	0	0	0	(-	-)	1	0	0	0	0	0	0	0	0	0	0	0	-	0	.333	.333	.333
2002 Tampa Bay	AL	59	157	34	8	2	0	(0	0)	46	17	9	12	3	0	44	7	3	1	7	2	.78	2	.217	.262	.293
2003 Tampa Bay	AL	10	27	5	2	0	0	(0	0)	7	2	2	3	2	0	6	0	0	0	1	0	1.00	0	.185	.241	.259
2 ML YEARS		69	184	39	10	2	0	(0	0)	53	19	11	15	5	0	50	7	3	1	8	2	.80	2	.212	.259	.288

Alex Escobar

Bats: R Throws: R Pos: RF-25; PH-3   Ht: 6'1" Wt: 180 Born: 9/6/78 Age: 25

							BATTING											BASERUNNING				AVERAGES		
Year Team	Lg	G	AB	H	2B	3B	HR	(Hm | Rd)	TB	R	RBI	RC	TBB	IBB	SO	HBP	SH	SF	SB	CS	SB%	GDP	Avg	OBP	Slg
1996 Mets	R	24	75	27	4	0	0	(- | -)	31	15	10	14	4	0	9	3	0	1	7	1	.88	0	.360	.410	.413
1997 Kingsport	R+	10	36	7	3	0	0	(- | -)	10	6	3	2	3	1	8	0	0	1	1	0	1.00	3	.194	.250	.278
1997 Mets	R	26	73	18	4	1	1	(- | -)	27	12	11	10	10	0	17	1	0	1	0	0	-	1	.247	.341	.370
1998 Capital City	A	112	416	129	23	5	27	(- | -)	243	90	91	100	54	1	133	5	5	3	49	7	.88	1	.310	.393	.584
1999 St.Lucie	A+	1	3	2	0	0	1	(- | -)	5	1	3	2	1	0	1	0	0	0	1	1	.50	0	.667	.750	1.667
1999 Mets	R	2	8	3	2	0	0	(- | -)	5	1	1	2	1	0	2	0	0	1	0	0	-	0	.375	.400	.625
2000 Binghamton	AA	122	437	126	25	7	16	(- | -)	213	79	67	80	57	5	114	0	0	5	24	5	.83	8	.288	.367	.487
2001 Norfolk	AAA	111	397	106	21	4	12	(- | -)	171	55	50	56	35	2	146	3	1	5	18	3	.86	10	.267	.327	.431
2003 Buffalo	AAA	118	439	110	21	2	24	(- | -)	207	63	78	59	24	3	133	7	0	6	8	3	.73	11	.251	.296	.472
2001 New York	NL	18	50	10	1	0	3	(3 | 0)	20	3	8	5	3	0	19	0	0	0	1	0	1.00	1	.200	.245	.400
2003 Cleveland	AL	28	99	27	2	0	5	(4 | 1)	44	16	14	9	7	1	33	1	0	1	1	0	1.00	0	.273	.324	.444
2 ML YEARS		46	149	37	3	0	8	(7 | 1)	64	19	22	14	10	1	52	1	0	1	2	0	1.00	1	.248	.298	.430

Kelvim Escobar

Pitches: R Bats: R Pos: SP-26; RP-15   Ht: 6'1" Wt: 210 Born: 4/11/76 Age: 28

		HOW MUCH HE PITCHED						WHAT HE GAVE UP										THE RESULTS						
Year Team	Lg	G	GS	CG	GF	IP	BFP	H	R	ER	HR	SH	SF	HB	TBB	IBB	SO	WP	Bk	W	L	Pct	ShO	Sv-Op	Hld	ERC	ERA
1997 Toronto	AL	27	0	0	23	31.0	139	28	12	10	1	2	0	0	19	2	36	0	0	3	2	.600	0	14-17	1	3.68	2.90
1998 Toronto	AL	22	10	0	2	79.2	342	72	37	33	5	0	3	0	35	0	72	0	0	7	3	.700	0	0-1	5	3.41	3.73
1999 Toronto	AL	33	30	1	2	174.0	795	203	118	110	19	2	8	10	81	2	129	6	1	14	11	.560	0	0-0	0	5.62	5.69
2000 Toronto	AL	43	24	3	8	180.0	794	186	118	107	26	5	4	3	85	3	142	4	0	10	15	.400	1	2-3	3	4.94	5.35
2001 Toronto	AL	59	11	1	15	126.0	517	93	51	49	8	2	5	3	52	5	121	2	0	6	8	.429	1	0-0	13	2.43	3.50
2002 Toronto	AL	76	0	0	68	78.0	355	75	39	37	10	1	0	5	44	6	85	4	0	5	7	.417	0	38-46	0	4.77	4.27
2003 Toronto	AL	41	26	1	12	180.1	797	189	94	86	15	5	5	9	78	3	159	9	0	13	9	.591	1	4-5	0	4.53	4.29
7 ML YEARS		301	101	6	130	849.0	3739	846	469	432	84	17	25	30	394	21	744	25	1	58	55	.513	3	58-72	22	4.39	4.58

Bobby Estalella

Bats: R Throws: R Pos: C-46   Ht: 6'1" Wt: 213 Born: 8/23/74 Age: 29

							BATTING											BASERUNNING				AVERAGES		
Year Team	Lg	G	AB	H	2B	3B	HR	(Hm	Rd)	TB	R	RBI	RC	TBB	IBB	SO	HBP	SH	SF	SB	CS	SB%	GDP	Avg	OBP	Slg
1996 Philadelphia	NL	7	17	6	0	0	2	(0	2)	12	5	4	4	1	0	6	0	0	0	1	0	1.00	0	.353	.389	.706
1997 Philadelphia	NL	13	29	10	1	0	4	(1	3)	23	9	9	9	7	0	7	0	0	0	0	0	-	2	.345	.472	.793
1998 Philadelphia	NL	47	165	31	6	1	8	(3	5)	63	16	20	15	13	0	49	1	0	3	0	0	-	4	.188	.247	.382
1999 Philadelphia	NL	9	18	3	0	0	0	(0	0)	3	2	1	1	4	0	7	0	0	0	0	1	.00	0	.167	.318	.167
2000 San Francisco	NL	106	299	70	22	3	14	(6	8)	140	45	53	52	57	9	92	2	0	3	3	0	1.00	4	.234	.357	.468
2001 SF-NYY		32	97	19	5	1	3	(2	1)	35	12	10	10	12	2	30	2	0	0	0	0	-	2	.196	.297	.361
2002 Colorado	NL	38	112	23	8	0	8	(6	2)	55	17	25	18	14	0	33	0	0	4	0	1	.00	1	.205	.285	.491
2003 Colorado	NL	46	140	28	7	0	7	(2	5)	56	17	21	18	19	0	55	1	2	3	2	0	1.00	4	.200	.294	.400
2001 San Francisco	NL	29	93	19	5	1	3	(2	1)	35	11	10	10	11	2	28	1	0	0	0	0	-	2	.204	.295	.376
2001 New York	AL	3	4	0	0	0	0	(0	0)	0	1	0	0	1	0	2	1	0	0	0	0	-	0	.000	.333	.000
8 ML YEARS		298	877	190	49	5	46	(20	26)	387	123	143	127	127	11	279	6	2	13	6	2	.75	17	.217	.316	.441

Shawn Estes

Pitches: L Bats: R Pos: SP-28; RP-1   Ht: 6'2" Wt: 200 Born: 2/18/73 Age: 31

		HOW MUCH HE PITCHED						WHAT HE GAVE UP										THE RESULTS						
Year Team	Lg	G	GS	CG	GF	IP	BFP	H	R	ER	HR	SH	SF	HB	TBB	IBB	SO	WP	Bk	W	L	Pct	ShO	Sv-Op	Hld	ERC	ERA
1995 San Francisco	NL	3	3	0	0	17.1	76	16	14	13	2	0	1	5	0	14	4	0	0	3	.000	0	0-0	0	3.37	6.75
1996 San Francisco	NL	11	11	0	0	70.0	305	63	30	28	3	5	0	2	39	3	60	4	0	3	5	.375	0	0-0	0	3.78	3.60
1997 San Francisco	NL	32	32	3	0	201.0	849	162	80	71	12	13	2	8	100	2	181	10	2	19	5	.792	2	0-0	0	3.28	3.18
1998 San Francisco	NL	25	25	1	0	149.1	661	150	89	84	14	15	4	5	80	6	136	6	1	7	12	.368	1	0-0	0	4.71	5.06
1999 San Francisco	NL	32	32	1	0	203.0	914	209	121	111	21	14	3	5	112	2	159	15	1	11	11	.500	1	0-0	0	4.96	4.92
2000 San Francisco	NL	30	30	4	0	190.1	829	194	99	90	11	7	6	3	108	1	136	11	0	15	6	.714	2	0-0	0	4.75	4.26
2001 San Francisco	NL	27	27	0	0	159.0	693	151	78	71	11	5	9	5	77	7	109	10	2	9	8	.529	0	0-0	0	3.96	4.02
2002 NYM-Cin	NL	29	29	1	0	160.2	713	171	94	91	13	7	6	9	83	9	109	3	1	5	12	.294	1	0-0	0	5.00	5.10
2003 Chicago	NL	29	28	1	0	152.1	699	182	113	97	20	11	7	1	83	1	103	6	0	8	11	.421	1	0-0	0	6.15	5.73
2002 New York	NL	23	23	1	0	132.2	580	133	70	67	12	7	4	5	66	9	92	2	1	4	9	.308	1	0-0	0	4.51	4.55
2002 Cincinnati	NL	6	6	0	0	28.0	133	38	24	24	1	0	2	4	17	0	17	1	0	1	3	.250	0	0-0	0	7.52	7.71
9 ML YEARS		218	217	11	0	1303.0	5739	1298	718	656	107	77	37	39	687	31	1007	69	7	77	73	.513	8	0-0	0	4.56	4.53

Johnny Estrada

Bats: B Throws: R Pos: C-14; PH-3   Ht: 5'11" Wt: 209 Born: 6/27/76 Age: 28

							BATTING											BASERUNNING				AVERAGES		
Year Team	Lg	G	AB	H	2B	3B	HR	(Hm	Rd)	TB	R	RBI	RC	TBB	IBB	SO	HBP	SH	SF	SB	CS	SB%	GDP	Avg	OBP	Slg
2003 Richmond*	AAA	106	354	116	29	0	10	(-	-)	175	40	66	66	30	5	30	12	0	6	0	0	-	11	.328	.393	.494
2001 Philadelphia	NL	89	298	68	15	0	8	(7	1)	107	26	37	25	16	6	32	4	2	4	0	0	-	15	.228	.273	.359
2002 Philadelphia	NL	10	17	2	1	0	0	(0	0)	3	0	2	0	2	1	2	0	0	0	0	0	-	0	.118	.211	.176
2003 Atlanta	NL	16	36	11	0	0	0	(0	0)	11	2	2	1	0	0	3	3	0	0	0	0	-	1	.306	.359	.306
3 ML YEARS		115	351	81	16	0	8	(7	1)	121	28	41	26	18	7	37	7	2	4	0	0	-	16	.231	.279	.345

Leo Estrella

Pitches: R Bats: R Pos: RP-58   Ht: 6'1" Wt: 185 Born: 2/20/75 Age: 29

Year Team	Lg	G	GS	CG	GF	IP	BFP	H	R	ER	HR	SH	SF	HB	TBB	IBB	SO	WP	Bk	W	L	Pct	ShO	Sv-Op	Hld	ERC	ERA
1996 Kingsport	R+	15	7	1	3	58.0	248	54	32	25	3	4	1	1	24	0	52	6	2	6	3	.667	0	0- -	-	3.48	3.88
1997 Pittsfield	A-	15	15	0	0	82.0	395	91	48	31	0	2	1	3	27	0	55	3	2	7	6	.538	0	0- -	-	3.42	3.40
1998 Capital City	A	20	20	3	0	119.0	502	120	66	52	10	7	3	8	23	0	97	1	1	10	8	.556	0	0- -	-	3.44	3.93
1998 Hagerstown	A	5	5	0	0	30.0	133	34	19	15	0	2	3	3	13	1	27	2	1	1	3	.250	0	0- -	-	4.67	4.50
1999 Dunedin	A+	27	24	2	0	168.0	696	166	74	60	11	6	5	17	47	0	116	6	1	14	7	.667	2	0- -	-	3.83	3.21
2000 Tennessee	AA	13	13	3	0	76.0	324	68	36	31	6	4	3	10	30	1	63	2	0	5	5	.500	2	0- -	-	3.88	3.67
2000 Syracuse	AAA	15	15	3	0	89.2	364	68	42	40	8	1	4	2	40	0	48	2	1	5	4	.556	1	0- -	-	3.05	4.01
2001 Chattanooga	AA	3	3	0	0	14.2	59	14	6	6	0	0	0	1	4	0	14	0	0	0	1	.000	0	0- -	-	2.68	3.68
2001 Norfolk	AAA	8	1	0	0	17.1	77	23	7	6	1	0	1	3	8	0	10	3	0	2	0	1.000	0	0- -	-	7.30	3.12
2001 Louisville	AAA	34	5	0	9	62.2	273	67	36	34	8	2	1	1	27	0	37	3	0	1	1	.500	0	1- -	-	4.94	4.88
2002 W Tennessee	AA	10	3	0	2	24.2	106	23	13	9	0	5	0	1	8	0	18	1	0	2	2	.500	0	0- -	-	2.82	3.28
2002 Iowa	AAA	8	0	0	4	10.2	51	10	8	7	0	0	1	1	7	0	9	1	0	0	0	-	0	1- -	-	4.10	5.91
2002 New Haven	AA	14	5	0	4	39.1	187	46	30	21	4	2	4	2	20	0	23	4	0	2	2	.500	0	0- -	-	5.55	4.81
2003 Indianapolis	AAA	7	0	0	2	15.0	59	9	2	2	1	0	0	0	6	0	12	0	0	1	0	1.000	0	0- -	-	1.86	1.20
2000 Toronto	AL	2	0	0	0	4.2	21	9	0	3	1	0	0	0	0	0	3	0	0	0	0	-	0	0-0	0	9.77	5.79
2003 Milwaukee	NL	58	0	0	18	66.0	290	75	32	32	10	4	3	3	21	5	25	2	1	7	3	.700	0	3-8	9	4.97	4.36
2 ML YEARS		60	0	0	18	70.2	311	84	32	35	11	4	3	3	21	5	28	2	1	7	3	.700	0	3-8	9	5.25	4.46

Seth Etherton

Pitches: R Bats: R Pos: SP-7   Ht: 6'1" Wt: 200 Born: 10/17/76 Age: 27

Year Team	Lg	G	GS	CG	GF	IP	BFP	H	R	ER	HR	SH	SF	HB	TBB	IBB	SO	WP	Bk	W	L	Pct	ShO	Sv-Op	Hld	ERC	ERA
1998 Midland	AA	9	7	1	1	48.1	211	57	36	33	9	2	1	1	12	0	35	1	1	1	5	.167	0	0- -	-	5.18	6.14
1999 Erie	AA	24	24	4	0	167.2	694	153	72	61	14	7	5	3	43	0	153	4	4	10	10	.500	1	0- -	-	2.99	3.27
1999 Edmonton	AAA	4	4	0	0	21.1	94	25	13	13	7	1	1	0	6	0	19	1	0	0	2	.000	0	0- -	-	6.17	5.48
2000 Edmonton	AAA	9	9	0	0	58.1	248	60	30	26	6	0	1	1	19	0	50	3	0	3	2	.600	0	0- -	-	4.06	4.01
2002 Dayton	A	1	1	0	0	1.0	4	1	0	0	0	0	0	0	0	0	2	0	0	0	0	-	0	0- -	-	1.95	0.00
2002 Chattanooga	AA	3	3	0	0	9.1	34	5	1	1	0	1	0	1	2	0	4	0	0	0	1	.000	0	0- -	-	1.24	0.96
2002 Louisville	AAA	5	5	0	0	15.1	71	21	16	14	4	0	1	0	6	0	10	2	0	0	1	.000	0	0- -	-	7.61	8.22
2002 Norwich	AA	1	1	0	0	2.0	9	1	1	0	0	1	0	0	1	0	2	0	0	0	0	-	0	0- -	-	1.26	0.00
2003 Louisville	AAA	21	21	2	0	123.1	523	144	62	59	11	2	7	3	26	1	69	1	0	7	7	.500	1	0- -	-	4.35	4.31
2000 Anaheim	AL	11	11	0	0	60.1	270	68	0	37	16	0	0	0	22	0	32	0	0	5	1	.833	0	0-0	0	5.77	5.52
2003 Cincinnati	NL	7	7	0	0	30.0	145	39	23	23	4	3	3	3	15	1	17	0	0	2	4	.333	0	0-0	0	6.85	6.90
2 ML YEARS		18	18	0	0	90.1	415	107	23	60	20	3	3	3	37	1	49	0	0	7	5	.583	0	0-0	0	6.15	5.98

Adam Everett

Bats: R Throws: R Pos: SS-128; PR-4; PH-1   Ht: 6'0" Wt: 156 Born: 2/2/77 Age: 27

Year Team	Lg	G	AB	H	2B	3B	HR	(Hm	Rd)	TB	R	RBI	RC	TBB	IBB	SO	HBP	SH	SF	SB	CS	SB%	GDP	Avg	OBP	Slg
2003 New Orleans*	AAA	25	100	25	6	1	1	(-	-)	36	23	9	11	7	0	16	1	3	0	3	1	.75	1	.250	.306	.360
2001 Houston	NL	9	3	0	0	0	0	(0	0)	0	1	0	0	0	0	1	0	0	0	1	0	1.00	0	.000	.000	.000
2002 Houston	NL	40	88	17	3	0	0	(0	0)	20	11	4	6	12	1	19	1	2	0	3	0	1.00	1	.193	.297	.227
2003 Houston	NL	128	387	99	18	3	8	(5	3)	147	51	51	49	28	6	66	9	11	1	8	1	.89	7	.256	.320	.380
3 ML YEARS		177	478	116	21	3	8	(5	3)	167	63	55	55	40	7	86	10	13	1	12	1	.92	8	.243	.314	.349

Carl Everett

Bats: B Throws: R Pos: CF-81; LF-48; RF-34; PH-9; DH-4   Ht: 6'0" Wt: 215 Born: 6/3/71 Age: 33

Year Team	Lg	G	AB	H	2B	3B	HR	(Hm	Rd)	TB	R	RBI	RC	TBB	IBB	SO	HBP	SH	SF	SB	CS	SB%	GDP	Avg	OBP	Slg
1993 Florida	NL	11	19	2	0	0	0	(0	0)	2	0	0	0	1	0	9	0	0	0	1	0	1.00	0	.105	.150	.105
1994 Florida	NL	16	51	11	1	0	2	(2	0)	18	7	6	5	3	0	15	0	0	0	4	0	1.00	0	.216	.259	.353
1995 New York	NL	79	289	75	13	1	12	(9	3)	126	48	54	41	39	2	67	2	1	0	2	5	.29	11	.260	.352	.436
1996 New York	NL	101	192	46	8	1	1	(1	0)	59	29	16	21	21	2	53	4	1	1	6	0	1.00	4	.240	.326	.307
1997 New York	NL	142	443	110	28	3	14	(11	3)	186	58	57	58	32	3	102	7	3	2	17	9	.65	3	.248	.308	.420
1998 Houston	NL	133	467	138	34	4	15	(5	10)	225	72	76	76	44	2	102	3	3	2	14	12	.54	11	.296	.359	.482
1999 Houston	NL	123	464	151	33	3	25	(11	14)	265	86	108	105	50	5	94	11	2	8	27	7	.79	5	.325	.398	.571
2000 Boston	AL	137	496	149	32	4	34	(17	17)	291	82	108	106	52	5	113	8	0	5	11	4	.73	4	.300	.373	.587
2001 Boston	AL	102	409	105	24	4	14	(6	8)	179	61	58	59	27	3	104	13	0	0	9	2	.82	3	.257	.323	.438
2002 Texas	AL	105	374	100	16	0	16	(11	5)	164	47	62	59	33	4	77	6	1	4	2	3	.40	7	.267	.333	.438
2003 Tex-CWS	AL	147	526	151	27	3	28	(15	13)	268	93	92	101	53	6	84	15	4	4	8	4	.67	7	.287	.366	.510
2003 Texas	AL	74	270	74	13	3	18	(10	8)	147	53	51	57	31	2	48	5	4	3	4	1	.80	2	.274	.356	.544
2003 Chicago	AL	73	256	77	14	0	10	(5	5)	121	40	41	44	22	4	36	10	0	1	4	3	.57	5	.301	.377	.473
11 ML YEARS		1096	3730	1038	216	23	161	(88	73)	1783	583	637	631	355	32	820	69	15	26	101	46	.69	55	.278	.350	.478

Scott Eyre

Pitches: L Bats: L Pos: RP-74   Ht: 6'1" Wt: 210 Born: 5/30/72 Age: 32

Year Team	Lg	G	GS	CG	GF	IP	BFP	H	R	ER	HR	SH	SF	HB	TBB	IBB	SO	WP	Bk	W	L	Pct	ShO	Sv-Op	Hld	ERC	ERA
1997 Chicago	AL	11	11	0	0	60.2	267	62	36	34	11	1	2	1	31	1	36	2	0	4	4	.500	0	0-0	0	5.37	5.04
1998 Chicago	AL	33	17	0	10	107.0	491	114	78	64	24	2	3	2	64	0	73	7	0	3	8	.273	0	0-0	0	6.31	5.38
1999 Chicago	AL	21	0	0	8	25.0	129	38	22	21	6	0	1	1	15	2	17	1	0	1	1	.500	0	0-0	1	9.23	7.56
2000 Chicago	AL	13	1	0	3	19.0	93	29	15	14	3	0	2	1	12	0	16	0	0	1	1	.500	0	0-0	0	9.49	6.63
2001 Toronto	AL	17	0	0	5	15.2	66	15	6	6	1	0	1	1	7	2	16	2	0	1	2	.333	0	2-3	3	3.96	3.45
2002 Tor-SF	AL	70	3	0	6	74.2	333	80	41	37	4	2	4	0	36	8	58	5	0	2	4	.333	0	0-1	18	4.26	4.46
2003 San Francisco	NL	74	0	0	10	57.0	256	60	23	21	4	2	3	1	26	0	35	6	0	2	1	.667	0	1-3	20	4.37	3.32

72

Year Team	Lg	G	GS	CG	GF	IP	BFP	H	R	ER	HR	SH	SF	HB	TBB	IBB	SO	WP	Bk	W	L	Pct	ShO	Sv-Op	Hld	ERC	ERA
2002 Toronto	AL	49	3	0	3	63.1	283	69	37	35	4	2	4	0	29	7	51	4	0	2	4	.333	0	0-1	12	4.32	4.97
2002 San Francisco	NL	21	0	0	3	11.1	50	11	4	2	0	0	0	0	7	1	7	1	0	0	0	.333	0	0-0	6	3.91	1.59
7 ML YEARS		239	32	0	42	359.0	1635	398	221	197	53	7	16	7	191	13	251	23	0	14	21	.400	0	3-7	42	5.63	4.94

Kyle Farnsworth

Pitches: R **Bats:** R **Pos:** RP-77   **Ht:** 6'4" **Wt:** 235 **Born:** 4/14/76 **Age:** 28

Year Team	Lg	G	GS	CG	GF	IP	BFP	H	R	ER	HR	SH	SF	HB	TBB	IBB	SO	WP	Bk	W	L	Pct	ShO	Sv-Op	Hld	ERC	ERA
1999 Chicago	NL	27	21	1	1	130.0	579	140	80	73	28	6	2	3	52	1	70	7	1	5	9	.357	1	0-0	0	5.39	5.05
2000 Chicago	NL	46	5	0	8	77.0	371	90	58	55	14	4	4	4	50	8	74	3	0	2	9	.182	0	1-6	6	6.72	6.43
2001 Chicago	NL	76	0	0	24	82.0	339	65	26	25	8	2	2	1	29	2	107	2	2	4	6	.400	0	2-3	24	2.76	2.74
2002 Chicago	NL	45	0	0	17	46.2	213	53	47	38	9	2	5	1	24	7	46	1	0	4	6	.400	0	1-7	6	5.89	7.33
2003 Chicago	NL	77	0	0	13	76.1	312	53	31	28	6	4	1	0	36	1	92	6	0	3	2	.600	0	0-3	19	2.58	3.30
5 ML YEARS		271	26	1	63	412.0	1814	401	242	219	65	18	14	9	191	19	389	19	3	18	32	.360	1	4-19	55	4.56	4.78

Jeff Fassero

Pitches: L **Bats:** L **Pos:** RP-56; SP-6   **Ht:** 6'1" **Wt:** 200 **Born:** 1/5/63 **Age:** 41

Year Team	Lg	G	GS	CG	GF	IP	BFP	H	R	ER	HR	SH	SF	HB	TBB	IBB	SO	WP	Bk	W	L	Pct	ShO	Sv-Op	Hld	ERC	ERA
1991 Montreal	NL	51	0	0	30	55.1	223	39	17	15	1	6	0	1	17	1	42	4	0	2	5	.286	0	8-11	7	1.75	2.44
1992 Montreal	NL	70	0	0	22	85.2	368	81	35	27	1	5	2	2	34	6	63	7	1	8	7	.533	0	1-7	12	3.10	2.84
1993 Montreal	NL	56	15	1	10	149.2	616	119	50	38	7	7	4	0	54	0	140	5	0	12	5	.706	0	1-3	6	2.48	2.29
1994 Montreal	NL	21	21	1	0	138.2	569	119	54	46	13	7	2	1	40	4	119	6	0	8	6	.571	0	0-0	0	2.82	2.99
1995 Montreal	NL	30	30	1	0	189.0	833	207	102	91	15	19	7	2	74	3	164	7	1	13	14	.481	0	0-0	0	4.43	4.33
1996 Montreal	NL	34	34	5	0	231.2	967	217	95	85	20	16	5	3	55	3	222	5	2	15	11	.577	1	0-0	0	3.00	3.30
1997 Seattle	AL	35	35	2	0	234.1	1010	226	108	94	21	7	10	3	84	6	189	13	2	16	9	.640	1	0-0	0	3.60	3.61
1998 Seattle	AL	32	32	7	0	224.2	954	223	115	99	33	8	8	10	66	2	176	12	0	13	12	.520	0	0-0	0	4.10	3.97
1999 Sea-Tex	AL	37	27	0	2	156.1	751	208	135	125	35	2	7	4	83	3	114	9	0	5	14	.263	0	0-0	2	7.69	7.20
2000 Boston	AL	38	23	0	4	130.0	577	153	72	69	16	7	2	1	50	2	97	2	0	8	8	.500	0	0-0	5	5.25	4.78
2001 Chicago	NL	82	0	0	30	73.2	308	66	31	28	6	1	2	1	23	5	79	3	0	4	4	.500	0	12-17	25	2.97	3.42
2002 ChC-StL	NL	73	0	0	18	69.0	315	81	43	41	9	7	1	3	27	5	56	2	1	8	6	.571	0	0-3	13	5.25	5.35
2003 St Louis	NL	62	6	0	15	77.2	354	93	51	49	17	3	1	2	34	4	55	2	0	1	7	.125	0	3-6	11	6.34	5.68
1999 Seattle	AL	30	24	0	1	139.0	669	188	123	114	34	1	6	4	73	3	101	7	0	4	14	.222	0	0-0	2	8.02	7.38
1999 Texas	AL	7	3	0	1	17.1	82	20	12	11	1	1	1	0	10	0	13	2	0	1	0	1.000	0	0-0	0	5.21	5.71
2002 Chicago	NL	57	0	0	17	51.0	240	65	37	35	5	6	1	3	22	5	44	2	1	5	6	.455	0	0-1	6	5.79	6.18
2002 St Louis	NL	16	0	0	1	18.0	75	16	6	6	4	1	0	0	5	0	12	0	0	3	0	1.000	0	0-2	7	3.70	3.00
13 ML YEARS		621	223	17	131	1815.2	7845	1832	908	807	194	95	51	33	641	44	1516	77	7	113	108	.511	2	25-47	81	3.99	4.00

Carlos Febles

Bats: R **Throws:** R **Pos:** 2B-67; PR-9; PH-3; SS-2; DH-2   **Ht:** 5'11" **Wt:** 185 **Born:** 5/24/76 **Age:** 28

Year Team	Lg	G	AB	H	2B	3B	HR	(Hm	Rd)	TB	R	RBI	RC	TBB	IBB	SO	HBP	SH	SF	SB	CS	SB%	GDP	Avg	OBP	Slg
2003 Omaha*	AAA	9	32	10	4	0	0	(-	-)	14	7	6	6	3	0	6	1	1	0	2	1	.67	0	.313	.389	.438
1998 Kansas City	AL	11	25	10	1	2	0	(0	0)	15	5	2	7	4	0	7	0	0	0	2	1	.67	0	.400	.483	.600
1999 Kansas City	AL	123	453	116	22	9	10	(5	5)	186	71	53	63	47	0	91	9	12	3	20	4	.83	16	.256	.336	.411
2000 Kansas City	AL	100	339	87	12	1	2	(2	0)	107	59	29	39	36	1	48	10	13	1	17	6	.74	10	.257	.345	.316
2001 Kansas City	AL	79	292	69	9	2	8	(6	2)	106	45	25	30	22	0	58	1	1	1	5	2	.71	7	.236	.291	.363
2002 Kansas City	AL	119	351	86	16	4	4	(2	2)	122	44	26	44	41	0	63	7	5	0	16	5	.76	8	.245	.336	.348
2003 Kansas City	AL	74	196	46	5	0	0	(0	0)	51	31	11	11	13	0	30	5	5	0	8	2	.80	8	.235	.299	.260
6 ML YEARS		506	1656	414	65	18	24	(15	9)	587	255	146	194	163	1	297	32	36	5	68	20	.77	49	.250	.328	.354

Pedro Feliciano

Pitches: L **Bats:** L **Pos:** RP-23   **Ht:** 5'10" **Wt:** 185 **Born:** 8/25/76 **Age:** 27

Year Team	Lg	G	GS	CG	GF	IP	BFP	H	R	ER	HR	SH	SF	HB	TBB	IBB	SO	WP	Bk	W	L	Pct	ShO	Sv-Op	Hld	ERC	ERA
1995 Great Falls	R+	6	0	0	3	6.2	43	12	12	10	0	0	2	0	7	1	9	4	2	0	0	-	0	0- -	-	9.44	13.50
1996 Great Falls	R+	22	1	0	10	41.0	206	50	36	26	1	0	5	3	26	2	39	4	3	2	3	.400	0	3- -	-	5.62	5.71
1997 Savannah	A	36	9	1	8	105.2	437	90	45	31	11	3	3	1	39	0	94	6	4	3	7	.300	0	4- -	-	3.24	2.64
1997 Vero Beach	A+	1	0	0	0	2.0	7	3	1	1	0	0	0	0	1	0	1	0	0	0	0	-	0	0- -	-	10.61	4.50
1998 Vero Beach	A+	22	10	0	8	68.1	300	68	44	35	8	0	1	2	30	1	51	2	0	2	5	.286	0	2- -	-	4.39	4.61
2000 Vero Beach	A+	25	2	0	7	61.1	289	76	31	26	4	4	4	5	24	1	48	3	0	4	5	.444	0	0- -	-	5.32	3.82
2000 San Antonio	AA	9	0	0	3	9.1	37	7	2	2	0	1	0	1	4	1	11	0	2	0	0	-	0	2- -	-	2.59	1.93
2000 Albuquerque	AAA	1	0	0	1	1.0	9	3	3	2	2	0	0	0	1	0	2	0	0	0	0	-	0	0- -	-	34.63	18.00
2001 Jacksonville	AA	54	0	0	38	60.1	229	41	14	13	3	4	0	3	11	1	55	2	0	5	4	.556	0	17- -	-	1.62	1.94
2001 Las Vegas	AAA	6	0	0	1	8.2	49	16	11	7	2	1	0	1	5	1	5	1	0	0	1	.000	0	0- -	-	11.36	7.27
2002 Chattanooga	AA	28	0	0	14	38.2	160	33	14	11	1	4	1	3	11	1	26	0	0	2	1	.667	0	4- -	-	2.62	2.56
2002 Louisville	AAA	20	0	0	6	26.2	116	35	10	9	3	1	3	1	4	0	19	0	0	1	1	.500	0	0- -	-	5.17	3.04
2002 Norfolk	AAA	5	0	0	3	9.0	41	14	7	7	1	0	1	0	1	0	6	0	0	0	0	-	0	2- -	-	6.26	7.00
2003 Norfolk	AAA	15	0	0	9	22.2	91	20	10	10	3	1	0	0	6	1	18	0	0	3	2	.600	0	1- -	-	3.12	3.97
2002 New York	NL	6	0	0	3	6.0	26	9	5	5	0	0	0	1	1	0	4	0	0	0	0	-	0	0-0	0	5.56	7.50
2003 New York	NL	23	0	0	8	48.1	218	52	21	18	5	0	1	3	21	3	43	3	1	0	0	-	0	0-0	0	4.77	3.35
2 ML YEARS		29	0	0	11	54.1	244	61	26	23	5	0	1	3	22	3	47	3	1	0	0	-	0	0-0	0	4.85	3.81

Pedro Feliz

Bats: R **Throws:** R **Pos:** 3B-49; PH-25; LF-14; 1B-12; PR-3; RF-1   **Ht:** 6'1" **Wt:** 205 **Born:** 4/27/77 **Age:** 27

Year Team	Lg	G	AB	H	2B	3B	HR	(Hm	Rd)	TB	R	RBI	RC	TBB	IBB	SO	HBP	SH	SF	SB	CS	SB%	GDP	Avg	OBP	Slg
2000 San Francisco	NL	8	7	2	0	0	0	(0	0)	2	1	0	1	0	0	1	0	0	0	0	0	-	0	.286	.286	.286
2001 San Francisco	NL	94	220	50	9	1	7	(3	4)	82	23	22	20	10	2	50	2	3	3	2	1	.67	5	.227	.264	.373
2002 San Francisco	NL	67	146	37	4	1	2	(1	1)	49	14	13	12	6	1	27	0	0	1	0	0	-	2	.253	.281	.336
2003 San Francisco	NL	95	235	58	9	3	16	(6	10)	121	31	48	35	10	0	53	1	1	2	2	2	.50	7	.247	.278	.515
4 ML YEARS		264	608	147	22	5	25	(10	15)	254	69	83	68	26	3	131	3	4	6	4	3	.57	14	.242	.274	.418

Jared Fernandez

Pitches: R **Bats:** R **Pos:** SP-6; RP-6   **Ht:** 6'2" **Wt:** 225 **Born:** 2/2/72 **Age:** 32

		HOW MUCH HE PITCHED						WHAT HE GAVE UP											THE RESULTS						
Year Team	Lg	G	GS	CG	GF	IP	BFP	H	R	ER	HR	SH	SF	HB	TBB	IBB	SO	WP	Bk	W	L	Pct	ShO	Sv-Op	Hld	ERC	ERA
2003 New Orleans*	AAA	26	23	2	0	156.0	660	164	73	66	16	6	3	7	37	1	51	2	0	7	10	.412	0	0--	-	3.92	3.81
2001 Cincinnati	NL	5	2	0	2	12.1	57	13	9	6	1	0	0	2	6	0	5	1	0	0	1	.000	0	0-0	0	5.21	4.38
2002 Cincinnati	NL	14	8	0	2	50.2	232	59	31	25	5	1	2	3	24	1	36	3	0	1	3	.250	0	0-0	0	5.54	4.44
2003 Houston	NL	12	6	0	3	38.1	161	37	17	17	2	3	1	2	12	2	19	3	0	3	3	.500	0	0-0	0	3.38	3.99
3 ML YEARS		31	16	0	7	101.1	450	109	57	48	8	4	3	7	42	3	60	7	0	4	7	.364	0	0-0	0	4.65	4.26

Anthony Ferrari

Pitches: L **Bats:** L **Pos:** RP-4   **Ht:** 5'9" **Wt:** 165 **Born:** 6/22/78 **Age:** 26

		HOW MUCH HE PITCHED						WHAT HE GAVE UP											THE RESULTS						
Year Team	Lg	G	GS	CG	GF	IP	BFP	H	R	ER	HR	SH	SF	HB	TBB	IBB	SO	WP	Bk	W	L	Pct	ShO	Sv-Op	Hld	ERC	ERA
2000 Vermont	A-	25	0	0	21	47.1	190	31	14	9	2	3	0	5	15	0	37	2	1	2	2	.500	0	5--	-	2.03	1.71
2001 Jupiter	A+	51	0	0	40	56.2	226	36	11	5	1	4	1	4	17	0	45	1	0	2	3	.400	0	21--	-	1.63	0.79
2002 Harrisburg	AA	44	0	0	29	75.1	339	79	35	34	2	1	3	8	34	1	53	5	0	7	4	.636	0	6--	-	4.39	4.06
2003 Harrisburg	AA	14	0	0	12	16.0	66	13	1	1	0	0	0	2	6	1	9	0	0	2	0	1.000	0	5--	-	2.74	0.56
2003 Edmonton	AAA	28	0	0	16	49.2	229	63	34	27	3	3	3	6	18	4	17	0	0	5	2	.714	0	0--	-	5.56	4.89
2003 Montreal	NL	4	0	0	1	4.0	24	4	3	3	1	0	0	1	5	1	1	1	0	0	0	-	0	0-0	1	8.54	6.75

Mike Fetters

Pitches: R **Bats:** R **Pos:** RP-5   **Ht:** 6'4" **Wt:** 239 **Born:** 12/19/64 **Age:** 39

		HOW MUCH HE PITCHED						WHAT HE GAVE UP											THE RESULTS						
Year Team	Lg	G	GS	CG	GF	IP	BFP	H	R	ER	HR	SH	SF	HB	TBB	IBB	SO	WP	Bk	W	L	Pct	ShO	Sv-Op	Hld	ERC	ERA
1989 Anaheim	AL	1	0	0	0	3.1	16	5	4	3	1	0	0	0	1	0	4	2	0	0	0	-	0	0-0	0	8.14	8.10
1990 Anaheim	AL	26	2	0	10	67.2	291	77	33	31	9	1	0	2	20	0	35	3	0	1	1	.500	0	1-1	1	4.88	4.12
1991 Anaheim	AL	19	4	0	8	44.2	206	53	29	24	4	1	0	3	28	2	24	4	0	2	5	.286	0	0-1	1	6.44	4.84
1992 Milwaukee	NL	50	0	0	11	62.2	243	38	15	13	3	5	2	7	24	2	43	4	1	5	1	.833	0	2-5	8	2.13	1.87
1993 Milwaukee	NL	45	0	0	14	59.1	246	59	29	22	4	5	5	2	22	4	23	0	0	3	3	.500	0	0-0	8	3.89	3.34
1994 Milwaukee	NL	42	0	0	31	46.0	202	41	16	13	0	2	3	1	27	5	31	3	1	1	4	.200	0	17-20	3	3.36	2.54
1995 Milwaukee	NL	40	0	0	34	34.2	163	40	16	13	3	2	1	0	20	4	33	5	0	0	3	.000	0	22-27	2	5.27	3.38
1996 Milwaukee	NL	61	0	0	55	61.1	268	65	28	23	4	0	4	1	26	4	53	5	0	3	3	.500	0	32-38	1	4.24	3.38
1997 Milwaukee	NL	51	0	0	20	70.1	298	62	30	27	4	6	4	1	33	3	62	2	1	1	5	.167	0	6-11	11	3.41	3.45
1998 Oak-Ana	AL	60	0	0	28	58.2	264	62	34	28	5	4	2	1	25	2	43	6	0	2	8	.200	0	5-9	11	4.29	4.30
1999 Baltimore	AL	27	0	0	10	31.0	151	35	23	20	5	1	0	2	22	2	22	1	1	1	0	1.000	0	0-3	2	6.66	5.81
2000 Los Angeles	NL	51	0	0	20	50.0	201	35	18	18	7	3	0	2	25	2	40	3	0	6	2	.750	0	5-7	11	3.34	3.24
2001 LA-Pit	NL	54	0	0	22	47.1	223	49	32	29	7	1	3	4	26	1	37	7	0	3	2	.600	0	9-12	14	5.37	5.51
2002 Pit-Ari	NL	65	0	0	22	55.0	252	53	31	25	4	0	2	3	37	6	53	8	0	3	3	.500	0	0-2	16	4.75	4.09
2003 Minnesota	AL	5	0	0	2	6.0	22	2	0	0	0	0	0	0	1	0	1	0	0	0	0	-	0	0-0	0	0.69	0.00
1998 Oakland	AL	48	0	0	22	47.1	214	48	26	21	3	4	2	1	21	2	34	3	0	1	6	.143	0	5-8	10	3.93	3.99
1998 Anaheim	AL	12	0	0	6	11.1	50	14	8	7	2	0	0	0	4	0	9	3	0	1	2	.333	0	0-1	1	5.95	5.56
2001 Los Angeles	NL	34	0	0	7	29.2	139	33	23	20	6	1	3	1	13	0	26	6	0	2	1	.667	0	1-3	14	5.53	6.07
2001 Pittsburgh	NL	20	0	0	14	17.2	84	16	9	9	1	0	0	3	13	1	11	1	0	1	1	.500	0	8-9	0	5.01	4.58
2002 Pittsburgh	NL	32	0	0	13	30.1	134	25	13	11	3	0	1	1	18	1	29	2	0	1	0	1.000	0	0-1	11	3.86	3.26
2002 Arizona	NL	33	0	0	9	24.2	118	28	18	14	1	0	1	2	19	5	24	6	0	2	3	.400	0	0-1	5	5.91	5.11
15 ML YEARS		597	6	0	286	698.0	3046	676	338	289	60	31	26	30	337	37	504	53	4	31	40	.437	0	99-136	88	4.24	3.73

Robert Fick

Bats: L **Throws:** R **Pos:** 1B-115; PH-13   **Ht:** 6'1" **Wt:** 200 **Born:** 3/15/74 **Age:** 30

Year Team	Lg	G	AB	H	2B	3B	HR	(Hm	Rd)	TB	R	RBI	RC	TBB	IBB	SO	HBP	SH	SF	SB	CS	SB%	GDP	Avg	OBP	Slg
1998 Detroit	AL	7	22	8	1	0	3	(0	3)	18	6	7	6	2	0	7	0	0	0	1	0	1.00	1	.364	.417	.818
1999 Detroit	AL	15	41	9	0	0	3	(1	2)	18	6	10	6	7	0	6	0	0	1	1	0	1.00	1	.220	.327	.439
2000 Detroit	AL	66	163	41	7	2	3	(0	3)	61	18	22	21	22	2	39	1	0	2	2	1	.67	6	.252	.340	.374
2001 Detroit	AL	124	401	109	21	2	19	(8	11)	191	62	61	62	39	3	62	4	0	4	0	3	.00	10	.272	.339	.476
2002 Detroit	AL	148	556	150	36	2	17	(12	5)	241	66	63	71	46	4	90	7	0	5	1	0	1.00	17	.270	.331	.433
2003 Atlanta	NL	126	409	110	26	1	11	(4	7)	171	52	80	67	42	4	47	2	0	7	1	0	1.00	9	.269	.335	.418
6 ML YEARS		486	1592	427	91	7	56	(25	31)	700	210	243	233	158	13	251	14	0	19	5	5	.50	42	.268	.336	.440

Nate Field

Pitches: R **Bats:** R **Pos:** RP-19   **Ht:** 6'2" **Wt:** 200 **Born:** 12/11/75 **Age:** 28

		HOW MUCH HE PITCHED						WHAT HE GAVE UP											THE RESULTS						
Year Team	Lg	G	GS	CG	GF	IP	BFP	H	R	ER	HR	SH	SF	HB	TBB	IBB	SO	WP	Bk	W	L	Pct	ShO	Sv-Op	Hld	ERC	ERA
1998 Vermont	A-	25	0	0	16	35.0	150	21	16	12	1	1	0	3	11	0	39	5	1	3	1	.750	0	2--	-	1.52	3.09
1999 Cape Fear	A	42	0	0	21	65.0	300	75	49	39	8	2	3	7	22	2	55	4	0	4	8	.333	0	2--	-	5.12	5.40
1999 Ottawa	AAA	2	0	0	0	3.0	16	4	1	1	0	0	0	0	4	0	4	0	0	0	0	-	0	0--	-	9.50	3.00
2000 Sioux City	IND	11	0	0	3	23.1	100	17	10	5	1	1	1	0	15	3	19	3	0	3	0	1.000	0	0--	-	2.91	1.93
2000 Christn - WV	A	17	0	0	4	36.1	152	28	10	9	2	4	1	2	15	0	31	3	1	1	2	.333	0	0--	-	2.79	2.23

Year Team	Lg	G	GS	CG	GF	IP	BFP	H	R	ER	HR	SH	SF	HB	TBB	IBB	SO	WP	Bk	W	L	Pct	ShO	Sv-Op	Hld	ERC	ERA
2001 Wichita	AA	52	0	0	44	73.0	300	61	16	12	3	3	2	2	18	3	67	5	0	4	2	.667	0	19- -	-	2.27	1.48
2002 Omaha	AAA	18	0	0	17	16.1	81	22	10	6	0	0	0	0	8	0	13	0	0	0	1	1.000	0	7- -	-	5.37	3.31
2002 Columbus	AAA	21	2	0	5	38.2	180	46	30	29	6	0	7	1	21	1	25	1	0	2	1	.667	0	0- -	-	6.28	6.75
2003 Wichita	AA	15	0	0	14	20.0	87	20	9	8	2	0	0	1	8	1	20	2	1	1	0	1.000	0	3- -	-	4.20	3.60
2003 Omaha	AAA	19	0	0	15	22.2	85	15	8	8	4	0	0	1	4	0	17	3	0	2	2	.500	0	4- -	-	2.18	3.18
2002 Kansas City	AL	5	0	0	0	5.0	26	8	5	5	2	1	0	0	3	1	3	2	0	0	0	-	0	0-0	0	10.82	9.00
2003 Kansas City	AL	19	0	0	7	21.2	97	19	10	10	3	0	1	1	14	1	19	0	0	1	1	.500	0	0-0	2	4.74	4.15
2 ML YEARS		24	0	0	7	26.2	123	27	15	15	5	1	1	1	17	2	22	2	0	1	1	.500	0	0-0	2	5.78	5.06

Chone Figgins

Bats: B **Throws:** R **Pos:** CF-44; 2B-14; SS-8; PR-4; LF-3; DH-1; PH-1   **Ht:** 5'9" **Wt:** 155 **Born:** 1/22/78 **Age:** 26

							BATTING												BASERUNNING				AVERAGES		
Year Team	Lg	G	AB	H	2B	3B	HR	(Hm Rd)	TB	R	RBI	RC	TBB	IBB	SO	HBP	SH	SF	SB	CS	SB%	GDP	Avg	OBP	Slg
1997 Rockies	R	53	210	59	5	6	1	(- -)	79	41	23	35	34	0	50	3	0	2	30	12	.71	2	.281	.386	.376
1998 Portland	A-	69	269	76	9	3	1	(- -)	94	41	26	37	24	0	56	2	6	1	25	4	.86	3	.283	.345	.349
1999 Salem	A+	123	444	106	12	3	0	(- -)	124	65	22	40	41	0	86	3	14	2	27	13	.68	5	.239	.306	.279
2000 Salem	A+	134	522	145	26	14	3	(- -)	208	92	48	77	67	0	107	1	6	5	37	19	.66	7	.278	.358	.398
2001 Carolina	AA	86	332	73	14	5	2	(- -)	103	41	25	37	40	2	73	2	6	2	27	8	.77	0	.220	.306	.310
2001 Arkansas	AA	39	138	37	12	2	0	(- -)	53	21	12	19	14	0	26	0	3	3	7	2	.78	0	.268	.329	.384
2002 Salt Lake	AAA	125	511	156	25	18	7	(- -)	238	100	62	90	53	1	83	0	6	6	39	8	.83	5	.305	.364	.466
2003 Salt Lake	AAA	68	285	89	14	15	4	(- -)	145	55	30	55	29	1	36	3	2	2	16	6	.73	4	.312	.379	.509
2002 Anaheim	AL	15	12	2	1	0	0	(0 0)	3	6	1	1	0	0	5	0	0	0	2	1	.67	1	.167	.167	.250
2003 Anaheim	AL	71	240	71	9	4	0	(0 0)	88	34	27	38	20	0	38	0	6	4	13	7	.65	1	.296	.345	.367
2 ML YEARS		86	252	73	10	4	0	(0 0)	91	40	28	39	20	0	43	0	6	4	15	8	.65	2	.290	.337	.361

Nelson Figueroa

Pitches: R **Bats:** R **Pos:** RP-9; SP-3   **Ht:** 6'1" **Wt:** 155 **Born:** 5/18/74 **Age:** 30

			HOW MUCH HE PITCHED					WHAT HE GAVE UP												THE RESULTS						
Year Team	Lg	G	GS	CG	GF	IP	BFP	H	R	ER	HR	SH	SF	HB	TBB	IBB	SO	WP	Bk	W	L	Pct	ShO	Sv-Op	Hld	ERC	ERA
2003 Nashville*	AAA	23	23	3	0	151.1	627	144	54	50	11	7	2	8	37	5	121	5	0	12	5	.706	1	0- -	-	3.21	2.97
2000 Arizona	NL	3	3	0	0	15.2	68	17	13	13	4	1	2	0	5	0	7	2	0	1	0	1.000	0	0-0	0	5.31	7.47
2001 Philadelphia	NL	19	13	0	1	89.0	393	95	40	39	8	4	0	7	37	3	61	2	0	4	5	.444	0	0-0	0	4.76	3.94
2002 Milwaukee	NL	30	11	0	4	93.0	412	96	59	52	18	11	5	4	37	6	51	5	0	1	7	.125	0	0-0	1	4.94	5.03
2003 Pittsburgh	NL	12	3	0	1	35.1	146	28	13	13	8	2	2	2	13	2	23	2	0	2	1	.667	0	0-0	0	3.80	3.31
4 ML YEARS		64	30	0	6	233.0	1019	236	125	117	38	18	9	13	92	11	142	11	0	7	14	.333	0	0-0	1	4.73	4.52

Jeremy Fikac

Pitches: R **Bats:** R **Pos:** RP-14   **Ht:** 6'2" **Wt:** 185 **Born:** 4/8/75 **Age:** 29

			HOW MUCH HE PITCHED					WHAT HE GAVE UP												THE RESULTS						
Year Team	Lg	G	GS	CG	GF	IP	BFP	H	R	ER	HR	SH	SF	HB	TBB	IBB	SO	WP	Bk	W	L	Pct	ShO	Sv-Op	Hld	ERC	ERA
2003 Sacramento*	AAA	42	0	0	19	56.0	218	40	19	14	4	0	2	4	13	1	50	1	0	3	3	.500	0	4- -	-	1.83	2.25
2001 San Diego	NL	23	0	0	5	26.1	99	15	6	4	2	2	0	1	5	1	19	0	0	2	0	1.000	0	0-2	6	1.33	1.37
2002 San Diego	NL	65	0	0	15	69.0	318	74	50	42	13	2	2	3	34	8	66	6	1	4	7	.364	0	0-6	12	5.39	5.48
2003 Oakland	AL	14	0	0	1	16.0	71	14	8	8	4	0	0	3	11	1	9	0	0	0	1	.000	0	0-0	2	6.69	4.50
3 ML YEARS		102	0	0	21	111.1	488	103	64	54	19	4	2	7	50	10	94	6	1	6	8	.429	0	0-8	20	4.42	4.37

Steve Finley

Bats: L **Throws:** L **Pos:** CF-140; PH-9   **Ht:** 6'2" **Wt:** 195 **Born:** 3/12/65 **Age:** 39

							BATTING												BASERUNNING				AVERAGES		
Year Team	Lg	G	AB	H	2B	3B	HR	(Hm Rd)	TB	R	RBI	RC	TBB	IBB	SO	HBP	SH	SF	SB	CS	SB%	GDP	Avg	OBP	Slg
1989 Baltimore	AL	81	217	54	5	2	2	(0 2)	69	35	25	23	15	1	30	1	6	2	17	3	.85	3	.249	.298	.318
1990 Baltimore	AL	142	464	119	16	4	3	(1 2)	152	46	37	47	32	3	53	2	10	5	22	9	.71	8	.256	.304	.328
1991 Houston	NL	159	596	170	28	10	8	(0 8)	242	84	54	80	42	5	65	2	10	6	34	18	.65	8	.285	.331	.406
1992 Houston	NL	162	607	177	29	13	5	(5 0)	247	84	55	93	58	6	63	3	16	2	44	9	.83	10	.292	.355	.407
1993 Houston	NL	142	545	145	15	13	8	(1 7)	210	69	44	64	28	1	65	3	6	3	19	6	.76	8	.266	.304	.385
1994 Houston	NL	94	373	103	16	5	11	(4 7)	162	64	33	54	28	0	52	0	13	1	13	7	.65	3	.276	.329	.434
1995 San Diego	NL	139	562	167	23	8	10	(4 6)	236	104	44	90	59	5	62	3	4	2	36	12	.75	8	.297	.366	.420
1996 San Diego	NL	161	655	195	45	9	30	(15 15)	348	126	95	117	56	5	87	4	1	5	22	8	.73	20	.298	.354	.531
1997 San Diego	NL	143	560	146	26	5	28	(5 23)	266	101	92	84	43	2	92	3	2	7	15	3	.83	10	.261	.313	.475
1998 San Diego	NL	159	619	154	40	6	14	(8 6)	248	92	67	76	45	0	103	3	3	4	12	3	.80	9	.249	.301	.401
1999 Arizona	NL	156	590	156	32	10	34	(17 17)	310	100	103	105	63	7	94	3	2	5	8	4	.67	4	.264	.336	.525
2000 Arizona	NL	152	539	151	27	5	35	(17 18)	293	100	96	104	65	7	87	8	2	9	12	6	.67	9	.280	.361	.544
2001 Arizona	NL	140	495	136	27	4	14	(8 6)	213	66	73	71	47	9	67	1	2	3	11	7	.61	8	.275	.337	.430
2002 Arizona	NL	150	505	145	24	4	25	(14 11)	252	82	89	85	65	7	73	3	1	3	16	4	.80	10	.287	.370	.499
2003 Arizona	NL	147	516	148	24	10	22	(10 12)	258	82	70	85	57	4	94	6	0	3	15	8	.65	6	.287	.363	.500
15 ML YEARS		2127	7843	2166	377	108	249	(109 140)	3506	1235	977	1188	703	62	1087	47	78	60	296	107	.73	124	.276	.337	.447

Tony Fiore

Pitches: R **Bats:** R **Pos:** RP-21   **Ht:** 6'4" **Wt:** 210 **Born:** 10/12/71 **Age:** 32

			HOW MUCH HE PITCHED					WHAT HE GAVE UP												THE RESULTS						
Year Team	Lg	G	GS	CG	GF	IP	BFP	H	R	ER	HR	SH	SF	HB	TBB	IBB	SO	WP	Bk	W	L	Pct	ShO	Sv-Op	Hld	ERC	ERA
2003 Rochester*	AAA	16	11	2	2	84.1	349	80	44	37	5	4	0	2	21	2	48	4	1	5	6	.455	0	1- -	-	3.01	3.95
2000 Tampa Bay	AL	11	0	0	3	15.0	74	21	16	14	3	0	0	2	9	2	8	1	0	1	1	.500	0	0-1	0	8.74	8.40
2001 TB-Min	AL	7	0	0	5	9.2	41	9	6	6	0	0	0	1	3	0	8	1	0	1	0	1.000	0	0-0	0	3.07	5.59
2002 Minnesota	AL	48	2	0	11	91.0	385	74	32	32	10	4	2	5	43	4	55	2	0	10	3	.769	0	0-0	5	3.57	3.16
2003 Minnesota	AL	21	0	0	10	36.0	161	32	25	22	5	2	3	3	21	1	23	3	0	1	1	.500	0	0-0	0	4.73	5.50

Year Team	Lg	G	GS	CG	GF	IP	BFP	H	R	ER	HR	SH	SF	HB	TBB	IBB	SO	WP	Bk	W	L	Pct	ShO	Sv-Op	Hld	ERC	ERA
2001 Tampa Bay	AL	3	0	0	3	3.1	15	4	2	2	0	0	0	1	1	0	3	1	0	0	0	-	0	0-0	0	5.47	5.40
2001 Minnesota	AL	4	0	0	2	6.1	26	5	4	4	0	0	0	0	2	0	5	0	0	0	1	.000	0	0-0	0	2.01	5.68
4 ML YEARS		87	2	0	29	151.2	661	136	79	74	18	6	5	11	76	7	94	7	0	12	6	.667	0	0-1	5	4.26	4.39

John Flaherty

Bats: R **Throws:** R **Pos:** C-40; PH-1; PR-1   **Ht:** 6'1" **Wt:** 196 **Born:** 10/21/67 **Age:** 36

Year Team	Lg	G	AB	H	2B	3B	HR	(Hm	Rd)	TB	R	RBI	RC	TBB	IBB	SO	HBP	SH	SF	SB	CS	SB%	GDP	Avg	OBP	Slg
1992 Boston	AL	35	66	13	2	0	0	(0	0)	15	3	2	3	3	0	7	0	1	1	0	0	-	0	.197	.229	.227
1993 Boston	AL	13	25	3	2	0	0	(0	0)	5	3	2	1	2	0	6	1	1	0	0	0	-	0	.120	.214	.200
1994 Detroit	AL	34	40	6	1	0	0	(0	0)	7	2	4	0	1	0	11	0	2	1	0	1	.00	1	.150	.167	.175
1995 Detroit	AL	112	354	86	22	1	11	(6	5)	143	39	40	39	18	0	47	3	8	2	0	0	-	8	.243	.284	.404
1996 Det-SD		119	416	118	24	0	13	(8	5)	181	40	64	53	17	2	61	3	4	4	3	3	.50	13	.284	.314	.435
1997 San Diego	NL	129	439	120	21	1	9	(4	5)	170	38	46	52	33	7	62	0	2	2	4	4	.50	11	.273	.323	.387
1998 Tampa Bay	AL	91	304	63	11	0	3	(1	2)	83	21	24	17	22	0	46	1	4	3	0	5	.00	9	.207	.261	.273
1999 Tampa Bay	AL	117	446	124	19	0	14	(3	11)	185	53	71	54	19	0	64	6	1	10	0	2	.00	14	.278	.310	.415
2000 Tampa Bay	AL	109	394	103	15	0	10	(7	3)	148	36	39	41	20	2	57	0	2	2	0	0	-	11	.261	.296	.376
2001 Tampa Bay	AL	78	248	59	17	1	4	(3	1)	90	20	29	22	10	1	33	1	5	1	1	0	1.00	9	.238	.269	.363
2002 Tampa Bay	AL	76	281	73	20	0	4	(4	0)	105	27	33	32	15	0	50	1	2	4	2	2	.50	6	.260	.296	.374
2003 New York	AL	40	105	28	8	0	4	(0	4)	48	16	14	12	4	1	19	1	5	1	0	0	-	6	.267	.297	.457
1996 Detroit	AL	47	152	38	12	0	4	(2	2)	62	18	23	17	8	1	25	1	3	1	1	0	1.00	5	.250	.290	.408
1996 San Diego	NL	72	264	80	12	0	9	(6	3)	119	22	41	36	9	1	36	2	1	3	2	3	.40	8	.303	.327	.451
12 ML YEARS		953	3118	796	162	3	72	(36	36)	1180	298	368	326	164	13	463	17	37	31	10	17	.37	88	.255	.293	.378

Cliff Floyd

Bats: L **Throws:** R **Pos:** LF-95; DH-9; PH-5   **Ht:** 6'4" **Wt:** 260 **Born:** 12/5/72 **Age:** 31

Year Team	Lg	G	AB	H	2B	3B	HR	(Hm	Rd)	TB	R	RBI	RC	TBB	IBB	SO	HBP	SH	SF	SB	CS	SB%	GDP	Avg	OBP	Slg
1993 Montreal	NL	10	31	7	0	0	1	(0	1)	10	3	2	2	0	0	9	0	0	0	0	0	-	0	.226	.226	.323
1994 Montreal	NL	100	334	94	19	4	4	(2	2)	133	43	41	46	24	0	63	3	2	3	10	3	.77	3	.281	.332	.398
1995 Montreal	NL	29	69	9	1	0	1	(1	0)	13	6	8	2	7	0	22	1	0	0	3	0	1.00	1	.130	.221	.188
1996 Montreal	NL	117	227	55	15	4	6	(3	3)	96	29	26	35	30	1	52	5	1	3	7	1	.88	3	.242	.340	.423
1997 Florida	NL	61	137	32	9	1	6	(2	4)	61	23	19	23	24	0	33	2	1	1	6	2	.75	3	.234	.354	.445
1998 Florida	NL	153	588	166	45	3	22	(10	12)	283	85	90	92	47	7	112	3	0	3	27	14	.66	10	.282	.337	.481
1999 Florida	NL	69	251	76	19	1	11	(4	7)	130	37	49	45	30	5	47	2	0	2	5	6	.45	8	.303	.379	.518
2000 Florida	NL	121	420	126	30	0	22	(13	9)	222	75	91	88	50	5	82	8	0	9	24	3	.89	4	.300	.378	.529
2001 Florida	NL	149	555	176	44	4	31	(16	15)	321	123	103	121	59	19	101	10	0	5	18	3	.86	9	.317	.390	.578
2002 Fla-Mon-Bos		146	520	150	43	0	28	(13	15)	277	86	79	95	76	19	106	10	0	5	15	5	.75	6	.288	.388	.533
2003 New York	NL	108	365	106	25	2	18	(10	8)	189	57	68	70	51	2	66	3	0	6	3	0	1.00	3	.290	.376	.518
2002 Florida	NL	84	296	85	20	0	18	(7	11)	159	49	57	65	58	18	68	7	0	1	10	5	.67	0	.287	.414	.537
2002 Montreal	NL	15	53	11	2	0	3	(3	0)	22	7	4	2	3	1	10	1	0	0	1	0	1.00	1	.208	.263	.415
2002 Boston	AL	47	171	54	21	0	7	(3	4)	96	30	18	28	15	0	28	2	0	2	4	0	1.00	6	.316	.374	.561
11 ML YEARS		1063	3497	997	250	19	150	(74	76)	1735	567	576	619	398	58	693	47	4	35	118	37	.76	57	.285	.363	.496

Josh Fogg

Pitches: R **Bats:** R **Pos:** SP-26   **Ht:** 6'0" **Wt:** 202 **Born:** 12/13/76 **Age:** 27

Year Team	Lg	G	GS	CG	GF	IP	BFP	H	R	ER	HR	SH	SF	HB	TBB	IBB	SO	WP	Bk	W	L	Pct	ShO	Sv-Op	Hld	ERC	ERA
2003 Nashville*	AAA	2	2	0	0	10.0	40	12	6	6	1	1	1	0	1	0	7	0	0	0	1	.000	0	0--	-	4.24	5.40
2001 Chicago	AL	11	0	0	4	13.1	53	10	3	3	0	0	1	1	3	1	17	0	0	0	0	-	0	0-0	2	1.73	2.03
2002 Pittsburgh	NL	33	33	0	0	194.1	832	199	102	94	28	6	3	8	69	12	113	2	0	12	12	.500	0	0-0	0	4.46	4.35
2003 Pittsburgh	NL	26	26	1	0	142.0	625	166	90	83	22	6	4	9	40	0	71	2	0	10	9	.526	0	0-0	0	5.25	5.26
3 ML YEARS		70	59	1	4	349.2	1510	375	195	180	50	12	8	18	112	13	201	4	0	22	21	.512	0	0-0	2	4.66	4.63

Jesse Foppert

Pitches: R **Bats:** R **Pos:** SP-21; RP-2   **Ht:** 6'6" **Wt:** 210 **Born:** 7/10/80 **Age:** 23

Year Team	Lg	G	GS	CG	GF	IP	BFP	H	R	ER	HR	SH	SF	HB	TBB	IBB	SO	WP	Bk	W	L	Pct	ShO	Sv-Op	Hld	ERC	ERA
2001 Salem-Keizer	A-	14	14	0	0	70.0	264	35	18	15	7	0	3	5	23	0	88	4	3	8	1	.889	0	0--	-	1.65	1.93
2002 Shreveport	AA	11	11	0	0	61.1	249	44	22	19	3	3	1	3	21	0	74	3	0	3	3	.500	0	0--	-	2.24	2.79
2002 Fresno	AAA	14	14	0	0	79.0	337	71	37	35	12	3	5	3	35	0	109	7	1	3	6	.333	0	0--	-	4.23	3.99
2003 San Jose	A+	1	1	0	0	3.0	14	5	3	3	0	0	1	0	0	0	3	0	0	0	1	.000	0	0--	-	5.42	9.00
2003 Fresno	AAA	1	1	0	0	5.0	19	3	1	1	0	0	0	1	0	0	9	3	0	0	0	-	0	0--	-	1.11	1.80
2003 San Francisco	NL	23	21	0	0	111.0	500	103	69	62	16	5	9	3	69	4	101	12	0	8	9	.471	0	0-0	1	4.89	5.03

Lew Ford

Bats: R **Throws:** R **Pos:** CF-13; LF-8; PH-8; RF-6; PR-4; DH-2   **Ht:** 6'0" **Wt:** 190 **Born:** 8/12/76 **Age:** 27

Year Team	Lg	G	AB	H	2B	3B	HR	(Hm	Rd)	TB	R	RBI	RC	TBB	IBB	SO	HBP	SH	SF	SB	CS	SB%	GDP	Avg	OBP	Slg
1999 Lowell	A-	62	250	70	17	4	7	(-	-)	116	48	34	41	19	1	35	5	0	3	15	2	.88	6	.280	.339	.464
2000 Augusta	A	126	514	162	35	11	9	(-	-)	246	122	74	102	52	3	83	12	3	2	52	4	.93	12	.315	.390	.479
2001 Fort Myers	A+	67	265	79	15	2	2	(-	-)	104	42	24	41	21	3	30	12	1	2	19	9	.68	3	.298	.373	.392
2001 New Britain	AA	62	252	55	9	3	7	(-	-)	91	30	25	26	20	0	35	6	1	2	5	5	.50	4	.218	.289	.361
2002 New Britain	AA	93	373	116	27	2	15	(-	-)	192	81	51	78	49	0	47	8	4	1	17	5	.77	5	.311	.401	.515
2002 Edmonton	AAA	47	193	64	11	2	5	(-	-)	94	40	24	38	13	0	21	6	1	1	11	1	.92	2	.332	.390	.487
2003 Rochester	AAA	53	211	64	18	2	3	(-	-)	95	33	31	33	10	1	28	8	0	1	4	5	.44	1	.303	.357	.450
2003 Minnesota	AL	34	73	24	7	1	3	(2	1)	42	16	15	17	8	0	9	1	1	0	2	0	1.00	1	.329	.402	.575

Matt Ford

Pitches: L **Bats:** B **Pos:** RP-21; SP-4   **Ht:** 6'1" **Wt:** 175 **Born:** 4/8/81 **Age:** 23

Year Team	Lg	G	GS	CG	GF	IP	BFP	H	R	ER	HR	SH	SF	HB	TBB	IBB	SO	WP	Bk	W	L	Pct	ShO	Sv-Op	Hld	ERC	ERA
1999 Medicine Hat	R+	13	7	0	0	48.1	193	31	11	11	0	0	0	0	23	0	68	1	0	4	0	1.000	0	0--	-	1.92	2.05
2000 Hagerstown	A	18	14	1	0	83.2	353	81	42	36	5	0	4	3	36	0	86	5	0	5	3	.625	0	0--	-	3.99	3.87
2001 Dunedin	A+	13	12	0	0	60.0	270	67	41	39	8	2	1	2	37	0	48	7	0	2	7	.222	0	0--	-	6.28	5.85
2001 Chrlstn - WV	A	11	11	1	0	70.2	287	62	28	19	2	0	3	0	22	0	69	8	1	4	4	.500	0	0--	-	2.66	2.42
2002 Dunedin	A+	21	18	0	1	114.0	466	100	43	30	7	3	2	2	42	0	85	2	1	9	5	.643	0	0--	-	3.18	2.37
2003 Milwaukee	NL	25	4	0	12	43.2	197	46	23	21	5	0	1	1	21	0	26	0	0	0	3	.000	0	0-0	1	4.84	4.33

Brook Fordyce

Bats: R **Throws:** R **Pos:** C-107; PH-1   **Ht:** 6'0" **Wt:** 190 **Born:** 5/7/70 **Age:** 34

Year Team	Lg	G	AB	H	2B	3B	HR	(Hm	Rd)	TB	R	RBI	RC	TBB	IBB	SO	HBP	SH	SF	SB	CS	SB%	GDP	Avg	OBP	Slg
1995 New York	NL	4	2	1	1	0	0	(0	0)	2	1	0	1	1	0	0	0	0	0	0	0	-	0	.500	.667	1.000
1996 Cincinnati	NL	4	7	2	1	0	0	(0	0)	3	0	1	2	3	0	1	0	0	0	0	0	-	0	.286	.500	.429
1997 Cincinnati	NL	47	96	20	5	0	1	(1	0)	28	7	8	8	8	1	15	0	0	1	2	0	1.00	0	.208	.267	.292
1998 Cincinnati	NL	57	146	37	9	0	3	(3	0)	55	8	14	16	11	3	28	0	1	0	0	1	.00	2	.253	.306	.377
1999 Chicago	AL	105	333	99	25	1	9	(5	4)	153	36	49	52	21	0	48	3	3	2	2	0	1.00	5	.297	.343	.459
2000 CWS-Bal	AL	93	302	91	18	1	14	(8	6)	153	41	49	51	17	0	50	4	2	5	0	0	-	4	.301	.341	.507
2001 Baltimore	AL	95	292	61	18	0	5	(0	5)	94	30	19	23	21	1	56	3	3	1	1	2	.33	7	.209	.268	.322
2002 Baltimore	AL	56	130	30	8	0	1	(1	0)	41	7	8	11	9	0	19	4	3	0	1	0	1.00	5	.231	.301	.315
2003 Baltimore	AL	108	348	95	12	2	6	(3	3)	129	28	31	30	19	1	44	1	6	2	2	3	.40	10	.273	.311	.371
2000 Chicago	AL	40	125	34	7	1	5	(3	2)	58	18	21	18	6	0	23	2	2	1	0	0	-	1	.272	.313	.464
2000 Baltimore	AL	53	177	57	11	0	9	(5	4)	95	23	28	33	11	0	27	2	0	4	0	0	-	3	.322	.361	.537
9 ML YEARS		569	1656	436	97	4	39	(21	18)	658	158	179	194	110	6	261	15	18	11	8	6	.57	33	.263	.313	.397

Casey Fossum

Pitches: L **Bats:** B **Pos:** SP-14; RP-5   **Ht:** 6'1" **Wt:** 165 **Born:** 1/6/78 **Age:** 26

Year Team	Lg	G	GS	CG	GF	IP	BFP	H	R	ER	HR	SH	SF	HB	TBB	IBB	SO	WP	Bk	W	L	Pct	ShO	Sv-Op	Hld	ERC	ERA
2003 Pawtucket*	AAA	5	4	0	1	13.0	53	11	5	5	1	0	0	1	5	0	14	0	0	1	0	1.000	0	1--	-	3.46	3.46
2003 Portland*	AA	3	2	0	0	4.0	21	5	3	3	1	0	0	1	3	0	7	0	0	1	0	1.000	0	0--	-	9.34	6.75
2001 Boston	AL	13	7	0	3	44.1	197	44	26	24	4	0	1	6	20	1	26	1	1	3	2	.600	0	0-0	-	4.70	4.87
2002 Boston	AL	43	12	0	13	106.2	461	113	54	41	12	2	4	4	30	0	101	3	0	5	4	.556	0	1-1	3	4.14	3.46
2003 Boston	AL	19	14	0	2	79.0	346	82	55	48	9	1	3	4	34	0	63	4	0	6	5	.545	0	1-1	0	4.77	5.47
3 ML YEARS		75	33	0	18	230.0	1004	239	137	113	25	3	8	14	84	1	190	8	1	14	11	.560	0	2-2	3	4.46	4.42

John Foster

Pitches: L **Bats:** L **Pos:** RP-23   **Ht:** 6'0" **Wt:** 200 **Born:** 5/17/78 **Age:** 26

Year Team	Lg	G	GS	CG	GF	IP	BFP	H	R	ER	HR	SH	SF	HB	TBB	IBB	SO	WP	Bk	W	L	Pct	ShO	Sv-Op	Hld	ERC	ERA
1999 Danville	R+	18	0	0	7	39.0	148	28	10	6	0	5	0	2	6	0	36	4	0	4	1	.800	0	1--	-	1.51	1.38
2000 Myrtle Beach	A+	38	0	0	17	48.2	204	48	13	10	2	4	2	2	14	4	46	4	0	2	1	.667	0	3--	-	3.22	1.85
2001 Greenville	AA	50	0	0	21	68.2	303	71	30	23	6	11	3	2	33	7	63	5	0	8	7	.533	0	7--	-	4.47	3.01
2002 Richmond	AAA	55	0	0	25	62.0	277	67	30	29	5	4	1	1	28	8	48	3	0	8	4	.667	0	8--	-	4.41	4.21
2003 Indianapolis	AAA	27	0	0	7	41.1	181	44	21	17	4	3	1	2	13	1	37	0	0	2	2	.500	0	1-1	-	4.18	3.70
2002 Atlanta	NL	5	0	0	0	5.0	28	6	6	6	3	0	0	1	6	0	6	0	0	1	0	1.000	0	0-0	0	14.44	10.80
2003 Milwaukee	NL	23	0	0	3	21.0	98	30	11	11	5	1	1	1	8	2	16	1	0	2	0	1.000	0	0-2	3	7.91	4.71
2 ML YEARS		28	0	0	3	26.0	126	36	17	17	8	1	1	2	14	2	22	1	0	3	0	1.000	0	0-2	3	9.10	5.88

Keith Foulke

Pitches: R **Bats:** R **Pos:** RP-72   **Ht:** 6'0" **Wt:** 210 **Born:** 10/19/72 **Age:** 31

Year Team	Lg	G	GS	CG	GF	IP	BFP	H	R	ER	HR	SH	SF	HB	TBB	IBB	SO	WP	Bk	W	L	Pct	ShO	Sv-Op	Hld	ERC	ERA
1997 SF-CWS	AL	27	8	0	5	73.1	326	88	52	52	13	3	1	4	23	2	54	1	0	4	5	.444	0	3-6	5	5.68	6.38
1998 Chicago	AL	54	0	0	18	65.1	267	51	31	30	9	2	2	4	20	3	57	3	1	3	2	.600	0	1-2	13	2.95	4.13
1999 Chicago	AL	67	0	0	31	105.1	411	72	28	26	11	3	0	3	21	4	123	1	0	3	3	.500	0	9-13	22	1.80	2.22
2000 Chicago	AL	72	0	0	58	88.0	350	66	31	29	9	5	2	2	22	2	91	1	0	3	1	.750	0	34-39	0	2.28	2.97
2001 Chicago	AL	72	0	0	69	81.0	322	57	21	21	3	4	1	8	22	1	75	1	0	4	9	.308	0	42-45	0	2.06	2.33
2002 Chicago	AL	65	0	0	35	77.2	306	65	26	25	7	2	0	2	13	2	58	1	0	2	4	.333	0	11-14	8	2.38	2.90
2003 Oakland	AL	72	0	0	67	86.2	338	57	21	20	10	1	1	7	20	2	88	0	1	9	1	.900	0	**43-48**	0	2.07	2.08
1997 San Francisco	NL	11	8	0	0	44.2	209	60	41	41	9	2	0	4	18	1	33	1	0	1	5	.167	0	0-1	0	7.41	8.26
1997 Chicago	AL	16	0	0	5	28.2	117	28	11	11	4	1	1	0	5	1	21	0	0	3	0	1.000	0	3-5	5	3.27	3.45
7 ML YEARS		429	8	0	283	577.1	2320	456	210	203	62	20	7	30	141	16	546	8	2	28	25	.528	0	143-167	51	2.59	3.16

Andy Fox

Bats: L **Throws:** R **Pos:** PH-37; 2B-15; SS-9; 3B-5; PR-5; 1B-2; LF-2   **Ht:** 6'4" **Wt:** 202 **Born:** 1/12/71 **Age:** 33

Year Team	Lg	G	AB	H	2B	3B	HR	(Hm	Rd)	TB	R	RBI	RC	TBB	IBB	SO	HBP	SH	SF	SB	CS	SB%	GDP	Avg	OBP	Slg
1996 New York	AL	113	189	37	4	0	3	(1	2)	50	26	13	15	20	0	28	1	9	0	11	3	.79	2	.196	.276	.265
1997 New York	AL	22	31	7	1	0	0	(0	0)	8	13	1	3	7	0	9	0	2	0	2	1	.67	1	.226	.368	.258
1998 Arizona	NL	139	502	139	21	6	9	(5	4)	199	67	44	74	43	0	97	18	0	1	14	7	.67	2	.277	.355	.396
1999 Arizona	NL	99	274	70	12	2	6	(4	2)	104	34	33	38	33	10	61	9	1	3	4	1	.80	4	.255	.351	.380
2000 Ari-Fla	NL	100	250	58	8	2	4	(2	2)	82	29	20	25	22	4	53	3	0	0	10	4	.71	2	.232	.302	.328
2001 Florida	NL	54	81	15	0	1	3	(3	0)	26	8	7	9	15	1	17	2	0	0	1	0	1.00	5	.185	.327	.321
2002 Florida	NL	133	435	109	14	5	4	(3	1)	145	55	41	57	49	6	94	10	5	3	31	7	.82	9	.251	.338	.333
2003 Florida	NL	70	108	21	5	1	0	(0	0)	28	12	8	8	7	0	29	4	1	0	1	2	.33	2	.194	.269	.259

	BATTING																			BASERUNNING				AVERAGES		
Year Team	Lg	G	AB	H	2B	3B	HR	(Hm Rd)	TB	R	RBI	RC	TBB	IBB	SO	HBP	SH	SF	SB	CS	SB%	GDP	Avg	OBP	Slg
2000 Arizona	NL	31	86	18	4	0	1	(1 0)	25	10	10	5	4	1	16	0	0	0	2	1	.67	1	.209	.244	.291
2000 Florida	NL	69	164	40	4	2	3	(1 2)	57	19	10	20	18	3	37	3	0	0	8	3	.73	1	.244	.330	.348
8 ML YEARS		730	1870	456	65	17	29	(18 11)	642	244	167	229	196	21	388	47	18	7	74	25	.75	24	.244	.330	.343

Chad Fox

Pitches: R **Bats:** R **Pos:** RP-38

Ht: 6'3" **Wt:** 206 **Born:** 9/3/70 **Age:** 33

		HOW MUCH HE PITCHED						WHAT HE GAVE UP												THE RESULTS							
Year Team	Lg	G	GS	CG	GF	IP	BFP	H	R	ER	HR	SH	SF	HB	TBB	IBB	SO	WP	Bk	W	L	Pct	ShO	Sv-Op	Hld	ERC	ERA
2003 Sarasota*	A+	2	1	0	0	2.0	9	2	1	1	0	0	0	0	1	0	1	0	0	0	0	-	0	0- -	-	3.63	4.50
2003 Portland*	AA	1	0	0	0	1.1	7	1	0	0	0	0	0	0	2	0	2	0	0	0	0	-	0	0- -	-	5.91	0.00
2003 Pawtucket*	AAA	1	0	0	1	1.1	8	3	3	2	1	1	0	0	1	0	2	1	0	0	0	-	0	0- -	-	20.88	13.50
2003 Albuquerque*	AAA	3	0	0	0	2.1	12	4	1	1	0	0	0	0	1	0	5	0	0	0	0	-	0	0- -	-	7.52	3.86
1997 Atlanta	NL	30	0	0	8	27.1	120	24	12	10	4	0	0	0	16	0	28	4	0	0	1	.000	0	0-1	7	4.44	3.29
1998 Milwaukee	NL	49	0	0	12	57.0	242	56	27	25	4	6	0	1	20	0	64	5	0	1	4	.200	0	0-2	20	3.66	3.95
1999 Milwaukee	NL	6	0	0	2	6.2	36	11	8	8	1	0	0	0	4	0	12	1	1	0	0	-	0	0-0	1	9.96	10.80
2001 Milwaukee	NL	65	0	0	9	66.2	287	44	16	14	6	2	1	5	36	7	80	5	1	5	2	.714	0	2-4	20	2.75	1.89
2002 Milwaukee	NL	3	0	0	0	4.2	25	6	3	3	0	1	0	0	5	1	3	0	0	1	0	1.000	0	0-0	0	7.03	5.79
2003 Bos-Fla		38	0	0	13	43.1	198	35	16	15	3	5	5	1	31	4	46	6	0	3	3	.500	0	3-5	7	3.80	3.12
2003 Boston	AL	17	0	0	10	18.0	93	19	10	9	2	2	1	1	17	2	19	1	0	1	2	.333	0	3-5	0	6.42	4.50
2003 Florida	NL	21	0	0	3	25.1	105	16	6	6	1	3	4	0	14	2	27	5	0	2	1	.667	0	0-0	7	2.18	2.13
6 ML YEARS		191	0	0	44	205.2	908	176	82	75	18	14	6	8	112	12	233	21	2	10	10	.500	0	5-12	55	3.73	3.28

John Franco

Pitches: L **Bats:** L **Pos:** RP-38

Ht: 5'10" **Wt:** 185 **Born:** 9/17/60 **Age:** 43

		HOW MUCH HE PITCHED						WHAT HE GAVE UP												THE RESULTS							
Year Team	Lg	G	GS	CG	GF	IP	BFP	H	R	ER	HR	SH	SF	HB	TBB	IBB	SO	WP	Bk	W	L	Pct	ShO	Sv-Op	Hld	ERC	ERA
2003 St.Lucie*	A+	4	3	0	0	4.1	20	6	3	3	1	0	0	0	1	0	5	0	0	0	1	.000	0	0- -	-	6.49	6.23
2003 Norfolk*	AAA	2	0	0	0	1.2	7	1	0	0	0	0	0	0	1	0	2	0	0	0	0	-	0	0- -	-	2.03	0.00
1984 Cincinnati	NL	54	0	0	30	79.1	335	74	28	23	3	4	4	2	36	4	55	2	0	6	2	.750	0	4-9	1	3.58	2.61
1985 Cincinnati	NL	67	0	0	33	99.0	407	83	27	24	5	11	1	1	40	8	61	4	0	12	3	.800	0	12-15	11	2.86	2.18
1986 Cincinnati	NL	74	0	0	52	101.0	429	90	40	33	7	8	3	2	44	12	84	4	2	6	6	.500	0	29-38	1	3.30	2.94
1987 Cincinnati	NL	68	0	0	60	82.0	344	76	26	23	6	5	2	0	27	6	61	1	0	8	5	.615	0	32-41	0	3.10	2.52
1988 Cincinnati	NL	70	0	0	61	86.0	336	60	18	15	3	5	1	0	27	3	46	1	2	6	6	.500	0	39-42	0	1.82	1.57
1989 Cincinnati	NL	60	0	0	50	80.2	345	77	35	28	3	7	3	0	36	8	60	3	2	4	8	.333	0	32-39	0	3.42	3.12
1990 New York	NL	55	0	0	48	67.2	287	66	22	19	4	3	1	1	21	2	56	7	2	5	3	.625	0	33-39	0	3.24	2.53
1991 New York	NL	52	0	0	48	55.1	247	61	27	18	2	3	0	1	18	4	45	6	0	5	9	.357	0	30-35	0	3.73	2.93
1992 New York	NL	31	0	0	30	33.0	128	24	6	6	1	0	2	0	11	2	20	0	0	6	2	.750	0	15-17	0	2.00	1.64
1993 New York	NL	35	0	0	30	36.1	172	46	24	21	6	4	1	1	19	3	29	5	0	4	3	.571	0	10-17	0	6.62	5.20
1994 New York	NL	47	0	0	43	50.0	216	47	20	15	2	2	1	1	19	0	42	1	0	1	4	.200	0	30-36	0	3.27	2.70
1995 New York	NL	48	0	0	41	51.2	213	48	17	14	4	4	1	0	17	2	41	0	0	5	3	.625	0	29-36	0	3.26	2.44
1996 New York	NL	51	0	0	44	54.0	235	54	15	11	2	6	0	0	21	0	48	2	0	4	3	.571	0	28-36	0	3.53	1.83
1997 New York	NL	59	0	0	53	60.0	244	49	18	17	3	5	1	1	20	2	53	0	0	5	3	.625	0	36-42	0	2.57	2.55
1998 New York	NL	61	0	0	54	64.2	289	66	28	26	4	4	5	4	29	7	59	2	0	0	8	.000	0	38-46	0	4.11	3.62
1999 New York	NL	46	0	0	34	40.2	182	40	14	13	1	3	1	2	19	1	41	0	0	0	2	.000	0	19-21	1	3.77	2.88
2000 New York	NL	62	0	0	14	55.2	239	46	24	21	6	3	0	2	26	6	56	2	0	5	4	.556	0	4-4	20	3.36	3.40
2001 New York	NL	58	0	0	16	53.1	232	55	25	24	8	2	1	2	19	2	50	4	1	6	2	.750	0	2-7	17	4.50	4.05
2003 New York	NL	38	0	0	13	34.1	148	35	11	10	5	1	1	1	13	2	16	2	0	0	3	.000	0	2-3	4	4.48	2.62
19 ML YEARS		1036	0	0	754	1184.2	5028	1097	425	361	75	80	29	20	462	74	923	52	9	88	79	.527	0	424-523	55	3.35	2.74

Julio Franco

Bats: R **Throws:** R **Pos:** 1B-75; PH-41

Ht: 6'1" **Wt:** 188 **Born:** 8/23/58 **Age:** 45

	BATTING																			BASERUNNING				AVERAGES		
Year Team	Lg	G	AB	H	2B	3B	HR	(Hm Rd)	TB	R	RBI	RC	TBB	IBB	SO	HBP	SH	SF	SB	CS	SB%	GDP	Avg	OBP	Slg
1982 Philadelphia	NL	16	29	8	1	0	0	(0 0)	9	3	3	2	2	1	4	0	1	0	0	2	.00	1	.276	.323	.310
1983 Cleveland	AL	149	560	153	24	8	8	(6 2)	217	68	80	62	27	1	50	2	3	6	32	12	.73	21	.273	.306	.388
1984 Cleveland	AL	160	658	188	22	5	3	(1 2)	229	82	79	72	43	1	68	6	1	10	19	10	.66	23	.286	.331	.348
1985 Cleveland	AL	160	636	183	33	4	6	(3 3)	242	97	90	78	54	2	74	4	0	9	13	9	.59	26	.288	.343	.381
1986 Cleveland	AL	149	599	183	30	5	10	(4 6)	253	80	74	76	32	1	66	0	0	5	10	7	.59	28	.306	.338	.422
1987 Cleveland	AL	128	495	158	24	3	8	(5 3)	212	86	52	81	57	2	56	3	0	5	32	9	.78	23	.319	.389	.428
1988 Cleveland	AL	152	613	186	23	6	10	(3 7)	251	88	54	89	56	4	72	2	1	4	25	11	.69	17	.303	.361	.409
1989 Texas	AL	150	548	173	31	5	13	(9 4)	253	80	92	93	66	11	69	1	0	6	21	3	.88	27	.316	.386	.462
1990 Texas	AL	157	582	172	27	1	11	(4 7)	234	96	69	94	82	3	83	2	2	2	31	10	.76	12	.296	.383	.402
1991 Texas	AL	146	589	201	27	3	15	(7 8)	279	108	78	113	65	8	78	3	0	2	36	9	.80	13	.341	.408	.474
1992 Texas	AL	35	107	25	7	0	2	(2 0)	38	19	8	12	15	2	17	0	1	0	1	1	.50	3	.234	.328	.355
1993 Texas	AL	144	532	154	31	3	14	(6 8)	233	84	84	83	62	4	95	1	5	7	9	3	.75	16	.289	.360	.438
1994 Chicago	AL	112	433	138	19	2	20	(10 10)	221	72	98	87	62	4	75	5	0	5	8	1	.89	14	.319	.406	.510
1996 Cleveland	AL	112	432	139	20	1	14	(7 7)	203	72	76	79	61	2	82	3	0	3	8	8	.50	14	.322	.407	.470
1997 Cle-Mil		120	430	116	16	1	7	(5 2)	155	68	44	58	69	4	116	1	1	4	15	6	.71	17	.270	.369	.360
1999 Tampa Bay	AL	1	1	0	0	0	0	(0 0)	0	0	0	0	0	0	1	0	0	0	0	0	-	0	.000	.000	.000
2001 Atlanta	NL	25	90	27	4	0	3	(2 1)	40	13	11	14	10	1	20	1	0	0	0	0	-	3	.300	.376	.444
2002 Atlanta	NL	125	338	96	13	1	6	(3 3)	129	51	30	38	39	3	75	1	2	3	5	1	.83	13	.284	.357	.382
2003 Atlanta	NL	103	197	58	12	2	5	(1 4)	89	28	31	31	25	5	43	0	0	1	0	1	.00	8	.294	.372	.452
1997 Cleveland	AL	78	289	82	13	1	3	(2 1)	106	46	25	37	38	2	75	0	1	0	8	5	.62	13	.284	.367	.367
1997 Milwaukee	NL	42	141	34	3	0	4	(3 1)	49	22	19	21	31	2	41	1	0	4	7	1	.88	4	.241	.373	.348
19 ML YEARS		2144	7869	2358	364	50	155	(78 77)	3287	1196	1053	1162	827	59	1144	35	17	72	265	103	.72	279	.300	.366	.418

Matt Franco

Bats: L **Throws:** R **Pos:** PH-92; 1B-15; DH-3; RF-2; LF-1   **Ht:** 6'1" **Wt:** 210 **Born:** 8/19/69 **Age:** 34

Year Team	Lg	G	AB	H	2B	3B	HR	(Hm	Rd)	TB	R	RBI	RC	TBB	IBB	SO	HBP	SH	SF	SB	CS	SB%	GDP	Avg	OBP	Slg
1995 Chicago	NL	16	17	5	1	0	0	(0	0)	6	3	1	2	0	0	4	0	0	0	0	0	-	0	.294	.294	.353
1996 New York	NL	14	31	6	1	0	1	(0	1)	10	3	2	2	1	0	5	1	0	1	0	0	-	1	.194	.235	.323
1997 New York	NL	112	163	45	5	0	5	(3	2)	65	21	21	21	13	4	23	0	0	0	1	0	1.00	6	.276	.330	.399
1998 New York	NL	103	161	44	7	2	1	(1	0)	58	20	13	20	23	6	26	1	1	1	0	1	.00	8	.273	.366	.360
1999 New York	NL	122	132	31	5	0	4	(0	4)	48	18	21	17	28	3	21	0	0	1	0	0	-	9	.235	.366	.364
2000 New York	NL	101	134	32	4	0	2	(1	1)	42	9	14	15	21	3	22	0	1	1	0	0	-	3	.239	.340	.313
2002 Atlanta	NL	81	205	65	15	4	6	(3	3)	106	25	30	39	27	2	31	0	0	1	1	0	1.00	5	.317	.395	.517
2003 Atlanta	NL	112	134	33	5	0	3	(3	0)	47	11	15	12	11	0	26	0	1	2	0	1	.00	4	.246	.299	.351
8 ML YEARS		661	977	261	43	6	22	(11	11)	382	110	117	128	124	18	158	2	3	7	2	2	.50	34	.267	.349	.391

Ryan Franklin

Pitches: R **Bats:** R **Pos:** SP-32   **Ht:** 6'3" **Wt:** 165 **Born:** 3/5/73 **Age:** 31

Year Team	Lg	G	GS	CG	GF	IP	BFP	H	R	ER	HR	SH	SF	HB	TBB	IBB	SO	WP	Bk	W	L	Pct	ShO	Sv-Op	Hld	ERC	ERA
1999 Seattle	AL	6	0	0	2	11.1	51	10	6	6	2	0	0	1	8	1	6	0	0	0	0	-	0	0-0	1	5.52	4.76
2001 Seattle	AL	38	0	0	14	78.1	335	76	32	31	13	1	2	4	24	4	60	2	0	5	1	.833	0	0-1	5	4.08	3.56
2002 Seattle	AL	41	12	0	10	118.2	495	117	62	53	14	5	5	5	22	1	65	0	0	7	5	.583	0	0-1	3	3.40	4.02
2003 Seattle	AL	32	32	2	0	212.0	877	199	93	84	34	8	5	9	61	3	99	1	2	11	13	.458	1	0-0	0	3.90	3.57
4 ML YEARS		117	44	2	26	420.1	1758	402	193	174	63	14	12	19	115	9	230	3	2	23	19	.548	1	0-2	9	3.83	3.73

Wayne Franklin

Pitches: L **Bats:** L **Pos:** SP-34; RP-2   **Ht:** 6'2" **Wt:** 205 **Born:** 3/9/74 **Age:** 30

Year Team	Lg	G	GS	CG	GF	IP	BFP	H	R	ER	HR	SH	SF	HB	TBB	IBB	SO	WP	Bk	W	L	Pct	ShO	Sv-Op	Hld	ERC	ERA
2000 Houston	NL	25	0	0	4	21.1	103	24	14	13	2	0	2	4	12	1	21	0	1	0	0	-	0	0-0	8	6.01	5.48
2001 Houston	NL	11	0	0	3	12.0	60	17	9	9	4	0	0	0	9	0	9	0	0	0	0	-	0	0-0	1	10.43	6.75
2002 Milwaukee	NL	4	4	0	0	24.0	103	16	8	7	1	1	0	0	17	1	17	0	0	2	1	.667	0	0-0	0	2.96	2.63
2003 Milwaukee	NL	36	34	1	1	194.2	870	201	129	119	36	12	3	10	94	2	116	3	4	10	13	.435	1	0-0	0	5.43	5.50
4 ML YEARS		76	38	1	8	252.0	1136	258	160	148	43	13	5	14	132	4	163	3	5	12	14	.462	1	0-0	9	5.44	5.29

Ryan Freel

Bats: R **Throws:** R **Pos:** CF-20; 2B-11; LF-5; PH-5; PR-3; 3B-2   **Ht:** 5'10" **Wt:** 178 **Born:** 3/8/76 **Age:** 28

Year Team	Lg	G	AB	H	2B	3B	HR	(Hm	Rd)	TB	R	RBI	RC	TBB	IBB	SO	HBP	SH	SF	SB	CS	SB%	GDP	Avg	OBP	Slg
1995 St. Ctharines	A-	65	243	68	10	5	3	(-	-)	97	30	29	35	22	0	49	7	7	5	12	7	.63	3	.280	.350	.399
1996 Dunedin	A+	104	381	97	23	3	4	(-	-)	138	64	41	44	33	0	76	5	14	2	19	15	.56	4	.255	.321	.362
1997 Knoxville	AA	33	94	19	1	1	0	(-	-)	22	18	4	9	19	0	13	2	1	0	5	3	.63	3	.202	.348	.234
1997 Dunedin	A+	61	181	51	8	2	3	(-	-)	72	42	17	40	46	2	28	9	6	1	24	5	.83	3	.282	.447	.398
1998 Knoxville	AA	66	252	72	17	3	4	(-	-)	107	47	36	41	33	0	32	1	3	4	18	9	.67	3	.286	.366	.425
1998 Syracuse	AAA	37	118	27	4	0	2	(-	-)	37	19	12	17	26	0	16	4	0	3	4	4	.69	3	.229	.377	.314
1999 Knoxville	AA	11	46	13	5	1	1	(-	-)	23	9	9	9	8	0	4	0	1	0	4	2	.67	0	.283	.382	.500
1999 Syracuse	AAA	20	77	23	3	2	1	(-	-)	33	15	11	13	8	0	13	4	1	0	10	3	.77	3	.299	.393	.429
2000 Dunedin	A+	4	18	9	1	0	3	(-	-)	19	7	6	7	0	0	1	0	0	0	0	0	-	0	.500	.500	1.056
2000 Tennessee	AA	12	44	13	3	1	0	(-	-)	18	11	8	6	8	0	6	1	0	2	2	3	.40	3	.295	.400	.409
2000 Syracuse	AAA	80	283	81	14	5	10	(-	-)	135	62	30	56	35	1	44	9	4	2	30	7	.81	3	.286	.380	.477
2001 Syracuse	AAA	85	319	83	21	3	5	(-	-)	125	60	33	47	42	0	42	7	6	2	22	9	.71	8	.260	.357	.392
2002 Durham	AAA	119	448	117	27	4	8	(-	-)	176	65	48	63	38	0	51	14	10	1	37	10	.79	10	.261	.337	.393
2003 Louisville	AAA	54	215	59	11	1	3	(-	-)	81	38	12	31	21	0	32	0	0	2	25	6	.81	2	.274	.336	.377
2001 Toronto	AL	9	22	6	1	0	0	(0	0)	7	1	3	3	1	0	4	1	0	0	2	1	.67	0	.273	.333	.318
2003 Cincinnati	NL	43	137	39	6	1	4	(0	4)	59	23	12	17	9	1	13	4	2	1	9	4	.69	2	.285	.344	.431
2 ML YEARS		52	159	45	7	1	4	(0	4)	66	24	15	20	10	1	17	5	2	1	11	5	.69	2	.283	.343	.415

Brian Fuentes

Pitches: L **Bats:** L **Pos:** RP-75   **Ht:** 6'4" **Wt:** 220 **Born:** 8/9/75 **Age:** 28

Year Team	Lg	G	GS	CG	GF	IP	BFP	H	R	ER	HR	SH	SF	HB	TBB	IBB	SO	WP	Bk	W	L	Pct	ShO	Sv-Op	Hld	ERC	ERA
2001 Seattle	AL	10	0	0	3	11.2	47	6	6	6	2	0	1	3	8	0	10	1	0	1	1	.500	0	0-1	1	4.39	4.63
2002 Colorado	NL	31	0	0	9	26.2	118	25	14	14	4	0	2	3	13	0	38	1	0	2	0	1.000	0	0-0	0	4.91	4.73
2003 Colorado	NL	75	0	0	23	75.1	320	64	24	23	7	0	3	6	34	2	82	2	1	3	3	.500	0	4-6	19	3.71	2.75
3 ML YEARS		116	0	0	35	113.2	485	95	44	43	13	0	6	12	55	2	130	4	1	6	4	.600	0	4-7	20	4.05	3.40

Brad Fullmer

Bats: L **Throws:** R **Pos:** DH-41; 1B-19; PH-5   **Ht:** 6'0" **Wt:** 220 **Born:** 1/17/75 **Age:** 29

Year Team	Lg	G	AB	H	2B	3B	HR	(Hm	Rd)	TB	R	RBI	RC	TBB	IBB	SO	HBP	SH	SF	SB	CS	SB%	GDP	Avg	OBP	Slg
1997 Montreal	NL	19	40	12	2	0	3	(1	2)	23	4	8	8	2	1	7	1	0	0	0	0	-	0	.300	.349	.575
1998 Montreal	NL	140	505	138	44	2	13	(3	10)	225	58	73	70	39	4	70	2	0	1	6	6	.50	12	.273	.327	.446
1999 Montreal	NL	100	347	96	34	2	9	(4	5)	161	38	47	47	22	6	35	2	0	3	2	3	.40	14	.277	.321	.464
2000 Toronto	AL	133	482	142	29	1	32	(16	16)	269	76	104	86	30	3	68	6	0	6	3	1	.75	14	.295	.340	.558
2001 Toronto	AL	146	522	143	31	2	18	(8	10)	232	71	83	73	38	8	88	6	0	7	5	2	.71	13	.274	.326	.444
2002 Anaheim	AL	130	429	124	35	6	19	(9	10)	228	75	59	73	32	6	44	15	0	3	10	3	.77	7	.289	.357	.531
2003 Anaheim	AL	63	206	63	9	2	9	(3	6)	103	32	35	40	26	4	31	2	0	1	5	4	.56	4	.306	.387	.500
7 ML YEARS		731	2531	718	184	15	103	(44	59)	1241	354	409	397	189	32	343	34	0	21	31	19	.62	64	.284	.339	.490

Aaron Fultz

Pitches: L **Bats:** L **Pos:** RP-64 **Ht:** 6'0" **Wt:** 200 **Born:** 9/4/73 **Age:** 30

Year Team	Lg	HOW MUCH HE PITCHED						WHAT HE GAVE UP										THE RESULTS					
		G	GS	CG	GF	IP	BFP	H	R	ER	HR	SH	SF	HB	TBB	IBB	SO	WP	Bk	W	L	Pct	ShO	Sv-Op	Hld	ERC	ERA
2003 Frisco*	AA	1	0	0	0	1.0	6	2	1	1	0	0	0	0	0	0	0	0	0	0	0		0	0- -		6.14	9.00
2003 Oklahoma*	AAA	1	0	0	0	1.0	6	2	3	3	2	0	0	0	1	0	2	0	0	0	0		0	0- -		34.00	27.00
2000 San Francisco	NL	58	0	0	18	69.1	299	67	38	36	8	7	6	3	28	0	62	0	2	5	2	.714	0	1-3	7	4.19	4.67
2001 San Francisco	NL	66	0	0	17	71.0	300	70	40	36	9	3	4	1	21	3	67	1	0	3	1	.750	0	1-2	12	3.75	4.56
2002 San Francisco	NL	43	0	0	12	41.1	185	47	22	22	4	2	1	3	19	3	31	1	0	2	2	.500	0	0-1	4	5.36	4.79
2003 Texas	AL	64	0	0	10	67.1	297	75	43	39	9	4	2	2	27	7	53	1	1	1	3	.250	0	0-0	19	4.97	5.21
4 ML YEARS		231	0	0	57	249.0	1081	259	143	133	30	16	13	9	95	13	213	3	3	11	8	.579	0	2-6	42	4.46	4.81

Rafael Furcal

Bats: B **Throws:** R **Pos:** SS-155; PH-2 **Ht:** 5'10" **Wt:** 165 **Born:** 10/24/77 **Age:** 26

Year Team	Lg	BATTING																	BASERUNNING				AVERAGES		
		G	AB	H	2B	3B	HR	(Hm | Rd)	TB	R	RBI	RC	TBB	IBB	SO	HBP	SH	SF	SB	CS	SB%	GDP	Avg	OBP	Slg
2000 Atlanta	NL	131	455	134	20	4	4	(1 | 3)	174	87	37	78	73	0	80	3	9	2	40	14	.74	2	.295	.394	.382
2001 Atlanta	NL	79	324	89	19	0	4	(3 | 1)	120	39	30	41	24	1	56	1	4	6	22	6	.79	5	.275	.321	.370
2002 Atlanta	NL	154	636	175	31	8	8	(4 | 4)	246	95	47	79	43	0	114	3	9	2	27	15	.64	8	.275	.323	.387
2003 Atlanta	NL	156	664	194	35	10	15	(4 | 11)	294	130	61	106	60	2	76	3	3	4	25	2	.93	1	.292	.352	.443
4 ML YEARS		520	2079	592	105	22	31	(12 | 19)	834	351	175	304	200	3	326	10	25	14	114	37	.75	16	.285	.348	.401

Eric Gagne

Pitches: R **Bats:** R **Pos:** RP-77 **Ht:** 6'2" **Wt:** 195 **Born:** 1/7/76 **Age:** 28

Year Team	Lg	HOW MUCH HE PITCHED						WHAT HE GAVE UP										THE RESULTS					
		G	GS	CG	GF	IP	BFP	H	R	ER	HR	SH	SF	HB	TBB	IBB	SO	WP	Bk	W	L	Pct	ShO	Sv-Op	Hld	ERC	ERA
1999 Los Angeles	NL	5	5	0	0	30.0	119	18	8	7	3	1	0	0	15	0	30	1	0	1	1	.500	0	0-0	0	2.42	2.10
2000 Los Angeles	NL	20	19	0	0	101.1	464	106	62	58	20	5	3	6	42	0	79	4	0	4	6	.400	0	0-0	0	5.97	5.15
2001 Los Angeles	NL	33	24	0	3	151.2	649	144	90	80	24	6	8	16	46	1	130	3	1	6	7	.462	0	0-0	0	4.22	4.75
2002 Los Angeles	NL	77	0	0	68	82.1	314	55	18	18	6	3	2	2	16	4	114	1	0	4	1	.800	0	52-56	1	1.60	1.97
2003 Los Angeles	NL	77	0	0	67	82.1	306	37	12	11	2	4	0	3	20	2	137	2	0	2	3	.400	0	55-55	1	0.93	1.20
5 ML YEARS		212	48	0	138	447.2	1852	360	190	174	55	19	13	24	157	8	490	11	1	17	18	.486	0	107-111	1	3.16	3.50

Andres Galarraga

Bats: R **Throws:** R **Pos:** 1B-69; PH-44; DH-2 **Ht:** 6'3" **Wt:** 250 **Born:** 6/18/61 **Age:** 43

Year Team	Lg	BATTING																	BASERUNNING				AVERAGES		
		G	AB	H	2B	3B	HR	(Hm | Rd)	TB	R	RBI	RC	TBB	IBB	SO	HBP	SH	SF	SB	CS	SB%	GDP	Avg	OBP	Slg
1985 Montreal	NL	24	75	14	1	0	2	(0 | 2)	21	9	4	4	3	0	18	1	0	0	1	2	.33	0	.187	.228	.280
1986 Montreal	NL	105	321	87	13	0	10	(4 | 6)	130	39	42	42	30	5	79	3	1	1	6	5	.55	8	.271	.338	.405
1987 Montreal	NL	147	551	168	40	3	13	(7 | 6)	253	72	90	86	41	13	127	10	0	4	7	10	.41	11	.305	.361	.459
1988 Montreal	NL	157	609	184	42	8	29	(14 | 15)	329	99	92	110	39	9	153	10	0	3	13	4	.76	12	.302	.352	.540
1989 Montreal	NL	152	572	147	30	1	23	(10 | 13)	248	76	85	79	48	10	158	13	0	3	12	5	.71	12	.257	.327	.434
1990 Montreal	NL	155	579	148	29	0	20	(6 | 14)	237	65	87	70	40	8	169	4	0	5	10	1	.91	14	.256	.306	.409
1991 Montreal	NL	107	375	82	13	2	9	(3 | 6)	126	34	33	30	23	5	86	2	0	1	5	6	.45	6	.219	.268	.336
1992 St Louis	NL	95	325	79	14	2	10	(4 | 6)	127	38	39	33	11	0	69	8	0	3	5	4	.56	8	.243	.282	.391
1993 Colorado	NL	120	470	174	35	4	22	(13 | 9)	283	71	98	102	24	12	73	6	0	6	2	4	.33	9	.370	.403	.602
1994 Colorado	NL	103	417	133	21	0	31	(16 | 15)	247	77	85	82	19	8	93	8	0	5	8	3	.73	10	.319	.356	.592
1995 Colorado	NL	143	554	155	29	3	31	(18 | 13)	283	89	106	90	32	6	146	13	0	5	12	2	.86	14	.280	.331	.511
1996 Colorado	NL	159	626	190	39	3	47	(32 | 15)	376	119	150	130	40	3	157	17	0	8	18	8	.69	6	.304	.357	.601
1997 Colorado	NL	154	600	191	31	3	41	(21 | 20)	351	120	140	126	54	2	141	17	0	3	15	8	.65	16	.318	.389	.585
1998 Atlanta	NL	153	555	169	27	1	44	(16 | 28)	330	103	121	124	63	11	146	25	0	5	7	6	.54	8	.305	.397	.595
2000 Atlanta	NL	141	494	149	25	1	28	(14 | 14)	260	67	100	88	36	5	126	17	0	1	3	5	.38	15	.302	.369	.526
2001 Tex-SF		121	399	102	28	1	17	(8 | 9)	183	50	69	56	31	2	117	12	0	3	1	3	.25	12	.256	.326	.459
2002 Montreal	NL	104	292	76	12	0	9	(7 | 2)	115	30	40	35	30	6	81	9	0	3	2	2	.50	8	.260	.344	.394
2003 San Francisco	NL	110	272	82	15	0	12	(6 | 6)	133	36	42	42	19	1	61	2	0	0	1	3	.25	9	.301	.352	.489
2001 Texas	AL	72	243	57	16	0	10	(5 | 5)	103	33	34	30	18	1	68	9	0	1	1	0	1.00	6	.235	.310	.424
2001 San Francisco	NL	49	156	45	12	1	7	(3 | 4)	80	17	35	26	13	1	49	3	0	2	0	3	.00	3	.288	.351	.513
18 ML YEARS		2250	8086	2330	444	32	398	(202 | 196)	4032	1194	1423	1329	583	106	2000	177	1	58	128	81	.61	178	.288	.347	.499

Mike Gallo

Pitches: L **Bats:** L **Pos:** RP-32 **Ht:** 6'0" **Wt:** 175 **Born:** 4/2/77 **Age:** 27

Year Team	Lg	HOW MUCH HE PITCHED						WHAT HE GAVE UP										THE RESULTS					
		G	GS	CG	GF	IP	BFP	H	R	ER	HR	SH	SF	HB	TBB	IBB	SO	WP	Bk	W	L	Pct	ShO	Sv-Op	Hld	ERC	ERA
1999 Auburn	A-	3	3	0	0	14.2	63	13	4	2	0	0	0	0	7	0	11	0	0	1	0	1.000	0	0- -		3.03	1.23
1999 Michigan	A	12	12	0	0	60.0	268	76	47	39	6	1	2	1	23	0	32	1	0	2	3	.400	0	0- -		5.76	5.85
2000 Michigan	A	24	13	0	3	90.2	406	104	58	49	6	5	6	3	27	1	56	4	1	8	3	.727	0	0- -		4.26	4.86
2001 Michigan	A	44	0	0	17	84.1	360	83	38	36	6	1	2	8	19	1	67	3	1	9	2	.818	0	4- -		3.26	3.84
2002 Lexington	A	42	2	0	25	88.1	359	69	29	18	6	3	2	1	26	4	93	2	0	4	4	.500	0	8- -		2.29	1.83
2002 Round Rock	AA	1	0	0	0	1.1	5	1	1	1	0	0	0	0	0	0	0	0	0	0	0		0	0- -		4.25	6.75
2003 New Orleans	AAA	16	0	0	3	17.1	64	13	4	4	0	0	1	0	3	0	11	0	0	3	0	1.000	0	0- -		1.75	2.08
2003 Round Rock	AA	17	0	0	8	19.2	78	17	3	3	1	2	1	0	6	2	22	0	0	1	1	.500	0	2- -		2.63	1.37
2003 Houston	NL	32	0	0	6	30.0	121	28	10	10	3	2	3	1	10	2	16	0	0	1	0	1.000	0	0-1	6	3.66	3.00

Ron Gant

Bats: R **Throws:** R **Pos:** LF-8; DH-6; PH-6; RF-1   **Ht:** 6'0" **Wt:** 195 **Born:** 3/2/65 **Age:** 39

Year Team	Lg	G	AB	H	2B	3B	HR	(Hm	Rd)	TB	R	RBI	RC	TBB	IBB	SO	HBP	SH	SF	SB	CS	SB%	GDP	Avg	OBP	Slg
1987 Atlanta	NL	21	83	22	4	0	2	(1	1)	32	9	9	8	1	0	11	0	1	1	4	2	.67	3	.265	.271	.386
1988 Atlanta	NL	146	563	146	28	8	19	(7	12)	247	85	60	78	46	4	118	3	2	4	19	10	.66	7	.259	.317	.439
1989 Atlanta	NL	75	260	46	8	3	9	(5	4)	87	26	25	20	20	0	63	1	2	2	9	6	.60	0	.177	.237	.335
1990 Atlanta	NL	152	575	174	34	3	32	(18	14)	310	107	84	107	50	0	86	1	1	4	33	16	.67	8	.303	.357	.539
1991 Atlanta	NL	154	561	141	35	3	32	(18	14)	278	101	105	96	71	8	104	5	0	5	34	15	.69	6	.251	.338	.496
1992 Atlanta	NL	153	544	141	22	6	17	(10	7)	226	74	80	74	45	5	101	7	0	6	32	10	.76	10	.259	.321	.415
1993 Atlanta	NL	157	606	166	27	4	36	(17	19)	309	113	117	105	67	2	117	2	0	7	26	9	.74	14	.274	.345	.510
1995 Cincinnati	NL	119	410	113	19	4	29	(12	17)	227	79	88	87	74	5	108	3	1	5	23	8	.74	11	.276	.386	.554
1996 St Louis	NL	122	419	103	14	2	30	(17	13)	211	74	82	77	73	5	98	3	1	4	13	4	.76	9	.246	.359	.504
1997 St Louis	NL	139	502	115	21	4	17	(11	6)	195	68	62	63	58	3	162	1	0	1	14	6	.70	2	.229	.310	.388
1998 St Louis	NL	121	383	92	17	1	26	(14	12)	189	60	67	64	51	2	92	2	0	2	8	0	1.00	6	.240	.331	.493
1999 Philadelphia	NL	138	516	134	27	5	17	(6	11)	222	107	77	86	85	0	112	1	0	3	13	3	.81	6	.260	.364	.430
2000 Phi-Ana		123	425	106	19	3	26	(14	12)	209	69	54	70	56	1	91	1	1	4	6	6	.50	7	.249	.335	.492
2001 Col-Oak		93	252	65	13	3	10	(7	3)	114	46	35	42	35	2	80	0	2	3	5	1	.83	0	.258	.345	.452
2002 San Diego	NL	102	309	81	14	1	18	(9	9)	151	58	59	50	36	1	59	2	1	5	4	6	.40	8	.262	.338	.489
2003 Oakland	AL	17	41	6	0	0	1	(0	1)	9	4	4	0	2	0	9	0	0	1	0	0	-	0	.146	.182	.220
2000 Philadelphia	NL	89	343	87	16	2	20	(9	11)	167	54	38	53	36	1	73	1	1	3	5	4	.56	7	.254	.324	.487
2000 Anaheim	AL	34	82	19	3	1	6	(5	1)	42	15	16	17	20	0	18	0	0	1	1	2	.33	0	.232	.379	.512
2001 Colorado	NL	59	171	44	8	2	8	(6	2)	80	31	22	29	24	2	56	0	2	2	3	1	.75	0	.257	.345	.468
2001 Oakland	AL	34	81	21	5	1	2	(1	1)	34	15	13	13	11	0	24	0	0	1	2	0	1.00	0	.259	.344	.420
16 ML YEARS		1832	6449	1651	302	50	321	(167	154)	3016	1080	1008	1027	770	38	1411	32	12	57	243	102	.70	98	.256	.336	.468

Danny Garcia

Bats: R **Throws:** R **Pos:** 2B-17; LF-1; PR-1   **Ht:** 6'1" **Wt:** 174 **Born:** 4/12/80 **Age:** 24

Year Team	Lg	G	AB	H	2B	3B	HR	(Hm	Rd)	TB	R	RBI	RC	TBB	IBB	SO	HBP	SH	SF	SB	CS	SB%	GDP	Avg	OBP	Slg
2001 Brooklyn	A-	15	56	18	2	0	1	(-	-)	23	10	6	9	4	0	10	2	0	0	3	2	.60	0	.321	.387	.411
2001 Capital City	A	30	103	31	12	1	2	(-	-)	51	25	16	23	15	0	18	6	4	3	7	3	.70	0	.301	.409	.495
2002 St.Lucie	A+	122	432	118	34	5	4	(-	-)	174	69	52	71	53	0	77	15	6	4	13	6	.68	0	.273	.369	.403
2003 Norfolk	AAA	101	388	102	23	3	4	(-	-)	143	45	54	48	22	1	60	9	2	6	11	1	.92	3	.263	.313	.369
2003 New York	NL	19	56	12	2	0	2	(1	1)	20	5	6	4	2	0	11	3	1	1	0	0	-	2	.214	.274	.357

Freddy Garcia

Pitches: R **Bats:** R **Pos:** SP-33   **Ht:** 6'4" **Wt:** 235 **Born:** 6/10/76 **Age:** 28

| | | HOW MUCH HE PITCHED | | | | | | WHAT HE GAVE UP | | | | | | | | | | | | THE RESULTS | | | | | |
Year Team	Lg	G	GS	CG	GF	IP	BFP	H	R	ER	HR	SH	SF	HB	TBB	IBB	SO	WP	Bk	W	L	Pct	ShO	Sv-Op	Hld	ERC	ERA
1999 Seattle	AL	33	33	2	0	201.1	888	205	96	91	18	3	6	10	90	4	170	12	3	17	8	.680	1	0-0	0	4.46	4.07
2000 Seattle	AL	21	20	0	0	124.1	538	112	62	54	16	6	1	2	64	4	79	4	2	9	5	.643	0	0-0	0	4.20	3.91
2001 Seattle	AL	34	34	4	0	**238.2**	971	199	88	81	16	8	5	5	69	6	163	3	1	18	6	.750	3	0-0	0	**2.61**	**3.05**
2002 Seattle	AL	34	34	1	0	223.2	955	227	110	109	30	4	8	6	63	3	181	8	1	16	10	.615	0	0-0	0	3.98	4.39
2003 Seattle	AL	33	33	1	0	201.1	862	196	109	101	31	2	8	11	71	2	144	11	0	12	14	.462	0	0-0	0	4.33	4.51
5 ML YEARS		155	154	8	0	989.1	4214	939	465	436	111	23	28	34	357	19	737	38	7	72	43	.626	4	0-0	0	3.83	3.97

Jesse Garcia

Bats: R **Throws:** R **Pos:** 2B-6; PR-5; PH-4; SS-3; 3B-2   **Ht:** 5'10" **Wt:** 171 **Born:** 9/24/73 **Age:** 30

Year Team	Lg	G	AB	H	2B	3B	HR	(Hm	Rd)	TB	R	RBI	RC	TBB	IBB	SO	HBP	SH	SF	SB	CS	SB%	GDP	Avg	OBP	Slg
2003 Richmond*	AAA	110	425	130	17	3	2	(-	-)	159	45	30	52	12	0	50	4	5	3	29	9	.76	9	.306	.329	.374
1999 Baltimore	AL	17	29	6	0	0	2	(1	1)	12	6	2	3	2	0	3	0	3	0	0	0	-	1	.207	.258	.414
2000 Baltimore	AL	14	17	1	0	0	0	(0	0)	1	2	0	0	2	0	2	0	0	0	0	0	-	0	.059	.158	.059
2001 Atlanta	NL	22	5	1	0	0	0	(0	0)	1	3	0	0	0	0	1	0	1	0	6	2	.75	0	.200	.200	.200
2002 Atlanta	NL	39	61	12	1	0	0	(0	0)	13	6	5	3	0	0	14	0	0	1	0	1	.00	1	.197	.197	.213
2003 Atlanta	NL	13	10	4	0	1	0	(0	0)	6	6	2	2	0	0	1	0	0	0	0	1	.00	0	.400	.400	.600
5 ML YEARS		105	122	24	1	1	2	(1	1)	33	23	9	8	4	0	21	0	4	0	6	4	.60	2	.197	.222	.270

Karim Garcia

Bats: L **Throws:** L **Pos:** RF-54; LF-13; CF-10; PR-3; PH-2; DH-1   **Ht:** 6'0" **Wt:** 195 **Born:** 10/29/75 **Age:** 28

Year Team	Lg	G	AB	H	2B	3B	HR	(Hm	Rd)	TB	R	RBI	RC	TBB	IBB	SO	HBP	SH	SF	SB	CS	SB%	GDP	Avg	OBP	Slg
2003 Buffalo*	AAA	14	60	16	6	0	0	(-	-)	22	6	7	6	2	1	17	0	0	0	2	1	.67	1	.267	.290	.367
1995 Los Angeles	NL	13	20	4	0	0	0	(0	0)	4	1	0	0	0	0	4	0	0	0	0	0	-	0	.200	.200	.200
1996 Los Angeles	NL	1	1	0	0	0	0	(0	0)	0	0	0	0	0	0	1	0	0	0	0	0	-	0	.000	.000	.000
1997 Los Angeles	NL	15	39	5	0	1	0	(0	1)	8	5	8	2	6	1	14	0	0	1	0	0	-	0	.128	.239	.205
1998 Arizona	NL	113	333	74	10	8	9	(4	5)	127	39	43	31	18	1	78	0	0	3	5	4	.56	6	.222	.260	.381
1999 Detroit	AL	96	288	69	10	3	14	(4	10)	127	38	32	36	20	1	67	0	0	1	2	4	.33	2	.240	.288	.441
2000 Det-Bal	AL	16	33	3	0	0	0	(0	0)	3	1	0	0	0	0	10	0	0	0	0	0	-	1	.091	.091	.091
2001 Cleveland	AL	20	45	14	3	0	5	(1	4)	32	8	9	11	3	0	13	1	0	1	0	0	-	0	.311	.360	.711
2002 NYY-Cle	AL	53	202	60	8	0	16	(7	9)	116	30	52	35	6	0	41	0	0	2	1	1	.50	6	.297	.314	.574
2003 Cle-NYY	AL	76	244	64	6	0	11	(4	7)	103	25	35	29	14	2	52	1	0	3	0	2	.00	8	.262	.302	.422
2000 Detroit	AL	8	17	3	0	0	0	(0	0)	3	1	0	0	0	0	4	0	0	0	0	0	-	1	.176	.176	.176
2000 Baltimore	AL	8	16	0	0	0	0	(0	0)	0	0	0	0	0	0	6	0	0	0	0	0	-	0	.000	.000	.000
2002 New York	AL	2	5	1	0	0	0	(0	0)	1	1	0	0	0	0	1	0	0	0	0	0	-	0	.200	.200	.200
2002 Cleveland	AL	51	197	59	8	0	16	(7	9)	115	29	52	35	6	0	40	0	0	2	1	1	.50	6	.299	.317	.584
2003 Cleveland	AL	24	93	18	1	0	5	(1	4)	34	8	14	7	5	1	20	1	0	2	0	0	-	4	.194	.238	.366
2003 New York	AL	52	151	46	5	0	6	(3	3)	69	17	21	22	9	1	32	0	0	1	0	2	.00	4	.305	.342	.457
9 ML YEARS		403	1205	293	37	11	56	(20	36)	520	147	179	144	67	5	280	2	0	11	7	13	.35	24	.243	.282	.432

Reynaldo Garcia

Pitches: R **Bats:** R **Pos:** RP-17   **Ht:** 6'3" **Wt:** 170 **Born:** 4/15/74 **Age:** 30

Year Team	Lg	G	GS	CG	GF	IP	BFP	H	R	ER	HR	SH	SF	HB	TBB	IBB	SO	WP	Bk	W	L	Pct	ShO	Sv-Op	Hld	ERC	ERA
1999 Rangers	R	12	11	0	0	64.0	268	55	30	23	3	2	4	0	26	0	42	4	3	4	4	.500	0	0- -	-	2.98	3.23
2000 Savannah	A	49	2	1	35	97.0	410	87	37	29	6	2	4	5	33	1	82	8	0	6	7	.462	0	14- -	-	3.19	2.69
2001 Charlotte	A+	35	16	0	9	116.1	499	107	62	46	7	6	4	8	45	3	111	8	1	5	10	.333	0	4- -	-	3.52	3.56
2002 Tulsa	AA	18	9	0	1	68.1	294	63	36	28	11	3	2	3	30	1	54	4	1	5	1	.833	0	0- -	-	4.39	3.69
2002 Oklahoma	AAA	25	0	0	10	31.2	135	23	12	10	2	1	2	2	14	1	33	2	0	2	2	.500	0	4- -	-	2.64	2.84
2003 Oklahoma	AAA	39	3	0	24	61.0	261	64	27	25	3	1	2	1	19	1	64	6	0	4	3	.571	0	9- -	-	3.69	3.69
2002 Texas	AL	3	0	0	1	2.0	14	7	7	7	3	0	0	0	1	0	2	1	0	0	0	-	0	0-0	0	39.83	31.50
2003 Texas	AL	17	0	0	4	18.0	87	19	18	18	6	1	1	2	14	0	15	3	0	0	0	-	0	0-0	1	8.46	9.00
2 ML YEARS		20	0	0	5	20.0	101	26	25	25	9	1	1	2	15	0	17	4	0	0	0	-	0	0-0	1	11.04	11.25

Rosman Garcia

Pitches: R **Bats:** R **Pos:** RP-46   **Ht:** 6'2" **Wt:** 160 **Born:** 1/3/79 **Age:** 25

Year Team	Lg	G	GS	CG	GF	IP	BFP	H	R	ER	HR	SH	SF	HB	TBB	IBB	SO	WP	Bk	W	L	Pct	ShO	Sv-Op	Hld	ERC	ERA
1998 Yankees	R	12	8	0	2	57.1	226	39	15	13	2	0	2	1	19	0	77	3	4	4	2	.667	0	0- -	-	1.88	2.04
1999 Greensboro	A	9	9	0	0	42.1	204	60	33	30	4	0	1	2	20	0	31	12	3	2	3	.400	0	0- -	-	7.05	6.38
1999 Staten Island	A-	18	10	0	1	69.2	310	86	40	33	3	3	3	4	14	2	40	4	1	2	6	.250	0	1- -	-	4.31	4.26
2000 Greensboro	A	23	15	1	1	104.1	454	115	67	53	12	3	1	4	35	0	73	5	1	6	6	.500	0	0- -	-	4.70	4.57
2000 Tampa	A+	4	3	0	1	18.0	77	18	13	11	1	0	3	2	4	0	6	0	1	0	2	.000	0	1- -	-	3.48	5.50
2001 Tampa	A+	26	7	0	4	59.2	263	56	30	23	2	4	2	5	22	6	42	4	0	2	6	.250	0	1- -	-	3.21	3.47
2001 Norwich	AA	1	1	0	0	6.0	28	5	4	0	0	0	0	1	2	0	6	2	0	1	0	1.000	0	0- -	-	2.55	0.00
2002 Tulsa	AA	53	0	0	28	74.2	326	75	34	25	1	10	3	3	32	9	38	3	2	8	5	.615	0	6- -	-	3.54	3.01
2003 Oklahoma	AAA	17	2	0	13	28.1	109	20	7	6	1	1	0	0	6	0	21	0	0	1	2	.333	0	10- -	-	1.60	1.91
2003 Texas	AL	46	0	0	7	46.1	224	63	33	31	4	1	1	2	23	0	25	1	1	1	2	.333	0	0-2	7	6.62	6.02

Nomar Garciaparra

Bats: R **Throws:** R **Pos:** SS-156; PH-1   **Ht:** 6'0" **Wt:** 190 **Born:** 7/23/73 **Age:** 30

Year Team	Lg	G	AB	H	2B	3B	HR	(Hm	Rd)	TB	R	RBI	RC	TBB	IBB	SO	HBP	SH	SF	SB	CS	SB%	GDP	Avg	OBP	Slg
1996 Boston	AL	24	87	21	2	3	4	(3	1)	41	11	16	13	4	0	14	0	1	1	5	0	1.00	0	.241	.272	.471
1997 Boston	AL	153	684	209	44	11	30	(11	19)	365	122	98	122	35	2	92	6	2	7	22	9	.71	9	.306	.342	.534
1998 Boston	AL	143	604	195	37	8	35	(17	18)	353	111	122	117	33	1	62	8	0	7	12	6	.67	20	.323	.362	.584
1999 Boston	AL	135	532	190	42	4	27	(14	13)	321	103	104	125	51	7	39	8	0	4	14	3	.82	11	.357	.418	.603
2000 Boston	AL	140	529	197	51	3	21	(7	14)	317	104	96	127	61	20	50	2	0	7	5	2	.71	8	.372	.434	.599
2001 Boston	AL	21	83	24	3	0	4	(3	1)	39	13	8	13	7	0	9	1	0	0	0	1	.00	1	.289	.352	.470
2002 Boston	AL	156	635	197	56	5	24	(10	14)	335	101	120	115	41	4	63	6	0	11	5	2	.71	17	.310	.352	.528
2003 Boston	AL	156	658	198	37	13	28	(18	10)	345	120	105	114	39	1	61	11	1	10	19	5	.79	10	.301	.345	.524
8 ML YEARS		928	3812	1231	272	47	173	(83	90)	2116	685	669	746	271	35	390	42	4	47	82	28	.75	76	.323	.370	.555

Jon Garland

Pitches: R **Bats:** R **Pos:** SP-32   **Ht:** 6'6" **Wt:** 205 **Born:** 9/27/79 **Age:** 24

Year Team	Lg	G	GS	CG	GF	IP	BFP	H	R	ER	HR	SH	SF	HB	TBB	IBB	SO	WP	Bk	W	L	Pct	ShO	Sv-Op	Hld	ERC	ERA
2000 Chicago	AL	15	13	0	0	69.2	324	82	55	50	10	0	2	1	40	0	42	4	0	4	8	.333	0	0-0	1	6.26	6.46
2001 Chicago	AL	35	16	0	8	117.0	510	123	59	48	16	2	5	4	55	2	61	3	0	6	7	.462	0	1-1	2	5.16	3.69
2002 Chicago	AL	33	33	1	0	192.2	827	188	109	98	23	3	4	9	83	1	112	5	0	12	12	.500	1	0-0	0	4.46	4.58
2003 Chicago	AL	32	32	0	0	191.2	813	188	103	96	28	4	8	4	74	1	108	8	0	12	13	.480	0	0-0	0	4.38	4.51
4 ML YEARS		115	94	1	9	571.0	2474	581	326	292	77	9	19	18	252	4	323	20	0	34	40	.459	1	1-1	3	4.79	4.60

Chad Gaudin

Pitches: R **Bats:** R **Pos:** RP-12; SP-3   **Ht:** 5'11" **Wt:** 165 **Born:** 3/24/83 **Age:** 21

Year Team	Lg	G	GS	CG	GF	IP	BFP	H	R	ER	HR	SH	SF	HB	TBB	IBB	SO	WP	Bk	W	L	Pct	ShO	Sv-Op	Hld	ERC	ERA
2002 Chrlstn - SC	A	26	17	0	5	119.1	491	106	43	30	5	3	5	11	37	0	106	4	3	4	6	.400	1	1- -	-	3.17	2.26
2003 Orlando	AA	3	3	1	0	19.0	64	8	1	1	0	0	0	0	3	0	23	0	0	2	0	1.000	1	0- -	-	0.65	0.47
2003 Bakersfield	A+	14	14	1	0	80.1	323	63	23	19	2	3	2	1	23	0	70	0	2	5	3	.625	0	0- -	-	2.12	2.13
2003 Tampa Bay	AL	15	3	0	5	40.0	173	37	18	16	4	0	2	1	16	0	23	1	0	2	0	1.000	0	0-0	0	3.70	3.60

Geoff Geary

Pitches: R **Bats:** R **Pos:** RP-5   **Ht:** 6'0" **Wt:** 175 **Born:** 8/26/76 **Age:** 27

Year Team	Lg	G	GS	CG	GF	IP	BFP	H	R	ER	HR	SH	SF	HB	TBB	IBB	SO	WP	Bk	W	L	Pct	ShO	Sv-Op	Hld	ERC	ERA
1998 Batavia	A-	16	16	1	1	95.1	368	78	20	17	6	3	0	0	14	0	101	3	0	9	1	.900	1	0- -	-	2.03	1.60
1999 Clearwater	A+	24	19	2	0	139.0	611	175	77	61	11	6	4	5	31	1	77	6	3	10	5	.667	0	0- -	-	4.85	3.95
2000 Reading	AA	22	22	1	0	129.1	553	141	66	59	15	2	4	7	22	0	112	1	2	7	6	.538	0	0- -	-	3.94	4.11
2001 Scrtn/WlksBr	AAA	7	3	0	0	22.0	101	35	17	17	2	1	0	1	6	1	21	0	1	0	3	.000	0	0- -	-	7.49	6.95
2001 Reading	AA	29	13	0	10	112.1	449	101	48	45	14	7	5	3	21	3	88	4	3	9	7	.563	0	2- -	-	2.98	3.61
2002 Scrtn/WlksBr	AAA	38	8	0	6	101.0	427	108	46	34	9	0	1	4	32	1	82	1	0	4	2	.667	0	1- -	-	4.31	3.03
2003 Scrtn/WlksBr	AAA	46	3	0	18	87.2	343	73	26	21	3	2	5	4	13	1	80	1	0	9	4	.692	0	5- -	-	2.08	2.16
2003 Philadelphia	NL	5	0	0	2	6.0	28	8	3	3	0	1	0	0	3	0	3	0	0	0	0	-	0	0-0	0	5.70	4.50

Chris George

Pitches: L Bats: L Pos: SP-18   Ht: 6'2" Wt: 200 Born: 9/16/79 Age: 24

Year Team	Lg	G	GS	CG	GF	IP	BFP	H	R	ER	HR	SH	SF	HB	TBB	IBB	SO	WP	Bk	W	L	Pct	ShO	Sv-Op	Hld	ERC	ERA
2003 Omaha*	AAA	10	10	0	0	54.1	251	71	49	44	8	0	2	1	22	0	28	2	0	3	5	.375	0	0--	-	6.37	7.29
2001 Kansas City	AL	13	13	1	0	74.0	313	83	48	46	14	3	4	0	18	0	32	3	2	4	8	.333	0	0-0	0	4.82	5.59
2002 Kansas City	AL	6	6	0	0	27.1	124	37	17	17	2	0	1	1	8	0	13	1	0	0	4	.000	0	0-0	0	5.70	5.60
2003 Kansas City	AL	18	18	0	0	93.2	441	120	75	74	22	2	4	3	44	2	39	5	3	9	6	.600	0	0-0	0	7.19	7.11
3 ML YEARS		37	37	1	0	195.0	878	240	140	137	38	5	9	4	70	2	84	9	5	13	18	.419	0	0-0	0	6.06	6.32

Esteban German

Bats: R Throws: R Pos: 2B-5; PH-1   Ht: 5'9" Wt: 165 Born: 1/26/78 Age: 26

Year Team	Lg	G	AB	H	2B	3B	HR	(Hm	Rd)	TB	R	RBI	RC	TBB	IBB	SO	HBP	SH	SF	SB	CS	SB%	GDP	Avg	OBP	Slg
1998 Athletics	R	55	202	62	3	10	2	(-	-)	91	52	28	44	33	0	43	4	2	1	40	8	.83	1	.307	.413	.450
1999 Modesto	A+	128	501	156	16	12	4	(-	-)	208	107	52	100	102	0	128	5	5	7	40	16	.71	3	.311	.428	.415
2000 Midland	AA	24	75	16	1	0	1	(-	-)	20	13	6	10	18	0	21	2	2	0	5	3	.63	1	.213	.379	.267
2000 Visalia	A+	109	428	113	14	10	2	(-	-)	153	82	35	72	61	0	86	5	4	2	78	8	.91	4	.264	.361	.357
2001 Midland	AA	92	335	95	20	3	6	(-	-)	139	79	30	64	63	0	66	12	4	0	31	11	.74	6	.284	.415	.415
2001 Sacramento	AAA	38	150	56	8	0	4	(-	-)	76	40	14	36	18	0	20	6	2	1	17	2	.89	4	.373	.457	.507
2002 Sacramento	AAA	121	458	126	16	4	2	(-	-)	156	72	43	68	78	1	66	8	7	0	26	14	.65	7	.275	.390	.341
2003 Sacramento	AAA	115	467	143	20	8	3	(-	-)	188	86	51	74	56	1	64	2	13	6	32	8	.80	17	.306	.379	.403
2002 Oakland	AL	9	35	7	0	0	0	(0	0)	7	4	0	2	4	0	11	1	0	0	1	0	1.00	0	.200	.300	.200
2003 Oakland	AL	5	4	1	0	0	0	(0	0)	1	0	1	1	0	0	1	0	0	0	0	0	-	1	.250	.250	.250
2 ML YEARS		14	39	8	0	0	0	(0	0)	8	4	1	3	4	0	12	1	0	0	1	0	1.00	1	.205	.295	.205

Franklyn German

Pitches: R Bats: R Pos: RP-45   Ht: 6'4" Wt: 265 Born: 1/20/80 Age: 24

Year Team	Lg	G	GS	CG	GF	IP	BFP	H	R	ER	HR	SH	SF	HB	TBB	IBB	SO	WP	Bk	W	L	Pct	ShO	Sv-Op	Hld	ERC	ERA
1998 Athletics	R	14	12	0	0	54.1	249	69	43	37	5	1	5	7	18	0	46	5	3	2	1	.667	0	0--	-	5.90	6.13
1999 Sth Oregon	A-	15	15	0	0	73.2	344	89	52	49	10	0	4	4	45	1	58	4	0	3	5	.375	0	0--	-	6.83	5.99
2000 Modesto	A+	17	14	0	2	72.0	333	88	55	44	4	0	3	6	37	0	52	7	2	5	5	.500	0	0--	-	5.94	5.50
2000 Vancouver	A-	9	2	0	2	20.1	86	13	4	4	0	0	0	1	10	0	20	4	0	1	0	1.000	0	0--	-	1.99	1.77
2001 Visalia	A+	53	0	0	45	63.1	294	67	34	28	7	3	2	2	31	1	93	11	0	2	4	.333	0	19--	-	4.75	3.98
2002 Midland	AA	37	0	0	28	41.1	174	28	14	14	0	0	3	0	27	2	59	7	0	1	1	.500	0	16--	-	2.56	3.05
2002 Toledo	AAA	23	0	0	21	22.2	88	15	4	4	0	0	1	0	7	0	31	1	1	1	1	.500	0	13--	-	1.54	1.59
2003 Toledo	AAA	24	0	0	10	29.1	118	21	9	8	2	3	1	6	9	1	32	6	0	1	4	.200	0	4--	-	2.83	2.45
2002 Detroit	AL	7	0	0	1	6.2	25	3	0	0	2	0	1	1	2	1	6	0	0	1	0	1.000	0	1-1	1	1.09	0.00
2003 Detroit	AL	45	0	0	15	44.2	222	47	32	30	5	2	1	2	45	3	41	8	0	2	4	.333	0	5-7	4	7.06	6.04
2 ML YEARS		52	0	0	16	51.1	247	50	32	30	5	4	1	3	47	4	47	8	0	3	4	.429	0	6-8	5	6.10	5.26

Jody Gerut

Bats: L Throws: L Pos: RF-63; LF-36; CF-14; DH-11; PH-4   Ht: 6'0" Wt: 190 Born: 9/18/77 Age: 26

Year Team	Lg	G	AB	H	2B	3B	HR	(Hm	Rd)	TB	R	RBI	RC	TBB	IBB	SO	HBP	SH	SF	SB	CS	SB%	GDP	Avg	OBP	Slg
1999 Salem	A+	133	499	144	33	11	11	(-	-)	232	80	63	85	61	4	65	3	1	3	25	12	.68	10	.289	.367	.465
2000 Carolina	AA	109	362	103	32	3	3	(-	-)	150	48	57	65	76	2	54	2	1	7	18	11	.62	9	.285	.405	.414
2002 Buffalo	AAA	55	183	59	7	2	1	(-	-)	73	31	21	28	23	0	20	1	0	0	3	5	.38	6	.322	.401	.399
2002 Akron	AA	65	256	72	15	2	9	(-	-)	118	44	39	42	34	3	30	1	0	0	17	8	.68	7	.281	.368	.461
2003 Buffalo	AAA	17	65	18	5	0	5	(-	-)	38	13	19	15	11	0	11	0	0	1	4	0	1.00	1	.277	.377	.585
2003 Cleveland	AL	127	480	134	33	2	22	(13	9)	237	66	75	74	35	4	70	7	1	2	4	5	.44	13	.279	.336	.494

Jason Giambi

Bats: L Throws: R Pos: 1B-85; DH-69; PH-2   Ht: 6'3" Wt: 235 Born: 1/8/71 Age: 33

Year Team	Lg	G	AB	H	2B	3B	HR	(Hm	Rd)	TB	R	RBI	RC	TBB	IBB	SO	HBP	SH	SF	SB	CS	SB%	GDP	Avg	OBP	Slg
1995 Oakland	AL	54	176	45	7	0	6	(3	3)	70	27	25	27	28	0	31	3	1	2	2	1	.67	4	.256	.364	.398
1996 Oakland	AL	140	536	156	40	1	20	(6	14)	258	84	79	88	51	3	95	5	1	5	0	1	.00	15	.291	.355	.481
1997 Oakland	AL	142	519	152	41	2	20	(16	4)	257	66	81	91	55	3	89	6	0	8	0	1	.00	11	.293	.362	.495
1998 Oakland	AL	153	562	166	28	0	27	(12	15)	275	92	110	103	81	7	102	5	0	9	2	2	.50	16	.295	.384	.489
1999 Oakland	AL	158	575	181	36	1	33	(17	16)	318	115	123	132	105	6	106	7	0	8	1	1	.50	11	.315	.422	.553
2000 Oakland	AL	152	510	170	29	1	43	(23	20)	330	108	137	152	137	6	96	9	0	8	2	0	1.00	9	.333	.476	.647
2001 Oakland	AL	154	520	178	47	2	38	(27	11)	343	109	120	153	129	24	83	13	0	9	2	0	1.00	17	.342	.477	.660
2002 New York	AL	155	560	176	34	1	41	(19	22)	335	120	122	140	109	4	112	15	0	5	2	2	.50	18	.314	.435	.598
2003 New York	AL	156	535	134	25	0	41	(12	29)	282	97	107	120	129	9	140	21	0	5	2	1	.67	9	.250	.412	.527
9 ML YEARS		1264	4493	1358	287	8	269	(133	136)	2468	818	904	1006	824	62	854	84	2	59	13	9	.59	110	.302	.415	.549

Jeremy Giambi

Bats: L Throws: L Pos: DH-29; PH-13; LF-9; RF-2   Ht: 5'11" Wt: 216 Born: 9/30/74 Age: 29

Year Team	Lg	G	AB	H	2B	3B	HR	(Hm	Rd)	TB	R	RBI	RC	TBB	IBB	SO	HBP	SH	SF	SB	CS	SB%	GDP	Avg	OBP	Slg
2003 Pawtucket*	AAA	10	35	8	4	0	1	(-	-)	15	6	4	6	7	0	15	0	0	0	0	0	-	0	.229	.357	.429
1998 Kansas City	AL	18	58	13	4	0	2	(0	2)	23	6	8	7	11	0	9	0	0	1	0	1	.00	3	.224	.343	.397
1999 Kansas City	AL	90	288	82	13	1	3	(2	1)	106	34	34	41	40	5	67	3	1	4	0	0	-	7	.285	.373	.368
2000 Oakland	AL	104	260	66	10	2	10	(3	7)	110	42	50	37	32	2	61	3	4	3	0	0	-	7	.254	.338	.423
2001 Oakland	AL	124	371	105	26	0	12	(5	7)	167	64	57	64	63	1	83	4	3	2	1	0	1.00	13	.283	.391	.450
2002 Oak-Phi	AL	124	313	81	17	0	20	(12	8)	158	58	45	59	79	2	94	4	1	0	1	0	1.00	5	.259	.414	.505
2003 Boston	AL	50	127	25	5	0	5	(2	3)	45	15	15	14	26	0	42	2	1	0	1	0	1.00	3	.197	.342	.354

Year Team	Lg	G	AB	H	2B	3B	HR	(Hm	Rd)	TB	R	RBI	RC	TBB	IBB	SO	HBP	SH	SF	SB	CS	SB%	GDP	Avg	OBP	Slg
								BATTING												BASERUNNING				AVERAGES		
2002 Oakland	AL	42	157	43	7	0	8	(6	2)	74	26	17	24	27	0	40	3	0	0	0	0	-	4	.274	.390	.471
2002 Philadelphia	NL	82	156	38	10	0	12	(6	6)	84	32	28	35	52	2	54	1	1	0	0	1	.00	1	.244	.435	.538
6 ML YEARS		510	1417	372	75	3	52	(24	28)	609	219	209	222	251	10	356	16	9	11	1	3	.25	38	.263	.377	.430

Jay Gibbons

Bats: L **Throws:** L **Pos:** RF-144; 1B-13; DH-5   **Ht:** 6'0" **Wt:** 200 **Born:** 3/2/77 **Age:** 27

Year Team	Lg	G	AB	H	2B	3B	HR	(Hm	Rd)	TB	R	RBI	RC	TBB	IBB	SO	HBP	SH	SF	SB	CS	SB%	GDP	Avg	OBP	Slg
								BATTING												BASERUNNING				AVERAGES		
2001 Baltimore	AL	73	225	53	10	0	15	(9	6)	108	27	36	31	17	0	39	4	0	0	0	1	.00	7	.236	.301	.480
2002 Baltimore	AL	136	490	121	29	1	28	(17	11)	236	71	69	72	45	3	66	2	0	4	1	3	.25	9	.247	.311	.482
2003 Baltimore	AL	160	625	173	39	2	23	(12	11)	285	80	100	96	49	11	89	3	0	5	0	1	.00	12	.277	.330	.456
3 ML YEARS		369	1340	347	78	3	66	(38	28)	629	178	205	199	111	14	194	9	0	9	1	5	.17	28	.259	.318	.469

Benji Gil

Bats: R **Throws:** R **Pos:** 2B-28; SS-20; PH-7; 1B-5; PR-5; 3B-4; DH-1   **Ht:** 6'2" **Wt:** 210 **Born:** 10/6/72 **Age:** 31

Year Team	Lg	G	AB	H	2B	3B	HR	(Hm	Rd)	TB	R	RBI	RC	TBB	IBB	SO	HBP	SH	SF	SB	CS	SB%	GDP	Avg	OBP	Slg
								BATTING												BASERUNNING				AVERAGES		
2003 Buffalo*	AAA	9	36	5	1	0	2	(-	-)	12	4	6	1	0	0	10	0	0	0	0	0	-	1	.139	.139	.333
1993 Texas	AL	22	57	7	0	0	0	(0	0)	7	3	2	0	5	0	22	0	4	0	1	2	.33	0	.123	.194	.123
1995 Texas	AL	130	415	91	20	3	9	(5	4)	144	36	46	36	26	0	147	1	10	2	2	4	.33	5	.219	.266	.347
1996 Texas	AL	5	5	2	0	0	0	(0	0)	2	0	1	1	1	0	1	0	1	0	0	1	.00	0	.400	.500	.400
1997 Texas	AL	110	317	71	13	2	5	(3	2)	103	35	31	26	17	0	96	1	6	4	1	2	.33	3	.224	.263	.325
2000 Anaheim	AL	110	301	72	14	1	6	(4	2)	106	28	23	33	30	0	59	5	5	2	10	6	.63	7	.239	.317	.352
2001 Anaheim	AL	104	260	77	15	4	8	(6	2)	124	33	39	38	14	0	57	0	2	2	3	4	.43	6	.296	.330	.477
2002 Anaheim	AL	61	130	37	8	1	3	(2	1)	56	11	20	19	5	0	33	0	2	2	1	1	.67	0	.285	.307	.431
2003 Anaheim	AL	62	125	24	5	1	1	(1	0)	34	12	9	2	4	1	33	0	4	2	5	1	.83	5	.192	.214	.272
8 ML YEARS		604	1610	381	75	12	32	(21	11)	576	158	171	155	102	1	448	7	34	14	24	21	.53	26	.237	.283	.358

Geronimo Gil

Bats: R **Throws:** R **Pos:** C-53; PH-1   **Ht:** 6'2" **Wt:** 195 **Born:** 8/7/75 **Age:** 28

Year Team	Lg	G	AB	H	2B	3B	HR	(Hm	Rd)	TB	R	RBI	RC	TBB	IBB	SO	HBP	SH	SF	SB	CS	SB%	GDP	Avg	OBP	Slg
								BATTING												BASERUNNING				AVERAGES		
2003 Ottawa*	AAA	36	134	47	10	0	1	(-	-)	60	15	17	22	7	0	28	2	3	2	0	3	.00	2	.351	.386	.448
2001 Baltimore	AL	17	58	17	2	0	0	(0	0)	19	3	6	7	5	0	7	2	1	0	0	0	-	1	.293	.369	.328
2002 Baltimore	AL	125	422	98	19	0	12	(5	7)	153	33	45	33	21	1	88	1	5	1	2	2	.50	17	.232	.270	.363
2003 Baltimore	AL	54	169	40	4	0	3	(2	1)	53	22	16	17	12	0	34	3	2	0	0	0	-	2	.237	.299	.314
3 ML YEARS		196	649	155	25	0	15	(7	8)	225	58	67	57	38	1	129	6	8	1	2	2	.50	20	.239	.287	.347

Brian Giles

Bats: L **Throws:** L **Pos:** LF-128; CF-16   **Ht:** 5'10" **Wt:** 202 **Born:** 1/20/71 **Age:** 33

Year Team	Lg	G	AB	H	2B	3B	HR	(Hm	Rd)	TB	R	RBI	RC	TBB	IBB	SO	HBP	SH	SF	SB	CS	SB%	GDP	Avg	OBP	Slg
								BATTING												BASERUNNING				AVERAGES		
1995 Cleveland	AL	6	9	5	0	0	1	(1	0)	8	6	3	3	0	0	1	0	0	0	0	0	-	0	.556	.556	.889
1996 Cleveland	AL	51	121	43	14	1	5	(2	3)	74	26	27	29	19	4	13	0	0	3	3	0	1.00	6	.355	.434	.612
1997 Cleveland	AL	130	377	101	15	3	17	(7	10)	173	62	61	66	63	2	50	1	3	7	13	3	.81	10	.268	.368	.459
1998 Cleveland	AL	112	350	94	19	0	16	(10	6)	161	56	66	66	73	8	75	3	1	3	10	5	.67	7	.269	.396	.460
1999 Pittsburgh	NL	141	521	164	33	3	39	(24	15)	320	109	115	127	95	7	80	3	0	8	6	2	.75	14	.315	.418	.614
2000 Pittsburgh	NL	156	559	176	37	7	35	(16	19)	332	111	123	139	114	13	69	7	0	8	6	0	1.00	15	.315	.432	.594
2001 Pittsburgh	NL	160	576	178	37	7	37	(18	19)	340	116	95	131	90	14	67	4	0	4	13	6	.68	10	.309	.404	.590
2002 Pittsburgh	NL	153	497	148	37	5	38	(15	23)	309	95	103	131	135	24	74	7	0	5	15	6	.71	10	.298	.450	.622
2003 Pit-SD	NL	134	492	147	34	6	20	(8	12)	253	93	88	103	105	12	58	8	0	4	4	3	.57	12	.299	.427	.514
2003 Pittsburgh	NL	105	388	116	30	4	16	(10	6)	202	70	70	80	85	11	48	6	0	2	0	3	.00	8	.299	.430	.521
2003 San Diego	NL	29	104	31	4	2	4	(2	2)	51	23	18	23	20	1	10	2	0	2	4	0	1.00	4	.298	.414	.490
9 ML YEARS		1043	3502	1056	226	32	208	(104	104)	1970	674	681	795	694	84	487	33	4	42	70	25	.74	84	.302	.417	.563

Marcus Giles

Bats: R **Throws:** R **Pos:** 2B-140; PH-7   **Ht:** 5'8" **Wt:** 180 **Born:** 5/18/78 **Age:** 26

Year Team	Lg	G	AB	H	2B	3B	HR	(Hm	Rd)	TB	R	RBI	RC	TBB	IBB	SO	HBP	SH	SF	SB	CS	SB%	GDP	Avg	OBP	Slg
								BATTING												BASERUNNING				AVERAGES		
2001 Atlanta	NL	68	244	64	10	2	9	(5	4)	105	36	31	33	28	0	37	0	1	0	2	5	.29	8	.262	.338	.430
2002 Atlanta	NL	68	213	49	10	1	8	(4	4)	85	27	23	23	25	3	41	2	1	1	1	1	.50	5	.230	.315	.399
2003 Atlanta	NL	145	551	174	49	2	21	(9	12)	290	101	69	102	59	2	80	11	10	4	14	4	.78	7	.316	.390	.526
3 ML YEARS		281	1008	287	69	5	38	(18	20)	480	164	123	158	112	5	158	13	12	5	17	10	.63	20	.285	.362	.476

Jason Gilfillan

Pitches: R **Bats:** R **Pos:** RP-13   **Ht:** 6'5" **Wt:** 220 **Born:** 8/31/76 **Age:** 27

Year Team	Lg	G	GS	CG	GF	IP	BFP	H	R	ER	HR	SH	SF	HB	TBB	IBB	SO	WP	Bk	W	L	Pct	ShO	Sv-Op	Hld	ERC	ERA
			HOW MUCH HE PITCHED								WHAT HE GAVE UP											THE RESULTS				
1997 Spokane	A-	16	0	0	5	16.0	82	16	13	9	0	1	0	1	16	1	22	3	0	2	1	.667	0	0- -	-	5.51	5.06
1998 Royals	R	7	6	0	0	9.0	42	10	8	8	1	0	1	1	4	0	6	1	0	1	1	.500	0	0- -	-	5.30	8.00
1998 Spokane	A-	6	0	0	0	7.1	36	7	5	4	0	0	1	1	6	0	8	0	0	0	0	-	0	0- -	-	5.04	4.91
1999 Chrlstn - WV	A	8	0	0	1	11.2	66	22	21	19	2	0	0	1	6	0	9	1	0	0	1	.000	0	0- -	-	10.75	14.66
1999 Spokane	A-	25	0	0	7	34.2	161	31	23	22	6	3	4	6	22	0	37	3	1	4	1	.800	0	1- -	-	5.62	5.71
2000 Chrlstn - WV	A	30	0	0	19	45.0	202	45	24	21	3	0	3	4	21	0	44	4	0	1	2	.333	0	7- -	-	4.40	4.20
2000 Wilmington	A+	12	0	0	3	15.1	74	13	6	3	0	0	0	1	13	1	20	2	0	3	1	.750	0	1- -	-	4.11	1.76

Year Team	Lg	G	GS	CG	GF	IP	BFP	H	R	ER	HR	SH	SF	HB	TBB	IBB	SO	WP	Bk	W	L	Pct	ShO	Sv-Op	Hld	ERC	ERA
		HOW MUCH HE PITCHED						**WHAT HE GAVE UP**												**THE RESULTS**							
2000 Omaha	AAA	1	0	0	1	1.0	4	0	0	0	0	0	0	0	1	0	2	0	0	0	0		0	0- -	-	0.95	0.00
2001 Wilmington	A+	33	0	0	23	55.0	219	35	8	6	0	3	0	4	17	1	68	3	0	4	1	.800	0	9- -	-	1.58	0.98
2001 Wichita	AA	11	0	0	3	17.1	89	23	13	12	0	0	1	1	13	2	13	4	0	0	0		0	0- -	-	6.44	6.23
2002 Wichita	AA	21	1	0	8	37.2	176	35	16	11	2	1	4	4	27	5	31	4	0	2	2	.500	0	0- -	-	4.69	2.63
2002 Omaha	AAA	33	0	0	24	39.0	158	32	16	16	5	1	2	3	14	0	28	1	0	2	2	.500	0	4- -	-	3.55	3.69
2003 Omaha	AAA	35	0	0	20	52.2	209	46	14	12	4	0	3	2	12	0	33	0	0	6	0	1.000	0	7- -	-	2.82	2.05
2003 Kansas City	AL	13	0	0	4	16.1	83	22	14	14	3	1	0	1	10	1	12	5	0	2	0	1.000	0	0-1	1	7.66	7.71

Keith Ginter

Bats: R **Throws:** R **Pos:** 2B-53; 3B-40; PH-32; SS-2; LF-2; PR-2   **Ht:** 5'10" **Wt:** 190 **Born:** 5/5/76 **Age:** 28

Year Team	Lg	G	AB	H	2B	3B	HR	(Hm	Rd)	TB	R	RBI	RC	TBB	IBB	SO	HBP	SH	SF	SB	CS	SB%	GDP	Avg	OBP	Slg
		BATTING																		**BASERUNNING**				**AVERAGES**		
2000 Houston	NL	5	8	2	0	0	1	(1	0)	5	3	3	2	1	0	3	0	0	0	0	0	-	0	.250	.300	.625
2001 Houston	NL	1	1	0	0	0	0	(0	0)	0	0	0	0	0	0	0	0	0	0	0	0	-	0	.000	.000	.000
2002 Hou-Mil	NL	28	81	19	9	0	1	(1	0)	31	7	8	13	17	0	15	1	0	0	0	0	-	0	.235	.374	.383
2003 Milwaukee	NL	127	358	92	15	2	14	(9	5)	153	51	44	51	37	1	87	17	0	3	1	1	.50	8	.257	.352	.427
2002 Seattle	NL	7	5	1	1	0	0	(0	0)	2	1	0	1	2	0	1	1	0	0	0	0	-	0	.200	.500	.400
2002 Milwaukee	NL	21	76	18	8	0	1	(1	0)	29	6	8	12	15	0	14	0	0	0	0	0	-	0	.237	.363	.382
4 ML YEARS		161	448	113	24	2	16	(11	5)	189	61	55	66	55	1	105	18	0	4	1	1	.50	8	.252	.354	.422

Matt Ginter

Pitches: R **Bats:** R **Pos:** RP-3   **Ht:** 6'1" **Wt:** 220 **Born:** 12/24/77 **Age:** 26

Year Team	Lg	G	GS	CG	GF	IP	BFP	H	R	ER	HR	SH	SF	HB	TBB	IBB	SO	WP	Bk	W	L	Pct	ShO	Sv-Op	Hld	ERC	ERA
		HOW MUCH HE PITCHED						**WHAT HE GAVE UP**												**THE RESULTS**							
2003 Charlotte*	AAA	49	0	0	27	68.1	298	66	27	23	2	5	2	4	22	3	52	1	0	3	5	.375	0	14- -	-	3.16	3.03
2000 Chicago	AL	7	0	0	3	9.1	52	18	14	14	5	0	1	0	7	0	6	1	0	1	0	1.000	0	0-1	0	16.24	13.50
2001 Chicago	AL	20	0	0	7	39.2	167	34	23	23	2	0	3	7	14	2	24	2	0	1	0	1.000	0	0-0	0	3.44	5.22
2002 Chicago	AL	33	0	0	15	54.1	236	59	34	27	6	0	2	1	21	0	37	2	0	1	0	1.000	0	1-1	0	4.72	4.47
2003 Chicago	AL	3	0	0	0	3.1	15	2	5	5	1	1	0	2	1	0	0	0	0	0	0	-	0	0-0	0	5.16	13.50
4 ML YEARS		63	0	0	25	106.2	470	113	76	69	14	1	6	10	43	2	67	5	0	3	0	1.000	0	1-2	0	5.07	5.82

Charles Gipson

Bats: R **Throws:** R **Pos:** PR-12; CF-8; PH-3; DH-2   **Ht:** 6'1" **Wt:** 195 **Born:** 12/16/72 **Age:** 31

Year Team	Lg	G	AB	H	2B	3B	HR	(Hm	Rd)	TB	R	RBI	RC	TBB	IBB	SO	HBP	SH	SF	SB	CS	SB%	GDP	Avg	OBP	Slg
		BATTING																		**BASERUNNING**				**AVERAGES**		
2003 Columbus*	AAA	31	120	33	6	1	0	(-	-)	41	17	5	14	9	0	18	5	1	0	5	6	.45	1	.275	.351	.342
1998 Seattle	AL	44	51	12	1	0	0	(0	0)	13	11	2	4	5	1	9	1	0	0	2	1	.67	1	.235	.316	.255
1999 Seattle	AL	55	80	18	5	2	0	(0	0)	27	16	9	6	6	0	13	1	2	0	3	4	.43	2	.225	.287	.338
2000 Seattle	AL	59	29	9	1	1	0	(0	0)	12	7	3	4	4	0	9	0	0	0	2	3	.40	0	.310	.394	.414
2001 Seattle	AL	94	64	14	2	2	0	(0	0)	20	16	5	5	4	0	20	2	1	1	1	1	.50	1	.219	.282	.313
2002 Seattle	AL	79	72	17	5	2	0	(0	0)	26	22	8	7	9	0	14	1	2	0	4	0	1.00	3	.236	.329	.361
2003 New York	AL	18	10	2	0	0	0	(0	0)	2	3	2	1	1	0	2	1	0	0	2	1	.67	0	.200	.273	.200
6 ML YEARS		349	306	72	14	7	0	(0	0)	100	75	29	27	29	1	67	5	6	1	14	10	.58	8	.235	.311	.327

Joe Girardi

Bats: R **Throws:** R **Pos:** C-13; PH-4   **Ht:** 5'11" **Wt:** 200 **Born:** 10/14/64 **Age:** 39

Year Team	Lg	G	AB	H	2B	3B	HR	(Hm	Rd)	TB	R	RBI	RC	TBB	IBB	SO	HBP	SH	SF	SB	CS	SB%	GDP	Avg	OBP	Slg
		BATTING																		**BASERUNNING**				**AVERAGES**		
2003 Tennessee*	AA	3	10	4	0	0	0	(-	-)	4	0	1	2	0	0	0	1	0	0	0	1	.00	0	.400	.455	.400
2003 Peoria*	A	3	9	1	0	0	0	(-	-)	1	0	1	0	0	0	2	1	0	0	0	0	-	0	.111	.200	.111
2003 Memphis*	AAA	18	65	19	1	0	0	(-	-)	20	3	4	6	5	0	6	1	0	0	0	0	-	4	.292	.352	.308
1989 Chicago	NL	59	157	39	10	0	1	(0	1)	52	15	14	15	11	5	26	2	1	1	2	1	.67	4	.248	.304	.331
1990 Chicago	NL	133	419	113	24	2	1	(1	0)	144	36	38	40	17	11	50	3	4	4	8	3	.73	13	.270	.300	.344
1991 Chicago	NL	21	47	9	2	0	0	(0	0)	11	3	6	3	6	1	6	0	1	0	0	0	-	0	.191	.283	.234
1992 Chicago	NL	91	270	73	3	1	1	(1	0)	81	19	12	24	19	3	38	1	0	1	0	2	.00	8	.270	.320	.300
1993 Colorado	NL	86	310	90	14	5	3	(2	1)	123	35	31	42	24	0	41	3	12	1	6	6	.50	6	.290	.346	.397
1994 Colorado	NL	93	330	91	9	4	4	(1	3)	120	47	34	35	21	1	48	2	6	2	3	3	.50	13	.276	.321	.364
1995 Colorado	NL	125	462	121	17	2	8	(6	2)	166	63	55	47	29	0	76	2	12	1	3	3	.50	15	.262	.308	.359
1996 New York	AL	124	422	124	22	3	2	(1	1)	158	55	45	55	30	1	55	5	11	3	13	4	.76	11	.294	.346	.374
1997 New York	AL	112	398	105	23	1	1	(1	0)	133	38	50	37	26	1	53	2	5	2	2	3	.40	15	.264	.311	.334
1998 New York	AL	78	254	70	11	4	3	(1	2)	98	31	31	27	14	1	38	2	4	0	1	2	.33	10	.276	.317	.386
1999 New York	AL	65	209	50	16	1	2	(1	1)	74	23	27	15	10	0	26	0	8	2	3	1	.75	16	.239	.271	.354
2000 Chicago	NL	106	363	101	15	1	6	(4	2)	136	47	40	45	32	3	61	3	6	3	1	0	1.00	12	.278	.339	.375
2001 Chicago	NL	78	229	58	10	1	3	(1	2)	79	22	25	25	21	4	50	0	2	1	0	1	.00	9	.253	.315	.345
2002 Chicago	NL	90	234	53	10	1	1	(0	1)	68	19	13	16	16	3	35	0	5	1	1	0	1.00	10	.226	.275	.291
2003 St Louis	NL	16	23	3	0	0	0	(0	0)	3	1	1	0	3	0	4	0	0	0	0	0	-	2	.130	.231	.130
15 ML YEARS		1277	4127	1100	186	26	36	(20	16)	1446	454	422	426	279	34	607	25	81	23	44	31	.59	137	.267	.315	.350

Doug Glanville

Bats: R **Throws:** R **Pos:** CF-67; PH-14; LF-3; RF-1   **Ht:** 6'2" **Wt:** 174 **Born:** 8/25/70 **Age:** 33

Year Team	Lg	G	AB	H	2B	3B	HR	(Hm	Rd)	TB	R	RBI	RC	TBB	IBB	SO	HBP	SH	SF	SB	CS	SB%	GDP	Avg	OBP	Slg
		BATTING																		**BASERUNNING**				**AVERAGES**		
2003 Frisco*	AA	4	15	2	0	0	0	(-	-)	2	2	0	0	1	0	4	0	0	0	0	0	-	0	.133	.188	.133
2003 Oklahoma*	AAA	9	37	6	0	0	0	(-	-)	6	4	3	1	2	1	3	1	0	0	1	0	1.00	1	.162	.225	.162
1996 Chicago	NL	49	83	20	5	1	1	(1	0)	30	10	10	9	3	0	11	0	2	1	2	0	1.00	0	.241	.264	.361
1997 Chicago	NL	146	474	142	22	5	4	(2	2)	186	79	35	60	24	0	46	1	9	2	19	11	.63	9	.300	.333	.392
1998 Philadelphia	NL	158	**678**	189	28	7	8	(3	5)	255	106	49	86	42	1	89	6	5	4	23	6	.79	7	.279	.325	.376
1999 Philadelphia	NL	150	628	204	38	6	11	(5	6)	287	101	73	112	48	1	82	6	5	5	34	2	**.94**	9	.325	.376	.457

Year Team	Lg	G	AB	H	2B	3B	HR	(Hm	Rd)	TB	R	RBI	RC	TBB	IBB	SO	HBP	SH	SF	SB	CS	SB%	GDP	Avg	OBP	Slg
										BATTING										**BASERUNNING**				**AVERAGES**		
2000 Philadelphia	NL	154	637	175	27	6	8	(3	5)	238	89	52	75	31	1	76	2	12	7	31	8	.79	11	.275	.307	.374
2001 Philadelphia	NL	153	634	166	24	3	14	(6	8)	238	74	55	70	19	1	91	4	10	7	28	6	.82	7	.262	.285	.375
2002 Philadelphia	NL	138	422	105	16	3	6	(3	3)	145	49	29	34	25	4	57	2	8	3	19	2	.90	5	.249	.292	.344
2003 Tex-ChC	AL	80	246	65	5	0	5	(3	2)	85	24	16	18	8	1	29	0	3	1	4	1	.80	2	.264	.286	.346
2003 Texas	AL	52	195	53	5	0	4	(2	2)	70	22	14	15	6	1	25	0	2	0	4	0	1.00	2	.272	.294	.359
2003 Chicago	NL	28	51	12	0	0	1	(1	0)	15	2	2	3	2	0	4	0	1	1	0	1	.00	0	.235	.259	.294
8 ML YEARS		1028	3802	1066	165	31	57	(26	31)	1464	532	319	464	200	9	481	21	54	30	160	36	.82	50	.280	.318	.385

Troy Glaus

Bats: R **Throws:** R **Pos:** 3B-87; DH-4   **Ht:** 6'5" **Wt:** 245 **Born:** 8/3/76 **Age:** 27

Year Team	Lg	G	AB	H	2B	3B	HR	(Hm	Rd)	TB	R	RBI	RC	TBB	IBB	SO	HBP	SH	SF	SB	CS	SB%	GDP	Avg	OBP	Slg
										BATTING										**BASERUNNING**				**AVERAGES**		
2003 R Cucamnga*	A+	2	6	2	0	0	0	(-	-)	2	1	1	2	3	0	2	0	0	0	0	0	-	0	.333	.556	.333
1998 Anaheim	AL	48	165	36	9	0	1	(0	1)	48	19	23	13	15	0	51	0	0	2	1	0	1.00	3	.218	.280	.291
1999 Anaheim	AL	154	551	132	29	0	29	(12	17)	248	85	79	84	71	1	143	6	0	3	5	1	.83	9	.240	.331	.450
2000 Anaheim	AL	159	563	160	37	1	47	(24	23)	340	120	102	129	112	6	163	2	0	1	14	11	.56	14	.284	.404	.604
2001 Anaheim	AL	161	588	147	38	2	41	(22	19)	312	100	108	114	107	7	158	6	0	7	10	3	.77	16	.250	.367	.531
2002 Anaheim	AL	156	569	142	24	1	30	(13	17)	258	99	111	100	88	4	144	6	0	8	10	3	.77	12	.250	.352	.453
2003 Anaheim	AL	91	319	79	17	2	16	(9	7)	148	53	50	49	46	4	73	1	0	1	7	2	.78	8	.248	.343	.464
6 ML YEARS		769	2755	696	154	6	164	(80	84)	1354	476	473	489	439	22	732	21	0	22	47	20	.70	62	.253	.357	.491

Mike Glavine

Bats: L **Throws:** L **Pos:** PH-4; 1B-3   **Ht:** 6'3" **Wt:** 210 **Born:** 1/24/73 **Age:** 31

Year Team	Lg	G	AB	H	2B	3B	HR	(Hm	Rd)	TB	R	RBI	RC	TBB	IBB	SO	HBP	SH	SF	SB	CS	SB%	GDP	Avg	OBP	Slg
										BATTING										**BASERUNNING**				**AVERAGES**		
1995 Burlington	R+	46	155	38	10	0	11	(-	-)	81	28	28	29	22	0	37	1	0	2	1	0	1.00	0	.245	.339	.523
1996 Columbus	A	38	119	33	5	0	6	(-	-)	56	17	16	24	28	2	33	1	0	1	0	0	-	2	.277	.416	.471
1997 Columbus	A	114	397	95	16	0	28	(-	-)	195	62	75	72	80	1	127	3	0	1	0	1	.00	9	.239	.370	.491
1998 Kinston	A+	125	398	87	23	1	22	(-	-)	178	61	76	64	73	4	117	5	2	6	1	4	.20	4	.219	.342	.447
1999 Greenville	AA	107	305	82	24	0	17	(-	-)	157	47	52	58	49	0	65	1	0	2	0	3	.00	3	.269	.370	.515
2000 Greenville	AA	128	423	99	26	0	11	(-	-)	158	37	81	47	36	3	83	5	0	7	1	1	.50	8	.234	.297	.374
2001 Richmond	AAA	23	44	6	2	0	0	(-	-)	8	1	4	1	6	2	11	0	0	1	0	0	-	1	.136	.235	.182
2001 Somerset	IND	68	254	62	14	0	11	(-	-)	109	24	41	33	27	0	55	1	1	4	2	3	.40	6	.244	.315	.429
2002 Somerset	IND	125	454	124	29	0	21	(-	-)	216	64	66	72	41	1	82	1	1	2	2	0	1.00	5	.273	.333	.476
2003 Norfolk	AAA	79	169	45	11	0	5	(-	-)	71	15	17	26	25	4	36	0	1	2	0	0	-	4	.266	.357	.420
2003 New York	NL	6	7	1	0	0	0	(0	0)	1	0	0	0	0	0	2	0	0	0	0	0	-	0	.143	.143	.143

Tom Glavine

Pitches: L **Bats:** L **Pos:** SP-32   **Ht:** 6'0" **Wt:** 185 **Born:** 3/25/66 **Age:** 38

Year Team	Lg	G	GS	CG	GF	IP	BFP	H	R	ER	HR	SH	SF	HB	TBB	IBB	SO	WP	Bk	W	L	Pct	ShO	Sv-Op	Hld	ERC	ERA
		HOW MUCH HE PITCHED						**WHAT HE GAVE UP**												**THE RESULTS**							
1987 Atlanta	NL	9	9	0	0	50.1	238	55	34	31	5	2	3	3	33	4	20	1	1	2	4	.333	0	0-0	0	5.70	5.54
1988 Atlanta	NL	34	34	1	0	195.1	844	201	111	99	12	17	11	8	63	7	84	2	2	7	17	.292	0	0-0	0	3.74	4.56
1989 Atlanta	NL	29	29	6	0	186.0	766	172	88	76	20	11	4	2	40	3	90	2	0	14	8	.636	4	0-0	0	2.99	3.68
1990 Atlanta	NL	33	33	1	0	214.1	929	232	111	102	18	21	2	1	78	10	129	8	1	10	12	.455	0	0-0	0	4.24	4.28
1991 Atlanta	NL	34	34	9	0	246.2	989	201	83	70	17	7	6	2	69	6	192	10	2	20	11	.645	1	0-0	0	2.47	2.55
1992 Atlanta	NL	33	33	7	0	225.0	919	197	81	69	6	2	6	2	70	7	129	5	0	20	8	.714	5	0-0	0	2.61	2.76
1993 Atlanta	NL	36	36	4	0	239.1	1014	236	91	85	16	10	2	2	90	7	120	4	0	22	6	.786	2	0-0	0	3.70	3.20
1994 Atlanta	NL	25	25	2	0	165.1	731	173	76	73	10	9	6	1	70	10	140	6	0	13	9	.591	0	0-0	0	4.02	3.97
1995 Atlanta	NL	29	29	3	0	198.2	822	182	76	68	9	7	5	5	66	0	127	3	0	16	7	.696	1	0-0	0	3.14	3.08
1996 Atlanta	NL	36	36	1	0	235.1	994	222	91	78	14	15	2	0	85	7	181	4	0	15	10	.600	0	0-0	0	3.29	2.98
1997 Atlanta	NL	33	33	5	0	240.0	970	197	86	79	20	11	6	4	79	9	152	3	0	14	7	.667	2	0-0	0	2.80	2.96
1998 Atlanta	NL	33	33	4	0	229.1	934	202	67	63	13	6	2	2	74	2	157	3	0	20	6	.769	3	0-0	0	2.93	2.47
1999 Atlanta	NL	35	35	2	0	234.0	1023	259	115	107	18	22	10	4	83	14	138	2	0	14	11	.560	0	0-0	0	4.31	4.12
2000 Atlanta	NL	35	35	4	0	241.0	992	222	101	91	24	9	5	4	65	6	152	0	0	21	9	.700	2	0-0	0	3.19	3.40
2001 Atlanta	NL	35	35	1	0	219.1	929	213	92	87	24	5	8	2	97	10	116	2	0	16	7	.696	1	0-0	0	4.21	3.57
2002 Atlanta	NL	36	36	2	0	224.2	936	210	85	74	21	12	6	8	78	8	127	2	0	18	11	.621	1	0-0	0	3.61	2.96
2003 New York	NL	32	32	0	0	183.1	790	205	94	92	21	7	4	2	66	7	82	2	0	9	14	.391	0	0-0	0	4.77	4.52
17 ML YEARS		537	537	52	0	3528.0	14820	3379	1482	1344	268	173	88	52	1206	117	2136	61	7	251	157	.615	22	0-0	0	3.49	3.43

Gary Glover

Pitches: R **Bats:** R **Pos:** RP-42   **Ht:** 6'5" **Wt:** 205 **Born:** 12/3/76 **Age:** 27

Year Team	Lg	G	GS	CG	GF	IP	BFP	H	R	ER	HR	SH	SF	HB	TBB	IBB	SO	WP	Bk	W	L	Pct	ShO	Sv-Op	Hld	ERC	ERA
		HOW MUCH HE PITCHED						**WHAT HE GAVE UP**												**THE RESULTS**							
1999 Toronto	AL	1	0	0	1	1.0	3	0	0	0	0	0	0	1	1	0	0	0	0	0	0	-	0	0-0	0	1.26	0.00
2001 Chicago	AL	46	11	0	10	100.1	429	98	61	55	16	2	2	4	32	3	63	4	0	5	5	.500	0	0-1	7	4.12	4.93
2002 Chicago	AL	41	22	0	10	138.1	604	136	86	80	21	6	2	7	52	1	70	6	0	7	8	.467	0	1-1	2	4.39	5.20
2003 CWS-Ana	AL	42	0	0	15	62.2	279	77	33	33	6	0	5	3	22	3	37	2	0	2	0	1.000	0	0-0	1	5.37	4.74
2003 Chicago	AL	24	0	0	8	35.2	160	43	18	18	3	0	3	2	14	2	23	1	0	1	0	1.000	0	0-0	1	5.32	4.54
2003 Anaheim	AL	18	0	0	7	27.0	119	34	15	15	3	0	2	1	8	1	14	1	0	1	0	1.000	0	0-0	0	5.44	5.00
4 ML YEARS		130	33	0	36	302.1	1315	311	180	168	43	8	9	14	107	7	170	12	0	14	13	.519	0	1-2	10	4.49	5.00

Jimmy Gobble

Pitches: L Bats: L Pos: SP-9　　　　　　　　　　Ht: 6'3" Wt: 190 Born: 7/19/81 Age: 22

		HOW MUCH HE PITCHED						WHAT HE GAVE UP										THE RESULTS						
Year Team	Lg	G	GS	CG	GF	IP	BFP	H	R	ER	HR	SH	SF	HB	TBB	IBB	SO	WP	Bk	W	L	Pct	ShO	Sv-Op	Hld	ERC	ERA
1999 Royals	R	4	1	0	0	6.2	32	6	3	2	0	0	0	0	5	0	8	1	1	0	0	-	0	0--	-	3.85	2.70
2000 Chrlstn - WV	A	25	25	3	0	145.0	604	144	75	59	10	1	2	4	34	0	115	1	1	12	10	.545	2	0--	-	3.30	3.66
2001 Wilmington	A	27	27	0	0	162.1	649	134	58	46	8	9	4	9	33	3	154	7	0	10	6	.625	0	0--	-	2.31	2.55
2002 Wichita	AA	13	13	0	0	69.1	291	71	29	26	3	2	2	2	19	2	52	5	0	5	7	.417	0	0--	-	3.43	3.38
2003 Wichita	AA	22	22	2	0	132.2	559	128	57	47	11	5	5	5	40	1	100	5	0	12	8	.600	1	0--	-	3.52	3.19
2003 Kansas City	AL	9	9	0	0	52.2	230	56	32	27	8	1	3	4	15	0	31	1	0	4	5	.444	0	0-0	0	4.61	4.61

Jonny Gomes

Bats: R Throws: R Pos: DH-6; PH-4　　　　　　　　　　Ht: 6'1" Wt: 205 Born: 11/22/80 Age: 23

		BATTING																		BASERUNNING				AVERAGES		
Year Team	Lg	G	AB	H	2B	3B	HR	(Hm	Rd)	TB	R	RBI	RC	TBB	IBB	SO	HBP	SH	SF	SB	CS	SB%	GDP	Avg	OBP	Slg
2001 Princeton	R+	62	206	60	11	2	16	(-	-)	123	58	44	57	33	0	73	26	1	4	15	4	.79	1	.291	.442	.597
2002 Bakersfield	A+	134	446	124	24	9	30	(-	-)	256	102	72	113	91	6	173	31	0	1	15	3	.83	4	.278	.432	.574
2003 Orlando	AA	120	442	110	28	3	17	(-	-)	195	68	56	74	53	1	148	16	0	4	23	2	.92	5	.249	.348	.441
2003 Durham	AAA	5	19	6	2	1	0	(-	-)	10	2	1	4	2	0	5	2	0	0	0	0	-	0	.316	.435	.526
2003 Tampa Bay	AL	8	15	2	1	0	0	(0	0)	3	1	0	0	0	0	6	1	0	0	0	0	-	0	.133	.188	.200

Chris Gomez

Bats: R Throws: R Pos: 2B-23; 3B-18; SS-17; PH-7; PR-2　　　　　　　　　　Ht: 6'1" Wt: 185 Born: 6/16/71 Age: 33

		BATTING																		BASERUNNING				AVERAGES		
Year Team	Lg	G	AB	H	2B	3B	HR	(Hm	Rd)	TB	R	RBI	RC	TBB	IBB	SO	HBP	SH	SF	SB	CS	SB%	GDP	Avg	OBP	Slg
1993 Detroit	AL	46	128	32	7	1	0	(0	0)	41	11	11	12	9	0	17	1	3	0	2	2	.50	2	.250	.304	.320
1994 Detroit	AL	84	296	76	19	0	8	(5	3)	119	32	53	39	33	0	64	3	3	1	5	3	.63	8	.257	.336	.402
1995 Detroit	AL	123	431	96	20	2	11	(5	6)	153	49	50	43	41	0	96	3	3	4	4	1	.80	13	.223	.292	.355
1996 Det-SD		137	456	117	21	1	4	(2	2)	152	53	45	52	57	1	84	7	6	2	3	3	.50	16	.257	.347	.333
1997 San Diego	NL	150	522	132	19	2	5	(2	3)	170	62	54	52	53	1	114	5	3	3	5	8	.38	16	.253	.326	.326
1998 San Diego	NL	145	449	120	32	3	4	(3	1)	170	55	39	58	51	7	87	5	7	3	1	3	.25	11	.267	.346	.379
1999 San Diego	NL	76	234	59	8	1	1	(1	0)	72	20	15	23	27	3	49	1	2	1	1	2	.33	6	.252	.331	.308
2000 San Diego	NL	33	54	12	0	0	0	(0	0)	12	4	3	4	7	0	5	0	1	1	0	0	-	1	.222	.306	.222
2001 SD-TB		98	301	78	19	0	8	(5	3)	121	37	43	36	17	0	38	2	6	5	4	0	1.00	6	.259	.298	.402
2002 Tampa Bay	AL	130	461	122	31	3	10	(2	8)	189	51	46	52	21	0	58	7	6	3	1	3	.25	8	.265	.305	.410
2003 Minnesota	AL	58	175	44	9	3	1	(0	1)	62	14	15	15	7	1	13	0	2	1	1	2	.67	10	.251	.279	.354
1996 Detroit	AL	48	128	31	5	0	1	(1	0)	39	21	16	13	18	0	20	1	3	0	1	1	.50	5	.242	.340	.305
1996 San Diego	NL	89	328	86	16	1	3	(1	2)	113	32	29	39	39	1	64	6	3	2	2	2	.50	11	.262	.349	.345
2001 San Diego	NL	40	112	21	3	0	0	(0	0)	24	6	7	4	9	0	14	0	2	2	1	0	1.00	5	.188	.244	.214
2001 Tampa Bay	AL	58	189	57	16	0	8	(5	3)	97	31	36	32	8	0	24	2	4	3	3	0	1.00	4	.302	.332	.513
11 ML YEARS		1080	3507	888	185	16	52	(25	27)	1261	388	374	386	323	13	625	34	42	24	28	26	.52	100	.253	.320	.360

Alex Gonzalez

Bats: R Throws: R Pos: SS-150　　　　　　　　　　Ht: 6'0" Wt: 200 Born: 2/15/77 Age: 27

		BATTING																		BASERUNNING				AVERAGES		
Year Team	Lg	G	AB	H	2B	3B	HR	(Hm	Rd)	TB	R	RBI	RC	TBB	IBB	SO	HBP	SH	SF	SB	CS	SB%	GDP	Avg	OBP	Slg
1998 Florida	NL	25	86	13	2	0	3	(1	2)	24	11	7	5	9	0	30	1	2	0	0	-	-	2	.151	.240	.279
1999 Florida	NL	136	560	155	28	8	14	(7	7)	241	81	59	69	15	0	113	12	1	3	3	5	.38	13	.277	.308	.430
2000 Florida	NL	109	385	77	17	4	7	(5	2)	123	35	42	26	13	0	77	2	5	2	7	1	.88	7	.200	.229	.319
2001 Florida	NL	145	515	129	36	1	9	(5	4)	194	57	48	56	30	6	107	10	3	3	2	2	.50	13	.250	.303	.377
2002 Florida	NL	42	151	34	7	1	2	(1	1)	49	15	18	14	12	1	32	4	3	2	3	1	.75	2	.225	.296	.325
2003 Florida	NL	150	528	135	33	6	18	(7	11)	234	52	77	68	33	13	106	13	3	5	0	4	.00	8	.256	.313	.443
6 ML YEARS		607	2225	543	123	20	53	(26	27)	865	251	251	238	112	20	465	42	17	15	15	13	.54	45	.244	.291	.389

Alex S Gonzalez

Bats: R Throws: R Pos: SS-150; PH-4　　　　　　　　　　Ht: 6'0" Wt: 200 Born: 4/8/73 Age: 31

		BATTING																		BASERUNNING				AVERAGES		
Year Team	Lg	G	AB	H	2B	3B	HR	(Hm	Rd)	TB	R	RBI	RC	TBB	IBB	SO	HBP	SH	SF	SB	CS	SB%	GDP	Avg	OBP	Slg
1994 Toronto	AL	15	53	8	3	1	0	(0	0)	13	7	1	2	4	0	17	1	1	0	3	0	1.00	1	.151	.224	.245
1995 Toronto	AL	111	367	89	19	4	10	(8	2)	146	51	42	47	44	1	114	1	9	4	4	4	.50	7	.243	.322	.398
1996 Toronto	AL	147	527	124	30	5	14	(3	11)	206	64	64	61	45	0	127	5	7	3	16	6	.73	12	.235	.300	.391
1997 Toronto	AL	126	426	102	23	2	12	(4	8)	165	46	35	50	34	1	94	5	11	2	15	6	.71	9	.239	.302	.387
1998 Toronto	AL	158	568	136	28	1	13	(7	6)	205	70	51	56	28	1	121	6	13	3	21	6	.78	13	.239	.281	.361
1999 Toronto	AL	38	154	45	13	0	2	(1	1)	64	22	12	23	16	0	23	3	0	0	4	2	.67	4	.292	.370	.416
2000 Toronto	AL	141	527	133	31	2	15	(5	10)	213	68	69	64	43	0	113	4	16	1	4	4	.50	14	.252	.313	.404
2001 Toronto	AL	154	636	161	25	5	17	(9	8)	247	79	76	72	43	0	149	7	7	10	18	11	.62	16	.253	.303	.388
2002 Chicago	NL	142	513	127	27	5	18	(13	5)	218	58	61	59	46	7	136	3	4	2	5	3	.63	11	.248	.312	.425
2003 Chicago	NL	152	536	122	37	0	20	(11	9)	219	71	59	59	47	1	123	6	8	4	3	3	.50	17	.228	.295	.409
10 ML YEARS		1184	4307	1047	236	25	121	(61	60)	1696	536	470	493	350	11	1017	41	76	29	93	45	.67	105	.243	.304	.394

Edgar Gonzalez

Pitches: R Bats: R Pos: RP-7; SP-2　　　　　　　　　　Ht: 6'0" Wt: 215 Born: 2/23/83 Age: 21

		HOW MUCH HE PITCHED						WHAT HE GAVE UP										THE RESULTS						
Year Team	Lg	G	GS	CG	GF	IP	BFP	H	R	ER	HR	SH	SF	HB	TBB	IBB	SO	WP	Bk	W	L	Pct	ShO	Sv-Op	Hld	ERC	ERA
2002 South Bend	A	23	23	4	0	151.1	625	141	66	49	4	4	7	7	34	0	110	10	1	11	8	.579	2	0--	-	2.73	2.91
2002 Lancaster	A+	4	4	0	0	23.0	97	24	7	2	1	0	1	2	3	0	21	0	0	3	0	1.000	0	0--	-	3.19	0.78
2003 El Paso	AA	6	6	0	0	36.0	155	40	18	14	1	1	0	1	11	0	30	3	0	2	2	.500	0	0--	-	3.96	3.50
2003 Tucson	AAA	20	19	1	1	129.2	542	126	65	54	4	6	5	8	28	0	69	5	1	8	7	.533	0	0--	-	2.98	3.75
2003 Arizona	NL	9	2	0	1	18.1	85	28	10	10	3	1	1	0	7	2	14	2	0	2	1	.667	0	0-1	0	7.81	4.91

Jeremi Gonzalez

Pitches: R **Bats:** R **Pos:** SP-25   **Ht:** 6'0" **Wt:** 220 **Born:** 1/8/75 **Age:** 29

Year Team	Lg	G	GS	CG	GF	IP	BFP	H	R	ER	HR	SH	SF	HB	TBB	IBB	SO	WP	Bk	W	L	Pct	ShO	Sv-Op	Hld	ERC	ERA
2003 Durham*	AAA	7	6	0	1	32.0	127	24	11	9	2	0	1	1	6	0	33	2	0	1	0	1.000	0	0--	-	1.88	2.53
1997 Chicago	NL	23	23	1	0	144.0	613	126	73	68	16	4	5	2	69	5	93	1	1	11	9	.550	1	0-0	0	3.79	4.25
1998 Chicago	NL	20	20	1	0	110.0	493	124	72	65	13	5	2	3	41	5	70	2	3	7	7	.500	1	0-0	0	4.80	5.32
2003 Tampa Bay	AL	25	25	2	0	156.1	668	131	71	68	18	3	9	12	69	1	97	3	2	6	11	.353	0	0-0	0	3.74	3.91
3 ML YEARS		68	68	4	0	410.1	1774	381	216	201	47	12	16	17	179	11	260	6	6	24	27	.471	2	0-0	0	4.03	4.41

Juan Gonzalez

Bats: R **Throws:** R **Pos:** RF-57; DH-24; PH-1   **Ht:** 6'3" **Wt:** 220 **Born:** 10/16/69 **Age:** 34

Year Team	Lg	G	AB	H	2B	3B	HR	(Hm	Rd)	TB	R	RBI	RC	TBB	IBB	SO	HBP	SH	SF	SB	CS	SB%	GDP	Avg	OBP	Slg
1989 Texas	AL	24	60	9	3	0	1	(1	0)	15	6	7	2	6	0	17	0	2	0	0	0	-	4	.150	.227	.250
1990 Texas	AL	25	90	26	7	1	4	(3	1)	47	11	12	14	2	0	18	2	0	1	0	1	.00	2	.289	.316	.522
1991 Texas	AL	142	545	144	34	1	27	(7	20)	261	78	102	81	42	7	118	5	0	3	4	4	.50	10	.264	.321	.479
1992 Texas	AL	155	584	152	24	2	43	(19	24)	309	77	109	90	35	1	143	5	0	8	0	1	.00	16	.260	.304	.529
1993 Texas	AL	140	536	166	33	1	46	(24	22)	339	105	118	116	37	7	99	13	0	1	4	1	.80	12	.310	.368	.632
1994 Texas	AL	107	422	116	18	4	19	(6	13)	199	57	85	60	30	10	66	7	0	4	6	4	.60	18	.275	.330	.472
1995 Texas	AL	90	352	104	20	2	27	(15	12)	209	57	82	61	17	3	66	0	0	5	0	0	-	15	.295	.324	.594
1996 Texas	AL	134	541	170	33	2	47	(23	24)	348	89	144	119	45	12	82	3	0	3	2	0	1.00	13	.314	.368	.643
1997 Texas	AL	133	533	158	24	3	42	(18	24)	314	87	131	100	33	7	107	3	0	10	0	0	-	12	.296	.335	.589
1998 Texas	AL	154	606	193	50	2	45	(21	24)	382	110	157	128	46	9	126	6	0	11	2	1	.67	20	.318	.366	.630
1999 Texas	AL	144	562	183	36	1	39	(14	25)	338	114	128	121	51	7	105	4	0	12	3	3	.50	10	.326	.378	.601
2000 Detroit	AL	115	461	133	30	2	22	(8	14)	233	69	67	73	32	3	84	2	0	1	1	2	.33	13	.289	.337	.505
2001 Cleveland	AL	140	532	173	34	1	35	(22	13)	314	97	140	108	41	5	94	6	0	16	1	0	1.00	18	.325	.370	.590
2002 Texas	AL	70	277	78	21	1	8	(4	4)	125	38	35	38	17	1	56	1	0	1	2	0	1.00	11	.282	.324	.451
2003 Texas	AL	82	327	96	17	1	24	(11	13)	187	49	70	55	14	1	73	4	0	1	1	1	.50	10	.294	.329	.572
15 ML YEARS		1655	6428	1901	384	24	429	(196	233)	3620	1044	1387	1166	448	73	1254	61	2	77	26	18	.59	181	.296	.344	.563

Luis Gonzalez

Bats: L **Throws:** R **Pos:** LF-154; PH-2   **Ht:** 6'2" **Wt:** 195 **Born:** 9/3/67 **Age:** 36

Year Team	Lg	G	AB	H	2B	3B	HR	(Hm	Rd)	TB	R	RBI	RC	TBB	IBB	SO	HBP	SH	SF	SB	CS	SB%	GDP	Avg	OBP	Slg
1990 Houston	NL	12	21	4	2	0	0	(0	0)	6	1	0	2	2	1	5	0	0	0	0	0	-	0	.190	.261	.286
1991 Houston	NL	137	473	120	28	9	13	(4	9)	205	51	69	64	40	4	101	8	1	4	10	7	.59	9	.254	.320	.433
1992 Houston	NL	122	387	94	19	3	10	(4	6)	149	40	55	41	24	3	52	2	1	2	7	7	.50	6	.243	.289	.385
1993 Houston	NL	154	540	162	34	3	15	(8	7)	247	82	72	90	47	7	83	10	3	10	20	9	.69	9	.300	.361	.457
1994 Houston	NL	112	392	107	29	4	8	(3	5)	168	57	67	57	49	6	57	3	0	6	15	13	.54	10	.273	.353	.429
1995 Hou-ChC	NL	133	471	130	29	8	13	(6	7)	214	69	69	72	57	8	63	6	1	6	6	8	.43	16	.276	.357	.454
1996 Chicago	NL	146	483	131	30	4	15	(6	9)	214	70	79	75	61	8	49	4	1	6	9	6	.60	13	.271	.354	.443
1997 Houston	NL	152	550	142	31	2	10	(4	6)	207	78	68	73	71	7	67	5	0	5	10	7	.59	12	.258	.345	.376
1998 Detroit	AL	154	547	146	35	5	23	(15	8)	260	84	71	89	57	7	62	8	0	3	12	7	.63	9	.267	.340	.475
1999 Arizona	NL	153	614	206	45	4	26	(10	16)	337	112	111	129	66	6	63	7	1	5	9	5	.64	13	.336	.403	.549
2000 Arizona	NL	162	618	192	47	2	31	(14	17)	336	106	114	128	78	6	85	12	2	12	2	4	.33	12	.311	.392	.544
2001 Arizona	NL	162	609	198	36	7	57	(26	31)	419	128	142	164	100	24	83	14	0	5	1	1	.50	14	.325	.429	.688
2002 Arizona	NL	148	524	151	19	3	28	(11	17)	260	90	103	113	97	8	76	5	0	7	9	2	.82	12	.288	.400	.496
2003 Arizona	NL	156	579	176	46	4	26	(16	10)	308	92	104	114	94	17	67	3	0	3	5	3	.63	19	.304	.402	.532
1995 Houston	NL	56	209	54	10	4	6	(1	5)	90	35	35	26	18	3	30	3	1	3	1	3	.25	8	.258	.322	.431
1995 Chicago	NL	77	262	76	19	4	7	(5	2)	124	34	34	46	39	5	33	3	0	3	5	5	.50	8	.290	.384	.473
14 ML YEARS		1903	6808	1959	430	58	275	(117	158)	3330	1060	1124	1211	843	112	913	87	10	79	115	79	.59	154	.288	.370	.489

Mike Gonzalez

Pitches: L **Bats:** R **Pos:** RP-16   **Ht:** 6'2" **Wt:** 213 **Born:** 5/23/78 **Age:** 26

Year Team	Lg	G	GS	CG	GF	IP	BFP	H	R	ER	HR	SH	SF	HB	TBB	IBB	SO	WP	Bk	W	L	Pct	ShO	Sv-Op	Hld	ERC	ERA
1997 Pirates	R	7	3	0	0	29.0	115	21	9	8	0	1	0	1	8	0	33	3	3	2	0	1.000	0	0--	-	1.75	2.48
1997 Augusta	A	4	3	0	1	19.1	76	11	5	4	1	1	0	0	8	0	22	3	0	1	1	.500	0	0--	-	1.68	1.86
1998 Lynchburg	A+	7	7	0	0	28.1	131	40	21	21	5	0	1	3	13	0	22	1	0	0	3	.000	0	0--	-	8.38	6.67
1998 Augusta	A	11	9	0	0	50.2	221	43	24	16	2	1	1	7	26	0	72	3	4	4	2	.667	0	0--	-	3.80	2.84
1999 Lynchburg	A+	20	20	0	0	112.0	478	98	55	50	10	2	1	4	63	0	119	10	0	10	4	.714	0	0--	-	4.19	4.02
1999 Altoona	AA	7	5	0	0	26.2	133	34	25	24	4	2	1	2	19	0	31	3	3	2	3	.400	0	0--	-	7.75	8.10
2000 Pirates	R	2	1	0	1	6.0	35	8	6	3	1	0	0	1	4	0	7	3	0	1	0	1.000	0	0--	-	7.34	4.50
2000 Lynchburg	A+	12	10	0	1	56.0	256	57	34	29	6	5	2	3	34	0	53	1	0	4	3	.571	0	0--	-	5.28	4.66
2001 Lynchburg	A+	14	2	0	7	30.2	127	28	14	10	3	3	1	0	7	1	32	5	1	2	2	.500	0	0--	-	2.83	2.93
2001 Altoona	AA	14	14	1	0	87.1	367	81	38	36	5	6	2	0	36	0	66	2	1	5	4	.556	1	0--	-	3.48	3.71
2002 Altoona	AA	16	16	0	0	85.1	367	77	38	36	4	0	0	4	47	2	82	7	1	8	4	.667	0	0--	-	3.97	3.80
2002 Pirates	R	2	2	0	0	13.1	47	5	1	0	0	0	0	0	3	0	14	0	0	2	0	1.000	0	0--	-	0.63	0.00
2003 Pawtucket	AAA	2	0	0	1	1.2	8	2	0	0	0	0	0	0	1	0	2	0	0	0	0	-	0	1--	-	5.10	0.00
2003 Lynchburg	A+	5	5	0	0	7.0	32	7	9	4	0	1	0	0	5	0	9	0	0	0	1	.000	0	0--	-	4.56	5.14
2003 Altoona	AA	5	0	0	0	7.1	28	4	1	1	1	0	0	0	2	0	10	0	0	0	0	-	0	1--	-	1.58	1.23
2003 Nashville	AAA	7	0	0	2	10.0	45	9	5	5	0	0	0	0	4	1	10	0	0	0	0	-	0	2--	-	3.30	4.50
2003 Pittsburgh	NL	16	0	0	2	8.1	38	7	7	7	4	1	1	0	6	0	6	1	0	0	1	.000	0	0-0	3	7.18	7.56

Raul Gonzalez

Bats: R **Throws:** R **Pos:** LF-45; RF-40; PH-36; CF-25   **Ht:** 5'9" **Wt:** 190 **Born:** 12/27/73 **Age:** 30

					BATTING														BASERUNNING				AVERAGES		
Year Team	Lg	G	AB	H	2B	3B	HR	(Hm	Rd)	TB	R	RBI	RC	TBB	IBB	SO	HBP	SH	SF	SB	CS	SB%	GDP	Avg	OBP	Slg
2003 Norfolk	AAA	32	120	43	3	1	3	(-	-)	57	18	19	24	16	1	23	0	0	1	5	2	.71	3	.358	.431	.475
2000 Chicago	NL	3	2	0	0	0	0	(0	0)	0	0	0	0	0	0	2	0	0	0	0	0	-	0	.000	.000	.000
2001 Cincinnati	NL	11	14	3	0	0	0	(0	0)	3	0	0	1	1	0	3	0	0	0	0	0	-	0	.214	.267	.214
2002 Cin-NYM	NL	40	104	27	3	0	3	(1	2)	39	13	12	13	6	0	22	0	0	1	4	2	.67	1	.260	.297	.375
2003 New York	NL	107	217	50	12	2	2	(1	1)	72	28	21	26	27	1	34	1	0	1	3	0	1.00	6	.230	.317	.332
2002 Cincinnati	NL	10	23	6	1	0	0	(0	0)	7	4	1	2	2	0	5	0	0	0	2	0	1.00	1	.261	.320	.304
2002 New York	NL	30	81	21	2	0	3	(1	2)	32	9	11	11	4	0	17	0	0	1	2	2	.50	2	.259	.291	.395
4 ML YEARS		161	337	80	15	2	5	(2	3)	114	41	33	40	34	1	61	1	0	2	7	2	.78	11	.237	.307	.338

Wiki Gonzalez

Bats: R **Throws:** R **Pos:** C-23; PH-2   **Ht:** 5'11" **Wt:** 203 **Born:** 5/17/74 **Age:** 30

					BATTING														BASERUNNING				AVERAGES		
Year Team	Lg	G	AB	H	2B	3B	HR	(Hm	Rd)	TB	R	RBI	RC	TBB	IBB	SO	HBP	SH	SF	SB	CS	SB%	GDP	Avg	OBP	Slg
2003 Portland*	AAA	44	149	42	8	1	4	(-	-)	64	17	20	25	21	0	12	3	1	1	1	0	1.00	5	.282	.379	.430
1999 San Diego	NL	30	83	21	2	1	3	(1	2)	34	7	12	7	1	0	8	1	0	0	0	0	-	5	.253	.271	.410
2000 San Diego	NL	95	284	66	15	1	5	(1	4)	98	25	30	30	30	4	31	3	1	1	1	2	.33	5	.232	.311	.345
2001 San Diego	NL	64	160	44	6	0	8	(5	3)	74	16	27	25	11	1	28	4	0	1	2	0	1.00	3	.275	.335	.463
2002 San Diego	NL	112	328	72	16	2	2	(2	0)	98	32	40	32	54	6	48	2	0	4	0	0	-	20	.220	.330	.299
2003 San Diego	NL	24	65	13	5	0	0	(0	0)	18	1	10	7	5	1	13	1	1	1	0	0	-	3	.200	.264	.277
2002 San Diego	NL	56	164	36	8	1	1	(1	0)	49	16	20	15	27	3	24	1	0	2	0	0	-	10	.220	.330	.299
2002 San Diego	NL	56	164	36	8	1	1	(1	0)	49	16	20	17	27	3	24	1	0	2	0	0	-	10	.220	.330	.299
5 ML YEARS		325	920	216	44	4	18	(9	9)	322	81	119	101	101	12	128	11	2	7	3	2	.60	36	.235	.316	.350

Andy Good

Pitches: R **Bats:** R **Pos:** SP-10; RP-6   **Ht:** 6'1" **Wt:** 209 **Born:** 9/19/79 **Age:** 24

		HOW MUCH HE PITCHED						WHAT HE GAVE UP										THE RESULTS					
Year Team	Lg	G	GS	CG	GF	IP	BFP	H	R	ER	HR	SH	SF	HB	TBB	IBB	SO	WP	Bk	W	L	Pct	ShO	Sv-Op	Hld	ERC	ERA
1998 Diamndbcks	R	9	8	0	0	33.2	152	46	25	16	1	0	1	2	7	0	25	3	0	1	3	.250	0	0- -	-	5.13	4.28
1998 South Bend	A	2	0	0	1	6.0	28	7	4	2	0	0	0	2	1	0	6	0	1	0	1	.000	0	0- -	-	4.53	3.00
1999 South Bend	A	27	27	0	0	153.2	662	160	80	70	9	3	9	9	42	0	146	7	0	11	10	.524	0	0- -	-	3.72	4.10
2001 Lancaster	A+	19	18	0	0	101.1	454	108	63	54	12	6	4	13	27	0	104	5	0	8	6	.571	0	0- -	-	4.43	4.80
2001 El Paso	AA	10	9	0	0	56.2	270	79	44	37	2	1	2	3	20	0	46	3	0	2	3	.400	0	0- -	-	5.80	5.88
2002 El Paso	AA	28	27	2	0	178.0	730	170	89	70	21	5	6	7	26	0	127	3	0	13	6	.684	1	0- -	-	3.09	3.54
2003 Tucson	AAA	11	11	0	0	63.0	276	78	36	35	12	1	0	2	13	0	45	1	0	4	4	.500	0	0- -	-	5.45	5.00
2003 Arizona	NL	16	10	0	0	66.1	289	74	42	39	15	3	4	3	16	2	42	3	0	4	2	.667	0	0- -	1	5.06	5.29

Tom Goodwin

Bats: L **Throws:** R **Pos:** PH-32; CF-27; LF-17; RF-15; PR-7   **Ht:** 6'1" **Wt:** 175 **Born:** 7/27/68 **Age:** 35

					BATTING														BASERUNNING				AVERAGES		
Year Team	Lg	G	AB	H	2B	3B	HR	(Hm	Rd)	TB	R	RBI	RC	TBB	IBB	SO	HBP	SH	SF	SB	CS	SB%	GDP	Avg	OBP	Slg
1991 Los Angeles	NL	16	7	1	0	0	0	(0	0)	1	3	0	0	0	0	0	0	0	0	1	1	.50	0	.143	.143	.143
1992 Los Angeles	NL	57	73	17	1	1	0	(0	0)	20	15	3	6	6	0	10	0	4	0	7	3	.70	0	.233	.291	.274
1993 Los Angeles	NL	30	17	5	1	0	0	(0	0)	6	6	1	1	1	0	4	0	0	0	1	2	.33	1	.294	.333	.353
1994 Kansas City	AL	2	2	0	0	0	0	(0	0)	0	0	0	0	0	0	1	0	0	0	0	0	-	0	.000	.000	.000
1995 Kansas City	AL	133	480	138	16	3	4	(2	2)	172	72	28	64	38	0	72	5	14	0	50	18	.74	7	.288	.346	.358
1996 Kansas City	AL	143	524	148	14	4	1	(0	1)	173	80	35	65	39	0	79	2	21	1	66	22	.75	3	.282	.334	.330
1997 KC-Tex	AL	150	574	149	26	6	2	(0	2)	193	90	39	65	44	1	88	3	11	3	50	16	.76	7	.260	.314	.336
1998 Texas	AL	154	520	151	13	3	2	(2	0)	176	102	33	74	73	0	90	2	10	3	38	20	.66	2	.290	.378	.338
1999 Texas	AL	109	405	105	12	6	3	(1	2)	138	63	33	49	40	0	61	0	7	3	39	11	.78	7	.259	.324	.341
2000 Col-LA	NL	147	528	139	11	9	6	(4	2)	186	94	58	74	68	2	117	1	5	4	55	10	.85	0	.263	.346	.352
2001 Los Angeles	NL	105	286	66	8	5	4	(1	3)	96	51	22	29	23	0	58	0	1	2	22	8	.73	3	.231	.286	.336
2002 San Francisco	NL	78	154	40	5	2	1	(0	1)	52	23	17	21	14	0	25	0	3	0	16	2	.89	3	.260	.321	.338
2003 Chicago	NL	87	171	49	10	0	1	(0	1)	62	26	12	19	11	0	33	0	1	1	19	5	.79	3	.287	.328	.363
1997 Kansas City	AL	97	367	100	13	4	2	(0	2)	127	51	22	42	19	0	51	2	11	1	34	10	.77	5	.272	.311	.346
1997 Texas	AL	53	207	49	13	2	0	(0	0)	66	39	17	23	25	1	37	1	0	2	16	6	.73	2	.237	.319	.319
2000 Colorado	NL	91	317	86	8	8	5	(4	1)	125	65	47	54	50	2	76	1	1	4	39	7	.85	3	.271	.368	.394
2000 Los Angeles	NL	56	211	53	3	1	1	(0	1)	61	29	11	20	18	0	41	0	0	0	16	3	.84	4	.251	.310	.289
13 ML YEARS		1211	3741	1008	117	39	24	(10	14)	1275	625	281	467	357	3	638	13	73	17	364	118	.76	43	.269	.334	.341

Tom Gordon

Pitches: R **Bats:** R **Pos:** RP-66   **Ht:** 5'10" **Wt:** 190 **Born:** 11/18/67 **Age:** 36

		HOW MUCH HE PITCHED						WHAT HE GAVE UP										THE RESULTS					
Year Team	Lg	G	GS	CG	GF	IP	BFP	H	R	ER	HR	SH	SF	HB	TBB	IBB	SO	WP	Bk	W	L	Pct	ShO	Sv-Op	Hld	ERC	ERA
1988 Kansas City	AL	5	2	0	0	15.2	67	16	9	9	1	0	0	0	9	0	18	0	0	0	2	.000	0	0-0	2	4.22	5.17
1989 Kansas City	AL	49	16	1	16	163.0	677	122	67	66	10	4	4	1	86	4	153	12	0	17	9	.654	1	1-7	3	2.97	3.64
1990 Kansas City	AL	32	32	6	0	195.1	858	192	99	81	17	8	2	3	99	1	175	11	0	12	11	.522	1	0-0	0	4.37	3.73
1991 Kansas City	AL	45	14	1	11	158.0	684	129	76	68	16	5	3	4	87	0	167	5	0	9	14	.391	0	1-4	3	3.67	3.87
1992 Kansas City	AL	40	11	0	13	117.2	516	116	60	60	9	2	6	4	55	4	98	5	2	6	10	.375	0	0-2	0	4.17	4.59
1993 Kansas City	AL	48	14	2	18	155.2	651	125	65	62	11	6	6	1	77	5	143	17	0	12	6	.667	0	1-6	2	3.18	3.58
1994 Kansas City	AL	24	24	0	0	155.1	675	136	79	75	15	3	8	3	87	3	126	12	1	11	7	.611	0	0-0	0	4.04	4.35
1995 Kansas City	AL	31	31	2	0	189.0	843	204	97	93	12	7	11	4	89	4	119	9	0	12	12	.500	0	0-0	0	4.59	4.43
1996 Boston	AL	34	34	4	0	215.2	998	249	143	134	28	2	11	6	105	5	171	6	1	12	9	.571	0	0-0	0	5.50	5.59
1997 Boston	AL	42	25	2	16	182.2	774	155	85	76	10	3	4	3	78	1	159	6	0	6	10	.375	1	11-13	0	3.08	3.74
1998 Boston	AL	73	0	0	69	79.1	317	55	24	24	2	2	2	0	25	1	78	9	0	7	4	.636	0	46-47	0	1.72	2.72
1999 Boston	AL	21	0	0	15	17.2	82	17	11	11	2	0	0	1	12	0	24	0	0	0	2	.000	0	11-13	6	5.04	5.60
2001 Chicago	NL	47	0	0	40	45.1	187	32	18	17	4	0	0	1	16	1	67	2	0	1	2	.333	0	27-31	5	2.27	3.38
2002 ChC-Hou	NL	34	0	0	10	42.2	181	42	19	16	3	3	0	1	16	3	48	1	0	1	3	.250	0	0-0	6	3.71	3.38

Year Team	Lg	G	GS	CG	GF	IP	BFP	H	R	ER	HR	SH	SF	HB	TBB	IBB	SO	WP	Bk	W	L	Pct	ShO	Sv-Op	Hld	ERC	ERA
				HOW MUCH HE PITCHED						WHAT HE GAVE UP												THE RESULTS				
2003 Chicago	AL	66	0	0	35	74.0	310	57	29	26	4	4	3	4	31	3	91	5	0	7	6	.538	0	12-17	7	2.74	3.16
2002 Chicago	NL	19	0	0	7	23.2	104	27	12	9	1	4	1	0	10	1	31	0	0	1	1	.500	0	0-0	2	4.75	3.42
2002 Houston	NL	15	0	0	3	19.0	77	15	7	7	2	2	0	0	6	2	17	0	0	0	2	.000	0	0-0	4	2.53	3.32
15 ML YEARS		591	203	18	243	1807.0	7820	1647	901	818	144	49	60	34	870	43	1637	98	4	113	107	.514	4	110-140	25	3.78	4.07

John Grabow

Pitches: L **Bats:** L **Pos:** RP-5

Ht: 6'3" **Wt:** 185 **Born:** 11/4/78 **Age:** 25

Year Team	Lg	G	GS	CG	GF	IP	BFP	H	R	ER	HR	SH	SF	HB	TBB	IBB	SO	WP	Bk	W	L	Pct	ShO	Sv-Op	Hld	ERC	ERA
				HOW MUCH HE PITCHED						WHAT HE GAVE UP												THE RESULTS				
1997 Pirates	R	11	8	0	0	45.1	204	57	32	23	0	1	2	0	14	0	28	3	0	2	7	.222	0	0--	-	4.38	4.57
1998 Augusta	A	17	16	0	0	71.2	329	84	59	46	7	1	5	3	34	0	67	9	0	4	2	.667	0	0--	-	5.52	5.78
1999 Hickory	A	26	26	0	0	156.1	654	152	82	66	16	3	3	5	32	0	164	3	0	9	10	.474	0	0--	-	3.26	3.80
2000 Altoona	AA	24	24	1	0	145.1	637	145	81	70	10	1	6	5	65	0	109	8	1	8	7	.533	0	0--	-	4.16	4.33
2001 Pirates	R	6	6	0	0	12.0	50	11	6	5	1	0	0	1	4	0	9	2	0	0	1	.000	0	0--	-	3.65	3.75
2001 Lynchburg	A+	7	7	0	0	36.2	174	42	30	26	3	3	0	2	26	0	35	2	0	1	3	.250	0	0--	-	6.34	6.38
2001 Altoona	AA	10	10	0	0	50.2	214	30	23	19	1	2	0	2	39	0	42	5	3	5	2	.286	0	0--	-	2.91	3.38
2002 Altoona	AA	28	27	1	1	146.1	653	181	94	89	10	6	6	6	47	0	97	9	5	8	13	.381	1	0--	-	5.09	5.47
2003 Nashville	AAA	17	0	0	4	24.2	112	31	17	13	0	1	0	1	7	2	26	0	0	0	2	.000	0	0--	-	4.07	4.74
2003 Altoona	AA	24	9	0	5	83.0	341	87	34	31	9	6	5	1	19	2	73	3	1	6	1	.857	0	1--	-	3.84	3.36
2003 Pittsburgh	NL	5	0	0	1	5.0	22	6	3	2	0	0	0	0	0	0	9	0	0	0	0	-	0	0-0	0	2.73	3.60

Jason Grabowski

Bats: L **Throws:** R **Pos:** PH-5; RF-3; 3B-1; DH-1

Ht: 6'3" **Wt:** 200 **Born:** 5/24/76 **Age:** 28

Year Team	Lg	G	AB	H	2B	3B	HR	(Hm	Rd)	TB	R	RBI	RC	TBB	IBB	SO	HBP	SH	SF	SB	CS	SB%	GDP	Avg	OBP	Slg
						BATTING														BASERUNNING				AVERAGES		
1997 Pulaski	R+	50	174	51	14	0	4	(-	-)	77	36	24	36	40	2	32	0	1	1	6	1	.86	2	.293	.423	.443
1998 Savannah	A	104	352	95	13	6	14	(-	-)	162	63	52	60	57	0	93	1	0	1	16	9	.64	7	.270	.372	.460
1999 Charlotte	A+	123	434	136	31	6	12	(-	-)	215	68	87	85	65	3	66	5	1	2	13	10	.57	8	.313	.407	.495
1999 Tulsa	AA	2	6	1	0	0	0	(-	-)	1	1	0	1	2	1	2	0	0	0	0	0	-	0	.167	.375	.167
2000 Tulsa	AA	135	493	135	33	5	19	(-	-)	235	93	90	90	81	1	106	4	0	7	8	7	.53	12	.274	.383	.477
2001 Tacoma	AAA	114	394	117	32	3	9	(-	-)	182	60	58	71	61	5	94	2	0	5	7	4	.64	9	.297	.390	.462
2002 Sacramento	AAA	73	265	78	22	3	12	(-	-)	142	50	52	52	39	2	56	1	0	6	6	4	.60	8	.294	.387	.536
2003 Sacramento	AAA	67	250	73	13	2	9	(-	-)	117	44	40	43	31	0	46	0	0	5	7	2	.78	5	.292	.364	.468
2002 Oakland	AL	4	8	3	1	1	0	(0	0)	6	3	1	3	3	0	1	0	0	0	0	0	-	0	.375	.545	.750
2003 Oakland	AL	8	8	0	0	0	0	(0	0)	0	0	0	0	1	0	5	0	0	0	0	0	-	0	.000	.111	.000
2 ML YEARS		12	16	3	1	1	0	(0	0)	6	3	1	3	4	0	6	0	0	0	0	0	-	0	.188	.350	.375

Mark Grace

Bats: L **Throws:** L **Pos:** 1B-39; PH-28; DH-1; PR-1

Ht: 6'2" **Wt:** 200 **Born:** 6/28/64 **Age:** 40

Year Team	Lg	G	AB	H	2B	3B	HR	(Hm	Rd)	TB	R	RBI	RC	TBB	IBB	SO	HBP	SH	SF	SB	CS	SB%	GDP	Avg	OBP	Slg
						BATTING														BASERUNNING				AVERAGES		
1988 Chicago	NL	134	486	144	23	4	7	(0	7)	196	65	57	73	60	5	43	0	0	4	3	3	.50	12	.296	.371	.403
1989 Chicago	NL	142	510	160	28	3	13	(8	5)	233	74	79	94	80	13	42	0	3	3	14	7	.67	13	.314	.405	.457
1990 Chicago	NL	157	589	182	32	1	9	(4	5)	243	72	82	93	59	5	54	5	1	8	15	6	.71	10	.309	.372	.413
1991 Chicago	NL	160	619	169	28	5	8	(5	3)	231	87	58	84	70	7	53	3	4	7	3	4	.43	6	.273	.346	.373
1992 Chicago	NL	158	603	185	37	5	9	(5	4)	259	72	79	100	72	8	36	4	2	8	6	1	.86	14	.307	.380	.430
1993 Chicago	NL	155	594	193	39	4	14	(5	9)	282	86	98	104	71	14	32	1	1	9	8	4	.67	25	.325	.393	.475
1994 Chicago	NL	106	403	120	23	3	6	(5	1)	167	55	44	61	48	5	41	0	0	3	0	1	.00	10	.298	.370	.414
1995 Chicago	NL	143	552	180	51	3	16	(4	12)	285	97	92	110	65	9	46	2	1	7	6	2	.75	10	.326	.395	.516
1996 Chicago	NL	142	547	181	39	1	9	(4	5)	249	88	75	94	62	8	41	1	0	6	2	3	.40	18	.331	.396	.455
1997 Chicago	NL	151	555	177	32	5	13	(6	7)	258	87	78	104	88	3	45	2	1	8	2	4	.33	18	.319	.409	.465
1998 Chicago	NL	158	595	184	39	3	17	(7	10)	280	92	89	109	93	8	56	3	0	7	4	7	.36	17	.309	.401	.471
1999 Chicago	NL	161	593	183	44	5	16	(8	8)	285	107	91	110	83	4	44	2	0	10	3	4	.43	14	.309	.390	.481
2000 Chicago	NL	143	510	143	41	1	11	(3	8)	219	75	82	92	95	11	28	6	2	8	1	2	.33	7	.280	.394	.429
2001 Arizona	NL	145	476	142	31	2	15	(6	9)	222	66	78	87	67	6	36	4	1	4	1	0	1.00	7	.298	.386	.466
2002 Arizona	NL	124	298	75	19	0	7	(4	3)	115	43	48	44	46	6	30	1	0	3	2	0	1.00	5	.252	.351	.386
2003 Arizona	NL	66	135	27	5	0	3	(2	1)	41	13	16	10	16	2	15	0	1	3	0	0	-	6	.200	.279	.304
16 ML YEARS		2245	8065	2445	511	45	173	(76	97)	3565	1179	1146	1369	1075	114	642	34	17	99	70	48	.59	192	.303	.383	.442

Tony Graffanino

Bats: R **Throws:** R **Pos:** SS-36; 2B-29; 3B-21; PH-16; PR-4; 1B-2; DH-1

Ht: 6'1" **Wt:** 190 **Born:** 6/6/72 **Age:** 32

Year Team	Lg	G	AB	H	2B	3B	HR	(Hm	Rd)	TB	R	RBI	RC	TBB	IBB	SO	HBP	SH	SF	SB	CS	SB%	GDP	Avg	OBP	Slg
						BATTING														BASERUNNING				AVERAGES		
1996 Atlanta	NL	22	46	8	1	1	0			11	7	2	3	4	0	13	1	0	1	0	0	-	0	.174	.250	.239
1997 Atlanta	NL	104	186	48	9	1	8	(5	3)	83	33	20	29	26	1	46	1	3	5	6	4	.60	3	.258	.344	.446
1998 Atlanta	NL	105	289	61	14	1	5	(3	2)	92	32	22	22	24	0	68	2	1	1	4	2	.20	7	.211	.275	.318
1999 Tampa Bay	AL	39	130	41	9	4	2	(0	2)	64	20	19	23	9	0	22	1	2	0	3	2	.60	1	.315	.364	.492
2000 TB-CWS	AL	70	168	46	6	1	2	(1	1)	60	33	17	23	22	0	27	2	1	1	7	4	.64	3	.274	.363	.357
2001 Chicago	AL	74	145	44	9	0	2	(1	1)	59	23	15	22	16	0	29	1	4	3	4	1	.80	4	.303	.370	.407
2002 Chicago	AL	70	229	60	12	4	6	(4	2)	98	35	31	34	22	1	38	2	4	2	2	1	.67	2	.262	.329	.428
2003 Chicago	AL	90	250	65	15	3	7	(4	3)	107	51	23	37	24	1	37	3	3	1	8	0	1.00	1	.260	.331	.428
2000 Tampa Bay	AL	13	20	6	1	0	0			7	8	1	2	1	0	2	1	1	0	0	0	-	1	.300	.364	.350
2000 Chicago	AL	57	148	40	5	1	2	(1	1)	53	25	16	21	21	0	25	1	1	1	7	4	.64	1	.270	.363	.358
8 ML YEARS		574	1443	373	75	15	32	(18	14)	574	234	149	193	147	3	280	13	18	14	31	16	.66	20	.258	.330	.398

Danny Graves

Pitches: R **Bats:** R **Pos:** SP-26; RP-4   **Ht:** 6'0" **Wt:** 185 **Born:** 8/7/73 **Age:** 30

		HOW MUCH HE PITCHED						WHAT HE GAVE UP											THE RESULTS						
Year Team	Lg	G	GS	CG	GF	IP	BFP	H	R	ER	HR	SH	SF	HB	TBB	IBB	SO	WP	Bk	W	L	Pct	ShO	Sv-Op	Hld	ERC	ERA
1996 Cleveland	AL	15	0	0	5	29.2	129	29	18	15	2	0	1	0	10	0	22	1	0	2	0	1.000	0	0-1	0	3.37	4.55
1997 Cle-Cin		15	0	0	3	26.0	134	41	22	16	2	3	2	0	20	1	11	1	0	0	0	-	0	0-0	1	9.10	5.54
1998 Cincinnati	NL	62	0	0	35	81.1	340	76	31	30	6	2	5	2	28	4	44	4	0	2	1	.667	0	8-8	6	3.38	3.32
1999 Cincinnati	NL	75	0	0	56	111.0	454	90	42	38	10	5	2	2	49	4	69	3	0	8	7	.533	0	27-36	0	3.25	3.08
2000 Cincinnati	NL	66	0	0	57	91.1	388	81	31	26	8	6	4	3	42	7	53	3	1	10	5	.667	0	30-35	0	3.64	2.56
2001 Cincinnati	NL	66	0	0	54	80.1	337	83	41	37	7	3	2	4	18	6	49	2	1	6	5	.545	0	32-39	0	3.59	4.15
2002 Cincinnati	NL	68	4	0	54	98.2	412	99	37	35	7	3	6	3	25	9	58	5	0	7	3	.700	0	32-39	0	3.33	3.19
2003 Cincinnati	NL	30	26	2	3	169.0	741	204	108	100	30	6	3	7	41	6	60	2	0	4	15	.211	1	2-2	0	5.32	5.33
1997 Cleveland	AL	5	0	0	2	11.1	56	15	8	6	2	0	1	0	9	0	4	0	0	0	0	-	0	0-0	0	8.52	4.76
1997 Cincinnati	NL	10	0	0	1	14.2	78	26	14	10	0	3	1	0	11	1	7	1	0	0	0	-	0	0-0	1	9.52	6.14
8 ML YEARS		397	30	2	267	687.1	2935	703	330	297	72	28	25	21	233	37	366	21	2	39	36	.520	1	131-160	7	4.06	3.89

Shawn Green

Bats: L **Throws:** L **Pos:** RF-157; DH-2; PH-1   **Ht:** 6'4" **Wt:** 200 **Born:** 11/10/72 **Age:** 31

								BATTING													BASERUNNING				AVERAGES		
Year Team	Lg	G	AB	H	2B	3B	HR	(Hm	Rd)	TB	R	RBI	RC	TBB	IBB	SO	HBP	SH	SF	SB	CS	SB%	GDP	Avg	OBP	Slg
1993 Toronto	AL	3	6	0	0	0	0	(0	0)	0	0	0	0	0	0	1	0	0	0	0	0	-	0	.000	.000	.000
1994 Toronto	AL	14	33	3	1	0	0	(0	0)	4	1	1	0	1	0	8	0	0	0	1	0	1.00	1	.091	.118	.121
1995 Toronto	AL	121	379	109	31	4	15	(5	10)	193	52	54	61	20	3	68	3	0	3	1	2	.33	4	.288	.326	.509
1996 Toronto	AL	132	422	118	32	3	11	(7	4)	189	52	45	64	33	3	75	8	0	2	5	1	.83	9	.280	.342	.448
1997 Toronto	AL	135	429	123	22	4	16	(10	6)	201	57	53	70	36	4	99	1	1	4	14	3	.82	6	.287	.340	.469
1998 Toronto	AL	158	630	175	33	4	35	(21	14)	321	106	100	108	50	2	142	5	1	3	35	12	.74	6	.278	.334	.510
1999 Toronto	AL	153	614	190	45	0	42	(20	22)	361	134	123	132	66	4	117	11	0	5	20	7	.74	13	.309	.384	.588
2000 Los Angeles	NL	162	610	164	44	4	24	(15	9)	288	98	99	107	90	9	121	8	0	6	24	5	.83	18	.269	.367	.472
2001 Los Angeles	NL	161	619	184	31	4	49	(19	30)	370	121	125	134	72	10	107	5	0	5	20	4	.83	10	.297	.372	.598
2002 Los Angeles	NL	158	582	166	31	1	42	(18	24)	325	110	114	108	93	22	112	5	0	5	8	5	.62	26	.285	.385	.558
2003 Los Angeles	NL	160	611	171	49	2	19	(10	9)	281	84	85	74	68	2	112	6	0	6	6	2	.75	18	.280	.355	.460
11 ML YEARS		1357	4935	1403	319	26	253	(125	128)	2533	815	799	878	529	59	962	52	2	39	134	41	.77	109	.284	.357	.513

Khalil Greene

Bats: R **Throws:** R **Pos:** SS-20; PH-1   **Ht:** 5'11" **Wt:** 210 **Born:** 10/21/79 **Age:** 24

								BATTING													BASERUNNING				AVERAGES		
Year Team	Lg	G	AB	H	2B	3B	HR	(Hm	Rd)	TB	R	RBI	RC	TBB	IBB	SO	HBP	SH	SF	SB	CS	SB%	GDP	Avg	OBP	Slg
2002 Eugene	A-	10	37	10	1	0	0	(-	-)	11	5	6	5	5	1	6	3	0	0	0	0	-	0	.270	.400	.297
2002 Lk Elsinore	A+	46	183	58	9	1	9	(-	-)	96	33	32	33	12	0	33	4	0	2	0	0	-	7	.317	.368	.525
2003 Portland	AAA	76	319	92	19	0	10	(-	-)	141	42	47	49	20	1	52	11	0	5	5	4	.56	3	.288	.346	.442
2003 Mobile	AA	59	229	63	17	2	3	(-	-)	93	20	20	28	16	0	55	2	0	1	2	3	.40	7	.275	.327	.406
2003 San Diego	NL	20	65	14	4	1	2	(0	2)	26	8	6	4	4	0	19	1	0	0	0	1	.00	3	.215	.271	.400

Todd Greene

Bats: R **Throws:** R **Pos:** C-51; PH-8; 1B-2; DH-2   **Ht:** 5'10" **Wt:** 208 **Born:** 5/8/71 **Age:** 33

								BATTING													BASERUNNING				AVERAGES		
Year Team	Lg	G	AB	H	2B	3B	HR	(Hm	Rd)	TB	R	RBI	RC	TBB	IBB	SO	HBP	SH	SF	SB	CS	SB%	GDP	Avg	OBP	Slg
2003 Frisco*	AA	3	9	3	0	0	2	(-	-)	9	3	4	3	2	0	2	0	0	0	0	0	-	1	.333	.455	1.000
1996 Anaheim	AL	29	79	15	1	0	2	(1	1)	22	9	9	4	4	0	11	1	0	0	2	0	1.00	4	.190	.238	.278
1997 Anaheim	AL	34	124	36	6	0	9	(5	4)	69	24	24	22	7	1	25	0	0	0	2	0	1.00	1	.290	.328	.556
1998 Anaheim	AL	29	71	18	4	0	1	(0	1)	25	3	7	7	2	0	20	0	0	0	0	0	-	0	.254	.274	.352
1999 Anaheim	AL	97	321	78	20	0	14	(7	7)	140	36	42	35	12	0	63	3	0	0	1	4	.20	8	.243	.275	.436
2000 Toronto	AL	34	85	20	2	0	5	(2	3)	37	11	10	9	5	0	18	0	0	0	0	0	-	4	.235	.278	.435
2001 New York	AL	35	96	20	4	0	1	(1	0)	27	9	11	5	3	0	21	1	0	0	0	0	-	3	.208	.240	.281
2002 Texas	AL	42	112	30	5	0	10	(6	4)	65	15	19	12	2	0	23	1	1	2	0	0	-	4	.268	.282	.580
2003 Texas	AL	62	205	47	10	1	10	(4	6)	89	25	20	14	2	0	47	2	0	1	0	0	-	2	.229	.243	.434
8 ML YEARS		362	1093	264	52	1	52	(26	26)	474	132	142	108	37	1	228	8	1	5	5	4	.56	26	.242	.270	.434

Kevin Gregg

Pitches: R **Bats:** R **Pos:** SP-3; RP-2   **Ht:** 6'6" **Wt:** 220 **Born:** 6/20/78 **Age:** 26

				HOW MUCH HE PITCHED					WHAT HE GAVE UP													THE RESULTS					
Year Team	Lg	G	GS	CG	GF	IP	BFP	H	R	ER	HR	SH	SF	HB	TBB	IBB	SO	WP	Bk	W	L	Pct	ShO	Sv-Op	Hld	ERC	ERA
1996 Athletics	R	11	9	0	0	40.2	169	30	14	14	1	1	1	2	21	0	48	11	0	3	3	.500	0	0--	-	2.83	3.10
1997 Visalia	A+	25	24	0	0	115.1	534	116	81	73	8	2	3	5	74	0	136	28	0	6	8	.429	0	0--	-	4.95	5.70
1998 Modesto	A+	30	24	0	3	144.0	640	139	72	61	7	9	2	6	76	2	141	7	0	8	7	.533	0	1--	-	4.13	3.81
1999 Visalia	A+	13	11	1	2	64.0	271	60	34	27	3	1	2	4	23	0	48	7	1	4	4	.500	1	0--	-	3.48	3.80
1999 Midland	AA	16	16	2	0	91.1	380	75	45	38	7	0	2	6	31	1	66	6	0	4	7	.364	0	0--	-	2.96	3.74
1999 Vancouver	AAA	1	1	0	0	5.0	21	6	2	2	0	0	0	0	2	0	4	2	0	1	0	1.000	0	0--	-	4.80	3.60
2000 Midland	AA	28	27	0	0	140.2	655	171	120	100	18	5	6	8	73	0	97	6	0	5	14	.263	0	0--	-	6.34	6.40
2001 Midland	AA	44	1	0	10	81.1	366	88	48	41	5	1	0	4	40	4	72	8	1	5	5	.500	0	1--	-	4.74	4.54
2002 Midland	AA	11	4	0	0	37.2	162	31	20	18	3	0	1	3	18	0	45	3	0	3	3	.500	0	0--	-	3.56	4.30
2002 Sacramento	AAA	16	8	0	2	58.2	280	82	56	49	7	0	4	6	23	0	45	3	1	2	5	.286	0	0--	-	7.04	7.52
2002 Visalia	A+	3	3	0	0	17.1	69	8	5	4	0	2	0	1	9	0	11	2	0	2	1	.667	0	0--	-	1.48	2.08
2003 Salt Lake	AAA	15	15	0	0	91.2	378	90	47	41	10	0	1	8	18	0	75	4	0	7	4	.636	0	0--	-	3.64	4.03
2003 Arkansas	AA	15	11	2	0	66.1	279	60	29	26	2	2	5	4	19	0	60	2	0	4	3	.571	0	0--	-	2.86	3.53
2003 Anaheim	AL	5	3	0	0	24.2	97	18	9	9	3	0	0	1	8	0	14	0	0	2	0	1.000	0	0-0	-	2.74	3.28

Tom Gregorio

Bats: R **Throws:** R **Pos:** C-12; PH-1 **Ht:** 6'2" **Wt:** 215 **Born:** 5/5/77 **Age:** 27

Year Team	Lg	G	AB	H	2B	3B	HR	(Hm Rd)	TB	R	RBI	RC	TBB	IBB	SO	HBP	SH	SF	SB	CS	SB%	GDP	Avg	OBP	Slg
1999 Boise	A-	52	186	55	10	1	5	(- -)	82	29	36	27	11	0	33	2	0	3	0	1	.00	3	.296	.338	.441
2000 Cedar Rpds	A	106	379	93	17	0	6	(- -)	128	46	41	39	35	4	79	7	3	2	2	1	.67	13	.245	.319	.338
2001 Angels	R	4	11	3	0	0	0	(- -)	3	1	1	2	3	0	2	0	0	0	0	0	-	0	.273	.429	.273
2001 Arkansas	AA	45	157	30	10	0	1	(- -)	43	15	23	9	7	0	31	4	2	1	0	0	-	3	.191	.243	.274
2002 Arkansas	AA	56	188	47	10	1	3	(- -)	68	18	15	20	9	0	33	2	3	0	2	0	1.00	3	.250	.291	.362
2002 Salt Lake	AAA	15	51	13	4	0	1	(- -)	20	7	3	6	2	0	14	2	0	0	0	1	.00	1	.255	.309	.392
2003 Salt Lake	AAA	54	181	40	10	0	5	(- -)	65	26	24	19	14	0	44	4	0	1	0	0	-	1	.221	.290	.359
2003 Anaheim	AL	12	19	3	0	0	0	(0 0)	3	1	2	1	1	0	8	1	0	0	0	0	-	0	.158	.238	.158

Ben Grieve

Bats: L **Throws:** R **Pos:** DH-36; RF-10; PH-9 **Ht:** 6'4" **Wt:** 216 **Born:** 5/4/76 **Age:** 28

Year Team	Lg	G	AB	H	2B	3B	HR	(Hm Rd)	TB	R	RBI	RC	TBB	IBB	SO	HBP	SH	SF	SB	CS	SB%	GDP	Avg	OBP	Slg
1997 Oakland	AL	24	93	29	6	0	3	(3 0)	44	12	24	18	13	1	25	1	1	0	0	0	-	1	.312	.402	.473
1998 Oakland	AL	155	583	168	41	2	18	(5 13)	267	94	89	101	85	3	123	9	0	1	2	2	.50	18	.288	.386	.458
1999 Oakland	AL	148	486	129	21	0	28	(13 15)	234	80	86	81	63	2	108	8	0	1	4	0	1.00	17	.265	.358	.481
2000 Oakland	AL	158	594	166	40	1	27	(13 14)	289	92	104	95	73	2	130	3	0	5	3	0	1.00	32	.279	.359	.487
2001 Tampa Bay	AL	154	542	143	30	2	11	(5 6)	210	72	72	82	87	2	159	8	0	2	7	1	.88	13	.264	.372	.387
2002 Tampa Bay	AL	136	482	121	30	0	19	(7 12)	208	62	64	69	69	5	121	8	0	2	8	2	.80	15	.251	.353	.432
2003 Tampa Bay	AL	55	165	38	7	0	4	(2 2)	57	28	17	19	32	1	41	6	0	2	0	0	-	3	.230	.371	.345
7 ML YEARS		830	2945	794	175	5	110	(48 62)	1309	440	456	465	422	16	707	43	1	13	24	5	.83	99	.270	.368	.444

Ken Griffey Jr.

Bats: L **Throws:** L **Pos:** CF-43; PH-7; DH-3 **Ht:** 6'3" **Wt:** 205 **Born:** 11/21/69 **Age:** 34

Year Team	Lg	G	AB	H	2B	3B	HR	(Hm Rd)	TB	R	RBI	RC	TBB	IBB	SO	HBP	SH	SF	SB	CS	SB%	GDP	Avg	OBP	Slg
1989 Seattle	AL	127	455	120	23	0	16	(10 6)	191	61	61	64	44	8	83	2	1	4	16	7	.70	4	.264	.329	.420
1990 Seattle	AL	155	597	179	28	7	22	(8 14)	287	91	80	101	63	12	81	2	0	4	16	11	.59	12	.300	.366	.481
1991 Seattle	AL	154	548	179	42	1	22	(16 6)	289	76	100	112	71	21	82	1	4	9	18	6	.75	10	.327	.399	.527
1992 Seattle	AL	142	565	174	39	4	27	(16 11)	302	83	103	102	44	15	67	5	0	3	10	5	.67	15	.308	.361	.535
1993 Seattle	AL	156	582	180	38	3	45	(21 24)	359	113	109	137	96	25	91	6	0	7	17	9	.65	14	.309	.408	.617
1994 Seattle	AL	111	433	140	24	4	40	(18 22)	292	94	90	107	56	19	73	2	0	2	11	3	.79	9	.323	.402	.674
1995 Seattle	AL	72	260	67	7	0	17	(13 4)	125	52	42	49	52	6	53	0	0	2	4	2	.67	4	.258	.379	.481
1996 Seattle	AL	140	545	165	26	2	49	(26 23)	342	125	140	131	78	13	104	7	1	7	16	1	.94	7	.303	.392	.628
1997 Seattle	AL	157	608	185	34	3	56	(27 29)	393	125	147	142	76	23	121	8	0	12	15	4	.79	12	.304	.382	.646
1998 Seattle	AL	161	633	180	33	3	56	(30 26)	387	120	146	136	76	11	121	7	0	4	20	5	.80	14	.284	.365	.611
1999 Seattle	AL	160	606	173	26	3	48	(27 21)	349	123	134	132	91	17	108	7	0	2	24	7	.77	8	.285	.384	.576
2000 Cincinnati	NL	145	520	141	22	3	40	(22 18)	289	100	118	111	94	17	117	9	0	8	6	4	.60	7	.271	.387	.556
2001 Cincinnati	NL	111	364	104	20	2	22	(12 10)	194	57	65	69	44	6	72	4	1	4	2	0	1.00	8	.286	.365	.533
2002 Cincinnati	NL	70	197	52	8	0	8	(4 4)	84	17	23	26	28	6	39	3	0	4	1	2	.33	6	.264	.358	.426
2003 Cincinnati	NL	53	166	41	12	1	13	(5 8)	94	34	26	27	27	5	44	6	1	1	1	0	1.00	3	.247	.370	.566
15 ML YEARS		1914	7079	2080	382	36	481	(255 226)	3977	1271	1384	1446	940	204	1256	69	8	73	177	66	.73	133	.294	.379	.562

Jeremy Griffiths

Pitches: R **Bats:** R **Pos:** SP-6; RP-3 **Ht:** 6'6" **Wt:** 240 **Born:** 3/22/78 **Age:** 26

Year Team	Lg	G	GS	CG	GF	IP	BFP	H	R	ER	HR	SH	SF	HB	TBB	IBB	SO	WP	Bk	W	L	Pct	ShO	Sv-Op	Hld	ERC	ERA
1999 Kingsport	R+	14	14	1	0	76.1	321	68	40	28	6	1	3	1	36	1	74	5	1	3	5	.375	0	0--	-	3.71	3.30
2000 Capital City	A	26	26	0	0	128.2	548	120	78	62	12	1	4	8	39	0	138	8	0	7	12	.368	0	0--	-	3.48	4.34
2001 St.Lucie	A+	23	20	2	0	132.0	551	126	63	55	9	9	3	5	35	1	95	11	3	7	8	.467	0	0--	-	3.23	3.75
2001 Binghamton	AA	2	2	1	0	13.0	51	8	3	1	0	1	0	0	4	0	12	1	0	2	0	1.000	0	0--	-	1.37	0.69
2002 Binghamton	AA	27	26	2	0	152.2	652	157	75	66	12	5	4	11	54	0	126	5	0	8	6	.571	0	0--	-	4.28	3.89
2003 Norfolk	AAA	21	19	1	1	115.0	459	94	43	35	6	1	4	9	26	0	78	5	0	7	6	.538	0	1--	-	2.50	2.74
2003 New York	NL	9	6	0	1	41.0	199	57	34	32	4	0	2	2	19	2	25	1	0	1	4	.200	0	0-0	0	6.88	7.02

Jason Grimsley

Pitches: R **Bats:** R **Pos:** RP-76 **Ht:** 6'3" **Wt:** 205 **Born:** 8/7/67 **Age:** 36

Year Team	Lg	G	GS	CG	GF	IP	BFP	H	R	ER	HR	SH	SF	HB	TBB	IBB	SO	WP	Bk	W	L	Pct	ShO	Sv-Op	Hld	ERC	ERA
1989 Philadelphia	NL	4	4	0	0	18.1	91	19	13	12	2	1	0	0	19	1	7	2	0	1	3	.250	0	0-0	0	6.86	5.89
1990 Philadelphia	NL	11	11	0	0	57.1	255	47	21	21	1	2	1	2	43	0	41	6	1	3	2	.600	0	0-0	0	3.98	3.30
1991 Philadelphia	NL	12	12	0	0	61.0	272	54	34	33	4	3	2	3	41	3	42	14	0	1	7	.125	0	0-0	0	4.39	4.87
1993 Cleveland	AL	10	6	0	0	42.1	194	52	26	25	3	1	0	1	20	1	27	2	0	3	4	.429	0	0-0	0	5.57	5.31
1994 Cleveland	AL	14	13	1	0	82.2	368	91	47	42	7	4	2	6	34	1	59	6	1	5	2	.714	0	0-0	0	4.89	4.57
1995 Cleveland	AL	15	2	0	2	34.0	165	37	24	23	4	2	2	2	32	1	25	7	0	0	0	-	0	1-1	0	7.37	6.09
1996 Anaheim	AL	35	20	2	4	130.1	620	150	110	99	14	4	5	13	74	5	82	11	0	5	7	.417	1	0-0	0	5.98	6.84
1999 New York	AL	55	0	0	25	75.0	336	66	39	30	7	3	3	4	40	5	49	8	0	7	2	.778	0	1-4	8	3.87	3.60
2000 New York	AL	63	4	0	18	96.1	428	100	58	54	10	2	6	5	42	1	53	16	0	3	2	.600	0	1-4	4	4.63	5.04
2001 Kansas City	AL	73	0	0	24	80.1	327	71	32	27	8	2	1	2	28	5	61	4	0	1	5	.167	0	0-7	26	3.34	3.02
2002 Kansas City	AL	70	0	0	26	71.1	310	64	32	31	4	1	0	1	37	8	59	8	0	4	7	.364	0	1-3	13	3.51	3.91
2003 Kansas City	AL	76	0	0	5	75.0	346	88	47	43	6	6	5	5	36	5	58	4	0	2	6	.250	0	0-7	28	5.40	5.16
12 ML YEARS		438	72	3	105	824.0	3712	839	483	440	70	30	27	44	446	36	563	88	2	35	47	.427	1	4-26	80	4.77	4.81

Marquis Grissom

Bats: R **Throws:** R **Pos:** CF-148; PH-2; PR-2   **Ht:** 5'11" **Wt:** 188 **Born:** 4/17/67 **Age:** 37

								BATTING													BASERUNNING				AVERAGES		
Year Team	Lg	G	AB	H	2B	3B	HR	(Hm	Rd)	TB	R	RBI	RC	TBB	IBB	SO	HBP	SH	SF	SB	CS	SB%	GDP	Avg	OBP	Slg
1989 Montreal	NL	26	74	19	2	0	1	(0	1)	24	16	2	10	12	0	21	0	1	0	1	0	1.00	1	.257	.360	.324
1990 Montreal	NL	98	288	74	14	2	3	(2	1)	101	42	29	37	27	2	40	0	4	1	22	2	.92	3	.257	.320	.351
1991 Montreal	NL	148	558	149	23	9	6	(3	3)	208	73	39	71	34	0	89	1	4	0	76	17	.82	8	.267	.310	.373
1992 Montreal	NL	159	653	180	39	6	14	(8	6)	273	99	66	96	42	6	81	5	3	4	78	13	.86	12	.276	.322	.418
1993 Montreal	NL	157	630	188	27	2	19	(9	10)	276	104	95	103	52	6	76	3	0	8	53	10	.84	9	.298	.351	.438
1994 Montreal	NL	110	475	137	25	4	11	(4	7)	203	96	45	73	41	4	66	1	0	4	36	6	.86	10	.288	.344	.427
1995 Atlanta	NL	139	551	142	23	3	12	(5	7)	207	80	42	68	47	4	61	3	1	4	29	9	.76	8	.258	.317	.376
1996 Atlanta	NL	158	671	207	32	10	23	(11	12)	328	106	74	111	41	6	73	3	4	4	28	11	.72	12	.308	.349	.489
1997 Cleveland	AL	144	558	146	27	6	12	(5	7)	221	74	66	69	43	1	89	6	6	9	22	13	.63	12	.262	.317	.396
1998 Milwaukee	NL	142	542	147	28	1	10	(2	8)	207	57	60	59	24	2	78	2	2	2	13	8	.62	12	.271	.304	.382
1999 Milwaukee	NL	154	603	161	27	1	20	(9	11)	250	92	83	81	49	4	109	0	4	5	24	6	.80	12	.267	.320	.415
2000 Milwaukee	NL	146	595	145	18	2	14	(4	10)	209	67	60	59	39	2	99	0	2	4	20	10	.67	9	.244	.288	.351
2001 Los Angeles	NL	135	448	99	17	1	21	(9	12)	181	56	60	41	16	0	107	2	0	2	7	5	.58	12	.221	.250	.404
2002 Los Angeles	NL	111	343	95	21	4	17	(10	7)	175	57	60	56	22	2	68	2	0	4	5	1	.83	6	.277	.321	.510
2003 San Francisco	NL	149	587	176	33	3	20	(10	10)	275	82	79	89	20	0	82	2	3	6	11	3	.79	14	.300	.322	.468
15 ML YEARS		1976	7576	2065	356	54	203	(91	112)	3138	1101	862	1023	509	39	1139	30	34	57	425	114	.79	140	.273	.319	.414

Buddy Groom

Pitches: L **Bats:** L **Pos:** RP-60   **Ht:** 6'2" **Wt:** 207 **Born:** 7/10/65 **Age:** 38

		HOW MUCH HE PITCHED						WHAT HE GAVE UP										THE RESULTS						
Year Team	Lg	G	GS	CG	GF	IP	BFP	H	R	ER	HR	SH	SF	HB	TBB	IBB	SO	WP	Bk	W	L	Pct	ShO	Sv-Op	Hld	ERC	ERA
1992 Detroit	AL	12	7	0	3	38.2	177	48	28	25	4	3	2	0	22	4	15	0	1	0	5	.000	0	1-2	0	6.20	5.82
1993 Detroit	AL	19	3	0	8	36.2	170	48	25	25	4	2	4	2	13	5	15	2	1	0	2	.000	0	0-0	1	5.72	6.14
1994 Detroit	AL	40	0	0	10	32.0	139	31	14	14	4	0	3	2	13	2	27	0	0	0	1	.000	0	1-1	11	4.25	3.94
1995 Det-Fla		37	4	0	11	55.2	274	81	47	46	8	2	2	2	32	4	35	3	0	2	5	.286	0	1-3	0	8.05	7.44
1996 Oakland	AL	72	1	0	16	77.1	341	85	37	33	8	2	0	3	34	3	57	5	0	5	0	1.000	0	2-4	10	5.00	3.84
1997 Oakland	AL	78	0	0	17	64.2	285	75	38	37	9	0	4	0	24	1	45	3	0	2	2	.500	0	3-5	12	5.18	5.15
1998 Oakland	AL	75	0	0	13	57.1	251	62	30	27	4	1	3	1	20	1	36	1	0	3	1	.750	0	0-6	16	4.12	4.24
1999 Oakland	AL	76	0	0	6	46.0	196	48	29	26	1	2	0	1	18	5	32	2	1	3	2	.600	0	0-3	27	3.71	5.09
2000 Baltimore	AL	70	0	0	14	59.1	260	63	37	32	5	5	5	0	21	2	44	1	0	6	3	.667	0	4-11	27	4.01	4.85
2001 Baltimore	AL	70	0	0	35	66.0	265	64	28	26	4	0	1	1	9	0	54	2	0	1	4	.200	0	11-13	16	2.75	3.55
2002 Baltimore	AL	70	0	0	17	62.0	239	44	11	11	4	0	1	2	12	3	48	0	0	3	2	.600	0	2-4	19	1.73	1.60
2003 Baltimore	AL	60	0	0	20	45.1	207	58	27	27	7	1	1	3	14	2	34	1	0	1	3	.250	0	1-3	16	5.93	5.36
1995 Detroit	AL	23	4	0	6	40.2	203	55	35	34	6	2	2	2	26	4	23	3	0	1	3	.250	0	1-3	0	7.54	7.52
1995 Florida	NL	14	0	0	5	15.0	71	26	12	12	2	0	0	0	6	0	12	0	0	1	2	.333	0	0-0	0	9.52	7.20
12 ML YEARS		679	15	0	160	641.0	2804	707	351	329	62	18	26	17	232	32	442	20	3	26	30	.464	0	26-55	155	4.53	4.62

Mark Grudzielanek

Bats: R **Throws:** R **Pos:** 2B-121; PH-2; PR-1   **Ht:** 6'1" **Wt:** 185 **Born:** 6/30/70 **Age:** 34

								BATTING													BASERUNNING				AVERAGES		
Year Team	Lg	G	AB	H	2B	3B	HR	(Hm	Rd)	TB	R	RBI	RC	TBB	IBB	SO	HBP	SH	SF	SB	CS	SB%	GDP	Avg	OBP	Slg
2003 Iowa*	AAA	2	10	5	0	0	0	(-	-)	5	1	1	3	1	0	1	0	0	0	0	0	-	0	.500	.545	.500
1995 Montreal	NL	78	269	66	12	2	1	(1	0)	85	27	20	24	14	4	47	7	3	0	8	3	.73	7	.245	.300	.316
1996 Montreal	NL	153	657	201	34	4	6	(5	1)	261	99	49	90	26	3	83	9	1	3	33	7	.83	10	.306	.340	.397
1997 Montreal	NL	156	649	177	54	3	4	(1	3)	249	76	51	75	23	0	76	10	3	3	25	9	.74	13	.273	.307	.384
1998 Mon-LA	NL	156	589	160	21	1	10	(5	5)	213	62	62	64	26	2	73	11	8	7	18	5	.78	18	.272	.311	.362
1999 Los Angeles	NL	123	488	159	23	5	7	(4	3)	213	72	46	76	31	1	65	10	2	3	6	6	.50	13	.326	.376	.436
2000 Los Angeles	NL	148	617	172	35	6	7	(4	3)	240	101	49	80	45	0	81	9	2	3	12	3	.80	16	.279	.335	.389
2001 Los Angeles	NL	133	539	146	21	3	13	(8	5)	212	83	55	66	28	0	83	11	3	5	4	4	.50	9	.271	.317	.393
2002 Los Angeles	NL	150	536	145	23	0	9	(5	4)	195	56	50	52	22	4	89	3	1	4	4	1	.80	17	.271	.301	.364
2003 Chicago	NL	121	481	151	38	1	3	(2	1)	200	73	38	70	30	0	64	11	7	2	6	2	.75	12	.314	.366	.416
1998 Montreal	NL	105	396	109	15	1	8	(3	5)	150	51	41	47	21	1	50	9	5	4	11	5	.69	11	.275	.323	.379
1998 Los Angeles	NL	51	193	51	6	0	2	(2	0)	63	11	21	17	5	1	23	2	3	3	7	0	1.00	7	.264	.286	.326
9 ML YEARS		1218	4825	1377	261	25	60	(35	25)	1868	649	420	597	245	14	661	81	30	30	116	40	.74	115	.285	.329	.387

Kevin Gryboski

Pitches: R **Bats:** R **Pos:** RP-64   **Ht:** 6'5" **Wt:** 235 **Born:** 11/15/73 **Age:** 30

		HOW MUCH HE PITCHED						WHAT HE GAVE UP										THE RESULTS						
Year Team	Lg	G	GS	CG	GF	IP	BFP	H	R	ER	HR	SH	SF	HB	TBB	IBB	SO	WP	Bk	W	L	Pct	ShO	Sv-Op	Hld	ERC	ERA
1995 Everett	A-	25	0	0	14	36.0	156	27	18	14	2	3	1	8	18	2	25	3	0	1	5	.167	1	2--	-	2.95	3.50
1996 Wisconsin	A	32	21	3	5	138.2	630	146	90	73	7	9	6	12	62	2	100	12	0	10	5	.667	1	1--	-	4.44	4.74
1997 Lancaster	A+	21	15	0	4	67.1	332	113	82	74	13	2	8	1	26	0	41	7	0	0	7	.000	0	0--	-	9.20	9.89
1998 Lancaster	A+	37	3	0	17	85.0	351	75	35	25	4	1	2	4	31	1	73	3	0	5	5	.500	0	8--	-	3.18	2.65
1998 Orlando	AA	2	0	0	0	5.0	23	8	5	5	1	0	0	0	1	0	4	2	0	0	0	-	0	0--	-	7.85	9.00
1999 New Haven	AA	47	0	0	32	62.1	267	67	27	20	5	5	2	3	20	4	41	3	0	2	5	.286	0	10--	-	4.19	2.89
2000 New Haven	AA	16	0	0	14	18.0	78	15	5	5	0	1	0	1	8	1	20	4	0	1	1	.500	0	9--	-	2.71	2.50
2000 Tacoma	AAA	31	0	0	18	41.0	181	45	23	22	3	2	0	0	23	4	35	7	0	2	2	.500	0	2--	-	5.07	4.83
2001 Tacoma	AAA	58	0	0	50	60.0	256	64	29	26	8	5	1	0	19	2	50	2	0	2	5	.286	0	22--	-	4.33	3.90
2002 Richmond	AAA	7	0	0	6	7.0	29	7	1	1	0	0	0	0	1	0	5	1	0	1	0	1.000	0	3--	-	2.41	1.29
2002 Macon	A	2	1	0	0	2.0	8	1	0	0	0	0	0	0	1	0	2	0	0	0	0	-	0	0--	-	3.21	0.00
2002 Atlanta	NL	57	0	0	10	51.2	238	50	20	20	6	1	0	5	37	5	33	2	0	2	1	.667	0	0-2	11	5.58	3.48
2003 Atlanta	NL	64	0	0	9	44.1	190	44	22	19	3	4	0	2	23	6	32	2	0	6	4	.600	0	0-4	12	4.39	3.86
2 ML YEARS		121	0	0	19	96.0	428	94	42	39	9	5	0	7	60	11	65	4	0	8	5	.615	0	0-6	23	5.02	3.66

Eddie Guardado

Pitches: L **Bats:** R **Pos:** RP-66   **Ht:** 6'0" **Wt:** 194 **Born:** 10/2/70 **Age:** 33

Year Team	Lg	HOW MUCH HE PITCHED						WHAT HE GAVE UP											THE RESULTS							
		G	GS	CG	GF	IP	BFP	H	R	ER	HR	SH	SF	HB	TBB	IBB	SO	WP	Bk	W	L	Pct	ShO	Sv-Op	Hld	ERC	ERA
1993 Minnesota	AL	19	16	0	2	94.2	426	123	68	65	13	1	3	1	36	2	46	0	0	3	8	.273	0	0-0	0	6.18	6.18
1994 Minnesota	AL	4	4	0	0	17.0	81	26	16	16	3	1	2	0	4	0	8	0	0	0	2	.000	0	0-0	0	7.01	8.47
1995 Minnesota	AL	51	5	0	10	91.1	410	99	54	52	13	6	5	0	45	2	71	5	1	4	9	.308	0	2-5	5	5.20	5.12
1996 Minnesota	AL	83	0	0	17	73.2	313	61	45	43	12	6	4	3	33	4	74	3	0	6	5	.545	0	4-7	18	3.81	5.25
1997 Minnesota	AL	69	0	0	20	46.0	201	45	23	20	7	2	1	2	17	2	54	2	0	0	4	.000	0	1-1	13	4.23	3.91
1998 Minnesota	AL	79	0	0	12	65.2	286	66	34	33	10	3	6	0	28	6	53	2	0	3	1	.750	0	0-4	16	4.42	4.52
1999 Minnesota	AL	63	0	0	13	48.0	197	37	25	25	6	2	1	2	25	4	50	0	0	2	5	.286	0	2-4	15	3.63	4.69
2000 Minnesota	AL	70	0	0	36	61.2	262	55	27	27	14	3	2	1	25	3	52	1	1	7	4	.636	0	9-11	8	4.34	3.94
2001 Minnesota	AL	67	0	0	26	66.2	270	47	27	26	5	5	3	1	23	4	67	4	0	7	1	.875	0	12-14	14	2.13	3.51
2002 Minnesota	AL	68	0	0	62	67.2	270	53	22	22	9	2	2	1	18	2	70	0	0	1	3	.250	0	45-51	0	2.66	2.93
2003 Minnesota	AL	66	0	0	60	65.1	261	50	22	21	7	3	2	0	14	2	60	5	0	3	5	.375	0	41-45	0	2.13	2.89
11 ML YEARS		639	25	0	258	697.2	2977	662	363	350	99	34	31	11	268	31	605	22	2	36	47	.434	0	116-142	89	4.01	4.52

Vladimir Guerrero

Bats: R **Throws:** R **Pos:** RF-112   **Ht:** 6'3" **Wt:** 210 **Born:** 2/9/76 **Age:** 28

Year Team	Lg	BATTING																		BASERUNNING				AVERAGES		
		G	AB	H	2B	3B	HR	(Hm	Rd)	TB	R	RBI	RC	TBB	IBB	SO	HBP	SH	SF	SB	CS	SB%	GDP	Avg	OBP	Slg
2003 Brevard Cnty*	A+	3	6	3	0	0	1			6	2	1	3	0	0	0	1	0	0	0	0	-	0	.500	.571	1.000
1996 Montreal	NL	9	27	5	0	0	1	(0	1)	8	2	1	1	0	0	3	0	0	0	0	0	-	0	.185	.185	.296
1997 Montreal	NL	90	325	98	22	2	11	(5	6)	157	44	40	51	19	2	39	7	0	3	3	4	.43	11	.302	.350	.483
1998 Montreal	NL	159	623	202	37	7	38	(19	19)	367	108	109	124	42	13	95	7	0	5	11	9	.55	15	.324	.371	.589
1999 Montreal	NL	160	610	193	37	5	42	(23	19)	366	102	131	127	55	14	62	7	0	2	14	7	.67	18	.316	.378	.600
2000 Montreal	NL	154	571	197	28	11	44	(25	19)	379	101	123	137	58	23	74	8	0	4	9	10	.47	15	.345	.410	.664
2001 Montreal	NL	159	599	184	45	4	34	(21	13)	339	107	108	116	60	24	88	9	0	5	37	16	.70	24	.307	.377	.566
2002 Montreal	NL	161	614	206	37	2	39	(20	19)	364	106	111	125	84	32	70	6	0	5	40	20	.67	20	.336	.417	.593
2003 Montreal	NL	112	394	130	20	3	25	(15	10)	231	71	79	83	63	21	53	6	0	4	9	5	.64	18	.330	.426	.586
8 ML YEARS		1004	3763	1215	226	34	234	(128	106)	2211	641	702	764	381	129	484	50	0	26	123	71	.63	122	.323	.390	.588

Aaron Guiel

Bats: L **Throws:** R **Pos:** RF-87; PH-10; DH-2; LF-1; CF-1   **Ht:** 5'10" **Wt:** 190 **Born:** 10/5/72 **Age:** 31

Year Team	Lg	BATTING																		BASERUNNING				AVERAGES		
		G	AB	H	2B	3B	HR	(Hm	Rd)	TB	R	RBI	RC	TBB	IBB	SO	HBP	SH	SF	SB	CS	SB%	GDP	Avg	OBP	Slg
1993 Boise	A-	35	104	31	6	4	2	(-	-)	51	24	12	25	26	1	21	4	2	0	3	0	1.00	1	.298	.455	.490
1994 Cedar Rpds	A	127	454	122	30	1	18	(-	-)	208	84	82	79	64	2	93	6	5	3	21	7	.75	7	.269	.364	.458
1995 Lk Elsinore	A+	113	409	110	25	7	7	(-	-)	170	73	58	68	69	0	96	7	4	4	7	6	.54	7	.269	.380	.416
1996 Midland	AA	129	439	118	29	7	10	(-	-)	191	72	48	71	56	0	71	10	2	1	11	7	.61	6	.269	.364	.435
1997 Midland	AA	116	419	138	37	7	22	(-	-)	255	91	85	102	59	3	94	18	2	3	14	10	.58	9	.329	.431	.609
1997 Mobile	AA	8	26	10	2	0	1	(-	-)	15	9	9	8	5	0	4	1	0	0	1	0	1.00	1	.385	.500	.577
1998 Las Vegas	AAA	60	183	57	15	4	5	(-	-)	95	33	31	39	28	2	51	4	1	2	5	1	.83	4	.311	.410	.519
1998 Padres	R	8	16	8	3	1	1	(-	-)	16	8	6	9	5	1	5	3	0	0	1	1	.50	0	.500	.667	1.000
1999 Las Vegas	AAA	84	257	63	25	2	12	(-	-)	128	46	39	46	44	3	86	5	0	3	5	4	.56	6	.245	.362	.498
2000 Omaha	AAA	73	258	74	15	2	13	(-	-)	132	47	40	52	35	0	54	8	0	0	6	0	1.00	3	.287	.389	.512
2001 Omaha	AAA	121	442	118	27	3	21	(-	-)	214	78	73	75	51	3	92	13	1	6	6	4	.60	12	.267	.355	.484
2002 Omaha	AAA	61	215	76	11	1	9	(-	-)	116	44	50	51	29	3	34	8	0	3	8	1	.89	6	.353	.443	.540
2003 Omaha	AAA	52	190	53	9	2	8	(-	-)	90	38	30	39	33	2	43	9	0	1	3	0	1.00	3	.279	.408	.474
2002 Kansas City	AL	70	240	56	13	0	4	(4	0)	81	30	38	33	19	1	61	4	2	4	1	5	.17	3	.233	.296	.338
2003 Kansas City	AL	99	354	98	30	0	15	(4	11)	173	63	52	60	27	0	63	13	2	5	3	5	.38	3	.277	.346	.489
2 ML YEARS		169	594	154	43	0	19	(8	11)	254	93	90	93	46	1	124	17	4	9	4	10	.29	6	.259	.326	.428

Carlos Guillen

Bats: B **Throws:** R **Pos:** SS-76; 3B-32; DH-1   **Ht:** 6'1" **Wt:** 202 **Born:** 9/30/75 **Age:** 28

Year Team	Lg	BATTING																		BASERUNNING				AVERAGES		
		G	AB	H	2B	3B	HR	(Hm	Rd)	TB	R	RBI	RC	TBB	IBB	SO	HBP	SH	SF	SB	CS	SB%	GDP	Avg	OBP	Slg
2003 Tacoma*	AAA	4	14	5	1	0	2	(-	-)	12	2	4	3	0	0	1	1	0	0	0	0	-	2	.357	.400	.857
1998 Seattle	AL	10	39	13	1	1	0	(1	0)	16	9	5	7	3	0	9	0	0	0	2	0	1.00	0	.333	.381	.410
1999 Seattle	AL	5	19	3	0	0	1	(1	0)	6	2	3	1	1	0	6	0	1	0	0	0	-	1	.158	.200	.316
2000 Seattle	AL	90	288	74	15	2	7	(3	4)	114	45	42	36	28	0	53	2	7	3	1	3	.25	6	.257	.324	.396
2001 Seattle	AL	140	456	118	21	4	5	(3	2)	162	72	53	56	53	0	89	1	7	6	4	1	.80	9	.259	.333	.355
2002 Seattle	AL	134	475	124	24	6	9	(4	5)	187	73	56	58	46	4	91	1	3	3	4	5	.44	8	.261	.326	.394
2003 Seattle	AL	109	388	107	19	3	7	(4	3)	153	63	52	52	52	2	64	1	5	5	4	4	.50	12	.276	.359	.394
6 ML YEARS		488	1665	439	80	16	29	(14	15)	638	264	211	210	183	6	312	5	23	17	15	13	.54	36	.264	.335	.383

Jose Guillen

Bats: R **Throws:** R **Pos:** RF-96; LF-31; PH-20; CF-5   **Ht:** 5'11" **Wt:** 195 **Born:** 5/17/76 **Age:** 28

Year Team	Lg	BATTING																		BASERUNNING				AVERAGES		
		G	AB	H	2B	3B	HR	(Hm	Rd)	TB	R	RBI	RC	TBB	IBB	SO	HBP	SH	SF	SB	CS	SB%	GDP	Avg	OBP	Slg
2003 Louisville*	AAA	4	15	5	1	0	0	(-	-)	6	4	3	2	1	0	3	0	0	1	1	0	1.00	1	.333	.353	.400
1997 Pittsburgh	NL	143	498	133	20	5	14	(5	9)	205	58	70	56	17	0	88	0	0	3	1	2	.33	16	.267	.300	.412
1998 Pittsburgh	NL	153	573	153	38	2	14	(10	4)	237	60	84	68	21	0	100	6	1	4	3	5	.38	7	.267	.298	.414
1999 Pit-TB		87	288	73	16	0	3	(1	2)	98	42	31	28	20	2	57	1	1	0	1	0	1.00	16	.253	.315	.340
2000 Tampa Bay	AL	105	316	80	16	5	10	(5	5)	136	40	41	41	18	1	65	13	2	0	3	1	.75	6	.253	.320	.430
2001 Tampa Bay	AL	41	135	37	5	0	3	(0	3)	51	14	11	15	6	2	26	3	0	1	2	3	.40	2	.274	.317	.378
2002 Ari-Cin	NL	85	240	57	7	0	8	(5	3)	88	25	31	16	14	1	43	3	1	1	4	5	.44	13	.238	.287	.367
2003 Cin-Oak		136	485	151	28	2	31	(14	17)	276	77	86	87	24	2	95	14	8	3	1	3	.25	16	.311	.359	.569
1999 Pittsburgh	NL	40	120	32	6	0	1	(0	1)	41	18	18	12	10	1	21	0	1	0	1	0	1.00	7	.267	.321	.342
1999 Tampa Bay	AL	47	168	41	10	0	2	(1	1)	57	24	13	16	10	1	36	1	0	0	0	0	-	9	.244	.312	.339
2002 Arizona	NL	54	131	30	4	0	4	(3	1)	46	13	15	7	7	1	25	2	0	1	3	4	.43	7	.229	.277	.351

Year Team	Lg	G	AB	H	2B	3B	HR	(Hm Rd)	TB	R	RBI	RC	TBB	IBB	SO	HBP	SH	SF	SB	CS	SB%	GDP	Avg	OBP	Slg
2002 Cincinnati	NL	31	109	27	3	0	4	(2 2)	42	12	16	9	7	0	18	1	1	0	1	1	.50	6	.248	.299	.385
2003 Cincinnati	NL	91	315	106	21	1	23	(10 13)	198	52	63	65	17	1	63	9	6	2	1	3	.25	8	.337	.385	.629
2003 Oakland	AL	45	170	45	7	1	8	(4 4)	78	25	23	22	7	1	32	5	2	1	0	0	-	8	.265	.311	.459
7 ML YEARS		750	2535	684	130	14	83	(40 43)	1091	316	354	313	120	8	474	54	13	14	15	19	.44	76	.270	.315	.430

Mark Guthrie

Pitches: L Bats: R Pos: RP-65   Ht: 6'4" Wt: 215 Born: 9/22/65 Age: 38

Year Team	Lg	G	GS	CG	GF	IP	BFP	H	R	ER	HR	SH	SF	HB	TBB	IBB	SO	WP	Bk	W	L	Pct	ShO	Sv-Op	Hld	ERC	ERA
1989 Minnesota	AL	13	8	0	2	57.1	254	66	32	29	7	1	5	1	21	1	38	1	0	2	4	.333	0	0-0	0	5.02	4.55
1990 Minnesota	AL	24	21	3	0	144.2	603	154	65	61	8	6	0	1	39	3	101	9	0	7	9	.438	1	0-0	0	3.69	3.79
1991 Minnesota	AL	41	12	0	13	98.0	432	116	52	47	11	4	3	1	41	2	72	7	0	7	5	.583	0	2-2	5	5.45	4.32
1992 Minnesota	AL	54	0	0	15	75.0	303	59	27	24	7	4	2	0	23	7	76	2	0	2	3	.400	0	5-7	19	2.43	2.88
1993 Minnesota	AL	22	0	0	2	21.0	94	20	11	11	2	1	2	0	16	2	15	1	3	2	1	.667	0	0-1	8	5.20	4.71
1994 Minnesota	AL	50	2	0	13	51.1	234	65	43	35	8	2	6	2	18	2	38	7	0	4	2	.667	0	1-3	12	5.95	6.14
1995 Min-LA		60	0	0	14	62.0	272	66	33	29	6	4	0	2	25	5	67	5	1	5	5	.500	0	0-2	15	4.44	4.21
1996 Los Angeles	NL	66	0	0	16	73.0	302	65	21	18	3	4	4	1	22	2	56	1	0	2	3	.400	0	1-3	12	2.73	2.22
1997 Los Angeles	NL	62	0	0	18	69.1	305	71	44	41	12	10	3	0	30	6	42	2	1	1	4	.200	0	1-4	13	4.69	5.32
1998 Los Angeles	NL	53	0	0	11	54.0	241	56	26	21	3	5	0	2	24	1	45	2	0	2	1	.667	0	0-1	8	4.20	3.50
1999 Bos-ChC		57	0	0	15	58.2	254	57	38	35	10	2	3	2	24	5	45	3	0	1	3	.250	0	2-2	14	4.45	5.37
2000 ChC-TB-Tor		76	0	0	15	71.1	315	70	41	37	8	4	4	2	37	9	63	13	0	3	6	.333	0	4-10	44	4.44	4.67
2001 Oakland	AL	54	0	0	11	52.1	225	49	29	26	7	1	3	4	20	1	52	3	0	6	2	.750	0	1-3	12	4.17	4.47
2002 New York	NL	68	0	0	13	48.0	190	35	13	13	3	0	1	1	19	3	44	4	0	5	3	.625	0	1-2	17	2.48	2.44
2003 Chicago	NL	65	0	0	10	42.2	187	40	14	13	6	6	2	3	22	4	24	3	0	2	3	.400	0	0-1	10	4.65	2.74
1995 Minnesota	AL	36	0	0	7	42.1	181	47	22	21	5	2	0	1	16	3	48	3	1	5	3	.625	0	0-2	10	4.89	4.46
1995 Los Angeles	NL	24	0	0	7	19.2	91	19	11	8	1	2	0	1	9	2	19	2	0	0	2	.000	0	0-0	5	3.54	3.66
1999 Boston	AL	46	0	0	15	46.1	207	50	32	30	9	0	3	2	20	3	36	2	0	1	1	.500	0	2-2	12	5.42	5.83
1999 Chicago	NL	11	0	0	0	12.1	47	7	6	5	1	2	0	0	4	2	9	1	0	0	2	.000	0	0-0	2	1.46	3.65
2000 Chicago	NL	19	0	0	3	18.2	82	17	11	10	1	2	3	1	10	4	17	4	0	2	3	.400	0	0-0	3	3.61	4.82
2000 Tampa Bay	AL	34	0	0	7	32.0	145	33	18	16	4	1	0	0	18	5	26	7	0	1	1	.500	0	0-3	4	4.77	4.50
2000 Toronto	AL	23	0	0	5	20.2	88	20	12	11	3	1	1	1	9	0	20	2	0	0	2	.000	0	0-1	3	4.68	4.79
15 ML YEARS		765	43	3	168	978.2	4211	989	489	440	101	54	38	22	381	53	778	63	5	51	54	.486	1	14-35	155	4.14	4.05

Ricky Gutierrez

Bats: R Throws: R Pos: SS-9; 3B-7; PH-2   Ht: 6'1" Wt: 190 Born: 5/23/70 Age: 34

Year Team	Lg	G	AB	H	2B	3B	HR	(Hm Rd)	TB	R	RBI	RC	TBB	IBB	SO	HBP	SH	SF	SB	CS	SB%	GDP	Avg	OBP	Slg
2003 Buffalo*	AAA	16	65	19	2	1	0	(- -)	23	8	5	8	4	0	5	1	0	1	4	1	.80	2	.292	.338	.354
1993 San Diego	NL	133	438	110	10	5	5	(5 0)	145	76	26	50	50	2	97	5	1	1	4	3	.57	7	.251	.334	.331
1994 San Diego	NL	90	275	66	11	2	1	(1 0)	84	27	28	25	32	1	54	2	2	3	6		.25	8	.240	.321	.305
1995 Houston	NL	52	156	43	6	0	0	(0 0)	49	22	12	16	10	3	33	1	1		5	0	1.00	4	.276	.321	.314
1996 Houston	NL	89	218	62	8	1	1	(1 0)	75	28	15	29	23	3	42	3	4	1	6	1	.86	4	.284	.359	.344
1997 Houston	NL	102	303	79	14	4	3	(0 3)	110	33	34	30	21	2	50	3	0	5	2		.71	17	.261	.315	.363
1998 Houston	NL	141	491	128	24	3	2	(1 1)	164	55	46	54	54	5	84	6	3	7	13	7	.65	20	.261	.337	.334
1999 Houston	NL	85	268	70	7	5	1	(1 0)	90	33	25	31	37	4	45	2	3	1	2	5	.29	9	.261	.354	.336
2000 Chicago	NL	125	449	124	19	2	11	(7 4)	180	73	56	72	66	0	58	7	16	4	2		.80	10	.276	.375	.401
2001 Chicago	NL	147	528	153	23	3	10	(7 3)	212	76	66	74	40	0	56	10	17	11	4	3	.57	13	.290	.345	.402
2002 Cleveland	AL	94	353	97	13	0	4	(2 2)	122	38	38	39	20	0	48	7	3	1	0	1	.00	14	.275	.325	.346
2003 Cleveland	AL	16	50	13	3	0	0	(0 0)	16	2	3	3	3	0	5	1	1	1	0	0	-	1	.260	.309	.320
11 ML YEARS		1074	3529	945	138	25	38	(25 13)	1247	463	349	423	356	20	572	47	51	31	49	30	.62	107	.268	.340	.353

Cristian Guzman

Bats: B Throws: R Pos: SS-141; PH-2; PR-1   Ht: 6'0" Wt: 195 Born: 3/21/78 Age: 26

Year Team	Lg	G	AB	H	2B	3B	HR	(Hm Rd)	TB	R	RBI	RC	TBB	IBB	SO	HBP	SH	SF	SB	CS	SB%	GDP	Avg	OBP	Slg
1999 Minnesota	AL	131	420	95	12	3	1	(1 0)	116	47	26	29	22	0	90	3	7	4	9	7	.56	5	.226	.267	.276
2000 Minnesota	AL	156	631	156	25	20	8	(3 5)	245	89	54	76	46	1	101	2	7	4	28	10	.74	5	.247	.299	.388
2001 Minnesota	AL	118	493	149	28	14	10	(7 3)	235	80	51	79	21	0	78	5	8	0	25	8	.76	6	.302	.337	.477
2002 Minnesota	AL	148	623	170	31	6	9	(6 3)	240	80	59	61	17	2	79	2	8	6	12	13	.48	12	.273	.292	.385
2003 Minnesota	AL	143	534	143	15	14	3	(1 2)	195	78	53	60	30	0	79	5	12	4	19	9	.67	4	.268	.311	.365
5 ML YEARS		696	2701	713	111	57	31	(18 13)	1031	374	243	305	136	3	427	17	42	18	92	47	.66	32	.264	.302	.382

Edwards Guzman

Bats: L Throws: R Pos: 3B-28; 1B-13; PH-10; C-4; DH-3   Ht: 5'11" Wt: 204 Born: 9/11/76 Age: 27

Year Team	Lg	G	AB	H	2B	3B	HR	(Hm Rd)	TB	R	RBI	RC	TBB	IBB	SO	HBP	SH	SF	SB	CS	SB%	GDP	Avg	OBP	Slg
2003 Edmonton*	AAA	55	213	75	12	1	3	(- -)	98	26	27	34	8	1	18	0	0	2	5	1	.83	6	.352	.372	.460
1999 San Francisco	NL	14	15	0	0	0	0	(0 0)	0	0	0	0	0	0	4	0	1	0	0	0	-	0	.000	.000	.000
2001 San Francisco	NL	61	115	28	6	0	3	(1 2)	43	8	7	11	5	2	16	0	0	1	0	0	-	2	.243	.273	.374
2003 Montreal	NL	52	146	35	5	0	1	(1 2)	43	15	14	7	5	2	17	0	3	1	0	0	-	6	.240	.263	.295
3 ML YEARS		127	276	63	11	0	4	(2 2)	86	23	21	18	10	4	37	0	4	2	0	0	-	8	.228	.253	.312

Luther Hackman

Pitches: R **Bats:** R **Pos:** RP-65   **Ht:** 6'4" **Wt:** 195 **Born:** 10/10/74 **Age:** 29

		HOW MUCH HE PITCHED				WHAT HE GAVE UP												THE RESULTS					
Year Team	Lg	G	GS	CG	GF	IP	BFP	H	R	ER	HR	SH	SF	HB	TBB	IBB	SO	WP	Bk	W	L	Pct	ShO	Sv-Op	Hld	ERC	ERA
1999 Colorado	NL	5	3	0	0	16.0	84	26	19	19	5	2	0	0	12	0	10	0	0	1	2	.333	0	0-0	0	11.65	10.69
2000 St Louis	NL	1	0	0	0	2.2	17	4	3	3	0	2	0	1	4	1	0	0	0	0	0	-	0	0-0	0	11.43	10.13
2001 St Louis	NL	35	0	0	8	35.2	149	28	18	17	7	1	0	2	14	0	24	1	1	1	2	.333	0	1-3	5	3.71	4.29
2002 St Louis	NL	43	6	0	9	81.0	366	90	42	37	7	3	6	4	39	3	46	7	1	5	4	.556	0	0-1	1	5.09	4.11
2003 San Diego	NL	65	0	0	16	76.2	347	78	51	44	7	2	2	8	36	2	48	6	0	2	2	.500	0	0-2	11	4.71	5.17
5 ML YEARS		149	9	0	33	212.0	963	226	133	120	26	10	8	15	105	6	128	14	2	9	10	.474	0	1-6	17	5.23	5.09

Travis Hafner

Bats: L **Throws:** R **Pos:** DH-43; 1B-42; PH-8   **Ht:** 6'3" **Wt:** 240 **Born:** 6/3/77 **Age:** 27

		BATTING												BASERUNNING				AVERAGES		
Year Team	Lg	G	AB	H	2B	3B	HR	(Hm	Rd)	TB	R	RBI	RC	TBB	IBB	SO	HBP	SH	SF	SB	CS	SB%	GDP	Avg	OBP	Slg
1997 Rangers	R	55	189	54	14	0	5	(-	-)	83	38	24	32	24	1	45	3	0	0	7	2	.78	3	.286	.375	.439
1998 Savannah	A	123	405	96	15	4	16	(-	-)	167	62	84	61	68	2	139	6	1	5	7	3	.70	8	.237	.351	.412
1999 Savannah	A	134	480	140	30	4	28	(-	-)	262	94	111	97	67	6	151	11	0	5	5	4	.56	11	.292	.387	.546
2000 Charlotte	A+	122	436	151	34	1	22	(-	-)	253	90	109	107	67	2	86	18	0	7	0	4	.00	9	.346	.447	.580
2001 Tulsa	AA	88	323	91	25	0	20	(-	-)	176	59	74	67	59	5	82	4	0	3	3	1	.75	10	.282	.396	.545
2002 Oklahoma	AAA	110	401	137	22	1	21	(-	-)	224	79	77	100	79	4	76	12	0	0	2	1	.67	9	.342	.463	.559
2003 Buffalo	AAA	29	100	27	4	0	2	(-	-)	37	15	10	17	25	2	26	1	0	0	2	1	.67	2	.270	.421	.370
2002 Texas	AL	23	62	15	4	1	1	(0	1)	24	6	6	7	8	1	15	0	0	0	0	1	.00	1	.242	.329	.387
2003 Cleveland	AL	91	291	74	19	3	14	(7	7)	141	35	40	44	22	2	81	10	0	1	2	1	.67	7	.254	.327	.485
2 ML YEARS		114	353	89	23	4	15	(7	8)	165	41	46	51	30	3	96	10	0	1	2	2	.50	7	.252	.327	.467

Jerry Hairston Jr.

Bats: R **Throws:** R **Pos:** 2B-48; DH-8; PH-1; PR-1   **Ht:** 5'10" **Wt:** 175 **Born:** 5/29/76 **Age:** 28

		BATTING												BASERUNNING				AVERAGES		
Year Team	Lg	G	AB	H	2B	3B	HR	(Hm	Rd)	TB	R	RBI	RC	TBB	IBB	SO	HBP	SH	SF	SB	CS	SB%	GDP	Avg	OBP	Slg
1998 Baltimore	AL	6	7	0	0	0	0	(-	-)	0	2	0	0	0	0	1	0	0	0	0	0	-	0	.000	.000	.000
1999 Baltimore	AL	50	175	47	12	1	4	(1	3)	73	26	17	24	11	0	24	3	4	0	9	4	.69	2	.269	.323	.417
2000 Baltimore	AL	49	180	46	5	0	5	(2	3)	66	27	19	22	21	0	22	6	5	0	8	5	.62	8	.256	.353	.367
2001 Baltimore	AL	159	532	124	25	5	8	(5	3)	183	63	47	57	44	0	73	13	9	4	29	11	.73	12	.233	.305	.344
2002 Baltimore	AL	122	426	114	25	3	5	(2	3)	160	55	32	54	34	0	55	7	8	4	21	6	.78	5	.268	.329	.376
2003 Baltimore	AL	58	218	59	12	2	2	(1	1)	81	25	21	32	23	0	25	6	10	2	14	5	.74	8	.271	.353	.372
6 ML YEARS		444	1538	390	79	11	24	(11	13)	563	198	136	189	133	0	200	35	36	10	81	31	.72	35	.254	.325	.366

John Halama

Pitches: L **Bats:** L **Pos:** RP-22; SP-13   **Ht:** 6'5" **Wt:** 210 **Born:** 2/22/72 **Age:** 32

		HOW MUCH HE PITCHED						WHAT HE GAVE UP												THE RESULTS					
Year Team	Lg	G	GS	CG	GF	IP	BFP	H	R	ER	HR	SH	SF	HB	TBB	IBB	SO	WP	Bk	W	L	Pct	ShO	Sv-Op	Hld	ERC	ERA
1998 Houston	NL	6	6	0	0	32.1	147	37	21	21	0	3	4	2	13	0	21	2	1	1	1	.500	0	0-0	0	4.34	5.85
1999 Seattle	AL	38	24	1	7	179.0	763	193	88	84	20	5	9	7	56	3	105	4	0	11	10	.524	1	0-0	1	4.47	4.22
2000 Seattle	AL	30	30	1	0	166.2	736	206	108	94	19	4	6	2	56	0	87	4	1	14	9	.609	1	0-0	0	5.42	5.08
2001 Seattle	AL	31	17	0	6	110.1	485	132	69	58	18	3	4	6	26	0	50	2	0	10	7	.588	0	0-0	1	5.21	4.73
2002 Seattle	AL	31	10	0	12	101.0	438	112	45	40	9	3	2	1	33	5	70	2	1	6	5	.545	0	0-0	0	4.29	3.56
2003 Oakland	AL	35	13	0	4	108.2	484	117	68	51	18	7	3	2	36	2	51	3	3	3	5	.375	0	0-0	3	4.61	4.22
6 ML YEARS		171	100	2	29	698.0	3053	797	399	348	84	25	28	20	220	10	384	17	6	45	37	.549	2	0-0	5	4.80	4.49

Bill Hall

Bats: R **Throws:** R **Pos:** 2B-18; SS-18; PH-18; 3B-1   **Ht:** 6'0" **Wt:** 175 **Born:** 12/28/79 **Age:** 24

		BATTING												BASERUNNING				AVERAGES		
Year Team	Lg	G	AB	H	2B	3B	HR	(Hm	Rd)	TB	R	RBI	RC	TBB	IBB	SO	HBP	SH	SF	SB	CS	SB%	GDP	Avg	OBP	Slg
1998 Helena	R+	29	85	15	3	0	0	(-	-)	18	11	5	3	9	0	27	1	1	0	5	5	.50	2	.176	.263	.212
1999 Ogden	R+	69	280	81	15	2	6	(-	-)	118	41	31	38	15	1	61	2	2	1	19	8	.70	6	.289	.329	.421
2000 Beloit	A	130	470	123	30	6	3	(-	-)	174	57	41	45	18	0	127	1	12	5	10	11	.48	12	.262	.287	.370
2001 High Desert	A+	89	346	105	21	6	15	(-	-)	183	61	51	62	22	0	78	3	4	3	18	9	.67	8	.303	.348	.529
2001 Huntsville	AA	41	160	41	8	1	3	(-	-)	60	14	14	15	5	0	46	0	3	0	5	3	.63	5	.256	.279	.375
2002 Indianapolis	AAA	134	465	106	20	1	4	(-	-)	140	35	31	34	25	0	105	4	4	2	17	10	.63	12	.228	.272	.301
2003 Indianapolis	AAA	89	354	100	25	2	5	(-	-)	144	57	32	45	27	2	79	1	9	0	10	11	.48	7	.282	.335	.407
2002 Milwaukee	NL	19	36	7	1	1	1	(0	1)	13	3	5	3	3	0	13	0	0	0	0	1	.00	1	.194	.256	.361
2003 Milwaukee	NL	52	142	37	9	2	5	(2	3)	65	23	20	18	7	0	28	1	4	1	1	2	.33	5	.261	.298	.458
2 ML YEARS		71	178	44	10	3	6	(2	4)	78	26	25	21	10	0	41	1	4	1	1	3	.25	6	.247	.289	.438

Josh Hall

Pitches: R **Bats:** R **Pos:** SP-5; RP-1   **Ht:** 6'2" **Wt:** 190 **Born:** 12/16/80 **Age:** 23

		HOW MUCH HE PITCHED						WHAT HE GAVE UP												THE RESULTS					
Year Team	Lg	G	GS	CG	GF	IP	BFP	H	R	ER	HR	SH	SF	HB	TBB	IBB	SO	WP	Bk	W	L	Pct	ShO	Sv-Op	Hld	ERC	ERA
1998 Billings	R+	14	14	1	0	81.0	363	89	53	45	6	2	2	4	33	0	50	14	2	5	4	.556	0	0--	-	4.64	5.00
2000 Reds	R	6	6	0	0	15.1	84	26	25	18	2	0	1	0	13	0	20	3	0	0	5	.000	0	0--	-	10.67	10.57
2001 Dayton	A	22	22	0	0	132.1	549	117	63	39	4	2	1	2	39	1	122	18	0	11	5	.688	0	0--	-	2.63	2.65
2002 Stockton	A+	7	7	1	0	43.2	176	31	13	11	1	1	0	2	13	0	51	5	0	4	0	1.000	0	0--	-	1.89	2.27
2002 Chattanooga	AA	22	22	1	0	132.0	575	142	75	55	7	6	5	6	50	0	116	9	0	7	8	.467	0	0--	-	4.20	3.75
2003 Chattanooga	AA	26	25	2	0	153.0	655	152	73	59	9	8	6	3	53	1	114	10	1	8	10	.444	0	0--	-	3.60	3.47
2003 Cincinnati	NL	6	5	0	1	24.2	121	33	22	18	4	0	1	0	15	1	18	0	0	0	2	.000	0	0-0	0	7.32	6.57

Toby Hall

Bats: R **Throws:** R **Pos:** C-130　　　　　　　**Ht:** 6'3" **Wt:** 240 **Born:** 10/21/75 **Age:** 28

Year Team	Lg	G	AB	H	2B	3B	HR	(Hm	Rd)	TB	R	RBI	RC	TBB	IBB	SO	HBP	SH	SF	SB	CS	SB%	GDP	Avg	OBP	Slg
2000 Tampa Bay	AL	4	12	2	0	0	1	(0	1)	5	1	1	1	1	0	0	0	0	0	0	0	-	0	.167	.231	.417
2001 Tampa Bay	AL	49	188	56	16	0	4	(1	3)	84	28	30	25	4	0	16	3	0	1	2	2	.50	5	.298	.321	.447
2002 Tampa Bay	AL	85	330	85	19	1	6	(2	4)	124	37	42	39	17	3	27	1	2	3	0	1	.00	14	.258	.293	.376
2003 Tampa Bay	AL	130	463	117	23	0	12	(4	8)	176	50	47	45	23	4	40	7	0	5	0	1	.00	14	.253	.295	.380
4 ML YEARS		268	993	260	58	1	23	(7	16)	389	116	120	110	45	7	83	11	2	9	2	4	.33	33	.262	.299	.392

Roy Halladay

Pitches: R **Bats:** R **Pos:** SP-36　　　　　　　**Ht:** 6'6" **Wt:** 230 **Born:** 5/14/77 **Age:** 27

Year Team	Lg	G	GS	CG	GF	IP	BFP	H	R	ER	HR	SH	SF	HB	TBB	IBB	SO	WP	Bk	W	L	Pct	ShO	Sv-Op	Hld	ERC	ERA
1998 Toronto	AL	2	2	1	0	14.0	53	9	4	3	2	0	0	0	2	0	13	0	0	1	0	1.000	0	0-0	0	1.61	1.93
1999 Toronto	AL	36	18	1	2	149.1	668	156	76	65	19	3	4	4	79	1	82	6	0	8	7	.533	1	1-1	2	5.19	3.92
2000 Toronto	AL	19	13	0	4	67.2	349	107	87	80	14	2	3	2	42	0	44	6	1	4	7	.364	0	0-0	0	9.70	10.64
2001 Toronto	AL	17	16	1	0	105.1	432	97	41	37	3	3	1	1	25	0	96	4	1	5	3	.625	1	0-0	0	2.61	3.16
2002 Toronto	AL	34	34	2	0	239.1	993	223	93	78	10	9	2	7	62	6	168	4	1	19	7	.731	1	0-0	0	2.85	2.93
2003 Toronto	AL	36	36	9	0	266.0	1071	253	111	96	26	3	2	9	32	1	204	6	1	22	7	.759	2	0-0	0	2.86	3.25
6 ML YEARS		144	119	14	6	841.2	3566	845	412	359	74	20	12	23	242	8	607	26	4	59	31	.656	5	1-1	2	3.66	3.84

Shane Halter

Bats: R **Throws:** R **Pos:** 3B-50; SS-27; 2B-24; 1B-12; PH-10; DH-4; LF-2; PR-2　　　　**Ht:** 6'0" **Wt:** 180 **Born:** 11/8/69 **Age:** 34

Year Team	Lg	G	AB	H	2B	3B	HR	(Hm	Rd)	TB	R	RBI	RC	TBB	IBB	SO	HBP	SH	SF	SB	CS	SB%	GDP	Avg	OBP	Slg
1997 Kansas City	AL	74	123	34	5	1	2	(1	1)	47	16	10	16	10	0	28	2	4	0	4	3	.57	1	.276	.341	.382
1998 Kansas City	AL	86	204	45	12	0	2	(0	2)	63	17	13	15	12	0	38	1	7	2	2	5	.29	3	.221	.265	.309
1999 New York	NL	7	0	0	0	0	0	(0	0)	0	0	0	0	0	0	0	0	0	0	0	0	-	0	-	-	-
2000 Detroit	AL	105	238	62	12	2	3	(0	3)	87	26	27	26	14	0	49	1	10	2	5	2	.71	5	.261	.302	.366
2001 Detroit	AL	136	450	128	32	7	13	(4	8)	210	53	65	69	37	2	100	7	7	5	3	3	.50	14	.284	.344	.467
2002 Detroit	AL	122	410	98	22	6	10	(4	6)	162	46	39	45	39	1	92	4	1	4	0	4	.00	12	.239	.309	.395
2003 Detroit	AL	114	360	78	5	2	12	(6	6)	123	33	30	24	27	0	77	0	3	3	2	3	.40	11	.217	.269	.342
7 ML YEARS		644	1785	445	88	18	41	(15	26)	692	191	184	195	139	3	384	15	32	17	16	20	.44	46	.249	.306	.388

Joey Hamilton

Pitches: R **Bats:** R **Pos:** RP-3　　　　　　　**Ht:** 6'4" **Wt:** 240 **Born:** 9/9/70 **Age:** 33

Year Team	Lg	G	GS	CG	GF	IP	BFP	H	R	ER	HR	SH	SF	HB	TBB	IBB	SO	WP	Bk	W	L	Pct	ShO	Sv-Op	Hld	ERC	ERA
2003 Louisville*	AAA	33	8	0	7	86.1	366	103	38	31	5	2	5	4	18	1	45	0	1	8	3	.727	0	1- -	-	4.39	3.23
1994 San Diego	NL	16	16	1	0	108.2	447	98	40	36	7	4	2	6	29	3	61	6	0	9	6	.600	1	0-0	0	3.00	2.98
1995 San Diego	NL	31	30	2	1	204.1	850	189	89	70	17	12	4	11	56	5	123	2	0	6	9	.400	2	0-0	0	3.25	3.08
1996 San Diego	NL	34	33	3	0	211.2	908	206	100	98	19	6	5	9	83	3	184	14	1	15	9	.625	1	0-0	0	3.99	4.17
1997 San Diego	NL	31	29	1	1	192.2	831	199	100	91	22	8	8	12	69	2	124	7	0	12	7	.632	0	0-0	0	4.48	4.25
1998 San Diego	NL	34	34	0	0	217.1	950	220	113	103	16	15	6	8	106	10	147	4	0	13	13	.500	0	0-0	0	4.36	4.27
1999 Toronto	AL	22	18	0	1	98.0	440	118	73	71	13	0	2	3	39	0	56	4	1	7	8	.467	0	0-0	0	5.69	6.52
2000 Toronto	AL	6	6	0	0	30.0	135	28	13	13	3	0	1	2	12	0	15	0	0	2	1	.667	0	0-0	0	3.38	3.55
2001 Tor-Cin		26	26	0	0	139.2	633	193	100	92	20	6	8	4	44	1	92	5	0	6	10	.375	0	0-0	0	6.57	5.93
2002 Cincinnati	NL	39	17	0	9	124.2	554	136	78	73	11	7	3	6	50	2	85	5	0	4	10	.286	0	1-2	4	4.67	5.27
2003 Cincinnati	NL	3	0	0	1	10.2	57	21	15	15	3	0	0	0	5	0	7	0	0	0	0	-	0	0-0	0	12.37	12.66
2001 Toronto	AL	22	22	0	0	122.1	554	170	88	80	17	4	8	3	38	1	82	5	0	5	8	.385	0	0-0	0	6.55	5.89
2001 Cincinnati	NL	4	4	0	0	17.1	79	23	12	12	3	2	0	1	6	0	10	0	0	1	2	.333	0	0-0	0	6.72	6.23
10 ML YEARS		242	209	7	13	1340.2	5813	1408	721	662	130	56	39	61	493	26	894	47	2	74	73	.503	4	1-2	6	4.39	4.44

Robby Hammock

Bats: R **Throws:** R **Pos:** C-36; 3B-16; RF-12; LF-5; PH-3; DH-1; PR-1　　　　**Ht:** 5'10" **Wt:** 187 **Born:** 5/13/77 **Age:** 27

Year Team	Lg	G	AB	H	2B	3B	HR	(Hm	Rd)	TB	R	RBI	RC	TBB	IBB	SO	HBP	SH	SF	SB	CS	SB%	GDP	Avg	OBP	Slg
1998 Lethbridge	R+	62	227	65	14	2	10	(-	-)	113	46	56	41	28	1	34	2	0	2	5	4	.56	3	.286	.367	.498
1999 High Desert	A+	114	379	26	20	7	9	(-	-)	87	80	72	6	47	2	63	2	0	6	3	6	.33	8	.069	.173	.230
2000 High Desert	A+	40	136	48	15	1	3	(-	-)	74	25	23	32	27	1	24	1	0	3	3	3	.50	5	.353	.455	.544
2000 El Paso	AA	45	140	35	5	1	1	(-	-)	45	22	15	14	11	1	25	1	0	2	1	2	.33	1	.250	.305	.321
2001 El Paso	AA	26	74	12	5	0	0	(-	-)	17	6	4	3	7	0	18	0	1	0	2	2	.50	1	.162	.235	.230
2001 South Bend	A	34	125	31	3	2	2	(-	-)	44	16	14	13	14	0	21	0	1	0	5	6	.45	2	.248	.324	.352
2001 Lancaster	A+	45	190	59	11	3	4	(-	-)	88	33	36	32	16	1	42	7	0	4	9	7	.56	8	.311	.378	.463
2002 El Paso	AA	122	441	128	28	4	11	(-	-)	197	68	73	69	43	0	68	8	1	8	5	4	.56	14	.290	.358	.447
2003 Tucson	AAA	33	116	31	6	2	2	(-	-)	47	14	17	16	11	0	24	0	0	4	1	0	1.00	2	.267	.321	.405
2003 Arizona	NL	65	195	55	10	2	8	(5	3)	93	30	28	28	17	3	44	2	0	2	3	2	.60	5	.282	.343	.477

Chris Hammond

Pitches: L **Bats:** L **Pos:** RP-62　　　　　　　**Ht:** 6'1" **Wt:** 195 **Born:** 1/21/66 **Age:** 38

Year Team	Lg	G	GS	CG	GF	IP	BFP	H	R	ER	HR	SH	SF	HB	TBB	IBB	SO	WP	Bk	W	L	Pct	ShO	Sv-Op	Hld	ERC	ERA
1990 Cincinnati	NL	3	3	0	0	11.1	56	19	8	8	2	1	0	0	12	1	4	1	3	0	2	.000	0	0-0	0	8.50	6.35
1991 Cincinnati	NL	20	18	0	0	99.2	425	92	51	45	4	6	1	2	48	3	50	3	0	7	7	.500	0	0-0	0	3.63	4.06
1992 Cincinnati	NL	28	26	0	1	147.1	627	149	75	69	13	5	3	3	55	6	79	6	0	7	10	.412	0	0-0	0	4.02	4.21
1993 Florida	NL	32	32	1	0	191.0	826	207	106	99	18	10	2	1	66	2	108	10	5	11	12	.478	1	0-0	0	4.31	4.66
1994 Florida	NL	13	13	1	0	73.1	312	79	30	25	5	5	2	1	23	1	40	3	0	4	4	.500	1	0-0	0	4.03	3.07
1995 Florida	NL	25	24	3	0	161.0	683	157	73	68	17	7	7	4	47	2	126	3	1	9	6	.600	2	0-0	0	3.75	3.80

Year Team	Lg	HOW MUCH HE PITCHED						WHAT HE GAVE UP										THE RESULTS						
		G	GS	CG	GF	IP	BFP	H	R	ER	HR	SF	SF	HB	TBB	IBB	SO	WP	Bk	W	L	Pct	ShO	Sv-Op	Hld	ERC	ERA
1996 Florida	NL	38	9	0	5	81.0	368	104	65	59	14	3	4	4	27	3	50	1	0	5	8	.385	0	0-0	5	6.21	6.56
1997 Boston	AL	29	8	0	6	65.1	293	81	45	43	5	0	3	2	27	4	48	2	0	3	4	.429	0	1-2	4	5.47	5.92
1998 Florida	NL	3	3	0	0	13.2	67	20	11	10	3	2	0	1	8	0	8	0	0	0	2	.000	0	0-0	0	9.33	6.59
2002 Atlanta	NL	63	0	0	6	76.0	311	53	15	8	1	5	2	1	31	9	63	1	0	7	2	.778	0	0-2	17	1.85	0.95
2003 New York	AL	62	0	0	16	63.0	262	65	23	20	5	5	3	2	11	0	45	1	0	3	2	.600	0	1-4	17	3.36	2.86
11 ML YEARS		316	136	5	34	982.2	4230	1020	503	454	87	49	27	26	355	31	621	31	9	56	59	.487	3	2-8	43	4.14	4.16

Jeffrey Hammonds

Bats: R **Throws:** R **Pos:** LF-17; CF-14; RF-14; PH-8; PR-1   **Ht:** 6'0" **Wt:** 200 **Born:** 3/5/71 **Age:** 33

Year Team	Lg	BATTING																		BASERUNNING				AVERAGES		
		G	AB	H	2B	3B	HR	(Hm	Rd)	TB	R	RBI	RC	TBB	IBB	SO	HBP	SH	SF	SB	CS	SB%	GDP	Avg	OBP	Slg
2003 Giants*	R	4	10	5	1	1	3	(-	-)	17	4	6	6	1	0	1	0	0	0	0	0	-	2	.500	.545	1.700
2003 Fresno*	AAA	11	36	12	1	0	2	(-	-)	19	7	2	7	3	0	3	0	0	0	1	0	1.00	1	.333	.385	.528
1993 Baltimore	AL	33	105	32	8	0	3	(2	1)	49	10	19	15	2	1	16	0	1	2	4	0	1.00	3	.305	.312	.467
1994 Baltimore	AL	68	250	74	18	2	8	(6	2)	120	45	31	42	17	1	39	2	0	5	5	0	1.00	3	.296	.339	.480
1995 Baltimore	AL	57	178	43	9	1	4	(2	2)	66	18	23	18	9	0	30	1	1	2	4	2	.67	3	.242	.279	.371
1996 Baltimore	AL	71	248	56	10	1	9	(3	6)	95	38	27	27	23	1	53	4	6	1	3	3	.50	7	.226	.301	.383
1997 Baltimore	AL	118	397	105	19	3	21	(9	12)	193	71	55	64	32	1	73	3	0	2	15	1	.94	6	.264	.323	.486
1998 Bal-Cin		89	257	72	16	2	6	(1	5)	110	50	39	45	39	1	56	3	3	4	8	3	.73	2	.280	.376	.428
1999 Cincinnati	NL	123	262	73	13	0	17	(5	12)	137	43	41	45	27	0	64	1	2	1	3	6	.33	4	.279	.347	.523
2000 Colorado	NL	122	454	152	24	2	20	(14	6)	240	94	106	90	44	4	83	5	2	6	14	7	.67	11	.335	.395	.529
2001 Milwaukee	NL	49	174	43	11	1	6	(3	3)	74	20	21	23	14	1	42	4	0	2	5	3	.63	2	.247	.314	.425
2002 Milwaukee	NL	128	448	115	26	5	9	(2	7)	178	47	41	53	52	0	86	2	1	7	4	5	.44	13	.257	.332	.397
2003 Mil-SF	NL	46	132	32	12	0	4	(3	1)	56	22	13	15	16	0	28	1	0	0	1	0	1.00	5	.242	.329	.424
1998 Baltimore	AL	63	171	46	12	1	6	(1	5)	78	36	28	31	26	1	38	3	0	3	7	2	.78	2	.269	.369	.456
1998 Cincinnati	NL	26	86	26	4	1	0	(0	0)	32	14	11	14	13	0	18	0	3	1	1	1	.50	0	.302	.390	.372
2003 Milwaukee	NL	10	38	6	2	0	1	(1	0)	11	2	3	0	3	0	7	0	0	0	0	0	-	2	.158	.220	.289
2003 San Francisco	NL	36	94	26	10	0	3	(2	1)	45	20	10	15	13	0	21	1	0	0	1	0	1.00	1	.277	.370	.479
11 ML YEARS		904	2905	797	166	17	107	(50	57)	1318	458	416	437	275	10	570	26	16	32	66	30	.69	57	.274	.339	.454

Mike Hampton

Pitches: L **Bats:** R **Pos:** SP-31   **Ht:** 5'10" **Wt:** 180 **Born:** 9/9/72 **Age:** 31

Year Team	Lg	HOW MUCH HE PITCHED						WHAT HE GAVE UP												THE RESULTS						
		G	GS	CG	GF	IP	BFP	H	R	ER	HR	SH	SF	HB	TBB	IBB	SO	WP	Bk	W	L	Pct	ShO	Sv-Op	Hld	ERC	ERA
1993 Seattle	AL	13	3	0	2	17.0	95	28	20	18	3	1	1	0	17	3	8	1	1	1	3	.250	0	1-1	2	11.09	9.53
1994 Houston	NL	44	0	0	7	41.1	181	46	19	17	4	0	0	2	16	1	24	5	1	2	1	.667	0	0-1	10	4.88	3.70
1995 Houston	NL	24	24	0	0	150.2	641	141	73	56	13	11	5	4	49	3	115	3	1	9	8	.529	0	0-0	0	3.37	3.35
1996 Houston	NL	27	27	2	0	160.1	691	175	79	64	12	10	3	3	49	1	101	7	2	10	10	.500	1	0-0	0	4.11	3.59
1997 Houston	NL	34	34	7	0	223.0	941	217	105	95	16	11	7	2	77	2	139	6	1	15	10	.600	2	0-0	0	3.56	3.83
1998 Houston	NL	32	32	1	0	211.2	917	227	92	79	18	7	7	5	81	1	137	4	2	11	7	.611	1	0-0	0	4.45	3.36
1999 Houston	NL	34	34	3	0	239.0	979	206	86	77	12	10	9	5	101	2	177	9	0	22	4	.846	2	0-0	0	3.25	2.90
2000 New York	NL	33	33	3	0	217.2	929	194	89	76	10	11	5	8	99	5	151	10	0	15	10	.600	1	0-0	0	3.44	3.14
2001 Colorado	NL	32	32	2	0	203.0	904	236	138	122	31	8	6	8	85	7	122	6	0	14	13	.519	1	0-0	0	5.69	5.41
2002 Colorado	NL	30	30	0	0	178.2	838	228	135	122	24	9	9	7	91	4	74	9	2	7	15	.318	0	0-0	0	6.61	6.15
2003 Atlanta	NL	31	31	1	0	190.0	823	186	91	81	14	10	5	1	78	4	110	10	1	14	8	.636	1	0-0	0	3.77	3.84
11 ML YEARS		334	280	19	9	1832.1	7939	1884	927	807	157	81	57	45	743	33	1158	70	11	120	89	.574	8	1-2	12	4.25	3.96

Josh Hancock

Pitches: R **Bats:** R **Pos:** RP-2   **Ht:** 6'3" **Wt:** 217 **Born:** 4/11/78 **Age:** 26

Year Team	Lg	HOW MUCH HE PITCHED						WHAT HE GAVE UP												THE RESULTS						
		G	GS	CG	GF	IP	BFP	H	R	ER	HR	SH	SF	HB	TBB	IBB	SO	WP	Bk	W	L	Pct	ShO	Sv-Op	Hld	ERC	ERA
1998 Red Sox	R	5	1	0	1	13.1	51	9	5	5	1	2	0	0	3	0	21	0	0	1	1	.500	0	0- -	-	1.69	3.38
1998 Lowell	A-	1	1	0	0	4.0	20	5	2	1	0	0	1	0	4	0	4	1	0	1	0	1.000	0	0- -	-	7.36	2.25
1999 Augusta	A	25	25	0	0	139.2	607	154	79	59	12	4	2	4	46	0	106	10	1	6	8	.429	0	0- -	-	4.41	3.80
2000 Sarasota	A+	26	24	1	0	143.2	628	164	89	71	9	5	6	6	37	0	95	8	2	5	10	.333	0	0- -	-	4.17	4.45
2001 Trenton	AA	24	24	0	0	130.2	553	138	60	53	8	3	2	4	37	0	119	11	0	8	6	.571	0	0- -	-	3.82	3.65
2002 Trenton	AA	15	14	2	1	84.2	351	82	40	34	9	0	0	5	18	0	69	5	0	3	4	.429	0	1- -	-	3.46	3.61
2002 Pawtucket	AAA	8	8	0	0	44.1	198	39	20	17	2	2	2	2	26	0	29	3	0	4	2	.667	0	0- -	-	3.85	3.45
2003 Scrtn/WlksBr	AAA	28	27	2	1	165.2	677	147	78	71	14	2	6	6	46	1	122	4	0	10	9	.526	2	0- -	-	3.06	3.86
2002 Boston	AL	3	1	0	2	7.1	28	5	3	3	1	1	0	0	2	0	6	0	0	0	0	1.000	0	0-0	0	2.25	3.68
2003 Philadelphia	NL	2	0	0	0	3.0	11	2	1	1	0	0	0	0	0	0	4	0	0	0	0	-	0	0-0	0	0.91	3.00
2 ML YEARS		5	1	0	2	10.1	39	7	4	4	1	1	0	0	2	0	10	0	0	0	1	.000	0	0-0	0	1.73	3.48

Dave Hansen

Bats: L **Throws:** R **Pos:** PH-78; 1B-20; 3B-11; DH-3; 2B-1   **Ht:** 6'0" **Wt:** 195 **Born:** 11/24/68 **Age:** 35

Year Team	Lg	BATTING																		BASERUNNING				AVERAGES		
		G	AB	H	2B	3B	HR	(Hm	Rd)	TB	R	RBI	RC	TBB	IBB	SO	HBP	SH	SF	SB	CS	SB%	GDP	Avg	OBP	Slg
1990 Los Angeles	NL	5	7	1	0	0	0	(0	0)	1	0	1	0	0	0	3	0	0	0	0	0	-	0	.143	.143	.143
1991 Los Angeles	NL	53	56	15	4	0	1	(0	1)	22	3	5	6	2	0	12	0	0	0	1	0	1.00	1	.268	.293	.393
1992 Los Angeles	NL	132	341	73	11	0	6	(1	5)	102	30	22	27	34	3	49	1	0	2	0	2	.00	9	.214	.286	.299
1993 Los Angeles	NL	84	105	38	3	0	4	(2	2)	53	13	30	25	21	3	13	0	0	1	0	1	.00	6	.362	.465	.505
1994 Los Angeles	NL	40	44	15	3	0	0	(0	0)	18	3	5	8	5	0	5	0	0	0	0	0	-	1	.341	.408	.409
1995 Los Angeles	NL	100	181	52	10	0	1	(0	1)	65	19	14	26	28	4	28	1	0	1	0	0	-	4	.287	.384	.359
1996 Los Angeles	NL	80	104	23	1	0	0	(0	0)	24	7	6	6	11	1	22	0	0	1	0	0	-	4	.221	.293	.231
1997 Chicago	NL	90	151	47	8	2	3	(1	2)	68	19	21	31	31	1	32	1	2	1	1	2	.33	4	.311	.429	.450
1999 Los Angeles	NL	100	107	27	8	1	2	(2	0)	43	14	17	19	26	0	20	2	0	1	0	0	-	2	.252	.404	.402
2000 Los Angeles	NL	102	121	35	6	2	8	(4	4)	69	18	26	27	26	0	32	0	0	0	0	1	.00	3	.289	.415	.570
2001 Los Angeles	NL	92	140	33	10	0	2	(1	1)	49	13	20	20	32	5	29	0	0	3	0	1	.00	3	.236	.371	.350

Year Team	Lg	G	AB	H	2B	3B	HR	(Hm	Rd)	TB	R	RBI	RC	TBB	IBB	SO	HBP	SH	SF	SB	CS	SB%	GDP	Avg	OBP	Slg
								BATTING												BASERUNNING				AVERAGES		
2002 Los Angeles	NL	96	120	35	6	0	2	(0	2)	47	15	17	17	14	3	22	0	0	1	1	0	1.00	2	.292	.363	.392
2003 San Diego	NL	110	135	33	4	1	2	(2	0)	45	13	15	17	23	3	25	1	0	0	1	0	1.00	1	.244	.358	.333
13 ML YEARS		1084	1612	427	74	6	31	(13	18)	606	167	199	229	253	23	292	6	2	11	4	7	.36	33	.265	.365	.376

Aaron Harang

Pitches: R **Bats:** R **Pos:** SP-15; RP-1 — **Ht:** 6'7" **Wt:** 240 **Born:** 5/9/78 **Age:** 26

Year Team	Lg	G	GS	CG	GF	IP	BFP	H	R	ER	HR	SH	SF	HB	TBB	IBB	SO	WP	Bk	W	L	Pct	ShO	Sv-Op	Hld	ERC	ERA
1999 Pulaski	R+	16	10	1	6	78.1	309	64	22	20	5	2	3	4	17	1	87	2	1	9	2	.818	1	1--	-	2.44	2.30
2000 Charlotte	A+	28	27	3	0	157.0	642	128	68	58	10	1	3	7	50	0	136	5	1	13	5	.722	2	0--	-	2.73	3.32
2001 Midland	AA	27	27	0	0	150.0	654	173	81	69	9	0	3	6	37	1	112	3	0	10	8	.556	0	0--	-	4.17	4.14
2002 Midland	AA	3	3	0	0	16.2	66	12	3	2	0	1	0	3	7	0	21	1	0	2	0	1.000	0	0--	-	2.86	1.08
2002 Sacramento	AAA	8	8	0	0	38.2	165	41	17	14	1	0	0	2	9	0	39	2	0	3	3	.500	0	0--	-	3.43	3.26
2003 Louisville	AAA	1	1	0	0	3.0	16	5	5	5	1	0	0	0	2	0	4	0	0	0	1	.000	0	0--	-	11.45	15.00
2003 Sacramento	AAA	12	12	0	0	69.2	287	62	24	21	5	1	0	4	17	0	60	1	0	8	2	.800	0	0--	-	2.92	2.71
2002 Oakland	AL	16	15	0	0	78.1	354	78	44	42	7	3	4	3	45	2	64	1	0	5	4	.556	0	0-0	0	4.76	4.83
2003 Oak-Cin		16	15	0	1	76.1	327	89	47	45	11	5	1	1	19	0	42	3	1	5	6	.455	0	0-0	0	4.84	5.31
2003 Oakland	AL	7	6	0	1	30.1	136	41	19	18	5	2	1	0	9	0	16	0	1	1	3	.250	0	0-0	0	6.32	5.34
2003 Cincinnati	NL	9	9	0	0	46.0	191	48	28	27	6	3	0	1	10	0	26	3	0	4	3	.571	0	0-0	0	3.94	5.28
2 ML YEARS		32	30	0	1	154.2	681	167	91	87	18	8	5	4	64	2	106	4	1	10	10	.500	0	0-0	0	4.81	5.06

Rich Harden

Pitches: R **Bats:** L **Pos:** SP-13; RP-2 — **Ht:** 6'1" **Wt:** 180 **Born:** 11/30/81 **Age:** 22

Year Team	Lg	G	GS	CG	GF	IP	BFP	H	R	ER	HR	SH	SF	HB	TBB	IBB	SO	WP	Bk	W	L	Pct	ShO	Sv-Op	Hld	ERC	ERA
2001 Vancouver	A-	18	14	0	3	74.1	309	47	29	28	3	3	1	4	38	0	100	8	1	2	4	.333	0	0--	-	2.35	3.39
2002 Visalia	A+	12	12	1	0	67.2	271	49	27	22	4	0	2	3	24	0	85	3	1	4	3	.571	0	0--	-	2.29	2.93
2002 Midland	AA	16	16	1	0	85.1	365	67	33	28	2	1	0	3	52	1	102	1	1	8	3	.727	0	0--	-	3.32	2.95
2003 Sacramento	AAA	16	14	0	0	88.2	357	72	34	31	6	1	1	1	35	0	91	5	0	9	4	.692	0	0--	-	2.98	3.15
2003 Midland	AA	2	2	0	0	13.0	39	0	0	0	0	0	0	0	0	0	17	0	0	2	0	1.000	0	0--	-	0.00	0.00
2003 Oakland	AL	15	13	0	0	74.2	324	72	38	37	5	2	3	1	40	1	67	6	0	5	4	.556	0	0-0	0	4.28	4.46

Danny Haren

Pitches: R **Bats:** R **Pos:** SP-14 — **Ht:** 6'5" **Wt:** 220 **Born:** 9/17/80 **Age:** 23

Year Team	Lg	G	GS	CG	GF	IP	BFP	H	R	ER	HR	SH	SF	HB	TBB	IBB	SO	WP	Bk	W	L	Pct	ShO	Sv-Op	Hld	ERC	ERA
2001 New Jersey	A-	12	8	0	1	52.1	210	47	22	18	6	0	0	5	8	0	57	1	0	3	3	.500	0	1--	-	3.10	3.10
2002 Peoria	A	14	14	1	0	101.2	399	89	32	22	6	0	4	2	12	0	89	4	2	7	3	.700	0	0--	-	2.23	1.95
2002 Potomac	A+	14	14	1	0	92.0	383	90	43	37	8	3	1	3	19	2	82	2	1	3	6	.333	0	0--	-	3.20	3.62
2003 Memphis	AAA	8	8	0	0	45.2	197	50	25	25	6	1	0	4	8	1	35	1	1	2	1	.667	0	0--	-	4.20	4.93
2003 Tennessee	AA	8	8	0	0	55.0	209	36	8	5	2	3	0	1	6	0	49	1	0	6	0	1.000	0	0--	-	1.24	0.82
2003 St Louis	NL	14	14	0	0	72.2	320	84	44	41	9	4	2	5	22	0	43	3	0	3	7	.300	0	0-0	0	5.07	5.08

Travis Harper

Pitches: R **Bats:** R **Pos:** RP-61 — **Ht:** 6'4" **Wt:** 192 **Born:** 5/21/76 **Age:** 28

Year Team	Lg	G	GS	CG	GF	IP	BFP	H	R	ER	HR	SH	SF	HB	TBB	IBB	SO	WP	Bk	W	L	Pct	ShO	Sv-Op	Hld	ERC	ERA
2000 Tampa Bay	AL	6	5	1	0	32.0	141	30	17	17	5	1	1	1	15	0	14	1	0	1	2	.333	1	0-0	0	4.46	4.78
2001 Tampa Bay	AL	2	2	0	0	7.0	36	15	11	6	5	0	0	0	3	0	2	1	0	2	.000	0	0-0	0	19.14	7.71
2002 Tampa Bay	AL	37	7	0	16	85.2	394	101	54	52	14	5	4	9	27	3	60	2	0	5	9	.357	0	1-2	3	5.49	5.46
2003 Tampa Bay	AL	61	0	0	14	93.0	388	86	45	39	9	7	3	6	31	8	64	6	0	4	8	.333	0	1-6	15	3.56	3.77
4 ML YEARS		106	14	1	30	217.2	959	232	127	114	33	13	8	16	76	11	140	10	0	10	21	.323	1	2-8	18	4.82	4.71

Lenny Harris

Bats: L **Throws:** R **Pos:** PH-47; 3B-35; LF-3; RF-3; 1B-2; PR-1 — **Ht:** 5'10" **Wt:** 220 **Born:** 10/28/64 **Age:** 39

Year Team	Lg	G	AB	H	2B	3B	HR	(Hm	Rd)	TB	R	RBI	RC	TBB	IBB	SO	HBP	SH	SF	SB	CS	SB%	GDP	Avg	OBP	Slg
2003 Albuquerque*	AAA	8	24	4	1	0	0	(-	-)	5	3	1	1	4	2	3	0	0	0	0	0	-	1	.167	.286	.208
1988 Cincinnati	NL	16	43	16	1	0	0	(0	0)	17	7	8	8	5	0	4	0	1	2	4	1	.80	1	.372	.420	.395
1989 Cin-LA	NL	115	335	79	10	1	3	(1	2)	100	36	26	23	20	0	33	2	1	0	14	9	.61	14	.236	.283	.299
1990 Los Angeles	NL	137	431	131	16	4	2	(0	2)	161	61	29	55	29	2	31	1	3	1	15	10	.60	8	.304	.348	.374
1991 Los Angeles	NL	145	429	123	16	1	3	(1	2)	150	59	38	52	37	5	32	5	12	2	12	3	.80	16	.287	.349	.350
1992 Los Angeles	NL	135	347	94	11	0	0	(0	0)	105	28	30	33	24	3	24	1	6	2	19	7	.73	10	.271	.318	.303
1993 Los Angeles	NL	107	160	38	6	1	2	(0	2)	52	20	11	15	15	4	15	0	1	0	3	1	.75	4	.238	.303	.325
1994 Cincinnati	NL	66	100	31	3	1	0	(0	0)	36	13	14	13	5	0	13	0	0	1	7	2	.78	0	.310	.340	.360
1995 Cincinnati	NL	101	197	41	8	3	2	(0	2)	61	32	16	15	14	0	20	0	3	1	10	1	.91	6	.208	.259	.310
1996 Cincinnati	NL	125	302	86	17	2	5	(2	3)	122	33	32	41	21	1	31	1	6	3	14	6	.70	3	.285	.330	.404
1997 Cincinnati	NL	120	238	65	13	1	3	(2	1)	89	32	28	27	18	1	18	2	3	2	4	3	.57	10	.273	.327	.374
1998 Cin-NYM	NL	132	290	75	15	0	6	(2	4)	108	30	27	29	17	3	21	2	4	4	6	5	.55	13	.259	.300	.372
1999 Col-Ari	NL	110	187	58	13	0	1	(1	0)	74	17	20	23	9	0	7	0	0	1	2	1	.67	7	.310	.330	.396
2000 Ari-NYM	NL	112	223	58	7	4	4	(2	2)	85	31	26	28	20	2	22	0	0	2	13	1	.93	7	.260	.317	.381
2001 New York	NL	110	135	30	5	1	0	(0	0)	37	12	9	9	8	0	9	0	0	0	3	2	.60	3	.222	.266	.274
2002 Milwaukee	NL	122	197	60	8	2	3	(2	1)	81	23	17	25	14	1	17	2	1	1	4	1	.80	4	.305	.355	.411
2003 ChC-Fla	NL	88	145	28	3	0	1	(0	1)	34	14	8	8	16	3	21	0	1	1	1	0	1.00	2	.193	.272	.234
1989 Cincinnati	NL	61	188	42	4	0	2	(0	2)	52	17	11	11	9	0	20	1	1	0	10	6	.63	5	.223	.263	.277
1989 Los Angeles	NL	54	147	37	6	1	1	(1	0)	48	19	15	12	11	0	13	1	0	0	4	3	.57	9	.252	.308	.327
1998 Cincinnati	NL	57	122	36	8	0	0	(0	0)	44	12	10	12	8	2	9	1	0	2	1	3	.25	8	.295	.338	.361
1998 New York	NL	75	168	39	7	0	6	(2	4)	64	18	17	17	9	1	12	1	4	2	5	2	.71	5	.232	.272	.381

Year Team	Lg	G	AB	H	2B	3B	HR	(Hm Rd)	TB	R	RBI	RC	TBB	IBB	SO	HBP	SH	SF	SB	CS	SB%	GDP	Avg	OBP	Slg
1999 Colorado	NL	91	158	47	12	0	0	(0 0)	59	15	13	17	6	0	6	0	0	0	1	1	.50	7	.297	.323	.373
1999 Arizona	NL	19	29	11	1	0	1	(1 0)	15	2	7	6	0	0	1	0	0	0	1	0	1.00	0	.379	.367	.517
2000 Arizona	NL	36	85	16	1	1	1	(1 0)	22	9	13	4	3	1	5	0	0	3	5	0	1.00	0	.188	.209	.259
2000 New York	NL	76	138	42	6	3	3	(1 2)	63	22	13	24	17	1	17	0	0	2	8	1	.89	4	.304	.381	.457
2003 Chicago	NL	75	131	24	3	0	1	(0 1)	30	11	7	6	13	3	20	0	1	1	1	0	1.00	1	.183	.255	.229
2003 Florida	NL	13	14	4	0	0	0	(0 0)	4	3	1	2	3	0	1	0	0	0	0	0	-	1	.286	.412	.286
16 ML YEARS		1741	3759	1013	152	21	35	(13 22)	1312	448	339	404	269	25	318	16	44	24	131	53	.71	107	.269	.319	.349

Willie Harris

Bats: L Throws: R Pos: CF-61; 2B-12; PR-12; PH-8   Ht: 5'9" Wt: 175 Born: 6/22/78 Age: 26

Year Team	Lg	G	AB	H	2B	3B	HR	(Hm Rd)	TB	R	RBI	RC	TBB	IBB	SO	HBP	SH	SF	SB	CS	SB%	GDP	Avg	OBP	Slg
2003 Charlotte*	AAA	28	100	38	6	1	6	(- -)	64	22	13	29	17	0	20	0	1	0	9	3	.75	0	.380	.470	.640
2001 Baltimore	AL	9	24	3	1	0	0	(- -)	4	3	0	0	0	0	7	0	1	0	0	0	-	0	.125	.125	.167
2002 Chicago	AL	49	163	38	4	0	2	(2 0)	48	14	12	15	9	0	21	0	3	2	8	0	1.00	3	.233	.270	.294
2003 Chicago	AL	79	137	33	3	1	0	(0 0)	33	19	5	11	10	0	28	0	3	0	12	2	.86	1	.204	.259	.241
3 ML YEARS		137	324	69	8	1	2	(2 0)	85	36	17	26	19	0	56	0	7	2	20	2	.91	4	.213	.255	.262

Bo Hart

Bats: R Throws: R Pos: 2B-69; PH-7; SS-3; PR-1   Ht: 5'11" Wt: 175 Born: 9/27/76 Age: 27

Year Team	Lg	G	AB	H	2B	3B	HR	(Hm Rd)	TB	R	RBI	RC	TBB	IBB	SO	HBP	SH	SF	SB	CS	SB%	GDP	Avg	OBP	Slg
1999 New Jersey	A-	50	163	30	3	3	3	(- -)	48	23	15	14	10	0	38	12	3	0	4	2	.67	1	.184	.281	.294
2000 Potomac	A+	75	273	70	25	4	0	(- -)	103	42	20	37	23	0	42	13	4	1	9	6	.60	2	.256	.342	.377
2001 Potomac	A+	81	279	85	23	3	5	(- -)	129	48	34	49	17	1	69	15	4	1	16	7	.70	3	.305	.375	.462
2002 New Haven	AA	104	405	101	17	6	4	(- -)	142	61	39	50	43	1	82	12	1	2	14	7	.67	6	.249	.338	.351
2003 Memphis	AAA	67	266	79	14	2	7	(- -)	118	30	31	39	15	1	55	0	0	3	4	2	.67	2	.297	.331	.444
2003 St Louis	NL	77	296	82	13	5	4	(1 3)	117	46	28	37	12	0	64	6	6	1	3	1	.75	3	.277	.317	.395

Ken Harvey

Bats: R Throws: R Pos: 1B-99; DH-32; PH-6   Ht: 6'2" Wt: 240 Born: 3/1/78 Age: 26

Year Team	Lg	G	AB	H	2B	3B	HR	(Hm Rd)	TB	R	RBI	RC	TBB	IBB	SO	HBP	SH	SF	SB	CS	SB%	GDP	Avg	OBP	Slg
1999 Spokane	A-	56	204	81	17	0	8	(- -)	122	49	41	54	23	4	30	8	0	0	7	1	.88	3	.397	.477	.598
2000 Wilmington	A+	46	164	55	10	0	4	(- -)	77	20	25	30	14	0	29	7	0	0	0	2	.00	4	.335	.411	.470
2001 Wilmington	A+	35	137	52	9	1	6	(- -)	81	22	27	33	13	0	21	6	0	0	3	1	.75	5	.380	.455	.591
2001 Wichita	AA	79	314	106	20	3	9	(- -)	159	54	63	55	18	0	60	4	0	0	3	0	1.00	12	.338	.372	.506
2002 Omaha	AAA	128	488	135	30	1	20	(- -)	227	75	75	72	42	1	87	8	0	3	8	3	.73	22	.277	.342	.465
2001 Kansas City	AL	4	12	3	1	0	0	(- -)	4	1	2	0	0	0	4	0	0	0	0	1	.00	1	.250	.250	.333
2003 Kansas City	AL	135	485	129	30	0	13	(5 8)	198	50	64	58	29	4	94	5	3	2	2	3	.40	15	.266	.313	.408
2 ML YEARS		139	497	132	31	0	13	(5 8)	202	51	66	58	29	4	98	5	3	2	2	4	.33	16	.266	.311	.406

Chad Harville

Pitches: R Bats: R Pos: RP-21   Ht: 5'9" Wt: 185 Born: 9/16/76 Age: 27

Year Team	Lg	G	GS	CG	GF	IP	BFP	H	R	ER	HR	SH	SF	HB	TBB	IBB	SO	WP	Bk	W	L	Pct	ShO	Sv-Op	Hld	ERC	ERA
2003 Sacramento*	AAA	48	0	0	44	57.0	232	42	16	13	5	3	0	0	21	2	57	5	0	3	5	.375	0	18- -	-	2.43	2.05
1999 Oakland	AL	15	0	0	0	14.1	69	18	0	11	2	0	0	0	10	0	15	0	0	0	2	.000	0	0-0	0	7.23	6.91
2001 Oakland	AL	3	0	0	0	3.0	11	2	0	0	0	0	0	0	0	0	2	0	0	0	0	-	0	0-0	0	0.91	0.00
2003 Oakland	AL	21	0	0	5	21.2	103	25	15	14	3	0	1	1	17	1	18	3	0	1	0	1.000	0	1-1	0	7.20	5.82
3 ML YEARS		39	0	0	5	39.0	183	45	15	25	5	0	1	1	27	1	35	3	0	1	2	.333	0	1-1	0	6.58	5.77

Shigetoshi Hasegawa

Pitches: R Bats: R Pos: RP-63   Ht: 5'11" Wt: 178 Born: 8/1/68 Age: 35

Year Team	Lg	G	GS	CG	GF	IP	BFP	H	R	ER	HR	SH	SF	HB	TBB	IBB	SO	WP	Bk	W	L	Pct	ShO	Sv-Op	Hld	ERC	ERA
1997 Anaheim	AL	50	7	0	17	116.2	497	118	60	51	14	5	5	3	46	6	83	2	1	3	7	.300	0	0-1	3	4.37	3.93
1998 Anaheim	AL	61	0	0	26	97.1	401	86	37	34	14	4	6	2	32	2	73	5	2	8	3	.727	0	5-7	10	3.54	3.14
1999 Anaheim	AL	64	1	0	26	77.0	333	80	45	42	14	3	4	2	34	2	44	4	0	4	6	.400	0	2-5	6	5.25	4.91
2000 Anaheim	AL	66	0	0	26	95.2	415	100	43	38	11	2	3	2	38	6	59	2	1	10	6	.625	0	9-18	19	4.44	3.57
2001 Anaheim	AL	46	0	0	10	55.2	235	52	28	25	5	1	2	2	20	5	41	2	0	5	6	.455	0	0-6	12	3.50	4.04
2002 Seattle	AL	53	0	0	20	70.1	288	60	26	25	4	3	1	2	30	8	39	0	1	8	3	.727	0	1-5	8	3.13	3.20
2003 Seattle	AL	63	0	0	36	73.0	282	62	12	12	5	1	0	0	18	3	32	0	0	2	4	.333	0	16-17	12	2.58	1.48
7 ML YEARS		403	8	0	155	585.2	2451	558	251	227	67	19	21	13	218	32	371	15	5	40	35	.533	0	33-59	70	3.88	3.49

Bill Haselman

Bats: R Throws: R Pos: C-2; DH-1; PH-1; PR-1   Ht: 6'3" Wt: 225 Born: 5/25/66 Age: 38

Year Team	Lg	G	AB	H	2B	3B	HR	(Hm Rd)	TB	R	RBI	RC	TBB	IBB	SO	HBP	SH	SF	SB	CS	SB%	GDP	Avg	OBP	Slg
2003 Pawtucket*	AAA	79	280	63	6	0	6	(- -)	87	37	24	15	9	0	46	0	0	2	1	1	.50	15	.225	.247	.311
1990 Texas	AL	7	13	2	0	0	0	(0 0)	2	0	3	0	1	0	5	0	0	0	0	0	-	0	.154	.214	.154
1992 Seattle	AL	8	19	5	0	0	0	(0 0)	5	1	0	1	0	0	7	0	0	0	0	0	-	1	.263	.263	.263
1993 Seattle	AL	58	137	35	8	0	5	(3 2)	58	21	16	18	12	0	19	1	2	2	2	1	.67	5	.255	.316	.423
1994 Seattle	AL	38	83	16	7	1	1	(1 0)	28	11	8	6	3	0	11	1	1	0	1	0	1.00	2	.193	.230	.337
1995 Boston	AL	64	152	37	6	1	5	(3 2)	60	22	23	19	17	0	30	2	0	3	2	0	.00	4	.243	.322	.395

BATTING | **BASERUNNING** | **AVERAGES**

Year Team	Lg	G	AB	H	2B	3B	HR	(Hm	Rd)	TB	R	RBI	RC	TBB	IBB	SO	HBP	SH	SF	SB	CS	SB%	GDP	Avg	OBP	Slg
1996 Boston	AL	77	237	65	13	1	8	(5	3)	104	33	34	30	19	3	52	1	0	0	4	2	.67	13	.274	.331	.439
1997 Boston	AL	67	212	50	15	0	6	(3	3)	83	22	26	21	15	2	44	2	1	2	0	2	.00	8	.236	.290	.392
1998 Boston	AL	40	105	33	6	0	6	(4	2)	57	11	17	18	3	0	17	0	0	2	0	0	-	2	.314	.327	.543
1999 Detroit	AL	48	143	39	8	0	4	(2	2)	59	13	14	18	10	1	26	0	0	0	2	0	1.00	4	.273	.320	.413
2000 Texas	AL	62	193	53	18	0	6	(3	3)	89	23	26	29	15	0	36	1	0	1	0	1	.00	1	.275	.329	.461
2001 Texas	AL	47	130	37	6	0	3	(2	1)	52	12	25	15	8	0	27	1	1	0	0	1	.00	5	.285	.331	.400
2002 Texas	AL	69	179	44	7	0	3	(1	2)	60	16	18	15	11	1	25	2	1	0	0	0	-	6	.246	.297	.335
2003 Boston	AL	4	3	0	0	0	0	(0	0)	0	0	0	0	0	0	0	0	0	0	0	0	-	0	.000	.000	.000
13 ML YEARS		589	1606	416	94	3	47	(27	20)	657	185	210	190	114	7	300	11	6	10	9	9	.50	51	.259	.311	.409

Scott Hatteberg

Bats: L **Throws:** R **Pos:** 1B-128; DH-13; PH-7   **Ht:** 6'1" **Wt:** 210 **Born:** 12/14/69 **Age:** 34

BATTING | **BASERUNNING** | **AVERAGES**

Year Team	Lg	G	AB	H	2B	3B	HR	(Hm	Rd)	TB	R	RBI	RC	TBB	IBB	SO	HBP	SH	SF	SB	CS	SB%	GDP	Avg	OBP	Slg
1995 Boston	AL	2	2	1	0	0	0	(0	0)	1	1	0	0	0	0	0	0	0	0	0	0	-	1	.500	.500	.500
1996 Boston	AL	10	11	2	1	0	0	(0	0)	3	3	0	1	3	0	2	0	0	0	0	0	-	2	.182	.357	.273
1997 Boston	AL	114	350	97	23	1	10	(5	5)	152	46	44	52	40	2	70	2	2	1	0	1	.00	11	.277	.354	.434
1998 Boston	AL	112	359	99	23	1	12	(4	8)	160	46	43	56	43	3	58	5	0	3	0	0	-	11	.276	.359	.446
1999 Boston	AL	30	80	22	5	0	1	(1	0)	30	12	11	14	18	0	14	1	0	1	0	0	-	2	.275	.410	.375
2000 Boston	AL	92	230	61	15	0	8	(2	6)	100	21	36	36	38	3	39	0	1	2	0	1	.00	8	.265	.367	.435
2001 Boston	AL	94	278	68	19	0	3	(2	1)	96	34	25	32	33	0	26	4	0	1	1	1	.50	7	.245	.332	.345
2002 Oakland	AL	136	492	138	22	4	15	(8	7)	213	58	61	76	68	1	56	6	1	1	0	1	.00	8	.280	.374	.433
2003 Oakland	AL	147	541	137	34	0	12	(6	6)	207	63	61	79	66	0	53	9	3	3	1	0	1.00	14	.253	.342	.383
9 ML YEARS		737	2343	625	142	6	61	(28	33)	962	284	281	346	309	9	318	27	7	12	1	4	.20	64	.267	.357	.411

LaTroy Hawkins

Pitches: R **Bats:** R **Pos:** RP-74   **Ht:** 6'5" **Wt:** 204 **Born:** 12/21/72 **Age:** 31

HOW MUCH HE PITCHED | **WHAT HE GAVE UP** | **THE RESULTS**

Year Team	Lg	G	GS	CG	GF	IP	BFP	H	R	ER	HR	SH	SF	HB	TBB	IBB	SO	WP	Bk	W	L	Pct	ShO	Sv-Op	Hld	ERC	ERA
1995 Minnesota	AL	6	6	1	0	27.0	131	39	29	26	3	0	3	1	12	0	9	1	1	2	3	.400	0	0-0	0	7.14	8.67
1996 Minnesota	AL	7	6	0	1	26.1	124	42	24	24	8	1	1	0	9	0	24	1	1	1	1	.500	0	0-0	0	9.49	8.20
1997 Minnesota	AL	20	20	0	0	103.1	478	134	71	67	19	2	2	4	47	0	58	6	3	6	12	.333	0	0-0	0	7.01	5.84
1998 Minnesota	AL	33	33	0	0	190.1	840	227	126	111	27	4	10	5	61	1	105	10	2	7	14	.333	0	0-0	0	5.31	5.25
1999 Minnesota	AL	33	33	1	0	174.1	803	238	136	129	29	1	5	1	60	2	103	9	0	10	14	.417	0	0-0	0	6.55	6.66
2000 Minnesota	AL	66	0	0	38	87.2	370	85	34	33	7	4	1	1	32	1	59	6	0	2	5	.286	0	14-14	1	3.70	3.39
2001 Minnesota	AL	62	0	0	51	51.1	248	59	34	34	3	1	4	1	39	3	36	7	0	1	5	.167	0	28-37	1	6.02	5.96
2002 Minnesota	AL	65	0	0	15	80.1	310	63	23	19	5	2	3	0	15	1	63	5	0	6	0	1.000	0	0-3	13	1.99	2.13
2003 Minnesota	AL	74	0	0	12	77.1	310	69	20	16	4	4	1	1	15	1	75	5	0	9	3	.750	0	2-8	28	2.48	1.86
9 ML YEARS		366	98	2	117	818.0	3614	956	497	459	105	19	30	14	290	9	532	50	7	44	57	.436	0	44-62	49	5.15	5.05

Jimmy Haynes

Pitches: R **Bats:** R **Pos:** SP-18   **Ht:** 6'4" **Wt:** 219 **Born:** 9/5/72 **Age:** 31

HOW MUCH HE PITCHED | **WHAT HE GAVE UP** | **THE RESULTS**

Year Team	Lg	G	GS	CG	GF	IP	BFP	H	R	ER	HR	SH	SF	HB	TBB	IBB	SO	WP	Bk	W	L	Pct	ShO	Sv-Op	Hld	ERC	ERA
2003 Louisville*	AAA	2	2	0	0	10.2	44	10	4	3	1	0	0	0	3	0	7	0	0	1	1	.500	0	0- -		3.25	2.53
2003 Dayton*	A	1	1	0	0	7.0	25	2	1	0	0	0	0	0	2	0	6	0	0	1	0	1.000	0	0- -		0.52	0.00
1995 Baltimore	AL	4	3	0	0	24.0	94	11	6	6	2	1	0	0	12	1	22	0	0	2	1	.667	0	0-0	0	1.61	2.25
1996 Baltimore	AL	26	11	0	8	89.0	435	122	84	82	14	4	5	2	58	1	65	5	0	3	6	.333	0	1-1	0	8.05	8.29
1997 Oakland	AL	13	13	0	0	73.1	329	74	38	36	7	1	4	2	40	1	65	4	1	3	6	.333	0	0-0	0	4.75	4.42
1998 Oakland	AL	33	33	1	0	194.1	875	229	124	110	25	5	9	5	88	4	134	11	0	11	9	.550	1	0-0	0	5.69	5.09
1999 Oakland	AL	30	25	0	2	142.0	652	158	112	100	21	4	5	2	80	3	93	7	2	7	12	.368	0	0-0	0	5.79	6.34
2000 Milwaukee	NL	33	33	0	0	199.1	897	228	128	118	21	10	6	7	100	7	88	7	0	12	13	.480	0	0-0	0	5.54	5.33
2001 Milwaukee	NL	31	29	0	0	172.2	756	182	98	93	20	14	7	4	78	17	112	8	0	8	17	.320	0	0-0	0	4.69	4.85
2002 Cincinnati	NL	34	34	0	0	196.2	852	210	97	91	21	7	6	3	81	4	126	6	0	15	10	.600	0	0-0	0	4.66	4.12
2003 Cincinnati	NL	18	18	1	0	94.1	448	118	74	66	14	7	2	3	57	3	49	2	0	2	12	.143	0	0-0	0	6.94	6.30
9 ML YEARS		222	199	2	10	1185.2	5338	1332	761	701	145	53	44	28	594	41	754	50	3	63	86	.423	1	1-1	0	5.46	5.32

Bryan Hebson

Pitches: R **Bats:** R **Pos:** RP-2   **Ht:** 6'5" **Wt:** 210 **Born:** 3/12/76 **Age:** 28

HOW MUCH HE PITCHED | **WHAT HE GAVE UP** | **THE RESULTS**

Year Team	Lg	G	GS	CG	GF	IP	BFP	H	R	ER	HR	SH	SF	HB	TBB	IBB	SO	WP	Bk	W	L	Pct	ShO	Sv-Op	Hld	ERC	ERA
1998 Expos	R	4	4	0	0	17.0	64	10	1	1	0	0	0	0	7	0	16	2	0	2	0	1.000	0	0- -		1.59	0.53
1998 Cape Fear	A	16	16	0	0	72.2	323	71	42	38	8	1	4	11	29	0	57	1	0	4	5	.444	0	0- -		4.60	4.71
1999 Cape Fear	A	6	6	0	0	33.2	142	22	13	10	2	1	1	3	17	0	34	2	0	0	1	.000	0	0- -		2.65	2.67
1999 Jupiter	A+	17	16	0	1	103.1	414	85	33	23	5	2	3	5	26	0	79	3	0	7	6	.538	0	0- -		2.48	2.00
2000 Harrisburg	AA	29	29	3	0	171.1	753	175	102	87	23	7	2	14	66	2	90	3	0	7	15	.318	0	0- -		4.69	4.57
2001 Harrisburg	AA	26	8	2	0	75.0	320	78	40	37	12	3	4	7	19	0	54	2	0	2	8	.200	0	0- -		4.55	4.44
2002 Harrisburg	AA	38	3	0	24	94.1	364	60	20	18	5	4	2	5	24	2	75	1	1	10	1	.909	0	7- -		1.65	1.72
2002 Ottawa	AAA	5	0	0	1	9.1	41	8	5	5	0	1	0	1	3	0	11	0	0	1	0	1.000	0	0- -		2.59	4.82
2003 Pawtucket	AAA	18	0	0	7	26.1	102	17	9	8	4	0	0	0	6	0	22	0	0	2	1	.667	0	0- -		1.92	2.73
2003 Edmonton	AAA	30	0	0	16	43.1	200	44	23	21	3	3	2	4	22	1	44	3	1	6	0	1.000	0	6- -		4.56	4.36
2003 Montreal	NL	2	0	0	1	2.0	12	4	3	3	1	0	1	1	1	0	1	0	0	0	0	-	0	0-0	0	17.51	13.50

Aaron Heilman

Pitches: R **Bats:** R **Pos:** SP-13; RP-1   **Ht:** 6'5" **Wt:** 220 **Born:** 11/12/78 **Age:** 25

Year Team	Lg	G	GS	CG	GF	IP	BFP	H	R	ER	HR	SH	SF	HB	TBB	IBB	SO	WP	Bk	W	L	Pct	ShO	Sv-Op	Hld	ERC	ERA
2001 St.Lucie	A+	7	7	0	0	38.1	153	26	11	10	0	1	1	1	13	0	39	1	0	0	0	.000	0	0--	-	1.70	2.35
2002 Binghamton	AA	17	17	0	0	96.2	397	85	43	41	7	2	2	6	28	2	97	5	0	4	4	.500	0	0--	-	3.07	3.82
2002 Norfolk	AAA	10	7	0	2	49.1	196	42	18	18	3	3	1	1	16	1	35	0	0	2	3	.400	0	0--	-	2.91	3.28
2003 Norfolk	AAA	16	16	0	0	94.1	399	99	37	34	5	3	1	2	32	0	71	1	0	6	4	.600	0	0--	-	3.95	3.24
2003 New York	NL	14	13	0	0	65.1	315	79	53	49	13	5	3	3	41	2	51	5	0	2	7	.222	0	0-0	0	7.16	6.75

Rick Helling

Pitches: R **Bats:** R **Pos:** SP-24; RP-11   **Ht:** 6'3" **Wt:** 220 **Born:** 12/15/70 **Age:** 33

Year Team	Lg	G	GS	CG	GF	IP	BFP	H	R	ER	HR	SH	SF	HB	TBB	IBB	SO	WP	Bk	W	L	Pct	ShO	Sv-Op	Hld	ERC	ERA
1994 Texas	AL	9	9	1	0	52.0	228	62	34	34	14	0	0	0	18	0	25	4	1	3	2	.600	1	0-0	0	6.33	5.88
1995 Texas	AL	3	3	0	0	12.1	62	17	11	9	2	0	2	2	8	0	5	0	0	0	2	.000	0	0-0	0	8.81	6.57
1996 Tex-Fla		11	6	0	2	48.0	198	37	23	23	9	1	1	0	16	0	42	1	1	3	3	.500	0	0-0	1	3.07	4.31
1997 Fla-Tex		41	16	0	9	131.0	550	108	67	65	17	3	9	6	69	2	99	3	0	5	9	.357	0	0-1	6	4.08	4.47
1998 Texas	AL	33	33	4	0	216.1	922	209	109	106	27	6	10	1	78	6	164	10	0	20	7	.741	2	0-0	0	3.86	4.41
1999 Texas	AL	35	35	3	0	219.1	943	228	127	118	41	5	10	6	85	5	131	4	0	13	11	.542	0	0-0	0	5.03	4.84
2000 Texas	AL	35	35	0	0	217.0	963	212	122	108	29	4	9	9	99	2	146	2	0	16	13	.552	0	0-0	0	4.50	4.48
2001 Texas	AL	34	34	2	0	215.2	941	256	134	124	38	3	10	4	63	2	154	6	0	12	11	.522	1	0-0	0	5.39	5.17
2002 Arizona	NL	30	30	0	0	175.2	751	180	94	88	31	10	6	4	48	6	120	7	1	10	12	.455	0	0-0	0	4.29	4.51
2003 Bal-Fla		35	24	0	5	155.0	665	167	91	89	31	4	2	12	45	0	98	5	1	8	8	.500	0	0-1	4	5.19	5.17
1996 Texas	AL	6	2	0	2	20.1	92	23	17	17	7	0	1	0	9	0	16	1	0	1	2	.333	0	0-0	1	6.80	7.52
1996 Bal	NL	5	4	0	0	27.2	106	14	6	6	2	1	0	0	7	0	26	0	1	2	1	.667	0	0-0	0	1.18	1.95
1997 Florida		31	8	0	8	76.0	324	61	38	37	12	2	7	4	48	2	53	0	0	2	6	.250	0	0-1	6	4.62	4.38
1997 Texas	AL	10	8	0	1	55.0	226	47	29	28	5	1	2	2	21	0	46	3	0	3	3	.500	0	0-0	0	3.37	4.58
2003 Baltimore	AL	24	24	0	0	138.2	603	156	90	88	30	4	2	12	40	0	86	4	1	7	8	.467	0	0-0	0	5.63	5.71
2003 Florida	NL	11	0	0	5	16.1	62	11	1	1	1	0	0	0	5	0	12	1	0	1	0	1.000	0	0-0	0	1.93	0.55
10 ML YEARS		266	225	10	16	1442.1	6223	1476	812	764	239	36	59	46	529	23	984	46	4	90	78	.536	4	0-1	8	4.67	4.77

Wes Helms

Bats: R **Throws:** R **Pos:** 3B-130; PH-4   **Ht:** 6'4" **Wt:** 230 **Born:** 5/12/76 **Age:** 28

Year Team	Lg	G	AB	H	2B	3B	HR	(Hm	Rd)	TB	R	RBI	RC	TBB	IBB	SO	HBP	SH	SF	SB	CS	SB%	GDP	Avg	OBP	Slg
2003 Indianapolis*	AAA	2	5	2	0	0	0	(-	-)	2	0	0	1	1	0	1	0	0	0	0	0	-	0	.400	.500	.400
1998 Atlanta	NL	7	13	4	1	0	1	(0	1)	8	2	2	2	0	0	4	0	0	0	0	0	-	0	.308	.308	.615
2000 Atlanta	NL	6	5	1	0	0	0	(0	0)	1	0	0	0	0	0	2	0	0	0	0	0	-	0	.200	.200	.200
2001 Atlanta	NL	100	216	48	10	3	10	(6	4)	94	28	36	27	21	2	56	1	0	1	1	1	.50	3	.222	.293	.435
2002 Atlanta	NL	85	210	51	16	0	6	(4	2)	85	20	22	16	11	2	57	3	1	6	1	1	.50	5	.243	.283	.405
2003 Milwaukee	NL	134	476	124	21	0	23	(16	7)	214	56	67	66	43	3	131	10	0	7	0	1	.00	10	.261	.330	.450
5 ML YEARS		332	920	228	48	3	40	(26	14)	402	106	127	111	75	7	250	14	1	14	2	3	.40	18	.248	.310	.437

Todd Helton

Bats: L **Throws:** L **Pos:** 1B-159; PH-1   **Ht:** 6'2" **Wt:** 204 **Born:** 8/20/73 **Age:** 30

Year Team	Lg	G	AB	H	2B	3B	HR	(Hm	Rd)	TB	R	RBI	RC	TBB	IBB	SO	HBP	SH	SF	SB	CS	SB%	GDP	Avg	OBP	Slg
1997 Colorado	NL	35	93	26	2	1	5	(3	2)	45	13	11	15	8	0	11	0	0	0	0	1	.00	1	.280	.337	.484
1998 Colorado	NL	152	530	167	37	1	25	(13	12)	281	78	97	101	53	5	54	6	1	5	3	3	.50	15	.315	.380	.530
1999 Colorado	NL	159	578	185	39	5	35	(23	12)	339	114	113	124	68	6	77	6	0	4	7	6	.54	14	.320	.395	.587
2000 Colorado	NL	160	580	216	59	2	42	(27	15)	405	138	147	169	103	22	61	4	0	10	5	3	.63	12	.372	.463	.698
2001 Colorado	NL	159	587	197	54	2	49	(27	22)	402	132	146	157	98	15	104	5	1	5	7	5	.58	14	.336	.432	.685
2002 Colorado	NL	156	553	182	39	4	30	(18	12)	319	107	109	128	99	21	91	5	0	10	5	1	.83	16	.329	.429	.577
2003 Colorado	NL	160	583	209	49	5	33	(23	10)	367	135	117	160	111	21	72	2	0	7	0	4	.00	19	.358	.458	.630
7 ML YEARS		981	3504	1182	279	20	219	(134	85)	2158	717	740	854	540	90	470	28	2	41	27	23	.54	85	.337	.425	.616

Rickey Henderson

Bats: R **Throws:** L **Pos:** LF-18; PH-13   **Ht:** 5'10" **Wt:** 190 **Born:** 12/25/58 **Age:** 45

Year Team	Lg	G	AB	H	2B	3B	HR	(Hm	Rd)	TB	R	RBI	RC	TBB	IBB	SO	HBP	SH	SF	SB	CS	SB%	GDP	Avg	OBP	Slg
1979 Oakland	AL	89	351	96	13	3	1	(1	0)	118	49	26	45	34	0	39	2	8	3	33	11	.75	4	.274	.338	.336
1980 Oakland	AL	158	591	179	22	4	9	(3	6)	236	111	53	119	117	7	54	5	6	3	100	26	.79	6	.303	.420	.399
1981 Oakland	AL	108	423	135	18	7	6	(5	1)	185	89	35	80	64	4	68	2	0	4	56	22	.72	7	.319	.408	.437
1982 Oakland	AL	149	536	143	24	4	10	(5	5)	205	119	51	100	116	1	94	2	0	2	130	42	.76	5	.267	.398	.382
1983 Oakland	AL	145	513	150	25	7	9	(5	4)	216	105	48	107	103	8	80	4	1	1	108	19	.85	11	.292	.414	.421
1984 Oakland	AL	142	502	147	27	4	16	(7	9)	233	113	58	101	86	1	81	5	1	3	66	18	.79	7	.293	.399	.458
1985 New York	AL	143	547	172	28	5	24	(8	16)	282	146	72	130	99	1	65	3	0	5	80	10	.89	8	.314	.419	.516
1986 New York	AL	153	608	160	31	5	28	(13	15)	285	130	74	112	89	2	81	2	0	5	87	18	.83	12	.263	.358	.469
1987 New York	AL	95	358	104	17	3	17	(10	7)	178	78	37	80	80	1	52	2	0	6	41	8	.84	10	.291	.423	.497
1988 New York	AL	140	554	169	30	2	6	(4	2)	221	118	50	106	82	1	54	3	2	6	93	13	.88	6	.305	.394	.399
1989 NYY-Oak	AL	150	541	148	26	3	12	(5	7)	216	113	57	108	126	5	68	3	0	8	77	14	.85	8	.274	.411	.399
1990 Oakland	AL	136	489	159	33	3	28	(8	20)	282	119	61	127	97	2	60	4	2	2	65	10	.87	13	.325	.439	.577
1991 Oakland	AL	134	470	126	17	1	18	(8	10)	199	105	57	90	98	7	73	7	0	3	58	18	.76	5	.268	.400	.423
1992 Oakland	AL	117	396	112	18	3	15	(10	5)	181	77	46	88	95	5	56	6	0	3	48	11	.81	5	.283	.426	.457
1993 Oak-Tor	AL	134	481	139	22	2	21	(10	11)	228	114	59	112	120	7	65	4	1	4	53	8	.87	4	.289	.432	.474
1994 Oakland	AL	87	296	77	13	0	6	(4	2)	108	66	20	55	72	1	45	5	1	2	22	7	.76	0	.260	.411	.365
1995 Oakland	AL	112	407	122	31	1	9	(6	3)	182	67	54	79	72	2	66	4	1	3	32	10	.76	8	.300	.407	.447
1996 San Diego	NL	148	465	112	17	2	9	(6	3)	160	110	29	81	125	2	90	10	0	2	37	15	.71	9	.241	.410	.344
1997 SD-Ana		120	403	100	14	0	8	(6	2)	138	84	34	68	97	2	85	6	1	2	45	8	.85	10	.248	.400	.342
1998 Oakland	AL	152	542	128	16	1	14	(6	8)	188	101	57	89	118	0	114	5	2	3	66	13	.84	5	.236	.376	.347

Year Team	Lg	G	AB	H	2B	3B	HR	(Hm	Rd)	TB	R	RBI	RC	TBB	IBB	SO	HBP	SH	SF	SB	CS	SB%	GDP	Avg	OBP	Slg
1999 New York	NL	121	438	138	30	0	12	(1	11)	204	89	42	92	82	1	82	2	1	3	37	14	.73	4	.315	.423	.466
2000 NYM-Sea		123	420	98	14	2	4	(2	2)	128	75	32	57	88	1	75	4	3	4	36	11	.77	11	.233	.368	.305
2001 San Diego	NL	123	379	86	17	3	8	(2	6)	133	70	42	56	81	0	84	3	0	2	25	7	.78	8	.227	.366	.351
2002 Boston	AL	72	179	40	6	1	5	(1	4)	63	40	16	24	38	0	47	4	0	1	8	2	.80	3	.223	.369	.352
2003 Los Angeles	NL	30	72	15	1	0	2	(2	0)	22	7	5	8	11	0	16	1	0	0	3	0	1.00	0	.208	.321	.306
1989 New York	AL	65	235	58	13	1	3	(1	2)	82	41	22	40	56	0	29	1	0	1	25	8	.76	0	.247	.392	.349
1989 Oakland	AL	85	306	90	13	2	9	(6	3)	134	72	35	68	70	5	39	2	0	3	52	6	.90	8	.294	.425	.438
1993 Oakland	AL	90	318	104	19	1	17	(8	9)	176	77	47	86	85	6	46	2	0	2	31	6	.84	8	.327	.469	.553
1993 Toronto	AL	44	163	35	3	1	4	(2	2)	52	37	12	26	35	1	19	2	1	2	22	2	.92	1	.215	.356	.319
1997 San Diego	NL	88	288	79	11	0	6	(5	1)	108	63	27	55	71	2	62	4	0	2	29	4	.88	7	.274	.422	.375
1997 Anaheim	AL	32	115	21	3	0	2	(1	1)	30	21	7	13	26	0	23	2	1	0	16	4	.80	3	.183	.343	.261
2000 New York	NL	31	96	21	1	0	0	(0	0)	22	17	2	12	25	1	20	2	0	1	5	2	.71	2	.219	.387	.229
2000 Seattle	AL	92	324	77	13	2	4	(2	2)	106	58	30	45	63	0	55	2	3	3	31	9	.78	9	.238	.362	.327
25 ML YEARS		3081	10961	3055	510	66	297	(135	162)	4588	2295	1115	2114	2190	61	1694	98	30	67	1406	335	.81	172	.279	.401	.419

Mark Hendrickson

Pitches: L **Bats:** L **Pos:** SP-30   **Ht:** 6'9" **Wt:** 230 **Born:** 6/23/74 **Age:** 30

		HOW MUCH HE PITCHED						WHAT HE GAVE UP										THE RESULTS							
Year Team	Lg	G	GS	CG	GF	IP	BFP	H	R	ER	HR	SH	SF	HB	TBB	IBB	SO	WP	Bk	W	L	Pct	ShO	Sv-Op	Hld	ERC	ERA
1998 Dunedin	A+	16	5	0	1	49.1	207	44	16	13	2	2	2	0	26	1	38	2	0	4	3	.571	0	1--		3.64	2.37
1999 Knoxville	AA	12	11	0	0	55.2	254	73	46	41	4	2	0	2	21	0	39	2	1	2	7	.222	0	0--		5.81	6.63
2000 Dunedin	A+	12	12	1	0	51.1	235	63	34	32	7	1	5	0	29	0	38	1	0	2	2	.500	0	0--		6.56	5.61
2000 Tennessee	AA	6	6	0	0	39.2	161	32	17	16	5	1	0	0	12	0	29	4	0	3	1	.750	0	0--		2.83	3.63
2001 Syracuse	AAA	38	6	0	7	73.1	315	80	43	38	13	2	0	3	18	1	33	2	0	2	9	.182	0	0--		4.65	4.66
2002 Syracuse	AAA	19	14	0	3	92.0	385	90	38	36	12	4	4	1	22	0	68	2	2	7	5	.583	0	0--		3.54	3.52
2003 Syracuse	AAA	1	1	0	0	6.0	25	8	4	3	1	0	0	1	0	0	5	0	0	0	0	-	0	0--		5.89	4.50
2003 Dunedin	A+	1	1	0	0	5.2	28	5	2	1	0	1	0	1	4	0	3	0	0	1	0	1.000	0	0--		4.20	1.59
2002 Toronto	AL	16	4	0	0	36.2	142	45	11	10	1	2	2	2	12	3	21	0	0	3	0	1.000	0	0-1	1	1.90	2.45
2003 Toronto	AL	30	30	1	0	158.1	703	207	111	97	24	1	8	0	40	3	76	4	0	9	9	.500	1	0-0		5.64	5.51
2 ML YEARS		46	34	1	0	195.0	845	232	122	107	25	3	10	2	52	6	97	4	0	12	9	.571	1	0-1	1	4.86	4.94

Drew Henson

Bats: R **Throws:** R **Pos:** 3B-3; PH-1; PR-1   **Ht:** 6'5" **Wt:** 222 **Born:** 2/13/80 **Age:** 24

								BATTING											BASERUNNING				AVERAGES		
Year Team	Lg	G	AB	H	2B	3B	HR	(Hm	Rd)	TB	R	RBI	RC	TBB	IBB	SO	HBP	SH	SF	SB	CS	SB%	GDP	Avg	OBP	Slg
1998 Yankees	R	10	38	12	3	0	1	(-	-)	18	5	2	6	3	1	9	0	0	0	0	0	-	1	.316	.366	.474
1999 Tampa	A+	69	254	71	12	0	13	(-	-)	122	37	37	41	26	0	71	1	0	3	3	1	.75	6	.280	.345	.480
2000 Tampa	A+	5	21	7	2	0	1	(-	-)	12	4	1	4	1	0	7	0	0	0	0	1	.00	0	.333	.364	.571
2000 Norwich	AA	59	223	64	9	2	7	(-	-)	98	39	39	31	20	1	75	1	0	1	0	5	.00	6	.287	.347	.439
2000 Chattanooga	AA	16	64	11	8	0	1	(-	-)	22	7	9	4	4	0	25	0	0	0	2	0	1.00	0	.172	.221	.344
2001 Tampa	A+	5	14	2	0	0	1	(-	-)	5	2	3	2	2	0	7	2	0	1	1	0	1.00	1	.143	.316	.357
2001 Norwich	AA	5	19	7	1	0	0	(-	-)	8	2	2	3	1	1	4	1	0	0	0	1	.00	1	.368	.429	.421
2001 Columbus	AAA	71	270	60	6	0	11	(-	-)	99	29	38	21	10	1	85	0	0	1	2	1	.67	8	.222	.249	.367
2002 Columbus	AAA	128	471	113	30	4	18	(-	-)	205	68	65	60	37	0	151	6	2	5	2	1	.67	11	.240	.301	.435
2003 Columbus	AAA	133	483	113	40	2	14	(-	-)	199	60	78	58	32	3	122	11	1	10	8	4	.67	8	.234	.291	.412
2002 New York	AL	3	1	0	0	0	0	(0	0)	0	1	0	0	0	0	1	0	0	0	0	0	-	0	.000	.000	.000
2003 New York	AL	5	8	1	0	0	0	(0	0)	1	2	0	0	0	0	2	0	0	0	0	0	-	0	.125	.125	.125
2 ML YEARS		8	9	1	0	0	0	(0	0)	1	3	0	0	0	0	3	0	0	0	0	0	-	0	.111	.111	.111

Pat Hentgen

Pitches: R **Bats:** R **Pos:** SP-22; RP-6   **Ht:** 6'2" **Wt:** 195 **Born:** 11/13/68 **Age:** 35

		HOW MUCH HE PITCHED						WHAT HE GAVE UP										THE RESULTS							
Year Team	Lg	G	GS	CG	GF	IP	BFP	H	R	ER	HR	SH	SF	HB	TBB	IBB	SO	WP	Bk	W	L	Pct	ShO	Sv-Op	Hld	ERC	ERA
1991 Toronto	AL	3	1	0	1	7.1	30	5	2	2	1	1	0	2	3	0	3	1	0	0	0	-	0	0-0		3.87	2.45
1992 Toronto	AL	28	2	0	10	50.1	229	49	30	30	7	2	2	0	32	5	39	2	1	5	2	.714	0	0-1	1	4.94	5.36
1993 Toronto	AL	34	32	3	0	216.1	926	215	103	93	27	6	5	7	74	0	122	11	1	19	9	.679	0	0-0		4.11	3.87
1994 Toronto	AL	24	24	6	0	174.2	728	158	74	66	21	6	3	3	59	1	147	5	1	13	8	.619	3	0-0		3.52	3.40
1995 Toronto	AL	30	30	2	0	200.2	913	236	129	114	24	2	1	5	90	6	135	7	2	10	14	.417	1	0-0		5.49	5.11
1996 Toronto	AL	35	35	10	0	265.2	1100	238	105	95	20	5	8	5	94	3	177	8	0	20	10	.667	3	0-0		3.26	3.22
1997 Toronto	AL	35	35	9	0	264.0	1085	253	116	108	31	9	3	7	71	2	160	6	2	15	10	.600	3	0-0		3.61	3.68
1998 Toronto	AL	29	29	0	0	177.2	795	208	109	102	28	5	7	5	69	1	94	7	1	12	11	.522	0	0-0		5.58	5.17
1999 Toronto	AL	34	34	1	0	199.0	869	225	115	106	32	3	11	3	65	1	118	8	1	11	12	.478	0	0-0		5.04	4.79
2000 St Louis	NL	33	33	1	0	194.1	846	202	107	102	24	13	8	3	89	4	118	4	0	15	12	.556	1	0-0		4.81	4.72
2001 Baltimore	AL	9	9	1	0	62.1	252	51	25	24	7	1	1	0	19	3	33	1	0	2	3	.400	0	0-0		2.77	3.47
2002 Baltimore	AL	4	4	0	0	22.0	103	31	20	19	6	0	1	0	10	0	11	1	0	0	4	.000	0	0-0		8.38	7.77
2003 Baltimore	AL	28	22	1	2	160.2	676	150	74	73	25	3	2	5	58	1	100	4	1	7	8	.467	1	1-1		4.09	4.09
13 ML YEARS		326	290	34	13	1995.0	8552	2021	1009	934	253	56	52	45	733	27	1257	65	10	129	103	.556	10	1-2	1	4.31	4.21

Felix Heredia

Pitches: L **Bats:** L **Pos:** RP-69   **Ht:** 6'0" **Wt:** 190 **Born:** 6/18/75 **Age:** 29

		HOW MUCH HE PITCHED						WHAT HE GAVE UP										THE RESULTS							
Year Team	Lg	G	GS	CG	GF	IP	BFP	H	R	ER	HR	SH	SF	HB	TBB	IBB	SO	WP	Bk	W	L	Pct	ShO	Sv-Op	Hld	ERC	ERA
1996 Florida	NL	21	0	0	5	16.2	78	21	8	8	1	0	1	0	10	1	10	2	0	1	1	.500	0	0-0	2	6.08	4.32
1997 Florida	NL	56	0	0	10	56.2	251	53	30	27	3	2	2	5	30	1	54	2	0	5	3	.625	0	0-1	7	4.06	4.29
1998 Fla-ChC	NL	71	2	0	18	58.2	268	57	33	33	2	1	2	1	38	3	54	6	1	3	3	.500	0	2-5	17	4.31	5.06
1999 Chicago	NL	69	0	0	15	52.0	237	56	35	28	7	1	4	1	25	2	50	2	0	3	1	.750	0	1-7	12	5.01	4.85
2000 Chicago	NL	74	0	0	24	58.2	250	46	31	31	6	4	2	2	33	4	52	5	0	7	3	.700	0	2-5	12	3.59	4.76
2001 Chicago	NL	48	0	0	9	35.0	165	45	27	24	6	1	3	2	16	1	28	3	0	2	2	.500	0	0-3	8	6.75	6.17
2002 Toronto	AL	53	0	0	15	52.1	232	51	29	21	5	3	2	2	26	3	31	5	0	1	2	.333	0	0-2	7	4.31	3.61
2003 Cin-NYY	AL	69	0	0	22	87.0	365	74	32	26	10	4	2	2	33	7	45	5	0	5	3	.625	0	1-5	8	3.23	2.69

Year Team	Lg	G	GS	CG	GF	IP	BFP	H	R	ER	HR	SH	SF	HB	TBB	IBB	SO	WP	Bk	W	L	Pct	ShO	Sv-Op	Hld	ERC	ERA
1998 Florida	NL	41	2	0	12	41.0	194	38	25	25	1	1	2	1	32	2	38	5	1	0	3	.000	0	2-3	9	4.44	5.49
1998 Chicago	NL	30	0	0	6	17.2	74	19	8	8	1	0	0	0	6	1	16	1	0	3	0	1.000	0	0-2	8	3.99	4.08
2003 Cincinnati	NL	57	0	0	18	72.0	303	61	27	24	9	4	2	2	28	5	41	5	0	5	2	.714	0	1-4	7	3.35	3.00
2003 New York	AL	12	0	0	4	15.0	62	13	5	5	2	1	0	0	5	2	4	0	0	0	1	.000	0	0-1	1	2.69	1.20
8 ML YEARS		461	2	0	118	417.0	1854	403	225	198	40	16	18	15	211	22	324	30	1	27	18	.600	0	6-28	73	4.29	4.27

Matt Herges

Pitches: R Bats: L Pos: RP-67   Ht: 6'0" Wt: 200 Born: 4/1/70 Age: 34

Year Team	Lg	G	GS	CG	GF	IP	BFP	H	R	ER	HR	SH	SF	HB	TBB	IBB	SO	WP	Bk	W	L	Pct	ShO	Sv-Op	Hld	ERC	ERA
2003 Portland*	AAA	4	0	0	2	5.0	18	1	1	1	0	0	0	0	2	0	5	0	0	0	0	--	0	0--	-	0.50	1.80
1999 Los Angeles	NL	17	0	0	9	24.1	104	24	13	11	5	1	0	1	8	0	18	0	0	0	2	.000	0	0-2	1	4.61	4.07
2000 Los Angeles	NL	59	4	0	17	110.2	461	100	43	39	7	9	4	6	40	5	75	4	0	11	3	.786	0	1-3	4	3.35	3.17
2001 Los Angeles	NL	75	0	0	22	99.1	435	97	39	38	8	4	3	8	46	12	76	2	0	9	8	.529	0	1-8	15	4.20	3.44
2002 Montreal	NL	62	0	0	25	64.2	298	80	33	29	10	6	2	2	26	8	50	3	0	2	5	.286	0	6-14	9	5.74	4.04
2003 SD-SF	NL	67	0	0	24	79.0	332	68	27	23	3	2	6	3	29	2	68	1	1	3	2	.600	0	3-6	9	2.87	2.62
2003 San Diego	NL	40	0	0	21	44.0	172	40	16	14	2	1	5	2	20	2	40	1	0	2	2	.500	0	3-5	4	3.45	2.86
2003 San Francisco	NL	27	0	0	3	35.0	140	28	11	9	1	1	1	1	9	0	28	0	1	1	0	1.000	0	0-1	5	2.18	2.31
5 ML YEARS		280	4	0	97	378.0	1630	369	155	140	33	22	15	20	149	27	287	10	1	25	20	.556	0	11-33	38	3.94	3.33

Chad Hermansen

Bats: R Throws: R Pos: LF-6; PH-5   Ht: 6'2" Wt: 192 Born: 9/10/77 Age: 26

Year Team	Lg	G	AB	H	2B	3B	HR	(Hm	Rd)	TB	R	RBI	RC	TBB	IBB	SO	HBP	SH	SF	SB	CS	SB%	GDP	Avg	OBP	Slg
2003 Vero Beach*	A+	17	63	15	4	0	1	(-	-)	22	12	7	6	6	0	7	0	0	2	0	1	.00	2	.238	.296	.349
2003 Las Vegas*	AAA	68	235	83	15	1	9	(-	-)	127	43	31	49	19	0	38	2	0	1	4	1	.80	4	.353	.405	.540
1999 Pittsburgh	NL	19	60	14	3	0	1	(0	1)	20	5	1	7	7	1	19	1	1	0	2	2	.50	0	.233	.324	.333
2000 Pittsburgh	NL	33	108	20	4	1	2	(2	0)	32	12	8	6	6	0	37	0	2	1	0	0	-	3	.185	.226	.296
2001 Pittsburgh	NL	22	55	9	1	0	2	(1	1)	16	5	5	2	1	0	18	0	0	0	0	1	.00	0	.164	.179	.291
2002 Pit-ChC	NL	100	237	49	14	1	8	(4	4)	89	25	18	20	22	0	82	1	4	1	7	5	.58	1	.207	.276	.376
2003 Los Angeles	NL	11	25	4	1	0	0	(0	0)	5	2	2	1	2	0	9	0	0	0	0	0	-	0	.160	.222	.200
2002 Pittsburgh	NL	65	194	40	11	1	7	(4	3)	74	22	15	17	17	0	68	1	3	1	7	5	.58	1	.206	.272	.381
2002 Chicago	NL	35	43	9	3	0	1	(0	1)	15	3	3	3	5	0	14	0	1	0	0	0	-	0	.209	.292	.349
5 ML YEARS		185	485	96	23	2	13	(7	6)	162	49	34	36	38	1	165	2	7	2	9	8	.53	4	.198	.258	.334

Dustin Hermanson

Pitches: R Bats: R Pos: RP-26; SP-6   Ht: 6'2" Wt: 200 Born: 12/21/72 Age: 31

Year Team	Lg	G	GS	CG	GF	IP	BFP	H	R	ER	HR	SH	SF	HB	TBB	IBB	SO	WP	Bk	W	L	Pct	ShO	Sv-Op	Hld	ERC	ERA
2003 Fresno*	AAA	4	4	0	0	26.0	109	29	16	14	2	1	4	1	3	1	17	1	0	0	1	.000	0	0--	-	3.52	4.85
1995 San Diego	NL	26	0	0	6	31.2	151	35	26	24	8	3	0	1	22	1	19	3	0	3	1	.750	0	0-0	1	7.19	6.82
1996 San Diego	NL	8	0	0	4	13.2	62	18	15	13	3	2	3	0	4	0	11	0	1	1	0	1.000	0	0-0	0	6.37	8.56
1997 Montreal	NL	32	28	1	0	158.1	656	134	68	65	15	10	6	1	66	2	136	4	1	8	8	.500	1	0-0	3	3.32	3.69
1998 Montreal	NL	32	30	1	0	187.0	768	163	80	65	21	9	3	3	56	3	154	4	3	14	11	.560	0	0-0	1	3.12	3.13
1999 Montreal	NL	34	34	0	0	216.1	928	225	110	101	20	16	7	7	69	4	145	4	1	9	14	.391	0	0-0	4	4.03	4.20
2000 Montreal	NL	38	30	2	7	198.0	876	226	128	105	26	10	9	4	75	5	94	5	0	12	14	.462	1	4-7	1	5.10	4.77
2001 St Louis	NL	33	33	0	0	192.1	830	195	106	95	34	7	2	8	73	3	123	6	0	14	13	.519	0	0-0	0	4.80	4.45
2002 Boston	AL	12	1	0	4	22.0	107	35	19	19	3	0	1	0	7	0	13	2	0	1	1	.500	0	0-1	2	7.52	7.77
2003 StL-SF	NL	32	6	0	12	68.2	291	70	32	31	9	4	2	3	24	4	39	3	0	3	3	.500	0	1-6	1	4.38	4.06
2003 St Louis	NL	23	0	0	10	29.2	129	35	18	18	4	2	1	1	14	2	12	1	0	1	2	.333	0	1-6	1	6.04	5.46
2003 San Francisco	NL	9	6	0	2	39.0	162	35	14	13	5	2	1	2	10	2	27	2	0	2	1	.667	0	0-0	0	3.25	3.00
9 ML YEARS		247	162	4	33	1088.0	4669	1101	584	518	139	61	33	27	396	22	734	31	6	65	65	.500	2	5-14	6	4.28	4.28

Jose Hernandez

Bats: R Throws: R Pos: 3B-75; SS-74; PH-6; CF-2; 1B-1; 2B-1   Ht: 6'1" Wt: 188 Born: 7/14/69 Age: 34

Year Team	Lg	G	AB	H	2B	3B	HR	(Hm	Rd)	TB	R	RBI	RC	TBB	IBB	SO	HBP	SH	SF	SB	CS	SB%	GDP	Avg	OBP	Slg
1991 Texas	AL	45	98	18	2	1	0	(0	0)	22	8	4	2	3	0	31	0	6	0	0	1	.00	2	.184	.208	.224
1992 Cleveland	AL	3	4	0	0	0	0	(0	0)	0	0	0	0	0	0	2	0	0	0	0	0	-	0	.000	.000	.000
1994 Chicago	NL	56	132	32	2	3	1	(0	1)	43	18	9	11	8	0	29	1	5	0	2	2	.50	4	.242	.291	.326
1995 Chicago	NL	93	245	60	11	4	13	(6	7)	118	37	40	31	13	3	69	0	2	3	1	0	1.00	6	.245	.281	.482
1996 Chicago	NL	131	331	80	14	1	10	(4	6)	126	52	41	35	24	4	97	1	5	2	4	0	1.00	10	.242	.293	.381
1997 Chicago	NL	121	183	50	8	5	7	(4	3)	89	33	26	26	14	2	42	0	1	1	2	5	.29	5	.273	.323	.486
1998 Chicago	NL	149	488	124	23	7	23	(11	12)	230	76	75	75	40	3	140	1	2	2	4	6	.40	12	.254	.311	.471
1999 ChC-Atl	NL	147	508	135	20	2	19	(6	13)	216	79	62	73	52	6	145	5	2	1	11	3	.79	10	.266	.339	.425
2000 Milwaukee	NL	124	446	109	22	1	11	(8	3)	166	51	59	48	41	3	125	6	0	3	3	7	.30	12	.244	.315	.372
2001 Milwaukee	NL	152	542	135	26	2	25	(9	16)	240	67	78	69	39	8	185	2	5	4	5	4	.56	9	.249	.300	.443
2002 Milwaukee	NL	152	525	151	24	2	24	(13	11)	251	72	73	76	52	5	188	4	0	1	3	5	.38	19	.288	.356	.478
2003 Col-ChC-Pit	NL	150	519	117	18	3	13	(7	6)	180	58	57	39	46	0	177	1	0	5	2	1	.67	16	.225	.287	.347
1999 Chicago	NL	99	342	93	12	2	15	(5	10)	154	57	43	55	40	3	101	5	1	0	7	2	.78	5	.272	.357	.450
1999 Atlanta	NL	48	166	42	8	0	4	(1	3)	62	22	19	18	12	3	44	0	1	1	4	1	.80	5	.253	.302	.373
2003 Colorado	NL	69	257	61	6	1	8	(4	4)	93	33	27	22	27	0	95	0	0	2	1	1	.50	6	.237	.308	.362
2003 Chicago	NL	23	69	13	3	1	2	(1	1)	24	6	9	4	3	0	26	0	0	1	0	0	-	1	.188	.222	.348
2003 Pittsburgh	NL	58	193	43	9	1	3	(2	1)	63	19	21	13	16	0	56	1	0	2	1	0	1.00	9	.223	.282	.326
12 ML YEARS		1323	4021	1011	170	31	146	(68	78)	1681	551	524	477	332	34	1230	21	34	21	37	34	.52	107	.251	.310	.418

Livan Hernandez

Pitches: R Bats: R Pos: SP-33   Ht: 6'2" Wt: 240 Born: 2/20/75 Age: 29

Year Team	Lg	G	GS	CG	GF	IP	BFP	H	R	ER	HR	SH	SF	HB	TBB	IBB	SO	WP	Bk	W	L	Pct	ShO	Sv-Op	Hld	ERC	ERA
1996 Florida	NL	1	0	0	0	3.0	13	3	0	0	0	0	0	0	2	0	2	0	0	0	0	-	0	0-0	0	4.60	0.00
1997 Florida	NL	17	17	0	0	96.1	405	81	39	34	5	4	7	3	38	1	72	0	0	9	3	.750	0	0-0	0	2.96	3.18
1998 Florida	NL	33	33	9	0	234.1	1040	265	133	123	37	8	5	6	104	8	162	4	3	10	12	.455	0	0-0	0	5.58	4.72
1999 Fla-SF	NL	30	30	2	0	199.2	886	227	110	103	23	7	6	2	76	5	144	2	2	8	12	.400	0	0-0	0	4.88	4.64
2000 San Francisco	NL	33	33	5	0	240.0	1030	254	114	100	22	12	9	4	73	3	165	3	0	17	11	.607	2	0-0	0	4.01	3.75
2001 San Francisco	NL	34	34	2	0	226.2	1008	266	143	132	24	12	12	3	85	7	138	7	0	13	15	.464	0	0-0	0	5.03	5.24
2002 San Francisco	NL	33	33	5	0	216.0	921	233	113	105	19	14	8	4	71	5	134	1	1	12	16	.429	3	0-0	0	4.26	4.38
2003 Montreal	NL	33	33	8	0	233.1	967	225	92	83	27	6	4	10	57	3	178	6	1	15	10	.600	0	0-0	0	3.55	3.20
1999 Florida	NL	20	20	2	0	136.0	612	161	78	72	17	3	4	2	55	3	97	2	1	5	9	.357	0	0-0	0	5.37	4.76
1999 San Francisco	NL	10	10	0	0	63.2	274	66	32	31	6	4	2	0	21	2	47	0	1	3	3	.500	0	0-0	0	3.88	4.38
8 ML YEARS		214	213	31	0	1449.1	6270	1554	744	680	157	63	51	32	506	32	995	23	7	84	79	.515	5	0-0	0	4.42	4.22

Michel Hernandez

Bats: R Throws: R Pos: C-5; PH-1   Ht: 6'0" Wt: 208 Born: 8/12/78 Age: 25

Year Team	Lg	G	AB	H	2B	3B	HR	(Hm	Rd)	TB	R	RBI	RC	TBB	IBB	SO	HBP	SH	SF	SB	CS	SB%	GDP	Avg	OBP	Slg
1998 Oneonta	A-	61	205	52	8	2	0	(-	-)	64	29	24	18	20	0	19	0	1	1	4	4	.50	10	.254	.319	.312
1999 Tampa	A+	82	281	69	10	1	2	(-	-)	87	26	23	24	18	0	49	3	3	2	2	2	.50	8	.246	.296	.310
2000 Norwich	AA	21	66	14	2	0	0	(-	-)	16	7	4	4	4	0	13	0	2	1	1	0	1.00	1	.212	.254	.242
2000 Tampa	A+	75	231	51	12	0	1	(-	-)	66	17	28	21	29	0	23	3	4	3	3	4	.43	4	.221	.312	.286
2001 Yankees	R	2	5	0	0	0	0	(-	-)	0	0	0	0	0	0	1	1	0	0	0	0	-	1	.000	.167	.000
2001 Norwich	AA	51	128	29	6	0	2	(-	-)	41	10	10	11	10	0	20	2	2	1	1	0	1.00	5	.227	.291	.320
2002 Norwich	AA	20	61	19	6	0	1	(-	-)	28	11	12	9	5	0	6	0	0	1	0	1	.00	2	.311	.358	.459
2002 Columbus	AAA	41	121	34	5	1	1	(-	-)	44	11	12	13	8	0	13	2	1	0	1	3	.25	5	.281	.336	.364
2003 Columbus	AAA	89	282	79	14	0	4	(-	-)	105	39	30	38	37	1	35	3	1	2	0	2	.00	9	.280	.367	.372
2003 New York	AL	5	4	1	0	0	0	(0	0)	1	0	0	1	1	0	1	0	0	0	0	0	-	0	.250	.400	.250

Orlando Hernandez

Pitches: R Bats: R Pos: SP   Ht: 6'2" Wt: 220 Born: 10/11/69 Age: 34

Year Team	Lg	G	GS	CG	GF	IP	BFP	H	R	ER	HR	SH	SF	HB	TBB	IBB	SO	WP	Bk	W	L	Pct	ShO	Sv-Op	Hld	ERC	ERA
1998 New York	AL	21	21	3	0	141.0	574	113	53	49	11	3	5	6	52	1	131	5	2	12	4	.750	1	0-0	0	2.96	3.13
1999 New York	AL	33	33	2	0	214.1	910	187	108	98	24	3	11	8	87	2	157	4	0	17	9	.654	1	0-0	0	3.60	4.12
2000 New York	AL	29	29	0	0	195.2	820	186	104	98	34	4	5	6	51	2	141	1	0	12	13	.480	0	0-0	0	3.82	4.51
2001 New York	AL	17	16	0	0	94.2	414	90	51	51	19	2	2	5	42	1	77	0	0	4	7	.364	0	0-0	0	4.87	4.85
2002 New York	AL	24	22	0	1	146.0	606	131	63	59	17	1	5	8	36	2	113	8	0	8	5	.615	0	1-1	1	3.20	3.64
5 ML YEARS		124	121	8	1	791.2	3324	707	379	355	105	13	28	33	268	8	619	18	2	53	38	.582	2	1-1	1	3.61	4.04

Ramon Hernandez

Bats: R Throws: R Pos: C-139; PH-5   Ht: 6'0" Wt: 210 Born: 5/20/76 Age: 28

Year Team	Lg	G	AB	H	2B	3B	HR	(Hm	Rd)	TB	R	RBI	RC	TBB	IBB	SO	HBP	SH	SF	SB	CS	SB%	GDP	Avg	OBP	Slg
1999 Oakland	AL	40	136	38	7	0	3	(1	2)	54	13	21	20	18	0	11	1	1	2	1	0	1.00	5	.279	.363	.397
2000 Oakland	AL	143	419	100	19	0	14	(7	7)	162	52	62	49	38	1	64	7	10	5	1	0	1.00	14	.241	.311	.387
2001 Oakland	AL	136	453	115	25	0	15	(5	10)	185	55	60	58	37	3	68	6	9	4	1	1	.50	10	.254	.316	.408
2002 Oakland	AL	136	403	94	20	0	7	(3	4)	135	51	42	41	43	1	64	5	3	3	0	0	-	11	.233	.313	.335
2003 Oakland	AL	140	483	132	24	1	21	(9	12)	221	70	78	69	33	2	79	12	2	6	0	0	-	14	.273	.331	.458
5 ML YEARS		595	1894	480	95	1	60	(25	35)	757	241	263	237	169	7	286	31	25	20	3	1	.75	54	.253	.322	.400

Roberto Hernandez

Pitches: R Bats: R Pos: RP-66   Ht: 6'4" Wt: 250 Born: 11/11/64 Age: 39

Year Team	Lg	G	GS	CG	GF	IP	BFP	H	R	ER	HR	SH	SF	HB	TBB	IBB	SO	WP	Bk	W	L	Pct	ShO	Sv-Op	Hld	ERC	ERA
2003 Richmond*	AAA	6	0	0	1	6.2	38	11	9	7	0	0	0	1	4	0	10	1	0	1	1	.500	0	0--	-	8.02	9.45
1991 Chicago	AL	9	3	0	1	15.0	69	18	15	13	1	0	0	0	7	0	6	1	0	1	0	1.000	0	0-0	0	5.19	7.80
1992 Chicago	AL	43	0	0	27	71.0	277	45	15	13	4	0	3	4	20	1	68	2	0	7	3	.700	0	12-16	6	1.74	1.65
1993 Chicago	AL	70	0	0	67	78.2	314	66	21	20	6	2	2	0	20	1	71	2	0	3	4	.429	0	38-44	0	2.54	2.29
1994 Chicago	AL	45	0	0	43	47.2	206	44	29	26	5	0	1	1	19	1	50	1	0	4	4	.500	0	14-20	0	3.66	4.91
1995 Chicago	AL	60	0	0	57	59.2	272	63	30	26	9	4	0	3	28	4	84	1	0	3	7	.300	0	32-42	0	5.04	3.92
1996 Chicago	AL	72	0	0	61	84.2	355	65	21	18	2	2	2	0	38	5	85	6	0	6	5	.545	0	38-46	0	2.40	1.91
1997 CWS-SF		74	0	0	50	80.2	340	67	24	22	7	2	1	1	38	5	82	3	0	10	3	.769	0	31-39	9	3.30	2.45
1998 Tampa Bay	AL	67	0	0	58	71.1	310	55	33	32	5	4	0	5	41	4	55	1	0	2	6	.250	0	26-35	0	3.43	4.04
1999 Tampa Bay	AL	72	0	0	66	73.1	321	68	27	25	1	2	3	4	33	1	69	3	0	2	3	.400	0	43-47	0	3.40	3.07
2000 Tampa Bay	AL	68	0	0	58	73.1	315	76	33	26	9	7	3	3	23	1	61	2	1	4	7	.364	0	32-40	1	4.24	3.19
2001 Kansas City	AL	63	0	0	55	67.2	287	69	34	31	7	1	0	1	26	3	46	6	0	5	6	.455	0	28-34	0	4.23	4.12
2002 Kansas City	AL	53	0	0	42	52.0	227	62	29	25	6	4	1	3	12	2	39	3	0	1	3	.250	0	26-33	0	4.79	4.33
2003 Atlanta	AL	66	0	0	12	60.0	282	61	36	29	10	4	0	3	43	7	45	0	0	5	6	.625	0	4-9	19	5.95	4.35
1997 Chicago	AL	46	0	0	43	48.0	203	38	15	13	5	1	1	1	24	4	47	2	0	5	1	.833	0	27-31	0	3.30	2.44
1997 San Francisco	NL	28	0	0	7	32.2	137	29	9	9	2	1	0	0	14	1	35	1	0	5	2	.714	0	4-8	9	3.29	2.48
13 ML YEARS		762	3	0	597	835.0	3575	759	347	306	72	32	16	28	348	35	761	31	1	53	54	.495	0	320-400	35	3.60	3.30

Runelvys Hernandez

Pitches: R Bats: R Pos: SP-16   Ht: 6'1" Wt: 205 Born: 4/27/78 Age: 26

Year	Team	Lg	G	GS	CG	GF	IP	BFP	H	R	ER	HR	SH	SF	HB	TBB	IBB	SO	WP	Bk	W	L	Pct	ShO	Sv-Op	Hld	ERC	ERA
2001	Burlington	A	17	17	0	0	100.2	426	94	46	38	5	2	2	3	29	0	100	6	3	7	5	.583	0	0--	-	3.01	3.40
2002	Wilmington	A+	2	2	0	0	12.0	46	12	6	5	0	1	0	1	1	0	9	0	0	1	1	.500	0	0--	-	2.40	3.75
2002	Wichita	AA	16	14	2	1	106.1	422	96	38	32	3	5	4	3	24	1	86	5	1	8	3	.727	0	0--	-	2.63	2.71
2003	Wichita	AA	2	2	0	0	9.1	40	9	4	4	0	0	0	1	5	0	5	0	0	2	0	.000	0	0--	-	3.78	3.86
2003	Omaha	AAA	1	1	0	0	5.0	20	3	1	1	0	0	0	1	2	0	5	0	0	1	0	1.000	0	0--	-	2.16	1.80
2002	Kansas City	AL	12	12	0	0	74.1	316	79	36	36	8	1	3	1	22	0	45	2	0	4	4	.500	0	0-0	0	4.16	4.36
2003	Kansas City	AL	16	16	0	0	91.2	397	87	51	47	9	1	4	6	37	0	48	2	1	7	5	.583	0	0-0	0	4.05	4.61
	2 ML YEARS		28	28	0	0	166.0	713	166	87	83	17	2	7	7	59	0	93	4	1	11	9	.550	0	0-0	0	4.10	4.50

Alex Herrera

Pitches: L Bats: L Pos: RP-10   Ht: 5'11" Wt: 175 Born: 11/5/76 Age: 27

Year	Team	Lg	G	GS	CG	GF	IP	BFP	H	R	ER	HR	SH	SF	HB	TBB	IBB	SO	WP	Bk	W	L	Pct	ShO	Sv-Op	Hld	ERC	ERA
2000	Columbus	A	20	0	0	2	42.0	186	41	25	16	1	3	3	3	21	1	41	2	1	4	3	.571	0	0--	-	4.02	3.43
2000	Kinston	A+	17	0	0	6	31.0	138	28	11	8	1	0	1	1	19	0	40	3	1	0	1	.000	0	1--	-	3.98	2.32
2000	Akron	AA	2	0	0	1	1.1	6	2	1	0	0	0	0	0	1	0	1	0	0	0	0	-	0	0--	-	8.87	0.00
2001	Kinston	A+	28	0	0	8	59.2	231	36	6	4	1	0	0	2	18	0	83	2	0	4	0	1.000	0	3--	-	1.48	0.60
2001	Akron	AA	15	0	0	9	28.2	114	24	9	9	1	0	0	0	9	0	22	2	0	3	0	1.000	0	2--	-	2.56	2.83
2002	Akron	AA	30	0	0	9	61.1	261	47	24	23	8	3	0	6	30	1	65	3	0	0	2	.000	0	5--	-	3.72	3.38
2002	Buffalo	AAA	5	0	0	1	7.0	39	10	9	9	0	1	0	1	8	0	5	2	0	0	1	.000	0	0--	-	9.59	11.57
2003	Buffalo	AAA	34	0	0	15	56.0	262	51	40	33	9	1	2	2	45	1	46	3	5	4	6	.400	0	1--	-	5.73	5.30
2002	Cleveland	AL	5	0	0	1	5.1	20	3	0	0	0	0	0	0	1	0	5	0	0	0	0	-	0	0-0	0	0.99	0.00
2003	Cleveland	AL	10	0	0	3	7.0	36	7	7	7	3	0	0	0	8	1	6	1	0	0	0	-	0	0-0	1	9.65	9.00
	2 ML YEARS		15	0	0	4	12.1	56	10	7	7	3	0	0	0	9	1	11	1	0	0	0	-	0	0-0	1	5.13	5.11

Mike Hessman

Bats: R Throws: R Pos: LF-7; PH-6; 1B-4; 3B-3; PR-2; RF-1   Ht: 6'5" Wt: 215 Born: 3/5/78 Age: 26

Year	Team	Lg	G	AB	H	2B	3B	HR	(Hm	Rd)	TB	R	RBI	RC	TBB	IBB	SO	HBP	SH	SF	SB	CS	SB%	GDP	Avg	OBP	Slg
1996	Braves	R	53	190	41	10	1	1	(-	-)	56	13	15	16	12	1	41	4	4	0	1	1	.50	6	.216	.277	.295
1997	Macon	A	122	459	108	25	0	21	(-	-)	196	69	74	59	41	0	167	6	0	2	0	2	.00	6	.235	.305	.427
1998	Danville	A+	118	445	89	21	0	20	(-	-)	170	47	63	42	30	0	172	6	0	2	3	3	.50	6	.200	.259	.382
1999	Myrtle Beach	A+	103	365	90	25	0	23	(-	-)	184	62	54	64	47	3	135	11	0	3	0	3	.00	3	.247	.347	.504
2000	Greenville	AA	127	437	80	23	1	19	(-	-)	162	52	50	40	37	0	178	8	0	2	3	1	.75	9	.183	.258	.371
2001	Greenville	AA	129	478	110	23	2	26	(-	-)	215	66	80	63	39	2	124	7	0	0	2	4	.33	5	.230	.298	.450
2002	Richmond	AAA	134	484	127	28	1	26	(-	-)	235	67	77	71	34	2	107	10	0	4	1	5	.17	13	.262	.321	.486
2003	Richmond	AAA	96	359	89	15	3	16	(-	-)	158	47	52	47	24	0	87	4	0	8	3	1	.75	6	.248	.296	.440
2003	Danville	R+	5	15	1	0	0	0	(-	-)	1	1	2	0	2	0	2	1	0	2	0	0	-	0	.067	.200	.067
2003	Atlanta	NL	19	21	6	2	0	2	(1	1)	14	2	3	5	5	1	6	0	0	0	0	0	-	2	.286	.423	.667

Richard Hidalgo

Bats: R Throws: R Pos: RF-137; PH-4; DH-1   Ht: 6'3" Wt: 220 Born: 7/2/75 Age: 28

Year	Team	Lg	G	AB	H	2B	3B	HR	(Hm	Rd)	TB	R	RBI	RC	TBB	IBB	SO	HBP	SH	SF	SB	CS	SB%	GDP	Avg	OBP	Slg
1997	Houston	NL	19	62	19	5	0	2	(0	2)	30	8	6	11	4	0	18	1	0	0	1	0	1.00	0	.306	.358	.484
1998	Houston	NL	74	211	64	15	0	7	(3	4)	100	31	35	34	17	0	37	2	0	4	3	3	.50	5	.303	.355	.474
1999	Houston	NL	108	383	87	25	2	15	(5	10)	161	49	56	55	56	2	73	4	0	5	8	5	.62	5	.227	.328	.420
2000	Houston	NL	153	558	175	42	3	44	(16	28)	355	118	122	130	56	3	110	21	0	9	13	6	.68	13	.314	.391	.636
2001	Houston	NL	146	512	141	29	3	19	(13	6)	233	70	80	81	54	3	107	16	0	11	3	5	.38	15	.275	.356	.455
2002	Houston	NL	114	388	91	17	4	15	(4	11)	161	54	48	42	43	1	85	6	0	2	6	2	.75	13	.235	.319	.415
2003	Houston	NL	141	514	159	43	4	28	(11	17)	294	91	88	89	58	8	104	8	0	5	9	7	.56	10	.309	.385	.572
	7 ML YEARS		755	2628	736	176	16	130	(52	78)	1334	421	435	442	288	17	534	58	0	36	43	28	.61	61	.280	.359	.508

Bobby Higginson

Bats: L Throws: R Pos: RF-117; DH-8; PH-6; CF-1   Ht: 5'11" Wt: 202 Born: 8/18/70 Age: 33

Year	Team	Lg	G	AB	H	2B	3B	HR	(Hm	Rd)	TB	R	RBI	RC	TBB	IBB	SO	HBP	SH	SF	SB	CS	SB%	GDP	Avg	OBP	Slg
1995	Detroit	AL	131	410	92	17	5	14	(10	4)	161	61	43	56	62	3	107	5	2	7	6	4	.60	5	.224	.329	.393
1996	Detroit	AL	130	440	141	35	0	26	(15	11)	254	75	81	99	65	7	66	1	3	6	6	3	.67	7	.320	.404	.577
1997	Detroit	AL	146	546	163	30	5	27	(16	11)	284	94	101	105	70	2	85	3	0	4	12	7	.63	10	.299	.379	.520
1998	Detroit	AL	157	612	174	37	4	25	(10	15)	294	92	85	100	63	2	101	6	0	4	3	3	.50	16	.284	.355	.480
1999	Detroit	AL	107	377	90	18	0	12	(8	4)	144	51	46	54	64	2	66	2	0	2	4	6	.40	2	.239	.351	.382
2000	Detroit	AL	154	597	179	44	4	30	(12	18)	321	104	102	121	74	6	99	2	2	3	15	3	.83	5	.300	.377	.538
2001	Detroit	AL	147	541	150	28	6	17	(7	10)	241	84	71	91	80	3	65	2	1	9	20	12	.63	8	.277	.367	.445
2002	Detroit	AL	119	444	125	24	3	10	(6	4)	185	50	63	72	41	3	45	6	1	7	12	5	.71	8	.282	.345	.417
2003	Detroit	AL	130	469	110	13	4	10	(6	4)	173	56	61	52	53	9	73	3	1	6	8	8	.50	12	.235	.320	.369
	9 ML YEARS		1221	4436	1224	246	31	175	(90	85)	2057	672	644	751	578	31	707	30	10	48	86	51	.63	73	.276	.360	.464

Bobby Hill

Bats: B Throws: R Pos: PH-4; 2B-3; PR-1   Ht: 5'10" Wt: 190 Born: 4/3/78 Age: 26

Year	Team	Lg	G	AB	H	2B	3B	HR	(Hm	Rd)	TB	R	RBI	RC	TBB	IBB	SO	HBP	SH	SF	SB	CS	SB%	GDP	Avg	OBP	Slg
2000	Newark	IND	132	481	157	22	9	13	(-	-)	236	109	82	118	101	2	57	4	1	7	81	15	.84	8	.326	.442	.491
2001	W Tennesse	AA	57	209	63	8	1	3	(-	-)	82	30	21	34	32	1	39	2	1	2	20	8	.71	7	.301	.396	.392
2001	Cubs	R	3	9	2	0	0	0	(-	-)	2	1	1	1	2	0	3	0	0	0	1	0	1.00	0	.222	.364	.222

Year Team	Lg	G	AB	H	2B	3B	HR	(Hm	Rd)	TB	R	RBI	RC	TBB	IBB	SO	HBP	SH	SF	SB	CS	SB%	GDP	Avg	OBP	Slg
2002 Iowa	AAA	92	354	99	23	3	8	(-	-)	152	80	39	64	49	0	66	11	3	2	29	5	.85	7	.280	.382	.429
2003 Iowa	AAA	92	361	104	23	4	6	(-	-)	153	53	40	56	37	0	65	8	3	2	8	7	.53	5	.288	.365	.424
2003 Nashville	AAA	17	66	11	2	1	1	(-	-)	18	5	4	4	8	0	8	0	1	0	1	2	.33	2	.167	.257	.273
2002 Chicago	NL	59	190	48	7	2	4	(1	3)	71	26	20	24	17	4	42	4	4	0	6	1	.86	0	.253	.327	.374
2003 ChC-Pit	NL	6	7	2	0	0	0	(0	0)	2	1	0	2	2	0	2	0	0	0	0	0	-	1	.286	.444	.286
2003 Chicago	NL	5	4	1	0	0	0	(0	0)	1	0	0	1	1	0	1	0	0	0	0	0	-	0	.250	.400	.250
2003 Pittsburgh	NL	1	3	1	0	0	0	(0	0)	1	1	0	1	1	0	0	0	0	0	0	0	-	0	.333	.500	.333
2 ML YEARS		65	197	50	7	2	4	(1	3)	73	27	20	26	19	4	44	4	4	0	6	1	.86	1	.254	.332	.371

Jeremy Hill

Pitches: R Bats: R Pos: RP-1   Ht: 5'10" Wt: 185 Born: 8/8/77 Age: 26

Year Team	Lg	G	GS	CG	GF	IP	BFP	H	R	ER	HR	SH	SF	HB	TBB	IBB	SO	WP	Bk	W	L	Pct	ShO	Sv-Op	Hld	ERC	ERA
2001 Burlington	A	40	0	0	31	47.2	190	22	11	8	2	2	0	3	25	0	66	6	0	0	2	.000	0	12--	-	1.68	1.51
2001 Wilmington	A+	9	0	0	7	12.1	52	10	2	1	0	1	0	0	8	1	13	2	0	4	0	1.000	0	2--	-	3.25	0.73
2002 Wichita	AA	56	0	0	46	76.1	317	61	26	20	4	6	2	1	32	5	80	3	0	7	.364	0	19--	-	2.71	2.36
2003 Binghamton	AA	11	0	0	4	13.0	72	14	15	15	3	2	0	1	15	2	10	7	0	0	2	.000	0	0--	-	8.58	10.38
2003 Wichita	AA	2	0	0	1	2.0	10	0	1	0	0	0	1	0	3	0	3	3	0	0	0	-	0	0--	-	1.71	0.00
2003 Omaha	AAA	26	1	0	7	40.1	202	42	38	35	5	2	1	4	42	0	41	9	0	1	3	.250	0	1--	-	7.69	7.81
2002 Kansas City	AL	10	0	0	6	9.1	43	8	4	4	1	0	1	0	8	1	7	1	0	0	0	1.000	0	0-0	0	4.93	3.86
2003 Kansas City	AL	1	0	0	1	1.0	4	1	0	0	0	0	0	0	0	0	0	0	0	0	0	-	0	0-0	0	1.95	0.00
2 ML YEARS		11	0	0	7	10.1	47	9	4	4	1	0	1	0	8	1	7	1	0	0	1	.000	0	0-0	0	4.61	3.48

Koyie Hill

Bats: B Throws: R Pos: PH-3   Ht: 6'0" Wt: 190 Born: 3/9/79 Age: 25

Year Team	Lg	G	AB	H	2B	3B	HR	(Hm	Rd)	TB	R	RBI	RC	TBB	IBB	SO	HBP	SH	SF	SB	CS	SB%	GDP	Avg	OBP	Slg
2000 Yakima	A-	64	251	65	13	1	2	(-	-)	86	26	29	25	25	2	47	0	5	2	0	7	.00	7	.259	.324	.343
2001 Wilmington	A+	134	498	150	20	2	8	(-	-)	198	65	79	74	49	14	82	7	2	6	21	12	.64	7	.301	.368	.398
2002 Jacksonville	AA	130	468	127	25	1	11	(-	-)	187	67	64	70	76	11	88	0	1	7	5	3	.63	14	.271	.368	.400
2003 Las Vegas	AAA	85	312	98	18	0	3	(-	-)	125	48	36	42	15	3	39	1	1	2	5	0	1.00	7	.314	.345	.401
2003 Jacksonville	AA	25	101	23	7	0	0	(-	-)	30	9	7	7	6	2	19	0	0	0	2	1	.67	3	.228	.271	.297
2003 Los Angeles	NL	3	3	1	1	0	0	(0	0)	2	0	0	1	0	0	2	0	0	0	0	0	-	0	.333	.333	.667

Shea Hillenbrand

Bats: R Throws: R Pos: 1B-84; 3B-63; PH-4; DH-1; PR-1   Ht: 6'1" Wt: 211 Born: 7/27/75 Age: 28

Year Team	Lg	G	AB	H	2B	3B	HR	(Hm	Rd)	TB	R	RBI	RC	TBB	IBB	SO	HBP	SH	SF	SB	CS	SB%	GDP	Avg	OBP	Slg
2003 Tucson*	AAA	3	10	3	1	0	0	(-	-)	4	0	1	1	0	0	1	0	0	0	0	0	-	0	.300	.300	.400
2001 Boston	AL	139	468	123	20	2	12	(5	7)	183	52	49	49	13	3	61	7	1	4	3	4	.43	12	.263	.291	.391
2002 Boston	AL	156	634	186	43	4	18	(5	13)	291	94	83	88	25	4	95	12	0	5	4	2	.67	18	.293	.330	.459
2003 Bos-Ari		134	515	144	35	1	20	(11	9)	241	60	97	67	24	4	70	6	0	9	1	0	1.00	22	.280	.314	.468
2003 Boston	AL	49	185	56	17	0	3	(0	3)	82	20	38	27	7	1	26	4	0	4	1	0	1.00	9	.303	.335	.443
2003 Arizona	NL	85	330	88	18	1	17	(11	6)	159	40	59	40	17	3	44	2	0	5	0	0	-	13	.267	.302	.482
3 ML YEARS		429	1617	453	98	7	50	(21	29)	715	206	229	204	62	11	226	25	1	18	8	6	.57	52	.280	.314	.442

A.J. Hinch

Bats: R Throws: R Pos: C-27; PH-1   Ht: 6'1" Wt: 205 Born: 5/15/74 Age: 30

Year Team	Lg	G	AB	H	2B	3B	HR	(Hm	Rd)	TB	R	RBI	RC	TBB	IBB	SO	HBP	SH	SF	SB	CS	SB%	GDP	Avg	OBP	Slg
2003 Toledo*	AAA	55	185	48	15	1	4	(-	-)	77	20	23	24	13	2	38	4	2	1	0	1	.00	2	.259	.320	.416
1998 Oakland	AL	120	337	78	10	0	9	(4	5)	115	34	35	36	30	0	89	4	13	7	3	0	1.00	6	.231	.296	.341
1999 Oakland	AL	76	205	44	4	1	7	(3	4)	71	26	24	18	11	0	41	2	9	1	6	2	.75	4	.215	.260	.346
2000 Oakland	AL	6	8	2	0	0	0	(0	0)	2	1	0	1	1	0	1	0	0	0	0	0	-	0	.250	.333	.250
2001 Kansas City	AL	45	121	19	3	0	6	(4	2)	40	10	15	7	8	1	26	3	1	1	1	1	.50	5	.157	.226	.331
2002 Kansas City	AL	72	197	49	7	1	7	(6	1)	79	25	27	26	18	0	35	3	2	0	3	3	.50	2	.249	.321	.401
2003 Detroit	AL	27	74	15	3	1	3	(1	2)	29	7	11	7	3	0	18	2	1	2	0	0	-	3	.203	.247	.392
6 ML YEARS		346	942	207	27	3	32	(18	14)	336	103	112	95	71	1	210	14	26	11	13	6	.68	20	.220	.281	.357

Eric Hinske

Bats: L Throws: R Pos: 3B-124; PH-3   Ht: 6'2" Wt: 225 Born: 8/5/77 Age: 26

Year Team	Lg	G	AB	H	2B	3B	HR	(Hm	Rd)	TB	R	RBI	RC	TBB	IBB	SO	HBP	SH	SF	SB	CS	SB%	GDP	Avg	OBP	Slg
1998 Williamsport	A-	68	248	74	20	0	9	(-	-)	121	48	57	50	35	3	61	2	0	4	19	3	.86	2	.298	.384	.488
1998 Rockford	A	6	20	9	4	0	1	(-	-)	16	8	4	8	5	0	6	0	0	1	1	0	1.00	0	.450	.538	.800
1999 Daytona	A+	130	445	132	28	6	19	(-	-)	229	76	79	87	62	7	90	5	1	5	16	10	.62	5	.297	.385	.515
1999 Iowa	AAA	4	15	4	0	1	1	(-	-)	9	3	2	3	1	0	4	0	0	0	0	0	-	0	.267	.313	.600
2000 W Tennessee	AA	131	436	113	21	9	20	(-	-)	212	76	73	81	78	3	133	3	0	3	14	5	.74	7	.259	.373	.486
2001 Sacramento	AAA	121	436	123	27	1	25	(-	-)	227	71	79	85	54	3	113	10	2	2	20	7	.74	6	.282	.373	.521
2003 Syracuse	AAA	2	8	4	1	0	0	(-	-)	5	4	2	4	2	0	0	0	0	0	0	0	-	0	.500	.500	1.000
2002 Toronto	AL	151	566	158	38	2	24	(15	9)	272	99	84	104	77	5	138	2	0	5	13	1	.93	12	.279	.365	.481
2003 Toronto	AL	124	449	109	45	3	12	(4	8)	196	74	63	69	59	1	104	1	0	1	12	2	.86	11	.243	.329	.437
2 ML YEARS		275	1015	267	83	5	36	(19	17)	468	173	147	173	136	6	242	3	0	10	25	3	.89	23	.263	.349	.461

Sterling Hitchcock

Pitches: L **Bats:** L **Pos:** RP-28; SP-7   **Ht:** 6'0" **Wt:** 205 **Born:** 4/29/71 **Age:** 33

Year Team	Lg	G	GS	CG	GF	IP	BFP	H	R	ER	HR	SH	SF	HB	TBB	IBB	SO	WP	Bk	W	L	Pct	ShO	Sv-Op	Hld	ERC	ERA
1992 New York	AL	3	3	0	0	13.0	68	23	12	12	2	0	0	1	6	0	6	0	0	0	2	.000	0	0-0	0	9.98	8.31
1993 New York	AL	6	6	0	0	31.0	135	32	18	16	4	0	2	1	14	1	26	3	2	1	2	.333	0	0-0	0	4.83	4.65
1994 New York	AL	23	5	1	4	49.1	218	48	24	23	3	1	7	0	29	1	37	5	0	4	1	.800	0	2-2	3	4.38	4.20
1995 New York	AL	27	27	4	0	168.1	719	155	91	88	22	5	9	5	68	1	121	5	2	11	10	.524	1	0-0	0	3.97	4.70
1996 Seattle	AL	35	35	0	0	196.2	885	245	131	117	27	3	8	7	73	4	132	4	1	13	9	.591	0	0-0	0	5.86	5.35
1997 San Diego	NL	32	28	1	1	161.0	693	172	102	93	24	7	4	4	55	2	106	6	2	10	11	.476	0	0-0	0	4.71	5.20
1998 San Diego	NL	39	27	2	3	176.1	743	169	83	77	29	9	3	9	48	2	158	11	1	9	7	.563	1	1-2	3	3.95	3.93
1999 San Diego	NL	33	33	1	0	205.2	892	202	99	94	29	9	6	5	76	6	194	15	2	12	14	.462	0	0-0	0	4.14	4.11
2000 San Diego	NL	11	11	0	0	65.2	292	69	38	36	12	2	1	5	26	1	61	4	0	1	6	.143	0	0-0	0	5.22	4.93
2001 SD-NYY		13	12	1	0	70.1	323	89	46	44	6	2	4	3	21	0	43	3	1	6	5	.545	0	0-0	0	5.15	5.63
2002 New York	AL	20	2	0	11	39.1	193	57	29	24	4	1	1	1	15	3	31	1	0	1	2	.333	0	0-0	0	6.43	5.49
2003 NYY-StL		35	7	0	8	87.2	383	91	50	46	14	4	3	1	32	4	68	3	0	6	4	.600	0	0-0	2	4.49	4.72
2001 San Diego	NL	3	3	0	0	19.0	85	22	9	7	1	1	0	1	3	0	15	1	0	2	1	.667	0	0-0	0	3.68	3.32
2001 New York	AL	10	9	1	0	51.1	238	67	37	37	5	1	4	2	18	0	28	2	1	4	4	.500	0	0-0	0	5.74	6.49
2003 New York	AL	27	1	0	8	49.2	221	57	33	30	6	1	2	0	18	3	36	1	0	1	3	.250	0	0-0	2	4.77	5.44
2003 St Louis	NL	8	6	0	0	38.0	162	34	17	16	8	3	1	1	14	1	32	2	0	5	1	.833	0	0-0	0	4.12	3.79
12 ML YEARS		277	196	10	27	1264.1	5544	1352	723	670	176	43	48	42	463	25	983	60	11	74	73	.503	2	3-4	8	4.71	4.77

Denny Hocking

Bats: B **Throws:** R **Pos:** 2B-25; 3B-24; SS-17; PR-11; 1B-10; PH-9; RF-4; LF-2; CF-2   **Ht:** 5'10" **Wt:** 183 **Born:** 4/2/70 **Age:** 34

Year Team	Lg	G	AB	H	2B	3B	HR	(Hm	Rd)	TB	R	RBI	RC	TBB	IBB	SO	HBP	SH	SF	SB	CS	SB%	GDP	Avg	OBP	Slg
1993 Minnesota	AL	15	36	5	1	0	0	(0	0)	6	7	0	1	6	0	8	0	0	0	1	0	1.00	1	.139	.262	.167
1994 Minnesota	AL	11	31	10	3	0	0	(0	0)	13	3	2	4	0	0	4	0	0	0	2	0	1.00	1	.323	.323	.419
1995 Minnesota	AL	9	25	5	0	2	0	(0	0)	9	4	3	2	2	1	2	0	1	0	1	0	1.00	1	.200	.259	.360
1996 Minnesota	AL	49	127	25	6	0	1	(0	1)	34	16	10	6	8	0	24	0	1	1	3	3	.50	3	.197	.243	.268
1997 Minnesota	AL	115	253	65	12	4	2	(0	2)	91	28	25	26	18	0	51	1	5	1	3	5	.38	6	.257	.308	.360
1998 Minnesota	AL	110	198	40	6	1	3	(1	2)	57	32	15	14	16	1	44	0	3	2	2	1	.67	2	.202	.259	.288
1999 Minnesota	AL	136	386	103	18	2	7	(2	5)	146	47	41	43	22	1	54	3	4	6	11	7	.61	10	.267	.307	.378
2000 Minnesota	AL	134	373	111	24	4	4	(1	3)	155	52	47	61	48	1	77	0	7	5	7	5	.58	2	.298	.373	.416
2001 Minnesota	AL	112	327	82	16	2	3	(1	2)	111	34	25	35	29	1	67	2	4	1	6	1	.86	7	.251	.315	.339
2002 Minnesota	AL	102	260	65	13	0	2	(1	1)	84	28	25	25	24	0	44	1	4	5	0	2	.00	3	.250	.310	.323
2003 Minnesota	AL	83	188	45	10	2	3	(0	3)	68	22	22	19	15	0	37	0	3	3	0	1	.00	3	.239	.291	.362
11 ML YEARS		876	2204	556	109	17	25	(6	19)	774	273	215	236	188	5	412	7	32	24	36	25	.59	39	.252	.310	.351

Trey Hodges

Pitches: R **Bats:** R **Pos:** RP-51; SP-1   **Ht:** 6'3" **Wt:** 187 **Born:** 6/29/78 **Age:** 26

Year Team	Lg	G	GS	CG	GF	IP	BFP	H	R	ER	HR	SH	SF	HB	TBB	IBB	SO	WP	Bk	W	L	Pct	ShO	Sv-Op	Hld	ERC	ERA
2000 Jamestown	A-	13	2	0	2	19.2	93	22	14	13	3	1	0	1	12	0	13	1	2	0	2	.000	0	0- -	-	6.19	5.95
2001 Myrtle Beach	A+	26	26	1	0	173.0	686	156	64	53	13	4	2	5	18	0	139	7	0	15	8	.652	0	0- -	-	2.41	2.76
2002 Richmond	AAA	28	28	1	0	172.1	716	158	66	61	9	7	5	8	56	1	116	2	1	15	9	.625	1	0- -	-	3.22	3.19
2002 Atlanta	NL	4	0	0	0	11.2	53	16	7	7	2	2	2	1	2	0	6	1	0	2	0	1.000	0	0-0	0	6.20	5.40
2003 Atlanta	NL	52	1	0	15	65.2	297	69	38	34	11	2	3	3	31	7	66	7	0	3	3	.500	0	0-2	4	5.10	4.66
2 ML YEARS		56	1	0	15	77.1	350	85	45	41	13	4	5	4	33	7	72	8	0	5	3	.625	0	0-2	4	5.26	4.77

Trevor Hoffman

Pitches: R **Bats:** R **Pos:** RP-9   **Ht:** 6'0" **Wt:** 205 **Born:** 10/13/67 **Age:** 36

Year Team	Lg	G	GS	CG	GF	IP	BFP	H	R	ER	HR	SH	SF	HB	TBB	IBB	SO	WP	Bk	W	L	Pct	ShO	Sv-Op	Hld	ERC	ERA
2003 Lk Elsinore*	A+	3	0	0	0	3.0	12	2	0	0	0	0	0	1	0	0	4	0	0	0	0	-	0	0- -	-	1.57	0.00
1993 Fla-SD	NL	67	0	0	26	90.0	391	80	43	39	10	4	5	1	39	13	79	5	0	4	6	.400	0	5-8	15	3.40	3.90
1994 San Diego	NL	47	0	0	41	56.0	225	39	16	16	4	1	2	0	20	6	68	3	0	4	4	.500	0	20-23	1	2.02	2.57
1995 San Diego	NL	55	0	0	51	53.1	218	48	25	23	10	0	0	0	14	3	52	1	0	7	4	.636	0	31-38	0	3.48	3.88
1996 San Diego	NL	70	0	0	62	88.0	348	50	23	22	6	2	2	2	31	5	111	2	0	9	5	.643	0	42-49	0	1.58	2.25
1997 San Diego	NL	70	0	0	59	81.1	322	59	25	24	9	2	1	0	24	4	111	7	0	6	4	.600	0	37-44	0	2.27	2.66
1998 San Diego	NL	66	0	0	61	73.0	274	41	12	12	2	3	0	1	21	2	86	8	0	4	2	.667	0	53-54	0	1.32	1.48
1999 San Diego	NL	64	0	0	54	67.1	263	48	23	16	5	1	3	0	15	2	73	4	0	2	3	.400	0	40-43	0	1.78	2.14
2000 San Diego	NL	70	0	0	59	72.1	291	61	29	24	7	3	5	0	11	4	85	4	0	4	7	.364	0	43-50	0	2.18	2.99
2001 San Diego	NL	62	0	0	55	60.1	248	48	25	23	10	2	2	1	21	2	63	3	0	3	4	.429	0	43-46	0	3.20	3.43
2002 San Diego	NL	61	0	0	52	59.1	245	52	20	18	2	2	2	1	18	2	69	3	0	2	5	.286	0	38-41	0	2.63	2.73
2003 San Diego	NL	9	0	0	7	9.0	36	7	2	2	1	0	0	0	3	0	11	0	0	0	0	-	0	0-0	0	2.76	2.00
1993 Florida	NL	28	0	0	13	35.2	152	24	13	13	5	2	1	0	19	7	26	3	0	2	2	.500	0	2-3	8	2.71	3.28
1993 San Diego	NL	39	0	0	13	54.1	239	56	30	26	5	2	4	1	20	6	53	2	0	2	4	.333	0	3-5	7	3.88	4.31
11 ML YEARS		641	0	0	527	710.0	2861	533	243	219	66	20	22	6	217	43	808	40	0	45	44	.506	0	352-396	16	2.31	2.78

Todd Hollandsworth

Bats: L **Throws:** L **Pos:** LF-61; PH-28; RF-3; DH-1   **Ht:** 6'2" **Wt:** 207 **Born:** 4/20/73 **Age:** 31

Year Team	Lg	G	AB	H	2B	3B	HR	(Hm	Rd)	TB	R	RBI	RC	TBB	IBB	SO	HBP	SH	SF	SB	CS	SB%	GDP	Avg	OBP	Slg
1995 Los Angeles	NL	41	103	24	2	0	5	(3	2)	41	16	13	13	10	2	29	1	0	1	2	1	.67	1	.233	.304	.398
1996 Los Angeles	NL	149	478	139	26	4	12	(2	10)	209	64	59	76	41	1	93	2	3	2	21	6	.78	5	.291	.348	.437
1997 Los Angeles	NL	106	296	73	20	2	4	(1	3)	109	39	31	28	17	2	60	0	2	2	5	5	.50	8	.247	.286	.368
1998 Los Angeles	NL	55	175	47	6	4	3	(1	2)	70	23	20	21	9	0	42	1	2	0	4	3	.57	2	.269	.308	.400
1999 Los Angeles	NL	92	261	74	12	2	9	(5	4)	117	39	32	41	24	1	61	1	0	1	5	2	.71	6	.284	.345	.448
2000 LA-Col	NL	137	428	115	20	0	19	(13	6)	192	81	47	63	41	3	99	1	0	1	18	7	.72	8	.269	.333	.449
2001 Colorado	NL	33	117	43	15	1	6	(3	3)	78	21	19	30	8	2	20	0	0	0	5	0	1.00	1	.368	.408	.667

108

BATTING | BASERUNNING | AVERAGES

Year Team	Lg	G	AB	H	2B	3B	HR	(Hm Rd)	TB	R	RBI	RC	TBB	IBB	SO	HBP	SH	SF	SB	CS	SB%	GDP	Avg	OBP	Slg
2002 Col-Tex		134	430	122	27	1	16	(11 5)	199	55	67	68	40	4	98	1	3	3	8	8	.50	8	.284	.344	.463
2003 Florida	NL	93	228	58	23	3	3	(1 2)	96	32	20	28	22	4	55	0	2	2	2	3	.40	2	.254	.317	.421
2000 Los Angeles	NL	81	261	61	12	0	8	(6 2)	97	42	24	31	30	2	61	1	0	1	11	4	.73	4	.234	.314	.372
2000 Colorado	NL	56	167	54	8	0	11	(7 4)	95	39	23	32	11	1	38	0	0	0	7	3	.70	4	.323	.365	.569
2002 Colorado	NL	95	298	88	21	1	11	(9 2)	144	39	48	46	26	4	71	1	1	2	7	8	.47	8	.295	.352	.483
2002 Texas	AL	39	132	34	6	0	5	(2 3)	55	16	19	22	14	0	27	0	2	1	1	0	1.00	6	.258	.327	.417
9 ML YEARS		840	2516	695	151	17	77	(40 37)	1111	370	308	368	212	19	557	7	12	12	70	35	.67	34	.276	.333	.442

Darren Holmes

Pitches: R Bats: R Pos: RP-48 Ht: 6'0" Wt: 202 Born: 4/25/66 Age: 38

HOW MUCH HE PITCHED | WHAT HE GAVE UP | THE RESULTS

Year Team	Lg	G	GS	CG	GF	IP	BFP	H	R	ER	HR	SH	SF	HB	TBB	IBB	SO	WP	Bk	W	L	Pct	ShO	Sv-Op	Hld	ERC	ERA
1990 Los Angeles	NL	14	0	0	1	17.1	77	15	10	10	1	1	2	0	11	3	19	1	0	0	1	.000	0	0-0	1	3.59	5.19
1991 Milwaukee	NL	40	0	0	9	76.1	344	90	43	40	6	8	3	1	27	1	59	6	0	1	4	.200	0	3-6	3	4.71	4.72
1992 Milwaukee	NL	41	0	0	25	42.1	173	35	12	12	1	4	0	2	11	4	31	0	0	4	4	.500	0	6-8	2	2.19	2.55
1993 Colorado	NL	62	0	0	51	66.2	274	56	31	30	6	0	0	2	20	1	60	2	1	3	3	.500	0	25-29	2	2.86	4.05
1994 Colorado	NL	29	0	0	14	28.1	142	35	25	20	5	4	1	1	24	4	33	2	0	0	3	.000	0	3-8	3	7.90	6.35
1995 Colorado	NL	68	0	0	33	66.2	286	59	26	24	3	5	3	1	28	3	61	7	1	6	1	.857	0	14-18	13	3.09	3.24
1996 Colorado	NL	62	0	0	21	77.0	333	78	41	34	8	2	1	1	28	2	73	2	0	5	4	.556	0	1-8	7	4.01	3.97
1997 Colorado	NL	42	6	0	10	89.1	406	113	58	53	12	6	4	0	36	3	70	4	0	9	2	.818	0	3-4	5	5.87	5.34
1998 New York	AL	34	0	0	13	51.1	215	53	19	19	4	0	3	2	14	3	31	1	0	0	3	.000	0	2-3	2	3.73	3.33
1999 Arizona	NL	44	0	0	9	48.2	219	50	21	20	3	2	0	1	25	8	35	0	2	4	3	.571	0	0-2	4	4.14	3.70
2000 Ari-StL-Bal		18	0	0	3	19.1	103	37	28	28	6	0	3	2	9	0	16	0	0	0	1	.000	0	1-2	1	12.92	13.03
2002 Atlanta	NL	55	0	0	10	54.2	214	41	12	11	3	4	1	2	12	4	47	0	0	2	2	.500	0	1-2	7	1.92	1.81
2003 Atlanta	NL	48	0	0	12	42.0	180	47	22	20	5	0	1	0	11	0	46	1	0	1	2	.333	0	0-1	11	4.33	4.29
2000 Arizona	NL	8	0	0	3	6.1	32	12	6	6	1	0	1	1	1	0	5	0	0	0	0	-	0	1-1	1	9.99	8.53
2000 St Louis	NL	5	0	0	1	8.1	39	12	9	9	2	0	2	1	3	0	5	0	0	0	1	.000	0	0-1	0	8.54	9.72
2000 Baltimore	AL	5	0	0	0	4.2	32	13	13	13	3	0	0	0	6	0	6	0	0	0	0	-	0	0-0	0	26.18	25.07
13 ML YEARS		557	6	0	212	680.0	2966	709	348	321	63	36	22	15	256	36	581	26	4	35	33	.515	0	59-91	60	4.15	4.25

J.R. House

Bats: R Throws: R Pos: PH-1 Ht: 5'10" Wt: 202 Born: 11/11/79 Age: 24

BATTING | BASERUNNING | AVERAGES

Year Team	Lg	G	AB	H	2B	3B	HR	(Hm Rd)	TB	R	RBI	RC	TBB	IBB	SO	HBP	SH	SF	SB	CS	SB%	GDP	Avg	OBP	Slg
1999 Pirates	R	33	113	37	9	3	5	(- -)	67	13	23	25	11	0	23	2	0	1	1	0	1.00	1	.327	.394	.593
1999 Williamsport	A-	26	100	30	6	0	1	(- -)	39	11	13	13	9	0	21	0	0	2	0	1	.00	2	.300	.358	.390
1999 Hickory	A	4	11	3	0	0	0	(- -)	3	1	0	1	0	0	3	0	0	0	0	0	-	0	.273	.273	.273
2000 Hickory	A	110	420	146	29	1	23	(- -)	246	78	90	96	46	2	91	6	0	6	1	2	.33	4	.348	.414	.586
2001 Altoona	AA	112	426	110	25	1	11	(- -)	170	51	56	53	37	2	103	5	0	2	1	1	.50	12	.258	.323	.399
2002 Altoona	AA	30	91	24	6	0	2	(- -)	36	9	11	12	13	0	21	0	0	2	0	0	-	4	.264	.349	.396
2003 Pirates	R	20	65	26	9	0	4	(- -)	47	16	23	21	12	1	5	1	0	0	0	0	-	1	.400	.476	.723
2003 Altoona	AA	20	63	21	6	0	2	(- -)	33	12	11	11	5	0	11	0	0	0	0	0	-	4	.333	.382	.524
2003 Pittsburgh	NL	1	1	1	0	0	0	(0 0)	1	0	0	0	0	0	0	0	0	0	0	0	-	0	1.000	1.000	1.000

Tyler Houston

Bats: L Throws: R Pos: PH-32; 3B-21; 1B-1 Ht: 6'1" Wt: 218 Born: 1/17/71 Age: 33

BATTING | BASERUNNING | AVERAGES

Year Team	Lg	G	AB	H	2B	3B	HR	(Hm Rd)	TB	R	RBI	RC	TBB	IBB	SO	HBP	SH	SF	SB	CS	SB%	GDP	Avg	OBP	Slg
2003 Scrtn/WlksBr*	AAA	6	23	4	1	1	0	(- -)	7	2	0	1	0	1	1	0	0	0	0	0	-	0	.174	.208	.304
1996 Atl-ChC	NL	79	142	45	9	1	3	(1 2)	65	21	27	21	9	1	27	0	0	0	3	2	.60	5	.317	.358	.458
1997 Chicago	NL	72	196	51	10	0	2	(0 2)	67	15	28	19	9	1	35	0	0	2	1	0	1.00	4	.260	.290	.342
1998 Chicago	NL	95	255	65	7	1	9	(4 5)	101	26	33	27	13	1	53	0	1	1	2	2	.50	6	.255	.290	.396
1999 ChC-Cle	NL	113	276	62	10	1	10	(2 8)	104	28	30	30	31	4	78	0	1	1	1	1	.50	7	.225	.302	.377
2000 Milwaukee	NL	101	284	71	15	0	18	(6 12)	140	30	43	37	17	3	72	0	4	0	2	1	.67	13	.250	.292	.493
2001 Milwaukee	NL	75	235	68	7	0	12	(6 6)	111	36	38	37	18	1	62	1	2	0	0	0	-	3	.289	.343	.472
2002 Mil-LA	NL	111	320	90	20	3	7	(6 1)	137	34	40	42	16	3	62	4	4	1	1	0	1.00	9	.281	.323	.428
2003 Philadelphia	NL	54	97	27	6	0	2	(0 2)	39	7	14	11	6	1	19	0	0	0	0	0	-	2	.278	.320	.402
1996 Atlanta	NL	33	27	6	2	1	1	(1 0)	13	3	8	3	1	0	9	0	0	0	0	0	-	1	.222	.250	.481
1996 Chicago	NL	46	115	39	7	0	2	(0 2)	52	18	19	18	8	1	18	0	0	0	3	2	.60	4	.339	.382	.452
1999 Chicago	NL	100	249	58	9	1	9	(2 7)	96	26	27	28	28	4	67	0	1	1	1	1	.50	7	.233	.309	.386
1999 Cleveland	AL	13	27	4	1	0	1	(0 1)	8	2	3	2	3	0	11	0	0	0	0	0	-	0	.148	.233	.296
2002 Milwaukee	NL	76	255	77	15	2	7	(6 1)	117	25	33	38	14	3	41	4	4	1	1	0	1.00	4	.302	.347	.459
2002 Los Angeles	NL	35	65	13	5	1	0	(0 0)	20	9	7	4	2	0	21	0	0	0	0	0	-	5	.200	.224	.308
8 ML YEARS		700	1805	479	84	6	63	(25 38)	764	197	253	224	119	15	408	5	12	5	10	6	.63	49	.265	.312	.423

Ben Howard

Pitches: R Bats: R Pos: SP-6 Ht: 6'2" Wt: 190 Born: 1/15/79 Age: 25

HOW MUCH HE PITCHED | WHAT HE GAVE UP | THE RESULTS

Year Team	Lg	G	GS	CG	GF	IP	BFP	H	R	ER	HR	SH	SF	HB	TBB	IBB	SO	WP	Bk	W	L	Pct	ShO	Sv-Op	Hld	ERC	ERA
1997 Padres	R	13	12	0	1	54.1	281	54	53	45	3	1	0	2	63	0	59	19	7	1	4	.200	0	0- -	-	6.74	7.45
1998 Idaho Falls	R+	15	15	0	0	68.2	354	61	46	42	4	1	4	4	87	0	79	17	6	5	4	.444	0	0- -	-	7.08	6.03
1999 Fort Wayne	A	28	28	0	0	144.2	666	123	100	76	17	4	3	5	110	0	131	19	1	6	10	.375	0	0- -	-	4.85	4.73
2000 R Cucamnga	A+	32	19	0	4	107.1	506	88	87	76	8	2	2	2	111	1	150	14	1	5	11	.313	0	0- -	-	5.45	6.37
2001 Lk Elsinore	A+	18	18	0	0	101.2	414	86	37	32	4	3	2	1	32	0	107	3	0	8	2	.800	0	0- -	-	2.60	2.83
2001 Mobile	AA	7	5	0	1	30.0	117	17	9	8	3	0	0	0	15	0	29	3	0	2	0	1.000	0	0- -	-	2.29	2.40
2002 Mobile	AA	6	6	0	0	33.0	135	26	10	8	2	1	0	1	16	0	30	0	0	3	1	.750	0	0- -	-	2.18	2.18
2002 Portland	AAA	11	7	0	2	45.0	195	47	34	31	10	1	0	2	15	0	25	3	0	4	0	.000	0	0- -	-	5.11	6.20
2003 Portland	AAA	22	22	0	0	130.2	550	118	69	66	17	6	3	6	49	0	68	7	0	7	9	.438	0	0- -	-	3.86	4.55

Year Team	Lg	G	GS	CG	GF	IP	BFP	H	R	ER	HR	SH	SF	HB	TBB	IBB	SO	WP	Bk	W	L	Pct	ShO	Sv-Op	Hld	ERC	ERA
2002 San Diego	NL	3	2	0	0	10.2	58	13	11	11	4	0	1	0	14	1	10	0	0	0	1	.000	0	0-0	0	11.84	9.28
2003 San Diego	NL	6	6	0	0	34.2	148	31	17	14	10	1	0	0	15	1	24	1	0	1	3	.250	0	0-0	0	4.84	3.63
2 ML YEARS		9	8	0	0	45.1	206	44	28	25	14	1	1	0	29	2	34	1	0	1	4	.200	0	0-0	0	6.37	4.96

Bob Howry

Pitches: R **Bats:** L **Pos:** RP-4   **Ht:** 6'5" **Wt:** 220 **Born:** 8/4/73 **Age:** 30

Year Team	Lg	G	GS	CG	GF	IP	BFP	H	R	ER	HR	SH	SF	HB	TBB	IBB	SO	WP	Bk	W	L	Pct	ShO	Sv-Op	Hld	ERC	ERA
2003 Pawtucket*	AAA	13	0	0	3	17.0	67	14	2	2	1	0	0	1	1	0	10	0	0	2	0	1.000	0	0- -	-	1.87	1.06
1998 Chicago	AL	44	0	0	15	54.1	217	37	20	19	7	2	3	2	19	2	51	2	0	0	3	.000	0	9-11	19	2.50	3.15
1999 Chicago	AL	69	0	0	54	67.2	298	58	34	27	8	3	1	3	38	3	80	3	1	5	3	.625	0	28-34	1	4.11	3.59
2000 Chicago	AL	65	0	0	29	71.0	289	54	26	25	6	2	4	4	29	2	60	2	0	2	4	.333	0	7-12	14	2.96	3.17
2001 Chicago	AL	69	0	0	23	78.2	346	85	41	41	11	4	3	4	30	9	64	6	0	4	5	.444	0	5-11	21	4.78	4.69
2002 CWS-Bos	AL	67	0	0	26	68.2	292	67	37	32	9	4	6	5	21	4	45	2	0	3	5	.375	0	0-1	15	4.00	4.19
2003 Boston	AL	4	0	0	3	4.1	27	11	6	6	1	0	1	0	3	1	4	0	0	0	0	-	0	0-1	0	16.51	12.46
2002 Chicago	AL	47	0	0	17	50.2	209	45	22	22	7	1	4	3	17	2	31	1	0	2	2	.500	0	0-0	10	3.72	3.91
2002 Boston	AL	20	0	0	9	18.0	83	22	15	10	2	3	2	2	4	2	14	1	0	1	3	.250	0	0-1	5	4.79	5.00
6 ML YEARS		318	0	0	150	344.2	1469	312	164	150	42	15	18	18	140	21	304	15	1	14	20	.412	0	49-70	70	3.85	3.92

Trenidad Hubbard

Bats: R **Throws:** R **Pos:** PH-6; CF-4; RF-1; PR-1   **Ht:** 5'9" **Wt:** 203 **Born:** 5/11/66 **Age:** 38

Year Team	Lg	G	AB	H	2B	3B	HR	(Hm	Rd)	TB	R	RBI	RC	TBB	IBB	SO	HBP	SH	SF	SB	CS	SB%	GDP	Avg	OBP	Slg
2003 Iowa*	AAA	91	348	111	16	2	5	(-	-)	146	65	29	60	47	3	29	5	0	2	24	7	.77	13	.319	.405	.420
1994 Colorado	NL	18	25	7	1	1	1	(1	0)	13	3	3	4	3	0	4	0	0	0	0	-	-	1	.280	.357	.520
1995 Colorado	NL	24	58	18	4	0	3	(2	1)	31	13	9	11	8	0	6	0	1	0	2	1	.67	2	.310	.394	.534
1996 Col-SF	NL	55	89	19	5	2	2	(2	0)	34	15	14	10	11	0	27	1	0	0	2	0	1.00	3	.213	.307	.382
1997 Cleveland	AL	7	12	3	1	0	0	(0	0)	4	3	0	2	1	0	3	0	0	0	2	0	1.00	0	.250	.308	.333
1998 Los Angeles	NL	94	208	62	9	1	7	(2	5)	94	29	18	33	18	0	46	3	3	3	9	5	.64	5	.298	.358	.452
1999 Los Angeles	NL	82	105	33	5	0	1	(0	1)	41	23	13	16	13	1	24	0	1	1	4	3	.57	2	.314	.387	.390
2000 Atl-Bal		92	108	20	2	2	1	(0	1)	29	18	6	7	11	0	23	1	3	0	4	2	.67	3	.185	.267	.269
2001 Kansas City	AL	5	12	3	0	1	0	(0	0)	5	2	0	1	0	0	2	0	0	0	0	0	-	0	.250	.250	.417
2002 San Diego	NL	89	129	27	5	0	1	(0	1)	35	16	7	9	14	0	28	0	0	1	9	6	.60	3	.209	.285	.271
2003 Chicago	NL	10	16	4	1	0	0	(0	0)	5	2	2	4	4	0	3	1	0	0	1	0	1.00	0	.250	.429	.313
1996 Colorado	NL	45	60	13	5	1	1	(1	0)	23	12	12	8	9	0	22	1	0	0	2	0	1.00	1	.217	.329	.383
1996 San Francisco	NL	10	29	6	0	1	1	(1	0)	11	3	2	2	2	0	5	0	0	0	0	0	-	2	.207	.258	.379
2000 Atlanta	NL	61	81	15	2	1	1	(0	1)	22	15	6	7	11	0	20	1	3	0	2	1	.67	1	.185	.290	.272
2000 Baltimore	AL	31	27	5	0	1	0	(0	0)	7	3	0	0	0	0	3	0	0	0	2	1	.67	2	.185	.185	.259
10 ML YEARS		476	762	196	33	7	16	(7	9)	291	124	72	97	83	1	166	6	8	5	33	17	.66	19	.257	.333	.382

Ken Huckaby

Bats: R **Throws:** R **Pos:** C-4; PH-1   **Ht:** 6'1" **Wt:** 205 **Born:** 1/27/71 **Age:** 33

Year Team	Lg	G	AB	H	2B	3B	HR	(Hm	Rd)	TB	R	RBI	RC	TBB	IBB	SO	HBP	SH	SF	SB	CS	SB%	GDP	Avg	OBP	Slg
2003 Syracuse*	AAA	75	267	78	14	0	3	(-	-)	101	24	25	30	15	2	30	0	3	3	1	1	.50	11	.292	.326	.378
2001 Arizona	NL	1	1	0	0	0	0	(0	0)	0	0	0	0	0	0	1	0	0	0	0	0	-	0	.000	.000	.000
2002 Toronto	AL	88	273	67	6	1	3	(1	2)	84	29	22	18	9	1	44	0	1	0	0	0	-	10	.245	.270	.308
2003 Toronto	AL	5	11	2	1	0	0	(0	0)	3	1	2	1	0	0	2	0	0	0	0	0	-	0	.182	.182	.273
3 ML YEARS		94	285	69	7	1	3	(1	2)	87	30	24	19	9	1	47	0	1	0	0	0	-	10	.242	.265	.305

Orlando Hudson

Bats: B **Throws:** R **Pos:** 2B-139; PH-4; PR-1   **Ht:** 6'0" **Wt:** 185 **Born:** 12/12/77 **Age:** 26

Year Team	Lg	G	AB	H	2B	3B	HR	(Hm	Rd)	TB	R	RBI	RC	TBB	IBB	SO	HBP	SH	SF	SB	CS	SB%	GDP	Avg	OBP	Slg
1998 Medicine Hat	R+	65	242	71	18	1	8	(-	-)	115	50	42	42	22	0	36	7	0	2	6	5	.55	3	.293	.366	.475
1999 Hagerstown	A	132	513	137	36	6	7	(-	-)	206	66	74	65	42	3	85	2	1	5	8	6	.57	10	.267	.322	.402
2000 Dunedin	A+	96	358	102	16	2	7	(-	-)	143	54	48	48	37	1	42	2	4	1	9	5	.64	15	.285	.354	.399
2000 Tennessee	AA	39	134	32	4	3	2	(-	-)	48	17	15	16	15	1	18	2	1	2	3	2	.60	3	.239	.320	.358
2001 Tennessee	AA	84	306	94	22	8	4	(-	-)	144	51	52	53	37	3	42	3	1	2	8	3	.73	12	.307	.385	.471
2001 Syracuse	AAA	55	194	59	14	3	4	(-	-)	91	31	27	36	23	1	34	2	2	3	11	3	.79	1	.304	.378	.469
2002 Syracuse	AAA	100	417	127	27	3	10	(-	-)	190	63	37	65	35	0	54	4	1	1	8	5	.62	14	.305	.363	.456
2002 Toronto	AL	54	192	53	10	5	4	(2	2)	85	20	23	30	11	0	27	2	0	2	0	1	.00	6	.276	.319	.443
2003 Toronto	AL	142	474	127	21	6	9	(5	4)	187	54	57	62	39	1	87	5	0	3	5	4	.56	13	.268	.328	.395
2 ML YEARS		196	666	180	31	11	13	(7	6)	272	74	80	92	50	1	114	7	0	5	5	5	.50	19	.270	.326	.408

Tim Hudson

Pitches: R **Bats:** R **Pos:** SP-34   **Ht:** 6'1" **Wt:** 164 **Born:** 7/14/75 **Age:** 28

Year Team	Lg	G	GS	CG	GF	IP	BFP	H	R	ER	HR	SH	SF	HB	TBB	IBB	SO	WP	Bk	W	L	Pct	ShO	Sv-Op	Hld	ERC	ERA
1999 Oakland	AL	21	21	1	0	136.1	580	121	56	49	8	1	2	4	62	2	132	6	0	11	2	.846	0	0-0	0	3.50	3.23
2000 Oakland	AL	32	32	2	0	202.1	847	169	100	93	24	5	7	7	82	5	169	7	0	20	6	.769	2	0-0	0	3.43	4.14
2001 Oakland	AL	35	35	3	0	235.0	980	216	100	88	20	12	8	6	71	5	181	9	1	18	9	.667	0	0-0	0	3.22	3.37
2002 Oakland	AL	34	34	4	0	238.1	983	237	87	79	19	6	5	8	62	9	152	7	1	15	9	.625	2	0-0	0	3.51	2.98
2003 Oakland	AL	34	34	3	0	240.0	967	197	84	72	15	11	2	10	61	9	162	6	0	16	7	.696	2	0-0	0	2.47	2.70
5 ML YEARS		156	156	13	0	1052.0	4357	940	427	381	86	35	24	35	338	30	796	35	2	80	33	.708	6	0-0	0	3.18	3.26

Aubrey Huff

Bats: L **Throws:** R **Pos:** RF-102; DH-33; 1B-22; 3B-8   **Ht:** 6'4" **Wt:** 231 **Born:** 12/20/76 **Age:** 27

Year	Team	Lg	G	AB	H	2B	3B	HR	(Hm	Rd)	TB	R	RBI	RC	TBB	IBB	SO	HBP	SH	SF	SB	CS	SB%	GDP	Avg	OBP	Slg
2000	Tampa Bay	AL	39	122	35	7	0	4	(3	1)	54	12	14	15	5	1	18	1	0	1	0	0	-	6	.287	.318	.443
2001	Tampa Bay	AL	111	411	102	25	1	8	(5	3)	153	42	45	37	23	2	72	0	0	0	1	3	.25	18	.248	.288	.372
2002	Tampa Bay	AL	113	454	142	25	0	23	(17	6)	236	67	59	67	37	7	55	1	0	2	4	1	.80	17	.313	.364	.520
2003	Tampa Bay	AL	162	636	198	47	3	34	(15	19)	353	91	107	114	53	17	80	8	0	9	2	3	.40	19	.311	.367	.555
	4 ML YEARS		425	1623	477	104	4	69	(40	29)	796	212	225	233	118	27	225	10	0	12	7	7	.50	60	.294	.343	.490

Tim Hummel

Bats: R **Throws:** R **Pos:** 3B-20; PH-6; SS-2; 2B-1   **Ht:** 6'2" **Wt:** 195 **Born:** 11/18/78 **Age:** 25

Year	Team	Lg	G	AB	H	2B	3B	HR	(Hm	Rd)	TB	R	RBI	RC	TBB	IBB	SO	HBP	SH	SF	SB	CS	SB%	GDP	Avg	OBP	Slg
2000	Burlington	A	33	144	47	9	1	1	(-	-)	61	22	21	27	21	0	20	1	0	2	8	3	.73	2	.326	.411	.424
2000	Winstn-Salm	A+	27	98	32	7	0	1	(-	-)	42	15	9	17	13	1	12	2	0	9	1	1	.50	4	.327	.385	.429
2001	Birmingham	AA	134	524	152	33	6	7	(-	-)	218	83	63	83	62	2	69	5	8	10	14	3	.82	12	.290	.364	.416
2002	Charlotte	AAA	142	523	136	33	0	4	(-	-)	181	55	41	63	51	0	95	10	10	9	6	5	.55	7	.260	.332	.346
2003	Charlotte	AAA	128	476	135	25	3	15	(-	-)	211	72	80	74	46	2	83	5	10	4	9	3	.75	10	.284	.350	.443
2003	Cincinnati	NL	26	84	19	5	0	2	(0	2)	30	9	10	9	8	0	13	0	1	1	0	0	-	1	.226	.290	.357

Todd Hundley

Bats: B **Throws:** R **Pos:** PH-13; C-10   **Ht:** 5'11" **Wt:** 200 **Born:** 5/27/69 **Age:** 35

Year	Team	Lg	G	AB	H	2B	3B	HR	(Hm	Rd)	TB	R	RBI	RC	TBB	IBB	SO	HBP	SH	SF	SB	CS	SB%	GDP	Avg	OBP	Slg
2003	Vero Beach*	A+	7	24	2	0	0	0	(-	-)	2	2	1	0	3	0	5	1	0	0	0	0	-	0	.083	.214	.083
1990	New York	NL	36	67	14	6	0	0	(0	0)	20	8	2	5	6	0	18	0	1	0	0	0	-	1	.209	.274	.299
1991	New York	NL	21	60	8	0	1	1	(1	0)	13	5	7	1	6	0	14	1	1	1	0	0	-	3	.133	.221	.217
1992	New York	NL	123	358	75	17	0	7	(2	5)	113	32	32	27	19	4	76	4	7	2	3	0	1.00	8	.209	.256	.316
1993	New York	NL	130	417	95	17	2	11	(5	6)	149	40	53	37	23	7	62	2	2	4	1	1	.50	10	.228	.269	.357
1994	New York	NL	91	291	69	10	1	16	(8	8)	129	45	42	39	25	4	73	3	3	1	2	1	.67	3	.237	.303	.443
1995	New York	NL	90	275	77	11	0	15	(6	9)	133	39	51	52	42	5	64	5	1	3	1	0	1.00	4	.280	.382	.484
1996	New York	NL	153	540	140	32	1	41	(20	21)	297	85	112	102	79	15	146	3	0	2	1	3	.25	9	.259	.356	.550
1997	New York	NL	132	417	114	21	2	30	(14	16)	229	78	86	87	83	16	116	3	0	5	2	3	.40	10	.273	.394	.549
1998	New York	NL	53	124	20	4	0	3	(1	2)	33	8	12	9	16	0	55	1	0	1	1	1	.50	1	.161	.261	.266
1999	Los Angeles	NL	114	376	78	14	0	24	(10	14)	164	49	55	50	44	3	113	4	1	3	3	0	1.00	5	.207	.295	.436
2000	Los Angeles	NL	90	299	85	16	0	24	(10	14)	173	49	70	63	45	6	69	2	1	6	0	1	.00	5	.284	.375	.579
2001	Chicago	NL	79	246	46	10	0	12	(4	8)	92	23	31	23	25	0	89	3	0	2	0	0	-	7	.187	.268	.374
2002	Chicago	NL	92	266	56	8	0	16	(8	8)	112	32	35	29	32	3	80	3	1	1	0	0	-	6	.211	.301	.421
2003	Los Angeles	NL	21	33	6	1	0	2	(1	1)	13	2	11	7	8	0	13	0	0	0	0	1	.00	0	.182	.341	.394
	14 ML YEARS		1225	3769	883	167	7	202	(90	112)	1670	495	599	531	453	63	988	34	18	31	14	11	.56	71	.234	.320	.443

Brian Hunter

Bats: R **Throws:** R **Pos:** PH-27; RF-15; CF-14; LF-5; PR-2   **Ht:** 6'3" **Wt:** 180 **Born:** 3/25/71 **Age:** 33

Year	Team	Lg	G	AB	H	2B	3B	HR	(Hm	Rd)	TB	R	RBI	RC	TBB	IBB	SO	HBP	SH	SF	SB	CS	SB%	GDP	Avg	OBP	Slg
1994	Houston	NL	6	24	6	1	0	0	(0	0)	7	2	0	2	1	0	6	0	1	0	2	1	.67	0	.250	.280	.292
1995	Houston	NL	78	321	97	14	5	2	(0	2)	127	52	28	47	21	0	52	2	2	3	24	7	.77	2	.302	.346	.396
1996	Houston	NL	132	526	145	27	2	5	(1	4)	191	74	35	59	17	0	92	2	1	7	35	9	.80	6	.276	.297	.363
1997	Detroit	AL	162	658	177	29	7	4	(2	2)	232	112	45	86	66	1	121	1	8	5	74	18	.80	13	.269	.334	.353
1998	Detroit	AL	142	595	151	29	3	4	(1	3)	198	67	36	61	36	0	94	2	2	1	42	12	.78	8	.254	.298	.333
1999	Det-Sea	AL	139	539	125	13	6	4	(0	4)	162	79	34	50	37	0	91	2	4	7	44	8	.85	8	.232	.280	.301
2000	Col-Cin	NL	104	240	64	5	1	1	(1	0)	74	47	14	30	27	0	40	1	5	1	20	3	.87	2	.267	.342	.308
2001	Philadelphia	NL	83	145	40	6	0	2	(2	0)	52	22	16	20	16	0	25	0	3	2	14	3	.82	3	.276	.344	.359
2002	Houston	NL	98	201	54	16	3	3	(0	3)	85	32	20	27	16	0	39	2	1	0	5	0	1.00	3	.269	.329	.423
2003	Houston	NL	56	98	23	6	1	0	(0	0)	31	13	13	10	6	0	21	1	0	3	0	0	-	1	.235	.278	.316
1999	Detroit	AL	18	55	13	2	1	0	(0	0)	17	8	0	5	5	0	11	1	1	0	0	3	.00	0	.236	.311	.309
1999	Seattle	AL	121	484	112	11	5	4	(0	4)	145	71	34	45	32	0	80	1	3	7	44	5	.90	8	.231	.277	.300
2000	Colorado	NL	72	200	55	4	1	1	(1	0)	64	36	13	25	21	0	31	1	4	0	15	3	.83	2	.275	.347	.320
2000	Cincinnati	NL	32	40	9	1	0	0	(0	0)	10	11	1	5	6	0	9	0	1	1	5	0	1.00	0	.225	.319	.250
	10 ML YEARS		1000	3347	882	146	28	25	(7	18)	1159	500	241	392	243	1	581	13	27	29	260	61	.81	46	.264	.313	.346

Torii Hunter

Bats: R **Throws:** R **Pos:** CF-151; DH-3; PH-1   **Ht:** 6'2" **Wt:** 205 **Born:** 7/18/75 **Age:** 28

Year	Team	Lg	G	AB	H	2B	3B	HR	(Hm	Rd)	TB	R	RBI	RC	TBB	IBB	SO	HBP	SH	SF	SB	CS	SB%	GDP	Avg	OBP	Slg
1997	Minnesota	AL	1	0	0	0	0	0	(0	0)	0	0	0	0	0	0	0	0	0	0	0	0	-	0	-	-	-
1998	Minnesota	AL	6	17	4	1	0	0	(0	0)	5	0	2	1	2	0	6	0	0	0	0	1	.00	1	.235	.316	.294
1999	Minnesota	AL	135	384	98	17	2	9	(2	7)	146	52	35	44	26	1	72	6	1	5	10	6	.63	9	.255	.309	.380
2000	Minnesota	AL	99	336	94	14	7	5	(4	1)	137	44	44	39	18	2	68	2	0	2	4	3	.57	13	.280	.318	.408
2001	Minnesota	AL	148	564	147	32	5	27	(13	14)	270	82	92	79	29	0	125	8	1	1	9	6	.60	12	.261	.306	.479
2002	Minnesota	AL	148	561	162	37	4	29	(13	16)	294	89	94	87	35	3	118	5	0	3	23	8	.74	17	.289	.334	.524
2003	Minnesota	AL	154	581	145	31	4	26	(12	14)	262	83	102	77	50	7	106	5	0	6	6	7	.46	15	.250	.312	.451
	7 ML YEARS		691	2443	650	132	22	96	(44	52)	1114	350	369	327	160	13	495	26	2	17	52	31	.63	67	.266	.316	.456

Adam Hyzdu

Bats: R Throws: R Pos: PH-21; CF-20; RF-11; PR-6; LF-3 Ht: 6'2" Wt: 205 Born: 12/6/71 Age: 32

Year Team	Lg	G	AB	H	2B	3B	HR	(Hm	Rd)	TB	R	RBI	RC	TBB	IBB	SO	HBP	SH	SF	SB	CS	SB%	GDP	Avg	OBP	Slg
2003 Nashville*	AAA	40	135	38	10	1	6	(-	-)	68	22	18	25	18	1	28	1	0	2	2	2	.50	2	.281	.365	.504
2000 Pittsburgh	NL	12	18	7	2	0	1	(0	1)	12	2	4	4	0	0	4	0	0	0	0	0	-	0	.389	.389	.667
2001 Pittsburgh	NL	51	72	15	1	0	5	(0	5)	31	7	9	8	4	0	18	1	0	0	0	1	.00	1	.208	.260	.431
2002 Pittsburgh	NL	59	155	36	6	0	11	(6	5)	75	24	34	27	21	0	44	1	0	1	0	0	-	1	.232	.324	.484
2003 Pittsburgh	NL	51	63	13	5	0	1	(0	1)	21	16	8	6	10	0	21	1	0	1	0	0	-	2	.206	.320	.333
4 ML YEARS		173	308	71	14	0	18	(6	12)	139	49	55	45	35	0	87	3	0	3	0	1	.00	4	.231	.312	.451

Raul Ibanez

Bats: L Throws: R Pos: LF-128; 1B-22; DH-12; RF-5; PH-1 Ht: 6'2" Wt: 200 Born: 6/2/72 Age: 32

Year Team	Lg	G	AB	H	2B	3B	HR	(Hm	Rd)	TB	R	RBI	RC	TBB	IBB	SO	HBP	SH	SF	SB	CS	SB%	GDP	Avg	OBP	Slg
1996 Seattle	AL	4	5	0	0	0	0	(0	0)	0	0	0	0	0	0	1	1	0	0	0	0	-	0	.000	.167	.000
1997 Seattle	AL	11	26	4	0	1	1	(1	0)	9	3	4	1	0	0	6	0	0	0	0	0	-	0	.154	.154	.346
1998 Seattle	AL	37	98	25	7	1	2	(1	1)	40	12	12	10	5	0	22	0	0	0	0	0	-	4	.255	.291	.408
1999 Seattle	AL	87	209	54	7	0	9	(3	6)	88	23	27	28	17	1	32	0	0	1	5	1	.83	4	.258	.313	.421
2000 Seattle	AL	92	140	32	8	0	2	(2	0)	46	21	15	15	14	1	25	1	0	1	2	0	1.00	1	.229	.301	.329
2001 Kansas City	AL	104	279	78	11	5	13	(5	8)	138	44	54	46	32	2	51	0	0	1	0	2	.00	6	.280	.353	.495
2002 Kansas City	AL	137	497	146	37	6	24	(14	10)	267	70	103	91	40	5	76	2	1	4	5	3	.63	11	.294	.346	.537
2003 Kansas City	AL	157	608	179	33	5	18	(8	10)	276	95	90	91	49	5	81	3	1	10	8	4	.67	10	.294	.345	.454
8 ML YEARS		629	1862	518	103	18	69	(34	35)	864	268	305	282	157	14	294	7	2	17	20	10	.67	36	.278	.334	.464

Omar Infante

Bats: R Throws: R Pos: SS-63; 3B-4; 2B-2; PR-2 Ht: 5'9" Wt: 150 Born: 12/26/81 Age: 22

Year Team	Lg	G	AB	H	2B	3B	HR	(Hm	Rd)	TB	R	RBI	RC	TBB	IBB	SO	HBP	SH	SF	SB	CS	SB%	GDP	Avg	OBP	Slg
1999 Tigers	R	21	75	20	0	0	0	(-	-)	20	9	4	6	3	0	9	0	0	1	4	0	1.00	1	.267	.291	.267
2000 Lakeland	A+	79	259	71	11	0	2	(-	-)	88	35	24	30	20	0	29	1	5	4	11	5	.69	4	.274	.324	.340
2000 W Michigan	A	12	48	11	0	0	0	(-	-)	11	7	5	4	5	0	7	2	0	0	1	0	1.00	2	.229	.327	.229
2001 Erie	AA	132	540	163	21	4	2	(-	-)	198	86	62	73	46	1	87	2	4	7	27	12	.69	9	.302	.355	.367
2002 Toledo	AAA	120	436	117	16	8	4	(-	-)	161	49	51	48	28	0	49	0	5	5	19	15	.56	5	.268	.309	.369
2003 Toledo	AAA	64	224	50	10	0	2	(-	-)	66	28	18	23	22	0	32	3	6	2	22	4	.85	3	.223	.299	.295
2002 Detroit	AL	18	72	24	3	0	1	(0	1)	30	4	6	11	3	0	10	0	0	0	1	0	.00	1	.333	.360	.417
2003 Detroit	AL	69	221	49	6	1	0	(0	0)	57	24	8	15	18	0	37	0	3	2	6	3	.67	1	.222	.278	.258
2 ML YEARS		87	293	73	9	1	1	(0	1)	87	28	14	26	21	0	47	0	3	2	6	4	.60	1	.249	.297	.297

Brandon Inge

Bats: R Throws: R Pos: C-104; PR-2 Ht: 5'11" Wt: 189 Born: 5/19/77 Age: 27

Year Team	Lg	G	AB	H	2B	3B	HR	(Hm	Rd)	TB	R	RBI	RC	TBB	IBB	SO	HBP	SH	SF	SB	CS	SB%	GDP	Avg	OBP	Slg
2003 Toledo*	AAA	39	142	39	9	0	5	(-	-)	63	15	15	19	11	1	23	0	1	0	3	1	.75	6	.275	.327	.444
2001 Detroit	AL	79	189	34	11	0	0	(0	0)	45	13	15	6	9	0	41	0	2	2	1	4	.20	2	.180	.215	.238
2002 Detroit	AL	95	321	65	15	3	7	(3	4)	107	27	24	25	24	0	101	4	1	1	1	3	.25	7	.202	.266	.333
2003 Detroit	AL	104	330	67	15	3	8	(4	4)	112	32	30	24	24	0	79	5	4	3	4	4	.50	9	.203	.265	.339
3 ML YEARS		278	840	166	41	6	15	(7	8)	264	72	69	55	57	0	221	9	7	6	6	11	.35	18	.198	.254	.314

Kazuhisa Ishii

Pitches: L Bats: L Pos: SP-27 Ht: 6'0" Wt: 190 Born: 9/9/73 Age: 30

		HOW MUCH HE PITCHED						WHAT HE GAVE UP										THE RESULTS						
Year Team	Lg	G	GS	CG	GF	IP	BFP	H	R	ER	HR	SH	SF	HB	TBB	IBB	SO	WP	Bk	W	L	Pct	ShO	Sv-Op	Hld	ERC	ERA
2002 Los Angeles	NL	28	28	0	0	154.0	692	137	82	73	20	6	5	4	106	3	143	7	0	14	10	.583	0	0-0	0	4.90	4.27
2003 Los Angeles	NL	27	27	0	0	147.0	656	129	72	63	16	6	2	6	101	4	140	10	2	9	7	.563	0	0-0	0	4.75	3.86
2 ML YEARS		55	55	0	0	301.0	1348	266	154	136	36	12	7	10	207	7	283	17	2	23	17	.575	0	0-0	0	4.83	4.07

Jason Isringhausen

Pitches: R Bats: R Pos: RP-40 Ht: 6'3" Wt: 230 Born: 9/7/72 Age: 31

		HOW MUCH HE PITCHED						WHAT HE GAVE UP										THE RESULTS						
Year Team	Lg	G	GS	CG	GF	IP	BFP	H	R	ER	HR	SH	SF	HB	TBB	IBB	SO	WP	Bk	W	L	Pct	ShO	Sv-Op	Hld	ERC	ERA
2003 Tennessee*	AA	2	2	0	0	2.0	7	1	0	0	0	0	0	0	0	0	3	0	0	0	0	-	0	0- -	0	0.54	0.00
1995 New York	NL	14	14	1	0	93.0	385	88	29	29	6	3	3	2	31	2	55	4	1	9	2	.818	0	0-0	0	3.40	2.81
1996 New York	NL	27	27	2	0	171.2	766	190	103	91	13	7	9	8	73	5	114	14	0	6	14	.300	1	0-0	0	4.75	4.77
1997 New York	NL	6	6	0	0	29.2	145	40	27	25	3	1	2	1	22	0	25	3	0	2	2	.500	0	0-0	0	7.99	7.58
1999 NYM-Oak		33	5	0	20	64.2	286	64	35	34	9	0	1	2	34	4	51	5	0	1	4	.200	0	9-9	0	4.86	4.73
2000 Oakland	AL	66	0	0	57	69.0	304	67	34	29	6	2	1	3	32	5	57	5	1	6	4	.600	0	33-40	0	4.09	3.78
2001 Oakland	AL	65	0	0	54	71.1	293	54	24	21	5	3	1	0	23	5	74	2	0	4	3	.571	0	34-43	0	2.18	2.65
2002 St Louis	NL	60	0	0	51	65.1	257	46	22	18	0	4	3	1	18	1	68	0	0	3	2	.600	0	32-37	0	1.61	2.48
2003 St Louis	NL	40	0	0	31	42.0	174	31	14	11	2	1	0	0	18	1	41	6	0	0	1	.000	0	22-25	1	2.40	2.36
1999 New York	NL	13	5	0	2	39.1	179	43	29	28	7	0	1	1	22	2	31	3	0	1	3	.250	0	1-1	0	5.93	6.41
1999 Oakland	AL	20	0	0	18	25.1	107	21	6	6	2	0	0	1	12	2	20	2	0	0	1	.000	0	8-8	0	3.33	2.13
8 ML YEARS		311	52	3	213	606.2	2610	580	288	258	44	21	20	17	251	23	485	39	2	31	32	.492	1	130-154	1	3.74	3.83

Cesar Izturis

Bats: B Throws: R Pos: SS-158; PH-2 Ht: 5'9" Wt: 175 Born: 2/10/80 Age: 24

Year Team	Lg	G	AB	H	2B	3B	HR	(Hm	Rd)	TB	R	RBI	RC	TBB	IBB	SO	HBP	SH	SF	SB	CS	SB%	GDP	Avg	OBP	Slg
2001 Toronto	AL	46	134	36	6	2	2	(1	1)	52	19	9	16	2	0	15	0	4	0	8	1	.89	0	.269	.279	.388
2002 Los Angeles	NL	135	439	102	24	2	1	(0	1)	133	43	31	26	14	1	39	0	10	5	7	7	.50	12	.232	.253	.303
2003 Los Angeles	NL	158	558	140	21	6	1	(0	1)	176	47	40	40	25	8	70	0	7	3	10	5	.67	8	.251	.282	.315
3 ML YEARS		339	1131	278	51	10	4	(1	3)	361	109	80	82	41	9	124	0	21	8	25	13	.66	20	.246	.270	.319

Damian Jackson

Bats: R Throws: R Pos: 2B-38; PR-37; SS-18; LF-13; CF-13; RF-12; PH-5; 3B-3; DH-3; 1B-2 Ht: 5'11" Wt: 185 Born: 8/16/73 Age: 30

Year Team	Lg	G	AB	H	2B	3B	HR	(Hm	Rd)	TB	R	RBI	RC	TBB	IBB	SO	HBP	SH	SF	SB	CS	SB%	GDP	Avg	OBP	Slg
1996 Cleveland	AL	5	10	3	2	0	0	(0	0)	5	2	1	2	1	0	4	0	0	0	0	0	-	0	.300	.364	.500
1997 Cle-Cin		20	36	7	2	1	1	(0	1)	14	8	2	4	4	1	8	1	1	0	2	1	.67	0	.194	.293	.389
1998 Cincinnati	NL	13	38	12	5	0	0	(0	0)	17	4	7	7	6	0	4	0	0	1	2	0	1.00	1	.316	.400	.447
1999 San Diego	NL	133	388	87	20	2	9	(6	3)	138	56	39	50	53	3	105	3	0	3	34	10	.77	2	.224	.320	.356
2000 San Diego	NL	138	470	120	27	6	6	(5	1)	177	68	37	66	62	2	108	3	4	2	28	6	.82	7	.255	.345	.377
2001 San Diego	NL	122	440	106	21	6	4	(1	3)	151	67	38	51	44	2	128	6	2	3	23	6	.79	6	.241	.316	.343
2002 Detroit	AL	81	245	63	20	1	1	(0	1)	88	31	25	33	21	0	36	3	2	1	12	3	.80	3	.257	.320	.359
2003 Boston	AL	109	161	42	7	0	1	(0	1)	52	34	13	12	8	0	28	0	2	1	16	8	.67	4	.261	.294	.323
1997 Cleveland	AL	8	9	1	0	0	0	(0	0)	1	2	0	0	0	0	1	1	0	0	1	0	1.00	0	.111	.200	.111
1997 Cincinnati	NL	12	27	6	2	1	1	(0	1)	13	6	2	4	4	1	7	0	1	0	1	1	.50	0	.222	.323	.481
8 ML YEARS		621	1788	440	104	16	22	(12	10)	642	270	162	225	199	8	421	16	11	13	117	34	.77	23	.246	.325	.359

Edwin Jackson

Pitches: R Bats: R Pos: SP-3; RP-1 Ht: 6'3" Wt: 190 Born: 9/9/83 Age: 20

Year Team	Lg	G	GS	CG	GF	IP	BFP	H	R	ER	HR	SH	SF	HB	TBB	IBB	SO	WP	Bk	W	L	Pct	ShO	Sv-Op	Hld	ERC	ERA
2001 Dodgers	R	12	2	0	1	22.0	106	14	12	6	1	3	0	3	19	0	23	2	0	2	1	.667	0	0--	-	3.66	2.45
2002 Sth Georgia	A	19	19	0	0	104.2	428	79	34	23	2	2	2	6	33	0	85	3	1	5	2	.714	0	0--	-	2.17	1.98
2003 Jacksonville	AA	27	27	0	0	148.1	619	121	68	61	9	4	3	8	53	0	157	9	1	7	7	.500	0	0--	-	2.85	3.70
2003 Los Angeles	NL	4	3	0	0	22.0	91	17	6	6	2	1	1	1	11	1	19	3	0	2	1	.667	0	0-0	0	3.36	2.45

Kevin Jarvis

Pitches: R Bats: L Pos: SP-16 Ht: 6'2" Wt: 200 Born: 8/1/69 Age: 34

Year Team	Lg	G	GS	CG	GF	IP	BFP	H	R	ER	HR	SH	SF	HB	TBB	IBB	SO	WP	Bk	W	L	Pct	ShO	Sv-Op	Hld	ERC	ERA
2003 Lk Elsinore*	A+	3	3	0	0	22.0	85	18	11	10	1	0	0	0	4	0	19	0	0	2	1	.667	0	0--	-	2.06	4.09
1994 Cincinnati	NL	6	3	0	0	17.2	79	22	14	14	4	1	0	0	5	0	10	1	0	1	1	.500	0	0-0	0	5.91	7.13
1995 Cincinnati	NL	19	11	1	2	79.0	354	91	56	50	13	2	5	3	32	2	33	2	0	3	4	.429	1	0-0	0	5.60	5.70
1996 Cincinnati	NL	24	20	2	2	120.1	552	152	93	80	17	6	2	2	43	5	63	3	0	8	9	.471	1	0-0	0	5.68	5.98
1997 Cin-Min-Det		32	5	0	13	68.0	329	99	62	58	17	2	1	1	29	0	48	4	0	0	4	.000	0	1-1	0	8.21	7.68
1999 Oakland	AL	4	1	0	0	14.0	75	28	19	18	6	0	1	1	6	0	11	0	0	0	1	.000	0	0-0	0	14.40	11.57
2000 Colorado	NL	24	19	0	0	115.0	505	138	83	76	26	6	2	4	33	3	60	2	0	3	4	.429	0	0-0	0	5.86	5.95
2001 San Diego	NL	32	32	1	0	193.1	809	189	107	103	37	7	4	5	49	4	133	1	0	12	11	.522	1	0-0	0	4.05	4.79
2002 San Diego	NL	7	7	0	0	35.0	146	36	19	17	5	0	1	1	10	1	24	2	0	2	4	.333	0	0-0	0	4.24	4.37
2003 San Diego	NL	16	16	0	0	92.0	413	113	65	60	15	2	5	2	32	5	49	2	0	4	8	.333	0	0-0	0	5.68	5.87
1997 Cincinnati	NL	9	0	0	3	13.1	70	21	16	15	4	1	0	1	7	0	12	2	0	0	1	.000	0	1-1	0	9.98	10.13
1997 Minnesota	AL	6	2	0	1	13.0	70	23	18	18	4	0	0	0	8	0	9	2	0	0	0	-	0	0-0	0	11.69	12.46
1997 Detroit	AL	17	3	0	9	41.2	189	55	28	25	9	1	1	0	14	0	27	0	0	0	3	.000	0	0-0	0	6.64	5.40
9 ML YEARS		164	114	4	17	734.1	3262	868	518	476	140	26	21	19	239	20	431	17	0	33	46	.418	3	1-1	0	5.55	5.83

Geoff Jenkins

Bats: L Throws: R Pos: LF-123; DH-1 Ht: 6'1" Wt: 213 Born: 7/21/74 Age: 29

Year Team	Lg	G	AB	H	2B	3B	HR	(Hm	Rd)	TB	R	RBI	RC	TBB	IBB	SO	HBP	SH	SF	SB	CS	SB%	GDP	Avg	OBP	Slg
2003 Huntsville*	AA	6	20	5	0	0	2	(-	-)	11	6	3	3	1	0	7	0	0	0	1	0	1.00	0	.250	.286	.550
1998 Milwaukee	NL	84	262	60	12	1	9	(4	5)	101	33	28	26	20	4	61	2	0	1	1	3	.25	7	.229	.288	.385
1999 Milwaukee	NL	135	447	140	43	3	21	(10	11)	252	70	82	88	35	7	87	7	3	1	5	1	.83	10	.313	.371	.564
2000 Milwaukee	NL	135	512	155	36	4	34	(15	19)	301	100	94	104	33	6	135	15	0	4	11	1	.92	9	.303	.360	.588
2001 Milwaukee	NL	105	397	105	21	1	20	(11	9)	188	60	63	60	36	7	120	8	0	5	4	2	.67	11	.264	.334	.474
2002 Milwaukee	NL	67	243	59	17	1	10	(4	6)	108	35	29	29	22	1	60	6	0	1	1	2	.33	8	.243	.320	.444
2003 Milwaukee	NL	124	487	144	30	2	28	(16	12)	262	81	95	90	58	10	120	6	0	3	0	0	-	12	.296	.375	.538
6 ML YEARS		650	2348	663	159	12	122	(60	62)	1212	379	391	397	204	35	583	44	3	15	22	9	.71	57	.282	.349	.516

Jason Jennings

Pitches: R Bats: L Pos: SP-32 Ht: 6'2" Wt: 242 Born: 7/17/78 Age: 25

Year Team	Lg	G	GS	CG	GF	IP	BFP	H	R	ER	HR	SH	SF	HB	TBB	IBB	SO	WP	Bk	W	L	Pct	ShO	Sv-Op	Hld	ERC	ERA
2001 Colorado	NL	7	7	1	0	39.1	174	42	21	20	2	1	1	1	19	0	26	1	0	4	1	.800	1	0-0	0	4.58	4.58
2002 Colorado	NL	32	32	0	0	185.1	808	201	102	93	26	9	3	8	70	2	127	10	0	16	8	.667	0	0-0	0	4.98	4.52
2003 Colorado	NL	32	32	1	0	181.1	820	212	115	103	20	11	6	5	88	7	119	7	0	12	13	.480	0	0-0	0	5.60	5.11
3 ML YEARS		71	71	2	0	406.0	1802	455	238	216	48	21	10	14	177	9	272	18	0	32	22	.593	1	0-0	0	5.22	4.79

Ryan Jensen

Pitches: R **Bats:** R **Pos:** RP-4; SP-2   **Ht:** 6'0" **Wt:** 205 **Born:** 9/17/75 **Age:** 28

Year Team	Lg	G	GS	CG	GF	IP	BFP	H	R	ER	HR	SH	SF	HB	TBB	IBB	SO	WP	Bk	W	L	Pct	ShO	Sv-Op	Hld	ERC	ERA
2003 Fresno*	AAA	27	18	0	1	103.2	463	114	70	61	14	11	9	6	36	2	50	4	1	1	10	.091	0	0--	-	4.82	5.30
2001 San Francisco	NL	10	7	0	2	42.1	193	44	21	20	5	0	4	0	25	0	26	2	0	1	2	.333	0	0-0	0	5.68	4.25
2002 San Francisco	NL	32	30	1	0	171.2	744	183	93	86	21	7	8	5	66	4	105	3	0	13	8	.619	0	0-0	0	4.69	4.51
2003 San Francisco	NL	6	2	0	3	13.1	64	21	16	16	6	4	2	1	5	0	3	0	0	0	0	-	0	0-0	0	11.25	10.80
3 ML YEARS		48	39	1	5	227.1	1001	248	130	122	32	11	10	10	96	4	134	5	0	14	10	.583	0	0-0	0	5.21	4.83

Derek Jeter

Bats: R **Throws:** R **Pos:** SS-118; PH-1   **Ht:** 6'3" **Wt:** 195 **Born:** 6/26/74 **Age:** 30

Year Team	Lg	G	AB	H	2B	3B	HR	(Hm	Rd)	TB	R	RBI	RC	TBB	IBB	SO	HBP	SH	SF	SB	CS	SB%	GDP	Avg	OBP	Slg
2003 Trenton*	AA	5	18	8	1	1	0	(-	-)	11	2	5	6	3	0	0	1	0	0	0	0	-	0	.444	.545	.611
1995 New York	AL	15	48	12	4	1	0	(0	0)	18	5	7	5	3	0	11	0	0	0	0	0	-	0	.250	.294	.375
1996 New York	AL	157	582	183	25	6	10	(3	7)	250	104	78	92	48	1	102	9	6	9	14	7	.67	13	.314	.370	.430
1997 New York	AL	159	654	190	31	7	10	(5	5)	265	116	70	99	74	0	125	10	8	2	23	12	.66	14	.291	.370	.405
1998 New York	AL	149	626	203	25	8	19	(9	10)	301	127	84	115	57	1	119	5	3	3	30	6	.83	13	.324	.384	.481
1999 New York	AL	158	627	**219**	37	9	24	(15	9)	346	134	102	146	91	5	116	12	3	6	19	8	.70	12	.349	.438	.552
2000 New York	AL	148	593	201	31	4	15	(8	7)	285	119	73	118	68	4	99	12	3	3	22	4	.85	14	.339	.416	.481
2001 New York	AL	150	614	191	35	3	21	(13	8)	295	110	74	112	56	3	99	10	5	1	27	3	.90	13	.311	.377	.480
2002 New York	AL	157	644	191	26	0	18	(8	10)	271	124	75	106	73	2	114	7	3	3	32	3	.91	14	.297	.373	.421
2003 New York	AL	119	482	156	25	3	10	(7	3)	217	87	52	84	43	2	88	13	3	1	11	5	.69	10	.324	.393	.450
9 ML YEARS		1212	4870	1546	239	41	127	(68	59)	2248	926	615	877	513	18	873	78	34	28	178	48	.79	103	.317	.389	.462

D'Angelo Jimenez

Bats: B **Throws:** R **Pos:** 2B-141; PH-5; 3B-4   **Ht:** 6'0" **Wt:** 194 **Born:** 12/21/77 **Age:** 26

Year Team	Lg	G	AB	H	2B	3B	HR	(Hm	Rd)	TB	R	RBI	RC	TBB	IBB	SO	HBP	SH	SF	SB	CS	SB%	GDP	Avg	OBP	Slg
1999 New York	AL	7	20	8	2	0	0	(0	0)	10	3	4	5	3	0	11	0	0	0	0	0	-	0	.400	.478	.500
2001 San Diego	NL	86	308	85	19	0	3	(2	1)	113	45	33	39	39	4	68	0	0	2	2	3	.40	9	.276	.355	.367
2002 SD-CWS	AL	114	429	108	15	7	4	(3	1)	149	61	44	53	50	1	73	1	0	2	6	3	.67	11	.252	.330	.347
2003 CWS-Cin		146	561	153	24	7	14	(6	8)	233	69	57	77	66	1	89	2	6	4	11	7	.61	7	.273	.349	.415
2002 San Diego	NL	87	321	77	11	4	3	(2	1)	105	39	33	34	34	1	63	0	0	2	4	2	.67	10	.240	.311	.327
2002 Chicago	AL	27	108	31	4	3	1	(1	0)	44	22	11	19	16	0	10	1	0	0	2	1	.67	1	.287	.384	.407
2003 Chicago	AL	73	271	69	11	5	7	(3	4)	111	35	26	34	32	1	46	0	4	1	4	3	.57	3	.255	.332	.410
2003 Cincinnati	NL	73	290	84	13	2	7	(3	4)	122	34	31	43	34	0	43	2	2	3	7	4	.64	4	.290	.365	.421
4 ML YEARS		353	1318	354	60	14	21	(11	10)	505	178	138	174	158	6	234	3	6	8	19	13	.59	27	.269	.346	.383

Jose Jimenez

Pitches: R **Bats:** R **Pos:** RP-56; SP-7   **Ht:** 6'3" **Wt:** 228 **Born:** 7/7/73 **Age:** 30

Year Team	Lg	G	GS	CG	GF	IP	BFP	H	R	ER	HR	SH	SF	HB	TBB	IBB	SO	WP	Bk	W	L	Pct	ShO	Sv-Op	Hld	ERC	ERA
1998 St Louis	NL	4	3	0	0	21.1	94	22	8	7	0	1	1	0	8	0	12	0	0	3	0	1.000	0	0-0	0	3.35	2.95
1999 St Louis	NL	29	28	2	0	163.0	727	173	114	106	16	10	6	11	71	2	113	10	1	5	14	.263	2	0-1	0	4.81	5.85
2000 Colorado	NL	72	0	0	55	70.2	301	63	27	25	4	4	2	3	28	6	44	5	0	5	2	.714	0	24-30	2	3.18	3.18
2001 Colorado	NL	56	0	0	49	55.0	237	56	27	25	6	2	1	0	22	4	37	3	0	6	1	.857	0	17-22	0	4.14	4.09
2002 Colorado	NL	74	0	0	**69**	73.1	307	76	34	29	7	4	3	6	11	4	47	0	0	2	10	.167	0	41-47	0	3.31	3.56
2003 Colorado	NL	63	7	0	40	101.2	471	137	62	59	7	4	3	6	32	5	45	4	0	2	10	.167	0	20-23	2	5.64	5.22
6 ML YEARS		298	38	2	213	485.0	2137	527	272	251	40	25	15	23	172	21	298	22	1	23	37	.383	2	102-123	4	4.35	4.66

Adam Johnson

Pitches: R **Bats:** R **Pos:** RP-2   **Ht:** 6'2" **Wt:** 210 **Born:** 7/12/79 **Age:** 24

Year Team	Lg	G	GS	CG	GF	IP	BFP	H	R	ER	HR	SH	SF	HB	TBB	IBB	SO	WP	Bk	W	L	Pct	ShO	Sv-Op	Hld	ERC	ERA
2000 Fort Myers	A+	13	12	1	0	69.1	267	45	21	19	2	0	2	3	20	1	92	2	1	5	4	.556	1	0--	-	1.67	2.47
2001 New Britain	AA	18	18	0	0	113.0	481	105	53	48	10	4	5	9	39	2	110	5	0	5	6	.455	0	0--	-	3.68	3.82
2001 Edmonton	AAA	4	4	0	0	23.2	98	19	15	15	0	2	1	1	10	0	25	0	0	1	1	.500	0	0--	-	2.63	5.70
2002 Edmonton	AAA	27	27	1	0	151.1	676	182	96	92	25	3	9	11	55	0	112	5	2	13	8	.619	1	0--	-	6.01	5.47
2003 Rochester	AAA	28	17	1	5	114.1	510	128	73	68	7	5	8	11	48	2	78	8	0	6	11	.353	0	0--	-	4.98	5.35
2001 Minnesota	AL	7	4	0	0	25.0	119	32	0	23	6	0	0	0	13	0	17	0	0	1	2	.333	0	0-0	0	7.29	8.28
2003 Minnesota	AL	2	0	0	1	1.1	13	8	8	7	1	0	0	0	1	0	0	1	0	0	1	.000	0	0-0	0	55.23	47.25
2 ML YEARS		9	4	0	1	26.1	132	40	8	30	7	0	0	0	14	0	17	1	0	1	3	.250	0	0-0	0	9.17	10.25

Charles Johnson

Bats: R **Throws:** R **Pos:** C-108   **Ht:** 6'3" **Wt:** 250 **Born:** 7/20/71 **Age:** 32

Year Team	Lg	G	AB	H	2B	3B	HR	(Hm	Rd)	TB	R	RBI	RC	TBB	IBB	SO	HBP	SH	SF	SB	CS	SB%	GDP	Avg	OBP	Slg
1994 Florida	NL	4	11	5	1	0	1	(1	0)	9	5	4	3	1	0	4	0	0	1	0	0	-	1	.455	.462	.818
1995 Florida	NL	97	315	79	15	1	11	(3	8)	129	40	39	44	46	2	71	4	4	2	0	2	.00	11	.251	.351	.410
1996 Florida	NL	120	386	84	13	1	13	(9	4)	138	34	37	35	40	6	91	2	2	0	1	0	1.00	20	.218	.292	.358
1997 Florida	NL	124	416	104	26	1	19	(7	12)	189	43	63	63	60	6	109	3	3	2	0	2	.00	13	.250	.347	.454
1998 Fla-LA	NL	133	459	100	18	0	19	(14	5)	175	44	58	48	45	1	129	1	0	1	0	2	.00	12	.218	.289	.381
1999 Baltimore	AL	135	426	107	19	1	16	(8	8)	176	58	54	59	55	2	107	4	4	3	0	0	-	13	.251	.340	.413
2000 Bal-CWS	AL	128	421	128	24	0	31	(19	12)	245	76	91	89	52	0	106	1	1	3	2	0	1.00	8	.304	.379	.582
2001 Florida	NL	128	451	117	32	0	18	(15	3)	203	51	75	64	38	2	133	4	0	3	0	0	-	8	.259	.321	.450
2002 Florida	NL	83	244	53	19	0	6	(2	4)	90	18	36	23	31	7	61	0	1	4	0	0	-	10	.217	.301	.369
2003 Colorado	NL	108	356	82	20	0	20	(12	8)	162	49	61	47	49	2	84	1	1	7	1	3	.25	8	.230	.320	.455

Year Team	Lg	G	AB	H	2B	3B	HR	(Hm	Rd)	TB	R	RBI	RC	TBB	IBB	SO	HBP	SH	SF	SB	CS	SB%	GDP	Avg	OBP	Slg
								BATTING												BASERUNNING				AVERAGES		
1998 Florida	NL	31	113	25	5	0	7	(5	2)	51	13	23	16	16	0	30	0	0	1	0	1	.00	3	.221	.315	.451
1998 Los Angeles	NL	102	346	75	13	0	12	(9	3)	124	31	35	32	29	1	99	1	0	0	0	1	.00	9	.217	.279	.358
2000 Baltimore	AL	84	286	84	16	0	21	(12	9)	163	52	55	56	32	0	69	0	1	1	2	0	1.00	8	.294	.364	.570
2000 Chicago	AL	44	135	44	8	0	10	(7	3)	82	24	36	33	20	0	37	1	0	2	0	0	-	0	.326	.411	.607
10 ML YEARS		1060	3485	859	187	4	154	(80	74)	1516	418	518	475	417	28	895	20	16	30	4	9	.31	104	.246	.328	.435

Gary Johnson

Bats: L **Throws:** L **Pos:** LF-2; RF-2; PH-2   **Ht:** 6'3" **Wt:** 210 **Born:** 10/29/75 **Age:** 28

Year Team	Lg	G	AB	H	2B	3B	HR	(Hm	Rd)	TB	R	RBI	RC	TBB	IBB	SO	HBP	SH	SF	SB	CS	SB%	GDP	Avg	OBP	Slg
								BATTING												BASERUNNING				AVERAGES		
1999 Boise	A-	71	264	83	17	1	2	(-	-)	108	56	48	44	34	3	44	2	0	3	6	2	.75	6	.314	.393	.409
2000 Lk Elsinore	A+	70	266	90	20	2	13	(-	-)	153	56	62	63	41	1	59	4	0	5	13	6	.68	6	.338	.427	.575
2000 Erie	AA	71	258	74	10	4	10	(-	-)	122	44	56	45	35	0	63	3	0	1	4	4	.50	4	.287	.377	.473
2001 Arkansas	AA	128	466	114	24	2	11	(-	-)	175	63	72	60	60	4	93	7	0	5	8	7	.53	8	.245	.336	.376
2002 Salt Lake	AAA	40	143	38	9	3	5	(-	-)	68	30	35	23	15	0	49	3	0	3	1	1	.50	3	.266	.341	.476
2002 W Tennesse	AA	121	389	100	15	2	6	(-	-)	137	48	45	53	50	2	77	14	2	8	13	8	.62	7	.257	.356	.352
2003 Salt Lake	AAA	121	447	114	23	7	12	(-	-)	187	65	74	68	61	2	112	4	0	6	4	2	.67	5	.255	.346	.418
2003 Anaheim	AL	5	8	3	1	0	0	(0	0)	4	1	0	1	1	0	1	0	0	0	0	1	.00	0	.375	.444	.500

Jason Johnson

Pitches: R **Bats:** R **Pos:** SP-32   **Ht:** 6'6" **Wt:** 235 **Born:** 10/27/73 **Age:** 30

Year Team	Lg	G	GS	CG	GF	IP	BFP	H	R	ER	HR	SH	SF	HB	TBB	IBB	SO	WP	Bk	W	L	Pct	ShO	Sv-Op	Hld	ERC	ERA
			HOW MUCH HE PITCHED						WHAT HE GAVE UP											THE RESULTS							
1997 Pittsburgh	NL	3	0	0	0	6.0	27	10	4	4	2	0	1	0	1	0	3	0	0	0	0	-	0	0-0	0	9.59	6.00
1998 Tampa Bay	AL	13	13	0	0	60.0	274	74	38	38	9	1	1	3	27	0	36	2	0	2	5	.286	0	0-0	0	6.35	5.70
1999 Baltimore	AL	22	21	0	0	115.1	515	120	74	70	16	2	4	3	55	0	71	5	1	8	7	.533	0	0-0	0	4.99	5.46
2000 Baltimore	AL	25	13	0	3	107.2	501	119	95	84	21	3	5	4	61	2	79	3	0	1	10	.091	0	0-0	2	6.18	7.02
2001 Baltimore	AL	32	32	2	0	196.0	856	194	109	89	28	6	6	13	77	3	114	9	0	10	12	.455	0	0-0	0	4.53	4.09
2002 Baltimore	AL	22	22	1	0	131.1	561	141	68	67	19	0	3	6	41	2	97	4	0	5	14	.263	0	0-0	0	4.70	4.59
2003 Baltimore	AL	32	32	0	0	189.2	858	216	100	88	22	3	1	10	80	8	118	7	0	10	10	.500	0	0-0	0	5.21	4.18
7 ML YEARS		149	133	3	3	806.0	3592	874	488	440	117	15	21	39	342	15	518	30	1	36	58	.383	0	0-0	2	5.16	4.91

Jonathan Johnson

Pitches: R **Bats:** R **Pos:** SP-3; RP-1   **Ht:** 6'0" **Wt:** 180 **Born:** 7/16/74 **Age:** 29

Year Team	Lg	G	GS	CG	GF	IP	BFP	H	R	ER	HR	SH	SF	HB	TBB	IBB	SO	WP	Bk	W	L	Pct	ShO	Sv-Op	Hld	ERC	ERA
			HOW MUCH HE PITCHED						WHAT HE GAVE UP											THE RESULTS							
2003 New Orleans*	AAA	13	13	1	0	78.0	333	74	38	34	4	3	2	2	27	0	62	9	0	5	4	.556	0	0--	-	3.32	3.92
1998 Texas	AL	1	1	0	0	4.1	22	5	4	4	0	0	1	0	5	0	3	0	0	0	0	-	0	0-0	0	7.36	8.31
1999 Texas	AL	1	0	0	0	3.0	21	9	5	5	0	0	1	1	2	0	3	0	0	0	0	-	0	0-0	0	19.55	15.00
2000 Texas	AL	15	0	0	3	29.0	144	34	23	20	3	0	2	6	19	2	23	2	0	1	1	.500	0	0-0	0	6.84	6.21
2001 Texas	AL	5	0	0	2	10.1	53	13	11	11	2	1	3	1	7	1	11	0	0	0	0	-	0	0-0	0	7.49	9.58
2002 SD-Ari	NL	16	0	0	5	15.1	67	15	8	7	2	1	0	1	5	1	21	0	0	1	2	.333	0	0-0	1	3.94	4.11
2003 Houston	NL	4	0	0	0	15.1	78	20	11	10	2	0	1	0	15	3	7	1	0	0	1	.000	0	0-0	0	8.38	5.87
2002 San Diego	NL	16	0	0	5	15.1	67	15	8	7	2	1	0	1	5	1	21	0	0	1	2	.333	0	0-0	1	3.94	4.11
2002 Arizona	NL	0	0	0	0	0.0	0	0	0	0	0	0	0	0	0	0	0	0	0	0	0	-	0	0-0	0	-	-
6 ML YEARS		42	4	0	10	77.1	385	96	62	57	9	2	8	9	53	7	68	3	0	2	4	.333	0	0-0	1	7.08	6.63

Mark L Johnson

Bats: L **Throws:** R **Pos:** C-13; PH-1   **Ht:** 6'0" **Wt:** 185 **Born:** 9/12/75 **Age:** 28

Year Team	Lg	G	AB	H	2B	3B	HR	(Hm	Rd)	TB	R	RBI	RC	TBB	IBB	SO	HBP	SH	SF	SB	CS	SB%	GDP	Avg	OBP	Slg
								BATTING												BASERUNNING				AVERAGES		
2003 Sacramento*	AAA	51	162	37	11	1	3	(-	-)	59	28	30	25	35	0	23	3	1	3	0	1	.00	2	.228	.369	.364
1998 Chicago	AL	7	23	2	0	2	0	(0	0)	6	2	1	0	1	0	8	0	0	0	0	0	-	0	.087	.125	.261
1999 Chicago	AL	73	207	47	11	0	4	(2	2)	70	27	16	27	36	0	58	2	1	2	3	1	.75	2	.227	.344	.338
2000 Chicago	AL	75	213	48	11	0	3	(2	1)	68	29	23	23	27	0	40	1	10	0	3	2	.60	3	.225	.315	.319
2001 Chicago	AL	61	173	43	6	1	5	(2	3)	66	21	18	25	23	1	31	2	10	3	2	1	.67	5	.249	.338	.382
2002 Chicago	AL	86	263	55	8	1	4	(1	3)	77	31	18	23	30	1	52	3	6	0	0	0	-	4	.209	.297	.293
2003 Oakland	AL	13	27	3	1	0	0	(0	0)	4	3	3	0	3	0	4	1	1	1	0	0	-	0	.111	.219	.148
6 ML YEARS		315	906	198	37	4	16	(7	9)	291	113	79	96	120	2	193	9	28	6	8	4	.67	14	.219	.314	.321

Nick Johnson

Bats: L **Throws:** L **Pos:** 1B-60; DH-32; PH-6   **Ht:** 6'3" **Wt:** 224 **Born:** 9/19/78 **Age:** 25

Year Team	Lg	G	AB	H	2B	3B	HR	(Hm	Rd)	TB	R	RBI	RC	TBB	IBB	SO	HBP	SH	SF	SB	CS	SB%	GDP	Avg	OBP	Slg
								BATTING												BASERUNNING				AVERAGES		
2003 Trenton*	AA	4	12	5	1	0	0	(-	-)	6	3	1	4	5	0	0	1	0	0	0	0	-	0	.417	.611	.500
2003 Columbus*	AAA	3	10	5	2	0	1	(-	-)	10	1	3	5	2	0	2	0	0	0	0	0	-	0	.500	.583	1.000
2001 New York	AL	23	67	13	2	0	2	(1	1)	21	6	8	6	7	0	15	4	0	0	0	0	-	3	.194	.308	.313
2002 New York	AL	129	378	92	15	0	15	(7	8)	152	56	58	58	48	5	98	12	3	0	1	3	.25	11	.243	.347	.402
2003 New York	AL	96	324	92	19	0	14	(8	6)	153	60	47	65	70	4	57	8	3	1	5	2	.71	9	.284	.422	.472
3 ML YEARS		248	769	197	36	0	31	(16	15)	326	122	113	129	125	9	170	24	6	1	6	5	.55	23	.256	.376	.424

Randy Johnson

Pitches: L Bats: R Pos: SP-18 **Ht: 6'10" Wt: 232 Born: 9/10/63 Age: 40**

Year Team	Lg	G	GS	CG	GF	IP	BFP	H	R	ER	HR	SH	SF	HB	TBB	IBB	SO	WP	Bk	W	L	Pct	ShO	Sv-Op	Hld	ERC	ERA
2003 Lancaster*	A+	1	1	0	0	6.0	32	11	5	4	1	0	0	2	0	0	6	0	0	0	1	.000	0	0--	-	9.10	6.00
2003 Tucson*	AAA	1	1	0	0	4.0	12	0	0	0	0	0	0	0	0	0	4	0	0	0	0	-	0	0--	-	0.00	0.00
2003 El Paso*	AA	1	1	0	0	4.0	18	3	2	0	0	0	2	2	1	0	5	0	0	0	0	-	0	0--	-	3.21	0.00
1988 Montreal	NL	4	4	1	0	26.0	109	23	8	7	3	0	0	0	7	0	25	3	0	3	0	1.000	0	0-0	-	2.96	2.42
1989 Mon-Sea		29	28	2	1	160.2	715	147	100	86	13	10	13	3	96	2	130	7	7	7	13	.350	0	0-0	0	4.26	4.82
1990 Seattle	AL	33	33	5	0	219.2	944	174	103	89	26	7	6	5	120	2	194	4	2	14	11	.560	2	0-0	0	3.68	3.65
1991 Seattle	AL	33	33	2	0	201.1	889	151	96	89	15	9	8	12	152	0	228	12	2	13	10	.565	1	0-0	0	4.15	3.98
1992 Seattle	AL	31	31	6	0	210.1	922	154	104	88	13	3	8	18	144	1	241	13	1	12	14	.462	2	0-0	0	3.75	3.77
1993 Seattle	AL	35	34	10	1	255.1	1043	185	97	92	22	8	7	16	99	1	308	0	2	19	8	.704	3	1-1	0	2.73	3.24
1994 Seattle	AL	23	23	9	0	172.0	694	132	65	61	14	3	1	6	72	2	204	5	0	13	6	.684	4	0-0	0	2.99	3.19
1995 Seattle	AL	30	30	6	0	214.1	866	159	65	59	12	2	1	6	65	1	294	5	2	18	2	.900	3	0-0	0	2.18	2.48
1996 Seattle	AL	14	8	0	2	61.1	256	48	27	25	8	1	0	2	25	0	85	3	1	5	0	1.000	0	1-2	0	3.24	3.67
1997 Seattle	AL	30	29	5	0	213.0	850	147	60	54	20	4	1	10	77	2	291	4	0	20	4	.833	2	0-0	0	2.47	2.28
1998 Sea-Hou		34	34	10	0	244.1	1014	203	102	89	23	5	2	14	86	1	329	7	2	19	11	.633	6	0-0	0	3.16	3.28
1999 Arizona	NL	35	35	12	0	271.2	1079	207	86	75	30	4	3	9	70	3	364	4	2	17	9	.654	2	0-0	0	2.49	2.48
2000 Arizona	NL	35	35	8	0	248.2	1001	202	89	73	23	14	5	6	76	1	347	5	2	19	7	.731	3	0-0	0	2.80	2.64
2001 Arizona	NL	35	34	3	1	249.2	994	181	74	69	19	10	5	18	71	2	372	8	1	21	6	.778	2	0-0	0	2.35	2.49
2002 Arizona	NL	35	35	8	0	260.0	1035	197	78	67	26	4	2	13	71	1	334	3	2	24	5	.828	4	0-0	0	2.54	2.32
2003 Arizona	NL	18	18	1	0	114.0	489	125	61	54	16	4	3	8	27	3	125	1	1	6	8	.429	1	0-0	0	4.52	4.26
1989 Montreal	NL	7	6	0	1	29.2	143	29	25	22	2	3	4	0	26	1	26	2	2	0	4	.000	0	0-0	0	5.42	6.67
1989 Seattle	AL	22	22	2	0	131.0	572	118	75	64	11	7	9	3	70	1	104	5	5	7	9	.438	0	0-0	0	4.01	4.40
1998 Seattle	AL	23	23	6	0	160.0	685	146	90	77	19	5	1	11	60	0	213	7	2	9	10	.474	2	0-0	0	3.88	4.33
1998 Houston	NL	11	11	4	0	84.1	329	57	12	12	4	0	1	3	26	1	116	0	0	10	1	.909	4	0-0	0	1.93	1.28
16 ML YEARS		454	444	88	5	3122.1	12900	2435	1215	1077	283	88	65	146	1258	22	3871	92	27	230	114	.669	35	2-3	0	3.03	3.10

Reed Johnson

Bats: R Throws: R Pos: RF-70; LF-53; PH-7; CF-5; PR-4 **Ht: 5'10" Wt: 180 Born: 12/8/76 Age: 27**

Year Team	Lg	G	AB	H	2B	3B	HR	(Hm	Rd)	TB	R	RBI	RC	TBB	IBB	SO	HBP	SH	SF	SB	CS	SB%	GDP	Avg	OBP	Slg
1999 St. Catharines	A-	60	191	46	8	2	2	(-	-)	64	24	23	21	24	1	31	2	4	4	5	5	.50	4	.241	.326	.335
2000 Hagerstown	A	95	324	94	24	5	8	(-	-)	152	66	70	68	62	1	49	14	2	3	14	2	.88	9	.290	.422	.469
2000 Dunedin	A+	36	133	42	9	2	4	(-	-)	67	26	28	29	14	0	27	11	1	3	3	2	.60	1	.316	.416	.504
2001 Tennessee	AA	136	554	174	29	4	13	(-	-)	250	104	74	98	45	2	79	18	5	2	42	12	.78	11	.314	.383	.451
2002 Dunedin	A+	8	33	9	3	0	0	(-	-)	12	7	6	5	3	0	3	2	0	0	0	1	.00	0	.273	.368	.364
2002 Rochester	AAA	44	159	37	8	3	2	(-	-)	57	27	10	18	12	0	23	8	3	1	1	4	.20	1	.233	.317	.358
2003 Syracuse	AAA	26	101	33	4	1	2	(-	-)	45	14	16	17	3	0	13	5	0	2	3	1	.75	2	.327	.369	.446
2003 Toronto	AL	114	412	121	21	2	10	(6	4)	176	79	52	62	20	1	67	20	1	4	5	3	.63	10	.294	.353	.427

Rontrez Johnson

Bats: R Throws: R Pos: CF-6; PR-3; PH-2; DH-1 **Ht: 5'10" Wt: 165 Born: 12/8/76 Age: 27**

Year Team	Lg	G	AB	H	2B	3B	HR	(Hm	Rd)	TB	R	RBI	RC	TBB	IBB	SO	HBP	SH	SF	SB	CS	SB%	GDP	Avg	OBP	Slg
1995 Red Sox	R	52	193	49	4	2	0	(-	-)	57	37	11	26	30	0	30	1	3	1	25	5	.83	1	.254	.356	.295
1996 Red Sox	R	28	85	25	6	0	0	(-	-)	31	20	9	14	17	0	11	0	1	0	6	2	.75	2	.294	.412	.365
1996 Lowell	A-	35	135	30	4	0	4	(-	-)	46	27	12	16	21	1	30	0	0	2	7	3	.70	2	.222	.323	.341
1997 Michigan	A	118	411	99	10	6	5	(-	-)	136	87	40	56	65	0	96	9	6	3	29	12	.71	4	.241	.355	.331
1998 Michigan	A	85	306	83	15	5	5	(-	-)	123	65	32	57	66	0	46	4	1	5	24	8	.75	4	.271	.402	.402
1999 Sarasota	A+	132	494	148	30	4	8	(-	-)	210	97	59	86	74	0	63	8	8	7	18	15	.55	7	.300	.395	.425
2000 Trenton	AA	134	524	141	21	2	6	(-	-)	184	83	53	63	55	1	73	6	3	4	30	19	.61	12	.269	.343	.351
2001 Trenton	AA	73	255	72	15	1	10	(-	-)	119	48	31	43	22	0	40	9	2	3	17	7	.71	4	.282	.356	.467
2001 Pawtucket	AAA	44	187	56	16	3	4	(-	-)	90	32	22	30	10	0	35	7	1	0	8	4	.67	7	.299	.358	.481
2002 Omaha	AAA	109	403	121	27	4	9	(-	-)	183	71	53	77	50	1	51	19	0	6	31	11	.74	6	.300	.397	.454
2003 Richmond	AAA	31	81	14	1	0	0	(-	-)	15	8	5	4	8	0	15	2	2	1	3	1	.75	2	.173	.261	.185
2003 Oklahoma	AAA	70	241	54	10	3	5	(-	-)	85	35	20	27	19	0	29	7	1	3	14	6	.70	1	.224	.296	.353
2003 Kansas City	AL	8	3	1	0	0	0	(0	0)	1	3	0	0	0	0	2	0	0	0	0	0	-	0	.333	.333	.333

Andruw Jones

Bats: R Throws: R Pos: CF-155; PH-3 **Ht: 6'1" Wt: 210 Born: 4/23/77 Age: 27**

Year Team	Lg	G	AB	H	2B	3B	HR	(Hm	Rd)	TB	R	RBI	RC	TBB	IBB	SO	HBP	SH	SF	SB	CS	SB%	GDP	Avg	OBP	Slg
1996 Atlanta	NL	31	106	23	7	1	5	(3	2)	47	11	13	13	7	0	29	0	0	0	3	0	1.00	1	.217	.265	.443
1997 Atlanta	NL	153	399	92	18	1	18	(5	13)	166	60	70	54	56	2	107	4	5	3	20	11	.65	11	.231	.329	.416
1998 Atlanta	NL	159	582	158	33	8	31	(16	15)	300	89	90	97	40	8	129	4	1	4	27	4	.87	10	.271	.321	.515
1999 Atlanta	NL	162	592	163	35	5	26	(10	16)	286	97	84	103	76	11	103	9	0	2	24	12	.67	12	.275	.365	.483
2000 Atlanta	NL	161	656	199	36	6	36	(15	21)	355	122	104	127	59	0	100	9	0	5	21	6	.78	12	.303	.366	.541
2001 Atlanta	NL	161	625	157	25	2	34	(16	18)	288	104	104	90	56	3	142	3	0	9	11	4	.73	10	.251	.312	.461
2002 Atlanta	NL	154	560	148	34	0	35	(18	17)	287	91	94	97	83	4	135	10	0	6	8	3	.73	14	.264	.366	.513
2003 Atlanta	NL	156	595	165	28	2	36	(16	20)	305	101	116	92	53	2	125	5	0	6	4	3	.57	18	.277	.338	.513
8 ML YEARS		1137	4115	1105	216	25	221	(99	122)	2034	675	675	673	430	30	870	44	6	35	118	43	.73	88	.269	.341	.494

Chipper Jones

Bats: B Throws: R Pos: LF-149; PH-3; DH-1 **Ht: 6'4" Wt: 210 Born: 4/24/72 Age: 32**

Year Team	Lg	G	AB	H	2B	3B	HR	(Hm	Rd)	TB	R	RBI	RC	TBB	IBB	SO	HBP	SH	SF	SB	CS	SB%	GDP	Avg	OBP	Slg
1993 Atlanta	NL	8	3	2	1	0	0	(0	0)	3	2	0	2	1	0	1	0	0	0	0	0	-	0	.667	.750	1.000
1995 Atlanta	NL	140	524	139	22	3	23	(15	8)	236	87	86	84	73	1	99	0	1	4	8	4	.67	10	.265	.353	.450
1996 Atlanta	NL	157	598	185	32	5	30	(18	12)	317	114	110	123	87	0	88	0	1	7	14	1	.93	14	.309	.393	.530

Year Team	Lg	G	AB	H	2B	3B	HR	(Hm	Rd)	TB	R	RBI	RC	TBB	IBB	SO	HBP	SH	SF	SB	CS	SB%	GDP	Avg	OBP	Slg
1997 Atlanta	NL	157	597	176	41	3	21	(7	14)	286	100	111	104	76	8	88	0	0	6	20	5	.80	19	.295	.371	.479
1998 Atlanta	NL	160	601	188	29	5	34	(17	17)	329	123	107	129	96	1	93	1	1	8	16	6	.73	17	.313	.404	.547
1999 Atlanta	NL	157	567	181	41	1	45	(25	20)	359	116	110	150	126	18	94	2	0	6	25	3	.89	20	.319	.441	.633
2000 Atlanta	NL	156	579	180	38	1	36	(18	18)	328	118	111	128	95	10	64	2	0	10	14	7	.67	14	.311	.404	.566
2001 Atlanta	NL	159	572	189	33	5	38	(19	19)	330	118	102	136	98	20	82	2	0	5	9	10	.47	13	.330	.427	.605
2002 Atlanta	NL	158	548	179	35	1	26	(17	9)	294	90	100	119	107	23	89	2	0	5	8	2	.80	18	.327	.435	.536
2003 Atlanta	NL	153	555	169	33	2	27	(16	11)	287	103	106	109	94	13	83	1	0	6	2	2	.50	10	.305	.402	.517
10 ML YEARS		1405	5144	1588	305	26	280	(152	128)	2785	966	943	1084	853	94	781	10	3	57	116	40	.74	135	.309	.404	.541

Greg Jones

Pitches: R **Bats:** R **Pos:** RP-18   **Ht:** 6'2" **Wt:** 195 **Born:** 11/15/76 **Age:** 27

Year Team	Lg	G	GS	CG	GF	IP	BFP	H	R	ER	HR	SH	SF	HB	TBB	IBB	SO	WP	Bk	W	L	Pct	ShO	Sv-Op	Hld	ERC	ERA
1997 Boise	A-	21	4	0	4	37.1	172	35	19	16	1	2	4	3	19	1	39	5	1	2	2	.500	0	2--	-	3.70	3.86
1998 Boise	A-	22	0	0	3	34.2	152	37	22	19	3	2	1	3	13	0	28	3	0	0	2	.000	0	1--	-	4.66	4.93
1999 Cedar Rpds	A	34	0	0	29	40.0	165	37	18	17	5	2	0	0	13	2	41	5	0	2	4	.333	0	13--	-	3.51	3.83
2000 Lk Elsinore	A+	16	0	0	12	17.2	81	19	9	8	0	2	1	1	10	3	12	3	0	0	0	-	0	3--	-	4.29	4.08
2000 Erie	AA	11	0	0	8	15.0	66	19	9	9	1	0	0	0	4	0	7	0	0	0	2	.000	0	2--	-	4.86	5.40
2000 Edmonton	AAA	25	0	0	13	42.1	217	57	42	36	5	1	3	4	33	1	21	6	0	2	2	.500	0	1--	-	8.28	7.65
2001 R Cucamnga	A+	6	6	0	0	27.2	118	25	15	13	2	1	1	0	11	0	27	3	0	1	3	.250	0	0--	-	3.31	4.23
2001 Angels	R	2	2	0	0	2.0	10	3	0	0	0	0	0	0	2	0	2	0	0	0	0	-	0	0--	-	9.50	0.00
2002 Salt Lake	AAA	39	0	0	9	62.2	274	68	35	30	5	0	2	1	22	0	55	3	0	7	4	.636	0	2--	-	4.26	4.31
2003 Salt Lake	AAA	33	0	0	14	47.0	184	36	24	23	4	0	1	0	9	0	56	2	0	2	3	.400	0	4--	-	2.02	4.40
2003 Anaheim	AL	18	0	0	7	27.2	127	29	15	15	3	0	0	2	14	0	28	5	0	0	0	-	0	0-0	2	5.05	4.88

Jacque Jones

Bats: L **Throws:** L **Pos:** LF-90; DH-29; RF-11; PH-9   **Ht:** 5'10" **Wt:** 176 **Born:** 4/25/75 **Age:** 29

Year Team	Lg	G	AB	H	2B	3B	HR	(Hm	Rd)	TB	R	RBI	RC	TBB	IBB	SO	HBP	SH	SF	SB	CS	SB%	GDP	Avg	OBP	Slg
1999 Minnesota	AL	95	322	93	24	2	9	(5	4)	148	54	44	46	17	1	63	4	1	3	3	4	.43	7	.289	.329	.460
2000 Minnesota	AL	154	523	149	26	5	19	(11	8)	242	66	76	70	26	4	111	0	1	0	7	5	.58	17	.285	.319	.463
2001 Minnesota	AL	149	475	131	25	0	14	(5	9)	198	57	49	63	39	2	92	3	2	0	12	9	.57	10	.276	.335	.417
2002 Minnesota	AL	149	577	173	37	2	27	(6	21)	295	96	85	100	37	2	129	2	4	6	6	7	.46	8	.300	.341	.511
2003 Minnesota	AL	136	517	157	33	1	16	(7	9)	240	76	69	74	21	2	105	4	1	5	13	1	.93	10	.304	.333	.464
5 ML YEARS		683	2414	703	145	10	85	(34	51)	1123	349	323	353	140	11	500	13	9	14	41	26	.61	52	.291	.332	.465

Jason Jones

Bats: B **Throws:** R **Pos:** LF-14; RF-13; PH-8; DH-6; 1B-3   **Ht:** 6'3" **Wt:** 210 **Born:** 10/17/76 **Age:** 27

Year Team	Lg	G	AB	H	2B	3B	HR	(Hm	Rd)	TB	R	RBI	RC	TBB	IBB	SO	HBP	SH	SF	SB	CS	SB%	GDP	Avg	OBP	Slg
1999 Pulaski	R+	69	262	93	24	1	11	(-	-)	152	65	58	62	33	1	55	7	0	5	1	2	.33	5	.355	.433	.580
2000 Savannah	A	132	466	125	34	6	9	(-	-)	198	59	61	70	65	4	97	4	1	5	9	5	.64	15	.268	.359	.425
2001 Tulsa	AA	30	107	23	6	0	2	(-	-)	35	8	8	7	3	1	17	1	0	0	0	0	-	4	.215	.243	.327
2001 Charlotte	A+	102	375	106	26	2	15	(-	-)	181	50	81	65	56	5	48	1	0	4	1	3	.25	12	.283	.374	.483
2002 Tulsa	AA	136	471	139	33	2	13	(-	-)	215	82	75	87	87	6	97	0	0	5	12	7	.63	12	.295	.401	.456
2003 Oklahoma	AAA	100	375	108	29	0	9	(-	-)	164	52	55	62	50	4	80	2	1	1	7	2	.78	8	.288	.374	.437
2003 Texas	AL	40	107	23	6	0	3	(3	0)	38	11	11	10	10	0	21	3	0	1	0	1	.00	1	.215	.298	.355

Todd Jones

Pitches: R **Bats:** B **Pos:** RP-58; SP-1   **Ht:** 6'3" **Wt:** 230 **Born:** 4/24/68 **Age:** 36

Year Team	Lg	G	GS	CG	GF	IP	BFP	H	R	ER	HR	SH	SF	HB	TBB	IBB	SO	WP	Bk	W	L	Pct	ShO	Sv-Op	Hld	ERC	ERA
1993 Houston	NL	27	0	0	8	37.1	150	28	14	13	4	2	1	1	15	2	25	1	1	1	2	.333	0	2-3	6	2.90	3.13
1994 Houston	NL	48	0	0	20	72.2	288	52	23	22	3	3	1	1	26	4	63	1	0	5	2	.714	0	5-9	8	2.10	2.72
1995 Houston	NL	68	0	0	40	99.2	442	89	38	34	8	5	4	6	52	17	96	5	0	6	5	.545	0	15-20	8	3.70	3.07
1996 Houston	NL	51	0	0	37	57.1	263	61	30	28	5	2	1	5	32	6	44	3	0	6	3	.667	0	17-23	1	5.16	4.40
1997 Detroit	AL	68	0	0	51	70.0	301	60	29	24	3	1	4	1	35	2	70	7	0	5	4	.556	0	31-36	5	3.27	3.09
1998 Detroit	AL	65	0	0	53	63.1	279	58	38	35	7	2	6	2	36	4	57	5	0	1	4	.200	0	28-32	0	4.37	4.97
1999 Detroit	AL	65	0	0	62	66.1	287	64	30	28	7	3	1	1	35	1	64	2	0	4	4	.500	0	30-35	0	4.55	3.80
2000 Detroit	AL	67	0	0	60	64.0	271	67	28	25	6	1	1	1	25	1	67	2	0	2	4	.333	0	42-46	0	4.43	3.52
2001 Det-Min	AL	69	0	0	36	68.0	314	87	39	32	9	3	3	0	29	1	54	3	0	5	5	.500	0	13-21	10	6.03	4.24
2002 Colorado	NL	79	0	0	20	82.1	352	84	43	43	10	6	3	3	28	3	73	1	0	1	4	.200	0	1-3	30	4.22	4.70
2003 Col-Bos		59	1	0	14	68.2	326	93	58	54	10	3	3	1	31	2	59	0	0	3	5	.375	0	0-5	4	6.73	7.08
2001 Detroit	AL	45	0	0	28	48.2	225	60	31	25	6	2	3	0	22	1	39	3	0	4	5	.444	0	11-17	5	5.74	4.62
2001 Minnesota	AL	24	0	0	8	19.1	89	27	8	7	3	1	0	0	7	0	15	0	0	1	0	1.000	0	2-4	7	6.80	3.26
2003 Colorado	NL	33	1	0	7	39.1	193	61	39	36	8	3	2	1	18	0	28	0	0	1	4	.200	0	0-5	3	8.77	8.24
2003 Boston	AL	26	0	0	7	29.1	133	32	19	18	2	0	1	0	13	2	31	0	0	2	1	.667	0	0-0	1	4.30	5.52
11 ML YEARS		666	1	0	401	749.2	3273	743	370	338	72	31	28	22	344	43	672	30	1	39	42	.481	0	184-233	72	4.27	4.06

Brian Jordan

Bats: R **Throws:** R **Pos:** LF-54; CF-14; RF-3; DH-2; PH-2; PR-1   **Ht:** 6'1" **Wt:** 205 **Born:** 3/29/67 **Age:** 37

Year Team	Lg	G	AB	H	2B	3B	HR	(Hm	Rd)	TB	R	RBI	RC	TBB	IBB	SO	HBP	SH	SF	SB	CS	SB%	GDP	Avg	OBP	Slg
1992 St Louis	NL	55	193	40	9	4	5	(3	2)	72	17	22	16	10	1	48	1	0	0	7	2	.78	6	.207	.250	.373
1993 St Louis	NL	67	223	69	10	6	10	(4	6)	121	33	44	39	12	0	35	4	0	3	6	6	.50	6	.309	.351	.543
1994 St Louis	NL	53	178	46	8	2	5	(4	1)	73	14	15	22	16	0	40	1	0	2	4	3	.57	6	.258	.320	.410
1995 St Louis	NL	131	490	145	20	4	22	(14	8)	239	83	81	80	22	4	79	11	0	2	24	9	.73	5	.296	.339	.488
1996 St Louis	NL	140	513	159	36	1	17	(3	14)	248	82	104	88	29	4	84	7	2	9	22	5	.81	6	.310	.349	.483

Year Team	Lg	G	AB	H	2B	3B	HR	(Hm	Rd)	TB	R	RBI	RC	TBB	IBB	SO	HBP	SH	SF	SB	CS	SB%	GDP	Avg	OBP	Slg
1997 St Louis	NL	47	145	34	5	0	0	(0	0)	39	17	10	13	10	1	21	6	0	0	6	1	.86	4	.234	.311	.269
1998 St Louis	NL	150	564	178	34	7	25	(9	16)	301	100	91	104	40	1	66	9	0	4	17	5	.77	18	.316	.368	.534
1999 Atlanta	NL	153	576	163	28	4	23	(11	12)	268	100	115	92	51	2	81	9	0	9	13	8	.62	9	.283	.346	.465
2000 Atlanta	NL	133	489	129	26	0	17	(7	10)	206	71	77	66	38	1	80	5	0	5	10	2	.83	12	.264	.320	.421
2001 Atlanta	NL	148	560	165	32	3	25	(14	11)	278	82	97	87	31	3	88	6	0	8	3	2	.60	18	.295	.334	.496
2002 Los Angeles	NL	128	471	134	27	3	18	(7	11)	221	65	80	73	34	3	86	6	0	4	2	2	.50	10	.285	.338	.469
2003 Los Angeles	NL	66	224	67	9	0	6	(3	3)	94	28	28	33	23	3	30	4	0	2	1	1	.50	3	.299	.372	.420
12 ML YEARS		1271	4626	1329	244	34	173	(79	94)	2160	692	764	713	316	23	738	69	2	48	115	46	.71	103	.287	.339	.467

Felix Jose

Bats: B Throws: R Pos: PH-16; RF-1; DH-1   Ht: 6'1" Wt: 220 Born: 5/2/65 Age: 39

Year Team	Lg	G	AB	H	2B	3B	HR	(Hm	Rd)	TB	R	RBI	RC	TBB	IBB	SO	HBP	SH	SF	SB	CS	SB%	GDP	Avg	OBP	Slg
1988 Oakland	AL	8	6	2	1	0	0	(0	0)	3	2	1	1	0	0	1	0	0	0	1	0	1.00	0	.333	.333	.500
1989 Oakland	AL	20	57	11	2	0	0	(0	0)	13	3	5	2	4	0	13	0	0	0	1	0	1.00	2	.193	.246	.228
1990 Oak-StL		126	426	113	16	1	11	(5	6)	164	54	52	49	24	0	81	5	2	1	12	6	.67	9	.265	.311	.385
1991 St Louis	NL	154	568	173	40	6	8	(3	5)	249	69	77	86	50	8	113	2	0	5	20	12	.63	12	.305	.360	.438
1992 St Louis	NL	131	509	150	22	3	14	(12	2)	220	62	75	75	40	8	100	1	0	1	28	12	.70	9	.295	.347	.432
1993 Kansas City	AL	149	499	126	24	3	6	(2	4)	174	64	43	54	36	5	95	1	1	2	31	13	.70	5	.253	.303	.349
1994 Kansas City	AL	99	366	111	28	1	11	(1	10)	174	56	55	57	35	6	75	0	0	2	10	12	.45	9	.303	.362	.475
1995 Kansas City	AL	9	30	4	1	0	0	(0	0)	5	2	1	2	2	0	9	0	0	0	0	0	-	1	.133	.188	.167
2000 New York	AL	20	29	7	0	0	1	(0	1)	10	4	5	2	2	0	9	0	0	1	0	1	.00	1	.241	.281	.345
2002 Arizona	NL	13	19	5	0	0	2	(2	0)	11	5	4	3	4	0	8	0	0	2	0	0	-	1	.263	.360	.579
2003 Arizona	NL	18	18	6	1	0	1	(0	1)	10	2	6	5	6	1	3	0	0	0	0	0	-	1	.333	.500	.556
1990 Oakland	AL	101	341	90	12	0	8	(3	5)	126	42	39	37	16	0	65	5	2	1	8	2	.80	8	.264	.306	.370
1990 St Louis	NL	25	85	23	4	1	3	(2	1)	38	12	13	12	8	0	16	0	0	0	4	4	.50	1	.271	.333	.447
11 ML YEARS		747	2527	708	135	14	54	(25	29)	1033	322	324	334	203	28	507	9	3	14	102	57	.64	50	.280	.334	.409

Jimmy Journell

Pitches: R Bats: R Pos: RP-7   Ht: 6'4" Wt: 205 Born: 12/29/77 Age: 26

Year Team	Lg	G	GS	CG	GF	IP	BFP	H	R	ER	HR	SH	SF	HB	TBB	IBB	SO	WP	Bk	W	L	Pct	ShO	Sv-Op	Hld	ERC	ERA
2000 New Jersey	A-	13	1	0	3	32.0	136	12	12	7	0	0	2	2	24	0	39	8	0	1	0	1.000	0	0--	-	1.65	1.97
2001 Potomac	A+	26	26	0	0	151.0	520	121	54	42	8	6	5	18	42	0	156	7	0	14	6	.700	0	0--	-	3.35	2.50
2001 New Haven	AA	1	1	1	0	7.0	21	0	0	0	0	0	0	0	3	0	6	0	0	1	0	1.000	1	0--	-	0.23	0.00
2002 New Haven	AA	10	10	2	0	66.2	269	50	22	20	3	2	0	6	18	0	66	2	0	3	3	.500	0	0--	-	2.29	2.70
2002 Memphis	AAA	7	7	0	0	36.2	166	38	16	15	3	1	1	2	18	0	32	3	0	2	4	.333	0	0--	-	4.67	3.68
2003 Memphis	AAA	40	7	0	16	78.0	343	80	38	34	3	5	1	6	32	2	70	5	0	6	6	.500	0	5--	-	4.08	3.92
2003 St Louis	NL	7	0	0	2	9.0	48	10	7	6	0	0	1	0	11	0	8	1	0	0	0	-	0	0-0	0	7.02	6.00

Jorge Julio

Pitches: R Bats: R Pos: RP-64   Ht: 6'1" Wt: 190 Born: 3/3/79 Age: 25

Year Team	Lg	G	GS	CG	GF	IP	BFP	H	R	ER	HR	SH	SF	HB	TBB	IBB	SO	WP	Bk	W	L	Pct	ShO	Sv-Op	Hld	ERC	ERA
2001 Baltimore	AL	18	0	0	8	21.1	99	25	13	9	2	2	0	1	9	0	22	1	0	1	1	.500	0	0-1	3	5.17	3.80
2002 Baltimore	AL	67	0	0	61	68.0	289	55	22	15	5	1	1	2	27	3	55	8	0	5	6	.455	0	25-31	1	2.83	1.99
2003 Baltimore	AL	64	0	0	51	61.2	273	60	36	30	10	2	1	2	34	4	52	0	0	0	7	.000	0	36-44	2	5.05	4.38
3 ML YEARS		149	0	0	120	151.0	661	140	71	54	17	5	2	5	70	7	129	9	0	6	14	.300	0	61-76	6	4.01	3.22

Eric Junge

Pitches: R Bats: R Pos: RP-6   Ht: 6'5" Wt: 215 Born: 1/5/77 Age: 27

Year Team	Lg	G	GS	CG	GF	IP	BFP	H	R	ER	HR	SH	SF	HB	TBB	IBB	SO	WP	Bk	W	L	Pct	ShO	Sv-Op	Hld	ERC	ERA
1999 Yakima	A-	15	15	0	0	82.0	363	98	60	53	10	3	6	0	31	0	55	3	0	5	7	.417	0	0--	-	5.34	5.82
2000 Sn Brnardino	A+	29	24	0	0	158.0	666	159	69	59	8	3	5	9	53	0	116	8	2	8	1	.889	0	1--	-	3.82	3.36
2001 Jacksonville	AA	27	27	1	0	164.0	686	143	72	63	19	11	3	13	56	2	116	6	0	10	11	.476	1	0--	-	3.57	3.46
2002 Scrtn/WlksBr	AAA	29	29	1	0	180.2	766	170	77	71	16	8	4	5	67	1	126	10	0	12	6	.667	0	0--	-	3.67	3.54
2003 Scrtn/WlksBr	AAA	10	8	0	0	47.0	196	38	20	16	2	1	0	3	16	1	42	1	0	1	0	1.000	0	0--	-	2.64	3.06
2002 Philadelphia	NL	4	1	0	2	12.2	57	14	3	2	0	2	0	0	5	0	11	0	0	2	0	1.000	0	0-0	0	3.81	1.42
2003 Philadelphia	NL	6	0	0	1	7.2	28	5	3	3	1	0	0	0	1	0	5	0	0	0	0	-	0	0-0	0	1.62	3.52
2 ML YEARS		10	1	0	3	20.1	85	19	6	5	1	2	0	0	6	0	16	0	0	2	0	1.000	0	0-0	0	2.96	2.21

Gabe Kapler

Bats: R Throws: R Pos: RF-43; LF-40; PH-26; PR-12; CF-10; 1B-1; DH-1   Ht: 6'2" Wt: 208 Born: 8/31/75 Age: 28

Year Team	Lg	G	AB	H	2B	3B	HR	(Hm	Rd)	TB	R	RBI	RC	TBB	IBB	SO	HBP	SH	SF	SB	CS	SB%	GDP	Avg	OBP	Slg
2003 Portland*	AA	1	3	1	1	0	0	(-	-)	2	1	0	1	0	0	1	0	0	0	0	0	-	0	.333	.333	.667
2003 Lowell*	A-	1	3	2	0	0	0	(-	-)	2	2	0	1	1	0	0	0	0	0	1	0	1.00	0	.667	.750	.667
2003 Co Springs*	AAA	13	35	6	2	1	0	(-	-)	10	5	2	5	8	0	10	1	0	1	4	0	1.00	0	.171	.333	.286
1998 Detroit	AL	7	25	5	0	1	0	(0	0)	7	3	0	2	1	0	4	0	0	0	2	0	1.00	0	.200	.231	.280
1999 Detroit	AL	130	416	102	22	4	18	(12	6)	186	60	49	59	42	0	74	2	4	4	11	5	.69	7	.245	.315	.447
2000 Texas	AL	116	444	134	32	1	14	(11	3)	210	59	66	72	42	2	57	0	2	3	8	4	.67	12	.302	.360	.473
2001 Texas	AL	134	483	129	29	1	17	(11	6)	211	77	72	77	61	2	70	3	2	7	23	6	.79	10	.267	.348	.437
2002 Tex-Col		112	315	88	16	4	2	(1	1)	118	37	34	43	16	0	53	1	7	3	11	4	.73	5	.279	.313	.375
2003 Col-Bos		107	225	61	13	1	4	(2	2)	88	39	27	28	22	1	41	0	0	0	6	2	.75	8	.271	.336	.391
2002 Texas	AL	72	196	51	12	1	0	(0	0)	65	25	17	20	8	0	30	0	7	3	5	2	.71	3	.260	.285	.332
2002 Colorado	NL	40	119	37	4	3	2	(1	1)	53	12	17	23	8	0	23	1	0	0	6	2	.75	2	.311	.359	.445

Year Team	Lg	G	AB	H	2B	3B	HR	(Hm	Rd)	TB	R	RBI	RC	TBB	IBB	SO	HBP	SH	SF	SB	CS	SB%	GDP	Avg	OBP	Slg
2003 Colorado	NL	39	67	15	2	0	0	(0	0)	17	10	4	5	8	1	18	0	0	0	2	0	1.00	3	.224	.307	.254
2003 Boston	AL	68	158	46	11	1	4	(2	2)	71	29	23	23	14	0	23	0	0	0	4	4	.67	5	.291	.349	.449
6 ML YEARS		606	1908	519	112	12	55	(37	18)	820	275	248	281	184	5	299	6	15	17	61	21	.74	42	.272	.335	.430

Eric Karros

Bats: R **Throws:** R **Pos:** 1B-97; PH-26   **Ht:** 6'4" **Wt:** 226 **Born:** 11/4/67 **Age:** 36

						BATTING														BASERUNNING				AVERAGES		
Year Team	Lg	G	AB	H	2B	3B	HR	(Hm	Rd)	TB	R	RBI	RC	TBB	IBB	SO	HBP	SH	SF	SB	CS	SB%	GDP	Avg	OBP	Slg
1991 Los Angeles	NL	14	14	1	1	0	0	(0	0)	2	0	1	0	1	0	6	0	0	0	0	0	-	0	.071	.133	.143
1992 Los Angeles	NL	149	545	140	30	1	20	(6	14)	232	63	88	66	37	3	103	2	0	5	2	4	.33	15	.257	.304	.426
1993 Los Angeles	NL	158	619	153	27	2	23	(13	10)	253	74	80	68	34	1	82	2	0	1	0	1	.00	17	.247	.287	.409
1994 Los Angeles	NL	111	406	108	21	1	14	(5	9)	173	51	46	52	29	1	53	2	0	11	2	0	1.00	13	.266	.310	.426
1995 Los Angeles	NL	143	551	164	29	3	32	(19	13)	295	83	105	103	61	4	115	4	0	4	4	4	.50	14	.298	.369	.535
1996 Los Angeles	NL	154	608	158	29	1	34	(16	18)	291	84	111	86	53	2	121	1	0	8	8	0	1.00	27	.260	.316	.479
1997 Los Angeles	NL	162	628	167	28	0	31	(13	18)	288	86	104	95	61	2	116	2	0	9	15	7	.68	10	.266	.329	.459
1998 Los Angeles	NL	139	507	150	20	1	23	(9	14)	241	59	87	86	47	1	93	3	0	7	7	2	.78	7	.296	.355	.475
1999 Los Angeles	NL	153	578	176	40	0	34	(17	17)	318	74	112	107	53	0	119	2	0	6	8	5	.62	18	.304	.362	.550
2000 Los Angeles	NL	155	584	146	29	0	31	(16	15)	268	84	106	84	63	2	122	4	0	12	4	3	.57	18	.250	.321	.459
2001 Los Angeles	NL	121	438	103	22	0	15	(7	8)	170	42	63	49	41	2	101	3	0	3	3	1	.75	15	.235	.303	.388
2002 Los Angeles	NL	142	524	142	26	1	13	(9	4)	209	52	73	72	37	1	74	6	0	6	4	2	.67	11	.271	.323	.399
2003 Chicago	NL	114	336	96	16	1	12	(7	5)	150	37	40	43	28	1	46	0	0	1	1	1	.50	14	.286	.340	.446
13 ML YEARS		1715	6338	1704	318	11	282	(137	145)	2890	789	1016	911	545	20	1151	31	0	75	58	30	.66	179	.269	.326	.456

Steve Karsay

Pitches: R **Bats:** R **Pos:** RP   **Ht:** 6'3" **Wt:** 215 **Born:** 3/24/72 **Age:** 32

		HOW MUCH HE PITCHED						WHAT HE GAVE UP										THE RESULTS							
Year Team	Lg	G	GS	CG	GF	IP	BFP	H	R	ER	HR	SH	SF	HB	TBB	IBB	SO	WP	Bk	W	L	Pct	ShO	Sv-Op	Hld	ERC	ERA
1993 Oakland	AL	8	8	0	0	49.0	210	49	23	22	4	0	2	2	16	1	33	1	0	3	3	.500	0	0-0	0	3.78	4.04
1994 Oakland	AL	4	4	1	0	28.0	115	26	8	8	1	2	1	1	8	0	15	0	0	1	1	.500	0	0-0	0	3.01	2.57
1997 Oakland	AL	24	24	0	0	132.2	609	166	92	85	20	2	5	9	47	3	92	7	0	3	12	.200	0	0-0	0	5.97	5.77
1998 Cleveland	AL	11	1	0	4	24.1	111	31	16	16	3	1	2	2	6	1	13	2	0	0	2	.000	0	0-0	2	5.40	5.92
1999 Cleveland	AL	50	3	0	13	78.2	324	71	29	26	6	2	3	2	30	3	68	5	0	10	2	.833	0	1-3	9	3.45	2.97
2000 Cleveland	AL	72	0	0	46	76.2	329	79	33	32	5	2	3	2	25	4	66	0	0	5	9	.357	0	20-29	11	3.79	3.76
2001 Cle-Atl	AL	74	0	0	29	88.0	356	73	27	23	5	6	4	1	25	10	83	3	0	3	5	.375	0	8-12	12	2.36	2.35
2002 New York	AL	78	0	0	38	88.1	379	87	33	32	7	7	3	2	30	14	65	3	0	6	4	.600	0	12-16	14	3.42	3.26
2001 Cleveland	AL	31	0	0	0	43.1	166	29	6	6	1	3	1	0	8	2	44	2	0	0	1	.000	0	1-1	8	1.33	1.25
2001 Atlanta	NL	43	0	0	21	44.2	190	44	21	17	4	3	3	1	17	8	39	1	0	3	4	.429	0	7-11	4	3.68	3.43
8 ML YEARS		321	40	1	130	565.2	2433	582	261	244	51	22	22	22	187	36	435	21	0	31	38	.449	0	41-60	48	3.95	3.88

Matt Kata

Bats: B **Throws:** R **Pos:** 2B-52; 3B-23; SS-6; PH-4; PR-4   **Ht:** 6'1" **Wt:** 185 **Born:** 3/14/78 **Age:** 26

						BATTING														BASERUNNING				AVERAGES		
Year Team	Lg	G	AB	H	2B	3B	HR	(Hm	Rd)	TB	R	RBI	RC	TBB	IBB	SO	HBP	SH	SF	SB	CS	SB%	GDP	Avg	OBP	Slg
1999 South Bend	A	78	318	83	14	5	3	(-	-)	116	40	33	37	28	0	46	4	1	1	5	6	.45	5	.261	.328	.365
2000 South Bend	A	133	521	133	22	9	6	(-	-)	191	82	59	66	52	2	58	6	3	5	38	12	.76	10	.255	.327	.367
2001 Lancaster	A+	119	494	146	19	6	10	(-	-)	207	80	54	77	41	3	79	5	4	1	30	8	.79	4	.296	.355	.419
2001 El Paso	AA	4	16	7	2	0	0	(-	-)	9	4	4	4	2	0	2	0	0	0	0	1	.00	0	.438	.500	.563
2002 El Paso	AA	136	578	172	33	9	11	(-	-)	256	95	57	87	37	4	79	4	4	5	12	7	.63	6	.298	.341	.443
2003 Tucson	AAA	48	201	58	13	5	3	(-	-)	90	31	25	29	9	1	29	3	0	1	2	3	.40	1	.289	.327	.448
2003 Arizona	NL	78	288	74	16	5	7	(3	4)	121	42	29	40	25	0	53	1	5	3	3	2	.60	4	.257	.315	.420

Austin Kearns

Bats: R **Throws:** R **Pos:** RF-50; CF-40; PH-4; LF-1   **Ht:** 6'3" **Wt:** 220 **Born:** 5/20/80 **Age:** 24

						BATTING														BASERUNNING				AVERAGES		
Year Team	Lg	G	AB	H	2B	3B	HR	(Hm	Rd)	TB	R	RBI	RC	TBB	IBB	SO	HBP	SH	SF	SB	CS	SB%	GDP	Avg	OBP	Slg
1998 Billings	R+	30	108	34	9	0	1	(-	-)	46	17	14	21	23	0	22	1	0	2	1	1	.50	4	.315	.433	.426
1999 Rockford	A	124	426	110	36	5	13	(-	-)	195	72	48	68	50	3	120	9	0	3	21	8	.72	9	.258	.346	.458
2000 Dayton	A	136	484	148	37	2	27	(-	-)	270	110	104	111	90	5	93	7	0	9	18	5	.78	14	.306	.415	.558
2001 Chattanooga	AA	59	205	55	11	2	6	(-	-)	88	30	36	32	26	0	43	6	2	2	7	5	.58	4	.268	.364	.429
2001 Reds	R	6	17	3	2	0	0	(-	-)	5	2	4	1	2	0	7	0	0	3	0	0	-	0	.176	.227	.294
2002 Chattanooga	AA	12	41	11	2	0	5	(-	-)	28	10	13	12	9	0	9	3	0	0	1	0	1.00	0	.268	.434	.683
2002 Louisville	AAA	1	4	3	2	0	0	(-	-)	5	3	2	3	1	0	0	0	0	0	0	0	-	0	.750	.800	1.250
2003 Chattanooga	AA	3	5	1	0	0	0	(-	-)	1	2	1	1	2	0	2	1	0	0	0	0	-	0	.200	.500	.200
2002 Cincinnati	NL	107	372	117	24	3	13	(7	6)	186	66	56	69	54	3	81	6	0	3	6	3	.67	11	.315	.407	.500
2003 Cincinnati	NL	82	292	77	11	0	15	(8	7)	133	39	58	51	41	1	68	5	0	0	5	2	.71	7	.264	.364	.455
2 ML YEARS		189	664	194	35	3	28	(15	13)	319	105	114	120	95	4	149	11	0	3	11	5	.69	18	.292	.388	.480

Randy Keisler

Pitches: L **Bats:** L **Pos:** SP-2   **Ht:** 6'3" **Wt:** 190 **Born:** 2/24/76 **Age:** 28

		HOW MUCH HE PITCHED						WHAT HE GAVE UP										THE RESULTS							
Year Team	Lg	G	GS	CG	GF	IP	BFP	H	R	ER	HR	SH	SF	HB	TBB	IBB	SO	WP	Bk	W	L	Pct	ShO	Sv-Op	Hld	ERC	ERA
2003 Portland*	AAA	8	6	0	0	41.1	166	33	12	12	6	0	1	0	12	0	24	2	0	5	1	.833	0	0--	-	2.88	2.61
2003 New Orleans*	AAA	9	9	0	0	48.1	211	53	24	23	3	6	2	1	21	2	27	1	0	2	3	.400	0	0--	-	4.58	4.28
2003 Oklahoma*	AAA	5	2	0	0	12.2	60	21	13	12	2	1	0	0	5	0	9	0	0	0	2	.000	0	0--	-	9.03	8.53
2000 New York	AL	4	1	0	0	10.2	52	16	9	14	1	0	0	0	8	0	6	0	0	1	0	1.000	0	0-0	0	9.10	11.81
2001 New York	AL	12	10	0	0	50.2	236	52	35	35	12	0	0	0	34	0	36	0	0	1	2	.333	0	0-0	0	4.51	6.22
2003 San Diego	NL	2	2	0	0	6.0	33	7	9	8	3	0	1	1	7	0	5	0	1	0	1	.000	0	0-0	0	12.82	12.00
3 ML YEARS		16	13	0	0	67.1	321	75	9	57	16	0	1	1	49	0	47	0	1	2	3	.400	0	0-0	0	7.29	7.62

Dave Kelton

Bats: R **Throws:** R **Pos:** PH-5; PR-3; LF-2

Ht: 6'3" Wt: 205 Born: 12/17/79 Age: 24

Year Team	Lg	G	AB	H	2B	3B	HR	(Hm	Rd)	TB	R	RBI	RC	TBB	IBB	SO	HBP	SH	SF	SB	CS	SB%	GDP	Avg	OBP	Slg
1998 Cubs	R	50	181	48	7	5	6	(-	-)	83	39	29	32	23	0	58	2	0	1	16	3	.84	2	.265	.353	.459
1999 Lansing	A	124	509	137	17	4	13	(-	-)	201	75	68	64	39	1	121	2	0	3	22	9	.71	11	.269	.322	.395
2000 Daytona	A+	132	523	140	30	7	18	(-	-)	238	75	84	72	38	4	120	2	1	5	7	8	.47	9	.268	.317	.455
2001 W Tennessee	AA	58	224	70	9	4	12	(-	-)	123	33	45	45	24	0	55	1	0	2	1	3	.25	1	.313	.378	.549
2002 W Tennessee	AA	129	498	130	28	6	20	(-	-)	230	68	79	75	52	2	129	2	0	3	12	6	.67	10	.261	.332	.462
2003 Iowa	AAA	121	442	119	24	3	16	(-	-)	197	62	67	67	46	1	115	2	1	4	8	2	.80	7	.269	.338	.446
2003 Chicago	NL	10	12	2	1	0	0	(0	0)	3	1	1	1	0	0	5	0	0	0	0	0	-	0	.167	.167	.250

Jason Kendall

Bats: R **Throws:** R **Pos:** C-146; PH-4

Ht: 6'0" Wt: 195 Born: 6/26/74 Age: 30

Year Team	Lg	G	AB	H	2B	3B	HR	(Hm	Rd)	TB	R	RBI	RC	TBB	IBB	SO	HBP	SH	SF	SB	CS	SB%	GDP	Avg	OBP	Slg
1996 Pittsburgh	NL	130	414	124	23	5	3	(2	1)	166	54	42	63	35	11	30	15	3	4	5	2	.71	7	.300	.372	.401
1997 Pittsburgh	NL	144	486	143	36	4	8	(5	3)	211	71	49	86	49	2	53	31	1	5	18	6	.75	11	.294	.391	.434
1998 Pittsburgh	NL	149	535	175	36	3	12	(6	6)	253	95	75	110	51	3	51	31	2	8	26	5	.84	6	.327	.411	.473
1999 Pittsburgh	NL	78	280	93	20	3	8	(5	3)	143	61	41	63	38	3	32	12	0	4	22	3	.88	8	.332	.428	.511
2000 Pittsburgh	NL	152	579	185	33	6	14	(7	7)	272	112	58	112	79	3	79	15	1	4	22	12	.65	13	.320	.412	.470
2001 Pittsburgh	NL	157	606	161	22	2	10	(3	7)	217	84	53	68	44	4	48	20	0	2	13	14	.48	18	.266	.335	.358
2002 Pittsburgh	NL	145	545	154	25	3	3	(1	2)	194	59	44	63	49	1	29	9	0	2	15	8	.65	11	.283	.350	.356
2003 Pittsburgh	NL	150	587	191	29	3	6	(3	3)	244	84	58	94	49	3	40	25	1	3	8	7	.53	9	.325	.399	.416
8 ML YEARS		1105	4032	1226	224	29	64	(32	32)	1700	620	420	659	394	30	362	158	8	32	129	57	.69	83	.304	.385	.422

Adam Kennedy

Bats: L **Throws:** R **Pos:** 2B-140; PH-10; PR-2

Ht: 6'1" Wt: 192 Born: 1/10/76 Age: 28

Year Team	Lg	G	AB	H	2B	3B	HR	(Hm	Rd)	TB	R	RBI	RC	TBB	IBB	SO	HBP	SH	SF	SB	CS	SB%	GDP	Avg	OBP	Slg
2003 R Cucamnga*	A+	3	11	3	1	0	1	(-	-)	7	3	1	2	0	0	2	1	0	0	0	0	-	0	.273	.333	.636
1999 St Louis	NL	33	102	26	10	1	1	(1	0)	41	12	16	12	3	0	8	2	1	2	0	1	.00	1	.255	.284	.402
2000 Anaheim	AL	156	598	159	33	11	9	(7	2)	241	82	72	72	28	5	73	3	8	4	22	8	.73	10	.266	.300	.403
2001 Anaheim	AL	137	478	129	25	3	6	(4	2)	178	44	40	57	27	3	71	11	7	9	12	7	.63	7	.270	.318	.372
2002 Anaheim	AL	144	474	148	32	6	7	(6	1)	213	65	52	70	19	1	80	7	5	4	17	4	.81	5	.312	.345	.449
2003 Anaheim	AL	143	449	121	17	1	13	(8	5)	179	71	49	61	45	4	73	9	2	5	22	9	.71	7	.269	.344	.399
5 ML YEARS		613	2101	583	117	22	36	(26	10)	852	278	229	272	122	13	305	32	23	24	73	29	.72	30	.277	.323	.406

Joe Kennedy

Pitches: L **Bats:** R **Pos:** SP-22; RP-10

Ht: 6'4" Wt: 237 Born: 5/24/79 Age: 25

Year Team	Lg	G	GS	CG	GF	IP	BFP	H	R	ER	HR	SH	SF	HB	TBB	IBB	SO	WP	Bk	W	L	Pct	ShO	Sv-Op	Hld	ERC	ERA
2003 Orlando*	AA	1	1	0	0	3.1	17	6	3	3	0	0	1	0	1	0	3	0	0	0	0	-	0	0--	-	7.51	8.10
2003 Durham*	AAA	1	1	0	0	6.1	24	6	1	1	0	0	0	0	0	0	4	0	0	1	0	1.000	0	0--	-	1.82	1.42
2001 Tampa Bay	AL	20	20	0	0	117.2	498	122	63	58	16	2	5	3	34	0	78	5	1	7	8	.467	0	0-0	0	4.23	4.44
2002 Tampa Bay	AL	30	30	5	0	196.2	840	204	114	99	23	2	9	16	55	0	109	4	0	8	11	.421	1	0-0	0	4.29	4.53
2003 Tampa Bay	AL	32	22	1	7	133.2	619	167	101	91	19	1	8	11	47	1	77	3	1	3	12	.200	1	1-2	1	5.92	6.13
3 ML YEARS		82	72	6	7	448.0	1957	493	278	248	58	5	22	30	136	1	264	12	2	18	31	.367	2	1-2	1	4.75	4.98

Jeff Kent

Bats: R **Throws:** R **Pos:** 2B-128; PH-3

Ht: 6'1" Wt: 220 Born: 3/7/68 Age: 36

Year Team	Lg	G	AB	H	2B	3B	HR	(Hm	Rd)	TB	R	RBI	RC	TBB	IBB	SO	HBP	SH	SF	SB	CS	SB%	GDP	Avg	OBP	Slg
2003 Round Rock*	AA	3	10	3	0	0	1	(-	-)	6	1	6	1	1	0	1	0	0	1	0	1	.00	1	.300	.333	.600
1992 Tor-NYM		102	305	73	21	2	11	(4	7)	131	52	50	40	27	0	76	7	0	4	2	3	.40	5	.239	.312	.430
1993 New York	NL	140	496	134	24	0	21	(9	12)	221	65	80	68	30	2	88	8	6	4	4	4	.50	11	.270	.320	.446
1994 New York	NL	107	415	121	24	5	14	(10	4)	197	53	68	64	23	3	84	10	1	3	1	4	.20	7	.292	.341	.475
1995 New York	NL	125	472	131	22	3	20	(11	9)	219	65	65	69	29	3	89	8	1	4	3	3	.50	9	.278	.327	.464
1996 NYM-Cle		128	437	124	27	1	12	(4	8)	189	61	55	61	31	1	78	2	1	6	6	4	.60	8	.284	.330	.432
1997 San Francisco	NL	155	580	145	38	2	29	(13	16)	274	90	121	86	48	6	133	13	0	10	11	3	.79	14	.250	.316	.472
1998 San Francisco	NL	137	526	156	37	3	31	(17	14)	292	94	128	100	48	4	110	9	1	10	9	4	.69	16	.297	.359	.555
1999 San Francisco	NL	138	511	148	40	2	23	(11	12)	261	86	101	93	61	3	112	5	0	8	13	6	.68	12	.290	.366	.511
2000 San Francisco	NL	159	587	196	41	7	33	(14	19)	350	114	125	138	90	6	107	9	0	9	12	9	.57	17	.334	.424	.596
2001 San Francisco	NL	159	607	181	49	6	22	(8	14)	308	84	106	112	65	4	96	11	0	13	7	6	.54	11	.298	.369	.507
2002 San Francisco	NL	152	623	195	42	2	37	(11	26)	352	102	108	106	52	3	101	4	0	3	5	1	.83	20	.313	.368	.565
2003 Houston	NL	130	505	150	39	1	22	(9	13)	257	77	93	93	39	2	85	5	0	3	6	2	.75	13	.297	.351	.509
1992 Toronto	AL	65	192	46	13	1	8	(2	6)	85	36	35	28	20	0	47	6	0	4	2	1	.67	3	.240	.324	.443
1992 New York	NL	37	113	27	8	1	3	(2	1)	46	16	15	12	7	0	29	1	0	0	0	2	.00	2	.239	.289	.407
1996 New York	NL	89	335	97	20	1	9	(2	7)	146	45	39	46	21	1	56	1	1	3	4	3	.57	7	.290	.331	.436
1996 Cleveland	AL	39	102	27	7	0	3	(2	1)	43	16	16	15	10	0	22	1	0	3	2	1	.67	1	.265	.328	.422
12 ML YEARS		1632	6064	1754	404	34	275	(121	154)	3051	943	1100	1030	543	37	1159	91	10	77	79	49	.62	143	.289	.352	.503

Jason Kershner

Pitches: L **Bats:** L **Pos:** RP-40

Ht: 6'2" Wt: 165 Born: 12/19/76 Age: 27

Year Team	Lg	G	GS	CG	GF	IP	BFP	H	R	ER	HR	SH	SF	HB	TBB	IBB	SO	WP	Bk	W	L	Pct	ShO	Sv-Op	Hld	ERC	ERA
1995 Martinsville	R+	13	13	0	0	63.0	278	67	42	36	10	0	2	5	29	0	64	4	2	0	0	-	0	0--	-	5.58	5.14
1996 Piedmont	A	28	28	2	0	168.0	703	154	81	70	12	5	4	3	59	0	156	12	1	11	9	.550	1	0--	-	3.33	3.75
1997 Clearwater	A+	22	16	0	3	99.1	417	113	49	43	9	2	4	4	21	0	51	2	0	5	10	.333	0	1--	-	4.30	3.90

120

Year Team	Lg	G	GS	CG	GF	IP	BFP	H	R	ER	HR	SH	SF	HB	TBB	IBB	SO	WP	Bk	W	L	Pct	ShO	Sv-Op	Hld	ERC	ERA
1998 Clearwater	A+	41	8	0	11	94.1	405	108	57	42	8	1	3	6	25	0	65	8	0	3	3	.500	0	3--	-	4.60	4.01
1999 Reading	AA	57	2	0	30	92.2	412	99	67	59	14	3	6	5	40	3	86	5	0	4	4	.500	0	8--	-	5.15	5.73
2000 Reading	AA	27	19	0	3	119.0	501	125	49	48	15	6	1	5	25	0	80	3	0	9	2	.818	0	1--	-	3.96	3.63
2000 Clearwater	A+	2	2	0	0	14.0	52	7	1	1	1	0	0	0	5	0	15	0	0	1	0	1.000	0	0--	-	1.45	0.64
2001 Reading	AA	26	19	0	2	123.2	525	147	75	66	18	5	5	3	26	1	70	4	0	5	9	.357	0	0--	-	4.90	4.80
2001 Scrtn/WlksBr	AAA	6	1	0	1	15.0	63	12	8	6	3	0	2	0	3	0	7	0	0	1	1	.500	0	0--	-	2.64	3.60
2002 Portland	AAA	31	12	0	3	86.0	339	65	30	29	8	3	0	1	26	0	83	2	0	7	2	.778	0	0--	-	2.49	3.03
2003 Syracuse	AAA	24	0	0	4	45.2	181	42	15	12	1	3	4	0	9	1	30	2	0	6	1	.857	0	0--	-	2.43	2.36
2002 SD-Tor	AL	25	0	0	4	24.0	107	20	16	13	3	0	0	2	14	1	18	3	0	0	1	.000	0	1-2	1	4.24	4.88
2003 Toronto	AL	40	0	0	8	54.0	220	43	21	19	5	2	3	2	15	2	32	2	0	3	3	.500	0	0-1	7	2.56	3.17
2002 San Diego	NL	15	0	0	2	18.2	81	15	14	12	2	0	0	2	11	0	11	0	0	1	0	.000	0	0-0	0	4.00	5.79
2002 Toronto	AL	10	0	0	2	5.1	26	5	2	1	1	0	0	0	4	1	7	3	0	0	0	-	0	1-2	1	5.11	1.69
2 ML YEARS		65	0	0	12	78.0	327	63	37	32	8	2	3	4	29	3	50	5	0	3	4	.429	0	1-3	8	3.05	3.69

Masao Kida

Pitches: R Bats: R Pos: SP-2; RP-1 Ht: 6'3" Wt: 210 Born: 9/12/68 Age: 35

Year Team	Lg	G	GS	CG	GF	IP	BFP	H	R	ER	HR	SH	SF	HB	TBB	IBB	SO	WP	Bk	W	L	Pct	ShO	Sv-Op	Hld	ERC	ERA
2003 Las Vegas*	AAA	21	12	0	2	84.1	365	89	53	47	9	2	5	6	23	1	57	6	1	2	4	.333	0	1--	-	4.17	5.02
1999 Detroit	AL	49	0	0	0	64.2	292	73	0	45	6	0	0	0	30	0	50	0	0	1	0	1.000	0	1-0	0	4.99	6.26
2000 Detroit	AL	2	0	0	0	2.2	13	5	0	3	1	0	0	0	0	0	0	0	0	0	0	-	0	0-0	0	9.86	10.13
2003 Los Angeles	NL	3	2	0	1	12.0	53	15	5	4	0	0	0	0	3	0	8	3	0	0	1	.000	0	0-0	0	4.14	3.00
3 ML YEARS		54	2	0	1	79.1	358	93	5	52	7	0	0	0	33	0	58	3	0	1	1	.500	0	1-0	0	5.01	5.90

Bobby Kielty

Bats: B Throws: R Pos: RF-89; DH-30; PH-17; LF-4; 1B-3; CF-3; PR-1 Ht: 6'1" Wt: 215 Born: 8/5/76 Age: 27

Year Team	Lg	G	AB	H	2B	3B	HR	(Hm	Rd)	TB	R	RBI	RC	TBB	IBB	SO	HBP	SH	SF	SB	CS	SB%	GDP	Avg	OBP	Slg
2001 Minnesota	AL	37	104	26	8	0	2	(1	1)	40	8	14	13	8	2	25	1	0	5	3	0	1.00	2	.250	.297	.385
2002 Minnesota	AL	112	289	84	14	3	12	(8	4)	140	49	46	58	52	4	66	5	0	2	4	1	.80	4	.291	.405	.484
2003 Min-Tor	AL	137	427	104	26	1	13	(6	7)	171	71	57	68	71	6	92	7	0	4	8	3	.73	11	.244	.358	.400
2003 Minnesota	AL	75	238	60	13	0	9	(4	5)	100	40	32	41	42	2	56	3	0	1	6	2	.75	5	.252	.370	.420
2003 Toronto	AL	62	189	44	13	1	4	(2	2)	71	31	25	27	29	4	36	4	0	3	2	1	.67	6	.233	.342	.376
3 ML YEARS		286	820	214	48	4	27	(15	12)	351	128	117	139	131	12	183	13	0	11	15	4	.79	17	.261	.367	.428

Brooks Kieschnick

Bats: L Throws: R Pos: RP-42; PH-24; DH-4; LF-3 Ht: 6'4" Wt: 230 Born: 6/6/72 Age: 32

Year Team	Lg	G	AB	H	2B	3B	HR	(Hm	Rd)	TB	R	RBI	RC	TBB	IBB	SO	HBP	SH	SF	SB	CS	SB%	GDP	Avg	OBP	Slg
2003 Indianapolis*	AAA	11	10	0	0	0	0	(-	-)	0	0	0	0	1	0	4	0	0	0	0	0	-	0	.000	.091	.000
1996 Chicago	NL	25	29	10	2	0	1	(0	1)	15	6	6	6	3	0	8	0	0	0	0	0	-	0	.345	.406	.517
1997 Chicago	NL	39	90	18	2	0	4	(3	1)	32	9	12	9	12	0	21	0	0	0	1	0	1.00	2	.200	.294	.356
2000 Cincinnati	NL	14	12	0	0	0	0	(0	0)	0	0	0	0	1	0	5	0	0	0	0	0	-	0	.000	.077	.000
2001 Colorado	NL	35	42	10	2	1	3	(1	2)	23	5	9	6	3	0	13	0	0	1	0	0	-	1	.238	.289	.548
2003 Milwaukee	NL	70	70	21	1	0	7	(2	5)	43	12	12	10	6	0	13	0	0	0	0	0	-	2	.300	.355	.614
5 ML YEARS		183	243	59	7	1	15	(6	9)	113	32	39	31	25	0	60	0	0	0	1	0	1.00	5	.243	.313	.465

Year Team	Lg	G	GS	CG	GF	IP	BFP	H	R	ER	HR	SH	SF	HB	TBB	IBB	SO	WP	Bk	W	L	Pct	ShO	Sv-Op	Hld	ERC	ERA
2003 Indianapolis*	AAA	8	0	0	4	13.2	68	17	15	13	3	0	1	1	10	2	14	0	0	1	0	1.000	0	0--	-	7.94	8.56
2003 Milwaukee	NL	42	0	0	15	53.0	242	66	32	31	5	2	0	6	13	4	39	2	0	1	1	.500	0	0-0	2	5.07	5.26

Byung-Hyun Kim

Pitches: R Bats: R Pos: RP-44; SP-12 Ht: 5'11" Wt: 177 Born: 1/19/79 Age: 25

Year Team	Lg	G	GS	CG	GF	IP	BFP	H	R	ER	HR	SH	SF	HB	TBB	IBB	SO	WP	Bk	W	L	Pct	ShO	Sv-Op	Hld	ERC	ERA
2003 Tucson*	AAA	3	3	0	0	17.2	69	17	5	5	2	1	1	3	1	0	8	0	0	1	1	.500	0	0--	-	3.49	2.55
1999 Arizona	NL	25	0	0	10	27.1	121	20	15	14	2	1	0	5	20	2	31	4	1	1	2	.333	0	1-4	5	4.35	4.61
2000 Arizona	NL	61	1	0	30	70.2	320	52	39	35	9	2	3	9	46	5	111	3	2	6	6	.500	0	14-20	5	4.04	4.46
2001 Arizona	NL	78	0	0	44	98.0	392	58	32	32	10	5	0	8	44	3	113	5	1	5	6	.455	0	19-23	11	2.45	2.94
2002 Arizona	NL	72	0	0	66	84.0	343	64	20	19	5	1	2	6	26	2	92	2	0	8	3	.727	0	36-42	6	2.45	2.04
2003 Ari-Bos		56	12	0	35	122.1	517	104	55	45	12	6	2	12	33	3	102	1	0	9	10	.474	0	16-19	1	3.02	3.31
2003 Arizona	NL	7	7	0	0	43.0	181	34	17	17	6	3	0	4	15	0	33	0	0	1	5	.167	0	0-0	0	3.32	3.56
2003 Boston	AL	49	5	0	35	79.1	336	70	38	28	6	3	2	8	18	3	69	1	0	8	5	.615	0	16-19	1	2.87	3.18
5 ML YEARS		292	13	0	185	402.1	1693	298	161	145	38	15	7	40	169	15	449	15	4	29	27	.518	0	86-108	20	3.02	3.24

Sun-Woo Kim

Pitches: R Bats: R Pos: SP-3; RP-1 Ht: 6'2" Wt: 188 Born: 9/4/77 Age: 26

Year Team	Lg	G	GS	CG	GF	IP	BFP	H	R	ER	HR	SH	SF	HB	TBB	IBB	SO	WP	Bk	W	L	Pct	ShO	Sv-Op	Hld	ERC	ERA
2003 Edmonton*	AAA	22	22	3	0	132.1	587	147	83	74	18	5	2	3	53	1	83	5	0	10	8	.556	2	0--	-	5.06	5.03
2001 Boston	AL	20	2	0	7	41.2	201	54	27	27	1	3	0	4	21	5	27	5	0	0	2	.000	0	0-0	1	5.72	5.83
2002 Bos-Mon		19	5	0	2	49.1	208	52	26	26	5	0	2	2	14	2	29	2	0	3	0	1.000	0	0-0	0	4.10	4.74
2003 Montreal	NL	4	3	0	1	14.0	72	24	13	13	6	0	1	4	8	0	5	0	0	0	1	.000	0	0-0	0	14.93	8.36

Year Team	Lg	G	GS	CG	GF	IP	BFP	H	R	ER	HR	SH	SF	HB	TBB	IBB	SO	WP	Bk	W	L	Pct	ShO	Sv-Op	Hld	ERC	ERA
2002 Boston	AL	15	2	0	7	29.0	128	34	24	24	5	0	2	1	7	0	18	2	0	2	0	1.000	0	0-0	2	5.01	7.45
2002 Montreal	NL	4	3	0	0	20.1	80	18	2	2	0	0	0	1	7	2	11	0	0	1	0	1.000	0	0-0	0	2.82	0.89
3 ML YEARS		43	10	0	15	105.0	481	130	66	66	12	3	3	10	43	7	61	7	0	3	3	.500	0	0-0	3	5.97	5.66

Ray King

Pitches: L **Bats:** L **Pos:** RP-80 **Ht:** 6'1" **Wt:** 242 **Born:** 1/15/74 **Age:** 30

Year Team	Lg	G	GS	CG	GF	IP	BFP	H	R	ER	HR	SH	SF	HB	TBB	IBB	SO	WP	Bk	W	L	Pct	ShO	Sv-Op	Hld	ERC	ERA
1999 Chicago	NL	10	0	0	0	10.2	50	11	8	7	2	1	0	1	10	0	5	1	0	0	0	—	0	0-0	2	8.10	5.91
2000 Milwaukee	NL	36	0	0	8	28.2	111	18	7	4	1	0	1	0	10	1	19	1	0	3	2	.600	0	0-1	5	1.64	1.26
2001 Milwaukee	NL	82	0	0	19	55.0	234	49	22	22	5	3	2	1	25	7	49	2	0	0	4	.000	0	1-4	18	3.51	3.60
2002 Milwaukee	NL	76	0	0	15	65.0	273	61	24	22	5	5	2	3	24	6	50	0	1	3	2	.600	0	0-1	15	3.55	3.05
2003 Atlanta	NL	80	0	0	9	59.0	247	46	30	23	3	1	2	1	27	2	43	4	0	3	4	.429	0	0-1	18	2.79	3.51
5 ML YEARS		284	0	0	51	218.1	915	185	91	78	16	10	7	6	96	16	166	8	1	9	12	.429	0	1-7	58	3.24	3.22

Gene Kingsale

Bats: B **Throws:** R **Pos:** CF-23; LF-8; PH-4; DH-3; PR-3 **Ht:** 6'3" **Wt:** 190 **Born:** 8/20/76 **Age:** 27

Year Team	Lg	G	AB	H	2B	3B	HR	(Hm	Rd)	TB	R	RBI	RC	TBB	IBB	SO	HBP	SH	SF	SB	CS	SB%	GDP	Avg	OBP	Slg
2003 Toledo*	AAA	46	160	39	6	5	0	(-	-)	55	19	12	17	11	0	24	2	3	2	9	5	.64	2	.244	.297	.344
1996 Baltimore	AL	3	0	0	0	0	0	(0	0)	0	0	0	0	0	0	0	0	0	0	0	0	—	0	-	-	-
1998 Baltimore	AL	11	2	0	0	0	0	(0	0)	0	1	0	0	0	0	1	0	0	0	0	0	-	0	.000	.000	.000
1999 Baltimore	AL	28	85	21	2	0	0	(0	0)	23	9	7	6	5	0	13	2	2	1	1	3	.25	3	.247	.301	.271
2000 Baltimore	AL	26	88	21	2	1	0	(0	0)	25	13	9	4	2	0	14	0	0	1	1	2	.33	4	.239	.253	.284
2001 Bal-Sea	AL	13	19	5	0	0	0	(0	0)	5	4	1	3	2	0	4	1	0	0	3	1	.75	1	.263	.364	.263
2002 Sea-SD		91	219	62	10	3	2	(0	2)	84	27	28	36	20	0	47	3	3	1	9	2	.82	6	.283	.350	.384
2003 Detroit	AL	39	120	25	3	1	1	(1	0)	33	11	8	11	10	0	17	0	8	2	1	3	.25	2	.208	.265	.275
2001 Baltimore	AL	3	4	0	0	0	0	(0	0)	0	0	0	0	0	0	2	0	0	0	1	1	.50	0	.000	.000	.000
2001 Seattle	AL	10	15	5	0	0	0	(0	0)	5	4	1	3	2	0	2	1	0	0	2	0	1.00	1	.333	.444	.333
2002 Seattle	AL	2	3	2	0	0	0	(0	0)	2	0	0	1	0	0	0	0	0	0	0	0	-	1	.667	.667	.667
2002 San Diego	NL	89	216	60	10	3	2	(0	2)	82	27	28	35	20	0	47	3	3	1	9	2	.82	5	.278	.346	.380
7 ML YEARS		211	533	134	17	5	3	(1	2)	170	65	53	60	39	0	96	6	13	5	15	11	.58	16	.251	.307	.319

Mike Kinkade

Bats: R **Throws:** R **Pos:** PH-41; LF-34; 1B-13; 3B-2; RF-2; DH-1 **Ht:** 6'1" **Wt:** 210 **Born:** 5/6/73 **Age:** 31

Year Team	Lg	G	AB	H	2B	3B	HR	(Hm	Rd)	TB	R	RBI	RC	TBB	IBB	SO	HBP	SH	SF	SB	CS	SB%	GDP	Avg	OBP	Slg
1998 New York	NL	3	2	0	0	0	0	(0	0)	0	2	0	0	0	0	0	0	0	0	0	0	-	0	.000	.000	.000
1999 New York	NL	28	46	9	2	1	2	(1	1)	19	3	6	5	3	0	9	2	0	0	1	0	1.00	1	.196	.275	.413
2000 NYM-Bal		5	9	3	1	0	0	(0	0)	4	0	1	2	0	0	1	1	0	0	0	0	-	0	.333	.400	.444
2001 Baltimore	AL	61	160	44	5	0	4	(2	2)	61	19	16	19	14	0	31	3	0	0	2	1	.67	8	.275	.345	.381
2002 Los Angeles	NL	37	50	19	5	0	2	(1	1)	30	7	11	12	4	0	10	6	0	0	1	0	1.00	0	.380	.483	.600
2003 Los Angeles	NL	88	162	35	7	0	5	(2	3)	57	25	14	18	13	2	38	16	0	0	1	3	.25	8	.216	.335	.352
2000 New York	NL	2	2	0	0	0	0	(0	0)	0	0	0	0	0	0	1	0	0	0	0	0	-	0	.000	.000	.000
2000 Baltimore	AL	3	7	3	1	0	0	(0	0)	4	0	1	2	0	0	1	0	0	0	0	0	-	0	.429	.500	.571
6 ML YEARS		222	429	110	20	1	13	(6	7)	171	56	48	56	34	2	89	28	0	0	5	4	.56	19	.256	.350	.399

Matt Kinney

Pitches: R **Bats:** R **Pos:** SP-31; RP-2 **Ht:** 6'5" **Wt:** 220 **Born:** 12/16/76 **Age:** 27

Year Team	Lg	G	GS	CG	GF	IP	BFP	H	R	ER	HR	SH	SF	HB	TBB	IBB	SO	WP	Bk	W	L	Pct	ShO	Sv-Op	Hld	ERC	ERA
2000 Minnesota	AL	8	8	0	0	42.1	186	41	26	24	7	0	4	0	25	1	24	4	0	2	2	.500	0	0-0	0	5.20	5.10
2002 Minnesota	AL	14	12	0	1	66.0	305	78	39	34	13	3	4	1	33	0	45	5	0	2	7	.222	0	0-0	0	6.35	4.64
2003 Milwaukee	NL	33	31	1	1	190.2	847	201	121	110	27	10	11	6	80	4	152	10	2	10	13	.435	0	0-0	0	4.82	5.19
3 ML YEARS		55	51	1	2	299.0	1338	320	186	168	47	13	19	7	138	5	221	19	2	14	22	.389	0	0-0	0	5.20	5.06

Danny Klassen

Bats: R **Throws:** R **Pos:** 3B-13; 2B-4; PH-4; SS-3; PR-1 **Ht:** 6'0" **Wt:** 190 **Born:** 9/22/75 **Age:** 28

Year Team	Lg	G	AB	H	2B	3B	HR	(Hm	Rd)	TB	R	RBI	RC	TBB	IBB	SO	HBP	SH	SF	SB	CS	SB%	GDP	Avg	OBP	Slg
2003 Toledo*	AAA	112	407	100	19	4	11	(-	-)	160	63	48	49	28	1	110	7	3	4	12	5	.71	5	.246	.303	.393
1998 Arizona	NL	29	108	21	2	1	3	(3	0)	34	12	8	7	9	0	33	1	0	0	1	1	.50	5	.194	.263	.315
1999 Arizona	NL	1	1	1	0	0	0	(0	0)	1	0	0	1	0	0	0	0	0	0	0	0	-	0	1.000	1.000	1.000
2000 Arizona	NL	29	76	18	3	0	2	(2	0)	27	13	8	9	8	0	24	1	2	0	1	1	.50	0	.237	.318	.355
2002 Arizona	NL	4	3	1	0	0	0	(0	0)	1	0	0	0	0	0	1	0	0	0	0	0	-	0	.333	.333	.333
2003 Detroit	AL	22	73	18	3	1	1	(0	1)	26	9	7	9	4	0	26	0	1	0	0	1	.00	1	.247	.286	.356
5 ML YEARS		85	261	59	8	2	6	(5	1)	89	34	23	26	21	0	84	2	3	0	2	3	.40	6	.226	.289	.341

Ryan Klesko

Bats: L **Throws:** L **Pos:** 1B-111; PH-17; DH-1 **Ht:** 6'3" **Wt:** 220 **Born:** 6/12/71 **Age:** 33

Year Team	Lg	G	AB	H	2B	3B	HR	(Hm	Rd)	TB	R	RBI	RC	TBB	IBB	SO	HBP	SH	SF	SB	CS	SB%	GDP	Avg	OBP	Slg
1992 Atlanta	NL	13	14	0	0	0	0	(0	0)	0	0	1	0	0	0	5	1	0	0	0	0	-	0	.000	.067	.000
1993 Atlanta	NL	22	17	6	1	0	2	(2	0)	13	3	5	5	3	1	4	0	0	0	0	0	-	0	.353	.450	.765
1994 Atlanta	NL	92	245	68	13	3	17	(7	10)	138	42	47	45	26	3	48	1	0	4	1	0	1.00	8	.278	.344	.563

						BATTING															BASERUNNING				AVERAGES		
Year Team	Lg	G	AB	H	2B	3B	HR	(Hm	Rd)	TB	R	RBI	RC	TBB	IBB	SO	HBP	SH	SF		SB	CS	SB%	GDP	Avg	OBP	Slg
1995 Atlanta	NL	107	329	102	25	2	23	(15	8)	200	48	70	73	47	10	72	2	0	3		5	4	.56	8	.310	.396	.608
1996 Atlanta	NL	153	528	149	21	4	34	(20	14)	280	90	93	99	68	10	129	2	0	4		6	3	.67	10	.282	.364	.530
1997 Atlanta	NL	143	467	122	23	6	24	(10	14)	229	67	84	73	48	5	130	4	1	2		4	4	.50	12	.261	.334	.490
1998 Atlanta	NL	129	427	117	29	1	18	(8	10)	202	69	70	72	56	5	66	3	0	4		5	3	.63	9	.274	.359	.473
1999 Atlanta	NL	133	404	120	28	2	21	(12	9)	215	55	80	80	53	8	69	2	0	7		5	2	.71	6	.297	.376	.532
2000 San Diego	NL	145	494	140	33	2	26	(9	17)	255	88	92	101	91	9	81	1	0	4		23	7	.77	10	.283	.393	.516
2001 San Diego	NL	146	538	154	34	6	30	(15	15)	290	105	113	111	88	7	89	3	0	9		23	4	.85	16	.286	.384	.539
2002 San Diego	NL	146	540	162	39	1	29	(11	18)	290	90	95	114	76	11	86	4	1	4		6	2	.75	7	.300	.388	.537
2003 San Diego	NL	121	397	100	18	0	21	(8	13)	181	47	67	60	65	5	83	3	0	9		2	5	.29	11	.252	.354	.456
12 ML YEARS		1350	4400	1240	264	27	245	(117	128)	2293	704	817	833	621	74	862	26	2	50		80	34	.70	97	.282	.370	.521

Steve Kline

Pitches: L **Bats:** B **Pos:** RP-78   **Ht:** 6'1" **Wt:** 215 **Born:** 8/22/72 **Age:** 31

		HOW MUCH HE PITCHED						WHAT HE GAVE UP											THE RESULTS						
Year Team	Lg	G	GS	CG	GF	IP	BFP	H	R	ER	HR	SH	SF	HB	TBB	IBB	SO	WP	Bk	W	L	Pct	ShO	Sv-Op	Hld	ERC	ERA
1997 Cle-Mon		46	1	0	7	52.2	248	73	37	35	10	4	2	3	23	4	37	4	1	4	4	.500	0	0-3	5	7.39	5.98
1998 Montreal	NL	78	0	0	18	71.2	319	62	25	22	4	1	2	3	41	7	76	5	0	3	6	.333	0	1-2	18	3.60	2.76
1999 Montreal	NL	82	0	0	18	69.2	297	56	32	29	8	3	1	3	33	6	69	2	0	7	4	.636	0	0-2	16	3.64	3.75
2000 Montreal	NL	83	0	0	42	82.1	349	88	36	32	8	2	1	3	27	2	64	4	0	1	5	.167	0	14-18	12	4.37	3.50
2001 St Louis	NL	89	0	0	26	75.0	303	53	16	15	3	4	5	4	29	7	54	1	0	3	3	.500	0	9-10	17	2.20	1.80
2002 St Louis	NL	66	0	0	17	58.1	241	54	23	22	3	2	2	1	21	2	41	1	0	2	1	.667	0	6-8	21	3.28	3.39
2003 St Louis	NL	78	0	0	22	63.2	275	56	29	27	5	3	2	3	30	5	31	2	0	5	5	.500	0	3-7	18	3.58	3.82
1997 Cleveland	AL	20	1	0	0	26.1	130	42	19	17	6	1	0	1	13	1	17	3	1	3	1	.750	0	0-2	4	9.58	5.81
1997 Montreal	NL	26	0	0	7	26.1	118	31	18	18	4	3	2	1	10	3	20	1	0	1	3	.250	0	0-1	1	5.39	6.15
7 ML YEARS		522	1	0	150	473.1	2032	442	198	182	41	19	15	19	204	33	372	19	1	25	28	.472	0	33-50	107	3.80	3.46

Eric Knott

Pitches: L **Bats:** L **Pos:** RP-12; SP-1   **Ht:** 6'1" **Wt:** 188 **Born:** 9/23/74 **Age:** 29

		HOW MUCH HE PITCHED						WHAT HE GAVE UP											THE RESULTS						
Year Team	Lg	G	GS	CG	GF	IP	BFP	H	R	ER	HR	SH	SF	HB	TBB	IBB	SO	WP	Bk	W	L	Pct	ShO	Sv-Op	Hld	ERC	ERA
1997 Lethbridge	R+	21	3	0	7	47.0	195	41	21	15	4	2	1	0	9	1	62	2	0	0	4	.000	0	3--	-	2.39	2.87
1998 High Desert	A+	28	22	1	3	143.1	616	175	84	72	16	3	4	1	28	1	96	3	3	12	7	.632	0	0--	-	4.64	4.52
1999 El Paso	AA	27	27	3	0	161.1	711	198	95	82	11	4	5	5	42	0	83	3	2	7	11	.389	0	0--	-	4.71	4.57
2000 Tucson	AAA	11	7	0	1	39.2	180	59	30	28	6	2	3	1	8	0	21	0	0	3	2	.600	0	0--	-	6.78	6.35
2001 El Paso	AA	17	0	0	2	26.0	116	29	13	9	2	2	0	1	8	2	20	1	0	4	1	.800	0	0--	-	4.11	3.12
2001 Tucson	AAA	25	8	0	9	73.1	303	82	34	31	6	4	3	0	8	1	43	1	1	6	2	.750	0	1--	-	3.46	3.80
2002 Tucson	AAA	31	23	1	2	150.0	650	188	91	81	12	6	6	1	23	1	96	2	0	8	10	.444	1	1--	-	4.38	4.86
2003 Edmonton	AAA	24	10	1	6	77.0	341	102	40	37	6	2	6	1	13	4	38	2	2	6	5	.545	1	0--	-	4.78	4.32
2001 Arizona	NL	3	1	0	0	4.2	25	8	0	1	0	0	0	0	0	0	4	0	0	0	1	.000	0	0-0	0	4.95	1.93
2003 Montreal	NL	13	1	0	1	19.1	86	23	12	11	2	1	1	0	6	0	17	0	0	1	2	.333	0	0-0	0	4.77	5.12
2 ML YEARS		16	2	0	1	24.0	111	31	12	12	2	1	1	0	6	0	21	0	0	1	3	.250	0	0-0	0	4.80	4.50

Gary Knotts

Pitches: R **Bats:** R **Pos:** SP-18; RP-2   **Ht:** 6'4" **Wt:** 200 **Born:** 2/12/77 **Age:** 27

		HOW MUCH HE PITCHED						WHAT HE GAVE UP											THE RESULTS						
Year Team	Lg	G	GS	CG	GF	IP	BFP	H	R	ER	HR	SH	SF	HB	TBB	IBB	SO	WP	Bk	W	L	Pct	ShO	Sv-Op	Hld	ERC	ERA
2003 Toledo*	AAA	13	13	0	0	79.0	361	98	54	45	15	4	1	6	28	3	63	5	0	4	6	.400	0	0--	-	6.25	5.13
2001 Florida	NL	2	1	0	0	6.0	28	7	4	4	1	0	0	2	1	0	9	0	0	0	1	.000	0	0-0	0	5.84	6.00
2002 Florida	NL	28	0	0	7	30.2	127	21	15	15	6	0	1	1	16	0	21	1	0	3	1	.750	0	0-1	5	3.62	4.40
2003 Detroit	AL	20	18	0	0	95.1	442	111	70	64	14	1	4	4	47	0	51	4	0	3	8	.273	0	0-0	0	5.90	6.04
3 ML YEARS		50	19	0	7	132.0	597	139	89	83	21	1	5	7	64	0	81	5	0	6	10	.375	0	0-1	5	5.35	5.66

Billy Koch

Pitches: R **Bats:** R **Pos:** RP-55   **Ht:** 6'3" **Wt:** 215 **Born:** 12/14/74 **Age:** 29

		HOW MUCH HE PITCHED						WHAT HE GAVE UP											THE RESULTS						
Year Team	Lg	G	GS	CG	GF	IP	BFP	H	R	ER	HR	SH	SF	HB	TBB	IBB	SO	WP	Bk	W	L	Pct	ShO	Sv-Op	Hld	ERC	ERA
2003 Charlotte*	AAA	4	0	0	0	3.2	19	5	2	2	0	0	0	0	3	0	2	0	0	0	1	.000	0	0--	-	6.95	4.91
1999 Toronto	AL	56	0	0	48	63.2	272	55	26	24	5	4	1	3	30	5	57	0	0	0	5	.000	0	31-35	0	3.53	3.39
2000 Toronto	AL	68	0	0	62	78.2	326	78	28	23	6	4	0	2	18	4	60	1	0	9	3	.750	0	33-38	0	3.25	2.63
2001 Toronto	AL	69	0	0	56	69.1	308	69	39	37	7	5	4	6	33	7	55	5	0	2	5	.286	0	36-44	0	4.54	4.80
2002 Oakland	AL	84	0	0	79	93.2	398	73	38	34	7	6	1	4	46	6	93	5	0	11	4	.733	0	44-50	0	3.10	3.27
2003 Chicago	AL	55	0	0	45	53.0	244	59	36	34	10	2	3	1	28	1	42	3	0	5	5	.500	0	11-15	1	5.93	5.77
5 ML YEARS		332	0	0	290	358.1	1548	334	167	152	35	21	9	16	155	23	307	14	0	27	22	.551	0	155-182	1	3.88	3.82

Danny Kolb

Pitches: R **Bats:** R **Pos:** RP-37   **Ht:** 6'4" **Wt:** 215 **Born:** 3/29/75 **Age:** 29

		HOW MUCH HE PITCHED						WHAT HE GAVE UP											THE RESULTS						
Year Team	Lg	G	GS	CG	GF	IP	BFP	H	R	ER	HR	SH	SF	HB	TBB	IBB	SO	WP	Bk	W	L	Pct	ShO	Sv-Op	Hld	ERC	ERA
2003 Indianapolis*	AAA	26	0	0	21	39.1	156	26	10	6	1	1	0	0	13	0	46	3	0	0	1	.000	0	4--	-	1.66	1.37
1999 Texas	AL	16	0	0	6	31.0	139	33	18	16	2	0	0	1	15	0	15	2	0	2	1	.667	0	0-0	0	4.63	4.65
2000 Texas	AL	1	0	0	0	0.2	9	5	5	5	0	0	1	0	2	0	0	0	0	0	0	-	0	0-0	0	69.84	67.50
2001 Texas	AL	17	0	0	1	15.1	70	15	8	8	2	1	1	0	10	1	15	3	0	0	0	-	0	0-0	7	5.03	4.70
2002 Texas	AL	34	0	0	14	32.0	145	27	17	15	1	1	2	1	22	2	20	6	0	3	6	.333	0	1-2	4	3.74	4.22
2003 Milwaukee	NL	37	0	0	25	41.1	175	34	10	9	2	1	0	1	19	3	39	1	0	1	2	.333	0	21-23	4	2.96	1.96
5 ML YEARS		105	0	0	46	120.1	538	114	58	53	7	3	4	3	68	6	89	12	0	6	9	.400	0	22-27	13	4.09	3.96

Paul Konerko

Bats: R **Throws:** R **Pos:** 1B-119; PH-15; DH-11   **Ht:** 6'2" **Wt:** 215 **Born:** 3/5/76 **Age:** 28

						BATTING															BASERUNNING				AVERAGES		
Year Team	Lg	G	AB	H	2B	3B	HR	(Hm	Rd)	TB	R	RBI	RC	TBB	IBB	SO	HBP	SH	SF		SB	CS	SB%	GDP	Avg	OBP	Slg
1997 Los Angeles	NL	6	7	1	0	0	0	(0	0)	1	0	0	0	1	0	2	0	0	0		0	0	-	1	.143	.250	.143
1998 LA-Cin	NL	75	217	47	4	0	7	(2	5)	72	21	29	17	16	0	40	3	0	3		0	1	.00	10	.217	.276	.332
1999 Chicago	AL	142	513	151	31	4	24	(16	8)	262	71	81	86	45	0	68	2	1	3		1	0	1.00	19	.294	.352	.511
2000 Chicago	AL	143	524	156	31	1	21	(10	11)	252	84	97	86	47	0	72	10	0	5		1	0	1.00	22	.298	.363	.481
2001 Chicago	AL	156	582	164	35	0	32	(19	13)	295	92	99	99	54	6	89	9	0	5		1	0	1.00	17	.282	.349	.507
2002 Chicago	AL	151	570	173	30	0	27	(13	14)	284	81	104	96	44	2	72	9	0	7		0	0	-	17	.304	.359	.498
2003 Chicago	AL	137	444	104	19	0	18	(9	9)	177	49	65	42	43	7	50	4	0	4		0	0	-	28	.234	.305	.399
1998 Los Angeles	NL	49	144	31	1	0	4	(2	2)	44	14	16	10	10	0	30	2	0	2		0	1	.00	5	.215	.272	.306
1998 Cincinnati	NL	26	73	16	3	0	3	(0	3)	28	7	13	7	6	0	10	1	0	1		0	0	-	5	.219	.284	.384
7 ML YEARS		810	2857	796	150	5	129	(69	60)	1343	398	475	426	250	15	393	37	1	27		3	1	.75	114	.279	.342	.470

Graham Koonce

Bats: L **Throws:** L **Pos:** 1B-5; PH-1; PR-1   **Ht:** 6'4" **Wt:** 225 **Born:** 5/15/75 **Age:** 29

						BATTING															BASERUNNING				AVERAGES		
Year Team	Lg	G	AB	H	2B	3B	HR	(Hm	Rd)	TB	R	RBI	RC	TBB	IBB	SO	HBP	SH	SF		SB	CS	SB%	GDP	Avg	OBP	Slg
1994 Bristol	R+	44	120	25	4	0	0	(-	-)	29	15	15	13	28	1	25	3	0	3		4	0	1.00	6	.208	.364	.242
1995 Jamestown	A-	73	289	81	16	1	3	(-	-)	108	37	34	43	35	0	63	2	0	12		8	3	.73	1	.280	.349	.374
1996 Fayetteville	A	133	487	116	22	3	8	(-	-)	168	61	59	55	58	2	97	5	2	4		7	7	.50	9	.238	.323	.345
1997 Tri-City	A-	89	286	82	15	3	3	(-	-)	112	46	34	53	67	4	55	3	2	4		13	6	.68	5	.287	.422	.392
1998 Chico	IND	69	242	80	15	0	10	(-	-)	125	50	41	51	38	4	41	3	0	1		0	0	-	6	.331	.426	.517
1999 R Cucamnga	A+	132	474	135	16	1	19	(-	-)	210	76	79	84	76	5	110	11	0	6		4	1	.80	12	.285	.392	.443
2000 R Cucamnga	A+	137	475	140	40	3	18	(-	-)	240	92	93	106	107	7	105	4	0	4		0	0	-	4	.295	.425	.505
2001 Mobile	AA	109	320	85	18	0	13	(-	-)	142	52	48	68	89	1	83	4	1	2		0	0	-	3	.266	.429	.444
2001 Portland	AAA	6	14	3	1	0	1	(-	-)	7	5	2	3	5	0	6	0	0	0		0	0	-	1	.214	.421	.500
2002 Midland	AA	140	470	129	28	0	24	(-	-)	229	86	96	107	133	12	117	10	0	5		2	0	1.00	6	.274	.440	.487
2003 Sacramento	AAA	138	480	133	23	1	34	(-	-)	260	82	115	106	98	3	119	11	0	12		0	0	-	11	.277	.403	.542
2003 Oakland	AL	6	8	1	1	0	0	(0	0)	2	0	0	0	0	0	6	0	0	0		0	0	-	0	.125	.125	.250

Mike Koplove

Pitches: R **Bats:** R **Pos:** RP-31   **Ht:** 6'0" **Wt:** 170 **Born:** 8/30/76 **Age:** 27

		HOW MUCH HE PITCHED						WHAT HE GAVE UP												THE RESULTS						
Year Team	Lg	G	GS	CG	GF	IP	BFP	H	R	ER	HR	SH	SF	HB	TBB	IBB	SO	WP	Bk	W	L	Pct	ShO	Sv-Op	Hld	ERC	ERA
2003 Tucson*	AAA	3	0	0	2	2.2	15	4	4	4	1	0	0	0	3	0	2	0	0	0	1	.000	0	1- -	-	12.97	13.50
2001 Arizona	NL	9	0	0	1	10.0	50	8	7	4	1	1	0	2	9	1	14	1	0	0	1	.000	0	0-0	1	5.25	3.60
2002 Arizona	NL	55	0	0	15	61.2	249	47	24	23	2	4	1	0	23	4	46	1	0	6	1	.857	0	0-0	10	2.23	3.36
2003 Arizona	NL	31	0	0	5	37.2	157	31	11	9	3	2	2	5	10	1	27	1	0	3	0	1.000	0	0-1	5	2.93	2.15
3 ML YEARS		95	0	0	21	109.1	456	86	42	36	6	7	3	7	42	6	87	3	0	9	2	.818	0	0-1	16	2.73	2.96

Corey Koskie

Bats: L **Throws:** R **Pos:** 3B-131   **Ht:** 6'3" **Wt:** 217 **Born:** 6/28/73 **Age:** 31

						BATTING															BASERUNNING				AVERAGES		
Year Team	Lg	G	AB	H	2B	3B	HR	(Hm	Rd)	TB	R	RBI	RC	TBB	IBB	SO	HBP	SH	SF		SB	CS	SB%	GDP	Avg	OBP	Slg
1998 Minnesota	AL	11	29	4	0	0	1	(1	0)	7	2	2	1	2	0	10	0	0	0		0	0	-	0	.138	.194	.241
1999 Minnesota	AL	117	342	106	21	0	11	(4	7)	160	42	58	61	40	4	72	5	2	3		4	4	.50	6	.310	.387	.468
2000 Minnesota	AL	146	474	142	32	4	9	(1	8)	209	79	65	84	77	7	104	4	1	3		5	4	.56	11	.300	.400	.441
2001 Minnesota	AL	153	562	155	37	2	26	(11	15)	274	100	103	99	68	9	118	12	0	7		27	6	.82	16	.276	.362	.488
2002 Minnesota	AL	140	490	131	37	4	15	(6	9)	219	71	69	73	72	4	127	9	0	5		10	11	.48	14	.267	.368	.447
2003 Minnesota	AL	131	469	137	29	2	14	(8	6)	212	76	69	84	77	5	113	7	0	9		11	5	.69	5	.292	.393	.452
6 ML YEARS		698	2366	675	156	11	76	(31	45)	1081	370	366	402	336	29	544	37	3	27		57	30	.66	52	.285	.379	.457

Mark Kotsay

Bats: L **Throws:** L **Pos:** CF-127; PH-1   **Ht:** 6'0" **Wt:** 201 **Born:** 12/2/75 **Age:** 28

						BATTING															BASERUNNING				AVERAGES		
Year Team	Lg	G	AB	H	2B	3B	HR	(Hm	Rd)	TB	R	RBI	RC	TBB	IBB	SO	HBP	SH	SF		SB	CS	SB%	GDP	Avg	OBP	Slg
1997 Florida	NL	14	52	10	1	1	0	(0	0)	13	5	4	3	4	0	7	0	1	0		3	0	1.00	1	.192	.250	.250
1998 Florida	NL	154	578	161	25	7	11	(5	6)	233	72	68	70	34	2	61	1	7	3		10	5	.67	17	.279	.318	.403
1999 Florida	NL	148	495	134	23	9	8	(5	3)	199	57	50	58	29	5	50	0	2	9		7	6	.54	11	.271	.306	.402
2000 Florida	NL	152	530	158	31	5	12	(5	7)	235	87	57	78	42	2	46	0	2	4		19	9	.68	17	.298	.347	.443
2001 San Diego	NL	119	406	118	29	1	10	(3	7)	179	67	58	65	48	1	58	2	1	3		13	5	.72	11	.291	.366	.441
2002 San Diego	NL	153	578	169	27	7	17	(11	6)	261	82	61	91	59	0	89	3	2	4		11	9	.55	10	.292	.359	.452
2003 San Diego	NL	128	482	128	28	4	7	(1	6)	185	64	38	59	56	3	82	1	1	1		6	3	.67	8	.266	.343	.384
7 ML YEARS		868	3121	878	164	34	65	(30	35)	1305	434	336	424	272	13	393	7	16	24		69	37	.65	75	.281	.338	.418

Chad Kreuter

Bats: B **Throws:** R **Pos:** C-7   **Ht:** 6'2" **Wt:** 200 **Born:** 8/26/64 **Age:** 39

						BATTING															BASERUNNING				AVERAGES		
Year Team	Lg	G	AB	H	2B	3B	HR	(Hm	Rd)	TB	R	RBI	RC	TBB	IBB	SO	HBP	SH	SF		SB	CS	SB%	GDP	Avg	OBP	Slg
1988 Texas	AL	16	51	14	2	1	1	(0	1)	21	3	5	8	7	0	13	0	0	0		0	0	-	1	.275	.362	.412
1989 Texas	AL	87	158	24	3	0	5	(2	3)	42	16	9	11	27	0	40	0	6	1		0	1	.00	4	.152	.274	.266
1990 Texas	AL	22	22	1	1	0	0	(0	0)	2	2	2	1	8	0	9	0	1	1		0	0	-	0	.045	.290	.091
1991 Texas	AL	3	4	0	0	0	0	(0	0)	0	0	0	0	0	0	1	0	0	0		0	0	-	0	.000	.000	.000
1992 Detroit	AL	67	190	48	9	0	2	(2	0)	63	22	16	19	20	1	38	0	3	2		0	1	.00	8	.253	.321	.332
1993 Detroit	AL	119	374	107	23	3	15	(9	6)	181	59	51	67	49	4	92	3	2	3		2	1	.67	5	.286	.371	.484
1994 Detroit	AL	65	170	38	8	0	1	(1	0)	49	17	19	18	28	0	36	0	2	4		0	1	.00	3	.224	.327	.288
1995 Seattle	AL	26	75	17	5	0	1	(0	1)	25	12	8	8	15	0	22	2	1	0		0	0	-	6	.227	.293	.333

124

Year Team	Lg	G	AB	H	2B	3B	HR	(Hm	Rd)	TB	R	RBI	RC	TBB	IBB	SO	HBP	SH	SF	SB	CS	SB%	GDP	Avg	OBP	Slg
1996 Chicago	AL	46	114	25	8	0	3	(2	1)	42	14	18	13	13	0	29	2	2	1	0	0	-	2	.219	.308	.368
1997 CWS-Ana	AL	89	255	59	9	2	5	(3	2)	87	25	21	25	29	0	66	0	1	0	3		.00	7	.231	.310	.341
1998 CWS-Ana	AL	96	252	63	10	1	2	(2	0)	81	27	33	28	33	1	49	3	5	1	1	0	1.00	8	.250	.343	.321
1999 Kansas City	AL	107	324	73	15	0	5	(2	3)	103	31	35	29	34	1	65	6	2	2	0	0	-	16	.225	.309	.318
2000 Los Angeles	NL	80	212	56	13	0	6	(4	2)	87	32	28	40	54	0	48	2	2	1	1	0	1.00	6	.264	.416	.410
2001 Los Angeles	NL	73	191	41	11	1	6	(4	2)	72	21	17	27	41	2	52	1	0	1	0	0	-	5	.215	.355	.377
2002 Los Angeles	NL	41	95	25	5	0	2	(2	0)	36	8	12	13	10	4	31	1	0	2	1	0	1.00	3	.263	.333	.379
2003 Texas	AL	7	18	2	1	0	0	(0	0)	3	0	0	0	3	0	2	0	0	0	0	0	-	0	.111	.238	.167
1997 Chicago	AL	19	37	8	2	1	1	(1	0)	15	6	3	6	8	0	9	0	0	0	0	1	.00	1	.216	.356	.405
1997 Anaheim	AL	70	218	51	7	1	4	(2	2)	72	19	18	19	21	0	57	0	1	0	0	2	.00	7	.234	.301	.330
1998 Chicago	AL	93	245	62	9	1	2	(2	0)	79	26	33	28	32	1	45	3	5	1	1	0	1.00	8	.253	.345	.322
1998 Anaheim	AL	3	7	1	1	0	0	(0	0)	2	1	0	0	1	0	4	0	0	0	0	0	-	0	.143	.250	.286
16 ML YEARS		944	2505	593	123	8	54	(33	21)	894	289	274	307	361	13	593	20	27	19	5	7	.42	68	.237	.335	.357

John Lackey

Pitches: R **Bats:** R **Pos:** SP-33 **Ht:** 6'6" **Wt:** 205 **Born:** 10/23/78 **Age:** 25

Year Team	Lg	G	GS	CG	GF	IP	BFP	H	R	ER	HR	SH	SF	HB	TBB	IBB	SO	WP	Bk	W	L	Pct	ShO	Sv-Op	Hld	ERC	ERA
1999 Boise	A-	15	15	1	0	81.1	372	81	59	45	7	5	2	8	50	1	77	14	1	6	2	.750	0	0--	-	5.21	4.98
2000 Cedar Rpds	A	5	5	0	0	30.1	115	20	7	7	1	0	0	2	5	0	21	4	0	3	2	.600	0	0--	-	1.50	2.08
2000 Lk Elsinore	A+	15	15	2	0	100.2	433	94	56	38	9	0	5	9	42	0	74	12	3	6	6	.500	1	0--	-	4.10	3.40
2000 Erie	AA	8	8	2	0	57.1	234	58	23	21	6	1	0	1	9	0	43	0	0	6	1	.857	0	0--	-	3.32	3.30
2001 Arkansas	AA	18	18	3	0	127.1	509	106	55	49	11	6	5	3	29	0	94	8	0	9	7	.563	2	0--	-	2.57	3.46
2001 Salt Lake	AAA	10	10	1	0	57.2	253	75	44	43	5	2	1	1	16	0	42	3	1	4	4	.429	0	0--	-	5.43	6.71
2002 Salt Lake	AAA	16	16	2	0	101.2	412	89	35	29	5	2	1	2	28	0	82	5	2	8	2	.800	1	0--	-	2.72	2.57
2002 Anaheim	AL	18	18	1	0	108.1	465	113	52	44	10	0	4	4	33	0	69	7	2	9	4	.692	0	0-0	0	4.03	3.66
2003 Anaheim	AL	33	33	2	0	204.0	885	223	117	105	31	2	6	10	66	4	151	11	1	10	16	.385	2	0-0	0	4.88	4.63
2 ML YEARS		51	51	3	0	312.1	1350	336	169	149	41	2	10	14	99	4	220	18	3	19	20	.487	2	0-0	0	4.58	4.29

Pete LaForest

Bats: L **Throws:** R **Pos:** DH-10; PH-6; C-4 **Ht:** 6'2" **Wt:** 208 **Born:** 1/27/78 **Age:** 26

Year Team	Lg	G	AB	H	2B	3B	HR	(Hm	Rd)	TB	R	RBI	RC	TBB	IBB	SO	HBP	SH	SF	SB	CS	SB%	GDP	Avg	OBP	Slg
1995 Expos	R	2	6	0	0	0	0	(-	-)	0	1	0	0	2	0	4	0	0	0	0	0	-	0	.000	.250	.000
1997 Devil Rays	R	34	107	28	7	2	3	(-	-)	48	21	21	16	10	0	18	1	0	1	4	3	.57	1	.262	.328	.449
1998 Princeton	R+	25	91	25	7	1	2	(-	-)	40	18	14	16	12	1	18	1	1	0	4	1	.80	0	.275	.365	.440
1999 Chrlstn - SC	A	125	445	114	21	3	13	(-	-)	180	64	53	62	55	6	97	5	6	3	9	3	.75	11	.256	.343	.404
2000 St.Pete	A+	129	474	128	28	7	14	(-	-)	212	85	70	75	56	4	108	6	1	5	2	4	.33	4	.270	.351	.447
2001 Orlando	AA	7	21	2	0	0	1	(-	-)	5	3	1	1	5	0	9	0	0	0	0	0	-	0	.095	.269	.238
2002 Orlando	AA	106	359	97	18	1	20	(-	-)	177	57	64	67	60	3	94	2	0	4	9	6	.60	4	.270	.374	.493
2002 Durham	AAA	17	66	17	3	0	3	(-	-)	29	7	15	8	3	0	28	0	0	0	0	1	.00	1	.258	.290	.439
2003 Orlando	AA	21	72	18	8	0	3	(-	-)	35	9	15	14	16	1	17	1	0	2	0	0	-	1	.250	.385	.486
2003 Durham	AAA	61	201	54	14	2	14	(-	-)	114	40	38	43	36	2	56	2	0	2	2	1	.67	2	.269	.382	.567
2003 Tampa Bay	AL	19	48	8	2	0	0	(0	0)	10	0	6	1	1	0	14	1	0	1	0	0	-	1	.167	.196	.208

Gerald Laird

Bats: R **Throws:** R **Pos:** C-16; PR-2; PH-1 **Ht:** 6'2" **Wt:** 195 **Born:** 11/3/79 **Age:** 24

Year Team	Lg	G	AB	H	2B	3B	HR	(Hm	Rd)	TB	R	RBI	RC	TBB	IBB	SO	HBP	SH	SF	SB	CS	SB%	GDP	Avg	OBP	Slg
1999 Sth Oregon	A-	60	228	65	7	2	2	(-	-)	82	45	39	32	28	0	43	2	2	5	10	5	.67	4	.285	.361	.360
2000 Visalia	A+	33	103	25	3	0	0	(-	-)	28	14	13	10	14	0	27	1	0	2	7	2	.78	3	.243	.333	.272
2000 Athletics	R	14	50	15	2	1	0	(-	-)	19	10	9	7	6	0	7	1	0	1	2	0	1.00	3	.300	.379	.380
2001 Modesto	A+	119	443	113	13	5	5	(-	-)	151	71	46	52	48	1	101	10	4	6	10	9	.53	9	.255	.337	.341
2002 Tulsa	AA	123	442	122	21	4	11	(-	-)	184	70	67	61	45	1	95	5	1	10	8	6	.57	14	.276	.343	.416
2003 Oklahoma	AAA	99	338	88	20	5	9	(-	-)	145	50	42	50	37	4	61	7	1	2	9	3	.75	7	.260	.344	.429
2003 Texas	AL	19	44	12	2	1	1	(0	1)	19	9	4	5	5	0	11	1	0	0	0	0	-	2	.273	.360	.432

Tim Laker

Bats: R **Throws:** R **Pos:** C-50; DH-2; PH-2 **Ht:** 6'3" **Wt:** 225 **Born:** 11/27/69 **Age:** 34

Year Team	Lg	G	AB	H	2B	3B	HR	(Hm	Rd)	TB	R	RBI	RC	TBB	IBB	SO	HBP	SH	SF	SB	CS	SB%	GDP	Avg	OBP	Slg
1992 Montreal	NL	28	46	10	3	0	0	(0	0)	13	8	4	2	2	0	14	0	0	0	1	1	.50	1	.217	.250	.283
1993 Montreal	NL	43	86	17	2	1	0	(0	0)	21	3	7	4	2	0	16	1	3	1	2	0	1.00	2	.198	.222	.244
1995 Montreal	NL	64	141	33	8	1	3	(1	2)	52	17	20	14	14	4	38	1	1	1	0	1	.00	5	.234	.306	.369
1997 Baltimore	AL	7	14	0	0	0	0	(0	0)	0	0	1	0	2	0	9	0	1	1	0	0	-	0	.000	.118	.000
1998 TB-Pit		17	29	10	1	0	1	(0	1)	14	3	2	5	2	0	4	0	0	1	0	1	.00	1	.345	.375	.483
1999 Pittsburgh	NL	6	9	3	0	0	0	(0	0)	3	0	0	1	0	0	2	0	0	0	0	0	-	0	.333	.333	.333
2001 Cleveland	AL	16	33	6	0	0	1	(0	1)	9	5	5	3	6	0	8	0	1	0	0	0	-	0	.182	.308	.273
2003 Cleveland	AL	52	162	39	11	0	3	(1	2)	59	17	21	18	9	1	38	0	5	0	2	2	.50	4	.241	.281	.364
1998 Tampa Bay	AL	3	5	1	0	0	0	(0	0)	1	1	0	1	0	1	0	1	0	0	1		.00	0	.200	.333	.200
1998 Pittsburgh	NL	14	24	9	1	0	1	(0	1)	13	2	2	5	1	0	3	0	0	1	0	0	-	0	.375	.385	.542
8 ML YEARS		233	520	118	25	2	8	(2	6)	171	53	60	47	37	5	129	2	11	4	5	5	.50	14	.227	.279	.329

Mike Lamb

Bats: L **Throws:** R **Pos:** PH-17; 1B-5; DH-5; LF-2; 3B-1; PR-1   **Ht:** 6'1" **Wt:** 195 **Born:** 8/9/75 **Age:** 28

Year Team	Lg	G	AB	H	2B	3B	HR	(Hm	Rd)	TB	R	RBI	RC	TBB	IBB	SO	HBP	SH	SF	SB	CS	SB%	GDP	Avg	OBP	Slg
2003 Oklahoma*	AAA	73	274	79	19	4	9	(-	-)	133	45	46	51	42	3	45	2	2	3	1	1	.50	4	.288	.383	.485
2000 Texas	AL	138	493	137	25	2	6	(4	2)	184	65	47	59	34	6	60	4	5	2	0	2	.00	10	.278	.328	.373
2001 Texas	AL	76	284	87	18	0	4	(1	3)	117	42	35	40	14	1	27	5	1	2	2	1	.67	6	.306	.348	.412
2002 Texas	AL	115	314	89	13	0	9	(7	2)	129	54	33	45	33	5	48	3	2	3	0	0	-	7	.283	.354	.411
2003 Texas	AL	28	38	5	0	0	0	(0	0)	5	3	2	0	2	0	7	1	0	1	1	0	1.00	1	.132	.190	.132
4 ML YEARS		357	1129	318	56	2	19	(12	7)	435	164	117	144	83	12	142	13	8	8	3	3	.50	24	.282	.336	.385

Jason Lane

Bats: R **Throws:** L **Pos:** PH-9; CF-6; LF-3; RF-2; PR-1   **Ht:** 6'2" **Wt:** 215 **Born:** 12/22/76 **Age:** 27

Year Team	Lg	G	AB	H	2B	3B	HR	(Hm	Rd)	TB	R	RBI	RC	TBB	IBB	SO	HBP	SH	SF	SB	CS	SB%	GDP	Avg	OBP	Slg
1999 Auburn	A-	74	283	79	18	5	13	(-	-)	146	46	59	54	38	2	46	3	0	4	6	4	.60	2	.279	.366	.516
2000 Michigan	A	133	511	153	38	0	23	(-	-)	260	98	104	99	62	7	91	8	0	13	20	7	.74	9	.299	.375	.509
2001 Round Rock	AA	137	526	166	36	2	38	(-	-)	320	103	124	126	61	11	98	21	1	1	14	2	.88	6	.316	.407	.608
2002 New Orleans	AAA	111	426	116	36	2	15	(-	-)	201	65	83	67	31	0	90	7	0	6	13	3	.81	6	.272	.328	.472
2003 New Orleans	AAA	71	248	74	17	0	7	(-	-)	112	37	39	42	30	1	26	3	1	5	2	1	.67	6	.298	.374	.452
2002 Houston	NL	44	69	20	3	1	4	(2	2)	37	12	10	11	10	1	12	0	0	1	1	1	.50	0	.290	.375	.536
2003 Houston	NL	18	27	8	2	0	4	(4	0)	22	5	10	6	0	0	2	0	0	0	0	0	-	0	.296	.296	.815
2 ML YEARS		62	96	28	5	1	8	(6	2)	59	17	20	17	10	1	14	0	0	1	1	1	.50	0	.292	.355	.615

Ryan Langerhans

Bats: L **Throws:** L **Pos:** RF-9; PR-6; CF-4; LF-3   **Ht:** 6'3" **Wt:** 195 **Born:** 2/20/80 **Age:** 24

Year Team	Lg	G	AB	H	2B	3B	HR	(Hm	Rd)	TB	R	RBI	RC	TBB	IBB	SO	HBP	SH	SF	SB	CS	SB%	GDP	Avg	OBP	Slg
1998 Braves	R	43	148	41	10	4	2	(-	-)	65	15	19	23	19	1	38	0	0	1	2	5	.29	0	.277	.357	.439
1999 Macon	A	121	448	120	30	1	9	(-	-)	179	66	49	64	52	2	99	7	2	2	19	11	.63	8	.268	.352	.400
2000 Myrtle Beach	A+	116	392	83	14	7	6	(-	-)	129	55	37	38	32	1	104	9	4	0	25	11	.69	3	.212	.286	.329
2001 Myrtle Beach	A+	125	450	129	30	3	7	(-	-)	186	66	48	71	55	3	104	8	2	0	22	13	.63	6	.287	.374	.413
2002 Greenville	AA	109	391	98	23	2	9	(-	-)	152	57	62	59	68	3	83	6	4	5	10	5	.67	9	.251	.366	.389
2003 Richmond	AAA	38	132	37	10	2	4	(-	-)	63	13	11	21	11	1	29	1	1	1	2	1	.67	2	.280	.348	.477
2003 Greenville	AA	94	336	85	23	2	6	(-	-)	130	42	38	44	46	3	85	3	2	0	10	10	.50	6	.253	.348	.387
2002 Atlanta	NL	1	1	0	0	0	0	(0	0)	0	0	0	0	0	0	0	0	0	0	0	0	-	0	.000	.000	.000
2003 Atlanta	NL	16	15	4	0	0	0	(0	0)	4	2	0	1	0	0	6	0	0	0	0	0	-	1	.267	.267	.267
2 ML YEARS		17	16	4	0	0	0	(0	0)	4	2	0	1	0	0	6	0	0	0	0	0	-	1	.250	.250	.250

Barry Larkin

Bats: R **Throws:** R **Pos:** SS-60; PH-10   **Ht:** 6'0" **Wt:** 185 **Born:** 4/28/64 **Age:** 40

Year Team	Lg	G	AB	H	2B	3B	HR	(Hm	Rd)	TB	R	RBI	RC	TBB	IBB	SO	HBP	SH	SF	SB	CS	SB%	GDP	Avg	OBP	Slg
1986 Cincinnati	NL	41	159	45	4	3	3	(3	0)	64	27	19	22	9	1	21	0	0	1	8	0	1.00	2	.283	.320	.403
1987 Cincinnati	NL	125	439	107	16	2	12	(6	6)	163	64	43	52	36	3	52	5	5	3	21	6	.78	8	.244	.306	.371
1988 Cincinnati	NL	151	588	174	32	5	12	(9	3)	252	91	56	94	41	3	24	8	10	5	40	7	.85	7	.296	.347	.429
1989 Cincinnati	NL	97	325	111	14	4	4	(1	3)	145	47	36	53	20	5	23	2	2	8	10	5	.67	7	.342	.375	.446
1990 Cincinnati	NL	158	614	185	25	6	7	(4	3)	243	85	67	90	49	3	49	7	7	4	30	5	.86	14	.301	.358	.396
1991 Cincinnati	NL	123	464	140	27	4	20	(16	4)	235	88	69	90	55	1	64	3	3	2	24	6	.80	7	.302	.378	.506
1992 Cincinnati	NL	140	533	162	32	6	12	(8	4)	242	76	78	92	63	8	58	4	2	7	15	4	.79	13	.304	.377	.454
1993 Cincinnati	NL	100	384	121	20	3	8	(4	4)	171	57	51	68	51	6	33	1	1	3	14	1	.93	13	.315	.394	.445
1994 Cincinnati	NL	110	427	119	23	5	9	(3	6)	179	78	52	73	64	3	58	0	5	5	26	2	.93	6	.279	.369	.419
1995 Cincinnati	NL	131	496	158	29	6	15	(8	7)	244	98	66	104	61	2	49	3	3	4	51	5	.91	6	.319	.394	.492
1996 Cincinnati	NL	152	517	154	32	4	33	(14	19)	293	117	89	118	96	3	52	7	0	7	36	10	.78	20	.298	.410	.567
1997 Cincinnati	NL	73	224	71	17	3	4	(0	4)	106	34	20	50	47	6	24	3	1	1	14	3	.82	3	.317	.440	.473
1998 Cincinnati	NL	145	538	166	34	10	17	(8	9)	271	93	72	109	79	5	69	2	4	3	26	3	.90	12	.309	.397	.504
1999 Cincinnati	NL	161	583	171	30	4	12	(7	5)	245	108	75	102	93	5	57	2	5	4	30	8	.79	12	.293	.390	.420
2000 Cincinnati	NL	102	396	124	26	5	11	(6	5)	193	71	41	73	48	0	31	1	2	0	14	6	.70	10	.313	.389	.487
2001 Cincinnati	NL	45	156	40	12	0	2	(1	1)	58	29	17	23	27	2	25	2	0	0	3	2	.60	2	.256	.373	.372
2002 Cincinnati	NL	145	507	124	37	2	7	(4	3)	186	72	47	54	44	9	57	3	6	7	13	4	.76	13	.245	.305	.367
2003 Cincinnati	NL	70	241	68	16	1	2	(2	0)	92	39	18	32	22	0	32	1	1	0	2	0	1.00	7	.282	.345	.382
18 ML YEARS		2069	7591	2240	426	73	190	(104	86)	3382	1274	916	1299	905	65	778	54	57	64	377	77	.83	162	.295	.371	.446

Greg LaRocca

Bats: R **Throws:** R **Pos:** 3B-2; PH-2; PR-1   **Ht:** 5'11" **Wt:** 185 **Born:** 11/10/72 **Age:** 31

Year Team	Lg	G	AB	H	2B	3B	HR	(Hm	Rd)	TB	R	RBI	RC	TBB	IBB	SO	HBP	SH	SF	SB	CS	SB%	GDP	Avg	OBP	Slg
2003 Buffalo*	AAA	132	500	145	33	2	10	(-	-)	212	63	68	75	40	2	53	6	1	6	5	3	.63	5	.290	.346	.424
2000 San Diego	NL	13	27	6	2	0	0	(0	0)	8	1	2	2	1	0	4	0	2	0	0	0	-	1	.222	.250	.296
2002 Cleveland	AL	21	52	14	3	1	0	(0	0)	19	12	4	8	6	0	6	2	0	0	1	0	1.00	1	.269	.367	.365
2003 Cleveland	AL	5	9	3	1	0	0	(0	0)	4	3	0	1	1	0	1	0	0	0	0	0	-	0	.333	.400	.444
3 ML YEARS		39	88	23	6	1	0	(0	0)	31	16	6	11	8	0	11	2	2	0	1	0	1.00	2	.261	.337	.352

Brandon Larson

Bats: R **Throws:** R **Pos:** 3B-24; PH-7; LF-3   **Ht:** 6'0" **Wt:** 210 **Born:** 5/24/76 **Age:** 28

Year Team	Lg	G	AB	H	2B	3B	HR	(Hm	Rd)	TB	R	RBI	RC	TBB	IBB	SO	HBP	SH	SF	SB	CS	SB%	GDP	Avg	OBP	Slg
2003 Louisville*	AAA	72	282	91	19	2	20	(-	-)	174	51	74	62	28	1	70	2	0	3	3	0	1.00	7	.323	.384	.617
2001 Cincinnati	NL	14	33	4	2	0	0	(0	0)	6	2	1	0	2	0	10	0	0	0	0	0	-	1	.121	.171	.182
2002 Cincinnati	NL	23	51	14	2	0	4	(4	0)	28	8	13	9	6	1	10	1	0	0	1	0	1.00	1	.275	.362	.549
2003 Cincinnati	NL	32	89	9	1	0	1	(0	1)	13	6	9	1	13	0	31	0	0	2	2	2	.50	2	.101	.212	.146
3 ML YEARS		69	173	27	5	0	5	(4	1)	47	16	23	10	21	1	51	1	0	2	3	2	.60	4	.156	.249	.272

Jason LaRue

Bats: R **Throws:** R **Pos:** C-114; PH-3; 1B-1; LF-1   **Ht:** 5'11" **Wt:** 200 **Born:** 3/19/74 **Age:** 30

Year Team	Lg	G	AB	H	2B	3B	HR	(Hm	Rd)	TB	R	RBI	RC	TBB	IBB	SO	HBP	SH	SF	SB	CS	SB%	GDP	Avg	OBP	Slg
1999 Cincinnati	NL	36	90	19	7	0	3	(1	2)	35	12	10	10	11	1	32	2	0	0	4	1	.80	4	.211	.311	.389
2000 Cincinnati	NL	31	98	23	3	0	5	(1	4)	41	12	12	12	5	2	19	4	0	0	0	0	-	1	.235	.299	.418
2001 Cincinnati	NL	121	364	86	21	2	12	(3	9)	147	39	43	42	27	4	106	9	1	2	3	3	.50	11	.236	.303	.404
2002 Cincinnati	NL	113	353	88	17	1	12	(5	7)	143	42	52	44	27	6	117	13	2	2	1	2	.33	13	.249	.324	.405
2003 Cincinnati	NL	118	379	87	23	1	16	(12	4)	160	52	50	48	33	4	111	20	1	4	3	3	.50	9	.230	.321	.422
5 ML YEARS		419	1284	303	71	4	48	(22	26)	526	157	167	156	103	17	385	48	4	8	11	9	.55	38	.236	.315	.410

Chris Latham

Bats: B **Throws:** R **Pos:** PR-3; CF-1; RF-1   **Ht:** 6'0" **Wt:** 205 **Born:** 5/26/73 **Age:** 31

Year Team	Lg	G	AB	H	2B	3B	HR	(Hm	Rd)	TB	R	RBI	RC	TBB	IBB	SO	HBP	SH	SF	SB	CS	SB%	GDP	Avg	OBP	Slg
1997 Minnesota	AL	15	22	4	1	0	0	(0	0)	5	4	1	0	0	0	8	0	0	0	0	0	-	0	.182	.182	.227
1998 Minnesota	AL	34	94	15	1	0	1	(1	0)	19	14	5	5	13	0	36	0	1	0	4	2	.67	0	.160	.262	.202
1999 Minnesota	AL	14	22	2	0	0	0	(0	0)	2	1	3	0	0	0	13	0	0	2	0	0	-	0	.091	.083	.091
2001 Toronto	AL	43	73	20	3	1	2	(1	1)	31	12	10	12	10	1	28	1	0	0	4	1	.80	1	.274	.369	.425
2003 New York	AL	4	2	2	0	0	0	(0	0)	2	3	0	1	0	0	0	0	0	0	1	0	1.00	0	1.000	1.000	1.000
5 ML YEARS		110	213	43	5	1	3	(2	1)	59	34	19	18	23	1	85	1	1	2	9	3	.75	1	.202	.280	.277

Brian Lawrence

Pitches: R **Bats:** R **Pos:** SP-33   **Ht:** 6'0" **Wt:** 195 **Born:** 5/14/76 **Age:** 28

Year Team	Lg	G	GS	CG	GF	IP	BFP	H	R	ER	HR	SH	SF	HB	TBB	IBB	SO	WP	Bk	W	L	Pct	ShO	Sv-Op	Hld	ERC	ERA
2001 San Diego	NL	27	15	1	5	114.2	484	107	44	10	4	3	5	84	1	5	.500		0	0-0	0	3.30	3.45				
2002 San Diego	NL	35	31	2	0	210.0	894	230	97	86	16	8	4	11	52	6	149	2	1	12	12	.500	2	0-0	0	4.05	3.69
2003 San Diego	NL	33	33	1	0	210.2	884	206	106	98	27	11	6	11	57	8	116	4	0	10	15	.400	0	0-0	0	3.81	4.19
3 ML YEARS		95	79	4	5	535.1	2262	543	256	228	53	23	13	27	143	19	349	7	1	27	32	.458	2	0-0	1	3.79	3.83

Matt Lawton

Bats: L **Throws:** R **Pos:** LF-62; DH-21; RF-13; PH-4   **Ht:** 5'10" **Wt:** 186 **Born:** 11/3/71 **Age:** 32

Year Team	Lg	G	AB	H	2B	3B	HR	(Hm	Rd)	TB	R	RBI	RC	TBB	IBB	SO	HBP	SH	SF	SB	CS	SB%	GDP	Avg	OBP	Slg
2003 Akron*	AA	5	19	1	0	0	0	(-	-)	1	1	1	0	2	0	6	0	0	0	0	0	-	1	.053	.143	.053
1995 Minnesota	AL	21	60	19	4	1	1	(1	0)	28	11	12	11	7	0	11	3	0	1	1	1	.50	1	.317	.414	.467
1996 Minnesota	AL	79	252	65	7	1	6	(1	5)	92	34	42	31	28	1	28	4	0	2	4	4	.50	6	.258	.339	.365
1997 Minnesota	AL	142	460	114	29	3	14	(8	6)	191	74	60	73	76	3	81	10	1	1	7	4	.64	7	.248	.366	.415
1998 Minnesota	AL	152	557	155	36	6	21	(11	10)	266	91	77	105	86	6	64	15	0	4	16	8	.67	10	.278	.387	.478
1999 Minnesota	AL	118	406	105	18	0	7	(2	5)	144	58	54	57	57	7	42	6	0	7	26	4	.87	11	.259	.353	.355
2000 Minnesota	AL	156	561	171	44	2	13	(8	5)	258	84	88	109	91	6	63	7	0	5	23	7	.77	10	.305	.405	.460
2001 Min-NYM		151	559	155	36	1	13	(5	8)	232	95	64	92	85	6	80	11	0	2	29	8	.78	16	.277	.382	.415
2002 Cleveland	AL	114	416	98	19	2	15	(8	7)	166	71	57	59	59	0	34	8	1	0	8	9	.47	13	.236	.342	.399
2003 Cleveland	AL	99	374	93	19	0	15	(6	9)	157	57	53	57	47	0	47	7	0	1	10	3	.77	8	.249	.343	.420
2001 Minnesota	AL	103	376	110	25	0	10	(4	6)	165	71	51	66	63	6	46	3	0	2	19	6	.76	14	.293	.396	.439
2001 New York	NL	48	183	45	11	1	3	(1	2)	67	24	13	26	22	0	34	8	0	0	10	2	.83	2	.246	.352	.366
9 ML YEARS		1032	3645	975	212	16	105	(50	55)	1534	575	507	594	536	31	450	71	2	22	124	48	.72	82	.267	.370	.421

Matt LeCroy

Bats: R **Throws:** R **Pos:** DH-60; C-22; 1B-17; PH-15   **Ht:** 6'2" **Wt:** 225 **Born:** 12/13/75 **Age:** 28

Year Team	Lg	G	AB	H	2B	3B	HR	(Hm	Rd)	TB	R	RBI	RC	TBB	IBB	SO	HBP	SH	SF	SB	CS	SB%	GDP	Avg	OBP	Slg
2000 Minnesota	AL	56	167	29	10	0	5	(2	3)	54	18	17	12	17	2	38	2	1	3	0	0	-	6	.174	.254	.323
2001 Minnesota	AL	15	40	17	5	0	3	(0	3)	31	6	12	11	0	0	8	1	0	1	0	1	.00	0	.425	.429	.775
2002 Minnesota	AL	63	181	47	11	1	7	(2	5)	81	19	27	24	13	1	38	0	0	2	0	2	.00	5	.260	.306	.448
2003 Minnesota	AL	107	345	99	19	0	17	(9	8)	169	39	64	60	25	1	82	4	0	0	0	1	.00	8	.287	.342	.490
4 ML YEARS		241	733	192	45	1	32	(13	19)	335	82	120	107	55	4	166	7	1	6	0	4	.00	19	.262	.317	.457

Ricky Ledee

Bats: L **Throws:** L **Pos:** PH-58; CF-42; LF-29; DH-2; RF-1   **Ht:** 6'1" **Wt:** 190 **Born:** 11/22/73 **Age:** 30

Year Team	Lg	G	AB	H	2B	3B	HR	(Hm	Rd)	TB	R	RBI	RC	TBB	IBB	SO	HBP	SH	SF	SB	CS	SB%	GDP	Avg	OBP	Slg
1998 New York	AL	42	79	19	5	2	1	(0	1)	31	13	12	9	7	0	29	0	0	1	3	1	.75	1	.241	.299	.392
1999 New York	AL	88	250	69	13	5	9	(4	5)	119	45	40	41	28	5	73	0	0	2	4	3	.57	2	.276	.346	.476
2000 NYY-Cle-Tex	AL	137	467	110	19	5	13	(6	7)	178	59	77	56	59	4	98	2	0	3	13	6	.68	17	.236	.322	.381

Year Team	Lg	G	AB	H	2B	3B	HR	(Hm	Rd)	TB	R	RBI	RC	TBB	IBB	SO	HBP	SH	SF	SB	CS	SB%	GDP	Avg	OBP	Slg
2001 Texas	AL	78	242	56	21	1	2	(1	1)	85	33	36	26	23	0	58	3	1	5	3	3	.50	3	.231	.303	.351
2002 Philadelphia	NL	96	203	46	13	1	8	(4	4)	85	33	23	24	35	0	50	1	1	1	1	2	.33	3	.227	.342	.419
2003 Philadelphia	NL	121	255	63	15	2	13	(6	7)	121	37	46	37	34	5	59	0	1	1	0	0	-	4	.247	.334	.475
2000 New York	AL	62	191	46	11	1	7	(2	5)	80	23	31	26	26	2	39	1	0	2	7	3	.70	7	.241	.332	.419
2000 Cleveland	AL	17	63	14	2	1	2	(2	0)	24	13	8	7	8	0	9	0	0	0	0	0	-	3	.222	.310	.381
2000 Texas	AL	58	213	50	6	3	4	(2	2)	74	23	38	23	25	2	50	1	0	1	6	3	.67	7	.235	.317	.347
6 ML YEARS		562	1496	363	86	16	46	(21	25)	619	220	234	193	186	14	367	6	3	11	24	15	.62	30	.243	.327	.414

Wil Ledezma

Pitches: L **Bats:** L **Pos:** RP-26; SP-8   **Ht:** 6'3" **Wt:** 150 **Born:** 1/21/81 **Age:** 23

Year Team	Lg	G	GS	CG	GF	IP	BFP	H	R	ER	HR	SH	SF	HB	TBB	IBB	SO	WP	Bk	W	L	Pct	ShO	Sv-Op	Hld	ERC	ERA
1999 Red Sox	R	13	6	0	2	57.1	242	51	28	21	2	1	1	1	20	0	52	3	1	5	1	.833	0	1--	-	2.88	3.30
2000 Augusta	A	14	14	0	0	52.2	240	51	33	30	3	1	1	2	36	0	60	5	0	2	4	.333	0	0--	-	4.86	5.13
2002 Red Sox	R	1	0	0	0	3.0	13	4	2	2	0	0	0	0	0	0	3	0	0	0	0	-	0	0--	-	3.56	6.00
2002 Augusta	A	5	5	0	0	23.2	101	23	10	10	0	0	0	1	8	0	38	2	0	2	2	.500	0	0--	-	3.14	3.80
2003 Detroit	AL	34	8	0	13	84.0	373	99	55	54	12	1	4	3	35	3	49	2	0	3	7	.300	0	0-1	1	5.72	5.79

Carlos Lee

Bats: R **Throws:** R **Pos:** LF-156; PH-2; DH-1   **Ht:** 6'2" **Wt:** 235 **Born:** 6/20/76 **Age:** 28

Year Team	Lg	G	AB	H	2B	3B	HR	(Hm	Rd)	TB	R	RBI	RC	TBB	IBB	SO	HBP	SH	SF	SB	CS	SB%	GDP	Avg	OBP	Slg
1999 Chicago	AL	127	492	144	32	2	16	(10	6)	228	66	84	68	13	0	72	4	1	7	4	2	.67	11	.293	.312	.463
2000 Chicago	AL	152	572	172	29	2	24	(12	12)	277	107	92	91	38	1	94	3	1	5	13	4	.76	17	.301	.345	.484
2001 Chicago	AL	150	558	150	33	3	24	(12	12)	261	75	84	81	38	2	85	6	1	2	17	7	.71	15	.269	.321	.468
2002 Chicago	AL	140	492	130	26	2	26	(14	12)	238	82	80	86	75	4	73	2	0	7	1	4	.20	5	.264	.359	.484
2003 Chicago	AL	158	623	181	35	1	31	(18	13)	311	100	113	106	37	2	91	4	0	7	18	4	.82	20	.291	.331	.499
5 ML YEARS		727	2737	777	155	10	121	(66	55)	1315	430	453	432	201	9	415	19	3	28	53	21	.72	68	.284	.334	.480

Cliff Lee

Pitches: L **Bats:** L **Pos:** SP-9   **Ht:** 6'3" **Wt:** 190 **Born:** 8/30/78 **Age:** 25

Year Team	Lg	G	GS	CG	GF	IP	BFP	H	R	ER	HR	SH	SF	HB	TBB	IBB	SO	WP	Bk	W	L	Pct	ShO	Sv-Op	Hld	ERC	ERA
2000 Cape Fear	A	11	11	0	0	44.2	217	50	39	26	1	1	1	1	36	0	63	3	2	1	4	.200	0	0--	-	5.82	5.24
2001 Jupiter	A+	21	20	0	1	109.2	451	78	43	34	13	5	5	4	46	0	129	2	3	6	7	.462	0	0--	-	2.86	2.79
2002 Buffalo	AAA	8	8	0	0	43.0	180	36	18	18	7	0	0	1	22	0	30	1	1	3	2	.600	0	0--	-	4.26	3.77
2002 Harrisburg	AA	15	15	0	0	86.1	336	61	31	31	12	1	1	1	23	0	105	2	0	7	2	.778	0	0--	-	2.36	3.23
2002 Akron	AA	3	3	0	0	16.2	72	11	11	10	1	0	0	1	10	0	18	1	0	2	1	.667	0	0--	-	2.89	5.40
2003 Buffalo	AAA	11	11	0	0	63.1	279	62	24	23	4	4	2	4	31	0	61	2	1	6	1	.857	0	0--	-	4.31	3.27
2003 Kinston	A+	1	1	0	0	4.1	17	0	1	0	0	1	0	0	3	0	4	0	0	0	0	-	0	0--	-	0.46	0.00
2003 Akron	AA	2	2	0	0	12.0	46	7	2	2	1	0	0	0	4	0	13	0	0	1	0	1.000	0	0--	-	1.68	1.50
2002 Cleveland	AL	2	2	0	0	10.1	44	6	2	2	0	1	0	0	8	1	6	0	1	1	0	1.000	0	0-0	0	2.38	1.74
2003 Cleveland	AL	9	9	0	0	52.1	210	41	28	21	7	1	1	2	20	1	44	3	0	3	3	.500	0	0-0	0	3.29	3.61
2 ML YEARS		11	11	0	0	62.2	254	47	30	23	7	2	1	2	28	2	50	3	1	4	3	.429	0	0-0	0	3.15	3.30

Dave Lee

Pitches: R **Bats:** R **Pos:** RP-8   **Ht:** 6'1" **Wt:** 202 **Born:** 3/12/73 **Age:** 31

Year Team	Lg	G	GS	CG	GF	IP	BFP	H	R	ER	HR	SH	SF	HB	TBB	IBB	SO	WP	Bk	W	L	Pct	ShO	Sv-Op	Hld	ERC	ERA
2003 Las Vegas*	AAA	56	0	0	30	60.1	264	47	22	21	4	1	3	2	36	3	61	0	1	3	2	.600	0	9- -	-	3.37	3.13
1999 Colorado	NL	36	0	0	0	49.0	212	43	0	20	4	0	0	0	29	0	38	0	0	3	2	.600	0	0-0	0	4.06	3.67
2000 Colorado	NL	7	0	0	0	5.2	35	10	0	7	3	0	0	0	6	0	6	0	0	0	0	-	0	1-0	0	15.31	11.12
2001 San Diego	NL	41	0	0	0	48.2	222	52	0	20	6	0	0	0	27	0	42	0	0	1	0	1.000	0	0-0	0	5.22	3.70
2003 Cleveland	AL	8	0	0	2	7.2	34	4	4	4	1	0	0	0	6	1	7	1	0	1	0	1.000	0	0-0	1	2.79	4.70
4 ML YEARS		92	0	0	2	111.0	503	109	4	51	14	0	0	0	68	1	93	1	0	5	2	.714	0	1-0	1	4.96	4.14

Derrek Lee

Bats: R **Throws:** R **Pos:** 1B-155   **Ht:** 6'5" **Wt:** 248 **Born:** 9/6/75 **Age:** 28

Year Team	Lg	G	AB	H	2B	3B	HR	(Hm	Rd)	TB	R	RBI	RC	TBB	IBB	SO	HBP	SH	SF	SB	CS	SB%	GDP	Avg	OBP	Slg
1997 San Diego	NL	22	54	14	3	0	1	(0	1)	20	9	4	8	9	0	24	0	0	0	0	0	-	1	.259	.365	.370
1998 Florida	NL	141	454	106	29	1	17	(4	13)	188	62	74	59	47	1	120	10	0	2	5	2	.71	12	.233	.318	.414
1999 Florida	NL	70	218	45	9	1	5	(0	5)	71	21	20	18	17	1	70	0	0	1	2	1	.67	3	.206	.263	.326
2000 Florida	NL	158	477	134	18	3	28	(9	19)	242	70	70	84	63	6	123	4	0	2	0	3	.00	14	.281	.368	.507
2001 Florida	NL	158	561	158	37	4	21	(8	13)	266	83	75	88	50	1	126	8	0	6	4	2	.67	18	.282	.346	.474
2002 Florida	NL	162	581	157	35	7	27	(9	18)	287	95	86	98	98	8	164	5	0	4	19	9	.68	14	.270	.378	.494
2003 Florida	NL	155	539	146	31	2	31	(11	20)	274	91	92	101	88	7	131	10	0	6	21	8	.72	9	.271	.379	.508
7 ML YEARS		866	2884	760	162	18	130	(41	89)	1348	431	421	456	372	24	758	37	0	21	51	25	.67	71	.264	.353	.467

Travis Lee

Bats: L **Throws:** L **Pos:** 1B-142; DH-2; PH-2   **Ht:** 6'3" **Wt:** 210 **Born:** 5/26/75 **Age:** 29

Year Team	Lg	G	AB	H	2B	3B	HR	(Hm	Rd)	TB	R	RBI	RC	TBB	IBB	SO	HBP	SH	SF	SB	CS	SB%	GDP	Avg	OBP	Slg
1998 Arizona	NL	146	562	151	20	2	22	(12	10)	241	71	72	83	67	5	123	0	0	1	8	1	.89	13	.269	.346	.429
1999 Arizona	NL	120	375	89	16	2	9	(7	2)	136	57	50	49	58	4	50	0	0	3	17	3	.85	10	.237	.337	.363
2000 Ari-Phi		128	404	95	24	1	9	(2	7)	148	53	54	53	65	1	79	2	0	2	8	1	.89	12	.235	.342	.366
2001 Philadelphia	NL	157	555	143	34	2	20	(11	9)	241	75	90	81	71	5	109	4	1	9	3	4	.43	15	.258	.341	.434
2002 Philadelphia	NL	153	536	142	26	2	13	(8	5)	211	55	70	64	54	10	104	0	0	2	5	3	.63	12	.265	.331	.394
2003 Tampa Bay	AL	145	542	149	37	3	19	(9	10)	249	75	70	78	64	4	97	0	1	6	6	2	.75	13	.275	.348	.459
2000 Arizona	NL	72	224	52	13	0	8	(1	7)	89	34	40	27	25	1	46	0	0	1	5	1	.83	6	.232	.308	.397
2000 Philadelphia	NL	56	180	43	11	1	1	(1	0)	59	19	14	26	40	0	33	2	0	1	3	0	1.00	6	.239	.381	.328
6 ML YEARS		849	2974	769	157	12	92	(49	43)	1226	386	406	408	379	29	562	6	2	23	47	14	.77	75	.259	.341	.412

Al Leiter

Pitches: L **Bats:** L **Pos:** SP-30   **Ht:** 6'3" **Wt:** 220 **Born:** 10/23/65 **Age:** 38

Year Team	Lg	G	GS	CG	GF	IP	BFP	H	R	ER	HR	SH	SF	HB	TBB	IBB	SO	WP	Bk	W	L	Pct	ShO	Sv-Op	Hld	ERC	ERA
1987 New York	AL	4	4	0	0	22.2	104	24	16	16	2	1	0	0	15	0	28	4	0	2	2	.500	0	0-0	0	5.41	6.35
1988 New York	AL	14	14	0	0	57.1	251	49	27	25	7	1	0	5	33	0	60	1	4	4	4	.500	0	0-0	0	4.51	3.92
1989 NYY-Tor	AL	5	5	0	0	33.1	154	32	23	21	2	1	1	2	23	0	26	2	1	1	2	.333	0	0-0	0	4.90	5.67
1990 Toronto	AL	4	0	0	2	6.1	22	1	0	0	0	0	0	0	2	0	5	0	0	0	0	-	0	0-0	0	0.33	0.00
1991 Toronto	AL	3	0	0	1	1.2	13	3	5	5	0	1	0	0	5	0	1	0	0	0	0	-	0	0-0	0	19.88	27.00
1992 Toronto	AL	1	0	0	0	1.0	7	1	1	1	0	0	0	0	2	0	0	0	0	0	0	-	0	0-0	0	8.07	9.00
1993 Toronto	AL	34	12	1	4	105.0	454	93	52	48	8	3	3	4	56	2	66	2	2	9	6	.600	1	2-3	3	3.94	4.11
1994 Toronto	AL	20	20	1	0	111.2	516	125	68	63	6	3	8	2	65	3	100	7	5	6	7	.462	0	0-0	0	5.14	5.08
1995 Toronto	AL	28	28	2	0	183.0	805	162	80	74	15	6	4	6	108	1	153	14	0	11	11	.500	1	0-0	0	4.18	3.64
1996 Florida	NL	33	33	2	0	215.1	896	153	74	70	14	7	3	11	119	3	200	5	0	16	12	.571	1	0-0	0	3.09	2.93
1997 Florida	NL	27	27	0	0	151.1	668	133	78	73	13	10	3	12	91	4	132	2	0	11	9	.550	0	0-0	0	4.39	4.34
1998 New York	NL	28	28	4	0	193.0	789	151	55	53	8	6	2	11	71	2	174	4	1	17	6	.739	2	0-0	0	2.65	2.47
1999 New York	NL	32	32	1	0	213.0	923	209	107	100	19	13	10	9	93	8	162	4	1	13	12	.520	1	0-0	0	4.17	4.23
2000 New York	NL	31	31	2	0	208.0	874	176	84	74	19	10	6	11	76	1	200	4	1	16	8	.667	1	0-0	0	3.23	3.20
2001 New York	NL	29	29	0	0	187.1	772	178	81	69	18	9	6	4	46	3	142	5	2	11	11	.500	0	0-0	0	3.26	3.31
2002 New York	NL	33	33	2	0	204.1	868	194	99	79	23	12	2	8	69	5	172	1	1	13	13	.500	2	0-0	0	3.75	3.48
2003 New York	NL	30	30	1	0	180.2	798	176	83	80	15	11	6	6	94	11	139	5	1	15	9	.625	1	0-0	0	4.40	3.99
1989 New York	AL	4	4	0	0	26.2	123	23	20	18	1	1	1	2	21	0	22	1	1	1	2	.333	0	0-0	0	4.62	6.08
1989 Toronto	AL	1	1	0	0	6.2	31	9	3	3	1	0	0	0	2	0	4	1	0	0	0	-	0	0-0	0	5.96	4.05
17 ML YEARS		356	326	16	7	2075.0	8914	1860	933	851	169	94	54	94	968	43	1760	60	19	145	112	.564	10	2-3	3	3.79	3.69

Jose Leon

Bats: R **Throws:** R **Pos:** 3B-10; 1B-7; PH-3; DH-2; PR-1   **Ht:** 6'0" **Wt:** 175 **Born:** 12/8/76 **Age:** 27

Year Team	Lg	G	AB	H	2B	3B	HR	(Hm	Rd)	TB	R	RBI	RC	TBB	IBB	SO	HBP	SH	SF	SB	CS	SB%	GDP	Avg	OBP	Slg
1994 Cardinals	R	46	161	37	3	2	0	(-	-)	44	16	17	11	11	0	51	3	1	4	1	4	.20	4	.230	.285	.273
1995 Savannah	A	41	133	22	4	1	0	(-	-)	28	15	11	3	10	1	46	1	1	0	0	1	.00	6	.165	.229	.211
1996 Johnson City	R+	59	222	55	9	3	10	(-	-)	100	29	36	31	17	0	92	2	2	1	5	3	.63	1	.248	.306	.450
1996 New Jersey	A-	7	28	8	3	1	1	(-	-)	16	4	3	5	0	0	7	2	0	0	0	0	-	0	.286	.333	.571
1997 Peoria	A	118	399	92	21	2	20	(-	-)	177	50	54	51	32	1	122	9	2	2	6	5	.55	10	.231	.301	.444
1998 Prnc William	A+	124	436	127	31	3	21	(-	-)	227	77	74	84	53	4	137	9	2	4	5	3	.63	6	.291	.376	.521
1999 Arkansas	AA	112	335	78	17	0	18	(-	-)	149	37	54	43	25	0	114	6	1	1	3	3	.50	5	.233	.297	.445
2000 Arkansas	AA	90	297	80	16	3	14	(-	-)	144	41	41	41	16	0	66	5	2	0	2	1	.67	7	.269	.318	.485
2000 Bowie	AA	18	68	17	1	0	1	(-	-)	21	7	6	6	4	0	13	2	0	0	5	2	.71	2	.250	.311	.309
2001 Bowie	AA	26	95	34	9	1	4	(-	-)	57	18	20	21	8	0	21	1	0	0	1	1	.50	2	.358	.413	.600
2001 Rochester	AAA	109	416	116	20	4	12	(-	-)	180	54	53	55	25	0	96	4	2	1	7	3	.70	14	.279	.325	.433
2002 Rochester	AAA	83	312	87	16	1	8	(-	-)	129	39	40	39	18	1	54	2	1	3	0	0	-	9	.279	.319	.413
2003 Ottawa	AAA	79	309	82	19	2	4	(-	-)	117	33	39	32	15	2	47	4	0	3	1	1	.50	12	.265	.305	.379
2002 Baltimore	AL	36	89	22	2	0	3	(1	2)	33	8	10	9	3	0	20	1	0	0	1	0	1.00	2	.247	.280	.371
2003 Baltimore	AL	21	54	13	1	0	0	(0	0)	14	6	0	2	3	0	18	2	0	0	0	0	-	1	.241	.305	.259
2 ML YEARS		57	143	35	3	0	3	(1	2)	47	14	10	11	6	0	38	3	0	0	1	0	1.00	3	.245	.289	.329

Curtis Leskanic

Pitches: R **Bats:** R **Pos:** RP-53   **Ht:** 6'0" **Wt:** 196 **Born:** 4/2/68 **Age:** 36

Year Team	Lg	G	GS	CG	GF	IP	BFP	H	R	ER	HR	SH	SF	HB	TBB	IBB	SO	WP	Bk	W	L	Pct	ShO	Sv-Op	Hld	ERC	ERA
1993 Colorado	NL	18	8	0	1	57.0	260	59	40	34	7	5	4	2	27	1	30	8	2	1	5	.167	0	0-0	0	4.71	5.37
1994 Colorado	NL	8	3	0	2	22.1	98	27	14	14	2	2	0	0	10	0	17	2	0	1	1	.500	0	0-0	0	5.62	5.64
1995 Colorado	NL	76	0	0	27	98.0	406	83	38	37	7	3	2	0	33	1	107	6	1	6	3	.667	0	10-16	19	2.79	3.40
1996 Colorado	NL	70	0	0	32	73.2	334	82	51	51	12	3	3	2	38	1	76	6	2	7	5	.583	0	6-10	9	5.81	6.23
1997 Colorado	NL	55	0	0	23	58.1	248	59	36	36	8	2	4	0	24	0	53	4	0	4	0	1.000	0	2-4	6	4.55	5.55
1998 Colorado	NL	66	0	0	20	75.2	332	75	37	37	9	0	0	1	40	2	55	3	1	6	4	.600	0	2-5	12	4.74	4.40
1999 Colorado	NL	63	0	0	3	85.0	382	87	54	48	7	5	3	5	49	4	77	5	0	6	2	.750	0	0-3	10	5.08	5.08
2000 Milwaukee	NL	73	0	0	39	77.1	333	58	23	22	7	1	4	3	51	5	75	5	0	9	3	.750	0	12-13	11	3.72	2.56
2001 Milwaukee	NL	70	0	0	58	69.1	297	63	30	28	11	3	0	2	31	5	64	2	0	2	6	.250	0	17-24	2	4.18	3.63
2003 Mil-KC		53	0	0	14	52.2	217	38	15	13	2	0	1	1	29	1	50	3	0	5	0	1.000	0	2-3	11	2.84	2.22
2003 Milwaukee	NL	26	0	0	5	26.2	116	22	8	8	1	0	1	0	18	0	28	2	0	4	0	1.000	0	0-0	4	3.93	2.70
2003 Kansas City	AL	27	0	0	9	26.0	101	16	7	5	1	0	1	0	11	1	22	1	0	1	0	1.000	0	2-3	7	1.84	1.73
10 ML YEARS		552	11	0	221	669.1	2907	631	338	320	72	24	21	16	332	20	604	44	6	47	29	.618	0	51-78	78	4.26	4.30

Al Levine

Pitches: R Bats: L Pos: RP-54   Ht: 6'3" Wt: 190 Born: 5/22/68 Age: 36

Year Team	Lg	G	GS	CG	GF	IP	BFP	H	R	ER	HR	SH	SF	HB	TBB	IBB	SO	WP	Bk	W	L	Pct	ShO	Sv-Op	Hld	ERC	ERA
1996 Chicago	AL	16	0	0	5	18.1	85	22	14	11	1	0	1	1	7	1	12	0	0	0	1	.000	0	0-1	3	4.80	5.40
1997 Chicago	AL	25	0	0	6	27.1	133	35	22	21	4	1	2	2	16	1	22	2	0	2	2	.500	0	0-1	3	7.10	6.91
1998 Texas	AL	30	0	0	11	58.0	251	68	30	29	6	1	3	0	16	1	19	5	0	1	1	.000	0	0-0	4	4.58	4.50
1999 Anaheim	AL	50	1	0	12	85.0	349	76	40	32	13	2	7	3	29	2	37	3	0	1	1	.500	0	0-1	3	3.81	3.39
2000 Anaheim	AL	51	5	0	12	95.1	426	98	44	41	10	3	3	2	49	5	42	1	0	3	4	.429	0	2-2	5	4.71	3.87
2001 Anaheim	AL	64	1	0	21	75.2	316	71	25	20	7	5	5	2	28	4	40	6	0	8	10	.444	0	2-6	17	3.66	2.38
2002 Anaheim	AL	52	0	0	21	63.2	286	61	35	30	8	2	7	2	34	3	40	2	0	4	4	.500	0	5-7	10	4.53	4.24
2003 TB-KC	AL	54	0	0	21	71.0	303	67	29	22	9	4	0	3	29	1	30	2	0	3	6	.333	0	1-4	10	4.17	2.79
2003 Tampa Bay	AL	36	0	0	14	49.2	208	45	23	16	7	3	0	2	18	0	25	2	0	3	5	.375	0	0-2	8	3.89	2.90
2003 Kansas City	AL	18	0	0	7	21.1	95	22	6	6	2	1	0	1	11	1	5	0	0	0	1	.000	0	1-2	2	4.82	2.53
8 ML YEARS		342	7	0	109	494.1	2149	498	239	206	58	18	28	15	208	18	242	21	0	21	29	.420	0	10-22	48	4.40	3.75

Allen Levrault

Pitches: R Bats: R Pos: RP-19   Ht: 6'3" Wt: 241 Born: 8/15/77 Age: 26

Year Team	Lg	G	GS	CG	GF	IP	BFP	H	R	ER	HR	SH	SF	HB	TBB	IBB	SO	WP	Bk	W	L	Pct	ShO	Sv-Op	Hld	ERC	ERA
2003 Albuquerque*	AAA	21	0	0	5	25.2	97	12	5	4	2	1	1	2	9	1	18	2	0	3	0	1.000	0	0- -	-	1.49	1.40
2000 Milwaukee	NL	5	1	0	2	12.0	51	10	7	6	0	1	1	0	7	0	9	0	0	1	1	.000	0	0-0	0	3.21	4.50
2001 Milwaukee	NL	32	20	1	0	130.2	593	146	93	88	27	3	4	7	59	7	80	2	1	6	10	.375	0	0-0	0	5.89	6.06
2003 Florida	NL	19	0	0	4	28.0	133	38	12	12	3	1	2	1	15	2	21	1	0	1	0	1.000	0	0-0	1	6.96	3.86
3 ML YEARS		56	21	1	6	170.2	777	194	112	106	30	5	7	8	81	9	110	3	1	7	11	.389	0	0-0	1	5.87	5.59

Colby Lewis

Pitches: R Bats: R Pos: SP-26   Ht: 6'4" Wt: 215 Born: 8/2/79 Age: 24

Year Team	Lg	G	GS	CG	GF	IP	BFP	H	R	ER	HR	SH	SF	HB	TBB	IBB	SO	WP	Bk	W	L	Pct	ShO	Sv-Op	Hld	ERC	ERA
1999 Pulaski	R+	14	11	1	0	64.2	280	46	24	14	3	0	3	7	27	0	84	3	4	7	3	.700	1	0- -	-	2.53	1.95
2000 Charlotte	A+	28	27	3	0	163.2	692	169	83	74	11	4	7	10	45	0	153	11	2	11	10	.524	1	0- -	-	3.83	4.07
2001 Charlotte	A+	1	0	0	0	4.1	13	0	0	0	0	0	0	0	0	0	8	0	0	1	0	1.000	0	0- -	-	0.00	0.00
2001 Tulsa	AA	25	25	1	0	156.0	686	150	85	78	15	8	6	16	62	2	162	16	0	10	10	.500	0	0- -	-	4.17	4.50
2002 Oklahoma	AAA	20	20	0	0	106.2	448	100	49	43	4	1	4	7	28	0	99	5	0	5	6	.455	0	0- -	-	3.03	3.63
2003 Oklahoma	AAA	7	7	0	0	47.2	195	36	16	16	6	0	1	0	19	0	43	3	2	5	1	.833	0	0- -	-	2.93	3.02
2002 Texas	AL	15	4	0	0	34.1	168	42	26	24	4	2	0	2	26	2	28	3	1	1	3	.250	0	0-2	1	7.22	6.29
2003 Texas	AL	26	26	0	0	127.0	594	163	104	103	23	2	2	5	70	1	88	5	0	10	9	.526	0	0-0	0	7.38	7.30
2 ML YEARS		41	30	0	4	161.1	762	205	130	127	27	4	2	7	96	3	116	8	1	11	12	.478	0	0-2	1	7.35	7.08

Brad Lidge

Pitches: R Bats: R Pos: RP-78   Ht: 6'5" Wt: 200 Born: 12/23/76 Age: 27

Year Team	Lg	G	GS	CG	GF	IP	BFP	H	R	ER	HR	SH	SF	HB	TBB	IBB	SO	WP	Bk	W	L	Pct	ShO	Sv-Op	Hld	ERC	ERA
1998 Quad City	A	4	4	0	0	16	50	10	5	4	0	0	0	1	5	0	6	1	0	0	1	.000	0	0- -	-	3.24	3.27
1999 Kissimmee	A+	6	6	0	0	21.1	82	13	8	8	0	0	0	0	11	0	19	2	0	0	2	.000	0	0- -	-	1.99	3.38
2000 Kissimmee	A+	8	8	0	0	41.2	164	28	14	13	3	1	0	1	15	0	46	1	2	2	1	.667	0	0- -	-	2.20	2.81
2001 Round Rock	AA	5	5	0	0	26.0	107	21	5	5	1	1	1	2	7	0	42	1	0	2	0	1.000	0	0- -	-	2.44	1.73
2002 Round Rock	AA	5	0	0	1	11.0	44	9	4	3	0	0	0	0	3	0	18	0	0	1	1	.500	0	0- -	-	2.06	2.45
2002 New Orleans	AAA	24	19	0	1	111.2	459	83	47	42	9	1	2	7	47	0	110	5	1	5	5	.500	0	0- -	-	2.93	3.39
2002 Houston	NL	6	1	0	2	8.2	48	12	6	6	0	1	0	2	9	1	12	0	0	1	0	1.000	0	0-0	0	8.90	6.23
2003 Houston	NL	78	0	0	9	85.0	349	60	36	34	6	2	3	5	42	7	97	4	1	6	3	.667	0	1-6	28	2.82	3.60
2 ML YEARS		84	1	0	11	93.2	397	72	42	40	6	3	3	7	51	8	109	4	1	7	3	.700	0	1-6	28	3.31	3.84

Cory Lidle

Pitches: R Bats: R Pos: SP-31   Ht: 5'11" Wt: 192 Born: 3/22/72 Age: 32

Year Team	Lg	G	GS	CG	GF	IP	BFP	H	R	ER	HR	SH	SF	HB	TBB	IBB	SO	WP	Bk	W	L	Pct	ShO	Sv-Op	Hld	ERC	ERA
2003 Syracuse*	AAA	1	1	0	0	4.0	16	5	0	0	0	0	0	0	0	0	3	0	0	0	0	-	0	0- -	-	3.37	0.00
1997 New York	NL	54	2	0	20	81.2	345	86	38	32	7	4	4	3	20	4	54	2	0	7	2	.778	0	2-3	9	3.75	3.53
1999 Tampa Bay	AL	5	1	0	1	5.0	24	8	4	4	0	0	0	0	2	0	4	0	0	1	0	1.000	0	0-0	0	6.98	7.20
2000 Tampa Bay	AL	31	15	0	5	96.2	424	114	61	54	13	3	1	3	28	2	62	6	0	4	6	.400	0	0-0	2	5.06	5.03
2001 Oakland	AL	29	29	1	0	188.0	762	170	84	75	23	2	1	10	47	7	118	5	0	13	6	.684	0	0-0	0	3.35	3.59
2002 Oakland	AL	31	30	2	0	192.0	796	191	90	83	17	5	6	6	39	3	111	6	1	8	10	.444	2	0-0	0	3.31	3.89
2003 Toronto	AL	31	31	2	0	192.2	840	216	133	123	24	5	5	5	60	3	112	9	0	12	15	.444	0	0-0	0	4.67	5.75
6 ML YEARS		181	104	5	26	756.0	3191	785	410	371	84	19	17	27	197	20	461	28	1	45	39	.536	2	2-3	11	3.94	4.42

Jon Lieber

Pitches: R Bats: L Pos: SP   Ht: 6'2" Wt: 230 Born: 4/2/70 Age: 34

Year Team	Lg	G	GS	CG	GF	IP	BFP	H	R	ER	HR	SH	SF	HB	TBB	IBB	SO	WP	Bk	W	L	Pct	ShO	Sv-Op	Hld	ERC	ERA
1994 Pittsburgh	NL	17	17	1	0	108.2	460	116	62	45	12	3	3	1	25	3	71	2	3	6	7	.462	0	0-0	0	3.83	3.73
1995 Pittsburgh	NL	21	12	0	3	72.2	327	103	56	51	7	5	6	4	14	0	45	3	0	4	7	.364	0	0-1	3	5.96	6.32
1996 Pittsburgh	NL	51	15	0	6	142.0	600	156	70	63	19	7	2	3	28	2	94	0	0	9	5	.643	0	1-4	9	4.12	3.99
1997 Pittsburgh	NL	33	32	1	0	188.1	799	193	102	94	23	6	7	1	51	8	160	3	1	11	14	.440	0	0-0	0	3.78	4.49
1998 Pittsburgh	NL	29	28	2	1	171.0	731	182	93	78	23	7	4	3	40	4	138	0	3	8	14	.364	0	1-1	0	4.00	4.11
1999 Chicago	NL	31	31	3	0	203.1	875	226	107	92	28	7	11	1	46	6	186	2	2	10	11	.476	1	0-0	0	4.19	4.07
2000 Chicago	NL	35	**35**	6	0	**251.0**	**1047**	248	130	123	36	9	7	10	54	3	192	2	2	12	11	.522	1	0-0	0	3.70	4.41

Year Team	Lg	G	GS	CG	GF	IP	BFP	H	R	ER	HR	SH	SF	HB	TBB	IBB	SO	WP	Bk	W	L	Pct	ShO	Sv-Op	Hld	ERC	ERA
2001 Chicago	NL	34	34	5	0	232.1	958	226	104	98	25	13	9	7	41	4	148	4	1	20	6	.769	1	0-0	0	3.19	3.80
2002 Chicago	NL	21	21	3	0	141.0	582	153	64	58	15	10	6	1	12	2	87	0	0	6	8	.429	0	0-0	0	3.33	3.70
9 ML YEARS		272	225	21	10	1510.1	6379	1603	788	702	188	67	55	31	311	32	1121	16	12	86	83	.509	3	2-6	12	3.84	4.18

Mike Lieberthal

Bats: R **Throws:** R **Pos:** C-131; PH-2　　　　　　　　　　**Ht:** 6'0" **Wt:** 190 **Born:** 1/18/72 **Age:** 32

					BATTING															BASERUNNING				AVERAGES		
Year Team	Lg	G	AB	H	2B	3B	HR	(Hm	Rd)	TB	R	RBI	RC	TBB	IBB	SO	HBP	SH	SF	SB	CS	SB%	GDP	Avg	OBP	Slg
1994 Philadelphia	NL	24	79	21	3	1	1	(1	0)	29	6	5	8	3	0	5	1	1	0	0	0	-	4	.266	.301	.367
1995 Philadelphia	NL	16	47	12	2	0	0	(0	0)	14	1	4	5	5	0	5	0	2	0	0	0	-	1	.255	.327	.298
1996 Philadelphia	NL	50	166	42	8	0	7	(4	3)	71	21	23	21	10	0	30	2	0	4	0	0	-	4	.253	.297	.428
1997 Philadelphia	NL	134	455	112	27	1	20	(11	9)	201	59	77	62	44	1	76	4	0	7	3	4	.43	10	.246	.314	.442
1998 Philadelphia	NL	86	313	80	15	3	8	(5	3)	125	39	45	39	17	1	44	7	0	5	2	1	.67	4	.256	.304	.399
1999 Philadelphia	NL	145	510	153	33	1	31	(10	21)	281	84	96	96	44	7	86	11	1	8	0	0	-	15	.300	.363	.551
2000 Philadelphia	NL	108	389	108	30	0	15	(8	7)	183	55	71	62	40	3	53	6	0	3	2	0	1.00	12	.278	.352	.470
2001 Philadelphia	NL	34	121	28	8	0	2	(2	0)	42	21	11	13	12	2	21	3	0	0	0	0	-	2	.231	.316	.347
2002 Philadelphia	NL	130	476	133	29	2	15	(7	8)	211	46	52	55	38	2	58	14	0	2	0	1	.00	16	.279	.349	.443
2003 Philadelphia	NL	131	508	159	30	1	13	(6	7)	230	68	81	79	38	2	59	12	0	3	0	0	-	14	.313	.373	.453
10 ML YEARS		858	3064	848	185	9	112	(52	60)	1387	400	465	440	251	18	437	60	4	32	7	6	.54	82	.277	.340	.453

Jeff Liefer

Bats: L **Throws:** R **Pos:** 1B-21; PH-15; 3B-6; DH-2; LF-1; PR-1　　　　**Ht:** 6'3" **Wt:** 210 **Born:** 8/17/74 **Age:** 29

					BATTING															BASERUNNING				AVERAGES		
Year Team	Lg	G	AB	H	2B	3B	HR	(Hm	Rd)	TB	R	RBI	RC	TBB	IBB	SO	HBP	SH	SF	SB	CS	SB%	GDP	Avg	OBP	Slg
2003 Durham*	AAA	44	157	41	10	3	7	(-	-)	78	20	24	25	14	0	49	1	1	0	0	0	-	2	.261	.326	.497
1999 Chicago	AL	45	113	28	7	1	0	(0	0)	37	8	14	11	8	0	28	0	0	1	2	0	1.00	3	.248	.295	.327
2000 Chicago	AL	5	11	2	0	0	0	(0	0)	2	0	0	0	0	0	4	0	0	0	0	0	-	0	.182	.182	.182
2001 Chicago	AL	83	254	65	13	0	18	(10	8)	132	36	39	40	20	1	69	2	1	2	0	1	.00	6	.256	.313	.520
2002 Chicago	AL	76	204	47	8	0	7	(4	3)	76	28	26	24	19	2	60	0	0	1	0	0	-	3	.230	.295	.373
2003 Mon-TB		44	113	20	4	0	4	(0	4)	36	10	21	13	6	1	39	0	0	1	0	1	.00	2	.177	.217	.319
2003 Montreal	NL	35	88	17	3	0	3	(0	3)	29	6	18	11	3	0	26	0	0	1	0	1	.00	2	.193	.217	.330
2003 Tampa Bay	AL	9	25	3	1	0	1	(0	1)	7	4	3	2	3	1	13	0	0	0	0	0	-	0	.120	.214	.280
5 ML YEARS		253	695	162	32	1	29	(14	15)	283	82	100	88	53	4	200	2	1	5	2	2	.50	14	.233	.287	.407

Kerry Ligtenberg

Pitches: R **Bats:** R **Pos:** RP-68　　　　　　　　　　**Ht:** 6'2" **Wt:** 215 **Born:** 5/11/71 **Age:** 33

					HOW MUCH HE PITCHED			WHAT HE GAVE UP												THE RESULTS					
Year Team	Lg	G	GS	CG	GF	IP	BFP	H	R	ER	HR	SH	SF	HB	TBB	IBB	SO	WP	Bk	W	L	Pct	ShO	Sv-Op	Hld	ERC	ERA
1997 Atlanta	NL	15	0	0	9	15.0	61	12	5	5	4	0	0	0	4	2	19	0	0	1	0	1.000	0	1-1	0	3.26	3.00
1998 Atlanta	NL	75	0	0	56	73.0	290	51	24	22	6	1	1	0	24	1	79	3	0	3	2	.600	0	30-34	11	2.13	2.71
2000 Atlanta	NL	59	0	0	19	52.1	217	43	21	21	7	2	1	0	24	5	51	0	0	2	3	.400	0	12-14	12	3.46	3.61
2001 Atlanta	NL	53	0	0	24	59.2	254	50	22	20	4	1	2	0	30	8	56	0	0	3	3	.500	0	1-2	0	3.14	3.02
2002 Atlanta	NL	52	0	0	25	66.2	281	52	23	22	6	3	1	0	33	3	51	1	1	3	4	.429	0	0-0	2	3.10	2.97
2003 Baltimore	AL	68	0	0	21	59.1	247	60	23	22	9	2	1	2	14	3	47	0	0	4	2	.667	0	1-4	14	3.93	3.34
6 ML YEARS		322	0	0	154	326.0	1350	268	118	112	36	9	6	2	129	22	303	7	1	16	14	.533	0	45-55	39	3.10	3.09

Ted Lilly

Pitches: L **Bats:** L **Pos:** SP-31; RP-1　　　　　　　　　　**Ht:** 6'0" **Wt:** 185 **Born:** 1/4/76 **Age:** 28

					HOW MUCH HE PITCHED			WHAT HE GAVE UP												THE RESULTS					
Year Team	Lg	G	GS	CG	GF	IP	BFP	H	R	ER	HR	SH	SF	HB	TBB	IBB	SO	WP	Bk	W	L	Pct	ShO	Sv-Op	Hld	ERC	ERA
1999 Montreal	NL	9	3	0	1	23.2	110	30	20	20	7	0	1	3	9	0	28	1	0	0	1	.000	0	0-0	0	7.76	7.61
2000 New York	AL	7	0	0	1	8.0	39	8	6	5	1	0	0	0	5	0	11	1	1	0	0	-	0	0-0	0	4.76	5.63
2001 New York	AL	26	21	0	2	120.2	537	126	81	72	20	2	5	7	51	1	112	9	2	5	6	.455	0	0-0	0	5.10	5.37
2002 NYY-Oak	AL	22	16	2	1	100.0	413	80	43	41	15	0	3	6	31	3	77	6	1	5	7	.417	1	0-0	0	3.14	3.69
2003 Oakland	AL	32	31	0	0	178.1	773	179	92	86	24	3	4	5	58	3	147	5	4	12	10	.545	0	0-0	0	4.06	4.34
2002 New York	AL	16	11	2	1	76.2	314	57	31	29	10	0	3	5	24	3	59	6	0	3	6	.333	1	0-0	0	2.74	3.40
2002 Oakland	AL	6	5	0	0	23.1	99	23	12	12	5	0	0	1	7	0	18	0	1	2	1	.667	0	0-0	0	4.56	4.63
5 ML YEARS		96	71	2	5	430.2	1872	423	242	224	67	5	13	21	154	7	375	22	8	22	24	.478	1	0-0	0	4.31	4.68

Jose Lima

Pitches: R **Bats:** R **Pos:** SP-14　　　　　　　　　　**Ht:** 6'2" **Wt:** 205 **Born:** 9/30/72 **Age:** 31

					HOW MUCH HE PITCHED			WHAT HE GAVE UP												THE RESULTS					
Year Team	Lg	G	GS	CG	GF	IP	BFP	H	R	ER	HR	SH	SF	HB	TBB	IBB	SO	WP	Bk	W	L	Pct	ShO	Sv-Op	Hld	ERC	ERA
1994 Detroit	AL	3	1	0	1	6.2	34	11	10	10	2	0	0	0	3	1	7	1	0	0	1	.000	0	0-0	0	9.61	13.50
1995 Detroit	AL	15	15	0	0	73.2	320	85	52	50	10	2	1	4	18	4	37	5	0	3	9	.250	0	0-0	0	4.73	6.11
1996 Detroit	AL	39	4	0	15	72.2	329	87	48	46	13	5	3	5	22	4	59	3	0	5	6	.455	0	3-7	6	5.53	5.70
1997 Houston	NL	52	1	0	15	75.0	321	79	45	44	9	6	3	5	16	2	63	2	0	1	6	.143	0	2-2	3	3.96	5.28
1998 Houston	NL	33	33	3	0	233.1	950	229	100	96	34	11	5	7	32	1	169	4	0	16	8	.667	1	0-0	0	3.36	3.70
1999 Houston	NL	35	35	3	0	246.1	1024	256	108	98	30	5	7	2	44	2	187	0	0	21	10	.677	0	0-0	0	3.58	3.58
2000 Houston	NL	33	33	0	0	196.1	895	251	152	145	48	12	12	2	68	3	124	3	0	7	16	.304	0	0-0	0	6.59	6.65
2001 Hou-Det		32	27	2	3	165.2	719	197	114	102	35	5	9	9	38	3	84	4	0	6	12	.333	0	0-0	0	5.53	5.54
2002 Detroit	AL	20	12	0	3	68.1	304	86	60	59	12	1	6	2	21	0	33	2	0	4	6	.400	0	0-0	0	5.97	7.77
2003 Kansas City	AL	14	14	0	0	73.1	321	80	40	40	7	1	3	5	26	0	32	2	2	8	3	.727	0	0-0	0	4.69	4.91
2001 Houston	NL	14	9	0	3	53.0	249	77	48	43	12	4	4	5	16	1	41	3	0	1	2	.333	0	0-0	0	7.90	7.30
2001 Detroit	AL	18	18	2	0	112.2	470	120	66	59	23	1	5	4	22	2	43	1	0	5	10	.333	0	0-0	0	4.49	4.71
10 ML YEARS		276	175	8	37	1211.1	5217	1361	729	690	200	48	49	41	288	20	795	34	2	71	77	.480	1	5-9	9	4.69	5.13

Mike Lincoln

Pitches: R **Bats:** R **Pos:** RP-36 **Ht:** 6'2" **Wt:** 203 **Born:** 4/10/75 **Age:** 29

Year Team	Lg	G	GS	CG	GF	IP	BFP	H	R	ER	HR	SH	SF	HB	TBB	IBB	SO	WP	Bk	W	L	Pct	ShO	Sv-Op	Hld	ERC	ERA
2003 Nashville*	AAA	8	0	0	1	12.2	52	8	2	1	1	3	1	1	4	0	9	1	0	1	1	.500	0	0- -		1.96	0.71
1999 Minnesota	AL	18	15	0	0	76.1	353	102	59	58	11	2	6	1	26	0	27	4	0	3	10	.231	0	0-0	1	6.16	6.84
2000 Minnesota	AL	8	4	0	1	20.2	109	36	25	25	10	0	0	2	13	0	15	1	0	0	3	.000	0	0-0	0	14.32	10.89
2001 Pittsburgh	NL	31	0	0	5	40.1	168	34	16	12	3	1	1	4	11	0	24	2	0	2	1	.667	0	0-2	7	2.94	2.68
2002 Pittsburgh	NL	55	0	0	9	72.1	309	80	28	25	7	2	4	0	27	8	50	2	0	2	4	.333	0	0-3	11	4.49	3.11
2003 Pittsburgh	NL	36	0	0	14	36.1	153	38	22	21	5	1	1	1	13	0	28	1	0	3	4	.429	0	5-8	5	4.70	5.20
5 ML YEARS		148	19	0	29	246.0	1092	290	150	141	36	6	12	8	90	8	144	10	0	10	22	.313	0	5-13	24	5.45	5.16

Todd Linden

Bats: B **Throws:** R **Pos:** LF-9; RF-6; PH-4; PR-2 **Ht:** 6'3" **Wt:** 210 **Born:** 6/30/80 **Age:** 24

Year Team	Lg	G	AB	H	2B	3B	HR	(Hm	Rd)	TB	R	RBI	RC	TBB	IBB	SO	HBP	SH	SF	SB	CS	SB%	GDP	Avg	OBP	Slg
2002 Shreveport	AA	111	392	123	26	2	12	(-	-)	189	64	52	77	61	7	101	12	1	3	9	5	.64	12	.314	.419	.482
2002 Fresno	AAA	29	100	25	2	1	3	(-	-)	38	18	10	16	20	0	35	1	0	0	2	0	1.00	2	.250	.380	.380
2003 Fresno	AAA	125	471	131	24	3	11	(-	-)	194	75	56	70	40	2	105	17	4	0	14	4	.78	9	.278	.356	.412
2003 San Francisco	NL	18	38	8	1	0	1	(0	1)	12	2	6	5	1	0	8	0	0	0	0	0	-	2	.211	.231	.316

Scott Linebrink

Pitches: R **Bats:** R **Pos:** RP-46; SP-6 **Ht:** 6'2" **Wt:** 200 **Born:** 8/4/76 **Age:** 27

Year Team	Lg	G	GS	CG	GF	IP	BFP	H	R	ER	HR	SH	SF	HB	TBB	IBB	SO	WP	Bk	W	L	Pct	ShO	Sv-Op	Hld	ERC	ERA
2003 New Orleans*	AAA	2	2	0	0	10.0	41	8	3	3	1	0	0	0	5	0	6	2	0	0	2	.000	0	0- -		3.49	2.70
2000 SF-Hou	NL	11	0	0	4	12.0	63	18	8	8	4	0	0	3	8	0	6	0	0	0	0	-	0	0-0	0	11.88	6.00
2001 Houston	NL	9	0	0	2	10.1	44	6	4	3	0	1	1	2	6	0	9	1	0	0	0	-	0	0-0	1	2.54	2.61
2002 Houston	NL	22	0	0	4	24.1	119	31	21	19	2	0	2	1	13	4	24	0	0	0	0	-	0	0-0	1	5.75	7.03
2003 Hou-SD	NL	52	6	0	8	92.1	397	93	37	34	9	4	6	6	36	4	68	11	0	3	2	.600	0	0-0	6	4.32	3.31
2000 San Francisco	NL	3	0	0	1	2.1	16	7	3	3	1	0	0	0	2	0	0	0	0	0	0	-	0	0-0	0	24.13	11.57
2000 Houston	NL	8	0	0	3	9.2	47	11	5	5	3	0	0	3	6	0	6	0	0	0	0	-	0	0-0	0	9.21	4.66
2003 Houston	NL	9	6	0	2	31.2	140	38	15	15	4	2	1	3	14	1	17	5	0	1	1	.500	0	0-0	0	6.27	4.26
2003 San Diego	NL	43	0	0	6	60.2	257	55	22	19	5	2	5	3	22	3	51	6	0	2	1	.667	0	0-0	6	3.41	2.82
4 ML YEARS		94	6	0	18	139.0	623	148	70	64	15	5	9	12	63	8	107	12	0	3	2	.600	0	0-0	7	4.99	4.14

Doug Linton

Pitches: R **Bats:** R **Pos:** RP-7 **Ht:** 6'1" **Wt:** 190 **Born:** 2/9/65 **Age:** 39

Year Team	Lg	G	GS	CG	GF	IP	BFP	H	R	ER	HR	SH	SF	HB	TBB	IBB	SO	WP	Bk	W	L	Pct	ShO	Sv-Op	Hld	ERC	ERA
2003 Syracuse*	AAA	32	13	1	8	109.0	467	133	67	64	13	2	3	5	19	2	79	5	0	2	10	.167	0	0- -		4.79	5.28
1992 Toronto	AL	8	3	0	2	24.0	116	31	23	23	5	1	2	0	17	0	16	2	0	1	3	.250	0	0-0	0	8.19	8.63
1993 Tor-Ana	AL	23	1	0	6	36.2	178	46	30	30	8	0	3	1	23	1	23	2	0	2	1	.667	0	0-1	0	7.53	7.36
1994 New York	NL	32	3	0	8	50.1	241	74	27	25	4	3	1	0	20	3	29	2	0	6	2	.750	0	0-0	0	6.55	4.47
1995 Kansas City	AL	7	2	0	0	22.1	98	22	21	18	4	0	0	2	10	1	13	0	0	0	1	.000	0	0-0	0	5.10	7.25
1996 Kansas City	AL	21	18	0	0	104.0	452	111	65	58	13	6	2	8	26	1	87	3	1	7	9	.438	0	0-0	1	4.28	5.02
1999 Baltimore	AL	14	8	0	0	59.0	264	69	41	39	14	4	0	2	25	1	31	4	0	1	4	.200	0	0-0	0	6.42	5.95
2003 Toronto	AL	7	0	0	7	9.0	35	7	3	3	2	0	0	0	4	0	7	0	0	0	0	-	0	0-0	0	4.14	3.00
1993 Toronto	AL	4	1	0	0	11.0	55	11	8	8	0	0	2	1	9	0	4	0	0	0	1	.000	0	0-0	0	5.03	6.55
1993 Anaheim	AL	19	0	0	6	25.2	123	35	22	22	8	0	1	0	14	1	19	2	0	2	0	1.000	0	0-1	0	8.65	7.71
7 ML YEARS		112	35	0	23	305.1	1384	360	210	196	50	14	8	13	125	7	206	13	1	17	20	.459	0	0-1	1	5.78	5.78

Graeme Lloyd

Pitches: L **Bats:** L **Pos:** RP-52 **Ht:** 6'7" **Wt:** 225 **Born:** 4/9/67 **Age:** 37

Year Team	Lg	G	GS	CG	GF	IP	BFP	H	R	ER	HR	SH	SF	HB	TBB	IBB	SO	WP	Bk	W	L	Pct	ShO	Sv-Op	Hld	ERC	ERA
1993 Milwaukee	NL	55	0	0	12	63.2	269	64	24	20	5	1	2	3	13	3	31	4	0	3	4	.429	0	0-4	6	3.26	2.83
1994 Milwaukee	NL	43	0	0	21	47.0	203	49	28	27	4	1	2	3	15	6	31	2	0	2	3	.400	0	3-6	3	3.94	5.17
1995 Milwaukee	NL	33	0	0	14	32.0	127	28	16	16	4	1	4	0	8	2	13	3	0	0	5	.000	0	4-6	9	2.98	4.50
1996 Mil-NYY		65	0	0	15	56.2	252	61	30	27	4	5	3	1	22	4	30	4	0	2	6	.250	0	0-5	17	4.13	4.29
1997 New York	AL	46	0	0	17	49.0	217	55	24	18	6	3	5	1	20	7	26	3	0	1	1	.500	0	1-1	2	4.84	3.31
1998 New York	AL	50	0	0	8	37.2	145	26	10	7	3	0	1	2	6	2	20	2	0	3	0	1.000	0	0-2	9	1.67	1.67
1999 Toronto	AL	74	0	0	25	72.0	301	68	36	29	11	1	1	4	23	4	47	1	0	5	3	.625	0	3-9	22	4.00	3.63
2001 Montreal	NL	84	0	0	28	70.1	303	74	38	34	6	2	2	6	21	2	44	1	0	9	5	.643	0	1-3	11	4.19	4.35
2002 Mon-Fla	NL	66	0	0	19	57.0	253	67	34	33	6	4	3	2	19	4	37	2	0	4	5	.444	0	5-8	11	4.88	5.21
2003 NYM-KC		52	0	0	16	47.2	223	68	34	28	2	1	4	1	14	2	25	1	0	0	1	.200	0	0-1	7	5.63	5.29
1996 Milwaukee	NL	52	0	0	15	51.0	217	49	19	16	3	5	1	1	17	3	24	0	0	2	4	.333	0	0-3	15	3.28	2.82
1996 New York	AL	13	0	0	0	5.2	35	12	11	11	1	0	2	0	5	1	6	4	0	0	2	.000	0	0-2	2	13.39	17.47
2002 Montreal	NL	41	0	0	14	30.2	138	41	21	20	5	2	1	2	8	3	17	1	0	2	3	.400	0	5-7	9	5.97	5.87
2002 Florida	NL	25	0	0	5	26.1	115	26	13	13	1	2	2	0	11	1	20	1	0	2	2	.500	0	0-1	2	3.69	4.44
2003 New York	NL	36	0	0	12	35.1	149	39	16	13	2	1	2	0	7	2	17	1	0	0	0		0	0-0	6	3.47	3.31
2003 Kansas City	AL	16	0	0	4	12.1	74	29	18	15	0	0	2	1	7	0	8	0	0	0	1	.000	0	0-1	1	12.89	10.95
10 ML YEARS		568	0	0	175	533.0	2293	560	274	239	51	19	27	23	161	36	304	23	0	30	36	.455	0	17-45	97	4.00	4.04

Paul Lo Duca

Bats: R **Throws:** R **Pos:** C-123; 1B-22; LF-6; PH-2   **Ht:** 5'10" **Wt:** 185 **Born:** 4/12/72 **Age:** 32

							BATTING												BASERUNNING				AVERAGES		
Year Team	Lg	G	AB	H	2B	3B	HR	(Hm | Rd)	TB	R	RBI	RC	TBB	IBB	SO	HBP	SH	SF	SB	CS	SB%	GDP	Avg	OBP	Slg
1998 Los Angeles	NL	6	14	4	1	0	0	(0 | 0)	5	2	1	1	0	0	1	0	0	0			-	0	.286	.286	.357
1999 Los Angeles	NL	36	95	22	1	0	3	(1 | 2)	32	11	11	9	10	4	9	2	1	2	1	2	.33	3	.232	.312	.337
2000 Los Angeles	NL	34	65	16	2	0	2	(0 | 2)	24	6	8	6	6	0	8	0	2	2			.00	2	.246	.301	.369
2001 Los Angeles	NL	125	460	147	28	0	25	(11 | 14)	250	71	90	89	39	2	30	6	5	9	2	4	.33	11	.320	.374	.543
2002 Los Angeles	NL	149	580	163	38	1	10	(5 | 5)	233	74	64	72	34	2	31	10	4	4	3	1	.75	20	.281	.330	.402
2003 Los Angeles	NL	147	568	155	34	2	7	(4 | 3)	214	64	52	66	44	6	54	10	7	1	0	2	.00	21	.273	.335	.377
6 ML YEARS		497	1782	507	104	3	47	(21 | 26)	758	228	226	243	133	14	133	28	19	18	6	11	.35	57	.285	.341	.425

Esteban Loaiza

Pitches: R **Bats:** R **Pos:** SP-34   **Ht:** 6'3" **Wt:** 205 **Born:** 12/31/71 **Age:** 32

		HOW MUCH HE PITCHED						WHAT HE GAVE UP											THE RESULTS						
Year Team	Lg	G	GS	CG	GF	IP	BFP	H	R	ER	HR	SH	SF	HB	TBB	IBB	SO	WP	Bk	W	L	Pct	ShO	Sv-Op	Hld	ERC	ERA
1995 Pittsburgh	NL	32	31	1	0	172.2	762	205	115	99	21	10	9	5	55	3	85	6	1	8	9	.471	0	0-0	0	5.10	5.16
1996 Pittsburgh	NL	10	10	1	0	52.2	236	65	32	29	11	3	1	2	19	2	32	0	0	2	3	.400	1	0-0	0	6.30	4.96
1997 Pittsburgh	NL	33	32	1	0	196.1	851	214	99	90	17	10	7	12	56	9	122	2	3	11	11	.500	0	0-0	0	4.20	4.13
1998 Pit-Tex		35	28	1	3	171.0	751	199	107	98	28	7	12	5	52	4	108	4	2	9	11	.450	1	0-1	0	5.19	5.16
1999 Texas	AL	30	15	0	4	120.1	517	128	65	61	10	7	4	0	40	2	77	2	0	9	5	.643	0	0-0	0	4.03	4.56
2000 Tex-Tor		34	31	1	2	199.1	871	228	112	101	29	4	5	13	57	1	137	1	0	10	13	.435	1	1-1	0	5.07	4.56
2001 Toronto	AL	36	30	1	1	190.0	837	239	113	106	27	6	4	9	40	1	110	1	1	11	11	.500	1	0-0	0	5.30	5.02
2002 Toronto	AL	25	25	3	0	151.1	670	192	102	96	18	1	6	4	38	3	87	1	0	9	10	.474	1	0-0	0	5.26	5.71
2003 Chicago	AL	34	34	1	0	226.1	922	196	75	73	17	7	6	10	56	2	207	3	1	21	9	.700	5	0-0	0	2.79	2.90
1998 Pittsburgh	NL	21	14	0	3	91.2	394	96	50	46	13	5	7	3	30	1	53	1	2	6	5	.545	0	0-1	0	4.48	4.52
1998 Texas	AL	14	14	1	0	79.1	357	103	57	52	15	2	5	2	22	3	55	3	0	3	6	.333	0	0-0	0	6.04	5.90
2000 Texas	AL	20	17	0	2	107.1	480	133	67	64	21	2	4	3	31	1	75	1	0	5	6	.455	0	1-1	0	5.81	5.37
2000 Toronto	AL	14	14	1	0	92.0	391	95	45	37	8	2	1	10	26	0	62	0	0	5	7	.417	1	0-0	0	4.22	3.62
9 ML YEARS		269	236	10	10	1480.0	6417	1666	820	753	178	55	54	60	413	27	965	20	8	90	82	.523	4	1-2	0	4.60	4.58

Keith Lockhart

Bats: L **Throws:** R **Pos:** PH-42; 2B-27; 3B-3   **Ht:** 5'10" **Wt:** 170 **Born:** 11/10/64 **Age:** 39

							BATTING												BASERUNNING				AVERAGES		
Year Team	Lg	G	AB	H	2B	3B	HR	(Hm	Rd)	TB	R	RBI	RC	TBB	IBB	SO	HBP	SH	SF	SB	CS	SB%	GDP	Avg	OBP	Slg
2003 Portland*	AAA	4	11	2	0	0	0	(-	-)	2	0	4	1	1	0	0	1	0	0			-	0	.182	.308	.182
1994 San Diego	NL	27	43	9	0	0	2	(2	0)	15	4	6	4	4	0	10	1	1	1	1	0	1.00	1	.209	.286	.349
1995 Kansas City	AL	94	274	88	19	3	6	(3	3)	131	41	33	48	14	2	21	4	1	7	8	1	.89	2	.321	.355	.478
1996 Kansas City	AL	138	433	118	33	3	7	(4	3)	178	49	55	56	30	4	40	2	1	5	11	6	.65	7	.273	.319	.411
1997 Atlanta	NL	96	147	41	5	3	6	(3	3)	70	25	32	23	14	0	17	1	3	4			-	4	.279	.337	.476
1998 Atlanta	NL	109	366	94	21	0	9	(4	5)	142	50	37	45	29	0	37	1	2	3	2	2	.50	2	.257	.311	.388
1999 Atlanta	NL	108	161	42	3	1	1	(0	1)	50	20	21	19	19	0	21	1	0	3	3	1	.75	2	.261	.337	.311
2000 Atlanta	NL	113	275	73	12	3	2	(1	1)	97	32	32	31	29	7	31	0	5	4	4	1	.80	10	.265	.331	.353
2001 Atlanta	NL	104	178	39	6	0	3	(3	0)	54	17	12	16	16	1	22	2	2	1	1	2	.33	1	.219	.289	.303
2002 Atlanta	NL	128	296	64	13	3	5	(3	2)	98	34	32	31	27	9	50	1	5	2	0	1	.00	4	.216	.282	.331
2003 San Diego	NL	62	95	23	5	1	3	(3	0)	39	18	8	11	13	0	19	1	2	0	0	1	.00	2	.242	.339	.411
10 ML YEARS		979	2268	591	117	17	44	(23	21)	874	290	268	284	195	23	268	14	22	30	30	15	.67	36	.261	.319	.385

Carlton Loewer

Pitches: R **Bats:** R **Pos:** SP-5   **Ht:** 6'6" **Wt:** 211 **Born:** 9/24/73 **Age:** 30

		HOW MUCH HE PITCHED						WHAT HE GAVE UP											THE RESULTS						
Year Team	Lg	G	GS	CG	GF	IP	BFP	H	R	ER	HR	SH	SF	HB	TBB	IBB	SO	WP	Bk	W	L	Pct	ShO	Sv-Op	Hld	ERC	ERA
2003 Portland*	AAA	23	23	0	0	125.0	554	161	84	75	9	5	8	10	28	0	57	1	0	7	8	.467	0	0- -	-	5.21	5.40
1998 Philadelphia	NL	21	21	1	0	122.2	549	154	86	83	18	5	8	3	39	1	58	4	0	7	8	.467	0	0-0	0	5.70	6.09
1999 Philadelphia	NL	20	13	2	2	89.2	385	100	54	51	9	5	6	0	26	0	48	3	0	2	6	.250	1	0-0	1	4.31	5.12
2001 San Diego	NL	2	2	0	0	4.1	29	13	12	12	2	1	0	0	3	0	1	0	0	0	2	.000	0	0-0	0	23.60	24.92
2003 San Diego	NL	5	5	0	0	21.2	105	35	17	16	3	0	1	1	8	1	11	1	0	1	2	.333	0	0-0	0	8.30	6.65
4 ML YEARS		48	41	3	2	238.1	1068	302	169	162	32	11	15	4	76	2	118	8	0	10	18	.357	1	0-0	1	5.64	6.12

Kenny Lofton

Bats: L **Throws:** L **Pos:** CF-137; PH-7   **Ht:** 6'0" **Wt:** 180 **Born:** 5/31/67 **Age:** 37

							BATTING												BASERUNNING				AVERAGES		
Year Team	Lg	G	AB	H	2B	3B	HR	(Hm	Rd)	TB	R	RBI	RC	TBB	IBB	SO	HBP	SH	SF	SB	CS	SB%	GDP	Avg	OBP	Slg
1991 Houston	NL	20	74	15	1	0	0	(0	0)	16	9	0	4	5	0	19	0	0	0	2	1	.67	0	.203	.253	.216
1992 Cleveland	AL	148	576	164	15	8	5	(3	2)	210	96	42	88	68	3	54	2	4	1	66	12	.85	7	.285	.362	.365
1993 Cleveland	AL	148	569	185	28	8	1	(1	0)	232	116	42	107	81	6	83	1	2	4	70	14	.83	8	.325	.408	.408
1994 Cleveland	AL	112	459	160	32	9	12	(10	2)	246	105	57	105	52	5	56	2	4	6	60	12	.83	5	.349	.412	.536
1995 Cleveland	AL	118	481	149	22	13	7	(5	2)	218	93	53	83	40	6	49	1	4	3	54	15	.78	6	.310	.362	.453
1996 Cleveland	AL	154	662	210	35	4	14	(7	7)	295	132	67	118	61	3	82	0	7	6	75	17	.82	7	.317	.372	.446
1997 Atlanta	NL	122	493	164	20	6	5	(3	2)	211	90	48	84	64	5	83	2	2	3	27	20	.57	10	.333	.409	.428
1998 Cleveland	AL	154	600	169	31	6	12	(6	6)	248	101	64	103	87	1	80	2	3	6	54	10	.84	7	.282	.371	.413
1999 Cleveland	AL	120	465	140	23	6	7	(1	6)	201	110	39	89	79	2	84	6	5	5	25	6	.81	6	.301	.405	.432
2000 Cleveland	AL	137	543	151	23	5	15	(10	5)	229	107	73	91	79	3	72	4	6	8	30	7	.81	11	.278	.369	.422
2001 Cleveland	AL	133	517	135	21	4	14	(9	5)	206	91	66	67	47	1	69	2	5	5	16	8	.67	8	.261	.322	.398
2002 CWS-SF		139	532	139	30	9	11	(8	3)	220	98	51	83	72	0	73	1	5	1	29	11	.73	1	.261	.350	.414
2003 Pit-ChC	NL	140	547	162	32	8	12	(5	7)	246	97	46	79	46	3	51	4	7	6	30	9	.77	6	.296	.352	.450
2002 Chicago	AL	93	352	91	20	6	8	(3	5)	147	68	42	57	49	0	51	0	4	1	22	8	.73	0	.259	.348	.418
2002 San Francisco	NL	46	180	48	10	3	3	(0	3)	73	30	9	26	23	0	22	1	1	0	7	3	.70	1	.267	.353	.406
2003 Pittsburgh	NL	84	339	94	19	4	9	(4	5)	148	58	26	43	28	1	29	2	2	3	18	5	.78	2	.277	.333	.437
2003 Chicago	NL	56	208	68	13	4	3	(1	2)	98	39	20	36	18	2	22	2	5	3	12	4	.75	4	.327	.381	.471
13 ML YEARS		1645	6518	1943	318	86	115	(63	52)	2778	1245	648	1101	781	38	855	27	54	54	538	142	.79	82	.298	.373	.426

Kyle Lohse

Pitches: R Bats: R Pos: SP-33   Ht: 6'2" Wt: 190 Born: 10/4/78 Age: 25

		HOW MUCH HE PITCHED						WHAT HE GAVE UP											THE RESULTS						
Year Team	Lg	G	GS	CG	GF	IP	BFP	H	R	ER	HR	SH	SF	HB	TBB	IBB	SO	WP	Bk	W	L	Pct	ShO	Sv-Op	Hld	ERC	ERA
2001 Minnesota	AL	19	16	0	2	90.1	402	102	60	57	16	1	5	8	29	0	64	5	0	4	7	.364	0	0-0	0	5.43	5.68
2002 Minnesota	AL	32	31	1	0	180.2	783	181	92	85	26	3	3	9	70	2	124	8	0	13	8	.619	1	0-1	0	4.55	4.23
2003 Minnesota	AL	33	33	2	0	201.0	850	211	107	103	28	8	5	5	45	1	130	10	1	14	11	.560	1	0-0	0	4.00	4.61
3 ML YEARS		84	80	3	2	472.0	2035	494	259	245	70	12	13	22	144	3	318	23	1	31	26	.544	2	0-1	0	4.47	4.67

George Lombard

Bats: L Throws: R Pos: RF-11; LF-3; PR-1   Ht: 6'0" Wt: 212 Born: 9/14/75 Age: 28

						BATTING															BASERUNNING				AVERAGES		
Year Team	Lg	G	AB	H	2B	3B	HR	(Hm	Rd)	TB	R	RBI	RC	TBB	IBB	SO	HBP	SH	SF	SB	CS	SB%	GDP	Avg	OBP	Slg
2003 Durham*	AAA	112	438	117	25	4	17	(-	-)	201	57	64	70	45	6	143	6	6	2	23	6	.79	6	.267	.342	.459
1998 Atlanta	NL	6	6	2	0	0	1	(0	1)	5	2	1	2	0	0	1	0	0	0	1	0	1.00	0	.333	.333	.833
1999 Atlanta	NL	6	6	2	0	0	0	(0	0)	2	1	0	1	1	0	2	0	0	0	2	0	1.00	0	.333	.429	.333
2000 Atlanta	NL	27	39	4	0	0	0	(0	0)	4	8	2	0	1	0	14	1	0	0	4	0	1.00	0	.103	.146	.103
2002 Detroit	AL	72	241	58	11	3	5	(2	3)	90	34	13	26	20	1	78	1	7	1	13	2	.87	0	.241	.300	.373
2003 Tampa Bay	AL	13	37	8	1	0	1	(0	1)	12	8	4	2	0	0	6	1	0	0	1	0	1.00	0	.216	.237	.324
5 ML YEARS		124	329	74	12	3	7	(2	5)	113	53	20	31	22	1	101	3	7	1	21	2	.91	2	.225	.279	.343

Terrence Long

Bats: L Throws: L Pos: LF-75; RF-74; PH-5; DH-1; PR-1   Ht: 6'1" Wt: 202 Born: 2/29/76 Age: 28

						BATTING															BASERUNNING				AVERAGES		
Year Team	Lg	G	AB	H	2B	3B	HR	(Hm	Rd)	TB	R	RBI	RC	TBB	IBB	SO	HBP	SH	SF	SB	CS	SB%	GDP	Avg	OBP	Slg
1999 New York	NL	3	3	0	0	0	0	(0	0)	0	0	0	0	0	0	2	0	0	0	0	0	-	1	.000	.000	.000
2000 Oakland	AL	138	584	168	34	4	18	(9	9)	264	104	80	85	43	1	77	1	0	3	5	0	1.00	18	.288	.336	.452
2001 Oakland	AL	162	629	178	37	4	12	(6	6)	259	90	85	84	52	8	103	0	0	6	9	3	.75	17	.283	.335	.412
2002 Oakland	AL	162	587	141	32	4	16	(9	7)	229	71	67	62	48	4	96	2	0	3	3	6	.33	17	.240	.298	.390
2003 Oakland	AL	140	486	119	22	2	14	(8	6)	187	64	61	60	31	4	67	3	0	2	4	1	.80	9	.245	.293	.385
5 ML YEARS		605	2289	606	125	14	60	(32	28)	939	329	293	291	174	19	345	6	0	14	21	10	.68	62	.265	.317	.410

Aaron Looper

Pitches: R Bats: R Pos: RP-6   Ht: 6'2" Wt: 185 Born: 9/7/76 Age: 27

				HOW MUCH HE PITCHED				WHAT HE GAVE UP												THE RESULTS						
Year Team	Lg	G	GS	CG	GF	IP	BFP	H	R	ER	HR	SH	SF	HB	TBB	IBB	SO	WP	Bk	W	L	Pct	ShO	Sv-Op	Hld	ERC	ERA
1998 Everett	A-	14	14	0	0	59.0	272	72	52	45	8	4	0	2	31	0	40	6	1	4	5	.444	0	0- -	-	6.41	6.86
1999 Wisconsin	A	38	7	0	10	90.0	391	89	47	41	8	1	3	6	26	0	73	6	1	9	6	.600	0	3- -	-	3.68	4.10
2000 Lancaster	A+	51	0	0	8	72.2	357	105	62	46	7	3	5	8	22	1	47	8	1	5	3	.625	0	0- -	-	6.49	5.70
2001 Sn Brnardino	A+	56	0	0	24	71.0	295	59	34	22	1	5	2	3	22	5	77	7	0	6	11	.353	0	5- -	-	2.31	2.79
2002 San Antonio	AA	57	0	0	9	90.2	377	76	33	23	4	6	1	9	30	6	73	4	0	1	.857	0	0- -	-	2.87	2.28
2003 Tacoma	AAA	46	0	0	20	75.1	324	72	27	26	10	3	1	2	26	2	67	2	0	5	2	.714	0	5- -	-	3.84	3.11
2003 Seattle	AL	6	0	0	3	7.0	29	7	4	4	1	0	0	1	2	0	6	0	0	0	0	-	0	0-0	0	4.73	5.14

Braden Looper

Pitches: R Bats: R Pos: RP-74   Ht: 6'3" Wt: 220 Born: 10/28/74 Age: 29

				HOW MUCH HE PITCHED				WHAT HE GAVE UP												THE RESULTS						
Year Team	Lg	G	GS	CG	GF	IP	BFP	H	R	ER	HR	SH	SF	HB	TBB	IBB	SO	WP	Bk	W	L	Pct	ShO	Sv-Op	Hld	ERC	ERA
1998 St Louis	NL	4	0	0	3	3.1	16	5	4	2	1	0	1	0	4	1	0	1	0	0	0	1.000	0	0-2	0	8.14	5.40
1999 Florida	NL	72	0	0	22	83.0	370	96	43	35	7	5	5	1	31	5	50	2	2	3	3	.500	0	0-4	8	4.67	3.80
2000 Florida	NL	73	0	0	23	67.1	311	71	41	33	3	3	2	5	36	6	29	5	0	5	1	.833	0	2-5	18	4.55	4.41
2001 Florida	NL	71	0	0	21	71.0	295	63	28	28	8	0	3	2	30	3	52	1	0	3	3	.500	0	3-6	16	3.77	3.55
2002 Florida	NL	78	0	0	40	86.0	349	73	31	30	8	3	0	1	28	3	55	1	0	2	5	.286	0	13-16	16	2.98	3.14
2003 Florida	NL	74	0	0	64	80.2	347	82	34	33	4	3	3	1	29	1	56	2	0	6	4	.600	0	28-34	0	3.67	3.68
6 ML YEARS		372	0	0	173	391.1	1688	390	181	161	31	14	14	10	155	18	246	11	2	19	17	.528	0	46-67	58	3.93	3.70

Albie Lopez

Pitches: R Bats: R Pos: RP-15   Ht: 6'2" Wt: 240 Born: 8/18/71 Age: 32

				HOW MUCH HE PITCHED				WHAT HE GAVE UP												THE RESULTS						
Year Team	Lg	G	GS	CG	GF	IP	BFP	H	R	ER	HR	SH	SF	HB	TBB	IBB	SO	WP	Bk	W	L	Pct	ShO	Sv-Op	Hld	ERC	ERA
2003 Omaha*	AAA	4	0	0	2	5.0	18	3	0	0	0	0	0	0	2	0	2	1	0	0	0	-	0	0- -	-	0.75	0.00
1993 Cleveland	AL	9	9	0	0	49.2	222	49	34	33	7	1	1	1	32	1	25	0	0	3	1	.750	0	0-0	0	5.45	5.98
1994 Cleveland	AL	4	4	1	0	17.0	76	20	11	8	3	0	0	1	6	0	18	3	0	1	2	.333	1	0-0	0	5.76	4.24
1995 Cleveland	AL	6	2	0	0	23.0	92	17	8	8	4	0	1	1	7	1	22	2	0	0	0	-	0	0-0	0	2.91	3.13
1996 Cleveland	AL	13	10	0	0	62.0	282	80	47	44	14	0	1	1	22	1	45	2	0	5	4	.556	0	0-0	0	6.74	6.39
1997 Cleveland	AL	37	6	0	10	76.2	364	101	61	59	11	3	2	4	40	9	63	5	0	3	7	.300	0	0-1	4	6.89	6.93
1998 Tampa Bay	AL	54	0	0	12	79.2	335	73	31	23	7	4	3	3	32	4	62	5	0	7	4	.636	0	1-5	4	3.66	2.60
1999 Tampa Bay	AL	51	0	0	14	64.0	281	66	40	33	8	1	4	1	24	2	37	3	0	3	2	.600	0	1-3	12	4.27	4.64
2000 Tampa Bay	AL	45	24	4	10	185.1	798	199	95	85	24	6	3	1	70	3	96	4	1	11	13	.458	1	2-4	1	4.68	4.13
2001 TB-Ari		33	33	3	0	205.2	896	226	123	110	26	8	5	4	75	3	136	2	1	9	19	.321	3	0-0	0	4.78	4.81
2002 Atlanta	NL	30	4	0	14	55.2	242	66	29	27	1	1	3	0	18	3	39	5	0	1	4	.200	0	0-0	1	4.19	4.37
2003 Kansas City	AL	15	0	0	3	22.2	125	41	32	32	7	1	0	0	17	1	15	3	0	4	2	.667	0	0-3	2	12.68	12.71
2001 Tampa Bay	AL	20	20	1	0	124.2	567	152	87	74	16	5	3	4	51	1	67	1	1	5	12	.294	1	0-0	0	5.74	5.34
2001 Arizona	NL	13	13	2	0	81.0	329	74	36	36	10	3	2	0	24	2	69	1	0	4	7	.364	2	0-0	0	3.39	4.00
11 ML YEARS		297	92	8	63	841.1	3713	938	511	462	112	25	23	18	343	28	558	34	2	47	58	.448	5	4-16	24	5.08	4.94

Aquilino Lopez

Pitches: R **Bats:** R **Pos:** RP-72 **Ht:** 6'3" **Wt:** 165 **Born:** 4/21/75 **Age:** 29

		HOW MUCH HE PITCHED							WHAT HE GAVE UP										THE RESULTS						
Year Team	Lg	G	GS	CG	GF	IP	BFP	H	R	ER	HR	SH	SF	HB	TBB	IBB	SO	WP	Bk	W	L	Pct	ShO	Sv-Op	Hld	ERC	ERA
1999 Everett	A-	15	15	1	0	87.2	365	76	44	37	8	1	2	2	30	2	93	2	0	7	6	.538	0	0--		3.12	3.80
2000 Wisconsin	A	39	5	1	29	68.0	268	47	16	14	1	0	1	4	20	4	67	3	0	6	1	.857	1	17--		1.76	1.85
2001 San Antonio	AA	42	0	0	13	62.2	265	48	24	21	4	2	2	6	25	2	79	5	0	4	3	.571	0	2--		2.85	3.02
2002 Tacoma	AAA	34	11	0	10	109.1	438	89	33	29	6	3	4	2	27	2	103	4	4	4	4	.500	0	5--		2.30	2.39
2003 Toronto	AL	72	0	0	34	73.2	315	58	31	28	5	2	2	5	34	5	64	2	1	1	3	.250	0	14-16	16	3.05	3.42

Felipe Lopez

Bats: B **Throws:** R **Pos:** SS-50; 3B-8; PH-4; 2B-3; PR-1 **Ht:** 6'0" **Wt:** 185 **Born:** 5/12/80 **Age:** 24

		BATTING																	BASERUNNING				AVERAGES		
Year Team	Lg	G	AB	H	2B	3B	HR	(Hm | Rd)	TB	R	RBI	RC	TBB	IBB	SO	HBP	SH	SF	SB	CS	SB%	GDP	Avg	OBP	Slg
2003 Louisville*	AAA	35	143	40	11	0	2	(- | -)	57	22	18	18	12	0	38	0	0	1	2	5	.29	0	.280	.333	.399
2001 Toronto	AL	49	177	46	5	4	5	(3 | 2)	74	21	23	22	12	1	39	0	1	2	4	3	.57	2	.260	.304	.418
2002 Toronto	AL	85	282	64	15	3	8	(5 | 3)	109	35	34	32	23	1	90	1	2	1	5	4	.56	4	.227	.287	.387
2003 Cincinnati	NL	59	197	42	7	2	2	(0 | 2)	59	28	13	21	28	1	59	1	2	1	8	5	.62	2	.213	.313	.299
3 ML YEARS		193	656	152	27	9	15	(8 | 7)	242	84	70	75	63	3	188	2	5	4	17	12	.59	8	.232	.299	.369

Javier Lopez

Pitches: L **Bats:** L **Pos:** RP-75 **Ht:** 6'4" **Wt:** 200 **Born:** 7/11/77 **Age:** 26

		HOW MUCH HE PITCHED							WHAT HE GAVE UP										THE RESULTS						
Year Team	Lg	G	GS	CG	GF	IP	BFP	H	R	ER	HR	SH	SF	HB	TBB	IBB	SO	WP	Bk	W	L	Pct	ShO	Sv-Op	Hld	ERC	ERA
1998 South Bend	A	16	9	0	1	44.0	218	60	36	32	2	2	3	0	30	0	31	7	0	2	4	.333	0	0--		6.93	6.55
1999 South Bend	A	20	20	0	0	99.0	458	122	74	66	9	1	4	3	43	0	70	9	0	4	6	.400	0	0--		5.58	6.00
2000 High Desert	A+	30	21	0	4	136.1	602	152	87	79	14	4	7	6	57	0	98	8	2	4	8	.333	0	2--		5.08	5.22
2001 Lancaster	A+	17	0	0	10	24.0	103	30	9	7	2	2	0	0	5	0	18	1	1	1	3	.250	0	1--		4.69	2.63
2001 El Paso	AA	22	1	0	4	40.0	191	64	39	33	6	2	1	0	14	2	21	1	0	1	0	1.000	0	0--		7.97	7.43
2002 El Paso	AA	61	0	0	25	46.1	186	34	16	14	3	2	1	0	16	1	47	1	0	2	2	.500	0	6--		2.24	2.72
2002 Vero Beach	A+	1	0	0	0	0.1	7	2	4	2	0	0	0	0	3	0	0	0	0	0	0	-	0	0--		74.92	54.00
2003 Colorado	NL	75	0	0	11	58.1	242	58	25	24	5	1	0	4	12	2	40	1	3	4	1	.800	0	1-2	15	3.44	3.70

Javy Lopez

Bats: R **Throws:** R **Pos:** C-120; PH-13; DH-3 **Ht:** 6'3" **Wt:** 225 **Born:** 11/5/70 **Age:** 33

		BATTING																	BASERUNNING				AVERAGES		
Year Team	Lg	G	AB	H	2B	3B	HR	(Hm | Rd)	TB	R	RBI	RC	TBB	IBB	SO	HBP	SH	SF	SB	CS	SB%	GDP	Avg	OBP	Slg
1992 Atlanta	NL	9	16	6	0	0	0	(0 | 0)	8	3	2	3	0	0	1	0	0	0	0	0	-	0	.375	.375	.500
1993 Atlanta	NL	8	16	6	1	1	1	(0 | 1)	12	1	2	4	0	0	2	1	0	0	0	0	-	0	.375	.412	.750
1994 Atlanta	NL	80	277	68	9	0	13	(4 | 9)	116	27	35	31	17	0	61	5	2	2	0	2	.00	2	.245	.299	.419
1995 Atlanta	NL	100	333	105	11	4	14	(8 | 6)	166	37	51	51	14	0	57	2	0	3	0	1	.00	13	.315	.344	.498
1996 Atlanta	NL	138	489	138	19	1	23	(10 | 13)	228	56	69	66	28	5	84	3	1	5	1	6	.14	17	.282	.322	.466
1997 Atlanta	NL	123	414	122	28	1	23	(11 | 12)	221	52	68	76	40	10	82	5	1	4	1	1	.50	9	.295	.361	.534
1998 Atlanta	NL	133	489	139	21	1	34	(18 | 16)	264	73	106	79	30	1	85	6	1	8	5	3	.63	22	.284	.328	.540
1999 Atlanta	NL	65	246	78	18	1	11	(1 | 10)	131	34	45	45	20	2	41	3	0	0	3	3	.00	6	.317	.375	.533
2000 Atlanta	NL	134	481	138	21	1	24	(12 | 12)	233	60	89	72	35	3	80	4	0	5	0	0	-	20	.287	.337	.484
2001 Atlanta	NL	128	438	117	16	1	17	(10 | 7)	186	45	66	58	28	3	82	10	1	5	1	0	1.00	12	.267	.322	.425
2002 Atlanta	NL	109	347	81	15	0	11	(1 | 10)	129	31	52	40	26	8	63	8	0	4	0	1	.00	15	.233	.299	.372
2003 Atlanta	NL	129	457	150	29	3	43	(26 | 17)	314	89	109	105	33	5	90	4	0	1	0	1	.00	10	.328	.378	.687
12 ML YEARS		1156	4003	1148	190	14	214	(101 | 113)	2008	508	694	630	271	37	728	51	6	37	8	18	.31	136	.287	.337	.502

Mendy Lopez

Bats: R **Throws:** R **Pos:** 1B-17; 3B-13; 2B-11; PH-6; PR-5; SS-4; RF-2; LF-1 **Ht:** 6'2" **Wt:** 200 **Born:** 10/15/74 **Age:** 29

		BATTING																	BASERUNNING				AVERAGES		
Year Team	Lg	G	AB	H	2B	3B	HR	(Hm | Rd)	TB	R	RBI	RC	TBB	IBB	SO	HBP	SH	SF	SB	CS	SB%	GDP	Avg	OBP	Slg
2003 Royals*	R	7	20	5	1	0	3	(- | -)	15	9	6	6	4	0	5	1	0	0	0	0	-	0	.250	.400	.750
1998 Kansas City	AL	74	206	50	10	2	1	(1 | 0)	67	18	15	18	12	0	40	1	5	1	5	2	.71	6	.243	.286	.325
1999 Kansas City	AL	7	20	8	0	1	0	(0 | 0)	10	2	3	4	0	0	5	1	0	0	0	0	-	0	.400	.429	.500
2000 Florida	NL	4	3	0	0	0	0	(0 | 0)	0	0	0	0	1	0	1	0	0	0	0	0	-	0	.000	.250	.000
2001 Hou-Pit	NL	32	58	14	3	1	1	(0 | 1)	22	8	7	8	6	1	20	1	0	1	0	0	-	1	.241	.318	.379
2002 Pittsburgh	NL	3	3	0	0	0	0	(0 | 0)	0	0	0	0	0	0	3	0	0	0	0	0	-	0	.000	.000	.000
2003 Kansas City	NL	52	94	26	5	1	3	(3 | 0)	42	13	11	12	4	0	28	0	2	0	2	0	1.00	3	.277	.306	.447
2001 Houston	NL	10	15	4	0	0	1	(0 | 1)	7	3	3	3	2	0	4	1	0	0	0	0	-	0	.267	.389	.467
2001 Pittsburgh	NL	22	43	10	3	1	0	(0 | 0)	15	5	4	5	4	1	16	0	0	1	0	0	-	1	.233	.292	.349
6 ML YEARS		172	384	98	18	5	5	(4 | 1)	141	41	36	42	23	1	97	3	7	2	7	2	.78	9	.255	.301	.367

Rodrigo Lopez

Pitches: R **Bats:** R **Pos:** SP-26 **Ht:** 6'1" **Wt:** 180 **Born:** 12/14/75 **Age:** 28

		HOW MUCH HE PITCHED							WHAT HE GAVE UP										THE RESULTS						
Year Team	Lg	G	GS	CG	GF	IP	BFP	H	R	ER	HR	SH	SF	HB	TBB	IBB	SO	WP	Bk	W	L	Pct	ShO	Sv-Op	Hld	ERC	ERA
2003 Bowie*	AA	1	1	0	0	6.1	21	3	0	0	0	0	0	0	0	0	13	0	0	1	0	1.000	0	0--		0.51	0.00
2000 San Diego	NL	6	6	0	0	24.2	120	40	24	24	5	0	1	0	13	0	17	0	0	0	3	.000	0	0-0	0	9.78	8.76
2002 Baltimore	AL	33	28	1	0	196.2	809	172	83	78	23	2	4	5	62	4	136	2	1	15	9	.625	1	0-0	0	3.27	3.57
2003 Baltimore	AL	26	26	3	0	147.0	663	188	101	95	24	3	7	10	43	6	103	2	1	7	10	.412	1	0-0	0	6.00	5.82
3 ML YEARS		65	60	4	0	368.1	1592	400	208	197	52	5	12	15	118	10	256	4	2	22	22	.500	1	0-0	0	4.70	4.81

Mark Loretta

Bats: R **Throws:** R **Pos:** 2B-150; PH-9; SS-3 **Ht:** 6'0" **Wt:** 186 **Born:** 8/14/71 **Age:** 32

							BATTING													**BASERUNNING**				**AVERAGES**			
Year Team	Lg	G	AB	H	2B	3B	HR	(Hm	Rd)	TB	R	RBI	RC	TBB	IBB	SO	HBP	SH	SF	SB	CS	SB%	GDP	Avg	OBP	Slg
1995 Milwaukee	NL	19	50	13	3	0	1	(0	1)	19	13	3	6	4	0	7	1	1	0	1	1	.50	1	.260	.327	.380
1996 Milwaukee	NL	73	154	43	3	0	1	(0	1)	49	20	13	16	14	0	15	0	2	0	2	1	.67	7	.279	.339	.318
1997 Milwaukee	NL	132	418	120	17	5	5	(2	3)	162	56	47	56	47	2	60	2	5	10	5	5	.50	15	.287	.354	.388
1998 Milwaukee	NL	140	434	137	29	0	6	(3	3)	184	55	54	68	42	1	47	7	4	4	9	6	.60	14	.316	.382	.424
1999 Milwaukee	NL	153	587	170	34	5	5	(2	3)	229	93	67	82	52	1	59	10	9	6	4	1	.80	14	.290	.354	.390
2000 Milwaukee	NL	91	352	99	21	1	7	(3	4)	143	49	40	48	37	2	38	1	8	1	0	3	.00	9	.281	.350	.406
2001 Milwaukee	NL	102	384	111	14	2	2	(0	2)	135	40	29	48	28	0	46	7	7	3	1	2	.33	6	.289	.346	.352
2002 Mil-Hou	NL	107	283	86	18	0	4	(2	2)	116	33	27	48	32	1	37	5	6	3	1	1	.50	7	.304	.381	.410
2003 San Diego	NL	154	589	185	28	4	13	(10	3)	260	74	72	92	54	2	62	3	3	4	5	4	.56	17	.314	.372	.441
2002 Milwaukee	NL	86	217	58	14	0	2	(1	1)	78	23	19	32	23	1	32	5	6	1	0	0	-	6	.267	.350	.359
2002 Houston	NL	21	66	28	4	0	2	(1	1)	38	10	8	16	9	0	5	0	0	2	1	1	.50	1	.424	.481	.576
9 ML YEARS		971	3251	964	167	17	44	(22	22)	1297	433	352	464	310	9	371	36	45	31	28	24	.54	90	.297	.361	.399

Shane Loux

Pitches: R **Bats:** R **Pos:** RP-7; SP-4 **Ht:** 6'2" **Wt:** 205 **Born:** 8/13/79 **Age:** 24

		HOW MUCH HE PITCHED						**WHAT HE GAVE UP**										**THE RESULTS**							
Year Team	Lg	G	GS	CG	GF	IP	BFP	H	R	ER	HR	SH	SF	HB	TBB	IBB	SO	WP	Bk	W	L	Pct	ShO	Sv-Op	Hld	ERC	ERA
1997 Tigers	R	10	9	1	0	43.0	158	19	7	4	0	0	0	1	10	0	33	2	1	4	1	.800	1	0--	-	0.82	0.84
1998 W Michigan	A	28	28	2	0	157.0	698	184	96	81	13	2	4	8	52	0	88	12	2	7	13	.350	1	0--	-	4.87	4.64
1999 W Michigan	A	8	8	0	0	47.1	215	55	39	33	5	1	2	8	16	1	43	4	0	1	3	.250	0	0--	-	5.49	6.27
1999 Lakeland	A+	17	17	0	0	91.0	412	92	48	41	8	2	5	10	47	0	52	7	1	6	5	.545	0	0--	-	4.96	4.05
2000 Lakeland	A+	1	1	0	0	5.0	19	2	1	1	0	1	0	0	3	0	6	0	0	0	1	.000	0	0--	-	1.39	1.80
2000 Jacksonville	AA	26	26	2	0	157.2	670	150	78	67	12	3	7	14	55	0	130	7	0	12	9	.571	0	0--	-	3.83	3.82
2001 Toledo	AAA	28	27	2	1	151.0	727	203	111	97	22	4	10	15	73	0	72	14	1	10	11	.476	0	0--	-	7.31	5.78
2002 Toledo	AAA	26	26	5	0	158.1	696	196	94	83	11	4	4	10	38	1	87	9	2	11	10	.524	3	0--	-	4.86	4.72
2003 Toledo	AAA	21	20	2	0	128.0	531	129	53	43	5	4	5	6	30	0	58	4	0	11	6	.647	1	0--	-	3.30	3.02
2002 Detroit	AL	3	3	0	0	14.0	64	19	16	14	4	0	0	1	3	0	7	1	0	0	3	.000	0	0-0	0	7.12	9.00
2003 Detroit	AL	11	4	0	1	30.1	140	37	24	24	4	1	1	4	12	1	8	1	0	1	1	.500	0	0-0	0	6.12	7.12
2 ML YEARS		14	7	0	1	44.1	204	56	40	38	8	1	1	5	15	1	15	2	0	1	4	.200	0	0-0	0	6.45	7.71

Derek Lowe

Pitches: R **Bats:** R **Pos:** SP-33 **Ht:** 6'6" **Wt:** 214 **Born:** 6/1/73 **Age:** 31

		HOW MUCH HE PITCHED						**WHAT HE GAVE UP**										**THE RESULTS**							
Year Team	Lg	G	GS	CG	GF	IP	BFP	H	R	ER	HR	SH	SF	HB	TBB	IBB	SO	WP	Bk	W	L	Pct	ShO	Sv-Op	Hld	ERC	ERA
1997 Sea-Bos	AL	20	9	0	1	69.0	298	74	49	47	11	4	2	4	23	3	52	2	0	2	6	.250	0	0-2	1	4.88	6.13
1998 Boston	AL	63	10	0	8	123.0	527	126	65	55	5	4	5	4	42	5	77	8	0	3	9	.250	0	4-9	12	3.64	4.02
1999 Boston	AL	74	0	0	32	109.1	436	84	35	32	7	1	2	4	25	1	80	1	0	6	3	.667	0	15-20	22	2.14	2.63
2000 Boston	AL	74	0	0	64	91.1	379	90	27	26	6	4	1	2	22	5	79	1	1	4	4	.500	0	42-47	1	3.17	2.56
2001 Boston	AL	67	0	0	50	91.2	404	103	39	36	7	5	1	5	29	9	82	4	0	5	10	.333	0	24-30	4	4.31	3.53
2002 Boston	AL	32	32	1	0	219.2	854	166	65	63	12	5	2	12	48	0	127	5	0	21	8	.724	1	0-0	0	2.13	2.58
2003 Boston	AL	33	33	1	0	203.1	886	216	113	101	17	3	5	11	72	4	110	3	0	17	7	.708	0	0-0	0	4.32	4.47
1997 Seattle	AL	12	9	0	1	53.0	234	59	43	41	11	2	1	2	20	2	39	2	0	2	4	.333	0	0-0	0	5.55	6.96
1997 Boston	AL	8	0	0	0	16.0	64	15	6	6	0	2	1	2	3	1	13	0	0	0	2	.000	0	0-2	1	2.78	3.38
7 ML YEARS		363	87	2	155	907.1	3784	859	393	360	65	26	18	42	261	27	607	24	1	58	47	.552	1	85-108	39	3.32	3.57

Sean Lowe

Pitches: R **Bats:** R **Pos:** RP-28 **Ht:** 6'2" **Wt:** 225 **Born:** 3/29/71 **Age:** 33

		HOW MUCH HE PITCHED						**WHAT HE GAVE UP**										**THE RESULTS**							
Year Team	Lg	G	GS	CG	GF	IP	BFP	H	R	ER	HR	SH	SF	HB	TBB	IBB	SO	WP	Bk	W	L	Pct	ShO	Sv-Op	Hld	ERC	ERA
2003 Omaha*	AAA	14	7	0	1	52.2	222	54	22	19	3	1	1	3	19	0	27	1	0	4	0	1.000	0	0--	-	4.12	3.25
1997 St Louis	NL	6	4	0	1	17.1	89	27	21	18	2	1	2	1	10	0	8	0	0	0	2	.000	0	0-0	0	8.57	9.35
1998 St Louis	NL	4	1	0	2	5.1	31	11	9	9	1	1	0	0	5	0	2	0	0	0	3	.000	0	0-0	0	14.71	15.19
1999 Chicago	AL	64	0	0	13	95.2	406	90	39	39	10	3	9	4	46	1	62	4	0	4	1	.800	0	0-3	6	4.38	3.67
2000 Chicago	AL	50	5	0	8	70.2	325	78	47	43	10	4	1	6	39	3	53	3	0	4	1	.800	0	0-0	6	5.95	5.48
2001 Chicago	AL	45	11	0	9	127.0	529	123	55	51	12	3	7	7	32	2	71	6	0	9	4	.692	0	3-3	3	3.51	3.61
2002 Pit-Col	NL	51	1	0	8	79.1	379	101	58	51	9	5	3	7	41	6	64	1	1	5	3	.625	0	0-2	10	6.50	5.79
2003 Kansas City	AL	28	0	0	6	44.2	208	55	32	31	7	1	1	2	21	5	28	3	0	1	1	.500	0	0-1	7	6.14	6.25
2002 Pittsburgh	NL	43	1	0	8	69.0	326	85	45	41	8	5	3	7	34	6	57	1	1	4	2	.667	0	0-2	9	6.20	5.35
2002 Colorado	NL	8	0	0	0	10.1	53	16	13	10	1	0	0	0	7	0	7	0	0	1	1	.500	0	0-0	1	8.60	8.71
7 ML YEARS		248	22	0	47	440.0	1967	485	261	242	51	18	23	27	194	17	288	17	1	23	15	.605	0	3-9	32	5.17	4.95

Mike Lowell

Bats: R **Throws:** R **Pos:** 3B-128; DH-2 **Ht:** 6'3" **Wt:** 217 **Born:** 2/24/74 **Age:** 30

							BATTING													**BASERUNNING**				**AVERAGES**		
Year Team	Lg	G	AB	H	2B	3B	HR	(Hm	Rd)	TB	R	RBI	RC	TBB	IBB	SO	HBP	SH	SF	SB	CS	SB%	GDP	Avg	OBP	Slg
1998 New York	AL	8	15	4	0	0	0	(0	0)	4	1	0	1	0	0	1	0	0	0	0	0	-	0	.267	.267	.267
1999 Florida	NL	97	308	78	15	0	12	(7	5)	129	32	47	40	26	1	69	5	0	5	0	0	-	8	.253	.317	.419
2000 Florida	NL	140	508	137	38	0	22	(11	11)	241	73	91	86	54	4	75	9	0	11	4	0	1.00	4	.270	.344	.474
2001 Florida	NL	146	551	156	37	0	18	(12	6)	247	65	100	84	43	3	79	10	0	10	1	2	.33	9	.283	.340	.448
2002 Florida	NL	160	597	165	44	0	24	(13	11)	281	88	92	86	65	5	92	4	0	11	4	3	.57	16	.276	.346	.471
2003 Florida	NL	130	492	136	27	1	32	(14	18)	261	76	105	90	56	6	78	3	0	6	3	1	.75	14	.276	.350	.530
6 ML YEARS		681	2471	676	161	1	108	(57	51)	1163	335	435	387	244	19	394	31	0	43	12	6	.67	51	.274	.341	.471

Noah Lowry

Pitches: L Bats: L Pos: RP-4   Ht: 6'2" Wt: 190 Born: 10/10/80 Age: 23

		HOW MUCH HE PITCHED						WHAT HE GAVE UP											THE RESULTS						
Year Team	Lg	G	GS	CG	GF	IP	BFP	H	R	ER	HR	SF	HB	TBB	IBB	SO	WP	Bk	W	L	Pct	ShO	Sv-Op	Hld	ERC	ERA
2001 Salem-Keizer	A-	8	7	0	0	25.0	109	26	15	10	2	0	2	8	0	28	2	0	1	1	.500	0	0- -		3.94	3.60
2002 San Jose	A+	15	12	0	0	58.2	229	38	21	14	4	1	3	20	0	62	1	0	6	5	.545	0	0- -		2.10	2.15
2003 Norwich	AA	23	23	2	0	118.1	509	127	66	62	7	7	5	47	0	97	3	2	9	6	.600	0	0- -		4.43	4.72
2003 Fresno	AAA	4	4	0	0	19.0	74	15	5	5	0	2	0	6	0	13	0	0	1	0	1.000	0	0- -		2.14	2.37
2003 San Francisco	NL	4	0	0	3	6.1	24	1	0	0	0	0	1	2	0	5	0	0	0	0	-	0	0-0	0	0.50	0.00

Ryan Ludwick

Bats: R Throws: L Pos: RF-25; LF-17; PH-5; DH-2; PR-1   Ht: 6'3" Wt: 203 Born: 7/13/78 Age: 25

		BATTING																BASERUNNING				AVERAGES		
Year Team	Lg	G	AB	H	2B	3B	HR	(Hm | Rd)	TB	R	RBI	RC	TBB	IBB	SO	HBP	SH	SF	SB	CS	SB%	GDP	Avg	OBP	Slg
1999 Modesto	A+	43	171	47	11	3	4	(- | -)	76	28	34	28	19	0	45	3	0	5	2	1	.67	0	.275	.348	.444
2000 Modesto	A+	129	493	130	26	3	29	(- | -)	249	86	102	90	68	0	128	9	1	7	10	6	.63	6	.264	.359	.505
2001 Midland	AA	119	443	119	23	3	25	(- | -)	223	82	96	78	56	1	113	7	1	5	9	10	.47	6	.269	.348	.503
2001 Sacramento	AAA	17	57	13	3	0	1	(- | -)	19	10	7	5	2	0	16	0	1	2	2	0	1.00	0	.228	.246	.333
2002 Oklahoma	AAA	78	305	87	27	4	15	(- | -)	167	62	52	60	38	1	76	5	1	3	2	2	.50	6	.285	.370	.548
2003 Oklahoma	AAA	81	317	96	24	3	17	(- | -)	177	51	63	62	33	3	71	5	0	5	1	1	.50	9	.303	.372	.558
2002 Texas	AL	23	81	19	6	0	1	(1 | 0)	28	10	9	6	7	0	24	0	0	0	2	1	.67	4	.235	.295	.346
2003 Tex-Cle		47	162	40	8	1	7	(2 | 5)	71	17	26	28	12	1	48	0	1	0	2	0	1.00	1	.247	.299	.438
2003 Texas	AL	8	26	4	1	0	0	(0 | 0)	5	3	0	1	4	0	9	0	0	0	0	0	-	0	.154	.267	.192
2003 Cleveland	AL	39	136	36	7	1	7	(2 | 5)	66	14	26	27	8	1	39	0	1	0	2	0	1.00	1	.265	.306	.485
2 ML YEARS		70	243	59	14	1	8	(3 | 5)	99	27	35	34	19	1	72	0	1	0	4	1	.80	5	.243	.298	.407

Julio Lugo

Bats: R Throws: R Pos: SS-139   Ht: 6'1" Wt: 170 Born: 11/16/75 Age: 28

		BATTING																BASERUNNING				AVERAGES		
Year Team	Lg	G	AB	H	2B	3B	HR	(Hm | Rd)	TB	R	RBI	RC	TBB	IBB	SO	HBP	SH	SF	SB	CS	SB%	GDP	Avg	OBP	Slg
2000 Houston	NL	116	420	119	22	5	10	(6 | 4)	181	78	40	62	37	0	93	4	3	1	22	9	.71	9	.283	.346	.431
2001 Houston	NL	140	513	135	20	3	10	(6 | 4)	191	93	37	63	46	0	116	5	15	7	12	11	.52	7	.263	.326	.372
2002 Houston	NL	88	322	84	15	1	8	(6 | 2)	125	45	35	43	28	3	74	2	4	2	9	3	.75	6	.261	.322	.388
2003 Hou-TB		139	498	135	16	4	15	(5 | 10)	204	64	55	67	44	1	100	4	7	3	12	4	.75	7	.271	.333	.410
2003 Houston	NL	22	65	16	3	0	0	(0 | 0)	19	6	2	7	9	1	12	0	1	0	2	1	.67	2	.246	.338	.292
2003 Tampa Bay	AL	117	433	119	13	4	15	(5 | 10)	185	58	53	60	35	0	88	4	7	3	10	3	.77	5	.275	.333	.427
4 ML YEARS		483	1753	473	73	13	43	(23 | 20)	701	280	167	235	155	4	383	15	29	13	55	27	.67	29	.270	.332	.400

Trey Lunsford

Bats: R Throws: R Pos: C-1   Ht: 6'1" Wt: 195 Born: 5/25/79 Age: 25

		BATTING																BASERUNNING				AVERAGES		
Year Team	Lg	G	AB	H	2B	3B	HR	(Hm | Rd)	TB	R	RBI	RC	TBB	IBB	SO	HBP	SH	SF	SB	CS	SB%	GDP	Avg	OBP	Slg
2000 Salem-Keizer	A-	120	438	110	24	2	15	(- | -)	183	61	61	63	43	1	106	10	3	2	10	1	.91	7	.251	.331	.418
2001 Hagerstown	A	114	396	94	19	0	5	(- | -)	128	53	50	41	45	1	89	5	4	4	10	5	.67	12	.237	.320	.323
2002 San Jose	A+	16	51	13	3	0	1	(- | -)	19	7	5	6	3	0	5	2	1	0	2	0	1.00	2	.255	.321	.373
2002 Shreveport	AA	66	210	59	13	0	1	(- | -)	75	26	20	31	29	1	42	4	5	0	5	2	.71	3	.281	.379	.357
2002 Fresno	AAA	19	57	10	0	0	2	(- | -)	16	3	9	4	6	0	15	1	0	2	0	0	-	2	.175	.258	.281
2003 Giants	R	5	13	6	0	1	0	(- | -)	8	5	3	5	7	0	3	0	0	1	1	1	.50	0	.462	.619	.615
2003 San Jose	A+	2	7	2	0	0	1	(- | -)	5	1	1	1	0	0	4	0	0	0	0	0	-	0	.286	.286	.714
2003 Salem-Keizer	A-	3	10	3	0	0	0	(- | -)	3	0	3	2	2	0	1	1	0	1	0	0	-	0	.300	.429	.300
2003 Fresno	AAA	69	206	59	10	1	2	(- | -)	77	20	20	26	17	0	33	1	4	2	0	1	.00	6	.286	.341	.374
2002 San Francisco	NL	3	3	2	1	0	0	(0 | 0)	3	0	1	1	0	0	1	0	0	0	0	0	-	0	.667	.667	1.000
2003 San Francisco	NL	1	1	0	0	0	0	(0 | 0)	0	0	0	0	0	0	0	0	0	0	0	0	-	0	.000	.000	.000
2 ML YEARS		4	4	2	1	0	0	(0 | 0)	3	0	1	1	0	0	1	0	0	0	0	0	-	0	.500	.500	.750

Brandon Lyon

Pitches: R Bats: R Pos: RP-49   Ht: 6'1" Wt: 185 Born: 8/10/79 Age: 24

		HOW MUCH HE PITCHED						WHAT HE GAVE UP											THE RESULTS						
Year Team	Lg	G	GS	CG	GF	IP	BFP	H	R	ER	HR	SF	HB	TBB	IBB	SO	WP	Bk	W	L	Pct	ShO	Sv-Op	Hld	ERC	ERA
2003 Pawtucket*	AAA	5	0	0	2	8.1	34	7	3	3	1	0	0	2	0	7	0	1	0	0	-	0	0- -		2.69	3.24
2001 Toronto	AL	11	11	0	0	63.0	261	63	31	30	6	2	6	15	0	35	0	1	5	4	.556	0	0-0	0	3.50	4.29
2002 Toronto	AL	15	10	0	0	62.0	279	78	47	45	14	3	2	19	2	30	2	0	1	4	.200	0	0-1	0	6.24	6.53
2003 Boston	AL	49	0	0	31	59.0	273	73	33	27	6	1	4	19	5	50	0	0	4	6	.400	0	9-12	2	4.96	4.12
3 ML YEARS		75	21	0	31	184.0	813	214	111	102	26	6	12	53	7	115	2	1	10	14	.417	0	9-13	2	4.86	4.99

John Mabry

Bats: L Throws: R Pos: PH-28; RF-14; 1B-9; DH-9; LF-8; PR-1   Ht: 6'4" Wt: 210 Born: 10/17/70 Age: 33

		BATTING																BASERUNNING				AVERAGES		
Year Team	Lg	G	AB	H	2B	3B	HR	(Hm | Rd)	TB	R	RBI	RC	TBB	IBB	SO	HBP	SH	SF	SB	CS	SB%	GDP	Avg	OBP	Slg
2003 Tacoma*	AAA	3	11	4	0	0	0	(- | -)	4	1	0	2	2	1	1	0	0	0	0	0	-	0	.364	.462	.364
1994 St Louis	NL	6	23	7	3	0	0	(0 | 0)	10	2	3	4	2	0	4	0	0	0	0	0	-	0	.304	.360	.435
1995 St Louis	NL	129	388	119	21	1	5	(2 | 3)	157	35	41	53	24	5	45	2	0	4	0	3	.00	9	.307	.347	.405
1996 St Louis	NL	151	543	161	30	2	13	(3 | 10)	234	63	74	74	37	11	84	3	3	5	3	2	.60	21	.297	.342	.431
1997 St Louis	NL	116	388	110	19	0	5	(5 | 0)	144	40	36	49	39	9	77	3	2	2	0	1	.00	11	.284	.352	.371
1998 St Louis	NL	142	377	94	22	0	9	(4 | 5)	143	41	46	42	30	6	76	1	3	6	2	0	1.00	6	.249	.305	.379
1999 Seattle	AL	87	262	64	14	0	9	(4 | 5)	105	34	33	30	20	1	60	0	2	1	2	1	.67	6	.244	.297	.401
2000 Sea-SD		95	226	53	13	0	8	(3 | 5)	90	35	32	25	15	0	69	2	0	1	0	1	.00	6	.235	.287	.398
2001 StL-Fla	NL	87	154	32	7	0	6	(2 | 4)	57	14	20	16	13	1	46	5	0	2	1	0	1.00	6	.208	.287	.370
2002 Phi-Oak		110	214	59	13	1	11	(8 | 3)	107	28	43	35	15	2	42	1	0	4	1	1	.50	7	.276	.321	.500

137

Year Team	Lg	G	AB	H	2B	3B	HR	(Hm	Rd)	TB	R	RBI	RC	TBB	IBB	SO	HBP	SH	SF	SB	CS	SB%	GDP	Avg	OBP	Slg
2003 Seattle	AL	64	104	22	6	0	3	(1	2)	37	12	16	12	15	2	21	3	0	0	0	0	-	3	.212	.328	.356
2000 Seattle	AL	47	103	25	5	0	1	(0	1)	33	18	7	11	10	0	31	2	0	0	0	1	.00	1	.243	.322	.320
2000 San Diego	NL	48	123	28	8	0	7	(3	4)	57	17	25	14	5	0	38	0	0	1	0	0	-	3	.228	.256	.463
2001 St Louis	NL	5	7	0	0	0	0	(0	0)	0	0	0	0	0	0	2	0	0	0	0	0	-	0	.000	.000	.000
2001 Florida	NL	82	147	32	7	0	6	(2	4)	57	14	20	16	13	1	44	5	0	2	1	0	1.00	6	.218	.299	.388
2002 Philadelphia	NL	21	21	6	0	0	0	(0	0)	6	1	3	3	1	1	5	0	0	1	0	0	-	0	.286	.304	.286
2002 Oakland	AL	89	193	53	13	1	11	(8	3)	101	27	40	32	14	1	37	1	0	3	1	1	.50	7	.275	.322	.523
10 ML YEARS		987	2679	721	148	4	69	(33	36)	1084	304	344	340	210	37	524	20	10	21	7	11	.39	70	.269	.325	.405

Mike MacDougal

Pitches: R Bats: B Pos: RP-68

Ht: 6'4" Wt: 195 Born: 3/5/77 Age: 27

Year Team	Lg	G	GS	CG	GF	IP	BFP	H	R	ER	HR	SH	SF	HB	TBB	IBB	SO	WP	Bk	W	L	Pct	ShO	Sv-Op	Hld	ERC	ERA
2001 Kansas City	AL	3	3	0	0	15.1	67	18	10	8	2	0	0	1	4	0	7	3	0	1	1	.500	0	0-0	0	5.04	4.70
2002 Kansas City	AL	6	0	0	1	9.0	38	5	5	5	0	0	0	0	7	1	10	1	0	0	1	.000	0	0-0	0	2.26	5.00
2003 Kansas City	AL	68	0	0	61	64.0	285	64	36	29	4	3	2	8	32	0	57	6	0	3	5	.375	0	27-35	1	4.76	4.08
3 ML YEARS		77	3	0	62	88.1	390	87	51	42	6	3	2	9	43	1	74	10	0	4	7	.364	0	27-35	1	4.54	4.28

Andy Machado

Bats: B Throws: R Pos: PR-1

Ht: 5'11" Wt: 165 Born: 1/25/81 Age: 23

Year Team	Lg	G	AB	H	2B	3B	HR	(Hm	Rd)	TB	R	RBI	RC	TBB	IBB	SO	HBP	SH	SF	SB	CS	SB%	GDP	Avg	OBP	Slg
1999 Phillies	R	68	143	37	6	3	2	(-	-)	55	26	12	19	15	2	38	2	7	1	6	3	.67	1	.259	.335	.385
1999 Clearwater	A+	1	2	0	0	0	0	(-	-)	0	0	0	0	0	0	1	0	0	0	0	0	-	0	.000	.000	.000
1999 Piedmont	A	20	60	14	4	2	0	(-	-)	22	7	7	8	7	0	20	1	1	0	2	1	.67	0	.233	.324	.367
2000 Clearwater	A+	117	417	102	19	7	1	(-	-)	138	55	35	47	54	0	103	0	5	2	32	18	.64	7	.245	.330	.331
2000 Reading	AA	3	11	4	1	0	1	(-	-)	8	2	2	3	0	0	4	0	0	0	0	0	-	0	.364	.364	.727
2001 Clearwater	A+	82	272	71	5	8	5	(-	-)	107	49	36	39	31	2	66	4	10	3	23	9	.72	3	.261	.342	.393
2001 Reading	AA	31	101	15	2	0	1	(-	-)	20	13	8	4	12	0	25	0	3	1	5	2	.71	1	.149	.237	.198
2002 Reading	AA	126	450	113	24	3	12	(-	-)	179	71	77	71	72	4	118	2	18	5	40	11	.78	5	.251	.353	.398
2003 Reading	AA	123	423	83	19	4	5	(-	-)	125	80	20	59	108	0	120	1	8	1	49	15	.77	2	.196	.360	.296
2003 Philadelphia	NL	1	0	0	0	0	0	(0	0)	0	0	0	0	0	0	0	0	0	0	1	0	1.00	0	-	-	-

Robert Machado

Bats: R Throws: R Pos: C-18; PH-1

Ht: 6'1" Wt: 210 Born: 6/3/73 Age: 31

Year Team	Lg	G	AB	H	2B	3B	HR	(Hm	Rd)	TB	R	RBI	RC	TBB	IBB	SO	HBP	SH	SF	SB	CS	SB%	GDP	Avg	OBP	Slg
2003 Ottawa*	AAA	59	221	74	17	0	8	(-	-)	115	30	38	42	17	2	36	3	1	0	0	0	-	6	.335	.390	.520
1996 Chicago	AL	4	6	4	1	0	0	(0	0)	5	1	2	2	0	0	0	0	0	0	0	0	-	1	.667	.667	.833
1997 Chicago	AL	10	15	3	0	1	0	(0	0)	5	1	2	1	1	0	6	0	1	0	0	0	-	0	.200	.250	.333
1998 Chicago	AL	34	111	23	6	0	3	(2	1)	38	14	15	9	7	0	22	0	3	0	0	0	-	3	.207	.254	.342
1999 Montreal	NL	17	22	4	1	0	0	(0	0)	5	3	0	1	2	0	6	0	0	0	0	0	-	0	.182	.250	.227
2000 Seattle	AL	8	14	3	0	0	1	(1	0)	6	2	1	2	1	0	4	0	0	0	0	0	-	0	.214	.267	.429
2001 Chicago	NL	52	135	30	10	0	2	(2	0)	46	13	13	11	7	3	26	1	3	0	0	0	-	0	.222	.266	.341
2003 Baltimore	AL	18	49	13	1	0	1	(1	0)	17	8	3	5	6	0	12	0	0	0	0	0	-	0	.265	.345	.347
2002 Chicago	NL	22	58	16	4	0	1	(0	1)	23	5	5	7	5	0	11	0	1	0	0	0	-	0	.276	.333	.397
2002 Milwaukee	NL	51	153	39	10	1	2	(1	1)	57	14	17	15	12	4	30	1	1	2	0	0	-	5	.255	.310	.373
8 ML YEARS		216	563	135	33	2	10	(7	3)	202	61	58	53	41	7	117	2	9	2	0	0	-	15	.240	.293	.359

Jose Macias

Bats: B Throws: R Pos: LF-41; PH-35; 3B-25; CF-15; RF-8; PR-5; 2B-4; DH-1

Ht: 5'10" Wt: 189 Born: 1/25/72 Age: 32

Year Team	Lg	G	AB	H	2B	3B	HR	(Hm	Rd)	TB	R	RBI	RC	TBB	IBB	SO	HBP	SH	SF	SB	CS	SB%	GDP	Avg	OBP	Slg
1999 Detroit	AL	5	4	1	0	0	0	(1	0)	4	2	2	1	0	0	1	0	0	0	0	0	-	0	.250	.250	1.000
2000 Detroit	AL	73	173	44	3	5	2	(2	0)	63	25	24	21	18	0	24	1	4	0	2	0	1.00	3	.254	.328	.364
2001 Detroit	AL	137	488	131	24	6	8	(7	1)	191	62	51	62	32	0	54	3	8	3	21	6	.78	7	.268	.316	.391
2002 Det-Mon		123	388	84	21	1	7	(4	3)	128	43	39	40	21	0	57	2	8	4	8	8	.50	6	.249	.293	.379
2003 Montreal	NL	111	272	65	15	2	4	(3	1)	96	31	22	23	11	1	45	2	2	1	4	3	.57	5	.239	.273	.353
2002 Detroit	AL	33	107	25	4	0	0	(0	0)	29	10	6	7	8	0	13	1	4	1	3	2	.60	4	.234	.291	.271
2002 Montreal	NL	90	231	59	17	1	7	(4	3)	99	33	33	33	13	0	44	1	4	3	5	6	.45	2	.255	.294	.429
5 ML YEARS		449	1275	325	63	14	22	(17	5)	482	163	138	147	82	1	181	8	22	8	35	17	.67	21	.255	.302	.378

Rob Mackowiak

Bats: L Throws: R Pos: PH-29; 3B-19; 2B-15; RF-14; LF-8; CF-8

Ht: 5'10" Wt: 190 Born: 6/20/76 Age: 28

Year Team	Lg	G	AB	H	2B	3B	HR	(Hm	Rd)	TB	R	RBI	RC	TBB	IBB	SO	HBP	SH	SF	SB	CS	SB%	GDP	Avg	OBP	Slg
2003 Nashville*	AAA	59	217	50	11	1	2	(-	-)	69	21	23	20	18	0	51	0	0	3	7	3	.70	3	.230	.286	.318
2001 Pittsburgh	NL	83	214	57	15	2	4	(3	1)	88	30	21	28	15	5	52	3	2	3	4	3	.57	3	.266	.319	.411
2002 Pittsburgh	NL	136	385	94	22	0	16	(9	7)	164	57	48	58	42	5	120	7	3	2	9	3	.75	0	.244	.328	.426
2003 Pittsburgh	NL	77	174	47	4	4	6	(1	5)	77	20	19	27	15	2	53	4	0	0	6	0	1.00	1	.270	.342	.443
3 ML YEARS		296	773	198	41	6	26	(13	13)	329	107	88	113	72	12	225	14	5	5	19	6	.76	4	.256	.329	.426

Greg Maddux

Pitches: R **Bats:** R **Pos:** SP-36　　　　　　　**Ht:** 6'0" **Wt:** 185 **Born:** 4/14/66 **Age:** 38

Year Team	Lg	G	GS	CG	GF	IP	BFP	H	R	ER	HR	SH	SF	HB	TBB	IBB	SO	WP	Bk	W	L	Pct	ShO	Sv-Op	Hld	ERC	ERA
1986 Chicago	NL	6	5	1	1	31.0	144	44	20	19	3	1	0	4	11	2	20	2	0	2	4	.333	0	0-0	0	6.45	5.52
1987 Chicago	NL	30	27	1	2	155.2	701	181	111	97	17	7	1	4	74	13	101	4	7	6	14	.300	1	0-0	0	5.42	5.61
1988 Chicago	NL	34	34	9	0	249.0	1047	230	97	88	13	11	2	9	81	16	140	3	6	18	8	.692	3	0-0	0	3.09	3.18
1989 Chicago	NL	35	35	7	0	238.1	1002	222	90	78	13	18	6	6	82	13	135	5	3	19	12	.613	1	0-0	0	3.20	2.95
1990 Chicago	NL	35	35	8	0	237.0	1011	242	116	91	11	18	5	4	71	10	144	3	3	15	15	.500	2	0-0	0	3.41	3.46
1991 Chicago	NL	37	37	7	0	263.0	1070	232	113	98	18	16	3	6	66	9	198	6	3	15	11	.577	2	0-0	0	2.73	3.35
1992 Chicago	NL	35	35	9	0	268.0	1061	201	68	65	7	15	3	14	70	7	199	5	3	20	11	.645	4	0-0	0	2.01	2.18
1993 Atlanta	NL	36	36	8	0	267.0	1064	228	85	70	14	15	7	6	52	7	197	5	1	20	10	.667	1	0-0	0	2.32	2.36
1994 Atlanta	NL	25	25	10	0	202.0	774	150	44	35	4	6	5	6	31	3	156	3	1	16	6	.727	3	0-0	0	1.59	1.56
1995 Atlanta	NL	28	28	10	0	209.2	785	147	39	38	8	9	1	4	23	3	181	1	0	19	2	.905	3	0-0	0	1.41	1.63
1996 Atlanta	NL	35	35	5	0	245.0	978	225	85	74	11	8	3	5	28	11	172	4	0	15	11	.577	1	0-0	0	2.22	2.72
1997 Atlanta	NL	33	33	5	0	232.2	893	200	58	57	9	11	7	6	20	6	177	0	0	19	4	.826	2	0-0	0	1.95	2.20
1998 Atlanta	NL	34	34	9	0	251.0	987	201	75	62	13	15	5	7	45	10	204	4	0	18	9	.667	5	0-0	0	2.01	2.22
1999 Atlanta	NL	33	33	4	0	219.1	940	258	103	87	16	15	5	4	37	8	136	1	0	19	9	.679	0	0-0	0	3.95	3.57
2000 Atlanta	NL	35	35	6	0	249.1	1012	225	91	83	19	8	5	10	42	12	190	1	2	19	9	.679	3	0-0	0	2.60	3.00
2001 Atlanta	NL	34	34	3	0	233.0	927	220	86	79	20	12	11	7	27	10	173	2	0	17	11	.607	3	0-0	0	3.05	3.05
2002 Atlanta	NL	34	34	0	0	199.1	820	194	67	58	14	13	4	4	45	7	118	1	0	16	6	.727	0	0-0	0	3.11	2.62
2003 Atlanta	NL	36	36	1	0	218.1	901	225	112	96	24	10	9	8	33	7	124	3	0	16	11	.593	0	0-0	0	3.44	3.96
18 ML YEARS		575	571	103	3	3968.2	16117	3625	1460	1275	234	208	84	109	838	154	2765	53	26	289	163	.639	34	0-0	0	2.70	2.89

Ryan Madson

Pitches: R **Bats:** L **Pos:** RP-1　　　　　　　**Ht:** 6'6" **Wt:** 180 **Born:** 8/28/80 **Age:** 23

Year Team	Lg	G	GS	CG	GF	IP	BFP	H	R	ER	HR	SH	SF	HB	TBB	IBB	SO	WP	Bk	W	L	Pct	ShO	Sv-Op	Hld	ERC	ERA
1998 Martinsville	R+	12	10	0	0	54.0	237	57	38	29	5	0	0	2	20	0	52	9	1	3	5	.375	0	0--	-	4.34	4.83
1999 Batavia	A-	15	15	0	0	87.2	383	80	51	46	5	2	4	10	43	0	75	10	0	5	5	.500	0	0--	-	4.12	4.72
2000 Piedmont	A	21	21	2	0	135.2	564	113	50	39	5	3	0	13	45	0	123	5	1	5	3	.625	1	0--	-	2.88	2.59
2001 Clearwater	A+	22	21	1	0	117.2	530	137	68	51	4	0	5	5	49	1	101	5	1	9	4	.692	0	0--	-	4.75	3.90
2002 Reading	AA	26	26	2	0	171.1	699	150	68	61	11	9	6	12	53	0	132	5	0	16	4	.800	0	0--	-	3.17	3.20
2003 Clearwater	A+	2	2	0	0	8.0	36	11	5	5	0	0	0	0	2	0	9	0	0	0	0	-	0	0--	-	4.89	5.63
2003 Scrtn/WlksBr	AAA	26	26	0	0	157.0	658	157	70	61	9	2	5	10	42	2	138	6	0	12	8	.600	0	0--	-	3.54	3.50
2003 Philadelphia	NL	1	0	0	0	2.0	6	0	0	0	0	0	0	0	0	0	0	0	0	0	0	-	0	0-0	0	0.00	0.00

Chris Magruder

Bats: B **Throws:** R **Pos:** LF-5; RF-3; PH-1　　　　　**Ht:** 5'11" **Wt:** 200 **Born:** 4/26/77 **Age:** 27

Year Team	Lg	G	AB	H	2B	3B	HR	(Hm	Rd)	TB	R	RBI	RC	TBB	IBB	SO	HBP	SH	SF	SB	CS	SB%	GDP	Avg	OBP	Slg
2003 Mahning VI*	A-	3	11	2	0	0	0	(-	-)	4	5	0	2	2	0	1	1	0	0	2	0	1.00	0	.182	.357	.364
2003 Buffalo*	AAA	41	137	45	7	2	3	(-	-)	65	20	15	26	15	1	27	1	0	3	5	1	.83	3	.328	.391	.474
2003 Akron*	AA	3	13	6	0	0	0	(-	-)	6	0	3	3	1	0	2	0	0	0	1	0	1.00	0	.462	.500	.462
2001 Texas	AL	17	29	5	0	0	0	(0	0)	5	3	1	0	1	0	5	1	0	0	0	0	-	1	.172	.226	.172
2002 Cleveland	AL	87	258	56	15	1	6	(3	3)	91	34	29	21	15	2	55	1	2	2	2	0	1.00	2	.217	.261	.353
2003 Cleveland	AL	9	26	9	2	1	1	(1	0)	16	3	3	6	3	0	6	1	0	0	0	1	.00	0	.346	.433	.615
3 ML YEARS		113	313	70	17	2	7	(4	3)	112	40	33	27	19	2	66	3	2	2	2	1	.67	8	.224	.273	.358

Ron Mahay

Pitches: L **Bats:** L **Pos:** RP-35　　　　　　　**Ht:** 6'2" **Wt:** 190 **Born:** 6/28/71 **Age:** 33

Year Team	Lg	G	GS	CG	GF	IP	BFP	H	R	ER	HR	SH	SF	HB	TBB	IBB	SO	WP	Bk	W	L	Pct	ShO	Sv-Op	Hld	ERC	ERA
2003 Oklahoma*	AAA	26	0	0	12	42.2	172	36	21	20	5	0	0	1	10	0	51	1	0	4	2	.667	0	3--	-	2.82	4.22
1997 Boston	AL	28	0	0	7	25.0	105	19	7	7	3	1	0	0	11	0	22	3	0	3	0	1.000	0	0-2	6	3.01	2.52
1998 Boston	AL	29	0	0	6	26.0	120	28	16	10	2	0	4	2	15	1	14	3	0	1	1	.500	0	1-2	7	4.76	3.46
1999 Oakland	AL	6	1	0	2	19.1	68	8	4	4	2	0	0	0	3	0	15	0	0	2	0	1.000	0	1-1	0	0.88	1.86
2000 Oak-Fla	AL	23	2	0	7	41.1	199	57	35	33	10	1	2	0	25	1	32	4	0	1	1	.500	0	0-0	2	8.55	7.19
2001 Chicago	NL	17	0	0	4	20.2	86	14	6	6	0	0	0	0	15	1	24	1	0	0	0	-	0	0-0	2	4.32	2.61
2002 Chicago	NL	11	0	0	1	14.2	65	13	14	14	6	0	0	0	8	0	14	0	0	2	0	1.000	0	0-0	4	6.11	8.59
2003 Texas	AL	35	0	0	5	45.1	189	33	19	16	3	0	0	0	20	7	38	4	0	3	3	.500	0	0-3	9	2.31	3.18
2000 Oakland	AL	5	2	0	0	16.0	82	26	18	16	4	1	1	0	9	0	5	2	0	1	0	1.000	0	0-0	0	9.97	9.00
2000 Florida	NL	18	0	0	6	25.1	117	31	17	17	6	0	1	0	16	1	27	2	0	1	0	1.000	0	0-0	2	7.67	6.04
7 ML YEARS		149	3	0	32	192.1	832	170	101	90	30	2	6	2	97	10	159	15	0	12	5	.706	0	2-8	26	4.18	4.21

Pat Mahomes

Pitches: R **Bats:** R **Pos:** RP-8; SP-1　　　　　　**Ht:** 6'4" **Wt:** 212 **Born:** 8/9/70 **Age:** 33

Year Team	Lg	G	GS	CG	GF	IP	BFP	H	R	ER	HR	SH	SF	HB	TBB	IBB	SO	WP	Bk	W	L	Pct	ShO	Sv-Op	Hld	ERC	ERA
2003 Nashville*	AAA	38	2	0	10	64.0	262	55	20	19	4	3	3	1	21	3	28	2	1	8	4	.667	0	2--	-	2.82	2.67
1992 Minnesota	AL	14	13	0	0	69.2	302	73	41	39	5	0	3	0	37	0	44	2	1	3	4	.429	0	0-0	0	4.83	5.04
1993 Minnesota	AL	12	5	0	4	37.1	173	47	34	32	8	1	1	3	16	0	23	3	0	1	5	.167	0	0-0	0	6.71	7.71
1994 Minnesota	AL	21	21	0	0	120.0	517	121	68	63	22	1	4	1	62	1	53	3	0	9	5	.643	0	0-0	0	5.41	4.73
1995 Minnesota	AL	47	7	0	16	94.2	423	100	74	67	22	3	2	2	47	1	67	6	0	4	10	.286	0	3-7	9	5.88	6.37
1996 Min-Bos	AL	31	5	0	10	57.1	271	72	46	44	13	2	2	0	33	0	36	2	0	3	4	.429	0	2-2	4	7.39	6.91
1997 Boston	AL	10	0	0	2	10.0	54	15	10	9	2	0	1	2	10	1	5	1	0	1	0	1.000	0	0-0	1	11.95	8.10
1999 New York	NL	39	0	0	12	63.2	265	44	26	26	7	1	2	2	37	5	51	2	0	8	0	1.000	0	0-1	1	3.22	3.68
2000 New York	NL	53	5	0	12	94.0	439	96	63	57	15	3	3	2	66	4	76	5	0	5	3	.625	0	0-1	5	5.87	5.46
2001 Texas	AL	56	4	0	14	107.1	475	115	71	68	17	2	7	0	55	9	61	3	0	7	6	.538	0	0-1	6	5.31	5.70
2002 Chicago	NL	16	2	0	2	32.2	147	36	15	14	3	3	0	1	17	3	23	1	0	1	1	.500	0	0-1	2	5.10	3.86
2003 Pittsburgh	NL	9	1	0	1	22.1	97	19	13	12	2	2	4	0	12	1	13	1	0	0	0	.000	0	0-0	0	3.60	4.84

Year Team	Lg	G	GS	CG	GF	IP	BFP	H	R	ER	HR	SH	SF	HB	TBB	IBB	SO	WP	Bk	W	L	Pct	ShO	Sv-Op	Hld	ERC	ERA
1996 Minnesota	AL	20	5	0	5	45.0	220	63	38	36	10	0	2	0	27	0	30	2	0	1	4	.200	0	0--	3	8.43	7.20
1996 Boston	AL	11	0	0	5	12.1	51	9	8	8	3	2	0	0	6	0	6	0	0	2	0	1.000	0	2-2	1	3.89	5.84
11 ML YEARS		308	63	0	74	709.0	3163	738	461	431	116	18	31	11	392	25	452	29	1	42	39	.519	0	5-13	26	5.48	5.47

Mark Malaska

Pitches: L Bats: L Pos: RP-22 **Ht: 6'3" Wt: 191 Born: 1/17/78 Age: 26**

Year Team	Lg	G	GS	CG	GF	IP	BFP	H	R	ER	HR	SH	SF	HB	TBB	IBB	SO	WP	Bk	W	L	Pct	ShO	Sv-Op	Hld	ERC	ERA
2000 Chrlstn - SC	A	2	0	0	0	2.0	8	3	2	2	1	0	0	0	0	0	3	0	0	0	0	-	0	0--	-	9.22	9.00
2000 Hudson Val	A-	10	5	0	0	40.1	176	44	27	22	1	0	0	1	14	2	36	8	0	0	2	.000	0	0--	-	3.84	4.91
2001 Chrlstn - SC	A	25	25	1	0	157.0	659	153	71	51	11	5	2	2	35	0	152	13	1	7	12	.368	0	0--	-	3.05	2.92
2001 Bakersfield	A+	3	3	0	0	17.2	70	14	8	8	1	1	0	0	5	0	13	1	0	2	1	.667	0	0--	-	2.33	4.08
2002 Bakersfield	A+	15	15	2	0	91.1	393	98	48	30	5	1	1	7	12	0	94	3	0	7	4	.636	2	0--	-	3.32	2.96
2002 Orlando	AA	12	11	1	1	70.2	314	82	37	29	4	2	1	2	28	2	49	4	0	4	5	.444	0	1--	-	4.76	3.69
2003 Durham	AAA	15	0	0	5	23.0	99	24	12	11	1	0	0	1	8	0	22	5	0	1	1	.500	0	0--	-	3.91	4.30
2003 Orlando	AA	19	0	0	5	25.0	96	21	6	6	2	2	1	0	4	1	22	0	0	1	1	.500	0	1--	-	2.25	2.16
2003 Tampa Bay	AL	22	0	0	3	16.0	70	13	7	5	0	1	0	1	12	3	17	0	0	2	1	.667	0	0-3	7	3.64	2.81

Jim Mann

Pitches: R Bats: R Pos: RP-2 **Ht: 6'3" Wt: 225 Born: 11/17/74 Age: 29**

Year Team	Lg	G	GS	CG	GF	IP	BFP	H	R	ER	HR	SH	SF	HB	TBB	IBB	SO	WP	Bk	W	L	Pct	ShO	Sv-Op	Hld	ERC	ERA
2003 Nashville	AAA	51	0	0	28	61.2	241	38	23	21	8	1	2	1	20	5	48	3	0	3	2	.600	0	5--	-	1.97	3.06
2000 New York	NL	2	0	0	2	2.2	15	6	3	3	1	0	0	0	1	0	0	0	0	0	0	-	0	0-0	0	14.72	10.13
2001 Houston	NL	4	0	0	1	5.1	23	3	2	2	0	0	0	2	4	0	5	0	0	0	0	-	0	0-0	0	3.87	3.38
2002 Houston	NL	17	0	0	12	22.0	94	19	10	10	3	1	0	5	7	1	19	0	0	0	1	.000	0	0-0	0	4.12	4.09
2003 Pittsburgh	NL	2	0	0	0	1.2	12	5	4	2	1	0	0	0	1	0	1	0	0	0	0	-	0	0-0	0	22.63	10.80
4 ML YEARS		25	0	0	15	31.2	144	33	19	17	5	1	0	7	13	1	25	0	0	0	1	.000	0	0-0	0	5.69	4.83

Dave Manning

Pitches: R Bats: R Pos: SP-2 **Ht: 6'3" Wt: 210 Born: 8/14/72 Age: 31**

Year Team	Lg	G	GS	CG	GF	IP	BFP	H	R	ER	HR	SH	SF	HB	TBB	IBB	SO	WP	Bk	W	L	Pct	ShO	Sv-Op	Hld	ERC	ERA
1992 Butte	R+	8	7	0	0	25.1	143	50	41	31	4	1	0	3	15	0	13	6	5	0	4	.000	0	0--	-	12.23	11.01
1992 Rangers	R	5	3	0	0	16.1	75	22	13	11	0	1	0	1	4	0	9	1	0	1	1	.500	0	0--	-	4.87	6.06
1993 Chrlstn - SC	A	37	10	0	8	116.0	495	112	54	39	3	5	5	7	39	4	83	11	3	6	7	.462	0	2--	-	3.30	3.03
1994 Charlotte	AAA	20	20	0	0	97.0	438	119	69	60	5	4	3	6	39	0	46	8	3	4	11	.267	0	0--	-	5.36	5.57
1995 Charlotte	AAA	26	20	0	2	128.2	545	127	56	50	7	3	3	3	46	0	66	0	5	9	5	.643	0	0--	-	3.65	3.50
1996 Tulsa	AA	39	5	0	13	91.0	394	89	35	33	5	3	5	2	45	6	48	5	0	6	5	.545	0	3--	-	4.03	3.26
1996 Oklahoma	AAA	1	1	0	0	5.0	21	6	3	3	0	0	1	0	2	0	1	0	0	0	0	-	0	0--	-	4.80	5.40
1997 Tulsa	AA	13	12	1	1	75.2	324	77	46	41	8	2	3	0	27	0	55	5	0	4	7	.364	0	0--	-	4.05	4.88
1997 Oklahoma	AAA	5	5	1	0	28.2	130	33	17	14	6	0	0	2	9	0	15	1	0	1	3	.250	0	0--	-	5.57	4.40
1997 Charlotte	AAA	1	1	0	0	6.0	26	4	1	1	1	0	0	0	4	0	4	0	0	0	0	-	0	0--	-	3.66	1.50
1998 Tulsa	AA	6	0	0	1	13.0	61	13	7	7	2	0	1	0	11	0	15	2	0	2	0	1.000	0	0--	-	6.40	4.85
1998 Oklahoma	AAA	6	0	0	0	9.0	36	11	1	1	1	0	0	0	0	0	9	0	0	0	0	-	0	1--	-	3.94	1.00
1999 W Tennesse	AA	23	18	6	0	123.1	518	113	59	54	7	5	4	3	51	1	78	7	0	8	5	.615	2	0--	-	3.51	3.94
1999 Iowa	AAA	7	0	0	0	9.2	44	9	6	5	2	0	3	0	8	0	7	0	0	0	0	-	0	0--	-	6.43	4.66
2000 Iowa	AAA	19	11	0	2	66.2	304	82	52	47	11	2	1	3	25	1	40	3	0	2	5	.286	0	0--	-	5.97	6.35
2002 New Britain	AA	11	10	0	0	62.1	275	69	37	32	3	8	2	5	27	0	38	6	0	3	3	.500	0	0--	-	4.87	4.62
2003 Indianapolis	AAA	23	17	0	1	99.0	455	103	57	54	7	3	5	3	60	0	76	8	0	6	8	.429	0	0--	-	4.99	4.91
2003 Milwaukee	NL	2	2	0	0	6.2	38	11	13	12	1	1	1	0	8	0	2	2	0	0	2	.000	0	0-0	0	12.41	16.20

Julio Manon

Pitches: R Bats: R Pos: RP-23 **Ht: 6'0" Wt: 200 Born: 7/10/73 Age: 30**

Year Team	Lg	G	GS	CG	GF	IP	BFP	H	R	ER	HR	SH	SF	HB	TBB	IBB	SO	WP	Bk	W	L	Pct	ShO	Sv-Op	Hld	ERC	ERA
1993 Cardinals	R	15	4	0	1	33.1	151	44	21	19	2	0	3	0	12	0	22	5	4	2	3	.400	0	0--	-	5.52	5.13
1994 Johnson City	R+	5	0	0	2	8.2	43	11	8	8	2	0	0	0	5	0	7	0	0	1	2	.333	0	0--	-	7.16	8.31
1994 Cardinals	R	14	0	0	4	16.0	69	20	9	9	0	0	0	0	1	0	18	1	2	0	1	.000	0	1--	-	3.36	5.06
1995 Huntington	R+	16	8	2	3	74.0	319	75	34	30	4	0	3	2	30	2	77	10	0	3	4	.429	0	1--	-	3.94	3.65
1997 Chrlstn - SC	A	27	9	0	4	88.2	392	95	53	44	8	5	3	3	22	1	98	7	0	3	5	.375	0	0--	-	3.76	4.47
1998 Orlando	AA	13	0	0	5	20.2	96	22	19	14	3	0	1	0	9	0	22	3	0	0	2	.000	0	0--	-	4.63	6.10
1998 St.Pete	A+	38	0	0	14	55.2	219	41	25	23	7	0	0	2	19	1	73	4	1	5	5	.500	0	1--	-	2.83	3.72
1999 Orlando	AA	30	5	0	8	67.0	303	80	43	38	9	0	1	2	23	0	53	3	0	3	3	.500	0	1--	-	5.27	5.10
1999 St.Paul	IND	4	3	0	0	20.1	85	18	9	5	0	0	1	0	7	0	21	1	0	1	1	.500	0	0--	-	2.57	2.21
2000 Expos	R	4	0	0	1	10.1	36	4	1	1	0	2	0	1	2	0	10	0	0	2	0	1.000	0	0--	-	0.78	0.87
2000 Harrisburg	AA	14	4	0	4	31.1	136	32	19	18	7	1	2	2	8	0	25	1	0	2	1	.667	0	1--	-	4.62	5.17
2001 Harrisburg	AA	10	7	0	3	52.0	207	50	20	18	6	1	1	0	16	0	44	1	0	4	3	.571	0	1--	-	3.83	3.12
2001 Ottawa	AAA	15	14	0	1	84.0	339	71	31	29	11	2	0	0	34	0	67	2	0	1	4	.200	0	0--	-	3.60	3.11
2002 Ottawa	AAA	28	13	2	9	105.1	436	83	42	41	8	5	2	2	45	0	81	3	0	8	6	.571	1	2--	-	2.97	3.50
2002 Harrisburg	AA	6	6	0	0	39.0	158	37	13	13	3	1	1	0	4	0	51	1	0	5	1	.833	0	0--	-	2.60	3.00
2003 Edmonton	AAA	35	0	0	32	42.0	180	33	12	10	4	0	0	0	19	1	48	2	0	3	1	.750	0	14--	-	2.95	2.14
2003 Montreal	NL	23	0	0	7	28.1	125	26	13	13	3	2	2	1	17	1	15	0	0	1	2	.333	0	1-1	6	4.57	4.13

Matt Mantei

Pitches: R **Bats:** R **Pos:** RP-50 **Ht:** 6'1" **Wt:** 200 **Born:** 7/7/73 **Age:** 30

Year Team	Lg	G	GS	CG	GF	IP	BFP	H	R	ER	HR	SH	SF	HB	TBB	IBB	SO	WP	Bk	W	L	Pct	ShO	Sv-Op	Hld	ERC	ERA
2003 Tucson*	AAA	3	0	0	1	4.0	13	2	1	1	1	0	0	0	0	4	4	0	0	0	0	-	0	0--	-	1.21	2.25
1995 Florida	NL	12	0	0	3	13.1	64	12	8	7	1	1	1	0	13	0	15	1	0	0	1	.000	0	0-0	0	5.54	4.73
1996 Florida	NL	14	0	0	1	18.1	89	13	13	13	2	1	0	1	21	1	25	2	0	1	0	1.000	0	0-1	0	5.46	6.38
1998 Florida	NL	42	0	0	23	54.2	224	38	19	18	1	3	4	7	23	3	63	0	0	3	4	.429	0	9-12	2	2.44	2.96
1999 Fla-Ari	NL	65	0	0	60	65.1	284	44	21	20	5	1	1	5	44	1	99	2	0	1	3	.250	0	32-37	6	3.42	2.76
2000 Arizona	NL	47	0	0	38	45.1	200	31	24	23	4	2	0	2	35	1	53	5	0	1	1	.500	0	17-20	0	3.80	4.57
2001 Arizona	NL	8	0	0	7	7.0	31	6	2	2	2	0	0	0	4	0	12	2	0	0	0	-	0	2-2	1	5.18	2.57
2002 Arizona	NL	31	0	0	6	26.2	122	28	15	14	3	0	0	1	12	0	26	1	0	2	2	.500	0	0-1	2	4.64	4.73
2003 Arizona	NL	50	0	0	44	55.0	220	37	17	16	6	4	2	2	18	1	68	1	0	5	4	.556	0	29-32	0	2.26	2.62
1999 Florida	NL	35	0	0	32	36.1	157	24	11	11	4	0	1	2	25	1	50	0	0	1	2	.333	0	10-12	0	3.55	2.72
1999 Arizona	NL	30	0	0	28	29.0	127	20	10	9	1	1	0	3	19	0	49	2	0	0	1	.000	0	22-25	0	3.25	2.79
8 ML YEARS		269	0	0	182	285.2	1234	209	119	113	24	12	8	18	170	7	361	14	0	13	15	.464	0	89-105	5	3.43	3.56

Josias Manzanillo

Pitches: R **Bats:** R **Pos:** RP-9 **Ht:** 6'0" **Wt:** 205 **Born:** 10/16/67 **Age:** 36

Year Team	Lg	G	GS	CG	GF	IP	BFP	H	R	ER	HR	SH	SF	HB	TBB	IBB	SO	WP	Bk	W	L	Pct	ShO	Sv-Op	Hld	ERC	ERA
2003 Louisville*	AAA	22	0	0	8	28.0	119	25	17	13	0	5	1	2	11	1	16	1	0	1	1	.500	0	0--	0		4.18
1991 Boston	AL	1	0	0	1	1.0	8	2	2	2	0	0	0	0	3	0	1	0	0	0	0	-	0	0-0	0	21.46	18.00
1993 Mil-NYM	NL	16	1	0	6	29.0	140	30	27	22	2	3	3	2	19	3	21	1	0	1	1	.500	0	1-2	0	4.92	6.83
1994 New York	NL	37	0	0	14	47.1	186	34	15	14	4	0	0	3	13	2	48	2	0	3	2	.600	0	2-5	11	2.28	2.66
1995 NYM-NYY		23	0	0	8	33.1	154	37	19	18	4	2	1	2	15	4	25	6	0	1	2	.333	0	0-0	0	4.97	4.86
1997 Seattle	AL	16	0	0	4	18.1	88	19	13	11	3	0	2	0	17	1	18	2	0	0	1	.000	0	0-1	1	6.97	5.40
1999 New York	NL	12	0	0	1	18.2	80	19	12	12	5	1	1	2	4	1	25	0	0	0	0	-	0	0-0	1	4.90	5.79
2000 Pittsburgh	NL	43	0	0	11	58.2	246	50	23	22	6	4	2	0	32	4	39	1	0	2	2	.500	0	0-2	5	3.85	3.38
2001 Pittsburgh	NL	71	0	0	25	79.2	329	60	32	30	4	5	8	5	26	3	80	4	0	3	2	.600	0	2-7	9	2.33	3.39
2002 Pittsburgh	NL	13	0	0	5	13.0	61	20	11	11	5	0	0	1	5	0	4	0	0	0	0	-	0	0-1	0	10.63	7.62
2003 Cincinnati	NL	9	0	0	1	10.2	59	21	20	15	7	1	0	0	4	0	12	0	0	0	2	.000	0	0-1	0	14.74	12.66
1993 Milwaukee	NL	10	1	0	4	17.0	86	22	20	18	1	2	2	2	10	3	10	1	0	1	1	.500	0	1-2	0	6.15	9.53
1993 New York	NL	6	0	0	2	12.0	54	8	7	4	1	1	1	0	9	0	11	0	0	0	0	-	0	0-0	0	3.32	3.00
1995 New York	NL	12	0	0	4	16.0	73	18	15	14	3	0	1	0	6	2	14	5	0	1	2	.333	0	0-0	0	4.93	7.88
1995 New York	AL	11	0	0	4	17.1	81	19	4	4	1	2	0	2	9	2	11	1	0	0	0	-	0	0-0	0	4.96	2.08
10 ML YEARS		241	1	0	76	309.2	1351	292	174	157	40	16	17	15	138	18	273	16	0	10	12	.455	0	5-19	27	4.22	4.56

Mike Maroth

Pitches: L **Bats:** L **Pos:** SP-33 **Ht:** 6'0" **Wt:** 180 **Born:** 8/17/77 **Age:** 26

Year Team	Lg	G	GS	CG	GF	IP	BFP	H	R	ER	HR	SH	SF	HB	TBB	IBB	SO	WP	Bk	W	L	Pct	ShO	Sv-Op	Hld	ERC	ERA
1998 Red Sox	R	4	2	0	1	12.2	49	9	3	0	0	0	0	0	2	0	14	0	0	1	1	.500	0	0--	-	1.34	0.00
1998 Lowell	A-	6	6	0	0	31.0	127	22	13	10	1	0	1	3	13	0	34	3	0	2	3	.400	0	0--	-	2.57	2.90
1999 Sarasota	A+	20	19	0	0	111.1	497	124	65	50	3	6	4	10	35	1	64	11	2	11	6	.647	0	0--	-	4.13	4.04
1999 Lakeland	A+	3	3	0	0	16.2	71	18	7	6	1	1	0	0	7	0	11	2	0	2	1	.667	0	0--	-	4.47	3.24
1999 Jacksonville	AA	4	4	0	0	20.2	96	27	15	11	2	1	1	0	7	0	10	1	0	1	2	.333	0	0--	-	5.45	4.79
2000 Jacksonville	AA	27	26	2	0	164.1	689	176	79	72	14	9	9	3	58	0	85	6	1	9	14	.391	1	0--	-	4.43	3.94
2001 Toledo	AAA	24	23	0	0	131.2	587	158	80	68	11	5	5	4	50	1	63	4	0	7	10	.412	0	0--	-	5.19	4.65
2002 Toledo	AAA	11	11	1	0	73.1	289	53	25	23	7	1	2	2	22	0	51	2	0	8	1	.889	0	0--	-	2.26	2.82
2002 Detroit	AL	21	21	0	0	128.2	538	136	68	64	7	5	3	2	36	1	58	4	0	6	10	.375	0	0-0	0	3.73	4.48
2003 Detroit	AL	33	33	1	0	193.1	847	231	131	123	34	9	8	8	50	2	87	7	0	9	21	.300	0	0-0	0	5.36	5.73
2 ML YEARS		54	54	1	0	322.0	1385	367	199	187	41	14	11	10	86	3	145	11	0	15	31	.326	0	0-0	0	4.69	5.23

Jason Marquis

Pitches: R **Bats:** L **Pos:** RP-19; SP-2 **Ht:** 6'1" **Wt:** 210 **Born:** 8/21/78 **Age:** 25

Year Team	Lg	G	GS	CG	GF	IP	BFP	H	R	ER	HR	SH	SF	HB	TBB	IBB	SO	WP	Bk	W	L	Pct	ShO	Sv-Op	Hld	ERC	ERA
2003 Richmond*	AAA	15	15	3	0	94.0	400	93	40	35	5	3	0	0	34	0	75	4	0	8	4	.667	1	0--	-	3.55	3.35
2000 Atlanta	NL	15	0	0	7	23.1	103	23	16	13	4	1	1	1	12	1	17	1	0	1	0	1.000	0	0-1	1	5.13	5.01
2001 Atlanta	NL	38	16	0	9	129.1	556	113	62	50	14	6	5	4	59	4	98	1	2	5	6	.455	0	0-2	2	3.70	3.48
2002 Atlanta	NL	22	22	0	0	114.1	507	127	66	64	19	4	3	3	49	3	84	4	0	8	9	.471	0	0-0	0	5.43	5.04
2003 Atlanta	NL	21	2	0	10	40.2	182	43	27	25	3	0	3	2	18	2	19	2	0	0	0	-	0	1-1	0	4.45	5.53
4 ML YEARS		96	40	0	26	307.2	1348	306	171	152	40	11	12	10	138	10	218	8	2	14	15	.483	0	1-4	3	4.53	4.45

Eli Marrero

Bats: R **Throws:** R **Pos:** RF-21; PH-12; LF-10; C-6; CF-6; 1B-2 **Ht:** 6'1" **Wt:** 180 **Born:** 11/17/73 **Age:** 30

Year Team	Lg	G	AB	H	2B	3B	HR	(Hm	Rd)	TB	R	RBI	RC	TBB	IBB	SO	HBP	SH	SF	SB	CS	SB%	GDP	Avg	OBP	Slg
2003 Memphis*	AAA	5	12	3	1	0	1	(-	-)	7	2	1	2	1	0	0	1	0	0	0	0	-	1	.250	.357	.583
1997 St Louis	NL	17	45	11	2	0	2	(0	2)	19	4	7	6	2	1	13	0	0	1	4	0	1.00	1	.244	.271	.422
1998 St Louis	NL	83	254	62	18	1	4	(2	2)	94	28	20	30	28	5	42	0	1	1	6	2	.75	5	.244	.318	.370
1999 St Louis	NL	114	317	61	13	1	6	(3	3)	94	32	34	18	18	4	56	1	4	3	11	2	.85	14	.192	.236	.297
2000 St Louis	NL	53	102	23	3	1	5	(2	3)	43	21	17	14	9	0	16	3	0	0	5	0	1.00	3	.225	.302	.422
2001 St Louis	NL	86	203	54	11	3	6	(2	4)	89	37	23	27	15	2	36	0	3	3	6	3	.67	4	.266	.312	.438
2002 St Louis	NL	131	397	104	19	1	18	(9	9)	179	63	66	60	40	11	72	0	5	4	14	2	.88	5	.262	.327	.451
2003 St Louis	NL	41	107	24	4	2	2	(1	1)	38	10	20	15	7	0	18	0	0	2	0	1	.00	0	.224	.267	.355
7 ML YEARS		525	1425	339	70	9	43	(19	24)	556	195	187	170	119	23	253	4	13	16	46	10	.82	32	.238	.295	.390

Damaso Marte

Pitches: L Bats: L Pos: RP-71　　　　Ht: 6'2" Wt: 200 Born: 2/14/75 Age: 29

Year Team	Lg	G	GS	CG	GF	IP	BFP	H	R	ER	HR	SH	SF	HB	TBB	IBB	SO	WP	Bk	W	L	Pct	ShO	Sv-Op	Hld	ERC	ERA
1999 Seattle	AL	5	0	0	2	8.2	47	16	9	9	3	0	0	0	6	0	3	0	0	0	1	.000	0	0-0	0	13.32	9.35
2001 Pittsburgh	NL	23	0	0	4	36.1	154	34	21	19	5	1	2	3	12	3	39	1	0	0	1	.000	0	0-0	0	3.93	4.71
2002 Chicago	AL	68	0	0	22	60.1	240	44	19	19	5	1	1	4	18	2	72	3	1	1	1	.500	0	10-12	14	2.42	2.83
2003 Chicago	AL	71	0	0	25	79.2	314	50	16	14	3	3	3	3	34	6	87	1	0	4	2	.667	0	11-18	14	1.96	1.58
4 ML YEARS		167	0	0	53	185.0	755	144	65	61	16	5	6	10	70	11	201	5	1	5	5	.500	0	21-30	28	2.88	2.97

Al Martin

Bats: L Throws: L Pos: DH-55; PH-40; LF-8; RF-5; 1B-1; PR-1　　　　Ht: 6'2" Wt: 214 Born: 11/24/67 Age: 36

Year Team	Lg	G	AB	H	2B	3B	HR	(Hm	Rd)	TB	R	RBI	RC	TBB	IBB	SO	HBP	SH	SF	SB	CS	SB%	GDP	Avg	OBP	Slg
1992 Pittsburgh	NL	12	12	2	0	1	0	(0	0)	4	1	2	1	0	0	5	0	0	1	0	0	-	0	.167	.154	.333
1993 Pittsburgh	NL	143	480	135	26	8	18	(15	3)	231	85	64	77	42	5	122	1	2	3	16	9	.64	5	.281	.338	.481
1994 Pittsburgh	NL	82	276	79	12	4	9	(6	3)	126	48	33	47	34	3	56	2	0	1	15	6	.71	3	.286	.367	.457
1995 Pittsburgh	NL	124	439	124	25	3	13	(8	5)	194	70	41	67	44	6	92	2	1	0	20	11	.65	5	.282	.351	.442
1996 Pittsburgh	NL	155	630	189	40	1	18	(8	10)	285	101	72	103	54	2	116	2	1	7	38	12	.76	9	.300	.345	.452
1997 Pittsburgh	NL	113	423	123	24	7	13	(8	5)	200	64	59	73	45	7	83	3	1	5	23	7	.77	7	.291	.359	.473
1998 Pittsburgh	NL	125	440	105	15	2	12	(5	7)	160	57	47	47	32	2	91	5	0	2	20	3	.87	13	.239	.296	.364
1999 Pittsburgh	NL	143	541	150	36	8	24	(12	12)	274	97	63	93	49	5	119	1	0	2	20	3	.87	8	.277	.337	.506
2000 SD-Sea	AL	135	480	137	15	10	15	(10	5)	217	81	36	73	36	5	85	4	0	3	10	9	.53	3	.285	.338	.452
2001 Seattle	AL	100	283	68	15	2	7	(2	5)	108	41	42	38	37	4	59	2	0	1	9	3	.75	2	.240	.330	.382
2003 Tampa Bay	AL	100	238	60	12	2	3	(2	1)	85	19	26	25	17	4	51	2	0	1	2	2	.50	8	.252	.306	.357
2000 San Diego	NL	93	346	106	13	6	11	(8	3)	164	62	27	57	28	5	54	2	0	2	6	8	.43	2	.306	.360	.474
2000	AL	42	134	31	2	4	4	(2	2)	53	19	9	16	8	0	31	2	0	1	4	1	.80	1	.231	.283	.396
11 ML YEARS		1232	4242	1172	220	48	132	(76	56)	1884	664	485	644	390	43	879	24	5	27	173	65	.73	63	.276	.339	.444

Tom Martin

Pitches: L Bats: L Pos: RP-80　　　　Ht: 6'1" Wt: 206 Born: 5/21/70 Age: 34

Year Team	Lg	G	GS	CG	GF	IP	BFP	H	R	ER	HR	SH	SF	HB	TBB	IBB	SO	WP	Bk	W	L	Pct	ShO	Sv-Op	Hld	ERC	ERA
1997 Houston	NL	55	0	0	18	56.0	236	52	13	13	2	6	1	1	23	2	36	3	0	5	3	.625	0	2-3	7	3.34	2.09
1998 Cleveland	AL	14	0	0	1	14.2	85	29	21	21	3	1	1	0	12	0	9	2	0	1	1	.500	0	0-0	3	13.19	12.89
1999 Cleveland	AL	6	0	0	0	9.1	44	13	9	9	2	0	1	0	3	1	8	0	0	0	1	.000	0	0-0	0	6.64	8.68
2000 Cleveland	AL	31	0	0	7	33.1	143	32	16	15	3	0	1	1	15	2	21	1	0	1	0	1.000	0	0-0	4	4.05	4.05
2001 New York	NL	14	0	0	2	17.0	85	23	22	19	4	1	1	1	10	2	12	0	0	1	0	1.000	0	0-0	1	8.02	10.06
2002 Tampa Bay	AL	2	0	0	2	1.2	11	5	3	3	0	0	0	0	1	0	1	0	0	0	0	-	0	0-0	-	17.54	16.20
2003 Los Angeles	NL	80	0	0	13	51.0	210	36	21	20	6	0	2	2	24	4	51	1	0	1	2	.333	0	0-1	28	2.94	3.53
7 ML YEARS		202	0	0	43	183.0	814	190	105	100	20	8	7	5	88	11	138	7	0	9	7	.563	0	2-4	39	4.69	4.92

Edgar Martinez

Bats: R Throws: R Pos: DH-139; PH-7　　　　Ht: 5'11" Wt: 210 Born: 1/2/63 Age: 41

Year Team	Lg	G	AB	H	2B	3B	HR	(Hm	Rd)	TB	R	RBI	RC	TBB	IBB	SO	HBP	SH	SF	SB	CS	SB%	GDP	Avg	OBP	Slg
1987 Seattle	AL	13	43	16	5	2	0	(0	0)	25	6	5	10	2	0	5	1	0	0	0	0	-	0	.372	.413	.581
1988 Seattle	AL	14	32	9	4	0	0	(0	0)	13	0	5	5	4	0	7	0	1	0	0	0	-	0	.281	.351	.406
1989 Seattle	AL	65	171	41	5	0	2	(0	2)	52	20	20	17	17	1	26	3	2	3	2	1	.67	3	.240	.314	.304
1990 Seattle	AL	144	487	147	27	2	11	(3	8)	211	71	49	83	74	3	62	5	1	3	1	4	.20	13	.302	.397	.433
1991 Seattle	AL	150	544	167	35	1	14	(6	8)	246	98	52	97	84	9	72	8	2	4	0	3	.00	19	.307	.405	.452
1992 Seattle	AL	135	528	181	46	3	18	(11	7)	287	100	73	110	54	2	61	4	1	5	14	4	.78	15	.343	.404	.544
1993 Seattle	AL	42	135	32	7	0	4	(1	3)	51	20	13	20	28	1	19	0	1	1	0	0	-	4	.237	.366	.378
1994 Seattle	AL	89	326	93	23	1	13	(4	9)	157	47	51	63	53	3	42	3	2	3	6	2	.75	2	.285	.387	.482
1995 Seattle	AL	145	511	182	52	0	29	(16	13)	321	121	113	144	116	19	87	8	0	4	4	3	.57	11	.356	.479	.628
1996 Seattle	AL	139	499	163	52	2	26	(14	12)	297	104	103	132	123	12	84	8	0	4	3	3	.50	15	.327	.464	.595
1997 Seattle	AL	155	542	179	35	1	28	(12	16)	300	104	108	130	119	11	86	11	0	6	4	4	.33	21	.330	.456	.554
1998 Seattle	AL	154	556	179	46	1	29	(17	12)	314	86	102	130	106	4	96	3	0	7	1	1	.50	13	.322	.429	.565
1999 Seattle	AL	142	502	169	35	1	24	(12	12)	278	86	86	121	97	6	99	6	0	3	7	2	.78	12	.337	.447	.554
2000 Seattle	AL	153	556	180	31	0	37	(19	18)	322	100	145	131	96	8	95	5	0	4	3	0	1.00	13	.324	.423	.579
2001 Seattle	AL	132	470	144	40	1	23	(10	13)	255	80	116	108	93	9	90	9	0	9	4	1	.80	11	.306	.423	.543
2002 Seattle	AL	97	328	91	23	0	15	(9	6)	159	42	59	61	67	8	69	6	0	6	1	1	.50	6	.277	.403	.485
2003 Seattle	AL	145	497	146	25	0	24	(8	16)	243	72	98	100	92	7	95	7	0	7	0	1	.00	17	.294	.406	.489
17 ML YEARS		1914	6727	2119	491	15	297	(144	153)	3531	1174	1198	1462	1225	103	1095	87	10	74	48	30	.62	175	.315	.423	.525

Luis Martinez

Pitches: L Bats: L Pos: SP-4　　　　Ht: 6'6" Wt: 200 Born: 1/20/80 Age: 24

Year Team	Lg	G	GS	CG	GF	IP	BFP	H	R	ER	HR	SH	SF	HB	TBB	IBB	SO	WP	Bk	W	L	Pct	ShO	Sv-Op	Hld	ERC	ERA
1998 Helena	R+	17	10	0	2	48.0	275	64	73	54	5	1	2	5	66	0	47	14	4	0	9	.000	0	0--	-	10.80	10.13
1999 Ogden	R+	15	7	0	4	50.1	259	66	65	39	3	1	3	3	34	0	43	13	0	0	7	.000	0	1--	-	6.68	6.97
2000 Beloit	A	28	13	0	7	92.2	412	71	49	39	8	0	6	5	61	1	77	7	1	5	7	.417	0	0--	-	3.81	3.79
2001 Huntsville	AA	7	0	0	0	9.1	48	13	7	7	0	0	0	0	9	0	13	0	0	0	0	-	0	0--	-	8.08	6.75
2001 High Desert	A+	22	22	0	0	112.2	498	112	67	65	9	2	2	4	64	0	121	9	1	8	9	.471	0	0--	-	4.79	5.19
2003 Huntsville	AA	20	20	1	0	115.0	489	93	46	33	4	11	1	7	54	0	116	6	1	8	5	.615	0	0--	-	3.08	2.58
2003 Indianapolis	AAA	7	7	0	0	45.2	177	37	5	5	0	2	0	0	19	0	46	2	0	4	0	1.000	0	0--	-	2.68	0.99
2003 Milwaukee	NL	4	4	0	0	16.1	86	25	18	18	3	4	0	0	15	2	10	3	1	0	3	.000	0	0-0	0	10.34	9.92

Pedro Martinez

Pitches: R **Bats:** R **Pos:** SP-29   **Ht:** 5'11" **Wt:** 180 **Born:** 10/25/71 **Age:** 32

Year Team	Lg	G	GS	CG	GF	IP	BFP	H	R	ER	HR	SH	SF	HB	TBB	IBB	SO	WP	Bk	W	L	Pct	ShO	Sv-Op	Hld	ERC	ERA
1992 Los Angeles	NL	2	1	0	1	8.0	31	6	2	2	0	0	0	0	1	0	8	0	0	0	1	.000	0	0-0	0	1.38	2.25
1993 Los Angeles	NL	65	2	0	20	107.0	444	76	34	31	5	0	5	4	57	4	119	3	1	10	5	.667	0	2-3	14	2.79	2.61
1994 Montreal	NL	24	23	1	1	144.2	584	115	58	55	11	2	3	11	45	3	142	6	0	11	5	.688	1	1-1	0	2.81	3.42
1995 Montreal	NL	30	30	2	0	194.2	784	158	79	76	21	7	3	11	66	1	174	5	2	14	10	.583	2	0-0	0	3.19	3.51
1996 Montreal	NL	33	33	4	0	216.2	901	189	100	89	19	9	6	3	70	3	222	6	0	13	10	.565	1	0-0	0	3.02	3.70
1997 Montreal	NL	31	31	13	0	241.1	947	158	65	51	16	9	1	9	67	5	305	3	1	17	8	.680	4	0-0	0	1.79	1.90
1998 Boston	AL	33	33	3	0	233.2	951	188	82	75	26	4	7	8	67	3	251	9	0	19	7	.731	2	0-0	0	2.78	2.89
1999 Boston	AL	31	29	5	1	213.1	835	160	56	49	9	3	6	9	37	1	313	6	0	23	4	.852	1	0-0	0	1.79	2.07
2000 Boston	AL	29	29	7	0	217.0	817	128	44	42	17	2	1	14	32	0	284	1	0	18	6	.750	4	0-0	0	1.39	1.74
2001 Boston	AL	18	18	1	0	116.2	456	84	33	31	5	2	0	6	25	0	163	4	0	7	3	.700	0	0-0	0	1.84	2.39
2002 Boston	AL	30	30	2	0	199.1	787	144	62	50	13	2	4	15	40	1	239	3	0	20	4	.833	0	0-0	0	1.98	2.26
2003 Boston	AL	29	29	3	0	186.2	749	147	52	46	7	4	4	9	47	0	206	5	0	14	4	.778	0	0-0	0	2.22	2.22
12 ML YEARS		355	288	41	23	2079.0	8286	1553	667	597	149	44	40	99	554	21	2426	51	4	166	67	.712	15	3-4	14	2.27	2.58

Ramon Martinez

Bats: R **Throws:** R **Pos:** 2B-41; 3B-37; SS-32; PH-10; 1B-2; PR-1   **Ht:** 6'1" **Wt:** 183 **Born:** 10/10/72 **Age:** 31

Year Team	Lg	G	AB	H	2B	3B	HR	Hm	Rd	TB	R	RBI	RC	TBB	IBB	SO	HBP	SH	SF	SB	CS	SB%	GDP	Avg	OBP	Slg
1998 San Francisco	NL	19	19	6	1	0	0	0	0	7	4	0	4	4	0	2	0	1	0	0	0	-	0	.316	.435	.368
1999 San Francisco	NL	61	144	38	6	0	5	3	2	59	21	19	19	14	0	17	0	6	1	1	2	.33	2	.264	.327	.410
2000 San Francisco	NL	88	189	57	13	2	6	4	2	92	30	25	31	15	1	22	1	4	1	3	2	.60	6	.302	.354	.487
2001 San Francisco	NL	128	391	99	18	3	5	1	4	138	48	37	44	38	6	52	5	6	6	1	2	.33	11	.253	.323	.353
2002 San Francisco	NL	72	181	49	10	2	4	0	4	75	26	25	32	14	2	26	4	0	1	2	0	1.00	1	.271	.335	.414
2003 Chicago	NL	108	293	83	16	1	3	3	0	110	30	34	33	24	1	50	2	6	8	0	1	.00	8	.283	.333	.375
6 ML YEARS		476	1217	332	64	8	23	15	8	481	159	140	163	109	10	169	12	23	17	7	7	.50	28	.273	.334	.395

Tino Martinez

Bats: L **Throws:** R **Pos:** 1B-126; PH-7; DH-5   **Ht:** 6'2" **Wt:** 210 **Born:** 12/7/67 **Age:** 36

Year Team	Lg	G	AB	H	2B	3B	HR	Hm	Rd	TB	R	RBI	RC	TBB	IBB	SO	HBP	SH	SF	SB	CS	SB%	GDP	Avg	OBP	Slg
1990 Seattle	AL	24	68	15	4	0	0	0	0	19	4	5	7	9	0	9	0	0	1	0	0	-	0	.221	.308	.279
1991 Seattle	AL	36	112	23	2	0	4	3	1	37	11	9	10	11	0	24	0	0	2	0	0	-	2	.205	.272	.330
1992 Seattle	AL	136	460	118	19	2	16	10	6	189	53	66	54	42	9	77	2	1	8	2	1	.67	24	.257	.316	.411
1993 Seattle	AL	109	408	108	25	1	17	9	8	186	48	60	62	45	9	56	5	3	3	0	3	.00	7	.265	.343	.456
1994 Seattle	AL	97	329	86	21	0	20	8	12	167	42	61	51	29	2	52	1	4	3	1	2	.33	9	.261	.320	.508
1995 Seattle	AL	141	519	152	35	3	31	14	17	286	92	111	102	62	15	91	4	2	6	0	0	-	10	.293	.369	.551
1996 New York	AL	155	595	174	28	0	25	9	16	277	82	117	97	68	4	85	2	1	5	2	1	.67	18	.292	.364	.466
1997 New York	AL	158	594	176	31	2	44	18	26	343	96	141	122	75	14	75	3	0	13	3	1	.75	15	.296	.371	.577
1998 New York	AL	142	531	149	33	1	28	12	16	268	92	123	92	61	3	83	6	0	10	2	1	.67	18	.281	.355	.505
1999 New York	AL	159	589	155	27	2	28	7	21	270	95	105	90	69	7	86	3	0	4	3	4	.43	14	.263	.341	.458
2000 New York	AL	155	569	147	37	4	16	12	4	240	69	91	76	52	9	74	8	0	3	4	1	.80	16	.258	.328	.422
2001 New York	AL	154	589	165	24	2	34	22	12	295	89	113	93	42	2	89	2	0	2	1	2	.33	12	.280	.329	.501
2002 St Louis	NL	150	511	134	25	1	21	12	9	224	63	75	70	58	9	71	2	1	4	3	2	.60	12	.262	.337	.438
2003 St Louis	NL	138	476	130	25	2	15	6	9	204	66	69	63	53	7	71	9	2	7	1	1	.50	14	.273	.352	.429
14 ML YEARS		1754	6350	1732	336	20	299	142	157	3005	902	1146	989	676	90	943	47	14	71	22	19	.54	171	.273	.344	.473

Victor Martinez

Bats: B **Throws:** R **Pos:** C-40; PH-6; DH-4   **Ht:** 6'2" **Wt:** 170 **Born:** 12/23/78 **Age:** 25

Year Team	Lg	G	AB	H	2B	3B	HR	Hm	Rd	TB	R	RBI	RC	TBB	IBB	SO	HBP	SH	SF	SB	CS	SB%	GDP	Avg	OBP	Slg
1999 Mahning VI	A-	64	235	65	9	0	4	-	-	86	37	36	31	27	0	31	1	0	6	0	1	.00	4	.277	.346	.366
2000 Kinston	A+	26	83	18	7	0	0	-	-	25	9	8	8	11	0	5	1	3	1	1	1	.50	3	.217	.313	.301
2000 Columbus	A	21	70	26	9	1	2	-	-	43	11	12	19	11	0	6	1	0	2	0	0	-	1	.371	.452	.614
2001 Kinston	A+	114	420	138	33	2	10	-	-	205	59	57	76	39	1	60	8	0	3	3	3	.50	12	.329	.394	.488
2002 Akron	AA	121	443	149	40	0	22	-	-	255	84	85	100	58	6	62	8	0	6	3	3	.50	10	.336	.417	.576
2003 Buffalo	AAA	73	274	90	19	0	7	-	-	130	42	45	47	26	1	32	8	0	6	3	5	.38	14	.328	.395	.474
2003 Akron	AA	3	12	4	2	0	0	-	-	6	1	2	2	0	0	1	0	0	0	0	0	-	1	.333	.333	.500
2002 Cleveland	AL	12	32	9	1	0	1	1	0	13	2	5	5	3	0	2	0	0	1	0	0	-	0	.281	.333	.406
2003 Cleveland	AL	49	159	46	4	0	1	0	1	53	15	16	15	13	0	21	1	0	1	1	1	.50	8	.289	.345	.333
2 ML YEARS		61	191	55	5	0	2	1	1	66	17	21	20	16	0	23	1	0	2	1	1	.50	9	.288	.343	.346

Henry Mateo

Bats: B **Throws:** R **Pos:** PH-49; 2B-43; PR-11; RF-6; SS-2; LF-2; CF-2; DH-2   **Ht:** 5'11" **Wt:** 170 **Born:** 10/14/76 **Age:** 27

Year Team	Lg	G	AB	H	2B	3B	HR	Hm	Rd	TB	R	RBI	RC	TBB	IBB	SO	HBP	SH	SF	SB	CS	SB%	GDP	Avg	OBP	Slg
2001 Montreal	NL	5	9	3	1	0	0	0	0	4	1	0	1	0	0	1	0	0	0	0	0	-	0	.333	.333	.444
2002 Montreal	NL	22	23	4	0	1	0	0	0	6	1	0	1	2	1	6	0	0	0	2	0	1.00	0	.174	.240	.261
2003 Montreal	NL	100	154	37	3	1	0	0	0	42	29	7	16	11	0	38	3	1	0	11	1	.92	0	.240	.304	.273
3 ML YEARS		127	186	44	4	2	0	0	0	52	31	7	18	13	1	45	3	1	0	13	1	.93	0	.237	.297	.280

Julio Mateo

Pitches: R **Bats:** R **Pos:** RP-50　　　　　　　　　　　　　　　　　　　**Ht:** 6'0" **Wt:** 177 **Born:** 8/2/77 **Age:** 26

Year Team	Lg	G	GS	CG	GF	IP	BFP	H	R	ER	HR	SH	SF	HB	TBB	IBB	SO	WP	Bk	W	L	Pct	ShO	Sv-Op	Hld	ERC	ERA
1997 Mariners	R	13	6	0	4	60.0	254	45	32	22	1	2	2	8	23	0	54	10	1	3	1	.750	0	1- -	-	2.58	3.30
1998 Lancaster	A+	1	0	0	0	1.1	6	1	1	1	1	0	0	1	1	0	1	0	0	0	0	-	0	0- -	-	15.24	6.75
1998 Everett	A-	28	0	0	13	38.1	170	40	25	20	6	3	2	2	17	1	37	6	0	3	3	.500	0	4- -	-	5.10	4.70
1999 Wisconsin	A	20	0	0	10	29.0	131	31	18	14	2	2	1	1	8	2	27	2	0	1	3	.250	0	4- -	-	3.56	4.34
2000 Wisconsin	A	36	1	0	15	68.2	295	63	38	32	12	4	1	6	23	1	73	9	0	4	8	.333	0	4- -	-	4.16	4.19
2001 Sn Brnardino	A+	56	0	0	47	66.0	273	58	28	21	5	2	1	2	16	5	79	1	1	5	4	.556	0	26- -	-	2.64	2.86
2002 San Antonio	AA	12	0	0	4	17.1	61	7	3	1	2	0	0	0	3	0	18	0	0	1	0	1.000	0	0- -	-	0.92	0.52
2002 Tacoma	AAA	20	0	0	16	31.0	137	39	15	14	2	1	2	4	7	1	23	2	0	4	2	.667	0	6- -	-	5.17	4.06
2002 Seattle	AL	12	0	0	7	21.0	94	20	10	10	2	0	0	1	12	0	15	1	0	0	0	-	0	0-0	2	4.63	4.29
2003 Seattle	AL	50	0	0	17	85.2	338	69	32	30	14	2	4	5	13	1	71	1	1	4	0	1.000	0	1-1	5	2.71	3.15
2 ML YEARS		62	0	0	24	106.2	432	89	42	40	16	2	4	6	25	1	86	2	1	4	0	1.000	0	1-1	4	3.08	3.38

Ruben Mateo

Bats: R **Throws:** R **Pos:** RF-39; PH-20; CF-14; LF-4　　　　　　　　　**Ht:** 6'0" **Wt:** 185 **Born:** 2/10/78 **Age:** 26

Year Team	Lg	G	AB	H	2B	3B	HR	(Hm	Rd)	TB	R	RBI	RC	TBB	IBB	SO	HBP	SH	SF	SB	CS	SB%	GDP	Avg	OBP	Slg
2003 Louisville*	AAA	57	217	71	15	1	9	(-	-)	115	36	50	46	26	1	34	5	0	2	3	1	.75	3	.327	.408	.530
1999 Texas	AL	32	122	29	9	1	5	(2	3)	55	16	18	15	4	0	28	1	0	0	3	0	1.00	2	.238	.268	.451
2000 Texas	AL	52	206	60	11	0	7	(3	4)	92	32	19	31	10	1	34	5	1	0	6	0	1.00	5	.291	.339	.447
2001 Texas	AL	40	129	32	5	2	1	(0	1)	44	18	13	14	9	0	28	6	1	2	1	0	1.00	4	.248	.322	.341
2002 Cincinnati	NL	46	86	22	6	0	2	(2	0)	34	11	7	7	6	0	20	2	0	0	0	0	-	1	.256	.319	.395
2003 Cincinnati	NL	74	207	50	9	0	3	(2	1)	68	16	18	21	12	1	53	3	0	2	0	0	-	4	.242	.290	.329
5 ML YEARS		244	750	193	40	3	18	(9	9)	293	93	75	88	41	2	163	17	2	4	10	0	1.00	16	.257	.309	.391

Mike Matheny

Bats: R **Throws:** R **Pos:** C-138; PH-5; 1B-4　　　　　　　　　　　**Ht:** 6'3" **Wt:** 205 **Born:** 9/22/70 **Age:** 33

Year Team	Lg	G	AB	H	2B	3B	HR	(Hm	Rd)	TB	R	RBI	RC	TBB	IBB	SO	HBP	SH	SF	SB	CS	SB%	GDP	Avg	OBP	Slg
1994 Milwaukee	NL	28	53	12	3	0	1	(1	0)	18	3	2	5	3	0	13	2	1	0	0	1	.00	1	.226	.293	.340
1995 Milwaukee	NL	80	166	41	9	1	0	(0	0)	52	13	21	16	12	0	28	2	1	0	2	1	.67	3	.247	.306	.313
1996 Milwaukee	NL	106	313	64	15	2	8	(5	3)	107	31	46	23	14	0	80	3	7	4	3	2	.60	9	.204	.243	.342
1997 Milwaukee	NL	123	320	78	16	1	4	(2	2)	108	29	32	30	17	0	68	7	9	3	1	0	1.00	9	.244	.294	.338
1998 Milwaukee	NL	108	320	76	13	0	6	(4	2)	107	24	27	28	11	0	63	7	3	0	1	0	1.00	9	.238	.278	.334
1999 Toronto	AL	57	163	35	6	0	3	(1	2)	50	16	17	13	12	0	37	1	2	1	0	0	-	3	.215	.271	.307
2000 St Louis	NL	128	417	109	22	1	6	(2	4)	151	43	47	46	32	8	96	4	7	4	0	0	-	11	.261	.317	.362
2001 St Louis	NL	121	381	83	12	0	7	(4	3)	116	40	42	29	28	5	76	4	8	3	0	1	.00	11	.218	.276	.304
2002 St Louis	NL	110	315	77	12	1	3	(1	2)	100	31	35	35	32	6	49	2	8	6	1	3	.25	3	.244	.313	.317
2003 St Louis	NL	141	441	111	18	2	8	(4	4)	157	43	47	50	44	16	81	2	8	3	1	1	.50	11	.252	.320	.356
10 ML YEARS		1002	2889	686	126	8	46	(24	22)	966	273	316	275	205	35	591	34	54	24	8	10	.44	67	.237	.293	.334

Julius Matos

Bats: R **Throws:** R **Pos:** 3B-13; 2B-11; PH-5; SS-2; RF-1; PR-1　　　　**Ht:** 5'11" **Wt:** 170 **Born:** 12/12/74 **Age:** 29

Year Team	Lg	G	AB	H	2B	3B	HR	(Hm	Rd)	TB	R	RBI	RC	TBB	IBB	SO	HBP	SH	SF	SB	CS	SB%	GDP	Avg	OBP	Slg
1994 Watertown	A-	43	138	34	2	2	0	(-	-)	40	13	18	11	13	0	33	0	0	2	3	2	.60	6	.246	.307	.290
1995 Columbus	A	52	155	38	7	3	0	(-	-)	51	16	13	13	11	1	21	3	1	0	2	2	.50	8	.245	.308	.329
1996 Thunder Bay	IND	82	295	81	13	0	3	(-	-)	103	33	32	29	14	0	48	2	5	1	8	7	.53	9	.275	.311	.349
1997 Sioux City	IND	83	353	94	12	3	6	(-	-)	130	64	44	40	20	0	38	4	1	2	8	7	.53	4	.266	.311	.368
1998 High Desert	A+	111	439	132	27	4	4	(-	-)	179	70	60	58	23	0	40	2	7	8	19	13	.59	9	.301	.333	.408
1999 El Paso	AA	120	425	119	17	5	5	(-	-)	161	54	41	46	13	0	37	1	4	3	5	2	.71	10	.280	.301	.379
2000 Mobile	AA	135	546	144	30	0	5	(-	-)	189	61	35	54	31	0	57	2	7	0	11	9	.55	13	.264	.306	.346
2001 Mobile	AA	19	67	22	6	0	0	(-	-)	28	13	2	9	1	0	5	1	2	1	1	2	.33	2	.328	.343	.418
2001 Portland	AAA	106	383	107	12	2	7	(-	-)	144	40	34	43	15	2	48	6	3	3	6	8	.43	6	.279	.314	.376
2002 Portland	AAA	50	186	58	17	0	4	(-	-)	87	20	26	28	9	0	20	2	5	3	1	2	.33	6	.312	.345	.468
2003 Omaha	AAA	92	371	107	19	0	7	(-	-)	147	44	48	47	13	0	32	8	8	3	10	5	.67	7	.288	.324	.396
2002 San Diego	NL	76	185	44	3	0	2	(0	2)	53	19	19	13	9	0	33	2	3	1	1	1	.50	5	.238	.279	.286
2003 Kansas City	AL	28	57	15	1	0	2	(0	2)	22	7	7	5	1	0	12	0	1	0	1	0	1.00	2	.263	.276	.386
2 ML YEARS		104	242	59	4	0	4	(0	4)	75	26	26	18	10	0	45	2	4	1	2	1	.67	7	.244	.278	.310

Luis Matos

Bats: R **Throws:** R **Pos:** CF-106; RF-4; DH-2; PH-1　　　　　　　　**Ht:** 6'0" **Wt:** 179 **Born:** 10/30/78 **Age:** 25

Year Team	Lg	G	AB	H	2B	3B	HR	(Hm	Rd)	TB	R	RBI	RC	TBB	IBB	SO	HBP	SH	SF	SB	CS	SB%	GDP	Avg	OBP	Slg
2003 Ottawa*	AAA	45	175	53	16	4	1	(Hm	Rd)	80	28	25	26	13	1	34	1	1	4	6	1	.86	6	.303	.347	.457
2000 Baltimore	AL	72	182	41	6	3	1	(1	0)	56	21	17	15	12	0	30	3	2	2	13	4	.76	7	.225	.281	.308
2001 Baltimore	AL	31	98	21	7	0	4	(1	3)	40	16	12	14	11	0	30	1	2	0	7	0	1.00	1	.214	.300	.408
2002 Baltimore	AL	17	31	4	1	0	0	(0	0)	5	0	1	0	1	0	6	0	1	0	1	0	1.00	1	.129	.156	.161
2003 Baltimore	AL	109	439	133	23	3	13	(6	7)	201	70	45	66	28	0	90	7	10	2	15	7	.68	9	.303	.353	.458
4 ML YEARS		229	750	199	37	6	18	(8	10)	302	107	75	95	52	0	156	11	15	4	36	11	.77	18	.265	.321	.403

Dave Matranga

Bats: R Throws: R Pos: PH-5; 2B-2   Ht: 6'0" Wt: 170 Born: 1/8/77 Age: 27

Year Team	Lg	G	AB	H	2B	3B	HR	(Hm	Rd)	TB	R	RBI	RC	TBB	IBB	SO	HBP	SH	SF	SB	CS	SB%	GDP	Avg	OBP	Slg
1998 Auburn	A-	40	144	44	13	1	4	(-	-)	71	34	24	33	25	1	38	5	1	1	16	3	.84	0	.306	.423	.493
1999 Kissimmee	A+	124	472	109	20	4	6	(-	-)	155	70	48	59	68	0	118	12	9	2	17	10	.63	3	.231	.341	.328
2000 Round Rock	AA	120	373	87	14	3	6	(-	-)	125	50	44	48	48	0	99	17	2	1	5	5	.50	1	.233	.346	.335
2001 Round Rock	AA	103	387	117	34	2	10	(-	-)	185	78	60	75	45	1	91	14	7	4	17	7	.71	2	.302	.391	.478
2001 New Orleans	AAA	4	16	5	1	0	1	(-	-)	9	3	3	3	0	0	5	1	0	1	1	0	1.00	0	.313	.333	.563
2002 New Orleans	AAA	101	300	82	15	3	7	(-	-)	124	47	40	44	27	0	79	6	5	3	7	2	.78	4	.273	.342	.413
2003 New Orleans	AAA	102	315	76	16	4	3	(-	-)	109	34	25	32	21	3	71	4	9	1	3	3	.50	3	.241	.296	.346
2003 Houston	NL	6	5	1	0	0	1	(1	0)	4	1	1	1	0	0	2	0	0	0	0	0	-	0	.200	.200	.800

Hideki Matsui

Bats: L Throws: R Pos: LF-118; CF-46; DH-2; PH-2; PR-1   Ht: 6'2" Wt: 210 Born: 6/12/74 Age: 30

Year Team	Lg	G	AB	H	2B	3B	HR	(Hm	Rd)	TB	R	RBI	RC	TBB	IBB	SO	HBP	SH	SF	SB	CS	SB%	GDP	Avg	OBP	Slg
1993 Yomiuri	Jap	57	184	41	9	0	11	(-	-)	83	27	27	25	17	0	50	2	0	0	1	0	1.00	1	.223	.296	.451
1994 Yomiuri	Jap	130	503	148	23	4	20	(-	-)	239	70	66	86	57	1	101	4	1	4	6	3	.67	12	.294	.368	.475
1995 Yomiuri	Jap	131	501	142	31	1	22	(-	-)	241	76	80	85	62	1	93	2	1	2	9	7	.56	12	.283	.363	.481
1996 Yomiuri	Jap	130	487	153	34	1	38	(-	-)	303	97	99	118	71	1	98	4	0	7	7	2	.78	5	.314	.401	.622
1997 Yomiuri	Jap	135	484	144	18	0	37	(-	-)	273	94	103	115	100	10	84	6	0	6	9	3	.75	5	.298	.419	.564
1998 Yomiuri	Jap	135	487	142	24	3	34	(-	-)	274	103	100	114	104	2	101	8	0	4	3	5	.38	7	.292	.421	.563
1999 Yomiuri	Jap	135	471	143	24	2	42	(-	-)	297	100	95	119	93	0	99	2	0	6	4	4	.00	3	.304	.416	.631
2000 Yomiuri	Jap	135	474	150	32	1	42	(-	-)	310	116	108	133	106	5	108	2	0	7	5	2	.71	1	.316	.438	.654
2001 Yomiuri	Jap	140	481	160	23	3	36	(-	-)	297	107	104	133	120	6	96	3	0	1	3	3	.50	9	.333	.463	.617
2002 Yomiuri	Jap	140	500	167	27	1	50	(-	-)	346	112	107	148	114	17	104	6	0	3	2	4	.43	4	.334	.461	.692
2003 New York	AL	163	623	179	42	1	16	(9	7)	271	82	106	96	63	5	86	3	0	6	2	2	.50	25	.287	.353	.435

Kazuo Matsui

Bats: B Throws: R Pos: SS   Ht: 5'10" Wt: 183 Born: 10/23/75 Age: 28

Year Team	Lg	G	AB	H	2B	3B	HR	(Hm	Rd)	TB	R	RBI	RC	TBB	IBB	SO	HBP	SH	SF	SB	CS	SB%	GDP	Avg	OBP	Slg
1995 Seibu	Jap	69	204	45	9	1	2	(-	-)	62	25	15	17	7	-	26	0	7	1	21	1	.95	4	.221	.245	.304
1996 Seibu	Jap	130	473	134	22	5	1	(-	-)	169	51	29	59	14	-	93	3	26	2	50	9	.85	2	.283	.307	.357
1997 Seibu	Jap	135	576	178	23	13	7	(-	-)	248	91	63	89	44	-	89	5	18	2	62	15	.81	4	.309	.362	.431
1998 Seibu	Jap	135	575	179	38	5	9	(-	-)	254	92	58	89	55	-	89	1	6	4	43	14	.75	10	.311	.370	.442
1999 Seibu	Jap	135	539	178	29	4	15	(-	-)	260	87	67	96	56	-	75	0	8	6	32	7	.82	7	.330	.389	.482
2000 Seibu	Jap	135	550	177	40	11	23	(-	-)	308	99	90	107	46	-	60	2	6	7	26	3	.90	8	.322	.372	.560
2001 Seibu	Jap	140	552	170	28	2	24	(-	-)	274	94	76	94	46	-	83	6	4	5	26	0	1.00	13	.308	.365	.496
2002 Seibu	Jap	140	582	193	46	6	36	(-	-)	359	119	87	127	53	-	112	4	9	3	33	11	.75	3	.332	.389	.617
2003 Seibu	Jap	140	587	179	36	4	33	(-	-)	322	104	84	118	55	-	124	4	-	1	13	-	-	4	.305	.368	.549

Mike Matthews

Pitches: L Bats: L Pos: RP-77   Ht: 6'2" Wt: 175 Born: 10/24/73 Age: 30

Year Team	Lg	G	GS	CG	GF	IP	BFP	H	R	ER	HR	SH	SF	HB	TBB	IBB	SO	WP	Bk	W	L	Pct	ShO	Sv-Op	Hld	ERC	ERA
2000 St Louis	NL	14	0	0	4	9.1	54	15	12	12	2	0	0	1	10	2	8	0	0	0	0	-	0	0-0	2	11.83	11.57
2001 St Louis	NL	51	10	0	4	89.0	368	74	32	32	11	4	1	4	33	4	72	4	1	3	4	.429	0	1-3	3	3.34	3.24
2002 StL-Mil	NL	47	0	0	10	45.2	205	43	23	20	5	2	4	2	29	3	34	5	1	2	1	.667	0	0-2	4	4.84	3.94
2003 San Diego	NL	77	0	0	20	64.2	282	65	34	32	4	3	5	4	29	5	44	4	0	6	4	.600	0	0-3	16	4.18	4.45
2002 St Louis	NL	43	0	0	10	41.2	184	40	21	18	5	2	4	2	22	2	32	5	0	2	1	.667	0	0-2	4	4.64	3.89
2002 Milwaukee	NL	4	0	0	0	4.0	21	3	2	2	0	0	0	0	7	1	2	0	1	0	0	-	0	0-0	0	6.63	4.50
4 ML YEARS		189	10	0	41	208.2	909	197	101	96	22	9	10	11	101	14	158	13	2	11	9	.550	0	1-8	25	4.26	4.14

Gary Matthews Jr.

Bats: B Throws: R Pos: CF-75; RF-35; LF-33; PH-19; DH-1   Ht: 6'3" Wt: 210 Born: 8/25/74 Age: 29

Year Team	Lg	G	AB	H	2B	3B	HR	(Hm	Rd)	TB	R	RBI	RC	TBB	IBB	SO	HBP	SH	SF	SB	CS	SB%	GDP	Avg	OBP	Slg
1999 San Diego	NL	23	36	8	0	0	0	(0	0)	8	4	7	4	9	0	9	0	0	0	2	0	1.00	1	.222	.378	.222
2000 San Diego	NL	80	158	30	1	2	4	(2	2)	47	24	14	13	15	1	28	1	1	0	3	0	1.00	3	.190	.264	.297
2001 ChC-Pit	NL	152	405	92	15	2	14	(4	10)	153	63	44	51	60	2	100	1	5	1	8	5	.62	8	.227	.328	.378
2002 NYM-Bal	NL	111	345	95	25	3	7	(6	1)	147	54	38	55	43	1	69	1	5	4	15	5	.75	8	.275	.354	.426
2003 Bal-SD	AL	144	468	116	31	4	7	(3	3)	169	71	42	51	43	0	95	2	0	0	12	8	.60	8	.248	.314	.361
2001 Chicago	NL	106	258	56	9	1	9	(2	7)	94	41	30	31	38	2	55	1	5	0	5	3	.63	4	.217	.320	.364
2001 Pittsburgh	NL	46	147	36	6	1	5	(2	3)	59	22	14	20	22	0	45	0	0	1	3	2	.60	4	.245	.341	.401
2002 New York	NL	2	1	0	0	0	0	(0	0)	0	0	0	0	0	0	0	0	0	0	0	0	-	0	.000	.000	.000
2002 Baltimore	AL	109	344	95	25	3	7	(6	1)	147	54	38	55	43	1	69	1	5	4	15	5	.75	4	.276	.355	.427
2003 Baltimore	AL	41	162	33	12	1	2	(2	0)	53	21	20	15	9	0	29	1	0	0	0	3	.00	4	.204	.250	.327
2003 San Diego	NL	103	306	83	19	1	4	(1	3)	116	50	22	36	34	0	66	1	0	0	12	5	.71	4	.271	.346	.379
5 ML YEARS		510	1412	341	72	9	31	(15	16)	524	216	145	174	170	4	301	5	11	5	40	18	.69	23	.242	.324	.371

Darrell May

Pitches: L Bats: L Pos: SP-32; RP-3   Ht: 6'2" Wt: 184 Born: 6/13/72 Age: 32

Year Team	Lg	G	GS	CG	GF	IP	BFP	H	R	ER	HR	SH	SF	HB	TBB	IBB	SO	WP	Bk	W	L	Pct	ShO	Sv-Op	Hld	ERC	ERA
1995 Atlanta	NL	2	0	0	1	4.0	21	10	5	5	0	0	1	0	0	0	1	0	0	0	0	-	0	0-0	0	11.41	11.25
1996 Pit-Ana		10	2	0	2	11.1	60	18	13	12	6	0	2	1	6	0	6	0	0	0	1	.000	0	0-0	1	12.24	9.53
1997 Anaheim	AL	29	2	0	7	51.2	234	56	31	30	6	3	4	0	25	2	42	2	0	2	1	.667	0	0-1	2	4.87	5.23
2002 Kansas City	AL	30	21	2	3	131.1	579	144	83	78	28	3	5	1	50	3	95	2	0	4	10	.286	1	0-1	0	5.35	5.35

Year Team	Lg	G	GS	CG	GF	IP	BFP	H	R	ER	HR	SH	SF	HB	TBB	IBB	SO	WP	Bk	W	L	Pct	ShO	Sv-Op	Hld	ERC	ERA
2003 Kansas City	AL	35	32	2	1	210.0	868	197	98	88	31	5	6	2	53	1	115	5	0	10	8	.556	1	0-1	0	3.50	3.77
1996 Pittsburgh	NL	5	2	0	0	8.2	47	15	10	9	5	0	0	1	4	0	5	0	0	0	1	.000	0	0-0	0	13.48	9.35
1996 Anaheim	AL	5	0	0	2	2.2	13	3	3	3	1	0	2	0	2	0	1	0	0	0	0	-	0	0-0	0	8.41	10.13
5 ML YEARS		106	57	4	14	408.1	1762	425	230	213	71	11	18	4	134	6	259	9	0	16	20	.444	2	0-3	3	4.53	4.69

Brent Mayne

Bats: L **Throws:** R **Pos:** C-112; PH-2   **Ht:** 6'1" **Wt:** 190 **Born:** 4/19/68 **Age:** 36

								BATTING										BASERUNNING				AVERAGES		
Year Team	Lg	G	AB	H	2B	3B	HR	(Hm Rd)	TB	R	RBI	RC	TBB	IBB	SO	HBP	SH	SF	SB	CS	SB%	GDP	Avg	OBP	Slg
1990 Kansas City	AL	5	13	3	0	0	0	(0 0)	3	2	1	1	3	0	3	0	0	0	0	1	.00	0	.231	.375	.231
1991 Kansas City	AL	85	231	58	8	0	3	(2 1)	75	22	31	22	23	4	42	0	2	3	4	4	.33	6	.251	.315	.325
1992 Kansas City	AL	82	213	48	10	0	0	(0 0)	58	16	18	12	11	0	26	0	2	3	0	4	.00	5	.225	.260	.272
1993 Kansas City	AL	71	205	52	9	1	2	(0 2)	69	22	22	20	18	7	31	1	3	0	3	2	.60	6	.254	.317	.337
1994 Kansas City	AL	46	144	37	5	1	2	(1 1)	50	19	20	16	14	1	27	0	0	0	1	0	1.00	3	.257	.323	.347
1995 Kansas City	AL	110	307	77	18	1	1	(1 0)	100	23	27	27	25	1	41	3	11	1	0	1	.00	16	.251	.313	.326
1996 New York	NL	70	99	26	6	0	1	(0 1)	35	9	6	11	12	1	22	0	2	0	0	1	.00	1	.263	.342	.354
1997 Oakland	AL	85	256	74	12	0	6	(4 2)	104	29	22	35	18	1	33	4	2	2	1	0	1.00	6	.289	.343	.406
1998 San Francisco	NL	94	275	75	15	0	3	(0 3)	99	26	32	36	37	3	47	1	2	2	2	1	.67	8	.273	.359	.360
1999 San Francisco	NL	117	322	97	32	0	2	(1 1)	135	39	39	50	43	5	65	5	1	3	2	2	.50	16	.301	.389	.419
2000 Colorado	NL	117	335	101	21	0	6	(3 3)	140	36	64	52	47	13	48	1	4	8	1	3	.25	12	.301	.381	.418
2001 Col-KC		100	326	93	11	1	2	(1 1)	112	28	40	35	26	5	41	1	0	6	1	2	.33	12	.285	.334	.344
2002 Kansas City	AL	101	326	77	8	2	4	(2 2)	101	35	30	31	34	1	54	2	4	4	4	4	.50	8	.236	.309	.310
2003 Kansas City	AL	113	372	91	17	1	6	(1 5)	128	39	36	40	32	5	59	3	4	3	0	2	.00	10	.245	.307	.344
2001 Colorado	NL	49	160	53	7	0	0	(0 0)	60	15	20	23	16	3	24	0	0	3	0	0	-	4	.331	.385	.375
2001 Kansas City	AL	51	166	40	4	1	2	(1 1)	52	13	20	12	10	2	17	1	0	3	1	2	.33	8	.241	.283	.313
14 ML YEARS		1196	3424	909	172	7	38	(16 22)	1209	345	388	388	343	47	539	21	37	35	17	27	.39	112	.265	.333	.353

Joe Mays

Pitches: R **Bats:** B **Pos:** SP-21; RP-10   **Ht:** 6'1" **Wt:** 185 **Born:** 12/10/75 **Age:** 28

Year Team	Lg	G	GS	CG	GF	IP	BFP	H	R	ER	HR	SH	SF	HB	TBB	IBB	SO	WP	Bk	W	L	Pct	ShO	Sv-Op	Hld	ERC	ERA
1999 Minnesota	AL	49	24	2	8	171.0	746	179	92	83	24	7	6	2	67	2	115	6	0	6	11	.353	1	0-0	2	4.62	4.37
2000 Minnesota	AL	31	28	2	1	160.1	723	193	105	99	20	3	5	2	67	1	102	11	0	7	15	.318	1	0-0	0	5.59	5.56
2001 Minnesota	AL	34	34	4	0	233.2	957	205	87	82	25	8	8	5	64	2	123	11	0	17	13	.567	2	0-0	0	3.05	3.16
2002 Minnesota	AL	17	17	1	0	95.1	418	113	60	57	14	2	2	2	25	0	38	6	0	4	8	.333	1	0-0	0	4.99	5.38
2003 Minnesota	AL	31	21	0	4	130.0	576	159	92	91	21	3	3	4	39	2	50	3	0	8	8	.500	0	0-1	1	5.55	6.30
5 ML YEARS		162	120	9	13	790.1	3420	849	436	412	104	23	24	15	262	7	428	37	0	42	55	.433	5	0-1	3	4.51	4.69

Dave McCarty

Bats: R **Throws:** R **Pos:** LF-12; 1B-8; PH-4; RF-1; DH-1; PR-1   **Ht:** 6'5" **Wt:** 215 **Born:** 11/23/69 **Age:** 34

								BATTING										BASERUNNING				AVERAGES		
Year Team	Lg	G	AB	H	2B	3B	HR	(Hm Rd)	TB	R	RBI	RC	TBB	IBB	SO	HBP	SH	SF	SB	CS	SB%	GDP	Avg	OBP	Slg
2003 Sacramento*	AAA	91	352	95	23	2	15	(- -)	167	69	72	57	44	0	71	3	0	5	4	1	.80	12	.270	.351	.474
1993 Minnesota	AL	98	350	75	15	2	2	(2 0)	100	36	21	18	19	0	80	1	1	0	2	6	.25	13	.214	.257	.286
1994 Minnesota	AL	44	131	34	8	2	1	(1 0)	49	21	12	15	7	1	32	5	0	0	2	1	.67	3	.260	.322	.374
1995 Min-SF		37	75	17	4	1	0	(0 0)	23	11	6	6	6	0	22	1	0	1	1	1	.50	1	.227	.289	.307
1996 San Francisco	NL	91	175	38	3	0	6	(5 1)	59	16	24	17	18	0	43	2	0	2	2	1	.67	5	.217	.294	.337
1998 Seattle	AL	8	18	5	0	0	1	(0 0)	8	1	2	4	5	0	4	0	0	0	1	0	1.00	0	.278	.435	.444
2000 Kansas City	AL	103	270	75	14	2	12	(6 6)	129	34	53	41	22	1	68	0	0	3	0	0	-	6	.278	.329	.478
2001 Kansas City	AL	98	200	50	10	0	7	(5 2)	81	26	26	26	24	1	45	1	1	4	0	0	-	8	.250	.328	.405
2002 KC-TB		25	66	9	1	0	2	(0 2)	16	5	4	2	6	0	19	2	0	0	0	0	-	3	.136	.230	.242
2003 Oak-Bos		24	53	18	5	0	1	(1 0)	26	6	8	10	3	0	14	0	0	1	0	0	-	0	.340	.368	.491
1995 Minnesota	AL	25	55	12	3	1	0	(0 0)	17	10	4	4	4	0	18	1	0	1	0	1	.00	1	.218	.279	.309
1995 San Francisco	NL	12	20	5	1	0	0	(0 0)	6	1	2	2	2	0	4	0	0	0	1	0	1.00	0	.250	.318	.300
2002 Kansas City	AL	13	32	3	1	0	1	(0 1)	7	3	2	2	2	0	10	0	0	0	0	0	-	1	.094	.147	.219
2002 Tampa Bay	AL	12	34	6	0	0	1	(0 1)	9	2	2	2	4	0	9	2	0	0	0	0	-	2	.176	.300	.265
2003 Oakland	AL	8	26	7	2	0	0	(0 0)	9	2	2	2	1	0	7	0	0	1	0	0	-	0	.269	.286	.346
2003 Boston	AL	16	27	11	3	0	1	(1 0)	17	4	6	8	2	0	7	0	0	0	0	0	-	0	.407	.448	.630
9 ML YEARS		528	1338	321	60	7	32	(21 11)	491	156	156	139	110	3	327	12	2	11	8	9	.47	37	.240	.301	.367

Seth McClung

Pitches: R **Bats:** L **Pos:** RP-7; SP-5   **Ht:** 6'6" **Wt:** 235 **Born:** 2/7/81 **Age:** 23

Year Team	Lg	G	GS	CG	GF	IP	BFP	H	R	ER	HR	SH	SF	HB	TBB	IBB	SO	WP	Bk	W	L	Pct	ShO	Sv-Op	Hld	ERC	ERA
1999 Princeton	R+	13	10	0	0	45.2	244	53	47	39	3	0	1	9	48	0	46	20	0	2	4	.333	0	0- -	-	8.19	7.69
2000 Hudson Val	A-	8	8	0	0	43.2	186	37	18	9	0	1	2	3	17	0	38	6	1	2	2	.500	0	0- -	-	2.76	1.85
2000 Chrlstn - SC	A	6	6	0	0	31.0	145	30	14	11	0	1	0	3	19	0	26	8	0	2	1	.667	0	0- -	-	4.21	3.19
2001 Chrlstn - SC	A	28	28	2	0	164.1	683	142	72	51	6	4	1	11	53	1	165	3	2	10	11	.476	1	0- -	-	2.88	2.79
2002 Bakersfield	A+	7	7	0	0	37.0	158	35	16	12	1	1	0	2	11	0	48	0	1	3	2	.600	0	0- -	-	3.05	2.92
2002 Orlando	AA	20	19	0	1	114.0	533	138	74	68	12	2	7	9	53	0	64	7	1	5	7	.417	0	0- -	-	5.90	5.37
2003 Tampa Bay	AL	12	5	0	2	38.2	167	33	23	23	6	1	1	3	25	1	25	2	0	4	1	.800	0	0-0	1	5.11	5.35

Quinton McCracken

Bats: B **Throws:** R **Pos:** PH-57; RF-34; CF-16; LF-11; PR-8; DH-1   **Ht:** 5'7" **Wt:** 173 **Born:** 3/16/70 **Age:** 34

							BATTING												BASERUNNING				AVERAGES		
Year Team	Lg	G	AB	H	2B	3B	HR	(Hm | Rd)	TB	R	RBI	RC	TBB	IBB	SO	HBP	SH	SF	SB	CS	SB%	GDP	Avg	OBP	Slg
1995 Colorado	NL	3	1	0	0	0	0	(0 | 0)	0	0	0	0	0	0	1	0	0	0	0	0	-	0	.000	.000	.000
1996 Colorado	NL	124	283	82	13	6	3	(2 | 1)	116	50	40	43	32	4	62	1	12	1	17	6	.74	5	.290	.363	.410
1997 Colorado	NL	147	325	95	11	1	3	(1 | 2)	117	69	36	47	42	0	62	1	6	1	28	11	.72	6	.292	.374	.360
1998 Tampa Bay	AL	155	614	179	38	7	7	(5 | 2)	252	77	59	83	41	1	107	3	9	8	19	10	.66	12	.292	.335	.410
1999 Tampa Bay	AL	40	148	37	6	1	1	(1 | 0)	48	20	18	13	14	0	23	1	1	1	6	5	.55	7	.250	.317	.324
2000 Tampa Bay	AL	15	31	4	0	0	0	(0 | 0)	4	5	2	0	6	0	4	0	0	0	0	1	.00	3	.129	.270	.129
2001 Minnesota	AL	24	64	14	2	2	0	(0 | 0)	20	7	3	5	5	0	13	0	1	0	0	1	.00	2	.219	.275	.313
2002 Arizona	NL	123	349	108	27	8	3	(1 | 2)	160	60	40	62	32	0	68	2	13	4	5	4	.56	3	.309	.367	.458
2003 Arizona	NL	115	203	46	5	2	0	(0 | 0)	55	17	18	15	15	2	34	0	5	3	5	1	.83	4	.227	.276	.271
9 ML YEARS		746	2018	565	102	27	17	(10 | 7)	772	305	216	268	187	7	374	8	47	18	80	39	.67	42	.280	.341	.383

John McDonald

Bats: R **Throws:** R **Pos:** 2B-37; SS-27; 3B-23; PR-7; PH-1   **Ht:** 5'11" **Wt:** 175 **Born:** 9/24/74 **Age:** 29

							BATTING												BASERUNNING				AVERAGES		
Year Team	Lg	G	AB	H	2B	3B	HR	(Hm	Rd)	TB	R	RBI	RC	TBB	IBB	SO	HBP	SH	SF	SB	CS	SB%	GDP	Avg	OBP	Slg
2003 Lake County*	A-	1	3	0	0	0	0	(-	-)	0	0	0	0	0	0	0	0	0	0	0	0	-	0	.000	.000	.000
2003 Mahning VI*	A-	1	2	0	0	0	0	(-	-)	0	1	0	0	1	0	0	0	0	0	0	0	-	0	.000	.333	.000
1999 Cleveland	AL	18	21	7	0	0	0	(0	0)	7	2	0	1	0	0	3	0	0	0	0	1	.00	2	.333	.333	.333
2000 Cleveland	AL	9	9	4	0	0	0	(0	0)	4	0	0	2	0	0	1	0	0	0	0	0	-	0	.444	.444	.444
2001 Cleveland	AL	17	22	2	1	0	0	(0	0)	3	1	0	0	1	0	7	1	1	0	0	0	-	0	.091	.167	.136
2002 Cleveland	AL	93	264	66	11	3	1	(0	1)	86	35	12	23	10	0	50	5	7	2	3	0	1.00	4	.250	.288	.326
2003 Cleveland	AL	82	214	46	9	1	1	(0	1)	60	21	14	17	11	0	31	2	4	2	3	3	.50	4	.215	.258	.280
5 ML YEARS		219	530	125	21	4	2	(0	2)	160	59	26	43	22	0	92	8	12	4	6	4	.60	10	.236	.275	.302

Joe McEwing

Bats: R **Throws:** R **Pos:** 2B-55; SS-42; LF-16; PH-14; PR-12; 1B-5; 3B-2; RF-2; CF-1   **Ht:** 5'11" **Wt:** 170 **Born:** 10/19/72 **Age:** 31

							BATTING												BASERUNNING				AVERAGES		
Year Team	Lg	G	AB	H	2B	3B	HR	(Hm	Rd)	TB	R	RBI	RC	TBB	IBB	SO	HBP	SH	SF	SB	CS	SB%	GDP	Avg	OBP	Slg
2003 Norfolk*	AAA	5	19	6	0	0	1	(-	-)	9	3	3	5	2	0	2	2	0	0	3	0	1.00	0	.316	.435	.474
1998 St Louis	NL	10	20	4	1	0	0	(0	0)	5	5	1	1	1	0	3	1	1	0	0	1	.00	0	.200	.273	.250
1999 St Louis	NL	152	513	141	28	4	9	(5	4)	204	65	44	70	41	8	87	6	9	5	7	4	.64	3	.275	.333	.398
2000 New York	NL	87	153	34	14	1	2	(1	1)	56	20	19	14	5	0	29	1	8	2	3	1	.75	2	.222	.248	.366
2001 New York	NL	116	283	80	17	3	8	(3	5)	127	41	30	44	17	0	57	10	6	3	8	5	.62	2	.283	.342	.449
2002 New York	NL	105	196	39	8	1	3	(2	1)	58	22	26	14	9	0	50	3	3	3	4	4	.50	0	.199	.242	.296
2003 New York	NL	119	278	67	11	0	1	(0	1)	81	31	16	25	25	4	57	3	6	1	3	0	1.00	6	.241	.309	.291
6 ML YEARS		589	1443	365	79	9	23	(11	12)	531	184	136	168	98	12	283	24	33	14	25	15	.63	13	.253	.308	.368

Fred McGriff

Bats: L **Throws:** L **Pos:** 1B-79; PH-7   **Ht:** 6'3" **Wt:** 225 **Born:** 10/31/63 **Age:** 40

							BATTING												BASERUNNING				AVERAGES		
Year Team	Lg	G	AB	H	2B	3B	HR	(Hm	Rd)	TB	R	RBI	RC	TBB	IBB	SO	HBP	SH	SF	SB	CS	SB%	GDP	Avg	OBP	Slg
2003 Dodgers*	R	1	3	2	1	0	0	(-	-)	3	1	0	1	0	0	0	0	0	0	0	0	-	0	.667	.667	1.000
2003 Vero Beach*	A+	2	6	1	0	0	0	(-	-)	1	0	0	0	1	0	2	0	0	0	0	0	-	0	.167	.286	.167
1986 Toronto	AL	3	5	1	0	0	0	(0	0)	1	1	0	0	0	0	2	0	0	0	0	0	-	0	.200	.200	.200
1987 Toronto	AL	107	295	73	16	0	20	(7	13)	149	58	43	57	60	4	104	1	0	0	3	2	.60	3	.247	.376	.505
1988 Toronto	AL	154	536	151	35	4	34	(18	16)	296	100	82	107	79	3	149	4	0	4	6	1	.86	15	.282	.376	.552
1989 Toronto	AL	161	551	148	27	3	36	(18	18)	289	98	92	115	119	12	132	4	1	5	7	4	.64	14	.269	.399	.525
1990 Toronto	AL	153	557	167	21	1	35	(14	21)	295	91	88	117	94	12	108	2	1	4	5	3	.63	7	.300	.400	.530
1991 San Diego	NL	153	528	147	19	1	31	(18	13)	261	84	106	102	105	26	135	2	0	7	4	1	.80	14	.278	.396	.494
1992 San Diego	NL	152	531	152	30	4	35	(21	14)	295	79	104	110	96	23	108	1	0	4	8	6	.57	14	.286	.394	.556
1993 SD-Atl	NL	151	557	162	29	2	37	(15	22)	306	111	101	110	76	6	106	2	0	5	5	3	.63	14	.291	.375	.549
1994 Atlanta	NL	113	424	135	25	1	34	(13	21)	264	81	94	96	50	8	76	1	0	3	7	3	.70	8	.318	.389	.623
1995 Atlanta	NL	144	528	148	27	1	27	(15	12)	258	85	93	87	65	6	99	5	0	6	3	6	.33	19	.280	.361	.489
1996 Atlanta	NL	159	617	182	37	1	28	(17	11)	305	81	107	105	68	12	116	2	0	4	7	3	.70	20	.295	.365	.494
1997 Atlanta	NL	152	564	156	25	1	22	(8	14)	249	77	97	85	68	4	112	4	0	5	5	0	1.00	22	.277	.356	.441
1998 Tampa Bay	AL	151	564	160	33	4	19	(14	5)	250	73	81	93	79	9	118	2	0	4	7	2	.78	14	.284	.371	.443
1999 Tampa Bay	AL	144	529	164	30	1	32	(18	14)	292	75	104	114	86	11	107	1	0	4	1	0	1.00	12	.310	.405	.552
2000 Tampa Bay	AL	158	566	157	18	0	27	(10	17)	256	82	106	95	91	10	120	0	0	4	2	0	1.00	16	.277	.373	.452
2001 TB-ChC		146	513	157	25	2	31	(17	14)	279	67	102	101	66	13	106	3	0	4	1	2	.33	13	.306	.386	.544
2002 Chicago	NL	146	523	143	27	2	30	(11	19)	264	67	103	88	63	6	99	4	0	5	1	2	.33	13	.273	.353	.505
2003 Los Angeles	NL	86	297	74	14	0	13	(7	6)	127	32	40	43	31	4	66	1	0	0	0	0	-	7	.249	.322	.428
1993 San Diego	NL	83	302	83	11	1	18	(7	11)	150	52	46	52	42	4	55	1	0	4	4	3	.57	9	.275	.361	.497
1993 Atlanta	NL	68	255	79	18	1	19	(8	11)	156	59	55	58	34	2	51	1	0	1	1	0	1.00	5	.310	.392	.612
2001 Tampa Bay	AL	97	343	109	18	0	19	(10	9)	184	40	61	67	40	9	69	0	0	2	1	1	.50	7	.318	.387	.536
2001 Chicago	NL	49	170	48	7	2	12	(7	5)	95	27	41	34	26	4	37	3	0	2	0	1	.00	6	.282	.383	.559
18 ML YEARS		2433	8685	2477	438	24	491	(241	250)	4436	1342	1543	1625	1296	169	1863	39	2	71	72	38	.65	225	.285	.378	.511

Mark McLemore

Bats: B **Throws:** R **Pos:** SS-38; 3B-29; LF-16; PH-7; 2B-6; DH-6; PR-6   **Ht:** 5'11" **Wt:** 207 **Born:** 10/4/64 **Age:** 39

							BATTING												BASERUNNING				AVERAGES		
Year Team	Lg	G	AB	H	2B	3B	HR	(Hm	Rd)	TB	R	RBI	RC	TBB	IBB	SO	HBP	SH	SF	SB	CS	SB%	GDP	Avg	OBP	Slg
1986 Anaheim	AL	5	4	0	0	0	0	(0	0)	0	0	0	0	1	0	2	0	1	0	0	1	.00	0	.000	.200	.000
1987 Anaheim	AL	138	433	102	13	3	3	(3	0)	130	61	41	44	48	0	72	0	15	3	25	8	.76	7	.236	.310	.300
1988 Anaheim	AL	77	233	56	11	2	2	(1	1)	77	38	16	24	25	0	28	0	5	2	13	7	.65	6	.240	.312	.330
1989 Anaheim	AL	32	103	25	3	1	0	(0	0)	30	12	14	9	7	0	19	1	3	1	6	1	.86	2	.243	.295	.291
1990 Ana-Cle	AL	28	60	9	2	0	0	(0	0)	11	6	2	1	4	0	15	0	1	0	1	0	1.00	1	.150	.203	.183
1991 Houston	NL	21	61	9	1	0	0	(0	0)	10	6	2	1	6	0	13	0	0	1	1	1	.00	1	.148	.221	.164

Year Team	Lg	G	AB	H	2B	3B	HR	(Hm	Rd)	TB	R	RBI	RC	TBB	IBB	SO	HBP	SH	SF	SB	CS	SB%	GDP	Avg	OBP	Slg
						BATTING																	**BASERUNNING**		**AVERAGES**		
1992 Baltimore	AL	101	228	56	7	2	0	(0	0)	67	40	27	20	21	1	26	0	6	1	11	5	.69	6	.246	.308	.294
1993 Baltimore	AL	148	581	165	27	5	4	(2	2)	214	81	72	72	64	4	92	1	11	6	21	15	.58	21	.284	.353	.368
1994 Baltimore	AL	104	343	88	11	1	3	(2	1)	110	44	29	44	51	3	50	1	4	1	20	5	.80	7	.257	.354	.321
1995 Texas	AL	129	467	122	20	5	5	(3	2)	167	73	41	59	59	6	71	3	10	3	21	11	.66	10	.261	.346	.358
1996 Texas	AL	147	517	150	23	4	5	(3	2)	196	84	46	81	87	5	69	0	2	5	27	10	.73	16	.290	.389	.379
1997 Texas	AL	89	349	91	17	2	1	(0	1)	115	47	25	41	40	1	54	2	6	2	7	5	.58	5	.261	.338	.330
1998 Texas	AL	126	461	114	15	1	5	(4	1)	146	79	53	60	89	1	64	2	12	3	12	4	.75	15	.247	.369	.317
1999 Texas	AL	144	566	155	20	7	6	(2	4)	207	105	45	81	83	2	79	0	9	6	16	8	.67	8	.274	.363	.366
2000 Seattle	AL	138	481	118	23	1	3	(2	1)	152	72	46	59	81	2	78	1	11	4	30	14	.68	12	.245	.353	.316
2001 Seattle	AL	125	409	117	16	9	5	(2	3)	166	78	57	73	69	0	84	0	3	6	39	7	.85	6	.286	.384	.406
2002 Seattle	AL	104	337	91	17	2	7	(4	3)	133	54	41	60	61	1	63	1	4	4	18	10	.64	3	.270	.380	.395
2003 Seattle	AL	99	309	72	15	2	2	(1	1)	97	34	37	35	38	0	71	2	0	3	5	5	.50	4	.233	.318	.314
1990 Anaheim	AL	20	48	7	2	0	0	(0	0)	9	4	2	1	4	0	9	0	1	0	1	0	1.00	1	.146	.212	.188
1990 Cleveland	AL	8	12	2	0	0	0	(0	0)	2	2	0	0	0	0	6	0	0	0	0	0	-	0	.167	.167	.167
18 ML YEARS		1755	5942	1540	241	47	51	(29	22)	2028	914	594	764	834	26	950	14	103	51	272	117	.70	130	.259	.349	.341

Billy McMillon

Bats: L **Throws:** L **Pos:** LF-35; PH-29; DH-8; 1B-3; RF-1   **Ht:** 5'11" **Wt:** 195 **Born:** 11/17/71 **Age:** 32

Year Team	Lg	G	AB	H	2B	3B	HR	(Hm	Rd)	TB	R	RBI	RC	TBB	IBB	SO	HBP	SH	SF	SB	CS	SB%	GDP	Avg	OBP	Slg
						BATTING																	**BASERUNNING**		**AVERAGES**		
2003 Sacramento*	AAA	38	153	51	10	0	8	(-	-)	85	31	35	32	17	0	30	1	0	1	1	1	.50	3	.333	.401	.556
1996 Florida	NL	28	51	11	0	0	0	(0	0)	11	4	4	3	5	1	14	0	0	0	0	0	-	1	.216	.286	.216
1997 Phi-Fla	NL	37	90	23	5	1	2	(0	2)	36	10	14	11	6	0	24	0	0	3	2	1	.67	1	.256	.293	.400
2000 Detroit	AL	46	123	37	7	1	4	(1	3)	58	20	24	24	19	0	19	1	2	4	1	0	1.00	2	.301	.388	.472
2001 Det-Oak	AL	40	92	20	8	1	1	(1	0)	33	7	14	10	7	0	25	2	0	1	1	0	1.00	1	.217	.284	.359
2003 Oakland	AL	66	153	41	11	0	6	(2	4)	70	15	26	26	19	1	36	2	0	1	0	0	-	3	.268	.354	.458
1997 Philadelphia	NL	24	72	21	4	1	2	(0	2)	33	10	13	11	6	0	17	0	0	3	2	1	.67	1	.292	.333	.458
1997 Florida	NL	13	18	2	1	0	0	(0	0)	3	0	1	0	0	0	7	0	0	0	0	0	-	0	.111	.111	.167
2001 Detroit	AL	20	34	3	1	0	1	(1	0)	7	1	4	0	2	0	12	1	0	0	0	0	-	1	.088	.162	.206
2001 Oakland	AL	20	58	17	7	1	0	(0	0)	26	6	10	10	5	0	13	1	0	1	1	0	1.00	0	.293	.354	.448
5 ML YEARS		217	509	132	31	3	13	(4	9)	208	56	82	74	56	2	118	5	2	9	4	1	.80	8	.259	.333	.409

Brian Meadows

Pitches: R **Bats:** R **Pos:** RP-27; SP-7   **Ht:** 6'4" **Wt:** 220 **Born:** 11/21/75 **Age:** 28

Year Team	Lg	G	GS	CG	GF	IP	BFP	H	R	ER	HR	SH	SF	HB	TBB	IBB	SO	WP	Bk	W	L	Pct	ShO	Sv-Op	Hld	ERC	ERA
			HOW MUCH HE PITCHED								**WHAT HE GAVE UP**											**THE RESULTS**					
2003 Nashville*	AAA	9	8	1	0	51.0	185	32	11	8	2	2	1	2	0	0	40	0	0	7	0	1.000	1	0- -	-	1.02	1.41
1998 Florida	NL	31	31	1	0	174.1	772	222	106	101	20	14	4	3	46	3	88	5	1	11	13	.458	0	0-0	0	5.29	5.21
1999 Florida	NL	31	31	0	0	178.1	795	214	117	111	31	16	8	5	57	5	72	4	1	11	15	.423	0	0-0	0	5.51	5.60
2000 SD-KC		33	32	2	0	196.1	869	234	119	112	32	7	5	8	64	6	79	3	0	13	10	.565	0	0-0	0	5.52	5.13
2001 Kansas City	AL	10	10	0	0	50.1	224	73	41	39	12	1	2	1	12	2	21	1	0	1	6	.143	0	0-0	0	7.47	6.97
2002 Pittsburgh	NL	11	11	0	0	62.2	259	62	29	27	7	2	0	1	14	8	31	2	0	1	6	.143	0	0-0	0	3.29	3.88
2003 Pittsburgh	NL	34	7	0	11	76.1	329	91	45	40	8	2	1	1	11	2	38	4	0	2	1	.667	0	1-1	5	4.12	4.72
2000 San Diego	NL	22	22	0	0	124.2	565	150	80	74	24	7	2	8	50	6	53	3	0	7	8	.467	0	0-0	0	6.23	5.34
2000 Kansas City	AL	11	10	2	0	71.2	304	84	39	38	8	0	3	0	14	0	26	0	0	6	2	.750	0	0-0	0	4.35	4.77
6 ML YEARS		150	122	3	11	738.1	3248	896	457	430	110	42	20	19	204	26	329	19	2	39	51	.433	0	1-1	5	5.23	5.24

Chris Mears

Pitches: R **Bats:** R **Pos:** RP-26; SP-3   **Ht:** 6'4" **Wt:** 190 **Born:** 1/20/78 **Age:** 26

Year Team	Lg	G	GS	CG	GF	IP	BFP	H	R	ER	HR	SH	SF	HB	TBB	IBB	SO	WP	Bk	W	L	Pct	ShO	Sv-Op	Hld	ERC	ERA
			HOW MUCH HE PITCHED								**WHAT HE GAVE UP**											**THE RESULTS**					
1996 Mariners	R	6	5	0	0	25.0	103	23	11	10	0	1	0	1	5	0	27	1	0	1	2	.333	0	0- -	-	2.38	3.60
1997 Everett	A-	12	12	0	0	62.1	283	82	47	37	5	3	1	1	20	0	47	3	1	3	5	.375	0	0- -	-	5.51	5.34
1998 Everett	A-	15	15	1	0	98.2	411	86	39	30	6	2	4	5	33	0	67	2	5	9	1	.900	0	0- -	-	3.07	2.74
1998 Orlando	AA	1	1	0	0	4.2	24	8	5	5	0	0	0	0	2	0	4	0	0	1	0	1.000	0	0- -	-	7.52	9.64
1999 Wisconsin	A	13	13	2	0	89.0	359	76	33	24	1	2	3	5	16	0	78	1	0	10	1	.909	1	0- -	-	2.15	2.43
1999 Lancaster	A+	10	10	0	0	54.2	250	71	44	43	12	1	1	3	18	0	45	3	2	3	6	.333	0	0- -	-	6.73	7.08
2000 Lancaster	A+	28	28	0	0	151.1	670	178	92	80	13	4	8	10	54	0	89	6	1	11	8	.579	0	0- -	-	5.16	4.76
2001 Sn Brnardino	A+	38	12	0	4	107.0	470	104	59	53	10	7	3	11	49	1	74	6	1	7	6	.538	0	0- -	-	4.54	4.46
2002 Sn Antonio	AA	30	20	1	4	143.1	597	138	57	50	16	1	2	9	38	2	103	2	1	6	9	.400	0	0- -	-	3.69	3.14
2003 Toledo	AAA	25	5	0	7	58.1	240	53	20	18	5	0	2	3	19	2	28	0	0	5	1	.833	0	2- -	-	3.42	2.78
2003 Detroit	AL	29	3	0	16	41.1	178	50	28	25	5	0	1	3	11	0	21	2	0	1	3	.250	0	5-5	1	5.38	5.44

Gil Meche

Pitches: R **Bats:** R **Pos:** SP-32   **Ht:** 6'3" **Wt:** 200 **Born:** 9/8/78 **Age:** 25

Year Team	Lg	G	GS	CG	GF	IP	BFP	H	R	ER	HR	SH	SF	HB	TBB	IBB	SO	WP	Bk	W	L	Pct	ShO	Sv-Op	Hld	ERC	ERA
			HOW MUCH HE PITCHED								**WHAT HE GAVE UP**											**THE RESULTS**					
1999 Seattle	AL	16	15	0	0	85.2	375	73	48	45	9	5	3	2	57	1	47	1	0	8	4	.667	0	0-0	0	4.47	4.73
2000 Seattle	AL	15	15	1	0	85.2	363	75	37	36	7	5	4	1	40	0	60	2	0	4	4	.500	1	0-0	0	3.60	3.78
2003 Seattle	AL	32	32	1	0	186.1	785	187	97	95	30	3	5	3	63	2	130	7	0	15	13	.536	0	0-0	0	4.39	4.59
3 ML YEARS		63	62	2	0	357.2	1523	335	182	176	46	13	12	6	160	3	237	10	0	27	21	.563	1	0-0	0	4.22	4.43

Jim Mecir

Pitches: R Bats: B Pos: RP-41   Ht: 6'1" Wt: 230 Born: 5/16/70 Age: 34

		HOW MUCH HE PITCHED							WHAT HE GAVE UP											THE RESULTS							
Year Team	Lg	G	GS	CG	GF	IP	BFP	H	R	ER	HR	SH	SF	HB	TBB	IBB	SO	WP	Bk	W	L	Pct	ShO	Sv-Op	Hld	ERC	ERA
2003 Sacramento*	AAA	3	2	0	0	3.1	18	5	4	2	0	0	0	0	2	0	3	0	0	0	0	-	0	0--	0	6.48	5.40
1995 Seattle	AL	2	0	0	1	4.2	21	5	1	0	0	0	0	0	2	0	3	0	0	0	0	-	0	0-0	0	3.75	0.00
1996 New York	AL	26	0	0	10	40.1	185	42	24	23	6	5	4	0	23	4	38	6	0	1	1	.500	0	0-0	0	5.10	5.13
1997 New York	AL	25	0	0	11	33.2	142	36	23	22	5	0	1	2	10	1	25	1	0	0	4	.000	0	0-1	1	4.73	5.88
1998 Tampa Bay	AL	68	0	0	23	84.0	343	68	30	29	6	3	2	3	33	5	77	2	0	7	2	.778	0	0-3	14	2.95	3.11
1999 Tampa Bay	AL	17	0	0	3	20.2	91	15	7	6	0	0	2	1	14	0	15	0	0	1	0	.000	0	0-2	6	3.05	2.61
2000 TB-Oak	AL	63	0	0	17	85.0	352	70	31	28	4	1	2	2	36	2	70	2	0	10	3	.769	0	5-13	21	2.95	2.96
2001 Oakland	AL	54	0	0	14	63.0	264	54	25	24	4	3	0	1	26	7	61	2	0	2	8	.200	0	3-8	17	3.00	3.43
2002 Oakland	AL	61	0	0	10	67.2	304	68	36	32	5	4	4	4	29	4	53	4	1	6	4	.600	0	1-6	20	4.05	4.26
2003 Oakland	AL	41	0	0	7	37.0	165	40	25	23	4	3	2	1	16	1	25	1	0	2	3	.400	0	1-2	12	4.77	5.59
2000 Tampa Bay	AL	38	0	0	10	49.2	199	35	17	17	2	1	1	1	22	0	33	0	0	7	2	.778	0	1-4	11	2.44	3.08
2000 Oakland	AL	25	0	0	7	35.1	153	35	14	11	2	0	1	1	14	2	37	2	0	3	1	.750	0	4-9	10	3.71	2.80
9 ML YEARS		357	0	0	96	436.0	1867	398	202	187	34	19	17	14	189	24	367	18	1	28	26	.519	0	10-35	91	3.61	3.86

Adam Melhuse

Bats: B Throws: R Pos: C-33; PH-6; 3B-2; PR-2; 1B-1   Ht: 6'2" Wt: 200 Born: 3/27/72 Age: 32

								BATTING												BASERUNNING				AVERAGES		
Year Team	Lg	G	AB	H	2B	3B	HR	(Hm	Rd)	TB	R	RBI	RC	TBB	IBB	SO	HBP	SH	SF	SB	CS	SB%	GDP	Avg	OBP	Slg
2003 Sacramento*	AAA	45	147	42	9	0	3	(-	-)	60	26	17	24	26	0	32	1	0	1	0	1	.00	5	.286	.394	.408
2000 LA-Col	NL	24	24	4	0	1	0	(0	0)	6	3	4	2	3	0	6	0	0	0	0	0	-	1	.167	.259	.250
2001 Colorado	NL	40	71	13	2	0	1	(0	1)	18	5	8	4	6	0	18	0	0	2	1	0	1.00	3	.183	.241	.254
2003 Oakland	AL	40	77	23	7	0	5	(2	3)	45	13	14	16	9	0	19	0	1	0	0	0	-	2	.299	.372	.584
2000 Los Angeles	NL	1	1	0	0	0	0	(0	0)	0	0	0	0	0	0	1	0	0	0	0	0	-	0	.000	.000	.000
2000 Colorado	NL	23	23	4	0	1	0	(0	0)	6	3	4	2	3	0	5	0	0	0	0	0	-	1	.174	.269	.261
3 ML YEARS		104	172	40	9	1	6	(2	4)	69	21	26	22	18	0	43	0	1	2	1	0	1.00	6	.233	.302	.401

Mitch Meluskey

Bats: B Throws: R Pos: PH-12   Ht: 6'0" Wt: 185 Born: 9/18/73 Age: 30

								BATTING												BASERUNNING				AVERAGES		
Year Team	Lg	G	AB	H	2B	3B	HR	(Hm	Rd)	TB	R	RBI	RC	TBB	IBB	SO	HBP	SH	SF	SB	CS	SB%	GDP	Avg	OBP	Slg
2003 Sacramento*	AAA	4	14	2	2	0	0	(-	-)	4	0	4	1	1	0	3	0	0	1	0	0	-	0	.143	.188	.286
2003 Round Rock*	AA	13	49	13	2	0	1	(-	-)	18	5	6	6	5	0	9	0	0	1	1	0	1.00	1	.265	.327	.367
1998 Houston	NL	8	8	2	1	0	0	(0	0)	3	1	0	1	1	0	4	0	0	0	0	0	-	0	.250	.333	.375
1999 Houston	NL	10	33	7	1	0	1	(0	1)	11	4	3	4	5	1	6	0	0	0	1	0	1.00	1	.212	.316	.333
2000 Houston	NL	117	337	101	21	0	14	(11	3)	164	47	69	65	55	10	74	4	1	3	1	0	1.00	7	.300	.401	.487
2002 Detroit	AL	8	27	6	0	0	0	(0	0)	6	3	1	3	5	0	3	1	0	1	0	0	-	0	.222	.353	.222
2003 Houston	NL	12	9	1	1	0	0	(0	0)	2	1	2	1	2	0	2	0	0	1	0	0	-	0	.111	.250	.222
5 ML YEARS		155	414	117	24	0	15	(11	4)	186	56	75	74	68	11	89	5	1	5	2	0	1.00	9	.283	.386	.449

Kevin Mench

Bats: R Throws: R Pos: LF-34; CF-3; PH-3; RF-2   Ht: 6'0" Wt: 215 Born: 1/7/78 Age: 26

								BATTING												BASERUNNING				AVERAGES		
Year Team	Lg	G	AB	H	2B	3B	HR	(Hm	Rd)	TB	R	RBI	RC	TBB	IBB	SO	HBP	SH	SF	SB	CS	SB%	GDP	Avg	OBP	Slg
1999 Pulaski	R+	65	260	94	22	1	16	(-	-)	166	63	60	67	28	0	48	2	0	5	12	2	.86	2	.362	.420	.638
1999 Savannah	A	6	23	7	1	1	2	(-	-)	16	4	8	6	2	0	4	2	0	0	0	0	-	1	.304	.407	.696
2000 Charlotte	A+	132	491	164	39	4	27	(-	-)	302	118	121	124	78	3	72	7	0	7	19	7	.73	9	.334	.427	.615
2001 Tulsa	AA	120	475	126	34	2	26	(-	-)	242	78	83	75	34	0	76	6	0	6	4	6	.40	7	.265	.319	.509
2002 Oklahoma	AAA	26	98	21	8	0	6	(-	-)	47	17	15	14	17	0	33	2	0	0	0	0	-	7	.214	.342	.480
2003 Frisco	AA	3	11	1	0	0	0	(-	-)	1	1	0	0	1	0	2	0	0	0	0	0	-	1	.091	.167	.091
2003 Oklahoma	AAA	29	105	28	8	0	4	(-	-)	48	16	21	20	19	0	15	1	0	6	2	0	1.00	1	.267	.366	.457
2002 Texas	AL	110	366	95	20	2	15	(8	7)	164	52	60	59	31	0	83	8	2	5	1	1	.50	4	.260	.327	.448
2003 Texas	AL	38	125	40	12	0	2	(1	1)	58	15	11	23	10	0	17	3	0	1	1	1	.50	2	.320	.381	.464
2 ML YEARS		148	491	135	32	2	17	(9	8)	222	67	71	82	41	0	100	11	2	6	2	2	.50	6	.275	.341	.452

Carlos Mendez

Bats: R Throws: R Pos: PH-11; 1B-9; DH-7   Ht: 6'0" Wt: 228 Born: 6/18/74 Age: 30

								BATTING												BASERUNNING				AVERAGES		
Year Team	Lg	G	AB	H	2B	3B	HR	(Hm	Rd)	TB	R	RBI	RC	TBB	IBB	SO	HBP	SH	SF	SB	CS	SB%	GDP	Avg	OBP	Slg
1992 Royals	R	49	200	61	16	1	3	(-	-)	88	34	33	29	8	2	13	2	0	3	2	1	.67	2	.305	.333	.440
1993 Royals	R	50	163	51	10	0	4	(-	-)	73	18	27	25	4	1	15	2	0	4	6	1	.86	2	.313	.329	.448
1994 Rockford	A	104	363	129	26	2	5	(-	-)	174	45	51	61	13	2	50	5	4	4	2	0	.00	11	.355	.382	.479
1995 Wilmington	A+	107	396	108	19	2	7	(-	-)	152	46	61	40	18	1	36	0	1	5	0	4	.00	17	.273	.301	.384
1996 Wilmington	A+	109	406	119	25	3	4	(-	-)	162	40	59	54	22	4	39	3	3	7	3	1	.75	6	.293	.329	.399
1997 Wichita	AA	129	507	165	32	1	12	(-	-)	235	72	90	73	19	2	43	1	0	8	4	7	.36	19	.325	.346	.464
1998 Omaha	AAA	50	173	47	13	0	2	(-	-)	66	23	18	21	10	0	24	1	0	2	3	0	1.00	4	.272	.312	.382
1998 Wichita	AA	52	207	66	14	0	9	(-	-)	107	37	39	32	7	1	20	0	1	5	4	1	.80	10	.319	.333	.517
1999 Omaha	AAA	84	293	82	25	0	10	(-	-)	137	38	37	37	6	0	32	0	3	3	4	3	.57	8	.280	.291	.468
2000 Toledo	AAA	100	374	108	21	0	19	(-	-)	186	49	72	55	12	0	37	3	0	7	0	0	-	11	.289	.311	.497
2001 Toledo	AAA	102	398	98	27	1	18	(-	-)	181	45	76	46	9	5	53	5	3	6	0	0	-	13	.246	.268	.455
2002 Sacramento	AAA	103	404	131	26	4	12	(-	-)	195	58	74	63	12	1	52	3	0	1	3	1	.75	11	.324	.348	.483
2003 Ottawa	AAA	61	248	86	18	4	4	(-	-)	124	32	42	42	11	5	28	1	0	1	1	2	.33	7	.347	.375	.500
2003 Baltimore	AL	26	45	10	2	0	0	(0	0)	12	3	5	2	0	0	12	0	0	1	0	0	-	0	.222	.217	.267

Donaldo Mendez

Bats: R **Throws:** R **Pos:** SS-26   **Ht:** 6'1" **Wt:** 155 **Born:** 6/7/78 **Age:** 26

Year Team	Lg	G	AB	H	2B	3B	HR	(Hm	Rd)	TB	R	RBI	RC	TBB	IBB	SO	HBP	SH	SF	SB	CS	SB%	GDP	Avg	OBP	Slg
1997 Kissimmee	A+	5	16	3	0	0	0	(-	-)	3	0	0	0	1	0	4	0	0	0	1	1	.50	0	.188	.235	.188
1997 Astros	R	48	150	29	4	0	1	(-	-)	36	16	13	9	13	0	32	2	3	3	9	6	.60	2	.193	.262	.240
1999 Auburn	A-	25	86	18	1	1	0	(-	-)	21	9	10	4	2	2	23	4	0	2	10	5	.67	3	.209	.255	.244
2000 Michigan	A	101	370	100	17	0	2	(-	-)	123	65	51	44	14	1	68	14	6	2	39	10	.80	3	.270	.320	.332
2002 Mobile	AA	56	224	49	16	0	4	(-	-)	77	36	18	24	19	1	53	6	1	0	15	5	.75	2	.219	.297	.344
2002 Portland	AAA	64	217	47	9	1	6	(-	-)	76	32	18	23	14	0	63	6	1	1	11	4	.73	0	.217	.282	.350
2003 Portland	AAA	102	358	81	17	0	6	(-	-)	116	49	36	32	25	1	83	7	1	3	10	7	.59	7	.226	.288	.324
2001 San Diego	NL	46	118	18	2	1	1	(0	1)	25	11	5	5	5	2	37	3	1	0	1	2	.33	2	.153	.206	.212
2003 San Diego	NL	26	84	19	6	0	2	(0	2)	31	10	9	9	7	1	32	2	0	1	1	0	1.00	0	.226	.298	.369
2 ML YEARS		72	202	37	8	1	3	(0	3)	56	21	14	14	12	3	69	5	1	1	2	2	.50	2	.183	.245	.277

Ramiro Mendoza

Pitches: R **Bats:** R **Pos:** RP-32; SP-5   **Ht:** 6'2" **Wt:** 195 **Born:** 6/15/72 **Age:** 32

Year Team	Lg	G	GS	CG	GF	IP	BFP	H	R	ER	HR	SH	SF	HB	TBB	IBB	SO	WP	Bk	W	L	Pct	ShO	Sv-Op	Hld	ERC	ERA
2003 Red Sox*	R	2	2	0	0	7.0	24	3	0	0	0	0	0	1	0	0	4	0	0	0	0	-	0	0- -	-	0.63	0.00
2003 Pawtucket*	AAA	4	0	0	1	9.0	33	8	2	2	1	0	0	0	1	0	8	0	0	0	0	-	0	1- -	-	2.20	2.00
2003 Sarasota*	A+	1	1	0	0	5.0	17	2	0	0	0	1	0	0	1	0	4	0	0	1	0	1.000	0	0- -	-	0.67	0.00
1996 New York	AL	12	11	0	0	53.0	249	80	43	40	5	1	1	4	10	1	34	2	1	4	5	.444	0	0-0	0	6.42	6.79
1997 New York	AL	39	15	0	9	133.2	578	157	67	63	15	3	5	5	28	2	82	2	1	8	6	.571	0	2-4	4	4.52	4.24
1998 New York	AL	41	14	1	6	130.1	548	131	50	47	9	6	7	9	30	6	56	3	0	10	2	.833	1	1-4	5	3.44	3.25
1999 New York	AL	53	6	0	15	123.2	536	141	68	59	13	6	4	3	27	3	80	2	0	9	9	.500	0	3-6	4	4.19	4.29
2000 New York	AL	14	9	1	0	65.2	281	66	32	31	9	1	2	4	20	1	30	0	0	7	4	.636	1	0-1	0	4.21	4.25
2001 New York	AL	56	2	0	11	100.2	401	89	44	42	9	4	3	2	23	3	70	2	0	8	4	.667	0	6-8	13	2.84	3.75
2002 New York	AL	62	0	0	14	91.2	394	102	43	35	8	1	4	2	16	2	61	1	0	8	4	.667	0	4-8	12	3.70	3.44
2003 Boston	AL	37	5	0	8	66.2	311	98	51	50	10	1	4	5	20	4	36	1	0	3	5	.375	0	0-1	3	7.22	6.75
8 ML YEARS		314	62	2	63	765.1	3298	864	398	367	78	23	30	34	174	22	449	13	2	57	39	.594	2	16-32	41	4.26	4.32

Frank Menechino

Bats: R **Throws:** R **Pos:** 2B-22; 3B-19; PH-12; SS-3   **Ht:** 5'8" **Wt:** 198 **Born:** 1/7/71 **Age:** 33

Year Team	Lg	G	AB	H	2B	3B	HR	(Hm	Rd)	TB	R	RBI	RC	TBB	IBB	SO	HBP	SH	SF	SB	CS	SB%	GDP	Avg	OBP	Slg
1999 Oakland	AL	9	9	2	0	0	0	(0	0)	2	0	0	0	0	0	4	0	0	0	0	0	-	0	.222	.222	.222
2000 Oakland	AL	66	145	37	9	1	6	(3	3)	66	31	26	22	20	0	45	1	1	2	1	4	.20	1	.255	.345	.455
2001 Oakland	AL	139	471	114	22	2	12	(4	8)	176	82	60	69	79	0	97	19	3	6	2	3	.40	13	.242	.369	.374
2002 Oakland	AL	38	132	27	7	0	3	(2	1)	43	22	15	14	20	0	32	1	0	1	0	0	-	4	.205	.312	.326
2003 Oakland	AL	43	83	16	0	0	2	(1	1)	22	10	9	10	19	1	16	4	2	1	0	0	-	2	.193	.364	.265
5 ML YEARS		295	840	196	38	3	23	(10	13)	309	145	110	115	138	1	194	25	6	10	3	7	.30	20	.233	.354	.368

Hector Mercado

Pitches: L **Bats:** L **Pos:** RP-13   **Ht:** 6'3" **Wt:** 235 **Born:** 4/29/74 **Age:** 30

Year Team	Lg	G	GS	CG	GF	IP	BFP	H	R	ER	HR	SH	SF	HB	TBB	IBB	SO	WP	Bk	W	L	Pct	ShO	Sv-Op	Hld	ERC	ERA
2003 Reading*	AA	1	1	0	0	2.0	6	0	0	0	0	0	0	0	1	0	0	0	0	0	0	-	0	0- -	-	0.32	0.00
2003 Scrtn/WlksBr*	AAA	14	2	0	2	32.0	136	34	12	5	2	3	2	0	11	0	20	0	0	0	3	.000	0	0- -	-	4.00	1.41
2000 Cincinnati	NL	12	0	0	4	14.0	60	12	7	7	2	1	1	0	8	0	13	2	0	0	0	-	0	0-0	1	4.32	4.50
2001 Cincinnati	NL	56	0	0	10	53.0	240	55	27	24	6	1	2	0	30	1	59	4	0	3	2	.600	0	0-2	5	4.99	4.08
2002 Philadelphia	NL	31	3	0	7	39.0	173	32	21	20	2	1	1	3	25	2	40	3	1	2	2	.500	0	0-0	3	3.86	4.62
2003 Philadelphia	NL	13	0	0	4	18.2	87	18	12	12	5	0	2	1	12	0	15	1	0	0	0	-	0	1-2	0	6.24	5.79
4 ML YEARS		112	3	0	25	124.2	560	117	67	63	15	3	6	4	75	3	127	10	1	5	4	.556	0	1-4	9	4.74	4.55

Orlando Merced

Bats: L **Throws:** R **Pos:** PH-78; RF-21; 1B-12; LF-10; DH-7; 3B-2   **Ht:** 6'1" **Wt:** 195 **Born:** 11/2/66 **Age:** 37

Year Team	Lg	G	AB	H	2B	3B	HR	(Hm	Rd)	TB	R	RBI	RC	TBB	IBB	SO	HBP	SH	SF	SB	CS	SB%	GDP	Avg	OBP	Slg
1990 Pittsburgh	NL	25	24	5	1	0	0	(0	0)	6	3	0	1	1	0	9	0	0	0	0	0	-	1	.208	.240	.250
1991 Pittsburgh	NL	120	411	113	17	2	10	(5	5)	164	83	50	64	64	4	81	1	1	1	8	4	.67	6	.275	.373	.399
1992 Pittsburgh	NL	134	405	100	28	5	6	(4	2)	156	50	60	53	52	8	63	2	1	5	5	4	.56	6	.247	.332	.385
1993 Pittsburgh	NL	137	447	140	26	4	8	(3	5)	198	68	70	83	77	10	64	1	0	2	3	3	.50	9	.313	.414	.443
1994 Pittsburgh	NL	108	386	105	21	3	9	(4	5)	159	48	51	51	42	5	58	1	0	2	4	1	.80	17	.272	.343	.412
1995 Pittsburgh	NL	132	487	146	29	4	15	(8	7)	228	75	83	82	52	9	74	1	0	5	7	2	.78	9	.300	.365	.468
1996 Pittsburgh	NL	120	453	130	24	1	17	(9	8)	207	69	80	73	51	5	74	0	0	3	8	4	.67	9	.287	.357	.457
1997 Toronto	AL	98	368	98	23	2	9	(3	6)	152	45	40	55	47	1	62	3	0	2	7	3	.70	6	.266	.352	.413
1998 Min-Bos-ChC		84	223	62	12	0	6	(3	3)	92	24	40	29	20	3	34	1	0	3	1	4	.20	6	.278	.336	.413
1999 Montreal	NL	93	194	52	12	1	8	(3	5)	90	25	26	31	26	0	27	0	0	1	2	1	.67	5	.268	.353	.464
2001 Houston	NL	94	137	36	6	1	6	(3	3)	62	19	29	21	14	1	32	1	0	1	5	1	.83	3	.263	.333	.453
2002 Houston	NL	123	251	72	13	3	6	(4	2)	109	35	30	36	26	5	50	0	1	3	4	0	1.00	9	.287	.350	.434
2003 Houston	NL	123	212	49	17	2	3	(1	2)	79	20	26	21	15	2	33	1	0	2	3	2	.60	3	.231	.283	.373
1998 Minnesota	AL	63	204	59	12	0	5	(3	2)	86	22	33	28	17	3	29	1	0	3	1	4	.20	4	.289	.345	.422
1998 Boston	AL	9	9	0	0	0	0	(0	0)	0	0	2	0	2	0	3	0	0	0	0	0	-	0	.000	.167	.000
1998 Chicago	NL	12	10	3	0	0	1	(0	0)	6	2	5	1	1	0	2	0	0	0	0	0	-	2	.300	.333	.600
13 ML YEARS		1391	3998	1108	229	28	103	(51	52)	1702	564	585	600	487	53	661	12	3	30	57	29	.66	89	.277	.355	.426

Jose Mercedes

Pitches: R **Bats:** R **Pos:** RP-5   **Ht:** 6'1" **Wt:** 180 **Born:** 3/5/71 **Age:** 33

| | | | HOW MUCH HE PITCHED | | | | | | WHAT HE GAVE UP | | | | | | | | | | | | THE RESULTS | | | | | | |
Year Team	Lg	G	GS	CG	GF	IP	BFP	H	R	ER	HR	SH	SF	HB	TBB	IBB	SO	WP	Bk	W	L	Pct	ShO	Sv-Op	Hld	ERC	ERA
1994 Milwaukee	NL	19	0	0	0	31.0	120	22	0	8	4	0	0	0	16	0	11	0	0	2	0	1.000	0	0-0	0	3.42	2.32
1995 Milwaukee	NL	5	0	0	0	7.1	42	12	0	8	1	0	0	0	8	0	6	0	0	0	1	.000	0	0-0	0	11.32	9.82
1996 Milwaukee	NL	11	0	0	0	16.2	74	20	0	17	6	0	0	0	5	0	6	0	0	0	2	.000	0	0-0	0	6.70	9.18
1997 Milwaukee	NL	29	23	2	0	159.0	653	146	0	67	24	0	0	0	53	0	80	0	0	7	10	.412	1	0-0	0	3.78	3.79
1998 Milwaukee	NL	7	5	0	0	32.0	146	42	0	24	5	0	0	0	9	0	11	0	0	2	2	.500	0	0-0	0	5.74	6.75
2000 Baltimore	AL	36	20	1	0	145.2	636	150	0	65	15	0	0	0	64	0	70	0	0	14	7	.667	0	0-0	0	4.43	4.02
2001 Baltimore	AL	33	31	2	0	184.0	828	219	0	119	20	0	0	0	63	0	123	0	0	8	17	.320	0	0-0	0	4.92	5.82
2003 Montreal	NL	5	0	0	0	7.1	31	6	3	0	0	0	0	0	5	0	3	1	0	0	0	-	0	0-0	0	3.58	0.00
8 ML YEARS		145	79	5	0	583.0	2530	617	3	308	75	0	0	0	223	0	310	1	0	33	39	.458	1	0-0	0	4.55	4.75

Kent Mercker

Pitches: L **Bats:** L **Pos:** RP-67   **Ht:** 6'2" **Wt:** 195 **Born:** 2/1/68 **Age:** 36

| | | | HOW MUCH HE PITCHED | | | | | | WHAT HE GAVE UP | | | | | | | | | | | | THE RESULTS | | | | | | |
Year Team	Lg	G	GS	CG	GF	IP	BFP	H	R	ER	HR	SH	SF	HB	TBB	IBB	SO	WP	Bk	W	L	Pct	ShO	Sv-Op	Hld	ERC	ERA
1989 Atlanta	NL	2	1	0	1	4.1	26	8	6	6	0	0	0	0	6	0	4	0	0	0	0	-	0	0-0	0	13.19	12.46
1990 Atlanta	NL	36	0	0	28	48.1	211	43	22	17	6	1	2	2	24	3	39	2	0	4	7	.364	0	7-10	0	4.04	3.17
1991 Atlanta	NL	50	4	0	28	73.1	306	56	23	21	5	2	2	1	35	3	62	4	1	5	3	.625	0	6-8	3	2.88	2.58
1992 Atlanta	NL	53	0	0	18	68.1	289	51	27	26	4	4	1	1	35	1	49	6	0	3	2	.600	0	6-9	6	2.99	3.42
1993 Atlanta	NL	43	6	0	9	66.0	283	52	24	21	2	0	0	2	36	3	59	5	1	3	1	.750	0	0-3	4	3.02	2.86
1994 Atlanta	NL	20	17	2	0	112.1	461	90	46	43	16	4	3	0	45	3	111	4	1	9	4	.692	1	0-0	0	3.27	3.45
1995 Atlanta	NL	29	26	0	1	143.0	622	140	73	66	16	8	7	3	61	2	102	6	2	7	8	.467	0	0-0	0	4.19	4.15
1996 Bal-Cle	AL	24	12	0	2	69.2	329	83	60	54	13	3	6	3	38	2	29	3	1	4	6	.400	0	0-2	0	6.56	6.98
1997 Cincinnati	NL	28	25	0	0	144.2	616	135	65	63	16	8	4	2	62	6	75	2	1	8	11	.421	0	0-0	0	3.91	3.92
1998 St Louis	NL	30	29	0	1	161.2	716	199	99	91	11	10	9	3	53	4	72	6	4	11	11	.500	0	0-0	0	4.96	5.07
1999 St Louis	NL	30	23	0	2	129.1	589	148	85	69	16	8	4	3	64	3	81	3	1	8	5	.615	0	0-0	0	5.54	4.80
2000 Anaheim	AL	21	7	0	2	48.1	225	57	35	35	12	3	1	2	29	3	30	2	0	1	3	.250	0	0-0	1	7.35	6.52
2002 Colorado	NL	58	0	0	8	44.0	208	55	33	30	12	0	0	2	22	2	37	1	0	3	1	.750	0	0-3	9	7.45	6.14
2003 Cin-Atl	NL	67	0	0	15	55.1	242	46	16	12	6	6	1	0	32	4	48	4	1	0	2	.000	0	1-5	11	3.72	1.95
1996 Baltimore	AL	14	12	0	0	58.0	283	73	56	50	12	3	4	3	35	1	22	3	1	3	6	.333	0	0-0	0	7.45	7.76
1996 Cleveland	AL	10	0	0	2	11.2	46	10	4	4	1	0	2	0	3	1	7	0	0	1	0	1.000	0	0-2	2	2.65	3.09
1999 St Louis	NL	25	18	0	2	103.2	476	125	73	59	16	8	3	2	51	3	64	3	1	6	5	.545	0	0-0	0	6.15	5.12
1999 Boston	AL	5	5	0	0	25.2	113	23	12	10	0	0	1	1	13	0	17	0	0	2	0	1.000	0	0-0	0	3.29	3.51
2003 Cincinnati	NL	49	0	0	8	38.1	169	31	13	10	5	6	0	0	25	2	41	2	1	0	2	.000	0	0-3	10	4.09	2.35
2003 Atlanta	NL	18	0	0	7	17.0	73	15	3	2	1	0	1	0	7	2	7	2	0	0	0	-	0	1-2	1	2.95	1.06
14 ML YEARS		491	150	2	115	1168.2	5123	1163	614	554	135	57	40	26	542	39	798	48	13	66	64	.508	1	20-38	36	4.45	4.27

Lou Merloni

Bats: R **Throws:** R **Pos:** 3B-32; SS-23; 2B-17; PH-16; LF-3; 1B-2; PR-2   **Ht:** 5'10" **Wt:** 201 **Born:** 4/6/71 **Age:** 33

| | | | | BATTING | | | | | | | | | | | | | | | | | BASERUNNING | | | | AVERAGES | | |
Year Team	Lg	G	AB	H	2B	3B	HR	(Hm	Rd)	TB	R	RBI	RC	TBB	IBB	SO	HBP	SH	SF	SB	CS	SB%	GDP	Avg	OBP	Slg
2003 Lk Elsinore*	A+	5	19	9	3	0	1	(-	-)	15	3	7	6	1	0	0	0	0	1	0	0	-	0	.474	.476	.789
1998 Boston	AL	39	96	27	6	0	1	(1	0)	36	10	15	13	7	1	20	2	1	0	1	0	1.00	1	.281	.343	.375
1999 Boston	AL	43	126	32	7	0	1	(0	1)	42	18	13	12	8	0	16	2	3	1	0	0	-	6	.254	.307	.333
2000 Boston	AL	40	128	41	11	2	0	(0	0)	56	10	18	17	4	1	22	1	4	2	1	0	1.00	8	.320	.341	.438
2001 Boston	AL	52	146	39	10	0	3	(0	3)	58	21	13	16	6	0	31	3	2	2	2	1	.67	6	.267	.306	.397
2002 Boston	AL	84	194	48	12	2	4	(1	3)	76	28	18	25	20	0	35	5	2	1	1	2	.33	4	.247	.332	.392
2003 SD-Bos	NL	80	181	48	8	2	1	(1	0)	63	24	18	21	26	2	41	1	2	3	2	3	.40	3	.265	.355	.348
2003 San Diego	NL	65	151	41	7	2	1	(0	0)	55	20	17	18	22	2	33	1	2	3	2	3	.40	3	.272	.362	.364
2003 Boston	AL	15	30	7	1	0	0	(0	0)	8	4	1	3	4	0	8	0	0	0	0	0	-	0	.233	.324	.267
6 ML YEARS		338	871	235	54	6	10	(3	7)	331	111	95	104	71	4	165	14	14	9	7	6	.54	28	.270	.332	.380

Jose Mesa

Pitches: R **Bats:** R **Pos:** RP-61   **Ht:** 6'3" **Wt:** 225 **Born:** 5/22/66 **Age:** 38

| | | | HOW MUCH HE PITCHED | | | | | | WHAT HE GAVE UP | | | | | | | | | | | | THE RESULTS | | | | | | |
Year Team	Lg	G	GS	CG	GF	IP	BFP	H	R	ER	HR	SH	SF	HB	TBB	IBB	SO	WP	Bk	W	L	Pct	ShO	Sv-Op	Hld	ERC	ERA
1987 Baltimore	AL	6	5	0	0	31.1	143	38	23	21	7	0	0	0	15	0	17	4	0	1	3	.250	0	0-0	1	6.67	6.03
1990 Baltimore	AL	7	7	0	0	46.2	202	37	20	20	2	2	2	1	27	2	24	1	1	3	2	.600	0	0-0	0	3.21	3.86
1991 Baltimore	AL	23	23	2	0	123.2	566	151	86	82	11	5	4	3	62	2	64	3	0	6	11	.353	1	0-0	0	5.85	5.97
1992 Bal-Cle	AL	28	27	1	1	160.2	700	169	86	82	14	2	5	4	70	1	62	2	0	7	12	.368	1	0-0	0	4.57	4.59
1993 Cleveland	AL	34	33	3	0	208.2	897	232	122	114	21	9	9	7	62	2	118	8	2	10	12	.455	0	0-0	0	4.48	4.92
1994 Cleveland	AL	51	0	0	22	73.0	315	71	33	31	3	3	4	3	26	7	63	3	0	7	5	.583	0	2-6	3	3.31	3.82
1995 Cleveland	AL	62	0	0	57	64.0	250	49	9	8	3	4	2	0	17	2	58	5	3	3	0	1.000	0	46-48	0	2.06	1.13
1996 Cleveland	AL	69	0	0	60	72.1	304	69	32	30	6	2	2	3	28	4	64	4	0	2	7	.222	0	39-44	0	3.81	3.73
1997 Cleveland	AL	66	0	0	38	82.1	356	83	28	22	7	2	2	3	28	3	69	1	0	4	4	.500	0	16-21	3	3.83	2.40
1998 Cle-SF		76	0	0	36	84.2	383	91	50	43	8	6	2	4	38	5	63	10	0	8	7	.533	0	1-4	13	4.68	4.57
1999 Seattle	AL	68	0	0	60	68.2	325	84	42	38	11	2	4	4	40	4	42	7	0	3	6	.333	0	33-38	1	6.83	4.98
2000 Seattle	AL	66	0	0	29	80.2	372	89	48	48	11	2	6	5	41	0	84	3	4	4	6	.400	0	1-3	11	5.60	5.36
2001 Philadelphia	AL	71	0	0	59	69.1	291	65	26	18	4	2	3	2	20	2	59	2	1	3	3	.500	0	42-46	1	3.07	2.34
2002 Philadelphia	NL	74	0	0	64	75.2	331	65	26	25	5	6	1	4	39	7	64	9	0	4	6	.400	0	45-54	0	3.51	2.97
2003 Philadelphia	NL	61	0	0	47	58.0	273	71	44	42	7	1	0	1	31	2	45	3	0	5	7	.417	0	24-28	2	6.07	6.52
1992 Baltimore	AL	13	12	0	0	67.2	300	77	41	39	9	0	3	2	27	1	22	2	0	3	8	.273	0	0-0	0	5.25	5.19
1992 Cleveland	AL	15	15	1	0	93.0	400	92	45	43	5	2	2	2	43	0	40	0	0	4	4	.500	1	0-0	0	4.09	4.16
1998 Cleveland	AL	44	0	0	18	54.0	244	61	36	31	7	2	2	4	20	3	35	2	0	1	3	.429	0	1-3	7	5.07	5.17
1998 San Francisco	NL	32	0	0	18	30.2	139	30	14	12	1	4	0	0	18	2	28	8	0	5	3	.625	0	0-1	6	3.99	3.52
15 ML YEARS		762	95	6	473	1299.2	5708	1364	675	624	120	48	46	44	544	43	896	65	4	70	91	.435	2	249-292	46	4.46	4.32

Chad Meyers

Bats: R Throws: R Pos: PR-6; LF-3; DH-2; PH-1   Ht: 5'11" Wt: 185 Born: 8/8/75 Age: 28

Year Team	Lg	G	AB	H	2B	3B	HR	(Hm	Rd)	TB	R	RBI	RC	TBB	IBB	SO	HBP	SH	SF	SB	CS	SB%	GDP	Avg	OBP	Slg
2003 Tacoma*	AAA	97	377	113	20	3	4	(-	-)	151	50	34	57	30	0	46	7	4	1	37	12	.76	7	.300	.361	.401
1999 Chicago	NL	43	142	33	9	0	0	(0	0)	42	17	4	12	9	1	27	3	2	0	4	2	.67	5	.232	.292	.296
2000 Chicago	NL	36	52	9	2	0	0	(0	0)	11	8	5	3	3	0	11	1	0	1	1	0	1.00	0	.173	.228	.212
2001 Chicago	NL	18	17	2	0	0	0	(0	0)	2	1	0	1	2	0	5	4	0	0	0	1	.00	0	.118	.348	.118
2003 Seattle	AL	9	1	0	0	0	0	(0	0)	0	1	0	0	0	0	0	0	0	0	1	0	1.00	0	.000	.000	.000
4 ML YEARS		106	212	44	11	0	0	(0	0)	55	27	9	16	14	1	43	8	2	1	6	3	.67	5	.208	.281	.259

Bart Miadich

Pitches: R Bats: R Pos: RP-1   Ht: 6'4" Wt: 205 Born: 2/3/76 Age: 28

Year Team	Lg	G	GS	CG	GF	IP	BFP	H	R	ER	HR	SH	SF	HB	TBB	IBB	SO	WP	Bk	W	L	Pct	ShO	Sv-Op	Hld	ERC	ERA
1998 Sarasota	A+	22	0	0	15	48.2	199	40	20	17	1	3	0	1	15	4	64	2	1	3	2	.600	0	7--	-	2.24	3.14
1998 Trenton	AA	22	8	0	4	54.1	253	66	39	36	4	1	2	5	26	1	33	3	0	1	6	.143	0	1--	-	5.81	5.96
1999 El Paso	AA	12	0	0	2	20.0	104	37	22	18	3	1	1	2	7	1	16	0	0	0	2	.000	0	1--	-	10.02	8.10
1999 High Desert	A+	21	16	0	1	98.0	448	125	71	59	9	2	4	12	40	0	85	1	1	3	8	.273	0	0--	-	6.36	5.42
2000 Erie	AA	28	0	0	17	40.1	171	27	16	15	2	1	2	4	21	0	38	4	0	3	1	.750	0	2--	-	2.77	3.35
2000 Edmonton	AAA	10	0	0	3	21.2	101	25	14	11	3	1	0	0	9	0	20	2	0	2	1	.667	0	1--	-	5.07	4.57
2001 Salt Lake	AAA	55	0	0	54	59.0	245	40	20	16	4	3	1	1	29	1	73	5	0	4	4	.500	0	27--	-	2.52	2.44
2002 Salt Lake	AAA	59	0	0	42	80.2	370	60	43	33	5	1	2	3	64	2	92	12	0	4	3	.571	0	14--	-	3.87	3.68
2003 Salt Lake	AAA	46	0	0	38	51.1	235	39	23	21	4	2	1	4	41	0	65	12	1	5	5	.500	0	16--	-	4.36	3.68
2001 Anaheim	AL	11	0	0	0	10.0	41	6	0	5	2	0	0	0	8	0	11	0	0	0	0	-	0	0-0	0	4.38	4.50
2003 Anaheim	AL	1	0	0	0	2.0	12	5	4	4	0	0	0	1	1	0	3	1	0	0	0	-	0	0-0	0	17.04	18.00
2 ML YEARS		12	0	0	0	12.0	53	11	4	9	2	0	0	1	9	0	14	1	0	0	0	-	0	0-0	0	6.21	6.75

Danny Miceli

Pitches: R Bats: R Pos: RP-57   Ht: 6'0" Wt: 216 Born: 9/9/70 Age: 33

Year Team	Lg	G	GS	CG	GF	IP	BFP	H	R	ER	HR	SH	SF	HB	TBB	IBB	SO	WP	Bk	W	L	Pct	ShO	Sv-Op	Hld	ERC	ERA
2003 Buffalo*	AAA	5	0	0	3	6.0	26	7	2	2	1	0	0	0	1	1	6	0	0	0	1	.000	0	0--	-	4.18	3.00
1993 Pittsburgh	NL	9	0	0	1	5.1	25	6	3	3	0	0	0	0	3	0	4	0	1	0	0	-	0	0-0	0	4.53	5.06
1994 Pittsburgh	NL	28	0	0	9	27.1	121	28	19	18	5	1	2	2	11	2	27	2	0	2	1	.667	0	2-3	4	4.98	5.93
1995 Pittsburgh	NL	58	0	0	51	58.0	264	61	30	30	7	2	4	4	28	5	56	4	0	4	4	.500	0	21-27	2	4.93	4.66
1996 Pittsburgh	NL	44	9	0	17	85.2	398	99	65	55	15	3	7	3	45	5	66	9	0	2	10	.167	0	1-1	4	6.09	5.78
1997 Detroit	AL	71	0	0	24	82.2	357	77	49	46	13	5	3	1	38	4	79	3	0	3	2	.600	0	3-8	11	4.30	5.01
1998 San Diego	NL	67	0	0	18	72.2	302	64	28	26	6	3	2	1	27	4	70	5	1	10	5	.667	0	2-8	20	3.20	3.22
1999 San Diego	NL	66	0	0	28	68.2	296	67	39	34	7	4	2	2	36	5	59	2	0	4	5	.444	0	2-4	9	4.57	4.46
2000 Florida	NL	45	0	0	9	48.2	207	45	23	23	4	1	1	1	18	2	40	3	0	6	4	.600	0	0-3	11	3.42	4.25
2001 Fla-Col	NL	51	0	0	15	45.0	199	47	29	24	7	2	2	0	16	2	48	4	0	2	5	.286	0	1-4	8	4.34	4.80
2002 Texas	AL	9	0	0	5	8.1	42	13	8	8	1	0	0	0	3	0	5	0	1	0	2	.000	0	0-1	0	7.11	8.64
2003 Col-Cle-NYY-Hou	NL	57	0	0	16	70.1	293	59	27	25	13	3	0	2	25	3	58	4	1	2	4	.333	0	1-2	5	3.61	3.20
2001 Florida	NL	29	0	0	9	24.2	114	29	21	19	5	1	1	0	11	2	31	3	0	0	5	.000	0	0-3	8	5.80	6.93
2001 Colorado	NL	22	0	0	6	20.1	85	18	8	5	2	1	1	0	5	0	17	1	0	2	0	1.000	0	1-1	0	2.77	2.21
2003 Colorado	NL	14	0	0	1	20.2	95	24	13	13	7	1	0	1	9	1	18	1	0	0	2	.000	0	0-0	1	7.07	5.66
2003 Cleveland	AL	13	0	0	4	15.0	61	9	4	2	1	0	0	0	6	1	19	1	0	1	1	.500	0	0-1	0	1.70	1.20
2003 New York	AL	7	0	0	3	4.2	21	4	3	3	2	0	0	0	3	0	1	0	0	0	0	-	0	1-1	1	6.53	5.79
2003 Houston	NL	23	0	0	8	30.0	116	22	7	7	3	2	0	1	7	1	20	2	1	1	1	.500	0	0-0	3	2.22	2.10
11 ML YEARS		505	9	0	193	572.2	2504	566	320	292	78	24	23	16	250	32	512	36	4	35	42	.455	0	33-61	74	4.42	4.59

Jason Michaels

Bats: R Throws: R Pos: PH-45; LF-23; RF-13; CF-5; PR-2   Ht: 6'0" Wt: 204 Born: 5/4/76 Age: 28

Year Team	Lg	G	AB	H	2B	3B	HR	(Hm	Rd)	TB	R	RBI	RC	TBB	IBB	SO	HBP	SH	SF	SB	CS	SB%	GDP	Avg	OBP	Slg
2003 Clearwater*	A+	4	14	0	0	0	0	(-	-)	0	1	0	0	2	0	4	0	0	0	0	0	-	0	.000	.125	.000
2001 Philadelphia	NL	6	6	1	0	0	0	(0	0)	1	0	1	0	0	0	2	0	0	0	0	0	-	0	.167	.167	.167
2002 Philadelphia	NL	81	105	28	10	3	2	(0	2)	50	16	11	15	13	1	33	1	0	2	1	1	.50	4	.267	.347	.476
2003 Philadelphia	NL	76	109	36	11	0	5	(1	4)	62	20	17	19	15	1	22	1	0	0	0	0	-	3	.330	.416	.569
3 ML YEARS		163	220	65	21	3	7	(1	6)	113	36	29	34	28	2	57	2	0	2	1	1	.50	4	.295	.377	.514

Jason Middlebrook

Pitches: R Bats: R Pos: RP-5   Ht: 6'3" Wt: 215 Born: 6/26/75 Age: 29

Year Team	Lg	G	GS	CG	GF	IP	BFP	H	R	ER	HR	SH	SF	HB	TBB	IBB	SO	WP	Bk	W	L	Pct	ShO	Sv-Op	Hld	ERC	ERA
2003 Norfolk*	AAA	23	23	0	0	118.1	497	121	64	59	21	5	4	1	33	0	91	3	1	7	10	.412	0	0--	-	4.31	4.49
2001 San Diego	NL	4	3	0	0	19.1	85	18	11	11	6	1	0	1	10	1	10	0	0	2	1	.667	0	0-0	0	5.85	5.12
2002 SD-NYM	NL	15	5	0	5	51.1	216	44	27	27	2	4	3	1	22	2	42	2	1	2	3	.400	0	0-0	1	3.02	4.73
2003 New York	NL	5	0	0	2	7.0	36	13	8	8	0	1	1	0	4	0	3	1	0	0	0	-	0	0-0	0	9.62	10.29
2002 San Diego	NL	12	2	0	5	35.1	149	31	20	20	1	3	3	1	15	2	28	2	0	1	3	.250	0	0-0	1	3.05	5.09
2002 New York	NL	3	3	0	0	16.0	67	13	7	7	1	1	0	0	7	0	14	0	1	1	0	1.000	0	0-0	0	2.95	3.94
3 ML YEARS		24	8	0	7	77.2	337	75	46	46	8	6	4	2	36	3	55	3	1	4	4	.500	0	0-0	1	4.22	5.33

Doug Mientkiewicz

Bats: L **Throws:** R **Pos:** 1B-139; RF-3; 2B-1; 3B-1; DH-1; PH-1; PR-1   **Ht:** 6'2" **Wt:** 200 **Born:** 6/19/74 **Age:** 30

Year Team	Lg	G	AB	H	2B	3B	HR	(Hm	Rd)	TB	R	RBI	RC	TBB	IBB	SO	HBP	SH	SF	SB	CS	SB%	GDP	Avg	OBP	Slg
1998 Minnesota	AL	8	25	5	1	0	0	(0	0)	6	1	2	2	4	0	3	0	0	0	1	1	.50	0	.200	.310	.240
1999 Minnesota	AL	118	327	75	21	3	2	(0	2)	108	34	32	34	43	3	51	4	3	2	1	1	.50	13	.229	.324	.330
2000 Minnesota	AL	3	14	6	0	0	0	(0	0)	6	0	4	2	0	0	0	0	0	1	0	0	-	1	.429	.400	.429
2001 Minnesota	AL	151	543	166	39	1	15	(11	4)	252	77	74	96	67	6	92	9	0	7	2	6	.25	10	.306	.387	.464
2002 Minnesota	AL	143	467	122	29	1	10	(6	4)	183	60	64	75	74	8	69	6	0	7	1	2	.33	7	.261	.365	.392
2003 Minnesota	AL	142	487	146	38	1	11	(6	5)	219	67	65	89	74	4	55	5	2	6	4	1	.80	9	.300	.393	.450
6 ML YEARS		565	1863	520	128	6	38	(23	15)	774	239	241	298	262	21	270	24	5	23	9	11	.45	40	.279	.371	.415

Aaron Miles

Bats: B **Throws:** R **Pos:** PH-4; 2B-3; DH-2; PR-1   **Ht:** 5'8" **Wt:** 170 **Born:** 12/15/76 **Age:** 27

Year Team	Lg	G	AB	H	2B	3B	HR	(Hm	Rd)	TB	R	RBI	RC	TBB	IBB	SO	HBP	SH	SF	SB	CS	SB%	GDP	Avg	OBP	Slg
1995 Astros	R	47	171	44	9	3	0	(-	-)	59	32	18	18	14	0	14	0	4	1	9	6	.60	3	.257	.312	.345
1996 Astros	R	55	214	63	3	2	0	(-	-)	70	48	15	26	20	0	18	1	5	0	14	7	.67	3	.294	.357	.327
1997 Quad City	A	97	370	97	13	2	1	(-	-)	117	55	35	37	30	0	45	2	7	4	18	11	.62	8	.262	.318	.316
1998 Quad City	A	108	369	90	22	6	2	(-	-)	130	42	37	38	25	3	52	1	7	1	28	13	.68	6	.244	.293	.352
1999 Michigan	A	112	470	149	28	8	10	(-	-)	223	72	71	76	28	3	33	2	6	7	17	12	.59	8	.317	.353	.474
2000 Kissimmee	A+	75	295	86	20	1	2	(-	-)	114	40	36	40	28	0	29	0	2	1	11	6	.65	7	.292	.352	.386
2001 Birmingham	AA	84	343	89	16	3	8	(-	-)	135	53	42	39	26	0	35	2	3	3	3	5	.38	10	.259	.313	.394
2002 Birmingham	AA	138	531	171	39	1	9	(-	-)	239	67	68	87	40	4	45	2	11	5	25	16	.61	4	.322	.369	.450
2003 Charlotte	AAA	133	546	166	34	5	11	(-	-)	243	80	50	82	40	2	52	1	5	3	8	9	.47	9	.304	.351	.445
2003 Chicago	AL	8	12	4	3	0	0	(0	0)	7	3	2	3	0	0	0	0	0	0	0	0	-	0	.333	.333	.583

Kevin Millar

Bats: R **Throws:** R **Pos:** 1B-101; LF-19; DH-18; RF-12; PH-7   **Ht:** 6'0" **Wt:** 210 **Born:** 9/24/71 **Age:** 32

Year Team	Lg	G	AB	H	2B	3B	HR	(Hm	Rd)	TB	R	RBI	RC	TBB	IBB	SO	HBP	SH	SF	SB	CS	SB%	GDP	Avg	OBP	Slg
1998 Florida	NL	2	2	1	0	0	0	(0	0)	1	1	0	1	1	0	0	0	0	0	0	0	-	0	.500	.667	.500
1999 Florida	NL	105	351	100	17	4	9	(3	6)	152	48	67	57	40	2	64	7	1	8	1	0	1.00	7	.285	.362	.433
2000 Florida	NL	123	259	67	14	3	14	(6	8)	129	36	42	47	36	0	47	8	0	2	0	0	-	5	.259	.364	.498
2001 Florida	NL	144	449	141	39	5	20	(13	7)	250	62	85	89	39	2	70	5	0	2	0	0	-	8	.314	.374	.557
2002 Florida	NL	126	438	134	41	0	16	(11	5)	223	58	57	64	40	0	74	5	0	6	0	2	.00	15	.306	.366	.509
2003 Boston	NL	148	544	150	30	1	25	(10	15)	257	83	96	87	60	5	108	5	0	9	3	2	.60	14	.276	.348	.472
6 ML YEARS		648	2043	593	141	13	84	(43	41)	1012	288	347	345	216	9	363	30	1	27	4	4	.50	49	.290	.362	.495

Corky Miller

Bats: R **Throws:** R **Pos:** C-11; PH-3   **Ht:** 6'1" **Wt:** 225 **Born:** 3/18/76 **Age:** 28

Year Team	Lg	G	AB	H	2B	3B	HR	(Hm	Rd)	TB	R	RBI	RC	TBB	IBB	SO	HBP	SH	SF	SB	CS	SB%	GDP	Avg	OBP	Slg
2003 Louisville*	AAA	103	354	88	28	0	11	(-	-)	149	49	43	47	35	2	58	7	1	3	0	0	-	12	.249	.326	.421
2001 Cincinnati	NL	17	49	9	2	0	3	(1	2)	20	5	7	6	4	0	16	2	0	2	1	0	1.00	1	.184	.263	.408
2002 Cincinnati	NL	39	114	29	10	0	3	(2	1)	48	9	15	15	9	2	20	4	1	1	0	0	-	6	.254	.328	.421
2003 Cincinnati	NL	14	30	8	0	0	0	(0	0)	8	4	1	4	5	0	7	2	0	1	0	0	-	1	.267	.395	.267
3 ML YEARS		70	193	46	12	0	6	(3	3)	76	18	23	25	18	2	43	8	1	4	1	0	1.00	9	.238	.323	.394

Damian Miller

Bats: R **Throws:** R **Pos:** C-114; PH-3   **Ht:** 6'2" **Wt:** 218 **Born:** 10/13/69 **Age:** 34

Year Team	Lg	G	AB	H	2B	3B	HR	(Hm	Rd)	TB	R	RBI	RC	TBB	IBB	SO	HBP	SH	SF	SB	CS	SB%	GDP	Avg	OBP	Slg
1997 Minnesota	AL	25	66	18	1	0	2	(1	1)	25	5	13	7	2	0	12	0	0	3	0	0	-	2	.273	.282	.379
1998 Arizona	NL	57	168	48	14	2	3	(2	1)	75	17	14	25	11	2	43	2	2	0	1	0	1.00	2	.286	.337	.446
1999 Arizona	NL	86	296	80	19	0	11	(3	8)	132	35	47	40	19	3	78	2	0	3	0	0	-	6	.270	.316	.446
2000 Arizona	NL	100	324	89	24	0	10	(6	4)	143	43	44	49	36	4	74	1	1	2	2	2	.50	6	.275	.347	.441
2001 Arizona	NL	123	380	103	19	0	13	(9	4)	161	45	47	52	35	9	80	4	4	2	0	1	.00	9	.271	.337	.424
2002 Arizona	NL	101	297	74	22	0	11	(4	7)	129	40	42	36	38	5	88	3	2	0	0	0	-	14	.249	.340	.434
2003 Chicago	NL	114	352	82	19	1	9	(6	3)	130	34	36	36	39	6	91	1	7	1	1	0	1.00	15	.233	.310	.369
7 ML YEARS		606	1883	494	118	3	59	(31	28)	795	219	243	245	180	29	466	13	16	11	4	3	.57	54	.262	.329	.422

Matt Miller

Pitches: R **Bats:** R **Pos:** RP-4   **Ht:** 6'3" **Wt:** 215 **Born:** 11/23/71 **Age:** 32

Year Team	Lg	G	GS	CG	GF	IP	BFP	H	R	ER	HR	SH	SF	HB	TBB	IBB	SO	WP	Bk	W	L	Pct	ShO	Sv-Op	Hld	ERC	ERA
1998 Savannah	A	17	0	0	10	35.1	137	25	9	9	0	2	1	2	10	0	46	2	0	3	1	.750	0	3--	-	1.82	2.29
1999 Charlotte	A+	22	0	0	20	29.2	132	25	9	9	0	1	1	1	13	1	39	2	0	1	2	.333	0	8--	-	2.60	2.73
1999 Tulsa	AA	34	0	0	25	56.0	235	42	24	21	2	4	5	1	28	2	83	5	0	6	4	.600	0	7--	-	2.69	3.38
2000 Rangers	R	1	0	0	0	2.0	9	2	1	1	0	0	0	0	1	0	4	0	0	0	0	-	0	0--	-	3.63	4.50
2000 Tulsa	AA	3	0	0	0	3.2	22	7	7	6	0	1	0	0	4	0	4	1	0	0	0	-	0	0--	-	11.78	14.73
2000 Oklahoma	AAA	39	0	0	25	60.1	276	61	29	24	6	4	4	3	34	4	69	4	0	3	3	.500	0	4--	-	4.80	3.58
2001 Portland	AAA	44	0	0	31	44.2	192	44	22	18	1	3	0	2	14	2	43	5	0	1	7	.125	0	17--	-	3.18	3.63
2002 Sacramento	AAA	54	0	0	39	71.0	322	81	42	34	5	2	5	2	28	8	63	3	0	3	7	.300	0	6--	-	4.68	4.31
2003 Co Springs	AAA	61	0	0	13	63.1	260	46	17	15	0	5	1	6	23	1	83	2	1	5	0	1.000	0	3--	-	2.19	2.13
2003 Colorado	NL	4	0	0	2	4.1	18	5	1	1	0	0	0	0	2	0	5	0	0	0	0	-	0	0-0	0	4.86	2.08

Trever Miller

Pitches: L **Bats:** R **Pos:** RP-79   **Ht:** 6'4" **Wt:** 195 **Born:** 5/29/73 **Age:** 31

Year Team	Lg	HOW MUCH HE PITCHED						WHAT HE GAVE UP												THE RESULTS						
		G	GS	CG	GF	IP	BFP	H	R	ER	HR	SH	SF	HB	TBB	IBB	SO	WP	Bk	W	L	Pct	ShO	Sv-Op	Hld	ERC	ERA
1996 Detroit	AL	5	4	0	0	16.2	88	28	17	17	3	2	2	2	9	0	8	0	0	0	4	.000	0	0-0	0	10.15	9.18
1998 Houston	NL	37	1	0	15	53.1	235	57	21	18	4	0	0	1	20	1	30	1	0	2	0	1.000	0	1-2	1	4.18	3.04
1999 Houston	NL	47	0	0	11	49.2	232	58	29	28	6	2	2	5	29	1	37	4	0	3	2	.600	0	1-1	4	6.48	5.07
2000 Phi-LA	NL	16	0	0	2	16.1	90	27	22	19	3	1	1	2	12	1	11	1	0	0	0	-	0	0-0	0	10.68	10.47
2003 Toronto	AL	**79**	0	0	18	52.2	234	46	30	27	7	1	0	5	28	3	44	2	0	2	2	.500	0	4-5	16	4.36	4.61
2000 Philadelphia	NL	14	0	0	2	14.0	72	19	16	13	3	1	1	1	9	1	10	1	0	0	0	-	0	0-0	0	8.14	8.36
2000 Los Angeles	NL	2	0	0	0	2.1	18	8	6	6	0	0	0	1	3	0	1	0	0	0	0	-	0	0-0	0	28.18	23.14
5 ML YEARS		184	5	0	46	188.2	879	216	119	109	23	6	5	15	98	6	130	8	0	7	8	.467	0	6-8	21	5.82	5.20

Wade Miller

Pitches: R **Bats:** R **Pos:** SP-33   **Ht:** 6'2" **Wt:** 210 **Born:** 9/13/76 **Age:** 27

Year Team	Lg	HOW MUCH HE PITCHED						WHAT HE GAVE UP												THE RESULTS						
		G	GS	CG	GF	IP	BFP	H	R	ER	HR	SH	SF	HB	TBB	IBB	SO	WP	Bk	W	L	Pct	ShO	Sv-Op	Hld	ERC	ERA
1999 Houston	NL	5	1	0	2	10.1	52	17	11	11	4	0	0	0	5	0	8	0	0	0	1	.000	0	0-0	0	11.07	9.58
2000 Houston	NL	16	16	2	0	105.0	453	104	66	60	14	3	1	3	42	1	89	1	0	6	6	.500	0	0-0	0	4.37	5.14
2001 Houston	NL	32	32	1	0	212.0	873	183	91	80	31	7	5	4	76	3	183	8	0	16	8	.667	0	0-0	0	3.57	3.40
2002 Houston	NL	26	26	1	0	164.2	688	151	63	60	14	8	5	6	62	9	144	4	0	15	4	.789	1	0-0	0	3.54	3.28
2003 Houston	NL	33	33	1	0	187.1	797	168	96	86	17	8	7	10	77	1	161	4	0	14	13	.519	0	0-0	0	3.70	4.13
5 ML YEARS		112	108	5	2	679.1	2863	623	327	297	80	26	18	23	262	14	585	17	0	51	32	.614	1	0-0	0	3.82	3.93

Kevin Millwood

Pitches: R **Bats:** R **Pos:** SP-35   **Ht:** 6'4" **Wt:** 220 **Born:** 12/24/74 **Age:** 29

Year Team	Lg	HOW MUCH HE PITCHED						WHAT HE GAVE UP												THE RESULTS						
		G	GS	CG	GF	IP	BFP	H	R	ER	HR	SH	SF	HB	TBB	IBB	SO	WP	Bk	W	L	Pct	ShO	Sv-Op	Hld	ERC	ERA
1997 Atlanta	NL	12	8	0	2	51.1	227	55	26	23	1	3	5	2	21	1	42	1	0	5	3	.625	0	0-0	1	4.03	4.03
1998 Atlanta	NL	31	29	3	1	174.1	748	175	86	79	18	8	3	3	56	3	163	6	1	17	8	.680	1	0-0	1	3.81	4.08
1999 Atlanta	NL	33	33	2	0	228.0	906	168	80	68	24	9	3	4	59	2	205	5	0	18	7	.720	0	0-0	0	2.26	2.68
2000 Atlanta	NL	36	**35**	0	0	212.2	903	213	115	110	26	8	5	3	62	2	168	4	0	10	13	.435	0	0-0	0	3.83	4.66
2001 Atlanta	NL	21	21	0	0	121.0	515	121	66	58	20	7	2	1	40	6	84	5	1	7	7	.500	0	0-0	0	4.20	4.31
2002 Atlanta	NL	35	34	1	0	217.0	895	186	83	78	16	9	4	8	65	7	178	4	0	18	8	.692	1	0-0	0	2.85	3.24
2003 Philadelphia	NL	35	35	5	0	222.0	930	210	103	99	19	12	5	4	68	6	169	2	0	14	12	.538	**3**	0-0	1	3.35	4.01
7 ML YEARS		203	195	11	3	1226.1	5124	1128	559	515	124	56	27	25	371	27	1009	27	2	89	58	.605	5	0-0	1	3.30	3.78

Eric Milton

Pitches: L **Bats:** L **Pos:** SP-3   **Ht:** 6'3" **Wt:** 220 **Born:** 8/4/75 **Age:** 28

Year Team	Lg	HOW MUCH HE PITCHED						WHAT HE GAVE UP												THE RESULTS						
		G	GS	CG	GF	IP	BFP	H	R	ER	HR	SH	SF	HB	TBB	IBB	SO	WP	Bk	W	L	Pct	ShO	Sv-Op	Hld	ERC	ERA
2003 Fort Myers*	A+	1	1	0	0	2.0	9	1	0	0	0	0	0	0	2	0	2	0	0	0	0	-	0	0- -	-	2.80	0.00
1998 Minnesota	AL	32	32	1	0	172.1	772	195	113	108	25	2	6	2	70	0	107	1	0	8	14	.364	0	0-0	0	5.21	5.64
1999 Minnesota	AL	34	34	4	0	206.1	858	190	111	103	28	3	6	3	63	2	163	2	0	7	11	.389	2	0-0	0	3.56	4.49
2000 Minnesota	AL	33	33	0	0	200.0	849	205	123	108	35	4	6	7	44	0	160	5	0	13	10	.565	0	0-0	0	4.09	4.86
2001 Minnesota	AL	35	34	2	0	220.2	944	222	109	106	35	8	6	5	61	0	157	2	0	15	7	.682	1	0-0	0	4.05	4.32
2002 Minnesota	AL	29	29	2	0	171.0	707	173	96	92	24	0	4	3	30	0	121	4	0	13	9	.591	1	0-0	0	3.59	4.84
2003 Minnesota	AL	3	3	0	0	17.0	66	15	5	5	2	0	1	0	1	0	7	0	0	1	0	1.000	0	0-0	0	2.29	2.65
6 ML YEARS		166	165	9	0	987.1	4196	1000	557	522	149	17	29	20	269	2	715	14	0	57	51	.528	4	0-0	0	4.04	4.76

Doug Mirabelli

Bats: R **Throws:** R **Pos:** C-55; PH-6; DH-3; 1B-2   **Ht:** 6'1" **Wt:** 227 **Born:** 10/18/70 **Age:** 33

Year Team	Lg	BATTING																	BASERUNNING				AVERAGES		
		G	AB	H	2B	3B	HR	(Hm	Rd)	TB	R	RBI	RC	TBB	IBB	SO	HBP	SH	SF	SB	CS	SB%	GDP	Avg	OBP	Slg
1996 San Francisco	NL	9	18	4	1	0	0	(0	0)	5	2	1	2	3	0	4	0	0	0	0	0	-	0	.222	.333	.278
1997 San Francisco	NL	6	7	1	0	0	0	(0	0)	1	0	0	0	1	0	3	0	0	0	0	0	-	0	.143	.250	.143
1998 San Francisco	NL	10	17	4	2	0	1	(1	0)	9	2	4	3	2	0	6	0	0	0	0	0	-	0	.235	.316	.529
1999 San Francisco	NL	33	87	22	6	0	1	(1	0)	31	10	10	10	9	1	25	1	0	1	0	0	-	1	.253	.327	.356
2000 San Francisco	NL	82	230	53	10	2	6	(2	4)	85	23	28	30	36	2	57	2	3	2	1	0	1.00	6	.230	.337	.370
2001 Tex-Bos	AL	77	190	43	10	0	11	(5	6)	86	20	29	29	27	2	57	4	1	2	0	0	-	3	.226	.332	.453
2002 Boston	AL	57	151	34	7	0	7	(5	2)	62	17	25	19	17	0	33	3	0	2	0	0	-	6	.225	.312	.411
2003 Boston	AL	62	163	42	13	0	6	(3	3)	73	23	18	16	11	0	36	1	0	1	0	0	-	4	.258	.307	.448
2001 Texas	AL	23	49	5	2	0	2	(1	1)	13	4	3	3	10	0	21	0	0	0	0	0	-	1	.102	.254	.265
2001 Boston	AL	54	141	38	8	0	9	(4	5)	73	16	26	26	17	2	36	4	1	2	0	0	-	2	.270	.360	.518
8 ML YEARS		336	863	203	49	2	32	(17	15)	352	97	115	109	106	5	221	11	4	8	1	0	1.00	19	.235	.324	.408

Sergio Mitre

Pitches: R **Bats:** R **Pos:** SP-2; RP-1   **Ht:** 6'4" **Wt:** 210 **Born:** 2/16/81 **Age:** 23

Year Team	Lg	HOW MUCH HE PITCHED						WHAT HE GAVE UP												THE RESULTS						
		G	GS	CG	GF	IP	BFP	H	R	ER	HR	SH	SF	HB	TBB	IBB	SO	WP	Bk	W	L	Pct	ShO	Sv-Op	Hld	ERC	ERA
2001 Boise	A-	15	15	1	0	91.0	371	85	37	31	2	0	0	3	18	1	71	3	3	8	4	.667	1	0- -	-	2.58	3.07
2002 Lansing	A	27	27	2	0	168.2	685	166	72	53	7	6	6	10	27	1	96	10	0	8	10	.444	0	0- -	-	2.96	2.83
2003 W Tennessee	AA	25	24	0	0	145.2	639	162	75	54	6	9	3	12	41	0	128	6	0	7	9	.438	0	0- -	-	4.12	3.34
2003 Chicago	NL	3	2	0	1	8.2	43	15	8	8	1	0	1	0	4	1	3	0	0	0	1	.000	0	0-0	0	9.02	8.31

Brian Moehler

Pitches: R Bats: R Pos: SP-3   Ht: 6'3" Wt: 235 Born: 12/31/71 Age: 32

		HOW MUCH HE PITCHED						WHAT HE GAVE UP											THE RESULTS						
Year Team	Lg	G	GS	CG	GF	IP	BFP	H	R	ER	HR	SH	SF	HB	TBB	IBB	SO	WP	Bk	W	L	Pct	ShO	Sv-Op	Hld	ERC	ERA
2003 New Orleans*	AAA	1	1	0	0	2.0	9	3	1	1	0	0	1	0	0	0	3	0	0	0	0	-	0	0--	0	4.47	4.50
1996 Detroit	AL	2	2	0	0	10.1	51	11	10	5	1	1	0	0	8	1	2	1	0	0	1	.000	0	0-0	0	5.49	4.35
1997 Detroit	AL	31	31	2	0	175.1	770	198	97	91	22	1	8	5	61	1	97	3	0	11	12	.478	1	0-0	0	4.92	4.67
1998 Detroit	AL	33	33	4	0	221.1	912	220	103	96	30	3	3	2	56	1	123	4	0	14	13	.519	3	0-0	0	3.79	3.90
1999 Detroit	AL	32	32	2	0	196.1	859	229	116	110	22	8	5	7	59	5	106	4	0	10	16	.385	2	0-0	0	4.85	5.04
2000 Detroit	AL	29	29	2	0	178.0	776	222	99	89	20	3	4	2	40	0	103	2	1	12	9	.571	0	0-0	0	4.95	4.50
2001 Detroit	AL	1	1	0	0	8.0	30	6	3	3	0	0	0	0	1	0	2	0	0	0	0	-	0	0-0	0	1.43	3.38
2002 Det-Cin		13	12	0	0	63.0	278	78	39	34	11	4	2	1	13	0	31	0	0	3	5	.375	0	0-0	0	5.20	4.86
2003 Houston	NL	3	3	0	0	13.2	66	22	12	12	4	1	1	0	6	0	5	0	0	0	0	-	0	0-0	0	9.97	7.90
2002 Detroit	AL	3	3	0	0	19.2	77	17	5	5	3	1	1	0	2	0	13	0	0	1	1	.500	0	0-0	0	2.54	2.29
2002 Cincinnati	NL	10	9	0	0	43.1	201	61	34	29	8	3	1	1	11	0	18	0	0	2	4	.333	0	0-0	0	6.56	6.02
8 ML YEARS		144	143	10	0	866.0	3742	986	479	440	110	21	23	17	244	8	469	14	1	50	56	.472	6	0-0	0	4.68	4.57

Chad Moeller

Bats: R Throws: R Pos: C-76; PH-2; PR-2   Ht: 6'3" Wt: 210 Born: 2/18/75 Age: 29

		BATTING																	BASERUNNING				AVERAGES		
Year Team	Lg	G	AB	H	2B	3B	HR	(Hm	Rd)	TB	R	RBI	RC	TBB	IBB	SO	HBP	SH	SF	SB	CS	SB%	GDP	Avg	OBP	Slg
2000 Minnesota	AL	48	128	27	3	1	1	(1	0)	35	13	9	8	9	0	33	0	1	1	1	0	1.00	4	.211	.261	.273
2001 Arizona	NL	25	56	13	0	1	1	(1	0)	18	8	2	5	6	1	12	0	1	0	0	0	-	2	.232	.306	.321
2002 Arizona	NL	37	105	30	11	1	2	(2	0)	49	10	16	18	17	3	23	0	1	0	1	0	1.00	6	.286	.385	.467
2003 Arizona	NL	78	239	64	17	1	7	(2	5)	104	29	29	29	23	11	59	2	3	2	1	2	.33	7	.268	.335	.435
4 ML YEARS		188	528	134	31	4	11	(6	5)	206	60	56	60	55	15	127	2	6	3	2	3	.40	19	.254	.325	.390

Dustan Mohr

Bats: R Throws: R Pos: RF-77; LF-30; CF-11; PR-8; PH-6; DH-3   Ht: 6'0" Wt: 210 Born: 6/19/76 Age: 28

		BATTING																	BASERUNNING				AVERAGES		
Year Team	Lg	G	AB	H	2B	3B	HR	(Hm	Rd)	TB	R	RBI	RC	TBB	IBB	SO	HBP	SH	SF	SB	CS	SB%	GDP	Avg	OBP	Slg
2001 Minnesota	AL	20	51	12	2	0	0	(0	0)	14	6	4	4	5	0	17	0	0	1	1	1	.50	0	.235	.298	.275
2002 Minnesota	AL	120	383	103	23	2	12	(3	9)	166	55	45	51	31	3	86	1	2	0	3	6	.33	7	.269	.325	.433
2003 Minnesota	AL	121	348	87	22	0	10	(4	6)	139	50	36	37	33	0	106	1	2	3	5	2	.71	10	.250	.314	.399
3 ML YEARS		261	782	202	47	2	22	(7	15)	319	111	85	92	69	3	209	2	4	4	12	6	.67	15	.258	.319	.408

Ben Molina

Bats: R Throws: R Pos: C-117; PH-4   Ht: 5'11" Wt: 210 Born: 7/20/74 Age: 29

		BATTING																	BASERUNNING				AVERAGES		
Year Team	Lg	G	AB	H	2B	3B	HR	(Hm	Rd)	TB	R	RBI	RC	TBB	IBB	SO	HBP	SH	SF	SB	CS	SB%	GDP	Avg	OBP	Slg
1998 Anaheim	AL	2	1	0	0	0	0	(0	0)	0	0	0	0	0	0	0	0	0	0	0	0	-	0	.000	.000	.000
1999 Anaheim	AL	31	101	26	5	0	1	(0	1)	34	8	10	9	6	0	6	2	0	0	0	1	.00	5	.257	.314	.337
2000 Anaheim	AL	130	473	133	20	2	14	(11	3)	199	59	71	60	23	0	33	6	4	7	0	1	1.00	17	.281	.318	.421
2001 Anaheim	AL	96	325	85	11	0	6	(6	0)	114	31	40	34	16	3	51	8	2	4	0	1	.00	8	.262	.309	.351
2002 Anaheim	AL	122	428	105	18	0	5	(2	3)	138	34	47	32	15	3	34	4	6	6	0	0	-	15	.245	.274	.322
2003 Anaheim	AL	119	409	115	24	0	14	(7	7)	181	37	71	57	13	2	31	2	2	4	1	1	.50	17	.281	.304	.443
6 ML YEARS		500	1737	464	78	2	40	(26	14)	666	169	239	192	73	8	155	22	14	21	2	3	.40	62	.267	.302	.383

Gabe Molina

Pitches: R Bats: R Pos: RP-3   Ht: 6'1" Wt: 220 Born: 5/3/75 Age: 29

		HOW MUCH HE PITCHED						WHAT HE GAVE UP											THE RESULTS						
Year Team	Lg	G	GS	CG	GF	IP	BFP	H	R	ER	HR	SH	SF	HB	TBB	IBB	SO	WP	Bk	W	L	Pct	ShO	Sv-Op	Hld	ERC	ERA
2003 Memphis*	AAA	57	0	0	35	63.2	288	73	40	36	9	6	0	1	31	8	47	7	1	2	9	.182	0	9--	-	5.47	5.09
1999 Baltimore	AL	20	0	0	7	16.1	102	22	19	17	4	0	0	0	16	1	14	4	0	1	2	.333	0	0-1	2	5.67	6.65
2000 Bal-Atl		11	0	0	4	15.0	85	28	18	15	3	0	3	1	10	0	9	0	0	0	0	-	0	0-0	1	11.76	9.00
2002 St Louis	NL	12	0	0	3	11.1	43	6	2	2	1	0	0	0	6	0	4	0	0	1	0	1.000	0	0-0	2	2.21	1.59
2003 St Louis	NL	3	0	0	1	2.2	14	5	4	4	1	0	0	0	1	0	1	0	0	0	0	-	0	0-0	0	11.86	13.50
2000 Baltimore	AL	9	0	0	3	13.0	74	25	14	13	2	0	2	0	9	0	8	0	0	0	0	-	0	0-0	1	11.48	9.00
2000 Atlanta	NL	2	0	0	1	2.0	11	3	4	2	1	0	1	1	1	0	1	0	0	0	0	-	0	0-0	0	13.58	9.00
4 ML YEARS		46	0	0	15	52.0	244	61	43	38	9	0	3	1	33	1	28	4	0	2	2	.500	0	0-1	5	6.76	6.58

Jose Molina

Bats: R Throws: R Pos: C-53; PH-2   Ht: 6'1" Wt: 215 Born: 6/3/75 Age: 29

		BATTING																	BASERUNNING				AVERAGES		
Year Team	Lg	G	AB	H	2B	3B	HR	(Hm	Rd)	TB	R	RBI	RC	TBB	IBB	SO	HBP	SH	SF	SB	CS	SB%	GDP	Avg	OBP	Slg
1999 Chicago	NL	10	19	5	1	0	0	(0	0)	6	3	1	2	2	1	4	0	0	0	0	0	-	0	.263	.333	.316
2001 Anaheim	AL	15	37	10	3	0	2	(0	2)	19	8	4	6	3	0	8	0	2	0	0	0	-	2	.270	.325	.514
2002 Anaheim	AL	29	70	19	3	0	0	(0	0)	22	5	5	4	5	0	15	0	4	2	0	2	.00	2	.271	.312	.314
2003 Anaheim	AL	53	114	21	4	0	0	(0	0)	25	12	6	5	1	0	26	3	4	1	0	0	-	1	.184	.210	.219
4 ML YEARS		107	240	55	11	0	2	(0	2)	72	28	16	17	11	1	53	3	10	3	0	2	.00	5	.229	.268	.300

Raul Mondesi

Bats: R **Throws:** R **Pos:** RF-139; PH-3; CF-2; DH-1   **Ht:** 5'11" **Wt:** 230 **Born:** 3/12/71 **Age:** 33

							BATTING											BASERUNNING				AVERAGES		
Year Team	Lg	G	AB	H	2B	3B	HR	(Hm Rd)	TB	R	RBI	RC	TBB	IBB	SO	HBP	SH	SF	SB	CS	SB%	GDP	Avg	OBP	Slg
1993 Los Angeles	NL	42	86	25	3	1	4	(2 2)	42	13	10	14	4	0	16	0	1	0	4	1	.80	1	.291	.322	.488
1994 Los Angeles	NL	112	434	133	27	8	16	(10 6)	224	63	56	69	16	5	78	2	0	2	11	8	.58	9	.306	.333	.516
1995 Los Angeles	NL	139	536	153	23	6	26	(13 13)	266	91	88	89	33	4	96	4	0	7	27	4	.87	7	.285	.328	.496
1996 Los Angeles	NL	157	634	188	40	7	24	(11 13)	314	98	88	102	32	9	122	5	0	2	14	7	.67	6	.297	.334	.495
1997 Los Angeles	NL	159	616	191	42	5	30	(16 14)	333	95	87	114	44	7	105	6	1	3	32	15	.68	11	.310	.360	.541
1998 Los Angeles	NL	148	580	162	26	5	30	(13 17)	288	85	90	88	30	4	112	3	0	4	16	10	.62	8	.279	.316	.497
1999 Los Angeles	NL	159	601	152	29	5	33	(18 15)	290	98	99	102	71	6	134	3	0	5	36	9	.80	3	.253	.332	.483
2000 Toronto	AL	96	388	105	22	2	24	(10 14)	203	78	67	67	32	0	73	3	0	3	22	6	.79	8	.271	.329	.523
2001 Toronto	AL	149	572	144	26	4	27	(10 17)	259	88	84	89	73	3	128	6	0	2	30	11	.73	13	.252	.342	.453
2002 Tor-NYY	AL	146	569	132	34	1	26	(16 10)	246	90	88	75	59	3	103	5	0	4	15	6	.71	11	.232	.308	.432
2003 NYY-Ari	AL	143	523	142	31	4	24	(14 10)	253	83	71	66	56	6	97	3	0	4	22	11	.67	9	.272	.343	.484
2002 Toronto	AL	75	299	67	16	1	15	(10 5)	130	51	45	39	31	1	57	3	0	2	9	2	.82	8	.224	.301	.435
2002 New York	AL	71	270	65	18	0	11	(6 5)	116	39	43	36	28	2	46	2	0	2	6	4	.60	3	.241	.315	.430
2003 New York	AL	98	361	93	23	3	16	(9 7)	170	56	49	43	38	6	66	2	0	2	17	7	.71	6	.258	.330	.471
2003 Arizona	NL	45	162	49	8	1	8	(5 3)	83	27	22	23	18	0	31	1	0	2	5	4	.56	3	.302	.372	.512
11 ML YEARS		1450	5539	1527	303	48	264	(133 131)	2718	882	828	875	450	47	1064	40	2	36	229	88	.72	86	.276	.333	.491

Craig Monroe

Bats: R **Throws:** R **Pos:** LF-75; RF-38; PH-18; DH-7; CF-2; PR-1   **Ht:** 6'1" **Wt:** 195 **Born:** 2/27/77 **Age:** 27

							BATTING											BASERUNNING				AVERAGES		
Year Team	Lg	G	AB	H	2B	3B	HR	(Hm Rd)	TB	R	RBI	RC	TBB	IBB	SO	HBP	SH	SF	SB	CS	SB%	GDP	Avg	OBP	Slg
2003 Toledo*	AAA	14	47	19	4	1	2	(- -)	31	14	6	13	4	0	10	0	0	0	1	0	1.00	0	.404	.451	.660
2001 Texas	AL	27	52	11	1	0	2	(1 1)	18	8	5	6	6	0	18	0	0	0	2	0	1.00	1	.212	.293	.346
2002 Detroit	AL	13	25	3	1	0	1	(0 1)	7	3	1	0	0	0	5	1	0	0	0	2	.00	1	.120	.154	.280
2003 Detroit	AL	128	425	102	18	1	23	(10 13)	191	51	70	62	27	2	89	2	1	3	4	2	.67	10	.240	.287	.449
3 ML YEARS		168	502	116	20	1	26	(11 15)	216	62	76	68	33	2	112	3	1	3	6	4	.60	12	.231	.281	.430

Melvin Mora

Bats: R **Throws:** R **Pos:** LF-56; RF-13; CF-12; SS-11; 2B-6; PH-2; PR-2; 1B-1   **Ht:** 5'10" **Wt:** 180 **Born:** 2/2/72 **Age:** 32

							BATTING											BASERUNNING				AVERAGES		
Year Team	Lg	G	AB	H	2B	3B	HR	(Hm Rd)	TB	R	RBI	RC	TBB	IBB	SO	HBP	SH	SF	SB	CS	SB%	GDP	Avg	OBP	Slg
2003 Bowie*	AA	6	21	6	0	0	2	(- -)	12	3	5	4	2	0	4	0	0	0	0	0	-	0	.286	.348	.571
1999 New York	NL	66	31	5	0	0	0	(0 0)	5	6	1	2	4	0	7	1	3	0	2	1	.67	0	.161	.278	.161
2000 NYM-Bal		132	414	114	22	5	8	(5 3)	170	60	47	56	35	3	80	6	4	5	12	11	.52	5	.275	.337	.411
2001 Baltimore	AL	128	436	109	28	0	7	(6 1)	158	49	48	55	41	2	91	14	5	7	11	4	.73	6	.250	.329	.362
2002 Baltimore	AL	149	557	130	30	4	19	(8 11)	225	86	64	78	70	2	108	20	1	4	16	10	.62	7	.233	.338	.404
2003 Baltimore	AL	96	344	109	17	1	15	(8 7)	173	68	48	67	49	0	71	12	6	2	6	3	.67	3	.317	.418	.503
2000 New York	NL	79	215	56	13	2	6	(4 2)	91	35	30	29	18	3	48	2	2	5	7	3	.70	3	.260	.317	.423
2000 Baltimore	AL	53	199	58	9	3	2	(1 1)	79	25	17	27	17	0	32	4	2	0	5	8	.38	2	.291	.359	.397
5 ML YEARS		571	1782	467	97	10	49	(27 22)	731	269	208	258	199	7	357	53	19	18	47	29	.62	21	.262	.350	.410

Jose Morban

Bats: B **Throws:** R **Pos:** PR-22; SS-14; 2B-12; PH-12; DH-8; 3B-1   **Ht:** 6'1" **Wt:** 170 **Born:** 12/2/79 **Age:** 24

							BATTING											BASERUNNING				AVERAGES		
Year Team	Lg	G	AB	H	2B	3B	HR	(Hm Rd)	TB	R	RBI	RC	TBB	IBB	SO	HBP	SH	SF	SB	CS	SB%	GDP	Avg	OBP	Slg
1999 Rangers	R	54	205	58	10	5	4	(- -)	90	45	18	34	31	2	70	2	4	3	19	14	.58	1	.283	.378	.439
2000 Pulaski	R+	30	120	27	3	2	3	(- -)	43	21	17	13	12	2	35	0	3	1	6	3	.67	0	.225	.293	.358
2000 Savannah	A	80	273	60	8	4	4	(- -)	88	44	28	31	41	0	79	4	5	0	27	13	.68	6	.220	.330	.322
2001 Savannah	A	122	474	119	20	11	8	(- -)	185	71	47	58	42	0	119	2	5	3	46	18	.72	11	.251	.313	.390
2002 Charlotte	A+	126	485	126	27	12	8	(- -)	201	75	66	69	46	1	111	3	10	3	21	9	.70	2	.260	.326	.414
2003 Baltimore	AL	61	71	10	0	0	2	(2 0)	16	14	5	1	3	0	21	1	2	0	8	0	1.00	0	.141	.187	.225

Mike Mordecai

Bats: R **Throws:** R **Pos:** PH-25; SS-14; 2B-12; 3B-12; PR-11; 1B-1   **Ht:** 5'10" **Wt:** 185 **Born:** 12/13/67 **Age:** 36

							BATTING											BASERUNNING				AVERAGES		
Year Team	Lg	G	AB	H	2B	3B	HR	(Hm Rd)	TB	R	RBI	RC	TBB	IBB	SO	HBP	SH	SF	SB	CS	SB%	GDP	Avg	OBP	Slg
1994 Atlanta	NL	4	4	1	0	0	1	(1 0)	4	1	3	1	1	0	0	0	0	0	0	0	-	0	.250	.400	1.000
1995 Atlanta	NL	69	75	21	6	0	3	(1 2)	36	10	11	13	9	0	16	0	2	1	0	0	-	0	.280	.353	.480
1996 Atlanta	NL	66	108	26	5	0	2	(0 2)	37	12	8	11	9	1	24	0	4	1	1	0	1.00	1	.241	.297	.343
1997 Atlanta	NL	61	81	14	2	1	0	(0 0)	18	8	3	2	6	0	16	0	1	1	0	1	.00	4	.173	.227	.222
1998 Montreal	NL	73	119	24	4	2	3	(1 2)	41	12	10	10	9	0	20	0	2	0	1	0	1.00	0	.202	.258	.345
1999 Montreal	NL	109	226	53	10	2	5	(4 1)	82	29	25	24	20	0	31	1	1	2	2	5	.29	1	.235	.297	.363
2000 Montreal	NL	86	169	48	16	0	4	(2 2)	76	20	16	25	12	0	34	1	1	0	2	2	.50	1	.284	.335	.450
2001 Montreal	NL	96	254	71	17	2	3	(1 2)	101	28	32	32	19	1	53	1	1	2	2	2	.50	6	.280	.330	.398
2002 Mon-Fla	NL	93	151	37	8	0	0	(0 0)	45	19	11	15	13	4	27	2	10	0	2	2	.50	3	.245	.313	.298
2003 Florida	NL	65	89	19	4	0	2	(1 1)	29	11	8	6	8	3	21	0	3	1	0	3	1.00	1	.213	.276	.326
2002 Montreal	NL	55	74	15	4	0	0	(0 0)	19	9	4	6	8	3	14	1	7	0	1	1	.50	2	.203	.289	.257
2002 Florida	NL	38	77	22	4	0	0	(0 0)	26	10	7	9	5	1	13	1	3	0	1	1	.50	1	.286	.337	.338
10 ML YEARS		722	1276	314	72	7	23	(11 12)	469	150	127	139	106	9	242	5	25	8	13	12	.52	18	.246	.305	.368

Orber Moreno

Pitches: R **Bats:** R **Pos:** RP-7 **Ht:** 6'3" **Wt:** 200 **Born:** 4/27/77 **Age:** 27

Year Team	Lg	G	GS	CG	GF	IP	BFP	H	R	ER	HR	SH	SF	HB	TBB	IBB	SO	WP	Bk	W	L	Pct	ShO	Sv-Op	Hld	ERC	ERA
1995 Royals	R	8	3	0	1	22.0	89	15	9	6	0	0	0	2	7	0	21	2	0	1	1	.500	0	0- -	-	1.84	2.45
1996 Royals	R	12	7	0	1	46.1	187	37	15	7	2	2	0	1	10	0	50	1	2	5	1	.833	0	1- -	-	2.05	1.36
1997 Lansing	A	27	25	0	0	138.1	603	150	83	74	15	6	4	8	45	0	128	9	0	4	8	.333	0	0- -	-	4.56	4.81
1998 Wilmington	A+	23	0	0	17	33.0	115	8	3	3	1	1	0	0	10	1	50	1	0	3	2	.600	0	7- -	-	0.53	0.82
1998 Wichita	AA	24	0	0	19	34.1	144	28	13	11	1	2	0	0	12	3	40	3	0	0	1	.000	0	7- -	-	2.26	2.88
1999 Omaha	AAA	16	0	0	15	25.2	97	17	6	6	2	0	0	0	4	0	30	0	0	3	1	.750	0	4- -	-	1.49	2.10
1999 Royals	R	1	1	0	0	1.0	3	0	0	0	0	0	0	0	0	0	1	0	0	0	0	-	0	0- -	-	0.00	0.00
2000 Wilmington	A+	8	1	0	2	10.2	48	12	5	3	1	0	0	1	1	0	16	1	0	1	1	.500	0	1- -	-	3.62	2.53
2000 Wichita	AA	5	0	0	2	8.2	31	3	0	0	0	0	0	1	2	0	10	0	1	0	0	-	0	1- -	-	0.76	0.00
2000 Omaha	AAA	17	0	0	11	21.0	90	19	11	11	4	0	0	0	8	0	25	1	0	1	1	.500	0	3- -	-	4.00	4.71
2003 Norfolk	AAA	38	0	0	32	52.0	206	36	11	11	1	0	0	1	17	0	58	2	0	5	1	.833	0	12- -	-	1.83	1.90
2003 Binghamton	AA	4	0	0	3	5.1	21	4	1	1	0	0	0	0	1	0	7	0	0	2	0	1.000	0	1- -	-	2.44	1.69
1999 Kansas City	AL	7	0	0	0	8.0	34	4	0	5	1	0	0	0	6	0	7	0	0	0	0	-	0	0-0	0	2.84	5.63
2003 New York	NL	7	0	0	4	8.0	36	10	7	7	1	1	0	0	3	0	5	0	0	0	0	-	0	0-0	0	5.65	7.88
2 ML YEARS		14	0	0	4	16.0	70	14	7	12	2	1	0	0	9	0	12	0	0	0	0	-	0	0-0	0	4.16	6.75

Justin Morneau

Bats: L **Throws:** R **Pos:** DH-21; PH-16; 1B-7; PR-1 **Ht:** 6'4" **Wt:** 225 **Born:** 5/15/81 **Age:** 23

Year Team	Lg	G	AB	H	2B	3B	HR	(Hm	Rd)	TB	R	RBI	RC	TBB	IBB	SO	HBP	SH	SF	SB	CS	SB%	GDP	Avg	OBP	Slg
1999 Twins	R	17	53	16	5	0	0	(-	-)	21	3	9	6	2	0	6	1	1	1	0	1	.00	2	.302	.333	.396
2000 Twins	R	52	194	78	21	0	10	(-	-)	129	47	58	55	30	7	18	0	0	2	3	1	.75	5	.402	.478	.665
2000 Elizabethton	R+	6	23	5	0	0	1	(-	-)	8	4	3	2	1	0	6	0	0	0	0	0	-	0	.217	.250	.348
2001 Quad City	A	64	236	84	17	2	12	(-	-)	141	50	53	56	26	1	38	3	0	4	0	0	-	4	.356	.420	.597
2001 Ft Myers	A+	53	197	58	10	3	4	(-	-)	86	25	40	34	24	1	41	8	0	5	0	0	-	4	.294	.385	.437
2001 New Britain	AA	10	38	6	1	0	0	(-	-)	7	3	4	1	3	0	8	0	0	1	0	1	.158	.214	.184
2002 New Britain	AA	126	494	147	31	4	16	(-	-)	234	72	80	83	42	5	88	6	0	6	7	0	1.00	6	.298	.356	.474
2003 Rochester	AAA	71	265	71	11	1	16	(-	-)	132	39	42	45	28	3	56	4	0	2	0	2	.00	2	.268	.344	.498
2003 New Britain	AA	20	79	26	3	1	6	(-	-)	49	14	13	18	7	2	14	0	0	0	0	0	-	0	.329	.384	.620
2003 Minnesota	AL	40	106	24	4	0	4	(1	3)	40	14	16	11	9	1	30	0	0	0	0	0	-	4	.226	.287	.377

Matt Morris

Pitches: R **Bats:** R **Pos:** SP-27 **Ht:** 6'5" **Wt:** 210 **Born:** 8/9/74 **Age:** 29

Year Team	Lg	G	GS	CG	GF	IP	BFP	H	R	ER	HR	SH	SF	HB	TBB	IBB	SO	WP	Bk	W	L	Pct	ShO	Sv-Op	Hld	ERC	ERA
1997 St Louis	NL	33	33	3	0	217.0	900	208	88	77	12	11	7	7	69	2	149	5	3	12	9	.571	0	0-0	0	3.41	3.19
1998 St Louis	NL	17	17	2	0	113.2	468	101	37	32	8	6	1	3	42	6	79	3	0	7	5	.583	1	0-0	0	3.25	2.53
2000 St Louis	NL	31	0	0	12	53.0	226	53	22	21	3	3	1	2	17	1	34	0	0	3	3	.500	0	4-7	7	3.58	3.57
2001 St Louis	NL	34	34	2	0	216.1	909	218	86	76	13	14	5	13	54	3	185	5	1	22	8	.733	1	0-0	0	3.50	3.16
2002 St Louis	NL	32	32	1	0	210.1	890	210	86	80	16	7	8	6	64	3	171	3	0	17	9	.654	1	0-0	0	3.63	3.42
2003 St Louis	NL	27	27	5	0	172.1	703	164	76	72	20	5	3	4	39	1	120	3	0	11	8	.579	3	0-0	0	3.37	3.76
6 ML YEARS		174	143	13	12	982.2	4096	954	395	358	72	46	25	35	285	16	738	19	4	72	42	.632	6	4-7	7	3.46	3.28

Warren Morris

Bats: L **Throws:** R **Pos:** 2B-89; PH-11; PR-1 **Ht:** 5'11" **Wt:** 180 **Born:** 1/11/74 **Age:** 30

Year Team*	Lg	G	AB	H	2B	3B	HR	(Hm	Rd)	TB	R	RBI	RC	TBB	IBB	SO	HBP	SH	SF	SB	CS	SB%	GDP	Avg	OBP	Slg
2003 Toledo*	AAA	56	206	57	13	4	2	(-	-)	84	26	19	28	16	1	26	1	5	1	4	1	.80	4	.277	.330	.408
1999 Pittsburgh	NL	147	511	147	20	3	15	(9	6)	218	65	73	76	59	3	88	2	4	5	3	7	.30	12	.288	.360	.427
2000 Pittsburgh	NL	144	528	137	31	3	3	(3	0)	181	68	43	63	65	3	78	2	8	3	7	10	.41	7	.259	.341	.343
2001 Pittsburgh	NL	48	103	21	6	0	2	(2	0)	33	6	11	6	3	0	9	2	0	1	2	3	.40	2	.204	.239	.320
2002 Minnesota	AL	4	7	0	0	0	0	(0	0)	0	0	0	0	0	1	1	0	0	0	0	0	-	0	.000	.000	.000
2003 Detroit	AL	97	346	94	13	2	6	(4	2)	129	37	37	42	23	1	42	1	4	3	4	2	.67	6	.272	.316	.373
5 ML YEARS		440	1495	399	70	7	26	(18	8)	561	176	164	187	150	7	218	7	16	12	16	22	.42	27	.267	.334	.375

Damian Moss

Pitches: L **Bats:** R **Pos:** SP-29; RP-2 **Ht:** 6'0" **Wt:** 187 **Born:** 11/24/76 **Age:** 27

Year Team	Lg	G	GS	CG	GF	IP	BFP	H	R	ER	HR	SH	SF	HB	TBB	IBB	SO	WP	Bk	W	L	Pct	ShO	Sv-Op	Hld	ERC	ERA
2001 Atlanta	NL	5	1	0	2	9.0	41	3	3	3	1	1	0	0	9	0	8	1	0	0	0	-	0	0-0	0	2.61	3.00
2002 Atlanta	NL	33	29	0	2	179.0	743	140	80	68	20	12	3	6	89	5	111	13	2	12	6	.667	0	0-0	0	3.51	3.42
2003 SF-Bal		31	29	0	0	165.2	762	184	102	95	24	5	6	11	92	5	79	12	3	10	12	.455	0	0-0	0	5.97	5.16
2003 San Francisco	NL	21	20	0	0	115.0	518	121	62	60	12	3	4	5	63	3	57	11	3	9	7	.563	0	0-0	0	5.18	4.70
2003 Baltimore	AL	10	9	0	0	50.2	244	63	40	35	12	2	2	6	29	2	22	1	0	1	5	.167	0	0-0	0	7.87	6.22
3 ML YEARS		69	59	0	4	353.2	1546	327	185	166	45	18	9	17	190	10	198	26	5	22	18	.550	0	0-0	0	4.59	4.22

Guillermo Mota

Pitches: R **Bats:** R **Pos:** RP-76 **Ht:** 6'4" **Wt:** 205 **Born:** 7/25/73 **Age:** 30

Year Team	Lg	G	GS	CG	GF	IP	BFP	H	R	ER	HR	SH	SF	HB	TBB	IBB	SO	WP	Bk	W	L	Pct	ShO	Sv-Op	Hld	ERC	ERA
1999 Montreal	NL	51	0	0	18	55.1	243	54	24	18	5	3	3	2	25	3	27	1	1	2	4	.333	0	0-1	3	4.10	2.93
2000 Montreal	NL	29	0	0	7	30.0	126	27	21	20	3	1	1	2	12	0	24	1	1	1	1	.500	0	0-0	5	3.86	6.00
2001 Montreal	NL	53	0	0	12	49.2	212	51	30	29	9	3	2	1	18	1	31	1	0	1	3	.250	0	0-3	12	4.77	5.26

Year Team	Lg	G	GS	CG	GF	IP	BFP	H	R	ER	HR	SH	SF	HB	TBB	IBB	SO	WP	Bk	W	L	Pct	ShO	Sv-Op	Hld	ERC	ERA
2002 Los Angeles	NL	43	0	0	11	60.2	256	45	30	28	4	3	1	2	27	6	49	3	0	1	3	.250	0	0-1	4	2.57	4.15
2003 Los Angeles	NL	76	0	0	18	105.0	410	78	23	23	7	3	1	1	26	4	99	0	0	6	3	.667	0	1-3	13	2.01	1.97
5 ML YEARS		252	0	0	66	300.2	1247	255	128	118	28	13	8	8	108	14	230	6	2	11	14	.440	0	1-8	37	3.09	3.53

Tony Mounce

Pitches: L **Bats:** L **Pos:** SP-11 **Ht:** 6'2" **Wt:** 170 **Born:** 2/8/75 **Age:** 29

Year Team	Lg	G	GS	CG	GF	IP	BFP	H	R	ER	HR	SH	SF	HB	TBB	IBB	SO	WP	Bk	W	L	Pct	ShO	Sv-Op	Hld	ERC	ERA
1994 Astros	R	11	11	0	0	59.2	246	56	24	18	1	2	1	1	18	0	72	2	2	4	2	.667	0	0- -	-	2.92	2.72
1995 Quad City	A	25	25	3	0	159.0	649	118	55	43	6	6	6	3	57	2	143	6	2	16	8	.667	1	0- -	-	2.22	2.43
1996 Kissimmee	A+	25	25	4	0	155.2	675	139	65	39	7	6	3	10	68	1	102	7	0	9	9	.500	2	0- -	-	3.45	2.25
1997 New Orleans	AAA	1	1	0	0	4.2	21	2	1	1	1	0	0	0	6	0	6	0	0	0	0	-	0	0- -	-	5.34	1.93
1997 Jackson	AA	25	25	1	0	145.0	645	165	91	81	18	6	5	2	66	3	116	7	0	8	9	.471	0	0- -	-	5.37	5.03
1998 Jackson	AA	32	17	1	3	109.2	498	128	73	62	14	3	5	2	48	0	82	5	0	6	6	.500	0	0- -	-	5.46	5.09
1998 Kissimmee	A+	5	5	0	0	26.0	122	35	22	20	2	2	0	2	13	1	15	1	0	0	1	.000	0	0- -	-	6.79	6.92
1999 New Orleans	AAA	14	0	0	2	11.0	55	10	3	3	0	0	1	0	13	0	10	2	0	1	0	1.000	0	0- -	-	5.75	2.45
1999 Jackson	AA	31	6	0	11	68.1	300	64	33	28	6	1	1	2	30	0	80	5	0	5	2	.714	0	0- -	-	3.83	3.69
2000 Oklahoma	AAA	32	4	0	6	62.0	287	74	49	39	4	2	6	1	30	1	48	4	0	1	4	.200	0	1- -	-	5.24	5.66
2002 Charlotte	AAA	11	5	0	2	39.1	153	32	12	9	1	1	2	0	11	0	31	1	0	3	0	1.000	0	0- -	-	2.29	2.06
2002 Savannah	A	4	1	0	3	11.0	42	7	1	1	0	1	0	0	2	0	16	0	0	2	0	1.000	0	1- -	-	1.18	0.82
2002 Oklahoma	AAA	2	1	0	0	5.0	23	10	5	5	1	0	0	0	1	0	2	0	0	1	0	1.000	0	0- -	-	11.64	9.00
2002 Tulsa	AA	11	11	0	0	57.2	238	59	28	25	7	3	0	2	15	0	47	2	0	5	3	.625	0	0- -	-	4.05	3.90
2003 Frisco	AA	9	7	0	2	50.1	197	41	13	8	2	3	0	1	12	0	31	0	1	7	1	.875	0	0- -	-	2.28	1.43
2003 Oklahoma	AAA	11	11	2	0	66.1	274	60	25	25	6	1	0	0	26	0	51	2	0	2	4	.333	0	0- -	-	3.54	3.39
2003 Texas	AL	11	11	0	0	50.2	238	65	42	40	9	2	1	5	25	0	30	1	0	1	5	.167	0	0-0	0	7.34	7.11

Jamie Moyer

Pitches: L **Bats:** L **Pos:** SP-33 **Ht:** 6'0" **Wt:** 175 **Born:** 11/18/62 **Age:** 41

Year Team	Lg	G	GS	CG	GF	IP	BFP	H	R	ER	HR	SH	SF	HB	TBB	IBB	SO	WP	Bk	W	L	Pct	ShO	Sv-Op	Hld	ERC	ERA
1986 Chicago	NL	16	16	1	0	87.1	395	107	52	49	10	3	3	3	42	1	45	3	3	7	4	.636	1	0-0	0	6.13	5.05
1987 Chicago	NL	35	33	1	1	201.0	899	210	127	114	28	14	7	5	97	9	147	11	2	12	15	.444	0	0-0	0	4.96	5.10
1988 Chicago	NL	34	30	3	1	202.0	855	212	84	78	20	14	4	4	55	7	121	4	0	9	15	.375	1	0-2	0	3.89	3.48
1989 Texas	AL	15	15	1	0	76.0	337	84	51	41	10	1	4	2	33	0	44	1	0	4	9	.308	0	0-0	0	5.20	4.86
1990 Texas	AL	33	10	1	6	102.1	447	115	59	53	6	1	7	4	39	4	58	1	0	2	6	.250	0	0-0	1	4.57	4.66
1991 St Louis	NL	8	7	0	1	31.1	142	38	21	20	5	4	2	1	16	0	20	2	1	0	5	.000	0	0-0	0	6.58	5.74
1993 Baltimore	AL	25	25	3	0	152.0	630	154	63	58	11	3	1	6	38	2	90	1	1	12	9	.571	1	0-0	0	3.58	3.43
1994 Baltimore	AL	23	23	0	0	149.0	631	158	81	79	23	5	2	2	38	3	87	1	0	5	7	.417	0	0-0	0	4.24	4.77
1995 Baltimore	AL	27	18	0	3	115.2	483	117	70	67	18	5	3	3	30	0	65	0	0	8	6	.571	0	0-0	0	4.11	5.21
1996 Bos-Sea	AL	34	21	0	1	160.2	703	177	86	71	23	7	6	2	46	5	79	3	1	13	3	**.813**	1	0-0	1	4.42	3.98
1997 Seattle	AL	30	30	2	0	188.2	787	187	82	81	21	6	1	7	43	2	113	3	0	17	5	.773	0	0-0	0	3.56	3.86
1998 Seattle	AL	34	34	4	0	234.1	974	234	99	92	23	4	3	10	42	2	158	3	1	15	9	.625	3	0-0	0	3.34	3.53
1999 Seattle	AL	32	32	4	0	228.0	945	235	108	98	23	6	2	9	48	1	137	3	0	14	8	.636	0	0-0	0	3.71	3.87
2000 Seattle	AL	26	26	0	0	154.0	678	173	103	94	22	3	3	3	53	2	98	4	1	13	10	.565	0	0-0	0	4.91	5.49
2001 Seattle	AL	33	33	1	0	209.2	851	187	84	80	24	5	11	10	44	4	119	1	0	20	6	.769	0	0-0	0	3.03	3.43
2002 Seattle	AL	34	34	4	0	230.2	931	198	89	85	28	5	7	9	50	4	147	3	0	13	8	.619	2	0-0	0	2.89	3.32
2003 Seattle	AL	33	33	1	0	215.0	897	199	83	78	19	7	6	8	66	3	129	0	0	21	7	.750	0	0-0	0	3.37	3.27
1996 Boston	AL	23	10	0	1	90.0	405	111	50	45	14	4	3	1	27	2	50	2	1	7	1	.875	0	0-0	1	5.37	4.50
1996 Seattle	AL	11	11	0	0	70.2	298	66	36	26	9	3	3	1	19	3	29	1	0	6	2	.750	0	0-0	0	3.31	3.31
17 ML YEARS		472	420	26	13	2737.2	11585	2785	1342	1238	314	93	72	88	780	49	1657	44	10	185	132	.584	8	0-2	2	3.94	4.07

Bill Mueller

Bats: B **Throws:** R **Pos:** 3B-135; 2B-10; PH-7; SS-1 **Ht:** 5'10" **Wt:** 180 **Born:** 3/17/71 **Age:** 33

Year Team	Lg	G	AB	H	2B	3B	HR	(Hm	Rd)	TB	R	RBI	RC	TBB	IBB	SO	HBP	SH	SF	SB	CS	SB%	GDP	Avg	OBP	Slg
1996 San Francisco	NL	55	200	66	15	1	0	(0	0)	83	31	19	35	24	0	26	1	1	2	0	0	-	1	.330	.401	.415
1997 San Francisco	NL	128	390	114	26	3	7	(5	2)	167	51	44	62	48	1	71	3	6	6	4	3	.57	10	.292	.369	.428
1998 San Francisco	NL	145	534	157	27	0	9	(1	8)	211	93	59	83	79	1	83	1	3	5	3	3	.50	12	.294	.383	.395
1999 San Francisco	NL	116	414	120	24	0	2	(1	1)	150	61	36	62	65	1	52	3	8	2	4	2	.67	11	.290	.388	.362
2000 San Francisco	NL	153	560	150	29	4	10	(3	7)	217	97	55	72	52	0	62	6	7	6	4	2	.67	16	.268	.333	.388
2001 Chicago	NL	70	210	62	12	1	6	(3	3)	94	38	23	39	37	3	19	0	4	3	1	1	.50	4	.295	.403	.448
2002 ChC-SF	NL	111	366	96	19	4	7	(4	3)	144	51	38	55	52	2	42	0	4	5	0	0	-	9	.262	.350	.393
2003 Boston	AL	146	524	171	45	5	19	(6	13)	283	85	85	102	59	2	77	7	4	6	1	4	.20	11	**.326**	.398	.540
2002 Chicago	NL	103	353	94	19	4	7	(4	3)	142	51	37	55	51	2	41	0	4	5	0	0	-	8	.266	.355	.402
2002 San Francisco	NL	8	13	2	0	0	0	(0	0)	2	0	1	0	1	0	1	0	0	0	0	0	-	1	.154	.214	.154
8 ML YEARS		924	3198	936	197	18	60	(23	37)	1349	507	359	510	416	10	432	24	37	35	17	15	.53	74	.293	.375	.422

Mark Mulder

Pitches: L **Bats:** L **Pos:** SP-26 **Ht:** 6'6" **Wt:** 215 **Born:** 8/5/77 **Age:** 26

Year Team	Lg	G	GS	CG	GF	IP	BFP	H	R	ER	HR	SH	SF	HB	TBB	IBB	SO	WP	Bk	W	L	Pct	ShO	Sv-Op	Hld	ERC	ERA
2000 Oakland	AL	27	27	0	0	154.0	705	191	106	93	22	3	8	4	69	3	88	6	0	9	10	.474	0	0-0	0	6.14	5.44
2001 Oakland	AL	34	34	6	0	229.1	927	214	92	88	16	8	3	5	51	4	153	4	0	**21**	8	.724	**4**	0-0	0	2.95	3.45
2002 Oakland	AL	30	30	2	0	207.1	862	182	88	80	21	6	4	11	55	3	159	7	1	19	7	.731	1	0-0	0	3.06	3.47
2003 Oakland	AL	26	26	**9**	0	186.2	747	180	66	65	15	7	2	2	40	2	128	7	0	15	9	.625	**2**	0-0	0	3.17	3.13
4 ML YEARS		117	117	17	0	777.1	3241	767	352	326	74	24	17	22	215	12	528	24	1	64	34	.653	7	0-0	0	3.61	3.77

158

Terry Mulholland

Pitches: L Bats: R Pos: RP-42; SP-3   Ht: 6'3" Wt: 220 Born: 3/9/63 Age: 41

Year Team	Lg	G	GS	CG	GF	IP	BFP	H	R	ER	HR	SH	SF	HB	TBB	IBB	SO	WP	Bk	W	L	Pct	ShO	Sv-Op	Hld	ERC	ERA
1986 San Francisco	NL	15	10	0	1	54.2	245	51	33	30	3	5	1	1	35	2	27	6	0	1	7	.125	0	0-0	0	4.31	4.94
1988 San Francisco	NL	9	6	2	1	46.0	191	50	20	19	3	5	0	1	7	0	18	1	0	2	1	.667	0	0-0	1	3.46	3.72
1989 SF-Phi	NL	25	18	2	4	115.1	513	137	66	63	8	7	1	4	36	3	66	3	0	4	7	.364	1	0-0	1	4.64	4.92
1990 Philadelphia	NL	33	26	6	2	180.2	746	172	78	67	15	7	12	2	42	7	75	7	2	9	10	.474	1	0-1	0	3.04	3.34
1991 Philadelphia	NL	34	34	8	0	232.0	956	231	100	93	15	11	6	3	49	2	142	3	0	16	13	.552	3	0-0	0	3.15	3.61
1992 Philadelphia	NL	32	32	12	0	229.0	937	227	101	97	14	10	7	3	46	3	125	3	0	13	11	.542	2	0-0	0	3.07	3.81
1993 Philadelphia	NL	29	28	7	0	191.0	786	177	80	69	20	5	4	3	40	2	116	5	0	12	9	.571	2	0-0	0	2.99	3.25
1994 New York	AL	24	19	2	4	120.2	542	150	94	87	24	3	4	3	37	1	72	5	0	6	7	.462	0	0-0	0	5.92	6.49
1995 San Francisco	NL	29	24	2	2	149.0	666	190	112	96	25	11	6	4	38	1	65	4	0	5	13	.278	0	0-0	0	5.67	5.80
1996 Phi-Sea		33	33	3	0	202.2	871	232	112	105	22	11	8	5	49	4	86	6	0	13	11	.542	0	0-0	0	4.41	4.66
1997 ChC-SF	NL	40	27	1	5	186.2	794	190	100	88	24	17	4	11	51	3	99	3	0	6	13	.316	0	0-0	0	4.09	4.24
1998 Chicago	NL	70	6	0	14	112.0	476	100	49	36	7	5	3	4	39	7	72	4	0	6	5	.545	0	3-5	19	3.04	2.89
1999 ChC-Atl	NL	42	24	0	7	170.1	736	201	95	83	21	9	4	1	45	6	83	3	0	10	8	.556	0	1-1	4	4.73	4.39
2000 Atlanta	NL	54	20	1	14	156.2	702	198	96	89	24	10	5	4	41	7	78	3	0	9	9	.500	0	1-3	2	5.43	5.11
2001 Pit-LA	NL	41	4	0	8	65.2	285	78	35	34	12	1	1	2	17	1	42	1	0	1	1	.500	0	0-0	7	5.34	4.66
2002 LA-Cle		37	3	0	17	79.0	358	101	56	50	15	2	6	6	21	3	38	1	0	3	2	.600	0	0-0	2	6.08	5.70
2003 Cleveland	AL	45	3	0	14	99.0	444	117	60	54	17	0	6	6	37	6	42	1	0	3	4	.429	0	0-2	5	5.76	4.91
1989 San Francisco	NL	5	1	0	2	11.0	51	15	5	5	0	0	0	0	4	0	6	0	0	0	0	-	0	0-0	1	5.23	4.09
1989 Philadelphia	NL	20	17	2	2	104.1	462	122	61	58	8	7	1	4	32	3	60	3	0	4	7	.364	1	0-0	0	4.58	5.00
1996 Philadelphia	NL	21	21	3	0	133.1	571	157	74	69	17	6	5	3	21	1	52	5	0	8	7	.533	0	0-0	0	4.36	4.66
1996 Seattle	AL	12	12	0	0	69.1	300	75	38	36	5	5	3	2	28	3	34	1	0	5	4	.556	0	0-0	0	4.49	4.67
1997 Chicago	NL	25	25	1	0	157.0	668	162	79	71	20	13	3	9	45	2	74	2	0	6	12	.333	0	0-0	0	4.24	4.07
1997 San Francisco	NL	15	2	0	5	29.2	126	28	21	17	4	4	1	2	6	1	25	1	0	0	1	.000	0	0-0	1	3.34	5.16
1999 Chicago	NL	26	16	0	4	110.0	485	137	71	63	16	6	3	1	32	4	44	2	0	6	6	.500	0	0-0	1	5.42	5.15
1999 Atlanta	NL	16	8	0	3	60.1	251	64	24	20	5	3	1	0	13	2	39	1	0	4	2	.667	0	1-1	3	3.55	2.98
2001 Pittsburgh	NL	22	1	0	3	36.1	150	38	15	15	5	1	1	1	10	1	17	1	0	0	0	-	0	0-0	3	4.32	3.72
2001 Los Angeles	NL	19	3	0	5	29.1	135	40	20	19	7	0	0	1	7	0	25	0	0	1	1	.500	0	0-0	4	6.67	5.83
2002 Los Angeles	AL	21	0	0	12	32.0	148	45	29	26	10	0	2	2	7	0	17	1	0	0	0	-	0	0-0	0	7.62	7.31
2002 Cleveland	AL	16	3	0	5	47.0	210	56	27	24	5	2	4	4	14	3	21	0	0	3	2	.600	0	0-0	2	5.05	4.60
17 ML YEARS		592	317	46	93	2390.1	10248	2602	1287	1160	269	119	78	63	630	58	1246	59	2	119	131	.476	10	5-12	39	4.18	4.37

Scott Mullen

Pitches: L Bats: R Pos: RP-2; SP-1   Ht: 6'2" Wt: 195 Born: 1/17/75 Age: 29

Year Team	Lg	G	GS	CG	GF	IP	BFP	H	R	ER	HR	SH	SF	HB	TBB	IBB	SO	WP	Bk	W	L	Pct	ShO	Sv-Op	Hld	ERC	ERA
2003 Omaha*	AAA	20	9	0	6	69.2	300	75	35	30	3	3	4	3	22	1	50	2	0	5	3	.625	0	1--	-	3.94	3.88
2003 Las Vegas*	AAA	7	7	0	0	41.0	177	50	22	18	4	2	1	1	14	0	23	0	0	4	2	.667	0	0--	-	5.41	3.95
2000 Kansas City	AL	11	0	0	5	10.1	44	10	5	5	2	0	0	0	3	0	7	0	0	0	0	-	0	0-0	2	4.00	4.35
2001 Kansas City	AL	17	0	0	2	10.0	52	13	6	5	0	0	1	0	9	0	3	0	0	0	0	-	0	0-0	1	6.89	4.50
2002 Kansas City	AL	44	0	0	10	40.0	171	40	16	14	5	4	2	2	13	2	21	1	0	4	5	.444	0	0-2	6	4.08	3.15
2003 KC-LA		3	1	0	0	7.1	46	13	11	11	2	0	1	1	10	0	4	1	0	0	0	-	0	0-0	0	15.81	13.50
2003 Kansas City	AL	2	0	0	0	4.1	29	11	8	8	2	0	0	0	5	0	3	1	0	0	0	-	0	0-0	0	22.33	16.62
2003 Los Angeles	NL	1	1	0	0	3.0	17	2	3	3	0	0	1	1	5	0	1	0	0	0	0	-	0	0-0	0	7.34	9.00
4 ML YEARS		75	1	0	17	67.2	313	76	38	35	9	4	4	3	35	2	35	2	0	4	5	.444	0	0-2	9	5.59	4.66

Pete Munro

Pitches: R Bats: R Pos: RP-38; SP-2   Ht: 6'2" Wt: 200 Born: 6/14/75 Age: 29

Year Team	Lg	G	GS	CG	GF	IP	BFP	H	R	ER	HR	SH	SF	HB	TBB	IBB	SO	WP	Bk	W	L	Pct	ShO	Sv-Op	Hld	ERC	ERA
2003 New Orleans*	AAA	5	4	0	0	22.1	106	28	16	15	1	2	1	0	12	1	12	0	0	0	4	.000	0	0--	-	5.50	6.04
1999 Toronto	AL	31	2	0	9	55.1	250	70	38	37	6	1	4	2	23	0	38	3	0	0	2	.000	0	0-1	4	6.04	6.02
2000 Toronto	AL	9	3	0	2	25.2	127	38	22	17	1	1	0	3	16	0	16	1	0	1	1	.500	0	0-0	0	8.18	5.96
2002 Houston	NL	19	14	0	0	80.2	347	89	37	32	5	7	0	3	23	3	45	2	0	5	5	.500	0	0-0	1	4.04	3.57
2003 Houston	NL	40	2	0	8	54.0	249	63	30	28	7	3	1	5	26	2	27	1	0	3	4	.429	0	0-1	3	5.97	4.67
4 ML YEARS		99	21	0	19	215.2	973	260	127	114	19	12	5	13	88	5	126	7	0	9	12	.429	0	0-2	8	5.49	4.76

Eric Munson

Bats: L Throws: R Pos: 3B-91; PH-8   Ht: 6'3" Wt: 228 Born: 10/3/77 Age: 26

								BATTING													BASERUNNING			AVERAGES		
Year Team	Lg	G	AB	H	2B	3B	HR	(Hm	Rd)	TB	R	RBI	RC	TBB	IBB	SO	HBP	SH	SF	SB	CS	SB%	GDP	Avg	OBP	Slg
2000 Detroit	AL	3	5	0	0	0	0	(0	0)	0	0	1	0	0	0	1	0	0	0	0	0	-	0	.000	.000	.000
2001 Detroit	AL	17	66	10	3	1	1	(1	0)	18	4	6	2	3	0	21	0	0	0	0	1	.00	2	.152	.188	.273
2002 Detroit	AL	18	59	11	0	0	2	(0	2)	17	3	5	2	6	0	11	1	0	1	0	0	-	1	.186	.269	.288
2003 Detroit	AL	99	313	75	9	0	18	(7	11)	138	28	50	45	35	1	61	1	1	7	3	0	1.00	4	.240	.312	.441
4 ML YEARS		137	443	96	12	1	21	(8	13)	173	35	62	49	44	1	94	2	1	8	3	1	.75	7	.217	.286	.391

Mike Mussina

Pitches: R Bats: L Pos: SP-31   Ht: 6'2" Wt: 185 Born: 12/8/68 Age: 35

Year Team	Lg	G	GS	CG	GF	IP	BFP	H	R	ER	HR	SH	SF	HB	TBB	IBB	SO	WP	Bk	W	L	Pct	ShO	Sv-Op	Hld	ERC	ERA
1991 Baltimore	AL	12	12	2	0	87.2	349	77	31	28	7	3	2	1	21	0	52	3	1	4	5	.444	0	0-0	0	2.80	2.87
1992 Baltimore	AL	32	32	8	0	241.0	957	212	70	68	16	13	6	2	48	2	130	6	0	18	5	.783	0	0-0	0	2.54	2.54
1993 Baltimore	AL	25	25	3	0	167.2	693	163	84	83	20	6	4	3	44	2	117	5	0	14	6	.700	2	0-0	0	3.61	4.46
1994 Baltimore	AL	24	24	3	0	176.1	712	163	63	60	19	3	9	1	42	1	99	0	0	16	5	.762	0	0-0	0	3.16	3.06
1995 Baltimore	AL	32	32	7	0	221.2	882	187	86	81	24	2	2	1	50	4	158	2	0	19	9	.679	4	0-0	0	2.66	3.29
1996 Baltimore	AL	36	36	4	0	243.1	1039	264	137	130	31	4	4	3	69	0	204	3	0	19	11	.633	1	0-0	0	4.36	4.81
1997 Baltimore	AL	33	33	4	0	224.2	905	197	87	80	27	3	2	3	54	3	218	5	0	15	8	.652	1	0-0	0	3.00	3.20

			HOW MUCH HE PITCHED						WHAT HE GAVE UP												THE RESULTS							
Year Team	Lg	G	GS	CG	GF	IP	BFP	H	R	ER	HR	SH	SF	HB	TBB	IBB	SO	WP	Bk	W	L	Pct	ShO	Sv-Op	Hld	ERC	ERA
1998 Baltimore	AL	29	29	4	0	206.1	835	189	85	80	22	6	3	4	41	3	175	10	0	13	10	.565	2	0-0	0	2.96	3.49
1999 Baltimore	AL	31	31	4	0	203.1	842	207	88	79	16	9	7	1	52	0	172	2	0	18	7	.720	0	0-0	0	3.54	3.50
2000 Baltimore	AL	34	34	6	0	**237.2**	987	236	105	100	28	**8**	6	3	46	0	210	3	0	11	15	.423	1	0-0	0	3.37	3.79
2001 New York	AL	34	34	4	0	228.2	909	202	87	80	20	5	6	4	42	2	214	6	0	17	11	.607	3	0-0	0	2.65	3.15
2002 New York	AL	33	33	2	0	215.2	886	208	103	97	27	5	5	5	48	1	182	7	0	18	10	.643	2	0-0	0	3.46	4.05
2003 New York	AL	31	31	2	0	214.2	855	192	86	81	21	1	4	3	40	4	195	4	0	17	8	.680	1	0-0	0	2.75	3.40
13 ML YEARS		386	386	53	0	2668.2	10851	2497	1112	1047	278	68	60	34	597	22	2126	56	1	199	110	.644	21	0-0	0	3.14	3.53

Brett Myers

Pitches: R Bats: R Pos: SP-32   Ht: 6'4" Wt: 215 Born: 8/17/80 Age: 23

			HOW MUCH HE PITCHED						WHAT HE GAVE UP												THE RESULTS							
Year Team	Lg	G	GS	CG	GF	IP	BFP	H	R	ER	HR	SH	SF	HB	TBB	IBB	SO	WP	Bk	W	L	Pct	ShO	Sv-Op	Hld	ERC	ERA
1999 Phillies	R	7	5	0	0	27.0	105	17	8	7	0	0	0	2	7	0	30	2	0	2	1	.667	0	0--	-	1.49	2.33
2000 Piedmont	A	27	27	2	0	175.1	738	165	78	62	7	1	4	9	69	0	140	8	0	13	7	.650	1	0--	-	3.58	3.18
2001 Reading	AA	26	23	1	0	156.0	661	156	71	67	21	3	1	10	43	1	130	5	0	13	4	.765	1	0--	-	4.09	3.87
2002 Scrtn/WlksBr	AAA	19	19	4	0	128.0	509	121	54	51	9	3	3	3	20	0	97	1	0	9	6	.600	1	0--	-	2.82	3.59
2002 Philadelphia	NL	12	12	1	0	72.0	307	73	38	34	11	6	2	6	29	1	34	2	1	4	5	.444	0	0-0	0	5.04	4.25
2003 Philadelphia	NL	32	32	1	0	193.0	848	205	99	95	20	6	3	9	76	8	143	9	0	14	9	.609	1	0-0	0	4.56	4.43
2 ML YEARS		44	44	2	0	265.0	1155	278	137	129	31	12	5	15	105	9	177	11	1	18	14	.563	1	0-0	0	4.69	4.38

Greg Myers

Bats: L Throws: R Pos: C-81; PH-33; DH-19   Ht: 6'2" Wt: 225 Born: 4/14/66 Age: 38

								BATTING													BASERUNNING				AVERAGES		
Year Team	Lg	G	AB	H	2B	3B	HR	(Hm Rd)	TB	R	RBI	RC	TBB	IBB	SO	HBP	SH	SF	SB	CS	SB%	GDP	Avg	OBP	Slg
1987 Toronto	AL	7	9	1	0	0	0	(0 0)	1	1	0	0	0	0	3	0	0	0	0	0	-	2	.111	.111	.111
1989 Toronto	AL	17	44	5	2	0	0	(0 0)	7	0	1	0	2	0	9	0	0	0	0	1	.00	2	.114	.152	.159
1990 Toronto	AL	87	250	59	7	1	5	(3 2)	83	33	22	21	22	0	33	0	1	4	0	1	.00	12	.236	.293	.332
1991 Toronto	AL	107	309	81	22	0	8	(5 3)	127	25	36	35	21	4	45	0	0	3	0	0	-	13	.262	.306	.411
1992 Tor-Ana	AL	30	78	18	7	0	1	(0 1)	28	4	13	7	5	0	11	0	1	2	0	0	-	2	.231	.271	.359
1993 Anaheim	AL	108	290	74	10	0	7	(4 3)	105	27	40	29	17	2	47	2	3	3	3	3	.50	8	.255	.298	.362
1994 Anaheim	AL	45	126	31	6	0	2	(1 1)	43	10	8	12	10	3	27	0	5	1	0	2	.00	3	.246	.299	.341
1995 Anaheim	AL	85	273	71	12	2	9	(6 3)	114	35	38	34	17	3	49	1	1	2	0	1	.00	4	.260	.304	.418
1996 Minnesota	AL	97	329	94	22	3	5	(3 2)	140	37	47	42	19	3	52	0	0	5	0	0	-	11	.286	.320	.426
1997 Min-Atl	AL	71	174	45	11	1	5	(3 2)	73	24	29	23	17	2	32	0	0	2	0	0	-	4	.259	.321	.420
1998 San Diego	NL	69	171	42	10	0	4	(1 3)	64	19	20	18	17	1	36	0	0	1	0	0	.00	6	.246	.312	.374
1999 SD-Atl	NL	84	200	53	6	0	5	(3 2)	74	19	24	26	26	4	30	0	0	1	0	0	-	6	.265	.348	.370
2000 Baltimore	AL	43	125	28	6	0	3	(1 2)	43	9	12	9	8	0	29	0	1	0	0	0	-	7	.224	.271	.344
2001 Bal-Oak	AL	58	161	36	3	0	11	(5 6)	72	24	31	22	21	1	38	0	0	0	0	0	-	5	.224	.313	.447
2002 Oakland	AL	65	144	32	5	0	6	(2 4)	55	15	21	17	26	3	36	0	0	0	0	0	-	4	.222	.341	.382
2003 Toronto	AL	121	329	101	19	0	15	(8 7)	165	51	52	51	37	2	57	0	0	3	0	3	.00	14	.307	.374	.502
1992 Toronto	AL	22	61	14	6	0	1	(0 1)	23	4	13	6	5	0	5	0	0	2	0	0	-	2	.230	.279	.377
1992 Anaheim	AL	8	17	4	1	0	0	(0 0)	5	0	0	1	0	0	6	0	0	0	0	0	-	0	.235	.235	.294
1997 Minnesota	AL	62	165	44	11	1	5	(3 2)	72	24	28	23	16	2	29	0	0	0	0	0	-	4	.267	.328	.436
1997 Atlanta	NL	9	9	1	0	0	0	(0 0)	1	0	1	0	1	0	3	0	0	0	0	0	-	0	.111	.200	.111
1999 San Diego	NL	50	128	37	4	0	3	(2 1)	50	9	15	17	13	2	14	0	0	0	0	0	-	5	.289	.355	.391
1999 Atlanta	NL	34	72	16	2	0	2	(1 1)	24	10	9	9	13	2	16	0	0	1	0	0	-	1	.222	.337	.333
2001 Baltimore	AL	25	74	20	2	0	4	(3 1)	34	11	18	11	8	0	17	0	0	0	0	0	-	3	.270	.341	.459
2001 Oakland	AL	33	87	16	1	0	7	(2 5)	38	13	13	11	13	1	21	0	0	0	0	0	-	2	.184	.290	.437
16 ML YEARS		1094	3012	771	148	7	87	(45 42)	1194	333	394	346	265	28	534	3	12	27	3	12	.20	103	.256	.314	.396

Mike Myers

Pitches: L Bats: L Pos: RP-64   Ht: 6'4" Wt: 212 Born: 6/26/69 Age: 35

			HOW MUCH HE PITCHED						WHAT HE GAVE UP												THE RESULTS							
Year Team	Lg	G	GS	CG	GF	IP	BFP	H	R	ER	HR	SH	SF	HB	TBB	IBB	SO	WP	Bk	W	L	Pct	ShO	Sv-Op	Hld	ERC	ERA
1995 Fla-Det		13	0	0	5	8.1	42	11	7	7	1	0	1	2	7	0	4	0	0	1	0	1.000	0	0-1	1	9.61	7.56
1996 Detroit	AL	**83**	0	0	25	64.2	298	70	41	36	6	2	1	4	34	8	69	2	0	1	5	.167	0	6-8	17	4.97	5.01
1997 Detroit	AL	**88**	0	0	23	53.2	246	58	36	34	12	4	3	2	25	2	50	0	0	0	4	.000	0	2-5	18	5.70	5.70
1998 Milwaukee	NL	70	0	0	14	50.0	211	44	19	15	5	4	2	6	22	1	40	2	1	2	2	.500	0	1-3	**23**	4.14	2.70
1999 Milwaukee	NL	71	0	0	14	41.1	179	46	24	24	7	5	0	3	13	1	35	1	0	2	1	.667	0	0-3	14	5.24	5.23
2000 Colorado	NL	78	0	0	22	45.1	177	24	10	10	2	1	0	2	24	3	41	1	0	0	1	.000	0	1-2	15	1.94	1.99
2001 Colorado	NL	73	0	0	14	40.0	169	32	17	16	2	1	1	1	24	7	36	0	0	2	3	.400	0	0-2	10	3.29	3.60
2002 Arizona	NL	69	0	0	15	37.0	171	39	18	18	2	3	1	8	17	0	31	0	0	4	3	.571	0	4-9	17	5.13	4.38
2003 Arizona	NL	64	0	0	17	36.1	172	38	23	23	4	1	0	5	21	1	21	1	0	1	0	1.000	0	0-3	6	5.54	5.70
1995 Florida	NL	2	0	0	2	2.0	9	1	0	0	0	0	0	0	3	0	0	0	0	0	0	-	0	0-0	0	5.03	0.00
1995 Detroit	AL	11	0	0	3	6.1	33	10	7	7	1	0	1	2	4	0	4	0	0	1	0	1.000	0	0-1	1	11.13	9.95
9 ML YEARS		609	0	0	149	376.2	1665	362	195	183	41	21	9	33	187	23	327	7	1	12	20	.375	0	14-36	121	4.58	4.37

Rodney Myers

Pitches: R Bats: R Pos: RP-4   Ht: 6'1" Wt: 215 Born: 6/26/69 Age: 35

			HOW MUCH HE PITCHED						WHAT HE GAVE UP												THE RESULTS							
Year Team	Lg	G	GS	CG	GF	IP	BFP	H	R	ER	HR	SH	SF	HB	TBB	IBB	SO	WP	Bk	W	L	Pct	ShO	Sv-Op	Hld	ERC	ERA
2003 Las Vegas*	AAA	46	1	0	10	71.0	299	66	32	26	4	2	2	5	22	1	48	3	1	9	1	.900	0	1--	-	3.31	3.30
1996 Chicago	NL	45	0	0	8	67.1	298	61	38	35	6	1	5	3	38	3	50	4	1	2	1	.667	0	0-0	4	4.20	4.68
1997 Chicago	NL	5	1	0	2	9.0	44	12	6	6	1	0	0	1	7	1	6	0	0	0	0	-	0	0-0	0	8.42	6.00
1998 Chicago	NL	12	0	0	3	18.0	82	26	14	14	3	0	0	6	6	0	15	1	0	0	1	.000	0	0-1	0	7.19	7.00
1999 Chicago	NL	46	0	0	5	63.2	278	71	34	31	10	4	2	1	25	2	41	2	0	3	1	.750	0	0-1	8	5.22	4.38
2000 San Diego	NL	3	0	0	1	2.0	8	2	1	1	0	0	0	0	0	0	3	1	0	0	0	-	0	0-0	0	1.95	4.50
2001 San Diego	NL	37	0	0	16	47.1	211	53	31	28	6	1	4	4	20	0	29	2	0	1	2	.333	0	1-2	3	5.50	5.32

HOW MUCH HE PITCHED								WHAT HE GAVE UP												THE RESULTS							
Year Team	Lg	G	GS	CG	GF	IP	BFP	H	R	ER	HR	SH	SF	HB	TBB	IBB	SO	WP	Bk	W	L	Pct	ShO	Sv-Op	Hld	ERC	ERA
2002 San Diego	NL	14	0	0	4	21.1	101	29	20	14	1	1	0	3	10	0	11	2	0	1	1	.500	0	0-0	2	6.83	5.91
2003 Los Angeles	NL	4	0	0	3	9.0	42	10	7	6	1	0	0	1	4	0	5	0	0	0	0	-	0	0-0	0	5.30	6.00
8 ML YEARS		166	1	0	42	237.2	1064	264	151	135	28	7	11	13	110	6	160	12	1	7	5	.583	0	1-4	14	5.35	5.11

Aaron Myette

Pitches: R **Bats:** R **Pos:** RP-2   **Ht:** 6'4" **Wt:** 210 **Born:** 9/26/77 **Age:** 26

HOW MUCH HE PITCHED								WHAT HE GAVE UP												THE RESULTS							
Year Team	Lg	G	GS	CG	GF	IP	BFP	H	R	ER	HR	SH	SF	HB	TBB	IBB	SO	WP	Bk	W	L	Pct	ShO	Sv-Op	Hld	ERC	ERA
2003 Akron*	AA	3	0	0	0	5.0	18	0	0	0	0	0	0	0	2	0	7	0	0	0	0	-	0	0- -	-	0.17	0.00
2003 Buffalo*	AAA	23	1	0	9	33.1	154	33	21	17	4	3	2	0	23	1	25	6	0	0	0	-	0	1- -	-	5.23	4.59
2003 Scrtn/WlksBr*	AAA	11	10	0	1	59.0	245	50	28	28	4	2	1	4	20	0	54	1	0	5	4	.556	0	0- -	-	3.08	4.27
1999 Chicago	AL	4	3	0	0	15.2	80	17	11	11	2	0	0	2	14	1	11	2	0	0	2	.000	0	0-0	0	7.09	6.32
2000 Chicago	AL	2	0	0	1	2.2	12	0	0	0	0	0	0	0	4	0	1	0	0	0	0	-	0	0-0	0	1.96	0.00
2001 Texas	AL	19	15	0	1	80.2	376	94	65	64	12	3	4	11	37	0	67	2	0	4	5	.444	0	0-0	0	6.23	7.14
2002 Texas	AL	15	12	0	2	48.1	248	64	57	54	11	1	4	6	41	0	48	5	0	2	5	.286	0	0-0	0	9.83	10.06
2003 Cleveland	AL	2	0	0	1	2.2	18	7	7	7	1	0	0	1	2	0	1	0	0	0	0	-	0	0-0	0	21.83	23.63
5 ML YEARS		42	30	0	5	150.0	734	182	140	136	26	4	8	20	98	1	128	9	0	6	12	.333	0	0-0	0	7.59	8.16

Xavier Nady

Bats: R **Throws:** R **Pos:** RF-105; PH-8; PR-3   **Ht:** 6'0" **Wt:** 180 **Born:** 11/14/78 **Age:** 25

BATTING																	BASERUNNING				AVERAGES		
Year Team	Lg	G	AB	H	2B	3B	HR	(Hm | Rd)	TB	R	RBI	RC	TBB	IBB	SO	HBP	SH	SF	SB	CS	SB%	GDP	Avg	OBP	Slg
2001 Lk Elsinore	A+	137	524	158	38	1	26	(- | -)	276	96	100	102	62	7	109	10	0	8	6	0	1.00	14	.302	.381	.527
2002 Lk Elsinore	A+	45	169	47	6	3	13	(- | -)	98	41	37	37	28	4	40	1	0	1	2	0	1.00	2	.278	.382	.580
2002 Portland	AAA	85	315	89	12	1	10	(- | -)	133	46	43	41	20	0	60	3	0	2	0	1	.00	11	.283	.329	.422
2003 Portland	AAA	37	136	36	7	0	7	(- | -)	64	19	23	21	12	0	28	2	0	2	0	0	-	2	.265	.329	.471
2000 San Diego	NL	1	1	1	0	0	0	(0 | 0)	1	1	0	1	0	0	0	0	0	0	0	0	-	0	1.000	1.000	1.000
2003 San Diego	NL	110	371	99	17	1	9	(5 | 4)	145	50	39	39	24	0	74	6	2	1	6	2	.75	14	.267	.321	.391
2 ML YEARS		111	372	100	17	1	9	(5 | 4)	146	51	39	40	24	0	74	6	2	1	6	2	.75	14	.269	.323	.392

Charles Nagy

Pitches: R **Bats:** L **Pos:** RP-5   **Ht:** 6'3" **Wt:** 200 **Born:** 5/5/67 **Age:** 37

HOW MUCH HE PITCHED								WHAT HE GAVE UP												THE RESULTS							
Year Team	Lg	G	GS	CG	GF	IP	BFP	H	R	ER	HR	SH	SF	HB	TBB	IBB	SO	WP	Bk	W	L	Pct	ShO	Sv-Op	Hld	ERC	ERA
2003 Portland*	AAA	3	1	0	1	7.1	28	8	1	1	1	0	0	1	0	0	5	0	0	1	0	1.000	0	1- -	-	4.15	1.23
1990 Cleveland	AL	9	8	0	1	45.2	208	58	31	30	7	1	1	1	21	1	26	1	1	2	4	.333	0	0-0	0	6.54	5.91
1991 Cleveland	AL	33	33	6	0	211.1	914	228	103	97	15	5	9	6	66	7	109	6	2	10	15	.400	1	0-0	0	4.02	4.13
1992 Cleveland	AL	33	33	10	0	252.0	1018	245	91	83	11	6	9	2	57	1	169	7	0	17	10	.630	3	0-0	0	2.99	2.96
1993 Cleveland	AL	9	9	1	0	48.2	223	66	38	34	6	2	1	2	13	1	30	2	0	2	6	.250	0	0-0	0	5.90	6.29
1994 Cleveland	AL	23	23	3	0	169.1	717	175	76	65	15	2	2	5	48	1	108	5	1	10	8	.556	0	0-0	0	3.86	3.45
1995 Cleveland	AL	29	29	2	0	178.0	771	194	95	90	20	2	5	6	61	0	139	2	0	16	6	.727	1	0-0	0	4.63	4.55
1996 Cleveland	AL	32	32	5	0	222.0	921	217	89	84	21	2	4	3	61	2	167	7	0	17	5	.773	0	0-0	0	3.50	3.41
1997 Cleveland	AL	34	34	1	0	227.0	991	253	115	108	27	5	6	7	77	4	149	5	0	15	11	.577	1	0-0	0	4.74	4.28
1998 Cleveland	AL	33	33	2	0	210.1	930	250	122	122	34	8	6	9	66	12	120	3	0	15	10	.600	0	0-0	0	5.39	5.22
1999 Cleveland	AL	33	32	1	0	202.0	887	238	120	111	26	5	4	6	59	4	126	3	0	17	11	.607	0	0-0	0	4.97	4.95
2000 Cleveland	AL	11	11	0	0	57.0	267	71	53	52	15	5	2	2	21	2	41	1	0	2	7	.222	0	0-0	0	6.54	8.21
2001 Cleveland	AL	15	13	0	1	70.1	325	102	53	50	10	3	4	0	20	1	29	2	0	5	6	.455	0	0-0	0	6.60	6.40
2002 Cleveland	AL	19	7	0	0	48.2	231	76	51	48	10	2	4	2	13	1	22	1	0	1	4	.200	0	0-0	0	7.98	8.88
2003 San Diego	NL	5	0	0	0	12.1	52	15	7	6	0	1	0	0	3	0	7	0	0	0	2	.000	0	0-0	0	4.10	4.38
14 ML YEARS		318	297	31	9	1954.2	8455	2188	1061	980	217	49	55	51	586	37	1242	45	4	129	105	.551	6	0-0	0	4.53	4.51

Mike Nakamura

Pitches: R **Bats:** R **Pos:** RP-12   **Ht:** 5'10" **Wt:** 178 **Born:** 9/6/76 **Age:** 27

HOW MUCH HE PITCHED								WHAT HE GAVE UP												THE RESULTS							
Year Team	Lg	G	GS	CG	GF	IP	BFP	H	R	ER	HR	SH	SF	HB	TBB	IBB	SO	WP	Bk	W	L	Pct	ShO	Sv-Op	Hld	ERC	ERA
1998 Fort Wayne	A	29	9	0	6	80.0	347	82	41	29	8	4	3	3	29	0	70	3	2	2	5	.286	0	1- -	-	4.21	3.26
1998 Fort Myers	A+	8	6	1	1	28.2	123	28	15	11	3	2	0	2	10	0	21	1	0	1	3	.250	0	0- -	-	4.07	3.45
1999 Fort Myers	A+	14	0	0	6	19.2	74	9	5	4	1	2	2	0	5	0	18	1	0	2	0	1.000	0	2- -	-	0.99	1.83
2000 Fort Myers	A+	32	0	0	19	41.1	162	33	9	7	0	2	1	1	11	1	46	2	0	1	0	1.000	0	12- -	-	2.13	1.52
2001 New Britain	AA	48	1	0	19	86.1	357	75	20	17	3	3	1	2	24	5	109	3	0	5	1	.833	0	5- -	-	2.47	1.77
2002 Edmonton	AAA	46	4	0	7	87.1	368	85	51	46	7	0	5	6	22	0	80	7	1	4	3	.571	0	2- -	-	3.48	4.74
2003 Minnesota	AL	12	0	0	7	12.2	62	20	11	11	4	0	0	1	2	0	14	0	0	0	0	-	0	1-1	1	8.35	7.82

Shane Nance

Pitches: L **Bats:** L **Pos:** RP-26   **Ht:** 5'8" **Wt:** 180 **Born:** 9/7/77 **Age:** 26

HOW MUCH HE PITCHED								WHAT HE GAVE UP												THE RESULTS							
Year Team	Lg	G	GS	CG	GF	IP	BFP	H	R	ER	HR	SH	SF	HB	TBB	IBB	SO	WP	Bk	W	L	Pct	ShO	Sv-Op	Hld	ERC	ERA
2000 Yakima	A-	12	9	0	0	58.0	228	41	19	16	1	2	0	2	22	0	66	2	0	2	4	.333	0	0- -	-	2.17	2.48
2001 Vero Beach	A+	21	0	0	13	48.0	196	28	15	14	3	1	0	3	21	1	63	2	0	6	3	.667	0	4- -	-	2.00	2.63
2001 Jacksonville	AA	28	0	0	11	45.1	179	31	11	8	4	2	1	0	17	1	44	1	0	7	0	1.000	0	1- -	-	2.28	1.59
2002 Las Vegas	AAA	37	0	0	10	58.1	255	58	32	27	5	2	2	2	26	1	53	1	0	11	3	.786	0	4- -	-	4.23	4.17
2002 Indianapolis	AAA	9	0	0	4	16.2	67	12	0	0	0	0	0	3	6	0	10	0	2	3	0	1.000	0	0- -	-	2.56	0.00
2003 Indianapolis	AAA	35	1	0	7	52.1	201	34	10	8	4	2	1	1	13	1	53	1	0	2	4	.333	0	3- -	-	1.70	1.38
2002 Milwaukee	NL	4	0	0	0	6.1	27	4	3	3	1	0	0	0	4	0	5	0	0	0	0	-	0	0- -	-	3.29	4.26
2003 Milwaukee	NL	26	0	0	6	24.1	118	34	16	13	5	1	2	1	10	1	25	1	0	0	2	.000	0	0-1	1	7.31	4.81
2 ML YEARS		30	0	0	6	30.2	145	38	19	16	6	1	2	1	14	1	30	1	0	0	2	.000	0	0-1	1	6.41	4.70

Joe Nathan

Pitches: R **Bats:** R **Pos:** RP-78 | **Ht:** 6'4" **Wt:** 195 **Born:** 11/22/74 **Age:** 29

Year Team	Lg	G	GS	CG	GF	IP	BFP	H	R	ER	HR	SH	SF	HB	TBB	IBB	SO	WP	Bk	W	L	Pct	ShO	Sv-Op	Hld	ERC	ERA
1999 San Francisco	NL	19	14	0	2	90.1	395	84	45	42	17	2	0	1	46	0	54	2	0	7	4	.636	0	1-1	0	4.78	4.18
2000 San Francisco	NL	20	15	0	0	93.1	426	89	63	54	12	5	5	4	63	4	61	5	0	5	2	.714	0	0-1	0	5.23	5.21
2002 San Francisco	NL	4	0	0	3	3.2	12	1	0	0	0	0	0	0	0	0	2	0	0	0	0	—	0	0-0	0	0.17	0.00
2003 San Francisco	NL	78	0	0	9	79.0	316	51	26	26	7	2	4	3	33	3	83	4	1	12	4	.750	0	0-3	20	2.34	2.96
4 ML YEARS		121	29	0	14	266.1	1149	225	134	122	36	9	9	8	142	7	200	11	1	24	10	.706	0	1-5	20	4.06	4.12

Denny Neagle

Pitches: L **Bats:** L **Pos:** SP-7 | **Ht:** 6'3" **Wt:** 225 **Born:** 9/13/68 **Age:** 35

Year Team	Lg	G	GS	CG	GF	IP	BFP	H	R	ER	HR	SH	SF	HB	TBB	IBB	SO	WP	Bk	W	L	Pct	ShO	Sv-Op	Hld	ERC	ERA
2003 Visalia*	A+	2	2	0	0	10.0	37	4	0	0	0	0	0	1	2	0	13	1	0	1	0	1.000	0	0--	-	0.79	0.00
2003 Co Springs*	AAA	4	4	0	0	24.0	101	28	10	9	2	1	0	0	4	0	16	0	0	3	0	1.000	0	0--	-	4.00	3.38
1991 Minnesota	AL	7	3	0	2	20.0	92	28	9	9	3	0	0	0	7	2	14	1	0	0	1	.000	0	0-0	0	6.53	4.05
1992 Pittsburgh	NL	55	6	0	8	86.1	380	81	46	43	9	4	3	2	43	8	77	3	2	4	6	.400	0	2-4	5	4.04	4.48
1993 Pittsburgh	NL	50	7	0	13	81.1	360	82	49	48	10	1	1	3	37	3	73	5	0	3	5	.375	0	1-1	6	4.57	5.31
1994 Pittsburgh	NL	24	24	2	0	137.0	587	135	80	78	18	7	6	3	49	3	122	2	0	9	10	.474	0	0-0	0	4.09	5.12
1995 Pittsburgh	NL	31	31	5	0	209.2	876	221	91	80	20	13	6	3	45	3	150	6	0	13	8	.619	1	0-0	0	3.67	3.43
1996 Pit-Atl	NL	33	33	2	0	221.1	910	226	93	86	26	10	4	3	48	2	149	3	1	16	9	.640	0	0-0	0	3.69	3.50
1997 Atlanta	NL	34	34	4	0	233.1	947	204	87	77	18	12	6	6	49	5	172	3	0	20	5	.800	4	0-0	0	2.60	2.97
1998 Atlanta	NL	32	31	5	0	210.1	861	196	91	83	25	7	3	6	60	3	165	6	1	16	11	.593	2	0-0	0	3.55	3.55
1999 Cincinnati	NL	20	19	0	0	111.2	467	95	54	53	23	3	5	4	40	3	76	4	0	9	5	.643	0	0-0	0	3.88	4.27
2000 Cin-NYY		34	33	1	0	209.0	906	210	109	105	31	8	6	5	81	4	146	7	1	15	9	.625	0	0-0	0	4.45	4.52
2001 Colorado	NL	30	30	0	0	170.2	760	192	107	102	29	8	9	7	60	3	139	2	0	9	8	.529	0	0-0	0	5.21	5.38
2002 Colorado	NL	35	28	1	0	164.1	724	170	101	96	26	5	6	10	63	5	111	4	1	8	11	.421	0	0-0	2	4.80	5.26
2003 Colorado	NL	7	7	0	0	35.1	161	47	31	31	12	1	0	1	12	0	21	1	0	2	4	.333	0	0-0	0	7.90	7.90
1996 Pittsburgh	NL	27	27	1	0	182.2	745	186	67	62	21	9	3	3	34	2	131	2	1	14	6	.700	0	0-0	0	3.55	3.05
1996 Atlanta	NL	6	6	1	0	38.2	165	40	26	24	5	1	1	0	14	0	18	1	0	2	3	.400	0	0-0	0	4.37	5.59
2000 Cincinnati	NL	18	18	0	0	117.2	506	111	48	46	15	2	1	3	50	3	88	3	0	8	2	.800	0	0-0	0	4.12	3.52
2000 New York	AL	16	15	1	0	91.1	400	99	61	59	16	6	5	2	31	1	58	4	1	7	7	.500	0	0-0	0	4.89	5.81
13 ML YEARS		392	286	20	23	1890.1	8031	1887	948	891	250	79	55	53	594	44	1415	47	6	124	92	.574	7	3-5	13	4.03	4.24

Blaine Neal

Pitches: R **Bats:** L **Pos:** RP-18 | **Ht:** 6'5" **Wt:** 240 **Born:** 4/6/78 **Age:** 26

Year Team	Lg	G	GS	CG	GF	IP	BFP	H	R	ER	HR	SH	SF	HB	TBB	IBB	SO	WP	Bk	W	L	Pct	ShO	Sv-Op	Hld	ERC	ERA
2003 Albuquerque*	AAA	40	0	0	30	46.1	202	55	22	12	1	2	1	2	16	2	32	3	0	3	2	.600	0	21--	-	4.55	2.33
2001 Florida	NL	4	0	0	0	5.1	28	7	4	4	0	0	0	0	5	0	3	1	0	0	0	—	0	0-0	0	7.12	6.75
2002 Florida	NL	32	0	0	6	33.0	144	32	12	10	1	1	0	0	14	2	33	4	0	3	0	1.000	0	0-0	2	3.35	2.73
2003 Florida	NL	18	0	0	6	21.0	108	38	20	19	2	1	5	1	9	1	10	1	0	0	0	—	0	0-0	2	9.42	8.14
3 ML YEARS		54	0	0	12	59.1	280	77	36	33	3	2	5	1	28	3	46	6	0	3	0	1.000	0	0-0	4	5.64	5.01

Jeff Nelson

Pitches: R **Bats:** R **Pos:** RP-70 | **Ht:** 6'8" **Wt:** 235 **Born:** 11/17/66 **Age:** 37

Year Team	Lg	G	GS	CG	GF	IP	BFP	H	R	ER	HR	SH	SF	HB	TBB	IBB	SO	WP	Bk	W	L	Pct	ShO	Sv-Op	Hld	ERC	ERA
1992 Seattle	AL	66	0	0	27	81.0	352	71	34	31	7	9	3	6	44	12	46	2	0	1	7	.125	0	6-14	6	3.93	3.44
1993 Seattle	AL	71	0	0	13	60.0	269	57	30	29	5	2	4	8	34	10	61	2	0	5	3	.625	0	1-11	17	4.62	4.35
1994 Seattle	AL	28	0	0	7	42.1	185	35	18	13	3	1	1	8	20	4	44	2	0	0	0	—	0	0-0	2	3.77	2.76
1995 Seattle	AL	62	0	0	24	78.2	318	58	21	19	4	5	3	6	27	5	96	1	0	7	3	.700	0	2-4	14	2.39	2.17
1996 New York	AL	73	0	0	27	74.1	328	75	38	36	6	3	1	2	36	1	91	4	0	4	4	.500	0	2-4	10	4.41	4.36
1997 New York	AL	77	0	0	22	78.2	327	53	32	25	7	7	2	4	37	12	81	4	0	3	7	.300	0	2-8	22	2.48	2.86
1998 New York	AL	45	0	0	13	40.1	192	44	18	17	1	1	3	8	22	4	35	2	0	5	3	.625	0	3-6	10	5.13	3.79
1999 New York	AL	39	0	0	8	30.1	139	27	14	14	2	2	2	3	22	2	35	2	1	2	1	.667	0	1-2	10	4.76	4.15
2000 New York	AL	73	0	0	13	69.2	296	44	24	19	2	6	2	2	45	1	71	4	0	8	4	.667	0	0-4	15	2.61	2.45
2001 Seattle	AL	69	0	0	16	65.1	273	30	21	20	3	2	4	3	44	1	88	2	0	4	3	.571	0	4-5	26	2.20	2.76
2002 Seattle	AL	41	0	0	12	45.2	199	36	20	20	4	2	4	3	27	3	55	5	0	3	2	.600	0	2-4	12	3.70	3.94
2003 Sea-NYY	AL	70	0	0	28	55.1	240	51	25	23	4	4	2	4	24	3	68	3	1	4	2	.667	0	8-14	14	3.76	3.74
2003 Seattle	AL	46	0	0	25	37.2	159	34	16	14	3	4	2	2	14	1	47	2	1	3	2	.600	0	7-11	6	3.48	3.35
2003 New York	AL	24	0	0	3	17.2	81	17	9	9	1	0	0	2	10	2	21	1	0	1	0	1.000	0	1-3	8	4.37	4.58
12 ML YEARS		714	0	0	210	721.2	3118	581	295	266	48	44	27	60	382	58	771	33	2	46	39	.541	0	31-76	158	3.46	3.32

Robb Nen

Pitches: R **Bats:** R **Pos:** RP | **Ht:** 6'5" **Wt:** 222 **Born:** 11/28/69 **Age:** 34

Year Team	Lg	G	GS	CG	GF	IP	BFP	H	R	ER	HR	SH	SF	HB	TBB	IBB	SO	WP	Bk	W	L	Pct	ShO	Sv-Op	Hld	ERC	ERA
1993 Tex-Fla		24	4	0	5	56.0	272	63	45	42	6	1	2	0	46	0	39	6	1	2	1	.667	0	0-0	0	6.58	6.75
1994 Florida	NL	44	0	0	28	58.0	228	46	20	19	6	3	1	0	17	2	60	3	2	5	5	.500	0	15-15	1	2.63	2.95
1995 Florida	NL	62	0	0	54	65.2	279	62	26	24	6	0	1	1	23	3	68	2	0	0	7	.000	0	23-29	0	3.48	3.29
1996 Florida	NL	75	0	0	66	83.0	326	67	21	18	2	5	1	1	21	6	92	4	0	5	1	.833	0	35-42	0	2.07	1.95
1997 Florida	NL	73	0	0	65	74.0	332	72	35	32	7	1	3	0	40	7	81	5	0	9	3	.750	0	35-42	0	3.73	3.89
1998 San Francisco	NL	78	0	0	67	88.2	357	59	21	15	4	2	2	1	25	5	110	3	0	7	7	.500	0	40-45	0	1.58	1.52
1999 San Francisco	NL	72	0	0	64	72.1	320	79	36	32	8	5	1	0	27	3	77	5	0	3	8	.273	0	37-46	0	4.44	3.98
2000 San Francisco	NL	68	0	0	63	66.0	256	37	15	11	4	4	3	2	19	1	92	5	0	4	3	.571	0	41-46	0	1.44	1.50
2001 San Francisco	NL	79	0	0	71	77.2	312	58	28	26	6	0	3	1	22	6	93	2	0	4	5	.444	0	45-52	0	2.12	3.01
2002 San Francisco	NL	68	0	0	66	73.2	301	64	19	18	2	4	0	1	20	8	81	1	0	6	2	.750	0	43-51	0	2.33	2.20

Year Team	Lg	G	GS	CG	GF	IP	BFP	H	R	ER	HR	SH	SF	HB	TBB	IBB	SO	WP	Bk	W	L	Pct	ShO	Sv-Op	Hld	ERC	ERA
1993 Texas	AL	9	3	0	3	22.2	113	28	17	16	1	0	1	0	26	0	12	2	1	1	1	.500	0	0-0	0	8.60	6.35
1993 Florida	NL	15	1	0	2	33.1	159	35	28	26	5	1	1	0	20	0	27	4	0	1	0	1.000	0	0-0	0	5.28	7.02
10 ML YEARS		643	4	0	549	715.0	2983	607	266	237	51	25	17	7	260	41	793	36	3	45	42	.517	0	314-368	1	2.87	2.98

Mike Neu

Pitches: R **Bats:** B **Pos:** RP-32　　　　**Ht:** 5'10" **Wt:** 175 **Born:** 3/9/78 **Age:** 26

Year Team	Lg	G	GS	CG	GF	IP	BFP	H	R	ER	HR	SH	SF	HB	TBB	IBB	SO	WP	Bk	W	L	Pct	ShO	Sv-Op	Hld	ERC	ERA
1999 Rockford	A	9	0	0	2	18.0	84	17	10	9	1	0	1	2	12	1	23	4	0	0	1	.000	0	1- -	-	4.74	4.50
2000 Clinton	A	58	0	0	54	69.0	306	47	27	24	5	4	3	1	52	8	95	10	0	7	7	.500	0	24- -	-	3.27	3.13
2001 Mudville	A+	53	0	0	44	64.2	277	50	21	17	3	4	1	3	30	4	102	5	1	3	2	.600	0	21- -	-	2.75	2.37
2002 Louisville	AAA	40	0	0	34	40.1	172	35	19	18	4	2	1	0	18	0	47	1	0	2	3	.400	0	16- -	-	3.49	4.02
2002 Chattanooga	AA	21	0	0	12	27.0	113	22	4	4	0	1	1	1	9	1	38	3	0	1	0	1.000	0	7- -	-	2.24	1.33
2003 Oakland	AL	32	0	0	26	42.0	194	43	18	17	2	1	0	2	26	2	20	4	0	0	0	-	0	1-1	0	4.73	3.64

Phil Nevin

Bats: R **Throws:** R **Pos:** 1B-31; RF-29　　　　**Ht:** 6'2" **Wt:** 231 **Born:** 1/19/71 **Age:** 33

								BATTING													BASERUNNING				AVERAGES		
Year Team	Lg	G	AB	H	2B	3B	HR	(Hm	Rd)	TB	R	RBI	RC	TBB	IBB	SO	HBP	SH	SF	SB	CS	SB%	GDP	Avg	OBP	Slg
2003 Portland*	AAA	6	18	2	0	0	0	(-	-)	2	0	1	0	1	0	1	0	0	0	0	0	-	2	.111	.158	.111
2003 Lk Elsinore*	A+	5	15	4	1	0	0	(-	-)	5	1	5	2	2	0	2	0	0	3	0	0	-	1	.267	.300	.333
1995 Hou-Det		47	156	28	4	1	2	(2	0)	40	13	13	10	18	1	40	4	1	0	1	0	1.00	5	.179	.281	.256
1996 Detroit	AL	38	120	35	5	0	8	(3	5)	64	15	19	21	8	0	39	1	0	1	1	0	1.00	1	.292	.338	.533
1997 Detroit	AL	93	251	59	16	1	9	(4	5)	104	32	35	31	25	1	68	1	0	1	0	1	.00	5	.235	.306	.414
1998 Anaheim	AL	75	237	54	8	1	8	(3	5)	88	27	27	25	17	0	67	5	0	2	0	0	-	6	.228	.291	.371
1999 San Diego	NL	128	383	103	27	0	24	(12	12)	202	52	85	71	51	1	82	1	1	5	1	0	1.00	7	.269	.352	.527
2000 San Diego	NL	143	538	163	34	1	31	(13	18)	292	87	107	102	59	9	121	4	0	4	2	0	1.00	17	.303	.374	.543
2001 San Diego	NL	149	546	167	31	0	41	(19	22)	321	97	126	116	71	7	147	4	0	3	4	4	.50	13	.306	.388	.588
2002 San Diego	NL	107	410	116	16	0	12	(5	7)	168	53	57	51	38	4	87	1	0	4	4	0	1.00	12	.285	.344	.413
2003 San Diego	NL	59	226	63	8	0	13	(6	7)	110	30	46	37	21	1	44	0	0	1	2	0	1.00	9	.279	.339	.487
1995 Houston	NL	18	60	7	1	0	0	(0	0)	8	4	1	0	7	1	13	1	1	0	1	0	1.00	2	.117	.221	.133
1995 Detroit	AL	29	96	21	3	1	2	(2	0)	32	9	12	10	11	0	27	3	0	0	0	0	-	3	.219	.314	.333
9 ML YEARS		839	2864	788	149	4	148	(67	81)	1389	406	515	464	308	24	695	21	2	21	15	5	.75	75	.275	.348	.485

Lance Niekro

Bats: R **Throws:** R **Pos:** 1B-3; PH-1; PR-1　　　　**Ht:** 6'3" **Wt:** 210 **Born:** 1/29/79 **Age:** 25

								BATTING													BASERUNNING				AVERAGES		
Year Team	Lg	G	AB	H	2B	3B	HR	(Hm	Rd)	TB	R	RBI	RC	TBB	IBB	SO	HBP	SH	SF	SB	CS	SB%	GDP	Avg	OBP	Slg
2000 Salem-Keizer	A-	49	196	71	14	4	5	(-	-)	108	27	44	40	11	2	25	4	0	2	0	1	.00	6	.362	.404	.551
2001 San Jose	A+	42	163	47	11	0	3	(-	-)	67	18	34	20	4	0	14	0	0	4	4	2	.67	2	.288	.298	.411
2002 Shreveport	AA	79	297	92	20	1	4	(-	-)	126	33	34	37	7	0	32	2	1	3	0	2	.00	11	.310	.327	.424
2003 Fresno	AAA	98	381	115	15	2	4	(-	-)	146	43	41	45	19	1	39	1	1	3	3	3	.50	12	.302	.334	.383
2003 San Francisco	NL	5	5	1	1	0	0	(0	0)	2	2	2	1	0	0	1	0	0	0	0	0	-	0	.200	.200	.400

C.J. Nitkowski

Pitches: L **Bats:** L **Pos:** RP-6　　　　**Ht:** 6'3" **Wt:** 205 **Born:** 3/9/73 **Age:** 31

Year Team	Lg	G	GS	CG	GF	IP	BFP	H	R	ER	HR	SH	SF	HB	TBB	IBB	SO	WP	Bk	W	L	Pct	ShO	Sv-Op	Hld	ERC	ERA
2003 Oklahoma*	AAA	33	6	0	12	81.1	356	88	40	37	6	4	3	5	31	2	53	5	1	5	4	.556	0	2- -	-	4.53	4.09
1995 Cin-Det		20	18	0	0	71.2	338	94	57	53	11	2	4	5	35	3	31	2	2	2	7	.222	0	0-1	0	7.04	6.66
1996 Detroit	AL	11	8	0	0	45.2	234	62	44	41	7	0	2	7	38	1	36	2	0	2	3	.400	0	0-0	0	9.44	8.08
1998 Houston	NL	43	0	0	11	59.2	250	49	27	25	4	4	2	6	23	2	44	3	1	3	3	.500	0	3-5	8	3.19	3.77
1999 Detroit	AL	68	7	0	7	81.2	349	63	44	39	11	1	4	3	45	3	66	4	3	4	5	.444	0	0-0	11	3.73	4.30
2000 Detroit	AL	67	11	0	7	109.2	497	124	79	64	13	3	8	4	49	3	81	3	1	4	9	.308	0	0-2	15	5.23	5.25
2001 Det-NYM		61	0	0	14	51.0	241	54	30	28	7	3	1	5	34	8	42	1	0	1	3	.250	0	0-6	6	5.89	4.94
2002 Texas	AL	12	0	0	2	13.2	63	11	4	4	0	1	0	0	13	0	14	0	0	0	1	.000	0	0-0	4	4.35	2.63
2003 Texas	AL	6	0	0	0	9.2	52	17	8	8	0	1	2	0	8	1	5	0	0	0	0	-	0	0-0	1	9.69	7.45
1995 Cincinnati	NL	9	7	0	0	32.1	154	41	25	22	4	2	1	2	15	1	18	1	2	1	3	.250	0	0-1	0	6.20	6.12
1995 Detroit	AL	11	11	0	0	39.1	184	53	32	31	7	0	3	3	20	2	13	1	0	1	4	.200	0	0-0	0	7.76	7.09
2001 Detroit	AL	56	0	0	12	45.1	220	51	30	28	7	3	1	5	31	7	38	1	0	0	3	.000	0	0-6	6	6.53	5.56
2001 New York	NL	5	0	0	2	5.2	21	3	0	0	0	0	0	0	3	1	4	0	0	1	0	1.000	0	0-0	0	1.52	0.00
8 ML YEARS		288	44	0	41	442.2	2024	474	293	262	53	15	23	30	245	21	319	15	7	16	31	.340	0	3-14	42	5.47	5.33

Ramon Nivar

Bats: R **Throws:** R **Pos:** CF-26; PR-2; DH-1; PH-1　　　　**Ht:** 5'10" **Wt:** 170 **Born:** 2/22/80 **Age:** 24

								BATTING													BASERUNNING				AVERAGES		
Year Team	Lg	G	AB	H	2B	3B	HR	(Hm	Rd)	TB	R	RBI	RC	TBB	IBB	SO	HBP	SH	SF	SB	CS	SB%	GDP	Avg	OBP	Slg
2003 Frisco	AA	79	317	110	17	4	4	(-	-)	147	53	37	54	20	0	23	2	8	2	9	9	.50	5	.347	.387	.464
2003 Oklahoma	AAA	23	89	30	2	2	2	(-	-)	42	11	12	15	5	0	5	0	1	1	6	1	.86	4	.337	.368	.472
2003 Texas	AL	28	90	19	1	2	0	(0	0)	24	9	7	6	4	0	10	1	2	0	4	2	.67	1	.211	.253	.267

Laynce Nix

Bats: L **Throws:** L **Pos:** RF-38; CF-20; LF-5; PH-3; DH-1; PR-1   **Ht:** 6'0" **Wt:** 190 **Born:** 10/30/80 **Age:** 23

Year Team	Lg	G	AB	H	2B	3B	HR	(Hm	Rd)	TB	R	RBI	RC	TBB	IBB	SO	HBP	SH	SF	SB	CS	SB%	GDP	Avg	OBP	Slg
2000 Rangers	R	51	199	45	7	1	2	(-	-)	60	34	25	20	23	1	37	2	2	4	4	2	.67	1	.226	.307	.302
2001 Savannah	A	104	407	113	26	8	8	(-	-)	179	50	59	59	37	2	94	2	1	5	9	6	.60	7	.278	.337	.440
2001 Charlotte	A+	9	37	11	3	1	0	(-	-)	16	4	2	4	1	0	13	0	0	0	0	0	-	2	.297	.316	.432
2002 Charlotte	A+	137	512	146	27	3	21	(-	-)	242	86	110	94	72	8	105	6	0	9	17	1	.94	9	.285	.374	.473
2003 Frisco	AA	87	335	95	23	0	15	(-	-)	163	52	63	57	34	6	68	0	0	6	9	2	.82	4	.284	.344	.487
2003 Texas	AL	53	184	47	10	0	8	(7	1)	81	25	30	26	9	0	53	0	1	1	3	0	1.00	1	.255	.289	.440

Trot Nixon

Bats: L **Throws:** L **Pos:** RF-129; PH-11; CF-1; PR-1   **Ht:** 6'2" **Wt:** 211 **Born:** 4/11/74 **Age:** 30

Year Team	Lg	G	AB	H	2B	3B	HR	(Hm	Rd)	TB	R	RBI	RC	TBB	IBB	SO	HBP	SH	SF	SB	CS	SB%	GDP	Avg	OBP	Slg
1996 Boston	AL	2	4	2	1	0	0	(0	0)	3	2	0	1	0	0	1	0	0	0	1	0	1.00	-	.500	.500	.750
1998 Boston	AL	13	27	7	1	0	0	(0	0)	8	3	0	2	1	0	3	0	0	0	0	0	-	-	.259	.286	.296
1999 Boston	AL	124	381	103	22	5	15	(3	12)	180	67	52	66	53	1	75	3	2	8	3	1	.75	7	.270	.357	.472
2000 Boston	AL	123	427	118	27	8	12	(4	8)	197	66	60	74	63	2	85	2	5	5	8	1	.89	11	.276	.368	.461
2001 Boston	AL	148	535	150	31	4	27	(14	13)	270	100	88	102	79	1	113	7	6	6	7	4	.64	8	.280	.376	.505
2002 Boston	AL	152	532	136	36	3	24	(8	16)	250	81	94	86	65	2	109	5	3	7	4	2	.67	7	.256	.338	.470
2003 Boston	AL	134	441	135	24	6	28	(10	18)	255	81	87	90	65	4	96	3	1	3	4	2	.67	3	.306	.396	.578
7 ML YEARS		696	2347	651	142	26	106	(39	67)	1163	400	381	421	326	10	482	20	17	29	27	10	.73	36	.277	.366	.496

Hideo Nomo

Pitches: R **Bats:** R **Pos:** SP-33   **Ht:** 6'2" **Wt:** 210 **Born:** 8/31/68 **Age:** 35

Year Team	Lg	G	GS	CG	GF	IP	BFP	H	R	ER	HR	SH	SF	HB	TBB	IBB	SO	WP	Bk	W	L	Pct	ShO	Sv-Op	Hld	ERC	ERA
1995 Los Angeles	NL	28	28	4	0	191.1	780	124	63	54	14	11	4	5	78	2	236	19	5	13	6	.684	3	0-0	0	2.16	2.54
1996 Los Angeles	NL	33	33	3	0	228.1	932	180	93	81	23	12	6	2	85	6	234	11	3	16	11	.593	2	0-0	0	2.86	3.19
1997 Los Angeles	NL	33	33	1	0	207.1	904	193	104	98	23	7	1	9	92	2	233	10	4	14	12	.538	0	0-0	0	4.06	4.25
1998 LA-NYM	NL	29	28	3	0	157.1	687	130	88	86	19	8	5	4	94	2	167	13	4	6	12	.333	0	0-0	0	4.10	4.92
1999 Milwaukee	NL	28	28	0	0	176.1	767	173	96	89	27	5	5	3	78	2	161	10	1	12	8	.600	0	0-0	0	4.57	4.54
2000 Detroit	AL	32	31	1	0	190.0	828	191	102	100	31	6	3	3	89	1	181	16	0	8	12	.400	0	0-0	0	4.95	4.74
2001 Boston	AL	33	33	2	0	198.0	849	171	105	99	26	4	7	3	96	2	220	6	0	13	10	.565	2	0-0	0	3.90	4.50
2002 Los Angeles	NL	34	34	0	0	220.1	926	189	92	83	26	17	4	2	101	5	193	6	0	16	6	.727	0	0-0	0	3.68	3.39
2003 Los Angeles	NL	33	33	2	0	218.1	897	175	82	75	24	11	3	1	98	6	177	11	0	16	13	.552	2	0-0	0	3.30	3.09
1998 Los Angeles	NL	12	12	2	0	67.2	295	57	39	38	8	2	2	3	38	0	73	4	1	2	7	.222	0	0-0	0	4.13	5.05
1998 New York	NL	17	16	1	0	89.2	392	73	49	48	11	6	3	1	56	2	94	9	3	4	5	.444	0	0-0	0	4.07	4.82
9 ML YEARS		283	281	16	0	1787.1	7570	1526	825	765	213	81	38	32	811	28	1802	102	17	114	90	.559	9	0-0	0	3.67	3.85

Greg Norton

Bats: B **Throws:** R **Pos:** PH-78; 3B-34; 1B-9; RF-3; PR-1   **Ht:** 6'1" **Wt:** 200 **Born:** 7/6/72 **Age:** 31

Year Team	Lg	G	AB	H	2B	3B	HR	(Hm	Rd)	TB	R	RBI	RC	TBB	IBB	SO	HBP	SH	SF	SB	CS	SB%	GDP	Avg	OBP	Slg
1996 Chicago	AL	11	23	5	0	0	2	(0	2)	11	4	3	3	4	0	6	0	0	0	0	1	.00	0	.217	.333	.478
1997 Chicago	AL	18	34	9	2	2	0	(0	0)	15	5	1	5	2	0	8	0	1	0	0	0	-	0	.265	.306	.441
1998 Chicago	AL	105	299	71	17	2	9	(6	3)	119	38	36	33	26	1	77	2	1	2	3	3	.50	11	.237	.301	.398
1999 Chicago	AL	132	436	111	26	0	16	(5	11)	185	62	50	66	69	3	93	2	1	2	4	4	.50	11	.255	.358	.424
2000 Chicago	AL	71	201	49	6	1	6	(4	2)	75	25	28	27	26	0	47	2	0	2	1	0	1.00	2	.244	.333	.373
2001 Colorado	NL	117	225	60	13	2	13	(7	6)	116	30	40	36	19	2	65	0	0	2	1	0	1.00	6	.267	.321	.516
2002 Colorado	NL	113	168	37	8	1	7	(3	4)	68	19	37	22	24	0	52	0	1	2	2	3	.40	4	.220	.314	.405
2003 Colorado	NL	114	179	47	15	0	6	(2	4)	80	19	31	27	16	0	47	1	0	1	2	1	.67	4	.263	.325	.447
8 ML YEARS		681	1565	389	87	8	59	(27	32)	669	202	226	219	186	6	395	7	4	11	13	12	.52	38	.249	.329	.427

Phil Norton

Pitches: L **Bats:** R **Pos:** RP-21   **Ht:** 6'0" **Wt:** 210 **Born:** 2/1/76 **Age:** 28

Year Team	Lg	G	GS	CG	GF	IP	BFP	H	R	ER	HR	SH	SF	HB	TBB	IBB	SO	WP	Bk	W	L	Pct	ShO	Sv-Op	Hld	ERC	ERA
1996 Cubs	R	1	0	0	1	3.0	10	1	0	0	0	0	0	0	0	0	6	0	1	0	0	-	0	0--	-	0.25	0.00
1996 Williamsport	A-	15	13	2	1	85.0	364	68	33	24	1	3	2	3	33	2	77	7	3	7	4	.636	1	0--	-	2.39	2.54
1997 Rockford	A	18	18	3	0	109.0	460	92	51	39	4	3	3	1	44	1	114	12	1	9	3	.750	0	0--	-	2.81	3.22
1997 Daytona	A+	7	6	3	0	42.1	171	40	14	11	5	1	0	0	12	0	44	0	0	3	2	.600	0	0--	-	3.55	2.34
1997 Orlando	AA	2	1	0	1	7.0	28	8	2	2	0	0	0	0	2	1	7	0	0	1	0	1.000	0	0--	-	3.80	2.57
1998 Daytona	A+	10	10	0	0	66.0	275	57	30	24	4	1	1	2	26	1	54	4	1	3	5	.571	0	0--	-	3.17	3.27
1998 W Tennessee	AA	19	19	1	0	120.1	515	118	60	47	11	4	3	5	50	1	119	6	1	6	6	.500	1	0--	-	4.19	3.52
1999 W Tennessee	AA	14	13	0	0	86.2	365	72	32	29	5	3	4	3	42	4	81	9	0	7	4	.636	0	0--	-	3.29	2.39
1999 Iowa	AAA	14	14	0	0	79.2	361	98	63	59	20	0	2	5	33	0	61	3	1	5	6	.455	0	0--	-	7.08	6.67
2000 Iowa	AAA	26	26	2	0	159.2	733	166	100	88	16	9	6	2	104	4	126	8	2	8	13	.381	1	0--	-	5.33	4.96
2001 Iowa	AAA	46	3	0	14	73.2	318	65	27	22	3	3	9	6	41	7	75	8	1	6	3	.667	0	2--	-	3.84	2.69
2003 Iowa	AAA	48	1	0	17	47.2	211	44	26	20	4	3	1	1	24	3	43	3	1	4	2	.667	0	1--	-	3.84	3.78
2000 Chicago	NL	2	2	0	0	8.2	47	14	0	9	5	0	0	0	7	0	6	0	0	0	1	.000	0	0-0	0	14.18	9.35
2003 ChC-Cin	NL	21	0	0	4	18.0	68	9	6	6	0	1	0	0	9	0	7	1	0	0	0	-	0	0-0	5	1.50	3.00
2003 Chicago	NL	4	0	0	2	3.1	14	2	2	2	0	0	0	0	3	0	5	1	0	0	0	-	0	0-0	0	3.21	5.40
2003 Cincinnati	NL	17	0	0	2	14.2	54	7	4	4	0	1	0	0	6	0	7	0	0	0	0	-	0	0-0	5	1.24	2.45
2 ML YEARS		23	2	0	4	26.2	115	23	6	15	5	1	0	0	16	0	13	1	0	0	1	.000	0	0-0	5	4.80	5.06

Abraham O Nunez

Bats: B **Throws:** R **Pos:** 2B-71; PH-32; SS-23; PR-2; 3B-1   **Ht:** 5'11" **Wt:** 185 **Born:** 3/16/76 **Age:** 28

						BATTING													BASERUNNING				AVERAGES		
Year Team	Lg	G	AB	H	2B	3B	HR	(Hm	Rd)	TB	R	RBI	RC	TBB	IBB	SO	HBP	SH	SF	SB	CS	SB%	GDP	Avg	OBP	Slg
1997 Pittsburgh	NL	19	40	9	2	2	0	(0	0)	15	3	6	4	3	0	10	1	0	1	1	0	1.00	1	.225	.289	.375
1998 Pittsburgh	NL	24	52	10	2	0	1	(0	1)	15	6	2	6	12	0	14	0	3	0	4	2	.67	1	.192	.344	.288
1999 Pittsburgh	NL	90	259	57	8	0	0	(0	0)	65	25	17	22	28	0	54	1	13	0	9	1	.90	2	.220	.299	.251
2000 Pittsburgh	NL	40	91	20	1	0	1	(0	1)	24	10	8	6	8	1	14	0	0	0	0	0	-	3	.220	.283	.264
2001 Pittsburgh	NL	115	301	79	11	4	1	(0	1)	101	30	21	36	28	1	53	1	4	1	8	2	.80	0	.262	.326	.336
2002 Pittsburgh	NL	112	253	59	14	1	2	(2	0)	81	28	15	25	27	1	44	2	3	1	3	4	.43	2	.233	.311	.320
2003 Pittsburgh	NL	118	311	77	8	7	4	(2	2)	111	37	35	28	26	1	53	3	9	2	9	3	.75	8	.248	.310	.357
7 ML YEARS		518	1307	311	46	14	9	(4	5)	412	139	104	127	132	4	242	8	32	5	34	12	.74	17	.238	.311	.315

Vladimir Nunez

Pitches: R **Bats:** R **Pos:** RP-14   **Ht:** 6'4" **Wt:** 240 **Born:** 3/15/75 **Age:** 29

		HOW MUCH HE PITCHED						WHAT HE GAVE UP										THE RESULTS							
Year Team	Lg	G	GS	CG	GF	IP	BFP	H	R	ER	HR	SH	SF	HB	TBB	IBB	SO	WP	Bk	W	L	Pct	ShO	Sv-Op	Hld	ERC	ERA
2003 Albuquerque*	AAA	46	3	0	26	68.0	290	67	36	36	13	3	2	6	20	0	54	4	0	4	1	.800	0	5--		4.58	4.76
1998 Arizona	NL	4	0	0	2	5.1	25	7	6	6	0	0	1	0	2	0	2	0	1	0	-	-	0	0-0		4.87	10.13
1999 Ari-Fla	NL	44	12	0	12	108.2	463	95	63	49	11	7	6	4	54	6	86	8	1	7	10	.412	0	1-3	4	3.88	4.06
2000 Florida	NL	17	12	0	3	68.1	322	88	63	60	12	5	5	2	34	2	45	5	0	0	6	.000	0	0-0	1	6.88	7.90
2001 Florida	NL	52	3	0	13	92.0	380	79	33	28	9	2	5	5	30	5	64	1	1	4	5	.444	0	0-1	4	3.17	2.74
2002 Florida	NL	77	0	0	43	97.2	404	80	38	37	8	6	4	0	37	1	73	2	0	6	5	.545	0	20-28	11	2.88	3.41
2003 Florida	NL	14	0	0	4	10.2	63	21	21	19	7	1	2	0	7	0	10	0	0	0	3	.000	0	0-3	2	16.12	16.03
1999 Arizona	NL	27	0	0	11	34.0	146	29	15	11	2	2	3	1	20	5	28	3	0	3	2	.600	0	1-2	3	3.63	2.91
1999 Florida	NL	17	12	0	1	74.2	317	66	48	38	9	5	3	3	34	1	58	5	1	4	8	.333	0	0-1	1	3.98	4.58
6 ML YEARS		208	27	0	77	382.2	1657	370	224	199	47	21	23	11	164	14	280	16	3	17	29	.370	0	21-35	22	4.22	4.68

Wes Obermueller

Pitches: R **Bats:** R **Pos:** SP-11; RP-1   **Ht:** 6'2" **Wt:** 195 **Born:** 12/22/76 **Age:** 27

		HOW MUCH HE PITCHED						WHAT HE GAVE UP										THE RESULTS							
Year Team	Lg	G	GS	CG	GF	IP	BFP	H	R	ER	HR	SH	SF	HB	TBB	IBB	SO	WP	Bk	W	L	Pct	ShO	Sv-Op	Hld	ERC	ERA
1999 Royals	R	11	7	0	2	38.1	159	33	16	11	2	0	1	1	12	1	39	2	1	2	1	.667	0	0--		2.73	2.58
2000 Chrlstn - WV	A	8	7	0	0	31.2	117	19	6	4	0	0	0	3	5	0	29	1	0	3	0	1.000	0	0--		1.26	1.14
2001 Wilmington	A+	20	6	0	1	38.0	163	38	15	13	3	2	1	1	16	1	28	2	0	2	0	.000	0	0--		4.13	3.08
2002 Wilmington	A+	8	4	0	1	45.2	182	38	14	14	1	0	1	0	14	0	44	4	0	5	0	1.000	0	0--		2.41	2.76
2002 Wichita	AA	17	17	0	0	105.2	443	98	39	34	6	3	3	4	40	3	65	6	2	9	5	.643	0	0--		3.46	2.90
2003 Indianapolis	AAA	3	3	0	0	15.1	66	18	9	8	1	0	0	0	6	0	11	1	0	2	0	.000	0	0--		4.97	4.70
2003 Omaha	AAA	17	17	2	0	106.1	466	108	61	52	11	3	2	7	42	1	62	0	0	10	5	.667	0	0--		4.41	4.40
2002 Kansas City	AL	2	2	0	0	7.2	39	14	10	10	3	0	0	0	2	0	5	0	0	0	2	.000	0	0-0	0	11.04	11.74
2003 Milwaukee	NL	12	11	0	0	65.2	303	81	40	37	10	1	2	6	25	2	34	5	0	2	5	.286	0	0-0	0	6.08	5.07
2 ML YEARS		14	13	0	0	73.1	342	95	50	47	13	1	2	6	27	2	39	5	0	2	7	.222	0	0-0	0	6.57	5.77

Tomo Ohka

Pitches: R **Bats:** R **Pos:** SP-34   **Ht:** 6'1" **Wt:** 180 **Born:** 3/18/76 **Age:** 28

		HOW MUCH HE PITCHED						WHAT HE GAVE UP										THE RESULTS							
Year Team	Lg	G	GS	CG	GF	IP	BFP	H	R	ER	HR	SH	SF	HB	TBB	IBB	SO	WP	Bk	W	L	Pct	ShO	Sv-Op	Hld	ERC	ERA
1999 Boston	AL	8	2	0	3	13.0	65	21	12	9	2	0	1	0	6	0	8	0	0	1	2	.333	0	0-0	0	8.56	6.23
2000 Boston	AL	13	12	0	1	69.1	297	70	25	24	7	1	2	2	26	0	40	3	0	3	6	.333	0	0-0	0	4.19	3.12
2001 Bos-Mon		22	21	0	1	107.0	469	134	70	65	15	2	2	3	29	0	68	2	1	3	9	.250	0	0-0	0	5.52	5.47
2002 Montreal	NL	32	31	2	1	192.2	806	194	83	68	19	13	6	7	45	7	118	2	1	13	8	.619	0	0-0	0	3.55	3.18
2003 Montreal	NL	34	34	2	0	199.0	864	233	106	92	24	8	3	9	45	11	118	8	0	10	12	.455	0	0-0	0	4.59	4.16
2001 Boston	AL	12	11	0	0	52.1	241	69	40	36	7	1	1	2	19	0	37	1	1	2	5	.286	0	0-0	0	6.24	6.19
2001 Montreal	NL	10	10	0	0	54.2	228	65	30	29	8	1	1	1	10	0	31	1	0	1	4	.200	0	0-0	0	4.83	4.77
5 ML YEARS		109	100	4	6	581.0	2501	652	296	258	67	24	14	21	151	18	352	15	2	30	37	.448	0	0-0	0	4.43	4.00

Kevin Ohme

Pitches: L **Bats:** L **Pos:** RP-2   **Ht:** 6'1" **Wt:** 180 **Born:** 4/13/71 **Age:** 33

		HOW MUCH HE PITCHED						WHAT HE GAVE UP										THE RESULTS							
Year Team	Lg	G	GS	CG	GF	IP	BFP	H	R	ER	HR	SH	SF	HB	TBB	IBB	SO	WP	Bk	W	L	Pct	ShO	Sv-Op	Hld	ERC	ERA
1993 Fort Wayne	A	15	4	0	6	46.1	184	38	19	13	1	2	2	1	15	1	45	5	1	3	2	.600	0	0--	-	2.48	2.53
1994 Fort Wayne	A	2	2	0	0	7.0	29	7	2	2	0	0	1	0	0	0	8	0	0	1	0	1.000	0	0--	-	2.41	2.57
1995 New Britain	AA	35	11	0	7	101.1	427	89	51	39	5	7	7	3	45	1	52	7	0	3	4	.429	0	0--	-	3.37	3.46
1996 New Britain	AA	51	0	0	22	81.0	363	83	49	39	7	6	4	6	33	5	42	5	2	5	6	.455	0	3--	-	4.25	4.33
1997 Salt Lake	AAA	56	0	0	34	73.2	324	70	49	46	6	5	1	6	34	4	45	4	1	2	5	.286	0	11--	-	4.13	5.62
1998 Salt Lake	AAA	51	0	0	23	82.2	361	90	48	46	5	3	4	6	31	3	47	3	1	4	3	.571	0	6--	-	4.49	5.01
1999 Salt Lake	AAA	51	3	0	15	82.1	368	94	44	35	8	1	6	8	31	2	48	4	1	5	3	.625	0	2--	-	5.18	3.83
2002 Memphis	AAA	56	5	0	19	87.2	376	103	44	44	10	6	4	7	21	1	56	2	0	4	3	.571	0	2--	-	4.97	4.52
2003 Memphis	AAA	49	0	0	13	66.2	296	77	34	32	8	0	3	2	21	4	32	4	1	5	5	.500	0	1--	-	4.74	4.32
2003 St Louis	NL	2	0	0	0	4.1	17	3	0	0	0	0	1	0	1	1	2	1	0	0	0	-	0	0-0	1	1.23	0.00

Augie Ojeda

Bats: B **Throws:** R **Pos:** SS-7; 2B-5; 3B-1   **Ht:** 5'8" **Wt:** 170 **Born:** 12/20/74 **Age:** 29

Year Team	Lg	G	AB	H	2B	3B	HR	(Hm	Rd)	TB	R	RBI	RC	TBB	IBB	SO	HBP	SH	SF	SB	CS	SB%	GDP	Avg	OBP	Slg
2003 Iowa*	AAA	106	283	71	10	3	2	(-	-)	93	42	23	36	34	3	25	10	6	1	4	0	1.00	6	.251	.351	.329
2000 Chicago	NL	28	77	17	3	1	2	(1	1)	28	10	8	9	10	1	9	0	1	1	0	1	.00	1	.221	.307	.364
2001 Chicago	NL	78	144	29	5	1	1	(0	1)	39	16	12	10	12	1	20	2	2	2	1	0	1.00	2	.201	.269	.271
2002 Chicago	NL	30	70	13	4	0	0	(0	0)	17	4	4	4	5	0	5	1	4	1	1	0	1.00	2	.186	.247	.243
2003 Chicago	NL	12	25	3	0	0	0	(0	0)	3	2	0	0	1	1	5	1	0	0	0	0	-	1	.120	.185	.120
4 ML YEARS		148	316	62	12	2	3	(2	1)	87	32	24	23	28	3	39	4	7	4	2	1	.67	6	.196	.267	.275

Miguel Ojeda

Bats: R **Throws:** R **Pos:** C-48; PH-14; 1B-2   **Ht:** 6'2" **Wt:** 190 **Born:** 1/29/75 **Age:** 29

Year Team	Lg	G	AB	H	2B	3B	HR	(Hm	Rd)	TB	R	RBI	RC	TBB	IBB	SO	HBP	SH	SF	SB	CS	SB%	GDP	Avg	OBP	Slg
1993 Pirates	R	27	97	27	3	1	3	(-	-)	41	9	11	15	10	0	18	0	1	2	2	0	1.00	1	.278	.339	.423
1998 Carolina	AA	18	58	9	2	0	1	(-	-)	14	4	4	2	3	0	12	1	2	0	0	0	-	0	.155	.210	.241
2003 San Diego	NL	61	141	33	6	0	4	(3	1)	51	13	22	20	18	2	26	3	0	1	1	1	.50	2	.234	.331	.362

Troy O'Leary

Bats: L **Throws:** L **Pos:** PH-46; LF-28; RF-24; PR-1   **Ht:** 6'0" **Wt:** 208 **Born:** 8/4/69 **Age:** 34

Year Team	Lg	G	AB	H	2B	3B	HR	(Hm	Rd)	TB	R	RBI	RC	TBB	IBB	SO	HBP	SH	SF	SB	CS	SB%	GDP	Avg	OBP	Slg
1993 Milwaukee	NL	19	41	12	3	0	0	(0	0)	15	3	3	6	5	0	9	0	3	0	0	0	-	1	.293	.370	.366
1994 Milwaukee	NL	27	66	18	1	1	2	(0	2)	27	9	7	9	5	0	12	1	0	1	1	1	.50	0	.273	.329	.409
1995 Boston	AL	112	399	123	31	6	10	(5	5)	196	60	49	66	29	4	64	1	3	2	5	3	.63	8	.308	.355	.491
1996 Boston	AL	149	497	129	28	5	15	(10	5)	212	68	81	67	47	3	80	4	1	3	3	2	.60	13	.260	.327	.427
1997 Boston	AL	146	499	154	32	4	15	(5	10)	239	65	80	79	39	7	70	2	1	4	0	5	.00	13	.309	.358	.479
1998 Boston	AL	156	611	165	36	8	23	(12	11)	286	95	83	85	36	2	108	5	0	5	2	2	.50	17	.270	.314	.468
1999 Boston	AL	157	596	167	36	4	28	(13	15)	295	84	103	95	56	5	91	4	0	5	1	2	.33	21	.280	.343	.495
2000 Boston	AL	138	513	134	30	4	13	(7	6)	211	68	70	65	44	2	76	2	0	4	0	2	.00	12	.261	.320	.411
2001 Boston	AL	104	341	82	16	6	13	(9	4)	149	50	50	42	25	2	73	5	0	5	1	3	.25	9	.240	.298	.437
2002 Montreal	NL	97	273	78	12	2	3	(1	2)	103	27	37	40	34	5	47	3	4	0	1	2	.33	6	.286	.371	.377
2003 Chicago	NL	93	174	38	9	0	5	(1	4)	62	18	28	16	14	1	31	1	1	4	3	0	1.00	8	.218	.275	.356
11 ML YEARS		1198	4010	1100	234	40	127	(63	64)	1795	547	591	570	334	31	661	28	13	33	17	22	.44	108	.274	.332	.448

John Olerud

Bats: L **Throws:** L **Pos:** 1B-152; PH-2   **Ht:** 6'5" **Wt:** 220 **Born:** 8/5/68 **Age:** 35

Year Team	Lg	G	AB	H	2B	3B	HR	(Hm	Rd)	TB	R	RBI	RC	TBB	IBB	SO	HBP	SH	SF	SB	CS	SB%	GDP	Avg	OBP	Slg
1989 Toronto	AL	6	8	3	0	0	0	(0	0)	3	2	0	1	0	0	1	0	0	0	0	0	-	0	.375	.375	.375
1990 Toronto	AL	111	358	95	15	1	14	(11	3)	154	43	48	57	57	6	75	1	1	4	0	2	.00	5	.265	.364	.430
1991 Toronto	AL	139	454	116	30	1	17	(7	10)	199	64	68	71	68	9	84	6	3	10	0	2	.00	12	.256	.353	.438
1992 Toronto	AL	138	458	130	28	0	16	(4	12)	206	68	66	76	70	11	61	1	1	7	1	0	1.00	15	.284	.375	.450
1993 Toronto	AL	158	551	200	54	2	24	(9	15)	330	109	107	146	114	33	65	7	0	7	0	2	.00	12	.363	.473	.599
1994 Toronto	AL	108	384	114	29	2	12	(6	6)	183	47	67	70	61	12	53	3	0	5	1	2	.33	11	.297	.393	.477
1995 Toronto	AL	135	492	143	32	0	8	(1	7)	199	72	54	80	84	10	54	4	0	1	0	0	-	17	.291	.398	.404
1996 Toronto	AL	125	398	109	25	0	18	(9	9)	188	59	61	72	60	6	37	10	0	1	1	0	1.00	10	.274	.382	.472
1997 New York	NL	154	524	154	34	1	22	(13	9)	256	90	102	101	85	5	67	13	0	8	0	0	-	19	.294	.400	.489
1998 New York	NL	160	557	197	36	4	22	(13	9)	307	91	93	131	96	11	73	4	1	7	2	2	.50	15	.354	.447	.551
1999 New York	NL	162	581	173	39	0	19	(11	8)	269	107	96	118	125	5	66	11	0	6	3	0	1.00	22	.298	.427	.463
2000 Seattle	AL	159	565	161	45	0	14	(8	6)	248	84	103	98	102	11	96	4	2	10	0	2	.00	17	.285	.392	.439
2001 Seattle	AL	159	572	173	32	1	21	(15	6)	270	91	95	106	94	19	70	5	1	7	3	1	.75	21	.302	.401	.472
2002 Seattle	AL	154	553	166	39	0	22	(9	13)	271	85	102	108	98	6	66	5	0	12	0	0	-	19	.300	.403	.490
2003 Seattle	AL	152	539	145	35	0	10	(8	2)	210	64	83	79	84	7	67	6	2	3	0	1	.00	20	.269	.372	.390
15 ML YEARS		2020	6994	2079	473	12	239	(124	115)	3293	1076	1145	1314	1198	151	935	80	11	88	11	14	.44	215	.297	.402	.471

Darren Oliver

Pitches: L **Bats:** R **Pos:** SP-32; RP-1   **Ht:** 6'2" **Wt:** 220 **Born:** 10/6/70 **Age:** 33

Year Team	Lg	G	GS	CG	GF	IP	BFP	H	R	ER	HR	SH	SF	HB	TBB	IBB	SO	WP	Bk	W	L	Pct	ShO	Sv-Op	Hld	ERC	ERA
1993 Texas	AL	2	0	0	0	3.1	14	2	1	1	1	0	0	0	1	1	4	0	0	0	0	-	0	0-0	0	2.15	2.70
1994 Texas	AL	43	0	0	10	50.0	226	40	24	19	4	6	0	6	35	4	50	2	2	4	0	1.000	0	2-3	9	4.29	3.42
1995 Texas	AL	17	7	0	2	49.0	222	47	25	23	3	5	1	1	32	1	39	4	0	4	2	.667	0	0-0	0	4.59	4.22
1996 Texas	AL	30	30	1	0	173.2	777	190	97	90	20	2	7	10	76	3	112	5	1	14	6	.700	0	0-0	0	5.10	4.66
1997 Texas	AL	32	32	3	0	201.1	887	213	111	94	29	2	5	11	82	3	104	7	0	13	12	.520	1	0-0	0	4.98	4.20
1998 Tex-StL		29	29	2	0	160.1	749	204	115	102	18	8	8	10	66	2	87	7	4	10	11	.476	0	0-0	0	6.01	5.73
1999 St Louis	NL	30	30	2	0	196.1	842	197	96	93	16	11	4	11	74	4	119	6	2	9	9	.500	1	0-0	0	4.11	4.26
2000 Texas	AL	21	21	0	0	108.0	501	151	95	89	16	5	4	4	42	3	49	4	1	2	9	.182	0	0-0	0	7.04	7.42
2001 Texas	AL	28	28	1	0	154.0	696	189	109	103	23	1	5	6	65	0	104	8	2	11	11	.500	0	0-0	0	6.14	6.02
2002 Boston	AL	14	9	1	0	58.0	258	70	30	30	7	1	3	6	27	0	32	1	0	4	5	.444	1	0-0	0	6.49	4.66
2003 Colorado	NL	33	32	1	0	180.1	786	201	108	101	21	4	5	8	61	3	88	0	0	13	11	.542	0	0-0	0	4.80	5.04
1998 Texas	AL	19	19	2	0	103.1	493	140	84	75	11	3	6	10	43	1	58	6	1	6	7	.462	0	0-0	0	6.68	6.53
1998 St Louis	NL	10	10	0	0	57.0	256	64	31	27	7	5	2	0	23	1	29	1	3	4	4	.500	0	0-0	0	4.85	4.26
11 ML YEARS		279	218	11	12	1334.1	5958	1504	811	745	158	45	42	73	561	24	788	44	12	84	76	.525	4	2-3	9	5.27	5.02

Miguel Olivo

Bats: R **Throws:** R **Pos:** C-113; PR-7; PH-1   **Ht:** 6'0" **Wt:** 180 **Born:** 7/15/78 **Age:** 25

Year Team	Lg	G	AB	H	2B	3B	HR	(Hm	Rd)	TB	R	RBI	RC	TBB	IBB	SO	HBP	SH	SF	SB	CS	SB%	GDP	Avg	OBP	Slg
1998 Athletics	R	46	164	51	11	3	2	(-	-)	74	30	23	24	8	0	43	4	0	1	2	2	.50	5	.311	.356	.451
1999 Modesto	A+	73	243	74	13	6	9	(-	-)	126	46	42	42	21	1	60	2	1	1	4	5	.44	6	.305	.363	.519
2000 Modesto	A+	58	227	64	11	5	5	(-	-)	100	40	35	31	16	0	53	2	0	2	5	2	.71	8	.282	.332	.441
2000 Midland	AA	19	59	14	2	0	1	(-	-)	19	8	9	5	5	0	15	0	1	0	0	0	-	3	.237	.297	.322
2001 Birmingham	AA	93	316	82	23	1	14	(-	-)	149	45	55	53	37	4	62	7	5	3	6	3	.67	4	.259	.347	.472
2002 Birmingham	AA	106	359	110	24	10	6	(-	-)	172	51	49	63	40	5	66	5	4	3	29	13	.69	11	.306	.381	.479
2002 Chicago	AL	6	19	4	1	0	1	(0	1)	8	2	5	4	2	0	5	0	0	0	0	0	-	1	.211	.286	.421
2003 Chicago	AL	114	317	75	19	1	6	(4	2)	114	37	27	32	19	0	80	4	4	2	6	4	.60	3	.237	.287	.360
2 ML YEARS		120	336	79	20	1	7	(4	3)	122	39	32	36	21	0	85	4	4	2	6	4	.60	4	.235	.287	.363

Ray Olmedo

Bats: B **Throws:** R **Pos:** SS-51; 2B-18; PH-13; PR-5   **Ht:** 5'11" **Wt:** 155 **Born:** 5/31/81 **Age:** 23

Year Team	Lg	G	AB	H	2B	3B	HR	(Hm	Rd)	TB	R	RBI	RC	TBB	IBB	SO	HBP	SH	SF	SB	CS	SB%	GDP	Avg	OBP	Slg
1999 Reds	R	54	195	46	12	1	1	(-	-)	63	30	19	18	12	0	28	1	1	2	13	7	.65	1	.236	.281	.323
2000 Dayton	A	111	369	94	19	1	4	(-	-)	127	50	41	37	30	1	70	1	14	4	17	11	.61	11	.255	.309	.344
2001 Mudville	A+	129	536	131	23	4	0	(-	-)	162	57	28	43	24	0	121	8	13	4	38	17	.69	15	.244	.285	.302
2002 Chattanooga	AA	132	478	118	21	1	3	(-	-)	150	62	30	50	53	2	86	7	14	0	15	16	.48	4	.247	.331	.314
2003 Louisville	AAA	9	25	6	1	0	1	(-	-)	10	4	4	3	2	0	6	0	4	0	0	0	-	0	.240	.296	.400
2003 Chattanooga	AA	49	160	47	11	0	2	(-	-)	64	23	15	22	14	1	29	0	7	1	3	3	.50	3	.294	.349	.400
2003 Cincinnati	NL	79	230	55	6	1	0	(0	0)	63	24	17	18	13	0	46	0	7	0	1	1	.50	4	.239	.280	.274

Kevin Olsen

Pitches: R **Bats:** R **Pos:** RP-7   **Ht:** 6'2" **Wt:** 196 **Born:** 7/26/76 **Age:** 27

Year Team	Lg	G	GS	CG	GF	IP	BFP	H	R	ER	HR	SH	SF	HB	TBB	IBB	SO	WP	Bk	W	L	Pct	ShO	Sv-Op	Hld	ERC	ERA
2003 Albuquerque*	AAA	7	7	0	0	38.1	151	36	12	9	1	0	2	0	7	1	28	0	0	2	1	.667	0	0--	-	2.52	2.11
2003 Jupiter*	A+	1	1	0	0	4.0	13	1	0	0	0	0	0	1	0	0	3	0	0	0	0	-	0	0--	-	0.44	0.00
2001 Florida	NL	4	2	0	0	15.0	56	11	2	2	0	0	0	0	2	1	13	0	0	0	0	-	0	0-0	0	1.34	1.40
2002 Florida	NL	17	8	0	0	55.2	250	57	31	28	5	5	2	1	31	1	38	3	1	0	5	.000	0	0-0	1	4.81	4.53
2003 Florida	NL	7	0	0	2	12.0	63	25	18	17	2	0	0	0	4	1	12	1	0	0	0	-	0	0-0	0	11.35	12.75
3 ML YEARS		28	10	0	5	82.2	369	93	51	47	7	5	2	1	37	3	63	4	1	0	5	.000	0	0-0	1	4.87	5.12

Magglio Ordonez

Bats: R **Throws:** R **Pos:** RF-154; CF-4; PH-3; DH-2   **Ht:** 6'0" **Wt:** 210 **Born:** 1/28/74 **Age:** 30

Year Team	Lg	G	AB	H	2B	3B	HR	(Hm	Rd)	TB	R	RBI	RC	TBB	IBB	SO	HBP	SH	SF	SB	CS	SB%	GDP	Avg	OBP	Slg
1997 Chicago	AL	21	69	22	6	0	4	(2	2)	40	12	11	12	2	0	8	0	1	0	1	2	.33	1	.319	.348	.580
1998 Chicago	AL	145	535	151	25	2	14	(8	6)	222	70	65	67	28	1	53	9	2	4	9	7	.56	19	.282	.326	.415
1999 Chicago	AL	157	624	188	34	3	30	(16	14)	318	100	117	102	47	4	64	1	0	5	13	6	.68	24	.301	.349	.510
2000 Chicago	AL	153	588	185	34	3	32	(21	11)	321	102	126	112	60	3	64	2	0	15	18	4	.82	28	.315	.371	.546
2001 Chicago	AL	160	593	181	40	1	31	(17	14)	316	97	113	117	70	7	70	5	0	3	25	7	.78	14	.305	.382	.533
2002 Chicago	AL	153	590	189	47	1	38	(24	14)	352	116	135	122	53	2	77	7	0	3	7	5	.58	21	.320	.381	.597
2003 Chicago	AL	160	606	192	46	3	29	(17	12)	331	95	99	110	57	1	73	7	0	4	9	5	.64	20	.317	.380	.546
7 ML YEARS		949	3605	1108	232	13	178	(105	73)	1900	592	666	642	317	18	409	31	3	34	82	36	.69	127	.307	.365	.527

Rey Ordonez

Bats: R **Throws:** R **Pos:** SS-34   **Ht:** 5'9" **Wt:** 159 **Born:** 1/11/71 **Age:** 33

Year Team	Lg	G	AB	H	2B	3B	HR	(Hm	Rd)	TB	R	RBI	RC	TBB	IBB	SO	HBP	SH	SF	SB	CS	SB%	GDP	Avg	OBP	Slg
1996 New York	NL	151	502	129	12	4	1	(0	1)	152	51	30	39	22	12	53	1	4	1	1	3	.25	12	.257	.289	.303
1997 New York	NL	120	356	77	5	3	1	(1	0)	91	35	33	19	18	3	36	1	14	2	11	5	.69	10	.216	.255	.256
1998 New York	NL	153	505	124	20	2	1	(0	1)	151	46	42	37	23	7	60	1	15	4	3	6	.33	11	.246	.278	.299
1999 New York	NL	154	520	134	24	2	1	(1	0)	165	49	60	51	49	12	59	1	11	7	8	4	.67	16	.258	.319	.317
2000 New York	NL	45	133	25	5	0	0	(0	0)	30	10	9	8	17	2	16	0	4	1	0	0	-	2	.188	.278	.226
2001 New York	NL	149	461	114	24	4	3	(0	3)	155	31	44	41	34	17	43	1	7	2	3	2	.60	17	.247	.299	.336
2002 New York	NL	144	460	117	25	2	1	(0	1)	149	53	42	36	24	11	46	2	9	4	2	2	.50	19	.254	.292	.324
2003 Tampa Bay	AL	34	117	37	11	0	3	(1	2)	57	14	22	17	2	0	12	1	2	2	0	2	.00	3	.316	.328	.487
8 ML YEARS		950	3054	757	126	17	11	(3	8)	950	289	282	248	189	64	325	8	66	23	28	24	.54	92	.248	.291	.311

Eddie Oropesa

Pitches: L **Bats:** L **Pos:** RP-47   **Ht:** 6'3" **Wt:** 215 **Born:** 11/23/71 **Age:** 32

Year Team	Lg	G	GS	CG	GF	IP	BFP	H	R	ER	HR	SH	SF	HB	TBB	IBB	SO	WP	Bk	W	L	Pct	ShO	Sv-Op	Hld	ERC	ERA
2003 Tucson*	AAA	15	0	0	5	15.1	63	14	4	4	0	1	0	1	7	1	9	1	0	0	1	.000	0	0--	-	2.60	2.35
2001 Philadelphia	NL	30	0	0	4	19.0	87	16	10	10	1	1	0	0	17	6	15	1	0	1	0	1.000	0	0-1	6	4.20	4.74
2002 Arizona	NL	32	0	0	5	25.1	132	39	30	29	6	2	1	2	15	0	18	1	1	2	0	1.000	0	0-1	7	9.65	10.30
2003 Arizona	NL	47	0	0	9	38.2	180	38	27	25	3	3	0	2	27	2	39	3	1	3	3	.500	0	0-0	10	5.06	5.82
3 ML YEARS		109	0	0	18	83.0	399	93	67	64	10	6	1	4	59	8	72	5	2	6	3	.667	0	0-2	23	6.19	6.94

Jesse Orosco

Pitches: L Bats: R Pos: RP-65   **Ht: 6'2" Wt: 205 Born: 4/21/57 Age: 47**

Year Team	Lg	G	GS	CG	GF	IP	BFP	H	R	ER	HR	SH	SF	HB	TBB	IBB	SO	WP	Bk	W	L	Pct	ShO	Sv-Op	Hld	ERC	ERA
1979 New York	NL	18	2	0	6	35.0	154	33	20	19	4	3	0	2	22	0	22	0	0	1	2	.333	0	0-0	0	5.16	4.89
1981 New York	NL	8	0	0	4	17.1	69	13	4	3	2	2	0	0	6	2	18	0	1	0	1	.000	0	1-1	0	2.53	1.56
1982 New York	NL	54	2	0	22	109.1	451	92	37	33	7	5	4	2	40	2	89	3	2	4	10	.286	0	4-5	5	2.92	2.72
1983 New York	NL	62	0	0	42	110.0	432	76	27	18	3	4	3	1	38	7	84	1	2	13	7	.650	0	17-22	1	1.84	1.47
1984 New York	NL	60	0	0	52	87.0	355	58	29	25	7	3	3	2	34	6	85	1	1	10	6	.625	0	31-39	0	2.14	2.59
1985 New York	NL	54	0	0	39	79.0	331	66	26	24	6	1	1	0	34	7	68	4	0	8	6	.571	0	17-25	1	3.00	2.73
1986 New York	NL	58	0	0	40	81.0	338	64	23	21	6	2	3	3	35	3	62	2	0	8	6	.571	0	21-29	1	2.99	2.33
1987 New York	NL	58	0	0	41	77.0	335	78	41	38	5	5	4	2	31	9	78	2	0	3	9	.250	0	16-22	4	3.81	4.44
1988 Los Angeles	NL	55	0	0	21	53.0	229	41	18	16	4	3	2	2	30	3	43	1	0	3	2	.600	0	9-15	11	3.33	2.72
1989 Cleveland	AL	69	0	0	29	78.0	312	54	20	18	7	8	3	2	26	4	79	0	0	3	4	.429	0	3-7	11	2.20	2.08
1990 Cleveland	AL	55	0	0	28	64.2	289	58	35	28	9	5	3	0	38	7	55	1	0	5	4	.556	0	2-3	2	4.25	3.90
1991 Cleveland	AL	47	0	0	20	45.2	202	52	20	19	4	1	3	1	15	8	36	1	1	2	0	1.000	0	0-0	3	4.24	3.74
1992 Milwaukee	NL	59	0	0	14	39.0	158	33	15	14	5	0	2	1	13	1	40	2	0	3	1	.750	0	1-2	11	3.31	3.23
1993 Milwaukee	NL	57	0	0	27	56.2	233	47	25	20	2	1	2	3	17	3	67	3	1	3	5	.375	0	8-13	11	2.50	3.18
1994 Milwaukee	NL	40	0	0	5	39.0	174	32	26	22	4	0	2	2	26	2	36	0	0	3	1	.750	0	0-4	8	4.22	5.08
1995 Baltimore	AL	65	0	0	23	49.2	200	28	19	18	4	2	4	1	27	7	58	2	1	2	4	.333	0	3-6	15	2.12	3.26
1996 Baltimore	AL	66	0	0	10	55.2	236	42	22	21	5	2	1	2	28	4	52	2	0	3	1	.750	0	0-3	19	3.07	3.40
1997 Baltimore	AL	71	0	0	12	50.1	205	29	13	13	6	1	2	0	30	0	46	1	1	6	3	.667	0	0-4	21	2.73	2.32
1998 Baltimore	AL	69	0	0	26	56.2	243	46	20	20	6	4	2	1	28	1	50	3	1	4	1	.800	0	7-9	9	3.45	3.18
1999 Baltimore	AL	65	0	0	12	32.0	144	28	21	19	5	2	3	2	20	3	35	2	0	0	2	.000	0	1-4	12	4.73	5.34
2000 St Louis	NL	6	0	0	0	2.1	16	3	3	1	1	0	0	2	3	2	4	0	0	0	0	-	0	0-0	3	13.85	3.86
2001 Los Angeles	NL	35	0	0	7	16.0	69	17	7	7	3	0	1	0	7	1	21	0	0	1	0	1.000	0	0-2	10	5.25	3.94
2002 Los Angeles	NL	56	0	0	8	27.0	119	24	10	9	4	1	1	0	12	1	22	2	0	1	2	.333	0	1-1	17	3.75	3.00
2003 SD-NYY-Min		65	0	0	13	34.0	166	41	31	29	4	1	4	3	21	3	29	7	0	2	2	.500	0	2-4	11	6.42	7.68
2003 San Diego	NL	42	0	0	10	25.0	118	33	22	21	4	0	2	2	10	0	22	4	0	1	1	.500	0	2-3	7	6.76	7.56
2003 New York	AL	15	0	0	0	4.1	24	4	6	5	0	1	1	0	6	3	4	0	0	0	0	-	0	0-1	4	4.76	10.38
2003 Minnesota	AL	8	0	0	3	4.2	24	4	3	3	0	0	1	1	5	0	3	3	0	1	1	.500	0	0-0	0	5.73	5.79
24 ML YEARS		1252	4	0	501	1295.1	5460	1055	512	455	113	56	54	34	581	86	1179	40	11	87	80	.521	0	144-220	186	3.16	3.16

David Ortiz

Bats: L Throws: L Pos: DH-74; 1B-45; PH-11   **Ht: 6'4" Wt: 230 Born: 11/18/75 Age: 28**

Year Team	Lg	G	AB	H	2B	3B	HR	(Hm	Rd)	TB	R	RBI	RC	TBB	IBB	SO	HBP	SH	SF	SB	CS	SB%	GDP	Avg	OBP	Slg
1997 Minnesota	AL	15	49	16	3	0	1	(0	1)	22	10	6	7	2	0	19	0	0	0	0	0	-	1	.327	.353	.449
1998 Minnesota	AL	86	278	77	20	0	9	(2	7)	124	47	46	46	39	3	72	5	0	4	1	0	1.00	8	.277	.371	.446
1999 Minnesota	AL	10	20	0	0	0	0	(0	0)	0	1	0	0	5	0	12	0	0	0	0	0	-	2	.000	.200	.000
2000 Minnesota	AL	130	415	117	36	1	10	(7	3)	185	59	63	66	57	2	81	0	0	6	1	0	1.00	13	.282	.364	.446
2001 Minnesota	AL	89	303	71	17	1	18	(6	12)	144	46	48	46	40	8	68	1	1	2	1	0	1.00	6	.234	.324	.475
2002 Minnesota	AL	125	412	112	32	1	20	(5	15)	206	52	75	63	43	0	87	3	0	8	1	2	.33	5	.272	.339	.500
2003 Boston	AL	128	448	129	39	2	31	(17	14)	265	79	101	82	58	8	83	1	0	2	0	0	-	9	.288	.369	.592
7 ML YEARS		583	1925	522	147	5	89	(37	52)	946	294	339	310	244	21	422	10	1	22	4	2	.67	44	.271	.353	.491

Ramon Ortiz

Pitches: R Bats: R Pos: SP-32   **Ht: 6'0" Wt: 170 Born: 3/23/73 Age: 31**

Year Team	Lg	G	GS	CG	GF	IP	BFP	H	R	ER	HR	SH	SF	HB	TBB	IBB	SO	WP	Bk	W	L	Pct	ShO	Sv-Op	Hld	ERC	ERA
1999 Anaheim	AL	9	9	0	0	48.1	218	50	35	35	7	0	2	2	25	0	44	2	2	2	3	.400	0	0-0	0	5.23	6.52
2000 Anaheim	AL	18	18	2	0	111.1	472	96	69	63	18	4	4	2	55	0	73	7	4	8	6	.571	0	0-0	0	4.24	5.09
2001 Anaheim	AL	32	32	0	0	208.2	916	223	114	101	25	9	6	12	76	6	135	7	0	13	11	.542	0	0-0	0	4.65	4.36
2002 Anaheim	AL	32	32	4	0	217.1	896	188	97	91	40	2	5	5	68	0	162	7	3	15	9	.625	1	0-0	0	3.64	3.77
2003 Anaheim	AL	32	32	1	0	180.0	814	209	121	104	28	3	7	12	63	0	94	4	0	16	13	.552	0	0-0	0	5.44	5.20
5 ML YEARS		123	123	9	0	765.2	3316	766	436	394	118	18	24	33	287	6	508	27	9	54	42	.563	1	0-0	0	4.52	4.63

Russ Ortiz

Pitches: R Bats: R Pos: SP-34   **Ht: 6'1" Wt: 208 Born: 6/5/74 Age: 30**

Year Team	Lg	G	GS	CG	GF	IP	BFP	H	R	ER	HR	SH	SF	HB	TBB	IBB	SO	WP	Bk	W	L	Pct	ShO	Sv-Op	Hld	ERC	ERA
1998 San Francisco	NL	22	13	0	3	88.1	394	90	51	49	11	5	4	4	46	1	75	3	0	4	4	.500	0	0-0	1	5.05	4.99
1999 San Francisco	NL	33	33	3	0	207.2	922	189	109	88	24	11	6	6	125	5	164	13	0	18	9	.667	0	0-0	0	4.56	3.81
2000 San Francisco	NL	33	32	0	0	195.2	871	192	117	109	28	10	6	7	112	1	167	8	0	14	12	.538	0	0-0	0	5.17	5.01
2001 San Francisco	NL	33	33	1	0	218.2	911	187	90	80	13	10	4	0	91	3	169	8	1	17	9	.654	1	0-0	0	3.08	3.29
2002 San Francisco	NL	33	33	2	0	214.1	911	191	89	86	15	15	6	4	94	5	137	5	0	14	10	.583	0	0-0	0	3.46	3.61
2003 Atlanta	NL	34	34	1	0	212.1	912	177	101	90	17	6	7	4	102	7	149	5	0	21	7	.750	1	0-0	1	3.32	3.81
6 ML YEARS		188	178	7	3	1137.0	4921	1026	557	502	108	57	33	25	570	22	861	42	1	88	51	.633	2	0-0	1	3.95	3.97

Keith Osik

Bats: R Throws: R Pos: C-78; PH-2   **Ht: 6'0" Wt: 200 Born: 10/22/68 Age: 35**

Year Team	Lg	G	AB	H	2B	3B	HR	(Hm	Rd)	TB	R	RBI	RC	TBB	IBB	SO	HBP	SH	SF	SB	CS	SB%	GDP	Avg	OBP	Slg
1996 Pittsburgh	NL	48	140	41	14	1	1	(0	1)	60	18	14	21	14	1	22	1	1	0	1	0	1.00	3	.293	.361	.429
1997 Pittsburgh	NL	49	105	27	9	1	0	(0	0)	38	10	7	12	9	1	21	1	2	0	0	1	.00	1	.257	.322	.362
1998 Pittsburgh	NL	39	98	21	4	0	0	(0	0)	25	8	7	7	13	2	16	2	2	1	2	3	.33	4	.214	.316	.255
1999 Pittsburgh	NL	66	167	31	3	1	2	(1	1)	42	12	13	7	11	0	30	1	1	1	0	0	-	8	.186	.239	.251
2000 Pittsburgh	NL	46	123	36	6	1	4	(1	3)	56	11	22	23	14	0	11	5	1	0	3	0	1.00	2	.293	.387	.455
2001 Pittsburgh	NL	56	120	25	4	0	2	(0	2)	35	9	13	11	13	0	24	3	0	1	1	0	1.00	1	.208	.299	.292

Year Team	Lg	G	AB	H	2B	3B	HR	(Hm	Rd)	TB	R	RBI	RC	TBB	IBB	SO	HBP	SH	SF	SB	CS	SB%	GDP	Avg	OBP	Slg
2002 Pittsburgh	NL	55	100	16	3	0	2	(1	1)	25	6	11	4	6	0	25	1	2	2	0	0	-	2	.160	.211	.250
2003 Milwaukee	NL	80	241	60	12	0	2	(1	1)	78	22	21	19	31	0	44	3	0	0	0	1	.00	7	.249	.342	.324
8 ML YEARS		439	1094	257	55	4	13	(4	9)	359	96	108	104	111	4	193	17	9	5	6	4	.60	28	.235	.314	.328

Antonio Osuna

Pitches: R **Bats:** R **Pos:** RP-48   **Ht:** 5'11" **Wt:** 205 **Born:** 4/12/73 **Age:** 31

	HOW MUCH HE PITCHED						WHAT HE GAVE UP												THE RESULTS							
Year Team	Lg	G	GS	CG	GF	IP	BFP	H	R	ER	HR	SH	SF	HB	TBB	IBB	SO	WP	Bk	W	L	Pct	ShO	Sv-Op	Hld	ERC	ERA
2003 Yankees*	R	1	1	0	0	1.0	4	1	0	0	0	0	0	0	0	0	2	0	0	0	0	-	0	0--	-	1.95	0.00
2003 Tampa*	A+	2	2	0	0	4.0	13	1	0	0	0	0	0	0	1	0	5	0	0	0	0	-	0	0--	-	0.44	0.00
1995 Los Angeles	NL	39	0	0	8	44.2	186	39	22	22	5	2	1	1	20	2	46	1	0	2	4	.333	0	0-2	11	3.76	4.43
1996 Los Angeles	NL	73	0	0	21	84.0	342	65	33	28	6	7	5	2	32	12	85	3	2	9	6	.600	0	4-9	16	2.53	3.00
1997 Los Angeles	NL	48	0	0	18	61.2	245	46	15	15	6	4	1	1	19	2	68	2	0	3	4	.429	0	0-0	10	2.43	2.19
1998 Los Angeles	NL	54	0	0	25	64.2	272	50	26	22	8	2	2	2	32	0	72	1	0	7	1	.875	0	6-11	12	3.50	3.06
1999 Los Angeles	NL	5	0	0	1	4.2	22	4	5	4	0	0	0	1	3	0	5	1	0	0	0	-	0	0-0	2	4.14	7.71
2000 Los Angeles	NL	46	0	0	16	67.1	293	57	30	28	7	4	3	2	35	2	70	1	2	3	6	.333	0	0-3	4	3.74	3.74
2001 Chicago	AL	4	0	0	0	4.1	23	8	10	10	3	0	1	0	2	1	6	0	0	0	0	-	0	0-1	0	16.71	20.77
2002 Chicago	AL	59	0	0	28	67.2	296	64	32	29	1	5	3	4	28	4	66	0	1	8	2	.800	0	11-14	9	3.31	3.86
2003 New York	AL	48	0	0	16	50.2	232	58	22	21	3	2	2	2	20	3	47	3	0	2	5	.286	0	0-1	9	4.51	3.73
9 ML YEARS		376	0	0	133	449.2	1911	391	195	179	39	26	18	16	191	26	465	12	5	34	28	.548	0	21-41	73	3.41	3.58

Roy Oswalt

Pitches: R **Bats:** R **Pos:** SP-21   **Ht:** 6'0" **Wt:** 175 **Born:** 8/29/77 **Age:** 26

	HOW MUCH HE PITCHED						WHAT HE GAVE UP												THE RESULTS							
Year Team	Lg	G	GS	CG	GF	IP	BFP	H	R	ER	HR	SH	SF	HB	TBB	IBB	SO	WP	Bk	W	L	Pct	ShO	Sv-Op	Hld	ERC	ERA
2003 New Orleans*	AAA	1	1	0	0	3.0	12	3	1	1	0	0	0	0	0	0	2	1	0	0	0	-	0	0--	-	1.95	3.00
2001 Houston	NL	28	20	3	4	141.2	575	126	48	43	13	4	4	6	24	2	144	0	0	14	3	.824	1	0-0	0	2.68	2.73
2002 Houston	NL	35	34	0	0	233.0	956	215	86	78	17	12	7	5	62	4	208	3	0	19	9	.679	0	0-0	0	3.05	3.01
2003 Houston	NL	21	21	0	0	127.1	514	116	48	42	15	7	1	5	29	0	108	1	0	10	5	.667	0	0-0	0	3.26	2.97
3 ML YEARS		84	75	3	4	502.0	2045	457	182	163	45	23	12	16	115	6	460	4	0	43	17	.717	1	0-0	0	3.00	2.92

Lyle Overbay

Bats: L **Throws:** L **Pos:** 1B-75; PH-11   **Ht:** 6'2" **Wt:** 215 **Born:** 1/28/77 **Age:** 27

							BATTING													BASERUNNING				AVERAGES		
Year Team	Lg	G	AB	H	2B	3B	HR	(Hm	Rd)	TB	R	RBI	RC	TBB	IBB	SO	HBP	SH	SF	SB	CS	SB%	GDP	Avg	OBP	Slg
2003 Tucson*	AAA	35	119	34	11	0	4	(-	-)	57	24	16	25	28	2	19	0	0	1	0	0	-	2	.286	.419	.479
2001 Arizona	NL	2	2	1	0	0	0	(0	0)	1	0	0	0	0	0	1	0	0	0	0	0	-	0	.500	.500	.500
2002 Arizona	NL	10	10	1	0	0	0	(0	0)	1	0	1	0	0	0	5	0	0	0	0	0	-	0	.100	.100	.100
2003 Arizona	NL	86	254	70	20	0	4	(2	2)	102	23	28	34	35	7	67	2	0	2	1	0	1.00	8	.276	.365	.402
3 ML YEARS		98	266	72	20	0	4	(2	2)	104	23	29	34	35	7	73	2	0	2	1	0	1.00	8	.271	.357	.391

Eric Owens

Bats: R **Throws:** R **Pos:** CF-48; RF-42; PR-14; PH-12; LF-10   **Ht:** 6'0" **Wt:** 208 **Born:** 2/3/71 **Age:** 33

							BATTING													BASERUNNING				AVERAGES		
Year Team	Lg	G	AB	H	2B	3B	HR	(Hm	Rd)	TB	R	RBI	RC	TBB	IBB	SO	HBP	SH	SF	SB	CS	SB%	GDP	Avg	OBP	Slg
1995 Cincinnati	NL	2	2	2	0	0	0	(0	0)	2	0	1	1	0	0	0	0	1	0	0	0	-	0	1.000	1.000	1.000
1996 Cincinnati	NL	88	205	41	6	0	0	(0	0)	47	26	9	16	23	1	38	1	1	2	16	2	.89	2	.200	.281	.229
1997 Cincinnati	NL	27	57	15	0	0	0	(0	0)	15	8	3	4	4	0	11	0	0	0	3	2	.60	2	.263	.311	.263
1998 Milwaukee	NL	34	40	5	2	0	1	(0	1)	10	5	4	0	2	0	6	0	0	1	0	0	-	3	.125	.167	.250
1999 San Diego	NL	149	440	117	22	3	9	(2	7)	172	55	61	58	38	2	50	3	2	2	33	7	.83	12	.266	.327	.391
2000 San Diego	NL	145	583	171	19	7	6	(4	2)	222	87	51	75	45	4	63	4	0	4	29	14	.67	16	.293	.346	.381
2001 Florida	NL	119	400	101	16	1	5	(4	1)	134	51	28	37	29	2	59	0	4	1	8	6	.57	13	.253	.302	.335
2002 Florida	NL	131	385	104	15	5	4	(2	2)	141	44	37	42	31	1	33	0	8	1	26	9	.74	11	.270	.324	.366
2003 Anaheim	AL	111	241	65	6	0	1	(0	1)	74	29	20	22	10	0	24	1	4	1	11	8	.58	4	.270	.300	.307
9 ML YEARS		806	2353	621	86	16	26	(12	14)	817	305	214	255	182	10	284	9	21	11	126	48	.72	63	.264	.318	.347

Pablo Ozuna

Bats: R **Throws:** R **Pos:** 2B-8; CF-5; SS-3; PH-3; PR-2   **Ht:** 6'0" **Wt:** 160 **Born:** 8/25/74 **Age:** 29

							BATTING													BASERUNNING				AVERAGES		
Year Team	Lg	G	AB	H	2B	3B	HR	(Hm	Rd)	TB	R	RBI	RC	TBB	IBB	SO	HBP	SH	SF	SB	CS	SB%	GDP	Avg	OBP	Slg
2003 Visalia*	A+	2	8	5	0	0	0	(-	-)	5	1	1	3	1	0	1	0	0	0	1	1	.50	0	.625	.667	.625
2003 Tulsa*	AA	12	59	15	3	0	0	(-	-)	18	4	4	5	2	1	5	0	0	0	4	2	.67	0	.254	.279	.305
2003 Co Springs*	AAA	56	219	59	13	7	1	(-	-)	89	30	17	26	9	0	23	1	5	1	12	6	.67	3	.269	.300	.406
2000 Florida	NL	14	24	8	1	0	0	(0	0)	9	2	0	3	0	0	2	0	2	0	1	0	1.00	0	.333	.333	.375
2002 Florida	NL	34	47	13	2	2	0	(0	0)	19	4	3	4	1	0	3	1	0	1	1	1	.50	2	.277	.300	.404
2003 Colorado	NL	17	40	8	1	0	0	(0	0)	9	5	2	4	2	0	6	2	1	0	3	0	1.00	1	.200	.273	.225
3 ML YEARS		65	111	29	4	2	0	(0	0)	37	11	5	11	3	0	11	3	3	1	5	1	.83	3	.261	.297	.333

Vicente Padilla

Pitches: R **Bats:** B **Pos:** SP-32   **Ht:** 6'2" **Wt:** 200 **Born:** 9/27/77 **Age:** 26

	HOW MUCH HE PITCHED						WHAT HE GAVE UP												THE RESULTS							
Year Team	Lg	G	GS	CG	GF	IP	BFP	H	R	ER	HR	SH	SF	HB	TBB	IBB	SO	WP	Bk	W	L	Pct	ShO	Sv-Op	Hld	ERC	ERA
1999 Arizona	NL	5	0	0	2	2.2	19	7	5	5	1	1	0	0	3	0	0	0	0	0	1	.000	0	0-1	1	20.65	16.88
2000 Ari-Phi	NL	55	0	0	16	65.1	291	72	33	27	3	5	3	1	28	7	51	1	0	4	7	.364	0	2-7	15	4.22	3.72
2001 Philadelphia	NL	23	0	0	5	34.0	144	36	18	16	1	0	0	0	12	0	29	1	0	3	1	.750	0	0-3	1	3.80	4.24

Year Team	Lg	G	GS	CG	GF	IP	BFP	H	R	ER	HR	SH	SF	HB	TBB	IBB	SO	WP	Bk	W	L	Pct	ShO	Sv-Op	Hld	ERC	ERA
		HOW MUCH HE PITCHED						WHAT HE GAVE UP												THE RESULTS						
2002 Philadelphia	NL	32	32	1	0	206.0	861	198	83	75	16	10	3	15	53	5	128	6	2	14	11	.560	1	0-0	0	3.43	3.28
2003 Philadelphia	NL	32	32	1	0	208.2	876	196	94	84	22	11	7	16	62	4	133	3	2	14	12	.538	1	0-0	0	3.68	3.62
2000 Arizona	NL	27	0	0	12	35.0	143	32	10	9	0	0	1	0	10	2	30	0	0	2	1	.667	0	0-1	7	2.48	2.31
2000 Philadelphia	NL	28	0	0	4	30.1	148	40	23	18	3	5	2	1	18	5	21	1	0	2	6	.250	0	2-6	8	6.52	5.34
5 ML YEARS		147	64	2	23	516.2	2191	509	233	207	43	27	13	32	158	16	341	11	4	35	32	.522	2	2-11	17	3.72	3.61

Lance Painter

Pitches: L **Bats:** L **Pos:** RP-22 **Ht:** 6'1" **Wt:** 200 **Born:** 7/21/67 **Age:** 36

Year Team	Lg	G	GS	CG	GF	IP	BFP	H	R	ER	HR	SH	SF	HB	TBB	IBB	SO	WP	Bk	W	L	Pct	ShO	Sv-Op	Hld	ERC	ERA
2003 Palm Beach*	A+	1	1	0	0	1.0	3	0	0	0	0	0	0	0	0	0	1	0	0	0	0	-	0	0--	-	0.00	0.00
2003 Memphis*	AAA	3	0	0	0	3.0	10	2	0	0	0	0	0	0	0	0	1	0	0	0	0	-	0	0--	-	1.01	0.00
1993 Colorado	NL	10	6	1	2	39.0	166	52	26	26	5	1	0	0	9	0	16	2	0	2	2	.500	0	0-0	0	5.83	6.00
1994 Colorado	NL	15	14	0	1	73.2	336	91	51	50	9	3	5	1	26	2	41	3	1	4	6	.400	0	0-0	0	5.35	6.11
1995 Colorado	NL	33	1	0	7	45.1	198	55	23	22	9	0	0	2	10	0	36	4	1	3	0	1.000	0	1-1	4	5.50	4.37
1996 Colorado	NL	34	1	0	4	50.2	234	56	37	33	12	3	3	3	25	3	48	1	0	4	2	.667	0	0-1	4	6.19	5.86
1997 St Louis	NL	14	0	0	4	17.0	69	13	9	9	1	0	0	0	8	2	11	0	0	1	1	.500	0	0-0	3	2.71	4.76
1998 St Louis	NL	65	0	0	9	47.1	207	42	24	21	5	4	2	4	28	3	39	2	0	4	0	1.000	0	1-2	21	4.56	3.99
1999 St Louis	NL	56	4	0	10	63.1	272	63	37	34	6	4	3	2	25	1	56	4	0	4	5	.444	0	1-3	10	4.12	4.83
2000 Toronto	AL	42	2	0	11	66.2	285	69	37	35	9	5	1	2	22	1	53	4	0	2	0	1.000	0	0-1	5	4.37	4.73
2001 Tor-Mil		23	0	0	7	29.0	139	38	22	21	7	0	0	1	18	2	20	0	0	1	1	.500	0	0-0	4	8.23	6.52
2003 St Louis	NL	22	0	0	1	18.0	76	17	12	11	3	1	0	0	7	1	11	0	0	0	1	.000	0	0-1	5	4.13	5.50
2001 Toronto	AL	10	0	0	3	18.1	91	27	17	16	4	0	0	1	11	0	14	0	0	0	1	.000	0	0-0	0	9.25	7.85
2001 Milwaukee	NL	13	0	0	4	10.2	48	11	5	5	3	0	0	0	7	2	6	0	0	1	0	1.000	0	0-0	4	6.53	4.22
10 ML YEARS		314	28	1	56	450.0	1982	496	278	262	66	21	14	15	178	15	331	20	2	25	18	.581	0	3-9	52	5.11	5.24

Orlando Palmeiro

Bats: L **Throws:** L **Pos:** RF-61; PH-56; LF-41; CF-17; PR-2 **Ht:** 5'10" **Wt:** 182 **Born:** 1/19/69 **Age:** 35

Year Team	Lg	G	AB	H	2B	3B	HR	(Hm	Rd)	TB	R	RBI	RC	TBB	IBB	SO	HBP	SH	SF	SB	CS	SB%	GDP	Avg	OBP	Slg
1995 Anaheim	AL	15	20	7	0	0	0	(0	0)	7	3	1	3	1	0	1	0	0	0	0	0	-	0	.350	.381	.350
1996 Anaheim	AL	50	87	25	6	1	0	(0	0)	33	6	6	12	8	1	13	2	1	0	1	0	1.00	1	.287	.361	.379
1997 Anaheim	AL	74	134	29	2	2	0	(0	0)	35	19	8	10	17	1	11	1	3	1	2	2	.50	4	.216	.307	.261
1998 Anaheim	AL	75	165	53	7	2	0	(0	0)	64	28	21	26	20	1	11	0	7	0	5	4	.56	2	.321	.395	.388
1999 Anaheim	AL	109	317	88	12	1	1	(0	1)	105	46	23	41	39	1	30	6	6	3	5	5	.50	4	.278	.364	.331
2000 Anaheim	AL	108	243	73	20	2	0	(0	0)	97	38	25	42	38	0	20	2	10	3	4	1	.80	4	.300	.395	.399
2001 Anaheim	AL	104	230	56	10	1	2	(0	2)	74	29	23	25	25	2	24	3	7	5	6	6	.50	3	.243	.319	.322
2002 Anaheim	AL	110	263	79	12	1	0	(0	0)	93	35	31	38	30	1	22	0	4	3	7	2	.78	5	.300	.368	.354
2003 St Louis	NL	141	317	86	13	1	3	(1	2)	110	37	33	36	32	3	31	2	7	6	3	3	.50	1	.271	.336	.347
9 ML YEARS		786	1776	496	82	11	6	(1	5)	618	241	171	233	210	10	163	16	45	21	32	24	.57	26	.279	.357	.348

Rafael Palmeiro

Bats: L **Throws:** L **Pos:** DH-95; 1B-55; PH-4 **Ht:** 6'0" **Wt:** 190 **Born:** 9/24/64 **Age:** 39

Year Team	Lg	G	AB	H	2B	3B	HR	(Hm	Rd)	TB	R	RBI	RC	TBB	IBB	SO	HBP	SH	SF	SB	CS	SB%	GDP	Avg	OBP	Slg
1986 Chicago	NL	22	73	18	4	0	3	(1	2)	31	9	12	8	4	0	6	1	0	0	1	1	.50	4	.247	.295	.425
1987 Chicago	NL	84	221	61	15	1	14	(5	9)	120	32	30	39	20	1	26	1	0	2	2	2	.50	4	.276	.336	.543
1988 Chicago	NL	152	580	178	41	5	8	(8	0)	253	75	53	88	38	6	34	3	2	6	12	2	.86	11	.307	.349	.436
1989 Texas	AL	156	559	154	23	4	8	(4	4)	209	76	64	73	63	3	48	6	2	2	4	3	.57	18	.275	.354	.374
1990 Texas	AL	154	598	191	35	6	14	(9	5)	280	72	89	93	40	6	59	3	2	8	3	3	.50	24	.319	.361	.468
1991 Texas	AL	159	631	203	49	3	26	(12	14)	336	115	88	123	68	10	72	6	2	7	4	3	.57	17	.322	.389	.532
1992 Texas	AL	159	608	163	27	4	22	(8	14)	264	84	85	94	72	8	83	10	5	6	2	3	.40	10	.268	.352	.434
1993 Texas	AL	160	597	176	40	2	37	(22	15)	331	124	105	123	73	22	85	5	2	9	22	3	.88	8	.295	.371	.554
1994 Baltimore	AL	111	436	139	32	0	23	(11	12)	240	82	76	90	54	1	63	2	0	6	7	3	.70	11	.319	.392	.550
1995 Baltimore	AL	143	554	172	30	2	39	(21	18)	323	89	104	116	62	5	65	3	0	5	3	1	.75	12	.310	.380	.583
1996 Baltimore	AL	162	626	181	40	2	39	(21	18)	342	110	142	130	95	12	96	3	0	9	8	0	1.00	9	.289	.381	.546
1997 Baltimore	AL	158	614	156	24	2	38	(20	18)	298	95	110	97	67	7	109	5	0	6	5	2	.71	14	.254	.329	.485
1998 Baltimore	AL	162	619	183	36	1	43	(25	18)	350	98	121	126	79	8	91	7	0	4	11	7	.61	14	.296	.379	.565
1999 Texas	AL	158	565	183	30	1	47	(28	19)	356	96	148	139	97	14	69	3	0	9	2	4	.33	13	.324	.420	.630
2000 Texas	AL	158	565	163	29	3	39	(26	13)	315	102	120	121	103	17	77	3	0	7	2	1	.67	14	.288	.397	.558
2001 Texas	AL	160	600	164	33	0	47	(23	24)	338	98	123	128	101	8	90	7	0	6	1	1	.50	8	.273	.381	.563
2002 Texas	AL	155	546	149	34	0	43	(20	23)	312	99	105	106	104	16	94	6	0	7	2	0	1.00	10	.273	.391	.571
2003 Texas	AL	154	561	146	21	2	38	(21	17)	285	92	112	106	84	9	77	5	0	4	2	0	1.00	7	.260	.359	.508
18 ML YEARS		2567	9553	2780	543	38	528	(288	240)	4983	1548	1687	1800	1224	153	1244	79	15	102	93	39	.70	208	.291	.373	.522

Dean Palmer

Bats: R **Throws:** R **Pos:** DH-22; PH-2; 1B-1; 3B-1 **Ht:** 6'1" **Wt:** 219 **Born:** 12/27/68 **Age:** 35

Year Team	Lg	G	AB	H	2B	3B	HR	(Hm	Rd)	TB	R	RBI	RC	TBB	IBB	SO	HBP	SH	SF	SB	CS	SB%	GDP	Avg	OBP	Slg
1989 Texas	AL	16	19	2	2	0	0	(0	0)	4	0	1	0	0	0	12	0	0	1	0	0	-	0	.105	.100	.211
1991 Texas	AL	81	268	50	9	2	15	(6	9)	108	38	37	30	32	0	98	3	1	0	2	2	.00	4	.187	.281	.403
1992 Texas	AL	152	541	124	25	0	26	(11	15)	227	74	72	71	62	2	154	4	2	4	10	4	.71	9	.229	.311	.420
1993 Texas	AL	148	519	127	31	2	33	(12	21)	261	88	96	83	53	4	154	8	0	5	11	10	.52	5	.245	.321	.503
1994 Texas	AL	93	342	84	14	2	19	(11	8)	159	50	59	46	26	0	89	2	0	1	3	4	.43	7	.246	.302	.465
1995 Texas	AL	36	119	40	6	0	9	(5	4)	73	30	24	31	21	1	21	4	0	1	1	1	.50	2	.336	.448	.613
1996 Texas	AL	154	582	163	26	2	38	(19	19)	307	98	107	103	59	4	145	5	0	6	2	2	.50	15	.280	.348	.527
1997 Tex-KC	AL	143	542	139	31	1	23	(10	13)	241	70	86	74	41	2	134	3	1	5	2	2	.50	7	.256	.310	.445
1998 Kansas City	AL	152	572	159	27	2	34	(21	13)	292	84	119	94	48	3	134	6	0	13	8	2	.80	18	.278	.333	.510
1999 Detroit	AL	150	560	147	25	2	38	(24	14)	290	92	100	95	57	3	153	10	0	4	3	3	.50	12	.263	.339	.518
2000 Detroit	AL	145	524	134	22	2	29	(15	14)	247	73	102	84	66	2	146	4	0	10	4	2	.67	9	.256	.338	.471

Year Team	Lg	G	AB	H	2B	3B	HR	(Hm Rd)	TB	R	RBI	RC	TBB	IBB	SO	HBP	SH	SF	SB	CS	SB%	GDP	Avg	OBP	Slg
2001 Detroit	AL	57	216	48	11	0	11	(5 6)	92	34	40	30	27	0	59	3	0	0	4	1	.80	3	.222	.317	.426
2002 Detroit	AL	4	12	0	0	0	0	(0 0)	0	0	0	0	1	0	5	0	0	0	0	0		1	.000	.077	.000
2003 Detroit	AL	26	86	12	2	0	0	(0 0)	14	3	6	2	9	0	28	2	0	1	0	0		2	.140	.235	.163
1997 Texas	AL	94	355	87	21	0	14	(6 8)	150	47	55	45	26	2	84	1	1	3	1	0	1.00	4	.245	.296	.423
1997 Kansas City	AL	49	187	52	10	1	9	(4 5)	91	23	31	29	15	0	50	2	0	2	1	2	.33	3	.278	.335	.487
14 ML YEARS		1357	4902	1229	231	15	275	(139 136)	2315	734	849	743	502	21	1332	54	4	51	48	31	.61	94	.251	.324	.472

Jose Paniagua

Pitches: R Bats: R Pos: RP-1

Ht: 6'2" Wt: 195 Born: 8/20/73 Age: 30

Year Team	Lg	G	GS	CG	GF	IP	BFP	H	R	ER	HR	SH	SF	HB	TBB	IBB	SO	WP	Bk	W	L	Pct	ShO	Sv-Op	Hld	ERC	ERA
2003 Charlotte*	AAA	3	0	0	0	2.1	12	4	2	2	0	0	0	0	2	0	2	1	0	0	0		0	0--	-	10.22	7.71
1996 Montreal	NL	13	11	0	0	51.0	223	55	24	20	7	1	1	3	23	0	27	2	2	2	4	.333	0	0-0	0	5.41	3.53
1997 Montreal	NL	9	3	0	0	18.0	100	29	24	24	2	1	1	4	16	1	8	1	0	1	2	.333	0	0-0	0	11.18	12.00
1998 Seattle	AL	18	0	0	2	22.0	83	15	5	5	3	0	0	3	5	0	16	2	0	2	0	1.000	0	1-2	6	2.68	2.05
1999 Seattle	AL	59	0	0	16	77.2	350	75	37	35	5	4	3	7	52	4	74	6	0	6	11	.353	0	3-12	16	5.06	4.06
2000 Seattle	AL	69	0	0	26	80.1	344	68	31	31	6	3	5	7	38	3	71	4	1	3	0	1.000	0	5-8	14	3.64	3.47
2001 Seattle	AL	60	0	0	24	66.0	296	59	35	32	7	0	1	4	38	2	46	3	0	4	3	.571	0	3-4	16	4.34	4.36
2002 Detroit	AL	41	0	0	15	41.2	191	50	30	27	10	0	3	3	15	1	34	2	0	0	1	.000	0	1-2	7	6.35	5.83
2003 Chicago	AL	1	0	0	0	0.1	5	3	4	4	0	0	0	0	1	0	0	0	0	0	0		0	0-0	0	83.91	108.0
8 ML YEARS		270	14	0	83	357.0	1592	354	190	178	40	9	14	31	188	11	276	20	3	18	21	.462	0	13-28	59	4.97	4.49

Craig Paquette

Bats: R Throws: R Pos: 1B-5; LF-3; PH-3; RF-2

Ht: 6'0" Wt: 190 Born: 3/28/69 Age: 35

Year Team	Lg	G	AB	H	2B	3B	HR	(Hm Rd)	TB	R	RBI	RC	TBB	IBB	SO	HBP	SH	SF	SB	CS	SB%	GDP	Avg	OBP	Slg
2003 Memphis*	AAA	11	49	13	1	0	0	(- -)	14	3	4	4	2	0	12	0	0	1	0	0	-	1	.265	.288	.286
1993 Oakland	AL	105	393	86	20	4	12	(8 4)	150	35	46	34	14	2	108	0	1	1	4	2	.67	7	.219	.245	.382
1994 Oakland	AL	14	49	7	2	0	0	(0 0)	9	0	0	0	0	0	14	0	1	0	1	0	1.00	6	.143	.143	.184
1995 Oakland	AL	105	283	64	13	1	13	(8 5)	118	42	49	30	12	0	88	1	3	5	5	2	.71	5	.226	.256	.417
1996 Kansas City	AL	118	429	111	15	1	22	(12 10)	194	61	67	55	23	2	101	2	3	5	5	3	.63	11	.259	.296	.452
1997 Kansas City	AL	77	252	58	15	1	8	(7 1)	99	26	33	21	10	0	57	2	1	2	2	2	.50	13	.230	.263	.393
1998 New York	NL	7	19	5	2	0	0	(0 0)	7	3	0	1	0	0	6	0	0	0	1	0	1.00	3	.263	.263	.368
1999 St Louis	NL	48	157	45	6	0	10	(7 3)	81	21	37	23	6	0	38	0	1	2	1	0	1.00	6	.287	.309	.516
2000 St Louis	NL	134	384	94	24	2	15	(13 2)	167	47	61	49	27	1	83	2	1	6	4	3	.57	5	.245	.294	.435
2001 St Louis	NL	123	340	96	17	0	15	(8 7)	158	47	64	48	18	1	67	5	5	2	3	1	.75	11	.282	.326	.465
2002 Detroit	AL	72	252	49	14	1	4	(0 4)	77	20	20	13	10	0	53	0	1	3	1	0	1.00	7	.194	.223	.306
2003 Detroit	AL	11	33	5	0	0	0	(0 0)	5	2	0	0	0	0	5	0	0	2	0	0	-	2	.152	.152	.152
11 ML YEARS		814	2591	620	128	10	99	(63 36)	1065	304	377	274	120	6	620	12	17	26	27	13	.68	70	.239	.274	.411

Chan Ho Park

Pitches: R Bats: R Pos: SP-7

Ht: 6'2" Wt: 204 Born: 6/30/73 Age: 31

Year Team	Lg	G	GS	CG	GF	IP	BFP	H	R	ER	HR	SH	SF	HB	TBB	IBB	SO	WP	Bk	W	L	Pct	ShO	Sv-Op	Hld	ERC	ERA
2003 Frisco*	AA	2	2	0	0	11.0	52	10	5	3	0	0	2	4	4	0	6	1	0	1	0	1.000	0	0--	-	3.87	2.45
2003 Oklahoma*	AAA	3	3	0	0	18.1	87	27	12	12	4	0	1	0	8	0	12	1	0	1	0	1.000	0	0--	-	8.21	5.89
1994 Los Angeles	NL	2	0	0	0	4.0	23	5	5	5	1	0	0	1	5	0	6	0	0	0	0		0	0-0	0	11.69	11.25
1995 Los Angeles	NL	2	1	0	0	4.0	16	2	2	2	1	0	0	0	2	0	7	0	1	0	0		0	0-0	0	2.70	4.50
1996 Los Angeles	NL	48	10	0	7	108.2	477	82	48	44	7	8	1	4	71	3	119	4	3	5	5	.500	0	0-0	4	3.50	3.64
1997 Los Angeles	NL	32	29	2	1	192.0	792	149	80	72	24	9	5	8	70	1	166	4	1	14	8	.636	0	0-0	0	3.04	3.38
1998 Los Angeles	NL	34	34	2	0	220.2	946	199	101	91	16	11	10	11	97	1	191	6	2	15	9	.625	0	0-0	0	3.69	3.71
1999 Los Angeles	NL	33	33	0	0	194.1	883	208	120	113	31	10	5	14	100	4	174	11	1	13	11	.542	0	0-0	0	5.68	5.23
2000 Los Angeles	NL	34	34	3	0	226.0	963	173	92	82	21	12	5	12	124	4	217	13	0	18	10	.643	1	0-0	0	3.51	3.27
2001 Los Angeles	NL	36	35	2	0	234.0	981	183	98	91	23	16	7	20	91	1	218	3	3	15	11	.577	1	0-0	0	3.15	3.50
2002 Texas	AL	25	25	0	0	145.2	666	154	95	93	20	4	3	17	78	2	121	9	0	9	8	.529	0	0-0	0	5.75	5.75
2003 Texas	AL	7	7	0	0	29.2	146	34	26	25	5	1	3	6	25	0	16	1	1	1	3	.250	0	0-0	0	8.56	7.58
10 ML YEARS		253	208	9	9	1359.0	5893	1189	667	618	149	71	39	93	663	16	1235	51	12	90	65	.581	2	0-0	4	4.04	4.09

Chad Paronto

Pitches: R Bats: R Pos: RP-6

Ht: 6'5" Wt: 250 Born: 7/28/75 Age: 28

Year Team	Lg	G	GS	CG	GF	IP	BFP	H	R	ER	HR	SH	SF	HB	TBB	IBB	SO	WP	Bk	W	L	Pct	ShO	Sv-Op	Hld	ERC	ERA
2003 Buffalo*	AAA	49	0	0	47	56.0	263	64	36	27	2	5	0	3	22	7	48	4	0	3	5	.375	0	18--	-	4.14	4.34
2001 Baltimore	AL	24	0	0	9	27.0	128	33	24	15	5	1	1	0	11	0	16	1	0	1	3	.250	0	0-1	5	5.98	5.00
2002 Cleveland	AL	29	0	0	11	35.2	154	34	19	16	3	0	4	2	11	1	23	2	0	0	2	.000	0	0-0	0	3.45	4.04
2003 Cleveland	AL	6	0	0	5	6.2	29	7	8	7	1	1	1	0	3	0	6	0	0	0	2	.000	0	0-0	0	5.00	9.45
3 ML YEARS		59	0	0	25	69.1	311	74	51	38	9	2	6	3	25	1	45	3	0	1	7	.125	0	0-1	5	4.54	4.93

Jim Parque

Pitches: L Bats: L Pos: SP-5

Ht: 5'11" Wt: 170 Born: 2/8/76 Age: 28

Year Team	Lg	G	GS	CG	GF	IP	BFP	H	R	ER	HR	SH	SF	HB	TBB	IBB	SO	WP	Bk	W	L	Pct	ShO	Sv-Op	Hld	ERC	ERA
2003 Durham*	AAA	21	21	1	0	121.1	524	132	62	55	13	3	3	9	47	1	49	5	0	5	7	.417	0	0--	-	5.03	4.08
1998 Chicago	AL	21	21	0	0	113.0	507	135	72	64	14	1	0	6	49	0	77	0	3	7	5	.583	0	0-0	0	5.88	5.10
1999 Chicago	AL	31	30	1	0	173.2	804	210	111	99	23	5	8	10	79	2	111	3	2	9	15	.375	0	0-0	0	5.98	5.13
2000 Chicago	AL	33	32	0	0	187.0	828	208	105	89	21	5	5	11	71	1	111	2	5	13	6	.684	0	0-0	0	4.99	4.28
2001 Chicago	AL	5	5	1	0	28.0	132	36	26	25	7	2	1	2	10	1	15	0	0	0	3	.000	0	0-0	0	6.86	8.04

Year Team	Lg	G	GS	CG	GF	IP	BFP	H	R	ER	HR	SH	SF	HB	TBB	IBB	SO	WP	Bk	W	L	Pct	ShO	Sv-Op	Hld	ERC	ERA
2002 Chicago	AL	8	4	0	0	25.1	126	34	29	28	11	0	2	1	16	0	13	0	0	1	4	.200	0	0-0	0	10.13	9.95
2003 Tampa Bay	AL	5	5	0	0	17.1	95	27	23	23	2	1	0	1	16	0	8	0	0	1	1	.500	0	0-0	0	10.16	11.94
6 ML YEARS		103	97	2	0	544.1	2492	650	366	328	78	14	16	31	241	4	335	5	10	31	34	.477	0	0-0	0	5.97	5.42

Steve Parris

Pitches: R **Bats:** R **Pos:** SP-7; RP-3   **Ht:** 6'0" **Wt:** 195 **Born:** 12/17/67 **Age:** 36

Year Team	Lg	G	GS	CG	GF	IP	BFP	H	R	ER	HR	SH	SF	HB	TBB	IBB	SO	WP	Bk	W	L	Pct	ShO	Sv-Op	Hld	ERC	ERA
1995 Pittsburgh	NL	15	15	1	0	82.0	360	89	49	49	12	3	2	7	33	1	61	4	0	6	6	.500	1	0-0	0	5.36	5.38
1996 Pittsburgh	NL	8	4	0	3	26.1	123	35	22	21	4	1	1	1	11	0	27	2	0	0	3	.000	0	0-0	0	6.70	7.18
1998 Cincinnati	NL	18	16	1	0	99.0	421	89	44	41	9	7	1	4	32	3	77	1	1	6	5	.545	1	0-0	0	3.22	3.73
1999 Cincinnati	NL	22	21	2	0	128.2	545	124	59	50	16	7	3	6	52	4	86	3	0	11	4	.733	1	0-0	0	4.29	3.50
2000 Cincinnati	NL	33	33	0	0	192.2	861	227	109	103	30	10	3	4	71	5	117	9	1	12	17	.414	0	0-0	0	5.44	4.81
2001 Toronto	AL	19	19	1	0	105.2	471	126	60	54	18	4	2	2	41	4	49	3	0	4	6	.400	0	0-0	0	5.75	4.60
2002 Toronto	AL	14	14	0	0	75.1	348	96	50	50	13	2	2	3	35	5	48	3	0	5	5	.500	0	0-0	0	6.68	5.97
2003 Tampa Bay	AL	10	7	0	1	43.2	200	60	32	30	12	2	2	0	13	0	14	2	0	0	3	.000	0	0-0	0	7.23	6.18
8 ML YEARS		139	129	5	4	753.1	3329	846	425	398	114	36	16	27	288	22	479	27	2	44	49	.473	3	0-0	0	5.22	4.75

John Parrish

Pitches: L **Bats:** L **Pos:** RP-14   **Ht:** 5'11" **Wt:** 181 **Born:** 11/26/77 **Age:** 26

Year Team	Lg	G	GS	CG	GF	IP	BFP	H	R	ER	HR	SH	SF	HB	TBB	IBB	SO	WP	Bk	W	L	Pct	ShO	Sv-Op	Hld	ERC	ERA
2003 Bowie*	AA	49	0	0	17	76.1	310	58	22	17	5	3	1	2	33	0	85	8	0	3	3	.500	0	6- -	-	2.86	2.00
2000 Baltimore	AL	8	8	0	0	36.1	180	40	0	29	6	0	0	0	35	0	28	0	0	2	4	.333	0	0-0	0	7.59	7.18
2001 Baltimore	AL	16	1	0	0	22.0	107	22	0	15	5	0	0	0	17	0	20	0	0	1	2	.333	0	0-0	0	6.34	6.14
2003 Baltimore	AL	14	0	0	2	23.2	93	17	7	5	2	0	1	1	8	2	15	2	0	0	1	.000	0	0-2	1	2.39	1.90
3 ML YEARS		38	9	0	2	82.0	380	79	7	49	13	0	1	1	60	2	63	2	0	3	7	.300	0	0-2	1	5.63	5.38

Corey Patterson

Bats: L **Throws:** R **Pos:** CF-82; PH-4   **Ht:** 5'9" **Wt:** 175 **Born:** 8/13/79 **Age:** 24

Year Team	Lg	G	AB	H	2B	3B	HR	(Hm	Rd)	TB	R	RBI	RC	TBB	IBB	SO	HBP	SH	SF	SB	CS	SB%	GDP	Avg	OBP	Slg
2000 Chicago	NL	11	42	7	1	0	2	(1	1)	14	9	2	3	3	0	14	1	1	0	1	1	.50	0	.167	.239	.333
2001 Chicago	NL	59	131	29	3	0	4	(1	3)	44	26	14	13	6	0	33	3	2	3	4	0	1.00	1	.221	.266	.336
2002 Chicago	NL	153	592	150	30	5	14	(7	7)	232	71	54	61	19	1	142	8	4	5	18	3	.86	8	.253	.284	.392
2003 Chicago	NL	83	329	98	17	7	13	(7	6)	168	49	55	56	15	2	77	1	0	2	16	5	.76	5	.298	.329	.511
4 ML YEARS		306	1094	284	51	12	33	(16	17)	458	155	125	133	43	3	266	13	7	10	39	9	.81	14	.260	.293	.419

Danny Patterson

Pitches: R **Bats:** R **Pos:** RP-19   **Ht:** 6'0" **Wt:** 185 **Born:** 2/17/71 **Age:** 33

Year Team	Lg	G	GS	CG	GF	IP	BFP	H	R	ER	HR	SH	SF	HB	TBB	IBB	SO	WP	Bk	W	L	Pct	ShO	Sv-Op	Hld	ERC	ERA
2003 Toledo*	AAA	10	0	0	2	11.0	45	8	3	3	0	1	0	1	5	1	6	2	0	1	0	1.000	0	0- -	-	2.43	2.45
1996 Texas	AL	7	0	0	5	8.2	38	10	4	0	0	0	0	0	3	1	5	0	0	0	0	-	0	0-0	0	3.81	0.00
1997 Texas	AL	54	0	0	17	71.0	296	70	29	27	3	4	3	0	23	4	69	7	1	10	6	.625	0	1-8	9	3.27	3.42
1998 Texas	AL	56	0	0	12	60.2	257	64	31	30	11	1	1	2	19	2	39	3	0	2	5	.286	0	2-2	19	4.79	4.45
1999 Texas	AL	53	0	0	18	60.1	275	77	38	38	5	0	2	1	19	3	43	2	0	2	0	1.000	0	0-1	4	5.11	5.67
2000 Detroit	AL	58	0	0	12	56.2	244	69	26	25	4	3	2	2	14	2	29	1	0	5	1	.833	0	0-2	12	4.68	3.97
2001 Detroit	AL	60	0	0	16	64.2	258	64	24	22	4	5	3	4	12	5	27	2	0	5	4	.556	0	1-5	16	3.21	3.06
2002 Detroit	AL	6	0	0	1	3.0	17	5	5	5	0	0	0	1	2	0	1	0	0	0	2	.000	0	0-1	0	9.70	15.00
2003 Detroit	AL	19	0	0	9	17.2	73	15	8	8	1	2	0	1	4	0	19	0	0	0	0	-	0	3-3	1	2.51	4.08
8 ML YEARS		313	0	0	99	342.2	1458	374	165	155	28	15	11	11	96	17	226	15	1	24	18	.571	0	7-22	61	4.09	4.07

Jarrod Patterson

Bats: L **Throws:** R **Pos:** 3B-4; DH-4; PH-4; 1B-2   **Ht:** 6'1" **Wt:** 195 **Born:** 9/7/73 **Age:** 30

Year Team	Lg	G	AB	H	2B	3B	HR	(Hm	Rd)	TB	R	RBI	RC	TBB	IBB	SO	HBP	SH	SF	SB	CS	SB%	GDP	Avg	OBP	Slg
1993 Mets	R	46	166	40	9	1	2	(-	-)	57	27	25	19	24	1	28	0	1	4	1	3	.25	5	.241	.330	.343
1994 Kingsport	R+	36	112	29	5	2	5	(-	-)	53	12	18	18	12	2	39	1	0	0	2	0	1.00	1	.259	.336	.473
1994 Pittsfield	A-	29	106	19	6	1	1	(-	-)	30	8	16	7	10	0	34	0	0	2	0	1	.00	1	.179	.246	.283
1995 Kingsport	R+	64	240	67	17	3	13	(-	-)	129	45	57	45	28	2	50	0	0	3	3	1	.75	2	.279	.351	.538
1996 St.Lucie	A+	17	61	11	2	0	1	(-	-)	16	6	6	4	3	0	19	1	0	1	1	0	1.00	0	.180	.227	.262
1996 Capital City	A	70	213	49	9	1	3	(-	-)	69	26	37	25	33	3	65	2	0	4	1	1	.50	3	.230	.333	.324
1997 Regina	IND	65	240	87	24	2	7	(-	-)	136	52	50	60	38	2	47	2	2	1	7	3	.70	1	.363	.452	.567
1998 High Desert	A+	131	492	165	34	9	18	(-	-)	271	89	102	108	66	4	97	2	0	3	9	2	.82	8	.335	.414	.551
1999 El Paso	AA	67	249	95	25	3	11	(-	-)	159	63	51	72	51	6	45	1	0	3	3	2	.60	3	.382	.484	.639
1999 Tucson	AAA	75	274	92	25	3	11	(-	-)	156	46	47	61	36	0	37	3	0	3	4	1	.80	9	.336	.415	.569
2000 Altoona	AA	11	36	5	1	0	0	(-	-)	6	1	4	1	3	0	11	1	0	1	0	0	-	1	.139	.220	.167
2000 Nashville	AAA	70	198	55	10	0	5	(-	-)	80	25	30	26	13	0	40	2	2	2	0	2	.00	2	.278	.326	.404
2000 Ottawa	AAA	25	92	25	6	1	0	(-	-)	33	9	16	9	4	0	13	0	0	1	1	0	1.00	4	.272	.299	.359
2001 Erie	AA	20	70	28	5	1	7	(-	-)	56	17	18	24	11	0	11	0	0	0	0	0	-	0	.400	.476	.800
2001 Toledo	AAA	69	213	63	15	2	7	(-	-)	103	41	25	37	30	1	47	1	0	3	2	1	.67	9	.296	.381	.484
2002 Toledo	AAA	117	447	132	34	6	13	(-	-)	217	66	70	78	46	4	71	4	2	3	3	1	.75	8	.295	.364	.485
2003 Omaha	AAA	123	478	123	33	2	18	(-	-)	214	74	91	70	51	5	92	2	1	4	4	1	.80	9	.257	.329	.448
2001 Detroit	AL	13	44	11	1	1	2	(0	0)	20	6	4	5	0	0	4	2	0	0	0	1	.00	0	.268	.302	.488
2003 Kansas City	AL	13	22	4	0	0	0	(0	0)	4	3	0	0	3	1	6	0	0	0	0	0	-	2	.182	.280	.182
2 ML YEARS		26	63	15	1	1	2	(0	1)	24	9	4	5	3	1	10	2	0	0	0	1	.00	2	.238	.294	.381

John Patterson

Pitches: R Bats: R Pos: SP-8; RP-8 — Ht: 6'5" Wt: 183 Born: 1/30/78 Age: 26

Year Team	Lg	G	GS	CG	GF	IP	BFP	H	R	ER	HR	SH	SF	HB	TBB	IBB	SO	WP	Bk	W	L	Pct	ShO	Sv-Op	Hld	ERC	ERA
1997 South Bend	A	18	18	0	0	78.0	327	63	32	28	3	1	2	5	34	0	95	8	0	1	9	.100	0	0--	-	3.02	3.23
1998 High Desert	A+	25	25	0	0	127.0	519	102	54	40	12	0	3	4	42	0	148	5	0	8	7	.533	0	0--	-	2.86	2.83
1999 El Paso	AA	18	18	2	0	100.0	429	98	61	53	16	3	1	0	42	0	117	3	0	8	6	.571	0	0--	-	4.49	4.77
1999 Tucson	AAA	7	6	0	0	30.2	148	43	26	24	3	0	0	0	18	0	29	0	0	1	5	.167	0	0--	-	7.36	7.04
2000 Tucson	AAA	3	2	0	0	15.0	76	21	14	13	1	1	1	0	9	0	10	2	0	0	2	.000	0	0--	-	6.77	7.80
2001 Lancaster	A+	2	2	0	0	9.1	40	9	6	6	3	0	0	0	3	0	9	0	0	0	0	-	0	0--	-	4.95	5.79
2001 El Paso	AA	5	5	0	0	25.1	112	30	15	12	2	0	0	2	9	0	19	1	0	1	2	.333	0	0--	-	5.23	4.26
2001 Tucson	AAA	13	12	0	0	67.2	313	82	50	44	9	2	5	3	31	3	40	2	1	2	7	.222	0	0--	-	5.89	5.85
2002 Tucson	AAA	19	18	0	0	112.2	496	117	59	53	14	3	3	4	45	1	104	6	1	10	5	.667	0	0--	-	4.57	4.23
2003 Tucson	AAA	18	18	2	0	109.1	474	100	48	32	6	3	7	5	43	0	74	6	0	10	5	.667	2	0--	-	3.38	2.63
2002 Arizona	NL	7	5	0	1	30.2	123	27	11	11	7	0	0	1	7	0	31	2	0	2	0	1.000	0	0-0	-	3.76	3.23
2003 Arizona	NL	16	8	0	3	55.0	252	61	39	37	7	1	2	2	30	5	43	4	0	1	4	.200	0	1-1	0	5.50	6.05
2 ML YEARS		23	13	0	4	85.2	375	88	50	48	14	1	2	3	37	5	74	6	0	3	4	.429	0	1-1	0	4.89	5.04

Josh Paul

Bats: R Throws: R Pos: C-14; PR-2 — Ht: 6'1" Wt: 200 Born: 5/19/75 Age: 29

Year Team	Lg	G	AB	H	2B	3B	HR	(Hm	Rd)	TB	R	RBI	RC	TBB	IBB	SO	HBP	SH	SF	SB	CS	SB%	GDP	Avg	OBP	Slg
2003 Iowa*	AAA	47	146	37	4	0	2	(-	-)	47	12	15	12	8	0	30	1	1	0	0	2	.00	5	.253	.297	.322
2003 Charlotte*	AAA	19	64	12	0	1	2	(-	-)	20	6	5	4	5	0	14	0	2	1	1	1	.50	1	.188	.243	.313
1999 Chicago	AL	6	18	4	1	0	0	(0	0)	5	2	1	1	0	0	4	0	0	0	0	0	-	0	.222	.222	.278
2000 Chicago	AL	36	71	20	3	2	1	(1	0)	30	15	8	9	5	0	17	1	2	0	1	0	1.00	3	.282	.338	.423
2001 Chicago	AL	57	139	37	11	0	3	(0	3)	57	20	18	19	13	0	25	0	1	1	6	2	.75	3	.266	.327	.410
2002 Chicago	AL	33	104	25	4	0	0	(0	0)	29	11	11	11	9	0	22	1	2	2	2	0	1.00	1	.240	.302	.279
2003 CWS-ChC		16	23	6	0	0	0	(0	0)	6	6	4	5	3	0	6	0	1	0	0	0	-	0	.261	.346	.261
2003 Chicago	AL	13	17	6	0	0	0	(0	0)	6	6	4	5	3	0	6	0	0	0	0	0	-	0	.353	.450	.353
2003 Chicago	NL	3	6	0	0	0	0	(0	0)	0	0	0	0	0	0	3	0	1	0	0	0	-	0	.000	.000	.000
5 ML YEARS		148	355	92	19	2	4	(1	3)	127	54	42	45	30	0	74	2	6	3	9	2	.82	7	.259	.318	.358

Carl Pavano

Pitches: R Bats: R Pos: SP-32; RP-1 — Ht: 6'5" Wt: 230 Born: 1/8/76 Age: 28

Year Team	Lg	G	GS	CG	GF	IP	BFP	H	R	ER	HR	SH	SF	HB	TBB	IBB	SO	WP	Bk	W	L	Pct	ShO	Sv-Op	Hld	ERC	ERA
1998 Montreal	NL	24	23	0	0	134.2	580	130	70	63	18	5	6	8	43	1	83	1	0	6	9	.400	0	0-0	0	3.97	4.21
1999 Montreal	NL	19	18	1	0	104.0	457	117	66	65	8	5	2	4	35	1	70	1	3	6	8	.429	1	0-0	0	4.51	5.63
2000 Montreal	NL	15	15	0	0	97.0	408	89	40	33	8	4	3	8	34	1	64	1	1	8	4	.667	0	0-0	0	3.67	3.06
2001 Montreal	NL	8	8	0	0	42.2	199	59	33	30	7	2	1	2	16	1	36	0	1	1	6	.143	0	0-0	0	6.99	6.33
2002 Mon-Fla	NL	37	22	0	2	136.0	618	174	88	78	19	4	4	10	45	4	92	3	2	6	10	.375	0	0-0	3	5.99	5.16
2003 Florida	NL	33	32	2	1	201.0	846	204	99	96	19	9	10	7	49	10	133	3	2	12	13	.480	0	0-0	0	3.57	4.30
2002 Montreal	NL	15	14	0	0	74.1	349	98	55	52	14	2	2	7	31	3	51	2	1	3	8	.273	0	0-0	0	7.09	6.30
2002 Florida	NL	22	8	0	2	61.2	269	76	33	26	5	2	2	3	14	3	41	1	1	3	2	.600	0	0-0	3	4.74	3.79
6 ML YEARS		136	118	3	3	715.1	3108	773	396	365	79	29	26	39	222	22	478	9	9	39	50	.438	1	0-0	3	4.42	4.59

Jay Payton

Bats: R Throws: R Pos: LF-149; CF-8; PH-7; RF-3 — Ht: 5'10" Wt: 185 Born: 11/22/72 Age: 31

Year Team	Lg	G	AB	H	2B	3B	HR	(Hm	Rd)	TB	R	RBI	RC	TBB	IBB	SO	HBP	SH	SF	SB	CS	SB%	GDP	Avg	OBP	Slg
1998 New York	NL	15	22	7	1	0	0	(0	0)	8	2	0	3	1	0	4	0	0	0	0	0	-	0	.318	.348	.364
1999 New York	NL	13	8	2	1	0	0	(0	0)	3	1	1	0	0	0	2	1	0	0	1	2	.33	0	.250	.333	.375
2000 New York	NL	149	488	142	23	1	17	(9	8)	218	63	62	68	30	0	60	3	0	8	5	11	.31	9	.291	.331	.447
2001 New York	NL	104	361	92	16	1	8	(6	2)	134	44	34	37	18	1	52	5	0	2	4	3	.57	11	.255	.298	.371
2002 NYM-Col	NL	134	445	135	20	7	16	(9	7)	217	69	59	71	29	0	54	4	2	1	7	4	.64	11	.303	.351	.488
2003 Colorado	NL	157	600	181	32	5	28	(13	15)	307	93	89	94	43	3	77	5	5	3	6	4	.60	27	.302	.354	.512
2002 New York	NL	87	275	78	6	3	8	(4	4)	114	33	31	37	21	0	34	1	2	1	4	1	.80	8	.284	.336	.415
2002 Colorado	NL	47	170	57	14	4	8	(5	3)	103	36	28	34	8	0	20	3	0	0	3	3	.50	3	.335	.376	.606
6 ML YEARS		572	1924	559	93	14	69	(37	32)	887	272	245	273	121	4	249	20	7	14	23	24	.49	58	.291	.337	.461

Josh Pearce

Pitches: R Bats: R Pos: RP-7 — Ht: 6'3" Wt: 215 Born: 8/20/77 Age: 26

Year Team	Lg	G	GS	CG	GF	IP	BFP	H	R	ER	HR	SH	SF	HB	TBB	IBB	SO	WP	Bk	W	L	Pct	ShO	Sv-Op	Hld	ERC	ERA
1999 New Jersey	A-	14	14	1	0	77.2	336	78	45	43	8	2	6	5	20	0	78	14	1	3	7	.300	1	0--	-	3.73	4.98
2000 Potomac	A+	10	10	1	0	62.2	259	70	25	24	5	0	1	1	10	0	42	0	0	5	3	.625	0	0--	-	3.78	3.45
2000 Arkansas	AA	17	17	0	0	97.1	441	117	68	59	13	6	2	6	35	2	63	5	1	5	6	.455	0	0--	-	5.54	5.46
2001 New Haven	AA	18	18	0	0	115.1	484	111	55	48	11	4	2	6	34	1	96	5	0	6	8	.429	0	0--	-	3.64	3.75
2001 Memphis	AAA	10	10	0	0	69.2	291	72	43	33	11	2	5	1	12	1	36	3	0	4	4	.500	0	0--	-	3.74	4.26
2002 Memphis	AAA	4	4	0	0	20.0	91	28	18	17	8	1	0	0	3	0	17	1	0	0	4	.000	0	0--	-	7.49	7.65
2003 Memphis	AAA	10	5	0	0	46.1	192	51	22	21	8	1	1	0	8	1	27	2	0	3	3	.500	0	0--	-	4.24	4.08
2003 Tennessee	AA	5	5	0	0	33.0	134	34	15	15	3	2	0	3	8	0	20	0	0	2	1	.667	0	0--	-	3.40	4.09
2003 Palm Beach	A+	6	5	0	0	28.0	108	28	10	10	2	2	0	1	2	0	15	1	0	1	4	.200	0	0--	-	2.93	3.21
2002 St Louis	NL	3	3	0	0	13.0	66	20	13	11	1	3	1	1	8	0	1	0	0	0	0	-	0	0-0	0	8.51	7.62
2003 St Louis	NL	7	0	0	2	9.0	39	11	3	3	0	0	1	0	2	0	4	1	0	0	0	-	0	0-0	1	4.45	3.00
2 ML YEARS		10	3	0	2	22.0	105	31	16	14	1	3	1	2	10	0	5	1	0	0	0	-	0	0-0	1	6.78	5.73

Jason Pearson

Pitches: L **Bats:** L **Pos:** RP-2   **Ht:** 6'0" **Wt:** 195 **Born:** 12/29/75 **Age:** 28

Year Team	Lg	G	GS	CG	GF	IP	BFP	H	R	ER	HR	SH	SF	HB	TBB	IBB	SO	WP	Bk	W	L	Pct	ShO	Sv-Op	Hld	ERC	ERA
1998 Marlins	R	11	3	0	5	34.1	134	28	8	6	0	0	0	1	5	0	36	2	0	4	0	1.000	0	2- -	-	1.74	1.57
1998 Kane County	A	2	0	0	2	2.2	14	3	3	1	0	0	1	1	1	0	1	0	0	0	0	-	0	0- -	-	4.83	3.38
1999 Sioux Falls	IND	27	2	0	11	63.1	271	57	29	21	6	3	5	3	28	2	48	2	0	2	3	.400	0	0- -	-	3.80	2.98
2000 Fargo-Mh	IND	18	16	1	0	107.2	455	90	45	36	6	3	2	3	49	1	82	4	1	10	2	.833	0	0- -	-	3.19	3.01
2001 Mobile	AA	54	5	0	16	86.1	371	88	40	40	5	4	6	3	30	3	67	3	0	5	5	.500	0	1- -	-	3.77	4.17
2002 Portland	AAA	23	0	0	5	30.0	125	25	5	5	3	0	0	2	9	0	18	0	0	3	0	1.000	0	0- -	-	3.02	1.50
2002 Fresno	AAA	34	0	0	8	36.0	155	35	20	15	5	2	1	2	16	1	28	3	0	0	0	-	0	0- -	-	4.64	3.75
2003 Memphis	AAA	44	0	0	8	52.1	207	41	21	18	3	0	2	2	9	1	36	1	0	4	4	.500	0	3- -	-	1.98	3.10
2003 Tennessee	AA	9	0	0	0	11.0	43	7	0	0	0	1	0	1	2	0	11	0	0	0	0	-	0	-	-	1.36	0.00
2002 San Diego	NL	2	0	0	1	1.2	6	1	0	0	0	0	0	0	0	0	3	0	0	0	0	-	0	0-0	0	0.75	0.00
2003 St Louis	NL	2	0	0	0	1.0	10	4	7	7	1	0	0	0	3	0	1	0	0	0	0	-	0	0-0	0	53.56	63.00
2 ML YEARS		4	0	0	1	2.2	16	5	7	7	1	0	0	0	3	0	4	0	0	0	0	-	0	0-0	0	15.82	23.63

Jake Peavy

Pitches: R **Bats:** R **Pos:** SP-32   **Ht:** 6'1" **Wt:** 180 **Born:** 5/31/81 **Age:** 23

Year Team	Lg	G	GS	CG	GF	IP	BFP	H	R	ER	HR	SH	SF	HB	TBB	IBB	SO	WP	Bk	W	L	Pct	ShO	Sv-Op	Hld	ERC	ERA
1999 Padres	R	13	11	1	0	73.2	286	52	16	11	4	2	0	3	23	0	90	5	3	7	1	.875	0	0- -	-	2.19	1.34
1999 Idaho Falls	R+	2	2	0	0	11.0	40	5	0	0	0	0	0	0	1	0	13	0	0	2	0	1.000	0	0- -	-	0.57	0.00
2000 Fort Wayne	A	26	25	0	0	133.2	565	107	61	43	6	4	3	9	53	0	164	8	2	13	8	.619	0	0- -	-	2.84	2.90
2001 Lk Elsinore	A+	19	19	0	0	105.1	422	76	41	36	6	2	1	6	33	1	144	5	0	7	5	.583	0	0- -	-	2.25	3.08
2001 Mobile	AA	5	5	0	0	28.0	114	19	8	8	3	0	0	3	12	1	44	1	0	2	1	.667	0	0- -	-	2.93	2.57
2002 Mobile	AA	14	14	0	0	80.1	335	65	26	25	4	3	1	5	30	0	89	1	1	4	5	.444	0	0- -	-	2.85	2.80
2002 San Diego	NL	17	17	0	0	97.2	430	106	54	49	11	5	2	3	33	4	90	4	1	6	7	.462	0	0-0	0	4.41	4.52
2003 San Diego	NL	32	32	0	0	194.2	827	173	94	89	33	7	5	6	82	3	156	2	0	12	11	.522	0	0-0	0	4.13	4.11
2 ML YEARS		49	49	0	0	292.1	1257	279	148	138	44	12	7	9	115	7	246	6	1	18	18	.500	0	0-0	0	4.22	4.25

Kit Pellow

Bats: R **Throws:** R **Pos:** C-7; PH-2; 1B-1; LF-1   **Ht:** 6'1" **Wt:** 200 **Born:** 8/28/73 **Age:** 30

Year Team	Lg	G	AB	H	2B	3B	HR	(Hm	Rd)	TB	R	RBI	RC	TBB	IBB	SO	HBP	SH	SF	SB	CS	SB%	GDP	Avg	OBP	Slg
1996 Spokane	A-	71	279	80	18	2	18	(-	-)	156	48	66	53	20	0	52	8	1	7	8	3	.73	5	.287	.344	.559
1997 Lansing	A	65	256	76	17	2	11	(-	-)	130	39	52	47	24	1	74	6	0	4	2	0	1.00	5	.297	.366	.508
1997 Wichita	AA	68	241	60	12	1	10	(-	-)	104	40	41	32	21	1	72	2	2	3	5	2	.71	5	.249	.311	.432
1998 Wichita	AA	103	374	100	24	3	29	(-	-)	217	70	73	70	27	2	107	6	1	3	4	3	.57	2	.267	.324	.580
1998 Omaha	AAA	14	54	10	3	0	2	(-	-)	19	8	6	4	2	0	19	0	0	2	2	0	1.00	1	.185	.207	.352
1999 Omaha	AAA	131	475	136	28	4	35	(-	-)	277	88	99	88	20	3	117	18	1	7	6	5	.55	11	.286	.335	.583
2000 Omaha	AAA	117	421	105	17	3	22	(-	-)	194	61	75	65	38	1	89	16	1	5	6	4	.60	5	.249	.331	.461
2001 Omaha	AAA	129	484	141	15	0	20	(-	-)	216	81	81	78	37	1	101	13	2	7	4	3	.57	5	.291	.353	.446
2002 Omaha	AAA	105	402	116	25	2	27	(-	-)	226	65	76	76	21	1	82	19	0	4	4	2	.67	7	.289	.350	.562
2003 Co Springs	AAA	89	320	93	15	1	19	(-	-)	167	48	57	59	25	2	75	12	0	1	2	1	.67	5	.291	.363	.522
2003 Asheville	A	6	20	9	2	0	1	(-	-)	14	3	8	8	5	0	5	2	0	1	0	0	-	0	.450	.571	.700
2002 Kansas City	AL	29	63	15	1	0	1	(0	1)	19	6	5	7	9	0	21	1	0	1	1	1	.50	2	.238	.342	.302
2003 Colorado	NL	11	18	8	3	1	1	(0	1)	16	6	4	6	0	0	4	2	0	1	0	0	-	0	.444	.476	.889
2 ML YEARS		40	81	23	4	1	2	(0	2)	35	12	9	13	9	0	25	3	0	1	1	1	.50	2	.284	.372	.432

Carlos Pena

Bats: L **Throws:** L **Pos:** 1B-128; PH-3; DH-1   **Ht:** 6'2" **Wt:** 210 **Born:** 5/17/78 **Age:** 26

Year Team	Lg	G	AB	H	2B	3B	HR	(Hm	Rd)	TB	R	RBI	RC	TBB	IBB	SO	HBP	SH	SF	SB	CS	SB%	GDP	Avg	OBP	Slg
2003 Toledo*	AAA	8	30	10	4	1	0	(-	-)	16	4	5	7	4	1	7	1	0	0	0	0	-	0	.333	.429	.533
2001 Texas	AL	22	62	16	4	1	3	(2	1)	31	6	12	11	10	0	17	0	0	0	0	0	-	1	.258	.361	.500
2002 Oak-Det	AL	115	397	96	17	4	19	(10	9)	178	43	52	57	41	0	111	3	0	2	2	2	.50	7	.242	.316	.448
2003 Detroit	AL	131	452	112	21	6	18	(8	10)	199	51	50	62	53	1	123	6	1	4	4	5	.44	6	.248	.332	.440
2002 Oakland	AL	40	124	27	4	0	7	(5	2)	52	12	16	17	15	0	38	1	0	1	0	0	-	2	.218	.305	.419
2002 Detroit	AL	75	273	69	13	4	12	(5	7)	126	31	36	40	26	0	73	2	0	1	2	2	.50	5	.253	.321	.462
3 ML YEARS		268	911	224	42	11	40	(20	20)	408	100	114	130	104	1	251	9	1	6	6	7	.46	14	.246	.327	.448

Wily Mo Pena

Bats: R **Throws:** R **Pos:** PH-27; CF-26; RF-14; PR-11; LF-8; 3B-1   **Ht:** 6'3" **Wt:** 215 **Born:** 1/23/82 **Age:** 22

Year Team	Lg	G	AB	H	2B	3B	HR	(Hm	Rd)	TB	R	RBI	RC	TBB	IBB	SO	HBP	SH	SF	SB	CS	SB%	GDP	Avg	OBP	Slg
1999 Yankees	R	45	166	41	10	1	7	(-	-)	74	21	26	24	12	0	54	7	0	1	3	2	.60	2	.247	.323	.446
2000 Greensboro	A	67	249	51	7	1	10	(-	-)	90	41	28	21	18	1	91	5	0	4	6	5	.55	9	.205	.268	.361
2000 Staten Island	A-	20	73	22	1	2	0	(-	-)	27	7	10	10	2	0	23	4	0	0	2	0	1.00	1	.301	.354	.370
2001 Dayton	A	135	511	135	25	5	26	(-	-)	248	87	113	82	33	1	177	17	0	4	26	10	.72	6	.264	.327	.485
2002 Chattanooga	AA	105	388	99	23	1	11	(-	-)	157	47	47	53	36	2	126	9	0	3	8	0	1.00	9	.255	.330	.405
2003 Louisville	AAA	14	51	19	3	0	4	(-	-)	34	16	14	14	5	1	13	3	0	1	0	0	-	0	.373	.450	.667
2002 Cincinnati	NL	13	18	4	0	1	0	(1	0)	7	1	1	1	0	0	11	0	0	0	0	0	-	0	.222	.222	.389
2003 Cincinnati	NL	80	165	36	6	1	5	(1	4)	59	20	16	14	12	2	53	3	1	0	3	2	.60	2	.218	.283	.358
2 ML YEARS		93	183	40	6	1	6	(2	4)	66	21	17	15	12	2	64	3	1	0	3	2	.60	2	.219	.278	.361

Brad Penny

Pitches: R **Bats:** R **Pos:** SP-32   **Ht:** 6'4" **Wt:** 247 **Born:** 5/24/78 **Age:** 26

			HOW MUCH HE PITCHED						WHAT HE GAVE UP										THE RESULTS						
Year Team	Lg	G	GS	CG	GF	IP	BFP	H	R	ER	HR	SH	SF	HB	TBB	IBB	SO	WP Bk	W	L	Pct	ShO	Sv-Op	Hld	ERC	ERA
2000 Florida	NL	23	22	0	0	119.2	529	120	70	64	13	6	2	5	60	4	80	4 1	8	7	.533	0	0-0	0	4.70	4.81
2001 Florida	NL	31	31	1	0	205.0	833	183	92	84	15	8	2	7	54	3	154	2 0	10	10	.500	1	0-0	0	2.96	3.69
2002 Florida	NL	24	24	1	0	129.1	574	148	76	67	18	6	4	1	50	7	93	4 0	8	7	.533	1	0-0	0	5.08	4.66
2003 Florida	NL	32	32	0	0	196.1	811	195	96	90	21	7	5	3	56	6	138	3 4	14	10	.583	0	0-0	0	3.73	4.13
4 ML YEARS		110	109	2	0	650.1	2747	646	334	305	67	27	13	16	220	20	465	13 5	40	34	.541	2	0-0	0	3.91	4.22

Jhonny Peralta

Bats: R **Throws:** R **Pos:** SS-72; 3B-6; PH-1; PR-1   **Ht:** 6'1" **Wt:** 180 **Born:** 5/28/82 **Age:** 22

								BATTING											BASERUNNING				AVERAGES		
Year Team	Lg	G	AB	H	2B	3B	HR	(Hm Rd)	TB	R	RBI	RC	TBB	IBB	SO	HBP	SH	SF	SB	CS	SB%	GDP	Avg	OBP	Slg
2000 Columbus	A	106	349	84	13	1	3	(- -)	108	52	34	38	59	0	102	2	1	2	7	6	.54	13	.241	.352	.309
2001 Kinston	A+	125	441	106	24	2	7	(- -)	155	57	47	50	58	0	148	1	2	3	4	8	.33	9	.240	.328	.351
2002 Akron	AA	130	470	132	28	5	15	(- -)	215	62	62	78	45	0	97	5	7	11	4	2	.67	0	.281	.343	.457
2003 Buffalo	AAA	63	237	61	12	1	1	(- -)	78	25	21	22	15	0	45	3	3	0	1	3	.25	6	.257	.310	.329
2003 Cleveland	AL	77	242	55	10	1	4	(3 1)	79	24	21	23	20	0	65	4	2	2	1	3	.25	5	.227	.295	.326

Troy Percival

Pitches: R **Bats:** R **Pos:** RP-52   **Ht:** 6'3" **Wt:** 235 **Born:** 8/9/69 **Age:** 34

				HOW MUCH HE PITCHED						WHAT HE GAVE UP								THE RESULTS							
Year Team	Lg	G	GS	CG	GF	IP	BFP	H	R	ER	HR	SH	SF	HB	TBB	IBB	SO	WP Bk	W	L	Pct	ShO	Sv-Op	Hld	ERC	ERA
1995 Anaheim	AL	62	0	0	16	74.0	284	37	19	16	6	4	1	1	26	2	94	2 2	3	2	.600	0	3-6	29	1.44	1.95
1996 Anaheim	AL	62	0	0	52	74.0	291	38	20	19	8	2	1	2	31	4	100	2 0	0	2	.000	0	36-39	2	1.76	2.31
1997 Anaheim	AL	55	0	0	46	52.0	224	40	20	20	6	1	2	4	22	2	72	5 0	5	5	.500	0	27-31	0	3.15	3.46
1998 Anaheim	AL	67	0	0	60	66.2	287	45	31	27	5	3	2	3	37	4	87	3 0	2	7	.222	0	42-48	0	2.74	3.65
1999 Anaheim	AL	60	0	0	50	57.0	230	38	24	24	9	0	1	3	22	0	58	3 0	4	6	.400	0	31-39	0	2.83	3.79
2000 Anaheim	AL	54	0	0	45	50.0	221	42	27	25	7	3	2	2	30	4	49	1 0	5	5	.500	0	32-42	0	4.24	4.50
2001 Anaheim	AL	57	0	0	50	57.2	230	39	19	17	3	1	0	2	18	1	71	2 0	4	2	.667	0	39-42	0	1.90	2.65
2002 Anaheim	AL	58	0	0	50	56.1	226	38	12	12	5	0	1	0	25	1	68	5 0	4	1	.800	0	40-44	0	2.47	1.92
2003 Anaheim	AL	52	0	0	49	49.1	206	33	22	19	7	0	1	3	23	1	48	1 0	0	5	.000	0	33-37	0	2.99	3.47
9 ML YEARS		527	0	0	418	537.0	2199	350	194	179	56	14	11	20	234	19	647	24 2	27	35	.435	0	283-328	31	2.48	3.00

Antonio Perez

Bats: R **Throws:** R **Pos:** 2B-31; 3B-6; SS-6; PR-6; PH-3; DH-2   **Ht:** 5'11" **Wt:** 175 **Born:** 1/26/80 **Age:** 24

								BATTING											BASERUNNING			AVERAGES		
Year Team	Lg	G	AB	H	2B	3B	HR	(Hm Rd)	TB	R	RBI	RC	TBB	IBB	SO	HBP	SH	SF	SB	CS	SB%	GDP	Avg	OBP	Slg
1999 Rockford	A	119	385	111	20	3	7	(- -)	158	69	41	61	43	0	80	13	8	3	35	24	.59	3	.288	.376	.410
2000 Lancaster	A+	98	395	109	36	6	17	(- -)	208	90	63	79	58	1	99	8	9	4	28	16	.64	5	.276	.376	.527
2001 San Antonio	AA	5	21	3	0	0	0	(- -)	3	3	0	0	0	0	7	0	0	0	0	0	-	0	.143	.143	.143
2002 San Antonio	AA	72	240	62	8	2	2	(- -)	80	30	24	25	11	0	64	10	8	5	15	9	.63	3	.258	.312	.333
2003 Orlando	AA	24	81	22	5	1	2	(- -)	35	16	10	17	18	0	18	4	1	1	3	1	.75	0	.272	.423	.432
2003 Durham	AAA	34	134	38	12	2	6	(- -)	72	27	20	24	10	0	38	3	1	1	3	1	.75	2	.284	.345	.537
2003 Tampa Bay	AL	48	125	31	6	1	2	(0 2)	45	19	12	19	18	0	34	1	2	1	4	1	.80	1	.248	.345	.360

Eddie Perez

Bats: R **Throws:** R **Pos:** C-102; PH-9   **Ht:** 6'1" **Wt:** 220 **Born:** 5/4/68 **Age:** 36

								BATTING											BASERUNNING			AVERAGES		
Year Team	Lg	G	AB	H	2B	3B	HR	(Hm Rd)	TB	R	RBI	RC	TBB	IBB	SO	HBP	SH	SF	SB	CS	SB%	GDP	Avg	OBP	Slg
1995 Atlanta	NL	7	13	4	1	0	1	(0 1)	8	1	4	2	0	0	2	0	0	0	0	0	-	0	.308	.308	.615
1996 Atlanta	NL	68	156	40	9	1	4	(2 2)	63	19	17	17	8	0	19	1	0	2	0	0	-	6	.256	.293	.404
1997 Atlanta	NL	73	191	41	5	0	6	(4 2)	64	20	18	14	10	0	35	2	1	2	0	1	.00	8	.215	.259	.335
1998 Atlanta	NL	61	149	50	12	0	6	(3 3)	80	18	32	30	15	0	28	2	1	0	1	1	.50	3	.336	.404	.537
1999 Atlanta	NL	104	309	77	17	0	7	(0 7)	115	30	30	32	17	4	40	6	4	3	0	1	.00	9	.249	.299	.372
2000 Atlanta	NL	7	22	4	1	0	0	(0 0)	5	0	3	1	0	0	2	0	0	0	0	0	-	0	.182	.182	.227
2001 Atlanta	NL	5	10	3	0	0	0	(0 0)	3	0	0	1	0	0	2	0	0	0	0	0	-	0	.300	.300	.300
2002 Cleveland	AL	42	117	25	9	0	0	(0 0)	34	6	4	4	5	0	25	1	2	0	0	0	-	6	.214	.252	.291
2003 Milwaukee	NL	107	350	95	17	1	11	(5 6)	147	26	45	37	17	3	47	0	6	2	0	0	-	16	.271	.304	.420
9 ML YEARS		474	1317	339	71	2	35	(14 21)	519	120	153	138	72	7	200	12	14	9	1	4	.20	48	.257	.300	.394

Eduardo Perez

Bats: R **Throws:** R **Pos:** RF-64; PH-42; 3B-12; LF-10; 1B-5; DH-1   **Ht:** 6'4" **Wt:** 215 **Born:** 9/11/69 **Age:** 34

								BATTING											BASERUNNING			AVERAGES		
Year Team	Lg	G	AB	H	2B	3B	HR	(Hm Rd)	TB	R	RBI	RC	TBB	IBB	SO	HBP	SH	SF	SB	CS	SB%	GDP	Avg	OBP	Slg
1993 Anaheim	AL	52	180	45	6	2	4	(2 2)	67	16	30	18	9	0	39	2	0	1	5	4	.56	4	.250	.292	.372
1994 Anaheim	AL	38	129	27	7	0	5	(3 2)	49	10	16	13	12	1	29	0	1	1	3	0	1.00	6	.209	.275	.380
1995 Anaheim	AL	29	71	12	4	1	1	(0 1)	21	9	7	6	12	0	9	2	0	1	0	2	.00	3	.169	.302	.296
1996 Cincinnati	NL	18	36	8	0	0	3	(3 0)	17	8	5	5	5	1	9	0	0	0	0	0	-	2	.222	.317	.472
1997 Cincinnati	NL	106	297	75	18	0	16	(7 9)	141	44	52	45	29	1	76	2	0	2	5	1	.83	6	.253	.321	.475
1998 Cincinnati	NL	84	172	41	4	0	4	(1 3)	57	20	30	19	21	2	45	2	1	2	0	1	.00	2	.238	.325	.331
1999 St Louis	NL	21	32	11	2	0	1	(1 0)	16	6	9	8	7	0	6	0	0	0	0	0	-	0	.344	.462	.500
2000 St Louis	NL	33	91	27	4	0	3	(0 3)	40	9	10	14	5	0	19	3	2	1	1	0	1.00	0	.297	.350	.440
2002 St Louis	NL	96	154	31	9	0	10	(4 6)	70	22	26	18	17	0	36	3	1	2	0	0	-	7	.201	.290	.455
2003 St Louis	NL	105	253	72	16	0	11	(5 6)	121	47	41	38	29	1	53	4	1	2	5	2	.71	7	.285	.365	.478
10 ML YEARS		584	1415	349	70	3	58	(25 33)	599	191	226	184	146	6	321	18	6	12	19	10	.66	38	.247	.322	.423

Neifi Perez

Bats: B **Throws:** R **Pos:** 2B-57; SS-45; PH-29; 3B-2; PR-2   **Ht:** 6'0" **Wt:** 175 **Born:** 6/2/73 **Age:** 31

Year Team	Lg	G	AB	H	2B	3B	HR	(Hm	Rd)	TB	R	RBI	RC	TBB	IBB	SO	HBP	SH	SF	SB	CS	SB%	GDP	Avg	OBP	Slg
1996 Colorado	NL	17	45	7	2	0	0	(0	0)	9	4	3	0	0	0	8	0	1	0	2	2	.50	2	.156	.156	.200
1997 Colorado	NL	83	313	91	13	10	5	(3	2)	139	46	31	46	21	4	43	1	5	4	4	3	.57	3	.291	.333	.444
1998 Colorado	NL	162	647	177	25	9	9	(6	3)	247	80	59	77	38	0	70	1	22	4	5	6	.45	8	.274	.313	.382
1999 Colorado	NL	157	690	193	27	11	12	(8	4)	278	108	70	87	28	0	54	1	9	4	13	5	.72	4	.280	.307	.403
2000 Colorado	NL	162	651	187	39	11	10	(7	3)	278	92	71	85	30	6	63	0	7	11	3	6	.33	9	.287	.314	.427
2001 Col-KC		136	581	162	26	9	8	(7	1)	230	83	59	69	26	1	68	1	11	4	9	6	.60	10	.279	.309	.396
2002 Kansas City	AL	145	554	131	20	4	3	(1	2)	168	65	37	36	20	2	53	0	5	6	8	9	.47	11	.236	.260	.303
2003 San Francisco	NL	120	328	84	19	4	1	(1	0)	114	27	31	29	14	3	23	0	9	2	3	2	.60	9	.256	.285	.348
2001 Colorado	NL	87	382	114	19	8	7	(7	0)	170	65	47	53	16	1	49	0	4	1	6	2	.75	8	.298	.326	.445
2001 Kansas City	AL	49	199	48	7	1	1	(0	1)	60	18	12	16	10	0	19	1	7	3	3	4	.43	2	.241	.277	.302
8 ML YEARS		982	3809	1032	171	58	48	(33	15)	1463	505	361	429	177	16	382	4	69	35	47	39	.55	56	.271	.301	.384

Odalis Perez

Pitches: L **Bats:** L **Pos:** SP-30   **Ht:** 6'0" **Wt:** 150 **Born:** 6/11/77 **Age:** 27

Year Team	Lg	G	GS	CG	GF	IP	BFP	H	R	ER	HR	SH	SF	HB	TBB	IBB	SO	WP	Bk	W	L	Pct	ShO	Sv-Op	Hld	ERC	ERA
1998 Atlanta	NL	10	0	0	0	10.2	45	10	5	5	1	0	0	0	4	0	5	0	0	0	1	.000	0	0-1	5	3.60	4.22
1999 Atlanta	NL	18	17	0	0	93.0	424	100	65	62	12	3	4	1	53	2	82	5	3	4	6	.400	0	0-0	0	5.42	6.00
2001 Atlanta	NL	24	16	0	1	95.1	418	108	55	52	7	3	3	1	39	0	71	2	3	7	8	.467	0	0-0	0	4.79	4.91
2002 Los Angeles	NL	32	32	4	0	222.1	869	182	76	74	21	3	7	4	38	5	155	2	3	15	10	.600	2	0-0	0	2.31	3.00
2003 Los Angeles	NL	30	30	0	0	185.1	772	191	98	93	28	5	3	3	46	4	141	2	1	12	12	.500	0	0-0	0	4.07	4.52
5 ML YEARS		114	95	4	1	606.2	2528	591	299	286	69	24	17	9	180	11	454	11	10	38	37	.507	2	0-1	5	3.69	4.24

Oliver Perez

Pitches: L **Bats:** L **Pos:** SP-24   **Ht:** 6'3" **Wt:** 160 **Born:** 8/15/81 **Age:** 22

Year Team	Lg	G	GS	CG	GF	IP	BFP	H	R	ER	HR	SH	SF	HB	TBB	IBB	SO	WP	Bk	W	L	Pct	ShO	Sv-Op	Hld	ERC	ERA
1999 Padres	R	15	2	0	7	28.1	133	28	20	16	1	1	0	1	16	0	37	0	2	1	2	.333	0	3--	-	4.09	5.08
2000 Idaho Falls	R+	5	5	0	0	24.1	100	24	14	11	1	0	1	1	9	0	27	3	0	3	1	.750	0	0--	-	3.82	4.07
2001 Fort Wayne	A	19	19	0	0	101.1	415	84	46	39	9	0	5	1	43	0	98	1	2	8	5	.615	0	0--	-	3.29	3.46
2001 Lk Elsinore	A+	9	9	0	0	53.0	231	45	25	16	4	3	2	1	25	0	62	6	0	2	4	.333	0	0--	-	3.33	2.72
2002 Lk Elsinore	A+	9	8	0	0	48.2	201	36	13	10	1	0	1	2	24	0	66	0	0	3	3	.500	0	0--	-	2.56	1.85
2002 Mobile	AA	4	4	0	0	23.0	93	11	3	3	1	2	0	0	16	0	34	4	0	1	0	1.000	0	0--	-	2.13	1.17
2003 Portland	AAA	8	8	0	0	47.2	200	44	20	16	6	3	2	4	12	0	48	1	1	3	3	.500	0	0--	-	3.56	3.02
2002 San Diego	NL	16	15	0	0	90.0	387	71	37	35	13	5	3	5	48	1	94	3	0	4	5	.444	0	0-0	0	3.93	3.50
2003 SD-Pit	NL	24	24	0	0	126.2	579	129	80	77	22	5	2	4	77	3	141	7	1	4	10	.286	0	0-0	0	5.66	5.47
2003 San Diego	NL	19	19	0	0	103.2	473	103	65	62	20	4	2	3	65	2	117	6	1	4	7	.364	0	0-0	0	5.74	5.38
2003 Pittsburgh	NL	5	5	0	0	23.0	106	26	15	15	2	1	0	1	12	1	24	1	0	0	3	.000	0	0-0	0	5.29	5.87
2 ML YEARS		40	39	0	0	216.2	966	200	117	112	35	10	5	9	125	4	235	10	1	8	15	.348	0	0-0	0	4.92	4.65

Timo Perez

Bats: L **Throws:** L **Pos:** LF-58; CF-49; PH-27; RF-14; PR-3   **Ht:** 5'9" **Wt:** 167 **Born:** 4/8/75 **Age:** 29

Year Team	Lg	G	AB	H	2B	3B	HR	(Hm	Rd)	TB	R	RBI	RC	TBB	IBB	SO	HBP	SH	SF	SB	CS	SB%	GDP	Avg	OBP	Slg
2003 Norfolk*	AAA	3	9	2	0	0	1	(-	-)	5	2	1	2	1	0	0	0	0	0	0	0	-	0	.222	.300	.556
2000 New York	NL	24	49	14	4	1	1	(0	1)	23	11	3	8	3	0	5	1	0	1	1	1	.50	0	.286	.333	.469
2001 New York	NL	85	239	59	9	1	5	(2	3)	85	26	22	23	12	0	25	2	6	1	1	6	.14	1	.247	.287	.356
2002 New York	NL	136	444	131	27	6	8	(3	5)	194	52	47	63	23	2	36	2	10	2	10	6	.63	10	.295	.331	.437
2003 New York	NL	127	346	93	21	0	4	(1	3)	126	32	42	38	18	1	29	2	7	9	5	6	.45	5	.269	.301	.364
4 ML YEARS		372	1078	297	61	8	18	(6	12)	428	121	114	132	56	3	95	7	23	13	17	19	.47	16	.276	.312	.397

Tomas Perez

Bats: B **Throws:** R **Pos:** 3B-58; PH-41; 2B-26; 1B-9; SS-4   **Ht:** 5'11" **Wt:** 177 **Born:** 12/29/73 **Age:** 30

Year Team	Lg	G	AB	H	2B	3B	HR	(Hm	Rd)	TB	R	RBI	RC	TBB	IBB	SO	HBP	SH	SF	SB	CS	SB%	GDP	Avg	OBP	Slg
1995 Toronto	AL	41	98	24	3	1	1	(1	0)	32	12	8	7	7	0	18	0	0	1	0	1	.00	6	.245	.292	.327
1996 Toronto	AL	91	295	74	13	4	1	(1	0)	98	24	19	28	25	0	29	1	6	1	1	2	.33	10	.251	.311	.332
1997 Toronto	AL	40	123	24	3	2	0	(0	0)	31	9	9	8	11	0	28	1	3	0	1	1	.50	2	.195	.267	.252
1998 Toronto	AL	6	9	1	0	0	0	(0	0)	1	1	0	0	1	0	3	0	0	0	0	0	-	0	.111	.200	.111
2000 Philadelphia	NL	45	140	31	7	1	1	(0	1)	43	17	13	11	11	2	30	0	1	0	1	1	.50	3	.221	.278	.307
2001 Philadelphia	NL	62	135	41	7	1	3	(1	2)	59	11	19	20	7	1	22	2	1	0	1	0	.00	6	.304	.347	.437
2002 Philadelphia	NL	92	212	53	13	1	5	(2	3)	83	22	20	20	21	6	40	1	2	1	1	0	1.00	6	.250	.319	.392
2003 Philadelphia	NL	125	298	79	18	1	5	(2	3)	114	39	33	29	23	11	54	0	4	2	0	1	.00	7	.265	.316	.383
8 ML YEARS		502	1310	327	64	11	16	(8	8)	461	135	121	123	106	20	224	5	18	5	4	7	.36	36	.250	.307	.352

Herbert Perry

Bats: R **Throws:** R **Pos:** 1B-5; PH-4; 3B-2   **Ht:** 6'2" **Wt:** 225 **Born:** 9/15/69 **Age:** 34

Year Team	Lg	G	AB	H	2B	3B	HR	(Hm	Rd)	TB	R	RBI	RC	TBB	IBB	SO	HBP	SH	SF	SB	CS	SB%	GDP	Avg	OBP	Slg
2003 Frisco*	AA	9	34	11	2	0	1	(-	-)	16	5	6	6	3	1	3	2	0	0	0	0	-	2	.324	.410	.471
1994 Cleveland	AL	4	9	1	0	0	0	(0	0)	1	1	1	1	3	1	1	1	0	1	0	0	-	0	.111	.357	.111
1995 Cleveland	AL	52	162	51	13	1	3	(3	0)	75	23	23	26	13	0	28	4	3	2	1	3	.25	5	.315	.376	.463
1996 Cleveland	AL	7	12	1	1	0	0	(0	0)	2	1	0	0	1	0	2	0	0	0	1	0	1.00	0	.083	.154	.167
1999 Tampa Bay	AL	66	209	53	10	1	6	(5	1)	83	29	32	25	16	1	42	10	0	4	0	0	-	13	.254	.331	.397
2000 TB-CWS	AL	116	411	124	30	1	12	(7	5)	192	71	62	64	24	1	75	9	2	4	4	1	.80	13	.302	.350	.467

Year Team	Lg	G	AB	H	2B	3B	HR	(Hm	Rd)	TB	R	RBI	RC	TBB	IBB	SO	HBP	SH	SF	SB	CS	SB%	GDP	Avg	OBP	Slg
2001 Chicago	AL	92	285	73	21	1	7	(5	2)	117	38	32	35	23	1	55	7	0	1	2	2	.50	11	.256	.326	.411
2002 Texas	AL	132	450	124	24	1	22	(9	13)	216	64	77	64	34	1	66	6	4	2	4	2	.67	17	.276	.333	.480
2003 Texas	AL	11	24	4	1	0	0	(0	0)	5	1	2	1	0	0	3	0	0	0	0	0	-	0	.167	.167	.208
2000 Tampa Bay	AL	7	28	6	1	0	0	(0	0)	7	2	1	2	2	0	7	0	0	0	0	0	-	0	.214	.267	.250
2000 Chicago	AL	109	383	118	29	1	12	(7	5)	185	69	61	62	22	1	68	9	2	4	4	1	.80	13	.308	.356	.483
8 ML YEARS		480	1562	431	100	5	50	(29	21)	691	228	229	216	114	5	272	37	9	14	12	8	.60	59	.276	.337	.442

Robert Person

Pitches: R **Bats:** R **Pos:** RP-7   **Ht:** 6'0" **Wt:** 193 **Born:** 10/6/69 **Age:** 34

		HOW MUCH HE PITCHED						WHAT HE GAVE UP											THE RESULTS							
Year Team	Lg	G	GS	CG	GF	IP	BFP	H	R	ER	HR	SH	SF	HB	TBB	IBB	SO	WP	Bk	W	L	Pct	ShO	Sv-Op	Hld	ERC	ERA
2003 Sarasota*	A+	7	7	0	0	24.2	102	27	12	8	1	0	0	0	6	0	17	0	0	1	1	.500	0	0- -	-	3.68	2.92
2003 Pawtucket*	AAA	6	1	0	3	7.2	33	5	4	4	0	0	0	0	5	0	6	2	0	0	0	-	0	1- -	-	2.42	4.70
1995 New York	NL	3	1	0	0	12.0	44	5	1	1	1	0	0	0	2	0	10	0	0	1	0	1.000	0	0-0	0	0.82	0.75
1996 New York	NL	27	13	0	1	89.2	390	86	50	45	16	1	4	2	35	3	76	3	0	4	5	.444	0	0-0	1	4.32	4.52
1997 Toronto	AL	23	22	0	0	128.1	566	125	86	80	19	4	6	5	60	2	99	7	0	5	10	.333	0	0-0	0	4.65	5.61
1998 Toronto	AL	27	0	0	14	38.1	184	45	31	30	9	2	5	2	22	1	31	0	0	3	1	.750	0	6-8	0	6.94	7.04
1999 Tor-Phi		42	22	0	8	148.0	659	139	84	77	24	7	6	6	85	2	139	5	1	10	7	.588	0	2-2	1	5.04	4.68
2000 Philadelphia	NL	28	28	1	0	173.1	743	144	73	70	13	4	9	6	95	1	164	10	1	7	7	.563	1	0-0	0	3.70	3.63
2001 Philadelphia	NL	33	33	3	0	208.1	867	179	103	97	34	8	6	8	80	3	183	10	1	15	7	.682	1	0-0	0	3.84	4.19
2002 Philadelphia	NL	16	16	0	0	87.2	388	79	58	53	13	2	2	5	51	0	61	2	0	4	5	.444	0	0-0	0	4.85	5.44
2003 Boston	AL	7	0	0	3	11.2	55	11	10	10	0	0	2	1	8	0	10	2	0	0	0	-	0	1-1	0	4.30	7.71
1999 Toronto	AL	11	0	0	7	11.0	60	9	12	12	1	0	2	4	15	1	12	2	0	0	2	.000	0	2-2	1	8.06	9.82
1999 Philadelphia	NL	31	22	0	1	137.0	599	130	72	65	23	7	4	2	70	1	127	3	1	10	5	.667	0	0-0	0	4.78	4.27
9 ML YEARS		206	135	4	26	897.1	3896	813	496	463	129	28	40	35	438	12	773	39	3	51	42	.548	2	9-11	2	4.34	4.64

Ben Petrick

Bats: R **Throws:** R **Pos:** LF-19; CF-15; C-7; PH-5; PR-5; RF-3; 1B-2   **Ht:** 6'0" **Wt:** 200 **Born:** 4/7/77 **Age:** 27

		BATTING																		BASERUNNING				AVERAGES		
Year Team	Lg	G	AB	H	2B	3B	HR	(Hm	Rd)	TB	R	RBI	RC	TBB	IBB	SO	HBP	SH	SF	SB	CS	SB%	GDP	Avg	OBP	Slg
2003 Co Springs*	AAA	80	228	59	16	3	11	(-	-)	114	38	40	35	26	1	53	1	0	3	4	4	.50	8	.259	.333	.500
1999 Colorado	NL	19	62	20	3	0	4	(4	0)	35	13	12	14	10	0	13	0	0	0	1	0	1.00	1	.323	.417	.565
2000 Colorado	NL	52	146	47	10	1	3	(2	1)	68	32	20	28	20	2	33	2	1	4	1	2	.33	1	.322	.401	.466
2001 Colorado	NL	85	244	58	15	3	11	(7	4)	112	41	39	36	31	3	67	3	1	3	3	3	.50	5	.238	.327	.459
2002 Colorado	NL	38	95	20	3	1	5	(4	1)	40	10	11	6	9	0	33	1	0	1	0	1	.00	1	.211	.283	.421
2003 Col-Det		46	122	27	6	0	4	(2	2)	45	18	12	11	8	0	31	0	1	0	0	0	-	3	.221	.269	.369
2003 Colorado	NL	3	2	0	0	0	0	(0	0)	0	0	0	0	0	0	1	0	0	0	0	0	-	0	.000	.000	.000
2003 Detroit	AL	43	120	27	6	0	4	(2	2)	45	18	12	11	8	0	30	0	1	0	0	0	-	3	.225	.273	.375
5 ML YEARS		240	669	172	37	5	27	(19	8)	300	114	94	95	78	5	177	6	3	8	5	6	.45	11	.257	.336	.448

Andy Pettitte

Pitches: L **Bats:** L **Pos:** SP-33   **Ht:** 6'5" **Wt:** 225 **Born:** 6/15/72 **Age:** 32

		HOW MUCH HE PITCHED						WHAT HE GAVE UP											THE RESULTS							
Year Team	Lg	G	GS	CG	GF	IP	BFP	H	R	ER	HR	SH	SF	HB	TBB	IBB	SO	WP	Bk	W	L	Pct	ShO	Sv-Op	Hld	ERC	ERA
1995 New York	AL	31	26	3	1	175.0	745	183	86	81	15	4	5	1	63	3	114	8	1	12	9	.571	0	0-0	0	4.13	4.17
1996 New York	AL	35	34	2	1	221.0	929	229	105	95	23	7	3	3	72	2	162	6	1	21	8	.724	0	0-0	0	4.14	3.87
1997 New York	AL	35	35	4	0	240.1	986	233	86	77	7	6	2	3	65	0	166	7	0	18	7	.720	1	0-0	0	3.05	2.88
1998 New York	AL	33	32	5	0	216.1	932	226	110	102	20	6	7	6	87	1	146	5	0	16	11	.593	0	0-0	0	4.46	4.24
1999 New York	AL	31	31	0	0	191.2	851	216	105	100	20	6	6	3	89	3	121	3	1	14	11	.560	0	0-0	0	5.22	4.70
2000 New York	AL	32	32	3	0	204.2	903	219	111	99	17	7	4	4	80	4	125	2	3	19	9	.679	1	0-0	0	4.32	4.35
2001 New York	AL	31	31	2	0	200.2	858	224	103	89	14	8	7	6	41	3	164	2	2	15	10	.600	0	0-0	0	3.82	3.99
2002 New York	AL	22	22	3	0	134.2	570	144	58	49	6	3	2	4	32	2	97	2	1	13	5	.722	1	0-0	0	3.55	3.27
2003 New York	AL	33	33	1	0	208.1	896	227	109	93	21	5	5	1	50	3	180	5	0	21	8	.724	0	0-0	0	3.89	4.02
9 ML YEARS		283	276	23	2	1792.2	7670	1901	873	785	143	52	41	31	579	21	1275	40	9	149	78	.656	3	0-0	0	4.05	3.94

Josh Phelps

Bats: R **Throws:** R **Pos:** DH-101; PH-14; 1B-8   **Ht:** 6'3" **Wt:** 220 **Born:** 5/12/78 **Age:** 26

		BATTING																		BASERUNNING				AVERAGES		
Year Team	Lg	G	AB	H	2B	3B	HR	(Hm	Rd)	TB	R	RBI	RC	TBB	IBB	SO	HBP	SH	SF	SB	CS	SB%	GDP	Avg	OBP	Slg
2003 Syracuse*	AAA	4	11	5	0	0	2	(-	-)	11	2	4	4	1	0	3	0	0	0	0	0	-	0	.455	.500	1.000
2000 Toronto	AL	1	1	0	0	0	0	(0	0)	0	0	0	0	0	0	1	0	0	0	0	0	-	0	.000	.000	.000
2001 Toronto	AL	8	12	0	0	0	0	(0	0)	0	3	1	0	2	0	5	0	0	0	1	0	1.00	0	.000	.143	.000
2002 Toronto	AL	74	265	82	20	1	15	(6	9)	149	41	58	53	19	0	82	3	0	0	0	0	-	7	.309	.362	.562
2003 Toronto	AL	119	396	106	18	1	20	(11	9)	186	57	66	64	39	3	115	17	0	1	1	2	.33	12	.268	.358	.470
4 ML YEARS		202	674	188	38	2	35	(17	18)	335	101	125	117	60	3	203	20	0	1	2	2	.50	20	.279	.355	.497

Tommy Phelps

Pitches: L **Bats:** L **Pos:** RP-20; SP-7   **Ht:** 6'3" **Wt:** 192 **Born:** 3/4/74 **Age:** 30

		HOW MUCH HE PITCHED						WHAT HE GAVE UP											THE RESULTS							
Year Team	Lg	G	GS	CG	GF	IP	BFP	H	R	ER	HR	SH	SF	HB	TBB	IBB	SO	WP	Bk	W	L	Pct	ShO	Sv-Op	Hld	ERC	ERA
1993 Burlington	A	8	8	0	0	41.0	173	36	18	17	4	1	1	1	13	0	33	2	0	2	4	.333	0	0- -	-	3.11	3.73
1993 Jamestown	A-	16	15	1	0	92.1	416	102	62	47	4	4	3	5	37	1	74	7	1	3	8	.273	0	0- -	-	4.39	4.58
1994 Burlington	A	23	23	1	0	118.1	534	143	91	73	9	7	7	5	48	1	82	7	0	8	8	.500	1	0- -	-	5.33	5.55
1995 W Palm Bch	A+	2	2	0	0	5.0	33	10	10	9	0	0	0	0	11	0	5	2	0	0	2	.000	0	0- -	-	19.29	16.20
1995 Albany	A	24	24	1	0	135.1	597	142	76	50	6	0	4	5	45	0	119	5	1	10	9	.526	0	0- -	-	3.74	3.33
1996 W Palm Bch	A+	18	18	1	0	112.0	468	105	42	36	5	4	1	2	35	0	71	8	0	10	2	.833	1	0- -	-	3.10	2.89
1996 Harrisburg	AA	8	8	2	0	47.1	195	43	16	13	3	2	0	1	19	2	23	0	0	2	2	.500	2	0- -	-	3.46	2.47
1997 Harrisburg	AA	18	18	0	0	101.1	462	115	68	53	14	8	5	5	39	1	86	3	1	10	6	.625	0	0- -	-	5.15	4.71

		HOW MUCH HE PITCHED						WHAT HE GAVE UP											THE RESULTS							
Year Team	Lg	G	GS	CG	GF	IP	BFP	H	R	ER	HR	SH	SF	HB	TBB	IBB	SO	WP	Bk	W	L	Pct	ShO	Sv-Op	Hld	ERC	ERA
1998 Jupiter	A+	7	7	0	0	41.0	181	42	21	20	3	0	2	2	15	0	21	1	0	2	2	.500	0	0- -	-	4.00	4.39
1998 Harrisburg	AA	12	10	0	0	59.2	247	57	29	24	5	4	3	0	26	0	26	2	0	5	4	.556	0	0- -	-	4.02	3.62
1999 Harrisburg	AA	13	13	1	0	64.2	306	76	53	41	13	3	6	7	26	0	36	2	0	3	6	.333	0	0- -	-	6.14	5.71
2000 Jacksonville	AA	38	11	0	7	102.0	435	111	59	56	17	1	0	7	26	2	62	1	0	6	6	.500	0	0- -	-	4.78	4.94
2001 Toledo	AAA	29	0	0	8	59.2	271	74	30	24	4	0	1	3	19	3	53	1	0	3	2	.600	0	1- -	-	4.95	3.62
2001 Erie	AA	15	2	0	5	32.2	139	33	14	13	1	3	2	3	8	2	31	2	0	1	1	.500	0	2- -	-	3.31	3.58
2002 Calgary	AAA	51	0	0	10	74.1	314	76	27	26	8	4	1	2	21	3	62	3	0	4	2	.667	0	2- -	-	3.85	3.15
2002 Calgary	AAA	51	0	0	10	74.1	314	76	27	26	8	4	1	2	21	3	62	3	0	4	2	.667	0	2- -	-	3.85	3.15
2003 Jupiter	A+	2	1	0	0	3.0	14	5	2	2	0	0	0	0	0	0	3	0	0	0	0	-	0	0- -	-	5.42	6.00
2003 Albuquerque	AAA	5	0	0	1	7.2	26	5	1	1	1	0	0	0	3	0	13	1	0	0	0	-	0	0- -	-	2.95	1.17
2003 Florida	NL	27	7	0	8	63.0	276	70	32	28	3	1	2	2	23	1	43	1	0	3	2	.600	0	0-0	1	4.31	4.00

Brandon Phillips

Bats: R Throws: R Pos: 2B-109; PH-4; PR-1   Ht: 5'11" Wt: 185 Born: 6/28/81 Age: 23

		BATTING																		BASERUNNING				AVERAGES		
Year Team	Lg	G	AB	H	2B	3B	HR	(Hm	Rd)	TB	R	RBI	RC	TBB	IBB	SO	HBP	SH	SF	SB	CS	SB%	GDP	Avg	OBP	Slg
1999 Expos	R	47	169	49	11	3	1	(-	-)	69	23	21	25	15	0	35	3	0	0	12	3	.80	6	.290	.358	.408
2000 Cape Fear	A	126	484	117	17	8	11	(-	-)	183	74	72	56	38	3	97	9	0	5	23	8	.74	11	.242	.306	.378
2001 Jupiter	A+	55	194	55	12	2	4	(-	-)	83	36	23	39	38	0	45	6	0	1	17	3	.85	3	.284	.414	.428
2001 Harrisburg	AA	67	265	79	19	0	7	(-	-)	119	35	36	37	12	0	42	4	1	1	13	6	.68	9	.298	.337	.449
2002 Harrisburg	AA	60	245	80	13	2	9	(-	-)	124	40	35	44	16	2	33	5	1	0	6	3	.67	1	.327	.380	.506
2002 Ottawa	AAA	10	35	9	4	0	1	(-	-)	16	1	5	5	2	0	6	0	0	0	0	0	-	0	.257	.297	.457
2002 Buffalo	AAA	55	223	63	14	0	8	(-	-)	101	30	27	32	14	0	39	1	4	5	8	2	.80	6	.283	.321	.453
2003 Buffalo	AAA	43	154	27	7	0	3	(-	-)	43	14	13	10	12	0	22	3	2	1	7	3	.70	3	.175	.247	.279
2002 Cleveland	AL	11	31	8	3	1	0	(0	0)	13	5	4	5	3	0	6	1	1	0	0	0	-	0	.258	.343	.419
2003 Cleveland	AL	112	370	77	18	1	6	(3	3)	115	36	33	23	14	0	77	3	5	1	4	5	.44	12	.208	.242	.311
2 ML YEARS		123	401	85	21	2	6	(3	3)	128	41	37	28	17	0	83	4	6	1	4	5	.44	12	.212	.251	.319

Jason Phillips

Bats: R Throws: R Pos: 1B-84; C-29; PH-10   Ht: 6'1" Wt: 177 Born: 9/27/76 Age: 27

		BATTING																		BASERUNNING				AVERAGES		
Year Team	Lg	G	AB	H	2B	3B	HR	(Hm	Rd)	TB	R	RBI	RC	TBB	IBB	SO	HBP	SH	SF	SB	CS	SB%	GDP	Avg	OBP	Slg
2003 Norfolk*	AAA	22	78	27	5	0	4	(1	3)	44	13	20	17	11	3	9	2	0	1	0	0	-	4	.346	.435	.564
2001 New York	NL	6	7	1	1	0	0	(0	0)	2	2	0	0	0	0	1	0	0	0	0	0	-	0	.143	.143	.286
2002 New York	NL	11	19	7	0	0	1	(0	1)	10	4	3	3	1	0	1	1	0	1	0	0	-	1	.368	.409	.526
2003 New York	NL	119	403	120	25	0	11	(7	4)	178	45	58	64	39	3	50	10	0	1	0	1	.00	21	.298	.373	.442
3 ML YEARS		136	429	128	26	0	12	(7	5)	190	51	61	67	40	3	52	11	0	2	0	1	.00	22	.298	.371	.443

Jason C Phillips

Pitches: R Bats: R Pos: RP-3   Ht: 6'6" Wt: 225 Born: 3/22/74 Age: 30

		HOW MUCH HE PITCHED						WHAT HE GAVE UP											THE RESULTS							
Year Team	Lg	G	GS	CG	GF	IP	BFP	H	R	ER	HR	SH	SF	HB	TBB	IBB	SO	WP	Bk	W	L	Pct	ShO	Sv-Op	Hld	ERC	ERA
2003 Buffalo*	AAA	13	12	1	0	85.0	334	68	24	20	4	3	1	5	19	0	56	0	0	10	1	.909	0	0- -	-	2.33	2.12
1999 Pittsburgh	NL	6	0	0	0	7.0	37	11	9	9	2	2	1	0	6	1	7	2	0	0	0	-	0	0-0	0	11.24	11.57
2002 Cleveland	AL	8	6	0	0	41.2	185	41	24	23	7	1	2	4	20	0	23	0	1	1	3	.250	0	0-0	0	5.23	4.97
2003 Cleveland	AL	3	0	0	2	5.0	25	9	5	5	1	0	1	0	2	0	2	0	0	0	1	.000	0	0-0	0	10.22	9.00
3 ML YEARS		17	6	0	2	53.2	247	61	38	37	10	3	4	4	28	1	32	2	1	1	4	.200	0	0-0	0	6.38	6.20

Adam Piatt

Bats: R Throws: R Pos: LF-33; PH-17; RF-13; DH-3; PR-3; 1B-1   Ht: 6'2" Wt: 205 Born: 2/8/76 Age: 28

		BATTING																		BASERUNNING				AVERAGES		
Year Team	Lg	G	AB	H	2B	3B	HR	(Hm	Rd)	TB	R	RBI	RC	TBB	IBB	SO	HBP	SH	SF	SB	CS	SB%	GDP	Avg	OBP	Slg
2000 Oakland	AL	60	157	47	5	5	5	(3	2)	77	24	23	30	23	0	44	1	1	0	0	1	.00	1	.299	.392	.490
2001 Oakland	AL	36	95	20	5	1	0	(0	0)	27	9	6	7	13	0	26	0	1	2	0	0	-	5	.211	.300	.284
2002 Oakland	AL	55	137	32	8	0	5	(3	2)	55	18	18	16	12	0	33	2	0	1	2	1	.67	1	.234	.303	.401
2003 Oak-TB	AL	61	132	30	13	0	6	(3	3)	61	11	18	13	9	0	46	0	0	2	1	2	.33	2	.227	.273	.462
2003 Oakland	AL	47	100	24	10	0	4	(1	3)	46	6	15	10	6	0	30	0	0	1	1	2	.33	2	.240	.280	.460
2003 Tampa Bay	AL	14	32	6	3	0	2	(2	0)	15	5	3	3	3	0	16	0	0	1	0	0	-	0	.188	.250	.469
4 ML YEARS		212	521	129	31	6	16	(9	7)	220	62	65	66	57	0	149	3	2	5	3	4	.43	9	.248	.323	.422

Mike Piazza

Bats: R Throws: R Pos: C-65; PH-5; 1B-1   Ht: 6'3" Wt: 215 Born: 9/4/68 Age: 35

		BATTING																		BASERUNNING				AVERAGES		
Year Team	Lg	G	AB	H	2B	3B	HR	(Hm	Rd)	TB	R	RBI	RC	TBB	IBB	SO	HBP	SH	SF	SB	CS	SB%	GDP	Avg	OBP	Slg
2003 Norfolk*	AAA	5	17	3	0	0	1	(-	-)	6	2	2	1	1	0	3	0	0	0	0	0	-	0	.176	.222	.353
1992 Los Angeles	NL	21	69	16	3	0	1	(1	0)	22	5	7	6	4	0	12	1	0	0	0	0	-	1	.232	.284	.319
1993 Los Angeles	NL	149	547	174	24	2	35	(21	14)	307	81	112	107	46	6	86	3	0	6	3	4	.43	10	.318	.370	.561
1994 Los Angeles	NL	107	405	129	18	0	24	(13	11)	219	64	92	74	33	10	65	1	0	3	1	3	.25	11	.319	.370	.541
1995 Los Angeles	NL	112	434	150	17	0	32	(9	23)	263	82	93	96	39	10	80	1	0	1	1	0	1.00	6	.346	.400	.606
1996 Los Angeles	NL	148	547	184	16	0	36	(14	22)	308	87	105	117	81	21	93	1	0	2	0	3	.00	21	.336	.422	.563
1997 Los Angeles	NL	152	556	201	32	1	40	(22	18)	355	104	124	137	69	11	77	3	0	5	5	1	.83	19	.362	.431	.638
1998 LA-Fla-NYM	NL	151	561	184	38	1	32	(15	17)	320	88	111	116	58	14	80	2	0	5	1	0	1.00	15	.328	.390	.570
1999 New York	NL	141	534	162	25	0	40	(18	22)	307	100	124	99	51	11	70	1	0	7	2	2	.50	27	.303	.361	.575
2000 New York	NL	136	482	156	26	0	38	(17	21)	296	90	113	107	58	10	69	3	0	2	4	2	.67	15	.324	.398	.614
2001 New York	NL	141	503	151	29	0	36	(16	20)	288	81	94	100	67	19	87	2	0	1	0	2	.00	20	.300	.384	.573
2002 New York	NL	135	478	134	23	2	33	(12	21)	260	69	98	84	57	9	82	3	0	2	0	0	.00	26	.280	.359	.544
2003 New York	NL	68	234	67	13	0	11	(4	7)	113	37	34	42	35	3	40	1	0	3	0	0	-	11	.286	.377	.483
1998 Los Angeles	NL	37	149	42	5	0	9	(5	4)	74	20	30	23	11	4	27	0	0	1	0	0	-	3	.282	.329	.497

Year Team	Lg	G	AB	H	2B	3B	HR	(Hm Rd)	TB	R	RBI	RC	TBB	IBB	SO	HBP	SH	SF	SB	CS	SB%	GDP	Avg	OBP	Slg
1998 Florida	NL	5	18	5	0	1	0	(0 0)	7	1	5	2	0	0	0	0	0	1	0	0	-	0	.278	.263	.389
1998 New York	NL	109	394	137	33	0	23	(10 13)	239	67	76	91	47	10	53	2	0	3	1	0	1.00	12	.348	.417	.607
12 ML YEARS		1461	5350	1708	264	6	358	(162 196)	3058	888	1107	1085	598	124	841	22	0	37	17	20	.46	186	.319	.388	.572

Juan Pierre

Bats: L **Throws:** L **Pos:** CF-161; PH-1 **Ht:** 6'0" **Wt:** 180 **Born:** 8/14/77 **Age:** 26

Year Team	Lg	G	AB	H	2B	3B	HR	(Hm Rd)	TB	R	RBI	RC	TBB	IBB	SO	HBP	SH	SF	SB	CS	SB%	GDP	Avg	OBP	Slg
2000 Colorado	NL	51	200	62	2	0	0	(0 0)	64	26	20	23	13	0	15	1	4	1	7	6	.54	2	.310	.353	.320
2001 Colorado	NL	156	617	202	26	11	2	(0 2)	256	108	55	101	41	1	29	10	14	1	46	17	.73	6	.327	.378	.415
2002 Colorado	NL	152	592	170	20	5	1	(0 1)	203	90	35	77	31	0	52	9	8	0	47	12	.80	7	.287	.332	.343
2003 Florida	NL	162	668	204	28	7	1	(1 0)	249	100	41	89	55	1	35	5	15	3	65	20	.76	9	.305	.361	.373
4 ML YEARS		521	2077	638	76	23	4	(1 3)	772	324	151	290	140	2	131	25	41	5	165	55	.75	24	.307	.357	.372

A.J. Pierzynski

Bats: L **Throws:** R **Pos:** C-135; PH-6 **Ht:** 6'3" **Wt:** 220 **Born:** 12/30/76 **Age:** 27

Year Team	Lg	G	AB	H	2B	3B	HR	(Hm Rd)	TB	R	RBI	RC	TBB	IBB	SO	HBP	SH	SF	SB	CS	SB%	GDP	Avg	OBP	Slg
1998 Minnesota	AL	7	14	3	0	0	0	(0 0)	3	1	1	2	1	0	2	1	0	1	0	0	-	0	.300	.385	.300
1999 Minnesota	AL	9	22	6	2	0	0	(0 0)	8	3	3	3	1	0	4	1	0	0	0	0	-	0	.273	.333	.364
2000 Minnesota	AL	33	88	27	5	1	2	(1 1)	40	12	11	14	5	0	14	2	0	1	1	0	1.00	1	.307	.354	.455
2001 Minnesota	AL	114	381	110	33	2	7	(3 4)	168	51	55	50	16	4	57	4	1	3	1	7	.13	7	.289	.322	.441
2002 Minnesota	AL	130	440	132	31	6	6	(2 4)	193	54	49	59	13	1	61	11	2	3	1	2	.33	14	.300	.334	.439
2003 Minnesota	AL	137	487	152	35	3	11	(6 5)	226	63	74	80	24	12	55	15	2	5	3	1	.75	13	.312	.360	.464
6 ML YEARS		430	1428	430	106	12	26	(12 14)	638	184	193	208	60	17	193	34	5	13	6	10	.38	35	.301	.341	.447

Joel Pineiro

Pitches: R **Bats:** R **Pos:** SP-32 **Ht:** 6'1" **Wt:** 180 **Born:** 9/25/78 **Age:** 25

Year Team	Lg	G	GS	CG	GF	IP	BFP	H	R	ER	HR	SH	SF	HB	TBB	IBB	SO	WP	Bk	W	L	Pct	ShO	Sv-Op	Hld	ERC	ERA
2000 Seattle	AL	8	1	0	5	19.1	94	25	13	12	3	0	2	0	13	0	10	0	0	1	0	1.000	0	0-0	0	7.44	5.59
2001 Seattle	AL	17	11	0	1	75.1	289	50	24	17	2	1	2	3	21	0	56	2	0	6	2	.750	0	0-0	2	1.71	2.03
2002 Seattle	AL	37	28	2	4	194.1	812	189	75	70	24	5	7	7	54	1	136	8	0	14	7	.667	1	0-0	3	3.77	3.24
2003 Seattle	AL	32	32	3	0	211.2	890	192	94	89	19	3	9	6	76	3	151	5	0	16	11	.593	2	0-0	0	3.43	3.78
4 ML YEARS		94	72	5	10	500.2	2085	456	206	188	48	9	20	16	164	4	353	15	0	37	20	.649	3	0-0	5	3.42	3.38

Dan Plesac

Pitches: L **Bats:** L **Pos:** RP-58 **Ht:** 6'5" **Wt:** 217 **Born:** 2/4/62 **Age:** 42

Year Team	Lg	G	GS	CG	GF	IP	BFP	H	R	ER	HR	SH	SF	HB	TBB	IBB	SO	WP	Bk	W	L	Pct	ShO	Sv-Op	Hld	ERC	ERA
1986 Milwaukee	NL	51	0	0	33	91.0	377	81	34	30	5	6	5	0	29	1	75	4	0	10	7	.588	0	14-18	6	2.86	2.97
1987 Milwaukee	NL	57	0	0	47	79.1	325	63	30	23	8	1	2	3	23	1	89	6	0	5	6	.455	0	23-36	0	2.67	2.61
1988 Milwaukee	NL	50	0	0	48	52.1	211	46	14	14	2	2	0	0	12	2	52	4	6	1	2	.333	0	30-35	0	2.36	2.41
1989 Milwaukee	NL	52	0	0	51	61.1	242	47	16	16	6	0	4	0	17	1	52	0	0	3	4	.429	0	33-40	0	2.39	2.35
1990 Milwaukee	NL	66	0	0	52	69.0	299	67	36	34	5	2	2	3	31	6	65	2	0	3	7	.300	0	24-34	2	3.97	4.43
1991 Milwaukee	NL	45	10	0	25	92.1	402	92	49	44	12	3	7	3	39	1	61	2	1	2	7	.222	0	8-12	1	4.48	4.29
1992 Milwaukee	NL	44	4	0	13	79.0	330	64	28	26	5	8	4	3	35	5	54	3	1	5	4	.556	0	1-3	1	3.04	2.96
1993 Chicago	NL	57	0	0	12	62.2	276	74	37	33	10	4	3	0	21	6	47	5	2	2	1	.667	0	0-2	12	5.15	4.74
1994 Chicago	NL	54	0	0	14	54.2	235	61	30	28	9	1	1	1	13	0	53	0	0	2	3	.400	0	1-3	14	4.59	4.61
1995 Pittsburgh	NL	58	0	0	16	60.1	259	53	26	24	3	4	3	1	27	7	57	1	0	4	4	.500	0	3-5	11	3.09	3.58
1996 Pittsburgh	NL	73	0	0	30	70.1	300	67	35	32	4	2	3	0	24	6	76	4	0	6	5	.545	0	11-17	11	3.12	4.09
1997 Toronto	AL	73	0	0	18	50.1	215	47	22	20	8	2	1	0	19	4	61	2	0	2	4	.333	0	1-5	27	3.86	3.58
1998 Toronto	AL	78	0	0	16	50.0	203	41	23	21	4	0	3	1	16	1	55	0	0	4	3	.571	0	4-5	27	2.76	3.78
1999 Toronto	AL	64	0	0	11	44.1	198	50	30	29	7	4	1	0	17	2	53	3	0	2	4	.333	0	1-3	15	5.03	5.89
2000 Arizona	NL	62	0	0	14	40.0	182	34	21	14	4	6	1	0	26	2	45	3	0	5	1	.833	0	0-4	9	3.98	3.15
2001 Toronto	AL	62	0	0	6	45.1	190	34	18	18	4	0	1	1	24	5	68	1	0	4	5	.444	0	1-2	16	3.07	3.57
2002 Tor-Phi		60	0	0	8	36.1	154	27	17	17	6	0	1	0	18	3	41	0	0	3	3	.500	0	1-4	18	3.29	4.21
2003 Philadelphia	NL	58	0	0	9	33.1	141	29	12	10	3	2	0	1	11	1	37	1	0	2	1	.667	0	2-4	10	3.04	2.70
1999 Toronto	AL	30	0	0	5	22.2	104	28	21	21	4	3	1	0	9	1	26	2	0	0	3	.000	0	0-2	9	5.87	8.34
1999 Arizona	NL	34	0	0	6	21.2	94	22	9	8	3	1	0	0	8	1	27	1	0	2	1	.667	0	1-1	6	4.19	3.32
2002 Toronto	AL	19	0	0	3	13.1	58	11	5	5	1	0	1	0	6	0	14	0	0	1	2	.333	0	0-1	5	3.02	3.38
2002 Philadelphia	NL	41	0	0	5	23.0	96	16	12	12	5	0	0	0	12	3	27	0	0	2	1	.667	0	1-3	13	3.45	4.70
18 ML YEARS		1064	14	0	422	1072.0	4539	977	478	433	105	47	42	17	402	54	1041	41	10	65	71	.478	0	158-232	180	3.45	3.64

Scott Podsednik

Bats: L **Throws:** L **Pos:** CF-123; PH-19; RF-13; LF-3 **Ht:** 6'0" **Wt:** 170 **Born:** 3/18/76 **Age:** 28

Year Team	Lg	G	AB	H	2B	3B	HR	(Hm Rd)	TB	R	RBI	RC	TBB	IBB	SO	HBP	SH	SF	SB	CS	SB%	GDP	Avg	OBP	Slg
2001 Seattle	AL	5	6	1	0	1	0	(0 0)	3	1	3	0	0	0	1	0	0	0	0	0	-	1	.167	.167	.500
2002 Seattle	AL	14	20	4	0	0	1	(0 1)	7	2	5	3	4	0	6	0	0	1	0	0	-	0	.200	.320	.350
2003 Milwaukee	NL	154	558	175	29	8	9	(7 2)	247	100	58	100	56	2	91	4	8	2	43	10	.81	11	.314	.379	.443
3 ML YEARS		173	584	180	29	9	10	(7 3)	257	103	66	103	60	2	98	4	8	3	43	10	.81	13	.308	.375	.440

Placido Polanco

Bats: R **Throws:** R **Pos:** 2B-99; 3B-21; PH-2   **Ht:** 5'10" **Wt:** 168 **Born:** 10/10/75 **Age:** 28

Year Team	Lg	G	AB	H	2B	3B	HR	(Hm Rd)	TB	R	RBI	RC	TBB	IBB	SO	HBP	SH	SF	SB	CS	SB%	GDP	Avg	OBP	Slg
1998 St Louis	NL	45	114	29	3	2	1	(1 0)	39	10	11	12	5	0	9	1	2	0	2	0	1.00	1	.254	.292	.342
1999 St Louis	NL	88	220	61	9	3	1	(0 1)	79	24	19	23	15	1	24	0	3	2	1	3	.25	7	.277	.321	.359
2000 St Louis	NL	118	323	102	12	3	5	(2 3)	135	50	39	44	16	0	26	1	7	3	4	4	.50	8	.316	.347	.418
2001 St Louis	NL	144	564	173	26	4	3	(1 2)	216	87	38	70	25	0	43	6	14	1	12	3	.80	22	.307	.342	.383
2002 StL-Phi	NL	147	548	158	32	2	9	(8 1)	221	75	49	64	26	1	41	8	13	0	5	3	.63	15	.288	.330	.403
2003 Philadelphia	NL	122	492	142	30	3	14	(7 7)	220	87	63	74	42	1	38	8	8	4	14	2	.88	16	.289	.352	.447
2002 St Louis	NL	94	342	97	19	1	5	(5 0)	133	47	27	38	12	1	27	4	9	0	3	1	.75	12	.284	.316	.389
2002 Philadelphia	NL	53	206	61	13	1	4	(3 1)	88	28	22	26	14	0	14	4	4	0	2	2	.50	3	.296	.353	.427
6 ML YEARS		664	2261	665	112	17	33	(19 14)	910	333	219	287	129	3	181	24	47	10	38	15	.72	69	.294	.337	.402

Cliff Politte

Pitches: R **Bats:** R **Pos:** RP-54   **Ht:** 5'11" **Wt:** 185 **Born:** 2/27/74 **Age:** 30

Year Team	Lg	G	GS	CG	GF	IP	BFP	H	R	ER	HR	SH	SF	HB	TBB	IBB	SO	WP	Bk	W	L	Pct	ShO	Sv-Op	Hld	ERC	ERA
2003 Syracuse*	AAA	1	0	0	0	1.0	3	0	0	0	0	0	0	0	0	0	1	0	0	0	0	-	0	0--		0.00	0.00
1998 St Louis	NL	8	8	0	0	37.0	172	45	32	26	6	3	1	1	18	0	22	2	1	2	3	.400	0	0-0	0	6.28	6.32
1999 Philadelphia	NL	13	0	0	0	17.2	85	19	14	14	2	1	0	0	15	0	15	2	0	1	0	1.000	0	0-0	1	6.47	7.13
2000 Philadelphia	NL	12	8	0	1	59.0	251	55	24	24	8	1	1	0	27	1	50	3	0	4	3	.571	0	0-0	0	4.20	3.66
2001 Philadelphia	NL	23	0	0	7	26.0	109	24	8	7	2	1	3	1	8	3	23	1	0	2	3	.400	0	0-0	1	3.11	2.42
2002 Phi-Tor		68	0	0	20	73.2	304	57	33	30	5	3	1	2	28	2	72	2	0	3	3	.500	0	1-4	25	2.64	3.67
2003 Toronto	AL	54	0	0	30	66.1	216	52	32	31	11	1	3	1	17	4	40	1	0	1	5	.167	0	12-18	8	4.93	5.66
2002 Philadelphia	NL	13	0	0	7	16.1	77	19	10	7	0	1	0	1	9	1	15	1	0	2	0	1.000	0	0-1	0	4.89	3.86
2002 Toronto	AL	55	0	0	13	57.1	227	38	23	23	5	2	1	1	19	1	57	1	0	1	3	.250	0	1-3	25	2.06	3.61
6 ML YEARS		178	16	0	58	262.2	1137	252	143	132	34	10	9	5	113	10	222	11	1	13	17	.433	0	13-22	35	4.18	4.52

Sidney Ponson

Pitches: R **Bats:** R **Pos:** SP-31   **Ht:** 6'1" **Wt:** 225 **Born:** 11/2/76 **Age:** 27

Year Team	Lg	G	GS	CG	GF	IP	BFP	H	R	ER	HR	SH	SF	HB	TBB	IBB	SO	WP	Bk	W	L	Pct	ShO	Sv-Op	Hld	ERC	ERA
1998 Baltimore	AL	31	20	0	5	135.0	588	157	82	79	19	3	4	3	42	2	85	4	1	8	9	.471	0	1-2	0	5.07	5.27
1999 Baltimore	AL	32	32	6	0	210.0	897	227	118	110	35	4	7	1	80	2	112	4	0	12	12	.500	0	0-0	0	5.08	4.71
2000 Baltimore	AL	32	32	6	0	222.0	953	223	125	119	30	3	3	1	83	0	152	5	0	9	13	.409	1	0-0	0	4.26	4.82
2001 Baltimore	AL	23	23	3	0	138.1	605	161	83	76	21	3	2	6	37	0	84	2	0	5	10	.333	1	0-0	0	5.04	4.94
2002 Baltimore	AL	28	28	3	0	176.0	736	172	84	80	26	2	3	2	63	1	120	3	0	7	9	.438	0	0-0	0	4.24	4.09
2003 Bal-SF		31	31	4	0	216.0	898	211	94	90	16	6	5	5	61	5	134	9	0	17	12	.586	0	0-0	0	3.41	3.75
2003 Baltimore	AL	21	21	4	0	148.0	622	147	65	62	10	2	3	4	43	2	100	6	0	14	6	.700	0	0-0	0	3.50	3.77
2003 San Francisco	NL	10	10	0	0	68.0	276	64	29	28	6	4	2	1	18	3	34	3	0	3	6	.333	0	0-0	0	3.23	3.71
6 ML YEARS		177	166	22	5	1097.1	4677	1151	586	554	147	21	24	18	366	10	687	27	1	58	65	.472	2	1-2	0	4.43	4.54

Colin Porter

Bats: L **Throws:** L **Pos:** PR-8; CF-7; RF-6; PH-5; LF-1   **Ht:** 6'2" **Wt:** 210 **Born:** 11/23/75 **Age:** 28

Year Team	Lg	G	AB	H	2B	3B	HR	(Hm Rd)	TB	R	RBI	RC	TBB	IBB	SO	HBP	SH	SF	SB	CS	SB%	GDP	Avg	OBP	Slg
1998 Auburn	A-	67	240	68	18	4	4	(- -)	106	40	30	35	19	0	61	5	2	1	14	11	.56	3	.283	.347	.442
1999 Michigan	A	127	453	132	28	9	18	(- -)	232	91	68	86	53	2	123	7	3	8	23	13	.64	4	.291	.369	.512
2000 Round Rock	AA	124	435	119	25	5	14	(- -)	196	76	57	71	56	4	130	6	0	1	17	9	.65	6	.274	.363	.451
2001 Round Rock	AA	25	100	32	5	5	2	(- -)	53	14	12	17	5	2	25	1	0	0	1	3	.25	0	.320	.358	.530
2001 New Orleans	AAA	101	312	74	14	1	7	(- -)	111	48	33	36	34	2	105	3	1	4	11	6	.65	2	.237	.314	.356
2002 New Orleans	AAA	134	461	122	30	5	6	(- -)	180	59	38	62	46	8	127	0	2	1	28	7	.80	5	.265	.331	.390
2003 New Orleans	AAA	102	356	114	23	6	11	(- -)	182	52	50	66	22	3	80	3	2	4	22	6	.79	3	.320	.361	.511
2003 Houston	NL	24	32	6	0	0	0	(0 0)	6	5	0	0	1	0	17	0	0	0	1	0	1.00	1	.188	.212	.188

Mike Porzio

Pitches: L **Bats:** L **Pos:** SP-3   **Ht:** 6'3" **Wt:** 190 **Born:** 8/20/72 **Age:** 31

Year Team	Lg	G	GS	CG	GF	IP	BFP	H	R	ER	HR	SH	SF	HB	TBB	IBB	SO	WP	Bk	W	L	Pct	ShO	Sv-Op	Hld	ERC	ERA
2003 Charlotte*	AAA	26	22	1	3	133.2	568	124	70	63	19	7	6	8	47	1	115	3	0	8	6	.571	0	0--		4.01	4.24
1999 Colorado	NL	16	0	0	3	14.2	75	21	14	14	5	1	0	0	10	0	10	0	0	0	0	-	0	0-0	0	9.91	8.59
2002 Chicago	AL	32	0	0	8	43.0	190	40	25	23	10	0	3	3	23	2	33	3	1	2	2	.500	0	0-0	3	5.44	4.81
2003 Chicago	AL	3	3	0	0	14.0	62	18	10	10	2	2	1	2	1	0	9	0	0	1	1	.500	0	0-0	0	5.25	6.43
3 ML YEARS		51	3	0	11	71.2	327	79	49	47	17	3	4	5	34	2	52	3	1	3	3	.500	0	0-0	3	6.26	5.90

Jorge Posada

Bats: B **Throws:** R **Pos:** C-137; PH-9; DH-2   **Ht:** 6'2" **Wt:** 205 **Born:** 8/17/71 **Age:** 32

Year Team	Lg	G	AB	H	2B	3B	HR	(Hm Rd)	TB	R	RBI	RC	TBB	IBB	SO	HBP	SH	SF	SB	CS	SB%	GDP	Avg	OBP	Slg
1995 New York	AL	1	0	0	0	0	0	(0 0)	0	0	0	0	0	0	0	0	0	0	0	0	-	0	-	-	-
1996 New York	AL	8	14	1	0	0	0	(0 0)	1	1	0	0	1	0	6	0	0	0	0	0	-	1	.071	.133	.071
1997 New York	AL	60	188	47	12	0	6	(2 4)	77	29	25	29	30	2	33	3	1	2	1	2	.33	2	.250	.359	.410
1998 New York	AL	111	358	96	23	0	17	(6 11)	170	56	63	56	47	7	92	0	4	4	0	1	.00	14	.268	.350	.475
1999 New York	AL	112	379	93	19	2	12	(4 8)	152	50	57	52	53	2	91	3	0	2	1	0	1.00	9	.245	.341	.401
2000 New York	AL	151	505	145	35	1	28	(18 10)	266	92	86	110	107	10	151	8	0	4	2	2	.50	11	.287	.417	.527
2001 New York	AL	138	484	134	28	1	22	(14 8)	230	59	95	80	62	10	132	6	0	5	2	6	.25	10	.277	.363	.475

Year Team	Lg	BATTING G	AB	H	2B	3B	HR	(Hm Rd)	TB	R	RBI	RC	TBB	IBB	SO	HBP	SH	SF	BASERUNNING SB	CS	SB%	GDP	AVERAGES Avg	OBP	Slg
2002 New York	AL	143	511	137	40	1	20	(12 8)	239	79	99	93	81	9	143	3	0	3	1	0	1.00	23	.268	.370	.468
2003 New York	AL	142	481	135	24	0	30	(15 15)	249	83	101	98	93	6	110	10	0	4	2	4	.33	13	.281	.405	.518
9 ML YEARS		866	2920	788	181	5	135	(71 64)	1384	449	526	518	474	46	758	33	1	24	9	15	.38	83	.270	.375	.474

Brian Powell

Pitches: R **Bats:** R **Pos:** SP-1   **Ht:** 6'2" **Wt:** 205 **Born:** 10/10/73 **Age:** 30

Year Team	Lg	HOW MUCH HE PITCHED G	GS	CG	GF	IP	BFP	WHAT HE GAVE UP H	R	ER	HR	SH	SF	HB	TBB	IBB	SO	WP	Bk	THE RESULTS W	L	Pct	ShO	Sv-Op	Hld	ERC	ERA
2003 Fresno*	AAA	23	15	0	1	101.0	444	118	57	47	10	3	3	0	32	2	59	1	0	7	8	.467	0	0--	-	4.65	4.19
2003 Scrtn/WlksBr*	AAA	8	7	2	0	52.2	223	57	33	27	1	2	2	0	12	2	36	3	0	2	4	.333	1	0--	-	3.23	4.61
1998 Detroit	AL	18	16	0	1	83.2	383	101	67	59	17	1	1	2	36	2	46	3	0	3	8	.273	0	0-0	0	6.25	6.35
2000 Houston	NL	9	5	0	1	31.1	140	34	21	20	8	2	2	1	13	0	14	0	0	2	1	.667	0	0-0	0	5.88	5.74
2001 Houston	NL	1	1	0	0	3.0	17	5	6	6	1	0	0	0	3	0	3	0	0	0	1	.000	0	0-0	0	13.15	18.00
2002 Detroit	AL	13	9	0	1	57.2	254	64	34	31	11	0	2	1	21	0	30	2	0	1	5	.167	0	0-0	0	5.29	4.84
2003 San Francisco	NL	1	1	0	0	4.2	22	8	7	7	3	0	0	0	1	0	3	0	0	0	1	.000	0	0-0	0	12.71	13.50
5 ML YEARS		42	32	0	3	180.1	816	212	135	123	40	3	5	4	74	2	96	5	0	6	16	.273	0	0-0	0	6.13	6.14

Jay Powell

Pitches: R **Bats:** R **Pos:** RP-51   **Ht:** 6'4" **Wt:** 225 **Born:** 1/9/72 **Age:** 32

Year Team	Lg	HOW MUCH HE PITCHED G	GS	CG	GF	IP	BFP	WHAT HE GAVE UP H	R	ER	HR	SH	SF	HB	TBB	IBB	SO	WP	Bk	THE RESULTS W	L	Pct	ShO	Sv-Op	Hld	ERC	ERA
2003 Frisco	AA	4	0	0	1	6.2	30	5	2	2	0	0	0	0	5	0	8	0	0	0	0	-	0	1--	-	3.21	2.70
1995 Florida	NL	9	0	0	1	8.1	38	7	2	1	0	1	0	2	6	1	4	0	0	0	0	-	0	0-0	2	4.44	1.08
1996 Florida	NL	67	0	0	16	71.1	321	71	41	36	5	2	1	4	36	1	52	3	0	4	3	.571	0	2-5	10	4.39	4.54
1997 Florida	NL	74	0	0	23	79.2	337	71	35	29	3	6	4	4	30	3	65	3	0	7	2	.778	0	2-4	24	3.10	3.28
1998 Fla-Hou	NL	62	0	0	35	70.1	302	58	28	26	6	3	1	3	37	9	62	1	0	7	7	.500	0	7-11	3	3.46	3.33
1999 Houston	NL	67	0	0	26	75.0	341	82	38	36	3	5	2	3	40	4	77	5	0	5	4	.556	0	4-7	16	4.75	4.32
2000 Houston	NL	29	0	0	10	27.0	127	29	18	17	1	1	0	0	19	1	16	0	0	1	1	.500	0	0-0	5	5.10	5.67
2001 Hou-Col	NL	74	0	0	20	75.0	327	75	36	27	9	5	1	2	31	3	54	0	1	5	3	.625	0	7-13	8	4.30	3.24
2002 Texas	AL	51	0	0	5	49.2	224	50	28	19	5	1	0	1	24	4	35	2	0	3	2	.600	0	0-4	12	4.28	3.44
2003 Texas	AL	51	0	0	20	58.2	279	75	58	51	7	1	6	2	34	3	40	6	0	3	0	1.000	0	0-0	2	6.72	7.82
1998 Florida	NL	33	0	0	26	36.1	165	36	19	17	5	3	1	2	22	6	24	1	0	4	4	.500	0	3-6	0	5.07	4.21
1998 Houston	NL	29	0	0	9	34.0	137	22	9	9	1	0	0	1	15	3	38	0	0	3	3	.500	0	4-5	3	1.96	2.38
2001 Houston	NL	35	0	0	5	36.1	170	41	18	15	4	1	1	0	19	0	28	0	1	2	2	.500	0	0-5	5	5.23	3.72
2001 Colorado	NL	39	0	0	15	38.2	157	34	18	12	5	4	0	2	12	3	26	0	0	3	1	.750	0	7-8	3	3.45	2.79
9 ML YEARS		484	0	0	156	515.0	2296	518	284	242	39	25	15	21	257	29	405	20	1	35	22	.614	0	22-44	82	4.37	4.23

Todd Pratt

Bats: R **Throws:** R **Pos:** C-35; 1B-6; PH-5   **Ht:** 6'3" **Wt:** 230 **Born:** 2/9/67 **Age:** 37

Year Team	Lg	BATTING G	AB	H	2B	3B	HR	(Hm Rd)	TB	R	RBI	RC	TBB	IBB	SO	HBP	SH	SF	BASERUNNING SB	CS	SB%	GDP	AVERAGES Avg	OBP	Slg
1992 Philadelphia	NL	16	46	13	1	0	2	(2 0)	20	6	10	6	4	0	12	0	0	0	0	0	-	2	.283	.340	.435
1993 Philadelphia	NL	33	87	25	6	0	5	(4 1)	46	8	13	15	5	0	19	1	1	1	0	0	-	2	.287	.330	.529
1994 Philadelphia	NL	28	102	20	6	1	2	(1 1)	34	10	9	9	12	0	29	0	0	0	0	1	.00	3	.196	.281	.333
1995 Chicago	NL	25	60	8	2	0	0	(0 0)	10	3	4	1	6	1	21	0	0	1	0	0	-	1	.133	.209	.167
1997 New York	NL	39	106	30	6	0	2	(1 1)	42	12	19	16	13	0	32	2	0	0	0	1	.00	1	.283	.372	.396
1998 New York	NL	41	69	19	9	1	2	(1 1)	36	9	18	11	2	0	20	0	0	0	0	0	-	1	.275	.296	.522
1999 New York	NL	71	140	41	4	0	3	(1 2)	54	18	21	22	15	0	32	3	0	2	2	0	1.00	4	.293	.369	.386
2000 New York	NL	80	160	44	6	0	8	(2 6)	74	33	25	28	22	1	31	5	2	1	0	0	-	5	.275	.378	.463
2001 NYM-Phi	NL	80	173	32	8	0	4	(0 4)	52	18	11	18	34	3	61	3	1	1	1	0	1.00	6	.185	.327	.301
2002 Philadelphia	NL	39	106	33	11	0	3	(2 1)	53	14	16	21	24	6	28	4	0	2	2	0	1.00	3	.311	.449	.500
2003 Philadelphia	NL	43	125	34	10	1	4	(3 1)	58	16	20	25	22	0	38	6	1	2	0	0	-	3	.272	.400	.464
2001 New York	NL	45	80	13	5	0	2	(0 2)	24	6	4	7	15	1	36	2	0	1	1	0	1.00	4	.163	.306	.300
2001 Philadelphia	NL	35	93	19	3	0	2	(0 2)	28	12	7	11	19	2	25	1	1	0	0	0	-	2	.204	.345	.301
11 ML YEARS		495	1174	299	69	3	35	(17 18)	479	147	166	172	159	11	323	24	5	10	5	2	.71	27	.255	.353	.408

Curtis Pride

Bats: L **Throws:** R **Pos:** RF-2; LF-1; PH-1   **Ht:** 6'0" **Wt:** 210 **Born:** 12/17/68 **Age:** 35

Year Team	Lg	BATTING G	AB	H	2B	3B	HR	(Hm Rd)	TB	R	RBI	RC	TBB	IBB	SO	HBP	SH	SF	BASERUNNING SB	CS	SB%	GDP	AVERAGES Avg	OBP	Slg
2003 Columbus*	AAA	55	225	65	11	4	7	(- -)	105	44	34	34	20	4	48	4	1	0	7	7	.50	7	.289	.357	.467
1993 Montreal	NL	10	9	4	1	1	1	(0 0)	10	3	5	5	0	0	3	0	0	0	1	0	1.00	0	.444	.444	1.111
1995 Montreal	NL	48	63	11	1	0	0	(0 0)	12	10	2	3	5	0	16	0	1	0	3	2	.60	2	.175	.235	.190
1996 Detroit	AL	95	267	80	17	5	10	(5 5)	137	52	31	52	31	1	63	0	3	0	11	6	.65	2	.300	.372	.513
1997 Det-Bos	AL	81	164	35	4	4	3	(3 0)	56	22	20	19	24	1	46	1	2	1	6	4	.60	4	.213	.316	.341
1998 Atlanta	NL	70	107	27	6	1	3	(1 2)	44	19	9	15	9	0	29	3	1	1	4	0	1.00	1	.252	.325	.411
2000 Boston	AL	9	20	5	1	0	0	(0 0)	6	4	0	2	1	0	7	0	0	0	0	0	-	0	.250	.286	.300
2001 Montreal	NL	36	76	19	3	1	1	(0 1)	27	8	9	9	9	0	22	2	0	0	3	2	.60	4	.250	.345	.355
2003 New York	AL	4	12	1	0	0	1	(0 1)	4	1	1	0	0	0	2	0	0	0	0	0	-	1	.083	.083	.333
1997 Detroit	AL	79	162	34	4	4	2	(2 0)	52	21	19	17	24	1	45	1	2	1	6	4	.60	4	.210	.314	.321
1997 Boston	AL	2	2	1	0	0	1	(1 0)	4	1	1	2	0	0	1	0	0	0	0	0	-	0	.500	.500	2.000
8 ML YEARS		353	718	182	33	12	19	(10 8)	296	119	77	105	79	2	188	6	7	2	28	14	.67	15	.253	.332	.412

Alex Prieto

Bats: R Throws: R Pos: 2B-5; PH-3; SS-1   Ht: 5'11" Wt: 200 Born: 6/19/76 Age: 28

Year Team	Lg	G	AB	H	2B	3B	HR	(Hm	Rd)	TB	R	RBI	RC	TBB	IBB	SO	HBP	SH	SF	SB	CS	SB%	GDP	Avg	OBP	Slg
1993 Royals	R	43	114	28	3	0	0	(-	-)	31	14	6	10	9	1	13	0	4	0	4	2	.67	1	.246	.301	.272
1994 Royals	R	18	60	18	5	0	2	(-	-)	29	15	17	11	2	1	5	4	1	4	1	0	1.00	0	.300	.343	.483
1995 Springfield	A	124	431	108	9	3	2	(-	-)	129	61	44	42	40	1	69	6	12	2	11	7	.61	10	.251	.322	.299
1996 Wilmington	A+	119	447	127	19	6	1	(-	-)	161	65	40	53	31	0	66	3	8	5	26	15	.63	7	.284	.331	.360
1997 Wilmington	A+	129	437	94	13	3	3	(-	-)	122	52	38	36	41	1	59	2	11	6	20	8	.71	6	.215	.282	.279
1998 Wichita	AA	113	384	101	18	7	2	(-	-)	139	61	35	41	31	0	54	2	8	0	4	6	.40	13	.263	.321	.362
1999 Wichita	AA	114	360	106	23	4	6	(-	-)	155	56	41	54	35	1	47	1	13	3	12	6	.67	10	.294	.356	.431
2000 Omaha	AAA	118	384	101	19	0	7	(-	-)	141	54	37	44	26	0	40	6	8	2	14	6	.70	12	.263	.318	.367
2001 Omaha	AAA	105	376	106	21	3	8	(-	-)	157	45	44	53	36	0	59	1	4	3	9	2	.82	12	.282	.344	.418
2002 Edmonton	AAA	80	276	73	14	1	7	(-	-)	110	38	29	33	19	1	47	2	0	1	4	4	.50	5	.264	.315	.399
2003 Rochester	AAA	69	234	62	9	1	5	(-	-)	88	27	21	25	12	1	49	0	4	2	6	3	.67	6	.265	.298	.376
2003 Minnesota	AL	8	11	1	0	0	0	(0	0)	1	1	0	0	0	0	4	0	0	0	0	0	-	0	.091	.091	.091

Tom Prince

Bats: R Throws: R Pos: C-29; PH-5; PR-2; DH-1   Ht: 5'11" Wt: 206 Born: 8/13/64 Age: 39

Year Team	Lg	G	AB	H	2B	3B	HR	(Hm	Rd)	TB	R	RBI	RC	TBB	IBB	SO	HBP	SH	SF	SB	CS	SB%	GDP	Avg	OBP	Slg
2003 Omaha*	AAA	29	91	28	10	0	1	(-	-)	41	16	6	17	14	0	15	4	0	1	0	1	.00	2	.308	.418	.451
1987 Pittsburgh	NL	4	9	2	1	0	1	(0	1)	6	1	2	1	0	0	2	0	0	0	0	0	-	0	.222	.222	.667
1988 Pittsburgh	NL	29	74	13	2	0	0	(0	0)	15	3	6	1	4	0	15	0	2	0	0	0	-	5	.176	.218	.203
1989 Pittsburgh	NL	21	52	7	4	0	0	(0	0)	11	1	5	1	6	1	12	0	0	1	1	1	.50	1	.135	.220	.212
1990 Pittsburgh	NL	4	10	1	0	0	0	(0	0)	1	1	0	0	1	0	2	0	0	0	0	1	.00	0	.100	.182	.100
1991 Pittsburgh	NL	26	34	9	3	0	1	(0	1)	15	4	2	6	7	0	3	1	0	0	0	0	-	3	.265	.405	.441
1992 Pittsburgh	NL	27	44	4	2	0	0	(0	0)	6	1	5	0	6	0	9	0	0	2	1	1	.50	0	.091	.192	.136
1993 Pittsburgh	NL	66	179	35	14	0	2	(2	0)	55	14	24	14	13	2	38	7	2	3	1	1	.50	5	.196	.272	.307
1994 Los Angeles	NL	3	6	2	0	0	0	(0	0)	2	2	1	1	1	0	3	0	0	0	0	0	-	0	.333	.429	.333
1995 Los Angeles	NL	18	40	8	2	1	1	(0	1)	15	3	4	4	4	0	10	0	0	0	0	0	-	0	.200	.273	.375
1996 Los Angeles	NL	40	64	19	6	0	1	(0	1)	28	6	11	11	6	2	15	2	3	2	0	0	-	0	.297	.365	.438
1997 Los Angeles	NL	47	100	22	5	0	3	(2	1)	36	17	14	10	5	0	15	3	4	1	0	0	-	2	.220	.275	.360
1998 Los Angeles	NL	37	81	15	5	1	0	(0	0)	22	7	5	6	7	1	24	2	2	0	0	0	-	0	.185	.267	.272
1999 Philadelphia	NL	4	6	1	0	0	0	(0	0)	1	1	0	0	1	0	1	0	0	0	0	0	-	0	.167	.286	.167
2000 Philadelphia	NL	46	122	29	9	0	2	(0	2)	44	14	16	13	13	0	31	2	3	0	1	0	1.00	6	.238	.321	.361
2001 Minnesota	AL	64	196	43	4	1	7	(3	4)	70	19	23	19	12	0	39	6	0	1	3	1	.75	5	.219	.284	.357
2002 Minnesota	AL	51	125	28	7	1	4	(3	1)	49	14	16	17	14	0	26	4	3	2	1	3	.25	4	.224	.317	.392
2003 Min-KC	AL	32	48	10	2	0	2	(1	1)	18	5	6	5	5	0	7	2	2	0	1	0	1.00	2	.208	.309	.375
2003 Minnesota	AL	24	40	8	2	0	2	(1	1)	16	5	5	5	5	0	7	2	2	0	1	0	1.00	0	.200	.319	.400
2003 Kansas City	AL	8	8	2	0	0	0	(0	0)	2	0	1	0	0	0	0	0	0	0	0	0	-	2	.250	.250	.250
17 ML YEARS		519	1190	248	66	4	24	(11	13)	394	113	140	109	105	6	252	29	21	12	9	8	.53	36	.208	.286	.331

Bret Prinz

Pitches: R Bats: R Pos: RP-3   Ht: 6'3" Wt: 185 Born: 6/15/77 Age: 27

Year Team	Lg	G	GS	CG	GF	IP	BFP	H	R	ER	HR	SH	SF	HB	TBB	IBB	SO	WP	Bk	W	L	Pct	ShO	Sv-Op	Hld	ERC	ERA
2003 Lancaster*	A+	1	1	0	0	1.0	3	0	0	0	0	0	0	0	0	0	2	0	0	0	0	-	0	0- -	-	0.00	0.00
2003 Columbus*	AAA	10	0	0	3	12.1	57	20	11	11	2	0	1	0	1	0	13	1	0	0	1	.000	0	0- -	-	6.91	8.03
2003 El Paso*	AA	2	0	0	0	2.0	10	3	1	1	0	0	0	0	1	0	2	0	0	0	0	-	0	0- -	-	6.48	4.50
2003 Tucson*	AAA	10	0	0	2	12.0	59	19	9	8	1	0	1	0	3	0	7	1	0	0	1	.000	0	0- -	-	6.53	6.00
2001 Arizona	NL	46	0	0	26	41.0	174	33	13	12	4	3	1	1	19	1	27	1	4	4	1	.800	0	9-12	6	3.27	2.63
2002 Arizona	NL	20	0	0	5	13.1	71	23	14	14	1	2	1	1	10	1	10	3	0	0	2	.000	0	0-2	5	10.34	9.45
2003 Ari-NYY		3	0	0	2	3.0	20	7	4	4	1	0	0	0	4	2	3	0	0	0	0	-	0	0-0	0	18.22	12.00
2003 Arizona	NL	1	0	0	0	1.0	5	1	0	0	0	0	0	0	1	1	1	0	0	0	0	-	0	0-0	0	3.46	0.00
2003 New York	AL	2	0	0	2	2.0	15	6	4	4	1	0	0	0	3	1	2	0	0	0	0	-	0	0-0	0	27.15	18.00
3 ML YEARS		69	0	0	33	57.1	265	63	31	30	6	5	2	2	33	4	40	4	1	4	3	.571	0	9-14	11	5.38	4.71

Mark Prior

Pitches: R Bats: R Pos: SP-30   Ht: 6'5" Wt: 225 Born: 9/7/80 Age: 23

Year Team	Lg	G	GS	CG	GF	IP	BFP	H	R	ER	HR	SH	SF	HB	TBB	IBB	SO	WP	Bk	W	L	Pct	ShO	Sv-Op	Hld	ERC	ERA
2002 W Tennesse	AA	6	6	0	0	34.2	145	26	16	10	0	2	0	2	10	0	55	3	1	4	1	.800	0	0- -	-	1.87	2.60
2002 Iowa	AAA	3	3	0	0	16.1	75	13	10	3	1	1	1	1	8	0	24	0	1	1	1	.500	0	0- -	-	3.00	1.65
2002 Chicago	NL	19	19	1	0	116.2	486	98	45	43	14	3	4	7	38	0	147	1	0	6	6	.500	0	0-0	0	3.27	3.32
2003 Chicago	NL	30	30	3	0	211.1	863	183	67	57	15	9	2	9	50	4	245	9	0	18	6	.750	1	0-0	0	2.69	2.43
2 ML YEARS		49	49	4	0	328.0	1349	281	112	100	29	12	6	16	88	4	392	10	0	24	12	.667	1	0-0	0	2.89	2.74

Brandon Puffer

Pitches: R Bats: R Pos: RP-13   Ht: 6'3" Wt: 190 Born: 10/5/75 Age: 28

Year Team	Lg	G	GS	CG	GF	IP	BFP	H	R	ER	HR	SH	SF	HB	TBB	IBB	SO	WP	Bk	W	L	Pct	ShO	Sv-Op	Hld	ERC	ERA
1994 Twins	R	18	0	0	16	35.1	157	33	18	12	1	0	1	4	19	0	40	6	1	2	2	.500	0	2- -	-	4.18	3.06
1995 Twins	R	14	5	0	6	40.2	175	29	21	13	0	0	0	6	21	0	35	5	0	0	3	.000	0	1- -	-	2.42	2.88
1996 Angels	R	1	1	0	0	5.0	23	7	2	2	0	0	0	1	0	3	1	0	0	0	1	.000	0	0- -	-	4.69	3.60
1996 Boise	A-	16	0	0	8	30.1	129	27	19	15	3	1	3	1	11	0	22	3	0	2	0	1.000	0	1- -	-	3.41	4.45
1997 Boise	A-	6	0	0	2	15.1	63	10	5	4	0	0	1	1	2	0	15	1	0	0	0	-	0	1- -	-	1.17	2.35
1997 Cedar Rpds	A	10	0	0	2	17.1	66	8	6	5	0	0	0	0	10	0	11	3	1	0	0	-	0	0- -	-	1.54	2.60
1998 Chrlstn - WV	A	29	0	0	12	50.2	242	68	45	39	4	2	1	7	23	4	36	5	0	2	7	.222	0	1- -	-	6.65	6.93
1998 Chattanooga	AA	7	0	0	4	8.2	32	2	3	3	2	0	0	1	3	0	6	0	0	1	0	-	0	0- -	-	1.37	3.12
1999 Clinton	A	59	0	0	55	63.1	277	53	20	14	2	2	1	11	24	3	60	4	1	1	2	.333	0	34- -	-	3.14	1.99

Year Team	Lg	G	GS	CG	GF	IP	BFP	H	R	ER	HR	SH	SF	HB	TBB	IBB	SO	WP	Bk	W	L	Pct	ShO	Sv-Op	Hld	ERC	ERA
2000 Asheville	A	14	0	0	9	14.1	75	19	16	13	3	2	0	3	11	3	15	3	0	0		5--	-	9.03	8.16
2000 Somerset	IND	15	0	0	7	23.0	104	25	12	9	1	0	1	1	9	2	21	2	1	2	2	.500	0	1--	-	4.03	3.52
2000 Kissimmee	A+	18	0	0	18	21.1	95	18	6	3	0	3	0	1	11	4	26	3	0	2	3	.400	0	9--	-	2.72	1.27
2001 Round Rock	AA	56	0	0	33	82.2	331	52	19	19	4	1	1	7	35	2	91	3	0	6	1	.857	0	8--	-	2.23	2.07
2002 New Orleans	AAA	11	0	0	4	15.0	57	8	3	3	1	0	0	2	4	0	13	1	0	2	1	.667	0	0--	-	1.63	1.80
2003 New Orleans	AAA	44	0	0	20	52.2	226	50	23	17	1	1	4	7	16	1	41	1	0	7	3	.700	0	5--	-	3.34	2.91
2002 Houston	NL	55	0	0	19	69.0	311	67	37	34	3	5	2	5	38	8	48	2	0	3	3	.500	0	0-0	2	4.13	4.43
2003 Houston	NL	13	0	0	4	21.0	100	24	13	12	2	2	0	1	16	3	10	1	0	0	0	-	0	0-1	1	6.39	5.14
2 ML YEARS		68	0	0	23	90.0	411	91	50	46	5	7	2	6	54	11	58	3	0	3	3	.500	0	0-1	3	4.63	4.60

Albert Pujols

Bats: R **Throws:** R **Pos:** LF-113; 1B-62; PH-7; DH-1 **Ht:** 6'3" **Wt:** 210 **Born:** 1/16/80 **Age:** 24

Year Team	Lg	G	AB	H	2B	3B	HR	(Hm	Rd)	TB	R	RBI	RC	TBB	IBB	SO	HBP	SH	SF	SB	CS	SB%	GDP	Avg	OBP	Slg
2001 St Louis	NL	161	590	194	47	4	37	(18	19)	360	112	130	132	69	6	93	9	1	7	1	3	.25	21	.329	.403	.610
2002 St Louis	NL	157	590	185	40	2	34	(14	20)	331	118	127	122	72	13	69	9	0	4	2	4	.33	20	.314	.394	.561
2003 St Louis	NL	157	591	212	51	1	43	(21	22)	394	137	124	162	79	12	65	10	0	5	5	1	.83	13	.359	.439	.667
3 ML YEARS		475	1771	591	138	7	114	(53	61)	1085	367	381	416	220	31	227	28	1	16	8	8	.50	54	.334	.412	.613

Carlos Pulido

Pitches: L **Bats:** L **Pos:** RP-6; SP-1 **Ht:** 6'0" **Wt:** 200 **Born:** 8/5/71 **Age:** 32

Year Team	Lg	G	GS	CG	GF	IP	BFP	H	R	ER	HR	SH	SF	HB	TBB	IBB	SO	WP	Bk	W	L	Pct	ShO	Sv-Op	Hld	ERC	ERA
1989 Twins	R	22	0	0	11	36.0	143	22	9	9	0	2	3	14	0	46	6	3	3	0	1.000	0	2--	-	1.76	2.25
1990 Kenosha	A	56	0	0	29	61.2	270	55	21	16	2	2	1	4	36	3	70	3	4	5	5	.500	0	6--	-	3.91	2.34
1991 Visalia	A+	57	0	0	32	80.2	334	77	34	18	2	5	2	0	23	2	102	3	1	1	5	.167	0	17--	-	2.87	2.01
1991 Portland	AA	2	0	0	2	1.2	10	4	3	3	1	0	0	0	1	0	2	0	0	0	0	-	0	0--	-	19.61	16.20
1992 Orlando	AA	52	5	0	20	100.1	432	99	52	49	7	1	6	3	37	0	87	4	1	6	2	.750	0	1--	-	3.77	4.40
1993 Portland	AA	33	22	1	5	146.0	625	169	74	68	8	3	4	2	45	1	79	8	1	10	6	.625	0	0--	-	4.43	4.19
1995 Salt Lake	AAA	43	3	0	9	71.1	321	87	42	37	10	1	0	2	20	4	32	3	2	8	1	.889	0	3--	-	5.08	4.67
1996 Iowa	AAA	28	17	0	3	101.2	461	133	64	60	17	6	3	3	36	3	48	5	1	2	8	.200	0	0--	-	6.38	5.31
1996 Orlando	AA	6	0	0	1	9.2	50	17	9	8	0	0	0	0	3	0	12	3	0	2	2	.500	0	0--	-	7.14	7.45
1997 Ottawa	AAA	44	5	0	17	76.1	333	84	47	46	10	0	2	2	25	2	44	2	0	5	2	.714	0	4--	-	4.64	5.42
1998 Somerset	IND	12	2	1	5	35.1	145	30	14	13	3	2	2	1	12	1	33	1	0	2	2	.500	0	0--	-	3.03	3.31
1998 Norfolk	AAA	3	0	0	1	5.1	20	6	1	1	1	0	0	0	0	0	6	0	0	0	0	-	0	0--	-	4.07	1.69
1999 Somerset	IND	22	22	4	0	148.2	607	137	77	73	20	5	4	2	36	0	105	7	0	9	4	.692	0	0--	-	3.33	4.42
2003 Rochester	AAA	25	25	1	0	149.1	611	145	65	59	13	8	7	2	40	0	87	3	0	12	5	.706	0	0--	-	3.45	3.56
1994 Minnesota	AL	19	14	0	0	84.1	366	87	0	56	17	0	0	0	40	0	32	1	0	3	7	.300	0	0-0	0	5.41	5.98
2003 Minnesota	AL	7	1	0	1	15.2	65	15	9	7	0	1	2	0	3	0	6	1	0	0	1	1.000	0	0-0	1	2.37	4.02
2 ML YEARS		26	15	0	1	100.0	431	102	9	63	17	1	2	0	43	0	38	1	0	3	8	.273	0	0-0	1	4.88	5.67

Nick Punto

Bats: B **Throws:** R **Pos:** PH-28; 2B-16; PR-12; 3B-9; SS-7 **Ht:** 5'9" **Wt:** 170 **Born:** 11/8/77 **Age:** 26

Year Team	Lg	G	AB	H	2B	3B	HR	(Hm	Rd)	TB	R	RBI	RC	TBB	IBB	SO	HBP	SH	SF	SB	CS	SB%	GDP	Avg	OBP	Slg
2003 Scrtn/WlksBr*	AAA	25	111	35	7	1	0	(-	-)	44	19	9	17	7	0	13	0	2	1	7	1	.88	0	.315	.353	.396
2001 Philadelphia	NL	4	5	2	0	0	0	(0	0)	2	0	0	1	0	0	0	0	0	0	0	0	-	0	.400	.400	.400
2002 Philadelphia	NL	9	6	1	0	0	0	(0	0)	1	0	0	0	0	0	3	0	1	0	0	0	-	0	.167	.167	.167
2003 Philadelphia	NL	64	92	20	2	0	1	(0	1)	25	14	4	7	7	1	22	0	0	0	2	1	.67	0	.217	.273	.272
3 ML YEARS		77	103	23	2	0	1	(0	1)	28	14	4	8	7	1	25	0	1	0	2	1	.67	0	.223	.273	.272

J.J. Putz

Pitches: R **Bats:** R **Pos:** RP-3 **Ht:** 6'5" **Wt:** 220 **Born:** 2/22/77 **Age:** 27

Year Team	Lg	G	GS	CG	GF	IP	BFP	H	R	ER	HR	SH	SF	HB	TBB	IBB	SO	WP	Bk	W	L	Pct	ShO	Sv-Op	Hld	ERC	ERA
1999 Everett	A-	10	0	0	3	22.1	99	23	13	12	2	1	4	2	11	1	17	0	1	0	0	-	0	2--	-	4.91	4.84
2000 Wisconsin	A	26	25	3	0	142.2	611	130	71	50	4	6	7	9	63	2	105	8	0	12	6	.667	2	0--	-	3.49	3.15
2001 San Antonio	AA	27	26	0	0	148.0	642	145	80	63	11	10	6	9	59	2	135	12	0	7	9	.438	0	0--	-	4.00	3.83
2002 San Antonio	AA	15	15	1	0	84.0	354	84	41	34	7	0	3	5	28	0	60	5	0	3	10	.231	1	0--	-	4.02	3.64
2002 Tacoma	AAA	9	9	0	0	54.0	225	51	23	23	4	1	1	4	21	0	39	8	0	2	4	.333	0	0--	-	3.99	3.83
2003 Tacoma	AAA	41	0	0	22	86.0	352	69	30	24	4	7	1	3	34	0	60	3	0	0	3	.000	0	11--	-	2.83	2.51
2003 Seattle	AL	3	0	0	0	3.2	18	4	2	2	0	0	0	0	3	0	3	0	0	0	0	-	0	0-0	0	5.31	4.91

Paul Quantrill

Pitches: R **Bats:** L **Pos:** RP-89 **Ht:** 6'1" **Wt:** 195 **Born:** 11/3/68 **Age:** 35

Year Team	Lg	G	GS	CG	GF	IP	BFP	H	R	ER	HR	SH	SF	HB	TBB	IBB	SO	WP	Bk	W	L	Pct	ShO	Sv-Op	Hld	ERC	ERA
1992 Boston	AL	27	0	0	10	49.1	213	55	18	12	1	4	2	1	15	5	24	1	0	2	3	.400	0	1-5	3	3.70	2.19
1993 Boston	AL	49	14	1	8	138.0	594	151	73	60	13	4	2	1	44	14	66	0	1	6	12	.333	1	1-2	3	4.16	3.91
1994 Bos-Phi		35	1	0	9	53.0	236	64	31	29	7	5	3	5	15	4	28	0	2	3	3	.500	0	1-4	3	5.34	4.92
1995 Philadelphia	NL	33	29	0	0	179.1	784	212	102	93	20	9	6	6	44	3	103	0	3	11	12	.478	0	0-0	0	4.67	4.67
1996 Toronto	AL	38	20	0	7	134.1	609	172	90	81	27	5	7	2	51	3	86	1	1	5	14	.263	0	0-2	1	6.52	5.43
1997 Toronto	AL	77	0	0	29	88.0	373	103	25	19	5	5	3	1	17	3	56	1	0	6	7	.462	0	5-10	16	3.94	1.94
1998 Toronto	AL	82	0	0	32	80.0	345	88	26	23	5	7	4	3	22	6	59	1	0	3	4	.429	0	7-14	27	3.90	2.59
1999 Toronto	AL	41	0	0	13	48.2	212	53	19	18	5	1	2	4	17	1	28	0	0	3	2	.600	0	0-4	8	4.77	3.33
2000 Toronto	AL	68	0	0	24	83.2	367	100	45	42	7	1	3	2	25	1	47	1	0	2	5	.286	0	1-3	13	4.78	4.52
2001 Toronto	AL	80	0	0	20	83.0	341	86	29	28	6	7	2	6	12	7	58	0	0	11	2	.846	0	2-9	21	3.31	3.04
2002 Los Angeles	NL	86	0	0	22	76.2	330	80	27	23	1	1	1	3	25	7	53	0	0	5	4	.556	0	1-3	33	3.42	2.70

Year Team	Lg	G	GS	CG	GF	IP	BFP	H	R	ER	HR	SH	SF	HB	TBB	IBB	SO	WP	Bk	W	L	Pct	ShO	Sv-Op	Hld	ERC	ERA
		HOW MUCH HE PITCHED						**WHAT HE GAVE UP**												**THE RESULTS**							
2003 Los Angeles	NL	**89**	0	0	21	77.1	291	61	18	15	2	4	0	3	15	2	44	0	0	2	5	.286	0	1-5	28	2.03	1.75
1994 Boston	AL	17	0	0	4	23.0	101	25	10	9	4	2	2	2	5	1	15	0	0	1	1	.500	0	0-2	2	4.53	3.52
1994 Philadelphia	NL	18	1	0	5	30.0	135	39	21	20	3	3	1	3	10	3	13	0	2	2	2	.500	0	1-2	1	5.97	6.00
12 ML YEARS		705	64	1	196	1091.1	4695	1225	503	443	99	53	35	38	302	56	652	5	7	59	73	.447	1	20-61	156	4.30	3.65

Ruben Quevedo

Pitches: R Bats: R Pos: SP-8; RP-1   Ht: 6'1" Wt: 257 Born: 1/5/79 Age: 25

Year Team	Lg	G	GS	CG	GF	IP	BFP	H	R	ER	HR	SH	SF	HB	TBB	IBB	SO	WP	Bk	W	L	Pct	ShO	Sv-Op	Hld	ERC	ERA
		HOW MUCH HE PITCHED						**WHAT HE GAVE UP**												**THE RESULTS**							
2003 Indianapolis*	AAA	5	5	0	0	25.2	106	24	7	6	1	1	1	0	8	1	23	0	0	2	1	.667	0	0- -		2.95	2.10
2000 Chicago	NL	21	15	1	1	88.0	418	96	81	73	21	4	3	3	54	4	65	2	0	3	10	.231	0	0-0		6.49	7.47
2001 Milwaukee	NL	10	10	0	0	56.2	253	56	30	29	9	3	2	0	30	4	60	1	0	4	5	.444	0	0-0		4.79	4.61
2002 Milwaukee	NL	26	25	1	0	139.0	634	159	100	89	28	6	3	4	68	3	93	6	0	6	11	.353	1	0-0		6.16	5.76
2003 Milwaukee	NL	9	8	0	0	42.2	196	53	32	32	12	1	3	0	23	1	19	0	0	1	4	.200	0	0-0		7.69	6.75
4 ML YEARS		66	58	2	1	326.1	1501	364	243	223	70	14	11	7	175	12	237	9	0	14	30	.318	1	0-0		6.19	6.15

Robb Quinlan

Bats: R Throws: R Pos: 1B-33; DH-3; PH-2; LF-1; PR-1   Ht: 6'1" Wt: 195 Born: 3/17/77 Age: 27

Year Team	Lg	G	AB	H	2B	3B	HR	(Hm	Rd)	TB	R	RBI	RC	TBB	IBB	SO	HBP	SH	SF	SB	CS	SB%	GDP	Avg	OBP	Slg
		BATTING												**BASERUNNING**										**AVERAGES**		
1999 Boise	A-	73	295	95	20	1	9	(-	-)	144	51	77	56	35	2	52	4	0	1	5	3	.63	5	.322	.400	.488
2000 Lk Elsinore	A+	127	482	153	35	5	5	(-	-)	213	79	85	87	67	1	82	2	2	9	6	4	.60	7	.317	.396	.442
2001 Arkansas	AA	129	492	145	33	7	14	(-	-)	234	82	79	82	53	9	84	6	0	7	0	4	.00	12	.295	.366	.476
2002 Salt Lake	AAA	136	528	176	31	13	20	(-	-)	293	95	112	104	41	2	93	4	0	15	8	2	.80	16	.333	.376	.555
2003 Salt Lake	AAA	95	393	122	18	4	9	(-	-)	175	55	68	60	25	2	59	1	0	2	10	3	.77	9	.310	.352	.445
2003 Anaheim	AL	38	94	27	4	2	0	(0	0)	35	13	4	7	6	0	16	0	1	0	1	2	.33	3	.287	.330	.372

Humberto Quintero

Bats: R Throws: R Pos: C-11; PH-2; PR-1   Ht: 6'1" Wt: 190 Born: 8/8/79 Age: 24

Year Team	Lg	G	AB	H	2B	3B	HR	(Hm	Rd)	TB	R	RBI	RC	TBB	IBB	SO	HBP	SH	SF	SB	CS	SB%	GDP	Avg	OBP	Slg
		BATTING												**BASERUNNING**										**AVERAGES**		
1999 Bristol	R+	48	155	43	5	2	0	(-	-)	52	30	15	18	9	0	19	6	3	0	11	1	.92	8	.277	.341	.335
2000 Burlington	A	75	248	59	12	2	0	(-	-)	75	23	24	19	15	1	31	3	4	2	10	6	.63	8	.238	.287	.302
2000 White Sox	R	15	56	22	2	2	0	(-	-)	28	13	8	10	0	0	3	2	0	0	1	0	1.00	2	.393	.414	.500
2001 Kannapolis	A	60	197	53	7	1	1	(-	-)	65	32	20	21	8	1	20	7	8	0	7	3	.70	5	.269	.321	.330
2001 Birmingham	AA	5	19	4	0	0	0	(-	-)	4	0	2	1	0	0	2	1	0	0	0	0	-	0	.211	.250	.211
2001 Winstn-Salm	A+	43	154	37	6	0	0	(-	-)	43	15	12	11	5	0	19	2	2	3	9	3	.75	3	.240	.268	.279
2002 Winstn-Salm	A+	52	160	31	1	1	0	(-	-)	34	15	12	6	8	0	23	4	7	2	2	3	.40	4	.194	.247	.213
2002 Birmingham	AA	4	12	6	0	0	0	(-	-)	6	1	3	3	0	0	1	1	1	0	1	0	1.00	1	.500	.538	.500
2002 Charlotte	AAA	15	41	9	1	0	0	(-	-)	10	2	5	2	3	0	8	0	0	0	0	3	.00	3	.220	.273	.244
2002 Mobile	AA	37	125	30	8	0	1	(-	-)	41	11	14	10	5	0	12	3	1	0	0	3	.00	3	.240	.286	.328
2003 Mobile	AA	110	386	115	26	0	3	(-	-)	150	37	52	47	19	5	41	9	4	3	0	0	-	17	.298	.343	.389
2003 San Diego	NL	12	23	5	0	0	0	(0	0)	5	1	2	1	1	1	6	0	0	0	0	0	-	0	.217	.250	.217

Brad Radke

Pitches: R Bats: R Pos: SP-33   Ht: 6'2" Wt: 188 Born: 10/27/72 Age: 31

Year Team	Lg	G	GS	CG	GF	IP	BFP	H	R	ER	HR	SH	SF	HB	TBB	IBB	SO	WP	Bk	W	L	Pct	ShO	Sv-Op	Hld	ERC	ERA
		HOW MUCH HE PITCHED						**WHAT HE GAVE UP**												**THE RESULTS**							
1995 Minnesota	AL	29	28	2	0	181.0	772	195	112	107	32	2	9	4	47	0	75	4	0	11	14	.440	1	0-0	0	4.58	5.32
1996 Minnesota	AL	35	35	3	0	232.0	973	231	125	115	40	5	8	4	57	2	148	1	0	11	16	.407	0	0-0	0	3.97	4.46
1997 Minnesota	AL	35	35	4	0	239.2	989	238	114	103	28	2	9	3	48	1	174	1	1	20	10	.667	1	0-0	0	3.41	3.87
1998 Minnesota	AL	32	32	5	0	213.2	904	238	109	102	23	9	3	9	43	1	146	3	1	12	14	.462	0	0-0	0	4.18	4.30
1999 Minnesota	AL	33	33	4	0	218.2	910	239	97	91	28	5	5	1	44	0	121	4	0	12	14	.462	0	0-0	0	4.07	3.75
2000 Minnesota	AL	34	34	4	0	226.2	978	261	119	112	27	7	4	5	51	0	141	5	0	12	16	.429	1	0-0	0	4.44	4.45
2001 Minnesota	AL	33	33	6	0	226.0	919	235	105	99	24	10	6	10	26	0	137	4	1	15	11	.577	2	0-0	0	3.45	3.94
2002 Minnesota	AL	21	21	2	0	118.1	490	124	64	62	12	2	5	7	20	0	62	0	0	9	5	.643	1	0-0	0	3.73	4.72
2003 Minnesota	AL	33	33	3	0	212.1	888	242	111	106	32	12	4	5	28	2	120	0	0	14	10	.583	1	0-0	0	4.24	4.49
9 ML YEARS		285	284	33	0	1868.1	7823	2003	956	897	246	54	51	48	364	7	1124	22	3	116	110	.513	8	0-0	0	4.00	4.32

Brady Raggio

Pitches: R Bats: R Pos: RP-10   Ht: 6'4" Wt: 210 Born: 9/17/72 Age: 31

Year Team	Lg	G	GS	CG	GF	IP	BFP	H	R	ER	HR	SH	SF	HB	TBB	IBB	SO	WP	Bk	W	L	Pct	ShO	Sv-Op	Hld	ERC	ERA
		HOW MUCH HE PITCHED						**WHAT HE GAVE UP**												**THE RESULTS**							
2003 Tucson*	AAA	18	7	0	3	56.2	235	60	27	22	4	1	2	0	8	0	32	2	0	4	4	.500	0	0- -		3.17	3.49
1997 St Louis	NL	15	4	0	0	31.1	151	44	24	24	1	0	0	0	16	0	21	0	0	1	2	.333	0	0-0	0	6.35	6.89
1998 St Louis	NL	4	1	0	0	7.0	43	22	12	12	1	0	0	0	3	0	3	0	0	1	1	.500	0	0-0	0	20.89	15.43
2003 Arizona	NL	10	0	0	4	8.1	38	9	6	6	1	1	0	0	6	1	8	0	0	0	0	-	0	1-1	3	5.96	6.48
3 ML YEARS		29	5	0	4	46.2	232	75	6	42	3	1	0	0	25	1	32	0	0	2	3	.400	0	1-1	3	8.13	8.10

Tim Raines Jr

Bats: B **Throws:** R **Pos:** CF-17; PH-4; PR-2; LF-1; DH-1   **Ht:** 5'10" **Wt:** 183 **Born:** 8/31/79 **Age:** 24

Year Team	Lg	G	AB	H	2B	3B	HR	(Hm	Rd)	TB	R	RBI	RC	TBB	IBB	SO	HBP	SH	SF	SB	CS	SB%	GDP	Avg	OBP	Slg
1998 Orioles	R	56	197	48	7	4	1	(-	-)	66	40	13	35	30	1	53	12	3	0	37	4	.90	0	.244	.377	.335
1999 Delmarva	A	117	415	103	24	8	2	(-	-)	149	80	49	63	71	1	130	3	3	4	49	16	.75	1	.248	.359	.359
2000 Frederick	A+	127	457	108	21	3	2	(-	-)	141	89	36	63	67	0	106	13	11	3	81	19	.81	8	.236	.348	.309
2001 Frederick	A+	23	84	21	3	1	3	(-	-)	35	15	13	13	13	0	23	0	1	0	14	4	.78	2	.250	.351	.417
2001 Bowie	AA	65	254	74	14	1	4	(-	-)	102	46	30	42	34	0	60	3	4	1	29	10	.74	3	.291	.380	.402
2001 Rochester	AAA	40	133	34	5	1	2	(-	-)	47	19	12	16	11	0	30	0	1	0	11	3	.79	2	.256	.313	.353
2002 Bowie	AA	123	491	128	17	4	5	(-	-)	168	66	25	52	34	0	101	2	10	2	33	15	.69	8	.261	.310	.342
2003 Ottawa	AAA	52	214	64	11	5	3	(-	-)	94	37	23	34	19	0	37	1	2	1	23	9	.72	3	.299	.357	.439
2003 Bowie	AA	66	247	76	15	4	4	(-	-)	111	44	26	45	21	0	40	5	8	2	28	6	.82	3	.308	.371	.449
2001 Baltimore	AL	7	23	4	2	0	0	(0	0)	6	6	0	2	3	0	8	0	1	0	3	0	1.00	0	.174	.269	.261
2003 Baltimore	AL	20	43	6	1	1	0	(0	0)	9	4	2	1	2	0	12	1	0	0	0	0	-	2	.140	.196	.209
2 ML YEARS		27	66	10	3	1	0	(0	0)	15	10	2	3	5	0	20	1	1	0	3	0	1.00	2	.152	.222	.227

Aramis Ramirez

Bats: R **Throws:** R **Pos:** 3B-159; PH-1   **Ht:** 6'1" **Wt:** 211 **Born:** 6/25/78 **Age:** 26

Year Team	Lg	G	AB	H	2B	3B	HR	(Hm	Rd)	TB	R	RBI	RC	TBB	IBB	SO	HBP	SH	SF	SB	CS	SB%	GDP	Avg	OBP	Slg
1998 Pittsburgh	NL	72	251	59	9	1	6	(3	3)	88	23	24	26	18	0	72	4	1	1	0	1	.00	3	.235	.296	.351
1999 Pittsburgh	NL	18	56	10	2	1	0	(0	0)	14	2	7	4	6	0	9	0	1	1	0	0	-	0	.179	.254	.250
2000 Pittsburgh	NL	73	254	65	15	2	6	(4	2)	102	19	35	28	10	0	36	5	1	4	0	0	-	9	.256	.293	.402
2001 Pittsburgh	NL	158	603	181	40	4	34	(16	18)	323	83	112	108	40	4	100	8	0	4	5	4	.56	9	.300	.350	.536
2002 Pittsburgh	NL	142	522	122	26	0	18	(7	11)	202	51	71	49	29	3	95	8	0	11	2	0	1.00	17	.234	.279	.387
2003 Pit-ChC	NL	159	607	165	32	2	27	(10	17)	282	75	106	88	42	3	99	10	0	11	2	2	.50	21	.272	.324	.465
2003 Pittsburgh	NL	96	375	105	25	1	12	(6	6)	168	44	67	49	25	3	68	7	0	8	1	1	.50	17	.280	.330	.448
2003 Chicago	NL	63	232	60	7	1	15	(4	11)	114	31	39	39	17	0	31	3	0	3	1	1	.50	4	.259	.314	.491
6 ML YEARS		622	2293	602	124	6	91	(40	51)	1011	253	355	303	145	10	411	35	3	32	9	7	.56	59	.263	.312	.441

Erasmo Ramirez

Pitches: L **Bats:** L **Pos:** RP-34   **Ht:** 6'0" **Wt:** 180 **Born:** 4/29/76 **Age:** 28

Year Team	Lg	G	GS	CG	GF	IP	BFP	H	R	ER	HR	SH	SF	HB	TBB	IBB	SO	WP	Bk	W	L	Pct	ShO	Sv-Op	Hld	ERC	ERA
1998 Bakersfield	A+	14	0	0	2	44.0	175	10	8	8	0	2	0	2	6	0	17	1	3	1	1	.500	0	3--	-	1.11	3.38
1998 Salem-Keizer	A-	9	2	0	0	19.1	81	19	11	8	3	1	0	1	2	0	23	0	0	1	1	.000	0	0--	-	3.26	3.72
1999 San Jose	A+	31	0	0	12	57.1	219	42	18	17	2	2	4	1	8	0	52	2	0	2	0	1.000	0	5--	-	1.56	2.67
2000 Shreveport	AA	39	2	0	13	58.2	269	80	45	42	7	6	4	3	21	5	46	0	0	5	0	.000	0	1--	-	6.39	6.44
2001 San Jose	A+	17	0	0	6	31.2	126	23	14	12	2	2	0	0	5	0	33	2	0	3	2	.600	0	1--	-	1.58	3.41
2001 Shreveport	AA	22	1	0	6	33.1	130	25	10	8	1	0	0	3	5	0	39	2	0	2	0	1.000	0	1--	-	1.83	2.16
2001 Tulsa	AA	12	0	0	6	16.1	68	17	8	8	3	0	0	0	5	0	18	0	0	2	1	.667	0	0--	-	4.63	4.41
2002 Tulsa	AA	34	0	0	3	54.0	215	51	23	18	1	2	0	4	8	0	34	1	0	4	2	.667	0	2--	-	2.67	3.00
2002 Oklahoma	AAA	25	0	0	7	21.0	83	15	5	3	0	0	1	4	1	1	17	1	0	4	1	.800	0	1--	-	1.47	1.29
2003 Frisco	AA	3	0	0	2	3.0	15	4	2	2	1	0	0	0	1	0	4	1	0	1	0	1.000	0	0--	-	6.91	6.00
2003 Oklahoma	AAA	22	0	0	11	35.1	147	36	8	6	0	4	1	0	2	0	20	0	0	2	1	.667	0	4--	-	2.16	1.53
2003 Texas	AL	34	0	0	9	49.0	199	46	21	21	4	2	2	4	9	0	28	1	0	3	1	.750	0	0-1	2	3.17	3.86

Horacio Ramirez

Pitches: L **Bats:** L **Pos:** SP-29   **Ht:** 6'1" **Wt:** 170 **Born:** 11/24/79 **Age:** 24

Year Team	Lg	G	GS	CG	GF	IP	BFP	H	R	ER	HR	SH	SF	HB	TBB	IBB	SO	WP	Bk	W	L	Pct	ShO	Sv-Op	Hld	ERC	ERA
1997 Braves	R	11	8	0	2	44.0	175	30	13	11	1	0	1	0	18	0	61	4	0	3	3	.500	0	0--	-	2.02	2.25
1998 Macon	A	12	12	0	0	55.1	249	70	50	36	8	2	3	2	16	0	38	2	0	1	7	.125	0	0--	-	5.64	5.86
1998 Eugene	A-	16	8	0	3	55.2	273	84	51	39	4	3	6	4	17	0	39	4	2	2	7	.222	0	0--	-	6.61	6.31
1999 Macon	A	17	14	1	0	77.2	316	70	30	23	6	2	5	2	25	0	43	1	1	6	3	.667	1	0--	-	3.28	2.67
2000 Myrtle Beach	A+	27	26	3	0	148.1	609	136	57	53	14	1	1	2	42	0	125	6	4	15	8	.652	2	0--	-	3.22	3.22
2001 Greenville	AA	3	3	0	0	14.2	66	17	8	8	2	2	0	1	8	0	17	0	0	1	1	.500	0	0--	-	6.43	4.91
2002 Greenville	AA	16	16	0	0	92.0	376	85	41	31	5	1	7	0	32	0	64	3	1	9	5	.643	0	0--	-	3.25	3.03
2003 Atlanta	NL	29	29	1	0	182.1	781	181	91	81	21	12	3	6	72	10	100	5	1	12	4	.750	0	0-0	0	4.21	4.00

Julio Ramirez

Bats: R **Throws:** R **Pos:** CF-3; RF-2; PR-2; DH-1   **Ht:** 5'11" **Wt:** 170 **Born:** 8/10/77 **Age:** 26

Year Team	Lg	G	AB	H	2B	3B	HR	(Hm	Rd)	TB	R	RBI	RC	TBB	IBB	SO	HBP	SH	SF	SB	CS	SB%	GDP	Avg	OBP	Slg
2003 Salt Lake*	AAA	110	402	112	17	6	10	(-	-)	171	50	48	51	12	0	86	5	0	5	16	6	.73	7	.279	.304	.425
1999 Florida	NL	15	21	3	1	0	0	(0	0)	4	3	2	0	1	0	6	0	0	0	1	0	1.00	0	.143	.182	.190
2001 Chicago	AL	22	37	3	0	0	0	(0	0)	3	2	1	0	2	0	15	0	0	0	2	0	1.00	0	.081	.128	.081
2002 Anaheim	AL	29	32	9	0	1	1	(1	0)	14	6	7	5	2	0	14	1	0	0	0	2	.00	0	.281	.343	.438
2003 Anaheim	AL	6	2	0	0	0	0	(0	0)	0	1	0	0	0	0	0	0	0	0	0	0	-	0	.000	.000	.000
4 ML YEARS		72	92	15	1	1	1	(1	0)	21	12	10	5	5	0	35	1	1	0	2	3	.40	0	.163	.214	.228

Manny Ramirez

Bats: R **Throws:** R **Pos:** LF-128; DH-26; PH-2   **Ht:** 6'0" **Wt:** 213 **Born:** 5/30/72 **Age:** 32

Year Team	Lg	G	AB	H	2B	3B	HR	(Hm	Rd)	TB	R	RBI	RC	TBB	IBB	SO	HBP	SH	SF	SB	CS	SB%	GDP	Avg	OBP	Slg
1993 Cleveland	AL	22	53	9	1	0	2	(0	2)	16	5	5	2	2	0	8	0	0	0	0	0	-	3	.170	.200	.302
1994 Cleveland	AL	91	290	78	22	0	17	(9	8)	151	51	60	53	42	4	72	0	0	4	4	2	.67	6	.269	.357	.521
1995 Cleveland	AL	137	484	149	26	1	31	(12	19)	270	85	107	103	75	6	112	5	2	5	6	6	.50	13	.308	.402	.558

Year Team	Lg	G	AB	H	2B	3B	HR	(Hm	Rd)	TB	R	RBI	RC	TBB	IBB	SO	HBP	SH	SF	SB	CS	SB%	GDP	Avg	OBP	Slg
1996 Cleveland	AL	152	550	170	45	3	33	(19	14)	320	94	112	120	85	8	104	3	0	9	8	5	.62	18	.309	.399	.582
1997 Cleveland	AL	150	561	184	40	0	26	(14	12)	302	99	88	117	79	5	115	7	0	4	2	3	.40	19	.328	.415	.538
1998 Cleveland	AL	150	571	168	35	2	45	(25	20)	342	108	145	121	76	6	121	6	0	10	5	3	.63	18	.294	.377	.599
1999 Cleveland	AL	147	522	174	34	4	44	(21	23)	346	131	165	141	96	9	131	13	0	9	2	4	.33	12	.333	.442	.663
2000 Cleveland	AL	118	439	154	34	2	38	(22	16)	306	92	122	127	86	9	117	3	0	4	1	1	.50	9	.351	.457	.697
2001 Boston	AL	142	529	162	33	2	41	(21	20)	322	93	125	122	81	25	147	8	0	2	0	1	.00	9	.306	.405	.609
2002 Boston	AL	120	436	152	31	0	33	(18	15)	282	84	107	126	73	14	85	8	0	1	0	0	-	13	.349	.450	.647
2003 Boston	AL	154	569	185	36	1	37	(18	19)	334	117	104	127	97	28	94	8	0	5	3	1	.75	22	.325	.427	.587
11 ML YEARS		1383	5004	1585	337	14	347	(179	168)	2991	959	1140	1159	792	114	1106	61	2	53	31	26	.54	142	.317	.413	.598

Mario Ramos

Pitches: L **Bats:** L **Pos:** SP-3

Ht: 5'11" **Wt:** 180 **Born:** 10/19/77 **Age:** 26

		HOW MUCH HE PITCHED						WHAT HE GAVE UP										THE RESULTS						
Year Team	Lg	G	GS	CG	GF	IP	BFP	H	R	ER	HR	SH	SF	HB	TBB	IBB	SO	WP	Bk	W	L	Pct	ShO	Sv-Op	Hld	ERA
2000 Modesto	A+	26	24	1	1	152.0	624	131	63	49	6	9	3	3	50	4	134	3	1	12	5	.706	1	0- -	-	2.73	2.90
2000 Midland	AA	4	4	0	0	27.1	107	24	6	4	0	1	1	0	6	0	19	0	0	2	0	1.000	0	0- -	-	2.22	1.32
2001 Midland	AA	15	15	0	0	93.2	384	71	37	32	7	3	1	4	28	0	82	4	0	8	1	.889	0	0- -	-	2.39	3.07
2001 Sacramento	AAA	13	1	3	1	81.1	340	74	32	28	5	2	2	2	27	0	82	4	0	3	8	.727	1	0- -	-	3.08	3.14
2002 Oklahoma	AAA	34	19	0	2	121.2	572	162	107	100	20	2	6	7	53	0	75	0	1	3	8	.273	0	0- -	-	7.00	7.40
2003 Oklahoma	AAA	5	5	0	0	32.1	142	39	24	23	1	1	1	0	12	0	22	0	1	0	3	.000	0	0- -	-	4.71	6.40
2003 Frisco	AA	19	19	0	0	121.1	509	130	59	52	9	4	5	2	28	1	103	1	3	8	7	.533	0	0- -	-	3.72	3.86
2003 Texas	AL	3	3	0	0	13.0	65	11	9	9	3	1	0	2	13	0	8	0	0	1	1	.500	0	0-0	0	7.20	6.23

Joe Randa

Bats: R **Throws:** R **Pos:** 3B-129; DH-2; PH-2

Ht: 5'11" **Wt:** 190 **Born:** 12/18/69 **Age:** 34

		BATTING																		BASERUNNING				AVERAGES		
Year Team	Lg	G	AB	H	2B	3B	HR	(Hm	Rd)	TB	R	RBI	RC	TBB	IBB	SO	HBP	SH	SF	SB	CS	SB%	GDP	Avg	OBP	Slg
1995 Kansas City	AL	34	70	12	2	0	1	(1	0)	17	6	5	3	6	0	17	0	0	0	0	1	.00	2	.171	.237	.243
1996 Kansas City	AL	110	337	102	24	1	6	(2	4)	146	36	47	50	26	4	47	1	2	4	13	4	.76	10	.303	.351	.433
1997 Pittsburgh	NL	126	443	134	27	9	7	(5	2)	200	58	60	72	41	1	64	6	4	5	4	2	.67	10	.302	.366	.451
1998 Detroit	AL	138	460	117	21	2	9	(3	6)	169	56	50	54	41	1	70	7	3	3	8	7	.53	9	.254	.323	.367
1999 Kansas City	AL	156	628	197	36	8	16	(7	9)	297	92	84	103	50	4	80	3	1	7	5	4	.56	15	.314	.363	.473
2000 Kansas City	AL	158	612	186	29	4	15	(9	6)	268	88	106	88	36	3	66	6	1	10	6	3	.67	19	.304	.343	.438
2001 Kansas City	AL	151	581	147	34	2	13	(8	5)	224	59	83	67	42	2	80	6	1	6	3	2	.60	15	.253	.307	.386
2002 Kansas City	AL	151	549	155	36	5	11	(6	5)	234	63	80	77	46	1	69	9	2	11	2	1	.67	13	.282	.341	.426
2003 Kansas City	AL	131	502	146	31	1	16	(9	7)	227	80	72	79	41	0	61	7	9	7	1	0	1.00	12	.291	.348	.452
9 ML YEARS		1155	4182	1196	240	32	94	(50	44)	1782	538	587	593	329	16	554	45	23	53	42	24	.64	105	.286	.341	.426

Scott Randall

Pitches: R **Bats:** R **Pos:** RP-13; SP-2

Ht: 6'3" **Wt:** 190 **Born:** 10/29/75 **Age:** 28

		HOW MUCH HE PITCHED						WHAT HE GAVE UP										THE RESULTS						
Year Team	Lg	G	GS	CG	GF	IP	BFP	H	R	ER	HR	SH	SF	HB	TBB	IBB	SO	WP	Bk	W	L	Pct	ShO	Sv-Op	Hld	ERA
1995 Portland	A-	15	15	1	0	95.0	391	76	35	21	2	2	2	8	28	1	78	7	2	7	3	.700	0	0- -	-	2.41	1.99
1996 Asheville	A	24	24	1	0	154.1	615	121	53	47	11	5	1	7	50	3	136	4	0	14	4	.778	1	0- -	-	2.69	2.74
1997 Salem	A+	27	26	2	1	176.0	763	167	93	75	8	8	6	11	66	3	128	14	0	9	10	.474	1	0- -	-	3.49	3.84
1998 New Haven	AA	29	29	7	0	202.0	863	210	104	86	14	9	10	9	62	1	135	10	1	10	14	.417	2	0- -	-	3.91	3.83
1999 Co Springs	AAA	9	9	0	0	42.0	205	62	41	37	5	3	1	1	22	1	25	5	1	1	4	.200	0	0- -	-	7.77	7.93
1999 Carolina	AA	16	16	3	0	99.2	432	101	52	38	6	3	5	8	34	2	102	3	0	5	8	.385	1	0- -	-	3.92	3.43
2000 Salt Lake	AAA	14	14	0	0	75.2	344	105	52	46	9	1	1	1	22	0	54	5	0	5	3	.625	0	0- -	-	6.17	5.47
2000 Oklahoma	AAA	16	10	0	2	74.2	339	96	49	45	8	3	6	4	33	1	35	2	0	2	3	.400	0	0- -	-	6.39	5.42
2001 Salem	A+	2	0	0	0	6.0	27	9	3	3	0	0	0	0	1	0	7	0	0	0	0	-	0	0- -	-	5.34	4.50
2001 Carolina	AA	1	1	0	0	6.0	21	5	0	0	0	0	0	0	3	0	3	0	0	0	0	-	0	0- -	-	1.50	0.00
2001 Co Springs	AAA	19	12	0	2	70.2	319	74	48	43	11	0	1	3	34	3	47	3	1	6	5	.545	0	0- -	-	5.14	5.48
2002 New Britain	AA	5	5	0	0	31.0	123	25	13	12	3	0	0	3	4	0	19	0	0	2	0	1.000	0	0- -	-	2.40	3.48
2002 Edmonton	AAA	19	15	2	1	105.1	444	110	47	38	6	2	5	1	24	0	54	10	0	12	0	1.000	0	0- -	-	3.38	3.25
2003 Louisville	AAA	30	20	0	3	136.0	611	170	76	70	9	3	5	14	39	0	86	9	0	10	4	.714	0	3- -	-	5.27	4.63
2003 Cincinnati	NL	15	2	0	2	27.2	127	34	20	20	1	2	0	2	11	3	25	1	0	2	5	.286	0	0-1	2	4.98	6.51

Stephen Randolph

Pitches: L **Bats:** L **Pos:** RP-50

Ht: 6'3" **Wt:** 202 **Born:** 5/1/74 **Age:** 30

		HOW MUCH HE PITCHED						WHAT HE GAVE UP										THE RESULTS						
Year Team	Lg	G	GS	CG	GF	IP	BFP	H	R	ER	HR	SH	SF	HB	TBB	IBB	SO	WP	Bk	W	L	Pct	ShO	Sv-Op	Hld	ERA
1995 Yankees	R	8	3	0	1	24.1	94	11	7	6	1	0	0	1	16	0	34	3	1	4	0	1.000	0	0- -	-	2.11	2.22
1995 Oneonta	A-	6	6	0	0	21.2	109	19	22	18	0	0	2	1	23	0	31	5	0	0	3	.000	0	0- -	-	5.12	7.48
1996 Greensboro	A	32	17	0	7	100.1	451	64	46	42	8	4	5	5	96	1	111	13	3	4	7	.364	0	0- -	-	4.27	3.77
1997 Tampa	A+	34	13	1	6	95.1	417	74	55	41	8	7	3	3	63	5	108	4	1	4	7	.364	0	1- -	-	3.76	3.87
1998 High Desert	A+	17	17	0	0	85.1	357	71	44	34	6	3	2	3	42	0	104	0	0	4	4	.500	0	0- -	-	3.52	3.59
1998 Tucson	AAA	17	1	0	3	22.2	99	16	11	8	1	0	2	0	19	2	23	3	0	1	3	.250	0	0- -	-	3.63	3.18
1999 El Paso	AA	8	8	0	0	44.1	186	39	14	13	1	2	0	1	23	0	38	1	1	2	2	.500	0	0- -	-	3.53	2.64
1999 Tucson	AAA	11	10	1	0	41.2	204	47	37	32	7	1	2	2	32	1	26	1	0	0	7	.000	0	0- -	-	6.99	6.91
1999 Diamndbcks	R	2	2	0	0	6.0	25	5	3	3	0	0	0	0	2	0	7	0	0	0	0	-	0	0- -	-	2.26	4.50
2000 Tucson	AAA	5	3	0	0	13.1	69	11	13	13	3	1	1	0	19	0	16	0	0	0	0	-	0	0- -	-	8.32	8.78
2001 El Paso	AA	18	14	1	0	75.0	342	69	50	43	11	4	2	2	53	1	66	7	1	5	6	.455	1	0- -	-	5.35	5.16
2001 Tucson	AAA	18	0	0	7	21.1	109	24	15	15	2	1	2	2	19	1	16	2	0	2	0	1.000	0	0- -	-	6.91	6.33
2002 Tucson	AAA	28	27	1	1	163.1	704	151	75	63	15	6	7	6	81	2	129	6	0	15	7	.682	1	0- -	-	4.15	3.47
2003 Arizona	NL	50	0	0	9	60.0	271	50	28	27	7	5	0	2	43	3	50	3	2	8	1	.889	0	0-0	2	4.51	4.05

Cody Ransom

Bats: R **Throws:** R **Pos:** SS-12; PR-5; PH-4 **Ht:** 6'2" **Wt:** 196 **Born:** 2/17/76 **Age:** 28

Year Team	Lg	G	AB	H	2B	3B	HR	(Hm	Rd)	TB	R	RBI	RC	TBB	IBB	SO	HBP	SH	SF	SB	CS	SB%	GDP	Avg	OBP	Slg
2003 Fresno*	AAA	112	396	100	16	4	12	(-	-)	160	56	50	52	45	1	91	3	3	3	14	4	.78	14	.253	.331	.404
2001 San Francisco	NL	9	7	0	0	0	0	(0	0)	0	1	0	0	0	0	5	0	0	0	0	0	-	0	.000	.000	.000
2002 San Francisco	NL	7	3	2	0	0	0	(0	0)	2	2	1	1	1	1	1	0	0	0	0	0	-	0	.667	.750	.667
2003 San Francisco	NL	20	27	6	1	0	1	(1	0)	10	7	1	1	1	0	11	0	0	0	0	0	-	0	.222	.250	.370
3 ML YEARS		36	37	8	1	0	1	(1	0)	12	10	2	2	2	1	17	0	0	0	0	0	-	0	.216	.256	.324

Britt Reames

Pitches: R **Bats:** R **Pos:** RP-2 **Ht:** 5'11" **Wt:** 175 **Born:** 8/19/73 **Age:** 30

Year Team	Lg	G	GS	CG	GF	IP	BFP	H	R	ER	HR	SH	SF	HB	TBB	IBB	SO	WP	Bk	W	L	Pct	ShO	Sv-Op	Hld	ERC	ERA
2003 Edmonton*	AAA	25	20	0	2	118.0	542	146	80	71	8	2	3	3	46	1	86	7	1	5	13	.278	0	0- -	-	5.19	5.42
2000 St.Louis	NL	8	7	0	0	40.2	170	30	17	13	4	0	1	1	23	1	31	2	1	2	1	.667	0	0-0	0	3.39	2.88
2001 Montreal	NL	41	13	0	3	95.0	432	101	68	59	16	7	2	5	48	3	86	2	0	4	8	.333	0	0-1	6	5.52	5.59
2002 Montreal	NL	42	6	0	7	68.0	308	70	42	38	8	3	1	3	38	6	76	2	0	1	4	.200	0	0-1	6	5.04	5.03
2003 Montreal	NL	2	0	0	0	1.1	10	4	4	4	0	0	0	0	2	0	1	0	0	0	0	-	0	0-0	0	22.07	27.00
4 ML YEARS		93	26	0	10	205.0	920	205	131	114	28	10	4	9	111	10	194	6	1	7	13	.350	0	0-2	12	5.01	5.00

Jeff Reboulet

Bats: R **Throws:** R **Pos:** 2B-76; PH-18; 3B-7; PR-1 **Ht:** 6'0" **Wt:** 175 **Born:** 4/30/64 **Age:** 40

Year Team	Lg	G	AB	H	2B	3B	HR	(Hm	Rd)	TB	R	RBI	RC	TBB	IBB	SO	HBP	SH	SF	SB	CS	SB%	GDP	Avg	OBP	Slg
2003 Nashville*	AAA	17	49	11	1	0	0	(-	-)	12	6	2	4	10	0	11	0	0	0	3	.00	1	.224	.356	.245
1992 Minnesota	AL	73	137	26	7	1	1	(1	0)	38	15	16	14	23	0	26	1	7	0	3	2	.60	0	.190	.311	.277
1993 Minnesota	AL	109	240	62	9	0	1	(0	1)	73	33	15	27	35	0	37	2	5	1	5	5	.50	6	.258	.356	.304
1994 Minnesota	AL	74	189	49	11	1	3	(2	1)	71	28	23	22	18	0	23	1	2	0	0	0	-	6	.259	.327	.376
1995 Minnesota	AL	87	216	63	11	0	4	(1	3)	86	39	23	33	27	0	34	1	2	0	1	2	.33	3	.292	.373	.398
1996 Minnesota	AL	107	234	52	9	0	0	(0	0)	61	20	23	16	25	1	34	1	4	2	4	2	.67	10	.222	.298	.261
1997 Baltimore	AL	99	228	54	9	0	4	(2	2)	75	26	27	25	23	0	44	1	11	2	3	0	1.00	3	.237	.307	.329
1998 Baltimore	AL	79	126	31	6	0	1	(1	0)	40	20	8	15	19	0	34	2	7	1	0	1	.00	3	.246	.351	.317
1999 Baltimore	AL	99	154	25	4	0	0	(0	0)	29	25	4	12	33	0	29	2	3	0	1	0	1.00	1	.162	.317	.188
2000 Kansas City	AL	66	182	44	7	0	0	(0	0)	51	29	14	16	23	0	32	0	6	1	3	1	.75	8	.242	.325	.280
2001 Los Angeles	NL	94	214	57	15	2	3	(3	0)	85	35	22	32	33	1	48	1	5	0	1	0	1.00	3	.266	.367	.397
2002 Los Angeles	NL	38	48	10	3	0	0	(0	0)	13	3	2	2	6	0	13	0	3	1	0	0	-	1	.208	.291	.271
2003 Pittsburgh	NL	93	261	63	10	2	3	(0	3)	86	37	25	29	27	3	47	4	6	1	2	1	.67	6	.241	.321	.330
12 ML YEARS		1018	2229	536	100	6	20	(10	10)	708	310	202	243	292	5	401	16	61	9	22	15	.59	50	.240	.332	.318

Tim Redding

Pitches: R **Bats:** R **Pos:** SP-32; RP-1 **Ht:** 6'0" **Wt:** 195 **Born:** 2/12/78 **Age:** 26

Year Team	Lg	G	GS	CG	GF	IP	BFP	H	R	ER	HR	SH	SF	HB	TBB	IBB	SO	WP	Bk	W	L	Pct	ShO	Sv-Op	Hld	ERC	ERA
2001 Houston	NL	13	9	0	1	55.2	249	62	38	34	11	2	3	3	24	0	55	2	0	3	1	.750	0	0-0	0	5.87	5.50
2002 Houston	NL	18	14	0	1	73.1	325	78	49	44	10	4	3	0	35	3	63	5	1	3	6	.333	0	0-0	0	4.96	5.40
2003 Houston	NL	33	32	0	0	176.0	769	179	85	72	16	7	3	7	65	4	116	3	0	10	14	.417	0	0-0	0	4.07	3.68
3 ML YEARS		64	55	0	2	305.0	1343	319	172	150	37	13	9	10	124	7	234	10	1	16	21	.432	0	0-0	0	4.59	4.43

Mark Redman

Pitches: L **Bats:** L **Pos:** SP-29 **Ht:** 6'5" **Wt:** 245 **Born:** 1/5/74 **Age:** 30

Year Team	Lg	G	GS	CG	GF	IP	BFP	H	R	ER	HR	SH	SF	HB	TBB	IBB	SO	WP	Bk	W	L	Pct	ShO	Sv-Op	Hld	ERC	ERA
1999 Minnesota	AL	5	1	0	0	12.2	65	17	13	12	3	0	0	1	7	0	11	0	0	1	0	1.000	0	0-0	0	7.86	8.53
2000 Minnesota	AL	32	24	0	3	151.1	651	168	81	80	22	3	2	3	45	0	117	6	0	12	9	.571	0	0-0	0	4.73	4.76
2001 Min-Det	AL	11	11	0	0	58.0	261	68	32	29	7	2	0	1	23	0	33	6	0	2	6	.250	0	0-0	0	5.26	4.50
2002 Detroit	AL	30	30	3	0	203.0	858	201	107	95	15	5	8	6	51	2	109	11	1	8	15	.348	0	0-0	0	3.64	4.21
2003 Florida	NL	29	29	3	0	190.2	802	172	82	76	16	10	5	5	61	3	151	7	2	14	9	.609	0	0-0	0	3.17	3.59
2001 Minnesota	AL	9	9	0	0	49.0	219	57	26	23	6	1	0	0	19	0	29	6	0	2	4	.333	0	0-0	0	5.11	4.22
2001 Detroit	AL	2	2	0	0	9.0	42	11	6	6	1	1	0	1	4	0	4	0	0	0	2	.000	0	0-0	0	6.12	6.00
5 ML YEARS		107	95	6	3	615.2	2637	636	315	292	63	20	15	16	187	5	421	30	3	37	39	.487	0	0-0	0	3.98	4.27

Prentice Redman

Bats: R **Throws:** R **Pos:** CF-9; PR-5; RF-2; PH-2 **Ht:** 6'3" **Wt:** 185 **Born:** 8/23/79 **Age:** 24

Year Team	Lg	G	AB	H	2B	3B	HR	(Hm	Rd)	TB	R	RBI	RC	TBB	IBB	SO	HBP	SH	SF	SB	CS	SB%	GDP	Avg	OBP	Slg
1999 Kingsport	R+	58	200	59	14	1	6	(-	-)	93	40	29	35	24	0	42	2	3	2	16	11	.59	0	.295	.373	.465
2000 Capital City	A	131	497	129	19	1	3	(-	-)	159	60	46	57	52	1	90	3	1	2	26	10	.72	5	.260	.332	.320
2001 St.Lucie	A+	132	495	129	18	1	9	(-	-)	176	70	65	61	42	0	91	6	4	6	29	8	.78	7	.261	.322	.356
2002 Binghamton	AA	135	491	139	35	2	11	(-	-)	211	79	63	87	59	1	112	9	6	5	43	9	.83	5	.283	.367	.430
2003 Norfolk	AAA	128	433	110	29	2	11	(-	-)	176	60	48	60	40	0	96	7	2	1	24	8	.75	5	.254	.326	.406
2003 New York	NL	15	24	3	1	0	1	(0	1)	7	3	2	1	1	0	9	1	1	0	2	0	1.00	1	.125	.192	.292

Tike Redman

Bats: L **Throws:** L **Pos:** CF-54; PH-4   **Ht:** 5'11" **Wt:** 166 **Born:** 3/10/77 **Age:** 27

Year Team	Lg	G	AB	H	2B	3B	HR	(Hm	Rd)	TB	R	RBI	RC	TBB	IBB	SO	HBP	SH	SF	SB	CS	SB%	GDP	Avg	OBP	Slg
2003 Nashville*	AAA	100	360	106	12	7	4	(-	-)	144	60	29	57	36	1	32	0	3	2	42	9	.82	5	.294	.357	.400
2000 Pittsburgh	NL	9	18	6	1	0	1	(0	1)	10	2	1	4	1	0	7	0	0	0	1	0	1.00		.333	.368	.556
2001 Pittsburgh	NL	37	125	28	4	1	1	(1	0)	37	8	4	8	4	0	25	0	0	1	3	5	.38	2	.224	.246	.296
2003 Pittsburgh	NL	56	230	76	16	5	3	(2	1)	111	36	19	40	14	0	18	2	2	0	7	3	.70	1	.330	.374	.483
3 ML YEARS		102	373	110	21	6	5	(3	2)	158	46	24	52	19	0	50	2	2	1	11	8	.58	3	.295	.332	.424

Mike Redmond

Bats: R **Throws:** R **Pos:** C-37; PH-24; 1B-1; 3B-1   **Ht:** 5'11" **Wt:** 208 **Born:** 5/5/71 **Age:** 33

Year Team	Lg	G	AB	H	2B	3B	HR	(Hm	Rd)	TB	R	RBI	RC	TBB	IBB	SO	HBP	SH	SF	SB	CS	SB%	GDP	Avg	OBP	Slg
1998 Florida	NL	37	118	39	9	0	2	(1	1)	54	10	12	18	5	2	16	2	4	0				6	.331	.368	.458
1999 Florida	NL	84	242	73	9	0	1	(0	1)	85	22	27	33	26	2	34	5	5	0				8	.302	.381	.351
2000 Florida	NL	87	210	53	8	1	0	(0	0)	63	17	15	20	13	3	19	8	1	3				5	.252	.316	.300
2001 Florida	NL	48	141	44	4	0	4	(3	1)	60	19	14	21	13	4	13	2	1	1				6	.312	.376	.426
2002 Florida	NL	89	256	78	15	0	2	(1	1)	99	19	28	36	21	8	34	8	2	3	0	2	.00	4	.305	.372	.387
2003 Florida	NL	59	125	30	7	1	0	(0	0)	39	12	11	10	7	0	16	5	2	2	0	0		2	.240	.302	.312
6 ML YEARS		404	1092	317	52	2	9	(5	4)	400	99	107	138	85	19	132	30	15	9	0	2	.00	31	.290	.355	.366

Rick Reed

Pitches: R **Bats:** R **Pos:** SP-21; RP-6   **Ht:** 6'1" **Wt:** 195 **Born:** 8/16/65 **Age:** 38

Year Team	Lg	G	GS	CG	GF	IP	BFP	H	R	ER	HR	SH	SF	HB	TBB	IBB	SO	WP	Bk	W	L	Pct	ShO	Sv-Op	Hld	ERC	ERA
1988 Pittsburgh	NL	2	2	0	0	12.0	47	10	4	4	1	2	0	0	2	0	6	0	0	1	0	1.000	0	0-0	1	2.26	3.00
1989 Pittsburgh	NL	15	7	0	2	54.2	232	62	35	34	5	2	3	2	11	3	34	0	3	1	4	.200	0	0-0	0	4.07	5.60
1990 Pittsburgh	NL	13	8	1	2	53.2	238	62	32	26	6	2	1	1	12	6	27	0	0	2	3	.400	1	1-1	1	4.08	4.36
1991 Pittsburgh	NL	1	1	0	0	4.1	21	8	6	5	1	0	0	0	1	0	2	0	0	0	0		0	0-0	0	10.07	10.38
1992 Kansas City	AL	19	18	1	0	100.1	419	105	47	41	10	2	5	5	20	3	49	0	0	3	7	.300	1	0-0	0	3.73	3.68
1993 KC-Tex	AL	3	0	0	0	7.2	36	12	5	5	1	0	0	0	2	0	5	0	0	1	0	1.000	0	0-0	0	8.88	5.87
1994 Texas	AL	4	3	0	0	16.2	75	17	13	11	3	0	0	1	7	0	12	0	0	1	1	.500	0	0-0	0	4.98	5.94
1995 Cincinnati	NL	4	3	0	1	17.0	70	18	12	11	5	1	0	0	3	0	10	0	0	0	0		0	0-0	0	4.84	5.82
1997 New York	NL	33	31	2	0	208.1	824	186	76	67	19	7	3	6	31	4	113	0	0	13	9	.591	0	0-0	0	2.61	2.89
1998 New York	NL	31	31	2	0	212.1	845	208	84	82	30	8	5	6	29	2	153	1	0	16	11	.593	1	0-0	0	3.39	3.48
1999 New York	NL	26	26	1	0	149.1	637	163	77	76	23	6	3	1	47	2	104	1	0	11	5	.688	1	0-0	0	4.71	4.58
2000 New York	NL	30	30	0	0	184.0	768	192	90	84	28	3	5	5	34	3	121	2	1	11	5	.688	0	0-0	0	3.90	4.11
2001 NYM-Min		32	32	3	0	202.1	834	211	98	91	28	3	5	3	31	3	142	3	0	12	12	.500	1	0-0	0	3.69	4.05
2002 Minnesota	AL	33	32	2	0	188.0	778	192	89	79	32	1	5	6	26	0	121	1	1	15	7	.682	1	0-0	1	3.72	3.78
2003 Minnesota	AL	27	21	2	1	135.0	583	155	80	76	21	2	4	5	29	2	71	3	0	6	12	.333	1	0-1	0	4.68	5.07
1993 Kansas City	AL	1	0	0	0	3.2	18	6	4	4	0	0	0	1	1	0	3	0	0		0		0	0-0	0	7.97	9.82
1993 Texas	AL	2	0	0	0	4.0	18	6	1	1	1	0	0	0	1	0	2	0	0	1	0	1.000	0	0-0	0	9.70	2.25
2001 New York	NL	20	20	3	0	134.2	531	119	53	52	16	8	1	1	17	3	99	2	0	8	6	.571	1	0-0	0	2.55	3.48
2001 Minnesota	AL	12	12	0	0	67.2	303	92	45	39	12	0	2	4	14	0	43	1	0	4	6	.400	0	0-0	0	6.30	5.19
15 ML YEARS		273	245	14	6	1545.2	6407	1601	748	692	213	44	37	44	285	28	970	11	5	93	76	.550	7	1-2	2	3.78	4.03

Steve Reed

Pitches: R **Bats:** R **Pos:** RP-67   **Ht:** 6'2" **Wt:** 212 **Born:** 3/11/66 **Age:** 38

Year Team	Lg	G	GS	CG	GF	IP	BFP	H	R	ER	HR	SH	SF	HB	TBB	IBB	SO	WP	Bk	W	L	Pct	ShO	Sv-Op	Hld	ERC	ERA
1992 San Francisco	NL	18	0	0	2	15.2	63	13	5	4	2	0	0	1	3	0	11	0	0	1	0	1.000	0	0-0	1	2.80	2.30
1993 Colorado	NL	64	0	0	14	84.1	347	80	47	42	13	2	3	3	30	5	51	1	0	9	5	.643	0	3-6	9	4.19	4.48
1994 Colorado	NL	61	0	0	11	64.0	297	79	33	28	9	0	7	6	26	3	51	1	0	3	2	.600	0	3-10	14	6.09	3.94
1995 Colorado	NL	71	0	0	15	84.0	327	61	24	20	8	3	1	1	21	3	79	0	2	5	2	.714	0	3-6	11	2.11	2.14
1996 Colorado	NL	70	0	0	7	75.0	307	66	38	33	11	2	4	6	19	0	51	1	0	4	3	.571	0	0-6	22	3.52	3.96
1997 Colorado	NL	63	0	0	23	62.1	260	49	28	28	10	3	1	5	27	1	43	0	0	4	6	.400	0	6-13	10	3.78	4.04
1998 SF-Cle		70	0	0	19	80.1	322	56	29	28	8	2	0	5	27	5	73	0	0	4	3	.571	0	1-6	21	2.42	3.14
1999 Cleveland	AL	63	0	0	15	61.2	274	69	33	29	10	4	5	3	20	5	44	2	0	3	2	.600	0	0-3	8	4.91	4.23
2000 Cleveland	AL	57	0	0	16	56.0	243	58	30	27	7	4	1	1	21	4	39	2	1	2	0	1.000	0	0-1	9	4.31	4.34
2001 Cle-Atl		70	0	0	14	58.1	250	52	25	23	6	3	1	3	23	5	46	0	0	3	3	.500	0	1-2	11	3.51	3.55
2002 SD-NYM	NL	64	0	0	15	67.0	269	56	15	15	2	6	0	8	14	3	50	2	0	2	5	.286	0	1-4	17	2.48	2.01
2003 Colorado	NL	67	0	0	22	63.1	269	59	24	23	9	2	1	8	26	3	39	1	2	5	3	.625	0	0-2	14	4.61	3.27
1998 San Francisco	NL	50	0	0	14	54.2	213	30	10	9	4	0	0	4	19	5	50	0	0	2	1	.667	0	1-5	13	1.64	1.48
1998 Cleveland	AL	20	0	0	5	25.2	109	26	19	19	4	0	0	1	8	0	23	0	0	2	2	.500	0	0-1	8	4.38	6.66
2001 San Diego	AL	31	0	0	8	27.1	116	22	11	11	3	0	0	2	10	2	21	0	0	1	1	.500	0	0-1	5	3.06	3.62
2001 Atlanta	NL	39	0	0	6	31.0	134	30	14	12	3	3	1	1	13	3	25	0	0	2	2	.500	0	1-1	5	3.92	3.48
2002 San Diego	NL	40	0	0	11	41.0	166	33	9	9	2	5	0	6	10	2	36	1	0	2	4	.333	0	1-3	11	2.65	1.98
2002 New York	NL	24	0	0	4	26.0	103	23	6	6	0	1	0	2	4	1	14	1	0	0	1	.000	0	0-1	6	2.22	2.08
12 ML YEARS		738	0	0	173	772.0	3228	698	331	300	95	31	24	50	257	37	577	10	5	45	34	.570	0	18-59	147	3.66	3.50

Pokey Reese

Bats: R **Throws:** R **Pos:** 2B-33; PH-5; PR-2   **Ht:** 5'11" **Wt:** 188 **Born:** 6/10/73 **Age:** 31

Year Team	Lg	G	AB	H	2B	3B	HR	(Hm	Rd)	TB	R	RBI	RC	TBB	IBB	SO	HBP	SH	SF	SB	CS	SB%	GDP	Avg	OBP	Slg
1997 Cincinnati	NL	128	397	87	15	4	4	(3	1)	114	48	26	35	31	2	82	5	4	0	25	7	.78	1	.219	.284	.287
1998 Cincinnati	NL	59	133	34	2	2	1	(0	1)	43	20	16	14	14	1	28	0	2	2	3	2	.60	3	.256	.322	.323
1999 Cincinnati	NL	149	585	167	37	5	10	(5	5)	244	85	52	84	35	3	81	6	5	5	38	7	.84	9	.285	.330	.417
2000 Cincinnati	NL	135	518	132	20	6	12	(3	9)	200	76	46	69	45	5	86	6	3	5	29	3	.91	8	.255	.319	.386
2001 Cincinnati	NL	133	428	96	20	2	9	(4	5)	147	50	40	44	34	4	82	3	5	4	25	4	.86	7	.224	.284	.343

Year Team	Lg	G	AB	H	2B	3B	HR	(Hm	Rd)	TB	R	RBI	RC	TBB	IBB	SO	HBP	SH	SF	SB	CS	SB%	GDP	Avg	OBP	Slg
								BATTING												**BASERUNNING**				**AVERAGES**		
2002 Pittsburgh	NL	119	421	111	25	0	4	(3	1)	148	46	50	60	41	4	81	3	5	5	12	1	.92	4	.264	.330	.352
2003 Pittsburgh	NL	37	107	23	2	0	1	(0	1)	28	9	12	9	9	1	31	0	2	2	6	0	1.00	2	.215	.271	.262
7 ML YEARS		760	2589	650	121	15	41	(18	23)	924	334	242	315	209	20	471	23	26	23	138	24	.85	34	.251	.310	.357

Dan Reichert

Pitches: R **Bats:** R **Pos:** RP-15   **Ht:** 6'3" **Wt:** 175 **Born:** 7/12/76 **Age:** 27

Year Team	Lg	G	GS	CG	GF	IP	BFP	H	R	ER	HR	SH	SF	HB	TBB	IBB	SO	WP	Bk	W	L	Pct	ShO	Sv-Op	Hld	ERC	ERA
				HOW MUCH HE PITCHED						**WHAT HE GAVE UP**											**THE RESULTS**					
2003 Syracuse*	AAA	41	0	0	10	58.0	259	55	26	23	2	5	1	2	35	1	60	7	0	4	3	.571	0	0- -	-	4.21	3.57
1999 Kansas City	AL	8	8	0	0	36.2	183	48	38	37	2	1	1	2	32	1	20	1	0	2	2	.500	0	0-0	0	7.91	9.08
2000 Kansas City	AL	44	18	1	11	153.1	690	157	92	80	15	5	7	7	91	1	94	18	0	8	10	.444	1	2-6	4	5.22	4.70
2001 Kansas City	AL	27	19	0	4	123.0	554	131	83	77	14	3	4	8	67	2	77	12	0	8	8	.500	0	0-0	1	5.46	5.63
2002 Kansas City	AL	30	6	0	3	66.0	290	77	48	39	10	6	3	4	25	2	36	3	0	3	5	.375	0	0-0	6	5.70	5.32
2003 Toronto	AL	15	0	0	2	16.1	82	28	12	11	2	0	0	2	8	3	13	0	0	0	0	-	0	0-1	2	9.67	6.06
5 ML YEARS		124	51	1	20	395.1	1799	441	273	244	43	15	15	23	223	9	240	34	0	21	25	.457	1	2-7	13	5.79	5.55

Brian Reith

Pitches: R **Bats:** R **Pos:** RP-41; SP-1   **Ht:** 6'5" **Wt:** 220 **Born:** 2/28/78 **Age:** 26

Year Team	Lg	G	GS	CG	GF	IP	BFP	H	R	ER	HR	SH	SF	HB	TBB	IBB	SO	WP	Bk	W	L	Pct	ShO	Sv-Op	Hld	ERC	ERA
				HOW MUCH HE PITCHED						**WHAT HE GAVE UP**											**THE RESULTS**					
1996 Yankees	R	10	4	0	1	32.2	143	31	16	15	1	2	2	1	16	0	21	3	0	2	3	.400	0	0- -	-	3.75	4.13
1997 Yankees	R	12	11	1	0	63.0	270	70	28	20	1	2	2	3	14	0	40	8	0	4	2	.667	0	0- -	-	3.59	2.86
1998 Greensboro	A	20	20	3	0	118.1	475	86	42	30	7	2	0	3	32	0	116	1	0	6	7	.462	1	0- -	-	2.01	2.28
1999 Tampa	A+	26	23	0	0	139.2	616	174	87	73	12	7	4	4	35	1	101	4	0	9	9	.500	0	0- -	-	4.90	4.70
2000 Tampa	A+	18	18	1	0	119.2	487	101	39	29	4	2	3	5	33	0	100	6	1	9	4	.692	1	0- -	-	2.53	2.18
2000 Dayton	A	5	5	0	0	34.1	139	33	12	11	2	0	0	0	8	0	30	2	0	2	1	.667	0	0- -	-	3.01	2.88
2000 Chattanooga	AA	5	5	0	0	30.0	128	31	14	13	3	2	2	1	11	0	29	2	0	1	3	.250	0	0- -	-	4.35	3.90
2001 Louisville	AAA	1	1	0	0	5.0	21	7	2	2	0	1	0	0	1	0	6	0	0	0	0	-	0	0- -	-	5.19	3.60
2001 Chattanooga	AA	18	18	1	0	104.1	448	103	63	46	10	2	5	1	42	1	89	1	0	6	4	.600	1	0- -	-	4.02	3.97
2002 Scrtn/WlksBr	AAA	4	4	0	0	18.0	94	26	18	14	1	1	1	2	11	0	13	0	0	0	4	.000	0	0- -	-	7.48	7.00
2002 Louisville	AAA	23	22	0	0	132.2	574	137	76	70	15	3	4	8	46	3	99	3	0	8	9	.471	0	0- -	-	4.37	4.75
2003 Louisville	AAA	16	0	0	6	23.0	91	12	9	5	1	1	0	2	9	2	28	1	0	3	1	.750	0	1- -	-	1.55	1.96
2001 Cincinnati	NL	9	8	0	0	40.1	192	56	0	35	13	0	0	0	16	0	22	0	0	0	7	.000	0	0- -	-	8.08	7.81
2003 Cincinnati	NL	42	1	0	15	61.1	277	61	32	28	8	3	5	1	36	6	39	1	0	2	3	.400	0	1-1	4	4.89	4.11
2 ML YEARS		51	9	0	15	101.2	469	117	32	63	21	3	5	1	52	6	61	1	0	2	10	.167	0	1-1	4	6.12	5.58

Chris Reitsma

Pitches: R **Bats:** R **Pos:** RP-54; SP-3   **Ht:** 6'5" **Wt:** 215 **Born:** 12/31/77 **Age:** 26

Year Team	Lg	G	GS	CG	GF	IP	BFP	H	R	ER	HR	SH	SF	HB	TBB	IBB	SO	WP	Bk	W	L	Pct	ShO	Sv-Op	Hld	ERC	ERA
				HOW MUCH HE PITCHED						**WHAT HE GAVE UP**											**THE RESULTS**					
2003 Louisville*	AAA	4	4	0	0	18.0	80	22	10	8	1	0	0	0	5	0	11	0	0	1	2	.333	0	0- -	-	4.47	4.00
2001 Cincinnati	NL	36	29	0	1	182.0	800	209	121	107	23	13	8	5	49	6	96	5	0	7	15	.318	0	0-0	1	4.59	5.29
2002 Cincinnati	NL	32	21	1	6	138.1	598	144	73	56	17	4	4	5	45	5	84	4	0	6	12	.333	1	0-0	4	3.24	3.64
2003 Cincinnati	NL	57	3	0	36	84.0	351	92	41	40	14	4	1	0	19	6	53	2	0	9	5	.643	0	12-18	3	4.33	4.29
3 ML YEARS		125	53	1	43	404.1	1749	445	235	203	54	21	13	10	113	17	233	11	0	22	32	.407	1	12-18	4	4.42	4.52

Desi Relaford

Bats: B **Throws:** R **Pos:** 2B-89; 3B-33; RF-15; PH-12; SS-6; CF-5; DH-3; PR-2; LF-1   **Ht:** 5'9" **Wt:** 174 **Born:** 9/16/73 **Age:** 30

Year Team	Lg	G	AB	H	2B	3B	HR	(Hm	Rd)	TB	R	RBI	RC	TBB	IBB	SO	HBP	SH	SF	SB	CS	SB%	GDP	Avg	OBP	Slg
								BATTING												**BASERUNNING**				**AVERAGES**		
1996 Philadelphia	NL	15	40	7	2	0	0	(0	0)	9	2	1	2	3	0	9	0	1	0	1	0	1.00	1	.175	.233	.225
1997 Philadelphia	NL	15	38	7	1	2	0	(0	0)	12	3	6	4	5	0	6	0	1	0	3	0	1.00	0	.184	.279	.316
1998 Philadelphia	NL	142	494	121	25	3	5	(4	1)	167	45	41	48	33	4	87	3	10	6	9	5	.64	9	.245	.293	.338
1999 Philadelphia	NL	65	211	51	11	2	1	(0	1)	69	31	26	22	19	2	34	6	6	0	4	3	.57	5	.242	.322	.327
2000 Phi-SD	NL	128	410	88	14	3	5	(0	5)	123	55	46	51	75	7	71	12	3	2	13	0	1.00	10	.215	.351	.300
2001 New York	NL	120	301	91	27	0	8	(4	4)	142	43	36	52	27	1	65	5	2	5	13	5	.72	4	.302	.364	.472
2002 Seattle	AL	112	329	88	13	2	6	(1	5)	123	55	43	42	33	2	51	6	1	3	10	3	.77	6	.267	.339	.374
2003 Kansas City	AL	141	500	127	27	5	8	(5	3)	188	70	59	68	40	1	70	6	8	3	20	4	.83	10	.254	.315	.376
2000 Philadelphia	NL	83	253	56	12	3	3	(0	3)	83	29	30	34	48	7	45	9	2	1	5	0	1.00	7	.221	.363	.328
2000 San Diego	NL	45	157	32	2	0	2	(0	2)	40	26	16	17	27	0	26	3	1	1	8	0	1.00	3	.204	.330	.255
8 ML YEARS		738	2323	580	120	17	33	(14	19)	833	304	258	289	235	17	393	38	32	23	73	20	.78	45	.250	.326	.359

Mike Remlinger

Pitches: L **Bats:** L **Pos:** RP-73   **Ht:** 6'1" **Wt:** 210 **Born:** 3/23/66 **Age:** 38

Year Team	Lg	G	GS	CG	GF	IP	BFP	H	R	ER	HR	SH	SF	HB	TBB	IBB	SO	WP	Bk	W	L	Pct	ShO	Sv-Op	Hld	ERC	ERA
				HOW MUCH HE PITCHED						**WHAT HE GAVE UP**											**THE RESULTS**					
1991 San Francisco	NL	8	6	1	1	35.0	155	36	17	17	5	1	1	0	20	1	19	2	1	2	1	.667	1	0-0	5	5.30	4.37
1994 New York	NL	10	9	0	0	54.2	252	55	30	28	9	2	3	1	35	4	33	3	0	1	5	.167	0	0-0	1	5.46	4.61
1995 NYM-Cin	NL	7	0	0	4	6.2	34	9	6	5	1	1	0	0	5	0	7	0	0	0	1	.000	0	0-1	0	7.94	6.75
1996 Cincinnati	NL	19	4	0	2	27.1	125	24	17	17	4	3	1	3	19	2	19	2	2	0	0	.000	0	0-0	1	5.23	5.60
1997 Cincinnati	NL	69	12	2	10	124.0	525	100	61	57	11	6	4	7	60	6	145	12	2	8	8	.500	0	2-2	14	3.43	4.14
1998 Cincinnati	NL	35	28	1	0	164.1	727	164	96	88	23	12	7	5	87	1	144	11	1	8	15	.348	0	0-0	0	5.04	4.82
1999 Atlanta	NL	73	0	0	14	83.2	346	66	24	22	9	2	1	1	35	5	81	5	0	10	1	.909	0	1-3	21	3.03	2.37
2000 Atlanta	NL	71	0	0	18	72.2	311	55	29	28	6	3	2	3	37	1	72	3	0	5	3	.625	0	12-16	23	3.15	3.47
2001 Atlanta	NL	74	0	0	6	75.0	313	67	25	23	9	2	0	2	23	4	93	4	0	3	3	.500	0	1-5	31	3.27	2.76
2002 Atlanta	NL	73	0	0	7	68.0	275	48	17	15	3	4	0	1	28	3	69	0	0	7	3	.700	0	0-5	30	2.24	1.99
2003 Chicago	NL	73	0	0	26	69.0	301	54	30	28	11	2	2	2	39	4	83	2	0	6	5	.545	0	1-1	17	3.88	3.65

Year Team	Lg	HOW MUCH HE PITCHED					WHAT HE GAVE UP											THE RESULTS						
		G	GS	CG	GF	IP	BFP	H	R	ER	HR	SH	SF	HB	TBB	IBB	SO	WP	Bk	W	L	Pct	ShO	Sv-Op	Hld	ERC	ERA
1995 New York	NL	5	0	0	4	5.2	27	7	5	4	1	1	0	0	2	0	6	0	0	0	1	.000	0	0-1	0	5.47	6.35
1995 Cincinnati	NL	2	0	0	0	1.0	7	2	1	1	0	0	0	0	3	0	1	0	0	0	0		0	0-0	0	24.60	9.00
11 ML YEARS		512	59	4	88	780.1	3364	678	352	328	91	38	21	25	388	31	765	44	6	50	46	.521	2	16-33	138	3.90	3.78

Edgar Renteria

Bats: R **Throws:** R **Pos:** SS-156; PH-1   **Ht:** 6'1" **Wt:** 180 **Born:** 8/7/75 **Age:** 28

Year Team	Lg	BATTING																		BASERUNNING				AVERAGES		
		G	AB	H	2B	3B	HR	(Hm	Rd)	TB	R	RBI	RC	TBB	IBB	SO	HBP	SH	SF	SB	CS	SB%	GDP	Avg	OBP	Slg
1996 Florida	NL	106	431	133	18	3	5	(2	3)	172	68	31	62	33	0	68	2	2	3	16	2	.89	12	.309	.358	.399
1997 Florida	NL	154	617	171	21	3	4	(3	1)	210	90	52	68	45	1	108	4	19	6	32	15	.68	17	.277	.327	.340
1998 Florida	NL	133	517	146	18	2	3	(2	1)	177	79	31	61	48	1	78	4	9	2	41	22	.65	13	.282	.347	.342
1999 St Louis	NL	154	585	161	36	2	11	(6	5)	234	92	63	81	53	0	82	2	6	7	37	8	.82	16	.275	.334	.400
2000 St Louis	NL	150	562	156	32	1	16	(4	12)	238	94	76	80	63	3	77	1	8	9	21	13	.62	19	.278	.346	.423
2001 St Louis	NL	141	493	128	19	3	10	(3	7)	183	54	57	57	39	4	73	3	8	6	17	4	.81	15	.260	.314	.371
2002 St Louis	NL	152	544	166	36	2	11	(4	7)	239	77	83	94	49	7	57	4	7	5	22	7	.76	17	.305	.364	.439
2003 St Louis	NL	157	587	194	47	1	13	(4	9)	282	96	100	104	65	12	54	1	3	7	34	7	.83	21	.330	.394	.480
8 ML YEARS		1147	4336	1255	227	17	73	(28	45)	1735	650	493	607	395	28	597	21	62	45	220	78	.74	130	.289	.348	.400

Mike Restovich

Bats: R **Throws:** R **Pos:** RF-14; DH-5; PR-5; LF-3; PH-2   **Ht:** 6'4" **Wt:** 233 **Born:** 1/3/79 **Age:** 25

Year Team	Lg	BATTING																		BASERUNNING				AVERAGES		
		G	AB	H	2B	3B	HR	(Hm	Rd)	TB	R	RBI	RC	TBB	IBB	SO	HBP	SH	SF	SB	CS	SB%	GDP	Avg	OBP	Slg
1998 Elizabethton	R+	65	242	86	20	1	13	(-	-)	147	68	64	67	54	0	58	9	0	0	5	2	.71	10	.355	.489	.607
1998 Fort Wayne	A	11	45	20	5	2	0	(-	-)	29	9	6	12	4	0	12	0	0	0	0	0	-	1	.444	.490	.644
1999 Quad City	A	131	493	154	30	6	19	(-	-)	253	91	107	101	74	4	100	13	0	5	7	9	.44	9	.312	.412	.513
2000 Fort Myers	A+	135	475	125	27	9	8	(-	-)	194	73	64	69	61	1	100	4	0	3	19	7	.73	11	.263	.350	.408
2001 New Britain	AA	140	501	135	33	4	23	(-	-)	245	69	84	84	54	8	125	6	0	4	15	7	.68	8	.269	.345	.489
2002 Edmonton	AAA	138	518	148	32	7	29	(-	-)	281	95	98	95	53	2	151	4	0	5	11	7	.61	10	.286	.353	.542
2003 Rochester	AAA	119	454	125	34	2	16	(-	-)	211	75	72	72	47	6	117	4	0	3	10	3	.77	10	.275	.346	.465
2002 Minnesota	AL	8	13	4	0	0	1	(0	1)	7	3	1	0	1	0	4	0	0	0	1	0	1.00	2	.308	.357	.538
2003 Minnesota	AL	24	53	15	3	2	0	(0	0)	22	10	4	8	10	0	12	1	0	0	0	0	-	3	.283	.406	.415
2 ML YEARS		32	66	19	3	2	1	(0	1)	29	13	5	8	11	0	16	1	0	0	1	0	1.00	5	.288	.397	.439

Al Reyes

Pitches: R **Bats:** R **Pos:** RP-13   **Ht:** 6'1" **Wt:** 206 **Born:** 4/10/71 **Age:** 33

Year Team	Lg	HOW MUCH HE PITCHED						WHAT HE GAVE UP											THE RESULTS						
		G	GS	CG	GF	IP	BFP	H	R	ER	HR	SH	SF	HB	TBB	IBB	SO	WP	Bk	W	L	Pct	ShO	Sv-Op	Hld	ERC	ERA
2003 Columbus*	AAA	15	0	0	13	17.0	72	16	7	7	1	0	0	0	5	0	21	0	0	1	1	.500	0	2- -	-	3.01	3.71
1995 Milwaukee	NL	27	0	0	13	33.1	138	19	9	9	3	1	2	3	18	2	29	0	0	1	1	.500	0	1-1	4	2.51	2.43
1996 Milwaukee	NL	5	0	0	2	5.2	27	8	5	5	1	0	0	0	2	0	2	2	0	1	0	1.000	0	0-0	0	6.79	7.94
1997 Milwaukee	NL	19	0	0	7	29.2	131	32	19	18	4	2	0	3	9	0	28	1	0	1	2	.333	0	1-1	1	4.76	5.46
1998 Milwaukee	NL	50	0	0	13	57.0	253	55	26	25	9	2	1	2	31	1	58	2	0	5	1	.833	0	0-1	10	5.01	3.95
1999 Mil-Bal		53	0	0	12	65.2	287	50	33	33	9	4	3	6	41	3	67	3	0	4	3	.571	0	0-4	6	4.19	4.52
2000 Bal-LA		19	0	0	6	19.2	86	15	10	10	2	1	2	0	12	1	18	0	0	1	0	1.000	0	0-1	3	3.43	4.58
2001 Los Angeles	NL	19	0	0	6	25.2	120	28	13	11	3	0	2	1	13	1	23	0	0	2	1	.667	0	1-2	0	5.07	3.86
2002 Pittsburgh	NL	15	0	0	6	17.0	67	9	5	5	1	1	1	2	7	0	21	1	0	0	0	-	0	0-1	3	1.93	2.65
2003 New York	AL	13	0	0	2	17.0	73	13	7	6	1	0	0	0	9	1	9	1	0	0	0	-	0	0-1	0	2.86	3.18
1999 Milwaukee	NL	26	0	0	6	36.0	161	27	17	17	5	1	1	3	25	1	39	2	0	2	0	1.000	0	0-1	2	4.35	4.25
1999 Baltimore	AL	27	0	0	6	29.2	126	23	16	16	4	3	2	3	16	2	28	1	0	2	3	.400	0	0-3	4	3.99	4.85
2000 Baltimore	AL	13	0	0	2	13.0	62	13	10	10	2	1	2	0	11	1	10	0	0	1	0	1.000	0	0-1	2	6.14	6.92
2000 Los Angeles	NL	6	0	0	4	6.2	24	2	0	0	0	0	0	0	1	0	8	0	0	0	0	-	0	0-0	1	0.35	0.00
9 ML YEARS		220	0	0	70	270.2	1182	229	127	122	33	11	11	17	142	9	255	10	1	15	8	.652	0	3-12	27	4.03	4.06

Carlos Reyes

Pitches: R **Bats:** B **Pos:** RP-7; SP-3   **Ht:** 6'0" **Wt:** 190 **Born:** 4/4/69 **Age:** 35

Year Team	Lg	HOW MUCH HE PITCHED						WHAT HE GAVE UP											THE RESULTS						
		G	GS	CG	GF	IP	BFP	H	R	ER	HR	SH	SF	HB	TBB	IBB	SO	WP	Bk	W	L	Pct	ShO	Sv-Op	Hld	ERC	ERA
2003 Durham*	AAA	22	21	1	0	132.1	522	124	47	42	9	2	1	1	14	1	78	7	0	10	3	.769	0	0- -	-	2.49	2.86
1994 Oakland	AL	27	9	0	8	74.0	344	71	38	36	10	2	3	2	44	1	57	3	0	3	4	.000	0	1-1	0	4.50	4.15
1995 Oakland	AL	40	1	0	19	69.0	306	71	43	39	10	4	0	5	28	4	48	5	0	4	6	.400	0	0-1	4	4.76	5.09
1996 Oakland	AL	46	10	0	14	122.1	550	134	71	65	19	2	8	2	61	8	78	2	1	7	10	.412	0	0-0	1	5.42	4.78
1997 Oakland	AL	37	6	0	9	77.1	352	101	52	50	13	3	2	2	25	2	43	2	1	3	4	.429	0	0-1	1	6.15	5.82
1998 SD-Bos		46	0	0	18	66.0	267	58	26	26	6	2	2	3	20	2	47	3	1	3	3	.500	0	1-2	3	3.21	3.55
1999 San Diego	NL	65	0	0	23	77.1	331	76	38	32	11	5	3	0	24	4	57	7	1	2	4	.333	0	1-2	6	3.76	3.72
2000 Phi-SD	NL	22	0	0	9	28.1	121	25	18	18	7	2	0	1	13	0	17	1	1	1	3	.250	0	1-3	2	4.85	5.72
2003 Tampa Bay	AL	10	3	0	5	39.2	161	40	23	23	10	1	2	2	5	0	13	1	1	0	0	.000	0	0-0	0	4.28	5.22
1998 San Diego	NL	22	0	0	8	27.2	109	23	11	11	4	2	1	2	6	0	24	0	1	2	2	.500	0	1-2	1	3.14	3.58
1998 Boston	AL	24	0	0	10	38.1	158	35	15	15	2	0	1	1	14	2	23	3	0	1	1	.500	0	0-0	2	3.25	3.52
2000 Philadelphia	NL	10	0	0	5	10.1	44	10	6	6	2	2	0	0	5	0	4	1	0	0	2	.000	0	0-0	0	5.04	5.23
2000 San Diego	NL	12	0	0	4	18.0	77	15	12	12	5	0	0	1	8	0	13	0	1	1	1	.500	0	1-3	2	4.74	6.00
8 ML YEARS		293	29	0	105	558.0	2432	576	309	289	86	21	20	17	220	21	360	24	6	20	36	.357	0	4-10	17	4.69	4.66

Dennys Reyes

Pitches: L Bats: R Pos: RP-15   **Ht: 6'3" Wt: 246 Born: 4/19/77 Age: 27**

Year Team	Lg	G	GS	CG	GF	IP	BFP	H	R	ER	HR	SH	SF	HB	TBB	IBB	SO	WP	Bk	W	L	Pct	ShO	Sv-Op	Hld	ERC	ERA
2003 Tucson*	AAA	33	0	0	12	31.2	140	24	16	10	0	0	0	1	22	2	30	6	0	2	1	.667	0	2- -	-	3.12	2.84
1997 Los Angeles	NL	14	5	0	0	47.0	207	51	21	20	4	5	1	1	18	3	36	2	1	2	3	.400	0	0-0	0	4.34	3.83
1998 LA-Cin	NL	19	10	0	4	67.1	300	62	36	34	3	7	2	1	47	5	77	6	1	3	5	.375	0	0-0	0	4.37	4.54
1999 Cincinnati	NL	65	1	0	12	61.2	277	53	30	26	5	4	3	3	39	1	72	5	1	2	2	.500	0	2-3	14	4.16	3.79
2000 Cincinnati	NL	62	0	0	15	43.2	200	43	31	22	5	3	3	1	29	0	36	6	0	2	1	.667	0	0-1	10	5.24	4.53
2001 Cincinnati	NL	35	6	0	2	53.0	246	51	35	29	5	2	2	1	35	1	52	5	0	2	6	.250	0	0-0	6	4.77	4.92
2002 Col-Tex		58	5	0	15	82.2	378	98	52	49	10	3	2	0	45	4	59	10	1	4	4	.500	0	0-0	4	5.90	5.33
2003 Pit-Ari		15	0	0	4	12.2	63	15	16	15	2	1	2	0	10	1	16	5	0	0	0		0	0-0	2	6.43	10.66
1998 Los Angeles	NL	11	3	0	4	28.2	130	27	17	15	1	3	1	0	20	4	33	1	1	0	4	.000	0	0-0	0	4.16	4.71
1998 Cincinnati	NL	8	7	0	0	38.2	170	35	19	19	2	4	1	1	27	1	44	5	0	3	1	.750	0	0-0	0	4.44	4.42
2002 Colorado	NL	43	0	0	13	40.1	182	43	19	19	1	2	2	0	24	3	30	4	0	0	1	.000	0	0-0	4	4.55	4.24
2002 Texas	AL	15	5	0	2	42.1	196	55	33	30	9	1	0	0	21	1	29	6	1	4	3	.571	0	0-0	0	7.24	6.38
2003 Pittsburgh	NL	12	0	0	4	10.1	50	10	13	12	1	1	2	0	9	1	11	5	0	0	0		0	0-0	2	5.43	10.45
2003 Arizona	NL	3	0	0	0	2.1	13	5	3	3	1	0	0	0	1	0	5	0	0	0	0		0	0-0	0	14.73	11.57
7 ML YEARS		268	27	0	52	368.0	1671	373	221	195	34	25	15	7	223	15	348	39	4	15	21	.417	0	2-4	36	4.91	4.77

Jose Reyes

Bats: B Throws: R Pos: SS-69   **Ht: 6'0" Wt: 160 Born: 6/11/83 Age: 21**

Year Team	Lg	G	AB	H	2B	3B	HR	(Hm	Rd)	TB	R	RBI	RC	TBB	IBB	SO	HBP	SH	SF	SB	CS	SB%	GDP	Avg	OBP	Slg
2000 Kingsport	R+	49	132	33	3	3	0	(-	-)	42	22	8	18	20	0	37	3	3	1	10	4	.71	1	.250	.359	.318
2001 Capital City	A	108	407	126	22	15	5	(-	-)	192	71	48	65	18	0	71	2	5	3	30	10	.75	4	.307	.337	.472
2002 St.Lucie	A+	69	288	83	10	11	6	(-	-)	133	58	38	48	30	1	35	1	4	4	31	13	.70	5	.288	.353	.462
2002 Binghamton	AA	65	275	79	16	8	2	(-	-)	117	46	24	40	16	1	42	2	2	0	27	11	.71	2	.287	.331	.425
2003 Norfolk	AAA	42	160	43	6	4	0	(-	-)	57	28	13	23	15	0	25	1	4	1	26	5	.84	2	.269	.333	.356
2003 New York	NL	69	274	84	12	4	5	(1	4)	119	47	32	45	13	0	36	0	2	3	13	3	.81	1	.307	.334	.434

Rene Reyes

Bats: B Throws: R Pos: RF-25; PH-18; LF-10; CF-5; PR-1   **Ht: 5'11" Wt: 213 Born: 2/21/78 Age: 26**

Year Team	Lg	G	AB	H	2B	3B	HR	(Hm	Rd)	TB	R	RBI	RC	TBB	IBB	SO	HBP	SH	SF	SB	CS	SB%	GDP	Avg	OBP	Slg
1998 Rockies	R	49	177	76	9	4	5	(-	-)	108	40	39	48	8	1	15	15	0	1	18	7	.72	5	.429	.493	.610
1999 Rockies	R	22	97	35	4	4	1	(-	-)	50	21	20	19	4	0	14	2	0	0	6	1	.86	2	.361	.398	.515
1999 Asheville	A	40	160	56	6	1	3	(-	-)	73	26	19	27	6	0	22	1	0	0	1	0	1.00	1	.350	.377	.456
2001 Asheville	A	128	484	156	27	2	11	(-	-)	220	71	61	85	28	2	80	12	0	4	53	12	.82	9	.322	.371	.455
2002 Carolina	AA	123	455	133	33	4	14	(-	-)	216	64	54	68	29	4	69	5	2	4	10	11	.48	10	.292	.339	.475
2003 Co Springs	AAA	98	370	127	23	3	6	(-	-)	174	60	50	61	22	0	56	2	1	3	12	8	.60	11	.343	.380	.470
2003 Colorado	NL	53	116	30	7	1	2	(2	0)	45	13	7	9	5	0	19	0	1	1	2	1	.67	3	.259	.287	.388

Shane Reynolds

Pitches: R Bats: R Pos: SP-29; RP-1   **Ht: 6'3" Wt: 215 Born: 3/26/68 Age: 36**

Year Team	Lg	G	GS	CG	GF	IP	BFP	H	R	ER	HR	SH	SF	HB	TBB	IBB	SO	WP	Bk	W	L	Pct	ShO	Sv-Op	Hld	ERC	ERA
1992 Houston	NL	8	5	0	0	25.1	122	42	22	20	2	6	1	0	6	1	10	1	1	1	3	.250	0	0-0	0	7.07	7.11
1993 Houston	NL	5	1	0	0	11.0	49	11	4	1	0	0	0	0	6	1	10	0	0	0	0	-	0	0-0	0	3.72	0.82
1994 Houston	NL	33	14	1	5	124.0	517	128	46	42	10	4	0	6	21	3	110	3	2	8	5	.615	1	0-0	5	3.38	3.05
1995 Houston	NL	30	30	3	0	189.1	792	196	87	73	15	8	0	2	37	6	175	7	1	10	11	.476	2	0-0	0	3.31	3.47
1996 Houston	NL	35	35	4	0	239.0	981	227	103	97	20	11	7	8	44	3	204	5	1	16	10	.615	1	0-0	0	2.97	3.65
1997 Houston	NL	30	30	2	0	181.0	773	189	92	85	19	9	5	3	47	5	152	5	2	9	10	.474	0	0-0	0	3.79	4.23
1998 Houston	NL	35	35	3	0	233.1	986	257	99	91	25	5	7	2	53	2	209	5	0	19	8	.704	1	0-0	0	4.05	3.51
1999 Houston	NL	35	35	4	0	231.2	963	250	108	99	23	11	5	1	37	0	197	4	0	16	14	.533	2	0-0	0	3.58	3.85
2000 Houston	NL	22	22	0	0	131.0	588	150	86	76	20	6	8	6	45	2	93	5	0	7	8	.467	0	0-0	0	5.17	5.22
2001 Houston	NL	28	28	3	0	182.2	772	208	95	88	24	13	2	4	36	2	102	2	0	14	11	.560	0	0-0	0	4.38	4.34
2002 Houston	NL	13	13	0	0	74.0	322	80	43	40	13	2	1	1	26	2	47	1	0	3	6	.333	0	0-0	0	4.90	4.86
2003 Atlanta	NL	30	29	0	0	167.1	731	191	104	101	20	10	3	8	59	6	94	0	1	11	9	.550	0	0-0	0	5.07	5.43
12 ML YEARS		304	277	20	5	1789.2	7596	1929	889	813	191	85	39	41	417	33	1403	38	8	114	95	.545	7	0-0	5	3.96	4.09

Arthur Rhodes

Pitches: L Bats: L Pos: RP-67   **Ht: 6'2" Wt: 205 Born: 10/24/69 Age: 34**

Year Team	Lg	G	GS	CG	GF	IP	BFP	H	R	ER	HR	SH	SF	HB	TBB	IBB	SO	WP	Bk	W	L	Pct	ShO	Sv-Op	Hld	ERC	ERA
1991 Baltimore	AL	8	8	0	0	36.0	174	47	35	32	4	1	3	0	23	0	23	2	0	0	3	.000	0	0-0	0	7.00	8.00
1992 Baltimore	AL	15	15	2	0	94.1	394	87	39	38	6	5	1	1	38	2	77	2	1	7	5	.583	1	0-0	0	3.48	3.63
1993 Baltimore	AL	17	17	0	0	85.2	387	91	62	62	16	2	3	1	49	1	49	2	0	5	6	.455	0	0-0	0	5.88	6.51
1994 Baltimore	AL	10	10	3	0	52.2	238	51	34	34	8	2	3	2	30	1	47	3	0	3	5	.375	2	0-0	0	5.03	5.81
1995 Baltimore	AL	19	9	0	3	75.1	336	68	53	52	13	4	0	0	48	1	77	3	1	2	5	.286	0	0-1	0	4.97	6.21
1996 Baltimore	AL	28	2	0	5	53.0	224	48	28	24	6	1	1	0	23	3	62	0	0	9	1	.900	0	1-1	2	3.72	4.08
1997 Baltimore	AL	53	0	0	6	95.1	378	75	32	32	9	0	4	4	26	5	102	2	0	10	3	.769	0	1-2	9	2.58	3.02
1998 Baltimore	AL	45	0	0	10	77.0	321	65	30	30	8	2	5	1	34	2	83	1	1	4	4	.500	0	4-8	10	3.47	3.51
1999 Baltimore	AL	43	0	0	11	53.0	244	43	37	32	9	2	2	0	45	6	59	4	0	3	4	.429	0	3-5	5	5.07	5.43
2000 Seattle	AL	72	0	0	9	69.1	281	51	34	33	6	1	0	1	29	3	77	4	0	5	8	.385	0	0-7	24	4.22	4.28
2001 Seattle	AL	71	0	0	16	68.0	258	46	14	13	5	1	0	1	12	0	83	3	0	8	0	1.000	0	3-7	32	1.61	1.72
2002 Seattle	AL	66	0	0	9	69.2	257	45	18	18	4	2	1	0	13	1	81	2	0	10	4	.714	0	2-7	27	1.46	2.33
2003 Seattle	AL	67	0	0	14	54.0	229	53	25	25	4	2	0	1	18	2	48	2	0	3	3	.500	0	3-6	18	3.55	4.17
13 ML YEARS		514	61	5	83	883.1	3721	770	441	425	98	25	25	11	388	27	868	30	3	69	51	.575	3	17-44	127	3.63	4.33

Chris Richard

Bats: L **Throws:** L **Pos:** PH-15; LF-3; 1B-1   **Ht:** 6'2" **Wt:** 190 **Born:** 6/7/74 **Age:** 30

Year Team	Lg	G	AB	H	2B	3B	HR	(Hm	Rd)	TB	R	RBI	RC	TBB	IBB	SO	HBP	SH	SF	SB	CS	SB%	GDP	Avg	OBP	Slg
2000 StL-Bal		62	215	57	14	2	14	(4	10)	117	39	37	36	17	3	40	4	0	3	7	5	.58	5	.265	.326	.544
2001 Baltimore	AL	136	483	128	31	3	15	(6	9)	210	74	61	66	45	4	100	8	2	4	11	9	.55	15	.265	.335	.435
2002 Baltimore	AL	50	155	36	11	0	4	(2	2)	59	15	21	16	12	0	30	2	0	2	0	3	.00	2	.232	.292	.381
2003 Colorado	NL	19	27	6	1	1	1	(0	1)	12	3	3	2	3	0	6	0	0	0	0	1	.00	1	.222	.300	.444
2000 St Louis	NL	6	16	2	0	0	1	(0	1)	5	1	1	1	2	0	2	0	0	0	0	0	-	0	.125	.222	.313
2000 Baltimore	AL	56	199	55	14	2	13	(4	9)	112	38	36	35	15	3	38	4	0	3	7	5	.58	5	.276	.335	.563
4 ML YEARS		267	880	227	57	6	34	(12	22)	398	131	122	120	77	7	176	14	2	9	18	18	.50	23	.258	.324	.452

John Riedling

Pitches: R **Bats:** R **Pos:** RP-47; SP-8   **Ht:** 5'11" **Wt:** 190 **Born:** 8/29/75 **Age:** 28

Year Team	Lg	G	GS	CG	GF	IP	BFP	H	R	ER	HR	SH	SF	HB	TBB	IBB	SO	WP	Bk	W	L	Pct	ShO	Sv-Op	Hld	ERC	ERA
2000 Cincinnati	NL	13	0	0	5	15.1	63	11	7	4	1	1	0	1	8	0	18	1	0	3	1	.750	0	1-2	2	3.12	2.35
2001 Cincinnati	NL	29	0	0	14	33.2	136	22	9	9	1	2	0	2	14	0	23	5	0	1	1	.500	0	1-3	5	2.13	2.41
2002 Cincinnati	NL	33	0	0	7	46.2	202	39	16	14	2	6	1	3	26	6	30	1	0	2	4	.333	0	0-0	8	3.42	2.70
2003 Cincinnati	NL	55	8	0	11	101.0	455	107	61	55	7	2	6	3	47	0	65	7	1	2	3	.400	0	1-4	6	4.50	4.90
4 ML YEARS		130	8	0	37	196.2	856	179	93	82	11	11	7	9	95	6	136	14	1	8	9	.471	0	3-9	21	3.70	3.75

Jerrod Riggan

Pitches: R **Bats:** R **Pos:** RP-2   **Ht:** 6'3" **Wt:** 197 **Born:** 5/16/74 **Age:** 30

Year Team	Lg	G	GS	CG	GF	IP	BFP	H	R	ER	HR	SH	SF	HB	TBB	IBB	SO	WP	Bk	W	L	Pct	ShO	Sv-Op	Hld	ERC	ERA
2003 Buffalo*	AAA	9	0	0	6	16.1	65	14	5	4	0	0	1	0	5	1	14	0	0	2	1	.667	0	0--	-	2.32	2.20
2003 Norfolk*	AAA	5	0	0	2	6.1	26	7	2	2	0	0	0	0	1	0	11	0	0	0	0	-	0	1--	-	3.10	2.84
2000 New York	NL	1	0	0	0	2.0	10	3	2	0	0	0	0	0	0	0	1	0	0	0	0	-	0	0-0	0	3.96	0.00
2001 New York	NL	35	0	0	12	47.2	202	42	19	18	5	2	3	0	24	7	41	4	0	3	3	.500	0	0-1	4	3.67	3.40
2002 Cleveland	AL	29	0	0	9	33.0	165	53	28	28	3	1	4	0	18	4	22	4	1	2	1	.667	0	0-0	0	8.17	7.64
2003 Cleveland	AL	2	0	0	0	4.0	19	7	4	4	0	0	1	0	1	0	2	0	1	0	0	-	0	0-0	0	7.38	9.00
4 ML YEARS		67	0	0	22	86.2	396	105	53	50	8	3	8	0	43	11	66	8	2	5	4	.556	0	0-1	4	5.45	5.19

Adam Riggs

Bats: R **Throws:** R **Pos:** 1B-10; LF-8; PH-4; 2B-3; DH-2; PR-1   **Ht:** 6'0" **Wt:** 190 **Born:** 10/4/72 **Age:** 31

Year Team	Lg	G	AB	H	2B	3B	HR	(Hm	Rd)	TB	R	RBI	RC	TBB	IBB	SO	HBP	SH	SF	SB	CS	SB%	GDP	Avg	OBP	Slg
2003 Salt Lake*	AAA	103	394	116	35	0	14	(-	-)	193	59	82	67	37	0	67	5	1	10	8	2	.80	13	.294	.354	.490
1997 Los Angeles	NL	9	20	4	1	0	0	(0	0)	5	3	1	2	4	1	3	0	0	0	1	0	1.00	0	.200	.333	.250
2001 San Diego	NL	12	36	7	1	0	0	(0	0)	8	2	1	2	2	0	8	0	0	0	1	1	.50	1	.194	.237	.222
2003 Anaheim	AL	24	61	15	4	1	3	(0	3)	30	11	5	6	9	0	9	0	2	0	3	1	.75	2	.246	.343	.492
3 ML YEARS		45	117	26	6	1	3	(0	3)	43	16	7	10	15	1	20	0	2	0	5	2	.71	3	.222	.311	.368

Matt Riley

Pitches: L **Bats:** L **Pos:** SP-2   **Ht:** 6'1" **Wt:** 201 **Born:** 8/2/79 **Age:** 24

Year Team	Lg	G	GS	CG	GF	IP	BFP	H	R	ER	HR	SH	SF	HB	TBB	IBB	SO	WP	Bk	W	L	Pct	ShO	Sv-Op	Hld	ERC	ERA
1998 Delmarva	A	16	14	0	0	83.0	324	42	19	11	0	2	1	0	44	0	136	9	3	5	4	.556	0	0--	-	1.54	1.19
1999 Frederick	A+	8	8	0	0	51.2	200	34	19	15	5	3	0	1	14	0	58	5	1	3	2	.600	0	0--	-	1.94	2.61
1999 Bowie	AA	20	20	3	0	125.2	520	113	53	42	13	2	3	5	42	0	131	10	4	10	6	.625	0	0--	-	3.50	3.01
2000 Rochester	AAA	2	2	0	0	7.0	41	15	12	11	3	0	0	1	3	0	8	2	0	0	2	.000	0	0--	-	16.30	14.14
2002 Bowie	AA	22	22	0	0	109.1	502	136	84	77	12	0	7	3	48	1	105	11	2	4	10	.286	0	0--	-	5.86	6.34
2003 Ottawa	AAA	13	13	0	0	70.1	300	70	30	28	4	0	4	0	28	1	77	4	2	4	2	.667	0	0--	-	3.75	3.58
2003 Bowie	AA	14	14	1	0	72.1	297	56	27	25	4	3	3	1	23	1	73	4	2	5	2	.714	1	0--	-	2.30	3.11
1999 Baltimore	AL	3	3	0	0	11.0	59	17	0	9	4	0	0	0	13	0	6	0	0	0	0	-	0	0-0	0	14.43	7.36
2003 Baltimore	AL	2	2	0	0	10.0	41	7	2	2	1	0	0	0	5	0	8	0	0	1	0	1.000	0	0-0	0	2.88	1.80
2 ML YEARS		5	5	0	0	21.0	100	24	2	11	5	0	0	0	18	0	14	0	0	1	0	1.000	0	0-0	0	8.28	4.71

Juan Rincon

Pitches: R **Bats:** R **Pos:** RP-58   **Ht:** 5'11" **Wt:** 190 **Born:** 1/23/79 **Age:** 25

Year Team	Lg	G	GS	CG	GF	IP	BFP	H	R	ER	HR	SH	SF	HB	TBB	IBB	SO	WP	Bk	W	L	Pct	ShO	Sv-Op	Hld	ERC	ERA
2003 Rochester*	AAA	2	2	0	0	8.1	39	12	7	7	0	0	1	0	5	0	8	0	0	0	2	.000	0	0--	-	7.07	7.56
2001 Minnesota	AL	4	0	0	1	5.2	28	7	5	4	1	1	0	0	5	0	4	0	0	0	0	-	0	0-0	0	8.33	6.35
2002 Minnesota	AL	10	3	0	0	28.2	135	44	23	20	5	0	1	0	9	0	21	2	0	0	2	.000	0	0-1	0	7.62	6.28
2003 Minnesota	AL	58	0	0	20	85.2	370	74	38	35	5	2	5	4	38	7	63	7	0	5	6	.455	0	0-1	5	3.21	3.68
3 ML YEARS		72	3	0	21	120.0	533	125	66	59	11	3	6	4	52	7	88	9	0	5	8	.385	0	0-2	5	4.38	4.43

Ricardo Rincon

Pitches: L **Bats:** L **Pos:** RP-64   **Ht:** 5'9" **Wt:** 187 **Born:** 4/13/70 **Age:** 34

Year Team	Lg	G	GS	CG	GF	IP	BFP	H	R	ER	HR	SH	SF	HB	TBB	IBB	SO	WP	Bk	W	L	Pct	ShO	Sv-Op	Hld	ERC	ERA
1997 Pittsburgh	NL	62	0	0	23	60.0	254	51	26	23	5	5	1	2	24	6	71	2	3	4	8	.333	0	4-6	18	3.10	3.45
1998 Pittsburgh	NL	60	0	0	27	65.0	272	50	31	21	6	1	2	0	29	2	64	2	0	0	2	.000	0	14-17	11	2.88	2.91
1999 Cleveland	AL	59	0	0	14	44.2	193	41	22	22	6	2	1	0	24	5	30	2	1	2	3	.400	0	0-2	11	4.38	4.43

Year Team	Lg	G	GS	CG	GF	IP	BFP	H	R	ER	HR	SH	SF	HB	TBB	IBB	SO	WP	Bk	W	L	Pct	ShO	Sv-Op	Hld	ERC	ERA
2000 Cleveland	AL	35	0	0	4	20.0	90	17	7	6	1	0	0	1	13	1	20	1	0	2	0	1.000	0	0-0	10	3.89	2.70
2001 Cleveland	AL	67	0	0	19	54.0	223	44	18	17	3	2	3	0	21	5	50	1	0	2	1	.667	0	2-4	12	2.62	2.83
2002 Cle-Oak	AL	71	0	0	9	56.0	222	47	28	26	4	2	4	1	11	1	49	0	0	1	4	.200	0	1-5	27	2.36	4.18
2003 Oakland	AL	64	0	0	16	55.1	241	45	21	20	4	8	2	3	32	4	40	0	0	8	4	.667	0	0-3	13	3.62	3.25
2002 Cleveland	AL	46	0	0	6	35.2	150	36	21	19	3	2	2	1	8	1	30	0	0	1	4	.200	0	0-3	11	3.38	4.79
2002 Oakland	AL	25	0	0	3	20.1	72	11	7	7	1	0	2	0	3	0	19	0	0	0	0	-	0	1-2	16	1.06	3.10
7 ML YEARS		418	0	0	112	355.0	1495	295	153	135	29	20	13	8	154	24	324	8	4	19	22	.463	0	21-37	102	3.14	3.42

Armando Rios

Bats: L **Throws:** L **Pos:** CF-23; PH-15; LF-9; RF-6; DH-3; PR-2 **Ht:** 5'9" **Wt:** 185 **Born:** 9/13/71 **Age:** 32

Year Team	Lg	G	AB	H	2B	3B	HR	(Hm	Rd)	TB	R	RBI	RC	TBB	IBB	SO	HBP	SH	SF	SB	CS	SB%	GDP	Avg	OBP	Slg
2003 Charlotte*	AAA	45	155	50	9	1	6	(-	-)	79	23	30	28	14	2	30	4	1	2	5	6	.45	4	.323	.389	.510
1998 San Francisco	NL	12	7	4	0	0	2	(0	2)	10	3	3	5	3	0	2	0	0	0	0	0	-	0	.571	.700	1.429
1999 San Francisco	NL	72	150	49	9	0	7	(4	3)	79	32	29	32	24	1	35	1	1	1	7	4	.64	3	.327	.420	.527
2000 San Francisco	NL	115	233	62	15	5	10	(2	8)	117	38	50	38	31	4	43	0	1	4	3	2	.60	9	.266	.347	.502
2001 SF-Pit	NL	95	319	83	17	3	14	(3	11)	148	38	50	50	36	6	74	0	1	3	3	2	.60	3	.260	.332	.464
2002 Pittsburgh	NL	76	208	55	11	0	1	(0	1)	69	20	24	17	16	1	39	1	0	1	1	1	.50	8	.264	.319	.332
2003 Chicago	NL	49	104	22	3	0	2	(2	0)	31	4	11	4	5	0	13	0	2	1	0	1	.00	6	.212	.245	.298
2001 San Francisco	NL	93	316	82	17	3	14	(3	11)	147	38	49	49	34	6	73	0	1	2	3	2	.60	2	.259	.330	.465
2001 Pittsburgh	NL	2	3	1	0	0	0	(0	0)	1	0	1	1	2	0	1	0	0	1	0	0	-	1	.333	.500	.333
6 ML YEARS		419	1021	275	55	8	36	(11	25)	454	135	167	146	115	12	206	2	5	10	14	10	.58	29	.269	.341	.445

David Riske

Pitches: R **Bats:** R **Pos:** RP-68 **Ht:** 6'2" **Wt:** 175 **Born:** 10/23/76 **Age:** 27

Year Team	Lg	G	GS	CG	GF	IP	BFP	H	R	ER	HR	SH	SF	HB	TBB	IBB	SO	WP	Bk	W	L	Pct	ShO	Sv-Op	Hld	ERC	ERA
1999 Cleveland	AL	12	0	0	3	14.0	68	20	15	13	2	1	1	0	6	0	16	0	0	1	1	.500	0	0-1	0	6.96	8.36
2001 Cleveland	AL	26	0	0	6	27.1	118	20	7	6	3	0	1	2	18	3	29	1	0	2	0	1.000	0	1-1	3	3.81	1.98
2002 Cleveland	AL	51	0	0	17	51.1	237	49	32	30	8	4	3	4	35	4	65	1	0	2	2	.500	0	1-1	5	5.55	5.26
2003 Cleveland	AL	68	0	0	24	74.2	294	52	21	19	9	4	1	3	20	3	82	1	0	2	2	.500	0	8-13	17	2.25	2.29
4 ML YEARS		157	0	0	50	167.1	717	141	75	68	22	9	6	9	79	10	192	3	0	7	5	.583	0	10-16	25	3.82	3.66

Todd Ritchie

Pitches: R **Bats:** R **Pos:** SP-5 **Ht:** 6'3" **Wt:** 210 **Born:** 11/7/71 **Age:** 32

Year Team	Lg	G	GS	CG	GF	IP	BFP	H	R	ER	HR	SH	SF	HB	TBB	IBB	SO	WP	Bk	W	L	Pct	ShO	Sv-Op	Hld	ERC	ERA
1997 Minnesota	AL	42	0	0	19	74.2	331	87	41	38	11	0	1	2	28	0	44	11	0	2	3	.400	0	0-2	3	5.44	4.58
1998 Minnesota	AL	15	0	0	7	24.0	113	30	17	15	1	0	0	0	9	0	21	3	0	0	0	-	0	0-0	0	4.75	5.63
1999 Pittsburgh	NL	28	26	3	0	172.2	715	169	79	67	17	3	2	4	54	3	107	7	0	15	9	.625	0	0-0	1	3.76	3.49
2000 Pittsburgh	NL	31	31	1	0	187.0	804	208	111	100	26	8	5	3	51	1	124	5	1	9	8	.529	1	0-0	0	4.55	4.81
2001 Pittsburgh	NL	33	33	4	0	207.1	887	211	118	103	23	9	5	7	52	7	124	7	0	11	15	.423	2	0-0	0	3.68	4.47
2002 Chicago	AL	26	23	0	1	133.2	623	176	104	90	18	6	7	5	52	2	77	10	0	5	15	.250	0	0-0	0	6.27	6.06
2003 Milwaukee	NL	5	5	0	0	28.1	132	36	17	16	4	2	2	4	10	0	15	3	0	1	2	.333	0	0-0	0	6.40	5.08
7 ML YEARS		180	118	7	27	827.2	3605	917	487	429	100	28	22	25	256	13	512	46	1	43	52	.453	3	0-2	4	4.57	4.66

Luis Rivas

Bats: R **Throws:** R **Pos:** 2B-134; PR-3 **Ht:** 5'11" **Wt:** 175 **Born:** 8/30/79 **Age:** 24

Year Team	Lg	G	AB	H	2B	3B	HR	(Hm	Rd)	TB	R	RBI	RC	TBB	IBB	SO	HBP	SH	SF	SB	CS	SB%	GDP	Avg	OBP	Slg
2000 Minnesota	AL	16	58	18	4	1	0	(0	0)	24	8	6	8	2	0	4	0	2	2	2	0	1.00	1	.310	.323	.414
2001 Minnesota	AL	153	563	150	21	6	7	(3	4)	204	70	47	65	40	0	99	6	5	5	31	11	.74	15	.266	.319	.362
2002 Minnesota	AL	93	316	81	23	4	4	(2	2)	124	46	35	35	19	2	51	3	8	0	9	4	.69	12	.256	.305	.392
2003 Minnesota	AL	135	475	123	16	9	8	(4	4)	181	69	43	45	30	0	65	5	8	3	17	7	.71	20	.259	.308	.381
4 ML YEARS		397	1412	372	64	20	19	(9	10)	533	193	131	153	91	2	219	14	23	10	59	22	.73	49	.263	.312	.377

Carlos Rivera

Bats: L **Throws:** L **Pos:** 1B-60; PH-29; PR-4 **Ht:** 6'1" **Wt:** 245 **Born:** 6/10/78 **Age:** 26

Year Team	Lg	G	AB	H	2B	3B	HR	(Hm	Rd)	TB	R	RBI	RC	TBB	IBB	SO	HBP	SH	SF	SB	CS	SB%	GDP	Avg	OBP	Slg
1996 Pirates	R	48	183	52	8	3	3	(-	-)	75	24	26	23	15	1	22	1	0	2	1	1	.50	8	.284	.338	.410
1997 Augusta	A	120	415	113	16	5	9	(-	-)	166	52	65	52	19	2	82	10	0	6	4	1	.80	9	.272	.316	.400
1998 Lynchburg	A+	29	113	26	4	0	4	(-	-)	42	11	16	8	0	0	19	1	0	1	0	1	.00	3	.230	.235	.372
1998 Augusta	A	87	316	90	17	1	5	(-	-)	124	38	53	36	11	2	46	6	0	3	3	5	.38	9	.285	.318	.392
1999 Hickory	A	119	457	147	16	1	13	(-	-)	218	63	86	73	15	2	45	11	0	4	2	1	.67	13	.322	.355	.477
2000 Pirates	R	6	24	7	0	0	0	(-	-)	7	2	0	2	1	0	2	0	0	0	0	0	-	1	.292	.320	.292
2000 Lynchburg	A+	64	233	63	17	0	5	(-	-)	95	20	47	36	6	1	34	2	0	9	0	1	.00	7	.270	.284	.408
2001 Altoona	AA	111	389	91	30	0	10	(-	-)	151	44	50	35	13	2	71	1	1	4	0	2	.00	11	.234	.258	.388
2002 Altoona	AA	128	494	149	28	2	22	(-	-)	247	67	84	78	27	3	75	8	0	4	1	1	.50	18	.302	.345	.500
2003 Nashville	AAA	72	262	69	18	0	9	(-	-)	114	28	31	34	13	3	38	1	0	1	3	1	.75	2	.263	.300	.435
2003 Pittsburgh	NL	78	95	21	5	0	3	(2	1)	35	12	10	8	8	2	28	1	1	2	0	0	-	2	.221	.283	.368

Juan Rivera

Bats: R **Throws:** R **Pos:** LF-34; RF-22; PH-6; PR-1   **Ht:** 6'2" **Wt:** 170 **Born:** 7/3/78 **Age:** 25

					BATTING														BASERUNNING				AVERAGES		
Year Team	Lg	G	AB	H	2B	3B	HR	(Hm | Rd)	TB	R	RBI	RC	TBB	IBB	SO	HBP	SH	SF	SB	CS	SB%	GDP	Avg	OBP	Slg
2003 Columbus*	AAA	79	308	100	21	0	7	(- | -)	142	47	37	50	26	1	37	0	0	3	1	3	.25	8	.325	.374	.461
2001 New York	AL	3	4	0	0	0	0	(0 | 0)	0	0	0	0	0	0	0	0	0	0	0	0	-	0	.000	.000	.000
2002 New York	AL	28	83	22	5	0	1	(0 | 1)	30	9	6	8	6	0	10	0	1	1	1	1	.50	4	.265	.311	.361
2003 New York	AL	57	173	46	14	0	7	(4 | 3)	81	22	26	24	10	1	27	0	0	0	0	0	-	8	.266	.304	.468
3 ML YEARS		88	260	68	19	0	8	(4 | 4)	111	31	32	32	16	1	37	0	2	2	1	1	.50	12	.262	.302	.427

Mariano Rivera

Pitches: R **Bats:** R **Pos:** RP-64   **Ht:** 6'2" **Wt:** 185 **Born:** 11/29/69 **Age:** 34

		HOW MUCH HE PITCHED						WHAT HE GAVE UP												THE RESULTS						
Year Team	Lg	G	GS	CG	GF	IP	BFP	H	R	ER	HR	SH	SF	HB	TBB	IBB	SO	WP	Bk	W	L	Pct	ShO	Sv-Op	Hld	ERC	ERA
1995 New York	AL	19	10	0	2	67.0	301	71	43	41	11	0	2	2	30	0	51	0	1	5	3	.625	0	0-1	0	5.14	5.51
1996 New York	AL	61	0	0	14	107.2	425	73	25	25	1	2	1	2	34	3	130	1	0	8	3	.727	0	5-8	27	1.65	2.09
1997 New York	AL	66	0	0	56	71.2	301	65	17	15	5	3	4	0	20	6	68	2	0	6	4	.600	0	43-52	0	2.73	1.88
1998 New York	AL	54	0	0	49	61.1	246	48	13	13	3	2	3	1	17	1	36	0	0	3	0	1.000	0	36-41	0	2.21	1.91
1999 New York	AL	66	0	0	63	69.0	268	43	15	14	2	0	2	3	18	3	52	2	1	4	3	.571	0	45-49	0	1.47	1.83
2000 New York	AL	66	0	0	61	75.2	311	58	26	24	4	5	2	0	25	3	58	2	0	7	4	.636	0	36-41	0	2.20	2.85
2001 New York	AL	71	0	0	66	80.2	310	61	24	21	5	4	1	1	12	2	83	1	0	4	6	.400	0	50-57	0	1.74	2.34
2002 New York	AL	45	0	0	37	46.0	187	35	16	14	3	2	0	2	11	2	41	1	1	1	4	.200	0	28-32	2	2.08	2.74
2003 New York	AL	64	0	0	57	70.2	279	61	15	13	3	1	2	4	10	1	63	0	0	5	2	.714	0	40-46	0	2.27	1.66
9 ML YEARS		512	10	0	405	649.2	2628	515	194	180	37	19	17	15	177	21	582	9	3	43	29	.597	0	283-327	29	2.28	2.49

Mike Rivera

Bats: R **Throws:** R **Pos:** C-19; 1B-1; PH-1   **Ht:** 6'0" **Wt:** 210 **Born:** 9/8/76 **Age:** 27

					BATTING														BASERUNNING				AVERAGES		
Year Team	Lg	G	AB	H	2B	3B	HR	(Hm	Rd)	TB	R	RBI	RC	TBB	IBB	SO	HBP	SH	SF	SB	CS	SB%	GDP	Avg	OBP	Slg
2003 Portland*	AAA	13	50	8	1	0	0	(-	-)	9	0	2	0	1	0	21	0	0	0	0	1	.00	1	.160	.176	.180
2003 Charlotte*	AAA	68	245	76	11	0	12	(-	-)	123	38	52	44	16	0	50	9	0	1	0	1	.00	4	.310	.373	.502
2001 Detroit	AL	4	12	4	2	0	0	(0	0)	6	2	1	2	0	0	2	0	0	0	0	0	-	0	.333	.333	.500
2002 Detroit	AL	39	132	30	8	1	1	(0	1)	43	11	11	8	4	0	35	1	0	1	0	0	-	5	.227	.254	.326
2003 San Diego	NL	19	53	9	1	0	1	(0	1)	13	2	2	0	5	0	11	0	0	0	0	0	-	4	.170	.241	.245
3 ML YEARS		62	197	43	11	1	2	(0	2)	62	15	14	10	9	0	48	1	0	1	0	0	-	9	.218	.255	.315

Ruben Rivera

Bats: R **Throws:** R **Pos:** CF-13; LF-9; RF-6; PH-4; PR-1   **Ht:** 6'3" **Wt:** 200 **Born:** 11/14/73 **Age:** 30

					BATTING														BASERUNNING				AVERAGES		
Year Team	Lg	G	AB	H	2B	3B	HR	(Hm	Rd)	TB	R	RBI	RC	TBB	IBB	SO	HBP	SH	SF	SB	CS	SB%	GDP	Avg	OBP	Slg
2003 Ottawa*	AAA	14	48	20	3	2	2	(-	-)	33	12	7	14	4	0	12	2	0	0	2	0	1.00	1	.417	.481	.688
2003 Bowie*	AA	41	128	25	5	1	6	(-	-)	50	17	20	13	12	0	35	2	0	1	0	1	.00	4	.195	.273	.391
1995 New York	AL	5	1	0	0	0	0	(0	0)	0	0	0	0	0	0	1	0	0	0	0	0	-	0	.000	.000	.000
1996 New York	AL	46	88	25	6	1	2	(0	2)	39	17	16	16	13	0	26	2	1	2	6	2	.75	1	.284	.381	.443
1997 San Diego	NL	17	20	5	1	0	0	(0	0)	6	2	1	2	2	0	9	0	0	0	2	1	.67	0	.250	.318	.300
1998 San Diego	NL	95	172	36	7	2	6	(2	4)	65	31	29	23	28	0	52	2	1	1	5	1	.83	1	.209	.325	.378
1999 San Diego	NL	147	411	80	16	1	23	(10	13)	167	65	48	50	55	1	143	5	0	4	18	7	.72	9	.195	.295	.406
2000 San Diego	NL	135	423	88	18	6	17	(8	9)	169	62	57	50	44	1	137	10	0	2	8	4	.67	8	.208	.296	.400
2001 Cincinnati	NL	117	263	67	13	1	10	(6	4)	112	37	34	34	21	1	83	5	0	1	6	3	.67	7	.255	.321	.426
2002 Texas	AL	69	158	33	4	0	4	(2	2)	49	17	14	15	17	0	45	5	4	2	4	2	.67	8	.209	.302	.310
2003 San Francisco	NL	31	50	9	2	0	2	(0	2)	17	6	4	4	5	1	14	0	0	1	1	0	1.00	0	.180	.255	.340
9 ML YEARS		662	1586	343	67	11	64	(28	36)	624	237	203	194	185	4	510	29	6	12	50	20	.71	28	.216	.307	.393

Joe Roa

Pitches: R **Bats:** R **Pos:** RP-24; SP-4   **Ht:** 6'1" **Wt:** 194 **Born:** 10/11/71 **Age:** 32

		HOW MUCH HE PITCHED						WHAT HE GAVE UP												THE RESULTS						
Year Team	Lg	G	GS	CG	GF	IP	BFP	H	R	ER	HR	SH	SF	HB	TBB	IBB	SO	WP	Bk	W	L	Pct	ShO	Sv-Op	Hld	ERC	ERA
2003 Indianapolis*	AAA	5	4	0	0	24.2	106	32	15	13	3	3	0	1	3	0	18	0	0	2	2	.500	0	0- -	-	5.05	4.74
1995 Cleveland	AL	1	1	0	0	6.0	28	9	4	4	1	1	0	0	2	0	0	0	0	0	1	.000	0	0-0	0	7.46	6.00
1996 Cleveland	AL	1	0	0	0	1.2	11	4	2	2	0	0	0	0	3	0	0	0	0	0	0	-	0	0-0	0	20.57	10.80
1997 San Francisco	NL	28	3	0	4	65.2	289	86	40	38	8	5	4	2	20	5	34	0	1	2	5	.286	0	0-0	2	5.85	5.21
2002 Philadelphia	NL	14	11	0	1	71.1	298	78	33	32	11	1	3	1	13	2	35	0	1	4	4	.500	0	0-0	0	4.14	4.04
2003 Phi-Col-SD	NL	28	4	0	9	51.1	232	69	36	35	10	3	1	2	10	0	38	1	0	1	3	.250	0	0-0	2	6.06	6.14
2003 Philadelphia	NL	6	3	0	1	19.1	88	28	13	13	3	1	0	1	4	0	16	1	0	0	2	.000	0	0-0	0	6.67	6.05
2003 Colorado	NL	4	0	0	3	6.2	26	7	3	3	2	0	0	0	0	0	4	0	0	0	0	-	0	0-0	0	4.06	4.05
2003 San Diego	NL	18	1	0	5	25.1	118	34	20	19	5	2	1	1	6	0	18	0	0	1	1	.500	0	0-0	2	6.12	6.75
5 ML YEARS		72	19	0	14	196.0	858	246	115	111	30	10	8	5	48	7	107	1	2	7	13	.350	0	0-0	2	5.42	5.10

Jason Roach

Pitches: R **Bats:** R **Pos:** SP-2   **Ht:** 6'4" **Wt:** 205 **Born:** 4/20/76 **Age:** 28

		HOW MUCH HE PITCHED						WHAT HE GAVE UP												THE RESULTS						
Year Team	Lg	G	GS	CG	GF	IP	BFP	H	R	ER	HR	SH	SF	HB	TBB	IBB	SO	WP	Bk	W	L	Pct	ShO	Sv-Op	Hld	ERC	ERA
1998 Capital City	A	1	0	0	1	1.0	5	1	0	0	0	0	0	0	1	0	1	0	0	0	0	-	0	0- -	-	5.48	0.00
1999 St.Lucie	A+	2	0	0	1	2.0	7	1	0	0	0	0	0	0	3	0	0	0	0	0	0	-	0	0- -	-	6.63	0.00
2000 Pittsfield	A-	5	5	0	0	26.2	108	18	11	7	0	0	0	2	7	0	26	0	1	1	1	.500	0	0- -	-	1.59	2.36
2000 Binghamton	AA	1	1	0	0	5.0	24	7	3	2	0	1	0	0	3	0	3	0	0	0	0	-	0	0- -	-	6.56	3.60
2000 St.Lucie	A+	9	9	0	0	48.2	191	42	15	14	2	1	2	0	12	0	22	1	0	5	3	.625	0	0- -	-	2.50	2.59
2001 Binghamton	AA	22	21	0	0	116.0	500	129	54	42	7	6	4	4	28	1	70	1	2	8	7	.533	0	0- -	-	3.90	3.26
2001 Norfolk	AAA	4	4	0	0	16.1	77	21	13	13	1	2	1	1	7	1	7	0	0	1	2	.333	0	0- -	-	5.63	7.16

Year Team	Lg	G	GS	CG	GF	IP	BFP	H	R	ER	HR	SH	SF	HB	TBB	IBB	SO	WP	Bk	W	L	Pct	ShO	Sv-Op	Hld	ERC	ERA
2002 Binghamton	AA	8	8	0	0	44.1	175	40	19	18	3	1	3	0	12	0	23	3	0	3	4	.429	0	0--	-	2.98	3.65
2002 Norfolk	AAA	19	17	0	1	106.1	456	117	41	33	9	1	0	3	31	2	64	0	1	6	6	.500	0	0--	-	4.22	2.79
2003 Norfolk	AAA	31	20	2	2	120.2	528	140	74	68	12	2	3	7	36	1	98	4	0	5	11	.313	0	0--	-	4.85	5.07
2003 New York	NL	2	2	0	0	9.0	46	14	12	12	3	1	0	1	4	0	2	2	0	0	2	.000	0	0-0	0	10.08	12.00

Brian Roberts

Bats: B **Throws:** R **Pos:** 2B-107; DH-3; SS-2; PH-1   **Ht:** 5'9" **Wt:** 170 **Born:** 10/9/77 **Age:** 26

Year Team	Lg	G	AB	H	2B	3B	HR	Hm	Rd	TB	R	RBI	RC	TBB	IBB	SO	HBP	SH	SF	SB	CS	SB%	GDP	Avg	OBP	Slg
2003 Ottawa*	AAA	44	178	56	13	1	0	(-	-)	71	36	15	32	27	1	12	0	4	2	19	6	.76	3	.315	.401	.399
2001 Baltimore	AL	75	273	69	12	3	2	(0	2)	93	42	17	27	13	0	36	0	3	3	12	3	.80	1	.253	.284	.341
2002 Baltimore	AL	38	128	29	6	0	1	(1	0)	38	18	11	12	15	0	21	1	3	2	9	2	.82	3	.227	.308	.297
2003 Baltimore	AL	112	460	124	22	4	5	(3	2)	169	65	41	61	46	1	58	1	4	1	23	6	.79	9	.270	.337	.367
3 ML YEARS		225	861	222	40	7	8	(4	4)	300	125	69	100	74	1	115	2	10	6	44	11	.80	15	.258	.316	.348

Dave Roberts

Bats: L **Throws:** L **Pos:** CF-105; PH-3; PR-3   **Ht:** 5'10" **Wt:** 180 **Born:** 5/31/72 **Age:** 32

Year Team	Lg	G	AB	H	2B	3B	HR	Hm	Rd	TB	R	RBI	RC	TBB	IBB	SO	HBP	SH	SF	SB	CS	SB%	GDP	Avg	OBP	Slg
2003 Ogden*	R+	3	10	4	0	0	0	(-	-)	4	4	0	2	1	0	0	0	1	0	1	0	1.00	0	.400	.455	.400
2003 Las Vegas*	AAA	2	5	0	0	0	0	(-	-)	0	2	0	0	1	0	0	0	0	0	0	0	-	0	.000	.167	.000
1999 Cleveland	AL	41	143	34	4	0	2	(1	1)	44	26	12	14	9	0	16	0	3	1	11	3	.79	0	.238	.281	.308
2000 Cleveland	AL	19	10	2	0	0	0	(0	0)	2	1	0	1	2	0	2	0	1	0	1	1	.50	0	.200	.333	.200
2001 Cleveland	AL	15	12	4	1	0	0	(0	0)	5	3	2	2	1	0	2	0	0	0	1	0	1.00	0	.333	.385	.417
2002 Los Angeles	NL	127	422	117	14	7	3	(0	3)	154	63	34	66	48	0	51	2	6	1	45	10	.82	1	.277	.353	.365
2003 Los Angeles	NL	107	388	97	6	5	2	(1	1)	119	56	16	41	43	1	39	4	5	0	40	14	.74	1	.250	.331	.307
5 ML YEARS		309	975	254	25	12	7	(2	5)	324	149	64	124	103	1	110	6	15	2	97	29	.77	1	.261	.334	.332

Grant Roberts

Pitches: R **Bats:** R **Pos:** RP-18   **Ht:** 6'3" **Wt:** 205 **Born:** 9/13/77 **Age:** 26

Year Team	Lg	G	GS	CG	GF	IP	BFP	H	R	ER	HR	SH	SF	HB	TBB	IBB	SO	WP	Bk	W	L	Pct	ShO	Sv-Op	Hld	ERC	ERA
2003 St.Lucie*	A+	5	2	0	0	9.0	36	5	4	0	0	0	0	0	3	0	5	0	0	1	0	1.000	0	0--	-	1.21	0.00
2003 Norfolk*	AAA	8	0	0	2	7.2	36	7	3	3	0	0	0	1	5	0	6	0	0	0	0	-	0	0--	-	4.18	3.52
2000 New York	NL	4	1	0	0	7.0	38	11	10	9	0	0	2	0	4	1	6	0	0	0	0	-	0	0-0	-	6.53	11.57
2001 New York	NL	16	0	0	2	26.0	110	24	11	11	2	1	1	0	8	1	29	0	1	1	0	1.000	0	0-1	1	3.03	3.81
2002 New York	NL	34	0	0	6	45.0	192	43	12	11	3	3	2	1	16	7	31	0	0	3	1	.750	0	0-0	0	3.25	2.20
2003 New York	NL	18	0	0	5	19.0	79	19	9	8	0	1	0	1	3	1	10	0	0	0	3	.000	0	1-1	4	2.60	3.79
4 ML YEARS		72	1	0	13	97.0	419	97	42	39	5	5	5	2	31	10	76	0	1	4	4	.500	0	1-2	5	3.28	3.62

Willis Roberts

Pitches: R **Bats:** R **Pos:** RP-26   **Ht:** 6'3" **Wt:** 175 **Born:** 6/19/75 **Age:** 29

Year Team	Lg	G	GS	CG	GF	IP	BFP	H	R	ER	HR	SH	SF	HB	TBB	IBB	SO	WP	Bk	W	L	Pct	ShO	Sv-Op	Hld	ERC	ERA
1999 Detroit	AL	1	0	0	0	1.1	8	3	4	2	0	0	1	1	0	0	0	0	0	0	0	-	0	0-0	0	12.64	13.50
2001 Baltimore	AL	46	18	1	20	132.0	593	142	75	72	15	5	4	11	55	1	95	3	2	9	10	.474	0	6-10	-	4.98	4.91
2002 Baltimore	AL	66	0	0	24	75.0	334	79	34	28	5	1	4	4	32	3	51	7	0	5	4	.556	0	1-3	13	4.35	3.36
2003 Baltimore	AL	26	0	0	9	39.1	174	41	26	25	7	1	0	7	16	2	26	2	0	3	1	.750	0	0-0	1	5.72	5.72
4 ML YEARS		139	18	1	53	247.2	1109	265	139	127	27	7	9	23	103	6	172	12	2	17	15	.531	0	7-13	15	4.94	4.62

Jeriome Robertson

Pitches: L **Bats:** L **Pos:** SP-31; RP-1   **Ht:** 6'1" **Wt:** 190 **Born:** 3/30/77 **Age:** 27

Year Team	Lg	G	GS	CG	GF	IP	BFP	H	R	ER	HR	SH	SF	HB	TBB	IBB	SO	WP	Bk	W	L	Pct	ShO	Sv-Op	Hld	ERC	ERA
1996 Astros	R	13	13	1	0	78.1	304	51	20	15	2	3	0	4	15	0	98	6	2	5	3	.625	1	0--	-	1.44	1.72
1996 Kissimmee	A+	1	1	0	0	7.0	27	4	4	2	0	0	0	1	0	2	0	0	0	0	0	-	0	0--	-	0.90	2.57
1997 Quad City	A	26	25	2	1	146.0	647	151	86	66	12	1	4	8	56	1	135	5	3	11	8	.579	1	1--	-	4.22	4.07
1998 Kissimmee	A+	28	28	2	0	175.0	740	185	83	72	13	3	5	7	53	3	131	6	4	10	10	.500	0	0--	-	4.04	3.70
1999 Jackson	AA	28	28	1	0	191.0	791	184	81	65	22	6	4	8	45	2	133	5	7	15	7	.682	0	0--	-	3.50	3.06
2000 Kissimmee	A+	5	5	1	0	29.0	121	28	19	15	1	1	0	2	5	0	13	0	0	2	1	.667	1	0--	-	2.82	4.66
2000 Round Rock	AA	11	10	0	1	61.0	265	62	36	28	8	3	1	2	18	1	30	4	1	2	2	.500	0	0--	-	3.98	4.13
2001 Round Rock	AAA	9	9	0	0	49.2	228	64	42	39	10	2	2	3	23	1	27	1	0	1	7	.125	0	0--	-	7.30	7.07
2002 New Orleans	AAA	57	0	0	11	73.2	326	89	33	32	10	2	1	1	21	0	72	6	0	5	1	.833	0	3--	-	5.10	3.91
2002 New Orleans	AAA	27	27	2	0	180.0	734	160	59	51	13	4	4	9	45	0	114	4	0	12	8	.600	1	0--	-	2.95	2.55
2003 New Orleans	AAA	1	1	0	0	6.2	28	7	5	5	2	0	0	0	2	0	6	1	0	1	0	1.000	0	0--	-	5.44	6.75
2002 Houston	NL	11	1	0	1	9.2	46	13	8	7	4	5	3	0	5	3	6	2	0	0	2	.000	0	0-0	-	8.70	6.52
2003 Houston	NL	32	31	0	0	160.2	711	180	98	91	23	8	5	6	64	8	99	1	2	15	9	.625	0	0-0	-	5.19	5.10
2 ML YEARS		43	32	0	1	170.1	757	193	106	98	27	13	8	6	69	11	105	3	2	15	11	.577	0	0-0	-	5.38	5.18

Nate Robertson

Pitches: L **Bats:** R **Pos:** SP-8   **Ht:** 6'2" **Wt:** 215 **Born:** 9/3/77 **Age:** 26

Year Team	Lg	G	GS	CG	GF	IP	BFP	H	R	ER	HR	SH	SF	HB	TBB	IBB	SO	WP	Bk	W	L	Pct	ShO	Sv-Op	Hld	ERC	ERA
1999 Utica	A-	5	5	0	0	26.0	101	22	9	8	0	1	2	0	8	0	26	0	0	2	0	1.000	0	0- -	-	2.43	2.77
1999 Kane County	A	8	8	1	0	51.0	197	42	14	13	1	0	2	0	12	0	33	0	0	6	1	.857	1	0- -	-	2.15	2.29
2000 Kane County	A	6	6	0	0	17.2	81	24	13	10	0	0	0	1	6	0	15	0	0	2	0	.000	0	0- -	-	5.43	5.09
2001 Brevard Cnty	A+	19	19	2	0	106.1	445	95	44	34	3	6	2	5	43	1	67	5	1	11	4	.733	0	0- -	-	3.24	2.88
2002 Portland	AA	27	27	3	0	163.0	670	156	77	62	12	6	8	7	50	2	109	0	2	10	9	.526	0	0- -	-	3.55	3.42
2003 Toledo	AAA	24	23	3	1	155.0	640	145	62	54	14	4	2	6	47	2	102	0	0	9	7	.563	1	0- -	-	3.48	3.14
2002 Florida	NL	6	1	0	1	8.1	46	15	11	11	3	0	0	2	4	1	3	0	0	0	1	.000	0	0-0	0	12.69	11.88
2003 Detroit	AL	8	8	0	0	44.2	203	55	27	27	6	0	0	0	23	2	33	3	0	1	2	.333	0	0-0	0	6.24	5.44
2 ML YEARS		14	9	0	1	53.0	249	70	38	38	9	0	0	2	27	3	36	3	0	1	3	.250	0	0-0	0	7.19	6.45

Kerry Robinson

Bats: L **Throws:** L **Pos:** PH-51; RF-39; LF-36; CF-20; PR-6   **Ht:** 6'0" **Wt:** 175 **Born:** 10/3/73 **Age:** 30

Year Team	Lg	G	AB	H	2B	3B	HR	(Hm	Rd)	TB	R	RBI	RC	TBB	IBB	SO	HBP	SH	SF	SB	CS	SB%	GDP	Avg	OBP	Slg
2003 Memphis*	AAA	16	61	21	2	1	0	(-	-)	25	14	3	10	1	0	7	0	1	0	5	0	1.00	0	.344	.355	.410
1998 Tampa Bay	AL	2	3	0	0	0	0	(0	0)	0	0	0	0	0	0	1	0	0	0	0	0	-	0	.000	.000	.000
1999 Cincinnati	NL	9	1	0	0	0	0	(0	0)	0	4	0	0	0	0	1	0	0	0	0	1	.00	0	.000	.000	.000
2001 St Louis	NL	114	186	53	6	1	1	(1	0)	64	34	15	24	12	0	20	2	4	3	11	2	.85	1	.285	.330	.344
2002 St Louis	NL	124	181	47	7	4	1	(0	1)	65	27	15	20	11	3	29	0	2	1	7	4	.64	1	.260	.301	.359
2003 St Louis	NL	116	208	52	6	3	1	(1	0)	67	19	16	20	8	3	27	1	4	0	6	1	.86	3	.250	.281	.322
5 ML YEARS		365	579	152	19	8	3	(2	1)	196	84	46	64	31	6	78	3	10	4	24	8	.75	5	.263	.301	.339

John Rocker

Pitches: L **Bats:** R **Pos:** RP-2   **Ht:** 6'4" **Wt:** 225 **Born:** 10/17/74 **Age:** 29

Year Team	Lg	G	GS	CG	GF	IP	BFP	H	R	ER	HR	SH	SF	HB	TBB	IBB	SO	WP	Bk	W	L	Pct	ShO	Sv-Op	Hld	ERC	ERA
2003 Orlando*	AA	17	0	0	4	19.2	105	23	23	20	4	0	0	1	26	0	20	2	1	0	1	.000	0	0- -	-	10.46	9.15
1998 Atlanta	NL	47	0	0	16	38.0	156	22	10	9	4	3	0	3	22	4	42	6	0	1	3	.250	0	2-4	15	2.73	2.13
1999 Atlanta	NL	74	0	0	61	72.1	301	47	24	20	5	2	0	1	37	4	104	7	0	4	5	.444	0	38-45	2	2.38	2.49
2000 Atlanta	NL	59	0	0	41	53.0	251	42	25	17	5	1	0	2	48	4	77	5	2	1	2	.333	0	24-27	4	4.72	2.89
2001 Atl-Cle	NL	68	0	0	48	66.2	300	58	36	32	4	4	2	5	41	4	79	11	2	5	9	.357	0	23-30	7	4.03	4.32
2002 Texas	AL	30	0	0	10	24.1	114	29	19	18	5	1	3	0	13	1	30	0	0	2	3	.400	0	1-4	10	6.43	6.66
2003 Tampa Bay	AL	2	0	0	0	1.0	8	2	1	1	0	0	0	1	3	0	0	0	0	0	0	-	0	0-0	0	29.64	9.00
2001 Atlanta	NL	30	0	0	28	32.0	135	25	13	11	2	0	1	2	16	1	36	5	0	2	2	.500	0	19-23	0	3.23	3.09
2001 Cleveland	AL	38	0	0	20	34.2	165	33	23	21	2	4	1	3	25	3	43	6	2	3	7	.300	0	4-7	7	4.79	5.45
6 ML YEARS		280	0	0	176	255.1	1130	200	115	97	23	11	5	12	164	17	332	29	4	13	22	.371	0	88-110	36	3.76	3.42

Fernando Rodney

Pitches: R **Bats:** R **Pos:** RP-27   **Ht:** 5'11" **Wt:** 170 **Born:** 3/18/77 **Age:** 27

Year Team	Lg	G	GS	CG	GF	IP	BFP	H	R	ER	HR	SH	SF	HB	TBB	IBB	SO	WP	Bk	W	L	Pct	ShO	Sv-Op	Hld	ERC	ERA
1999 Tigers	R	22	0	0	20	30.0	129	20	8	8	1	3	2	3	21	0	39	1	1	3	3	.500	0	9- -	-	3.35	2.40
1999 Lakeland	A+	4	0	0	4	6.1	25	7	1	1	0	0	0	1	1	0	5	0	0	1	0	1.000	0	2- -	-	4.01	1.42
2000 W Michigan	A	22	10	0	1	82.2	353	74	34	27	2	5	0	2	35	0	56	3	0	6	4	.600	0	0- -	-	3.15	2.94
2001 Lakeland	A+	16	9	0	4	55.1	235	53	26	21	2	2	0	1	19	1	44	1	1	4	2	.667	0	0- -	-	3.22	3.42
2001 Tigers	R	1	1	0	0	1.0	3	0	0	0	0	0	0	0	1	0	1	0	0	0	0	-	0	0- -	-	1.26	0.00
2002 Erie	AA	4	0	0	2	6.1	30	7	3	3	1	0	1	2	3	0	8	0	0	0	1	.000	0	1- -	-	6.86	4.26
2002 Erie	AA	21	0	0	19	20.1	77	14	4	3	0	0	0	0	5	0	18	3	0	1	0	1.000	0	11- -	-	1.51	1.33
2002 Toledo	AAA	20	0	0	11	22.1	90	13	4	2	1	1	3	1	9	0	25	2	2	1	1	.500	0	4- -	-	1.76	0.81
2003 Toledo	AAA	38	0	0	35	40.2	156	22	6	6	0	1	3	4	13	0	58	3	0	1	1	.500	0	23- -	-	1.41	1.33
2002 Detroit	AL	20	0	0	10	18.0	89	25	15	12	2	2	1	0	10	2	10	0	1	1	3	.250	0	0-4	0	6.77	6.00
2003 Detroit	AL	27	0	0	11	29.2	143	35	20	20	2	3	3	1	17	1	33	0	0	1	3	.250	0	3-6	3	5.46	6.07
2 ML YEARS		47	0	0	21	47.2	232	60	35	32	4	5	4	1	27	3	43	0	1	2	6	.250	0	3-10	3	5.94	6.04

Alex Rodriguez

Bats: R **Throws:** R **Pos:** SS-158; PH-2; DH-1   **Ht:** 6'3" **Wt:** 210 **Born:** 7/27/75 **Age:** 28

Year Team	Lg	G	AB	H	2B	3B	HR	(Hm	Rd)	TB	R	RBI	RC	TBB	IBB	SO	HBP	SH	SF	SB	CS	SB%	GDP	Avg	OBP	Slg
1994 Seattle	AL	17	54	11	0	0	0	(0	0)	11	4	2	3	3	0	20	0	1	1	3	0	1.00	0	.204	.241	.204
1995 Seattle	AL	48	142	33	6	2	5	(1	4)	58	15	19	15	6	0	42	0	1	0	4	2	.67	0	.232	.264	.408
1996 Seattle	AL	146	601	215	54	1	36	(18	18)	379	141	123	144	59	1	104	4	6	7	15	4	.79	15	.358	.414	.631
1997 Seattle	AL	141	587	176	40	3	23	(16	7)	291	100	84	100	41	1	99	5	4	1	29	6	.83	14	.300	.350	.496
1998 Seattle	AL	161	686	213	35	5	42	(18	24)	384	123	124	135	45	0	121	10	3	4	46	13	.78	12	.310	.360	.560
1999 Seattle	AL	129	502	143	25	0	42	(20	22)	294	110	111	102	56	2	109	5	1	8	21	7	.75	12	.285	.357	.586
2000 Seattle	AL	148	554	175	34	2	41	(13	28)	336	134	132	138	100	5	121	7	0	11	15	4	.79	10	.316	.420	.606
2001 Texas	AL	162	632	201	34	1	52	(26	26)	393	133	135	148	75	6	131	16	0	9	18	3	.86	17	.318	.399	.622
2002 Texas	AL	162	624	187	27	2	57	(34	23)	389	125	142	153	87	12	122	10	0	4	9	4	.69	14	.300	.392	.623
2003 Texas	AL	161	607	181	30	6	47	(26	21)	364	124	118	133	87	10	126	15	0	6	17	3	.85	16	.298	.396	.600
10 ML YEARS		1275	4989	1535	285	22	345	(172	173)	2899	1009	990	1071	559	37	995	72	16	51	177	46	.79	110	.308	.382	.581

Felix Rodriguez

Pitches: R **Bats:** R **Pos:** RP-68   **Ht:** 6'1" **Wt:** 198 **Born:** 9/9/72 **Age:** 31

		HOW MUCH HE PITCHED						WHAT HE GAVE UP												THE RESULTS							
Year Team	Lg	G	GS	CG	GF	IP	BFP	H	R	ER	HR	SH	SF	HB	TBB	IBB	SO	WP	Bk	W	L	Pct	ShO	Sv-Op	Hld	ERC	ERA
1995 Los Angeles	NL	11	0	0	5	10.2	45	11	3	3	2	0	0	0	5	0	5	0	0	1	1	.500	0	0-1	0	5.43	2.53
1997 Cincinnati	NL	26	1	0	13	46.0	212	48	23	22	2	0	1	6	28	2	34	4	1	0	0	-	0	0-0	0	5.22	4.30
1998 Arizona	NL	43	0	0	23	44.0	207	44	31	30	5	4	3	1	29	1	36	5	2	0	2	.000	0	5-8	0	5.11	6.14
1999 San Francisco	NL	47	0	0	26	66.1	292	67	32	28	6	2	3	2	29	2	55	2	0	2	3	.400	0	0-1	3	4.25	3.80
2000 San Francisco	NL	76	0	0	19	81.2	346	65	29	24	5	2	3	3	42	2	95	3	1	4	2	.667	0	3-8	30	3.26	2.64
2001 San Francisco	NL	80	0	0	13	80.1	314	53	16	15	5	1	3	1	27	2	91	1	0	9	1	.900	0	0-3	32	1.92	1.68
2002 San Francisco	NL	71	0	0	12	69.0	288	53	33	32	5	2	3	4	29	1	58	4	0	8	6	.571	0	0-6	24	2.92	4.17
2003 San Francisco	NL	68	0	0	24	61.0	265	59	21	21	5	3	1	4	29	2	46	5	1	8	2	.800	0	2-3	19	4.33	3.10
8 ML YEARS		422	1	0	135	459.0	1969	400	188	175	35	14	17	21	218	12	420	24	5	32	17	.653	0	10-30	108	3.64	3.43

Francisco Rodriguez

Pitches: R **Bats:** R **Pos:** RP-59   **Ht:** 6'0" **Wt:** 175 **Born:** 1/7/82 **Age:** 22

		HOW MUCH HE PITCHED						WHAT HE GAVE UP												THE RESULTS							
Year Team	Lg	G	GS	CG	GF	IP	BFP	H	R	ER	HR	SH	SF	HB	TBB	IBB	SO	WP	Bk	W	L	Pct	ShO	Sv-Op	Hld	ERC	ERA
1999 Butte	R+	12	9	1	0	51.2	211	33	21	19	1	3	0	3	21	1	69	10	3	1	1	.500	0	0--	-	1.90	3.31
1999 Boise	A-	1	1	0	0	5.0	22	3	4	3	0	0	1	0	1	0	6	0	0	1	0	1.000	0	0--	-	0.96	5.40
2000 Lk Elsinore	A+	43	29	0	0	64.0	265	43	29	20	2	2	2	1	32	0	79	12	1	4	4	.500	0	0--	-	2.32	2.81
2001 R Cucamnga	A+	20	20	1	0	113.2	523	127	72	68	13	2	1	6	55	1	147	17	4	5	7	.417	1	0--	-	5.34	5.38
2002 Arkansas	AA	23	0	0	16	41.1	170	32	13	9	2	0	0	0	15	0	61	7	1	3	3	.500	0	9--	-	2.39	1.96
2002 Salt Lake	AAA	27	0	0	23	42.0	164	30	13	12	1	1	0	3	13	0	59	2	0	2	3	.400	0	6--	-	2.14	2.57
2002 Anaheim	AL	5	0	0	4	5.2	21	3	0	0	0	0	0	1	2	1	13	0	0	0	0	-	0	0-0	0	1.52	0.00
2003 Anaheim	AL	59	0	0	23	86.0	334	50	30	29	12	2	4	2	35	5	95	7	0	8	3	.727	0	2-6	7	2.25	3.03
2 ML YEARS		64	0	0	27	91.2	355	53	30	29	12	2	4	3	37	6	108	7	0	8	3	.727	0	2-6	7	2.21	2.85

Ivan Rodriguez

Bats: R **Throws:** R **Pos:** C-138; PH-8; DH-1; PR-1   **Ht:** 5'9" **Wt:** 205 **Born:** 11/30/71 **Age:** 32

		BATTING																		BASERUNNING				AVERAGES		
Year Team	Lg	G	AB	H	2B	3B	HR	(Hm	Rd)	TB	R	RBI	RC	TBB	IBB	SO	HBP	SH	SF	SB	CS	SB%	GDP	Avg	OBP	Slg
1991 Texas	AL	88	280	74	16	0	3	(3	0)	99	24	27	23	5	0	42	0	2	1	0	1	.00	10	.264	.276	.354
1992 Texas	AL	123	420	109	16	1	8	(4	4)	151	39	37	41	24	2	73	1	7	2	0	0	-	15	.260	.300	.360
1993 Texas	AL	137	473	129	28	4	10	(7	3)	195	56	66	57	29	3	70	4	5	8	8	7	.53	16	.273	.315	.412
1994 Texas	AL	99	363	108	19	1	16	(7	9)	177	56	57	61	31	5	42	7	0	4	6	3	.67	10	.298	.360	.488
1995 Texas	AL	130	492	149	32	2	12	(5	7)	221	56	67	68	16	2	48	4	0	5	0	2	.00	11	.303	.327	.449
1996 Texas	AL	153	639	192	47	3	19	(10	9)	302	116	86	99	38	7	55	4	0	4	5	0	1.00	15	.300	.342	.473
1997 Texas	AL	150	597	187	34	4	20	(12	8)	289	98	77	98	38	7	89	8	1	4	7	3	.70	18	.313	.360	.484
1998 Texas	AL	145	579	186	40	4	21	(12	9)	297	88	91	100	32	4	88	3	0	3	9	0	1.00	18	.321	.358	.513
1999 Texas	AL	144	600	199	29	1	35	(12	23)	335	116	113	104	24	2	64	1	0	5	25	12	.68	31	.332	.356	.558
2000 Texas	AL	91	363	126	27	4	27	(16	11)	242	66	83	78	19	5	48	1	0	6	5	5	.50	17	.347	.375	.667
2001 Texas	AL	111	442	136	24	2	25	(16	9)	239	70	65	77	23	3	73	4	0	1	10	3	.77	13	.308	.347	.541
2002 Texas	AL	108	408	128	32	2	19	(15	4)	221	67	60	64	25	2	71	2	1	4	5	4	.56	13	.314	.353	.542
2003 Florida	NL	144	511	152	36	3	16	(8	8)	242	90	85	91	55	6	92	6	1	5	10	6	.63	18	.297	.369	.474
13 ML YEARS		1623	6167	1875	380	31	231	(127	104)	3010	942	914	961	359	48	855	45	17	52	90	46	.66	205	.304	.344	.488

Ricardo Rodriguez

Pitches: R **Bats:** R **Pos:** SP-15   **Ht:** 6'3" **Wt:** 165 **Born:** 5/21/78 **Age:** 26

		HOW MUCH HE PITCHED						WHAT HE GAVE UP												THE RESULTS							
Year Team	Lg	G	GS	CG	GF	IP	BFP	H	R	ER	HR	SH	SF	HB	TBB	IBB	SO	WP	Bk	W	L	Pct	ShO	Sv-Op	Hld	ERC	ERA
2000 Great Falls	R+	15	15	2	0	95.2	374	66	32	20	2	3	3	1	23	0	129	4	0	10	3	.769	0	0--	-	1.56	1.88
2001 Vero Beach	A+	26	26	2	0	154.1	645	133	67	55	13	7	2	3	60	0	154	18	1	14	6	.700	0	0--	-	3.26	3.21
2002 Jacksonville	AA	11	11	2	0	68.0	268	56	21	15	4	2	1	2	13	0	44	5	0	5	4	.556	0	0--	-	2.27	1.99
2002 Las Vegas	AAA	2	2	0	0	11.2	51	13	5	5	1	0	1	1	5	0	7	0	0	1	0	1.000	0	0--	-	5.28	3.86
2002 Buffalo	AAA	4	4	0	0	25.0	106	26	16	10	1	1	0	2	7	0	14	0	0	3	1	.750	0	0--	-	3.78	3.60
2003 Buffalo	AAA	2	2	0	0	8.1	34	6	4	4	2	0	0	1	3	0	7	1	0	0	1	.000	0	0--	-	3.83	4.32
2002 Cleveland	AL	7	7	0	0	41.1	183	40	27	26	5	0	0	8	18	3	24	1	0	2	2	.500	0	0-0	0	4.92	5.66
2003 Cleveland	AL	15	15	0	0	81.2	360	89	57	52	16	3	2	3	28	1	41	4	1	3	9	.250	0	0-0	0	5.14	5.73
2 ML YEARS		22	22	0	0	123.0	543	129	84	78	21	3	2	11	46	4	65	5	1	5	11	.313	0	0-0	0	5.08	5.71

Rich Rodriguez

Pitches: L **Bats:** L **Pos:** RP-3   **Ht:** 6'0" **Wt:** 205 **Born:** 3/1/63 **Age:** 41

		HOW MUCH HE PITCHED						WHAT HE GAVE UP												THE RESULTS							
Year Team	Lg	G	GS	CG	GF	IP	BFP	H	R	ER	HR	SH	SF	HB	TBB	IBB	SO	WP	Bk	W	L	Pct	ShO	Sv-Op	Hld	ERC	ERA
2003 Salt Lake*	AAA	34	0	0	12	43.2	181	47	14	12	3	0	3	0	12	0	18	3	0	3	2	.600	0	1--	-	3.91	2.47
1990 San Diego	NL	32	0	0	15	47.2	201	52	17	15	2	2	1	1	16	4	22	1	1	1	1	.500	0	1-1	3	3.99	2.83
1991 San Diego	NL	64	1	0	19	80.0	335	66	31	29	8	7	2	0	44	8	40	4	1	3	1	.750	0	0-2	8	3.63	3.26
1992 San Diego	NL	61	1	0	15	91.0	369	77	28	24	4	2	2	0	29	4	64	1	1	6	3	.667	0	0-1	5	2.56	2.37
1993 SD-Fla	NL	70	0	0	21	76.0	331	73	38	32	10	5	0	2	33	8	43	3	0	2	4	.333	0	3-7	10	4.12	3.79
1994 St Louis	NL	56	0	0	15	60.1	260	62	30	27	6	2	1	1	26	4	43	4	0	3	5	.375	0	0-3	15	4.38	4.03
1995 St Louis	NL	1	0	0	0	1.2	4	0	0	0	0	0	0	0	0	0	0	0	0	0	0	-	0	0-0	0	0.00	0.00
1997 San Francisco	NL	71	0	0	15	65.1	271	65	24	23	7	3	0	1	21	4	32	0	0	4	3	.571	0	1-5	14	3.85	3.17
1998 San Francisco	NL	68	0	0	11	65.2	278	69	28	27	7	2	2	0	20	5	44	3	0	4	0	1.000	0	2-6	22	3.94	3.70
1999 San Francisco	NL	62	0	0	6	56.2	255	60	33	33	8	5	2	1	28	5	44	1	0	3	0	1.000	0	0-2	11	4.98	5.24
2000 New York	NL	32	0	0	13	37.0	185	59	40	32	7	0	5	3	15	0	18	2	1	0	1	.000	0	0-0	0	8.86	7.78
2001 Cleveland	AL	53	0	0	6	39.0	174	41	24	18	2	2	1	2	17	3	31	1	1	2	2	.500	0	0-2	8	4.19	4.15
2002 Texas	AL	36	0	0	6	16.2	72	14	10	10	1	1	0	1	11	1	12	0	0	3	2	.600	0	1-3	4	4.17	5.40
2003 Anaheim	AL	3	0	0	2	3.2	15	4	1	1	0	0	1	0	1	0	3	0	0	0	0	-	0	0-0	0	3.55	2.45

		HOW MUCH HE PITCHED		WHAT HE GAVE UP		THE RESULTS	
Year Team	Lg	G GS CG GF	IP BFP	H R ER HR SH SF HB	TBB IBB SO WP Bk	W L Pct ShO	Sv-Op Hld ERC ERA
1993 San Diego	NL	34 0 0 10	30.0 133	34 15 11 2 2 0 1	9 3 22 1 0	2 3 .400 0	2-5 8 4.08 3.30
1993 Florida	NL	36 0 0 11	46.0 198	39 23 21 8 3 0 1	24 5 21 2 0	0 1 .000 0	1-2 2 4.14 4.11
13 ML YEARS		609 2 0 146	640.2 2750	642 304 271 62 31 17 12	261 46 396 20 5	31 22 .585 0	8-32 100 4.09 3.81

Kenny Rogers

Pitches: L **Bats:** L **Pos:** SP-31; RP-2   **Ht:** 6'1" **Wt:** 217 **Born:** 11/10/64 **Age:** 39

		HOW MUCH HE PITCHED		WHAT HE GAVE UP		THE RESULTS	
Year Team	Lg	G GS CG GF	IP BFP	H R ER HR SH SF HB	TBB IBB SO WP Bk	W L Pct ShO	Sv-Op Hld ERC ERA
1989 Texas	AL	73 0 0 24	73.2 314	60 28 24 2 6 3 4	42 9 63 6 0	3 4 .429 0	2-5 15 3.26 2.93
1990 Texas	AL	69 3 0 46	97.2 428	93 40 34 6 7 4 1	42 5 74 5 0	10 6 .625 0	15-23 6 3.53 3.13
1991 Texas	AL	63 9 0 20	109.2 511	121 80 66 14 9 5 6	61 7 73 3 1	10 10 .500 0	5-6 11 5.57 5.42
1992 Texas	AL	81 0 0 38	78.2 337	80 32 27 7 4 1 0	26 8 70 4 1	3 6 .333 0	6-10 16 3.63 3.09
1993 Texas	AL	35 33 5 0	208.1 885	210 108 95 18 7 5 4	71 2 140 6 1	16 10 .615 0	0-0 1 3.88 4.10
1994 Texas	AL	24 24 6 0	167.1 714	169 93 83 24 3 6 3	52 1 120 3 1	11 8 .579 2	0-0 0 4.12 4.46
1995 Texas	AL	31 31 3 0	208.0 877	192 87 78 26 3 5 2	76 1 140 8 1	17 7 .708 1	0-0 0 3.72 3.38
1996 New York	AL	30 30 2 0	179.0 786	179 97 93 16 6 3 8	83 2 92 5 0	12 8 .600 1	0-0 0 4.43 4.68
1997 New York	AL	31 22 1 4	145.0 651	161 100 91 18 2 4 7	62 1 78 2 2	6 7 .462 0	0-0 1 5.18 5.65
1998 Oakland	AL	34 34 7 0	238.2 970	215 96 84 19 4 5 7	67 0 138 5 2	16 8 .667 1	0-0 0 3.13 3.17
1999 Oak-NYM	AL	31 31 5 0	195.1 845	206 101 91 16 7 7 13	69 1 126 4 1	10 4 .714 0	0-0 0 4.38 4.19
2000 Texas	AL	34 34 2 0	227.1 998	257 126 115 20 3 4 11	78 2 127 1 1	13 13 .500 0	0-0 0 4.72 4.55
2001 Texas	AL	20 20 0 0	120.2 552	150 88 83 18 1 6 8	49 2 74 4 1	5 7 .417 0	0-0 0 6.22 6.19
2002 Texas	AL	33 33 2 0	210.2 892	212 101 90 21 3 1 6	70 1 107 5 1	13 8 .619 1	0-0 0 3.99 3.84
2003 Minnesota	AL	33 31 0 0	195.0 851	227 108 99 22 9 3 11	50 5 116 6 4	13 8 .619 0	0-0 0 4.73 4.57
1999 Oakland	AL	19 19 3 0	119.1 528	135 66 57 8 4 6 9	41 0 68 3 1	5 3 .625 0	0-0 0 4.68 4.30
1999 New York	NL	12 12 2 0	76.0 317	71 35 34 8 3 1 4	28 1 58 1 0	5 1 .833 1	0-0 0 3.91 4.03
15 ML YEARS		622 335 33 132	2455.0 10611	2532 1285 1153 247 74 62 91	898 47 1538 67 21	158 114 .581 7	28-44 50 4.26 4.23

Scott Rolen

Bats: R **Throws:** R **Pos:** 3B-153; PH-1   **Ht:** 6'4" **Wt:** 226 **Born:** 4/4/75 **Age:** 29

		BATTING														BASERUNNING				AVERAGES		
Year Team	Lg	G	AB	H	2B	3B	HR	(Hm Rd)	TB	R	RBI	RC	TBB	IBB	SO	HBP	SH	SF	SB	CS	SB%	GDP	Avg	OBP	Slg
1996 Philadelphia	NL	37	130	33	7	0	4	(2 2)	52	10	18	16	13	0	27	1	0	2	0	2	.00	4	.254	.322	.400
1997 Philadelphia	NL	156	561	159	35	3	21	(11 10)	263	93	92	103	76	4	138	13	0	7	16	6	.73	6	.283	.377	.469
1998 Philadelphia	NL	160	601	174	45	4	31	(19 12)	320	120	110	124	93	6	141	11	0	6	14	7	.67	10	.290	.391	.532
1999 Philadelphia	NL	112	421	113	28	1	26	(9 17)	221	74	77	83	67	2	114	3	0	6	12	2	.86	8	.268	.368	.525
2000 Philadelphia	NL	128	483	144	32	6	26	(12 14)	266	88	89	97	51	9	99	5	0	2	8	1	.89	4	.298	.370	.551
2001 Philadelphia	NL	151	554	160	39	1	25	(11 13)	276	96	107	108	74	6	127	13	0	12	16	5	.76	6	.289	.378	.498
2002 Phi-StL	NL	155	580	154	29	8	31	(14 17)	292	89	110	99	72	4	102	12	0	3	8	4	.67	22	.266	.357	.503
2003 St Louis	NL	154	559	160	49	1	28	(12 16)	295	98	104	106	82	5	104	9	0	7	13	3	.81	19	.286	.382	.528
2002 Philadelphia	NL	100	375	97	21	4	17	(9 8)	177	52	66	60	52	2	68	8	0	3	5	2	.71	12	.259	.358	.472
2002 St Louis	NL	55	205	57	8	4	14	(6 8)	115	37	44	39	20	2	34	4	0	0	3	2	.60	10	.278	.354	.561
8 ML YEARS		1053	3889	1097	264	24	192	(91 101)	1985	668	707	736	528	36	852	67	0	45	87	30	.74	79	.282	.374	.510

Jimmy Rollins

Bats: B **Throws:** R **Pos:** SS-154; PH-2   **Ht:** 5'8" **Wt:** 165 **Born:** 11/27/78 **Age:** 25

		BATTING														BASERUNNING				AVERAGES		
Year Team	Lg	G	AB	H	2B	3B	HR	(Hm Rd)	TB	R	RBI	RC	TBB	IBB	SO	HBP	SH	SF	SB	CS	SB%	GDP	Avg	OBP	Slg
2000 Philadelphia	NL	14	53	17	1	1	0	(0 0)	20	5	5	8	2	0	7	0	0	0	3	0	1.00	0	.321	.345	.377
2001 Philadelphia	NL	158	656	180	29	12	14	(8 6)	275	97	54	96	48	2	108	2	9	5	46	8	.85	5	.274	.323	.419
2002 Philadelphia	NL	154	637	156	33	10	11	(3 8)	242	82	60	71	54	3	103	4	6	4	31	13	.70	14	.245	.306	.380
2003 Philadelphia	NL	156	628	165	42	6	8	(5 3)	243	85	62	76	54	4	113	0	5	2	20	12	.63	9	.263	.320	.387
4 ML YEARS		482	1974	518	105	29	33	(16 17)	780	269	181	251	158	9	331	6	20	11	100	33	.75	28	.262	.317	.395

Damian Rolls

Bats: R **Throws:** R **Pos:** 3B-73; RF-33; LF-6; PH-4; PR-3; 2B-2   **Ht:** 6'2" **Wt:** 215 **Born:** 9/15/77 **Age:** 26

		BATTING														BASERUNNING				AVERAGES		
Year Team	Lg	G	AB	H	2B	3B	HR	(Hm Rd)	TB	R	RBI	RC	TBB	IBB	SO	HBP	SH	SF	SB	CS	SB%	GDP	Avg	OBP	Slg
2003 Durham*	AAA	18	77	19	4	1	0	(- -)	25	11	9	7	4	0	15	0	2	0	4	2	.67	0	.247	.284	.325
2000 Tampa Bay	AL	4	3	1	0	0	0	(0 0)	1	0	0	0	0	0	1	0	0	0	0	0	-	0	.333	.333	.333
2001 Tampa Bay	AL	81	237	62	11	1	2	(2 0)	81	33	12	23	10	0	47	0	2	0	12	4	.75	5	.262	.291	.342
2002 Tampa Bay	AL	21	89	26	6	1	0	(0 0)	34	15	6	7	3	0	16	2	1	0	2	5	.29	1	.292	.330	.382
2003 Tampa Bay	AL	107	373	95	20	0	7	(4 3)	136	43	46	43	19	1	84	7	2	3	11	3	.79	5	.255	.301	.365
4 ML YEARS		213	702	184	37	2	9	(6 3)	252	91	64	73	32	1	148	9	5	3	25	12	.68	11	.262	.302	.359

Jason Romano

Bats: R **Throws:** R **Pos:** CF-17; LF-9; PH-8; PR-7; RF-2; 2B-1; DH-1   **Ht:** 6'0" **Wt:** 185 **Born:** 6/24/79 **Age:** 25

		BATTING														BASERUNNING				AVERAGES		
Year Team	Lg	G	AB	H	2B	3B	HR	(Hm Rd)	TB	R	RBI	RC	TBB	IBB	SO	HBP	SH	SF	SB	CS	SB%	GDP	Avg	OBP	Slg
1997 Rangers	R	34	109	28	5	3	2	(- -)	45	27	11	18	13	0	19	3	1	1	13	4	.76	1	.257	.349	.413
1998 Savannah	A	134	524	142	19	4	7	(- -)	190	72	52	68	46	1	94	8	5	5	40	17	.70	6	.271	.336	.363
1998 Charlotte	A+	7	24	5	1	0	0	(- -)	6	3	1	1	2	0	2	0	1	1	1	2	.33	0	.208	.259	.250
1999 Charlotte	A+	120	459	143	27	14	13	(- -)	237	84	71	89	39	2	72	13	4	7	34	16	.68	4	.312	.376	.516
2000 Tulsa	AA	131	535	145	35	2	8	(- -)	208	87	70	73	56	0	84	6	16	7	25	10	.71	13	.271	.343	.389
2001 Tulsa	AA	46	186	45	9	1	1	(- -)	59	19	19	17	16	0	31	1	3	1	8	3	.73	8	.242	.304	.317
2001 Oklahoma	AAA	41	149	47	6	1	4	(- -)	67	32	13	25	20	1	28	0	6	1	3	4	.43	4	.315	.394	.450
2001 Rangers	R	5	21	3	0	0	0	(- -)	3	2	0	0	1	0	1	0	0	0	1	0	1.00	0	.143	.182	.143
2001 Charlotte	A+	3	10	4	2	0	0	(- -)	6	3	1	4	4	0	1	0	0	0	1	0	1.00	0	.400	.571	.600
2002 Oklahoma	AAA	48	196	53	8	1	4	(- -)	75	28	28	26	19	0	41	0	8	4	10	3	.77	5	.270	.329	.383

Year Team	Lg	G	AB	H	2B	3B	HR	(Hm Rd)	TB	R	RBI	RC	TBB	IBB	SO	HBP	SH	SF	SB	CS	SB%	GDP	Avg	OBP	Slg
2002 Co Springs	AAA	31	129	40	7	2	0	(- -)	51	20	9	18	6	0	27	0	3	1	8	3	.73	1	.310	.338	.395
2003 Las Vegas	AAA	57	216	66	18	4	4	(- -)	104	45	23	34	11	2	32	0	5	2	10	6	.63	3	.306	.336	.481
2002 Tex-Col		47	91	23	4	1	0	(0 0)	29	17	5	10	7	0	24	0	2	1	6	1	.86	0	.253	.303	.319
2003 Los Angeles	NL	37	36	3	0	0	0	(0 0)	3	3	0	0	1	0	8	0	0	0	2	0	1.00	0	.083	.108	.083
2002 Texas	AL	29	54	11	4	0	0	(0 0)	15	8	4	5	4	0	13	0	1	1	2	0	1.00	1	.204	.254	.278
2002 Colorado	NL	18	37	12	0	1	0	(0 0)	14	9	1	5	3	0	11	0	1	0	4	1	.80	0	.324	.375	.378
2 ML YEARS		84	127	26	4	1	0	(0 0)	32	20	5	10	8	0	32	0	2	1	8	1	.89	2	.205	.250	.252

J.C. Romero

Pitches: L Bats: B Pos: RP-73 **Ht: 5'11" Wt: 195 Born: 6/4/76 Age: 28**

Year Team	Lg	G	GS	CG	GF	IP	BFP	H	R	ER	HR	SH	SF	HB	TBB	IBB	SO	WP	Bk	W	L	Pct	ShO	Sv-Op	Hld	ERC	ERA
1999 Minnesota	AL	5	0	0	3	9.2	39	13	4	4	0	0	0	0	4	0	0	0	0	0	0	—	0	0-0	0	3.95	3.72
2000 Minnesota	AL	12	11	0	3	57.2	268	72	51	45	8	4	2	1	30	0	50	2	1	2	7	.222	0	0-0	0	6.48	7.02
2001 Minnesota	AL	14	11	0	1	65.0	286	71	48	45	10	3	2	1	24	1	39	1	0	1	4	.200	0	0-0	0	4.89	6.23
2002 Minnesota	AL	81	0	0	15	81.0	332	62	17	17	3	1	4	6	36	4	76	9	0	9	2	.818	0	1-5	33	2.74	1.89
2003 Minnesota	AL	73	0	0	17	63.0	295	66	37	35	7	4	0	6	42	7	50	9	2	2	0	1.000	0	0-4	22	5.72	5.00
5 ML YEARS		185	22	0	36	276.1	1220	284	157	146	28	12	4	12	132	12	219	21	3	14	13	.519	0	1-9	55	4.69	4.76

Mandy Romero

Bats: B Throws: R Pos: C-2; PH-1 **Ht: 5'11" Wt: 196 Born: 10/29/67 Age: 36**

Year Team	Lg	G	AB	H	2B	3B	HR	(Hm Rd)	TB	R	RBI	RC	TBB	IBB	SO	HBP	SH	SF	SB	CS	SB%	GDP	Avg	OBP	Slg
2003 Co Springs*	AAA	81	250	74	11	1	4	(- -)	99	30	31	33	18	0	38	2	1	6	0	0	—	7	.296	.341	.396
1997 San Diego	NL	21	48	10	0	0	2	(1 1)	16	7	4	4	2	0	18	0	0	0	1	0	1.00	1	.208	.240	.333
1998 SD-Bos		18	22	3	1	0	0	(0 0)	4	3	1	1	4	0	6	0	0	0	0	0	—	1	.136	.269	.182
2003 Colorado	NL	3	7	3	1	0	0	(0 0)	4	2	0	2	0	0	1	2	0	0	0	0	—	1	.429	.556	.571
1998 San Diego	NL	6	9	0	0	0	0	(0 0)	0	1	0	0	1	0	3	0	0	0	0	0	—	0	.000	.100	.000
1998 Boston	AL	12	13	3	1	0	0	(0 0)	4	2	1	1	3	0	3	0	0	0	0	0	—	1	.231	.375	.308
3 ML YEARS		42	77	16	2	0	2	(1 1)	24	12	5	7	6	0	25	2	0	0	1	0	1.00	3	.208	.282	.312

Matt Roney

Pitches: R Bats: R Pos: RP-34; SP-11 **Ht: 6'3" Wt: 230 Born: 1/10/80 Age: 24**

Year Team	Lg	G	GS	CG	GF	IP	BFP	H	R	ER	HR	SH	SF	HB	TBB	IBB	SO	WP	Bk	W	L	Pct	ShO	Sv-Op	Hld	ERC	ERA
1998 Rockies	R	9	9	1	0	40.1	187	50	31	26	1	1	0	3	11	0	49	4	2	1	1	.500	1	0- -	-	4.49	5.80
2000 Portland	A-	15	15	1	0	80.1	360	75	35	28	6	1	1	7	44	0	85	8	2	7	5	.583	0	0- -	-	4.42	3.14
2001 Asheville	A	23	23	1	0	121.0	540	131	74	67	16	2	5	13	43	0	115	6	1	8	10	.444	0	0- -	-	5.02	4.98
2002 Asheville	A	14	14	1	0	82.2	349	82	39	32	7	3	2	5	25	1	88	1	1	4	6	.400	1	0- -	-	3.80	3.48
2002 Carolina	AA	13	13	0	0	70.2	312	73	52	48	6	1	1	2	33	0	61	2	1	3	6	.333	0	0- -	-	4.54	6.11
2003 Detroit	AL	45	11	0	12	100.2	450	102	67	61	17	4	4	4	48	4	47	2	2	1	9	.100	0	0-2	6	5.02	5.45

Rodrigo Rosario

Pitches: R Bats: R Pos: SP-2 **Ht: 6'2" Wt: 165 Born: 12/14/77 Age: 26**

Year Team	Lg	G	GS	CG	GF	IP	BFP	H	R	ER	HR	SH	SF	HB	TBB	IBB	SO	WP	Bk	W	L	Pct	ShO	Sv-Op	Hld	ERC	ERA
1998 Astros	R	13	12	0	1	67.2	286	63	36	31	6	1	2	4	30	0	65	4	1	2	2	.500	0	0- -	-	4.13	4.12
1998 Auburn	A-	2	0	0	2	2.0	9	0	0	0	0	0	0	0	3	0	2	1	0	0	0	—	0	0- -	-	1.96	0.00
1999 Martinsville	R+	14	14	0	0	78.2	345	78	46	41	9	7	3	11	32	0	72	8	7	5	5	.500	0	0- -	-	4.78	4.69
2000 Auburn	A-	14	14	0	0	75.2	330	67	36	29	3	2	1	6	32	1	67	2	0	5	6	.455	0	0- -	-	3.33	3.45
2001 Lexington	A	30	21	1	5	147.0	584	105	46	35	8	7	2	10	36	1	131	3	0	13	4	.765	0	2- -	-	2.00	2.14
2002 Round Rock	AA	26	23	0	0	130.1	561	106	56	45	5	2	4	19	59	1	94	2	0	11	6	.647	0	0- -	-	3.37	3.11
2003 New Orleans	AAA	15	15	1	0	87.0	364	71	40	39	7	4	1	7	32	0	68	3	0	5	7	.417	1	0- -	-	3.14	4.03
2003 Houston	NL	2	2	0	0	8.0	33	5	2	1	0	0	0	1	3	1	6	1	0	1	0	1.000	0	0-0	0	1.67	1.13

Cody Ross

Bats: R Throws: L Pos: RF-6 **Ht: 5'11" Wt: 180 Born: 12/23/80 Age: 23**

Year Team	Lg	G	AB	H	2B	3B	HR	(Hm Rd)	TB	R	RBI	RC	TBB	IBB	SO	HBP	SH	SF	SB	CS	SB%	GDP	Avg	OBP	Slg
1999 Tigers	R	42	142	31	8	3	4	(Hm Rd)	57	19	18	18	16	0	28	2	2	1	3	1	.75	3	.218	.304	.401
2000 W Michigan	A	122	434	116	17	9	7	(- -)	172	71	68	63	55	0	83	9	2	1	11	3	.79	14	.267	.356	.396
2001 Lakeland	A+	127	482	133	34	5	15	(- -)	222	84	80	78	44	0	96	5	6	9	28	5	.85	9	.276	.337	.461
2002 Erie	AA	105	400	112	28	3	19	(- -)	203	73	72	71	44	1	86	3	2	5	16	2	.89	11	.280	.352	.508
2003 Toledo	AAA	124	470	135	35	6	20	(- -)	242	74	61	78	32	0	86	5	4	9	15	6	.71	12	.287	.333	.515
2003 Detroit	AL	6	19	4	1	0	1	(1 0)	8	5	4	5	1	0	3	1	1	0	0	0	—	2	.211	.286	.421

Dave Ross

Bats: R Throws: R Pos: C-38; PH-3 **Ht: 6'2" Wt: 205 Born: 3/19/77 Age: 27**

Year Team	Lg	G	AB	H	2B	3B	HR	(Hm Rd)	TB	R	RBI	RC	TBB	IBB	SO	HBP	SH	SF	SB	CS	SB%	GDP	Avg	OBP	Slg
1998 Yakima	A-	59	159	59	14	1	6	(- -)	93	31	25	38	34	0	49	1	2	2	2	2	.50	5	.309	.412	.487
1999 Vero Beach	A+	114	375	85	19	1	7	(- -)	127	47	39	38	46	1	111	7	1	6	5	10	.33	10	.227	.318	.339
2000 Sn Brnardino	A+	51	191	49	11	1	7	(- -)	83	27	21	26	17	1	43	1	3	1	3	2	.60	3	.257	.319	.435
2000 San Antonio	AA	24	67	14	2	1	3	(- -)	27	11	12	9	9	1	17	1	1	1	1	0	1.00	3	.209	.308	.403
2001 Jacksonville	AA	74	146	65	13	1	11	(- -)	113	35	45	55	34	0	72	10	0	3	1	1	.50	5	.445	.565	.774

Year Team	Lg	G	AB	H	2B	3B	HR	(Hm	Rd)	TB	R	RBI	RC	TBB	IBB	SO	HBP	SH	SF	SB	CS	SB%	GDP	Avg	OBP	Slg
								BATTING												**BASERUNNING**				**AVERAGES**		
2002 Las Vegas	AAA	92	293	87	16	2	15	(-	-)	152	48	68	58	35	0	86	9	5	4	1	1	.50	4	.297	.384	.519
2003 Las Vegas	AAA	24	86	19	4	0	5	(-	-)	38	12	16	12	11	0	27	1	1	1	0	2	.00	0	.221	.313	.442
2002 Los Angeles	NL	8	10	2	1	0	1	(0	1)	6	2	2	2	2	0	4	1	0	0	0	0	-	0	.200	.385	.600
2003 Los Angeles	NL	40	124	32	7	0	10	(5	5)	69	19	18	19	13	0	42	2	0	1	0	0	-	4	.258	.336	.556
2 ML YEARS		48	134	34	8	0	11	(5	6)	75	21	20	21	15	0	46	3	0	1	0	0	-	4	.254	.340	.560

Aaron Rowand

Bats: R Throws: R Pos: CF-65; LF-24; RF-12; PH-5; PR-4   **Ht: 6'1" Wt: 200 Born: 8/29/77 Age: 26**

Year Team	Lg	G	AB	H	2B	3B	HR	(Hm	Rd)	TB	R	RBI	RC	TBB	IBB	SO	HBP	SH	SF	SB	CS	SB%	GDP	Avg	OBP	Slg
								BATTING												**BASERUNNING**				**AVERAGES**		
2003 Charlotte*	AAA	32	120	29	9	0	3	(-	-)	47	15	13	15	11	0	12	2	6	0	0	0	-	3	.242	.316	.392
2001 Chicago	AL	63	123	36	5	0	4	(5	2)	53	21	20	22	15	0	28	4	5	1	5	1	.83	2	.293	.385	.431
2002 Chicago	AL	126	302	78	16	2	7	(5	2)	119	41	29	37	12	1	54	6	9	2	0	1	.00	8	.258	.298	.394
2003 Chicago	AL	93	157	45	8	0	6	(5	1)	71	22	24	28	7	0	21	3	2	1	0	0	-	1	.287	.327	.452
3 ML YEARS		282	582	159	29	2	17	(13	4)	243	84	73	87	34	1	103	13	16	4	5	2	.71	11	.273	.325	.418

Wilkin Ruan

Bats: R Throws: R Pos: CF-20; PR-2; PH-1   **Ht: 6'0" Wt: 170 Born: 11/18/79 Age: 24**

Year Team	Lg	G	AB	H	2B	3B	HR	(Hm	Rd)	TB	R	RBI	RC	TBB	IBB	SO	HBP	SH	SF	SB	CS	SB%	GDP	Avg	OBP	Slg
								BATTING												**BASERUNNING**				**AVERAGES**		
1998 Jupiter	A+	5	18	3	0	0	0	(-	-)	3	2	0	1	1	0	3	0	0	0	2	0	1.00	0	.167	.211	.167
1998 Expos	R	54	201	48	9	3	1	(-	-)	66	22	19	15	5	0	43	2	3	2	13	13	.50	1	.239	.262	.328
1999 Cape Fear	A	112	397	89	16	4	1	(-	-)	116	43	47	28	18	0	79	6	7	0	29	17	.63	5	.224	.268	.292
2000 Cape Fear	A	134	574	165	29	10	0	(-	-)	214	95	51	78	24	1	75	8	2	3	64	10	.86	4	.287	.323	.373
2001 Jupiter	A+	72	293	83	8	2	2	(-	-)	101	41	26	31	10	2	35	3	7	1	25	14	.64	3	.283	.313	.345
2001 Harrisburg	AA	30	117	29	7	0	0	(-	-)	36	14	6	11	3	0	18	2	1	0	6	0	1.00	1	.248	.279	.308
2002 Jacksonville	AA	78	324	82	16	6	3	(-	-)	119	44	34	40	17	0	33	8	5	1	23	3	.88	4	.253	.306	.367
2002 Las Vegas	AAA	40	153	50	7	3	0	(-	-)	63	18	29	21	2	0	17	0	2	0	12	0	1.00	7	.327	.335	.412
2003 Las Vegas	AAA	108	403	124	6	3	0	(-	-)	136	58	40	50	10	0	38	7	7	2	41	7	.85	6	.308	.334	.337
2002 Los Angeles	NL	12	11	3	1	0	0	(0	0)	4	2	3	2	0	0	2	0	0	0	0	0	-	0	.273	.273	.364
2003 Los Angeles	NL	21	41	9	2	1	0	(0	0)	13	2	2	3	0	0	7	0	0	0	1	0	1.00	0	.220	.220	.317
2 ML YEARS		33	52	12	3	1	0	(0	0)	17	4	5	5	0	0	9	0	0	0	1	0	1.00	0	.231	.231	.327

Kirk Rueter

Pitches: L Bats: L Pos: SP-27   **Ht: 6'3" Wt: 212 Born: 12/1/70 Age: 33**

Year Team	Lg	G	GS	CG	GF	IP	BFP	H	R	ER	HR	SH	SF	HB	TBB	IBB	SO	WP	Bk	W	L	Pct	ShO	Sv-Op	Hld	ERC	ERA
						HOW MUCH HE PITCHED						**WHAT HE GAVE UP**										**THE RESULTS**					
2003 Fresno*	AAA	1	1	0	0	4.2	16	1	0	0	0	0	0	0	2	0	6	0	0	0	0	-	0	0- -	-	0.61	0.00
1993 Montreal	NL	14	14	1	0	85.2	341	85	33	26	5	1	0	0	18	1	31	0	0	8	0	1.000	0	0-0	0	3.14	2.73
1994 Montreal	NL	20	20	0	0	92.1	397	106	60	53	11	6	6	2	23	1	50	2	0	7	3	.700	0	0-0	0	4.54	5.17
1995 Montreal	NL	9	9	1	0	47.1	184	38	17	17	3	4	1	2	9	0	28	0	0	5	3	.625	1	0-0	0	2.19	3.23
1996 Mon-SF	NL	20	19	0	0	102.0	430	109	50	45	12	4	1	2	27	0	46	2	0	6	8	.429	0	0-0	0	4.18	3.97
1997 San Francisco	NL	32	32	0	0	190.2	802	194	83	73	17	10	6	1	51	8	115	3	0	13	6	.684	0	0-0	0	3.54	3.45
1998 San Francisco	NL	33	33	1	0	187.2	806	193	100	91	27	5	8	7	57	3	102	6	0	16	9	.640	0	0-0	0	4.27	4.36
1999 San Francisco	NL	33	33	1	0	184.2	804	219	118	111	28	6	4	2	55	2	94	2	0	15	10	.600	0	0-0	0	5.19	5.41
2000 San Francisco	NL	32	31	0	0	184.0	799	205	92	81	23	**19**	9	2	62	5	71	1	0	11	9	.550	0	0-0	0	4.68	3.96
2001 San Francisco	NL	34	34	0	0	195.1	840	213	105	96	25	11	6	4	66	4	83	1	0	14	12	.538	0	0-0	0	4.65	4.42
2002 San Francisco	NL	33	33	0	0	203.2	846	204	83	73	22	6	6	1	54	7	76	3	0	14	8	.636	0	0-0	0	3.61	3.23
2003 San Francisco	NL	27	27	0	0	147.0	631	170	77	74	14	9	2	1	47	2	41	0	0	10	5	.667	0	0-0	0	4.72	4.53
1996 Montreal	NL	16	16	0	0	78.2	338	91	44	40	12	4	1	2	22	0	30	0	0	5	6	.455	0	0-0	0	5.06	4.58
1996 San Francisco	NL	4	3	0	0	23.1	92	18	6	5	0	0	0	0	5	0	16	2	0	1	2	.333	0	0-0	0	1.66	1.93
11 ML YEARS		287	285	4	0	1620.1	6880	1736	818	740	187	81	48	23	469	33	737	20	0	119	73	.620	1	0-0	0	4.21	4.11

Ryan Rupe

Pitches: R Bats: R Pos: RP-3; SP-1   **Ht: 6'5" Wt: 248 Born: 3/31/75 Age: 29**

Year Team	Lg	G	GS	CG	GF	IP	BFP	H	R	ER	HR	SH	SF	HB	TBB	IBB	SO	WP	Bk	W	L	Pct	ShO	Sv-Op	Hld	ERC	ERA
						HOW MUCH HE PITCHED						**WHAT HE GAVE UP**										**THE RESULTS**					
2003 Pawtucket*	AAA	20	18	0	0	102.0	421	93	50	37	11	4	4	4	19	1	77	3	0	8	4	.667	0	0- -	-	2.92	3.26
1999 Tampa Bay	AL	24	24	0	0	142.1	614	136	81	72	17	1	7	12	57	2	97	4	1	8	9	.471	0	0-0	0	4.32	4.55
2000 Tampa Bay	AL	18	18	0	0	91.0	425	121	75	70	19	2	6	9	31	3	61	4	0	5	6	.455	0	0-0	0	7.02	6.92
2001 Tampa Bay	AL	28	26	0	0	143.1	635	161	111	105	30	3	5	11	48	0	123	7	1	5	12	.294	0	0-1	0	5.67	6.59
2002 Tampa Bay	AL	15	15	2	0	90.0	382	83	60	56	11	2	4	10	25	0	67	6	0	5	10	.333	0	0-0	0	3.74	5.60
2003 Boston	AL	4	1	0	0	10.0	45	13	9	7	4	1	0	0	1	0	7	0	0	1	1	.500	0	0-1	0	6.40	6.30
5 ML YEARS		89	84	2	0	476.2	2101	514	336	310	81	9	22	42	162	5	355	21	2	24	38	.387	0	0-2	0	5.14	5.85

Glendon Rusch

Pitches: L Bats: L Pos: SP-19; RP-13   **Ht: 6'1" Wt: 200 Born: 11/7/74 Age: 29**

Year Team	Lg	G	GS	CG	GF	IP	BFP	H	R	ER	HR	SH	SF	HB	TBB	IBB	SO	WP	Bk	W	L	Pct	ShO	Sv-Op	Hld	ERC	ERA
						HOW MUCH HE PITCHED						**WHAT HE GAVE UP**										**THE RESULTS**					
2003 Indianapolis*	AAA	4	3	1	0	21.0	84	17	9	9	4	0	2	0	4	0	20	0	0	1	1	.500	0	0- -	-	3.21	3.86
1997 Kansas City	AL	30	27	1	0	170.1	758	206	111	104	28	8	7	7	52	0	116	0	1	6	9	.400	0	0-0	0	5.56	5.50
1998 Kansas City	AL	29	24	1	2	154.2	686	191	104	101	22	1	2	4	50	0	94	1	0	6	15	.286	1	1-1	0	5.62	5.88
1999 KC-NYM		4	0	0	2	5.0	26	8	7	7	1	0	0	1	3	0	4	0	0	1	0	1.000	0	0-0	0	10.75	12.60
2000 New York	NL	31	30	2	0	190.2	802	196	91	85	18	10	7	6	44	2	157	2	0	11	11	.500	0	0-0	0	3.64	4.01
2001 New York	NL	33	33	1	0	179.0	785	216	101	92	23	11	5	7	43	2	156	3	2	8	12	.400	0	0-0	0	4.97	4.63
2002 Milwaukee	NL	34	34	4	0	210.2	913	227	118	110	30	14	5	5	76	1	140	6	0	10	**16**	.385	1	0-0	0	4.80	4.70
2003 Milwaukee	NL	32	19	1	1	123.1	573	171	93	88	11	5	2	4	45	3	93	3	0	1	12	.077	0	1-1	7	6.27	6.42

Year Team	Lg	G	GS	CG	GF	IP	BFP	H	R	ER	HR	SH	SF	HB	TBB	IBB	SO	WP	Bk	W	L	Pct	ShO	Sv-Op	Hld	ERC	ERA
1999 Kansas City	AL	3	0	0	1	4.0	23	7	7	7	1	0	0	1	3	0	4	0	0	0	1	.000	0	0-0	0	12.89	15.75
1999 New York	NL	1	0	0	1	1.0	3	1	0	0	0	0	0	0	0	0	0	0	0	0	0	-	0	0-0	0	2.79	0.00
7 ML YEARS		193	167	10	5	1033.2	4543	1215	625	587	133	49	28	34	313	8	760	15	3	42	76	.356	2	2-2	7	5.04	5.11

B.J. Ryan

Pitches: L **Bats:** L **Pos:** RP-76   **Ht:** 6'6" **Wt:** 230 **Born:** 12/28/75 **Age:** 28

Year Team	Lg	G	GS	CG	GF	IP	BFP	H	R	ER	HR	SH	SF	HB	TBB	IBB	SO	WP	Bk	W	L	Pct	ShO	Sv-Op	Hld	ERC	ERA
1999 Cin-Bal		14	0	0	3	20.1	82	13	7	7	0	0	1	0	13	1	29	1	0	1	0	1.000	0	0-0	0	2.42	3.10
2000 Baltimore	AL	42	0	0	9	42.2	193	36	29	28	7	1	1	0	31	1	41	2	1	2	3	.400	0	0-3	7	4.87	5.91
2001 Baltimore	AL	61	0	0	9	53.0	237	47	31	25	6	1	2	2	30	4	54	0	0	2	4	.333	0	2-4	14	4.13	4.25
2002 Baltimore	AL	67	0	0	13	57.2	252	51	31	30	7	3	0	4	33	4	56	4	0	2	1	.667	0	1-2	12	4.48	4.68
2003 Baltimore	AL	76	0	0	17	50.1	219	42	19	19	1	1	3	3	27	0	63	2	0	4	1	.800	0	0-2	19	3.33	3.40
1999 Cincinnati	NL	1	0	0	0	2.0	9	4	1	1	0	0	0	0	1	0	1	0	0	0	0	-	0	0-0	0	12.01	4.50
1999 Baltimore	AL	13	0	0	3	18.1	73	9	6	6	0	0	1	0	12	1	28	1	0	1	0	1.000	0	0-0	0	1.73	2.95
5 ML YEARS		260	0	0	51	224.0	983	189	117	109	21	6	7	9	134	10	243	9	1	11	9	.550	0	3-11	52	4.01	4.38

Mike Ryan

Bats: L **Throws:** R **Pos:** RF-12; PH-10; LF-4; DH-4   **Ht:** 6'0" **Wt:** 185 **Born:** 7/6/77 **Age:** 26

Year Team	Lg	G	AB	H	2B	3B	HR	(Hm	Rd)	TB	R	RBI	RC	TBB	IBB	SO	HBP	SH	SF	SB	CS	SB%	GDP	Avg	OBP	Slg
1996 Twins	R	43	157	31	8	2	0	(-	-)	43	12	13	11	13	1	20	1	1	2	3	0	1.00	3	.197	.260	.274
1997 Elizabethton	R+	62	220	66	10	4	3	(-	-)	85	44	29	35	38	3	39	3	1	4	2	2	.50	8	.300	.404	.386
1998 Fort Wayne	A	113	412	131	24	6	9	(-	-)	194	69	71	73	44	2	92	2	3	5	7	3	.70	8	.318	.382	.471
1999 Fort Myers	A+	131	507	139	26	5	8	(-	-)	199	85	71	72	63	2	60	5	4	6	3	4	.43	11	.274	.356	.393
2000 New Britain	AA	122	481	133	23	8	11	(-	-)	205	64	69	64	34	1	79	2	3	6	4	3	.57	13	.277	.323	.426
2000 Salt Lake	AAA	3	9	2	0	0	0	(-	-)	2	1	2	1	3	0	2	0	0	0	0	0	-	1	.222	.417	.222
2001 Edmonton	AAA	135	527	152	36	7	18	(-	-)	256	89	73	83	52	1	121	2	1	3	1	6	.14	17	.288	.353	.486
2002 Edmonton	AAA	131	540	141	36	6	31	(-	-)	282	92	101	90	55	6	124	2	0	3	4	5	.44	9	.261	.330	.522
2003 Rochester	AAA	115	408	92	20	4	15	(-	-)	165	56	60	48	38	5	89	1	1	6	6	1	.86	8	.225	.289	.404
2002 Minnesota	AL	7	11	1	0	0	0	(0	0)	1	3	0	0	0	0	2	0	0	0	0	0	-	0	.091	.091	.091
2003 Minnesota	AL	27	61	24	7	0	5	(4	1)	46	13	13	16	6	0	12	0	0	1	2	1	.67	4	.393	.441	.754
2 ML YEARS		34	72	25	7	0	5	(4	1)	47	16	13	16	6	0	14	0	0	1	2	1	.67	4	.347	.392	.653

Kirk Saarloos

Pitches: R **Bats:** R **Pos:** RP-32; SP-4   **Ht:** 6'0" **Wt:** 185 **Born:** 5/23/79 **Age:** 25

Year Team	Lg	G	GS	CG	GF	IP	BFP	H	R	ER	HR	SH	SF	HB	TBB	IBB	SO	WP	Bk	W	L	Pct	ShO	Sv-Op	Hld	ERC	ERA
2001 Lexington	A	22	0	0	19	30.2	119	18	5	4	1	2	0	1	7	0	40	2	0	1	1	.500	0	11- -	-	1.30	1.17
2002 Round Rock	AA	13	13	1	0	83.1	315	48	17	13	1	3	2	4	21	0	82	1	0	10	1	.909	1	0- -	-	1.32	1.40
2002 New Orleans	AAA	4	2	0	2	16.0	65	12	4	4	1	1	0	5	2	0	19	0	0	2	0	1.000	0	0- -	-	2.69	2.25
2003 New Orleans	AAA	13	7	2	1	61.1	239	54	22	21	4	2	0	3	11	1	34	0	0	5	0	1.000	1	0- -	-	2.67	3.08
2002 Houston	NL	17	17	1	0	85.1	372	100	59	57	12	5	2	6	27	5	54	1	0	6	7	.462	1	0-0	0	5.35	6.01
2003 Houston	NL	36	4	0	11	49.1	218	55	31	27	4	1	1	3	17	3	43	0	0	2	1	.667	0	0-0	4	4.51	4.93
2 ML YEARS		53	21	1	11	134.2	590	155	90	84	16	6	3	9	44	8	97	1	0	8	8	.500	1	0-0	4	5.03	5.61

C.C. Sabathia

Pitches: L **Bats:** L **Pos:** SP-30   **Ht:** 6'7" **Wt:** 270 **Born:** 7/21/80 **Age:** 23

Year Team	Lg	G	GS	CG	GF	IP	BFP	H	R	ER	HR	SH	SF	HB	TBB	IBB	SO	WP	Bk	W	L	Pct	ShO	Sv-Op	Hld	ERC	ERA
2001 Cleveland	AL	33	33	0	0	180.1	763	149	93	88	19	3	5	7	95	1	171	7	3	17	5	.773	0	0-0	0	3.86	4.39
2002 Cleveland	AL	33	33	2	0	210.0	891	198	109	102	17	5	10	1	88	2	149	6	3	13	11	.542	0	0-0	0	3.74	4.37
2003 Cleveland	AL	30	30	2	0	197.2	832	190	85	79	19	10	4	6	66	3	141	4	2	13	9	.591	1	0-0	0	3.70	3.60
3 ML YEARS		96	96	4	0	588.0	2486	537	287	269	55	18	19	14	249	6	461	17	8	43	25	.632	1	0-0	0	3.77	4.12

Carl Sadler

Pitches: L **Bats:** L **Pos:** RP-18   **Ht:** 6'2" **Wt:** 180 **Born:** 10/11/76 **Age:** 27

Year Team	Lg	G	GS	CG	GF	IP	BFP	H	R	ER	HR	SH	SF	HB	TBB	IBB	SO	WP	Bk	W	L	Pct	ShO	Sv-Op	Hld	ERC	ERA
1996 Expos	R	17	3	0	6	37.0	170	41	24	16	2	2	0	2	12	0	24	3	3	2	2	.500	0	1- -	-	4.05	3.89
1997 Expos	R	9	3	0	0	20.2	91	26	11	10	0	0	1	2	5	0	14	2	0	0	2	.000	0	0- -	-	4.65	4.35
1997 Vermont	A-	7	6	0	0	36.1	167	33	20	17	2	1	2	2	23	0	27	4	1	2	2	.500	0	0- -	-	4.24	4.21
1999 Burlington	R+	5	5	0	0	23.0	93	18	10	8	0	1	0	0	10	0	22	5	0	1	0	1.000	0	0- -	-	2.47	3.13
1999 Mahning VI	A-	1	1	0	0	2.0	17	8	7	7	0	0	0	0	3	0	3	1	0	1	0	1.000	0	0- -	-	30.35	31.50
2000 Mahning VI	A-	5	0	0	1	6.0	25	5	2	2	0	1	0	0	3	0	3	0	0	0	0	-	0	0- -	-	2.93	3.00
2000 Columbus	A	10	0	0	3	16.1	73	20	13	12	0	0	0	0	7	0	21	5	0	1	3	.250	0	0- -	-	4.79	6.61
2001 Kinston	A+	27	2	0	10	62.1	258	51	19	13	2	0	0	3	18	1	78	1	0	6	0	1.000	0	2- -	-	2.38	1.88
2001 Akron	AA	11	0	0	6	18.0	85	23	16	13	1	0	0	0	9	0	14	0	1	2	3	.400	0	0- -	-	5.68	6.50
2002 Akron	AA	21	0	0	7	46.1	185	39	12	12	0	0	1	2	12	1	37	2	0	4	1	.800	0	2- -	-	2.27	2.33
2002 Buffalo	AAA	12	0	0	8	18.2	81	19	7	4	1	2	0	0	8	1	13	0	0	1	1	.500	0	1- -	-	3.87	1.93
2003 Buffalo	AAA	31	0	0	14	53.0	247	62	41	37	4	1	4	3	31	3	32	3	0	1	2	.667	0	3- -	-	5.80	6.28
2002 Cleveland	AL	24	0	0	5	20.1	82	15	10	10	2	0	0	0	11	0	23	3	0	1	2	.333	0	0-1	5	3.34	4.43
2003 Cleveland	AL	18	0	0	5	9.2	45	11	2	2	0	1	1	2	5	0	10	1	0	0	0	-	0	0-0	3	5.48	1.86
2 ML YEARS		42	0	0	10	30.0	127	26	12	12	2	1	1	2	16	0	33	4	0	1	2	.333	0	0-1	8	4.01	3.60

Donnie Sadler

Bats: R **Throws:** R **Pos:** 3B-23; CF-22; SS-19; LF-19; PR-14; RF-7; PH-3; 2B-1   **Ht:** 5'6" **Wt:** 175 **Born:** 6/17/75 **Age:** 29

Year Team	Lg	G	AB	H	2B	3B	HR	(Hm	Rd)	TB	R	RBI	RC	TBB	IBB	SO	HBP	SH	SF	SB	CS	SB%	GDP	Avg	OBP	Slg
2003 Oklahoma*	AAA	19	66	20	4	1	1	(-	-)	29	14	6	13	10	0	9	2	2	1	6	1	.86	1	.303	.405	.439
1998 Boston	AL	58	124	28	4	4	3	(0	3)	49	21	15	15	6	0	28	3	5	1	4	0	1.00	1	.226	.276	.395
1999 Boston	AL	49	107	30	5	1	0	(0	0)	37	18	4	12	5	0	20	0	3	0	2	1	.67	1	.280	.313	.346
2000 Boston	AL	49	99	22	5	0	1	(0	1)	30	14	10	8	5	0	18	1	5	2	3	1	.75	1	.222	.262	.303
2001 Cin-KC		93	185	30	6	0	1	(0	1)	39	28	5	8	18	0	37	2	5	1	7	4	.64	3	.162	.243	.211
2002 KC-Tex	AL	73	98	16	2	1	0	(0	0)	20	16	7	3	7	0	19	2	1	1	5	3	.63	1	.163	.231	.204
2003 Texas	AL	77	131	26	5	2	1	(0	1)	38	27	5	10	13	0	34	2	2	2	4	3	.57	1	.198	.277	.290
2001 Cincinnati	NL	39	84	17	3	0	1	(0	1)	23	9	3	5	9	0	20	0	2	0	3	3	.50	3	.202	.280	.274
2001 Kansas City	AL	54	101	13	3	0	0	(0	0)	16	19	2	3	9	0	17	2	3	1	4	1	.80	0	.129	.212	.158
2002 Kansas City	AL	35	68	13	1	1	0	(0	0)	16	10	5	3	4	0	12	0	0	1	3	1	.75	0	.191	.233	.235
2002 Texas	AL	38	30	3	1	0	0	(0	0)	4	6	2	0	3	0	7	2	1	0	2	2	.50	1	.100	.229	.133
6 ML YEARS		399	744	152	27	8	6	(0	6)	213	124	46	56	54	0	156	10	21	7	25	12	.68	8	.204	.265	.286

Tim Salmon

Bats: R **Throws:** R **Pos:** RF-78; DH-68; PH-3   **Ht:** 6'3" **Wt:** 225 **Born:** 8/24/68 **Age:** 35

Year Team	Lg	G	AB	H	2B	3B	HR	(Hm	Rd)	TB	R	RBI	RC	TBB	IBB	SO	HBP	SH	SF	SB	CS	SB%	GDP	Avg	OBP	Slg
1992 Anaheim	AL	23	79	14	1	0	2	(1	1)	21	8	6	6	11	1	23	1	0	1	1	1	.50	1	.177	.283	.266
1993 Anaheim	AL	142	515	146	35	1	31	(23	8)	276	93	95	104	82	5	135	5	0	8	5	6	.45	6	.283	.382	.536
1994 Anaheim	AL	100	373	107	18	2	23	(12	11)	198	67	70	75	54	2	102	5	0	3	1	3	.25	3	.287	.382	.531
1995 Anaheim	AL	143	537	177	34	3	34	(15	19)	319	111	105	130	91	2	111	6	0	4	5	5	.50	9	.330	.429	.594
1996 Anaheim	AL	156	581	166	27	4	30	(18	12)	291	90	98	113	93	7	125	4	0	3	4	2	.67	8	.286	.386	.501
1997 Anaheim	AL	157	582	172	28	1	33	(17	16)	301	95	129	117	95	5	142	7	0	11	9	12	.43	7	.296	.394	.517
1998 Anaheim	AL	136	463	139	28	1	26	(13	13)	247	84	88	103	90	5	100	3	0	10	1	0	1.00	4	.300	.410	.533
1999 Anaheim	AL	98	353	94	24	2	17	(7	10)	173	60	69	66	63	2	82	0	0	6	4	1	.80	7	.266	.372	.490
2000 Anaheim	AL	158	568	165	36	2	34	(17	17)	307	108	97	120	104	5	139	6	0	2	2	0	.00	14	.290	.404	.540
2001 Anaheim	AL	137	475	108	21	1	17	(11	6)	182	63	49	72	96	4	121	8	0	2	9	3	.75	11	.227	.365	.383
2002 Anaheim	AL	138	483	138	37	1	22	(10	12)	243	84	88	100	71	3	102	7	0	7	6	3	.67	6	.286	.380	.503
2003 Anaheim	AL	148	528	145	35	4	19	(10	9)	245	78	72	92	77	3	93	10	0	6	3	1	.75	12	.275	.374	.464
12 ML YEARS		1536	5537	1571	324	22	288	(154	134)	2803	941	966	1098	927	44	1275	62	0	63	47	40	.54	88	.284	.389	.506

Alex Sanchez

Bats: L **Throws:** L **Pos:** CF-135; PH-12; PR-2   **Ht:** 5'10" **Wt:** 159 **Born:** 8/26/76 **Age:** 27

Year Team	Lg	G	AB	H	2B	3B	HR	(Hm	Rd)	TB	R	RBI	RC	TBB	IBB	SO	HBP	SH	SF	SB	CS	SB%	GDP	Avg	OBP	Slg
2001 Milwaukee	NL	30	68	14	3	2	0	(0	0)	21	7	4	6	5	0	13	0	0	0	6	2	.75	0	.206	.260	.309
2002 Milwaukee	NL	112	394	114	10	7	1	(0	1)	141	55	33	53	31	0	62	2	6	2	37	14	.73	4	.289	.343	.358
2003 Mil-Det		144	557	160	23	9	1	(0	1)	202	58	32	59	25	0	74	3	9	5	52	24	.68	5	.287	.319	.363
2003 Milwaukee	NL	43	163	46	10	3	0	(0	0)	62	15	10	17	7	0	28	2	2	2	8	6	.57	1	.282	.316	.380
2003 Detroit	AL	101	394	114	13	5	1	(0	1)	140	43	22	42	18	0	46	1	7	3	44	18	.71	4	.289	.320	.355
3 ML YEARS		286	1019	288	36	17	2	(0	2)	364	120	69	118	61	0	149	5	15	7	95	40	.70	9	.283	.324	.357

Duaner Sanchez

Pitches: R **Bats:** R **Pos:** RP-6   **Ht:** 6'0" **Wt:** 190 **Born:** 10/14/79 **Age:** 24

Year Team	Lg	G	GS	CG	GF	IP	BFP	H	R	ER	HR	SH	SF	HB	TBB	IBB	SO	WP	Bk	W	L	Pct	ShO	Sv-Op	Hld	ERC	ERA
1999 High Desert	A+	3	3	0	0	14.1	63	15	13	12	2	0	1	1	9	0	9	0	0	0	0	-	0	0- -		6.23	7.53
1999 Missoula	R+	13	11	0	0	63.1	269	54	34	22	3	1	1	3	23	0	51	8	0	5	3	.625	0	0- -		2.91	3.13
2000 South Bend	A	28	28	4	0	165.1	700	152	80	67	6	5	5	11	54	1	121	6	2	8	9	.471	0	0- -		3.16	3.65
2001 El Paso	AA	13	13	0	0	70.1	323	92	56	53	5	1	7	6	25	1	41	5	0	3	7	.300	0	0- -		5.86	6.78
2001 Lancaster	A+	10	10	1	0	59.0	270	65	44	30	7	4	4	7	18	0	49	3	4	2	4	.333	0	0- -		4.71	4.58
2002 El Paso	AA	31	0	0	29	35.2	155	31	16	12	1	0	1	2	13	1	37	3	0	4	3	.571	0	13- -		2.80	3.03
2002 Tucson	AAA	4	0	0	4	5.1	24	6	4	4	1	0	0	0	1	0	9	0	0	1	1	.500	0	1- -		4.22	6.75
2002 Nashville	AAA	20	0	0	17	22.2	100	23	12	12	2	2	2	1	11	2	20	2	0	0	3	.000	0	6- -		4.47	4.76
2003 Nashville	AAA	41	1	0	11	61.0	269	63	28	25	3	1	2	1	27	5	34	1	1	4	4	.500	0	1- -		3.96	3.69
2002 Ari-Pit	NL	9	0	0	5	6.0	31	6	6	6	2	0	0	0	7	0	6	0	0	0	0	-	0	0-1		9.19	9.00
2003 Pittsburgh	NL	6	0	0	2	6.0	34	15	11	11	2	0	1	2	1	0	3	0	0	1	0	1.000	0	0-0	0	17.96	16.50
2002 Arizona	NL	6	0	0	3	3.2	19	3	2	2	1	0	0	0	5	0	4	0	0	0	0	-	0	0-1		8.32	4.91
2002 Pittsburgh	NL	3	0	0	2	2.1	12	3	4	4	1	0	0	0	2	0	2	0	0	0	0	-	0	0-0	0	10.55	15.43
2 ML YEARS		15	0	0	7	12.0	65	21	17	17	4	0	1	2	8	0	9	0	0	1	0	1.000	0	0-1	1	13.33	12.75

Felix Sanchez

Pitches: L **Bats:** R **Pos:** RP-3   **Ht:** 6'3" **Wt:** 180 **Born:** 8/3/81 **Age:** 22

Year Team	Lg	G	GS	CG	GF	IP	BFP	H	R	ER	HR	SH	SF	HB	TBB	IBB	SO	WP	Bk	W	L	Pct	ShO	Sv-Op	Hld	ERC	ERA
2001 Boise	A-	3	3	0	0	17.1	71	11	4	3	0	0	0	0	10	0	16	5	1	0	0	1.000	0	0- -		2.19	1.56
2002 Lansing	A	26	21	0	4	119.1	514	130	67	55	7	7	3	6	44	0	101	5	1	6	6	.500	0	2- -		4.47	4.15
2003 Cubs	R	1	1	0	0	2.0	8	2	0	0	0	0	0	0	0	0	3	0	0	0	0	-	0	0- -		1.95	0.00
2003 W Tennessee	AA	30	8	0	4	64.0	284	57	30	23	3	3	3	4	31	0	55	5	2	2	2	.500	0	0-0		3.57	3.23
2003 Chicago	NL	3	0	0	0	1.2	9	2	2	1	0	0	0	0	3	0	2	0	0	0	0	-	0	0-0	0	18.51	10.80

Freddy Sanchez

Bats: R **Throws:** R **Pos:** 3B-7; SS-6; PH-5; PR-4; 2B-3   **Ht:** 5'11" **Wt:** 185 **Born:** 12/21/77 **Age:** 26

Year Team	Lg	G	AB	H	2B	3B	HR	(Hm	Rd)	TB	R	RBI	RC	TBB	IBB	SO	HBP	SH	SF	SB	CS	SB%	GDP	Avg	OBP	Slg
2000 Lowell	A-	34	132	38	13	2	1	(-	-)	58	24	14	19	9	0	16	3	2	0	2	4	.33	1	.288	.347	.439
2000 Augusta	A	30	109	33	7	0	0	(-	-)	40	17	15	16	11	0	19	1	4	0	4	0	1.00	1	.303	.372	.367
2001 Sarasota	A+	69	280	95	19	4	1	(-	-)	125	40	24	48	22	1	30	2	3	3	5	3	.63	3	.339	.388	.446
2001 Trenton	AA	44	178	58	20	0	2	(-	-)	84	25	19	29	9	0	21	2	2	1	3	1	.75	6	.326	.363	.472
2002 Trenton	AA	80	311	102	23	1	3	(-	-)	136	60	38	57	37	0	45	5	5	4	19	3	.86	9	.328	.403	.437
2002 Pawtucket	AAA	45	183	55	10	1	4	(-	-)	79	25	28	28	12	0	21	3	5	2	5	3	.63	3	.301	.350	.432
2003 Pawtucket	AAA	58	211	72	17	0	5	(-	-)	104	46	25	44	31	0	36	2	5	0	8	0	1.00	7	.341	.430	.493
2003 Nashville	AAA	1	5	2	1	0	0	(-	-)	3	1	0	1	0	0	1	0	0	0	0	0	-	0	.400	.400	.600
2002 Boston	AL	12	16	3	0	0	0	(0	0)	3	3	2	1	2	0	3	0	0	0	0	0	-	0	.188	.278	.188
2003 Boston	AL	20	34	8	2	0	0	(0	0)	10	6	2	1	0	0	8	0	0	0	0	0	-	0	.235	.235	.294
2 ML YEARS		32	50	11	2	0	0	(0	0)	13	9	4	2	2	0	11	0	0	0	0	0	-	0	.220	.250	.260

Jesus Sanchez

Pitches: L **Bats:** L **Pos:** RP-9   **Ht:** 5'11" **Wt:** 175 **Born:** 10/11/74 **Age:** 29

Year Team	Lg	G	GS	CG	GF	IP	BFP	H	R	ER	HR	SH	SF	HB	TBB	IBB	SO	WP	Bk	W	L	Pct	ShO	Sv-Op	Hld	ERC	ERA
2003 Co Springs*	AAA	46	3	0	12	63.1	269	61	28	28	4	2	1	3	26	1	52	6	0	2	0	1.000	0	2--	-	3.89	3.98
1998 Florida	NL	35	29	0	1	173.0	765	178	98	86	18	12	4	4	91	2	137	8	5	7	9	.438	0	0-1	0	4.91	4.47
1999 Florida	NL	59	10	0	8	76.1	362	84	53	51	16	2	7	4	60	11	62	5	2	5	7	.417	0	0-2	11	7.28	6.01
2000 Florida	NL	32	32	2	0	182.0	805	197	118	108	32	9	12	4	76	4	123	4	0	9	12	.429	2	0-0	0	5.24	5.34
2001 Florida	NL	16	9	0	3	62.2	274	61	33	33	7	2	1	2	31	2	46	0	0	2	4	.333	0	0-0	0	4.49	4.74
2002 Chicago	NL	8	0	0	2	8.1	51	15	12	12	4	0	2	1	10	1	6	3	0	0	0	-	0	0-0	0	17.13	12.96
2003 Colorado	NL	9	0	0	4	8.0	38	11	8	8	1	0	0	0	4	2	2	1	0	0	0	-	0	0-0	1	6.48	9.00
6 ML YEARS		159	80	2	18	510.1	2295	546	322	298	78	25	26	15	272	22	376	21	7	23	32	.418	2	0-3	12	5.51	5.26

Rey Sanchez

Bats: R **Throws:** R **Pos:** SS-88; 2B-12; PH-2; PR-2   **Ht:** 5'9" **Wt:** 175 **Born:** 10/5/67 **Age:** 36

Year Team	Lg	G	AB	H	2B	3B	HR	(Hm	Rd)	TB	R	RBI	RC	TBB	IBB	SO	HBP	SH	SF	SB	CS	SB%	GDP	Avg	OBP	Slg
2003 Binghamton*	AA	3	9	1	0	0	0	(-	-)	1	1	0	0	1	0	1	0	2	0	0	0	-	3	.111	.200	.111
1991 Chicago	NL	13	23	6	0	0	0	(0	0)	6	1	2	3	4	0	3	0	0	0	0	0	-	0	.261	.370	.261
1992 Chicago	NL	74	255	64	14	3	1	(1	0)	87	24	19	23	10	1	17	3	5	2	2	1	.67	5	.251	.285	.341
1993 Chicago	NL	105	344	97	11	2	0	(0	0)	112	35	28	34	15	7	22	3	9	2	1	1	.50	8	.282	.316	.326
1994 Chicago	NL	96	291	83	13	1	0	(0	0)	98	26	24	32	20	4	29	7	4	1	2	5	.29	9	.285	.345	.337
1995 Chicago	NL	114	428	119	22	2	3	(0	3)	154	57	27	44	14	2	48	1	8	2	6	4	.60	9	.278	.301	.360
1996 Chicago	NL	95	289	61	9	0	1	(1	0)	73	28	12	19	22	6	42	3	8	2	7	1	.88	6	.211	.272	.253
1997 ChC-NYY		135	343	94	21	0	2	(1	1)	121	35	27	34	16	2	47	1	9	1	4	6	.40	8	.274	.307	.353
1998 San Francisco	NL	109	316	90	14	2	2	(0	2)	114	44	30	35	16	0	47	4	1	2	0	0	-	11	.285	.325	.361
1999 Kansas City	AL	134	479	141	18	6	2	(1	1)	177	66	56	56	22	2	48	4	10	3	11	5	.69	14	.294	.329	.370
2000 Kansas City	AL	143	509	139	18	2	1	(1	0)	164	68	38	49	28	0	55	4	11	3	7	3	.70	17	.273	.314	.322
2001 KC-Atl		149	544	153	18	6	0	(0	0)	183	56	37	52	15	1	49	2	13	5	11	1	.92	20	.281	.300	.336
2002 Boston	AL	107	357	102	12	3	1	(1	0)	123	46	38	40	17	1	31	2	5	5	2	2	.50	9	.286	.318	.345
2003 NYM-Sea		102	344	86	8	2	0	(0	0)	98	33	23	23	16	3	39	2	4	3	2	1	.67	10	.250	.285	.285
1997 Chicago	NL	97	205	51	9	0	1	(1	0)	63	14	12	16	11	2	26	0	4	0	4	2	.67	7	.249	.287	.307
1997 New York	AL	38	138	43	12	0	1	(0	1)	58	21	15	18	5	0	21	1	5	1	0	4	.00	1	.312	.338	.420
2001 Kansas City	AL	100	390	118	14	5	0	(0	0)	142	46	28	45	11	0	34	2	9	4	9	1	.90	11	.303	.322	.364
2001 Atlanta	NL	49	154	35	4	1	0	(0	0)	41	10	9	7	4	1	15	0	4	1	2	0	1.00	9	.227	.245	.266
2003 New York	NL	56	174	36	3	1	0	(0	0)	41	11	12	6	8	2	18	0	0	1	1	1	.50	7	.207	.240	.236
2003 Seattle	AL	46	170	50	5	1	0	(0	0)	57	22	11	17	8	1	21	2	4	2	1	0	1.00	3	.294	.330	.335
13 ML YEARS		1376	4522	1235	178	29	13	(6	7)	1510	519	361	444	215	29	477	36	87	31	55	30	.65	128	.273	.309	.334

Jared Sandberg

Bats: R **Throws:** R **Pos:** 3B-50; PH-6; 1B-1; SS-1   **Ht:** 6'3" **Wt:** 226 **Born:** 3/2/78 **Age:** 26

Year Team	Lg	G	AB	H	2B	3B	HR	(Hm	Rd)	TB	R	RBI	RC	TBB	IBB	SO	HBP	SH	SF	SB	CS	SB%	GDP	Avg	OBP	Slg
2003 Durham*	AAA	74	272	63	17	1	12	(-	-)	118	40	37	37	30	1	95	2	1	0	1	0	1.00	4	.232	.313	.434
2001 Tampa Bay	AL	39	136	28	7	0	1	(1	0)	38	13	15	9	10	0	45	1	2	0	1	0	1.00	6	.206	.265	.279
2002 Tampa Bay	AL	102	358	82	21	1	18	(10	8)	159	55	54	47	39	3	139	1	1	2	3	2	.60	7	.229	.305	.444
2003 Tampa Bay	AL	55	136	29	10	1	6	(0	6)	59	15	23	18	16	1	52	2	2	0	0	0	-	3	.213	.305	.434
3 ML YEARS		196	630	139	38	2	25	(11	14)	256	83	92	74	65	4	236	4	5	2	4	2	.67	12	.221	.297	.406

Dave Sanders

Pitches: L **Bats:** L **Pos:** RP-20   **Ht:** 6'0" **Wt:** 200 **Born:** 8/29/79 **Age:** 24

Year Team	Lg	G	GS	CG	GF	IP	BFP	H	R	ER	HR	SH	SF	HB	TBB	IBB	SO	WP	Bk	W	L	Pct	ShO	Sv-Op	Hld	ERC	ERA
1999 Tucson	AAA	7	1	0	2	16.1	66	12	3	2	0	1	0	1	6	3	26	1	0	1	0	1.000	0	1--	-	1.92	1.10
2000 Winstn-Salm	A+	51	0	0	20	48.1	228	39	35	28	4	2	2	4	39	1	50	12	1	3	5	.600	0	6--	-	4.59	5.21
2001 Birmingham	AA	36	0	0	12	34.0	150	27	12	10	1	1	2	3	25	1	25	2	0	3	0	1.000	0	0--	-	4.07	2.65
2002 Birmingham	AA	47	0	0	10	63.2	272	56	17	13	3	1	1	3	28	7	61	4	0	3	1	.750	0	0--	-	3.21	1.84
2003 Charlotte	AAA	19	0	0	10	22.0	97	23	9	9	3	0	0	4	6	0	25	1	0	1	1	.500	0	4--	-	4.81	3.68
2003 Chicago	AL	20	0	0	7	22.0	103	25	16	15	5	0	1	1	11	0	14	0	0	0	0	-	0	0-0	0	6.33	6.14

Reggie Sanders

Bats: R **Throws:** R **Pos:** RF-91; LF-39; PH-15; DH-2; PR-1   **Ht:** 6'1" **Wt:** 205 **Born:** 12/1/67 **Age:** 36

		BATTING																	BASERUNNING				AVERAGES		
Year Team	Lg	G	AB	H	2B	3B	HR	(Hm	Rd)	TB	R	RBI	RC	TBB	IBB	SO	HBP	SH	SF	SB	CS	SB%	GDP	Avg	OBP	Slg
1991 Cincinnati	NL	9	40	8	0	0	1	(0	1)	11	6	3	1	0	0	9	0	0	0	1	1	.50	1	.200	.200	.275
1992 Cincinnati	NL	116	385	104	26	6	12	(6	6)	178	62	36	64	48	2	98	4	0	1	16	7	.70	6	.270	.356	.462
1993 Cincinnati	NL	138	496	136	16	4	20	(8	12)	220	90	83	76	51	7	118	5	3	8	27	10	.73	10	.274	.343	.444
1994 Cincinnati	NL	107	400	105	20	8	17	(10	7)	192	66	62	65	41	1	114	2	1	3	21	9	.70	2	.263	.332	.480
1995 Cincinnati	NL	133	484	148	36	6	28	(9	19)	280	91	99	109	69	4	122	8	0	6	36	12	.75	9	.306	.397	.579
1996 Cincinnati	NL	81	287	72	17	1	14	(7	7)	133	49	33	47	44	4	86	2	0	1	24	8	.75	8	.251	.353	.463
1997 Cincinnati	NL	86	312	79	19	2	19	(11	8)	159	52	56	53	42	3	93	3	1	0	13	7	.65	9	.253	.347	.510
1998 Cincinnati	NL	135	481	129	18	6	14	(7	7)	201	83	59	69	51	2	137	7	4	2	20	9	.69	10	.268	.346	.418
1999 San Diego	NL	133	478	136	24	7	26	(11	15)	252	92	72	94	65	1	108	6	0	1	36	13	.73	10	.285	.376	.527
2000 Atlanta	NL	103	340	79	23	1	11	(4	7)	137	43	37	42	32	2	78	2	3	0	21	4	.84	9	.232	.302	.403
2001 Arizona	NL	126	441	116	21	3	33	(19	14)	242	84	90	80	46	7	126	5	1	3	14	10	.58	2	.263	.337	.549
2002 San Francisco	NL	140	505	126	23	6	23	(12	11)	230	75	85	66	47	3	121	12	0	7	18	6	.75	10	.250	.324	.455
2003 Pittsburgh	NL	130	453	129	27	4	31	(17	14)	257	74	87	81	38	4	110	5	0	2	15	5	.75	10	.285	.345	.567
13 ML YEARS		1437	5102	1367	270	54	249	(121	128)	2492	867	802	847	574	40	1320	61	13	34	262	101	.72	96	.268	.347	.488

Johan Santana

Pitches: L **Bats:** L **Pos:** RP-27; SP-18   **Ht:** 6'0" **Wt:** 195 **Born:** 3/13/79 **Age:** 25

		HOW MUCH HE PITCHED						WHAT HE GAVE UP											THE RESULTS						
Year Team	Lg	G	GS	CG	GF	IP	BFP	H	R	ER	HR	SH	SF	HB	TBB	IBB	SO	WP	Bk	W	L	Pct	ShO	Sv-Op	Hld	ERC	ERA
2000 Minnesota	AL	30	5	0	9	86.0	398	102	64	62	11	1	3	2	54	0	64	5	2	2	3	.400	0	0-0	0	6.59	6.49
2001 Minnesota	AL	15	4	0	5	43.2	195	50	25	23	6	2	3	3	16	0	28	3	0	1	0	1.000	0	0-0	0	5.36	4.74
2002 Minnesota	AL	27	14	0	2	108.1	452	84	41	36	7	3	3	1	49	0	137	15	2	8	6	.571	0	1-1	3	2.86	2.99
2003 Minnesota	AL	45	18	0	7	158.1	643	127	56	54	17	2	4	3	47	1	169	6	2	12	3	.800	0	0-0	5	2.74	3.07
4 ML YEARS		117	41	0	23	396.1	1688	363	186	175	41	8	13	9	166	1	398	29	6	23	12	.657	0	1-1	8	3.80	3.97

Benito Santiago

Bats: R **Throws:** R **Pos:** C-106; PH-2   **Ht:** 6'1" **Wt:** 200 **Born:** 3/9/65 **Age:** 39

		BATTING																	BASERUNNING				AVERAGES		
Year Team	Lg	G	AB	H	2B	3B	HR	(Hm	Rd)	TB	R	RBI	RC	TBB	IBB	SO	HBP	SH	SF	SB	CS	SB%	GDP	Avg	OBP	Slg
1986 San Diego	NL	17	62	18	2	0	3	(2	1)	29	10	6	9	2	0	12	0	0	1	0	1	.00	0	.290	.308	.468
1987 San Diego	NL	146	546	164	33	2	18	(11	7)	255	64	79	77	16	2	112	5	1	4	21	12	.64	12	.300	.324	.467
1988 San Diego	NL	139	492	122	22	2	10	(3	7)	178	49	46	45	24	2	82	1	5	5	15	7	.68	18	.248	.282	.362
1989 San Diego	NL	129	462	109	16	3	16	(8	8)	179	50	62	47	26	6	89	1	3	2	11	6	.65	9	.236	.277	.387
1990 San Diego	NL	100	344	93	8	5	11	(6	5)	144	42	53	47	27	2	55	3	1	7	5	5	.50	4	.270	.323	.419
1991 San Diego	NL	152	580	155	22	3	17	(6	11)	234	60	87	61	23	5	114	4	0	7	8	10	.44	21	.267	.296	.403
1992 San Diego	NL	106	386	97	21	0	10	(8	2)	148	37	42	37	21	1	52	0	0	4	2	5	.29	14	.251	.287	.383
1993 Florida	NL	139	469	108	19	6	13	(6	7)	178	49	50	50	37	2	88	5	0	4	10	7	.59	9	.230	.291	.380
1994 Florida	NL	101	337	92	14	2	11	(4	7)	143	35	41	43	25	1	57	1	2	4	1	2	.33	11	.273	.322	.424
1995 San Diego	NL	81	266	76	20	0	11	(7	4)	129	40	44	43	24	1	48	4	0	2	2	2	.50	7	.286	.351	.485
1996 Philadelphia	NL	136	481	127	21	2	30	(8	22)	242	71	85	79	49	7	104	1	0	2	2	0	1.00	8	.264	.332	.503
1997 Toronto	AL	97	341	83	10	0	13	(7	6)	132	31	42	35	17	1	80	2	1	5	1	0	1.00	10	.243	.279	.387
1998 Toronto	AL	15	29	9	5	0	0	(0	0)	14	3	4	4	1	0	6	0	0	0	0	0	–	1	.310	.333	.483
1999 Chicago	NL	109	350	87	18	3	7	(2	5)	132	28	36	39	32	6	71	2	0	4	1	1	.50	12	.249	.313	.377
2000 Cincinnati	NL	89	252	66	11	1	8	(7	1)	103	22	45	30	19	8	45	1	0	5	2	2	.50	7	.262	.310	.409
2001 San Francisco	NL	133	477	125	25	4	6	(3	3)	176	39	45	46	23	0	78	2	7	6	5	4	.56	19	.262	.295	.369
2002 San Francisco	NL	126	478	133	24	5	16	(6	10)	215	56	74	57	27	8	73	2	3	7	4	2	.67	19	.278	.315	.450
2003 San Francisco	NL	108	401	112	21	2	11	(2	9)	170	53	56	50	29	0	69	2	0	2	0	1	.00	13	.279	.329	.424
18 ML YEARS		1923	6753	1776	312	40	211	(95	116)	2801	739	897	799	422	52	1235	36	23	69	90	67	.57	194	.263	.307	.415

Jose Santiago

Pitches: R **Bats:** R **Pos:** RP-25   **Ht:** 6'3" **Wt:** 215 **Born:** 11/5/74 **Age:** 29

		HOW MUCH HE PITCHED						WHAT HE GAVE UP											THE RESULTS						
Year Team	Lg	G	GS	CG	GF	IP	BFP	H	R	ER	HR	SH	SF	HB	TBB	IBB	SO	WP	Bk	W	L	Pct	ShO	Sv-Op	Hld	ERC	ERA
2003 Buffalo*	AAA	25	4	0	5	66.2	291	79	35	18	1	0	2	2	22	1	33	0	0	3	3	.500	0	2--	–	4.39	2.43
1997 Kansas City	AL	4	0	0	3	4.2	24	7	2	1	0	0	0	0	2	1	1	0	0	0	0	–	0	0-0	0	6.62	1.93
1998 Kansas City	AL	2	0	0	2	2.0	9	4	2	2	0	0	0	0	2	0	0	0	0	0	0	–	0	0-0	0	8.38	9.00
1999 Kansas City	AL	34	0	0	15	47.1	203	46	23	18	7	1	3	2	14	2	15	2	1	3	4	.429	0	2-3	4	3.87	3.42
2000 Kansas City	AL	45	0	0	20	69.0	302	70	33	30	7	1	3	3	26	3	44	0	0	8	6	.571	0	2-8	5	4.14	3.91
2001 KC-Phi		73	0	0	11	91.2	397	106	47	47	5	4	5	3	22	2	43	1	0	4	6	.400	0	0-2	9	4.09	4.61
2002 Philadelphia	AL	42	0	0	7	47.0	214	56	35	35	7	1	2	3	15	1	30	1	0	1	3	.250	0	0-1	5	5.34	6.70
2003 Cleveland	AL	25	0	0	4	31.2	138	37	11	10	2	0	0	0	14	3	15	0	0	1	3	.250	0	0-2	4	4.94	2.84
2001 Kansas City	AL	20	0	0	6	29.1	136	40	22	22	2	3	3	1	9	1	15	1	0	2	2	.500	0	0-1	0	5.60	6.75
2001 Philadelphia	NL	53	0	0	5	62.1	261	66	25	25	3	1	2	2	13	1	28	0	0	2	4	.333	0	0-1	9	3.42	3.61
7 ML YEARS		225	0	0	62	293.1	1287	326	153	143	28	7	13	12	93	12	150	4	1	17	22	.436	0	4-16	31	4.42	4.39

Ramon Santiago

Bats: B **Throws:** R **Pos:** SS-85; 2B-53; PH-4   **Ht:** 5'11" **Wt:** 150 **Born:** 8/31/79 **Age:** 24

		BATTING																	BASERUNNING				AVERAGES		
Year Team	Lg	G	AB	H	2B	3B	HR	(Hm	Rd)	TB	R	RBI	RC	TBB	IBB	SO	HBP	SH	SF	SB	CS	SB%	GDP	Avg	OBP	Slg
1999 Tigers	R	35	134	43	9	2	0	(-	-)	56	25	11	21	9	0	17	1	4	3	20	7	.74	3	.321	.361	.418
1999 Oneonta	A-	12	50	17	1	2	1	(-	-)	25	9	8	10	2	0	12	1	1	0	5	0	1.00	0	.340	.377	.500
2000 W Michigan	A	98	379	103	15	1	1	(-	-)	123	69	42	47	34	1	60	12	15	6	39	12	.76	11	.272	.346	.325
2001 Lakeland	A+	120	429	115	15	3	2	(-	-)	142	64	46	60	54	0	60	11	14	4	34	8	.81	7	.268	.361	.331
2002 Erie	AA	22	75	21	0	2	1	(-	-)	28	9	7	10	3	0	12	3	2	1	6	0	1.00	0	.280	.329	.373
2002 Toledo	AAA	9	28	12	1	0	2	(-	-)	19	6	6	8	3	0	4	2	0	0	0	2	.00	0	.429	.515	.679

Year Team	Lg	G	AB	H	2B	3B	HR	(Hm Rd)	TB	R	RBI	RC	TBB	IBB	SO	HBP	SH	SF	SB	CS	SB%	GDP	Avg	OBP	Slg
2002 Detroit	AL	65	222	54	5	5	4	(3 1)	81	33	20	23	13	0	48	8	4	2	8	5	.62	2	.243	.306	.365
2003 Detroit	AL	141	444	100	18	1	2	(1 1)	126	41	29	37	33	0	66	10	**18**	2	10	4	.71	9	.225	.292	.284
2 ML YEARS		206	666	154	23	6	6	(4 2)	207	74	49	60	46	0	114	18	22	4	18	9	.67	11	.231	.297	.311

Angel Santos

Bats: B Throws: R Pos: 2B-28; 3B-4; PH-2; PR-2
Ht: 5'11" Wt: 178 Born: 8/14/79 Age: 24

Year Team	Lg	G	AB	H	2B	3B	HR	(Hm Rd)	TB	R	RBI	RC	TBB	IBB	SO	HBP	SH	SF	SB	CS	SB%	GDP	Avg	OBP	Slg
1997 Red Sox	R	17	60	11	1	0	0	(- -)	12	8	7	4	7	0	11	0	1	2	8	3	.73	0	.183	.261	.200
1998 Red Sox	R	23	77	27	5	1	0	(- -)	34	14	13	16	13	0	19	0	1	2	7	3	.70	1	.351	.435	.442
1998 Lowell	A-	28	102	25	4	1	1	(- -)	34	19	12	10	9	0	12	0	2	0	2	1	.67	4	.245	.306	.333
1999 Augusta	A	130	466	126	30	2	15	(- -)	205	83	55	74	62	4	88	5	2	3	25	10	.71	12	.270	.360	.440
2000 Trenton	AA	80	275	71	17	2	3	(- -)	101	32	32	35	32	0	60	2	1	4	18	8	.69	7	.258	.335	.367
2001 Trenton	AA	129	510	138	32	0	14	(- -)	212	75	52	77	54	2	106	5	3	5	26	9	.74	7	.271	.343	.416
2001 Pawtucket	AAA	4	15	3	1	0	0	(- -)	4	1	2	1	1	0	4	0	0	1	1	0	1.00	0	.200	.235	.267
2002 Pawtucket	AAA	102	350	91	15	2	10	(- -)	140	40	50	46	38	3	70	2	10	5	12	8	.60	8	.260	.332	.400
2003 Pawtucket	AAA	70	214	51	8	0	5	(- -)	74	25	20	26	32	2	50	1	4	1	9	4	.69	6	.238	.339	.346
2003 Buffalo	AAA	13	46	11	2	0	2	(- -)	19	10	8	7	5	0	8	0	0	0	5	0	1.00	0	.239	.314	.413
2001 Boston	AL	9	16	2	1	0	0	(0 0)	3	2	1	0	2	0	7	0	0	1	0	0	-	2	.125	.211	.188
2003 Cleveland	AL	32	76	17	3	1	3	(1 2)	31	9	6	6	3	0	18	0	1	0	1	1	.50	0	.224	.253	.408
2 ML YEARS		41	92	19	4	1	3	(1 2)	34	11	7	6	5	0	25	0	1	1	1	1	.50	2	.207	.245	.370

Francisco Santos

Bats: L Throws: L Pos: PH-5; RF-3; 1B-1
Ht: 6'1" Wt: 175 Born: 3/9/74 Age: 30

Year Team	Lg	G	AB	H	2B	3B	HR	(Hm Rd)	TB	R	RBI	RC	TBB	IBB	SO	HBP	SH	SF	SB	CS	SB%	GDP	Avg	OBP	Slg
2003 Fresno	AAA	87	301	72	15	5	6	(- -)	115	23	42	30	10	0	38	0	0	3	1	0	1.00	3	.239	.261	.382
2003 San Francisco	NL	8	15	3	2	0	1	(1 0)	8	2	1	0	0	0	3	0	0	0	0	0	-	0	.200	.200	.533

Victor Santos

Pitches: R Bats: R Pos: SP-4; RP-4
Ht: 6'3" Wt: 195 Born: 10/2/76 Age: 27

Year Team	Lg	G	GS	CG	GF	IP	BFP	H	R	ER	HR	SH	SF	HB	TBB	IBB	SO	WP	Bk	W	L	Pct	ShO	Sv-Op	Hld	ERC	ERA
2003 Oklahoma*	AAA	20	16	1	2	108.1	470	112	54	41	6	6	2	2	35	0	65	2	0	5	4	.556	1	1- -	-	3.67	3.41
2001 Detroit	AL	33	7	0	6	76.1	335	62	33	28	9	1	3	3	49	4	52	0	0	2	2	.500	0	0-0	2	4.18	3.30
2002 Colorado	NL	24	2	0	6	26.0	140	41	30	30	3	3	1	0	22	3	25	2	0	4	0	.000	0	0-0	1	9.37	10.38
2003 Texas	AL	8	4	0	2	25.2	117	29	21	20	5	1	1	1	16	1	15	0	0	0	2	.000	0	0-0	0	6.82	7.01
3 ML YEARS		65	13	0	14	128.0	592	132	84	78	17	5	5	4	87	8	92	2	0	2	8	.200	0	0-0	3	5.68	5.48

Dane Sardinha

Bats: R Throws: R Pos: C-1; PH-1
Ht: 6'0" Wt: 215 Born: 4/8/79 Age: 25

Year Team	Lg	G	AB	H	2B	3B	HR	(Hm Rd)	TB	R	RBI	RC	TBB	IBB	SO	HBP	SH	SF	SB	CS	SB%	GDP	Avg	OBP	Slg
2001 Mudville	A+	109	422	99	24	2	9	(- -)	154	45	55	36	12	2	9	3	4	4	0	1	.00	12	.235	.259	.365
2002 Chattanooga	AA	106	394	81	20	0	4	(- -)	113	0	40	33	14	0	114	0	0	2	0	0	.00	0	.206	.233	.287
2003 Chattanooga	AA	72	246	63	15	0	3	(- -)	87	21	32	29	22	3	61	1	0	6	5	3	.63	1	.256	.313	.354
2003 Cincinnati	NL	1	2	0	0	0	0	(0 0)	0	0	0	0	0	0	1	0	0	0	0	0	-	0	.000	.000	.000

Kazuhiro Sasaki

Pitches: R Bats: R Pos: RP-35
Ht: 6'4" Wt: 220 Born: 2/22/68 Age: 36

Year Team	Lg	G	GS	CG	GF	IP	BFP	H	R	ER	HR	SH	SF	HB	TBB	IBB	SO	WP	Bk	W	L	Pct	ShO	Sv-Op	Hld	ERC	ERA
2003 Tacoma*	AAA	3	2	0	1	3.2	17	5	4	4	0	0	0	0	1	0	5	0	0	0	1	.000	0	1- -	-	4.76	9.82
2003 Everett*	A-	2	2	0	0	2.0	11	5	5	5	3	0	0	0	0	0	5	0	0	0	1	.000	0	0- -	-	25.85	22.50
2003 InlandEmpire*	A+	1	1	0	0	1.0	4	0	0	0	0	0	0	0	1	0	2	0	0	0	0	-	0	0- -	-	0.95	0.00
2000 Seattle	AL	63	0	0	58	62.2	265	42	25	22	10	2	2	2	31	5	78	1	0	2	5	.286	0	37-40	0	2.98	3.16
2001 Seattle	AL	69	0	0	63	66.2	261	48	24	24	6	0	4	0	11	2	62	4	0	0	4	.000	0	45-52	0	1.90	3.24
2002 Seattle	AL	61	0	0	55	60.2	249	44	24	17	6	3	5	2	20	4	73	6	0	4	5	.444	0	37-45	0	2.35	2.52
2003 Seattle	AL	35	0	0	25	33.1	150	31	17	15	2	2	2	1	15	2	29	4	0	1	2	.333	0	10-14	0	3.45	4.05
4 ML YEARS		228	0	0	201	223.1	925	165	90	78	24	7	9	9	77	13	242	15	0	7	16	.304	0	129-151	0	2.54	3.14

Scott Sauerbeck

Pitches: L Bats: R Pos: RP-79
Ht: 6'3" Wt: 197 Born: 11/9/71 Age: 32

Year Team	Lg	G	GS	CG	GF	IP	BFP	H	R	ER	HR	SH	SF	HB	TBB	IBB	SO	WP	Bk	W	L	Pct	ShO	Sv-Op	Hld	ERC	ERA
1999 Pittsburgh	NL	65	0	0	16	67.2	287	53	19	15	6	4	0	4	38	5	55	3	0	4	1	.800	0	2-5	10	3.60	2.00
2000 Pittsburgh	NL	75	0	0	13	75.2	349	76	36	34	4	3	3	1	61	8	83	9	2	5	4	.556	0	1-4	13	5.31	4.04
2001 Pittsburgh	NL	70	0	0	14	62.2	281	61	41	39	4	2	0	2	40	6	79	3	0	2	2	.500	0	2-4	19	4.60	5.60
2002 Pittsburgh	NL	78	0	0	21	62.2	255	50	18	16	4	0	0	1	27	4	70	2	1	5	4	.556	0	0-0	28	2.91	2.30
2003 Pit-Bos		79	0	0	13	56.2	261	47	34	30	6	2	1	5	43	5	52	1	0	3	5	.375	0	0-5	18	4.71	4.76
2003 Pittsburgh	NL	53	0	0	11	40.0	174	30	20	18	5	2	0	1	25	2	32	0	0	3	4	.429	0	0-4	16	3.72	4.05
2003 Boston	AL	26	0	0	2	16.2	87	17	14	12	1	0	1	4	18	3	18	1	0	0	1	.000	0	0-1	2	7.20	6.48
5 ML YEARS		367	0	0	77	325.1	1433	287	148	134	24	11	4	13	209	28	337	18	3	19	16	.543	0	5-18	88	4.23	3.71

Curt Schilling

Pitches: R Bats: R Pos: SP-24   Ht: 6'4" Wt: 231 Born: 11/14/66 Age: 37

Year Team	Lg	G	GS	CG	GF	IP	BFP	H	R	ER	HR	SH	SF	HB	TBB	IBB	SO	WP	Bk	W	L	Pct	ShO	Sv-Op	Hld	ERC	ERA
2003 Tucson*	AAA	2	2	0	0	10.0	42	10	5	5	3	0	0	0	3	0	15	0	0	1	0	1.000	0	0- -		5.06	4.50
1988 Baltimore	AL	4	4	0	0	14.2	76	22	19	16	3	0	3	1	10	1	4	2	0	0	3	.000	0	0-0	0	9.43	9.82
1989 Baltimore	AL	5	1	0	0	8.2	38	10	6	6	2	0	0	0	3	0	6	1	0	0	1	.000	0	0-0	0	5.74	6.23
1990 Baltimore	AL	35	0	0	16	46.0	191	38	13	13	1	2	4	0	19	0	32	0	0	1	2	.333	0	3-9	5	2.68	2.54
1991 Houston	NL	56	0	0	34	75.2	336	79	35	32	2	5	1	0	39	7	71	4	1	3	5	.375	0	8-11	5	4.08	3.81
1992 Philadelphia	NL	42	26	10	10	226.1	895	165	67	59	11	7	8	1	59	4	147	4	0	14	11	.560	4	2-3	0	1.86	2.35
1993 Philadelphia	NL	34	34	7	0	235.1	982	234	114	105	23	9	7	4	57	6	186	9	3	16	7	.696	2	0-0	0	3.44	4.02
1994 Philadelphia	NL	13	13	1	0	82.1	360	87	42	41	10	6	1	3	28	3	58	3	1	2	8	.200	0	0-0	0	4.36	4.48
1995 Philadelphia	NL	17	17	1	0	116.0	473	96	52	46	12	5	2	3	26	2	114	0	1	7	5	.583	0	0-0	0	2.55	3.57
1996 Philadelphia	NL	26	26	8	0	183.1	732	149	69	65	16	6	4	3	50	5	182	5	0	9	10	.474	2	0-0	0	2.59	3.19
1997 Philadelphia	NL	35	35	7	0	254.1	1009	208	96	84	25	8	8	5	58	3	319	5	1	17	11	.607	2	0-0	0	2.55	2.97
1998 Philadelphia	NL	35	35	15	0	268.2	1089	236	101	97	23	14	7	6	61	3	300	12	0	15	14	.517	2	0-0	0	2.75	3.25
1999 Philadelphia	NL	24	24	8	0	180.1	735	159	74	71	25	11	3	5	44	0	152	4	0	15	6	.714	1	0-0	0	3.20	3.54
2000 Phi-Ari	NL	29	29	8	0	210.1	862	204	90	89	27	11	4	1	45	4	168	4	0	11	12	.478	2	0-0	0	3.38	3.81
2001 Arizona	NL	35	35	6	0	256.2	1021	237	86	85	37	8	5	1	39	0	293	4	0	22	6	.786	1	0-0	0	3.03	2.98
2002 Arizona	NL	36	35	5	0	259.1	1017	218	95	93	29	4	3	3	33	1	316	6	0	23	7	.767	1	0-0	0	2.33	3.23
2003 Arizona	NL	24	24	3	0	168.0	673	144	58	55	17	11	1	3	32	2	194	4	0	8	9	.471	2	0-0	0	2.59	2.95
2000 Philadelphia	NL	16	16	4	0	112.2	474	110	49	49	17	5	1	1	32	4	96	4	0	6	6	.500	1	0-0	0	3.79	3.91
2000 Arizona	NL	13	13	4	0	97.2	388	94	41	40	10	6	3	0	13	0	72	0	0	5	6	.455	1	0-0	0	2.91	3.69
16 ML YEARS		450	338	79	60	2586.0	10489	2286	1017	957	263	107	61	39	603	41	2542	67	7	163	117	.582	19	13-23	10	2.87	3.33

Brian Schmack

Pitches: R Bats: R Pos: RP-11   Ht: 6'2" Wt: 190 Born: 12/7/73 Age: 30

Year Team	Lg	G	GS	CG	GF	IP	BFP	H	R	ER	HR	SH	SF	HB	TBB	IBB	SO	WP	Bk	W	L	Pct	ShO	Sv-Op	Hld	ERC	ERA
1995 Newark	IND	7	4	0	2	30.1	135	40	21	18	3	5	0	2	10	0	16	1	0	2	1	.667	0	0- -	-	6.15	5.34
1996 Hickory	A	43	0	0	25	62.1	264	61	24	16	4	9	0	4	16	5	56	3	1	6	4	.600	0	5- -	-	3.26	2.31
1997 Winstn-Salm	A+	42	0	0	18	75.1	325	65	32	23	0	5	3	2	36	4	71	6	1	2	5	.286	0	1- -	-	2.91	2.75
1998 Winstn-Salm	A+	42	0	0	34	61.1	256	48	23	15	3	5	0	9	17	0	52	2	1	5	5	.500	0	10- -	-	2.64	2.20
1999 Birmingham	A+	43	0	0	26	63.0	270	60	31	24	3	2	1	8	18	0	56	6	0	4	4	.500	0	6- -	-	3.49	3.43
2000 Charlotte	AAA	51	0	0	13	90.2	379	82	32	28	10	4	1	1	29	5	84	4	0	11	7	.611	0	1- -	-	3.25	2.78
2001 Oklahoma	AAA	40	0	0	15	53.0	231	56	31	24	5	1	1	1	14	1	34	0	0	2	2	.500	0	1- -	-	3.75	4.08
2002 Oklahoma	AAA	29	1	0	11	54.2	241	66	35	30	6	2	2	4	18	0	45	5	0	0	4	.000	0	1- -	-	5.49	4.94
2002 Tulsa	AA	12	7	0	0	37.1	162	45	26	24	1	1	2	3	7	0	20	2	0	1	3	.250	0	0- -	-	4.21	5.79
2003 Erie	AA	53	0	0	48	57.0	231	53	15	13	2	6	2	0	10	2	47	4	0	3	3	.500	0	29- -	-	2.39	2.05
2003 Detroit	AL	11	0	0	1	13.0	55	14	6	5	1	0	2	1	4	0	4	1	0	1	0	1.000	0	0-0	2	4.43	3.46

Jason Schmidt

Pitches: R Bats: R Pos: SP-29   Ht: 6'5" Wt: 205 Born: 1/29/73 Age: 31

Year Team	Lg	G	GS	CG	GF	IP	BFP	H	R	ER	HR	SH	SF	HB	TBB	IBB	SO	WP	Bk	W	L	Pct	ShO	Sv-Op	Hld	ERC	ERA
1995 Atlanta	NL	9	2	0	1	25.0	119	27	17	16	2	2	4	1	18	3	19	1	0	2	2	.500	0	0-1	0	5.56	5.76
1996 Atl-Pit	NL	19	17	1	0	96.1	445	108	67	61	10	4	9	2	53	0	74	8	1	5	6	.455	0	0-0	0	5.46	5.70
1997 Pittsburgh	NL	32	32	2	0	187.2	825	193	106	96	16	10	3	9	76	2	136	8	0	10	9	.526	0	0-0	0	4.31	4.60
1998 Pittsburgh	NL	33	33	0	0	214.1	916	228	106	97	24	10	3	4	71	3	158	15	1	11	14	.440	0	0-0	0	4.35	4.07
1999 Pittsburgh	NL	33	33	2	0	212.2	937	219	110	99	24	7	7	3	85	4	148	6	4	13	11	.542	0	0-0	0	4.30	4.19
2000 Pittsburgh	NL	11	11	0	0	63.1	295	70	43	38	6	1	2	1	41	2	51	1	0	2	5	.286	0	0-0	0	5.77	5.40
2001 Pit-SF	NL	25	25	1	0	150.1	641	138	75	68	13	5	3	7	61	3	142	8	1	13	7	.650	0	0-0	0	3.72	4.07
2002 San Francisco	NL	29	29	2	0	185.1	769	148	78	71	15	11	5	2	73	1	196	12	0	13	8	.619	2	0-0	0	2.87	3.45
2003 San Francisco	NL	29	29	5	0	207.2	819	152	56	54	14	6	3	5	46	1	208	7	1	17	5	.773	3	0-0	0	1.93	2.34
1996 Atlanta	NL	13	11	0	0	58.2	274	69	48	44	8	3	6	0	32	0	48	5	1	3	4	.429	0	0-0	0	5.92	6.75
1996 Pittsburgh	NL	6	6	1	0	37.2	171	39	19	17	2	1	3	2	21	0	26	3	0	2	2	.500	0	0-0	0	4.75	4.06
2001 Pittsburgh	NL	14	14	1	0	84.0	357	81	46	43	11	3	2	7	28	2	77	3	1	6	6	.500	0	0-0	0	4.17	4.61
2001 San Francisco	NL	11	11	0	0	66.1	284	57	29	25	2	2	1	0	33	1	65	5	0	7	1	.875	0	0-0	0	3.16	3.39
9 ML YEARS		220	211	13	1	1342.2	5766	1284	658	600	124	56	39	34	524	19	1132	66	8	86	67	.562	5	0-1	0	3.81	4.02

Brian Schneider

Bats: L Throws: R Pos: C-98; PH-9; DH-2   Ht: 6'1" Wt: 200 Born: 11/26/76 Age: 27

Year Team	Lg	G	AB	H	2B	3B	HR	(Hm	Rd)	TB	R	RBI	RC	TBB	IBB	SO	HBP	SH	SF	SB	CS	SB%	GDP	Avg	OBP	Slg
2000 Montreal	NL	45	115	27	6	0	0	(0	0)	33	6	11	8	7	2	24	0	0	1	0	1	.00	1	.235	.276	.287
2001 Montreal	NL	27	41	13	3	0	1	(1	0)	19	4	6	8	6	1	3	0	0	1	0	0	-	0	.317	.396	.463
2002 Montreal	NL	73	207	57	19	2	5	(3	2)	95	21	29	30	21	8	41	0	2	2	1	2	.33	7	.275	.339	.459
2003 Montreal	NL	108	335	77	26	1	9	(9	0)	132	34	46	37	37	8	75	2	1	2	0	2	.00	12	.230	.309	.394
4 ML YEARS		253	698	174	54	3	15	(13	2)	279	65	92	83	71	19	143	2	3	6	1	5	.17	20	.249	.318	.400

Scott Schoeneweis

Pitches: L Bats: L Pos: RP-59   Ht: 6'0" Wt: 185 Born: 10/2/73 Age: 30

Year Team	Lg	G	GS	CG	GF	IP	BFP	H	R	ER	HR	SH	SF	HB	TBB	IBB	SO	WP	Bk	W	L	Pct	ShO	Sv-Op	Hld	ERC	ERA
1999 Anaheim	AL	31	0	0	6	39.1	175	47	27	24	4	0	1	0	14	1	22	1	0	1	1	.500	0	0-0	3	4.99	5.49
2000 Anaheim	AL	27	27	1	0	170.0	742	183	112	103	21	2	5	6	67	2	78	4	3	7	10	.412	1	0-0	0	4.84	5.45
2001 Anaheim	AL	32	32	1	0	205.1	910	227	122	116	21	3	8	14	77	2	104	4	1	10	11	.476	0	0-0	0	4.87	5.08
2002 Anaheim	AL	54	15	0	4	118.0	510	119	68	64	17	1	5	5	49	4	65	1	1	9	8	.529	0	1-4	11	4.68	4.88
2003 Ana-CWS	AL	59	0	0	19	64.2	276	63	35	30	3	2	1	4	19	5	56	3	0	3	2	.600	0	0-2	4	3.25	4.18

Year Team	Lg	G	GS	CG	GF	IP	BFP	H	R	ER	HR	SH	SF	HB	TBB	IBB	SO	WP	Bk	W	L	Pct	ShO	Sv-Op	Hld	ERC	ERA
2003 Anaheim	AL	39	0	0	12	38.2	163	37	19	17	2	1	1	3	10	3	29	1	0	1	1	.500	0	0-1	4	3.14	3.96
2003 Chicago	AL	20	0	0	7	26.0	113	26	16	13	1	1	0	1	9	2	27	2	0	2	1	.667	0	0-1	0	3.41	4.50
5 ML YEARS		203	74	2	29	597.1	2613	639	364	337	66	8	20	29	226	14	325	13	5	30	32	.484	1	1-6	18	4.65	5.08

Marco Scutaro

Bats: R Throws: R Pos: 2B-39; PR-9; PH-8; SS-1 Ht: 5'10" Wt: 170 Born: 10/30/75 Age: 28

Year Team	Lg	G	AB	H	2B	3B	HR	(Hm	Rd)	TB	R	RBI	RC	TBB	IBB	SO	HBP	SH	SF	SB	CS	SB%	GDP	Avg	OBP	Slg
1996 Columbus	A	85	315	79	12	3	10	(-	-)	127	66	45	44	38	0	86	4	4	5	6	3	.67	6	.251	.334	.403
1997 Kinston	A+	97	378	103	17	6	10	(-	-)	162	58	59	60	35	0	72	9	2	3	23	7	.77	3	.272	.346	.429
1997 Buffalo	AAA	21	57	15	3	0	1	(-	-)	21	8	6	6	6	0	8	0	1	1	0	1	.00	4	.263	.328	.368
1998 Akron	AA	124	462	146	27	6	11	(-	-)	218	68	62	84	47	0	71	10	4	6	33	16	.67	8	.316	.387	.472
1998 Buffalo	AAA	8	26	6	3	0	0	(-	-)	9	3	4	2	0	0	2	0	1	0	0	0	-	0	.231	.231	.346
1999 Buffalo	AAA	129	462	126	24	2	8	(-	-)	178	76	51	71	61	2	69	6	6	4	21	6	.78	5	.273	.362	.385
2000 Buffalo	AAA	124	425	117	20	5	5	(-	-)	162	67	54	65	61	0	53	9	7	7	9	6	.60	8	.275	.373	.381
2000 Indianapolis	AAA	4	13	7	1	1	1	(-	-)	13	5	3	5	1	0	2	0	0	0	1	0	1.00	1	.538	.571	1.000
2001 Indianapolis	AAA	132	495	146	29	3	11	(-	-)	214	87	50	81	62	2	83	10	5	3	11	11	.50	9	.295	.382	.432
2002 Norfolk	AAA	97	354	113	22	6	7	(-	-)	168	48	28	59	30	3	61	2	7	1	7	8	.47	7	.319	.375	.475
2003 Norfolk	AAA	70	244	76	18	3	9	(-	-)	127	42	32	50	33	0	34	6	9	4	11	6	.65	6	.311	.401	.520
2002 New York	NL	27	36	8	0	1	1	(1	0)	13	2	6	2	0	0	11	0	1	1	0	1	.00	1	.222	.216	.361
2003 New York	NL	48	75	16	4	0	2	(0	2)	26	10	6	10	13	2	14	1	1	1	2	0	1.00	1	.213	.333	.347
2 ML YEARS		75	111	24	4	1	3	(1	2)	39	12	12	12	13	2	25	1	2	2	2	1	.67	2	.216	.299	.351

Rudy Seanez

Pitches: R Bats: R Pos: RP-9 Ht: 5'11" Wt: 205 Born: 10/20/68 Age: 35

Year Team	Lg	G	GS	CG	GF	IP	BFP	H	R	ER	HR	SH	SF	HB	TBB	IBB	SO	WP	Bk	W	L	Pct	ShO	Sv-Op	Hld	ERC	ERA
2003 Pawtucket*	AAA	17	0	0	10	20.2	90	20	14	14	5	0	1	0	10	1	24	2	0	2	2	.500	0	3- -		5.19	6.10
2003 Oklahoma*	AAA	5	0	0	2	4.1	23	3	4	1	0	1	0	0	5	0	7	2	1	0	1	.000	0	0- -		3.88	2.08
2003 Iowa*	AAA	13	0	0	5	13.0	62	12	10	5	1	1	1	0	9	2	13	0	0	1	2	.333	0	2- -		4.08	3.46
1989 Cleveland	AL	5	0	0	2	5.0	20	1	2	2	0	0	2	0	4	1	7	1	1	0	0	-	0	0-0	0	0.94	3.60
1990 Cleveland	AL	24	0	0	12	27.1	127	22	17	17	2	0	1	1	25	1	24	5	0	2	1	.667	0	0-0	3	4.85	5.60
1991 Cleveland	AL	5	0	0	0	5.0	33	10	12	9	2	0	0	0	7	0	7	2	0	0	0	-	0	0-1	0	17.96	16.20
1993 San Diego	NL	3	0	0	3	3.1	20	8	6	5	1	1	0	0	2	0	1	0	0	0	0	-	0	0-0	0	16.31	13.50
1994 Los Angeles	NL	17	0	0	6	23.2	104	24	7	7	2	4	2	1	9	1	18	3	0	1	1	.500	0	0-1	1	4.01	2.66
1995 Los Angeles	NL	37	0	0	12	34.2	159	39	27	26	5	3	0	1	18	3	29	0	0	1	3	.250	0	3-4	6	5.57	6.75
1998 Atlanta	NL	34	0	0	8	36.0	148	25	13	11	2	1	2	1	16	0	50	2	0	4	1	.800	0	2-4	8	2.44	2.75
1999 Atlanta	NL	56	0	0	13	53.2	225	47	21	20	3	0	2	1	21	1	41	3	0	6	1	.857	0	3-8	18	3.12	3.35
2000 Atlanta	NL	23	0	0	8	21.0	89	15	11	10	3	1	0	1	9	1	20	0	0	2	4	.333	0	2-3	6	2.95	4.29
2001 SD-Atl	NL	38	0	0	8	36.0	150	23	12	11	4	0	1	1	19	0	41	4	0	0	2	.000	0	1-3	9	2.78	2.75
2002 Texas	AL	33	0	0	4	33.0	150	28	25	21	5	3	1	0	24	1	40	6	0	1	3	.250	0	0-4	10	4.77	5.73
2003 Boston	AL	9	0	0	4	8.2	44	11	7	6	2	0	1	0	6	1	9	3	0	0	1	.000	0	0-1	0	7.45	6.23
2001 San Diego	NL	26	0	0	8	24.0	102	15	8	7	3	0	1	1	15	0	24	1	0	0	2	.000	0	1-3	5	3.21	2.63
2001 Atlanta	NL	12	0	0	0	12.0	48	8	4	4	1	0	0	0	4	0	17	3	0	0	0	-	0	0-0	4	1.99	3.00
12 ML YEARS		284	0	0	80	287.1	1269	253	160	145	31	13	12	7	160	10	287	29	1	17	17	.500	0	11-29	61	4.07	4.54

Todd Sears

Bats: L Throws: R Pos: 1B-15; PH-15; DH-5 Ht: 6'5" Wt: 215 Born: 10/23/75 Age: 28

Year Team	Lg	G	AB	H	2B	3B	HR	(Hm	Rd)	TB	R	RBI	RC	TBB	IBB	SO	HBP	SH	SF	SB	CS	SB%	GDP	Avg	OBP	Slg
1997 Portland	A-	55	200	54	13	1	2	(-	-)	75	37	29	32	41	7	49	0	1	1	2	0	1.00	4	.270	.393	.375
1998 Asheville	A	130	459	133	26	2	11	(-	-)	196	71	82	79	72	1	89	5	1	6	10	4	.71	9	.290	.387	.427
1999 Salem	A+	109	385	108	21	0	14	(-	-)	171	58	59	66	58	1	99	4	0	1	11	2	.85	9	.281	.379	.444
2000 Carolina	AA	86	299	90	21	0	12	(-	-)	147	54	72	66	72	11	76	2	0	5	12	3	.80	7	.301	.434	.492
2000 New Britain	AA	40	140	44	8	1	3	(-	-)	63	15	15	24	18	1	40	1	0	0	1	0	1.00	5	.314	.396	.450
2000 Salt Lake	AAA	3	11	4	1	0	1	(-	-)	8	2	4	3	1	0	2	0	0	0	0	0	-	1	.364	.417	.727
2001 Edmonton	AAA	118	408	127	25	2	13	(-	-)	195	61	50	68	41	2	71	3	1	3	2	1	.67	16	.311	.376	.478
2002 Edmonton	AAA	129	484	150	36	4	20	(-	-)	254	88	100	96	59	4	142	5	0	4	2	1	.67	6	.310	.388	.525
2003 Rochester	AAA	80	283	72	12	1	7	(-	-)	107	35	41	38	37	6	90	4	0	2	6	1	.86	6	.254	.347	.378
2002 Minnesota	AL	7	12	4	2	0	0	(0	0)	6	1	1	1	0	0	1	0	0	0	0	0	-	0	.333	.333	.500
2003 Min-SD		33	73	18	3	0	2	(2	0)	27	9	11	10	7	0	18	1	0	1	0	0	-	4	.247	.317	.370
2003 Minnesota	AL	24	65	16	2	0	2	(2	0)	24	7	11	10	7	0	15	1	0	1	0	0	-	4	.246	.324	.369
2003 San Diego	NL	9	8	2	1	0	0	(0	0)	3	2	0	0	0	0	3	0	0	0	0	0	-	0	.250	.250	.375
2 ML YEARS		40	85	22	5	0	2	(2	0)	33	11	11	11	7	0	19	1	0	1	0	0	-	4	.259	.319	.388

Bobby Seay

Pitches: L Bats: L Pos: RP-12 Ht: 6'2" Wt: 235 Born: 6/20/78 Age: 26

Year Team	Lg	G	GS	CG	GF	IP	BFP	H	R	ER	HR	SH	SF	HB	TBB	IBB	SO	WP	Bk	W	L	Pct	ShO	Sv-Op	Hld	ERC	ERA
1997 Chrlstn - SC	A	13	1	3	0	61.1	269	56	35	31	2	2	2	3	37	0	64	6	0	3	4	.429	0	0- -		4.14	4.55
1998 Chrlstn - SC	A	15	15	0	0	69.0	289	59	40	33	10	3	2	5	29	0	74	7	2	1	7	.125	0	0- -		4.03	4.30
1999 St.Pete	A+	12	11	0	1	57.0	238	56	25	19	0	2	2	4	23	0	45	2	0	2	6	.250	0	0- -		3.72	3.00
1999 Orlando	AA	6	6	0	0	17.0	85	22	15	15	2	0	1	0	15	0	16	4	2	1	2	.333	0	0- -		8.16	7.94
2000 Orlando	AA	24	24	0	0	132.1	568	132	64	57	13	4	5	8	53	1	106	4	0	8	7	.533	0	0- -		4.36	3.88
2001 Orlando	AA	15	13	0	0	64.2	288	81	48	43	9	2	4	3	20	0	49	2	0	2	5	.286	0	0- -		6.10	5.98
2002 Orlando	AA	15	3	0	2	35.2	150	31	16	13	2	0	1	3	15	0	24	2	0	2	0	1.000	0	0- -		3.53	3.28
2003 Durham	AAA	25	0	0	7	30.0	131	23	10	7	1	0	1	3	15	0	29	1	0	3	0	1.000	0	0- -		3.03	2.10
2001 Tampa Bay	AL	12	0	0	2	13.0	58	13	0	9	3	0	0	0	5	0	12	0	0	1	1	.500	0	0-0	0	4.74	6.23
2003 Tampa Bay	AL	12	0	0	2	9.0	39	7	3	3	0	0	2	0	6	0	5	0	0	0	0	-	0	0-1	0	3.17	3.00
2 ML YEARS		24	0	0	2	22.0	97	20	3	12	3	0	2	0	11	0	17	0	0	1	1	.500	0	0-1	0	4.12	4.91

David Segui

Bats: B **Throws:** L **Pos:** DH-52; PH-9; 1B-8; PR-1   **Ht:** 6'1" **Wt:** 202 **Born:** 7/19/66 **Age:** 37

Year Team	Lg	G	AB	H	2B	3B	HR	(Hm	Rd)	TB	R	RBI	RC	TBB	IBB	SO	HBP	SH	SF	SB	CS	SB%	GDP	Avg	OBP	Slg
2003 Frederick*	A+	1	4	1	0	0	0	(-	-)	1	0	0	0	0	0	1	0	0	0	0	0	-	0	.250	.250	.250
1990 Baltimore	AL	40	123	30	7	0	2	(1	1)	43	14	15	10	11	2	15	1	1	0	0	0	-	12	.244	.311	.350
1991 Baltimore	AL	86	212	59	7	0	2	(1	1)	72	15	22	21	12	2	19	0	3	1	1	1	.50	7	.278	.316	.340
1992 Baltimore	AL	115	189	44	9	0	1	(1	0)	56	21	17	17	20	3	23	0	2	0	1	0	1.00	4	.233	.306	.296
1993 Baltimore	AL	146	450	123	27	0	10	(6	4)	180	54	60	62	58	4	53	0	3	8	2	1	.67	18	.273	.351	.400
1994 New York	NL	92	336	81	17	1	10	(5	5)	130	46	43	40	33	6	43	1	1	3	0	0	-	6	.241	.308	.387
1995 NYM-Mon	NL	130	456	141	25	4	12	(6	6)	210	68	68	73	40	5	47	3	8	3	2	7	.22	10	.309	.367	.461
1996 Montreal	NL	115	416	119	30	1	11	(6	5)	184	69	58	69	60	4	54	0	0	5	4	4	.50	8	.286	.375	.442
1997 Montreal	NL	125	459	141	22	3	21	(10	11)	232	75	68	86	57	12	66	1	0	6	1	0	1.00	9	.307	.380	.505
1998 Seattle	AL	143	522	159	36	1	19	(10	9)	254	79	84	89	49	4	80	0	0	9	3	1	.75	12	.305	.359	.487
1999 Sea-Tor	AL	121	440	131	27	3	14	(5	9)	206	57	52	70	40	4	60	1	1	4	1	2	.33	10	.298	.355	.468
2000 Tex-Cle	AL	150	574	192	42	1	19	(8	11)	293	93	103	105	53	2	84	1	0	0	1	0	-	20	.334	.388	.510
2001 Baltimore	AL	82	292	88	18	1	10	(5	5)	138	48	46	57	49	5	61	4	0	2	1	1	.50	4	.301	.406	.473
2002 Baltimore	AL	26	95	25	4	0	2	(1	1)	35	10	16	14	11	0	22	0	0	1	0	0	-	0	.263	.336	.368
2003 Baltimore	AL	67	224	59	10	1	5	(2	3)	86	26	25	28	26	2	47	1	0	1	1	0	1.00	8	.263	.341	.384
1995 New York	NL	33	73	24	3	1	2	(2	0)	35	9	11	14	12	1	9	1	4	2	1	3	.25	2	.329	.420	.479
1995 Montreal	NL	97	383	117	22	3	10	(4	6)	175	59	57	59	28	4	38	2	4	1	1	4	.20	8	.305	.355	.457
1999 Seattle	AL	90	345	101	22	3	9	(4	5)	156	43	39	52	32	4	43	1	1	3	1	2	.33	9	.293	.352	.452
1999 Toronto	AL	31	95	30	5	0	5	(1	4)	50	14	13	18	8	0	17	0	0	1	0	0	-	1	.316	.365	.526
2000 Texas	AL	93	351	118	29	1	11	(4	7)	182	52	57	66	34	1	51	0	0	0	0	1	.00	12	.336	.391	.519
2000 Cleveland	AL	57	223	74	13	0	8	(4	4)	111	41	46	39	19	1	33	1	0	0	0	0	-	8	.332	.384	.498
14 ML YEARS		1438	4788	1392	281	16	138	(67	71)	2119	675	677	741	519	55	674	13	19	45	17	18	.49	128	.291	.359	.443

Fernando Seguignol

Bats: B **Throws:** R **Pos:** 1B-3; PH-3   **Ht:** 6'5" **Wt:** 230 **Born:** 1/19/75 **Age:** 29

Year Team	Lg	G	AB	H	2B	3B	HR	(Hm	Rd)	TB	R	RBI	RC	TBB	IBB	SO	HBP	SH	SF	SB	CS	SB%	GDP	Avg	OBP	Slg
2003 Tampa*	A+	3	13	5	0	0	0	(-	-)	5	1	1	2	0	0	2	0	0	0	0	0	-	1	.385	.385	.385
2003 Columbus*	AAA	106	402	137	28	1	28	(-	-)	251	78	87	88	34	3	81	8	0	2	0	0	-	19	.341	.401	.624
1998 Montreal	NL	16	42	11	4	0	2	(2	0)	21	6	3	6	3	0	15	0	0	1	0	0	-	0	.262	.304	.500
1999 Montreal	NL	35	105	27	9	0	5	(3	2)	51	14	10	17	5	1	33	7	0	2	0	0	-	5	.257	.328	.486
2000 Montreal	NL	76	162	45	8	0	10	(1	9)	83	22	22	25	9	0	46	3	0	1	0	1	.00	5	.278	.326	.512
2001 Montreal	NL	46	50	7	2	0	0	(0	0)	9	0	5	1	2	1	17	1	0	1	0	0	-	1	.140	.185	.180
2003 New York	AL	5	7	1	0	0	0	(0	0)	1	0	0	0	1	0	3	0	0	0	0	0	-	0	.143	.250	.143
5 ML YEARS		178	366	91	23	0	17	(6	11)	165	42	40	49	20	2	114	11	0	5	0	1	.00	11	.249	.303	.451

Bill Selby

Bats: L **Throws:** R **Pos:** PH-18; 3B-10; DH-2; PR-2; 1B-1; 2B-1; LF-1   **Ht:** 5'10" **Wt:** 195 **Born:** 6/11/70 **Age:** 34

Year Team	Lg	G	AB	H	2B	3B	HR	(Hm	Rd)	TB	R	RBI	RC	TBB	IBB	SO	HBP	SH	SF	SB	CS	SB%	GDP	Avg	OBP	Slg
2003 Memphis*	AAA	76	279	73	12	6	9	(-	-)	124	33	41	40	24	1	32	0	1	0	5	1	.83	5	.262	.319	.444
1996 Boston	AL	40	95	26	4	0	3	(0	3)	39	12	6	12	9	1	11	0	1	0	1	1	.50	3	.274	.337	.411
2000 Cleveland	AL	30	46	11	1	0	0	(0	0)	12	8	4	3	1	0	9	1	0	0	0	0	-	1	.239	.271	.261
2001 Cincinnati	NL	36	92	21	7	1	2	(1	1)	36	7	12	10	5	1	13	1	1	1	0	0	-	4	.228	.273	.391
2002 Cleveland	AL	65	159	34	7	2	6	(2	4)	63	15	21	21	15	2	27	0	0	4	0	1	.00	4	.214	.278	.396
2003 Cleveland	AL	27	39	4	1	0	0	(0	0)	5	3	5	1	3	0	11	0	0	1	0	0	-	0	.103	.163	.128
5 ML YEARS		198	431	96	20	3	11	(3	8)	155	45	48	47	33	4	71	2	3	4	1	2	.33	9	.223	.279	.360

Aaron Sele

Pitches: R **Bats:** R **Pos:** SP-25   **Ht:** 6'5" **Wt:** 220 **Born:** 6/25/70 **Age:** 34

Year Team	Lg	G	GS	CG	GF	IP	BFP	H	R	ER	HR	SH	SF	HB	TBB	IBB	SO	WP	Bk	W	L	Pct	ShO	Sv-Op	Hld	ERC	ERA
2003 R Cucamnga*	A+	3	2	0	0	8.0	35	12	4	4	0	0	0	0	3	0	7	0	0	0	0	-	0	0--	-	6.71	4.50
2003 Salt Lake*	AAA	3	3	0	0	14.0	63	16	10	10	2	0	0	0	9	0	8	1	0	1	2	.333	0	0--	-	6.53	6.43
1993 Boston	AL	18	18	0	0	111.2	484	100	42	34	5	2	5	7	48	2	93	5	0	7	2	.778	0	0-0	0	3.40	2.74
1994 Boston	AL	22	22	2	0	143.1	615	140	68	61	13	4	5	9	60	2	105	4	0	8	7	.533	0	0-0	0	4.26	3.83
1995 Boston	AL	6	6	0	0	32.1	146	32	14	11	3	1	1	3	14	0	21	3	0	3	1	.750	0	0-0	0	4.35	3.06
1996 Boston	AL	29	29	1	0	157.1	722	192	110	93	14	6	7	8	67	2	137	2	0	7	11	.389	0	0-0	0	5.56	5.32
1997 Boston	AL	33	33	1	0	177.1	810	196	115	106	25	5	7	15	80	4	122	7	0	13	12	.520	0	0-0	0	5.47	5.38
1998 Texas	AL	33	33	3	0	212.2	954	239	116	100	14	5	7	13	84	6	167	4	0	19	11	.633	2	0-0	0	4.69	4.23
1999 Texas	AL	33	33	2	0	205.0	920	244	115	109	21	1	3	12	70	3	186	4	0	18	9	.667	2	0-0	0	5.17	4.79
2000 Seattle	AL	34	34	2	0	211.2	908	221	110	106	17	5	8	5	74	7	137	5	0	17	10	.630	2	0-0	0	4.06	4.51
2001 Seattle	AL	34	33	2	0	215.0	899	216	93	86	25	5	9	7	51	2	114	1	0	15	5	.750	1	0-0	0	3.70	3.60
2002 Anaheim	AL	26	26	1	0	160.0	706	190	92	87	21	5	10	7	49	2	82	5	0	8	9	.471	1	0-0	0	5.20	4.89
2003 Anaheim	AL	25	25	0	0	121.2	552	135	82	78	17	2	5	12	58	1	53	5	0	7	11	.389	0	0-0	0	5.78	5.77
11 ML YEARS		293	292	14	0	1748.0	7716	1905	957	871	175	41	67	98	655	31	1217	45	0	122	88	.581	8	0-0	0	4.69	4.48

Jae Seo

Pitches: R **Bats:** R **Pos:** SP-31; RP-1   **Ht:** 6'1" **Wt:** 215 **Born:** 5/24/77 **Age:** 27

Year Team	Lg	G	GS	CG	GF	IP	BFP	H	R	ER	HR	SH	SF	HB	TBB	IBB	SO	WP	Bk	W	L	Pct	ShO	Sv-Op	Hld	ERC	ERA
1998 St.Lucie	A+	8	7	0	0	35.0	141	26	13	9	2	2	0	3	10	0	37	1	6	3	1	.750	0	0--	-	2.37	2.31
1998 Mets	R	2	0	0	0	5.0	17	4	0	0	0	0	0	0	0	0	6	0	0	0	0	-	0	0--	-	1.42	0.00
1999 St.Lucie	A+	3	3	0	0	14.2	55	8	3	3	0	0	1	0	2	0	14	0	0	2	0	1.000	0	0--	-	0.84	1.84
2001 St.Lucie	A+	4	5	0	0	25.1	104	21	11	10	2	0	1	1	6	0	19	0	0	2	3	.400	0	0--	-	2.53	3.55
2001 Binghamton	AA	12	10	0	0	60.1	235	44	14	13	3	3	1	6	11	1	47	0	1	5	1	.833	0	0--	-	1.97	1.94
2001 Norfolk	AAA	9	9	0	0	47.1	191	53	18	18	4	4	0	2	6	1	25	0	1	2	2	.500	0	0--	-	3.87	3.42

Year Team	Lg	G	GS	CG	GF	IP	BFP	H	R	ER	HR	SH	SF	HB	TBB	IBB	SO	WP	Bk	W	L	Pct	ShO	Sv-Op	Hld	ERC	ERA
2002 Norfolk	AAA	26	24	1	0	128.2	548	145	66	57	14	6	6	3	22	1	87	0	0	6	9	.400	0	0- -	-	3.99	3.99
2002 New York	NL	1	0	0	1	1.0	3	0	0	0	0	0	0	0	0	0	1	0	0	0	0	-	0	0-0	0	0.00	0.00
2003 New York	NL	32	31	0	0	188.1	806	193	94	80	18	8	4	6	46	11	110	2	0	9	12	.429	0	0-0	0	3.54	3.82
2 ML YEARS		33	31	0	1	189.1	809	193	94	80	18	8	4	6	46	11	111	2	0	9	12	.429	0	0-0	0	3.51	3.80

Dan Serafini

Pitches: L **Bats:** B **Pos:** RP-6; SP-4   **Ht:** 6'1" **Wt:** 195 **Born:** 1/25/74 **Age:** 30

Year Team	Lg	G	GS	CG	GF	IP	BFP	H	R	ER	HR	SH	SF	HB	TBB	IBB	SO	WP	Bk	W	L	Pct	ShO	Sv-Op	Hld	ERC	ERA
2003 Memphis*	AAA	3	2	0	0	8.0	43	19	9	8	0	0	0	1	2	0	2	0	0	0	1	.000	0	0- -	-	12.62	9.00
1996 Minnesota	AL	1	1	0	0	4.1	23	7	0	5	1	0	0	0	2	0	1	0	0	0	1	.000	0	0-0	0	8.69	10.38
1997 Minnesota	AL	6	4	1	0	26.1	111	27	0	10	1	0	0	0	11	0	15	0	0	2	1	.667	0	0-0	0	3.98	3.42
1998 Minnesota	AL	28	9	0	0	75.0	345	95	0	54	10	0	0	0	29	0	46	0	0	7	4	.636	0	0-0	0	5.77	6.48
1999 Chicago	NL	42	4	0	0	62.1	302	86	0	48	9	0	0	0	32	0	17	0	0	3	2	.600	0	1-0	0	7.11	6.93
2000 SD-Pit	NL	14	11	0	0	65.1	300	79	0	40	11	0	0	0	28	0	35	0	0	2	5	.286	0	0-0	0	5.87	5.51
2003 Cincinnati	NL	10	4	0	0	30.0	141	41	23	18	5	3	2	0	14	1	13	1	0	1	3	.250	0	0-0	0	7.08	5.40
2000 San Diego	NL	3	0	0	0	3.0	20	9	0	6	2	0	0	0	2	0	3	0	0	0	0	-	0	0-0	0	25.94	18.00
2000 Pittsburgh	NL	11	11	0	0	62.1	280	70	0	34	9	0	0	0	26	0	32	0	0	2	5	.286	0	0-0	0	5.12	4.91
6 ML YEARS		101	33	1	2	263.1	1222	335	23	175	37	3	2	0	116	1	127	1	0	15	16	.484	0	1-0	0	6.11	5.98

Scott Service

Pitches: R **Bats:** R **Pos:** RP-33   **Ht:** 6'6" **Wt:** 240 **Born:** 2/26/67 **Age:** 37

Year Team	Lg	G	GS	CG	GF	IP	BFP	H	R	ER	HR	SH	SF	HB	TBB	IBB	SO	WP	Bk	W	L	Pct	ShO	Sv-Op	Hld	ERC	ERA
2003 Louisville*	AAA	4	0	0	1	3.2	14	3	1	1	0	0	0	0	0	0	7	0	0	0	0	-	0	0- -	-	1.32	2.45
2003 Tucson*	AAA	9	0	0	7	12.1	49	6	2	0	0	0	1	1	2	0	13	1	0	0	0	-	0	3- -	-	0.84	0.00
1988 Philadelphia	NL	5	0	0	1	5.1	23	7	1	1	0	0	0	1	1	0	6	0	0	0	0	-	0	0-0	1	5.34	1.69
1992 Montreal	NL	5	0	0	0	7.0	41	15	11	11	1	0	0	0	5	0	11	0	0	0	0	-	0	0-0	1	13.24	14.14
1993 Col-Cin	NL	29	0	0	7	46.0	197	44	24	22	6	2	4	2	16	4	43	0	0	2	2	.500	0	2-3	3	3.85	4.30
1994 Cincinnati	NL	6	0	0	2	7.1	35	8	9	6	2	2	0	0	3	0	*	5	0	0	1	2	.333	0	0-0	0	5.42	7.36
1995 San Francisco	NL	28	0	0	6	31.0	129	18	11	11	4	3	2	2	20	4	30	3	0	3	1	.750	0	0-0	7	3.04	3.19
1996 Cincinnati	NL	34	1	0	5	48.0	213	51	21	21	7	4	1	6	18	4	46	5	0	1	0	1.000	0	0-0	3	5.07	3.94
1997 Cin-KC		16	0	0	3	22.1	95	28	16	16	2	2	1	0	6	0	22	2	0	0	3	.000	0	0-1	5	5.14	6.45
1998 Kansas City	AL	73	0	0	26	82.2	353	70	35	32	7	2	5	9	34	4	95	10	1	6	4	.600	0	4-8	18	3.52	3.48
1999 Kansas City	AL	68	0	0	29	75.1	352	87	51	51	13	4	7	3	42	8	68	3	0	5	5	.500	0	8-15	8	6.14	6.09
2000 Oakland	AL	20	0	0	6	36.2	172	45	31	26	5	1	2	1	19	1	35	0	0	1	2	.333	0	1-1	1	6.22	6.38
2003 Ari-Tor		33	0	0	11	34.1	146	38	18	18	4	1	2	0	8	1	35	1	0	0	2	.000	0	1-2	3	4.08	4.72
1993 Colorado	NL	3	0	0	0	4.2	24	8	5	5	1	0	2	1	1	0	3	0	0	0	0	-	0	0-0	0	9.48	9.64
1993 Cincinnati	NL	26	0	0	7	41.1	173	36	19	17	5	2	2	1	15	4	40	0	0	2	2	.500	0	2-3	3	3.31	3.70
1997 Cincinnati	NL	4	0	0	2	5.1	26	11	7	7	1	1	0	0	1	0	3	2	0	0	0	-	0	0-0	1	11.35	11.81
1997 Kansas City	AL	12	0	0	1	17.0	69	17	9	9	1	1	1	0	5	0	19	0	0	0	3	.000	0	0-1	2	3.53	4.76
2003 Arizona	NL	18	0	0	7	18.1	77	21	10	10	1	1	0	0	2	1	18	1	0	0	2	.000	0	1-1	0	3.32	4.91
2003 Toronto	AL	15	0	0	4	16.0	69	17	8	8	3	0	1	0	6	0	17	0	0	0	0	-	0	0-1	3	5.00	4.50
11 ML YEARS		317	1	0	96	396.0	1756	411	228	215	51	21	24	24	172	26	396	24	1	19	21	.475	0	16-29	47	4.77	4.89

Richie Sexson

Bats: R **Throws:** R **Pos:** 1B-162   **Ht:** 6'8" **Wt:** 227 **Born:** 12/29/74 **Age:** 29

Year Team	Lg	G	AB	H	2B	3B	HR	(Hm	Rd)	TB	R	RBI	RC	TBB	IBB	SO	HBP	SH	SF	SB	CS	SB%	GDP	Avg	OBP	Slg
1997 Cleveland	AL	5	11	3	0	0	0	(0	0)	3	1	0	0	0	0	2	0	0	0	0	0	-	2	.273	.273	.273
1998 Cleveland	AL	49	174	54	14	1	11	(9	2)	103	28	35	33	6	0	42	3	0	0	1	1	.50	3	.310	.344	.592
1999 Cleveland	AL	134	479	122	17	7	31	(18	13)	246	72	116	70	34	0	117	4	0	8	3	3	.50	19	.255	.305	.514
2000 Cle-Mil		148	537	146	30	4	30	(15	15)	268	89	91	91	59	2	159	7	0	4	2	1	1.00	11	.272	.349	.499
2001 Milwaukee	NL	158	598	162	24	3	45	(28	17)	327	94	125	103	60	5	178	6	0	3	2	4	.33	20	.271	.342	.547
2002 Milwaukee	NL	157	570	159	37	2	29	(13	16)	287	86	102	100	70	7	136	8	0	4	0	-	17	.279	.363	.504
2003 Milwaukee	NL	162	606	165	28	2	45	(23	22)	332	97	124	117	98	7	151	9	0	5	2	3	.40	18	.272	.379	.548
2000 Cleveland	AL	91	324	83	16	1	16	(8	8)	149	45	44	45	25	0	96	4	0	3	1	0	1.00	8	.256	.315	.460
2000 Milwaukee	NL	57	213	63	14	0	14	(7	7)	119	44	47	46	34	2	63	3	0	1	1	0	1.00	3	.296	.398	.559
7 ML YEARS		813	2975	811	150	16	191	(106	85)	1566	467	593	514	327	21	785	37	0	24	10	11	.48	90	.273	.349	.526

Ben Sheets

Pitches: R **Bats:** R **Pos:** SP-34   **Ht:** 6'1" **Wt:** 203 **Born:** 7/18/78 **Age:** 25

Year Team	Lg	G	GS	CG	GF	IP	BFP	H	R	ER	HR	SH	SF	HB	TBB	IBB	SO	WP	Bk	W	L	Pct	ShO	Sv-Op	Hld	ERC	ERA
2001 Milwaukee	NL	25	25	1	0	151.1	653	166	89	80	23	8	5	5	48	6	94	3	0	11	10	.524	1	0-0	0	4.78	4.76
2002 Milwaukee	NL	34	34	1	0	216.2	934	237	105	100	21	10	0	10	70	10	170	9	0	11	16	.407	0	0-0	0	4.45	4.15
2003 Milwaukee	NL	34	34	1	0	220.2	931	232	122	109	29	11	6	6	43	2	157	7	0	11	13	.458	0	0-0	0	3.83	4.45
3 ML YEARS		93	93	3	0	588.2	2518	635	316	289	73	29	11	21	161	18	421	19	0	33	39	.458	1	0-0	0	4.30	4.42

Gary Sheffield

Bats: R **Throws:** R **Pos:** RF-154; PH-1   **Ht:** 6'0" **Wt:** 205 **Born:** 11/18/68 **Age:** 35

Year Team	Lg	G	AB	H	2B	3B	HR	(Hm	Rd)	TB	R	RBI	RC	TBB	IBB	SO	HBP	SH	SF	SB	CS	SB%	GDP	Avg	OBP	Slg
1988 Milwaukee	NL	24	80	19	1	0	4	(1	3)	32	12	12	8	7	0	7	0	1	1	3	1	.75	5	.238	.295	.400
1989 Milwaukee	NL	95	368	91	18	0	5	(2	3)	124	34	32	38	27	0	33	4	3	3	10	6	.63	4	.247	.303	.337
1990 Milwaukee	NL	125	487	143	30	1	10	(3	7)	205	67	67	73	44	1	41	3	4	9	25	10	.71	11	.294	.350	.421
1991 Milwaukee	NL	50	175	34	12	2	2	(2	0)	56	25	22	15	19	1	15	3	1	5	5	5	.50	3	.194	.277	.320
1992 San Diego	NL	146	557	184	34	3	33	(23	10)	323	87	100	113	48	5	40	6	0	7	5	6	.45	19	.330	.385	.580

Year Team	Lg	G	AB	H	2B	3B	HR	(Hm Rd)	TB	R	RBI	RC	TBB	IBB	SO	HBP	SH	SF	SB	CS	SB%	GDP	Avg	OBP	Slg
								BATTING											**BASERUNNING**				**AVERAGES**		
1993 SD-Fla	NL	140	494	145	20	5	20	(10 10)	235	67	73	84	47	6	64	9	0	7	17	5	.77	11	.294	.361	.476
1994 Florida	NL	87	322	89	16	1	27	(15 12)	188	61	78	68	51	11	50	6	0	5	12	6	.67	10	.276	.380	.584
1995 Florida	NL	63	213	69	8	0	16	(4 12)	125	46	46	60	55	8	45	4	0	2	19	4	.83	3	.324	.467	.587
1996 Florida	NL	161	519	163	33	1	42	(19 23)	324	118	120	144	142	19	66	10	0	6	16	9	.64	16	.314	**.465**	.624
1997 Florida	NL	135	444	111	22	1	21	(13 8)	198	86	71	90	121	11	79	15	0	2	11	7	.61	7	.250	.424	.446
1998 Fla-LA	NL	130	437	132	27	2	22	(11 11)	229	73	85	102	95	12	46	8	0	9	22	7	.76	7	.302	.428	.524
1999 Los Angeles	NL	152	549	165	20	0	34	(15 19)	287	103	101	118	101	4	64	4	0	9	11	5	.69	10	.301	.407	.523
2000 Los Angeles	NL	141	501	163	24	3	43	(23 20)	322	105	109	131	101	7	71	4	0	6	4	6	.40	13	.325	.438	.643
2001 Los Angeles	NL	143	515	160	28	2	36	(16 20)	300	98	100	120	94	13	67	4	0	5	10	4	.71	12	.311	.417	.583
2002 Atlanta	NL	135	492	151	26	0	25	(10 15)	252	82	84	102	72	2	53	11	0	4	12	2	.86	16	.307	.404	.512
2003 Atlanta	NL	155	576	190	31	2	39	(20 19)	348	126	132	135	86	6	55	8	0	8	18	4	.82	16	.330	.419	.604
1993 San Diego	NL	68	258	76	12	2	10	(6 4)	122	34	36	40	18	0	30	3	0	3	5	1	.83	9	.295	.344	.473
1993 Florida	NL	72	236	69	8	3	10	(4 6)	113	33	37	44	29	6	34	6	0	4	12	4	.75	2	.292	.378	.479
1998 Florida	NL	40	136	37	11	1	6	(6 0)	68	21	28	27	26	1	16	2	0	2	4	2	.67	3	.272	.392	.500
1998 Los Angeles	NL	90	301	95	16	1	16	(5 11)	161	52	57	75	69	11	30	6	0	7	18	5	.78	4	.316	.444	.535
16 ML YEARS		1882	6729	2009	356	23	379	(187 192)	3548	1190	1232	1403	1110	106	796	99	9	88	200	87	.70	163	.299	.401	.527

Scot Shields

Pitches: R **Bats:** R **Pos:** RP-31; SP-13   **Ht:** 6'1" **Wt:** 175 **Born:** 7/22/75 **Age:** 28

Year Team	Lg	G	GS	CG	GF	IP	BFP	H	R	ER	HR	SH	SF	HB	TBB	IBB	SO	WP	Bk	W	L	Pct	ShO	Sv-Op	Hld	ERC	ERA
				HOW MUCH HE PITCHED							**WHAT HE GAVE UP**												**THE RESULTS**				
2001 Anaheim	AL	8	0	0	6	11.0	48	8	1	0	0	0	0	1	7	0	7	2	0	0	0	-	0	0-0	0	3.10	0.00
2002 Anaheim	AL	29	1	0	13	49.0	188	31	13	12	4	1	0	1	21	1	30	3	0	5	3	.625	0	0-0	3	2.35	2.20
2003 Anaheim	AL	44	13	0	5	148.1	609	138	56	47	12	3	4	5	38	6	111	4	0	5	6	.455	0	1-1	3	3.12	2.85
3 ML YEARS		81	14	0	24	208.1	845	177	70	59	16	4	4	7	66	7	148	9	0	10	9	.526	0	1-1	6	2.94	2.55

Jason Shiell

Pitches: R **Bats:** R **Pos:** RP-17   **Ht:** 6'0" **Wt:** 180 **Born:** 10/19/76 **Age:** 27

Year Team	Lg	G	GS	CG	GF	IP	BFP	H	R	ER	HR	SH	SF	HB	TBB	IBB	SO	WP	Bk	W	L	Pct	ShO	Sv-Op	Hld	ERC	ERA
				HOW MUCH HE PITCHED							**WHAT HE GAVE UP**												**THE RESULTS**				
1995 Braves	R	12	0	0	9	22.1	101	23	16	11	0	0	0	2	10	1	13	3	0	1	3	.250	0	2--	-	3.89	4.43
1996 Danville	R+	12	12	0	0	59.1	231	44	14	13	1	0	1	1	19	0	57	3	0	3	1	.750	0	0--	-	2.08	1.97
1997 Macon	A	27	24	0	0	129.0	523	113	53	41	12	3	5	8	32	0	101	6	0	10	5	.667	0	0--	-	3.07	2.86
1998 Macon	A	4	3	0	0	8.0	32	7	4	4	2	0	0	0	1	0	8	1	0	0	1	.000	0	0--	-	3.17	4.50
1999 Myrtle Beach	A+	26	17	0	1	114.2	485	118	51	48	5	4	2	3	36	0	90	9	0	6	7	.462	0	0--	-	3.65	3.77
2000 R Cucamnga	A+	16	14	0	0	81.0	356	73	54	48	9	0	3	6	41	0	80	10	2	7	5	.583	0	0--	-	4.30	5.33
2001 Mobile	AA	45	2	0	8	81.0	353	91	46	40	5	4	8	1	32	2	60	4	0	2	3	.400	0	0--	-	4.56	4.44
2002 Portland	AAA	56	0	0	22	74.1	315	62	26	23	6	0	1	2	29	0	74	2	1	4	3	.571	0	6--	-	3.06	2.78
2003 Pawtucket	AAA	20	0	0	13	26.0	107	26	11	7	0	0	2	0	6	0	22	0	0	3	2	.600	0	2--	-	2.79	2.42
2002 San Diego	NL	3	0	0	0	1.1	13	7	4	4	0	0	0	0	3	0	1	0	0	0	0	-	0	0-0	0	48.76	27.00
2003 Boston	AL	17	0	0	6	23.1	111	23	13	12	4	0	0	2	17	2	23	2	0	2	0	1.000	0	1-2	0	6.00	4.63
2 ML YEARS		20	0	0	6	24.2	124	30	17	16	4	0	0	2	20	2	24	2	0	2	0	1.000	0	1-2	0	7.78	5.84

Tsuyoshi Shinjo

Bats: R **Throws:** R **Pos:** CF-50; PH-15; LF-7; PR-5; RF-1   **Ht:** 6'1" **Wt:** 185 **Born:** 1/28/72 **Age:** 32

Year Team	Lg	G	AB	H	2B	3B	HR	(Hm Rd)	TB	R	RBI	RC	TBB	IBB	SO	HBP	SH	SF	SB	CS	SB%	GDP	Avg	OBP	Slg
								BATTING											**BASERUNNING**				**AVERAGES**		
2003 Norfolk*	AAA	36	111	36	5	2	3	(- -)	54	12	9	19	9	1	17	1	4	1	0	1	.00	2	.324	.377	.486
2001 New York	NL	123	400	107	23	1	10	(4 6)	162	46	56	50	25	3	70	7	4	2	4	5	.44	8	.268	.320	.405
2002 San Francisco	NL	118	362	86	15	3	9	(4 5)	134	42	37	36	24	2	46	6	3	3	5	0	1.00	5	.238	.294	.370
2003 New York	NL	62	114	22	3	0	1	(1 0)	28	10	7	3	6	1	12	1	2	1	0	1	.00	0	.193	.238	.246
3 ML YEARS		303	876	215	41	4	20	(9 11)	324	98	100	89	55	6	128	14	9	6	9	6	.60	13	.245	.299	.370

Brian Shouse

Pitches: L **Bats:** L **Pos:** RP-62   **Ht:** 5'11" **Wt:** 180 **Born:** 9/26/68 **Age:** 35

Year Team	Lg	G	GS	CG	GF	IP	BFP	H	R	ER	HR	SH	SF	HB	TBB	IBB	SO	WP	Bk	W	L	Pct	ShO	Sv-Op	Hld	ERC	ERA
				HOW MUCH HE PITCHED							**WHAT HE GAVE UP**												**THE RESULTS**				
2003 Oklahoma*	AAA	6	0	0	3	7.1	32	8	3	3	0	0	0	1	3	0	2	1	0	0	1	.000	0	1--	-	4.58	3.68
1993 Pittsburgh	NL	6	0	0	1	4.0	22	7	4	4	1	0	1	0	2	0	3	1	0	0	0	-	0	0-0	0	9.92	9.00
1998 Boston	AL	7	0	0	4	8.0	36	9	5	5	2	0	0	0	4	0	5	0	0	0	1	.000	0	0-0	1	6.42	5.63
2002 Kansas City	AL	23	0	0	7	14.2	71	15	10	10	3	1	1	2	9	1	11	2	0	0	0	-	0	0-0	2	6.11	6.14
2003 Texas	AL	62	0	0	14	61.0	253	62	24	21	1	3	0	4	14	6	40	2	0	0	1	.000	0	1-1	10	3.10	3.10
4 ML YEARS		98	0	0	26	87.2	382	93	43	40	7	4	2	6	29	7	59	5	0	0	2	.000	0	1-1	13	4.14	4.11

Paul Shuey

Pitches: R **Bats:** R **Pos:** RP-62   **Ht:** 6'3" **Wt:** 215 **Born:** 9/16/70 **Age:** 33

Year Team	Lg	G	GS	CG	GF	IP	BFP	H	R	ER	HR	SH	SF	HB	TBB	IBB	SO	WP	Bk	W	L	Pct	ShO	Sv-Op	Hld	ERC	ERA
				HOW MUCH HE PITCHED							**WHAT HE GAVE UP**												**THE RESULTS**				
2003 Las Vegas*	AAA	1	1	0	0	1.0	6	2	3	3	1	0	0	0	1	0	1	0	0	0	1	.000	0	0--	-	23.01	27.00
1994 Cleveland	AL	14	0	0	7	11.2	62	14	11	11	1	0	0	0	12	1	16	4	0	0	1	.000	0	5-5	1	7.28	8.49
1995 Cleveland	AL	7	0	0	3	6.1	28	5	4	3	0	2	0	0	5	0	5	1	0	0	2	.000	0	0-0	0	3.70	4.26
1996 Cleveland	AL	42	0	0	18	53.2	225	45	19	17	6	1	3	0	26	3	44	3	1	5	2	.714	0	4-7	7	3.56	2.85
1997 Cleveland	AL	40	0	0	16	45.0	212	52	31	31	5	4	2	1	28	3	46	2	0	4	2	.667	0	2-3	4	5.92	6.20
1998 Cleveland	AL	43	0	0	16	51.0	229	44	19	17	6	2	0	3	25	5	58	3	0	5	4	.556	0	2-5	12	3.83	3.00
1999 Cleveland	AL	72	0	0	28	81.2	351	68	37	32	8	4	1	1	40	7	103	8	0	8	5	.615	0	6-12	19	3.36	3.53
2000 Cleveland	AL	57	0	0	12	63.2	270	51	25	24	4	1	3	3	30	3	69	0	0	4	2	.667	0	0-5	28	3.11	3.39
2001 Cleveland	AL	47	0	0	11	54.1	244	53	25	17	1	4	2	1	26	5	70	6	0	5	3	.625	0	2-5	9	3.46	2.82
2002 Cle-LA	AL	67	0	0	18	68.0	288	56	29	25	3	1	2	1	31	2	63	3	0	8	2	.800	0	1-5	19	2.95	3.31

Year Team	Lg	G	GS	CG	GF	IP	BFP	H	R	ER	HR	SH	SF	HB	TBB	IBB	SO	WP	Bk	W	L	Pct	ShO	Sv-Op	Hld	ERC	ERA
2003 Los Angeles	NL	62	0	0	18	69.0	281	50	24	23	6	2	0	4	33	3	60	3	0	6	4	.600	0	0-1	10	3.06	3.00
2002 Cleveland	AL	39	0	0	12	37.1	150	31	11	10	1	1	1	0	10	1	39	2	0	3	0	1.000	0	0-2	12	2.21	2.41
2002 Los Angeles	NL	28	0	0	6	30.2	138	25	18	15	2	0	1	1	21	1	24	1	0	5	2	.714	0	1-3	7	3.89	4.40
10 ML YEARS		451	0	0	151	504.1	2183	438	224	200	40	21	13	14	256	32	534	33	1	45	27	.625	0	22-48	109	3.61	3.57

Terry Shumpert

Bats: R **Throws:** R **Pos:** PH-23; 2B-14; 3B-11; RF-9; PR-7; LF-5; DH-5; SS-1   **Ht:** 6'0" **Wt:** 198 **Born:** 8/16/66 **Age:** 37

Year Team	Lg	G	AB	H	2B	3B	HR	(Hm	Rd)	TB	R	RBI	RC	TBB	IBB	SO	HBP	SH	SF	SB	CS	SB%	GDP	Avg	OBP	Slg
2003 Orlando*	AA	2	9	2	0	0	0	(-	-)	2	1	1	1	0	0	2	1	0	0	0	0	-	0	.222	.300	.222
1990 Kansas City	AL	32	91	25	6	1	0	(0	0)	33	7	8	8	2	0	17	1	0	2	3	3	.50	4	.275	.292	.363
1991 Kansas City	AL	144	369	80	16	4	5	(1	4)	119	45	34	31	30	0	75	5	10	3	17	11	.61	10	.217	.283	.322
1992 Kansas City	AL	36	94	14	5	1	1	(0	1)	24	6	11	2	3	0	17	0	2	0	2	2	.50	2	.149	.175	.255
1993 Kansas City	AL	8	10	1	0	0	0	(0	0)	1	0	0	0	2	0	2	0	0	0	1	0	1.00	0	.100	.250	.100
1994 Kansas City	AL	64	183	44	6	2	8	(2	6)	78	28	24	26	13	0	39	0	5	1	18	3	.86	0	.240	.289	.426
1995 Boston	AL	21	47	11	3	0	0	(0	0)	14	6	3	4	4	0	13	0	0	0	3	1	.75	0	.234	.294	.298
1996 Chicago	NL	27	31	7	1	0	2	(2	0)	14	5	6	4	2	0	11	1	0	1	0	1	.00	0	.226	.286	.452
1997 San Diego	NL	13	33	9	3	0	1	(0	1)	15	4	6	5	3	0	4	0	0	1	0	0	-	1	.273	.324	.455
1998 Colorado	NL	23	26	6	1	0	1	(0	1)	10	3	2	3	2	0	8	0	0	0	0	0	-	0	.231	.286	.385
1999 Colorado	NL	92	262	91	26	3	10	(8	2)	153	58	37	64	31	2	61	2	4	5	14	0	1.00	3	.347	.413	.584
2000 Colorado	NL	115	263	68	11	7	9	(7	2)	120	52	40	42	28	1	40	6	0	3	8	4	.67	3	.259	.340	.456
2001 Colorado	NL	114	242	70	14	5	4	(3	1)	106	37	24	37	15	2	44	3	4	1	14	3	.82	2	.289	.337	.438
2002 Colorado	NL	106	234	55	12	1	6	(4	2)	87	30	21	21	21	0	41	4	5	4	4	1	.80	9	.235	.304	.372
2003 Tampa Bay	AL	59	84	16	5	2	2	(1	1)	31	14	7	9	10	0	17	2	2	1	1	0	1.00	0	.190	.289	.369
14 ML YEARS		854	1969	497	109	26	49	(28	21)	805	295	223	256	166	5	369	24	32	22	85	29	.75	33	.252	.315	.409

Ruben Sierra

Bats: B **Throws:** R **Pos:** DH-42; PH-30; LF-26; RF-15; PR-1   **Ht:** 6'1" **Wt:** 215 **Born:** 10/6/65 **Age:** 38

Year Team	Lg	G	AB	H	2B	3B	HR	(Hm	Rd)	TB	R	RBI	RC	TBB	IBB	SO	HBP	SH	SF	SB	CS	SB%	GDP	Avg	OBP	Slg
1986 Texas	AL	113	382	101	13	10	16	(8	8)	182	50	55	52	22	3	65	1	1	5	7	8	.47	8	.264	.302	.476
1987 Texas	AL	158	643	169	35	4	30	(15	15)	302	97	109	86	39	4	114	2	0	12	16	11	.59	18	.263	.302	.470
1988 Texas	AL	156	615	156	32	2	23	(15	8)	261	77	91	78	44	10	91	1	0	8	18	4	.82	15	.254	.301	.424
1989 Texas	AL	162	634	194	35	14	29	(21	8)	344	101	119	118	43	2	82	2	0	10	8	2	.80	7	.306	.347	.543
1990 Texas	AL	159	608	170	37	2	16	(10	6)	259	70	96	84	49	13	86	1	0	8	9	0	1.00	15	.280	.330	.426
1991 Texas	AL	161	661	203	44	5	25	(12	13)	332	110	116	114	56	7	91	0	0	9	16	4	.80	17	.307	.357	.502
1992 Tex-Oak	AL	151	601	167	34	7	17	(10	7)	266	83	87	66	45	12	68	0	0	10	14	4	.78	11	.278	.323	.443
1993 Oakland	AL	158	630	147	23	5	22	(9	13)	246	77	101	70	52	16	97	0	0	10	25	5	.83	17	.233	.288	.390
1994 Oakland	AL	110	426	114	21	1	23	(11	12)	206	71	92	58	23	4	64	0	0	11	8	5	.62	15	.268	.298	.484
1995 Oak-NYY	AL	126	479	126	32	0	19	(8	11)	215	73	86	69	46	4	76	0	0	8	5	4	.56	8	.263	.323	.449
1996 NYY-Det	AL	142	518	128	26	2	12	(4	8)	194	61	72	62	60	12	83	0	0	9	4	4	.50	12	.247	.320	.375
1997 Cin-Tor	AL	39	138	32	5	3	3	(3	0)	52	10	12	14	9	2	34	0	0	1	0	0	-	1	.232	.277	.377
1998 Chicago	AL	27	74	16	4	1	4	(0	4)	34	7	11	8	3	0	11	0	0	0	2	0	1.00	0	.216	.247	.459
2000 Texas	AL	20	60	14	0	0	1	(0	1)	17	5	7	5	4	0	9	0	0	0	1	0	1.00	1	.233	.281	.283
2001 Texas	AL	94	344	100	22	1	23	(13	10)	193	55	67	58	19	0	52	0	0	6	2	0	1.00	13	.291	.322	.561
2002 Seattle	AL	122	419	113	23	0	13	(6	7)	175	47	60	47	31	5	66	0	0	2	4	0	1.00	17	.270	.319	.418
2003 Tex-NYY	AL	106	307	83	17	1	9	(7	2)	129	33	43	35	27	3	47	0	0	2	2	1	.67	9	.270	.327	.420
1992 Texas	AL	124	500	139	30	6	14	(8	6)	223	66	70	70	31	6	59	0	0	8	12	4	.75	9	.278	.315	.446
1992 Oakland	AL	27	101	28	4	1	3	(2	1)	43	17	17	16	14	6	9	0	0	2	2	0	1.00	2	.277	.359	.426
1995 Oakland	AL	70	264	70	17	0	12	(3	9)	123	40	42	40	24	2	42	0	0	3	4	4	.50	2	.265	.323	.466
1995 New York	AL	56	215	56	15	0	7	(5	2)	92	33	44	29	22	2	34	0	0	5	1	0	1.00	6	.260	.322	.428
1996 New York	AL	96	360	93	17	1	11	(4	7)	145	39	52	46	40	11	58	0	0	7	1	3	.25	10	.258	.327	.403
1996 Detroit	AL	46	158	35	9	1	1	(0	1)	49	22	20	16	20	1	25	0	0	2	3	1	.75	2	.222	.306	.310
1997 Cincinnati	NL	25	90	22	5	1	2	(2	0)	35	6	7	10	6	1	21	0	0	0	0	0	-	1	.244	.292	.389
1997 Toronto	AL	14	48	10	0	2	1	(1	0)	17	4	5	4	3	1	13	0	0	1	0	0	-	0	.208	.250	.354
2003 Texas	AL	43	133	35	9	0	3	(2	1)	53	14	12	15	14	1	27	0	0	0	1	1	.50	2	.263	.333	.398
2003 New York	AL	63	174	48	8	1	6	(5	1)	76	19	31	20	13	2	20	0	0	2	1	0	1.00	7	.276	.323	.437
17 ML YEARS		2004	7539	2033	403	58	285	(152	133)	3407	1027	1224	1044	572	97	1136	7	1	111	141	52	.73	186	.270	.317	.452

Carlos Silva

Pitches: R **Bats:** R **Pos:** RP-61; SP-1   **Ht:** 6'4" **Wt:** 225 **Born:** 4/23/79 **Age:** 25

Year Team	Lg	G	GS	CG	GF	IP	BFP	H	R	ER	HR	SH	SF	HB	TBB	IBB	SO	WP	Bk	W	L	Pct	ShO	Sv-Op	Hld	ERC	ERA
1996 Martinsville	R+	7	1	0	1	18.0	78	20	11	8	1	4	1	1	5	0	16	0	0	0	0	-	0	0--	-	4.13	4.00
1997 Martinsville	R+	11	11	0	0	57.2	252	66	46	33	9	3	2	1	14	0	31	6	3	2	2	.500	0	0--	-	4.66	5.15
1998 Martinsville	R+	7	7	1	0	41.0	180	48	24	23	2	2	3	2	4	0	21	3	2	1	4	.200	0	0--	-	3.51	5.05
1998 Batavia	A-	9	7	0	0	45.1	206	61	37	32	4	0	1	2	9	0	27	2	0	2	3	.400	0	0--	-	5.27	6.35
1999 Piedmont	A	26	26	3	0	164.1	708	176	79	57	6	8	6	9	41	2	99	8	2	11	8	.579	1	0--	-	3.60	3.12
2000 Clearwater	A+	26	24	4	0	176.1	778	229	99	70	7	6	5	11	26	1	82	4	2	8	13	.381	0	0--	-	4.55	3.57
2001 Reading	AA	28	28	4	0	180.0	740	197	85	78	20	6	2	11	27	0	100	3	0	15	8	.652	1	0--	-	4.05	3.90
2002 Reading	AA	2	0	0	1	3.0	10	0	0	0	0	0	0	0	0	0	0	1	0	0	0	-	0	1--	-	0.00	0.00
2002 Philadelphia	NL	68	0	0	21	84.0	350	88	34	30	4	9	3	4	22	6	41	3	0	5	0	1.000	0	1-5	8	3.60	3.21
2003 Philadelphia	NL	62	1	0	16	87.1	380	92	43	43	7	6	1	8	37	5	48	12	1	3	1	.750	0	1-3	4	4.73	4.43
2 ML YEARS		130	1	0	36	171.1	730	180	77	73	11	15	4	12	59	11	89	15	1	8	1	.889	0	2-8	12	4.16	3.83

Randall Simon

Bats: L **Throws:** L **Pos:** 1B-109; PH-20 **Ht:** 6'0" **Wt:** 230 **Born:** 5/26/75 **Age:** 29

Year Team	Lg	G	AB	H	2B	3B	HR	(Hm	Rd)	TB	R	RBI	RC	TBB	IBB	SO	HBP	SH	SF	SB	CS	SB%	GDP	Avg	OBP	Slg
2003 Nashville*	AAA	2	8	3	1	0	1	(-	-)	7	3	2	2	0	0	0	0	0	0	0	0	-	1	.375	.375	.875
1997 Atlanta	NL	13	14	6	1	0	0	(0	0)	7	2	1	3	1	0	2	0	0	0	0	0	-	1	.429	.467	.500
1998 Atlanta	NL	7	16	3	0	0	0	(0	0)	3	2	4	0	0	0	1	0	0	1	0	0	-	0	.188	.176	.188
1999 Atlanta	NL	90	218	69	16	0	5	(2	3)	100	26	25	33	17	6	25	1	0	1	2	2	.50	10	.317	.367	.459
2001 Detroit	AL	81	256	78	14	2	6	(1	5)	114	28	37	36	15	2	28	0	1	2	0	1	.00	9	.305	.341	.445
2002 Detroit	AL	130	482	145	17	1	19	(13	6)	221	51	82	68	13	5	30	4	0	7	0	1	.00	13	.301	.320	.459
2003 Pit-ChC	NL	124	410	113	17	0	16	(4	12)	178	47	72	61	16	2	37	4	0	1	0	0	-	7	.276	.309	.434
2003 Pittsburgh	NL	91	307	84	14	0	10	(4	6)	128	34	51	40	12	1	30	2	0	0	0	0	-	6	.274	.305	.417
2003 Chicago	NL	33	103	29	3	0	6	(0	6)	50	13	21	21	4	1	7	2	0	1	0	0	-	1	.282	.318	.485
6 ML YEARS		445	1396	414	65	3	46	(20	26)	623	156	221	201	62	15	123	9	1	12	2	4	.33	40	.297	.328	.446

Jason Simontacchi

Pitches: R **Bats:** R **Pos:** RP-30; SP-16 **Ht:** 6'2" **Wt:** 185 **Born:** 11/13/73 **Age:** 30

Year Team	Lg	G	GS	CG	GF	IP	BFP	H	R	ER	HR	SH	SF	HB	TBB	IBB	SO	WP	Bk	W	L	Pct	ShO	Sv-Op	Hld	ERC	ERA
1996 Spokane	A-	14	6	0	3	47.0	214	59	37	27	8	3	3	3	15	0	43	1	0	2	5	.286	0	2- -	-	6.02	5.17
1997 Lansing	A	29	1	0	11	60.2	295	93	56	47	7	3	4	4	15	1	38	1	2	3	7	.300	0	2- -	-	6.82	6.97
1998 Springfield	IND	16	16	3	0	110.0	451	103	43	36	14	7	0	6	21	3	92	4	1	10	2	.833	1	0- -	-	3.28	2.95
1999 Hickory	A	23	7	0	8	69.1	297	71	34	31	8	2	1	6	19	1	66	5	3	4	6	.400	0	1- -	-	4.15	4.02
2001 Edmonton	AAA	32	18	2	3	143.1	627	192	97	85	21	3	7	6	23	1	83	4	0	7	13	.350	0	0- -	-	5.67	5.34
2002 Memphis	AAA	6	6	0	0	42.1	170	44	12	11	2	3	0	1	5	1	28	0	0	5	1	.833	0	0- -	-	2.99	2.34
2002 St Louis	NL	24	24	0	0	143.1	600	134	68	64	18	6	4	6	54	4	72	1	0	11	5	.688	0	0-0	0	4.01	4.02
2003 St Louis	NL	46	16	1	7	126.1	563	153	82	78	21	2	4	5	41	0	74	4	0	9	5	.643	0	1-3	7	5.68	5.56
2 ML YEARS		70	40	1	7	269.2	1163	287	150	142	39	8	8	11	95	4	146	5	0	20	10	.667	0	1-3	7	4.77	4.74

Chris Singleton

Bats: L **Throws:** L **Pos:** CF-102; PR-13; PH-10; RF-8; LF-4 **Ht:** 6'2" **Wt:** 210 **Born:** 8/15/72 **Age:** 31

Year Team	Lg	G	AB	H	2B	3B	HR	(Hm	Rd)	TB	R	RBI	RC	TBB	IBB	SO	HBP	SH	SF	SB	CS	SB%	GDP	Avg	OBP	Slg
1999 Chicago	AL	133	496	149	31	6	17	(5	12)	243	72	72	79	22	1	45	1	4	6	20	5	.80	10	.300	.328	.490
2000 Chicago	AL	147	511	130	22	5	11	(5	6)	195	83	62	61	35	2	85	1	12	4	22	7	.76	6	.254	.301	.382
2001 Chicago	AL	140	392	117	21	5	7	(4	3)	169	57	45	54	20	2	61	1	14	4	12	11	.52	5	.298	.331	.431
2002 Baltimore	AL	136	466	122	30	6	9	(4	5)	191	67	50	56	21	0	83	4	6	5	20	2	.91	8	.262	.296	.410
2003 Oakland	AL	120	306	75	24	1	1	(0	1)	104	38	36	32	26	4	55	1	2	6	7	2	.78	2	.245	.301	.340
5 ML YEARS		676	2171	593	128	23	45	(18	27)	902	317	265	282	124	9	329	8	38	25	81	27	.75	31	.273	.311	.415

Dan Smith

Pitches: R **Bats:** R **Pos:** RP-32 **Ht:** 6'3" **Wt:** 210 **Born:** 9/15/75 **Age:** 28

Year Team	Lg	G	GS	CG	GF	IP	BFP	H	R	ER	HR	SH	SF	HB	TBB	IBB	SO	WP	Bk	W	L	Pct	ShO	Sv-Op	Hld	ERC	ERA
1999 Montreal	NL	20	17	0	0	89.2	407	104	64	60	12	7	2	4	39	0	72	3	0	4	9	.308	0	0-1	0	5.59	6.02
2000 Boston	AL	2	0	0	0	3.1	15	2	3	3	0	1	3	0	3	0	1	0	0	0	0	-	0	0-0	0	2.96	8.10
2002 Montreal	NL	33	0	0	13	46.2	188	34	18	18	6	2	2	1	21	0	34	1	0	1	1	.500	0	2-2	2	3.17	3.47
2003 Montreal	NL	32	0	0	8	37.2	170	42	23	22	11	0	0	2	18	2	35	5	0	2	2	.500	0	0-1	2	6.75	5.26
4 ML YEARS		87	17	0	21	177.1	780	182	108	103	29	10	7	7	81	2	142	9	0	7	12	.368	0	2-4	4	5.10	5.23

Jason Smith

Bats: L **Throws:** R **Pos:** 3B-1 **Ht:** 6'3" **Wt:** 199 **Born:** 7/24/77 **Age:** 26

Year Team	Lg	G	AB	H	2B	3B	HR	(Hm	Rd)	TB	R	RBI	RC	TBB	IBB	SO	HBP	SH	SF	SB	CS	SB%	GDP	Avg	OBP	Slg
2003 Durham*	AAA	130	515	147	20	14	15	(-	-)	240	76	71	73	11	0	128	5	8	5	14	9	.61	1	.285	.304	.466
2001 Chicago	NL	2	1	0	0	0	0	(0	0)	0	0	0	0	0	0	1	0	0	0	0	0	-	0	.000	.000	.000
2002 Tampa Bay	AL	26	65	13	1	2	1	(0	1)	21	9	6	5	2	0	24	0	2	0	3	0	1.00	0	.200	.224	.323
2003 Tampa Bay	AL	1	4	1	0	0	0	(0	0)	1	0	0	0	0	0	0	0	0	0	0	0	-	0	.250	.250	.250
3 ML YEARS		29	70	14	1	2	1	(0	1)	22	9	6	5	2	0	25	0	2	0	3	0	1.00	0	.200	.222	.314

Mark Smith

Bats: R **Throws:** R **Pos:** PH-19; LF-12; RF-3 **Ht:** 6'3" **Wt:** 225 **Born:** 5/7/70 **Age:** 34

Year Team	Lg	G	AB	H	2B	3B	HR	(Hm	Rd)	TB	R	RBI	RC	TBB	IBB	SO	HBP	SH	SF	SB	CS	SB%	GDP	Avg	OBP	Slg
2003 Indianapolis*	AAA	103	388	114	25	2	15	(-	-)	188	46	62	58	21	2	58	5	0	2	3	2	.60	14	.294	.337	.485
1994 Baltimore	AL	3	7	1	0	0	0	(0	0)	1	0	2	0	0	0	2	0	0	0	0	0	-	0	.143	.143	.143
1995 Baltimore	AL	37	104	24	5	0	3	(1	2)	38	11	15	12	12	2	22	1	2	1	3	0	1.00	4	.231	.314	.365
1996 Baltimore	AL	27	78	19	2	0	4	(1	3)	33	9	10	9	3	0	20	3	0	0	2	0	.00	0	.244	.298	.423
1997 Pittsburgh	NL	71	193	55	13	1	9	(6	3)	97	29	35	37	28	1	36	0	0	1	3	1	.75	3	.285	.374	.503
1998 Pittsburgh	NL	59	128	25	6	0	2	(1	1)	37	18	13	12	10	0	26	3	0	3	7	0	1.00	1	.195	.264	.289
2000 Florida	NL	104	192	47	8	1	5	(2	3)	72	22	27	23	17	1	54	2	0	2	2	0	1.00	3	.245	.310	.375
2001 Montreal	NL	80	194	47	13	1	6	(3	3)	80	28	18	26	23	0	38	2	1	2	0	2	.00	3	.242	.326	.412
2003 Milwaukee	NL	33	63	15	4	0	3	(1	2)	28	8	10	7	4	0	13	0	0	2	0	0	-	5	.238	.275	.444
8 ML YEARS		414	959	233	51	3	32	(17	15)	386	125	130	126	97	4	211	11	3	11	15	5	.75	18	.243	.316	.403

Stephen Smitherman

Bats: R **Throws:** R **Pos:** LF-14; PH-8; PR-1   **Ht:** 6'4" **Wt:** 235 **Born:** 9/1/78 **Age:** 25

							BATTING												BASERUNNING				AVERAGES		
Year Team	Lg	G	AB	H	2B	3B	HR	(Hm | Rd)	TB	R	RBI	RC	TBB	IBB	SO	HBP	SH	SF	SB	CS	SB%	GDP	Avg	OBP	Slg
2000 Billings	R+	70	301	95	16	5	15	(- | -)	166	61	65	59	23	2	67	6	0	2	14	1	.93	10	.316	.373	.551
2001 Dayton	A	134	497	139	45	2	20	(- | -)	248	89	73	84	43	1	113	10	0	2	16	7	.70	9	.280	.348	.499
2002 Stockton	A+	128	482	151	36	1	19	(- | -)	246	78	99	88	39	2	126	6	0	14	17	2	.89	14	.313	.362	.510
2003 Louisville	AAA	17	63	8	0	0	0	(- | -)	8	1	5	0	4	0	19	1	0	1	0	0	-	2	.127	.188	.127
2003 Chattanooga	AA	105	365	113	21	2	19	(- | -)	195	60	73	78	54	6	95	6	0	5	11	3	.79	7	.310	.402	.534
2003 Cincinnati	NL	21	44	7	2	0	1	(1 | 0)	12	3	6	4	3	0	9	0	0	0	1	0	1.00	0	.159	.213	.273

John Smoltz

Pitches: R **Bats:** R **Pos:** RP-62   **Ht:** 6'3" **Wt:** 220 **Born:** 5/15/67 **Age:** 37

		HOW MUCH HE PITCHED						WHAT HE GAVE UP											THE RESULTS					
Year Team	Lg	G	GS	CG	GF	IP	BFP	H	R	ER	HR	SH	SF	HB	TBB	IBB	SO	WP	Bk	W	L	Pct	ShO	Sv-Op	Hld	ERC	ERA
1988 Atlanta	NL	12	12	0	0	64.0	297	74	40	39	10	2	0	3	33	4	37	2	1	2	7	.222	0	0-0	0	5.86	5.48
1989 Atlanta	NL	29	29	5	0	208.0	847	160	79	68	15	10	7	2	72	3	168	8	3	12	11	.522	0	0-0	0	2.50	2.94
1990 Atlanta	NL	34	34	6	0	231.1	966	206	109	99	20	9	8	1	90	3	170	14	3	14	11	.560	2	0-0	0	3.37	3.85
1991 Atlanta	NL	36	36	5	0	229.2	947	206	101	97	16	9	9	3	77	1	148	20	2	14	13	.519	0	0-0	0	3.15	3.80
1992 Atlanta	NL	35	35	9	0	246.2	1021	206	90	78	17	7	8	5	80	5	215	17	1	15	12	.556	3	0-0	0	2.73	2.85
1993 Atlanta	NL	35	35	3	0	243.2	1028	208	104	98	23	13	4	6	100	12	208	13	1	15	11	.577	1	0-0	0	3.29	3.62
1994 Atlanta	NL	21	21	1	0	134.2	568	120	69	62	15	7	6	4	48	4	113	7	0	6	10	.375	0	0-0	0	3.44	4.14
1995 Atlanta	NL	29	29	2	0	192.2	808	166	76	68	15	13	5	4	72	8	193	13	0	12	7	.632	1	0-0	0	3.08	3.18
1996 Atlanta	NL	35	35	6	0	253.2	995	199	93	83	19	12	4	2	55	3	276	10	1	24	8	.750	2	0-0	0	2.17	2.94
1997 Atlanta	NL	35	35	7	0	256.0	1043	234	97	86	21	10	3	1	63	9	241	10	1	15	12	.556	2	0-0	0	2.89	3.02
1998 Atlanta	NL	26	26	2	0	167.2	681	145	58	54	10	4	2	4	44	2	173	3	1	17	3	.850	2	0-0	0	2.67	2.90
1999 Atlanta	NL	29	29	1	0	186.1	746	168	70	66	14	10	5	4	40	2	156	2	0	11	8	.579	1	0-0	0	2.81	3.19
2001 Atlanta	NL	36	5	0	20	59.0	238	53	24	22	7	1	2	2	10	2	57	0	0	3	3	.500	0	10-11	5	2.85	3.36
2002 Atlanta	NL	75	0	0	68	80.1	314	59	30	29	4	2	1	0	24	1	85	1	1	3	2	.600	0	55-59	0	2.06	3.25
2003 Atlanta	NL	62	0	0	55	64.1	244	48	9	8	2	0	1	0	8	1	73	2	0	0	2	.000	0	45-49	0	1.50	1.12
15 ML YEARS		529	361	47	143	2618.0	10743	2252	1049	957	208	109	65	40	816	59	2313	122	15	163	120	.576	14	110-119	5	2.89	3.29

J.T. Snow

Bats: L **Throws:** L **Pos:** 1B-98; PH-5   **Ht:** 6'2" **Wt:** 209 **Born:** 2/26/68 **Age:** 36

							BATTING												BASERUNNING				AVERAGES		
Year Team	Lg	G	AB	H	2B	3B	HR	(Hm	Rd)	TB	R	RBI	RC	TBB	IBB	SO	HBP	SH	SF	SB	CS	SB%	GDP	Avg	OBP	Slg
1992 New York	AL	7	14	2	1	0	0	(0	0)	3	1	2	2	5	1	5	0	0	0	0	0	-	0	.143	.368	.214
1993 Anaheim	AL	129	419	101	18	2	16	(10	6)	171	60	57	57	55	4	88	2	7	6	3	0	1.00	10	.241	.328	.408
1994 Anaheim	AL	61	223	49	4	0	8	(7	1)	77	22	30	22	19	1	48	3	2	1	0	1	.00	2	.220	.289	.345
1995 Anaheim	AL	143	544	157	22	1	24	(14	10)	253	80	102	85	52	4	91	3	5	2	2	1	.67	16	.289	.353	.465
1996 Anaheim	AL	155	575	148	20	1	17	(8	9)	221	69	67	67	56	6	96	5	2	3	1	6	.14	19	.257	.327	.384
1997 San Francisco	NL	157	531	149	36	1	28	(14	14)	271	81	104	105	96	13	124	1	2	7	6	4	.60	8	.281	.387	.510
1998 San Francisco	NL	138	435	108	29	1	15	(9	6)	184	65	79	60	58	3	84	0	0	7	1	2	.33	12	.248	.332	.423
1999 San Francisco	NL	161	570	156	25	2	24	(7	17)	257	93	98	93	86	7	121	5	1	6	0	4	.00	16	.274	.370	.451
2000 San Francisco	NL	155	536	152	33	2	19	(10	9)	246	82	96	87	66	6	129	11	0	14	1	3	.25	20	.284	.365	.459
2001 San Francisco	NL	101	285	70	12	1	8	(3	5)	108	43	34	44	55	10	81	4	0	4	0	0	-	2	.246	.371	.379
2002 San Francisco	NL	143	422	104	26	2	6	(1	5)	152	47	53	53	59	5	90	7	0	6	0	0	-	11	.246	.344	.360
2003 San Francisco	NL	103	330	90	18	3	8	(2	6)	138	48	51	58	55	0	55	8	1	2	1	2	.33	7	.273	.387	.418
12 ML YEARS		1453	4884	1286	244	16	173	(85	88)	2081	691	773	733	662	60	1012	49	20	58	15	23	.39	123	.263	.353	.426

Kyle Snyder

Pitches: R **Bats:** B **Pos:** SP-15   **Ht:** 6'8" **Wt:** 220 **Born:** 9/9/77 **Age:** 26

		HOW MUCH HE PITCHED						WHAT HE GAVE UP											THE RESULTS					
Year Team	Lg	G	GS	CG	GF	IP	BFP	H	R	ER	HR	SH	SF	HB	TBB	IBB	SO	WP	Bk	W	L	Pct	ShO	Sv-Op	Hld	ERC	ERA
1999 Spokane	A-	7	7	0	0	24.0	103	20	13	11	1	2	1	2	7	0	25	1	0	1	0	1.000	0	0--	-	2.59	4.13
2000 Royals	R	1	1	0	0	2.0	7	1	0	0	0	0	0	0	0	0	4	0	0	0	0	-	0	0--	-	0.54	0.00
2000 Wilmington	A+	1	1	0	0	0.0	1	0	1	0	0	0	0	0	1	0	0	0	0	0	0	-	0	0--	-	-	-
2002 Wilmington	A+	15	15	0	0	48.1	207	49	19	16	1	1	2	5	11	0	48	2	0	0	2	.000	0	0--	-	3.31	2.98
2002 Wichita	AA	6	6	0	0	25.2	101	21	12	12	4	0	0	1	7	1	18	3	0	2	2	.500	0	0--	-	3.18	4.21
2003 Wichita	AA	1	1	0	0	5.0	17	2	0	0	0	0	0	0	0	0	2	0	0	0	0	-	0	0--	-	0.67	0.00
2003 Omaha	AAA	5	5	0	0	29.0	116	28	9	9	3	0	1	1	6	0	15	0	0	3	0	1.000	0	0--	-	3.42	2.79
2003 Royals	R	1	1	0	0	2.0	8	3	1	1	0	0	0	0	0	0	1	0	0	0	0	-	0	0--	-	5.09	4.50
2003 Kansas City	AL	15	15	0	0	85.1	364	94	52	49	11	0	9	2	21	3	39	4	0	1	6	.143	0	0-0	0	4.29	5.17

Luis Sojo

Bats: R **Throws:** R **Pos:** 1B-1; 2B-1; PH-1   **Ht:** 5'11" **Wt:** 185 **Born:** 1/3/66 **Age:** 38

							BATTING												BASERUNNING				AVERAGES		
Year Team	Lg	G	AB	H	2B	3B	HR	(Hm	Rd)	TB	R	RBI	RC	TBB	IBB	SO	HBP	SH	SF	SB	CS	SB%	GDP	Avg	OBP	Slg
1990 Toronto	AL	33	80	18	3	0	1	(0	1)	24	14	9	6	5	0	5	0	0	0	1	1	.50	1	.225	.271	.300
1991 Anaheim	AL	113	364	94	14	1	3	(1	2)	119	38	20	33	14	0	26	5	19	0	4	2	.67	12	.258	.295	.327
1992 Anaheim	AL	106	368	100	12	3	7	(2	5)	139	37	43	35	14	0	24	1	7	1	7	11	.39	14	.272	.299	.378
1993 Toronto	AL	19	47	8	2	0	0	(0	0)	10	5	6	2	4	0	2	0	2	1	0	0	-	3	.170	.231	.213
1994 Seattle	AL	63	213	59	9	2	6	(4	2)	90	32	22	28	8	0	25	2	1	1	2	1	.67	2	.277	.308	.423
1995 Seattle	AL	102	339	98	18	2	7	(4	3)	141	50	39	46	23	0	19	1	6	1	4	2	.67	9	.289	.335	.416
1996 Sea-NYY	AL	95	287	63	10	1	1	(1	0)	78	23	21	17	11	0	17	1	8	1	2	2	.50	10	.220	.250	.272
1997 New York	AL	77	215	66	6	1	2	(2	0)	80	27	25	29	16	0	14	1	5	2	3	1	.75	5	.307	.355	.372
1998 New York	AL	54	147	34	3	1	0	(3	0)	39	16	14	9	4	0	15	0	1	1	1	0	1.00	5	.231	.250	.265
1999 New York	AL	49	127	32	6	0	2	(1	1)	44	20	16	11	4	0	17	0	2	0	1	0	1.00	4	.252	.275	.346
2000 Pit-NYY		95	301	86	18	1	7	(4	3)	127	33	37	38	17	3	22	1	3	1	2	0	1.00	11	.286	.325	.422
2001 New York	AL	39	79	13	2	0	0	(0	0)	15	5	9	4	4	0	12	1	0	0	1	0	1.00	0	.165	.214	.190
2003 New York	AL	3	4	0	0	0	0			0	0	0	0	0	0	0	0	0	0	0	0	-	0	.000	.000	.000

213

Year Team	Lg	G	AB	H	2B	3B	HR	(Hm Rd)	TB	R	RBI	RC	TBB	IBB	SO	HBP	SH	SF	SB	CS	SB%	GDP	Avg	OBP	Slg
1996 Seattle	AL	77	247	52	8	1	1	(0 0)	65	20	16	14	10	0	13	1	6	0	2	2	.50	8	.211	.244	.263
1996 New York	AL	18	40	11	2	0	0	(1 0)	13	3	5	3	1	0	4	0	2	1	0	0	-	2	.275	.286	.325
2000 Pittsburgh	NL	61	176	50	11	0	5	(2 3)	76	14	20	23	11	3	16	1	0	1	1	0	1.00	6	.284	.328	.432
2000 New York	AL	34	125	36	7	1	2	(2 0)	51	19	17	15	6	0	6	0	3	0	1	0	1.00	5	.288	.321	.408
13 ML YEARS		848	2571	671	103	12	36	(22 17)	906	300	261	258	124	3	198	13	56	9	28	20	.58	76	.261	.297	.352

Zach Sorensen

Bats: B Throws: R Pos: 2B-14; PR-13; PH-11; SS-3; 3B-1; LF-1 **Ht: 6'0" Wt: 190 Born: 1/3/77 Age: 27**

Year Team	Lg	G	AB	H	2B	3B	HR	(Hm Rd)	TB	R	RBI	RC	TBB	IBB	SO	HBP	SH	SF	SB	CS	SB%	GDP	Avg	OBP	Slg
1998 Watertown	A-	53	200	60	7	8	4	(- -)	95	38	26	41	35	0	35	0	2	0	14	4	.78	2	.300	.404	.475
1999 Kinston	A+	130	508	121	16	7	7	(- -)	172	79	59	58	62	1	126	2	8	2	24	12	.67	6	.238	.322	.339
2000 Akron	AA	96	382	99	17	4	6	(- -)	142	62	38	49	42	0	62	2	4	3	16	6	.73	8	.259	.333	.372
2000 Buffalo	AAA	12	38	10	1	1	0	(- -)	13	5	2	4	3	0	9	0	0	1	1	0	1.00	2	.263	.310	.342
2001 Akron	AA	46	194	45	6	1	5	(- -)	68	24	16	17	11	1	30	0	3	0	10	8	.56	3	.232	.273	.351
2001 Mahning VI	A-	14	53	13	0	1	1	(- -)	18	10	11	5	2	0	8	0	1	2	2	0	1.00	1	.245	.263	.340
2001 Buffalo	AAA	2	7	2	0	0	0	(- -)	2	1	1	1	0	0	0	0	0	0	0	0	-	0	.286	.286	.286
2002 Buffalo	AAA	120	455	120	12	12	7	(- -)	177	55	54	52	24	1	72	1	15	4	13	6	.68	9	.264	.300	.389
2003 Buffalo	AAA	61	238	57	12	3	3	(- -)	84	39	29	26	22	0	42	0	5	4	12	5	.71	3	.239	.299	.353
2003 Cleveland	AL	36	37	5	1	0	1	(0 1)	9	2	2	1	7	0	13	0	0	0	0	3	.00	0	.135	.273	.243

Alfonso Soriano

Bats: R Throws: R Pos: 2B-155; PR-2 **Ht: 6'1" Wt: 180 Born: 1/7/78 Age: 26**

Year Team	Lg	G	AB	H	2B	3B	HR	(Hm Rd)	TB	R	RBI	RC	TBB	IBB	SO	HBP	SH	SF	SB	CS	SB%	GDP	Avg	OBP	Slg
1999 New York	AL	9	8	1	0	0	1	(1 0)	4	2	1	0	0	0	3	0	0	0	0	1	.00	0	.125	.125	.500
2000 New York	AL	22	50	9	3	0	2	(0 2)	18	5	3	4	1	0	15	0	2	0	2	0	1.00	0	.180	.196	.360
2001 New York	AL	158	574	154	34	3	18	(8 10)	248	77	73	77	29	0	125	3	3	5	43	14	.75	7	.268	.304	.432
2002 New York	AL	156	696	209	51	2	39	(17 22)	381	128	102	125	23	1	157	14	1	7	41	13	.76	8	.300	.332	.547
2003 New York	AL	156	682	198	36	5	38	(15 23)	358	114	91	112	38	7	130	12	0	2	35	8	.81	6	.290	.338	.525
5 ML YEARS		501	2010	571	124	10	98	(41 57)	1009	326	270	318	91	8	430	29	6	14	121	36	.77	23	.284	.322	.502

Rafael Soriano

Pitches: R Bats: R Pos: RP-40 **Ht: 6'1" Wt: 175 Born: 12/19/79 Age: 24**

Year Team	Lg	G	GS	CG	GF	IP	BFP	H	R	ER	HR	SH	SF	HB	TBB	IBB	SO	WP	Bk	W	L	Pct	ShO	Sv-Op	Hld	ERC	ERA
1999 Everett	A-	14	14	0	0	75.1	323	56	34	26	8	1	0	4	49	0	83	2	0	5	4	.556	0	0--	-	3.95	3.11
2000 Wisconsin	A	21	21	1	0	122.1	500	97	41	39	3	2	5	12	50	0	90	5	2	8	4	.667	0	0--	-	2.96	2.87
2001 Sn Brnardino	A+	15	15	2	0	89.0	346	49	28	25	4	2	2	4	39	0	98	2	0	6	3	.667	1	0--	-	1.82	2.53
2001 San Antonio	AA	8	8	0	0	48.1	193	34	18	18	5	0	0	2	14	0	53	2	1	2	2	.500	0	0--	-	2.29	3.35
2002 San Antonio	AA	10	8	0	0	46.2	185	32	13	12	6	0	1	1	15	0	52	0	0	2	3	.400	0	0--	-	2.41	2.31
2003 Tacoma	AAA	11	10	0	0	62.0	241	43	24	22	2	0	1	1	12	0	63	0	1	4	3	.571	0	0--	-	1.65	3.19
2002 Seattle	AL	10	8	0	1	47.1	202	45	25	24	8	1	0	0	16	1	32	2	0	0	3	.000	0	1-1	0	3.93	4.56
2003 Seattle	AL	40	0	0	12	53.0	201	30	9	9	2	0	1	3	12	1	68	0	0	3	0	1.000	0	1-2	5	1.32	1.53
2 ML YEARS		50	8	0	13	100.1	403	75	34	33	10	1	1	3	28	2	100	2	0	3	3	.500	0	2-3	5	2.38	2.96

Jorge Sosa

Pitches: R Bats: B Pos: SP-19; RP-10 **Ht: 6'2" Wt: 177 Born: 4/28/77 Age: 27**

Year Team	Lg	G	GS	CG	GF	IP	BFP	H	R	ER	HR	SH	SF	HB	TBB	IBB	SO	WP	Bk	W	L	Pct	ShO	Sv-Op	Hld	ERC	ERA
2001 Everett	A-	21	7	0	11	58.2	247	45	22	11	2	2	3	2	19	0	57	8	1	3	1	.750	0	7--	-	2.18	1.69
2001 Wisconsin	A	2	0	0	0	2.0	9	3	2	2	1	0	0	0	0	0	4	0	0	0	0	-	0	0--	-	8.13	9.00
2002 Orlando	AA	2	2	0	0	7.0	25	4	2	0	1	0	0	0	1	0	3	0	0	0	0	-	0	0--	-	1.44	0.00
2003 Durham	AAA	4	4	0	0	24.2	112	32	15	15	3	0	0	1	9	0	17	3	0	1	1	.500	0	0--	-	6.10	5.47
2002 Tampa Bay	AL	31	14	0	10	99.1	434	88	63	61	16	0	5	2	54	0	48	5	0	2	7	.222	0	0-0	1	4.54	5.53
2003 Tampa Bay	AL	29	19	1	4	128.2	566	137	71	66	14	4	5	4	60	4	72	8	1	5	12	.294	1	0-0	0	4.93	4.62
2 ML YEARS		60	33	1	14	228.0	1000	225	134	127	30	4	10	6	114	4	120	13	1	7	19	.269	1	0-0	1	4.75	5.01

Sammy Sosa

Bats: R Throws: R Pos: RF-137 **Ht: 6'0" Wt: 220 Born: 11/12/68 Age: 35**

Year Team	Lg	G	AB	H	2B	3B	HR	(Hm Rd)	TB	R	RBI	RC	TBB	IBB	SO	HBP	SH	SF	SB	CS	SB%	GDP	Avg	OBP	Slg
1989 Tex-CWS	AL	58	183	47	8	0	4	(1 3)	67	27	13	18	11	2	47	2	5	2	7	5	.58	6	.257	.303	.366
1990 Chicago	AL	153	532	124	26	10	15	(10 5)	215	72	70	59	33	4	150	6	2	6	32	16	.67	10	.233	.282	.404
1991 Chicago	AL	116	316	64	10	1	10	(3 7)	106	39	33	23	14	2	98	2	5	1	13	6	.68	5	.203	.240	.335
1992 Chicago	NL	67	262	68	7	2	8	(4 4)	103	41	25	33	19	1	63	4	4	2	15	7	.68	4	.260	.317	.393
1993 Chicago	NL	159	598	156	25	5	33	(23 10)	290	92	93	88	38	6	135	4	0	5	36	11	.77	14	.261	.309	.485
1994 Chicago	NL	105	426	128	17	6	25	(11 14)	232	59	70	75	25	1	92	2	1	4	22	13	.63	7	.300	.339	.545
1995 Chicago	NL	144	564	151	17	3	36	(19 17)	282	89	119	98	58	11	134	5	0	7	34	7	.83	8	.268	.340	.500
1996 Chicago	NL	124	498	136	21	2	40	(26 14)	281	84	100	87	34	6	134	5	0	4	18	5	.78	5	.273	.323	.564
1997 Chicago	NL	162	642	161	31	4	36	(25 11)	308	90	119	88	45	9	174	2	0	5	22	12	.65	9	.251	.300	.480
1998 Chicago	NL	159	643	198	20	0	66	(35 31)	416	134	158	142	73	14	171	1	0	5	18	9	.67	20	.308	.377	.647
1999 Chicago	NL	162	625	180	24	2	63	(33 30)	397	114	141	134	78	8	171	3	0	6	7	8	.47	9	.288	.367	.635
2000 Chicago	NL	156	604	193	38	1	50	(22 28)	383	106	138	144	91	19	168	2	0	7	7	4	.64	12	.320	.406	.634
2001 Chicago	NL	160	577	189	34	5	64	(34 30)	425	146	160	170	116	37	153	6	0	12	0	2	.00	16	.328	.437	.737
2002 Chicago	NL	150	556	160	19	2	49	(24 25)	330	122	108	122	103	15	144	3	0	4	2	0	1.00	6	.288	.399	.594
2003 Chicago	NL	137	517	144	22	0	40	(19 21)	286	99	103	95	62	9	143	5	0	5	0	1	.00	14	.279	.358	.553

Year Team	Lg	G	AB	H	2B	3B	HR	(Hm	Rd)	TB	R	RBI	RC	TBB	IBB	SO	HBP	SH	SF	SB	CS	SB%	GDP	Avg	OBP	Slg
1989 Texas	AL	25	84	20	3	0	1	(0	1)	26	8	3	4	0	0	20	0	4	0	0	2	.00	3	.238	.238	.310
1989 Chicago	AL	33	99	27	5	0	3	(1	2)	41	19	10	14	11	2	27	2	1	2	7	3	.70	3	.273	.351	.414
15 ML YEARS		2012	7543	2099	319	43	539	(289	250)	4121	1314	1450	1376	800	144	1977	52	17	67	233	106	.69	167	.278	.349	.546

Steve Sparks

Pitches: R **Bats:** R **Pos:** RP-51   **Ht:** 6'0" **Wt:** 195 **Born:** 7/2/65 **Age:** 38

| | | HOW MUCH HE PITCHED | | | | | | WHAT HE GAVE UP | | | | | | | | | | | | THE RESULTS | | | | | | |
Year Team	Lg	G	GS	CG	GF	IP	BFP	H	R	ER	HR	SH	SF	HB	TBB	IBB	SO	WP	Bk	W	L	Pct	ShO	Sv-Op	Hld	ERC	ERA
1995 Milwaukee	NL	33	27	3	2	202.0	875	210	111	104	17	5	12	5	86	1	96	5	1	9	11	.450	0	0-0	0	4.44	4.63
1996 Milwaukee	NL	20	13	1	2	88.2	406	103	66	65	19	3	1	3	52	0	21	6	0	4	7	.364	0	0-0	0	7.03	6.60
1998 Anaheim	AL	22	20	0	1	128.2	562	130	66	62	14	2	3	5	58	0	90	6	0	9	4	.692	0	0-0	0	4.60	4.34
1999 Anaheim	AL	28	26	0	1	147.2	688	165	101	89	21	2	8	9	82	0	73	8	0	5	11	.313	0	0-0	0	5.94	5.42
2000 Detroit	AL	20	15	1	5	104.0	446	108	55	47	7	1	4	4	29	0	53	6	0	7	5	.583	1	1-1	0	3.71	4.07
2001 Detroit	AL	35	33	8	2	232.0	982	244	110	94	22	4	9	6	64	1	116	8	2	14	9	.609	1	0-0	0	3.97	3.65
2002 Detroit	AL	32	30	3	0	189.0	868	238	134	116	23	3	8	12	67	3	98	8	3	8	16	.333	0	0-0	0	5.78	5.52
2003 Det-Oak	AL	51	0	0	26	107.0	460	114	68	58	13	1	7	3	37	4	54	3	0	0	6	.000	0	2-4	0	4.49	4.88
2003 Detroit	AL	42	0	0	24	89.2	385	95	57	47	11	1	6	3	34	4	49	3	0	0	6	.000	0	2-4	0	4.65	4.72
2003 Oakland	AL	9	0	0	2	17.1	75	19	11	11	2	0	1	0	3	0	5	0	0	0	0	-	0	0-0	0	3.67	5.71
8 ML YEARS		241	164	16	39	1199.0	5287	1312	711	635	136	21	49	47	475	9	601	50	6	56	69	.448	2	3-5	0	4.87	4.77

Justin Speier

Pitches: R **Bats:** R **Pos:** RP-72   **Ht:** 6'4" **Wt:** 205 **Born:** 11/6/73 **Age:** 30

| | | HOW MUCH HE PITCHED | | | | | | WHAT HE GAVE UP | | | | | | | | | | | | THE RESULTS | | | | | | |
Year Team	Lg	G	GS	CG	GF	IP	BFP	H	R	ER	HR	SH	SF	HB	TBB	IBB	SO	WP	Bk	W	L	Pct	ShO	Sv-Op	Hld	ERC	ERA
1998 ChC-Fla	NL	19	0	0	10	20.2	99	27	20	20	7	2	1	0	13	1	17	3	0	0	3	.000	0	0-1	1	8.94	8.71
1999 Atlanta	NL	19	0	0	8	28.2	127	28	18	18	8	0	1	0	13	1	22	0	0	0	0	-	0	0-0	0	5.27	5.65
2000 Cleveland	AL	47	0	0	12	68.1	290	57	27	25	9	2	4	4	28	3	69	7	1	5	2	.714	0	0-1	6	3.56	3.29
2001 Cle-Col		54	0	0	10	76.2	324	71	40	39	13	2	7	8	20	3	62	6	1	6	3	.667	0	0-1	4	3.93	4.58
2002 Colorado	NL	63	0	0	7	62.1	259	51	31	30	9	0	1	3	19	4	47	1	2	5	1	.833	0	1-4	18	3.06	4.33
2003 Colorado	NL	72	0	0	31	73.1	319	73	37	33	11	1	4	7	23	6	66	0	0	3	1	.750	0	9-12	12	4.27	4.05
1998 Chicago	NL	1	0	0	0	1.1	7	2	2	2	0	0	0	0	1	0	2	1	0	0	0	-	0	0-0	0	7.52	13.50
1998 Florida	NL	18	0	0	10	19.1	92	25	18	18	7	2	1	0	12	1	15	2	0	0	3	.000	0	0-1	1	9.02	8.38
2001 Cleveland	AL	12	0	0	2	20.2	96	24	16	16	5	0	3	3	8	0	15	2	0	2	0	1.000	0	0-0	0	6.61	6.97
2001 Colorado	NL	42	0	0	8	56.0	228	47	24	23	8	2	4	5	12	3	47	4	1	4	3	.571	0	0-1	4	3.04	3.70
6 ML YEARS		274	0	0	78	330.0	1418	307	173	165	57	7	18	22	116	18	283	17	4	19	10	.655	0	10-19	41	4.14	4.50

Shane Spencer

Bats: R **Throws:** R **Pos:** LF-66; RF-42; 1B-11; PH-10; DH-7; PR-2   **Ht:** 5'11" **Wt:** 225 **Born:** 2/20/72 **Age:** 32

| | | | | | | | | BATTING | | | | | | | | | | | | BASERUNNING | | | | AVERAGES | | |
Year Team	Lg	G	AB	H	2B	3B	HR	(Hm	Rd)	TB	R	RBI	RC	TBB	IBB	SO	HBP	SH	SF	SB	CS	SB%	GDP	Avg	OBP	Slg
1998 New York	AL	27	67	25	6	0	10	(8	2)	61	18	27	22	5	0	12	0	0	1	0	1	.00	0	.373	.411	.910
1999 New York	AL	71	205	48	8	0	8	(2	6)	80	25	20	23	18	0	51	2	0	1	0	4	.00	1	.234	.301	.390
2000 New York	AL	73	248	70	11	3	9	(4	5)	114	33	40	37	19	0	45	2	0	7	1	2	.33	4	.282	.330	.460
2001 New York	AL	80	283	73	14	2	10	(6	4)	121	40	46	39	21	0	58	4	0	3	4	1	.80	4	.258	.315	.428
2002 New York	AL	94	288	71	15	2	6	(5	1)	108	32	34	34	31	4	62	4	2	4	0	3	.00	5	.247	.324	.375
2003 Cle-Tex	AL	119	395	99	20	0	12	(5	7)	155	39	49	53	45	0	92	3	0	5	2	0	1.00	8	.251	.328	.392
2003 Cleveland	AL	64	210	57	10	0	8	(2	6)	91	23	26	31	18	0	52	1	0	3	2	0	1.00	6	.271	.328	.433
2003 Texas	AL	55	185	42	10	0	4	(3	1)	64	16	23	22	27	0	40	2	0	2	0	0	-	2	.227	.329	.346
6 ML YEARS		464	1486	386	74	7	55	(30	25)	639	187	216	208	139	4	320	15	2	21	7	11	.39	22	.260	.325	.430

Scott Spiezio

Bats: B **Throws:** R **Pos:** 1B-114; 3B-52; PH-11; RF-7; LF-3; PR-1   **Ht:** 6'2" **Wt:** 225 **Born:** 9/21/72 **Age:** 31

| | | | | | | | | BATTING | | | | | | | | | | | | BASERUNNING | | | | AVERAGES | | |
Year Team	Lg	G	AB	H	2B	3B	HR	(Hm	Rd)	TB	R	RBI	RC	TBB	IBB	SO	HBP	SH	SF	SB	CS	SB%	GDP	Avg	OBP	Slg
1996 Oakland	AL	9	29	9	2	0	2	(1	1)	17	6	8	6	4	1	4	0	2	0	0	1	.00	0	.310	.394	.586
1997 Oakland	AL	147	538	131	28	4	14	(6	8)	209	58	65	61	44	2	75	1	3	4	9	3	.75	13	.243	.300	.388
1998 Oakland	AL	114	406	105	19	1	9	(6	3)	153	54	50	50	44	3	56	2	7	2	1	3	.25	10	.259	.333	.377
1999 Oakland	AL	89	247	60	24	0	8	(3	5)	108	31	33	35	29	3	36	2	1	3	0	0	-	5	.243	.324	.437
2000 Anaheim	AL	123	297	72	11	2	17	(10	7)	138	47	49	47	40	2	56	3	1	4	1	2	.33	5	.242	.334	.465
2001 Anaheim	AL	139	457	124	29	4	13	(8	5)	200	57	54	65	34	4	65	5	3	4	5	2	.71	6	.271	.326	.438
2002 Anaheim	AL	157	491	140	34	2	12	(7	5)	214	80	82	86	67	7	52	4	3	6	6	7	.46	12	.285	.371	.436
2003 Anaheim	AL	158	521	138	36	7	16	(7	9)	236	69	83	73	46	8	66	5	2	7	6	3	.67	12	.265	.326	.453
8 ML YEARS		932	2986	779	183	20	91	(48	43)	1275	402	424	423	308	30	410	22	22	30	28	21	.57	63	.261	.331	.427

Junior Spivey

Bats: R **Throws:** R **Pos:** 2B-98; PH-9; PR-2; CF-1   **Ht:** 6'0" **Wt:** 185 **Born:** 1/28/75 **Age:** 29

| | | | | | | | | BATTING | | | | | | | | | | | | BASERUNNING | | | | AVERAGES | | |
Year Team	Lg	G	AB	H	2B	3B	HR	(Hm	Rd)	TB	R	RBI	RC	TBB	IBB	SO	HBP	SH	SF	SB	CS	SB%	GDP	Avg	OBP	Slg
2003 Tucson*	AAA	4	15	4	2	0	0	(-	-)	6	3	1	2	1	0	1	0	0	0	0	0	-	0	.267	.313	.400
2003 El Paso*	AA	4	11	5	1	0	0	(-	-)	6	2	1	3	2	1	1	1	0	1	2	0	1.00	1	.455	.533	.545
2001 Arizona	NL	72	163	42	6	3	5	(4	1)	69	33	21	26	23	0	47	2	6	1	3	0	1.00	3	.258	.354	.423
2002 Arizona	NL	143	538	162	34	6	16	(9	7)	256	103	78	94	65	5	100	16	1	6	11	6	.65	10	.301	.389	.476
2003 Arizona	NL	106	365	93	22	2	13	(10	3)	158	52	50	48	33	1	95	7	0	3	4	3	.57	7	.255	.326	.433
3 ML YEARS		321	1066	297	62	11	34	(23	11)	483	188	149	168	121	6	242	25	7	10	18	9	.67	20	.279	.363	.453

Tim Spooneybarger

Pitches: R **Bats:** R **Pos:** RP-33   **Ht:** 6'3" **Wt:** 190 **Born:** 10/21/79 **Age:** 24

Year Team	Lg	G	GS	CG	GF	IP	BFP	H	R	ER	HR	SH	SF	HB	TBB	IBB	SO	WP	Bk	W	L	Pct	ShO	Sv-Op	Hld	ERC	ERA
2001 Atlanta	NL	4	0	0	3	4.0	19	5	1	1	0	0	1	0	2	1	3	0	0	0	1	.000	0	0-0	0	4.53	2.25
2002 Atlanta	NL	51	0	0	14	51.1	214	38	16	15	4	1	1	2	26	5	33	4	0	1	0	1.000	0	1-1	11	2.96	2.63
2003 Florida	NL	33	0	0	9	42.0	159	27	21	19	1	2	3	1	11	0	32	5	0	1	2	.333	0	0-1	6	1.55	4.07
3 ML YEARS		88	0	0	26	97.1	392	70	38	35	5	3	5	3	39	6	68	9	0	2	3	.400	0	1-2	17	2.36	3.24

Russ Springer

Pitches: R **Bats:** R **Pos:** RP-17   **Ht:** 6'4" **Wt:** 211 **Born:** 11/7/68 **Age:** 35

Year Team	Lg	G	GS	CG	GF	IP	BFP	H	R	ER	HR	SH	SF	HB	TBB	IBB	SO	WP	Bk	W	L	Pct	ShO	Sv-Op	Hld	ERC	ERA
2003 Memphis*	AAA	7	0	0	6	6.1	23	2	1	1	0	0	0	0	4	0	5	0	0	0	0	-	0	0- -	-	2.00	1.42
1992 New York	AL	14	0	0	5	16.0	75	18	11	11	0	0	0	1	10	0	12	0	0	0	0	-	0	0-0	2	5.15	6.19
1993 Anaheim	AL	14	9	1	3	60.0	278	73	48	48	11	1	1	3	32	1	31	6	0	1	6	.143	0	0-0	0	6.87	7.20
1994 Anaheim	AL	18	5	0	6	45.2	198	53	28	28	9	1	0	3	14	0	28	2	0	2	2	.500	0	2-3	1	5.38	5.52
1995 Ana-Phi		33	6	0	6	78.1	350	82	48	46	16	2	2	7	35	4	70	2	0	1	2	.333	0	1-2	1	5.63	5.29
1996 Philadelphia	NL	51	7	0	12	96.2	437	106	60	50	12	5	3	1	38	6	94	5	0	3	10	.231	0	0-3	6	4.57	4.66
1997 Houston	NL	54	0	0	13	55.1	241	48	28	26	4	1	2	4	27	2	74	4	0	3	3	.500	0	3-7	9	3.69	4.23
1998 Ari-Atl		48	0	0	14	52.2	232	51	26	24	4	2	1	1	30	4	56	5	0	5	4	.556	0	0-4	7	4.38	4.10
1999 Atlanta	NL	49	0	0	8	47.1	194	31	20	18	5	0	2	2	22	2	49	0	0	2	1	.667	0	1-1	8	2.63	3.42
2000 Arizona	NL	52	0	0	10	62.0	282	63	36	35	11	2	3	2	34	6	59	3	0	2	3	.400	0	0-2	3	5.25	5.08
2001 Arizona	NL	18	0	0	9	17.2	79	20	16	14	5	1	1	0	4	0	12	2	0	0	0	-	0	1-1	2	5.13	7.13
2003 St Louis	NL	17	0	0	4	17.1	77	19	16	16	8	0	0	1	6	0	11	1	0	1	1	.500	0	0-1	5	7.27	8.31
1995 Anaheim	AL	19	6	0	3	51.2	238	60	37	35	11	1	0	5	25	1	38	1	0	1	2	.333	0	1-2	0	6.69	6.10
1995 Philadelphia	NL	14	0	0	3	26.2	112	22	11	11	5	1	2	2	10	3	32	1	0	0	0	-	0	0-0	0	3.73	3.71
1998 Arizona	NL	26	0	0	13	32.2	140	29	16	15	4	0	0	1	14	1	37	3	0	4	3	.571	0	0-3	1	3.77	4.13
1998 Atlanta	NL	22	0	0	1	20.0	92	22	10	9	0	2	1	0	16	3	19	2	0	1	1	.500	0	0-1	6	5.36	4.05
11 ML YEARS		368	27	1	90	549.0	2443	564	337	316	85	15	16	22	252	25	496	30	0	20	33	.377	0	8-24	43	4.93	5.18

Chris Spurling

Pitches: R **Bats:** R **Pos:** RP-66   **Ht:** 6'6" **Wt:** 240 **Born:** 6/28/77 **Age:** 27

Year Team	Lg	G	GS	CG	GF	IP	BFP	H	R	ER	HR	SH	SF	HB	TBB	IBB	SO	WP	Bk	W	L	Pct	ShO	Sv-Op	Hld	ERC	ERA
1998 Yankees	R	13	6	0	2	51.1	219	57	21	13	3	0	2	2	11	0	44	2	0	2	1	.667	0	1- -	-	3.83	2.28
1998 Greensboro	A	1	1	0	0	6.0	25	7	2	2	1	0	0	0	1	0	5	0	0	1	0	1.000	0	0- -	-	4.63	3.00
1999 Greensboro	A	49	0	0	26	76.1	332	78	34	31	8	4	9	2	23	3	68	7	0	4	6	.400	0	4- -	-	3.79	3.66
2000 Tampa	A+	34	0	0	15	57.0	239	50	27	24	1	2	3	1	22	5	55	3	0	4	6	.400	0	1- -	-	2.74	3.79
2000 Lynchburg	A+	9	0	0	6	18.1	66	8	2	2	1	0	1	0	3	0	17	0	0	1	0	1.000	0	5- -	-	0.80	0.98
2001 Altoona	AA	34	15	0	11	121.2	512	133	48	42	9	1	3	4	28	1	63	2	0	5	7	.417	0	1- -	-	3.92	3.11
2002 Altoona	AA	51	0	0	45	70.0	275	54	18	17	8	2	1	2	12	1	60	1	0	4	3	.571	0	20- -	-	2.21	2.19
2003 Detroit	AL	66	0	0	18	77.0	327	78	42	40	9	3	5	3	22	1	38	2	1	1	3	.250	0	3-6	5	3.95	4.68

Matt Stairs

Bats: L **Throws:** R **Pos:** RF-47; PH-43; 1B-31; LF-8; DH-2   **Ht:** 5'9" **Wt:** 215 **Born:** 2/27/68 **Age:** 36

Year Team	Lg	G	AB	H	2B	3B	HR	(Hm	Rd)	TB	R	RBI	RC	TBB	IBB	SO	HBP	SH	SF	SB	CS	SB%	GDP	Avg	OBP	Slg
2003 Nashville*	AAA	7	18	3	0	0	2	(-	-)	9	4	3	4	7	0	2	2	0	0	0	0	-	1	.167	.444	.500
1992 Montreal	NL	13	30	5	2	0	0	(0	0)	7	2	5	3	7	0	7	0	0	1	0	0	-	0	.167	.316	.233
1993 Montreal	NL	6	8	3	1	0	0	(0	0)	4	1	2	1	0	0	1	0	0	0	0	0	-	1	.375	.375	.500
1995 Boston	AL	39	88	23	7	1	1	(0	1)	35	8	17	9	4	0	14	1	1	1	0	1	.00	4	.261	.298	.398
1996 Oakland	AL	61	137	38	5	1	10	(5	5)	75	21	23	27	19	2	23	1	0	1	1	1	.50	2	.277	.367	.547
1997 Oakland	AL	133	352	105	19	0	27	(20	7)	205	62	73	77	50	1	60	3	1	4	3	2	.60	6	.298	.386	.582
1998 Oakland	AL	149	523	154	33	1	26	(16	10)	267	88	106	96	59	4	93	6	1	4	8	3	.73	13	.294	.370	.511
1999 Oakland	AL	146	531	137	26	3	38	(15	23)	283	94	102	101	89	6	124	2	0	1	2	7	.22	8	.258	.366	.533
2000 Oakland	AL	143	476	108	26	0	21	(9	12)	197	74	81	69	78	4	122	1	1	6	5	2	.71	7	.227	.333	.414
2001 Chicago	NL	128	340	85	21	0	17	(5	12)	157	48	61	57	52	7	76	7	1	3	2	3	.40	4	.250	.358	.462
2002 Milwaukee	NL	107	270	66	15	0	16	(6	10)	129	41	41	39	36	4	50	8	0	1	2	0	1.00	7	.244	.349	.478
2003 Pittsburgh	NL	121	305	89	20	1	20	(13	7)	171	49	57	59	45	3	64	5	0	2	0	1	.00	7	.292	.389	.561
11 ML YEARS		1046	3060	813	175	7	176	(89	87)	1530	488	568	538	439	31	634	34	5	24	23	20	.53	59	.266	.362	.500

Jason Standridge

Pitches: R **Bats:** R **Pos:** SP-7; RP-1   **Ht:** 6'4" **Wt:** 230 **Born:** 11/9/78 **Age:** 25

Year Team	Lg	G	GS	CG	GF	IP	BFP	H	R	ER	HR	SH	SF	HB	TBB	IBB	SO	WP	Bk	W	L	Pct	ShO	Sv-Op	Hld	ERC	ERA
2003 Durham*	AAA	12	10	0	2	60.0	265	62	32	30	5	3	3	1	28	0	37	1	0	2	4	.333	0	1- -	-	4.47	4.50
2001 Tampa Bay	AL	9	1	0	6	19.1	87	19	10	10	5	0	0	0	14	1	9	0	0	0	0	-	0	0-0	0	6.63	4.66
2002 Tampa Bay	AL	1	0	0	0	3.0	18	7	3	3	1	0	0	0	4	0	1	0	0	0	0	-	0	0-0	0	22.36	9.00
2003 Tampa Bay	AL	8	7	1	1	35.1	157	38	25	25	7	1	1	1	16	0	20	4	0	0	5	.000	0	0-0	0	5.60	6.37
3 ML YEARS		18	8	1	7	57.2	262	64	38	38	13	1	1	1	34	1	30	4	0	0	5	.000	0	0-0	0	6.65	5.93

Jason Stanford

Pitches: L **Bats:** L **Pos:** SP-8; RP-5   **Ht:** 6'2" **Wt:** 200 **Born:** 1/27/77 **Age:** 27

Year Team	Lg	G	GS	CG	GF	IP	BFP	H	R	ER	HR	SH	SF	HB	TBB	IBB	SO	WP	Bk	W	L	Pct	ShO	Sv-Op	Hld	ERC	ERA
2000 Columbus	A	14	14	0	0	79.0	335	82	32	24	3	1	3	2	20	0	72	3	0	7	4	.636	0	0- -	-	3.37	2.73
2000 Kinston	A+	11	11	1	0	70.0	294	68	22	20	2	1	2	2	17	0	58	0	0	4	3	.571	0	0- -	-	2.92	2.57
2000 Akron	AA	1	1	0	0	5.2	23	5	1	1	0	0	0	1	1	0	5	0	0	1	0	1.000	0	0- -	-	2.68	1.59

Year Team	Lg	G	GS	CG	GF	IP	BFP	H	R	ER	HR	SH	SF	HB	TBB	IBB	SO	WP	Bk	W	L	Pct	ShO	Sv-Op	Hld	ERC	ERA
2001 Akron	AA	24	24	0	0	141.2	602	152	71	64	11	3	7	10	32	4	108	2	1	6	11	.353	0	0--	-	3.90	4.07
2001 Buffalo	AAA	1	1	1	0	9.0	29	3	0	0	0	0	0	0	0	0	10	0	0	1	0	1.000	1	0--	-	0.26	0.00
2002 Akron	AA	18	18	1	0	102.1	440	108	44	39	3	4	5	6	33	0	86	2	2	7	6	.538	1	0--	-	3.84	3.43
2003 Buffalo	AAA	20	20	1	0	126.0	515	124	57	48	13	4	4	5	25	1	108	2	2	10	4	.714	0	0--	-	3.42	3.43
2003 Cleveland	AL	13	8	0	1	50.0	213	48	20	20	5	0	1	1	16	1	30	0	0	1	3	.250	0	0-0	0	3.55	3.60

Mike Stanton

Pitches: L Bats: L Pos: RP-50 **Ht:** 6'1" **Wt:** 215 **Born:** 6/2/67 **Age:** 37

Year Team*	Lg	G	GS	CG	GF	IP	BFP	H	R	ER	HR	SH	SF	HB	TBB	IBB	SO	WP	Bk	W	L	Pct	ShO	Sv-Op	Hld	ERC	ERA
2003 Brooklyn*	A-	1	1	0	0	2.0	6	1	0	0	0	0	0	0	0	0	1	1	0	0	0	-	0	0--	-	0.63	0.00
2003 Binghamton*	AA	1	1	0	0	1.0	9	6	3	1	0	0	1	0	0	0	1	0	0	0	1	.000	0	0--	-	39.65	9.00
1989 Atlanta	NL	20	0	0	10	24.0	94	17	4	4	0	4	0	0	8	1	27	1	0	0	1	.000	0	7-8	2	1.72	1.50
1990 Atlanta	NL	7	0	0	4	7.0	42	16	16	14	1	1	0	1	4	2	7	1	0	0	3	.000	0	2-3	0	13.58	18.00
1991 Atlanta	NL	74	0	0	20	78.0	314	62	27	25	6	6	0	1	21	6	54	0	0	5	5	.500	0	7-10	15	2.31	2.88
1992 Atlanta	NL	65	0	0	23	63.2	264	59	32	29	6	1	2	2	20	2	44	3	0	5	4	.556	0	8-11	15	3.42	4.10
1993 Atlanta	NL	63	0	0	41	52.0	236	51	35	27	4	5	2	0	29	7	43	1	0	4	6	.400	0	27-33	5	4.08	4.67
1994 Atlanta	NL	49	0	0	15	45.2	197	41	18	18	2	2	1	3	26	3	35	1	0	3	1	.750	0	3-4	10	4.01	3.55
1995 Atl-Bos		48	0	0	22	40.1	178	48	23	19	6	2	1	1	14	2	23	2	1	2	1	.667	0	1-3	8	5.41	4.24
1996 Bos-Tex	AL	81	0	0	28	78.2	327	78	32	32	11	4	2	0	27	5	60	3	2	4	4	.500	0	1-6	22	4.08	3.66
1997 New York	AL	64	0	0	15	66.2	283	50	19	19	3	2	0	3	34	2	70	3	2	6	1	.857	0	3-5	26	2.88	2.57
1998 New York	AL	67	0	0	26	79.0	330	71	51	48	13	1	2	4	26	1	69	0	0	4	1	.800	0	6-10	18	3.88	5.47
1999 New York	AL	73	1	0	10	62.1	271	71	30	30	5	4	2	1	18	4	59	2	0	2	2	.500	0	0-5	21	4.23	4.33
2000 New York	AL	69	0	0	20	68.0	291	68	32	31	5	2	4	2	24	2	75	1	0	2	3	.400	0	0-4	15	3.78	4.10
2001 New York	AL	76	0	0	16	80.1	342	80	25	23	4	2	3	4	29	9	78	3	1	9	4	.692	0	0-1	23	3.61	2.58
2002 New York	AL	79	0	0	25	78.0	324	73	29	26	4	4	7	0	28	3	44	4	0	7	1	.875	0	6-9	17	3.23	3.00
2003 New York	NL	50	0	0	24	45.1	194	37	25	23	6	1	3	2	19	4	34	2	1	2	7	.222	0	5-7	10	3.33	4.57
1995 Atlanta	NL	26	0	0	10	19.1	94	31	14	12	3	2	1	1	6	2	13	1	1	1	1	.500	0	1-2	4	7.86	5.59
1995 Boston	AL	22	0	0	12	21.0	84	17	9	7	3	0	0	0	8	0	10	1	0	0	1	1.000	0	0-1	4	3.37	3.00
1996 Boston	AL	59	0	0	19	56.1	239	58	24	24	9	3	2	0	23	4	46	3	2	4	3	.571	0	1-5	15	4.71	3.83
1996 Texas	AL	22	0	0	9	22.1	88	20	8	8	2	1	0	0	4	1	14	0	0	0	1	.000	0	0-1	7	2.62	3.22
15 ML YEARS		885	1	0	299	869.0	3687	822	398	368	76	41	29	24	327	53	722	27	7	55	44	.556	0	76-119	207	3.63	3.81

Denny Stark

Pitches: R Bats: R Pos: SP-13; RP-4 **Ht:** 6'2" **Wt:** 210 **Born:** 10/27/74 **Age:** 29

Year Team	Lg	G	GS	CG	GF	IP	BFP	H	R	ER	HR	SH	SF	HB	TBB	IBB	SO	WP	Bk	W	L	Pct	ShO	Sv-Op	Hld	ERC	ERA
2003 Co Springs*	AAA	4	4	0	0	19.2	90	22	14	13	1	1	0	0	9	0	10	2	0	0	2	.000	0	0--	-	4.49	5.95
2003 Tulsa*	AA	1	1	0	0	4.1	23	4	5	3	0	0	2	1	4	0	3	0	0	0	1	.000	0	0--	-	5.35	6.23
1999 Seattle	AL	5	0	0	2	6.1	31	10	8	7	0	0	0	0	4	0	4	0	0	0	0	-	0	0-0	0	8.05	9.95
2001 Seattle	AL	4	3	0	0	14.2	68	21	15	15	3	0	1	0	4	0	12	0	0	1	1	.500	0	0-0	0	7.99	9.20
2002 Colorado	NL	32	20	0	1	128.1	554	108	69	57	25	2	4	5	64	4	64	2	0	11	4	.733	0	0-1	1	4.33	4.00
2003 Colorado	NL	17	13	0	0	78.2	364	98	57	51	12	2	7	3	33	2	30	2	1	3	3	.500	0	0-0	0	6.09	5.83
4 ML YEARS		58	36	0	3	228.0	1017	237	149	130	42	4	12	8	105	6	110	4	1	15	8	.652	0	0-1	1	5.24	5.13

Dernell Stenson

Bats: L Throws: L Pos: LF-18; PH-14; RF-7; 1B-1 **Ht:** 6'1" **Wt:** 230 **Born:** 6/17/78 **Age:** 26

Year Team	Lg	G	AB	H	2B	3B	HR	(Hm	Rd)	TB	R	RBI	RC	TBB	IBB	SO	HBP	SH	SF	SB	CS	SB%	GDP	Avg	OBP	Slg
1996 Red Sox	R	32	97	21	3	1	2	(-	-)	32	16	15	14	16	0	26	7	0	3	4	3	.57	0	.216	.358	.330
1997 Michigan	A	131	471	137	35	2	15	(-	-)	221	79	80	90	72	6	105	19	0	6	6	4	.60	10	.291	.401	.469
1998 Trenton	AA	138	505	130	21	1	24	(-	-)	225	90	71	89	84	3	135	14	1	4	5	3	.63	6	.257	.376	.446
1999 Red Sox	R	6	23	5	0	0	2	(-	-)	11	2	7	4	3	0	5	0	0	0	0	0	-	0	.217	.308	.478
1999 Pawtucket	AAA	121	440	119	28	2	18	(-	-)	205	64	82	73	55	5	119	6	2	5	2	1	.67	7	.270	.356	.466
2000 Pawtucket	AAA	98	380	102	14	0	23	(-	-)	185	59	71	63	45	6	99	4	0	4	0	0	-	8	.268	.349	.487
2001 Pawtucket	AAA	122	464	110	18	1	16	(-	-)	178	53	69	54	43	3	116	2	0	5	0	0	-	6	.237	.302	.384
2002 Pawtucket	AAA	107	368	92	20	1	9	(-	-)	141	44	36	45	37	2	96	2	1	1	4	3	.57	6	.250	.321	.383
2003 Louisville	AAA	17	59	14	3	0	5	(-	-)	32	9	14	9	5	0	10	0	0	1	0	0	-	1	.237	.292	.542
2003 Chattanooga	AA	101	356	109	28	0	14	(-	-)	179	51	76	63	39	4	74	2	1	7	4	5	.44	10	.306	.371	.503
2003 Cincinnati	NL	37	81	20	5	0	3	(3	0)	34	14	13	11	11	0	24	0	0	1	0	0	-	0	.247	.333	.420

Garrett Stephenson

Pitches: R Bats: R Pos: SP-27; RP-5 **Ht:** 6'5" **Wt:** 208 **Born:** 1/2/72 **Age:** 32

Year Team	Lg	G	GS	CG	GF	IP	BFP	H	R	ER	HR	SH	SF	HB	TBB	IBB	SO	WP	Bk	W	L	Pct	ShO	Sv-Op	Hld	ERC	ERA
1996 Baltimore	AL	3	0	0	2	6.1	35	13	9	9	1	1	0	1	3	1	3	0	0	0	1	.000	0	0-0	0	12.31	12.79
1997 Philadelphia	NL	20	18	2	0	117.0	474	104	45	41	11	2	5	3	38	0	81	1	0	8	6	.571	0	0-0	0	3.35	3.15
1998 Philadelphia	NL	6	6	0	0	23.0	118	31	24	23	3	1	0	0	19	0	17	0	1	0	2	.000	0	0-0	0	8.16	9.00
1999 St Louis	NL	18	12	0	1	85.1	371	90	43	40	11	5	5	5	29	1	59	0	0	6	3	.667	0	0-0	0	4.58	4.22
2000 St Louis	NL	32	31	3	0	200.1	858	209	105	100	31	6	7	7	63	0	123	2	2	16	9	.640	2	0-0	1	4.53	4.49
2002 St Louis	NL	12	10	0	0	45.0	205	48	27	27	4	4	1	5	25	0	34	2	0	2	5	.286	0	0-0	0	5.54	5.40
2003 St Louis	NL	32	27	1	3	174.1	747	167	94	89	30	11	9	13	60	3	91	5	0	7	13	.350	0	0-0	1	4.40	4.59
7 ML YEARS		123	104	6	6	651.1	2808	662	347	329	91	30	27	34	237	5	408	10	3	39	39	.500	2	0-0	1	4.54	4.55

Josh Stewart

Pitches: L Bats: L Pos: SP-5　　　　　　　　　　　　　　　　　　Ht: 6'3" Wt: 205 Born: 12/5/78 Age: 25

		HOW MUCH HE PITCHED				WHAT HE GAVE UP								THE RESULTS						
Year Team	Lg	G GS CG GF	IP	BFP	H R ER	HR SH SF HB	TBB IBB	SO	WP Bk	W L	Pct	ShO	Sv-Op	Hld	ERC	ERA
1999 Bristol	R+	5 0 0 2	18.0	71	13 5 3	0 1 0 2	5 0	25	0 0	1 0	1.000	0	1- -	-	2.04	1.50
1999 Burlington	A	16 0 0 3	29.2	138	32 25 24	6 0 1 2	21 0	35	1 0	2 0	1.000	0	1- -	-	7.09	7.28
2000 Burlington	A	25 25 1 0	138.0	617	157 84 70	14 5 3 10	58 2	82	9 0	9 9	.500	1	0- -	-	5.30	4.57
2001 Winstn-Salm	A+	12 12 1 0	63.2	287	64 41 27	6 3 4 4	28 1	38	3 0	4 6	.400	0	0- -	-	4.33	3.82
2001 Birmingham	AA	16 16 0 0	82.1	388	110 68 61	7 2 3 8	42 0	47	2 2	3 4	.429	0	0- -	-	7.01	6.67
2002 Birmingham	AA	26 26 1 0	150.1	630	145 65 59	11 2 0 2	56 1	92	7 0	11 7	.611	1	0- -	-	3.70	3.53
2003 Charlotte	AAA	5 5 0 0	26.1	121	38 18 18	4 1 2 2	6 0	10	0 1	0 3	.000	0	0- -	-	6.81	6.15
2003 Bristol	R+	2 2 0 0	6.0	24	5 0 0	0 0 0 0	2 0	5	1 0	0 0	-	0	0- -	-	2.37	0.00
2003 Chicago	AL	5 5 0 0	25.2	121	28 18 17	4 1 1 0	16 0	13	0 0	1 2	.333	0	0-0	0	5.82	5.96

Scott Stewart

Pitches: L Bats: R Pos: RP-51　　　　　　　　　　　　　　　　　Ht: 6'2" Wt: 225 Born: 8/14/75 Age: 28

		HOW MUCH HE PITCHED				WHAT HE GAVE UP								THE RESULTS						
Year Team	Lg	G GS CG GF	IP	BFP	H R ER	HR SH SF HB	TBB IBB	SO	WP Bk	W L	Pct	ShO	Sv-Op	Hld	ERC	ERA
2003 Brevard Cnty*	A+	2 2 0 0	3.2	13	1 0 0	0 0 0 0	1 0	4	0 0	0 0	-	0	0- -	-	0.47	0.00
2001 Montreal	NL	62 0 0 0	47.2	199	43 20 20	5 2 4 3	13 0	39	2 0	3 1	.750	0	3-4	8	3.31	3.78
2002 Montreal	NL	67 0 0 28	64.0	263	49 29 22	4 2 2 1	22 5	67	1 0	4 2	.667	0	17-19	14	2.31	3.09
2003 Montreal	NL	51 0 0 0	43.0	187	52 22 19	5 1 1 1	13 4	29	1 1	3 1	.750	0	0-1	13	5.05	3.98
3 ML YEARS		180 0 0 46	154.2	649	144 71 61	14 5 7 5	48 9	135	4 1	10 4	.714	0	20-24	35	3.32	3.55

Shannon Stewart

Bats: R Throws: R Pos: LF-115; RF-14; DH-8; PH-1　　　　　　Ht: 6'1" Wt: 210 Born: 2/25/74 Age: 30

		BATTING														BASERUNNING				AVERAGES		
Year Team	Lg	G	AB	H	2B 3B HR	(Hm Rd)	TB	R RBI RC	TBB IBB	SO	HBP SH SF	SB CS SB% GDP	Avg OBP Slg
2003 Syracuse*	AAA	1	3	0	0 0 0	(- -)	0	0 0 0	1 0	0	0 0 0	0 0 - 0	.000 .250 .000
1995 Toronto	AL	12	38	8	0 0 0	(0 0)	8	2 1 3	5 0	5	1 0 0	2 0 1.00 0	.211 .318 .211
1996 Toronto	AL	7	17	3	1 0 0	(0 0)	4	2 2 1	1 0	4	0 0 0	1 0 1.00 1	.176 .222 .235
1997 Toronto	AL	44	168	48	13 7 0	(0 0)	75	25 22 29	19 1	24	4 0 2	10 3 .77 3	.286 .368 .446
1998 Toronto	AL	144	516	144	29 3 12	(6 6)	215	90 55 88	67 1	77	15 6 1	51 18 .74 5	.279 .377 .417
1999 Toronto	AL	145	608	185	28 2 11	(4 7)	250	102 67 95	59 0	83	8 3 4	37 14 .73 12	.304 .371 .411
2000 Toronto	AL	136	583	186	43 5 21	(12 9)	302	107 69 106	37 1	79	6 1 4	20 5 .80 12	.319 .363 .518
2001 Toronto	AL	155	640	202	44 7 12	(6 6)	296	103 60 109	46 1	72	11 0 1	27 10 .73 9	.316 .371 .463
2002 Toronto	AL	141	577	175	38 6 10	(4 6)	255	103 45 91	54 2	60	9 0 1	14 2 .88 17	.303 .371 .442
2003 Tor-Min	AL	136	573	176	44 2 13	(7 6)	263	90 73 93	52 3	66	6 2 11	4 6 .40 10	.307 .364 .459
2003 Toronto	AL	71	303	89	22 2 7	(3 4)	136	47 35 51	27 2	30	2 0 8	1 2 .33 6	.294 .347 .449
2003 Minnesota	AL	65	270	87	22 0 6	(4 2)	127	43 38 42	25 1	36	4 2 3	3 4 .43 4	.322 .384 .470
9 ML YEARS		920	3720	1127	240 32 79	(39 40)	1668	624 394 615	340 9	470	60 12 24	166 58 .74 69	.303 .368 .448

Kelly Stinnett

Bats: R Throws: R Pos: C-51; PH-18; PR-1　　　　　　　　　　Ht: 5'11" Wt: 225 Born: 2/4/70 Age: 34

		BATTING														BASERUNNING				AVERAGES		
Year Team	Lg	G	AB	H	2B 3B HR	(Hm Rd)	TB	R RBI RC	TBB IBB	SO	HBP SH SF	SB CS SB% GDP	Avg OBP Slg
1994 New York	NL	47	150	38	6 2 2	(0 2)	54	20 14 18	11 1	28	5 0 1	2 0 1.00 3	.253 .323 .360
1995 New York	NL	77	196	43	8 1 4	(1 3)	65	23 18 24	29 3	65	6 0 0	2 0 1.00 3	.219 .338 .332
1996 Milwaukee	NL	14	26	2	0 0 0	(0 0)	2	1 0 0	2 0	11	1 0 0	0 0 - 0	.077 .172 .077
1997 Milwaukee	NL	30	36	9	4 0 0	(0 0)	13	2 3 4	3 0	9	0 0 0	0 0 - 0	.250 .308 .361
1998 Arizona	NL	92	274	71	14 1 11	(5 6)	120	35 34 41	35 3	74	6 1 2	0 1 .00 9	.259 .353 .438
1999 Arizona	NL	88	284	66	13 0 14	(3 11)	121	36 38 37	24 2	83	5 2 2	2 1 .67 4	.232 .302 .426
2000 Arizona	NL	76	240	52	7 0 8	(2 6)	83	22 33 23	19 4	56	6 0 0	1 0 1.00 5	.217 .291 .346
2001 Cincinnati	NL	63	187	48	11 0 9	(6 3)	86	27 25 27	17 3	61	5 1 1	2 2 .50 5	.257 .333 .460
2002 Cincinnati	NL	34	93	21	5 0 3	(1 2)	35	10 13 13	15 1	25	0 0 0	2 0 1.00 1	.226 .333 .376
2003 Cin-Phi	NL	67	186	44	13 0 3	(2 1)	66	14 19 20	14 3	52	4 2 1	0 0 - 3	.237 .302 .355
2003 Cincinnati	NL	60	179	41	13 0 3	(2 1)	63	14 19 18	13 3	51	4 2 1	0 0 - 3	.229 .294 .352
2003 Philadelphia	NL	7	7	3	0 0 0	(0 0)	3	0 0 2	1 0	1	0 0 0	0 0 - 0	.429 .500 .429
10 ML YEARS		588	1672	394	81 4 54	(20 34)	645	190 197 207	169 20	464	38 6 7	10 5 .67 33	.236 .319 .386

Ricky Stone

Pitches: R Bats: R Pos: RP-65　　　　　　　　　　　　　　　　Ht: 6'1" Wt: 190 Born: 2/28/75 Age: 29

		HOW MUCH HE PITCHED				WHAT HE GAVE UP								THE RESULTS						
Year Team	Lg	G GS CG GF	IP	BFP	H R ER	HR SH SF HB	TBB IBB	SO	WP Bk	W L	Pct	ShO	Sv-Op	Hld	ERC	ERA
2001 Houston	NL	6 0 0 3	7.2	33	8 3 2	1 0 0 0	2 1	4	0 0	0 0	-	0	0-0	0	3.69	2.35
2002 Houston	NL	78 0 0 16	77.1	335	78 36 31	9 5 2 1	34 3	63	1 0	3 3	.500	0	1-2	12	4.43	3.61
2003 Houston	NL	65 0 0 20	83.0	350	76 36 34	11 4 1 6	31 4	47	1 0	6 4	.600	0	1-1	7	4.00	3.69
3 ML YEARS		149 0 0 39	168.0	718	162 75 67	21 9 3 7	67 8	114	2 0	9 7	.563	0	2-3	19	4.18	3.59

Pat Strange

Pitches: R Bats: R Pos: RP-6　　　　　　　　　　　　　　　　Ht: 6'5" Wt: 243 Born: 8/23/80 Age: 23

		HOW MUCH HE PITCHED				WHAT HE GAVE UP								THE RESULTS						
Year Team	Lg	G GS CG GF	IP	BFP	H R ER	HR SH SF HB	TBB IBB	SO	WP Bk	W L	Pct	ShO	Sv-Op	Hld	ERC	ERA
1998 Mets	R	4 4 0 0	18.0	79	18 3 3	0 0 0 1	7 0	19	0 0	1 1	.500	0	0- -	-	3.49	1.50
1999 Capital City	A	28 21 2 1	154.0	627	138 57 45	4 4 3 10	29 1	113	7 0	12 5	.706	0	1- -	-	2.50	2.63
2000 St.Lucie	A+	19 13 2 1	88.0	374	78 48 35	4 2 5 9	32 0	77	9 1	10 1	.909	0	0- -	-	3.34	3.58
2000 Binghamton	AA	10 10 0 0	55.1	252	62 30 28	2 3 2 4	30 0	36	3 0	4 3	.571	0	0- -	-	4.93	4.55
2001 Binghamton	AA	26 24 1 1	153.1	669	171 94 83	18 5 6 12	52 1	106	7 0	11 6	.647	0	0- -	-	5.01	4.87
2001 Norfolk	AAA	1 1 0 0	6.0	23	4 0 0	0 0 0 0	1 0	6	0 0	1 0	1.000	0	0- -	-	1.23	0.00

Year Team	Lg	G	GS	CG	GF	IP	BFP	H	R	ER	HR	SH	SF	HB	TBB	IBB	SO	WP	Bk	W	L	Pct	ShO	Sv-Op	Hld	ERC	ERA
2002 Norfolk	AAA	29	25	2	1	165.0	699	165	77	70	12	6	4	7	59	2	109	3	0	10	10	.500	0	0- -	-	3.94	3.82
2003 Norfolk	AAA	31	10	0	4	89.1	407	111	61	57	8	2	4	2	44	1	64	4	0	5	4	.556	0	1- -	-	6.00	5.74
2002 New York	NL	5	0	0	4	8.0	30	6	1	1	0	0	0	0	1	1	4	0	1	0	0	-	0	0-0	-	1.32	1.13
2003 New York	NL	6	0	0	1	9.0	49	13	11	11	4	0	0	0	11	0	5	0	0	0	0	-	0	0-0	1	14.36	11.00
2 ML YEARS		11	0	0	5	17.0	79	19	12	12	4	0	0	0	12	1	9	0	1	0	0	-	0	0-0	1	7.16	6.35

Scott Strickland

Pitches: R Bats: R Pos: RP-19　　　　　　　　　　**Ht: 5'11" Wt: 180 Born: 4/26/76 Age: 28**

Year Team	Lg	G	GS	CG	GF	IP	BFP	H	R	ER	HR	SH	SF	HB	TBB	IBB	SO	WP	Bk	W	L	Pct	ShO	Sv-Op	Hld	ERC	ERA
1999 Montreal	NL	17	0	0	5	18.0	78	15	10	9	3	2	0	0	11	0	23	0	0	0	1	.000	0	0-0	2	4.48	4.50
2000 Montreal	NL	49	0	0	20	48.0	200	38	18	16	3	3	3	1	16	2	48	2	0	4	3	.571	0	9-13	6	2.44	3.00
2001 Montreal	NL	77	0	0	31	81.1	351	67	36	29	9	3	1	4	41	5	85	4	0	2	6	.250	0	9-12	12	3.65	3.21
2002 Mon-NYM	NL	69	0	0	21	68.2	299	61	29	27	7	1	2	2	33	9	69	3	0	6	9	.400	0	2-6	15	3.64	3.54
2003 New York	NL	19	0	0	3	20.0	84	16	6	5	1	0	0	1	10	1	16	1	0	0	2	.000	0	0-1	4	3.19	2.25
2002 Montreal	NL	1	0	0	0	1.0	3	0	0	0	0	0	0	0	0	0	2	0	0	0	0	-	0	0-0	0	0.00	0.00
2002 New York	NL	68	0	0	21	67.2	296	61	29	27	7	1	2	2	33	9	67	3	0	6	9	.400	0	2-6	15	3.74	3.59
5 ML YEARS		231	0	0	80	236.0	1012	197	99	86	23	9	6	8	111	17	241	10	0	12	21	.364	0	20-32	39	3.41	3.28

Jamal Strong

Bats: R Throws: R Pos: PR-9; CF-2; DH-2; PH-1　　　　　　　　　　**Ht: 5'10" Wt: 175 Born: 8/5/78 Age: 25**

Year Team	Lg	G	AB	H	2B	3B	HR	(Hm	Rd)	TB	R	RBI	RC	TBB	IBB	SO	HBP	SH	SF	SB	CS	SB%	GDP	Avg	OBP	Slg
2000 Everett	A-	75	296	93	7	3	1	(-	-)	109	63	28	59	52	1	29	4	5	1	60	14	.81	0	.314	.422	.368
2001 Wisconsin	A	51	184	65	12	1	0	(-	-)	79	41	19	47	40	2	27	5	1	1	35	4	.90	2	.353	.478	.429
2001 Sn Brnardino	A+	81	331	103	11	2	0	(-	-)	118	74	32	59	51	2	60	5	6	0	47	8	.85	4	.311	.411	.356
2002 San Antonio	AA	127	503	140	16	5	1	(-	-)	169	63	31	70	62	1	87	10	2	5	46	16	.74	7	.278	.366	.336
2003 Tacoma	AAA	56	210	64	6	1	2	(-	-)	78	38	19	33	25	0	38	5	3	1	26	11	.70	3	.305	.390	.371
2003 Mariners	R	2	7	5	0	1	0	(-	-)	7	5	4	5	3	0	1	1	0	2	3	0	1.00	0	.714	.692	1.000
2003 Seattle	AL	12	2	0	0	0	0	(0	0)	0	2	0	0	0	0	0	0	0	0	0	0	-	0	.000	.000	.000

Tanyon Sturtze

Pitches: R Bats: R Pos: RP-32; SP-8　　　　　　　　　　**Ht: 6'5" Wt: 221 Born: 10/12/70 Age: 33**

Year Team	Lg	G	GS	CG	GF	IP	BFP	H	R	ER	HR	SH	SF	HB	TBB	IBB	SO	WP	Bk	W	L	Pct	ShO	Sv-Op	Hld	ERC	ERA
1995 Chicago	NL	2	0	0	0	2.0	9	2	2	2	1	0	0	0	1	0	0	0	0	0	0	-	0	0-0	0	7.30	9.00
1996 Chicago	NL	6	0	0	3	11.0	51	16	11	11	3	0	0	0	5	0	7	0	0	1	0	1.000	0	0-0	0	8.87	9.00
1997 Texas	AL	9	5	0	1	32.2	155	45	30	30	6	0	4	0	18	0	18	1	1	1	1	.500	0	0-0	0	7.84	8.27
1999 Chicago	AL	1	1	0	0	6.0	22	4	0	0	0	0	0	0	2	0	2	0	0	0	0	-	0	0-0	0	1.73	0.00
2000 CWS-TB	AL	29	6	0	9	68.1	300	72	39	36	8	1	2	3	29	1	44	2	0	5	2	.714	0	0-0	0	4.80	4.74
2001 Tampa Bay	AL	39	27	0	6	195.1	837	200	98	96	23	2	10	9	79	0	110	11	0	11	12	.478	0	1-3	3	4.65	4.42
2002 Tampa Bay	AL	33	33	4	0	224.0	1008	271	141	129	33	7	6	9	89	2	137	7	2	4	18	.182	0	0-0	0	5.87	5.18
2003 Toronto	AL	40	8	0	7	89.1	415	107	67	59	14	2	2	7	43	3	54	6	0	7	6	.538	0	0-0	1	6.30	5.94
2000 Chicago	AL	10	1	0	2	15.2	85	25	23	21	4	0	2	2	15	0	6	1	0	1	2	.333	0	0-0	0	12.84	12.06
2000 Tampa Bay	AL	19	5	0	7	52.2	215	47	16	15	4	1	0	1	14	1	38	1	0	4	0	1.000	0	0-0	0	2.89	2.56
8 ML YEARS		159	80	4	26	628.2	2797	717	388	363	88	12	24	28	266	6	372	27	3	29	39	.426	0	1-3	4	5.53	5.20

Chris Stynes

Bats: R Throws: R Pos: 3B-120; PH-17; 2B-5　　　　　　　　　　**Ht: 5'10" Wt: 205 Born: 1/19/73 Age: 31**

Year Team	Lg	G	AB	H	2B	3B	HR	(Hm	Rd)	TB	R	RBI	RC	TBB	IBB	SO	HBP	SH	SF	SB	CS	SB%	GDP	Avg	OBP	Slg
1995 Kansas City	AL	22	35	6	1	0	0	(0	0)	7	7	2	1	4	0	3	0	0	0	0	0	-	3	.171	.256	.200
1996 Kansas City	AL	36	92	27	6	0	0	(0	0)	33	8	6	10	2	0	5	0	1	0	5	2	.71	1	.293	.309	.359
1997 Cincinnati	NL	49	198	69	7	1	6	(2	4)	96	31	28	37	11	1	13	4	2	0	11	2	.85	5	.348	.394	.485
1998 Cincinnati	NL	123	347	88	10	1	6	(3	3)	118	52	27	42	32	1	36	4	4	1	15	1	.94	5	.254	.323	.340
1999 Cincinnati	NL	73	113	27	1	0	2	(1	1)	34	18	14	11	12	1	13	0	3	1	5	2	.71	2	.239	.310	.301
2000 Cincinnati	NL	119	380	127	24	1	12	(8	4)	189	71	40	71	32	2	54	2	3	3	5	2	.71	5	.334	.386	.497
2001 Boston	AL	96	361	101	19	2	8	(3	5)	148	52	33	43	20	0	56	3	1	1	4	5	.44	12	.280	.322	.410
2002 Chicago	NL	98	195	47	9	1	5	(4	1)	73	25	26	27	21	1	29	1	5	3	1	1	.50	5	.241	.314	.374
2003 Colorado	NL	138	443	113	31	3	11	(10	1)	183	71	73	65	48	1	76	6	3	2	3	1	.75	8	.255	.335	.413
9 ML YEARS		754	2164	605	108	9	50	(28	22)	881	335	249	307	182	7	285	20	22	11	49	16	.75	46	.280	.340	.407

Scott Sullivan

Pitches: R Bats: R Pos: RP-65　　　　　　　　　　**Ht: 6'3" Wt: 210 Born: 3/13/71 Age: 33**

Year Team	Lg	G	GS	CG	GF	IP	BFP	H	R	ER	HR	SH	SF	HB	TBB	IBB	SO	WP	Bk	W	L	Pct	ShO	Sv-Op	Hld	ERC	ERA
1995 Cincinnati	NL	3	0	0	1	3.2	17	4	2	2	0	1	0	0	2	0	2	0	0	0	0	-	0	0-0	0	4.28	4.91
1996 Cincinnati	NL	7	0	0	4	8.0	35	7	2	2	0	1	0	1	5	0	3	1	0	0	0	-	0	0-0	0	4.11	2.25
1997 Cincinnati	NL	59	0	0	15	97.1	402	79	36	35	12	3	3	7	30	8	96	7	1	5	3	.625	0	1-2	13	3.01	3.24
1998 Cincinnati	NL	67	0	0	13	102.0	440	98	62	59	14	3	4	9	36	4	86	4	0	5	5	.500	0	1-4	5	4.22	5.21
1999 Cincinnati	NL	79	0	0	16	113.2	470	88	41	38	10	4	4	8	47	4	78	6	1	5	4	.556	0	3-5	13	3.08	3.01
2000 Cincinnati	NL	79	0	0	22	106.1	439	87	44	41	14	2	5	9	38	8	96	7	0	3	6	.333	0	3-6	22	3.40	3.47
2001 Cincinnati	NL	79	0	0	16	103.1	437	94	44	38	10	1	5	8	36	8	82	0	0	7	1	.875	0	0-3	20	3.55	3.31
2002 Cincinnati	NL	71	0	0	16	78.2	358	93	60	53	15	2	3	5	31	11	78	2	0	6	5	.545	0	1-3	19	5.81	6.06
2003 Cin-CWS		65	0	0	8	64.0	276	48	28	26	6	1	3	6	32	4	56	1	0	6	0	1.000	0	0-1	12	3.27	3.66
2003 Cincinnati	NL	50	0	0	6	49.2	218	39	22	20	4	0	2	5	26	4	43	1	0	6	0	1.000	0	0-1	10	3.42	3.62
2003 Chicago	AL	15	0	0	2	14.1	58	9	6	6	2	1	1	1	6	0	13	0	0	0	0	-	0	0-0	2	2.71	3.77
9 ML YEARS		509	0	0	111	677.0	2874	598	319	294	81	18	27	53	257	47	577	28	2	37	24	.607	0	9-24	104	3.70	3.91

Jeff Suppan

Pitches: R **Bats:** R **Pos:** SP-31; RP-1 **Ht:** 6'2" **Wt:** 210 **Born:** 1/2/75 **Age:** 29

			HOW MUCH HE PITCHED						WHAT HE GAVE UP											THE RESULTS						
Year Team	Lg	G	GS	CG	GF	IP	BFP	H	R	ER	HR	SH	SF	HB	TBB	IBB	SO	WP	Bk	W	L	Pct	ShO	Sv-Op	Hld	ERC	ERA
1995 Boston	AL	8	3	0	1	22.2	100	29	15	15	4	1	1	0	5	1	19	0	0	1	2	.333	0	0-0	1	5.43	5.96
1996 Boston	AL	8	4	0	2	22.2	107	29	19	19	3	1	4	1	13	0	13	3	0	1	1	.500	0	0-0	0	7.03	7.54
1997 Boston	AL	23	22	0	1	112.1	503	140	75	71	12	0	4	4	36	1	67	5	0	7	3	.700	0	0-0	0	5.39	5.69
1998 Ari-KC		17	14	1	2	78.2	345	91	56	50	13	3	2	1	22	1	51	2	0	1	7	.125	0	0-0	0	4.95	5.72
1999 Kansas City	AL	32	32	4	0	208.2	887	222	113	105	28	7	5	3	62	4	103	5	1	10	12	.455	1	0-0	0	4.33	4.53
2000 Kansas City	AL	35	33	3	0	217.0	948	240	121	119	36	5	6	7	84	3	128	7	1	10	9	.526	1	0-0	0	5.31	4.94
2001 Kansas City	AL	34	34	1	0	218.1	946	227	120	106	26	5	6	12	74	3	120	6	0	10	14	.417	0	0-0	0	4.40	4.37
2002 Kansas City	AL	33	33	3	0	208.0	912	229	134	123	32	4	11	7	68	3	109	10	1	9	16	.360	1	0-0	0	4.84	5.32
2003 Pit-Bos		32	31	3	0	204.0	873	217	98	95	23	11	6	8	51	5	110	7	0	13	11	.542	2	0-0	0	4.03	4.19
1998 Arizona	NL	13	13	1	0	66.0	299	82	55	49	12	3	2	1	21	1	39	2	0	1	7	.125	0	0-0	0	5.73	6.68
1998 Kansas City	NL	4	1	0	2	12.2	46	9	1	1	1	0	0	0	1	0	12	0	0	0	0	—	0	0-0	0	1.51	0.71
2003 Pittsburgh	NL	21	21	3	0	141.0	597	147	57	56	11	10	2	6	31	5	78	3	0	10	7	.588	2	0-0	0	3.55	3.57
2003 Boston	AL	11	10	0	0	63.0	276	70	41	39	12	1	4	2	20	0	32	4	0	3	4	.429	0	0-0	0	5.15	5.57
9 ML YEARS		222	206	15	6	1292.1	5621	1424	751	703	177	37	45	43	415	21	720	45	3	62	75	.453	5	0-0	1	4.73	4.90

B.J. Surhoff

Bats: L **Throws:** R **Pos:** DH-39; LF-24; 1B-22; PH-10; RF-3 **Ht:** 6'1" **Wt:** 200 **Born:** 8/4/64 **Age:** 39

								BATTING													BASERUNNING				AVERAGES		
Year Team	Lg	G	AB	H	2B	3B	HR	(Hm	Rd)	TB	R	RBI	RC	TBB	IBB	SO	HBP	SH	SF	SB	CS	SB%	GDP	Avg	OBP	Slg
1987 Milwaukee	NL	115	395	118	22	3	7	(5	2)	167	50	68	56	36	1	30	0	5	9	11	10	.52	13	.299	.350	.423
1988 Milwaukee	NL	139	493	121	21	0	5	(2	3)	157	47	38	45	31	9	49	3	11	3	21	6	.78	12	.245	.292	.318
1989 Milwaukee	NL	126	436	108	17	4	5	(3	2)	148	42	55	41	25	1	29	3	3	10	14	12	.54	8	.248	.287	.339
1990 Milwaukee	NL	135	474	131	21	4	6	(4	2)	178	55	59	61	41	5	37	1	7	7	18	7	.72	8	.276	.331	.376
1991 Milwaukee	NL	143	505	146	19	4	5	(3	2)	188	57	68	53	26	2	33	0	13	9	5	8	.38	21	.289	.319	.372
1992 Milwaukee	NL	139	480	121	19	1	4	(3	1)	154	63	62	50	46	8	41	2	5	10	14	8	.64	9	.252	.314	.321
1993 Milwaukee	NL	148	552	151	38	3	7	(4	3)	216	66	79	67	36	5	47	2	4	5	12	9	.57	9	.274	.318	.391
1994 Milwaukee	NL	40	134	35	11	2	5	(2	3)	65	20	22	21	16	0	14	0	2	2	0	1	.00	5	.261	.336	.485
1995 Milwaukee	NL	117	415	133	26	3	13	(7	6)	204	72	73	75	37	4	43	4	2	4	7	3	.70	7	.320	.378	.492
1996 Baltimore	AL	143	537	157	27	6	21	(12	9)	259	74	82	89	47	8	79	3	2	1	0	1	.00	7	.292	.352	.482
1997 Baltimore	AL	147	528	150	30	4	18	(10	8)	242	80	88	84	49	14	60	5	3	10	1	1	.50	7	.284	.345	.458
1998 Baltimore	AL	162	573	160	34	1	22	(9	13)	262	79	92	84	49	9	81	1	1	10	9	7	.56	13	.279	.332	.457
1999 Baltimore	AL	162	673	207	38	1	28	(9	19)	331	104	107	111	43	1	78	2	1	8	5	1	.83	15	.308	.347	.492
2000 Bal-Atl		147	539	157	36	2	14	(7	7)	239	69	68	81	41	3	58	3	2	2	10	2	.83	10	.291	.344	.443
2001 Atlanta	NL	141	484	131	33	1	10	(5	5)	196	68	58	65	38	5	48	1	1	7	9	3	.75	5	.271	.321	.405
2002 Atlanta	NL	25	75	22	5	0	0	(0	0)	27	5	9	9	9	0	5	0	1	0	1	3	.25	1	.293	.369	.360
2003 Atlanta	NL	93	319	94	20	0	5	(4	1)	129	32	41	51	29	3	29	1	3	2	2	2	.50	4	.295	.353	.404
2000 Baltimore	AL	103	411	120	27	0	13	(6	7)	186	56	57	63	29	3	46	2	1	1	7	2	.78	5	.292	.341	.453
2000 Atlanta	NL	44	128	37	9	2	1	(1	0)	53	13	11	18	12	0	12	1	1	1	3	0	1.00	5	.289	.352	.414
17 ML YEARS		2122	7612	2142	417	39	175	(89	86)	3162	983	1069	1043	599	78	761	31	66	99	139	84	.62	154	.281	.332	.415

Ichiro Suzuki

Bats: L **Throws:** R **Pos:** RF-159; PH-2 **Ht:** 5'9" **Wt:** 160 **Born:** 10/22/73 **Age:** 30

								BATTING													BASERUNNING				AVERAGES		
Year Team	Lg	G	AB	H	2B	3B	HR	(Hm	Rd)	TB	R	RBI	RC	TBB	IBB	SO	HBP	SH	SF	SB	CS	SB%	GDP	Avg	OBP	Slg
2001 Seattle	AL	157	692	242	34	8	8	(5	3)	316	127	69	124	30	10	53	8	4	4	56	14	.80	3	.350	.381	.457
2002 Seattle	AL	157	647	208	27	8	8	(4	4)	275	111	51	108	68	27	62	5	3	5	31	15	.67	8	.321	.388	.425
2003 Seattle	AL	159	679	212	29	8	13	(8	5)	296	111	62	106	36	7	69	6	3	1	34	8	.81	3	.312	.352	.436
3 ML YEARS		473	2018	662	90	24	29	(17	12)	887	349	182	338	134	44	184	19	10	10	121	37	.77	14	.328	.374	.440

Pedro Swann

Bats: L **Throws:** R **Pos:** LF-6; PH-2; DH-1 **Ht:** 6'0" **Wt:** 200 **Born:** 10/27/70 **Age:** 33

								BATTING													BASERUNNING				AVERAGES		
Year Team	Lg	G	AB	H	2B	3B	HR	(Hm	Rd)	TB	R	RBI	RC	TBB	IBB	SO	HBP	SH	SF	SB	CS	SB%	GDP	Avg	OBP	Slg
2003 Ottawa*	AAA	121	418	117	21	2	10	(-	-)	172	62	53	52	35	3	73	2	2	1	4	6	.40	17	.280	.338	.411
2000 Atlanta	NL	4	2	0	0	0	0	(0	0)	0	0	0	0	0	0	2	0	0	0	0	0	—	0	.000	.000	.000
2002 Toronto	AL	13	12	1	0	0	0	(0	0)	1	3	1	0	1	0	6	0	0	0	0	0	—	0	.083	.154	.083
2003 Baltimore	AL	8	14	3	1	0	1	(1	0)	7	3	2	1	1	0	4	0	0	0	0	0	—	1	.214	.267	.500
3 ML YEARS		25	28	4	1	0	1	(1	0)	8	6	3	1	2	0	12	0	0	0	0	0	—	1	.143	.200	.286

Brian Sweeney

Pitches: R **Bats:** R **Pos:** RP-5 **Ht:** 6'2" **Wt:** 185 **Born:** 6/13/74 **Age:** 30

				HOW MUCH HE PITCHED						WHAT HE GAVE UP											THE RESULTS						
Year Team	Lg	G	GS	CG	GF	IP	BFP	H	R	ER	HR	SH	SF	HB	TBB	IBB	SO	WP	Bk	W	L	Pct	ShO	Sv-Op	Hld	ERC	ERA
1997 Lancaster	A+	40	0	0	13	85.1	358	83	39	36	11	2	4	2	21	1	73	8	0	6	3	.667	0	1--	-	3.56	3.80
1998 Lancaster	A+	17	4	0	3	52.0	211	41	26	21	6	0	1	1	21	1	48	2	1	6	0	1.000	0	0--	-	3.17	3.63
1999 Lancaster	A+	5	0	0	1	9.1	44	14	7	7	4	0	0	0	3	0	14	1	0	0	0	—	0	0--	-	9.53	6.75
1999 Tacoma	AAA	5	1	0	2	16.0	75	26	17	12	5	2	0	0	2	0	10	1	0	0	2	.000	0	0--	-	8.34	6.75
1999 New Haven	AA	23	18	0	3	111.1	478	125	65	58	18	1	3	4	31	1	83	4	0	4	6	.400	0	1--	-	4.92	4.69
2000 Tacoma	AAA	2	1	0	0	6.0	26	9	4	4	2	0	0	0	1	0	1	1	0	1	0	1.000	0	0--	-	8.38	6.00
2000 New Haven	AA	19	7	0	5	47.2	207	49	20	18	3	1	2	2	19	0	27	5	0	4	3	.571	0	0--	-	4.15	3.40
2001 San Antonio	AA	37	9	0	8	104.1	448	117	47	44	8	3	3	5	23	1	96	7	0	4	4	.636	0	1--	-	4.06	3.80
2002 Tacoma	AAA	30	23	1	4	142.0	606	157	67	60	16	3	1	3	28	0	113	5	0	9	5	.643	1	2--	-	4.00	3.80
2003 Tacoma	AAA	29	21	0	2	141.0	613	165	80	67	17	4	3	2	32	0	115	4	0	11	10	.524	0	0--	-	4.51	4.28
2003 Seattle	AL	5	0	0	0	9.1	35	7	2	2	0	0	1	0	1	0	7	0	0	0	0	—	0	0-0	0	1.66	1.93

Mark Sweeney

Bats: L **Throws:** L **Pos:** PH-47; RF-11; 1B-8; LF-7; DH-1   **Ht:** 6'1" **Wt:** 215 **Born:** 10/26/69 **Age:** 34

					BATTING																BASERUNNING				AVERAGES		
Year Team	Lg	G	AB	H	2B	3B	HR	(Hm	Rd)	TB	R	RBI	RC	TBB	IBB	SO	HBP	SH	SF		SB	CS	SB%	GDP	Avg	OBP	Slg
2003 Co Springs*	AAA	51	165	49	10	1	5	(-	-)	76	24	35	30	34	5	32	0	1	5		1	4	.20	5	.297	.407	.461
1995 St Louis	NL	37	77	21	2	0	2	(0	2)	29	5	13	10	10	0	15	0	1	2		1	1	.50	3	.273	.348	.377
1996 St Louis	NL	98	170	45	9	0	3	(0	3)	63	32	22	27	33	2	29	1	5	0		3	0	1.00	4	.265	.387	.371
1997 StL-SD	NL	115	164	46	7	0	2	(0	0)	59	16	23	22	20	1	32	1	1	2		2	3	.40	3	.280	.358	.360
1998 San Diego	NL	122	192	45	8	3	2	(1	1)	65	17	15	21	26	0	37	1	0	3		1	2	.33	5	.234	.324	.339
1999 Cincinnati	NL	37	31	11	3	0	2	(1	1)	20	6	7	7	4	1	9	0	0	0		0	0	-	2	.355	.429	.645
2000 Milwaukee	NL	71	73	16	6	0	1	(0	1)	25	9	6	9	12	1	18	1	1	0		0	0	-	1	.219	.337	.342
2001 Milwaukee	NL	48	89	23	3	1	3	(1	2)	37	9	11	14	12	0	23	0	2	0		2	1	.67	0	.258	.347	.416
2002 San Diego	NL	48	65	11	3	0	1	(0	1)	17	3	4	4	4	0	19	0	0	0		0	0	-	1	.169	.217	.262
2003 Colorado	NL	67	97	25	9	0	2	(1	1)	40	13	14	16	9	1	27	0	0	1		0	1	.00	1	.258	.321	.412
1997 St Louis	NL	44	61	13	3	0	0	(0	0)	16	5	4	5	9	1	14	1	1	1		0	1	.00	2	.213	.319	.262
1997 San Diego	NL	71	103	33	4	0	2	(0	0)	43	11	19	17	11	0	18	0	0	1		2	2	.50	1	.320	.383	.417
9 ML YEARS		643	958	243	50	4	18	(6	12)	355	110	115	127	130	6	209	4	10	7		9	8	.53	21	.254	.343	.371

Mike Sweeney

Bats: R **Throws:** R **Pos:** DH-62; 1B-45; PH-1   **Ht:** 6'3" **Wt:** 225 **Born:** 7/22/73 **Age:** 30

					BATTING																BASERUNNING				AVERAGES		
Year Team	Lg	G	AB	H	2B	3B	HR	(Hm	Rd)	TB	R	RBI	RC	TBB	IBB	SO	HBP	SH	SF		SB	CS	SB%	GDP	Avg	OBP	Slg
2003 Omaha*	AAA	2	8	2	1	0	1	(-	-)	6	3	1	2	1	0	1	0	0	0		0	0	-	0	.250	.333	.750
1995 Kansas City	AL	4	4	1	0	0	0	(0	0)	1	1	0	0	0	0	0	0	0	0		0	0	-	0	.250	.250	.250
1996 Kansas City	AL	50	165	46	10	0	4	(1	3)	68	23	24	23	18	0	21	4	0	3		1	2	.33	7	.279	.358	.412
1997 Kansas City	AL	84	240	58	8	0	7	(5	2)	87	30	31	25	17	0	33	6	1	2		3	2	.60	8	.242	.306	.363
1998 Kansas City	AL	92	282	73	18	0	8	(6	2)	115	32	35	35	24	1	38	2	2	1		2	3	.40	7	.259	.320	.408
1999 Kansas City	AL	150	575	185	44	2	22	(10	12)	299	101	102	109	54	0	48	10	0	4		6	1	.86	21	.322	.387	.520
2000 Kansas City	AL	159	618	206	30	0	29	(17	12)	323	105	144	128	71	5	67	15	0	13		8	3	.73	15	.333	.407	.523
2001 Kansas City	AL	147	559	170	46	0	29	(14	15)	303	97	99	109	64	13	64	2	1	6		10	3	.77	13	.304	.374	.542
2002 Kansas City	AL	126	471	160	31	1	24	(14	10)	265	81	86	113	61	10	46	6	0	7		9	7	.56	9	.340	.417	.563
2003 Kansas City	AL	108	392	115	18	1	16	(7	9)	183	62	83	82	64	5	56	2	0	5		3	2	.60	13	.293	.391	.467
9 ML YEARS		920	3306	1014	205	4	139	(74	65)	1644	532	604	624	373	34	373	47	4	41		42	23	.65	93	.307	.381	.497

Jon Switzer

Pitches: L **Bats:** L **Pos:** RP-5   **Ht:** 6'3" **Wt:** 191 **Born:** 8/13/79 **Age:** 24

		HOW MUCH HE PITCHED						WHAT HE GAVE UP											THE RESULTS							
Year Team	Lg	G	GS	CG	GF	IP	BFP	H	R	ER	HR	SH	SF	HB	TBB	IBB	SO	WP	Bk	W	L	Pct	ShO	Sv-Op	Hld	ERC	ERA
2001 Hudson Val	A-	5	0	0	2	14.1	57	9	3	1	0	1	0	2	2	0	20	2	0	2	0	1.000	0	0--	-	1.32	0.63
2002 Bakersfield	A+	20	20	0	0	103.1	441	108	55	49	8	4	1	8	26	0	129	4	0	7	5	.583	0	0--	-	3.91	4.27
2003 Orlando	AA	22	22	2	0	126.0	522	117	63	48	10	5	4	5	32	1	100	9	1	8	8	.500	0	0--	-	3.13	3.43
2003 Durham	AAA	1	1	0	0	5.0	19	6	1	1	1	0	0	0	0	0	3	0	0	1	0	1.000	0	0--	-	4.64	1.80
2003 Tampa Bay	AL	5	0	0	1	9.2	46	13	8	8	2	0	1	4	3	0	7	1	0	0	0	-	0	0-0	0	8.88	7.45

So Taguchi

Bats: R **Throws:** R **Pos:** CF-16; RF-13; PH-13; LF-11; PR-5; 2B-1   **Ht:** 5'10" **Wt:** 163 **Born:** 7/2/69 **Age:** 34

					BATTING																BASERUNNING				AVERAGES		
Year Team	Lg	G	AB	H	2B	3B	HR	(Hm	Rd)	TB	R	RBI	RC	TBB	IBB	SO	HBP	SH	SF		SB	CS	SB%	GDP	Avg	OBP	Slg
2002 Memphis	AAA	91	304	75	17	0	5	(-	-)	107	37	36	30	13	0	44	5	11	3		6	3	.67	5	.247	.286	.352
2002 New Haven	AA	26	107	33	10	0	1	(-	-)	46	21	15	18	9	0	15	3	0	1		3	1	.75	1	.308	.375	.430
2003 Memphis	AAA	90	258	66	8	2	2	(-	-)	84	31	24	28	22	0	36	2	5	1		14	5	.74	5	.256	.318	.326
2002 St Louis	NL	19	15	6	0	0	0	(0	0)	6	4	2	4	2	0	1	0	2	0		1	0	1.00	0	.400	.471	.400
2003 St Louis	NL	43	54	14	3	1	3	(1	2)	28	9	13	11	4	1	11	0	1	0		0	0	-	2	.259	.310	.519
2 ML YEARS		62	69	20	3	1	3	(1	2)	34	13	15	15	6	1	12	0	3	0		1	0	1.00	2	.290	.347	.493

Brian Tallet

Pitches: L **Bats:** L **Pos:** SP-3; RP-2   **Ht:** 6'7" **Wt:** 208 **Born:** 9/21/77 **Age:** 26

		HOW MUCH HE PITCHED						WHAT HE GAVE UP											THE RESULTS							
Year Team	Lg	G	GS	CG	GF	IP	BFP	H	R	ER	HR	SH	SF	HB	TBB	IBB	SO	WP	Bk	W	L	Pct	ShO	Sv-Op	Hld	ERC	ERA
2000 Mahning Vl	A-	6	6	0	0	15.2	62	10	2	2	0	0	0	1	3	0	20	0	0	0	0	-	0	0--	-	1.30	1.15
2001 Kinston	A+	27	27	2	0	160.0	644	134	62	54	12	3	2	4	38	0	164	2	0	9	7	.563	0	0--	-	2.55	3.04
2002 Akron	AA	18	16	1	0	102.1	425	93	41	35	9	1	1	9	32	0	73	2	1	10	1	.909	0	0--	-	3.57	3.08
2002 Buffalo	AAA	8	7	0	1	44.0	189	47	17	15	1	3	2	1	16	0	25	4	0	2	3	.400	0	0--	-	3.90	3.07
2003 Buffalo	AAA	15	15	0	0	84.0	377	89	50	48	10	3	5	5	34	1	67	6	0	4	4	.500	0	0--	-	4.72	5.14
2002 Cleveland	AL	2	2	0	0	12.0	47	9	3	2	0	0	0	1	4	0	5	0	0	1	0	1.000	0	0-0	0	2.31	1.50
2003 Cleveland	AL	5	3	0	1	19.0	87	23	14	10	2	2	0	1	8	0	9	0	0	0	2	.000	0	0-0	0	5.65	4.74
2 ML YEARS		7	5	0	1	31.0	134	32	17	12	2	2	0	2	12	0	14	0	0	1	2	.333	0	0-0	0	4.27	3.48

Jeff Tam

Pitches: R **Bats:** R **Pos:** RP-44   **Ht:** 6'1" **Wt:** 219 **Born:** 8/19/70 **Age:** 33

		HOW MUCH HE PITCHED						WHAT HE GAVE UP											THE RESULTS							
Year Team	Lg	G	GS	CG	GF	IP	BFP	H	R	ER	HR	SH	SF	HB	TBB	IBB	SO	WP	Bk	W	L	Pct	ShO	Sv-Op	Hld	ERC	ERA
2003 Syracuse*	AAA	17	0	0	10	17.2	74	16	3	3	1	1	0	1	3	0	11	1	0	1	0	1.000	0	4--	-	2.55	1.53
1998 New York	NL	15	0	0	5	14.1	60	13	10	10	2	0	0	2	4	1	8	0	0	1	1	.500	0	0-1	1	3.86	6.28
1999 NYM-Cle		10	0	0	4	11.2	47	8	7	7	3	1	0	0	4	1	8	0	0	0	0	-	0	0-0	0	2.97	5.40
2000 Oakland	AL	72	0	0	23	85.2	351	86	30	25	3	2	4	1	23	8	46	3	0	3	3	.500	0	3-6	19	3.14	2.63
2001 Oakland	AL	70	0	0	15	74.2	310	68	27	25	3	3	3	3	29	9	44	0	0	2	4	.333	0	3-6	25	3.18	3.01
2002 Oakland	AL	40	0	0	14	40.1	188	56	25	23	2	3	2	2	13	5	14	3	0	1	2	.333	0	0-4	5	5.59	5.13
2003 Toronto*	AL	44	0	0	9	44.2	214	58	30	28	5	2	1	1	25	7	26	2	0	4	4	.000	0	1-2	6	6.37	5.64

Year Team	Lg	G	GS	CG	GF	IP	BFP	H	R	ER	HR	SH	SF	HB	TBB	IBB	SO	WP	Bk	W	L	Pct	ShO	Sv-Op	Hld	ERC	ERA
1999 New York	NL	9	0	0	3	11.1	43	6	4	4	3	0	0	0	3	0	8	0	0	0	0	-	0	0-0	0	2.05	3.18
1999 Cleveland	AL	1	0	0	0	0.1	4	2	3	3	0	1	0	0	1	1	0	0	0	0	0	-	0	0-0	0	44.68	81.00
6 ML YEARS		251	0	0	69	271.1	1170	289	129	118	18	11	10	9	98	31	146	8	0	7	14	.333	0	7-19	54	4.04	3.91

Dennis Tankersley

Pitches: R **Bats:** R **Pos:** SP-1

Ht: 6'2" **Wt:** 185 **Born:** 2/24/79 **Age:** 25

Year Team	Lg	G	GS	CG	GF	IP	BFP	H	R	ER	HR	SH	SF	HB	TBB	IBB	SO	WP	Bk	W	L	Pct	ShO	Sv-Op	Hld	ERC	ERA
1999 Red Sox	R	11	6	0	2	35.2	133	14	7	3	2	0	0	3	9	1	57	0	0	1	0	1.000	0	1--	-	0.99	0.76
2000 Augusta	A	15	15	1	0	75.1	326	73	41	34	4	0	0	4	32	0	74	1	1	5	3	.625	1	0--	-	3.89	4.06
2000 Fort Wayne	A	12	12	0	0	66.1	265	48	25	21	5	2	2	2	25	0	87	2	0	5	2	.714	0	0--	-	2.55	2.85
2001 Lk Elsinore	A+	9	8	0	0	52.1	196	29	5	3	1	1	0	0	12	0	68	0	0	5	1	.833	0	0--	-	1.12	0.52
2001 Mobile	AA	13	13	0	0	69.2	282	44	23	16	6	1	0	4	24	1	89	2	1	4	1	.800	0	0--	-	2.04	2.07
2001 Portland	AAA	3	3	0	0	14.1	68	16	13	11	2	2	2	0	8	0	16	0	0	1	2	.333	0	0--	-	5.48	6.91
2002 Mobile	AA	10	10	0	0	50.2	218	47	20	17	1	2	1	2	21	0	56	0	1	3	3	.500	0	0--	-	3.31	3.02
2002 Portland	AAA	9	9	0	0	51.0	223	43	29	22	6	2	2	1	30	0	51	2	1	3	4	.429	0	0--	-	4.13	3.88
2003 Portland	AAA	27	27	0	0	151.0	660	149	82	78	15	1	4	9	67	0	148	7	0	8	11	.421	0	0--	-	4.43	4.65
2002 San Diego	NL	17	9	0	3	51.1	245	59	46	46	10	3	2	6	40	3	39	3	0	1	4	.200	0	0-0	0	8.04	8.06
2003 San Diego	NL	1	1	0	0	0.0	7	3	7	7	0	0	0	0	4	0	0	0	0	0	1	.000	0	0-0	0		
2 ML YEARS		18	10	0	3	51.1	252	62	53	53	10	3	2	6	44	3	39	3	0	1	5	.167	0	0-0	0	8.79	9.29

Fernando Tatis

Bats: R **Throws:** R **Pos:** 3B-49; PH-4

Ht: 5'10" **Wt:** 180 **Born:** 1/1/75 **Age:** 29

Year Team	Lg	G	AB	H	2B	3B	HR	(Hm	Rd)	TB	R	RBI	RC	TBB	IBB	SO	HBP	SH	SF	SB	CS	SB%	GDP	Avg	OBP	Slg
1997 Texas	AL	60	223	57	9	0	8	(6	2)	90	29	29	26	14	0	42	0	2	2	3	0	1.00	6	.256	.297	.404
1998 Tex-StL		150	532	147	33	4	11	(6	5)	221	69	58	69	36	3	123	6	4	1	13	5	.72	16	.276	.329	.415
1999 St Louis	NL	149	537	160	31	2	34	(16	18)	297	104	107	117	82	4	128	16	0	4	21	9	.70	11	.298	.404	.553
2000 St Louis	NL	96	324	82	21	1	18	(11	7)	159	59	64	58	57	1	94	10	1	2	2	3	.40	13	.253	.379	.491
2001 Montreal	NL	41	145	37	9	0	2	(0	2)	52	20	11	18	16	0	43	4	0	3	0	0	-	5	.255	.339	.359
2002 Montreal	NL	114	381	87	18	1	15	(5	10)	152	43	55	39	35	1	90	8	1	5	2	2	.50	15	.228	.303	.399
2003 Montreal	NL	53	175	34	6	0	2	(1	1)	46	15	15	14	18	0	40	3	0	0	2	1	.67	7	.194	.281	.263
1998 Texas	AL	95	330	89	17	2	3	(1	2)	119	41	32	33	12	2	66	4	4	0	6	2	.75	10	.270	.303	.361
1998 St Louis	NL	55	202	58	16	2	8	(5	3)	102	28	26	36	24	1	57	2	0	1	7	3	.70	6	.287	.367	.505
7 ML YEARS		663	2317	604	127	8	90	(45	45)	1017	339	339	341	258	9	560	47	8	17	43	20	.68	73	.261	.344	.439

Julian Tavarez

Pitches: R **Bats:** L **Pos:** RP-64

Ht: 6'2" **Wt:** 195 **Born:** 5/22/73 **Age:** 31

Year Team	Lg	G	GS	CG	GF	IP	BFP	H	R	ER	HR	SH	SF	HB	TBB	IBB	SO	WP	Bk	W	L	Pct	ShO	Sv-Op	Hld	ERC	ERA
1993 Cleveland	AL	8	7	0	0	37.0	172	53	29	27	7	0	1	2	13	2	19	3	1	2	2	.500	0	0-0	0	7.48	6.57
1994 Cleveland	AL	1	1	0	0	1.2	14	6	8	4	1	0	1	0	1	1	0	0	0	0	1	.000	0	0-0	0	24.13	21.60
1995 Cleveland	AL	57	0	0	15	85.0	350	76	36	23	7	0	2	3	21	0	68	3	2	10	2	.833	0	0-4	19	2.93	2.44
1996 Cleveland	AL	51	4	0	13	80.2	353	101	49	48	9	5	4	1	22	5	46	1	0	4	7	.364	0	0-0	13	5.12	5.36
1997 San Francisco	NL	89	0	0	39	88.1	378	91	43	38	6	3	8	4	34	5	38	4	0	6	4	.600	0	0-3	26	4.13	3.87
1998 San Francisco	NL	60	0	0	12	85.1	374	96	41	36	5	5	3	8	36	11	52	1	1	5	3	.625	0	1-6	10	4.89	3.80
1999 San Francisco	NL	47	0	0	12	54.2	258	65	39	36	7	3	2	8	25	3	33	4	1	2	0	1.000	0	0-2	5	6.10	5.93
2000 Colorado	NL	51	12	1	8	120.0	530	124	68	59	11	3	4	7	53	9	62	2	1	11	5	.688	0	1-1	6	4.49	4.43
2001 Chicago	NL	34	28	0	1	161.1	712	172	98	81	13	8	4	11	69	4	107	2	1	10	9	.526	0	0-0	2	4.70	4.52
2002 Florida	NL	29	27	0	1	153.2	714	188	100	92	9	13	2	15	74	7	67	7	2	10	12	.455	0	0-1	0	5.75	5.39
2003 Pittsburgh	NL	64	0	0	29	83.2	350	75	37	34	1	9	1	5	27	8	39	3	0	3	3	.500	0	11-14	9	2.72	3.66
11 ML YEARS		491	79	1	104	951.1	4205	1047	547	478	76	49	32	64	375	55	531	30	9	63	48	.568	0	13-31	90	4.69	4.52

Aaron Taylor

Pitches: R **Bats:** R **Pos:** RP-10

Ht: 6'7" **Wt:** 230 **Born:** 8/20/77 **Age:** 26

Year Team	Lg	G	GS	CG	GF	IP	BFP	H	R	ER	HR	SH	SF	HB	TBB	IBB	SO	WP	Bk	W	L	Pct	ShO	Sv-Op	Hld	ERC	ERA
1996 Braves	R	13	9	0	3	52.1	259	68	54	45	0	7	2	6	28	0	33	14	2	0	9	.000	0	0--	-	5.87	7.74
1997 Danville	R+	15	1	0	2	55.1	261	65	49	34	4	1	1	2	31	0	38	11	1	1	8	.111	0	0--	-	5.60	5.53
1998 Danville	R+	14	14	1	0	72.0	334	87	60	50	9	1	3	3	36	0	55	3	1	3	6	.333	0	0--	-	6.09	6.25
1999 Macon	A	27	8	0	6	79.1	360	86	56	43	9	2	5	7	27	2	78	17	0	6	7	.462	0	1--	-	4.58	4.88
2000 Everett	A-	15	14	0	1	63.0	298	76	54	52	5	0	2	7	37	0	57	10	1	1	4	.200	0	0--	-	6.63	7.43
2001 Wisconsin	A	28	0	0	26	29.1	119	19	9	8	1	2	1	2	11	2	50	4	2	3	1	.750	0	9--	-	1.90	2.45
2002 San Antonio	AA	61	0	0	48	77.0	323	64	28	20	5	3	3	6	34	0	93	2	0	4	3	.571	0	24--	-	2.46	2.34
2003 Tacoma	AAA	33	0	0	31	40.1	164	30	11	11	3	3	2	2	13	1	34	2	0	1	3	.250	0	16--	-	2.42	2.45
2002 Seattle	AL	5	0	0	2	5.0	23	8	5	5	2	0	0	0	6	0	6	0	0	0	0	-	0	0-1	0	8.09	9.00
2003 Seattle	AL	10	0	0	4	12.2	62	17	12	12	0	0	1	1	6	0	9	2	0	0	0	-	0	0-0	0	5.74	8.53
2 ML YEARS		15	0	0	6	17.2	85	25	17	17	2	0	1	1	12	0	15	2	0	0	0	-	0	0-1	0	6.48	8.66

Reggie Taylor

Bats: L **Throws:** R **Pos:** CF-49; PH-49; LF-13; PR-6; RF-3

Ht: 6'1" **Wt:** 178 **Born:** 1/12/77 **Age:** 27

Year Team	Lg	G	AB	H	2B	3B	HR	(Hm	Rd)	TB	R	RBI	RC	TBB	IBB	SO	HBP	SH	SF	SB	CS	SB%	GDP	Avg	OBP	Slg
2000 Philadelphia	NL	9	11	1	0	0	0	(0	0)	1	1	0	0	0	0	8	0	0	0	1	0	1.00	0	.091	.091	.091
2001 Philadelphia	NL	5	7	0	0	0	0	(0	0)	0	1	0	0	1	0	1	0	0	0	0	0	-	0	.000	.125	.000
2002 Cincinnati	NL	135	287	73	15	4	9	(6	3)	123	41	38	33	14	3	79	2	5	3	11	8	.58	6	.254	.291	.429
2003 Cincinnati	NL	100	180	39	5	2	5	(3	2)	63	17	19	12	11	0	68	1	2	0	7	0	1.00	4	.217	.266	.350
4 ML YEARS		249	485	113	20	6	14	(9	5)	187	60	57	45	26	3	156	3	7	3	19	8	.70	10	.233	.275	.386

Mark Teixeira

Bats: B Throws: R Pos: 1B-116; 3B-15; LF-14; RF-11; DH-5; PH-3; PR-3   Ht: 6'2" Wt: 215 Born: 4/11/80 Age: 24

Year Team	Lg	G	AB	H	2B	3B	HR	(Hm	Rd)	TB	R	RBI	RC	TBB	IBB	SO	HBP	SH	SF	SB	CS	SB%	GDP	Avg	OBP	Slg
2002 Charlotte	A+	38	150	48	10	2	9	(-	-)	89	32	41	35	21	2	24	3	0	1	2	0	1.00	4	.320	.411	.593
2002 Tulsa	AA	48	171	54	11	3	10	(-	-)	101	31	28	40	25	0	36	4	0	0	3	2	.60	2	.316	.415	.591
2003 Texas	AL	146	529	137	29	5	26	(19	7)	254	66	84	79	44	5	120	14	0	2	1	2	.33	14	.259	.331	.480

Miguel Tejada

Bats: R Throws: R Pos: SS-162   Ht: 5'9" Wt: 200 Born: 5/25/76 Age: 28

Year Team	Lg	G	AB	H	2B	3B	HR	(Hm	Rd)	TB	R	RBI	RC	TBB	IBB	SO	HBP	SH	SF	SB	CS	SB%	GDP	Avg	OBP	Slg
1997 Oakland	AL	26	99	20	3	2	2	(1	1)	33	10	10	7	2	0	22	3	0	0	2	0	1.00	3	.202	.240	.333
1998 Oakland	AL	105	365	85	20	1	11	(5	6)	140	53	45	40	28	0	86	7	4	3	5	6	.45	8	.233	.298	.384
1999 Oakland	AL	159	593	149	33	4	21	(12	9)	253	93	84	82	57	3	94	10	9	5	8	7	.53	11	.251	.325	.427
2000 Oakland	AL	160	607	167	32	1	30	(16	14)	291	105	115	99	66	6	102	4	2	2	6	0	1.00	15	.275	.349	.479
2001 Oakland	AL	162	622	166	31	3	31	(17	14)	296	107	113	94	43	5	89	13	1	4	11	5	.69	14	.267	.326	.476
2002 Oakland	AL	162	662	204	30	0	34	(17	17)	336	108	131	122	38	3	84	11	0	4	7	2	.78	21	.308	.354	.508
2003 Oakland	AL	162	636	177	42	0	27	(15	12)	300	98	106	104	53	7	65	6	0	8	10	0	1.00	12	.278	.336	.472
7 ML YEARS		936	3584	968	191	11	156	(83	73)	1649	574	604	548	287	24	542	54	16	26	49	20	.71	84	.270	.331	.460

Michael Tejera

Pitches: L Bats: L Pos: RP-44; SP-6   Ht: 5'9" Wt: 175 Born: 10/18/76 Age: 27

| | | HOW MUCH HE PITCHED | | | | | | WHAT HE GAVE UP | | | | | | | | | | THE RESULTS | | | | | | |
Year Team	Lg	G	GS	CG	GF	IP	BFP	H	R	ER	HR	SH	SF	HB	TBB	IBB	SO	WP	Bk	W	L	Pct	ShO	Sv-Op	Hld	ERC	ERA
1999 Florida	NL	3	1	0	1	6.1	31	10	8	8	1	0	0	0	5	0	7	0	0	0	0	-	0	0-0	0	10.73	11.37
2002 Florida	NL	47	18	0	2	139.2	611	144	71	69	17	5	4	6	60	3	95	3	0	8	8	.500	0	1-3	8	4.70	4.45
2003 Florida	NL	50	6	0	10	81.0	353	82	44	42	6	8	1	1	36	3	58	0	0	3	4	.429	0	2-2	5	4.13	4.67
3 ML YEARS		100	25	0	13	227.0	995	236	123	119	24	13	5	7	101	6	160	3	0	11	12	.478	0	3-5	13	4.64	4.72

Amaury Telemaco

Pitches: R Bats: R Pos: SP-8   Ht: 6'3" Wt: 222 Born: 1/19/74 Age: 30

| | | HOW MUCH HE PITCHED | | | | | | WHAT HE GAVE UP | | | | | | | | | | THE RESULTS | | | | | | |
Year Team	Lg	G	GS	CG	GF	IP	BFP	H	R	ER	HR	SH	SF	HB	TBB	IBB	SO	WP	Bk	W	L	Pct	ShO	Sv-Op	Hld	ERC	ERA
2003 Scrtn/WlksBr*	AAA	25	24	3	0	155.1	599	125	59	56	15	6	4	3	22	1	116	5	0	10	9	.526	2	0- -	-	2.19	3.24
1996 Chicago	NL	25	17	0	0	97.1	427	108	0	59	20	0	0	0	31	0	64	0	0	5	7	.417	0	0-0	0	5.06	5.46
1997 Chicago	NL	10	5	0	0	38.0	169	47	0	26	4	0	0	0	11	0	29	0	0	1	3	.000	0	0-0	0	5.00	6.16
1998 ChC-Ari	NL	41	18	0	0	148.2	637	150	0	65	18	0	0	0	46	0	78	0	0	7	10	.412	0	0-0	0	3.86	3.93
1999 Ari-Phi	NL	49	0	0	0	53.0	234	52	0	34	10	0	0	0	26	0	43	0	0	4	0	1.000	0	0-0	0	4.93	5.77
2000 Philadelphia	NL	13	2	0	0	24.1	107	25	0	18	6	0	0	0	14	0	22	0	0	1	3	.250	0	0-0	0	6.24	6.66
2001 Philadelphia	NL	24	14	1	0	89.1	388	93	0	55	15	0	0	0	32	0	59	0	0	5	5	.500	0	0-0	0	4.58	5.54
2003 Philadelphia	NL	8	8	0	0	45.1	194	47	22	20	5	3	1	7	11	2	29	3	0	1	4	.200	0	0-0	0	3.48	3.97
1998 Chicago	NL	14	0	0	0	27.2	118	23	0	12	5	0	0	0	13	0	18	0	0	1	1	.500	0	0-0	0	3.92	3.90
1998 Arizona	NL	27	18	0	0	121.0	519	127	0	53	13	0	0	0	33	0	60	0	0	6	9	.400	0	0-0	0	3.84	3.94
1999 Arizona	NL	5	0	0	0	6.0	28	7	0	5	2	0	0	0	6	0	2	0	0	1	0	1.000	0	0-0	0	10.63	7.50
1999 Philadelphia	NL	44	0	0	0	47.0	206	45	0	29	8	0	0	0	20	0	41	0	0	3	0	1.000	0	0-0	0	4.33	5.55
7 ML YEARS		170	64	1	0	496.0	2156	516	22	277	78	3	1	7	171	2	324	3	0	23	32	.418	0	0-0	0	4.49	5.03

Luis Terrero

Bats: R Throws: R Pos: PH-3; CF-2; RF-1   Ht: 6'2" Wt: 206 Born: 5/18/80 Age: 24

Year Team	Lg	G	AB	H	2B	3B	HR	(Hm	Rd)	TB	R	RBI	RC	TBB	IBB	SO	HBP	SH	SF	SB	CS	SB%	GDP	Avg	OBP	Slg
1999 Missoula	R+	71	272	78	13	7	8	(-	-)	129	74	40	50	32	1	91	5	3	6	27	10	.73	2	.287	.365	.474
2000 High Desert	A+	19	79	15	3	1	0	(-	-)	20	10	1	2	3	0	16	1	0	0	5	5	.50	2	.190	.229	.253
2000 Missoula	R+	68	276	72	10	4	8	(-	-)	106	48	44	31	10	0	75	8	1	1	23	11	.68	5	.261	.305	.384
2001 South Bend	A	24	89	14	2	0	1	(-	-)	19	4	8	1	0	0	29	2	0	0	3	0	1.00	2	.157	.176	.213
2001 Yakima	A-	11	41	13	2	1	0	(-	-)	17	7	0	5	2	0	8	0	0	0	0	3	.00	0	.317	.349	.415
2001 Lancaster	A+	19	71	32	9	1	4	(-	-)	55	16	11	21	1	1	14	1	0	0	5	0	1.00	3	.451	.466	.775
2002 El Paso	AA	34	147	44	13	3	3	(-	-)	72	29	8	24	4	0	45	3	2	0	9	2	.82	2	.299	.331	.490
2003 Tucson	AAA	118	467	134	20	15	3	(-	-)	193	83	46	64	31	0	103	11	2	1	23	19	.55	6	.287	.345	.413
2003 Arizona	NL	5	4	1	0	0	0	(0	0)	1	0	0	1	0	0	1	0	0	0	0	0	-	0	.250	.400	.250

Marcus Thames

Bats: R Throws: R Pos: RF-19; LF-4; DH-4; PR-4; PH-3; CF-1   Ht: 6'2" Wt: 205 Born: 3/6/77 Age: 27

Year Team	Lg	G	AB	H	2B	3B	HR	(Hm	Rd)	TB	R	RBI	RC	TBB	IBB	SO	HBP	SH	SF	SB	CS	SB%	GDP	Avg	OBP	Slg
1997 Yankees	R	57	195	67	17	4	7	(-	-)	113	51	36	42	16	0	26	3	1	4	6	4	.60	3	.344	.394	.579
1997 Greensboro	A	4	16	5	1	0	0	(-	-)	6	2	2	2	0	0	3	0	0	0	1	0	1.00	0	.313	.313	.375
1998 Tampa	A+	122	457	130	18	3	11	(-	-)	187	62	59	62	24	1	78	8	1	5	13	6	.68	5	.284	.328	.409
1999 Norwich	AA	51	182	41	6	2	4	(-	-)	63	25	26	21	22	0	40	3	1	2	0	1	.00	2	.225	.316	.346
1999 Tampa	A+	69	266	65	12	4	11	(-	-)	118	47	38	42	33	1	58	3	1	2	3	0	1.00	5	.244	.332	.444
2000 Norwich	AA	131	474	114	30	2	15	(-	-)	193	72	79	58	50	1	89	4	0	8	1	5	.17	13	.241	.313	.407
2001 Norwich	AA	139	520	167	43	4	31	(-	-)	311	106	97	122	73	8	101	7	0	3	10	4	.71	6	.321	.410	.598
2002 Columbus	AAA	107	386	80	21	3	13	(-	-)	146	51	45	43	43	0	71	7	0	2	5	4	.56	8	.207	.297	.378
2003 Oklahoma	AAA	18	66	17	4	0	2	(-	-)	27	9	7	9	8	0	12	0	0	0	1	0	1.00	2	.258	.338	.409
2003 Columbus	AAA	52	194	54	15	2	2	(-	-)	79	26	28	25	17	0	48	1	0	5	3	4	.43	4	.278	.332	.407

		BATTING																			BASERUNNING				AVERAGES		
Year Team	Lg	G	AB	H	2B	3B	HR	(Hm	Rd)	TB	R	RBI	RC	TBB	IBB	SO	HBP	SH	SF	SB	CS	SB%	GDP	Avg	OBP	Slg
2002 New York	AL	7	13	3	1	0	1	(1	0)	7	2	2	2	0	0	4	0	0	0	0	0	-	0	.231	.231	.538
2003 Texas	AL	30	73	15	2	0	1	(0	1)	20	12	4	5	8	0	18	2	0	1	0	1	.00	2	.205	.298	.274
2 ML YEARS		37	86	18	3	0	2	(1	1)	27	14	6	7	8	0	22	2	0	1	0	1	.00	2	.209	.289	.314

Brad Thomas

Pitches: L **Bats:** L **Pos:** RP-3   **Ht:** 6'4" **Wt:** 220 **Born:** 10/22/77 **Age:** 26

		HOW MUCH HE PITCHED						WHAT HE GAVE UP												THE RESULTS						
Year Team	Lg	G	GS	CG	GF	IP	BFP	H	R	ER	HR	SH	SF	HB	TBB	IBB	SO	WP	Bk	W	L	Pct	ShO	Sv-Op	Hld	ERC	ERA
1996 Great Falls	R+	11	5	0	3	35.2	163	48	27	25	2	1	1	0	11	0	28	5	4	3	2	.600	0	0- -		5.35	6.31
1997 Elizabethton	R+	14	13	0	0	70.1	307	78	43	35	5	3	0	3	21	0	53	8	2	3	4	.429	0	0- -		4.23	4.48
1998 Fort Wayne	A	27	26	1	1	152.1	650	146	68	50	9	4	5	8	45	1	125	11	3	11	8	.579	1	0- -		3.31	2.95
1999 Fort Myers	A+	27	27	1	0	152.2	666	182	99	81	11	4	3	6	46	0	108	8	1	8	11	.421	1	0- -		4.81	4.78
2000 Fort Myers	A+	12	12	0	0	65.0	279	62	33	12	3	1	0	3	16	0	57	3	0	6	2	.750	0	0- -		2.95	1.66
2000 New Britain	AA	14	13	1	0	75.1	346	80	47	34	3	3	4	4	46	1	66	9	2	6	6	.500	1	0- -		5.01	4.06
2001 New Britain	AA	19	19	1	0	119.1	474	91	37	26	4	1	2	4	26	0	97	7	0	10	3	.769	0	0- -		1.91	1.96
2002 Edmonton	AAA	28	27	1	1	152.0	682	175	112	97	20	2	8	17	54	0	97	1	2	6	12	.333	0	0- -		5.51	5.74
2003 Rochester	AAA	15	11	0	2	58.2	244	68	23	23	3	1	0	0	10	0	50	3	2	0	3	.000	0	0- -		3.80	3.53
2003 Twins	R	2	2	0	0	10.0	38	6	0	0	0	1	0	0	1	0	12	0	0	0	0	-	0	0- -		0.90	0.00
2001 Minnesota	AL	5	5	0	0	16.1	82	20	0	17	6	0	0	0	14	0	6	0	0	0	2	.000	0	0-0	0	9.68	9.37
2003 Minnesota	AL	3	0	0	1	4.2	22	6	4	4	1	0	0	0	3	1	2	0	0	0	1	.000	0	0-0	0	7.54	7.71
2 ML YEARS		8	5	0	1	21.0	104	26	4	21	7	0	0	0	17	1	8	0	0	0	3	.000	0	0-0	0	9.20	9.00

Frank Thomas

Bats: R **Throws:** R **Pos:** DH-124; 1B-27; PH-2   **Ht:** 6'5" **Wt:** 275 **Born:** 5/27/68 **Age:** 36

		BATTING																			BASERUNNING				AVERAGES		
Year Team	Lg	G	AB	H	2B	3B	HR	(Hm	Rd)	TB	R	RBI	RC	TBB	IBB	SO	HBP	SH	SF	SB	CS	SB%	GDP	Avg	OBP	Slg
1990 Chicago	AL	60	191	63	11	3	7	(2	5)	101	39	31	46	44	0	54	2	0	3	0	1	.00	5	.330	.454	.529
1991 Chicago	AL	158	559	178	31	2	32	(24	8)	309	104	109	134	138	13	112	1	0	2	1	2	.33	20	.318	.453	.553
1992 Chicago	AL	160	573	185	46	2	24	(10	14)	307	108	115	132	122	6	88	5	0	11	6	3	.67	19	.323	.439	.536
1993 Chicago	AL	153	549	174	36	0	41	(26	15)	333	106	128	137	112	23	54	2	0	13	4	2	.67	10	.317	.426	.607
1994 Chicago	AL	113	399	141	34	1	38	(22	16)	291	106	101	127	109	12	61	2	0	7	2	3	.40	15	.353	.487	.729
1995 Chicago	AL	145	493	152	27	0	40	(15	25)	299	102	111	132	136	29	74	6	0	12	3	2	.60	14	.308	.454	.606
1996 Chicago	AL	141	527	184	26	0	40	(16	24)	330	110	134	137	109	26	70	5	0	8	1	1	.50	25	.349	.459	.626
1997 Chicago	AL	146	530	184	35	0	35	(16	19)	324	110	125	139	109	9	69	3	0	7	1	1	.50	15	.347	.456	.611
1998 Chicago	AL	160	585	155	35	2	29	(15	14)	281	109	109	111	110	2	93	6	0	11	7	0	1.00	14	.265	.381	.480
1999 Chicago	AL	135	486	148	36	0	15	(9	6)	229	74	77	95	87	13	66	9	0	8	3	3	.50	13	.305	.414	.471
2000 Chicago	AL	159	582	191	44	0	43	(30	13)	364	115	143	148	112	18	94	5	0	8	1	3	.25	13	.328	.436	.625
2001 Chicago	AL	20	68	15	3	0	4	(2	2)	30	8	10	10	10	2	12	0	0	1	0	0	-	0	.221	.316	.441
2002 Chicago	AL	148	523	132	29	1	28	(24	4)	247	77	92	96	88	2	115	7	0	10	3	0	1.00	10	.252	.361	.472
2003 Chicago	AL	153	546	146	35	0	42	(29	13)	307	87	105	116	100	4	115	12	0	4	0	0	-	11	.267	.390	.562
14 ML YEARS		1851	6611	2048	428	11	418	(240	178)	3752	1255	1390	1560	1386	159	1077	65	0	105	32	21	.60	186	.310	.428	.568

Jim Thome

Bats: L **Throws:** R **Pos:** 1B-156; DH-2; PH-2   **Ht:** 6'4" **Wt:** 220 **Born:** 8/27/70 **Age:** 33

		BATTING																			BASERUNNING				AVERAGES		
Year Team	Lg	G	AB	H	2B	3B	HR	(Hm	Rd)	TB	R	RBI	RC	TBB	IBB	SO	HBP	SH	SF	SB	CS	SB%	GDP	Avg	OBP	Slg
1991 Cleveland	AL	27	98	25	4	2	1	(0	1)	36	7	9	9	5	1	16	1	0	0	1	1	.50	4	.255	.298	.367
1992 Cleveland	AL	40	117	24	3	1	2	(1	1)	35	8	12	9	10	2	34	2	0	2	2	0	1.00	3	.205	.275	.299
1993 Cleveland	AL	47	154	41	11	0	7	(5	2)	73	28	22	30	29	1	36	4	0	5	2	1	.67	3	.266	.385	.474
1994 Cleveland	AL	98	321	86	20	1	20	(10	10)	168	58	52	56	46	5	84	0	1	1	3	3	.50	11	.268	.359	.523
1995 Cleveland	AL	137	452	142	29	3	25	(13	12)	252	92	73	109	97	3	113	5	0	3	4	3	.57	8	.314	.438	.558
1996 Cleveland	AL	151	505	157	28	5	38	(16	22)	309	122	116	132	123	8	141	6	0	2	2	2	.50	13	.311	.450	.612
1997 Cleveland	AL	147	496	142	25	0	40	(17	23)	287	104	102	120	120	9	146	3	0	8	1	1	.50	9	.286	.423	.579
1998 Cleveland	AL	123	440	129	34	2	30	(18	12)	257	89	85	104	89	8	141	4	0	4	1	0	1.00	7	.293	.413	.584
1999 Cleveland	AL	146	494	137	27	2	33	(19	14)	267	101	108	116	127	13	171	4	0	4	0	0	-	6	.277	.426	.540
2000 Cleveland	AL	158	557	150	33	1	37	(21	16)	296	106	106	119	118	4	171	4	0	5	1	0	1.00	3	.269	.398	.531
2001 Cleveland	AL	156	526	153	26	1	49	(30	19)	328	101	124	130	111	14	185	4	0	3	0	1	.00	9	.291	.416	.624
2002 Cleveland	AL	147	480	146	19	2	52	(30	22)	325	101	118	140	122	18	139	5	0	6	1	2	.33	5	.304	.445	.677
2003 Philadelphia	NL	159	578	154	30	3	47	(28	19)	331	111	131	127	111	11	182	4	0	5	0	3	.00	5	.266	.385	.573
13 ML YEARS		1536	5218	1486	289	23	381	(210	171)	2964	1028	1058	1201	1108	97	1559	46	1	48	18	17	.51	91	.285	.411	.568

John Thomson

Pitches: R **Bats:** R **Pos:** SP-35   **Ht:** 6'3" **Wt:** 190 **Born:** 10/1/73 **Age:** 30

		HOW MUCH HE PITCHED						WHAT HE GAVE UP												THE RESULTS						
Year Team	Lg	G	GS	CG	GF	IP	BFP	H	R	ER	HR	SH	SF	HB	TBB	IBB	SO	WP	Bk	W	L	Pct	ShO	Sv-Op	Hld	ERC	ERA
1997 Colorado	NL	27	27	2	0	166.1	721	193	94	87	15	10	3	5	51	0	106	2	0	7	9	.438	1	0-0	0	4.74	4.71
1998 Colorado	NL	26	26	2	0	161.0	680	174	86	86	21	8	5	0	49	0	106	4	2	8	11	.421	0	0-0	0	4.45	4.81
1999 Colorado	NL	14	13	1	1	62.2	305	85	62	56	11	4	2	1	36	1	34	2	0	1	10	.091	0	0-0	0	7.60	8.04
2001 Colorado	NL	14	14	1	0	93.2	386	84	46	42	15	3	3	4	25	3	68	1	0	4	5	.444	1	0-0	0	3.52	4.04
2002 Col-NYM	NL	30	30	0	0	181.2	800	201	116	95	28	13	10	2	44	9	107	2	0	9	14	.391	0	0-0	0	4.24	4.71
2003 Texas	AL	35	35	3	0	217.0	910	234	125	117	27	2	7	4	42	2	136	5	0	13	14	.481	1	0-0	0	4.10	4.85
2002 Colorado	NL	21	21	0	0	127.1	550	136	77	69	21	7	7	2	27	6	76	2	0	7	8	.467	0	0-0	0	4.02	4.88
2002 New York	NL	9	9	0	0	54.1	250	65	39	26	7	6	3	0	17	3	31	0	0	2	6	.250	0	0-0	0	4.74	4.31
6 ML YEARS		146	145	9	1	882.1	3802	971	529	483	117	40	30	16	254	15	557	16	2	42	63	.400	3	0-0	0	4.48	4.93

Corey Thurman

Pitches: R **Bats:** R **Pos:** SP-3; RP-3   **Ht:** 6'1" **Wt:** 215 **Born:** 11/5/78 **Age:** 25

			HOW MUCH HE PITCHED					WHAT HE GAVE UP										THE RESULTS						
Year Team	Lg	G	GS	CG	GF	IP	BFP	H	R	ER	HR	SH	SF	HB	TBB	IBB	SO	WP	Bk	W	L	Pct	ShO	Sv-Op	Hld	ERC	ERA
1996 Royals	R	11	11	1	0	47.1	221	53	32	32	2	0	2	3	28	0	52	8	1	1	6	.143	0	0--	-	5.33	6.08
1997 Royals	R	8	8	1	0	34.0	149	28	12	9	1	1	0	2	22	0	42	1	0	2	1	.667	0	0--	-	3.80	2.38
1997 Spokane	A-	5	5	0	0	22.2	106	23	19	13	2	0	2	2	13	0	24	2	1	1	2	.333	0	0--	-	4.99	5.16
1998 Lansing	A	14	11	0	2	62.1	261	47	31	25	6	0	1	4	30	0	61	10	0	5	6	.455	0	0--	-	3.30	3.61
1998 Spokane	A-	12	11	0	0	60.0	278	72	35	27	3	1	3	5	31	0	49	6	0	3	3	.500	0	0--	-	5.73	4.05
1999 Wilmington	A+	27	27	0	0	149.1	667	160	89	81	11	4	5	9	64	0	131	11	1	8	11	.421	0	0--	-	4.63	4.88
2000 Wilmington	A+	19	19	1	0	115.2	468	97	33	29	6	1	5	4	46	0	96	7	0	10	5	.667	0	0--	-	3.13	2.26
2000 Wichita	AA	9	9	0	0	50.1	222	46	34	27	10	2	1	3	24	0	47	4	1	4	5	.444	0	0--	-	4.79	4.83
2001 Wichita	AA	25	25	0	0	155.0	636	117	66	58	16	2	2	1	65	1	148	8	0	13	5	.722	0	0--	-	2.88	3.37
2001 Omaha	AAA	1	1	0	0	5.0	24	6	4	3	0	0	0	0	2	0	4	1	0	0	0	-	0	0--	-	4.13	5.40
2003 Syracuse	AAA	17	16	0	0	86.1	373	90	45	41	8	0	5	6	26	0	72	6	0	6	4	.600	0	0--	-	4.15	4.27
2002 Toronto	AL	43	1	0	5	68.0	310	65	34	33	11	1	0	2	45	2	56	4	0	2	3	.400	0	0-2	4	5.40	4.37
2003 Toronto	AL	6	3	0	0	15.1	76	21	11	11	3	0	0	0	9	1	11	0	0	1	1	.500	0	0-0	0	7.61	6.46
2 ML YEARS		**49**	**4**	**0**	**5**	**83.1**	**386**	**86**	**45**	**44**	**14**	**1**	**0**	**2**	**54**	**3**	**67**	**4**	**0**	**3**	**4**	**.429**	**0**	**0-2**	**4**	**5.79**	**4.75**

Joe Thurston

Bats: L **Throws:** R **Pos:** PH-9; 2B-3; PR-1   **Ht:** 5'11" **Wt:** 175 **Born:** 9/29/79 **Age:** 24

								BATTING										BASERUNNING				AVERAGES		
Year Team	Lg	G	AB	H	2B	3B	HR	(Hm | Rd)	TB	R	RBI	RC	TBB	IBB	SO	HBP	SH	SF	SB	CS	SB%	GDP	Avg	OBP	Slg
1999 Yakima	A-	71	277	79	10	3	0	(- | -)	95	48	32	41	27	1	34	21	6	3	27	17	.61	3	.285	.387	.343
1999 Sn Brnardino	A+	2	3	0	0	0	0	(- | -)	0	0	0	0	0	0	1	1	0	0	0	0	-	0	.000	.250	.000
2000 Sn Brnardino	A+	138	551	167	31	8	4	(- | -)	226	97	70	89	56	1	61	17	9	8	43	25	.63	8	.303	.380	.410
2001 Jacksonville	AA	134	544	145	25	7	7	(- | -)	205	80	46	70	48	0	65	12	9	3	20	18	.53	5	.267	.338	.377
2002 Las Vegas	AAA	136	587	196	39	13	12	(- | -)	297	106	55	106	25	1	60	12	5	2	22	9	.71	10	.334	.372	.506
2003 Las Vegas	AAA	132	538	156	27	6	7	(- | -)	216	77	68	71	31	0	48	18	11	8	1	12	.08	10	.290	.345	.401
2002 Los Angeles	NL	8	13	6	1	0	0	(0 | 0)	7	1	1	2	0	0	1	0	1	0	0	0	-	0	.462	.429	.538
2003 Los Angeles	NL	12	10	2	0	0	0	(0 | 0)	2	2	0	0	1	0	1	0	0	0	0	0	-	0	.200	.273	.200
2 ML YEARS		**20**	**23**	**8**	**1**	**0**	**0**	**(0** | **0)**	**9**	**3**	**1**	**2**	**1**	**0**	**2**	**0**	**1**	**0**	**0**	**0**	**-**	**0**	**.348**	**.360**	**.391**

Mike Timlin

Pitches: R **Bats:** R **Pos:** RP-72   **Ht:** 6'4" **Wt:** 210 **Born:** 3/10/66 **Age:** 38

					HOW MUCH HE PITCHED				WHAT HE GAVE UP										THE RESULTS						
Year Team	Lg	G	GS	CG	GF	IP	BFP	H	R	ER	HR	SH	SF	HB	TBB	IBB	SO	WP	Bk	W	L	Pct	ShO	Sv-Op	Hld	ERC	ERA
1991 Toronto	AL	63	3	0	17	108.1	463	94	43	38	6	6	2	1	50	11	85	5	0	11	6	.647	0	3-8	9	3.14	3.16
1992 Toronto	AL	26	0	0	14	43.2	190	45	23	20	0	2	1	1	20	5	35	0	0	0	2	.000	0	1-1	1	3.68	4.12
1993 Toronto	AL	54	0	0	27	55.2	254	63	32	29	7	1	3	1	27	3	49	1	0	4	2	.667	0	1-4	9	5.32	4.69
1994 Toronto	AL	34	0	0	16	40.0	179	41	25	23	5	0	0	2	20	0	38	3	0	0	1	.000	0	2-4	5	5.01	5.18
1995 Toronto	AL	31	0	0	19	42.0	179	38	13	10	1	3	0	2	17	5	36	3	1	4	3	.571	0	5-9	4	3.04	2.14
1996 Toronto	AL	59	0	0	56	56.2	230	47	25	23	4	2	3	2	18	4	52	3	0	1	6	.143	0	31-38	2	2.74	3.65
1997 Tor-Sea	AL	64	0	0	31	72.2	297	69	30	26	8	6	1	1	20	5	45	1	1	6	4	.600	0	10-18	3	3.40	3.22
1998 Seattle	AL	70	0	0	40	79.1	321	78	26	26	5	4	2	3	16	2	60	0	0	3	3	.500	0	19-24	6	3.17	2.95
1999 Baltimore	AL	62	0	0	52	63.0	261	51	30	25	9	1	1	5	23	3	50	1	0	3	9	.250	0	27-36	0	3.46	3.57
2000 Bal-StL		62	0	0	40	64.2	295	67	33	30	8	7	2	4	35	6	52	0	0	5	4	.556	0	12-18	6	5.08	4.18
2001 St Louis	NL	67	0	0	19	72.2	307	78	35	33	6	1	2	3	19	4	47	3	1	4	5	.444	0	3-7	12	3.95	4.09
2002 StL-Phi	NL	72	1	0	17	96.2	376	75	35	32	15	2	1	5	14	2	50	3	0	4	6	.400	0	0-4	20	2.46	2.98
2003 Boston	NL	72	0	0	13	83.2	340	77	37	33	11	4	1	4	9	3	65	0	0	6	4	.600	0	2-6	17	2.81	3.55
1997 Toronto	AL	38	0	0	26	47.0	190	41	17	15	6	4	1	1	15	4	36	1	1	3	2	.600	0	9-13	2	3.30	2.87
1997 Seattle	AL	26	0	0	5	25.2	107	28	13	11	2	2	0	0	5	1	9	0	0	3	2	.600	0	1-5	1	3.59	3.86
2000 Baltimore	AL	37	0	0	31	35.0	157	37	22	19	6	5	1	2	15	3	26	0	0	2	3	.400	0	11-15	1	5.08	4.89
2000 St Louis	NL	25	0	0	9	29.2	138	30	11	11	2	2	1	2	20	3	26	0	0	3	1	.750	0	1-3	5	5.05	3.34
2002 St Louis	NL	42	1	0	10	61.0	236	48	19	17	9	2	0	4	7	2	35	1	0	1	3	.250	0	0-2	12	2.41	2.51
2002 Philadelphia	NL	30	0	0	7	35.2	140	27	16	15	6	0	1	1	7	0	15	2	0	3	3	.500	0	0-2	8	2.55	3.79
13 ML YEARS		**736**	**4**	**0**	**361**	**879.0**	**3692**	**823**	**387**	**348**	**85**	**39**	**19**	**34**	**288**	**53**	**664**	**23**	**3**	**51**	**55**	**.481**	**0**	**116-177**	**100**	**3.50**	**3.56**

Kevin Tolar

Pitches: L **Bats:** R **Pos:** RP-6   **Ht:** 6'3" **Wt:** 230 **Born:** 1/28/71 **Age:** 33

					HOW MUCH HE PITCHED				WHAT HE GAVE UP										THE RESULTS						
Year Team	Lg	G	GS	CG	GF	IP	BFP	H	R	ER	HR	SH	SF	HB	TBB	IBB	SO	WP	Bk	W	L	Pct	ShO	Sv-Op	Hld	ERC	ERA
2003 Pawtucket*	AAA	47	0	0	17	31.2	125	19	9	8	3	0	0	1	17	2	34	1	0	5	1	.833	0	4--	-	2.60	2.27
2000 Detroit	AL	5	0	0	0	3.0	12	1	0	1	0	0	0	0	1	0	3	0	0	0	0	-	0	0-0	0	0.63	3.00
2001 Detroit	AL	9	0	0	4	10.2	50	7	8	8	0	0	0	0	13	0	11	0	0	0	0	-	0	0-0	0	4.54	6.75
2003 Boston	AL	6	0	0	0	4.0	18	5	5	4	1	0	0	0	2	0	3	0	0	0	0	-	0	0-0	1	7.44	9.00
3 ML YEARS		**20**	**0**	**0**	**0**	**17.2**	**80**	**13**	**5**	**13**	**1**	**0**	**0**	**0**	**16**	**0**	**17**	**0**	**0**	**0**	**0**	**-**	**0**	**0-0**	**1**	**4.23**	**6.62**

Brian Tollberg

Pitches: R **Bats:** R **Pos:** SP-3   **Ht:** 6'3" **Wt:** 195 **Born:** 9/16/72 **Age:** 31

					HOW MUCH HE PITCHED				WHAT HE GAVE UP										THE RESULTS						
Year Team	Lg	G	GS	CG	GF	IP	BFP	H	R	ER	HR	SH	SF	HB	TBB	IBB	SO	WP	Bk	W	L	Pct	ShO	Sv-Op	Hld	ERC	ERA
2003 Portland*	AAA	20	12	0	2	82.1	353	94	52	48	12	2	4	2	13	0	45	0	0	5	3	.625	0	0--	-	4.26	5.25
2000 San Diego	NL	19	19	1	0	118.0	506	126	58	47	13	6	0	5	35	4	76	2	1	4	5	.444	0	0-0	0	4.26	3.58
2001 San Diego	NL	19	19	0	0	117.1	503	133	58	56	15	5	7	2	25	3	71	1	0	10	4	.714	0	0-0	0	4.29	4.30
2002 San Diego	NL	12	11	0	0	61.2	288	88	47	42	11	5	6	1	19	2	33	4	0	1	5	.167	0	0-0	0	6.84	6.13
2003 San Diego	NL	3	3	0	0	10.1	45	9	11	8	1	1	1	0	4	0	2	0	0	0	2	.000	0	0-0	0	3.15	6.97
4 ML YEARS		**53**	**52**	**1**	**0**	**307.1**	**1342**	**356**	**174**	**153**	**40**	**17**	**14**	**8**	**83**	**9**	**182**	**7**	**1**	**15**	**16**	**.484**	**0**	**0-0**	**0**	**4.72**	**4.48**

Brett Tomko

Pitches: R **Bats:** R **Pos:** SP-32; RP-1   **Ht:** 6'4" **Wt:** 215 **Born:** 4/7/73 **Age:** 31

Year Team	Lg	G	GS	CG	GF	IP	BFP	H	R	ER	HR	SH	SF	HB	TBB	IBB	SO	WP	Bk	W	L	Pct	ShO	Sv-Op	Hld	ERC	ERA
1997 Cincinnati	NL	22	19	0	1	126.0	519	106	50	48	14	5	9	4	47	4	95	5	0	11	7	.611	0	0-0	0	3.31	3.43
1998 Cincinnati	NL	34	34	1	0	210.2	887	198	111	104	22	12	2	7	64	3	162	9	1	13	12	.520	0	0-0	0	3.50	4.44
1999 Cincinnati	NL	33	26	1	1	172.0	744	175	103	94	31	9	5	4	60	10	132	8	0	5	7	.417	0	0-0	1	4.51	4.92
2000 Seattle	AL	32	8	0	10	92.1	401	92	53	48	12	5	5	3	40	4	59	1	1	7	5	.583	0	1-2	3	4.49	4.68
2001 Seattle	AL	11	4	0	1	34.2	164	42	24	20	9	1	2	0	15	2	22	1	0	3	1	.750	0	0-1	0	6.31	5.19
2002 San Diego	NL	32	32	3	0	204.1	871	212	107	102	31	6	8	2	60	9	126	3	0	10	10	.500	0	0-0	0	4.18	4.49
2003 St Louis	NL	33	32	2	0	202.2	903	252	126	119	35	12	3	5	57	2	114	6	0	13	9	.591	0	0-0	0	5.63	5.28
7 ML YEARS		197	155	7	13	1042.2	4489	1077	574	535	154	50	34	25	343	34	710	33	2	62	51	.549	0	1-3	4	4.35	4.62

Tony Torcato

Bats: L **Throws:** R **Pos:** PH-9; LF-4; RF-2   **Ht:** 6'1" **Wt:** 195 **Born:** 10/25/79 **Age:** 24

Year Team	Lg	G	AB	H	2B	3B	HR	(Hm	Rd)	TB	R	RBI	RC	TBB	IBB	SO	HBP	SH	SF	SB	CS	SB%	GDP	Avg	OBP	Slg
1998 Salem-Keizer	A-	59	220	64	15	2	3	(-	-)	92	31	43	32	14	0	38	3	0	6	4	2	.67	0	.291	.333	.418
1999 Bakersfield	A+	110	422	123	25	0	4	(-	-)	160	50	58	55	30	3	67	3	1	7	2	1	.67	6	.291	.338	.379
2000 San Jose	A+	119	490	159	37	2	7	(-	-)	221	77	88	87	41	8	62	6	0	1	19	4	.83	2	.324	.379	.451
2000 Shreveport	AA	2	8	4	0	0	0	(-	-)	4	1	2	2	0	0	1	0	0	0	0	0	-	0	.500	.500	.500
2001 San Jose	A+	67	258	88	21	2	2	(-	-)	119	38	47	45	17	3	40	4	0	7	9	3	.75	5	.341	.381	.461
2001 Shreveport	AA	36	147	43	9	1	1	(-	-)	57	13	23	18	9	3	15	4	0	3	0	1	.00	6	.293	.344	.388
2001 Fresno	AAA	35	150	48	8	1	2	(-	-)	64	20	8	19	2	0	20	0	0	1	1	0	1.00	5	.320	.329	.427
2002 Fresno	AAA	130	490	142	23	3	13	(-	-)	210	64	64	67	29	3	65	2	2	4	4	6	.40	6	.290	.330	.429
2003 Fresno	AAA	107	423	125	18	2	3	(-	-)	156	36	48	43	6	2	33	2	2	7	4	0	1.00	18	.296	.304	.369
2002 San Francisco	NL	5	11	3	1	0	0	(0	0)	4	0	0	0	0	0	0	0	0	0	0	0	-	0	.273	.273	.364
2003 San Francisco	NL	14	16	3	1	0	0	(0	0)	4	0	1	1	0	0	4	1	1	0	0	0	-	0	.188	.235	.250
2 ML YEARS		19	27	6	2	0	0	(0	0)	8	0	1	1	0	0	6	1	1	0	0	0	-	0	.222	.250	.296

Yorvit Torrealba

Bats: R **Throws:** R **Pos:** C-66; LF-1; PH-1   **Ht:** 5'11" **Wt:** 180 **Born:** 7/19/78 **Age:** 25

Year Team	Lg	G	AB	H	2B	3B	HR	(Hm	Rd)	TB	R	RBI	RC	TBB	IBB	SO	HBP	SH	SF	SB	CS	SB%	GDP	Avg	OBP	Slg
2001 San Francisco	NL	3	4	2	0	1	0	(0	0)	4	0	2	2	0	0	0	0	0	0	0	0	-	0	.500	.500	1.000
2002 San Francisco	NL	53	136	38	10	0	2	(0	2)	54	17	14	15	14	2	20	2	3	0	0	0	-	11	.279	.355	.397
2003 San Francisco	NL	66	200	52	10	2	4	(3	1)	78	22	29	25	14	1	39	2	3	2	1	0	1.00	3	.260	.312	.390
3 ML YEARS		122	340	92	20	3	6	(3	3)	136	39	45	42	28	3	59	4	6	2	1	0	1.00	14	.271	.332	.400

Andres Torres

Bats: B **Throws:** R **Pos:** CF-36; RF-16; PH-7; PR-4; LF-1; DH-1   **Ht:** 5'10" **Wt:** 175 **Born:** 1/26/78 **Age:** 26

Year Team	Lg	G	AB	H	2B	3B	HR	(Hm	Rd)	TB	R	RBI	RC	TBB	IBB	SO	HBP	SH	SF	SB	CS	SB%	GDP	Avg	OBP	Slg
1998 Jamestown	A-	48	192	45	2	6	1	(-	-)	62	28	21	24	25	0	50	1	1	2	13	2	.87	1	.234	.323	.323
1999 W Michigan	A	117	407	96	20	5	2	(-	-)	132	72	34	63	92	1	116	10	9	5	39	18	.68	2	.236	.385	.324
2000 Lakeland	A+	108	398	118	11	11	3	(-	-)	160	82	33	72	63	2	82	5	10	0	65	16	.80	10	.296	.399	.402
2000 Jacksonville	AA	14	54	8	0	0	0	(-	-)	8	3	0	1	5	0	14	0	0	0	2	0	1.00	1	.148	.220	.148
2001 Erie	AA	64	252	74	16	3	1	(-	-)	99	54	23	41	36	1	50	5	0	1	19	11	.63	1	.294	.391	.393
2002 Toledo	AAA	115	462	123	17	8	4	(-	-)	168	80	42	66	53	0	116	5	14	4	42	12	.78	3	.266	.345	.364
2003 Toledo	AAA	70	271	69	13	3	2	(-	-)	94	36	16	30	18	0	61	0	10	0	27	11	.71	1	.255	.301	.347
2002 Detroit	AL	19	70	14	1	1	0	(0	0)	17	7	3	1	6	0	16	1	0	2	2	2	.50	2	.200	.266	.243
2003 Detroit	AL	59	168	37	4	3	1	(1	0)	50	23	9	9	10	0	35	0	6	1	5	5	.50	5	.220	.263	.298
2 ML YEARS		78	238	51	5	4	1	(1	0)	67	30	12	10	16	0	51	1	6	3	7	7	.50	7	.214	.264	.282

Salomon Torres

Pitches: R **Bats:** R **Pos:** RP-25; SP-16   **Ht:** 5'11" **Wt:** 165 **Born:** 3/11/72 **Age:** 32

Year Team	Lg	G	GS	CG	GF	IP	BFP	H	R	ER	HR	SH	SF	HB	TBB	IBB	SO	WP	Bk	W	L	Pct	ShO	Sv-Op	Hld	ERC	ERA
2003 Nashville*	AAA	1	1	0	0	5.0	19	2	1	1	0	0	0	1	1	0	4	0	0	1	0	1.000	0	0--	-	0.95	1.80
1993 San Francisco	NL	8	8	0	0	44.2	196	37	21	20	5	7	1	1	27	3	23	3	1	3	5	.375	0	0-0	0	3.95	4.03
1994 San Francisco	NL	16	14	1	2	84.1	378	95	55	51	10	4	8	7	34	2	42	4	1	2	8	.200	0	0-0	0	5.29	5.44
1995 SF-Sea		20	14	1	4	80.0	384	100	61	56	16	1	0	2	49	3	47	1	2	3	9	.250	0	0-0	0	7.30	6.30
1996 Seattle	AL	10	7	1	1	49.0	212	44	27	25	5	3	1	2	23	2	36	1	0	3	3	.500	1	0-0	0	3.98	4.59
1997 Sea-Mon		14	0	0	4	25.2	127	32	29	28	2	3	1	3	15	0	11	3	0	0	0	-	0	0-0	0	6.44	9.82
2002 Pittsburgh	NL	5	5	0	0	30.0	127	28	10	9	2	2	0	3	13	1	12	0	0	2	1	.667	0	0-0	0	4.07	2.70
2003 Pittsburgh	NL	41	16	0	7	121.0	519	128	65	64	19	4	1	7	42	5	84	3	0	7	5	.583	0	2-3	6	4.87	4.76
1995 San Francisco	NL	4	1	0	2	8.0	40	13	8	8	4	0	0	0	7	0	2	0	0	1	0	1.000	0	0-0	0	15.31	9.00
1995 Seattle	AL	16	13	1	2	72.0	344	87	53	48	12	1	0	2	42	3	45	1	2	3	8	.273	0	0-0	0	6.55	6.00
1997 Seattle	AL	2	0	0	1	3.1	21	7	10	10	0	0	0	1	3	0	0	0	0	0	0	-	0	0-0	0	13.67	27.00
1997 Montreal	NL	12	0	0	3	22.1	106	25	19	18	2	3	1	2	12	0	11	3	0	0	0	-	0	0-0	0	5.47	7.25
7 ML YEARS		114	64	3	18	434.2	1943	464	268	253	59	24	12	26	203	16	255	15	4	20	31	.392	1	2-3	6	5.21	5.24

Josh Towers

Pitches: R **Bats:** R **Pos:** SP-8; RP-6   **Ht:** 6'1" **Wt:** 165 **Born:** 2/26/77 **Age:** 27

Year Team	Lg	G	GS	CG	GF	IP	BFP	H	R	ER	HR	SH	SF	HB	TBB	IBB	SO	WP	Bk	W	L	Pct	ShO	Sv-Op	Hld	ERC	ERA
2003 Syracuse*	AAA	21	20	1	0	132.2	545	133	55	49	10	4	5	2	20	1	76	3	0	5	7	.417	1	0--	-	3.00	3.32
2001 Baltimore	AL	24	20	1	2	140.1	586	165	74	70	21	3	4	6	16	0	58	1	0	8	10	.444	1	0-0	0	4.51	4.49

226

Year Team	Lg	G	GS	CG	GF	IP	BFP	H	R	ER	HR	SH	SF	HB	TBB	IBB	SO	WP	Bk	W	L	Pct	ShO	Sv-Op	Hld	ERC	ERA
2002 Baltimore	AL	5	3	0	1	27.1	124	42	24	24	11	1	2	0	5	0	13	1	0	0	3	.000	0	0-0	0	9.00	7.90
2003 Toronto	AL	14	8	1	2	64.1	265	67	34	32	15	0	2	4	7	1	42	1	0	8	1	.889	0	1-1	0	4.26	4.48
3 ML YEARS		43	31	2	5	232.0	975	274	132	126	47	4	8	10	28	1	113	3	0	16	14	.533	1	1-1	0	4.92	4.89

Billy Traber

Pitches: L **Bats:** L **Pos:** SP-18; RP-15　　　　　　　　**Ht:** 6'5" **Wt:** 205 **Born:** 9/18/79 **Age:** 24

Year Team	Lg	G	GS	CG	GF	IP	BFP	H	R	ER	HR	SH	SF	HB	TBB	IBB	SO	WP	Bk	W	L	Pct	ShO	Sv-Op	Hld	ERC	ERA
2001 St.Lucie	A+	18	18	0	0	101.2	415	85	36	30	2	3	2	5	23	0	79	4	1	6	5	.545	0	0--	-	2.22	2.66
2001 Binghamton	AA	8	8	0	0	42.2	188	50	25	21	4	1	3	2	13	1	45	4	1	4	3	.571	0	0--	-	4.80	4.43
2001 Norfolk	AAA	1	1	0	0	7.0	26	5	3	1	0	0	0	0	0	0	0	1	1	0	1	.000	0	0--	-	1.04	1.29
2002 Akron	AA	18	17	2	0	107.2	436	99	38	33	8	1	0	7	20	0	82	2	0	13	2	.867	2	0--	-	2.95	2.76
2002 Buffalo	AAA	9	9	0	0	54.2	229	58	22	20	3	1	4	2	12	0	33	1	1	4	3	.571	0	0--	-	3.58	3.29
2003 Cleveland	AL	33	18	1	0	111.2	503	132	67	65	15	4	3	5	40	4	88	5	0	6	9	.400	1	0-0	1	5.31	5.24

Steve Trachsel

Pitches: R **Bats:** R **Pos:** SP-33　　　　　　　　**Ht:** 6'4" **Wt:** 205 **Born:** 10/31/70 **Age:** 33

Year Team	Lg	G	GS	CG	GF	IP	BFP	H	R	ER	HR	SH	SF	HB	TBB	IBB	SO	WP	Bk	W	L	Pct	ShO	Sv-Op	Hld	ERC	ERA
1993 Chicago	NL	3	3	0	0	19.2	78	16	10	10	4	1	1	0	3	0	14	1	0	0	2	.000	0	0-0	0	2.71	4.58
1994 Chicago	NL	22	22	1	0	146.0	612	133	57	52	19	3	3	3	54	4	108	6	0	9	7	.563	0	0-0	0	3.74	3.21
1995 Chicago	NL	30	29	2	0	160.2	722	174	104	92	25	12	5	0	76	8	117	2	1	7	13	.350	0	0-0	0	5.13	5.15
1996 Chicago	NL	31	31	3	0	205.0	845	181	82	69	30	3	3	8	62	3	132	5	2	13	9	.591	2	0-0	0	3.52	3.03
1997 Chicago	NL	34	34	0	0	201.1	878	225	110	101	32	8	11	5	69	6	160	4	1	8	12	.400	0	0-0	0	5.04	4.51
1998 Chicago	NL	33	33	1	0	208.0	894	204	107	103	27	9	7	8	84	5	149	3	2	15	8	.652	0	0-0	0	4.35	4.46
1999 Chicago	NL	34	34	4	0	205.2	894	226	133	127	32	6	14	3	64	4	149	8	3	8	18	.308	0	0-0	0	4.69	5.56
2000 TB-Tor	AL	34	34	3	0	200.2	882	232	116	107	26	6	6	6	74	2	110	4	0	8	15	.348	1	0-0	0	5.25	4.80
2001 New York	NL	28	28	1	0	173.2	726	168	90	86	28	8	7	3	47	7	144	4	0	11	13	.458	1	0-0	0	3.80	4.46
2002 New York	NL	30	30	1	0	173.2	741	170	80	65	16	9	3	0	69	4	105	4	0	11	11	.500	1	0-0	0	3.88	3.37
2003 New York	NL	33	33	2	0	204.2	857	204	90	86	26	8	8	3	65	9	111	5	2	16	10	.615	2	0-0	0	3.97	3.78
2000 Tampa Bay	AL	23	23	3	0	137.2	606	160	76	70	16	2	5	6	49	1	78	3	0	6	10	.375	1	0-0	0	5.19	4.58
2000 Toronto	AL	11	11	0	0	63.0	276	72	40	37	10	4	1	0	25	1	32	1	0	2	5	.286	0	0-0	0	5.38	5.29
11 ML YEARS		312	311	18	0	1899.0	8129	1933	979	898	265	73	68	39	667	52	1299	46	11	106	118	.473	7	0-0	0	4.32	4.26

Bubba Trammell

Bats: R **Throws:** R **Pos:** DH-14; PH-7; LF-3　　　　　　　　**Ht:** 6'2" **Wt:** 220 **Born:** 11/6/71 **Age:** 32

Year Team	Lg	G	AB	H	2B	3B	HR	(Hm	Rd)	TB	R	RBI	RC	TBB	IBB	SO	HBP	SH	SF	SB	CS	SB%	GDP	Avg	OBP	Slg
1997 Detroit	AL	44	123	28	5	0	4	(2	2)	45	14	13	14	15	0	35	0	0	2	3	1	.75	2	.228	.307	.366
1998 Tampa Bay	AL	59	199	57	18	1	12	(6	6)	113	28	35	36	16	0	45	0	0	1	0	2	.00	4	.286	.338	.568
1999 Tampa Bay	AL	82	283	82	19	0	14	(6	8)	143	49	39	53	43	1	37	1	0	1	0	2	.00	7	.290	.384	.505
2000 TB-NYM		102	245	65	13	2	10	(6	4)	112	28	45	38	29	0	49	2	0	2	4	0	1.00	6	.265	.345	.457
2001 San Diego	NL	142	490	128	20	3	25	(11	14)	229	66	92	74	48	2	78	4	0	4	2	2	.50	10	.261	.330	.467
2002 San Diego	NL	133	403	98	16	1	17	(5	12)	167	54	56	55	53	2	71	3	3	3	1	3	.25	6	.243	.333	.414
2003 New York	AL	22	55	11	5	0	0	(0	0)	16	4	5	3	6	0	10	0	0	0	0	0	-	1	.200	.279	.291
2000 Tampa Bay	AL	66	189	52	11	2	7	(5	2)	88	19	33	31	21	0	30	2	0	1	3	0	1.00	5	.275	.352	.466
2000 New York	NL	36	56	13	2	0	3	(1	2)	24	9	12	7	8	0	19	0	0	1	1	0	1.00	3	.232	.323	.429
7 ML YEARS		584	1798	469	96	7	82	(36	46)	825	243	285	273	210	5	325	10	3	13	10	10	.50	38	.261	.339	.459

Chris Truby

Bats: R **Throws:** R **Pos:** 3B-13　　　　　　　　**Ht:** 6'2" **Wt:** 215 **Born:** 12/9/73 **Age:** 30

Year Team	Lg	G	AB	H	2B	3B	HR	(Hm	Rd)	TB	R	RBI	RC	TBB	IBB	SO	HBP	SH	SF	SB	CS	SB%	GDP	Avg	OBP	Slg
2003 Durham*	AAA	112	430	113	27	6	16	(-	-)	188	57	48	61	44	4	77	7	0	3	4	6	.40	11	.263	.339	.437
2000 Houston	NL	78	258	67	15	4	11	(9	2)	123	28	59	36	10	1	56	5	1	5	2	1	.67	4	.260	.295	.477
2001 Houston	NL	48	136	28	6	1	8	(4	4)	60	11	23	17	13	2	38	1	0	2	1	2	.33	1	.206	.276	.441
2002 Mon-Det		124	382	82	18	4	4	(1	3)	120	35	22	17	10	1	98	3	4	5	2	2	.50	7	.215	.238	.314
2003 Tampa Bay	AL	13	43	12	3	0	0	(0	0)	15	4	3	6	5	0	13	0	1	0	0	0	-	1	.279	.354	.349
2002 Montreal	NL	35	105	27	5	2	2	(1	1)	42	12	7	8	5	1	27	1	1	0	1	1	.50	2	.257	.297	.400
2002 Detroit	AL	89	277	55	13	2	2	(0	2)	78	23	15	9	5	0	71	2	3	5	1	1	.50	5	.199	.215	.282
4 ML YEARS		263	819	189	42	9	23	(14	9)	318	78	107	76	38	4	205	9	6	12	5	5	.50	13	.231	.269	.388

Chin-hui Tsao

Pitches: R **Bats:** R **Pos:** SP-8; RP-1　　　　　　　　**Ht:** 6'2" **Wt:** 177 **Born:** 6/2/81 **Age:** 23

Year Team	Lg	G	GS	CG	GF	IP	BFP	H	R	ER	HR	SH	SF	HB	TBB	IBB	SO	WP	Bk	W	L	Pct	ShO	Sv-Op	Hld	ERC	ERA
2000 Asheville	A	24	24	0	0	145.0	591	119	54	44	8	3	2	5	40	0	187	6	1	11	8	.579	0	0--	-	2.50	2.73
2001 Salem	A+	4	4	0	0	17.1	78	23	11	9	1	2	1	1	5	0	18	1	1	0	4	.000	0	0--	-	5.52	4.67
2002 Tri-City	A-	3	3	0	0	11.0	42	6	2	0	0	0	0	0	2	0	16	2	1	0	0	-	0	0--	-	0.91	0.00
2002 Salem	A+	9	9	0	0	47.1	180	34	13	11	3	1	0	0	12	0	45	2	1	4	2	.667	0	0--	-	1.97	2.09
2003 Tulsa	AA	18	18	0	0	113.1	446	88	34	31	7	2	2	5	26	0	125	3	3	11	4	.733	0	0--	-	2.25	2.46
2003 Colorado	NL	9	8	0	1	43.1	196	48	30	29	11	3	0	4	20	1	29	0	0	3	3	.500	0	0-0	0	6.56	6.02

Michael Tucker

Bats: L **Throws:** R **Pos:** RF-47; CF-30; LF-21; DH-14; PH-5 **Ht:** 6'2" **Wt:** 195 **Born:** 6/25/71 **Age:** 33

Year Team	Lg	G	AB	H	2B	3B	HR	Hm	Rd	TB	R	RBI	RC	TBB	IBB	SO	HBP	SH	SF	SB	CS	SB%	GDP	Avg	OBP	Slg
1995 Kansas City	AL	62	177	46	10	0	4	1	3	68	23	17	22	18	2	51	1	2	0	2	3	.40	3	.260	.332	.384
1996 Kansas City	AL	108	339	88	18	4	12	2	10	150	55	53	53	40	1	69	7	3	4	10	4	.71	7	.260	.346	.442
1997 Atlanta	NL	138	499	141	25	7	14	5	9	222	80	56	76	44	0	116	6	4	1	12	7	.63	7	.283	.347	.445
1998 Atlanta	NL	130	414	101	27	3	13	10	3	173	54	46	58	49	10	112	3	1	2	8	3	.73	4	.244	.327	.418
1999 Cincinnati	NL	133	296	75	8	5	11	5	6	126	55	44	44	37	3	81	3	0	4	11	4	.73	5	.253	.338	.426
2000 Cincinnati	NL	148	270	72	13	4	15	7	8	138	55	36	53	44	1	64	7	0	2	13	6	.68	6	.267	.381	.511
2001 Cin-ChC	NL	149	436	110	19	8	12	4	8	181	62	61	59	46	4	102	2	10	6	16	8	.67	8	.252	.322	.415
2002 Kansas City	AL	144	475	118	27	6	12	10	2	193	65	56	64	56	1	105	3	7	2	23	9	.72	5	.248	.330	.406
2003 Kansas City	AL	104	389	102	20	5	13	8	5	171	61	55	61	39	3	88	2	6	2	9	10	.44	8	.262	.331	.440
2001 Cincinnati	NL	86	231	56	10	1	7	1	6	89	31	30	28	23	1	55	1	5	5	12	5	.71	4	.242	.308	.385
2001 Chicago	NL	63	205	54	9	7	5	3	2	92	31	31	31	23	3	47	1	5	1	4	3	.57	4	.263	.339	.449
9 ML YEARS		1116	3295	853	167	42	106	52	54	1422	510	424	490	373	25	788	34	33	23	103	54	.66	53	.259	.338	.432

T.J. Tucker

Pitches: R **Bats:** R **Pos:** RP-38; SP-7 **Ht:** 6'3" **Wt:** 245 **Born:** 8/20/78 **Age:** 25

Year Team	Lg	G	GS	CG	GF	IP	BFP	H	R	ER	HR	SH	SF	HB	TBB	IBB	SO	WP	Bk	W	L	Pct	ShO	Sv-Op	Hld	ERC	ERA
2003 Edmonton*	AAA	3	3	0	0	16.1	68	16	5	5	2	0	0	0	7	0	6	0	0	1	0	1.000	0	0--	-	4.41	2.76
2000 Montreal	NL	2	2	0	0	7.0	35	11	9	9	5	0	0	0	3	0	2	1	0	0	1	.000	0	0-0	0	12.90	11.57
2002 Montreal	NL	57	0	0	19	61.1	278	69	32	28	5	5	2	0	31	9	42	4	0	6	3	.667	0	4-7	17	4.80	4.11
2003 Montreal	NL	45	7	0	7	80.0	349	90	49	42	8	0	1	4	20	1	47	1	0	2	3	.400	0	0-2	3	4.33	4.73
3 ML YEARS		104	9	0	26	148.1	662	170	90	79	18	5	3	4	54	10	91	6	0	8	7	.533	0	4-9	20	4.89	4.79

Derrick Turnbow

Pitches: R **Bats:** R **Pos:** RP-11 **Ht:** 6'3" **Wt:** 200 **Born:** 1/25/78 **Age:** 26

Year Team	Lg	G	GS	CG	GF	IP	BFP	H	R	ER	HR	SH	SF	HB	TBB	IBB	SO	WP	Bk	W	L	Pct	ShO	Sv-Op	Hld	ERC	ERA
1997 Martinsville	R+	7	7	0	0	24.1	121	34	29	20	5	0	6	3	16	1	7	5	0	1	3	.250	0	0--	-	9.20	7.40
1998 Martinsville	R+	13	13	1	0	70.0	300	66	44	39	7	3	5	1	26	1	45	5	0	2	6	.250	0	0--	-	3.64	5.01
1999 Piedmont	A	26	26	4	0	161.0	651	130	67	60	10	1	2	7	53	0	149	8	0	12	8	.600	1	0--	-	2.76	3.35
2001 Arkansas	AA	3	3	0	0	14.0	56	12	4	4	0	1	0	0	5	0	11	0	1	0	0	-	0	0--	-	2.60	2.57
2002 R Cucamnga	A+	13	0	0	4	12.0	59	16	11	7	1	0	0	0	9	0	14	2	1	0	0	-	0	0--	-	7.50	5.25
2003 Arkansas	AA	7	0	0	5	14.0	51	4	0	0	0	0	0	0	5	0	19	1	0	1	0	1.000	0	3--	-	0.62	0.00
2003 Salt Lake	AAA	35	0	0	15	55.0	255	68	36	35	5	2	1	1	24	0	63	7	0	1	2	.333	0	2--	-	5.54	5.73
2000 Anaheim	AL	24	1	0	0	38.0	181	36	0	20	7	0	0	0	36	0	25	0	0	0	0	-	0	0-0	0	6.74	4.74
2003 Anaheim	AL	11	0	0	7	15.1	53	7	1	1	0	0	0	0	3	0	15	0	0	2	0	1.000	0	0-0	0	0.79	0.59
2 ML YEARS		35	1	0	7	53.1	234	43	1	21	7	0	0	0	39	0	40	0	0	2	0	1.000	0	0-0	0	4.58	3.54

Jason Tyner

Bats: L **Throws:** L **Pos:** RF-23; PH-14; LF-9; PR-6; CF-2; DH-2 **Ht:** 6'1" **Wt:** 168 **Born:** 4/23/77 **Age:** 27

Year Team	Lg	G	AB	H	2B	3B	HR	Hm	Rd	TB	R	RBI	RC	TBB	IBB	SO	HBP	SH	SF	SB	CS	SB%	GDP	Avg	OBP	Slg
2003 Durham*	AAA	65	275	89	11	5	0	-	-	110	34	24	41	22	1	25	1	6	3	10	7	.59	5	.324	.372	.400
2000 NYM-TB		50	124	28	4	0	0	0	0	32	9	13	9	5	0	16	2	8	3	7	2	.78	2	.226	.261	.258
2001 Tampa Bay	AL	105	396	111	8	5	0	0	0	129	51	21	43	15	0	42	3	5	1	31	6	.84	6	.280	.311	.326
2002 Tampa Bay	AL	44	168	36	2	1	0	0	0	40	17	9	7	7	0	19	1	3	1	7	1	.88	1	.214	.249	.238
2003 Tampa Bay	AL	46	90	25	7	0	0	0	0	32	12	6	12	10	0	12	0	2	0	2	1	.67	1	.278	.350	.356
2000 New York	NL	13	41	8	2	0	0	0	0	10	3	5	2	1	0	4	1	3	2	1	1	.50	1	.195	.222	.244
2000 Tampa Bay	AL	37	83	20	2	0	0	0	0	22	6	8	7	4	0	12	1	5	1	6	1	.86	1	.241	.281	.265
4 ML YEARS		245	778	200	21	6	0	0	0	233	89	49	71	37	0	89	6	18	5	47	10	.82	10	.257	.294	.299

Luis Ugueto

Bats: B **Throws:** R **Pos:** PR-6; 2B-4; PH-2; 3B-1; SS-1; DH-1 **Ht:** 5'11" **Wt:** 170 **Born:** 2/15/79 **Age:** 25

Year Team	Lg	G	AB	H	2B	3B	HR	Hm	Rd	TB	R	RBI	RC	TBB	IBB	SO	HBP	SH	SF	SB	CS	SB%	GDP	Avg	OBP	Slg
1998 Brevard Cnty	A+	3	11	2	0	0	0	-	-	2	0	0	0	0	0	5	0	1	0	0	0	-	0	.182	.182	.182
1998 Marlins	R	50	166	38	8	2	0	-	-	50	20	15	14	8	0	37	2	2	2	7	1	.88	2	.229	.270	.301
1999 Brevard Cnty	A+	12	30	4	0	0	0	-	-	4	1	3	1	7	0	5	0	1	0	1	0	1.00	3	.133	.297	.133
1999 Marlins	R	1	3	0	0	0	0	-	-	0	0	2	0	1	0	0	0	0	1	0	0	-	0	.000	.200	.000
1999 Utica	A-	56	217	60	11	2	1	-	-	78	33	26	26	18	0	46	1	3	0	9	4	.69	4	.276	.335	.359
2000 Kane County	A	114	393	92	13	2	1	-	-	112	43	32	28	28	0	83	5	7	4	12	14	.46	10	.234	.291	.285
2001 Brevard Cnty	A+	121	392	103	12	5	3	-	-	134	53	43	46	38	0	96	2	9	1	22	7	.76	7	.263	.330	.342
2002 Tacoma	AAA	12	51	13	1	0	0	-	-	14	5	5	4	3	0	13	0	1	1	2	1	.67	0	.255	.291	.275
2003 Tacoma	AAA	8	26	8	3	0	2	-	-	17	9	4	7	5	0	4	0	1	0	2	0	1.00	0	.308	.419	.654
2003 San Antonio	AA	89	350	91	12	2	1	-	-	110	53	40	35	27	0	75	1	3	3	25	10	.71	7	.260	.312	.314
2002 Seattle	AL	62	23	5	0	0	1	0	1	8	19	1	2	2	0	8	0	0	0	8	4	.67	0	.217	.280	.348
2003 Seattle	AL	12	5	1	0	0	0	0	0	1	4	1	1	1	0	0	0	0	0	2	0	1.00	0	.200	.333	.200
2 ML YEARS		74	28	6	0	0	1	0	1	9	23	2	3	3	0	8	0	0	0	10	4	.71	0	.214	.290	.321

Ugueth Urbina

Pitches: R Bats: R Pos: RP-72   Ht: 6'0" Wt: 205 Born: 2/15/74 Age: 30

Year Team	Lg	G	GS	CG	GF	IP	BFP	H	R	ER	HR	SH	SF	HB	TBB	IBB	SO	WP	Bk	W	L	Pct	ShO	Sv-Op	Hld	ERC	ERA
1995 Montreal	NL	7	4	0	0	23.1	109	26	17	16	6	2	0	0	14	1	15	2	0	2	2	.500	0	0-0	6	6.66	6.17
1996 Montreal	NL	33	17	0	2	114.0	484	102	54	47	18	1	3	1	44	4	108	3	1	10	5	.667	0	0-1	6	3.78	3.71
1997 Montreal	NL	63	0	0	50	64.1	276	52	29	27	9	3	0	1	29	2	84	2	0	5	8	.385	0	27-32	1	3.42	3.78
1998 Montreal	NL	64	0	0	59	69.1	272	37	11	10	2	2	1	0	33	2	94	3	2	6	3	.667	0	34-38	0	1.59	1.30
1999 Montreal	NL	71	0	0	62	75.2	323	59	35	31	6	1	2	0	36	6	100	6	0	6	6	.500	0	**41-50**	0	2.85	3.69
2000 Montreal	NL	13	0	0	11	13.1	54	11	6	6	1	0	0	0	5	0	22	1	0	0	1	.000	0	8-10	0	2.95	4.05
2001 Mon-Bos		64	0	0	53	66.2	278	58	29	27	9	2	1	0	24	1	89	2	1	2	2	.500	0	24-28	3	3.41	3.65
2002 Boston	AL	61	0	0	55	60.0	242	44	21	20	8	1	3	0	20	5	71	3	1	1	6	.143	0	40-46	0	2.50	3.00
2003 Tex-Fla		72	0	0	48	77.0	316	56	25	24	8	6	5	0	31	2	78	4	1	3	4	.429	0	32-38	11	2.60	2.81
2001 Montreal	NL	45	0	0	40	46.2	201	42	24	22	8	1	1	0	21	1	57	2	1	2	1	.667	0	15-18	1	4.13	4.24
2001 Boston	AL	19	0	0	13	20.0	77	16	5	5	1	1	0	0	3	0	32	0	0	0	1	.000	0	9-10	2	1.88	2.25
2003 Texas	AL	39	0	0	37	38.2	167	33	19	18	6	4	3	0	18	2	41	2	1	0	4	.000	0	26-30	0	3.74	4.19
2003 Florida	NL	33	0	0	11	38.1	149	23	6	6	2	2	2	0	13	0	37	2	0	3	0	1.000	0	6-8	11	1.61	1.41
9 ML YEARS		448	21	0	340	563.2	2354	445	227	208	67	18	15	2	236	23	661	26	6	35	37	.486	0	206-243	21	3.06	3.32

Juan Uribe

Bats: R Throws: R Pos: SS-74; 2B-11; PH-3; CF-1; PR-1   Ht: 5'11" Wt: 173 Born: 7/22/79 Age: 24

Year Team	Lg	G	AB	H	2B	3B	HR	(Hm	Rd)	TB	R	RBI	RC	TBB	IBB	SO	HBP	SH	SF	SB	CS	SB%	GDP	Avg	OBP	Slg
2003 Visalia*	A+	2	9	5	1	0	0	(-	-)	6	4	1	3	1	0	0	0	0	0	0	0	-	1	.556	.600	.667
2003 Tulsa*	AA	5	20	5	2	0	1	(-	-)	10	3	4	3	0	0	2	0	0	1	0	0	-	0	.250	.238	.500
2001 Colorado	NL	72	273	82	15	11	8	(3	5)	143	32	53	44	8	1	55	2	0	0	3	0	1.00	6	.300	.325	.524
2002 Colorado	NL	155	566	136	25	7	6	(4	2)	193	69	49	53	34	1	120	5	7	6	9	2	.82	17	.240	.286	.341
2003 Colorado	NL	87	316	80	19	3	10	(6	4)	135	45	33	45	17	0	60	3	6	1	7	2	.78	5	.253	.297	.427
3 ML YEARS		314	1155	298	59	21	24	(13	11)	471	146	135	142	59	2	235	10	13	7	19	4	.83	26	.258	.298	.408

Chase Utley

Bats: L Throws: R Pos: 2B-37; PH-6; PR-1   Ht: 6'1" Wt: 170 Born: 12/17/78 Age: 25

Year Team	Lg	G	AB	H	2B	3B	HR	(Hm	Rd)	TB	R	RBI	RC	TBB	IBB	SO	HBP	SH	SF	SB	CS	SB%	GDP	Avg	OBP	Slg
2000 Batavia	A-	40	153	47	13	1	2	(-	-)	68	21	22	26	18	1	23	2	0	2	5	3	.63	3	.307	.383	.444
2001 Clearwater	A+	122	467	120	25	2	16	(-	-)	197	65	59	65	37	4	88	12	1	6	19	8	.70	6	.257	.324	.422
2002 Scrtn/WlksBr	AAA	125	464	122	39	1	17	(-	-)	214	73	70	78	46	2	89	20	0	4	8	3	.73	5	.263	.352	.461
2003 Scrtn/WlksBr	AAA	113	431	139	26	2	18	(-	-)	223	80	77	87	41	6	75	11	0	7	10	4	.71	3	.323	.390	.517
2003 Philadelphia	NL	43	134	32	10	1	2	(1	1)	50	13	21	19	11	0	22	6	0	1	2	0	1.00	3	.239	.322	.373

Carlos Valderrama

Bats: R Throws: R Pos: LF-4; CF-2; PH-1; PR-1   Ht: 5'11" Wt: 175 Born: 11/30/77 Age: 26

Year Team	Lg	G	AB	H	2B	3B	HR	(Hm	Rd)	TB	R	RBI	RC	TBB	IBB	SO	HBP	SH	SF	SB	CS	SB%	GDP	Avg	OBP	Slg
1997 Salem-Keizer	A-	41	138	44	7	3	3	(-	-)	66	21	28	28	12	0	29	0	0	2	22	0	1.00	2	.319	.368	.478
1998 Salem-Keizer	A-	7	29	10	1	0	0	(-	-)	11	5	4	4	1	0	7	0	0	0	4	0	1.00	2	.345	.367	.379
1999 San Jose	A+	26	90	23	2	0	0	(-	-)	25	12	12	7	4	0	19	0	2	0	8	4	.67	1	.256	.287	.278
1999 Salem-Keizer	A-	40	134	39	3	1	2	(-	-)	50	27	18	21	12	0	34	0	3	0	17	2	.89	0	.291	.349	.373
2000 Bakersfield	A+	121	435	137	21	5	13	(-	-)	207	78	81	83	39	1	96	4	5	8	54	11	.83	4	.315	.370	.476
2001 Shreveport	AA	41	159	49	12	2	1	(-	-)	68	29	8	27	18	0	29	0	2	0	11	5	.69	1	.308	.379	.428
2002 San Jose	A+	74	299	94	19	6	15	(-	-)	170	65	45	62	34	4	60	0	0	0	14	5	.74	5	.314	.384	.569
2003 Norwich	AA	65	240	74	15	3	1	(-	-)	98	37	18	36	25	1	34	1	5	1	13	6	.68	7	.308	.375	.408
2003 Fresno	AAA	54	202	56	5	0	3	(-	-)	70	20	10	21	12	0	28	2	5	0	7	8	.47	3	.277	.324	.347
2003 San Francisco	NL	7	7	1	0	0	0	(0	0)	1	0	0	1	0	0	3	0	0	0	1	0	1.00	0	.143	.143	.143

Ismael Valdes

Pitches: R Bats: R Pos: SP-22   Ht: 6'4" Wt: 225 Born: 8/21/73 Age: 30

Year Team	Lg	G	GS	CG	GF	IP	BFP	H	R	ER	HR	SH	SF	HB	TBB	IBB	SO	WP	Bk	W	L	Pct	ShO	Sv-Op	Hld	ERC	ERA
2003 Frisco*	AA	3	3	0	0	13.1	55	12	5	3	0	0	1	0	2	0	6	0	0	1	2	.333	0	0- -	-	1.94	2.03
1994 Los Angeles	NL	21	1	0	7	28.1	115	21	10	10	2	3	0	0	10	2	28	1	2	3	1	.750	0	0-0	4	2.25	3.18
1995 Los Angeles	NL	33	27	6	1	197.2	804	168	76	67	17	10	5	1	51	5	150	1	3	13	11	.542	2	1-1	2	2.62	3.05
1996 Los Angeles	NL	33	33	0	0	225.0	945	219	94	83	20	7	7	3	54	10	173	1	5	15	7	.682	0	0-0	0	3.18	3.32
1997 Los Angeles	NL	30	30	0	0	196.2	795	171	68	58	16	11	3	3	43	1	140	3	2	10	11	.476	0	0-0	0	2.72	2.65
1998 Los Angeles	NL	27	27	2	0	174.0	745	171	82	77	17	5	3	2	66	4	122	4	2	11	10	.524	2	0-0	0	3.89	3.98
1999 Los Angeles	NL	32	32	2	0	203.1	871	213	97	90	32	9	8	6	58	2	143	6	0	9	14	.391	1	0-0	0	4.38	3.98
2000 ChC-LA	NL	21	20	0	1	107.0	469	124	69	67	22	0	4	3	40	2	74	0	0	7	7	.222	0	0-0	0	5.89	5.64
2001 Anaheim	AL	27	27	1	0	163.2	699	177	82	81	20	3	0	8	50	3	100	3	0	9	13	.409	0	0-0	0	4.57	4.45
2002 Tex-Sea	AL	31	31	1	0	196.0	818	194	94	91	26	6	4	9	47	1	102	0	2	8	12	.400	0	0-0	0	3.80	4.18
2003 Texas	AL	22	22	0	0	115.0	511	148	83	78	23	4	7	5	29	0	47	2	0	8	8	.500	0	0-0	0	6.14	6.10
2000 Chicago	NL	12	12	0	0	67.0	291	71	40	40	17	0	2	2	27	2	45	0	0	2	4	.333	0	0-0	0	5.72	5.37
2000 Los Angeles	NL	9	8	0	1	40.0	178	53	29	27	5	0	2	1	13	0	29	0	0	5	3	.625	0	0-0	0	6.15	6.08
2002 Texas	AL	23	23	0	0	146.2	608	135	65	64	19	2	2	8	36	1	75	0	2	6	9	.400	0	0-0	0	3.47	3.93
2002 Seattle	AL	8	8	1	0	49.1	210	59	29	27	7	0	2	1	11	0	27	0	0	2	3	.400	0	0-0	6	4.86	4.93
10 ML YEARS		277	250	12	9	1606.2	6772	1606	755	702	195	54	41	40	452	30	1079	21	16	88	94	.484	5	1-1	6	3.83	3.93

Eric Valent

Bats: L **Throws:** L **Pos:** PH-9; RF-8; PR-1   **Ht:** 6'0" **Wt:** 191 **Born:** 4/4/77 **Age:** 27

Year Team	Lg	G	AB	H	2B	3B	HR	(Hm	Rd)	TB	R	RBI	RC	TBB	IBB	SO	HBP	SH	SF	SB	CS	SB%	GDP	Avg	OBP	Slg
2003 Scrtn/WlksBr*	AAA	134	450	98	27	2	12	(-	-)	165	62	51	53	60	5	102	1	4	5	0	0	-	5	.218	.308	.367
2001 Philadelphia	NL	22	41	4	2	0	0	(0	0)	6	3	1	0	4	0	11	1	0	0	0	0	-	0	.098	.196	.146
2002 Philadelphia	NL	7	10	2	0	0	0	(0	0)	2	1	0	0	0	0	3	0	0	0	0	0	-	1	.200	.200	.200
2003 Cincinnati	NL	18	42	9	0	0	0	(0	0)	9	3	1	2	2	0	9	0	0	0	0	0	-	0	.214	.250	.214
3 ML YEARS		47	93	15	2	0	0	(0	0)	17	7	2	2	6	0	23	1	0	0	0	0	-	1	.161	.220	.183

Javier Valentin

Bats: B **Throws:** R **Pos:** C-42; PH-5; DH-4   **Ht:** 5'10" **Wt:** 192 **Born:** 9/19/75 **Age:** 28

Year Team	Lg	G	AB	H	2B	3B	HR	(Hm	Rd)	TB	R	RBI	RC	TBB	IBB	SO	HBP	SH	SF	SB	CS	SB%	GDP	Avg	OBP	Slg
1997 Minnesota	AL	4	7	2	0	0	0	(0	0)	2	1	0	1	0	0	3	0	0	0	0	0	-	0	.286	.286	.286
1998 Minnesota	AL	55	162	32	7	1	3	(1	2)	50	11	18	10	11	1	30	0	3	1	0	0	-	7	.198	.247	.309
1999 Minnesota	AL	78	218	54	12	1	5	(2	3)	83	22	28	27	22	0	39	1	1	5	0	0	-	2	.248	.313	.381
2002 Minnesota	AL	4	4	2	0	0	0	(0	0)	2	0	0	0	0	0	0	0	0	0	0	0	-	0	.500	.500	.500
2003 Tampa Bay	AL	49	135	30	7	1	3	(2	1)	48	13	15	11	5	0	31	1	0	1	0	0	-	0	.222	.254	.356
5 ML YEARS		190	526	120	26	3	11	(5	6)	185	47	61	49	38	1	103	2	4	7	0	0	-	16	.228	.279	.352

Jose Valentin

Bats: B **Throws:** R **Pos:** SS-143; PH-7   **Ht:** 5'10" **Wt:** 185 **Born:** 10/12/69 **Age:** 34

Year Team	Lg	G	AB	H	2B	3B	HR	(Hm	Rd)	TB	R	RBI	RC	TBB	IBB	SO	HBP	SH	SF	SB	CS	SB%	GDP	Avg	OBP	Slg
1992 Milwaukee	NL	4	3	0	0	0	0	(0	0)	0	1	1	0	0	0	0	0	0	1	0	0	-	0	.000	.000	.000
1993 Milwaukee	NL	19	53	13	1	2	1	(1	0)	21	10	7	8	7	1	16	1	2	0	1	0	1.00	1	.245	.344	.396
1994 Milwaukee	NL	97	285	68	19	0	11	(8	3)	120	47	46	43	38	1	75	2	4	2	12	3	.80	1	.239	.330	.421
1995 Milwaukee	NL	112	338	74	23	3	11	(3	8)	136	62	49	42	37	0	83	0	7	4	16	8	.67	0	.219	.293	.402
1996 Milwaukee	NL	154	552	143	33	7	24	(10	14)	262	90	95	91	66	9	145	0	6	4	17	4	.81	4	.259	.336	.475
1997 Milwaukee	NL	136	494	125	23	1	17	(4	13)	201	58	58	64	39	4	109	4	4	5	18	8	.70	5	.253	.310	.407
1998 Milwaukee	NL	151	428	96	24	0	16	(7	9)	168	65	49	57	63	8	105	1	2	3	10	7	.59	2	.224	.323	.393
1999 Milwaukee	NL	89	256	58	9	5	10	(3	7)	107	45	38	40	48	7	52	2	2	5	3	2	.60	3	.227	.347	.418
2000 Chicago	AL	144	568	155	37	6	25	(16	9)	279	107	92	97	59	1	106	4	13	4	19	2	.90	11	.273	.343	.491
2001 Chicago	AL	124	438	113	22	2	28	(14	14)	223	74	68	74	50	2	114	3	8	3	9	6	.60	7	.258	.336	.509
2002 Chicago	AL	135	474	118	26	4	25	(15	10)	227	70	75	76	43	2	99	2	3	5	3	3	.50	9	.249	.311	.479
2003 Chicago	AL	144	503	119	26	4	28	(14	14)	233	79	74	74	54	4	114	3	7	2	8	3	.73	6	.237	.313	.463
12 ML YEARS		1309	4392	1082	243	32	196	(95	101)	1977	708	652	666	504	39	1018	22	58	38	117	46	.72	49	.246	.324	.450

Joe Valentine

Pitches: R **Bats:** R **Pos:** RP-2   **Ht:** 6'2" **Wt:** 195 **Born:** 12/24/79 **Age:** 24

Year Team	Lg	G	GS	CG	GF	IP	BFP	H	R	ER	HR	SH	SF	HB	TBB	IBB	SO	WP	Bk	W	L	Pct	ShO	Sv-Op	Hld	ERC	ERA
1999 Bristol	R+	11	0	0	7	16.2	90	27	17	13	2	0	3	3	9	0	14	1	1	0	0	-	0	0- -	-	9.21	7.02
1999 White Sox	R	3	0	0	0	4.0	14	2	0	0	0	0	0	0	1	0	2	0	0	0	0	-	0	0- -	-	1.01	0.00
2000 Bristol	R+	19	0	0	16	25.0	104	14	10	8	1	2	2	2	12	1	30	9	0	2	1	.667	0	7- -	-	1.90	2.88
2001 Kannapolis	A	30	0	0	29	30.2	123	21	10	10	0	2	0	3	10	1	33	1	1	2	2	.500	0	14- -	-	1.89	2.93
2001 Winstn-Salm	A+	27	0	0	18	44.2	179	18	7	5	0	3	0	1	27	3	50	2	0	5	1	.833	0	8- -	-	1.32	1.01
2003 Louisville	AAA	9	0	0	6	11.1	41	5	1	1	0	0	0	0	3	0	8	0	1	1	0	1.000	0	1- -	-	0.84	0.79
2003 Sacramento	AAA	40	0	0	23	52.1	239	44	33	28	5	1	1	2	37	3	53	9	1	1	3	.250	0	4- -	-	4.31	4.82
2003 Cincinnati	NL	2	0	0	1	2.0	12	5	4	4	1	0	0	0	1	0	1	0	0	0	0	-	0	0-0	0	18.76	18.00

Jose Valverde

Pitches: R **Bats:** R **Pos:** RP-54   **Ht:** 6'4" **Wt:** 254 **Born:** 7/24/79 **Age:** 24

Year Team	Lg	G	GS	CG	GF	IP	BFP	H	R	ER	HR	SH	SF	HB	TBB	IBB	SO	WP	Bk	W	L	Pct	ShO	Sv-Op	Hld	ERC	ERA
1999 Diamndbcks	R	20	0	0	17	28.2	138	34	21	13	1	0	0	4	10	0	47	1	1	1	2	.333	0	8- -	-	4.71	4.08
1999 South Bend	A	2	0	0	2	2.2	11	2	0	0	0	0	0	1	2	0	3	1	1	0	0	-	0	0- -	-	5.44	0.00
2000 South Bend	A	31	0	0	21	31.2	152	31	20	19	1	2	0	3	25	0	39	8	0	0	5	.000	0	14- -	-	5.26	5.40
2000 Missoula	R+	12	0	0	11	11.2	44	3	0	0	0	0	0	0	4	0	24	2	0	1	0	1.000	0	4- -	-	0.51	0.00
2001 El Paso	AA	39	0	0	28	41.1	193	36	19	18	1	1	1	4	27	0	72	6	1	2	2	.500	0	13- -	-	3.98	3.92
2002 Tucson	AAA	49	0	0	24	47.2	214	45	33	31	8	3	3	5	23	1	65	4	2	2	4	.333	0	5- -	-	4.91	5.85
2003 Tucson	AAA	22	0	0	14	29.0	127	26	11	10	1	1	2	0	14	1	26	3	0	1	1	.500	0	5- -	-	3.23	3.10
2003 Arizona	NL	54	0	0	33	50.1	204	24	16	12	4	0	1	2	26	2	71	2	0	2	1	.667	0	10-11	8	1.77	2.15

Todd Van Poppel

Pitches: R **Bats:** R **Pos:** RP-11; SP-5   **Ht:** 6'5" **Wt:** 240 **Born:** 12/9/71 **Age:** 32

Year Team	Lg	G	GS	CG	GF	IP	BFP	H	R	ER	HR	SH	SF	HB	TBB	IBB	SO	WP	Bk	W	L	Pct	ShO	Sv-Op	Hld	ERC	ERA
2003 Frisco*	AA	2	2	0	0	9.0	37	8	2	2	0	0	0	1	2	0	7	0	0	0	0	-	0	0- -	-	2.60	2.00
2003 Louisville*	AAA	20	5	0	6	54.0	214	49	23	19	4	4	1	0	11	1	45	4	0	4	3	.571	0	1- -	-	2.72	3.17
1991 Oakland	AL	1	1	0	0	4.2	21	7	5	5	1	0	0	0	2	0	6	0	0	0	0	-	0	0-0	0	8.85	9.64
1993 Oakland	AL	16	16	0	0	84.0	380	76	50	47	10	1	2	2	62	0	47	3	0	6	6	.500	0	0-0	0	5.17	5.04
1994 Oakland	AL	23	23	0	0	116.2	532	108	80	79	20	4	4	3	89	2	83	3	1	7	10	.412	0	0-0	0	5.82	6.09
1995 Oakland	AL	36	14	1	10	138.1	582	125	77	75	16	3	6	4	56	1	122	4	0	4	8	.333	0	0-0	0	3.82	4.88
1996 Oak-Det	AL	37	15	1	8	99.1	491	139	107	100	24	4	7	3	62	3	53	7	0	3	9	.250	1	1-2	0	8.80	9.06
1998 Tex-Pit		22	11	0	3	66.1	303	79	52	47	9	3	3	1	28	3	42	7	3	2	4	.333	0	0-0	0	5.47	6.38
2000 Chicago	NL	51	2	0	13	86.1	378	80	38	36	10	4	3	2	48	2	77	5	0	4	5	.444	0	2-5	7	4.48	3.75
2001 Chicago	NL	59	0	0	18	75.0	324	63	23	21	9	4	0	1	38	4	90	5	1	4	1	.800	0	0-0	5	3.61	2.52

Year Team	Lg	G	GS	CG	GF	IP	BFP	H	R	ER	HR	SH	SF	HB	TBB	IBB	SO	WP	Bk	W	L	Pct	ShO	Sv-Op	Hld	ERC	ERA
2002 Texas	AL	50	0	0	19	72.2	326	80	44	44	14	1	1	3	29	1	85	8	0	3	2	.600	0	1-2	3	5.44	5.45
2003 Tex-Cin		16	5	0	1	48.1	211	51	32	30	8	1	0	1	15	2	34	0	1	3	1	.750	0	0-0	1	4.43	5.59
1996 Oakland	AL	28	6	0	8	63.0	301	86	56	54	13	3	5	2	33	3	37	4	0	1	5	.167	0	1-2	0	7.81	7.71
1996 Detroit	AL	9	9	1	0	36.1	190	53	51	46	11	1	2	1	29	0	16	3	0	2	4	.333	1	0-0	0	10.57	11.39
1998 Texas	AL	4	4	0	0	19.1	95	26	20	19	5	0	1	1	10	0	10	2	0	1	2	.333	0	0-0	0	8.04	8.84
1998 Pittsburgh	NL	18	7	0	3	47.0	208	53	32	28	4	3	2	0	18	3	32	5	3	1	2	.333	0	0-0	0	4.50	5.36
2003 Texas	AL	7	1	0	0	12.2	67	20	14	12	1	0	0	0	9	2	9	0	0	0	1	0 1.000	0	0-0	0	8.27	8.53
2003 Cincinnati	NL	9	4	0	1	35.2	144	31	18	18	7	1	0	1	6	0	25	0	1	2	1	.667	0	0-0	1	3.15	4.54
10 ML YEARS		311	87	2	72	791.2	3548	808	507	484	121	25	26	19	429	18	639	42	6	36	46	.439	1	4-9	17	5.23	5.50

Cory Vance

Pitches: L **Bats:** L **Pos:** RP-6; SP-3
Ht: 6'1" **Wt:** 195 **Born:** 6/20/79 **Age:** 25

Year Team	Lg	G	GS	CG	GF	IP	BFP	H	R	ER	HR	SH	SF	HB	TBB	IBB	SO	WP	Bk	W	L	Pct	ShO	Sv-Op	Hld	ERC	ERA
2000 Portland	A-	7	3	0	1	24.1	93	11	5	3	1	3	0	2	8	0	26	1	0	0	2	.000	0	0--	1	1.27	1.11
2001 Salem	A+	26	26	1	0	154.0	641	129	65	53	9	3	2	14	65	0	142	4	4	10	8	.556	0	0--	0	3.43	3.10
2002 Carolina	AA	25	25	1	0	150.1	646	142	73	63	8	9	5	2	76	1	114	5	1	10	8	.556	0	0--	1	3.95	3.77
2003 Co Springs	AAA	24	24	3	0	157.1	680	179	89	81	18	9	6	6	50	2	96	1	10	9	11	.450	2	0--	1	4.86	4.63
2002 Colorado	NL	2	1	0	0	4.0	20	4	3	3	2	0	0	1	4	0	1	0	0	0	0	-	0	0-0	0	11.75	6.75
2003 Colorado	NL	9	3	0	1	27.1	121	31	19	17	6	0	2	1	10	0	12	0	1	1	3	.250	0	0-1	1	5.78	5.60
2 ML YEARS		11	4	0	1	31.1	141	35	22	20	8	0	2	2	14	0	13	0	1	1	3	.250	0	0-1	1	6.46	5.74

John Vander Wal

Bats: L **Throws:** L **Pos:** RF-83; PH-30; LF-6
Ht: 6'1" **Wt:** 197 **Born:** 4/29/66 **Age:** 38

Year Team	Lg	G	AB	H	2B	3B	HR	(Hm	Rd)	TB	R	RBI	RC	TBB	IBB	SO	HBP	SH	SF	SB	CS	SB%	GDP	Avg	OBP	Slg
1991 Montreal	NL	21	61	13	4	1	1	(0	1)	22	4	8	4	1	0	18	0	0	1	0	0	-	2	.213	.222	.361
1992 Montreal	NL	105	213	51	8	2	4	(2	2)	75	21	20	25	24	2	36	0	0	0	3	0	1.00	2	.239	.316	.352
1993 Montreal	NL	106	215	50	7	4	5	(1	4)	80	34	30	26	27	2	30	1	0	1	6	3	.67	4	.233	.320	.372
1994 Colorado	NL	91	110	27	3	1	5	(1	4)	47	12	15	15	16	0	31	0	0	1	2	1	.67	4	.245	.339	.427
1995 Colorado	NL	105	101	35	8	1	5	(2	3)	60	15	21	24	16	5	23	0	0	1	1	1	.50	2	.347	.432	.594
1996 Colorado	NL	104	151	38	6	2	5	(5	0)	63	20	31	22	19	2	38	1	0	2	2	2	.50	1	.252	.335	.417
1997 Colorado	NL	76	92	16	2	0	1	(0	1)	21	7	11	4	10	0	33	0	0	0	1	1	.50	2	.174	.255	.228
1998 Col-SD	NL	109	129	36	13	1	5	(3	2)	66	21	20	26	22	0	34	0	0	1	0	0	-	2	.279	.382	.512
1999 San Diego	NL	132	246	67	18	0	6	(2	4)	103	26	41	39	37	1	59	2	0	3	2	1	.67	5	.272	.368	.419
2000 Pittsburgh	NL	134	384	115	29	0	24	(13	11)	216	74	94	88	72	5	92	2	0	3	11	2	.85	7	.299	.410	.563
2001 Pit-SF	NL	146	452	122	28	4	14	(6	8)	200	58	70	72	68	9	122	1	2	4	8	6	.57	10	.270	.364	.442
2002 New York	AL	84	219	57	17	1	6	(2	4)	94	30	20	20	23	3	58	0	0	3	1	1	.50	2	.260	.327	.429
2003 Milwaukee	NL	117	327	84	25	1	14	(7	7)	153	50	45	46	46	3	104	1	0	0	1	2	.33	5	.257	.350	.468
1998 Colorado	NL	89	104	30	10	1	5	(3	2)	57	18	20	22	16	0	29	0	0	0	0	0	-	1	.288	.380	.548
1998 San Diego	NL	20	25	6	3	0	0	(0	0)	9	3	0	4	6	0	5	0	0	1	0	0	-	1	.240	.387	.360
2001 Pittsburgh	NL	97	313	87	22	3	11	(5	6)	148	39	50	52	42	6	84	1	0	4	7	4	.64	7	.278	.361	.473
2001 San Francisco	NL	49	139	35	6	1	3	(1	2)	52	19	20	20	26	3	38	0	2	0	1	2	.33	3	.252	.370	.374
13 ML YEARS		1330	2700	711	168	18	95	(44	51)	1200	372	426	411	381	32	678	8	2	20	38	20	.66	53	.263	.354	.444

Claudio Vargas

Pitches: R **Bats:** R **Pos:** SP-20; RP-3
Ht: 6'3" **Wt:** 225 **Born:** 6/19/78 **Age:** 26

Year Team	Lg	G	GS	CG	GF	IP	BFP	H	R	ER	HR	SH	SF	HB	TBB	IBB	SO	WP	Bk	W	L	Pct	ShO	Sv-Op	Hld	ERC	ERA
1998 Brevard Cnty	A+	2	2	0	0	9.2	46	15	5	5	5	1	1	0	4	1	9	0	0	0	1	.000	0	0--	1	11.23	4.66
1998 Marlins	R	5	4	0	0	28.2	117	24	15	13	1	0	1	3	7	0	27	2	0	0	4	.000	0	0--	0	2.62	4.08
1999 Kane County	A	19	19	1	0	99.2	426	97	47	43	8	2	3	0	41	0	88	2	2	5	5	.500	0	0--	0	3.85	3.88
2000 Brevard Cnty	A+	24	23	0	0	145.1	596	126	64	53	10	4	2	7	44	3	143	3	0	10	5	.667	0	0--	0	2.97	3.28
2000 Portland	AA	3	2	0	0	15.0	68	16	9	6	1	1	2	1	6	0	13	0	0	1	1	.500	0	0--	0	4.36	3.60
2001 Portland	AA	27	27	0	0	159.0	666	122	77	74	25	8	2	11	67	1	151	2	1	8	9	.471	0	0--	0	3.53	4.19
2002 Calgary	AAA	17	16	1	0	76.1	349	88	63	57	18	6	2	4	35	0	61	3	1	4	11	.267	0	0--	0	6.48	6.72
2002 Harrisburg	AA	8	8	0	0	33.0	146	38	17	17	2	1	0	3	9	0	34	3	0	2	2	.500	0	0--	0	4.49	4.64
2003 Edmonton	AAA	2	2	0	0	9.2	43	7	3	3	1	0	0	1	5	2	12	0	0	0	0	-	0	0--	0	2.96	2.79
2003 Harrisburg	AA	2	2	0	0	12.0	46	7	1	1	0	0	1	1	3	0	13	0	0	1	0	1.000	0	0--	0	1.35	0.75
2003 Montreal	NL	23	20	0	0	114.0	491	111	59	55	16	5	4	7	41	5	62	2	0	6	8	.429	0	0-0	0	4.22	4.34

Jason Varitek

Bats: B **Throws:** R **Pos:** C-137; PH-15; DH-3
Ht: 6'2" **Wt:** 237 **Born:** 4/11/72 **Age:** 32

Year Team	Lg	G	AB	H	2B	3B	HR	(Hm	Rd)	TB	R	RBI	RC	TBB	IBB	SO	HBP	SH	SF	SB	CS	SB%	GDP	Avg	OBP	Slg
1997 Boston	AL	1	1	1	0	0	0	(0	0)	1	0	0	1	0	0	0	0	0	0	0	0	-	0	1.000	1.000	1.000
1998 Boston	AL	86	221	56	13	0	7	(1	6)	90	31	33	26	17	1	45	2	4	3	2	2	.50	8	.253	.309	.407
1999 Boston	AL	144	483	130	39	2	20	(12	8)	233	70	76	75	46	2	85	2	5	8	1	2	.33	13	.269	.330	.482
2000 Boston	AL	139	448	111	31	1	10	(2	8)	174	55	65	59	60	3	84	6	1	4	1	1	.50	16	.248	.342	.388
2001 Boston	AL	51	174	51	11	1	7	(2	5)	85	19	25	30	21	3	35	1	1	1	0	0	-	6	.293	.371	.489
2002 Boston	AL	132	467	124	27	1	10	(6	4)	183	58	61	52	41	3	95	1	1	3	4	3	.57	13	.266	.332	.392
2003 Boston	AL	142	451	123	31	1	25	(13	12)	231	63	85	80	51	8	106	7	5	7	3	2	.60	10	.273	.351	.512
7 ML YEARS		695	2245	596	152	6	79	(36	43)	997	296	345	323	236	20	450	25	17	26	11	10	.52	66	.265	.338	.444

Greg Vaughn

Bats: R **Throws:** R **Pos:** PH-14; LF-6; DH-3; RF-1　　　**Ht:** 6'0" **Wt:** 206 **Born:** 7/3/65 **Age:** 38

Year Team	Lg	G	AB	H	2B	3B	HR	(Hm	Rd)	TB	R	RBI	RC	TBB	IBB	SO	HBP	SH	SF	SB	CS	SB%	GDP	Avg	OBP	Slg
2003 Co Springs*	AAA	35	116	35	7	1	12	(-	-)	80	26	35	29	16	1	28	1	0	1	1	0	1.00	2	.302	.388	.690
1989 Milwaukee	NL	38	113	30	3	0	5	(1	4)	48	18	23	18	13	0	23	0	0	2	4	1	.80	0	.265	.336	.425
1990 Milwaukee	NL	120	382	84	26	2	17	(9	8)	165	51	61	45	33	1	91	1	7	6	7	4	.64	11	.220	.280	.432
1991 Milwaukee	NL	145	542	132	24	5	27	(16	11)	247	81	98	81	62	2	125	1	2	7	2	2	.50	5	.244	.319	.456
1992 Milwaukee	NL	141	501	114	18	2	23	(11	12)	205	77	78	63	60	1	123	5	2	5	15	15	.50	8	.228	.313	.409
1993 Milwaukee	NL	154	569	152	28	2	30	(12	18)	274	97	97	102	89	14	118	5	0	4	10	7	.59	6	.267	.369	.482
1994 Milwaukee	NL	95	370	94	24	1	19	(9	10)	177	59	55	61	51	6	93	1	0	1	9	5	.64	6	.254	.345	.478
1995 Milwaukee	NL	108	392	88	19	1	17	(8	9)	160	67	59	51	55	3	89	0	0	4	10	4	.71	10	.224	.317	.408
1996 Mil-SD	NL	145	516	134	19	1	41	(22	19)	278	98	117	101	82	6	130	6	0	5	9	3	.75	7	.260	.365	.539
1997 San Diego	NL	120	361	78	10	0	18	(11	7)	142	60	57	47	56	1	110	2	0	3	7	4	.64	7	.216	.322	.393
1998 San Diego	NL	158	573	156	28	4	50	(23	27)	342	112	119	122	79	6	121	5	0	4	11	4	.73	7	.272	.363	.597
1999 Cincinnati	NL	153	550	135	20	2	45	(20	25)	294	104	118	104	85	3	137	3	0	5	15	2	.88	5	.245	.347	.535
2000 Tampa Bay	AL	127	461	117	27	1	28	(15	13)	230	83	74	85	80	3	128	2	0	2	8	1	.89	10	.254	.365	.499
2001 Tampa Bay	AL	136	485	113	25	0	24	(12	12)	210	74	82	70	71	7	130	3	0	3	11	5	.69	10	.233	.333	.433
2002 Tampa Bay	AL	69	251	41	10	2	8	(1	7)	79	28	29	23	41	1	82	0	0	1	3	2	.60	5	.163	.286	.315
2003 Colorado	NL	22	37	7	3	0	3	(1	2)	19	8	5	6	8	0	13	0	0	0	0	0	-	0	.189	.326	.514
1996 Milwaukee	NL	102	375	105	16	0	31	(16	15)	214	78	95	79	58	4	99	4	0	5	5	2	.71	6	.280	.378	.571
1996 San Diego	NL	43	141	29	3	1	10	(6	4)	64	20	22	22	24	2	31	2	0	0	4	1	.80	1	.206	.329	.454
15 ML YEARS		1731	6103	1475	284	23	355	(169	186)	2870	1017	1072	979	865	54	1513	37	11	54	121	59	.67	101	.242	.337	.470

Mo Vaughn

Bats: L **Throws:** R **Pos:** 1B-25; PH-2　　　**Ht:** 6'1" **Wt:** 275 **Born:** 12/15/67 **Age:** 36

Year Team	Lg	G	AB	H	2B	3B	HR	(Hm	Rd)	TB	R	RBI	RC	TBB	IBB	SO	HBP	SH	SF	SB	CS	SB%	GDP	Avg	OBP	Slg
1991 Boston	AL	74	219	57	12	0	4	(1	3)	81	21	32	27	26	2	43	2	0	4	2	1	.67	7	.260	.339	.370
1992 Boston	AL	113	355	83	16	2	13	(8	5)	142	42	57	46	47	7	67	3	0	3	3	3	.50	8	.234	.326	.400
1993 Boston	AL	152	539	160	34	1	29	(13	16)	283	86	101	106	79	23	130	8	0	7	4	3	.57	14	.297	.390	.525
1994 Boston	AL	111	394	122	25	1	26	(15	11)	227	65	82	87	57	20	112	10	0	2	4	4	.50	7	.310	.408	.576
1995 Boston	AL	140	550	165	28	3	39	(15	24)	316	98	126	115	68	17	150	14	0	4	11	4	.73	17	.300	.388	.575
1996 Boston	AL	161	635	207	29	1	44	(27	17)	370	118	143	146	95	19	154	14	0	8	2	0	1.00	17	.326	.420	.583
1997 Boston	AL	141	527	166	24	0	35	(20	15)	295	91	96	118	86	17	154	12	0	3	2	2	.50	10	.315	.420	.560
1998 Boston	AL	154	609	205	31	2	40	(19	21)	360	107	115	134	61	13	144	8	0	3	0	0	-	13	.337	.402	.591
1999 Anaheim	AL	139	524	147	20	0	33	(16	17)	266	63	108	92	54	7	127	11	0	3	0	0	-	11	.281	.358	.508
2000 Anaheim	AL	161	614	167	31	0	36	(18	18)	306	93	117	110	79	0	181	14	0	5	2	0	1.00	14	.272	.365	.498
2002 New York	NL	139	487	126	18	0	26	(16	10)	222	67	72	74	59	6	145	10	0	2	0	1	.00	15	.259	.349	.456
2003 New York	NL	27	79	15	2	0	3	(1	2)	26	10	15	8	14	2	22	2	0	1	0	0	-	2	.190	.323	.329
12 ML YEARS		1512	5532	1620	270	10	328	(169	159)	2894	861	1064	1063	725	144	1429	108	0	45	30	18	.63	135	.293	.383	.523

Javier Vazquez

Pitches: R **Bats:** R **Pos:** SP-34　　　**Ht:** 6'2" **Wt:** 195 **Born:** 7/25/76 **Age:** 27

Year Team	Lg	G	GS	CG	GF	IP	BFP	H	R	ER	HR	SH	SF	HB	TBB	IBB	SO	WP	Bk	W	L	Pct	ShO	Sv-Op	Hld	ERC	ERA
1998 Montreal	NL	33	32	0	1	172.1	764	196	121	116	31	9	4	11	68	2	139	2	0	5	15	.250	1	0-0	0	5.79	6.06
1999 Montreal	NL	26	26	3	0	154.2	667	154	98	86	20	3	3	4	52	4	113	2	0	9	8	.529	1	0-0	0	4.02	5.00
2000 Montreal	NL	33	33	2	0	217.2	945	247	104	98	24	11	3	5	61	10	196	3	0	11	9	.550	1	0-0	0	4.45	4.05
2001 Montreal	NL	32	32	5	0	223.2	898	197	92	85	24	9	2	3	44	4	208	3	1	16	11	.593	3	0-0	0	2.75	3.42
2002 Montreal	NL	34	34	2	0	230.1	971	243	111	100	28	15	7	4	49	6	179	3	0	10	13	.435	0	0-0	0	3.80	3.91
2003 Montreal	NL	34	34	4	0	230.2	938	198	93	83	28	6	6	4	57	5	241	11	1	13	12	.520	1	0-0	0	2.90	3.24
6 ML YEARS		192	191	16	1	1229.1	5183	1235	619	568	155	53	25	31	331	31	1076	24	2	64	68	.485	6	0-0	0	3.82	4.16

Ramon Vazquez

Bats: L **Throws:** R **Pos:** SS-108; PH-5; 3B-4; 2B-3　　　**Ht:** 5'11" **Wt:** 170 **Born:** 8/21/76 **Age:** 27

Year Team	Lg	G	AB	H	2B	3B	HR	(Hm	Rd)	TB	R	RBI	RC	TBB	IBB	SO	HBP	SH	SF	SB	CS	SB%	GDP	Avg	OBP	Slg
2003 Lk Elsinore*	A+	5	16	3	0	0	1	(-	-)	6	3	4	2	3	0	3	1	0	0	0	1	.00	1	.188	.350	.375
2001 Seattle	AL	17	35	8	0	0	0	(0	0)	8	5	4	2	0	0	3	0	1	1	0	0	-	0	.229	.222	.229
2002 San Diego	NL	128	423	116	21	5	2	(0	2)	153	50	32	54	45	3	79	1	3	2	7	2	.78	6	.274	.344	.362
2003 San Diego	NL	116	422	110	17	4	3	(1	2)	144	56	30	48	52	2	88	2	5	3	10	3	.77	4	.261	.342	.341
3 ML YEARS		261	880	234	38	9	5	(1	4)	305	111	66	104	97	5	170	3	9	6	17	5	.77	10	.266	.339	.347

Jorge Velandia

Bats: R **Throws:** R **Pos:** SS-23; PR-1　　　**Ht:** 5'9" **Wt:** 185 **Born:** 1/12/75 **Age:** 29

Year Team	Lg	G	AB	H	2B	3B	HR	(Hm	Rd)	TB	R	RBI	RC	TBB	IBB	SO	HBP	SH	SF	SB	CS	SB%	GDP	Avg	OBP	Slg
2003 Norfolk*	AAA	111	374	88	22	2	11	(-	-)	147	45	48	43	37	2	90	4	6	6	2	5	.29	9	.235	.306	.393
1997 San Diego	NL	14	29	3	2	0	0	(0	0)	5	0	0	1	1	0	7	0	0	0	0	0	-	0	.103	.133	.172
1998 Oakland	AL	8	4	1	0	0	0	(0	0)	1	0	0	0	0	0	1	0	0	0	0	0	-	0	.250	.250	.250
1999 Oakland	AL	63	48	9	1	0	0	(0	0)	10	4	2	3	2	0	13	1	0	0	2	0	1.00	0	.188	.235	.208
2000 Oak-NYM		33	31	3	1	0	0	(0	0)	4	2	2	1	2	0	8	1	0	0	0	0	-	0	.097	.176	.129
2001 New York	NL	9	9	0	0	0	0	(0	0)	0	1	0	0	2	0	1	0	0	0	0	0	-	0	.000	.182	.000
2003 New York	NL	23	58	11	3	1	0	(0	0)	16	6	8	6	10	1	15	0	3	1	0	0	-	0	.190	.304	.276
2000 Oakland	AL	18	24	3	1	0	0	(0	0)	4	1	2	1	0	0	6	1	0	0	0	0	-	1	.125	.160	.167
2000 New York	NL	15	7	0	0	0	0	(0	0)	0	1	0	0	2	0	2	0	0	0	0	0	-	0	.000	.222	.000
6 ML YEARS		150	179	27	7	1	0	(0	0)	36	13	12	11	17	1	45	2	3	1	2	0	1.00	1	.151	.231	.201

Mike Venafro

Pitches: L **Bats:** L **Pos:** RP-24   **Ht:** 5'10" **Wt:** 180 **Born:** 8/2/73 **Age:** 30

Year Team	Lg	G	GS	CG	GF	IP	BFP	H	R	ER	HR	SH	SF	HB	TBB	IBB	SO	WP	Bk	W	L	Pct	ShO	Sv-Op	Hld	ERC	ERA
2003 New Orleans*	AAA	23	0	0	9	28.0	121	35	11	11	0	2	0	1	5	1	11	2	0	2	1	.667	0	0- -	-	4.00	3.54
1999 Texas	AL	65	0	0	11	68.1	283	63	29	25	4	5	2	3	22	0	37	0	0	3	2	.600	0	0-1	19	3.30	3.29
2000 Texas	AL	77	0	0	21	56.1	248	64	27	24	2	2	4	4	21	4	32	1	0	3	1	.750	0	1-2	17	4.49	3.83
2001 Texas	AL	70	0	0	20	60.0	266	54	35	32	2	2	4	7	28	4	29	3	0	5	5	.500	0	4-8	21	3.58	4.80
2002 Oakland	AL	47	0	0	8	37.0	168	45	23	19	5	4	2	2	14	2	16	1	0	2	2	.500	0	0-0	15	5.65	4.62
2003 Tampa Bay	AL	24	0	0	6	19.0	85	24	10	10	1	0	1	3	3	0	9	1	0	1	0	1.000	0	0-0	4	4.89	4.74
5 ML YEARS		283	0	0	66	240.2	1050	250	124	110	14	13	13	19	88	10	123	6	0	14	10	.583	0	5-11	76	4.12	4.11

Robin Ventura

Bats: L **Throws:** R **Pos:** 3B-83; 1B-42; PH-20; 2B-1; DH-1   **Ht:** 6'1" **Wt:** 198 **Born:** 7/14/67 **Age:** 36

								BATTING												BASERUNNING				AVERAGES		
Year Team	Lg	G	AB	H	2B	3B	HR	(Hm	Rd)	TB	R	RBI	RC	TBB	IBB	SO	HBP	SH	SF	SB	CS	SB%	GDP	Avg	OBP	Slg
1989 Chicago	AL	16	45	8	3	0	0	(0	0)	11	5	7	4	8	0	6	1	1	3	0	0	-	1	.178	.298	.244
1990 Chicago	AL	150	493	123	17	1	5	(2	3)	157	48	54	53	55	2	53	1	13	3	1	4	.20	5	.249	.324	.318
1991 Chicago	AL	157	606	172	25	1	23	(16	7)	268	92	100	95	80	3	67	4	8	7	2	4	.33	22	.284	.367	.442
1992 Chicago	AL	157	592	167	38	1	16	(7	9)	255	85	93	96	93	9	71	0	1	8	2	4	.33	14	.282	.375	.431
1993 Chicago	AL	157	554	145	27	1	22	(12	10)	240	85	94	90	105	16	82	3	1	6	1	6	.14	18	.262	.379	.433
1994 Chicago	AL	109	401	113	15	1	18	(8	10)	184	57	78	70	61	15	69	2	2	8	3	1	.75	8	.282	.373	.459
1995 Chicago	AL	135	492	145	22	0	26	(8	18)	245	79	93	94	75	11	98	1	1	8	4	3	.57	8	.295	.384	.498
1996 Chicago	AL	158	586	168	31	2	34	(13	21)	305	96	105	107	78	10	81	2	0	8	1	3	.25	18	.287	.368	.520
1997 Chicago	AL	54	183	48	10	1	6	(2	4)	78	27	26	31	34	5	21	0	0	3	0	0	-	3	.262	.373	.426
1998 Chicago	AL	161	590	155	31	4	21	(15	6)	257	84	91	90	79	15	111	1	1	3	1	1	.50	10	.263	.349	.436
1999 New York	NL	161	588	177	38	0	32	(13	19)	311	88	120	113	74	10	109	3	1	5	1	1	.50	14	.301	.379	.529
2000 New York	NL	141	469	109	23	1	24	(12	12)	206	61	84	68	75	12	91	2	1	4	3	5	.38	14	.232	.338	.439
2001 New York	NL	142	456	108	20	0	21	(9	12)	191	70	61	68	88	10	101	1	0	4	2	5	.29	13	.237	.359	.419
2002 New York	AL	141	465	115	17	0	27	(9	18)	213	68	93	78	90	9	101	2	0	5	3	1	.75	14	.247	.368	.458
2003 NYY-LA		138	392	95	18	1	14	(8	6)	157	42	55	48	58	4	87	0	3	0	-	-	-	11	.242	.340	.401
2003 New York	AL	89	283	71	13	0	9	(4	5)	111	31	42	39	40	2	62	0	3	0	0	0	-	8	.251	.344	.392
2003 Los Angeles	NL	49	109	24	5	1	5	(4	1)	46	11	13	9	18	2	25	0	0	0	0	0	-	3	.220	.331	.422
15 ML YEARS		1977	6912	1848	335	14	289	(134	155)	3078	987	1154	1105	1053	131	1148	23	33	75	24	38	.39	173	.267	.363	.445

Dave Veres

Pitches: R **Bats:** R **Pos:** RP-31   **Ht:** 6'2" **Wt:** 220 **Born:** 10/19/66 **Age:** 37

Year Team	Lg	G	GS	CG	GF	IP	BFP	H	R	ER	HR	SH	SF	HB	TBB	IBB	SO	WP	Bk	W	L	Pct	ShO	Sv-Op	Hld	ERC	ERA
2003 Iowa*	AAA	11	4	0	2	16.0	63	15	5	5	2	0	0	0	1	0	13	2	0	0	1	.000	0	0- -	-	2.61	2.81
1994 Houston	NL	32	0	0	7	41.0	168	39	13	11	4	0	2	1	7	3	28	2	0	3	3	.500	0	1-1	3	2.89	2.41
1995 Houston	NL	72	0	0	15	103.1	418	89	29	26	5	6	8	4	30	6	94	4	0	5	1	.833	0	1-3	19	2.70	2.26
1996 Montreal	NL	68	0	0	22	77.2	351	85	39	36	10	3	3	6	32	2	81	3	2	6	3	.667	0	4-6	15	5.11	4.17
1997 Montreal	NL	53	0	0	11	62.0	281	68	28	24	5	6	1	2	27	3	47	7	0	2	3	.400	0	1-4	10	4.59	3.48
1998 Colorado	NL	63	0	0	26	76.1	319	67	26	24	6	0	2	2	27	2	74	2	2	3	1	.750	0	8-13	8	3.15	2.83
1999 Colorado	NL	73	0	0	63	77.0	349	88	46	44	14	5	2	2	37	7	71	8	1	4	8	.333	0	31-39	0	5.84	5.14
2000 St Louis	NL	71	0	0	61	75.2	310	65	26	24	6	5	2	6	25	2	67	3	1	3	5	.375	0	29-36	1	3.25	2.85
2001 St Louis	NL	71	0	0	44	65.2	279	57	29	27	12	2	1	2	28	1	61	6	0	3	2	.600	0	15-19	8	4.11	3.70
2002 St Louis	NL	71	0	0	26	82.2	346	67	34	32	12	3	3	2	39	4	68	7	0	5	8	.385	0	4-8	16	3.68	3.48
2003 Chicago	NL	31	0	0	9	32.2	136	36	17	17	4	2	4	1	5	0	26	3	1	2	1	.667	0	1-2	4	3.98	4.68
10 ML YEARS		605	0	0	284	694.0	2957	661	287	265	78	32	28	28	257	30	617	45	7	36	35	.507	0	95-131	84	3.89	3.44

Shane Victorino

Bats: B **Throws:** R **Pos:** CF-16; LF-15; PR-6; RF-3; PH-2   **Ht:** 5'9" **Wt:** 160 **Born:** 11/30/80 **Age:** 23

								BATTING												BASERUNNING				AVERAGES		
Year Team	Lg	G	AB	H	2B	3B	HR	(Hm	Rd)	TB	R	RBI	RC	TBB	IBB	SO	HBP	SH	SF	SB	CS	SB%	GDP	Avg	OBP	Slg
1999 Great Falls	R+	55	225	63	7	6	2	(-	-)	88	53	25	32	20	0	31	0	6	3	20	5	.80	3	.280	.335	.391
2000 Yakima	A-	61	236	58	7	2	2	(-	-)	75	32	20	25	20	1	44	3	12	2	21	9	.70	3	.246	.310	.318
2001 Wilmington	A+	112	435	123	21	9	4	(-	-)	174	71	32	66	36	0	61	5	13	1	47	13	.78	5	.283	.344	.400
2001 Vero Beach	A+	2	6	1	0	0	0	(-	-)	1	2	0	1	3	0	1	0	0	0	0	0	-	0	.167	.444	.167
2002 Jacksonville	AA	122	481	124	15	1	4	(-	-)	153	61	34	56	47	0	49	4	16	2	45	16	.74	6	.258	.328	.318
2003 Las Vegas	AAA	11	41	16	1	2	1	(-	-)	24	6	9	8	1	0	5	0	2	1	0	1	.00	1	.390	.395	.585
2003 Jacksonville	AA	66	266	75	9	4	2	(-	-)	98	37	15	35	21	1	41	3	2	1	16	7	.70	3	.282	.340	.368
2003 San Diego	NL	36	73	11	2	0	0	(0	0)	13	8	4	1	7	0	17	1	1	1	7	2	.78	5	.151	.232	.178

Jose Vidro

Bats: B **Throws:** R **Pos:** 2B-137; PH-7   **Ht:** 5'11" **Wt:** 195 **Born:** 8/27/74 **Age:** 29

								BATTING												BASERUNNING				AVERAGES		
Year Team	Lg	G	AB	H	2B	3B	HR	(Hm	Rd)	TB	R	RBI	RC	TBB	IBB	SO	HBP	SH	SF	SB	CS	SB%	GDP	Avg	OBP	Slg
1997 Montreal	NL	67	169	42	12	1	2	(0	2)	62	19	17	19	11	0	20	2	0	3	1	0	1.00	1	.249	.297	.367
1998 Montreal	NL	83	205	45	12	0	0	(0	0)	57	24	18	19	27	0	33	4	6	3	2	2	.50	5	.220	.318	.278
1999 Montreal	NL	140	494	150	45	0	12	(5	7)	235	67	59	76	29	2	51	4	2	2	0	4	.00	12	.304	.346	.476
2000 Montreal	NL	153	606	200	51	2	24	(11	13)	327	101	97	115	49	4	69	2	0	6	5	4	.56	17	.330	.379	.540
2001 Montreal	NL	124	486	155	34	1	15	(6	9)	236	82	59	81	31	2	49	10	2	2	4	1	.80	18	.319	.371	.486
2002 Montreal	NL	152	604	190	43	3	19	(11	8)	296	103	96	112	60	1	70	3	11	3	2	1	.67	12	.315	.378	.490
2003 Montreal	NL	144	509	158	36	0	15	(7	8)	239	77	65	89	69	6	50	7	2	5	3	2	.60	16	.310	.397	.470
7 ML YEARS		863	3073	940	233	9	87	(40	47)	1452	473	411	511	276	15	342	32	23	24	17	14	.55	81	.306	.367	.473

Brandon Villafuerte

Pitches: R Bats: R Pos: RP-31
Ht: 5'11" Wt: 165 Born: 12/17/75 Age: 28

Year Team	Lg	G	GS	CG	GF	IP	BFP	H	R	ER	HR	SH	SF	HB	TBB	IBB	SO	WP	Bk	W	L	Pct	ShO	Sv-Op	Hld	ERC	ERA
2003 Lk Elsinore	A+	2	0	0	2	2.0	8	1	0	0	0	0	0	0	1	0	2	0	0	0	0	-	0	2- -	-	1.41	0.00
2003 Portland	AAA	37	0	0	23	44.0	183	42	10	9	1	2	1	3	14	1	40	0	0	3	1	.750	0	12- -	-	3.29	1.84
2000 Detroit	AL	3	0	0	2	4.1	20	4	5	5	0	0	0	0	4	0	1	1	0	0	0	-	0	0-0	0	5.01	10.38
2001 Texas	AL	6	0	0	4	5.2	35	12	9	9	3	0	1	1	4	0	4	1	0	0	0	-	0	0-0	0	17.59	14.29
2002 San Diego	NL	31	0	0	11	32.0	133	29	5	5	2	1	1	2	12	2	25	0	0	1	2	.333	0	1-1	8	3.44	1.41
2003 San Diego	NL	31	0	0	11	40.2	187	39	20	19	7	2	1	3	26	2	34	2	0	0	2	.000	0	2-5	2	5.54	4.20
4 ML YEARS		71	0	0	28	82.2	375	84	39	38	12	3	3	6	46	4	64	4	0	1	4	.200	0	3-6	10	5.36	4.14

Oscar Villarreal

Pitches: R Bats: L Pos: RP-85; SP-1
Ht: 6'0" Wt: 205 Born: 11/22/81 Age: 22

Year Team	Lg	G	GS	CG	GF	IP	BFP	H	R	ER	HR	SH	SF	HB	TBB	IBB	SO	WP	Bk	W	L	Pct	ShO	Sv-Op	Hld	ERC	ERA
1999 Diamndbcks	R	14	11	0	1	64.1	286	64	39	27	1	2	3	10	25	0	51	6	4	1	5	.167	0	0- -	-	3.97	3.78
2000 Tucson	AAA	2	0	0	0	4.1	19	6	1	1	0	0	0	0	2	0	4	0	0	1	0	1.000	0	0- -	-	6.28	2.08
2000 South Bend	A	13	5	0	5	32.2	155	37	19	16	0	0	1	3	17	3	30	2	1	1	3	.250	0	0- -	-	4.59	4.41
2000 Diamndbcks	R	1	0	0	0	1.0	5	2	1	1	0	0	0	3	0	0	1	0	0	0	0	-	0	0- -	-	7.48	9.00
2000 High Desert	A+	9	4	0	0	24.2	117	24	20	10	4	4	1	3	14	0	18	2	0	0	2	.000	0	0- -	-	5.33	3.65
2001 El Paso	AA	27	27	0	0	140.2	644	154	96	69	10	4	7	8	63	1	108	14	11	6	9	.400	0	0- -	-	4.71	4.41
2002 El Paso	AA	14	12	1	0	84.1	344	73	36	35	2	0	1	4	26	0	85	3	0	6	3	.667	0	0- -	-	2.74	3.74
2002 Tucson	AAA	10	10	0	0	64.0	272	68	33	31	8	0	1	4	22	0	40	5	2	3	3	.500	0	0- -	-	4.79	4.36
2003 Arizona	NL	86	1	0	14	98.0	422	80	40	28	6	9	3	3	46	10	80	3	2	10	7	.588	0	0-4	10	2.97	2.57

Ron Villone

Pitches: L Bats: L Pos: SP-19
Ht: 6'4" Wt: 235 Born: 1/16/70 Age: 34

Year Team	Lg	G	GS	CG	GF	IP	BFP	H	R	ER	HR	SH	SF	HB	TBB	IBB	SO	WP	Bk	W	L	Pct	ShO	Sv-Op	Hld	ERC	ERA
2003 Tucson*	AAA	15	0	0	6	25.1	104	20	14	10	2	3	2	1	12	1	22	0	0	1	1	.500	0	1- -	-	3.27	3.55
2003 New Orleans*	AAA	5	5	0	0	29.1	115	24	5	4	0	1	1	0	10	0	18	0	0	3	1	.750	0	0- -	-	2.38	1.23
1995 Sea-SD		38	0	0	15	45.0	212	44	31	29	11	3	1	1	34	0	63	3	0	2	3	.400	0	1-5	6	6.57	5.80
1996 SD-Mil	NL	44	0	0	19	43.0	182	31	15	15	6	0	2	5	25	0	38	2	0	1	1	.500	0	2-3	9	4.08	3.14
1997 Milwaukee	NL	50	0	0	15	52.2	238	54	23	20	4	2	0	1	36	2	40	3	0	1	0	1.000	0	0-2	8	5.30	3.42
1998 Cleveland	AL	25	0	0	6	27.0	129	30	18	18	3	2	2	2	22	0	15	0	0	0	0	-	0	0-0	1	7.01	6.00
1999 Cincinnati	NL	29	22	0	2	142.2	610	114	70	67	8	9	3	5	73	2	97	6	0	9	7	.563	0	2-2	0	3.20	4.23
2000 Cincinnati	NL	35	23	2	5	141.0	643	154	95	85	22	10	8	9	78	3	77	7	0	10	10	.500	0	0-0	1	5.97	5.43
2001 Col-Hou	NL	53	12	0	12	114.2	523	133	81	75	18	1	1	5	53	5	113	4	1	6	10	.375	0	0-0	6	5.81	5.89
2002 Pittsburgh	NL	45	7	0	6	93.0	399	95	63	60	8	5	3	5	34	3	55	1	0	4	6	.400	0	0-1	0	4.18	5.81
2003 Houston	NL	19	19	0	0	106.2	448	91	51	49	16	3	3	5	48	1	91	1	0	6	6	.500	0	0-0	0	4.05	4.13
1995 Seattle	AL	19	0	0	7	19.1	101	20	19	17	6	3	0	1	23	0	26	1	0	0	2	.000	0	0-3	3	9.67	7.91
1995 San Diego	NL	19	0	0	8	25.2	111	24	12	12	5	0	1	0	11	0	37	2	0	2	1	.667	0	1-2	3	4.44	4.21
1996 San Diego	NL	21	0	0	9	18.1	78	17	6	6	2	0	0	1	7	0	19	0	0	1	1	.500	0	0-1	4	3.90	2.95
1996 Milwaukee	NL	23	0	0	10	24.2	104	14	9	9	4	0	2	4	18	0	19	2	0	0	0	-	0	2-2	5	4.21	3.28
2001 Colorado	NL	22	6	0	6	46.2	222	56	35	33	6	1	1	1	29	4	48	2	0	1	3	.250	0	0-0	2	6.30	6.30
2001 Houston	NL	31	6	0	6	68.0	301	77	46	42	12	0	0	4	24	1	65	2	1	5	7	.417	0	0-0	1	5.46	5.56
9 ML YEARS		338	83	2	80	765.2	3384	746	447	418	96	35	23	38	403	16	589	27	1	39	43	.476	0	5-13	31	4.82	4.91

Fernando Vina

Bats: L Throws: R Pos: 2B-60; PH-1
Ht: 5'9" Wt: 174 Born: 4/16/69 Age: 35

Year Team	Lg	G	AB	H	2B	3B	HR	(Hm Rd)	TB	R	RBI	RC	TBB	IBB	SO	HBP	SH	SF	SB	CS	SB%	GDP	Avg	OBP	Slg
2003 Memphis*	AAA	5	17	3	0	0	0	(- -)	3	1	1	0	2	0	2	0	0	1	0	0	-	1	.176	.250	.176
1993 Seattle	AL	24	45	10	2	0	0	(0 0)	12	5	2	6	4	0	3	1	0	0	6	0	1.00	0	.222	.327	.267
1994 New York	NL	79	124	31	6	0	0	(0 0)	37	20	6	15	12	2	11	**12**	2	0	3	1	.75	4	.250	.372	.298
1995 Milwaukee	NL	113	288	74	7	7	3	(1 2)	104	46	29	35	22	0	28	9	4	2	6	3	.67	6	.257	.327	.361
1996 Milwaukee	NL	140	554	157	19	10	7	(4 3)	217	94	46	73	38	3	35	13	6	4	16	7	.70	15	.283	.342	.392
1997 Milwaukee	NL	79	324	89	12	2	4	(1 3)	117	37	28	36	12	1	23	7	2	3	8	7	.53	4	.275	.312	.361
1998 Milwaukee	NL	159	637	198	39	7	7	(2 5)	272	101	45	106	54	2	46	25	5	1	22	16	.58	7	.311	.386	.427
1999 Milwaukee	NL	37	154	41	7	0	1	(0 1)	51	17	16	19	14	0	6	4	3	2	5	2	.71	1	.266	.339	.331
2000 St Louis	NL	123	487	146	24	6	4	(1 3)	194	81	31	76	36	0	36	**28**	2	1	10	8	.56	5	.300	.380	.398
2001 St Louis	NL	154	631	191	30	8	9	(5 4)	264	95	56	96	32	3	35	22	3	7	17	7	.71	7	.303	.357	.418
2002 St Louis	NL	150	622	168	29	5	1	(0 1)	210	75	54	70	44	2	36	18	1	7	17	11	.61	11	.270	.333	.338
2003 St Louis	NL	61	259	65	14	4	4	(2 2)	99	35	23	27	11	0	24	11	3	1	4	4	.50	5	.251	.309	.382
11 ML YEARS		1119	4125	1170	189	49	40	(15 25)	1577	606	336	559	279	11	283	152	32	23	114	66	.63	65	.284	.350	.382

Joe Vitiello

Bats: R Throws: R Pos: LF-15; 1B-12; PH-11; DH-1
Ht: 6'3" Wt: 220 Born: 4/11/70 Age: 34

Year Team	Lg	G	AB	H	2B	3B	HR	(Hm Rd)	TB	R	RBI	RC	TBB	IBB	SO	HBP	SH	SF	SB	CS	SB%	GDP	Avg	OBP	Slg
2003 Fresno*	AAA	23	75	16	5	0	0	(- -)	21	9	3	5	8	0	9	0	0	0	0	0	-	3	.213	.289	.280
2003 Edmonton*	AAA	27	96	26	7	0	2	(- -)	39	11	14	13	10	1	17	0	0	2	0	0	-	2	.271	.333	.406
1995 Kansas City	AL	53	130	33	4	0	7	(3 4)	58	13	21	17	8	0	25	4	0	0	0	0	-	4	.254	.317	.446
1996 Kansas City	AL	85	257	62	15	1	8	(3 5)	103	29	40	34	38	2	69	3	0	3	2	0	1.00	12	.241	.342	.401
1997 Kansas City	AL	51	130	31	6	0	5	(4 1)	52	11	18	17	14	1	37	2	0	0	0	0	-	0	.238	.322	.400
1998 Kansas City	AL	3	7	1	0	0	0	(0 0)	1	0	0	0	1	0	2	0	0	0	0	0	-	0	.143	.250	.143
1999 Kansas City	AL	13	41	6	1	0	1	(0 1)	10	4	4	2	2	0	9	0	0	0	0	0	-	0	.146	.222	.244
2000 San Diego	NL	39	52	13	3	0	2	(1 1)	22	7	7	9	10	0	19	2	0	0	0	0	-	1	.250	.365	.423
2003 Montreal	NL	38	76	26	6	0	3	(2 1)	41	12	13	14	7	0	14	2	0	1	0	0	-	1	.342	.407	.539
7 ML YEARS		282	693	172	35	1	26	(13 13)	287	76	104	82	80	3	165	13	0	5	2	0	1.00	22	.248	.335	.414

Jose Vizcaino

Bats: B **Throws:** R **Pos:** PH-48; SS-32; 2B-20; 3B-2; 1B-1   **Ht:** 6'1" **Wt:** 185 **Born:** 3/26/68 **Age:** 36

Year Team	Lg	G	AB	H	2B	3B	HR	(Hm	Rd)	TB	R	RBI	RC	TBB	IBB	SO	HBP	SH	SF	SB	CS	SB%	GDP	Avg	OBP	Slg
2003 New Orleans*	AAA	2	8	2	0	0	1	(-	-)	5	1	1	2	1	0	0	0	0	0	0	0	-	0	.250	.333	.625
1989 Los Angeles	NL	7	10	2	0	0	0	(0	0)	2	2	0	0	0	0	1	0	1	0	0	0	-	0	.200	.200	.200
1990 Los Angeles	NL	37	51	14	1	1	0	(0	0)	17	3	2	5	4	1	8	0	0	0	1	1	.50	1	.275	.327	.333
1991 Chicago	NL	93	145	38	5	0	0	(0	0)	43	7	10	12	5	0	18	0	2	2	2	1	.67	1	.262	.283	.297
1992 Chicago	NL	86	285	64	10	4	1	(0	1)	85	25	17	21	14	2	35	0	5	1	3	0	1.00	4	.225	.260	.298
1993 Chicago	NL	151	551	158	19	4	4	(1	3)	197	74	54	68	46	2	71	3	8	9	12	9	.57	9	.287	.340	.358
1994 New York	NL	103	410	105	13	3	3	(1	2)	133	47	33	39	33	3	62	2	5	6	1	11	.08	5	.256	.310	.324
1995 New York	NL	135	509	146	21	5	3	(2	1)	186	66	56	60	35	4	76	1	13	3	8	3	.73	14	.287	.332	.365
1996 NYM-Cle		144	542	161	17	8	1	(1	0)	197	70	45	68	35	0	82	3	10	3	15	7	.68	8	.297	.341	.363
1997 San Francisco	NL	151	568	151	19	7	5	(1	4)	199	77	50	62	48	1	87	0	13	1	8	8	.50	13	.266	.323	.350
1998 Los Angeles	NL	67	237	62	9	0	3	(0	3)	80	30	29	25	17	0	35	1	10	2	7	3	.70	4	.262	.311	.338
1999 Los Angeles	NL	94	266	67	9	0	1	(0	1)	79	27	29	23	20	0	23	1	9	2	2	1	.67	9	.252	.304	.297
2000 LA-NYY		113	267	67	10	2	0	(0	0)	81	32	14	23	22	3	43	1	5	2	6	7	.46	6	.251	.308	.303
2001 Houston	NL	107	256	71	8	3	1	(1	0)	88	38	14	29	15	0	33	2	9	0	3	2	.60	6	.277	.322	.344
2002 Houston	NL	125	406	123	19	2	5	(4	1)	161	53	37	52	24	2	40	1	5	2	3	5	.38	5	.303	.342	.397
2003 Houston	NL	91	189	47	7	3	3	(2	1)	69	14	26	23	8	3	22	1	4	1	0	1	.00	5	.249	.281	.365
1996 New York	NL	96	363	110	12	6	1	(1	0)	137	47	32	49	28	0	58	3	6	2	9	5	.64	6	.303	.356	.377
1996 Cleveland	AL	48	179	51	5	2	0	(0	0)	60	23	13	19	7	0	24	0	4	1	6	2	.75	2	.285	.310	.335
2000 Los Angeles	NL	40	93	19	2	1	0	(0	0)	23	9	4	6	10	3	15	1	2	0	1	0	1.00	3	.204	.288	.247
2000 New York	AL	73	174	48	8	1	0	(0	0)	58	23	10	17	12	0	28	0	3	2	5	7	.42	3	.276	.319	.333
15 ML YEARS		1504	4692	1276	167	42	30	(14	16)	1617	565	416	509	326	21	636	16	99	34	71	59	.55	90	.272	.319	.345

Luis Vizcaino

Pitches: R **Bats:** R **Pos:** RP-75   **Ht:** 5'11" **Wt:** 174 **Born:** 8/6/74 **Age:** 29

Year Team	Lg	G	GS	CG	GF	IP	BFP	H	R	ER	HR	SH	SF	HB	TBB	IBB	SO	WP	Bk	W	L	Pct	ShO	Sv-Op	Hld	ERC	ERA
1999 Oakland	AL	1	0	0	1	3.1	16	3	2	2	1	0	0	0	3	0	2	1	0	0	0	-	0	0-0	0	7.01	5.40
2000 Oakland	AL	12	0	0	1	19.1	96	25	17	16	2	0	1	2	11	0	18	1	0	0	1	.000	0	0-0	0	6.83	7.45
2001 Oakland	AL	36	0	0	15	36.2	156	38	19	19	8	0	1	0	12	1	31	3	0	2	1	.667	0	1-1	3	4.80	4.66
2002 Milwaukee	NL	76	0	0	30	81.1	326	55	27	27	6	3	3	3	30	4	79	3	2	5	3	.625	0	5-6	19	2.20	2.99
2003 Milwaukee	NL	75	0	0	21	62.0	272	64	45	44	16	2	1	1	25	3	61	3	0	4	3	.571	0	0-6	9	5.37	6.39
5 ML YEARS		200	0	0	68	202.2	866	185	110	108	33	5	6	6	81	8	191	11	2	11	8	.579	0	6-13	31	4.06	4.80

Omar Vizquel

Bats: B **Throws:** R **Pos:** SS-64; PH-1   **Ht:** 5'9" **Wt:** 175 **Born:** 4/24/67 **Age:** 37

Year Team	Lg	G	AB	H	2B	3B	HR	(Hm	Rd)	TB	R	RBI	RC	TBB	IBB	SO	HBP	SH	SF	SB	CS	SB%	GDP	Avg	OBP	Slg
2003 Lake County*	A-	4	14	1	0	0	0	(-	-)	1	0	0	0	1	0	2	0	0	0	1	0	1.00	0	.071	.133	.071
1989 Seattle	AL	143	387	85	7	3	1	(1	0)	101	45	20	25	28	0	40	1	13	2	1	4	.20	6	.220	.273	.261
1990 Seattle	AL	81	255	63	3	2	2	(0	2)	76	19	18	22	18	0	22	0	10	2	4	1	.80	7	.247	.295	.298
1991 Seattle	AL	142	426	98	16	4	1	(1	0)	125	42	41	39	45	0	37	0	8	3	7	2	.78	8	.230	.302	.293
1992 Seattle	AL	136	483	142	20	4	0	(0	0)	170	49	21	54	32	0	38	2	9	1	15	13	.54	14	.294	.340	.352
1993 Seattle	AL	158	560	143	14	2	2	(1	1)	167	68	31	53	50	2	71	4	13	3	12	14	.46	7	.255	.319	.298
1994 Cleveland	AL	69	286	78	10	1	1	(0	1)	93	39	33	32	23	0	23	0	11	2	13	4	.76	4	.273	.325	.325
1995 Cleveland	AL	136	542	144	28	0	6	(3	3)	190	87	56	70	59	0	59	1	10	10	29	11	.73	4	.266	.333	.351
1996 Cleveland	AL	151	542	161	36	1	9	(2	7)	226	98	64	87	56	0	42	4	12	9	35	9	.80	10	.297	.362	.417
1997 Cleveland	AL	153	565	158	23	6	5	(3	2)	208	89	49	75	57	1	58	2	16	2	43	12	.78	16	.280	.347	.368
1998 Cleveland	AL	151	576	166	30	6	2	(0	2)	214	86	50	82	62	1	64	4	12	6	37	12	.76	10	.288	.358	.372
1999 Cleveland	AL	144	574	191	36	4	5	(3	2)	250	112	66	106	65	0	50	1	17	7	42	9	.82	8	.333	.397	.436
2000 Cleveland	AL	156	613	176	27	3	7	(1	6)	230	101	66	92	87	0	72	5	7	5	22	10	.69	13	.287	.377	.375
2001 Cleveland	AL	155	611	156	26	8	2	(2	0)	204	84	50	66	61	0	72	2	15	4	13	9	.59	14	.255	.323	.334
2002 Cleveland	AL	151	582	160	31	5	14	(9	5)	243	85	72	91	56	3	64	8	7	10	18	10	.64	7	.275	.341	.418
2003 Cleveland	AL	64	250	61	13	2	2	(2	0)	84	43	19	25	29	0	20	0	5	1	8	3	.73	11	.244	.321	.336
15 ML YEARS		1990	7252	1982	320	51	59	(28	31)	2581	1047	656	919	728	7	732	34	165	67	299	123	.71	139	.273	.340	.356

Ryan Vogelsong

Pitches: R **Bats:** R **Pos:** SP-5; RP-1   **Ht:** 6'3" **Wt:** 205 **Born:** 7/22/77 **Age:** 26

Year Team	Lg	G	GS	CG	GF	IP	BFP	H	R	ER	HR	SH	SF	HB	TBB	IBB	SO	WP	Bk	W	L	Pct	ShO	Sv-Op	Hld	ERC	ERA
2003 Nashville*	AAA	26	26	1	0	149.0	643	142	75	71	12	9	5	6	54	5	146	6	0	12	8	.600	1	0- -	0	3.59	4.29
2000 San Francisco	NL	4	0	0	0	6.0	24	4	0	0	0	0	0	0	2	0	6	0	0	0	0	-	0	0-0	0	1.57	0.00
2001 SF-Pit		15	2	0	0	34.2	164	39	0	26	6	0	0	0	20	0	24	0	0	0	5	.000	0	0-0	0	5.92	6.75
2003 Pittsburgh	NL	6	5	0	0	22.0	108	30	19	16	1	3	1	2	9	3	15	1	0	2	2	.500	0	0-0	0	5.72	6.55
2001 San Francisco	NL	13	0	0	0	28.2	130	29	0	18	5	0	0	0	14	0	17	0	0	0	3	.000	0	0-0	0	4.89	5.65
2001 Pittsburgh	NL	2	2	0	0	6.0	34	10	0	8	1	0	0	0	6	0	7	0	0	0	2	.000	0	0-0	0	11.42	12.00
3 ML YEARS		25	7	0	0	62.2	296	73	19	42	7	3	1	2	31	3	45	1	0	2	7	.222	0	0-0	0	5.38	6.03

Brad Voyles

Pitches: R **Bats:** R **Pos:** RP-8; SP-3   **Ht:** 6'0" **Wt:** 195 **Born:** 12/30/76 **Age:** 27

Year Team	Lg	G	GS	CG	GF	IP	BFP	H	R	ER	HR	SH	SF	HB	TBB	IBB	SO	WP	Bk	W	L	Pct	ShO	Sv-Op	Hld	ERC	ERA
2003 Omaha*	AAA	29	9	1	14	81.1	326	68	27	27	5	5	2	1	24	0	69	2	1	2	2	.500	0	2- -	-	2.67	2.99
2001 Kansas City	AL	7	0	0	3	9.1	40	5	4	4	1	0	0	1	8	0	6	0	0	0	0	-	0	0-0	1	3.85	3.86
2002 Kansas City	AL	22	0	0	6	27.2	131	31	21	20	5	2	0	2	18	1	26	1	0	0	2	.000	0	1-2	1	6.72	6.51
2003 Kansas City	AL	11	3	0	4	31.1	158	47	29	26	6	2	2	1	18	1	24	3	0	0	2	.000	0	0-0	0	8.71	7.47
3 ML YEARS		40	3	0	13	68.1	329	83	54	50	12	4	2	4	44	2	56	4	0	0	4	.000	0	1-2	2	7.19	6.59

Doug Waechter

Pitches: R **Bats:** R **Pos:** SP-5; RP-1   **Ht:** 6'4" **Wt:** 209 **Born:** 1/28/81 **Age:** 23

Year Team	Lg	G	GS	CG	GF	IP	BFP	H	R	ER	HR	SH	SF	HB	TBB	IBB	SO	WP	Bk	W	L	Pct	ShO	Sv-Op	Hld	ERC	ERA
1999 Princeton	R+	11	7	0	0	35.0	189	46	45	38	2	0	5	4	35	0	38	21	1	0	5	.000	0	0- -	-	8.47	9.77
2000 Hudson Val	A-	14	14	2	0	72.2	302	53	23	19	2	2	1	4	37	0	58	7	3	4	4	.500	2	0- -	-	2.80	2.35
2001 Chrlstn - SC	A	26	26	1	0	153.1	684	179	97	74	14	7	6	5	38	1	107	12	3	8	11	.421	0	0- -	-	4.35	4.34
2002 Chrlstn - SC	A	7	7	0	0	36.1	162	39	20	14	2	2	1	2	16	3	36	1	2	3	3	.500	0	0- -	-	4.39	3.47
2002 Bakersfield	A+	17	17	0	0	108.1	466	114	43	32	9	7	2	1	29	0	101	8	0	6	3	.667	0	0- -	-	3.70	2.66
2002 Orlando	AA	4	4	1	0	18.0	93	27	20	18	4	0	0	0	13	0	18	3	1	1	3	.250	0	0- -	-	9.59	9.00
2003 Durham	AAA	10	10	0	0	51.1	210	51	25	19	9	2	1	0	12	0	35	3	0	3	3	.500	0	0- -	-	3.95	3.33
2003 Orlando	AA	13	12	0	0	76.1	314	74	39	35	6	3	3	1	19	0	45	1	0	5	3	.625	0	0- -	-	3.27	4.13
2003 Tampa Bay	AL	6	5	1	0	35.1	145	29	13	13	4	0	0	1	15	0	29	0	0	3	2	.600	1	0-0	-	3.48	3.31

Billy Wagner

Pitches: L **Bats:** L **Pos:** RP-78   **Ht:** 5'11" **Wt:** 195 **Born:** 7/25/71 **Age:** 32

Year Team	Lg	G	GS	CG	GF	IP	BFP	H	R	ER	HR	SH	SF	HB	TBB	IBB	SO	WP	Bk	W	L	Pct	ShO	Sv-Op	Hld	ERC	ERA
1995 Houston	NL	1	0	0	0	0.1	1	0	0	0	0	0	0	0	0	0	0	0	0	0	0	-	0	0- -	0	0.00	0.00
1996 Houston	NL	37	0	0	20	51.2	212	28	16	14	6	7	2	3	30	2	67	1	0	2	2	.500	0	9-13	3	2.61	2.44
1997 Houston	NL	62	0	0	49	66.1	277	49	23	21	5	3	1	3	30	1	106	3	0	7	8	.467	0	23-29	1	2.85	2.85
1998 Houston	NL	58	0	0	50	60.0	247	46	19	18	6	4	0	0	25	1	97	2	0	4	3	.571	0	30-35	1	2.87	2.70
1999 Houston	NL	66	0	0	55	74.2	286	35	14	13	5	2	1	1	23	1	124	2	0	4	1	.800	0	39-42	1	1.20	1.57
2000 Houston	NL	28	0	0	19	27.2	129	28	19	19	6	0	0	1	18	0	28	7	0	2	4	.333	0	6-15	0	6.15	6.18
2001 Houston	NL	64	0	0	58	62.2	251	44	19	19	5	3	1	5	20	0	79	3	0	2	5	.286	0	39-41	0	2.42	2.73
2002 Houston	NL	70	0	0	61	75.0	289	51	21	21	7	2	3	2	22	5	88	6	0	4	2	.667	0	35-41	0	2.08	2.52
2003 Houston	NL	78	0	0	67	86.0	335	52	18	17	8	1	0	3	23	5	105	4	0	1	4	.200	0	44-47	0	1.63	1.78
9 ML YEARS		464	0	0	379	504.1	2027	333	149	142	48	22	8	18	191	15	694	28	0	26	29	.473	0	225-263	6	2.29	2.53

Ryan Wagner

Pitches: R **Bats:** R **Pos:** RP-17   **Ht:** 6'4" **Wt:** 210 **Born:** 7/15/82 **Age:** 21

Year Team	Lg	G	GS	CG	GF	IP	BFP	H	R	ER	HR	SH	SF	HB	TBB	IBB	SO	WP	Bk	W	L	Pct	ShO	Sv-Op	Hld	ERC	ERA
2003 Chattanooga	AA	5	0	0	1	5.0	19	2	1	0	0	0	0	0	2	0	6	0	0	1	0	1.000	0	0- -	-	0.95	0.00
2003 Louisville	AAA	4	0	0	0	4.0	16	5	2	2	0	0	0	0	0	0	4	0	0	0	1	.000	0	0- -	-	3.37	4.50
2003 Cincinnati	NL	17	0	0	3	21.2	88	13	4	4	2	0	1	0	12	1	25	4	0	2	0	1.000	0	0-1	6	2.46	1.66

Tim Wakefield

Pitches: R **Bats:** R **Pos:** SP-33; RP-2   **Ht:** 6'2" **Wt:** 214 **Born:** 8/2/66 **Age:** 37

Year Team	Lg	G	GS	CG	GF	IP	BFP	H	R	ER	HR	SH	SF	HB	TBB	IBB	SO	WP	Bk	W	L	Pct	ShO	Sv-Op	Hld	ERC	ERA
1992 Pittsburgh	NL	13	13	4	0	92.0	373	76	26	22	3	6	4	1	35	1	51	3	1	8	1	.889	1	0-0	0	2.72	2.15
1993 Pittsburgh	NL	24	20	3	1	128.1	595	145	83	80	14	7	5	9	75	2	59	6	0	6	11	.353	2	0-0	0	5.97	5.61
1995 Boston	AL	27	27	6	0	195.1	804	163	76	64	22	3	7	9	68	0	119	11	0	16	8	.667	1	0-0	0	3.28	2.95
1996 Boston	AL	32	32	6	0	211.2	963	238	151	121	38	1	9	12	90	0	140	4	1	14	13	.519	0	0-0	0	5.68	5.14
1997 Boston	AL	35	29	4	2	201.1	866	193	109	95	24	3	7	16	87	5	151	6	0	12	15	.444	2	0-0	1	4.47	4.25
1998 Boston	AL	36	33	2	1	216.0	939	211	123	110	30	1	8	14	79	1	146	6	1	17	8	.680	0	0-0	0	4.30	4.58
1999 Boston	AL	49	17	0	28	140.0	635	146	93	79	19	1	8	5	72	2	104	1	0	6	11	.353	0	15-18	0	5.12	5.08
2000 Boston	AL	51	17	0	13	159.1	706	170	107	97	31	4	8	4	65	3	102	4	0	6	10	.375	0	0-1	3	5.23	5.48
2001 Boston	AL	45	17	0	5	168.2	732	156	84	73	13	3	9	18	73	5	148	5	1	9	12	.429	0	3-5	3	4.02	3.90
2002 Boston	AL	45	15	0	10	163.1	657	121	57	51	15	1	4	9	51	2	134	5	2	11	5	.688	0	3-5	5	2.54	2.81
2003 Boston	AL	35	33	0	2	202.1	872	193	106	92	23	2	4	12	71	0	169	8	0	11	7	.611	0	1-1	0	3.92	4.09
11 ML YEARS		392	253	25	62	1878.1	8142	1812	1015	884	232	32	73	109	766	21	1323	59	6	116	101	.535	6	22-30	12	4.29	4.24

Matt Walbeck

Bats: B **Throws:** R **Pos:** C-55; PH-5; PR-2   **Ht:** 5'11" **Wt:** 188 **Born:** 10/2/69 **Age:** 34

Year Team	Lg	G	AB	H	2B	3B	HR	(Hm	Rd)	TB	R	RBI	RC	TBB	IBB	SO	HBP	SH	SF	SB	CS	SB%	GDP	Avg	OBP	Slg
2003 Toledo*	AAA	4	12	5	0	0	0	(-	-)	5	2	1	3	3	0	2	0	0	0	0	0	-	0	.417	.533	.417
1993 Chicago	NL	11	30	6	2	0	1	(1	0)	11	2	6	2	1	0	6	0	0	0	0	0	-	0	.200	.226	.367
1994 Minnesota	AL	97	338	69	12	0	5	(0	5)	96	31	35	20	17	1	37	2	1	1	1	1	.50	7	.204	.246	.284
1995 Minnesota	AL	115	393	101	18	1	1	(1	0)	124	40	44	35	25	2	71	1	1	2	3	1	.75	11	.257	.302	.316
1996 Minnesota	AL	63	215	48	10	0	2	(1	1)	64	25	24	14	9	0	34	0	1	2	3	1	.75	6	.223	.252	.298
1997 Detroit	AL	47	137	38	3	0	3	(1	2)	50	18	10	16	12	0	19	0	0	2	3	3	.50	4	.277	.331	.365
1998 Anaheim	AL	108	338	87	15	2	6	(3	3)	124	41	46	39	30	0	68	2	5	5	1	1	.50	9	.257	.317	.367
1999 Anaheim	AL	107	288	69	8	1	3	(1	2)	88	26	22	24	26	1	46	3	3	1	2	3	.40	12	.240	.308	.306
2000 Anaheim	AL	47	146	29	5	0	6	(2	4)	52	17	12	11	7	0	22	1	1	0	0	1	.00	2	.199	.240	.356
2001 Philadelphia	NL	1	1	1	0	0	0	(0	0)	1	0	0	1	0	0	0	0	0	0	0	0	-	0	1.000	1.000	1.000
2002 Detroit	AL	27	85	20	2	0	0	(0	0)	22	4	3	4	3	0	14	0	0	1	0	0	-	2	.235	.258	.259
2003 Detroit	AL	59	138	24	4	1	1	(1	0)	33	11	6	2	3	0	26	1	2	0	1	1	.00	3	.174	.197	.239
11 ML YEARS		682	2109	492	79	5	28	(11	17)	665	215	208	168	133	4	343	10	14	14	13	12	.52	56	.233	.280	.315

Jamie Walker

Pitches: L **Bats:** L **Pos:** RP-78   **Ht:** 6'2" **Wt:** 190 **Born:** 7/1/71 **Age:** 32

Year Team	Lg	G	GS	CG	GF	IP	BFP	H	R	ER	HR	SH	SF	HB	TBB	IBB	SO	WP	Bk	W	L	Pct	ShO	Sv-Op	Hld	ERC	ERA
1997 Kansas City	AL	50	0	0	15	43.0	197	46	28	26	6	2	2	3	20	3	24	2	0	3	3	.500	0	0-1	3	5.10	5.44
1998 Kansas City	AL	6	2	0	2	17.1	86	30	20	19	5	1	1	2	3	0	15	0	0	0	1	.000	0	0-0	1	9.69	9.87

Year Team	Lg	G	GS	CG	GF	IP	BFP	H	R	ER	HR	SH	SF	HB	TBB	IBB	SO	WP	Bk	W	L	Pct	ShO	Sv-Op	Hld	ERC	ERA
2002 Detroit	AL	57	0	0	16	43.2	175	32	19	18	9	0	1	4	9	1	40	1	1	1	1	.500	0	1-4	5	2.86	3.71
2003 Detroit	AL	78	0	0	19	65.0	273	61	30	24	9	5	2	2	17	1	45	1	0	4	3	.571	0	3-7	12	3.51	3.32
4 ML YEARS		191	2	0	52	169.0	731	169	97	87	29	8	6	11	49	5	124	4	1	8	8	.500	0	4-12	21	4.28	4.63

Kevin Walker

Pitches: L Bats: L Pos: RP-11   Ht: 6'4" Wt: 190 Born: 9/20/76 Age: 27

Year Team	Lg	G	GS	CG	GF	IP	BFP	H	R	ER	HR	SH	SF	HB	TBB	IBB	SO	WP	Bk	W	L	Pct	ShO	Sv-Op	Hld	ERC	ERA
2003 Portland*	AAA	34	1	0	7	46.1	198	53	24	21	5	1	3	2	10	1	43	2	0	3	1	.750	0	0--	-	4.39	4.08
2003 Lk Elsinore*	A+	4	0	0	0	4.0	21	6	6	6	1	0	0	1	2	0	3	0	0	0	0	-	0	0--	-	9.88	13.50
2000 San Diego	NL	70	0	0	14	66.2	287	49	35	31	5	4	2	5	38	6	56	2	1	7	1	.875	0	0-0	19	3.23	4.19
2001 San Diego	NL	16	0	0	5	12.0	49	5	4	4	0	0	0	0	8	2	17	0	1	0	0	-	0	0-1	4	1.33	3.00
2002 San Diego	NL	11	0	0	1	8.0	42	12	6	5	2	1	0	0	5	1	11	1	0	0	1	.000	0	0-1	1	8.79	5.63
2003 San Diego	NL	11	0	0	2	6.2	30	5	4	4	1	0	0	0	5	0	5	0	0	0	0	-	0	0-0	0	4.31	5.40
4 ML YEARS		108	0	0	22	93.1	408	71	49	44	8	5	2	5	56	9	89	3	2	7	2	.778	0	0-2	24	3.43	4.24

Larry Walker

Bats: L Throws: R Pos: RF-132; PH-12; DH-2   Ht: 6'3" Wt: 233 Born: 12/1/66 Age: 37

Year Team	Lg	G	AB	H	2B	3B	HR	(Hm	Rd)	TB	R	RBI	RC	TBB	IBB	SO	HBP	SH	SF	SB	CS	SB%	GDP	Avg	OBP	Slg
1989 Montreal	NL	20	47	8	0	0	0	(0	0)	8	4	4	2	5	0	13	1	3	0	1	1	.50	0	.170	.264	.170
1990 Montreal	NL	133	419	101	18	3	19	(9	10)	182	59	51	60	49	5	112	5	3	2	21	7	.75	8	.241	.326	.434
1991 Montreal	NL	137	487	141	30	2	16	(5	11)	223	59	64	77	42	2	102	5	1	4	14	9	.61	7	.290	.349	.458
1992 Montreal	NL	143	528	159	31	4	23	(13	10)	267	85	93	93	41	10	97	6	0	8	18	6	.75	9	.301	.353	.506
1993 Montreal	NL	138	490	130	24	5	22	(13	9)	230	85	86	89	80	20	76	6	0	6	29	7	.81	8	.265	.371	.469
1994 Montreal	NL	103	395	127	44	2	19	(7	12)	232	76	86	88	47	5	74	4	0	6	15	5	.75	8	.322	.394	.587
1995 Colorado	NL	131	494	151	31	5	36	(24	12)	300	96	101	108	49	13	72	14	0	5	16	3	.84	13	.306	.381	.607
1996 Colorado	NL	83	272	75	18	4	18	(12	6)	155	58	58	53	20	2	58	9	0	3	18	2	.90	7	.276	.342	.570
1997 Colorado	NL	153	568	208	46	4	49	(20	29)	409	143	130	166	78	14	90	14	0	4	33	8	.80	15	.366	.452	.720
1998 Colorado	NL	130	454	165	46	3	23	(17	6)	286	113	67	117	64	2	61	4	2	4	14	4	.78	11	.363	.445	.630
1999 Colorado	NL	127	438	166	26	4	37	(26	11)	311	108	115	127	57	8	52	12	0	6	11	4	.73	12	.379	.458	.710
2000 Colorado	NL	87	314	97	21	7	9	(7	2)	159	64	51	61	46	4	40	9	0	3	5	5	.50	12	.309	.409	.506
2001 Colorado	NL	142	497	174	35	3	38	(20	18)	329	107	123	138	82	6	103	14	0	8	14	5	.74	9	.350	.449	.662
2002 Colorado	NL	136	477	161	40	4	26	(18	8)	287	95	104	114	65	6	73	7	0	4	6	5	.55	8	.338	.421	.602
2003 Colorado	NL	143	454	129	25	7	16	(8	8)	216	86	79	97	98	14	87	11	0	1	4	7	.64	9	.284	.422	.476
15 ML YEARS		1806	6334	1992	435	57	351	(199	152)	3594	1238	1212	1390	823	111	1110	121	7	62	222	75	.75	136	.314	.400	.567

Pete Walker

Pitches: R Bats: R Pos: RP-16; SP-7   Ht: 6'2" Wt: 195 Born: 4/8/69 Age: 35

Year Team	Lg	G	GS	CG	GF	IP	BFP	H	R	ER	HR	SH	SF	HB	TBB	IBB	SO	WP	Bk	W	L	Pct	ShO	Sv-Op	Hld	ERC	ERA
2003 Syracuse*	AAA	5	5	0	0	13.1	57	15	10	10	2	0	0	0	3	0	8	0	0	0	1	.000	0	0--	-	4.41	6.75
2003 New Haven*	AA	2	2	0	0	2.0	8	3	2	2	0	0	0	1	0	0	1	0	0	0	1	.000	0	0--	-	5.09	9.00
1995 New York	NL	13	0	0	10	17.2	79	24	9	9	3	0	1	0	5	0	5	0	0	1	0	1.000	0	0-0	1	6.35	4.58
1996 San Diego	NL	1	0	0	0	0.2	5	0	0	0	0	0	0	0	3	0	1	0	0	0	0	-	0	0-0	0	13.05	0.00
2000 Colorado	NL	3	0	0	1	4.2	27	10	9	9	1	0	0	0	4	0	2	0	0	0	0	-	0	0-0	0	15.29	17.36
2001 New York	NL	2	0	0	1	6.2	25	6	2	2	0	0	0	0	0	0	4	0	0	0	0	-	0	0-0	0	1.63	2.70
2002 NYM-Tor		38	20	0	4	140.1	599	145	73	68	18	4	6	3	51	5	80	2	1	10	5	.667	0	1-1	3	4.41	4.36
2003 Toronto	AL	23	7	0	2	55.1	242	59	31	30	11	2	1	2	24	2	29	2	0	2	2	.500	0	0-0	2	5.51	4.88
2002 New York	NL	1	0	0	0	1.0	5	2	1	1	0	0	0	0	0	0	0	0	0	0	0	-	0	0-0	0	7.48	9.00
2002 Toronto	AL	37	20	0	4	139.1	594	143	72	67	18	4	6	3	51	5	80	2	1	10	5	.667	0	1-1	3	4.39	4.33
6 ML YEARS		80	27	0	18	225.1	977	244	124	118	33	6	8	5	87	7	121	4	1	13	7	.650	0	1-1	6	4.94	4.71

Todd Walker

Bats: L Throws: R Pos: 2B-139; PH-7; DH-2   Ht: 6'0" Wt: 190 Born: 5/25/73 Age: 31

Year Team	Lg	G	AB	H	2B	3B	HR	(Hm	Rd)	TB	R	RBI	RC	TBB	IBB	SO	HBP	SH	SF	SB	CS	SB%	GDP	Avg	OBP	Slg
1996 Minnesota	AL	25	82	21	6	0	0	(0	0)	27	8	6	7	4	0	13	0	0	3	2	0	1.00	4	.256	.281	.329
1997 Minnesota	AL	52	156	37	7	1	3	(1	2)	55	15	16	16	11	1	30	1	1	2	7	0	1.00	5	.237	.288	.353
1998 Minnesota	AL	143	528	167	41	3	12	(7	5)	250	85	62	90	47	9	65	2	0	4	19	7	.73	13	.316	.372	.473
1999 Minnesota	AL	143	531	148	37	4	6	(4	2)	211	62	46	70	52	5	83	1	0	2	18	10	.64	15	.279	.343	.397
2000 Min-Col		80	248	72	11	4	9	(5	4)	118	42	44	43	27	0	29	1	1	6	7	1	.88	5	.290	.355	.476
2001 Col-Cin	NL	151	551	163	35	2	17	(13	4)	253	93	75	84	51	1	82	1	4	3	8	5	.11	14	.296	.355	.459
2002 Cincinnati	NL	155	612	183	42	3	11	(7	4)	264	79	64	89	50	7	81	3	7	3	8	5	.50	17	.299	.353	.431
2003 Boston	AL	144	587	166	38	4	13	(6	7)	251	92	85	83	48	0	54	1	1	10	1	1	.50	17	.283	.333	.428
2000 Minnesota	AL	23	77	18	1	0	2	(0	2)	25	14	8	7	7	0	10	0	0	3	3	0	1.00	3	.234	.287	.325
2000 Colorado	NL	57	171	54	10	4	7	(5	2)	93	28	36	36	20	0	19	1	1	3	4	1	.80	2	.316	.385	.544
2001 Colorado	NL	85	290	86	18	2	12	(10	2)	144	52	43	47	25	1	40	0	3	3	1	3	.25	8	.297	.349	.497
2001 Cincinnati	NL	66	261	77	17	0	5	(3	2)	109	41	32	37	26	0	42	1	1	0	0	5	.00	6	.295	.361	.418
8 ML YEARS		893	3295	957	217	21	71	(43	28)	1429	476	398	482	290	23	437	10	14	33	63	32	.66	82	.290	.346	.434

Les Walrond

Pitches: L Bats: L Pos: RP-7   Ht: 6'0" Wt: 195 Born: 11/7/76 Age: 27

Year Team	Lg	G	GS	CG	GF	IP	BFP	H	R	ER	HR	SH	SF	HB	TBB	IBB	SO	WP	Bk	W	L	Pct	ShO	Sv-Op	Hld	ERC	ERA
1998 New Jersey	A-	13	10	0	0	51.2	228	52	31	23	1	1	2	0	24	0	52	3	0	2	4	.333	0	0--	-	3.73	4.01
1999 Peoria	A	21	20	0	0	109.0	489	115	77	69	12	2	5	3	59	0	78	6	0	7	10	.412	0	0--	-	5.19	5.70
2000 Potomac	A+	27	27	0	0	151.0	632	134	66	56	9	1	3	7	54	0	153	12	1	10	5	.667	0	0--	-	3.23	3.34

Year Team	Lg	G	GS	CG	GF	IP	BFP	H	R	ER	HR	SH	SF	HB	TBB	IBB	SO	WP	Bk	W	L	Pct	ShO	Sv-Op	Hld	ERC	ERA
2001 New Haven	AA	16	16	1	0	81.1	354	68	41	35	5	3	3	2	46	0	67	6	0	2	8	.200	0	0--	-	3.61	3.87
2002 New Haven	AA	4	4	0	0	22.1	96	19	8	6	2	0	0	0	10	0	31	3	0	2	1	.667	0	0--	-	3.30	2.42
2002 Memphis	AAA	28	18	0	2	123.0	538	127	75	68	20	3	1	1	63	2	111	8	0	8	7	.533	0	0--	-	5.30	4.98
2003 Tennessee	AA	4	0	0	0	6.2	28	4	2	2	1	0	0	0	4	0	7	0	0	-	-	-	0	0--	-	2.97	2.70
2003 Wichita	AA	2	2	0	0	11.0	43	7	4	2	2	0	0	0	2	0	9	2	0	2	0	1.000	0	0--	-	1.81	3.27
2003 Memphis	AAA	10	1	0	2	17.1	71	12	2	2	0	0	1	0	7	1	14	0	0	0	0	-	0	0--	-	1.77	1.04
2003 Omaha	AAA	18	0	0	5	25.2	109	19	9	7	1	1	1	1	9	0	20	4	1	3	1	.750	0	2--	-	2.17	2.45
2003 Kansas City	AL	7	0	0	2	8.0	41	11	9	9	2	0	0	0	7	1	6	1	0	0	2	.000	0	0-0	1	9.58	10.13

Daryle Ward

Bats: L **Throws:** L **Pos:** PH-29; 1B-13; LF-11   **Ht:** 6'2" **Wt:** 240 **Born:** 6/27/75 **Age:** 29

Year Team	Lg	G	AB	H	2B	3B	HR	(Hm	Rd)	TB	R	RBI	RC	TBB	IBB	SO	HBP	SH	SF	SB	CS	SB%	GDP	Avg	OBP	Slg
2003 Las Vegas*	AAA	34	128	38	9	0	4	(-	-)	59	16	24	20	10	1	22	0	0	2	0	0	-	3	.297	.343	.461
2003 Jacksonville*	AA	4	16	2	0	0	0	(-	-)	2	0	1	0	0	0	3	0	0	0	0	0	-	0	.125	.125	.125
1998 Houston	NL	4	3	1	0	0	0	(0	0)	1	1	0	1	1	0	2	0	0	0	0	0	-	0	.333	.500	.333
1999 Houston	NL	64	150	41	6	0	8	(2	6)	71	11	30	21	9	0	31	0	0	2	0	0	-	3	.273	.311	.473
2000 Houston	NL	119	264	68	10	2	20	(13	7)	142	36	47	40	15	2	61	0	0	2	0	0	-	6	.258	.295	.538
2001 Houston	NL	95	213	56	15	0	9	(5	4)	98	21	39	31	19	4	48	1	0	2	0	0	-	3	.263	.323	.460
2002 Houston	NL	136	453	125	31	0	12	(9	3)	192	41	72	61	33	5	82	1	0	4	1	3	.25	9	.276	.324	.424
2003 Los Angeles	NL	52	109	20	1	0	0	(0	0)	21	6	9	0	3	0	19	1	0	1	0	0	-	4	.183	.211	.193
6 ML YEARS		470	1192	311	63	2	49	(29	20)	525	116	197	154	80	11	243	3	0	11	1	3	.25	25	.261	.306	.440

John Wasdin

Pitches: R **Bats:** R **Pos:** SP-2; RP-1   **Ht:** 6'2" **Wt:** 196 **Born:** 8/5/72 **Age:** 31

Year Team	Lg	G	GS	CG	GF	IP	BFP	H	R	ER	HR	SH	SF	HB	TBB	IBB	SO	WP	Bk	W	L	Pct	ShO	Sv-Op	Hld	ERC	ERA
2003 Syracuse*	AAA	10	1	0	3	20.2	91	28	13	12	1	1	0	1	9	0	21	2	0	2	1	.667	0	0--	-	4.44	5.23
2003 Nashville*	AAA	18	18	3	0	112.1	462	101	46	38	4	4	7	3	24	4	116	1	0	8	4	.667	1	0--	-	2.45	3.04
1995 Oakland	AL	5	2	0	0	17.1	69	14	0	9	4	0	0	0	3	0	6	0	0	1	1	.500	0	0-0	0	2.91	4.67
1996 Oakland	AL	25	21	1	0	131.1	575	145	0	87	24	0	0	0	50	0	75	0	0	8	7	.533	0	0-0	0	5.22	5.96
1997 Boston	AL	53	7	0	0	124.2	534	121	0	61	18	0	0	0	38	0	84	0	0	4	6	.400	0	0-0	0	3.75	4.40
1998 Boston	AL	47	8	0	0	96.0	424	111	0	56	14	0	0	0	27	0	59	0	0	6	4	.600	0	0-0	0	4.73	5.25
1999 Boston	AL	45	0	0	0	74.1	302	66	0	34	14	0	0	0	18	0	57	0	0	8	3	.727	0	2-0	0	3.41	4.12
2000 Bos-Col		39	4	1	0	80.1	352	90	0	48	14	0	0	0	24	0	71	0	0	1	6	.143	0	1-0	0	4.82	5.38
2001 Col-Bal		44	0	0	0	74.0	330	86	0	42	11	0	0	0	24	0	64	0	0	3	2	.600	0	0-0	0	4.97	5.11
2003 Toronto	AL	3	2	0	0	5.0	35	16	13	13	2	0	1	0	4	0	5	0	0	0	1	.000	0	0-0	0	25.15	23.40
2000 Oakland	AL	25	1	0	0	44.2	198	48	0	25	8	0	0	0	15	0	36	0	0	1	3	.250	0	1-0	0	4.67	5.04
2000 Colorado	NL	14	3	1	0	35.2	154	42	0	23	6	0	0	0	9	0	35	0	0	0	3	.000	0	0-0	0	5.01	5.80
2001 Colorado	NL	18	0	0	0	24.1	110	32	0	19	7	0	0	0	8	0	17	0	0	2	1	.667	0	0-0	0	7.15	7.03
2001 Baltimore	AL	26	0	0	0	49.2	220	54	0	23	4	0	0	0	16	0	47	0	0	1	1	.500	0	0-0	0	4.00	4.17
8 ML YEARS		261	44	2	0	603.0	2621	649	13	350	101	0	1	0	188	0	421	0	0	31	30	.508	0	3-0	0	4.57	5.22

Jarrod Washburn

Pitches: L **Bats:** L **Pos:** SP-32   **Ht:** 6'1" **Wt:** 187 **Born:** 8/13/74 **Age:** 29

Year Team	Lg	G	GS	CG	GF	IP	BFP	H	R	ER	HR	SH	SF	HB	TBB	IBB	SO	WP	Bk	W	L	Pct	ShO	Sv-Op	Hld	ERC	ERA
1998 Anaheim	AL	15	11	0	0	74.0	317	70	40	38	11	2	3	3	27	1	48	0	0	6	3	.667	0	0-0	1	4.09	4.62
1999 Anaheim	AL	16	10	0	3	61.2	264	61	36	36	6	1	2	1	26	0	39	2	0	4	5	.444	0	0-0	1	4.20	5.25
2000 Anaheim	AL	14	14	0	0	84.1	340	64	38	35	16	1	3	1	37	0	49	1	0	7	2	.778	0	0-0	0	3.66	3.74
2001 Anaheim	AL	30	30	1	0	193.1	813	196	89	81	25	4	4	7	54	4	126	3	0	11	10	.524	0	0-0	0	4.03	3.77
2002 Anaheim	AL	32	32	1	0	206.0	852	183	75	72	19	4	7	3	59	1	139	5	1	18	6	.750	0	0-0	0	3.02	3.15
2003 Anaheim	AL	32	32	2	0	207.1	876	205	106	102	34	5	6	11	54	4	118	4	1	10	15	.400	0	0-0	0	4.07	4.43
6 ML YEARS		139	129	4	3	826.2	3462	779	384	364	111	17	25	26	257	10	519	15	2	56	41	.577	0	0-0	2	3.76	3.96

Mark Watson

Pitches: L **Bats:** R **Pos:** RP-2   **Ht:** 6'4" **Wt:** 215 **Born:** 1/23/74 **Age:** 30

Year Team	Lg	G	GS	CG	GF	IP	BFP	H	R	ER	HR	SH	SF	HB	TBB	IBB	SO	WP	Bk	W	L	Pct	ShO	Sv-Op	Hld	ERC	ERA
2003 Louisville*	AAA	44	0	0	23	53.2	226	53	30	26	1	6	7	1	14	1	46	3	0	4	4	.500	0	4--	-	2.95	4.36
2000 Cleveland	AL	6	0	0	1	6.1	33	12	7	6	0	0	0	1	2	0	4	0	0	0	1	.000	0	0-0	0	9.18	8.53
2002 Seattle	AL	3	0	0	1	4.0	24	8	8	8	1	0	1	0	4	0	1	1	0	1	0	1.000	0	0-0	0	14.76	18.00
2003 Cincinnati	NL	2	0	0	2	2.0	9	2	1	1	0	0	0	0	1	0	2	0	0	0	0	-	0	0-0	0	3.63	4.50
3 ML YEARS		11	0	0	4	12.1	66	22	16	15	1	0	1	1	7	0	7	1	0	1	1	.500	0	0-0	0	9.89	10.95

Matt Watson

Bats: L **Throws:** R **Pos:** PH-11; LF-5   **Ht:** 5'9" **Wt:** 200 **Born:** 11/5/78 **Age:** 25

Year Team	Lg	G	AB	H	2B	3B	HR	(Hm	Rd)	TB	R	RBI	RC	TBB	IBB	SO	HBP	SH	SF	SB	CS	SB%	GDP	Avg	OBP	Slg
1999 Vermont	A-	70	284	108	13	3	7	(-	-)	147	55	47	62	30	1	27	3	2	4	17	7	.71	6	.380	.439	.518
2000 Jupiter	A+	40	137	24	5	2	0	(-	-)	33	10	8	7	18	2	23	1	0	0	4	3	.57	6	.175	.276	.241
2001 Jupiter	A+	124	446	147	33	4	5	(-	-)	203	70	74	84	63	4	45	1	0	4	17	9	.65	11	.330	.417	.455
2002 Binghamton	AA	127	438	122	26	2	10	(-	-)	182	55	67	59	39	4	52	3	2	5	12	8	.60	14	.279	.339	.416
2002 Harrisburg	AA	1	4	1	0	0	0	(-	-)	1	1	0	0	0	0	0	0	0	0	0	0	-	0	.250	.250	.250
2003 St.Lucie	A+	2	7	2	0	1	0	(-	-)	4	2	2	2	1	0	2	0	0	1	1	0	1.00	0	.286	.333	.571
2003 Norfolk	AAA	74	254	75	18	1	11	(-	-)	128	40	55	47	23	1	23	8	1	5	2	2	.50	4	.295	.366	.504

BATTING

Year Team	Lg	G	AB	H	2B	3B	HR	(Hm Rd)	TB	R	RBI	RC	TBB	IBB	SO	HBP	SH	SF	SB	CS	SB%	GDP	Avg	OBP	Slg
2003 Brooklyn	A-	4	14	2	1	0	0	(- -)	3	0	0	1	2	0	3	1	0	0	2	1	.67	0	.143	.294	.214
2003 Binghamton	AA	8	28	11	3	0	1	(- -)	17	6	1	7	2	0	2	1	0	0	1	1	.50	0	.393	.452	.607
2003 New York	NL	15	23	4	2	0	0	(0 0)	6	0	2	1	1	0	5	0	1	0	0	0	-	1	.174	.208	.261

Justin Wayne

Pitches: R Bats: R Pos: SP-2   Ht: 6'3" Wt: 200 Born: 4/16/79 Age: 25

		HOW MUCH HE PITCHED						WHAT HE GAVE UP												THE RESULTS							
Year Team	Lg	G	GS	CG	GF	IP	BFP	H	R	ER	HR	SH	SF	HB	TBB	IBB	SO	WP	Bk	W	L	Pct	ShO	Sv-Op	Hld	ERC	ERA
2000 Jupiter	A+	5	5	0	0	26.1	112	26	22	17	2	1	1	0	11	0	24	1	0	0	3	.000	0	0--	-	3.97	5.81
2001 Jupiter	A+	8	7	0	0	41.2	166	31	16	14	0	0	2	3	9	0	35	2	0	2	3	.400	0	0--	-	1.75	3.02
2001 Harrisburg	AA	14	14	2	0	92.2	398	87	28	27	4	3	1	9	34	0	70	5	0	9	2	.818	0	0--	-	3.60	2.62
2002 Calgary	AAA	2	2	0	0	11.1	48	8	8	8	3	0	0	1	6	0	10	0	0	1	1	.000	0	0--	-	4.45	6.35
2002 Harrisburg	AA	17	17	0	0	98.2	401	74	41	26	7	6	9	6	32	0	47	5	2	5	2	.714	0	0--	-	2.52	2.37
2002 Portland	AA	7	7	1	0	42.2	184	43	26	23	3	2	4	5	13	0	30	2	1	3	3	.500	1	0--	-	4.02	4.85
2003 Jupiter	A+	1	1	0	0	6.0	24	6	0	0	0	0	0	0	0	0	4	0	0	0	0	-	0	0--	-	1.95	0.00
2003 Albuquerque	AAA	23	23	2	0	136.0	573	138	81	64	10	4	3	6	40	0	82	2	1	4	12	.250	0	0--	-	3.78	4.24
2002 Florida	NL	5	5	0	0	23.2	105	22	16	14	3	0	2	0	13	0	16	2	1	2	3	.400	0	0-0	0	4.41	5.32
2003 Florida	NL	2	2	0	0	5.1	31	9	7	7	1	0	1	1	5	0	1	1	0	0	2	.000	0	0-0	0	12.39	11.81
2 ML YEARS		7	7	0	0	29.0	136	31	23	21	4	0	3	1	18	0	17	3	1	2	5	.286	0	0-0	0	5.72	6.52

David Weathers

Pitches: R Bats: R Pos: RP-77   Ht: 6'3" Wt: 230 Born: 9/25/69 Age: 34

		HOW MUCH HE PITCHED						WHAT HE GAVE UP												THE RESULTS							
Year Team	Lg	G	GS	CG	GF	IP	BFP	H	R	ER	HR	SH	SF	HB	TBB	IBB	SO	WP	Bk	W	L	Pct	ShO	Sv-Op	Hld	ERC	ERA
1991 Toronto	AL	15	0	0	4	14.2	79	15	9	8	1	2	1	2	17	3	13	0	0	1	0	1.000	0	0-0	1	6.88	4.91
1992 Toronto	AL	2	0	0	0	3.1	15	5	3	3	1	0	0	0	2	0	3	0	0	0	0	-	0	0-0	0	10.97	8.10
1993 Florida	NL	14	6	0	2	45.2	202	57	26	26	3	2	0	1	13	1	34	6	0	2	3	.400	0	0-0	0	4.86	5.12
1994 Florida	NL	24	24	0	0	135.0	621	166	87	79	13	12	4	4	59	9	72	7	1	8	12	.400	0	0-0	0	5.52	5.27
1995 Florida	NL	28	15	0	0	90.1	419	104	68	60	8	7	3	5	52	3	60	3	0	4	5	.444	0	0-0	1	5.79	5.98
1996 Fla-NYY		42	12	0	9	88.2	409	108	60	54	8	5	2	6	42	5	53	3	0	2	4	.333	0	0-0	3	5.80	5.48
1997 NYY-Cle	AL	19	1	0	5	25.2	126	38	24	24	3	2	1	1	15	0	18	3	0	1	3	.250	0	0-1	0	8.27	8.42
1998 Cin-Mil	NL	44	9	0	9	110.0	492	130	69	60	6	6	6	2	41	3	94	7	2	6	5	.545	0	0-1	3	4.73	4.91
1999 Milwaukee	NL	63	0	0	14	93.0	414	102	49	48	14	4	4	2	38	3	74	1	1	7	4	.636	0	2-6	9	5.04	4.65
2000 Milwaukee	NL	69	0	0	23	76.1	320	73	29	26	7	4	1	2	32	8	50	0	0	3	5	.375	0	1-7	14	3.90	3.07
2001 Mil-ChC	NL	80	0	0	25	86.0	351	65	24	23	6	10	3	3	34	8	66	0	0	4	5	.444	0	4-10	16	2.59	2.41
2002 New York	NL	71	0	0	12	77.1	331	69	30	25	6	4	3	0	36	7	61	2	0	6	3	.667	0	0-5	18	3.60	2.91
2003 New York	NL	77	0	0	20	87.2	384	87	33	30	6	8	0	6	40	6	75	1	0	1	6	.143	0	7-9	26	4.21	3.08
1996 Florida	NL	31	8	0	8	71.1	319	85	41	36	7	5	1	4	28	4	40	2	0	2	2	.500	0	0-0	3	5.35	4.54
1996 New York	AL	11	4	0	1	17.1	90	23	19	18	1	0	1	2	14	1	13	1	0	0	2	.000	0	0-0	0	7.66	9.35
1997 New York	AL	10	0	0	3	9.0	47	15	10	10	1	0	0	0	7	0	4	2	0	0	1	.000	0	0-1	0	10.26	10.00
1997 Cleveland	AL	9	1	0	2	16.2	79	23	14	14	2	2	1	1	8	0	14	1	0	1	2	.333	0	0-0	0	7.23	7.56
1998 Cincinnati	NL	16	9	0	0	62.1	294	86	47	43	3	4	1	1	27	2	51	5	1	2	4	.333	0	0-0	3	6.04	6.21
1998 Milwaukee	NL	28	0	0	9	47.2	198	44	22	17	3	2	1	2	14	1	43	2	1	4	1	.800	0	0-1	3	3.15	3.21
2001 Milwaukee	NL	52	0	0	21	57.2	233	37	14	13	3	8	1	2	25	7	46	0	0	3	4	.429	0	4-7	10	2.01	2.03
2001 Chicago	NL	28	0	0	4	28.1	118	28	10	10	3	2	2	1	9	1	20	0	0	1	1	.500	0	0-3	6	3.90	3.18
13 ML YEARS		548	67	0	123	933.2	4163	1019	511	466	82	68	25	38	421	56	673	33	4	45	55	.450	0	14-39	91	4.79	4.49

Jeff Weaver

Pitches: R Bats: R Pos: SP-24; RP-8   Ht: 6'5" Wt: 200 Born: 8/22/76 Age: 27

		HOW MUCH HE PITCHED						WHAT HE GAVE UP												THE RESULTS							
Year Team	Lg	G	GS	CG	GF	IP	BFP	H	R	ER	HR	SH	SF	HB	TBB	IBB	SO	WP	Bk	W	L	Pct	ShO	Sv-Op	Hld	ERC	ERA
1999 Detroit	AL	30	29	0	1	163.2	717	176	104	101	27	5	5	17	56	2	114	0	0	9	12	.429	0	0-0	0	5.21	5.55
2000 Detroit	AL	31	30	2	0	200.0	849	205	102	96	26	3	9	15	52	2	136	3	2	11	15	.423	0	0-0	0	4.18	4.32
2001 Detroit	AL	33	33	5	0	229.1	985	235	116	104	19	12	7	14	68	4	152	3	3	13	16	.448	0	0-0	0	3.89	4.08
2002 Det-NYY	AL	32	25	3	3	199.2	840	193	88	78	16	4	3	11	48	4	132	6	0	11	11	.500	3	2-2	0	3.30	3.52
2003 New York	AL	32	24	0	0	159.1	735	211	113	106	16	9	9	11	47	2	93	2	0	7	9	.438	0	0-0	1	5.77	5.99
2002 Detroit	AL	17	17	3	0	121.2	509	112	50	43	4	5	2	8	33	3	75	4	0	6	8	.429	3	0-0	0	2.94	3.18
2002 New York	AL	15	8	0	3	78.0	331	81	38	35	12	1	1	3	15	3	57	2	0	5	3	.625	0	2-2	0	3.86	4.04
5 ML YEARS		158	141	10	7	952.0	4126	1020	523	485	104	35	33	68	271	14	627	14	2	51	63	.447	3	2-2	1	4.35	4.59

Brandon Webb

Pitches: R Bats: R Pos: SP-28; RP-1   Ht: 6'2" Wt: 228 Born: 5/9/79 Age: 25

		HOW MUCH HE PITCHED						WHAT HE GAVE UP												THE RESULTS							
Year Team	Lg	G	GS	CG	GF	IP	BFP	H	R	ER	HR	SH	SF	HB	TBB	IBB	SO	WP	Bk	W	L	Pct	ShO	Sv-Op	Hld	ERC	ERA
2000 Diamndbcks	R	1	1	0	0	1.0	5	2	1	1	0	0	0	0	0	0	3	0	0	0	0	-	0	0--	-	7.48	9.00
2000 South Bend	A	12	0	0	7	16.2	69	10	7	6	0	0	0	2	9	1	18	1	0	0	0	-	0	2--	-	2.20	3.24
2001 Lancaster	A+	29	28	0	0	162.1	711	174	90	72	9	3	5	27	44	0	158	11	1	6	10	.375	0	0--	-	4.33	3.99
2002 El Paso	AA	26	25	1	1	152.0	647	141	66	53	4	2	3	13	59	1	122	12	1	10	6	.625	1	0--	-	3.48	3.14
2002 Tucson	AAA	1	1	0	0	7.0	31	5	3	3	0	1	0	1	4	0	5	0	0	1	0	1.000	0	0--	-	2.92	3.86
2003 Tucson	AAA	3	3	0	0	18.0	84	18	17	12	0	0	2	3	9	0	17	2	0	1	1	.500	0	0--	-	4.23	6.00
2003 Arizona	NL	29	28	1	1	180.2	750	140	65	57	12	9	1	13	68	4	172	9	1	10	9	.526	1	0-0	0	2.80	2.84

Ben Weber

Pitches: R **Bats:** R **Pos:** RP-62

Ht: 6'4" **Wt:** 210 **Born:** 11/17/69 **Age:** 34

Year Team	Lg	G	GS	CG	GF	IP	BFP	H	R	ER	HR	SH	SF	HB	TBB	IBB	SO	WP	Bk	W	L	Pct	ShO	Sv-Op	Hld	ERC	ERA
2000 SF-Ana		19	0	0	3	22.2	103	28	19	16	0	0	1	0	6	1	14	2	0	1	1	.500	0	0-2	5	3.91	6.35
2001 Anaheim	AL	56	0	0	19	68.1	299	66	28	26	4	0	0	5	31	8	40	0	1	6	2	.750	0	0-1	6	3.90	3.42
2002 Anaheim	AL	63	0	0	16	78.0	314	70	25	22	4	4	2	3	22	3	43	2	0	7	2	.778	0	7-11	18	2.94	2.54
2003 Anaheim	AL	62	0	0	20	80.1	333	84	26	24	7	4	1	0	22	7	46	4	0	5	1	.833	0	0-2	11	3.70	2.69
2000 San Francisco	NL	9	0	0	2	8.0	44	16	13	13	0	0	0	0	4	0	6	1	0	0	1	.000	0	0-2	1	9.72	14.63
2000 Anaheim	AL	10	0	0	1	14.2	59	12	6	3	0	0	1	0	2	1	8	1	0	1	0	1.000	0	0-0	1	1.52	1.84
4 ML YEARS		**200**	**0**	**0**	**58**	**249.1**	**1049**	**248**	**98**	**88**	**15**	**8**	**4**	**8**	**81**	**19**	**143**	**8**	**1**	**19**	**6**	**.760**	**0**	**7-16**	**37**	**3.53**	**3.18**

Rickie Weeks

Bats: R **Throws:** R **Pos:** 2B-4; PH-3

Ht: 6'0" **Wt:** 195 **Born:** 9/13/82 **Age:** 21

Year Team	Lg	G	AB	H	2B	3B	HR	(Hm	Rd)	TB	R	RBI	RC	TBB	IBB	SO	HBP	SH	SF	SB	CS	SB%	GDP	Avg	OBP	Slg
2003 Brewers	R	1	4	2	0	0	0	(-	-)	2	0	4	1	0	0	2	1	0	0	1	0	1.00	0	.500	.600	.500
2003 Beloit	A	20	63	22	8	1	1	(-	-)	35	13	16	19	15	0	9	6	0	3	2	0	1.00	1	.349	.494	.556
2003 Milwaukee	NL	7	12	2	1	0	0	(0	0)	3	1	0	0	1	0	6	1	0	0	0	0	-	0	.167	.286	.250

Todd Wellemeyer

Pitches: R **Bats:** R **Pos:** RP-15

Ht: 6'3" **Wt:** 205 **Born:** 8/30/78 **Age:** 25

Year Team	Lg	G	GS	CG	GF	IP	BFP	H	R	ER	HR	SH	SF	HB	TBB	IBB	SO	WP	Bk	W	L	Pct	ShO	Sv-Op	Hld	ERC	ERA
2000 Eugene	A-	15	15	0	0	76.0	315	62	35	31	3	1	1	4	33	2	85	3	1	4	4	.500	0	0--	-	3.02	3.67
2001 Lansing	A	27	27	1	0	147.0	667	165	85	68	14	4	5	11	74	0	167	10	1	13	9	.591	0	0--	-	5.55	4.16
2002 Daytona	A+	14	14	0	0	73.2	301	63	33	31	7	1	3	4	19	1	87	3	0	4	4	.333	0	0--	-	2.92	3.79
2002 W Tennesse	AA	8	8	1	0	46.0	187	33	25	24	2	0	4	3	18	0	37	2	0	3	3	.500	1	0--	-	2.46	4.70
2003 Iowa	AAA	13	12	0	0	66.0	291	68	39	38	7	2	4	2	33	4	56	1	0	5	5	.500	0	0--	-	4.77	5.18
2003 W Tennesse	AA	4	4	0	0	21.1	95	19	13	13	1	0	2	3	10	0	34	0	0	1	1	.500	0	0--	-	3.84	5.48
2003 Chicago	NL	15	0	0	8	27.2	122	25	22	20	5	1	0	0	19	1	30	0	0	1	1	.500	0	1-1	1	5.33	6.51

David Wells

Pitches: L **Bats:** L **Pos:** SP-30; RP-1

Ht: 6'4" **Wt:** 240 **Born:** 5/20/63 **Age:** 41

Year Team	Lg	G	GS	CG	GF	IP	BFP	H	R	ER	HR	SH	SF	HB	TBB	IBB	SO	WP	Bk	W	L	Pct	ShO	Sv-Op	Hld	ERC	ERA
1987 Toronto	AL	18	2	0	6	29.1	132	37	14	13	0	1	0	0	12	0	32	4	0	4	3	.571	0	1-2	2	4.91	3.99
1988 Toronto	AL	41	0	0	15	64.1	279	65	36	33	12	2	2	2	31	9	56	6	2	3	5	.375	0	4-6	8	5.11	4.62
1989 Toronto	AL	54	0	0	19	86.1	352	66	25	23	5	3	2	2	28	7	78	6	3	7	4	.636	0	2-9	8	2.16	2.40
1990 Toronto	AL	43	25	0	8	189.0	759	165	72	66	14	9	2	2	45	3	115	7	1	11	6	.647	0	3-3	3	2.67	3.14
1991 Toronto	AL	40	28	2	3	198.1	811	188	88	82	24	6	6	2	49	1	106	10	3	15	10	.600	0	1-2	3	3.41	3.72
1992 Toronto	AL	41	14	0	14	120.0	529	138	84	72	16	3	4	8	36	6	62	3	1	7	9	.438	0	2-4	3	4.98	5.40
1993 Detroit	AL	32	30	0	0	187.0	776	183	93	87	26	3	3	7	42	6	139	13	0	11	9	.550	0	0-0	1	3.64	4.19
1994 Detroit	AL	16	16	5	0	111.1	464	113	54	49	13	3	1	2	24	6	71	5	0	5	7	.417	1	0-0	0	3.54	3.96
1995 Det-Cin		29	29	6	0	203.0	839	194	88	73	23	7	3	2	53	9	133	7	2	16	8	.667	0	0-0	0	3.37	3.24
1996 Baltimore	AL	34	34	3	0	224.1	946	247	132	128	32	8	14	7	51	7	130	4	2	11	14	.440	0	0-0	0	4.39	5.14
1997 New York	AL	32	32	5	0	218.0	922	239	109	102	24	7	3	6	45	0	156	8	0	16	10	.615	2	0-0	0	4.04	4.21
1998 New York	AL	30	30	8	0	214.1	851	195	86	83	29	2	2	1	29	0	163	2	0	18	4	.818	5	0-0	0	2.83	3.49
1999 Toronto	AL	34	34	7	0	231.2	987	246	132	124	32	6	6	6	62	2	169	1	0	17	10	.630	1	0-0	0	4.26	4.82
2000 Toronto	AL	35	35	9	0	229.2	972	266	115	105	23	6	7	8	31	0	166	9	1	20	8	.714	1	0-0	0	4.05	4.11
2001 Chicago	AL	16	16	1	0	100.2	432	120	55	50	12	2	2	3	21	1	59	2	0	5	7	.417	0	0-0	0	4.69	4.47
2002 New York	AL	31	31	2	0	206.1	873	210	100	86	21	6	5	5	45	2	137	4	0	19	7	.731	0	0-0	0	3.50	3.75
2003 New York	AL	31	30	4	0	213.0	887	242	101	98	24	6	7	8	20	0	101	3	0	15	7	.682	1	0-0	0	3.87	4.14
1995 Detroit	AL	18	18	3	0	130.1	539	120	54	44	17	3	2	2	37	5	83	6	1	10	3	.769	0	0-0	0	3.40	3.04
1995 Cincinnati	NL	11	11	3	0	72.2	300	74	34	29	6	4	1	0	16	4	50	1	1	6	5	.545	0	0-0	0	3.31	3.59
17 ML YEARS		**557**	**386**	**52**	**65**	**2826.2**	**11811**	**2914**	**1384**	**1274**	**330**	**80**	**69**	**69**	**624**	**59**	**1873**	**94**	**15**	**200**	**128**	**.610**	**12**	**13-26**	**28**	**3.73**	**4.06**

Kip Wells

Pitches: R **Bats:** R **Pos:** SP-31

Ht: 6'3" **Wt:** 205 **Born:** 4/21/77 **Age:** 27

Year Team	Lg	G	GS	CG	GF	IP	BFP	H	R	ER	HR	SH	SF	HB	TBB	IBB	SO	WP	Bk	W	L	Pct	ShO	Sv-Op	Hld	ERC	ERA
1999 Chicago	AL	7	7	0	0	35.2	153	33	17	16	2	0	2	3	15	0	29	1	2	4	1	.800	0	0-0	0	3.80	4.04
2000 Chicago	AL	20	20	0	0	98.2	468	126	76	66	15	1	3	2	58	4	71	7	0	6	9	.400	0	0-0	0	7.01	6.02
2001 Chicago	AL	40	20	0	3	133.1	603	145	80	71	14	8	6	12	61	5	99	14	0	10	11	.476	0	0-2	6	5.16	4.79
2002 Pittsburgh	NL	33	33	1	0	198.1	844	197	92	79	21	7	5	7	71	11	134	7	0	12	14	.462	1	0-0	0	4.01	3.58
2003 Pittsburgh	NL	31	31	1	0	197.1	835	171	77	72	24	15	2	7	76	7	147	6	0	10	9	.526	0	0-0	0	3.49	3.28
5 ML YEARS		**131**	**111**	**2**	**3**	**663.1**	**2903**	**672**	**342**	**304**	**76**	**31**	**18**	**31**	**281**	**27**	**480**	**35**	**2**	**42**	**44**	**.488**	**1**	**0-2**	**6**	**4.48**	**4.12**

Vernon Wells

Bats: R **Throws:** R **Pos:** CF-161

Ht: 6'1" **Wt:** 225 **Born:** 12/8/78 **Age:** 25

Year Team	Lg	G	AB	H	2B	3B	HR	(Hm	Rd)	TB	R	RBI	RC	TBB	IBB	SO	HBP	SH	SF	SB	CS	SB%	GDP	Avg	OBP	Slg
1999 Toronto	AL	24	88	23	5	0	1	(1	0)	31	8	8	7	4	0	18	0	0	1	1	1	.50	6	.261	.293	.352
2000 Toronto	AL	3	2	0	0	0	0	(0	0)	0	0	0	0	0	0	0	0	0	0	0	0	-	0	.000	.000	.000
2001 Toronto	AL	30	96	30	8	0	1	(1	0)	41	14	6	16	5	0	15	1	0	1	5	0	1.00	6	.313	.350	.427
2002 Toronto	AL	159	608	167	34	4	23	(10	13)	278	87	100	89	27	0	85	3	2	8	9	4	.69	15	.275	.305	.457
2003 Toronto	AL	161	678	215	49	5	33	(13	20)	373	118	117	125	42	2	80	7	0	8	4	1	.80	21	.317	.359	.550
5 ML YEARS		**377**	**1472**	**435**	**96**	**9**	**58**	**(25**	**33)**	**723**	**227**	**231**	**237**	**78**	**2**	**198**	**11**	**2**	**17**	**19**	**6**	**.76**	**42**	**.296**	**.332**	**.491**

Turk Wendell

Pitches: R Bats: L Pos: RP-56   Ht: 6'2" Wt: 205 Born: 5/19/67 Age: 37

		HOW MUCH HE PITCHED						WHAT HE GAVE UP												THE RESULTS							
Year Team	Lg	G	GS	CG	GF	IP	BFP	H	R	ER	HR	SH	SF	HB	TBB	IBB	SO	WP	Bk	W	L	Pct	ShO	Sv-Op	Hld	ERC	ERA
2003 Clearwater*	A+	5	5	0	0	6.0	21	3	0	0	0	0	0	0	0	0	5	0	0	0	0	0--	-	0	-	0.54	0.00
1993 Chicago	NL	7	4	0	1	22.2	98	24	13	11	0	2	0	0	8	1	15	1	1	1	2	.333	0	0-0	0	3.42	4.37
1994 Chicago	NL	6	2	0	1	14.1	76	22	20	19	3	2	1	0	10	1	9	1	0	0	1	.000	0	0-0	0	9.21	11.93
1995 Chicago	NL	43	0	0	17	60.1	270	71	35	33	11	3	3	2	24	4	50	1	0	3	1	.750	0	0-0	3	5.79	4.92
1996 Chicago	NL	70	0	0	49	79.1	339	58	26	25	8	3	1	3	44	4	75	3	2	4	5	.444	0	18-21	6	3.25	2.84
1997 ChC-NYM	NL	65	0	0	21	76.1	345	68	42	37	7	4	3	2	53	6	64	4	0	3	5	.375	0	5-7	2	4.51	4.36
1998 New York	NL	66	0	0	17	76.2	319	62	25	25	4	2	1	2	33	9	58	1	0	5	1	.833	0	4-8	11	2.78	2.93
1999 New York	NL	80	0	0	14	85.2	369	80	31	29	9	2	1	2	37	8	77	2	1	5	4	.556	0	3-6	21	3.80	3.05
2000 New York	NL	77	0	0	17	82.2	346	60	36	33	9	6	3	5	41	7	73	0	1	8	6	.571	0	1-5	16	3.14	3.59
2001 NYM-Phi	NL	70	0	0	22	67.0	297	63	36	33	12	2	4	3	34	9	56	2	0	4	5	.444	0	1-3	16	4.74	4.43
2003 Philadelphia	NL	56	0	0	20	64.0	273	54	24	24	6	6	3	6	28	5	27	1	0	3	3	.500	0	1-5	8	3.57	3.38
1997 Chicago	NL	52	0	0	18	60.0	269	53	32	28	4	3	3	1	39	5	54	4	0	3	5	.375	0	4-5	2	4.03	4.20
1997 New York	NL	13	0	0	3	16.1	76	15	10	9	3	1	0	1	14	1	10	0	0	0	0	-	0	1-2	0	6.38	4.96
2001 New York	NL	49	0	0	14	51.1	218	42	23	20	8	2	3	3	22	6	41	1	0	4	3	.571	0	1-3	6	3.59	3.51
2001 Philadelphia	NL	21	0	0	8	15.2	79	21	13	13	4	0	1	1	12	3	15	1	0	0	2	.000	0	0-0	2	9.04	7.47
10 ML YEARS		540	6	0	179	629.0	2732	562	288	269	69	32	20	26	312	54	504	16	5	36	33	.522	0	33-55	75	3.94	3.85

Jayson Werth

Bats: R Throws: R Pos: RF-19; PR-4; PH-3; CF-1; DH-1   Ht: 6'5" Wt: 190 Born: 5/20/79 Age: 25

								BATTING												BASERUNNING				AVERAGES		
Year Team	Lg	G	AB	H	2B	3B	HR	(Hm	Rd)	TB	R	RBI	RC	TBB	IBB	SO	HBP	SH	SF	SB	CS	SB%	GDP	Avg	OBP	Slg
1997 Orioles	R	32	88	26	6	0	1	(-	-)	35	16	8	19	22	0	22	0	0	1	7	1	.88	0	.295	.432	.398
1998 Delmarva	A	120	408	108	20	3	8	(-	-)	158	71	53	59	50	0	92	15	1	2	21	6	.78	14	.265	.364	.387
1998 Bowie	AA	5	19	3	2	0	0	(-	-)	5	2	1	1	2	0	6	0	0	0	1	0	1.00	0	.158	.238	.263
1999 Frederick	A+	66	236	72	10	1	3	(-	-)	93	41	30	42	37	2	37	3	1	2	16	3	.84	4	.305	.403	.394
1999 Bowie	AA	35	121	33	5	1	1	(-	-)	43	18	11	18	17	0	26	2	1	3	7	1	.88	1	.273	.364	.355
2000 Bowie	AA	85	276	63	16	2	5	(-	-)	98	47	26	38	54	1	50	4	4	1	9	3	.75	10	.228	.361	.355
2000 Frederick	A+	24	83	23	3	0	2	(-	-)	32	16	18	12	10	1	15	0	1	2	5	1	.83	3	.277	.347	.386
2001 Dunedin	A+	85	70	14	3	0	2	(-	-)	23	9	14	9	17	0	19	0	0	0	1	1	.50	2	.200	.356	.329
2001 Tennessee	AA	104	369	105	23	1	18	(-	-)	184	51	69	74	63	0	93	3	1	7	12	3	.80	5	.285	.387	.499
2002 Syracuse	AAA	127	443	114	25	2	18	(-	-)	197	65	82	74	67	2	125	4	0	9	24	7	.77	7	.257	.354	.445
2003 Syracuse	AAA	64	236	56	19	1	9	(-	-)	104	37	34	30	15	1	68	2	0	3	11	1	.92	7	.237	.285	.441
2003 Dunedin	A+	18	62	23	5	0	4	(-	-)	40	10	18	14	3	0	14	0	0	2	1	0	1.00	3	.371	.388	.645
2002 Toronto	AL	15	46	12	2	1	0	(0	0)	16	4	6	5	6	0	11	0	0	0	1	0	1.00	4	.261	.340	.348
2003 Toronto	AL	26	48	10	4	0	2	(0	2)	20	7	10	6	3	0	22	0	0	0	1	0	1.00	0	.208	.255	.417
2 ML YEARS		41	94	22	6	1	2	(0	2)	36	11	16	11	9	0	33	0	0	0	2	0	1.00	4	.234	.298	.383

Barry Wesson

Bats: R Throws: R Pos: LF-5; RF-4; PR-1   Ht: 6'2" Wt: 210 Born: 4/6/77 Age: 27

								BATTING												BASERUNNING				AVERAGES		
Year Team	Lg	G	AB	H	2B	3B	HR	(Hm	Rd)	TB	R	RBI	RC	TBB	IBB	SO	HBP	SH	SF	SB	CS	SB%	GDP	Avg	OBP	Slg
1995 Astros	R	45	138	26	2	2	2	(-	-)	38	14	18	12	19	0	40	1	1	1	4	0	1.00	2	.188	.289	.275
1995 Jackson	AA	4	3	2	0	1	0	(-	-)	4	2	1	2	0	0	0	0	0	0	0	0	-	0	.667	.667	1.333
1996 Auburn	A-	55	176	28	7	0	0	(-	-)	35	11	12	4	12	1	46	1	1	3	5	3	.63	5	.159	.214	.199
1997 Auburn	A-	58	208	54	7	3	3	(-	-)	76	24	26	23	10	0	45	1	1	1	8	4	.67	1	.260	.295	.365
1998 Quad City	A	138	493	124	21	2	7	(-	-)	170	71	43	49	32	1	90	5	2	0	22	12	.65	10	.252	.304	.345
1999 Kissimmee	A+	115	352	76	15	1	4	(-	-)	105	32	34	28	26	0	84	4	2	2	8	7	.53	3	.216	.276	.298
2000 Round Rock	AA	39	110	26	1	2	2	(-	-)	37	12	15	11	10	0	32	0	0	2	6	2	.75	2	.236	.295	.336
2000 Kissimmee	A+	81	308	84	21	3	5	(-	-)	126	50	35	48	33	0	66	2	4	1	24	5	.83	2	.273	.346	.409
2001 Round Rock	AA	133	472	119	23	7	16	(-	-)	204	67	54	66	41	0	135	6	7	4	20	10	.67	4	.252	.317	.432
2002 New Orleans	AAA	111	413	121	25	5	11	(-	-)	189	43	61	57	16	0	100	5	2	3	4	7	.36	9	.293	.325	.458
2003 Salt Lake	AAA	123	475	133	27	6	8	(-	-)	196	62	53	67	38	0	86	3	0	5	17	3	.85	10	.280	.334	.413
2002 Houston	NL	15	20	4	0	1	0	(0	0)	6	1	1	1	1	0	5	0	0	0	0	0	-	2	.200	.238	.300
2003 Anaheim	AL	10	11	2	0	0	1	(1	0)	5	2	3	1	0	0	4	0	0	0	1	0	1.00	0	.182	.182	.455
2 ML YEARS		25	31	6	0	1	1	(1	0)	11	3	4	2	1	0	9	0	0	0	1	0	1.00	2	.194	.219	.355

Jake Westbrook

Pitches: R Bats: R Pos: SP-22; RP-12   Ht: 6'3" Wt: 185 Born: 9/29/77 Age: 26

		HOW MUCH HE PITCHED						WHAT HE GAVE UP												THE RESULTS							
Year Team	Lg	G	GS	CG	GF	IP	BFP	H	R	ER	HR	SH	SF	HB	TBB	IBB	SO	WP	Bk	W	L	Pct	ShO	Sv-Op	Hld	ERC	ERA
2003 Buffalo*	AAA	2	2	0	0	10.0	35	0	0	0	0	1	0	0	4	0	7	1	0	1	0	1.000	0	0--	-	0.17	0.00
2000 New York	AL	3	2	0	1	6.2	38	15	10	10	1	0	2	0	4	1	1	0	0	0	2	.000	0	0-0	0	13.53	13.50
2001 Cleveland	AL	23	6	0	3	64.2	290	79	43	42	6	1	5	4	22	4	48	4	0	4	4	.500	0	0-0	5	5.25	5.85
2002 Cleveland	AL	11	4	0	1	41.2	185	50	30	27	6	2	1	1	12	1	20	1	0	1	3	.250	0	0-2	1	5.12	5.83
2003 Cleveland	AL	34	22	1	4	133.0	580	142	70	64	9	4	3	12	56	1	58	3	0	7	10	.412	0	0-0	1	4.78	4.33
4 ML YEARS		71	34	1	9	246.0	1093	286	153	143	22	7	11	17	94	7	127	8	0	12	19	.387	0	0-2	7	5.17	5.23

Dan Wheeler

Pitches: R Bats: R Pos: RP-35   Ht: 6'3" Wt: 222 Born: 12/10/77 Age: 26

		HOW MUCH HE PITCHED						WHAT HE GAVE UP												THE RESULTS							
Year Team	Lg	G	GS	CG	GF	IP	BFP	H	R	ER	HR	SH	SF	HB	TBB	IBB	SO	WP	Bk	W	L	Pct	ShO	Sv-Op	Hld	ERC	ERA
2003 Norfolk*	AAA	22	5	0	10	45.2	199	48	20	20	4	1	0	1	16	3	44	0	0	4	2	.667	0	4--	-	4.03	3.94
1999 Tampa Bay	AL	6	6	0	0	30.2	136	35	0	20	7	0	0	0	13	0	32	0	0	0	4	.000	0	0-0	0	6.01	5.87
2000 Tampa Bay	AL	11	2	0	0	23.0	111	29	0	14	2	0	0	0	11	0	17	0	0	1	1	.500	0	0-0	0	5.57	5.48
2001 Tampa Bay	AL	13	0	0	0	17.2	87	30	0	17	3	0	0	0	5	0	12	0	0	1	0	1.000	0	0-0	0	8.38	8.66
2003 New York	NL	35	0	0	10	51.0	215	49	23	21	6	0	3	1	17	4	35	1	0	1	3	.250	0	2-3	6	3.69	3.71
4 ML YEARS		65	8	0	10	122.1	549	143	23	72	18	0	3	1	46	4	96	1	0	3	8	.273	0	2-3	7	5.24	5.30

Gabe White

Pitches: L **Bats:** L **Pos:** RP-46   **Ht:** 6'2" **Wt:** 204 **Born:** 11/20/71 **Age:** 32

Year Team	Lg	G	GS	CG	GF	IP	BFP	H	R	ER	HR	SH	SF	HB	TBB	IBB	SO	WP	Bk	W	L	Pct	ShO	Sv-Op	Hld	ERC	ERA
2003 Tampa*	A+	1	1	0	0	0.2	3	1	0	0	0	0	0	0	0	0	0	0	0	0	0	-	0	0--	-	4.47	0.00
2003 Yankees*	R	1	1	0	0	1.0	4	0	0	0	0	0	0	0	1	0	1	0	0	0	0	-	0	0--	-	0.95	0.00
2003 Louisville*	AAA	1	1	0	0	1.0	6	2	1	1	0	0	0	0	1	0	0	0	0	0	0	-	0	0--	-	12.01	9.00
2003 Trenton*	AA	2	2	0	0	2.1	10	3	2	2	1	0	0	0	0	0	2	0	0	0	0	-	0	0--	-	6.14	7.71
1994 Montreal	NL	7	5	0	2	23.2	106	24	16	16	4	1	1	1	11	0	17	0	0	1	1	.500	0	1-1	0	5.03	6.08
1995 Montreal	NL	19	1	0	8	25.2	115	26	21	20	7	2	3	1	9	0	25	0	0	1	2	.333	0	0-0	0	5.12	7.01
1997 Cincinnati	NL	12	6	0	2	41.0	168	39	20	20	6	3	2	1	8	1	25	0	0	2	2	.500	0	1-1	3	3.37	4.39
1998 Cincinnati	NL	69	3	0	29	98.2	404	86	46	44	17	2	2	1	27	6	83	3	0	5	5	.500	0	9-13	6	3.30	4.01
1999 Cincinnati	NL	50	0	0	18	61.0	261	68	31	30	13	2	1	2	14	1	61	0	0	1	2	.333	0	0-1	3	4.95	4.43
2000 Cin-Col	NL	68	0	0	17	84.0	329	64	23	22	6	2	6	3	15	2	84	1	0	11	2	.846	0	5-9	19	1.98	2.36
2001 Colorado	NL	69	0	0	16	67.2	290	70	47	47	18	2	2	1	26	5	47	1	0	1	7	.125	0	0-2	8	5.42	6.25
2002 Cincinnati	NL	62	0	0	7	54.1	220	49	19	18	3	1	0	2	10	2	41	0	0	6	1	.857	0	0-1	19	2.55	2.98
2003 Cin-NYY		46	0	0	5	46.2	190	44	22	21	7	2	3	2	8	4	29	0	0	5	1	.833	0	0-2	12	3.26	4.05
2000 Colorado	NL	1	0	0	0	1.0	6	2	2	2	1	0	0	0	1	0	2	0	0	0	0	-	0	0-0	0	23.01	18.00
2000 Colorado	NL	67	0	0	17	83.0	323	62	21	20	5	2	6	3	14	2	82	1	0	11	2	.846	0	5-9	19	1.82	2.17
2003 Cincinnati	NL	34	0	0	4	34.1	141	36	15	15	5	1	2	1	6	3	23	0	0	3	0	1.000	0	0-1	6	3.81	3.93
2003 New York	AL	12	0	0	1	12.1	49	8	7	6	2	1	1	1	2	1	6	0	0	2	1	.667	0	0-1	6	1.89	4.38
9 ML YEARS		402	15	0	104	502.2	2083	470	245	238	81	17	20	14	128	21	412	5	0	33	23	.589	0	16-30	70	3.60	4.26

Matt White

Pitches: L **Bats:** R **Pos:** RP-6   **Ht:** 6'5" **Wt:** 234 **Born:** 8/19/77 **Age:** 26

Year Team	Lg	G	GS	CG	GF	IP	BFP	H	R	ER	HR	SH	SF	HB	TBB	IBB	SO	WP	Bk	W	L	Pct	ShO	Sv-Op	Hld	ERC	ERA
1998 Burlington	R+	8	8	0	0	46.1	190	34	14	10	0	2	2	0	24	0	47	4	4	4	1	.800	0	0--	-	2.49	1.94
1998 Watertown	A-	6	6	0	0	27.1	120	31	19	13	4	0	2	2	11	1	24	1	2	3	2	.600	0	0--	-	5.61	4.28
1999 Columbus	A	19	18	1	0	95.1	414	99	67	56	12	3	3	5	31	0	75	7	1	3	10	.231	0	0--	-	4.37	5.29
2000 Kinston	A+	28	26	2	1	143.2	616	136	76	65	14	7	7	10	63	0	115	7	1	11	9	.550	0	0--	-	4.26	4.07
2001 Akron	AA	25	25	0	0	144.0	618	151	84	77	18	6	3	3	60	1	72	7	2	8	10	.444	0	0--	-	4.79	4.81
2002 Akron	AA	27	11	0	5	89.1	392	97	42	39	9	6	0	0	39	0	63	3	0	6	2	.750	0	1--	-	4.76	3.93
2002 Buffalo	AAA	7	1	0	2	17.0	81	23	13	9	1	0	1	2	6	0	12	0	0	0	0	-	0	0--	-	6.05	4.76
2003 Sarasota	A+	2	2	0	0	5.0	22	6	1	0	0	0	0	0	1	0	2	0	0	0	0	-	0	0--	-	3.60	0.00
2003 Portland	AA	2	1	0	1	3.0	13	1	1	1	0	1	0	1	2	0	3	1	0	0	0	-	0	0--	-	2.02	0.00
2003 Pawtucket	AAA	2	0	0	0	3.1	12	1	1	1	0	0	0	0	0	0	5	0	0	0	0	-	0	0--	-	0.19	0.00
2003 Buffalo	AAA	19	1	0	7	42.1	177	36	12	10	3	4	1	0	16	0	34	2	0	2	3	.400	0	0--	-	2.97	2.13
2003 Bos-Sea	AL	6	0	0	3	5.2	33	13	14	14	3	0	1	0	5	0	0	0	0	0	1	.000	0	0-0	0	20.79	22.24
2003 Boston	AL	3	0	0	1	3.2	23	10	11	11	1	0	1	0	3	0	0	0	0	0	1	.000	0	0-0	0	20.66	27.00
2003 Seattle	AL	3	0	0	2	2.0	10	3	3	3	2	0	0	0	2	0	0	0	0	0	0	-	0	0-0	0	20.49	13.50

Rick White

Pitches: R **Bats:** R **Pos:** RP-49   **Ht:** 6'4" **Wt:** 230 **Born:** 12/23/68 **Age:** 35

Year Team	Lg	G	GS	CG	GF	IP	BFP	H	R	ER	HR	SH	SF	HB	TBB	IBB	SO	WP	Bk	W	L	Pct	ShO	Sv-Op	Hld	ERC	ERA
1994 Pittsburgh	NL	43	5	0	23	75.1	317	79	35	32	9	7	5	6	17	3	38	2	2	4	5	.444	0	6-9	3	4.11	3.82
1995 Pittsburgh	NL	15	9	0	2	55.0	247	66	33	29	3	3	3	2	18	0	29	2	0	2	3	.400	0	0-0	2	4.70	4.75
1998 Tampa Bay	AL	38	3	0	12	68.2	289	66	32	29	8	0	3	2	23	2	39	3	0	2	6	.250	0	0-0	2	3.82	3.80
1999 Tampa Bay	AL	63	1	0	11	108.0	480	132	56	49	8	2	5	1	38	5	81	3	0	5	3	.625	0	0-2	4	4.96	4.08
2000 TB-NYM		66	0	0	14	99.2	420	83	44	39	9	1	3	7	38	5	67	3	0	5	9	.357	0	3-7	4	3.21	3.52
2001 New York	NL	55	0	0	15	69.2	299	71	38	30	7	2	2	2	17	4	51	1	0	4	5	.444	0	2-4	10	3.52	3.88
2002 Col-StL	NL	61	0	0	10	62.2	264	62	33	30	4	3	4	1	21	5	41	3	0	5	7	.417	0	0-1	16	3.49	4.31
2003 CWS-Hou		49	0	0	15	67.0	293	74	48	43	13	2	2	4	21	2	54	2	0	1	2	.333	0	1-1	4	5.22	5.78
2000 Tampa Bay	AL	44	0	0	8	71.1	293	57	30	27	7	1	2	5	26	3	47	3	0	3	6	.333	0	2-5	2	3.09	3.41
2000 New York	NL	22	0	0	6	28.1	127	26	14	12	2	0	1	2	12	2	20	0	0	2	3	.400	0	1-2	2	3.51	3.81
2002 Colorado	NL	41	0	0	8	40.2	182	49	30	28	4	1	4	1	18	4	27	3	0	2	6	.250	0	0-1	9	5.47	6.20
2002 St Louis	NL	20	0	0	2	22.0	82	13	3	2	0	2	0	0	3	1	14	0	0	3	1	.750	0	0-0	7	0.94	0.82
2003 Chicago	AL	34	0	0	12	47.2	207	56	39	35	11	1	2	1	13	2	37	0	0	1	2	.333	0	1-1	5	5.58	6.61
2003 Houston	NL	15	0	0	3	19.1	86	18	9	8	2	1	0	3	8	0	17	2	0	0	0	-	0	0-0	1	4.33	3.72
8 ML YEARS		390	18	0	102	606.0	2609	633	319	281	61	20	27	25	193	26	400	19	2	28	40	.412	0	12-24	43	4.11	4.17

Rondell White

Bats: R **Throws:** R **Pos:** LF-121; PH-9; DH-7   **Ht:** 6'1" **Wt:** 225 **Born:** 2/23/72 **Age:** 32

Year Team	Lg	G	AB	H	2B	3B	HR	(Hm	Rd)	TB	R	RBI	RC	TBB	IBB	SO	HBP	SH	SF	SB	CS	SB%	GDP	Avg	OBP	Slg
1993 Montreal	NL	23	73	19	3	1	2	(1	1)	30	9	15	9	7	0	16	0	2	1	1	2	.33	2	.260	.321	.411
1994 Montreal	NL	40	97	27	10	1	2	(1	1)	45	16	13	16	9	0	18	3	0	0	1	1	.50	1	.278	.358	.464
1995 Montreal	NL	130	474	140	33	4	13	(6	7)	220	87	57	79	41	1	87	6	0	4	25	5	.83	11	.295	.356	.464
1996 Montreal	NL	88	334	98	19	4	6	(2	4)	143	35	41	46	22	0	53	2	0	1	14	6	.70	11	.293	.340	.428
1997 Montreal	NL	151	592	160	29	5	28	(9	19)	283	84	82	84	31	3	111	10	1	4	16	8	.67	18	.270	.316	.478
1998 Montreal	NL	97	357	107	21	2	17	(8	9)	183	54	58	65	30	2	57	7	0	3	16	7	.70	7	.300	.363	.513
1999 Montreal	NL	138	539	168	26	6	22	(10	12)	272	83	64	91	32	2	85	11	0	6	10	6	.63	17	.312	.359	.505
2000 Mon-ChC	NL	94	357	111	26	0	13	(3	10)	176	59	61	64	33	0	79	4	0	2	5	3	.63	4	.311	.374	.493
2001 Chicago	NL	95	323	99	19	1	17	(7	10)	171	43	50	57	26	4	56	7	1	0	1	0	1.00	14	.307	.371	.529
2002 New York	AL	126	455	109	21	0	14	(5	9)	172	59	62	42	25	1	86	8	1	5	1	2	.33	11	.240	.288	.378
2003 SD-KC		137	488	141	23	4	22	(5	17)	238	62	77	73	31	2	79	10	0	5	1	4	.20	13	.289	.341	.488
2000 Montreal	NL	75	290	89	24	0	11	(3	8)	146	52	54	53	28	0	67	2	0	2	5	1	.83	4	.307	.370	.503
2000 Chicago	NL	19	67	22	2	0	2	(0	2)	30	7	7	11	5	0	12	2	0	0	0	2	.00	0	.328	.392	.448
2003 San Diego	NL	115	413	115	17	3	18	(4	14)	192	49	66	54	25	2	71	8	0	3	1	4	.20	11	.278	.330	.465
2003 Kansas City	AL	22	75	26	6	1	4	(1	3)	46	13	21	19	6	0	8	2	0	2	0	0	-	2	.347	.400	.613
11 ML YEARS		1119	4089	1179	230	28	156	(58	98)	1933	591	590	626	287	15	727	68	5	31	91	44	.67	109	.288	.343	.473

Bob Wickman

Pitches: R **Bats:** R **Pos:** RP **Ht:** 6'1" **Wt:** 240 **Born:** 2/6/69 **Age:** 35

Year Team	Lg	HOW MUCH HE PITCHED						WHAT HE GAVE UP												THE RESULTS							
		G	GS	CG	GF	IP	BFP	H	R	ER	HR	SH	SF	HB	TBB	IBB	SO	WP	Bk	W	L	Pct	ShO	Sv-Op	Hld	ERC	ERA
1992 New York	AL	8	8	0	0	50.1	213	51	25	23	2	1	3	2	20	0	21	3	0	6	1	.857	0	0-0	0	3.99	4.11
1993 New York	AL	41	19	1	9	140.0	629	156	82	72	13	4	1	5	69	7	70	2	0	14	4	.778	1	4-8	2	5.16	4.63
1994 New York	AL	53	0	0	19	70.0	286	54	26	24	3	0	5	1	27	3	56	2	0	5	4	.556	0	6-10	11	2.45	3.09
1995 New York	AL	63	1	0	14	80.0	347	77	38	36	6	4	1	5	33	3	51	2	0	2	4	.333	0	1-10	21	3.92	4.05
1996 NYY-Mil		70	0	0	18	95.2	429	106	50	47	10	2	4	5	44	3	75	4	0	7	1	.875	0	0-4	10	5.17	4.42
1997 Milwaukee	NL	74	0	0	20	95.2	405	89	32	29	8	6	2	3	41	7	78	8	0	7	6	.538	0	1-5	28	3.76	2.73
1998 Milwaukee	NL	72	0	0	51	82.1	357	79	38	34	5	10	3	4	39	2	71	1	0	6	9	.400	0	25-32	4	4.05	3.72
1999 Milwaukee	NL	71	0	0	63	74.1	331	75	31	28	6	3	2	2	38	6	60	2	0	3	8	.273	0	37-45	0	4.38	3.39
2000 Mil-Cle		69	0	0	60	72.2	309	64	30	25	1	3	1	1	32	5	55	2	0	3	5	.375	0	30-37	0	2.92	3.10
2001 Cleveland	AL	70	0	0	56	67.2	270	61	18	18	4	0	0	2	14	2	66	2	0	5	0	1.000	0	32-35	4	2.69	2.39
2002 Cleveland	AL	36	0	0	30	34.1	159	42	22	17	3	0	1	0	10	0	36	0	0	1	3	.250	0	20-22	0	4.72	4.46
1996 New York	AL	58	0	0	14	79.0	358	94	41	41	7	1	4	5	34	1	61	3	0	4	1	.800	0	0-3	6	5.51	4.67
1996 Milwaukee	NL	12	0	0	4	16.2	71	12	9	6	3	1	0	0	10	2	14	1	0	3	0	1.000	0	0-1	4	3.66	3.24
2000 Milwaukee	NL	43	0	0	36	46.0	194	37	18	15	1	0	1	1	20	2	44	2	0	2	2	.500	0	16-20	0	2.62	2.93
2000 Cleveland	AL	26	0	0	24	26.2	115	27	12	10	0	3	0	0	12	3	11	0	0	1	3	.250	0	14-17	0	3.47	3.38
11 ML YEARS		627	28	1	340	863.0	3735	854	392	353	61	33	22	31	367	38	639	28	0	59	45	.567	1	156-208	85	4.00	3.68

Chris Widger

Bats: R **Throws:** R **Pos:** C-41; PH-3; 1B-1; RF-1 **Ht:** 6'3" **Wt:** 215 **Born:** 5/21/71 **Age:** 33

Year Team	Lg	BATTING								TB	R	RBI	RC	TBB	IBB	SO	HBP	SH	SF	BASERUNNING				AVERAGES		
		G	AB	H	2B	3B	HR	(Hm	Rd)											SB	CS	SB%	GDP	Avg	OBP	Slg
2003 Memphis*	AAA	23	71	17	7	0	2	(-	-)	30	8	10	10	7	0	12	0	1	1	1	0	1.00	0	.239	.304	.423
1995 Seattle	AL	23	45	9	0	0	1	(1	0)	12	2	2	3	3	0	11	0	0	1	0	0	-	0	.200	.245	.267
1996 Seattle	AL	8	11	2	0	0	0	(0	0)	2	1	0	0	0	0	5	1	0	0	0	0	-	0	.182	.250	.182
1997 Montreal	NL	91	278	65	20	3	7	(4	3)	112	30	37	32	22	1	59	1	2	2	2	0	1.00	7	.234	.290	.403
1998 Montreal	NL	125	417	97	18	1	15	(6	9)	162	36	53	46	29	2	85	0	0	2	6	1	.86	5	.233	.281	.388
1999 Montreal	NL	124	383	101	24	1	14	(11	3)	169	42	56	53	28	0	86	7	0	1	1	4	.20	5	.264	.325	.441
2000 Mon-Sea		96	292	68	17	2	13	(6	7)	128	32	35	39	30	3	63	1	0	1	1	2	.33	5	.233	.306	.438
2002 New York	AL	21	64	19	5	0	0	(0	0)	24	4	5	8	2	0	9	2	0	0	0	0	-	0	.297	.338	.375
2003 St Louis	NL	44	102	24	9	0	0	(0	0)	33	9	14	10	6	1	20	1	1	2	0	0	-	5	.235	.279	.324
2000 Montreal	NL	86	281	67	17	2	12	(6	6)	124	31	34	38	29	3	61	1	0	1	1	2	.33	5	.238	.311	.441
2000 Seattle	AL	10	11	1	0	0	1	(0	1)	4	1	1	1	1	0	2	0	0	0	0	0	-	0	.091	.167	.364
8 ML YEARS		532	1592	385	93	7	50	(28	22)	642	156	202	191	120	7	338	13	3	9	10	7	.59	27	.242	.299	.403

Ty Wigginton

Bats: R **Throws:** R **Pos:** 3B-155; PH-1 **Ht:** 6'0" **Wt:** 200 **Born:** 10/11/77 **Age:** 26

Year Team	Lg	BATTING								TB	R	RBI	RC	TBB	IBB	SO	HBP	SH	SF	BASERUNNING				AVERAGES		
		G	AB	H	2B	3B	HR	(Hm	Rd)											SB	CS	SB%	GDP	Avg	OBP	Slg
1998 Pittsfield	A-	70	272	65	14	4	8	(-	-)	111	39	29	32	16	0	72	1	1	0	11	2	.85	4	.239	.284	.408
1999 St.Lucie	A+	123	456	133	23	5	21	(-	-)	229	69	73	82	56	4	82	4	4	2	9	12	.43	5	.292	.373	.502
2000 Binghamton	AA	122	453	129	27	3	20	(-	-)	222	64	77	70	24	0	107	2	1	7	5	5	.50	4	.285	.319	.490
2001 Norfolk	AAA	78	260	65	12	0	7	(-	-)	98	29	24	32	27	0	66	2	1	2	3	3	.50	4	.250	.323	.377
2001 St.Lucie	A+	3	9	3	1	0	0	(-	-)	4	1	1	3	4	0	2	1	0	0	0	0	-	0	.333	.571	.444
2001 Binghamton	AA	8	28	8	3	0	0	(-	-)	11	5	0	5	5	0	5	0	1	0	1	0	1.00	0	.286	.394	.393
2002 Norfolk	AAA	104	383	115	26	3	6	(-	-)	165	49	48	61	43	4	50	1	0	8	5	3	.63	7	.300	.366	.431
2002 New York	NL	46	116	35	8	0	6	(4	2)	61	18	18	16	8	0	19	2	0	1	2	1	.67	4	.302	.354	.526
2003 New York	NL	156	573	146	36	6	11	(4	7)	227	73	71	77	46	2	124	9	1	4	12	2	.86	15	.255	.318	.396
2 ML YEARS		202	689	181	44	6	17	(8	9)	288	91	89	93	54	2	143	11	1	5	14	3	.82	19	.263	.324	.418

Brad Wilkerson

Bats: L **Throws:** L **Pos:** LF-95; CF-42; 1B-27; RF-16; PH-2 **Ht:** 6'0" **Wt:** 200 **Born:** 6/1/77 **Age:** 27

Year Team	Lg	BATTING								TB	R	RBI	RC	TBB	IBB	SO	HBP	SH	SF	BASERUNNING				AVERAGES		
		G	AB	H	2B	3B	HR	(Hm	Rd)											SB	CS	SB%	GDP	Avg	OBP	Slg
2001 Montreal	NL	47	117	24	7	2	1	(1	0)	38	11	5	12	17	1	41	0	1	1	2	1	.67	2	.205	.304	.325
2002 Montreal	NL	153	507	135	27	8	20	(12	8)	238	92	59	83	81	7	161	5	6	4	7	8	.47	5	.266	.370	.469
2003 Montreal	NL	146	504	135	34	4	19	(9	10)	234	78	77	91	89	0	155	4	2	3	13	10	.57	5	.268	.380	.464
3 ML YEARS		346	1128	294	68	14	40	(22	18)	510	181	141	186	187	8	357	9	9	8	22	19	.54	12	.261	.368	.452

Bernie Williams

Bats: B **Throws:** R **Pos:** CF-115; DH-3; PH-2 **Ht:** 6'2" **Wt:** 205 **Born:** 9/13/68 **Age:** 35

Year Team	Lg	BATTING								TB	R	RBI	RC	TBB	IBB	SO	HBP	SH	SF	BASERUNNING				AVERAGES		
		G	AB	H	2B	3B	HR	(Hm	Rd)											SB	CS	SB%	GDP	Avg	OBP	Slg
2003 Trenton*	AA	5	15	5	2	0	0	(-	-)	7	4	4	3	4	1	1	1	0	1	0	1	.00	1	.333	.476	.467
1991 New York	AL	85	320	76	19	4	3	(1	2)	112	43	34	41	48	0	57	1	2	3	10	5	.67	4	.238	.336	.350
1992 New York	AL	62	261	73	14	2	5	(3	2)	106	39	26	37	29	1	36	1	2	0	7	6	.54	5	.280	.354	.406
1993 New York	AL	139	567	152	31	4	12	(5	7)	227	67	68	71	53	4	106	4	1	3	9	9	.50	17	.268	.333	.400
1994 New York	AL	108	408	118	29	1	12	(4	8)	185	80	57	70	61	2	54	3	1	2	16	9	.64	11	.289	.384	.453
1995 New York	AL	144	563	173	29	9	18	(7	11)	274	93	82	105	75	1	98	5	2	3	8	6	.57	12	.307	.392	.487
1996 New York	AL	143	551	168	26	7	29	(12	17)	295	108	102	113	82	8	72	0	1	7	17	4	.81	15	.305	.391	.535
1997 New York	AL	129	509	167	35	6	21	(13	8)	277	107	100	109	73	7	80	1	0	8	15	8	.65	10	.328	.408	.544
1998 New York	AL	128	499	169	30	5	26	(12	14)	287	101	97	110	74	9	81	1	0	4	15	9	.63	19	**.339**	.422	.575
1999 New York	AL	158	591	202	28	6	25	(11	14)	317	116	115	131	100	**17**	95	1	0	11	9	10	.47	11	.342	.435	.536
2000 New York	AL	141	537	165	37	6	30	(15	15)	304	108	121	112	71	11	84	5	0	3	13	5	.72	15	.307	.391	.566
2001 New York	AL	146	540	166	38	0	26	(14	12)	282	102	94	108	78	11	67	6	0	9	11	5	.69	15	.307	.395	.522
2002 New York	AL	154	612	204	37	2	19	(13	6)	302	102	102	122	83	7	97	3	0	1	8	4	.67	19	.333	.415	.493
2003 New York	AL	119	445	117	19	1	15	(5	10)	183	77	64	65	71	8	61	3	0	2	5	0	1.00	21	.263	.367	.411
13 ML YEARS		1656	6403	1950	372	53	241	(117	124)	3151	1143	1062	1194	898	86	988	34	9	50	143	80	.64	174	.305	.390	.492

Gerald Williams

Bats: R **Throws:** R **Pos:** LF-11; PR-9; PH-6; RF-3; CF-2   **Ht:** 6'2" **Wt:** 187 **Born:** 8/10/66 **Age:** 37

Year Team	Lg	G	AB	H	2B	3B	HR	(Hm Rd)	TB	R	RBI	RC	TBB	IBB	SO	HBP	SH	SF	SB	CS	SB%	GDP	Avg	OBP	Slg
2003 Albuquerque*	AAA	85	327	99	22	5	14	(- -)	173	59	50	59	24	2	45	4	1	2	15	11	.58	2	.303	.356	.529
1992 New York	AL	15	27	8	2	0	3	(2 1)	19	7	6	6	0	0	3	0	0	0	2	0	1.00	0	.296	.296	.704
1993 New York	AL	42	67	10	2	3	0	(0 0)	18	11	6	2	1	0	14	2	0	1	2	0	1.00	1	.149	.183	.269
1994 New York	AL	57	86	25	8	0	4	(2 2)	45	19	13	11	4	0	17	0	0	1	1	3	.25	6	.291	.319	.523
1995 New York	AL	100	182	45	18	2	6	(4 2)	85	33	28	28	22	1	34	1	0	3	4	2	.67	4	.247	.327	.467
1996 NYY-Mil		125	325	82	19	4	5	(3 2)	124	43	34	34	19	3	57	5	3	5	10	9	.53	8	.252	.299	.382
1997 Milwaukee	NL	155	566	143	32	2	10	(3 7)	209	73	41	58	19	1	90	6	5	5	23	9	.72	9	.253	.282	.369
1998 Atlanta	NL	129	266	81	19	2	10	(5 5)	134	46	44	45	17	1	48	3	2	1	11	5	.69	5	.305	.352	.504
1999 Atlanta	NL	143	422	116	24	1	17	(7 10)	193	76	68	63	33	1	67	6	4	2	19	11	.63	8	.275	.335	.457
2000 Tampa Bay	AL	146	632	173	30	2	21	(6 15)	270	87	89	83	34	0	103	3	9	4	12	12	.50	5	.274	.312	.427
2001 TB-NYY	AL	100	279	56	18	0	4	(3 1)	86	42	19	20	18	0	55	5	4	0	13	5	.72	9	.201	.262	.308
2002 New York	AL	33	17	0	0	0	0	(0 0)	0	6	0	0	2	0	4	0	0	0	2	0	1.00	1	.000	.105	.000
2003 Florida	NL	27	31	4	1	0	0	(0 0)	5	5	3	1	2	0	5	1	2	0	3	0	1.00	0	.129	.182	.161
1996 New York	AL	99	233	63	15	4	5	(3 2)	101	37	30	29	15	2	39	4	1	5	7	8	.47	7	.270	.319	.433
1996 Milwaukee	NL	26	92	19	4	0	0	(0 0)	23	6	4	5	4	1	18	1	2	0	3	1	.75	1	.207	.247	.250
2001 Tampa Bay	AL	62	232	48	17	0	4	(3 1)	77	30	17	18	13	0	42	4	3	0	10	4	.71	8	.207	.261	.332
2001 New York	AL	38	47	8	1	0	0	(0 0)	9	12	2	2	5	0	13	1	1	0	3	1	.75	1	.170	.264	.191
12 ML YEARS		1072	2900	743	173	16	80	(35 45)	1188	448	351	351	171	7	497	31	29	22	102	56	.65	57	.256	.302	.410

Jerome Williams

Pitches: R **Bats:** R **Pos:** SP-21   **Ht:** 6'1" **Wt:** 189 **Born:** 12/4/81 **Age:** 22

Year Team	Lg	G	GS	CG	GF	IP	BFP	H	R	ER	HR	SH	SF	HB	TBB	IBB	SO	WP	Bk	W	L	Pct	ShO	Sv-Op	Hld	ERC	ERA
1999 Salem-Keizer	A-	7	7	1	0	37.0	151	29	13	9	1	0	1	3	11	0	34	1	0	1	1	.500	1	0- -	-	2.40	2.19
2000 San Jose	A+	23	19	0	2	125.2	512	89	53	41	6	5	6	10	48	3	115	9	2	7	6	.538	0	0- -	-	2.42	2.94
2001 Shreveport	AA	23	23	2	0	130.0	542	116	69	57	14	2	3	9	34	0	84	6	1	9	7	.563	1	0- -	-	3.26	3.95
2002 Fresno	AAA	28	28	0	0	160.2	671	140	76	64	16	8	5	9	50	1	130	5	3	6	11	.353	0	0- -	-	3.23	3.59
2003 Fresno	AAA	10	10	1	0	57.0	242	52	19	17	3	2	1	4	16	0	40	2	0	4	2	.667	0	0- -	-	3.04	2.68
2003 San Francisco	NL	21	21	2	0	131.0	545	116	54	48	10	6	3	7	49	3	88	2	1	7	5	.583	1	0-0	0	3.42	3.30

Matt Williams

Bats: R **Throws:** R **Pos:** 3B-42; PH-6   **Ht:** 6'2" **Wt:** 219 **Born:** 11/28/65 **Age:** 38

Year Team	Lg	G	AB	H	2B	3B	HR	(Hm Rd)	TB	R	RBI	RC	TBB	IBB	SO	HBP	SH	SF	SB	CS	SB%	GDP	Avg	OBP	Slg
1987 San Francisco	NL	84	245	46	9	2	8	(5 3)	83	28	21	17	16	4	68	1	3	1	4	3	.57	5	.188	.240	.339
1988 San Francisco	NL	52	156	32	6	1	8	(7 1)	64	17	19	14	8	0	41	2	3	1	0	1	.00	7	.205	.251	.410
1989 San Francisco	NL	84	292	59	18	1	18	(10 8)	133	31	50	31	14	1	72	2	1	2	1	2	.33	5	.202	.242	.455
1990 San Francisco	NL	159	617	171	27	2	33	(20 13)	301	87	122	92	33	9	138	7	2	5	7	4	.64	13	.277	.319	.488
1991 San Francisco	NL	157	589	158	24	5	34	(17 17)	294	72	98	88	33	6	128	6	0	7	5	5	.50	11	.268	.310	.499
1992 San Francisco	NL	146	529	120	13	5	20	(9 11)	203	58	66	53	39	11	109	6	0	2	7	7	.50	15	.227	.286	.384
1993 San Francisco	NL	145	579	170	33	4	38	(19 19)	325	105	110	100	27	4	80	4	0	9	1	3	.25	12	.294	.325	.561
1994 San Francisco	NL	112	445	119	16	3	43	(20 23)	270	74	96	82	33	7	87	2	0	3	1	0	1.00	11	.267	.319	.607
1995 San Francisco	NL	76	283	95	17	1	23	(9 14)	183	53	65	66	30	8	58	2	0	3	2	0	1.00	8	.336	.399	.647
1996 San Francisco	NL	105	404	122	16	1	22	(13 9)	206	69	85	72	39	9	91	6	0	6	1	2	.33	10	.302	.367	.510
1997 Cleveland	AL	151	596	157	32	3	32	(7 25)	291	86	105	86	34	4	108	4	0	2	12	4	.75	14	.263	.307	.488
1998 Arizona	NL	135	510	136	26	1	20	(11 9)	224	72	71	68	43	8	102	3	0	1	5	1	.83	19	.267	.327	.439
1999 Arizona	NL	154	627	190	37	2	35	(17 18)	336	98	142	109	41	9	93	2	0	8	2	0	1.00	17	.303	.344	.536
2000 Arizona	NL	96	371	102	18	2	12	(5 7)	160	43	47	47	20	1	51	3	0	3	1	2	.33	11	.275	.315	.431
2001 Arizona	NL	106	408	112	30	0	16	(7 9)	190	58	65	55	22	3	70	3	0	3	1	0	1.00	15	.275	.314	.466
2002 Arizona	NL	60	215	56	7	2	12	(7 5)	103	29	40	31	21	1	41	0	0	2	3	1	.75	8	.260	.324	.479
2003 Arizona	NL	44	134	33	9	0	4	(1 3)	54	17	16	15	16	1	26	2	0	4	0	0	-	1	.246	.327	.403
17 ML YEARS		1866	7000	1878	338	35	378	(184 194)	3420	997	1218	1026	469	86	1363	55	9	62	53	35	.60	182	.268	.317	.489

Mike Williams

Pitches: R **Bats:** R **Pos:** RP-68   **Ht:** 6'2" **Wt:** 200 **Born:** 7/29/68 **Age:** 35

Year Team	Lg	G	GS	CG	GF	IP	BFP	H	R	ER	HR	SH	SF	HB	TBB	IBB	SO	WP	Bk	W	L	Pct	ShO	Sv-Op	Hld	ERC	ERA
1992 Philadelphia	NL	5	5	1	0	28.2	121	29	20	17	3	1	1	0	7	0	5	0	0	1	1	.500	0	0-0	0	3.52	5.34
1993 Philadelphia	NL	17	4	0	2	51.0	221	50	32	30	5	1	0	0	22	2	33	2	0	1	3	.250	0	0-0	0	4.00	5.29
1994 Philadelphia	NL	12	8	0	2	50.1	222	61	31	28	7	2	3	0	20	3	29	0	0	2	4	.333	0	0-0	0	5.62	5.01
1995 Philadelphia	NL	33	8	0	1	87.2	367	78	37	32	10	5	3	3	29	2	57	7	0	3	3	.500	0	0-0	1	3.39	3.29
1996 Philadelphia	NL	32	29	0	1	167.0	732	188	107	101	25	6	5	6	67	6	103	16	1	6	14	.300	0	0-0	0	5.37	5.44
1997 Kansas City	AL	10	0	0	4	14.0	70	20	11	10	1	0	1	1	8	1	10	0	0	0	2	.000	0	1-1	0	7.23	6.43
1998 Pittsburgh	NL	37	1	0	9	51.0	204	39	12	11	1	1	2	0	16	4	59	3	0	4	2	.667	0	0-1	7	1.95	1.94
1999 Pittsburgh	NL	58	0	0	50	58.1	269	63	36	33	9	2	1	1	37	7	76	4	0	3	4	.429	0	23-28	1	5.80	5.09
2000 Pittsburgh	NL	72	0	0	63	72.0	307	56	34	28	8	2	4	4	40	3	71	1	0	3	4	.429	0	24-29	0	3.72	3.50
2001 Pit-Hou	NL	65	0	0	48	64.0	285	60	28	27	9	3	1	0	35	3	59	2	0	6	4	.600	0	22-25	3	4.45	3.80
2002 Pittsburgh	NL	59	0	0	59	61.1	258	54	24	20	6	4	0	1	21	3	43	2	0	2	6	.250	0	46-50	0	3.14	2.93
2003 Pit-Phi	NL	68	0	0	47	63.0	299	66	44	43	5	6	2	4	41	6	39	2	0	1	7	.125	0	28-35	2	5.16	6.14
2001 Pittsburgh	NL	40	0	0	38	41.2	183	39	18	17	6	2	0	0	21	2	43	1	0	2	4	.333	0	22-24	3	4.32	3.67
2001 Houston	NL	25	0	0	10	22.1	102	21	10	10	3	1	1	0	14	1	16	1	0	4	0	1.000	0	0-1	3	4.70	4.03
2003 Pittsburgh	NL	40	0	0	33	37.1	175	42	26	26	5	1	2	1	22	1	20	1	0	1	3	.250	0	25-30	0	5.84	6.27
2003 Philadelphia	NL	28	0	0	14	25.2	124	24	18	17	0	5	0	3	19	5	19	1	0	0	4	.000	0	3-5	2	4.17	5.96
12 ML YEARS		468	55	0	292	768.1	3355	764	416	380	89	33	23	20	343	40	584	39	1	32	54	.372	0	144-169	15	4.37	4.45

Woody Williams

Pitches: R **Bats:** R **Pos:** SP-33; RP-1 · **Ht:** 6'0" **Wt:** 195 **Born:** 8/19/66 **Age:** 37

		HOW MUCH HE PITCHED					WHAT HE GAVE UP										THE RESULTS				
Year Team	Lg	G	GS	CG	GF	IP	BFP	H	R	ER	HR	SH	SF	HB	TBB	IBB	SO	WP	Bk	W	L	Pct	ShO	Sv-Op	Hld	ERC	ERA
1993 Toronto	AL	30	0	0	9	37.0	172	40	18	18	2	2	1	1	22	3	24	2	1	3	1	.750	0	0-2	4	4.85	4.38
1994 Toronto	AL	38	0	0	14	59.1	253	44	24	24	5	1	2	2	33	1	56	4	0	1	3	.250	0	0-0	5	3.25	3.64
1995 Toronto	AL	23	3	0	10	53.2	232	44	23	22	6	2	0	2	28	1	41	0	0	1	2	.333	0	0-1	1	3.72	3.69
1996 Toronto	AL	12	10	1	0	59.0	255	64	33	31	8	2	1	1	21	1	43	2	0	4	5	.444	0	0-0	0	4.73	4.73
1997 Toronto	AL	31	31	0	0	194.2	833	201	98	94	31	6	8	5	66	3	124	7	0	9	14	.391	0	0-0	0	4.55	4.35
1998 Toronto	AL	32	32	1	0	209.2	894	196	112	104	36	5	6	2	81	3	151	2	1	10	9	.526	1	0-0	0	4.15	4.46
1999 San Diego	NL	33	33	0	0	208.1	887	213	106	102	33	9	9	2	73	5	137	9	0	12	12	.500	0	0-0	0	4.46	4.41
2000 San Diego	NL	23	23	4	0	168.0	700	152	74	70	23	4	3	3	54	2	111	4	0	10	8	.556	0	0-0	0	3.55	3.75
2001 SD-StL	NL	34	34	3	0	220.0	922	224	110	99	35	13	8	8	56	5	154	5	0	15	9	.625	1	0-0	0	4.15	4.05
2002 St Louis	NL	17	17	1	0	103.1	412	84	30	29	10	3	1	4	25	2	76	2	0	9	4	.692	0	0-0	0	2.63	2.53
2003 St Louis	NL	34	33	0	1	220.2	944	220	101	95	20	11	6	11	55	2	153	3	0	18	9	.667	0	0-1	0	3.52	3.87
2001 San Diego	NL	23	23	0	0	145.0	632	170	88	80	28	8	8	5	37	4	102	4	0	8	8	.500	0	0-0	0	5.26	4.97
2001 St Louis	NL	11	11	3	0	75.0	290	54	22	19	7	5	0	3	19	1	52	1	0	7	1	.875	1	0-0	0	2.24	2.28
11 ML YEARS		307	216	10	34	1533.2	6504	1482	729	688	209	58	45	41	514	28	1070	40	2	92	76	.548	2	0-4	10	3.96	4.04

Scott Williamson

Pitches: R **Bats:** R **Pos:** RP-66 · **Ht:** 6'0" **Wt:** 185 **Born:** 2/17/76 **Age:** 28

		HOW MUCH HE PITCHED					WHAT HE GAVE UP										THE RESULTS				
Year Team	Lg	G	GS	CG	GF	IP	BFP	H	R	ER	HR	SH	SF	HB	TBB	IBB	SO	WP	Bk	W	L	Pct	ShO	Sv-Op	Hld	ERC	ERA
1999 Cincinnati	NL	62	0	0	40	93.1	366	54	29	25	8	5	2	1	43	6	107	13	0	12	7	.632	0	19-26	5	2.05	2.41
2000 Cincinnati	NL	48	10	0	13	112.0	495	92	45	41	7	4	2	3	75	7	136	21	1	5	8	.385	0	6-8	6	3.85	3.29
2001 Cincinnati	NL	2	0	0	0	0.2	6	1	0	0	0	0	0	1	2	0	0	1	0	0	0	—	0	0-0	1	24.61	0.00
2002 Cincinnati	NL	63	0	0	23	74.0	299	46	27	24	5	5	2	2	36	5	84	8	1	3	4	.429	0	8-12	8	2.24	2.92
2003 Cin-Bos		66	0	0	40	62.2	276	54	30	29	7	2	1	1	34	6	74	11	0	5	4	.556	0	21-28	5	3.78	4.16
2003 Cincinnati	NL	42	0	0	34	42.1	187	34	15	15	6	2	0	1	25	4	53	7	0	5	3	.625	0	21-26	0	3.87	3.19
2003 Boston	AL	24	0	0	6	20.1	89	20	15	14	1	0	1	0	9	2	21	4	0	0	1	.000	0	0-2	5	3.58	6.20
5 ML YEARS		241	10	0	116	342.2	1442	247	131	119	27	16	7	8	190	24	401	54	2	25	23	.521	0	54-74	25	3.00	3.13

Dontrelle Willis

Pitches: L **Bats:** L **Pos:** SP-27 · **Ht:** 6'4" **Wt:** 200 **Born:** 1/12/82 **Age:** 22

		HOW MUCH HE PITCHED					WHAT HE GAVE UP										THE RESULTS				
Year Team	Lg	G	GS	CG	GF	IP	BFP	H	R	ER	HR	SH	SF	HB	TBB	IBB	SO	WP	Bk	W	L	Pct	ShO	Sv-Op	Hld	ERC	ERA
2000 Cubs	R	9	1	0	3	28.0	118	26	15	12	0	1	2	1	8	1	22	0	0	3	1	.750	0	0--	-	2.64	3.86
2001 Boise	A-	15	15	0	0	93.2	374	76	36	31	1	0	1	3	19	0	77	5	1	8	2	.800	0	0--	-	1.95	2.98
2002 Kane County	A	19	19	3	0	127.2	491	91	29	26	3	5	2	8	21	0	101	9	3	10	2	.833	2	0--	-	1.62	1.83
2002 Jupiter	A+	5	5	0	0	30.0	115	24	7	6	2	0	0	1	3	0	27	0	0	2	0	1.000	0	0--	-	1.92	1.80
2003 Carolina	AA	6	6	0	0	36.1	133	24	6	6	2	0	0	0	9	0	32	1	0	4	0	1.000	0	0--	-	1.70	1.49
2003 Florida	NL	27	27	2	0	160.2	668	148	61	59	13	3	1	3	58	0	142	7	1	14	6	.700	2	0-0	0	3.49	3.30

Craig Wilson

Bats: R **Throws:** R **Pos:** RF-40; 1B-36; PH-26; C-21; LF-7; DH-3; PR-1 · **Ht:** 6'2" **Wt:** 225 **Born:** 11/30/76 **Age:** 27

		BATTING																BASERUNNING				AVERAGES		
Year Team	Lg	G	AB	H	2B	3B	HR	(Hm | Rd)	TB	R	RBI	RC	TBB	IBB	SO	HBP	SH	SF	SB	CS	SB%	GDP	Avg	OBP	Slg
2001 Pittsburgh	NL	88	158	49	3	1	13	(8 | 5)	93	27	32	34	15	1	53	7	1	2	3	1	.75	4	.310	.390	.589
2002 Pittsburgh	NL	131	368	97	16	1	16	(3 | 13)	163	48	57	54	32	0	116	21	1	2	2	3	.40	10	.264	.355	.443
2003 Pittsburgh	NL	116	309	81	15	4	18	(9 | 9)	158	49	48	50	35	4	89	13	0	1	3	1	.75	6	.262	.360	.511
3 ML YEARS		335	835	227	34	6	47	(20 | 27)	414	124	137	138	82	5	258	41	2	5	8	5	.62	20	.272	.363	.496

Dan Wilson

Bats: R **Throws:** R **Pos:** C-96 · **Ht:** 6'3" **Wt:** 214 **Born:** 3/25/69 **Age:** 35

		BATTING																BASERUNNING				AVERAGES		
Year Team	Lg	G	AB	H	2B	3B	HR	(Hm | Rd)	TB	R	RBI	RC	TBB	IBB	SO	HBP	SH	SF	SB	CS	SB%	GDP	Avg	OBP	Slg
2003 San Antonio*	AA	2	7	0	0	0	0	(- | -)	0	0	0	0	0	0	3	0	0	0	0	0	-	0	.000	.000	.000
1992 Cincinnati	NL	12	25	9	1	0	0	(0 | 0)	10	2	3	4	3	0	8	0	0	0	0	0	-	2	.360	.429	.400
1993 Cincinnati	NL	36	76	17	3	0	0	(0 | 0)	20	6	8	6	9	4	16	0	2	1	0	0	-	2	.224	.302	.263
1994 Seattle	AL	91	282	61	14	2	3	(1 | 2)	88	24	27	17	10	0	57	1	8	2	1	2	.33	11	.216	.244	.312
1995 Seattle	AL	119	399	111	22	3	9	(5 | 4)	166	40	51	53	33	1	63	2	5	1	2	1	.67	12	.278	.336	.416
1996 Seattle	AL	138	491	140	24	0	18	(7 | 11)	218	51	83	68	32	2	88	3	9	5	1	2	.33	15	.285	.330	.444
1997 Seattle	AL	146	508	137	31	1	15	(9 | 6)	215	66	74	69	39	1	72	5	8	3	7	2	.78	12	.270	.326	.423
1998 Seattle	AL	96	325	82	17	1	9	(6 | 3)	128	39	44	40	24	0	56	5	4	8	2	1	.67	6	.252	.308	.394
1999 Seattle	AL	123	414	110	23	2	7	(3 | 4)	158	46	38	49	29	4	83	2	10	2	5	0	1.00	16	.266	.315	.382
2000 Seattle	AL	90	268	63	12	0	5	(2 | 3)	90	31	27	24	22	0	51	0	11	2	1	2	.33	8	.235	.291	.336
2001 Seattle	AL	123	377	100	20	1	10	(4 | 6)	152	44	42	45	20	0	69	2	8	1	3	2	.60	6	.265	.305	.403
2002 Seattle	AL	115	359	106	16	1	6	(3 | 3)	142	35	44	41	18	1	81	2	7	8	1	0	1.00	8	.295	.326	.396
2003 Seattle	AL	96	316	76	15	2	4	(1 | 3)	107	32	43	28	15	0	52	0	3	3	0	0	-	8	.241	.272	.339
12 ML YEARS		1185	3840	1012	198	13	86	(41 | 45)	1494	416	484	444	254	13	696	22	79	34	23	12	.66	100	.264	.310	.389

Enrique Wilson

Bats: B **Throws:** R **Pos:** SS-33; 3B-17; PR-12; 2B-10; PH-4; DH-1 · **Ht:** 5'11" **Wt:** 195 **Born:** 7/27/73 **Age:** 30

		BATTING																BASERUNNING				AVERAGES		
Year Team	Lg	G	AB	H	2B	3B	HR	(Hm | Rd)	TB	R	RBI	RC	TBB	IBB	SO	HBP	SH	SF	SB	CS	SB%	GDP	Avg	OBP	Slg
1997 Cleveland	AL	5	15	5	0	0	0	(0 | 0)	5	2	1	2	0	0	2	0	0	0	0	0	-	0	.333	.333	.333
1998 Cleveland	AL	32	90	29	6	0	2	(1 | 1)	41	13	12	13	4	0	8	1	1	1	2	4	.33	1	.322	.354	.456
1999 Cleveland	AL	113	332	87	22	1	2	(1 | 1)	117	41	24	34	25	1	41	1	4	6	5	4	.56	12	.262	.310	.352

Year Team	Lg	G	AB	H	2B	3B	HR	(Hm Rd)	TB	R	RBI	RC	TBB	IBB	SO	HBP	SH	SF	SB	CS	SB%	GDP	Avg	OBP	Slg
2000 Cle-Pit		80	239	70	15	1	5	(3 2)	102	27	27	34	18	2	24	0	4	2	2	2	.50	6	.293	.340	.427
2001 Pit-NYY		94	228	48	8	1	2	(1 1)	64	17	20	9	9	0	37	0	2	2	0	5	.00	10	.211	.238	.281
2002 New York	AL	60	105	19	2	2	2	(2 0)	31	17	11	8	8	0	22	0	6	0	1	1	.50	2	.181	.239	.295
2003 New York	AL	63	135	31	9	0	3	(1 2)	49	18	15	13	7	0	14	2	2	1	3	1	.75	3	.230	.276	.363
2000 Cleveland	AL	40	117	38	9	0	2	(2 0)	53	16	12	19	7	0	11	0	2	1	2	1	.67	2	.325	.360	.453
2000 Pittsburgh	NL	40	122	32	6	1	3	(1 2)	49	11	15	15	11	2	13	0	2	1	0	1	.00	4	.262	.321	.402
2001 Pittsburgh	NL	46	129	24	3	0	1	(0 1)	30	7	8	1	3	0	23	0	0	1	0	3	.00	7	.186	.203	.233
2001 New York	AL	48	99	24	5	1	1	(1 0)	34	10	12	8	6	0	14	0	2	1	0	2	.00	3	.242	.283	.343
7 ML YEARS		447	1144	289	62	5	16	(9 7)	409	135	110	113	71	3	148	4	19	12	13	17	.43	34	.253	.296	.358

Jack Wilson

Bats: R **Throws:** R **Pos:** SS-149; PH-2   **Ht:** 6'0" **Wt:** 195 **Born:** 12/29/77 **Age:** 26

Year Team	Lg	G	AB	H	2B	3B	HR	(Hm Rd)	TB	R	RBI	RC	TBB	IBB	SO	HBP	SH	SF	SB	CS	SB%	GDP	Avg	OBP	Slg
2001 Pittsburgh	NL	108	390	87	17	1	3	(0 3)	115	44	25	27	16	2	70	1	17	1	1	3	.25	4	.223	.255	.295
2002 Pittsburgh	NL	147	527	133	22	4	4	(2 2)	175	77	47	58	37	2	74	4	17	1	5	2	.71	7	.252	.306	.332
2003 Pittsburgh	NL	150	558	143	21	3	9	(2 7)	197	58	62	61	36	3	74	4	11	6	5	5	.50	11	.256	.303	.353
3 ML YEARS		405	1475	363	60	8	16	(4 12)	487	179	134	146	89	7	218	9	45	8	11	10	.52	22	.246	.292	.330

Kris Wilson

Pitches: R **Bats:** R **Pos:** RP-25; SP-4   **Ht:** 6'4" **Wt:** 225 **Born:** 8/6/76 **Age:** 27

Year Team	Lg	G	GS	CG	GF	IP	BFP	H	R	ER	HR	SH	SF	HB	TBB	IBB	SO	WP	Bk	W	L	Pct	ShO	Sv-Op	Hld	ERC	ERA
2003 Omaha*	AAA	5	0	0	3	12.1	61	21	12	11	2	1	1	1	3	0	9	0	1	0	2	.000	0	0--	-	8.59	8.03
2000 Kansas City	AL	20	0	0	5	34.1	145	38	16	16	3	1	1	0	11	3	17	0	0	1	0	1.000	0	0-1	0	4.25	4.19
2001 Kansas City	AL	29	15	0	6	109.1	487	132	78	63	26	1	3	7	32	0	67	1	0	6	5	.545	0	1-1	0	6.17	5.19
2002 Kansas City	AL	12	0	0	4	18.2	91	29	18	17	7	0	2	2	5	0	10	0	0	2	0	1.000	0	0-2	0	9.63	8.20
2003 Kansas City	AL	29	4	0	7	72.2	328	92	49	43	13	0	4	6	16	3	42	0	1	6	3	.667	0	0-1	1	5.69	5.33
4 ML YEARS		90	19	0	22	235.0	1051	291	161	139	49	2	10	15	64	6	136	1	1	14	9	.609	0	1-5	1	5.99	5.32

Paul Wilson

Pitches: R **Bats:** R **Pos:** SP-28   **Ht:** 6'5" **Wt:** 214 **Born:** 3/28/73 **Age:** 31

Year Team	Lg	G	GS	CG	GF	IP	BFP	H	R	ER	HR	SH	SF	HB	TBB	IBB	SO	WP	Bk	W	L	Pct	ShO	Sv-Op	Hld	ERC	ERA
1996 New York	NL	26	26	1	0	149.0	677	157	102	89	15	7	3	10	71	11	109	3	3	5	12	.294	0	0-0	0	4.77	5.38
2000 Tampa Bay	AL	11	7	0	0	51.0	206	38	20	19	1	2	2	4	16	2	40	1	0	1	4	.200	0	0-0	1	2.17	3.35
2001 Tampa Bay	AL	37	24	0	6	151.1	674	165	94	82	21	3	12	13	52	2	119	7	0	8	9	.471	0	0-1	0	4.94	4.88
2002 Tampa Bay	AL	30	30	1	0	193.2	851	219	113	104	29	2	6	13	67	2	111	4	1	6	12	.333	0	0-0	0	5.30	4.83
2003 Cincinnati	NL	28	28	0	0	166.2	730	190	97	86	24	7	0	7	50	5	93	1	0	8	10	.444	0	0-0	1	4.92	4.64
5 ML YEARS		132	115	2	6	711.2	3138	769	426	380	90	21	23	47	256	22	472	16	4	28	47	.373	0	0-1	1	4.78	4.81

Preston Wilson

Bats: R **Throws:** R **Pos:** CF-155; PH-1   **Ht:** 6'2" **Wt:** 213 **Born:** 7/19/74 **Age:** 29

Year Team	Lg	G	AB	H	2B	3B	HR	(Hm Rd)	TB	R	RBI	RC	TBB	IBB	SO	HBP	SH	SF	SB	CS	SB%	GDP	Avg	OBP	Slg
1998 NYM-Fla	NL	22	51	8	2	0	1	(1 0)	13	7	3	3	6	0	21	1	2	0	1	1	.50	0	.157	.259	.255
1999 Florida	NL	149	482	135	21	4	26	(8 18)	242	67	71	81	46	3	156	9	0	6	11	4	.73	15	.280	.350	.502
2000 Florida	NL	161	605	160	35	3	31	(12 19)	294	94	121	97	55	1	187	8	0	6	36	14	.72	11	.264	.331	.486
2001 Florida	NL	123	468	128	30	2	23	(9 14)	231	70	71	73	36	2	107	6	0	3	20	8	.71	14	.274	.331	.494
2002 Florida	NL	141	510	124	22	2	23	(8 15)	219	80	65	59	58	3	140	9	2	3	20	11	.65	17	.243	.329	.429
2003 Colorado	NL	155	600	169	43	1	36	(21 15)	322	94	141	113	54	1	139	4	0	3	14	7	.67	23	.282	.343	.537
1998 New York	NL	8	20	6	2	0	0	(0 0)	8	3	2	3	2	0	8	0	0	0	1	1	.50	0	.300	.364	.400
1998 Florida	NL	14	31	2	0	0	1	(1 0)	5	4	1	0	4	0	13	1	2	0	0	0	-	0	.065	.194	.161
6 ML YEARS		751	2716	724	153	12	140	(59 81)	1321	412	472	426	255	10	750	37	4	21	102	45	.69	80	.267	.335	.486

Tom Wilson

Bats: R **Throws:** R **Pos:** C-76; PH-17; 1B-14; LF-1; RF-1; DH-1   **Ht:** 6'3" **Wt:** 220 **Born:** 12/19/70 **Age:** 33

Year Team	Lg	G	AB	H	2B	3B	HR	(Hm Rd)	TB	R	RBI	RC	TBB	IBB	SO	HBP	SH	SF	SB	CS	SB%	GDP	Avg	OBP	Slg
2001 Oakland	AL	9	21	4	0	0	2	(1 1)	10	4	4	2	1	0	5	1	0	1	0	0	-	1	.190	.250	.476
2002 Toronto	AL	96	265	68	10	0	8	(6 2)	102	33	37	37	28	0	79	5	0	4	0	0	-	6	.257	.334	.385
2003 Toronto	AL	96	256	66	19	0	5	(2 3)	100	37	35	29	28	0	80	1	0	2	0	0	-	4	.258	.331	.391
3 ML YEARS		201	542	138	29	0	15	(9 6)	212	74	76	68	57	0	164	7	0	7	0	0	-	11	.255	.330	.391

Vance Wilson

Bats: R **Throws:** R **Pos:** C-89; PH-8; PR-5   **Ht:** 5'11" **Wt:** 190 **Born:** 3/17/73 **Age:** 31

Year Team	Lg	G	AB	H	2B	3B	HR	(Hm Rd)	TB	R	RBI	RC	TBB	IBB	SO	HBP	SH	SF	SB	CS	SB%	GDP	Avg	OBP	Slg
1999 New York	NL	1	0	0	0	0	0	(0 0)	0	0	0	0	0	0	0	0	0	0	0	0	-	0	-	-	-
2000 New York	NL	4	4	0	0	0	0	(0 0)	0	0	0	0	0	0	2	0	0	0	0	0	-	0	.000	.000	.000
2001 New York	NL	32	57	17	3	0	0	(0 0)	20	3	6	6	2	0	16	2	0	1	0	1	.00	1	.298	.339	.351
2002 New York	NL	74	163	40	7	0	5	(3 2)	62	19	26	21	5	0	32	8	2	0	0	1	.00	4	.245	.301	.380
2003 New York	NL	96	268	65	9	1	8	(3 5)	100	28	39	30	15	1	56	5	2	2	1	2	.33	6	.243	.293	.373
5 ML YEARS		207	492	122	19	1	13	(6 7)	182	50	71	57	22	1	106	15	4	3	1	4	.20	11	.248	.299	.370

Randy Winn

Bats: B Throws: R Pos: LF-139; CF-20; RF-4   Ht: 6'2" Wt: 197 Born: 6/9/74 Age: 30

								BATTING										BASERUNNING				AVERAGES		
Year Team	Lg	G	AB	H	2B	3B	HR	(Hm | Rd)	TB	R	RBI	RC	TBB	IBB	SO	HBP	SH	SF	SB	CS	SB%	GDP	Avg	OBP	Slg
1998 Tampa Bay	AL	109	338	94	9	9	1	(0 | 1)	124	51	17	44	29	0	69	1	11	0	26	12	.68	2	.278	.337	.367
1999 Tampa Bay	AL	79	303	81	16	4	2	(2 | 0)	111	44	24	32	17	0	63	1	1	2	9	9	.50	3	.267	.307	.366
2000 Tampa Bay	AL	51	159	40	5	0	1	(1 | 0)	48	28	16	18	26	0	25	2	2	1	6	7	.46	2	.252	.362	.302
2001 Tampa Bay	AL	128	429	117	25	6	6	(3 | 3)	172	54	50	56	38	0	81	6	5	2	12	10	.55	10	.273	.339	.401
2002 Tampa Bay	AL	152	607	181	39	9	14	(9 | 5)	280	87	75	105	55	3	109	6	1	5	27	8	.77	9	.298	.360	.461
2003 Seattle	AL	157	600	177	37	4	11	(6 | 5)	255	103	75	97	41	0	108	8	6	5	23	5	.82	9	.295	.346	.425
6 ML YEARS		676	2436	690	131	32	35	(21 | 14)	990	367	257	352	206	3	455	24	26	15	103	51	.67	35	.283	.343	.406

Jay Witasick

Pitches: R Bats: R Pos: RP-46   Ht: 6'4" Wt: 235 Born: 8/28/72 Age: 31

			HOW MUCH HE PITCHED					WHAT HE GAVE UP										THE RESULTS						
Year Team	Lg	G	GS	CG	GF	IP	BFP	H	R	ER	HR	SH	SF	HB	TBB	IBB	SO	WP	Bk	W	L	Pct	ShO	Sv-Op	Hld	ERC	ERA
2003 Portland*	AAA	5	0	0	3	6.0	24	4	2	2	0	0	1	0	1	0	8	1	0	0	0	-	0	1--	-	1.18	3.00
2003 Lk Elsinore*	A+	4	0	0	4	4.2	20	6	4	3	0	0	0	0	0	0	7	0	0	0	0	-	0	0--	-	3.32	5.79
1996 Oakland	AL	12	0	0	6	13.0	55	12	9	9	5	0	1	0	5	0	12	2	0	1	1	.500	0	0-1	0	5.52	6.23
1997 Oakland	AL	8	0	0	4	11.0	53	14	7	7	2	1	0	0	6	0	8	0	0	0	0	-	0	0-0	1	6.81	5.73
1998 Oakland	AL	7	3	0	1	27.0	131	36	24	19	9	0	0	0	15	1	29	2	0	1	3	.250	0	0-0	0	8.53	6.33
1999 Kansas City	AL	32	28	1	2	158.1	732	191	108	98	23	4	8	8	83	1	102	4	2	9	12	.429	1	0-0	0	6.45	5.57
2000 KC-SD		33	25	2	2	150.0	697	178	107	97	24	8	4	7	73	5	121	5	1	6	10	.375	0	0-0	0	6.09	5.82
2001 SD-NYY		63	0	0	17	79.0	352	78	41	29	8	3	2	6	33	4	106	4	0	8	2	.800	0	1-4	10	4.22	3.30
2002 San Francisco	NL	44	0	0	9	68.1	276	58	19	18	3	2	1	4	21	3	54	3	0	1	0	1.000	0	0-0	4	2.78	2.37
2003 San Diego	NL	46	0	0	14	45.2	202	42	24	23	6	3	1	1	25	4	42	5	0	3	7	.300	0	2-7	12	4.34	4.53
2000 Kansas City	AL	22	14	2	2	89.1	410	109	65	59	15	3	3	4	38	0	67	3	0	3	8	.273	0	0-0	0	6.19	5.94
2000 San Diego	NL	11	11	0	0	60.2	287	69	42	38	9	5	1	3	35	5	54	2	1	3	2	.600	0	0-0	0	5.94	5.64
2001 San Diego	NL	31	0	0	9	38.2	164	31	14	8	3	3	0	4	15	3	53	3	0	5	2	.714	0	1-3	5	3.05	1.86
2001 New York	AL	32	0	0	8	40.1	188	47	27	21	5	0	2	2	18	1	53	1	0	3	0	1.000	0	0-1	5	5.43	4.69
8 ML YEARS		245	56	3	52	552.1	2498	609	339	300	80	21	17	26	261	18	474	25	3	29	35	.453	1	3-12	27	5.44	4.89

Kevin Witt

Bats: L Throws: R Pos: DH-36; 1B-27; PH-20; LF-13; 3B-5   Ht: 6'4" Wt: 220 Born: 1/5/76 Age: 28

								BATTING										BASERUNNING				AVERAGES		
Year Team	Lg	G	AB	H	2B	3B	HR	(Hm	Rd)	TB	R	RBI	RC	TBB	IBB	SO	HBP	SH	SF	SB	CS	SB%	GDP	Avg	OBP	Slg
2003 Toledo*	AAA	39	133	42	10	0	9	(-	-)	79	22	28	29	16	1	36	1	0	1	0	0	-	2	.316	.391	.594
1998 Toronto	AL	5	7	1	0	0	0	(0	0)	1	0	0	0	0	0	3	0	0	0	0	0	-	0	.143	.143	.143
1999 Toronto	AL	15	34	7	1	0	1	(1	0)	11	3	5	3	2	0	9	0	1	0	0	0	-	0	.206	.250	.324
2001 San Diego	NL	14	27	5	0	0	2	(1	1)	11	5	5	3	2	0	7	0	0	1	0	0	-	0	.185	.233	.407
2003 Detroit	AL	93	270	71	9	0	10	(4	6)	110	25	26	24	15	0	68	1	0	3	1	1	.50	5	.263	.301	.407
4 ML YEARS		127	338	84	10	0	13	(6	7)	133	33	36	30	19	0	87	1	1	4	1	1	.50	5	.249	.287	.393

Mark Wohlers

Pitches: R Bats: R Pos: RP   Ht: 6'4" Wt: 207 Born: 1/23/70 Age: 34

			HOW MUCH HE PITCHED					WHAT HE GAVE UP										THE RESULTS						
Year Team	Lg	G	GS	CG	GF	IP	BFP	H	R	ER	HR	SH	SF	HB	TBB	IBB	SO	WP	Bk	W	L	Pct	ShO	Sv-Op	Hld	ERC	ERA
1991 Atlanta	NL	17	0	0	4	19.2	89	17	7	7	1	2	1	2	13	3	13	0	0	3	1	.750	0	2-4	2	4.07	3.20
1992 Atlanta	NL	32	0	0	16	35.1	140	28	11	10	0	5	1	1	14	4	17	1	0	1	2	.333	0	4-6	2	2.37	2.55
1993 Atlanta	NL	46	0	0	13	48.0	199	37	25	24	2	5	1	1	22	3	45	0	0	6	2	.750	0	0-0	12	2.69	4.50
1994 Atlanta	NL	51	0	0	15	51.0	236	51	35	26	1	4	6	0	33	9	58	2	0	7	2	.778	0	1-2	7	4.02	4.59
1995 Atlanta	NL	65	0	0	49	64.2	269	51	16	15	2	2	0	1	24	3	90	4	0	7	3	.700	0	25-29	2	2.36	2.09
1996 Atlanta	NL	77	0	0	64	77.1	323	71	30	26	8	2	2	2	21	3	100	10	0	2	4	.333	0	39-44	0	3.17	3.03
1997 Atlanta	NL	71	0	0	55	69.1	300	57	29	27	4	4	4	0	38	0	92	6	0	5	7	.417	0	33-40	1	3.33	3.50
1998 Atlanta	NL	27	0	0	17	20.1	113	18	23	23	2	1	0	1	33	0	22	7	0	0	1	.000	0	8-8	0	8.41	10.18
1999 Atlanta	NL	2	0	0	0	0.2	10	1	2	2	0	1	0	0	6	0	0	0	0	0	0	-	0	0-0	0	41.75	27.00
2000 Cincinnati	NL	20	0	0	7	28.0	119	19	14	14	3	2	1	0	17	0	20	2	0	1	2	.333	0	0-0	0	3.14	4.50
2001 Cin-NYY		61	0	0	25	67.2	298	69	40	32	8	5	3	2	25	2	54	11	0	4	1	.800	0	0-1	13	4.18	4.26
2002 Cleveland	AL	64	0	0	28	71.1	304	71	41	38	6	1	2	3	26	3	46	7	0	3	4	.429	0	7-11	10	3.94	4.79
2001 Cincinnati	NL	30	0	0	11	32.0	139	36	20	14	5	4	1	1	7	2	21	4	0	3	1	.750	0	0-1	8	4.41	3.94
2001 New York	AL	31	0	0	14	35.2	159	33	20	18	3	1	2	1	18	0	33	7	0	1	0	1.000	0	0-0	5	3.96	4.54
12 ML YEARS		533	0	0	293	553.1	2400	490	273	244	37	34	21	13	272	30	557	50	0	39	29	.574	0	119-145	49	3.54	3.97

Randy Wolf

Pitches: L Bats: L Pos: SP-33   Ht: 6'0" Wt: 194 Born: 8/22/76 Age: 27

			HOW MUCH HE PITCHED					WHAT HE GAVE UP										THE RESULTS						
Year Team	Lg	G	GS	CG	GF	IP	BFP	H	R	ER	HR	SH	SF	HB	TBB	IBB	SO	WP	Bk	W	L	Pct	ShO	Sv-Op	Hld	ERC	ERA
1999 Philadelphia	NL	22	21	0	0	121.2	552	126	78	75	20	5	1	5	67	0	116	4	0	6	9	.400	0	0-0	0	5.54	5.55
2000 Philadelphia	NL	32	32	1	0	206.1	889	210	107	100	25	10	8	8	83	2	160	4	0	11	9	.550	0	0-0	0	4.54	4.36
2001 Philadelphia	NL	28	25	4	1	163.0	684	150	74	67	15	11	7	10	51	4	152	1	0	10	11	.476	2	0-0	0	3.46	3.70
2002 Philadelphia	NL	31	31	3	0	210.2	855	172	77	75	23	7	6	7	63	5	172	4	0	11	9	.550	2	0-0	0	2.88	3.20
2003 Philadelphia	NL	33	33	2	0	200.0	850	176	101	94	27	8	4	6	78	4	177	6	0	16	10	.615	2	0-0	0	3.67	4.23
5 ML YEARS		146	142	10	1	901.2	3830	834	437	411	110	41	26	36	342	15	777	16	0	54	48	.529	6	0-0	0	3.87	4.10

Tony Womack

Bats: L **Throws:** R **Pos:** SS-73; 2B-21; PH-10; PR-5; CF-1 **Ht:** 5'9" **Wt:** 170 **Born:** 9/25/69 **Age:** 34

Year Team	Lg	G	AB	H	2B	3B	HR	(Hm	Rd)	TB	R	RBI	RC	TBB	IBB	SO	HBP	SH	SF	SB	CS	SB%	GDP	Avg	OBP	Slg
2003 El Paso*	AA	4	17	5	0	0	0	(-	-)	5	3	2	3	2	1	2	0	0	0	3	0	1.00	0	.294	.368	.294
1993 Pittsburgh	NL	15	24	2	0	0	0	(0	0)	2	5	0	0	3	0	3	0	1	0	2	1	1.00	0	.083	.185	.083
1994 Pittsburgh	NL	5	12	4	0	0	0	(0	0)	4	4	1	2	2	0	3	0	0	0	0	0	-	0	.333	.429	.333
1996 Pittsburgh	NL	17	30	10	3	1	0	(0	0)	15	11	7	8	6	0	1	1	3	0	2	0	1.00	0	.333	.459	.500
1997 Pittsburgh	NL	155	641	178	26	9	6	(5	1)	240	85	50	87	43	2	109	3	2	0	60	7	.90	6	.278	.326	.374
1998 Pittsburgh	NL	159	655	185	26	7	3	(2	1)	234	85	45	84	38	1	94	0	6	5	58	8	.88	4	.282	.319	.357
1999 Arizona	NL	144	614	170	25	10	4	(1	3)	227	111	41	88	52	0	68	2	9	7	72	13	.85	4	.277	.332	.370
2000 Arizona	NL	146	617	167	21	14	7	(4	3)	237	95	57	78	30	0	74	5	2	5	45	11	.80	6	.271	.307	.384
2001 Arizona	NL	125	481	128	19	5	3	(2	1)	166	66	30	54	23	2	54	6	7	1	28	7	.80	4	.266	.307	.345
2002 Arizona	NL	153	590	160	23	5	5	(4	1)	208	90	57	74	46	2	80	4	6	6	29	12	.71	9	.271	.325	.353
2003 Ari-Col-ChC	NL	103	349	79	14	4	2	(2	0)	107	43	22	23	9	0	47	3	2	1	13	5	.72	7	.226	.251	.307
2003 Arizona	NL	61	219	52	10	3	2	(2	0)	74	30	15	16	8	0	27	2	1	1	8	3	.73	6	.237	.270	.338
2003 Colorado	NL	21	79	15	2	0	0	(0	0)	17	9	5	3	0	0	9	1	1	0	3	1	.75	1	.190	.200	.215
2003 Chicago	NL	21	51	12	2	1	0	(0	0)	16	4	2	4	1	0	11	0	0	0	2	1	.67	0	.235	.250	.314
10 ML YEARS		1022	4013	1083	157	55	30	(20	10)	1440	595	310	498	252	7	533	24	38	25	309	63	.83	40	.270	.315	.359

Kerry Wood

Pitches: R **Bats:** R **Pos:** SP-32 **Ht:** 6'5" **Wt:** 230 **Born:** 6/16/77 **Age:** 27

Year Team	Lg	G	GS	CG	GF	IP	BFP	H	R	ER	HR	SH	SF	HB	TBB	IBB	SO	WP	Bk	W	L	Pct	ShO	Sv-Op	Hld	ERC	ERA
1998 Chicago	NL	26	26	1	0	166.2	699	117	69	63	14	2	4	11	85	1	233	6	3	13	6	.684	1	0-0	0	3.03	3.40
2000 Chicago	NL	23	23	1	0	137.0	603	112	77	73	17	7	5	9	87	0	132	5	1	8	7	.533	0	0-0	0	4.43	4.80
2001 Chicago	NL	28	28	1	0	174.1	740	127	70	65	16	4	5	10	92	3	217	9	0	12	6	.667	1	0-0	0	3.22	3.36
2002 Chicago	NL	33	33	4	0	213.2	895	169	92	87	22	13	5	16	97	5	217	8	1	12	11	.522	1	0-0	0	3.46	3.66
2003 Chicago	NL	32	32	4	0	211.0	887	152	77	75	24	11	6	21	100	2	266	10	0	14	11	.560	2	0-0	0	3.31	3.20
5 ML YEARS		142	142	11	0	902.2	3824	677	385	363	93	37	25	67	461	11	1065	38	5	59	41	.590	5	0-0	0	3.44	3.62

Mike Wood

Pitches: R **Bats:** R **Pos:** RP-6; SP-1 **Ht:** 6'3" **Wt:** 180 **Born:** 4/26/80 **Age:** 24

Year Team	Lg	G	GS	CG	GF	IP	BFP	H	R	ER	HR	SH	SF	HB	TBB	IBB	SO	WP	Bk	W	L	Pct	ShO	Sv-Op	Hld	ERC	ERA
2001 Vancouver	A-	5	2	0	2	21.2	86	17	4	3	0	0	1	0	4	0	24	2	0	2	0	1.000	0	0- -	-	1.61	1.25
2001 Modesto	A+	10	9	0	0	58.1	233	46	22	20	6	3	0	2	10	3	52	2	0	4	3	.571	0	0- -	-	2.17	3.09
2002 Modesto	A+	7	7	0	0	41.1	170	41	17	16	4	3	3	3	6	0	50	4	1	3	3	.500	0	0- -	-	3.32	3.48
2002 Midland	AA	17	17	0	0	105.2	443	103	41	37	8	5	5	7	29	0	63	1	0	11	3	.786	0	0- -	-	3.58	3.15
2003 Sacramento	AAA	16	16	0	0	91.1	373	87	34	31	5	5	2	4	23	1	59	3	1	9	3	.750	0	0- -	-	3.17	3.05
2003 Oakland	AL	7	1	0	2	13.2	72	24	17	16	1	1	0	2	7	2	15	2	0	2	1	.667	0	0-0	0	9.45	10.54

Steve Woodard

Pitches: R **Bats:** L **Pos:** RP-7 **Ht:** 6'4" **Wt:** 217 **Born:** 5/15/75 **Age:** 29

Year Team	Lg	G	GS	CG	GF	IP	BFP	H	R	ER	HR	SH	SF	HB	TBB	IBB	SO	WP	Bk	W	L	Pct	ShO	Sv-Op	Hld	ERC	ERA
2003 Pawtucket*	AAA	31	11	0	9	94.0	393	103	55	49	9	4	6	3	12	1	58	3	0	6	7	.462	0	2- -	-	3.60	4.69
1997 Milwaukee	NL	7	7	0	0	36.2	153	39	25	21	5	0	0	2	6	0	32	0	0	3	3	.500	0	0-0	0	3.98	5.15
1998 Milwaukee	NL	34	26	0	2	165.2	692	170	83	77	19	2	4	9	33	4	135	3	2	10	12	.455	0	0-0	0	3.73	4.18
1999 Milwaukee	NL	31	29	2	0	185.0	801	219	101	93	23	9	4	6	36	7	119	4	1	11	8	.579	0	0-0	0	4.52	4.52
2000 Mil-Cle		40	22	1	7	147.2	659	182	105	96	26	8	4	6	44	5	100	8	0	4	10	.286	0	0-0	0	5.71	5.85
2001 Cleveland	AL	29	10	0	4	97.0	429	129	59	56	10	7	3	5	17	1	52	4	3	3	3	.500	0	0-0	0	5.33	5.20
2002 Texas	AL	14	0	0	4	17.2	83	20	13	13	4	0	0	2	8	1	14	0	1	0	0	-	0	0-1	1	6.28	6.62
2003 Boston	AL	7	0	0	1	17.2	81	23	10	10	3	0	1	1	5	2	12	1	0	1	0	1.000	0	0-0	0	5.87	5.09
2000 Milwaukee	NL	27	11	1	6	93.2	432	125	70	62	16	7	3	4	33	4	65	5	0	1	7	.125	0	0-0	0	6.55	5.96
2000 Cleveland	AL	13	11	0	1	54.0	227	57	35	34	10	1	1	2	11	1	35	3	0	3	3	.500	0	0-0	0	4.31	5.67
7 ML YEARS		162	94	3	15	667.1	2898	782	396	366	90	26	16	31	149	20	464	20	7	32	36	.471	0	0-1	2	4.74	4.94

Chris Woodward

Bats: R **Throws:** R **Pos:** SS-103; PR-2 **Ht:** 6'0" **Wt:** 185 **Born:** 6/27/76 **Age:** 28

Year Team	Lg	G	AB	H	2B	3B	HR	(Hm	Rd)	TB	R	RBI	RC	TBB	IBB	SO	HBP	SH	SF	SB	CS	SB%	GDP	Avg	OBP	Slg
1999 Toronto	AL	14	26	6	1	0	0	(0	0)	7	1	2	2	2	0	6	0	0	1	0	0	-	1	.231	.276	.269
2000 Toronto	AL	37	104	19	7	0	3	(1	2)	35	16	14	9	10	3	28	0	1	0	1	0	1.00	1	.183	.254	.337
2001 Toronto	AL	37	63	12	3	2	2	(2	0)	25	9	5	4	1	0	14	0	2	0	0	1	.00	1	.190	.203	.397
2002 Toronto	AL	90	312	86	13	4	13	(9	4)	146	48	45	45	26	0	72	3	1	8	3	0	1.00	8	.276	.330	.468
2003 Toronto	AL	104	349	91	22	2	7	(4	3)	138	49	45	41	28	0	72	3	0	6	1	2	.33	6	.261	.316	.395
5 ML YEARS		282	854	214	46	8	25	(16	9)	351	123	111	101	67	3	192	6	4	15	5	3	.63	17	.251	.305	.411

Shawn Wooten

Bats: R **Throws:** R **Pos:** 1B-32; PH-23; DH-20; C-19; 3B-17 **Ht:** 5'10" **Wt:** 225 **Born:** 7/24/72 **Age:** 31

Year Team	Lg	G	AB	H	2B	3B	HR	(Hm	Rd)	TB	R	RBI	RC	TBB	IBB	SO	HBP	SH	SF	SB	CS	SB%	GDP	Avg	OBP	Slg
2000 Anaheim	AL	7	9	5	1	0	0	(0	0)	6	2	1	3	0	0	0	0	0	0	0	0	-	0	.556	.556	.667
2001 Anaheim	AL	79	221	69	8	1	8	(3	5)	103	24	32	33	5	0	42	3	0	3	2	0	1.00	5	.312	.332	.466
2002 Anaheim	AL	49	113	33	8	0	3	(2	1)	50	13	19	17	6	1	24	1	0	1	2	0	1.00	3	.292	.331	.442
2003 Anaheim	AL	98	272	66	8	0	7	(5	2)	95	25	32	21	24	5	45	1	0	3	0	4	.00	7	.243	.303	.349
4 ML YEARS		233	615	173	25	1	18	(10	8)	254	64	84	74	35	6	111	5	0	7	4	4	.50	15	.281	.322	.413

Tim Worrell

Pitches: R **Bats:** R **Pos:** RP-76   **Ht:** 6'4" **Wt:** 230 **Born:** 7/5/67 **Age:** 36

Year Team	Lg	G	GS	CG	GF	IP	BFP	H	R	ER	HR	SH	SF	HB	TBB	IBB	SO	WP	Bk	W	L	Pct	ShO	Sv-Op	Hld	ERC	ERA
1993 San Diego	NL	21	16	0	1	100.2	443	104	63	55	11	8	5	0	43	5	52	3	0	2	7	.222	0	0-0	1	4.31	4.92
1994 San Diego	NL	3	3	0	0	14.2	59	9	7	6	0	0	1	0	5	0	14	0	0	0	1	.000	0	0-0	0	1.40	3.68
1995 San Diego	NL	9	0	0	4	13.1	63	16	7	7	2	1	0	1	6	0	13	1	0	1	0	1.000	0	0-0	0	6.01	4.73
1996 San Diego	NL	50	11	0	8	121.0	510	109	45	41	9	3	1	6	39	1	99	0	0	9	7	.563	0	1-2	10	3.22	3.05
1997 San Diego	NL	60	10	0	14	106.1	483	116	67	61	14	6	6	7	50	2	81	2	1	4	8	.333	0	3-7	16	5.34	5.16
1998 Det-Cle-Oak	AL	43	9	0	5	103.0	440	106	62	60	16	2	3	1	29	3	82	2	0	2	7	.222	0	0-3	6	4.10	5.24
1999 Oakland	AL	53	0	0	17	69.1	309	69	38	32	6	1	1	3	34	1	62	1	0	2	2	.500	0	0-5	5	4.42	4.15
2000 Bal-ChC		59	0	0	29	69.1	307	72	26	23	10	4	1	1	29	11	57	1	0	5	6	.455	0	3-6	12	4.42	2.99
2001 San Francisco	NL	73	0	0	12	78.1	339	71	33	30	4	3	4	3	33	4	63	2	0	2	5	.286	0	0-3	13	3.32	3.45
2002 San Francisco	NL	80	0	0	23	72.0	296	55	21	18	3	3	4	0	30	2	55	0	0	8	2	.800	0	0-1	23	2.47	2.25
2003 San Francisco	NL	76	0	0	64	78.1	335	74	35	25	5	3	3	0	28	6	65	5	0	4	4	.500	0	38-45	1	3.19	2.87
1998 Detroit	AL	15	9	0	0	61.2	265	66	42	41	11	0	1	1	19	2	47	0	0	2	6	.250	0	0-1	0	4.68	5.98
1998 Cleveland	AL	3	0	0	1	5.1	24	6	3	3	0	0	2	0	2	0	2	0	0	0	0	-	0	0-0	0	3.84	5.06
1998 Oakland	AL	25	0	0	4	36.0	151	34	17	16	5	2	0	0	8	1	33	2	0	0	1	.000	0	0-2	6	3.20	4.00
2000 Baltimore	AL	5	0	0	2	7.1	39	12	6	6	3	0	0	0	5	3	5	0	0	2	2	.500	0	0-0	0	11.13	7.36
2000 Chicago	NL	54	0	0	27	62.0	268	60	20	17	7	4	1	1	24	8	52	1	0	3	4	.429	0	3-6	12	3.75	2.47
11 ML YEARS		**527**	**49**	**0**	**177**	**826.1**	**3584**	**801**	**404**	**358**	**80**	**34**	**29**	**22**	**326**	**35**	**643**	**17**	**1**	**39**	**49**	**.443**	**0**	**45-72**	**87**	**3.86**	**3.90**

Dan Wright

Pitches: R **Bats:** R **Pos:** SP-15; RP-5   **Ht:** 6'5" **Wt:** 225 **Born:** 12/14/77 **Age:** 26

Year Team	Lg	G	GS	CG	GF	IP	BFP	H	R	ER	HR	SH	SF	HB	TBB	IBB	SO	WP	Bk	W	L	Pct	ShO	Sv-Op	Hld	ERC	ERA
2001 Chicago	AL	13	12	0	1	66.1	307	72	45	42	12	1	5	2	39	1	36	5	0	5	3	.625	0	0-0	0	6.74	5.70
2002 Chicago	AL	33	33	0	0	196.1	855	200	124	113	32	7	10	6	71	1	136	10	1	14	12	.538	1	0-0	0	4.55	5.18
2003 Chicago	AL	20	15	0	1	86.1	387	91	63	59	16	6	4	3	46	2	47	6	0	1	7	.125	0	1-1	0	5.74	6.15
3 ML YEARS		**66**	**60**	**1**	**2**	**349.0**	**1549**	**369**	**232**	**214**	**60**	**14**	**19**	**11**	**156**	**4**	**219**	**21**	**1**	**20**	**22**	**.476**	**1**	**1-1**	**0**	**5.24**	**5.52**

Jamey Wright

Pitches: R **Bats:** R **Pos:** SP-4   **Ht:** 6'5" **Wt:** 234 **Born:** 12/24/74 **Age:** 29

Year Team	Lg	G	GS	CG	GF	IP	BFP	H	R	ER	HR	SH	SF	HB	TBB	IBB	SO	WP	Bk	W	L	Pct	ShO	Sv-Op	Hld	ERC	ERA
2003 Indianapolis*	AAA	7	4	0	0	22.0	108	32	21	18	5	1	1	3	10	0	17	1	0	1	3	.250	0	0--	-	8.86	7.36
2003 Oklahoma*	AAA	7	7	2	0	39.1	172	38	18	18	1	1	1	3	21	0	40	2	0	2	1	.667	0	0--	-	4.25	4.12
2003 Omaha*	AAA	13	12	1	0	76.2	330	70	35	31	10	3	1	3	38	0	65	2	0	3	5	.375	0	0--	-	4.40	3.64
1996 Colorado	NL	16	15	0	0	91.1	406	105	60	50	8	4	2	7	41	1	45	1	2	4	4	.500	0	0-0	1	5.50	4.93
1997 Colorado	NL	26	26	1	0	149.2	698	198	113	104	19	8	3	11	71	3	59	6	2	8	12	.400	0	0-0	0	6.96	6.25
1998 Colorado	NL	34	34	1	0	206.1	919	235	143	130	24	8	6	11	95	3	86	6	3	9	14	.391	0	0-0	0	5.57	5.67
1999 Colorado	NL	16	16	0	0	94.1	423	110	52	51	10	3	4	4	54	3	49	3	0	4	3	.571	0	0-0	0	6.19	4.87
2000 Milwaukee	NL	26	25	0	1	164.2	718	157	81	75	12	4	6	18	88	5	96	9	2	7	9	.438	0	0-0	0	4.67	4.10
2001 Milwaukee	NL	33	33	1	0	194.2	868	201	115	106	26	7	5	20	98	10	129	6	1	11	12	.478	1	0-0	0	5.36	4.90
2002 Mil-StL	NL	23	22	1	0	129.1	585	130	80	76	17	9	6	11	75	9	77	9	0	7	13	.350	1	0-0	0	5.35	5.29
2003 Kansas City	AL	4	4	2	0	25.1	106	23	14	12	1	0	0	1	11	0	19	0	0	1	2	.333	1	0-0	0	3.53	4.26
2002 Milwaukee	NL	19	19	1	0	114.1	515	115	72	68	15	9	6	11	63	8	69	8	0	5	13	.278	1	0-0	0	5.28	5.35
2002 St Louis	NL	4	3	0	0	15.0	70	15	8	8	2	0	0	0	12	1	8	1	0	2	0	1.000	0	0-0	0	5.87	4.80
8 ML YEARS		**178**	**175**	**6**	**1**	**1055.2**	**4723**	**1159**	**658**	**604**	**117**	**43**	**32**	**83**	**533**	**34**	**560**	**40**	**10**	**51**	**69**	**.425**	**3**	**0-0**	**1**	**5.55**	**5.15**

Jaret Wright

Pitches: R **Bats:** R **Pos:** RP-50   **Ht:** 6'2" **Wt:** 230 **Born:** 12/29/75 **Age:** 28

Year Team	Lg	G	GS	CG	GF	IP	BFP	H	R	ER	HR	SH	SF	HB	TBB	IBB	SO	WP	Bk	W	L	Pct	ShO	Sv-Op	Hld	ERC	ERA
2003 Portland*	AAA	12	1	0	1	19.0	81	16	7	3	0	0	0	2	7	0	21	2	0	2	1	.667	0	0--	-	2.79	1.42
1997 Cleveland	AL	16	16	0	0	90.1	388	81	45	44	9	3	4	5	35	0	63	1	0	8	3	.727	0	0-0	0	3.63	4.38
1998 Cleveland	AL	32	32	1	0	192.2	855	207	109	101	22	4	6	11	87	4	140	6	0	12	10	.545	1	0-0	0	5.07	4.72
1999 Cleveland	AL	26	26	0	0	133.2	609	144	99	90	18	3	3	7	77	1	91	4	0	8	10	.444	0	0-0	0	5.77	6.06
2000 Cleveland	AL	9	9	1	0	51.2	217	44	27	27	6	0	1	1	28	0	36	2	0	3	4	.429	1	0-0	0	4.13	4.70
2001 Cleveland	AL	7	7	0	0	29.0	140	36	23	21	2	2	1	0	22	0	18	1	1	2	2	.500	0	0-0	0	6.82	6.52
2002 Cleveland	AL	8	6	0	1	18.1	116	40	34	32	3	0	3	2	19	0	12	1	0	2	3	.400	0	0-0	0	15.90	15.71
2003 SD-Atl	NL	50	0	0	17	56.1	269	76	46	46	9	2	4	3	31	2	50	12	0	2	5	.286	0	2-5	4	7.59	7.35
2003 San Diego	NL	39	0	0	14	47.1	233	69	44	44	9	1	4	2	28	2	41	10	0	1	5	.167	0	2-4	1	8.71	8.37
2003 Atlanta	NL	11	0	0	3	9.0	36	7	2	2	0	1	0	1	3	0	9	2	0	1	0	1.000	0	0-1	3	2.51	2.00
7 ML YEARS		**148**	**96**	**2**	**18**	**572.0**	**2594**	**628**	**383**	**361**	**69**	**14**	**22**	**29**	**299**	**7**	**410**	**27**	**1**	**37**	**37**	**.500**	**2**	**2-5**	**4**	**5.53**	**5.68**

Kelly Wunsch

Pitches: L **Bats:** L **Pos:** RP-43   **Ht:** 6'5" **Wt:** 225 **Born:** 7/12/72 **Age:** 31

Year Team	Lg	G	GS	CG	GF	IP	BFP	H	R	ER	HR	SH	SF	HB	TBB	IBB	SO	WP	Bk	W	L	Pct	ShO	Sv-Op	Hld	ERC	ERA
2003 Charlotte*	AAA	3	0	0	0	3.1	17	6	3	2	1	0	1	2	0	0	4	0	0	0	1	.000	0	0--	-	12.48	5.40
2000 Chicago	AL	83	0	0	12	61.1	259	50	22	20	4	0	2	2	29	1	51	0	0	6	3	.667	0	1-5	25	3.22	2.93
2001 Chicago	AL	33	0	0	2	22.1	105	21	19	19	4	3	2	6	9	1	16	0	0	2	1	.667	0	0-2	3	5.11	7.66
2002 Chicago	AL	50	0	0	9	31.2	138	26	12	12	3	1	0	5	19	1	22	1	0	2	1	.667	0	0-1	9	4.51	3.41
2003 Chicago	AL	43	0	0	6	36.0	160	17	13	11	1	1	5	7	25	4	33	1	0	0	0	-	0	0-0	5	2.28	2.75
4 ML YEARS		**209**	**0**	**0**	**29**	**151.1**	**662**	**114**	**66**	**62**	**12**	**5**	**9**	**20**	**82**	**7**	**122**	**2**	**0**	**10**	**5**	**.667**	**0**	**1-8**	**42**	**3.51**	**3.69**

Esteban Yan

Pitches: R Bats: R Pos: RP-54　　　　Ht: 6'4" Wt: 255 Born: 6/22/75 Age: 29

Year Team	Lg	G	GS	CG	GF	IP	BFP	H	R	ER	HR	SH	SF	HB	TBB	IBB	SO	WP	Bk	W	L	Pct	ShO	Sv-Op	Hld	ERC	ERA
1996 Baltimore	AL	4	0	0	2	9.1	42	13	7	6	3	0	0	0	3	1	7	0	0	0	0	-	0	0-0	0	7.88	5.79
1997 Baltimore	AL	3	2	0	0	9.2	58	20	18	17	3	0	1	2	7	0	4	1	0	0	1	.000	0	0-0	0	15.60	15.83
1998 Tampa Bay	AL	64	0	0	18	88.2	381	78	41	38	11	1	3	5	41	2	77	6	0	5	4	.556	0	1-5	8	4.02	3.86
1999 Tampa Bay	AL	50	1	0	15	61.0	286	77	41	40	8	6	3	9	32	4	46	2	0	3	4	.429	0	0-3	7	7.13	5.90
2000 Tampa Bay	AL	43	20	0	8	137.2	618	158	98	95	26	4	6	11	42	0	111	7	1	7	8	.467	0	0-2	3	5.46	6.21
2001 Tampa Bay	AL	54	0	0	51	62.1	264	64	34	27	7	3	1	5	11	1	64	5	0	4	6	.400	0	22-31	0	3.68	3.90
2002 Tampa Bay	AL	55	0	0	47	69.0	305	70	35	33	10	2	1	3	29	1	53	5	1	7	8	.467	0	19-27	0	4.67	4.30
2003 Tex-StL		54	0	0	23	66.2	309	84	48	47	13	2	4	7	23	5	53	9	0	2	1	.667	0	1-1	4	6.39	6.35
2003 Texas	AL	15	0	0	6	23.1	110	31	19	18	5	0	0	2	7	1	25	5	0	0	1	.000	0	0-0	1	6.64	6.94
2003 St Louis	NL	39	0	0	17	43.1	199	53	29	29	8	2	4	5	16	4	28	4	0	2	0	1.000	0	1-1	3	6.26	6.02
8 ML YEARS		327	23	0	164	504.1	2263	564	322	303	81	18	19	42	188	14	415	35	2	28	32	.467	0	43-69	22	5.38	5.41

Dmitri Young

Bats: B Throws: R Pos: DH-74; LF-61; 3B-16; PH-6; 1B-1; PR-1　　　　Ht: 6'2" Wt: 235 Born: 10/11/73 Age: 30

Year Team	Lg	G	AB	H	2B	3B	HR	Hm	Rd	TB	R	RBI	RC	TBB	IBB	SO	HBP	SH	SF	SB	CS	SB%	GDP	Avg	OBP	Slg
1996 St Louis	NL	16	29	7	0	0	0	(0	0)	7	3	2	2	4	0	5	1	0	0	0	1	.00	1	.241	.353	.241
1997 St Louis	NL	110	333	86	14	3	5	(2	3)	121	38	34	40	38	3	63	2	1	3	6	5	.55	8	.258	.335	.363
1998 Cincinnati	NL	144	536	166	48	1	14	(3	11)	258	81	83	88	47	4	94	2	0	5	2	4	.33	16	.310	.364	.481
1999 Cincinnati	NL	127	373	112	30	2	14	(9	5)	188	63	56	63	30	1	71	2	0	4	3	1	.75	11	.300	.352	.504
2000 Cincinnati	NL	152	548	166	37	6	18	(6	12)	269	68	88	86	36	6	80	3	1	5	0	3	.00	16	.303	.346	.491
2001 Cincinnati	NL	142	540	163	28	3	21	(8	13)	260	68	69	83	37	10	77	5	1	3	8	5	.62	22	.302	.350	.481
2002 Detroit	AL	54	201	57	14	0	7	(5	2)	92	25	27	28	12	5	39	2	0	1	2	0	1.00	12	.284	.329	.458
2003 Detroit	AL	155	562	167	34	7	29	(10	19)	302	78	85	103	58	16	130	11	0	4	2	1	.67	16	.297	.372	.537
8 ML YEARS		900	3122	924	205	22	108	(43	65)	1497	424	444	493	262	45	559	28	3	25	23	20	.53	102	.296	.353	.480

Eric Young

Bats: R Throws: R Pos: 2B-117; PH-14; PR-4; CF-2; DH-1　　　　Ht: 5'8" Wt: 180 Born: 5/18/67 Age: 37

Year Team	Lg	G	AB	H	2B	3B	HR	Hm	Rd	TB	R	RBI	RC	TBB	IBB	SO	HBP	SH	SF	SB	CS	SB%	GDP	Avg	OBP	Slg
1992 Los Angeles	NL	49	132	34	1	0	1	(0	1)	38	9	11	12	8	0	9	0	4	0	6	1	.86	3	.258	.300	.288
1993 Colorado	NL	144	490	132	16	3	3	(0	0)	173	82	42	66	63	3	41	4	4	4	42	19	.69	9	.269	.355	.353
1994 Colorado	NL	90	228	62	13	1	7	(6	1)	98	37	30	40	38	1	17	2	5	2	18	7	.72	3	.272	.378	.430
1995 Colorado	NL	120	366	116	21	9	6	(5	1)	173	68	36	73	49	3	29	5	3	1	35	12	.74	4	.317	.404	.473
1996 Colorado	NL	141	568	184	23	4	8	(7	1)	239	113	74	99	47	1	31	21	2	5	53	19	.74	9	.324	.393	.421
1997 Col-LA	NL	155	622	174	33	4	8	(2	6)	247	106	61	93	71	1	54	9	10	6	45	14	.76	18	.280	.359	.397
1998 Los Angeles	NL	117	452	129	24	1	8	(7	1)	179	78	43	70	45	0	32	5	9	2	42	13	.76	4	.285	.355	.396
1999 Los Angeles	NL	119	456	128	24	2	2	(2	0)	162	73	41	65	63	0	26	5	6	4	51	22	.70	12	.281	.371	.355
2000 Chicago	NL	153	607	180	40	2	6	(5	1)	242	98	47	99	63	1	39	8	7	5	54	7	.89	12	.297	.367	.399
2001 Chicago	NL	149	603	168	43	4	6	(4	2)	237	98	42	78	42	1	45	9	15	3	31	14	.69	15	.279	.333	.393
2002 Milwaukee	NL	138	496	139	29	3	3	(2	1)	183	57	28	52	39	0	38	6	8	4	31	11	.74	14	.280	.338	.369
2003 Mil-SF	NL	135	475	119	20	1	15	(7	8)	186	80	34	54	57	2	44	5	2	2	28	12	.70	12	.251	.336	.392
1997 Colorado	NL	118	468	132	29	6	6	(2	4)	191	78	45	71	57	0	37	5	8	5	32	12	.73	16	.282	.363	.408
1997 Los Angeles	NL	37	154	42	4	2	2	(0	2)	56	28	16	22	14	1	17	4	2	1	13	2	.87	2	.273	.347	.364
2003 Milwaukee	NL	109	404	105	18	1	15	(7	8)	170	71	31	51	48	2	34	4	2	1	25	7	.78	9	.260	.344	.421
2003 San Francisco	NL	26	71	14	2	0	0	(0	0)	16	9	3	3	9	0	10	1	0	1	3	5	.38	3	.197	.293	.225
12 ML YEARS		1510	5495	1565	287	43	73	(50	23)	2157	899	489	801	585	13	405	79	75	38	436	151	.74	115	.285	.360	.393

Ernie Young

Bats: R Throws: R Pos: DH-4; PH-1　　　　Ht: 6'1" Wt: 234 Born: 7/8/69 Age: 34

Year Team	Lg	G	AB	H	2B	3B	HR	Hm	Rd	TB	R	RBI	RC	TBB	IBB	SO	HBP	SH	SF	SB	CS	SB%	GDP	Avg	OBP	Slg
2003 Toledo*	AAA	128	454	120	22	0	21	(-	-)	205	56	84	69	50	1	119	6	0	5	10	6	.63	10	.264	.342	.452
1994 Oakland	AL	11	30	2	1	0	0	(0	0)	3	2	3	0	1	0	8	0	0	0	0	0	-	1	.067	.097	.100
1995 Oakland	AL	26	50	10	3	0	2	(2	0)	19	9	5	6	8	0	12	0	0	0	0	0	-	1	.200	.310	.380
1996 Oakland	AL	141	462	112	19	4	19	(10	9)	196	72	64	62	52	1	118	7	3	4	7	5	.58	13	.242	.326	.424
1997 Oakland	AL	71	175	39	7	0	5	(3	2)	61	22	15	17	19	0	57	2	2	2	1	3	.25	6	.223	.303	.349
1998 Kansas City	AL	25	53	10	3	0	1	(0	1)	16	2	3	3	2	0	9	1	0	0	2	1	.67	3	.189	.232	.302
1999 Arizona	NL	6	11	2	0	0	0	(0	0)	2	1	0	1	3	0	2	1	0	0	0	0	-	0	.182	.400	.182
2003 Detroit	AL	5	11	2	0	0	0	(0	0)	2	0	0	0	4	0	5	0	0	0	0	2	.00	1	.182	.400	.182
7 ML YEARS		285	792	177	33	4	27	(15	12)	299	108	90	89	89	1	211	11	5	6	10	11	.48	25	.223	.308	.378

Jason Young

Pitches: R Bats: R Pos: RP-5; SP-3　　　　Ht: 6'5" Wt: 214 Born: 9/28/79 Age: 24

Year Team	Lg	G	GS	CG	GF	IP	BFP	H	R	ER	HR	SH	SF	HB	TBB	IBB	SO	WP	Bk	W	L	Pct	ShO	Sv-Op	Hld	ERC	ERA
2001 Salem	A+	17	17	2	0	104.2	439	104	47	40	8	0	0	10	28	0	91	5	0	6	7	.462	1	0- -	3	3.81	3.44
2002 Carolina	AA	14	14	1	0	88.2	359	71	30	26	1	1	1	3	30	0	76	0	2	7	4	.636	1	0- -	0	2.39	2.64
2002 Co Springs	AAA	13	13	0	0	79.2	362	87	52	44	10	1	0	3	38	0	74	3	0	6	5	.545	0	0- -	0	5.21	4.97
2003 Co Springs	AAA	23	21	2	0	116.1	525	128	63	51	10	6	2	8	37	0	99	3	0	6	7	.462	0	0- -	0	4.35	3.95
2003 Colorado	NL	8	3	0	1	21.1	108	34	22	20	8	1	1	1	9	0	18	2	0	0	2	.000	0	0-0	0	10.29	8.44

Kevin Young

Bats: R **Throws:** R **Pos:** 1B-44; PH-13; RF-1; PR-1   **Ht:** 6'3" **Wt:** 225 **Born:** 6/16/69 **Age:** 35

Year Team	Lg	G	AB	H	2B	3B	HR	(Hm	Rd)	TB	R	RBI	RC	TBB	IBB	SO	HBP	SH	SF	SB	CS	SB%	GDP	Avg	OBP	Slg
2003 Rochester*	AAA	4	7	1	1	0	0	(-	-)	2	0	1	1	3	0	3	0	0	0			-	1	.143	.400	.286
1992 Pittsburgh	NL	10	7	4	0	0	0	(0	0)	4	2	4	3	2	0	0	0	0	0	1	0	1.00		.571	.667	.571
1993 Pittsburgh	NL	141	449	106	24	3	6	(6	0)	154	38	47	46	36	3	82	9	5	9	2	2	.50	10	.236	.300	.343
1994 Pittsburgh	NL	59	122	25	7	2	1	(1	0)	39	15	11	8	8	2	34	1	2	1	0	2	.00	3	.205	.258	.320
1995 Pittsburgh	NL	56	181	42	9	0	6	(5	1)	69	13	22	16	8	0	53	2	1	3	1	3	.25	5	.232	.268	.381
1996 Kansas City	AL	55	132	32	6	0	8	(4	4)	62	20	23	18	11	0	32	0	0	0	3	3	.50	2	.242	.301	.470
1997 Pittsburgh	NL	97	333	100	18	3	18	(11	7)	178	59	74	59	16	1	89	4	1	8	11	2	.85	6	.300	.332	.535
1998 Pittsburgh	NL	159	592	160	40	2	27	(15	12)	285	88	108	89	44	1	127	11	0	9	15	7	.68	20	.270	.328	.481
1999 Pittsburgh	NL	156	584	174	41	6	26	(20	6)	305	103	106	115	75	5	124	12	0	4	22	10	.69	13	.298	.387	.522
2000 Pittsburgh	NL	132	496	128	27	0	20	(11	9)	215	77	88	64	32	1	96	8	0	5	8	3	.73	15	.258	.311	.433
2001 Pittsburgh	NL	142	449	104	33	0	14	(7	7)	179	53	65	51	42	3	119	11	0	5	15	11	.58	17	.232	.310	.399
2002 Pittsburgh	NL	146	468	115	26	1	16	(7	9)	191	60	51	51	50	2	101	4	0	3	4	6	.40	13	.246	.322	.408
2003 Pittsburgh	NL	52	84	17	4	0	2	(0	2)	27	8	7	8	12	0	25	0	0	0	1	0	1.00	1	.202	.302	.321
12 ML YEARS		1205	3897	1007	235	17	144	(83	61)	1708	536	606	528	336	18	882	62	9	47	83	49	.63	105	.258	.324	.438

Michael Young

Bats: R **Throws:** R **Pos:** 2B-159; SS-7   **Ht:** 6'1" **Wt:** 190 **Born:** 10/19/76 **Age:** 27

Year Team	Lg	G	AB	H	2B	3B	HR	(Hm	Rd)	TB	R	RBI	RC	TBB	IBB	SO	HBP	SH	SF	SB	CS	SB%	GDP	Avg	OBP	Slg
2000 Texas	AL	2	2	0	0	0	0	(0	0)	0	0	0	0	0	0	1	0	0	0	0	0	-	0	.000	.000	.000
2001 Texas	AL	106	386	96	18	4	11	(7	4)	155	57	49	45	26	0	91	3	9	5	3	1	.75	9	.249	.298	.402
2002 Texas	AL	156	573	150	26	8	9	(3	6)	219	77	62	62	41	1	112	0	13	6	6	7	.46	14	.262	.308	.382
2003 Texas	AL	160	666	204	33	9	14	(9	5)	297	106	72	104	36	1	103	1	3	7	13	2	.87	14	.306	.339	.446
4 ML YEARS		424	1627	450	77	21	34	(19	15)	671	240	183	211	103	2	307	4	25	18	22	10	.69	37	.277	.318	.412

Carlos Zambrano

Pitches: R **Bats:** B **Pos:** SP-32   **Ht:** 6'5" **Wt:** 250 **Born:** 6/1/81 **Age:** 23

Year Team	Lg	G	GS	CG	GF	IP	BFP	H	R	ER	HR	SH	SF	HB	TBB	IBB	SO	WP	Bk	W	L	Pct	ShO	Sv-Op	Hld	ERC	ERA
2001 Chicago	NL	6	1	0	1	7.2	42	11	13	13	2	1	1	0	8	0	4	1	0	1	2	.333	0	0-1	0	11.86	15.26
2002 Chicago	NL	32	16	0	3	108.1	477	94	53	44	9	9	1	4	63	2	93	6	0	4	8	.333	0	0-0	0	4.02	3.66
2003 Chicago	NL	32	32	3	0	214.0	907	188	88	74	9	11	6	10	94	12	168	6	1	13	11	.542	1	0-0	0	3.28	3.11
3 ML YEARS		70	49	3	4	330.0	1426	293	154	131	20	21	8	15	165	14	265	13	1	18	21	.462	1	0-1	0	3.68	3.57

Victor Zambrano

Pitches: R **Bats:** R **Pos:** SP-28; RP-6   **Ht:** 6'0" **Wt:** 203 **Born:** 8/6/75 **Age:** 28

Year Team	Lg	G	GS	CG	GF	IP	BFP	H	R	ER	HR	SH	SF	HB	TBB	IBB	SO	WP	Bk	W	L	Pct	ShO	Sv-Op	Hld	ERC	ERA
2003 Durham*	AAA	1	1	0	0	4.0	20	4	6	2	0	0	0	0	2	0	6	1	0	0	1	.000	0	0--		3.21	4.50
2001 Tampa Bay	AL	36	0	0	19	51.1	212	38	21	18	6	2	0	3	18	0	58	4	0	6	2	.750	0	2-6	5	2.80	3.16
2002 Tampa Bay	AL	42	11	0	11	114.0	519	120	77	70	15	7	8	4	68	5	73	10	0	8	8	.500	0	1-3	6	5.52	5.53
2003 Tampa Bay	AL	34	28	1	2	188.1	836	165	97	88	21	3	10	20	106	2	132	15	3	12	10	.545	0	0-0	2	4.51	4.21
3 ML YEARS		112	39	1	32	353.2	1567	323	195	176	42	12	18	27	192	7	263	29	3	26	20	.565	0	3-9	13	4.56	4.48

Gregg Zaun

Bats: B **Throws:** R **Pos:** C-45; PH-33; PR-1   **Ht:** 5'10" **Wt:** 190 **Born:** 4/14/71 **Age:** 33

Year Team	Lg	G	AB	H	2B	3B	HR	(Hm	Rd)	TB	R	RBI	RC	TBB	IBB	SO	HBP	SH	SF	SB	CS	SB%	GDP	Avg	OBP	Slg
1995 Baltimore	AL	40	104	27	5	0	3	(1	2)	41	18	14	15	16	0	14	0	2	0	1	1	.50	2	.260	.358	.394
1996 Bal-Fla		60	139	34	9	1	2	(1	1)	51	20	15	16	14	3	20	2	1	2	1	0	1.00	5	.245	.318	.367
1997 Florida	NL	58	143	43	10	2	2	(0	2)	63	21	20	27	26	4	18	2	1	0	1	0	1.00	3	.301	.415	.441
1998 Florida	NL	106	298	56	12	2	5	(2	3)	87	19	24	23	35	2	52	1	2	2	5	2	.71	7	.188	.274	.292
1999 Texas	AL	43	93	23	2	1	1	(0	1)	30	12	12	10	10	0	7	0	1	2	1	0	1.00	2	.247	.314	.323
2000 Kansas City	AL	83	234	64	11	0	7	(2	5)	96	36	33	40	43	3	34	3	0	2	7	3	.70	4	.274	.390	.410
2001 Kansas City	AL	39	125	40	9	0	6	(1	5)	67	15	18	24	12	0	16	0	0	1	1	2	.33	2	.320	.377	.536
2002 Houston	NL	76	185	41	7	1	3	(3	0)	59	18	24	16	12	1	36	2	2	1	1	0	1.00	4	.222	.275	.319
2003 Hou-Col	NL	74	166	38	8	0	4	(1	3)	58	15	21	19	19	0	21	1	1	2	1	1	.50	5	.229	.309	.349
1996 Baltimore	AL	50	108	25	8	1	1	(1	0)	38	16	13	12	11	2	15	2	0	2	0	0	-	3	.231	.309	.352
1996 Florida	NL	10	31	9	1	0	1	(0	1)	13	4	2	4	3	1	5	0	1	0	1	0	1.00	2	.290	.353	.419
2003 Houston	NL	59	120	26	7	0	1	(1	0)	36	9	13	11	14	0	14	1	1	2	1	0	1.00	5	.217	.299	.300
2003 Colorado	NL	15	46	12	1	0	3	(0	3)	22	6	8	8	5	0	7	0	0	0	0	1	.00	0	.261	.333	.478
9 ML YEARS		579	1487	366	73	7	33	(11	22)	552	174	186	190	187	13	218	11	10	12	19	9	.68	34	.246	.332	.371

Todd Zeile

Bats: R **Throws:** R **Pos:** 3B-64; 1B-23; PH-12; DH-8; PR-1   **Ht:** 6'1" **Wt:** 200 **Born:** 9/9/65 **Age:** 38

Year Team	Lg	G	AB	H	2B	3B	HR	(Hm	Rd)	TB	R	RBI	RC	TBB	IBB	SO	HBP	SH	SF	SB	CS	SB%	GDP	Avg	OBP	Slg
1989 St Louis	NL	28	82	21	3	1	1	(Hm	Rd)	29	7	8	10	9	1	14	0	1	1	0	1	.00	2	.256	.326	.354
1990 St Louis	NL	144	495	121	25	3	15	(8	7)	197	62	57	66	67	3	77	2	0	6	2	4	.33	11	.244	.333	.398
1991 St Louis	NL	155	565	158	36	3	11	(7	4)	233	76	81	81	62	3	94	5	0	6	17	11	.61	15	.280	.353	.412
1992 St Louis	NL	126	439	113	18	4	7	(4	3)	160	51	48	56	68	4	70	0	0	7	7	10	.41	11	.257	.352	.364
1993 St Louis	NL	157	571	158	36	1	17	(8	9)	247	82	103	86	70	5	76	0	0	6	5	4	.56	15	.277	.352	.433
1994 St Louis	NL	113	415	111	25	1	19	(10	9)	195	62	75	66	52	3	56	3	0	7	1	3	.25	13	.267	.348	.470
1995 StL-ChC	NL	113	426	105	22	0	14	(8	6)	169	50	52	50	34	4	76	4	4	5	1	0	1.00	13	.246	.305	.397
1996 Phi-Bal		163	617	162	32	0	25	(10	15)	269	78	99	92	82	4	104	1	0	4	1	1	.50	18	.263	.348	.436

Year Team	Lg	G	AB	H	2B	3B	HR	(Hm	Rd)	TB	R	RBI	RC	TBB	IBB	SO	HBP	SH	SF	SB	CS	SB%	GDP	Avg	OBP	Slg
																				BATTING			**BASERUNNING**		**AVERAGES**	
1997 Los Angeles	NL	160	575	154	17	0	31	(17	14)	264	89	90	94	85	7	112	6	0	6	8	7	.53	18	.268	.365	.459
1998 LA-Fla-Tex		158	572	155	32	3	19	(7	12)	250	85	94	87	69	2	90	4	1	7	4	4	.50	12	.271	.350	.437
1999 Texas	AL	156	588	172	41	1	24	(13	11)	287	80	98	96	56	3	94	4	1	7	1	2	.33	20	.293	.354	.488
2000 New York	NL	153	544	146	36	3	22	(8	14)	254	67	79	88	74	4	85	2	0	3	3	4	.43	15	.268	.356	.467
2001 New York	NL	151	531	141	25	1	10	(4	6)	198	66	62	72	73	3	102	6	0	2	1	0	1.00	15	.266	.359	.373
2002 Colorado	NL	144	506	138	23	0	18	(11	7)	215	61	87	76	66	3	92	1	0	7	1	1	.50	27	.273	.353	.425
2003 NYY-Mon		100	299	68	10	2	11	(7	4)	115	40	42	33	34	0	54	3	0	5	1	0	1.00	6	.227	.308	.385
1995 St Louis	NL	34	127	37	6	0	5	(2	3)	58	16	22	23	18	1	23	1	0	2	1	0	1.00	2	.291	.378	.457
1995 Chicago	NL	79	299	68	16	0	9	(6	3)	111	34	30	27	16	0	53	3	4	3	0	0	-	11	.227	.271	.371
1996 Philadelphia	NL	134	500	134	24	0	20	(9	11)	218	61	80	75	67	4	88	1	0	4	1	1	.50	16	.268	.353	.436
1996 Baltimore	AL	29	117	28	8	0	5	(1	4)	51	17	19	17	15	0	16	0	0	0	0	0	-	2	.239	.326	.436
1998 Los Angeles	NL	40	158	40	6	1	7	(1	6)	69	22	27	19	10	0	24	1	0	1	1	1	.50	5	.253	.300	.437
1998 Florida	NL	66	234	68	12	1	6	(2	4)	100	37	39	38	31	2	34	2	0	3	2	3	.40	4	.291	.374	.427
1998 Texas	AL	52	180	47	14	1	6	(4	2)	81	26	28	30	28	0	32	1	1	3	1	0	1.00	3	.261	.358	.450
2003 New York	AL	66	186	39	8	0	6	(4	2)	65	29	23	18	24	0	36	0	0	4	0	0	-	3	.210	.294	.349
2003 Montreal	NL	34	113	29	2	2	5	(3	2)	50	11	19	15	10	0	18	3	0	1	1	0	1.00	3	.257	.331	.442
15 ML YEARS		2021	7225	1923	381	23	244	(121	123)	3082	956	1075	1053	901	46	1196	41	7	79	53	51	.51	210	.266	.347	.427

Chad Zerbe

Pitches: L **Bats:** L **Pos:** RP-32; SP-1

Ht: 6'0" **Wt:** 200 **Born:** 4/27/72 **Age:** 32

Year Team	Lg	G	GS	CG	GF	IP	BFP	H	R	ER	HR	SH	SF	HB	TBB	IBB	SO	WP	Bk	W	L	Pct	ShO	Sv-Op	Hld	ERC	ERA
					HOW MUCH HE PITCHED					**WHAT HE GAVE UP**												**THE RESULTS**				
2003 San Jose*	A+	2	2	0	0	3.0	15	3	2	0	0	1	0	2	0	1	0	0	0	0	0	-	0	0- -	-	3.91	0.00
2003 Fresno*	AAA	7	0	0	2	10.1	42	11	6	3	3	0	1	0	1	0	7	0	0	1	1	.500	0	2- -	-	4.46	2.61
2000 San Francisco	NL	4	0	0	2	6.0	24	6	3	3	1	1	0	0	1	0	5	0	0	0	0	-	0	0-0	0	3.69	4.50
2001 San Francisco	NL	27	1	0	9	39.0	162	41	21	17	3	3	2	1	10	0	22	2	0	3	0	1.000	0	0-0	0	3.83	3.92
2002 San Francisco	NL	50	0	0	16	56.1	240	52	22	19	3	4	1	4	21	2	26	1	0	2	0	1.000	0	0-1	5	3.45	3.04
2003 San Francisco	NL	33	1	0	14	49.2	218	60	26	26	3	3	7	1	14	2	17	1	0	1	1	.500	0	0-1	2	4.53	4.71
4 ML YEARS		114	2	0	41	151.0	644	159	72	65	10	11	10	6	46	4	70	4	0	6	1	.857	0	0-2	7	3.91	3.87

Barry Zito

Pitches: L **Bats:** L **Pos:** SP-35

Ht: 6'4" **Wt:** 215 **Born:** 5/13/78 **Age:** 26

Year Team	Lg	G	GS	CG	GF	IP	BFP	H	R	ER	HR	SH	SF	HB	TBB	IBB	SO	WP	Bk	W	L	Pct	ShO	Sv-Op	Hld	ERC	ERA
					HOW MUCH HE PITCHED					**WHAT HE GAVE UP**												**THE RESULTS**				
2000 Oakland	AL	14	14	1	0	92.2	376	64	30	28	6	1	0	2	45	2	78	2	0	7	4	.636	1	0-0	0	2.63	2.72
2001 Oakland	AL	35	35	3	0	214.1	902	184	92	83	18	5	4	13	80	0	205	6	1	17	8	.680	2	0-0	0	3.33	3.49
2002 Oakland	AL	35	35	1	0	229.1	939	182	79	70	24	9	7	9	78	2	182	2	1	23	5	.821	1	0-0	0	2.92	2.75
2003 Oakland	AL	35	35	4	0	231.2	957	186	98	85	19	7	7	6	88	3	146	4	0	14	12	.538	1	0-0	0	2.91	3.30
4 ML YEARS		119	119	9	0	768.0	3174	616	299	266	67	22	18	30	291	7	611	14	2	61	29	.678	4	0-0	0	2.99	3.12

Pete Zoccolillo

Bats: L **Throws:** R **Pos:** PH-13; RF-4; LF-3

Ht: 6'2" **Wt:** 200 **Born:** 2/6/77 **Age:** 27

Year Team	Lg	G	AB	H	2B	3B	HR	(Hm	Rd)	TB	R	RBI	RC	TBB	IBB	SO	HBP	SH	SF	SB	CS	SB%	GDP	Avg	OBP	Slg
																				BATTING			**BASERUNNING**		**AVERAGES**	
1999 Eugene	A-	64	183	43	7	1	1	(-	-)	55	20	15	19	22	1	26	2	0	2	3	2	.60	2	.235	.321	.301
2000 Lansing	A	109	358	104	22	2	8	(-	-)	154	58	56	61	46	5	47	8	0	4	5	2	.71	4	.291	.380	.430
2001 Daytona	A+	96	326	86	18	4	2	(-	-)	118	42	35	41	35	1	57	1	2	6	7	5	.58	4	.264	.332	.362
2001 Beloit	A	31	123	41	8	0	6	(-	-)	67	16	23	23	10	0	19	1	0	1	0	2	.00	3	.333	.385	.545
2002 High Desert	A+	44	161	55	10	0	8	(-	-)	89	31	37	38	28	1	24	2	0	4	2	1	.67	3	.342	.436	.553
2002 Huntsville	AA	75	227	67	12	1	12	(-	-)	117	43	45	44	40	1	50	1	0	3	6	7	.46	7	.295	.399	.515
2003 Indianapolis	AAA	132	443	124	36	1	12	(-	-)	198	57	73	70	51	1	70	10	0	10	3	5	.38	14	.280	.360	.447
2003 Milwaukee	NL	20	37	4	1	0	0	(0	0)	5	0	3	0	2	0	13	0	0	0	0	0	-	1	.108	.154	.135

2003 Fielding Statistics

SBA is Total Stolen Bases Attempted.

CS is Total Caught Stealing.

PCS is Number of the Total Caught Stealing attributed to the pitcher, not the catcher in question (e.g. the pitcher throws to first, the runner makes a move towards second, and is thrown out without the catcher involved).

CS% is the percentage of runners caught stealing not including PCS.

In other words, the formula for CS% is:

$$\frac{(CS - PCS)}{(SBA - PCS)}$$

You may find many of our catcher ERAs (CERA—which, like pitcher ERAs, tracks runs each catcher "gave up" while he was behind the plate) to be different from other sources. However, we have solid statistical reasons to believe ours are the most accurate catcher ERAs available.

These fielding stats are not official. You will certainly find some differences when the official Major League Baseball numbers arrive later this year. However, we hope you'll agree that having an unofficial statistical fielding record in this November book is better than holding up the entire process for the official totals.

First Basemen - Regulars

Player	Tm	G	GS	Inn	PO	A	E	DP	Pct.	Rng
Konerko,Paul	CWS	119	105	938.2	889	79	2	102	.998	-
Lee,Travis	TB	142	141	1244.1	1220	100	3	117	.998	-
Olerud,John	Sea	152	143	1287.0	1096	125	3	126	.998	-
Martinez,Tino	StL	126	126	1065.0	1026	85	3	90	.997	-
Overbay,Lyle	Ari	75	69	604.0	644	57	2	48	.997	-
Thome,Jim	Phi	156	155	1361.2	1372	86	5	131	.997	-
Mientkiewicz,D	Min	139	133	1159.1	1092	67	4	86	.997	-
Lee,Derrek	Fla	155	153	1353.2	1279	97	5	131	.996	-
Teixeira,Mark	Tex	116	104	932.2	931	70	4	95	.996	-
Millar,Kevin	Bos	101	96	853.0	857	80	4	80	.996	-
Cordero,Wil	Mon	123	117	1004.0	1064	65	5	89	.996	-
Casey,Sean	Cin	144	144	1251.2	1259	75	6	111	.996	-
Giambi,Jason	NYY	85	85	742.2	747	19	4	62	.995	-
Snow,J.T.	SF	98	94	812.1	812	74	5	79	.994	-
Spiezio,Scott	Ana	113	89	791.1	722	57	5	61	.994	-
Bagwell,Jeff	Hou	158	158	1375.2	1290	112	9	124	.994	-
Klesko,Ryan	SD	111	103	908.0	849	82	6	65	.994	-
Simon,Randall	TOT	109	99	812.0	852	70	6	71	.994	-
Delgado,Carlos	Tor	147	147	1278.0	1355	103	10	134	.993	-
Helton,Todd	Col	159	159	1369.0	1418	156	11	148	.993	-
Sexson,Richie	Mil	162	162	1452.0	1361	130	11	130	.993	-
Hillenbrand,S	TOT	84	69	624.2	632	39	5	45	.993	-
Conine,Jeff	TOT	118	118	1037.2	1062	80	9	105	.992	-
Hatteberg,S	Oak	128	126	1111.1	1177	81	10	101	.992	-
Karros,Eric	ChC	97	84	730.2	676	47	6	79	.992	-
Broussard,Ben	Cle	114	101	925.0	955	62	9	85	.991	-
Phillips,Jason	NYM	84	82	682.1	667	44	7	69	.990	-
Pena,Carlos	Det	128	124	1094.2	1134	90	13	126	.989	-
McGriff,Fred	LA	79	79	672.0	667	40	8	65	.989	-
Harvey,Ken	KC	99	94	816.1	805	80	11	76	.988	-
Fick,Robert	Atl	115	111	915.2	1001	51	14	89	.987	-

First Basemen - The Rest

Player	Tm	G	GS	Inn	PO	A	E	DP	Pct.	Rng
Abad,Andy	Bos	7	3	38.0	35	1	1	2	.973	-
Baerga,Carlos	Ari	19	13	118.1	124	8	2	12	.985	-
Banks,Brian	Fla	12	6	63.1	72	0	0	10	1.000	-
Barnes,Larry	LA	8	5	48.2	43	2	0	4	1.000	-
Bell,Jay	NYM	14	3	36.1	33	0	1	3	.971	-
Bellhorn,Mark	Col	1	0	1.0	1	1	0	0	1.000	-
Berg,Dave	Tor	2	1	9.0	15	0	0	2	1.000	-
Blake,Casey	Cle	31	12	140.2	132	12	0	22	1.000	-
Bloomquist,W	Sea	3	0	6.1	6	1	0	0	1.000	-
Blum,Geoff	Hou	6	0	10.0	11	0	0	1	1.000	-
Branyan,R	Cin	14	10	99.0	97	7	1	13	.990	-
Buchanan,Brian	SD	24	19	152.0	137	9	2	19	.986	-
Burke,Jamie	CWS	1	0	2.0	1	1	0	0	1.000	-
Burkhart,M	KC	2	1	14.0	10	0	0	2	1.000	-
Cabrera,Jol	LA	8	4	31.1	25	2	0	2	1.000	-
Cairo,Miguel	StL	3	0	7.2	9	0	0	1	1.000	-
Castro,Juan	Cin	1	0	1.0	0	0	0	0		-
Catalanotto,F	Tex	5	2	23.0	20	3	2	3	.920	-
Choi,Hee Seop	ChC	69	55	504.2	523	40	5	46	.991	-
Cirillo,Jeff	Sea	1	0	2.0	2	0	0	1	1.000	-
Clark,Howie	Tor	2	0	4.0	4	0	0	1	1.000	-
Clark,Tony	NYM	80	50	499.2	465	25	4	42	.992	-
Colbrunn,Greg	Sea	14	13	92.0	83	5	1	5	.989	-
Coomer,Ron	LA	24	15	121.0	106	10	0	10	1.000	-
Counsell,Craig	Ari	2	0	4.0	3	0	0	1	1.000	-
Cuddyer,Mike	Min	5	3	27.0	30	1	1	2	.969	-
Daubach,Brian	CWS	45	30	278.1	245	20	1	21	.996	-
DeRosa,Mark	Atl	1	0	1.0	1	0	0	1	1.000	-
Dunn,Adam	Cin	19	7	84.2	81	8	1	10	.989	-
Durazo,Erubiel	Oak	33	33	283.1	298	8	6	26	.981	-
Feliz,Pedro	SF	12	9	83.0	81	4	0	9	1.000	-
Fox,Andy	Fla	2	2	17.0	14	1	0	3	1.000	-
Franco,Julio	Atl	75	38	412.0	432	32	1	46	.998	-
Franco,Matt	Atl	15	10	100.2	122	6	3	13	.977	-
Fullmer,Brad	Ana	19	17	148.2	142	11	0	17	1.000	-
Galarraga,A	SF	69	57	527.0	502	29	3	55	.994	-
Gibbons,Jay	Bal	13	11	97.0	91	7	1	16	.990	-
Gil,Benji	Ana	5	1	21.0	15	4	0	2	1.000	-
Glavine,Mike	NYM	3	1	9.0	10	1	0	1	1.000	-

Player	Tm	G	GS	Inn	PO	A	E	DP	Pct.	Rng
Grace,Mark	Ari	39	28	268.0	257	19	2	24	.993	-
Graffanino,T	CWS	2	0	3.0	6	0	0	0	1.000	-
Greene,Todd	Tex	2	0	3.0	5	3	0	1	1.000	-
Guzman,Edwards	Mon	13	9	73.1	70	3	2	7	.973	-
Hafner,Travis	Cle	42	40	329.2	369	18	6	46	.985	-
Halter,Shane	Det	12	7	76.0	84	4	2	13	.978	-
Hansen,Dave	SD	20	9	94.2	105	10	0	14	1.000	-
Harris,Lenny	ChC	2	0	4.0	5	1	0	0	1.000	-
Hernandez,Jose	Col	1	1	7.0	8	1	0	0	1.000	-
Hessman,Mike	Atl	4	3	27.0	30	1	0	3	1.000	-
Hillenbrand,S	Bos	28	17	164.0	193	12	0	13	1.000	-
Hillenbrand,S	Ari	56	52	460.2	439	27	5	32	.989	-
Hocking,Denny	Min	10	1	38.2	44	4	1	3	.980	-
Houston,Tyler	Phi	1	0	5.0	6	0	0	1	1.000	-
Huff,Aubrey	TB	22	20	181.1	166	12	0	23	1.000	-
Ibanez,Raul	KC	22	18	167.0	164	19	1	15	.995	-
Jackson,Damian	Bos	2	0	3.0	4	0	0	0	1.000	-
Johnson,Nick	NYY	60	60	529.0	509	34	5	44	.991	-
Jones,Jason	Tex	3	0	3.0	3	0	0	0	1.000	-
Kapler,Gabe	Bos	1	0	2.2	3	0	0	0	1.000	-
Kielty,Bobby	Tor	3	2	16.0	19	2	0	2	1.000	-
Kinkade,Mike	LA	13	6	73.0	71	10	0	7	1.000	-
Koonce,Graham	Oak	5	1	20.0	22	2	0	3	1.000	-
Lamb,Mike	Tex	5	0	6.0	6	1	0	0	1.000	-
LaRue,Jason	Cin	1	1	9.0	7	1	0	0	1.000	-
LeCroy,Matt	Min	17	12	105.1	99	3	1	7	.990	-
Leon,Jose	Bal	7	5	46.2	44	2	1	7	.979	-
Liefer,Jeff	Mon	21	19	154.2	143	7	3	19	.980	-
Lo Duca,Paul	LA	22	17	160.2	157	11	1	14	.994	-
Lopez,Mendy	KC	17	4	59.0	57	9	0	3	1.000	-
Mabry,John	Sea	9	6	53.2	43	8	0	7	1.000	-
Marrero,Eli	StL	2	0	4.0	6	0	0	0	1.000	-
Martin,Al	TB	1	0	3.0	2	0	0	0	1.000	-
Martinez,Ramon	ChC	2	0	2.1	1	0	0	0	1.000	-
Matheny,Mike	StL	4	0	7.0	7	0	0	1	1.000	-
McCarty,Dave	Oak	3	2	20.0	26	1	1	2	.964	-
McCarty,Dave	Bos	5	2	19.0	23	2	1	2	.962	-
McEwing,Joe	NYM	5	0	8.2	8	1	0	1	1.000	-
McMillon,Billy	Oak	3	0	3.0	5	0	0	0	1.000	-
Melhuse,Adam	Oak	1	0	1.0	2	0	0	0	1.000	-
Mendez,Carlos	Bal	9	3	34.0	28	3	2	1	.939	-
Merced,Orlando	Hou	12	4	59.1	50	4	1	6	.982	-
Merloni,Lou	SD	2	0	5.2	5	0	0	1	1.000	-
Mirabelli,Doug	Bos	2	0	7.0	5	1	1	0	.857	-
Mora,Melvin	Bal	1	0	4.0	2	0	0	0	1.000	-
Mordecai,Mike	Fla	1	1	9.0	10	0	0	1	1.000	-
Morneau,Justin	Min	7	2	34.2	28	4	1	1	.970	-
Nevin,Phil	SD	31	30	261.0	239	21	1	25	.996	-
Niekro,Lance	SF	3	0	7.0	4	0	0	1	1.000	-
Norton,Greg	Col	9	0	16.0	20	2	0	0	1.000	-
Ojeda,Miguel	SD	2	1	8.0	12	0	0	1	1.000	-
Ortiz,David	Bos	45	44	378.0	343	30	3	20	.992	-
Palmeiro,R	Tex	55	55	462.2	445	49	2	53	.996	-
Palmer,Dean	Det	1	1	8.0	9	1	0	0	1.000	-
Paquette,Craig	Det	5	4	34.0	43	0	0	4	1.000	-
Patterson,J	KC	2	0	6.1	9	1	0	0	1.000	-
Pellow,Kit	Col	1	1	8.0	9	0	0	0	1.000	-
Perez,Eduardo	StL	5	0	9.1	9	2	0	1	1.000	-
Perez,Tomas	Phi	9	3	37.0	35	3	0	5	1.000	-
Perry,Herbert	Tex	5	3	26.0	18	3	0	2	1.000	-
Petrick,Ben	Det	2	0	2.0	3	0	0	0	1.000	-
Phelps,Josh	Tor	8	8	61.0	55	4	2	2	.967	-
Piatt,Adam	Oak	1	0	3.0	6	0	0	1	1.000	-
Piazza,Mike	NYM	1	0	1.0	3	0	0	0	1.000	-
Pratt,Todd	Phi	6	4	40.0	44	2	0	3	1.000	-
Pujols,Albert	StL	62	36	369.2	341	33	1	35	.997	-
Quinlan,Robb	Ana	33	19	185.1	146	13	2	15	.988	-
Redmond,Mike	Fla	1	0	2.1	1	0	0	1	1.000	-
Richard,Chris	Col	1	0	3.0	3	0	0	1	1.000	-
Riggs,Adam	Ana	10	9	73.0	71	9	2	5	.976	-
Rivera,Carlos	Pit	60	14	205.2	229	16	4	22	.984	-
Rivera,Mike	SD	1	0	1.0	2	0	0	0	1.000	-
Sandberg,Jared	TB	1	1	8.0	7	0	0	2	1.000	-
Santos,F	SF	1	1	8.0	5	0	0	2	1.000	-
Sears,Todd	Min	14	11	97.0	94	6	1	7	.990	-
Sears,Todd	SD	1	0	1.0	1	0	0	1	1.000	-
Segui,David	Bal	8	6	58.0	52	6	0	7	1.000	-
Seguignol,F	NYY	3	1	14.0	9	3	0	0	1.000	-
Selby,Bill	Cle	1	0	0.0	0	0	0	0	-	-

Player	Tm	G	GS	Inn	PO	A	E	DP	Pct.	Rng
Simon,Randall	Pit	80	76	597.1	655	51	4	55	.994	-
Simon,Randall	ChC	29	23	214.2	197	19	2	16	.991	-
Sojo,Luis	NYY	1	0	1.0	0	0	0	0	-	-
Spencer,Shane	Cle	11	9	64.0	66	1	0	3	1.000	-
Stairs,Matt	Pit	31	27	214.0	213	10	2	16	.991	-
Stenson,D	Cin	1	0	1.0	1	0	0	0	1.000	-
Surhoff,B.J.	Bal	22	20	172.1	156	10	1	14	.994	-
Sweeney,Mark	Col	8	1	16.0	12	0	0	2	1.000	-
Sweeney,Mike	KC	45	45	376.0	381	35	4	30	.990	-
Thomas,Frank	CWS	27	27	209.0	206	9	1	19	.995	-
Vaughn,Mo	NYM	25	25	176.1	178	8	5	21	.974	-
Ventura,Robin	LA	42	25	255.2	252	16	2	26	.993	-
Vitiello,Joe	Mon	12	6	74.1	75	7	2	7	.976	-
Vizcaino,Jose	Hou	1	0	5.0	6	0	0	0	1.000	-
Ward,Daryle	LA	13	11	95.1	108	10	1	14	.992	-
Widger,Chris	StL	1	0	1.0	2	1	0	0	1.000	-
Wilkerson,Brad	Mon	27	11	131.1	148	9	0	8	1.000	-
Wilson,Craig	Pit	36	29	227.2	230	20	3	32	.988	-
Wilson,Tom	Tor	14	2	44.0	46	4	1	4	.980	-
Witt,Kevin	Det	27	26	220.0	214	20	0	31	1.000	-
Wooten,Shawn	Ana	32	27	212.0	210	14	1	21	.996	-
Young,Dmitri	Det	1	0	4.0	5	0	0	0	1.000	-
Young,Kevin	Pit	44	16	199.2	203	18	1	25	.995	-
Zeile,Todd	NYY	23	17	175.1	181	15	1	10	.995	-

Second Basemen - Regulars

Player	Tm	G	GS	Inn	PO	A	E	DP	Pct.	Rng
Hudson,Orlando	Tor	139	129	1146.2	267	477	12	98	.984	5.84
Giles,Marcus	Atl	140	137	1213.2	279	471	14	85	.982	5.56
Morris,Warren	Det	89	85	734.2	181	270	6	82	.987	5.52
Phillips,B	Cle	109	104	925.1	236	325	11	76	.981	5.46
Cora,Alex	LA	141	122	1103.0	286	377	15	109	.978	5.41
Ellis,Mark	Oak	153	147	1297.2	323	455	14	93	.982	5.40
Belliard,R	Col	113	105	909.1	225	312	15	78	.973	5.31
Polanco,P	Phi	99	99	873.2	213	300	4	70	.992	5.28
Relaford,Desi	KC	89	83	705.1	182	223	8	48	.981	5.17
Durham,Ray	SF	105	101	867.2	186	308	5	65	.990	5.12
Kent,Jeff	Hou	128	127	1113.0	277	354	11	82	.983	5.10
Roberts,Brian	Bal	107	105	925.0	198	321	7	67	.987	5.05
Young,Michael	Tex	159	158	1389.1	307	471	10	115	.987	5.04
Grudzielanek,M	ChC	121	115	1011.2	233	330	8	91	.986	5.01
Loretta,Mark	SD	150	144	1247.1	273	412	7	84	.990	4.94
Castillo,Luis	Fla	152	151	1312.1	287	433	10	99	.986	4.94
Young,Eric	TOT	117	113	976.1	230	305	16	65	.971	4.93
Jimenez,D	TOT	141	139	1226.0	282	388	11	97	.984	4.92
Spivey,Junior	Ari	98	90	808.2	169	268	6	54	.982	4.86
Kennedy,Adam	Ana	139	125	1119.2	234	371	6	75	.990	4.86
Soriano,A	NYY	155	154	1376.0	292	445	19	87	.975	4.82
Walker,Todd	Bos	139	134	1187.1	234	391	16	78	.975	4.74
Alomar,Roberto	TOT	139	134	1141.0	257	342	9	86	.985	4.72
Anderson,Mar	TB	134	117	1060.1	194	349	15	89	.973	4.61
Vidro,Jose	Mon	137	137	1158.1	199	393	10	75	.983	4.60
Boone,Bret	Sea	159	159	1375.0	267	425	7	106	.990	4.53
Rivas,Luis	Min	134	131	1144.0	218	326	10	64	.982	4.28

Second Basemen - The Rest

Player	Tm	G	GS	Inn	PO	A	E	DP	Pct.	Rng
Abernathy,B	TB	2	1	15.0	1	8	1	0	.900	5.40
Abernathy,B	KC	9	6	61.1	12	20	0	4	1.000	4.70
Alfonzo,E	SF	6	6	49.2	10	14	0	3	1.000	4.35
Alomar,Roberto	NYM	72	69	583.2	138	171	6	49	.981	4.76
Alomar,Roberto	CWS	67	65	557.1	119	171	3	37	.990	4.68
Baerga,Carlos	Ari	15	15	113.0	21	40	1	11	.984	4.86
Bell,David	Phi	3	3	19.0	3	8	0	1	1.000	5.21
Bell,Jay	NYM	14	10	84.0	15	24	2	7	.951	4.18
Bellhorn,Mark	Col	20	12	118.1	31	41	2	6	.973	5.48
Berg,Dave	Tor	24	20	171.1	39	53	2	8	.979	4.83
Blalock,Hank	Tex	4	1	12.0	2	7	1	1	.900	6.75
Bloomquist,W	Sea	7	0	18.0	3	3	0	0	1.000	3.00
Blum,Geoff	Hou	25	18	162.1	34	42	1	8	.987	4.21
Boone,Aaron	Cin	19	19	161.1	44	63	0	14	1.000	5.97
Bordick,Mike	Tor	13	10	93.0	29	37	0	6	1.000	6.39
Bruntlett,Eric	Hou	9	3	41.1	12	14	0	4	1.000	5.66

Player	Tm	G	GS	Inn	PO	A	E	DP	Pct.	Rng
Butler,Brent	Col	20	18	156.0	32	51	1	10	.988	4.79
Cabrera,Jol	LA	59	40	346.1	94	95	1	22	.995	4.91
Cairo,Miguel	StL	40	33	294.2	58	88	2	17	.986	4.46
Carroll,Jamey	Mon	11	5	51.1	12	14	0	5	1.000	4.56
Castro,Juan	Cin	56	45	421.1	100	154	4	33	.984	5.43
Cintron,Alex	Ari	9	5	56.1	14	17	0	4	1.000	4.95
Clark,Howie	Tor	3	3	24.0	4	13	1	1	.944	6.38
Clark,Jermaine	Tex	7	2	24.0	5	6	0	2	1.000	4.13
Counsell,Craig	Ari	10	7	67.2	8	22	0	5	1.000	3.99
Cromer,Tripp	Hou	1	0	3.0	1	2	0	1	1.000	9.00
Cruz,Enrique	Mil	6	1	22.0	3	7	0	0	1.000	4.09
Cuddyer,Mike	Min	1	0	1.0	0	0	0	0	-	.00
Dawkins,Gookie	KC	3	1	11.0	4	4	0	0	1.000	6.55
Delgado,Wilson	StL	12	6	50.1	12	20	0	3	1.000	5.72
Delgado,Wilson	Ana	1	1	7.0	4	3	0	1	1.000	9.00
DeRosa,Mark	Atl	29	25	229.1	49	77	2	20	.984	4.94
Durrington,T	Ana	5	1	21.0	1	5	0	0	1.000	2.57
Easley,Damion	TB	4	3	24.2	4	7	0	1	1.000	4.01
Escalona,Felix	TB	1	1	8.0	3	4	0	3	1.000	7.88
Febles,Carlos	KC	67	57	517.1	98	162	3	34	.989	4.52
Figgins,Chone	Ana	14	12	105.0	24	27	1	6	.981	4.37
Fox,Andy	Fla	15	8	86.0	14	22	3	6	.923	3.77
Freel,Ryan	Cin	11	10	76.2	14	20	1	2	.971	3.99
Garcia,Danny	NYM	17	16	130.2	36	40	4	9	.950	5.23
Garcia,Jesse	Atl	6	0	13.1	6	4	0	1	1.000	6.75
German,Esteban	Oak	5	0	13.0	5	6	0	1	1.000	7.62
Gil,Benji	Ana	28	22	168.2	32	61	2	13	.979	4.96
Ginter,Keith	Mil	53	49	446.1	102	128	2	35	.991	4.64
Gomez,Chris	Min	23	16	159.2	37	50	1	10	.989	4.90
Graffanino,T	CWS	29	22	202.0	53	77	3	22	.977	5.79
Hairston Jr.,J	Bal	48	48	418.1	103	136	5	34	.980	5.14
Hall,Bill	Mil	18	14	134.2	41	46	4	14	.956	5.81
Halter,Shane	Det	24	22	196.0	40	74	0	12	1.000	5.23
Hansen,Dave	SD	1	0	1.0	0	0	0	0	-	.00
Harris,Willie	CWS	12	7	71.0	13	24	0	5	1.000	4.69
Hart,Bo	StL	69	65	586.0	167	180	4	36	.989	5.33
Hernandez,Jose	ChC	1	0	1.0	0	0	0	0	-	.00
Hill,Bobby	ChC	2	0	5.0	1	0	0	0	1.000	1.80
Hill,Bobby	Pit	1	0	6.0	0	2	0	0	1.000	3.00
Hocking,Denny	Min	25	14	137.2	32	36	0	9	1.000	4.45
Hummel,Tim	Cin	1	1	4.0	2	3	0	1	1.000	11.25
Infante,Omar	Det	2	1	13.0	5	9	0	3	1.000	9.69
Jackson,Damian	Bos	38	14	147.1	18	54	3	6	.960	4.40
Jimenez,D	CWS	68	67	586.2	118	174	7	41	.977	4.48
Jimenez,D	Cin	73	72	639.1	164	214	4	56	.990	5.32
Kata,Matt	Ari	52	45	409.1	107	131	3	27	.988	5.23
Klassen,Danny	Det	4	4	34.0	12	16	1	3	.966	7.41
Lockhart,Keith	SD	27	14	129.0	37	33	1	8	.986	4.88
Lopez,Felipe	Cin	3	3	24.2	3	4	1	1	.875	2.55
Lopez,Mendy	KC	11	10	84.2	22	15	0	4	1.000	3.93
Macias,Jose	Mon	4	0	6.0	0	2	0	0	1.000	3.00
Mackowiak,Rob	Pit	15	11	87.1	21	30	0	3	1.000	5.26
Martinez,Ramon	ChC	41	33	310.2	55	84	3	26	.979	4.03
Mateo,Henry	Mon	43	20	222.0	48	83	4	22	.970	5.31
Matos,Julius	KC	11	5	59.0	10	22	1	4	.970	4.88
Matranga,Dave	Hou	2	0	3.0	2	0	0	0	1.000	6.00
McDonald,John	Cle	37	31	274.0	48	94	3	27	.979	4.66
McEwing,Joe	NYM	55	42	357.1	100	101	1	23	.995	5.06
McLemore,Mark	Sea	6	3	39.0	10	10	1	3	.952	4.62
Menechino,F	Oak	22	15	131.0	29	42	1	11	.986	4.88
Merloni,Lou	SD	10	2	34.0	9	10	1	1	.950	5.03
Merloni,Lou	Bos	7	2	27.0	5	5	0	3	1.000	3.33
Mientkiewicz,D	Min	1	0	1.0	0	0	0	0	-	.00
Miles,Aaron	CWS	3	1	14.0	1	6	0	0	1.000	4.50
Mora,Melvin	Bal	6	5	49.1	14	16	0	6	1.000	5.47
Morban,Jose	Bal	12	5	57.0	14	23	1	4	.974	5.84
Mordecai,Mike	Fla	12	3	47.0	5	10	1	4	.938	2.87
Mueller,Bill	Bos	10	10	83.0	22	17	0	7	1.000	4.23
Nunez,A O	Pit	71	60	526.2	125	196	7	42	.979	5.49
Ojeda,Augie	ChC	5	4	37.0	8	9	0	2	1.000	4.14
Olmedo,Ray	Cin	18	12	119.0	35	36	0	9	1.000	5.37
Ozuna,Pablo	Col	8	8	67.0	21	31	1	9	.981	6.99
Perez,Antonio	TB	31	30	246.1	35	65	1	11	.990	3.65
Perez,Neifi	SF	57	37	371.2	97	134	3	35	.987	5.59
Perez,Tomas	Phi	26	17	165.0	52	54	2	11	.981	5.78
Prieto,Alex	Min	5	1	18.2	6	6	0	1	1.000	5.79
Punto,Nick	Phi	16	7	83.0	35	29	1	6	.985	6.94
Reboulet,Jeff	Pit	76	62	565.1	131	214	4	49	.989	5.49
Reese,Pokey	Pit	33	29	259.0	65	120	6	24	.969	6.43

Player	Tm	G	GS	Inn	PO	A	E	DP	Pct.	Rng
Riggs,Adam	Ana	3	1	10.0	5	3	0	0	1.000	7.20
Rolls,Damian	TB	2	0	3.0	0	0	0	0	-	.00
Romano,Jason	LA	1	0	2.1	0	0	0	0	-	.00
Sadler,Donnie	Tex	1	1	8.0	1	0	0	0	1.000	1.13
Sanchez,Freddy	Bos	3	2	20.0	9	2	0	1	1.000	4.95
Sanchez,Rey	NYM	12	6	62.0	16	23	2	8	.951	5.66
Santiago,Ramon	Det	53	50	461.0	105	153	10	43	.963	5.04
Santos,Angel	Cle	28	21	188.0	39	65	2	16	.981	4.98
Scutaro,Marco	NYM	38	18	195.2	53	51	2	12	.981	4.78
Selby,Bill	Cle	1	0	1.0	0	1	0	0	1.000	9.00
Shumpert,Terry	TB	14	10	79.1	·21	24	1	3	.978	5.11
Sojo,Luis	NYY	1	1	7.0	0	3	0	0	1.000	3.86
Sorensen,Zach	Cle	14	6	71.0	14	20	2	5	.944	4.31
Stynes,Chris	Col	5	4	34.0	7	10	0	3	1.000	4.50
Taguchi,So	StL	1	0	2.0	0	0	0	0	-	.00
Thurston,Joe	LA	3	0	6.0	2	4	1	2	.857	9.00
Ugueto,Luis	Sea	4	0	9.0	2	3	0	2	1.000	5.00
Uribe,Juan	Col	11	10	89.0	25	40	1	10	.985	6.57
Utley,Chase	Phi	37	36	303.0	66	107	3	30	.983	5.14
Vazquez,Ramon	SD	3	2	20.0	6	9	0	5	1.000	6.75
Ventura,Robin	NYY	1	0	7.0	0	2	0	0	1.000	2.57
Vina,Fernando	StL	60	58	530.2	148	156	8	43	.974	5.16
Vizcaino,Jose	Hou	20	14	127.1	35	44	2	9	.975	5.58
Weeks,Rickie	Mil	4	2	21.0	1	1	1	0	.667	.86
Wilson,Enrique	NYY	10	8	72.0	14	19	0	2	1.000	4.13
Womack,Tony	Col	6	5	46.1	11	13	0	4	1.000	4.66
Womack,Tony	ChC	13	10	91.1	19	25	0	4	1.000	4.34
Young,Eric	Mil	99	96	828.0	196	250	15	53	.967	4.85
Young,Eric	SF	18	17	148.1	34	55	1	12	.989	5.40

Third Basemen - Regulars

Player	Tm	G	GS	Inn	PO	A	E	DP	Pct.	Rng
Chavez,Eric	Oak	154	153	1333.1	125	341	14	33	.971	3.15
Rolls,Damian	TB	73	68	609.0	75	135	6	15	.972	3.10
Stynes,Chris	Col	120	111	948.2	91	223	9	22	.972	2.98
Boone,Aaron	TOT	137	133	1178.0	99	290	20	26	.951	2.97
Bell,David	Phi	85	81	703.2	62	168	8	17	.966	2.94
Blake,Casey	Cle	140	136	1184.0	91	290	19	27	.953	2.90
Castilla,Vinny	Atl	147	144	1266.1	98	307	19	25	.955	2.88
Ensberg,Morgan	Hou	111	89	818.0	76	185	9	16	.967	2.87
Randa,Joe	KC	129	127	1073.1	102	237	7	12	.980	2.84
Beltre,Adrian	LA	157	150	1346.0	111	308	19	30	.957	2.80
Wigginton,Ty	NYM	155	153	1329.0	118	294	16	26	.963	2.79
Ramirez,Aramis	TOT	159	156	1397.2	97	333	33	24	.929	2.77
Rolen,Scott	StL	153	152	1339.0	109	299	13	24	.969	2.74
Burroughs,Sean	SD	137	132	1144.2	104	239	12	22	.966	2.70
Blalock,Hank	Tex	141	131	1167.0	110	236	15	31	.958	2.67
Lowell,Mike	Fla	128	128	1109.2	84	242	9	27	.973	2.64
Koskie,Corey	Min	131	130	1128.0	90	233	9	15	.973	2.58
Helms,Wes	Mil	130	130	1137.2	88	236	19	20	.945	2.56
Crede,Joe	CWS	151	149	1306.0	107	262	14	28	.963	2.54
Ventura,Robin	TOT	83	78	682.2	45	147	6	9	.970	2.53
Batista,Tony	Bal	154	154	1364.1	91	290	20	32	.950	2.51
Munson,Eric	Det	91	88	781.0	68	150	19	12	.920	2.51
Mueller,Bill	Bos	135	124	1118.1	76	234	16	22	.951	2.49
Hinske,Eric	Tor	124	120	1063.2	80	214	22	12	.930	2.49
Blum,Geoff	Hou	83	72	617.0	33	135	5	18	.971	2.45
Alfonzo,E	SF	133	133	1143.0	79	232	11	16	.966	2.45
Glaus,Troy	Ana	87	86	732.1	56	135	16	10	.923	2.35
Cirillo,Jeff	Sea	85	76	672.2	66	108	4	7	.978	2.33

Third Basemen - The Rest

Player	Tm	G	GS	Inn	PO	A	E	DP	Pct.	Rng
Amezaga,A	Ana	13	11	94.1	12	20	2	1	.941	3.05
Atkins,Garrett	Col	19	16	134.0	9	25	6	0	.850	2.28
Baerga,Carlos	Ari	4	4	40.0	6	7	0	0	1.000	2.93
Bell,Jay	NYM	14	7	73.0	7	13	1	2	.952	2.47
Bellhorn,Mark	ChC	42	39	340.1	18	72	6	4	.938	2.38
Bellhorn,Mark	Col	15	8	90.2	6	22	1	0	.966	2.78
Berg,Dave	Tor	17	15	128.0	7	23	2	0	.938	2.11
Bloomquist,W	Sea	37	29	268.0	21	44	2	3	.970	2.18
Boone,Aaron	Cin	83	81	715.2	62	179	14	19	.945	3.03
Boone,Aaron	NYY	54	52	462.1	37	111	6	7	.961	2.88

Player	Tm	G	GS	Inn	PO	A	E	DP	Pct.	Rng
Borders,Pat	Sea	2	0	3.0	0	1	0	0	1.000	3.00
Bordick,Mike	Tor	22	17	159.0	20	32	1	4	.981	2.94
Branyan,R	Cin	20	18	145.0	11	50	2	5	.968	3.79
Bruntlett,Eric	Hou	1	0	1.0	0	0	0	0	-	.00
Butler,Brent	Col	8	0	17.1	1	4	2	0	.714	2.60
Cabrera,Jol	LA	5	3	27.0	1	7	0	2	1.000	2.67
Cabrera,Miguel	Fla	34	30	275.0	17	53	1	2	.986	2.29
Cairo,Miguel	StL	12	2	33.0	3	6	2	1	.818	2.45
Carroll,Jamey	Mon	67	46	421.1	43	114	5	8	.969	3.35
Castro,Juan	Cin	30	20	188.1	17	42	1	6	.983	2.82
Chamblee,Jim	Cin	1	0	1.0	0	0	0	0	-	.00
Chapman,Travis	Phi	1	0	3.0	0	0	0	0	-	.00
Cintron,Alex	Ari	16	14	117.0	14	22	3	0	.923	2.77
Clark,Howie	Tor	13	10	84.1	2	20	1	4	.957	2.35
Collier,Lou	Bos	2	0	3.0	1	1	0	1	1.000	6.00
Conine,Jeff	Bal	1	1	9.0	0	4	0	0	1.000	4.00
Coomer,Ron	LA	11	6	60.2	4	10	0	2	1.000	2.08
Counsell,Craig	Ari	57	49	429.0	32	103	2	9	.985	2.83
Cruz,Enrique	Mil	2	0	7.0	0	2	1	0	.667	2.57
Cuddyer,Mike	Min	7	5	52.1	2	7	0	0	1.000	1.55
Delgado,Wilson	StL	11	2	42.2	2	6	0	1	1.000	1.69
Delgado,Wilson	Ana	9	4	50.0	3	10	2	1	.867	2.34
DeRosa,Mark	Atl	25	18	169.1	12	43	4	4	.932	2.92
Durrington,T	Ana	4	1	7.0	1	1	0	0	1.000	2.57
Easley,Damion	TB	23	22	188.2	12	35	4	1	.922	2.24
Escalona,Felix	TB	1	0	2.0	0	0	0	0	-	.00
Feliz,Pedro	SF	49	28	293.0	24	81	3	8	.972	3.23
Fox,Andy	Fla	5	3	30.2	4	5	1	1	.900	2.64
Freel,Ryan	Cin	2	1	10.0	0	2	0	2	1.000	1.80
Garcia,Jesse	Atl	2	0	9.2	2	1	0	1	1.000	2.79
Gil,Benji	Ana	4	1	18.0	2	2	0	0	1.000	2.00
Ginter,Keith	Mil	40	32	303.1	19	51	6	6	.921	2.08
Gomez,Chris	Min	18	15	141.2	14	31	1	3	.978	2.86
Grabowski,J	Oak	1	0	1.1	0	0	0	0	-	.00
Graffanino,T	CWS	21	12	115.0	5	18	1	2	.958	1.80
Guillen,Carlos	Sea	32	32	280.2	39	44	3	3	.965	2.66
Gutierrez,R	Cle	7	5	47.0	5	5	0	0	1.000	1.91
Guzman,Edwards	Mon	28	18	181.2	5	37	2	3	.955	2.08
Hall,Bill	Mil	1	0	4.0	0	0	0	0	.000	.00
Halter,Shane	Det	50	42	368.0	36	96	2	11	.985	3.23
Hammock,Robby	Ari	16	11	107.0	8	45	4	4	.930	4.46
Hansen,Dave	SD	11	8	73.1	6	16	1	0	.957	2.70
Harris,Lenny	ChC	34	26	227.0	10	44	3	4	.947	2.14
Henson,Drew	NYY	3	2	17.0	4	3	0	1	1.000	3.71
Hernandez,Jose	ChC	17	13	116.2	5	25	1	5	.968	2.31
Hernandez,Jose	Pit	58	51	449.0	34	133	8	14	.954	3.35
Hessman,Mike	Atl	3	0	11.0	0	3	0	0	1.000	2.45
Hillenbrand,S	Bos	29	28	242.0	26	42	3	3	.958	2.53
Hillenbrand,S	Ari	34	30	265.0	15	54	7	4	.908	2.34
Hocking,Denny	Min	24	12	139.0	19	33	2	1	.963	3.37
Houston,Tyler	Phi	21	21	139.2	15	28	3	0	.935	2.77
Huff,Aubrey	TB	8	7	71.0	7	8	3	2	.833	1.90
Hummel,Tim	Cin	20	18	160.2	10	32	5	0	.894	2.35
Infante,Omar	Det	4	3	27.0	1	8	1	1	.900	3.00
Jackson,Damian	Bos	3	2	18.0	1	7	1	0	.889	4.00
Jimenez,D	CWS	2	1	10.0	0	4	2	0	.667	3.60
Jimenez,D	Cin	2	0	4.0	0	2	0	0	1.000	4.50
Kata,Matt	Ari	23	19	173.1	10	41	1	2	.981	2.65
Kinkade,Mike	LA	2	1	8.0	0	0	1	0	.000	.00
Klassen,Danny	Det	13	12	108.0	15	24	0	3	1.000	3.25
Lamb,Mike	Tex	1	0	1.2	0	0	0	0	-	.00
LaRocca,Greg	Cle	2	2	17.0	0	6	0	0	1.000	3.18
Larson,Brandon	Cin	24	22	184.2	18	48	4	7	.943	3.22
Leon,Jose	Bal	10	8	75.1	10	16	1	3	.963	3.11
Liefer,Jeff	TB	6	6	44.0	5	8	1	0	.929	2.66
Lockhart,Keith	SD	3	2	24.0	2	6	1	0	.889	3.00
Lopez,Felipe	Cin	8	2	32.0	3	4	0	0	1.000	1.97
Lopez,Mendy	KC	13	5	57.0	3	15	0	0	1.000	2.84
Macias,Jose	Mon	25	16	159.1	9	35	3	1	.936	2.49
Mackowiak,Rob	Pit	19	17	132.1	11	24	2	4	.946	2.38
Martinez,Ramon	ChC	37	22	217.1	12	48	5	5	.923	2.48
Matos,Julius	KC	13	7	74.0	3	9	0	0	1.000	1.46
McDonald,John	Cle	23	9	112.0	10	17	3	2	.900	2.17
McEwing,Joe	NYM	2	1	11.1	2	5	0	1	1.000	5.56
McLemore,Mark	Sea	29	25	215.2	16	48	2	8	.970	2.67
Melhuse,Adam	Oak	2	0	2.2	0	1	1	0	.500	3.38
Menechino,F	Oak	19	9	104.1	6	21	2	2	.931	2.33
Merced,Orlando	Hou	2	0	5.0	0	1	0	0	1.000	1.80
Merloni,Lou	SD	25	17	162.1	12	37	4	3	.925	2.72

Player	Tm	G	GS	Inn	PO	A	E	DP	Pct.	Rng
Merloni,Lou	Bos	7	4	45.0	6	14	0	1	1.000	4.00
Mientkiewicz,D	Min	1	0	1.0	0	0	0	0	-	.00
Morban,Jose	Bal	1	0	1.0	0	0	0	0	-	.00
Mordecai,Mike	Fla	12	1	28.0	5	3	1	0	.889	2.57
Norton,Greg	Col	34	27	229.1	24	49	6	3	.924	2.86
Nunez,A O	Pit	1	0	1.0	0	1	0	0	1.000	9.00
Ojeda,Augie	ChC	1	0	3.0	0	0	0	0	-	.00
Palmer,Dean	Det	1	1	8.0	0	4	0	0	1.000	4.50
Patterson,J	KC	4	0	10.0	0	0	1	0	.000	.00
Pena,Wily Mo	Cin	1	0	5.0	0	1	0	0	1.000	1.80
Peralta,Jhonny	Cle	6	3	32.0	2	6	0	1	1.000	2.25
Perez,Antonio	TB	6	3	31.0	1	7	1	0	.889	2.32
Perez,Eduardo	StL	12	6	49.0	3	7	3	1	.769	1.84
Perez,Neifi	SF	2	0	1.1	0	0	0	0	-	.00
Perez,Tomas	Phi	58	36	387.1	37	85	6	12	.953	2.83
Perry,Herbert	Tex	2	2	14.0	2	2	0	1	1.000	2.57
Polanco,P	Phi	21	21	179.0	10	37	2	5	.959	2.36
Punto,Nick	Phi	9	3	31.0	5	5	1	0	.909	2.90
Ramirez,Aramis	Pit	96	94	845.2	62	213	23	10	.923	2.93
Ramirez,Aramis	ChC	63	62	552.0	35	120	10	14	.939	2.53
Reboulet,Jeff	Pit	7	0	16.1	3	3	0	1	1.000	3.31
Redmond,Mike	Fla	1	0	2.0	0	0	0	0	-	.00
Relaford,Desi	KC	33	23	224.1	11	59	6	5	.921	2.81
Sadler,Donnie	Tex	23	18	151.0	15	30	2	3	.957	2.68
Sanchez,Freddy	Bos	7	4	38.1	4	12	0	1	1.000	3.76
Sandberg,Jared	TB	50	41	349.1	34	75	5	4	.956	2.81
Santos,Angel	Cle	4	1	13.0	0	3	0	0	1.000	2.08
Selby,Bill	Cle	10	6	53.1	6	19	2	2	.926	4.22
Shumpert,Terry	TB	11	1	19.1	1	1	0	1	1.000	.93
Smith,Jason	TB	1	1	8.0	0	2	2	1	.500	2.25
Sorensen,Zach	Cle	1	0	1.0	0	0	0	0	-	.00
Spiezio,Scott	Ana	52	43	396.1	31	61	6	8	.939	2.09
Tatis,Fernando	Mon	49	48	403.2	32	88	4	8	.968	2.68
Teixeira,Mark	Tex	15	11	99.2	10	20	7	0	.811	2.71
Truby,Chris	TB	13	13	114.1	9	31	1	4	.976	3.15
Ugueto,Luis	Sea	1	0	1.0	0	0	0	0	-	.00
Vazquez,Ramon	SD	4	3	27.0	2	3	1	0	.833	1.67
Ventura,Robin	NYY	80	76	666.2	44	146	5	9	.974	2.57
Ventura,Robin	LA	3	2	16.0	1	1	1	0	.667	1.13
Vizcaino,Jose	Hou	2	1	9.0	0	0	0	0	-	.00
Williams,Matt	Ari	42	35	323.2	21	71	4	5	.958	2.56
Wilson,Enrique	NYY	17	9	95.2	6	26	2	4	.941	3.01
Witt,Kevin	Det	5	0	17.2	1	4	0	0	1.000	2.55
Wooten,Shawn	Ana	17	16	133.1	12	26	1	1	.974	2.57
Young,Dmitri	Det	16	16	129.0	8	37	8	5	.849	3.14
Zeile,Todd	NYY	30	24	220.1	16	49	6	8	.915	2.66
Zeile,Todd	Mon	34	34	271.2	22	67	5	4	.947	2.95

Shortstops - Regulars

Player	Tm	G	GS	Inn	PO	A	E	DP	Pct.	Rng
Everett,Adam	Hou	128	116	1000.2	206	343	17	70	.970	4.94
Santiago,Ramon	Det	85	84	724.0	140	249	10	68	.975	4.84
Berroa,Angel	KC	158	158	1381.2	264	472	24	106	.968	4.79
Furcal,Rafael	Atl	155	154	1350.0	237	478	31	106	.958	4.77
Lugo,Julio	TOT	139	137	1198.0	240	393	20	82	.969	4.76
Woodward,Chris	Tor	103	98	871.0	159	300	17	69	.964	4.74
Peralta,Jhonny	Cle	72	69	624.0	104	223	8	41	.976	4.72
Wilson,Jack	Pit	149	148	1294.2	218	452	17	103	.975	4.66
Cabrera,O	Mon	162	160	1385.2	259	457	18	99	.975	4.65
Valentin,Jose	CWS	143	136	1200.0	224	396	20	96	.969	4.65
Tejada,Miguel	Oak	162	162	1417.2	241	490	21	94	.972	4.64
Hernandez,Jose	TOT	74	68	603.1	118	192	5	48	.984	4.62
Rodriguez,Alex	Tex	158	158	1369.2	227	464	8	110	.989	4.54
Gonzalez,Alex	Fla	150	150	1315.2	235	457	16	105	.976	4.53
Cruz,Deivi	Bal	147	144	1261.1	221	409	16	95	.975	4.50
Izturis,Cesar	LA	158	154	1365.1	198	481	16	92	.977	4.48
Gonzalez,A S	ChC	150	141	1237.0	193	422	10	93	.984	4.47
Garciaparra,N	Bos	156	155	1364.2	218	455	20	82	.971	4.44
Eckstein,David	Ana	116	114	985.0	193	292	8	64	.984	4.43
Rollins,Jimmy	Phi	154	153	1357.2	203	461	14	91	.979	4.40
Sanchez,Rey	TOT	88	84	735.2	134	223	6	56	.983	4.37
Clayton,Royce	Mil	141	137	1217.2	193	395	14	76	.977	4.35
Cintron,Alex	Ari	93	90	795.2	138	235	8	55	.979	4.22
Renteria,Edgar	StL	156	154	1367.1	191	438	16	83	.975	4.14
Aurilia,Rich	SF	123	123	1064.0	173	315	13	78	.974	4.13
Guillen,Carlos	Sea	76	70	620.0	121	162	11	55	.963	4.11

Player	Tm	G	GS	Inn	PO	A	E	DP	Pct.	Rng
Vazquez,Ramon	SD	108	102	904.2	131	274	13	57	.969	4.03
Guzman,C	Min	141	137	1232.1	195	352	11	67	.980	3.99
Jeter,Derek	NYY	118	118	1033.2	160	271	14	51	.969	3.75

Shortstops - The Rest

Player	Tm	G	GS	Inn	PO	A	E	DP	Pct.	Rng
Almonte,Erick	NYY	31	29	252.1	50	66	12	13	.906	4.14
Amezaga,A	Ana	24	21	193.0	39	57	3	9	.970	4.48
Barmes,Clint	Col	12	8	75.0	19	27	2	6	.958	5.52
Bell,Jay	NYM	12	6	51.0	11	19	1	6	.968	5.29
Bellhorn,Mark	Col	6	2	22.2	1	9	0	1	1.000	3.97
Beltre,Adrian	LA	1	0	1.0	0	0	0	0	-	.00
Berg,Dave	Tor	1	0	1.0	0	0	0	0	-	.00
Bloomquist,W	Sea	18	14	123.2	24	37	2	8	.968	4.44
Blum,Geoff	Hou	11	3	45.2	3	18	1	6	.955	4.14
Boone,Aaron	Cin	5	3	31.0	3	15	3	1	.857	5.23
Bordick,Mike	Tor	69	64	562.0	112	179	4	52	.986	4.66
Bruntlett,Eric	Hou	10	5	63.1	12	14	1	3	.963	3.69
Butler,Brent	Col	4	2	22.0	4	7	0	2	1.000	4.50
Cabrera,Jol	LA	9	3	36.0	8	11	2	4	.905	4.75
Cairo,Miguel	StL	7	4	39.2	5	10	1	2	.938	3.40
Carroll,Jamey	Mon	14	2	50.0	7	15	0	4	1.000	3.96
Castro,Juan	Cin	24	18	154.0	28	43	0	14	1.000	4.15
Clark,Howie	Tor	1	0	1.0	0	0	0	0	-	.00
Cora,Alex	LA	15	5	55.1	10	18	0	4	1.000	4.55
Counsell,Craig	Ari	26	18	167.2	23	66	1	9	.989	4.78
Crosby,Bobby	Oak	9	0	20.0	5	11	2	2	.889	7.20
Cruz,Enrique	Mil	13	6	72.0	8	20	0	3	1.000	3.50
Delgado,Wilson	StL	11	3	42.2	5	13	1	1	.947	3.80
Delgado,Wilson	Ana	9	8	71.2	20	17	1	6	.974	4.65
DeRosa,Mark	Atl	20	8	100.0	21	42	0	9	1.000	5.67
Escalona,Felix	TB	8	8	69.0	15	21	0	8	1.000	4.70
Febles,Carlos	KC	2	0	4.0	0	0	0	0	-	.00
Figgins,Chone	Ana	8	6	56.0	11	18	2	4	.935	4.66
Fox,Andy	Fla	9	3	37.0	5	10	0	3	1.000	3.65
Garcia,Jesse	Atl	3	0	6.1	0	1	0	0	1.000	1.42
Gil,Benji	Ana	20	13	125.2	25	35	4	12	.938	4.30
Ginter,Keith	Mil	2	1	9.1	4	3	0	1	1.000	6.75
Gomez,Chris	Min	17	11	103.0	13	21	1	3	.971	2.97
Graffanino,T	CWS	36	26	231.0	41	78	4	17	.967	4.64
Greene,Khalil	SD	20	18	155.0	28	51	3	11	.963	4.59
Gutierrez,R	Cle	9	9	77.0	12	26	3	4	.927	4.44
Hall,Bill	Mil	18	18	153.0	31	49	4	11	.952	4.71
Halter,Shane	Det	27	18	171.0	33	62	5	14	.950	5.00
Hart,Bo	StL	3	1	14.0	2	5	0	1	1.000	4.50
Hernandez,Jose	Col	69	67	584.0	116	182	5	47	.983	4.59
Hernandez,Jose	ChC	5	1	19.1	2	10	0	1	1.000	5.59
Hocking,Denny	Min	17	14	121.2	23	41	0	8	1.000	4.73
Hummel,Tim	Cin	2	1	11.0	1	4	0	0	1.000	4.09
Infante,Omar	Det	63	59	525.2	117	211	13	52	.962	5.62
Jackson,Damian	Bos	18	6	82.0	19	18	5	4	.881	4.06
Kata,Matt	Ari	6	4	37.2	7	5	0	1	1.000	2.87
Klassen,Danny	Det	3	1	18.0	5	8	2	0	.867	6.50
Larkin,Barry	Cin	60	58	469.2	71	159	9	36	.962	4.41
Lopez,Felipe	Cin	50	42	397.1	60	131	15	20	.927	4.33
Lopez,Mendy	KC	4	0	11.0	2	8	1	1	.909	8.18
Loretta,Mark	SD	3	0	6.1	2	0	0	0	1.000	2.84
Lugo,Julio	Hou	22	21	173.1	29	57	3	10	.966	4.47
Lugo,Julio	TB	117	116	1024.2	211	336	17	72	.970	4.80
Martinez,Ramon	ChC	32	18	169.1	29	57	2	15	.977	4.57
Mateo,Henry	Mon	2	0	2.0	1	1	0	1	1.000	9.00
Matos,Julius	KC	2	0	3.0	0	1	0	0	1.000	3.00
McDonald,John	Cle	27	20	195.0	39	53	4	16	.958	4.25
McEwing,Joe	NYM	42	24	242.2	51	92	5	26	.966	5.30
McLemore,Mark	Sea	38	34	304.0	46	95	4	25	.972	4.17
Mendez,Donaldo	SD	26	26	224.0	26	71	5	9	.951	3.90
Menechino,F	Oak	3	0	4.0	1	1	1	1	.667	4.50
Merloni,Lou	SD	23	16	141.1	35	43	1	11	.987	4.97
Mora,Melvin	Bal	11	10	98.1	19	30	1	5	.980	4.48
Morban,Jose	Bal	14	7	74.0	13	12	0	7	1.000	3.04
Mordecai,Mike	Fla	14	9	92.2	14	27	1	7	.976	3.98
Mueller,Bill	Bos	1	0	1.0	1	0	0	0	1.000	9.00
Nunez,A O	Pit	23	14	149.2	29	44	1	9	.986	4.39
Ojeda,Augie	ChC	7	2	30.0	8	8	0	2	1.000	4.80
Olmedo,Ray	Cin	51	40	383.1	60	121	14	20	.928	4.25
Ordonez,Rey	TB	34	24	294.0	60	101	5	30	.970	4.93

257

Player	Tm	G	GS	Inn	PO	A	E	DP	Pct.	Rng
Ozuna,Pablo	Col	3	2	15.0	3	6	1	0	.900	5.40
Perez,Antonio	TB	6	5	41.0	13	13	0	2	1.000	5.71
Perez,Neifi	SF	45	33	311.0	71	129	2	33	.990	5.79
Perez,Tomas	Phi	4	4	34.0	4	8	1	3	.923	3.18
Prieto,Alex	Min	1	0	5.0	1	1	0	0	1.000	3.60
Punto,Nick	Phi	7	5	52.0	5	17	0	2	1.000	3.81
Ransom,Cody	SF	12	5	62.1	9	17	1	7	.963	3.75
Relaford,Desi	KC	6	4	39.0	6	11	0	2	1.000	3.92
Reyes,Jose	NYM	69	69	596.1	107	212	9	40	.973	4.81
Roberts,Brian	Bal	2	2	16.0	1	8	2	1	.818	5.06
Sadler,Donnie	Tex	19	3	46.2	6	15	2	3	.913	4.05
Sanchez,Freddy	Bos	6	1	17.0	2	9	0	1	1.000	5.82
Sanchez,Rey	NYM	42	40	344.1	57	114	2	23	.988	4.47
Sanchez,Rey	Sea	46	44	391.1	77	109	4	33	.979	4.28
Sandberg,Jared	TB	1	0	1.0	1	1	0	0	1.000	18.00
Scutaro,Marco	NYM	1	0	2.0	1	1	0	0	1.000	9.00
Shumpert,Terry	TB	1	1	7.0	0	3	0	0	1.000	3.86
Sorensen,Zach	Cle	3	1	12.0	2	6	0	1	1.000	6.00
Ugueto,Luis	Sea	1	0	2.0	0	0	0	0	-	.00
Uribe,Juan	Col	74	69	598.1	143	243	11	57	.972	5.81
Velandia,Jorge	NYM	23	22	177.0	40	65	3	13	.972	5.34
Vizcaino,Jose	Hou	32	17	167.0	31	48	3	12	.963	4.26
Vizquel,Omar	Cle	64	63	551.1	115	202	7	58	.978	5.17
Wilson,Enrique	NYY	33	16	176.0	32	45	1	8	.987	3.94
Womack,Tony	Ari	58	50	454.0	70	130	7	27	.966	3.96
Womack,Tony	Col	14	12	103.0	16	31	2	5	.959	4.11
Young,Michael	Tex	7	1	17.0	4	5	0	1	1.000	4.76

Left Fielders - Regulars

Player	Tm	G	GS	Inn	PO	A	E	DP	Pct.	Rng
Crawford,Carl	TB	137	131	1158.2	317	10	3	1	.991	2.54
Anderson,G	Ana	144	144	1241.1	326	13	1	2	.997	2.46
Stewart,Sh	TOT	115	113	986.1	247	6	4	0	.984	2.31
Dunn,Adam	Cin	99	98	828.2	206	6	9	2	.959	2.30
Monroe,Craig	Det	75	70	602.2	148	6	4	1	.975	2.30
Winn,Randy	Sea	139	134	1188.0	300	3	3	1	.990	2.30
Jones,Jacque	Min	90	87	754.1	189	2	5	0	.974	2.28
Wilkerson,Brad	Mon	95	80	702.1	167	8	4	1	.978	2.24
Payton,Jay	Col	149	143	1230.0	298	7	3	1	.990	2.23
Bigbie,Larry	Bal	76	74	648.1	153	3	1	0	.994	2.17
Lee,Carlos	CWS	156	155	1328.2	308	9	7	1	.978	2.15
Giles,Brian	TOT	128	120	1060.1	247	5	4	0	.984	2.14
White,Rondell	TOT	121	119	969.1	218	6	5	2	.978	2.08
Ibanez,Raul	KC	128	119	1042.0	231	8	3	1	.988	2.06
Floyd,Cliff	NYM	95	94	728.2	159	8	5	4	.971	2.06
Pujols,Albert	StL	113	113	904.1	199	7	3	0	.986	2.05
Matsui,Hideki	NYY	118	110	997.1	210	11	7	3	.969	1.99
Jenkins,Geoff	Mil	123	122	1088.1	224	11	0	0	1.000	1.94
Ramirez,Manny	Bos	128	126	1073.0	206	12	4	1	.982	1.83
Burrell,Pat	Phi	140	138	1186.2	234	7	6	0	.976	1.83
Berkman,Lance	Hou	153	153	1348.1	253	10	3	0	.989	1.76
Gonzalez,Luis	Ari	154	154	1359.1	249	9	3	0	.989	1.71
Alou,Moises	ChC	142	140	1219.0	203	4	6	1	.972	1.53
Jones,Chipper	Atl	149	149	1282.1	202	9	7	1	.968	1.48

Left Fielders - The Rest

Player	Tm	G	GS	Inn	PO	A	E	DP	Pct.	Rng
Allen,Chad	Fla	6	4	40.0	10	1	0	0	1.000	2.48
Anderson,Mar	TB	3	3	27.0	4	0	0	0	1.000	1.33
Banks,Brian	Fla	23	17	154.0	27	1	0	0	1.000	1.64
Barnes,Larry	LA	2	0	2.0	2	0	0	0	1.000	9.00
Bautista,Danny	Ari	3	2	20.0	2	0	0	0	1.000	.90
Bay,Jay	Pit	24	20	180.1	33	0	1	0	.971	1.65
Benard,Marvin	SF	17	11	105.2	31	0	0	0	1.000	2.64
Berg,Dave	Tor	1	0	1.0	0	0	0	0	-	.00
Bloomquist,W	Sea	10	7	63.0	18	0	0	0	1.000	2.57
Blum,Geoff	Hou	1	0	2.0	0	1	0	0	1.000	4.50
Bocachica,H	Det	1	1	8.0	2	0	0	0	1.000	2.25
Bragg,Darren	Atl	29	12	140.2	28	0	0	0	1.000	1.79
Branyan,R	Cin	17	13	118.2	30	0	0	0	1.000	2.28
Brown,Adrian	Bos	3	0	4.0	0	0	0	0	-	.00
Brown,Dee	KC	17	8	93.2	22	0	0	0	1.000	2.11

Player	Tm	G	GS	Inn	PO	A	E	DP	Pct.	Rng
Bruntlett,Eric	Hou	1	0	2.1	0	0	0	0	-	.00
Buchanan,Brian	SD	15	5	64.0	14	0	0	0	1.000	1.97
Burks,Ellis	Cle	2	2	14.0	5	0	0	0	1.000	3.21
Burnitz,Jeromy	NYM	10	8	66.0	12	1	1	0	.929	1.77
Burnitz,Jeromy	LA	54	48	409.0	69	3	3	0	.960	1.58
Byrnes,Eric	Oak	44	31	283.1	49	3	0	0	1.000	1.65
Cabrera,Jol	LA	31	4	91.0	8	0	0	0	1.000	.79
Cabrera,Miguel	Fla	55	55	481.0	99	6	3	1	.972	1.96
Cairo,Miguel	StL	22	14	129.2	27	1	1	1	.966	1.94
Calloway,Ron	Mon	50	42	374.1	93	4	2	0	.980	2.33
Catalanotto,F	Tor	61	55	460.1	91	4	1	0	.990	1.86
Cepicky,Matt	Mon	3	1	13.2	1	0	0	0	1.000	.66
Clark,Brady	Mil	25	15	151.2	26	1	1	0	.964	1.60
Clark,Howie	Tor	4	2	18.0	3	0	0	0	1.000	1.50
Clark,Jermaine	Tex	16	11	102.2	29	2	0	0	1.000	2.72
Clark,Jermaine	SD	1	1	9.0	2	0	0	0	1.000	2.00
Clark,Tony	NYM	1	0	2.0	1	0	0	0	1.000	4.50
Collier,Lou	Bos	1	0	2.2	0	0	0	0	-	.00
Conine,Jeff	Bal	6	5	48.0	8	0	0	0	1.000	1.50
Conine,Jeff	Fla	25	25	208.0	44	3	0	3	1.000	2.03
Conti,Jason	Mil	1	0	2.0	1	0	0	0	1.000	4.50
Cordero,Wil	Mon	1	0	1.0	0	0	0	0	-	.00
Cordova,Marty	Bal	4	4	35.0	7	2	0	0	1.000	2.31
Crisp,Coco	Cle	39	38	347.0	88	4	1	0	.989	2.39
Crosby,Bubba	LA	1	1	9.0	2	0	1	0	.667	2.00
Cuddyer,Mike	Min	1	0	1.0	0	0	0	0	-	.00
Cust,Jack	Bal	1	0	4.2	3	0	0	0	1.000	5.79
Daubach,Brian	CWS	3	3	25.0	7	0	0	0	1.000	2.52
DaVanon,Jeff	Ana	8	4	39.0	12	1	1	0	.929	3.00
Dellucci,David	Ari	4	0	9.1	1	0	0	0	1.000	.96
Dellucci,David	NYY	2	2	12.0	1	0	0	0	1.000	.75
DeRosa,Mark	Atl	2	1	11.0	2	0	0	0	1.000	1.64
Diaz,Matt	TB	1	1	9.0	6	0	1	0	.857	6.00
Drew,J.D.	StL	2	1	5.1	1	0	0	0	1.000	1.69
Duncan,Jeff	NYM	1	0	2.0	0	0	0	0	-	.00
Durrington,T	Ana	1	0	2.0	0	0	0	0	-	.00
Dye,Jermaine	Oak	1	0	5.0	0	0	0	0	-	.00
Edmonds,Jim	StL	1	0	6.0	1	0	0	0	1.000	1.50
Edwards,Mike	Oak	2	0	4.0	0	0	0	0	-	.00
Ellison,Jason	SF	3	2	17.0	2	0	0	0	1.000	1.06
Everett,Carl	Tex	40	28	256.0	56	3	1	1	.983	2.07
Everett,Carl	CWS	8	2	26.0	8	0	0	0	1.000	2.77
Feliz,Pedro	SF	14	11	92.2	22	0	1	0	.957	2.14
Figgins,Chone	Ana	3	1	13.0	5	0	0	0	1.000	3.46
Ford,Lew	Min	8	4	43.0	8	0	0	0	1.000	1.67
Fox,Andy	Fla	2	1	10.0	1	0	0	0	1.000	.90
Franco,Matt	Atl	1	0	5.0	0	0	0	0	-	.00
Freel,Ryan	Cin	5	3	27.1	8	0	0	0	1.000	2.63
Gant,Ron	Oak	8	4	42.0	6	0	0	0	1.000	1.29
Garcia,Danny	NYM	1	0	0.2	0	0	0	0	-	.00
Garcia,Karim	NYY	13	12	98.0	32	1	1	0	.971	3.03
Gerut,Jody	Cle	36	35	317.0	81	2	3	0	.965	2.36
Giambi,Jeremy	Bos	9	6	57.0	13	0	1	0	.929	2.05
Giles,Brian	Pit	99	91	808.1	192	3	2	0	.990	2.17
Giles,Brian	SD	29	29	252.0	55	2	2	0	.966	2.04
Ginter,Keith	Mil	2	2	18.0	1	0	0	0	1.000	.50
Glanville,Doug	ChC	3	0	4.0	0	0	0	0	-	.00
Gonzalez,Raul	NYM	45	15	172.0	55	1	1	0	.982	2.93
Goodwin,Tom	ChC	17	6	74.1	16	0	0	0	1.000	1.94
Guiel,Aaron	KC	1	0	1.0	0	0	0	0	-	.00
Guillen,Jose	Cin	22	13	131.1	34	0	4	0	.895	2.33
Guillen,Jose	Oak	10	8	63.0	12	0	0	0	1.000	1.71
Halter,Shane	Det	2	0	7.0	0	0	0	0	-	.00
Hammock,Robby	Ari	5	0	10.0	2	0	0	0	1.000	1.80
Hammonds,J	SF	17	9	82.2	21	0	0	0	1.000	2.29
Harris,Lenny	ChC	1	0	1.0	0	0	0	0	-	.00
Harris,Lenny	Fla	2	0	7.0	2	0	0	0	1.000	2.57
Henderson,R	LA	18	17	139.2	20	1	1	1	.955	1.35
Hermansen,Chad	LA	6	5	42.0	8	0	0	0	1.000	1.71
Hessman,Mike	Atl	7	0	12.1	4	0	1	0	.800	2.92
Hocking,Denny	Min	2	0	2.2	0	0	0	0	-	.00
Hollandsworth,T	Fla	61	56	491.1	106	5	2	0	.982	2.03
Hunter,Brian	Hou	5	2	25.1	4	0	0	0	1.000	1.42
Hyzdu,Adam	Pit	3	0	5.0	2	0	0	0	1.000	3.60
Jackson,Damian	Bos	13	1	31.0	9	1	0	0	1.000	2.90
Johnson,Gary	Ana	2	0	4.0	3	0	0	0	1.000	6.75
Johnson,Reed	Tor	53	33	326.2	74	2	1	0	.987	2.09
Jones,Jason	Tex	14	13	93.0	17	2	0	0	1.000	1.84
Jordan,Brian	LA	54	43	399.2	62	2	0	0	1.000	1.44

Player	Tm	G	GS	Inn	PO	A	E	DP	Pct.	Rng
Kapler,Gabe	Col	15	3	40.0	6	1	0	1	1.000	1.58
Kapler,Gabe	Bos	25	9	110.0	21	1	1	0	.957	1.80
Kearns,Austin	Cin	1	0	1.2	0	0	0	0	-	.00
Kelton,Dave	ChC	2	2	13.0	4	0	0	0	1.000	2.77
Kielty,Bobby	Min	1	1	9.0	1	0	0	0	1.000	1.00
Kielty,Bobby	Tor	3	3	27.0	4	0	0	0	1.000	1.33
Kieschnick,B	Mil	3	3	26.0	2	0	1	0	.667	.69
Kingsale,Gene	Det	8	7	70.0	14	0	0	0	1.000	1.80
Kinkade,Mike	LA	33	27	225.2	30	0	3	0	.909	1.20
Lamb,Mike	Tex	2	1	6.0	1	0	0	0	1.000	1.50
Lane,Jason	Hou	3	1	14.0	3	0	0	0	1.000	1.93
Langerhans,R	Atl	3	0	5.0	1	0	0	0	1.000	1.80
Larson,Brandon	Cin	3	3	22.0	9	1	0	0	1.000	4.09
LaRue,Jason	Cin	1	0	0.2	0	0	0	0	-	.00
Lawton,Matt	Cle	62	61	532.2	116	3	1	0	.992	2.01
Ledee,Ricky	Phi	29	19	174.2	34	1	0	0	1.000	1.80
Liefer,Jeff	TB	1	0	2.0	2	0	0	0	1.000	9.00
Linden,Todd	SF	9	4	45.0	10	0	1	0	.909	2.00
Lo Duca,Paul	LA	6	6	46.0	10	1	0	0	1.000	2.15
Lombard,George	TB	3	3	25.0	5	1	0	0	1.000	2.16
Long,Terrence	Oak	75	62	567.2	106	0	0	0	1.000	1.70
Lopez,Mendy	KC	1	1	8.0	5	0	0	0	1.000	5.63
Ludwick,Ryan	Tex	4	4	32.0	5	0	0	0	1.000	1.41
Ludwick,Ryan	Cle	13	11	100.0	31	0	0	0	1.000	2.79
Mabry,John	Sea	8	7	57.0	14	0	1	0	.933	2.21
Macias,Jose	Mon	41	25	252.1	48	2	2	1	.962	1.78
Mackowiak,Rob	Pit	8	3	36.0	6	0	0	0	1.000	1.50
Magruder,Chris	Cle	5	5	43.0	10	0	0	0	1.000	2.09
Marrero,Eli	StL	10	4	37.2	12	0	0	0	1.000	2.87
Martin,Al	TB	8	7	62.2	19	0	0	0	1.000	2.73
Mateo,Henry	Mon	2	1	9.0	2	0	0	0	1.000	2.00
Mateo,Ruben	Cin	4	1	15.2	5	0	0	0	1.000	2.87
Matthews Jr.,G	SD	32	20	195.2	37	0	1	0	.974	1.70
McCarty,Dave	Oak	5	5	41.0	5	0	0	0	1.000	1.10
McCarty,Dave	Bos	7	4	41.0	7	0	0	0	1.000	1.54
McCracken,Q	LA	10	6	56.1	7	0	0	0	1.000	1.12
McEwing,Joe	NYM	14	4	50.2	17	0	0	0	1.000	3.02
McLemore,Mark	Sea	16	14	129.0	28	1	0	0	1.000	2.02
McMillon,Billy	Oak	36	27	213.2	47	0	1	0	.979	1.98
Mench,Kevin	Tex	34	30	267.0	56	1	1	0	.983	1.92
Merced,Orlando	Hou	10	6	54.0	14	1	1	1	.938	2.50
Merloni,Lou	SD	2	0	3.0	2	0	0	0	1.000	6.00
Merloni,Lou	Bos	1	0	1.0	0	0	0	0	-	.00
Meyers,Chad	Sea	3	0	4.0	0	0	0	0	-	.00
Michaels,Jason	Phi	23	5	82.1	13	3	0	0	1.000	1.75
Millar,Kevin	Bos	19	16	145.0	33	1	1	0	.971	2.11
Mohr,Dustan	Min	30	23	220.1	55	1	2	0	.966	2.29
Mora,Melvin	Bal	56	54	468.0	118	8	0	2	1.000	2.42
Nix,Laynce	Tex	5	4	28.0	14	0	2	0	.875	4.50
O'Leary,Troy	ChC	28	14	145.0	18	1	0	0	1.000	1.18
Owens,Eric	Ana	10	4	46.0	9	0	1	0	.900	1.76
Palmeiro,O	StL	42	19	209.2	50	3	0	0	1.000	2.28
Paquette,Craig	Det	3	3	27.0	8	0	0	0	1.000	2.67
Pellow,Kit	Col	1	1	5.0	1	0	0	0	1.000	1.80
Pena,Wily Mo	Cin	8	4	38.2	6	0	0	0	1.000	1.40
Perez,Eduardo	StL	10	5	43.2	13	0	1	0	.929	2.68
Perez,Timo	NYM	58	36	340.1	66	1	1	0	.985	1.77
Petrick,Ben	Col	1	0	2.0	1	0	0	0	1.000	4.50
Petrick,Ben	Det	18	12	127.0	34	0	1	0	.971	2.41
Piatt,Adam	Oak	32	24	209.0	37	2	1	0	.975	1.68
Piatt,Adam	TB	1	1	9.0	3	0	0	0	1.000	3.00
Podsednik,S	Mil	2	0	8.1	0	0	0	0	-	.00
Porter,Colin	Hou	1	0	4.0	1	0	0	0	1.000	2.25
Pride,Curtis	NYY	1	1	8.0	3	0	0	0	1.000	3.38
Quinlan,Robb	Ana	1	1	12.1	5	0	0	0	1.000	3.65
Raines Jr,Tim	Bal	1	1	9.0	3	0	0	0	1.000	3.00
Relaford,Desi	KC	1	0	8.0	1	0	0	0	1.000	1.13
Restovich,Mike	Min	3	2	26.1	10	0	0	0	1.000	3.42
Reyes,Rene	Col	10	5	53.2	10	1	1	0	.917	1.84
Richard,Chris	Col	3	3	21.0	5	0	0	0	1.000	2.14
Riggs,Adam	Ana	8	7	49.2	13	1	0	0	1.000	2.54
Rios,Armando	CWS	9	2	26.0	6	1	0	0	1.000	2.42
Rivera,Juan	NYY	34	30	289.2	65	0	2	0	.970	2.02
Rivera,Ruben	SF	9	1	26.1	12	0	0	0	1.000	4.10
Robinson,Kerry	StL	36	4	100.1	18	0	0	0	1.000	1.61
Rolls,Damian	TB	6	5	40.1	18	0	0	0	1.000	4.02
Romano,Jason	LA	9	0	14.2	3	0	0	0	1.000	1.84
Rowand,Aaron	CWS	24	0	25.1	6	0	0	0	1.000	2.13
Ryan,Mike	Min	4	1	20.0	8	0	0	0	1.000	3.60
Sadler,Donnie	Tex	19	1	42.0	8	1	0	0	1.000	1.93
Sanders,Reggie	Pit	39	36	311.2	67	1	2	1	.971	1.96
Selby,Bill	Cle	1	0	2.0	1	0	0	0	1.000	4.50
Shinjo,T	NYM	7	2	22.0	8	0	0	0	1.000	3.27
Shumpert,Terry	TB	5	3	27.0	7	0	0	0	1.000	2.33
Sierra,Ruben	Tex	20	18	138.2	21	1	0	0	1.000	1.43
Sierra,Ruben	NYY	6	5	35.0	6	0	0	0	1.000	1.54
Singleton,C	Oak	4	1	13.0	0	0	0	0	-	.00
Smith,Mark	Mil	12	11	88.0	22	0	1	0	.957	2.25
Smitherman,S	Cin	14	9	93.1	17	0	0	0	1.000	1.64
Sorensen,Zach	Cle	1	0	2.0	0	0	0	0	-	.00
Spencer,Shane	Cle	16	10	101.2	26	1	0	1	1.000	2.39
Spencer,Shane	Tex	50	40	369.1	76	2	2	1	.975	1.90
Spiezio,Scott	Ana	3	0	7.0	1	0	0	0	1.000	1.29
Stairs,Matt	Pit	8	8	59.0	18	0	1	0	.947	2.75
Stenson,D	Cin	18	16	131.1	37	1	1	0	.974	2.60
Stewart,Sh	Tor	69	69	601.0	145	2	4	0	.974	2.20
Stewart,Sh	Min	46	44	385.1	102	4	0	0	1.000	2.48
Surhoff,B.J.	Bal	24	22	209.2	40	0	1	0	.976	1.72
Swann,Pedro	Bal	6	3	27.0	6	0	0	0	1.000	2.00
Sweeney,Mark	Col	7	4	37.1	6	0	0	0	1.000	1.45
Taguchi,So	StL	11	2	27.1	6	0	0	0	1.000	1.98
Taylor,Reggie	Cin	13	2	37.0	9	0	0	0	1.000	2.19
Teixeira,Mark	Tex	14	10	79.2	14	0	1	0	.933	1.58
Thames,Marcus	Tex	4	2	19.0	5	0	0	0	1.000	2.37
Torcato,Tony	SF	4	1	18.0	5	0	1	0	.833	2.50
Torrealba,Y	SF	1	0	1.0	0	0	0	0	-	.00
Torres,Andres	Det	1	1	8.0	2	0	0	0	1.000	2.25
Trammell,Bubba	NYY	3	3	22.0	9	0	0	0	1.000	3.68
Tucker,Michael	KC	21	17	154.0	31	2	0	0	1.000	1.93
Tyner,Jason	TB	9	8	76.0	16	0	1	0	.941	1.89
Valderrama,C	SF	4	0	5.0	1	0	0	0	1.000	1.80
Vander Wal,J	Mil	6	6	44.2	16	0	1	0	.941	3.22
Vaughn,Greg	Col	6	3	30.0	9	0	0	0	1.000	2.70
Victorino,S	SD	15	5	70.1	17	2	0	0	1.000	2.43
Vitiello,Joe	Mon	15	13	85.0	14	0	0	0	1.000	1.48
Ward,Daryle	LA	11	11	79.0	10	0	0	0	1.000	1.14
Watson,Matt	NYM	5	2	29.0	11	0	2	0	.846	3.41
Wesson,Barry	Ana	5	1	17.0	6	0	0	0	1.000	3.18
White,Rondell	SD	104	102	837.1	173	6	4	2	.978	1.92
White,Rondell	KC	17	17	132.0	45	0	1	0	.978	3.07
Williams,G	Fla	11	4	54.0	12	0	1	0	.923	2.00
Wilson,Craig	Pit	7	4	44.0	9	1	1	0	.909	2.05
Wilson,Tom	Tor	1	0	1.0	0	0	0	0	-	.00
Witt,Kevin	Det	13	9	77.0	20	0	0	0	1.000	2.34
Young,Dmitri	Det	61	59	512.0	126	5	2	2	.985	2.30
Zoccolillo,P	Mil	3	3	25.0	5	0	0	0	1.000	1.80

Center Fielders - Regulars

Player	Tm	G	GS	Inn	PO	A	E	DP	Pct.	Rng
Cameron,Mike	Sea	147	145	1284.0	484	3	4	2	.992	3.41
Sanchez,Alex	TOT	135	128	1118.2	378	4	7	1	.982	3.07
Baldelli,Rocco	TB	154	149	1322.2	437	14	5	4	.989	3.07
Beltran,Carlos	KC	130	129	1123.0	371	10	5	1	.987	3.05
Edmonds,Jim	StL	128	118	1017.1	333	11	5	4	.986	3.04
Hunter,Torii	Min	151	149	1299.1	424	5	4	1	.991	2.97
Matos,Luis	Bal	106	105	920.0	298	5	4	1	.987	2.96
Kotsay,Mark	SD	127	121	1055.1	324	13	3	3	.991	2.87
Bradley,Milton	Cle	93	93	838.2	245	6	2	2	.992	2.69
Jones,Andruw	Atl	155	153	1329.0	389	7	3	1	.992	2.68
Williams,B	NYY	115	113	1001.1	291	3	1	1	.997	2.64
Podsednik,S	Mil	123	122	1090.0	315	3	1	1	.991	2.63
Damon,Johnny	Bos	144	141	1265.0	361	7	1	1	.997	2.62
Pierre,Juan	Fla	161	161	1433.1	402	6	3	5	.993	2.56
Grissom,M	SF	148	141	1236.2	341	3	8	0	.977	2.50
Chavez,Endy	Mon	134	112	1033.1	278	9	3	2	.990	2.50
Lofton,Kenny	TOT	137	133	1170.0	312	9	3	2	.991	2.47
Wells,Vernon	Tor	161	161	1416.0	383	3	4	0	.990	2.45
Byrd,Marlon	Phi	131	124	1100.1	295	4	5	1	.984	2.45
Wilson,Preston	Col	155	153	1307.1	331	8	7	0	.980	2.33
Biggio,Craig	Hou	150	150	1313.0	327	9	1	1	.997	2.30
Byrnes,Eric	Oak	82	77	672.1	164	2	2	1	.988	2.22
Singleton,C	Oak	102	82	737.1	175	1	5	1	.972	2.15
Roberts,Dave	LA	105	98	870.1	202	4	5	1	.976	2.13
Finley,Steve	Ari	140	130	1168.1	257	9	5	1	.982	2.05
Patterson,C	ChC	82	79	710.1	151	3	4	1	.975	1.95

Center Fielders - The Rest

Player	Tm	G	GS	Inn	PO	A	E	DP	Pct.	Rng
Allen,Chad	Fla	1	0	2.0	1	0	0	0	1.000	4.50
Bautista,Danny	Ari	18	16	135.0	31	0	1	0	.969	2.07
Bay,Jay	SD	3	3	19.0	8	0	0	0	1.000	3.79
Bay,Jay	Pit	2	2	17.0	4	0	0	0	1.000	2.12
Bellhorn,Mark	Col	3	0	4.0	2	0	0	0	1.000	4.50
Berkman,Lance	Hou	1	0	2.0	1	0	0	0	1.000	4.50
Bigbie,Larry	Bal	2	1	10.0	6	0	0	0	1.000	5.40
Bocachica,H	Det	5	4	37.0	9	1	0	0	1.000	2.43
Borchard,Joe	CWS	16	15	133.0	32	0	0	0	1.000	2.17
Bragg,Darren	Atl	21	9	113.0	23	0	0	0	1.000	1.83
Brown,Adrian	Bos	6	2	33.0	9	0	0	0	1.000	2.45
Bruntlett,Eric	Hou	1	0	2.0	0	0	0	0	-	.00
Budzinski,Mark	Cin	1	1	8.0	3	0	0	0	1.000	3.38
Burnitz,Jeromy	NYM	21	20	156.0	46	0	0	0	1.000	2.65
Burnitz,Jeromy	LA	12	11	90.2	14	0	2	0	.875	1.39
Cabrera,Jol	LA	38	28	245.2	48	3	2	0	.962	1.87
Calloway,Ron	Mon	2	0	6.0	2	0	0	0	1.000	3.00
Cedeno,Roger	NYM	17	15	131.1	31	3	0	0	1.000	2.33
Christenson,R	Tex	59	46	424.0	134	0	0	1	1.000	2.84
Clark,Brady	Mil	6	4	49.0	17	3	0	2	1.000	3.67
Clark,Jermaine	Tex	1	0	2.0	0	0	0	0	-	.00
Collier,Lou	Bos	1	0	1.0	0	0	0	0	-	.00
Conti,Jason	Mil	1	0	3.0	3	0	0	0	1.000	9.00
Crawford,Carl	TB	13	12	103.2	34	0	0	0	1.000	2.95
Crisp,Coco	Cle	53	51	462.0	123	1	0	1	1.000	2.42
Cruz,Jose	SF	3	1	13.1	4	0	0	0	1.000	2.70
DaVanon,Jeff	Ana	31	25	215.0	80	0	0	0	1.000	3.35
DeJesus,David	KC	8	0	21.0	2	0	0	0	1.000	.86
Dellucci,David	Ari	9	4	39.2	13	0	0	0	1.000	2.95
Dellucci,David	NYY	1	0	1.0	1	0	0	0	1.000	9.00
Drew,J.D.	StL	26	22	190.2	52	2	0	0	1.000	2.55
Duncan,Jeff	NYM	52	41	366.0	137	1	0	0	1.000	3.39
Dye,Jermaine	Oak	3	1	12.0	4	0	0	0	1.000	3.00
Ellison,Jason	SF	1	0	1.0	1	0	0	0	1.000	9.00
Erstad,Darin	Ana	66	66	559.1	191	2	0	0	1.000	3.11
Everett,Carl	Tex	15	13	97.0	25	0	0	0	1.000	2.32
Everett,Carl	CWS	66	63	482.2	136	1	2	0	.986	2.55
Figgins,Chone	Ana	44	40	354.2	108	1	0	0	1.000	2.77
Ford,Lew	Min	13	5	74.2	17	1	2	1	.900	2.17
Freel,Ryan	Cin	20	19	164.2	51	2	0	0	1.000	2.90
Garcia,Karim	Cle	7	6	48.0	14	1	1	0	.938	2.81
Garcia,Karim	NYY	3	2	22.0	8	1	0	0	1.000	3.68
Gerut,Jody	Cle	14	12	110.2	29	1	0	0	1.000	2.44
Giles,Brian	Pit	16	14	124.2	40	1	0	0	1.000	2.96
Gipson,Charles	NYY	8	2	31.0	8	0	0	0	1.000	2.32
Glanville,Doug	Tex	52	47	417.2	117	1	0	0	1.000	2.54
Glanville,Doug	ChC	15	8	82.0	27	1	0	1	1.000	3.07
Gonzalez,Raul	NYM	25	13	109.1	38	3	0	0	1.000	3.38
Goodwin,Tom	ChC	27	18	165.0	33	0	0	0	1.000	1.80
Griffey Jr.,K	Cin	43	43	355.2	89	3	1	0	.989	2.33
Guiel,Aaron	KC	1	1	9.0	6	0	0	0	1.000	6.00
Guillen,Jose	Cin	1	0	2.1	1	0	0	0	1.000	3.86
Guillen,Jose	Oak	4	2	20.0	4	0	0	0	1.000	1.80
Hammonds,J	SF	14	12	103.2	26	1	0	0	1.000	2.34
Harris,Willie	CWS	61	23	258.2	83	3	2	0	.977	2.99
Hernandez,Jose	ChC	2	2	15.0	1	0	0	0	1.000	.60
Higginson,B	Det	1	1	8.0	1	0	0	0	1.000	1.13
Hocking,Denny	Min	2	1	9.0	3	0	0	0	1.000	3.00
Hubbard,T	ChC	4	3	28.0	5	0	0	0	1.000	1.61
Hunter,Brian	Hou	14	7	77.0	11	1	0	0	1.000	1.40
Hyzdu,Adam	Pit	20	11	103.1	32	1	0	0	1.000	2.87
Jackson,Damian	Bos	13	12	101.0	22	2	0	1	1.000	2.14
Johnson,Reed	Tor	5	0	8.0	1	0	0	0	1.000	1.13
Johnson,R	KC	6	0	9.0	0	0	1	0	.000	.00
Jordan,Brian	LA	14	13	96.0	31	0	1	0	.969	2.91
Kapler,Gabe	Col	2	2	16.0	6	0	0	0	1.000	3.38
Kapler,Gabe	Bos	8	7	62.2	16	2	2	0	.900	2.59
Kearns,Austin	Cin	40	37	323.2	105	3	1	0	.991	3.00
Kielty,Bobby	Min	2	2	18.0	5	0	1	0	.833	2.50
Kielty,Bobby	Tor	1	0	2.0	2	0	0	0	1.000	9.00
Kingsale,Gene	Det	23	22	192.0	52	0	1	0	.981	2.44
Lane,Jason	Hou	6	2	23.0	2	0	0	0	1.000	.78
Langerhans,R	Atl	4	0	14.1	3	0	0	0	1.000	1.88
Latham,Chris	NYY	1	0	3.0	2	0	0	0	1.000	6.00
Ledee,Ricky	Phi	42	35	314.1	64	4	0	0	1.000	1.95
Lofton,Kenny	Pit	82	81	714.0	202	6	0	2	1.000	2.62
Lofton,Kenny	ChC	55	52	456.0	110	3	3	0	.974	2.23
Macias,Jose	Mon	15	10	91.0	27	2	0	0	1.000	2.87
Mackowiak,Rob	Pit	8	3	36.0	10	0	0	0	1.000	2.50
Marrero,Eli	StL	6	2	27.0	7	1	0	0	1.000	2.67
Mateo,Henry	Mon	2	0	4.0	1	0	0	0	1.000	2.25
Mateo,Ruben	Cin	14	12	103.0	26	1	0	1	1.000	2.36
Matsui,Hideki	NYY	46	46	403.2	110	2	1	1	.991	2.50
Matthews Jr.,G	Bal	40	38	346.2	99	2	0	0	1.000	2.62
Matthews Jr.,G	SD	35	27	247.0	65	1	0	0	1.000	2.40
McCracken,Q	Ari	16	11	93.0	18	1	1	1	.950	1.84
McEwing,Joe	NYM	1	1	7.0	4	0	0	0	1.000	5.14
Mench,Kevin	Tex	3	3	18.0	3	0	0	0	1.000	1.50
Michaels,Jason	Phi	5	3	29.0	8	0	0	0	1.000	2.48
Mohr,Dustan	Min	11	5	61.0	22	0	0	0	1.000	3.25
Mondesi,Raul	Ari	2	1	10.0	6	0	0	0	1.000	5.40
Monroe,Craig	Det	2	2	17.0	1	0	0	0	1.000	.53
Mora,Melvin	Bal	12	11	82.0	23	1	0	0	1.000	2.63
Nivar,Ramon	Tex	26	23	218.0	70	3	3	1	.961	3.01
Nix,Laynce	Tex	20	17	137.0	53	0	0	0	1.000	3.48
Nixon,Trot	Bos	1	0	2.0	1	0	0	0	1.000	4.50
Ordonez,M	CWS	4	3	25.0	5	0	0	0	1.000	1.80
Owens,Eric	Ana	47	31	298.1	100	0	1	0	.990	3.02
Ozuna,Pablo	Col	5	0	12.0	1	0	0	0	1.000	.75
Palmeiro,O	StL	17	10	95.2	24	1	0	0	1.000	2.35
Payton,Jay	Col	8	4	45.0	8	0	0	0	1.000	1.60
Pena,Wily Mo	Cin	26	24	205.1	55	1	0	1	1.000	2.45
Perez,Timo	NYM	49	41	332.2	98	4	1	1	.990	2.76
Petrick,Ben	Col	1	0	2.0	1	1	0	0	1.000	9.00
Petrick,Ben	Det	14	13	107.0	26	2	1	0	.966	2.36
Porter,Colin	Hou	7	3	33.0	9	0	0	0	1.000	2.45
Raines Jr,Tim	Bal	17	8	91.0	34	1	1	1	.972	3.46
Ramirez,Julio	Ana	3	0	4.0	2	0	1	0	.667	4.50
Redman,P	NYM	9	5	55.2	15	0	0	0	1.000	2.43
Redman,Tike	Pit	54	51	449.1	126	1	2	0	.984	2.54
Relaford,Desi	KC	5	4	37.0	12	2	1	1	.933	3.41
Reyes,Rene	Col	5	2	21.2	1	0	0	0	1.000	.42
Rios,Armando	CWS	23	19	153.0	39	0	0	0	1.000	2.29
Rivera,Ruben	SF	13	6	68.2	28	0	0	0	1.000	3.67
Robinson,Kerry	StL	20	5	74.1	19	0	0	0	1.000	2.30
Romano,Jason	LA	17	4	60.0	14	0	0	0	1.000	2.10
Rowand,Aaron	CWS	65	39	378.2	100	6	0	0	1.000	2.52
Ruan,Wilkin	LA	20	8	95.0	22	1	0	0	1.000	2.18
Sadler,Donnie	Tex	22	12	111.2	33	1	0	0	1.000	2.74
Sanchez,Alex	Mil	36	36	310.0	99	3	1	1	.990	2.96
Sanchez,Alex	Det	99	92	808.2	279	1	6	0	.979	3.12
Shinjo,T	NYM	50	25	255.1	90	5	3	1	.969	3.35
Spivey,Junior	Ari	1	0	4.0	0	0	0	0	-	.00
Strong,Jamal	Sea	2	0	3.0	0	0	0	0	-	.00
Taguchi,So	StL	16	5	58.2	19	2	0	0	1.000	3.22
Taylor,Reggie	Cin	49	26	284.2	81	2	1	0	.988	2.62
Terrero,Luis	Ari	2	0	5.0	1	0	0	0	1.000	1.80
Thames,Marcus	Tex	1	1	8.0	2	0	0	0	1.000	2.25
Torres,Andres	Det	36	28	269.0	81	0	0	0	.988	2.74
Tucker,Michael	KC	30	28	239.2	60	0	0	0	1.000	2.25
Tyner,Jason	TB	2	1	11.0	3	0	0	0	1.000	2.45
Uribe,Juan	Col	1	1	9.0	3	0	0	0	1.000	3.00
Valderrama,C	SF	2	1	11.0	5	0	0	0	1.000	4.09
Victorino,S	SD	16	11	110.0	21	1	0	0	1.000	1.80
Werth,Jayson	Tor	1	1	9.0	6	0	0	0	1.000	6.00
Wilkerson,Brad	Mon	42	40	305.1	72	2	1	0	.987	2.18
Williams,G	Fla	1	1	10.0	3	0	0	0	1.000	2.70
Winn,Randy	Sea	20	17	154.0	60	0	0	0	1.000	3.51
Womack,Tony	Col	1	0	3.0	1	0	0	0	1.000	3.00
Young,Eric	SF	2	0	3.0	2	0	0	0	1.000	6.00

Right Fielders - Regulars

Player	Tm	G	GS	Inn	PO	A	E	DP	Pct.	Rng
Cruz,Jose	SF	157	151	1332.2	337	18	2	7	.994	2.40
Guiel,Aaron	KC	87	83	744.1	184	8	3	1	.985	2.32
Suzuki,Ichiro	Sea	159	156	1367.0	336	12	2	3	.994	2.29
Higginson,B	Det	117	115	996.2	248	4	5	0	.981	2.28
Cedeno,Roger	NYM	111	100	803.0	199	2	3	0	.985	2.25
Hidalgo,R	Hou	137	136	1200.0	276	22	4	3	.987	2.24
Encarnacion,J	Fla	155	155	1355.1	329	7	0	2	1.000	2.23
Vander Wal,J	Mil	83	81	663.1	160	4	2	1	.988	2.23
Ordonez,M	CWS	154	154	1324.2	316	7	2	1	.994	2.19

Player	Tm	G	GS	Inn	PO	A	E	DP	Pct.	Rng
Sanders,Reggie	Pit	91	76	666.1	156	5	2	1	.988	2.17
Guerrero,V	Mon	112	112	949.2	218	10	7	0	.970	2.16
Guillen,Jose	TOT	96	92	802.2	181	9	8	0	.960	2.13
Mondesi,Raul	TOT	139	137	1216.0	272	9	6	1	.979	2.08
Huff,Aubrey	TB	102	102	849.2	190	5	6	1	.970	2.07
Gibbons,Jay	Bal	144	144	1274.2	284	8	5	0	.983	2.06
Salmon,Tim	Ana	78	78	604.1	133	4	6	1	.958	2.04
Abreu,Bobby	Phi	158	156	1373.1	304	6	6	0	.981	2.03
Sheffield,Gary	Atl	154	154	1288.1	283	7	4	2	.986	2.03
Nixon,Trot	Bos	129	119	1078.2	230	4	4	0	.983	1.95
Walker,Larry	Col	132	128	1102.2	230	8	4	1	.983	1.94
Nady,Xavier	SD	105	98	846.2	170	12	6	2	.968	1.93
Kielty,Bobby	TOT	89	76	690.1	143	3	2	0	.986	1.90
Green,Shawn	LA	157	157	1397.2	260	8	5	0	.982	1.73
Sosa,Sammy	ChC	137	136	1178.2	213	2	5	1	.977	1.64

Right Fielders - The Rest

Player	Tm	G	GS	Inn	PO	A	E	DP	Pct.	Rng
Abad,Andy	Bos	1	1	7.0	0	0	0	0	-	.00
Allen,Chad	Fla	2	0	3.0	2	0	0	0	1.000	6.00
Banks,Brian	Fla	10	5	53.2	11	0	1	0	.917	1.84
Bautista,Danny	Ari	59	54	485.0	91	1	4	0	.958	1.71
Bay,Jay	Pit	1	1	8.0	2	1	0	0	1.000	3.38
Bellhorn,Mark	Col	2	0	4.0	0	0	0	0	-	.00
Benard,Marvin	SF	4	2	17.2	6	2	0	0	1.000	4.08
Berg,Dave	Tor	5	4	38.0	5	0	1	0	.833	1.18
Berger,Brandon	KC	11	8	69.2	17	1	0	0	1.000	2.33
Bigbie,Larry	Bal	5	3	27.2	6	1	0	0	1.000	2.28
Bloomquist,W	Sea	1	0	1.0	1	0	0	0	1.000	9.00
Blum,Geoff	Hou	1	0	3.0	0	0	0	0	-	.00
Bragg,Darren	Atl	35	7	132.0	28	1	1	0	.967	1.98
Brown,Dee	KC	17	15	124.0	40	2	1	1	.977	3.05
Buchanan,Brian	SD	29	12	129.1	33	2	0	1	1.000	2.44
Burnitz,Jeromy	NYM	48	36	327.0	80	1	1	0	.988	2.23
Burnitz,Jeromy	LA	2	1	15.0	1	0	0	0	1.000	.60
Byrnes,Eric	Oak	2	0	2.2	0	0	0	0	-	.00
Cabrera,Jol	LA	4	0	6.0	0	0	0	0	-	.00
Cairo,Miguel	StL	6	1	15.0	4	0	0	0	1.000	2.40
Calloway,Ron	Mon	47	37	346.1	71	0	1	0	.986	1.85
Catalanotto,F	Tor	43	40	340.0	55	0	0	0	1.000	1.46
Cepicky,Matt	Mon	1	0	3.0	0	0	0	0	-	.00
Clark,Brady	Mil	82	50	472.1	129	1	4	1	.970	2.48
Clark,Howie	Tor	1	1	7.0	1	0	0	0	1.000	1.29
Conine,Jeff	Bal	2	0	1.0	0	0	0	0	-	.00
Conti,Jason	Mil	19	7	89.2	25	1	3	0	.897	2.61
Cuddyer,Mike	Min	17	16	139.0	24	1	0	0	1.000	1.62
Daubach,Brian	CWS	9	6	53.1	6	0	1	0	.857	1.01
DaVanon,Jeff	Ana	91	53	538.0	136	1	3	0	.979	2.29
Davis,J.J.	Pit	10	8	66.2	13	1	0	0	1.000	1.89
DeJesus,David	KC	1	0	1.0	0	0	0	0	-	.00
Dellucci,David	Ari	43	34	312.0	65	0	2	0	.970	1.88
Dellucci,David	NYY	16	13	121.0	29	1	0	1	1.000	2.23
Drew,J.D.	StL	53	47	391.0	101	5	1	1	.991	2.44
Dunn,Adam	Cin	5	2	26.0	3	0	1	0	.750	1.04
Dye,Jermaine	Oak	60	59	500.1	102	1	0	0	1.000	1.85
Escobar,Alex	Cle	25	25	221.0	59	3	2	1	.969	2.52
Everett,Carl	Tex	33	26	240.1	56	3	1	1	.983	2.21
Everett,Carl	CWS	1	0	7.2	1	2	0	0	1.000	3.52
Feliz,Pedro	SF	1	0	2.0	0	0	0	0	-	.00
Ford,Lew	Min	6	3	34.0	9	0	1	0	.900	2.38
Franco,Matt	Atl	2	0	7.0	1	0	0	0	1.000	1.29
Gant,Ron	Oak	1	1	8.0	2	0	0	0	1.000	2.25
Garcia,Karim	Cle	17	16	148.2	22	1	3	0	.885	1.39
Garcia,Karim	NYY	37	32	266.2	59	3	1	0	.984	2.09
Gerut,Jody	Cle	63	61	542.2	125	6	1	2	.992	2.17
Giambi,Jeremy	Bos	2	1	8.0	4	0	0	0	1.000	4.50
Glanville,Doug	ChC	1	1	6.0	3	0	0	0	1.000	4.50
Gonzalez,Juan	Tex	57	57	471.0	97	10	0	1	1.000	2.04
Gonzalez,Raul	NYM	40	17	197.1	41	0	0	0	1.000	1.87
Goodwin,Tom	ChC	15	8	84.2	17	0	0	0	1.000	1.81
Grabowski,J	Oak	3	0	7.0	3	0	0	0	1.000	3.86
Grieve,Ben	TB	10	10	85.0	17	1	1	1	.947	1.91
Guillen,Jose	Cin	63	59	512.2	133	9	4	0	.973	2.49
Guillen,Jose	Oak	33	33	290.0	48	0	4	0	.923	1.49
Hammock,Robby	Ari	12	9	81.2	13	0	1	0	.929	1.43
Hammonds,J	Mil	10	10	82.0	17	0	0	0	1.000	1.87

Player	Tm	G	GS	Inn	PO	A	E	DP	Pct.	Rng
Hammonds,J	SF	4	3	24.0	2	0	0	0	1.000	.75
Harris,Lenny	ChC	1	0	3.0	0	0	0	0	-	.00
Harris,Lenny	Fla	2	1	11.0	3	0	0	0	1.000	2.45
Hessman,Mike	Atl	1	0	3.0	0	0	0	0	-	.00
Hocking,Denny	Min	4	3	26.0	7	0	0	0	1.000	2.42
Hollandsworth,T	Fla	3	1	17.1	8	0	0	0	1.000	4.15
Hubbard,T	ChC	1	0	2.0	0	0	0	0	-	.00
Hunter,Brian	Hou	15	7	71.2	18	0	2	0	.900	2.26
Hyzdu,Adam	Pit	11	1	34.0	4	0	0	0	1.000	1.06
Ibanez,Raul	KC	5	5	41.0	12	1	0	0	1.000	2.85
Jackson,Damian	Bos	12	6	57.2	20	1	0	0	1.000	3.28
Johnson,Gary	Ana	2	2	15.0	3	0	0	0	1.000	1.80
Johnson,Reed	Tor	71	61	532.1	88	4	3	1	.968	1.56
Jones,Jacque	Min	10	10	81.0	23	0	0	0	1.000	2.56
Jones,Jason	Tex	13	12	93.0	24	1	1	0	.962	2.42
Jordan,Brian	LA	3	3	26.0	5	0	0	0	1.000	1.73
Jose,Felix	Ari	1	1	6.0	0	0	0	0	-	.00
Kapler,Gabe	Col	13	7	76.0	17	2	1	0	.950	2.25
Kapler,Gabe	Bos	30	25	226.0	40	2	3	1	.933	1.67
Kearns,Austin	Cin	50	40	364.2	95	2	1	0	.990	2.39
Kielty,Bobby	Min	33	31	277.2	62	1	1	0	.984	2.04
Kielty,Bobby	Tor	56	45	412.2	81	2	1	0	.988	1.81
Kinkade,Mike	LA	2	1	8.0	2	0	0	0	1.000	2.25
Lane,Jason	Hou	2	0	6.0	2	0	0	0	1.000	3.00
Langerhans,R	Atl	9	1	26.0	8	1	0	0	1.000	3.12
Latham,Chris	NYY	1	0	3.0	1	0	0	0	1.000	3.00
Lawton,Matt	Cle	13	12	110.1	17	1	0	0	1.000	1.47
Ledee,Ricky	Phi	1	0	2.0	0	0	0	0	-	.00
Linden,Todd	SF	6	3	28.1	3	0	0	0	1.000	.95
Lombard,George	TB	11	6	66.0	21	0	1	0	.955	2.86
Long,Terrence	Oak	74	62	559.1	135	2	4	0	.972	2.20
Lopez,Mendy	KC	2	1	8.2	0	0	0	0	-	.00
Ludwick,Ryan	Tex	6	4	40.0	11	0	0	0	1.000	2.48
Ludwick,Ryan	Cle	19	19	175.0	40	2	0	0	1.000	2.16
Mabry,John	Sea	14	3	49.0	7	1	0	0	1.000	1.47
Macias,Jose	Mon	8	2	26.0	6	0	0	0	1.000	2.08
Mackowiak,Rob	Pit	14	5	61.0	14	0	0	0	1.000	2.07
Magruder,Chris	Cle	3	2	19.0	1	0	0	0	1.000	.47
Marrero,Eli	StL	21	11	117.0	28	0	1	0	.966	2.15
Martin,Al	TB	5	3	22.0	4	0	0	0	1.000	1.64
Mateo,Henry	Mon	6	2	17.2	6	0	0	0	1.000	3.06
Mateo,Ruben	Cin	39	36	313.0	77	1	2	0	.975	2.24
Matos,Julius	KC	1	0	1.0	0	0	0	0	-	.00
Matos,Luis	Bal	4	1	18.0	5	0	0	0	1.000	2.50
Matthews Jr.,G	SD	35	22	215.0	47	1	0	0	1.000	2.01
McCarty,Dave	Bos	1	0	1.0	0	0	0	0	-	.00
McCracken,Q	Ari	34	22	207.1	32	0	0	0	1.000	1.39
McEwing,Joe	NYM	2	0	8.2	0	0	0	0	-	.00
McMillon,Billy	Oak	1	0	2.0	0	0	0	0	-	.00
Mench,Kevin	Tex	2	0	3.0	0	0	0	0	-	.00
Merced,Orlando	Hou	21	16	135.1	28	3	1	0	.969	2.06
Michaels,Jason	Phi	13	6	68.1	16	0	1	0	.941	2.11
Mientkiewicz,D	Min	3	2	18.0	3	0	0	0	1.000	1.50
Millar,Kevin	Bos	12	10	86.1	17	1	0	0	1.000	1.88
Mohr,Dustan	Min	77	62	574.1	161	4	1	4	.976	2.54
Mondesi,Raul	NYY	97	95	854.0	198	7	3	1	.986	2.16
Mondesi,Raul	Ari	42	42	362.0	74	2	3	0	.962	1.89
Monroe,Craig	Det	38	30	280.0	71	2	3	0	.961	2.35
Mora,Melvin	Bal	13	12	103.1	21	0	1	0	.955	1.83
Nevin,Phil	SD	29	29	228.0	47	1	1	0	.980	1.89
Nix,Laynce	Tex	38	36	259.2	64	1	3	0	.956	2.25
Norton,Greg	Col	3	0	5.2	0	0	0	0	-	.00
O'Leary,Troy	ChC	24	17	182.0	41	2	0	0	1.000	2.13
Owens,Eric	Ana	42	25	232.1	55	3	3	2	.951	2.25
Palmeiro,O	StL	61	36	317.1	91	2	0	1	1.000	2.64
Paquette,Craig	Det	2	1	9.0	2	0	0	0	1.000	2.00
Payton,Jay	Col	3	1	9.0	0	0	0	0	-	.00
Pena,Wily Mo	Cin	14	11	102.0	21	0	2	0	.913	1.85
Perez,Eduardo	StL	64	46	386.2	99	2	3	0	.971	2.35
Perez,Timo	NYM	14	8	71.1	16	0	0	0	1.000	2.02
Petrick,Ben	Det	3	0	6.0	1	0	0	0	1.000	1.50
Piatt,Adam	Oak	7	4	36.0	6	0	0	0	1.000	1.50
Piatt,Adam	TB	6	5	45.0	4	0	0	0	1.000	.80
Podsednik,S	Mil	13	8	92.2	30	2	0	0	1.000	3.11
Porter,Colin	Hou	6	3	34.0	7	0	0	0	1.000	1.85
Pride,Curtis	NYY	2	2	18.0	2	0	0	0	1.000	1.00
Ramirez,Julio	Ana	2	0	3.0	1	0	0	0	1.000	3.00
Redman,P	NYM	2	0	4.0	1	0	0	0	1.000	2.25
Relaford,Desi	KC	15	10	94.0	24	2	1	0	.963	2.49

Player	Tm	G	GS	Inn	PO	A	E	DP	Pct.	Rng
Restovich,Mike	Min	14	11	105.0	19	1	0	0	1.000	1.71
Reyes,Rene	Col	25	16	149.2	39	2	1	0	.976	2.47
Rios,Armando	CWS	6	2	22.2	6	0	1	0	.857	2.38
Rivera,Juan	NYY	22	13	128.1	25	3	0	0	1.000	1.96
Rivera,Ruben	SF	6	1	15.0	2	0	0	0	1.000	1.20
Robinson,Kerry	StL	39	20	206.2	56	0	0	0	1.000	2.44
Rolls,Damian	TB	33	23	213.0	46	0	1	0	.979	1.94
Romano,Jason	LA	2	0	5.0	1	0	0	0	1.000	1.80
Ross,Cody	Det	6	6	49.0	15	0	2	0	.882	2.76
Rowand,Aaron	CWS	12	0	22.2	7	0	0	0	1.000	2.78
Ryan,Mike	Min	12	10	87.1	25	2	0	1	1.000	2.78
Sadler,Donnie	Tex	7	0	10.0	2	0	0	0	1.000	1.80
Santos,F	SF	3	1	13.1	3	0	0	0	1.000	2.03
Shinjo,T	NYM	1	0	2.0	0	0	0	0	-	.00
Shumpert,Terry	TB	9	4	40.1	10	0	1	0	.909	2.23
Sierra,Ruben	Tex	4	2	19.0	3	0	1	0	.750	1.42
Sierra,Ruben	NYY	11	8	71.0	14	0	0	0	1.000	1.77
Singleton,C	Oak	8	3	36.1	11	0	1	0	.917	2.72
Smith,Mark	Mil	3	2	20.0	3	0	0	0	1.000	1.35
Spencer,Shane	Cle	30	27	242.2	49	1	1	0	.980	1.85
Spencer,Shane	Tex	12	9	78.2	29	0	0	0	1.000	3.32
Spiezio,Scott	Ana	7	3	25.2	5	0	0	0	1.000	1.75
Stairs,Matt	Pit	47	42	335.1	56	4	0	0	1.000	1.61
Stenson,D	Cin	7	4	41.2	7	0	0	0	1.000	1.51
Stewart,Sh	Min	14	14	119.2	33	0	1	0	.971	2.48
Surhoff,B.J.	Bal	3	3	25.0	4	0	0	0	1.000	1.44
Sweeney,Mark	Col	11	9	66.0	12	0	0	0	1.000	1.64
Taguchi,So	StL	13	1	28.2	5	0	0	0	1.000	1.57
Taylor,Reggie	Cin	3	2	15.0	6	0	0	0	1.000	3.60
Teixeira,Mark	Tex	11	8	65.0	15	0	0	0	1.000	2.08
Terrero,Luis	Ari	1	0	1.0	0	0	0	0	-	.00
Thames,Marcus	Tex	19	18	153.2	29	1	0	0	1.000	1.76
Torcato,Tony	SF	2	0	4.1	0	0	0	0	-	.00
Torres,Andres	Det	16	10	98.0	20	3	0	1	1.000	2.11
Tucker,Michael	KC	47	40	355.0	81	5	2	0	.977	2.18
Tyner,Jason	TB	23	9	115.0	30	1	1	0	.969	2.43
Valent,Eric	Cin	8	8	71.0	20	1	0	0	1.000	2.66
Vaughn,Greg	Col	1	1	8.0	3	0	0	0	1.000	3.38
Victorino,S	SD	3	1	12.1	3	0	0	0	1.000	2.19
Werth,Jayson	Tor	19	10	99.0	21	1	0	0	1.000	2.00
Wesson,Barry	Ana	4	1	13.0	3	0	0	0	1.000	2.08
Widger,Chris	StL	1	0	1.0	1	0	0	0	1.000	9.00
Wilkerson,Brad	Mon	16	9	95.0	18	1	0	0	1.000	1.80
Williams,G	Fla	3	0	5.0	1	0	0	0	1.000	1.80
Wilson,Craig	Pit	40	28	265.0	78	2	1	0	.988	2.72
Wilson,Tom	Tor	1	1	6.0	1	0	0	0	1.000	1.50
Winn,Randy	Sea	4	3	24.0	4	0	0	0	1.000	1.50
Young,Kevin	Pit	1	1	8.0	1	0	1	0	.500	1.13
Zoccolillo,P	Mil	4	4	32.0	11	0	0	0	1.000	3.09

Catchers - Regulars

Player	Tm	G	GS	Inn	PO	A	E	DP	PB	Pct.
Matheny,Mike	StL	138	121	1096.2	776	49	0	4	5	1.000
Wilson,Dan	Sea	96	92	817.1	588	19	1	3	4	.998
Ausmus,Brad	Hou	143	129	1158.0	984	75	3	10	3	.997
Miller,Damian	ChC	114	103	929.2	940	73	3	3	8	.997
Inge,Brandon	Det	104	98	867.1	500	68	2	6	5	.996
Bennett,Gary	SD	91	87	747.0	536	24	2	4	6	.996
Schneider,B	Mon	98	95	841.0	662	44	3	9	3	.996
Fordyce,Brook	Bal	107	100	884.2	624	41	3	5	6	.996
Posada,Jorge	NYY	137	131	1165.0	937	71	6	2	13	.994
Mayne,Brent	KC	112	107	948.0	594	42	4	3	5	.994
Lopez,Javy	Atl	120	114	992.0	720	52	5	5	6	.994
Johnson,C	Col	108	103	897.2	561	33	4	4	6	.993
Pierzynski,A	Min	135	131	1165.2	843	44	6	6	5	.993
Molina,Ben	Ana	117	109	949.2	673	62	5	2	4	.993
Santiago,B	SF	106	106	902.2	629	34	5	2	8	.993
Rodriguez,Ivan	Fla	138	134	1132.1	916	46	8	6	10	.992
Hernandez,Ra	Oak	139	133	1172.2	864	52	8	7	8	.991
Bard,Josh	Cle	87	80	715.2	487	54	5	6	4	.991
Perez,Eddie	Mil	102	91	821.2	614	31	6	5	8	.991
Osik,Keith	Mil	78	71	630.1	480	42	5	5	6	.991
Lieberthal,M	Phi	131	129	1143.2	868	44	9	1	11	.990
Varitek,Jason	Bos	137	119	1075.1	854	43	9	6	4	.990
Wilson,Vance	NYM	89	71	650.2	442	43	5	4	4	.990
Kendall,Jason	Pit	146	145	1176.0	842	49	10	2	9	.989

Player	Tm	G	GS	Inn	PO	A	E	DP	PB	Pct.
Diaz,Einar	Tex	101	95	842.0	650	50	8	7	4	.989
Hall,Toby	TB	130	126	1107.0	687	59	9	8	7	.988
Olivo,Miguel	CWS	113	98	848.0	692	39	9	4	8	.988
Lo Duca,Paul	LA	123	120	1080.0	1014	99	15	7	6	.987
LaRue,Jason	Cin	114	109	954.1	649	45	11	6	6	.984

Catchers - The Rest

Player	Tm	G	GS	Inn	PO	A	E	DP	PB	Pct.
Alomar Jr.,S	CWS	75	57	511.0	372	15	1	2	3	.997
Bako,Paul	ChC	69	57	507.2	440	32	6	2	4	.987
Barajas,Rod	Ari	79	65	595.0	543	40	0	4	8	1.000
Barrett,M	Mon	68	63	562.2	391	21	1	4	7	.998
Blanco,Henry	Atl	52	42	388.0	256	24	1	2	1	.996
Borders,Pat	Sea	7	4	36.0	29	1	0	0	0	1.000
Bowen,Rob	Min	7	0	23.1	16	1	1	0	1	.944
Burke,Jamie	CWS	4	2	18.0	7	1	0	0	1	1.000
Cash,Kevin	Tor	34	31	278.0	179	13	1	0	5	.995
Castillo,A	SF	10	3	38.0	38	1	1	0	0	.975
Castro,Ramon	Fla	18	2	65.2	51	3	1	0	1	.982
Chavez,Raul	Hou	16	7	77.2	55	3	0	0	0	1.000
Cota,Humberto	Pit	4	2	23.0	18	0	0	0	0	1.000
Davis,Ben	Sea	73	66	587.2	421	24	4	8	8	.991
DePastino,Joe	NYM	1	0	1.0	1	0	0	0	0	1.000
DiFelice,Mike	KC	58	54	469.2	304	35	2	0	2	.994
Estalella,B	Col	46	43	374.1	248	19	4	1	3	.985
Estrada,Johnny	Atl	14	6	76.1	47	1	0	0	0	1.000
Flaherty,John	NYY	40	31	284.0	200	10	2	0	0	.991
Gil,Geronimo	Bal	53	49	435.2	326	34	6	1	3	.984
Girardi,Joe	StL	13	5	52.0	23	0	1	0	0	.958
Gonzalez,Wiki	SD	23	17	151.0	128	7	1	0	1	.993
Greene,Todd	Tex	51	49	430.1	288	25	4	3	6	.987
Gregorio,Tom	Ana	12	6	60.0	44	2	1	0	3	.979
Guzman,Edwards	Mon	4	4	34.0	23	0	0	1	0	1.000
Hammock,Robby	Ari	36	28	264.0	264	17	2	1	4	.993
Haselman,Bill	Bos	2	0	2.0	2	0	0	0	0	1.000
Hernandez,M	NYY	5	1	13.0	10	0	0	0	0	1.000
Hinch,A.J.	Det	27	23	197.2	110	6	2	0	0	.983
Huckaby,Ken	Tor	4	3	27.0	17	3	0	0	0	1.000
Hundley,Todd	LA	10	7	63.2	49	3	1	0	0	.981
Johnson,Mark L	Oak	13	10	83.0	65	4	0	0	0	1.000
Kreuter,Chad	Tex	7	6	50.0	31	3	0	0	0	1.000
LaForest,Pete	TB	4	3	24.0	16	1	0	0	1	1.000
Laird,Gerald	Tex	16	12	111.0	65	8	1	2	1	.986
Laker,Tim	Cle	50	42	401.2	266	18	5	5	4	.983
LeCroy,Matt	Min	22	20	158.0	95	4	2	0	2	.980
Lunsford,Trey	SF	1	0	1.0	0	0	0	0	0	-
Machado,Robert	Bal	18	14	129.1	84	13	1	3	3	.990
Marrero,Eli	StL	6	4	36.1	29	4	0	0	0	1.000
Martinez,V	Cle	40	40	342.0	231	22	1	2	3	.996
Melhuse,Adam	Oak	33	19	186.0	130	9	1	1	1	.993
Miller,Corky	Cin	11	9	78.2	60	5	0	0	0	1.000
Mirabelli,Doug	Bos	55	43	387.1	319	21	4	3	14	.988
Moeller,Chad	Ari	76	69	596.0	491	37	7	3	3	.987
Molina,Jose	Ana	53	39	332.0	221	17	1	0	3	.996
Myers,Greg	Tor	81	67	583.2	405	21	8	3	2	.982
Ojeda,Miguel	SD	48	35	336.0	293	14	6	1	4	.981
Paul,Josh	CWS	11	5	54.0	27	4	0	0	1	1.000
Paul,Josh	ChC	3	2	19.0	20	2	0	1	0	1.000
Pellow,Kit	Col	7	2	24.0	14	0	0	0	1	1.000
Petrick,Ben	Col	1	0	1.0	0	0	0	0	0	-
Petrick,Ben	Det	6	3	35.0	25	0	0	0	0	1.000
Phillips,Jason	NYM	29	26	229.1	148	6	1	0	0	.994
Piazza,Mike	NYM	65	64	532.1	347	30	7	5	1	.982
Pratt,Todd	Phi	35	33	296.0	231	9	1	4	5	.996
Prince,Tom	Min	22	11	115.0	84	5	0	0	2	1.000
Prince,Tom	KC	7	1	21.0	8	1	0	0	1	1.000
Quintero,H	SD	11	7	58.1	52	2	1	1	2	.982
Redmond,Mike	Fla	37	26	247.1	195	10	1	1	0	.995
Rivera,Mike	SD	19	16	139.0	133	7	2	0	2	.986
Romero,Mandy	Col	2	2	17.0	13	1	1	0	0	.933
Ross,Dave	LA	38	35	314.0	260	26	4	3	2	.986
Sardinha,Dane	Cin	1	0	4.0	2	0	0	0	0	1.000
Stinnett,Kelly	Cin	50	44	409.1	261	21	2	1	3	.993
Stinnett,Kelly	Phi	1	0	4.0	6	0	0	0	0	1.000
Torrealba,Y	SF	66	52	495.2	365	29	1	2	0	.997
Valentin,Ja	TB	42	33	305.2	213	12	0	0	1	1.000

Player	Tm	G	GS	Inn	PO	A	E	DP	PB	Pct.
Walbeck,Matt	Det	55	38	338.2	172	16	4	0	4	.979
Widger,Chris	StL	41	32	278.2	185	14	1	1	2	.995
Wilson,Craig	Pit	21	15	143.0	87	11	1	1	1	.990
Wilson,Tom	Tor	76	61	546.1	401	26	4	3	7	.991
Wooten,Shawn	Ana	19	8	89.2	65	4	0	0	1	1.000
Zaun,Gregg	Hou	31	26	214.1	152	8	4	0	1	.976
Zaun,Gregg	Col	14	12	106.0	71	2	2	0	1	.973

Catchers Special - Regulars

Player	Tm	G	GS	Inn	SBA	CS	PCS	CS%	ER	CERA
Lo Duca,Paul	LA	123	120	1080.0	140	57	14	.34	327	2.73
Hernandez,Ra	Oak	139	133	1172.2	109	36	11	.26	453	3.48
Santiago,B	SF	106	106	902.2	54	10	2	.15	354	3.53
Ausmus,Brad	Hou	143	129	1158.0	105	37	6	.31	471	3.66
Schneider,B	Mon	98	95	841.0	51	27	6	.47	351	3.76
Wilson,Dan	Sea	96	92	817.1	40	12	4	.22	344	3.79
Olivo,Miguel	CWS	113	98	848.0	53	19	0	.36	358	3.80
Rodriguez,Ivan	Fla	138	134	1132.1	60	20	1	.32	483	3.84
Bennett,Gary	SD	91	87	747.0	60	12	1	.19	322	3.88
Miller,Damian	ChC	114	103	929.2	69	27	1	.38	401	3.88
Lopez,Javy	Atl	120	114	992.0	75	23	3	.28	436	3.96
Lieberthal,M	Phi	131	129	1143.2	103	19	1	.18	522	4.11
Posada,Jorge	NYY	137	131	1165.0	100	28	2	.27	535	4.13
Pierzynski,A	Min	135	131	1165.2	66	20	3	.27	537	4.15
Bard,Josh	Cle	87	80	715.2	64	23	4	.32	343	4.31
Molina,Jose	Ana	117	109	949.2	81	36	5	.41	456	4.32
Kendall,Jason	Pit	146	145	1278.1	86	23	8	.19	635	4.47
Varitek,Jason	Bos	137	119	1075.1	84	23	4	.24	539	4.51
Osik,Keith	Mil	78	71	630.1	57	18	4	.26	322	4.60
Matheny,Mike	StL	138	121	1096.2	55	15	3	.23	561	4.60
Mayne,Brent	KC	112	107	948.0	83	26	4	.28	494	4.69
Wilson,Vance	NYM	89	71	650.2	56	25	11	.31	342	4.73
Fordyce,Brook	Bal	107	100	884.2	90	20	5	.18	471	4.79
Hall,Toby	TB	130	126	1107.0	78	34	3	.41	614	4.99
LaRue,Jason	Cin	114	109	954.1	64	17	1	.25	541	5.10
Inge,Brandon	Det	104	98	867.1	110	40	10	.30	499	5.18
Johnson,C	Col	108	103	897.2	62	26	11	.29	523	5.24
Perez,Eddie	Mil	102	91	821.2	80	19	3	.21	489	5.36
Diaz,Einar	Tex	101	95	842.0	72	23	1	.31	515	5.50

Catchers Special - The Rest

Player	Tm	G	GS	Inn	SBA	CS	PCS	CS%	ER	CERA
Alomar Jr.,S	CWS	75	57	511.0	26	6	2	.17	268	4.72
Bako,Paul	ChC	69	57	507.2	40	13	1	.31	215	3.81
Barajas,Rod	Ari	79	65	595.0	43	17	1	.38	239	3.62
Barrett,M	Mon	68	63	562.2	26	10	0	.38	266	4.25
Blanco,Henry	Atl	52	42	388.0	44	11	1	.23	193	4.48
Borders,Pat	Sea	7	4	36.0	5	3	2	.33	5	1.25
Bowen,Rob	Min	7	0	23.1	8	0	0	.00	17	6.56
Burke,Jamie	CWS	4	2	18.0	2	0	0	.00	14	7.00
Cash,Kevin	Tor	34	31	278.0	20	6	1	.26	129	4.18
Castillo,A	SF	10	3	38.0	1	0	0	.00	13	3.08
Castro,Ramon	Fla	18	2	65.2	2	0	0	.00	23	3.15
Chavez,Raul	Hou	16	7	77.2	5	3	1	.50	38	4.40
Cota,Humberto	Pit	4	2	23.0	2	1	1	.00	15	5.87
Davis,Ben	Sea	73	66	587.2	49	17	2	.32	253	3.87
DePastino,Joe	NYM	1	0	1.0	0	0	0	-	0	0.00
DiFelice,Mike	KC	58	54	469.2	52	16	1	.29	305	5.84
Estalella,B	Col	46	43	374.1	37	12	2	.29	197	4.74
Estrada,Johnny	Atl	14	6	76.1	6	0	0	.00	34	4.01
Flaherty,John	NYY	40	31	284.0	28	9	3	.24	117	3.71
Gil,Geronimo	Bal	53	49	435.2	48	10	0	.21	235	4.85
Girardi,Joe	StL	13	5	52.0	3	0	0	.00	32	5.54
Gonzalez,Wiki	SD	23	17	151.0	18	4	2	.13	117	6.97
Greene,Todd	Tex	51	49	430.1	57	19	3	.30	283	5.92
Gregorio,Tom	Ana	12	6	60.0	5	2	1	.25	37	5.55
Guzman,Edwards	Mon	4	4	34.0	1	1	1	-	24	6.35
Hammock,Robby	Ari	36	28	264.0	25	7	1	.25	120	4.09
Haselman,Bill	Bos	2	0	2.0	1	0	0	.00	0	0.00
Hernandez,M	NYY	5	1	13.0	1	0	0	.00	3	2.08
Hinch,A.J.	Det	27	23	197.2	26	3	1	.08	109	4.96
Huckaby,Ken	Tor	4	3	27.0	5	0	0	.00	11	3.67
Hundley,Todd	LA	10	7	63.2	7	2	0	.29	24	3.39

Player	Tm	G	GS	Inn	SBA	CS	PCS	CS%	ER	CERA
Johnson,Mark L	Oak	13	10	83.0	7	2	1	.17	32	3.47
Kreuter,Chad	Tex	7	6	50.0	5	0	0	.00	37	6.66
LaForest,Pete	TB	4	3	24.0	5	0	0	.00	11	4.13
Laird,Gerald	Tex	16	12	111.0	7	3	0	.43	71	5.76
Laker,Tim	Cle	50	42	401.2	34	11	3	.26	179	4.01
LeCroy,Matt	Min	22	20	158.0	18	4	1	.18	87	4.96
Lunsford,Trey	SF	1	0	1.0	0	0	0	-	0	0.00
Machado,Robert	Bal	18	14	129.1	20	7	1	.32	61	4.24
Marrero,Eli	StL	6	4	36.1	3	3	1	1.00	22	5.45
Martinez,V	Cle	40	40	342.0	29	9	1	.29	160	4.21
Melhuse,Adam	Oak	33	19	186.0	18	5	1	.24	97	4.69
Miller,Corky	Cin	11	9	78.2	12	2	1	.09	39	4.46
Mirabelli,Doug	Bos	55	43	387.1	51	12	3	.19	192	4.46
Moeller,Chad	Ari	76	69	596.0	54	14	2	.23	262	3.96
Molina,Jose	Ana	53	39	332.0	25	7	1	.25	150	4.07
Myers,Greg	Tor	81	67	583.2	62	12	2	.17	274	4.23
Ojeda,Miguel	SD	48	35	336.0	26	5	1	.16	206	5.52
Paul,Josh	CWS	11	5	54.0	6	4	1	.60	23	3.83
Paul,Josh	ChC	3	2	19.0	3	2	1	.50	3	1.42
Pellow,Kit	Col	7	2	24.0	2	0	0	.00	16	6.00
Petrick,Ben	Col	1	0	1.0	1	0	0	.00	4	36.00
Petrick,Ben	Det	6	3	35.0	4	1	0	.25	20	5.14
Phillips,Jason	NYM	29	26	229.1	12	4	0	.33	128	5.02
Piazza,Mike	NYM	65	64	532.1	82	23	6	.22	236	3.99
Pratt,Todd	Phi	35	34	296.0	33	5	1	.13	126	3.83
Prince,Tom	Min	22	11	115.0	5	3	0	.60	75	5.87
Prince,Tom	KC	7	1	21.0	2	0	0	.00	11	4.71
Quintero,H	SD	11	7	58.1	3	1	1	.00	42	6.48
Redmond,Mike	Fla	37	26	247.1	33	5	1	.13	143	5.20
Rivera,Mike	SD	19	16	139.0	13	3	1	.17	88	5.70
Romero,Mandy	Col	2	2	17.0	3	1	0	.33	16	8.47
Ross,Dave	LA	38	35	314.0	45	16	3	.31	160	4.59
Sardinha,Dane	Cin	1	0	4.0	0	0	0	-	3	6.75
Stinnett,Kelly	Cin	50	44	409.1	29	9	2	.26	235	5.17
Stinnett,Kelly	Phi	1	0	4.0	0	0	0	-	3	6.75
Torrealba,Y	SF	66	52	495.2	41	19	5	.39	228	4.14
Valentin,Ja	TB	42	33	305.2	23	7	1	.27	162	4.77
Walbeck,Matt	Det	55	38	338.2	42	10	4	.16	222	5.90
Widger,Chris	StL	41	32	278.2	18	6	1	.29	136	4.39
Wilson,Craig	Pit	21	15	143.0	7	2	0	.29	96	6.04
Wilson,Tom	Tor	76	61	546.1	71	14	2	.17	334	5.50
Wooten,Shawn	Ana	19	8	89.2	17	3	1	.13	38	3.81
Zaun,Gregg	Hou	31	26	214.1	24	8	5	.16	114	4.79
Zaun,Gregg	Col	14	12	106.0	10	3	2	.13	70	5.94

Pitchers Hitting, Fielding & Holding Runners,

and Hitters Pitching

Pitchers Hitting, Fielding and Holding Runners

Pitcher	2003 Hitting						Career Hitting										2003 Fielding and Holding Runners											
	Avg	AB	H	HR	RBI	SH	Avg	AB	H	2B	3B	HR	RBI	BB	SO	SH	G	Inn	PO	A	E	DP	Pct	SBA	CS	PCS	PPO	CS%
Abbott,Paul, KC	-	0	0	0	0	0	.333	9	3	1	0	0	0	0	2	2	10	47.2	8	6	1	0	.933	10	3	0	0	.30
Acevedo,Jose, Cin	.000	9	0	0	0	2	.100	50	5	2	0	0	3	1	29	6	5	27.0	1	3	0	1	1.000	1	1	0	0	1.00
Acevedo,Juan, NYY-Tor	-	0	0	0	0	0	.092	65	6	2	0	0	0	3	33	6	39	38.1	6	2	1	0	.889	4	0	0	0	.00
Adams,Terry, Phi	.000	1	0	0	0	0	.051	78	4	1	0	0	2	7	41	12	66	68.0	10	9	1	1	.950	1	1	0	0	1.00
Adkins,Jon, CWS	-	0	0	0	0	0	-	0	0	0	0	0	0	0	0	0	4	9.1	2	1	0	1	1.000	0	0	0	0	-
Affeldt,Jeremy, KC	.333	6	2	0	2	0	.333	6	2	0	0	0	2	1	1	0	36	126.0	4	19	1	2	.958	20	6	4	0	.30
Ainsworth,Kurt, SF-Bal	.045	22	1	0	0	4	.071	28	2	1	0	0	0	0	8	5	14	68.1	5	6	0	0	1.000	5	2	1	1	.40
Alfonseca,A, ChC	-	0	0	0	0	1	.167	12	2	0	0	0	2	0	7	1	60	66.1	2	7	1	0	.900	16	1	0	0	.06
Almanza,A, Fla	-	0	0	0	0	0	.000	4	0	0	0	0	0	0	2	1	51	50.1	1	5	1	0	.857	5	1	1	0	.20
Almonte,Edwin, NYM	.000	1	0	0	0	0	.000	1	0	0	0	0	0	0	0	0	12	11.1	0	3	0	0	1.000	2	0	0	0	.00
Almonte,Hector, Bos-Mon	.000	1	0	0	0	0	.000	1	0	0	0	0	0	0	1	0	35	36.2	2	3	0	0	1.000	3	2	0	0	.67
Alvarez,Juan, Fla	-	0	0	0	0	0	-	0	0	0	0	0	0	0	0	0	9	11.2	1	2	0	0	1.000	2	0	0	1	.00
Alvarez,Victor, LA	-	0	0	0	0	0	.000	2	0	0	0	0	0	0	2	0	5	5.2	0	0	0	0	-	0	0	0	0	-
Alvarez,Wilson, LA	.172	29	5	0	0	1	.123	65	8	0	0	0	1	3	20	2	21	95.0	4	17	0	2	1.000	4	3	2	1	.75
Anderson,Bri, Cle-KC	.000	1	0	0	0	0	.138	254	35	5	3	1	10	7	57	21	32	197.2	8	38	2	2	.958	9	8	5	1	.89
Anderson,Ja, NYY-NYM	-	0	0	0	0	0	-	0	0	0	0	0	0	0	0	0	28	31.1	1	2	0	0	1.000	3	0	0	1	.00
Anderson,Ji, Cin	.111	9	1	0	0	2	.136	169	23	3	0	0	6	8	44	15	8	38.2	0	10	0	0	1.000	3	0	0	0	.00
Anderson,Mat, Det	-	0	0	0	0	0	-	0	0	0	0	0	0	0	0	0	23	25.1	1	3	2	0	.667	3	0	0	0	.00
Appier,Kevin, Ana-KC	.000	5	0	0	0	0	.096	83	8	0	0	0	4	1	39	5	23	111.2	4	6	0	0	1.000	10	3	0	0	.30
Armas Jr.,Tony, Mon	.200	10	2	0	0	0	.113	141	16	1	1	0	7	2	48	14	5	31.0	0	4	0	0	1.000	1	0	0	0	.00
Arroyo,Bronson, Bos	-	0	0	0	0	0	.083	48	4	2	0	0	1	1	27	2	6	17.1	2	0	0	0	1.000	0	0	0	0	-
Asencio,Miguel, KC	-	0	0	0	0	0	.000	2	0	0	0	0	0	0	1	0	48	83.1	2	7	1	1	.900	4	2	0	0	.50
Ashby,Andy, LA	.000	14	0	0	0	3	.134	521	70	13	0	1	26	16	218	83	21	73.0	4	10	0	0	1.000	14	5	1	0	.36
Astacio,Pedro, NYM	.091	11	1	0	0	3	.132	634	84	7	1	0	27	4	243	77	7	36.2	2	2	0	0	1.000	2	2	0	0	1.00
Austin,Jeff, Cin	.125	8	1	0	0	2	.125	8	1	0	0	0	0	0	5	2	7	28.1	2	5	0	1	1.000	0	0	0	1	-
Avery,Steve, Det	1.000	1	1	0	0	0	.174	437	76	14	4	4	32	12	135	41	19	16.0	4	3	0	1	1.000	1	0	0	0	.00
Ayala,Luis, Mon	.000	1	0	0	0	0	.000	1	0	0	0	0	0	0	1	0	65	71.0	8	18	1	0	.963	3	2	1	0	.67
Aybar,Manny, SF	-	0	0	0	0	0	.186	70	13	0	0	1	5	2	28	4	3	3.0	0	0	0	0	-	0	0	0	0	-
Backe,Brandon, TB	-	0	0	0	0	0	-	0	0	0	0	0	0	0	0	0	28	44.2	3	3	0	1	1.000	4	4	0	0	1.00
Bacsik,Mike, NYM	.000	3	0	0	0	0	.095	21	2	1	0	0	2	0	4	3	5	17.2	0	3	0	0	1.000	3	2	1	0	.67
Baez,Danys, Cle	.000	1	0	0	0	0	.000	3	0	0	0	0	0	0	0	0	73	75.2	4	12	1	0	.941	6	0	0	0	.00
Baldwin,James, Min	-	0	0	0	0	0	.098	41	4	1	1	0	2	0	19	3	10	15.0	3	3	1	0	.857	1	0	0	0	.00
Bale,John, Cin	.118	17	2	0	0	0	.118	17	2	0	0	0	0	0	8	0	10	46.1	1	7	0	0	1.000	8	2	0	0	.25
Balfour,Grant, Min	-	0	0	0	0	0	-	0	0	0	0	0	0	0	0	0	17	26.0	0	4	0	0	1.000	3	1	0	0	.33
Batista,Miguel, Ari	.070	57	4	0	0	4	.096	219	21	4	0	2	5	9	126	14	36	193.1	9	31	3	2	.930	16	8	1	0	.50
Bauer,Rick, Bal	-	0	0	0	0	0	-	0	0	0	0	0	0	0	0	0	35	61.1	2	9	0	1	1.000	10	1	0	0	.10
Beck,Rod, SD	-	0	0	0	0	0	.211	19	4	0	0	0	1	0	10	1	36	35.1	1	6	0	0	1.000	2	0	0	0	.00
Beckett,Josh, Fla	.152	46	7	0	3	5	.119	84	10	4	0	0	3	1	36	12	24	142.0	6	18	1	0	.960	10	5	0	0	.50
Beimel,Joe, Pit	.000	5	0	0	0	0	.244	41	10	1	0	0	1	2	15	6	69	62.0	2	11	0	0	1.000	6	5	5	2	.83
Belisle,Matt, Cin	.000	1	0	0	0	0	.000	1	0	0	0	0	0	0	1	0	6	8.2	2	2	0	0	1.000	0	0	0	0	-
Bell,Rob, TB	.000	2	0	0	0	0	.073	55	4	1	0	0	0	3	32	5	19	101.0	9	10	1	0	.950	8	4	1	0	.50
Benes,Alan, ChC-Tex	.000	1	0	0	0	0	.158	139	22	6	0	0	8	3	53	9	7	23.1	3	1	0	0	1.000	1	1	0	0	1.00
Benitez,A, NYM-NYY-Sea	.000	1	0	0	0	0	.000	7	0	0	0	0	2	0	3	0	69	73.0	6	1	0	0	1.000	11	1	0	0	.09
Benoit,Joaquin, Tex	.000	2	0	0	0	0	.000	2	0	0	0	0	0	0	0	0	25	105.0	8	14	1	0	.957	9	5	0	0	.56
Benson,Kris, Pit	.000	30	0	0	0	6	.115	200	23	6	0	0	9	8	75	25	18	105.0	6	10	1	2	.941	8	3	0	0	.38
Bere,Jason, Cle	-	0	0	0	0	0	.186	161	30	6	1	0	5	3	60	17	2	6.2	0	2	0	0	1.000	0	0	0	0	-
Bernero,Adam, Det-Col	.000	6	0	0	0	0	.000	10	0	0	0	0	0	0	6	1	49	133.1	9	17	0	2	1.000	12	3	1	0	.25
Betancourt,R, Cle	-	0	0	0	0	0	-	0	0	0	0	0	0	0	0	0	33	38.0	1	2	1	0	.750	3	0	0	0	.00
Biddle,Rocky, Mon	.000	1	0	0	0	0	.000	3	0	0	0	0	0	0	3	1	72	69.2	0	4	0	0	1.000	3	1	0	0	.33
Bierbrodt,Nick, TB-Cle	-	0	0	0	0	0	.667	6	4	1	0	0	0	2	0	2	18	43.1	1	2	0	1	1.000	6	1	0	0	.17
Bland,Nate, Hou	-	0	0	0	0	0	-	0	0	0	0	0	0	0	0	0	22	20.1	0	4	2	0	.667	3	0	0	0	.00
Boehringer,B, Pit	-	0	0	0	0	0	.067	30	2	1	0	0	2	3	15	3	62	62.1	3	3	0	0	1.000	6	1	0	0	.17
Bonderman,J, Det	.000	5	0	0	0	0	.000	5	0	0	0	0	0	0	2	0	33	162.0	14	24	1	2	.974	34	9	0	1	.26
Bong,Jung, Atl	.000	5	0	0	0	1	.000	7	0	0	0	0	0	1	3	1	44	57.0	2	13	0	4	1.000	1	0	0	1	.00
Bootcheck,C, Ana	-	0	0	0	0	0	-	0	0	0	0	0	0	0	0	0	4	10.1	0	0	0	0	-	0	0	0	0	-
Borbon,Pedro, StL	-	0	0	0	0	0	.143	7	1	0	0	0	0	0	4	1	7	4.0	1	1	0	0	1.000	1	0	0	0	.00
Borland,Toby, Fla	-	0	0	0	0	0	.083	12	1	0	0	0	2	0	3	1	7	9.2	2	1	0	0	1.000	1	0	0	0	.00
Borowski,Joe, ChC	-	0	0	0	0	0	.222	9	2	0	0	0	0	0	7	0	68	68.1	5	11	0	0	1.000	8	0	0	1	.00
Bottalico,R, Ari	-	0	0	0	0	0	.133	15	2	2	0	0	1	0	8	1	2	1.2	0	0	0	0	-	0	0	0	0	-
Bowie,Micah, Oak	-	0	0	0	0	0	.214	14	3	0	0	0	3	1	3	0	6	8.1	0	2	0	0	1.000	1	1	1	0	1.00
Bowles,Brian, Tor	-	0	0	0	0	0	-	0	0	0	0	0	0	0	0	0	5	7.0	0	1	0	0	1.000	0	0	0	0	-
Boyd,Jason, Cle	-	0	0	0	0	0	.000	1	0	0	0	0	0	0	1	0	44	52.1	2	11	1	1	.929	5	1	0	0	.20
Bradford,Chad, Oak	-	0	0	0	0	0	-	0	0	0	0	0	0	0	0	0	71	76.0	2	20	1	1	.957	4	2	1	0	.50
Brazelton,D, TB	.000	1	0	0	0	0	.000	1	0	0	0	0	0	0	1	0	10	48.1	3	7	1	1	.909	3	0	0	0	.00
Brohawn,Troy, LA	1.000	1	1	0	0	0	.500	2	1	0	0	0	0	0	1	0	12	11.2	0	1	0	0	1.000	4	1	0	0	.25
Brower,Jim, SF	.176	17	3	0	1	1	.200	55	11	1	0	0	4	0	18	4	51	100.0	5	13	0	1	1.000	7	3	0	0	.43
Brown,Kevin, LA	.159	63	10	0	2	6	.128	493	63	9	0	2	29	19	186	54	32	211.0	14	43	3	2	.950	23	9	1	2	.39
Buehrle,Mark, CWS	.167	6	1	0	1	0	.133	15	2	0	0	0	1	1	9	0	35	230.1	15	38	0	3	1.000	5	4	2	3	.80
Bukvich,Ryan, KC	-	0	0	0	0	0	-	0	0	0	0	0	0	0	0	0	9	10.1	0	4	0	0	1.000	1	0	0	0	.00
Bullinger,Kirk, Hou	-	0	0	0	0	0	-	0	0	0	0	0	0	0	0	0	7	8.0	1	1	0	0	1.000	1	0	0	0	.00
Bump,Nate, Fla	-	0	0	0	0	0	-	0	0	0	0	0	0	0	0	1	32	36.1	2	8	0	0	1.000	2	0	0	0	.00
Burba,Dave, Mil	.000	10	0	0	0	1	.137	190	26	1	0	3	12	10	83	22	17	43.1	5	7	0	0	1.000	5	1	0	0	.20

Pitchers Hitting, Fielding and Holding Runners

Pitcher	2003 Hitting						Career Hitting										2003 Fielding and Holding Runners											
	Avg	AB	H	HR	RBI	SH	Avg	AB	H	2B	3B	HR	RBI	BB	SO	SH	G	Inn	PO	A	E	DP	Pct	SBA	CS	PCS	PPO	CS%
Burkett,John, Bos	.000	1	0	0	0	1	.093	540	50	6	0	0	18	26	226	62	32	181.2	7	19	1	4	.963	13	7	0	0	.54
Burnett,A.J., Fla	.143	7	1	0	0	0	.128	156	20	4	1	2	6	11	78	16	4	23.0	3	4	0	0	1.000	2	1	0	0	.50
Bynum,Mike, SD	.300	10	3	0	0	1	.167	18	3	0	0	0	0	0	7	1	13	36.0	4	4	1	0	.889	5	2	2	0	.40
Calero,Kiko, StL	.250	4	1	0	1	0	.250	4	1	0	0	0	1	0	0	0	26	38.1	1	3	0	0	1.000	5	1	1	0	.20
Callaway,M, Ana-Tex	-	0	0	0	0	0	.667	3	2	0	0	0	1	0	0	0	23	60.2	8	5	1	1	.929	6	1	0	0	.17
Capuano,Chris, Ari	.000	8	0	0	0	0	.000	8	0	0	0	0	0	0	5	0	9	33.0	1	8	1	1	.900	3	0	0	2	.00
Carrara,G, Sea	-	0	0	0	0	0	.107	28	3	0	0	0	0	1	9	3	23	29.0	4	4	0	1	1.000	4	2	0	0	.50
Carrasco,D.J., KC	.000	2	0	0	0	0	.000	2	0	0	0	0	0	0	1	0	50	80.1	4	9	1	1	.929	4	2	0	0	.50
Carrasco,H, Bal	-	0	0	0	0	0	.056	18	1	0	0	0	0	0	12	0	40	38.1	5	4	0	0	1.000	1	1	0	0	1.00
Carter,Lance, TB	-	0	0	0	0	0	-	0	0	0	0	0	0	0	0	0	62	79.0	4	5	0	0	1.000	3	1	0	0	.33
Cerda,Jaime, NYM	.000	1	0	0	0	0	.000	2	0	0	0	0	0	0	1	0	27	32.1	0	6	0	0	1.000	1	1	0	0	1.00
Cerros,Juan, Cin	-	0	0	0	0	0	-	0	0	0	0	0	0	0	0	0	11	13.0	2	1	0	0	1.000	2	0	0	0	.00
Chacon,Shawn, Col	.196	46	9	1	5	2	.156	128	20	3	0	1	8	0	52	11	23	137.0	14	18	1	1	.970	7	2	1	0	.29
Chen,Bruce, Hou-Bos	.000	1	0	0	0	0	.117	111	13	1	0	0	3	1	53	17	16	24.1	0	1	0	0	1.000	2	0	0	0	.00
Choate,Randy, NYY	-	0	0	0	0	0	.000	4	0	0	0	0	0	0	2	0	5	3.2	0	1	0	0	1.000	0	0	0	0	-
Christiansen,J, SF	-	0	0	0	0	0	.100	10	1	0	0	0	1	0	7	1	39	25.0	2	3	0	0	1.000	0	0	0	0	-
Chulk,Vinnie, Tor	-	0	0	0	0	0	-	0	0	0	0	0	0	0	0	0	3	5.1	0	3	0	0	1.000	0	0	0	0	-
Claussen,B, NYY	.250	4	1	0	1	0	.250	4	1	0	0	0	1	0	1	0	1	6.1	0	1	0	0	1.000	0	0	0	0	-
Clemens,Roger, NYY	.000	1	0	0	0	1	.200	20	4	2	0	0	1	2	8	3	33	211.2	7	32	1	2	.975	28	8	0	0	.29
Clement,Matt, ChC	.145	62	9	0	3	8	.084	287	24	4	1	0	10	12	141	39	32	201.2	20	24	4	0	.917	11	5	0	0	.45
Colome,Jesus, TB	-	0	0	0	0	0	-	0	0	0	0	0	0	0	0	0	54	74.0	6	10	0	1	.941	3	2	1	0	.67
Colon,Bartolo, CWS	.000	6	0	0	0	1	.123	73	9	0	0	0	4	0	43	4	34	242.0	12	16	3	3	.903	7	6	0	1	.86
Colyer,Steve, LA	-	0	0	0	0	0	-	0	0	0	0	0	0	1	0	0	13	19.2	1	2	0	1	1.000	2	1	0	0	.50
Condrey,Clay, SD	.200	10	2	0	0	0	.125	16	2	0	0	0	0	0	9	0	9	34.0	1	8	1	0	.900	3	0	0	0	.00
Cone,David, NYM	.250	4	1	0	0	0	.155	412	64	9	0	0	22	16	91	38	5	18.0	0	3	0	0	1.000	2	1	1	0	.50
Contreras,Jose, NYY	.000	3	0	0	0	0	.000	3	0	0	0	0	0	0	2	0	18	71.0	1	9	1	1	.909	7	0	0	0	.00
Cook,Aaron, Col	.172	29	5	0	3	6	.150	40	6	0	0	0	4	2	10	7	43	124.0	14	24	1	3	.974	9	1	0	1	.11
Corcoran,Roy, Mon	.000	1	0	0	0	0	.000	1	0	0	0	0	0	0	1	0	5	7.1	2	1	0	1	1.000	0	0	0	0	-
Cordero,Chad, Mon	-	0	0	0	0	1	-	0	0	0	0	0	0	0	0	1	12	11.0	2	0	0	0	1.000	0	0	0	0	-
Cordero,F, Tex	-	0	0	0	0	0	.000	1	0	0	0	0	0	0	1	0	73	82.2	8	10	1	0	.947	10	5	1	1	.50
Corey,Mark, Pit	-	0	0	0	0	0	.000	2	0	0	0	0	0	0	2	0	22	30.1	1	3	1	0	.800	4	1	1	0	.25
Cormier,Rheal, Phi	.500	2	1	0	0	0	.189	190	36	4	1	0	12	5	43	28	64	83.1	2	29	0	1	1.000	3	1	1	0	.33
Cornejo,Nate, Det	.000	4	0	0	0	0	.000	4	0	0	0	0	0	0	4	1	32	194.2	15	35	1	4	.980	15	8	2	4	.53
Correia,Kevin, SF	.154	13	2	0	2	1	.154	13	2	0	0	0	2	0	6	1	10	39.1	3	4	0	0	1.000	6	2	0	0	.33
Cortes,David, Cle	-	0	0	0	0	0	-	0	0	0	0	0	0	0	0	0	2	3.0	0	0	0	0	-	1	0	0	0	.00
Cotts,Neal, CWS	-	0	0	0	0	0	-	0	0	0	0	0	0	0	0	0	4	13.1	1	1	0	1	1.000	0	0	0	0	-
Creek,Doug, Tor	-	0	0	0	0	0	.200	5	1	0	0	0	0	0	3	3	21	13.2	2	1	1	1	.750	1	0	0	0	.00
Cressend,Jack, Cle	-	0	0	0	0	0	-	0	0	0	0	0	0	0	0	0	33	43.0	2	0	1	0	.667	6	4	0	0	.67
Crudale,Mike, StL-Mil	-	0	0	0	0	0	.000	2	0	0	0	0	0	0	1	0	22	20.2	1	2	0	0	1.000	2	0	0	0	.00
Cruz,Juan, ChC	.250	12	3	0	1	1	.167	42	7	0	1	0	2	0	14	5	25	61.0	2	8	2	0	.833	4	1	0	0	.25
Cruz,Nelson, Col	.154	13	2	0	1	2	.091	33	3	1	0	0	2	1	12	4	20	54.0	7	6	0	2	1.000	7	3	0	0	.43
Cunnane,Will, Atl	-	0	0	0	0	0	.200	35	7	1	1	0	4	3	9	1	20	20.1	1	2	0	0	1.000	1	0	0	0	.00
Daal,Omar, Bal	-	0	0	0	0	0	.196	275	54	8	0	2	22	14	61	31	19	93.2	8	25	1	3	.971	4	2	2	0	.50
D'Amico,Jeff, Pit	.125	48	6	1	3	9	.101	148	15	2	1	2	5	13	72	21	29	175.1	5	16	1	2	.955	9	1	0	0	.11
Darensbourg,V, Col-Mon	.000	1	0	0	0	0	.111	18	2	0	0	0	0	2	6	1	9	9.0	3	3	1	0	.857	1	0	0	0	.00
Davis,Doug, Tex-Tor-Mil	.095	21	2	0	0	1	.083	24	2	0	0	0	0	0	12	2	21	109.1	6	10	0	1	1.000	7	3	1	0	.43
Davis,Jason, Cle	.000	2	0	0	0	0	.000	2	0	0	0	0	0	0	1	1	27	165.1	10	28	6	3	.864	11	8	1	3	.73
Dawley,Joe, Atl	.000	1	0	0	0	0	.000	1	0	0	0	0	0	0	1	0	5	7.0	0	0	0	0	-	0	0	0	0	-
Day,Zach, Mon	.043	47	2	0	2	1	.057	53	3	0	0	0	2	2	26	3	23	131.1	8	22	1	1	.968	6	2	0	0	.33
de los Santos,V, Mil-Phi	.000	1	0	0	0	0	.000	9	0	0	0	0	0	1	6	2	51	52.0	1	13	2	1	.875	8	1	0	0	.13
Deago,Roger, SD	.000	4	0	0	0	0	.000	4	0	0	0	0	0	0	3	0	2	10.1	0	4	0	0	1.000	0	0	0	0	-
DeHart,Rick, KC	.000	1	0	0	0	0	.000	1	0	0	0	0	0	0	1	0	4	4.0	0	1	0	0	1.000	0	0	0	0	-
DeJean,Mike, Mil-StL	-	0	0	0	0	0	.063	16	1	1	0	0	0	0	9	2	76	82.2	9	15	0	2	1.000	13	1	0	0	.08
Dempster,Ryan, Cin	.030	33	1	0	0	1	.078	296	23	5	1	0	7	6	127	32	22	115.2	4	14	3	1	.857	4	3	1	0	.75
DePaula,Jorge, NYY	-	0	0	0	0	0	-	0	0	0	0	0	0	0	0	0	4	11.1	2	0	0	0	1.000	0	0	0	0	-
Dessens,Elmer, Ari	.196	46	9	0	6	10	.174	201	35	2	1	0	16	17	54	33	34	175.2	8	18	0	2	1.000	11	4	0	0	.36
Dickey,R.A., Tex	1.000	1	1	0	0	0	1.000	1	1	0	0	0	0	0	0	0	38	16.1	0	1	0	0	1.000	4	2	0	1	.22
Dominguez,Juan, Tex	-	0	0	0	0	0	-	0	0	0	0	0	0	0	0	0	6	16.1	0	1	0	0	1.000	4	2	0	0	.50
Donnelly,B, Ana	-	0	0	0	0	0	-	0	0	0	0	0	0	0	0	0	63	74.0	4	3	2	0	.778	2	0	0	0	.00
Dotel,Octavio, Hou	.000	6	0	0	0	0	.068	74	5	0	0	0	1	5	42	9	76	87.0	0	6	0	0	1.000	3	0	0	0	.00
Douglass,Sean, Bal	-	0	0	0	0	0	-	0	0	0	0	0	0	0	0	0	8	8.0	0	0	0	0	-	0	0	0	0	-
Downs,Scott, Mon	.000	1	0	0	0	0	.069	29	2	0	0	0	1	2	10	4	1	3.0	0	0	0	0	-	0	0	0	0	-
Dreifort,D, LA	.133	15	2	0	0	1	.185	238	44	10	0	6	23	8	106	17	10	60.1	9	15	1	1	.960	4	1	0	0	.25
Drese,Ryan, Tex	-	0	0	0	0	0	.000	3	0	0	0	0	0	1	0	1	11	46.0	1	4	0	2	1.000	7	1	0	0	.14
Drew,Tim, Mon	.000	1	0	0	0	0	.000	5	0	0	0	0	0	0	4	1	6	8.2	1	1	0	0	1.000	2	0	0	0	.00
Driskill,T, Bal	.000	1	0	0	0	0	.000	1	0	0	0	0	0	1	3	0	20	48.0	3	6	0	1	1.000	1	1	0	0	1.00
DuBose,Eric, Bal	-	0	0	0	0	0	-	0	0	0	0	0	0	0	0	0	17	73.2	4	10	0	1	1.000	8	5	2	0	.63
Duchscherer,J, Oak	-	0	0	0	0	0	-	0	0	0	0	0	0	0	0	0	4	16.1	0	3	0	0	1.000	0	0	0	0	.00
Duckworth,B, Phi	.185	27	5	0	2	1	.196	97	19	2	0	0	7	9	20	9	24	93.0	7	11	2	0	.900	14	3	0	0	.21
Durbin,Chad, Cle	-	0	0	0	0	0	.000	1	0	0	0	0	0	0	3	1	8	8.2	0	1	1	0	.500	1	1	0	0	.00
Durocher,J, Mil	-	0	0	0	0	0	.000	2	0	0	0	0	0	0	1	0	6	7.1	0	2	0	0	1.000	3	1	1	0	.33
Eaton,Adam, SD	.196	56	11	2	3	7	.191	141	27	6	0	2	9	15	51	9	31	183.1	19	28	3	1	.940	12	2	0	0	.17
Eckenstahler,E, Det	-	0	0	0	0	0	-	0	0	0	0	0	0	0	0	0	20	15.2	0	0	1	0	.000	4	0	0	0	.00
Eischen,Joey, Mon	.250	4	1	0	0	0	.100	20	2	1	0	0	0	1	8	0	70	53.0	1	13	2	1	.875	5	4	2	0	.80
Elarton,Scott, Col	.077	13	1	0	0	2	.129	147	19	2	0	0	3	4	48	23	11	51.2	3	11	0	1	1.000	5	0	0	0	.00

Pitchers Hitting, Fielding and Holding Runners

Pitcher	Avg	AB	H	HR	RBI	SH	Avg	AB	H	2B	3B	HR	RBI	BB	SO	SH	G	Inn	PO	A	E	DP	Pct	SBA	CS	PCS	PPO	CS%
		2003 Hitting						Career Hitting										2003 Fielding and Holding Runners										
Elder,Dave, Cle	-	0	0	0	0	0	-	0	0	0	0	0	0	0	0	0	4	2.1	0	1	0	0	1.000	0	0	0	0	-
Eldred,Cal, StL	.500	2	1	0	0	0	.123	65	8	2	0	0	4	6	34	10	62	67.1	3	10	0	0	1.000	6	1	0	0	.17
Ellis,Robert, Tex	-	0	0	0	0	0	.154	26	4	0	0	0	1	1	12	1	4	18.1	0	2	0	0	1.000	3	2	0	0	.67
Embree,Alan, Bos	-	0	0	0	0	0	.000	2	0	0	0	0	0	1	1	0	65	55.0	4	8	0	0	1.000	8	3	2	0	.38
Escobar,Kelvim, Tor	.167	6	1	0	1	0	.071	14	1	0	0	0	1	0	8	0	41	180.1	15	18	2	2	.943	26	2	0	1	.08
Estes,Shawn, ChC	.179	39	7	1	3	9	.150	387	58	11	0	4	26	13	145	64	29	152.1	10	29	3	6	.929	16	4	1	0	.25
Estrella,Leo, Mil	-	0	0	0	0	0	-	0	0	0	0	0	0	0	0	0	58	66.0	8	14	1	1	.957	0	0	0	0	-
Etherton,Seth, Cin	.143	7	1	0	0	3	.091	11	1	0	0	0	0	2	2	3	7	30.0	1	2	0	0	1.000	2	0	0	0	.00
Eyre,Scott, SF	.500	2	1	0	0	0	.286	7	2	0	0	0	0	0	3	0	74	57.0	2	11	2	1	.867	2	1	1	0	.50
Farnsworth,K, ChC	.000	1	0	0	0	0	.075	53	4	1	0	0	3	2	18	8	77	76.1	5	12	0	0	1.000	12	4	0	0	.33
Fassero,Jeff, StL	.000	9	0	0	0	1	.076	238	18	2	1	0	5	17	135	41	62	77.2	5	12	1	1	.944	5	1	1	0	.20
Feliciano,P, NYM	.000	3	0	0	0	0	.000	3	0	0	0	0	0	1	1	0	23	48.1	2	7	1	0	.900	1	0	0	0	.00
Fernandez,J, Hou	.000	9	0	0	0	1	.095	21	2	0	0	0	1	1	10	3	12	38.1	2	11	0	1	1.000	8	4	2	0	.50
Ferrari,A, Mon	-	0	0	0	0	0	-	0	0	0	0	0	0	0	0	4	4	6.0	0	1	0	0	1.000	0	0	0	0	-
Fetters,Mike, Min	-	0	0	0	0	0	-	0	0	0	0	0	0	0	0	0	5	6.0	0	0	0	0	-	0	0	0	0	-
Field,Nate, KC	-	0	0	0	0	0	-	0	0	0	0	0	0	0	0	0	19	21.2	1	8	0	0	1.000	2	2	0	0	1.00
Figueroa,N, Pit	.000	7	0	0	0	0	.184	49	9	1	0	0	4	2	22	6	12	35.1	1	6	1	0	.875	2	0	0	0	.00
Fikac,Jeremy, Oak	-	0	0	0	0	0	.000	2	0	0	0	0	0	0	1	0	14	16.0	0	2	0	0	1.000	2	1	0	0	.50
Fiore,Tony, Min	.000	1	0	0	0	0	.000	4	0	0	0	0	0	0	2	0	21	36.0	3	5	0	2	1.000	4	1	0	0	.25
Fogg,Josh, Pit	.190	42	8	0	1	7	.150	100	15	0	0	2	4	4	37	9	26	142.0	13	16	1	1	.967	12	4	0	0	.33
Foppert,Jesse, SF	.081	37	3	0	1	0	.081	37	3	1	1	0	1	0	19	0	23	111.0	3	13	0	0	1.000	9	4	0	0	.44
Ford,Matt, Mil	.143	7	1	0	1	0	.143	7	1	1	0	0	1	1	3	0	25	43.2	2	4	1	0	.857	1	1	0	0	1.00
Fossum,Casey, Bos	-	0	0	0	0	0	-	0	0	0	0	0	0	0	0	0	19	79.0	1	8	0	0	1.000	11	6	3	0	.55
Foster,John, Mil	-	0	0	0	0	0	-	0	0	0	0	0	0	0	0	0	23	23.0	1	1	0	0	1.000	5	0	0	0	.00
Foulke,Keith, Oak	-	0	0	0	0	0	.125	16	2	0	0	0	0	0	5	2	72	86.2	3	12	0	1	1.000	12	3	1	0	.25
Fox,Chad, Bos-Fla	-	0	0	0	0	0	.000	7	0	0	0	0	0	0	3	1	38	43.1	0	5	1	0	.833	6	0	0	0	.00
Franco,John, NYM	-	0	0	0	0	0	.088	34	3	0	0	0	1	0	14	3	38	34.1	1	10	0	0	1.000	3	1	1	0	.33
Franklin,Ryan, Sea	.250	4	1	0	0	0	.250	4	1	0	0	0	0	0	1	0	32	212.0	10	18	0	2	1.000	12	6	1	5	.50
Franklin,Wayne, Mil	.169	59	10	0	3	12	.149	67	10	1	0	0	3	2	22	12	36	194.2	8	24	0	2	1.000	13	4	2	0	.31
Fuentes,Brian, Col	.000	1	0	0	0	0	.000	1	0	0	0	0	0	0	0	0	75	75.1	3	9	1	1	.923	5	4	4	0	.80
Fultz,Aaron, Tex	-	0	0	0	0	0	.333	12	4	0	0	0	0	1	1	1	64	68.2	7	11	0	3	1.000	3	1	0	0	.33
Gagne,Eric, LA	-	0	0	0	0	0	.145	83	12	2	1	3	1	22	12		77	82.1	4	11	0	0	1.000	3	1	0	0	.33
Gallo,Mike, Hou	.000	2	0	0	0	0	.000	2	0	0	0	0	0	0	1	0	32	30.0	3	6	1	1	.900	4	2	2	0	.50
Garcia,Freddy, Sea	.200	5	1	0	1	0	.280	25	7	1	0	0	2	0	6	8	33	203.0	21	22	1	2	.977	13	7	2	1	.54
Garcia,R, Tex	-	0	0	0	0	0	-	0	0	0	0	0	0	0	0	0	17	18.0	2	1	0	0	1.000	0	0	0	0	-
Garcia,Rosman, Tex	-	0	0	0	0	0	-	0	0	0	0	0	0	0	0	0	46	46.1	5	4	0	0	1.000	4	0	0	0	.00
Garland,Jon, CWS	.000	2	0	0	0	1	.000	6	0	0	0	0	0	1	1	2	32	191.2	15	29	0	1	1.000	15	6	0	1	.40
Gaudin,Chad, TB	-	0	0	0	0	0	-	0	0	0	0	0	0	0	0	0	15	40.0	4	2	0	0	1.000	1	0	0	0	.00
Geary,Geoff, Phi	-	0	0	0	0	0	-	0	0	0	0	0	0	0	0	0	9	6.0	0	0	0	0	-	1	1	0	0	1.00
George,Chris, KC	1.000	1	1	0	1	2	1.000	1	1	0	0	0	1	0	0	2	18	93.2	9	11	1	1	.952	8	2	0	0	.25
German,F, Det	-	0	0	0	0	0	-	0	0	0	0	0	0	0	0	0	45	44.2	1	5	0	1	1.000	7	1	0	0	.14
Gilfillan,J, KC	-	0	0	0	0	0	-	0	0	0	0	0	0	0	0	0	13	16.1	2	0	0	0	1.000	0	0	0	0	-
Ginter,Matt, CWS	-	0	0	0	0	0	-	0	0	0	0	0	0	0	0	0	3	3.1	1	0	0	0	1.000	0	0	0	0	-
Glavine,Tom, NYM	.151	53	8	0	3	10	.185	1077	199	21	2	1	72	73	278	178	32	183.1	6	41	2	5	.959	20	8	5	1	.40
Glover,Gary, CWS-Ana	-	0	0	0	0	0	.000	1	0	0	0	0	0	0	1	0	42	62.2	2	6	1	2	.889	8	2	0	1	.25
Gobble,Jimmy, KC	-	0	0	0	0	0	-	0	0	0	0	0	0	0	0	0	9	52.2	3	4	0	0	1.000	6	1	0	0	.17
Gonzalez,Edgar, Ari	.250	4	1	0	0	1	.250	4	1	0	0	0	0	0	0	1	9	18.1	1	3	0	0	1.000	1	1	0	0	1.00
Gonzalez,J, TB	.000	6	0	0	0	0	.128	78	10	1	0	0	3	3	26	16	25	156.1	15	11	1	0	.963	9	3	1	4	.33
Gonzalez,Mike, Pit	-	0	0	0	0	0	-	0	0	0	0	0	0	0	0	0	16	8.1	0	3	0	0	1.000	0	0	0	0	-
Good,Andy, Ari	.125	16	2	0	1	4	.125	16	2	0	0	0	1	0	5	4	16	66.1	4	10	1	0	.933	9	2	1	1	.22
Gordon,Tom, CWS	-	0	0	0	0	0	.000	1	0	0	0	0	0	0	0	0	66	74.0	6	10	0	1	1.000	1	0	0	0	.00
Grabow,John, Pit	-	0	0	0	0	0	-	0	0	0	0	0	0	0	0	0	5	5.0	0	0	0	0	-	0	0	0	0	-
Graves,Danny, Cin	.111	54	6	0	0	0	.105	76	8	0	0	2	3	1	25	5	30	169.0	12	36	0	2	1.000	10	3	0	0	.30
Gregg,Kevin, Ana	-	0	0	0	0	0	-	0	0	0	0	0	0	0	0	0	5	24.2	1	1	0	0	1.000	3	2	0	0	.67
Griffiths,J, NYM	.000	9	0	0	0	1	.000	9	0	0	0	0	0	1	3	1	9	41.0	2	7	1	1	.900	7	1	0	0	.14
Grimsley,Jason, KC	-	0	0	0	0	0	.103	39	4	0	0	0	2	5	11	5	76	75.0	17	14	1	2	.969	9	2	0	0	.22
Groom,Buddy, Bal	-	0	0	0	0	0	-	0	0	0	0	0	0	0	0	0	60	45.1	2	6	0	0	1.000	5	0	0	0	.00
Gryboski,Kevin, Atl	.000	1	0	0	0	0	.000	1	0	0	0	0	0	0	1	0	64	45.1	3	5	1	0	.889	2	0	0	0	.00
Guardado,Eddie, Min	-	0	0	0	0	0	-	0	0	0	0	0	0	0	0	0	66	68.1	3	2	1	0	.833	3	0	0	0	.00
Guthrie,Mark, ChC	.000	1	0	0	0	0	.071	14	1	0	0	0	0	0	2	1	65	42.2	2	12	0	1	1.000	3	3	2	1	1.00
Hackman,Luther, SD	.000	2	0	0	0	0	.083	24	2	0	0	0	0	1	11	0	65	76.2	7	11	1	1	.947	5	0	0	0	.00
Halama,John, Oak	-	0	0	0	0	0	.111	18	2	1	0	0	0	3	10	3	35	108.2	9	19	1	1	.966	6	3	0	0	.50
Hall,Josh, Cin	.167	6	1	0	0	1	.167	6	1	0	0	0	0	0	4	0	16	24.2	4	1	0	0	1.000	2	1	0	0	.50
Halladay,Roy, Tor	.111	9	1	0	0	0	.056	18	1	0	0	0	0	0	6	2	36	266.1	23	50	1	4	.986	27	4	0	0	.15
Hamilton,Joey, Cin	.000	3	0	0	0	0	.127	339	43	8	1	4	22	8	167	36	3	10.2	0	0	0	0	-	0	0	0	0	-
Hammond,Chris, NYY	-	0	0	0	0	0	.204	235	48	7	1	4	14	28	95	19	62	63.0	2	6	0	1	1.000	1	1	0	0	1.00
Hampton,Mike, Atl	.183	60	11	2	8	9	.247	575	142	15	5	12	60	40	144	52	31	190.0	15	51	1	4	.985	9	6	1	0	.67
Hancock,Josh, Phi	-	0	0	0	0	0	-	0	0	0	0	0	0	0	0	0	2	3.0	0	0	0	0	-	0	0	0	0	-
Harang,Aaron, Oak-Cin	.056	18	1	0	0	0	.048	21	1	0	0	0	0	0	15	0	16	76.1	2	7	0	0	1.000	10	2	0	0	.20
Harden,Rich, Oak	-	0	0	0	0	0	-	0	0	0	0	0	0	0	0	0	15	74.2	5	11	3	0	.941	11	2	0	1	.18
Haren,Danny, StL	.080	25	2	0	1	1	.080	25	2	0	0	0	1	1	10	1	14	72.2	3	5	0	0	1.000	3	1	0	0	.33
Harper,Travis, TB	-	0	0	0	0	0	-	0	0	0	0	0	0	0	0	0	61	93.0	11	6	0	0	1.000	6	2	0	0	.33
Harville,Chad, Oak	-	0	0	0	0	0	-	0	0	0	0	0	0	0	0	0	21	21.2	0	0	0	0	-	1	1	0	0	1.00
Hasegawa,S, Sea	-	0	0	0	0	0	.000	1	0	0	0	0	0	0	0	0	62	73.0	10	13	0	3	1.000	2	2	0	0	1.00
Hawkins,LaTroy, Min	-	0	0	0	0	1	.000	5	0	0	0	0	0	0	4	1	74	77.1	4	2	0	0	1.000	4	2	0	0	.50

Pitchers Hitting, Fielding and Holding Runners

Pitcher	2003 Hitting						Career Hitting										2003 Fielding and Holding Runners											
	Avg	AB	H	HR	RBI	SH	Avg	AB	H	2B	3B	HR	RBI	BB	SO	SH	G	Inn	PO	A	E	DP	Pct	SBA	CS	PCS	PPO	CS%
Haynes,Jimmy, Cin	.261	23	6	0	3	7	.153	209	32	9	0	0	13	5	67	28	18	94.1	11	16	1	4	.964	11	4	0	0	.36
Hebson,Bryan, Mon	-	0	0	0	0	0	-	0	0	0	0	0	0	0	0	0	2	2.0	0	0	0	0	-	0	0	0	0	-
Heilman,Aaron, NYM	.045	22	1	0	1	0	.045	22	1	0	0	0	1	1	13	0	14	65.1	3	12	2	0	.882	5	1	0	0	.20
Helling,Rick, Bal-Fla	.333	3	1	0	0	0	.071	99	7	1	0	0	1	8	37	9	35	155.0	4	14	3	0	.857	11	3	0	3	.27
Hendrickson,M, Tor	.250	4	1	1	1	0	.250	4	1	0	0	1	1	0	1	0	30	158.1	8	22	2	2	.938	28	8	3	0	.29
Hentgen,Pat, Bal	.000	5	0	0	0	0	.108	83	9	0	0	0	0	4	25	9	28	161.0	7	20	1	1	.964	9	4	1	0	.44
Heredia,Felix, Cin-NYY	.333	3	1	0	0	0	.267	15	4	0	0	0	1	0	4	1	69	87.0	4	8	1	0	.923	7	1	0	0	.14
Herges,Matt, SD-SF	.333	3	1	0	0	0	.222	27	6	0	0	0	1	1	14	2	67	79.0	2	9	2	0	.846	5	1	0	0	.17
Hermanson,D, StL-SF	.000	11	0	0	0	3	.092	292	27	5	0	2	9	20	149	34	32	69.1	8	7	0	1	1.000	6	2	0	1	.33
Hernandez,L, Mon	.189	74	14	0	6	6	.234	483	113	19	1	4	45	4	77	40	33	233.1	15	47	1	6	.984	12	5	1	1	.42
Hernandez,Ro, Atl	-	0	0	0	0	0	.500	2	1	0	0	0	0	0	1	0	66	59.1	3	11	1	1	.933	6	2	0	0	.33
Hernandez,Ru, KC	-	0	0	0	0	0	-	0	0	0	0	0	0	0	0	0	16	91.2	6	10	0	2	1.000	11	7	0	0	.64
Herrera,Alex, Cle	-	0	0	0	0	0	-	0	0	0	0	0	0	0	0	0	10	7.0	0	1	0	0	1.000	2	0	0	0	.00
Hill,Jeremy, KC	-	0	0	0	0	0	-	0	0	0	0	0	0	0	0	0	1	1.0	0	0	0	0	-	0	0	0	0	-
Hitchcock,S, NYY-StL	.083	12	1	0	0	2	.094	203	19	0	0	0	5	7	108	23	35	87.2	3	5	2	1	.800	13	3	2	0	.23
Hodges,Trey, Atl	.000	5	0	0	0	1	.000	8	0	0	0	0	0	0	6	1	51	65.1	8	7	0	1	1.000	6	1	0	0	.17
Hoffman,Trevor, SD	-	0	0	0	0	0	.121	33	4	2	0	0	5	0	10	2	9	9.0	2	1	0	1	1.000	0	0	0	0	-
Holmes,Darren, Atl	-	0	0	0	0	0	.107	28	3	0	0	1	2	1	14	6	48	43.0	2	2	1	1	.800	4	1	0	0	.25
Howard,Ben, SD	.091	11	1	0	0	0	.067	15	1	0	0	0	0	0	7	1	6	34.2	3	3	0	1	1.000	5	1	1	0	.20
Howry,Bob, Bos	-	0	0	0	0	0	-	0	0	0	0	0	0	0	0	0	4	4.1	0	0	0	0	-	2	0	0	0	.00
Hudson,Tim, Oak	.333	3	1	0	1	0	.130	23	3	1	0	0	1	2	8	0	34	240.0	20	52	2	1	.973	13	6	0	2	.46
Ishii,Kazuhisa, LA	.029	34	1	0	0	9	.071	84	6	0	1	0	2	2	37	13	27	147.0	4	14	0	0	1.000	31	13	4	0	.42
Isringhausen,J, StL	.500	2	1	0	3	0	.202	99	20	4	1	2	14	5	33	8	40	42.0	0	6	0	0	1.000	4	0	0	0	.00
Jackson,Edwin, LA	.000	6	0	0	0	1	.000	6	0	0	0	0	0	1	2	1	4	22.0	0	3	0	0	1.000	1	0	0	0	.00
Jarvis,Kevin, SD	.136	22	3	0	2	3	.160	188	30	6	0	1	14	13	62	23	16	92.0	13	15	0	0	1.000	13	2	0	0	.15
Jennings,Jason, Col	.222	54	12	0	3	5	.267	131	35	8	0	1	16	9	32	8	32	181.1	8	23	2	2	.939	15	6	1	0	.40
Jensen,Ryan, SF	.400	5	2	0	2	0	.137	73	10	2	0	0	6	1	21	9	6	13.1	0	2	0	0	1.000	1	1	0	1	1.00
Jimenez,Jose, Col	.176	17	3	0	0	2	.123	81	10	0	1	0	4	0	38	7	63	101.2	9	16	3	1	.893	3	1	0	0	.33
Johnson,Adam, Min	-	0	0	0	0	0	-	0	0	0	0	0	0	0	0	0	2	1.1	0	0	0	0	-	0	0	0	0	-
Johnson,Jason, Bal	.200	5	1	0	0	0	.105	19	2	0	0	0	0	2	13	2	32	189.2	8	24	3	0	.914	38	6	0	0	.16
Johnson,Jon, Hou	.000	4	0	0	0	0	.000	4	0	0	0	0	0	0	2	0	4	15.1	4	2	0	0	1.000	3	1	0	0	.33
Johnson,Randy, Ari	.194	36	7	1	3	2	.130	440	57	10	0	1	29	9	204	32	18	114.0	2	13	0	0	1.000	19	6	1	0	.32
Jones,Greg, Ana	-	0	0	0	0	0	-	0	0	0	0	0	0	0	0	0	18	27.2	0	1	0	0	1.000	4	0	0	0	.00
Jones,Todd, Col-Bos	.000	2	0	0	0	0	.188	16	3	1	0	0	0	0	4	0	59	68.2	9	7	1	1	.941	8	3	0	0	.38
Journell,Jimmy, StL	-	0	0	0	0	0	-	0	0	0	0	0	0	0	0	0	7	9.0	0	1	1	0	.500	0	0	0	0	-
Julio,Jorge, Bal	-	0	0	0	0	0	-	0	0	0	0	0	0	0	0	0	64	61.2	3	4	0	0	1.000	14	1	0	0	.07
Junge,Eric, Phi	-	0	0	0	0	0	.000	3	0	0	0	0	0	0	0	0	6	7.2	1	0	0	0	1.000	1	0	0	0	.00
Keisler,Randy, SD	.000	2	0	0	0	0	.000	6	0	0	0	0	0	0	1	0	2	6.0	0	1	0	0	1.000	3	0	0	0	.00
Kennedy,Joe, TB	-	0	0	0	0	0	.364	11	4	0	0	0	1	0	3	0	32	133.2	13	20	1	1	.971	14	4	1	1	.29
Kershner,Jason, Tor	-	0	0	0	0	0	-	0	0	0	0	0	0	0	0	1	40	54.0	7	5	0	1	1.000	1	0	0	0	.00
Kida,Masao, LA	.250	4	1	0	0	0	.250	4	1	0	0	0	0	0	2	0	3	12.0	0	1	0	0	1.000	0	0	0	0	-
Kim,Byung-Hyun, Ari-Bos	.200	20	4	0	1	2	.188	32	6	1	0	0	3	1	6	2	56	122.1	14	23	2	0	.949	16	1	0	0	.06
Kim,Sun-Woo, Mon	.000	3	0	0	0	0	.182	11	2	0	0	0	0	3	3	0	14	14.0	1	1	0	0	1.000	0	0	0	1	-
King,Ray, Atl	-	0	0	0	0	0	.000	3	0	0	0	0	0	0	0	2	80	58.2	3	12	0	0	1.000	2	1	1	0	.50
Kinney,Matt, Mil	.036	55	2	0	0	5	.035	57	2	1	0	0	0	2	28	5	33	190.2	13	23	1	4	.973	28	4	0	0	.14
Kline,Steve, StL	.500	2	1	0	2	1	.154	13	2	1	0	0	2	0	5	3	78	63.0	1	16	0	3	1.000	4	1	1	0	.25
Knott,Eric, Mon	.000	5	0	0	0	0	.000	6	0	0	0	0	0	0	3	0	13	19.1	0	2	1	0	.667	2	0	0	0	.00
Knotts,Gary, Det	.000	1	0	0	0	0	.250	4	1	0	0	0	0	0	0	0	20	95.1	7	16	0	1	1.000	15	2	0	0	.13
Koch,Billy, CWS	-	0	0	0	0	0	.000	2	0	0	0	0	0	0	2	0	55	53.0	6	3	0	0	1.000	10	1	0	0	.10
Kolb,Danny, Mil	-	0	0	0	0	0	-	0	0	0	0	0	0	0	0	0	37	41.1	2	4	0	0	1.000	2	1	0	0	.50
Koplove,Mike, Ari	-	0	0	0	0	0	.000	2	0	0	0	0	0	0	1	0	30	36.2	0	10	0	0	1.000	3	3	0	0	1.00
Lackey,John, Ana	.000	3	0	0	0	0	.000	3	0	0	0	0	0	0	2	0	33	204.1	14	22	3	1	.923	22	8	2	0	.36
Lawrence,Brian, SD	.224	67	15	1	5	2	.154	156	24	6	0	1	14	8	39	7	33	210.2	14	41	3	2	.948	17	6	0	0	.35
Ledezma,Wil, Det	-	0	0	0	0	0	-	0	0	0	0	0	0	0	0	0	33	81.2	4	5	0	0	1.000	3	2	0	0	.25
Lee,Cliff, Cle	-	0	0	0	0	0	-	0	0	0	0	0	0	0	0	0	9	52.1	1	5	1	0	.857	6	2	0	0	.33
Lee,Dave, Cle	-	0	0	0	0	0	-	0	0	0	0	0	0	0	0	0	8	7.2	0	0	0	0	-					
Leiter,Al, NYM	.019	53	1	0	0	5	.087	458	40	6	1	0	16	32	248	42	30	180.2	4	26	0	4	1.000	32	11	5	0	.34
Leskanic,C, Mil-KC	-	0	0	0	0	0	.179	39	7	3	0	1	7	1	17	5	52	50.2	11	4	0	2	1.000	8	3	0	0	.38
Levine,Al, TB-KC	-	0	0	0	0	0	-	0	0	0	0	0	0	0	0	0	54	71.0	4	11	0	0	1.000	8	6	0	0	.75
Levrault,Allen, Fla	.000	2	0	0	0	0	.053	38	2	0	0	0	1	1	17	6	19	28.0	0	2	0	1	1.000	0	0	0	0	.00
Lewis,Colby, Tex	.000	1	0	0	0	0	.000	1	0	0	0	0	0	0	0	0	26	127.0	7	13	0	1	1.000	11	6	0	0	.55
Lidge,Brad, Hou	.000	4	0	0	0	0	.333	6	2	1	0	0	2	0	4	0	78	85.0	2	4	0	0	1.000	11	6	0	0	.55
Lidle,Cory, Tor	.333	6	2	0	0	0	.125	16	2	0	0	0	0	1	7	1	31	192.2	15	30	0	4	1.000	22	6	0	1	.27
Ligtenberg,K, Bal	-	0	0	0	0	0	-	0	0	0	0	0	0	0	0	0	68	59.1	1	7	0	0	1.000	7	2	0	0	.29
Lilly,Ted, Oak	.000	5	0	0	0	0	.071	14	1	0	0	0	0	0	5	3	32	178.1	5	14	0	1	1.000	25	1	1	0	.04
Lima,Jose, KC	.500	2	1	0	0	1	.119	236	28	4	0	0	8	6	77	34	14	73.1	7	5	0	0	1.000	10	0	0	0	.00
Lincoln,Mike, Pit	-	0	0	0	0	0	.100	10	1	0	0	0	0	0	5	1	36	36.1	4	1	0	0	.833	4	2	0	0	.50
Linebrink,S, Hou-SD	.167	12	2	0	0	1	.231	13	3	1	0	0	0	0	7	1	52	92.0	6	4	0	0	1.000	13	4	0	0	.31
Linton,Doug, Tor	-	0	0	0	0	0	.000	7	0	0	0	0	0	0	3	2	7	9.0	1	2	0	0	1.000	1	1	0	0	1.00
Lloyd,Graeme, NYM-KC	-	0	0	0	0	0	.000	6	0	0	0	0	0	0	1	2	52	47.2	4	6	0	0	1.000	6	0	0	0	.00
Loaiza,Esteban, CWS	.200	5	1	0	0	0	.178	174	31	2	1	0	11	3	38	20	34	226.1	16	31	2	2	.959	15	9	0	1	.60
Loewer,Carlton, SD	.000	5	0	0	1	1	.129	62	8	0	0	0	3	5	22	8	5	21.2	0	1	1	0	.500	7	2	0	0	.29
Lohse,Kyle, Min	.333	3	1	0	0	3	.333	12	4	1	0	0	1	0	4	3	33	201.0	16	21	1	1	.974	15	3	0	1	.20
Looper,Aaron, Sea	-	0	0	0	0	0	-	0	0	0	0	0	0	0	0	0	6	7.0	0	1	0	0	1.000	0	0	0	0	-
Looper,Braden, Fla	1.000	1	1	0	0	1	.167	6	1	0	0	0	0	0	4	1	74	80.2	1	10	0	0	1.000	2	0	0	0	.00

Pitchers Hitting, Fielding and Holding Runners

Pitcher	2003 Hitting						Career Hitting										2003 Fielding and Holding Runners											
	Avg	AB	H	HR	RBI	SH	Avg	AB	H	2B	3B	HR	RBI	BB	SO	SH	G	Inn	PO	A	E	DP	Pct	SBA	CS	PCS	PPO	CS%
Lopez,Albie, KC	-	0	0	0	0	0	.043	46	2	0	0	0	0	2	25	3	15	22.2	1	3	0	0	1.000	2	0	0	0	.00
Lopez,Aquilino, Tor	-	0	0	0	0	0	-	0	0	0	0	0	0	0	0	0	72	73.2	2	7	2	0	.818	7	0	0	0	.00
Lopez,Javier, Col	.200	5	1	0	1	0	.200	5	1	0	0	0	1	0	1	0	75	58.1	5	13	0	0	1.000	5	3	2	0	.60
Lopez,Rodrigo, Bal	.000	2	0	0	0	0	.071	14	1	0	0	0	0	0	8	0	26	147.0	8	14	2	1	.917	27	6	0	1	.22
Loux,Shane, Det	-	0	0	0	0	0	-	0	0	0	0	0	0	0	0	0	11	30.1	3	5	0	0	1.000	4	2	0	0	.50
Lowe,Derek, Bos	.000	4	0	0	0	1	.063	16	1	0	0	0	0	2	7	2	33	203.1	20	44	0	0	1.000	17	3	1	0	.18
Lowe,Sean, KC	-	0	0	0	0	0	.136	22	3	0	0	0	0	0	8	2	28	44.2	3	5	1	0	.889	7	3	0	0	.43
Lowry,Noah, SF	.500	2	1	0	0	0	.500	2	1	0	0	0	0	0	1	0	4	6.1	0	1	0	0	1.000	0	0	0	0	-
Lyon,Brandon, Bos	-	0	0	0	0	0	-	0	0	0	0	0	0	0	0	0	49	59.0	3	7	1	0	.909	5	0	0	0	.00
MacDougal,Mike, KC	-	0	0	0	0	0	-	0	0	0	0	0	0	0	0	0	68	64.0	5	8	3	0	.813	1	0	0	0	.00
Maddux,Greg, Atl	.147	68	10	0	2	8	.178	1261	224	31	2	4	64	29	336	143	36	218.1	13	58	2	5	.973	34	8	0	1	.24
Madson,Ryan, Phi	-	0	0	0	0	0	-	0	0	0	0	0	0	0	0	0	1	2.0	0	0	0	0	-	0	0	0	0	-
Mahay,Ron, Tex	-	0	0	0	0	0	.333	6	2	1	0	0	0	0	2	0	35	45.1	4	5	2	0	.818	5	1	0	0	.20
Mahomes,Pat, Pit	.250	4	1	0	0	0	.256	43	11	4	0	0	4	1	16	2	9	22.1	4	4	0	0	1.000	1	0	0	0	.00
Malaska,Mark, TB	-	0	0	0	0	0	-	0	0	0	0	0	0	0	0	0	22	16.0	1	3	0	2	1.000	0	0	0	0	-
Mann,Jim, Pit	-	0	0	0	0	0	.000	1	0	0	0	0	0	0	1	0	2	1.2	0	0	0	0	-	0	0	0	0	-
Manning,Dave, Mil	.000	1	0	0	0	0	.000	1	0	0	0	0	0	0	1	0	2	6.2	0	1	0	0	1.000	2	1	0	0	.50
Manon,Julio, Mon	.000	1	0	0	0	0	.000	1	0	0	0	0	0	0	1	0	23	28.1	1	2	1	0	.750	2	1	0	0	.50
Mantei,Matt, Ari	-	0	0	0	0	0	.200	5	1	0	0	0	0	0	2	0	50	55.0	1	4	0	0	1.000	3	0	0	0	.00
Manzanillo,J, Cin	-	0	0	0	0	0	.091	11	1	0	0	0	0	0	5	2	9	10.2	0	1	1	0	.500	1	0	0	0	.00
Maroth,Mike, Det	.500	2	1	0	0	1	.250	8	2	0	0	0	0	1	5	1	33	193.2	9	42	2	2	.962	19	11	7	1	.58
Marquis,Jason, Atl	.500	2	1	0	1	2	.096	73	7	1	0	1	2	2	26	7	21	40.2	3	8	1	0	.917	1	0	0	0	.00
Marte,Damaso, CWS	-	0	0	0	0	0	.000	4	0	0	0	0	0	0	1	0	71	79.2	2	9	0	1	1.000	6	0	0	1	.00
Martin,Tom, LA	.000	1	0	0	0	0	.000	7	0	0	0	0	0	0	3	0	80	51.0	3	7	0	2	1.000	4	1	1	0	.25
Martinez,Luis, Mil	.000	4	0	0	0	0	.000	4	0	0	0	0	0	0	3	0	4	16.1	0	3	0	0	1.000	1	1	1	0	1.00
Martinez,Pedro, Bos	.000	3	0	0	0	0	.095	263	25	3	2	0	11	11	120	38	29	186.2	14	19	0	0	1.000	8	3	0	0	.38
Mateo,Julio, Sea	-	0	0	0	0	0	-	0	0	0	0	0	0	0	0	0	48	84.0	4	4	2	0	.800	9	0	0	0	.00
Matthews,Mike, SD	.000	2	0	0	0	1	.120	25	3	0	0	1	1	0	9	3	77	64.2	2	12	0	1	1.000	8	4	2	1	.50
May,Darrell, KC	.000	4	0	0	0	1	.077	13	1	0	0	0	0	1	7	1	35	210.0	9	18	2	1	.931	9	5	0	0	.56
Mays,Joe, Min	.333	3	1	0	0	1	.250	12	3	1	0	0	0	3	5	3	30	128.1	6	19	1	3	.962	4	1	0	0	.25
McClung,Seth, TB	-	0	0	0	0	0	-	0	0	0	0	0	0	0	0	0	12	38.2	2	2	0	1	1.000	3	3	0	0	1.00
Meadows,Brian, Pit	.071	14	1	0	0	3	.119	176	21	3	0	0	7	7	73	19	34	76.1	5	10	2	0	.882	4	1	0	0	.25
Mears,Chris, Det	-	0	0	0	0	0	-	0	0	0	0	0	0	0	0	0	29	41.1	3	5	0	2	1.000	9	3	0	0	.33
Meche,Gil, Sea	.200	5	1	0	0	0	.200	5	1	0	0	0	0	0	1	0	32	186.1	15	20	1	2	.972	8	4	0	0	.50
Mecir,Jim, Oak	-	0	0	0	0	0	.000	1	0	0	0	0	0	0	0	0	41	37.0	2	8	0	0	1.000	3	1	0	0	.33
Mendoza,Ramiro, Bos	-	0	0	0	0	0	.000	3	0	0	0	0	0	0	3	1	37	66.2	4	9	0	1	1.000	6	1	0	0	.17
Mercado,Hector, Phi	.000	2	0	0	0	0	.111	9	1	0	0	0	0	0	4	0	13	18.2	0	3	0	0	1.000	2	0	0	0	.00
Mercedes,Jose, Mon	-	0	0	0	0	0	-	0	0	0	0	0	0	0	0	0	5	7.1	0	1	0	0	1.000	0	0	0	0	-
Mercker,Kent, Cin-Atl	.000	1	0	0	0	0	.114	246	28	5	2	1	18	11	115	22	67	55.1	6	6	1	0	.923	6	1	1	0	.17
Mesa,Jose, Phi	-	0	0	0	0	0	-	0	0	0	0	0	0	1	0	0	61	58.0	4	2	1	0	.857	4	0	0	0	.00
Miadich,Bart, Ana	-	0	0	0	0	0	-	0	0	0	0	0	0	0	0	0	1	2.0	1	0	0	0	1.000	0	0	0	0	-
Miceli,Danny, Col-Cle-NYY-Hou	.000	1	0	0	0	0	.050	20	1	0	0	0	0	0	9	0	57	70.1	7	9	1	0	.941	10	2	0	0	.20
Middlebrook,J, NYM	-	0	0	0	0	0	.167	18	3	0	0	0	1	1	9	1	5	7.0	1	0	0	0	1.000	1	0	0	0	.00
Miller,Matt, Col	-	0	0	0	0	0	-	0	0	0	0	0	0	0	0	0	4	4.1	1	1	0	0	1.000	1	1	1	0	1.00
Miller,Trever, Tor	-	0	0	0	0	0	.167	6	1	1	0	0	0	0	1	2	78	52.1	5	2	0	0	1.000	0	0	0	0	.00
Miller,Wade, Hou	.159	63	10	0	6	5	.155	232	36	9	0	0	14	4	74	22	33	187.1	13	21	1	1	.971	14	5	0	0	.36
Millwood,Kevin, Phi	.059	68	4	0	1	6	.118	380	45	12	0	2	23	17	166	45	35	222.0	11	22	2	0	.943	45	4	0	0	.09
Milton,Eric, Min	-	0	0	0	0	0	.300	20	6	0	0	2	1	7	0	3	17.0	0	0	0	0	-	3	2	0	0	.67
Mitre,Sergio, ChC	.500	2	1	0	0	0	.500	2	1	0	0	0	0	0	1	0	3	8.2	0	3	0	0	1.000	0	0	0	0	-
Moehler,Brian, Hou	.000	4	0	0	0	0	.000	30	0	0	0	0	0	2	12	1	3	13.2	0	5	0	0	1.000	0	0	0	0	-
Molina,Gabe, StL	-	0	0	0	0	0	-	0	0	0	0	0	0	0	0	0	3	2.2	0	0	0	0	-	0	0	0	0	-
Moreno,Orber, NYM	.000	1	0	0	0	0	.000	1	0	0	0	0	0	0	1	0	7	8.0	0	2	0	0	1.000	1	0	0	0	.00
Morris,Matt, StL	.192	52	10	1	3	12	.167	300	50	10	0	1	20	17	125	40	27	172.1	15	17	0	0	1.000	6	3	0	0	.00
Moss,Damian, SF-Bal	.241	29	7	0	1	7	.150	80	12	1	0	0	3	6	37	13	31	165.2	6	25	1	0	.969	12	6	3	1	.50
Mota,Guillermo, LA	.222	9	2	1	2	0	.278	18	5	0	0	2	5	0	7	0	76	105.0	6	14	1	0	.952	13	5	0	0	.38
Mounce,Tony, Tex	.000	2	0	0	0	0	.000	2	0	0	0	0	0	0	1	0	11	50.2	2	8	0	0	1.000	11	4	1	0	.36
Moyer,Jamie, Sea	.400	5	2	0	0	1	.152	171	26	2	0	0	4	15	56	22	33	215.0	18	29	1	2	.979	17	6	4	0	.35
Mulder,Mark, Oak	.000	4	0	0	1	1	.056	18	1	0	0	0	1	0	8	1	26	186.2	14	31	0	2	1.000	20	10	6	1	.50
Mulholland,T, Cle	.000	1	0	0	0	0	.112	617	69	13	1	2	23	13	281	53	45	99.0	4	12	0	1	1.000	1	0	0	3	.00
Mullen,Scott, KC-LA	.000	1	0	0	0	0	.000	1	0	0	0	0	0	0	1	0	3	7.1	0	0	0	0	-	1	0	0	0	.00
Munro,Pete, Hou	.000	1	0	0	0	2	.125	24	3	0	0	0	2	2	7	3	40	54.0	4	10	0	2	1.000	8	2	0	0	.25
Mussina,Mike, NYY	.000	2	0	0	0	0	.216	37	8	1	0	0	5	0	6	1	31	214.2	14	33	0	2	1.000	19	10	0	0	.53
Myers,Brett, Phi	.145	62	9	0	1	5	.141	85	12	2	0	0	2	2	27	8	32	193.0	12	28	2	1	.952	21	5	0	0	.24
Myers,Mike, Ari	-	0	0	0	0	0	.000	1	0	0	0	0	0	0	1	0	64	37.1	4	8	0	0	1.000	1	0	0	0	.00
Myers,Rodney, LA	.000	2	0	0	0	0	.167	18	3	1	0	0	1	0	9	0	4	9.0	0	1	0	1	1.000	0	0	0	0	-
Myette,Aaron, Cle	-	0	0	0	0	0	-	0	0	0	0	0	0	0	0	0	2	2.2	0	0	0	0	-	1	0	0	0	.00
Nagy,Charles, SD	.000	2	0	0	0	0	.105	19	2	0	0	0	0	0	10	1	5	12.1	1	2	0	0	1.000	1	0	0	0	.00
Nakamura,Mike, Min	-	0	0	0	0	0	-	0	0	0	0	0	0	0	0	0	12	12.2	0	2	0	0	1.000	1	0	0	0	.00
Nance,Shane, Mil	-	0	0	0	0	0	.333	3	1	0	0	0	1	0	2	0	26	24.1	4	3	1	1	.875	4	0	0	0	.00
Nathan,Joe, SF	.000	1	0	0	0	1	.164	61	10	3	0	2	4	3	16	10	78	79.0	5	5	0	0	1.000	6	1	0	0	.17
Neagle,Denny, Col	.000	11	0	0	0	2	.164	531	87	17	0	5	44	19	155	75	7	35.1	3	0	1	1	1.000	2	1	0	0	.50
Neal,Blaine, Fla	-	0	0	0	0	0	-	0	0	0	0	0	0	0	0	0	18	21.0	1	1	0	0	1.000	1	1	0	0	1.00
Nelson,Jeff, Sea-NYY	-	0	0	0	0	0	.000	2	0	0	0	0	0	0	0	1	70	56.1	0	4	0	0	1.000	3	1	0	0	.33
Neu,Mike, Oak	-	0	0	0	0	0	-	0	0	0	0	0	0	0	0	0	32	42.0	3	11	0	0	1.000	2	1	1	0	.50
Nitkowski,C.J., Tex	-	0	0	0	0	0	.133	15	2	0	0	0	1	0	10	1	6	9.2	5	0	1	1	1.000	3	0	0	0	.00

Pitchers Hitting, Fielding and Holding Runners

Pitcher	2003 Hitting Avg	AB	H	HR	RBI	SH	Career Hitting Avg	AB	H	2B	3B	HR	RBI	BB	SO	SH	2003 Fielding and Holding Runners G	Inn	PO	A	E	DP	Pct	SBA	CS	PCS	PPO	CS%
Nomo,Hideo, LA	.138	65	9	0	1	3	.136	455	62	14	1	3	25	13	204	43	33	218.1	14	29	1	4	.977	33	14	0	0	.42
Norton,Phil, ChC-Cin	.000	1	0	0	0	0	.571	7	4	0	0	0	0	0	1	2	21	18.0	1	2	0	1	1.000	3	1	1	0	.33
Nunez,Vladimir, Fla	-	0	0	0	0	0	.136	59	8	0	0	1	5	1	19	8	14	10.2	1	0	1	0	.500	0	0	0	0	-
Obermueller,W, Mil	.130	23	3	0	1	2	.130	23	3	0	0	0	1	0	6	2	12	65.2	13	12	0	1	1.000	5	1	0	0	.20
Ohka,Tomo, Mon	.182	55	10	0	3	8	.156	128	20	1	0	0	6	6	46	18	34	199.0	9	36	4	2	.918	10	8	2	0	.80
Ohme,Kevin, StL	1.000	1	1	0	0	0	1.000	1	1	0	0	0	0	0	0	0	2	4.1	1	0	0	0	1.000	0	0	0	0	-
Oliver,Darren, Col	.254	67	17	1	8	2	.239	180	43	10	0	1	17	7	58	12	33	180.1	6	27	0	3	1.000	20	6	4	0	.30
Olsen,Kevin, Fla	-	0	0	0	0	0	.067	15	1	0	0	0	0	0	10	1	7	12.0	0	0	0	0	-	0	0	0	0	-
Oropesa,Eddie, Ari	-	0	0	0	0	0	-	0	0	0	0	0	0	0	0	0	47	38.2	2	11	1	1	.929	5	2	1	0	.40
Orosco,Jesse, SD-NYY-Min	-	0	0	0	0	0	.169	59	10	0	0	0	4	8	25	7	65	34.0	5	5	0	1	1.000	7	0	0	0	.00
Ortiz,Ramon, Ana	.000	5	0	0	0	0	.000	19	0	0	0	0	0	0	7	1	32	180.0	12	19	4	1	.886	16	2	0	0	.13
Ortiz,Russ, Atl	.257	70	18	2	10	6	.223	363	81	19	0	6	40	28	95	39	34	212.1	13	25	1	5	.974	27	5	1	1	.19
Osuna,Antonio, NYY	-	0	0	0	0	0	.111	9	1	0	0	0	0	1	1	0	47	50.0	2	7	0	0	1.000	2	1	0	0	.50
Oswalt,Roy, Hou	.179	39	7	0	0	7	.160	163	26	4	0	0	7	7	53	17	21	127.1	10	13	0	1	1.000	6	5	1	0	.83
Padilla,V, Phi	.060	67	4	0	1	3	.070	129	9	2	0	0	6	7	67	11	32	208.2	12	35	4	1	.922	9	4	0	0	.44
Painter,Lance, StL	.000	1	0	0	0	0	.154	65	10	2	1	0	5	2	33	8	22	18.0	2	5	0	1	1.000	0	0	0	0	-
Paniagua,Jose, CWS	-	0	0	0	0	0	.000	18	0	0	0	0	0	2	11	1	1	0.1	0	0	0	0	-	0	0	0	0	-
Park,Chan Ho, Tex	-	0	0	0	0	0	.168	345	58	15	1	2	23	17	125	39	7	29.2	3	6	1	2	.900	1	0	0	0	.00
Paronto,Chad, Cle	-	0	0	0	0	0	-	0	0	0	0	0	0	0	0	0	6	6.2	0	0	0	0	-	0	0	0	0	-
Parque,Jim, TB	-	0	0	0	0	0	.200	10	2	0	0	0	0	0	4	3	5	17.1	0	2	0	0	1.000	1	0	0	0	.00
Parris,Steve, TB	.000	1	0	0	0	0	.154	162	25	4	0	0	15	3	53	16	10	43.2	6	2	0	0	1.000	2	0	0	0	.00
Parrish,John, Bal	-	0	0	0	0	0	-	0	0	0	0	0	0	0	0	0	14	23.2	1	3	2	0	.667	0	0	0	2	-
Patterson,D, Det	-	0	0	0	0	0	.000	1	0	0	0	0	0	0	0	0	19	18.0	3	3	1	0	.857	1	1	1	1	1.00
Patterson,John, Ari	.083	12	1	0	1	1	.091	22	2	0	0	0	1	1	8	2	16	55.0	3	2	0	0	1.000	8	1	0	0	.13
Pavano,Carl, Fla	.098	61	6	0	1	5	.127	220	28	5	2	0	8	3	88	25	33	201.0	12	28	0	2	1.000	20	3	0	0	.15
Pearce,Josh, StL	-	0	0	0	0	0	.250	4	1	0	0	0	1	0	0	2	7	9.0	1	1	0	0	1.000	0	0	0	0	-
Pearson,Jason, StL	-	0	0	0	0	0	-	0	0	0	0	0	0	0	0	0	2	1.0	0	0	0	0	-	0	0	0	0	-
Peavy,Jake, SD	.073	55	4	0	1	8	.125	98	11	3	0	0	3	3	34	10	32	194.2	17	20	3	3	.925	8	1	0	0	.13
Penny,Brad, Fla	.132	68	9	2	8	5	.143	223	32	4	2	2	12	1	77	10	32	196.1	19	12	1	1	.969	14	3	0	0	.21
Percival,Troy, Ana	-	0	0	0	0	0	.000	1	0	0	0	0	0	0	1	0	52	49.1	2	0	0	0	1.000	4	0	0	0	.00
Perez,Odalis, LA	.096	52	5	0	0	10	.140	172	24	6	0	1	8	2	43	26	30	185.1	5	41	1	3	.979	34	9	7	0	.26
Perez,Oliver, SD-Pit	.179	39	7	0	4	3	.159	69	11	0	0	4	1	22	6	24	126.2	1	15	1	0	.941	2	1	1	0	.50
Person,Robert, Bos	.000	1	0	0	0	0	.117	214	25	5	0	4	16	10	119	25	7	11.2	0	2	0	0	1.000	0	0	0	0	-
Pettitte,Andy, NYY	.143	7	1	0	1	0	.107	28	3	1	0	0	2	1	11	3	33	208.1	7	27	6	1	.850	14	1	0	0	.07
Phelps,Tommy, Fla	.091	11	1	0	0	1	.091	11	1	0	0	0	0	2	3	1	27	63.0	3	7	0	0	1.000	4	2	0	0	.50
Phillips,J C, Cle	-	0	0	0	0	0	-	0	0	0	0	0	0	0	0	0	3	5.0	2	1	0	0	1.000	1	1	0	1	1.00
Pineiro,Joel, Sea	.000	4	0	0	0	1	.091	11	1	0	0	0	2	0	5	1	32	211.2	20	24	1	2	.978	13	2	0	0	.15
Plesac,Dan, Phi	-	0	0	0	0	0	.067	15	1	0	0	0	0	0	10	0	58	33.1	0	5	0	0	1.000	5	0	0	0	.00
Politte,Cliff, Tor	-	0	0	0	0	0	.094	32	3	1	0	0	2	3	14	3	54	49.1	2	1	0	0	1.000	7	2	0	0	.29
Ponson,Sidney, Bal-SF	.074	27	2	0	0	3	.122	41	5	2	0	0	0	0	10	6	31	216.0	21	27	1	5	.980	16	4	1	0	.25
Porzio,Mike, CWS	-	0	0	0	0	0	-	0	0	0	0	0	0	0	0	0	3	14.0	0	4	0	0	1.000	2	0	0	0	.00
Powell,Brian, SF	.000	2	0	0	0	0	.154	13	2	1	0	0	1	6	0	1	4	4.2	3	2	0	0	1.000	0	0	0	0	-
Powell,Jay, Tex	-	0	0	0	0	0	.167	12	2	1	0	0	1	0	8	1	51	58.2	6	4	0	0	1.000	7	2	1	0	.29
Prinz,Bret, Ari-NYY	-	0	0	0	0	0	-	0	0	0	0	0	0	0	0	0	3	3.0	1	0	0	0	1.000	0	0	0	0	-
Prior,Mark, ChC	.250	72	18	1	6	7	.224	107	24	8	0	1	10	4	42	9	30	211.1	8	13	3	0	.870	16	9	0	0	.56
Puffer,Brandon, Hou	.000	3	0	0	0	0	.000	9	0	0	0	0	0	1	7	1	13	21.0	0	8	0	0	1.000	3	1	0	0	.33
Pulido,Carlos, Min	-	0	0	0	0	0	-	0	0	0	0	0	0	0	0	0	7	15.2	0	2	0	0	1.000	1	0	0	0	.00
Putz,J.J., Sea	-	0	0	0	0	0	-	0	0	0	0	0	0	0	0	0	3	3.2	1	0	0	0	1.000	0	0	0	0	-
Quantrill,Paul, LA	.000	1	0	0	0	0	.108	65	7	0	0	0	4	29	7	89	77.1	2	19	0	2	1.000	12	4	1	0	.33
Quevedo,Ruben, Mil	.300	10	3	0	0	1	.153	98	15	0	0	5	2	44	9	9	42.2	2	8	0	0	1.000	4	2	0	1	.50
Radke,Brad, Min	.200	5	1	0	0	1	.143	21	3	0	0	0	0	6	1	33	212.1	16	31	1	0	.979	21	6	0	2	.29
Raggio,Brady, Ari	-	0	0	0	0	0	-	0	0	0	0	0	0	0	0	0	10	8.1	0	1	0	0	.000	2	0	0	0	.00
Ramirez,Erasmo, Tex	-	0	0	0	0	0	-	0	0	0	0	0	0	0	0	0	33	47.2	0	3	0	0	1.000	4	3	1	0	.75
Ramirez,H, Atl	.098	61	6	0	2	6	.098	61	6	0	1	0	2	0	12	6	29	182.1	7	32	3	4	.929	17	4	1	0	.24
Ramos,Mario, Tex	.000	1	0	0	0	0	.000	1	0	0	0	0	0	0	1	0	3	13.0	1	1	0	0	1.000	2	0	0	0	.00
Randall,Scott, Cin	.250	4	1	0	0	0	.250	4	1	0	0	0	0	0	0	0	15	27.2	2	4	0	0	1.000	2	0	0	0	.00
Randolph,S, Ari	.000	3	0	0	0	1	.000	3	0	0	0	0	0	2	1	50	60.0	3	5	0	1	1.000	2	2	1	1.00
Reames,Britt, Mon	.000	1	0	0	0	0	.128	39	5	0	0	1	3	4	11	6	2	1.1	0	0	0	0	-	0	0	0	0	-
Redding,Tim, Hou	.200	50	10	0	2	8	.179	84	15	3	0	0	5	2	42	11	33	176.0	6	29	2	2	.946	19	2	0	0	.11
Redman,Mark, Fla	.016	62	1	0	1	4	.028	71	2	0	0	0	1	1	35	5	29	191.2	5	24	1	0	.967	4	1	0	0	.25
Reed,Rick, Min	-	0	0	0	0	0	.172	297	51	9	0	2	24	13	93	47	27	135.0	5	10	1	0	.938	10	5	1	0	.50
Reed,Steve, Col	-	0	0	0	1	0	.154	26	4	0	0	0	1	0	8	2	67	63.1	4	14	0	2	1.000	5	3	1	0	.60
Reichert,Dan, Tor	-	0	0	0	0	0	.111	9	1	0	0	0	0	6	1	15	16.1	1	1	0	0	1.000	1	0	0	0	.00
Reith,Brian, Cin	.000	7	0	0	0	0	.194	31	6	0	0	0	4	0	12	0	42	61.1	1	6	1	0	.875	7	3	0	0	.43
Reitsma,Chris, Cin	.125	8	1	0	2	0	.105	86	9	1	0	0	5	3	42	14	57	84.0	1	9	2	0	.833	1	0	0	0	.00
Remlinger,Mike, ChC	.000	1	0	0	0	0	.073	109	8	3	0	0	8	8	36	19	73	69.0	2	4	0	0	1.000	0	0	0	0	.00
Reyes,Al, NYY	-	0	0	0	0	0	.200	10	2	0	0	0	0	5	1	13	17.0	1	0	0	0	1.000	1	0	0	0	.00
Reyes,Carlos, TB	.000	1	0	0	0	0	.000	3	0	0	0	0	0	1	1	0	10	39.2	3	3	0	1	1.000	3	3	0	0	1.00
Reyes,Dennys, Pit-Ari	-	0	0	0	0	0	.070	43	3	1	0	0	0	2	20	2	15	12.2	1	2	1	0	.750	2	1	0	0	.50
Reynolds,Shane, Atl	.093	54	5	0	3	10	.141	546	77	15	0	5	43	14	247	97	30	167.1	7	20	0	2	1.000	12	5	0	0	.42
Rhodes,Arthur, Sea	-	0	0	0	0	0	.250	4	1	0	0	0	0	3	0	67	54.0	1	6	0	0	1.000	1	0	0	0	.00
Riedling,John, Cin	.222	18	4	0	2	1	.182	22	4	0	0	0	2	0	14	1	55	101.0	11	12	1	1	.958	4	2	0	0	.50
Riggan,Jerrod, Cle	-	0	0	0	0	0	.000	2	0	0	0	0	0	0	2	0	2	4.0	0	2	0	0	1.000	0	0	0	0	-
Riley,Matt, Bal	-	0	0	0	0	0	-	0	0	0	0	0	0	0	0	0	2	10.0	1	0	0	0	1.000	0	0	0	0	-
Rincon,Juan, Min	-	0	0	0	0	0	1.000	1	1	0	0	0	0	0	0	0	58	87.1	15	10	0	0	1.000	9	1	0	0	.11

271

Pitchers Hitting, Fielding and Holding Runners

Pitcher	2003 Hitting						Career Hitting										2003 Fielding and Holding Runners											
	Avg	AB	H	HR	RBI	SH	Avg	AB	H	2B	3B	HR	RBI	BB	SO	SH	G	Inn	PO	A	E	DP	Pct	SBA	CS	PCS	PPO	CS%
Rincon,Ricardo, Oak	-	0	0	0	0	0	.000	4	0	0	0	0	0	0	1	0	64	55.1	2	9	0	0	1.000	7	3	0	0	.43
Riske,David, Cle	-	0	0	0	0	0	-	0	0	0	0	0	0	0	0	0	68	74.2	2	5	0	2	1.000	6	2	0	0	.33
Ritchie,Todd, Mil	.222	9	2	0	0	2	.176	187	33	5	0	0	6	7	69	20	5	28.1	1	5	1	0	.857	6	2	0	0	.33
Rivera,Mariano, NYY	-	0	0	0	0	0	-	0	0	0	0	0	0	0	0	0	64	70.1	4	15	2	0	.905	5	2	0	0	.40
Roa,Joe, Phi-Col-SD	.286	7	2	0	1	0	.213	47	10	1	0	0	3	2	13	3	28	51.1	4	9	0	2	1.000	6	0	0	0	.00
Roach,Jason, NYM	1.000	2	2	0	0	0	1.000	2	2	0	0	0	0	0	0	0	2	9.0	0	3	0	0	1.000	0	0	0	0	-
Roberts,Grant, NYM	-	0	0	0	0	0	.250	4	1	0	0	0	0	0	3	1	18	19.0	1	7	0	0	1.000	3	0	0	0	.00
Roberts,Willis, Bal	-	0	0	0	0	0	.250	4	1	0	0	0	0	0	3	1	26	39.1	4	4	0	0	1.000	6	1	0	0	.17
Robertson,J, Hou	.154	52	8	0	3	5	.154	52	8	0	1	0	3	1	14	5	32	160.2	11	35	4	2	.920	12	7	6	1	.58
Robertson,Nate, Det	-	0	0	0	0	0	.000	2	0	0	0	0	0	0	1	0	8	44.1	1	6	0	1	1.000	4	3	1	0	.75
Rocker,John, TB	-	0	0	0	0	0	-	0	0	0	0	0	0	0	0	0	2	1.0	0	0	0	0	-	0	0	0	0	-
Rodney,F, Det	-	0	0	0	0	0	-	0	0	0	0	0	0	0	0	0	27	29.2	0	3	0	0	1.000	11	1	0	0	.09
Rodriguez,Fe, SF	1.000	1	1	0	0	0	.267	15	4	1	0	1	3	0	4	2	68	61.0	0	9	1	2	.900	3	2	0	1	.67
Rodriguez,Fr, Ana	-	0	0	0	0	0	-	0	0	0	0	0	0	0	0	0	59	86.0	2	9	0	2	1.000	10	4	1	0	.40
Rodriguez,Rica, Cle	.000	3	0	0	0	0	.000	3	0	0	0	0	0	0	0	0	15	81.2	7	15	2	0	.917	11	1	0	0	.09
Rodriguez,Rich, Ana	-	0	0	0	0	0	.107	28	3	0	0	0	1	3	9	4	3	3.2	0	0	0	0	-	0	0	0	0	-
Rogers,Kenny, Min	.000	4	0	0	0	0	.146	48	7	0	0	0	3	4	17	4	33	195.0	20	37	2	4	.966	6	2	1	3	.33
Romero,J.C., Min	.000	1	0	0	0	0	.333	3	1	1	0	0	0	0	1	0	73	63.0	7	12	2	1	.905	2	1	1	0	.50
Roney,Matt, Det	.500	2	1	0	0	0	.500	2	1	0	0	0	0	0	1	0	45	100.2	7	11	2	0	.900	12	5	1	0	.42
Rosario,R, Hou	-	0	0	0	0	0	-	0	0	0	0	0	0	0	0	0	2	8.0	0	2	0	0	1.000	2	0	0	0	.00
Rueter,Kirk, SF	.132	53	7	0	3	6	.154	531	82	6	0	0	37	23	96	77	27	147.0	10	33	0	5	1.000	3	1	0	1	.33
Rupe,Ryan, Bos	-	0	0	0	0	0	.111	9	1	1	0	0	0	0	3	0	10	10.0	3	1	0	0	1.000	0	0	0	0	-
Rusch,Glendon, Mil	.206	34	7	0	2	4	.152	210	32	0	0	1	16	8	75	28	32	123.1	3	15	0	1	1.000	7	6	3	1	.86
Ryan,B.J., Bal	-	0	0	0	0	0	.000	2	0	0	0	0	0	0	0	0	76	50.0	3	6	1	2	.900	6	1	0	0	.17
Saarloos,Kirk, Hou	.000	5	0	0	1	3	.057	35	2	1	0	0	3	1	11	8	36	49.1	2	6	2	1	.800	5	1	0	0	.20
Sabathia,C.C., Cle	.500	6	3	0	0	0	.267	15	4	0	0	0	1	2	1	1	30	197.2	7	19	2	2	.929	14	9	2	0	.64
Sadler,Carl, Cle	-	0	0	0	0	0	-	0	0	0	0	0	0	0	0	0	18	9.2	0	2	0	0	1.000	1	0	0	0	.00
Sanchez,Duaner, Pit	-	0	0	0	0	0	-	0	0	0	0	0	0	0	0	0	6	6.0	0	0	0	0	-	0	0	0	0	-
Sanchez,Felix, ChC	-	0	0	0	0	0	-	0	0	0	0	0	0	0	0	0	3	1.2	0	0	0	0	-	1	0	0	0	.00
Sanchez,Jesus, Col	-	0	0	0	0	0	.181	138	25	0	1	0	6	3	38	11	9	8.0	0	2	0	0	1.000	1	1	1	0	1.00
Sanders,Dave, CWS	-	0	0	0	0	0	-	0	0	0	0	0	0	0	0	0	20	22.0	0	0	0	0	-	0	0	0	0	-
Santana,Johan, Min	.333	3	1	0	0	0	.250	8	2	0	0	0	0	0	1	0	44	155.1	3	9	3	1	.800	6	2	1	1	.33
Santiago,Jose, Cle	-	0	0	0	0	0	.000	5	0	0	0	0	0	2	4	0	25	31.2	1	3	2	0	.667	2	2	0	0	.50
Santos,Victor, Tex	.000	2	0	0	0	1	.250	4	1	0	0	0	0	0	1	1	8	25.2	1	3	1	0	.800	2	1	0	0	.50
Sasaki,K, Sea	-	0	0	0	0	0	-	0	0	0	0	0	0	0	0	0	35	33.1	2	3	0	0	1.000	4	0	0	0	.00
Sauerbeck,S, Pit-Bos	.000	1	0	0	0	0	.000	7	0	0	0	0	0	0	0	0	56	42.2	4	12	1	2	.941	4	0	0	0	.00
Schilling,Curt, Ari	.058	52	3	0	0	4	.150	762	114	13	1	0	29	25	266	102	24	168.0	8	13	5	1	.808	6	3	0	0	.50
Schmack,Brian, Det	-	0	0	0	0	0	-	0	0	0	0	0	0	0	0	0	11	13.0	1	0	0	0	1.000	0	0	0	0	-
Schmidt,Jason, SF	.066	61	4	0	0	15	.095	399	38	6	0	2	14	18	190	63	29	207.2	13	14	2	1	.931	17	0	0	0	.00
Schoeneweis,S, Ana-CWS	-	0	0	0	0	0	.200	5	1	0	0	0	1	2	2	0	59	64.1	3	7	2	1	.833	3	1	0	0	.33
Seanez,Rudy, Bos	-	0	0	0	0	0	.000	4	0	0	0	0	0	0	1	4	9	8.2	1	1	0	0	1.000	0	0	0	0	-
Seay,Bobby, TB	-	0	0	0	0	0	-	0	0	0	0	0	0	0	0	0	12	9.0	0	1	0	0	1.000	1	0	0	0	.00
Sele,Aaron, Ana	.333	3	1	0	0	0	.167	24	4	1	0	0	1	1	4	4	25	121.2	6	14	1	0	.952	7	6	0	0	.86
Seo,Jae, NYM	.098	51	5	0	0	4	.098	51	5	1	0	0	0	3	19	4	32	188.1	11	35	1	0	.979	11	7	0	1	.64
Serafini,Dan, Cin	.000	6	0	0	0	1	.070	43	3	0	0	0	2	3	19	5	10	30.0	1	4	1	0	.833	1	1	1	0	1.00
Service,Scott, Ari-Tor	-	0	0	0	0	0	.063	16	1	0	0	0	1	0	9	0	33	34.1	3	2	0	0	1.000	5	0	0	0	.00
Sheets,Ben, Mil	.076	66	5	0	2	5	.080	176	14	1	0	0	6	9	103	11	34	220.2	22	19	2	0	.953	18	4	0	1	.22
Shields,Scot, Ana	-	0	0	0	0	0	-	0	0	0	0	0	0	0	0	0	44	148.1	18	26	1	0	.978	17	8	2	1	.47
Shiell,Jason, Bos	-	0	0	0	0	0	-	0	0	0	0	0	0	0	0	0	17	23.1	1	2	1	0	.750	2	0	0	0	.00
Shouse,Brian, Tex	-	0	0	0	0	0	-	0	0	0	0	0	0	0	0	0	62	61.0	6	18	0	1	1.000	1	0	0	0	.00
Shuey,Paul, LA	.000	2	0	0	0	0	.143	7	1	0	0	0	0	0	3	0	62	69.0	11	12	0	0	1.000	10	8	0	0	.80
Silva,Carlos, Phi	.222	9	2	0	1	1	.182	11	2	1	0	0	1	1	3	1	62	87.1	2	19	1	2	.955	5	1	0	0	.20
Simontacchi,J, StL	.132	38	5	0	0	0	.193	88	17	1	0	0	2	2	29	4	46	126.1	13	15	2	1	.933	1	1	1	0	1.00
Smith,Dan, Mon	.000	2	0	0	0	0	.069	29	2	0	0	0	1	3	18	3	32	37.2	1	1	0	0	1.000	3	3	0	0	1.00
Smoltz,John, Atl	.000	1	0	0	0	0	.172	737	127	20	1	5	51	70	282	92	61	63.1	4	6	0	1	1.000	2	1	0	0	.50
Snyder,Kyle, KC	.000	2	0	0	0	0	.000	2	0	0	0	0	0	0	1	0	15	85.1	10	13	0	2	1.000	10	2	0	0	.20
Soriano,Rafael, Sea	-	0	0	0	0	0	.000	4	0	0	0	0	0	0	0	0	40	53.0	2	4	0	0	1.000	5	1	0	0	.20
Sosa,Jorge, TB	-	0	0	0	0	0	-	0	0	0	0	0	0	0	0	0	29	128.2	4	9	0	0	1.000	9	4	0	0	.44
Sparks,Steve, Det-Oak	-	0	0	0	0	0	.100	10	1	1	0	0	2	1	3	1	51	107.0	8	16	0	6	1.000	7	3	0	0	.43
Speier,Justin, Col	.000	1	0	0	0	0	.188	16	3	0	0	0	0	0	7	0	72	73.1	4	5	0	0	1.000	8	3	0	0	.38
Spooneybarger,T, Fla	.000	3	0	0	0	0	.000	4	0	0	0	0	0	0	0	0	33	42.0	6	5	0	0	1.000	6	1	0	0	.17
Springer,Russ, StL	.000	1	0	0	0	1	.077	26	2	0	0	0	0	0	16	0	17	17.1	3	3	0	1	1.000	0	0	0	0	-
Spurling,Chris, Det	-	0	0	0	0	0	-	0	0	0	0	0	0	0	0	0	66	77.0	1	7	0	0	1.000	12	0	0	0	.00
Standridge,J, TB	-	0	0	0	0	0	-	0	0	0	0	0	0	1	0	0	8	35.1	2	2	0	0	1.000	3	2	0	0	.67
Stanford,Jason, Cle	-	0	0	0	0	0	-	0	0	0	0	0	0	0	0	0	13	50.0	3	1	0	1	1.000	5	0	0	0	.00
Stanton,Mike, NYM	.000	1	0	0	0	0	.412	17	7	1	0	0	2	1	2	1	50	45.1	2	8	3	0	.769	2	0	0	0	.00
Stark,Denny, Col	.000	22	0	0	4	1	.111	63	7	3	0	1	8	4	25	4	17	78.1	5	9	0	0	1.000	5	1	0	0	.20
Stephenson,G, StL	.205	44	9	0	2	7	.100	180	18	2	0	0	7	9	71	31	32	174.1	7	20	0	2	1.000	13	4	0	0	.31
Stewart,Josh, CWS	-	0	0	0	0	0	-	0	0	0	0	0	0	0	0	0	5	25.2	1	7	1	0	.889	2	0	0	0	.00
Stewart,Scott, Mon	.000	2	0	0	0	0	.000	4	0	0	0	0	0	0	3	0	51	43.0	0	7	0	0	1.000	3	2	0	0	.67
Stone,Ricky, Hou	.000	3	0	0	0	0	.000	7	0	0	0	0	0	0	3	1	65	83.0	9	8	1	0	.944	8	2	0	0	.25
Strange,Pat, NYM	.000	1	0	0	0	0	.000	1	0	0	0	0	0	0	0	0	6	9.0	2	0	0	0	1.000	0	0	0	0	-
Strickland,S, NYM	.000	1	0	0	0	1	.000	6	0	0	0	0	0	0	4	1	19	20.0	2	2	0	0	1.000	4	0	0	0	.00
Sturtze,Tanyon, Tor	-	0	0	0	0	0	.077	13	1	0	0	0	0	4	0	2	40	89.1	6	14	0	1	1.000	12	3	0	0	.25
Sullivan,Scott, Cin-CWS	-	0	0	0	0	0	.083	48	4	0	0	0	1	0	28	3	65	64.0	3	6	1	0	.900	5	0	0	0	.00

Pitchers Hitting, Fielding and Holding Runners

Pitcher	2003 Hitting						Career Hitting											2003 Fielding and Holding Runners											
	Avg	AB	H	HR	RBI	SH	Avg	AB	H	2B	3B	HR	RBI	BB	SO	SH	G	Inn	PO	A	E	DP	Pct	SBA	CS	PCS	PPO	CS%
Suppan,Jeff, Pit-Bos	.286	42	12	0	2	10	.263	80	21	1	0	0	4	3	22	14	32	204.0	18	30	1	1	.980	13	4	1	0	.31
Sweeney,Brian, Sea	-	0	0	0	0	0	-	0	0	0	0	0	0	0	0	0	4	7.1	3	0	0	0	1.000	0	0	0	0	-
Switzer,Jon, TB	-	0	0	0	0	0	-	0	0	0	0	0	0	0	0	0	5	9.2	0	0	0	0	-	0	0	0	0	-
Tallet,Brian, Cle	.000	2	0	0	0	0	.000	2	0	0	0	0	0	0	1	0	5	19.0	0	5	1	0	.833	4	1	0	0	.25
Tam,Jeff, Tor	1.000	1	1	0	1	0	.500	2	1	1	0	0	1	0	0	0	44	44.2	3	8	1	3	.917	3	0	0	0	.00
Tankersley,D, SD	-	0	0	0	0	1	.308	13	4	1	0	1	1	0	2	1	1	0.0	0	0	0	0	-	1	0	0	0	.00
Tavarez,Julian, Pit	.000	4	0	0	0	0	.111	135	15	0	0	0	8	6	57	20	64	84.0	6	20	0	3	1.000	0	0	0	0	-
Taylor,Aaron, Sea	-	0	0	0	0	0	-	0	0	0	0	0	0	0	0	0	10	14.2	0	2	0	0	1.000	0	0	0	0	-
Tejera,Michael, Fla	.071	14	1	0	0	1	.157	51	8	0	0	1	5	1	6	3	50	80.0	2	19	1	2	.955	7	2	1	0	.29
Telemaco,A, Phi	.286	14	4	0	0	1	.125	112	14	4	1	0	3	6	50	8	8	45.1	7	5	0	0	1.000	2	1	0	0	.50
Thomas,Brad, Min	-	0	0	0	0	0	-	0	0	0	0	0	0	0	0	0	3	4.2	1	1	0	0	1.000	1	0	0	1	1.00
Thomson,John, Tex	.000	1	0	0	0	0	.188	197	37	1	1	0	12	10	87	27	35	217.0	17	36	2	2	.964	17	4	0	0	.24
Thurman,Corey, Tor	-	0	0	0	0	0	.000	1	0	0	0	0	0	0	0	1	6	15.1	0	0	0	0	-	0	0	0	0	-
Timlin,Mike, Bos	-	0	0	0	0	0	.000	7	0	0	0	0	0	0	0	4	0	72	83.2	8	14	2	0	.917	6	2	0	0	.33
Tolar,Kevin, Bos	-	0	0	0	0	0	-	0	0	0	0	0	0	0	0	0	6	4.0	0	1	0	0	1.000	0	0	0	0	-
Tollberg,Brian, SD	.000	2	0	0	0	1	.151	93	14	1	0	0	2	4	33	13	3	10.1	4	2	0	0	1.000	1	0	0	0	.00
Tomko,Brett, StL	.286	63	18	0	9	11	.188	277	52	7	0	0	23	13	95	38	33	202.2	18	30	0	0	1.000	9	5	1	0	.56
Torres,Salomon, Pit	.063	32	2	0	1	6	.121	91	11	0	0	1	0	2	40	12	41	121.0	11	19	0	1	1.000	6	3	1	0	.50
Towers,Josh, Tor	.000	1	0	0	0	0	.000	3	0	0	0	0	0	0	0	0	14	64.1	9	10	1	0	.950	6	3	1	0	.50
Traber,Billy, Cle	.000	4	0	0	0	0	.000	4	0	0	0	0	0	0	0	2	0	33	111.2	7	10	0	2	1.000	13	2	1	0	.15
Trachsel,Steve, NYM	.190	58	11	0	4	11	.167	515	86	15	1	2	33	21	159	72	33	204.2	16	30	2	2	.958	25	8	2	3	.32
Tsao,Chin-hui, Col	.154	13	2	0	0	2	.154	13	2	1	0	0	0	1	9	2	9	43.1	3	8	0	2	1.000	2	0	0	0	.00
Tucker,T.J., Mon	.263	19	5	0	0	1	.375	24	9	1	0	0	0	0	6	1	45	80.0	9	13	1	0	.957	4	1	0	0	.25
Turnbow,D, Ana	-	0	0	0	0	0	-	0	0	0	0	0	0	0	0	0	11	15.1	3	1	0	1	1.000	0	0	0	0	-
Urbina,Ugueth, Tex-Fla	-	0	0	0	0	1	.094	53	5	0	0	1	3	2	32	0	72	77.0	3	4	0	0	1.000	14	2	0	0	.14
Valdes,Ismael, Tex	.000	4	0	0	0	2	.120	334	40	5	0	1	12	10	107	55	22	115.0	4	21	4	1	.862	13	3	0	1	.23
Valentine,Joe, Cin	-	0	0	0	0	0	-	0	0	0	0	0	0	0	0	0	2	2.0	0	0	0	0	-	3	0	0	0	.00
Valverde,Jose, Ari	1.000	1	1	0	0	0	1.000	1	1	1	0	0	0	0	0	0	54	50.1	3	1	0	0	1.000	6	0	0	0	.00
Van Poppel,T, Tex-Cin	.111	9	1	0	0	1	.150	40	6	1	0	0	1	1	16	6	16	48.1	3	3	1	0	.857	4	0	0	0	.00
Vance,Cory, Col	.286	7	2	0	0	2	.250	8	2	1	0	0	0	0	2	2	9	27.1	3	5	1	0	.889	2	0	0	0	.00
Vargas,Claudio, Mon	.000	30	0	0	0	4	.000	30	0	0	0	0	0	1	15	4	23	114.0	5	13	1	1	.947	14	5	0	0	.36
Vazquez,Javier, Mon	.154	65	10	0	6	12	.209	359	75	8	2	0	22	14	58	65	34	230.2	10	33	2	3	.956	5	2	1	0	.40
Venafro,Mike, TB	-	0	0	0	0	0	-	0	0	0	0	0	0	0	0	0	24	19.0	2	0	0	0	1.000	1	1	0	1	1.00
Veres,Dave, ChC	-	0	0	0	0	0	.259	27	7	1	0	0	1	1	12	3	31	32.2	1	2	0	0	1.000	1	1	0	0	1.00
Villafuerte,B, SD	.000	1	0	0	0	0	.000	1	0	0	0	0	0	0	1	0	31	40.2	6	7	0	0	1.000	3	0	0	0	.00
Villarreal,O, Ari	.000	3	0	0	0	0	.000	3	0	0	0	0	0	0	2	0	86	98.0	5	17	2	1	.917	5	2	0	0	.40
Villone,Ron, Hou	.167	42	7	1	2	1	.131	168	22	3	1	1	7	1	49	12	19	106.2	14	16	0	1	1.000	5	4	0	3	.80
Vizcaino,Luis, Mil	-	0	0	0	0	0	.000	2	0	0	0	0	0	0	0	2	0	75	62.0	5	6	0	0	1.000	4	1	0	0	.25
Vogelsong,Ryan, Pit	.167	6	1	0	0	0	.115	26	3	2	0	0	0	8	2	6	22.0	2	4	1	1	.857	1	0	0	0	.00
Voyles,Brad, KC	.000	1	0	0	0	0	.000	1	0	0	0	0	0	0	0	1	0	11	31.1	1	5	0	0	1.000	2	0	0	0	.00
Waechter,Doug, TB	-	0	0	0	0	0	-	0	0	0	0	0	0	0	0	0	6	35.1	2	1	0	0	1.000	2	0	0	0	.00
Wagner,Billy, Hou	.000	2	0	0	1	0	.067	15	1	0	0	0	1	1	8	0	78	86.0	5	11	0	0	1.000	6	2	1	0	.33
Wagner,Ryan, Cin	-	0	0	0	0	0	-	0	0	0	0	0	0	0	0	0	17	21.2	3	0	1	0	.750	1	0	0	0	.00
Wakefield,Tim, Bos	-	0	0	0	0	0	.122	82	10	2	0	1	3	2	29	12	35	202.1	16	20	1	0	.973	31	8	0	0	.26
Walker,Jamie, Det	-	0	0	0	0	0	-	0	0	0	0	0	0	0	0	0	78	65.0	4	10	1	1	.933	3	0	0	0	.00
Walker,Kevin, SD	-	0	0	0	0	0	.250	4	1	0	0	0	0	0	1	0	11	6.2	0	2	0	0	1.000	1	0	0	0	.00
Walker,Pete, Tor	-	0	0	0	0	0	.000	1	0	0	0	0	0	0	0	1	1	23	55.1	2	9	1	0	.917	5	2	0	0	.40
Walrond,Les, KC	-	0	0	0	0	0	-	0	0	0	0	0	0	0	0	0	7	8.0	1	2	0	0	1.000	1	1	0	0	1.00
Wasdin,John, Tor	-	0	0	0	0	0	.273	11	3	1	0	0	1	1	2	1	3	5.0	0	0	0	0	-	0	0	0	0	-
Washburn,J, Ana	.200	5	1	0	0	0	.316	19	6	0	0	0	2	2	7	4	32	207.1	6	17	1	1	.958	17	6	3	0	.35
Watson,Mark, Cin	-	0	0	0	0	0	-	0	0	0	0	0	0	0	0	0	2	2.0	0	0	0	0	-	0	0	0	0	-
Wayne,Justin, Fla	.000	2	0	0	0	0	.000	9	0	0	0	0	0	0	4	1	2	5.1	0	1	0	0	1.000	0	0	0	0	-
Weathers,David, NYM	.000	3	0	0	0	0	.104	135	14	0	0	2	4	7	83	16	77	87.2	14	4	2	2	.800	7	5	0	1	.71
Weaver,Jeff, NYY	-	0	0	0	0	0	.211	19	4	1	0	0	1	0	7	2	32	159.1	8	18	1	1	.963	9	5	0	0	.56
Webb,Brandon, Ari	.100	50	5	0	0	7	.100	50	5	1	0	0	2	2	21	7	29	180.2	14	31	3	0	.938	14	3	0	0	.21
Weber,Ben, Ana	-	0	0	0	0	0	-	0	0	0	0	0	0	0	0	0	62	80.1	5	17	2	0	.917	9	7	0	2	.78
Wellemeyer,T, ChC	.000	1	0	0	0	1	.000	1	0	0	0	0	0	0	1	0	15	27.2	1	2	0	0	1.000	1	1	0	0	1.00
Wells,David, NYY	.167	6	1	0	0	0	.125	56	7	1	0	0	0	0	13	0	31	213.0	7	32	0	2	1.000	21	5	3	1	.24
Wells,Kip, Pit	.191	68	13	1	5	4	.187	139	26	5	0	2	10	1	58	17	31	197.1	8	28	5	0	.878	16	2	1	0	.13
Wendell,Turk, Phi	.000	2	0	0	0	0	.073	41	3	0	0	0	5	19	1	56	64.0	3	11	0	1	1.000	4	1	1	0	.25
Westbrook,Jake, Cle	-	0	0	0	0	0	.000	1	0	0	0	0	0	0	1	1	34	133.0	6	23	1	3	.967	15	4	0	1	.27
Wheeler,Dan, NYM	.000	2	0	0	0	0	.000	2	0	0	0	0	0	0	0	0	35	51.0	1	4	0	0	1.000	7	4	2	0	.57
White,Gabe, Cin-NYY	.000	2	0	0	0	0	.105	38	4	0	0	1	3	1	26	10	46	46.2	1	5	1	1	.857	2	0	0	0	.00
White,Matt, Bos-Sea	-	0	0	0	0	0	-	0	0	0	0	0	0	0	0	0	6	5.2	0	1	0	0	1.000	1	1	1	0	1.00
White,Rick, CWS-Hou	-	0	0	0	0	0	.100	40	4	1	0	0	1	0	12	2	49	67.0	3	7	0	2	1.000	7	1	0	0	.14
Williams,J, SF	.108	37	4	0	1	6	.108	37	4	1	0	0	1	0	19	6	21	132.0	12	14	3	3	.897	13	4	1	1	.31
Williams,Mike, Pit-Phi	-	0	0	0	0	0	.157	108	17	2	0	0	7	3	33	24	68	63.0	8	14	2	1	.917	8	0	0	0	.00
Williams,Woody, StL	.243	70	17	1	7	9	.219	320	70	20	1	3	32	14	104	21	34	220.2	16	34	1	1	.980	12	4	0	1	.33
Williamson,S, Cin-Bos	-	0	0	0	0	0	.043	23	1	0	0	0	0	3	14	7	66	62.2	1	4	1	0	.833	6	0	0	0	.00
Willis,D, Fla	.241	58	14	1	4	2	.241	58	14	2	0	1	4	3	8	2	27	160.2	2	17	4	2	.826	6	3	0	3	.50
Wilson,Kris, KC	-	0	0	0	0	0	.333	3	1	0	0	0	0	0	0	0	29	72.2	12	8	4	0	.833	6	2	0	1	.33
Wilson,Paul, Cin	.115	52	6	0	1	4	.093	107	10	1	0	1	5	3	65	11	28	166.2	8	18	1	1	.963	10	4	0	0	.40
Witasick,Jay, SD	-	0	0	0	0	0	.081	37	3	0	0	0	3	1	21	2	46	45.2	0	7	1	0	.875	1	1	0	0	1.00
Wolf,Randy, Phi	.200	70	14	0	11	6	.184	261	48	13	0	1	21	17	86	40	33	201.1	14	23	3	0	.925	10	2	0	0	.20
Wood,Kerry, ChC	.164	61	10	2	6	8	.175	275	48	2	0	6	25	8	95	39	32	211.0	18	18	1	2	.973	13	8	0	3	.62

273

Pitchers Hitting, Fielding and Holding Runners

Pitcher	2003 Hitting						Career Hitting										2003 Fielding and Holding Runners											
	Avg	AB	H	HR	RBI	SH	Avg	AB	H	2B	3B	HR	RBI	BB	SO	SH	G	Inn	PO	A	E	DP	Pct	SBA	CS	PCS	PPO	CS%
Wood,Mike, Oak	-	0	0	0	0	0	-	0	0	0	0	0	0	0	0	0	7	13.2	0	4	1	0	.800	0	0	0	0	-
Woodard,Steve, Bos	-	0	0	0	0	0	.119	126	15	3	0	0	6	7	34	14	7	17.2	0	1	0	0	1.000	2	0	0	0	.00
Worrell,Tim, SF	.000	3	0	0	0	0	.101	79	8	1	0	0	4	4	42	10	76	78.1	6	8	1	0	.933	3	0	0	0	.00
Wright,Dan, CWS	.000	2	0	0	0	0	.000	6	0	0	0	0	0	0	2	0	20	86.1	12	8	1	0	.952	9	2	1	1	.22
Wright,Jamey, KC	-	0	0	0	0	0	.137	314	43	11	1	1	13	11	130	34	4	25.1	1	3	0	0	1.000	5	0	0	1	.00
Wright,Jaret, SD-Atl	.250	4	1	0	0	0	.278	18	5	1	0	0	1	0	8	3	50	56.1	7	9	0	3	1.000	7	0	0	0	.00
Wunsch,Kelly, CWS	-	0	0	0	0	0	-	0	0	0	0	0	0	0	0	0	43	36.0	4	2	1	0	.857	6	0	0	0	.00
Yan,Esteban, Tex-StL	1.000	1	1	0	0	0	1.000	2	2	0	0	1	1	0	0	1	54	66.2	9	3	2	0	.857	2	1	0	0	.50
Young,Jason, Col	.286	7	2	0	0	0	.286	7	2	1	0	0	0	1	1	0	8	21.1	0	3	0	0	1.000	3	1	0	0	.33
Zambrano,C, ChC	.240	75	18	2	6	4	.178	107	19	6	0	2	6	1	41	6	32	214.0	19	45	4	2	.941	8	5	0	1	.63
Zambrano,V, TB	.000	3	0	0	0	2	.000	4	0	0	0	0	0	0	3	2	34	188.1	10	16	2	2	.929	18	2	0	0	.11
Zerbe,Chad, SF	.000	5	0	0	0	1	.150	20	3	0	0	0	2	0	5	4	33	49.2	3	13	0	1	1.000	3	1	1	0	.33
Zito,Barry, Oak	.000	6	0	0	0	0	.000	15	0	0	0	0	0	0	8	2	35	232.2	12	29	1	1	.976	20	7	2	0	.35

Hitters Pitching

Player	2003 Pitching											Career Pitching										
	G	W	L	Sv	IP	H	R	ER	BB	SO	ERA	G	W	L	Sv	IP	H	R	ER	BB	SO	ERA
Finley,Steve, Ari	0	0	0	0	0.0	0	0	0	0	0	-	1	0	0	0	1.0	0	0	0	1	0	0.00
Franco,Matt, Atl	0	0	0	0	0.0	0	0	0	0	0	-	2	0	0	0	1.1	3	2	2	3	2	13.50
Gonzalez,Wiki, SD	1	0	0	0	1.0	0	0	0	1	0	0.00	1	0	0	0	1.0	0	0	0	1	0	0.00
Grace,Mark, Ari	0	0	0	0	0.0	0	0	0	0	0	-	1	0	0	0	1.0	1	1	1	0	0	9.00
Halter,Shane, Det	0	0	0	0	0.0	0	0	0	0	0	-	2	0	0	0	1.0	1	0	0	1	0	0.00
Harris,Lenny, ChC-Fla	0	0	0	0	0.0	0	0	0	0	0	-	1	0	0	0	1.0	0	0	0	0	1	0.00
Jimenez,D, CWS-Cin	0	0	0	0	0.0	0	0	0	0	0	-	1	0	0	0	1.1	0	0	0	0	0	0.00
Laker,Tim, Cle	0	0	0	0	0.0	0	0	0	0	0	-	1	0	0	0	1.0	1	0	0	1	1	0.00
Loretta,Mark, SD	0	0	0	0	0.0	0	0	0	0	0	-	1	0	0	0	1.0	1	0	0	1	2	0.00
Mabry,John, Sea	0	0	0	0	0.0	0	0	0	0	0	-	2	0	0	0	1.0	6	7	7	4	0	63.00
Mayne,Brent, KC	0	0	0	0	0.0	0	0	0	0	0	-	1	1	0	0	1.0	1	0	0	1	0	0.00
Menechino,F, Oak	0	0	0	0	0.0	0	0	0	0	0	-	1	0	0	0	1.0	6	4	4	0	0	36.00
Osik,Keith, Mil	0	0	0	0	0.0	0	0	0	0	0	-	2	0	0	0	2.0	7	9	9	2	2	40.50
Perez,Tomas, Phi	0	0	0	0	0.0	0	0	0	0	0	-	1	0	0	0	0.1	0	0	0	0	0	0.00
Relaford,Desi, KC	0	0	0	0	0.0	0	0	0	0	0	-	1	0	0	0	1.0	0	0	0	0	1	0.00
Zeile,Todd, NYY-Mon	0	0	0	0	0.0	0	0	0	0	0	-	1	0	0	0	1.0	1	0	0	0	1	0.00

The Manager's Record

Many years ago, in writing a *Baseball Abstract*, I was struck by the fact that the discussion of baseball managers proceeds in a vacuum of organized information. Take two baseball players—let's say Paul Konerko and Orlando Hudson. If you ask a baseball fan a series of comparative questions about those two, like "Which one has more power?", "Which one runs faster?", and "Which one has a better throwing arm?" he will know the answers. Even if the difference between the two is very slight, like the difference between Jay Gibbons' speed and Jason Giambi's or the difference between Jason Giambi and a potted plant, he will still know.

But if you ask parallel questions about two managers, he will not know the answers. Who is quicker to go to the bullpen: Mike Hargrove or Tony Pena? Who platoons more: Bobby Cox or Tony LaRussa? Who uses the Intentional Walk more often: Grady Little or Joe Torre? The average baseball fan most likely doesn't have a clue.

What do you put on the back of a manager's baseball card? Take one and flip it over. We have thousands of statistics about hitters, but we know how to summarize a player's abilities into a simple chart. Same thing with a pitcher's card—we condense his performance into 10 or 12 categories which tell you how much he pitched, how well he pitched, and a little bit about what type of pitcher he is. You look at the back of a manager's card, and it will tell you that he hit .247 in the Sally League in 1974. It doesn't have anything to do with how he manages.

What, specifically, does one manager do that another manager might not do? Does he pinch hit a lot, and if so, under what conditions? Does he like to platoon? Does he prefer to use his bench for speed, defense or something else? Does he like to push his starting pitcher, or get to the bullpen? These are simple, objective questions which have simple, objective answers.

I began addressing this subject about fifteen years ago—during which time, for various reasons, little progress has been made. Some things have been done. Old records have been compiled which will tell us how many relievers each manager used each season. A few people have begun printing scattered records about related issues, such as hit-and-run plays and attempted bunts by different managers.

But the discussion has not moved forward as much as it should have because that information has not yet been put into a form that the average fan can use. In a 1997 book about baseball managers, I wrote an article explaining how a manager's record could be constructed to make this kind of information generally accessible. At that time nobody picked up on the plan. But when I was meeting with John Dewan and Steve Moyer, outlining the contents of this book, the subject of creating a better record for managers came up again, and . . . here it is.

The record we have for you here contains eighteen columns of information, the first four of which require no explanation:

> Year
> Team
> League
> Games

The next two categories are LUp and PL%, which probably require some explanation. LUp is "Lineups Used". Bob Brenly this year (2003) used 160 different lineups; Bobby Cox used only 98. PL% is "Platoon Percentage". Of all the hitters in the starting lineup for Bob Brenly in 2003, 66% had the platoon edge on the opposition pitcher; for Bobby Cox, the same percentage was 52%. These two facts are related; obviously, Cox didn't juggle his lineup to get platoon advantages, while Brenly did; see, already we are learning something from doing this.

The next four categories list the number of substitutes used in five different categories:

> PH   Pinch Hitters Used
> PR   Pinch Runners Used
> DS   Defensive Substitutes
> Rel   Relief Pitchers Used
> LO   Long Outings

In 2002, managing the Mets, Bobby Valentine used 312 pinch hitters, while Luis Pujols, managing the Tigers or attempting to do so, used only 47. In 2003 the Tigers mantle was assumed by (Hah! They *wish* they had Mantle) Alan Trammell, who upped the Tigers to 125 pinch hitters (who incidentally hit .301 and had a .395 on-base percentage, believe it or not).

Art Howe in 2002 used 81 pinch runners, mostly Jason Christianson running for Matt Stairs or Jeremy Giambi, I would guess, but anyway, he always uses a bunch of pinch runners—54 last year with the Mets, which was the highest total in the National League. The 81 was surely nowhere near the major league record, but probably nobody knows what the major league record is, since nobody historically has paid attention to this stuff.

Of course, how you use your bench depends on who you have. Lou Piniella in 2002, managing the Mariners with Edgar Martinez, John Olerud, and Dan Wilson in the lineup, used 96 pinch runners. In 2003, managing the Devil Rays, he used only 29 pinch runners. Art Howe in 2001 used only 18 defensive substitutes. In 2003, managing the Mets, he used 67, and no doubt could have used another 800 if roster space had permitted. But who is on the team is not the ONLY thing that determines bench usage, either. Jeff Torborg, managing the Marlins in early 2003, used 115 relief pitchers in 38 games—more than three per game, one of the highest rates in the league. Jack McKeon, taking over the same team, used only 280 relievers in 124 games, a very low rate in modern baseball.

"LO" is a count of "Long Outings" by starting pitchers, a long outing being defined as most than 120 pitches. Frank Robinson's starters in Montreal had 23 Long Outings; Mike Scioscia's starters had only one, and Alan Trammell had only two (although they had a lot of outings that SEEMED like they lasted for a long time.) Jimy Williams had only one

Long Outing from his starting pitchers; Dusty Baker had 26. It is interesting to note how similar Baker's entire line is from 2003, managing the Cubs, to his line from 2002, managing the Giants. Very little changed for him, other than the uniform and that BB vs. SS thing.

Under the general heading of "tactics" we have four more categories:

SBA   Stolen Base Attempts
SacA   Sacrifice Attempts (Sac Bunt Attempts. . .can't call them both SBA)
IBB   Intentional Walks
PO   Pitch Outs

Bruce Bochy, managing the Padres to 91 wins in 1996, ordered 65 pitchouts. In 2003, managing them to 96 losses, he called only 6 pitchouts. Like Earl Weaver on the bunt (Weaver actually bunted quite a bit when he first came to the majors), he may simply have decided that it doesn't work—but on the other hand, it's a different team; the 1996 team allowed 135 stolen bases, which is a lot; this team allowed only 95, which is still quite a few. (Incidentally, did you know that the average American League team last year stole 91 bases and grounded into 128 double plays, whereas the average National League team stole only 81 bases and grounded into 129 double plays. I don't know when the last time was that the American League was more of a base-stealing league.)

Who were the most active major league managers in 2003, in terms of ordering a stolen base, a sac bunt, an intentional walk or a pitchout?

1. Jeff Torborg	109 in 38 games	2.87
2. Jack McKeon	284 in 124 games	2.29
3. Lloyd McClendon	356 in 162 games	2.20
4. Alan Trammell	318 in 162 games	1.96
Mike Scioscia	318 in 162 games	1.96

Who were the most in-active?

1. Ken Macha	144 in 162 games	0.89
2. Carlos Tosca	171 in 162 games	1.06
3. Buck Showalter	186 in 162 games	1.15
4. Jerry Manuel	219 in 162 games	1.35
5. Grady Little	224 in 162 games	1.38

Three obvious conclusions:

1. The NL is still more "active" in these regards than the AL,
2. Losing teams are generally more active at this stuff than winning teams,
3. Some of this data is not a revelation to those of you who read "Moneyball".

Which major league managers most preferred the bunt to the stolen base? Ratios given are bunt attempts to stolen base attempts:

1. Felipe Alou	97 to 90	1.08-1
2. Dave Miley	29 to 28	1.04-1
3. Art Howe	103 to 101	1.02-1
4. Bobby Cox	87 to 90	0.97-1
5. Tony LaRussa	110 to 114	0.96-1

The managers most preferring steal attempts to bunt attempts:

1. Carlos Tosca	13 to 62	0.21-1
2. Joe Torre	33 to 131	0.25-1
3. Grady Little	32 to 123	0.26-1
4. Lou Piniella	50 to 184	0.27-1
5. Jeff Torborg	21 to 74	0.28-1

The American League manager most favoring the bunt to the stolen base was Jerry Manuel (63 to 106).

The major league managers most fond of the Intentional Walk: 1. Art Howe (71 in 161 games), 2. Bobby Cox, 3. Bob Boone. Least fond of the Intentional Walk: 1. Bob Melvin (24 in 162 games), 2. Jerry Manuel, 3. Tony Pena.

Finally, of course, there is the manager's won-lost record, or the team's won-lost record, which we are going to credit to the manager. When I was designing this record, I was worrying quite a bit about not overloading the reader, creating more information than we could use. But as I see it on the page, I realize that we actually could (should) flesh it out a little more. But that's fine; it is easier to start with a sparse record and fill it in when we see what is needed than it would be to start with a crowded line and force ourselves to push something out later on. If you have thoughts about what should be added, you know where to find me, or if you don't, I'm not telling. Thanks for reading. It seems to me that this is pretty basic information about the game of baseball that any student of the game would want, and we probably should have gotten ourselves organized to make it available years ago.

Bill James
Lawrence, Kansas
October 10, 2003

Felipe Alou

Year	Team	Lg	G	LUp	PL%	PH	PR	DS	Rel	LO	SBA	SacA	IBB	PO	W	L	Pct
				LINEUPS		**SUBSTITUTIONS**					**TACTICS**				**RESULTS**		
1994	Expos	NL	114	72	.48	143	33	7	259	0	173	72	24	20	74	40	.649
1995	Expos	NL	144	116	.49	200	36	10	396	7	169	74	20	22	66	78	.458
1996	Expos	NL	162	113	.49	240	31	30	433	13	142	97	25	25	88	74	.543
1997	Expos	NL	162	138	.58	205	22	40	390	15	121	91	33	30	78	84	.481
1998	Expos	NL	162	133	.50	235	27	37	443	2	137	111	30	18	65	97	.401
1999	Expos	NL	162	143	.49	247	33	55	432	5	121	84	28	26	68	94	.420
2000	Expos	NL	162	120	.61	211	24	32	452	5	106	103	29	18	67	95	.414
2001	Expos	NL	53	40	.58	84	4	5	171	1	39	28	10	7	21	32	.396
2003	Giants	NL	161	150	.56	195	26	41	461	8	90	98	34	9	100	61	.621
	162-Game Average			130	.53	222	30	32	434	7	139	96	29	22	79	83	.489

Dusty Baker

Year	Team	Lg	G	LUp	PL%	PH	PR	DS	Rel	LO	SBA	SacA	IBB	PO	W	L	Pct
				LINEUPS		**SUBSTITUTIONS**					**TACTICS**				**RESULTS**		
1994	Giants	NL	115	76	.53	177	16	9	288	2	154	88	24	78	55	60	.478
1995	Giants	NL	144	96	.41	230	36	13	381	8	184	101	33	77	67	77	.465
1996	Giants	NL	162	129	.51	250	17	15	425	15	166	103	45	96	68	94	.420
1997	Giants	NL	162	114	.71	212	17	22	481	17	170	85	37	93	90	72	.556
1998	Giants	NL	163	130	.62	224	20	12	433	8	153	111	51	41	89	74	.546
1999	Giants	NL	162	120	.62	233	16	16	450	27	165	113	28	40	86	76	.531
2000	Giants	NL	162	82	.56	233	26	22	384	25	118	86	16	37	97	65	.599
2001	Giants	NL	162	122	.48	261	22	19	439	10	99	95	32	45	90	72	.556
2002	Giants	NL	161	143	.43	204	28	37	417	21	95	94	44	40	95	66	.590
2003	Cubs	NL	162	147	.49	239	20	42	420	26	104	100	36	24	88	74	.543
	162-Game Average			121	.54	236	23	22	429	17	147	102	36	59	86	76	.531

Bruce Bochy

Year	Team	Lg	G	LUp	PL%	PH	PR	DS	Rel	LO	SBA	SacA	IBB	PO	W	L	Pct
				LINEUPS		**SUBSTITUTIONS**					**TACTICS**				**RESULTS**		
1995	Padres	NL	144	96	.59	262	30	23	337	17	170	68	26	38	70	74	.486
1996	Padres	NL	162	114	.52	289	29	15	411	10	164	73	42	65	91	71	.562
1997	Padres	NL	162	111	.60	291	26	9	426	3	200	84	24	58	76	86	.469
1998	Padres	NL	162	110	.65	280	62	44	369	9	116	84	30	27	98	64	.605
1999	Padres	NL	162	137	.60	298	51	21	403	4	241	60	39	29	74	88	.457
2000	Padres	NL	162	134	.52	285	44	14	443	14	184	52	40	27	76	86	.469
2001	Padres	NL	162	116	.60	255	54	27	422	6	173	43	40	23	79	83	.488
2002	Padres	NL	162	151	.66	241	29	56	459	2	115	62	61	12	66	96	.407
2003	Padres	NL	162	155	.58	307	16	29	473	3	115	74	52	6	64	98	.395
	162-Game Average			126	.59	282	38	27	421	8	166	68	40	32	78	84	.482

Bob Boone

Year	Team	Lg	G	LUp	PL%	PH	PR	DS	Rel	LO	SBA	SacA	IBB	PO	W	L	Pct
				LINEUPS		**SUBSTITUTIONS**					**TACTICS**				**RESULTS**		
1995	Royals	AL	144	127	.70	222	44	17	308	15	173	98	24	32	70	74	.486
1996	Royals	AL	161	152	.69	172	53	28	322	26	280	93	21	38	75	86	.466
1997	Royals	AL	82	61	.64	80	34	7	174	10	126	43	20	29	36	46	.439
2001	Reds	NL	162	132	.53	313	46	19	461	1	157	88	27	25	66	96	.407
2002	Reds	NL	162	154	.52	294	35	37	462	3	168	121	63	20	78	84	.481
2003	Reds	NL	104	101	.50	177	23	14	303	1	86	73	40	4	46	58	.442
	162-Game Average			145	.60	250	47	24	404	11	197	103	39	29	74	88	.455

Larry Bowa

Year	Team	Lg	G	LUp	PL%	PH	PR	DS	Rel	LO	SBA	SacA	IBB	PO	W	L	Pct
				LINEUPS		**SUBSTITUTIONS**					**TACTICS**				**RESULTS**		
2001	Phillies	NL	162	81	.59	232	15	5	473	6	200	87	43	38	86	76	.531
2002	Phillies	NL	161	145	.61	261	15	31	450	9	147	97	54	14	80	81	.497
2003	Phillies	NL	162	155	.57	244	17	26	437	5	101	78	51	31	86	76	.531
	162-Game Average			127	.59	246	16	21	454	7	150	88	49	28	84	78	.520

Bob Brenly

Year	Team	Lg	G	LUp	PL%	PH	PR	DS	Rel	LO	SBA	SacA	IBB	PO	W	L	Pct
				LINEUPS		**SUBSTITUTIONS**					**TACTICS**				**RESULTS**		
2001	Diamondbacks	NL	162	123	.55	321	35	20	421	22	109	89	23	43	92	70	.568
2002	Diamondbacks	NL	162	153	.66	305	25	41	422	14	138	89	30	24	98	64	.605
2003	Diamondbacks	NL	162	160	.66	270	27	29	452	7	114	89	52	41	84	78	.519
	162-Game Average			145	.62	299	29	30	432	14	120	89	35	36	91	71	.564

Bobby Cox

Year	Team	Lg	G	LINEUPS		SUBSTITUTIONS					TACTICS				RESULTS		
				LUp	PL%	PH	PR	DS	Rel	LO	SBA	SacA	IBB	PO	W	L	Pct
1994	Braves	NL	114	64	.60	163	30	25	244	5	79	83	39	44	68	46	.596
1995	Braves	NL	144	59	.56	224	48	40	339	13	116	77	38	41	90	54	.625
1996	Braves	NL	162	162	.62	254	32	27	408	19	126	90	48	34	96	66	.593
1997	Braves	NL	162	87	.64	276	58	29	374	23	166	112	46	13	101	62	.620
1998	Braves	NL	162	80	.64	245	28	25	354	14	141	97	26	40	106	56	.654
1999	Braves	NL	162	76	.58	272	51	34	394	13	214	89	37	54	103	59	.636
2000	Braves	NL	162	103	.59	252	72	11	376	6	204	109	34	59	95	67	.586
2001	Braves	NL	162	113	.57	278	50	23	412	4	131	84	55	90	88	74	.543
2002	Braves	NL	160	138	.48	263	27	43	469	5	115	95	63	46	101	59	.631
2003	Braves	NL	162	98	.52	251	36	43	489	5	90	87	69	49	101	61	.623
	162-Game Average			102	.58	259	45	31	403	11	144	96	47	49	99	63	.611

Ron Gardenhire

Year	Team	Lg	G	LINEUPS		SUBSTITUTIONS					TACTICS				RESULTS		
				LUp	PL%	PH	PR	DS	Rel	LO	SBA	SacA	IBB	PO	W	L	Pct
2002	Twins	AL	161	111	.69	124	30	43	435	4	141	48	24	11	94	67	.584
2003	Twins	AL	162	131	.63	124	40	25	399	2	138	62	35	14	90	72	.556
	162-Game Average			121	.66	124	35	34	418	3	140	55	30	13	92	70	.570

Mike Hargrove

Year	Team	Lg	G	LINEUPS		SUBSTITUTIONS					TACTICS				RESULTS		
				LUp	PL%	PH	PR	DS	Rel	LO	SBA	SacA	IBB	PO	W	L	Pct
1994	Indians	AL	113	53	.67	79	18	31	222	3	179	43	22	40	66	47	.584
1995	Indians	AL	144	64	.66	101	34	21	335	12	185	40	12	22	100	44	.694
1996	Indians	AL	161	96	.56	115	20	25	382	14	210	58	31	41	99	62	.615
1997	Indians	AL	162	109	.58	86	17	14	429	14	177	60	30	37	86	75	.534
1998	Indians	AL	162	108	.62	88	21	32	423	19	203	53	39	47	89	73	.549
1999	Indians	AL	162	123	.66	99	25	22	466	15	197	82	36	28	97	65	.599
2000	Orioles	AL	162	107	.54	77	42	19	396	24	191	36	21	31	74	88	.457
2001	Orioles	AL	162	139	.53	82	27	20	392	3	186	57	17	71	63	98	.391
2002	Orioles	AL	162	131	.52	105	20	22	407	7	158	62	34	39	67	95	.414
2003	Orioles	AL	163	126	.52	73	30	14	425	11	125	66	43	16	71	91	.438
	162-Game Average			110	.58	94	26	23	404	13	189	58	30	39	85	77	.524

Art Howe

Year	Team	Lg	G	LINEUPS		SUBSTITUTIONS					TACTICS				RESULTS		
				LUp	PL%	PH	PR	DS	Rel	LO	SBA	SacA	IBB	PO	W	L	Pct
1996	Athletics	AL	162	124	.46	121	74	40	419	7	93	49	49	37	78	84	.481
1997	Athletics	AL	162	133	.61	198	62	38	481	8	107	66	40	43	65	97	.401
1998	Athletics	AL	162	129	.59	136	47	40	408	12	178	75	19	26	74	88	.457
1999	Athletics	AL	162	129	.62	144	62	56	406	5	107	53	32	43	87	75	.537
2000	Athletics	AL	161	119	.59	162	81	39	381	9	55	40	45	38	91	70	.565
2001	Athletics	AL	162	116	.60	131	30	18	416	4	97	40	41	43	102	60	.630
2002	Athletics	AL	162	110	.56	126	57	54	408	3	66	30	45	16	103	59	.636
2003	Mets	NL	161	153	.61	271	54	67	412	6	101	104	71	14	66	95	.410
	162-Game Average			127	.58	161	58	44	417	7	101	57	43	33	83	79	.515

Clint Hurdle

Year	Team	Lg	G	LINEUPS		SUBSTITUTIONS					TACTICS				RESULTS		
				LUp	PL%	PH	PR	DS	Rel	LO	SBA	SacA	IBB	PO	W	L	Pct
2002	Rockies	NL	140	129	.52	247	19	41	437	3	139	47	38	13	67	73	.479
2003	Rockies	NL	162	139	.47	287	13	31	500	0	100	81	51	16	74	88	.457
	162-Game Average			144	.49	286	17	39	503	2	128	69	48	16	76	86	.467

Ray Knight

Year	Team	Lg	G	LINEUPS		SUBSTITUTIONS					TACTICS				RESULTS		
				LUp	PL%	PH	PR	DS	Rel	LO	SBA	SacA	IBB	PO	W	L	Pct
1996	Reds	NL	162	147	.55	313	17	27	425	9	234	96	50	36	81	81	.500
1997	Reds	NL	99	88	.63	215	21	16	269	1	178	69	31	13	43	56	.434
2003	Reds	NL	1	1	.75	2	0	0	4	0	1	1	0	0	1	0	1.000
	162-Game Average			146	.58	328	23	27	432	6	255	103	50	30	77	85	.477

Tony LaRussa

Year	Team	Lg	G	LUp	PL%	PH	PR	DS	Rel	LO	SBA	SacA	IBB	PO	W	L	Pct
				LINEUPS		**SUBSTITUTIONS**					**TACTICS**				**RESULTS**		
1994	Athletics	AL	114	97	.62	89	28	14	308	5	130	31	23	32	51	63	.447
1995	Athletics	AL	144	120	.54	113	38	24	358	19	158	42	17	42	67	77	.465
1996	Cardinals	NL	162	120	.52	246	25	13	413	24	207	117	38	41	88	74	.543
1997	Cardinals	NL	162	146	.54	307	17	18	399	16	224	77	26	79	73	89	.451
1998	Cardinals	NL	162	146	.52	259	7	18	429	13	174	85	32	34	83	79	.512
1999	Cardinals	NL	161	138	.47	264	32	28	454	13	182	103	31	30	75	86	.466
2000	Cardinals	NL	162	137	.53	240	35	25	386	11	138	107	21	34	95	67	.586
2001	Cardinals	NL	162	117	.47	256	26	13	485	7	126	102	31	25	93	69	.574
2002	Cardinals	NL	162	141	.52	302	23	42	472	6	128	117	39	13	97	65	.599
2003	Cardinals	NL	162	153	.50	296	20	50	460	10	114	111	36	9	85	77	.525
	162-Game Average			137	.52	247	26	26	434	13	165	93	31	35	84	78	.520

Grady Little

Year	Team	Lg	G	LUp	PL%	PH	PR	DS	Rel	LO	SBA	SacA	IBB	PO	W	L	Pct
				LINEUPS		**SUBSTITUTIONS**					**TACTICS**				**RESULTS**		
2002	Red Sox	AL	162	130	.59	114	40	23	338	2	108	31	29	46	93	69	.574
2003	Red Sox	AL	162	127	.64	113	62	31	437	4	123	32	41	28	95	67	.586
	162-Game Average			129	.62	114	51	27	388	3	116	32	35	37	94	68	.580

Ken Macha

Year	Team	Lg	G	LUp	PL%	PH	PR	DS	Rel	LO	SBA	SacA	IBB	PO	W	L	Pct
				LINEUPS		**SUBSTITUTIONS**					**TACTICS**				**RESULTS**		
2003	Athletics	AL	162	119	.57	117	25	23	364	4	62	31	42	9	96	66	.593
	162-Game Average			119	.57	117	25	23	364	4	62	31	42	9	96	66	.593

Jerry Manuel

Year	Team	Lg	G	LUp	PL%	PH	PR	DS	Rel	LO	SBA	SacA	IBB	PO	W	L	Pct
				LINEUPS		**SUBSTITUTIONS**					**TACTICS**				**RESULTS**		
1998	White Sox	AL	162	110	.56	65	19	31	405	6	173	54	13	26	80	82	.494
1999	White Sox	AL	161	109	.58	79	35	39	409	9	160	69	22	22	75	86	.466
2000	White Sox	AL	162	84	.53	84	35	20	466	8	161	75	26	32	95	67	.586
2001	White Sox	AL	162	115	.53	104	34	50	406	5	182	95	30	41	83	79	.512
2002	White Sox	AL	162	108	.55	76	10	39	423	2	106	72	31	16	81	81	.500
2003	White Sox	AL	162	107	.57	128	32	67	361	5	106	64	30	20	86	76	.531
	162-Game Average			106	.55	89	28	41	412	6	148	72	25	26	83	79	.515

Lloyd McClendon

Year	Team	Lg	G	LUp	PL%	PH	PR	DS	Rel	LO	SBA	SacA	IBB	PO	W	L	Pct
				LINEUPS		**SUBSTITUTIONS**					**TACTICS**				**RESULTS**		
2001	Pirates	NL	162	131	.51	255	17	32	410	2	166	83	49	52	62	100	.383
2002	Pirates	NL	161	149	.45	248	32	65	458	0	135	102	93	65	72	89	.447
2003	Pirates	NL	162	156	.57	285	21	58	457	4	123	103	58	73	75	87	.463
	162-Game Average			146	.51	263	23	52	443	2	142	96	67	63	70	92	.431

Jack McKeon

Year	Team	Lg	G	LUp	PL%	PH	PR	DS	Rel	LO	SBA	SacA	IBB	PO	W	L	Pct
				LINEUPS		**SUBSTITUTIONS**					**TACTICS**				**RESULTS**		
1997	Reds	NL	63	50	.46	102	18	7	154	5	79	42	12	18	33	30	.524
1998	Reds	NL	162	132	.55	288	30	25	366	10	137	98	31	7	77	85	.475
1999	Reds	NL	163	95	.50	251	30	38	381	9	218	88	43	14	96	67	.589
2000	Reds	NL	163	117	.51	270	31	41	387	10	137	82	43	24	85	77	.525
2003	Marlins	NL	124	93	.43	160	23	13	280	7	150	89	28	17	75	49	.605
	162-Game Average			117	.50	257	32	30	376	10	173	96	38	19	88	74	.543

Bob Melvin

Year	Team	Lg	G	LUp	PL%	PH	PR	DS	Rel	LO	SBA	SacA	IBB	PO	W	L	Pct
				LINEUPS		**SUBSTITUTIONS**					**TACTICS**				**RESULTS**		
2003	Mariners	AL	162	112	.62	74	48	33	366	7	145	51	24	5	93	69	.574
	162-Game Average			112	.62	74	48	33	366	7	145	51	24	5	93	69	.574

Dave Miley

Year	Team	Lg	G	LINEUPS		SUBSTITUTIONS					TACTICS				RESULTS		
				LUp	PL%	PH	PR	DS	Rel	LO	SBA	SacA	IBB	PO	W	L	Pct
2003	Reds	NL	57	57	.61	94	9	17	168	0	27	29	21	7	22	35	.386
	162-Game Average			162	.61	267	26	48	477	0	77	82	60	20	63	99	.386

Tony Pena

Year	Team	Lg	G	LINEUPS		SUBSTITUTIONS					TACTICS				RESULTS		
				LUp	PL%	PH	PR	DS	Rel	LO	SBA	SacA	IBB	PO	W	L	Pct
2002	Royals	AL	126	113	.66	80	22	13	339	8	160	57	43	7	49	77	.389
2003	Royals	AL	162	132	.60	88	24	15	407	1	162	76	33	8	83	79	.512
	162-Game Average			138	.63	95	26	16	420	5	181	75	43	8	74	88	.458

Lou Piniella

Year	Team	Lg	G	LINEUPS		SUBSTITUTIONS					TACTICS				RESULTS		
				LUp	PL%	PH	PR	DS	Rel	LO	SBA	SacA	IBB	PO	W	L	Pct
1994	Mariners	AL	112	98	.49	113	24	6	252	4	69	54	28	37	49	63	.438
1995	Mariners	AL	145	98	.56	137	41	22	324	30	151	66	32	40	79	66	.545
1996	Mariners	AL	161	99	.55	190	28	14	403	15	129	65	40	40	85	76	.528
1997	Mariners	AL	162	84	.57	147	35	27	392	25	129	61	30	32	90	72	.556
1998	Mariners	AL	161	111	.53	99	38	43	368	32	154	58	18	20	76	85	.472
1999	Mariners	AL	162	130	.46	122	38	30	346	21	175	49	27	31	79	83	.488
2000	Mariners	AL	162	130	.50	109	43	52	383	1	178	73	32	22	91	71	.562
2001	Mariners	AL	162	115	.64	121	44	64	392	5	216	62	23	33	116	46	.716
2002	Mariners	AL	162	133	.64	89	96	50	343	8	195	66	34	25	93	69	.574
2003	Devil Rays	AL	162	129	.60	159	29	24	372	9	184	50	37	23	63	99	.389
	162-Game Average			118	.56	134	43	35	373	16	165	63	31	32	86	76	.529

Frank Robinson

Year	Team	Lg	G	LINEUPS		SUBSTITUTIONS					TACTICS				RESULTS		
				LUp	PL%	PH	PR	DS	Rel	LO	SBA	SacA	IBB	PO	W	L	Pct
2002	Expos	NL	162	154	.60	239	37	40	437	9	182	130	80	23	83	79	.512
2003	Expos	NL	162	157	.63	228	44	29	437	23	139	84	51	8	83	79	.512
	162-Game Average			156	.61	234	41	35	437	16	161	107	66	16	83	79	.512

Mike Scioscia

Year	Team	Lg	G	LINEUPS		SUBSTITUTIONS					TACTICS				RESULTS		
				LUp	PL%	PH	PR	DS	Rel	LO	SBA	SacA	IBB	PO	W	L	Pct
2000	Angels	AL	162	75	.62	110	41	4	441	6	145	63	32	40	82	80	.506
2001	Angels	AL	162	130	.62	118	30	8	384	5	168	66	33	50	75	87	.463
2002	Angels	AL	162	108	.64	142	46	26	400	5	168	60	24	29	99	63	.611
2003	Angels	AL	162	134	.64	114	47	40	375	1	190	65	38	25	77	85	.475
	162-Game Average			112	.63	121	41	20	400	4	168	64	32	36	83	79	.514

Buck Showalter

Year	Team	Lg	G	LINEUPS		SUBSTITUTIONS					TACTICS				RESULTS		
				LUp	PL%	PH	PR	DS	Rel	LO	SBA	SacA	IBB	PO	W	L	Pct
1994	Yankees	AL	113	79	.59	95	31	3	241	0	95	34	18	22	70	43	.619
1995	Yankees	AL	145	107	.68	124	30	20	302	37	80	27	15	29	79	65	.549
1998	Diamondbacks	NL	162	124	.62	252	17	15	368	7	111	68	18	13	65	97	.401
1999	Diamondbacks	NL	162	97	.63	220	20	17	382	25	176	75	34	15	100	62	.617
2000	Diamondbacks	NL	162	99	.60	250	32	11	390	18	141	89	36	10	85	77	.525
2003	Rangers	AL	162	142	.61	81	40	39	494	4	90	39	45	12	71	91	.438
	162-Game Average			116	.62	183	30	19	389	16	124	59	30	18	84	78	.519

Jeff Torborg

Year	Team	Lg	G	LINEUPS		SUBSTITUTIONS					TACTICS				RESULTS		
				LUp	PL%	PH	PR	DS	Rel	LO	SBA	SacA	IBB	PO	W	L	Pct
2001	Expos	NL	109	73	.61	167	12	3	320	5	113	52	21	13	47	62	.431
2002	Marlins	NL	162	156	.44	257	27	31	461	13	250	87	46	20	79	83	.488
2003	Marlins	NL	38	35	.52	68	6	4	115	2	74	21	12	2	16	22	.421
	162-Game Average			138	.51	258	24	20	470	10	229	84	41	18	74	88	.460

Joe Torre

Year Team	Lg	G	LINEUPS LUp	PL%	SUBSTITUTIONS PH	PR	DS	Rel	LO	TACTICS SBA	SacA	IBB	PO	RESULTS W	L	Pct
1994 Cardinals	NL	115	79	.68	192	9	0	330	6	122	57	13	33	53	61	.465
1995 Cardinals	NL	47	36	.51	99	6	4	146	1	42	26	11	14	20	27	.426
1996 Yankees	AL	162	131	.57	92	62	55	411	22	142	53	27	19	92	70	.568
1997 Yankees	AL	162	118	.61	75	70	23	368	19	157	54	29	14	96	66	.593
1998 Yankees	AL	162	96	.62	94	36	28	334	27	216	44	18	9	114	48	.704
1999 Yankees	AL	162	76	.63	103	57	10	276	26	129	31	15	12	98	64	.605
2000 Yankees	AL	161	112	.63	86	49	27	382	27	147	22	16	8	87	74	.540
2001 Yankees	AL	161	94	.56	76	33	14	362	10	214	44	22	21	95	65	.594
2002 Yankees	AL	161	127	.62	84	48	31	334	10	138	33	44	17	103	58	.640
2003 Yankees	AL	163	119	.65	101	39	18	367	13	131	33	36	33	101	61	.623
162-Game Average			110	.61	111	46	23	368	18	160	44	26	20	96	66	.591

Carlos Tosca

Year Team	Lg	G	LINEUPS LUp	PL%	SUBSTITUTIONS PH	PR	DS	Rel	LO	TACTICS SBA	SacA	IBB	PO	RESULTS W	L	Pct
2002 Blue Jays	AL	109	91	.49	56	20	22	303	1	54	12	35	20	58	51	.532
2003 Blue Jays	AL	162	129	.60	129	23	29	443	4	62	13	46	50	86	76	.531
162-Game Average			132	.56	111	26	30	446	3	69	15	48	42	86	76	.531

Jim Tracy

Year Team	Lg	G	LINEUPS LUp	PL%	SUBSTITUTIONS PH	PR	DS	Rel	LO	TACTICS SBA	SacA	IBB	PO	RESULTS W	L	Pct
2001 Dodgers	NL	162	111	.50	264	34	20	409	8	131	81	25	10	86	76	.531
2002 Dodgers	NL	162	145	.52	281	34	35	423	3	133	96	45	18	92	70	.568
2003 Dodgers	NL	162	147	.64	242	18	63	438	6	116	102	35	10	85	77	.525
162-Game Average			134	.56	262	29	39	423	6	127	93	35	13	88	74	.541

Alan Trammell

Year Team	Lg	G	LINEUPS LUp	PL%	SUBSTITUTIONS PH	PR	DS	Rel	LO	TACTICS SBA	SacA	IBB	PO	RESULTS W	L	Pct
2003 Tigers	AL	162	135	.72	124	25	14	451	2	161	94	35	28	43	119	.265
162-Game Average			135	.72	124	25	14	451	2	161	94	35	28	43	119	.265

Eric Wedge

Year Team	Lg	G	LINEUPS LUp	PL%	SUBSTITUTIONS PH	PR	DS	Rel	LO	TACTICS SBA	SacA	IBB	PO	RESULTS W	L	Pct
2003 Indians	AL	162	148	.67	104	32	26	428	1	147	66	37	12	68	94	.420
162-Game Average			148	.67	104	32	26	428	1	147	66	37	12	68	94	.420

Jimy Williams

Year Team	Lg	G	LINEUPS LUp	PL%	SUBSTITUTIONS PH	PR	DS	Rel	LO	TACTICS SBA	SacA	IBB	PO	RESULTS W	L	Pct
1997 Red Sox	AL	162	97	.56	123	48	16	417	13	116	30	40	108	78	84	.481
1998 Red Sox	AL	162	95	.60	165	53	14	432	14	111	48	23	75	92	70	.568
1999 Red Sox	AL	162	111	.62	123	35	9	412	13	106	47	15	75	94	68	.580
2000 Red Sox	AL	162	140	.67	158	52	30	425	9	73	49	28	114	85	77	.525
2001 Red Sox	AL	118	93	.63	69	22	26	315	5	48	31	29	106	65	53	.551
2002 Astros	NL	162	143	.58	251	34	48	480	3	98	89	78	38	84	78	.519
2003 Astros	NL	162	116	.43	291	19	29	502	1	96	80	53	38	87	75	.537
162-Game Average			118	.58	175	39	26	443	9	96	56	40	82	87	75	.537

Ned Yost

Year Team	Lg	G	LINEUPS LUp	PL%	SUBSTITUTIONS PH	PR	DS	Rel	LO	TACTICS SBA	SacA	IBB	PO	RESULTS W	L	Pct
2003 Brewers	NL	162	127	.44	286	15	31	460	5	138	88	43	23	68	94	.420
162-Game Average			127	.44	286	15	31	460	5	138	88	43	23	68	94	.420

2003 American League Managers

Manager	G	LINEUPS		SUBSTITUTIONS					TACTICS				RESULTS		
		LUp	PL%	PH	PR	DS	Rel	LO	SBA	SacA	IBB	PO	W	L	Pct
Ron Gardenhire, Min	162	131	.63	124	40	25	399	2	138	62	35	14	90	72	.556
Mike Hargrove, Bal	163	126	.52	73	30	14	425	11	125	66	43	16	71	91	.438
Grady Little, Bos	162	127	.64	113	62	31	437	4	123	32	41	28	95	67	.586
Ken Macha, Oak	162	119	.57	117	25	23	364	4	62	31	42	9	96	66	.593
Jerry Manuel, CWS	162	107	.57	128	32	67	361	5	106	64	30	20	86	76	.531
Bob Melvin, Sea	162	112	.62	74	48	33	366	7	145	51	24	5	93	69	.574
Tony Pena, KC	162	132	.60	88	24	15	407	1	162	76	33	8	83	79	.512
Lou Piniella, TB	162	129	.60	159	29	24	372	9	184	50	37	23	63	99	.389
Mike Scioscia, Ana	162	134	.64	114	47	40	375	1	190	65	38	25	77	85	.475
Buck Showalter, Tex	162	142	.61	81	40	39	494	4	90	39	45	12	71	91	.438
Joe Torre, NYY	163	119	.65	101	39	18	367	13	131	33	36	33	101	61	.623
Carlos Tosca, Tor	162	129	.60	129	23	29	443	4	62	13	46	50	86	76	.531
Alan Trammell, Det	162	135	.72	124	25	14	451	2	161	94	35	28	43	119	.265
Eric Wedge, Cle	162	148	.67	104	32	26	428	1	147	66	37	12	68	94	.420

2003 National League Managers

Manager	G	LINEUPS		SUBSTITUTIONS					TACTICS				RESULTS		
		LUp	PL%	PH	PR	DS	Rel	LO	SBA	SacA	IBB	PO	W	L	Pct
Felipe Alou, SF	161	150	.56	195	26	41	461	8	90	98	34	9	100	61	.621
Dusty Baker, ChC	162	147	.49	239	20	42	420	26	104	100	36	24	88	74	.543
Bruce Bochy, SD	162	155	.58	307	16	29	473	3	115	74	52	6	64	98	.395
Bob Boone, Cin	104	101	.50	177	23	14	303	1	86	73	40	4	46	58	.442
Larry Bowa, Phi	162	155	.57	244	17	26	437	5	101	78	51	31	86	76	.531
Bob Brenly, Ari	162	160	.66	270	27	29	452	7	114	89	52	41	84	78	.519
Bobby Cox, Atl	162	98	.52	251	36	43	489	5	90	87	69	49	101	61	.623
Art Howe, NYM	161	153	.61	271	54	67	412	6	101	104	71	14	66	95	.410
Clint Hurdle, Col	162	139	.47	287	13	31	500	0	100	81	51	16	74	88	.457
Ray Knight, Cin	1	1	.75	2	0	0	4	0	1	1	0	0	1	0	1.000
Tony LaRussa, StL	162	153	.50	296	20	50	460	10	114	111	36	9	85	77	.525
Lloyd McClendon, Pit	162	156	.57	285	21	58	457	4	123	103	58	73	75	87	.463
Jack McKeon, Fla	124	93	.43	160	23	13	280	7	150	89	28	17	75	49	.605
Dave Miley, Cin	57	57	.61	94	9	17	168	0	27	29	21	7	22	35	.386
Frank Robinson, Mon	162	157	.63	228	44	29	437	23	139	84	51	8	83	79	.512
Jeff Torborg, Fla	38	35	.52	68	6	4	115	2	74	21	12	2	16	22	.421
Jim Tracy, LA	162	147	.64	242	18	63	438	6	116	102	35	10	85	77	.525
Jimy Williams, Hou	162	116	.43	291	19	29	502	1	96	80	53	38	87	75	.537
Ned Yost, Mil	162	127	.44	286	15	31	460	5	138	88	43	23	68	94	.420

2003 Park Indices

Park Indices are calculated in a way that neutralizes the effect of a team's makeup and isolates the effects of the park. This isolation is accomplished by comparing what both the team and its opponents accomplished at home, and comparing that to what the same team and its opponents accomplished on the road. To calculate the Park Index for Home Runs in Bank One Ballpark, take the total Home Runs of the Diamondbacks and their opponents at Bank One (73+79=152), and compare it to the total Home Runs of the Diamondbacks and their opponents in other games (69+65=134). We divide each of these totals by the At Bats in the equivalent situations (5129 and 4897) so that if there are more at bats in either situation, the index is not skewed. The result, (152/5129) / (134/4897) = 1.08, is multiplied by 100 to yield the familiar form, 108. In 2003, it was 8% easier to hit home runs in Bank One Ballpark than in other National League parks.

The Park Indices for Doubles, Triples, Walks, Strikeouts and Home Runs by Lefties and Righties are determined like Home Runs, above—relative to At Bats. Indices of At Bats, Runs, Hits, Errors, and Infield Fielding Errors (E-Infield) are calculated relative to Games. The three Batting Average Indices are calculated as-is, as these are already relative to At Bats.

Additionally, interleague games are not included in the underlying Park Index data, both because the interleague schedules are significantly imbalanced, and because the Designated Hitter rule, only used in the American League parks, would artificially skew AL parks towards appearing to be Hitters' Parks and all NL parks towards appearing to be Pitchers' Parks.

Anaheim Angels - Edison International Field Surface: Grass

| | 2003 Season | | | | | | | 2002-2003 | | | | | | |
| | Home Games | | | Away Games | | | | Home Games | | | Away Games | | | |
	Angels	Opp	Total	Angels	Opp	Total	Index	Angels	Opp	Total	Angels	Opp	Total	Index
G	73	73	146	71	71	142		145	145	290	143	143	286	
Avg	.268	.264	.266	.266	.269	.268	99	.273	.253	.263	.276	.257	.267	98
AB	2398	2565	4963	2451	2355	4806	100	4865	5054	9919	5054	4708	9762	100
R	320	312	632	323	367	690	89	678	596	1274	722	651	1373	92
H	643	677	1320	652	634	1286	100	1326	1280	2606	1397	1208	2605	99
2B	122	132	254	131	111	242	102	264	246	510	287	209	496	101
3B	12	8	20	14	17	31	62	29	12	41	23	29	52	78
HR	59	76	135	62	94	156	84	121	143	264	135	175	310	84
BB	203	224	427	224	222	446	93	401	458	859	434	451	885	96
SO	348	472	820	392	398	790	101	700	931	1631	756	832	1588	101
E	44	32	76	44	36	80	92	84	78	162	87	98	185	86
E-Infield	18	10	28	15	12	27	101	36	28	64	38	33	71	89
LHB-Avg	.281	.246	.262	.286	.272	.279	94	.280	.243	.262	.291	.254	.274	96
LHB-HR	28	36	64	34	46	80	75	56	66	122	69	80	149	79
RHB-Avg	.257	.282	.270	.250	.267	.258	105	.265	.262	.264	.263	.259	.261	101
RHB-HR	31	40	71	28	48	76	93	65	77	142	66	95	161	89

Arizona Diamondbacks - Bank One Ballpark Surface: Grass

| | 2003 Season | | | | | | | 2002-2003 | | | | | | |
| | Home Games | | | Away Games | | | | Home Games | | | Away Games | | | |
	D'Backs	Opp	Total	D'Backs	Opp	Total	Index	D'Backs	Opp	Total	D'Backs	Opp	Total	Index
G	75	75	150	72	72	144		147	147	294	144	144	288	
Avg	.273	.253	.263	.247	.244	.245	107	.279	.250	.264	.247	.246	.247	107
AB	2521	2608	5129	2514	2383	4897	101	4934	5157	10091	4999	4744	9743	101
R	365	349	714	264	280	544	126	780	662	1442	583	564	1147	123
H	689	659	1348	620	582	1202	108	1375	1291	2666	1237	1166	2403	109
2B	150	144	294	113	100	213	132	281	271	552	229	201	430	124
3B	27	15	42	16	7	23	174	52	37	89	30	15	45	191
HR	73	79	152	69	65	134	108	152	152	304	139	136	275	107
BB	276	241	517	217	239	456	108	607	436	1043	472	418	890	113
SO	448	605	1053	479	578	1057	95	880	1228	2108	965	1119	2084	98
E	44	41	85	52	44	96	85	87	86	173	89	103	192	88
E-Infield	18	20	38	25	21	46	79	43	41	84	39	50	89	92
LHB-Avg	.281	.288	.284	.256	.245	.251	113	.283	.277	.281	.258	.252	.256	110
LHB-HR	32	38	70	40	25	65	104	77	63	140	81	57	138	100
RHB-Avg	.265	.230	.244	.236	.244	.240	102	.273	.235	.250	.235	.241	.239	105
RHB-HR	41	41	82	29	40	69	113	75	89	164	58	79	137	113

Atlanta Braves - Turner Field Surface: Grass

| | 2003 Season | | | | | | | 2002-2003 | | | | | | |
| | Home Games | | | Away Games | | | | Home Games | | | Away Games | | | |
	Braves	Opp	Total	Braves	Opp	Total	Index	Braves	Opp	Total	Braves	Opp	Total	Index
G	75	75	150	72	72	144		147	147	294	143	143	286	
Avg	.286	.249	.267	.285	.270	.278	96	.274	.246	.260	.269	.257	.263	99
AB	2530	2586	5116	2631	2460	5091	96	4891	5066	9957	5127	4810	9937	97
R	392	340	732	437	347	784	90	713	597	1310	723	605	1328	96
H	723	643	1366	751	664	1415	93	1340	1246	2586	1379	1237	2616	96
2B	138	122	260	160	156	316	82	256	241	497	282	251	533	93
3B	15	11	26	15	10	25	103	28	23	51	24	26	50	102
HR	101	64	165	112	75	187	88	175	122	297	180	130	310	96
BB	254	264	518	236	242	478	108	497	500	997	486	510	996	100
SO	413	443	856	443	456	899	95	846	893	1739	928	925	1853	94
E	58	54	112	54	46	100	108	110	106	216	104	94	198	106
E-Infield	28	25	53	31	16	47	108	54	56	110	54	27	81	132
LHB-Avg	.285	.245	.263	.270	.251	.261	101	.279	.248	.262	.265	.244	.254	103
LHB-HR	23	19	42	21	26	47	87	47	35	82	33	43	76	107
RHB-Avg	.286	.251	.269	.292	.280	.287	94	.271	.245	.258	.271	.265	.268	96
RHB-HR	78	45	123	91	49	140	88	128	87	215	147	87	234	92

Baltimore Orioles - Oriole Park at Camden Yards Surface: Grass

| | 2003 Season | | | | | | | 2002-2003 | | | | | | |
| | Home Games | | | Away Games | | | | Home Games | | | Away Games | | | |
	Orioles	Opp	Total	Orioles	Opp	Total	Index	Orioles	Opp	Total	Orioles	Opp	Total	Index
G	72	72	144	73	73	146		144	144	288	145	145	290	
Avg	.276	.262	.269	.258	.287	.272	99	.261	.261	.261	.253	.283	.268	97
AB	2431	2523	4954	2566	2507	5073	99	4837	5066	9903	5049	4968	10017	100
R	325	330	655	332	380	712	93	617	661	1278	632	754	1386	93
H	671	662	1333	663	719	1382	98	1263	1323	2586	1277	1407	2684	97
2B	130	124	254	115	146	261	100	241	233	474	275	275	550	87
3B	6	8	14	13	17	30	48	16	13	29	25	36	61	48
HR	68	90	158	63	85	148	109	149	191	340	129	176	305	113
BB	199	236	435	189	223	412	108	406	477	883	384	465	849	105
SO	368	440	808	415	432	847	98	793	866	1659	847	880	1727	97
E	36	56	92	54	50	104	90	78	110	188	90	88	178	106
E-Infield	18	22	40	25	21	46	88	33	42	75	37	37	74	102
LHB-Avg	.267	.281	.275	.266	.272	.269	102	.260	.264	.263	.263	.276	.271	97
LHB-HR	23	45	68	22	44	66	103	53	92	145	42	93	135	106
RHB-Avg	.281	.245	.265	.254	.300	.275	96	.261	.258	.260	.248	.289	.266	98
RHB-HR	45	45	90	41	41	82	115	96	99	195	87	83	170	118

Boston Red Sox - Fenway Park Surface: Grass

| | 2003 Season | | | | | | | 2002-2003 | | | | | | |
| | Home Games | | | Away Games | | | | Home Games | | | Away Games | | | |
	Red Sox	Opp	Total	Red Sox	Opp	Total	Index	Red Sox	Opp	Total	Red Sox	Opp	Total	Index
G	72	72	144	72	72	144		144	144	288	144	144	288	
Avg	.308	.259	.284	.259	.263	.261	109	.294	.255	.274	.273	.250	.262	105
AB	2480	2530	5010	2587	2507	5094	98	4895	5008	9903	5221	4886	10107	98
R	445	343	788	365	362	727	108	810	655	1465	796	645	1441	102
H	765	656	1421	671	660	1331	107	1441	1277	2718	1426	1222	2648	103
2B	178	146	324	138	150	288	114	337	291	628	301	247	548	117
3B	17	17	34	9	20	29	119	31	23	54	23	36	59	93
HR	95	61	156	108	64	172	92	166	119	285	199	140	339	86
BB	288	191	479	230	241	471	103	536	364	900	479	443	922	100
SO	359	479	838	481	536	1017	84	759	1023	1782	901	1024	1925	94
E	49	44	93	48	35	83	112	102	98	200	86	82	168	119
E-Infield	25	24	49	19	16	35	140	50	41	91	35	35	70	130
LHB-Avg	.301	.258	.279	.251	.267	.259	108	.289	.245	.267	.262	.256	.259	103
LHB-HR	41	28	69	53	38	91	73	70	49	119	97	80	177	68
RHB-Avg	.317	.261	.288	.267	.260	.264	109	.299	.265	.282	.284	.244	.265	106
RHB-HR	54	33	87	55	26	81	115	96	70	166	102	60	162	105

Chicago Cubs - Wrigley Field Surface: Grass

| | 2003 Season | | | | | | | 2002-2003 | | | | | | |
| | Home Games | | | Away Games | | | | Home Games | | | Away Games | | | |
	Cubs	Opp	Total	Cubs	Opp	Total	Index	Cubs	Opp	Total	Cubs	Opp	Total	Index
G	72	72	144	72	72	144		147	147	294	147	147	294	
Avg	.255	.236	.245	.260	.239	.250	98	.246	.239	.242	.256	.253	.255	95
AB	2392	2464	4856	2509	2358	4867	100	4859	5032	9891	5127	4831	9958	99
R	306	305	611	343	299	642	95	611	647	1258	679	657	1336	94
H	610	581	1191	653	564	1217	98	1193	1204	2397	1315	1223	2538	94
2B	126	106	232	139	113	252	92	233	231	464	268	243	511	91
3B	8	9	17	11	9	20	85	21	19	40	27	28	55	73
HR	79	60	139	81	63	144	97	167	153	320	171	121	292	110
BB	241	283	524	207	254	461	114	527	548	1075	462	543	1005	108
SO	560	664	1224	493	601	1094	112	1140	1344	2484	1084	1150	2234	112
E	51	52	103	49	51	100	103	109	94	203	98	102	200	102
E-Infield	22	24	46	20	24	44	105	44	46	90	45	52	97	93
LHB-Avg	.241	.238	.239	.261	.239	.250	96	.237	.243	.240	.255	.260	.258	93
LHB-HR	14	23	37	23	28	51	75	50	58	108	66	58	124	89
RHB-Avg	.261	.234	.248	.260	.239	.250	99	.251	.237	.244	.257	.248	.253	96
RHB-HR	65	37	102	58	35	93	108	117	95	212	105	63	168	126

Chicago White Sox - U.S. Cellular Field Surface: Grass

| | 2003 Season | | | | | | | 2002-2003 | | | | | | |
| | Home Games | | | Away Games | | | | Home Games | | | Away Games | | | |
	White Sox	Opp	Total	White Sox	Opp	Total	Index	White Sox	Opp	Total	White Sox	Opp	Total	Index
G	72	72	144	72	72	144		144	144	288	144	144	288	
Avg	.266	.249	.257	.264	.258	.261	98	.275	.252	.263	.263	.261	.262	100
AB	2358	2448	4806	2535	2341	4876	99	4750	4895	9645	5054	4734	9788	99
R	363	297	660	346	344	690	96	790	628	1418	688	712	1400	101
H	628	609	1237	670	605	1275	97	1307	1232	2539	1331	1236	2567	99
2B	132	122	254	143	126	269	96	252	249	501	283	250	533	95
3B	9	12	21	10	11	21	101	19	19	38	25	20	45	86
HR	115	79	194	82	65	147	134	235	158	393	156	150	306	130
BB	219	217	436	228	247	475	93	456	458	914	461	476	937	99
SO	373	511	884	425	429	854	105	760	926	1686	860	845	1705	100
E	30	46	76	52	38	90	84	62	95	157	105	87	192	82
E-Infield	11	17	28	22	14	36	78	28	38	66	44	28	72	92
LHB-Avg	.256	.256	.256	.259	.275	.269	95	.277	.261	.267	.245	.281	.267	100
LHB-HR	25	40	65	22	30	52	126	55	86	141	44	73	117	124
RHB-Avg	.270	.241	.258	.266	.242	.257	101	.274	.243	.261	.271	.241	.259	101
RHB-HR	90	39	129	60	35	95	138	180	72	252	112	77	189	134

Cincinnati Reds - Great American Ballpark Surface: Grass

| | 2003 Season | | | | | | | 2002 (Cinergy Field) | | | | | | |
| | Home Games | | | Away Games | | | | Home Games | | | Away Games | | | |
	Reds	Opp	Total	Reds	Opp	Total	Index	Reds	Opp	Total	Reds	Opp	Total	Index
G	75	75	150	75	75	150		75	75	150	75	75	150	
Avg	.248	.271	.260	.244	.289	.266	98	.267	.279	.273	.244	.259	.252	109
AB	2505	2675	5180	2618	2585	5203	100	2487	2681	5168	2586	2505	5091	102
R	322	405	727	330	425	755	96	372	383	755	302	321	623	121
H	622	725	1347	638	746	1384	97	664	747	1411	632	649	1281	110
2B	117	154	271	107	159	266	102	165	148	313	114	127	241	128
3B	5	6	11	16	27	43	26	3	11	14	18	13	31	44
HR	88	110	198	79	89	168	118	83	103	186	79	57	136	135
BB	241	255	496	243	283	526	95	316	241	557	236	271	507	108
SO	586	449	1035	646	398	1044	100	522	486	1008	588	430	1018	98
E	72	52	124	60	50	110	113	49	43	92	64	50	114	81
E-Infield	30	25	55	17	19	36	153	20	14	34	28	18	46	74
LHB-Avg	.255	.264	.260	.253	.283	.268	97	.277	.283	.280	.263	.266	.264	106
LHB-HR	39	39	78	34	38	72	113	36	44	80	34	31	65	125
RHB-Avg	.244	.275	.260	.238	.292	.265	98	.260	.275	.268	.230	.254	.242	111
RHB-HR	49	71	120	45	51	96	123	47	59	106	45	26	71	144

Cleveland Indians - Jacobs Field Surface: Grass

| | 2003 Season | | | | | | | 2002-2003 | | | | | | |
| | Home Games | | | Away Games | | | | Home Games | | | Away Games | | | |
	Indians	Opp	Total	Indians	Opp	Total	Index	Indians	Opp	Total	Indians	Opp	Total	Index
G	72	72	144	72	72	144		144	144	288	144	144	288	
Avg	.251	.253	.252	.260	.274	.267	95	.249	.264	.257	.258	.275	.266	96
AB	2420	2526	4946	2519	2410	4929	100	4792	5059	9851	5009	4807	9816	100
R	297	315	612	331	374	705	87	634	703	1337	672	749	1421	94
H	607	640	1247	654	660	1314	95	1195	1334	2529	1293	1321	2614	97
2B	132	125	257	133	135	268	96	252	276	528	247	270	517	102
3B	7	11	18	16	12	28	64	15	24	39	30	37	67	58
HR	63	66	129	86	94	180	71	148	137	285	179	154	333	85
BB	204	223	427	193	224	417	102	413	510	923	457	480	937	98
SO	457	461	918	474	370	844	108	892	994	1886	927	768	1695	111
E	50	60	110	61	38	99	111	93	125	218	116	70	186	117
E-Infield	30	26	56	24	17	41	137	50	60	110	45	34	79	139
LHB-Avg	.251	.248	.249	.263	.284	.272	92	.251	.269	.259	.258	.280	.268	97
LHB-HR	41	24	65	42	34	76	87	99	59	158	105	59	164	96
RHB-Avg	.251	.257	.254	.256	.268	.262	97	.248	.260	.255	.259	.271	.265	96
RHB-HR	22	42	64	44	60	104	60	49	78	127	74	95	169	75

Colorado Rockies - Coors Field Surface: Grass

	2003 Season							2002-2003						
	Home Games			Away Games				Home Games			Away Games			
	Rockies	Opp	Total	Rockies	Opp	Total	Index	Rockies	Opp	Total	Rockies	Opp	Total	Index
G	72	72	144	75	75	150		144	144	288	147	147	294	
Avg	.294	.288	.291	.236	.287	.261	112	.302	.283	.292	.236	.278	.257	114
AB	2450	2600	5050	2558	2485	5043	104	4892	5143	10035	5005	4890	9895	104
R	458	397	855	305	405	710	125	893	816	1709	564	766	1330	131
H	721	749	1470	603	712	1315	116	1477	1458	2935	1180	1361	2541	118
2B	169	142	311	137	150	287	108	310	284	594	245	271	516	114
3B	23	21	44	5	14	19	231	49	38	87	17	30	47	183
HR	98	104	202	74	77	151	134	181	224	405	125	157	282	142
BB	291	218	509	277	288	565	90	523	461	984	481	555	1036	94
SO	439	416	855	608	360	968	88	842	840	1682	1149	741	1890	88
E	48	54	102	59	53	112	95	97	105	202	101	92	193	107
E-Infield	23	26	49	30	26	56	91	47	46	93	51	42	93	102
LHB-Avg	.336	.301	.316	.247	.312	.284	111	.334	.294	.312	.257	.300	.279	112
LHB-HR	30	44	74	25	27	52	150	71	92	163	52	57	109	148
RHB-Avg	.276	.279	.278	.230	.267	.247	113	.285	.277	.281	.224	.264	.243	115
RHB-HR	68	60	128	49	50	99	125	110	132	242	73	100	173	137

Detroit Tigers - Comerica Park Surface: Grass

	2003 Season							2002-2003						
	Home Games			Away Games				Home Games			Away Games			
	Tigers	Opp	Total	Tigers	Opp	Total	Index	Tigers	Opp	Total	Tigers	Opp	Total	Index
G	72	72	144	72	72	144		143	143	286	144	144	288	
Avg	.237	.271	.255	.239	.302	.270	94	.242	.275	.259	.245	.297	.271	96
AB	2409	2612	5021	2448	2422	4870	103	4756	5162	9918	4913	4858	9771	102
R	252	391	643	275	441	716	90	501	747	1248	554	877	1431	88
H	571	709	1280	584	731	1315	97	1150	1422	2572	1205	1444	2649	98
2B	84	123	207	96	155	251	80	176	267	443	249	317	566	77
3B	18	26	44	14	20	34	126	44	57	101	20	41	61	163
HR	62	87	149	74	90	164	88	119	142	261	130	187	317	81
BB	178	256	434	219	243	462	91	340	448	788	386	466	852	91
SO	464	370	834	510	313	823	98	860	733	1593	1013	665	1678	94
E	54	57	111	65	36	101	110	117	90	207	136	71	207	101
E-Infield	29	25	54	26	15	41	132	53	38	91	58	32	90	102
LHB-Avg	.257	.294	.273	.246	.314	.275	99	.262	.287	.273	.256	.306	.279	98
LHB-HR	33	45	78	45	44	89	89	76	79	155	75	87	162	96
RHB-Avg	.209	.255	.237	.228	.292	.264	90	.217	.267	.246	.233	.290	.264	93
RHB-HR	29	42	71	29	46	75	88	43	63	106	55	100	155	67

Florida Marlins - Pro Player Stadium Surface: Grass

	2003 Season							2002-2003						
	Home Games			Away Games				Home Games			Away Games			
	Marlins	Opp	Total	Marlins	Opp	Total	Index	Marlins	Opp	Total	Marlins	Opp	Total	Index
G	72	72	144	75	75	150		144	144	288	147	147	294	
Avg	.273	.240	.256	.260	.267	.263	97	.271	.247	.259	.256	.270	.263	99
AB	2403	2501	4904	2589	2466	5055	101	4801	5023	9824	5077	4868	9945	101
R	340	264	604	327	337	664	95	682	586	1268	605	710	1315	98
H	656	599	1255	672	659	1331	98	1303	1243	2546	1299	1315	2614	99
2B	113	122	235	151	147	298	81	243	255	498	268	277	545	93
3B	23	21	44	16	10	26	174	45	41	86	24	26	50	174
HR	64	45	109	78	67	145	77	127	103	230	145	151	296	79
BB	240	237	477	230	243	473	104	534	528	1062	456	520	976	110
SO	425	571	996	473	473	946	109	922	1127	2049	990	910	1900	109
E	33	46	79	42	59	101	81	76	93	169	91	115	206	84
E-Infield	9	13	22	18	27	45	51	24	31	55	41	43	84	67
LHB-Avg	.303	.231	.262	.261	.266	.264	99	.282	.244	.259	.258	.285	.274	95
LHB-HR	4	16	20	3	20	23	87	15	36	51	15	56	71	70
RHB-Avg	.261	.245	.253	.259	.268	.263	96	.267	.250	.259	.255	.261	.258	101
RHB-HR	60	29	89	75	47	122	76	112	67	179	130	95	225	82

Houston Astros - Minute Maid Park Surface: Grass

| | 2003 Season | | | | | | | 2002-2003 | | | | | | |
| | Home Games | | | Away Games | | | | Home Games | | | Away Games | | | |
	Astros	Opp	Total	Astros	Opp	Total	Index	Astros	Opp	Total	Astros	Opp	Total	Index
G	72	72	144	72	72	144		147	147	294	147	147	294	
Avg	.266	.244	.255	.253	.254	.253	101	.275	.250	.263	.245	.257	.251	105
AB	2388	2432	4820	2560	2388	4948	97	4912	5028	9940	5118	4846	9964	100
R	365	301	666	331	299	630	106	745	613	1358	649	613	1262	108
H	635	593	1228	647	607	1254	98	1352	1258	2610	1255	1244	2499	104
2B	131	103	234	137	123	260	92	273	246	519	269	266	535	97
3B	18	18	36	6	7	13	284	36	28	64	19	29	48	134
HR	82	79	161	82	66	148	112	165	139	304	155	138	293	104
BB	251	222	473	250	273	523	93	540	440	980	501	548	1049	94
SO	417	507	924	493	500	993	96	905	1082	1987	1042	1039	2081	96
E	40	45	85	39	54	93	91	81	94	175	77	97	174	101
E-Infield	19	13	32	21	28	49	65	35	32	67	37	51	88	76
LHB-Avg	.255	.251	.253	.241	.271	.259	98	.282	.262	.271	.253	.270	.263	103
LHB-HR	16	21	37	16	26	42	89	58	46	104	42	58	100	103
RHB-Avg	.269	.239	.256	.257	.244	.251	102	.272	.243	.258	.242	.248	.244	106
RHB-HR	66	58	124	66	40	106	121	107	93	200	113	80	193	104

Kansas City Royals - Ewing M. Kauffman Stadium Surface: Grass

| | 2003 Season | | | | | | | 2002-2003 | | | | | | |
| | Home Games | | | Away Games | | | | Home Games | | | Away Games | | | |
	Royals	Opp	Total	Royals	Opp	Total	Index	Royals	Opp	Total	Royals	Opp	Total	Index
G	71	71	142	73	73	146		143	143	286	145	145	290	
Avg	.281	.292	.286	.264	.264	.264	108	.276	.291	.284	.250	.265	.258	110
AB	2388	2583	4971	2542	2414	4956	103	4854	5220	10074	4986	4811	9797	104
R	382	458	840	351	307	658	131	754	891	1645	627	654	1281	130
H	671	753	1424	671	638	1309	112	1342	1520	2862	1248	1276	2524	115
2B	135	142	277	111	135	246	112	267	301	568	225	265	490	113
3B	15	16	31	18	14	32	97	38	30	68	34	30	64	103
HR	60	102	162	80	70	150	108	135	211	346	127	154	281	120
BB	215	248	463	203	242	445	104	451	491	942	432	486	918	100
SO	350	373	723	464	401	865	83	689	772	1461	939	838	1777	80
E	36	59	95	54	55	109	90	88	114	202	116	97	213	96
E-Infield	17	24	41	23	27	50	84	30	48	78	49	49	98	81
LHB-Avg	.276	.297	.286	.256	.279	.267	107	.275	.296	.285	.243	.273	.257	111
LHB-HR	28	41	69	43	29	72	94	64	90	154	68	65	133	112
RHB-Avg	.286	.288	.287	.271	.253	.262	109	.278	.287	.283	.257	.259	.258	110
RHB-HR	32	61	93	37	41	78	120	71	121	192	59	89	148	127

Los Angeles Dodgers - Dodger Stadium Surface: Grass

| | 2003 Season | | | | | | | 2002-2003 | | | | | | |
| | Home Games | | | Away Games | | | | Home Games | | | Away Games | | | |
	Dodgers	Opp	Total	Dodgers	Opp	Total	Index	Dodgers	Opp	Total	Dodgers	Opp	Total	Index
G	72	72	144	72	72	144		144	144	288	144	144	288	
Avg	.241	.222	.231	.252	.247	.250	93	.246	.227	.237	.266	.248	.257	92
AB	2316	2373	4689	2551	2378	4929	95	4688	4836	9524	5148	4743	9891	96
R	243	222	465	279	281	560	83	513	487	1000	642	581	1223	82
H	557	526	1083	643	587	1230	88	1153	1100	2253	1368	1175	2543	89
2B	114	74	188	119	111	230	86	217	172	389	273	238	511	79
3B	8	4	12	14	20	34	37	19	7	26	29	35	64	42
HR	59	62	121	54	51	105	121	119	137	256	131	117	248	107
BB	170	230	400	201	246	447	94	372	481	853	388	510	898	99
SO	425	607	1032	450	534	984	110	825	1137	1962	898	1022	1920	106
E	55	46	101	52	52	104	97	100	103	203	84	108	192	106
E-Infield	18	21	39	18	23	41	95	34	51	85	33	42	75	113
LHB-Avg	.249	.214	.234	.245	.237	.242	97	.244	.218	.232	.255	.245	.250	93
LHB-HR	29	19	48	27	15	42	117	45	40	85	55	38	93	96
RHB-Avg	.231	.226	.228	.260	.252	.256	89	.247	.233	.240	.275	.249	.262	92
RHB-HR	30	43	73	27	36	63	124	74	97	171	76	79	155	114

Milwaukee Brewers - Miller Park Surface: Grass

	2003 Season							2002-2003						
	Home Games			Away Games			Index	Home Games			Away Games			Index
	Brewers	Opp	Total	Brewers	Opp	Total		Brewers	Opp	Total	Brewers	Opp	Total	
G	75	75	150	75	75	150		150	150	300	150	150	300	
Avg	.255	.273	.264	.252	.285	.268	98	.252	.264	.258	.252	.281	.266	97
AB	2531	2741	5272	2585	2546	5131	103	4948	5320	10268	5165	5019	10184	101
R	318	426	744	329	387	716	104	595	780	1375	634	775	1409	98
H	646	747	1393	651	726	1377	101	1249	1405	2654	1300	1410	2710	98
2B	120	144	264	126	141	267	96	242	285	527	252	268	520	101
3B	8	20	28	13	20	33	83	20	34	54	27	33	60	89
HR	100	110	210	82	87	169	121	158	205	363	153	175	328	110
BB	260	282	542	257	254	511	103	502	566	1068	495	594	1089	97
SO	545	497	1042	583	461	1044	97	1030	1016	2046	1133	892	2025	100
E	58	38	96	49	60	109	88	104	78	182	102	104	206	88
E-Infield	27	19	46	20	27	47	98	48	37	85	38	42	80	106
LHB-Avg	.280	.284	.282	.271	.260	.266	106	.264	.276	.270	.259	.272	.266	102
LHB-HR	30	41	71	24	24	48	138	50	88	138	45	65	110	119
RHB-Avg	.244	.266	.255	.242	.298	.270	94	.246	.257	.252	.248	.286	.266	94
RHB-HR	70	69	139	58	63	121	114	108	117	225	108	110	218	105

Minnesota Twins - Hubert H. Humphrey Metrodome Surface: AstroTurf

	2003 Season							2002-2003						
	Home Games			Away Games			Index	Home Games			Away Games			Index
	Twins	Opp	Total	Twins	Opp	Total		Twins	Opp	Total	Twins	Opp	Total	
G	72	72	144	72	72	144		144	144	288	143	143	286	
Avg	.274	.266	.270	.277	.264	.270	100	.276	.259	.268	.274	.269	.271	99
AB	2436	2624	5060	2577	2425	5002	101	4868	5145	10013	5100	4860	9960	100
R	353	341	694	360	324	684	101	710	628	1338	696	672	1368	97
H	668	699	1367	713	640	1353	101	1346	1333	2679	1397	1306	2703	98
2B	139	142	281	143	122	265	105	313	274	587	280	244	524	111
3B	24	13	37	16	8	24	152	46	30	76	25	21	46	164
HR	71	85	156	69	81	150	103	134	151	285	158	177	335	85
BB	245	178	423	210	178	388	108	462	373	835	414	375	789	105
SO	452	485	937	444	389	833	111	904	957	1861	949	806	1755	105
E	32	55	87	46	55	101	86	62	106	168	85	108	193	86
E-Infield	8	22	30	21	21	42	71	22	38	60	41	40	81	74
LHB-Avg	.286	.267	.276	.294	.258	.277	100	.286	.261	.274	.284	.276	.281	98
LHB-HR	34	44	78	25	31	56	134	64	79	143	79	80	159	90
RHB-Avg	.262	.266	.264	.260	.269	.264	100	.265	.258	.261	.262	.263	.262	99
RHB-HR	37	41	78	44	50	94	84	70	72	142	79	97	176	80

Montreal Expos - Olympic Stadium Surface: AstroTurf

	2003 Season							2002-2003						
	Home Games			Away Games			Index	Home Games			Away Games			Index
	Expos	Opp	Total	Expos	Opp	Total		Expos	Opp	Total	Expos	Opp	Total	
G	56	56	112	72	72	144		128	128	256	144	144	288	
Avg	.280	.260	.270	.239	.266	.252	107	.275	.260	.267	.245	.269	.257	104
AB	1856	1963	3819	2441	2372	4813	102	4252	4483	8735	4933	4806	9739	101
R	307	251	558	237	287	524	137	648	560	1208	552	628	1180	115
H	520	511	1031	583	630	1213	109	1169	1167	2336	1210	1294	2504	105
2B	135	121	256	99	127	226	143	280	271	551	227	250	477	129
3B	14	6	20	8	12	20	126	29	21	50	24	28	52	107
HR	50	62	112	57	54	111	127	126	133	259	126	133	259	111
BB	179	149	328	223	214	437	95	445	350	795	476	470	946	94
SO	306	366	672	477	439	916	92	764	858	1622	1022	906	1928	94
E	31	33	64	42	46	88	94	95	93	188	103	100	203	104
E-Infield	9	16	25	22	18	40	80	32	38	70	50	41	91	87
LHB-Avg	.267	.255	.261	.231	.290	.259	101	.278	.262	.270	.238	.280	.258	105
LHB-HR	17	20	37	21	21	42	117	51	51	102	46	55	101	115
RHB-Avg	.291	.264	.276	.246	.248	.247	112	.272	.259	.265	.251	.262	.257	103
RHB-HR	33	42	75	36	33	69	131	75	82	157	80	78	158	109

Montreal Expos - Hiram Bithorn Stadium Surface: AstroTurf

	2003 Season						
	Home Games			Away Games			
	Expos	Opp	Total	Expos	Opp	Total	Index
G	16	16	32	72	72	144	
Avg	.261	.251	.256	.239	.266	.252	102
AB	528	574	1102	2441	2372	4813	103
R	80	75	155	237	287	524	133
H	138	144	282	583	630	1213	105
2B	34	22	56	99	127	226	108
3B	1	2	3	8	12	20	66
HR	20	26	46	57	54	111	181
BB	56	43	99	223	214	437	99
SO	101	115	216	477	439	916	103
E	14	11	25	42	46	88	128
E-Infield	7	5	12	22	18	40	135
LHB-Avg	.262	.260	.261	.231	.290	.259	101
LHB-HR	8	5	13	21	21	42	144
RHB-Avg	.261	.245	.252	.246	.248	.247	102
RHB-HR	12	21	33	36	33	69	199

New York Mets - Shea Stadium Surface: Grass

	2003 Season							2002-2003						
	Home Games			Away Games				Home Games			Away Games			
	Mets	Opp	Total	Mets	Opp	Total	Index	Mets	Opp	Total	Mets	Opp	Total	Index
G	74	74	148	72	72	144		146	146	292	143	143	286	
Avg	.256	.266	.261	.236	.275	.255	102	.250	.260	.255	.252	.267	.259	98
AB	2415	2564	4979	2411	2371	4782	101	4807	5119	9926	4907	4723	9630	101
R	291	336	627	284	330	614	99	581	647	1228	610	643	1253	96
H	618	683	1301	569	651	1220	104	1201	1331	2532	1235	1263	2498	99
2B	128	155	283	111	129	240	113	224	259	483	230	251	481	97
3B	9	14	23	14	25	39	57	20	27	47	22	42	64	71
HR	48	71	119	57	77	134	85	120	145	265	124	145	269	96
BB	229	266	495	233	246	479	99	451	496	947	455	490	945	97
SO	447	458	905	496	372	868	100	906	973	1879	972	832	1804	101
E	59	50	109	45	55	100	106	127	96	223	108	107	215	102
E-Infield	32	20	52	21	27	48	105	63	44	107	44	50	94	111
LHB-Avg	.270	.254	.262	.254	.249	.252	104	.262	.258	.260	.256	.247	.252	103
LHB-HR	24	23	47	28	17	45	97	63	53	116	51	37	88	128
RHB-Avg	.246	.273	.261	.223	.287	.257	101	.241	.261	.252	.249	.278	.264	95
RHB-HR	24	48	72	29	60	89	79	57	92	149	73	108	181	80

New York Yankees - Yankee Stadium Surface: Grass

	2003 Season							2002-2003						
	Home Games			Away Games				Home Games			Away Games			
	Yankees	Opp	Total	Yankees	Opp	Total	Index	Yankees	Opp	Total	Yankees	Opp	Total	Index
G	73	73	146	72	72	144		144	144	288	144	144	288	
Avg	.263	.265	.264	.277	.267	.272	97	.268	.255	.262	.276	.265	.271	97
AB	2410	2585	4995	2583	2500	5083	97	4817	5091	9908	5162	4988	10150	98
R	349	336	685	426	309	735	92	735	634	1369	837	614	1451	94
H	633	686	1319	715	667	1382	94	1293	1300	2593	1426	1320	2746	94
2B	120	132	252	143	163	306	84	245	265	510	292	304	596	88
3B	5	10	15	9	13	22	69	11	19	30	13	26	39	79
HR	94	66	160	107	56	163	100	189	132	321	211	113	324	101
BB	277	177	454	321	172	493	94	558	331	889	609	362	971	94
SO	443	509	952	473	475	948	102	937	1059	1996	1010	948	1958	104
E	54	50	104	49	41	90	114	104	104	208	109	79	188	111
E-Infield	24	21	45	26	18	44	101	41	44	85	50	34	84	101
LHB-Avg	.254	.273	.263	.274	.265	.270	97	.263	.253	.259	.275	.253	.265	98
LHB-HR	49	29	78	58	23	81	105	101	61	162	115	45	160	106
RHB-Avg	.272	.260	.265	.280	.269	.274	97	.273	.257	.264	.277	.273	.275	96
RHB-HR	45	37	82	49	33	82	96	88	71	159	96	68	164	98

Oakland Athletics - Network Associates Coliseum Surface: Grass

	2003 Season							2002-2003						
	Home Games			Away Games			Index	Home Games			Away Games			Index
	Athletics	Opp	Total	Athletics	Opp	Total		Athletics	Opp	Total	Athletics	Opp	Total	
G	72	72	144	72	72	144		144	144	288	144	144	288	
Avg	.257	.226	.241	.253	.255	.254	95	.260	.237	.248	.253	.258	.256	97
AB	2378	2439	4817	2518	2366	4884	99	4779	4915	9694	5065	4808	9873	98
R	333	234	567	355	313	668	85	696	536	1232	689	613	1302	95
H	612	551	1163	636	604	1240	94	1243	1164	2407	1283	1240	2523	95
2B	141	112	253	141	106	247	104	264	235	499	258	229	487	104
3B	8	7	15	13	9	22	69	23	16	39	24	26	50	79
HR	75	57	132	84	57	141	95	179	118	297	163	119	282	107
BB	227	214	441	263	228	491	91	514	410	924	515	460	975	97
SO	380	472	852	416	434	850	102	814	955	1769	863	861	1724	105
E	36	55	91	57	38	95	96	79	104	183	102	77	179	102
E-Infield	11	22	33	20	25	45	73	26	50	76	37	38	75	101
LHB-Avg	.264	.224	.247	.252	.251	.251	98	.271	.240	.257	.247	.253	.250	103
LHB-HR	36	15	51	46	25	71	75	95	40	135	90	50	140	100
RHB-Avg	.251	.227	.237	.253	.258	.256	93	.249	.235	.241	.260	.261	.260	93
RHB-HR	39	42	81	38	32	70	114	84	78	162	73	69	142	115

Philadelphia Phillies - Veterans Stadium Surface: NexTurf

	2003 Season							2002-2003						
	Home Games			Away Games			Index	Home Games			Away Games			Index
	Phillies	Opp	Total	Phillies	Opp	Total		Phillies	Opp	Total	Phillies	Opp	Total	
G	72	72	144	75	75	150		143	143	286	147	147	294	
Avg	.264	.235	.250	.259	.273	.266	94	.258	.234	.246	.265	.274	.269	91
AB	2379	2446	4825	2625	2482	5107	98	4717	4848	9565	5196	4934	10130	97
R	349	266	615	373	369	742	86	644	553	1197	720	734	1454	85
H	628	576	1204	681	678	1359	92	1216	1136	2352	1376	1351	2727	89
2B	148	135	283	145	157	302	99	282	245	527	305	304	609	92
3B	15	11	26	12	15	27	102	35	24	59	28	34	62	101
HR	68	54	122	76	76	152	85	141	121	262	153	149	302	92
BB	302	233	535	282	247	529	107	576	475	1051	573	511	1084	103
SO	496	555	1051	539	403	942	118	983	1079	2062	1027	828	1855	118
E	38	34	72	54	42	96	78	71	73	144	99	94	193	77
E-Infield	15	12	27	18	19	37	76	24	23	47	41	39	80	60
LHB-Avg	.269	.231	.252	.262	.282	.271	93	.255	.234	.246	.273	.285	.278	88
LHB-HR	40	13	53	38	27	65	83	72	38	110	71	58	129	89
RHB-Avg	.259	.238	.248	.257	.268	.263	94	.260	.234	.246	.258	.267	.263	94
RHB-HR	28	41	69	38	49	87	86	69	83	152	82	91	173	94

Pittsburgh Pirates - PNC Park Surface: Grass

	2003 Season							2002-2003						
	Home Games			Away Games			Index	Home Games			Away Games			Index
	Pirates	Opp	Total	Pirates	Opp	Total		Pirates	Opp	Total	Pirates	Opp	Total	
G	75	75	150	75	75	150		149	149	298	150	150	300	
Avg	.279	.269	.274	.257	.267	.262	105	.265	.271	.268	.246	.265	.256	105
AB	2509	2655	5164	2615	2482	5097	101	4898	5231	10129	5138	4912	10050	101
R	342	357	699	343	356	699	100	659	719	1378	629	677	1306	106
H	699	714	1413	671	663	1334	106	1297	1415	2712	1266	1302	2568	106
2B	135	139	274	111	138	249	109	257	284	541	232	264	496	108
3B	17	10	27	23	12	35	76	23	26	49	37	24	61	80
HR	74	73	147	76	86	162	90	131	154	285	154	157	311	91
BB	231	224	455	248	234	482	93	500	478	978	491	512	1003	97
SO	442	436	878	534	426	960	90	893	881	1774	1127	849	1976	89
E	66	43	109	47	52	99	110	125	93	218	98	92	190	116
E-Infield	40	22	62	20	23	43	144	68	46	114	43	38	81	142
LHB-Avg	.298	.294	.296	.273	.276	.274	108	.284	.287	.285	.265	.273	.269	106
LHB-HR	34	26	60	29	32	61	98	59	55	114	60	66	126	90
RHB-Avg	.267	.251	.259	.246	.261	.253	102	.255	.260	.257	.237	.260	.248	104
RHB-HR	40	47	87	47	54	101	84	72	99	171	94	91	185	92

San Diego Padres - Qualcomm Stadium Surface: Grass

	2003 Season							2002-2003						
	Home Games			Away Games				Home Games			Away Games			
	Padres	Opp	Total	Padres	Opp	Total	Index	Padres	Opp	Total	Padres	Opp	Total	Index
G	72	72	144	72	72	144		144	144	288	144	144	288	
Avg	.256	.256	.256	.264	.277	.270	95	.263	.259	.261	.251	.284	.267	98
AB	2404	2527	4931	2508	2394	4902	101	4844	5058	9902	4987	4806	9793	101
R	270	342	612	331	415	746	82	577	654	1231	608	834	1442	85
H	615	647	1262	661	664	1325	95	1273	1308	2581	1253	1363	2616	99
2B	96	115	211	126	125	251	84	198	235	433	239	284	523	82
3B	18	17	35	12	20	32	109	34	34	68	22	39	61	110
HR	48	87	135	63	101	164	82	105	160	265	127	192	319	82
BB	265	272	537	238	281	519	103	514	499	1013	465	564	1029	97
SO	484	513	997	482	473	955	104	911	1037	1948	1008	939	1947	99
E	46	47	93	41	39	80	116	99	99	198	99	87	186	106
E-Infield	17	18	35	14	19	33	106	42	37	79	36	48	84	94
LHB-Avg	.243	.264	.253	.278	.293	.284	89	.270	.270	.270	.258	.302	.278	97
LHB-HR	17	33	50	28	38	66	74	48	61	109	62	83	145	74
RHB-Avg	.266	.251	.258	.251	.267	.260	99	.256	.250	.253	.245	.271	.259	98
RHB-HR	31	54	85	35	63	98	87	57	99	156	65	109	174	89

San Francisco Giants - Pacific Bell Park Surface: Grass

	2003 Season							2002-2003						
	Home Games			Away Games				Home Games			Away Games			
	Giants	Opp	Total	Giants	Opp	Total	Index	Giants	Opp	Total	Giants	Opp	Total	Index
G	72	72	144	71	71	142		144	144	288	143	143	286	
Avg	.275	.243	.259	.249	.252	.250	103	.267	.244	.255	.262	.254	.258	99
AB	2391	2487	4878	2434	2304	4738	102	4720	4930	9650	4979	4650	9629	100
R	353	259	612	309	296	605	100	673	508	1181	697	596	1293	91
H	658	605	1263	605	581	1186	105	1259	1204	2463	1305	1179	2484	98
2B	120	116	236	128	111	239	96	239	221	460	277	219	496	93
3B	17	13	30	9	11	20	146	39	30	69	20	21	41	168
HR	70	55	125	86	63	149	81	132	89	221	202	130	332	66
BB	278	233	511	259	244	503	99	555	449	1004	543	497	1040	96
SO	412	481	893	474	416	890	97	811	921	1732	934	827	1761	98
E	42	53	95	29	37	66	142	86	109	195	70	82	152	127
E-Infield	20	22	42	11	16	27	153	42	44	86	32	37	69	124
LHB-Avg	.263	.231	.246	.254	.263	.259	95	.262	.240	.250	.275	.264	.269	93
LHB-HR	27	15	42	35	20	55	75	50	28	78	74	47	121	64
RHB-Avg	.281	.252	.267	.245	.244	.245	109	.269	.247	.259	.256	.246	.252	103
RHB-HR	43	40	83	51	43	94	85	82	61	143	128	83	211	68

Seattle Mariners - Safeco Field Surface: Grass

	2003 Season							2002-2003						
	Home Games			Away Games				Home Games			Away Games			
	Mariners	Opp	Total	Mariners	Opp	Total	Index	Mariners	Opp	Total	Mariners	Opp	Total	Index
G	72	72	144	72	72	144		144	144	288	144	144	288	
Avg	.271	.235	.253	.275	.265	.270	93	.268	.245	.256	.282	.265	.274	94
AB	2387	2437	4824	2570	2411	4981	97	4778	4948	9726	5124	4846	9970	98
R	370	271	641	355	315	670	96	697	577	1274	758	663	1421	90
H	646	573	1219	708	639	1347	90	1279	1214	2493	1444	1285	2729	91
2B	109	84	193	153	116	269	74	214	210	424	298	251	549	79
3B	16	10	26	15	4	19	141	33	13	46	25	15	40	118
HR	64	81	145	66	78	144	104	119	154	273	144	169	313	89
BB	278	208	486	245	209	454	111	586	425	1011	502	399	901	115
SO	422	455	877	462	429	891	102	864	961	1825	908	863	1771	106
E	28	45	73	34	33	67	109	65	101	166	74	85	159	104
E-Infield	11	22	33	16	13	29	114	28	47	75	31	34	65	115
LHB-Avg	.269	.247	.257	.277	.277	.277	93	.271	.256	.263	.293	.277	.285	92
LHB-HR	26	50	76	16	47	63	124	47	91	138	56	84	140	100
RHB-Avg	.272	.223	.249	.274	.252	.264	94	.264	.235	.250	.273	.254	.264	95
RHB-HR	38	31	69	50	31	81	88	72	63	135	88	85	173	80

St Louis Cardinals - Busch Stadium Surface: Grass

| | 2003 Season | | | | | | | 2002-2003 | | | | | | |
| | Home Games | | | Away Games | | | | Home Games | | | Away Games | | | |
	Cardinals	Opp	Total	Cardinals	Opp	Total	Index	Cardinals	Opp	Total	Cardinals	Opp	Total	Index
G	72	72	144	72	72	144		147	147	294	147	147	294	
Avg	.283	.251	.267	.267	.284	.276	97	.274	.247	.260	.268	.274	.271	96
AB	2433	2525	4958	2572	2497	5069	98	4928	5093	10021	5187	4939	10126	99
R	368	314	682	387	356	743	92	730	587	1317	752	689	1441	91
H	688	634	1322	688	709	1397	95	1349	1256	2605	1390	1352	2742	95
2B	161	133	294	138	148	286	105	287	267	554	274	265	539	104
3B	5	13	18	21	12	33	56	13	14	27	38	22	60	45
HR	77	79	156	94	102	196	81	157	142	299	175	170	345	88
BB	253	219	472	270	229	499	97	529	478	1007	501	489	990	103
SO	373	449	822	462	429	891	94	812	949	1761	902	872	1774	100
E	33	49	82	34	48	82	100	75	102	177	83	100	183	97
E-Infield	18	19	37	14	19	33	112	32	44	76	31	50	81	94
LHB-Avg	.256	.257	.256	.263	.295	.279	92	.266	.251	.258	.265	.275	.270	96
LHB-HR	30	30	60	33	30	63	100	67	52	119	63	59	122	100
RHB-Avg	.297	.247	.273	.270	.277	.273	100	.279	.244	.261	.270	.273	.271	96
RHB-HR	47	49	96	61	72	133	73	90	90	180	112	111	223	81

Tampa Bay Devil Rays - Tropicana Field Surface: NexTurf

| | 2003 Season | | | | | | | 2002-2003 | | | | | | |
| | Home Games | | | Away Games | | | | Home Games | | | Away Games | | | |
	Devil Rays	Opp	Total	Devil Rays	Opp	Total	Index	Devil Rays	Opp	Total	Devil Rays	Opp	Total	Index
G	72	72	144	72	72	144		144	144	288	143	143	286	
Avg	.269	.259	.264	.266	.274	.270	98	.267	.264	.265	.253	.284	.268	99
AB	2486	2533	5019	2570	2391	4961	101	4978	5118	10096	5015	4774	9789	102
R	319	370	689	331	391	722	95	627	776	1403	618	812	1430	97
H	669	655	1324	684	656	1340	99	1328	1349	2677	1269	1354	2623	101
2B	133	136	269	128	147	275	97	258	284	542	254	297	551	95
3B	17	13	30	15	12	27	110	33	27	60	28	20	48	121
HR	53	86	139	76	93	169	81	107	174	281	139	198	337	81
BB	195	275	470	165	289	454	102	401	563	964	366	559	925	101
SO	450	420	870	450	364	814	106	938	875	1813	953	728	1681	105
E	51	57	108	40	41	81	133	100	96	196	100	86	186	105
E-Infield	23	22	45	17	19	36	125	43	38	81	36	36	72	112
LHB-Avg	.274	.255	.265	.277	.268	.273	97	.274	.272	.273	.265	.287	.275	99
LHB-HR	35	35	70	37	44	81	86	70	85	155	69	94	163	92
RHB-Avg	.263	.262	.263	.254	.280	.267	98	.259	.256	.258	.241	.281	.261	99
RHB-HR	18	51	69	39	49	88	77	37	89	126	70	104	174	70

Texas Rangers - The Ballpark in Arlington Surface: Grass

| | 2003 Season | | | | | | | 2002-2003 | | | | | | |
| | Home Games | | | Away Games | | | | Home Games | | | Away Games | | | |
	Rangers	Opp	Total	Rangers	Opp	Total	Index	Rangers	Opp	Total	Rangers	Opp	Total	Index
G	72	72	144	72	72	144		144	144	288	144	144	288	
Avg	.287	.287	.287	.244	.285	.264	109	.285	.283	.284	.248	.275	.261	109
AB	2465	2591	5056	2570	2439	5009	101	4905	5170	10075	5119	4856	9975	101
R	443	435	878	301	410	711	123	864	860	1724	623	774	1397	123
H	707	743	1450	626	694	1320	110	1396	1461	2857	1271	1334	2605	110
2B	125	168	293	119	138	257	113	266	335	601	251	283	534	111
3B	22	17	39	10	16	26	149	35	37	72	22	35	57	125
HR	129	92	221	89	89	178	123	252	191	443	172	161	333	132
BB	223	262	485	201	278	479	100	481	548	1029	432	586	1018	100
SO	450	480	930	486	425	911	101	879	966	1845	968	856	1824	100
E	39	49	88	50	45	95	93	78	93	171	98	92	190	90
E-Infield	16	25	41	17	22	39	105	29	41	70	37	43	80	88
LHB-Avg	.287	.288	.288	.237	.290	.266	108	.286	.279	.282	.245	.279	.264	107
LHB-HR	62	44	106	36	44	80	129	105	87	192	64	81	145	128
RHB-Avg	.287	.285	.286	.247	.279	.262	109	.284	.286	.285	.250	.271	.259	110
RHB-HR	67	48	115	53	45	98	118	147	104	251	108	80	188	135

Toronto Blue Jays - SkyDome Surface: NexTurf

| | 2003 Season | | | | | | | 2002-2003 | | | | | | |
| | Home Games | | | Away Games | | | | Home Games | | | Away Games | | | |
	Blue Jays	Opp	Total	Blue Jays	Opp	Total	Index	Blue Jays	Opp	Total	Blue Jays	Opp	Total	Index
G	72	72	144	72	72	144		144	144	288	144	144	288	
Avg	.283	.282	.282	.273	.265	.269	105	.277	.275	.276	.264	.269	.267	103
AB	2471	2608	5079	2568	2429	4997	102	4903	5141	10044	5121	4873	9994	101
R	406	404	810	386	320	706	115	776	778	1554	758	699	1457	107
H	699	735	1434	701	643	1344	107	1356	1412	2768	1354	1312	2666	104
2B	182	157	339	151	112	263	127	333	311	644	277	241	518	124
3B	14	17	31	13	17	30	102	33	26	59	29	34	63	93
HR	76	99	175	81	68	149	116	168	177	345	156	148	304	113
BB	255	218	473	236	210	446	104	481	481	962	466	478	944	101
SO	461	486	947	521	382	903	103	944	941	1885	1065	819	1884	100
E	44	46	90	57	42	99	91	91	97	188	107	83	190	99
E-Infield	23	15	38	26	24	50	76	44	37	81	52	40	92	88
LHB-Avg	.294	.273	.282	.271	.249	.260	109	.279	.276	.277	.266	.269	.267	104
LHB-HR	42	40	82	37	24	61	134	84	83	167	74	68	142	120
RHB-Avg	.275	.290	.282	.275	.280	.277	102	.275	.274	.274	.264	.270	.266	103
RHB-HR	34	59	93	44	44	88	103	84	94	178	82	80	162	107

2003 American League Ballpark Index Rankings - Runs

Team	TOTALS											LHB		RHB	
	Avg	AB	R	H	2B	3B	HR	BB	SO	E	E-Inf	Avg	HR	Avg	HR
Kansas City - Ewing M. Kauffman Stadium	108	103	131	112	112	97	108	104	83	90	84	107	94	109	120
Texas - The Ballpark in Arlington	109	101	123	110	113	149	123	100	101	93	105	108	129	109	118
Toronto - SkyDome	105	102	115	107	127	102	116	104	103	91	76	109	134	102	103
Boston - Fenway Park	109	98	108	107	114	119	92	103	84	112	140	108	73	109	115
Minnesota - Hubert H. Humphrey Metrodome	100	101	101	101	105	152	103	108	111	86	71	100	134	100	84
Seattle - Safeco Field	93	97	96	90	74	141	104	111	102	109	114	93	124	94	88
Chicago - U.S. Cellular Field	98	99	96	97	96	101	134	93	105	84	78	95	126	101	138
Tampa Bay - Tropicana Field	98	101	95	99	97	110	81	102	106	133	125	97	86	98	77
Baltimore - Oriole Park at Camden Yards	99	99	93	98	100	48	109	108	98	90	88	102	103	96	115
New York - Yankee Stadium	97	97	92	94	84	69	100	94	102	114	101	97	105	97	96
Detroit - Comerica Park	94	103	90	97	80	126	88	91	98	110	132	99	89	90	88
Anaheim - Edison International Field	99	100	89	100	102	62	84	93	101	92	101	94	75	105	93
Cleveland - Jacobs Field	95	100	87	95	96	64	71	102	108	111	137	92	87	97	60
Oakland - Network Associates Coliseum	95	99	85	94	104	69	95	91	102	96	73	98	75	93	114

2003 American League Ballpark Index Rankings - Home Runs

Team	TOTALS											LHB		RHB	
	Avg	AB	R	H	2B	3B	HR	BB	SO	E	E-Inf	Avg	HR	Avg	HR
Chicago - U.S. Cellular Field	98	99	96	97	96	101	134	93	105	84	78	95	126	101	138
Texas - The Ballpark in Arlington	109	101	123	110	113	149	123	100	101	93	105	108	129	109	118
Toronto - SkyDome	105	102	115	107	127	102	116	104	103	91	76	109	134	102	103
Baltimore - Oriole Park at Camden Yards	99	99	93	98	100	48	109	108	98	90	88	102	103	96	115
Kansas City - Ewing M. Kauffman Stadium	108	103	131	112	112	97	108	104	83	90	84	107	94	109	120
Seattle - Safeco Field	93	97	96	90	74	141	104	111	102	109	114	93	124	94	88
Minnesota - Hubert H. Humphrey Metrodome	100	101	101	101	105	152	103	108	111	86	71	100	134	100	84
New York - Yankee Stadium	97	97	92	94	84	69	100	94	102	114	101	97	105	97	96
Oakland - Network Associates Coliseum	95	99	85	94	104	69	95	91	102	96	73	98	75	93	114
Boston - Fenway Park	109	98	108	107	114	119	92	103	84	112	140	108	73	109	115
Detroit - Comerica Park	94	103	90	97	80	126	88	91	98	110	132	99	89	90	88
Anaheim - Edison International Field	99	100	89	100	102	62	84	93	101	92	101	94	75	105	93
Tampa Bay - Tropicana Field	98	101	95	99	97	110	81	102	106	133	125	97	86	98	77
Cleveland - Jacobs Field	95	100	87	95	96	64	71	102	108	111	137	92	87	97	60

2003 National League Ballpark Index Rankings - Runs

Team	TOTALS											LHB		RHB	
	Avg	AB	R	H	2B	3B	HR	BB	SO	E	E-Inf	Avg	HR	Avg	HR
Montreal - Olympic Stadium	107	102	137	109	143	126	127	95	92	94	80	101	117	112	131
Montreal - Hiram Bithorn Stadium	102	103	133	105	108	66	181	99	103	128	135	101	144	102	199
Arizona - Bank One Ballpark	107	101	126	108	132	174	108	108	95	85	79	113	104	102	113
Colorado - Coors Field	112	104	125	116	108	231	134	90	88	95	91	111	150	113	125
Houston - Minute Maid Park	101	97	106	98	92	284	112	93	96	91	65	98	89	102	121
Milwaukee - Miller Park	98	103	104	101	96	83	121	103	97	88	98	106	138	94	114
Pittsburgh - PNC Park	105	101	100	106	109	76	90	93	90	110	144	108	98	102	84
San Francisco - Pacific Bell Park	103	102	100	105	96	146	81	99	97	142	153	95	75	109	85
New York - Shea Stadium	102	101	99	104	113	57	85	99	100	106	105	104	97	101	79
Cincinnati - Great American Ballpark	98	100	96	97	102	26	118	95	100	113	153	97	113	98	123
Chicago - Wrigley Field	98	100	95	98	92	85	97	114	112	103	105	96	75	99	108
Florida - Pro Player Stadium	97	101	95	98	81	174	77	104	109	81	51	99	87	96	76
St Louis - Busch Stadium	97	98	92	95	105	56	81	97	94	100	112	92	100	100	73
Atlanta - Turner Field	96	96	90	93	82	103	88	108	95	108	108	101	87	94	88
Philadelphia - Veterans Stadium	94	98	86	92	99	102	85	107	118	78	76	93	83	94	86
Los Angeles - Dodger Stadium	93	95	83	88	86	37	121	94	110	97	95	97	117	89	124
San Diego - Qualcomm Stadium	95	101	82	95	84	109	82	103	104	116	106	89	74	99	87

2003 National League Ballpark Index Rankings - Home Runs

Team	TOTALS											LHB		RHB	
	Avg	AB	R	H	2B	3B	HR	BB	SO	E	E-Inf	Avg	HR	Avg	HR
Montreal - Hiram Bithorn Stadium	102	103	133	105	108	66	181	99	103	128	135	101	144	102	199
Colorado - Coors Field	112	104	125	116	108	231	134	90	88	95	91	111	150	113	125
Montreal - Olympic Stadium	107	102	137	109	143	126	127	95	92	94	80	101	117	112	131
Los Angeles - Dodger Stadium	93	95	83	88	86	37	121	94	110	97	95	97	117	89	124
Milwaukee - Miller Park	98	103	104	101	96	83	121	103	97	88	98	106	138	94	114
Cincinnati - Great American Ballpark	98	100	96	97	102	26	118	95	100	113	153	97	113	98	123
Houston - Minute Maid Park	101	97	106	98	92	284	112	93	96	91	65	98	89	102	121
Arizona - Bank One Ballpark	107	101	126	108	132	174	108	108	95	85	79	113	104	102	113
Chicago - Wrigley Field	98	100	95	98	92	85	97	114	112	103	105	96	75	99	108
Pittsburgh - PNC Park	105	101	100	106	109	76	90	93	90	110	144	108	98	102	84
Atlanta - Turner Field	96	96	90	93	82	103	88	108	95	108	108	101	87	94	88
New York - Shea Stadium	102	101	99	104	113	57	85	99	100	106	105	104	97	101	79
Philadelphia - Veterans Stadium	94	98	86	92	99	102	85	107	118	78	76	93	83	94	86
San Diego - Qualcomm Stadium	95	101	82	95	84	109	82	103	104	116	106	89	74	99	87
San Francisco - Pacific Bell Park	103	102	100	105	96	146	81	99	97	142	153	95	75	109	85
St Louis - Busch Stadium	97	98	92	95	105	56	81	97	94	100	112	92	100	100	73
Florida - Pro Player Stadium	97	101	95	98	81	174	77	104	109	81	51	99	87	96	76

2002-2003 American League Ballpark Index Rankings - Runs

Team	TOTALS											LHB		RHB	
	Avg	AB	R	H	2B	3B	HR	BB	SO	E	E-Inf	Avg	HR	Avg	HR
Kansas City - Ewing M. Kauffman Stadium	110	104	130	115	113	103	120	100	80	96	81	111	112	110	127
Texas - The Ballpark in Arlington	109	101	123	110	111	125	132	100	100	90	88	107	128	110	135
Toronto - SkyDome	103	101	107	104	124	93	113	101	100	99	88	104	120	103	107
Boston - Fenway Park	105	98	102	103	117	93	86	100	94	119	130	103	68	106	105
Chicago - U.S. Cellular Field	100	99	101	99	95	86	130	99	100	82	92	100	124	101	134
Tampa Bay - Tropicana Field	99	102	97	101	95	121	81	101	105	105	112	99	92	99	70
Minnesota - Hubert H. Humphrey Metrodome	99	100	97	98	111	164	85	105	105	86	74	98	90	99	80
Oakland - Network Associates Coliseum	97	98	95	95	104	79	107	97	105	102	101	103	100	93	115
New York - Yankee Stadium	97	98	94	94	88	79	101	94	104	111	101	98	106	96	98
Cleveland - Jacobs Field	96	100	94	97	102	58	85	98	111	117	139	97	96	96	75
Baltimore - Oriole Park at Camden Yards	97	100	93	97	87	48	113	105	97	106	102	97	106	98	118
Anaheim - Edison International Field	98	100	92	99	101	78	84	96	101	86	89	96	79	101	89
Seattle - Safeco Field	94	98	90	91	79	118	89	115	106	104	115	92	100	95	80
Detroit - Comerica Park	96	102	88	98	77	163	81	91	94	101	102	98	96	93	67

2002-2003 American League Ballpark Index Rankings - Home Runs

Team	TOTALS											LHB		RHB	
	Avg	AB	R	H	2B	3B	HR	BB	SO	E	E-Inf	Avg	HR	Avg	HR
Texas - The Ballpark in Arlington	109	101	123	110	111	125	132	100	100	90	88	107	128	110	135
Chicago - U.S. Cellular Field	100	99	101	99	95	86	130	99	100	82	92	100	124	101	134
Kansas City - Ewing M. Kauffman Stadium	110	104	130	115	113	103	120	100	80	96	81	111	112	110	127
Toronto - SkyDome	103	101	107	104	124	93	113	101	100	99	88	104	120	103	107
Baltimore - Oriole Park at Camden Yards	97	100	93	97	87	48	113	105	97	106	102	97	106	98	118
Oakland - Network Associates Coliseum	97	98	95	95	104	79	107	97	105	102	101	103	100	93	115
New York - Yankee Stadium	97	98	94	94	88	79	101	94	104	111	101	98	106	96	98
Seattle - Safeco Field	94	98	90	91	79	118	89	115	106	104	115	92	100	95	80
Boston - Fenway Park	105	98	102	103	117	93	86	100	94	119	130	103	68	106	105
Cleveland - Jacobs Field	96	100	94	97	102	58	85	98	111	117	139	97	96	96	75
Minnesota - Hubert H. Humphrey Metrodome	99	100	97	98	111	164	85	105	105	86	74	98	90	99	80
Anaheim - Edison International Field	98	100	92	99	101	78	84	96	101	86	89	96	79	101	89
Detroit - Comerica Park	96	102	88	98	77	163	81	91	94	101	102	98	96	93	67
Tampa Bay - Tropicana Field	99	102	97	101	95	121	81	101	105	105	112	99	92	99	70

2002-2003 National League Ballpark Index Rankings - Runs

Team	TOTALS											LHB		RHB	
	Avg	AB	R	H	2B	3B	HR	BB	SO	E	E-Inf	Avg	HR	Avg	HR
Montreal - Hiram Bithorn Stadium*	102	103	133	105	108	66	181	99	103	128	135	101	144	102	199
Colorado - Coors Field	114	104	131	118	114	183	142	94	88	107	102	112	148	115	137
Arizona - Bank One Ballpark	107	101	123	109	124	191	107	113	98	88	92	110	100	105	113
Montreal - Olympic Stadium	104	101	115	105	129	107	111	94	94	104	87	105	115	103	109
Houston - Minute Maid Park	105	100	108	104	97	134	104	94	96	101	76	103	103	106	104
Pittsburgh - PNC Park	105	101	106	106	108	80	91	97	89	116	142	106	90	104	92
Florida - Pro Player Stadium	99	101	98	99	93	174	79	110	109	84	67	95	70	101	82
Milwaukee - Miller Park	97	101	98	98	101	89	110	97	100	88	106	102	119	94	105
Cincinnati - Great American Ballpark*	98	100	96	97	102	26	118	95	100	113	153	97	113	98	123
New York - Shea Stadium	98	101	96	99	97	71	96	97	101	102	111	103	128	95	80
Atlanta - Turner Field	99	97	96	96	93	102	96	100	94	106	132	103	107	96	92
Chicago - Wrigley Field	95	99	94	94	91	73	110	108	112	102	93	93	89	96	126
St Louis - Busch Stadium	96	99	91	95	104	45	88	103	100	97	94	96	100	96	81
San Francisco - Pacific Bell Park	99	100	91	98	93	168	66	96	98	127	124	93	64	103	68
San Diego - Qualcomm Stadium	98	101	85	99	82	110	82	97	99	106	94	97	74	98	89
Philadelphia - Veterans Stadium	91	97	85	89	92	101	92	103	118	77	60	88	89	94	94
Los Angeles - Dodger Stadium	92	96	82	89	79	42	107	99	106	106	113	93	96	92	114

2002-2003 National League Ballpark Index Rankings - Home Runs

Team	TOTALS											LHB		RHB	
	Avg	AB	R	H	2B	3B	HR	BB	SO	E	E-Inf	Avg	HR	Avg	HR
Montreal - Hiram Bithorn Stadium*	102	103	133	105	108	66	181	99	103	128	135	101	144	102	199
Colorado - Coors Field	114	104	131	118	114	183	142	94	88	107	102	112	148	115	137
Cincinnati - Great American Ballpark*	98	100	96	97	102	26	118	95	100	113	153	97	113	98	123
Montreal - Olympic Stadium	104	101	115	105	129	107	111	94	94	104	87	105	115	103	109
Chicago - Wrigley Field	95	99	94	94	91	73	110	108	112	102	93	93	89	96	126
Milwaukee - Miller Park	97	101	98	98	101	89	110	97	100	88	106	102	119	94	105
Los Angeles - Dodger Stadium	92	96	82	89	79	42	107	99	106	106	113	93	96	92	114
Arizona - Bank One Ballpark	107	101	123	109	124	191	107	113	98	88	92	110	100	105	113
Houston - Minute Maid Park	105	100	108	104	97	134	104	94	96	101	76	103	103	106	104
Atlanta - Turner Field	99	97	96	96	93	102	96	100	94	106	132	103	107	96	92
New York - Shea Stadium	98	101	96	99	97	71	96	97	101	102	111	103	128	95	80
Philadelphia - Veterans Stadium	91	97	85	89	92	101	92	103	118	77	60	88	89	94	94
Pittsburgh - PNC Park	105	101	106	106	108	80	91	97	89	116	142	106	90	104	92
St Louis - Busch Stadium	96	99	91	95	104	45	88	103	100	97	94	96	100	96	81
San Diego - Qualcomm Stadium	98	101	85	99	82	110	82	97	99	106	94	97	74	98	89
Florida - Pro Player Stadium	99	101	98	99	93	174	79	110	109	84	67	95	70	101	82
San Francisco - Pacific Bell Park	99	100	91	98	93	168	66	96	98	127	124	93	64	103	68

* - Data since 2003

2003 Lefty/Righty Statistics

Batters vs. Left-Handed and Right-Handed Pitchers

Batter	vs	Avg	AB	H	2B	3B	HR	RBI	BB	SO	OBP	Slg
Abad,Andy	L	.000	2	0	0	0	0	0	0	1	.000	.000
Bats Left	R	.133	15	2	0	0	0	0	2	4	.235	.133
Abernathy,Brent	L	.000	13	0	0	0	0	0	0	3	.000	.000
Bats Right	R	.095	21	2	0	0	0	0	1	0	.136	.095
Abreu,Bobby	L	.272	180	49	10	0	3	31	17	41	.330	.378
Bats Left	R	.312	397	124	25	1	17	70	92	85	.440	.509
Alfonzo,Edgardo	L	.236	106	25	3	0	4	13	17	6	.339	.377
Bats Right	R	.265	408	108	22	2	9	68	41	35	.333	.395
Allen,Chad	L	.250	12	3	1	0	0	0	0	5	.250	.333
Bats Right	R	.167	12	2	0	1	0	0	0	0	.231	.333
Allen,Luke	L	-	0	0	0	0	0	0	0	0	-	-
Bats Left	R	.000	0	0	0	0	0	0	0	0	.000	.000
Almonte,Erick	L	.280	25	7	1	0	0	3	4	8	.379	.320
Bats Right	R	.253	75	19	5	0	1	8	4	16	.300	.360
Alomar,Roberto	L	.189	148	28	5	1	2	10	10	21	.250	.277
Bats Both	R	.285	368	105	23	1	3	29	49	56	.364	.378
Alomar Jr.,Sandy	L	.233	60	14	4	0	0	6	1	4	.242	.300
Bats Right	R	.284	134	38	8	0	5	20	3	13	.299	.455
Alou,Moises	L	.346	127	44	8	1	6	28	10	11	.399	.567
Bats Right	R	.260	438	114	27	0	16	63	53	56	.346	.432
Amezaga,Alfredo	L	.214	28	6	0	0	0	1	1	7	.241	.214
Bats Both	R	.208	77	16	3	2	2	6	8	16	.291	.377
Anderson,Garret	L	.310	232	72	19	1	8	39	8	34	.329	.504
Bats Left	R	.318	406	129	30	3	21	77	23	49	.353	.562
Anderson,Marlon	L	.315	73	23	7	0	2	15	5	7	.370	.493
Bats Left	R	.262	409	107	20	3	4	52	36	53	.320	.355
Atkins,Garrett	L	.063	16	1	1	0	0	2	2	7	.167	.125
Bats Right	R	.189	53	10	1	0	0	2	1	7	.218	.208
Aurilia,Rich	L	.277	112	31	8	1	8	21	12	15	.347	.580
Bats Right	R	.277	393	109	18	0	5	37	24	67	.318	.361
Ausmus,Brad	L	.237	76	18	5	1	1	11	17	14	.383	.368
Bats Right	R	.227	374	85	7	1	3	36	29	52	.285	.275
Baerga,Carlos	L	.302	43	13	4	0	1	6	1	4	.340	.465
Bats Both	R	.354	164	58	9	0	3	33	17	16	.410	.463
Bagwell,Jeff	L	.327	107	35	5	0	7	20	24	16	.450	.570
Bats Right	R	.267	498	133	23	2	32	80	64	103	.356	.514
Bako,Paul	L	.200	25	5	2	0	0	0	2	5	.259	.280
Bats Left	R	.233	163	38	11	3	0	17	20	42	.319	.337
Baldelli,Rocco	L	.298	188	56	11	4	4	21	9	24	.333	.463
Bats Right	R	.285	449	128	21	4	7	57	21	104	.323	.396
Banks,Brian	L	.196	51	10	2	0	2	9	9	11	.311	.353
Bats Both	R	.255	98	25	4	2	2	14	16	27	.368	.398
Barajas,Rod	L	.244	41	10	4	0	1	6	5	7	.326	.415
Bats Right	R	.212	179	38	11	0	2	22	9	36	.250	.307
Bard,Josh	L	.289	83	24	3	0	2	13	3	9	.310	.398
Bats Both	R	.227	220	50	10	1	6	23	19	44	.286	.364
Barnes,Clint	L	.429	14	6	2	0	0	1	0	4	.429	.571
Bats Right	R	.182	11	2	0	0	0	1	0	6	.286	.182
Barnes,Larry	L	.000	2	0	0	0	0	0	0	1	.000	.000
Bats Left	R	.222	36	8	2	0	0	2	1	8	.243	.278
Barrett,Michael	L	.205	78	16	4	1	3	11	11	15	.303	.397
Bats Right	R	.209	148	31	5	1	7	19	10	22	.267	.399
Batista,Tony	L	.193	161	31	2	0	9	22	8	28	.283	.373
Bats Right	R	.249	470	117	18	1	17	77	20	74	.281	.400
Bautista,Danny	L	.267	101	27	10	0	1	11	10	17	.339	.396
Bats Right	R	.279	183	51	6	3	3	25	11	33	.325	.393
Bay,Jay	L	.281	32	9	4	0	1	1	5	7	.378	.500
Bats Right	R	.291	55	16	3	1	3	13	14	22	.443	.545
Bell,David	L	.169	71	12	2	0	3	10	3	11	.213	.324
Bats Right	R	.204	226	46	12	0	1	27	38	29	.319	.270
Bell,Jay	L	.139	36	5	0	0	0		9	12	.326	.139
Bats Right	R	.200	80	16	1	0	0	3	13	26	.316	.213
Bellhorn,Mark	L	.211	71	15	3	1	1	11	10	20	.310	.324
Bats Both	R	.225	178	40	7	0	1	15	40	58	.369	.281
Belliard,Ronnie	L	.345	113	39	15	0	4	20	15	18	.426	.584
Bats Right	R	.254	334	85	16	2	4	30	34	53	.324	.350
Beltran,Carlos	L	.325	151	49	4	4	7	25	25	19	.416	.543
Bats Both	R	.300	370	111	10	6	19	75	47	62	.377	.514
Beltre,Adrian	L	.232	138	32	5	1	7	21	16	23	.312	.435
Bats Right	R	.242	421	102	25	1	16	59	21	80	.283	.420
Benard,Marvin	L	.000	6	0	0	0	0	0	0	0	.000	.000
Bats Left	R	.215	65	14	3	1	0	4	4	9	.257	.292
Bennett,Gary	L	.218	101	22	6	0	1	15	7	11	.266	.307
Bats Right	R	.248	206	51	9	0	1	27	17	37	.310	.306
Berg,Dave	L	.304	79	24	5	1	3	14	6	15	.353	.506
Bats Right	R	.207	82	17	1	0	1	4	6	25	.250	.256
Berger,Brandon	L	.045	22	1	0	0	0	0	5	1	.222	.045
Bats Right	R	.600	10	6	0	0	0	3	0	3	.600	.600
Berkman,Lance	L	.282	117	33	5	1	4	26	22	18	.403	.444
Bats Both	R	.290	421	122	30	5	21	67	85	90	.415	.534
Berroa,Angel	L	.313	179	56	12	1	9	26	8	24	.339	.542
Bats Right	R	.276	388	107	16	6	8	47	21	76	.337	.410
Bigbie,Larry	L	.324	71	23	2	0	1	7	8	11	.388	.394
Bats Left	R	.296	216	64	13	1	8	24	21	49	.357	.477
Biggio,Craig	L	.267	120	32	11	0	2	10	16	18	.367	.408
Bats Right	R	.264	508	134	33	2	13	52	41	98	.346	.413
Blake,Casey	L	.245	159	39	12	0	7	21	12	25	.307	.453
Bats Right	R	.251	398	104	23	0	10	46	26	84	.314	.394
Blalock,Hank	L	.209	139	29	3	0	3	11	7	32	.245	.295
Bats Left	R	.329	428	141	30	3	26	79	37	65	.382	.596
Blanco,Henry	L	.281	32	9	2	0	0	4	3	3	.343	.344
Bats Right	R	.176	119	21	6	0	1	9	7	18	.227	.252
Bloomquist,Willie	L	.242	91	22	6	1	0	3	9	15	.307	.330
Bats Right	R	.257	105	27	1	1	1	11	10	24	.325	.314
Blum,Geoff	L	.135	37	5	1	0	0	6	3	11	.200	.162
Bats Both	R	.274	383	105	24	0	10	46	17	39	.305	.399
Bocachica,Hiram	L	.143	7	1	1	0	0	0	0	4	.143	.286
Bats Both	R	.000	15	0	0	0	0	0	0	3	.000	.000
Bonds,Barry	L	.363	124	45	5	0	16	30	36	22	.509	.790
Bats Left	R	.331	266	88	17	1	29	60	112	36	.537	.729
Boone,Aaron	L	.216	153	33	7	1	5	16	18	22	.306	.373
Bats Right	R	.285	439	125	25	2	19	80	28	82	.335	.481
Boone,Bret	L	.257	167	43	11	1	8	35	26	26	.352	.479
Bats Right	R	.308	455	140	24	4	27	82	42	99	.372	.556
Borchard,Joe	L	.176	17	3	0	0	0	1	0	9	.176	.176
Bats Both	R	.188	32	6	1	0	1	4	5	9	.275	.313
Borders,Pat	L	.333	3	1	1	0	0	1	0	0	.333	.667
Bats Right	R	.091	11	1	0	0	0	0	1	5	.167	.091
Bordick,Mike	L	.347	95	33	8	2	2	23	15	16	.441	.537
Bats Right	R	.246	248	61	10	0	3	31	18	44	.299	.323
Bowen,Rob	L	.500	2	1	0	0	0	0	0	0	.500	.500
Bats Both	R	.000	8	0	0	0	0	1	0	4	.000	.000
Bradley,Milton	L	.402	112	45	14	0	4	19	20	20	.500	.634
Bats Both	R	.287	265	76	20	2	6	37	44	53	.387	.445
Bragg,Darren	L	.292	48	14	2	1	0	3	5	9	.382	.375
Bats Left	R	.219	114	25	3	0	0	6	8	29	.270	.246
Branyan,Russell	L	.250	44	11	4	0	2	9	4	18	.306	.477
Bats Left	R	.205	132	27	8	0	7	17	23	51	.327	.424
Broussard,Ben	L	.175	103	18	2	1	2	12	10	22	.250	.272
Bats Left	R	.276	283	78	19	2	14	43	22	53	.335	.505
Brown,Adrian	L	.000	1	0	0	0	0	0	0	0	.000	.000
Bats Both	R	.214	14	3	0	0	0	1	1	4	.267	.214
Brown,Dee	L	.259	27	7	2	0	1	5	1	6	.310	.444
Bats Left	R	.219	105	23	5	0	1	9	7	31	.272	.295
Bruntlett,Eric	L	.190	21	4	0	0	0	1	0	5	.182	.190
Bats Right	R	.303	33	10	3	0	1	3	0	5	.303	.485
Buchanan,Brian	L	.302	106	32	6	0	6	18	21	27	.415	.528
Bats Right	R	.217	92	20	4	2	2	11	3	24	.255	.370
Budzinski,Mark	L	-	0	0	0	0	0	0	0	0	-	-
Bats Left	R	.000	7	0	0	0	0	0	0	4	.000	.000
Burke,Jamie	L	.333	6	2	0	0	0	1	0	0	.333	.333
Bats Right	R	.500	2	1	0	0	0	1	0	0	.500	.500
Burkhart,Morgan	L	.111	9	1	0	0	0	0	0	2	.111	.111
Bats Both	R	.333	6	2	0	0	0	1	1	0	.429	.333
Burks,Ellis	L	.322	59	19	4	1	3	11	13	8	.444	.576
Bats Right	R	.237	139	33	7	0	3	17	14	38	.321	.353
Burnitz,Jeromy	L	.250	136	34	3	0	8	24	7	39	.299	.449
Bats Left	R	.235	328	77	19	0	23	53	28	73	.299	.503
Burrell,Pat	L	.198	111	22	5	1	4	6	10	30	.305	.369
Bats Right	R	.212	411	87	26	3	17	58	56	112	.310	.414
Burroughs,Sean	L	.260	146	38	7	2	3	23	12	17	.335	.397
Bats Left	R	.296	371	110	20	4	4	35	32	58	.359	.404
Butler,Brent	L	.154	26	4	0	0	0	0	0	2	.154	.154
Bats Right	R	.234	64	15	3	1	1	4	7	11	.319	.359
Byrd,Marlon	L	.315	111	35	6	1	1	10	11	25	.381	.414
Bats Right	R	.299	384	115	22	3	6	35	33	69	.362	.419
Byrnes,Eric	L	.286	147	42	9	4	6	33	10	19	.340	.524
Bats Right	R	.251	267	67	18	5	6	33	31	49	.329	.423
Cabrera,Jolbert	L	.307	137	42	17	1	2	12	5	16	.336	.489
Bats Right	R	.267	210	56	15	1	4	25	12	46	.329	.405
Cabrera,Miguel	L	.364	55	20	5	1	3	11	3	10	.397	.655
Bats Right	R	.247	259	64	16	2	9	51	22	74	.310	.429

Batters vs. Left-Handed and Right-Handed Pitchers

Batter	vs	Avg	AB	H	2B	3B	HR	RBI	BB	SO	OBP	Slg
Cabrera,Orlando	L	.311	148	46	15	0	2	20	17	18	.376	.453
Bats Right	R	.293	478	140	32	2	15	60	35	46	.338	.462
Cairo,Miguel	L	.247	77	19	4	1	2	11	2	7	.256	.403
Bats Right	R	.245	184	45	11	1	3	21	11	23	.302	.364
Calloway,Ron	L	.169	59	10	1	0	1	7	4	27	.219	.237
Bats Left	R	.253	281	71	16	1	8	45	16	53	.296	.402
Cameron,Mike	L	.286	147	42	7	2	4	22	17	26	.365	.442
Bats Right	R	.240	387	93	24	3	14	54	53	111	.336	.426
Carroll,Jamey	L	.268	82	22	5	0	1	3	7	18	.326	.366
Bats Right	R	.255	145	37	5	1	0	7	12	21	.321	.303
Casey,Sean	L	.320	181	58	4	1	4	22	13	22	.367	.420
Bats Left	R	.278	392	109	15	2	10	58	38	36	.342	.403
Cash,Kevin	L	.100	30	3	1	0	1	3	1	7	.125	.233
Bats Right	R	.158	76	12	2	0	0	5	3	15	.200	.184
Castilla,Vinny	L	.290	124	36	5	0	5	17	9	14	.333	.452
Bats Right	R	.273	418	114	23	3	17	59	17	72	.303	.464
Castillo,Alberto	L	.500	2	1	0	0	1	4	0	0	.500	2.000
Bats Right	R	.154	13	2	1	0	0	0	0	5	.154	.231
Castillo,Luis	L	.320	172	55	8	2	6	13	19	13	.391	.494
Bats Both	R	.312	423	132	11	4	0	26	44	47	.377	.357
Castro,Juan	L	.193	88	17	4	0	0	2	11	17	.283	.239
Bats Right	R	.276	232	64	10	1	9	31	7	41	.293	.444
Castro,Ramon	L	.409	22	9	1	0	3	3	1	4	.435	.864
Bats Right	R	.194	31	6	1	0	2	5	3	7	.265	.419
Catalanotto,Frank	L	.176	68	12	3	1	1	6	7	13	.250	.294
Bats Left	R	.318	421	134	31	5	12	53	28	49	.368	.501
Cedeno,Roger	L	.241	108	26	4	2	3	12	9	23	.299	.398
Bats Both	R	.274	376	103	21	2	4	25	29	63	.326	.372
Cepicky,Matt	L	-	0	0	0	0	0	0	0	0	-	
Bats Left	R	.250	8	2	1	0	0	0	0	2	.250	.375
Chamblee,Jim	L	.000	1	0	0	0	0	0	0	1	.000	.000
Bats Both	R	.000	1	0	0	0	0	0	0	1	.000	.000
Chapman,Travis	L	.000	1	0	0	0	0	0	0	0	.000	.000
Bats Right	R	-	0	0	0	0	0	0	0	0	-	
Chavez,Endy	L	.304	92	28	8	0	0	13	10	7	.373	.391
Bats Left	R	.238	391	93	17	5	5	34	21	52	.275	.345
Chavez,Eric	L	.220	191	42	6	1	9	29	14	36	.271	.403
Bats Left	R	.312	397	124	33	4	20	72	48	53	.387	.567
Chavez,Raul	L	.429	14	6	1	1	0	2	1	3	.467	.643
Bats Right	R	.174	23	4	0	0	1	2	0	3	.174	.304
Chen,Chin-Feng	L	-	0	0	0	0	0	0	0	0	-	
Bats Right	R	.000	1	0	0	0	0	0	0	0	.000	.000
Choi,Hee Seop	L	.059	17	1	1	0	0	1	7	9	.360	.118
Bats Left	R	.232	185	43	16	0	8	27	30	62	.349	.449
Christenson,Ryan	L	.109	55	6	2	0	0	5	5	15	.197	.145
Bats Right	R	.209	110	23	5	0	2	11	10	29	.285	.309
Cintron,Alex	L	.365	137	50	8	3	5	19	12	7	.418	.577
Bats Both	R	.296	311	92	18	3	8	32	17	26	.331	.450
Cirillo,Jeff	L	.227	88	20	3	0	1	6	9	7	.313	.295
Bats Right	R	.194	170	33	8	0	1	17	15	25	.268	.259
Clark,Brady	L	.263	114	30	7	1	3	14	7	11	.320	.421
Bats Right	R	.279	201	56	14	0	3	26	14	29	.335	.393
Clark,Howie	L	.000	1	0	0	0	0	0	0	0	.000	.000
Bats Left	R	.362	69	25	3	1	0	7	3	5	.405	.435
Clark,Jermaine	L	-	0	0	0	0	0	0	0	0	-	
Bats Left	R	.167	48	8	2	0	0	7	6	5	.250	.208
Clark,Tony	L	.279	68	19	3	0	4	10	7	19	.355	.500
Bats Both	R	.215	186	40	10	0	12	33	17	54	.279	.462
Clayton,Royce	L	.240	96	23	4	0	1	8	16	15	.348	.313
Bats Right	R	.225	387	87	12	1	10	31	33	77	.288	.339
Colbrunn,Greg	L	.250	48	12	1	1	3	6	3	13	.294	.500
Bats Right	R	.400	10	4	0	0	0	1	1	3	.455	.400
Collier,Lou	L	.000	1	0	0	0	0	0	0	0	.000	.000
Bats Right	R	-	0	0	0	0	0	0	0	0	-	
Conine,Jeff	L	.288	125	36	7	0	3	13	17	23	.368	.416
Bats Right	R	.281	452	127	29	3	17	82	33	47	.329	.471
Conti,Jason	L	.000	4	0	0	0	0	0	1	4	.200	.000
Bats Left	R	.250	44	11	2	0	2	7	1	14	.261	.432
Coomer,Ron	L	.355	62	22	4	0	4	11	3	5	.379	.613
Bats Right	R	.127	63	8	0	0	0	4	7	14	.225	.127
Cora,Alex	L	.308	65	20	3	2	0	5	2	7	.348	.415
Bats Left	R	.240	412	99	21	1	4	29	14	52	.278	.325
Cordero,Wil	L	.324	108	35	10	0	4	19	17	19	.421	.528
Bats Right	R	.262	328	86	17	0	12	52	32	71	.331	.424
Cordova,Marty	L	.375	8	3	1	0	0	0		3	.545	.500
Bats Right	R	.182	22	4	0	0	1	4	5	5	.357	.318
Cota,Humberto	L	.250	4	1	1	0	0	0	1	1	.400	.500
Bats Right	R	.250	12	3	0	0	0	1	0	4	.250	.250
Counsell,Craig	L	.219	73	16	1	0	1	8	7	10	.301	.274
Bats Left	R	.239	230	55	5	3	2	13	34	22	.336	.313
Crawford,Carl	L	.263	179	47	5	1	0	12	5	30	.283	.302
Bats Left	R	.288	451	130	13	8	5	42	21	72	.319	.386
Crede,Joe	L	.300	150	45	9	2	6	23	10	21	.344	.507
Bats Right	R	.246	386	95	22	0	13	52	22	54	.294	.404
Crisp,Coco	L	.321	112	36	4	2	0	8	5	15	.347	.393
Bats Both	R	.245	302	74	11	4	3	19	18	36	.286	.338
Cromer,Tripp	L	-	0	0	0	0	0	0	0	0	-	
Bats Right	R	.250	4	1	0	1	0	1	0	0	.250	.750
Crosby,Bobby	L	.000	6	0	0	0	0	0	0	2	.000	.000
Bats Right	R	.000	6	0	0	0	0	0	1	3	.250	.000
Crosby,Bubba	L	-	0	0	0	0	0	0	0	0	-	
Bats Left	R	.083	12	1	0	0	0	0	0	3	.083	.083
Cruz,Deivi	L	.286	140	40	5	0	7	23	6	11	.320	.471
Bats Right	R	.238	408	97	19	2	7	42	7	38	.251	.346
Cruz,Enrique	L	.000	11	0	0	0	0	0	1	3	.083	.000
Bats Right	R	.100	60	6	1	0	0	2	3	27	.156	.117
Cruz,Jose	L	.304	135	41	8	0	7	17	23	20	.405	.519
Bats Both	R	.233	404	94	18	1	13	51	79	101	.353	.379
Cuddyer,Mike	L	.220	41	9	0	0	1	2	6	6	.319	.293
Bats Right	R	.262	61	16	1	3	3	6	6	13	.328	.525
Cust,Jack	L	.364	11	4	1	0	0	0		2	.364	.455
Bats Left	R	.242	62	15	6	0	4	11	10	23	.356	.532
Damon,Johnny	L	.275	193	53	7	4	3	23	18	26	.333	.399
Bats Left	R	.272	415	113	25	2	9	44	50	48	.350	.407
Daubach,Brian	L	.188	16	3	1	0	1	3	0	6	.188	.438
Bats Left	R	.234	167	39	10	0	5	18	34	48	.365	.383
DaVanon,Jeff	L	.342	38	13	3	0	2	7	8	12	.457	.579
Bats Both	R	.274	292	80	13	1	10	36	34	47	.346	.428
Davis,Ben	L	.281	57	16	7	0	3	12	5	13	.333	.561
Bats Both	R	.222	189	42	11	0	3	30	13	48	.268	.328
Davis,J.J.	L	.211	19	4	0	0	1	2	3	8	.318	.368
Bats Right	R	.188	16	3	0	0	0	2	0	5	.188	.188
Dawkins,Gookie	L	-	0	0	0	0	0	0	1	0	1.000	
Bats Right	R	.000	2	0	0	0	0	0	0	2	.000	.000
DeJesus,David	L	-	0	0	0	0	0	0	0	0	-	
Bats Left	R	.286	7	2	0	1	0	0	1	2	.444	.571
Delgado,Carlos	L	.284	183	52	14	0	7	46	29	48	.395	.475
Bats Left	R	.310	387	120	24	1	35	99	80	89	.439	.649
Delgado,Wilson	L	.195	41	8	1	0	0	0	2	7	.233	.220
Bats Both	R	.244	86	21	2	0	0	7	9	11	.320	.267
Dellucci,David	L	.132	38	5	1	0	1	6	4	18	.227	.237
Bats Left	R	.247	178	44	11	3	2	17	19	40	.332	.376
DePastino,Joe	L	-	0	0	0	0	0	0	0	0	-	
Bats Right	R	.000	2	0	0	0	0	0	0	1	.000	.000
DeRosa,Mark	L	.277	83	23	4	0	3	12	5	10	.322	.434
Bats Right	R	.257	183	47	10	0	3	10	11	39	.313	.361
Diaz,Einar	L	.253	79	20	3	0	1	11	2	9	.274	.329
Bats Right	R	.259	255	66	11	1	3	24	7	23	.300	.345
Diaz,Matt	L	.000	3	0	0	0	0	0	1	2	.250	.000
Bats Right	R	.167	6	1	0	0	0	0	0	1	.167	.167
DiFelice,Mike	L	.313	64	20	7	1	1	7	5	9	.371	.500
Bats Right	R	.224	125	28	9	0	2	18	4	21	.261	.344
Drew,J.D.	L	.218	55	12	2	0	3	7	6	15	.308	.418
Bats Left	R	.306	232	71	11	3	12	35	30	33	.390	.534
Duncan,Jeff	L	.067	15	1	0	0	0	3	5	5	.333	.067
Bats Left	R	.210	124	26	0	2	1	7	12	36	.285	.266
Dunn,Adam	L	.202	119	24	3	0	9	25	19	41	.333	.454
Bats Left	R	.221	262	58	9	1	18	32	55	85	.363	.469
Durazo,Erubiel	L	.283	173	49	9	0	7	27	28	39	.380	.457
Bats Left	R	.247	364	90	20	0	14	50	72	66	.373	.418
Durham,Ray	L	.370	100	37	9	2	1	10	12	16	.439	.530
Bats Both	R	.258	310	80	21	3	7	23	38	66	.342	.413
Durrington,Trent	L	.000	2	0	0	0	0	1	3	0	.600	.000
Bats Right	R	.167	12	2	0	0	0	1	0	6	.167	.167
Dye,Jermaine	L	.260	50	13	1	0	2	5	9	9	.377	.400
Bats Right	R	.146	171	25	5	0	2	15	16	33	.224	.211
Easley,Damion	L	.184	38	7	1	1	0	1	0	5	.184	.263
Bats Right	R	.188	69	13	2	0	1	6	2	13	.211	.261
Eckstein,David	L	.256	133	34	6	0	2	12	8	13	.324	.346
Bats Right	R	.251	319	80	16	1	1	19	28	32	.326	.317
Edmonds,Jim	L	.225	111	25	6	0	11	22	15	39	.320	.577
Bats Left	R	.292	336	98	26	2	28	67	62	88	.405	.631

Batters vs. Left-Handed and Right-Handed Pitchers

Batter	vs	Avg	AB	H	2B	3B	HR	RBI	BB	SO	OBP	Slg
Edwards,Mike	L	.333	3	1	0	0	0	0	0	1	.333	.333
Bats Right	R	.000	1	0	0	0	0	0	0	2	.667	.000
Ellis,Mark	L	.217	152	33	11	1	2	13	13	20	.279	.342
Bats Right	R	.259	401	104	20	4	7	39	35	74	.326	.382
Ellison,Jason	L	.000	8	0	0	0	0	0	0	0	.000	.000
Bats Right	R	.500	2	1	0	0	0	0	0	1	.500	.500
Encarnacion,Juan	L	.267	116	31	8	1	2	19	11	13	.331	.405
Bats Right	R	.270	485	131	29	5	17	75	26	69	.309	.456
Ensberg,Morgan	L	.316	98	31	6	0	7	20	19	15	.429	.592
Bats Right	R	.282	287	81	9	1	18	40	29	45	.358	.509
Erstad,Darin	L	.302	86	26	1	0	2	7	6	12	.362	.384
Bats Left	R	.227	172	39	6	1	2	10	12	28	.282	.308
Escalona,Felix	L	.250	4	1	0	0	0	0	0	1	.250	.250
Bats Right	R	.174	23	4	2	0	0	2	2	5	.240	.261
Escobar,Alex	L	.350	40	14	2	0	3	8	4	14	.413	.625
Bats Right	R	.220	59	13	0	0	2	6	3	19	.258	.322
Estalella,Bobby	L	.294	17	5	1	0	3	8	1	6	.316	.882
Bats Right	R	.187	123	23	6	0	4	13	18	49	.292	.333
Estrada,Johnny	L	.167	6	1	0	0	0	0	0	1	.167	.167
Bats Both	R	.333	30	10	0	0	0	2	0	2	.394	.333
Everett,Adam	L	.324	74	24	3	0	3	16	11	12	.425	.486
Bats Right	R	.240	313	75	15	3	5	35	17	54	.293	.355
Everett,Carl	L	.254	138	35	5	0	4	19	9	28	.320	.377
Bats Both	R	.299	388	116	22	3	24	73	44	56	.382	.557
Febles,Carlos	L	.333	63	21	3	0	0	6	6	7	.391	.381
Bats Right	R	.188	133	25	2	0	0	5	7	23	.255	.203
Feliz,Pedro	L	.231	52	12	2	0	4	14	3	12	.273	.500
Bats Right	R	.251	183	46	7	3	12	34	7	41	.280	.519
Fick,Robert	L	.135	52	7	1	0	2	8	3	12	.182	.269
Bats Left	R	.289	357	103	25	1	9	72	39	35	.356	.440
Figgins,Chone	L	.284	88	25	4	2	0	13	8	9	.340	.375
Bats Both	R	.303	152	46	5	2	0	14	12	37	.347	.362
Finley,Steve	L	.245	163	40	8	3	7	25	14	28	.309	.460
Bats Left	R	.306	353	108	16	7	15	45	43	66	.387	.518
Flaherty,John	L	.297	37	11	2	0	2	6	1	7	.316	.514
Bats Right	R	.250	68	17	6	0	2	8	3	12	.288	.426
Floyd,Cliff	L	.262	122	32	6	0	7	19	14	27	.340	.484
Bats Left	R	.305	243	74	19	2	11	49	37	39	.394	.535
Ford,Lew	L	.297	37	11	4	1	1	5	4	3	.366	.541
Bats Right	R	.361	36	13	3	0	2	10	4	6	.439	.611
Fordyce,Brook	L	.345	84	29	4	1	3	8	4	7	.371	.524
Bats Right	R	.250	264	66	8	1	3	23	15	37	.292	.322
Fox,Andy	L	.364	11	4	0	0	0	2	0	4	.364	.364
Bats Left	R	.175	97	17	5	1	0	6	7	25	.259	.247
Franco,Julio	L	.351	94	33	6	1	3	19	17	16	.446	.532
Bats Right	R	.243	103	25	6	1	2	12	8	27	.299	.379
Franco,Matt	L	.333	9	3	0	0	1	1	3	2	.500	.667
Bats Left	R	.240	125	30	5	0	2	14	8	24	.281	.328
Freel,Ryan	L	.326	43	14	2	0	4	5	3	2	.370	.651
Bats Right	R	.266	94	25	4	1	0	7	6	11	.333	.330
Fullmer,Brad	L	.267	30	8	1	0	1	6	2	4	.324	.400
Bats Left	R	.313	176	55	8	2	8	29	24	27	.398	.517
Furcal,Rafael	L	.247	154	38	14	0	5	18	19	21	.328	.435
Bats Both	R	.306	510	156	21	10	10	43	41	55	.359	.445
Galarraga,Andres	L	.309	94	29	4	0	7	17	8	15	.369	.574
Bats Right	R	.298	178	53	11	0	5	25	11	46	.342	.444
Gant,Ron	L	.185	27	5	0	0	1	2	1	3	.214	.296
Bats Right	R	.071	14	1	0	0	0	2	1	6	.125	.071
Garcia,Danny	L	.333	18	6	1	0	1	1	0	3	.333	.556
Bats Right	R	.158	38	6	1	0	1	5	2	8	.250	.263
Garcia,Jesse	L	.000	1	0	0	0	0	0	0	0	.000	.000
Bats Right	R	.444	9	4	0	1	0	2	0	1	.444	.667
Garcia,Karim	L	.164	55	9	1	0	1	3	1	15	.179	.236
Bats Left	R	.291	189	55	6	0	10	32	13	37	.335	.476
Garciaparra,Nomar	L	.357	171	61	7	3	7	29	8	14	.390	.556
Bats Right	R	.281	487	137	30	10	21	76	31	47	.330	.513
German,Esteban	L	.000	0	0	0	0	0	0	0	0	.000	.000
Bats Right	R	.333	3	1	0	0	0	1	0	1	.333	.333
Gerut,Jody	L	.209	134	28	5	0	3	14	7	30	.274	.313
Bats Left	R	.306	346	106	28	2	19	61	28	40	.360	.564
Giambi,Jason	L	.192	146	28	6	0	6	30	30	46	.362	.356
Bats Left	R	.272	389	106	19	0	35	77	99	94	.430	.591
Giambi,Jeremy	L	.125	24	3	1	0	0	2	2	12	.192	.167
Bats Left	R	.214	103	22	4	0	5	13	24	30	.372	.398
Gibbons,Jay	L	.273	187	51	10	0	5	19	12	34	.320	.406
Bats Left	R	.279	438	122	29	2	18	81	37	55	.334	.477
Gil,Benji	L	.177	79	14	5	1	0	5	3	17	.202	.266
Bats Right	R	.217	46	10	0	0	1	4	1	16	.234	.283
Gil,Geronimo	L	.293	41	12	1	0	0	6	3	6	.341	.317
Bats Right	R	.219	128	28	3	0	3	10	9	28	.286	.313
Giles,Brian	L	.286	161	46	11	4	3	31	33	21	.416	.460
Bats Left	R	.305	331	101	23	2	17	57	72	37	.432	.541
Giles,Marcus	L	.283	127	36	4	0	8	20	15	17	.361	.504
Bats Right	R	.325	424	138	45	2	13	49	44	63	.399	.533
Ginter,Keith	L	.224	85	19	3	0	4	6	13	23	.340	.400
Bats Right	R	.267	273	73	12	2	10	38	24	64	.356	.436
Gipson,Charles	L	.000	3	0	0	0	0	1	1	1	.250	.000
Bats Right	R	.286	7	2	0	0	0	1	0	1	.286	.286
Girardi,Joe	L	.000	4	0	0	0	0	0	1	1	.200	.000
Bats Right	R	.158	19	3	0	0	0	1	2	3	.238	.158
Glanville,Doug	L	.280	93	26	3	0	1	7	4	8	.306	.344
Bats Right	R	.255	153	39	2	0	4	9	4	21	.274	.346
Glaus,Troy	L	.303	89	27	6	1	2	10	16	18	.410	.461
Bats Right	R	.226	230	52	11	1	14	40	30	55	.317	.465
Glavine,Mike	L	-	0	0	0	0	0	0	0	0	-	-
Bats Left	R	.143	7	1	0	0	0	0	0	2	.143	.143
Gomes,Jonny	L	.250	8	2	1	0	0	0	0	2	.333	.375
Bats Right	R	.000	7	0	0	0	0	0	0	4	.000	.000
Gomez,Chris	L	.250	56	14	4	1	1	7	2	4	.276	.411
Bats Right	R	.252	119	30	5	2	0	8	5	9	.280	.328
Gonzalez,Alex	L	.274	113	31	9	2	4	18	8	19	.333	.496
Bats Right	R	.251	415	104	24	4	14	59	25	87	.307	.429
Gonzalez,Alex S	L	.228	123	28	10	0	3	11	13	27	.301	.382
Bats Right	R	.228	413	94	27	0	17	48	34	96	.293	.416
Gonzalez,Juan	L	.273	99	27	4	0	4	8	7	16	.321	.434
Bats Right	R	.303	228	69	13	1	20	62	7	57	.333	.632
Gonzalez,Luis	L	.223	220	49	9	3	8	30	24	36	.302	.400
Bats Left	R	.354	359	127	37	1	18	74	70	31	.459	.613
Gonzalez,Raul	L	.240	96	23	6	0	0	7	7	12	.291	.302
Bats Right	R	.223	121	27	2	0	2	14	20	22	.336	.355
Gonzalez,Wiki	L	.214	14	3	1	0	0	4	3	2	.333	.286
Bats Right	R	.196	51	10	4	0	0	6	2	11	.241	.275
Goodwin,Tom	L	.238	42	10	1	0	1	3	2	12	.273	.333
Bats Left	R	.302	129	39	9	0	0	9	9	21	.345	.372
Grabowski,Jason	L	-	0	0	0	0	0	0	0	0	-	-
Bats Left	R	.000	8	0	0	0	0	0	1	5	.111	.000
Grace,Mark	L	.217	23	5	2	0	0	0	6	1	.379	.304
Bats Left	R	.196	112	22	3	0	3	16	10	14	.256	.304
Graffanino,Tony	L	.303	165	50	14	3	6	21	14	20	.356	.533
Bats Right	R	.176	85	15	1	0	1	2	10	17	.286	.224
Green,Shawn	L	.252	214	54	17	1	8	41	18	43	.319	.453
Bats Left	R	.295	397	117	32	1	11	44	50	69	.373	.463
Greene,Khalil	L	.318	22	7	1	1	0	1	2	5	.375	.455
Bats Right	R	.163	43	7	3	0	2	5	2	14	.217	.372
Greene,Todd	L	.211	76	16	2	1	3	6	1	10	.231	.382
Bats Right	R	.240	129	31	8	0	7	14	1	37	.250	.465
Gregorio,Tom	L	.000	1	0	0	0	0	0	0	0	.500	.000
Bats Right	R	.167	18	3	0	0	0	2	1	8	.211	.167
Grieve,Ben	L	.208	53	11	3	0	0	7	8	13	.348	.264
Bats Left	R	.241	112	27	4	0	4	10	24	28	.381	.384
Griffey Jr.,Ken	L	.250	56	14	0	0	4	7	11	14	.400	.536
Bats Left	R	.245	110	27	8	1	9	19	16	30	.354	.582
Grissom,Marquis	L	.364	140	51	12	1	9	25	8	12	.399	.657
Bats Right	R	.280	447	125	21	2	11	54	12	70	.298	.409
Grudzielanek,Mark	L	.360	100	36	11	0	0	4	15	14	.444	.470
Bats Right	R	.302	381	115	27	1	3	34	15	50	.344	.402
Guerrero,Vladimir	L	.393	84	33	6	1	9	22	15	9	.485	.810
Bats Right	R	.313	310	97	14	2	16	57	48	44	.410	.526
Guiel,Aaron	L	.275	102	28	9	0	2	15	10	25	.358	.422
Bats Left	R	.278	252	70	21	0	13	37	17	38	.341	.516
Guillen,Carlos	L	.265	113	30	4	1	2	15	10	18	.323	.372
Bats Both	R	.280	275	77	15	2	5	37	42	46	.373	.404
Guillen,Jose	L	.315	130	41	10	0	7	20	8	26	.371	.554
Bats Both	R	.310	355	110	18	2	24	66	16	69	.355	.575
Gutierrez,Ricky	L	.313	16	5	0	0	0	0	0	0	.313	.313
Bats Right	R	.235	34	8	3	0	0	3	3	5	.308	.324
Guzman,Cristian	L	.250	164	41	9	2	1	14	12	23	.302	.348
Bats Both	R	.276	370	102	6	12	2	39	18	56	.315	.373
Guzman,Edwards	L	.200	25	5	0	0	0	3	1	4	.231	.200
Bats Right	R	.248	121	30	5	0	1	11	4	13	.270	.314
Hafner,Travis	L	.190	142	27	7	0	2	12	8	29	.284	.345
Bats Left	R	.280	207	58	12	3	12	28	14	52	.345	.541

Batters vs. Left-Handed and Right-Handed Pitchers

Batter	vs	Avg	AB	H	2B	3B	HR	RBI	BB	SO	OBP	Slg
Hairston Jr.,Jerry	L	.255	55	14	5	0	0	7	5	3	.311	.345
Bats Right	R	.276	163	45	7	2	2	14	18	22	.367	.380
Hall,Bill	L	.185	27	5	1	0	0	1	4	9	.290	.222
Bats Right	R	.278	115	32	8	2	5	19	3	19	.300	.513
Hall,Toby	L	.253	150	38	9	0	3	11	12	8	.307	.373
Bats Right	R	.252	313	79	14	0	9	36	11	32	.290	.383
Halter,Shane	L	.243	152	37	3	1	6	15	15	30	.310	.395
Bats Right	R	.197	208	41	2	1	6	15	12	47	.239	.303
Hammock,Robby	L	.308	78	24	4	2	2	10	5	10	.345	.487
Bats Right	R	.265	117	31	6	0	6	18	12	34	.341	.470
Hammonds,Jeffrey	L	.360	25	9	1	0	0	3	3	5	.429	.400
Bats Right	R	.215	107	23	11	0	4	13	13	23	.306	.430
Hansen,Dave	L	.500	6	3	0	0	1	2	3	1	.667	1.000
Bats Right	R	.233	129	30	4	1	1	13	20	24	.340	.302
Harris,Lenny	L	.050	20	1	0	0	0	1	2	5	.130	.050
Bats Left	R	.216	125	27	3	0	1	7	14	16	.295	.264
Harris,Willie	L	.105	19	2	0	0	0	0	1	8	.150	.105
Bats Left	R	.220	118	26	3	1	0	5	9	20	.276	.263
Hart,Bo	L	.300	90	27	6	3	0	8	6	19	.344	.433
Bats Right	R	.267	206	55	7	2	4	20	6	45	.306	.379
Harvey,Ken	L	.333	156	52	15	0	7	27	10	22	.377	.564
Bats Right	R	.234	329	77	15	0	6	37	19	72	.282	.334
Haselman,Bill	L	-	0	0	0	0	0	0	0	0	-	-
Bats Right	R	.000	3	0	0	0	0	0	1	0	.000	.000
Hatteberg,Scott	L	.255	149	38	10	0	2	15	15	18	.351	.362
Bats Left	R	.253	392	99	24	0	10	46	51	35	.339	.390
Helms,Wes	L	.314	86	27	5	0	6	18	16	24	.425	.581
Bats Right	R	.249	390	97	16	0	17	49	27	107	.307	.421
Helton,Todd	L	.387	199	77	17	2	10	49	34	24	.470	.643
Bats Left	R	.344	384	132	32	3	23	68	77	48	.452	.622
Henderson,Rickey	L	.167	36	6	1	0	0	1	8	8	.333	.194
Bats Right	R	.250	36	9	0	0	2	4	3	8	.308	.417
Henson,Drew	L	.250	4	1	0	0	0	0	0	1	.250	.250
Bats Right	R	.000	4	0	0	0	0	0	0	1	.000	.000
Hermansen,Chad	L	.000	3	0	0	0	0	0	1	3	.250	.000
Bats Right	R	.182	22	4	1	0	0	2	1	6	.217	.227
Hernandez,Jose	L	.235	153	36	4	2	9	29	14	54	.299	.464
Bats Right	R	.221	366	81	14	1	4	28	32	123	.282	.298
Hernandez,Michel	L	-	0	0	0	0	0	0	1	0	1.000	-
Bats Right	R	.250	4	1	0	0	0	0	0	1	.250	.250
Hernandez,Ramon	L	.208	149	31	5	1	6	13	8	20	.255	.376
Bats Right	R	.302	334	101	19	0	15	65	25	59	.365	.494
Hessman,Mike	L	.333	12	4	2	0	1	1	3	2	.467	.750
Bats Right	R	.222	9	2	0	0	1	2	2	4	.364	.556
Hidalgo,Richard	L	.307	88	27	4	0	7	14	14	26	.394	.591
Bats Right	R	.310	426	132	39	4	21	74	44	78	.383	.568
Higginson,Bobby	L	.227	154	35	6	1	3	19	18	29	.305	.338
Bats Left	R	.238	315	75	7	3	11	33	41	44	.328	.384
Hill,Bobby	L	.250	4	1	0	0	0	0	2	1	.500	.250
Bats Both	R	.333	3	1	0	0	0	0	0	1	.333	.333
Hill,Koyie	L	.000	1	0	0	0	0	0	0	1	.000	.000
Bats Both	R	.500	2	1	1	0	0	0	0	1	.500	1.000
Hillenbrand,Shea	L	.298	161	48	12	1	6	32	9	22	.331	.497
Bats Right	R	.271	354	96	23	0	14	65	15	48	.306	.455
Hinch,A.J.	L	.190	21	4	1	0	0	2	0	3	.217	.238
Bats Right	R	.208	53	11	2	1	2	3	9	15	.259	.453
Hinske,Eric	L	.256	133	34	18	0	2	26	11	36	.309	.436
Bats Left	R	.237	316	75	27	3	10	37	48	68	.337	.437
Hocking,Denny	L	.172	64	11	4	0	1	4	2	16	.197	.281
Bats Both	R	.274	124	34	6	2	2	18	13	21	.336	.403
Hollandsworth,Todd	L	.250	32	8	2	1	0	1	2	14	.294	.375
Bats Left	R	.255	196	50	21	2	3	19	20	41	.321	.429
House,J.R.	L	-	0	0	0	0	0	0	0	0	-	-
Bats Right	R	1.000	1	1	0	0	0	0	0	0	1.000	1.000
Houston,Tyler	L	.333	3	1	0	0	0	1	0	2	.333	.333
Bats Left	R	.277	94	26	6	0	2	13	6	17	.320	.404
Hubbard,Trenidad	L	.333	12	4	1	0	0	2	3	1	.467	.417
Bats Right	R	.000	4	0	0	0	0	0	1	2	.333	.000
Huckaby,Ken	L	.333	3	1	0	0	0	0	0	0	.333	.333
Bats Right	R	.125	8	1	1	0	0	2	0	2	.125	.250
Hudson,Orlando	L	.160	100	16	3	0	0	4	8	19	.222	.190
Bats Both	R	.297	374	111	18	6	9	53	31	68	.356	.449
Huff,Aubrey	L	.318	220	70	12	1	7	29	11	30	.353	.477
Bats Left	R	.308	416	128	35	2	27	78	42	50	.374	.596
Hummel,Tim	L	.259	27	7	1	0	2	4	5	4	.375	.519
Bats Right	R	.211	57	12	4	0	0	6	3	9	.246	.281
Hundley,Todd	L	.000	6	0	0	0	0	0	1	3	.143	.000
Bats Both	R	.222	27	6	1	0	2	11	7	10	.382	.481
Hunter,Brian	L	.263	38	10	0	0	0	5	2	9	.301	.263
Bats Right	R	.217	60	13	6	1	0	8	4	12	.258	.350
Hunter,Torii	L	.251	167	42	6	2	9	35	21	28	.330	.473
Bats Right	R	.249	414	103	25	2	17	67	29	78	.304	.442
Hyzdu,Adam	L	.188	32	6	2	0	1	5	6	9	.308	.344
Bats Right	R	.226	31	7	3	0	0	3	4	12	.333	.323
Ibanez,Raul	L	.245	204	50	7	1	7	29	11	33	.291	.392
Bats Left	R	.319	404	129	26	4	11	61	38	48	.371	.485
Infante,Omar	L	.155	71	11	2	1	0	3	5	10	.208	.211
Bats Right	R	.253	150	38	4	0	0	5	13	27	.311	.280
Inge,Brandon	L	.245	110	27	6	1	5	12	10	24	.306	.455
Bats Right	R	.182	220	40	9	2	3	18	14	55	.245	.282
Izturis,Cesar	L	.263	156	41	8	3	0	12	3	14	.275	.353
Bats Both	R	.246	402	99	13	3	1	28	22	56	.284	.301
Jackson,Damian	L	.241	87	21	4	0	0	7	3	14	.264	.287
Bats Right	R	.284	74	21	3	0	1	6	5	14	.329	.365
Jenkins,Geoff	L	.270	159	43	8	0	4	22	10	48	.322	.396
Bats Left	R	.308	328	101	22	2	24	73	48	72	.400	.607
Jeter,Derek	L	.370	100	37	4	0	3	13	10	14	.442	.500
Bats Right	R	.312	382	119	21	3	7	39	33	74	.380	.437
Jimenez,D'Angelo	L	.273	154	42	6	1	2	12	18	15	.345	.364
Bats Both	R	.273	407	111	18	6	12	45	48	74	.351	.435
Johnson,Charles	L	.250	96	24	5	0	2	10	20	19	.381	.365
Bats Right	R	.223	260	58	15	0	18	51	29	65	.295	.488
Johnson,Gary	L	-	0	0	0	0	0	0	0	0	-	-
Bats Left	R	.375	8	3	1	0	0	1	1	1	.444	.500
Johnson,Mark L	L	.500	2	1	0	0	0	0	1	1	.667	.500
Bats Left	R	.080	25	2	1	0	0	3	2	3	.172	.120
Johnson,Nick	L	.282	71	20	5	0	2	9	10	15	.393	.437
Bats Left	R	.285	253	72	14	0	12	38	60	42	.429	.482
Johnson,Reed	L	.328	122	40	10	0	5	17	6	14	.366	.533
Bats Right	R	.279	290	81	11	2	5	35	14	53	.348	.383
Johnson,Rontrez	L	.000	1	0	0	0	0	0	0	1	.000	.000
Bats Right	R	.500	2	1	0	0	0	0	0	0	.500	.500
Jones,Andruw	L	.260	131	34	7	0	11	27	13	24	.329	.565
Bats Right	R	.282	464	131	21	2	25	89	40	101	.341	.498
Jones,Chipper	L	.306	121	37	3	0	2	18	25	17	.425	.380
Bats Both	R	.304	434	132	30	2	25	88	69	66	.396	.555
Jones,Jacque	L	.269	145	39	12	0	2	14	6	41	.310	.393
Bats Left	R	.317	372	118	21	1	14	55	15	64	.342	.492
Jones,Jason	L	.182	22	4	1	0	1	2	2	2	.240	.364
Bats Both	R	.224	85	19	5	0	2	9	8	19	.313	.353
Jordan,Brian	L	.397	58	23	2	0	4	12	12	5	.493	.638
Bats Right	R	.265	166	44	7	0	2	16	11	25	.324	.343
Jose,Felix	L	.400	5	2	1	0	0	3	2	1	.571	.600
Bats Both	R	.308	13	4	0	0	1	4	2	4	.471	.538
Kapler,Gabe	L	.326	92	30	9	1	0	6	9	13	.386	.446
Bats Right	R	.233	133	31	4	0	4	21	13	28	.301	.353
Karros,Eric	L	.366	112	41	9	1	3	10	15	11	.441	.545
Bats Right	R	.246	224	55	7	0	9	30	13	35	.286	.397
Kata,Matt	L	.299	97	29	7	1	4	15	6	15	.333	.515
Bats Both	R	.236	191	45	9	4	3	14	19	38	.307	.372
Kearns,Austin	L	.266	79	21	2	0	1	8	11	17	.356	.329
Bats Right	R	.263	213	56	9	0	14	50	30	51	.367	.502
Kelton,Dave	L	.125	8	1	0	0	0	0	0	4	.125	.125
Bats Right	R	.250	4	1	1	0	0	1	0	1	.250	.500
Kendall,Jason	L	.310	158	49	11	0	1	14	12	11	.376	.399
Bats Right	R	.331	429	142	18	3	5	44	37	29	.407	.422
Kennedy,Adam	L	.235	115	27	3	0	2	13	5	23	.268	.313
Bats Left	R	.281	334	94	14	1	11	36	40	50	.369	.428
Kent,Jeff	L	.361	97	35	12	1	2	17	11	12	.422	.567
Bats Right	R	.282	408	115	27	0	20	76	28	73	.334	.495
Kielty,Bobby	L	.300	140	42	11	0	8	27	24	20	.417	.550
Bats Both	R	.216	287	62	15	1	5	30	47	72	.328	.328
Kieschnick,Brooks	L	.125	8	1	0	0	1	2	0	1	.125	.500
Bats Left	R	.323	62	20	1	0	6	10	6	12	.382	.629
Kingsale,Gene	L	.270	37	10	3	0	0	3	2	6	.293	.351
Bats Both	R	.181	83	15	0	1	1	5	8	11	.253	.241
Kinkade,Mike	L	.370	54	20	6	0	3	10	5	11	.507	.648
Bats Right	R	.139	108	15	1	0	2	4	8	27	.238	.204
Klassen,Danny	L	.281	32	9	1	0	1	5	2	12	.324	.406
Bats Right	R	.220	41	9	2	1	0	2	2	14	.256	.317
Klesko,Ryan	L	.194	103	20	3	0	4	11	10	28	.270	.340
Bats Left	R	.272	294	80	15	0	17	56	55	55	.382	.497

305

Batters vs. Left-Handed and Right-Handed Pitchers

Batter	vs	Avg	AB	H	2B	3B	HR	RBI	BB	SO	OBP	Slg
Konerko,Paul	L	.327	150	49	10	0	10	28	11	10	.373	.593
Bats Right	R	.187	294	55	9	0	8	37	32	40	.272	.299
Koonce,Graham	L	.000	3	0	0	0	0	0	0	2	.000	.000
Bats Right	R	.200	5	1	1	0	0	0	0	4	.200	.400
Koskie,Corey	L	.224	170	38	9	0	3	20	17	46	.306	.329
Bats Left	R	.331	299	99	20	2	11	49	60	67	.440	.522
Kotsay,Mark	L	.236	140	33	6	2	1	9	16	20	.316	.329
Bats Left	R	.278	342	95	22	2	6	29	40	62	.353	.406
Kreuter,Chad	L	.000	1	0	0	0	0	0	0	0	.000	.000
Bats Both	R	.118	17	2	1	0	0	0	3	2	.250	.176
LaForest,Pete	L	-	0	0	0	0	0	0	0	0	-	
Bats Left	R	.167	48	8	2	0	0	6	1	14	.196	.208
Laird,Gerald	L	.294	17	5	1	1	0	2	1	4	.333	.471
Bats Right	R	.259	27	7	1	0	1	2	4	7	.375	.407
Laker,Tim	L	.189	53	10	1	0	1	6	4	12	.246	.264
Bats Right	R	.266	109	29	10	0	2	15	5	26	.298	.413
Lamb,Mike	L	.000	2	0	0	0	0	0	0	1	.000	.000
Bats Left	R	.139	36	5	0	0	0	2	2	6	.200	.139
Lane,Jason	L	.273	11	3	1	0	1	4	0	1	.273	.636
Bats Right	R	.313	16	5	1	0	3	6	0	1	.313	.938
Langerhans,Ryan	L	.400	5	2	0	0	0	0	0	2	.400	.400
Bats Left	R	.200	10	2	0	0	0	0	0	2	.200	.200
Larkin,Barry	L	.200	60	12	4	1	0	3	10	6	.314	.300
Bats Right	R	.309	181	56	12	0	2	15	12	26	.356	.409
LaRocca,Greg	L	.200	5	1	1	0	0	0	1	1	.333	.400
Bats Right	R	.500	4	2	0	0	0	0	0	0	.500	.500
Larson,Brandon	L	.143	28	4	1	0	0	3	4	7	.242	.179
Bats Right	R	.082	61	5	0	0	1	6	9	24	.197	.131
LaRue,Jason	L	.210	105	22	6	0	4	16	12	31	.288	.381
Bats Right	R	.237	274	65	17	1	12	34	21	80	.333	.438
Latham,Chris	L	-	0	0	0	0	0	0	0	0	-	
Bats Both	R	1.000	2	2	0	0	0	0	0	0	1.000	1.000
Lawton,Matt	L	.183	93	17	3	0	3	15	8	8	.269	.312
Bats Left	R	.270	281	76	16	0	12	38	39	39	.366	.456
LeCroy,Matt	L	.298	131	39	6	0	7	20	14	35	.370	.504
Bats Right	R	.280	214	60	13	0	10	44	11	47	.325	.481
Ledee,Ricky	L	.250	20	5	1	0	0	4	3	5	.348	.300
Bats Left	R	.247	235	58	14	2	13	42	31	54	.333	.489
Lee,Carlos	L	.218	165	36	8	0	5	20	11	25	.274	.333
Bats Right	R	.317	458	145	27	1	26	93	26	66	.352	.550
Lee,Derrek	L	.333	105	35	8	1	6	23	25	24	.462	.600
Bats Right	R	.256	434	111	23	1	25	69	63	107	.358	.486
Lee,Travis	L	.285	193	55	15	2	3	25	10	42	.316	.430
Bats Left	R	.269	349	94	22	1	16	45	54	55	.365	.476
Leon,Jose	L	.286	35	10	1	0	0	0	2	8	.342	.314
Bats Right	R	.158	19	3	0	0	0	0	1	10	.238	.158
Lieberthal,Mike	L	.319	116	37	7	0	1	12	10	9	.378	.405
Bats Right	R	.311	392	122	23	1	12	69	28	50	.371	.467
Liefer,Jeff	L	.125	16	2	1	0	0	4	0	4	.125	.188
Bats Left	R	.186	97	18	3	0	4	17	6	35	.231	.340
Linden,Todd	L	.667	3	2	0	0	1	3	1	0	.750	1.667
Bats Both	R	.171	35	6	1	0	0	3	6	8	.171	.200
Lo Duca,Paul	L	.281	153	43	9	1	3	13	15	12	.357	.412
Bats Right	R	.270	415	112	25	1	4	39	29	42	.327	.364
Lockhart,Keith	L	.100	10	1	0	1	0	0	3	2	.308	.300
Bats Left	R	.259	85	22	5	0	3	8	10	17	.344	.424
Lofton,Kenny	L	.244	135	33	7	3	1	11	5	17	.283	.363
Bats Left	R	.313	412	129	25	5	11	35	41	34	.373	.478
Lombard,George	L	.000	4	0	0	0	0	0	0	2	.000	.000
Bats Left	R	.242	33	8	1	0	1	4	0	4	.265	.364
Long,Terrence	L	.236	140	33	7	0	2	16	5	29	.270	.329
Bats Left	R	.249	346	86	15	2	12	45	26	38	.302	.408
Lopez,Felipe	L	.196	51	10	0	1	0	0	8	17	.305	.235
Bats Both	R	.219	146	32	7	1	2	13	20	42	.315	.322
Lopez,Javy	L	.336	110	37	9	0	11	30	6	22	.373	.718
Bats Right	R	.326	347	113	20	3	32	79	27	68	.379	.677
Lopez,Mendy	L	.316	38	12	1	1	0	4	3	9	.366	.395
Bats Right	R	.250	56	14	4	0	3	7	1	19	.263	.482
Loretta,Mark	L	.307	189	58	9	3	4	20	27	14	.394	.450
Bats Right	R	.318	400	127	19	1	9	52	27	48	.361	.438
Lowell,Mike	L	.295	112	33	8	0	12	35	12	14	.363	.688
Bats Right	R	.271	380	103	19	1	20	70	44	64	.346	.484
Ludwick,Ryan	L	.220	59	13	3	0	4	8	4	21	.270	.475
Bats Right	R	.262	103	27	5	1	3	8	8	27	.315	.417
Lugo,Julio	L	.240	146	35	4	2	5	12	11	33	.304	.397
Bats Right	R	.284	352	100	12	2	10	43	33	67	.345	.415

Batter	vs	Avg	AB	H	2B	3B	HR	RBI	BB	SO	OBP	Slg
Lunsford,Trey	L	.000	1	0	0	0	0	0	0	0	.000	.000
Bats Right	R	-	0	0	0	0	0	0	0	0	-	
Mabry,John	L	.000	6	0	0	0	0	0	0	1	.143	.000
Bats Left	R	.224	98	22	6	0	3	16	15	20	.339	.378
Machado,Andy	L	-	0	0	0	0	0	0	0	0	-	
Bats Both	R	-	0	0	0	0	0	0	0	0	-	
Machado,Robert	L	.600	10	6	0	0	1	3	2	1	.667	.900
Bats Right	R	.179	39	7	1	0	0		4	11	.256	.205
Macias,Jose	L	.250	112	28	7	0	2	11	2	15	.270	.366
Bats Both	R	.231	160	37	8	2	2	11	9	30	.275	.344
Mackowiak,Rob	L	.257	35	9	0	2	1	2	0	7	.257	.457
Bats Left	R	.273	139	38	4	2	5	17	15	46	.361	.439
Magruder,Chris	L	.400	5	2	0	1	1	1	0	1	.400	1.400
Bats Both	R	.333	21	7	2	0	0	2	3	5	.440	.429
Marrero,Eli	L	.231	26	6	1	1	0	4	3	3	.310	.346
Bats Right	R	.222	81	18	3	1	2	16	4	15	.253	.358
Martin,Al	L	.333	6	2	0	0	0	0	2	3	.500	.333
Bats Left	R	.250	232	58	12	2	3	26	15	48	.300	.358
Martinez,Edgar	L	.301	123	37	10	0	8	32	37	19	.457	.577
Bats Right	R	.291	374	109	15	0	16	66	55	76	.388	.460
Martinez,Ramon	L	.346	81	28	6	0	2	14	8	16	.391	.494
Bats Right	R	.259	212	55	10	1	1	20	16	34	.311	.330
Martinez,Tino	L	.235	81	19	3	0	2	12	10	15	.323	.346
Bats Left	R	.281	395	111	22	2	13	57	43	56	.358	.446
Martinez,Victor	L	.271	59	16	1	0	1	8	6	9	.333	.339
Bats Both	R	.300	100	30	3	0	0	8	7	12	.352	.330
Mateo,Henry	L	.241	58	14	3	1	0	3	0	10	.254	.328
Bats Right	R	.240	96	23	0	0	0	4	11	28	.330	.240
Mateo,Ruben	L	.257	74	19	2	0	1	9	5	24	.296	.324
Bats Right	R	.233	133	31	7	0	2	9	7	29	.287	.331
Matheny,Mike	L	.340	100	34	5	0	3	15	9	13	.384	.480
Bats Right	R	.226	341	77	13	2	5	32	35	68	.302	.320
Matos,Julius	L	.421	19	8	0	0	1	4	0	1	.421	.579
Bats Right	R	.184	38	7	1	0	1	3	1	11	.205	.289
Matos,Luis	L	.269	108	29	5	1	1	9	10	21	.336	.361
Bats Right	R	.314	331	104	18	2	12	36	18	69	.359	.489
Matranga,Dave	L	.000	1	0	0	0	0	0	0	1	.000	.000
Bats Right	R	.250	4	1	0	0	1	1	0	1	.250	1.000
Matsui,Hideki	L	.287	195	56	9	0	3	24	13	31	.335	.379
Bats Left	R	.287	428	123	33	1	13	82	50	55	.360	.460
Matthews Jr.,Gary	L	.287	129	37	14	1	1	9	9	28	.343	.434
Bats Both	R	.233	339	79	17	1	5	33	34	67	.303	.333
Mayne,Brent	L	.236	106	25	2	0	3	13	8	26	.291	.340
Bats Left	R	.248	266	66	15	1	3	23	24	33	.314	.346
McCarty,Dave	L	.400	25	10	3	0	1	5	2	6	.444	.640
Bats Right	R	.286	28	8	2	0	0	3	1	8	.300	.357
McCracken,Quinton	L	.215	79	17	2	0	0	5	4	17	.247	.241
Bats Both	R	.234	124	29	3	2	0	13	11	17	.294	.290
McDonald,John	L	.215	65	14	1	0	0	4	2	7	.246	.231
Bats Both	R	.215	149	32	8	1	1	10	9	24	.263	.302
McEwing,Joe	L	.247	77	19	3	0	0	8	10	17	.330	.286
Bats Right	R	.239	201	48	8	0	1	8	15	40	.301	.294
McGriff,Fred	L	.194	93	18	4	0	5	11	3	22	.219	.398
Bats Left	R	.275	204	56	10	0	8	29	28	44	.365	.441
McLemore,Mark	L	.433	30	13	0	0	0	8	6	5	.541	.533
Bats Left	R	.211	279	59	12	2	2	29	32	66	.292	.290
McMillon,Billy	L	.118	17	2	0	0	1	0	1	8	.118	.294
Bats Left	R	.287	136	39	11	0	5	25	19	28	.380	.478
Melhuse,Adam	L	.333	24	8	3	0	2	3	0	6	.333	.708
Bats Both	R	.283	53	15	4	0	3	11	9	13	.387	.528
Meluskey,Mitch	L	1.000	1	1	1	0	0	1	0	0	1.000	2.000
Bats Both	R	.000	8	0	0	0	0	0	2	2	.182	.000
Mench,Kevin	L	.346	52	18	4	0	1	2	2	3	.370	.481
Bats Right	R	.301	73	22	8	0	1	9	8	14	.388	.452
Mendez,Carlos	L	.350	20	7	0	0	0	5	0	3	.333	.350
Bats Right	R	.120	25	3	2	0	0	0	0	9	.120	.200
Mendez,Donaldo	L	.176	17	3	2	0	0	1	2	5	.300	.294
Bats Right	R	.239	67	16	4	0	2	8	5	27	.297	.388
Menechino,Frank	L	.250	36	9	0	0	2	3	7	6	.386	.417
Bats Right	R	.149	47	7	0	0	0	6	12	10	.349	.149
Merced,Orlando	L	.296	27	8	2	0	1	6	0	7	.296	.481
Bats Left	R	.222	185	41	15	2	2	20	15	26	.281	.357
Merloni,Lou	L	.196	92	18	2	1	1	8	15	20	.308	.272
Bats Right	R	.337	89	30	6	1	0	10	11	21	.404	.427
Meyers,Chad	L	-	0	0	0	0	0	0	0	0	-	
Bats Right	R	.000	1	0	0	0	0	0	0	0	.000	.000

Batters vs. Left-Handed and Right-Handed Pitchers

Batter	vs	Avg	AB	H	2B	3B	HR	RBI	BB	SO	OBP	Slg
Michaels,Jason	L	.382	55	21	6	0	3	12	10	11	.477	.655
Bats Right	R	.278	54	15	5	0	2	5	5	11	.350	.481
Mientkiewicz,Doug	L	.280	168	47	10	0	8	26	20	20	.363	.482
Bats Left	R	.310	319	99	28	1	3	39	54	35	.408	.433
Miles,Aaron	L	.667	3	2	1	0	0	0	0	0	.667	1.000
Bats Both	R	.222	9	2	2	0	0	2	0	0	.222	.444
Millar,Kevin	L	.289	149	43	9	0	5	25	20	24	.370	.450
Bats Right	R	.271	395	107	21	1	20	71	40	84	.339	.481
Miller,Corky	L	.250	4	1	0	0	0	0	1	1	.400	.250
Bats Right	R	.269	26	7	0	0	0	1	4	6	.394	.269
Miller,Damian	L	.248	109	27	8	0	0	9	14	17	.333	.321
Bats Right	R	.226	243	55	11	1	9	27	25	74	.300	.391
Mirabelli,Doug	L	.250	52	13	2	0	0	4	4	8	.298	.288
Bats Right	R	.261	111	29	11	0	6	14	7	28	.311	.523
Moeller,Chad	L	.284	81	23	2	0	2	14	8	15	.348	.383
Bats Right	R	.259	158	41	15	1	5	15	15	44	.328	.462
Mohr,Dustan	L	.265	117	31	10	0	4	12	15	35	.348	.453
Bats Right	R	.242	231	56	12	0	6	24	18	71	.296	.372
Molina,Ben	L	.289	114	33	8	0	7	19	6	7	.322	.544
Bats Right	R	.278	295	82	16	0	7	52	7	24	.296	.403
Molina,Jose	L	.240	50	12	2	0	0	3	1	10	.269	.280
Bats Right	R	.141	64	9	2	0	0	3	0	16	.164	.172
Mondesi,Raul	L	.262	122	32	9	4	5	18	11	22	.319	.525
Bats Right	R	.274	401	110	22	0	19	53	45	75	.350	.471
Monroe,Craig	L	.293	157	46	9	1	14	34	11	28	.337	.631
Bats Right	R	.209	268	56	9	0	9	36	16	61	.257	.343
Mora,Melvin	L	.324	74	24	3	0	5	12	13	10	.440	.568
Bats Right	R	.315	270	85	14	1	10	36	36	61	.411	.485
Morban,Jose	L	.100	20	2	0	0	1	1	0	5	.100	.250
Bats Both	R	.157	51	8	0	0	1	4	3	16	.218	.216
Mordecai,Mike	L	.263	38	10	1	0	1	2	4	6	.333	.368
Bats Right	R	.176	51	9	3	0	1	6	4	15	.232	.294
Morneau,Justin	L	.154	26	4	1	0	0	1	1	7	.185	.192
Bats Left	R	.250	80	20	3	0	4	15	8	23	.318	.438
Morris,Warren	L	.286	77	22	3	0	0	7	4	17	.329	.325
Bats Left	R	.268	269	72	10	2	6	30	19	25	.313	.387
Mueller,Bill	L	.295	173	51	15	0	8	27	21	21	.375	.520
Bats Both	R	.342	351	120	30	5	11	58	38	56	.409	.550
Munson,Eric	L	.208	77	16	4	0	3	8	10	17	.299	.377
Bats Left	R	.250	236	59	5	0	15	42	25	44	.316	.462
Myers,Greg	L	.333	42	14	5	0	0	6	3	9	.370	.452
Bats Left	R	.303	287	87	14	0	15	46	34	48	.375	.509
Nady,Xavier	L	.311	106	33	8	0	1	8	8	24	.365	.415
Bats Right	R	.249	265	66	9	1	8	31	16	50	.303	.381
Nevin,Phil	L	.349	63	22	3	0	9	27	5	12	.397	.825
Bats Right	R	.252	163	41	5	0	4	19	16	32	.317	.356
Niekro,Lance	L	-	0	0	0	0	0	0	0	0	-	-
Bats Right	R	.200	5	1	1	0	0	2	0	1	.200	.400
Nivar,Ramon	L	.147	34	5	0	0	0	1	1	4	.171	.147
Bats Right	R	.250	56	14	1	2	0	6	3	6	.300	.339
Nix,Laynce	L	.150	20	3	0	0	1	3	2	7	.227	.300
Bats Left	R	.268	164	44	10	0	7	27	7	46	.297	.457
Nixon,Trot	L	.219	96	21	4	1	3	10	9	21	.296	.375
Bats Left	R	.330	345	114	20	5	25	77	56	75	.423	.635
Norton,Greg	L	.273	22	6	2	0	0	5	2	8	.333	.364
Bats Both	R	.261	157	41	13	0	6	26	14	39	.324	.459
Nunez,Abraham O	L	.163	43	7	1	0	0	3	6	12	.302	.186
Bats Both	R	.261	268	70	7	7	4	32	20	41	.311	.384
Ojeda,Augie	L	.200	5	1	0	0	0	0	0	1	.200	.200
Bats Both	R	.100	20	2	0	0	0	0	1	4	.182	.100
Ojeda,Miguel	L	.233	43	10	2	0	2	6	4	5	.292	.419
Bats Right	R	.235	98	23	4	0	2	16	14	21	.348	.337
O'Leary,Troy	L	.214	28	6	0	0	1	2	4	8	.313	.321
Bats Left	R	.219	146	32	9	0	4	26	10	23	.267	.363
Olerud,John	L	.239	155	37	11	0	0	23	15	30	.318	.310
Bats Left	R	.281	384	108	24	0	10	60	69	37	.392	.422
Olivo,Miguel	L	.302	86	26	9	0	4	12	2	17	.315	.547
Bats Right	R	.212	231	49	10	1	2	15	17	63	.277	.290
Olmedo,Ray	L	.215	65	14	2	0	0	5	3	15	.250	.246
Bats Both	R	.248	165	41	4	1	0	12	10	31	.291	.285
Ordonez,Magglio	L	.317	164	52	12	1	12	35	11	14	.358	.622
Bats Right	R	.317	442	140	34	2	17	64	46	59	.388	.518
Ordonez,Rey	L	.308	26	8	4	0	0	6	0	1	.296	.462
Bats Right	R	.319	91	29	7	0	3	16	2	11	.337	.495
Ortiz,David	L	.216	116	25	9	1	4	22	7	26	.260	.414
Bats Left	R	.313	332	104	30	1	27	79	51	57	.404	.654

Batter	vs	Avg	AB	H	2B	3B	HR	RBI	BB	SO	OBP	Slg
Osik,Keith	L	.378	37	14	5	0	0	7	6	3	.465	.514
Bats Right	R	.225	204	46	7	0	2	14	25	41	.319	.289
Overbay,Lyle	L	.291	86	25	10	0	0	9	4	29	.326	.407
Bats Left	R	.268	168	45	10	0	4	19	31	38	.383	.399
Owens,Eric	L	.308	143	44	4	0	1	18	5	12	.329	.357
Bats Right	R	.214	98	21	2	0	0	2	5	12	.260	.235
Ozuna,Pablo	L	.125	8	1	0	0	0	0	0	2	.125	.125
Bats Right	R	.219	32	7	1	0	0	2	2	4	.306	.250
Palmeiro,Orlando	L	.182	55	10	1	0	0	3	2	4	.224	.200
Bats Left	R	.290	262	76	12	1	3	30	30	27	.358	.378
Palmeiro,Rafael	L	.282	170	48	5	1	15	43	24	18	.374	.588
Bats Left	R	.251	391	98	16	1	23	69	60	59	.353	.473
Palmer,Dean	L	.189	37	7	1	0	0	0	4	9	.268	.216
Bats Right	R	.102	49	5	1	0	0	6	5	19	.211	.122
Paquette,Craig	L	.000	16	0	0	0	0	0	0	2	.000	.000
Bats Right	R	.294	17	5	0	0	0	0	0	3	.294	.294
Patterson,Corey	L	.289	90	26	2	1	4	22	3	25	.316	.467
Bats Left	R	.301	239	72	15	6	9	33	12	52	.333	.527
Patterson,Jarrod	L	.000	5	0	0	0	0	0	2	1	.286	.000
Bats Left	R	.235	17	4	0	0	0	0	1	5	.278	.235
Paul,Josh	L	.333	9	3	0	0	0	0	0	2	.333	.333
Bats Right	R	.214	14	3	0	0	0	4	3	4	.353	.214
Payton,Jay	L	.288	160	46	9	1	11	27	16	23	.354	.563
Bats Right	R	.307	440	135	23	4	17	62	27	54	.354	.493
Pellow,Kit	L	.250	8	2	0	0	1	1	0	2	.333	.625
Bats Right	R	.600	10	6	3	1	0	3	0	2	.583	1.100
Pena,Carlos	L	.208	149	31	5	1	5	18	14	49	.284	.356
Bats Left	R	.267	303	81	16	5	13	32	39	74	.355	.482
Pena,Wily Mo	L	.204	54	11	2	0	2	5	5	19	.283	.352
Bats Right	R	.225	111	25	4	1	3	11	7	34	.283	.360
Peralta,Jhonny	L	.260	73	19	3	1	3	9	4	21	.316	.452
Bats Right	R	.213	169	36	7	0	1	12	16	44	.286	.272
Perez,Antonio	L	.237	59	14	3	1	0	2	15	18	.392	.322
Bats Right	R	.258	66	17	3	0	2	10	3	16	.296	.394
Perez,Eddie	L	.342	76	26	6	0	2	11	6	11	.386	.500
Bats Right	R	.252	274	69	11	1	9	34	11	36	.280	.398
Perez,Eduardo	L	.353	102	36	8	0	8	17	18	20	.459	.667
Bats Right	R	.238	151	36	8	0	3	24	11	33	.295	.351
Perez,Neifi	L	.253	75	19	6	0	1	14	3	6	.278	.373
Bats Both	R	.257	253	65	13	4	0	17	11	17	.287	.340
Perez,Timo	L	.172	29	5	2	0	0	3	1	4	.200	.241
Bats Left	R	.278	317	88	19	0	4	39	17	25	.310	.375
Perez,Tomas	L	.266	79	21	6	0	3	9	4	12	.301	.456
Bats Both	R	.265	219	58	12	1	2	24	19	42	.321	.356
Perry,Herbert	L	.154	13	2	0	0	0	1	0	1	.154	.154
Bats Right	R	.182	11	2	1	0	0	1	0	2	.182	.273
Petrick,Ben	L	.259	58	15	4	0	1	7	4	11	.306	.379
Bats Right	R	.188	64	12	2	0	3	5	4	20	.235	.359
Phelps,Josh	L	.317	145	46	3	0	7	20	15	34	.393	.483
Bats Right	R	.239	251	60	15	1	13	46	24	81	.338	.462
Phillips,Brandon	L	.179	95	17	3	0	2	8	6	20	.228	.274
Bats Right	R	.218	275	60	15	1	4	25	8	57	.247	.324
Phillips,Jason	L	.308	117	36	8	0	2	18	20	12	.406	.427
Bats Right	R	.294	286	84	17	0	9	40	19	38	.359	.448
Piatt,Adam	L	.263	95	25	10	0	4	13	6	26	.301	.495
Bats Right	R	.135	37	5	3	0	2	5	3	20	.200	.378
Piazza,Mike	L	.265	49	13	6	0	1	7	10	8	.390	.449
Bats Right	R	.292	185	54	7	0	10	27	25	32	.374	.492
Pierre,Juan	L	.311	206	64	7	2	0	8	10	9	.346	.364
Bats Left	R	.303	462	140	21	5	1	33	45	26	.368	.377
Pierzynski,A.J.	L	.281	135	38	9	1	4	22	2	22	.333	.452
Bats Left	R	.324	352	114	26	2	7	52	22	33	.370	.469
Podsednik,Scott	L	.270	148	40	3	4	4	22	13	26	.333	.426
Bats Left	R	.329	410	135	26	4	5	36	43	65	.395	.449
Polanco,Placido	L	.292	96	28	5	1	5	14	12	8	.364	.521
Bats Right	R	.288	396	114	25	2	9	49	30	30	.349	.429
Porter,Colin	L	.111	9	1	0	0	0	0	0	5	.111	.111
Bats Left	R	.217	23	5	0	0	0	0	1	12	.250	.217
Posada,Jorge	L	.295	122	36	6	0	8	27	19	23	.403	.541
Bats Both	R	.276	359	99	18	0	22	74	74	87	.405	.510
Pratt,Todd	L	.267	30	8	3	0	1	4	6	8	.378	.467
Bats Right	R	.274	95	26	7	1	3	16	16	30	.407	.463
Pride,Curtis	L	-	0	0	0	0	0	0	0	0	-	-
Bats Left	R	.083	12	1	0	0	1	1	0	2	.083	.333
Prieto,Alex	L	.200	5	1	0	0	0	0	0	1	.200	.200
Bats Right	R	.000	6	0	0	0	0	0	0	3	.000	.000

Batters vs. Left-Handed and Right-Handed Pitchers

Batter	vs	Avg	AB	H	2B	3B	HR	RBI	BB	SO	OBP	Slg
Prince,Tom	L	.316	19	6	0	0	1	1	0	4	.316	.474
Bats Right	R	.138	29	4	2	0	1	5	5	3	.306	.310
Pujols,Albert	L	.387	142	55	16	0	11	32	21	8	.458	.732
Bats Right	R	.350	449	157	35	1	32	92	58	57	.434	.646
Punto,Nick	L	.278	36	10	2	0	0	1	2	6	.316	.333
Bats Both	R	.179	56	10	0	0	1	3	5	16	.246	.232
Quinlan,Robb	L	.286	35	10	1	1	0	2	3	3	.342	.371
Bats Right	R	.288	59	17	3	1	0	2	3	13	.323	.373
Quintero,Humberto	L	.286	7	2	0	0	0	0	0	2	.286	.286
Bats Right	R	.188	16	3	0	0	0	2	1	4	.235	.188
Raines Jr,Tim	L	.143	21	3	1	0	0	1	1	6	.182	.190
Bats Both	R	.136	22	3	0	1	0	1	1	6	.208	.227
Ramirez,Aramis	L	.285	137	39	8	0	10	28	7	17	.322	.562
Bats Right	R	.268	470	126	24	2	17	78	35	82	.324	.436
Ramirez,Julio	L	-	0	0	0	0	0	0	0	0	-	
Bats Right	R	.000	2	0	0	0	0	0	0	0	.000	.000
Ramirez,Manny	L	.385	143	55	11	0	8	23	25	16	.476	.629
Bats Both	R	.305	426	130	25	1	29	81	72	78	.411	.573
Randa,Joe	L	.311	151	47	10	0	6	21	10	18	.356	.497
Bats Right	R	.282	351	99	21	1	10	51	31	43	.345	.433
Ransom,Cody	L	.250	4	1	1	0	0	0	0	1	.250	.500
Bats Right	R	.217	23	5	0	0	1	1	1	10	.250	.348
Reboulet,Jeff	L	.220	100	22	3	1	2	4	10	11	.297	.330
Bats Right	R	.255	161	41	7	1	1	21	17	36	.335	.329
Redman,Prentice	L	.167	12	2	1	0	0	1	1	4	.231	.250
Bats Right	R	.083	12	1	0	0	1	1	0	5	.154	.333
Redman,Tike	L	.329	73	24	5	1	0	6	3	6	.372	.425
Bats Left	R	.331	157	52	11	4	3	13	11	12	.375	.510
Redmond,Mike	L	.314	35	11	3	1	0	4	0	5	.324	.457
Bats Right	R	.211	90	19	4	0	0	7	7	11	.294	.256
Reese,Pokey	L	.161	31	5	0	0	1	4	4	6	.257	.258
Bats Right	R	.237	76	18	2	0	0	8	5	25	.277	.263
Relaford,Desi	L	.300	130	39	7	1	3	19	22	19	.409	.438
Bats Both	R	.238	370	88	20	4	5	40	18	51	.278	.354
Renteria,Edgar	L	.391	115	45	17	0	5	34	27	8	.503	.670
Bats Right	R	.316	472	149	30	1	8	66	38	46	.364	.434
Restovich,Mike	L	.227	22	5	0	1	0	1	1	2	.261	.318
Bats Right	R	.323	31	10	3	1	0	3	9	10	.488	.484
Reyes,Jose	L	.225	80	18	5	0	3	17	5	13	.267	.400
Bats Both	R	.340	194	66	7	4	2	15	8	23	.363	.448
Reyes,Rene	L	.289	38	11	3	0	1	3	3	7	.341	.447
Bats Both	R	.244	78	19	4	1	1	4	2	12	.259	.359
Richard,Chris	L	.500	2	1	0	0	0	0	0	0	.500	.500
Bats Left	R	.200	25	5	1	1	1	3	3	6	.286	.440
Riggs,Adam	L	.350	20	7	3	0	0	1	5	2	.480	.500
Bats Right	R	.195	41	8	1	1	3	4	4	7	.267	.488
Rios,Armando	L	.214	14	3	0	0	0	0	0	2	.214	.214
Bats Left	R	.211	90	19	3	0	2	11	5	11	.250	.311
Rivas,Luis	L	.200	130	26	1	1	1	9	10	18	.259	.246
Bats Right	R	.281	345	97	15	8	7	34	20	47	.327	.432
Rivera,Carlos	L	.188	16	3	1	0	1	2	0	6	.188	.438
Bats Left	R	.228	79	18	4	0	2	8	8	22	.300	.354
Rivera,Juan	L	.340	50	17	4	0	4	10	2	5	.358	.660
Bats Right	R	.236	123	29	10	0	3	16	8	22	.282	.390
Rivera,Mike	L	.000	9	0	0	0	0	0	2	3	.182	.000
Bats Right	R	.205	44	9	1	0	1	2	3	8	.255	.295
Rivera,Ruben	L	.182	11	2	1	0	1	1	1	1	.250	.545
Bats Right	R	.179	39	7	1	0	1	3	4	13	.256	.282
Roberts,Brian	L	.264	129	34	7	0	2	8	6	16	.296	.364
Bats Both	R	.272	331	90	15	4	3	33	40	42	.351	.369
Roberts,Dave	L	.265	83	22	3	0	0	3	14	6	.378	.301
Bats Left	R	.246	305	75	3	5	2	13	29	33	.318	.308
Robinson,Kerry	L	.238	21	5	0	1	1	1	0	2	.238	.476
Bats Left	R	.251	187	47	6	2	0	15	8	25	.286	.305
Rodriguez,Alex	L	.305	187	57	11	3	16	37	31	40	.404	.652
Bats Right	R	.295	420	124	19	3	31	81	56	86	.392	.576
Rodriguez,Ivan	L	.376	117	44	12	1	3	18	19	18	.460	.573
Bats Right	R	.274	394	108	24	2	13	67	36	74	.340	.444
Rolen,Scott	L	.283	113	32	12	0	7	27	28	24	.427	.575
Bats Right	R	.287	446	128	37	1	21	77	54	88	.370	.516
Rollins,Jimmy	L	.262	145	38	9	0	2	11	10	24	.308	.366
Bats Both	R	.263	483	127	33	6	6	51	44	89	.324	.393
Rolls,Damian	L	.273	121	33	3	0	3	11	4	25	.294	.372
Bats Right	R	.246	252	62	17	0	4	35	15	59	.304	.361
Romano,Jason	L	.050	20	1	0	0	0	0	0	3	.050	.050
Bats Right	R	.125	16	2	0	0	0	0	1	5	.176	.125
Romero,Mandy	L	1.000	1	1	0	0	0	0	0	0	1.000	1.000
Bats Both	R	.333	6	2	1	0	0	0	0	1	.333	.500
Ross,Cody	L	.286	7	2	0	0	1	4	0	1	.286	.714
Bats Right	R	.167	12	2	1	0	0	1	1	2	.286	.250
Ross,Dave	L	.258	31	8	0	0	3	6	4	10	.333	.548
Bats Right	R	.258	93	24	7	0	7	12	9	32	.337	.559
Rowand,Aaron	L	.338	65	22	4	0	1	7	2	9	.380	.446
Bats Right	R	.250	92	23	4	0	5	17	5	12	.289	.457
Ruan,Wilkin	L	.100	10	1	0	1	0	0	0	4	.100	.300
Bats Right	R	.258	31	8	2	0	0	2	0	3	.258	.323
Ryan,Mike	L	.438	16	7	4	0	0	2	1	4	.471	.688
Bats Left	R	.378	45	17	3	0	5	11	5	8	.431	.778
Sadler,Donnie	L	.203	59	12	1	0	1	4	7	13	.290	.271
Bats Right	R	.194	72	14	4	2	0	11	6	21	.266	.306
Salmon,Tim	L	.157	157	43	10	1	7	26	33	20	.400	.484
Bats Right	R	.275	371	102	25	3	12	46	44	73	.362	.456
Sanchez,Alex	L	.309	152	47	6	2	0	9	7	16	.335	.375
Bats Left	R	.279	405	113	17	6	1	23	18	58	.312	.358
Sanchez,Freddy	L	.462	13	6	0	0	0	1	0	1	.462	.462
Bats Right	R	.095	21	2	2	0	0	1	0	7	.095	.190
Sanchez,Rey	L	.292	89	26	2	1	0	5	8	9	.347	.371
Bats Right	R	.235	255	60	6	1	0	18	8	30	.262	.267
Sandberg,Jared	L	.209	67	14	4	1	2	8	7	28	.284	.388
Bats Right	R	.217	69	15	6	0	4	15	9	24	.325	.478
Sanders,Reggie	L	.301	136	41	7	2	12	33	15	26	.368	.647
Bats Right	R	.278	317	88	20	2	19	54	23	84	.335	.533
Santiago,Benito	L	.290	100	29	5	0	4	12	7	22	.336	.460
Bats Right	R	.276	301	83	16	2	7	44	22	47	.327	.412
Santiago,Ramon	L	.187	134	25	5	0	1	4	7	10	.232	.246
Bats Both	R	.242	310	75	13	1	1	25	26	56	.317	.300
Santos,Angel	L	.231	13	3	0	0	1	1	1	7	.286	.462
Bats Both	R	.222	63	14	3	1	2	5	2	11	.246	.397
Santos,Francisco	L	.000	2	0	0	0	0	0	0	0	.000	.000
Bats Left	R	.231	13	3	0	0	1	1	0	3	.231	.615
Sardinha,Dane	L	.000	1	0	0	0	0	0	0	0	.000	.000
Bats Right	R	.000	1	0	0	0	0	0	0	1	.000	.000
Schneider,Brian	L	.179	67	12	3	0	3	9	10	20	.282	.358
Bats Left	R	.243	268	65	23	1	6	37	27	55	.315	.403
Scutaro,Marco	L	.095	21	2	1	0	0	0	3	2	.174	.143
Bats Right	R	.259	54	14	3	0	2	6	11	11	.388	.426
Sears,Todd	L	.167	6	1	0	0	0	1	0	2	.167	.167
Bats Left	R	.254	67	17	3	0	2	10	7	16	.329	.388
Segui,David	L	.200	50	10	2	0	0	4	3	7	.259	.240
Bats Both	R	.282	174	49	8	1	5	21	23	40	.364	.425
Seguignol,Fernando	L	.000	3	0	0	0	0	0	0	2	.000	.000
Bats Both	R	.250	4	1	0	0	0	0	1	1	.400	.250
Selby,Bill	L	.000	2	0	0	0	0	0	0	0	.000	.000
Bats Left	R	.108	37	4	1	0	0	5	3	11	.171	.135
Sexson,Richie	L	.279	122	34	2	1	10	23	38	25	.448	.557
Bats Right	R	.271	484	131	26	1	35	101	60	126	.359	.545
Sheffield,Gary	L	.341	123	42	9	1	10	32	25	10	.450	.675
Bats Right	R	.327	453	148	28	1	29	100	61	45	.410	.585
Shinjo,Tsuyoshi	L	.247	81	20	3	0	1	6	1	10	.295	.321
Bats Right	R	.061	33	2	0	0	0	1	1	2	.088	.061
Shumpert,Terry	L	.203	69	14	4	2	2	6	7	14	.282	.406
Bats Right	R	.133	15	2	1	0	0	1	3	3	.316	.200
Sierra,Ruben	L	.236	89	21	6	0	3	13	6	14	.281	.404
Bats Both	R	.284	218	62	11	1	6	30	21	33	.346	.427
Simon,Randall	L	.269	52	14	0	0	2	10	2	6	.296	.385
Bats Left	R	.277	358	99	17	0	14	62	14	31	.310	.441
Singleton,Chris	L	.167	48	8	4	0	0	6	7	12	.276	.250
Bats Left	R	.260	258	67	20	1	1	30	19	43	.306	.357
Smith,Jason	L	-	0	0	0	0	0	0	0	0	-	
Bats Left	R	.250	4	1	0	0	0	0	0	0	.250	.250
Smith,Mark	L	.241	29	7	2	0	0	1	2	5	.290	.310
Bats Right	R	.235	34	8	2	0	3	9	2	8	.263	.559
Smitherman,Stephen	L	.190	21	4	2	0	0	2	1	3	.227	.286
Bats Right	R	.130	23	3	0	0	1	4	2	6	.200	.261
Snow,J.T.	L	.208	48	10	1	0	0	6	10	12	.387	.229
Bats Left	R	.284	282	80	17	3	8	45	45	43	.387	.450
Sojo,Luis	L	.000	1	0	0	0	0	0	0	0	.000	.000
Bats Right	R	.000	3	0	0	0	0	0	0	0	.000	.000
Sorensen,Zach	L	.111	9	1	1	0	0	0	3	1	.333	.222
Bats Both	R	.143	28	4	0	0	1	2	4	12	.250	.250
Soriano,Alfonso	L	.312	138	43	10	2	7	16	14	25	.379	.565
Bats Right	R	.285	544	155	26	3	31	75	24	105	.327	.515

Batters vs. Left-Handed and Right-Handed Pitchers

Batter	vs	Avg	AB	H	2B	3B	HR	RBI	BB	SO	OBP	Slg
Sosa,Sammy	L	.333	105	35	4	0	7	14	20	23	.440	.571
Bats Right	R	.265	412	109	18	0	33	89	42	120	.336	.549
Spencer,Shane	L	.277	166	46	7	0	7	26	15	33	.335	.446
Bats Right	R	.231	229	53	13	0	5	23	30	59	.323	.354
Spiezio,Scott	L	.223	148	33	6	1	3	22	11	22	.282	.338
Bats Both	R	.282	373	105	30	6	13	61	35	44	.344	.499
Spivey,Junior	L	.288	125	36	11	1	5	19	15	21	.366	.512
Bats Right	R	.238	240	57	11	1	8	31	18	74	.305	.392
Stairs,Matt	L	.188	32	6	0	0	2	4	3	7	.278	.375
Bats Left	R	.304	273	83	20	1	18	53	42	57	.402	.582
Stenson,Dernell	L	.200	5	1	0	0	0	0	1	4	.333	.200
Bats Left	R	.250	76	19	5	0	3	13	10	20	.333	.434
Stewart,Shannon	L	.331	139	46	10	1	4	16	14	19	.389	.504
Bats Right	R	.300	434	130	34	1	9	57	38	47	.357	.445
Stinnett,Kelly	L	.193	57	11	6	0	0	2	5	16	.270	.298
Bats Right	R	.256	129	33	7	0	3	17	9	36	.317	.380
Strong,Jamal	L	.000	1	0	0	0	0	0	0	0	.000	.000
Bats Right	R	.000	1	0	0	0	0	0	0	0	.000	.000
Stynes,Chris	L	.284	134	38	11	3	2	22	17	26	.373	.455
Bats Right	R	.243	309	75	20	0	9	51	31	50	.318	.395
Surhoff,B.J.	L	.284	74	21	2	0	0	9	8	11	.357	.311
Bats Left	R	.298	245	73	18	0	5	32	21	18	.352	.433
Suzuki,Ichiro	L	.359	209	75	13	2	0	17	9	19	.391	.440
Bats Left	R	.291	470	137	16	6	13	45	27	50	.335	.434
Swann,Pedro	L	1.000	1	1	0	0	0	1	0	0	1.000	1.000
Bats Left	R	.154	13	2	1	0	1	1	1	4	.214	.462
Sweeney,Mark	L	.000	6	0	0	0	0	0	0	4	.000	.000
Bats Left	R	.275	91	25	9	0	2	14	9	23	.340	.440
Sweeney,Mike	L	.277	112	31	6	0	5	20	18	14	.374	.464
Bats Right	R	.300	280	84	12	1	11	63	46	42	.398	.468
Taguchi,So	L	.259	27	7	0	0	2	6	3	2	.333	.481
Bats Right	R	.259	27	7	3	1	1	7	1	9	.286	.556
Tatis,Fernando	L	.240	50	12	0	0	2	6	2	9	.296	.360
Bats Right	R	.176	125	22	6	0	0	9	16	31	.275	.224
Taylor,Reggie	L	.167	30	5	0	0	2	5	1	9	.194	.367
Bats Left	R	.227	150	34	5	2	3	14	10	59	.280	.347
Teixeira,Mark	L	.295	173	51	8	2	11	32	17	38	.368	.555
Bats Both	R	.242	356	86	21	3	15	52	27	82	.313	.444
Tejada,Miguel	L	.269	167	45	9	0	8	25	24	7	.361	.467
Bats Right	R	.281	469	132	33	0	19	81	29	58	.326	.473
Terrero,Luis	L	.000	2	0	0	0	0	0	0	0	.000	.000
Bats Right	R	.500	2	1	0	0	0	0	0	1	.667	.500
Thames,Marcus	L	.250	52	13	1	0	1	3	3	10	.304	.327
Bats Right	R	.095	21	2	1	0	0	1	5	8	.286	.143
Thomas,Frank	L	.315	149	47	11	0	17	35	34	22	.446	.732
Bats Right	R	.249	397	99	24	0	25	70	66	93	.368	.499
Thome,Jim	L	.254	177	45	6	0	10	34	24	62	.338	.458
Bats Left	R	.272	401	109	24	3	37	97	87	120	.405	.623
Thurston,Joe	L	-	0	0	0	0	0	0	0	0	-	-
Bats Left	R	.200	10	2	0	0	0	0	1	1	.273	.200
Torcato,Tony	L	.000	2	0	0	0	0	0	0	0	.000	.000
Bats Left	R	.214	14	3	1	0	0	1	0	4	.267	.286
Torrealba,Yorvit	L	.212	33	7	2	2	0	2	5	5	.333	.394
Bats Right	R	.269	167	45	8	0	4	27	9	34	.307	.389
Torres,Andres	L	.258	62	16	3	1	1	5	3	5	.288	.387
Bats Both	R	.198	106	21	1	2	0	4	7	30	.248	.245
Trammell,Bubba	L	.188	32	6	2	0	0	4	4	5	.278	.250
Bats Right	R	.217	23	5	3	0	0	1	2	5	.280	.348
Truby,Chris	L	.385	13	5	0	0	0	1	2	4	.467	.385
Bats Right	R	.233	30	7	3	0	0	2	3	9	.303	.333
Tucker,Michael	L	.236	123	29	6	2	2	11	11	29	.307	.366
Bats Left	R	.274	266	73	14	3	11	44	28	59	.342	.474
Tyner,Jason	L	.167	12	2	0	0	0	0	1	2	.231	.167
Bats Left	R	.295	78	23	7	0	0	6	9	10	.368	.385
Ugueto,Luis	L	.250	4	1	0	0	0	0	0	0	.250	.250
Bats Both	R	.000	1	0	0	0	0	1	1	0	.500	.000
Uribe,Juan	L	.301	83	25	5	1	2	7	4	14	.341	.458
Bats Right	R	.236	233	55	14	2	8	26	13	46	.281	.416
Utley,Chase	L	.333	12	4	2	0	0	2	1	2	.500	.500
Bats Left	R	.230	122	28	8	1	2	19	10	20	.301	.361
Valderrama,Carlos	L	.000	3	0	0	0	0	0	0	1	.000	.000
Bats Right	R	.250	4	1	0	0	0	0	0	2	.250	.250
Valent,Eric	L	.286	7	2	0	0	0	0	0	1	.286	.286
Bats Left	R	.200	35	7	0	0	0	1	2	8	.243	.200
Valentin,Javier	L	.231	13	3	0	0	0	0	1	2	.286	.231
Bats Both	R	.221	122	27	7	1	3	15	4	29	.250	.369

Batter	vs	Avg	AB	H	2B	3B	HR	RBI	BB	SO	OBP	Slg
Valentin,Jose	L	.131	107	14	1	0	2	6	8	28	.190	.196
Bats Both	R	.265	396	105	25	2	26	68	46	86	.345	.535
Vander Wal,John	L	.158	38	6	2	0	0	2	4	18	.256	.211
Bats Left	R	.270	289	78	23	1	14	43	42	86	.363	.502
Varitek,Jason	L	.309	136	42	9	1	10	33	17	24	.387	.610
Bats Both	R	.257	315	81	22	0	15	52	34	82	.335	.470
Vaughn,Greg	L	.250	12	3	1	0	2	3	4	3	.438	.833
Bats Right	R	.160	25	4	2	0	1	2	4	10	.267	.360
Vaughn,Mo	L	.133	15	2	0	0	0	4	1	6	.235	.133
Bats Left	R	.203	64	13	2	0	3	11	13	16	.342	.375
Vazquez,Ramon	L	.224	116	26	5	0	0	7	11	24	.292	.267
Bats Left	R	.275	306	84	12	4	3	23	41	64	.361	.369
Velandia,Jorge	L	.250	8	2	0	0	0	5	2	3	.364	.250
Bats Right	R	.180	50	9	3	1	0	3	8	12	.293	.280
Ventura,Robin	L	.216	51	11	3	0	3	5	6	16	.298	.451
Bats Left	R	.246	341	84	15	1	11	50	52	71	.346	.393
Victorino,Shane	L	.133	15	2	0	0	0	0	2	2	.235	.133
Bats Both	R	.155	58	9	2	0	0	4	5	15	.231	.190
Vidro,Jose	L	.315	127	40	7	0	7	22	15	14	.389	.535
Bats Both	R	.309	382	118	29	0	8	43	54	36	.399	.448
Vina,Fernando	L	.163	49	8	2	1	0	5	2	10	.236	.245
Bats Left	R	.271	210	57	12	3	4	18	9	14	.326	.414
Vitiello,Joe	L	.375	56	21	6	0	2	10	6	9	.435	.589
Bats Right	R	.250	20	5	0	0	1	3	1	5	.333	.400
Vizcaino,Jose	L	.222	36	8	0	0	0	0	0	5	.243	.222
Bats Both	R	.255	153	39	7	3	3	26	8	17	.290	.399
Vizquel,Omar	L	.224	67	15	5	0	0	3	8	5	.303	.299
Bats Both	R	.251	183	46	8	2	2	16	21	15	.328	.350
Walbeck,Matt	L	.269	26	7	1	0	1	4	1	5	.296	.423
Bats Both	R	.152	112	17	3	1	0	2	2	21	.174	.196
Walker,Larry	L	.321	156	50	9	3	4	32	23	26	.422	.494
Bats Left	R	.265	298	79	16	4	12	47	75	61	.422	.466
Walker,Todd	L	.234	158	37	10	0	4	25	12	10	.282	.373
Bats Left	R	.301	429	129	28	4	9	60	36	44	.352	.448
Ward,Daryle	L	.400	5	2	0	0	0	0	0	1	.500	.400
Bats Left	R	.173	104	18	1	0	0	9	3	18	.194	.183
Watson,Matt	L	.000	2	0	0	0	0	0	0	1	.000	.000
Bats Left	R	.190	21	4	2	0	0	2	1	4	.227	.286
Weeks,Rickie	L	.000	2	0	0	0	0	0	1	2	.333	.000
Bats Right	R	.200	10	2	1	0	0	0	0	4	.273	.300
Wells,Vernon	L	.347	173	60	18	3	4	26	17	12	.402	.555
Bats Right	R	.307	505	155	31	2	29	91	25	68	.344	.549
Werth,Jayson	L	.056	18	1	1	0	0	4	2	7	.150	.111
Bats Right	R	.300	30	9	3	0	2	6	1	15	.323	.600
Wesson,Barry	L	.000	4	0	0	0	0	0	0	2	.000	.000
Bats Right	R	.286	7	2	0	0	1	3	0	2	.286	.714
White,Rondell	L	.299	137	41	7	1	4	20	8	19	.351	.453
Bats Right	R	.285	351	100	16	3	18	67	23	60	.337	.501
Widger,Chris	L	.227	22	5	2	0	0	5	1	6	.250	.318
Bats Right	R	.238	80	19	7	0	0	9	5	14	.287	.325
Wigginton,Ty	L	.297	155	46	11	1	4	17	20	34	.377	.458
Bats Right	R	.239	418	100	25	5	7	54	26	90	.295	.373
Wilkerson,Brad	L	.281	128	36	11	1	3	19	27	44	.405	.453
Bats Left	R	.263	376	99	23	3	16	58	62	111	.371	.468
Williams,Bernie	L	.280	132	37	5	1	4	18	28	17	.414	.424
Bats Both	R	.256	313	80	14	0	11	46	43	44	.345	.406
Williams,Gerald	L	.167	18	3	1	0	0	3	0	2	.167	.222
Bats Right	R	.077	13	1	0	0	0	0	2	3	.200	.077
Williams,Matt	L	.302	43	13	3	0	3	8	7	5	.396	.581
Bats Right	R	.220	91	20	6	0	1	8	9	21	.291	.319
Wilson,Craig	L	.308	107	33	6	1	11	26	21	24	.431	.692
Bats Right	R	.238	202	48	9	3	7	22	14	65	.320	.416
Wilson,Dan	L	.264	106	28	7	0	2	20	6	16	.304	.387
Bats Right	R	.229	210	48	8	2	2	23	9	36	.257	.314
Wilson,Enrique	L	.133	30	4	0	0	1	2	4	3	.235	.233
Bats Both	R	.257	105	27	9	0	2	13	3	11	.288	.400
Wilson,Jack	L	.261	134	35	4	1	2	11	13	9	.324	.351
Bats Right	R	.255	424	108	17	2	7	51	23	65	.296	.354
Wilson,Preston	L	.274	179	49	7	0	5	25	25	43	.361	.397
Bats Right	R	.285	421	120	36	1	31	116	29	96	.336	.596
Wilson,Tom	L	.299	107	32	10	0	1	9	16	22	.387	.421
Bats Right	R	.228	149	34	9	0	4	26	12	58	.288	.369
Wilson,Vance	L	.243	74	18	2	0	2	8	3	15	.273	.351
Bats Right	R	.242	194	47	7	1	6	31	12	41	.300	.381
Winn,Randy	L	.314	169	53	15	3	3	16	13	22	.368	.491
Bats Both	R	.288	431	124	22	1	8	59	28	86	.337	.399

Batters vs. Left-Handed and Right-Handed Pitchers

Batter	vs	Avg	AB	H	2B	3B	HR	RBI	BB	SO	OBP	Slg
Witt,Kevin	L	.241	29	7	1	0	0	2	2	11	.290	.276
Bats Left	R	.266	241	64	8	0	10	24	13	57	.302	.423
Womack,Tony	L	.268	56	15	4	1	0	6	1	7	.293	.375
Bats Left	R	.218	293	64	10	3	2	16	8	40	.243	.294
Woodward,Chris	L	.307	101	31	10	1	2	16	10	19	.360	.485
Bats Right	R	.242	248	60	12	1	5	29	18	53	.298	.359
Wooten,Shawn	L	.238	151	36	6	0	5	21	14	20	.304	.377
Bats Right	R	.248	121	30	2	0	2	11	10	25	.303	.314
Young,Dmitri	L	.293	191	56	11	1	9	27	24	45	.382	.503
Bats Both	R	.299	371	111	23	6	20	58	34	85	.366	.555
Young,Eric	L	.246	114	28	4	0	6	8	19	10	.356	.439
Bats Right	R	.252	361	91	16	1	9	26	38	34	.329	.377
Young,Ernie	L	.167	6	1	0	0	0	0	2	4	.375	.167
Bats Right	R	.200	5	1	0	0	0	0	2	1	.429	.200
Young,Kevin	L	.167	48	8	1	0	1	4	4	12	.231	.250
Bats Right	R	.250	36	9	3	0	1	3	8	13	.386	.417
Young,Michael	L	.308	198	61	13	2	5	23	8	33	.332	.470
Bats Right	R	.306	468	143	20	7	9	49	28	70	.343	.436
Zaun,Gregg	L	.308	39	12	2	0	0	3	5	5	.378	.359
Bats Both	R	.205	127	26	6	0	4	18	14	16	.287	.346
Zeile,Todd	L	.235	98	23	4	1	7	21	14	14	.319	.510
Bats Right	R	.224	201	45	6	1	4	21	20	40	.302	.323
Zoccolillo,Pete	L	.000	1	0	0	0	0	0	0	0	.000	.000
Bats Left	R	.111	36	4	1	0	0	3	2	13	.158	.139

Pitchers vs. Left-Handed and Right-Handed Batters

Pitcher	vs	Avg	AB	H	2B	3B	HR	RBI	BB	SO	OBP	Slg
Abbott,Paul	L	.305	105	32	5	0	5	16	18	17	.413	.495
Throws Right	R	.192	78	15	4	0	3	6	8	15	.267	.359
Acevedo,Jose	L	.136	44	6	3	0	2	3	4	8	.204	.341
Throws Right	R	.224	49	11	3	1	1	5	2	15	.264	.388
Acevedo,Juan	L	.292	72	21	8	0	2	12	8	16	.370	.486
Throws Right	R	.341	91	31	5	1	4	18	10	12	.400	.549
Adams,Terry	L	.264	110	29	7	0	0	9	10	23	.331	.327
Throws Right	R	.271	144	39	6	1	1	15	13	28	.331	.347
Adkins,Jon	L	.176	17	3	3	0	0	2	2	2	.250	.353
Throws Right	R	.333	15	5	0	0	1	3	5	1	.524	.533
Affeldt,Jeremy	L	.223	112	25	5	1	2	16	13	24	.302	.339
Throws Left	R	.272	371	101	23	1	10	37	25	74	.323	.420
Ainsworth,Kurt	L	.286	105	30	7	1	2	9	15	19	.372	.429
Throws Right	R	.261	161	42	8	0	6	19	12	33	.314	.422
Alfonseca,Antonio	L	.340	100	34	1	1	3	16	14	11	.417	.460
Throws Right	R	.259	162	42	7	1	4	38	13	40	.322	.389
Almanza,Armando	L	.277	65	18	2	0	3	12	11	24	.385	.446
Throws Left	R	.306	134	41	8	0	7	21	14	25	.371	.522
Almonte,Edwin	L	.385	13	5	0	0	1	2	2	2	.467	.615
Throws Right	R	.421	38	16	5	1	2	10	3	5	.463	.763
Almonte,Hector	L	.326	46	15	3	1	1	7	12	12	.466	.500
Throws Right	R	.280	100	28	4	0	4	19	12	20	.362	.440
Alvarez,Juan	L	.222	9	2	0	0	1	2	2	2	.417	.556
Throws Left	R	.214	28	6	1	0	1	2	6	4	.353	.357
Alvarez,Victor	L	.500	4	2	0	0	0	1	0	1	.500	.500
Throws Left	R	.368	19	7	3	0	1	7	6	2	.538	.684
Alvarez,Wilson	L	.235	68	16	3	0	1	7	4	9	.288	.324
Throws Left	R	.230	278	64	7	1	4	17	19	73	.288	.306
Anderson,Brian	L	.258	182	47	10	0	9	20	9	27	.293	.462
Throws Left	R	.286	576	165	29	8	18	80	34	60	.324	.458
Anderson,Jason	L	.354	48	17	3	0	4	9	10	2	.467	.667
Throws Right	R	.219	73	16	3	0	1	9	9	14	.310	.301
Anderson,Jimmy	L	.357	42	15	6	1	2	11	1	4	.372	.690
Throws Left	R	.360	125	45	9	1	6	26	13	9	.411	.592
Anderson,Matt	L	.286	35	10	2	0	2	7	1	3	.297	.514
Throws Right	R	.263	57	15	1	0	3	10	8	10	.364	.439
Appier,Kevin	L	.253	249	63	13	1	14	34	26	26	.336	.482
Throws Right	R	.289	197	57	10	3	7	31	17	29	.353	.477
Armas Jr.,Tony	L	.250	44	11	3	1	0	4	2	7	.271	.364
Throws Right	R	.209	67	14	1	0	4	5	6	16	.284	.403
Arroyo,Bronson	L	.161	31	5	1	1	0	1	4	3	.257	.258
Throws Right	R	.167	30	5	3	0	0	2	0	11	.194	.267
Asencio,Miguel	L	.344	96	33	7	2	2	18	11	15	.396	.521
Throws Right	R	.241	87	21	2	1	2	9	10	12	.337	.356
Ashby,Andy	L	.336	131	44	4	1	6	22	9	13	.389	.519
Throws Right	R	.291	158	46	7	3	2	17	8	28	.323	.411
Astacio,Pedro	L	.324	71	23	7	1	4	10	14	7	.442	.620
Throws Right	R	.300	80	24	4	0	4	18	4	13	.345	.500
Austin,Jeff	L	.205	39	8	1	0	2	5	10	7	.367	.385
Throws Right	R	.282	71	20	3	0	7	16	11	15	.378	.620
Avery,Steve	L	.348	23	8	0	1	1	7	3	2	.423	.565
Throws Left	R	.275	40	11	2	0	4	8	4	4	.341	.625
Ayala,Luis	L	.337	101	34	2	3	5	14	9	14	.398	.564
Throws Right	R	.188	165	31	4	0	3	14	4	32	.221	.267
Aybar,Manny	L	-	0	0	0	0	0	0	2	0	1.000	-
Throws Right	R	.333	12	4	1	0	1	3	1	2	.357	.667
Backe,Brandon	L	.302	53	16	1	1	2	7	14	6	.456	.472
Throws Right	R	.220	109	24	4	0	4	18	11	30	.295	.367
Bacsik,Mike	L	.500	20	10	1	1	2	7	2	6	.545	.950
Throws Left	R	.321	56	18	5	1	3	13	6	6	.381	.607
Baez,Danys	L	.285	151	43	11	0	4	16	12	32	.341	.437
Throws Right	R	.165	133	22	6	0	5	18	11	34	.243	.323
Baldwin,James	L	.361	36	13	1	1	3	8	2	1	.385	.694
Throws Right	R	.296	27	8	1	0	3	5	2	6	.333	.667
Bale,John	L	.103	29	3	1	0	0	0	1	8	.133	.138
Throws Left	R	.315	149	47	10	4	7	22	11	29	.366	.577
Balfour,Grant	L	.229	48	11	2	0	1	6	11	14	.367	.333
Throws Right	R	.240	50	12	3	0	3	8	3	16	.283	.480
Batista,Miguel	L	.297	347	103	12	5	6	40	29	60	.355	.412
Throws Right	R	.241	390	94	20	2	7	42	31	82	.301	.356
Bauer,Rick	L	.247	93	23	6	0	2	12	17	21	.375	.376
Throws Right	R	.261	134	35	7	1	3	33	7	22	.301	.396
Beck,Rod	L	.159	69	11	1	0	2	4	10	18	.275	.261
Throws Right	R	.241	58	14	2	0	2	6	1	14	.254	.379
Beckett,Josh	L	.220	241	53	14	0	3	15	32	89	.310	.315
Throws Right	R	.267	296	79	12	2	6	29	24	63	.326	.382

Pitcher	vs	Avg	AB	H	2B	3B	HR	RBI	BB	SO	OBP	Slg
Beimel,Joe	L	.308	107	33	5	1	3	22	16	28	.405	.458
Throws Left	R	.290	124	36	6	2	4	23	17	14	.374	.468
Belisle,Matt	L	.250	12	3	1	0	0	1	1	1	.286	.333
Throws Right	R	.333	21	7	1	0	1	4	1	5	.391	.524
Bell,Rob	L	.247	215	53	16	1	9	28	23	24	.318	.456
Throws Right	R	.282	177	50	14	2	6	30	16	20	.357	.486
Benes,Alan	L	.438	48	21	6	1	2	10	9	10	.526	.729
Throws Right	R	.308	52	16	3	1	0	9	5	10	.362	.404
Benitez,Armando	L	.214	140	30	4	0	5	23	28	38	.345	.350
Throws Right	R	.221	131	29	7	0	1	8	13	37	.290	.298
Benoit,Joaquin	L	.222	212	47	6	6	13	34	30	48	.314	.491
Throws Right	R	.272	191	52	15	2	10	30	21	39	.352	.529
Benson,Kris	L	.339	189	64	14	0	9	37	19	22	.396	.556
Throws Right	R	.260	242	63	13	1	5	26	17	46	.308	.384
Bere,Jason	L	.294	17	5	2	0	0	1	2	0	.350	.412
Throws Right	R	.000	7	0	0	0	0	0	0	1	.000	.000
Bernero,Adam	L	.306	265	81	16	6	10	42	31	28	.377	.525
Throws Right	R	.225	249	56	10	3	9	38	23	52	.301	.398
Betancourt,Rafael	L	.270	63	17	4	1	3	14	11	17	.373	.508
Throws Right	R	.133	75	10	1	1	2	3	2	19	.167	.253
Biddle,Rocky	L	.244	119	29	5	0	3	15	19	23	.357	.361
Throws Right	R	.263	160	42	10	1	7	29	21	31	.360	.469
Bierbrodt,Nick	L	.393	56	22	7	1	3	15	6	13	.439	.714
Throws Left	R	.328	128	42	9	0	6	31	21	16	.432	.539
Bland,Nate	L	.273	44	12	1	0	0	7	5	13	.340	.295
Throws Left	R	.303	33	10	2	1	3	6	7	5	.452	.697
Boehringer,Brian	L	.193	88	17	3	0	3	11	17	24	.330	.330
Throws Right	R	.309	152	47	10	1	8	29	13	23	.367	.546
Bonderman,Jeremy	L	.306	382	117	28	2	14	60	38	46	.369	.500
Throws Right	R	.277	274	76	16	3	9	39	20	62	.329	.456
Bong,Jung	L	.264	72	19	3	1	4	15	7	22	.341	.500
Throws Left	R	.268	138	37	8	1	4	20	24	25	.377	.428
Bootcheck,Chris	L	.286	21	6	1	0	1	3	4	3	.400	.476
Throws Right	R	.385	26	10	2	0	4	8	2	4	.429	.923
Borbon,Pedro	L	.556	9	5	0	0	1	4	1	0	.636	.889
Throws Left	R	.563	16	9	4	0	1	8	1	0	.588	1.000
Borland,Toby	L	.077	13	1	0	0	0	1	6	1	.368	.077
Throws Right	R	.111	18	2	0	0	0	2	2	3	.190	.111
Borowski,Joe	L	.212	104	22	4	0	4	12	4	35	.248	.365
Throws Right	R	.204	152	31	3	0	1	13	15	31	.275	.243
Bottalico,Ricky	L	.000	2	0	0	0	0	0	2	0	.500	.000
Throws Right	R	.500	6	3	1	0	0	0	0	2	.500	.667
Bowie,Micah	L	.364	11	4	2	0	0	3	1	0	.417	.545
Throws Left	R	.360	25	9	1	1	1	4	1	4	.385	.600
Bowles,Brian	L	.200	10	2	1	0	0	0	2	1	.333	.300
Throws Right	R	.300	20	6	1	0	1	3	0	1	.364	.500
Boyd,Jason	L	.232	82	19	1	0	2	14	18	12	.370	.317
Throws Right	R	.176	108	19	9	0	2	14	8	19	.248	.315
Bradford,Chad	L	.326	95	31	9	0	5	17	19	11	.458	.579
Throws Right	R	.190	189	36	2	2	2	16	11	51	.246	.254
Brazelton,Dewon	L	.287	108	31	7	2	5	26	11	14	.347	.528
Throws Right	R	.299	87	26	8	1	4	14	12	10	.402	.552
Brohawn,Troy	L	.000	15	0	0	0	0	0	2	6	.118	.000
Throws Left	R	.345	29	10	3	0	2	8	2	7	.387	.655
Brower,Jim	L	.291	148	43	8	2	4	18	23	16	.384	.453
Throws Right	R	.220	214	47	11	1	4	28	16	49	.274	.336
Brown,Kevin	L	.254	374	95	10	4	0	23	36	76	.319	.302
Throws Right	R	.219	407	89	11	1	11	37	20	109	.263	.332
Buehrle,Mark	L	.263	274	72	13	0	7	38	8	39	.291	.387
Throws Left	R	.285	624	178	35	3	15	75	53	80	.340	.423
Bukvich,Ryan	L	.235	17	4	1	0	1	4	4	5	.364	.471
Throws Right	R	.333	24	8	2	0	1	6	5	3	.448	.542
Bullinger,Kirk	L	.300	10	3	0	0	1	2	1	1	.364	.600
Throws Right	R	.182	22	4	1	2	1	5	0	4	.182	.545
Bump,Nate	L	.229	48	11	3	0	2	5	10	8	.362	.417
Throws Right	R	.258	89	23	5	1	1	18	10	9	.374	.371
Burba,Dave	L	.219	64	14	5	0	1	1	8	12	.315	.344
Throws Right	R	.269	104	28	5	0	4	16	11	23	.356	.433
Burkett,John	L	.273	384	105	30	0	9	51	29	56	.327	.422
Throws Right	R	.290	335	97	23	0	11	53	18	51	.334	.457
Burnett,A.J.	L	.234	47	11	2	2	1	5	8	14	.345	.426
Throws Right	R	.194	36	7	1	0	1	8	10	7	.388	.306
Bynum,Mike	L	.278	36	10	0	1	1	5	4	9	.350	.417
Throws Left	R	.304	112	34	4	0	13	33	11	26	.371	.688
Calero,Kiko	L	.222	54	12	2	0	1	3	7	17	.323	.315
Throws Right	R	.205	83	17	4	1	4	14	13	34	.303	.422

Pitchers vs. Left-Handed and Right-Handed Batters

Pitcher	vs	Avg	AB	H	2B	3B	HR	RBI	BB	SO	OBP	Slg
Callaway,Mickey	L	.358	137	49	10	1	4	26	12	16	.412	.533
Throws Right	R	.307	114	35	4	0	3	15	12	25	.364	.421
Capuano,Chris	L	.129	31	4	0	0	0	4	1	7	.229	.129
Throws Left	R	.271	85	23	6	0	3	12	10	16	.364	.447
Carrara,Giovanni	L	.387	62	24	3	1	5	16	9	5	.472	.710
Throws Right	R	.276	58	16	2	0	1	5	5	8	.344	.362
Carrasco,D.J.	L	.290	138	40	5	0	5	22	28	24	.415	.435
Throws Right	R	.255	165	42	8	0	3	25	12	33	.317	.358
Carrasco,Hector	L	.288	66	19	1	1	5	10	7	13	.356	.561
Throws Right	R	.256	82	21	4	1	0	7	13	14	.371	.329
Carter,Lance	L	.222	162	36	10	2	5	23	10	29	.272	.401
Throws Right	R	.265	136	36	8	0	7	18	9	18	.313	.478
Cerda,Jaime	L	.242	33	8	3	0	1	8	8	4	.390	.424
Throws Left	R	.276	87	24	4	1	3	14	12	15	.356	.448
Cerros,Juan	L	.250	16	4	0	0	1	4	4	1	.400	.438
Throws Right	R	.212	33	7	1	1	0	6	1	8	.270	.303
Chacon,Shawn	L	.254	272	69	17	3	6	29	32	42	.330	.404
Throws Right	R	.230	239	55	14	1	6	36	26	51	.332	.372
Chen,Bruce	L	.323	31	10	2	1	2	11	2	6	.368	.645
Throws Left	R	.262	61	16	3	0	4	9	8	14	.348	.508
Choate,Randy	L	.600	5	3	1	0	0	1	0	0	.600	.800
Throws Left	R	.400	10	4	1	0	0	3	1	0	.455	.500
Christiansen,Jason	L	.208	48	10	2	1	0	8	3	10	.255	.292
Throws Left	R	.273	55	15	4	1	3	4	8	12	.375	.545
Chulk,Vinnie	L	.231	13	3	0	1	0	3	1	2	.286	.385
Throws Right	R	.333	9	3	0	0	0	1	2	0	.455	.333
Claussen,Brandon	L	.250	4	1	0	0	0	0	0	2	.250	.250
Throws Left	R	.304	23	7	0	0	1	2	1	3	.333	.435
Clemens,Roger	L	.215	455	98	14	2	12	44	37	106	.276	.334
Throws Right	R	.288	351	101	28	1	12	39	21	84	.330	.476
Clement,Matt	L	.246	358	88	19	1	12	45	45	84	.337	.405
Throws Right	R	.209	388	81	14	0	10	41	34	87	.288	.322
Colome,Jesus	L	.218	119	26	7	0	4	14	27	24	.367	.378
Throws Right	R	.269	160	43	8	0	5	31	19	45	.346	.413
Colon,Bartolo	L	.250	509	127	30	2	16	54	33	111	.294	.411
Throws Right	R	.246	390	96	14	0	14	45	34	62	.311	.390
Colyer,Steve	L	.364	22	8	1	0	0	1	4	4	.462	.409
Throws Left	R	.269	52	14	2	0	0	5	5	12	.333	.308
Condrey,Clay	L	.309	55	17	7	1	3	16	9	6	.415	.636
Throws Right	R	.302	86	26	3	0	4	13	12	19	.400	.477
Cone,David	L	.281	32	9	3	0	2	7	8	3	.425	.563
Throws Right	R	.282	39	11	1	0	2	5	5	10	.364	.462
Contreras,Jose	L	.203	143	29	7	0	2	15	19	44	.299	.294
Throws Right	R	.202	114	23	6	0	2	7	11	28	.295	.307
Cook,Aaron	L	.342	219	75	13	2	6	44	34	16	.424	.502
Throws Right	R	.298	285	85	16	0	2	32	23	27	.365	.375
Corcoran,Roy	L	.083	12	1	1	0	0	0	2	1	.214	.167
Throws Right	R	.375	16	6	1	1	0	2	1	1	.412	.563
Cordero,Chad	L	.111	9	1	0	0	0	0	2	4	.273	.111
Throws Right	R	.111	27	3	0	0	1	2	1	8	.143	.222
Cordero,Francisco	L	.236	148	35	4	0	1	13	24	43	.343	.284
Throws Right	R	.223	157	35	4	1	3	26	14	47	.287	.318
Corey,Mark	L	.316	38	12	2	2	2	13	4	8	.372	.632
Throws Right	R	.221	77	17	6	0	0	9	7	19	.287	.299
Cormier,Rheal	L	.119	84	10	3	0	0	5	11	22	.229	.155
Throws Left	R	.207	213	44	9	1	4	15	14	45	.256	.315
Cornejo,Nate	L	.309	375	116	25	4	12	53	41	20	.374	.493
Throws Right	R	.305	393	120	22	1	6	42	17	26	.337	.412
Correia,Kevin	L	.280	75	21	2	0	4	10	9	11	.353	.467
Throws Right	R	.270	74	20	4	0	2	8	9	17	.379	.405
Cortes,David	L	.667	9	6	3	0	0	2	0	1	.667	1.000
Throws Right	R	.250	8	2	0	0	1	3	0	0	.222	.625
Cotts,Neal	L	.250	4	1	0	0	0	0	4	1	.625	.250
Throws Left	R	.298	47	14	5	0	1	10	13	9	.450	.468
Creek,Doug	L	.269	26	7	1	0	1	7	5	2	.375	.423
Throws Left	R	.259	27	7	2	0	1	4	7	9	.432	.444
Cressend,Jack	L	.253	75	19	8	0	1	3	5	12	.300	.400
Throws Right	R	.250	84	21	6	0	0	9	4	16	.300	.321
Crudale,Mike	L	.105	19	2	2	0	0	3	11	4	.419	.211
Throws Right	R	.189	53	10	2	1	1	6	7	9	.295	.321
Cruz,Juan	L	.292	89	26	3	1	2	13	12	28	.382	.416
Throws Right	R	.265	151	40	9	1	5	24	16	37	.354	.437
Cruz,Nelson	L	.308	104	32	5	2	8	25	7	15	.360	.625
Throws Right	R	.295	112	33	4	0	7	21	4	23	.322	.518
Cunnane,Will	L	.200	30	6	2	0	1	2	2	5	.250	.367
Throws Right	R	.182	44	8	1	0	1	4	4	15	.250	.273

Pitcher	vs	Avg	AB	H	2B	3B	HR	RBI	BB	SO	OBP	Slg
Daal,Omar	L	.296	81	24	4	0	1	12	7	15	.356	.383
Throws Left	R	.355	310	110	33	2	10	48	23	38	.399	.571
D'Amico,Jeff	L	.294	309	91	21	3	7	33	27	39	.350	.450
Throws Right	R	.289	391	113	26	1	16	56	15	61	.324	.483
Darensbourg,Vic	L	.545	11	6	0	0	1	1	0	0	.545	.818
Throws Left	R	.333	33	11	4	0	1	8	1	4	.353	.545
Davis,Doug	L	.293	92	27	8	1	5	11	13	18	.381	.565
Throws Left	R	.283	339	96	10	1	11	34	38	44	.355	.416
Davis,Jason	L	.259	344	89	16	2	14	49	30	47	.320	.439
Throws Right	R	.289	287	83	16	1	11	38	17	38	.341	.467
Dawley,Joe	L	.444	18	8	3	0	3	9	1	2	.500	1.111
Throws Right	R	.368	19	7	2	1	0	4	2	6	.429	.579
Day,Zach	L	.286	231	66	14	0	4	24	22	22	.352	.398
Throws Right	R	.242	273	66	18	2	4	32	37	39	.345	.366
de los Santos,Valerio	L	.267	60	16	1	0	2	8	4	15	.324	.383
Throws Left	R	.228	127	29	4	1	6	17	21	24	.346	.417
Deago,Roger	L	.000	5	0	0	0	0	1	0	3	.000	.000
Throws Left	R	.324	34	11	3	1	0	6	8	7	.452	.471
DeHart,Rick	L	.444	9	4	2	0	1	3	0	0	.444	1.000
Throws Left	R	.400	10	4	2	0	0	2	2	1	.500	.600
DeJean,Mike	L	.329	149	49	7	2	9	28	19	22	.400	.584
Throws Right	R	.216	171	37	8	0	4	20	20	49	.304	.333
Dempster,Ryan	L	.300	207	62	17	1	7	36	41	42	.415	.493
Throws Right	R	.288	250	72	14	1	7	46	29	42	.368	.436
DePaula,Jorge	L	.056	18	1	0	0	0	0	1	2	.105	.056
Throws Right	R	.111	18	2	1	0	1	1	0	5	.158	.333
Dessens,Elmer	L	.364	332	121	25	2	12	50	29	41	.414	.560
Throws Right	R	.242	376	91	18	0	10	49	28	72	.300	.370
Dickey,R.A.	L	.279	251	70	11	2	11	31	20	52	.333	.470
Throws Right	R	.307	212	65	16	1	5	34	18	42	.369	.462
Dominguez,Juan	L	.346	26	9	2	0	2	6	6	8	.455	.654
Throws Right	R	.212	33	7	1	0	3	6	6	5	.333	.515
Donnelly,Brendan	L	.199	146	29	2	2	2	11	14	32	.272	.281
Throws Right	R	.202	129	26	10	1	0	5	10	47	.275	.295
Dotel,Octavio	L	.152	132	20	4	0	3	10	23	33	.287	.250
Throws Right	R	.186	177	33	5	2	6	20	8	64	.225	.339
Douglass,Sean	L	.421	19	8	2	0	1	8	4	1	.522	.684
Throws Right	R	.333	18	6	0	0	1	3	2	2	.429	.500
Downs,Scott	L	.000	1	0	0	0	0	0	0	1	.000	.000
Throws Left	R	.385	13	5	2	0	2	4	3	3	.500	1.000
Dreifort,Darren	L	.306	108	33	8	0	3	14	18	27	.402	.463
Throws Right	R	.202	124	25	6	0	3	11	7	40	.244	.323
Drese,Ryan	L	.438	89	39	9	0	4	18	13	8	.519	.674
Throws Right	R	.210	105	22	3	0	4	13	11	18	.303	.352
Drew,Tim	L	.429	14	6	4	0	1	3	2	2	.500	.929
Throws Right	R	.286	21	6	1	0	2	10	6	1	.414	.619
Driskill,Travis	L	.313	96	30	6	0	5	20	4	15	.340	.531
Throws Right	R	.308	104	32	8	0	3	19	5	18	.339	.471
DuBose,Eric	L	.305	82	25	5	0	1	7	9	16	.383	.402
Throws Left	R	.186	188	35	8	2	5	18	16	28	.258	.330
Duchscherer,Justin	L	.225	40	9	1	0	1	5	3	9	.279	.325
Throws Right	R	.320	25	8	2	0	0	2	0	6	.370	.400
Duckworth,Brandon	L	.246	175	43	11	0	4	20	15	39	.311	.377
Throws Right	R	.297	185	55	17	3	8	30	29	29	.414	.551
Durbin,Chad	L	.368	19	7	0	0	1	3	2	6	.429	.526
Throws Right	R	.478	23	11	5	1	1	8	1	2	.500	.913
Durocher,Jayson	L	.333	9	3	0	0	2	5	2	3	.455	1.000
Throws Right	R	.286	21	6	3	0	2	6	0	4	.318	.714
Eaton,Adam	L	.276	315	87	20	3	10	40	45	48	.364	.454
Throws Right	R	.222	388	86	24	1	10	41	23	98	.275	.366
Eckenstahler,Eric	L	.185	27	5	2	0	0	3	8	6	.405	.259
Throws Left	R	.148	27	4	1	0	0	1	7	6	.324	.185
Eischen,Joey	L	.255	98	25	4	2	3	12	5	25	.305	.429
Throws Left	R	.308	104	32	4	0	4	24	8	15	.363	.462
Elarton,Scott	L	.320	128	41	4	3	9	26	13	8	.380	.609
Throws Right	R	.340	94	32	5	4	4	16	7	12	.398	.606
Elder,Dave	L	.400	5	2	1	0	1	4	2	2	.571	1.200
Throws Right	R	.429	7	3	1	0	1	2	2	1	.556	1.000
Eldred,Cal	L	.295	78	23	2	1	2	11	9	25	.378	.423
Throws Right	R	.227	172	39	8	1	7	21	22	42	.318	.407
Ellis,Robert	L	.450	40	18	5	0	2	5	8	2	.531	.725
Throws Right	R	.222	36	8	1	0	5	10	2	6	.275	.667
Embree,Alan	L	.263	99	26	4	0	4	20	2	20	.272	.424
Throws Left	R	.221	104	23	5	1	1	7	14	25	.314	.317
Escobar,Kelvim	L	.233	356	83	17	1	8	45	38	86	.311	.354
Throws Right	R	.308	344	106	16	0	7	39	40	73	.387	.416

Pitchers vs. Left-Handed and Right-Handed Batters

Pitcher	vs	Avg	AB	H	2B	3B	HR	RBI	BB	SO	OBP	Slg
Estes,Shawn	L	.276	116	32	4	0	4	19	12	24	.346	.414
Throws Left	R	.312	481	150	28	0	16	80	71	79	.396	.470
Estrella,Leo	L	.290	107	31	10	0	5	20	12	8	.358	.523
Throws Right	R	.289	152	44	9	0	5	16	9	17	.337	.447
Etherton,Seth	L	.452	42	19	5	1	3	11	3	7	.500	.833
Throws Right	R	.253	79	20	8	0	1	9	12	10	.354	.392
Eyre,Scott	L	.219	96	21	2	0	1	13	9	15	.283	.271
Throws Left	R	.305	128	39	6	0	3	13	17	20	.385	.422
Farnsworth,Kyle	L	.189	90	17	3	0	1	8	14	28	.298	.256
Throws Right	R	.199	181	36	4	1	5	19	22	64	.284	.315
Fassero,Jeff	L	.337	98	33	8	0	3	11	8	20	.398	.510
Throws Left	R	.278	216	60	11	0	14	31	26	35	.354	.523
Feliciano,Pedro	L	.304	46	14	1	0	1	5	7	14	.407	.391
Throws Left	R	.259	147	38	7	0	4	19	14	29	.329	.388
Fernandez,Jared	L	.305	59	18	2	0	0	5	5	6	.373	.339
Throws Right	R	.226	84	19	5	0	2	10	7	13	.286	.357
Ferrari,Anthony	L	.143	7	1	0	0	0	0	3	1	.455	.143
Throws Left	R	.375	8	3	1	0	1	2	2	0	.500	.875
Fetters,Mike	L	.100	10	1	0	0	0	0	1	0	.182	.100
Throws Right	R	.100	10	1	0	0	0	0	0	1	.182	.100
Field,Nate	L	.214	42	9	0	0	1	2	8	6	.340	.286
Throws Right	R	.256	39	10	2	0	2	8	6	13	.362	.462
Figueroa,Nelson	L	.190	42	8	2	0	2	2	4	7	.277	.381
Throws Right	R	.235	85	20	2	0	6	12	9	16	.309	.471
Fikac,Jeremy	L	.227	22	5	2	0	0	6	5	4	.370	.318
Throws Right	R	.257	35	9	0	0	4	6	6	5	.409	.600
Fiore,Tony	L	.237	59	14	1	1	2	11	15	11	.387	.390
Throws Right	R	.247	73	18	4	0	3	16	6	12	.321	.425
Fogg,Josh	L	.320	247	79	16	3	8	38	17	30	.367	.506
Throws Right	R	.273	319	87	23	0	14	44	23	41	.332	.476
Foppert,Jesse	L	.267	206	55	7	3	9	27	31	46	.363	.461
Throws Right	R	.231	208	48	11	0	7	35	38	55	.345	.385
Ford,Matt	L	.304	46	14	4	1	0	3	7	3	.396	.435
Throws Left	R	.250	128	32	5	0	5	19	14	23	.326	.406
Fossum,Casey	L	.230	87	20	4	1	1	11	7	22	.299	.333
Throws Left	R	.286	217	62	21	3	8	35	27	41	.367	.521
Foster,John	L	.391	23	9	1	1	4	11	1	3	.440	1.043
Throws Left	R	.328	64	21	3	0	1	7	7	13	.389	.422
Foulke,Keith	L	.158	152	24	4	1	5	12	14	50	.243	.296
Throws Right	R	.210	157	33	7	1	5	13	6	38	.256	.363
Fox,Chad	L	.205	73	15	4	0	2	7	16	23	.352	.342
Throws Right	R	.241	83	20	3	0	1	19	15	23	.343	.313
Franco,John	L	.267	45	12	3	0	2	7	2	9	.298	.467
Throws Left	R	.264	87	23	3	0	3	6	11	7	.350	.402
Franklin,Ryan	L	.267	408	109	12	2	23	57	44	52	.341	.475
Throws Right	R	.233	386	90	13	0	11	33	17	47	.274	.352
Franklin,Wayne	L	.255	145	37	7	1	8	32	11	31	.317	.483
Throws Left	R	.271	606	164	43	7	28	87	83	85	.364	.503
Fuentes,Brian	L	.238	105	25	2	2	1	7	9	34	.319	.324
Throws Left	R	.227	172	39	8	0	6	24	25	48	.328	.378
Fultz,Aaron	L	.218	119	26	5	0	2	13	13	28	.295	.311
Throws Left	R	.345	142	49	13	1	7	28	14	25	.406	.599
Gagne,Eric	L	.130	138	18	2	0	1	2	13	55	.216	.167
Throws Right	R	.135	141	19	4	0	1	8	7	82	.181	.184
Gallo,Mike	L	.227	44	10	1	0	1	3	3	6	.265	.318
Throws Left	R	.295	61	18	2	0	2	9	7	10	.371	.426
Garcia,Freddy	L	.281	420	118	20	1	23	69	43	61	.352	.498
Throws Right	R	.223	350	78	17	1	8	27	28	83	.288	.346
Garcia,Reynaldo	L	.333	30	10	1	0	5	15	7	7	.474	.867
Throws Right	R	.231	39	9	0	0	1	3	7	8	.354	.308
Garcia,Rosman	L	.333	72	24	6	0	1	10	13	6	.435	.458
Throws Right	R	.312	125	39	10	0	3	23	10	19	.370	.464
Garland,Jon	L	.278	432	120	21	2	16	51	48	56	.351	.447
Throws Right	R	.234	290	68	14	1	12	41	26	52	.296	.414
Gaudin,Chad	L	.269	67	18	5	0	0	5	7	8	.329	.343
Throws Right	R	.218	87	19	3	0	4	11	9	15	.299	.391
Geary,Geoff	L	.273	11	3	1	0	0	3	2	3	.385	.364
Throws Right	R	.385	13	5	2	1	0	2	1	0	.429	.692
George,Chris	L	.280	100	28	3	1	7	22	6	9	.333	.540
Throws Left	R	.319	288	92	15	0	15	44	38	30	.396	.528
German,Franklyn	L	.238	80	19	6	1	2	13	27	20	.430	.413
Throws Right	R	.304	92	28	3	1	3	12	18	21	.425	.457
Gilfillan,Jason	L	.370	27	10	4	0	1	6	4	5	.469	.630
Throws Right	R	.273	44	12	3	0	2	8	6	7	.360	.477
Ginter,Matt	L	.333	6	2	0	0	1	4	0	0	.500	.833
Throws Right	R	.000	5	0	0	0	0	0	1	0	.167	.000

Pitcher	vs	Avg	AB	H	2B	3B	HR	RBI	BB	SO	OBP	Slg
Glavine,Tom	L	.285	144	41	6	3	0	16	14	14	.348	.368
Throws Left	R	.289	567	164	31	7	21	71	52	68	.349	.480
Glover,Gary	L	.360	125	45	11	1	4	22	15	20	.430	.560
Throws Right	R	.258	124	32	5	1	2	18	7	17	.299	.363
Gobble,Jimmy	L	.263	57	15	2	0	1	6	3	7	.333	.351
Throws Left	R	.273	150	41	10	1	7	26	12	24	.325	.493
Gonzalez,Edgar	L	.407	27	11	4	0	1	2	5	6	.500	.667
Throws Right	R	.347	49	17	3	0	2	10	2	8	.365	.531
Gonzalez,Jeremi	L	.235	293	69	17	3	9	31	37	51	.322	.406
Throws Right	R	.220	282	62	17	1	9	31	32	46	.316	.383
Gonzalez,Mike	L	.222	9	2	0	1	1	5	4	4	.429	.778
Throws Left	R	.238	21	5	0	0	3	6	2	2	.304	.667
Good,Andy	L	.337	104	35	6	0	5	17	8	16	.395	.538
Throws Right	R	.245	159	39	10	1	10	21	8	26	.279	.509
Gordon,Tom	L	.231	130	30	4	0	3	17	17	41	.315	.331
Throws Right	R	.196	138	27	5	0	1	6	14	50	.287	.254
Grabow,John	L	.444	9	4	0	0	0	3	0	3	.444	.444
Throws Left	R	.154	13	2	0	0	0	0	0	6	.154	.154
Graves,Danny	L	.297	293	87	23	4	11	43	27	27	.358	.515
Throws Right	R	.299	391	117	33	2	19	57	14	33	.331	.540
Gregg,Kevin	L	.205	44	9	2	2	1	6	3	7	.271	.409
Throws Right	R	.205	44	9	2	0	2	2	5	7	.286	.386
Griffiths,Jeremy	L	.346	81	28	4	2	3	21	8	13	.411	.556
Throws Right	R	.312	93	29	5	1	2	11	11	12	.390	.452
Grimsley,Jason	L	.316	152	48	11	3	2	33	21	23	.403	.467
Throws Right	R	.282	142	40	4	2	4	33	15	35	.354	.423
Groom,Buddy	L	.270	89	24	4	1	2	13	5	17	.320	.404
Throws Left	R	.343	99	34	4	2	5	12	9	17	.404	.576
Gryboski,Kevin	L	.227	44	10	3	1	0	5	10	7	.370	.341
Throws Right	R	.288	118	34	5	1	3	24	13	25	.368	.424
Guardado,Eddie	L	.175	63	11	3	0	0	5	2	21	.197	.222
Throws Left	R	.219	178	39	8	0	7	19	12	39	.267	.382
Guthrie,Mark	L	.280	75	21	4	1	3	15	12	14	.393	.480
Throws Left	R	.241	79	19	4	0	3	9	10	10	.326	.405
Hackman,Luther	L	.238	122	29	4	1	4	12	19	19	.340	.385
Throws Right	R	.277	177	49	11	1	3	34	17	29	.363	.401
Halama,John	L	.216	111	24	4	0	4	14	11	18	.287	.360
Throws Left	R	.286	325	93	19	0	14	44	25	33	.338	.474
Hall,Josh	L	.317	41	13	2	1	1	6	8	5	.429	.488
Throws Right	R	.313	64	20	3	0	3	12	7	13	.375	.500
Halladay,Roy	L	.262	610	160	30	3	17	69	22	105	.291	.405
Throws Right	R	.224	415	93	24	4	9	35	10	99	.252	.366
Hamilton,Joey	L	.529	17	9	5	0	1	2	5	3	.636	1.000
Throws Right	R	.343	35	12	5	0	2	10	0	4	.343	.657
Hammond,Chris	L	.289	90	26	4	1	3	13	7	12	.337	.456
Throws Left	R	.258	151	39	12	0	2	16	4	33	.282	.377
Hampton,Mike	L	.164	146	24	2	0	3	9	16	32	.248	.240
Throws Left	R	.278	583	162	35	2	11	65	62	78	.346	.401
Hancock,Josh	L	.200	5	1	0	0	0	1	0	2	.200	.200
Throws Right	R	.167	6	1	0	0	0	0	0	2	.167	.167
Harang,Aaron	L	.272	158	43	8	0	7	27	13	23	.329	.456
Throws Right	R	.322	143	46	10	0	4	17	6	19	.349	.476
Harden,Rich	L	.271	166	45	6	0	4	24	26	37	.367	.380
Throws Right	R	.241	112	27	6	1	1	9	14	30	.325	.339
Haren,Danny	L	.278	126	35	10	1	7	16	14	18	.348	.540
Throws Right	R	.304	161	49	8	2	2	18	8	25	.354	.416
Harper,Travis	L	.287	157	45	7	1	4	23	18	32	.370	.420
Throws Right	R	.223	184	41	5	0	5	19	13	32	.280	.332
Harville,Chad	L	.303	33	10	3	1	1	5	10	5	.465	.545
Throws Right	R	.288	52	15	3	0	2	9	7	13	.377	.462
Hasegawa,Shigetoshi	L	.246	142	35	4	0	2	10	11	13	.301	.317
Throws Right	R	.221	122	27	8	0	3	6	7	19	.264	.361
Hawkins,LaTroy	L	.205	122	25	2	0	4	12	10	33	.263	.320
Throws Right	R	.263	167	44	10	0	0	11	5	42	.289	.323
Haynes,Jimmy	L	.299	154	46	12	1	4	33	25	16	.392	.468
Throws Right	R	.320	225	72	9	1	10	32	32	33	.412	.502
Hebson,Bryan	L	.500	2	1	1	0	0	1	0	0	.333	1.000
Throws Right	R	.429	7	3	0	0	1	2	1	1	.556	.857
Heilman,Aaron	L	.299	117	35	7	1	8	23	14	27	.376	.581
Throws Right	R	.301	146	44	8	1	5	27	27	24	.412	.473
Helling,Rick	L	.281	302	85	20	2	16	49	27	59	.353	.520
Throws Right	R	.273	300	82	13	1	15	32	18	39	.324	.473
Hendrickson,Mark	L	.269	167	45	14	0	1	18	11	21	.311	.371
Throws Left	R	.333	487	162	33	2	23	83	29	55	.366	.550
Hentgen,Pat	L	.237	333	79	14	3	15	41	33	59	.315	.432
Throws Right	R	.258	275	71	13	2	10	29	25	41	.319	.429

Pitchers vs. Left-Handed and Right-Handed Batters

Pitcher	vs	Avg	AB	H	2B	3B	HR	RBI	BB	SO	OBP	Slg
Heredia,Felix	L	.233	133	31	7	1	7	21	9	25	.290	.459
Throws Left	R	.225	191	43	10	1	3	14	24	20	.310	.335
Herges,Matt	L	.209	115	24	3	0	1	9	11	30	.277	.261
Throws Right	R	.249	177	44	8	0	2	23	18	38	.320	.328
Hermanson,Dustin	L	.286	112	32	9	0	2	13	9	18	.333	.420
Throws Right	R	.260	146	38	6	0	7	21	15	21	.341	.445
Hernandez,Livan	L	.278	388	108	17	1	11	37	28	73	.333	.412
Throws Right	R	.233	502	117	17	2	16	49	29	105	.281	.371
Hernandez,Roberto	L	.248	105	26	5	2	5	20	23	17	.383	.476
Throws Right	R	.276	127	35	8	0	5	21	20	28	.387	.457
Hernandez,Runelvys	L	.267	180	48	14	3	5	27	22	26	.346	.461
Throws Right	R	.231	169	39	9	0	4	18	15	22	.309	.355
Herrera,Alex	L	.167	12	2	1	0	1	1	3	4	.333	.500
Throws Left	R	.313	16	5	1	0	2	5	5	2	.476	.750
Hill,Jeremy	L	.333	3	1	0	0	0	1	0	0	.333	.333
Throws Right	R	.000	1	0	0	0	0	0	0	0	.000	.000
Hitchcock,Sterling	L	.202	99	20	5	0	1	13	9	17	.269	.283
Throws Left	R	.291	244	71	11	0	13	29	23	51	.351	.496
Hodges,Trey	L	.269	104	28	8	0	6	22	16	25	.374	.519
Throws Right	R	.268	153	41	11	0	5	26	15	41	.333	.438
Hoffman,Trevor	L	.182	22	4	1	0	1	1	2	9	.250	.364
Throws Right	R	.273	11	3	3	0	0	1	1	2	.333	.545
Holmes,Darren	L	.355	62	22	3	0	2	10	7	8	.420	.500
Throws Right	R	.236	106	25	6	0	3	12	4	38	.261	.377
Howard,Ben	L	.227	66	15	1	1	3	4	9	11	.320	.409
Throws Right	R	.242	66	16	5	0	7	11	6	13	.306	.636
Howry,Bob	L	.500	10	5	0	0	0	3	2	1	.583	.500
Throws Right	R	.462	13	6	1	0	1	3	1	3	.467	.769
Hudson,Tim	L	.229	524	120	17	1	9	45	35	91	.286	.317
Throws Right	R	.214	359	77	9	1	6	31	26	71	.272	.295
Ishii,Kazuhisa	L	.192	125	24	3	1	4	12	17	41	.299	.328
Throws Left	R	.252	416	105	23	4	12	45	84	99	.381	.413
Isringhausen,Jason	L	.254	67	17	2	0	2	6	6	12	.315	.373
Throws Right	R	.159	88	14	4	0	0	5	12	29	.260	.205
Jackson,Edwin	L	.143	35	5	0	0	2	2	7	7	.302	.314
Throws Right	R	.286	42	12	2	1	0	3	4	12	.340	.381
Jarvis,Kevin	L	.288	163	47	7	1	5	18	17	15	.355	.436
Throws Right	R	.316	209	66	14	0	10	40	15	34	.360	.526
Jennings,Jason	L	.324	377	122	30	2	9	58	48	40	.400	.485
Throws Right	R	.270	333	90	21	2	11	49	40	79	.352	.444
Jensen,Ryan	L	.438	16	7	2	0	2	5	4	2	.524	.938
Throws Right	R	.389	36	14	0	1	4	10	1	1	.410	.778
Jimenez,Jose	L	.382	204	78	18	1	3	34	22	19	.439	.525
Throws Right	R	.266	222	59	14	3	4	30	10	26	.314	.410
Johnson,Adam	L	.600	5	3	1	0	0	2	0	0	.600	.800
Throws Right	R	.714	7	5	0	0	1	3	1	0	.750	1.143
Johnson,Jason	L	.283	407	115	24	2	12	48	51	58	.366	.440
Throws Right	R	.283	357	101	9	0	10	39	29	60	.349	.392
Johnson,Jonathan	L	.241	29	7	3	0	0	2	9	4	.410	.345
Throws Right	R	.394	33	13	1	1	2	6	6	3	.487	.667
Johnson,Randy	L	.303	66	20	5	1	3	9	6	13	.382	.545
Throws Left	R	.276	380	105	24	0	13	47	21	112	.321	.442
Jones,Greg	L	.283	53	15	4	0	2	14	6	15	.367	.472
Throws Right	R	.241	58	14	2	0	1	5	8	13	.343	.328
Jones,Todd	L	.321	131	42	8	1	3	21	15	23	.385	.466
Throws Right	R	.325	157	51	9	2	7	33	16	36	.389	.541
Journell,Jimmy	L	.357	14	5	0	0	0	2	5	2	.526	.357
Throws Right	R	.227	22	5	1	0	0	5	6	6	.379	.273
Julio,Jorge	L	.273	121	33	6	1	5	17	19	26	.371	.463
Throws Right	R	.239	113	27	2	0	5	19	15	26	.336	.389
Junge,Eric	L	.111	9	1	0	0	1	1	0	2	.111	.444
Throws Right	R	.222	18	4	1	0	0	1	1	3	.263	.278
Keisler,Randy	L	.600	5	3	1	0	2	6	2	1	.625	2.000
Throws Left	R	.211	19	4	2	0	1	3	5	4	.400	.474
Kennedy,Joe	L	.230	126	29	7	0	3	19	15	21	.329	.357
Throws Left	R	.324	426	138	28	6	16	78	32	56	.375	.531
Kershner,Jason	L	.178	90	16	2	0	2	5	6	21	.229	.267
Throws Left	R	.250	108	27	6	0	3	14	9	11	.311	.389
Kida,Masao	L	.300	20	6	1	1	0	1	0	5	.300	.450
Throws Right	R	.300	30	9	2	0	0	3	3	3	.364	.367
Kim,Byung-Hyun	L	.221	222	49	9	0	6	28	20	54	.319	.342
Throws Right	R	.227	242	55	9	0	6	25	13	48	.265	.339
Kim,Sun-Woo	L	.400	30	12	1	1	5	9	6	1	.500	1.000
Throws Right	R	.414	29	12	0	0	1	4	2	4	.500	.517
King,Ray	L	.200	95	19	1	1	1	11	8	17	.260	.263
Throws Left	R	.223	121	27	7	0	2	25	19	26	.331	.331

Pitcher	vs	Avg	AB	H	2B	3B	HR	RBI	BB	SO	OBP	Slg
Kinney,Matt	L	.284	359	102	19	4	12	47	40	64	.355	.460
Throws Right	R	.260	381	99	14	3	15	63	40	88	.332	.430
Kline,Steve	L	.243	107	26	5	1	1	12	10	17	.314	.336
Throws Left	R	.233	129	30	6	2	4	15	20	14	.340	.403
Knott,Eric	L	.286	21	6	1	0	0	1	3	4	.375	.333
Throws Left	R	.298	57	17	5	0	2	7	3	13	.328	.491
Knotts,Gary	L	.323	201	65	13	2	12	43	29	19	.410	.587
Throws Right	R	.249	185	46	8	1	2	17	18	32	.319	.335
Koch,Billy	L	.294	109	32	7	0	5	17	16	26	.386	.495
Throws Right	R	.267	101	27	8	1	5	22	12	16	.339	.515
Kolb,Danny	L	.209	67	14	4	0	1	3	10	15	.312	.313
Throws Right	R	.230	87	20	2	1	1	7	9	24	.309	.310
Koplove,Mike	L	.224	58	13	2	1	2	4	5	17	.288	.397
Throws Right	R	.225	80	18	2	0	1	6	5	10	.303	.288
Lackey,John	L	.286	448	128	26	1	15	61	40	85	.346	.449
Throws Right	R	.269	353	95	17	0	16	45	26	66	.329	.453
Lawrence,Brian	L	.275	360	99	19	2	12	35	33	38	.341	.439
Throws Right	R	.244	439	107	16	2	15	60	24	78	.291	.392
Ledezma,Wil	L	.316	95	30	5	0	4	22	14	15	.400	.495
Throws Left	R	.290	238	69	13	4	8	39	21	34	.351	.479
Lee,Cliff	L	.278	54	15	2	0	4	11	1	12	.304	.537
Throws Left	R	.197	132	26	3	1	3	13	19	32	.301	.303
Lee,Dave	L	.000	8	0	0	0	0	0	3	2	.273	.000
Throws Right	R	.200	20	4	0	0	1	4	3	5	.304	.350
Leiter,Al	L	.299	117	35	3	2	3	11	13	29	.376	.436
Throws Left	R	.252	560	141	38	1	12	61	81	110	.351	.388
Leskanic,Curtis	L	.176	85	15	6	0	0	5	16	23	.307	.247
Throws Right	R	.228	101	23	7	0	2	13	13	27	.319	.356
Levine,Al	L	.218	133	29	5	0	5	19	20	10	.329	.368
Throws Right	R	.284	134	38	8	0	4	13	9	20	.333	.433
Levrault,Allen	L	.383	47	18	4	0	2	10	12	10	.500	.596
Throws Right	R	.299	67	20	3	2	1	8	3	11	.333	.448
Lewis,Colby	L	.319	285	91	19	4	12	41	44	43	.411	.540
Throws Right	R	.313	230	72	22	1	11	48	26	45	.391	.561
Lidge,Brad	L	.230	135	31	8	2	3	18	20	34	.335	.385
Throws Right	R	.179	162	29	6	0	3	14	22	63	.286	.272
Lidle,Cory	L	.265	427	113	30	6	11	61	31	53	.317	.440
Throws Right	R	.305	338	103	17	5	13	55	29	59	.361	.500
Ligtenberg,Kerry	L	.356	87	31	3	0	4	13	11	12	.424	.529
Throws Right	R	.206	141	29	7	0	5	21	3	35	.233	.362
Lilly,Ted	L	.235	162	38	9	0	2	11	8	33	.277	.327
Throws Left	R	.261	541	141	31	2	22	71	50	114	.325	.447
Lima,Jose	L	.329	167	55	11	1	6	27	24	16	.418	.515
Throws Right	R	.210	119	25	5	2	1	10	2	16	.238	.311
Lincoln,Mike	L	.333	45	15	3	0	0	2	9	10	.444	.400
Throws Right	R	.250	92	23	5	0	5	15	4	18	.286	.467
Linebrink,Scott	L	.275	149	41	3	0	3	13	18	27	.359	.356
Throws Right	R	.265	196	52	14	1	6	28	18	41	.332	.439
Linton,Doug	L	.231	13	3	1	0	0	3	2	1	.333	.308
Throws Right	R	.222	18	4	0	0	2	5	2	6	.300	.556
Lloyd,Graeme	L	.338	68	23	4	0	0	12	1	5	.347	.397
Throws Left	R	.333	135	45	12	0	2	25	13	20	.387	.467
Loaiza,Esteban	L	.258	515	133	26	1	11	46	42	135	.321	.377
Throws Right	R	.192	328	63	14	3	6	22	14	72	.230	.308
Loewer,Carlton	L	.432	44	19	2	0	2	7	3	5	.479	.614
Throws Right	R	.314	51	16	1	0	1	8	5	6	.368	.392
Lohse,Kyle	L	.283	446	126	27	0	16	64	26	61	.323	.451
Throws Right	R	.249	341	85	17	0	12	33	19	69	.293	.405
Looper,Aaron	L	.286	14	4	0	0	1	3	2	4	.375	.500
Throws Right	R	.250	12	3	0	0	0	1	0	2	.308	.250
Looper,Braden	L	.280	143	40	8	2	3	22	12	28	.331	.427
Throws Right	R	.250	168	42	3	2	1	16	17	28	.321	.310
Lopez,Albie	L	.411	56	23	6	0	4	16	9	8	.492	.732
Throws Right	R	.353	51	18	6	0	3	9	8	7	.441	.647
Lopez,Aquilino	L	.250	112	28	6	0	4	16	18	12	.359	.411
Throws Right	R	.186	161	30	7	0	1	15	16	52	.273	.248
Lopez,Javier	L	.250	116	29	6	0	2	15	3	30	.269	.353
Throws Left	R	.266	109	29	3	0	3	6	9	10	.344	.376
Lopez,Rodrigo	L	.308	318	98	20	0	16	45	27	54	.364	.522
Throws Right	R	.319	282	90	20	2	8	48	16	49	.367	.489
Loux,Shane	L	.352	71	25	8	3	2	18	4	4	.403	.634
Throws Right	R	.235	51	12	3	0	2	9	8	4	.355	.412
Lowe,Derek	L	.276	431	119	17	4	13	52	42	52	.345	.425
Throws Right	R	.266	364	97	18	3	4	43	30	58	.331	.365
Lowe,Sean	L	.267	90	24	5	0	4	11	16	12	.377	.456
Throws Right	R	.333	93	31	8	0	3	22	5	16	.376	.516

Pitchers vs. Left-Handed and Right-Handed Batters

Pitcher	vs	Avg	AB	H	2B	3B	HR	RBI	BB	SO	OBP	Slg
Lowry,Noah	L	.000	5	0	0	0	0	0	2	1	.286	.000
Throws Left	R	.063	16	1	0	0	0	0	0	4	.118	.063
Lyon,Brandon	L	.317	120	38	9	2	5	21	11	21	.381	.550
Throws Right	R	.276	127	35	10	0	1	15	8	29	.312	.378
MacDougal,Mike	L	.230	135	31	4	1	2	16	20	32	.333	.319
Throws Right	R	.314	105	33	7	0	2	17	12	25	.413	.438
Maddux,Greg	L	.271	391	106	23	5	9	40	21	56	.311	.425
Throws Right	R	.264	450	119	21	1	15	64	12	68	.287	.416
Madson,Ryan	L	.000	2	0	0	0	0	0	0	0	.000	.000
Throws Right	R	.000	4	0	0	0	0	0	0	0	.000	.000
Mahay,Ron	L	.208	53	11	4	0	1	8	6	13	.288	.340
Throws Left	R	.190	116	22	10	0	2	11	14	25	.277	.328
Mahomes,Pat	L	.192	26	5	1	1	0	4	8	5	.361	.308
Throws Right	R	.264	53	14	2	1	2	11	4	8	.305	.453
Malaska,Mark	L	.219	32	7	0	0	0	4	5	12	.342	.219
Throws Left	R	.250	24	6	1	0	0	5	7	5	.419	.292
Mann,Jim	L	.500	4	2	0	0	0	0	1	0	.600	.500
Throws Right	R	.429	7	3	0	0	1	3	0	1	.429	.857
Manning,Dave	L	.300	10	3	0	1	0	4	6	1	.563	.500
Throws Right	R	.444	18	8	1	0	1	8	2	1	.476	.667
Manon,Julio	L	.195	41	8	1	1	0	4	8	5	.320	.268
Throws Right	R	.290	62	18	3	0	3	14	9	10	.384	.484
Mantei,Matt	L	.155	84	13	1	0	4	6	8	28	.237	.310
Throws Right	R	.218	110	24	2	1	2	8	10	40	.285	.309
Maroth,Mike	L	.257	171	44	11	1	5	22	10	24	.303	.421
Throws Left	R	.311	601	187	26	8	29	93	40	63	.357	.526
Marquis,Jason	L	.250	72	18	3	0	0	11	6	6	.309	.292
Throws Right	R	.287	87	25	5	1	3	12	12	13	.376	.471
Marte,Damaso	L	.168	125	21	6	0	1	12	11	42	.245	.240
Throws Left	R	.199	146	29	5	1	2	16	23	45	.308	.288
Martin,Tom	L	.190	105	20	3	0	3	7	9	31	.250	.305
Throws Left	R	.208	77	16	3	0	3	9	15	20	.351	.364
Martinez,Luis	L	.231	13	3	0	0	0	0	1	2	.286	.231
Throws Left	R	.407	54	22	8	0	3	17	14	8	.529	.722
Martinez,Pedro	L	.238	412	98	24	3	7	38	25	114	.289	.362
Throws Right	R	.179	273	49	13	2	0	10	22	92	.248	.242
Mateo,Julio	L	.220	168	37	5	0	8	22	5	28	.237	.393
Throws Right	R	.219	146	32	4	0	6	12	8	43	.283	.370
Matthews,Mike	L	.294	102	30	5	1	2	25	10	22	.362	.422
Throws Left	R	.254	138	35	8	3	2	15	19	22	.346	.399
May,Darrell	L	.217	203	44	9	0	6	18	9	28	.252	.350
Throws Left	R	.255	599	153	36	7	25	68	44	87	.305	.464
Mays,Joe	L	.346	295	102	21	5	16	62	22	25	.393	.614
Throws Right	R	.246	232	57	9	0	5	29	17	25	.302	.349
McClung,Seth	L	.281	64	18	3	0	2	8	14	14	.418	.422
Throws Right	R	.205	73	15	2	1	4	10	11	11	.322	.425
Meadows,Brian	L	.276	127	35	5	1	4	20	7	21	.311	.425
Throws Right	R	.299	187	56	7	0	4	20	4	17	.318	.401
Mears,Chris	L	.395	76	30	5	1	4	18	5	10	.432	.645
Throws Right	R	.230	87	20	4	0	1	10	6	11	.299	.310
Meche,Gil	L	.275	385	106	14	4	17	38	44	67	.350	.465
Throws Right	R	.248	326	81	11	1	13	41	19	63	.291	.408
Mecir,Jim	L	.311	61	19	3	0	3	11	7	9	.380	.508
Throws Right	R	.256	82	21	4	1	1	7	9	16	.330	.366
Mendoza,Ramiro	L	.320	125	40	10	1	5	17	13	15	.387	.536
Throws Right	R	.372	156	58	9	1	5	29	7	21	.405	.538
Mercado,Hector	L	.158	19	3	0	0	0	2	6	4	.346	.158
Throws Left	R	.288	52	15	2	1	5	12	6	11	.367	.654
Mercedes,Jose	L	.222	9	2	0	0	0	1	2	0	.364	.222
Throws Right	R	.235	17	4	0	0	0	2	3	3	.350	.235
Mercker,Kent	L	.222	81	18	6	1	1	14	17	20	.354	.358
Throws Left	R	.230	122	28	5	0	5	12	15	28	.314	.393
Mesa,Jose	L	.213	94	20	6	1	1	9	15	17	.327	.330
Throws Right	R	.349	146	51	3	2	6	29	16	28	.414	.521
Miadich,Bart	L	.250	4	1	0	0	0	0	0	2	.400	.250
Throws Right	R	.667	6	4	2	0	0	4	1	1	.714	1.000
Miceli,Danny	L	.194	108	21	6	1	7	9	11	16	.275	.463
Throws Right	R	.244	156	38	5	1	6	21	14	42	.310	.404
Middlebrook,Jason	L	.375	8	3	1	0	0	2	1	0	.400	.500
Throws Right	R	.455	22	10	3	0	0	5	3	3	.520	.591
Miller,Matt	L	.400	5	2	0	0	0	2	0	1	.571	.400
Throws Right	R	.273	11	3	0	0	0	1	0	5	.273	.273
Miller,Trever	L	.226	106	24	3	0	6	16	12	28	.328	.425
Throws Left	R	.237	93	22	1	1	1	9	16	16	.355	.301

Pitcher	vs	Avg	AB	H	2B	3B	HR	RBI	BB	SO	OBP	Slg
Miller,Wade	L	.258	329	85	23	2	10	39	40	71	.343	.432
Throws Right	R	.227	366	83	11	2	7	41	37	90	.305	.325
Millwood,Kevin	L	.246	362	89	17	3	6	40	36	79	.315	.359
Throws Right	R	.253	479	121	28	4	13	55	32	90	.301	.409
Milton,Eric	L	.389	18	7	2	0	1	3	1	0	.400	.667
Throws Left	R	.174	46	8	0	0	1	2	0	7	.174	.239
Mitre,Sergio	L	.467	15	7	2	1	0	3	2	1	.529	.733
Throws Right	R	.348	23	8	2	0	1	5	2	2	.385	.565
Moehler,Brian	L	.600	20	12	4	1	3	8	4	2	.667	1.350
Throws Right	R	.263	38	10	1	0	1	4	2	3	.293	.368
Molina,Gabe	L	.333	6	2	1	0	1	3	0	1	.333	1.000
Throws Right	R	.429	7	3	1	0	0	1	1	0	.500	.571
Moreno,Orber	L	.333	15	5	1	1	0	4	0	0	.333	.533
Throws Right	R	.294	17	5	3	0	1	6	3	5	.400	.647
Morris,Matt	L	.255	271	69	17	0	4	22	19	45	.306	.362
Throws Right	R	.249	381	95	21	2	16	48	20	75	.290	.441
Moss,Damian	L	.342	184	63	15	1	7	27	24	35	.433	.549
Throws Left	R	.261	464	121	26	0	17	63	68	54	.358	.427
Mota,Guillermo	L	.181	138	25	1	1	3	18	19	37	.278	.268
Throws Right	R	.220	241	53	8	1	4	17	7	62	.245	.311
Mounce,Tony	L	.310	58	18	4	0	2	8	7	4	.429	.483
Throws Left	R	.320	147	47	8	1	7	29	18	26	.392	.531
Moyer,Jamie	L	.278	248	69	14	0	7	29	23	25	.345	.419
Throws Left	R	.231	562	130	25	1	12	49	43	104	.289	.343
Mulder,Mark	L	.252	119	30	5	0	3	7	9	22	.305	.370
Throws Left	R	.260	577	150	31	4	12	57	31	106	.299	.390
Mulholland,Terry	L	.252	131	33	4	0	3	13	14	17	.329	.351
Throws Left	R	.317	265	84	18	1	14	47	23	25	.375	.551
Mullen,Scott	L	.429	7	3	0	0	0	2	1	1	.556	.429
Throws Left	R	.370	27	10	2	0	2	11	9	3	.514	.667
Munro,Pete	L	.293	82	24	4	1	3	15	8	9	.370	.476
Throws Right	R	.295	132	39	4	1	4	19	18	18	.390	.432
Mussina,Mike	L	.229	419	96	19	1	10	37	28	110	.278	.351
Throws Right	R	.247	388	96	22	1	11	43	12	85	.272	.394
Myers,Brett	L	.270	333	90	22	1	10	40	48	64	.363	.432
Throws Right	R	.273	421	115	21	5	10	48	29	79	.329	.418
Myers,Mike	L	.237	76	18	5	0	3	15	8	14	.318	.421
Throws Left	R	.290	69	20	3	0	1	15	13	7	.430	.377
Myers,Rodney	L	.200	15	3	1	0	0	1	2	3	.294	.267
Throws Right	R	.318	22	7	0	0	1	7	3	3	.400	.455
Myette,Aaron	L	.800	5	4	1	1	0	3	2	0	.875	1.400
Throws Right	R	.300	10	3	2	0	1	4	0	1	.300	.800
Nagy,Charles	L	.368	19	7	3	0	0	5	1	2	.400	.526
Throws Right	R	.276	29	8	1	0	0	2	2	5	.323	.310
Nakamura,Mike	L	.385	26	10	1	1	1	4	2	6	.429	.615
Throws Right	R	.303	33	10	3	0	3	10	0	8	.324	.667
Nance,Shane	L	.256	39	10	0	1	2	9	3	9	.318	.462
Throws Left	R	.369	65	24	2	0	3	9	7	16	.425	.538
Nathan,Joe	L	.276	98	27	4	0	2	14	17	31	.385	.378
Throws Right	R	.136	176	24	6	0	5	22	16	52	.213	.256
Neagle,Denny	L	.415	41	17	4	0	5	12	0	3	.415	.878
Throws Left	R	.283	106	30	7	2	7	19	12	18	.361	.585
Neal,Blaine	L	.447	38	17	3	0	1	12	4	4	.478	.605
Throws Right	R	.389	54	21	5	1	1	14	5	6	.426	.574
Nelson,Jeff	L	.273	77	21	4	0	2	16	14	23	.404	.403
Throws Right	R	.233	129	30	3	1	2	21	10	45	.289	.318
Neu,Mike	L	.214	70	15	5	0	0	8	12	11	.337	.286
Throws Right	R	.295	95	28	6	2	2	14	14	9	.391	.463
Nitkowski,C.J.	L	.550	20	11	1	0	0	4	1	4	.545	.600
Throws Left	R	.286	21	6	1	0	0	2	7	1	.448	.333
Nomo,Hideo	L	.214	355	76	12	0	10	27	54	78	.317	.332
Throws Right	R	.231	429	99	19	1	14	43	44	99	.302	.378
Norton,Phil	L	.214	28	6	0	0	0	1	1	3	.241	.214
Throws Left	R	.100	30	3	0	0	0	0	8	4	.289	.100
Nunez,Vladimir	L	.368	19	7	1	1	1	9	3	5	.417	.684
Throws Right	R	.412	34	14	3	0	6	12	4	5	.474	1.029
Obermueller,Wes	L	.301	103	31	5	2	3	11	15	13	.398	.476
Throws Right	R	.301	166	50	7	2	7	24	10	21	.352	.494
Ohka,Tomo	L	.311	318	99	22	2	6	26	18	44	.356	.450
Throws Right	R	.279	481	134	30	0	18	57	27	74	.322	.453
Ohme,Kevin	L	.000	5	0	0	0	0	1	0	0	.000	.000
Throws Left	R	.300	10	3	1	0	0	1	1	1	.364	.400
Oliver,Darren	L	.255	157	40	14	3	5	27	16	21	.333	.478
Throws Left	R	.292	551	161	30	4	16	69	45	67	.349	.449
Olsen,Kevin	L	.560	25	14	2	1	1	11	3	4	.607	.840
Throws Right	R	.333	33	11	3	0	1	6	1	8	.353	.515

315

Pitchers vs. Left-Handed and Right-Handed Batters

Pitcher	vs	Avg	AB	H	2B	3B	HR	RBI	BB	SO	OBP	Slg
Oropesa,Eddie	L	.206	63	13	3	1	1	6	11	21	.333	.333
Throws Left	R	.294	85	25	2	0	2	19	16	18	.412	.388
Orosco,Jesse	L	.231	78	18	3	1	2	14	10	20	.330	.372
Throws Left	R	.390	59	23	5	0	2	11	11	9	.473	.576
Ortiz,Ramon	L	.291	378	110	21	4	16	54	42	32	.366	.495
Throws Right	R	.282	351	99	14	0	12	57	21	62	.332	.425
Ortiz,Russ	L	.265	366	97	25	1	7	41	54	54	.355	.396
Throws Right	R	.187	427	80	16	2	10	45	48	95	.274	.304
Osuna,Antonio	L	.305	82	25	9	0	0	15	12	24	.389	.415
Throws Right	R	.266	124	33	11	0	3	14	8	23	.319	.427
Oswalt,Roy	L	.263	198	52	4	1	3	13	15	43	.315	.338
Throws Right	R	.234	274	64	10	0	12	33	14	65	.282	.401
Padilla,Vicente	L	.267	344	92	26	4	7	40	34	51	.333	.427
Throws Right	R	.239	436	104	26	0	15	45	28	82	.303	.401
Painter,Lance	L	.290	31	9	3	0	2	7	3	4	.353	.581
Throws Left	R	.211	38	8	2	0	1	4	4	7	.286	.342
Paniagua,Jose	L	1.000	2	2	0	1	0	2	1	0	1.000	2.000
Throws Right	R	.500	2	1	1	0	0	0	0	0	.500	1.000
Park,Chan Ho	L	.367	60	22	2	0	3	15	17	8	.494	.550
Throws Right	R	.235	51	12	2	0	2	7	8	8	.391	.392
Paronto,Chad	L	.429	7	3	0	0	0	2	1	1	.500	.429
Throws Right	R	.235	17	4	0	0	1	3	2	5	.300	.412
Parque,Jim	L	.294	17	5	1	0	0	3	3	2	.429	.353
Throws Left	R	.367	60	22	4	2	2	17	13	6	.479	.600
Parris,Steve	L	.290	93	27	4	0	5	14	7	5	.333	.495
Throws Right	R	.367	90	33	11	1	7	18	6	9	.406	.744
Parrish,John	L	.194	31	6	3	0	0	5	3	6	.278	.290
Throws Left	R	.212	52	11	1	0	2	2	5	9	.281	.346
Patterson,Danny	L	.176	34	6	2	0	1	4	3	12	.243	.324
Throws Right	R	.281	32	9	1	1	0	4	1	7	.324	.375
Patterson,John	L	.281	89	25	3	3	2	7	20	20	.409	.449
Throws Right	R	.281	128	36	15	0	5	28	10	23	.340	.516
Pavano,Carl	L	.267	341	91	26	2	7	31	27	53	.322	.416
Throws Right	R	.263	430	113	28	1	12	56	22	80	.302	.416
Pearce,Josh	L	.333	15	5	1	0	0	2	1	0	.375	.400
Throws Right	R	.286	21	6	3	0	0	1	1	4	.348	.429
Pearson,Jason	L	.500	4	2	0	0	0	2	1	0	.600	.500
Throws Left	R	.667	3	2	0	0	1	2	2	1	.800	1.667
Peavy,Jake	L	.246	362	89	16	4	16	40	42	70	.327	.445
Throws Right	R	.230	365	84	9	1	17	46	40	86	.310	.400
Penny,Brad	L	.269	360	97	15	6	8	40	32	72	.334	.411
Throws Right	R	.258	380	98	28	1	13	52	24	66	.298	.439
Percival,Troy	L	.165	91	15	0	0	3	11	19	27	.313	.264
Throws Right	R	.205	88	18	2	1	4	9	4	21	.255	.386
Perez,Odalis	L	.201	149	30	7	1	3	12	9	35	.261	.322
Throws Left	R	.284	566	161	26	3	25	81	37	106	.327	.473
Perez,Oliver	L	.292	72	21	4	0	3	8	8	21	.370	.472
Throws Left	R	.258	419	108	21	4	19	65	69	120	.365	.463
Person,Robert	L	.200	15	3	2	1	0	4	5	2	.429	.467
Throws Right	R	.276	29	8	2	0	0	5	3	8	.324	.345
Pettitte,Andy	L	.321	224	72	7	1	5	25	11	46	.356	.429
Throws Left	R	.254	611	155	27	5	16	66	39	134	.296	.393
Phelps,Tommy	L	.233	60	14	2	0	1	6	7	13	.333	.317
Throws Left	R	.298	188	56	13	1	2	23	16	30	.350	.410
Phillips,Jason C	L	.308	13	4	0	0	0	2	0	1	.286	.308
Throws Right	R	.556	9	5	1	0	1	3	2	1	.636	1.000
Pineiro,Joel	L	.234	441	103	23	0	11	53	49	85	.310	.361
Throws Right	R	.251	355	89	12	1	8	35	27	66	.308	.358
Plesac,Dan	L	.224	76	17	3	0	2	9	6	21	.289	.342
Throws Left	R	.235	51	12	1	0	1	4	5	16	.304	.314
Politte,Cliff	L	.287	101	29	5	0	3	17	12	19	.360	.426
Throws Right	R	.250	92	23	6	1	8	21	5	21	.290	.598
Ponson,Sidney	L	.271	410	111	19	4	5	40	35	61	.328	.373
Throws Right	R	.243	411	100	33	0	11	42	26	73	.293	.404
Porzio,Mike	L	.538	13	7	4	0	0	4	0	0	.571	.846
Throws Left	R	.256	43	11	2	0	2	6	1	9	.283	.442
Powell,Brian	L	.143	7	1	0	0	0	0	1	1	.250	.143
Throws Right	R	.500	14	7	2	0	3	7	0	2	.500	1.286
Powell,Jay	L	.255	94	24	11	0	3	28	18	20	.365	.468
Throws Right	R	.362	141	51	12	1	4	33	16	20	.426	.546
Prinz,Bret	L	.200	5	1	0	0	0	0	3	2	.500	.200
Throws Right	R	.545	11	6	4	0	1	8	1	1	.583	1.182
Prior,Mark	L	.240	362	87	12	3	6	29	31	103	.307	.340
Throws Right	R	.223	431	96	27	3	9	35	19	142	.263	.362
Puffer,Brandon	L	.313	32	10	3	0	2	5	9	4	.463	.594
Throws Right	R	.292	48	14	3	0	0	9	7	6	.393	.354

Pitcher	vs	Avg	AB	H	2B	3B	HR	RBI	BB	SO	OBP	Slg
Pulido,Carlos	L	.250	16	4	0	0	0	2	0	1	.250	.250
Throws Left	R	.256	43	11	5	0	0	5	3	5	.292	.372
Putz,J.J.	L	.444	9	4	2	0	0	2	2	1	.545	.667
Throws Right	R	.000	6	0	0	0	0	0	1	2	.143	.000
Quantrill,Paul	L	.198	96	19	3	0	1	6	11	21	.287	.260
Throws Right	R	.243	173	42	8	0	1	19	4	23	.268	.306
Quevedo,Ruben	L	.297	74	22	4	1	7	15	10	4	.376	.662
Throws Right	R	.326	95	31	4	2	5	13	13	15	.400	.568
Radke,Brad	L	.297	465	138	20	4	18	53	17	68	.326	.473
Throws Right	R	.278	374	104	23	0	14	46	11	52	.299	.452
Raggio,Brady	L	.333	9	3	1	0	0	3	4	2	.538	.444
Throws Right	R	.273	22	6	0	0	1	6	2	6	.333	.409
Ramirez,Erasmo	L	.250	64	16	2	0	2	11	3	10	.300	.375
Throws Left	R	.252	119	30	4	0	2	9	6	18	.297	.336
Ramirez,Horacio	L	.206	141	29	7	1	2	12	12	25	.282	.312
Throws Left	R	.278	547	152	40	2	19	66	60	75	.351	.463
Ramos,Mario	L	.211	19	4	0	0	1	1	4	5	.375	.368
Throws Left	R	.233	30	7	2	0	2	7	9	3	.425	.500
Randall,Scott	L	.375	32	12	2	0	0	6	3	6	.429	.438
Throws Right	R	.275	80	22	3	0	1	9	8	19	.356	.350
Randolph,Stephen	L	.222	90	20	3	1	3	14	13	20	.327	.378
Throws Left	R	.229	131	30	8	1	4	14	30	30	.377	.397
Reames,Britt	L	.000	1	0	0	0	0	0	2	0	.667	.000
Throws Right	R	.571	7	4	2	0	0	3	0	1	.571	.857
Redding,Tim	L	.297	316	94	23	3	8	41	38	51	.375	.465
Throws Right	R	.229	371	85	17	2	8	34	27	65	.289	.350
Redman,Mark	L	.200	140	28	4	1	4	13	9	42	.257	.329
Throws Left	R	.248	581	144	32	2	12	64	52	109	.311	.372
Reed,Rick	L	.264	295	78	13	1	8	34	20	44	.309	.397
Throws Right	R	.310	248	77	18	1	13	39	9	27	.345	.548
Reed,Steve	L	.374	99	37	5	0	7	19	14	15	.456	.636
Throws Right	R	.165	133	22	4	0	2	10	12	24	.268	.241
Reichert,Dan	L	.436	39	17	1	1	1	9	5	4	.511	.590
Throws Right	R	.333	33	11	3	0	1	10	3	9	.405	.515
Reith,Brian	L	.206	68	14	6	0	2	12	17	13	.360	.382
Throws Right	R	.287	164	47	13	1	6	20	19	26	.356	.488
Reitsma,Chris	L	.298	131	39	5	1	9	19	14	25	.363	.557
Throws Right	R	.270	196	53	10	0	5	20	5	28	.289	.398
Remlinger,Mike	L	.263	95	25	2	0	5	16	11	27	.343	.442
Throws Left	R	.180	161	29	3	1	6	17	28	56	.304	.323
Reyes,Al	L	.192	26	5	2	0	1	5	5	2	.323	.385
Throws Right	R	.211	38	8	3	0	0	6	4	7	.286	.289
Reyes,Carlos	L	.243	70	17	1	0	6	13	3	5	.286	.514
Throws Right	R	.284	81	23	6	0	4	10	2	8	.301	.506
Reyes,Dennys	L	.111	18	2	0	0	1	2	1	8	.158	.278
Throws Left	R	.406	32	13	3	0	1	11	9	8	.512	.594
Reynolds,Shane	L	.254	264	67	15	1	4	28	34	37	.342	.364
Throws Right	R	.320	387	124	24	1	16	63	25	57	.369	.512
Rhodes,Arthur	L	.269	104	28	2	0	2	9	7	25	.321	.346
Throws Left	R	.243	103	25	8	1	2	19	11	23	.316	.398
Riedling,John	L	.245	159	39	8	3	2	27	17	23	.320	.371
Throws Right	R	.286	238	68	11	0	5	34	30	42	.364	.395
Riggan,Jerrod	L	.444	9	4	0	0	0	1	0	1	.444	.444
Throws Right	R	.375	8	3	2	0	0	2	1	1	.400	.625
Riley,Matt	L	.143	7	1	0	0	0	0	2	3	.333	.143
Throws Left	R	.207	29	6	1	0	1	2	3	5	.281	.345
Rincon,Juan	L	.222	158	35	6	0	2	15	24	27	.332	.297
Throws Right	R	.239	163	39	9	0	3	20	14	36	.299	.350
Rincon,Ricardo	L	.200	80	16	3	0	1	6	7	20	.273	.275
Throws Left	R	.250	116	29	7	0	3	16	25	20	.386	.388
Riske,David	L	.145	124	18	5	0	5	12	12	44	.225	.306
Throws Right	R	.241	141	34	5	0	4	14	8	38	.291	.362
Ritchie,Todd	L	.409	44	18	3	0	2	8	5	4	.471	.614
Throws Right	R	.257	70	18	1	1	2	6	5	11	.329	.386
Rivera,Mariano	L	.199	146	29	1	0	1	12	2	39	.219	.226
Throws Right	R	.281	114	32	5	1	2	18	8	24	.336	.395
Roa,Joe	L	.434	76	33	3	2	3	18	7	12	.488	.645
Throws Right	R	.257	140	36	10	1	7	20	3	26	.273	.493
Roach,Jason	L	.389	18	7	1	0	2	7	2	0	.450	.778
Throws Right	R	.318	22	7	1	0	1	5	2	2	.400	.500
Roberts,Grant	L	.231	26	6	1	0	0	1	2	4	.286	.269
Throws Right	R	.271	48	13	2	2	0	4	1	6	.300	.396
Roberts,Willis	L	.298	57	17	1	0	5	13	7	11	.375	.579
Throws Right	R	.258	93	24	1	2	2	18	9	15	.367	.376
Robertson,Jeriome	L	.243	152	37	5	2	3	19	16	30	.335	.362
Throws Left	R	.300	476	143	37	0	20	64	48	69	.362	.504

Pitchers vs. Left-Handed and Right-Handed Batters

Pitcher	vs	Avg	AB	H	2B	3B	HR	RBI	BB	SO	OBP	Slg
Robertson,Nate	L	.300	30	9	3	0	0	2	5	11	.400	.400
Throws Left	R	.307	150	46	5	0	6	19	18	22	.381	.460
Rocker,John	L	.333	3	1	0	0	0	1	2	0	.600	.333
Throws Left	R	1.000	1	1	0	0	0	0	1	0	1.000	1.000
Rodney,Fernando	L	.345	58	20	3	0	1	15	10	14	.423	.448
Throws Right	R	.246	61	15	3	0	1	9	7	19	.333	.344
Rodriguez,Felix	L	.264	91	24	3	1	1	4	15	28	.374	.352
Throws Right	R	.255	137	35	7	1	4	21	14	18	.335	.409
Rodriguez,Francisco	L	.186	156	29	1	0	8	29	24	35	.293	.346
Throws Right	R	.156	135	21	5	0	4	12	11	60	.225	.281
Rodriguez,Ricardo	L	.300	160	48	10	1	9	31	13	13	.354	.544
Throws Right	R	.250	164	41	9	0	7	22	15	28	.319	.433
Rodriguez,Rich	L	.143	7	1	0	0	0	1	0	2	.125	.143
Throws Left	R	.500	6	3	0	0	0	1	1	1	.571	.500
Rogers,Kenny	L	.251	215	54	12	1	6	22	18	55	.311	.400
Throws Left	R	.307	563	173	34	5	16	74	32	61	.354	.471
Romero,J.C.	L	.214	103	22	3	1	1	13	15	24	.336	.291
Throws Left	R	.314	140	44	8	0	6	25	27	26	.432	.500
Roney,Matt	L	.297	182	54	6	1	10	32	32	28	.402	.505
Throws Right	R	.232	207	48	8	1	7	21	16	19	.292	.382
Rosario,Rodrigo	L	.286	14	4	3	0	0	0	1	3	.333	.500
Throws Right	R	.067	15	1	0	0	0	1	2	3	.222	.067
Rueter,Kirk	L	.212	146	31	8	0	1	13	9	13	.256	.288
Throws Left	R	.326	427	139	25	2	13	51	38	28	.381	.485
Rupe,Ryan	L	.231	13	3	1	0	1	3	1	2	.286	.538
Throws Right	R	.333	30	10	1	0	3	6	0	5	.333	.667
Rusch,Glendon	L	.307	127	39	10	1	2	21	6	23	.348	.449
Throws Left	R	.338	390	132	25	2	9	57	39	70	.400	.482
Ryan,B.J.	L	.186	97	18	3	0	0	14	13	45	.283	.216
Throws Left	R	.273	88	24	3	1	1	14	14	18	.381	.364
Saarloos,Kirk	L	.270	74	20	7	2	1	11	10	17	.357	.459
Throws Right	R	.287	122	35	6	0	3	18	7	26	.338	.410
Sabathia,C.C.	L	.275	178	49	8	2	1	17	13	34	.330	.360
Throws Left	R	.248	568	141	30	5	18	59	53	107	.315	.414
Sadler,Carl	L	.333	18	6	1	0	0	2	2	5	.435	.389
Throws Left	R	.278	18	5	1	0	0	5	3	5	.381	.333
Sanchez,Duaner	L	.500	10	5	0	0	1	3	1	1	.500	.800
Throws Right	R	.500	20	10	2	0	1	8	0	2	.545	.750
Sanchez,Felix	L	.333	3	1	0	0	1	4	2	0	.600	1.333
Throws Left	R	.333	3	1	1	0	0	0	1	2	.500	.667
Sanchez,Jesus	L	.250	8	2	1	0	0	0	2	0	.400	.375
Throws Left	R	.346	26	9	5	0	1	7	2	2	.393	.654
Sanders,Dave	L	.375	40	15	1	1	3	12	5	4	.444	.675
Throws Left	R	.204	49	10	2	0	2	9	6	10	.298	.367
Santana,Johan	L	.191	178	34	6	0	5	14	14	57	.256	.309
Throws Left	R	.227	410	93	26	3	12	37	33	112	.284	.393
Santiago,Jose	L	.353	34	12	0	0	0	1	6	4	.450	.353
Throws Right	R	.278	90	25	4	0	2	13	8	11	.337	.389
Santos,Victor	L	.346	52	18	4	0	2	16	10	7	.444	.538
Throws Right	R	.244	45	11	3	0	3	10	6	8	.346	.511
Sasaki,Kazuhiro	L	.235	68	16	4	0	1	8	10	19	.325	.338
Throws Right	R	.242	62	15	2	0	1	8	5	10	.309	.323
Sauerbeck,Scott	L	.192	104	20	1	1	3	14	18	28	.325	.308
Throws Left	R	.257	105	27	2	1	3	18	25	22	.409	.381
Schilling,Curt	L	.255	278	71	9	1	7	26	16	75	.303	.371
Throws Right	R	.210	348	73	18	0	10	28	16	119	.244	.348
Schmack,Brian	L	.296	27	8	2	0	1	6	4	0	.375	.481
Throws Right	R	.286	21	6	0	0	0	5	0	4	.304	.286
Schmidt,Jason	L	.197	401	79	14	3	7	27	31	95	.256	.299
Throws Right	R	.204	358	73	18	4	7	23	15	113	.243	.335
Schoeneweis,Scott	L	.229	118	27	6	0	0	20	8	27	.298	.280
Throws Left	R	.273	132	36	4	0	3	16	11	29	.329	.371
Seanez,Rudy	L	.200	15	3	1	0	0	1	5	3	.400	.267
Throws Right	R	.364	22	8	1	0	2	7	1	6	.375	.682
Seay,Bobby	L	.250	16	4	2	1	0	2	4	1	.364	.500
Throws Left	R	.200	15	3	1	0	0	2	2	4	.294	.267
Sele,Aaron	L	.252	262	66	11	3	7	41	34	28	.350	.397
Throws Right	R	.322	214	69	13	1	10	34	24	25	.399	.533
Seo,Jae	L	.223	337	75	23	3	6	37	30	61	.286	.362
Throws Right	R	.291	405	118	38	2	12	51	16	49	.325	.484
Serafini,Dan	L	.423	26	11	2	0	1	4	1	2	.429	.615
Throws Left	R	.313	96	30	5	3	4	17	13	11	.391	.552
Service,Scott	L	.327	55	18	2	3	1	9	6	12	.387	.527
Throws Right	R	.250	80	20	3	0	3	14	2	23	.265	.400
Sheets,Ben	L	.247	396	98	18	4	9	40	20	72	.286	.381
Throws Right	R	.286	469	134	25	1	20	76	23	85	.321	.471

Pitcher	vs	Avg	AB	H	2B	3B	HR	RBI	BB	SO	OBP	Slg
Shields,Scot	L	.229	271	62	15	0	9	27	28	61	.307	.384
Throws Right	R	.264	288	76	16	1	3	25	10	50	.290	.358
Shiell,Jason	L	.195	41	8	1	1	2	5	7	10	.327	.415
Throws Right	R	.300	50	15	4	0	2	12	10	13	.426	.500
Shouse,Brian	L	.195	133	26	7	0	1	18	2	31	.230	.271
Throws Left	R	.364	99	36	9	2	0	10	12	9	.432	.495
Shuey,Paul	L	.219	105	23	5	1	2	9	20	23	.349	.343
Throws Right	R	.197	137	27	6	2	4	14	13	37	.281	.358
Silva,Carlos	L	.300	130	39	8	2	2	22	17	16	.381	.438
Throws Right	R	.266	199	53	11	1	5	32	20	32	.355	.407
Simontacchi,Jason	L	.307	215	66	15	1	11	36	20	30	.367	.540
Throws Right	R	.294	296	87	22	2	10	42	21	44	.346	.483
Smith,Dan	L	.273	55	15	4	0	4	7	11	10	.394	.564
Throws Right	R	.284	95	27	1	0	7	18	7	25	.346	.516
Smoltz,John	L	.189	111	21	5	0	0	6	4	37	.217	.234
Throws Right	R	.218	124	27	7	0	2	10	4	36	.240	.323
Snyder,Kyle	L	.273	194	53	8	3	5	23	16	21	.324	.423
Throws Right	R	.297	138	41	9	0	6	25	5	18	.318	.493
Soriano,Rafael	L	.191	94	18	6	0	1	6	6	32	.248	.287
Throws Right	R	.132	91	12	2	0	1	3	6	36	.200	.187
Sosa,Jorge	L	.315	248	78	17	2	7	38	39	29	.402	.484
Throws Right	R	.241	245	59	10	0	7	34	21	43	.310	.367
Sparks,Steve	L	.290	176	51	13	0	5	38	21	33	.362	.449
Throws Right	R	.267	236	63	13	1	8	41	16	21	.315	.432
Speier,Justin	L	.273	121	33	12	0	3	10	9	31	.338	.446
Throws Right	R	.245	163	40	5	1	8	27	14	35	.313	.436
Spooneybarger,Tim	L	.152	66	10	0	1	1	7	4	13	.197	.227
Throws Right	R	.224	76	17	2	1	0	9	7	19	.291	.276
Springer,Russ	L	.240	25	6	1	0	2	7	2	2	.296	.520
Throws Right	R	.289	45	13	2	0	6	13	4	9	.360	.733
Spurling,Chris	L	.352	128	45	9	3	4	30	14	10	.413	.563
Throws Right	R	.200	165	33	8	0	5	22	8	28	.244	.339
Standridge,Jason	L	.250	64	16	5	0	1	5	11	9	.368	.375
Throws Right	R	.297	74	22	5	1	6	15	5	11	.338	.635
Stanford,Jason	L	.260	50	13	5	0	0	5	1	12	.269	.360
Throws Left	R	.241	145	35	6	1	5	14	15	18	.317	.400
Stanton,Mike	L	.206	63	13	3	0	0	4	7	15	.296	.254
Throws Left	R	.226	106	24	4	0	6	19	12	19	.303	.434
Stark,Denny	L	.346	153	53	9	2	8	28	24	8	.433	.588
Throws Right	R	.268	168	45	6	2	4	29	9	22	.306	.399
Stephenson,Garrett	L	.280	268	75	19	2	12	38	25	33	.348	.500
Throws Right	R	.238	386	92	21	1	18	49	35	58	.311	.438
Stewart,Josh	L	.333	18	6	3	0	0	1	4	0	.455	.500
Throws Left	R	.259	85	22	4	2	4	13	12	13	.347	.494
Stewart,Scott	L	.283	60	17	2	0	2	7	4	13	.328	.417
Throws Left	R	.318	110	35	9	0	3	16	9	16	.372	.482
Stone,Ricky	L	.290	124	36	5	1	6	24	10	14	.343	.492
Throws Right	R	.217	184	40	6	0	5	26	21	33	.316	.332
Strange,Pat	L	.500	12	6	0	0	2	10	5	3	.647	1.000
Throws Right	R	.280	25	7	0	0	2	4	6	2	.419	.520
Strickland,Scott	L	.222	27	6	1	0	1	4	3	5	.323	.370
Throws Right	R	.217	46	10	0	0	0	3	7	11	.321	.217
Sturtze,Tanyon	L	.271	177	48	10	1	5	28	30	23	.385	.424
Throws Right	R	.321	184	59	10	1	9	31	13	31	.375	.533
Sullivan,Scott	L	.238	84	20	8	0	2	11	10	17	.333	.405
Throws Right	R	.187	150	28	7	0	4	18	22	39	.302	.313
Suppan,Jeff	L	.310	374	116	29	4	12	54	28	52	.364	.505
Throws Right	R	.239	423	101	24	5	11	38	23	58	.281	.397
Sweeney,Brian	L	.250	20	5	0	0	0	1	0	4	.250	.250
Throws Right	R	.154	13	2	0	0	0	1	1	3	.267	.154
Switzer,Jon	L	.176	17	3	0	0	0	1	0	6	.250	.176
Throws Left	R	.476	21	10	2	0	2	10	3	1	.577	.857
Tallet,Brian	L	.143	14	2	1	1	0	1	1	3	.250	.357
Throws Left	R	.339	62	21	8	1	2	13	7	6	.406	.597
Tam,Jeff	L	.303	66	20	5	0	2	8	16	12	.439	.470
Throws Right	R	.319	119	38	4	2	3	24	9	14	.369	.462
Tankersley,Dennis	L	-	0	0	0	0	0	2	4	0	1.000	-
Throws Right	R	1.000	3	3	1	0	0	3	0	0	1.000	1.333
Tavarez,Julian	L	.292	113	33	7	0	0	12	19	14	.398	.354
Throws Right	R	.215	195	42	10	0	1	26	8	25	.260	.282
Taylor,Aaron	L	.320	25	8	2	0	0	4	4	5	.400	.400
Throws Right	R	.310	29	9	0	1	0	4	2	4	.375	.379
Tejera,Michael	L	.392	79	31	8	1	2	21	11	10	.467	.595
Throws Left	R	.224	228	51	12	0	4	24	25	48	.302	.329
Telemaco,Amaury	L	.288	73	21	9	0	2	5	3	10	.325	.493
Throws Right	R	.202	99	20	4	0	3	12	8	19	.298	.333

Pitchers vs. Left-Handed and Right-Handed Batters

Pitcher	vs	Avg	AB	H	2B	3B	HR	RBI	BB	SO	OBP	Slg
Thomas,Brad	L	.167	6	1	0	0	0	0	0	0	.167	.167
Throws Left	R	.385	13	5	3	0	1	4	3	2	.500	.846
Thomson,John	L	.281	455	128	27	3	13	54	29	69	.326	.440
Throws Right	R	.270	393	106	24	2	14	56	20	67	.305	.448
Thurman,Corey	L	.389	36	14	3	1	3	6	6	5	.476	.778
Throws Right	R	.226	31	7	2	0	0	3	3	6	.294	.290
Timlin,Mike	L	.287	150	43	9	1	7	25	4	24	.308	.500
Throws Right	R	.198	172	34	4	0	4	18	5	41	.233	.291
Tolar,Kevin	L	.222	9	2	0	0	1	3	1	3	.300	.556
Throws Left	R	.429	7	3	1	0	0	1	1	0	.500	.571
Tollberg,Brian	L	.192	26	5	0	0	1	3	4	0	.300	.308
Throws Right	R	.308	13	4	1	0	0	3	0	2	.286	.385
Tomko,Brett	L	.325	329	107	24	3	14	47	24	41	.372	.544
Throws Right	R	.292	496	145	30	3	21	72	33	73	.340	.492
Torres,Salomon	L	.307	202	62	11	0	10	36	20	32	.368	.510
Throws Right	R	.252	262	66	14	0	9	25	22	52	.326	.408
Towers,Josh	L	.281	128	36	3	4	6	18	5	20	.316	.508
Throws Right	R	.250	124	31	5	1	9	20	2	22	.271	.524
Traber,Billy	L	.219	114	25	6	0	1	14	15	29	.318	.298
Throws Left	R	.318	337	107	20	0	14	46	25	59	.368	.501
Trachsel,Steve	L	.199	327	65	13	2	6	18	29	46	.266	.306
Throws Right	R	.312	446	139	35	5	20	65	36	65	.361	.547
Tsao,Chin-hui	L	.309	68	21	2	0	3	9	11	9	.413	.471
Throws Right	R	.267	101	27	4	0	8	18	9	20	.345	.545
Tucker,T.J.	L	.258	128	33	9	0	5	22	5	11	.289	.445
Throws Right	R	.291	196	57	13	0	3	24	15	36	.350	.403
Turnbow,Derrick	L	.167	24	4	0	0	0	1	1	6	.200	.167
Throws Right	R	.115	26	3	0	0	0	0	2	9	.179	.115
Urbina,Ugueth	L	.182	143	26	10	0	2	15	21	32	.280	.294
Throws Right	R	.229	131	30	7	1	6	21	10	46	.282	.435
Valdes,Ismael	L	.283	223	63	11	3	8	33	16	27	.331	.466
Throws Right	R	.350	243	85	10	1	15	46	13	20	.385	.584
Valentine,Joe	L	1.000	1	1	1	0	0	0	0	0	1.000	2.000
Throws Right	R	.400	10	4	0	1	1	4	1	1	.455	.900
Valverde,Jose	L	.169	77	13	2	0	2	7	8	22	.247	.273
Throws Right	R	.112	98	11	3	0	2	11	18	49	.261	.204
Van Poppel,Todd	L	.225	80	18	2	1	5	16	11	13	.319	.463
Throws Right	R	.289	114	33	6	2	3	15	4	21	.319	.456
Vance,Cory	L	.161	31	5	2	0	0	2	4	4	.250	.226
Throws Left	R	.338	77	26	8	1	6	18	6	8	.388	.701
Vargas,Claudio	L	.270	196	53	14	2	4	16	22	24	.348	.423
Throws Right	R	.243	239	58	18	0	12	37	19	38	.308	.469
Vazquez,Javier	L	.233	377	88	20	4	10	35	29	100	.290	.387
Throws Right	R	.225	488	110	19	0	18	53	28	141	.269	.375
Venafro,Mike	L	.265	34	9	2	0	0	4	2	6	.342	.324
Throws Left	R	.341	44	15	3	0	1	8	1	3	.362	.477
Veres,Dave	L	.174	46	8	4	0	1	6	1	13	.188	.326
Throws Right	R	.359	78	28	5	0	3	17	4	13	.384	.538
Villafuerte,Brandon	L	.200	60	12	2	1	3	9	7	10	.290	.417
Throws Right	R	.284	95	27	1	0	4	15	19	24	.414	.421
Villarreal,Oscar	L	.252	135	34	7	0	4	16	19	24	.340	.393
Throws Right	R	.204	226	46	7	0	2	22	27	56	.296	.261
Villone,Ron	L	.267	101	27	4	1	5	9	10	26	.345	.475
Throws Left	R	.221	289	64	13	1	11	30	38	65	.315	.388
Vizcaino,Luis	L	.253	83	21	4	2	5	16	11	21	.340	.530
Throws Right	R	.269	160	43	6	1	11	30	14	40	.330	.525
Vogelsong,Ryan	L	.295	44	13	0	0	0	6	7	6	.392	.295
Throws Right	R	.347	49	17	2	0	1	8	2	9	.389	.449
Voyles,Brad	L	.357	84	30	9	0	5	17	13	16	.439	.643
Throws Right	R	.333	51	17	6	1	1	8	5	8	.397	.549
Waechter,Doug	L	.182	66	12	2	0	1	1	10	14	.289	.258
Throws Right	R	.270	63	17	4	0	3	10	5	15	.333	.476
Wagner,Billy	L	.216	74	16	1	0	1	1	2	27	.247	.270
Throws Left	R	.154	234	36	3	1	7	16	21	78	.230	.265
Wagner,Ryan	L	.240	25	6	1	0	0	1	6	9	.387	.280
Throws Right	R	.140	50	7	0	0	2	4	6	16	.228	.260
Wakefield,Tim	L	.269	376	101	25	2	7	39	44	69	.347	.402
Throws Right	R	.226	407	92	11	3	16	53	27	100	.289	.386
Walker,Jamie	L	.216	111	24	6	1	6	14	7	28	.267	.450
Throws Left	R	.272	136	37	6	0	3	27	10	17	.324	.382
Walker,Kevin	L	.300	10	3	1	0	0	1	3	1	.462	.400
Throws Left	R	.133	15	2	1	0	1	2	2	4	.235	.400
Walker,Pete	L	.278	115	32	9	2	3	13	15	16	.364	.470
Throws Right	R	.276	98	27	3	0	8	14	9	13	.343	.551
Walrond,Les	L	.250	8	2	1	0	1	2	3	1	.455	.750
Throws Left	R	.346	26	9	3	0	1	4	4	5	.433	.577

Pitcher	vs	Avg	AB	H	2B	3B	HR	RBI	BB	SO	OBP	Slg
Wasdin,John	L	.533	15	8	3	2	0	4	2	3	.588	1.000
Throws Right	R	.533	15	8	3	0	2	8	2	2	.556	1.133
Washburn,Jarrod	L	.230	191	44	12	1	6	23	12	41	.284	.398
Throws Left	R	.264	609	161	28	3	28	78	42	77	.318	.458
Watson,Mark	L	.000	1	0	0	0	0	0	1	0	.500	.000
Throws Left	R	.286	7	2	1	0	0	1	0	2	.286	.429
Wayne,Justin	L	.182	11	2	1	0	0	2	2	1	.357	.273
Throws Right	R	.538	13	7	2	0	1	5	3	0	.588	.923
Weathers,David	L	.239	109	26	3	1	2	10	21	36	.366	.339
Throws Right	R	.276	221	61	11	1	4	23	19	39	.347	.389
Weaver,Jeff	L	.342	383	131	33	4	11	62	27	48	.389	.535
Throws Right	R	.290	276	80	13	2	5	38	20	45	.344	.406
Webb,Brandon	L	.256	336	86	17	2	10	35	38	71	.337	.408
Throws Right	R	.167	323	54	5	0	2	20	30	101	.258	.201
Weber,Ben	L	.268	149	40	8	0	1	9	16	15	.339	.342
Throws Right	R	.282	156	44	4	2	6	22	6	31	.307	.449
Wellemeyer,Todd	L	.219	32	7	1	0	3	8	6	10	.342	.531
Throws Right	R	.257	70	18	6	1	2	13	13	20	.373	.457
Wells,David	L	.274	201	55	14	1	8	25	5	30	.307	.473
Throws Left	R	.290	645	187	40	2	16	72	15	71	.306	.433
Wells,Kip	L	.252	314	79	9	2	10	34	48	51	.350	.389
Throws Right	R	.219	421	92	18	1	14	36	28	96	.278	.366
Wendell,Turk	L	.302	86	26	6	0	3	11	10	9	.381	.477
Throws Right	R	.194	144	28	5	0	3	19	18	18	.300	.292
Westbrook,Jake	L	.276	275	76	16	1	5	28	46	26	.387	.396
Throws Right	R	.287	230	66	12	0	4	33	10	32	.335	.391
Wheeler,Dan	L	.197	71	14	3	1	1	8	7	12	.275	.310
Throws Right	R	.285	123	35	4	0	5	22	10	23	.333	.439
White,Gabe	L	.247	77	19	5	0	2	15	3	9	.268	.390
Throws Left	R	.255	98	25	8	0	5	16	5	20	.302	.490
White,Matt	L	.700	10	7	4	0	1	6	1	0	.727	1.400
Throws Left	R	.353	17	6	2	1	2	6	4	0	.455	.941
White,Rick	L	.223	112	25	8	3	1	18	10	28	.285	.375
Throws Right	R	.322	152	49	7	0	12	32	11	26	.381	.605
Williams,Jerome	L	.215	228	49	7	1	1	13	31	40	.309	.268
Throws Right	R	.266	252	67	10	2	9	28	18	48	.329	.429
Williams,Mike	L	.277	112	31	8	0	3	19	23	17	.394	.429
Throws Right	R	.261	134	35	10	0	2	26	18	22	.365	.381
Williams,Woody	L	.267	386	103	22	2	8	36	25	65	.315	.396
Throws Right	R	.246	475	117	25	4	12	55	30	88	.300	.392
Williamson,Scott	L	.200	95	19	2	0	4	8	19	27	.336	.347
Throws Right	R	.245	143	35	7	0	3	25	15	47	.316	.357
Willis,Dontrelle	L	.216	88	19	3	1	1	6	10	28	.296	.307
Throws Left	R	.250	515	129	30	5	12	49	48	114	.317	.398
Wilson,Kris	L	.355	152	54	13	1	7	24	12	20	.411	.592
Throws Right	R	.253	150	38	5	1	6	25	4	22	.281	.420
Wilson,Paul	L	.290	269	78	13	1	12	36	29	46	.361	.480
Throws Right	R	.282	397	112	27	2	12	54	21	47	.328	.451
Witasick,Jay	L	.292	65	19	5	2	1	11	15	18	.420	.477
Throws Right	R	.215	107	23	2	0	5	20	10	24	.288	.374
Wolf,Randy	L	.232	125	29	6	0	7	13	13	39	.304	.448
Throws Left	R	.234	629	147	40	2	20	74	65	138	.310	.399
Wood,Kerry	L	.198	313	62	12	1	10	30	53	109	.328	.339
Throws Right	R	.206	436	90	18	1	14	38	47	157	.299	.349
Wood,Mike	L	.344	32	11	4	0	0	7	5	6	.432	.469
Throws Right	R	.433	30	13	3	0	1	8	2	9	.500	.633
Woodard,Steve	L	.355	31	11	6	0	2	7	2	4	.394	.742
Throws Right	R	.279	43	12	2	1	1	6	3	8	.333	.442
Worrell,Tim	L	.241	145	35	5	0	2	22	15	30	.313	.317
Throws Right	R	.250	156	39	6	0	3	23	13	35	.302	.346
Wright,Dan	L	.280	189	53	10	3	10	37	25	26	.367	.524
Throws Right	R	.271	140	38	9	0	6	15	21	21	.366	.464
Wright,Jamey	L	.296	54	16	1	1	1	7	6	11	.367	.407
Throws Right	R	.175	40	7	3	0	0	6	5	8	.283	.250
Wright,Jaret	L	.365	85	31	3	3	4	21	14	14	.462	.612
Throws Right	R	.313	144	45	9	1	5	33	17	36	.380	.493
Wunsch,Kelly	L	.127	63	8	2	0	1	11	14	18	.301	.206
Throws Left	R	.153	59	9	3	0	0	7	11	15	.316	.203
Yan,Esteban	L	.309	94	29	11	0	2	21	12	12	.376	.489
Throws Right	R	.307	179	55	9	0	11	35	11	41	.369	.542
Young,Jason	L	.366	41	15	4	1	3	8	5	9	.438	.732
Throws Right	R	.345	55	19	0	0	5	10	4	9	.390	.618
Zambrano,Carlos	L	.245	314	77	19	1	5	28	41	75	.335	.360
Throws Right	R	.235	472	111	24	0	4	44	53	93	.320	.311
Zambrano,Victor	L	.263	373	98	15	2	11	49	64	62	.371	.402
Throws Right	R	.207	324	67	24	1	10	40	42	70	.325	.380

Pitchers vs. Left-Handed and Right-Handed Batters

Pitcher	vs	Avg	AB	H	2B	3B	HR	RBI	BB	SO	OBP	Slg
Zerbe,Chad	L	.365	74	27	9	2	1	17	6	6	.395	.581
Throws Left	R	.277	119	33	8	1	2	11	8	11	.318	.412
Zito,Barry	L	.223	197	44	7	1	5	29	19	37	.291	.345
Throws Left	R	.218	652	142	21	1	14	62	69	109	.296	.317

2003 Leader Boards

You'll find a higher quantity and higher quality of Leader Boards in this section than you've ever seen before in print. Each Board has the Top 10 players, giving a more complete picture of the best (or worst) players in each category.

You'll also find some Boards containing the complex pitching data we charted in 2003. Look out for a lot more of it from Baseball Info Solutions in the future.

And what the heck is "Best BPS on OutZ" you're very likely to ask?

OutZ stands for "Pitches Outside The Strike Zone" and BPS is Batting Average Plus Slugging, a combination we felt made more sense than OPS (On-Base Plus Slugging) when evaluating a player's hitting abilities outside the strike zone. (In this case, we're not all that interested in knowing who walks the most—we know that already. OPS outside the strike zone would be heavily populated with the league's most frequent walkers.)

2003 American League Batting Leaders

Batting Average (minimum 502 PA)		On Base Percentage (minimum 502 PA)		Slugging Average (minimum 502 PA)		Home Runs	
Mueller,Bill, Bos	.326	Ramirez,Manny, Bos	.427	Rodriguez,Alex, Tex	.600	Rodriguez,Alex, Tex	47
Ramirez,Manny, Bos	.325	Delgado,Carlos, Tor	.426	Delgado,Carlos, Tor	.593	Delgado,Carlos, Tor	42
Jeter,Derek, NYY	.324	Giambi,Jason, NYY	.412	Ortiz,David, Bos	.592	Thomas,Frank, CWS	42
Wells,Vernon, Tor	.317	Martinez,Edgar, Sea	.406	Ramirez,Manny, Bos	.587	Giambi,Jason, NYY	41
Ordonez,M, CWS	.317	Posada,Jorge, NYY	.405	Nixon,Trot, Bos	.578	Palmeiro,R, Tex	38
Anderson,G, Ana	.315	Mueller,Bill, Bos	.398	Thomas,Frank, CWS	.562	Soriano,A, NYY	38
Suzuki,Ichiro, Sea	.312	Nixon,Trot, Bos	.396	Huff,Aubrey, TB	.555	Ramirez,Manny, Bos	37
Pierzynski,A, Min	.312	Rodriguez,Alex, Tex	.396	Wells,Vernon, Tor	.550	Boone,Bret, Sea	35
Huff,Aubrey, TB	.311	Mientkiewicz,D, Min	.393	Ordonez,M, CWS	.546	Huff,Aubrey, TB	34
Stewart,Sh, Tor-Min	.307	Jeter,Derek, NYY	.393	Anderson,G, Ana	.541	Wells,Vernon, Tor	33

Games		Plate Appearances		At Bats		Hits	
Matsui,Hideki, NYY	163	Wells,Vernon, Tor	735	Soriano,A, NYY	682	Wells,Vernon, Tor	215
Huff,Aubrey, TB	162	Soriano,A, NYY	734	Suzuki,Ichiro, Sea	679	Suzuki,Ichiro, Sea	212
Tejada,Miguel, Oak	162	Suzuki,Ichiro, Sea	725	Wells,Vernon, Tor	678	Young,Michael, Tex	204
Batista,Tony, Bal	161	Garciaparra,N, Bos	719	Young,Michael, Tex	666	Anderson,G, Ana	201
Delgado,Carlos, Tor	161	Rodriguez,Alex, Tex	715	Garciaparra,N, Bos	658	Garciaparra,N, Bos	198
Rodriguez,Alex, Tex	161	Young,Michael, Tex	713	Anderson,G, Ana	638	Huff,Aubrey, TB	198
Wells,Vernon, Tor	161	Huff,Aubrey, TB	706	Baldelli,Rocco, TB	637	Soriano,A, NYY	198
Gibbons,Jay, Bal	160	Boone,Bret, Sea	705	Huff,Aubrey, TB	636	Ordonez,M, CWS	192
Ordonez,M, CWS	160	Delgado,Carlos, Tor	705	Tejada,Miguel, Oak	636	Ramirez,Manny, Bos	185
Young,Michael, Tex	160	Tejada,Miguel, Oak	703	Batista,Tony, Bal	631	Baldelli,Rocco, TB	184

Singles		Doubles		Triples		Total Bases	
Suzuki,Ichiro, Sea	162	Anderson,G, Ana	49	Guzman,C, Min	14	Wells,Vernon, Tor	373
Young,Michael, Tex	148	Wells,Vernon, Tor	49	Garciaparra,N, Bos	13	Rodriguez,Alex, Tex	364
Crawford,Carl, TB	145	Huff,Aubrey, TB	47	Beltran,Carlos, KC	10	Soriano,A, NYY	358
Baldelli,Rocco, TB	133	Ordonez,M, CWS	46	Byrnes,Eric, Oak	9	Huff,Aubrey, TB	353
Wells,Vernon, Tor	128	Hinske,Eric, Tor	45	Crawford,Carl, TB	9	Anderson,G, Ana	345
Winn,Randy, Sea	125	Mueller,Bill, Bos	45	Rivas,Luis, Min	9	Garciaparra,N, Bos	345
Ibanez,Raul, KC	123	Stewart,Sh, Tor-Min	44	Young,Michael, Tex	9	Delgado,Carlos, Tor	338
Garciaparra,N, Bos	120	Matsui,Hideki, NYY	42	Baldelli,Rocco, TB	8	Ramirez,Manny, Bos	334
Matsui,Hideki, NYY	120	Tejada,Miguel, Oak	42	Suzuki,Ichiro, Sea	8	Boone,Bret, Sea	333
2 tied with	119	3 tied with	39	3 tied with	7	Ordonez,M, CWS	331

Runs Scored		RBI		Walks		Strikeouts	
Rodriguez,Alex, Tex	124	Delgado,Carlos, Tor	145	Giambi,Jason, NYY	129	Giambi,Jason, NYY	140
Garciaparra,N, Bos	120	Rodriguez,Alex, Tex	118	Delgado,Carlos, Tor	109	Cameron,Mike, Sea	137
Wells,Vernon, Tor	118	Boone,Bret, Sea	117	Durazo,Erubiel, Oak	100	Delgado,Carlos, Tor	137
Delgado,Carlos, Tor	117	Wells,Vernon, Tor	117	Thomas,Frank, CWS	100	Soriano,A, NYY	130
Ramirez,Manny, Bos	117	Anderson,G, Ana	116	Ramirez,Manny, Bos	97	Young,Dmitri, Det	130
Soriano,A, NYY	114	Lee,Carlos, CWS	113	Posada,Jorge, NYY	93	Baldelli,Rocco, TB	128
Boone,Bret, Sea	111	Palmeiro,R, Tex	112	Martinez,Edgar, Sea	92	Rodriguez,Alex, Tex	126
Suzuki,Ichiro, Sea	111	Giambi,Jason, NYY	107	Rodriguez,Alex, Tex	87	Boone,Bret, Sea	125
Young,Michael, Tex	106	Huff,Aubrey, TB	107	Olerud,John, Sea	84	Pena,Carlos, Det	123
2 tied with	103	2 tied with	106	Palmeiro,R, Tex	84	Teixeira,Mark, Tex	120

2003 American League Batting Leaders

Sacrifice Hits		Sacrifice Flies		Stolen Bases		Caught Stealing	
Santiago,Ramon, Det	18	Conine,Jeff, Bal	12	Crawford,Carl, TB	55	Sanchez,Alex, Det	18
Berroa,Angel, KC	13	Stewart,Sh, Tor-Min	11	Sanchez,Alex, Det	44	Baldelli,Rocco, TB	10
Guzman,C, Min	12	Garciaparra,N, Bos	10	Beltran,Carlos, KC	41	Crawford,Carl, TB	10
Eckstein,David, Ana	10	Ibanez,Raul, KC	10	Soriano,A, NYY	35	Tucker,Michael, KC	10
Hairston Jr.,J, Bal	10	Walker,Todd, Bos	10	Suzuki,Ichiro, Sea	34	Blake,Casey, Cle	9
Matos,Luis, Bal	10	Huff,Aubrey, TB	9	Damon,Johnny, Bos	30	Crisp,Coco, Cle	9
Ellis,Mark, Oak	9	Koskie,Corey, Min	9	Baldelli,Rocco, TB	27	Guzman,C, Min	9
Randa,Joe, KC	9	Millar,Kevin, Bos	9	Roberts,Brian, Bal	23	Kennedy,Adam, Ana	9
5 tied with	8	4 tied with	8	Winn,Randy, Sea	23	5 tied with	8
				Kennedy,Adam, Ana	22		

Intentional Walks		Hit By Pitch		Grounded Into DP		Grounded Into DP Pct (minimum 50 GIDP Ops)	
Ramirez,Manny, Bos	28	Giambi,Jason, NYY	21	Konerko,Paul, CWS	28	Singleton,C, Oak	0.03
Delgado,Carlos, Tor	23	Johnson,Reed, Tor	20	Matsui,Hideki, NYY	25	Suzuki,Ichiro, Sea	0.03
Huff,Aubrey, TB	17	Delgado,Carlos, Tor	19	Ramirez,Manny, Bos	22	Nixon,Trot, Bos	0.03
Young,Dmitri, Det	16	Berroa,Angel, KC	18	Wells,Vernon, Tor	21	Guzman,C, Min	0.03
Durazo,Erubiel, Oak	12	Phelps,Josh, Tor	17	Williams,B, NYY	21	Bigbie,Larry, Bal	0.04
Pierzynski,A, Min	12	Eckstein,David, Ana	15	Batista,Tony, Bal	20	Mora,Melvin, Bal	0.04
Gibbons,Jay, Bal	11	Everett,Carl, Tex-CWS	15	Lee,Carlos, CWS	20	Koskie,Corey, Min	0.04
Anderson,G, Ana	10	Pierzynski,A, Min	15	Olerud,John, Sea	20	Guiel,Aaron, KC	0.04
Chavez,Eric, Oak	10	Rodriguez,Alex, Tex	15	Ordonez,M, CWS	20	Byrnes,Eric, Oak	0.05
Rodriguez,Alex, Tex	10	Teixeira,Mark, Tex	14	Rivas,Luis, Min	20	Crawford,Carl, TB	0.05

Leadoff Hitters OBP (minimum 150 PA)		Cleanup Hitters SLG (minimum 150 PA)		BA vs. LHP (minimum 125 PA)		BA vs. RHP (minimum 377 PA)	
Hairston Jr.,J, Bal	.389	Delgado,Carlos, Tor	.593	Bradley,Milton, Cle	.402	Mueller,Bill, Bos	.342
Guiel,Aaron, KC	.387	Ramirez,Manny, Bos	.587	Ramirez,Manny, Bos	.385	Nixon,Trot, Bos	.330
Stewart,Sh, Tor-Min	.363	Anderson,G, Ana	.583	Suzuki,Ichiro, Sea	.359	Blalock,Hank, Tex	.329
Johnson,Reed, Tor	.353	Bradley,Milton, Cle	.564	Garciaparra,N, Bos	.357	Pierzynski,A, Min	.324
Suzuki,Ichiro, Sea	.352	Tejada,Miguel, Oak	.544	Wells,Vernon, Tor	.347	Ibanez,Raul, KC	.319
Graffanino,T, CWS	.352	Ordonez,M, CWS	.544	Harvey,Ken, KC	.333	Catalanotto,F, Tor	.318
Figgins,Chone, Ana	.351	Young,Dmitri, Det	.536	Stewart,Sh, Tor-Min	.331	Anderson,G, Ana	.318
Jimenez,D, CWS	.344	Giambi,Jason, NYY	.526	Johnson,Reed, Tor	.328	Jones,Jacque, Min	.317
Soriano,A, NYY	.342	Chavez,Eric, Oak	.513	Konerko,Paul, CWS	.327	Ordonez,M, CWS	.317
Lawton,Matt, Cle	.337	LeCroy,Matt, Min	.509	Beltran,Carlos, KC	.325	Lee,Carlos, CWS	.317

Home BA (minimum 251 PA)		Away BA (minimum 251 PA)		OBP vs. LHP (minimum 125 PA)		OBP vs. RHP (minimum 377 PA)	
Garciaparra,N, Bos	.359	Martinez,Edgar, Sea	.339	Bradley,Milton, Cle	.500	Delgado,Carlos, Tor	.439
Young,Michael, Tex	.353	Anderson,G, Ana	.339	Ramirez,Manny, Bos	.476	Giambi,Jason, NYY	.430
Matos,Luis, Bal	.350	Jeter,Derek, NYY	.330	Martinez,Edgar, Sea	.457	Nixon,Trot, Bos	.423
Blalock,Hank, Tex	.342	Wells,Vernon, Tor	.329	Thomas,Frank, CWS	.446	Ramirez,Manny, Bos	.411
Mueller,Bill, Bos	.342	Pierzynski,A, Min	.328	Kielty,Bobby, Min-Tor	.417	Mueller,Bill, Bos	.409
Delgado,Carlos, Tor	.337	Mientkiewicz,D, Min	.325	Beltran,Carlos, KC	.416	Mientkiewicz,D, Min	.408
Beltran,Carlos, KC	.333	Huff,Aubrey, TB	.320	Williams,B, NYY	.414	Posada,Jorge, NYY	.405
Ramirez,Manny, Bos	.331	Ramirez,Manny, Bos	.320	Relaford,Desi, KC	.409	Ortiz,David, Bos	.404
Ordonez,M, CWS	.324	Anderson,Mar, TB	.312	Rodriguez,Alex, Tex	.404	Rodriguez,Alex, Tex	.392
Walker,Todd, Bos	.323	Suzuki,Ichiro, Sea	.311	Posada,Jorge, NYY	.403	Olerud,John, Sea	.392

323

2003 American League Batting Leaders

BA Close & Late
(minimum 50 PA)

Bigbie,Larry, Bal	.426
Ordonez,M, CWS	.425
Mientkiewicz,D, Min	.397
Anderson,G, Ana	.370
Hatteberg,S, Oak	.361
Sierra,Ruben, Tex-NYY	.358
Huff,Aubrey, TB	.354
Delgado,Carlos, Tor	.351
Harvey,Ken, KC	.351
2 tied with	.339

BA Bases Loaded
(minimum 10 PA)

Sweeney,Mike, KC	.667
Baldelli,Rocco, TB	.600
Bordick,Mike, Tor	.600
Delgado,Carlos, Tor	.588
Jeter,Derek, NYY	.533
Gerut,Jody, Cle	.500
Hillenbrand,S, Bos	.500
Martinez,Edgar, Sea	.500
Cruz,Deivi, Bal	.467
2 tied with	.455

SLG vs. LHP
(minimum 125 PA)

Thomas,Frank, CWS	.732
Rodriguez,Alex, Tex	.652
Bradley,Milton, Cle	.634
Monroe,Craig, Det	.631
Ramirez,Manny, Bos	.629
Ordonez,M, CWS	.622
Varitek,Jason, Bos	.610
Konerko,Paul, CWS	.593
Palmeiro,R, Tex	.588
Martinez,Edgar, Sea	.577

SLG vs. RHP
(minimum 377 PA)

Ortiz,David, Bos	.654
Delgado,Carlos, Tor	.649
Nixon,Trot, Bos	.635
Huff,Aubrey, TB	.596
Blalock,Hank, Tex	.596
Giambi,Jason, NYY	.591
Rodriguez,Alex, Tex	.576
Ramirez,Manny, Bos	.573
Chavez,Eric, Oak	.567
Gerut,Jody, Cle	.564

Batting Average w/ RISP
(minimum 100 PA)

Sweeney,Mike, KC	.398
Delgado,Carlos, Tor	.357
Martinez,Edgar, Sea	.352
Winn,Randy, Sea	.349
Beltran,Carlos, KC	.347
Lee,Carlos, CWS	.346
Molina,Ben, Ana	.346
Catalanotto,F, Tor	.344
Suzuki,Ichiro, Sea	.343
Anderson,Mar, TB	.341

At Bats Per Home Run
(minimum 502 PA)

Rodriguez,Alex, Tex	12.9
Thomas,Frank, CWS	13.0
Giambi,Jason, NYY	13.0
Delgado,Carlos, Tor	13.6
Ortiz,David, Bos	14.5
Palmeiro,R, Tex	14.8
Ramirez,Manny, Bos	15.4
Nixon,Trot, Bos	15.8
Posada,Jorge, NYY	16.0
Boone,Bret, Sea	17.8

Pitches Seen

Giambi,Jason, NYY	2913
Damon,Johnny, Bos	2842
Thomas,Frank, CWS	2817
Delgado,Carlos, Tor	2804
Young,Michael, Tex	2791
Boone,Bret, Sea	2773
Rodriguez,Alex, Tex	2747
Tejada,Miguel, Oak	2694
Palmeiro,R, Tex	2664
Ramirez,Manny, Bos	2660

Pitches Per Plate App
(minimum 502 PA)

Martinez,Edgar, Sea	4.32
Thomas,Frank, CWS	4.26
Giambi,Jason, NYY	4.22
Damon,Johnny, Bos	4.12
Koskie,Corey, Min	4.09
Hinske,Eric, Tor	4.08
Palmeiro,R, Tex	4.07
Ellis,Mark, Oak	4.07
Ortiz,David, Bos	4.06
Valentin,Jose, CWS	4.01

Pct Pitches Taken
(minimum 1500 Pitches)

Hatteberg,S, Oak	66.9
Martinez,Edgar, Sea	64.9
Olerud,John, Sea	64.3
Johnson,Nick, NYY	64.2
Thomas,Frank, CWS	63.3
Giambi,Jason, NYY	63.1
Matsui,Hideki, NYY	62.5
Higginson,B, Det	62.3
Kielty,Bobby, Min-Tor	61.4
Durazo,Erubiel, Oak	61.2

Highest GB/FB Ratio
(minimum 502 PA)

Jones,Jacque, Min	2.78
Jeter,Derek, NYY	2.54
Harvey,Ken, KC	2.46
Rivas,Luis, Min	2.34
Matsui,Hideki, NYY	2.30
Crawford,Carl, TB	2.28
Suzuki,Ichiro, Sea	1.85
Winn,Randy, Sea	1.76
Santiago,Ramon, Det	1.73
Guzman,C, Min	1.71

Lowest GB/FB Ratio
(minimum 502 PA)

Thomas,Frank, CWS	0.44
Giambi,Jason, NYY	0.52
Nixon,Trot, Bos	0.60
Valentin,Jose, CWS	0.68
Batista,Tony, Bal	0.70
Palmeiro,R, Tex	0.71
Garciaparra,N, Bos	0.71
Blalock,Hank, Tex	0.74
Kennedy,Adam, Ana	0.75
Soriano,A, NYY	0.75

Stolen Base Success Pct
(minimum 20 SBA)

Beltran,Carlos, KC	91.1
Anderson,Mar, TB	86.4
Rodriguez,Alex, Tex	85.0
Crawford,Carl, TB	84.6
Damon,Johnny, Bos	83.3
Relaford,Desi, KC	83.3
Winn,Randy, Sea	82.1
Lee,Carlos, CWS	81.8
Soriano,A, NYY	81.4
Suzuki,Ichiro, Sea	81.0

Steals of Third

Suzuki,Ichiro, Sea	12
Crawford,Carl, TB	9
Sanchez,Alex, Det	7
Beltran,Carlos, KC	6
Berroa,Angel, KC	6
Soriano,A, NYY	5
Winn,Randy, Sea	5
6 tied with	4

Pct CS by Catchers
(minimum 50 SBA)

Hall,Toby, TB	41.3
Molina,Ben, Ana	40.8
Olivo,Miguel, CWS	35.8
Bard,Josh, Cle	31.7
Diaz,Einar, Tex	31.0
Inge,Brandon, Det	30.0
Greene,Todd, Tex	29.6
DiFelice,Mike, KC	29.4
Mayne,Brent, KC	27.8
Pierzynski,A, Min	27.0

Best BPS on OutZ
(minimum 502 PA)

Pierzynski,A, Min	.564
Conine,Jeff, Bal	.500
Chavez,Eric, Oak	.460
Long,Terrence, Oak	.447
Walker,Todd, Bos	.424
Ordonez,M, CWS	.417
Suzuki,Ichiro, Sea	.415
Crede,Joe, CWS	.391
Lee,Carlos, CWS	.389
Anderson,G, Ana	.385

Worst BPS on OutZ
(minimum 502 PA)

Posada,Jorge, NYY	.000
Salmon,Tim, Ana	.000
Teixeira,Mark, Tex	.000
Young,Dmitri, Det	.034
Varitek,Jason, Bos	.037
Durazo,Erubiel, Oak	.041
Guzman,C, Min	.045
Hunter,Torii, Min	.066
Beltran,Carlos, KC	.074
2 tied with	.077

2003 American League Batting Leaders

Best OPS vs Fastballs
(minimum 251 PA)

Nixon,Trot, Bos	1.184
Delgado,Carlos, Tor	1.137
Ortiz,David, Bos	1.129
Anderson,G, Ana	1.060
Boone,Bret, Sea	1.053
Rodriguez,Alex, Tex	1.037
Posada,Jorge, NYY	1.030
Ordonez,M, CWS	1.029
Huff,Aubrey, TB	1.024
Thomas,Frank, CWS	1.020

Best OPS vs Curveballs
(minimum 50 PA)

Rodriguez,Alex, Tex	1.131
Ordonez,M, CWS	1.050
Wells,Vernon, Tor	1.048
Giambi,Jason, NYY	.995
Everett,Carl, Tex-CWS	.979
Valentin,Jose, CWS	.954
Mueller,Bill, Bos	.945
Gibbons,Jay, Bal	.945
Walker,Todd, Bos	.935
Anderson,Mar, TB	.903

Best OPS vs Changeups
(minimum 50 PA)

Pierzynski,A, Min	1.111
LeCroy,Matt, Min	1.106
Bradley,Milton, Cle	1.104
Millar,Kevin, Bos	.995
Lee,Carlos, CWS	.959
Blalock,Hank, Tex	.950
Tejada,Miguel, Oak	.944
Hudson,Orlando, Tor	.928
Giambi,Jason, NYY	.926
Ortiz,David, Bos	.921

Best OPS vs Sliders
(minimum 32 PA)

Mueller,Bill, Bos	1.162
Giambi,Jason, NYY	1.117
Williams,B, NYY	1.095
Young,Dmitri, Det	1.093
Posada,Jorge, NYY	1.073
Ramirez,Manny, Bos	1.035
Matos,Luis, Bal	.969
Millar,Kevin, Bos	.944
Ibanez,Raul, KC	.940
Beltran,Carlos, KC	.930

OPS
(minimum 502 PA)

Delgado,Carlos, Tor	1.019
Ramirez,Manny, Bos	1.014
Rodriguez,Alex, Tex	.995
Nixon,Trot, Bos	.975
Ortiz,David, Bos	.961
Thomas,Frank, CWS	.952
Giambi,Jason, NYY	.939
Mueller,Bill, Bos	.938
Ordonez,M, CWS	.926
Posada,Jorge, NYY	.922

OPS First Half
(minimum 251 PA)

Delgado,Carlos, Tor	1.053
Mora,Melvin, Bal	1.003
Ramirez,Manny, Bos	.984
Sweeney,Mike, KC	.979
Giambi,Jason, NYY	.966
Boone,Bret, Sea	.963
Varitek,Jason, Bos	.958
Nixon,Trot, Bos	.958
Mueller,Bill, Bos	.956
Martinez,Edgar, Sea	.954

OPS Second Half
(minimum 251 PA)

Rodriguez,Alex, Tex	1.105
Ramirez,Manny, Bos	1.060
Ortiz,David, Bos	.991
Ordonez,M, CWS	.972
Beltran,Carlos, KC	.968
Delgado,Carlos, Tor	.965
Thomas,Frank, CWS	.951
Huff,Aubrey, TB	.950
Chavez,Eric, Oak	.940
Wells,Vernon, Tor	.933

2003 National League Batting Leaders

Batting Average (minimum 502 PA)	
Pujols,Albert, StL	.359
Helton,Todd, Col	.358
Bonds,Barry, SF	.341
Renteria,Edgar, StL	.330
Sheffield,Gary, Atl	.330
Kendall,Jason, Pit	.325
Giles,Marcus, Atl	.316
Castillo,Luis, Fla	.314
Loretta,Mark, SD	.314
Grudzielanek,M, ChC	.314

On Base Percentage (minimum 502 PA)	
Bonds,Barry, SF	.529
Helton,Todd, Col	.458
Pujols,Albert, StL	.439
Giles,Brian, Pit-SD	.427
Walker,Larry, Col	.422
Sheffield,Gary, Atl	.419
Berkman,Lance, Hou	.412
Abreu,Bobby, Phi	.409
Jones,Chipper, Atl	.402
Gonzalez,Luis, Ari	.402

Slugging Average (minimum 502 PA)	
Bonds,Barry, SF	.749
Pujols,Albert, StL	.667
Helton,Todd, Col	.630
Edmonds,Jim, StL	.617
Sheffield,Gary, Atl	.604
Thome,Jim, Phi	.573
Hidalgo,R, Hou	.572
Sosa,Sammy, ChC	.553
Sexson,Richie, Mil	.548
Jenkins,Geoff, Mil	.538

Home Runs	
Thome,Jim, Phi	47
Bonds,Barry, SF	45
Sexson,Richie, Mil	45
Lopez,Javy, Atl	43
Pujols,Albert, StL	43
Sosa,Sammy, ChC	40
Bagwell,Jeff, Hou	39
Edmonds,Jim, StL	39
Sheffield,Gary, Atl	39
2 tied with	36

Games	
Cabrera,O, Mon	162
Pierre,Juan, Fla	162
Sexson,Richie, Mil	162
Bagwell,Jeff, Hou	160
Green,Shawn, LA	160
Helton,Todd, Col	160
Ramirez,A, Pit-ChC	159
Thome,Jim, Phi	159
4 tied with	158

Plate Appearances	
Pierre,Juan, Fla	747
Furcal,Rafael, Atl	734
Sexson,Richie, Mil	718
Biggio,Craig, Hou	717
Helton,Todd, Col	703
Bagwell,Jeff, Hou	702
Thome,Jim, Phi	698
Abreu,Bobby, Phi	695
Cabrera,O, Mon	691
Green,Shawn, LA	691

At Bats	
Pierre,Juan, Fla	668
Furcal,Rafael, Atl	664
Biggio,Craig, Hou	628
Rollins,Jimmy, Phi	628
Cabrera,O, Mon	626
Green,Shawn, LA	611
Ramirez,A, Pit-ChC	607
Sexson,Richie, Mil	606
Bagwell,Jeff, Hou	605
Encarnacion,J, Fla	601

Hits	
Pujols,Albert, StL	212
Helton,Todd, Col	209
Pierre,Juan, Fla	204
Furcal,Rafael, Atl	194
Renteria,Edgar, StL	194
Kendall,Jason, Pit	191
Sheffield,Gary, Atl	190
Castillo,Luis, Fla	187
Cabrera,O, Mon	186
Loretta,Mark, SD	185

Singles	
Pierre,Juan, Fla	168
Castillo,Luis, Fla	156
Kendall,Jason, Pit	153
Loretta,Mark, SD	140
Furcal,Rafael, Atl	134
Renteria,Edgar, StL	133
Casey,Sean, Cin	131
Podsednik,S, Mil	129
Helton,Todd, Col	122
2 tied with	120

Doubles	
Pujols,Albert, StL	51
Giles,Marcus, Atl	49
Green,Shawn, LA	49
Helton,Todd, Col	49
Rolen,Scott, StL	49
Cabrera,O, Mon	47
Renteria,Edgar, StL	47
Gonzalez,Luis, Ari	46
Biggio,Craig, Hou	44
2 tied with	43

Triples	
Finley,Steve, Ari	10
Furcal,Rafael, Atl	10
Lofton,Kenny, Pit-ChC	8
Podsednik,S, Mil	8
Nunez,A O, Pit	7
Patterson,C, ChC	7
Pierre,Juan, Fla	7
Walker,Larry, Col	7
10 tied with	6

Total Bases	
Pujols,Albert, StL	394
Helton,Todd, Col	367
Sheffield,Gary, Atl	348
Sexson,Richie, Mil	332
Thome,Jim, Phi	331
Wilson,Preston, Col	322
Bagwell,Jeff, Hou	317
Lopez,Javy, Atl	314
Gonzalez,Luis, Ari	308
Payton,Jay, Col	307

Runs Scored	
Pujols,Albert, StL	137
Helton,Todd, Col	135
Furcal,Rafael, Atl	130
Sheffield,Gary, Atl	126
Bonds,Barry, SF	111
Thome,Jim, Phi	111
Berkman,Lance, Hou	110
Bagwell,Jeff, Hou	109
Jones,Chipper, Atl	103
Biggio,Craig, Hou	102

RBI	
Wilson,Preston, Col	141
Sheffield,Gary, Atl	132
Thome,Jim, Phi	131
Pujols,Albert, StL	124
Sexson,Richie, Mil	124
Helton,Todd, Col	117
Jones,Andruw, Atl	116
Lopez,Javy, Atl	109
Jones,Chipper, Atl	106
Ramirez,A, Pit-ChC	106

Walks	
Bonds,Barry, SF	148
Helton,Todd, Col	111
Thome,Jim, Phi	111
Abreu,Bobby, Phi	109
Berkman,Lance, Hou	107
Giles,Brian, Pit-SD	105
Cruz,Jose, SF	102
Sexson,Richie, Mil	98
Walker,Larry, Col	98
2 tied with	94

Strikeouts	
Thome,Jim, Phi	182
Hernandez, Col-ChC-Pit	177
Wilkerson,Brad, Mon	155
Sexson,Richie, Mil	151
Sosa,Sammy, ChC	143
Burrell,Pat, Phi	142
Wilson,Preston, Col	139
Helms,Wes, Mil	131
Lee,Derrek, Fla	131
Edmonds,Jim, StL	127

2003 National League Batting Leaders

Sacrifice Hits		Sacrifice Flies		Stolen Bases		Caught Stealing	
Castillo,Luis, Fla	15	Ramirez,A, Pit-ChC	11	Pierre,Juan, Fla	65	Pierre,Juan, Fla	20
Pierre,Juan, Fla	15	Cabrera,O, Mon	9	Podsednik,S, Mil	43	Castillo,Luis, Fla	19
Schmidt,Jason, SF	15	Klesko,Ryan, SD	9	Roberts,Dave, LA	40	Roberts,Dave, LA	14
Franklin,Wayne, Mil	12	Perez,Timo, NYM	9	Renteria,Edgar, StL	34	Rollins,Jimmy, Phi	12
Morris,Matt, StL	12	Martinez,Ramon, ChC	8	Lofton,Kenny, Pit-ChC	30	Young,Eric, Mil-SF	12
Vazquez,Javier, Mon	12	Sheffield,Gary, Atl	8	Young,Eric, Mil-SF	28	Podsednik,S, Mil	10
Everett,Adam, Hou	11	12 tied with	7	Furcal,Rafael, Atl	25	Wilkerson,Brad, Mon	10
Tomko,Brett, StL	11			Cabrera,O, Mon	24	Abreu,Bobby, Phi	9
Trachsel,Steve, NYM	11			Abreu,Bobby, Phi	22	Cedeno,Roger, NYM	9
Wilson,Jack, Pit	11			2 tied with	21	Lofton,Kenny, Pit-ChC	9

Intentional Walks		Hit By Pitch		Grounded Into DP		Grounded Into DP Pct (minimum 50 GIDP Ops)	
Bonds,Barry, SF	61	Biggio,Craig, Hou	27	Payton,Jay, Col	27	Furcal,Rafael, Atl	0.01
Guerrero,V, Mon	21	Kendall,Jason, Pit	25	Bagwell,Jeff, Hou	25	Palmeiro,O, StL	0.02
Helton,Todd, Col	21	LaRue,Jason, Cin	20	Clayton,Royce, Mil	25	Reyes,Jose, NYM	0.02
Gonzalez,Luis, Ari	17	Ginter,Keith, Mil	17	Wilson,Preston, Col	23	Thome,Jim, Phi	0.03
Matheny,Mike, StL	16	Kinkade,Mike, LA	16	Castilla,Vinny, Atl	22	Bellhorn,Mark, ChC-Col	0.05
Walker,Larry, Col	14	Gonzalez,Alex, Fla	13	Lo Duca,Paul, LA	21	Burnitz,J, NYM-LA	0.05
Abreu,Bobby, Phi	13	Wilson,Craig, Pit	13	Phillips,Jason, NYM	21	Dunn,Adam, Cin	0.05
Berkman,Lance, Hou	13	Lieberthal,M, Phi	12	Ramirez,A, Pit-ChC	21	Wilkerson,Brad, Mon	0.05
Gonzalez,Alex, Fla	13	5 tied with	11	Renteria,Edgar, StL	21	Uribe,Juan, Col	0.05
Jones,Chipper, Atl	13			4 tied with	19	Biggio,Craig, Hou	0.05

Leadoff Hitters OBP (minimum 150 PA)		Cleanup Hitters SLG (minimum 150 PA)		BA vs. LHP (minimum 125 PA)		BA vs. RHP (minimum 377 PA)	
Grissom,M, SF	.412	Bonds,Barry, SF	.769	Renteria,Edgar, StL	.391	Gonzalez,Luis, Ari	.354
Podsednik,S, Mil	.399	Sanders,Reggie, Pit	.679	Pujols,Albert, StL	.387	Pujols,Albert, StL	.350
Byrd,Marlon, Phi	.374	Thome,Jim, Phi	.655	Helton,Todd, Col	.387	Helton,Todd, Col	.344
Redman,Tike, Pit	.367	Edmonds,Jim, StL	.624	Rodriguez,Ivan, Fla	.376	Kendall,Jason, Pit	.331
Counsell,Craig, Ari	.360	Guerrero,V, Mon	.607	Karros,Eric, ChC	.366	Bonds,Barry, SF	.331
Durham,Ray, SF	.359	Abreu,Bobby, Phi	.594	Cintron,Alex, Ari	.365	Podsednik,S, Mil	.329
Pierre,Juan, Fla	.359	Rolen,Scott, StL	.579	Grissom,M, SF	.364	Sheffield,Gary, Atl	.327
Grudzielanek,M, ChC	.358	Floyd,Cliff, NYM	.574	Bonds,Barry, SF	.363	Lopez,Javy, Atl	.326
Lofton,Kenny, Pit-ChC	.354	Gonzalez,Luis, Ari	.571	Alou,Moises, ChC	.346	Giles,Marcus, Atl	.325
Furcal,Rafael, Atl	.353	Sexson,Richie, Mil	.568	Belliard,R, Col	.345	Loretta,Mark, SD	.318

Home BA (minimum 251 PA)		Away BA (minimum 251 PA)		OBP vs. LHP (minimum 125 PA)		OBP vs. RHP (minimum 377 PA)	
Helton,Todd, Col	.391	Sheffield,Gary, Atl	.343	Bonds,Barry, SF	.509	Bonds,Barry, SF	.537
Pujols,Albert, StL	.388	Gonzalez,Luis, Ari	.342	Renteria,Edgar, StL	.503	Gonzalez,Luis, Ari	.459
Bonds,Barry, SF	.369	Giles,Marcus, Atl	.342	Helton,Todd, Col	.470	Helton,Todd, Col	.452
Renteria,Edgar, StL	.356	Kendall,Jason, Pit	.336	Lee,Derrek, Fla	.462	Abreu,Bobby, Phi	.440
Abreu,Bobby, Phi	.349	Pujols,Albert, StL	.331	Rodriguez,Ivan, Fla	.460	Pujols,Albert, StL	.434
Grudzielanek,M, ChC	.343	Casey,Sean, Cin	.330	Pujols,Albert, StL	.458	Giles,Brian, Pit-SD	.432
Walker,Larry, Col	.338	Podsednik,S, Mil	.326	Bagwell,Jeff, Hou	.450	Walker,Larry, Col	.422
Byrd,Marlon, Phi	.333	Helton,Todd, Col	.324	Sheffield,Gary, Atl	.450	Berkman,Lance, Hou	.415
Vidro,Jose, Mon	.333	Loretta,Mark, SD	.315	Sexson,Richie, Mil	.448	Sheffield,Gary, Atl	.410
Cabrera,O, Mon	.332	Bonds,Barry, SF	.313	Karros,Eric, ChC	.441	Kendall,Jason, Pit	.407

2003 National League Batting Leaders

BA Close & Late
(minimum 50 PA)

Baerga,Carlos, Ari	.407
Podsednik,S, Mil	.398
Pujols,Albert, StL	.390
Jimenez,D, Cin	.377
Kendall,Jason, Pit	.374
Casey,Sean, Cin	.358
Loretta,Mark, SD	.357
Pierre,Juan, Fla	.351
Sheffield,Gary, Atl	.347
Snow,J.T., SF	.340

BA Bases Loaded
(minimum 10 PA)

Belliard,R, Col	.625
Stynes,Chris, Col	.615
Kent,Jeff, Hou	.600
Lieberthal,M, Phi	.563
Kendall,Jason, Pit	.556
Podsednik,S, Mil	.556
Reyes,Jose, NYM	.556
Aurilia,Rich, SF	.545
4 tied with	.500

SLG vs. LHP
(minimum 125 PA)

Bonds,Barry, SF	.790
Pujols,Albert, StL	.732
Wilson,Craig, Pit	.692
Sheffield,Gary, Atl	.675
Renteria,Edgar, StL	.670
Grissom,M, SF	.657
Sanders,Reggie, Pit	.647
Helton,Todd, Col	.643
Lee,Derrek, Fla	.600
Belliard,R, Col	.584

SLG vs. RHP
(minimum 377 PA)

Bonds,Barry, SF	.729
Lopez,Javy, Atl	.677
Pujols,Albert, StL	.646
Edmonds,Jim, StL	.631
Thome,Jim, Phi	.623
Helton,Todd, Col	.622
Gonzalez,Luis, Ari	.613
Jenkins,Geoff, Mil	.607
Wilson,Preston, Col	.596
Sheffield,Gary, Atl	.585

Batting Average w/ RISP
(minimum 100 PA)

Helton,Todd, Col	.414
Podsednik,S, Mil	.381
Sheffield,Gary, Atl	.379
Cabrera,Miguel, Fla	.375
Rodriguez,Ivan, Fla	.375
Pujols,Albert, StL	.374
Abreu,Bobby, Phi	.361
Kent,Jeff, Hou	.358
Loretta,Mark, SD	.346
2 tied with	.342

At Bats Per Home Run
(minimum 502 PA)

Bonds,Barry, SF	8.7
Edmonds,Jim, StL	11.5
Thome,Jim, Phi	12.3
Sosa,Sammy, ChC	12.9
Sexson,Richie, Mil	13.5
Pujols,Albert, StL	13.7
Sheffield,Gary, Atl	14.8
Burnitz,J, NYM-LA	15.0
Lowell,Mike, Fla	15.4
Bagwell,Jeff, Hou	15.5

Pitches Seen

Abreu,Bobby, Phi	2999
Thome,Jim, Phi	2869
Furcal,Rafael, Atl	2849
Sexson,Richie, Mil	2847
Helton,Todd, Col	2826
Rolen,Scott, StL	2730
Bagwell,Jeff, Hou	2669
Gonzalez,Luis, Ari	2645
Wilkerson,Brad, Mon	2625
Lee,Derrek, Fla	2621

Pitches Per Plate App
(minimum 502 PA)

Wilkerson,Brad, Mon	4.36
Abreu,Bobby, Phi	4.32
Rolen,Scott, StL	4.16
Burrell,Pat, Phi	4.14
Edmonds,Jim, StL	4.13
Thome,Jim, Phi	4.11
Belliard,R, Col	4.08
Lee,Derrek, Fla	4.08
Helton,Todd, Col	4.02
Podsednik,S, Mil	4.01

Pct Pitches Taken
(minimum 1500 Pitches)

Bonds,Barry, SF	65.9
Abreu,Bobby, Phi	65.5
Counsell,Craig, Ari	64.2
Roberts,Dave, LA	64.1
Podsednik,S, Mil	62.9
Kendall,Jason, Pit	62.7
Ginter,Keith, Mil	62.3
Castillo,Luis, Fla	60.9
Berkman,Lance, Hou	60.8
Lee,Derrek, Fla	60.7

Highest GB/FB Ratio
(minimum 502 PA)

Castillo,Luis, Fla	3.07
Pierre,Juan, Fla	2.96
Chavez,Endy, Mon	2.37
Cedeno,Roger, NYM	2.15
Byrd,Marlon, Phi	1.98
Izturis,Cesar, LA	1.96
Belliard,R, Col	1.87
Grudzielanek,M, ChC	1.86
Vidro,Jose, Mon	1.85
Abreu,Bobby, Phi	1.84

Lowest GB/FB Ratio
(minimum 502 PA)

Bonds,Barry, SF	0.66
Edmonds,Jim, StL	0.72
Lowell,Mike, Fla	0.73
Burnitz,J, NYM-LA	0.73
Hidalgo,R, Hou	0.75
Gonzalez,Alex, Fla	0.77
Giles,Brian, Pit-SD	0.78
Rolen,Scott, StL	0.79
Ramirez,A, Pit-ChC	0.79
Burrell,Pat, Phi	0.79

Stolen Base Success Pct
(minimum 20 SBA)

Furcal,Rafael, Atl	92.6
Cabrera,O, Mon	92.3
Renteria,Edgar, StL	82.9
Sheffield,Gary, Atl	81.8
Podsednik,S, Mil	81.1
Goodwin,Tom, ChC	79.2
Lofton,Kenny, Pit-ChC	76.9
Pierre,Juan, Fla	76.5
Patterson,C, ChC	76.2
Sanders,Reggie, Pit	75.0

Steals of Third

Pierre,Juan, Fla	11
Renteria,Edgar, StL	8
Sanders,Reggie, Pit	7
Cabrera,O, Mon	6
Lofton,Kenny, Pit-ChC	5
Mateo,Henry, Mon	5
Podsednik,S, Mil	4
Rolen,Scott, StL	4
13 tied with	3

Pct CS by Catchers
(minimum 50 SBA)

Miller,Damian, ChC	38.2
Lo Duca,Paul, LA	34.1
Rodriguez,Ivan, Fla	32.2
Ausmus,Brad, Hou	31.3
Johnson,C, Col	29.4
Lopez,Javy, Atl	27.8
Osik,Keith, Mil	26.4
LaRue,Jason, Cin	25.4
Matheny,Mike, StL	23.1
Moeller,Chad, Ari	23.1

Best BPS on OutZ
(minimum 502 PA)

Pierre,Juan, Fla	.667
Lo Duca,Paul, LA	.625
Helton,Todd, Col	.622
Kendall,Jason, Pit	.615
Sheffield,Gary, Atl	.614
Grissom,M, SF	.596
Giles,Marcus, Atl	.588
Loretta,Mark, SD	.548
Renteria,Edgar, StL	.538
Castillo,Luis, Fla	.515

Worst BPS on OutZ
(minimum 502 PA)

Helms,Wes, Mil	.000
Lee,Derrek, Fla	.000
Sexson,Richie, Mil	.000
Hernandez, Col-ChC-Pit	.056
Walker,Larry, Col	.074
Burnitz,J, NYM-LA	.080
Jones,Chipper, Atl	.083
Sosa,Sammy, ChC	.083
Young,Eric, Mil-SF	.087
Wigginton,Ty, NYM	.088

2003 National League Batting Leaders

Best OPS vs Fastballs
(minimum 251 PA)

Bonds,Barry, SF	1.393
Pujols,Albert, StL	1.185
Lopez,Javy, Atl	1.172
Sheffield,Gary, Atl	1.137
Helton,Todd, Col	1.108
Edmonds,Jim, StL	1.072
Thome,Jim, Phi	1.064
Jenkins,Geoff, Mil	1.060
Abreu,Bobby, Phi	1.035
Sanders,Reggie, Pit	1.031

Best OPS vs Curveballs
(minimum 50 PA)

Payton,Jay, Col	1.120
Helton,Todd, Col	1.057
Sheffield,Gary, Atl	1.043
Encarnacion,J, Fla	1.029
Wilson,Preston, Col	.938
Lofton,Kenny, Pit-ChC	.933
Castilla,Vinny, Atl	.929
Sexson,Richie, Mil	.900
Cordero,Wil, Mon	.896
Gonzalez,Alex, Fla	.892

Best OPS vs Changeups
(minimum 50 PA)

Rodriguez,Ivan, Fla	1.288
Jones,Andruw, Atl	1.100
Helton,Todd, Col	1.053
Lowell,Mike, Fla	1.044
Berkman,Lance, Hou	1.023
Ramirez,A, Pit-ChC	1.005
Grissom,M, SF	.974
Giles,Brian, Pit-SD	.973
Lee,Derrek, Fla	.970
Lieberthal,M, Phi	.956

Best OPS vs Sliders
(minimum 32 PA)

Helton,Todd, Col	1.090
Galarraga,A, SF	1.083
Grissom,M, SF	1.064
Guillen,Jose, Cin	1.048
Kent,Jeff, Hou	1.047
Hidalgo,R, Hou	1.022
Giles,Brian, Pit-SD	1.011
Ensberg,Morgan, Hou	1.007
Kata,Matt, Ari	.999
Giles,Marcus, Atl	.999

OPS
(minimum 502 PA)

Bonds,Barry, SF	1.278
Pujols,Albert, StL	1.106
Helton,Todd, Col	1.088
Sheffield,Gary, Atl	1.023
Edmonds,Jim, StL	1.002
Thome,Jim, Phi	.958
Hidalgo,R, Hou	.957
Giles,Brian, Pit-SD	.941
Gonzalez,Luis, Ari	.934
Berkman,Lance, Hou	.927

OPS First Half
(minimum 251 PA)

Bonds,Barry, SF	1.214
Pujols,Albert, StL	1.121
Helton,Todd, Col	1.078
Edmonds,Jim, StL	1.066
Sheffield,Gary, Atl	1.019
Guillen,Jose, Cin	1.005
Lopez,Javy, Atl	.988
Sosa,Sammy, ChC	.985
Giles,Brian, Pit-SD	.956
Gonzalez,Luis, Ari	.952

OPS Second Half
(minimum 251 PA)

Helton,Todd, Col	1.102
Guerrero,V, Mon	1.095
Pujols,Albert, StL	1.084
Sheffield,Gary, Atl	1.028
Giles,Marcus, Atl	1.027
Thome,Jim, Phi	.994
Bagwell,Jeff, Hou	.989
Sexson,Richie, Mil	.980
Hidalgo,R, Hou	.969
Jones,Chipper, Atl	.963

2003 American League Pitching Leaders

Earned Run Average
(minimum 162 IP)

Martinez,Pedro, Bos	2.22
Hudson,Tim, Oak	2.70
Loaiza,Esteban, CWS	2.90
Mulder,Mark, Oak	3.13
Halladay,Roy, Tor	3.25
Moyer,Jamie, Sea	3.27
Zito,Barry, Oak	3.30
Mussina,Mike, NYY	3.40
Franklin,Ryan, Sea	3.57
Sabathia,C.C., Cle	3.60

Winning Percentage
(minimum 15 Decisions)

Santana,Johan, Min	.800
Martinez,Pedro, Bos	.778
Halladay,Roy, Tor	.759
Moyer,Jamie, Sea	.750
Pettitte,Andy, NYY	.724
Lowe,Derek, Bos	.708
Loaiza,Esteban, CWS	.700
Ponson,Sidney, Bal	.700
Hudson,Tim, Oak	.696
Wells,David, NYY	.682

Opponent Batting Average
(minimum 162 IP)

Martinez,Pedro, Bos	.215
Zito,Barry, Oak	.219
Hudson,Tim, Oak	.223
Loaiza,Esteban, CWS	.233
Zambrano,V, TB	.237
Mussina,Mike, NYY	.238
Pineiro,Joel, Sea	.241
May,Darrell, KC	.246
Moyer,Jamie, Sea	.246
Wakefield,Tim, Bos	.246

Baserunners Per 9 IP
(minimum 162 IP)

Martinez,Pedro, Bos	9.79
Mussina,Mike, NYY	9.85
Halladay,Roy, Tor	9.95
Hudson,Tim, Oak	10.05
Loaiza,Esteban, CWS	10.42
Mulder,Mark, Oak	10.70
May,Darrell, KC	10.80
Zito,Barry, Oak	10.88
Colon,Bartolo, CWS	10.97
Clemens,Roger, NYY	11.14

Games

Miller,Trever, Tor	79
Walker,Jamie, Det	78
Grimsley,Jason, KC	76
Ryan,B.J., Bal	76
Hawkins,LaTroy, Min	74
Baez,Danys, Cle	73
Cordero,F, Tex	73
Romero,J.C., Min	73
4 tied with	72

Games Started

Halladay,Roy, Tor	36
Buehrle,Mark, CWS	35
Thomson,John, Tex	35
Zito,Barry, Oak	35
Colon,Bartolo, CWS	34
Hudson,Tim, Oak	34
Loaiza,Esteban, CWS	34
10 tied with	33

Complete Games

Colon,Bartolo, CWS	9
Halladay,Roy, Tor	9
Mulder,Mark, Oak	9
Ponson,Sidney, Bal	4
Wells,David, NYY	4
Zito,Barry, Oak	4
6 tied with	3

Shutouts

Halladay,Roy, Tor	2
Hudson,Tim, Oak	2
Lackey,John, Ana	2
Mulder,Mark, Oak	2
Pineiro,Joel, Sea	2
21 tied with	1

Wins

Halladay,Roy, Tor	22
Loaiza,Esteban, CWS	21
Moyer,Jamie, Sea	21
Pettitte,Andy, NYY	21
Clemens,Roger, NYY	17
Lowe,Derek, Bos	17
Mussina,Mike, NYY	17
Hudson,Tim, Oak	16
Ortiz,Ramon, Ana	16
Pineiro,Joel, Sea	16

Losses

Maroth,Mike, Det	21
Bonderman,J, Det	19
Cornejo,Nate, Det	17
Lackey,John, Ana	16
Lidle,Cory, Tor	15
Washburn,J, Ana	15
Buehrle,Mark, CWS	14
Garcia,Freddy, Sea	14
Thomson,John, Tex	14
5 tied with	13

Innings Pitched

Halladay,Roy, Tor	266.0
Colon,Bartolo, CWS	242.0
Hudson,Tim, Oak	240.0
Zito,Barry, Oak	231.2
Buehrle,Mark, CWS	230.1
Loaiza,Esteban, CWS	226.1
Thomson,John, Tex	217.0
Moyer,Jamie, Sea	215.0
Mussina,Mike, NYY	214.2
Wells,David, NYY	213.0

Batters Faced

Halladay,Roy, Tor	1071
Colon,Bartolo, CWS	984
Buehrle,Mark, CWS	978
Hudson,Tim, Oak	967
Zito,Barry, Oak	957
Loaiza,Esteban, CWS	922
Thomson,John, Tex	910
Moyer,Jamie, Sea	897
Pettitte,Andy, NYY	896
Pineiro,Joel, Sea	890

Strikeouts

Loaiza,Esteban, CWS	207
Martinez,Pedro, Bos	206
Halladay,Roy, Tor	204
Mussina,Mike, NYY	195
Clemens,Roger, NYY	190
Pettitte,Andy, NYY	180
Colon,Bartolo, CWS	173
Santana,Johan, Min	169
Wakefield,Tim, Bos	169
Hudson,Tim, Oak	162

Walks Allowed

Zambrano,V, TB	106
Zito,Barry, Oak	88
Johnson,Jason, Bal	80
Escobar,Kelvim, Tor	78
Pineiro,Joel, Sea	76
Garland,Jon, CWS	74
Lowe,Derek, Bos	72
Garcia,Freddy, Sea	71
Wakefield,Tim, Bos	71
Lewis,Colby, Tex	70

Hit Batters

Zambrano,V, TB	20
Gonzalez,J, TB	12
Helling,Rick, Bal	12
Ortiz,Ramon, Ana	12
Sele,Aaron, Ana	12
Wakefield,Tim, Bos	12
Westbrook,Jake, Cle	12
6 tied with	11

Wild Pitches

Zambrano,V, TB	15
Bonderman,J, Det	12
Garcia,Freddy, Sea	11
Lackey,John, Ana	11
Lohse,Kyle, Min	10
Davis,Jason, Cle	9
Escobar,Kelvim, Tor	9
Lidle,Cory, Tor	9
Romero,J.C., Min	9
5 tied with	8

2003 American League Pitching Leaders

Runs Allowed	
Lidle,Cory, Tor	133
Maroth,Mike, Det	131
Thomson,John, Tex	125
Buehrle,Mark, CWS	124
Ortiz,Ramon, Ana	121
Bonderman,J, Det	118
Lackey,John, Ana	117
Lowe,Derek, Bos	113
Weaver,Jeff, NYY	113
4 tied with	111

Hits Allowed	
Halladay,Roy, Tor	253
Buehrle,Mark, CWS	250
Radke,Brad, Min	242
Wells,David, NYY	242
Cornejo,Nate, Det	236
Thomson,John, Tex	234
Maroth,Mike, Det	231
Pettitte,Andy, NYY	227
Rogers,Kenny, Min	227
2 tied with	223

Doubles Allowed	
Halladay,Roy, Tor	54
Wells,David, NYY	54
Burkett,John, Bos	53
Thomson,John, Tex	51
Buehrle,Mark, CWS	48
Cornejo,Nate, Det	47
Hendrickson,M, Tor	47
Lidle,Cory, Tor	47
Rogers,Kenny, Min	46
Weaver,Jeff, NYY	46

Home Runs Allowed	
Franklin,Ryan, Sea	34
Maroth,Mike, Det	34
Washburn,J, Ana	34
Radke,Brad, Min	32
Garcia,Freddy, Sea	31
Lackey,John, Ana	31
May,Darrell, KC	31
Colon,Bartolo, CWS	30
Helling,Rick, Bal	30
Meche,Gil, Sea	30

Run Support Per Nine IP (minimum 162 IP)	
Lowe,Derek, Bos	7.26
Pettitte,Andy, NYY	7.04
Anderson,Bri, Cle-KC	6.42
Ortiz,Ramon, Ana	6.35
Wells,David, NYY	6.34
Garland,Jon, CWS	6.06
Halladay,Roy, Tor	6.06
Martinez,Pedro, Bos	6.03
Pineiro,Joel, Sea	6.00
Meche,Gil, Sea	5.99

% Pitches In Strike Zone (minimum 162 IP)	
Wells,David, NYY	68.1
Mussina,Mike, NYY	64.6
Halladay,Roy, Tor	64.5
Loaiza,Esteban, CWS	64.1
Radke,Brad, Min	63.6
Colon,Bartolo, CWS	63.4
Sabathia,C.C., Cle	63.1
Martinez,Pedro, Bos	63.0
Wakefield,Tim, Bos	62.6
Washburn,J, Ana	62.5

Pitches Per Start (minimum 30 GS)	
Pineiro,Joel, Sea	109.2
Zito,Barry, Oak	107.2
Sabathia,C.C., Cle	104.8
Clemens,Roger, NYY	104.8
Moyer,Jamie, Sea	104.5
Mussina,Mike, NYY	104.5
Colon,Bartolo, CWS	103.6
Loaiza,Esteban, CWS	103.0
Hudson,Tim, Oak	102.8
Pettitte,Andy, NYY	102.6

Pitches Per Batter (minimum 162 IP)	
Wells,David, NYY	3.38
Halladay,Roy, Tor	3.39
Mulder,Mark, Oak	3.51
Lidle,Cory, Tor	3.52
Radke,Brad, Min	3.52
Bonderman,J, Det	3.53
Lowe,Derek, Bos	3.54
Davis,Jason, Cle	3.54
Cornejo,Nate, Det	3.55
Buehrle,Mark, CWS	3.57

Quality Starts	
Hudson,Tim, Oak	27
Loaiza,Esteban, CWS	27
Buehrle,Mark, CWS	24
Halladay,Roy, Tor	23
Zito,Barry, Oak	23
Colon,Bartolo, CWS	22
Moyer,Jamie, Sea	22
Clemens,Roger, NYY	21
Martinez,Pedro, Bos	21
5 tied with	20

Easy Saves	
Foulke,Keith, Oak	28
Guardado,Eddie, Min	28
Percival,Troy, Ana	24
Rivera,Mariano, NYY	23
Baez,Danys, Cle	19
Julio,Jorge, Bal	19
MacDougal,Mike, KC	18
Urbina,Ugueth, Tex	17
Carter,Lance, TB	16
2 tied with	9

Regular Saves	
Julio,Jorge, Bal	16
Guardado,Eddie, Min	13
Rivera,Mariano, NYY	12
Foulke,Keith, Oak	11
Lopez,Aquilino, Tor	9
MacDougal,Mike, KC	9
Percival,Troy, Ana	9
Urbina,Ugueth, Tex	9
Carter,Lance, TB	8
2 tied with	7

Tough Saves	
Rivera,Mariano, NYY	5
Foulke,Keith, Oak	4
Marte,Damaso, CWS	4
Acevedo,Juan, NYY-Tor	2
Affeldt,Jeremy, KC	2
Carter,Lance, TB	2
Hasegawa,S, Sea	2
Lopez,Aquilino, Tor	2
Riske,David, Cle	2
Rodney,F, Det	2

Stolen Bases Allowed	
Johnson,Jason, Bal	32
Bonderman,J, Det	25
Escobar,Kelvim, Tor	24
Lilly,Ted, Oak	24
Halladay,Roy, Tor	23
Wakefield,Tim, Bos	23
Lopez,Rodrigo, Bal	21
Clemens,Roger, NYY	20
Hendrickson,M, Tor	20
3 tied with	16

Caught Stealing Off	
Maroth,Mike, Det	11
Mulder,Mark, Oak	10
Mussina,Mike, NYY	10
Bonderman,J, Det	9
Loaiza,Esteban, CWS	9
Sabathia,C.C., Cle	9
8 tied with	8

Stolen Base Pct Allowed (minimum 162 IP)	
Anderson,Bri, Cle-KC	11.1
Colon,Bartolo, CWS	14.3
Buehrle,Mark, CWS	20.0
Davis,Jason, Cle	27.3
Sabathia,C.C., Cle	35.7
Loaiza,Esteban, CWS	40.0
Maroth,Mike, Det	42.1
May,Darrell, KC	44.4
Burkett,John, Bos	46.2
Garcia,Freddy, Sea	46.2

Pickoffs	
Maroth,Mike, Det	8
Mulder,Mark, Oak	7
Anderson,Bri, Cle-KC	6
Cornejo,Nate, Det	6
Franklin,Ryan, Sea	6
Buehrle,Mark, CWS	5
Gonzalez,J, TB	5
5 tied with	4

2003 American League Pitching Leaders

Strikeouts Per 9 IP
(minimum 162 IP)

Martinez,Pedro, Bos	9.93
Loaiza,Esteban, CWS	8.23
Mussina,Mike, NYY	8.18
Clemens,Roger, NYY	8.08
Escobar,Kelvim, Tor	7.94
Pettitte,Andy, NYY	7.78
Wakefield,Tim, Bos	7.52
Lilly,Ted, Oak	7.42
Halladay,Roy, Tor	6.90
Lackey,John, Ana	6.66

Opp On-Base Percentage
(minimum 162 IP)

Martinez,Pedro, Bos	.272
Mussina,Mike, NYY	.275
Halladay,Roy, Tor	.275
Hudson,Tim, Oak	.280
Loaiza,Esteban, CWS	.286
May,Darrell, KC	.292
Zito,Barry, Oak	.295
Clemens,Roger, NYY	.299
Mulder,Mark, Oak	.300
Colon,Bartolo, CWS	.301

Opp Slugging Average
(minimum 162 IP)

Hudson,Tim, Oak	.308
Martinez,Pedro, Bos	.314
Zito,Barry, Oak	.324
Loaiza,Esteban, CWS	.350
Pineiro,Joel, Sea	.359
Moyer,Jamie, Sea	.367
Mussina,Mike, NYY	.372
Escobar,Kelvim, Tor	.384
Mulder,Mark, Oak	.386
Halladay,Roy, Tor	.389

Hits Per Nine Innings
(minimum 162 IP)

Martinez,Pedro, Bos	7.09
Zito,Barry, Oak	7.23
Hudson,Tim, Oak	7.39
Loaiza,Esteban, CWS	7.79
Zambrano,V, TB	7.88
Mussina,Mike, NYY	8.05
Pineiro,Joel, Sea	8.16
Colon,Bartolo, CWS	8.29
Moyer,Jamie, Sea	8.33
May,Darrell, KC	8.44

Home Runs Per Nine IP
(minimum 162 IP)

Martinez,Pedro, Bos	0.34
Hudson,Tim, Oak	0.56
Loaiza,Esteban, CWS	0.68
Mulder,Mark, Oak	0.72
Zito,Barry, Oak	0.74
Escobar,Kelvim, Tor	0.75
Lowe,Derek, Bos	0.75
Moyer,Jamie, Sea	0.80
Pineiro,Joel, Sea	0.81
Cornejo,Nate, Det	0.83

Batting Average vs. LHB
(minimum 125 BF)

Riske,David, Cle	.145
Foulke,Keith, Oak	.158
Marte,Damaso, CWS	.168
Rodriguez,Fr, Ana	.186
Santana,Johan, Min	.191
Shouse,Brian, Tex	.195
Donnelly,B, Ana	.199
Rivera,Mariano, NYY	.199
Contreras,Jose, NYY	.203
Hawkins,LaTroy, Min	.205

Batting Average vs. RHB
(minimum 225 BF)

Martinez,Pedro, Bos	.179
Loaiza,Esteban, CWS	.192
Zambrano,V, TB	.207
Hudson,Tim, Oak	.214
Zito,Barry, Oak	.218
Gonzalez,J, TB	.220
Garcia,Freddy, Sea	.223
Halladay,Roy, Tor	.224
Wakefield,Tim, Bos	.226
Santana,Johan, Min	.227

Opp BA w/ RISP
(minimum 125 BF)

Santana,Johan, Min	.165
Clemens,Roger, NYY	.186
Loaiza,Esteban, CWS	.192
Martinez,Pedro, Bos	.200
Gonzalez,J, TB	.209
Sabathia,C.C., Cle	.213
Zambrano,V, TB	.214
Meche,Gil, Sea	.214
Hentgen,Pat, Bal	.220
Affeldt,Jeremy, KC	.227

OBP vs. Leadoff Hitter
(minimum 150 BF)

Clemens,Roger, NYY	.243
Martinez,Pedro, Bos	.245
Zito,Barry, Oak	.253
Halladay,Roy, Tor	.261
Mussina,Mike, NYY	.264
Hudson,Tim, Oak	.276
Santana,Johan, Min	.277
Wakefield,Tim, Bos	.278
Washburn,J, Ana	.279
Radke,Brad, Min	.288

Strikeouts / Walks Ratio
(minimum 162 IP)

Halladay,Roy, Tor	6.38
Wells,David, NYY	5.05
Mussina,Mike, NYY	4.88
Martinez,Pedro, Bos	4.38
Radke,Brad, Min	4.29
Loaiza,Esteban, CWS	3.70
Pettitte,Andy, NYY	3.60
Clemens,Roger, NYY	3.28
Mulder,Mark, Oak	3.20
Lohse,Kyle, Min	2.89

Highest GB/FB Ratio
(minimum 162 IP)

Lowe,Derek, Bos	4.38
Halladay,Roy, Tor	2.62
Hudson,Tim, Oak	2.49
Mulder,Mark, Oak	2.22
Pettitte,Andy, NYY	2.00
Lidle,Cory, Tor	1.77
Cornejo,Nate, Det	1.73
Escobar,Kelvim, Tor	1.56
Thomson,John, Tex	1.49
Loaiza,Esteban, CWS	1.48

Lowest GB/FB Ratio
(minimum 162 IP)

May,Darrell, KC	0.69
Washburn,J, Ana	0.71
Franklin,Ryan, Sea	0.77
Lilly,Ted, Oak	0.85
Colon,Bartolo, CWS	0.90
Moyer,Jamie, Sea	0.90
Ortiz,Ramon, Ana	0.92
Zito,Barry, Oak	0.93
Lohse,Kyle, Min	0.95
Meche,Gil, Sea	0.96

Rel Opp BA w/ Runners On
(minimum 50 IP)

Hasegawa,S, Sea	.134
Foulke,Keith, Oak	.138
Lopez,Aquilino, Tor	.162
Soriano,Rafael, Sea	.164
Donnelly,B, Ana	.176
Roney,Matt, Det	.179
Riske,David, Cle	.181
Rodriguez,Fr, Ana	.183
Miller,Trever, Tor	.187
Mateo,Julio, Sea	.192

Relief Opp BA w/ RISP
(minimum 50 IP)

Roney,Matt, Det	.111
Soriano,Rafael, Sea	.111
Donnelly,B, Ana	.134
Miller,Trever, Tor	.150
Lopez,Aquilino, Tor	.164
Foulke,Keith, Oak	.171
Marte,Damaso, CWS	.187
Baez,Danys, Cle	.189
Shields,Scot, Ana	.190
Hasegawa,S, Sea	.196

GIDP Induced

Colon,Bartolo, CWS	31
Cornejo,Nate, Det	30
Westbrook,Jake, Cle	26
Anderson,Bri, Cle-KC	25
Buehrle,Mark, CWS	24
Thomson,John, Tex	24
Halladay,Roy, Tor	23
Hudson,Tim, Oak	23
Franklin,Ryan, Sea	21
Lowe,Derek, Bos	21

GIDP Per Nine IP
(minimum 162 IP)

Cornejo,Nate, Det	1.39
Colon,Bartolo, CWS	1.15
Anderson,Bri, Cle-KC	1.14
Thomson,John, Tex	1.00
Davis,Jason, Cle	0.98
Mulder,Mark, Oak	0.96
Bonderman,J, Det	0.94
Burkett,John, Bos	0.94
Garland,Jon, CWS	0.94
Buehrle,Mark, CWS	0.94

2003 American League Pitching Leaders

Saves

Foulke,Keith, Oak	43
Guardado,Eddie, Min	41
Rivera,Mariano, NYY	40
Julio,Jorge, Bal	36
Percival,Troy, Ana	33
MacDougal,Mike, KC	27
Carter,Lance, TB	26
Urbina,Ugueth, Tex	26
Baez,Danys, Cle	25
2 tied with	16

Blown Saves

Baez,Danys, Cle	10
Cordero,F, Tex	10
Julio,Jorge, Bal	8
MacDougal,Mike, KC	8
Carter,Lance, TB	7
Grimsley,Jason, KC	7
Marte,Damaso, CWS	7
5 tied with	6

Save Pct
(minimum 20 Save Ops)

Guardado,Eddie, Min	91.1
Foulke,Keith, Oak	89.6
Percival,Troy, Ana	89.2
Rivera,Mariano, NYY	87.0
Urbina,Ugueth, Tex	86.7
Julio,Jorge, Bal	81.8
Carter,Lance, TB	78.8
MacDougal,Mike, KC	77.1
Baez,Danys, Cle	71.4
Cordero,F, Tex	60.0

Relief Earned Run Average
(minimum 50 IP)

Hasegawa,S, Sea	1.48
Soriano,Rafael, Sea	1.53
Donnelly,B, Ana	1.58
Marte,Damaso, CWS	1.58
Rivera,Mariano, NYY	1.66
Shields,Scot, Ana	1.68
Hawkins,LaTroy, Min	1.86
Foulke,Keith, Oak	2.08
Riske,David, Cle	2.29
Weber,Ben, Ana	2.69

Relief Wins

Foulke,Keith, Oak	9
Hawkins,LaTroy, Min	9
Rincon,Ricardo, Oak	8
Rodriguez,Fr, Ana	8
Bradford,Chad, Oak	7
Carter,Lance, TB	7
Gordon,Tom, CWS	7
Carrasco,D.J., KC	6
Kim,Byung-Hyun, Bos	6
Timlin,Mike, Bos	6

Relief Losses

Baez,Danys, Cle	9
Cordero,F, Tex	8
Harper,Travis, TB	8
Colome,Jesus, TB	7
Julio,Jorge, Bal	7
7 tied with	6

Holds

Donnelly,B, Ana	29
Grimsley,Jason, KC	28
Hawkins,LaTroy, Min	28
Bradford,Chad, Oak	23
Romero,J.C., Min	22
Fultz,Aaron, Tex	19
Ryan,B.J., Bal	19
Cordero,F, Tex	18
Rhodes,Arthur, Sea	18
3 tied with	17

Relief Games

Miller,Trever, Tor	79
Walker,Jamie, Det	78
Grimsley,Jason, KC	76
Ryan,B.J., Bal	76
Hawkins,LaTroy, Min	74
Baez,Danys, Cle	73
Cordero,F, Tex	73
Romero,J.C., Min	73
4 tied with	72

Relief Innings

Sparks,Steve, Det-Oak	107.0
Harper,Travis, TB	93.0
Foulke,Keith, Oak	86.2
Rodriguez,Fr, Ana	86.0
Mateo,Julio, Sea	85.2
Rincon,Juan, Min	85.2
Timlin,Mike, Bos	83.2
Cordero,F, Tex	82.2
Mulholland,T, Cle	81.1
Weber,Ben, Ana	80.1

Relief Opp Batting Average
(minimum 50 IP)

Soriano,Rafael, Sea	.162
Rodriguez,Fr, Ana	.172
Foulke,Keith, Oak	.184
Marte,Damaso, CWS	.185
Riske,David, Cle	.196
Boyd,Jason, Cle	.200
Donnelly,B, Ana	.200
Guardado,Eddie, Min	.207
Lopez,Aquilino, Tor	.212
Gordon,Tom, CWS	.213

Relief Opp On Base Pct
(minimum 50 IP)

Soriano,Rafael, Sea	.224
Guardado,Eddie, Min	.249
Foulke,Keith, Oak	.249
Mateo,Julio, Sea	.259
Riske,David, Cle	.260
Rodriguez,Fr, Ana	.262
Timlin,Mike, Bos	.268
Rivera,Mariano, NYY	.272
Donnelly,B, Ana	.273
Kershner,Jason, Tor	.275

Relief Opp Slugging Avg
(minimum 50 IP)

Soriano,Rafael, Sea	.238
Marte,Damaso, CWS	.266
Ryan,B.J., Bal	.286
Donnelly,B, Ana	.287
Gordon,Tom, CWS	.291
Kim,Byung-Hyun, Bos	.293
Rivera,Mariano, NYY	.300
Cordero,F, Tex	.302
Shields,Scot, Ana	.310
Lopez,Aquilino, Tor	.315

Inherited Runners Scrd %
(minimum 30 IR)

Groom,Buddy, Bal	14.6
Bradford,Chad, Oak	16.4
Hasegawa,S, Sea	16.7
Gordon,Tom, CWS	18.9
Rincon,Ricardo, Oak	20.0
Embree,Alan, Bos	20.5
Miller,Trever, Tor	23.0
Riske,David, Cle	23.7
Hawkins,LaTroy, Min	24.4
Shouse,Brian, Tex	25.9

Rel OBP 1st Batter Faced
(minimum 40 BF)

Kershner,Jason, Tor	.179
Timlin,Mike, Bos	.181
Gordon,Tom, CWS	.197
Soriano,Rafael, Sea	.200
Guardado,Eddie, Min	.212
Sparks,Steve, Det-Oak	.213
Embree,Alan, Bos	.215
Donnelly,B, Ana	.238
Shouse,Brian, Tex	.242
Ligtenberg,K, Bal	.242

Relief Opp BA Vs LHB
(minimum 50 AB)

Riske,David, Cle	.145
Foulke,Keith, Oak	.158
Marte,Damaso, CWS	.168
Guardado,Eddie, Min	.175
Kershner,Jason, Tor	.178
Ryan,B.J., Bal	.186
Rodriguez,Fr, Ana	.186
Soriano,Rafael, Sea	.191
Shouse,Brian, Tex	.195
2 tied with	.199

Relief Opp BA Vs RHB
(minimum 50 AB)

Soriano,Rafael, Sea	.132
Rodriguez,Fr, Ana	.156
Baez,Danys, Cle	.165
Boyd,Jason, Cle	.176
Lopez,Aquilino, Tor	.186
Bradford,Chad, Oak	.190
Kim,Byung-Hyun, Bos	.193
Gordon,Tom, CWS	.196
Timlin,Mike, Bos	.198
Marte,Damaso, CWS	.199

2003 American League Pitching Leaders

Fastest Average Fastball
(minimum 162 IP)

Sabathia,C.C., Cle	93.9
Colon,Bartolo, CWS	93.4
Escobar,Kelvim, Tor	93.3
Bonderman,J, Det	93.3
Meche,Gil, Sea	92.8
Lohse,Kyle, Min	92.8
Davis,Jason, Cle	92.6
Zambrano,V, TB	92.3
Halladay,Roy, Tor	92.3
Thomson,John, Tex	92.0

Slowest Average Fastball
(minimum 162 IP)

Wakefield,Tim, Bos	75.9
Moyer,Jamie, Sea	82.9
Burkett,John, Bos	83.6
Rogers,Kenny, Min	85.3
Maroth,Mike, Det	85.3
May,Darrell, KC	86.1
Buehrle,Mark, CWS	86.4
Anderson,Bri, Cle-KC	87.0
Lowe,Derek, Bos	87.2
Cornejo,Nate, Det	87.5

Pitches 100+ Velocity

Colon,Bartolo, CWS	12
Julio,Jorge, Bal	4
Colome,Jesus, TB	3
Cordero,F, Tex	2
Gordon,Tom, CWS	2
Halladay,Roy, Tor	1
Soriano,Rafael, Sea	1
Zambrano,V, TB	1

Pitches 95+ Velocity

Colon,Bartolo, CWS	636
Cordero,F, Tex	597
Colome,Jesus, TB	546
Percival,Troy, Ana	418
Julio,Jorge, Bal	402
MacDougal,Mike, KC	380
Sabathia,C.C., Cle	336
Hawkins,LaTroy, Min	310
Escobar,Kelvim, Tor	298
Sosa,Jorge, TB	265

Pitches Less Than 80 MPH

Wakefield,Tim, Bos	2307
Moyer,Jamie, Sea	1165
Sparks,Steve, Det-Oak	1010
Zito,Barry, Oak	877
Appier,Kevin, Ana-KC	724
Halladay,Roy, Tor	681
Maroth,Mike, Det	650
Traber,Billy, Cle	627
Burkett,John, Bos	609
Lidle,Cory, Tor	557

Lowest % Fastballs
(minimum 162 IP)

Wakefield,Tim, Bos	9.0
Rogers,Kenny, Min	48.9
Moyer,Jamie, Sea	49.5
Lilly,Ted, Oak	51.1
Escobar,Kelvim, Tor	52.6
Hudson,Tim, Oak	52.7
Maroth,Mike, Det	54.2
Mulder,Mark, Oak	55.2
Franklin,Ryan, Sea	55.3
Zito,Barry, Oak	55.3

Highest % Fastballs
(minimum 162 IP)

Lowe,Derek, Bos	79.6
Colon,Bartolo, CWS	75.4
Davis,Jason, Cle	72.9
Thomson,John, Tex	71.2
Cornejo,Nate, Det	68.3
Garland,Jon, CWS	68.1
Burkett,John, Bos	67.5
Johnson,Jason, Bal	67.3
Washburn,J, Ana	66.7
Bonderman,J, Det	66.1

Highest % Curveballs
(minimum 162 IP)

Halladay,Roy, Tor	28.5
Mussina,Mike, NYY	26.8
Wells,David, NYY	26.4
Johnson,Jason, Bal	25.9
Lackey,John, Ana	23.1
Zito,Barry, Oak	22.0
Pettitte,Andy, NYY	18.4
Lidle,Cory, Tor	18.1
Garcia,Freddy, Sea	17.0
Meche,Gil, Sea	16.7

Highest % Changeups
(minimum 162 IP)

Moyer,Jamie, Sea	32.2
Rogers,Kenny, Min	24.1
Anderson,Bri, Cle-KC	21.1
Radke,Brad, Min	19.4
Martinez,Pedro, Bos	19.2
Lilly,Ted, Oak	18.9
May,Darrell, KC	18.3
Maroth,Mike, Det	17.9
Buehrle,Mark, CWS	16.7
Ortiz,Ramon, Ana	16.0

Highest % Sliders
(minimum 162 IP)

Loaiza,Esteban, CWS	29.8
Franklin,Ryan, Sea	20.4
Thomson,John, Tex	18.3
Zambrano,V, TB	18.1
Bonderman,J, Det	17.6
Ortiz,Ramon, Ana	16.7
Lohse,Kyle, Min	16.3
Maroth,Mike, Det	14.7
Anderson,Bri, Cle-KC	12.3
Cornejo,Nate, Det	12.0

2003 National League Pitching Leaders

Earned Run Average
(minimum 162 IP)

Schmidt,Jason, SF	2.34
Brown,Kevin, LA	2.39
Prior,Mark, ChC	2.43
Webb,Brandon, Ari	2.84
Schilling,Curt, Ari	2.95
Nomo,Hideo, LA	3.09
Zambrano,C, ChC	3.11
Wood,Kerry, ChC	3.20
Hernandez,L, Mon	3.20
Vazquez,Javier, Mon	3.24

Winning Percentage
(minimum 15 Decisions)

Schmidt,Jason, SF	.773
Nathan,Joe, SF	.750
Ortiz,Russ, Atl	.750
Prior,Mark, ChC	.750
Ramirez,H, Atl	.750
Willis,D, Fla	.700
Oswalt,Roy, Hou	.667
Rueter,Kirk, SF	.667
Williams,Woody, StL	.667
Hampton,Mike, Atl	.636

Opponent Batting Average
(minimum 162 IP)

Schmidt,Jason, SF	.200
Wood,Kerry, ChC	.203
Webb,Brandon, Ari	.212
Ortiz,Russ, Atl	.223
Nomo,Hideo, LA	.223
Clement,Matt, ChC	.227
Vazquez,Javier, Mon	.229
Schilling,Curt, Ari	.230
Prior,Mark, ChC	.231
Wells,Kip, Pit	.233

Baserunners Per 9 IP
(minimum 162 IP)

Schmidt,Jason, SF	8.80
Schilling,Curt, Ari	9.59
Vazquez,Javier, Mon	10.11
Prior,Mark, ChC	10.31
Brown,Kevin, LA	10.45
Morris,Matt, StL	10.81
Maddux,Greg, Atl	10.96
Webb,Brandon, Ari	11.01
Redman,Mark, Fla	11.23
Hernandez,L, Mon	11.26

Games

Quantrill,Paul, LA	89
Villarreal,O, Ari	86
King,Ray, Atl	80
Martin,Tom, LA	80
Kline,Steve, StL	78
Lidge,Brad, Hou	78
Nathan,Joe, SF	78
Wagner,Billy, Hou	78
4 tied with	77

Games Started

Maddux,Greg, Atl	36
Millwood,Kevin, Phi	35
Franklin,Wayne, Mil	34
Ohka,Tomo, Mon	34
Ortiz,Russ, Atl	34
Sheets,Ben, Mil	34
Vazquez,Javier, Mon	34
7 tied with	33

Complete Games

Hernandez,L, Mon	8
Millwood,Kevin, Phi	5
Morris,Matt, StL	5
Schmidt,Jason, SF	5
Vazquez,Javier, Mon	4
Wood,Kerry, ChC	4
5 tied with	3

Shutouts

Millwood,Kevin, Phi	3
Morris,Matt, StL	3
Schmidt,Jason, SF	3
Nomo,Hideo, LA	2
Schilling,Curt, Ari	2
Suppan,Jeff, Pit	2
Trachsel,Steve, NYM	2
Willis,D, Fla	2
Wolf,Randy, Phi	2
Wood,Kerry, ChC	2

Wins

Ortiz,Russ, Atl	21
Prior,Mark, ChC	18
Williams,Woody, StL	18
Schmidt,Jason, SF	17
Maddux,Greg, Atl	16
Nomo,Hideo, LA	16
Trachsel,Steve, NYM	16
Wolf,Randy, Phi	16
3 tied with	15

Losses

D'Amico,Jeff, Pit	16
Graves,Danny, Cin	15
Lawrence,Brian, SD	15
Glavine,Tom, NYM	14
Redding,Tim, Hou	14
8 tied with	13

Innings Pitched

Hernandez,L, Mon	233.1
Vazquez,Javier, Mon	230.2
Millwood,Kevin, Phi	222.0
Sheets,Ben, Mil	220.2
Williams,Woody, StL	220.2
Maddux,Greg, Atl	218.1
Nomo,Hideo, LA	218.1
Zambrano,C, ChC	214.0
Ortiz,Russ, Atl	212.1
Prior,Mark, ChC	211.1

Batters Faced

Hernandez,L, Mon	967
Williams,Woody, StL	944
Vazquez,Javier, Mon	938
Sheets,Ben, Mil	931
Millwood,Kevin, Phi	930
Ortiz,Russ, Atl	912
Zambrano,C, ChC	907
Tomko,Brett, StL	903
Maddux,Greg, Atl	901
Nomo,Hideo, LA	897

Strikeouts

Wood,Kerry, ChC	266
Prior,Mark, ChC	245
Vazquez,Javier, Mon	241
Schmidt,Jason, SF	208
Schilling,Curt, Ari	194
Brown,Kevin, LA	185
Hernandez,L, Mon	178
Nomo,Hideo, LA	177
Wolf,Randy, Phi	177
Webb,Brandon, Ari	172

Walks Allowed

Ortiz,Russ, Atl	102
Ishii,Kazuhisa, LA	101
Wood,Kerry, ChC	100
Nomo,Hideo, LA	98
Franklin,Wayne, Mil	94
Leiter,Al, NYM	94
Zambrano,C, ChC	94
Jennings,Jason, Col	88
Estes,Shawn, ChC	83
Peavy,Jake, SD	82

Hit Batters

Wood,Kerry, ChC	21
Padilla,V, Phi	16
Clement,Matt, ChC	14
Stephenson,G, StL	13
Webb,Brandon, Ari	13
Chacon,Shawn, Col	12
Lawrence,Brian, SD	11
Williams,Woody, StL	11
6 tied with	10

Wild Pitches

Clement,Matt, ChC	13
Day,Zach, Mon	13
Foppert,Jesse, SF	12
Silva,Carlos, Phi	12
Wright,Jaret, SD-Atl	12
Linebrink,S, Hou-SD	11
Moss,Damian, SF	11
Nomo,Hideo, LA	11
Vazquez,Javier, Mon	11
5 tied with	10

2003 National League Pitching Leaders

Runs Allowed	
Franklin,Wayne, Mil	129
Tomko,Brett, StL	126
Sheets,Ben, Mil	122
Kinney,Matt, Mil	121
Jennings,Jason, Col	115
Estes,Shawn, ChC	113
Maddux,Greg, Atl	112
Graves,Danny, Cin	108
Oliver,Darren, Col	108
Dessens,Elmer, Ari	107

Hits Allowed	
Tomko,Brett, StL	252
Ohka,Tomo, Mon	233
Sheets,Ben, Mil	232
Hernandez,L, Mon	225
Maddux,Greg, Atl	225
Williams,Woody, StL	220
Dessens,Elmer, Ari	212
Jennings,Jason, Col	212
Millwood,Kevin, Phi	210
Lawrence,Brian, SD	206

Doubles Allowed	
Seo,Jae, NYM	61
Graves,Danny, Cin	56
Pavano,Carl, Fla	54
Tomko,Brett, StL	54
Ohka,Tomo, Mon	52
Padilla,V, Phi	52
Jennings,Jason, Col	51
Franklin,Wayne, Mil	50
Trachsel,Steve, NYM	48
3 tied with	47

Home Runs Allowed	
Franklin,Wayne, Mil	36
Tomko,Brett, StL	35
Peavy,Jake, SD	33
Graves,Danny, Cin	30
Stephenson,G, StL	30
Sheets,Ben, Mil	29
Perez,Odalis, LA	28
Vazquez,Javier, Mon	28
4 tied with	27

Run Support Per Nine IP (minimum 162 IP)	
Williams,Woody, StL	6.97
Tomko,Brett, StL	6.75
Wolf,Randy, Phi	6.71
Ortiz,Russ, Atl	6.49
Reynolds,Shane, Atl	6.45
Oliver,Darren, Col	6.14
Penny,Brad, Fla	6.05
Ramirez,H, Atl	5.97
Hampton,Mike, Atl	5.59
Miller,Wade, Hou	5.48

% Pitches In Strike Zone (minimum 162 IP)	
Millwood,Kevin, Phi	65.3
Maddux,Greg, Atl	64.4
Seo,Jae, NYM	64.4
Padilla,V, Phi	63.9
Myers,Brett, Phi	63.5
Graves,Danny, Cin	63.4
Pavano,Carl, Fla	63.4
Penny,Brad, Fla	63.4
Schmidt,Jason, SF	63.2
Ohka,Tomo, Mon	63.2

Pitches Per Start (minimum 30 GS)	
Prior,Mark, ChC	113.3
Wood,Kerry, ChC	110.7
Williams,Woody, StL	110.0
Vazquez,Javier, Mon	109.8
Hernandez,L, Mon	108.2
Leiter,Al, NYM	108.2
Zambrano,C, ChC	106.4
Ortiz,Russ, Atl	104.9
Wells,Kip, Pit	103.3
Trachsel,Steve, NYM	100.8

Pitches Per Batter (minimum 162 IP)	
Maddux,Greg, Atl	3.26
Graves,Danny, Cin	3.35
Ohka,Tomo, Mon	3.44
D'Amico,Jeff, Pit	3.47
Oliver,Darren, Col	3.49
Batista,Miguel, Ari	3.50
Lawrence,Brian, SD	3.52
Wilson,Paul, Cin	3.55
Myers,Brett, Phi	3.55
Morris,Matt, StL	3.56

Quality Starts	
Brown,Kevin, LA	25
Millwood,Kevin, Phi	23
Prior,Mark, ChC	23
Hernandez,L, Mon	22
Ohka,Tomo, Mon	22
Vazquez,Javier, Mon	22
Wood,Kerry, ChC	22
7 tied with	21

Easy Saves	
Gagne,Eric, LA	28
Smoltz,John, Atl	27
Wagner,Billy, Hou	24
Worrell,Tim, SF	22
Biddle,Rocky, Mon	21
Williams,Mike, Pit-Phi	19
Mesa,Jose, Phi	17
Borowski,Joe, ChC	16
Looper,Braden, Fla	15
Mantei,Matt, Ari	15

Regular Saves	
Gagne,Eric, LA	25
Wagner,Billy, Hou	16
Borowski,Joe, ChC	15
Smoltz,John, Atl	15
Worrell,Tim, SF	14
Mantei,Matt, Ari	13
Biddle,Rocky, Mon	12
Looper,Braden, Fla	12
Jimenez,Jose, Col	10
Kolb,Danny, Mil	10

Tough Saves	
Tavarez,Julian, Pit	4
Wagner,Billy, Hou	4
Smoltz,John, Atl	3
Borowski,Joe, ChC	2
Gagne,Eric, LA	2
Isringhausen,J, StL	2
Lincoln,Mike, Pit	2
Speier,Justin, Col	2
Weathers,David, NYM	2
Worrell,Tim, SF	2

Stolen Bases Allowed	
Millwood,Kevin, Phi	41
Maddux,Greg, Atl	26
Perez,Odalis, LA	25
Kinney,Matt, Mil	24
Ortiz,Russ, Atl	22
Leiter,Al, NYM	21
Nomo,Hideo, LA	19
Ishii,Kazuhisa, LA	18
4 tied with	17

Caught Stealing Off	
Nomo,Hideo, LA	14
Ishii,Kazuhisa, LA	13
Leiter,Al, NYM	11
Brown,Kevin, LA	9
Perez,Odalis, LA	9
Prior,Mark, ChC	9
7 tied with	8

Stolen Base Pct Allowed (minimum 162 IP)	
Ohka,Tomo, Mon	20.0
Hampton,Mike, Atl	33.3
Seo,Jae, NYM	36.4
Zambrano,C, ChC	37.5
Wood,Kerry, ChC	38.5
Prior,Mark, ChC	43.8
Tomko,Brett, StL	44.4
Batista,Miguel, Ari	50.0
Morris,Matt, StL	50.0
Schilling,Curt, Ari	50.0

Pickoffs	
Beimel,Joe, Pit	7
Perez,Odalis, LA	7
Robertson,J, Hou	7
Glavine,Tom, NYM	6
Leiter,Al, NYM	5
Trachsel,Steve, NYM	5
Fuentes,Brian, Col	4
Ishii,Kazuhisa, LA	4
Oliver,Darren, Col	4
Rusch,Glendon, Mil	4

2003 National League Pitching Leaders

Strikeouts Per 9 IP	
(minimum 162 IP)	
Wood,Kerry, ChC	11.35
Prior,Mark, ChC	10.43
Schilling,Curt, Ari	10.39
Vazquez,Javier, Mon	9.40
Schmidt,Jason, SF	9.01
Webb,Brandon, Ari	8.57
Wolf,Randy, Phi	7.97
Brown,Kevin, LA	7.89
Miller,Wade, Hou	7.73
Clement,Matt, ChC	7.63

Opp On-Base Percentage	
(minimum 162 IP)	
Schmidt,Jason, SF	.250
Schilling,Curt, Ari	.270
Vazquez,Javier, Mon	.278
Prior,Mark, ChC	.283
Brown,Kevin, LA	.290
Morris,Matt, StL	.297
Webb,Brandon, Ari	.298
Maddux,Greg, Atl	.299
Redman,Mark, Fla	.301
Hernandez,L, Mon	.304

Opp Slugging Average	
(minimum 162 IP)	
Webb,Brandon, Ari	.307
Schmidt,Jason, SF	.316
Brown,Kevin, LA	.318
Zambrano,C, ChC	.331
Wood,Kerry, ChC	.344
Ortiz,Russ, Atl	.347
Prior,Mark, ChC	.352
Nomo,Hideo, LA	.357
Schilling,Curt, Ari	.358
Clement,Matt, ChC	.362

Hits Per Nine Innings	
(minimum 162 IP)	
Wood,Kerry, ChC	6.48
Schmidt,Jason, SF	6.59
Webb,Brandon, Ari	6.97
Nomo,Hideo, LA	7.21
Ortiz,Russ, Atl	7.50
Clement,Matt, ChC	7.54
Schilling,Curt, Ari	7.71
Vazquez,Javier, Mon	7.73
Prior,Mark, ChC	7.79
Wells,Kip, Pit	7.80

Home Runs Per Nine IP	
(minimum 162 IP)	
Zambrano,C, ChC	0.38
Brown,Kevin, LA	0.47
Webb,Brandon, Ari	0.60
Batista,Miguel, Ari	0.61
Schmidt,Jason, SF	0.61
Prior,Mark, ChC	0.64
Hampton,Mike, Atl	0.66
Ortiz,Russ, Atl	0.72
Leiter,Al, NYM	0.75
Redman,Mark, Fla	0.76

Batting Average vs. LHB	
(minimum 125 BF)	
Gagne,Eric, LA	.130
Dotel,Octavio, Hou	.152
Hampton,Mike, Atl	.164
Mota,Guillermo, LA	.181
Ishii,Kazuhisa, LA	.192
Schmidt,Jason, SF	.197
Wood,Kerry, ChC	.198
Trachsel,Steve, NYM	.199
Redman,Mark, Fla	.200
Perez,Odalis, LA	.201

Batting Average vs. RHB	
(minimum 225 BF)	
Wagner,Billy, Hou	.154
Webb,Brandon, Ari	.167
Ortiz,Russ, Atl	.187
Villarreal,O, Ari	.204
Schmidt,Jason, SF	.204
Wood,Kerry, ChC	.206
Cormier,Rheal, Phi	.207
Clement,Matt, ChC	.209
Schilling,Curt, Ari	.210
Wells,Kip, Pit	.219

Opp BA w/ RISP	
(minimum 125 BF)	
Wood,Kerry, ChC	.157
Ishii,Kazuhisa, LA	.166
Wells,Kip, Pit	.169
Brown,Kevin, LA	.178
Prior,Mark, ChC	.183
Beckett,Josh, Fla	.192
Nomo,Hideo, LA	.202
Hernandez,L, Mon	.204
Webb,Brandon, Ari	.205
Stephenson,G, StL	.213

OBP vs. Leadoff Hitter	
(minimum 150 BF)	
Seo,Jae, NYM	.227
Willis,D, Fla	.251
Schilling,Curt, Ari	.254
Schmidt,Jason, SF	.258
Williams,Woody, StL	.272
Peavy,Jake, SD	.275
Padilla,V, Phi	.276
Perez,Odalis, LA	.279
Pavano,Carl, Fla	.280
Hernandez,L, Mon	.282

Strikeouts / Walks Ratio	
(minimum 162 IP)	
Schilling,Curt, Ari	6.06
Prior,Mark, ChC	4.90
Schmidt,Jason, SF	4.52
Vazquez,Javier, Mon	4.23
Maddux,Greg, Atl	3.76
Sheets,Ben, Mil	3.65
Brown,Kevin, LA	3.30
Hernandez,L, Mon	3.12
Morris,Matt, StL	3.08
Perez,Odalis, LA	3.07

Highest GB/FB Ratio	
(minimum 162 IP)	
Webb,Brandon, Ari	3.92
Brown,Kevin, LA	3.57
Zambrano,C, ChC	2.38
Perez,Odalis, LA	2.13
Hampton,Mike, Atl	2.08
Clement,Matt, ChC	2.06
Maddux,Greg, Atl	1.97
Batista,Miguel, Ari	1.96
Myers,Brett, Phi	1.81
Ramirez,H, Atl	1.71

Lowest GB/FB Ratio	
(minimum 162 IP)	
Stephenson,G, StL	0.72
Franklin,Wayne, Mil	0.73
Vazquez,Javier, Mon	0.83
Kinney,Matt, Mil	0.85
Schmidt,Jason, SF	0.91
Trachsel,Steve, NYM	0.92
Williams,Woody, StL	0.97
Seo,Jae, NYM	0.98
Redman,Mark, Fla	0.99
Leiter,Al, NYM	1.00

Rel Opp BA w/ Runners On	
(minimum 50 IP)	
Gagne,Eric, LA	.121
Mantei,Matt, Ari	.132
Mercker,Kent, Cin-Atl	.157
Wagner,Billy, Hou	.167
Smoltz,John, Atl	.169
Dotel,Octavio, Hou	.186
Randolph,S, Ari	.192
Nathan,Joe, SF	.195
Cormier,Rheal, Phi	.198
Farnsworth,K, ChC	.198

Relief Opp BA w/ RISP	
(minimum 50 IP)	
Mantei,Matt, Ari	.088
Wagner,Billy, Hou	.094
Gagne,Eric, LA	.118
Shuey,Paul, LA	.149
Smoltz,John, Atl	.152
Mercker,Kent, Cin-Atl	.154
Borowski,Joe, ChC	.164
Herges,Matt, SD-SF	.165
Reed,Steve, Col	.182
Valverde,Jose, Ari	.183

GIDP Induced	
Ramirez,H, Atl	29
Estes,Shawn, ChC	27
Penny,Brad, Fla	26
Rueter,Kirk, SF	24
Zambrano,C, ChC	24
Brown,Kevin, LA	23
Glavine,Tom, NYM	23
Lawrence,Brian, SD	23
Padilla,V, Phi	23
3 tied with	22

GIDP Per Nine IP	
(minimum 162 IP)	
Ramirez,H, Atl	1.43
Penny,Brad, Fla	1.19
Glavine,Tom, NYM	1.13
Oliver,Darren, Col	1.10
Jennings,Jason, Col	1.09
Reynolds,Shane, Atl	1.08
Batista,Miguel, Ari	1.02
Zambrano,C, ChC	1.01
Padilla,V, Phi	0.99
Lawrence,Brian, SD	0.98

2003 National League Pitching Leaders

Saves

Gagne,Eric, LA	55
Smoltz,John, Atl	45
Wagner,Billy, Hou	44
Worrell,Tim, SF	38
Biddle,Rocky, Mon	34
Borowski,Joe, ChC	33
Mantei,Matt, Ari	29
Looper,Braden, Fla	28
Williams,Mike, Pit-Phi	28
Mesa,Jose, Phi	24

Blown Saves

DeJean,Mike, Mil-StL	8
Benitez,A, NYM	7
Biddle,Rocky, Mon	7
Williams,Mike, Pit-Phi	7
Worrell,Tim, SF	7
Eldred,Cal, StL	6
Looper,Braden, Fla	6
Reitsma,Chris, Cin	6
Vizcaino,Luis, Mil	6
7 tied with	5

Save Pct
(minimum 20 Save Ops)

Beck,Rod, SD	100.0
Gagne,Eric, LA	100.0
Wagner,Billy, Hou	93.6
Smoltz,John, Atl	91.8
Kolb,Danny, Mil	91.3
Mantei,Matt, Ari	90.6
Borowski,Joe, ChC	89.2
Isringhausen,J, StL	88.0
Jimenez,Jose, Col	87.0
Mesa,Jose, Phi	85.7

Relief Earned Run Average
(minimum 50 IP)

Smoltz,John, Atl	1.12
Gagne,Eric, LA	1.20
Cormier,Rheal, Phi	1.70
Quantrill,Paul, LA	1.75
Wagner,Billy, Hou	1.78
Mercker,Kent, Cin-Atl	1.95
Mota,Guillermo, LA	1.97
Valverde,Jose, Ari	2.15
Villarreal,O, Ari	2.46
Dotel,Octavio, Hou	2.48

Relief Wins

Nathan,Joe, SF	12
Ayala,Luis, Mon	10
Villarreal,O, Ari	10
Cormier,Rheal, Phi	8
Randolph,S, Ari	8
Reitsma,Chris, Cin	8
Rodriguez,Fe, SF	8
Eldred,Cal, StL	7
Estrella,Leo, Mil	7
11 tied with	6

Relief Losses

Biddle,Rocky, Mon	8
DeJean,Mike, Mil-StL	8
Mesa,Jose, Phi	7
Stanton,Mike, NYM	7
Villarreal,O, Ari	7
Williams,Mike, Pit-Phi	7
Witasick,Jay, SD	7
Jimenez,Jose, Col	6
Weathers,David, NYM	6
6 tied with	5

Holds

Dotel,Octavio, Hou	33
Lidge,Brad, Hou	28
Martin,Tom, LA	28
Quantrill,Paul, LA	28
Weathers,David, NYM	26
Eyre,Scott, SF	20
Nathan,Joe, SF	20
5 tied with	19

Relief Games

Quantrill,Paul, LA	89
Villarreal,O, Ari	85
King,Ray, Atl	80
Martin,Tom, LA	80
Kline,Steve, StL	78
Lidge,Brad, Hou	78
Nathan,Joe, SF	78
Wagner,Billy, Hou	78
4 tied with	77

Relief Innings

Mota,Guillermo, LA	105.0
Villarreal,O, Ari	95.0
Weathers,David, NYM	87.2
Dotel,Octavio, Hou	87.0
Wagner,Billy, Hou	86.0
Lidge,Brad, Hou	85.0
Cormier,Rheal, Phi	84.2
Tavarez,Julian, Pit	83.2
Silva,Carlos, Phi	83.1
Stone,Ricky, Hou	83.0

Relief Opp Batting Average
(minimum 50 IP)

Gagne,Eric, LA	.133
Valverde,Jose, Ari	.137
Wagner,Billy, Hou	.169
Dotel,Octavio, Hou	.172
Cormier,Rheal, Phi	.182
Nathan,Joe, SF	.186
Mantei,Matt, Ari	.191
Farnsworth,K, ChC	.196
Martin,Tom, LA	.198
Lidge,Brad, Hou	.202

Relief Opp On Base Pct
(minimum 50 IP)

Gagne,Eric, LA	.199
Smoltz,John, Atl	.230
Wagner,Billy, Hou	.234
Cormier,Rheal, Phi	.248
Dotel,Octavio, Hou	.253
Valverde,Jose, Ari	.255
Mota,Guillermo, LA	.258
Mantei,Matt, Ari	.264
Borowski,Joe, ChC	.264
Quantrill,Paul, LA	.275

Relief Opp Slugging Avg
(minimum 50 IP)

Gagne,Eric, LA	.176
Valverde,Jose, Ari	.234
Wagner,Billy, Hou	.266
Cormier,Rheal, Phi	.269
Smoltz,John, Atl	.281
Quantrill,Paul, LA	.290
Borowski,Joe, ChC	.293
Farnsworth,K, ChC	.295
Mota,Guillermo, LA	.296
Nathan,Joe, SF	.299

Inherited Runners Scrd %
(minimum 30 IR)

Martin,Tom, LA	11.9
Cormier,Rheal, Phi	13.9
Ayala,Luis, Mon	16.7
Lopez,Javier, Col	18.6
Reed,Steve, Col	20.5
Plesac,Dan, Phi	21.3
Eyre,Scott, SF	22.0
Adams,Terry, Phi	22.4
Myers,Mike, Ari	22.6
2 tied with	23.3

Rel OBP 1st Batter Faced
(minimum 40 BF)

Smoltz,John, Atl	.180
Cormier,Rheal, Phi	.185
Riedling,John, Cin	.191
Martin,Tom, LA	.200
Williamson,S, Cin	.214
Nathan,Joe, SF	.218
Reitsma,Chris, Cin	.222
Mantei,Matt, Ari	.224
Borowski,Joe, ChC	.235
Mota,Guillermo, LA	.237

Relief Opp BA Vs LHB
(minimum 50 AB)

Cormier,Rheal, Phi	.119
Gagne,Eric, LA	.130
Dotel,Octavio, Hou	.152
Mantei,Matt, Ari	.155
Valverde,Jose, Ari	.169
Mota,Guillermo, LA	.181
Farnsworth,K, ChC	.189
Smoltz,John, Atl	.189
Martin,Tom, LA	.190
Boehringer,B, Pit	.193

Relief Opp BA Vs RHB
(minimum 50 AB)

Valverde,Jose, Ari	.112
Gagne,Eric, LA	.135
Nathan,Joe, SF	.136
Wagner,Billy, Hou	.154
Reed,Steve, Col	.165
Lidge,Brad, Hou	.179
Remlinger,Mike, ChC	.180
Tejera,Michael, Fla	.186
Dotel,Octavio, Hou	.186
Ayala,Luis, Mon	.188

2003 National League Pitching Leaders

Fastest Average Fastball
(minimum 162 IP)

Wood,Kerry, ChC	95.3
Schmidt,Jason, SF	95.0
Wells,Kip, Pit	93.8
Penny,Brad, Fla	93.7
Prior,Mark, ChC	92.9
Zambrano,C, ChC	92.7
Schilling,Curt, Ari	92.3
Eaton,Adam, SD	92.1
Miller,Wade, Hou	91.9
Padilla,V, Phi	91.9

Slowest Average Fastball
(minimum 162 IP)

Lawrence,Brian, SD	83.6
Redman,Mark, Fla	85.4
Maddux,Greg, Atl	85.4
Glavine,Tom, NYM	85.9
Reynolds,Shane, Atl	86.0
Oliver,Darren, Col	86.0
Stephenson,G, StL	86.7
Nomo,Hideo, LA	87.1
D'Amico,Jeff, Pit	87.2
Franklin,Wayne, Mil	87.5

Pitches 100+ Velocity

Wagner,Billy, Hou	159
Farnsworth,K, ChC	8
Beckett,Josh, Fla	3
Looper,Braden, Fla	2
7 tied with	1

Pitches 95+ Velocity

Wood,Kerry, ChC	1138
Schmidt,Jason, SF	894
Wagner,Billy, Hou	766
Farnsworth,K, ChC	510
Penny,Brad, Fla	471
Lidge,Brad, Hou	469
Hernandez,Ro, Atl	438
Zambrano,C, ChC	432
Mota,Guillermo, LA	431
Beckett,Josh, Fla	423

Pitches Less Than 80 MPH

Nomo,Hideo, LA	1055
Redman,Mark, Fla	907
Wolf,Randy, Phi	898
Ishii,Kazuhisa, LA	805
Seo,Jae, NYM	724
Reynolds,Shane, Atl	703
Penny,Brad, Fla	643
Morris,Matt, StL	632
Lawrence,Brian, SD	612
Robertson,J, Hou	566

Lowest % Fastballs
(minimum 162 IP)

Perez,Odalis, LA	48.3
Vazquez,Javier, Mon	48.7
Schilling,Curt, Ari	50.0
Hernandez,L, Mon	50.9
Stephenson,G, StL	51.1
Ohka,Tomo, Mon	51.2
D'Amico,Jeff, Pit	51.7
Nomo,Hideo, LA	54.1
Morris,Matt, StL	54.1
Lawrence,Brian, SD	55.0

Highest % Fastballs
(minimum 162 IP)

Brown,Kevin, LA	79.8
Padilla,V, Phi	79.3
Ortiz,Russ, Atl	78.3
Hampton,Mike, Atl	78.2
Zambrano,C, ChC	76.5
Webb,Brandon, Ari	73.1
Maddux,Greg, Atl	72.4
Schmidt,Jason, SF	71.1
Leiter,Al, NYM	69.6
Batista,Miguel, Ari	69.1

Highest % Curveballs
(minimum 162 IP)

Morris,Matt, StL	31.0
Sheets,Ben, Mil	30.7
Myers,Brett, Phi	29.5
Prior,Mark, ChC	27.7
Penny,Brad, Fla	27.0
D'Amico,Jeff, Pit	24.9
Wolf,Randy, Phi	21.1
Graves,Danny, Cin	20.3
Eaton,Adam, SD	20.1
Williams,Woody, StL	18.2

Highest % Changeups
(minimum 162 IP)

Glavine,Tom, NYM	29.7
Redman,Mark, Fla	26.2
Perez,Odalis, LA	22.7
Seo,Jae, NYM	21.7
Maddux,Greg, Atl	20.7
Ramirez,H, Atl	15.4
Franklin,Wayne, Mil	13.7
Webb,Brandon, Ari	13.6
Vazquez,Javier, Mon	13.5
Wilson,Paul, Cin	12.7

Highest % Sliders
(minimum 162 IP)

Clement,Matt, ChC	34.0
Lawrence,Brian, SD	24.6
Jennings,Jason, Col	22.9
Pavano,Carl, Fla	21.6
Ramirez,H, Atl	18.2
Dessens,Elmer, Ari	18.0
Wood,Kerry, ChC	17.7
Perez,Odalis, LA	17.6
Peavy,Jake, SD	17.2
Millwood,Kevin, Phi	16.9

2003 Active Career Batting Leaders

Batting Average		On Base Percentage		Slugging Average		Home Runs	
(minimum 1000 PA)		(minimum 1000 PA)		(minimum 1000 PA)			
Helton,Todd	.337	Bonds,Barry	.433	Helton,Todd	.616	Bonds,Barry	658
Pujols,Albert	.334	Thomas,Frank	.428	Pujols,Albert	.613	Sosa,Sammy	539
Suzuki,Ichiro	.328	Helton,Todd	.425	Bonds,Barry	.602	Palmeiro,R	528
Garciaparra,N	.323	Martinez,Edgar	.423	Ramirez,Manny	.598	McGriff,Fred	491
Guerrero,V	.323	Giles,Brian	.417	Guerrero,V	.588	Griffey Jr.,K	481
Piazza,Mike	.319	Giambi,Jason	.415	Rodriguez,Alex	.581	Gonzalez,Juan	429
Jeter,Derek	.317	Ramirez,Manny	.413	Piazza,Mike	.572	Bagwell,Jeff	419
Ramirez,Manny	.317	Pujols,Albert	.412	Thome,Jim	.568	Thomas,Frank	418
Martinez,Edgar	.315	Thome,Jim	.411	Thomas,Frank	.568	Galarraga,A	398
Walker,Larry	.314	Bagwell,Jeff	.411	Walker,Larry	.567	Thome,Jim	381

Games		At Bats		Hits		Total Bases	
Henderson,R	3081	Henderson,R	10961	Henderson,R	3055	Bonds,Barry	5253
Bonds,Barry	2569	Palmeiro,R	9553	Palmeiro,R	2780	Palmeiro,R	4983
Palmeiro,R	2567	Alomar,Roberto	8902	Alomar,Roberto	2679	Henderson,R	4588
McGriff,Fred	2433	Bonds,Barry	8725	Bonds,Barry	2595	McGriff,Fred	4436
Alomar,Roberto	2323	McGriff,Fred	8685	McGriff,Fred	2477	Sosa,Sammy	4121
Biggio,Craig	2253	Biggio,Craig	8588	Biggio,Craig	2461	Galarraga,A	4032
Galarraga,A	2250	Galarraga,A	8086	Grace,Mark	2445	Griffey Jr.,K	3977
Grace,Mark	2245	Grace,Mark	8065	Franco,Julio	2358	Alomar,Roberto	3951
Franco,Julio	2144	Franco,Julio	7869	Galarraga,A	2330	Bagwell,Jeff	3909
Finley,Steve	2127	Finley,Steve	7843	Larkin,Barry	2240	Thomas,Frank	3752

Doubles		Triples		Runs Scored		RBI	
Palmeiro,R	543	Finley,Steve	108	Henderson,R	2295	Bonds,Barry	1742
Bonds,Barry	536	Lofton,Kenny	86	Bonds,Barry	1941	Palmeiro,R	1687
Biggio,Craig	517	Alomar,Roberto	78	Palmeiro,R	1548	McGriff,Fred	1543
Grace,Mark	511	Bonds,Barry	74	Biggio,Craig	1503	Sosa,Sammy	1450
Henderson,R	510	Larkin,Barry	73	Alomar,Roberto	1490	Galarraga,A	1423
Alomar,Roberto	498	Damon,Johnny	68	Bagwell,Jeff	1402	Bagwell,Jeff	1421
Martinez,Edgar	491	Bell,Jay	67	McGriff,Fred	1342	Thomas,Frank	1390
Olerud,John	473	Henderson,R	66	Sosa,Sammy	1314	Gonzalez,Juan	1387
Bagwell,Jeff	455	Burks,Ellis	63	Larkin,Barry	1274	Griffey Jr.,K	1384
Galarraga,A	444	Durham,Ray	62	Griffey Jr.,K	1271	Sheffield,Gary	1232

Walks		Intentional Walks		Hit By Pitch		Strikeouts	
Henderson,R	2190	Bonds,Barry	484	Biggio,Craig	241	Galarraga,A	2000
Bonds,Barry	2070	Griffey Jr.,K	204	Galarraga,A	177	Sosa,Sammy	1977
Thomas,Frank	1386	McGriff,Fred	169	Kendall,Jason	158	McGriff,Fred	1863
McGriff,Fred	1296	Thomas,Frank	159	Vina,Fernando	152	Henderson,R	1694
Bagwell,Jeff	1287	Palmeiro,R	153	Walker,Larry	121	Thome,Jim	1559
Martinez,Edgar	1225	Olerud,John	151	Bagwell,Jeff	119	Vaughn,Greg	1513
Palmeiro,R	1224	Bagwell,Jeff	148	Delgado,Carlos	109	Bell,Jay	1443
Olerud,John	1198	Sosa,Sammy	144	Vaughn,Mo	108	Vaughn,Mo	1429
Sheffield,Gary	1110	Vaughn,Mo	144	Easley,Damion	103	Gant,Ron	1411
Thome,Jim	1108	Ventura,Robin	131	Sheffield,Gary	99	Bagwell,Jeff	1406

2003 Active Career Batting Leaders

Sacrifice Hits		Sacrifice Flies		Stolen Bases		Seasons Played	
Glavine,Tom	178	Sierra,Ruben	111	Henderson,R	1406	Henderson,R	25
Vizquel,Omar	165	Thomas,Frank	105	Lofton,Kenny	538	Orosco,Jesse	24
Bell,Jay	159	Palmeiro,R	102	Bonds,Barry	500	Clemens,Roger	20
Alomar,Roberto	145	Grace,Mark	99	Alomar,Roberto	474	Franco,John	19
Maddux,Greg	143	Surhoff,B.J.	99	Young,Eric	436	Franco,Julio	19
McLemore,Mark	103	Alomar,Roberto	96	Grissom,M	425	10 tied with	18
Schilling,Curt	102	Bagwell,Jeff	95	Biggio,Craig	389		
Vizcaino,Jose	99	Olerud,John	88	Larkin,Barry	377		
Bordick,Mike	97	Sheffield,Gary	88	Goodwin,Tom	364		
Reynolds,Shane	97	Bonds,Barry	84	Womack,Tony	309		

At Bats Per Home Run		Grounded Into DP		Stolen Base Success Pct		At Bats Per RBI	
(minimum 1000 AB)				(minimum 100 SBA)		(minimum 1000 AB)	
Bonds,Barry	13.3	Franco,Julio	279	Beltran,Carlos	88.2	Ramirez,Manny	4.4
Thome,Jim	13.7	McGriff,Fred	225	Reese,Pokey	85.2	Gonzalez,Juan	4.6
Sosa,Sammy	14.0	Olerud,John	215	Womack,Tony	83.1	Pujols,Albert	4.6
Ramirez,Manny	14.4	Zeile,Todd	210	Larkin,Barry	83.0	Helton,Todd	4.7
Rodriguez,Alex	14.5	Palmeiro,R	208	Glanville,Doug	81.6	Delgado,Carlos	4.7
Griffey Jr.,K	14.7	Bagwell,Jeff	207	Hunter,Brian	81.0	Thomas,Frank	4.8
Piazza,Mike	14.9	Rodriguez,Ivan	205	Alomar,Roberto	80.9	Piazza,Mike	4.8
Delgado,Carlos	15.0	Alomar,Roberto	202	Henderson,R	80.8	Thome,Jim	4.9
Gonzalez,Juan	15.0	Santiago,B	194	Boone,Aaron	80.5	Giambi,Jason	5.0
Pujols,Albert	15.5	Grace,Mark	192	Rodriguez,Alex	79.4	Berkman,Lance	5.0

Strikeouts / Walks Ratio		At Bats Per GIDP		OPS	
(minimum 1000 AB)		(minimum 1000 AB)		(minimum 1000 PA)	
Grace,Mark	.597	Maddux,Greg	180.1	Helton,Todd	1.041
Bonds,Barry	.670	Suzuki,Ichiro	144.1	Bonds,Barry	1.035
Young,Eric	.692	Furcal,Rafael	129.9	Pujols,Albert	1.025
Giles,Brian	.702	Sanchez,Alex	113.2	Ramirez,Manny	1.010
Sheffield,Gary	.717	McEwing,Joe	111.0	Thomas,Frank	.996
Henderson,R	.774	Branyan,R	110.4	Giles,Brian	.980
Palmeiro,O	.776	Glavine,Tom	107.7	Thome,Jim	.979
Thomas,Frank	.777	Damon,Johnny	100.7	Guerrero,V	.978
Olerud,John	.780	Womack,Tony	100.3	Berkman,Lance	.970
Lawton,Matt	.840	Wilkerson,Brad	94.0	Walker,Larry	.967

2003 Active Career Pitching Leaders

Earned Run Average (minimum 750 IP)	
Martinez,Pedro	2.58
Franco,John	2.74
Maddux,Greg	2.89
Johnson,Randy	3.10
Zito,Barry	3.12
Orosco,Jesse	3.16
Brown,Kevin	3.16
Clemens,Roger	3.19
Hudson,Tim	3.26
Morris,Matt	3.28

Winning Percentage (minimum 100 Decisions)	
Martinez,Pedro	.712
Hudson,Tim	.708
Johnson,Randy	.669
Clemens,Roger	.660
Pettitte,Andy	.656
Mussina,Mike	.644
Maddux,Greg	.639
Ortiz,Russ	.633
Morris,Matt	.632
Garcia,Freddy	.626

Opponent Batting Average (minimum 750 IP)	
Martinez,Pedro	.206
Wood,Kerry	.209
Johnson,Randy	.215
Zito,Barry	.219
Orosco,Jesse	.223
Clemens,Roger	.231
Nomo,Hideo	.231
Smoltz,John	.232
Cone,David	.232
Remlinger,Mike	.234

Baserunners Per 9 IP (minimum 750 IP)	
Martinez,Pedro	9.55
Schilling,Curt	10.19
Maddux,Greg	10.37
Mussina,Mike	10.55
Smoltz,John	10.68
Clemens,Roger	10.93
Zito,Barry	10.98
Johnson,Randy	11.07
Millwood,Kevin	11.18
Hudson,Tim	11.23

Games	
Orosco,Jesse	1252
Plesac,Dan	1064
Franco,John	1036
Stanton,Mike	885
Guthrie,Mark	765
Hernandez,Ro	762
Mesa,Jose	762
Reed,Steve	738
Timlin,Mike	736
Nelson,Jeff	714

Games Started	
Clemens,Roger	606
Maddux,Greg	571
Glavine,Tom	537
Johnson,Randy	444
Brown,Kevin	441
Burkett,John	423
Moyer,Jamie	420
Cone,David	419
Appier,Kevin	400
2 tied with	386

Complete Games	
Clemens,Roger	117
Maddux,Greg	103
Johnson,Randy	88
Schilling,Curt	79
Brown,Kevin	72
Cone,David	56
Mussina,Mike	53
Glavine,Tom	52
Wells,David	52
Smoltz,John	47

Shutouts	
Clemens,Roger	46
Johnson,Randy	35
Maddux,Greg	34
Cone,David	22
Glavine,Tom	22
Mussina,Mike	21
Schilling,Curt	19
Brown,Kevin	17
Martinez,Pedro	15
Smoltz,John	14

Wins	
Clemens,Roger	310
Maddux,Greg	289
Glavine,Tom	251
Johnson,Randy	230
Wells,David	200
Mussina,Mike	199
Brown,Kevin	197
Cone,David	194
Moyer,Jamie	185
Appier,Kevin	169

Losses	
Maddux,Greg	163
Clemens,Roger	160
Glavine,Tom	157
Appier,Kevin	136
Burkett,John	136
Moyer,Jamie	132
Brown,Kevin	131
Mulholland,T	131
Wells,David	128
Cone,David	126

Innings Pitched	
Clemens,Roger	4278.2
Maddux,Greg	3968.2
Glavine,Tom	3528.0
Johnson,Randy	3122.1
Brown,Kevin	3051.0
Cone,David	2898.2
Wells,David	2826.2
Moyer,Jamie	2737.2
Mussina,Mike	2668.2
Burkett,John	2648.1

Batters Faced	
Clemens,Roger	17653
Maddux,Greg	16117
Glavine,Tom	14820
Johnson,Randy	12900
Brown,Kevin	12644
Cone,David	12184
Wells,David	11811
Moyer,Jamie	11585
Burkett,John	11324
Appier,Kevin	10936

Strikeouts	
Clemens,Roger	4099
Johnson,Randy	3871
Maddux,Greg	2765
Cone,David	2668
Schilling,Curt	2542
Martinez,Pedro	2426
Smoltz,John	2313
Brown,Kevin	2264
Glavine,Tom	2136
Mussina,Mike	2126

Walks Allowed	
Clemens,Roger	1379
Johnson,Randy	1258
Glavine,Tom	1206
Cone,David	1137
Leiter,Al	968
Appier,Kevin	930
Rogers,Kenny	898
Gordon,Tom	870
Brown,Kevin	847
Maddux,Greg	838

Hit Batters	
Johnson,Randy	146
Clemens,Roger	141
Brown,Kevin	129
Maddux,Greg	109
Wakefield,Tim	109
Astacio,Pedro	108
Cone,David	106
Martinez,Pedro	99
Sele,Aaron	98
Leiter,Al	94

Wild Pitches	
Cone,David	149
Clemens,Roger	125
Smoltz,John	122
Appier,Kevin	104
Nomo,Hideo	102
Gordon,Tom	98
Brown,Kevin	96
Wells,David	94
Johnson,Randy	92
Grimsley,Jason	88

2003 Active Career Pitching Leaders

Saves		Save Pct (minimum 50 Save Ops)		Home Runs Allowed		Strikeouts Per 9 IP (minimum 750 IP)	
Franco,John	424	Gagne,Eric	96.4	Wells,David	330	Johnson,Randy	11.16
Hoffman,Trevor	352	Smoltz,John	92.4	Clemens,Roger	321	Wood,Kerry	10.62
Hernandez,Ro	320	Hoffman,Trevor	88.9	Moyer,Jamie	314	Martinez,Pedro	10.50
Beck,Rod	286	Rivera,Mariano	86.5	Johnson,Randy	283	Nomo,Hideo	9.07
Percival,Troy	283	Percival,Troy	86.3	Mussina,Mike	278	Schilling,Curt	8.85
Rivera,Mariano	283	Foulke,Keith	85.6	Mulholland,T	269	Rhodes,Arthur	8.84
Mesa,Jose	249	Wagner,Billy	85.6	Glavine,Tom	268	Remlinger,Mike	8.82
Wagner,Billy	225	Sasaki,K	85.4	Trachsel,Steve	265	Plesac,Dan	8.74
Urbina,Ugueth	206	Mesa,Jose	85.3	Schilling,Curt	263	Clemens,Roger	8.62
Benitez,A	197	Williams,Mike	85.2	2 tied with	258	Cone,David	8.28

Opp On-Base Percentage (minimum 750 IP)		Opp Slugging Average (minimum 750 IP)		Hits Per Nine Innings (minimum 750 IP)		Home Runs Per Nine IP (minimum 750 IP)	
Martinez,Pedro	.268	Martinez,Pedro	.315	Martinez,Pedro	6.72	Maddux,Greg	0.53
Schilling,Curt	.282	Zito,Barry	.333	Wood,Kerry	6.75	Brown,Kevin	0.56
Maddux,Greg	.287	Orosco,Jesse	.335	Johnson,Randy	7.02	Franco,John	0.57
Mussina,Mike	.290	Johnson,Randy	.338	Zito,Barry	7.22	Adams,Terry	0.57
Smoltz,John	.292	Franco,John	.339	Orosco,Jesse	7.33	Lowe,Derek	0.64
Clemens,Roger	.296	Maddux,Greg	.339	Nomo,Hideo	7.68	Martinez,Pedro	0.65
Zito,Barry	.297	Brown,Kevin	.343	Clemens,Roger	7.73	Morris,Matt	0.66
Johnson,Randy	.300	Clemens,Roger	.344	Smoltz,John	7.74	Clemens,Roger	0.68
Millwood,Kevin	.301	Wood,Kerry	.345	Cone,David	7.77	Glavine,Tom	0.68
Reed,Rick	.303	Smoltz,John	.351	Remlinger,Mike	7.82	Smoltz,John	0.72

Strikeouts / Walks Ratio (minimum 750 IP)		Stolen Base Pct Allowed (minimum 750 IP)		GIDP Induced		GIDP Per Nine IP (minimum 750 IP)	
Martinez,Pedro	4.38	Rueter,Kirk	35.6	Maddux,Greg	338	Estes,Shawn	1.24
Schilling,Curt	4.22	Mulholland,T	42.1	Glavine,Tom	336	Wright,Jamey	1.24
Mussina,Mike	3.56	Daal,Omar	42.2	Brown,Kevin	309	Tavarez,Julian	1.20
Reed,Rick	3.40	Rogers,Kenny	42.5	Clemens,Roger	283	Hampton,Mike	1.13
Reynolds,Shane	3.36	Weaver,Jeff	48.4	Rogers,Kenny	248	Pettitte,Andy	1.06
Maddux,Greg	3.30	Park,Chan Ho	49.5	Mulholland,T	239	Quantrill,Paul	1.03
Vazquez,Javier	3.25	Alvarez,Wilson	49.7	Hampton,Mike	231	Grimsley,Jason	1.03
Radke,Brad	3.09	Anderson,Bri	50.5	Moyer,Jamie	228	Rueter,Kirk	1.02
Johnson,Randy	3.08	Hammond,Chris	50.8	Burkett,John	224	Lowe,Derek	1.01
Wells,David	3.00	Dempster,Ryan	51.9	Pettitte,Andy	212	Adams,Terry	1.01

Complete Game % (minimum 100 GS)		Quality Start Pct (minimum 100 GS)		Walks Per 9 IP (minimum 750 IP)		Games Finished	
Schilling,Curt	0.23	Zito,Barry	71.4	Reed,Rick	1.66	Franco,John	754
Johnson,Randy	0.20	Martinez,Pedro	70.8	Radke,Brad	1.75	Hernandez,Ro	597
Clemens,Roger	0.19	Johnson,Randy	70.0	Anderson,Bri	1.87	Hoffman,Trevor	527
Maddux,Greg	0.18	Maddux,Greg	68.3	Maddux,Greg	1.90	Beck,Rod	509
Brown,Kevin	0.16	Schilling,Curt	68.0	Wells,David	1.99	Orosco,Jesse	501
Hernandez,L	0.15	Hudson,Tim	67.9	Mussina,Mike	2.01	Mesa,Jose	473
Mulder,Mark	0.15	Brown,Kevin	67.8	Mendoza,Ramiro	2.05	Plesac,Dan	422
Mulholland,T	0.15	Wood,Kerry	66.9	Reynolds,Shane	2.10	Percival,Troy	418
Martinez,Pedro	0.14	Morris,Matt	65.7	Schilling,Curt	2.10	Rivera,Mariano	405
Mussina,Mike	0.14	Buehrle,Mark	65.4	Lima,Jose	2.14	Jones,Todd	401

2003 American League Bill James Leaders

Top Game Scores

Pitcher	Date	Opp	IP	H	R	ER	BB	SO	GS
Halladay,Roy, Tor	9/6	Det	10.0	3	0	0	1	5	90
Kennedy,Joe, TB	5/2	Det	9.0	1	0	0	1	6	90
Mussina,Mike, NYY	8/17	Bal	9.0	3	0	0	0	9	90
Traber,Billy, Cle	7/8	NYY	9.0	1	0	0	0	5	90
Hudson,Tim, Oak	8/11	Bos	9.0	2	0	0	1	7	89
Hudson,Tim, Oak	7/11	Bal	9.0	3	0	0	1	9	89
Pineiro,Joel, Sea	5/30	Min	9.0	4	0	0	2	12	89
Waechter,Doug, TB	9/3	Sea	9.0	2	0	0	2	7	88
3 tied with									87

Worst Game Scores

Pitcher	Date	Opp	IP	H	R	ER	BB	SO	GS
Kennedy,Joe, TB	5/7	Min	4.0	13	10	10	2	1	-5
Buehrle,Mark, CWS	5/16	Min	3.1	10	10	9	2	0	0
Washburn,J, Ana	7/23	Tex	3.1	9	10	10	3	1	0
Daal,Omar, Bal	6/23	Tor	2.1	10	9	8	1	0	2
George,Chris, KC	6/29	StL	5.1	11	10	10	6	2	2
Reed,Rick, Min	4/21	NYY	4.1	10	11	9	3	4	2
Hernandez,Ru, KC	8/16	Min	3.1	9	9	9	3	1	4
Mulder,Mark, Oak	6/3	Fla	3.2	12	8	8	2	2	5
Martinez,Pedro, Bos	4/12	Bal	4.1	9	10	10	4	5	6
6 tied with									7

Runs Created

Delgado,Carlos, Tor	147
Rodriguez,Alex, Tex	133
Ramirez,Manny, Bos	127
Wells,Vernon, Tor	125
Giambi,Jason, NYY	120
Anderson,G, Ana	117
Beltran,Carlos, KC	117
Thomas,Frank, CWS	116
3 tied with	114

Runs Created Per 27 Outs

Delgado,Carlos, Tor	9.5
Ramirez,Manny, Bos	8.2
Beltran,Carlos, KC	8.2
Rodriguez,Alex, Tex	7.9
Giambi,Jason, NYY	7.7
Nixon,Trot, Bos	7.6
Thomas,Frank, CWS	7.5
Mueller,Bill, Bos	7.2
Posada,Jorge, NYY	7.1
Martinez,Edgar, Sea	7.1

Offensive Winning %

Delgado,Carlos, Tor	.793
Ramirez,Manny, Bos	.742
Beltran,Carlos, KC	.742
Rodriguez,Alex, Tex	.725
Giambi,Jason, NYY	.716
Nixon,Trot, Bos	.712
Thomas,Frank, CWS	.703
Mueller,Bill, Bos	.688
Posada,Jorge, NYY	.684
Martinez,Edgar, Sea	.682

Secondary Average
(minimum 502 PA)

Giambi,Jason, NYY	.520
Delgado,Carlos, Tor	.482
Thomas,Frank, CWS	.478
Rodriguez,Alex, Tex	.468
Ramirez,Manny, Bos	.436
Ortiz,David, Bos	.433
Posada,Jorge, NYY	.426
Beltran,Carlos, KC	.424
Nixon,Trot, Bos	.424
Palmeiro,R, Tex	.401

Isolated Power
(minimum 502 PA)

Ortiz,David, Bos	.304
Rodriguez,Alex, Tex	.301
Thomas,Frank, CWS	.295
Delgado,Carlos, Tor	.291
Giambi,Jason, NYY	.277
Nixon,Trot, Bos	.272
Ramirez,Manny, Bos	.262
Palmeiro,R, Tex	.248
Huff,Aubrey, TB	.244
Boone,Bret, Sea	.241

Power / Speed Number

Soriano,A, NYY	36.4
Beltran,Carlos, KC	31.8
Rodriguez,Alex, Tex	25.0
Lee,Carlos, CWS	22.8
Garciaparra,N, Bos	22.6
Boone,Bret, Sea	22.0
Suzuki,Ichiro, Sea	18.8
Berroa,Angel, KC	18.8
Cameron,Mike, Sea	17.5
Damon,Johnny, Bos	17.1

Speed Scores (2002-2003)

Crawford,Carl, TB	8.47
Beltran,Carlos, KC	8.03
Damon,Johnny, Bos	7.98
Erstad,Darin, Ana	7.52
Guzman,C, Min	7.26
Suzuki,Ichiro, Sea	7.20
Winn,Randy, Sea	7.07
Cameron,Mike, Sea	6.91
Tucker,Michael, KC	6.69
Soriano,A, NYY	6.69

Cheap Wins

Ortiz,Ramon, Ana	8
Lidle,Cory, Tor	6
Maroth,Mike, Det	6
George,Chris, KC	5
Lowe,Derek, Bos	5
Pettitte,Andy, NYY	5
Rogers,Kenny, Min	5
4 tied with	4

Tough Losses

Gonzalez,J, TB	7
Maroth,Mike, Det	7
Bernero,Adam, Det	6
Cornejo,Nate, Det	5
Franklin,Ryan, Sea	5
Garland,Jon, CWS	5
Lackey,John, Ana	5
Wakefield,Tim, Bos	5
Washburn,J, Ana	5
Zito,Barry, Oak	5

2003 National League Bill James Leaders

Top Game Scores

Pitcher	Date	Opp	IP	H	R	ER	BB	SO	GS
Johnson,Randy, Ari	9/14	Col	9.0	1	0	0	1	12	96
Schilling,Curt, Ari	5/14	Phi	9.0	2	0	0	1	14	96
Millwood,Kevin, Phi	4/27	SF	9.0	0	0	0	3	10	94
Miller,Wade, Hou	5/30	ChC	9.0	2	1	1	1	14	92
Willis,D, Fla	6/16	NYM	9.0	1	0	0	1	8	92
Prior,Mark, ChC	4/9	Mon	9.0	4	0	0	0	12	91
Schmidt,Jason, SF	4/30	ChC	9.0	3	0	0	2	12	91
Schilling,Curt, Ari	8/17	Atl	8.0	1	0	0	2	12	90
Schmidt,Jason, SF	6/19	LA	9.0	3	0	0	2	11	90
Vazquez,Javier, Mon	8/23	SD	9.0	3	0	0	1	10	90

Worst Game Scores

Pitcher	Date	Opp	IP	H	R	ER	BB	SO	GS
Chacon,Shawn, Col	6/7	KC	3.2	9	12	12	6	2	-9
Anderson,Ji, Cin	6/26	StL	5.0	15	11	11	3	2	-8
Tomko,Brett, StL	6/11	Bos	2.0	10	9	9	2	0	-2
Fogg,Josh, Pit	9/19	ChC	2.1	9	9	9	3	0	0
Haynes,Jimmy, Cin	4/17	ChC	4.2	10	10	10	6	2	0
Leiter,Al, NYM	5/15	SF	4.2	13	10	10	1	3	0
Lawrence,Brian, SD	5/8	Mon	2.2	9	10	9	3	2	1
Reynolds,Shane, Atl	4/25	Mil	3.1	10	10	10	2	3	1
Perez,Odalis, LA	5/29	Col	3.0	11	9	9	1	2	2
Rusch,Glendon, Mil	5/12	ChC	3.1	13	8	8	2	2	2

Runs Created

Pujols,Albert, StL	162
Helton,Todd, Col	160
Sheffield,Gary, Atl	135
Bonds,Barry, SF	131
Thome,Jim, Phi	127
Abreu,Bobby, Phi	120
Bagwell,Jeff, Hou	117
Sexson,Richie, Mil	117
Berkman,Lance, Hou	115
Gonzalez,Luis, Ari	114

Runs Created Per 27 Outs

Bonds,Barry, SF	13.2
Pujols,Albert, StL	10.9
Helton,Todd, Col	10.6
Sheffield,Gary, Atl	8.7
Thome,Jim, Phi	7.8
Berkman,Lance, Hou	7.7
Walker,Larry, Col	7.7
Giles,Brian, Pit-SD	7.6
Abreu,Bobby, Phi	7.4
Jones,Chipper, Atl	7.3

Offensive Winning %

Bonds,Barry, SF	.893
Pujols,Albert, StL	.850
Helton,Todd, Col	.843
Sheffield,Gary, Atl	.785
Thome,Jim, Phi	.743
Berkman,Lance, Hou	.739
Walker,Larry, Col	.737
Giles,Brian, Pit-SD	.733
Abreu,Bobby, Phi	.725
Jones,Chipper, Atl	.718

Secondary Average
(minimum 502 PA)

Bonds,Barry, SF	.805
Edmonds,Jim, StL	.510
Thome,Jim, Phi	.493
Helton,Todd, Col	.455
Pujols,Albert, StL	.448
Sheffield,Gary, Atl	.448
Sexson,Richie, Mil	.436
Giles,Brian, Pit-SD	.431
Berkman,Lance, Hou	.429
Lee,Derrek, Fla	.425

Isolated Power
(minimum 502 PA)

Bonds,Barry, SF	.408
Edmonds,Jim, StL	.342
Pujols,Albert, StL	.308
Thome,Jim, Phi	.306
Sexson,Richie, Mil	.276
Sosa,Sammy, ChC	.275
Sheffield,Gary, Atl	.274
Helton,Todd, Col	.271
Hidalgo,R, Hou	.263
Wilson,Preston, Col	.255

Power / Speed Number

Lee,Derrek, Fla	25.0
Sheffield,Gary, Atl	24.6
Abreu,Bobby, Phi	21.0
Sanders,Reggie, Pit	20.2
Wilson,Preston, Col	20.2
Cabrera,O, Mon	19.9
Young,Eric, Mil-SF	19.5
Encarnacion,J, Fla	19.0
Renteria,Edgar, StL	18.8
Furcal,Rafael, Atl	18.8

Speed Scores (2002-2003)

Roberts,Dave, LA	8.22
Pierre,Juan, Fla	7.85
Furcal,Rafael, Atl	7.75
Patterson,C, ChC	7.03
Wilkerson,Brad, Mon	6.88
Biggio,Craig, Hou	6.76
Womack,Tony, Ari-Col-ChC	6.73
Rollins,Jimmy, Phi	6.59
Castillo,Luis, Fla	6.54
Finley,Steve, Ari	6.54

Cheap Wins

Tomko,Brett, StL	7
Fogg,Josh, Pit	5
Trachsel,Steve, NYM	5
Williams,Woody, StL	5
Hampton,Mike, Atl	4
Myers,Brett, Phi	4
Ramirez,H, Atl	4
8 tied with	3

Tough Losses

Lawrence,Brian, SD	6
Nomo,Hideo, LA	6
Redding,Tim, Hou	6
Sheets,Ben, Mil	6
8 tied with	5

Additional Bill James Leaders

AL Batters Win Shares
(2003)

Delgado,Carlos, Tor	32
Rodriguez,Alex, Tex	32
Boone,Bret, Sea	30
Beltran,Carlos, KC	28
Giambi,Jason, NYY	28
Posada,Jorge, NYY	28
Ramirez,Manny, Bos	28
Soriano,A, NYY	27
Wells,Vernon, Tor	26
4 tied with	25

NL Batters Win Shares
(2003)

Pujols,Albert, StL	41
Bonds,Barry, SF	39
Sheffield,Gary, Atl	35
Helton,Todd, Col	34
Lopez,Javy, Atl	30
Thome,Jim, Phi	30
Abreu,Bobby, Phi	28
Giles,Marcus, Atl	28
Jones,Chipper, Atl	26
Sexson,Richie, Mil	26

AL Pitchers Win Shares
(2003)

Halladay,Roy, Tor	23
Hudson,Tim, Oak	23
Loaiza,Esteban, CWS	23
Foulke,Keith, Oak	21
Martinez,Pedro, Bos	20
Mussina,Mike, NYY	19
Moyer,Jamie, Sea	18
Rivera,Mariano, NYY	18
Zito,Barry, Oak	18
3 tied with	17

NL Pitchers Win Shares
(2003)

Gagne,Eric, LA	25
Hernandez,L, Mon	22
Prior,Mark, ChC	22
Schmidt,Jason, SF	22
Vazquez,Javier, Mon	21
Brown,Kevin, LA	20
Wagner,Billy, Hou	19
Wood,Kerry, ChC	18
Zambrano,C, ChC	18
2 tied with	17

Batters Win Shares
(Career)

Bonds,Barry	611
Henderson,R	535
Biggio,Craig	377
Alomar,Roberto	372
Bagwell,Jeff	363
Palmeiro,R	363
Thomas,Frank	347
Sheffield,Gary	337
Larkin,Barry	336
McGriff,Fred	326

Pitchers Win Shares
(Career)

Clemens,Roger	378
Maddux,Greg	347
Glavine,Tom	261
Johnson,Randy	261
Brown,Kevin	232
Smoltz,John	222
Mussina,Mike	215
Martinez,Pedro	208
Cone,David	205
Schilling,Curt	202

2003 AL Component ERA
(minimum 162 IP)

Martinez,Pedro, Bos	2.22
Hudson,Tim, Oak	2.47
Mussina,Mike, NYY	2.75
Loaiza,Esteban, CWS	2.79
Halladay,Roy, Tor	2.86
Zito,Barry, Oak	2.91
Mulder,Mark, Oak	3.17
Moyer,Jamie, Sea	3.37
Pineiro,Joel, Sea	3.43
Clemens,Roger, NYY	3.44

2003 NL Component ERA
(minimum 162 IP)

Schmidt,Jason, SF	1.93
Schilling,Curt, Ari	2.59
Brown,Kevin, LA	2.68
Prior,Mark, ChC	2.69
Webb,Brandon, Ari	2.80
Vazquez,Javier, Mon	2.90
Redman,Mark, Fla	3.17
Zambrano,Carlos, ChC	3.28
Nomo,Hideo, LA	3.30
Wood,Kerry, ChC	3.31

Win Shares

The following chart summarizes each major league player's Win Shares over the course of his major league career.

A Win Share is one-third of a team's win, credited to an individual player. The Win Shares credited to the players on a team always total up to exactly three times the team's win total. If the team wins 100 games, the players on their team will be credited with 300 Win Shares—300 thirds of a win. If the team wins 80 games, the players on the team will be credited with 240 Win Shares, always and without exception. Nothing—not even a rounding error—is allowed to disrupt this relationship.

In attributing shares of the team's success to individual players, we follow two guiding principles.

     1) A player's value should be exactly the same whether he plays for a good team or a bad team. No player deserves to—or does—rate better than another based on the accomplishments of his teammates.
     2) All kinds of accomplishments—hitting, fielding, pitching and base running—should be given credit in proportion to their impact on the team's won-lost record.

As to standards, generally speaking, 40 Win Shares is a historic season. Barry Bonds has cracked the 40-Win Share standard so often in recent years that the feat no longer seems quite so remarkable, but generally, there have been only a handful of players in each decade who earned 40 Win Shares in a season.

     30 Win Shares is, generally, the type of season which makes a player an MVP candidate.
     20 Win Shares can be loosely described as an All-Star type season, and as a season roughly equivalent in value to a starting pitcher winning 20 games.
     15 Win Shares is a run-of-the-mill total for a regular player, a high total for a bench player.
     10 Win Shares is a low total for an everyday player.
     5 Win Shares would be a bench player. Even a late-season callup, if he plays very well, can occasionally earn 5 win Shares for the season.

In a career, historically, 400 Win Shares means absolute enshrinement in the Hall of Fame. 300 Win Shares makes a player more likely than not to be a Hall of Famer. However, while those standards describe the PAST, they are not likely to describe the future as accurately. Players with 300 to 350 Win Shares in the past have generally gone into the Hall of Fame. In the future, they more often will not.

Bill James
Lawrence, Kansas
October 15, 2003

	WIN SHARES BY YEAR											
Player	<94	94	95	96	97	98	99	00	01	02	03	Career
Abad,Andy											0	0
Abbott,Paul	3				2	7	11	9	0	2		34
Abernathy,B									10	7	0	17
Abreu,Bobby				0	6	26	26	23	26	29	28	164
Acevedo,Jose									2	0	2	4
Acevedo,Juan			1		3	13	3	6	4	12	1	43
Adams,Terry			0	9	5	5	9	6	8	5	7	54
Adkins,Jon											0	0
Affeldt,Jeremy										5	12	17
Ainsworth,Kurt									0	2	3	5
Alfonseca,A				0	3	11	10	9	7	1		41
Alfonzo,E			8	6	28	22	29	36	15	25	17	186
Allen,Chad						7	1	2	0		0	10
Allen,Luke										0	0	0
Almanza,A					2	3	2	3	0			10
Almonte,Edwin											0	0
Almonte,Erick							1				1	2
Almonte,Hector											0	0
Alomar,Roberto	153	13	16	31	21	19	35	20	37	15	12	372
Alomar Jr.,S	33	12	7	8	18	6	4	8	4	5	4	109
Alou,Moises	36	22	11	20	23	29		17	21	9	20	208
Alvarez,Juan							0	0		2	1	3
Alvarez,Victor										0	0	0
Alvarez,Wilson	22	12	8	13	15	7	10			2	10	99
Amezaga,A										2	1	3
Anderson,Bri	1	6	3	3	2	9	7	14	2	5	12	64
Anderson,G		0	11	6	16	18	16	15	17	24	25	148
Anderson,Ja											1	1
Anderson,Ji					3	4	7	3	0			17
Anderson,Mar					2	8	2	16	10	12		50
Anderson,Mat					5	1	4	8	0		1	19
Appier,Kevin	74	13	16	19	18	0	9	11	15	11	3	189
Armas Jr.,Tony							0	5	12	7	4	28
Arroyo,Bronson								0	3	2	2	7
Asencio,Miguel										6	3	9
Ashby,Andy	1	9	14	11	6	15	13	8	1	7	0	85
Astacio,Pedro	12	6	5	13	10	6	19	11	7	5	0	94
Atkins,Garrett											0	0
Aurilia,Rich			2	5	5	13	18	20	33	14	13	123
Ausmus,Brad	3	5	13	8	13	14	17	16	10	9	12	120
Austin,Jeff									1	1	0	2
Avery,Steve	48	9	8	7	1	5	0				1	79
Ayala,Luis											11	11
Aybar,Manny				3	1	4	5	1	1	0		15
Backe,Brandon										0	1	1
Bacsik,Mike								0	2	0		2
Baerga,Carlos	82	13	23	6	11	10	2			2	7	156
Baez,Danys									6	11	9	26
Bagwell,Jeff	74	30	20	41	32	29	37	25	30	23	22	363
Bako,Paul						5	5	5	3	3	5	26
Baldelli,Rocco											14	14
Baldwin,James			0	10	6	6	9	11	8	3	0	53
Bale,John						0	0	2			2	4
Balfour,Grant								0			2	2
Banks,Brian				1	0	1	3			1	3	9
Barajas,Rod							1	0	1	3	5	10
Bard,Josh										1	7	8
Barnes,Larry							0			1		1
Barrett,M					1	11	1	2	12	7	34
Batista,Miguel	0			0	0	6	6	0	11	9	14	46
Batista,Tony				9	2	10	21	18	12	16	11	99
Bauer,Rick									0	5	2	7
Bautista,Danny	1	1	1	1	2	2	3	10	6	6	5	38
Bay,Jay											5	5
Beck,Rod	35	7	7	10	12	13	3	5	7		7	106
Beckett,Josh									3	5	11	19
Beimel,Joe									4	3	2	9
Bell,David			2	1	2	10	16	8	14	19	5	77
Bell,Jay	101	19	13	15	21	20	23	19	12	1	1	245
Bell,Rob							5	1	2	3	11
Bellhorn,Mark					5	0		0	1	19	4	29
Belliard,R					0	0	17	13	1	11	42
Beltran,Carlos						2	18	5	27	22	28	102
Beltre,Adrian						4	15	22	12	16	15	84
Benard,Marvin			2	8	2	10	20	14	11	3	1	71
Benes,Alan			0	5	12		0	1	0	1	1	20
Benitez,A		1	1	3	11	10	19	17	14	12	10	98
Bennett,Gary			0	0		1	2	3	1	4	6	17

	WIN SHARES BY YEAR											
Player	<94	94	95	96	97	98	99	00	01	02	03	Career
Benoit,Joaquin									0	3	5	8
Benson,Kris					12	14			5	2	33
Bere,Jason	11	10	0	0	2	2	1	7	9	0	0	42
Berg,Dave			9	6	5	3	8	1		32
Berger,Brandon								1	2	1	4
Berkman,Lance							1	10	32	30	25	98
Bernero,Adam							2	0	1	1	4
Berroa,Angel								1	1	16	18
Betancourt,R									4		4
Biddle,Rocky							0	4	4	8	16
Bierbrodt,Nick								3		0	3
Bigbie,Larry								2	0	9	11
Biggio,Craig	115	26	29	32	38	35	31	11	25	15	20	377
Blake,Casey							1	0	1	0	11	13
Blalock,Hank									1	17	18
Blanco,Henry			0		6	9	6	4	2	27
Bland,Nate										0	0
Bloomquist,W									3	3	6
Blum,Geoff					3	10	8	15	5	41
Bocachica,H					0	3	1	0		4
Boehringer,B		0	2	4	4	7	0	4	9	2	32
Bonderman,J										2	2
Bonds,Barry	248	25	36	39	36	34	19	32	54	49	39	611
Bong,Jung									0	3	3
Boone,Aaron				0	6	15	10	13	19	23	86
Boone,Bret	9	15	15	10	8	18	17	15	32	25	30	194
Borbon,Pedro	0		4	5		4	0	4	1	0	18
Borchard,Joe									1	0	1
Borders,Pat	45	4	2	4	3	1	1		0	0	1	61
Bordick,Mike	42	8	10	10	7	13	17	16	6	12	11	152
Borland,Toby			3	5	6	0	0		0	1	1	16
Borowski,Joe			1	1	2	0		0	8	14	26
Bottalico,R		0	11	13	10	0	0	8	6	0	0	48
Bowen,Rob										0	0
Bowie,Micah						0			2	0	2
Bowles,Brian								1	1	1	3
Boyd,Jason							0	0		0	3	3
Bradford,Chad						3	0	2	3	9	9	26
Bradley,Milton								3	3	6	18	30
Bragg,Darren		0	2	10	11	11	7	2	2	6	1	52
Branyan,R					0	1	5	10	8	6	30
Brazelton,D									1	0	1
Brohawn,Troy									2	0	1	3
Broussard,Ben									0	9	9
Brower,Jim					2	1	8	5	7	23
Brown,Dee						0	0	4	0	2	6
Brown,Kevin	66	7	13	26	23	26	19	20	11	1	20	232
Bruntlett,Eric										1	1
Buchanan,Brian							0	5	5	5	15
Budzinski,Mark										0	0
Buehrle,Mark							4	18	17	13	52
Bukvich,Ryan									1	0	1
Bump,Nate										2	2
Burba,Dave	7	3	7	10	7	15	15	13	3	6	3	89
Burke,Jamie							0		1	1
Burkett,John	38	8	8	12	10	7	6	7	17	8	8	129
Burkhart,M								2	0	0	2
Burks,Ellis	105	5	8	28	15	14	24	21	14	21	5	260
Burnett,A.J.							3	5	9	14	0	31
Burnitz,Jeromy	8	2	1	6	20	19	19	16	18	7	12	128
Burrell,Pat								12	17	25	9	63
Burroughs,Sean										2	16	18
Butler,Brent								1	6	0		7
Bynum,Mike									0	0	0
Byrd,Marlon									0	16	16
Byrnes,Eric							0	1	2	16	19
Cabrera,Jol						0	0	2	6	1	9	18
Cabrera,Miguel										12	12
Cabrera,O					0	6	8	9	26	14	20	83
Cairo,Miguel			0	0	10	10	10	4	3	3	40
Calero,Kiko										3	3
Callaway,M				0		0	2	0		2
Calloway,Ron										5	5
Cameron,Mike		0	0	17	6	19	19	29	19	21	130
Capuano,Chris									1	1
Carrara,G		0	0	0			0	8	7	0	15
Carrasco,D.J.									6		6
Carrasco,H	7	5	5	4	5	3	6	4		2	41

WIN SHARES BY YEAR

Player	<94	94	95	96	97	98	99	00	01	02	03	Career
Carroll,Jamey										3	3	6
Carter,Lance							0			3	10	13
Casey,Sean				0	10	23	17	18		5	17	90
Cash,Kevin										0	0	0
Castilla,Vinny	4	5	13	23	21	21	11	3	13	2	14	130
Castillo,A			0	1	1	3	7	4	3	0	1	20
Castillo,Luis			3	3	3	14	18	14	19	22		96
Castro,Juan			0	2	1	3	0	3	1	2	8	20
Castro,Ramon							1	3	0	4	2	10
Catalanotto,F				1	4	5	8	17	7	15		57
Cedeno,Roger		1	7	9	3	17	5	14	10	8		74
Cepicky,Matt										1	0	1
Cerda,Jaime										2	0	2
Chacon,Shawn									7	4	9	20
Chamblee,Jim											0	0
Chavez,Endy									0	3	10	13
Chavez,Eric					2	9	16	26	25	25		103
Chavez,Raul			0	0	0		0			0	1	1
Chen,Bruce					1	1	11	4	2	0		19
Chen,Chin-Feng										0	0	0
Choate,Randy								1	4	0	0	5
Choi,Hee Seop										0	6	6
Christenson,R					9	3	3	0	0	1		16
Christiansen,J			4	0	4	9	4	4	4	0	1	30
Cintron,Alex								0	1	14		15
Cirillo,Jeff		2	10	20	24	26	22	19	14	9	3	149
Clark,Brady							0	4	1	7		12
Clark,Howie										0	3	3
Clark,Jermaine							0			1		1
Clark,Tony			2	8	24	15	19	6	16	1	4	95
Claussen,B											1	1
Clayton,Royce	20	9	12	12	13	12	15	8	10	8	7	126
Clemens,Roger	204	16	10	20	32	25	10	16	19	11	15	378
Clement,Matt						1	6	5	4	11	10	37
Colbrunn,Greg	5	5	14	10	4	4	5	12	3	7	1	70
Collier,Lou					1	8	2	0	4	0		15
Colome,Jesus								4	0	4		8
Colon,Bartolo					2	16	16	15	14	22	17	102
Colyer,Steve										2		2
Condrey,Clay										2	0	2
Cone,David	102	20	19	8	16	17	15	0	8		0	205
Conine,Jeff	18	15	20	17	9	6	10	9	24	10	16	154
Conti,Jason								3	0	4	1	8
Contreras,Jose											7	7
Cook,Aaron										2	3	5
Coomer,Ron			2	5	14	6	8	9	6	1	0	51
Cora,Alex						1	0	6	6	13	13	39
Corcoran,Roy											1	1
Cordero,Chad											2	2
Cordero,F							2	3	0	8	12	25
Cordero,Wil	17	17	12	5	11	8	5	10	1	6	11	103
Cordova,Marty			17	18	6	8	9	1	11	9	2	81
Corey,Mark								0	0	1		1
Cormier,Rheal	15	2	8	8	0		5	4	4	1	14	61
Cornejo,Nate									0	1	8	9
Correia,Kevin											3	3
Cortes,David							0				0	0
Cota,Humberto									0	0	0	0
Cotts,Neal											0	0
Counsell,Craig			0		8	13	2	5	14	15	5	62
Crawford,Carl										6	13	19
Crede,Joe							0	1	6	13		20
Creek,Doug				1	0	0		0	4	3	2	11
Cressend,Jack								1	5	0	4	10
Crisp,Coco										3	7	10
Cromer,Tripp	0	0	4		5	0	1	0			0	10
Crosby,Bobby											0	0
Crosby,Bubba											0	0
Crudale,Mike										6	2	8
Cruz,Deivi					7	7	13	15	8	7	10	67
Cruz,Enrique											0	0
Cruz,Jose					11	12	11	15	16	14	17	96
Cruz,Juan									4	3	0	7
Cruz,Nelson				0		2	4	6	3	0		15
Cuddyer,Mike									0	3	1	4
Cunnane,Will				2	0	1	2	1	1	3		10
Cust,Jack									0	0	4	4
Daal,Omar	1	1	0	6	2	12	16	5	11	8	0	62

WIN SHARES BY YEAR

Player	<94	94	95	96	97	98	99	00	01	02	03	Career
D'Amico,Jeff				4	6		0	15	0	3	6	34
Damon,Johnny			6	9	11	17	18	26	17	21	18	143
Darensbourg,V						3	0	5	3	0	0	11
Daubach,Brian						0	14	10	13	14	4	55
DaVanon,Jeff							0		1	1	12	14
Davis,Ben						0	3	3	15	10	7	38
Davis,Doug							0	5	8	3	7	23
Davis,J.J.										0	0	0
Davis,Jason										2	5	7
Dawkins,Gookie								0	1	0	0	1
Dawley,Joe										0	0	0
Day,Zach										3	8	11
de los Santos,V					2	0	3	0	4	4		13
Deago,Roger											0	0
DeHart,Rick											0	0
DeJean,Mike					7	9	0	4	8	8	6	42
DeJesus,David											0	0
Delgado,Carlos	0	3	0	12	18	24	21	36	23	26	32	195
Delgado,Wilson				1	0	0	1	3	0	0	1	6
Dellucci,David				1	10	5	1	7	4	4		32
Dempster,Ryan						0	6	17	7	4	0	34
DePastino,Joe											0	0
DePaula,Jorge											2	2
DeRosa,Mark						0	0	1	6	7	5	19
Dessens,Elmer			1	1	1		10	10	15	7		45
Diaz,Einar			0	0	1	8	6	15	4	5		39
Diaz,Matt										0	0	0
Dickey,R.A.									0		6	6
DiFelice,Mike				0	6	5	8	2	1	4	6	32
Dominguez,Juan											0	0
Donnelly,B										6	12	18
Dotel,Octavio							3	7	12	17	12	51
Downs,Scott										0	0	0
Dreifort,D		0		0	7	9	8	9	1		3	37
Drese,Ryan										3	2	5
Drew,J.D.						3	10	18	22	15	13	81
Drew,Tim							0	0	2	0		2
Driskill,T										5	1	6
DuBose,Eric										1	5	6
Duckworth,B									5	2	2	9
Duncan,Jeff											3	3
Dunn,Adam									10	21	13	44
Durazo,Erubiel							9	5	7	10	17	48
Durbin,Chad							0	0	8	0	0	8
Durham,Ray			8	17	13	25	20	19	21	20	16	159
Durocher,J										4	0	4
Durrington,T								1	0		0	1
Dye,Jermaine				5	2	2	16	21	18	13	2	79
Easley,Damion	11	3	4	3	18	23	13	14	15	5	0	109
Eaton,Adam								9	5	0	7	21
Eckenstahler,E									0	1		1
Eckstein,David									12	20	11	43
Edmonds,Jim	1	7	21	18	19	24	5	29	30	29	22	205
Eischen,Joey		0	1	3	0				1	9	5	19
Elarton,Scott						5	10	11	0		0	26
Elder,Dave										2	0	2
Eldred,Cal	28	11	2	5	9	3	0	7	0		6	71
Ellis,Mark										14	18	32
Ellis,Robert			1						2	0	0	3
Ellison,Jason											0	0
Embree,Alan	0		1	0	6	3	6	3	2	7	5	33
Encarnacion,J				1	4	8	14	5	14	15		61
Ensberg,Morgan								0		2	15	17
Erstad,Darin				3	19	21	9	30	14	17	3	116
Escalona,Felix										1	1	2
Escobar,Alex									1		1	2
Escobar,Kelvim					6	7	7	8	11	9	12	60
Estalella,B				1	2	1	0	15	3	4	4	30
Estes,Shawn			0	4	16	3	6	10	7	4	0	50
Estrada,Johnny									5	0	0	5
Estrella,Leo								0			6	6
Etherton,Seth								3			0	3
Everett,Adam									0	1	11	12
Everett,Carl	0	0	8	2	13	16	25	24	11	9	21	129
Eyre,Scott					2	2	0	0	2	4	5	15
Farnsworth,K						5	0	9	0	0	7	21
Fassero,Jeff	29	10	8	18	17	14	1	8	10	2	0	117
Febles,Carlos						2	10	7	5	7	1	32

WIN SHARES BY YEAR

Player	<94	94	95	96	97	98	99	00	01	02	03	Career
Feliciano,P										0	3	3
Feliz,Pedro								0	0	2	8	10
Fernandez,J									0	2	2	4
Ferrari,A											0	0
Fetters,Mike	16	8	5	10	7	4	1	7	2	4	1	65
Fick,Robert						2	2	4	10	12	14	44
Field,Nate										0	2	2
Figgins,Chone										0	8	8
Figueroa,N								0	6	1	3	10
Fikac,Jeremy									3	0	1	4
Finley,Steve	73	9	19	27	19	15	24	21	15	23	18	263
Fiore,Tony									0	9	1	10
Flaherty,John	0	1	7	10	11	5	12	8	4	7	3	68
Floyd,Cliff	1	9	1	6	5	18	9	19	26	22	15	131
Fogg,Josh									2	10	4	16
Foppert,Jesse											2	2
Ford,Lew											4	4
Ford,Matt											2	2
Fordyce,Brook			0	1	1	2	12	11	2	1	5	35
Fossum,Casey									2	6	3	11
Foster,John										0	1	1
Foulke,Keith					4	5	16	16	17	10	21	89
Fox,Andy				2	1	15	7	4	1	14	1	45
Fox,Chad				2	4	0			9	0	5	20
Franco,John	113	8	10	10	12	8	6	7	5			182
Franco,Julio	204	15		13	9			0	3	6	6	256
Franco,Matt			0	0	4	3	3	3		9	1	23
Franklin,Ryan							1		5	6	13	25
Franklin,Wayne								1	0	2	4	7
Freel,Ryan										0	3	3
Fuentes,Brian									1	2	10	13
Fullmer,Brad					2	15	5	15	9	13	8	67
Fultz,Aaron								3	3	1	3	10
Furcal,Rafael								17	9	20	25	71
Gagne,Eric							3	2	4	19	25	53
Galarraga,A	111	13	14	25	20	27		16	11	5	9	251
Gallo,Mike											3	3
Gant,Ron	106		21	18	11	11	16	7	4	12	0	206
Garcia,Danny											0	0
Garcia,Freddy							16	8	18	11	8	61
Garcia,Jesse							0	0	0	1	1	2
Garcia,Karim			0	0	1	4	4	0	3	7	5	24
Garcia,R										0	0	0
Garcia,Rosman											1	1
Garciaparra,N				2	26	27	32	29	3	27	25	171
Garland,Jon								1	8	9	10	28
Gaudin,Chad											3	3
Geary,Geoff											0	0
George,Chris									2	1	2	5
German,F										2	0	2
Gerut,Jody											14	14
Giambi,Jason			5	15	18	23	30	38	38	34	28	229
Giambi,Jeremy						0	4	6	12	14	1	37
Gibbons,Jay									4	12	18	34
Gil,Benji	1		8	0	4			4	6	5	2	30
Gil,Geronimo									2	6	3	11
Giles,Brian			1	6	13	14	27	27	29	32	25	174
Giles,Marcus									9	5	28	42
Gilfillan,J											0	0
Ginter,Keith								0	0	2	9	11
Ginter,Matt								0	2	2	0	4
Gipson,Charles						1	1	1	1	1	0	5
Girardi,Joe	29	8	10	11	9	7	3	9	8	3	0	97
Glanville,Doug				2	9	17	23	10	11	5	2	79
Glaus,Troy						3	16	25	21	22	9	96
Glavine,Tom	87	12	20	22	21	23	14	21	16	18	7	261
Glover,Gary								0	4	5	3	12
Gobble,Jimmy											3	3
Gomez,Chris	2	8	6	11	7	15	6	1	8	11	2	77
Gonzalez,Alex						1	11	3	10	3	20	48
Gonzalez,A S		1	7	14	10	9	6	11	16	13	16	103
Gonzalez,Edgar											1	1
Gonzalez,J				9	2						8	19
Gonzalez,Juan	72	11	11	21	19	25	24	9	23	6	10	231
Gonzalez,Luis	46	13	15	17	12	12	26	27	37	26	24	255
Gonzalez,Mike											0	0
Gonzalez,Raul								0	0	2	4	6
Gonzalez,Wiki							1	6	7	4	1	19

WIN SHARES BY YEAR

Player	<94	94	95	96	97	98	99	00	01	02	03	Career
Good,Andy										2		2
Goodwin,Tom	1	0	10	9	9	13	5	14	5	5	3	74
Gordon,Tom	49	12	11	10	15	17	2		8	3	11	138
Grabowski,J										1	0	1
Grace,Mark	128	12	23	20	20	27	21	18	16	8	1	294
Graffanino,T				1	6	4	7	6	3	7	9	43
Graves,Danny				2	0	8	16	18	11	17	3	75
Green,Shawn	0	0	10	8	14	21	24	22	34	30	20	183
Greene,Khalil											1	1
Greene,Todd			1	4	1	3	0	0	1	1		11
Gregg,Kevin										2		2
Grieve,Ben					4	22	16	17	17	12	2	90
Griffey Jr.,K	122	20	9	28	36	29	31	24	14	5	6	324
Griffiths,J											0	0
Grimsley,Jason	5	5	0	1			6	5	8	7	4	41
Grissom,M	86	17	18	24	14	11	13	8	6	15	22	234
Groom,Buddy	0	3	0	7	3	4	3	6	8	10	1	45
Grudzielanek,M			3	17	14	13	13	15	17	13	18	123
Gryboski,Kevin										4	3	7
Guardado,Eddie	1	0	4	6	3	5	4	8	12	14	15	72
Guerrero,V				0	10	29	28	29	23	29	18	166
Guiel,Aaron										4	12	16
Guillen,Carlos						2	0	8	14	12	12	48
Guillen,Jose					7	11	3	6	2	2	20	51
Guthrie,Mark	25	2	4	8	1	3	3	4	3	6	4	63
Gutierrez,R	8	3	3	4	4	12	6	15	16	8	0	79
Guzman,C							5	12	18	13	13	61
Guzman,Edwards									0	1	1	2
Hackman,Luther							0	0	2	3	1	6
Hafner,Travis										1	7	8
Hairston Jr.,J						0	5	4	10	12	7	38
Halama,John						0	13	6	4	6	4	33
Hall,Bill										1	4	5
Hall,Josh											0	0
Hall,Toby								0	6	7	10	23
Halladay,Roy						2	10	0	9	21	23	65
Halter,Shane					1	3	0	3	16	8	2	33
Hamilton,Joey		8	12	11	6	8	2	3	2	3	0	55
Hammock,Robby											6	6
Hammond,Chris	19	6	10	0	2	0				13	7	57
Hammonds,J	4	6	4	3	14	9	8	14	5	8	4	79
Hampton,Mike	0	3	8	11	11	15	26	19	11	5	11	120
Hansen,Dave	13	1	5	0	6		3	6	4	4	3	45
Harang,Aaron										4	2	6
Harden,Rich											4	4
Haren,Danny											1	1
Harper,Travis								2	0	3	6	11
Harris,Lenny	47	3	2	10	3	3	4	5	0	4	1	82
Harris,Willie									0	2	2	4
Hart,Bo											7	7
Harvey,Ken										0	7	7
Harville,Chad									0	1	0	1
Hasegawa,S					7	11	5	11	5	7	13	59
Haselman,Bill	2	1	4	4	1	5	3	7	5	1	0	33
Hatteberg,S			0	0	6	11	4	5	5	16	14	61
Hawkins,LaTroy			0	0	2	6	3	12	3	11	13	50
Haynes,Jimmy			3	0	4	7	1	6	6	12	0	39
Hebson,Bryan											0	0
Heilman,Aaron										0	0	0
Helling,Rick		2	0	3	6	15	12	15	7	8	6	74
Helms,Wes						1		0	5	1	12	19
Helton,Todd					2	17	19	29	26	27	34	154
Henderson,R	413	11	19	16	15	20	16	8	12	4	1	535
Hendrickson,M										4	4	8
Henson,Drew										0	0	0
Hentgen,Pat	19	15	7	24	19	8	10	10	4	0	10	126
Heredia,Felix				1	3	3	3	4	0	3	9	26
Herges,Matt							1	10	9	4	7	31
Hermansen,Chad							0	0	0	3	0	3
Hermanson,D			0	0	10	13	12	9	8	0	4	56
Hernandez,Jose	1	1	6	4	16	16	9	13	19	6	6	97
Hernandez,L				1	8	6	9	14	5	7	22	72
Hernandez,M											0	0
Hernandez,Ra							6	10	13	12	19	60
Hernandez,Ro	29	5	6	17	15	10	14	12	9	7	3	127
Hernandez,Ru										5	6	11
Herrera,Alex										1	0	1
Hessman,Mike											1	1

Player	<94	94	95	96	97	98	99	00	01	02	03	Career
Hidalgo,R					2	6	9	21	17	7	20	82
Higginson,B			8	21	25	16	9	26	18	15	6	144
Hill,Bobby										5	0	5
Hill,Jeremy										1	0	1
Hillenbrand,S									5	17	11	33
Hinch,A.J.						5	3	0	2	4	1	15
Hinske,Eric										22	12	34
Hitchcock,S	1	4	9	8	3	9	10	1	2	1	3	51
Hocking,Denny	0	1	0	1	6	2	8	11	5	5	4	43
Hodges,Trey										1	2	3
Hollandsworth,T			2	19	7	6	7	8	4	12	5	70
Holmes,Darren	20	0	12	7	5	4	4	0		7	2	61
Houston,Tyler				6	4	7	3	5	8	7	2	42
Howard,Ben										0	1	1
Howry,Bob					7	10	9	5	3	0		34
Hubbard,T		1	1	2	0	6	4	1	0	0	1	16
Huckaby,Ken									0	2	0	2
Hudson,Orlando										7	18	25
Hudson,Tim							12	15	17	23	23	90
Huff,Aubrey								3	5	12	21	41
Hummel,Tim											2	2
Hundley,Todd	15	8	13	24	22	1	6	17	4	6	2	118
Hunter,Brian		0	10	7	17	9	4	4	5	6	1	63
Hunter,Torii					0	0	5	8	19	21	15	68
Hyzdu,Adam								1	1	6	1	9
Ibanez,Raul					0	1	4	1	9	13	15	43
Infante,Omar										3	3	6
Inge,Brandon									3	5	5	13
Ishii,Kazuhisa										6	6	12
Isringhausen,J			8	6	0		4	10	14	13	7	62
Izturis,Cesar									4	4	11	19
Jackson,Damian				1	1	2	11	15	11	7	2	50
Jarvis,Kevin			0	0	0	1	0	4	7	1	0	13
Jenkins,Geoff						1	18	20	11	5	20	75
Jennings,Jason									3	14	9	26
Jensen,Ryan									2	5	0	7
Jeter,Derek			1	18	19	27	35	23	28	24	18	193
Jimenez,D							1		8	11	17	37
Jimenez,Jose						2	2	15	8	13	6	46
Johnson,Adam									0			0
Johnson,C		1	12	10	21	15	12	20	17	6	10	124
Johnson,Gary											0	0
Johnson,Jason					0	2	4	0	9	5	10	30
Johnson, Jon						0	0	1	0	1	0	2
Johnson,Mark L						0	5	5	5	3	1	19
Johnson,Nick									0	11	14	25
Johnson,Randy	64	15	22	5	23	19	26	26	26	29	6	261
Johnson,Reed											11	11
Johnson,R											0	0
Jones,Andruw				3	13	26	28	30	22	28	23	173
Jones,Chipper	0		20	26	23	29	32	27	29	31	26	243
Jones,Greg											1	1
Jones,Jacque							9	11	10	25	14	69
Jones,Jason											1	1
Jones,Todd	3	9	9	5	13	7	10	10	5	6	1	78
Jordan,Brian	12	1	18	27	1	21	22	14	19	19	7	161
Jose,Felix	64	11	0						0	0	1	76
Journell,Jimmy											0	0
Julio,Jorge									1	13	6	20
Junge,Eric										2	1	3
Kapler,Gabe						0	8	10	13	8	4	43
Karros,Eric	23	7	25	20	18	22	20	14	8	18	8	183
Kata,Matt											8	8
Kearns,Austin										16	12	28
Keisler,Randy									0	0		0
Kelton,Dave											0	0
Kendall,Jason				12	22	26	13	24	9	13	20	139
Kennedy,Adam							2	11	8	17	14	52
Kennedy,Joe									6	9	0	15
Kent,Jeff	23	18	11	11	22	25	23	37	27	29	20	246
Kershner,Jason										1	5	6
Kida,Masao							2	0			1	3
Kielty,Bobby									1	15	12	28
Kieschnick,B			1	2					0	1	4	8
Kim,Byung-Hyun						2	8	16	20	14		60
Kim,Sun-Woo									1	3	0	4
King,Ray							0	4	5	5	5	19
Kingsale,Gene				0		0	1	1	1	8	1	12

Player	<94	94	95	96	97	98	99	00	01	02	03	Career
Kinkade,Mike						0	0	1	2	3	2	8
Kinney,Matt								2		2	4	8
Klassen,Danny						0	0	2		0	1	3
Klesko,Ryan	2	8	17	20	16	13	18	23	29	31	13	190
Kline,Steve					1	6	7	9	12	6	5	46
Knott,Eric										0	0	0
Knotts,Gary									0	2	1	3
Koch,Billy							10	16	8	19	2	55
Kolb,Danny							2	0	1	2	9	14
Konerko,Paul					0	1	14	15	17	17	4	68
Koplove,Mike									0	7	5	12
Koskie,Corey						0	13	17	24	19	21	94
Kotsay,Mark					1	13	6	12	16	22	14	84
Kreuter,Chad	25	3	2	3	5	7	3	9	8	4	0	69
Lackey,John										7	8	15
LaForest,Pete											0	0
Laird,Gerald											1	1
Laker,Tim	1		3		0	1	0		1		4	10
Lamb,Mike								6	8	7	0	21
Lane,Jason										3	1	4
Langerhans,R										0	0	0
Larkin,Barry	161	19	30	31	12	25	24	13	5	9	7	336
Larson,Brandon									0	2	1	3
LaRue,Jason							2	3	9	11	10	35
Latham,Chris					0	0	0	3			0	3
Lawrence,Brian									6	8	8	22
Lawton,Matt			4	7	14	21	8	20	20	9	10	113
LeCroy,Matt								2	3	4	12	21
Ledee,Ricky						2	9	10	4	5	7	37
Ledezma,Wil											2	2
Lee,Carlos							10	14	15	17	20	76
Lee,Cliff									1	3		4
Lee,Derrek					2	10	1	16	16	23	25	93
Lee,Travis						13	8	6	15	12	13	67
Leiter,Al	12	5	14	19	7	21	11	17	14	11	9	140
Leon,Jose									1	0		1
Leskanic,C	2	1	14	5	4	7	8	12	7		9	69
Levine,Al				0	0	3	7	7	10	4	7	38
Levrault,Allen								0	1		2	3
Lewis,Colby										0	1	1
Lidge,Brad										1	8	9
Lidle,Cory					6		0	4	13	13	5	41
Lieberthal,M		0	1	3	15	8	20	14	3	14	16	94
Liefer,Jeff							1	0	6	3	1	11
Ligtenberg,K					2	15		8	5	6	6	42
Lilly,Ted							0	0	3	6	10	19
Lima,Jose		0	2	3	1	14	18	2	4	0	5	49
Lincoln,Mike							1	0	4	6	2	13
Linden,Todd											1	1
Linebrink,S								1	1	0	5	7
Linton,Doug	0	3	0	5		1					1	10
Lloyd,Graeme	5	3	3	6	3	5	7		6	2	2	42
Lo Duca,Paul						0	2	2	28	19	19	70
Loaiza,Esteban			5	2	11	6	8	12	8	4	23	79
Lockhart,Keith		0	11	10	5	10	3	7	2	7	2	57
Loewer,Carlton						1	3	0			0	4
Lofton,Kenny	49	21	21	23	21	21	16	17	13	19	18	239
Lohse,Kyle									3	11	11	25
Lombard,George							0	0	0	4	0	4
Long,Terrence							0	18	17	12	11	58
Looper,Aaron											0	0
Looper,Braden						0	5	5	7	11	12	40
Lopez,Albie	1	1	2	2	0	9	4	13	8	2	0	42
Lopez,Aquilino											10	10
Lopez,Felipe									5	6	3	14
Lopez,Javier											7	7
Lopez,Javy	2	5	12	15	19	25	11	16	13	10	30	158
Lopez,Mendy						5	1	0	2	0	2	10
Lopez,Rodrigo								0	15	2		17
Loretta,Mark			1	2	12	16	14	12	9	10	0	76
Loux,Shane										0	0	0
Lowe,Derek					1	7	19	19	11	22	12	91
Lowe,Sean					0	0	8	3	10	2	1	24
Lowell,Mike						0	8	20	20	21	23	92
Ludwick,Ryan										0	6	6
Lugo,Julio								9	9	9	14	41
Lunsford,Trey										0	0	0
Lyon,Brandon									4	0	5	9

WIN SHARES BY YEAR

Player	<94	94	95	96	97	98	99	00	01	02	03	Career
Mabry,John		1	9	13	8	5	3	3	1	8	2	53
MacDougal,Mike								1	0	9		10
Machado,Robert				1	0	1	0	0	3	4	1	10
Macias,Jose						0	5	12	8	2		27
Mackowiak,Rob									4	12	6	22
Maddux,Greg	126	26	30	23	26	25	17	24	20	19	11	347
Mahay,Ron			0		3	2	3	1	2	0	5	16
Mahomes,Pat	2	8	2	1	0		7	2	3	2	1	28
Malaska,Mark										2		2
Mann,Jim							0	0	1	0		1
Manning,Dave										0		0
Manon,Julio										2		2
Mantei,Matt			0	0		5	12	6	1	1	14	39
Manzanillo,J	1	6	2		0		1	5	8	0	0	23
Maroth,Mike										6	4	10
Marquis,Jason								1	8	3	1	13
Marrero,Eli				1	6	5	5	7	14	3		41
Marte,Damaso						0		1	8	15		24
Martin,Al	16	11	11	17	13	5	14	10	8		2	107
Martin,Tom					7	0	0	2	0	0	5	14
Martinez,Edgar	72	11	32	23	27	24	22	28	25	13	20	297
Martinez,Pedro	13	11	14	14	26	21	27	29	12	21	20	208
Martinez,Ramon						0	5	7	9	9	7	37
Martinez,Tino	20	7	20	21	27	21	19	12	21	15	11	194
Martinez,V										1	3	4
Mateo,Henry								0	0	2		2
Mateo,Julio										1	7	8
Mateo,Ruben						3	3	1	1	3		11
Matheny,Mike		0	3	4	8	4	3	14	8	9	13	66
Matos,Julius										2	0	2
Matos,Luis								2	3	0	14	19
Matranga,Dave											0	0
Matsui,Hideki											19	19
Matthews,Mike							0	7	2	3		12
Matthews Jr.,G							1	1	10	10	9	31
May,Darrell				0	0	2				5	17	24
Mayne,Brent	17	4	7	1	6	9	13	8	6	5	10	86
Mays,Joe							10	6	22	2	2	42
McCarty,Dave	2	2	1	2		1		7	2	0	2	19
McClung,Seth										2		2
McCracken,Q			0	7	8	12	2	0	0	15	1	45
McDonald,John							0	0	0	5	2	7
McEwing,Joe						0	11	2	8	2	5	28
McGriff,Fred	166	22	20	19	14	13	24	0	22	18	8	326
McLemore,Mark	36	9	11	16	5	12	15	13	18	13	8	156
McMillon,Billy				0	2			5	2		5	14
Meadows,Brian					4	4	7	0	3	3		21
Mears,Chris											1	1
Meche,Gil					6	6					8	20
Mecir,Jim			1	2	0	9	2	12	6	6	1	39
Melhuse,Adam							0	0			4	4
Meluskey,Mitch					0	0	13		0	0		13
Mench,Kevin										10	4	14
Mendez,Carlos								0				0
Mendez,Donaldo								0		2		2
Mendoza,Ramiro				1	7	12	8	5	10	8	0	51
Menechino,F						0	6	18	3	2		29
Mercado,Hector									1	3	2	6
Merced,Orlando	51	10	18	16	8	4	5		4	7	2	125
Mercedes,Jose										1		1
Mercker,Kent	26	9	7	1	9	5	6	1		1	6	71
Merloni,Lou						4	2	3	2	6	5	22
Mesa,Jose	14	7	17	12	11	5	5	3	14	13	0	101
Meyers,Chad							1	0	0		0	1
Miadich,Bart								0	0			0
Miceli,Danny	0	1	6	0	5	8	4	5	3	0	6	38
Michaels,Jason									0	3	5	8
Middlebrook,J								1	2	0		3
Mientkiewicz,D					0	3		0	18	17	20	58
Millar,Kevin						0	12	10	20	14	16	72
Miller,Corky									2	5	1	8
Miller,Damian					2	6	10	11	10	10	10	59
Miller,Matt											1	1
Miller,Trever				0		4	2	0			4	10
Miller,Wade							0	4	17	13	9	43
Millwood,Kevin					3	10	22	10	5	19	11	80
Mirabelli,Doug				1	0	1	3	6	7	4	2	24
Mitre,Sergio											0	0

Player	<94	94	95	96	97	98	99	00	01	02	03	Career
Moehler,Brian				0	9	17	10	10	1	2	0	49
Moeller,Chad								2	0	6	6	14
Mohr,Dustan									1	11	6	18
Molina,Ben						0	3	13	7	9	16	48
Molina,Gabe							0	0		2	0	2
Molina,Jose							0		1	2	2	5
Mondesi,Raul	3	15	22	25	24	20	21	11	15	12	11	179
Monroe,Craig									1	0	10	11
Mora,Melvin							0	12	11	16	16	55
Morban,Jose											1	1
Mordecai,Mike		1	4	1	0	1	4	3	6	2	1	23
Morneau,Justin											1	1
Morris,Matt				16	10			6	17	13	10	72
Morris,Warren							16	10	1	0	7	34
Moss,Damian									1	12	5	18
Mota,Guillermo							5	1	2	2	14	24
Mounce,Tony										0		0
Moyer,Jamie	39	8	5	11	14	18	18	5	15	16	18	167
Mueller,Bill				9	14	18	12	10	8	12	23	106
Mulder,Mark								5	18	18	17	58
Mulholland,T	50	1	0	9	8	12	11	7	3	3	3	107
Mullen,Scott								1	0	4	0	5
Munro,Pete							1	0		5	2	8
Munson,Eric								0	0	0	7	7
Mussina,Mike	41	18	20	13	19	15	17	18	20	15	19	215
Myers,Brett										3	9	12
Myers,Greg	13	2	6	6	3	4	6	1	6	4	8	59
Myers,Mike			0	3	1	6	2	7	4	3	1	27
Myers,Rodney				3	0	0	5	0	1	0	0	9
Myette,Aaron								0	0	0	0	0
Nady,Xavier								0			7	7
Nagy,Charles	30	13	11	21	13	9	11	0	1	0	0	109
Nakamura,Mike											0	0
Nance,Shane										1	0	1
Nathan,Joe							5	2		1	11	19
Neagle,Denny	5	6	16	17	21	14	7	13	8	8	0	115
Neal,Blaine									0	3	0	3
Nelson,Jeff	9	3	10	6	8	4	2	9	8	4	6	69
Neu,Mike											3	3
Nevin,Phil			2	5	6	2	19	22	31	12	9	108
Nitkowski,C.J.			0	0		4	6	3	2	1	0	16
Nivar,Ramon											1	1
Nix,Laynce											4	4
Nixon,Trot				0		0	10	14	20	17	19	80
Nomo,Hideo			17	16	9	3	10	10	11	13	17	106
Norton,Greg				0	1	4	11	3	3	2	4	28
Norton,Phil								0		2		2
Nunez,A O					1	1	4	1	6	5	4	22
Nunez,Vladimir						0	5	0	8	14	0	27
Obermueller,W										0	2	2
Ohka,Tomo							0	6	2	14	12	34
Ohme,Kevin											1	1
Ojeda,Augie								2	2	1	0	5
Ojeda,Miguel											4	4
O'Leary,Troy	1	1	12	12	15	14	19	11	6	8	2	101
Olerud,John	77	14	11	10	27	34	26	22	21	27	15	284
Oliver,Darren	0	5	4	12	12	4	13	0	3	3	10	66
Olivo,Miguel										1	8	9
Olmedo,Ray											2	2
Olsen,Kevin									2	1	0	3
Ordonez,M					3	13	20	22	25	26	23	132
Ordonez,Rey				7	6	9	13	1	12	9	4	61
Oropesa,Eddie									1	0	1	2
Orosco,Jesse	108	2	6	6	7	7	1	0	1	3	0	141
Ortiz,David					2	9	0	8	7	11	15	52
Ortiz,Ramon							1	6	12	14	5	38
Ortiz,Russ						3	12	7	15	13	16	66
Osik,Keith				4	3	1	3	5	1	1	4	22
Osuna,Antonio			2	10	7	8	0	4	0	8	4	43
Oswalt,Roy									15	20	10	45
Overbay,Lyle									0	0	6	6
Owens,Eric			0	1	0	0	11	0	3	8	3	26
Ozuna,Pablo								1		0	1	2
Padilla,V							0	6	3	14	13	36
Painter,Lance	2	2	4	3	1	4	4	4	1		0	25
Palmeiro,O			1	2	1	5	6	7	4	7	6	39
Palmeiro,R	145	17	21	30	18	24	31	23	25	10	19	363
Palmer,Dean	39	7	7	15	11	12	17	15	6	0	0	129

Player	<94	94	95	96	97	98	99	00	01	02	03	Career
Paquette,Craig	5	0	4	5	2	0	5	8	12	1	0	42
Park,Chan Ho		0	0	7	13	13	6	18	16	5	0	78
Paronto,Chad									0	2	0	2
Parque,Jim						4	7	11	0	0	0	22
Parris,Steve			4	0		6	9	9	5	2	0	35
Parrish,John								0	0		2	2
Patterson,C								0	3	8	13	24
Patterson,D			1	8	5	3	5	7	0	2		31
Patterson,J								0	0		0	0
Patterson,John										3	0	3
Paul,Josh							0	3	4	2	1	10
Pavano,Carl						6	3	8	0	3	9	29
Payton,Jay						0	0	14	3	15	15	47
Pearce,Josh										0	1	1
Pearson,Jason										0	0	0
Peavy,Jake										3	7	10
Pena,Carlos									3	11	9	23
Pena,Wily Mo									0		1	1
Penny,Brad								5	12	4	10	31
Peralta,Jhonny											4	4
Percival,Troy			12	16	10	12	11	8	14	13	8	104
Perez,Antonio											3	3
Perez,Eddie			1	5	2	10	8	0	0	2	7	35
Perez,Eduardo	4	1	0	1	0	4	2	1		3	7	23
Perez,Neifi			0	9	12	14	15	11	6	8		75
Perez,Odalis					1	1		3	16	6		27
Perez,Oliver										4	1	5
Perez,Timo							2	4	14	5		25
Perez,Tomas			1	3	2	0		1	5	4	5	21
Perry,Herbert		0	5	0		3	13	5	10		0	36
Person,Robert			2	3	2	0	8	13	12	1	0	41
Petrick,Ben						2	3	4	1		1	11
Pettitte,Andy			11	18	20	13	10	14	13	12	15	126
Phelps,Josh								0	0	10	10	20
Phelps,Tommy											3	3
Phillips,B										1	4	5
Phillips,Jason								0	1	13		14
Phillips,J C					0				2	0		2
Piatt,Adam							6	1	3	1		11
Piazza,Mike	32	21	27	33	39	33	21	28	21	19	11	285
Pierre,Juan								3	17	15	20	55
Pierzynski,A				1		0	3	15	17	22		58
Pineiro,Joel							0	7	14	13		34
Plesac,Dan	67	2	6	8	5	7	2	4	5	3	4	113
Podsednik,S								0	1	22		23
Polanco,P						2	3	11	14	16	18	64
Politte,Cliff						0	0	5	3	7	3	18
Ponson,Sidney						5	10	11	4	10	15	55
Porter,Colin											0	0
Porzio,Mike							0			2	0	2
Posada,Jorge			0	0	6	15	10	29	23	22	28	133
Powell,Brian						1		1	0	2	0	4
Powell,Jay			1	4	9	7	6	1	9	4	0	41
Pratt,Todd	6	2	1		5	2	5	5	2	7	5	40
Pride,Curtis	2		0	9	2	2		0	1		0	16
Prieto,Alex											0	0
Prince,Tom	6	1	1	3	3	2	0	2	6	5	1	30
Prinz,Bret									7	0	0	7
Prior,Mark										7	22	29
Puffer,Brandon										3	0	3
Pujols,Albert									29	32	41	102
Pulido,Carlos											1	1
Punto,Nick									0	0	1	1
Putz,J.J.											0	0
Quantrill,Paul	13	2	7	4	12	11	5	6	11	8	11	90
Quevedo,Ruben							0	3	0	0		3
Quinlan,Robb											0	0
Quintero,H											0	0
Radke,Brad			7	14	16	14	17	15	17	6	12	118
Raggio,Brady											0	0
Raines Jr,Tim							0			0		0
Ramirez,Aramis					2	0	3	27	6	19		57
Ramirez,Erasmo										4		4
Ramirez,H										9		9
Ramirez,Julio							0		1	1	0	2
Ramirez,Manny	0	11	25	23	21	25	35	27	25	29	28	249
Ramos,Mario											0	0
Randa,Joe			1	9	16	9	17	18	11	11	14	106

Player	<94	94	95	96	97	98	99	00	01	02	03	Career
Randall,Scott										0	0	0
Randolph,S										6		6
Ransom,Cody								0	0	0		0
Reames,Britt								3	2	1	0	6
Reboulet,Jeff	12	5	7	2	5	2	2	3	10	0	6	54
Redding,Tim									2	1	10	13
Redman,Mark							0	10	3	10	11	34
Redman,P											0	0
Redman,Tike									1	1	9	11
Redmond,Mike					4	12	5	6	12	1		40
Reed,Rick	8	0	0		17	16	8	11	13	14	5	92
Reed,Steve	9	6	12	8	7	8	4	4	5	7	7	77
Reese,Pokey				0	3	18	11	7	15	2		56
Reichert,Dan							0	9	4	2	0	15
Reith,Brian							0			3	3	3
Reitsma,Chris									3	7	8	18
Relaford,Desi			0	1	5	4	12	13	9	11		55
Remlinger,Mike	1	1	0	0	9	5	12	12	9	11	6	66
Renteria,Edgar			15	15	11	13	15	13	26	25		133
Restovich,Mike										0	2	2
Reyes,Al		4	0	1	4	5	1	2	2	1		20
Reyes,Carlos	4	2	7	2	5	5	1					26
Reyes,Dennys				2	2	5	2	1	4	0		16
Reyes,Jose											12	12
Reyes,Rene										0	0	0
Reynolds,Shane	1	9	9	15	7	16	16	6	10	2	3	94
Rhodes,Arthur	8	2	1	5	10	7	2	6	12	11	4	68
Richard,Chris								6	12	1	0	19
Riedling,John								2	4	5	4	15
Riggan,Jerrod								0	4	0	0	4
Riggs,Adam					0				0		1	1
Rincon,Juan									0	0	7	7
Rincon,Ricardo					7	9	3	3	6	6	6	40
Rios,Armando						2	7	11	10	2	1	33
Riske,David							0		3	2	10	15
Ritchie,Todd				3	0	14	8	10	0	1		36
Rivas,Luis								1	8	6	6	21
Rivera,Carlos										0		0
Rivera,Juan									0	1	4	5
Rivera,Mariano			2	18	15	14	17	16	19	9	18	128
Rivera,Mike									0	1	0	1
Rivera,Ruben			0	4	1	6	6	10	5	3	1	36
Roa,Joe		0	0	1					4	0		5
Roach,Jason										0		0
Roberts,Brian									3	2	13	18
Roberts,Dave						2	0	0	19	8		29
Roberts,Grant								0	2	5	1	8
Roberts,Willis							0		6	6	1	13
Robertson,J									0	5		5
Robertson,Nate									0	1	1	1
Robinson,Kerry							0	0	4	4	3	11
Rocker,John						5	16	8	8	0	0	37
Rodney,F									0	1		1
Rodriguez,Alex		0	2	34	22	30	23	37	37	35	32	252
Rodriguez,Fe			1		2	1	4	9	12	5	8	42
Rodriguez,Fr										1	9	10
Rodriguez,Ivan	34	15	16	23	26	27	28	19	18	11	23	240
Rodriguez,Rica										1	1	2
Rodriguez,Rich	23	4	0		6	5	3	0	2	1	0	44
Rogers,Kenny	39	9	21	11	2	19	12	12	15	11	15	156
Rolen,Scott				2	29	30	15	18	29	28	25	176
Rollins,Jimmy								1	20	16	19	56
Rolls,Damian								0	2	0	8	10
Romano,Jason										2	0	2
Romero,J.C.							1	0	1	14	3	19
Romero,Mandy			1	0						0		1
Roney,Matt											2	2
Rosario,R										1		1
Ross,Cody										1		1
Ross,Dave									1	4		5
Rowand,Aaron									5	7	6	18
Ruan,Wilkin										1	1	2
Rueter,Kirk	8	2	4	5	12	8	5	9	7	12	6	78
Rupe,Ryan							8	1	1	2	0	12
Rusch,Glendon			5	5	0	11	6	7	0			34
Ryan,B.J.							2	2	3	3	6	16
Ryan,Mike									0	4		4
Saarloos,Kirk										0	2	2

WIN SHARES BY YEAR											
Player	<94	94	95	96	97	98	99	00	01	02	03	Career
Sabathia,C.C.									12	13	13	38
Sadler,Carl										2	1	3
Sadler,Donnie					3	1	2	2	1	1		10
Salmon,Tim	24	13	29	22	29	22	14	23	11	22	17	226
Sanchez,Alex									0	11	9	20
Sanchez,Duaner											0	0
Sanchez,Felix											0	0
Sanchez,Freddy											0	0
Sanchez,Jesus					4	0	6	2	0	0		12
Sanchez,Rey	15	7	7	5	7	8	12	9	13	9	6	98
Sandberg,Jared									1	9	3	13
Sanders,Dave											0	0
Sanders,Reggie	31	13	27	7	13	14	19	6	14	14	18	176
Santana,Johan								2	2	10	16	30
Santiago,B	83	12	12	19	9	1	7	6	10	15	13	187
Santiago,Jose			0	0	4	7	5	0	2			18
Santiago,Ramon										4	5	9
Santos,Angel								0		1		1
Santos,F							0					0
Santos,Victor									5	0	0	5
Sasaki,K								11	12	11	4	38
Sauerbeck,S							9	6	3	9	3	30
Schilling,Curt	40	2	8	14	22	22	15	16	24	24	15	202
Schmack,Brian											1	1
Schmidt,Jason			0	2	8	11	13	1	9	10	22	76
Schneider,B								1	2	8	13	24
Schoeneweis,S						1	6	9	5	3		24
Scutaro,Marco										0	2	2
Seanez,Rudy	1	2	0			5	7	2	3	1	0	21
Sears,Todd										0	2	2
Seay,Bobby								0			1	1
Segui,David	17	5	13	15	16	15	10	18	14	2	4	129
Seguignol,F									0			0
Selby,Bill				1				0	1	3	0	5
Sele,Aaron	11	11	3	6	7	14	13	12	14	5	2	98
Seo,Jae										0	9	9
Serafini,Dan				0	2	2	0	2			0	6
Service,Scott	4	0	3	3	1	11	3	0			2	27
Sexson,Richie					0	5	10	16	19	22	26	98
Sheets,Ben									6	8	9	23
Sheffield,Gary	77	15	13	34	22	30	24	31	30	26	35	337
Shields,Scot									2	6	12	20
Shiell,Jason										0	1	1
Shinjo,T									11	9	1	21
Shouse,Brian	0						0			0	6	6
Shuey,Paul		0	0	7	1	6	10	8	6	7	7	52
Shumpert,Terry	9	5	1	1	1	0	10	5	5	2	1	40
Sierra,Ruben	159	13	13	6	1	1		1	6	7	5	212
Silva,Carlos										7	5	12
Simon,Randall				1	0	4		7	12	11		35
Simontacchi,J										8	2	10
Singleton,C							0	11	12	9	6	38
Smith,Dan						2	0			4	1	7
Smith,Jason								0	0	0		0
Smith,Mark			0	3	1	9	1		4	3	1	22
Smitherman,S										0		0
Smoltz,John	76	6	17	27	21	16	18		8	17	16	222
Snow,J.T.	9	3	15	7	28	13	18	16	6	11	14	140
Snyder,Kyle											4	4
Sojo,Luis										0		0
Sorensen,Zach											0	0
Soriano,A							0	0	16	30	27	73
Soriano,Rafael										1	7	8
Sosa,Jorge										2	5	7
Sosa,Sammy	41	15	25	18	14	35	26	30	42	27	22	295
Sparks,Steve			11	2		8	5	7	16	3	3	55
Speier,Justin						0	1	7	5	6	8	27
Spencer,Shane						6	3	6	8	5	8	36
Spiezio,Scott				2	10	10	6	6	9	17	12	72
Spivey,Junior									6	23	10	39
Spooneybarger,T									0	6	3	9
Springer,Russ		0	3	3	3	3	3	5	3	0		23
Spurling,Chris											4	4
Stairs,Matt	1		1	4	15	20	20	10	11	7	13	102
Standridge,J									1	0	0	1
Stanford,Jason											3	3
Stanton,Mike	25	5	2	9	9	4	4	6	10	10	3	87
Stark,Denny								0		0	10	2	12

WIN SHARES BY YEAR											
Player	<94	94	95	96	97	98	99	00	01	02	03	Career
Stenson,D											2	2
Stephenson,G			0	10	0	5	11			0	5	31
Stewart,Josh											0	0
Stewart,Scott									6	12	4	22
Stewart,Sh			0	0	7	18	17	17	18	17	19	113
Stinnett,Kelly		4	4	0	1	10	6	21	5	4	4	59
Stone,Ricky									1	5	6	12
Strange,Pat									1	0		1
Strickland,S							0	8	10	5	2	25
Strong,Jamal										0		0
Sturtze,Tanyon			0	0	0		1	6	11	6	2	26
Stynes,Chris			1	1	10	5	2	13	8	5	10	55
Sullivan,Scott			0	1	9	3	11	10	9	1	6	50
Suppan,Jeff			1	0	4	2	12	12	12	9	14	66
Surhoff,B.J.	94	4	16	17	19	13	17	14	12	2	9	217
Suzuki,Ichiro									36	25	23	84
Sweeney,Brian											1	1
Sweeney,Mark		1	7	5	3	0	0	1	0	2		19
Sweeney,Mike			0	4	5	8	16	26	18	19	15	111
Switzer,Jon											0	0
Taguchi,So										1	3	4
Tallet,Brian										2	0	2
Tam,Jeff					0	1	10	8	1	1		21
Tankersley,D										0	0	0
Tatis,Fernando					3	9	23	11	2	5	1	54
Tavarez,Julian	0	0	10	4	6	5	1	10	6	2	10	54
Taylor,Aaron										0	0	0
Taylor,Reggie								0	0	5	1	6
Teixeira,Mark											13	13
Tejada,Miguel					1	7	20	23	25	32	25	133
Tejera,Michael							0			7	3	10
Telemaco,A				1	0	8	2	0	2		2	15
Terrero,Luis											0	0
Thames,Marcus										0	0	0
Thomas,Brad										0		0
Thomas,Frank	112	25	28	28	39	25	16	34	1	16	23	347
Thome,Jim	8	10	24	28	26	19	26	20	31	34	30	256
Thomson,John					10	9	0		7	7	11	44
Thurman,Corey										4	0	4
Thurston,Joe									1	0		1
Timlin,Mike	16	2	6	10	9	12	9	6	5	8	8	91
Tolar,Kevin								0	0	0	0	0
Tollberg,Brian								6	6	0	0	12
Tomko,Brett					10	9	6	5	1	6	6	43
Torcato,Tony										0	0	0
Torrealba,Y									1	4	7	12
Torres,Andres										0	1	1
Torres,Salomon	2	0	1	3	0					3	5	14
Towers,Josh									6	0	5	11
Traber,Billy											3	3
Trachsel,Steve	1	10	4	15	9	13	6	11	8	10	13	100
Trammell,Bubba					2	4	9	8	17	11	0	51
Truby,Chris								7	3	3	1	14
Tsao,Chin-hui										1	1	1
Tucker,Michael			3	9	15	11	10	7	10	8	9	82
Tucker,T.J.								0	5	4		9
Turnbow,D								2			2	4
Tyner,Jason								1	6	1	2	10
Ugueto,Luis										0	0	0
Urbina,Ugueth			0	8	10	17	14	2	11	11	15	88
Uribe,Juan									7	10	9	26
Utley,Chase											5	5
Valderrama,C										0		0
Valdes,Ismael		3	15	16	15	9	10	2	10	11	3	94
Valent,Eric									1	0	0	1
Valentin,Ja					0	2	5			0	2	9
Valentin,Jose	2	12	8	20	13	15	8	24	15	16	18	151
Valentine,Joe											0	0
Valverde,Jose											11	11
Van Poppel,T	3	2	5	0		1		6	8	3	2	30
Vance,Cory										0	1	1
Vander Wal,J	11	3	4	4	0	4	8	19	13	2	8	76
Vargas,Claudio										6		6
Varitek,Jason					0	5	12	7	8	12	17	61
Vaughn,Greg	74	9	5	17	7	30	24	16	15	1	1	199
Vaughn,Mo	32	17	24	29	22	25	19	17		15	1	201
Vazquez,Javier						0	8	14	21	12	21	76
Vazquez,Ramon									0	14	10	24

WIN SHARES BY YEAR												
Player	<94	94	95	96	97	98	99	00	01	02	03	Career
Velandia,Jorge											2	2
Venafro,Mike							7	6	4	2	1	20
Ventura,Robin	92	16	17	20	8	21	30	15	17	20	10	266
Veres,Dave		4	10	6	5	11	11	14	7	6	2	76
Victorino,S											0	0
Vidro,Jose					3	2	11	25	18	29	19	107
Villafuerte,B								0	0	3	1	4
Villarreal,O											11	11
Villone,Ron			2	5	4	1	8	5	3	1	5	34
Vina,Fernando	1	3	8	13	7	30	4	18	22	16	5	127
Vitiello,Joe			2	4	2	0	0	1			3	12
Vizcaino,Jose	22	7	16	14	17	8	4	3	4	11	4	110
Vizcaino,Luis							0	0	2	8	1	11
Vizquel,Omar	44	7	17	16	14	18	22	16	12	21	5	192
Vogelsong,Ryan								1	0		0	1
Voyles,Brad									1	0	0	1
Waechter,Doug											3	3
Wagner,Billy			0	8	11	11	20	1	13	16	19	99
Wagner,Ryan											3	3
Wakefield,Tim	11		18	10	12	11	8	5	11	15	12	113
Walbeck,Matt	1	5	5	3	2	9	4	2	0	1	0	32
Walker,Jamie					2	0				4	7	13
Walker,Larry	82	21	18	10	32	17	24	11	25	26	18	284
Walker,Pete			1	0			0	1	9	3	14
Walker,Todd				1	2	19	9	5	12	21	15	84
Walrond,Les											0	0
Ward,Daryle						0	3	3	5	10	0	21
Wasdin,John			1	4	7	4	7	3	3		0	29
Washburn,J						4	3	7	15	18	10	57
Watson,Mark								0		0	0	0
Wayne,Justin										0	0	0
Weathers,David	2	3	0	3	0	4	6	7	10	7	8	50
Weaver,Jeff							7	12	13	14	2	48
Webb,Brandon											17	17
Weber,Ben								2	7	11	8	28
Wellemeyer,T											0	0
Wells,David	53	7	17	10	12	18	13	18	5	15	14	182
Wells,Kip							3	2	6	13	16	40
Wells,Vernon							1	0	3	17	26	47
Wendell,Turk	1	0	2	12	4	10	9	8	5		6	57
Werth,Jayson										1	1	2
Wesson,Barry										0	0	0
Westbrook,Jake							0	2	1	6	9
Wheeler,Dan							1	1	0		3	5
White,Gabe		0	0		3	8	3	15	2	7	4	42
White,Matt											0	0
White,Rick		7	2			5	7	9	5	5	1	41
White,Rondell	3	4	14	10	17	16	15	14	12	6	15	126
Widger,Chris			0	0	5	10	8	4		2	2	31
Wigginton,Ty									1	4	15	19
Wilkerson,Brad									1	17	18	36
Williams,B	32	14	27	26	24	27	33	26	24	30	13	276
Williams,G	1	0	7	5	9	12	13	14	2	0	0	63
Williams,J											9	9
Williams,Matt	103	18	20	18	18	12	26	7	10	6	3	241
Williams,Mike	2	1	6	3	0	7	5	11	8	12	2	57
Williams,Woody	2	5	4	3	11	12	10	12	11	10	13	93
Williamson,S							17	11	0	10	7	45
Willis,D											14	14
Wilson,Craig									8	10	10	28
Wilson,Dan	2	4	16	15	21	7	9	4	14	12	7	111
Wilson,Enrique					1	3	3	5	3	1	2	18
Wilson,Jack									5	12	11	28
Wilson,Kris						2	4	0	4	10
Wilson,Paul				1			4	6	7	5	23
Wilson,Preston					1	13	20	10	11	20	75
Wilson,Tom									0	7	3	10
Wilson,Vance							0	0	1	5	7	13
Winn,Randy					5	4	2	10	23	21	65
Witasick,Jay			0	0	0	5	3	6	6	2	22
Witt,Kevin					0	0			1		2	3
Wolf,Randy						4	13	11	15	12	55
Womack,Tony	0	1		2	18	17	14	16	10	14	3	95
Wood,Kerry					14		7	13	12	18	64
Wood,Mike											0	0
Woodard,Steve				1	9	9	2	4	0	1	26
Woodward,Chris					0	2	1	10	9	22
Wooten,Shawn						0	6	3	2	11

WIN SHARES BY YEAR												
Player	<94	94	95	96	97	98	99	00	01	02	03	Career
Worrell,Tim	2	1	1	10	3	3	4	7	5	9	13	58
Wright,Dan									2	7	0	9
Wright,Jaret				6	11	3	3	0	0	1	24
Wunsch,Kelly							8	0	3	4	15
Yan,Esteban			0	0	7	2	4	8	7	1	29
Young,Dmitri			0	5	16	10	14	13	5	19	82
Young,Eric	14	6	12	17	17	17	14	18	16	9	9	149
Young,Ernie		0	1	10	1	1	0			0	13
Young,Jason										0	0
Young,Kevin	6	1	2	3	12	13	21	7	7	1	80
Young,Michael							0	7	11	21	39
Zambrano,C								0	5	18	23
Zambrano,V								6	4	10	20
Zaun,Gregg			3	3	9	3	3	9	4	2	2	38
Zeile,Todd	66	15	8	16	18	21	19	18	18	12	6	217
Zerbe,Chad							0	2	4	2	8
Zito,Barry								9	15	25	18	67
Zoccolillo,P										0	0

Career Assessments

Even though the 2003 season had fewer big season home run totals than recent years, it was still a big season for career home run milestones. Sammy Sosa and Rafael Palmeiro both slugged their 500th career home run. During his continued assault on Hank Aaron's career home run record, Barry Bonds fell just two home runs short of passing his godfather, Willie Mays, for third on the all-time list.

Bonds continues to wow fans at his advanced baseball age of 39. With another solid season of 45 home runs, he is clearly the frontrunner to break Aaron's record of 756 home runs out of the current cast of players. Bonds has a 52% chance of surpassing Aaron by the time his career is done, up from 47% last year. Sammy Sosa had an "off" year with "only" 40 home runs, compared to his prolific output of recent years and his chance of breaking the record dropped 8% to 37%. Alex Rodriguez remained nearly steady at 43%, rounding out the three serious record-breaking contenders.

Along with Bonds, Sosa and Rodriguez, Jim Thome (15%), Albert Pujols (8%) and Andruw Jones (3%) make the chance of Aaron's record withstanding the current onslaught low. There is an 87% chance that an active player will break Aaron's record, which is unchanged from last year.

At least Aaron can be more confident that his RBI record will still be standing for the time being. Rodriguez and Pujols lead a short list of players with a chance to knock in 2,298 runs. The chance that someone will shatter the career RBI record is at 41% this year, down from 47% last season.

Pujols also joins Rodriguez as the only two players with any discernable chance of challenging Pete Rose's record of 4,257 career hits. While Rose's spot in the Hall of Fame may still be in limbo, his grasp on the Hit King crown is firm. Pujols has only a 2% chance of breaking the record, while Rodriguez has only a 1% chance. The fact that very good, young players like Rodriguez and Pujols aren't close to the hit record just reiterates how a player needs to play at a high level for a long time to achieve such a big career record.

The upcoming season should provide more home run milestones. Barring injury, Bonds will surpass Willie Mays and only have Babe Ruth and Aaron ahead of him on the all-time home run list. Fred McGriff needs nine more home runs for 500. Hopefully, Ken Griffey Jr. can recover from his bout with the injury bug to slug the remaining 19 home runs he needs for 500. With 55 home runs, Rodriguez can be the youngest player to reach the 400 home run plateau. And with the way home runs fly off the bat these days, anything is possible.

Career Assessments

Player	Age	HOME RUN GOALS						HIT GOALS				RBI GOALS		
		Current	500	600	700	756	800	Current	3000	4000	4257	Current	2000	2298
Barry Bonds	38	658	4/17/2001	8/9/2002	97%	52%	20%	2595	20%	0%	0%	1742	31%	0%
Sammy Sosa	34	539	4/4/2003	96%	67%	37%	22%	2099	20%	0%	0%	1450	33%	4%
Rafael Palmeiro	38	528	5/11/2003	64%	0%	0%	0%	2780	86%	0%	0%	1687	21%	0%
Fred McGriff	39	491	99%	0%	0%	0%	0%	2477	0%	0%	0%	1543	0%	0%
Ken Griffey Jr.	33	481	96%	0%	0%	0%	0%	2080	0%	0%	0%	1384	0%	0%
Jeff Bagwell	35	419	93%	20%	0%	0%	0%	2137	18%	0%	0%	1421	13%	0%
Jim Thome	32	381	93%	62%	27%	15%	8%	1486	0%	0%	0%	1058	17%	1%
Alex Rodriguez	27	345	91%	86%	58%	43%	34%	1535	45%	7%	1%	990	46%	24%
Frank Thomas	35	418	84%	11%	0%	0%	0%	2048	0%	0%	0%	1390	0%	0%
Manny Ramirez	31	347	81%	29%	7%	0%	0%	1585	16%	0%	0%	1140	19%	2%
Juan Gonzalez	33	429	80%	4%	0%	0%	0%	1901	0%	0%	0%	1387	1%	0%
Gary Sheffield	34	379	62%	11%	0%	0%	0%	2009	19%	0%	0%	1232	8%	0%
Carlos Delgado	31	304	58%	22%	3%	0%	0%	1290	1%	0%	0%	959	16%	2%
Andruw Jones	26	221	51%	25%	9%	3%	0%	1105	17%	0%	0%	675	14%	3%
Albert Pujols	23	114	46%	26%	13%	8%	4%	591	29%	6%	2%	381	24%	12%
Richie Sexson	28	191	40%	18%	5%	0%	0%	811	2%	0%	0%	593	8%	0%
Vladimir Guerrero	27	234	38%	14%	0%	0%	0%	1215	19%	0%	0%	702	5%	0%
Jason Giambi	32	269	38%	11%	0%	0%	0%	1358	0%	0%	0%	904	2%	0%
Todd Helton	29	219	30%	9%	0%	0%	0%	1182	21%	0%	0%	740	11%	0%
Shawn Green	30	253	27%	5%	0%	0%	0%	1403	14%	0%	0%	799	1%	0%
Alfonso Soriano	25	98	24%	9%	0%	0%	0%	571	18%	0%	0%	270	0%	0%
Eric Chavez	25	134	22%	7%	0%	0%	0%	727	11%	0%	0%	466	9%	0%
Chipper Jones	31	280	21%	0%	0%	0%	0%	1588	18%	0%	0%	943	4%	0%
Miguel Tejada	27	156	15%	1%	0%	0%	0%	968	18%	0%	0%	604	12%	1%
Magglio Ordonez	29	178	15%	0%	0%	0%	0%	1108	15%	0%	0%	666	5%	0%
Scott Rolen	28	192	15%	0%	0%	0%	0%	1097	8%	0%	0%	707	8%	0%
Lance Berkman	27	126	15%	1%	0%	0%	0%	642	3%	0%	0%	429	3%	0%
Jim Edmonds	33	260	13%	0%	0%	0%	0%	1346	0%	0%	0%	798	0%	0%
Troy Glaus	26	164	9%	0%	0%	0%	0%	696	0%	0%	0%	473	0%	0%
Preston Wilson	28	140	7%	0%	0%	0%	0%	724	0%	0%	0%	472	0%	0%
Derrek Lee	27	130	7%	0%	0%	0%	0%	760	1%	0%	0%	421	0%	0%
Adam Dunn	23	72	6%	0%	0%	0%	0%	279	0%	0%	0%	171	0%	0%
Tony Batista	29	182	6%	0%	0%	0%	0%	932	0%	0%	0%	571	0%	0%
Carlos Lee	27	121	6%	0%	0%	0%	0%	777	4%	0%	0%	453	0%	0%
Pat Burrell	26	103	5%	0%	0%	0%	0%	519	0%	0%	0%	348	0%	0%
Carlos Beltran	26	108	4%	0%	0%	0%	0%	825	12%	0%	0%	465	3%	0%
Raul Mondesi	32	264	3%	0%	0%	0%	0%	1527	0%	0%	0%	828	0%	0%
Aramis Ramirez	25	91	2%	0%	0%	0%	0%	602	4%	0%	0%	355	0%	0%
Garret Anderson	31	193	2%	0%	0%	0%	0%	1633	30%	0%	0%	872	8%	0%
Vernon Wells	24	58	0%	0%	0%	0%	0%	435	9%	0%	0%	231	0%	0%
Rickey Henderson	44	297	0%	0%	0%	0%	0%	3055	10/8/2001	0%	0%	1115	0%	0%
Roberto Alomar	35	206	0%	0%	0%	0%	0%	2679	94%	0%	0%	1110	0%	0%
Derek Jeter	29	127	0%	0%	0%	0%	0%	1546	28%	0%	0%	615	0%	0%
Craig Biggio	37	210	0%	0%	0%	0%	0%	2461	25%	0%	0%	931	0%	0%
Edgar Renteria	27	73	0%	0%	0%	0%	0%	1255	25%	0%	0%	493	0%	0%
Juan Pierre	25	4	0%	0%	0%	0%	0%	638	19%	0%	0%	151	0%	0%
Johnny Damon	29	100	0%	0%	0%	0%	0%	1403	19%	0%	0%	531	0%	0%
John Olerud	34	239	0%	0%	0%	0%	0%	2079	18%	0%	0%	1145	0%	0%
Luis Castillo	27	14	0%	0%	0%	0%	0%	977	16%	0%	0%	194	0%	0%
Shannon Stewart	29	79	0%	0%	0%	0%	0%	1127	12%	0%	0%	394	0%	0%
Nomar Garciaparra	29	173	0%	0%	0%	0%	0%	1231	12%	0%	0%	669	0%	0%
Rafael Furcal	25	31	0%	0%	0%	0%	0%	592	10%	0%	0%	175	0%	0%
Ichiro Suzuki	29	29	0%	0%	0%	0%	0%	662	10%	0%	0%	182	0%	0%
Jimmy Rollins	24	33	0%	0%	0%	0%	0%	518	10%	0%	0%	181	0%	0%
Bobby Abreu	29	136	0%	0%	0%	0%	0%	1091	9%	0%	0%	569	0%	0%
Bernie Williams	34	241	0%	0%	0%	0%	0%	1950	9%	0%	0%	1062	0%	0%
Luis Gonzalez	35	275	0%	0%	0%	0%	0%	1959	8%	0%	0%	1124	0%	0%
Jose Vidro	28	87	0%	0%	0%	0%	0%	940	7%	0%	0%	411	0%	0%
Cristian Guzman	25	31	0%	0%	0%	0%	0%	713	7%	0%	0%	243	0%	0%
Adrian Beltre	24	99	0%	0%	0%	0%	0%	749	5%	0%	0%	389	0%	0%
Orlando Cabrera	28	62	0%	0%	0%	0%	0%	781	4%	0%	0%	350	0%	0%
Michael Young	26	34	0%	0%	0%	0%	0%	450	3%	0%	0%	183	0%	0%
Aubrey Huff	26	69	0%	0%	0%	0%	0%	477	2%	0%	0%	225	0%	0%
Rocco Baldelli	21	11	0%	0%	0%	0%	0%	184	1%	0%	0%	78	0%	0%
Edgardo Alfonzo	29	133	0%	0%	0%	0%	0%	1269	1%	0%	0%	619	0%	0%
Juan Encarnacion	27	96	0%	0%	0%	0%	0%	770	1%	0%	0%	403	0%	0%
Carl Crawford	21	7	0%	0%	0%	0%	0%	244	1%	0%	0%	84	0%	0%

358

Baseball Glossary

% Inherited Scored
The percentage of inherited baserunners a relief pitcher allows to score.

% Pitches Taken
The percentage of pitches that a batter does not swing at out of the total number of pitches thrown to him.

1st Batter Average
The Batting Average that a relief pitcher allows to the first batter he faces when he enters a game.

1st Batter OBP
The On-Base Percentage that a relief pitcher allows to the first batter he faces when he enters a game.

Active Career Batting Leaders
A list of batting leaders among active (appearing in 2003) players. An active player is eligible when he meets the minimum requirements for the following categories:

1,000 At Bats—Batting Average, On-Base Percentage, Slugging Average, At Bats Per HR, At Bats Per GDP, At Bats Per RBI, Strikeout to Walk Ratio
100 Stolen Base Attempts—Stolen Base Success Percentage

Active Career Pitching Leaders
A list of pitching leaders among active (appearing in 2003) players. An active player is eligible when he meets the minimum requirements for the following categories:

750 Innings Pitched—Earned Run Average, Opponent Batting Average, all "Per 9 Innings" categories, Strikeout to Walk Ratio
250 Games Started—Complete Game Frequency
100 Decisions—Win-Loss Percentage

AVG Allowed ScPos
The Batting Average allowed by a pitcher while pitching with runners in scoring position.

AVG Bases Loaded
The Batting Average of a hitter while batting with the bases loaded.

Batting Average
Hits divided by at bats.

Blown Save
When a relief pitcher enters a game in a Save Situation (see definition for Save Situation) and allows the other team to score the tying or go-ahead run.

Career Assessments

This method, once called the Favorite Toy, is a way to estimate the probability that a player will achieve a specific career goal. In this example, 3,000 hits will be used. The four components of the formula are Needed Hits, Years Remaining, Established Hit Level and Projected Remaining Hits.

Needed Hits. This is the number of Hits (or any statistic) that a player needs to reach a desired goal.

Years Remaining. This is the estimated number of years remaining in the player's career. It is determined using the player's age (on June 30th of the previous year; use 2003 when making the calculation after the 2003 season is complete). The formula is (42 - age) divided by two. This means a player who is 20 years old will have 11 remaining seasons, a player who is 25 years old will have 8.5 remaining seasons and a player who is 35 years old will have 3.5 remaining seasons. If the player is a catcher, then multiply his remaining seasons by .7. If a player is older than 39 (the Years Remaining calculation yields less than 1.5), consult the player's statistics for the most recent year. If the player either had 100 Hits or an Offensive Winning Percentage of .500 or greater, then the player will have 1.0 remaining seasons. If the player has both, he has 1.5 remaining seasons. If he has neither, he has .5 remaining seasons.

Established Hit Level. The Established Hit Level is a weighted average of the player's hits over the past three seasons. To calculate the Established Hit Level after the 2003 season is complete, add 2001 Hits, (2002 Hits multiplied by two) and (2003 Hits multiplied by three), then divide by six. If the Established Hit Level is less than 75% of the most recent performance (2003 Hits in this case), then the Established Hit Level is equal to .75 times the most recent performance.

Projected Remaining Hits. This is calculated by multiplying Years Remaining by the Established Hit Level.

The probability of achieving the specified goal is found by dividing Projected Remaining Hits by Need Hits, then subtracting .5. The maximum chance that any player has of achieving a goal is .97 raised to the power of (Need Hits / Established Hit Level). This prevents the possibility of a player reaching a goal from being higher than 100 percent, which is impossible.

Catcher's ERA

The ERA for a catcher is equal to the ERA of pitchers pitching while the catcher is playing behind the plate. It is calculated exactly like ERA for pitchers. Take the number of earned runs allowed while the catcher is playing, multiply it by 9 and then divide it by the total number of defensive innings that the catcher was behind the plate.

Cleanup Slugging Average

The Slugging Average of a batter when he bats in the cleanup spot, or fourth, in the batting order.

Component ERA (ERC)

A statistic that estimates what a pitcher's ERA should have been, based on his pitching performance. The ERC formula is calculated as follows:

1. Subtract the pitcher's Home Runs Allowed from his Hits Allowed.
2. Multiply Step 1 by 1.255.
3. Multiply his Home Runs Allowed by four.
4. Add Steps 2 and 3 together.
5. Multiply Step 4 by .89.
6. Add his Walks and Hit Batsmen.
7. Multiply Step 6 by .475.
8. Add Steps 5 and 7 together.

This yields the pitcher's total base estimate (PTB), which is:

$$PTB = 0.89 \times (1.255 \times (H - HR) + 4 \times HR) + 0.475 \times (BB + HB)$$

For those pitchers for whom there is intentional walk data, use this formula instead:

$$PTB = 0.89 \times (1.255 \times (H - HR) + 4 \times HR) + 0.56 \times (BB + HB - IBB)$$

9. Add Hits and Walks and Hit Batsmen.
10. Multiply Step 9 by PTB.
11. Divide Step 10 by Batters Facing Pitcher. If BFP data is unavailable, approximate it by multiplying Innings Pitched by 2.9, then adding Step 9.
12. Multiply Step 11 by 9.
13. Divide Step 12 by Innings Pitched.
14. Subtract .56 from Step 13.

This is the pitcher's ERC, which is:

$$\frac{(H + BB + HBP) \times PTB}{BFP \times IP} \times 9 - 0.56$$

If the result after Step 13 is less than 2.24, adjust the formula as follows:

$$\frac{(H + BB + HBP) \times PTB}{BFP \times IP} \times 9 \times 0.75$$

Earned Run Average

The number of earned runs that a pitcher surrenders per nine innings that he pitches. It is calculated by multiplying the total earned runs allowed by nine and dividing by the total number of innings pitched.

Easy Save

This label is used to separate Saves by difficulty level (Easy or Tough). A Save is considered Easy if the relief pitcher enters the game, pitches one inning or less, and the first batter he faces does not at least represent the tying run.

Fielding Percentage

The percentage of plays a player makes in the field without making an error out of the total number of opportunities. It is calculated by adding (Putouts plus Assists) and dividing by (Putouts plus Assists plus Errors).

Games Finished

The relief pitcher who is in the game for each team when the game ends is credited with a Game Finished.

Game Score

To determine the starting pitcher's Game Score:
Start with 50.
Add 1 point for each out recorded by the starting pitcher.
Add 2 points for each inning the pitcher completes after the fourth inning.
Add 1 point for each strikeout.
Subtract 2 points for each hit allowed.
Subtract 4 points for each earned run allowed.
Subtract 2 points for an unearned run.
Subtract 1 point for each walk.

GDP

Grounded into Double Play

GDP Opportunity

This is a situation where the batter has a chance to ground into a double play. It occurs with at least a runner on first base and less than two outs.

Ground / Fly Ratio (Grd/Fly, GB/FB)

Calculated for both batters and pitchers. For batters, it is the number of groundballs hit divided by the number of flyballs hit. For pitchers, it is exactly the same but uses the number of groundballs and flyballs allowed. Every fair batted ball is included except for bunts and line drives.

Hold

A relief pitcher is given a Hold anytime he enters a game in a Save Situation (see definition for Save Situation), records one out or more, and exits the game without giving up the lead. If the pitcher finishes the game, then he will only earn credit for a Save. He cannot receive credit for both a Hold and a Save.

Inherited Runner

When a relief pitcher enters the game, any runner who is on base at the time is considered an Inherited Runner.

Isolated Power
Slugging Average minus Batting Average.

K/BB Ratio
Strikeouts divided by Walks.

Late & Close
A situation in a game that is very similar to a Save Situation. The following requirements are necessary for a Late & Close game:
1. The game is in the seventh inning or later AND
2. The batting team is either leading by one run or tied OR
3. The tying run is on base, at bat, or on deck.

Leadoff On-Base Percentage
The On-Base Percentage of a batter when he bats leadoff, or first, in the batting order.

Offensive Winning Percentage (OWP)
A player's Offensive Winning Percentage is the winning percentage of a hypothetical team which has an offense consisting of nine of that player, and pitching and defense which is average for the player's league. It is calculated by taking the square of RC/27 (see the definition for Runs Created per 27 Outs), dividing it by the sum of RC/27 and the square of the average runs scored per game in the league.

On-Base Percentage
(Hits plus Walks plus Hit by Pitcher) divided by (At Bats plus Walks plus Hit by Pitcher plus Sacrifice Flies).

$$\frac{H + BB + HBP}{AB + BB + HBP + SF}$$

Opponent Batting Average
Hits Allowed divided by (Batters Faced minus Walks minus Hit Batsmen minus Sacrifice Hits minus Sacrifice Flies minus Catcher's Interference).

$$\frac{H}{BFP - BB - HBP - SH - SF - CI}$$

PA*
Used in the denominator for the calculation of On-Base Percentage. It is calculated by subtracting (Sacrifice Hits plus Times Reached Base on Defensive Interference) from Plate Appearances (see definition for Plate Appearances).

Park Index

The Park Index of a given ballpark is the amount that the ballpark influences a given statistic. The following is a calculation of a park index using runs as the statistic:

1. Add Runs and Opponent Runs in home games.
2. Add At Bats and Opponent At Bats in home games. (If At Bats are unavailable, use home games.)
3. Divide Step 1 by Step 2.
4. Add Runs and Opponent Runs in road games.
5. Add At Bats and Opponent At Bats in road games. (If At Bats are unavailable, use road games.)
6. Divide Step 4 by Step 5.
7. Divide Step 3 by Step 6.
8. Multiply Step 7 by 100.

An index of 100 means the park is completely neutral and does not influence the particular statistic at all. A park index of 112 for runs indicates that teams score 12 percent more runs in this ballpark than a neutral park. A park index of 92 for runs means that teams tend to score 8 percent fewer runs in this ballpark than a neutral park.

PCS (Pitchers' Caught Stealing)

The number of runners officially scored as Caught Stealing where the pitcher initiated the play. The normal Caught Stealing is when a runner is out attempting to steal a base but the play was initiated by the catcher. PCS plays are often referred to as pickoffs, but differ when the runner breaks towards the next base as opposed to returning to the base he was currently on. Pickoffs occur when the pitcher throws to a base that a runner is leading from, and the runner is out attempting to return to that base. Pickoffs are not an official statistic.

Pitches per PA

The total number of pitches a hitter sees divided by his total Plate Appearances.

Plate Appearances

At Bats plus Total Walks plus Hit By Pitcher plus Sacrifice Hits plus Sacrifice Flies plus Times Reached on Defensive Interference.

Power/Speed Number

A single number that reflects a combination of power and speed. To achieve a high Power/Speed Number, a player must score high in both power and speed. To calculate the Power/Speed Number, multiply Home Runs by Stolen Bases by two, and divide by the sum of Home Runs and Stolen Bases.

$$\frac{2 \times HR \times SB}{HR + SB}$$

PPO (Pitcher Pickoff)

The number of baserunners thrown out when a pitcher throws to a base with a leading baserunner, and the runner is tagged out attempting to return to the base. PPO is not an official statistic and does not count toward Caught Stealing totals.

Quality Start

A game where the starting pitcher pitches for at least six innings and allows no more than three earned runs.

Quality Start Percentage

Quality Starts divided by Games Started (see the definition for Quality Start).

Range Factor

The number of Successful Chances (Putouts plus Assists) times nine divided by the number of Defensive Innings Played. The average for a Regular Player at each position in 2003:

Second Base: 5.03
Third Base: 2.70
Shortstop: 4.52
Left Field: 2.03
Center Field: 2.63
Right Field: 2.10

RHS

Righthanded Starting Pitcher.

Run Support Per 9 IP

The total number of runs scored by a pitcher's team while he is in the game multiplied by nine and divided by total Innings Pitched.

Runs Created

Bill James has devised many different Runs Created formulas, based on the statistics available and the time period of the statistics. The current method is as follows:

1. Add hits plus walks plus hit by pitcher.
2. Subtract caught stealings and grounded into double plays from Step 1. This is the A factor.
3. Add unintentional walks plus hit by pitcher.
4. Multiply Step 3 by .24.
5. Multiply stolen bases by .62.
6. Add sacrifice hits plus sacrifice flies.
7. Multiply Step 6 by .5.
8. Add total bases plus Step 4 plus Step 5 plus Step 7.
9. Multiply strikeouts by .03.
10. Subtract Step 9 from Step 8. This is the B factor.
11. Add at-bats plus walks plus hit by pitcher plus sacrifice hits plus sacrifice flies. This is the C factor.

To summarize:

$$A = H + BB + HBP - CS - GDP$$
$$B = 0.24 \times (BB - IBB + HBP) + 0.62 \times SB + 0.5 \times (SH + SF) + TB - 0.03 \times SO$$
$$C = AB + BB + HBP + SH + SF$$

Each player's runs created is determined as if he were operating in a context of eight other players of average skill. The final steps are:

12. Multiply C by 2.4.
13. Add A plus Step 12.
14. Multiply C by 3.
15. Add B plus Step 14.
16. Multiply Step 13 by Step 15.
17. Multiply C by 9.
18. Divide Step 16 by Step 17.
19. Multiply C by .9.
20. Subtract Step 19 from Step 18.

Expressed as an equation, that's:

$$\frac{(2.4 \times C + A) \times (3 \times C + B)}{9 \times C} - (0.9 \times C)$$

When there is available data for home runs with men on base (HRmob) and batting average with runners in scoring position (AVGrsp), we can make further adjustments to the Runs Created formula.

The first adjustment deals with HRmob. It comes from the fact that the Runs Created formula assumes that a player hits home runs at the same frequency with men on base as he does with no men on base. If a player hits home runs at a higher frequency with men on base, then he creates more runs. If he hits home runs at a lower frequency, he will have created less runs than the original formula gives him. To figure out the HRmob adjustment, first divide home runs by total at bats to calculate the player's overall home run frequency. Then, multiply the frequency by the player's at bats with men on base (ABmob) to get the expected number of home runs with men on base. Subtract this expected number from the players actual HRmob and add the result to the player's Runs Created.

The other adjustment deals with AVGrsp. The adjustment is needed to deal with the fact that the Runs Created formula assumes that a player has the same batting average with runners in scoring position as he does without. If this is not the case, Runs Created needs to be adjusted. The calculation is similar to the HRmob adjustment. First multiply the player's overall batting average by at bats with runners in scoring position (ABrsp) to get the number of expected hits with runners in scoring position. Then subtract the expected hits from the actual hits with runners in scoring position (AVGrsp x ABrsp) and add it to Runs Created.

The adjustment formulas written are:

$$HRmob - \frac{HR \times ABmob}{AB}$$

$$(AVGrsp \times ABrsp) - (AVG \times ABrsp)$$

The last step is an adjustment to reconcile the results of the Runs Created formula with actual runs scored. Add up all of a team's players' runs created and compare it to the team's actual number of runs scored and reconcile the difference proportionally. For example, if the sum of the Runs Created for the team is 800 runs and the team in reality scored 848 runs, increase each player's Runs Created by 6 percent (848 / 800 = 1.06). Finally, each player's Runs Created can be rounded to the nearest integer value.

Runs Created per 27 Outs (RC/27)
This statistic estimates the number of runs per game that a team made up of nine of the same player would score. The name is a bit deceiving, because Bill James' current formula is based upon each league's average outs per team game instead of the standard 27. To calculate RC/27, multiply Runs Created by league outs per team game, divide the result by outs made by the player (the sum of at bats plus sacrifice hits plus sacrifice flies plus caught stealing plus grounded into double plays, minus hits). The formula written out is:

$$\frac{\frac{RC \times 3 \times LgIP}{2 \times LgG}}{AB - H + SH + SF + CS + GDP}$$

Save Percentage
A pitcher's Saves divided by the total number of Save Situations he faces (see definition for Save Situation).

Save Situation
A relief pitcher is in a Save Situation when he enters the game with his team in the lead, has the opportunity to finish the game, is not the winning pitcher of record at the time, and meets any one of the three following conditions:
  1. The pitcher's team is leading by no more than three runs and the pitcher has the chance to pitch for at least one inning, OR
  2. The pitcher enters the game with the potential tying run on base, at bat, or on deck, OR
  3. The pitcher pitches three or more effective innings regardless of the lead. The determination of a save in this situation is made by the official scorer.
It is not possible to have more than one save credited to a single team in a game.

SB Success Percentage

Stolen Bases divided by the number of Stolen Base attempts (Stolen Bases plus Caught Stealing).

$$\frac{SB}{SB + CS}$$

Secondary Average

A number meant to reflect everything else except for batting average. A player will have a high Secondary Average if he hits for power, takes walks and steals bases. It is calculated with the following formula:

$$\frac{TB - H + BB + SB - CS}{AB}$$

Similarity Score

A number which reflects the similarity between two different statistical lines, either for a player or for a team. A score of 1,000 means that the statistical lines are identical.

Slugging Average

Total Bases divided by At Bats.

$$\frac{TB}{AB}$$

Speed Score

Speed Score is a number which evaluates how fast a player is. To calculate the Speed Score, start with the player's statistics over the last two seasons combined. A value will be found for each of the following six categories and will be combined for a final score at the end:

1. Stolen Base Percentage. The value of this category is:

$$\left(\frac{SB + 3}{SB + CS + 7} - 0.4\right) \times 20$$

2. Frequency of Stolen Base Attempts. The value of this category is:

$$\frac{\sqrt{\dfrac{SB + CS}{Singles + BB + HBP}}}{0.07}$$

3. Percentage of Triples. This is calculated by taking the percentage of triples out of the number of balls put in play. To get the percentage, use this formula:

$$\frac{3B}{AB - HR - SO}$$

From this assign an integer from 0 to 10, based on the following chart:

Less than .001	0
.001 - .0023	1
.0023 - .0039	2
.0039 - .0058	3
.0058 - .0080	4
.0080 - .0105	5
.0105 - .013	6
.013 - .0158	7
.0158 - .0189	8
.0189 - .0223	9
.0223 or more	10

4. Runs Scored Percentage. This is calculated by taking the percentage of times the player scores a run out of the number of times the player is on base. To get the percentage, use this formula:

$$\frac{\left(\dfrac{R - HR}{H + HBP + BB - HR} - 0.1\right)}{0.04}$$

5. Grounded Into Double Play Frequency. To get the frequency, use this formula:

$$\frac{0.055 - \left(\dfrac{GIDP}{AB - HR - SO}\right)}{0.005}$$

6. Range Factor. The value of this category depends on the players position:

Catcher—1
First Baseman—2
Designated Hitter—1.5
Second Baseman—1.25 x Range Factor
Third Baseman—1.51 x Range Factor
Shortstop—1.52 x Range Factor
Outfield—3 x Range Factor
For an explanation on Range Factor, consult the definition in this glossary. Remember to figure range factors over a two-year period.

If any category value is greater than 10, then reduce it to 10. If any value is less than zero, then increase the value to zero. All category values must fall within the zero to 10 range. The Speed Score is then calculated by discarding the lowest of the six values, and taking the average of the remaining five.

Total Bases
Hits plus Doubles plus (2 times Triples) plus (3 times Home Runs).

$$H + 2B + (2 \times 3B) + (3 \times HR)$$

Tough Save
This label is used to separate Saves by difficulty level (Easy or Tough). A Save is considered Tough if the relief pitcher enters the game with the tying run on base.

Winning Percentage
Wins divided by (Wins plus Losses).

Baseball Info Solutions

BIS has been a baseball data provider for two straight seasons and has roots that run deep within the industry.

Owner and founder John Dewan is a former President and CEO of STATS, Inc. and even before that was the Executive Director of Project Scoresheet, the Bill James-led effort that pioneered the new wave of baseball statistics that are now common baseball terminology.

President Steve Moyer met up with John as one of the first full-time employees at STATS. Steve went on to become the first Director of Operations at STATS and, since then, has also worked for Broadband Sports and RotoSports, Inc. He brings more than 10 years of experience in the sports industry to BIS. Steve saw a need to collect a statistical snapshot of *every* important moment of *every* Major League Baseball game with the most advanced technology, resulting in a database that includes traditional data, pitch-by-pitch data, spray-chart hit location data and brand new pitch-charting data (type, location and velocity).

BIS is equipped to service any client with relevant baseball data - for teams, sports agents, fantasy services, baseball card companies, computer game companies, and private individuals. We can handle almost any data request, big or small, in a timely manner. Because we're still small, we can offer the kind of personal attention you may be missing from the larger data providers. (Phone and you're very likely to connect directly to the company President.)

Ventures into other sports are not planned for the immediate future, but will probably be a reality in a matter of time.

Contact us so we can service your baseball data needs:

Baseball Info Solutions
224 Nazareth Pike
Bethlehem, PA 18020
610-746-3965
www.baseballinfosolutions.com
info@baseballinfosolutions.com